Oxford Dictionary of
National Biography

Volume 46

Oxford Dictionary of National Biography

IN ASSOCIATION WITH
The British Academy

From the earliest times to the year 2000

Edited by
H. C. G. Matthew
and
Brian Harrison

Volume 46
Randolph–Rippingille

OXFORD
UNIVERSITY PRESS

OXFORD

UNIVERSITY PRESS

Great Clarendon Street, Oxford OX2 6DP

Oxford University Press is a department of the University of Oxford.
It furthers the University's objective of excellence in research, scholarship,
and education by publishing worldwide in

Oxford New York

Auckland Bangkok Buenos Aires Cape Town
Chennai Dar es Salaam Delhi Hong Kong Istanbul Karachi
Kolkata Kuala Lumpur Madrid Melbourne Mexico City Mumbai Nairobi
São Paulo Shanghai Taipei Tokyo Toronto

Oxford is a registered trade mark of Oxford University Press
in the UK and in certain other countries

Published in the United States
by Oxford University Press Inc., New York

British Library Cataloguing in Publication Data
Data available

Library of Congress Cataloging in Publication Data
Data available: for details see volume 1, p. iv

ISBN 0-19-861396-2 (this volume)
ISBN 0-19-861411-X (set of sixty volumes)

Text captured by Alliance Phototypesetters, Pondicherry
Illustrations reproduced and archived by
Alliance Graphics Ltd, UK
Typeset in OUP Swift by Interactive Sciences Limited, Gloucester
Printed in Great Britain on acid-free paper by
Butler and Tanner Ltd,
Frome, Somerset

LIST OF ABBREVIATIONS

1 General abbreviations

AB	bachelor of arts
ABC	Australian Broadcasting Corporation
ABC TV	ABC Television
act.	active
A$	Australian dollar
AD	*anno domini*
AFC	Air Force Cross
AIDS	acquired immune deficiency syndrome
AK	Alaska
AL	Alabama
A level	advanced level [examination]
ALS	associate of the Linnean Society
AM	master of arts
AMICE	associate member of the Institution of Civil Engineers
ANZAC	Australian and New Zealand Army Corps
appx *pl.* appxs	appendix(es)
AR	Arkansas
ARA	associate of the Royal Academy
ARCA	associate of the Royal College of Art
ARCM	associate of the Royal College of Music
ARCO	associate of the Royal College of Organists
ARIBA	associate of the Royal Institute of British Architects
ARP	air-raid precautions
ARRC	associate of the Royal Red Cross
ARSA	associate of the Royal Scottish Academy
art.	article / item
ASC	Army Service Corps
Asch	Austrian Schilling
ASDIC	Antisubmarine Detection Investigation Committee
ATS	Auxiliary Territorial Service
ATV	Associated Television
Aug	August
AZ	Arizona
b.	born
BA	bachelor of arts
BA (Admin.)	bachelor of arts (administration)
BAFTA	British Academy of Film and Television Arts
BAO	bachelor of arts in obstetrics
bap.	baptized
BBC	British Broadcasting Corporation / Company
BC	before Christ
BCE	before the common (*or* Christian) era
BCE	bachelor of civil engineering
BCG	bacillus of Calmette and Guérin [inoculation against tuberculosis]
BCh	bachelor of surgery
BChir	bachelor of surgery
BCL	bachelor of civil law

BCnL	bachelor of canon law
BCom	bachelor of commerce
BD	bachelor of divinity
BEd	bachelor of education
BEng	bachelor of engineering
bk *pl.* bks	book(s)
BL	bachelor of law / letters / literature
BLitt	bachelor of letters
BM	bachelor of medicine
BMus	bachelor of music
BP	before present
BP	British Petroleum
Bros.	Brothers
BS	(1) bachelor of science; (2) bachelor of surgery; (3) British standard
BSc	bachelor of science
BSc (Econ.)	bachelor of science (economics)
BSc (Eng.)	bachelor of science (engineering)
bt	baronet
BTh	bachelor of theology
bur.	buried
C.	command [identifier for published parliamentary papers]
c.	*circa*
c.	*capitulum pl. capitula*: chapter(s)
CA	California
Cantab.	Cantabrigiensis
cap.	*capitulum pl. capitula*: chapter(s)
CB	companion of the Bath
CBE	commander of the Order of the British Empire
CBS	Columbia Broadcasting System
cc	cubic centimetres
C$	Canadian dollar
CD	compact disc
Cd	command [identifier for published parliamentary papers]
CE	Common (*or* Christian) Era
cent.	century
cf.	compare
CH	Companion of Honour
chap.	chapter
ChB	bachelor of surgery
CI	Imperial Order of the Crown of India
CIA	Central Intelligence Agency
CID	Criminal Investigation Department
CIE	companion of the Order of the Indian Empire
Cie	Compagnie
CLit	companion of literature
CM	master of surgery
cm	centimetre(s)

Cmd	command [identifier for published parliamentary papers]
CMG	companion of the Order of St Michael and St George
Cmnd	command [identifier for published parliamentary papers]
CO	Colorado
Co.	company
co.	county
col. *pl.* cols.	column(s)
Corp.	corporation
CSE	certificate of secondary education
CSI	companion of the Order of the Star of India
CT	Connecticut
CVO	commander of the Royal Victorian Order
cwt	hundredweight
$	(American) dollar
d.	(1) penny (pence); (2) died
DBE	dame commander of the Order of the British Empire
DCH	diploma in child health
DCh	doctor of surgery
DCL	doctor of civil law
DCnL	doctor of canon law
DCVO	dame commander of the Royal Victorian Order
DD	doctor of divinity
DE	Delaware
Dec	December
dem.	demolished
DEng	doctor of engineering
des.	destroyed
DFC	Distinguished Flying Cross
DipEd	diploma in education
DipPsych	diploma in psychiatry
diss.	dissertation
DL	deputy lieutenant
DLitt	doctor of letters
DLittCelt	doctor of Celtic letters
DM	(1) Deutschmark; (2) doctor of medicine; (3) doctor of musical arts
DMus	doctor of music
DNA	dioxyribonucleic acid
doc.	document
DOL	doctor of oriental learning
DPH	diploma in public health
DPhil	doctor of philosophy
DPM	diploma in psychological medicine
DSC	Distinguished Service Cross
DSc	doctor of science
DSc (Econ.)	doctor of science (economics)
DSc (Eng.)	doctor of science (engineering)
DSM	Distinguished Service Medal
DSO	companion of the Distinguished Service Order
DSocSc	doctor of social science
DTech	doctor of technology
DTh	doctor of theology
DTM	diploma in tropical medicine
DTMH	diploma in tropical medicine and hygiene
DU	doctor of the university
DUniv	doctor of the university
dwt	pennyweight
EC	European Community
ed. *pl.* eds.	edited / edited by / editor(s)
Edin.	Edinburgh
edn	edition
EEC	European Economic Community
EFTA	European Free Trade Association
EICS	East India Company Service
EMI	Electrical and Musical Industries (Ltd)
Eng.	English
enl.	enlarged
ENSA	Entertainments National Service Association
ep. *pl.* epp.	*epistola(e)*
ESP	extra-sensory perception
esp.	especially
esq.	esquire
est.	estimate / estimated
EU	European Union
ex	sold by (*lit.* out of)
excl.	excludes / excluding
exh.	exhibited
exh. cat.	exhibition catalogue
f. *pl.* ff.	following [pages]
FA	Football Association
FACP	fellow of the American College of Physicians
facs.	facsimile
FANY	First Aid Nursing Yeomanry
FBA	fellow of the British Academy
FBI	Federation of British Industries
FCS	fellow of the Chemical Society
Feb	February
FEng	fellow of the Fellowship of Engineering
FFCM	fellow of the Faculty of Community Medicine
FGS	fellow of the Geological Society
fig.	figure
FIMechE	fellow of the Institution of Mechanical Engineers
FL	Florida
fl.	*floruit*
FLS	fellow of the Linnean Society
FM	frequency modulation
fol. *pl.* fols.	folio(s)
Fr	French francs
Fr.	French
FRAeS	fellow of the Royal Aeronautical Society
FRAI	fellow of the Royal Anthropological Institute
FRAM	fellow of the Royal Academy of Music
FRAS	(1) fellow of the Royal Asiatic Society; (2) fellow of the Royal Astronomical Society
FRCM	fellow of the Royal College of Music
FRCO	fellow of the Royal College of Organists
FRCOG	fellow of the Royal College of Obstetricians and Gynaecologists
FRCP(C)	fellow of the Royal College of Physicians of Canada
FRCP (Edin.)	fellow of the Royal College of Physicians of Edinburgh
FRCP (Lond.)	fellow of the Royal College of Physicians of London
FRCPath	fellow of the Royal College of Pathologists
FRCPsych	fellow of the Royal College of Psychiatrists
FRCS	fellow of the Royal College of Surgeons
FRGS	fellow of the Royal Geographical Society
FRIBA	fellow of the Royal Institute of British Architects
FRICS	fellow of the Royal Institute of Chartered Surveyors
FRS	fellow of the Royal Society
FRSA	fellow of the Royal Society of Arts

FRSCM	fellow of the Royal School of Church Music		ISO	companion of the Imperial Service Order
FRSE	fellow of the Royal Society of Edinburgh		It.	Italian
FRSL	fellow of the Royal Society of Literature		ITA	Independent Television Authority
FSA	fellow of the Society of Antiquaries		ITV	Independent Television
ft	foot *pl.* feet		Jan	January
FTCL	fellow of Trinity College of Music, London		JP	justice of the peace
ft-lb per min.	foot-pounds per minute [unit of horsepower]		jun.	junior
FZS	fellow of the Zoological Society		KB	knight of the Order of the Bath
GA	Georgia		KBE	knight commander of the Order of the British Empire
GBE	knight or dame grand cross of the Order of the British Empire		KC	king's counsel
GCB	knight grand cross of the Order of the Bath		kcal	kilocalorie
GCE	general certificate of education		KCB	knight commander of the Order of the Bath
GCH	knight grand cross of the Royal Guelphic Order		KCH	knight commander of the Royal Guelphic Order
GCHQ	government communications headquarters		KCIE	knight commander of the Order of the Indian Empire
GCIE	knight grand commander of the Order of the Indian Empire		KCMG	knight commander of the Order of St Michael and St George
GCMG	knight or dame grand cross of the Order of St Michael and St George		KCSI	knight commander of the Order of the Star of India
GCSE	general certificate of secondary education		KCVO	knight commander of the Royal Victorian Order
GCSI	knight grand commander of the Order of the Star of India		keV	kilo-electron-volt
GCStJ	bailiff or dame grand cross of the order of St John of Jerusalem		KG	knight of the Order of the Garter
			KGB	[Soviet committee of state security]
GCVO	knight or dame grand cross of the Royal Victorian Order		KH	knight of the Royal Guelphic Order
			KLM	Koninklijke Luchtvaart Maatschappij (Royal Dutch Air Lines)
GEC	General Electric Company		km	kilometre(s)
Ger.	German		KP	knight of the Order of St Patrick
GI	government (*or* general) issue		KS	Kansas
GMT	Greenwich mean time		KT	knight of the Order of the Thistle
GP	general practitioner		kt	knight
GPU	[Soviet special police unit]		KY	Kentucky
GSO	general staff officer		£	pound(s) sterling
Heb.	Hebrew		£E	Egyptian pound
HEICS	Honourable East India Company Service		L	lira *pl.* lire
HI	Hawaii		l. *pl.* ll.	line(s)
HIV	human immunodeficiency virus		LA	Lousiana
HK$	Hong Kong dollar		LAA	light anti-aircraft
HM	his / her majesty('s)		LAH	licentiate of the Apothecaries' Hall, Dublin
HMAS	his / her majesty's Australian ship		Lat.	Latin
HMNZS	his / her majesty's New Zealand ship		lb	pound(s), unit of weight
HMS	his / her majesty's ship		LDS	licence in dental surgery
HMSO	His / Her Majesty's Stationery Office		*lit.*	literally
HMV	His Master's Voice		LittB	bachelor of letters
Hon.	Honourable		LittD	doctor of letters
hp	horsepower		LKQCPI	licentiate of the King and Queen's College of Physicians, Ireland
hr	hour(s)		LLA	lady literate in arts
HRH	his / her royal highness			
HTV	Harlech Television		LLB	bachelor of laws
IA	Iowa		LLD	doctor of laws
ibid.	*ibidem*: in the same place		LLM	master of laws
ICI	Imperial Chemical Industries (Ltd)		LM	licentiate in midwifery
ID	Idaho		LP	long-playing record
IL	Illinois		LRAM	licentiate of the Royal Academy of Music
illus.	illustration		LRCP	licentiate of the Royal College of Physicians
illustr.	illustrated		LRCPS (Glasgow)	licentiate of the Royal College of Physicians and Surgeons of Glasgow
IN	Indiana			
in.	inch(es)		LRCS	licentiate of the Royal College of Surgeons
Inc.	Incorporated		LSA	licentiate of the Society of Apothecaries
incl.	includes / including		LSD	lysergic acid diethylamide
IOU	I owe you		LVO	lieutenant of the Royal Victorian Order
IQ	intelligence quotient		M. *pl.* MM.	Monsieur *pl.* Messieurs
Ir£	Irish pound		m	metre(s)
IRA	Irish Republican Army			

m. *pl.* mm.	membrane(s)	ND	North Dakota
MA	(1) Massachusetts; (2) master of arts	n.d.	no date
MAI	master of engineering	NE	Nebraska
MB	bachelor of medicine	*nem. con.*	*nemine contradicente*: unanimously
MBA	master of business administration	new ser.	new series
MBE	member of the Order of the British Empire	NH	New Hampshire
MC	Military Cross	NHS	National Health Service
MCC	Marylebone Cricket Club	NJ	New Jersey
MCh	master of surgery	NKVD	[Soviet people's commissariat for internal affairs]
MChir	master of surgery		
MCom	master of commerce	NM	New Mexico
MD	(1) doctor of medicine; (2) Maryland	nm	nanometre(s)
MDMA	methylenedioxymethamphetamine	no. *pl.* nos.	number(s)
ME	Maine	Nov	November
MEd	master of education	n.p.	no place [of publication]
MEng	master of engineering	NS	new style
MEP	member of the European parliament	NV	Nevada
MG	Morris Garages	NY	New York
MGM	Metro-Goldwyn-Mayer	NZBS	New Zealand Broadcasting Service
Mgr	Monsignor	OBE	officer of the Order of the British Empire
MI	(1) Michigan; (2) military intelligence	obit.	obituary
MI1c	[secret intelligence department]	Oct	October
MI5	[military intelligence department]	OCTU	officer cadets training unit
MI6	[secret intelligence department]	OECD	Organization for Economic Co-operation and Development
MI9	[secret escape service]		
MICE	member of the Institution of Civil Engineers	OEEC	Organization for European Economic Co-operation
MIEE	member of the Institution of Electrical Engineers		
		OFM	order of Friars Minor [Franciscans]
min.	minute(s)	OFMCap	Ordine Frati Minori Cappucini: member of the Capuchin order
Mk	mark		
ML	(1) licentiate of medicine; (2) master of laws	OH	Ohio
MLitt	master of letters	OK	Oklahoma
Mlle	Mademoiselle	O level	ordinary level [examination]
mm	millimetre(s)	OM	Order of Merit
Mme	Madame	OP	order of Preachers [Dominicans]
MN	Minnesota	op. *pl.* opp.	opus *pl.* opera
MO	Missouri	OPEC	Organization of Petroleum Exporting Countries
MOH	medical officer of health	OR	Oregon
MP	member of parliament	orig.	original
m.p.h.	miles per hour	OS	old style
MPhil	master of philosophy	OSB	Order of St Benedict
MRCP	member of the Royal College of Physicians	OTC	Officers' Training Corps
MRCS	member of the Royal College of Surgeons	OWS	Old Watercolour Society
MRCVS	member of the Royal College of Veterinary Surgeons	Oxon.	Oxoniensis
		p. *pl.* pp.	page(s)
MRIA	member of the Royal Irish Academy	PA	Pennsylvania
MS	(1) master of science; (2) Mississippi	p.a.	per annum
MS *pl.* MSS	manuscript(s)	para.	paragraph
MSc	master of science	PAYE	pay as you earn
MSc (Econ.)	master of science (economics)	pbk *pl.* pbks	paperback(s)
MT	Montana	*per.*	[during the] period
MusB	bachelor of music	PhD	doctor of philosophy
MusBac	bachelor of music	pl.	(1) plate(s); (2) plural
MusD	doctor of music	priv. coll.	private collection
MV	motor vessel	pt *pl.* pts	part(s)
MVO	member of the Royal Victorian Order	pubd	published
n. *pl.* nn.	note(s)	PVC	polyvinyl chloride
NAAFI	Navy, Army, and Air Force Institutes	q. *pl.* qq.	(1) question(s); (2) quire(s)
NASA	National Aeronautics and Space Administration	QC	queen's counsel
NATO	North Atlantic Treaty Organization	R	rand
NBC	National Broadcasting Corporation	R.	Rex / Regina
NC	North Carolina	*r*	recto
NCO	non-commissioned officer	*r.*	reigned / ruled
		RA	Royal Academy / Royal Academician

RAC	Royal Automobile Club
RAF	Royal Air Force
RAFVR	Royal Air Force Volunteer Reserve
RAM	[member of the] Royal Academy of Music
RAMC	Royal Army Medical Corps
RCA	Royal College of Art
RCNC	Royal Corps of Naval Constructors
RCOG	Royal College of Obstetricians and Gynaecologists
RDI	royal designer for industry
RE	Royal Engineers
repr. *pl.* reprs.	reprint(s) / reprinted
repro.	reproduced
rev.	revised / revised by / reviser / revision
Revd	Reverend
RHA	Royal Hibernian Academy
RI	(1) Rhode Island; (2) Royal Institute of Painters in Water-Colours
RIBA	Royal Institute of British Architects
RIN	Royal Indian Navy
RM	Reichsmark
RMS	Royal Mail steamer
RN	Royal Navy
RNA	ribonucleic acid
RNAS	Royal Naval Air Service
RNR	Royal Naval Reserve
RNVR	Royal Naval Volunteer Reserve
RO	Record Office
r.p.m.	revolutions per minute
RRS	royal research ship
Rs	rupees
RSA	(1) Royal Scottish Academician; (2) Royal Society of Arts
RSPCA	Royal Society for the Prevention of Cruelty to Animals
Rt Hon.	Right Honourable
Rt Revd	Right Reverend
RUC	Royal Ulster Constabulary
Russ.	Russian
RWS	Royal Watercolour Society
S4C	Sianel Pedwar Cymru
s.	shilling(s)
s.a.	*sub anno*: under the year
SABC	South African Broadcasting Corporation
SAS	Special Air Service
SC	South Carolina
ScD	doctor of science
S$	Singapore dollar
SD	South Dakota
sec.	second(s)
sel.	selected
sen.	senior
Sept	September
ser.	series
SHAPE	supreme headquarters allied powers, Europe
SIDRO	Société Internationale d'Énergie Hydro-Électrique
sig. *pl.* sigs.	signature(s)
sing.	singular
SIS	Secret Intelligence Service
SJ	Society of Jesus

Skr	Swedish krona
Span.	Spanish
SPCK	Society for Promoting Christian Knowledge
SS	(1) Santissimi; (2) Schutzstaffel; (3) steam ship
STB	bachelor of theology
STD	doctor of theology
STM	master of theology
STP	doctor of theology
supp.	supposedly
suppl. *pl.* suppls.	supplement(s)
s.v.	*sub verbo* / *sub voce*: under the word / heading
SY	steam yacht
TA	Territorial Army
TASS	[Soviet news agency]
TB	tuberculosis (*lit.* tubercle bacillus)
TD	(1) *teachtaí dála* (member of the Dáil); (2) territorial decoration
TN	Tennessee
TNT	trinitrotoluene
trans.	translated / translated by / translation / translator
TT	tourist trophy
TUC	Trades Union Congress
TX	Texas
U-boat	*Unterseeboot*: submarine
Ufa	Universum-Film AG
UMIST	University of Manchester Institute of Science and Technology
UN	United Nations
UNESCO	United Nations Educational, Scientific, and Cultural Organization
UNICEF	United Nations International Children's Emergency Fund
unpubd	unpublished
USS	United States ship
UT	Utah
v	verso
v.	versus
VA	Virginia
VAD	Voluntary Aid Detachment
VC	Victoria Cross
VE-day	victory in Europe day
Ven.	Venerable
VJ-day	victory over Japan day
vol. *pl.* vols.	volume(s)
VT	Vermont
WA	Washington [state]
WAAC	Women's Auxiliary Army Corps
WAAF	Women's Auxiliary Air Force
WEA	Workers' Educational Association
WHO	World Health Organization
WI	Wisconsin
WRAF	Women's Royal Air Force
WRNS	Women's Royal Naval Service
WV	West Virginia
WVS	Women's Voluntary Service
WY	Wyoming
¥	yen
YMCA	Young Men's Christian Association
YWCA	Young Women's Christian Association

2 Institution abbreviations

All Souls Oxf.	All Souls College, Oxford
AM Oxf.	Ashmolean Museum, Oxford
Balliol Oxf.	Balliol College, Oxford
BBC WAC	BBC Written Archives Centre, Reading
Beds. & Luton ARS	Bedfordshire and Luton Archives and Record Service, Bedford
Berks. RO	Berkshire Record Office, Reading
BFI	British Film Institute, London
BFI NFTVA	British Film Institute, London, National Film and Television Archive
BGS	British Geological Survey, Keyworth, Nottingham
Birm. CA	Birmingham Central Library, Birmingham City Archives
Birm. CL	Birmingham Central Library
BL	British Library, London
BL NSA	British Library, London, National Sound Archive
BL OIOC	British Library, London, Oriental and India Office Collections
BLPES	London School of Economics and Political Science, British Library of Political and Economic Science
BM	British Museum, London
Bodl. Oxf.	Bodleian Library, Oxford
Bodl. RH	Bodleian Library of Commonwealth and African Studies at Rhodes House, Oxford
Borth. Inst.	Borthwick Institute of Historical Research, University of York
Boston PL	Boston Public Library, Massachusetts
Bristol RO	Bristol Record Office
Bucks. RLSS	Buckinghamshire Records and Local Studies Service, Aylesbury
CAC Cam.	Churchill College, Cambridge, Churchill Archives Centre
Cambs. AS	Cambridgeshire Archive Service
CCC Cam.	Corpus Christi College, Cambridge
CCC Oxf.	Corpus Christi College, Oxford
Ches. & Chester ALSS	Cheshire and Chester Archives and Local Studies Service
Christ Church Oxf.	Christ Church, Oxford
Christies	Christies, London
City Westm. AC	City of Westminster Archives Centre, London
CKS	Centre for Kentish Studies, Maidstone
CLRO	Corporation of London Records Office
Coll. Arms	College of Arms, London
Col. U.	Columbia University, New York
Cornwall RO	Cornwall Record Office, Truro
Courtauld Inst.	Courtauld Institute of Art, London
CUL	Cambridge University Library
Cumbria AS	Cumbria Archive Service
Derbys. RO	Derbyshire Record Office, Matlock
Devon RO	Devon Record Office, Exeter
Dorset RO	Dorset Record Office, Dorchester
Duke U.	Duke University, Durham, North Carolina
Duke U., Perkins L.	Duke University, Durham, North Carolina, William R. Perkins Library
Durham Cath. CL	Durham Cathedral, chapter library
Durham RO	Durham Record Office
DWL	Dr Williams's Library, London
Essex RO	Essex Record Office
E. Sussex RO	East Sussex Record Office, Lewes
Eton	Eton College, Berkshire
FM Cam.	Fitzwilliam Museum, Cambridge
Folger	Folger Shakespeare Library, Washington, DC
Garr. Club	Garrick Club, London
Girton Cam.	Girton College, Cambridge
GL	Guildhall Library, London
Glos. RO	Gloucestershire Record Office, Gloucester
Gon. & Caius Cam.	Gonville and Caius College, Cambridge
Gov. Art Coll.	Government Art Collection
GS Lond.	Geological Society of London
Hants. RO	Hampshire Record Office, Winchester
Harris Man. Oxf.	Harris Manchester College, Oxford
Harvard TC	Harvard Theatre Collection, Harvard University, Cambridge, Massachusetts, Nathan Marsh Pusey Library
Harvard U.	Harvard University, Cambridge, Massachusetts
Harvard U., Houghton L.	Harvard University, Cambridge, Massachusetts, Houghton Library
Herefs. RO	Herefordshire Record Office, Hereford
Herts. ALS	Hertfordshire Archives and Local Studies, Hertford
Hist. Soc. Penn.	Historical Society of Pennsylvania, Philadelphia
HLRO	House of Lords Record Office, London
Hult. Arch.	Hulton Archive, London and New York
Hunt. L.	Huntington Library, San Marino, California
ICL	Imperial College, London
Inst. CE	Institution of Civil Engineers, London
Inst. EE	Institution of Electrical Engineers, London
IWM	Imperial War Museum, London
IWM FVA	Imperial War Museum, London, Film and Video Archive
IWM SA	Imperial War Museum, London, Sound Archive
JRL	John Rylands University Library of Manchester
King's AC Cam.	King's College Archives Centre, Cambridge
King's Cam.	King's College, Cambridge
King's Lond.	King's College, London
King's Lond., Liddell Hart C.	King's College, London, Liddell Hart Centre for Military Archives
Lancs. RO	Lancashire Record Office, Preston
L. Cong.	Library of Congress, Washington, DC
Leics. RO	Leicestershire, Leicester, and Rutland Record Office, Leicester
Lincs. Arch.	Lincolnshire Archives, Lincoln
Linn. Soc.	Linnean Society of London
LMA	London Metropolitan Archives
LPL	Lambeth Palace, London
Lpool RO	Liverpool Record Office and Local Studies Service
LUL	London University Library
Magd. Cam.	Magdalene College, Cambridge
Magd. Oxf.	Magdalen College, Oxford
Man. City Gall.	Manchester City Galleries
Man. CL	Manchester Central Library
Mass. Hist. Soc.	Massachusetts Historical Society, Boston
Merton Oxf.	Merton College, Oxford
MHS Oxf.	Museum of the History of Science, Oxford
Mitchell L., Glas.	Mitchell Library, Glasgow
Mitchell L., NSW	State Library of New South Wales, Sydney, Mitchell Library
Morgan L.	Pierpont Morgan Library, New York
NA Canada	National Archives of Canada, Ottawa
NA Ire.	National Archives of Ireland, Dublin
NAM	National Army Museum, London
NA Scot.	National Archives of Scotland, Edinburgh
News Int. RO	News International Record Office, London
NG Ire.	National Gallery of Ireland, Dublin

NG Scot.	National Gallery of Scotland, Edinburgh
NHM	Natural History Museum, London
NL Aus.	National Library of Australia, Canberra
NL Ire.	National Library of Ireland, Dublin
NL NZ	National Library of New Zealand, Wellington
NL NZ, Turnbull L.	National Library of New Zealand, Wellington, Alexander Turnbull Library
NL Scot.	National Library of Scotland, Edinburgh
NL Wales	National Library of Wales, Aberystwyth
NMG Wales	National Museum and Gallery of Wales, Cardiff
NMM	National Maritime Museum, London
Norfolk RO	Norfolk Record Office, Norwich
Northants. RO	Northamptonshire Record Office, Northampton
Northumbd RO	Northumberland Record Office
Notts. Arch.	Nottinghamshire Archives, Nottingham
NPG	National Portrait Gallery, London
NRA	National Archives, London, Historical Manuscripts Commission, National Register of Archives
Nuffield Oxf.	Nuffield College, Oxford
N. Yorks. CRO	North Yorkshire County Record Office, Northallerton
NYPL	New York Public Library
Oxf. UA	Oxford University Archives
Oxf. U. Mus. NH	Oxford University Museum of Natural History
Oxon. RO	Oxfordshire Record Office, Oxford
Pembroke Cam.	Pembroke College, Cambridge
PRO	National Archives, London, Public Record Office
PRO NIre.	Public Record Office for Northern Ireland, Belfast
Pusey Oxf.	Pusey House, Oxford
RA	Royal Academy of Arts, London
Ransom HRC	Harry Ransom Humanities Research Center, University of Texas, Austin
RAS	Royal Astronomical Society, London
RBG Kew	Royal Botanic Gardens, Kew, London
RCP Lond.	Royal College of Physicians of London
RCS Eng.	Royal College of Surgeons of England, London
RGS	Royal Geographical Society, London
RIBA	Royal Institute of British Architects, London
RIBA BAL	Royal Institute of British Architects, London, British Architectural Library
Royal Arch.	Royal Archives, Windsor Castle, Berkshire [by gracious permission of her majesty the queen]
Royal Irish Acad.	Royal Irish Academy, Dublin
Royal Scot. Acad.	Royal Scottish Academy, Edinburgh
RS	Royal Society, London
RSA	Royal Society of Arts, London
RS Friends, Lond.	Religious Society of Friends, London
St Ant. Oxf.	St Antony's College, Oxford
St John Cam.	St John's College, Cambridge
S. Antiquaries, Lond.	Society of Antiquaries of London
Sci. Mus.	Science Museum, London
Scot. NPG	Scottish National Portrait Gallery, Edinburgh
Scott Polar RI	University of Cambridge, Scott Polar Research Institute
Sheff. Arch.	Sheffield Archives
Shrops. RRC	Shropshire Records and Research Centre, Shrewsbury
SOAS	School of Oriental and African Studies, London
Som. ARS	Somerset Archive and Record Service, Taunton
Staffs. RO	Staffordshire Record Office, Stafford
Suffolk RO	Suffolk Record Office
Surrey HC	Surrey History Centre, Woking
TCD	Trinity College, Dublin
Trinity Cam.	Trinity College, Cambridge
U. Aberdeen	University of Aberdeen
U. Birm.	University of Birmingham
U. Birm. L.	University of Birmingham Library
U. Cal.	University of California
U. Cam.	University of Cambridge
UCL	University College, London
U. Durham	University of Durham
U. Durham L.	University of Durham Library
U. Edin.	University of Edinburgh
U. Edin., New Coll.	University of Edinburgh, New College
U. Edin., New Coll. L.	University of Edinburgh, New College Library
U. Edin. L.	University of Edinburgh Library
U. Glas.	University of Glasgow
U. Glas. L.	University of Glasgow Library
U. Hull	University of Hull
U. Hull, Brynmor Jones L.	University of Hull, Brynmor Jones Library
U. Leeds	University of Leeds
U. Leeds, Brotherton L.	University of Leeds, Brotherton Library
U. Lond.	University of London
U. Lpool	University of Liverpool
U. Lpool L.	University of Liverpool Library
U. Mich.	University of Michigan, Ann Arbor
U. Mich., Clements L.	University of Michigan, Ann Arbor, William L. Clements Library
U. Newcastle	University of Newcastle upon Tyne
U. Newcastle, Robinson L.	University of Newcastle upon Tyne, Robinson Library
U. Nott.	University of Nottingham
U. Nott. L.	University of Nottingham Library
U. Oxf.	University of Oxford
U. Reading	University of Reading
U. Reading L.	University of Reading Library
U. St Andr.	University of St Andrews
U. St Andr. L.	University of St Andrews Library
U. Southampton	University of Southampton
U. Southampton L.	University of Southampton Library
U. Sussex	University of Sussex, Brighton
U. Texas	University of Texas, Austin
U. Wales	University of Wales
U. Warwick Mod. RC	University of Warwick, Coventry, Modern Records Centre
V&A	Victoria and Albert Museum, London
V&A NAL	Victoria and Albert Museum, London, National Art Library
Warks. CRO	Warwickshire County Record Office, Warwick
Wellcome L.	Wellcome Library for the History and Understanding of Medicine, London
Westm. DA	Westminster Diocesan Archives, London
Wilts. & Swindon RO	Wiltshire and Swindon Record Office, Trowbridge
Worcs. RO	Worcestershire Record Office, Worcester
W. Sussex RO	West Sussex Record Office, Chichester
W. Yorks. AS	West Yorkshire Archive Service
Yale U.	Yale University, New Haven, Connecticut
Yale U., Beinecke L.	Yale University, New Haven, Connecticut, Beinecke Rare Book and Manuscript Library
Yale U. CBA	Yale University, New Haven, Connecticut, Yale Center for British Art

3 Bibliographic abbreviations

Adams, *Drama* — W. D. Adams, *A dictionary of the drama*, 1: *A–G* (1904); 2: *H–Z* (1956) [vol. 2 microfilm only]

AFM — J O'Donovan, ed. and trans., *Annala rioghachta Eireann / Annals of the kingdom of Ireland by the four masters*, 7 vols. (1848–51); 2nd edn (1856); 3rd edn (1990)

Allibone, *Dict.* — S. A. Allibone, *A critical dictionary of English literature and British and American authors*, 3 vols. (1859–71); suppl. by J. F. Kirk, 2 vols. (1891)

ANB — J. A. Garraty and M. C. Carnes, eds., *American national biography*, 24 vols. (1999)

Anderson, *Scot. nat.* — W. Anderson, *The Scottish nation, or, The surnames, families, literature, honours, and biographical history of the people of Scotland*, 3 vols. (1859–63)

Ann. mon. — H. R. Luard, ed., *Annales monastici*, 5 vols., Rolls Series, 36 (1864–9)

Ann. Ulster — S. Mac Airt and G. Mac Niocaill, eds., *Annals of Ulster (to AD 1131)* (1983)

APC — *Acts of the privy council of England*, new ser., 46 vols. (1890–1964)

APS — *The acts of the parliaments of Scotland*, 12 vols. in 13 (1814–75)

Arber, *Regs. Stationers* — F. Arber, ed., *A transcript of the registers of the Company of Stationers of London, 1554–1640 AD*, 5 vols. (1875–94)

ArchR — *Architectural Review*

ASC — D. Whitelock, D. C. Douglas, and S. I. Tucker, ed. and trans., *The Anglo-Saxon Chronicle: a revised translation* (1961)

AS chart. — P. H. Sawyer, *Anglo-Saxon charters: an annotated list and bibliography*, Royal Historical Society Guides and Handbooks (1968)

AusDB — D. Pike and others, eds., *Australian dictionary of biography*, 16 vols. (1966–2002)

Baker, *Serjeants* — J. H. Baker, *The order of serjeants at law*, SeldS, suppl. ser., 5 (1984)

Bale, *Cat.* — J. Bale, *Scriptorum illustrium Maioris Brytannie, quam nunc Angliam et Scotiam vocant: catalogus*, 2 vols. in 1 (Basel, 1557–9); facs. edn (1971)

Bale, *Index* — J. Bale, *Index Britanniae scriptorum*, ed. R. L. Poole and M. Bateson (1902); facs. edn (1990)

BBCS — *Bulletin of the Board of Celtic Studies*

BDMBR — J. O. Baylen and N. J. Gossman, eds., *Biographical dictionary of modern British radicals*, 3 vols. in 4 (1979–88)

Bede, *Hist. eccl.* — *Bede's Ecclesiastical history of the English people*, ed. and trans. B. Colgrave and R. A. B. Mynors, OMT (1969); repr. (1991)

Bénézit, *Dict.* — E. Bénézit, *Dictionnaire critique et documentaire des peintres, sculpteurs, dessinateurs et graveurs*, 3 vols. (Paris, 1911–23); new edn, 8 vols. (1948–66), repr. (1966); 3rd edn, rev. and enl., 10 vols. (1976); 4th edn, 14 vols. (1999)

BIHR — *Bulletin of the Institute of Historical Research*

Birch, *Seals* — W. de Birch, *Catalogue of seals in the department of manuscripts in the British Museum*, 6 vols. (1887–1900)

Bishop Burnet's History — *Bishop Burnet's History of his own time*, ed. M. J. Routh, 2nd edn, 6 vols. (1833)

Blackwood — *Blackwood's [Edinburgh] Magazine*, 328 vols. (1817–1980)

Blain, Clements & Grundy, *Feminist comp.* — V. Blain, P. Clements, and I. Grundy, eds., *The feminist companion to literature in English* (1990)

BL cat. — *The British Library general catalogue of printed books* [in 360 vols. with suppls., also CD-ROM and online]

BMJ — *British Medical Journal*

Boase & Courtney, *Bibl. Corn.* — G. C. Boase and W. P. Courtney, *Bibliotheca Cornubiensis: a catalogue of the writings … of Cornishmen*, 3 vols. (1874–82)

Boase, *Mod. Eng. biog.* — F. Boase, *Modern English biography: containing many thousand concise memoirs of persons who have died since the year 1850*, 6 vols. (privately printed, Truro, 1892–1921); repr. (1965)

Boswell, *Life* — *Boswell's Life of Johnson: together with Journal of a tour to the Hebrides and Johnson's Diary of a journey into north Wales*, ed. G. B. Hill, enl. edn, rev. L. F. Powell, 6 vols. (1934–50); 2nd edn (1964); repr. (1971)

Brown & Stratton, *Brit. mus.* — J. D. Brown and S. S. Stratton, *British musical biography* (1897)

Bryan, *Painters* — M. Bryan, *A biographical and critical dictionary of painters and engravers*, 2 vols. (1816); new edn, ed. G. Stanley (1849); new edn, ed. R. E. Graves and W. Armstrong, 2 vols. (1886–9); [4th edn], ed. G. C. Williamson, 5 vols. (1903–5) [various reprs.]

Burke, *Gen. GB* — J. Burke, *A genealogical and heraldic history of the commoners of Great Britain and Ireland*, 4 vols. (1833–8); new edn as *A genealogical and heraldic dictionary of the landed gentry of Great Britain and Ireland*, 3 vols. [1843–9] [many later edns]

Burke, *Gen. Ire.* — J. B. Burke, *A genealogical and heraldic history of the landed gentry of Ireland* (1899); 2nd edn (1904); 3rd edn (1912); 4th edn (1958); 5th edn as *Burke's Irish family records* (1976)

Burke, *Peerage* — J. Burke, *A general [later edns A genealogical] and heraldic dictionary of the peerage and baronetage of the United Kingdom* [later edns *the British empire*] (1829–)

Burney, *Hist. mus.* — C. Burney, *A general history of music, from the earliest ages to the present period*, 4 vols. (1776–89)

Burtchaell & Sadleir, *Alum. Dubl.* — G. D. Burtchaell and T. U. Sadleir, *Alumni Dublinenses: a register of the students, graduates, and provosts of Trinity College* (1924); [2nd edn], with suppl., in 2 pts (1935)

Calamy rev. — A. G. Matthews, *Calamy revised* (1934); repr. (1988)

CCI — *Calendar of confirmations and inventories granted and given up in the several commissariots of Scotland* (1876–)

CClR — *Calendar of the close rolls preserved in the Public Record Office*, 47 vols. (1892–1963)

CDS — J. Bain, ed., *Calendar of documents relating to Scotland*, 4 vols., PRO (1881–8); suppl. vol. 5, ed. G. G. Simpson and J. D. Galbraith [1986]

CEPR letters — W. H. Bliss, C. Johnson, and J. Twemlow, eds., *Calendar of entries in the papal registers relating to Great Britain and Ireland: papal letters* (1893–)

CGPLA — *Calendars of the grants of probate and letters of administration* [in 4 ser.: *England & Wales, Northern Ireland, Ireland,* and *Éire*]

Chambers, *Scots.* — R. Chambers, ed., *A biographical dictionary of eminent Scotsmen*, 4 vols. (1832–5)

Chancery records — chancery records pubd by the PRO

Chancery records (RC) — chancery records pubd by the Record Commissions

CIPM	*Calendar of inquisitions post mortem*, [20 vols.], PRO (1904–); also *Henry VII*, 3 vols. (1898–1955)
Clarendon, *Hist. rebellion*	E. Hyde, earl of Clarendon, *The history of the rebellion and civil wars in England*, 6 vols. (1888); repr. (1958) and (1992)
Cobbett, *Parl. hist.*	W. Cobbett and J. Wright, eds., *Cobbett's Parliamentary history of England*, 36 vols. (1806–1820)
Colvin, *Archs.*	H. Colvin, *A biographical dictionary of British architects, 1600–1840*, 3rd edn (1995)
Cooper, *Ath. Cantab.*	C. H. Cooper and T. Cooper, *Athenae Cantabrigienses*, 3 vols. (1858–1913); repr. (1967)
CPR	*Calendar of the patent rolls preserved in the Public Record Office* (1891–)
Crockford	*Crockford's Clerical Directory*
CS	Camden Society
CSP	*Calendar of state papers* [in 11 ser.: domestic, Scotland, Scottish series, Ireland, colonial, Commonwealth, foreign, Spain [at Simancas], Rome, Milan, and Venice]
CYS	Canterbury and York Society
DAB	*Dictionary of American biography*, 21 vols. (1928–36), repr. in 11 vols. (1964); 10 suppls. (1944–96)
DBB	D. J. Jeremy, ed., *Dictionary of business biography*, 5 vols. (1984–6)
DCB	G. W. Brown and others, *Dictionary of Canadian biography*, [14 vols.] (1966–)
Debrett's Peerage	*Debrett's Peerage* (1803–) [sometimes *Debrett's Illustrated peerage*]
Desmond, *Botanists*	R. Desmond, *Dictionary of British and Irish botanists and horticulturists* (1977); rev. edn (1994)
Dir. Brit. archs.	A. Felstead, J. Franklin, and L. Pinfield, eds., *Directory of British architects, 1834–1900* (1993); 2nd edn, ed. A. Brodie and others, 2 vols. (2001)
DLB	J. M. Bellamy and J. Saville, eds., *Dictionary of labour biography*, [10 vols.] (1972–)
DLitB	Dictionary of Literary Biography
DNB	*Dictionary of national biography*, 63 vols. (1885–1900), suppl., 3 vols. (1901); repr. in 22 vols. (1908–9); 10 further suppls. (1912–96); *Missing persons* (1993)
DNZB	W. H. Oliver and C. Orange, eds., *The dictionary of New Zealand biography*, 5 vols. (1990–2000)
DSAB	W. J. de Kock and others, *Dictionary of South African biography*, 5 vols. (1968–87)
DSB	C. C. Gillispie and F. L. Holmes, eds., *Dictionary of scientific biography*, 16 vols. (1970–80); repr. in 8 vols. (1981); 2 vol. suppl. (1990)
DSBB	A. Slaven and S. Checkland, eds., *Dictionary of Scottish business biography, 1860–1960*, 2 vols. (1986–90)
DSCHT	N. M. de S. Cameron and others, eds., *Dictionary of Scottish church history and theology* (1993)
Dugdale, *Monasticon*	W. Dugdale, *Monasticon Anglicanum*, 3 vols. (1655–72); 2nd edn, 3 vols. (1661–82); new edn, ed. J. Caley, J. Ellis, and B. Bandinel, 6 vols. in 8 pts (1817–30); repr. (1846) and (1970)
DWB	J. E. Lloyd and others, eds., *Dictionary of Welsh biography down to 1940* (1959) [Eng. trans. of *Y bywgraffiadur Cymreig hyd 1940*, 2nd edn (1954)]
EdinR	*Edinburgh Review, or, Critical Journal*
EETS	Early English Text Society
Emden, *Cam.*	A. B. Emden, *A biographical register of the University of Cambridge to 1500* (1963)
Emden, *Oxf.*	A. B. Emden, *A biographical register of the University of Oxford to AD 1500*, 3 vols. (1957–9); also *A biographical register of the University of Oxford, AD 1501 to 1540* (1974)
EngHR	*English Historical Review*
Engraved Brit. ports.	F. M. O'Donoghue and H. M. Hake, *Catalogue of engraved British portraits preserved in the department of prints and drawings in the British Museum*, 6 vols. (1908–25)
ER	*The English Reports*, 178 vols. (1900–32)
ESTC	*English short title catalogue, 1475–1800* [CD-ROM and online]
Evelyn, *Diary*	*The diary of John Evelyn*, ed. E. S. De Beer, 6 vols. (1955); repr. (2000)
Farington, *Diary*	*The diary of Joseph Farington*, ed. K. Garlick and others, 17 vols. (1978–98)
Fasti Angl. (Hardy)	J. Le Neve, *Fasti ecclesiae Anglicanae*, ed. T. D. Hardy, 3 vols. (1854)
Fasti Angl., 1066–1300	[J. Le Neve], *Fasti ecclesiae Anglicanae, 1066–1300*, ed. D. E. Greenway and J. S. Barrow, [8 vols.] (1968–)
Fasti Angl., 1300–1541	[J. Le Neve], *Fasti ecclesiae Anglicanae, 1300–1541*, 12 vols. (1962–7)
Fasti Angl., 1541–1857	[J. Le Neve], *Fasti ecclesiae Anglicanae, 1541–1857*, ed. J. M. Horn, D. M. Smith, and D. S. Bailey, [9 vols.] (1969–)
Fasti Scot.	H. Scott, *Fasti ecclesiae Scoticanae*, 3 vols. in 6 (1871); new edn, [11 vols.] (1915–)
FO List	*Foreign Office List*
Fortescue, *Brit. army*	J. W. Fortescue, *A history of the British army*, 13 vols. (1899–1930)
Foss, *Judges*	E. Foss, *The judges of England*, 9 vols. (1848–64); repr. (1966)
Foster, *Alum. Oxon.*	J. Foster, ed., *Alumni Oxonienses: the members of the University of Oxford, 1715–1886*, 4 vols. (1887–8); later edn (1891); also *Alumni Oxonienses … 1500–1714*, 4 vols. (1891–2); 8 vol. repr. (1968) and (2000)
Fuller, *Worthies*	T. Fuller, *The history of the worthies of England*, 4 pts (1662); new edn, 2 vols., ed. J. Nichols (1811); new edn, 3 vols., ed. P. A. Nuttall (1840); repr. (1965)
GEC, *Baronetage*	G. E. Cokayne, *Complete baronetage*, 6 vols. (1900–09); repr. (1983) [microprint]
GEC, *Peerage*	G. E. C. [G. E. Cokayne], *The complete peerage of England, Scotland, Ireland, Great Britain, and the United Kingdom*, 8 vols. (1887–98); new edn, ed. V. Gibbs and others, 14 vols. in 15 (1910–98); microprint repr. (1982) and (1987)
Genest, *Eng. stage*	J. Genest, *Some account of the English stage from the Restoration in 1660 to 1830*, 10 vols. (1832); repr. [New York, 1965]
Gillow, *Lit. biog. hist.*	J. Gillow, *A literary and biographical history or bibliographical dictionary of the English Catholics, from the breach with Rome, in 1534, to the present time*, 5 vols. [1885–1902]; repr. (1961); repr. with preface by C. Gillow (1999)
Gir. Camb. opera	*Giraldi Cambrensis opera*, ed. J. S. Brewer, J. F. Dimock, and G. F. Warner, 8 vols., Rolls Series, 21 (1861–91)
GJ	*Geographical Journal*

Gladstone, *Diaries* — *The Gladstone diaries: with cabinet minutes and prime-ministerial correspondence*, ed. M. R. D. Foot and H. C. G. Matthew, 14 vols. (1968–94)

GM — *Gentleman's Magazine*

Graves, *Artists* — A. Graves, ed., *A dictionary of artists who have exhibited works in the principal London exhibitions of oil paintings from 1760 to 1880* (1884); new edn (1895); 3rd edn (1901); facs. edn (1969); repr. [1970], (1973), and (1984)

Graves, *Brit. Inst.* — A. Graves, *The British Institution, 1806–1867: a complete dictionary of contributors and their work from the foundation of the institution* (1875); facs. edn (1908); repr. (1969)

Graves, *RA exhibitors* — A. Graves, *The Royal Academy of Arts: a complete dictionary of contributors and their work from its foundation in 1769 to 1904*, 8 vols. (1905–6); repr. in 4 vols. (1970) and (1972)

Graves, *Soc. Artists* — A. Graves, *The Society of Artists of Great Britain, 1760–1791, the Free Society of Artists, 1761–1783: a complete dictionary* (1907); facs. edn (1969)

Greaves & Zaller, *BDBR* — R. L. Greaves and R. Zaller, eds., *Biographical dictionary of British radicals in the seventeenth century*, 3 vols. (1982–4)

Grove, *Dict. mus.* — G. Grove, ed., *A dictionary of music and musicians*, 5 vols. (1878–90); 2nd edn, ed. J. A. Fuller Maitland (1904–10); 3rd edn, ed. H. C. Colles (1927); 4th edn with suppl. (1940); 5th edn, ed. E. Blom, 9 vols. (1954); suppl. (1961) [see also *New Grove*]

Hall, *Dramatic ports.* — L. A. Hall, *Catalogue of dramatic portraits in the theatre collection of the Harvard College library*, 4 vols. (1930–34)

Hansard — *Hansard's parliamentary debates*, ser. 1–5 (1803–)

Highfill, Burnim & Langhans, *BDA* — P. H. Highfill, K. A. Burnim, and E. A. Langhans, *A biographical dictionary of actors, actresses, musicians, dancers, managers, and other stage personnel in London, 1660–1800*, 16 vols. (1973–93)

Hist. U. Oxf. — T. H. Aston, ed., *The history of the University of Oxford*, 8 vols. (1984–2000) [1: *The early Oxford schools*, ed. J. I. Catto (1984); 2: *Late medieval Oxford*, ed. J. I. Catto and R. Evans (1992); 3: *The collegiate university*, ed. J. McConica (1986); 4: *Seventeenth-century Oxford*, ed. N. Tyacke (1997); 5: *The eighteenth century*, ed. L. S. Sutherland and L. G. Mitchell (1986); 6–7: *Nineteenth-century Oxford*, ed. M. G. Brock and M. C. Curthoys (1997–2000); 8: *The twentieth century*, ed. B. Harrison (2000)]

HJ — *Historical Journal*

HMC — Historical Manuscripts Commission

Holdsworth, *Eng. law* — W. S. Holdsworth, *A history of English law*, ed. A. L. Goodhart and H. L. Hanbury, 17 vols. (1903–72)

HoP, *Commons* — *The history of parliament: the House of Commons* [1386–1421, ed. J. S. Roskell, L. Clark, and C. Rawcliffe, 4 vols. (1992); 1509–1558, ed. S. T. Bindoff, 3 vols. (1982); 1558–1603, ed. P. W. Hasler, 3 vols. (1981); 1660–1690, ed. B. D. Henning, 3 vols. (1983); 1690–1715, ed. D. W. Hayton, E. Cruickshanks, and S. Handley, 5 vols. (2002); 1715–1754, ed. R. Sedgwick, 2 vols. (1970); 1754–1790, ed. L. Namier and J. Brooke, 3 vols. (1964), repr. (1985); 1790–1820, ed. R. G. Thorne, 5 vols. (1986); in draft (used with permission): 1422–1504, 1604–1629, 1640–1660, and 1820–1832]

IGI — *International Genealogical Index*, Church of Jesus Christ of the Latterday Saints

ILN — *Illustrated London News*

IMC — Irish Manuscripts Commission

Irving, *Scots.* — J. Irving, ed., *The book of Scotsmen eminent for achievements in arms and arts, church and state, law, legislation and literature, commerce, science, travel and philanthropy* (1881)

JCS — *Journal of the Chemical Society*

JHC — *Journals of the House of Commons*

JHL — *Journals of the House of Lords*

John of Worcester, *Chron.* — *The chronicle of John of Worcester*, ed. R. R. Darlington and P. McGurk, trans. J. Bray and P. McGurk, 3 vols., OMT (1995–) [vol. 1 forthcoming]

Keeler, *Long Parliament* — M. F. Keeler, *The Long Parliament, 1640–1641: a biographical study of its members* (1954)

Kelly, *Handbk* — *The upper ten thousand: an alphabetical list of all members of noble families*, 3 vols. (1875–7); continued as *Kelly's handbook of the upper ten thousand for 1878* [1879], 2 vols. (1878–9); continued as *Kelly's handbook to the titled, landed and official classes*, 94 vols. (1880–1973)

LondG — *London Gazette*

LP Henry VIII — J. S. Brewer, J. Gairdner, and R. H. Brodie, eds., *Letters and papers, foreign and domestic, of the reign of Henry VIII*, 23 vols. in 38 (1862–1932); repr. (1965)

Mallalieu, *Watercolour artists* — H. L. Mallalieu, *The dictionary of British watercolour artists up to 1820*, 3 vols. (1976–90); vol. 1, 2nd edn (1986)

Memoirs FRS — *Biographical Memoirs of Fellows of the Royal Society*

MGH — Monumenta Germaniae Historica

MT — *Musical Times*

Munk, *Roll* — W. Munk, *The roll of the Royal College of Physicians of London*, 2 vols. (1861); 2nd edn, 3 vols. (1878)

N&Q — *Notes and Queries*

New Grove — S. Sadie, ed., *The new Grove dictionary of music and musicians*, 20 vols. (1980); 2nd edn, 29 vols. (2001) [also online edn; see also Grove, *Dict. mus.*]

Nichols, *Illustrations* — J. Nichols and J. B. Nichols, *Illustrations of the literary history of the eighteenth century*, 8 vols. (1817–58)

Nichols, *Lit. anecdotes* — J. Nichols, *Literary anecdotes of the eighteenth century*, 9 vols. (1812–16); facs. edn (1966)

Obits. FRS — *Obituary Notices of Fellows of the Royal Society*

O'Byrne, *Naval biog. dict.* — W. R. O'Byrne, *A naval biographical dictionary* (1849); repr. (1990); [2nd edn], 2 vols. (1861)

OHS — Oxford Historical Society

Old Westminsters — *The record of Old Westminsters*, 1–2, ed. G. F. R. Barker and A. H. Stenning (1928); suppl. 1, ed. J. B. Whitmore and G. R. Y. Radcliffe [1938]; 3, ed. J. B. Whitmore, G. R. Y. Radcliffe, and D. C. Simpson (1963); suppl. 2, ed. F. E. Pagan (1978); 4, ed. F. E. Pagan and H. E. Pagan (1992)

OMT — Oxford Medieval Texts

Ordericus Vitalis, *Eccl. hist.* — *The ecclesiastical history of Orderic Vitalis*, ed. and trans. M. Chibnall, 6 vols., OMT (1969–80); repr. (1990)

Paris, *Chron.* — *Matthaei Parisiensis, monachi sancti Albani, chronica majora*, ed. H. R. Luard, Rolls Series, 7 vols. (1872–83)

Parl. papers — *Parliamentary papers* (1801–)

PBA — *Proceedings of the British Academy*

Pepys, *Diary*	*The diary of Samuel Pepys*, ed. R. Latham and W. Matthews, 11 vols. (1970–83); repr. (1995) and (2000)
Pevsner	N. Pevsner and others, Buildings of England series
PICE	*Proceedings of the Institution of Civil Engineers*
Pipe rolls	*The great roll of the pipe for . . .*, PRSoc. (1884–)
PRO	Public Record Office
PRS	*Proceedings of the Royal Society of London*
PRSoc.	Pipe Roll Society
PTRS	*Philosophical Transactions of the Royal Society*
QR	*Quarterly Review*
RC	Record Commissions
Redgrave, *Artists*	S. Redgrave, *A dictionary of artists of the English school* (1874); rev. edn (1878); repr. (1970)
Reg. Oxf.	C. W. Boase and A. Clark, eds., *Register of the University of Oxford*, 5 vols., OHS, 1, 10–12, 14 (1885–9)
Reg. PCS	J. H. Burton and others, eds., *The register of the privy council of Scotland*, 1st ser., 14 vols. (1877–98); 2nd ser., 8 vols. (1899–1908); 3rd ser., [16 vols.] (1908–70)
Reg. RAN	H. W. C. Davis and others, eds., *Regesta regum Anglo-Normannorum, 1066–1154*, 4 vols. (1913–69)
RIBA Journal	*Journal of the Royal Institute of British Architects* [later *RIBA Journal*]
RotP	J. Strachey, ed., *Rotuli parliamentorum ut et petitiones, et placita in parliamento*, 6 vols. (1767–77)
RotS	D. Macpherson, J. Caley, and W. Illingworth, eds., *Rotuli Scotiae in Turri Londinensi et in domo capitulari Westmonasteriensi asservati*, 2 vols., RC, 14 (1814–19)
RS	Record(s) Society
Rymer, *Foedera*	T. Rymer and R. Sanderson, eds., *Foedera, conventiones, literae et cuiuscunque generis acta publica inter reges Angliae et alios quosvis imperatores, reges, pontifices, principes, vel communitates*, 20 vols. (1704–35); 2nd edn, 20 vols. (1726–35); 3rd edn, 10 vols. (1739–45); facs. edn (1967); new edn, ed. A. Clarke, J. Caley, and F. Holbrooke, 4 vols., RC, 50 (1816–30)
Sainty, *Judges*	J. Sainty, ed., *The judges of England, 1272–1990*, SeldS, suppl. ser., 10 (1993)
Sainty, *King's counsel*	J. Sainty, ed., *A list of English law officers and king's counsel*, SeldS, suppl. ser., 7 (1987)
SCH	Studies in Church History
Scots peerage	J. B. Paul, ed. *The Scots peerage, founded on Wood's edition of Sir Robert Douglas's Peerage of Scotland, containing an historical and genealogical account of the nobility of that kingdom*, 9 vols. (1904–14)
SeldS	Selden Society
SHR	*Scottish Historical Review*
State trials	T. B. Howell and T. J. Howell, eds., *Cobbett's Complete collection of state trials*, 34 vols. (1809–28)
STC, 1475–1640	A. W. Pollard, G. R. Redgrave, and others, eds., *A short-title catalogue of . . . English books . . . 1475–1640* (1926); 2nd edn, ed. W. A. Jackson, F. S. Ferguson, and K. F. Pantzer, 3 vols. (1976–91) [see also Wing, *STC*]
STS	Scottish Text Society
SurtS	Surtees Society
Symeon of Durham, *Opera*	*Symeonis monachi opera omnia*, ed. T. Arnold, 2 vols., Rolls Series, 75 (1882–5); repr. (1965)
Tanner, *Bibl. Brit.-Hib.*	T. Tanner, *Bibliotheca Britannico-Hibernica*, ed. D. Wilkins (1748); repr. (1963)
Thieme & Becker, *Allgemeines Lexikon*	U. Thieme, F. Becker, and H. Vollmer, eds., *Allgemeines Lexikon der bildenden Künstler von der Antike bis zur Gegenwart*, 37 vols. (Leipzig, 1907–50); repr. (1961–5), (1983), and (1992)
Thurloe, *State papers*	*A collection of the state papers of John Thurloe*, ed. T. Birch, 7 vols. (1742)
TLS	*Times Literary Supplement*
Tout, *Admin. hist.*	T. F. Tout, *Chapters in the administrative history of mediaeval England: the wardrobe, the chamber, and the small seals*, 6 vols. (1920–33); repr. (1967)
TRHS	*Transactions of the Royal Historical Society*
VCH	H. A. Doubleday and others, eds., *The Victoria history of the counties of England*, [88 vols.] (1900–)
Venn, *Alum. Cant.*	J. Venn and J. A. Venn, *Alumni Cantabrigienses: a biographical list of all known students, graduates, and holders of office at the University of Cambridge, from the earliest times to 1900*, 10 vols. (1922–54); repr. in 2 vols. (1974–8)
Vertue, *Note books*	[G. Vertue], *Note books*, ed. K. Esdaile, earl of Ilchester, and H. M. Hake, 6 vols., Walpole Society, 18, 20, 22, 24, 26, 30 (1930–55)
VF	*Vanity Fair*
Walford, *County families*	E. Walford, *The county families of the United Kingdom, or, Royal manual of the titled and untitled aristocracy of Great Britain and Ireland* (1860)
Walker rev.	A. G. Matthews, *Walker revised: being a revision of John Walker's Sufferings of the clergy during the grand rebellion, 1642–60* (1948); repr. (1988)
Walpole, *Corr.*	*The Yale edition of Horace Walpole's correspondence*, ed. W. S. Lewis, 48 vols. (1937–83)
Ward, *Men of the reign*	T. H. Ward, ed., *Men of the reign: a biographical dictionary of eminent persons of British and colonial birth who have died during the reign of Queen Victoria* (1885); repr. (Graz, 1968)
Waterhouse, *18c painters*	E. Waterhouse, *The dictionary of 18th century painters in oils and crayons* (1981); repr. as *British 18th century painters in oils and crayons* (1991), vol. 2 of *Dictionary of British art*
Watt, *Bibl. Brit.*	R. Watt, *Bibliotheca Britannica, or, A general index to British and foreign literature*, 4 vols. (1824) [many reprs.]
Wellesley index	W. E. Houghton, ed., *The Wellesley index to Victorian periodicals, 1824–1900*, 5 vols. (1966–89); new edn (1999) [CD-ROM]
Wing, *STC*	D. Wing, ed., *Short-title catalogue of . . . English books . . . 1641–1700*, 3 vols. (1945–51); 2nd edn (1972–88); rev. and enl. edn, ed. J. J. Morrison, C. W. Nelson, and M. Seccombe, 4 vols. (1994–8) [see also *STC, 1475–1640*]
Wisden	*John Wisden's Cricketer's Almanack*
Wood, *Ath. Oxon.*	A. Wood, *Athenae Oxonienses . . . to which are added the Fasti*, 2 vols. (1691–2); 2nd edn (1721); new edn, 4 vols., ed. P. Bliss (1813–20); repr. (1967) and (1969)
Wood, *Vic. painters*	C. Wood, *Dictionary of Victorian painters* (1971); 2nd edn (1978); 3rd edn as *Victorian painters*, 2 vols. (1995), vol. 4 of *Dictionary of British art*
WW	*Who's who* (1849–)
WWBMP	M. Stenton and S. Lees, eds., *Who's who of British members of parliament*, 4 vols. (1976–81)
WWW	*Who was who* (1929–)

Randolph, Bernard (*bap.* **1643**, *d.* after **1689**?). *See under* Randolph, Edward (*bap.* 1632, *d.* 1703).

Randolph [*formerly* Randall]**, Charles** (1809–1878), marine engineer and shipbuilder, was born on 26 June 1809 in Stirling, the son of Charles Randall, bookseller, printer, and stationer, and his wife, Mary, *née* Steadman. He was educated at Stirling high school, Glasgow high school, the University of Glasgow, and at Anderson's Institution in Glasgow where he attended lectures by the chemist Dr Andrew Ure, brother of Isabella Ure, the wife of John Elder [*see below*]. He was then apprenticed as a wright (engineer) in William Kinross's coachworks in Stirling, subsequently transferring to Robert Napier's works at Camlachie where he was trained by David Elder [*see below*].

David Elder (1784–1866), born at Little Seggie, Kinross-shire, had been apprenticed in the works of his father, Charles Elder, whose family had been wrights in Fife for generations. Like others of his contemporaries he had supplemented his training with much private study, particularly in hydraulics and hydrodynamics. He left the family business at the turn of the century to gain experience in the construction industry, particularly in building and fitting out large cotton mills in the Glasgow area. In the late 1810s he supervised the commissioning of Mile End factory for J. Clark & Co. of Paisley and James Dunlop's Broomward mill. In 1821 he went to work for Robert Napier. The following year he helped Napier build his first marine engine and went on to make many improvements in the design of the engines built by the firm. He also developed special machine tools for turning and boring the large cylinders and other components, training cartwrights and joiners in their use. The reputation of Napier's engines for reliability in service owed much to Elder's skill in design and production.

During his apprenticeship Charles Randall changed his name back to the original Randolph, which the family had not used since his grandfather's participation in the Jacobite rising of 1745. On becoming a journeyman he worked in two Manchester firms: Omerods, and Fairbairn and Lillie. He returned to Glasgow in 1834 to open a millwright's business in Centre Street in partnership with his cousin Richard Cunliffe, a yarn merchant with contacts in the local textile trades. The new firm soon won fame for the accuracy of its gear-cutting and machining. In 1839 John Elliot (*d.* 1842), a manager with Fairbairn and Lillie, joined the partnership, which then traded as Randolph, Elliot & Co., and extended its activities to England, Ireland, and mainland Europe.

John Elder (1824–1869) was born at Glasgow on 8 March 1824, the third son of David Elder, who was then manager of Robert Napier's Lancefield and Vulcan engine works. He was educated at Glasgow high school and subsequently attended classes at the University of Glasgow under Lewis Gordon, newly appointed professor of civil engineering. Elder was a premium apprentice for five years at Robert Napier & Sons in Glasgow, where he was trained by his father. He showed an extraordinary talent as a marine engineer and man of business. He then worked for a year as a pattern maker at Messrs Hick of Bolton-le-Moors, Lancashire, before being appointed draughtsman to Great Grimsby docks. He returned to Glasgow to become Napier's drawing-office manager and chief draughtsman in 1848. While there he assisted his father in the design and construction of six vessels for the Cunard Company. Later the firm became involved in a dispute with the Pacific Steam Navigation Company over a contract for four paddle-steamers, which needed to be modified to meet the specification. When Napier incurred penalties for late delivery, John Elder reputedly decided to leave and accept a partnership with Randolph, Elliot & Co., which was rechristened Randolph, Elder & Co. His real motive in moving was probably because he realized that there was little prospect of his gaining a partnership in Napier's firm when James R. Napier, Robert Napier's son and himself a brilliant engineer, was managing the shipyard. David Elder continued to work for Napier until his death at the age of eighty-two in Glasgow on 31 January 1866. A deeply religious man, he was a member of the Scottish Episcopal church and was well known for his interest in theology. He was a keen musician, and he not only played organs but also built them.

Randolph, Elder & Co. diversified at once into the fast-expanding marine engineering business and with the help of W. J. Macquorn Rankine, then professor of civil engineering at the University of Glasgow, began experimenting with a two-cylinder compound engine following the example of other marine engineers. John Elder had for some time been concerned to improve the efficiency of marine engines by reducing friction of the moving parts, which would increase the power and cut coal consumption. Where others had failed Elder succeeded, because, according to Macquorn Rankine, he 'had thoroughly studied and understood the principles of the then almost new science of thermodynamics' (Macquorn Rankine, 29–30). The partners took out their first patent for a compound engine in 1853. The pistons of the high- and low-pressure cylinders were diametrically opposed so as to balance and largely neutralize strain and friction on the bearings, an aspect of engineering previously neglected. The new engines installed in the *Brandon* for the London and Limerick Steamship Company in 1854 reduced coal consumption per indicated hp from 4½ lb to 3½ lb. By experimenting with James Watt's proposal for steam-jacketing cylinders they were able to further reduce coal consumption to between 2 lb and 2½ lb.

Despite suspicion of the high piston speeds which these engines achieved, success was almost immediate and orders flowed in to the firm, notably from the Pacific Steam Navigation Company. John Elder described these developments in a series of scientific papers read at meetings of the British Association for the Advancement of Science between 1858 and 1860. In 1858 the partners began iron shipbuilding at a yard in Govan. Early in 1859 their engine works was burnt down and an imposing new shop with an Egyptian façade was constructed, capable of handling the massive cylinders for their engines. At the height of this success Elder, who was a man of striking good looks, was married on 28 March 1857 by his close friend the Revd Norman Macleod to Isabella Ure (1830–1905) [*see* Elder, Isabella], who later helped pioneer the higher education of women in the west of Scotland.

Randolph Elder continued to develop its engines, experimenting in the 1860s with both triple and quadruple expansion and water-tube boilers. To the frustration of their competitors they either together or separately patented all their innovations. In 1863 they built their first high-speed naval compound engine, which when demonstrated in HMS *Constance* totally outperformed competitors with conventional engines. During the American Civil War the firm constructed in five months in 1864 five blockade runners fitted with these engines. This must have strained relations with Macleod, a fervent supporter of anti-slavery. During that year Randolph Elder moved to a new, large shipyard at Fairfield, further down the River Clyde in Govan, which was considered to be about as complete and convenient a shipbuilding establishment as any in the world. By now the firm was undoubtedly the most successful shipbuilding and marine engineering business on the Clyde, employing some 4000 people, and the three partners were very rich men. Randolph and Richard Cunliffe withdrew from the partnership in 1868 but remained as investors. In the previous fifteen years the firm had supplied 111 sets of marine engines with an aggregate 20,145 indicated hp and had built 106 ships. John Elder continued as sole partner and began building a new engine works, which farsightedly included a boiler shop, separate from and to the west of the engine works, as well as a floating dock and repair slip. In his first year in business Elder constructed fourteen steamships and three sailing-ships of a total of over 25,000 tons, nearly double the production of any other Clyde yard. He attributed this achievement to a willingness to innovate continuously. During the late 1860s he devoted a great deal of time to experiments with the use for naval monitors of round hulls propelled by water-jets that could be used safely in shallow water.

Like his father, Elder was a deeply committed Christian and keenly interested in schemes to foster the social, intellectual, and religious welfare of his workforce. He organized and contributed to an accident and sick fund and in 1869 was planning to build new model houses and schools near the works. He was prevented from realizing this scheme by a serious liver complaint, which led to his death in London at the early age of forty-five on 17 September 1869. His funeral, according to Norman Macleod, who conducted the service,

> was one of the most impressive sights I ever witnessed. The busy works south of the Clyde were shut, forge and hammer at rest, and silent as the grave. The forest of masts along the river were draped in flags, lowered half mast in sign of mourning.

Of the man, he recalled:

> His religion was a life, not confined to the church or to Sunday, but carried out every day in the family, in the counting house, in society, and in business, manifested in untarnished honour, in the sweetest temper, in gentle words and most remarkable and most unselfish considerations for the feelings and the wants of others.   (Craig, 36–7)

He had only recently been elected president of the Institution of Engineers and Shipbuilders of Glasgow. With Macquorn Rankine, he served as an officer in the 1st (Lanarkshire) rifle volunteers. As he had no heir, his wife inherited his large estate.

On his retirement in 1868 Charles Randolph turned his attention to the improvement of the River Clyde, and he presented a long and unsolicited report on its development to the Clyde Navigation trustees in the same year. With a barrage of statistics he forecast with some accuracy that the trust's existing plans would be unable to cope with demand over the next fifty years. As a trustee he played an important part in its affairs over the next decade, particularly in the construction of Queen's Dock at Stobcross on the north bank of the river. He was also concerned to improve Glasgow's sewage disposal, helping to found the Glasgow Sanitary Association and supporting the construction of outfall sewers. Parsimony and competing priorities delayed action until after his death.

Randolph remained active in business, and in 1868 he helped establish the British and African Steam Navigation Company in partnership with Glasgow and Liverpool investors, including James Buchanan Mirrlees, Thomas Coats, and S. R. Wilson; he served as its first chairman. He was a director of the Glasgow-based Tharsis Sulphur and Copper Company, the Glasgow and South Western Railway Company, the Lochgelly Coal Company in Fife, the Bent Colliery Company at Hamilton, the Scottish Commercial Insurance Company, Nobel's Explosives Ltd, and the British Dynamite Company, the last of which he was also chairman. He never lost his appetite for invention, and in his later years he built a steam carriage that, unlike most others, was successful. He was an active member of the Philosophical Society of Glasgow and was much interested in education. He married Margaretta Sainte Pierre; the marriage was childless but they adopted a daughter, Agnes, who at the time of her father's death was married to Andrew Rintoul, a Glasgow merchant. Randolph died at his home, 14 Park Terrace, Glasgow, on 11 November 1878 and was buried in the old Holyrood churchyard, Stirling. He left £60,000, almost half of his estate, to the University of Glasgow to complete the Common, or Bute, Hall; the antechamber and the grand south staircase were named in his honour. In recognition of his munificence the university commissioned a portrait by the artist Duncan Macnee. There is no doubt that John Elder and Charles Randolph, by pioneering the compound engine, ensured the Clyde's continuing technical domination of the world shipbuilding industry in the second half of the nineteenth century. They were atypical in that, unlike many leading-edge firms in Britain at the time, they took great care to protect all their inventions and innovations by patent, which frustrated other shipbuilders throughout the world who had themselves been trying to design similar two-cylinder engines. In their lives they reflected the liberal Christian ideas of Norman Macleod and John Caird that dominated Glasgow society at the time.

MICHAEL S. MOSS

Sources A. Slaven, 'Randolph, Charles', *DSBB* · P. N. Davies, 'Elder, Alexander', *DSBB* · *Glasgow Herald* (12 Nov 1878) · *Stirling Journal* (17 Nov 1878) · *Proceedings of the Philosophical Society of Glasgow*, 11 (1877–9), 521–2 · J. MacLehose, ed., *Memoirs and portraits of one hundred Glasgow men who have died during the last thirty years*, 2 vols. (1886) · J. McAlpine, 'Biography of Isabella Elder', U. Glas., archives, Ure Elder MSS, DC 122 · W. J. Macquorn Rankine, *A memoir of John Elder, engineer and shipbuilder* (1883) · P. N. Davies, *The trade makers: Elder Dempster in West Africa, 1852–1972* (1973) · A. Craig, *The Elder Park, Govan* (1891) · J. R. Napier, 'Memoir of the late David Elder, engineer', *Transactions of the Institution of Engineers and Shipbuilders in Scotland*, 9 (1865–6), 92–105 · *The 'building of the ship': being an historical and descriptive narrative of the works of the Fairfield Shipbuilding & Engineering Co. Ltd* (privately printed, London, 1891) · *Historical and descriptive account of the works of the Fairfield Shipbuilding and Engineering Company (Limited)* [1898] · J. F. Riddell, *Clyde navigation: a history of development and deepening of the River Clyde* (1979) · D. D. Napier, *David Napier, engineer, 1790–1869: an autobiographical sketch with notes*, ed. D. Bell (1912) · d. cert. · *CGPLA Eng. & Wales* (1879) · *DNB*
Archives Mitchell L., Glas., Strathclyde Regional Archives, records of Fairfield Shipbuilding and Engineering Co. previously John Elder & Co. and Randolph Elder & Co., UCS2 · U. Glas., Archives and Business Record Centre
Likenesses D. Macnee, portrait, U. Glas.
Wealth at death £114,305 16s. 5d.: confirmation, 29 Jan 1879, *CCI* · £12,955 5s. 3d.: eik additional estate, 30 June 1879, *CCI* · £188,028 15s. 1d.—John Elder: confirmation, 29 Oct 1869, *CCI* · £9817 3s. 6d.—David Elder: confirmation, 14 March 1866, *CCI*

Randolph, Edmund (1753–1813), revolutionary army officer and politician in the United States of America, was born on 10 August 1753 in Williamsburg, Virginia, the son of John Randolph (d. 1784), lawyer, and Arianna Vanderheyden Jennings (d. 1782). By all odds Edmund should have achieved an important place in American history. Since the 1680s, when his great-grandfather had emigrated from England, his forebears had played a prominent part in Virginia's affairs. His grandfather Sir John *Randolph, the only native Virginian ever knighted, his father, John, and his uncle, Peyton Randolph, had all been king's attorneys and members of the Virginia house of burgesses. Peyton was also speaker of the house in the 1770s. After leaving the College of William and Mary in 1771, Randolph followed family tradition by reading law in his father's office in Williamsburg and being admitted to the bar in 1774. On 29 August 1776 he married Elizabeth (1753–1810), daughter of Robert Carter *Nicholas, the first Virginia state treasurer. They had five children.

Not only was Randolph born into the charmed circle, but he came to manhood during the American War of Independence, a time when reputations could be made on a Virginian and a national stage. Even his father's loyalism and exile did not prevent him from assuming a high place in the inner circle of the American patriot leadership. Peyton Randolph adopted Edmund as his heir and George Washington appointed him as an aide-de-camp in 1775. But he had served only a few months when his uncle's death forced him to return to Virginia. During the next several years Randolph was elected mayor of Williamsburg, was chosen as a delegate to the May Virginia convention where he was assigned to the committee that drafted the declaration of rights and the state constitution, and was selected to be the state's first attorney-general, a post he held for ten years (1776–86). Randolph also served two terms (1779, 1781) in the continental congress.

In 1786 the 33-year-old Randolph was elected governor of Virginia. As the governor of the most populous state he was in a position to shape events. A leading advocate of a new national constitution, he was instrumental in persuading Washington to attend the constitutional convention in 1787. It was Governor Randolph who opened the proceedings with a lengthy speech denouncing the defects of the articles of confederation, the temporary document that bound the states together, and the existing state constitutions. Yet, despite his early advocacy, Randolph refused to sign the completed document because he thought it insufficiently republican. By the time the battle for ratification began in Virginia, Randolph had reversed his position once again. Responding to charges of inconsistency, he insisted that his objections were as strong on 4 June 1788 as they had been in September 1787. But he had come to believe that if Virginia did not accept the constitution, the union would be disrupted, perhaps dismembered. 'The accession of eight states', he declared to the convention, has 'reduced our deliberations to the single question of Union or no Union' (Elliot, 652).

With the formation of the new federal government, Randolph was appointed the nation's attorney-general. Then, when Thomas Jefferson resigned as secretary of state, Washington appointed Randolph to the post in 1794. Randolph's most serious problem as attorney-general and secretary of state was the growing conflict between Alexander Hamilton and Jefferson within the cabinet. Holding tenaciously to the tradition that a public man should take a stand on specific issues, but never tie himself permanently to any faction, proved extremely difficult. Caught in a crossfire between warring elements in Washington's cabinet, his friend Jefferson felt that Randolph should always support him, and on most issues he did. However, he did not hesitate to differ whenever the occasion seemed to justify it. In frustration Jefferson characterized Randolph as 'the poorest chameleon I ever saw, having no colour of his own, and reflecting that nearest him' (Bemis, 100).

The problem was that Randolph was hardly the 'chameleon' Jefferson imagined him to be. With the rest of the cabinet aligned with Hamilton, and with Randolph determined to play the non-partisan, disaster was assured. He had advised the president against acceptance of the controversial Jay treaty (1794), which attempted to ease post-war British–American tensions, while the rest of the cabinet urged acceptance. Naturally both the Hamilton faction and the British government were anxious to discredit Randolph. In July 1795 a British man-of-war intercepted a letter written by the French minister Joseph Fauchet to his government, a rambling account in which he seemed to imply that Randolph had made improper revelations to him and had indicated that French money would be welcome. The British minister George Hammond delivered it in July 1795 to the secretary of the treasury, Oliver Wolcott. When Randolph was called in and questioned by Washington and the cabinet under humiliating circumstances, he angrily resigned. There can be little doubt that Randolph was innocent of any wrongdoing, but there was no one willing to defend him. It was James Madison who most accurately summarized Randolph's political obituary: 'His greatest enemies will not easily persuade themselves that he was under a corrupt influence of France, and his best friends can't save him from the self-condemnation of his political career' (Brant, 197).

With his resignation from office, Randolph returned to Virginia and re-established his law practice. He concentrated primarily on cases in the Virginia court of appeals, although he also helped to represent Aaron Burr in Burr's 1807 treason trial. Much of his free time Randolph spent on writing his *History of Virginia*. Although not published in its entirety until 1970, the work was read by many in manuscript. Although not represented as autobiographical, his story of the Virginia past and present was a personal tale. The story of the Randolph family, as he told it, was the story of Virginia in microcosm as the story of Edmund Randolph was that of revolutionary Virginia. As he outlined it, his ideal system of 'responsible' politics depended upon conditions peculiar to Virginia, a set of social circumstances 'favorable to the propagating' of a 'spirit of freedom'. That 'spirit' was enhanced by an extensive social intercourse. According to Randolph, there was in Virginia an easy intimacy between governors and governed. Social rank was fluid. Frequent elections 'afforded opportunities or unreserved interchange of ideas between candidates and electors and among electors themselves'.

Randolph drew, then, from Virginia's past and his personal experience a metaphor for contemporary Virginia. He had gone from an honoured career in Virginia to a disastrous failure at the national level. Virginia's excellence—its remarkable political system, within which he and his family had been such successful practitioners—depended on a social geography and an intimacy that, according to Randolph, was being undermined by national politics. From his perspective the Virginians' tenure on the federal stage represented a systematic if unwitting abandonment of their ideals in practice but not in principle. The characteristics of Virginia's ruling gentry that he celebrated in his history were the very characteristics that were being compromised at the federal level. Increasingly the Virginians' concern for a viable federal republic cut them off from their roots in the local community. The demands of professional political organization also made untenable their commitment to amateur politics. The addition of new political processes served to elevate the 'representative' style of politics over the 'responsible' style. Ultimately, the very qualities of statesmanship which had hitherto been the prerequisites for office in Virginia became a disqualification at the federal

level. Randolph died on 12 September 1813 in Millwood, Virginia, and was buried there in the Old Chapel graveyard.   ARTHUR H. SHAFFER

Sources E. Randolph, *History of Virginia*, ed. A. H. Schaffer (1970) • J. J. Reardon, *Edmund Randolph: a biography* (1974) • I. Brant, 'Edmund Randolph, not guilty!', *William and Mary Quarterly*, 7 (1950), 179–98 • S. Elkins and E. McKitrick, *The age of federalism* (1993), 424–31 • J. G. Clifford, 'A muddy middle of the road: the politics of Edmund Randolph, 1790–1795', *Virginia Magazine of History and Biography*, 80 (1972), 286–311 • M. K. Bunsteel Tachan, 'George Washington and the reputation of Randolph', *Journal of American History*, 73 (1986), 15–34 • J. Elliot, ed., *Debates in the several state conventions on the adoption of the federal constitution* (Philadelphia, 1861), vol. 3 • S. F. Bemis, ed., *The American secretaries of state and their diplomacy*, 2 (1927)
Archives L. Cong., Jefferson papers • L. Cong., Madison papers • L. Cong., Washington papers
Likenesses C. Brumidi, portrait, L. Cong. • F. J. Fisher, portrait (after original portrait, now lost), State Capitol, Richmond, Virginia

Randolph, Edward (*d.* 1566), soldier and military administrator, was one of at least three sons and two daughters of Avery Randolph (*d.* 1561), landowner, of Badlesmere, Kent, and his wife, Anne (*d.* in or after 1561), daughter of Sir John Gaynsford of Crowhurst, Surrey, and his wife, Katherine. Thomas *Randolph (1525/6–1590), a diplomat, was one of his brothers. His wife was Sybil Croft, sister of Sir James *Croft. Born in Kent, he was one of Sir Thomas Wyatt's 'alise neighbours companions in the same profession of armes' (Loades, 50), and possibly one of his proposed militia in 1549. Not surprisingly, Randolph was involved in Wyatt's rebellion of November 1553 to February 1554, when, like many others, he escaped punishment by fleeing abroad. Two months later he was in Paris with his brother Thomas, distancing himself from the rebels there and seeking pardon from Mary's government. That was promised on condition that he remained in France and sent useful information home. Consequently, Randolph estimated rebel numbers abroad—his figure, real or imagined, was 150—spied on the French army, and acted as intermediary for Sir Peter Carew. His official pardon came in October, and in the following April (1555) he received an annual pension of 200 crowns from Philip II with the designation of colonel of infantry. It was a rare distinction, recognizing his military talent perhaps, but certainly intended to bind him to the Marian regime. A show of outward conformity masked Randolph's continuing opposition; he met with other sympathizers at Arundel's tavern and kept in touch with the French ambassador. He was 'vehemently suspected', with his brother-in-law ('Croft and he all one'), of complicity in the Dudley conspiracy of March 1556 (*CSP dom., 1553–8*, 325–6).

Hence Randolph was one of the 'young heads' (Loades, 245), allied by marriage and limited prospects, who opposed Mary's government both openly and surreptitiously. His credentials thus established, like 'other gentlemen that be soldiers' (Loades, 207–8), his talents were put to good use by the Elizabethan regime. Her accession brought the rewards of military recognition and office: Randolph became a valued field commander and lieutenant of the office of ordnance. In November 1559 he was sent to Scotland with 300 men to counter the French threat and £3000 'to comfort the Protestants' (*CSP for., 1559–60*, 262). He won golden opinions at Leith: 'He is wise, painful, skilful and no pillar or robber', wrote Cecil to Norfolk (*CSP for., 1560–61*, 242(4)).

In 1563 Randolph was appointed high marshal of the garrison at Le Havre, under Ambrose Dudley, earl of Warwick, and between June and July subscribed to a series of letters, describing the inadequacies of the fortifications, the equipment, the victuals, and the pay, then, finally, the enemy trenches closing to arquebus range, the windmills lost, the ovens broken, and the bakers dead of the plague. Randolph, 'of whom they have great want' (*CSP for., 1563*, 1042(3)), was seriously ill by 18 July, and the constable of France gave permission for an English messenger to see him.

After the fall of the garrison and his own repatriation, Randolph was appointed lieutenant of the ordnance, once again second in command to Warwick. (His predecessor, William Bromefield, had succumbed to wounds suffered at Le Havre.) At the Minories, Randolph carried out routine commissariat work and sat on boards of commission to inspect accounts, including those of Le Havre, Berwick, Admiral William Winter, and Lieutenant Bromefield. In July 1566 he headed an expeditionary force to Ireland. As the leaseholder of an estate in Queen's county, he may have had a particular interest. Shane O'Neill's attack on the Derry garrison in November was defeated with heavy losses, but Randolph was one of the few English casualties. After his death, which may have occurred on 12 November, his account books were put in safe custody, and his debts to the ordnance office were listed. A year later his widow had her annuity confirmed—an appropriate recompense from a government now firmly established.   ROGER ASHLEY

Sources *CSP for., 1553–68* • *CSP Ire., 1509–73, 74–85* • *CPR, 1554–69* • *CSP dom., 1553–8* • *Calendar of the manuscripts of the most hon. the marquis of Salisbury*, 1–2, HMC, 9 (1883–8) • D. M. Loades, *Two Tudor conspiracies* (1965) • R. Bagwell, *Ireland under the Tudors*, 2 (1885) • S. G. Ellis, *Tudor Ireland: crown, community, and the conflict of cultures, 1470–1603* (1985) • N. P. Canny, *The Elizabethan conquest of Ireland: a pattern established, 1565–76* (1976) • PRO, PROB 11/49, sig. 2 • *The autobiography of Thomas Whythorne*, ed. J. M. Osborn (1961); another edn (1962), 101 n. 3, 120–23, 122n., 123n.

Randolph, Edward (*bap.* 1632, *d.* 1703), colonial administrator in America, was born in Canterbury, and baptized on 9 July 1632, the son of Dr Edmund Randolph (1600–1649), physician and a graduate of the University of Padua and University College, Oxford, and his wife, Deborah (*d.* 1666?), daughter of Giles Master. The family owned lands around Biddenden, south-west of Canterbury. Randolph was admitted to Gray's Inn in 1650 and to Queens' College, Cambridge, in 1651, but is not recorded as having graduated or been called to the bar. By 1660 he had married Jane (1640–1679), the daughter of Thomas Gibbon of West Cliffe, Kent, and his wife, Alice Taylor, with whom he had

four daughters. The marriage connected him with the family of Robert Tufton Mason, claimant to the proprietorship of New Hampshire, opening the way to government employment and his subsequent career in North America.

For several years Randolph served as muster master for the Cinque Ports and supplied timber for the Royal Navy. By the 1670s, however, he was in dire financial straits, and in the spring of 1676 Mason procured his appointment to carry a royal letter to the Massachusetts government requiring a response to Mason's claims, at which time he was also to gather information on New England's condition and its people's loyalty to the crown. He reached Boston in June, and returned to London in September, submitting several lengthy papers charging the Massachusetts government with abuse of its charter powers, tolerance of illegal trade, and tyranny over both its own citizens and its New England neighbours. Later he proposed plans for royal intervention. The detailed, if strongly partisan, information he provided and the forensic skills he displayed in its presentation were essential to the legal processes that culminated in the crown's 1684 annulment of the Massachusetts charter of government.

Randolph now began a long career as royal office holder in America. In June 1678 he was commissioned collector of customs in New England, a post that, following his return to Boston in December 1679, gave him abundant opportunity to experience and report back further instances of the colonists' disdain for royal authority. He served as councillor and attorney-general in the royal government set up in New Hampshire in 1679. In 1681 he married Grace Grenville, who died in December the following year. He married, third, in 1684, Sarah Platt, *née* Backhouse (*b. c.*1650), who predeceased him and with whom he had a fifth daughter. In alliance with a small group of colonists he identified as willing to collaborate with the crown, he played a major role in planning the new form of government, the dominion of New England, which was created in 1685 to replace the puritan regime in Massachusetts and also included the other New England colonies and later New York. Within the dominion Randolph accumulated the further offices of councillor, secretary and register, deputy postmaster, surveyor of woods, and deputy to William Blathwayt, auditor-general for the American colonies.

Randolph worked busily to advance his own fortunes in tandem with royal authority. But his sweeping plans to regulate trade, reissue land titles, and further the cause of the Church of England in America were intensely unpopular. He found himself increasingly excluded from power by his fellow royalists, especially after the dominion passed in 1686 under the rule of a new and autocratic royal governor, Sir Edmund Andros. As news of the revolution of 1688 reached Boston, popular discontent exploded into revolt. On 18 April 1689 Randolph and other members of the dominion government were seized and imprisoned before being sent back to England in February 1690. There they were exonerated from charges of misgovernment after a hearing before the committee of trade and plantations, and Randolph was given new employment in October 1691 as surveyor-general of customs throughout the American colonies.

Randolph landed in Virginia in April 1692 and began a three-year inspection of almost every eastern port between Maine and North Carolina. Throughout he uncovered evidence of inadequate record-keeping and official connivance with illegal trade, touching off several sharp conflicts with local authorities. When summarized in a formal report to the customs commissioners on his return to England in September 1695, his information led directly to the 1696 enactment, largely drafted by Randolph and sustained by his testimony before parliament, that significantly tightened regulation of colonial trade. From December 1697 until the summer of 1700 he was again in America, supervising enforcement of the new regulations and sniffing out local malfeasance. In Bermuda, in consequence, he spent nine months in prison before securing his release and the governor's dismissal. He repeatedly proposed the consolidation of the American colonies under direct royal authority, a plan adopted by the Board of Trade in a bill placed before parliament in 1701 but never enacted. In the autumn of 1702 he travelled once more to America—his seventeenth transatlantic voyage. He died in Virginia in April 1703 and was buried in Accomack county, Virginia.

Randolph typified a new species of emigrant to America in these years, of men who identified their own advancement with that of royal authority, farming the colonists rather than the land. But he was exceptional in his tireless zeal and grasp of larger issues of policy, his refusal to compromise with friend and foe alike, and the rigour and accuracy of his countless letters and reports. Though generously salaried by the crown and given many opportunities for personal profit, he did not die a wealthy man. His legacy was rather the tightening of imperial control and an enduring suspicion among the colonists of the men and methods deemed necessary to secure it.

Bernard Randolph (*bap.* 1643, *d.* after 1689?), writer, the son of Edmund Randolph and Deborah Master and Edward Randolph's younger brother, was born in Canterbury and baptized in October 1643. By 1664 he was living in Smyrna and he traded extensively through the Aegean region of the Ottoman empire until after 1680. Between 1683 and 1684 he travelled three times to Massachusetts to assist his elder brother Edward as deputy collector of customs. Back in England he published in 1686 *The Present State of the Morea*, a brief account of the port cities of the Peloponnese. A year later followed a longer, more anecdotal work, *The Present State of the Islands in the Archipelago*, in which Randolph interwove his own travels with descriptions of trading conditions and the conflict between Ottoman and Venetian rule in the lands around the Aegean. He died probably after 1689.

RICHARD R. JOHNSON

Sources *Edward Randolph: including his letters and official papers*, ed. R. N. Toppan and A. T. Goodrick, 7 vols. (1898–1909) • M. G. Hall, *Edward Randolph and the American colonies, 1676–1703* (1960) • *CSP col.*, vols. 7, 9–21 • B. Randolph, *The present state of the islands in the archipelago* (1687) • C. W. Tuttle, *Capt. Francis Champernowne, the Dutch conquest of Acadia, and other historical papers*, ed. A. H. Hoyt (1889) • *DNB* • B. Randolph, *The present state of the Morea, called anciently Peloponnesus* (1686); 2nd edn (1686); 3rd edn (1689) • B. Randolph, *The present state of the Morea, called anciently Peloponnesus* (1686); 2nd edn (1686); 3rd edn (1689) • R. R. Johnson, *Adjustment to empire: the New England colonies, 1675–1715* (1981) • I. K. Steele, *Politics of colonial policy: the board of trade in colonial administration, 1696–1720* (1968) • T. C. Barrow, *Trade and empire: the British customs service in colonial America, 1660–1715* (1967) • V. F. Barnes, *The dominion of New England: a study in British colonial policy* (1923)

Archives American Antiquarian Society, Worcester, Massachusetts, report on New England to privy council [contemporary copy] • HLRO, papers on colonial matters | Colonial Williamsburg Foundation, Virginia, Blathwayt papers • Hunt. L., letters to William Blathwayt • PRO, Colonial Office papers, classes 1, 5

Wealth at death seemingly small: will, Toppan and Goodrick, eds., *Edward Randolph*, vol. 5, pp. 288–90

Randolph, Francis (1752–1831), Church of England clergyman, was born at Bristol on 29 December 1752, the son of George Randolph, a Bristol doctor. He was king's scholar at Eton College in 1771 and was admitted at King's College, Cambridge, in 1772. He graduated BA (1777) and MA (1780) and was a fellow of the college from 1775 to 1787. He was made DD at Lambeth in 1795 and at Dublin in 1806. Having taken holy orders he held an impressive range of clerical posts. He was appointed vicar of Broad Chalke, Wiltshire, in 1786 and rector of Chenies, Buckinghamshire, in 1788; he was also rector of Aston until 1804, when he obtained the rectory of Watton, Hertfordshire. In addition to these posts he was English teacher to the duchess of York at the court in Bavaria and chaplain to the duke of York; he was prebendary of Bristol from 24 December 1791. Among his patrons was Francis Russell, fifth duke of Bedford, who in 1817 presented him to the living of St Paul's, Covent Garden; in the same year he was appointed vicar of Banwell, Somerset. He was a proprietor of Laura Chapel, Bathwick, Bath, which had sittings for one thousand people and opened in 1796.

In 1788 Randolph published a letter to William Pitt on the slave trade, in which he advocated partial and progressive emancipation. He gained fame as a theologian by contributing to the Socinian controversy. His tract *Scriptural Revision of Socinian Arguments, in a Letter to Dr Priestley* (1792) prompted a response from Benjamin Hobhouse; Randolph rejoined with a vindication of his *Scriptural Revision* in 1793. In 1800 he published a collection of sermons.

Randolph became embroiled in scandal when, in August 1795, he was entrusted with some letters of the princess of Wales to carry to Brunswick but, being prevented from going, he sent them back by coach from London to the princess at Brighton. They were lost on the way. Lady Jersey was accused in the press of having intercepted them and of sending some of them to Queen Charlotte, whom they supposedly maligned. In 1796 the earl of Jersey published the correspondence between Randolph and Lady Jersey in an attempt to clear his wife's name. However, the princess was unconvinced and her friends suggested that Randolph had been promised a bishopric for parting with the papers. Thomas James Mathias published several satirical pieces on the incident.

In 1808 Randolph issued *A Few Observations on the State of the Nation*, addressed to the duke of Bedford, in which he revived a plan propounded by Richard Watson, bishop of Llandaff, for a redemption of the national debt. Randolph, who was married, died at his prebendal house, Bristol, on 14 June 1831 and was buried in the churchyard of Bristol Cathedral. In the north aisle of Banwell church there is a mural tablet to his memory.

G. LE G. NORGATE, *rev.* EMMA MAJOR

Sources Venn, *Alum. Cant.* • *GM*, 1st ser., 101/1 (1831), 648 • *ESTC* • G. B. Villiers, fourth earl of Jersey, *The correspondence between the earl and countess of Jersey and the Rev Dr Randolph* (1796) • Allibone, *Dict.* **Likenesses** J. Downman, chalk drawing, 1777, FM Cam. • W. Bradley, portrait • T. G. Lupton, engraving (after W. Bradley)

Randolph, Francis Charles Hingeston- (1833–1910), antiquary, born Francis Charles Hingeston at Truro on 31 March 1833, was the son of Francis Hingeston (1796–1841), controller of customs at Truro, who belonged to a family long established in St Ives. His father had literary tastes and wrote poems which the son edited and published in 1857. Hingeston's mother was Jane Matilda, daughter of Captain William Kirkness of Kernick. From Truro grammar school Hingeston entered Exeter College, Oxford, in November 1851 as Elliott exhibitioner. He graduated BA in 1855 with an honorary fourth class in the final pass school, and proceeded MA in 1858. Ordained deacon in 1856, he served as curate of Holywell, Oxford, until 1858, when he moved to Hampton Gay, in the same county; he succeeded to the incumbency of the parish next year and was ordained priest in 1859.

From an early age Hingeston had developed antiquarian interests: when only seventeen years old he published *Specimens of Ancient Cornish Crosses and Fonts* (1850). During the late 1850s he became an editor for the Rolls Series; his involvement probably arose from his position as the accepted suitor of the eldest daughter of Joseph Stevenson, who—with Sir John Romilly and Sir Thomas Duffus Hardy—initiated the project to publish sources for early British history. He edited two works by the fifteenth-century historian and theologian John Capgrave, *The Chronicle of England* (1858) and the *Liber de illustribus Henricis* (1858), neither of which met with a favourable reception from reviewers. He was nevertheless commissioned to edit a two-volume collection of royal and historical letters of the reign of Henry IV. The first volume, published in 1860, failed to cover more than the first five years and contained such a voluminous amount of material that the master of the rolls calculated that the publication would run to thirty volumes for the whole reign if continued on this scale. In addition, the inaccuracies which had been apparent in Capgrave's volumes were also here present: Hingeston had taken no care to produce a correct text, either of Latin, French, or English.

Hingeston's connection with the Rolls Series was further weakened in the same year when he jilted Stevenson's daughter to marry, on 26 July, Martha Jane (*d.* 1904), only

daughter of Herbert Randolph, minister of Melrose, Roxburghshire: Stevenson, outraged by Hingston's 'base, treacherous and untruthful' conduct, commented that he 'could not congratulate the Lady did I know her' (Knowles, 113, n. 3). At the wish of his father-in-law, Hingston added the name Randolph to his and also adopted Hingeston, an older spelling of his family name. This circumstance—coupled with the fact that he also became vicar of Ringmore, near Kingsbridge, Devon, in the same year, the patronage of which living afterwards became invested in his family—suggests that the young clergyman might have discarded Stevenson's daughter in favour of an heiress. Certainly, on the expectation of plenty, he pledged some £200 in 1863 to a local builder and for the purchase of an organ. When in 1864 the second volume of *Royal and Historical Letters during the Reign of Henry IV* was in type form, Romilly arranged for the manuscripts to be recollated and the translation checked: it was found necessary to cancel and reprint sixty-two pages of text and add sixteen pages of errata. Romilly decided to suppress the volume; eight copies only were preserved and the rest of the edition was pulped. In 1965, however, Kraus Reprint published the second volume, together with the critics' amendments.

In 1885 Frederick Temple, then bishop of Exeter, made Hingeston-Randolph a prebendary of Exeter Cathedral; at the bishop's suggestion he began editing the *Episcopal Registers* of the diocese. Between 1886 and 1909 he completed those of eight late medieval bishops. He restricted himself largely to indexing the contents of the registers, a method which limited the historical value of his scheme. Hingeston-Randolph was also interested in church architecture, and was often consulted about the restoration of west country churches. He wrote on *The Architectural History of St. Germans Church, Cornwall* (1903), and contributed many architectural articles to *Building News* and *The Ecclesiologist*. He was also a contributor to *Devon and Cornwall Notes and Queries*, *Notes and Gleanings*, the *Western Antiquary*, and the *Journal of the Royal Institution of Cornwall*. For ten years (1879–90) he was rural dean of Woodleigh, and brought the work of the district to a high state of efficiency. In his articles 'Up and down the deanery', which he contributed to the *Salcombe Parish Magazine*, he included a historical account of every parish under his charge. He died at the rectory, Ringmore, on 27 August 1910, and was buried in the churchyard there. He left four sons and six daughters.

HARRY TAPLEY-SOPER, *rev.* CHRISTINE NORTH

Sources *WWW, 1897–1915* • Crockford (1902) • Boase & Courtney, *Bibl. Corn.*, 1.251 • G. C. Boase, *Collectanea Cornubiensia: a collection of biographical and topographical notes relating to the county of Cornwall* (1890) • Foster, *Alum. Oxon.* • D. Knowles, *Great historical enterprises and problems in monastic history* (1963), 112–14 • J. D. Cantwell, *The Public Record Office, 1838–1958* (1991), 217 • d. cert. • m. cert. • parish register, Truro, St Mary's, 8 June 1833, Cornwall RO [baptism] **Archives** BL, letters to F. J. Baigent and others • Devon RO, corresp. with F. J. Baigent and others and notes relating to Exeter episcopal registers; undergraduate notes • LPL, corresp. with A. C. Tait • St George's Chapel, Windsor, letters to J. N. Dalton **Wealth at death** £1076 0s. 5d.: administration, 7 Jan 1911, CGPLA Eng. & Wales

Randolph, Sir George Granville (1818–1907), naval officer, born in London on 26 January 1818, was the son of Thomas Randolph, prebendary of St Paul's Cathedral from 1812 until his death in 1875, chaplain-in-ordinary to Queen Victoria, and rector of Hadham, Hertfordshire. Dr John *Randolph, bishop of London, was his grandfather. George Randolph entered the navy as a first-class volunteer on 7 December 1830. He was commissioned lieutenant on 27 June 1838. In the following September he was appointed to the frigate *North Star* (26 guns), under Captain Lord John Hay, commodore on the north coast of Spain. He next (from 1840 to 1844) served on the *Vernon* (50 guns) in the Mediterranean, latterly as first lieutenant. In October 1844 he became first lieutenant of the *Daedalus* (20 guns), on the East India station, and on 19 August 1845 commanded her barge at the destruction of Malloodoo, a pirate stronghold in Borneo.

On 9 November 1846 Randolph was promoted, and a year later was appointed to the *Bellerophon* (78 guns); in this ship and in the *Rodney* he served for six years in the Mediterranean. In 1851 Randolph married Eleanor Harriet, daughter of the Revd Joseph Arkwright of Mark Hall, near Harlow, Essex; she died in April 1907. He was present in the *Rodney* at the attack on Fort Constantine, Sevastopol, took part in other operations in the Black Sea, and served ashore in the naval brigade; he received the fourth class of the Mejidiye. He was made a chevalier of the Légion d'honneur, and promoted captain on 18 November 1854. He commanded the *Cornwallis*, coastguard ship in the Humber, and afterwards the screw frigates *Diadem* and *Orlando* on the North American station.

The *Orlando* was transferred to the Mediterranean in 1863, and Randolph remained in her until May 1865, when he was appointed to the guardship at Sheerness. He was awarded a good service pension in March 1867, and from September 1867 until March 1869 was commodore at the Cape of Good Hope. He received the CB in June 1869, and was promoted to his flag on 24 April 1872. From December 1873 to June 1875 he commanded the detached squadron, his last active employment. He was promoted vice-admiral on 16 September 1877, retired on 26 July 1881, and was promoted admiral on 8 July 1884. At the 1897 diamond jubilee celebrations he was made KCB.

Randolph published in 1867 *The Rule of the Road at Sea*, and in 1879, *Problems in Naval Tactics*; he was a corresponding member of the Royal United Service Institution and a fellow of the Royal Geographical Society. He died on 16 May 1907 at his home, 70 Brunswick Place, Hove, Brighton, and was buried at Hove.

A fine seaman and a brave officer, Randolph reached an appropriate peak in his career, commanding one of the last squadrons principally powered by sail.

L. G. C. LAUGHTON, rev. ANDREW LAMBERT

Sources J. W. D. Dundas and C. Napier, *Russian war, 1854, Baltic and Black Sea: official correspondence*, ed. D. Bonner-Smith and A. C. Dewar, Navy RS, 83 (1943) · A. D. Lambert, *The Crimean War: British grand strategy, 1853–56* (1990) · O'Byrne, *Naval biog. dict.* · *The Times* (18 May 1907) · Burke, *Peerage* · CGPLA Eng. & Wales (1907) **Archives** Sandon Hall, Staffordshire, Harrowby Manuscript Trust, letters to Admiral Sir Alfred Ryder

Wealth at death £54,972 0s. 11d.: probate, 15 June 1907, CGPLA Eng. & Wales

Randolph, John, **third earl of Moray** (*d.* 1346), magnate, was the second son of Thomas *Randolph, first earl of Moray. The identity of his mother is not certain, but she may have been Isabella Stewart, a daughter of Sir John Stewart of Bonkill—in 1329 John Stewart's grandson, also John, was described as Thomas Randolph's nephew. John Randolph's elder brother, another Thomas *Randolph [*see under* Randolph, Thomas, first earl of Moray], became second earl of Moray on the death of their father on 20 July 1332, but died at the battle of Dupplin Moor on 11 August that year. Succeeding his brother in the earldom, and also in the lordships of Annandale and Man, Moray immediately assumed an active military role in the conflict between the supporters of David II and those of Edward Balliol, the English-backed claimant to the Scottish crown. Moray played a leading part in a successful attack by Bruce partisans on Balliol at Annan in December 1332, which forced Balliol to flee the kingdom. On 19 July 1333 Moray was present at the disastrous defeat of pro-David II forces at the battle of Halidon Hill near Berwick, but managed to escape death or capture. The defeat, and the military ascendancy achieved in its aftermath by Balliol and Edward III, caused David's followers to reconsider the position of their young king. Some time in the winter of 1333–4 Moray seems to have been entrusted with a mission to the French court to arrange for David's transfer there from his bolt-hole in Dumbarton Castle. He returned to Scotland in the spring of 1334 with ships and money from the French king to pay for the expenses involved in moving David II from Dumbarton, which was safely effected in May 1334.

On Moray's return he and Robert the Steward, David II's nephew and heir apparent, co-operated in attacks on Balliol supporters in Clydesdale, and by July 1334 they had become joint guardians. Moray's claim to exercise guardianship may have been partly justified by his own blood relationship to David II, for his grandmother was a sister of Robert I. The Steward apparently resented Moray's role as joint guardian, and the legacy of the personal animosity between the two men was to be an important feature of the politics of the kingdom throughout David II's reign.

On 27 September 1334 Moray forced the submission of David Strathbogie, titular earl of Atholl, one of the disinherited who had accompanied Edward Balliol to Scotland in 1332, and who had since been occupying Moray's own lordships of Lochaber and Badenoch. In April 1335 Strathbogie and Moray had a further falling out at a parliament held by the guardians at Dairsie in Fife. The Steward seems to have supported Strathbogie's position against Moray's, and an entry in the exchequer rolls indicates that the adherents of the two guardians were soon engaged in a struggle for control of the king's fermes and customs revenues from the burghs north of the Forth.

In July 1335 Edward III and Edward Balliol launched a renewed assault on David II's supporters in Scotland and swiftly established their campaign headquarters in Perth. In August Moray defeated a force under the command of

Gui, count of Namur, who was bringing his troops to the assistance of Edward III, in a series of running battles in and around Edinburgh. Gui and his men surrendered to Moray, who agreed to free the count under the condition that he took no further active part in Edward III's campaign. While escorting Gui to the English border, Moray was himself surprised and captured by a force from the English border garrisons. By 13 August 1335 he was recorded as being a prisoner at York, and he was subsequently held in a number of English gaols, including Nottingham Castle, Windsor, Winchester, and the Tower of London. He remained a prisoner until February 1342, when he was ransomed by Edward III in exchange for William Montagu, earl of Salisbury, who had been captured by the French early in 1340.

In June 1341, not long before Moray's release, David II had returned to Scotland from France. The earl's close political relationship with the young king was immediately restored, and David is reputed to have served under his command in a raid on northern England about 1342 (the precise date of this expedition is difficult to determine). Moray's interest and prominence in Anglo-Scottish warfare rested partly on his status as lord of Annandale. The chief castle of the lordship, Lochmaben, was garrisoned by English forces, and much of Annandale remained subject to the authority of agents of the English crown. In domestic politics, the affinities and allies of Moray and the Steward continued their rivalry from the 1330s. In 1342 Sir Alexander Ramsay, an active figure in Anglo-Scottish warfare and an associate of Moray, was appointed sheriff of Teviotdale by David II. The previous holder of the office, one of Ramsay's local rivals, Sir William Douglas of Liddesdale, promptly seized Ramsay and allowed him to die in his custody. Douglas was saved from the king's revenge by the Steward, although the incident provoked a long and bitter feud between the followers of Douglas and Moray. The latter still played an important role in border warfare and accompanied the king during his invasion of northern England in October 1346. On 17 October Moray was killed while commanding one of the three Scottish divisions at the battle of Nevilles Cross near Durham.

Randolph married *Euphemia (d. 1388/9), daughter of Hugh Ross, fourth earl of Ross, but the marriage seems to have produced no children. On 2 May 1355 Euphemia, as countess of Moray, received a dispensation to marry Robert the Steward (the future Robert II). Although the earldom of Moray had been granted to John's father in a male entail, after 1346 the husband of John's sister Agnes, Patrick, earl of Dunbar, assumed the title of earl of Moray. David II reclaimed the earldom for the crown in 1367–8; in 1372, however, David's successor, Robert II, granted the comital title to John Dunbar, the son of Sir Patrick Dunbar and John Randolph's younger sister Isabella. Title to the lordships of Annandale and Man passed to John Dunbar's elder brother, George, earl of March.

S. I. BOARDMAN

Sources W. Bower, *Scotichronicon*, ed. D. E. R. Watt and others, new edn, 9 vols. (1987–98), vol. 7 · *John of Fordun's Chronicle of the Scottish nation*, ed. W. F. Skene, trans. F. J. H. Skene (1872) · *The 'Original chronicle' of Andrew of Wyntoun*, ed. F. J. Amours, 5, STS, 1st ser., 56 (1907); 6, STS, 1st ser., 57 (1908) · G. W. S. Barrow and others, eds., *Regesta regum Scottorum*, 6, ed. B. Webster (1982) · G. Burnett and others, eds., *The exchequer rolls of Scotland*, 1 (1878) · A. Theiner, *Vetera monumenta Hibernorum et Scotorum historiam illustrantia* (Rome, 1864) · G. F. Warner and others, eds., *Miscellany … I*, Scottish History Society, 15 (1893) · W. Fraser, ed., *The Douglas book*, 4 vols. (1885), vol. 3 · C. Innes, ed., *Registrum episcopatus Moraviensis*, Bannatyne Club, 58 (1837) · *CDS*, vol. 3 · R. Nicholson, *Scotland: the later middle ages* (1974), vol. 2 of *The Edinburgh history of Scotland*, ed. G. Donaldson (1965–75).

Randolph, Sir John (1693–1737), lawyer and politician in America, was born on Turkey Island plantation on the James River, Virginia, the son of William *Randolph (1650–1711), colonist and planter, and his wife, Mary, daughter of Henry Isham, of Bermuda Hundred, a neighbouring plantation. Before travelling to England to pursue his law studies, Randolph was tutored at home by a Huguenot clergyman and for a time attended the College of William and Mary, among whose founders and trustees was his father. He entered Gray's Inn on 17 May 1715 and was called to the bar on 25 November 1717.

Randolph returned to Virginia and embarked on a distinguished career in public office, being appointed in 1718 as clerk to the house of burgesses, an office he would hold until his resignation sixteen years later. In 1736 he was selected to represent the College of William and Mary in the house of burgesses and in a matter of days was elected speaker. Later in the same session he was made treasurer of the colony and that year he also became recorder of the newly incorporated borough of Norfolk. Following his return from England he also built up a lucrative law practice in Williamsburg, residing at Tazewell Hall and serving as vestryman at Bruton parish church. In 1721 he married Susanna (c.1692–1768), daughter of Peter Beverley and his wife, Elizabeth, née Peyton. Forty of his legal cases have survived. They include numerous cases of ejectment, bills of chancery and actions for trespass, slander, and detinue, the latter often relating to slaves when widows remarried.

Randolph's activities, however, were not confined to Virginia. As clerk to the colony's Indian treaty commission in 1722, he accompanied Lieutenant-Governor Alexander Spotswood to New York to treat with the Iroquois Confederacy at Albany. Two missions to England followed in 1728 and 1732 which reflected both his stature among the ruling gentry of Virginia and his transatlantic connections. On the first of these occasions he was empowered by the Virginia assembly to seek the repeal of the act of parliament which had prohibited the export of tobacco stripped from the stalk; this measure exacerbated the poor state of Virginia's economy which had been depressed for the better part of three decades. He was also successful in obtaining the repeal of the offending legislation, though details of how this was accomplished are obscure. While in England Randolph also assumed responsibility for negotiating the transfer of the charter of the College of William and Mary from the trustees to the president and faculty and for boosting the college's finances. Facilitated by the death of the principal opponent of the transfer, former Virginia governor Francis Nicholson, and improvements to the college made by its president, James Blair, Randolph successfully returned with the charter which he presented to the president and faculty on 15 August 1729. The college, exercising its new powers under the charter, voted Randolph 50 guineas for his services; the Virginia assembly voted him £1000. In 1732 Randolph returned to England as agent for the colony to campaign against abuses in the tobacco trade. The assembly's petition, set forth in *The Case of the Planters of Tobacco in Virginia* and sent to the king and the lords of the Treasury, was published in London in 1733 together with *A Vindication of the Said Representation* which is attributed to Randolph. His arrival in England and the plan to put tobacco under an excise duty were considered sufficiently noteworthy to be mentioned in the *Gentleman's Magazine* in January 1733. Though the scheme appealed to the prime minister, Robert Walpole, it failed owing to the strong opposition of merchants. Randolph, none the less, received the honour of a knighthood for his efforts. He died on 2 March 1737, still only in his early forties, and was buried at the chapel of the College of William and Mary. He did not live long enough to write the history of Virginia that he had planned. He was survived by his wife and four children, one of whom, Peyton *Randolph, became a patriot serving as president of the first continental congress. Another, John, Virginia's last attorney-general before the American War of Independence, was a loyalist who fled to England.   GWENDA MORGAN

Sources R. T. Barton, ed., *Virginia colonial decisions: the reports by Sir John Randolph and by Edward Barradall of decisions of the general court of Virginia, 1728–1741*, 2 vols. (Boston, MA, 1909) • H. J. Eckenrode, *The Randolphs: the story of a Virginia family* (Indianapolis and New York, 1946) • R. L. Morton, *Colonial Virginia*, 2: *Westward expansion and prelude to revolution* (1960) • W. M. Billings, J. E. Selby, and T. W. Tate, *Colonial Virginia: a history* (1986) • M. N. Wooffin, 'Randolph, John', *DAB* • S. Crompton, 'Randolph, John', *ANB* • C. Dowdey, *The Virginia dynasty: the emergence of 'King' Carter and the golden age* (Boston, MA, 1969) • H. R. McIlwaine and J. P. Kennedy, eds., *Journals of the house of burgesses of Virginia, 1619–1776*, 13 vols. (1905–15) • V. C. Hall, ed., *Portraits in the collection of the Virginia Historical Society: a catalogue* (Charlottesville, VA, 1981) • S. H. Godson and others, eds., *The College of William and Mary: a history*, 1: *1693–1888* (Williamsburg, VA, 1993) • H. Brewer, 'Entailing aristocracy in colonial Virginia: "antient feudal restraints" and revolutionary reform', *William and Mary Quarterly*, 54 (1997), 307–46 • *Virginia Historical Register*, 4 (1851), 136–7, 138–41 • E. Lonn, *The colonial agents in the southern colonies* (Chapel Hill, NC, 1945) • J. Daniels, *The Randolphs of Virginia, America's foremost family* (Garden City, NJ, 1972)

Likenesses J. W. Günther, portraits, 1955 (after portraits by J. Randolph and E. P. Bruce), Virginia Historical Society, Richmond • E. P. Bruce, oils (after contemporary miniatures), College of William and Mary, Williamsburg, Virginia

Randolph, John (1749–1813), bishop of London, was born in Oxford on 6 July 1749, the third son of Thomas *Randolph (1701–1783), president of Corpus Christi College, Oxford, and Thomazine Honywood (1707/8–1783). He was educated at Westminster School and matriculated from Christ Church, Oxford, on 17 June 1767. He graduated BA (1771), MA (1774), BD (1782), and DD by diploma on 30 October 1783. From 1779 to 1783 he was a tutor and censor at Christ Church where he helped the dean, Lewis Bagot, to enforce discipline; he was appointed proctor in 1781. He was tutor to William Wyndham, later Baron Grenville, and to Richard Polwhele, who complained that, entrenched behind forms and ceremonies, Randolph's 'manner was frigid, and his words were few' (Polwhele 1.84). On 13 September 1785 he married Jane Lambarde (d. 1836), the daughter of Thomas Lambarde of Sevenoaks, Kent.

His father's influence at Oxford enabled Randolph to become a 'professorial pluralist' (*Hist. U. Oxf.* 5: *18th-cent. Oxf.*, 517) as professor of poetry (1776–83), regius professor of Greek (1782–3), professor of moral philosophy (1782–6), and regius professor of divinity (1783–1807). He delivered one lecture a term, in Latin, on the poetry of Homer and the course was still incomplete after seven years. The regius chair in Greek was a sinecure which normally went to a man from Christ Church and Randolph resigned it when he was promoted to the regius chair in divinity. He sought in his lectures on divinity to provide ordinands with a thorough instruction in the theology of the established church and a clear understanding of how it differed from that of Rome. However, as Cox remembered, the lectures were

> given late in the evening by candle-light; one effect of this (and not a very surprising one, considering the hour, the subject, and the audience) was, that many of the class slept through the lecture … the only things really carried away by the majority of the class, were the Syllabus given to each one at the commencement of the course, and a formidable printed list of authors recommended for future reading, presented at the close of the lectures. (Cox, 140)

Randolph was a conscientious and assiduous teacher who kept, in his own hand, a list of all students who attended each lecture. But his colleagues were critical of the appropriateness of these discourses; later Cyril Jackson, dean of Christ Church, commenting on over-long lectures, complained that Randolph 'used to write complete doctrinal treatises, which is absurd' (letter to Howley, 20 Oct 1810, LPL, MS 2186 fol. 24). His library, which was sold after his death, consisted of 1623 items that reflected his wide interests in theology, classical literature, history, natural science, and travel.

Randolph's clerical career was as successful as his academic one; his limited experience as a parish priest did not bar his route to the episcopate. He held the prebend of Chute and Chisenbury in Salisbury Cathedral for twelve months from October 1782, was rector of Ewelme and canon of Christ Church Cathedral, Oxford (1783–1807), and sinecure rector of Darowen in Montgomeryshire (1797–1800). He was consecrated bishop of Oxford on 1 September 1799, translated to Bangor on 6 January 1807, and thence to London on 9 August 1809. The charges issued on his primary visitation of each diocese reflect his consistent concerns: a profound distrust of Catholics and protestant dissenters, especially the Methodists; his opposition to clerical non-residence; his support for the education of the children of the poor; and his concern to keep his clergy well informed of clerical legislation in parliament. As bishop of London his correspondence reveals a conscientious bishop, much concerned to enforce the clergy residence act of 1803 and aware of the need for new church buildings to accommodate the rapidly growing population. His politics were traditional: he believed it was the duty of the clergy 'to promote the good order of society … by stifling every seed of discontent' (J. Randolph, *A Charge Delivered to the Clergy of the Diocese of Bangor*, 1808, 6), and warned 'the spirit of democracy is not easily subdued … it again rears its head wherever it can find or create the seeds of discontent; the dog returns to its own vomit again' (ibid., 9). Earlier a staunch opponent of the principles of the French Revolution, in 1813, as bishop of London, he rejected a proposal by the duke of Bedford to erect a statue of Charles James Fox in the porch of St Paul's Church, Covent Garden, commenting 'It looks like dedicating the Church to him.—If the Porch has been the scene of popular Elections for Westminster I can only lament the abuse, but this is no reason for augmenting it' (letter to Mr Embry, 22 May 1813, LPL, Randolph MSS 3, fol. 43).

As well as sermons and charges Randolph published the heads of his divinity lectures in 1784 (the whole course being published posthumously by his son in 1869–70) and engaged in controversy with Herbert Marsh on the synoptic gospels. He edited *The Clergyman's Instructor*, a collection of tracts on clerical duties, in 1807; his son published his lectures on Homer in 1870. He was a leading supporter of the National Society, a Busby trustee of Westminster School (1804), a governor of Charterhouse, and an official trustee of the British Museum. Sworn of the privy council on 27 September 1809, he was elected a fellow of the Royal Society on 19 December 1811.

Randolph died suddenly on a visit to one of his sons, Thomas, rector of Much Hadham in Hertfordshire, on 28 July 1813, following an apoplectic fit while on horseback. He was buried in Fulham churchyard on 5 August.

ROBERT HOLE

Sources *Hist. U. Oxf. 5: 18th-cent. Oxf.* · *Old Westminsters*, vol. 2 · Foster, *Alum. Oxon.* · *GM*, 1st ser., 83/2 (1813), 187–8 · *GM*, 2nd ser., 5 (1836), 332 · G. V. Cox, *Recollections of Oxford*, 2nd edn (1870) · R. Polwhele, *Traditions and recollections; domestic, clerical and literary*, 2 vols. (1826) · *Fasti Angl., 1541–1857*, [Bristol] · M. Barber, 'Catalogue of the Papers of John Randolph, Bishop of London, 1808–1813', 1988, LPL [typescript] · J. Randolph, 'Lecture register, 1784–89', LPL, MS 1819 · *A catalogue of the library of the late Right Rev. Dr. Randolph* (1814) · H. L. Thompson, *Christ Church* (1900) · *DNB*

Archives LPL, corresp. and papers | BL, corresp. with Lord Grenville, Add. MS 59002 · Bodl. Oxf., letters to his brother-in-law, Thomas Lambarde, rector of Ash, and other Randolph papers · Bodl. Oxf., MSS Clar Press, papers relating to Hero of Alexandria

Likenesses C. Turner, mezzotint, pubd 1810 (after J. Hoppner), BM, NPG · W. Owen, oils, 1811–12, Christ Church Oxf. · W. Owen, oils, 1812, Fulham Palace, London

Randolph, Peyton (1721/2–1775), planter and revolutionary politician in America, was probably born in Williamsburg, Virginia, the second of the three sons and one of the four children of Sir John *Randolph (1693–1737), planter and speaker of the Virginia house of burgesses in 1734 and 1736, and Susanna Beverley (c.1692–1768). He attended the College of William and Mary in 1733, entered the Middle

Peyton Randolph (1721/2–1775), by John Wollaston

Temple in London on 13 October 1739, and was called to the bar on 10 February 1744.

Randolph was appointed attorney-general of Virginia on 7 May 1744, an appointment which reflected the importance and influence of his family connections, and became judge of the colonial court of vice-admiralty in November, an appointment customarily linked with the attorney-general's office. He returned to Virginia and on 8 March 1746 married Elizabeth Harrison (c.1724–1783), of Berkeley plantation. They had no children. Randolph lived in a large, elegant frame house in Williamsburg. As a prominent young man closely related by blood and marriage to many other influential Virginia families, he was able to speculate heavily in unsettled western land and was a partner in the New River Company that between 1749 and the mid-1750s obtained grants for a total of more than 200,000 acres. At the time of his death Randolph owned several plantations and 109 slaves.

Randolph rose rapidly in politics. He was recorder (chief legal officer) of the borough of Norfolk and of the city of Williamsburg and became a Church of England vestryman of Bruton parish in Williamsburg in 1749. He represented Williamsburg in the house of burgesses from 1748 to 1752. Elected to the board of visitors of the College of William and Mary, he represented the college in the house from 1752 to 1758. He represented Williamsburg in the house again from 1758 until his death.

Randolph was not a timid politician. At the end of 1753 the house of burgesses sent him to England to oppose the imposition by the lieutenant-governor, Robert Dinwiddie, of a fee of 1 pistole for affixing the colonial seal to official documents. Dinwiddie suspended Randolph as attorney-general, but after the case was settled the privy council restored him to office on 13 May 1755. Randolph again defended the power of the assembly as chairman of its committee of correspondence to direct lobbying in London to secure approval for the second of two emergency measures, the so-called Two-Penny Acts of 1755 and 1758, that without prior permission amended Virginia statutes that had received royal approval. A political protégé of the most powerful of all colonial Virginia's native-born politicians, speaker of the house and colonial treasurer John Robinson, Randolph presided over the committee of the whole house in May 1765 when Patrick Henry pushed through inflammatory resolutions questioning the right of parliament to tax the colonies. The older generation opposed the tone of the resolutions and by close votes rescinded two of them, but in exasperation Randolph exclaimed: 'By God, I would have given 500 guineas for a single vote' to defeat the others (*The Confidential Letters from Thomas Jefferson to William Wirt. Being Reminiscences of Patrick Henry*, 1911, 5).

Randolph served as attorney-general until he was elected speaker of the house of burgesses on 6 November 1766 following the death of Robinson. Randolph then gave up the practice of law. He presided over the house during its final decade and won praise for his fairness as presiding officer and the dignity he lent to the proceedings. The members included some of the greatest eighteenth-century Virginia statesmen, including Richard Bland, Archibald Cary, Patrick Henry, Richard Henry Lee, George Washington, and Randolph's protégé Thomas Jefferson. During the tumultuous years prior to the American War of Independence, Randolph presided over a series of extra-legal meetings when members were forced to meet out of doors after royal governors repeatedly dissolved the assembly for adopting resolutions critical of parliamentary and ministerial measures. In 1773 he became chairman of the Virginia committee of correspondence to co-ordinate protests with the other colonies, and he presided at the first three Virginia revolutionary conventions that met after parliament passed the so-called Coercive or Intolerable Acts of 1774, in response to the Boston tea party.

The Virginia convention of August 1774 issued the call for the first continental congress. Randolph was chairman of the Virginia delegation and was elected president of congress when it met in Philadelphia on 5 September 1774. One member wrote:

> Our President seems designed by Nature, for the Business; of an affable, open, & majestic deportment, large in size, though not out of Proportion, he commands respect, & Esteem by his very aspect, independent of the high Character he sustains. (Smith, 1.23)

Randolph was elected president of the second continental congress on 10 May 1775, but he resigned and returned to Williamsburg to preside over what turned out to be the final meeting of the house of burgesses in June. The Williamsburg militia escorted Randolph into the city, where the citizens addressed him as 'the father of your country' years before George Washington received that title (*Virginia Gazette*, 1 June 1775).

Randolph's younger brother John Randolph (c.1729–1784) had succeeded him as attorney-general in 1766 but remained loyal during the war and fled to England early in the autumn of 1775. Although ill, Peyton Randolph presided over the third Virginia convention in Richmond in July 1775, then in September resumed his seat in congress in Philadelphia, where he died of a stroke on 22 October 1775. He was interred in the yard of Christ Episcopal Church in Philadelphia until November 1776, when his corpse was returned to Virginia and buried in the chapel of the College of William and Mary, Williamsburg.

BRENT TARTER

Sources J. J. Reardon, *Peyton Randolph, 1722–1775: one who presided* (Durham, North Carolina, 1982) · J. Kukla, *Speakers and clerks of the Virginia house of burgesses, 1643–1776* (1981), 129–33 · A. C. Edwards and others, *A view from the top: archaeological investigations of Peyton Randolph's urban plantation* (Williamsburg, Virginia, 1988) · J. P. Greene, ed., 'The case of the pistole fee: the report of a hearing on the pistole fee dispute before the privy council, June 18, 1754', *Virginia Magazine of History and Biography*, 66 (1958), 399–424 · Virginia Historical Society, Richmond, Virginia, Randolph family papers · L. Cong., manuscript division, Peyton Randolph estate MSS · *Pennsylvania Gazette* (26 Oct 1775) · *Pinkney's Virginia Gazette* (9 Nov 1775) · *Parks's Virginia Gazette* (13 March 1746) · *Purdie's Virginia Gazette* (10 Nov 1775) · *Dixon and Hunter's Virginia Gazette* (11 Nov 1775) · P. H. Smith and others, eds., *Letters of delegates to congress, 1774–1789*, 26 vols. (1976–2000) · PRO, CO 324/50; CO 5/1328, fols. 41–2; CO 391/61, fols. 166–7; CO 324/51; CO 5/1345, fol. 152; HCA 30/827, no. 800 · H. R. McIlwaine and J. P. Kennedy, eds., *Journals of the house of burgesses of Virginia, 1619–1776*, 13 vols. (1905–15) · W. J. Van Schreeven, R. L. Scribner, and B. Tarter, eds., *Revolutionary Virginia, the road to independence: a documentary record*, 7 vols. (1973–83) · W. C. Ford and others, eds., *Journals of the continental congress, 1774–1789*, 34 vols. (1904–37) · H. A. C. Sturgess, ed., *Register of admissions to the Honourable Society of the Middle Temple, from the fifteenth century to the year 1944*, 1 (1949), 326
Archives L. Cong., estate papers · Virginia Historical Society, Richmond, family papers
Likenesses J. Wollaston, portrait, Virginia Historical Society, Richmond [*see illus.*]
Wealth at death owned several plantations, part interest in vast speculative western land companies, and 109 slaves: will and inventory, York County, Virginia, wills and inventories no. 22 (1771–1783); 308–310, 337–346 [microfilm], Library of Virginia, Richmond

Randolph, Thomas, first earl of Moray (d. 1332), soldier and guardian of Scotland, was the son of Sir Thomas Randolph of Stichill, Roxburghshire, and of a daughter of Marjory, countess of Carrick, and her first husband, Adam of Kilconquhar. Thomas's mother was half-sister to Robert I, and he was 'our dearest nephew', but had no claim to the throne. His father (who probably died soon after 1296) and grandfather had held public office, including the chamberlainship; neither Thomas nor his father appears in the first phase of the wars of independence (1296–1304).

Fighting for Scottish independence When Robert Bruce seized the throne on 25 March 1306, Randolph was probably with him, and he was certainly there when incompetence lost the battle of Methven on 19 June to Aymer de Valence. He was taken prisoner, and only the fact that he switched allegiance and was promised his heritage before the arrival of Edward I's orders that the prisoners were to be sent for trial and execution saved his life. He was, however, imprisoned for a year or so, first at Inverkip and then in the custody of the earl of Lincoln, but in September 1307 he is found in the party which pursued Sir James Douglas near Paisley. Late in the following year he was captured in Peeblesshire, surprised in a house by a force under Douglas, and was sent to his uncle the king, whom he is said to have reproached for fighting a war of hit and run. They quarrelled, but in March 1309 Randolph was at parliament with the style of lord of Nithsdale—an obvious invitation to drive the English from their strongholds there. This he seems not to have attempted, but on 19 February 1310 he is described in the same way and as 'then lieutenant of the illustrious prince of Scotland from Forth to Orkney' (*Liber sancte Marie de Lundoris*, no. 10), which was more than the king then controlled. Clearly he was now in the innermost counsels of Robert I.

Randolph's value was recognized when the king conferred upon him a huge earldom, the first new one for almost a century and one which revived a title extinct since 1130. Between 12 April and 29 October 1312 he was made earl of Moray, with territory stretching from the western sea to the Moray Firth and south to the border of Perthshire; his judicial privileges of 'regality' were all-encompassing, and the king's tenants and vassals now owed homage to him—and this before the king conferred a much smaller earldom on his own brother and heir, Edward. The limitation to heirs male was probably a bonus in the earl's eyes, not a disadvantage. In 1328 he paid £275 as the tenth of rents of himself and his tenants within the regality for one term, representing annual rents totalling £5500; his share of that is not discoverable.

Moray is not mentioned in connection with the taking of Dundee or Perth, but early in 1314, in anticipation of Edward II's promised invasion to recover Scotland, he set siege to Edinburgh Castle. Eventually, as Barbour tells it, a former member of the garrison showed a way up the castle rock; Moray and a small party climbed it at night with ladders which took them to the top of the wall, and the castle fell. Another source adds that his army had launched a major diversionary assault, which must be correct, for the few on the wall cannot have overcome the garrison by themselves. The date was 14 March 1314; when Edward II came there in June 1314 and in August 1322, the castle on Edinburgh Rock was a heap of rubble.

In the preparations for Edward's attempt to relieve Stirling Castle, Robert I made Moray and Edward Bruce commanders of the two forward divisions, or 'battles', of his army, while he commanded the rear. On 23 June 1314 a group broke away from the English army as it went through the Torwood, and made for the castle. The king is said (by Barbour) to have reproached Moray that a rose had fallen from his chaplet, but the remark may have been borrowed from the chivalrous court of Edward III in France (1340s); it is not in doubt that Moray with a force of infantry stopped the English knights, killed many, and

put great heart into the main Scottish army. On the following day, according to Barbour, after the English van rode at Edward Bruce's division, Moray and his division attacked the main English force. The progress of the battle is obscure, but the English defeat was complete save for the escape of Edward II.

War in Ireland and England The disaster did not put the English in a peace-making frame of mind, and the Scots had to turn the screw by direct attacks on England and by seeking to drive them from Ireland. Moray crossed to Ulster with Edward Bruce in May 1315, and campaigned with him to Louth in the summer. He returned for reinforcements to Scotland, rejoining Edward at Dundalk to ravage as far south as Castledermot in the winter of 1315–16, then went back to Scotland, where he appears on 16 July 1316 for the first time as lord of Man. He was then at the unsuccessful siege of Berwick, but at an assembly at Cupar, Fife, on 30 September 1316 the king confirmed Moray and Man to him in a wholly exceptional act carrying not only the great seal, but also the seals of Edward (Bruce), king of Ireland, and of the prelates and magnates. What lies behind this is uncertain, but most probably it records Edward's reluctant agreement to Moray's title to Man, which the Scots had regained and lost once more; it was recovered by Moray, apparently late in 1317.

In the first half of 1317 Moray was with King Robert in Ireland, ravaging as far as Tipperary, before returning in May. In the following years he was active in northern England, offering the alternative of paying blackmail or suffering destruction. He secured the surrender of a number of Northumberland castles in 1318, and in 1319 commanded the force which defeated the men of Yorkshire at Myton and drew Edward II from the siege of Berwick. After the truce of 1320–21 he commanded under the king in the invasion of October 1322, when Edward was humiliated at Byland; Moray led the uphill assault which drove the English to flight. The military abilities he showed in these years have to be read between the lines of Barbour's poem, which is much concerned to advance the repute of Douglas, often at the expense of Moray.

When Edward Bruce went to Ireland, it was as King Robert's designated heir presumptive; none the less if Robert had an under-age son, Moray, not Edward, was to be guardian. In December 1318, when Edward had been killed, the succession of a child became more likely and Moray was confirmed as designated guardian (failing him, now, Douglas), and was given the valuable lordship of Annandale, formerly of the Bruce family. His position as second in the kingdom after an ailing king was as apparent as his unswerving loyalty, and in marked contrast to the royal home life south of the border. It was he who swore on the king's behalf to the truce of 1319 and to the extraordinary agreement with Andrew Harclay on 3 January 1323; he had negotiated with the earl of Lancaster in January 1322 as 'lieutenant' on behalf of a king in declining health who would not allow him to act as ambassador in England in 1323 without receiving very important English hostages in return. Once they had been received, he made the thirteen-year truce of Bishopthorpe, which effectively recognized the stalemate of the war, on 30 May 1323.

Diplomatic services Moray now entered the international stage, for that truce permitted the Scots to seek the lifting of ecclesiastical sanctions imposed on them as warmongers, and he wrote to John XXII (doubtless the wording came from the royal chancery) seeking his recognition of Robert as king. By mid-January 1324 he was at Avignon, where he so far prevailed that John XXII agreed to write to Robert as king, if only to tell him that this did not mean that he was recognized as king; the pope also fell silent about the censures of 1317–20. On his return in 1324 Moray was supposed to go to York for peace negotiations, but there was no serious English will for them; he had to make do with a renewal of royal charters of his three lordships. None the less his time abroad was clearly not wasted, for he was given letters of credence to Charles IV of France in April 1325 and was at the French court with an embassy by June. From there he went to the papal court, where he is recorded on 1 October, and where he may have stayed for some months. In February 1326 the pope wrote to him urging him to return from France to Scotland, but the Anglo-French war of St Sardos in 1324–5 had produced a much more favourable climate at the French court. There in April 1326 he made the treaty of Corbeil, a Franco-Scottish alliance which, after twenty-three years of French indifference or hostility, became the cornerstone of Scottish foreign policy for the remainder of the fourteenth century.

Moray returned with this remarkable achievement to obtain his king's confirmation in the parliament of July 1326. Six months later the Scots broke the truce, and in the summer of 1327 launched a highly successful attack on northern England. Moray was in command, but Douglas brought tactical skill and is depicted by Barbour as saving Moray from the folly of fighting their way out of a tight corner; that is as may be. What is clear is that first they drew Edward III himself into responding, and then humiliated the king and his divided Anglo-Hainaultese force, before escaping unnoticed at night from Stanhope Park. They were home by 9 August 1327. A month later King Robert was in Northumberland, besieging castles and distributing lands there to his followers; the bankrupt English government had no option but peace, which was concluded at Edinburgh in March 1328. In July Moray took the child David Bruce to Berwick for his marriage to Joan of the Tower, and negotiated again with Queen Isabella, agreeing that four English magnates, Thomas Wake, Henry de Beaumont, Henry Percy, and William Zouche, should have restitution of the lands they claimed in Scotland. This departure from the determined policy of Robert I is difficult to explain, and the failure to carry it out certainly gave Edward III his excuse to interfere again in Scotland.

Guardian of Scotland The death of King Robert on 7 June 1329 made Moray guardian or regent for David II, an office

he fulfilled with determination and distinction for a miserable 100 merks per annum. The government lost the annual tenth of rents granted to Robert for life, but persisted with the three-year tenth granted in 1328 to pay off the English for the peace. The last instalment of the £20,000 was paid in November 1331, the penalty documents destroyed, and the new king, knighted by Moray, crowned and anointed, received the homage of his magnates; the peace and above all the recognition of independence now seemed secure. Credit for the extraordinary achievements of the years 1327–31 belongs to Robert I and Moray, though the greater share must go to the earl. The guardianship was not untroubled, however, for Douglas had been killed in Spain, and the disinherited were nagging for their rights. The chronicler Bower depicts Moray active throughout the kingdom as justiciar, enforcing a stern justice, and then falling ill, poisoned by a friar, but struggling to appear fit as, swollen and flushed, with his army he received an English herald, whom he convinced that the Scots could still win a war, so that hostile plans were dropped. Moray died at Musselburgh, near Edinburgh, on 20 July 1332; presumably he had been nauseous for some time, suggesting liver cancer rather than food poisoning. On 6 August the disinherited invaded.

According to Barbour, Moray was of middling height and build, with a broad pleasant face; courteous and debonair, he loved loyalty, generosity, and honour. The few royal accounts show him close to King Robert in his final illness, and he was buried near him in Dunfermline Abbey. He married Isabel, daughter of Sir John Stewart of Bunkle, and they had two sons and two daughters. The elder son, **Thomas Randolph**, second earl of Moray (d. 1332), was killed within weeks of succeeding to his father's title, fighting the disinherited at Dupplin Moor, Perthshire, on 12 August 1332, and was succeeded by the third earl, his brother, John *Randolph, who was killed at Nevilles Cross. Both brothers were childless, and the earldom passed, despite the entail of 1312, to the earl of Dunbar, husband of their elder sister Agnes *Dunbar [see under Dunbar, Patrick (1285–1369)]. The extinction of the Randolph name and male lineage explains, at least in part, Barbour's subordination, in repute, of the first earl to Sir James Douglas.   A. A. M. DUNCAN

Sources J. Barbour, *The Bruce*, ed. A. A. M. Duncan (1997) · J. Stevenson, ed., *Chronicon de Lanercost, 1201–1346*, Bannatyne Club, 65 (1839) · *Scalacronica, by Sir Thomas Gray of Heton, knight: a chronical of England and Scotland from AD MLXVI to AD MCCCLXII*, ed. J. Stevenson, Maitland Club, 40 (1836) · W. Bower, *Scotichronicon*, ed. D. E. R. Watt and others, new edn, 9 vols. (1987–98), vol. 7 · G. W. S. Barrow, *Robert Bruce and the community of the realm of Scotland*, 3rd edn (1988) · G. W. S. Barrow and others, eds., *Regesta regum Scottorum*, 5, ed. A. A. M. Duncan (1988) · *Scots peerage*, 6.286–97 · G. Burnett and others, eds., *The exchequer rolls of Scotland*, 1 (1878) · [W. B. D. D. Turnbull], ed., *Liber sancte Marie de Balmorinach*, Abbotsford Club, 22 (1841)

Randolph, Thomas, second earl of Moray (d. 1332). See under Randolph, Thomas, first earl of Moray (d. 1332).

Randolph, Thomas (1525/6–1590), diplomat, was born at Badlesmere, Kent, the second son of Avery Randolph (d.

1561), landowner, of Badlesmere, Kent, and his wife, Anne (*d.* in or after 1561), daughter of Sir John Gaynsford of Crowhurst, Surrey, and his first wife, Katherine. One brother was Edward *Randolph (*d.* 1566), a soldier; a sister, Mary, married William Crispe, lieutenant of Dover Castle. Apparently he had at least one more sibling of each sex. Randolph described his Kentish birthplace as a farm, not apparently his father's since he himself bought it later.

Oxford, 'exile', and first journey to Scotland, 1545–1561 Randolph was schooled at Canterbury and went to Oxford with an exhibition from the chapter there. He proceeded BA in October 1545 and BCL in early 1548, when he was twenty-two. On 5 April 1548 the faculty office licensed him as a public notary. After migrating to Christ Church, he acted in this capacity as chapter clerk and also maintained a law studentship there, apparently even after acquiring on 21 November 1549 the (possibly ill-paid) post of principal of Broadgates Hall, the precursor of Pembroke College, specializing in civil law. He supplicated for DCL in October 1566 and June 1575, but did not complete the process. Anthony Wood thought he perhaps got the degree 'on one of his embassies', but lack of reference to him as doctor makes this unlikely (Wood, *Ath. Oxon.: Fasti*, 1.178).

Randolph was the subject of complaints in June 1550 by a Broadgates faction led by Thomas Darbyshire, who became principal under Mary I. Not being a theologian, Randolph was not so blatantly protestant as to suffer immediate expulsion after her accession. He gave shelter to John Jewel, ejected from Corpus Christi. Randolph did resign on 14 October 1553, but three months later Jewel was still with him at Broadgates. The idea that Randolph was a protestant exile is a half-truth. He was the conventional travelling gentleman, with protestant contacts and sympathies. His contacts at Paris were also significantly Scottish, such as George Buchanan, William Kirkcaldy of Grange, and James Melville of Halhill. Melville depicted Randolph as a religious exile in need of his financial help. By Randolph's own account, however, he was openly subsidized by his father.

Dr Nicholas Wotton, Mary's ambassador in France, procured a pardon for Edward Randolph (implicated in the rebellion of Sir Thomas Wyatt the younger) and employed Thomas Randolph occasionally. Following his return to England, in January 1558 Thomas Randolph was elected to parliament for both New Romney in Kent and St Ives in Cornwall, probably under the respective sponsorship of Sir Thomas Cheyne, lord warden of the Cinque Ports and a friend of his father, and Francis Russell, second earl of Bedford. Randolph was again selected by Bedford for St Ives in 1572 and witnessed his will in 1584.

Randolph did not stay in England. In 1561 he claimed that in the previous eight years he had never been able to see his parents two days together. Elizabeth I's accession found him already acting as a diplomatic, if unaccredited, agent in Germany. In December 1558 he said he would accompany the returning exiles Sir Anthony Cooke and Sir Thomas Wroth from Strasbourg to Antwerp. In the new year he was again elected to parliament, this time for

Grantham, Lincolnshire, through the influence of Sir William Cecil. Sir Nicholas Throckmorton proposed Randolph as clerk to the privy council. Instead he was sent in June 1559 to Throckmorton's embassy in France before undertaking the delicate task of secretly escorting James Hamilton, earl of Arran, via Geneva and Antwerp to Scotland. Oddly Randolph adopted the alias Thomas Barnaby or Barnabe, a former informant of Cecil.

In late November 1559 the lords of the congregation sent Randolph himself with William Maitland of Lethington south to seek English support, though the Berwick authorities tried too late to persuade him to stay in Scotland after having 'so discovered himself' as to compromise Elizabeth's bogus neutrality (Clifford, 1.588). The French complained about the activities of Barnaby, rather than Randolph, despite his carelessness with his alias. Randolph returned to Glasgow on 25 December, 'utterly destitute of anie maner of aide of one of my armes, by reason of a great fluxe of humours that is descended into the same, and also greved with a burnynge fever' (ibid., 1.665). He continued to press Cecil for a commitment to back Scottish protestantism, having helped encourage the successful intervention of 1560.

Randolph and the failure of the amity, 1561–1566 Randolph's expansive and gossipy correspondence serves as a major source for the period after Mary, queen of Scots, returned to Scotland. To an appreciable extent he was seduced by life at Mary's court, an environment for which he was unprepared by experience and in which he occupied a more prominent place than an English diplomat ever could have done in France. His lack of formal ambassadorial rank made him especially susceptible to the flattery of being seated with lords at feasts. His identification with his host government was at times considerable, as in the suppression of the rebellion of George Gordon, fourth earl of Huntly, in 1562 while he was touring Aberdeenshire with Mary. Randolph cultivated a courtly, perhaps even genuine, attachment to one of Mary's ladies, Mary *Beaton (*c.*1543–1597) [*see under* Queen's Maries (*act.* 1548–1567)]. Even as late as 1586 it was worth teasing him about the possibility of marriage to 'Mrs Beeton' (BL, Harley MS 6994, fol. 29r).

Randolph was not at this stage naturally allied to Calvinist critics of Mary. Although he helped introduce Scottish reforming ministers to English patrons, his sympathy was rather with his old visitor Jewel, now bishop of Salisbury, whose *Apologia pro ecclesiae Anglicanae* (1562) he presented to James Stewart, first earl of Moray, and which he rather optimistically asserted could be generally accepted by Scottish reformers. Randolph was sceptical of the 'exact severity' of John Knox, 'thoughe I acknowledge his doctryne to be sounde'. He was 'as wylfull as lerned' and acted 'as thoughe he were … of Godes previe consell, that knewe howe he had determined of her [Mary] from the begynnynge' (*CSP Scot.*, 1547–63, 564, 597, 672).

Randolph could not be accredited to the Scottish queen in her absence, but even on Mary's return he was not officially titled ambassador and was only allowed £1 6s. 8d. per day (later in his career he received £2 per day). The idea of a cheap posting was doubtful given Randolph's activity as a correspondent and courtier, but he was never paid the kind of allowance an ambassador of higher status would expect. Shortly before being expelled from Scotland in 1566 he claimed to be too indebted to 'depart with honeste [honesty]' ('A letter of Thomas Randolph to the earl of Leicester', 139). His old friend Throckmorton, visiting the previous year as a fully accredited ambassador, stressed the expense of Randolph's networking in Scotland: 'faire promises heretofore have drawen him to spend largely & to execute his charge carefully', but he had become discouraged 'since the fructes of his service worke him soe smalle advantage' (BL, Cotton MS Caligula B.x, fol. 297r).

In 1563 Randolph was instructed to dangle before Mary the prospect of recognition as Elizabeth's successor. This was to be done in return for dependence on Elizabeth's approval in Mary's marriage. Uncertainty over it damaged Randolph's position, giving him a reputation in Scotland for deceit. Elizabeth used him as a convenient scapegoat for her own dithering. Typical was the queen's instruction to Randolph in October 1565, when she had second thoughts about promising a special embassy, placing the blame with him for the misunderstanding.

Elizabeth's sincerity in offering Robert Dudley, earl of Leicester, as a bridegroom for Mary may have been very doubtful, but Randolph took it seriously and insistently urged him to show more enthusiasm, 'not to offend, but in all dutyfull service duly to serve your lordship duringe my life' (BL, Harley MS 787, fol. 121v). He genuinely wanted a settlement between Mary and Elizabeth, for 'to have them all wayes lyve in thys sorte and dowte th'one of th'other, is unprofitable to them bothe' (CSP Scot., 1563–9, 222). However, after the abortive meeting at Berwick of Randolph and Bedford with Moray and Lethington in November 1564, there was little chance of progress. In March 1565 Elizabeth declined to guarantee concessions even if Mary did marry to her liking and precipitated her objectionable marriage to Henry Stewart, Lord Darnley. This surprised Randolph, who completely failed to anticipate it.

The embitterment of Elizabeth's and Mary's relationship extended to Randolph, who found himself caught in the middle. It was not merely that a welcoming court changed to a suspicious one, but the débâcle seemed likely to ruin his diplomatic career. Randolph blamed his situation on Mary and Scotland in general, reversing his former liking for them and concluding that the Scottish queen's accession to the English throne would be 'as greate a plague unto our nation as cane come owte of Hell' ('A letter of Thomas Randolph to the earl of Leicester', 139). He tended to a lurid view of Catholic plots supposedly conducted through David Riccio. Randolph egged on Moray to revolt in summer 1565 and viewed favourably the genesis of the plot to kill Riccio, a deed accomplished after his own withdrawal to Berwick.

The animus was reciprocated. In October 1565 two harquebusiers shot into Randolph's lodgings, and in February 1566 he was expelled over the payment of 3000 crowns sent to Moray, although the money never actually passed through his hands. With some reluctance he finally departed on 2 March after the provost of Edinburgh told Randolph's landlord to throw out his belongings. The anti-Marian satire Mr Randolph's Fantasy was also blamed on him, though he clearly featured as dedicatee rather than author. The author, Thomas Jenye, was his clerk. Elizabeth was annoyed enough with Mary and (for once) supported rather than repudiated her servant. Randolph still considered himself 'unfortunate that ever I sette my foote in this countrie, whear so lyttle succes insuethe of so maynie yeres spent in yt as I have done', having 'gotten graye heares [hairs], not so hable a boddie for travaile as I brought with me, nor farther inriched in substance that yor honour knowethe, of whom I have byne a contynuall begger and shamles craver' (PRO, SP 52/11/49; SP 52/11/84). The last complaint was partly addressed. On his return to England, Elizabeth started giving Randolph significant grants of royal lands in Kent, for instance at Milton and Badlesmere. This created the local landed base that qualified him for appointment as JP for Kent by 1573. He also became constable of Queenborough Castle in Kent in 1567. He consolidated his position around the Medway estuary by becoming steward of the estates of the bishop of Rochester.

Randolph became master of the posts in May 1567, something apparently promised when he was in Scotland. In February 1566 Bedford had requested Leicester to assist Randolph:

> great and earnest suit hath been made for the postmastership … that Sir John Mason could admit a joint patent with him. You know Mr Randolph's service and how that he hath deserved a better thing than this, which if he miss in … his absence, would discourage any one to serve. (Pepys MSS, 76)

This served to enhance Randolph's diplomatic status—it was as postmaster that he was often introduced to foreigners. The department was also a vital auxiliary to the diplomatic service: though Randolph did most administration by deputy, he was an active regulator. From 1572 he was also (less actively) chamberlain of the exchequer.

Russia, 1568–1569 The postmastership seems to have brought with it at least the honorary status of gentleman of the privy chamber. Randolph was described as a gentleman of the privy chamber when accredited to Ivan IV. Russian specialists undertaking previous negotiations had been handicapped by lack of status; Randolph was supposed to provide this through his position as a courtier, while still being too junior to evade the most arduous journey in the Elizabethan diplomatic world. He landed on the White Sea coast on 23 July 1568, and arrived at Moscow on 15 October, but had to wait four months for an audience. Differences in custom enhanced the impression of offhand treatment.

The two monarchs' expectations were fundamentally incompatible. Ivan was interested in an answer to previous proposals of his for a reciprocal guarantee of asylum, in case Russia became too dangerous for him to remain there, and an offensive alliance, which he sought to direct against Poland. Elizabeth instructed Randolph to 'passe these matters with silence', conceding the simpler point of asylum if he must (Tolstoy, 43). Randolph's purpose in being there, she concurred with the London merchants, was to secure confirmation and extension of trading privileges for the Russia Company. They actually paid the £1527 cost of the mission. This had become more urgent with the incursion into Russia of non-company interlopers, who tried to defend their position by accusing Randolph of treachery 'as yf all the divles in hell were confederate to overthrowe this intercourse' (Willan, 105). He managed to refute the charge, a dangerous one where so unpredictable a monarch as Ivan the Terrible was concerned.

Randolph fulfilled the Russia Company's requests concerning White Sea, Baltic, and Persian trade. The grant was good enough that its reaffirmation was sought for another twenty years. Ivan, though, was disappointed that Elizabeth would not sign the treaty he sent back with Andrei Grigorievitch Savin on Randolph's return in October 1569. He complained to her that Randolph's 'talke was of bowrishnes and affaires of marchaunts … of our princelie affaires he made them of none effect' and 'whosoever was trusted in our affaires, and did deceave us, it were not meete that you should creditt them' (Tolstoy, 110, 114). Accusations of duplicity echo Randolph's career in Scotland; but it was probably true that he never 'did agree … otherwise then it should please the queen her majestie to like of at his returne home' and 'the true meaning … for want of a good interpretor, was not well understood' (ibid., 130). Randolph retained enough interest in the east to have considerable 'goodes adventured … into Persia [and] Media' to bequeath in his will (PRO, PROB 11/76, sig. 75). He was given supervisory commissions over, and invested in, voyages directed to the north-east and north-west passages.

Return to Scotland and France, 1570–1576 When news arrived that the Scottish regent Moray had been shot in January 1570, Randolph was sent north again, in the first instance to discover whether he was dead and, if so, to determine what would happen next. He shuttled between Edinburgh and Berwick for a year, and then returned in early 1572 with Sir William Drury, the marshal of Berwick, attempting to effect Elizabeth's incoherent desire for a Scottish settlement favourable to England that nevertheless did not openly reject Mary's sovereign rights.

Archibald Campbell, fifth earl of Argyll, himself no model of political consistency, was later reported as trying to exclude Randolph from negotiations in February 1570—'it wes not for the wele of the cuntrie that sic ane personage as he sould be permittit … to remayne thairin, to mak tumult and discord amangis the nobilitie of this realme' (Thomson, 160–61). At the time he certainly told Randolph another story. Melville's autobiography accused Randolph of acting as 'a double dealer and sower of discord' and encouraging the recalcitrance of his old acquaintances Maitland and Kirkcaldy in Edinburgh Castle, while claiming to support the regency for James VI (Melville, 198). At the time Melville had claimed to believe

Randolph was 'utterly myndit till peacefy our troublit estait, wherby ye may wyp away the wicked oppinion of the vulgaire that beleves the contrary' (*CSP Scot.*, 1571–4, 163). Frequently cited though Melville's statements have been since his autobiography was discovered, they are best considered as 'simply … paranoid', aggravated because he blamed Randolph for losing him a land grant (Pollitt, 17).

Maitland's and Kirkcaldy's attacks on Randolph's bias towards the regency, not to mention Mary's, were so vehement that the king's party believed that Maitland and Kirkcaldy had persuaded Elizabeth to have Drury take over negotiations from him. Kirkcaldy attempted to capture the regent, Matthew Stewart, fourth earl of Lennox, on 4 September 1571, supposedly to try to extricate him from Randolph's malign influence. It went wrong and Lennox was killed. Randolph's disillusionment with the queen's party was more outspoken from this point—'yff they weare hable to sett all the devilles in hell loose to make myscheif they wold not leave on [one] of them untyed' (PRO, SP 52/22/34). He certainly desired a more decisively partisan English policy and was frustrated in its absence. Indeed, 'yf I were ons qwyte of this countrie I wyll see Muscovia before that I come here agayne' though he conceded that the Scots were 'the honester men' (PRO, SP 52/18/75; BL, Cotton MS Caligula C.ii, fol. 396*v*).

Despite his Scottish missions, Randolph attended the parliament of 1572, sitting on committees on Mary (12 May) and on church ceremonies (20 May). In 1571 he married Anne (d. 1572x5), daughter of Thomas Walsingham of Chislehurst, Kent, and his wife, Dorothy. Thomas *Walsingham (1560/61–1630), the literary patron, became his brother-in-law. An alliance to the protestant gentry of north-western Kent was of wider significance because of the Walsingham connection to Francis *Walsingham (c.1532–1590). By 1575, and probably as early as 1572, Anne Randolph had died in childbirth and Randolph had married Ursula (d. in or after 1592), daughter of Henry Copinger of Buxhall, Suffolk, who was of Kentish origin. The couple had three sons, Thomas (*bap.* 1575), Ambrose, and Robert, and three daughters, Frances (1576–1618), Ursula, and Elizabeth. Considerable sense of kinship between Randolph and Francis Walsingham survived this change of wife. Walsingham, inaccurately but deferring to Randolph's slight seniority, called him 'uncle'. Randolph probably expected more promotion from this connection than actually occurred. His political and religious views and personal connections developed in parallel—in the 1570s he did join the so-called 'ideologues of the left' (MacCaffrey, *Queen Elizabeth and the Making of Policy*, 189). He became a close friend of William Davison and also grew closer to Leicester. In 1578 he appealed to the earl as 'th'onlye mayntayner in Englande of honeste and godlye men' on behalf of a preacher imprisoned over 'prophesyings', with an incidental repudiation of 'those that beare the name of puritans yf anye be so wicked as to calenge that to themselves' (BL, Cotton MS Titus B.vii, fol. 18*r*). Two years later he recommended Leicester support the return to Scotland of his Christ Church contemporary Christopher Goodman. Far more unequivocal than in his attitude to Knox two decades before, he praised Goodman's 'greate testimonie of his trewe service in Chryste's churche' (PRO, SP 12/144/34). In 1584 he was involved in the Kentish gentry's petitions against Archbishop Whitgift's antipuritan measures. His antipathy to Mary also led Randolph, who possibly had had some influence on Buchanan's political ideas in the 1560s, to encourage the Scottish scholar to write *De jure regni apud Scotos* (1579) and to arrange for the printing of his play *Baptises* with its stress on the tyranny of Herod.

In October 1573 Randolph went to France on a two-month mission to assess François, duc d'Alençon, as a marital prospect for the queen. According to the French ambassador, Bertrand de Salignac de la Mothe Fénélon, he was only named because Sir Henry Killigrew was ill. Fénélon described him as 'entirely depending' on Leicester: the earl had to counteract Randolph's 'doubts and fears into which the importance of the matter put him' as it concerned 'too closely the persons of very great princes with whom he had never before negotiated anything' (*Correspondance*, 5.427, 431). Randolph's diffidence may have been increased by his earlier abortive foray into royal marital questions. Between March and May 1576 he was back in France, but the mission's aim was superseded by 'the peace of Monsieur' (6 May 1576).

Scottish revolutions, 1578–1587 Randolph returned to Scotland in early 1578 for more troubleshooting when, as in Russia in 1568 and Scotland in 1570, 'all the divels in Hell were sturringe and in great rage in this countrye' (*CSP Scot., 1574–80*, 283). He concluded that the Anglophile regency of James Douglas, fourth earl of Morton, was unsustainable and his voluntary retirement was wise. Three years later he was sent back to see if Morton's life could be saved—he had the remarkable responsibility of delegated authority to call for invasion of Scotland by Henry Hastings, third earl of Huntingdon, and Henry Carey, first Baron Hunsdon. Walsingham, however, thought Morton doomed and wanted to concentrate on removing the sinister influence of Esmé Stewart, sieur d'Aubigny, now duke of Lennox. The latter was a point on which Randolph required Walsingham's urging:

> Yor putting of us in hope that D'Aubigny mighte easely be wonne to be at her majestes devotion was at the first interpreted to have ben *ironice* spoken by youe, but since yt seemith youe insist uppon yt, I could wish youe were ether otherwies perswadid of the man or at least keapt this opinion to yor self. (BL, Cotton MS Caligula C.vi, fol. 128r)

Randolph was, however, more dedicated to his own opinion than two decades before. He insisted that both aspects of English policy—seeking to stir up putatively Anglophile and pro-Morton Scots, and threatening military action—were useless. On the one hand, those 'heretofore … familiar are all nowe as strange unto me as if I had set fire in their chief city', a crime of which not even the Marians had yet accused him (BL, Cotton MS Caligula C.vi, fol. 124r). As for d'Aubigny, Randolph determined 'not for

all that to leave him desperate except I found you more resolute then I doe and better prepared to maynteyne so great a quarrell as this wil be if it be not looked to' (BL, Harley MS 6999, fol. 81r); 'an honourable peace is to be preferred to the most just war' (*Hastings MSS*, 2.23). Randolph did, however, finally burn his boats with Lennox by denouncing him at length on 20 February 1581 before the Scottish estates as an agent of the international Catholic conspiracy. This may have 'helped to seal Morton's fate', but less so than the plots of Archibald Douglas, earl of Angus, which seemed in Scotland to be more of Randolph's 'craftie conspiracies' (*DNB*; Moysie, 31).

Hunsdon, with whom Randolph had been at cross purposes in 1572, meanwhile insisted that a military demonstration could work and that if there was no sign from Anglophile Scots this was owing to Randolph's incompetence. Randolph's old friend Bedford reported considerable argument in the privy council:

> I tould my lords that youe having so much experience of this countrie I sawe no cause why youe should not have as good instruccons as he, but I thinke my lord hath no great goad [good] lykinge of youe, and I could wish he were more circumspecte then he is. Mr Secretarie Walsingham and others held verie harde for youe … my lord of Leycester is your very good frend … so that her majestie hath a verie good opinion of all youre dealings there. (PRO, SP 52/29/40)

Hunsdon did make a point of writing to Randolph as 'assurid ffrind' to 'lovinge friend' (BL, Lansdowne MS 31, fols. 93r–94r). Probably more sincere was his next denunciation of Randolph in 1587, this time for allegedly extorting the wages of newly appointed posts from them and causing the Berwick–London service to deteriorate.

Though Randolph's opposition to extreme measures was probably objective, he was also personally nervous at the anti-English feeling in Scotland. He asked Walsingham to 'vouchesauf me in yor superscriptions the name of an embassadeur to save my throte from cutting yf it be other wyse taken', and sent him some testamentary directions (PRO, SP 52/29/13). Shots through his window, as in 1566, did finally cause him to retire to Berwick on 28 March 1581.

Despite Randolph's failure in 1581, he was entrusted with the organization of the subsequent Anglo-Scottish border meeting. He missed Lennox's fall in 1582, though the prospect made him actually volunteer to return to Scotland, lest others 'repe the glorie of that for which I have adventured my bodie and spent of my owne, almoste to extreme beggerrie' (PRO, SP 52/30/28). In 1586 Randolph succeeded in forging a stronger amity and even convinced James finally to sign an alliance with Elizabeth with a last-minute cut in the financial offer. Memories of 1581 had made Randolph's welcome doubtful: Elizabeth, however, took pains to assure James that he 'in your childesche yeres sought all menes of your preservation' and 'hathe no other scope than to kipe us frendes' (*Letters of Queen Elizabeth and King James VI*, 28). James concurred, though after his mother's execution the following year, when there was an abortive rumour that Randolph would be sent back to excuse it, the young king sneered at 'dotinge Randalle' (*Extracts … Courcelles*, 41).

Randolph then made 'speede … to be owte of thys countrye', even though this 'haste … agayne distempered my boddie' (BL, Cotton MS Caligula C.ix, fol. 397r). Walsingham probably helped him back into parliament as MP for Maidstone, Kent, in 1584, 1586, and 1589. He was on the parliamentary committee on Mary (4 November 1586), and set off with Walsingham to her trial at Fotheringhay Castle, Northamptonshire, 'bycause of the knowledge I have of that woman's formar dealing agaynste her majestie' but was forced to 'retorne home … so miserablye I was tormented with the collicke' (PRO, SP 12/194/16; SP 12/194/39). It is likely that a knighthood was finally in the offing. Davison's disgrace after Mary's execution, however, put paid to any chance of such reward for Randolph, his close friend and a notorious anti-Marian.

Death and assessment Randolph's will expressed 'assured hope and confidence' in salvation, and also showed that he had no more cause to complain of poverty. Besides leases of lands for his wife and sons, he left £500 of 'plate, jewells, housholde stuffe, and readie mony' to his wife, portions of £500 for each of his three daughters once eighteen, and speculative trading investments for Ambrose Randolph, which he considered might come to exceed £500 in value. Randolph was supposedly 'well in health' when he made this will on 1 April 1589; when he added a codicil requiring his eldest son to guarantee his mother's jointure on 15 May 1590 he was probably less so, and on 8 June he died at his London house in St Peter's Hill. On 6 July he was buried in the local church, St Peter Paul's Wharf—his monument was doubtless, as requested, 'without great charge, voide of superstition' but perished in 1666 (PRO, PROB 11/76, sig. 75). Randolph asked Walsingham, William Brooke, tenth Lord Cobham, and Sir Walter Mildmay to acquire his heir's wardship for his widow. His relationship with the Kentish magnate Cobham was equivocal. He sent Walsingham nervous secret denunciations of Cobham's relatives—though not him—for corruption, but in 1591 Ursula Randolph did, as envisaged, turn to the only survivor of 'those honorable personnes my husband did so specially affect' (BL, Lansdowne MS 67, fol. 82r).

Randolph's broad and distinguished range of connections in both England and Scotland was remarkable. Though some Scottish friendships—such as with Maitland and Kirkcaldy—did not endure, he participated significantly in bringing Scottish and English political classes into an unprecedented degree of sympathy, though his efforts to develop an active Anglophile faction contributed only slightly to the Marian defeats of 1567, 1573, and 1582, in each case after his own departure.

Randolph was 'one of the first in England whom we can possibly identify as a career diplomat', spending over ten years abroad and, even at home, being frequently called upon to receive distinguished foreigners (Bell, 'Elizabethan diplomacy', 268). He showed that the profession could be worthwhile financially, though commercial investment seems to have supplemented direct rewards. He was, according to Thomas Morgan, 'both dogged and craftye'. Morgan attributed to James the remark 'that he never came thither [to Scotland] to do good, so as I am gladde that he knoweth Randolphe' (Murdin, 500, 505). The claims of the scarcely more reliable Melville have received more attention than they deserve. Inconsistencies in Randolph's negotiations generally emanated from Elizabeth: his own instinct was to be a partisan, not a duplicitous middleman. JULIAN LOCK

Sources K. P. Frescoln, 'Thomas Randolph: an Elizabethan in Scotland', PhD diss., University of West Virginia, 1971 · G. M. Bell, 'Men and their rewards in Elizabethan diplomatic service, 1558–85', PhD diss., U. Cal., Los Angeles, 1974, 25, 28, 34, 44–5, 49ff., 63, 77, 98–9, 118–19, 132–8, 369–76 · G. M. Bell, 'Elizabethan diplomacy: a subtle revolution', *Politics, religion, and diplomacy in early modern Europe: essays in honor of De Lamar Jensen*, ed. M. R. Thorp and A. J. Slavin, Sixteenth-Century Essays and Studies, 27 (1994), 267–88 · HoP, *Commons, 1509–58*, 3.176 · HoP, *Commons, 1558–1603*, 3.276–7 · *CSP Scot., 1547–93* · state papers domestic, Elizabeth I, PRO, SP 12 · BL, Cotton MSS Caligula B.ix, B.x, C.ii, C.iii, C.vi–C.–ix; Titus B.vii · BL, Harley MSS 289, 787, 6994, 6999 · BL, Lansdowne MSS 5, 6, 8, 13, 15, 31, 67, 69 · S. Haynes, ed., *Collection of state papers … 1542–70 … left by William Cecil, Lord Burghley … at Hatfield House* (1740) · W. Murdin, ed., *Collection of state papers … left by William Cecil, Lord Burghley … 1572–96* (1759) · *The state papers and letters of Sir Ralph Sadler*, ed. A. Clifford, 2 vols. (1809) · *Letters of Queen Elizabeth and King James VI of Scotland*, ed. J. Bruce, CS, 46 (1849) · J. Melville, *Memoirs of his own life, 1549–1593*, ed. A. F. Steuart (1929) · *Correspondance diplomatique de Bertrand de Salignac de la Mothe Fénélon*, ed. A. Teulet, 7 vols., Bannatyne Club, 67 (1838–40) · T. Thomson, ed., *A diurnal of remarkable occurrents that have passed within the country of Scotland*, Bannatyne Club, 43 (1833) · *Extracts from the despatches of M. Courcelles, French ambassador at the court of Scotland*, ed. R. Bell, Bannatyne Club, 22 (1828) · state papers Scottish, Elizabeth I, PRO, SP 52 · state papers foreign, Elizabeth I, PRO, SP 70 · D. Moysie, *Memoirs of the affairs of Scotland, 1577–1603*, ed. J. Dennistoun, Bannatyne Club, 39 (1830) · *Report on the manuscripts of the late Reginald Rawdon Hastings*, 4 vols., HMC, 78 (1928–47) · *Report on the Pepys manuscripts*, HMC, 70 (1911) · private information (2004) [J. Curthoys, archivist, Christ Church, Oxf.] · Wood, *Ath. Oxon.*, new edn, 1.563–4 · C. H. Garrett, *The Marian exiles: a study in the origins of Elizabethan puritanism* (1938), 266–7 · I. D. McFarlane, *Buchanan* (1981) · G. Tolstoy, *The first forty years of the intercourse between England and Russia, 1553–1593* (1875) · T. S. Willan, *The early history of the Russia Company, 1553–1603* (1956) · W. T. MacCaffrey, *The shaping of the Elizabethan regime, 1558–1571* (1969) · W. T. MacCaffrey, *Queen Elizabeth and the making of policy, 1572–1588* (1981) · *DNB* · 'A letter from Thomas Randolph to the earl of Leicester', ed. K. P. Frescoln, *Huntington Library Quarterly*, 37 (1973–4), 83–8 · 'A letter of Thomas Randolph to the earl of Leicester', ed. W. Park, SHR, 34 (1955), 135–9 · R. Pollitt, 'The defeat of the northern rebellion and the shaping of Anglo-Scottish relations', SHR, 64 (1985), 1–21 · W. B. Bannerman, ed., *The visitations of the county of Surrey … 1530 … 1572 … 1623*, Harleian Society, 43 (1899) · will, PRO, PROB 11/76, sig. 75

Archives BL, corresp. and papers, Add. MSS 33591–33592 | BL, corresp. with Robert Dudley, earl of Leicester, Egerton MS 1818 · BL, corresp. with Sir Nicholas Throckmorton and others, Add. MSS 35830–35832 · BL, Cotton MSS, corresp. with Sir Francis Walsingham and others, Caligula B.ix, B.x, C.ii, C.iii, C.vi–C.ix · BL, corresp. with Sir Francis Walsingham and others, Harley MS 6999 · BL, corresp. with William Cecil, Lord Burghley, and others, Lansdowne MSS 6, 8, 13, 15 · Hatfield House, Hertfordshire, corresp. with William Cecil, Lord Burghley · Hunt. L., corresp. with Henry Hastings, earl of Huntingdon · NL Scot., corresp. with Robert Dudley, earl of Leicester, MS 3657 · PRO, corresp. with Sir William

Cecil, Sir Francis Walsingham, and others, SP 52 · PRO, corresp. with Sir Francis Walsingham, William Davison and others, SP 12 **Wealth at death** £500 'plate, jewells, housholde stuffe, and readie mony' left to widow; plus £500 to each of three daughters at eighteen; Ambrose to receive max. £500 of 'shares, partes, freedome, stocke, and goodes adventured beyond the seas into Percia, Meida, Flanders, or elsewhere': will, PRO, PROB 11/76/75 · over £600 p.a.; granted duchy of Lancaster lands (value over £110 p.a.) in 1587–8; received £66 13s. 4d. p.a. as postmaster; was also chamberlain of exchequer; London house valued at £2 p.a.: PRO, SO 3/1; Fry, *Abstract of inquisitions*, 147–8; *CSP Borders*, 1.299

Randolph, Thomas (*bap.* 1605, *d.* 1635), poet and playwright, eldest son of William Randolph (1572–1660) and his first wife, Elizabeth, daughter of Thomas Smith of Newnham, near Daventry, in Northamptonshire, was born in his maternal grandfather's house and baptized in Newnham church on 15 June 1605.

Family background and early life Randolph's father originated from Hamsey, near Lewes, in Sussex. According to Aubrey, who had most of his information from a brother of the poet, William Randolph had been 'very wild in his youth', was disinherited, and became steward to a local landowner, Sir George Goring (*Brief Lives*, 2.195–8). Later he settled at Little Houghton, near Northampton, and served in the same capacity Edward, eleventh Baron Zouche (*d.* 1625), who had a house at Harringworth in the north of the county. His younger children William (*b.* 1607), Robert (1611–1671), and Elizabeth (*b.* 1613) were baptized at Little Houghton, as were the seven children of his subsequent marriage, on 30 March 1619, to Dorothy West, sister of Sir Richard Lane, lord keeper under Charles I.

At the age of nine Thomas Randolph wrote a 'History of the incarnation of our Saviour' in English verse, the manuscript of which, says Aubrey, was 'kept as a rarity' by his half-brother John (1620–1680). At an unknown date he was elected a king's scholar at Westminster School, where contemporaries included William Cartwright, the younger Donne, William Hemminges, son of the editor of the first folio, the Grecian James Duport, and Richard Busby, the future headmaster. He proved a brilliant student. Archdeacon Thomas Plume records a story told him by John Hacket that John Williams, when dean of Westminster, had singled out the ten-year-old Randolph to make extempore verses on subjects set by the dukes of Richmond and Buckingham and Sir Fulke Greville (*Essex Review*, 14, 1905, 19). The occasion is likely to have been one of the annual Rogation week election dinners held after Williams became dean in July 1620. Latin verse-composition formed an important element of the curriculum, and Duport long after placed Randolph, with Cartwright and Abraham Cowley, among its leading practitioners (Duport, *Musae subsecivae*, 1676, 75–7). The school maintained a strong dramatic tradition, and the headmaster, Lambert Osbaldeston, had himself recently acted in Robert Burton's *Philosophaster*. Some verses prefaced to the posthumous *Poems* of 1638 by Randolph's stepbrother Richard West assert that he:

> had not long of Playes Spectatour beene
> But his small Feete wore *Socks* fit for the Scene.

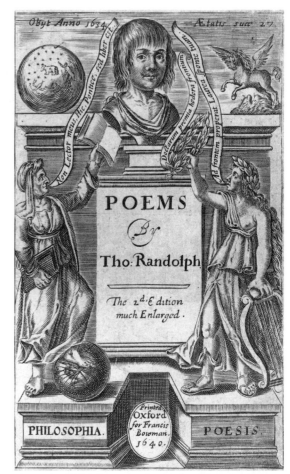

Thomas Randolph (*bap.* 1605, *d.* 1635), by William Marshall, pubd 1640

Here also he seems to have begun writing occasional verse, supplying two monumental epitaphs for the abbey cloisters on the surveyor William Laurence and the organist John Parsons. In May 1623 he was elected as head of the school to a scholarship at Trinity College, Cambridge, which, following the current practice, he took up a year later, entering on 9 April 1624 and matriculating as pensioner on 8 July (CUL, UA, Matr. 2).

University and literary career In 1625 Randolph framed the first of several contributions in Latin verse to university congratulatory volumes on royal events and in the following year the longest of the elegies published in *Manes Verulamianae*, the Trinity-inspired memorial volume for Bacon. Thomas Fuller attributes to him some lost verses on the discovery of a book in the belly of a cod-fish at Cambridge market on midsummer eve 1626 (Fuller, *Worthies*, 1662, 359). Above all, Randolph found ample scope to develop his talent for drama. His first attempt may have been the free rendering of Aristophanes' *Plutus* which, as *Hey for honesty, down with knavery*, was to form the basis for the version published by Francis Jacques in 1651. *Aristippus*, described as 'A Private shewe presented on a Fast night to the Seniours and fellowes of Trinitie' (Washington, DC, Folger Shakespeare Library, MS V.b.320), recommends to young students not the cyrenaic sage but the canary wine colloquially known by his name. Contemporary printed editions, where it is subtitled *The Joviall Philosopher*, follow it with *The Conceited Pedlar*, a witty monologue dated in one manuscript to All Saints' day 1627 (BL, Add. MS 27406).

In the same term of this, his third, year Randolph presided as 'father' at the informal initiation ceremony or 'salting' of freshmen in the college hall, delivering in verse a series of comic sketches of each of his 'sons'. By the time that his name appeared eighth in the *ordo senioritatis* of BAs in the following Lent all available college fellowships had been filled. On 11 August 1629 he was sent by the retiring master, Leonard Mawe, to the chancellor of the university, Lord Holland, with a letter of recommendation citing the support of Williams, then lord keeper, for a fellowship by royal mandate. This describes him as a person 'of those extraordinary parts of wit and learning … that scarce an age doth bring forth a better or the like' (*Poems*, ed. Thorn-Drury, xi–xii); he was admitted minor fellow on 22 September. In the same year he contributed prefatory Latin lines to Huntingdon Plumptre's *Epigrammatōn opusculum* and an epithalamium on the marriage of Lord Goring with Lettice Boyle on 25 July.

It is uncertain when Randolph first made the acquaintance of Ben Jonson, an old Westminster of an earlier generation, though a possible connection was through his father's employer and Jonson's friend, Lord Zouche (Bridges, 2.320). 'A gratulatory to Mʳ Ben Johnson for his adopting of him to be his Son' was probably written after the older man's disabling stroke in the winter of 1628–9. However, the circumstances of his adoption as described by William Winstanley (*Poor Robin's Jests*, 1667) in the famous anecdote of Randolph's paying his reckoning at the Devil tavern not in coin but with the extempore epigram 'I John Bo-peep' are elsewhere applied to Drummond of Hawthornden (*The Works of William Drummond*, 1711, ix). Randolph's mollifying answer to the 'Ode to Himself' that Jonson wrote in response to the hostile reception of *The New Inn* probably belongs to early spring 1629. In the following year his prospects suddenly broadened. No sooner had rival editions of *Aristippus* and *The Conceited Pedlar* been entered in the Stationers' register in March and April than plague forced the closure of both the Cambridge colleges and the London theatres until the autumn. According to notes taken by Malone from a lost office-book of Sir Henry Herbert, the King's Revels company produced Randolph's *The Entertainment* that summer in the provinces; its more familiar title is given in some verses on the '*Play called the* Entertainment, *printed by the name of the* Muses' looking-glass' (1638) in Sir Aston Cokayne's *Chayne of Golden Poems* (1658). This series of portraits of the virtues and vices, paraded before two puritan critics to persuade them of the moral seriousness of drama, was licensed on 25 November to the Children of the Revels, probably for performance at the reopening of the Salisbury Court theatre. A similar licence was granted on 26 November to the pastoral

drama *Amyntas*, a blend of high-flown Italian pastoral with English humour and farce which, subtitled 'the impossible dowry', was later acted before the king and queen at Whitehall, probably in 1631. A third piece, 'Praeludium', a brief dialogue between an actor and a theatregoer ascribed by the future Chancellor Hyde to 'T. Randall after the last Plague' (BL, Add. MS 37425, fols. 54–5), was probably written for the same occasion.

On 5 July 1631 Randolph figured sixth in the *ordo* of MAs and incorporated at Oxford in the same year. On 10 February 1632 the college conclusion book recorded the grant of 'allowances … agaynst the Kyngs coming, for comedyes', and Randolph's *The Jealous Lovers*, later dedicated to the master, Thomas Comber, as 'a thing born at your command', was ready by 7 March (Nelson, 1.636–43). This Jonsonian comedy in blank verse draws on his earlier play, 'The drinking academy', which survives anonymously in manuscript. In the event the royal visit was postponed to 19 February, when Trinity's offering was obliged to take second place to the Queens' College comedy, Peter Hausted's *The Rival Friends*, which was poorly received. Though the edition of Hausted's play published in London in June ascribes its failure to inter-collegiate rivalry— 'Cryed downe by Boyes, Factions, Envie, and confident Ignorance'—rumour put down to royal displeasure the suicide of the vice-chancellor, Dr Henry Butts, who had granted it precedence. Randolph, whose *Jealous Lovers* staged on the following day was pronounced 'not onely more compendious, but more facetious' (ibid., 1.636), could not resist a gloating allusion in the satirical Latin speech that he delivered at Great St Mary's in July as prevaricator during the commencement ceremonies. The text of his play, printed soon after by the university press, includes commendatory verses by Francis Meres and Duport alongside dedicatory poems to Thomas Riley, the principal actor, Sir Christopher, later Lord, Hatton, Anthony Stafford, Lane, and Osbaldeston. Oldys records a highly improbable story that the royal visit was the occasion of an exchange with Henrietta Maria in Latin verse (BL, MS C.45.d.14, p. 413).

Final years, death, and reputation Five days after the performance the college elected Randolph to a major fellowship, but from this point his career enters an uncertain phase. In the 'Eglogue to Mʳ Johnson', written at some time after the success of *The Jealous Lovers*, he laments leaving the university and his Aristotelian studies for the unruliness of theatrical life: the intriguing phrase 'Call'd hence to keep the flock of Corydon' has been taken to indicate a role in the management of the Salisbury Court, though hard evidence is wanting. It is commonly assumed that he 'indulged with increasing ardour in the dissipations of London literary life' (*DNB*), though the loss of his finger in a tavern brawl had already been mentioned in his Latin speech of July. If an undated anecdote is to be believed he was forced to adopt a clever subterfuge by which he:

> being thrust out of his fellowship desired a *bene discessit* [honourable discharge], which being obtained, he presented to the King, saying he could prove under the hands of the

head & all the fellowes that he was expelled undeservingly, whereupon he was reestablished in his place againe. (Bodl. Oxf., MS Wood F.31, fol. 104v)

In July 1633 he contributed a Latin hexastich to the Cambridge congratulatory volume on the king's return from Scotland, and sixty hexameters to the fourteen Latin pieces collected there in September for the *Mausoleum Mauritianum* in memory of Landgraf Moritz of Hesse-Cassel.

Randolph met his end in his native county, to which he had retained a deep attachment. Following a period allegedly spent in his 'delightful studies' at his father's house at Little Houghton (Wood, *Ath. Oxon.*, 1.566) he was offered the generous sum of £100 per year to take a post some 25 miles to the north-west as tutor to Edward (d. 1638), eldest son of the William Stafford (d. 1637) of Blatherwycke whose second marriage he celebrated in 1634 with a pastoral eclogue. Some undated verses to his 'Aunt' Lane mention an attack by smallpox, and his constitution may already have been undermined. Without doubt he was popular and gregarious: both Duport and Wood attribute his death in the following year to a readiness to match the conviviality of admiring friends. Thomas Bancroft wrote that:

he dranke too greedily
O' th'Muses Spring
(Bancroft, *Two Bookes of Epigrammes*, 1639, bk 1, no. 8)

and the charge was repeated by the sneering poet in the first act of his contemporary Robert Wild's comedy *The Benefice*, who likened Randolph to Tom a Bedlam, concluding:

Pitty! So rare a Fancy should have found
An *Helicon* so deep as to be drown'd.

Randolph was buried on 17 March 1635 in Blatherwyck church, on the south side, at the lower end of the north chancel, the register describing him as 'one of the fellowes of Trinity Colledge' (*Poems*, ed. Thorn-Drury, xix, n. 3). In the summer of 1640 Hatton, Stafford's neighbour at Kirby Hall, paid £10 to Nicholas Stone the younger for the mural tablet of white marble that incorporated the English verses by Hausted which Aubrey dismisses as 'puerile'. The posthumous collection of *Poems with the Muses Looking Glasse and Amyntas* (1638), brought out at Oxford by Randolph's brother Robert—himself promoted by Wood as 'a most ingenious poet' (Wood, *Ath. Oxon.: Fasti*, 1.430)—was said by West to comprise 'but's Ashes, which were throwne about'. Owen Felltham was among the ten writers who contributed commendary verses, and a copy of 'the late *R*'s Poems' had apparently reached Sir Henry Wotton bound up with Milton's *Comus* by April 1638. The enlarged edition that followed in 1640 incorporates an engraved portrait, the unsigned work of William Marshall, that was validated by Aubrey from the testimony of contemporaries:

From Mr. Needler:—his haire was of a very light flaxen, almost white … It was flaggy, as by his picture before his booke appeares. He was of a pale ill complexion and pock-pitten—from Mr. Thomas Fludd, his scholefellow at Westminster, who sayes he was of about my stature or scarce so tall.

The collection proved popular, and was reissued no fewer than five times between 1643 and 1668. Among its strengths are its epithalamia, love poems, songs, and above all pastoral pieces, from amatory dialogues like 'A pastorall courtship' to the rustic eclogue on Robert Dover's Cotswold games (*Annalia Dubrensia*, 1636). The style is throughout fluent and fertile and the tone good-humoured. In the field of drama some contemporaries, rather too eagerly, hailed him as Jonson's natural successor; the major plays were frequently reprinted at the time and continued to attract praise from Langbaine (1691) to the *Biographia dramatica* (1812). The first substantial collection of Randolph's works was brought out by W. C. Hazlitt in 1875, and modern scholarly interest began with editions of the poems by Parry (1917) and Thorn-Drury (1929) and the researches of G. C. Moore-Smith in the intervening years. The canon, nevertheless, remains fluid (Beal, 189–92): the Latin comedy *Cornelianum dolium*, published in 1638 as by 'T. R.', has been proposed as a refashioning of Randolph's work by Richard Braithwait, while forty-two poems not printed in the 1640 edition are attributed to him in manuscript verse anthologies of the time.

W. H. KELLIHER

Sources *Brief lives, chiefly of contemporaries, set down by John Aubrey, between the years 1669 and 1696*, ed. A. Clark, 2 vols. (1898) · Wood, *Ath. Oxon.*, new edn · Wood, *Ath. Oxon.: Fasti*, new edn · W. Winstanley, *The lives of the most famous English poets* (1687) · G. Langbaine, *An account of the English dramatick poets* (1691) [annotated copy in BL, C.45.d.14] · J. Bridges, *The history and antiquities of Northamptonshire*, 2 vols. (1762–91) · G. Baker, *The history and antiquities of the county of Northampton*, 2 vols. (1822–41) · H. I. Longden, *The visitation of the county of Northampton in the year 1681*, Harleian Society, 87 (1935) · G. E. Bentley, *The Jacobean and Caroline stage*, 7 vols. (1941–68) · A. H. Nelson, *Records of early English drama: Cambridge*, 2 vols. (1989) · N. W. Bawcutt, *The control and censorship of Caroline drama* (1996) · P. Beal and others, *Index of English literary manuscripts*, ed. P. J. Croft and others, [4 vols. in 11 pts] (1980–), vol. 2, pt 2 · *The poetical and dramatic works of Thomas Randolph*, ed. W. C. Hazlitt, 2 vols. (1875) · *The poems and Amintas of Thomas Randolph*, ed. J. J. Parry (1917) · *The poems of Thomas Randolph*, ed. G. Thorn-Drury (1929) · R. Richek, 'Thomas Randolph's "salting" (1627), its text, and John Milton's sixth prolusion as another salting', *English Literary Renaissance*, 12/1 (winter 1982), 103–31 · G. C. Moore Smith, 'The canon of Randolph's dramatic works', *Review of English Studies*, 1 (1925) · G. C. Moore Smith, 'Thomas Randolph', 1927 [British Academy Wharton Lecture] · L. J. Mills, *Peter Hausted, playwright, poet and preacher*, Indiana University Publications, Humanities Series, 12 (1944)

Archives University of Sheffield, papers of G. C. Moore Smith relating to Randolph

Likenesses W. Marshall, line engraving, BM, NPG; repro. in T. Randolph, *Poems, with the muses looking glasse, and Amyntas* (1640), frontispiece [*see illus.*]

Randolph, Thomas (1701–1783), college head, was born on 30 August 1701 in Canterbury, Kent, the eldest of three sons of Herbert Randolph (1657–1726), recorder of Canterbury, and his wife, Grace (1674–1750), daughter of John Blowe. He was educated at King's School, Canterbury, and elected to a Kent scholarship at Corpus Christi College, Oxford, on 19 November 1715; he graduated BA (1719), MA (1723), BD (1730), and DD (1735). On 22 August 1738 he married Thomasina (1706/7–1783), daughter of William Honywood, of Cherdon, and Frances Raleigh, and sister of Sir John Honywood, third baronet. There were six children of the marriage, three sons and three daughters, of whom one daughter, Thomasina, and three sons, Thomas, Herbert, and John *Randolph, survived into adulthood.

The early years of Randolph's career in the Church of England followed a conventional path and, while still pursuing his studies and publishing, notably *The Christian's Faith a Rational Assent* (1744–5), he attracted the attention of the bishop of Oxford and regius professor of divinity, John Potter, through whose influence he was made rector of Petham and Waltham in Kent. On 23 April 1748, however, he was elected to the presidency of Corpus Christi College, Oxford, where his younger brother, Francis, was still a fellow. His working life in Oxford as president of a small college was enhanced by public office as vice-chancellor of the university from 1756 to 1759, archdeacon of Oxford from 1767, and Lady Margaret professor of divinity from 1768.

Assiduous and methodical in his work, Randolph's legacy to his college persists in numerous handwritten notebooks covering college business and the history and management of its estates. Letters from tenants are often endorsed with notes of his replies, and the large volume of estate material is digested into a compendious survey. Typical of his interest is the notebook on Mapledurwell estate, 'Notes on manorial customs, with notes on copyholds, rents, fines and tenants' (Corpus Christi College archives, Cb 9/1). Similarly, when the Cheltenham school needed investigation in 1761 the president made a précis of the school statutes. Randolph's presidency also inaugurated regular dated notes of the decisions of the senior members; these minutes, or acts and proceedings, have proved a valuable source for historians of collegiate life in eighteenth-century Oxford. From the earliest months of his presidency the grant books are written up in Randolph's hand. The important collections of William Fulman and Lord Coleraine were bound, with their contents listed and foliated, by the president himself.

Orthodoxy and tradition governed Randolph's attitude to church and state. Apart from theological sermons preached and published in the middle years of his life he came to grips with public controversy in his publications over the question of subscription at matriculation to the Thirty-Nine Articles. His two most trenchant pieces were *An answer to a pamphlet entitled Reflections on the impropriety and inexpediency of lay-subscription to the XXXIX articles in the University of Oxford* (1772) and *An answer to a pamphlet, entitled, Considerations on the propriety of requiring a subscription to articles of faith* (1774). However, having put up a stout defence of the soundness of the established position, he bowed to the majority, mindful perhaps of his own previous position when he had preached against party zeal in January 1752. Though his part in the expulsion of the sixteen Methodist dissenters from St Edmund Hall in 1768 had caused unpopularity he was not intolerant of dissent when practised within the framework of the law; his concern was to preserve the perceived orthodoxy of the university.

During his term as vice-chancellor Randolph faced up to two notable controversies: the reorganization of the delegacy of the university press in 1757–8 and the skirmishes preceding the election of the new chancellor, Lord Westmorland, in 1759. These events have been well documented in print because they were closely connected to the career of the eminent lawyer William Blackstone. Blackstone's campaign for a radical overhaul of the management structure and business methods of the press was sharply focused on Randolph, who, as vice-chancellor, was chairman of the delegates.

Evidence of Randolph's benign and just leadership in his college is clear from the earliest days of his administration. The acts and proceedings reveal patient but firm dealings with the misdemeanours of junior (and sometimes senior) members; time is always offered to both parties to consider their position and to reconvene for further meetings, punishment is never summarily enforced, negotiation seems endlessly patient. Having come from a family with a strong affection for the college where he and his brothers had been educated and subsequent generations were to follow, and with his own wider contacts, Randolph raised the status of the college in academic terms through judicious selection; subsequently it became associated with good teaching and firm discipline. As one of the least well paid of Oxford heads of houses he was also a prudent manager of his money. His private accounts, which he kept with the same meticulous detail and care as the college records, give a privileged view of his domestic life. The records show a simple, well-ordered life; donations to charity feature frequently and provision for his family is consistently generous.

Randolph died at Corpus on 24 March 1783 and was buried there on 2 April, after a funeral oration in the chapel preached by John Buckland, fellow of the college. In his will it is his family, his servants, his circle of relatives, and the poor of the parishes of Petham and Waltham, Salwood and Hythe who benefit from the modest fruits of his orderly life. His widow died later in the same year, on 11 December aged seventy-six.   CHRISTINE BUTLER

Sources *Hist. U. Oxf.* 5: *18th-cent. Oxf.* • T. Fowler, *The history of Corpus Christi College*, OHS, 25 (1893) • Foster, *Alum. Oxon.* • W. R. Ward, *Georgian Oxford: university politics in the eighteenth century* (1958) • I. G. Philip, *William Blackstone and the reform of the university press in the eighteenth century* (1957) • CCC Oxf. • T. Randolph, accounts, Bodl. Oxf., MS Dep. e.173, Dep. e.174 • burial register, 1750, Canterbury Cathedral archives • memorial inscription, 11 Dec 1783, CCC Oxf. [Thomasina Randolph] • will, PRO, PROB 11/1102, fols. 354a–357r • GEC, *Baronetage* • DNB

Archives Bodl. Oxf., account books, MSS Dep. e. 173–174 • CCC Oxf., Add. 107/1 | CCC Oxf., archives

Likenesses J. K. Sherwin, line engraving, pubd 1783 (after J. Taylor), CCC Oxf. • J. K. Sherwin, line engraving (after J. Taylor), BM, NPG; repro. in T. Randolph, *A view of our blessed saviour's ministry*, 2 vols. (1784)

Wealth at death approx. £3500; also messuages, tenements, lands, and woodlands: will, PRO, PROB 11/1102, sig. 198

Randolph, William (1650–1711), colonist in America, was born on 7 November 1650 at Morton Morell, Warwickshire, the second son of Richard Randolph (1620–1671) and his wife, Elizabeth Ryland (1625–1699). During the interregnum the family moved to Dublin, where Richard Randolph later died. William was educated at home, becoming proficient in Greek and Latin, and studied law privately, although he never practised as a lawyer and was never called to the bar. His father was the half-brother of Thomas *Randolph, the noted poet, and the brother of Henry Randolph (1623–1673), who emigrated to Virginia in 1642, marrying Judith Somes, daughter of the speaker of the house of burgesses. It was a visit from this successful relative that caused William himself to leave Britain, arriving in Virginia between 1669 and 1673.

Randolph may have spent the earliest part of his residency in Jamestown engaged in building houses and barns, but by 1674 he was sufficiently wealthy to bring over twelve indentured servants and purchase 500 acres on Swift Creek, Virginia. He took a great interest in horse-racing, and was a favourite of Governor William and Lady Berkeley, although his high spirits once caused him to be charged with public profanity. During the traumatic period of Bacon's rebellion in 1676 Randolph remained neutral, although his property was scavenged by Bacon's men, causing considerable damage, and he was close friends with William Byrd and Captain Henry Isham of Bermuda Hundred, both Baconites. Randolph, however, profited handsomely from Bacon's defeat by purchasing plantations forfeited by the rebels, Turkey Island in 1684, and two others in 1698.

Perhaps as early as 1675 Randolph married Mary (1652–1735), heir of Captain Henry Isham and Katherine Banks, with whom he had nine surviving children, the first born in 1681. From his family seat at Turkey Island, he was now close to the new colonial capital at Williamsburg, which had replaced Jamestown, and became a local political figure, serving as county sheriff, coroner, justice of the peace, member of the house of burgesses, lieutenant-colonel of the militia, and escheator-general, a position which aided his accumulation of more than 10,000 acres of tobacco land. Randolph also inherited his uncle's position as court clerk of Henrico county, and served as speaker of the house of burgesses.

Randolph's estates soon made him a very wealthy man, with a large population of slaves who worked on his tobacco plantations, and his own ship, which took the produce of his lands to England to be sold through Micajah Perry, his agent in Britain. As was common among colonial planters, Randolph consistently owed enormous debts to Perry for the luxury goods with which he furnished his mansion and fitted out his family. Always keenly interested in education, especially for Native Americans, he was a major proponent of a university for Virginia, and was a generous donor when the College of William and Mary was finally established in 1693, serving as one of its trustees.

A particular friend of the Byrd family, Randolph kept watch at William Byrd's deathbed and acted as adviser to Byrd's sons when they served on the colonial council and ran the family estates. Randolph himself, however, was increasingly plagued by melancholia and gout, finally dying at his home on Turkey Island on 21 April 1711; he was buried in Turkey Island cemetery. He had established the Randolph family as an American dynasty that would be integral to the history of Virginia. One of his sons, John *Randolph, the colonial lawyer and legislator, was knighted during a visit to England in 1730. His wife died on 29 December 1735. MARGARET D. SANKEY

Sources J. Daniels, *The Randolphs of Virginia* (Garden City, NY, 1972) · H. J. Eckenrode, *The Randolphs* (1946) · W. M. Billings, J. E. Selby, and T. W. Tate, *Colonial Virginia: a history* (1986) · W. F. Craven, *The southern colonies in the seventeenth century, 1607–1689* (1949) · E. S. Morgan, *American slavery, American freedom: the ordeal of colonial Virginia* (1975)
Archives University of Virginia, Charlottesville, family MSS
Wealth at death 10,000 acres in Virginia: Daniels, *The Randolphs*

Rands, William Brighty [*pseuds.* Henry Holbeach, Matthew Browne] (1823–1882), parliamentary reporter and writer, was born on 24 December 1823 in Keppel Street, Chelsea, London, the son of a small shopkeeper, George Rands. He received a very limited education, and derived much of what he knew from reading at secondhand bookstalls. He had a varied career, worked for some years in a warehouse, went on the stage, and then became a clerk in an attorney's office. Having taught himself stenography, in May 1857 he entered the employment of Messrs Gurney, and was soon appointed a reporter in the committee rooms of the House of Commons. He proved very efficient, and after attending, during a session of the house, a committee on the merits of the Armstrong and Whitworth ordnance, he received a vote of thanks from the committee. Ill health compelled his resignation in August 1875.

When parliament was not sitting, Rands spent his time in literary work by special arrangement with his employers. At an early period he became a member of the staff of the *Illustrated Times*, and he also contributed to many other journals, such as *St. Pauls Magazine* and *Good Words for the Young*. In 1867, under the name Henry Holbeach, he contributed a tale entitled 'Shoemaker's Village' to *The Argosy*. He wrote many articles for the *Contemporary Review*, contributed to the *Saturday Journal*, and also wrote for *Tait's Edinburgh Magazine*. He was a reviewer for the *Pall Mall Gazette* and also wrote for *The Spectator*. In 1878 he helped to found *The Citizen* newspaper in the City of London.

Rands was in many ways an eccentric character, and his domestic life was apparently somewhat irregular. On 5 October 1846, he had married Mary Ditton (d. 1881), the daughter of Benjamin Ditton, a cheesemonger, at the parish church of St Mary Lambeth, and they had three children. But after some years, Rands left his wife to live with Hannah Rolls (b. 1831/2), the daughter of John Rolls, a member of the Curriers' Company and of the court of aldermen of the City of London. Rands and Hannah had four children, and after the death of his first wife he married Hannah on 25 March 1881 at Camberwell register office. Rands was also for some time a preacher at a chapel in Brixton, and composed hymns, one of which, beginning 'One Lord there is all lords above', achieved considerable popularity in the nineteenth century.

Rands was in fact a considerable all-round man of letters, poet, writer of fiction, literary critic, essayist, and children's writer. His adult poetry, such as *The Chain of Lilies* (1857), is typically Victorian sub-Tennysonian. The Christmas tale *The Frost upon the Pane* (1854) is almost equally sub-Dickensian, although his story of simple village folk is not without its own charm. His literary criticism is rather more robust. As well as essays on such American writers as Hawthorne and Poe, Rands produced a sketch of the life and writings of Robert Bloomfield in 1855, and in 1869 as Matthew Browne published a two-volume study, *Chaucer's England*, in which he reveals himself as an enthusiastic and informed advocate of the medieval poet. His essays on miscellaneous subjects, for example, in *Henry Holbeach: Student in Life and Philosophy* (1865), also retain some vitality in their lively, quirky opinions.

But it is as a children's writer that Rands is most likely to be remembered, principally for three books: *Lilliput Levee* (1864, 1867), *Lilliput Lectures* (1871), and *Lilliput Legends* (1872). *Lilliput Levee* contains some delightful verse, from the opening poem, in which children take over control of the world from adults, to such near-classics as 'Topsyturvey-world' and 'The Dream of a Girl who Lived at Seven-Oaks'. *Lilliput Lectures* combines talks for children on such topics as 'The world' and 'The family' with such poems as 'Great, Wide, Beautiful, Wonderful World'. But *Lilliput Legends* is all stories, sometimes fables or fairy-tales like 'Prince Hydrangea', which mix fantasy and realism in ways that remind one of George MacDonald. William Brighty Rands is a writer who often memorably catches the mind, the voice, and the imagination of the child. Rands died on 23 April 1882, at his home, Luton Villa, 67 Ondine Road, East Dulwich, London, and was buried in the Forest Hill cemetery.   DENNIS BUTTS

Sources DNB · F. J. Harvey Darton, *Children's books in England: five centuries of social life*, rev. B. Alderson, 3rd edn (1982) · *Wellesley index* · W. B. Rands, *Lilliput lectures*, ed. R. B. Johnson (1897) [with preface by R. B. Johnson] · d. cert. · m. certs. · *CGPLA Eng. & Wales* (1882) · private information (2004) [Allan J. Rands, grandson; David A. Rands, great-grandson]
Wealth at death £42 4s. 6d.: probate, 30 May 1882, *CGPLA Eng. & Wales*

Randulf. *See* Ranulf (II), fourth earl of Chester (d. 1153).

Ranelagh. For this title name *see* Jones, Katherine, Viscountess Ranelagh (1615–1691); Jones, Richard, earl of Ranelagh (1641–1712).

Ranew, Nathanael (1602?–1677), clergyman and ejected minister, was admitted to Emmanuel College, Cambridge, on 10 June 1617, graduated BA in 1621, and proceeded MA in 1624. He was incorporated at Oxford on 10 July 1627 and ordained deacon and priest in Peterborough in September of that year.

About 1644 Ranew became minister of St Andrew Hubbard, Little Eastcheap, London, a rectory that had been sequestered from Richard Chambers. The following year he was named as rector of West Hanningfield, Essex. On 29 February 1648 he was instituted under parliamentary order to the vicarage of Felsted, Essex, vacant after the death of Samuel Wharton. There he was 'well beloved' by the earl and countess of Warwick, who lived at Leighs Priory, near Felsted (Kennet, 890). They bestowed upon Ranew £20 per annum during his lifetime. On the division of Essex into classes the same year Ranew was placed in the eleventh, or East Hinckford, classis. He also subscribed to *A Testimony of the ministers in the province of Essex, to the trueth of Jesus Christ, and to the solemn league and covenant; as also against the errors, heresies, and blasphemies of these times* (1648) and in 1649 he signed *The Essex Watchmen's Watchword*, which sought to explain the ministers' original opposition to the crown and their current opposition to sectaries and the *Agreement of the People*. In 1650 Ranew was reported by the triers as 'an able, godly minister' (Davids, 389).

Following the Restoration, on 1 March 1661 Ranew secured the vicarage of Coggeshall, Essex, as a precaution in case of difficulties at Felsted, but did not take up the living. After being ejected from Felsted in September 1662, Ranew settled in Billericay. His *Solitude Improved by Divine Meditation* (1670), dedicated to the countess of Warwick, reflects his concern for proper preparation for death. On 30 April 1672 he took out a licence as a presbyterian teacher in the house of a Mr Finch, in Billericay, which was the same day licensed as a presbyterian meeting-house. Ranew died in Billericay in 1677 and was buried there on 17 March. His widow, Susanna, renounced administration of the estate in favour of Ranew's son, also Nathanael, bookseller and stationer, of the King's Arms, St Paul's Churchyard, who had published his father's book. Richard Ranew, who proceeded MA from Emmanuel College, Cambridge, in 1660, was possibly another son.   CHARLOTTE FELL-SMITH, *rev.* MARK ROBERT BELL

Sources *Calamy rev.*, 329, 403, 554 · T. W. Davids, *Annals of evangelical nonconformity in Essex* (1863), 389–90 · W. Kennett, *A register and chronicle ecclesiastical and civil* (1728), 789, 890 · *The division of the county of Essex into severall classes: together with the names of the ministers and orders fit to be of each classis* (1648), 16 · Venn, *Alum. Cant.* · *JHL*, 10 (1647–8), 82 · Foster, *Alum. Oxon.* · R. Newcourt, *Repertorium ecclesiasticum parochiale Londinense*, 2 (1710), 160

Ranger, William (1799–1863), civil engineer and sanitary inspector, was the son of Richard Ranger (d. 1839), a builder and later town commissioner, and his wife, Mary, née Martin, who were married on 21 October 1798. He was born in 1799 and baptized on 23 November at St Mary's, Ringmer, near Lewes, Sussex. His father had established himself as a builder in Brighton during the prosperous Regency period, and was town commissioner before and after the New Town Act of 1824.

Details of Ranger's childhood are not known, but he joined in his father's building firm, Ranger & Son, established at 13 Crescent Street and 4 New Road, Brighton. When Charles Barry won the competition for building the new church of St Peter, Ranger was appointed contractor in 1823, the church opening in 1828. Again, when Barry was appointed the architect of the Sussex County Hospital in Brighton, Ranger received the contract to build it in

1825. He also secured the contract for building the Esplanade, which Henry Edward Kendal jun. had designed, and for landscaping the beach and building a tunnel under the Marine Parade. This work was undertaken between 1828 and 1830, and finished by Thomas Cubitt, the builder of Kemp Town.

From the late 1820s Ranger also practised as a surveyor. He began by working for the commissioners of the Pevensey Level, and then gave advice about the draining of marshes in the neighbourhood of Worthing, though the Worthing town commissioners rejected his plans for their own town drainage. He provided the masonry for the Norfolk suspension bridge, designed by W. Tierney Clarke, which opened in 1833 at New Shoreham in the Adur valley, to carry the main Brighton to Worthing road.

In 1832 Ranger patented a kind of cement known as Ranger's artificial stone. The principal ingredient was 'grey lime' from the South Downs. The invention was reported in *The Times*, and he moved to London about 1833 to set up a patent stone manufactory in Lambeth Palace Road. He secured a further patent in 1834 for improvements to the original invention. Barry used his artificial stone in the building of the College of Surgeons in Lincoln's Inn Square in 1836, and it was used earlier for the Wellington barracks.

Between 1836 and 1838 Ranger was employed by the Great Western Railway to carry out three contracts, two at Bristol and one near Reading, which included tunnelling, earthworks, and a bridge over the Avon. The contracts overstretched his financial resources and, despite borrowing from the railway company, he failed to meet deadlines. The company took possession of his machinery and materials in July 1838 for non-completion of contract, whereupon he filed a bill against it for fraud, claiming he was misled over the nature of the rock and over Brunel's dual role as engineer and shareholder. The court of chancery dismissed his initial injunction with costs and he was no more successful on appeal. The case of *Ranger v. the Great Western Railway* was heard twice before the House of Lords, in 1847 and in 1854, but no judgment was given until 1854 because of the death of Lord Chancellor Cottenham.

Ranger was also employed by the marquess of Bristol to make alterations at his country seat at Ickworth, Suffolk, and to design two modest churches in Early English style, both afterwards listed buildings: the first was St Mary's, Westley (1835), and the second St John's, Bury St Edmunds (1841), the opening of which was attended by a duke, an earl, and a lord, as well as by the marquess.

Noble patronage probably accounts for Ranger's appointment in 1841 as professor of architecture and engineering at Putney College, founded in 1839 at Gordon House, near Hampstead, as the College of Civil Engineers. The college migrated via Battersea to Putney House in 1841, surviving until 1851. He was also a lecturer at the Royal Engineers establishment at Chatham.

In December 1848 Ranger was appointed one of the General Board of Health's six superintending inspectors, who were paid 3 guineas a day. Their principal task was to carry out preliminary inquiries, holding open court to hear evidence about the sanitary state of the places they visited and making recommendations about drainage, sanitation, and water supply. Among the first places he investigated were Barnard Castle, Cambridge, Darlington, Southampton, and Tottenham. He was also consulting engineer for the local boards of Dartford and Croydon. He earned unstinted praise at the general board, especially for his dual role at Croydon, the board's showpiece, since it was the first completed scheme. But a typhoid epidemic there in 1852–3 lay both the general board and its inspectors open to charges of incompetence, resulting in a Home Office inquiry in which Neil Arnott and Thomas Page criticized the alterations Ranger had made to the local board's original plan, and also the division of responsibilities which had allowed Ranger to act as both superintending and consultant engineer. When the general board was reconstituted in 1854, its role much diminished, T. W. Rammel and Robert Rawlinson both declined the offer of becoming superintending inspectors, thus enabling Ranger to retain the position. Although he was forbidden to undertake consultancy work, Ranger was given a salary of £800 a year, and he continued to write reports until the board's demise in 1858. He was married to Sarah, who died in 1860. Ranger died three years after his wife, at his home at 39 St George's Square, Pimlico, on 12 September 1863.

BRIAN LANCASTER

Sources *The Builder*, 21 (1863), 672 · A. Dale, *Fashionable Brighton, 1820–1860*, 2nd edn (1967) · minutes of the General Board of Health, PRO, MH/5–6 · *Ranger v. the Great Western Railway* [1854] 5 House of Lords Cases, 10 ER 824 · H. Smail, *The Worthing map story* (1947) · *Suffolk*, Pevsner (1974) · A. Burton, *The railway builders* (1992) · H. Hobhouse, *Thomas Cubitt: master builder* (1971) · *The Times* (29 Oct 1839) · *The Times* (30 July 1841) · D. Gerhold, ed., *Putney and Roehampton past* (1994) · 'Metropolitan sanitary commission: first report', *Parl. papers* (1847–8), 32.149–55, no. 895 · d. cert. · parish register (baptism), 23 Nov 1799, St Mary's, Ringmer, East Sussex · census returns, 1851

Ranjitsinhji Vibhaji, maharaja jam sahib of Navanagar [*known as* Ranjitsinhji or Ranji] (1872–1933), ruler in India and cricketer, was born on 10 September 1872 in Sarodar, a village on the Kathiawar peninsula in north-west India, the first son of Jiwansinhji, a farmer, and his second wife. The family was related to ruling houses in the region—including Navanagar, in whose territory Sarodar lay—but had fallen on hard times. Ranjitsinhji was physically frail and suffered from smallpox as a child; his father sought relief in alcohol and tyrannizing those around him. Perhaps because of this, Ranjitsinhji was lodged as a small boy with an uncle, the raja sahib of Dhrangadhara, who gave him the rudiments of his education. Ranjitsinhji was six when he experienced a great, though short-lived, stroke of fortune. It proved the seminal event of his life. He was selected as temporary heir to his distant relative Vibhaji, the jam sahib of Navanagar, as a precaution against the ruler's failure to produce a successor. However, Vibhaji and Ranjitsinhji's father soon fell out and the jam sahib shrank from formally endorsing the adoption. Four years later an heir, Jaswantsinhji, was born and the matter, as far as the ruler was concerned, was at an end.

Ranjitsinhji Vibhaji, maharaja jam sahib of Navanagar
[Ranjitsinhji or Ranji] (1872–1933), by George W. Beldam, 1901

It was not at an end for Ranjitsinhji's family, who had almost been within a heartbeat of the throne. They sought to discredit the alliance between Vibhaji and Jaswantsinhji's Muslim mother and gathered the support of Hindu fundamentalist relations in nearby states. The seeds of a dispute were sown, a dispute that underpinned much that Ranjitsinhji later did. The need to prove that he would have been a worthy heir found expression in his determination to make himself the prince of cricket; the need to extract reparation for what had been denied him found a less pleasant outlet in his brazen accumulation of debts and relentless pursuit of the Navanagar throne. Fully formed, Ranjitsinhji's personality was complex. A steely resolve was wrapped in clothes of charm. Some who dealt with claimant and ruler thought him ruthless and uncompromising; many who encountered the famous batsman found him enchanting and generous. Pleading poverty to some, he lavished gifts on others. Essentially, he was a solitary man. His childhood was rootless and lonely, his formative years in England scarred with racial injustice, and the facts told in his emotional insecurity. He achieved his broader aims but not happiness, as fear at offending sensibilities prevented him from following Vibhaji into forming a mixed marriage, in his case to a Westerner.

All hopes might have been derailed had Ranjitsinhji not enjoyed a second stroke of fortune. Even after the jam sahib fell foul of his father, Ranjitsinhji was allowed to continue his education along lines set out by the ruler. It was a demanding and friendless routine, but one that benefited him. From the age of six he spent eighteen months living and receiving personal tuition in a Rajkot bungalow before entering the princes' college, Rajkumar College, at Rajkot. He showed sporting and academic promise at the college, run by an Englishman, Chester Macnaghten, on the lines of an English public school, and by the time Ranjitsinhji left in 1888 Macnaghten, who said that 'a better or manlier boy has never resided within this college', had arranged for him to go to Cambridge, supported by an allowance from the Navanagar state.

Ranji: cricket for Cambridge, Sussex, and England Ranjitsinhji entered Trinity College in November 1889. Concentrating his energies on sport, he became fascinated by cricket, which he had learned in Rajkot from the age of eleven. He joined the university club but few took his early, faltering steps seriously and for three summers he played mainly for local clubs on Parker's Piece. After hours of practice against some of the best bowlers in the country, and armed with a stroke of his own invention, the leg glance, he scored heavily for town sides in 1892. In the following year he forced his way into the Cambridge eleven, where he proved a valuable team member with his capable batting and outstanding fielding. He became the first Indian to win a cricket blue. Though there is no contemporary evidence supporting the claim that he once scored three centuries in three matches on the same day, his enthusiasm was apparent and he won the hearts of fellow undergraduates. Their interest was heightened by the impression, which he did nothing to scotch, that royal blood coursed his veins (Ranjitsinhji had attached the princely prefix Kumar Shri after reaching England). It was at this time that he gained his lasting nickname, Ranji.

Ranjitsinhji had been expected to return to India after sitting bar examinations but, burdened by debt, left Cambridge in 1894 and chose to stay in England, even though his Navanagar allowance was stopped. He was friendly with some Sussex cricketers and began playing for the county in 1895, despite not having fulfilled the two-year residential qualification. His first appearance, against MCC at Lord's, was such a sensational success—with audacious strokeplay he scored 77 not out and 150—that no one made an issue of the matter. The season was a triumph, as he amassed 1775 runs at an average of 49.31, exceeded by only three players. Ranjitsinhji's sporting rise was now swift, testimony to his mastery of the art of batsmanship. Within five years of first playing seriously, he had become the world's leading batsman and forced a general reappraisal of tactics. In 1896 he scored 2780 runs, then a record for an English season, and his average of 57.91 was the highest of the summer. His ten centuries—two of which, uniquely, came on the same day of the match against Yorkshire at Brighton—equalled the existing record. Controversially, he was chosen for England against Australia in the second test match at Old Trafford after being omitted, no less contentiously, from the first at Lord's. The team was then selected by ground authorities and opinion was divided as to whether he should be regarded as eligible. The brilliance of his batting again silenced debate as he narrowly failed to turn the match in England's favour with innings of 62 and 154 not out.

The following year Ranjitsinhji published a technical treatise, *The Jubilee Book of Cricket*, which rapidly went through several editions and survives with its reputation intact. Ranjitsinhji's explanation of the book's production in the *Windsor Magazine* (October 1897) suggests later speculation that he was substantially assisted in the project was incorrect. Publicly, Ranjitsinhji built on his reputation steadily over the following years, continuing to set new standards in run-scoring which were unsurpassed until the era of Donald Bradman and Walter Hammond. He never finished outside the top five in the averages between 1895 and 1904, when he stopped playing regular county cricket. He visited Australia with Andrew Stoddart's team in 1897-8 and on an unsuccessful mission was one of the few individual successes, amassing 1157 runs, 457 of them in the five tests. He scored 189 in his first match against South Australia and a heroic 175 in the first test in Sydney (December 1897) while recovering from illness. He did not play in 1898 but in 1899, when he became Sussex captain, became the first player to score 3000 runs in a season and repeated the feat in 1900 (when his average was 87.57), at which stage the three highest aggregates stood to his name. His nearest rival was C. B. Fry, a close friend and Sussex team-mate, with whom he formed one of the most effective and famous sporting partnerships.

Ranjitsinhji's approach to the Englishman's summer game was significantly different from that of his predecessors. He felt no compunction to follow convention or style. Like Arthur Shrewsbury, the Nottinghamshire and England professional, but unlike W. G. Grace, who had set standards that appeared unbeatable, he based his technique on back-foot play, which he felt inherently safest. Other key components were placement, control of the strike, and economy of effort, which more than compensated for his lack of physical robustness (he stood about 5 feet 10 inches). The lateness with which he executed his swift, explosive cuts and glances caused general wonder—batsmen had not scored runs behind the wicket with such facility before—and gave life to the legend of an oriental magician. 'No man now living has ever seen finer batting than Ranjitsinhji showed us in this match', the *Manchester Guardian* (20 July 1896) reported after his England début. 'Grace has nothing to teach him as a batsman; and none of the men of renown of 30 years ago could have exhibited a more thorough mastery of every point in the game'. He became more orthodox later, as opponents countered his original methods.

Ranjitsinhji's achievements were the greater for the fact that he played, for the most part, on the brink of poor health and penury. But the man who put India on the map for many Englishmen knew that sporting success would assist his prospects of successfully contesting the Navanagar throne. He thought his chance had come after the tour of Australia in 1897-8, when he formally applied to the government of India for a review of his case, but after much debate—and questions in the House of Commons—his application was rejected. Four years later the struggle

had nearly got the better of him. He only narrowly avoided being declared bankrupt and the strain showed during the 1902 season, when his batting wore a distracted air and he contributed only 19 runs in four test innings against Australia before being dropped. He had played fifteen times for England but never appeared again. With help from friends and relations he bought himself two years' grace but in 1904 was forced to return to India, where he was kept by threats of legal action from an old schoolfriend who had given him £10,000.

Ruler of Navanagar Then, in August 1906, Ranjitsinhji had his third and greatest stroke of luck—or was it luck?—when Vibhaji's son, who had become the new jam sahib on the death of his father in 1895, died mysteriously and unexpectedly, without an heir. His death was attributed in some quarters to typhoid but there were rumours of foul play. With the assistance of Devisinhji, a half-brother, Ranjitsinhji had long prepared for such an opportunity and after an inordinate six months of deliberations was chosen ahead of other claimants by the government of India as the next jam sahib. As ruler, he took to terming himself Ranjitsinhji Vibhaji; years later, after lobbying, he was permitted by the government to use the term maharaja.

Ill-equipped for his new role and having spent little time in his native land since his youth, Ranjitsinhji found the early years of his reign demanding. As ruler of a small princely state, he was expected to exhibit loyalty towards Britain, and was disposed to do so, but in return wanted licence to live extravagantly. That Navanagar was crippled by drought, poverty, and disease did not deter him and he made full use of an agreement that he could visit Europe every four years. Both in 1908 and 1912 he delighted his cricket admirers by turning out for Sussex and, despite his increased weight by the second occasion, showing glimpses of his old magic, but created intense ill feeling by using diplomatic privilege to renege on debts. His levels of spending led the government of India to attach an administrator, Lieutenant-Colonel Henry Berthon, to his court. The British authorities encouraged Ranjitsinhji to stabilize his regime by marrying and producing an heir, but his talk on this subject came to nothing. Unbeknown to them, he had since 1902 been engaged tacitly, if not formally, to Edith Borissow (1873-1942), one of the daughters of his guardian at Cambridge, and their relationship continued clandestinely and possibly incompletely for long afterwards. It was eventually broken off by her a few years after the death in 1917 of her father, Louis Borissow, a clergyman, whose feelings had been one of the chief reasons for their secrecy. Late in life Ranjitsinhji embarked on another relationship with an Irish woman. In the absence of children, he took under his wing his many nephews and nieces.

When war came in Europe in 1914 Ranjitsinhji put the resources of his state at the empire's disposal. These included a house in Staines, purchased for £30,000 two years earlier, that was converted into a hospital for wounded officers. Ranjitsinhji went to the front but, like other Indian princes, was given frustratingly little to do. It was during one of several spells of leave that, on the last day of August 1915, he lost his right eye in a shooting accident on the Yorkshire moors. He returned to India a few months later and did not revisit Europe until the war ended; he played his last game for Sussex in 1920. His career figures in first-class cricket (1893–1920) were 24,692 runs scored (average 56.37), including seventy-two centuries; as a slow right-arm bowler he took 133 wickets (average 34.59). He was appointed KCSI in 1917, GBE in 1919, and GCSI in 1923.

Under Berthon's stewardship, and with Ranjitsinhji growing into his responsibilities, Navanagar slowly moved towards prosperity. Irrigation schemes were put in place, railways laid, and a rebuilding programme undertaken in the capital, Jamnagar. Most importantly, a port was developed at Bedi, which the British launched by suspending its customs line. Bedi proved so successful at taking trade from the imperial ports of Bombay and Karachi that the line was reinstated, causing a long-running dispute, but Bedi remained highly profitable. Thus were the conditions of his people improved and Ranjitsinhji guaranteed his opulent lifestyle, if one more in tune with occident than orient. At one time or another he owned in India two main palaces in Jamnagar—he invariably lived in the smaller one, Vibha Villas—a summer house and shooting lodge; in Britain he had a house in Staines and a lakeside castle at Ballynahinch, on the west coast of Ireland, ideal for another of his hobbies, fishing. He also possessed a yacht. He delighted in entertaining friends from the tweedy British aristocracy and his preferences were further apparent when he encouraged Duleepsinhji, the best cricketer among his nephews, to play for England rather than help India to form its first national team.

This was not a time to invite resentment among fellow Indians, and as one of the British empire's best-known figures Ranjitsinhji presented an easy target for Congress in its campaign for a democratic and independent country. In 1927 it issued a pamphlet attacking his performance as ruler. Alive to the threats, Ranjitsinhji played an active part in the formation and affairs of the chamber of princes, formed in 1920; he twice represented India at the League of Nations assembly at Geneva, and was a delegate to the earlier sessions of the round-table conference (1930) on the government of India. He also published detailed but unconvincing defences of his record in India and England. One of these was a biography, commissioned shortly before his death, in which he was closely involved. Written by Roland Wild and published in 1934, it told a fanciful account of the route by which he came to his throne. His incomplete adoption and his father's true character were ignored, and his financial misdemeanours suppressed. It was accepted as the definitive biography for more than fifty years.

Ranjitsinhji died of heart failure on 2 April 1933 in Vibha Villas, five days after returning from Delhi. He had suffered from heart and bronchial trouble for several years but his final illness was sudden; preparations for a trip to Britain were advanced. Later in the day, the people of Jamnagar lined the 4 mile route to his funeral pyre; five

months later his ashes were scattered on the Ganges near Allahabad. He was succeeded by another nephew, Digvijaysinhji. His bedroom in Vibha Villas is preserved as it was the day he died.　　　　　　　　SIMON WILDE

Sources S. Wilde, *Ranji: a genius rich and strange* (1990) · BL OIOC, Jamnagar: Ranjitsinhji's file, 1896–1901, R/2/575/12 · Ranji's claim to the throne, BL OIOC, R/2/575/15 · Nawanagar, 1908, BL OIOC, L/P+S/10/157 · R. Wild, *The biography of Colonel His Highness ShriSir Ranjitsinhji* (1934) · *Wisden* · school records, Rajkot, India · E. H. D. Sewell, *An outdoor wallah* (1945)
Archives BL OIOC, Jamnagar: Ranjitsinhji's file, 1896–1901, R/2/575/12 · BL OIOC, Nawanagar, 1908, L/P+S/10/157 · priv. coll. | CUL, corresp. with Lord Hardinge | FILM BFI NFTVA, actuality footage; documentary footage
Likenesses G. W. Beldam, photograph, 1901, priv. coll. [*see illus.*] · H. S. Tuke, portrait, exh. RA 1909, Jamnagar · H. Haseldine, statue, 1936, Jamnagar
Wealth at death £ 129,654 8s. 1d. in England: resworn administration, 13 July 1933, *CGPLA Eng. & Wales*

Rank, (Joseph) Arthur, Baron Rank (1888–1972), flour miller and film-maker, was born on 22 December 1888, at Chesnut Villas, Holderness Road, Drypool, near Kingston upon Hull, the youngest of three sons and sixth of eight children of Joseph *Rank (1854–1943), and his wife, Emily Voase (c.1855–1916).

Origins and early career　Rank's father was born in a cottage attached to the family windmill and began work as a miller at the age of fourteen. He gradually amassed a huge business and commensurate fortune. From the 1890s Rank senior built modern flour mills at major ports, ably embraced mechanization, mastered new marketing techniques, and was a canny dealer in commodities. He was a stern, driven man who abundantly increased his wealth during the First World War and justified his ruthlessness by declaring that survival of the fittest was a natural law. His business was converted into a public company, Joseph Rank Ltd, capitalized at over £7 million, in 1933. Joseph Rank made large, judicious gifts to his sons to avoid death duties (including £1 million to Arthur in 1920); as a fervent Wesleyan Methodist he donated £2,411,376 to the Methodist Missionary Society (1920–39).

Arthur Rank had a profound respect for his father, who was an exemplary influence throughout his life. Arthur was considered a dunce at The Leys, Cambridge, a Methodist boarding-school he attended from 1901 to 1906 (and of which he was later a governor, 1919–28). He joined Joseph Rank Ltd from school, working for six months in its London head office before six months on the London corn exchange, a year's apprenticeship in Luton, eighteen months working on all the milling processes at his father's new mill in London, and finally a year on production at his Clarence mills in Hull. He became a director in 1915.

Shortly after the outbreak of war in 1914 Rank enlisted in an army ambulance unit, and drove a converted Panhard taxi on the western front. He was promoted sergeant, in charge of twenty ambulances, before becoming a signalling expert and reaching the rank of captain in the

(Joseph) **Arthur Rank, Baron Rank (1888–1972)**, by Yousuf Karsh, 1949

Royal Field Artillery. Even as a soldier he remained a resolute teetotaller but he became a lurid, if never blasphemous, swearer, and retained this habit (to the distress of his fellow Methodists) in civilian life. He was withdrawn from the army in 1917 to organize women's labour in his father's mills, and on 18 October married Laura Ellen (1890–1971), elder daughter and coheir of a leading Methodist, Sir Horace Marshall, newsagent and lord mayor of London (1918–19), who in 1921 was created Baron Marshall. Arthur and Nell Rank were devoted and according to Noël Coward 'very sweet' (*Coward Diaries*, 170); they had one son, who died at birth, and two daughters. At the time of his marriage Rank was initiated as a freemason in Streatham at the instigation of his father-in-law; he ceased attendance after Marshall's death in 1936 (when he took over the chairmanship of Marshall's company) but was a member of the Old Leysian Lodge from 1923 to 1952. It was partly through Marshall's influence that he was a deputy lieutenant of the City of London (1927).

After the war Rank's father bought for him a firm known as Peterkin's Self-Raising Flour, which sold pastries and jams, but this venture was unsuccessful. After selling out Arthur worked in the milling side of his father's business and took charge of its diversification into the production and sale of branded animal feeds. On the flotation of the company in 1933 he became joint managing director.

> In appearance he was completely ordinary: black hair brilliantined back flat, and a nondescript tweaky moustache; quick moving but slow talking, so that any conversation

with him was liable to degenerate to a series of wordless gaps; tall, but stooping slightly from the waist. (Wood, 38)

He had a superb memory for detail and a great power of compartmentalizing his life and interests. He enjoyed practical jokes and his banter could be cruel, but he had a continuous sense of life's fun.

Rank shared his father's ardent Methodism. From 1919 he taught at the Methodist Sunday school at Reigate, he bought the *Methodist Times* (1925), and became president of the National Sunday School Union (1929). He had a strong, simple faith: he walked round his garden every morning of his life saying his prayers and had a profound personal sense of revealed religion. He would take no decision, domestic or public, without talking to God, and believed his decisions were sanctioned by a higher force. As his sometime employee Michael Balcon recalled, 'Lord Rank once told me that he prayed for me nightly' (Balcon, 186). Dismayed at the quality of religious films available to show children, Rank founded the Religious Films Society in 1933 to promote films with a religious and moral message.

Film producer Rank's family and associates warned him against involvement in cinema, but 'I felt called to the work' (Wood, 83). Rank and W. H. Lax, a slum minister, collaborated on a film called *Mastership* costing £2700, which opened in 1934. Next Rank commissioned a film adaptation of Tolstoy's *Let there be Love* and a biographical film, *St Francis of Assisi*, starring Donald Wolfit and Greer Garson (whose fees together amounted to under £10). Though Rank always found flour-milling stimulating, he was in the early 1930s an understretched man with a great fortune to spend and a taste for risks. Films provided him with a way to be both evangelical and grandly entrepreneurial. In association with his fellow plutocrat Lady *Yule, Rank formed a new film production company, British National (1934), and produced a film costing £30,000, called *The Turn of the Tide*, describing the rivalry between two Yorkshire fishing families. It was never widely exhibited, owing to its special religious themes, and yielded only £18,000. Rank's conflict with the film distributors convinced him that he must become his own exhibitor as well as film-maker.

British film production had been fatally retarded in the First World War. Audiences, seeing only Hollywood productions, had acquired a taste for these; British film-makers could never hope to rival the lavishness of Hollywood and their stars were lured away by higher Hollywood pay. Rank determined to redress these disadvantages. In 1935 he formed the General Cinema Finance Corporation, holding a 25 per cent stake in Universal Pictures, an American production company, and a controlling interest in General Film Distributors (GFD) headed by Charles Woolf. Rank was chairman of GFD from 1937 and of General Cinema Finance from 1938. He also bought the Leicester Square Theatre cinema in central London. In association with Lady Yule, he acquired Heatherden Hall, the sumptuously vulgar house at Iver in Buckinghamshire of the disgraced speculator, W. Grant

Morden MP. After an outlay of about £1 million, a reconstructed Heatherden opened in 1936 as Pinewood Studios (its name intended to evoke its rivalry with Hollywood). Characteristically the opening ceremony focused on a blessing from the Revd Benjamin Gregory, editor of the *Methodist Times* and honorary secretary of the Religious Films Society. Rank withdrew from British National in 1937 when he bought out Lady Yule's interest in Pinewood, of which he became chairman. As a result of complex negotiations (1938–9) a new company called D and P Studios was formed to run Pinewood (which was soon closed) and Alexander Korda's Denham Studios, where production was concentrated. Lord Grantley, who first met 'Rank the Methodist miller and millionaire' in this period, 'grew to like him, as everybody does, more and more. Never a talkative man, what he did say was always sound Yorkshire sense' (Grantley, 174).

Films as a force for good Rank declared, 'I am in films because of the Holy Spirit' (Wood, 67), and he meant it. He was determined to make good films, but more importantly, to make films a force for good. He believed that he was serving the will of God. Kind and scrupulous in his personal dealings, he was capable of bold, calm, and decisive action. He had nothing of the showman about him: punctual, methodical, and discreet, quietly working long hours, he was an incongruous leader in the feverish, illogical, extravagant, disjointed, and fantastic world of film-makers. He represented an extreme philistinism: he had never heard of Thomas Hardy, was alarmed at meeting George Bernard Shaw, disliked music, had the plain man's love of plain food, hung his houses with pictures of gun dogs and dead pheasants, and added a bedroom wing to Sutton Manor which was notably hideous. Yet this philistinism saved him, for he was consequently modest, giving money to his producers without the arbitrary interference that made other film tycoons insufferable. 'One of the most remarkable things about Arthur is his capacity to make you like him in spite of his appalling virtues', as one friend said.

From the outset Rank wished to rid Wardour Street of Hollywood values. He produced the excellent news documentaries *This Modern Age* to redress the Americanism of *March of Time*. After the declaration of hostilities in 1939 his patriotism was supported by the government, which valued his contribution to national morale. 'Arthur was a big man, and his father … had taught him to think big', wrote Michael Powell. He thus built 'an empire of entertainment, instruction and communication [that was] only rivalled by the BBC for the rest of the war' (Powell, 398). Partly by the chance deaths of his nearest rivals Rank acquired control of the Gaumont-British Picture Corporation production company for about £750,000 (1941) and of the exhibitors' Odeon Theatres (1942). In 1941 he formed a religious films unit GHW, and later an organization of independent producers. From 1941 Rank oversaw Gaumont-British newsreels and from 1943 Universal News newsreels. He thus came to control the Denham,

Pinewood, Gainsborough, and Gaumont-British film studios together with their stars and technicians. Ealing Studios, associated with Michael Balcon and best known for its post-war comedies, became a satellite of the Rank Organisation in 1944. This power, combined with his cinema ownership, was reviled in some quarters for its monopolistic tendencies. Yet it can be countered that Rank spent money when no one else dared, that he contributed enthusiasm and organizing ability, and always desired to make prestige films that could be exported in the national interest.

Wartime propagandist It was Rank's achievement that British cinema did not collapse in the Second World War as it had in 1914–18. Instead, during 1939–45, as cinema attendance peaked, British film-making broke free of Hollywood's shackles and reached its apotheosis in films heralded by the Rank trademark of Bombadier Billy Wells beating a gong. He became so much a national figure that cockney rhyming slang added a 'J. Arthur' to the sexual synonyms used by fighting men and civilians. Between 1935 and 1942 Woolf advised Rank to finance comedies, musicals, and spy thrillers as a safe way to make profits. Following Woolf's death in 1942, Rank pursued more ambitious, expensive ventures. Encouraged by his devout wife, who had a strong sense of right and wrong, he discouraged prurient or sensational subjects. These could only be approached obliquely in historical melodramas like *The Man in Grey* (1943), in which James Mason played a sadistic Regency buck who bludgeoned Margaret Lockwood to death, and *The Wicked Lady* (1945), featuring an eighteenth-century highwaywoman whore, which had a moralistic ending but nevertheless scandalized some public moralists.

Rank's films were central to British wartime propaganda. They embraced the realistic, historic, and comic. *In which we Serve* (1942) was a morale-boosting film in which the survivors of a torpedoed destroyer recalled their past lives. *The Gentle Sex* (1943) was a pleasant film about seven girls conscripted into the Auxiliary Territorial Service. *Henry V* (1944) starring Laurence Olivier with music by William Walton was a triumph of Shakespearian film-making mixed with rousing patriotism. *The Way to the Stars* (1945) was a comedy by Terence Rattigan in which the guests at a small country hotel near an airfield followed the progress of the war.

Challenging Hollywood's monopoly In 1946 Rank's companies owned 5 studios, 2 newsreels, and 650 cinemas, and employed 24 managing directors and a staff of 31,000, with a turnover of £45 million. 'No frills on Rank, who was obviously well disposed, and struck me as possessed of unusual understanding', noted James Agate in April 1946 (Agate, *Ego 9*, 68). Rank knew that Hollywood's big budget pictures depended upon $80 million a year received from Britain by the US movie industry, and urged that the British must seek a corresponding sum by the exhibition of their films in the USA. His purpose was as much missionary as mercenary. He wanted to promote the British way of life exemplified by *This Happy Breed* (1944), a film extolling the quiet pluck of an inter-war suburban family. After the war he and his ambitious young coadjutor John Davis devised a worldwide distribution network to market British films and challenge Hollywood's hegemony. Their strategy was, however, knocked awry by the vagaries of Clement Attlee's government. In August 1947, after minimal consultation with Rank, Hugh Dalton (later Lord Dalton) imposed customs duties of 75 per cent on the value of all imported films. The day afterwards the Motion Picture Association of America indefinitely suspended all further film shipments to the United Kingdom. Rank had just spent two months in the USA persuading big circuits to show his films. ('Is it true that you're dumb?', asked an American reporter; after pondering slowly, and rubbing his chin, Rank replied, 'No, just dull' (Wood, 223).) Overnight all Rank's efforts were ruined. His remonstrances to Herbert Morrison (later Lord Morrison of Lambeth) were received with bland insouciance. Yet shortly afterwards Rank (perhaps naively) responded to an appeal from Sir Stafford Cripps to increase British film production in the national interest by announcing on 3 November a programme to make forty-seven British feature films costing £9,250,000. Harold Wilson, the president of the Board of Trade, whose puritanism was offended by Rank's reputed profligacy in film-making, in 1947 set up the National Film Production Council to achieve by socialism what Rank was endeavouring by capitalism: this collision of means and duplication of effort was disastrous. When the 75 per cent levy was terminated in 1948, as the result of US negotiations with the British government from which the Rank Organisation was excluded, a torrent of the best US films flooded into Britain and swamped Rank's efforts. In a move that further alienated American film-makers Harold Wilson raised the quota on British-made films shown in Britain from 20 per cent to 45 per cent (1948), although it was reduced to 30 per cent by 1950. Rank's companies were also damaged by the entertainment tax on box office receipts. Bank loans and overdrafts with National Provincial exceeded £13.5 million in October 1948 and reached £16,286,581 in 1949.

Though the Rank Organisation failed to capture the US market, it produced some fine films while the attack was on. *Great Expectations* (1946) has enduring value and significance in British film history. Rank had to abandon his projected forty-seven feature films but still financed a few prestige movies in 1948 including Olivier's *Hamlet* (costing £580,000 on projected budget of £250,000) and *Red Shoes* (which cost £750,000 and grossed $5 million over six years). Balcon's Ealing Studios in 1949 produced a trio of great films: *Passport to Pimlico*, with Margaret Rutherford; *Whisky Galore* from Compton Mackenzie's novel; and *Kind Hearts and Coronets* with Alec Guinness.

Return to milling Following the death of his only surviving brother in 1952, Rank was obliged to concentrate on the family milling business. He and his wife settled their controlling interest in the film companies on the newly formed Rank Foundation imposing conditions to prevent an American takeover of the Rank Organisation (1953). This foundation was one of the richest charities in Britain

disbursing an estimated £100 million during his lifetime. It maintained the Methodist philanthropy of his father and supported Christian causes, and animal, educational, and medical activities. The Rank Organisation was sustained in the early 1950s by formulaic comedies until John Davis diversified the business into photocopying equipment (1956). The superb profits of Rank Xerox Ltd eclipsed Arthur Rank, who retired as chairman of the Rank Organisation in 1962. He was increasingly remote from the film world, where he was liked by those who knew him; strangers were often patronizing.

Bread was 'the stuff of life' to Rank. As chairman of Joseph Rank Ltd (1952–69) he helped to regulate competition among millers. Though his approach sometimes seemed old-fashioned he retained a strong strategic sense. He superintended diversification with the super-optimism that had characterized him as a film financier. During the 1950s the company bought over a hundred businesses which were consolidated into a new division, British Bakeries. The agricultural division extended its interests from animal feed into cereal and herbage seed production and sales, grain trading, and fertilizer merchandising. In 1962 Joseph Rank Ltd acquired the flour-milling company of Hovis-McDougall and was renamed Rank Hovis McDougall (RHM), capitalized at £45 million. By the acquisition in 1968 of Cerebos Ltd, RHM developed a fourth line of business, in grocery products, and expanded overseas. Rank was a paternalist employer who sometimes overindulged nonentities and sycophants.

Methodism and final years Throughout his life Rank strove for unity between the Methodist church and the Church of England. He was treasurer of the Methodist home mission department (1933–72) and general treasurer of Westminster Central Hall (1967–72). Until 1970 he continued financing religious films which were often ponderous or syrupy. He perpetuated the work of the Joseph Rank Benevolent Trust established by his father to build and restore Methodist church property. His subsidies increasingly maintained Methodism, although the conversion of Odeon cinemas into bingo halls deeply offended his co-religionists in the 1960s. Rank desired to take Methodism to the masses but had little understanding of the sacramental side of Christianity. Reliance on funding from Rank's charities affected the church's theology, directing it to evangelical charismatic work (Rank always responded favourably to phrasifying about the Holy Spirit) and diverting it from its more political tradition of social responsibility. Rank experienced a religious vision around 1967, and to the distress of his family and advisers supported the Oklahoma evangelist Oral Roberts, whose faith-healing struck others as charlatanism.

Rank was a tall, burly but agile man with a hawk-like nose, shrewd brown eyes and who resembled an avuncular Charles de Gaulle. He had a forgiving nature and chain-smoked. He bred pointers and labradors, was chairman of the Animal Health Trust, president of the Royal Agricultural Society of England (1969), founder-president of the Southern and Western Counties Field Trial Society and of the International Gun Dog League. Living on a millionaire's model estate of 300 acres by Reigate Heath (1919–53), he became a magistrate in Surrey (1923). For shooting he rented Tichborne Park near Alresford (1929–34) and then bought Sutton Manor in Hampshire, where he accumulated an estate of 14,000 acres. Having refused a peerage from Attlee he was created Baron Rank, of Sutton Scotney, in 1957. He died of a ruptured abdominal aneurysm on 29 March 1972 at Royal Hampshire County Hospital, Winchester, and was buried at Sutton Scotney. His barony became extinct.

Rank's nephew **Joseph McArthur Rank** (1918–1999), industrialist and philanthropist, was born on 24 April 1918 at Reigate, the son of Captain Rowland Rank (1885–1939), flour-mill owner, and his wife, Margaret, only daughter of David Jamieson McArthur, of Montreal, Canada. Joseph Rank (1854–1943) was his grandfather. Educated at Loretto School, Musselburgh, in 1936 he started work in his father's mill in Battersea. During the Second World War he was a flight lieutenant with the RAF transport command in Europe and later in Burma. On 14 February 1946 he married the Hon. Moira Woodwark (b. 1919), widow of one of his fellow officers, Flight Lieutenant Peter Anthony Woodwark, and daughter of Francis John Hopwood, third Baron Southborough. She already had a young daughter; a son and another daughter were born to this union. After the war the milling industry was in disarray, with flour rationed and many mills damaged. On the death of J. Arthur Rank's eldest brother, James Voase Rank (1881–1952), Joseph was brought in as his right-hand man in the milling business. Joseph expanded the business, buying up bakeries and related firms, and then acquiring other groups with different foods and agricultural products. He succeeded his uncle as chairman of Rank Hovis McDougall Ltd in 1969. By the time of his retirement in 1981 (he remained president until 1993) he was heading a global food conglomerate with 52,000 employees. He served on various trade associations, was the first high sheriff of East Sussex when that county was created in 1974, and lived for many years at Landhurst, a regency-style mansion on the edge of Ashdown Forest. He was a governor of the Royal College of Physicians, and a generous donor to charities. He died in Westminster on 10 February 1999, survived by his wife, their two children, and his stepdaughter.   RICHARD DAVENPORT-HINES

Sources A. Wood, *Mr Rank: a study of J. Arthur Rank and British films* (1952) · M. Wakelin, *J. Arthur Rank: the man behind the gong* (1996) · G. Macnab, *J. Arthur Rank and the British film industry* (1993) · M. Sissons and P. French, eds., *Age of austerity* (1963), 279–94 · *The Noël Coward diaries*, ed. G. Payn and S. Morley (1982) · M. Balcon, *Michael Balcon presents ... a lifetime of films* (1969) · R. H. B. N. Grantley, *Silver Spoon* (1954) · M. Powell, *A life in movies* (1986) · J. Agate, *Ego 8: continuing the autobiography of James Agate* (1946) · J. Agate, *Ego 9: concluding the autobiography of James Agate* (1948) · *CGPLA Eng. & Wales* (1972) · b. cert. · d. cert. · *Daily Telegraph* (11 March 1993) · *The Times* (18 March 1999) · *The Scotsman* (24 March 1999) · Burke, *Peerage* (1967) [Joseph McArthur Rank]

Archives U. Warwick Mod. RC, corresp. with Lady Allen relating to children's films

Likenesses photographs, 1935–59, Hult. Arch. · Y. Karsh, photograph, 1949, NPG [*see illus.*] · W. Stoneman, photograph, 1957, NPG · H. Coster, photographs, NPG · photographs, repro. in Wakelin, *J. Arthur Rank*

Wealth at death £5,993,323: probate, 28 June 1972, *CGPLA Eng. & Wales* · £704,915 gross, £692,324 net—Joseph McArthur Rank: probate, 10 Sept 1999, *CGPLA Eng. & Wal.*

Rank, James Voase (1881–1952). *See under* Rank, Joseph (1854–1943).

Rank, Joseph (1854–1943), flour miller and philanthropist, was born at Holderness Road in Hull on 28 March 1854, the second of four sons (the eldest died in infancy) of James Rank (1829–1874), miller, and his first wife, Mary Ann (d. 1858), daughter of Joseph Parrott, a Hull shipowner. He showed little promise at the Revd Haynes's school at Swinefleet near Goole. When at fourteen he joined the family mill, his father rated him good for nothing, and on James Rank's death in 1874, the executors handed him £500 and told him to look elsewhere. Rank set up his own mill, and on 15 June 1880 married Emily (d. 1916), daughter of Robert Voase, farmer, of Ellerby, near Hull. Gentle and industrious, she was the ideal helpmate for a man resolved to make good by living on a shoestring. She brought up their three sons (there were also three daughters) to become achievers despite their father's domineering behaviour towards them, the result of his own unhappy childhood.

While his subsequent pre-eminence as a flour miller undoubtedly owed a lot to good fortune, Rank had a shrewd understanding of his industry. Quick to exploit new technology, he was a first-rate dealer in commodities, being able to make a profit even in conditions of overcapacity and depressed trading. In 1885 he built the Alexandra mill at Hull, incorporating the latest technology of roller-milling, and six years later the Clarence mills, among the most modern in Britain. He increased his profits by importing wheat direct rather than through dealers. He subsequently erected other mills close to English and Welsh ports which had deep water access and could receive shipments of foreign grain. In 1899 the company became Joseph Rank Ltd, with a capital of £700,000. Five years later Rank moved the head office to London.

During the early 1880s Rank underwent a religious conversion to strict Methodism. Almost his whole life thereafter was devoted to living his simple and childlike faith: he once told his employees that he did not put down all his success to himself, much being due to God and much to themselves. He made his family attend services three times on Sundays, and forbade liquor and tobacco, theatregoing, and dancing in public. Energetic dances at home, however, were permitted, as were visits to the circus.

A lifelong cricketing addict, Rank took the family to Scarborough annually for the cricket festival. In later years, he often slipped away to Lord's on summer afternoons, with a packet of sandwiches and some ginger pop. Parsimonious to a fault, he avoided eating out, and walked rather than using transport. He did exercises every morning, had an excellent digestion, slept soundly, and to the end remained lithe and energetic. He was a Victorian at heart, paternalistic and mildly eccentric. As an ardent phrenologist, he kept a plaster head in his office, and selected employees by their cranial characteristics.

Having resisted the temptation in the 1890s to sell his firm and become an evangelist, Rank did the next best thing and gave away most of his wealth. He supported Hull Royal Infirmary and in 1934 endowed the Joseph Rank Benevolent Fund with £300,000 to relieve poverty in the city. Between 1920 and his death he gave over £3.5 million to Methodist causes. His wife died in 1916, and on 3 October 1918 he married her widowed sister, Annie Maria Witty (d. 1940).

In the First World War, Rank served on the Wheat Control Board. After 1918 his sons James Voase Rank and Joseph Arthur *Rank were in day-to-day charge. Ranks, the largest milling combine in Britain and one of the largest in the world, continued to expand. The Second World War brought Rank both personal sorrow, with the death of his second wife in 1940, and commercial setbacks when eight mills were wrecked by bombing. Rank himself died at his Surrey home, Colley Corner, Reigate Heath, on 13 November 1943.

His eldest son, **James Voase Rank** (1881–1952), was born at Wilton Street in Hull on 10 May 1881. He was educated at Hymers College, Hull, and at Weston College, Harrogate. He trained with a firm of wheat merchants, and then joined the company on the commercial side, becoming a prominent wheat buyer on the Baltic exchange. In 1907 he was made a director, and on 9 April that year he married Ursula Mary, daughter of Evan Tadman Ferrier, with whom he had a daughter.

As his father's right-hand man, and later as managing director, James Voase Rank steadily increased the number of the company's mills, and became a national figure in the milling business. In 1928–9, as president of its national association, he devised a scheme for rationalizing the industry, which involved quotas and buying in redundant capacity.

From 1938 onwards the government employed Rank's skills, first to build up a strategic reserve of wheat, and later as director of the Ministry of Food's imported cereals division, a post he continued to hold until his death. In a typically unbureaucratic manner, he oversaw the purchase, importation, and distribution of all cereals and cereal products in Britain, and subsequently for India, other British colonies, and various allied countries. As he was simultaneously president of the millers' national association, he came under criticism for the conflicts of interest the holding of these two posts entailed.

With an enjoyment of life and abundant energy, in sharp contrast to his father, James Voase Rank was a twentieth-century man through and through. Although still a Methodist, in 1926 he divorced his wife and on 10 May the following year married a divorcée, Mrs Patricia Edytha Morgan (d. 1954). There were no children of the marriage. A director of the International Horse Show and a member of the Kennel Club committee, in Surrey he bred horses and dogs. He won awards for his shorthorn cattle. He became a racehorse owner and—to his father's

consternation—bought a stud near Salisbury in 1934, winning the St Leger four years later. His philanthropy, mainly to hospitals and charitable institutions, was unostentatiously exercised. He died in the London Clinic, 20 Devonshire Place, London, on 3 January 1952.

T. A. B. CORLEY

Sources J. Brown, 'Rank, Joseph', *DBB* · R. G. Burnett, *Through the mill: the life of Joseph Rank* (1945) · J. Rank Ltd, *The master millers: the story of the house of Rank* (1956) · *The Times* (15 Nov 1943) · W. Beveridge, *British food control* (1928) · *WWW, 1941–50* · D. J. Jeremy, *Capitalists and Christians: business leaders and the churches in Britain, 1900–1960* (1990) · R. J. Hammond, *Food*, 1 (1951); 3 (1962) · *The Times* (4 Jan 1952) [obit. of James Voase Rank] · *The Times* (8 Jan 1952) [obit. of James Voase Rank] · *CGPLA Eng. & Wales* (1944) · *CGPLA Eng. & Wales* (1952) [James Voase Rank] · d. cert. [James Voase Rank]
Archives Rank Hovis Macdougall | BLPES, letters to tariff commission
Likenesses Vandyk, two photographs, *c.*1930–1934, repro. in Burnett, *Through the mill*, frontispiece, 192
Wealth at death £70,954 7*s.* 8*d.*: probate, 5 April 1944, *CGPLA Eng. & Wales* · £1,622,915 15*s.* 7*d.*—James Voase Rank: probate, 1952, *CGPLA Eng. & Wales*

Rank, Joseph McArthur (1918–1999). *See under* Rank, (Joseph) Arthur, Baron Rank (1888–1972).

Rankeillor. For this title name *see* Hope, Archibald, Lord Rankeillor (1639–1706) [*see under* Hope, Sir John, Lord Craighall (1603x5–1654)].

Rankeillour. For this title name *see* Hope, James Fitzalan, first Baron Rankeillour (1870–1949).

Ranken, Alexander (1755–1827), Church of Scotland minister and author, was born in Edinburgh on 28 February 1755. At the age of fifteen he entered the university of his native city and after graduating in arts began to study divinity in 1775. On 28 April 1779 he was licensed to preach, and in the same year became assistant to the pastor of St Cuthbert's, Edinburgh. He remained there two years, when, on 17 August 1781, he was appointed minister of the parish of Cambusnethan, Lanarkshire. On 12 November 1782 he married Euphemia Thomson (d. 1822); they had two children, Margaret (1783–1786) and Andrew (1785–1851). In July 1785, he was invited by the provost and magistrates of Glasgow to become minister of St David's in the town. There he received praise for the insight, chasteness, and simplicity of his sermons. In April 1801 Glasgow University gave him the degree of DD.

Besides topical homilies and memorial sermons for members of the royal family, Ranken was chiefly known for two published works, *Institutes of Theology* (1822), and especially his nine-volume *History of France from the Time of its Conquest by Clovis to the Death of Louis XVI* (1802–22). The *History* is organized thematically, with separate chapters on topics such as the arts, laws, and political affairs. The first three volumes received strong but fair criticism from Henry Hallam in the *Edinburgh Review* for the arrangement and Ranken's poor understanding of his Latin sources, as well as for being 'shamefully destitute of references' (*EdinR*, 6.220). Marking his prominence in the kirk, in 1811

Ranken was appointed moderator of the general assembly of the Church of Scotland. He died in Glasgow on 23 February 1827 and was buried there.

MICHAEL KUGLER

Sources *Fasti Scot.*, new edn · Allibone, *Dict.* · [H. Hallam], review of Alexander Ranken, *The history of France from the time of its conquest, EdinR*, 6 (1805), 209–28 · J. Marshall, *A sermon preached in St David's Church, Glasgow* (1827)

Ranken, George (1828–1856), army officer, was born in London on 4 January 1828, the eldest son of George Ranken of London. After education at private schools, in 1844 he passed into the Royal Military Academy, Woolwich. He was commissioned second-lieutenant, Royal Engineers, on 1 October 1847, and was promoted first-lieutenant on 29 December 1849. On 6 April 1850 Ranken embarked for Canada, arriving in Montreal early in May; he went to Quebec, returning to Montreal in March 1852. In July he took a prominent part in trying to extinguish the great fire at Montreal, when over 10,000 people were made homeless. In February and March 1853 Ranken travelled through the United States and to the West Indies. During the tour he made the acquaintance of W. M. Thackeray, who was lecturing, and travelled with him. Ranken's journal of his travels was edited by his brother, W. B. Ranken, and published as *Canada and the Crimea, or, Sketches of a Soldier's Life* (1862). In summer 1853 Ranken was again at Quebec, and during the cholera epidemic tried to mitigate the sufferings of the poor. He advocated in the local press the formation of a society to help distressed immigrants. In 1854 he distinguished himself in extinguishing the fire which destroyed the parliament buildings at Quebec, and received the thanks of the Canadian legislature for his role in saving the library of the Literary and Historical Society.

Ranken returned to England early in 1855, and was quartered at first in Edinburgh and then at Fort George, near Inverness. At this time he contributed letters, signed Delta, on military topics to the *Morning Post*. He urged increased pay for soldiers in the Crimea to induce the militia to volunteer for the line, a suggestion adopted by Lord Panmure. He proposed the formation, later carried out, of camps of instruction, and also the reorganization of the Royal Artillery and of the Royal Engineers.

While at Fort George, Ranken volunteered for active service, and was ordered to the Crimea, arriving at Balaklava on 12 August 1855. He served in the trenches. On 8 September the British assault on the Redan took place, with Ranken in the van. The assault, though unsuccessful, led later to Russian evacuation. On 10 September Ranken rode into Sevastopol to see the ruins of the burning city.

After the siege Ranken was placed in charge of the waterworks for the army. He was promoted second-captain on 25 September 1855 and brevet major on 2 November for distinguished service in the field. On 28 February 1856 he was accidentally killed while, under Lieutenant-Colonel Lloyd, demolishing the Korabelnaya barracks, Sevastopol, known as the White Buildings. General Codrington in his dispatch praised 'this excellent and gallant officer'. Ranken was buried on 2 March 1856 at the Right Attack burial-ground of the Royal Engineers in the Crimea, where eleven of his fellow officers had been buried. A memorial window was placed in the church of Valcartier, north of Quebec, a church towards the building of which he had largely contributed, and a monument was erected in the cathedral of Quebec. Ranken was unmarried. He kept a journal when in the Crimea, from which extracts were selected by W. B. Ranken and published in 1857 as *Six Months at Sebastopol*.

R. H. VETCH, *rev.* ROGER T. STEARN

Sources PRO, War Office MSS · W. Porter, *History of the corps of royal engineers*, 2 vols. (1889) · *Six months at Sebastopol: being selections from the journal and correspondence of … Major George Ranken*, ed. W. B. Ranken (1857) · Major Ranken [G. Ranken], *Canada and the Crimea, or, Sketches of a soldier's life*, ed. W. B. Ranken (1862) · A. D. Lambert, *The Crimean War: British grand strategy, 1853–56* (1990) · *GM*, 2nd ser., 45 (1856), 545 · Boase, *Mod. Eng. biog.*

Likenesses engraving (after photograph), repro. in Ranken, ed., *Six months at Sebastopol*

Rankin, Sir George Claus (1877–1946), judge, was born on 12 August 1877 at Lamington in Lanarkshire, the second son of the Revd Robert Rankin, minister of Lamington, and his wife, Theresa Margaret, daughter of George John Claus, shipowner, of Liverpool. He was educated at George Watson's College, Edinburgh, and at the University of Edinburgh, where he graduated in 1897 with first-class honours in philosophy. He was awarded the Bruce of Grangehill and Falkland prize and won the Vans Dunlop (1897) and Ferguson (1899) scholarships. In October 1897 he entered Trinity College, Cambridge, as a sizar, becoming a scholar the following year, and was placed in the first class of both parts of the moral sciences tripos (1899, 1900). He twice won a Hooper declamation prize and in 1901 was awarded a Whewell scholarship to which he was re-elected in 1903. In 1901 he was also president of the union.

In 1904 Rankin was called to the bar by Lincoln's Inn and entered the chambers of William Pickford, where he became acquainted with Lancelot Sanderson. He practised mainly in bankruptcy and commercial cases. In 1910 Rankin married Alice Maud Amy (*d.* 1924), daughter of Geoffrey Sayer, of Bromley, Kent; they had two daughters.

In 1916 Rankin received a commission in the Royal Garrison Artillery and served until 1918. On returning to the bar he found his practice dispersed and was faced with the uncertainty of regaining it, without the advantage of private means and with the anxieties of family responsibilities. So at the suggestion of Sanderson, then chief justice of Bengal, he accepted appointment as a puisne judge of the high court of Calcutta. In 1919 he served as a member of the Hunter commission appointed to report on the disturbances at Amritsar and the action taken by General R. E. H. Dyer. In 1924 he served as chairman of the civil justice committee appointed to make recommendations for the reform of legal procedure in British India, particularly with reference to the law's delays. In recognition of these services he was knighted in 1925, and a year later, on Sanderson's retirement, he was appointed chief justice of

Bengal, the first puisne judge of the Calcutta high court to be so promoted. Early in 1934 his health failed; he returned to England on long leave and eventually resigned his office.

In the following year Rankin's health was sufficiently restored for him to be able to resume work. He was appointed to inquire into the disorders at Barlinnie prison, Glasgow, was sworn of the privy council, and later in 1935 succeeded Sanderson in one of the two paid posts on the judicial committee of that body created by the Appellate Jurisdiction Act, 1929. He was elected a bencher of his inn and in 1937 received the honorary degree of LLD from Edinburgh University. In 1944 his health again broke down and he was forced to retire.

In both his private and his professional life Rankin was remarkable for his unassuming modesty and natural courtesy. The latter quality in particular endeared him to his colleagues and to the bar, both in India and in Downing Street. It was a friendly courtesy, recognized by practitioners as no mere conventional politeness. But it did not permit the abuse of the time of the court: persistence too prolix in an unacceptable argument met with observations containing more than a touch of acerbity.

Early in his tenure of office in India, Rankin applied himself to an exhaustive study of Hindu and Muslim law in both of which systems he attained a profound knowledge. His judgments delivered in India in cases governed by these laws were acknowledged to be of the greatest assistance to the judicial committee of the privy council in dealing with appeals from Indian courts. He also became thoroughly versed in all the complexities of the Bengal Tenancy Act, probably the most intricate code of law relating to land tenure ever devised by human wit. In dealing with cases which came before him, of whatever nature, Rankin excelled in quickly sifting out the essential questions of fact or law involved. His judgments were distinguished by great clarity of expression: only in rare instances did subtlety of thought find expression in a passage of some seeming obscurity.

When he became a member of the judicial committee, it was soon apparent that Rankin was a real addition of strength. However modestly he expressed his views, however seldom he intervened during argument, he proved himself capable of great tenacity in upholding his own opinion. Lord Maugham, on the occasion of his death, wrote of him: 'there has been no judge of my time who more greatly impressed me in a sphere he may be said to have made his own' (private information). He was probably the greatest judicial authority on Indian jurisprudence of his time. Rankin's authoritative *Background to Indian Law* appeared in 1946. Rankin died at the Beach Hotel, at Elie, Fife, on 8 April 1946.

W. W. K. PAGE, *rev.*

Sources *The Times* (9 April 1946) · *The Times* (12 April 1946) · personal knowledge (1959) · private information (1959) · *Scottish biographies* (1938) · *CGPLA Eng. & Wales* (1946)

Likenesses W. Stoneman, photograph, 1939, NPG

Wealth at death £13,456 15s. 4d.: probate, 10 Oct 1946, *CGPLA Eng. & Wales*

Rankin, Thomas (1738–1810), Methodist minister, was born in Dunbar, Haddingtonshire. Taught the 'principles of religion' by his parents (details of whom are unknown) and at school, he wandered as an adolescent into the 'trifling amusements' of the genteel life, particularly music and dancing (Rankin, 'Life', 5.136–7). He questioned the innocence of such practices and the security of his own spiritual estate after hearing Methodist preachers and the testimony of Methodists among troops garrisoned in Dunbar. Drawn into the Methodist orbit, Rankin attended class meetings, heard sermons by George Whitefield in Edinburgh while residing there with an uncle, and experienced the spiritual highs and lows that typified an evangelical conversion, culminating in his sense of forgiveness of sin. The ordeal produced a collapse that gave 'the appearance of a rapid consumption'. The spiritual ordeal also produced in Rankin aspirations for the ministry, 'thoughts of preaching' as he and other Methodists termed it. He entertained taking orders in the Church of Scotland, and sought Whitefield's advice on that possibility. Further schooling proving impractical, Rankin went on business to Charles Town, South Carolina, for an Edinburgh firm. He returned after several months and heard more Whitefield sermons, but gradually moved away from the Calvinistic towards the Wesleyan wing of the Methodist movement.

In 1759 Rankin began ministerial apprenticeship in the Methodist pattern, travelling with Wesley's lay preachers. In the first years of preaching he experienced doubts about his call, feelings of worthlessness, and temptations at the hand of 'Satan', but was sustained in the faith by fatherly counsel from Wesley, the support of brother preachers, and encouragement from pious sisters. Wesley appointed him to the Sussex circuit and in subsequent years to the Sheffield, Devonshire, and Cornwall circuits (1762–4). By 1765, when the printed conference *Minutes* first specify appointments, Rankin numbered among the handful of Wesley's assistants and headed the Dales circuit. He continued in that capacity for Epworth, Cornwall, and Sussex circuits. In 1769–70 Wesley had Rankin 'accompany him in his tour through the kingdom' (Rankin, 'Life', 5.181). Thereafter the relations between the two remained close, and when Wesley became concerned about the good order of the infant American movement, he turned to Rankin first for counsel and then as his general assistant for America.

Rankin arrived in June 1773 as tensions between the colonies and Britain were increasing, and came commissioned to replace Francis Asbury and to rectify the discipline among American Methodists. Relations with Asbury proved testy from the start. Rankin's name comes in for regular criticism in Asbury's journal, while Asbury's name appears frequently in Wesley's letters to Rankin. Asbury's resistant attitude, subversive actions, questioning of appointments, and undermining of policy—none of which Asbury tolerated against his own leadership—had some effect on Rankin's modest success and popularity. However, Asbury's judgement that Rankin proved too strict a disciplinarian, too loyal to Britain, and too subservient to Wesley for American Methodism has prevailed.

At issue in the exercise of discipline were Methodism's indigenization, adaptation to a slave-holding colonial culture, and adherence to British Wesleyan practices. Rankin was not the first nor last immigrant to experience difficulty in grasping the subtle changes that American culture had wrought on imported patterns. Rankin convened the first American conference, itinerated across the eastern seaboard, welcomed African Americans into the Methodist movement, presided over countless quarterly meetings, and brought what had been quite centrifugal evangelical impulses into Methodist order. He departed in October of 1777.

Rankin took regular appointments in Britain until 1783 when he retired, but remained an active supernumerary in London until 1795. In 1789 Wesley selected him as one of the few to be ordained for England and he continued preaching until his last illness. He died on 17 May 1810 at North-Green, in Finsbury, London, and was accorded the honour of burial near Wesley at the City Road Chapel.

RUSSELL E. RICHEY

Sources 'Journal of Thomas Rankin, 1773–1778', Drew University Methodist Collection, Madison, New Jersey [original in the library of Garrett-Evangelical Theological Seminary] [transcribed by F. H. Tees] • T. Rankin, 'The life of Mr. Thomas Rankin', *The lives of early Methodist preachers, chiefly written by themselves*, ed. T. Jackson, 4th edn, 5 (1873), 135–217 • 'A short account of Mr Thomas Rankin: in a letter to the Rev. Mr John Wesley', *Arminian Magazine*, 2 (1779), 182–98 • R. K. MacMaster, 'Thomas Rankin and the American colonists', *Proceedings of the Wesleyan Historical Society*, 39 (1973), 25–33 • A. Godbold, 'Francis Asbury and his difficulties with John Wesley and Thomas Rankin', *Methodist History*, 3 (1965), 3–19 • *The journal and letters of Francis Asbury*, ed. E. T. Clark, J. M. Potts, and J. S. Payton, 3 vols. (1958) • F. Mills, 'Thomas Rankin to Lord Dartmouth on the state of religion and political affairs in America', *Methodist History*, 23 (1985), 116–20 • K. B. Garlick, 'Thomas Rankin', *Proceedings of the Wesley Historical Society*, 38 (1971–2), 30–31 • *The letters of the Rev. John Wesley*, ed. J. Telford, 8 vols. (1931) • *Minutes of the Methodist conferences, from the first, held in London by the late Rev. John Wesley …*, 3 vols. (1812–13) • *Methodist Magazine*, 33 (1810), 281 • *Journal of Joseph Pilmore, Methodist itinerant, 1769–1774*, ed. F. E. Maser and H. T. Maag (1969) • W. B. Sprague, 'Thomas Rankin, of the Philadelphia conference', *Annals of the American pulpit*, 7 (1860); repr. (New York, 1969) • J. B. Wakeley, *Lost chapters recovered from the early history of American Methodism* (1858) • P. P. Sandford, *Memoirs of Mr. Wesley's missionaries to America, compiled from authentic sources* (1843)

Archives Garrett-Evangelical Theological Seminary, Evanston, Illinois

Rankine, Sir John (1846–1922), jurist, was born at Sorn, Ayrshire, on 18 February 1846, the eldest of the seven surviving children of the Revd John Rankine DD (1816–1885), Church of Scotland minister at Sorn, and his wife, Jane (1819–1879), daughter of Charles Simson of Threepwood, Langshaw, Roxburghshire. After schooling at Sorn and at Ayr Academy, he attended Edinburgh Academy from 1859 to 1861. He matriculated at the University of Edinburgh in 1861 and graduated MA in 1865. He embarked on legal study in the University of Edinburgh in 1866 before proceeding to Heidelberg, where he studied Roman law under C. A. von Vangerow, whom, according to Logan

Turner, he was always later to refer to as 'my revered teacher'.

After returning to Edinburgh Rankine was admitted as an advocate on 17 December 1869, joining a bar which was enjoying an intellectual revival and to which he was to make a distinguished contribution. According to Sir James Balfour Paul, Rankine 'had never a great forensic practice, but as a chamber counsel his opinion was much sought after and valued' (Paul, 306). A conservative in politics, he served briefly as an advocate-depute in 1885.

Rankine was elected professor of Scottish law in the University of Edinburgh early in 1888. He held this office with great distinction until his retirement in 1922 and was reputed to be an excellent teacher. A factor in this appointment was his important scholarly publications, the first of which was *The Law of Landownership in Scotland* (1879). An epoch-making work, it was the first authoritative survey of the law in this field; a fourth edition appeared in 1909, and was regularly used throughout the twentieth century. In 1887 Rankine published *The Law of Leases*. This also became a standard authority in its own day and reached a third edition in 1916. In 1921, towards the end of his life, Rankine published *A Treatise on the Law of Personal Bar in Scotland*, which, though it was the fruit of five years' research, was not a success. Rankine used as his textbook John Erskine's *Principles of the Law of Scotland*, which he edited four times between 1890 and 1911. He was also a general editor of the *Scottish Revised Reports*. A lighter side is revealed by his contributions to *Ballads of the Bench and Bar* in 1882.

Rankine's academic excellence was recognized in 1891 when he was elected a fellow of the Royal Society of Edinburgh and again in 1892 when the University of Glasgow conferred on him the honorary degree of LLD. When a Scottish roll of queen's counsel was instituted in 1897 Rankine was one of the first appointed. He served as a governor of the Royal Infirmary, the Royal Veterinary College, Donaldson's Hospital, and the Edinburgh Royal Asylum. As one might expect of a man with three brothers-in-law who were ministers, one of whom was professor of divinity in the University of Glasgow, Rankine was active in the Church of Scotland though he never became an elder. He served on the church's foreign mission committee, travelling abroad on its behalf to India in 1884 and to South Africa in 1902. His public services were recognized in 1921, when he was knighted.

Rankine had comfortable personal means. Genial and impressively whiskered, he was very fond of cigars and shooting. He never married but lived with his unmarried brother, Charles Rankine Simson, writer to the signet, whose estate of Threepwood (inherited through their mother) Rankine in turn inherited on his brother's death in 1911. He divided his time between his estate of 1000 acres and his house at 23 Ainslie Place, Edinburgh. Shortly after retirement from the chair, Rankine died suddenly at Threepwood on 8 August 1922.   JOHN W. CAIRNS

Sources J. B. Paul, 'The late Sir John Rankine', *Juridical Review*, 34 (1922), 305–9 • *Scots Law Times: News* (19 Aug 1922), 123–4 • Lord Johnston, *Proceedings of the Royal Society of Edinburgh*, 42 (1921–2), 371–5 •

Scots Law Times: News (11 June 1921), 97–8 · [T. Henderson and P. F. Hamilton-Grierson], eds., *The Edinburgh Academy register* (1914), 219 · *WWW* · matriculation albums, U. Edin. L., special collections division, university archives · *Edinburgh University Calendars* (1888–1922) · *Alphabetical list of graduates of the University of Edinburgh from 1859 to 1888*, University of Edinburgh (1889), 71 · W. I. Addison, *A roll of graduates of the University of Glasgow from 31st December 1727 to 31st December 1897* (1898), 509 · A. L. Turner, *History of the University of Edinburgh, 1883–1933* (1933), 97 · *Register of the Society of Writers to Her Majesty's Signet* (1983), 289 · *Fasti Scot.*, 3. 69 · F. J. Grant, ed., *The Faculty of Advocates in Scotland, 1532–1943*, Scottish RS, 145 (1944) · old parish record index, NA Scot. · d. cert., NA Scot., 799/2/6
Archives NL Scot., notes on Scots law in the Waverley novels · U. Edin. L., special collections division, lecture notes
Likenesses D. Alison, oils, 1919?, Edinburgh Royal Asylum · D. Alison, oils, U. Edin. L., Law Library · photograph, repro. in *Scots Law Times*, 1 (1893), 147 · photograph, repro. in *Scots Law Times (News)* (1922), 123 · photograph, repro. in Paul, 'The late Sir John Rankine'
Wealth at death £98,774 17s. 4d.: confirmation, 17 Oct 1922, *CCI*

Rankine, (William John) Macquorn (1820–1872), civil engineer and physicist, was born in Edinburgh on 5 July 1820, the second son of David Rankine (*d.* 1870), rifle brigade lieutenant and civil engineer, and his wife, Barbara (*d.* 1871), the elder daughter of Archibald Grahame (or Graham), a Glasgow banker. Tracing his ancestry to Robert the Bruce, Rankine could claim to be a Scot of Scots. His only sibling, David, died young. In early childhood Rankine's parents guided his religious education; his father taught him arithmetic and elementary mechanics. Between 1828 and 1829 he studied at Ayr Academy; in the autumn of 1830 he briefly attended Glasgow high school; later he studied geometry with George Lees in Edinburgh. During prolonged periods of confinement due to illness Rankine was privately educated. He exhibited a keen interest in the theory of music and read deeply in higher mathematics, including number theory. In December 1834 his uncle Archibald Graham gave him Newton's *Principia* in Latin: Rankine devoured the book, citing it later as the foundation of his natural philosophy.

The civil engineer Between 1836 and 1838 Rankine attended classes in natural philosophy, natural history, and botany at the University of Edinburgh. He had matriculated but did not register for a degree. Outside the university he studied chemistry with David Boswell Reid. James David Forbes awarded Rankine gold medals for prize essays on the wave theory of light (1836) and on methods in physical investigation (1838). At college Rankine read widely in empiricist and Scottish commonsense philosophy, explored French and German scientific literature, but did not attend mathematics classes, or progress to the exacting Cambridge mathematics tripos. Opting, instead, for the fashionable profession of the engineer, Rankine helped out on the new Leith branch (1837–8) of the Edinburgh and Dalkeith Railway which his father superintended. In 1838 he became a pupil of John Benjamin MacNeill, a prominent engineer with extensive commitments in the north of Ireland and a clutch of talented apprentices including Le Fanu and Bazalgette. Between 1839 and 1841 Rankine learned his trade implementing river improvements, waterworks and harbour works in

(William John) Macquorn Rankine (1820–1872), by Thomas Annan, pubd 1871

Ireland. At work on MacNeill's Dublin and Drogheda Railway (1841) he developed 'Rankine's method' for setting out curves.

Back in Edinburgh Rankine published a series of investigations conducted with his father as *An experimental inquiry into the advantages attending the use of cylindrical wheels on railways* (1842). He dedicated the work to his former teacher Forbes, a vociferous advocate of science applied to practice. In December 1842 Rankine became a fellow of Edinburgh's Royal Scottish Society of Arts. In July 1843 he entered the Institution of Civil Engineers (ICE) in London as an associate. During 1843 he read papers to the institution: one explained the fracture of axles by referring to molecular structure; others developed David Rankine's suggestions or publicized his mechanical contrivances; some received prizes, including a premium of the institution's president James Walker. Between 1844 and 1848 Rankine worked for Locke and Errington constructing the Clydesdale Junction Railway and on projects sponsored by the Caledonian Railway Company, of which his father had become secretary. In 1845–6 he projected the Edinburgh and Leith Waterworks, only to have the scheme defeated by the Edinburgh Water Company. In 1848 the Institution of Civil Engineers showed itself wary of Rankine's programme to reform the practice of sea defence construction, and of engineering practice generally, as an inductive science.

Thermodynamics Rankine made his scientific début in 1840 with a neat and topical mathematical analysis of the cooling of the earth. In 1842, after reading Clapeyron's discussion of Carnot's heat theory, Rankine started to write on molecular physics, elasticity, and, especially, the mechanical action of heat. From July 1849 he published results linking the temperature, pressure and density of gases, vapours (especially steam), and liquids, much encouraged by the close agreement between his theoretical deductions and Regnault's new experimental data. Rankine became a fellow of the Royal Society of Edinburgh in 1849. Shortly thereafter, in February 1850, he matched William Thomson's account of Carnot (1849) with an idiosyncratic theory of the mechanical action of heat. Here Rankine considered heat not as Carnot's indestructible caloric but, following Joule, as motion equivalent to work.

During the early 1850s Rankine, Thomson, and Rudolf Clausius elaborated a new thermodynamics which supplemented Joule's first law with a second law characterizing the potential efficiency of engines and, later, the order and decay of physical systems. Rankine's work had two distinguishing features. First, he quickly perceived and elaborated the links between the new science and thermodynamic engines, especially the ubiquitous steam engine, and its serious contemporary rivals like the air engine. By April 1851 he had constructed a simple law governing the potential efficiency of any heat engine in terms of its upper and lower working temperatures. Here was a perfect theoretical standard against which actual engine economy and the efficient practice of the engineer were to be assessed. Between 1853 and 1857 Rankine collaborated with the Glaswegian shipbuilder James Robert Napier in the development of a marketable hot-air engine (with regenerator), convinced on theoretical grounds that its efficiency would be greater than the maximum attainable by any condensing steam engine. Despite initial hopes that air would supersede steam they abandoned their patent when practical problems proved insurmountable. Second, rather than treat macroscopic phenomena, Rankine exploited what Maxwell termed scientific imagination to create a complex mechanical model of the unobservable whirling motions in which he believed heat to consist. He had designed this versatile hypothesis of molecular vortices to unify the study of heat, elasticity, light, and, ultimately, electromagnetism. Although Rankine was fêted by contemporaries as a founder of thermodynamics, Maxwell, Thomson, and others questioned his tenacious adherence to a hypothesis beyond the test of direct observation, accused him, not without justification, of obscurity in his statements of the second law, and claimed that the phrase 'molecular vortices' was of far greater import than the detail of the model itself (published December 1851).

Rankine nevertheless established himself as a significant scientific voice. As secretary of section A of the British Association for the Advancement of Science (BAAS) from 1850 he met Cambridge mathematical physicists like George Gabriel Stokes. He was president of section A in Newcastle (1863). Countering William Thomson's universal dissipation of the energy available to humanity, Rankine proposed in November 1852 a cyclic cosmology in which energy might be reconcentrated. Rankine had joined the Glasgow Philosophical Society early in 1852 and soon became prominent on its council. In January 1853 he presented the society with a set of general laws of the transformation between 'actual' and 'potential' forms of energy. This Aristotelian dichotomy engineered a succinct statement of an empirical law of energy conservation. Rankine's penchant for patenting scientific constructs expressed itself in many such coinages: some ('stress', 'strain', 'adiabatic') endured; others ('actual energy') fell into disuse or were so cumbersome ('platythliptic') as to cause mirth among tongue-tied colleagues.

Shortly after his election to the Royal Society of London (2 June 1853) Rankine refashioned the science of thermodynamics in geometrical terms: his diagram of energy (a theorized indicator diagram) linked the science of energy and heat-engine practice in a visual form ideal for teaching. In March 1854 the Royal Society of Edinburgh awarded him its Keith prize for his work on heat. In May 1855 he outlined the science of energetics in which he treated the laws of physical energy in an abstract and general manner, eschewing mechanical complexities and, in particular, treating heat phenomenologically. Positivists would subsequently champion Rankine's suggestion that energy—rather than matter—constituted a secure ontology for all physics. But Rankine had not abandoned the hypothesis of molecular vortices. As president of the Glasgow Philosophical Society (elected November 1861) he drew upon Scottish common-sense philosophy to argue for the legitimacy and probability of his model by virtue of its predictive capacity and its use of mechanical analogy. Having increasingly relaxed the conditions of the model, Rankine finally claimed that all that he required was a steady circulation of streams. Nevertheless scientists abandoned the hypothesis on which his claim to scientific originality largely rested in preference for a new orthodoxy of Maxwellian statistical physics.

The Glasgow engineering chair From 1849 Rankine balanced a burgeoning scientific career with engineering commitments. By the beginning of 1851 he had transferred his Scottish base from Edinburgh to Glasgow. There he worked at the core of the Glasgow Philosophical Society, establishing himself as an engineer concerned to promote the city's improvement. In partnership with John Thomson, son of medical professor Dr William Thomson, Rankine surveyed the Glasgow College grounds, promoted a submarine telegraph between Britain and Ireland, and, jointly with the professor of natural philosophy, lodged a patent for improvements in telegraph conductors (1854). Their most ambitious project (1852) revived the audacious scheme of Lawrence Hill and Rankine's friend the engineering professor Lewis Gordon to bring water to Glasgow from Loch Katrine.

Although Glasgow was to be the centre of Rankine's scientific and engineering business, in 1853 and 1854 he frequented Gordon's Westminster offices. Their proximity provided the opportunity to plan the relaunch of the all but abandoned engineering chair. The year 1855 saw these plans in operation: an appointment as visitor of the Edinburgh observatory enhanced Rankine's scientific status; from January to April Rankine lectured to aspirant civil engineers on applied mechanics and the science and practice of heat engines; they left the classroom with commercially valuable results. In September the British Association visited Glasgow, responding to the invitation of Rankine, the Philosophical Society, and other local bodies. Gordon resigned his commission during the meeting; Rankine used his address as president of section G (mechanical science) to make a thinly concealed bid for the chair.

On 7 November 1855 Rankine succeeded Gordon in the regius chair of civil engineering and mechanics, despite eleventh-hour attempts by some incumbent professors to have the government endowment of £275 per annum redirected. Rankine allied himself with a reforming whig faction in the college, including anatomy professor Allen Thomson. His widely reported inaugural address espoused the harmony of theory with practice in mechanics, and outlined a tripartite theory of knowledge—theory, practice, and the application of theory to practice—which left room for a new breed of engineering scientists to bridge theoretical and practical domains. A second introductory address (November 1856) likened the Christian's quest for spiritual perfection to the sacred duty of the engineer to perfect himself in the liberal and noble art of engineering.

Firmly ensconced in the college, Rankine promulgated a programme of engineering science in three interrelated ways. The first was institutional. Rankine was appointed consulting engineer to the Highland and Agricultural Society of Scotland (1865) and elected to bodies like the American Academy of Sciences (1856) and the Royal Academy of Sweden (1868). But the institution which gave him greatest scope for immediate action was closer to home. In 1856 Rankine supported a Glaswegian association temporarily constituted to host a summer meeting of the Institution of Mechanical Engineers. Collaborating thereafter with Walter Neilson and J. R. Napier, Rankine built upon the successes of the summer to create a permanent professional body for Scottish engineers independent of the Institution of Civil Engineers. Recently honoured with the degree of LLD from Trinity College, Dublin (1857), Rankine resigned his associateship of the Institution of Civil Engineers—never having been granted full membership—and was elected president (1857–9) of a new and dynamic Institution of Engineers in Scotland. The institution encouraged engineering science and practice in and beyond the Glaswegian 'metropolis of mechanics', worked closely with the Philosophical Society, and brought together academics, engineers, shipbuilders, and ironmasters like William Baird and Henry Dunlop.

No less important was the dissemination of Rankine's engineering science in literary form. Building upon the recent technical pedagogy of Moseley, Willis, and Whewell, Rankine repeatedly developed in his lectures new analytical techniques. His 'reciprocal diagrams' of frames and forces (1856) allowed an engineering designer more scope in studying the stresses in structures. Rankine issued lithographs of lecture notes in 1855 and 1856. Thereafter he arranged with Richard Griffin in Glasgow to publish a series of exhaustive manuals suitable for teaching and reference alike. The central pillar—*A Manual of Applied Mechanics* (1858)—had been extensively sketched in the *Encyclopaedia metropolitana*. The *Steam Engine and other Prime Movers* (1859) extended an article on the mechanical action of heat in Nichol's *Cyclopaedia* and offered a typically anglocentric historiography of thermodynamics; contemporaries applauded this work as the first systematic treatise of the new science. *Civil Engineering* (1862) put Rankine's applied mechanics to work in engineering practice. Completing the best-selling series with *Machinery and Millwork* (1869), Rankine wrote with the authority of an experienced juror of 'machinery in general' at the London International Exhibition (1862). With a companion volume of *Useful Rules and Tables* (1866) the manuals were standard texts. Some remained in print well into the twentieth century. Rankine's former student and assistant in his final years, E. F. Bamber, completed the *Mechanical Textbook* (1873) as a much-needed light introduction to the weighty matter of the manuals.

Rankine structured his books to suggest that engineering knowledge had its roots in scientific principle: he stated a general problem, solved it, and only then treated the special cases encountered in practice. Where no principles were yet accessible he was a natural historian of an artefactual world, provisionally collecting the data of engineering with the ultimate intention of subsuming them under scientific law. Consequently his works were exhaustive rather than elegant and they were hard reading for the bulk of the profession. Contemporaries nevertheless recognized a rare combination of practical sense, scientific breadth, original investigation, and literary workmanship in a permanent *Principia* of engineering. In order to respond to topical matters—from the stability of chimneys to the dynamics of the new velocipede—Rankine made almost weekly contributions to *The Engineer* from 1858. Even in popular works Rankine channelled his energies to promote or reflect practical and especially scientific engineering. A keen cellist, pianist, and vocalist, his one published composition was a piano accompaniment to a song entitled the 'Iron Horse'; as a British Association red lion, hailed as lion-king in 1871, he penned quirky and humorous poems like 'The Mathematician in Love' and 'The Three-Foot Rule' (a protest against the metric system). These *Songs and Fables* (1874) appeared posthumously with illustrations by Jemima Blackburn, wife of Glasgow College's mathematics professor. Thus his model of a systematic and responsive body of engineering theory escaped the Glasgow classroom to endure in literary form and, through his college students, in practice.

Finally, Rankine increased the purchase of engineering science by, quite literally, raising the profile of the university and of his own subject within it. From the late 1860s he worked to raise funds for the new college buildings—a cathedral of science—at Gilmorehill. Although in 1855 engineering was not recognized as a subject qualifying for a degree, and the university commissioners disallowed Rankine's suggestion (approved by senate in 1859) that college engineers be granted diplomas, by 1862 Rankine had at last ensured that a systematically educated Glasgow engineer could leave the university with a certificate of proficiency in engineering science. Rankine seriously considered moving to Edinburgh and its chair of engineering in 1868, and the following year admitted his aspirations to succeed Thomas Graham, a distant relation, as master of the Royal Mint. But he remained in Glasgow to press for a full degree in engineering. In 1872 the university began to offer the degree of BSc for science subjects, including engineering.

The science of the ship In July 1859 Rankine had taken a leading part in raising and organizing the second Lanarkshire, or Glasgow University corps, of the rifle volunteers. He attended a course at Hythe to qualify himself to instruct the corps in musketry. He became captain (October 1859) and then major of the corps (May 1860–June 1864). Later Rankine was the first convenor of the Glasgow University senate committee on the education of candidates for commissions in the army.

One of the reasons Rankine resigned his commission in 1864 was the increasing burden of work related to naval architecture. From the mid-1850s Rankine collaborated closely with men like J. R. Napier and the partners John Elder and Charles Randolph who combined craft skills with an overtly scientific approach to marine engineering and shipbuilding. In the autumn of 1857 Napier provided Rankine, in confidence, with a body of raw data from experiments relating engine power, size, shape, and speed of steamships. By December 1857 Rankine had deduced a general formula for the resistance of ships of the designs usually given to steamers. Unable to divulge a result which was commercially sensitive and, in Napier's *Admiral*, practically proven, Rankine published a letter in the *Philosophical Magazine* (September 1858) disguising the formula as an anagram.

Thereafter Rankine was ubiquitous on British Association committees, gathering and reducing data on the design, propulsion, and resistance of ships in commercial practice, and thereby seeking to remould shipbuilding as an exact science. He was a member of the Institution of Naval Architects from 1862. In 1864, in order to gather data on sea waves and the rolling of ships, he made observations in the Western Isles. He lectured to the Royal School of Naval Architecture in the years 1865–8 and was an examiner at the school. Rankine worked with Isaac Watts, chief constructor of the navy, Frederick K. Barnes of the controller's department, and Napier as corresponding editor and principal contributor to *Shipbuilding, Theoretical and Practical* (1866).

Rankine's numerous papers in hydrodynamics usually deployed his favoured strategy of stating simple principles and then following even the most difficult of investigations through with elementary mathematics. The topics he chose were almost invariably of practical relevance: he developed a theoretical description of waves of finite height (sea waves) on the surface of deep water; he applied his theory of streamlines to find good forms of lines for real ships; he investigated the causes of and remedies for ship resistance; in 1865 he produced a theory of the propeller. In these writings, always undertaken in dialogue with men of practice like Napier, Rankine successfully combined considerations of the fluid flow and the geometry of actual ships with engine propulsion, hull resistance, and, most importantly, work: that is, he had found a new practical object for energy physics in a science, jointly developed with William Froude and others, of naval dynamics. As a recognized expert, in December 1870 he accompanied William Thomson on a scientific sub-committee of the government committee on designs for ships of war, created after the loss of the *Captain*.

The death of John Elder precipitated Rankine once again into the presidency of the Institution of Engineers in Scotland (1869–70). Drawing upon his experience as co-editor and contributor in the area of engineering, mathematics, and natural philosophy to *The Imperial Dictionary of Universal Biography* (3 vols., 1857–63) Rankine wrote in 1870 and published in 1871 a memoir of his intimate friend and confidant. In May 1872, at the end of the university session, Elder's widow significantly enhanced the value of Rankine's professorship with a donation of £5000. Although in August 1872 Rankine was fit enough to work with Stevenson Macadam on a study of an explosion at the Tradeston Flour Mills, he did not teach again. Failing sight proved to be a symptom of deeper illness (possibly heart disease). Rankine's health deteriorated rapidly in October; during his last days he lost the power of speech and then of motion on his right side. He died, unmarried, at 59 St Vincent Street, Glasgow, on 24 December 1872 and was buried at Sighthill cemetery, Glasgow, four days later after a public service in the university chapel. The city mourned a chameleon—engineer, natural philosopher, and engineering scientist—who had brought the minute and orderly habits of a businessman to science and practice alike, worked to create a new science of thermodynamics, and fostered the philosophical reform of commerce and industry in the second city of the empire.

BEN MARSDEN

Sources B. Marsden, 'Engineering science in Glasgow: W. J. M. Rankine and the motive power of air', PhD diss., University of Kent at Canterbury, 1992 · B. Marsden, 'Engineering science in Glasgow: economy, efficiency and measurement as prime movers in the differentiation of an academic discipline', *British Journal for the History of Science*, 25 (1992), 319–46 · H. B. Sutherland, *Rankine, his life and times* (1973) · K. Hutchison, 'W. J. M. Rankine and the rise of thermodynamics', *British Journal for the History of Science*, 14 (1981), 1–26 · D. F. Channell, *William John Macquorn Rankine, FRSE, FRS* (1986) · P. G. Tait, 'Memoir', *Miscellaneous scientific papers by W. J. Macquorn Rankine*, ed. W. J. Millar (1881), xix–xxxvi · L. Gordon, *Proceedings of the Royal Society of Edinburgh*, 8 (1872–5), 296–306 · P. G. Tait, *Glasgow Herald* (26 Dec 1872) · P. G. Tait, *Glasgow Herald* (28 Dec 1872) · *Engineering* (3 Jan 1873) · *PRS*, 21 (1872–3), i–iv · *Proceedings of the American Academy of Arts and Science*, 1 (1873–4), 276–8 · Boase, *Mod. Eng. biog.* · inventory, NA Scot., SC36/48/70

Archives BL, James Croll MSS, Add. MS 41077 · CUL, Greenwich Royal Observatory archive, Airy MSS · CUL, letters to Lord Kelvin · Inst. EE, Faraday MSS · Mitchell L., Glas., Henry Dyer collection · NL Scot., Blackwood MSS · NL Scot., Royal Society of Edinburgh archives · Queen's University, Belfast, letters to T. Andrews and

J. Thomson • RS, Herschel letters, Lubbock letters, corresp., and referees' reports • U. Glas., Adam Smith Business Record Centre, Institution of Shipbuilders and Engineers in Scotland archives • U. Glas., special collections department, Kelvin MSS • U. Glas., J. R. Napier MSS • U. St Andr. L., James David Forbes MSS • Wellcome L., autograph letters series

Likenesses group portrait, photograph, 1870 (with the Glasgow University Senate), repro. in Channell, *William John Macquorn Rankine* • T. Annan, carte-de-visite, pubd 1871, NPG [*see illus.*] • statue, 1950, Virginia Polytechnic Institute, Blackburg, department of engineering • T. Annan?, photograph, Mitchell L., Glas. • Crawford (after photograph by Annan), Institution of Engineers and Shipbuilders in Scotland • bust replica (after Ewing), U. Glas., Hunterian Library • engraving, repro. in *Popular Science Monthly*, 12 (1877–8), facing p. 129 • portrait, repro. in Millar, ed., *Miscellaneous scientific papers*, frontispiece • portrait, repro. in *Memoirs and portraits of one hundred Glasgow men who have died in the last thirty years* (1886), 2.269–72

Wealth at death £2088 17s. 11d.: inventory, 1873, Scotland

Rankins, William

Rankins, William (*bap.* 1565, *d.* in or after 1609), writer, was baptized on 24 November 1565 at St Gregory by Paul, London, the son of Henry Rankyn and Mary Robynson (*d.* 1584). Two years after his son's birth Henry was elected to the livery of the Barber–Surgeons' Company, and he eventually became master of that company in 1587. During his lengthy career the elder Rankins seems to have earned a tidy sum. When he wrote his will in March 1597 he bequeathed to his elder son, William, £160; however, he also stipulated expressly that William was to have nothing to do with the administration of the estate. In fact, Henry set up his will so that his younger son (also named Henry) would inherit most of the estate if William were to 'mislike or refuse to accept' the bequest initially set forth in the will. (In retrospect, it would seem that William did indeed 'mislike' the arrangements made by his father. Over time, and upon arrival at adulthood, William's younger brother collected most of what the estate was valued at, a portion of £145.)

Such opposition seems to have been commonplace throughout Rankins's life. He began his literary career attacking plays in a polemic entitled *A mirrour of monsters: wherein is plainly described the manifold vices, and spotted enormities, that are caused by the infectious sight of plays* (1587). Also, early on, he published *My Roughcast Conceit of Hell* (n.d.) and a forceful denunciation of the Englishman's habit of imitating foreign fashions (*The English Ape*, 1588), both dedicated to Sir Christopher Hatton.

Ten years later, however, Rankins had reversed his position on the theatre and was writing plays for the Lord Admiral's Men at the Rose Playhouse. Philip Henslowe, the playhouse owner and company financier, paid Rankins for 'Mulmutius Dunwallow' (October 1598), 'Hannibal and Scipio' (January 1601), 'Scogan and Skelton' (January–March 1601), and 'The Conquest of Spain by John of Gaunt' (March–April 1601). The first play was apparently based on Raphael Holinshed's chronicles. (The last three were co-written with Richard Hathway, whose career as a playwright for the Admiral's Men produced at least eight other plays written between 1598 and 1602, including *1,2 Sir John Oldcastle*.) In addition, some theatre historians conjecture that Rankins was part-author of a play entitled

Leire (entered into the Stationers' register in 1594) which was revived by the Queen's and Sussex's Men for Henslowe on 6 and 8 April 1594 shortly before the Stationers' entry.

In 1598 Rankins published *Seaven Satyres Applied to the Weeke, Including the Worlds Ridiculous Follyes*. Dedicated to his friend John Salisbury of Lleweni, esquire, the book stands as Rankins's last substantial work. The preface to John Bodenham's *Belvedere* (1600) contains but three short stanzas ('A Sonnet to the Muses Garden') signed 'W. Rankins, Gent'; and in 1604 he contributed some miscellaneous verses to the anonymous *Plato's Cap*. By this time Rankins's professional career had subsided. A note of ownership inscribed in a copy of Holinshed, dated 4 June 1609 and perhaps written by Rankins himself, is possibly the last mention of him while he lived. Throughout his life his output was steady; but he seems generally to have drawn little attention, although in 1598 Frances Meres mentioned Rankins in his *Paladis Tamia* (along with Joseph Hall and John Marston) as one of the three best satirists of his age.

A 'William Rankyns of Clifford's Inn, gent', who bound himself to appear at the Middlesex sessions on 15 September 1587 might, or might not be the writer. If he is synonymous with the author, then Rankins's literary career was launched, like those of so many contemporary writers, during his time at the inns of court.

S. P. CERASANO

Sources E. K. Chambers, *The Elizabethan stage*, 4 vols. (1923), vols. 3–4 • M. Eccles, *Brief lives: Tudor and Stuart authors* (1982), 111–12 • W. W. Greg, *Henslowe papers: being documents supplementary to Henslowe's diary* (1907) • DNB

Rankley, Alfred

Rankley, Alfred (1819–1872), genre painter, had a brother, William, but of his parents nothing is known. He attended the Royal Academy Schools and began to exhibit at the academy in 1841, when he sent a scene from Shakespeare's *Macbeth*. Next year *Palamon and Lavinia* was exhibited at the Society of British Artists, and in 1844 a scene from *Othello* was shown at the academy. Rankley has been described as being 'caught up in the early Victorian craze for ambitious historical pieces' (Reynolds, 110). He was one of many artists who searched pre-Norman English history for episodes that could be used as vehicles for dramatic effect: his *Edith and the Monks Finding the Body of Harold* was exhibited at the Society of British Artists in 1846. In 1847 he sent *Cordelia* to the British Institution, and *The Village Church* to the Royal Academy, a painting that was well received and later engraved. From then until 1867 he exhibited regularly at the academy, generally sending a single work, and never more than two.

Rankley's contemporary subjects have proved more enduring than his historical ones. In *Contentment* (1850) he explored the effects of education on social class, through a painting of a young scholar 'ill at ease in his family's simple cottage', an early treatment of this subject (Boase, 279). Among his best works were *Old Schoolfellows* (1854) and *The Doctor's Coming* (1864), the latter depicting a scene from a Gypsy encampment. *Old Schoolfellows* in particular shows to good effect the technical ability that Rankley acquired through his earlier works. The painting depicts a prosperous young man alleviating the penury of a schoolfriend, who lies on his sickbed; when shown at the Royal Academy the catalogue entry included a quotation from the book of Proverbs, chapter 17: 'A friend loveth at all times, and a brother is born for adversity'. Such sentimentalism was characteristic of Rankley's work and the painting displays 'that clarity of anecdote and simplicity of moral appeal which was the strength as well as the limitation of mid-Victorian subject painting' (Reynolds, 110).

Rankley's paintings—'conscientiously finished, and inculcating some healthful thought' (Redgrave)—were popular, and among those engraved were *The Parish Beauty* and *The Pastor's Pet*, by Robert Mitchell; *Reading the Litany*, *Sunday Afternoon*, and *The Sunday School*, by James Scott; *Refreshment, Sir?* by W. H. Egleton; and *The Scoffers*, by H. T. Ryall. His last exhibited works were *Following the Trail* and *The Hearth of his Home* (1870), and *The Benediction* (1871). Rankley died, unmarried, at his home, Clifton Villa, Campden Hill, Kensington, London, on 7 December 1872, and was buried in the St Marylebone cemetery, East Finchley. His studio sale was held at Christies on 3 February 1873.   R. E. GRAVES, rev. MARK POTTLE

Sources Wood, *Vic. painters*, 2nd edn · G. Reynolds, *Victorian painting* (1966) · T. S. R. Boase, *English art, 1800–1870* (1959) · Redgrave, *Artists* · B. Stewart and M. Cutten, *The dictionary of portrait painters in Britain up to 1920* (1997) · *The exhibition of the Royal Academy* (1841–71) [exhibition catalogues] · *Art Journal*, 35 (1873), 44 · *The Athenaeum* (14 Dec 1872), 776 · CGPLA *Eng. & Wales* (1873)
Wealth at death under £800: resworn administration with will, July 1874, CGPLA *Eng. & Wales* (1873)

Rann, John [*nicknamed* Sixteen String Jack] (*c*.**1750–1774**), highwayman, is of obscure origins. A contemporary biographer asserts that he was born in the parish of St George, Hanover Square, Westminster, on 15 April 1752 (*Account*, 5), but this is not substantiated by the parish register. According to the Revd John Villette, ordinary of Newgate, he was born in a village near Bath about 1750, and at the age of twelve was in the service of a lady who visited the city in order to take the waters at the spa. Rann grew up in service and was at one time employed as a coachman by John Montagu, fourth earl of Sandwich, but at some point he lost his character and drifted into crime, possibly in a bid to emulate the lifestyle of his masters.

The true total of Rann's robberies is unknown, but his career as a highwayman was comparatively brief. On 13 November 1773 he was one of five men apprehended in London at the Three Tuns tavern near Knave's Acre, Soho, for the robbery, earlier in the day, of the Hampstead stagecoach. One of the men, John Scott, agreed to give evidence for the crown and in December the other four—Rann, William Davis (alias Scarlet), David Monro, and John Saunders—were tried at the Old Bailey on two indictments connected with the hold-up. Unfortunately for the prosecution neither the coachman nor the passengers could positively identify the robbers. This meant that the only serious evidence incriminating Rann and his co-defendants was that of Scott, and all were acquitted. Undeterred by this experience, Rann returned to his chosen trade and in April 1774 was once again tried and acquitted at the Old Bailey on two indictments for highway robbery. On 21 May John Deval's chaise was stopped by two highwaymen near the nine-mile stone on the Hounslow Road and he was robbed of his watch and 7 guineas. The watch was subsequently handed in to the maker, Mr Allam, by Eleanor Roache, one of Rann's female acquaintances, and when Rann was indicted for the robbery and Catherine Smith, his mistress, for receiving the watch, at the Old Bailey in July, Roache was the principal witness against them. She testified that she had been at Smith's house when, on the night of the robbery, Rann had returned and given 5 guineas and the watch to Smith. But Rann told the court that Roache's testimony was malicious because he had refused to accept her as his mistress and, once more, he was acquitted.

Rann's celebrity and self-esteem were now at their zenith. He appeared at Bagnigge Wells splendidly dressed in scarlet coat, tambour waistcoat, silk stockings, laced hat, and other finery, and, losing a ring there, brazenly boasted that 'it was but a hundred guineas gone, which one evening's work would replace' (*Account*, 16). Later, attending Barnet races and attired like a sporting peer of the first rank, he was followed about by hundreds of admirers from one side of the course to the other. Rann was a handsome man, 5 feet 5 inches in height, straight, and of 'genteel carriage'. His dress, when not engaged in criminal activities, was extravagant and distinctive. He wore an extraordinary hat with strings and a button on the crown and acquired the nickname Sixteen String Jack from his habit of attaching eight silk strings to each knee of his breeches. Although courageous and steadfast to his comrades, Rann was dissolute and self-indulgent and an unrepentant thief.

After the Deval trial Rann and Eleanor Roache mended their quarrel and, apparently, she became his mistress. Their liaison, however, was short-lived. On 26 September Rann stopped William Bell, chaplain to Princess Amelia, on the road between Ealing and Gunnersbury and robbed him of his watch, a stone seal set in gold, and 18*d*. in money. Roache's attempts to pawn the watch led the Bow Street officers to Rann, and on the night of 26 September he was arrested at her lodgings in Berners Street. He was tried, convicted, and sentenced to death at the Old Bailey in October. Eleanor Roache, convicted at the same time for receiving Bell's watch knowing it to have been stolen, received a sentence of fourteen years' transportation.

Rann was executed at Tyburn on 30 November 1774. John Thomas Smith, taken by Joseph Nollekens, the sculptor, to see Rann pass along Oxford Street to the gallows, remembered that the highwayman was dressed for the occasion in a bright pea-green coat and that an immense nosegay was affixed in the buttonhole. Samuel Johnson once remarked that Sixteen String Jack 'towered above the common mark' in his calling as Thomas Gray, the poet, did in his (Boswell, *Life*, 3.38). He was, indeed, a competent highwayman, but he owed his celebrity more to his flamboyant personality than to his exploits on the road. His fame was perpetuated into the nineteenth century through chapbook lives and collections of criminal biography. In the 1870s the young James Barrie was dubbed Sixteen String Jack by one of his schoolfriends because of his taste for such blood and thunder literature.

PHILIP SUGDEN

Sources *An account of John Rann, commonly called Sixteen String Jack* (1774) • J. Villette, *The annals of Newgate* (1776), vol. 4 • *The whole proceedings on the king's commission of the peace* (1773–4) [Old Bailey sessions papers, 8–14 Dec 1773, 13–20 April, 6–13 July, 19–25 Oct 1774] • J. T. Smith, *A book for a rainy day, or, Recollections of the events of the years 1766–1833*, ed. W. Whitten (1905) • J. T. Smith, *Nollekens and his times*, ed. W. Whitten, new edn, 2 vols. (1920) • *London Chronicle* (20 Oct 1774) • *London Chronicle* (1 Dec 1774) • H. Bleackley, 'Sir John Lade', *N&Q*, 11th ser., 10 (1914), 316 • P. Pringle, *Stand and deliver* (1951) • Boswell, *Life*
Archives LMA, gaol delivery rolls and books
Likenesses AR, etching, 1774, BM; repro. in H. Scott, ed., *Concise encyclopaedia of crime and criminals* (1961), pl. 73 • engraving, 1774, repro. in *An account of John Rann*, frontispiece • engraving, repro. in C. Gordon, *The Old Bailey and Newgate* (1902), 196

Ransford, Edwin (1805–1876), singer and composer, was born on 13 March 1805 at Bourton on the Water, Gloucestershire. He first appeared on the stage as an extra in the chorus at the King's Theatre, Haymarket, and was afterwards employed in the same capacity at Covent Garden. In March 1825 he married; his wife's name was Hannah (1804/5–1876). During Charles Kemble's management of Covent Garden, Ransford sang the baritone role of Don Caesar in Samuel James Arnold's *The Castle of Andalusia* (27 May 1829), and was engaged soon afterwards by Arnold for the English Opera House (later the Lyceum). During the autumn seasons of 1829 and 1830 he was at Covent Garden, and in 1831 he played leading characters under R. W. Elliston at the Surrey Theatre, where he won great acclaim. Later that same year he appeared at Sadler's Wells as Captain Cannonade in John Barnett's opera *The Convent, or, The Pet of the Petticoats* and on 3 November he played Giacomo in the first English production of Auber's *Fra Diavolo* at Drury Lane. In 1832 he was with Joe Grimaldi at Sadler's Wells, playing Tom Tuck in Andrew V. Campbell's nautical drama *The Battle of Trafalgar*, in which he made a great hit with S. C. Neukomm's song 'The Sea'. He afterwards fulfilled important engagements at Drury Lane, the Lyceum, and Covent Garden. At the last-named theatre he played the Doge of Venice in *Othello* on 25 March 1833, when Edmund Kean made his last appearance on the stage; he was also in the cast, as Sir Harry, when Charles Kemble made his last appearance, as Charles Surface in *The School for Scandal*. His own final theatrical engagement was with W. C. Macready at Covent Garden in 1837–8.

After his retirement from the stage, Ransford sang for a time at concerts, and then, from 1845 onwards, produced a series of popular musical entertainments in which he took the leading roles. Among these ventures were *Illustrations of Gipsy Life and Character* (with the words to the songs by Eliza Cook), *Tales of the Sea*, and *Songs of Dibdin*. Ransford was also well known as a composer of songs and glees, and between 1835 and 1876 had more than fifty pieces published. Under the name of Aquila he composed thirteen *Sacred Ballads* (1862–9) and wrote the words to the popular song 'In the days when we went Gipsying'. He was also the author of *Jottings—Music in Verse* (1863).

For some years Ransford was in business as a music-seller and publisher, and during the 1840s and 1850s he issued many popular songs. His business began in Charles Street, Soho Square, and moved to 461 Oxford Street in 1850. When he went into partnership with his son William Edwin (d. 1890), a talented singer, in 1869, the business was based at 2 Princes Street, Cavendish Square, where it continued to be managed by William after his father's death. A genial and popular man, Ransford died at his home, 59 Welbeck Street, Cavendish Square, on 11 July 1876, and was buried at Bourton on the Water on 15 July. His wife died four months later, aged seventy-one.

G. C. BOASE, *rev.* DAVID J. GOLBY

Sources W. Henderson and F. Kidson, 'Ransford, Edwin', Grove, *Dict. mus.* • *The Era* (16 July 1876), 10
Likenesses J. Bacon, lithograph, BM
Wealth at death under £2000: resworn probate, May 1877, CGPLA Eng. & Wales (1876)

Ransom, William Henry (1823–1907), physician and embryologist, was born on 19 November 1823 at Cromer, Norfolk, the younger son of Henry Ransom (1793–1832), a master mariner and shipowner, and his wife, Maria (*bap.* 1793, *d.* 1861), daughter of the Revd Richard Jones (1756?–1814). Brought up in an evangelical atmosphere, Ransom was educated at a private school at Norwich and at sixteen was apprenticed for four years to a medical practitioner at King's Lynn. In 1843 he went to University College, London, where Thomas Huxley was a fellow student. He competed with Huxley for an exhibition in 1845. Huxley, writing to Herbert Spencer in 1886, said, 'If Ransom had worked less hard I might have been first and he second, … in which case I should have obtained the Exhibition, should not have gone into the navy and should have forsaken science for practice' (Huxley, 142). After gaining his MB in 1847 Ransom held residential posts at University College Hospital. He then studied in Paris and Germany, and developed a continuing interest in continental medical and scientific literature. He graduated MD from the University of London in 1850.

Ransom settled in Nottingham at 26 Low Pavement, and, while waiting for patients to arrive, he undertook chemical and physiological studies in two rooms he had fitted out as laboratories. He was interested in the embryology of fish, and the development of galls and tumours in plants. On 14 August 1860 Ransom married Elizabeth Bramwell (*bap.* 1830, *d.* 1889), daughter of William Bramwell (1790?–1854), surgeon, who was related to the distinguished Edinburgh physician Sir Byrom Bramwell, and his wife, Elizabeth Tate (1789–1856); they had four sons and one daughter. Their eldest son, W. D. Ransom (1861–1909), succeeded his father as physician at the Nottingham General Hospital.

W. H. Ransom was physician to the Nottingham General Hospital from 1854 to 1890, and later honorary consultant physician. He was a first-rate diagnostician and inspired confidence in his patients, although he could sometimes appear brusque. He emphasized hygienic principles when the Nottingham General Hospital was enlarged. The death of two of his children from scarlet fever directed his attention to infectious diseases, and in 1870 he devised a gas-heated, disinfecting stove for sterilizing infected clothing and bedding from fever patients. It was widely used until replaced by steam sterilization. Ransom became a fellow of the Royal College of Physicians in 1869 and also of the Medical and Chirurgical Society and of University College, London. He was elected FRS in 1870 for his studies on the fertilization of fish ova, with the support of famous names such as Thomas Huxley, Joseph Lister, and James Paget. Ransom was president of the section of medicine at the British Medical Association meeting in Nottingham in 1892, where his address dealt with aspects of plant pathology, and in particular gall formation, which he regarded as relevant to human pathology.

Ransom was active in the civic life of Nottingham. He was one of the first to join the Robin Hood 1st Notts rifle corps in 1857 and continued as a private for fifteen years. He was involved in the formation of the Nottingham Literary and Philosophic Society and Nottingham University College. He was on the governing board of the college and the high school, and campaigned for the Liberal Party during the 1860s. Ransom was also interested in geology and assisted in the exploration of Nottinghamshire and Derbyshire caves. He read a paper at the first meeting of the British Association for the Advancement of Science at Nottingham in 1866: 'On the occurrence of *Felis lynx* as a British fossil'. Ransom's only book, *The Inflammation Idea in General Pathology* (1905), was reviewed disparagingly in *Nature* and the *BMJ*.

After being ill for three years, Ransom died from heart failure at his home, 17 Park Valley, Nottingham, on 16 April 1907. He was commemorated by a marble medallion by F. W. Pomeroy in the entrance hall of the Nottingham General Hospital. The medallion was later removed to the Ransom Hospital, Mansfield. In 1923 the Ransom Memorial Committee gave several thousand pounds to establish a pathology laboratory in the Nottingham General Hospital in memory of the Ransoms, father and son.

GEOFFREY L. ASHERSON

Sources *BMJ* (27 April 1907), 1032–3 · *The Lancet* (27 April 1907), 1196 · R. Mellors, *Men of Nottingham and Nottinghamshire* (1924) · L. Huxley, *Life and letters of T. H. Huxley*, 2 vols. (New York, 1901) · private information (1912) · Munk, *Roll* · *DNB* · *CGPLA Eng. & Wales* (1907)

Likenesses F. W. Pomeroy, marble medallion, Ransom Hospital, Mansfield · photograph, repro. in W. H. Jacob, *A history of the general hospital near Nottingham* (1951)

Wealth at death £15,760 1s. 6d.: probate, 6 May 1907, *CGPLA Eng. & Wales*

Ransome family (*per. c.1785–1875*), agricultural machinery manufacturers, came to prominence with **Robert Ransome** (1753–1830), who was born at Wells, Norfolk, son of Richard Ransome, a schoolmaster there. His grandfather, Richard Ransome, was a miller of North Walsham, Norfolk, and an early Quaker, who suffered frequent imprisonment while on preaching journeys in various parts of England, Ireland, and the Low Countries. He died at Bristol on 8 November 1716. On leaving school Robert

Ransome was apprenticed to an ironmonger, and he commenced business for himself at Norwich with a small brass foundry. Shortly afterwards he added iron founding. He married Mary Raven in 1782, and they had two sons.

Ransome possessed inventive skill, and as early as 1783 he took out a patent for cast-iron roofing plates, and published *Directions for Laying Ransome's Patent Cast-Iron coverings*, printed for the patentees in 1784. On 18 March 1785 he took out his first patent for tempering cast-iron plough-shares by wetting the mould with salt water. In 1803 he was responsible for one of the most important developments ever made in the manufacture of ploughs. This was the chilling process, whereby the underside of the share was made extra hard, while the upper part remained soft and tough. The upper part thus wore away faster than the lower, so that a sharp cutting edge was maintained and less draught was required. By the use of these shares, the continual laying and sharpening of wrought-iron shares was avoided. This invention was at once adopted and was not superseded. In 1808 Ransome took out a further patent for the manufacture of interchangeable plough parts. This development enabled him to offer farmers easier maintenance and replacement of worn parts, and to achieve a measure of standardization.

In 1789 Ransome moved to Ipswich, establishing there the business that became successful in manufacturing a wide range of agricultural and industrial implements. Ransome was joined in business by his two sons, and the firm traded as Ransome & Sons from 1818. During the period after the Napoleonic wars, as well as manufacturing ploughs the firm undertook general iron-founding and engineering work. William Cubitt was engineer to the business from 1812 to 1826, and he made the firm a pioneer in the construction of cast-iron bridges, the most notable of which was Stoke Bridge, Ipswich, built in 1818.

Upon retiring from business in 1825, Ransome learned copperplate-engraving as an amusement, and constructed a telescope for his own use, for which he ground the speculum himself. The later years of his life were spent at Woodbridge in Suffolk, where he died on 7 March 1830.

Robert Ransome's elder son, **James Ransome** (1782–1849), entered his father's business in 1795. With his brother Robert he took out several patents for improvements in ploughs. Threshing machines, scarifiers, and other agricultural implements were also improved by his firm. The brothers were among the earliest members of the Royal Agricultural Society of England, which was founded in 1838, and they gained in later years many of the society's chief medals and prizes. From the 1830s to the 1860s Ransomes also became leading manufacturers of railway equipment, especially of chairs and fastenings, and of chilled-iron crossings. Patents were taken out covering the manufacture of each of these. James Ransome died at Rushmere, near Ipswich, on 22 November 1849, his wife Hannah, daughter of Samuel Hunton of Southwold, having predeceased him on 8 December 1826. They had a large family.

Their eldest son, **James Allen Ransome** (1806–1875),

born in July 1806, was, after being educated at Colchester, apprenticed to the firm of Ransome & Sons; he became a partner in 1829, the firm then taking the style J. R. and A. Ransome. Between 1826 and 1829, and again from 1833 to 1839, he resided at Yoxford, Suffolk, where a branch of the business was established. He started a farmers' club there which was the precursor of many similar institutions, notably the London Farmers' Club, of which Ransome was one of the founders. In 1839 he moved permanently to Ipswich, and under his direction the business assumed huge proportions. In 1843 he published *The Implements of Agriculture*, part of which had been prepared as a prize essay for the Royal Agricultural Society of England. This was the most important book on its subject published in the mid-nineteenth century. Ransome had joined the Royal Agricultural Society in 1838, served two terms on its council (1844–6 and 1855–7), and was one of the most popular figures at its annual shows. He was an alderman of Ipswich from 1865 until his death. He married Catherine (*d.* 17 April 1868), daughter of James Neave of Fordingbridge, Hampshire, on 4 September 1829; and they had two sons, Robert James and Allen Ransome, and three daughters, one of whom married J. R. Jefferies, an active member of the firm. James Allen Ransome died at his house in Carr Street, Ipswich, on 29 April 1875.

The small brass foundry established by the elder Robert Ransome in the latter half of the eighteenth century had, by the 1850s, become one of Britain's leading agricultural engineering firms, employing more than 1000 workers. From producing and sharpening ploughs and other agricultural implements, the firm had diversified widely, especially into railway equipment. It was one of the first companies to build cast-iron bridges and later it also became renowned for its lawnmowers, when it was under the direction of Robert Charles *Ransome and James Edward *Ransome [*see under* Ransome, Robert Charles]. Members of the family retained their Quaker affiliation, and were active civic and philanthropic figures in Ipswich, where their works were based.

JONATHAN BROWN

Sources D. R. Grace and D. C. Phillips, *Ransomes of Ipswich: a history of the firm and guide to its records* (1975) · patents, 1783–1849 · 'James Allen Ransome', *Farmers' Magazine*, 3rd ser., 11 (1857), 1–2 · R. N. Bacon, *The report on the agriculture of Norfolk* (1844) · J. A. Ransome, *The implements of agriculture* (1843) · *Suffolk Chronicle* (15 Nov 1864) · *Suffolk Chronicle* (1 May 1875) · *Suffolk Chronicle* (8 May 1875) · *DBB* · d. certs. [James Ransome, James Allen Ransome]
Archives U. Reading, Rural History Centre, Ransomes collection
Likenesses oils, *c*.1800 (Robert Ransome), Ransomes, Sims, and Jefferies plc · T. H. Maguire, lithograph, 1849, BM, NPG; repro. in T. H. Maguire, *Portraits of honorary members of the Ipswich Museum* (1852) · Maguire?, engraving, 1849 (James Ransome), U. Reading, Rural History Centre, Ransome collection, 6 RAN PH 3/3 · engraving (James Allen Ransome), U. Reading, Rural History Centre, Ransome collection, 6 RAN PH 3/4
Wealth at death under £70,000—James Allen Ransome: probate, 1875, *CGPLA Eng. & Wales*

Ransome, Arthur (1834–1922), physician and expert on tuberculosis, was born on 11 February 1834 in Manchester, the son of Joseph Atkinson Ransome (1805–1867), honorary surgeon to Manchester Royal Infirmary between 1843

and 1866, and Eliza Brookhouse. His grandparents were John Atkinson Ransome (1779–1837), honorary surgeon to Manchester Infirmary from 1806 to 1837, and his first wife, Mary Hunton. His namesake, the author Arthur Ransome (1884–1967), was a great-grandson of John Atkinson Ransome and his second wife, Susannah Hoyle.

Ransome trained as a doctor. After a period in apprenticeship to his father he studied at Manchester, Trinity College, Dublin, and Gonville and Caius College, Cambridge, where he won scholarships in anatomy and chemistry and graduated BA (first class) in natural sciences in 1857. He became MA in 1860 and an honorary fellow of Caius College in 1892. He gained clinical experience at Dublin, St George's Hospital, London, and Paris. He qualified MRCS in 1855, LSA in 1856, MB (Cantab.) in 1858, MD (Cantab.) in 1869, MRCP in 1895, and FRCP in 1899.

In 1858 Ransome began general practice in Bowdon, Cheshire, where he quickly prospered. He took on a partner, W. O. Jones, in 1866. He also retained his father's surgery at 1 St Peter's Square, Manchester. He became medical officer to the Lloyd's Hospital and Dispensary in Altrincham, Cheshire, which he reorganized on provident lines. On 5 August 1862 he married Lucy Elizabeth (1840–1906), daughter of John Alexander Fullarton, iron merchant, and his wife, Sarah. In 1868 he had a house, Devisdale, designed for him in Bowdon by Alfred Waterhouse, a schoolboy friend. The Ransome household employed five servants in 1881.

Ransome's great interest was in public health. He joined the Manchester and Salford Sanitary Association in 1859, and he became its leading spirit, serving on its committee for nearly forty years, fourteen of them as chairman. He had a particular interest in the use of medical statistics, and he persuaded the association in 1860 to institute an innovative system of published weekly statistical returns of diseases from local medical institutions, which would provide a source for analysis. These returns were published continuously for twelve years, and the practice was widely imitated, greatly influencing the later campaign for a national system of notification and registration of diseases. Ransome was a regular lecturer in the association's courses entitled 'Health lectures for the people'. He encouraged the association to promote nursing services and training in Manchester and Salford by establishing Nightingale nurses within some of the medical institutions, thus originating the Manchester District Nursing Service.

Ransome was an active member of the Manchester Medical Society, the Manchester Literary and Philosophical Society, and the Manchester Statistical Society. In 1876 he was appointed lecturer in hygiene and medical jurisprudence at Owens College, Manchester. After the creation of the Victoria University in Manchester, he occupied the chair of public health. He was examiner in hygiene to both Cambridge and Victoria universities, and he was responsible for suggesting the idea of the Cambridge diploma in public health.

Ransome's most important work was in the study of tuberculosis. Early in his career he invented a stethometer, which he used in the scientific measurement of respiration. This gained him fellowship of the Royal Society in 1884. In the late 1870s he was appointed physician to the struggling Manchester Hospital for Consumption and Diseases of the Throat, for which he encouraged the move to salubrious Bowdon. The appointment gave him the opportunity to study many tuberculosis cases. Ransome was one of the first to take up Robert Koch's work, after the latter's discovery of the tubercle bacillus in 1882, and sent his son to Berlin to study Koch's research methods.

Ransome stressed the role of external and environmental factors in the spread of tuberculosis. Although he remained convinced that both the 'soil' and the 'seed' were essential in the genesis of the disease, he believed that if external factors were not present the disease would not develop. He linked infection to insanitary, dark, and poorly ventilated environments, and demonstrated that in warm parts of the year the tubercle bacillus could grow on damp wallpaper. Ransome experimented with specimens of infected sputum, showing that fresh air and sunlight caused them to lose their power, while in dark confined spaces they remained virulent for between three and five weeks. His published works included *On Stethometry* (1876), *On the Relation of Chest Movements to Prognosis in Lung Disease* (1882), *On the Causes of Consumption* (1885), *The Treatment of Phthisis* (1896), and *The Principles of 'Open Air' Treatment of Phthisis and of Sanatorium Construction* (1903). His collected papers on tuberculosis appeared as *A Campaign Against Consumption* (1915). His lectures as the first Milroy lecturer on tuberculosis at the Royal College of Physicians in 1890 were published as *The Causes and Prevention of Phthisis* (1890). He won the first Weber Parkes prize in 1897 with his essay *Researches in Tuberculosis* (1898). Ransome's work had a cosmopolitan reputation. In Germany he was recognized as a pioneer in the study of tuberculosis, and he was for many years an associate editor of *Zeitschrift für Tuberkulose*.

In 1894 Ransome retired to Sunnyhurst, Dean Park, Bournemouth, and he became consulting physician to the Royal Boscombe and West Hampshire Hospital. He died at 43 Portchester Road, Bournemouth, on 25 July 1922. His two elder sons Herbert Fullarton (1863–1917) and Arthur Cyril (*b*. 1868) became doctors, and his third son, John Theodore (*b*. 1878), became an engineer. His daughters were Lucy Helen, Mary Evelyn, Edith, Amy Gertrude, and Ethel.   K. A. WEBB

Sources K. A. Webb, 'Arthur Ransome, 1834–1922', *Some Manchester doctors: a biographical collection to mark the 150th anniversary of the Manchester Medical Society, 1834–1984*, ed. W. J. Elwood and A. F. Tuxford (1984), 93–7, 219 • *The Lancet* (5 Aug 1922), 301–2 • *BMJ* (12 Aug 1922), 285–6 • Munk, *Roll* • Venn, *Alum. Cant.* • A. Ransome, 'Some great and good men and women whom I have known', [n.d.], JRL, Manchester collection • *London and Provincial Medical Directory* (1856–1922) • census returns for Devisdale, Dunham Massey, Cheshire, 1881 • m. cert. • d. cert. • baptismal register, Manchester Cathedral, 31 Dec 1840 [Lucy Fullarton] • *The record of the Royal Society of London*, 4th edn (1940)
Archives JRL, Manchester collection, published papers, articles, and books by Arthur Ransome, and Arthur Ransome's undated typescript biography 'Some great and good men and women whom I have known'
Wealth at death £18,005 0*s*. 6*d*.: probate, 25 Sept 1922, *CGPLA Eng. & Wales*

Ransome, Arthur Michell (1884–1967), journalist and writer, was born at 6 Ash Grove, Headingley, Leeds, on 18 January 1884, the eldest in the family of two sons and two daughters of Cyril Ransome, professor of history at the Yorkshire College (later Leeds University), who died in 1897, when Arthur was thirteen, and his wife, Edith (*d*. 1945), daughter of Edward Baker Boulton, who had been a sheep farmer in Australia. He was educated at the Old College, Windermere, and then at Rugby School (1897–1901), but he was a reluctant pupil. Doggedly determined from early adolescence that he was going to be a writer, he spent two unprofitable terms at the Yorkshire College reading science before he threw in his hand and left for London, where he found a job for 8*s*. a week at Grant Richards, the publishers. He was then seventeen.

Ransome's bohemian life in London, with a brief period in Paris, lasted for some twelve years. He scratched a living by writing stories and articles, some of which appeared in book form; he reviewed and ghosted. His literary friends included Edward Thomas (who once described him as 'exuberant, rash, and Protean'), Lascelles Abercrombie, Gordon Bottomley, Robert Lynd and his wife, Sylvia, and Cecil Chesterton, brother of G. K. Chesterton. There were also actors and artists with whom he would celebrate the sale of an article or a picture by a flagon of Australian burgundy and a meal of macaroni cheese. Many of these met at the studio 'evenings' of Pamela Colman Smith (Pixie); he later said that it was from her telling of Jamaican folkstories that he learned so much of the art of narration. He was very poor but nevertheless avidly bought books, and he later attributed his chronic digestive troubles to the meagre and erratic meals of that period.

If there was time for a brief holiday and he could scrape together the fare, Ransome found himself hurrying 'through the big grey archway at Euston that was the gate to the enchanted North' on his way to the Lake District, where, before his father had died, his family had spent blissful summer holidays. There he passed much of his time with the family of W. G. Collingwood, adopted as an honorary nephew by the parents, camping and boating with the children, one of whom was Robin Collingwood. In 1928 he taught the next generation, Taqui, Susie, Mavis (1920–1998, known as Titty), and Roger Altounyan, children of the eldest daughter, Dora, to sail their dinghy *Swallow*. From the idyllic summer that he spent with them on Coniston Water the story of *Swallows and Amazons* evolved, although he later chose to disclaim this. Childlike himself, he did not much care for children unless they could share the activities he enjoyed, but those that did often found themselves featuring in one of his stories of holiday adventure. He hoped to marry Barbara, the second Collingwood daughter, but this never came about, and it was to escape the unhappy marriage that he did make, to Ivy Constance (1882–1939), daughter of George Graves Walker, on 13 March 1909, that he went to Russia in 1913.

The winter of 1912–13 had been one of continual nightmare. A book commissioned by Martin Secker on Oscar Wilde had landed Ransome in a suit for libel issued by Lord Alfred Douglas; although judgment was given against Douglas in April 1913, it was a scarring experience. Meanwhile, seeing Russian folk-stories as the material for a new book, he decided to visit Russia itself. Arriving there in June 1913, he taught himself Russian, collected folk-lore, and busied himself with writing a guide to St Petersburg commissioned by an English firm. He completed *Old Peter's Russian Tales* in 1915, during a bad bout of illness. These skilful retellings of traditional stories were published the following year, by which time he had taken on the post of Petrograd correspondent of the *Daily News*. Paying regular brief visits to England, he was to stay in Russia until 1919, becoming friendly with Lenin (whom he habitually sentimentalized in his writing) and other Bolshevik leaders, especially Karl Radek, and making himself unpopular with the British Foreign Office by his pro-Bolshevik stance and opposition to foreign intervention in Russian affairs. Robert Bruce Lockhart, who headed a British mission in Moscow in 1918, described him as 'a sentimentalist, who could always be relied upon to champion the under-dog, and a visionary, whose imagination had been fired by the revolution'. In *Six Weeks in Russia in 1919* (1919) he gave a picture of Moscow in those days of starvation and high hopes, and in *The Crisis in Russia* (1921) he defended the Russian Revolution and pleaded for a more balanced view of its aims. Yet documents discovered in 2002 showed that Ransome was in fact a British secret agent working for MI6 and that he filed regular reports back to his superiors at the secret intelligence service (SIS), who were working to crush the revolution in Russia. It is likely that Ransome was recruited by Clifford Sharp, editor of the *New Statesman*, who ran the British propaganda bureau in Stockholm during the war, with the aim of infiltrating Russian revolutionary organizations.

By that time Ransome was living in Estonia with Yevgeniya Petrovna Shelepina (1894–1975), daughter of Pyotr Shelepin. When he had first met her in 1917 she had been Trotsky's secretary. He was to marry her on 8 May 1924, after the dissolution of his first marriage. His connection with the *Daily News* ended in 1919 after a change in editorship brought a change in its political viewpoint. But C. P. Scott recruited him for the *Manchester Guardian*, for which he was to continue to write until 1930. From Estonia he reported on the scene in Russia, and such time as he could spare from newspaper articles he spent in the fishing and sailing that all his life were an absorbing passion. In the *Racundra*, a 30 ton ketch, built to his specifications at Riga, he cruised round the Baltic in 1922, accompanied by his superior from SIS, Ernest Boyce. The log of this holiday was published in *'Racundra's' First Cruise* (1923), the first book that is characteristic of the sort of writing for which he is now remembered.

At the end of 1924 Scott sent Ransome as correspondent to Egypt and then in 1925–6 to China, but Ransome was growing increasingly weary of political journalism and longing to settle to his own writing, in particular 'a brat book' as he himself termed it. (By this time he had bought a cottage, Low Ludderburn, on the fells above Windermere.) In March 1929 he began to write *Swallows and*

Arthur Michell Ransome (1884–1967), by John Gilroy, 1958 [*The Fly Dresser*]

Amazons. Published in 1930, it was slow to sell. Jonathan Cape, the publisher, had received it politely but was more interested in his fishing essays, *Rod and Line* (1929), originally published in the *Manchester Guardian*. Nevertheless he persisted, following it up with a further account of the Walker children and their allies the Blacketts sailing Lake Windermere and exploring the fells—*Swallowdale* (1931). But only with his third story, *Peter Duck* (1932), did he soar into the popularity that made his nine other books for children best-sellers. (It was in *Peter Duck* that he first attempted his own illustrations, a practice he was to continue.) *Winter Holiday* (1933) recalled a winter he had spent in the Lakes when he was at preparatory school. There were books such as *Coot Club* (1934) about bird-watching and sailing on the Norfolk broads, near which he lived for a time from 1935 on the River Orwell, in Suffolk. For *Pigeon Post* (1936) he received the Library Association's first Carnegie medal for the best children's book of the year. He became an honorary DLitt of Leeds University in 1952 and was appointed CBE in 1953. He published his last book, *Mainly about Fishing*, in 1959.

Bald, vastly moustached as he became in later life, habitually dressed in a fisherman's sagging tweeds and a thimble of a tweed hat, Ransome still contrived to retain much of the appearance of the round, rosy, bright-eyed schoolboy that can be seen in early photographs. With it went a boyish charm of manner with its mingling of enthusiasm and fierce indignation; a deftness of fingers—especially where tying flies was concerned—and a stimulating ability to say something new and unexpected about almost any subject.

Ransome died on 3 June 1967 at the Royal Hospital, Cheadle, Manchester, and was buried in Rusland church, Lancashire. His first wife had died in 1939, and his second wife died in 1975. He had one daughter from his first marriage, Tabitha (*b.* 1910).   GILLIAN AVERY

Sources H. Brogan, *The life of Arthur Ransome* (1984) · *The autobiography of Arthur Ransome*, ed. R. Hart-Davis (1967) · *The Times* (6 June 1967) · private information (1981) [J. Bell] · *BBC History Magazine* (20 Aug 2002)
Archives U. Leeds, Brotherton L., corresp. and papers, incl. literary MSS | JRL, letters to *Manchester Guardian* · King's Lond., Liddell Hart C., corresp. of him and Eugenie Ransome with Sir B. H. Liddell Hart · LUL, letters to Thomas Sturge Moore · U. Birm., letters to Francis Brett Young
Likenesses D. Collingwood, oils, 1930, Abbot Hall Art Gallery, Kendal · pencil drawing, 1930, repro. in Brogan, *Life* · H. Coster, photographs, 1932, NPG · J. Gilroy, oils, 1958 (*The fly dresser*), Garr. Club [*see illus.*] · R. Lutyens, lithograph, *c.*1961–1962, NPG
Wealth at death £71,264: probate, 2 Oct 1967, *CGPLA Eng. & Wales*

Ransome, James (1782–1849). *See under* Ransome family (*per. c.*1785–1875).

Ransome, James Allen (1806–1875). *See under* Ransome family (*per. c.*1785–1875).

Ransome, James Edward (1839–1905). *See under* Ransome, Robert Charles (1830–1886).

Ransome, Robert (1753–1830). *See under* Ransome family (*per. c.*1785–1875).

Ransome, Robert Charles (1830–1886), agricultural engineer, was born on 1 June 1830, at Carr Street, Ipswich, Suffolk, the eldest son of Robert Ransome (1795–1864), agricultural engineer, and his wife, Sarah Coleby (1794–1863). He was the grandson of Robert *Ransome (1753–1830) [*see under* Ransome family], the founder of the well-known firm of ironfounders and makers of agricultural implements in Ipswich.

Educated at the Friends' schools in Hitchin and York, at the age of sixteen Robert Charles entered the Ransome firm as an apprentice. He was made a partner in 1856. During the 1860s he took over most of the general management of the firm as the health of his uncle James Allen Ransome, then senior partner, began to deteriorate. Subsequently Robert Charles became senior partner, until the business was converted into a limited liability company in 1884, when he became the first chairman of Ransomes, Sims, and Jefferies Ltd.

Ransome's contributions to the firm's development were in general commercial management. He was credited by the *Implement and Machinery Review* for 1885–6 with being 'the first of his firm to cultivate the foreign export'. There had been sales overseas before his time, but he actively sought them out. One of his first jobs after being admitted to the partnership was an extensive tour of Europe and Egypt. He subsequently travelled widely, visiting such countries as Russia, Austria, Hungary, Italy, and the United States. The strength of the contacts established by his efforts was reflected by the fact that his death was reported in newspapers and magazines in Europe and America. He was similarly assiduous in promoting the firm's business at home, and took a lead in establishing its main strengths in ploughs and cultivating implements, steam engines, and threshing machines.

Ransome was a member of the council of the Smithfield Club and also of the council of the Royal Agricultural Society of England (1875–86). He was a founder member of the Agricultural Engineers' Association, established in 1875. Prominent in the local affairs of Ipswich, he was first elected to the borough council in 1859, served as mayor in 1867, and in 1877 became an alderman. He was president of the Ipswich Liberal Association from its foundation in 1873, and was invited on several occasions to stand for parliament but refused on the grounds that he would not be able to find time for parliamentary duties as well as managing his business. In his home town, however, Ransome was able to be chairman of the Ipswich school board for twelve years from its inception in 1871. A governor and a founder trustee of Framlingham College, he was also active in the founding of Ipswich middle school. He was a member of the Ipswich docks committee. He was appointed a justice of the peace for the borough in 1877, and for the county of Suffolk in 1883.

In 1854 Ransome married Sarah Jane, daughter of Richard W. Baker of Cottesmore, and they had a daughter. His wife died in 1856. In 1864 he married Elizabeth, daughter of James Gibb of London and Calcutta. They had three daughters and two sons. Deteriorating health caused Ransome to take nine months away from work in 1879–80, which included a recuperative visit to Australia. He died, from aneurysm and asphyxia, at Belstead Road, Ipswich, on 5 March 1886, and was buried at Ipswich cemetery on 11 March. He was survived by his second wife.

Ransome's successor as head of the firm was his younger brother **James Edward Ransome** (1839–1905), who was born on 13 July 1839 in Norwich Road, Ipswich. In 1856, aged seventeen, he entered upon his apprenticeship at the firm's Orwell works, and in 1868 he became one of the managing directors. On the death of his brother in 1886 he became joint chairman, with J. R. Jefferies, and was sole chairman from 1900 when Jefferies died. Ransome married Alice, daughter of Samuel Gross of Woodbridge, in 1863. The couple had four sons and three daughters.

Whereas his brother was noted for his commercial achievements in the business, James Edward Ransome was more involved in the engineering side. There are several patents for improvements to ploughs, harrows, and lawnmowers in his name, and he presented papers on ploughs and their development, two of which were published. He was recognized also as a shrewd man of business. His first responsibilities within the firm after completing his apprenticeship were with the plough and implement department. He worked on the development of new designs of plough and the promotion of them through agricultural shows and ploughing matches. One of the early successes with which he was associated was the winning of the top prizes at the Royal Agricultural Society's show at Newcastle in 1864. The 'Newcastle' design of plough subsequently became one of the most celebrated and commercially successful of the firm's ploughs. Ransome retained active interest and managerial control of the plough and implement department throughout his career, and took responsibility for the design of the new plough and implement shops at the Orwell works in 1900.

James Edward Ransome's other particular contribution to the firm's development was his promotion of the lawnmower from a 'plaything' to a serious part of the firm's activities. New models were introduced from the late 1860s, and in 1876 Ransome oversaw the construction of a new lawnmower works. The culmination of his efforts was the successful introduction of the motor mower in 1902. The result of the commercial and technical leadership of Robert Charles and James Edward Ransome, together with J. R. Jefferies, was the success of their firm in withstanding the effects of the commercial and agricultural depression of the late nineteenth century. By the time James Edward Ransome died the company's workforce had grown to more than 2000.

A member of the Institution of Mechanical Engineers from 1886 onwards, James Edward Ransome was also a member of the council of the Agricultural Engineers' Association. In addition he served on the councils of the Royal Agricultural Society of England (1886–1905), and of the Bath and West of England and Southern Counties Society; and he belonged to the Suffolk chamber of agriculture. He was a member of Ipswich borough council and devoted his energies in local affairs particularly to sanitary improvements and education. Chairman of the governors of Ipswich endowed schools, he gave strong support (including financial contributions) to the building of a new science block at the grammar school. He was appointed a magistrate for the borough of Ipswich, but died before he could take the oath.

Ransome's political allegiances at first were with the Liberal Party, but he later became a Conservative. He was chairman of the Suffolk branch of the Tariff Reform League, and was elected president of the Ipswich Conservative Club a few weeks before he died. A keen huntsman, he was associated with the duke of Hamilton's harriers for some years. His other recreations included skating and golf.

James Edward Ransome died from cancer on 30 January 1905 at 4 Upper Wimpole Street, London. He was survived by his wife.   JONATHAN BROWN

Sources *Implement and Machinery Review*, 11 (1885–6), 8135–6 · *Implement and Machinery Review*, 30 (1904–5), 1257–8 · *The Engineer*, 61 (1886), 213 · *The Engineer* (3 Feb 1905), 120 · *East Anglian Daily Times* (6 March 1886) · *East Anglian Daily Times* (1 Feb 1905) · U. Reading, Rural History Centre, records of Ransomes Sims and Jefferies, TR RAN SP1/1 [typescript company history with family tree etc.] · U. Reading, Rural History Centre, records of Ransomes Sims and Jefferies, TR RAN SP4/160 · U. Reading, Rural History Centre, records of Ransomes Sims and Jefferies, TR RAN SP4/176 [vol. of press notices from around the world relating to R. C. Ransome's death] · R. Trow-Smith, *Power on the land: a centenary history of the Agricultural Engineers Association, 1875–1975* (1975) · D. C. Phillips, 'Ransome, James Edward', *DBB* · D. C. Phillips, 'Ransome, Robert Charles', *DBB* · *CGPLA Eng. & Wales* (1886) · *CGPLA Eng. & Wales* (1905) · b. cert. [James Edward Ransome] · d. cert. [James Edward Ransome] · d. cert.

Archives U. Reading, Rural History Centre, business records of Ransomes Sims and Jefferies | Wellcome L., corresp. with John Hodgkin

Likenesses photograph, 1890–99 (Ransome, James Edward), U. Reading, Rural History Centre, Ransomes Sims and Jefferies archives · engraving, U. Reading, Rural History Centre, Ransomes Sims and Jefferies archives · engraving (Ransome, James Edward), U. Reading, Rural History Centre, Ransomes Sims and Jefferies archives · line drawing, repro. in *Agricultural Gazette* (15 March 1886) · photograph, repro. in *Implement and Machinery Review*, 11 (1885–6), 8135

Wealth at death £57,768 16s.: probate, 9 June 1886, *CGPLA Eng. & Wales* · £163,349 10s. 2d.—James Edward Ransome: probate, 22 Feb 1905, *CGPLA Eng. & Wales*

Ranson, Thomas Fryer (1784–1828), engraver, was born on 19 July 1784 in Sunderland, co. Durham, the son of Thomas Ranson and his wife, Mary. He was apprenticed to an engraver in Newcastle and in 1814 gained a Society of Arts medal. In February 1818 he was charged at Marlborough Street magistrates' court with possessing a forged £5 note and briefly imprisoned. Despite having refused to surrender the note he was bailed, and at a subsequent hearing the Bank of England decided not to prosecute. A year later he published an engraving of himself seated in a cell at Coldbath Fields prison.

Ranson is best known for his engraved portraits, especially that of Duncan Gray, after Sir David Wilkie, for which he won a Society of Arts gold medal in 1822. He was employed to work on the long-running publication *Ancient*

Marbles in the British Museum (1812–61) and engraved topographical subjects, such as the doorway of South Weald church, after J. A. Repton. He died, unmarried, at his residence, 23 Blandford Street, Portman Square, London, before 27 August 1828, when administration of his goods was granted to his brother Cuthbert.

ELEANOR TOLLFREE

Sources Redgrave, *Artists*, 348 · administration, PRO, PROB 6/204, fol. 229v · *Engraved Brit. ports.*, 3.544 · parish register, Sunderland, Durham RO · *DNB* · *The Times* (2 Feb 1818), 3e · *The Times* (9 Feb 1818), 4b
Archives NPG, Heinz Archive and Library, sitters' files
Likenesses T. F. Ranson, self-portrait, line engraving, pubd 1818, BM, NPG
Wealth at death £100: administration, PRO, PROB 6/204, fol. 229v

Rant, William (1603/4–1653), physician, the second of the five sons of William Rant (1564–1627), a physician of Norwich, and his first wife, Mary, daughter of Edward Ward, of Kirby, Norfolk, was born in Norwich, and attended school there for five years under Matthew Stonham. In 1619 Rant and his younger brother, Thomas, matriculated as pensioners at Gonville and Caius College, Cambridge, William Rant gaining his MB in 1625 and MD in 1630. On his father's death in 1627, he was bequeathed 'all my great books of physicke', and given a special charge 'that he be helpful (to the best of his power) to my sonne Edward in the study of physicke'. Edward (*d.* 1636) was almost certainly the son of a second marriage; his mother was also provided for in the will. As a reward for this service to his half-brother, Rant received 'all Avicen with comment in three great volumes' and other especially prized medical books. In addition, he inherited a house in Needham Street, Norwich, and lands outside the city's St Giles's Gate (PRO, PROB 11/152, sig. 108).

In 1630 Rant moved to London and built a thriving medical practice. He presented himself for examination at the College of Physicians in 1632; was elected a candidate in the college on 30 September 1633; and became a fellow on 30 September 1634. In the same year, Rant and his brother Thomas purchased a pedigree from the College of Arms during the heraldic visitation of London.

Rant soon became an active and highly respected fellow of the College of Physicians. As a second-generation Caius physician, he was more steeped than most in the traditions of academic medicine. He was admired for his elegant library and for his generous benefactions to the college coffers. In October 1639 he delivered the first Goulstonian lecture in morbid anatomy, a lecture endowed by Theodore Goulston's will of 1632. Around 1640 he married Jane Dingley (*d.* 1656), third daughter of Sir John Dingley, of Wolverton, Hampshire; they had a son, William (*b. c.*1642), and a daughter, Jane.

Despite having strong royalist sympathies, which led him to contribute financially to Charles I's cause, Rant faithfully attended college meetings in London throughout the civil war years, from 1642 to 1649, and was crucial in the college's functioning. He was a censor on four occasions, in 1640, 1645, 1647, and 1650, and was still active in

the college in 1651, when he volunteered to give the anatomy lecture in place of a delinquent Edmund Smith. Some of Rant's prescriptions, dating from 1652 and 1653, were preserved in the Sloane MSS in the British Library.

Rant was seriously ill in 1653 from what was called a 'marasmus', a general weakening or wasting away of the body, a body which, in Rant's case, was already tall and thin by nature. In his last days, he retired to Thorpe Market, in his native county of Norfolk, where he was reunited with his brother Thomas, who had himself withdrawn from London in disaffection with the Commonwealth. Rant died on 15 September 1653, and was buried in the parish church of Thorpe Market. His death was duly noted by the London obituarist Richard Smyth, who managed to confuse him with another college fellow, John Raven. Three years after Rant's death, on 1 February 1656, Thomas Rant presented the College of Physicians with six Arabic books which had been bequeathed to it by his brother.

WILLIAM BIRKEN

Sources Munk, *Roll* · Venn, *Alum. Cant.* · J. Venn and others, eds., *Biographical history of Gonville and Caius College*, 1: *1349–1713* (1897) · BL, Sloane MS 1055, fols. 91b–92a · B. Hamey, 'Bustorum aliquot reliquiae …', RCP Lond. · will, PRO, PROB 11/152, sig. 108 [father] · annals, RCP Lond. · *The visitation of London, anno Domini 1633, 1634, and 1635, made by Sir Henry St George*, 2, ed. J. J. Howard, Harleian Society, 17 (1883) · HoP, *Commons* · private information (2004) · *The obituary of Richard Smyth … being a catalogue of all such persons as he knew in their life*, ed. H. Ellis, CS, 44 (1849)

Ranulf [Ralph] (*d.* 1123), administrator, was a man of uncertain background, whom Henry I appointed his chancellor in 1107. The chancellor was the king's principal domestic servant, a clerk in charge of the court's secretarial and religious services and in receipt of the top pay and allowances. There were also pickings. Some time after 1106 Ranulf was granted by the king custody of the escheated honour of Berkhamsted. But, possibly because of poor health, lack of a suitable vacancy, or simply choice, he did not, like his predecessor and successor, retire to a bishopric. He attested over 160 royal acts, and probably accompanied Henry I for at least part of all the king's visits to Normandy during the years of his chancellorship. But he was also sometimes involved in the government of England during the king's absences, serving as a member of the regency council that assisted Queen Matilda and Prince William, and being recorded as a justice in the exchequer in 1119. According to Henry, archdeacon of Huntingdon, the chancellor also employed his lively intelligence, shrewdness, and cunning to the disinheritance and impoverishment of the unworldly. And as his health declined—he suffered from some unspecified illness for twenty years—so his cupidity and deceit increased.

The moralist had found a good subject, and would not have given Ranulf credit for the good education he gave to his sons. Ranulf sent them to school at Laon under the patronage of his predecessor, Waldric, in 1107 elected bishop of that city, and employed as their tutor William de Corbeil, later archbishop of Canterbury, who was attending the lectures of the great Master Anselm. The archdeacon regarded Ranulf's death, of which he may have been an eyewitness, as suitably ignoble. In January 1123, after spending Christmas with the king at Dunstable, the two set off for Berkhamsted, where Ranulf was to entertain his master. When they reached the top of the hill from which his castle came into view, Ranulf was so jubilant that he fell from his horse and was ridden over by a monk—at St Albans remembered as one of theirs. A few days later Ranulf died of his injuries. Clearly a trusted servant, even perhaps a friend, of the king, he could have shared not only Henry I's wealth but also some of his virtues and vices.   FRANK BARLOW

Sources Henry, archdeacon of Huntingdon, *Historia Anglorum*, ed. D. E. Greenway, OMT (1996) · Herman, 'De miraculis S. Mariae Laudunensis', *Patrologia Latina*, 156 (1853), 961–88 · Paris, *Chron.*, 2.150 · I. J. Sanders, *English baronies: a study of their origin and descent, 1086–1327* (1960), 14 · *Reg. RAN*, vol. 2

Ranulf (I) [Ranulf le Meschin], **third earl of Chester** (d. **1129**), magnate, was son of Ranulf (Ralph) de Briquessart, vicomte of the Bessin (the area around Bayeux), and Matilda, daughter of Richard, vicomte of the Avranchin (the area around Avranches). The name Meschin ('younger' or 'junior') was presumably first employed to distinguish him from his father.

Family and early career in the borders In the Durham book of fraternity (the *liber vitae*), in addition to Ranulf there are listed his parents, an elder brother, Richard, who died young, and a younger brother, William; and he had also a sister, Agnes, who was the first wife of Robert de Grandmesnil (d. c.1136). Ranulf (I) was a member of the military household first of William II and then of Henry I. He is first recorded as Ranulf, son of Ranulf *le vicomte*, on 24 April 1089 when he authenticated with his cross a grant of Robert Curthose, duke of Normandy, to the cathedral of Bayeux. In 1093–4, as nephew of Hugh d'Avranches, earl of Chester (d. 1101), he witnessed the charter which recorded the establishment of a monastic community at Chester. About 1098 he became the third husband of Lucy (d. c.1138), heir of the honour of Bolingbroke, who had earlier been married first to Ivo Taillebois and then to Roger fitz Gerold (the father of her son William de Roumare). This made him a major landowner in Lincolnshire. It also either originated or strengthened his ties with what would become the English shires of Cumberland and Westmorland, centred on Carlisle. In succession to Ivo Taillebois he was for a time lord of Appleby, for he later referred to 'my castle' in that place, which controlled the road from north Yorkshire to Carlisle (Prescott, no. 3). William Rufus had captured Carlisle in 1092, and it became the centre of Anglo-Norman settlement in the region. Ranulf was long remembered as the first lord of this region, and his lordship was for a time visible on the ground. An interesting charter of David, king of Scots, granting Annandale to Robert (I) de Brus (c.1124), defined his territory as being north of 'the boundary of Ranulf Meschin' (*divisam Randulphi Meschin*), and his rights as those 'which Ranulf Meschin once had in Carlisle and in his land of Cumberland' (Lawrie, 48–9). It is possible that Ranulf's involvement at Carlisle predated 1100, for one of his charters describes William Rufus as his lord, but firm

dates come from the reign of Henry I. Close to Carlisle, at Wetherhal, c.1106, Ranulf founded a Benedictine priory, a colony of St Mary's Abbey, York. The earliest baronies, according to the memory of the shire in 1212, were granted by Ranulf in the reign of Henry I, and the more significant of these were held by his relatives and dependants. His brother-in-law Robert de Trivers was given the lordship of Burgh by Sands. His Norman tenant Richer de Boiville received Kirklinton and served as sheriff.

William le Meschin The most important member of a tightly knit family group was Ranulf's younger brother **William le Meschin** (d. 1129x35). William went on the first crusade, where he is mentioned, as 'William son of Ranulf *le vicomte*' at the siege of Nicaea in 1097 (Ordericus Vitalis, *Eccl. hist.*, 5.59). In Cumbria William le Meschin was first given charge of Gilsland, which he failed to hold against the Scots, and then Egremont (the barony of Copeland). He built the castle at Egremont, and close by on the coast he founded the priory of St Bees, a further daughter house of St Mary's, York. William le Meschin married Cecily de Rumilly, the daughter of Robert de Rumilly and heir to the barony of Skipton in Craven, west Yorkshire, thus creating a substantial cross-Pennine estate. William and Cecily were the founders of the priory of Embsay, which later removed to Bolton in Wharfedale. In addition to the two baronies of Egremont and Skipton, William le Meschin acquired tenancies in several counties, the more significant held of his brother in Lincolnshire (where the Lindsey survey of 1115–18 provides detailed record) and in Cheshire. William remained closely linked with Ranulf, whom he survived by just a few years, dying before 1135. An elder son, Matthew, having predeceased him, William's heirs were successively his younger son, also called Ranulf le Meschin, and three sisters, Amice, Alice, and Matilda, who in the course of a total of seven marriages comprehensively dismembered the estate.

Earl of Chester Ranulf was in regular though not frequent attendance at the court of Henry I: he is found at various times at the palaces at Westminster, Winchester, and Rouen, at the hunting lodges at Brampton and Woodstock, and at the monastery at Reading. Most significantly, he was one of the commanders of Henry's forces at the battle of Tinchebrai in late September 1106, the others being Robert, count of Meulan, and William (II) de Warenne, earl of Surrey (d. 1138), all three men described by Orderic Vitalis as officers of the royal household. Ranulf was one of the magnates who witnessed the treaty of Dover made with the count of Flanders on 17 May 1110; and he was present at the Christmas court at St Albans in 1115. He occurs twice as a royal justice, first in 1106, then c.1116, and it may be significant that in each case one of his fellow justices was Geoffrey Ridel, whose wife was an illegitimate daughter of Hugh d'Avranches, earl of Chester. Even with his substantial English lordships, Ranulf was frequently in Normandy, particularly at times of military threat.

In 1119 Orderic Vitalis mentioned 'Richard, earl of Chester, and his kinsman and successor Ralph of Briquessart' as pre-eminent among those who remained loyal to the king (Ordericus Vitalis, *Eccl. hist.*, 6.223). The chronicler here looked ahead to the last and most crucial of the events that determined Ranulf's career. On 21 November 1120 Richard of Chester and Ranulf were together at Barfleur and witnessed a charter in favour of the abbey of Cerisy. Just four days later Richard died in the *White Ship* disaster. Ranulf was appointed earl of Chester in succession to his cousin, and occurs as such in a charter issued at London early in January 1121. The precise terms of his succession are not clear, but certainly some of Lucy's Lincolnshire lands were surrendered to the king, and seemingly also Ranulf's lordships in Cumbria. According to later tradition, on succeeding to the earldom Ranulf 'gave back to the lord king the county (*comitatus*) of Cumbria, on condition that each of those he had enfeoffed should hold of the king in chief' (Wilson, 492): this is from the *Chronicon Cumbrie*, a 'special source of error' according to J. H. Round (*DNB*), but with regard to the timing of the transfer probably accurate. He promised the king a substantial relief, for in 1129/30 his son Earl Ranulf (II) owed £1000 'for his father's debt for the land of Earl Hugh' (*Pipe rolls*, 31 Henry I, 110). This may well represent the full total of the original debt, for good connections at court and loyal service in the field would temper the king's demands for payment.

At court in the early 1120s Earl Ranulf (I) was named as chief among the kinsfolk who arranged a marriage that linked the Basset and Ridel families: named also in an agreement ratified by the king at Woodstock were his brother William le Meschin, his constable William, his chancellor Geoffrey, and Nigel d'Aubigny. All the while the old campaigner remained on military alert. In March 1123 the king at Woodstock received news of a threat from supporters of William Clito (*d.* 1128), and immediately the earls of Gloucester and Chester were sent over to Normandy 'to guard that territory' (Symeon of Durham, 267–8). Throughout the winter of 1123–4 Ranulf had charge of the garrison of Évreux. Good intelligence of the movements of the enemy led to the ambush at Bourgthéroulde on 25 March 1124, which led to the capture of Waleran, count of Meulan, and others, and gained Ranulf much credit.

Death and legacy The earldom of Chester gave Ranulf his title, but in the county itself he may not have had time to put down strong roots. His own grants as earl were all confirmations, to St Evroult in Normandy, to St Werburgh's, Chester, and to his wife's foundation at Spalding in Lincolnshire. He did, however, establish a second generation of his family in English lordship. His daughter Alice married the marcher lord Richard de Clare who was killed by the Welsh in late April 1136. Among the witnesses to his son's charters occur Richard Bacun, who married an illegitimate daughter, an illegitimate son, Benedict, and Fulk de Briquessart, who was possibly his nephew. Ranulf died in January 1129, and was buried in the chapter house of Chester Abbey. A long series of agreements made by his son *Ranulf (II) (de Gernons) and his widow, the Countess

Lucy, are entered on the pipe roll of 1129/30. Among these the countess offered the king 500 marks that she not be required to marry again.   EDMUND KING

Sources *Reg. RAN*, vols. 1–2 · Ordericus Vitalis, *Eccl. hist.* · G. Barraclough, ed., *The charters of the Anglo-Norman earls of Chester, c.1071–1237*, Lancashire and Cheshire RS, 126 (1988) · *Journal of the Chester Archaeological Society*, 71 (1991) [G. Barraclough issue, *The earldom of Chester and its charters*, ed. A. T. Thacker] · W. Farrer and others, eds., *Early Yorkshire charters*, 12 vols. (1914–65), vol. 7 · J. E. Prescott, ed., *Register of the priory of Wetherhal*, Cumberland and Westmorland Antiquarian and Archaeological Society, record series, 1 (1897) · H. Summerson, *Medieval Carlisle: the city and the borders from the late eleventh to the mid-sixteenth century*, 2 vols., Cumberland and Westmorland Antiquarian and Archaeological Society, extra ser., 25 (1993) · *Pipe rolls*, 31 Henry I · [J. Wilson], ed., *The register of the priory of St Bees*, SurtS, 126 (1915) · A. C. Lawrie, ed., *Early Scottish charters prior to AD 1153* (1905) · G. W. S. Barrow, 'The pattern of lordship and feudal settlement in Cumbria', *Journal of Medieval History*, 1 (1975), 117–38 · J. C. Holt, 'Politics and property in early medieval England', *Past and Present*, 57 (1972), appx 2, D, 51–2 · M. V. Taylor, 'Some obits of abbots and founders of St Werburgh's Abbey, Chester', *Liber Luciani de laude Cestrie*, ed. M. V. Taylor, Lancashire and Cheshire RS, 64 (1912), 90 · Dugdale, *Monasticon*, 3.217–18 · C. W. Foster and T. Longley, eds., *The Lincolnshire Domesday and the Lindsey Survey*, Lincoln RS, 19 (1924) · Symeon of Durham, *Opera*, vol. 2 · GEC, *Peerage*
Wealth at death earldom of Chester valued at approx. £800 in 1086

Ranulf (II) [Ranulf de Gernon], **fourth earl of Chester** (*d.* 1153), magnate, was the son of *Ranulf (I), third earl of Chester (*d.* 1129), and his wife, Lucy of Bolingbroke (*d.* c.1138). He had a half-brother, William de *Roumare, Lucy's son from a previous marriage to Roger fitz Gerold, and a sister, Alice, who married Richard de Clare (*d.* 1136). Among those who witnessed his charters were Benedict 'brother of the earl' (presumably an illegitimate son of Ranulf (I)), Foulque de Bricquessart (probably either a nephew of Ranulf (I) or another illegitimate son), and Richard Bacun, founder c.1143 of Rocester Abbey, Staffordshire, who described Ranulf (II) as his uncle (*avunculus*).

Succession to the earldom On his father's death in January in 1129 Ranulf (II) succeeded to his lands and titles in England and Normandy. He had evidently attained his majority, so would probably have been born during the first decade of the twelfth century. His Norman interests lay in the Bessin (the area around Bayeux) and the Avranchin (the area around Avranches), and included the hereditary *vicomté* of Bayeux. In England his honour as earl of Chester lay principally in the north and midlands, with the most important demesnes in north and east Cheshire (such as Eastham and Macclesfield), in Warwickshire (Coventry), Leicestershire (Barrow upon Soar), and Lincolnshire (Greetham). On or after becoming earl of Chester, Ranulf (I) had surrendered to the crown his lordship of Carlisle and most of his wife's Lincolnshire inheritance based upon Bolingbroke, none of which came later to Ranulf (II). However, about one-third of Lucy's Lincolnshire estate, largely within the soke of Belchford, had remained with Ranulf (I), was retained by Lucy until her death c.1138, and did subsequently pass to their son. The disposition of these holdings was clearly the subject of negotiation with Henry I, for among the accounts charged to Ranulf (II) in the 1130 pipe roll was a debt of £1000 left by his father 'for the land of Earl Hugh [of Chester]' and another debt of 500 marks for a concord over his mother's dower. Lucy herself rendered further accounts, including one of 400 marks 'for her father's land'.

Relations with Henry I and Stephen During the closing years of Henry I's reign Ranulf (II) was present at royal councils in Northampton (8 September 1131, when magnates were required to swear fealty to the Empress Matilda), Westminster (29 April 1132), and Windsor (Christmas 1132). Although favoured by geld pardons in 1130 in Leicestershire, Lincolnshire, Nottinghamshire and Derbyshire, Staffordshire, and Warwickshire, totalling £21 4s. 0d., there is no sign that he enjoyed the king's familiarity as his father had done. On the other hand, his marriage (not later than 1135) to *Matilda, daughter of *Robert, earl of Gloucester, associated him with the party favouring the empress's succession (after his death, his widow issued a charter referring to the empress as her aunt). Despite this, in common with nearly every other Anglo-Norman magnate, he accepted King Stephen's accession, attending the royal council at Westminster at Easter (22 March) 1136 and witnessing the Oxford charter of liberties (which signalled the earl of Gloucester's submission to Stephen) in April of that year. To all appearances Ranulf remained a loyal subject until 1140, despite his father-in-law's formal defiance of the king (May 1138) and military leadership of the Angevins in England following the empress's invasion (September 1139).

An early test of Ranulf's allegiance came in February 1136, when Stephen granted Carlisle to Henry of Scotland in the first treaty of Durham. The terms were confirmed in a second treaty of 9 April 1139. Ranulf's resentment at the alienation of a lordship formerly held by his father explains, at least in part, his withdrawal from the royal council at Easter 1136 in protest at the elevated position enjoyed there by Henry of Scotland, and his attempt in 1140 to capture Henry and his wife on their return from Stephen's court. However, the significance of Carlisle in motivating Ranulf's behaviour should not be exaggerated. It lay far from his main territorial interests, and he seems to have played no part in the military campaigns against the Scots which reached a climax with their defeat at the battle of the Standard in August 1138. The earl of Chester's principal ambitions were focused instead on the north midlands, especially in Lincolnshire where his mother's inheritance lay.

Having antagonized the king through his bid to capture Henry of Scotland, Ranulf compounded his offence later in 1140 by contriving the seizure of the royal castle at Lincoln. He arrived unarmed with three knights, ostensibly to collect his wife, and the wife of William de Roumare, who had been paying a social visit. On being allowed in, they seized weapons, expelled the royal garrison, and admitted Roumare and his men. The king's response was to visit Lincolnshire, but instead of taking reprisals against the half-brothers he treated them with favour: William of Malmesbury said that he 'added to [their] honours' (Malmesbury, 80–81), the *Gesta Stephani* that he

peaceably renewed a pact with Ranulf while intending to watch whether the promises were kept. Stephen left for London before Christmas, but made a surprise return during the festival to lay siege to Lincoln Castle. Ranulf managed to escape, obtained the armed assistance of his father-in-law, Robert, earl of Gloucester, and other Angevin adherents, raised soldiers from Cheshire and Wales, and marched back to Lincoln, where his wife and half-brother were continuing to resist the siege. At the battle of Lincoln on 2 February 1141 both Stephen and Ranulf fought on foot. The king was captured, and the earl followed up his victory with sack and slaughter in the city itself.

Ranulf and the Empress Matilda Although he played a leading role in the king's downfall, an event which looked set to bring the Empress Matilda to power, it seems clear that Ranulf fought primarily not on behalf of a contender for the throne, but for himself and his family. According to William of Malmesbury 'he seemed ambivalent in his loyalty' (Malmesbury, 82–3), and promised fealty to the empress only on condition that the earl of Gloucester would help him relieve Lincoln Castle. The speeches before the battle, put into the mouths of the protagonists by Henry of Huntingdon, have Ranulf perceiving the conflict in personal terms, to avenge the wrong done to himself, in contrast to Robert of Gloucester for whom the crown was at stake. Ranulf's ambivalence over the succession dispute, and consequent distrust by both parties, was repeatedly illustrated during the years which followed. He is not known to have attested any of the empress's charters after Stephen's accession. At the siege of Winchester in September 1141 he initially joined the queen's army, only to encounter such suspicion and hostility that he switched to the empress's camp; here, according to William of Malmesbury, his arrival was 'late and ineffective' (ibid., 102–03). His Norman castle at Bricquessart fell to the Angevins in 1142, and the castle he had taken at Lincoln withstood a siege by Stephen two years later. Although he subsequently met Stephen at Stamford (probably early in 1146, when the royalist cause was gaining ground) and apparently renewed his fealty to the king, even this reconciliation did not persist. He duly helped Stephen to capture Bedford town and besiege Wallingford Castle, but the king and the royalist magnates remained deeply suspicious of his failure to restore revenues from royal lands and castles he had seized, and thought he should give hostages to secure his good faith. He was again with the king at Northampton on 29 August 1146, but here his request that Stephen help him to campaign against the Welsh was seen as an attempted entrapment, and his refusal to give hostages or restore royal property led to his sudden arrest and imprisonment. He was released after agreeing to Stephen's terms and taking an oath not to resist the king in future, whereupon he set about trying to recover by force what he had been obliged to surrender. Subsequent campaigns led to armed confrontations with Stephen's son Eustace, and on at least two occasions, near Coventry (probably early in 1147) and Lincoln (1149), with the king himself.

Extension of Ranulf's basis of power In the years following the battle of Lincoln Ranulf was also involved in a series of conflicts and negotiations with northern and midlands barons, including Alan, earl of Richmond, William, count of Aumale, Robert Marmion, and Gilbert de Gant, who was captured in the battle and forced to marry the earl's niece Rohese de Clare. His consistent purpose was to strengthen his authority from the west coast to the east, and to this end he kept a house in Lincoln with separate household officials, refined his honorial administration especially for financial affairs, and employed a scribe as accomplished as those in royal service. A charter issued by Stephen, undated but probably attributable to the brief reconciliation of 1146, demonstrates the extent of his ambitions. He was granted royal manors in Warwickshire, Leicestershire, Nottinghamshire, and Lincolnshire, the towns of Newcastle under Lyme, and Derby, land in Grimsby, and the soke of Grantham, plus the honours of William d'Aubigny Brito (Belvoir), Roger de Bully (Tickhill), and Roger de Poitou (Lancaster, although that which lay north of the Ribble was under Scottish control). He was also confirmed in his tenure of Lincoln Castle, including the right to retain 'Lucy's tower', a reference which hints at the hereditary claims which had underlain his seizure of the castle. Much of this may already have been encroached upon by Ranulf, and much was presumably surrendered as the price of his release following his arrest at Northampton: Lincoln, for example, was in Stephen's hands by Christmas 1146, and, despite attacks on the castle in 1147 and 1149, Ranulf failed to regain it.

The death of Robert, earl of Gloucester, in October 1147, followed by the retirement of the Empress Matilda to Normandy early in 1148, brought a change in the political context, and with it Ranulf's closer association with the Angevin party. There is charter evidence of a gathering at Chester of the king's principal baronial opponents, such as Roger, earl of Hereford, and Gilbert fitz Richard, earl of Hertford, some time in 1147 or 1148, and also of a visit by Ranulf during this period to the Angevin headquarters at Bristol. Most significantly, when the future Henry II (then aged sixteen) was knighted by David, king of Scots, at Carlisle on Whitsunday (22 May) 1149, Ranulf was in attendance. He did homage to King David, who granted him the honour of Lancaster (including lands north of the Ribble) in exchange for a renunciation of claims to Carlisle; it was also agreed that Ranulf's son would marry one of the daughters of Henry of Scotland. Ranulf almost certainly did homage to the future Henry II on this occasion also, for he addressed him as 'his lord' in a charter of March 1150 at the latest. The immediate consequences of this meeting were slight: a plan to launch a combined assault on York was thwarted by Stephen's arrival, Ranulf was blamed by the king of Scots for failing to deliver his promises, and the proposed marriage never took place. But the earl of Chester had clearly made a firmer commitment to the Angevin cause than at any previous time in the civil war, and he was prepared to be a witness to Henry's charters both on this visit and on his return to England in 1153.

Even so, Ranulf continued to put his own interests first. Some time between 1149 and 1153 he made a formal agreement with Robert, earl of Leicester, whereby each pledged to bring only twenty knights if obliged by his liege lord to fight against the other, and generally to limit the impact of the war upon their estates. In the event, both earls joined the Angevin campaign in 1153, but Ranulf still struck a hard bargain, securing from Henry (not later than April) a charter issued at Devizes attested by ten men 'on the part of earl Ranulf' to complement the eleven other witnesses. This made lavish grants in the north midlands, many repeating those given by Stephen probably in 1146 but also including the estates of several royalist barons which the earl was effectively being invited to seize. Among these were the holdings of William Peverel of Nottingham, who was widely believed to have been responsible for Ranulf's death, and who in 1155 was disinherited for the crime.

As a marcher earl, Ranulf had to cope with a resurgence of Welsh aggression. In 1136 or 1137 he led a disastrous expedition into Wales from which he was one of the few to escape alive. In 1146 raids into Tegeingl east of the River Clwyd by Owain, king of Gwynedd, prompted Ranulf's appeal to Stephen for military assistance; within days of the earl's arrest, the Welsh were invading Cheshire, and reached Nantwich before being driven out by his seneschal Robert de Montalt on 3 September. Four years later, in alliance with Madog ap Maredudd, king of Powys, he prepared an attack on Owain Gwynedd, but the enterprise collapsed after defeat at Coleshill. As this episode demonstrates, Ranulf fully appreciated the value of co-operation as well as confrontation with the Welsh princes. Cadwaladr, brother of Owain Gwynedd, was a son-in-law of Ranulf's sister Alice. He accompanied Ranulf to the battle of Lincoln, where Welsh forces figured prominently, and was welcomed to the earl's court in the late 1140s and early 1150s, when he witnessed charters as 'king of Wales' in defiance of his brother. A Welsh prince referred to by Orderic Vitalis as Maredudd—probably Cadwaladr's brother-in-law Madog ap Maredudd of Powys, but possibly Cadwaladr's son Maredudd—was also with Ranulf at the battle of Lincoln.

Despite Ranulf's interests in Normandy, none of his charters is known to have been issued there, and the focus of his attention was clearly upon the English side of the channel. He certainly lost his Norman estates during the civil war: Bricquessart fell to the Angevins in 1142, and the lands Ranulf held from the bishop and cathedral of Bayeux featured in a charter of Robert, earl of Gloucester, in September 1146. At Devizes in 1153 the future Henry II duly restored Ranulf's 'Norman inheritance', interpreting this liberally to include Breuil, the castle of Vire, and other holdings once associated with his family, together with comital status and extensive lordship in the Avranchin. As with Henry's other promises to Ranulf in 1153, however, these did not survive the earl's death, and his son succeeded, in Normandy as in England, substantially to the position enjoyed at Stephen's accession.

Philanthropy, death, and reputation Ranulf founded four religious houses, an abbey for Savignac monks at Basingwerk, Flintshire, in 1131, priories for Benedictine monks and nuns at Minting, Lincolnshire, and Chester respectively (both at uncertain dates), and a priory for Augustinian canons at Trentham, Staffordshire. The last foundation, made on his deathbed in 1153, was probably the restoration of a house originally established by Hugh d'Avranches. At the end of his life he also compensated Lincoln Cathedral and the abbeys at Burton and Chester for the evils inflicted upon them, and soon after his death his widow and son made a grant to Walter, bishop of Chester, specifically for his absolution. The author of the *Gesta Stephani* suggests that he was excommunicated some time in the late 1140s, but, if so, reconciliation with the church seems apparent from a gift he made to Bordesley Abbey, Worcestershire, between 1149 and 1153, at the instigation, and in the presence, of Bishop Walter, and also from the fact that, according to later tradition, he was buried next to his father in Chester Abbey. Ranulf died on 17 December 1153 at Gresley, Derbyshire. According to the *Gesta Stephani*, the earl was given poisoned wine while a guest at the house of William Peverel. In this version, he 'just recovered, only because he had not drunk much', but in any event he did not survive for long. Ranulf's wife, Matilda, who in 1172 founded Repton Priory, Derbyshire, died on 29 July 1189. Their son *Hugh of Cyfeiliog, born in 1147, succeeded him as earl of Chester, taking seisin of the lands in 1162.

Most contemporary verdicts upon Ranulf were unfavourable. Although Orderic Vitalis acknowledged his resourcefulness and daring, the *Gesta Stephani* criticized 'the cunning devices of his accustomed bad faith' (*Gesta Stephani*, 192–3), and Henry of Huntingdon, through a speech supposedly by the royalist spokesman at the battle of Lincoln, called him 'a man of reckless daring, ready for conspiracy … panting for the impossible', prone to defeat or, at best, to Pyrrhic victories (*Historia Anglorum*, 734–5). Clearly, his strategy during the civil war was to take every opportunity to enhance his territorial position, especially in the north midlands, and such commitments as he made, either to the king or to the Angevins, were calculated to that end. Other magnates followed similar policies, but Ranulf (II) was exceptionally ruthless in pursuit of his ambitions, and accordingly he was hated by many and trusted by none.   GRAEME WHITE

Sources G. Barraclough, ed., *The charters of the Anglo-Norman earls of Chester, c.1071–1237*, Lancashire and Cheshire RS, 126 (1988) · *Reg. RAN*, vols. 2–3 · K. R. Potter and R. H. C. Davis, eds., *Gesta Stephani*, OMT (1976) · Henry, archdeacon of Huntingdon, *Historia Anglorum*, ed. D. E. Greenway, OMT (1996) · William of Malmesbury, *Historia novella: the contemporary history*, ed. E. King, trans. K. R. Potter, OMT (1998) · Ordericus Vitalis, *Eccl. hist.*, vol. 6 · R. C. Christie, ed. and trans., *Annales Cestrienses, or, Chronicle of the abbey of S. Werburg at Chester*, Lancashire and Cheshire RS, 14 (1887) · *Pipe rolls*, 31 Henry I · M. V. Taylor, 'Some obits of abbots and founders of St Werburgh's Abbey, Chester', *Liber Luciani de laude Cestrie*, ed. M. V. Taylor, Lancashire and Cheshire RS, 64 (1912) · Dugdale, *Monasticon*, new edn, vols. 3, 6 · *Journal of the Chester Archaeological Society*, 71 (1991) [G. Barraclough issue, *The earldom of Chester and its charters*, ed. A. T. Thacker] · P. Dalton, '*In neutro latere*: the armed neutrality of Ranulf II, earl of Chester in King Stephen's reign', *Anglo-Norman Studies*, 14 (1991), 39–59 · F. M. Stenton, *The first century of English feudalism, 1066–1166*, 2nd edn (1961)

Ranulf (**III**) [Ranulf de Blundeville], **sixth earl of Chester and first earl of Lincoln** (1170–1232), magnate, was the elder son of *Hugh, earl of Chester (1147–1181), and Bertrada de Montfort.

Birth and family Ranulf was born in 1170 according to the Chester annals, a source compiled after 1265 but usually reliable for events of importance to the comital house. Like other dates in the annals—the birth of Hugh (1147), his marriage (1169), and the birth of his second child, Matilda (1171)—it is compatible with record evidence. Ranulf's mother, Bertrada, is now thought to have been sister rather than daughter of Simon de Montfort (d. 1188), and hence aunt rather than sister of Simon de Montfort (d. 1218), father of Simon de Montfort, earl of Leicester. Born c.1155, Bertrada lived until 1227 without remarrying. Ranulf had a younger brother, Richard, who is mentioned in his father's acts, but his disappearance after 1181 suggests he died in childhood. The name by which Ranulf has hitherto been known, de Blundeville, has been taken as a reference to his birth at Oswestry on the Shropshire–Wales border. But B. E. Harris demonstrated in 1971 that the name occurs first in the (perhaps late fourteenth-century) Dieulacres annals, and is linked with Oswestry only from the sixteenth century. His birthplace must therefore be regarded as unknown. Ranulf's two marriages, in 1188 or 1189 to Constance of Brittany and in 1200 to Clemence de Fougères, produced no children. Because of this, his great inheritance was divided between his four sisters, who had all made important dynastic marriages, and their descendants on his death in 1232.

Duke of Brittany Little is known of Ranulf's upbringing, apparently in Chester. His nurse, Wymarc, came from a local family, and Earl Hugh gave a Cheshire heiress in marriage to 'Alexander my son's tutor' c.1177–81 (Barraclough, *Charters*, 193–4). Hugh's death on 30 June 1181 made Ranulf a royal ward; incomplete accounts of Chester appear on the pipe rolls down to Michaelmas 1187. Why did the minority end then? The answer must lie in Henry II's ambitious plans for Ranulf, who was soon married to *Constance (c.1161–1201), daughter and heir of *Conan (IV), duke of Brittany (c.1135–1171), widow of Henry's son Geoffrey since 1186, and custodian of the duchy on behalf of Geoffrey's posthumous son, Arthur. According to the Chester annals, Ranulf was knighted by the king on 1 January 1189 and the wedding followed on 3 February (St Werburgh's day) 1189, but the text is confused at this point and 1188 is more likely for both events. Henry II thus brought the young earl into the forefront of Angevin continental politics, charged with helping to resist French intervention in Brittany. The marriage also augmented Ranulf's English possessions with the honour and earldom of Richmond held in right of his wife. Perhaps by 1190 he celebrated his new status by commissioning a second seal modelled on those of his Breton predecessors, and he also used the titles duke of Brittany and earl of Richmond in his charters, though never consistently.

Ranulf's political activity between 1189 and 1194 did not match this potential importance. He did not accompany Richard I on crusade, despite later legends to this effect, and avoided entanglement in the contests for power among Richard's deputies in England and his brother John. Nor is Ranulf known to have played an important role in Normandy or Brittany. The distribution of charters he issued in this period, many of them in Chester, suggests that the earl's first priority was to take a firm grip of his inheritance after his minority. But in 1194 Ranulf helped to capture Nottingham Castle for the recently released Richard, and then carried a ceremonial sword at the formal crown wearing that followed. By September 1194 he had joined the king in France and spent much of the period from 1194 to 1199 there, mostly in Normandy to judge from his attestations of royal charters. One substantial reward he received was royal acceptance of his claim to the Lincolnshire barony of Bolingbroke on the death of his cousin (they had a common great-grandmother in Countess Lucy, wife of *Ranulf (I), third earl of Chester) William de Roumare in 1198. But however useful Ranulf's support was to Richard I, his success was limited by the token nature of his marriage. Since 1189 Constance had presided over an effectively independent duchy, with little documented influence from her husband. In 1196 Ranulf imprisoned her in his castle of St Jacques de Beuvron on the Norman frontier, driving the Breton nobility into open revolt, while Constance's son, Arthur, took refuge with Philip Augustus of France. Richard may well have supported the earl's actions, and was prepared to back his claims by invading the duchy, but in retrospect the episode seems a last unsuccessful attempt to assert an authority over his wife and her lands that Ranulf had never really possessed.

King John: loyalty under strain On Richard's death in 1199 Ranulf thus saw no advantage in the succession of his stepson Arthur, the latter backed by his own alienated wife, now freed from captivity. He supported John, and Constance reacted by terminating their marriage (though there is no formal record of this) and making a second alliance at once with the French noble Gui de Thouars. Ranulf accepted, perhaps even welcomed, the inevitable, and in 1200 he married Clemence (d. 1252), daughter of Guillaume de Fougères and widow of Alain de Dinan. This second Breton alliance must, in a more modest way, have had similar aims to the first: bolstering the earl's position in western Normandy where he was hereditary vicomte of the Bessin and Avranchin, and hence his influence over the Norman–Breton frontier. Clemence brought him some dower lands in England and Normandy, and the possibility at least of a more successful marriage and the birth of an heir. The fact remains that Ranulf had lost the honour of Richmond, which went to Gui de Thouars on Constance's death in 1201, and then to Robert de Breteuil, earl of Leicester (d. 1204), on Gui's defection in 1203. The French conquest of Normandy in 1204 caused him further

heavy losses. Nor did Ranulf receive any substantial compensation elsewhere in the early years of John's reign. Some historians have argued that this put great strain on his relations with the king. All that is known for certain is that on two occasions John demanded surrender of lands or castles and security for the earl's loyalty: the first in Normandy in April 1203 just after the defection of the Fougères family, the second in England in December 1204, when Ranulf was in alliance with the king's Welsh enemy Gwenwynwyn of Powys. Each time the earl convinced the king of his allegiance and the threatened sanctions were soon lifted. The evidence of charter attestations shows that Ranulf was frequently in attendance on the king, especially during John's last months in Normandy early in 1204. Nevertheless he had suffered heavy losses, and even if there is no real evidence that he was on the verge of rebellion, John seems to have decided not to test his loyalty too far. In March 1205, with Leicester dead, the king granted most of the Richmond lands in Yorkshire to the earl of Chester, along with substantial remissions of debt.

Having devoted much of the first phase of his career, from 1187 to 1204, to the defence of the continental lands of the Angevin empire, Ranulf now embarked on a second phase, from 1205 to 1218, in which he became more and more prominent in domestic politics as a loyal supporter of John, and later of John's son Henry III. He regularly witnessed royal charters, and received a steady flow of the gifts usual for a noble in royal favour. In 1205 and 1209 he was deputed to escort the king of Scots south. He took a leading role in successive Welsh campaigns between 1209 and 1212. At the same time Ranulf systematically consolidated his local rule in Cheshire, where the appearance of a chancellor by 1190 and a justiciar by 1202, as well as the earlier evolution of an 'exchequer' modelled on that of the king, give some indication of its exceptional independence. Both the Chester annals and Lucian, a monk of St Werburgh's Abbey writing in the 1190s, call the earl a 'prince' (princeps). The comital charters illustrate further development of this distinctive regional autonomy under John, even as the king was putting great pressure on many other magnates' local powers. In the decade 1205–15 both king and earl seem to have concluded that it was in their own interest to treat Cheshire as a special case; this was one reason for Ranulf's loyalism.

In 1214 Ranulf returned to France to participate in John's Poitou campaign, acting as one of the negotiators of the eventual truce with Philip Augustus. In January 1215 he was among the very few magnates to defend John against the initial demands of the baronial dissidents, and no contemporary source suggests any wavering of Ranulf's support through to the promulgation of Magna Carta and the slide into civil war. Probably in the aftermath of John's grant the earl issued his own Magna Carta of Cheshire, defining local customs, apparently in response to a petition from the honorial baronage. But Ranulf also received great rewards from the king: half of the honour of Leicester in custody for the younger Simon de Montfort in July 1215 (presumably because of his mother), the shrievalties of Lancashire, Shropshire, and Staffordshire in April 1216, and other grants of castles and rebel possessions. Chester's support was crucial to the king once civil war broke out in October 1215: with William (I) Marshal he kept the Welsh march largely loyal; with his brother-in-law William de Ferrers he set up a power bloc in the midlands which helped to neutralize the threat of the northern rebels, and divide them from their allies in the south. Even so, there were limits to the earl's power, and the patterns of allegiance in his lordships was mixed. While his Cheshire tenants followed him almost without exception in supporting the king, the tenants of Richmond in Yorkshire with equal unanimity rebelled, rejecting the influence of their (probably largely absentee) lord. In Lincolnshire the response of tenants was rather more mixed.

The minority of Henry III On John's death in October 1216 Ranulf and William Marshal were the two leading magnate supporters of the young prince Henry. Within days the Marshal had accepted the role of regent, but even the eulogistic *Histoire de Guillaume le Maréchal* makes it clear that he needed, and received, the consent and support of the earl of Chester to do so. Ranulf's role in the subsequent struggle against Louis of France can be traced through formal actions, like his attestation of the revised Magna Carta in November 1216, and also through the piecemeal process of local campaigning and bargaining with individual rebels that followed. In spring 1217 he raised a large force to attack Mountsorrel Castle near Leicester, on which he had a claim, and drew part of Louis's army north in response, precipitating the decisive battle of Lincoln in May. William Marshal and several others played major parts in this victory but Ranulf received the greatest reward: a grant of the earldom of Lincoln, made within days of the battle. In September 1217 he was among those who ratified the peace agreement by which Louis left England. Tensions between the royalist leaders appeared occasionally: some time early in 1217 it was proposed to Pope Honorius III (not necessarily by Ranulf himself) that Chester should be made co-regent with the elderly Marshal. But winning a civil war and then imposing peace without the influence of an adult king was bound to be a delicate process; on balance it is remarkable how little evidence suggests that the earl did anything that destabilized the minority government. Nor did his decision to depart on crusade in June 1218 indicate any lingering ambitions to succeed the Marshal. Ranulf did all he could to safeguard his position, by a private agreement with Llywelyn ab Iorwerth of Gwynedd, and by obtaining quittances of his shrieval accounts, but he was still prepared to take a risk in leaving England for what turned out to be over two years. In doing so, he discharged the crusading vow he had taken with John back in March 1215. He travelled with many relatives and allies, including the earls of Derby and Arundel, and what evidence there is suggests that other participants saw him as the most important of the English leaders. *L'estoire de Eracles empereur*, for instance, credits him with leading 100 knights. Ranulf joined the forces of the fifth crusade in Egypt and participated in the capture of Damietta in November 1219, leaving on the return journey in spring 1220 before the crusade ended in disastrous defeat.

Back in England by July 1220 Ranulf went first to Chester where he was received, according to the Chester annals, 'with the greatest veneration' (*Annales Cestrienses*, 50–51). He embarked on a third phase of his career in which, without ever threatening rebellion, he became ambivalent towards a royal government increasingly dominated, after the Marshal's death, by the justiciar Hubert de Burgh. Faced with pressure to surrender castles and custodies he had been granted in the civil war Ranulf gave ground gradually, conceding in 1221, for instance, that he would account for the revenues of his shrievalties outside Cheshire. The nearest approach to conflict came at Christmas 1223, when de Burgh demanded a general resumption of royal rights and property. Ranulf first took the lead in opposing this, then assessed the balance of forces on both sides and yielded, surrendering his custodies and royal castles on 30 December. In 1224, when Falkes de Bréauté openly rebelled against the minority regime, Chester was sympathetic enough to give him refuge and intercede for him, but again, not to compromise his own allegiance. This was easier for him because, unlike some of the other old royalists who had now lost ground, he had much to fall back on, including his power base in Cheshire. From 1225 he constructed there a great new castle at Beeston, all too obviously defending the county from England rather than Wales, and intended perhaps as a symbol of the power he still retained. Ranulf also buttressed his position by strengthening the alliance with Llywelyn initiated in 1218. In 1222 he married his nephew John the Scot, son of his sister Mabel and David, earl of Huntingdon, whose custody he had taken over after David's death in 1219, to the Welsh prince's daughter Helen.

Last years: the succession to Chester Ranulf gave only the most grudging support to royal campaigns against Llywelyn launched by Hubert de Burgh in 1223 and 1231. But on their side de Burgh and his allies did not want to alienate the powerful earl too seriously, so even his ambivalent loyalty was acknowledged. The custody of half of the honour of Leicester returned to him in 1220 became a grant for life in 1227. The Yorkshire lands of the honour of Richmond were regranted in 1227, a grant of royal demesne between Ribble and Mersey in Lancashire was added in 1229. The wardship of John the Scot, retained until John came of age in 1227, was another important concession, all the more so because Ranulf, his second marriage now childless for over twenty years, may already have intended this son of his eldest sister to be his heir for the earldom of Chester. The problem was that his other three sisters also had claims to a share of his property, so creating the risk that Cheshire would have to be divided. This provides an additional motive for the earl's acquisitiveness in his latter years; some of these gains went to swell the shares of the coheirs outside Cheshire to an acceptable size. It may also explain his willingness late in his life to cede custodies which would in any case lapse with his death and could not benefit his heirs. In 1230 he gave up his Richmond lands to the king's unreliable ally Pierre de Dreux, duke of Brittany, and by 1231 he had agreed to transfer his honour of Leicester lands to the king's French protégé, Simon de Montfort (d. 1265). In May 1232, when Ranulf fell ill while at court, the king undertook to observe the terms of his will. Probably after this he conveyed his earldom of Lincoln to his sister Hawise de Quincy, who in turn granted it to her son John de *Lacy (c.1192–1240), an arrangement that must have required royal consent. This final manoeuvre meant that all Ranulf's heirs held an earldom.

In 1230–31, perhaps also to maintain good relations with the young king, Ranulf took an active role in his French campaign, eventually taking over command of the English forces in 1231 after Henry's return to England, and negotiating a truce with the French. He was also able to reoccupy his family castle of St Jacques, and revisit the border areas he had contested in the 1190s. On his return to England he quarrelled briefly with the king, probably because he still resented Hubert de Burgh's influence over royal policy towards France, Wales, and domestic patronage. The following year Chester helped to bring about de Burgh's fall from power in July 1232, though in September 1232 he intervened with others to protect the former justiciar from the extreme of royal vengeance. Earl Ranulf died at Wallingford on 26 October 1232. His heart was buried at Dieulacres Abbey in Staffordshire, a Cistercian house which he had refounded in 1214 (it was previously at Poulton in Cheshire), in accordance with the terms of his charter. His body was interred at St Werburgh's Abbey in Chester on 3 November. His properties were divided, with John the Scot installed as earl of Chester by the end of the month, which confirms the impression of a prior agreement, though if so the coheirs subsequently changed their minds, and had issued writs to contest the division by 1235. But even after Ranulf's great earldom was absorbed by the crown after 1237, his reputation persisted and legends about him occur in late medieval sources. Despite an attempt to argue the contrary, there can be little doubt that he was the subject of the 'rymes of Randolf erl of chestre' alluded to in *Piers Plowman* (Langland, 49).

RICHARD EALES

Sources G. Barraclough, ed., *The charters of the Anglo-Norman earls of Chester, c.1071–1237*, Lancashire and Cheshire RS, 126 (1988) · *Journal of the Chester Archaeological Society*, 71 (1991) [G. Barraclough issue, *The earldom of Chester and its charters*, ed. A. T. Thacker] · B. E. Harris, 'Ranulph III earl of Chester', *Journal of the Chester Archaeological Society*, 58 (1975), 99–114 · J. W. Alexander, *Ranulf of Chester* (1983) · R. Eales, 'Henry III and the end of the Norman earldom of Chester', *Thirteenth century England: proceedings of the Newcastle upon Tyne conference* [Newcastle upon Tyne 1985], ed. P. R. Coss and S. D. Lloyd, 1 (1986), 100–13 · R. C. Christie, ed. and trans., *Annales Cestrienses, or, Chronicle of the abbey of S. Werburg at Chester*, Lancashire and Cheshire RS, 14 (1887) · G. Barraclough, ed., *Facsimiles of early Cheshire charters* (1957) · *VCH Cheshire*, vols. 2–3 · G. Barraclough, 'The earldom and county palatine of Chester', *Transactions of the Historic Society of Lancashire and Cheshire*, 103 (1951), 23–39 · D. A. Carpenter, *The minority of Henry III* (1990) · N. Vincent, *Peter des Roches: an alien in English politics, 1205–38*, Cambridge Studies in Medieval Life and Thought, 4th ser., 31 (1996) · J. C. Holt, *The northerners: a study in the reign of King John*, new edn (1992) · W. Langland, *Piers Plowman*, ed. J. A. W. Bennett (1972) · W. Farrer, *Honors and knights' fees … from the eleventh to the fourteenth century*, 2 (1924) · *L'estoire de Eracles empereur* (1841) · PRO

Archives PRO, Chester palatinate records

Ranyard, Arthur Cowper (1845–1894), astronomer, born at Swanscombe, Kent, on 21 June 1845, was the son of Benjamin Ranyard (1792/3–1879), a barge owner, and his wife, Ellen Henrietta White (1810–1879), the founder of the Biblewoman Movement [see Ranyard, Ellen Henrietta]. He attended University College School, London, from 1857 to 1860, then went on to University College. Here the influence of Professor Augustus De Morgan led him to concentrate his attention on mathematics and astronomy, and he formed a close friendship with the professor's son George. In 1864 the two young men formed the plan for a society for the special study of mathematics, and issued a circular inviting attendance at the first meeting of 'the University College Mathematical Society' on 7 November 1864. The first meeting was actually held on 16 January 1865, when, after Professor De Morgan's presidential address, Ranyard read the first paper, 'On determinants'. The new association received the support of eminent mathematicians, and ultimately developed into the London Mathematical Society.

Ranyard entered Pembroke College, Cambridge, in October 1865 and graduated MA in 1868. Having adopted the law as his profession he was called to the bar at Lincoln's Inn in 1871, but his tastes lay in the direction of science, and his means enabled him to devote much of his time to astronomy. He became a fellow of the Royal Astronomical Society in 1863, and served on its council (1872–88 and 1892–4) and as secretary (1874–80). He was assistant secretary of the expedition for observing the total solar eclipse of 1870, and made a successful series of polariscopic observations at Villasmunda in Sicily. In 1878 he went to Colorado to view the solar eclipse of that year, which he observed and photographed at a station near Denver. In 1882 he observed and photographed the total solar eclipse at Sohag in Upper Egypt. His most extensive work in astronomy was the eclipse volume of the Royal Astronomical Society (commenced in 1871 and completed in 1879), in which are systematized and discussed the observations of all solar eclipses down to 1878. It was originally begun in conjunction with Sir George Airy, but soon devolved on Ranyard alone.

In 1888 Ranyard's friend Richard Anthony Proctor died, leaving his great work, *Old and New Astronomy*, incomplete. Ranyard generously undertook to finish it for the benefit of the author's family, and wrote chapters on the universe of stars, the construction of the Milky Way, and the distribution of nebulae, which he discussed with much ability and thoroughness. He also succeeded Proctor as editor of *Knowledge*, a popular journal dealing with astronomy and natural sciences, to which he contributed a long series of articles on astronomy, giving his mature views on many intricate problems. His most important investigations were those on nebulae, the density of which he concluded to be extremely low, even as compared with the earth's atmosphere, and on star clusters, which he regarded as showing evidence of the ejection of matter from a centre, and not gradual condensation, as supposed by Laplace.

Although mainly engaged in scientific pursuits, Ranyard took much interest in public affairs, and in 1892 was elected a member of the London county council, where he sat on the committee dealing with the new (London) Building Act, which passed into law in the summer of 1894. Ranyard resigned that year due to ill health.

In 1872, in conjunction with Lord Lindsay (twenty-sixth earl of Crawford), Ranyard undertook experiments on photographic irradiation, and in 1886 he investigated the relation between brightness of object, time of exposure, and intensity of photographic action.

Ranyard, who was unmarried, lived a somewhat retired life of laborious industry. He was a man of generous spirit, extremely conscientious and completely devoted to duty. He died of stomach cancer at his home, 13 Hunter Street, Brunswick Square, London, on 14 December 1894, and was buried in the cemetery at Kingston upon Thames on 19 December.　　　　W. H. WESLEY, rev. ANITA McCONNELL

Sources Boase, *Mod. Eng. biog.* • *The Times* (18 Dec 1894), 6c • E. F. Collingwood, 'A century of the London Mathematical Society', *Journal of the London Mathematical Society*, 41 (1966), 577–94 • *Minutes of proceedings*, London County Council (1892), 302 • *Minutes of proceedings*, London County Council (1894), 1189 • b. cert. • d. cert.
Archives RAS, corresp. and papers | RAS, letters to Royal Astronomical Society
Likenesses portrait, repro. in *Knowledge* (Feb 1895)
Wealth at death £12,537 4s. 3d.: resworn probate, July 1896, CGPLA Eng. & Wales

Ranyard [*née* White], **Ellen Henrietta** (1810–1879), home mission worker, was born on 9 January 1810 in the district of Nine Elms, London, the eldest daughter of John Bazley White, maker of cement. She was a member of the Congregational church in Walworth, and after attending a Bible meeting at Wanstead when she was sixteen she accompanied her friend Elizabeth Saunders on a mission to supply Bibles to poor families. The two discovered that thirty-five families were without Bibles, and they collected 35 pennies towards supplying each family with the scriptures. She recollected:

> I came home having seen for the first time how the poor live; their ignorance, their dirt, their smells. ... She [Elizabeth] spoke to them, but the spirit of God carried the message home to *me*. ... When I went to bed at night I took up my Bible to read my usual chapter with a new feeling for it ... my hard young heart was softened, and a quiet new affection drawn out to this new and gentle friend. (Alldridge, 106–7)

Both girls caught typhoid fever after their missionary visit. Elizabeth died; but Ellen recovered and believed that she had found her life's work. 'I remember thinking', Ellen wrote a few years later, 'that the Bible work was the one work to which I had been called by God, and to which I must keep faithful as one who had been baptised for the dead' (Alldridge, 108). Once recovered from typhoid, Ellen returned to the thirty-five homes, collected the remaining money, which amounted to £6, and took it to a women's Bible committee meeting at the British and Foreign Bible Society, of which her grandmother was president, and

from which the thirty-five Bibles were procured and distributed by Ellen. She eventually became a secretary of the Bible committee, and canvassed other districts in addition to her own.

In her early twenties Ellen and her family moved to Swanscombe in Kent, where she met Benjamin Ranyard of Millibank Street, Westminster. They married at York Street Chapel, in Surrey, on 10 January 1839. They had two sons and two daughters, including Arthur Cowper *Ranyard. Ellen Ranyard combined her maternal responsibilities with philanthropic ones, primarily her work with the Bible Society. In her spare time she painted in oils as well as creating woodland scenes out of dried seaweed and watercolour. She also wrote edifying poems with titles such as 'Bear ye one another's burdens' and 'On Self-Regulation', which were collected and published in 1855 in *Leaves from Life* and in *The Border Land and other Poems* under the pseudonym LNR. She also wrote texts for the Bible Society, the first of these being a children's book about the Bible, *The Book and its Story* (1852), to celebrate the society's jubilee. Two years later she edited the society's journal, *The Book and its Missions, Past and Present*.

In 1857 the Ranyards left Kent for Bloomsbury, London. They settled at 13 Hunter Street, not far from slum areas which Ellen Ranyard, after visiting with a retired physician friend, decided to 'civilize'. She planned to accomplish this, as did many a Victorian philanthropist, by bringing the inhabitants both spiritual and material assistance since, as she remarked in a later publication, 'If Jesus makes our hearts clean, our homes will soon be clean too' (*Life Work*, 108). Her prime concern was how to supply London's poor with Bibles and she decided that this would best be accomplished not by city missionaries, but by working-class women. She asked St Giles's resident missionary in Bloomsbury whether he could recommend a suitable candidate; he suggested a woman named Marian, and so the Biblewoman movement, formally called the London Bible and Domestic Female Mission, was born. Characterized by its reliance on the poor as the dispensers as well as the recipients of charity and missionary endeavour, the movement spread not only to other English towns, but also to south-east Asia, Australia, and North America.

Over the years Ellen Ranyard expanded her operations to include mothers' meetings, at which working-class mothers would listen to Bible readings, sew, and converse; bed and clothing clubs; a dormitory for young watercress-sellers and needlewomen; a rescue home; and, in 1868, a district nursing scheme. Like the Biblewomen, the nurses dispensed spiritual aid and were expected to carry a Bible with their medical supplies. The combination of spiritual and medical assistance, which the Ranyard nurses dispensed, continued well into the mid-twentieth century.

Ellen Ranyard wrote extensively on her mission and its workers. Principal among her publications were *The Missing Link, or, Bible-Women in the Homes of the London Poor* (1859); *Life Work, or, The Link and the Rivet* (1861); *London and Ten Years' Work in it* (1868); and *Nurses for the Needy, or, Bible-Women*

Nurses in the Homes of the London Poor (1875). She also edited the mission's journal, the *Missing Link Magazine*.

Ellen Ranyard died from bronchitis at her home, 13 Hunter Street, on 11 February 1879, and was buried in Norwood cemetery. Her husband survived her.

LORI WILLIAMSON

Sources L. N. R. [E. H. Ranyard], *The missing link, or, Bible-women in the homes of the London poor* (1860) · LNR [E. H. Ranyard], *Life work, or, The link and the rivet* (1861); repr. (1868) · L. N. R. [E. H. Ranyard], *The true institution of sisterhood, or, A message and its messengers* [1862] · L. N. R. [E. H. Ranyard], *London, and ten years' work in it* (1868) · E. Alldridge, *The world's workers* (1890) · E. Platt, *The story of the Ranyard mission, 1857–1937* (1937) · B. Heeney, *The women's movement in the Church of England, 1850–1930* (1988) · d. cert. · m. cert.
Archives LMA, papers of the Ranyard mission and Ranyard nurses
Likenesses portrait, LMA, Records of the Ranyard Mission and Ranyard Nurses, 194/1–17

Raper, (William) Augustus (1845–1940), lawyer and defender of commoners' rights, was born on 11 January 1845, one of two surviving children of seven born to William Augustus Raper (1816–1904), of Curzon House, Portsmouth, the medical officer of health for Portsmouth, and his wife, Mary Hobbs (*bap.* 1805). He attended Portsmouth grammar school in 1857–8 as a private pupil, and Queenwood College, Hampshire, and was articled at Portsmouth. His first position was in Liverpool with Messrs Hull, Stone and Fletcher. He qualified as a solicitor by 1866 but, refusing a partnership, he moved to Battle, Sussex, in 1870. He married Mary Anna Ellis (1848–1922), from Binsted, Sussex, on 14 June 1871. They had four sons, three of whom died before reaching the age of forty, including the third son and Augustus's junior partner, Robert, who was killed at the battle of the Somme. They also had four daughters, of whom one predeceased him, and numerous grandchildren.

Raper began his professional career in Sussex by practising alone but soon entered into partnership with Frederick Ellman in a business which flourished and which he later purchased. His son Robert and later R. W. Fovargue entered the partnership, the latter having married Robert's widow. During his long years of legal practice at Battle Raper became vigorously associated with many of the town's activities. His was a powerful personality; he was a strong churchman and a churchwarden at Battle, continuing to read the lessons there until over ninety years of age. He was described as inquisitive and witty, with a professional manner heightened by a touch of what an obituarist called 'courtly arrogance' (*Sussex Daily News*, 1 Jan 1941, 8). He was a member of the local board of health, chaired Battle urban district council (1894–1918), was a member of the Battle Abbey masonic lodge, and was registrar of the deanery of Battle. For fifty-five years he was honorary clerk and treasurer to the Battle Charities, reorganizing them in 1879 to provide for a better distribution of the funds. He was also steward of estates and of up to twenty manors in the vicinity. In politics he was a 'staunch, even militant, Conservative' (ibid.), a local agent and, from 1907, an East Sussex county councillor. He was a keen historian and archaeologist, being an early member of the Sussex Archaeological Society by 1872, becoming a member of its council by 1877, and cataloguing a hoard of silver coins from the reign of Edward the Confessor at Battle. He was an early member of the Sussex Record Society, founded in 1901.

The 'Grand Old Man of Battle', Raper is best remembered in association with Ashdown Forest, a 13,000 acre area of wood, pasture, and heathland in northern Sussex. Having in 1874 become the first clerk to the conservators of the common rights of Ashdown Forest, a body of landowners and commoners who joined to protect the forest against encroachments and the illegal removal of turf and litter (heather, bracken, gorse, coarse grasses, and so on), he went on to represent the Ashdown commoners in defending their rights to cut and cart away litter, against Reginald Sackville, seventh Earl De La Warr, in the prolonged and complex Ashdown Forest case (1876–82). He amassed evidence dating back to the thirteenth century, and toured the forest collecting, in five small books, over a hundred verbatim testimonies to litter cutting. These accounts by working people give excellent insight into their life histories, stretching back to the late eighteenth century. The judge initially found for Earl De La Warr but the judgment was overturned on appeal in 1881. The Ashdown case was important in the history of commons preservation, and P. H. Lawrence and Sir Robert Hunter, legal advisers to the Commons Preservation Society, were involved in the case. In 1885 Ashdown was regulated under the Commons Act of 1876. A board of conservators was established, with Raper as its very active clerk, from its first meeting in May 1887 until December 1929. He was thus fundamentally involved with the conservation of open heathland at Ashdown (now the largest continuous area of heathland in south-east England), and with the preservation of commoners' interests. He deposited his notebooks and other papers with the Sussex Archaeological Society in 1934, and they form a valuable source of reference in the East Sussex Record Office.

Raper retired on the last day of 1934, aged ninety and with failing sight. He died on 31 December 1940 at his daughter's home, Winstowe, Charles Road, Hastings, and was buried two days later in the family plot at Battle cemetery.

BRIAN SHORT

Sources B. Short, *The Ashdown Forest case, 1876–1882: environmental politics and custom* (1997) · 'Modern South Saxons: no. 88, Mr William Augustus Raper', *Sussex County Magazine*, 10/4 (April 1936), 224–5 · *Sussex Daily News* (1 Jan 1941); (6 Jan 1941) · *Sussex Express* (3 Jan 1941) · *Hastings and St Leonards Observer* (4 Jan 1941) · parish register, Battle, E. Sussex RO, PAR 236/1/2/4-5 [baptism] · parish register, Battle, E. Sussex RO, PAR 236/1/5/4 [burial] · The Ashdown Forest case, legal papers, E. Sussex RO, AMS 3780-4140 · minute books, E. Sussex RO, Ashdown Forest conservators · W. A. Raper, 'The school in Penny Street', *The Portmuthian* (summer 1936), 4–5 · *CGPLA Eng. & Wales* (1941) · private information (2004) [family] · IGI · gravestone, Battle
Archives E. Sussex RO, Ashdown Forest case, legal papers · E. Sussex RO, Ashdown Forest conservators' minute books · E. Sussex RO, Battle parish registers
Likenesses portrait, repro. in 'Modern South Saxons', *Sussex County Magazine*, 224

Raper, George Frederick (1909–1973), mechanical engineer and inventor of wool textile machinery, was born at Bradford on 4 April 1909, the son of Arthur E. Raper and his wife, Maggie Maud, *née* Smith. Arthur Raper was chairman and managing director of the long-established woolcombers Isaac Holden & Sons Ltd, Bradford, where his father had also been managing director. George attended the Leys School, Cambridge. He initially proposed to read medicine, and went to Jesus College, Cambridge, but he graduated in 1930 with a third-class honours degree in mechanical engineering. His early practical experience included a period as an engineer with the Cunard Line. He then joined Isaac Holden & Sons as a machine operator, the usual way for members of mill-owning families to learn the business. At this time he was also attending Bradford Technical College to learn about textiles. In 1937 he went on a world tour to study the wool textile industry and on his return to Holdens in 1938 he was appointed manager; in 1939 he was made a director.

During his early years at Holdens Raper made several improvements on the chemical and engineering side of wool-combing. He then turned his attention to the design and building of a new wool-combing machine. An experimental room was provided for him to work in, but the outbreak of war halted these activities. Raper was commissioned into the Territorial Army before the war, and during it his activities included work on the searchlight-aided interception of enemy aircraft; later he lectured on the subject. On demobilization in 1945 he held the rank of lieutenant-colonel.

Raper returned to the Holden factory as mill manager, but the idea of a new approach to the preparation of wool slivers for the combing operation, later called the 'autoleveller', had remained in his mind since 1938, and took much of his effort and interest. In early 1948 his father died, and his cousin was appointed managing director. Support for his experiments was no longer so readily available and that same year he resigned from his £4000 a year position, although he retained his seat on the board. His annual income was now £400, and he took a cottage where he fitted out a bedroom as an engineering workshop. He worked single-handedly, taking responsibility for all calculations, designs, and patents. Friends in the industry provided facilities for proving his ideas, and in 1951 he perfected his machine.

The autoleveller unit, originally intended for use in the wool-combing sector of the industry, was also employed in worsted yarn manufacture. The autoleveller measured the volume of wool entering the machine and recorded any variations on a memory wheel, which, at the appropriate time, controlled the subsequent attenuation given to the material. This significantly improved the uniformity of the product. Consequently the number of operations required to produce a yarn was reduced from eight to three, with savings in labour, energy, and floorspace, and when used in conjunction with Ambler's 'superdraft

unit' it achieved one of the greatest advances in wool textile machinery of the century.

Inventive success did not bring Raper riches, and he complained that the bulk of his income went in taxes. It did, however, bring him considerable respect. In 1955 he was awarded the Hoffman Wood Yorkshire gold medal for invention and was made an honorary member of the Wool Industries Research Association. In 1960 he was made an honorary fellow of the Textile Institute. He was also an honorary lecturer in textile engineering at Leeds University. After leaving Bradford he lived at Masham, North Riding of Yorkshire, Windermere, and Ross-on-Wye. Raper was a rare example of a businessman who, from a managerial perspective, identified a technical opportunity and shifted from management to engineering in order to seize that opportunity. At the time of his death he was working on an automated weaving device. He died on 7 September 1973 at Verlands, Llangarron, Ross-on-Wye, Herefordshire, leaving £16,790 gross. He was survived by his wife, Constance Joan (Nan), and three children.   JOHN A. IREDALE

Sources 'George F. Raper—a biographical and personal note', *Journal of the Bradford Textile Society* (1955–6), 59–60 · file of cuttings, library of *Telegraph and Argus*, Bradford · private information (2004) [Mrs Nan Raper]

Archives Bradford Industrial Museum | SOUND Bradford Industrial Museum, tape recording by Raper

Likenesses S. Eram, black and white sketch, repro. in 'George F. Raper', 58

Wealth at death £16,790: probate, 25 Dec 1973, *CGPLA Eng. & Wales*

Raper, Henry (1767–1845), naval officer, entered the navy in February 1780, on board the *Berwick* (74 guns), which in July joined Sir George Rodney in the West Indies. After returning in 1781, he took part in the battle on the Doggerbank on 5 August and was wounded. He afterwards served in the *Cambridge* (74 guns), and in her was at the relief of Gibraltar by Lord Howe in October 1782. He then joined the sloop *Marquis de Seignelay* (14 guns), a captured French privateer, with Commander John Hunter (1738–1821), his former shipmate in the *Berwick*, and remained in her until 1785. From 1785 to 1788 he was in the *Salisbury*, the flagship of Rear-Admiral John Elliot, at Newfoundland, and afterwards in the *Impregnable* (98 guns) and *Queen Charlotte* (100 guns) in the channel until 22 November 1790, when he was promoted lieutenant. Through 1791 he served in the bomb (i.e. mortar) vessel *Vesuvius*, and in October 1793 he was appointed to the *Queen Charlotte*, flagship of Earl Howe, to whom he acted as signal lieutenant in May and on 1 June 1794. On 4 July he was promoted commander, and in September, on the recommendation of Howe, he was appointed signal officer on the staff of Vice-Admiral A. J. de Valle, of the Portuguese squadron serving with Howe. On resigning this post in December, he was presented with a diamond-hilted sword. In November 1795 he commanded the brig-sloop *Racoon* (16 guns) in the Thames; and on 1 February 1796 he was posted to the small frigate *Champion* (24 guns), employed on the coast of Ireland and afterwards in the North Sea. In January 1798 he assisted in the seizure of a Swedish convoy, which was brought into the Downs; and the following May he took part in the attempt to destroy the locks and sluice-gates of the Bruges and Ostend Canal.

From January 1799 to September 1802 Raper commanded the frigate *Aimable* (32 guns) in the West Indies and on 1 February 1799 he was promoted captain. In 1810 he declined an offer of the rank of vice-admiral in the Portuguese service; and in November that year he was appointed to the *Mars* (74 guns), which he commanded until February 1813, on the Lisbon station and in the Baltic. Despite repeated applications he had no further employment, but was promoted in due course rear-admiral on 12 August 1819, vice-admiral on 22 July 1830, and admiral on 23 November 1841. He published *A New System of Signals, by which Colours may be Wholly Dispensed with* (1828). He married, in 1798, a Miss Craig, and they had children. He died, after a very protracted illness, at South Audley Street, London, on 5 April 1845. His eldest son was Henry *Raper (1799–1859).   J. K. LAUGHTON, *rev.* ROGER T. STEARN

Sources O'Byrne, *Naval biog. dict.* · J. Marshall, *Royal naval biography*, 1/2 (1823), 713–15 · *GM*, 2nd ser., 23 (1845) · service book, PRO · P. Mackesy, *The war in the Mediterranean, 1803–1810* (1957); repr. (1981) · J. J. Colledge, *Ships of the Royal Navy: an historical index*, 1 (1969) · R. Muir, *Britain and the defeat of Napoleon, 1807–1815* (1996) · B. Lavery, *Nelson's navy: the ships, men, and organisation, 1793–1815*, rev. edn (1990)

Raper, Henry (1799–1859), naval officer and writer on navigation, was the eldest son of Admiral Henry *Raper (1767–1845) and his wife, formerly a Miss Craig. After attending Charterhouse School he entered the navy in November 1811 on board the *Mars*, his father's ship. He joined the Royal Naval College at Portsmouth in March 1812, passing out with distinction in 1814, and being awarded the silver medal for proficiency in mathematics. After a short time in the frigate *Nymphen* as a midshipman, he was appointed in October 1815 to the *Alceste* with Captain Murray Maxwell, conveying William Pitt Amherst, Earl Amherst, as envoy to the emperor of China. The mission was not a success; and on the homeward passage, on 18 February 1817, the *Alceste* struck a rock in the Strait of Gaspar, off the south-east coast of Sumatra. Raper bore his full share of the hardships experienced by the crew from weather, thirst and pirates. Between 1817 and 1820 he was a midshipman in the *Tyne* (26 guns) on the South American station, and the frigate *Seringapatam* at home and in the Mediterranean. In January 1821 he was appointed to the sloop *Adventure*, with Commander William Henry Smyth, surveying in the Mediterranean, though he did not join her until the spring of 1822; he was placed in charge of the chronometers, and had exceptional opportunities for the scientific study of navigation, nautical astronomy, and surveying. On 17 May 1823 he was promoted to lieutenant, and was appointed to the *Euryalus*, and then to the brig *Dispatch*. In January 1825, when Captain Frederick William Beechey commissioned the *Blossom* for hydrographic surveys in the northern Pacific, he offered Raper the post of first lieutenant at the suggestion of Smyth, all three having served together in the *Adventure*. Raper, however, imagined that his father had been undeservedly slighted

by the Admiralty, and declined Beechey's offer, thus virtually retiring from active service.

From that time Raper devoted himself to nautical science, greatly encouraged by Smyth. He became a fellow of the Royal Geographical and Royal Astronomical societies, repeatedly served on their councils, and was secretary of the latter society from 1839 to 1842. In 1832 he was appointed by the Admiralty to a committee that was to consider the method of measuring the tonnage of ships, and the report was drawn up principally by him. In 1840 he published his *Practice of Navigation and Nautical Astronomy*, for which he was awarded the gold medal of the Royal Geographical Society; the East India Company supplied copies to their ships, and—an unusual distinction—the Admiralty in January 1843 ordered a copy to be supplied to each of her majesty's ships. It remained a standard work for many years, the twenty-first edition being published in 1920. Other published works were *Rules for Finding Distances and Heights at Sea* (1831), and *Sailing Directions for the Western Coast of Africa* (1849).

Raper married in November 1850 the daughter of the Revd Frederick Ekins of Morpeth. He suffered severely from rheumatism and neuralgia during the last eighteen months of his life, but continued his labours up to the last, submitting a paper, 'An improvement in clearing the lunar distance', to the Royal Astronomical Society shortly before he died at Torquay, Devon, on 6 January 1859. His wife survived him.

J. K. LAUGHTON, *rev.* DEREK HOWSE

Sources *Monthly Notices of the Royal Astronomical Society*, 19 (1858–9), 128–31 · W. S. Smyth, *Journal of the Royal Geographical Society*, 29 (1859), 116–18 · RAS, fellowship records · *GM*, 3rd ser., 6 (1859), 221 · *BL cat.* · Boase, *Mod. Eng. biog.*
Archives RAS, letters and papers · RGS, letters and papers
Likenesses miniature, repro. in *R. N. Exhibition, Chelsea, Catalogue* (1891), no. 1915, p. 211
Wealth at death under £8000: probate, 17 June 1859, *CGPLA Eng. & Wales*

Raper, James Hayes (1820–1897), temperance reformer, was born on 6 October 1820 at Carlisle, the last of the twelve children of George Raper (*d.* 1820), a stonemason, and his wife, Jane (1780–1860), the daughter of Edgar Thomas Pattinson. George Raper was killed before James's birth, and the boy was brought up by his mother and maternal grandmother, who were committed Wesleyans. He received some schooling, but the details of it are unknown.

On leaving school Raper worked for one of his brothers, a builder and sculptor, and then for a short period in a draper's shop, before being apprenticed at the locomotive engine works at New Shildon. In 1836 he attended a temperance meeting addressed by Thomas Whittaker (1813–1899), and the following year he signed a pledge of total abstinence. A Sunday school teacher, he went on to help organize the New Shildon Juvenile Temperance Society.

Finding engineering uncongenial, Raper decided to become a schoolteacher, and after completing his apprenticeship he moved to London, where he qualified at the Borough Road Training College of the British and Foreign

School Society. In 1843 he became headmaster of the Fletcher Street Wesleyan schools, Bolton. On 24 December 1844 he married a colleague, Mrs Hannah Kenny (1809–1867), the daughter of John Hunter of Bacup. Together they helped form a branch of the Peace Society in Bolton. Raper was also active in the Bolton Temperance Society and was involved with the Anti-Corn Law movement. In 1846 he was elected a member of the mechanics' institute committee. He took a leading part in the Wesleyan reform agitation in Bolton in 1848, chairing a meeting to discuss changing the connexion's rules to allow lay representatives to take part in the annual conferences. This led to his expulsion by the quarterly district meeting; he subsequently resigned from the Fletcher Street School and with his wife started a private school at nearby Lark Hill.

Raper became involved with the prohibitionist United Kingdom Alliance at its foundation in 1853, and in 1860 he was appointed its first full-time parliamentary agent, a Manchester-based position which involved lobbying of MPs and paid a salary of £500 per annum. That year he assisted Wilfrid Lawson, MP for Carlisle, to draft the Permissive Bill (providing for a local veto on licensing drink outlets), which the alliance aimed to have enacted as a first step towards total prohibition. A popular orator, Raper spoke widely on the temperance question and represented the alliance at major conventions. In 1873 he visited Sweden to study the licensing system there, and in 1875 he toured Canada and the United States to investigate the working of prohibition, which he deemed a political success. In 1878 he stood as a Liberal candidate in a parliamentary by-election in Peterborough, but failed to win the seat. In the same year he resigned his position as parliamentary agent and joined the executive of the alliance; he continued lobbying MPs and speaking at temperance meetings.

Raper's first wife died on 4 March 1867. On 22 November 1879 he married Amelia Eliza Tisdall of Tunbridge Wells, the third daughter of Edmund Tisdall, a dyer, of Kensington. The couple settled permanently in London at 33 Pembroke Square, Kensington, where Raper died from complications of influenza on 19 May 1897. A funeral service was held at Brompton cemetery on 24 May, and various memorial services followed over the next few days. Raper was survived by his wife; he had no children.

Raper was one of the most popular orators of the temperance movement. He was very knowledgeable on the drink question and a respected and effective lobbyist. In December 1897 a memorial fund was set up to finance an annual lecture on temperance known as the Lees–Raper lectureship. (The temperance reformer F. R. Lees had also died in May of that year.) During his life Raper had also been involved with a range of other social and political reform causes, including anti-slavery, anti-smoking, vegetarianism, peace, free trade, parliamentary reform, purity, and sabbatarianism. MARK CLEMENT

Sources J. D. Hilton, *A brief memoir of James Hayes Raper: temperance reformer, 1820–1897* (1898) • A. E. Dingle, *The campaign for prohibition in Victorian England: the United Kingdom Alliance, 1872–1895* (1980) • B. Harrison, *Drink and the Victorians: the temperance question in England, 1815–1872*, 2nd edn (1994) • P. T. Winskill, *The temperance movement and its workers*, 4 vols. (1891–2) • m. cert.

Likenesses photograph, repro. in Hilton, *Brief memoir of James Hayes Raper*, frontispiece

Wealth at death £3609 8s. 7d.: probate, 14 Aug 1897, CGPLA Eng. & Wales

Raper, Robert William (1842–1915), college teacher and founder of university careers service, was born at Llanwenarth, Monmouthshire, on 9 March 1842, the second son of Lieutenant-Colonel Timothy Raper (1790?–1862), of the 19th foot regiment, and his wife, Christian Mary (d. 1858), daughter of Robert Steavenson MD of Newcastle upon Tyne. After being highly successful in the Ceylon expedition of 1815 his father settled at Hoe Court, Colwall, Herefordshire, on the west side of the Malvern hills. Raper's youngest brother, Allan Graeme Raper (1843–1906), followed his father's career to become major-general of the 98th foot and North Staffordshire regiments and assistant quartermaster-general at the War Office from 1895 to 1900. Raper had four sisters, all of whom remained unmarried.

After spending two years at Cheltenham College from 1857 to 1859, Raper proceeded to Balliol College, Oxford, in 1861, but in his first term was elected to a scholarship at Trinity College. There in 1862 he obtained the university prizes for Greek and Latin verse and a first class in moderations, and in 1865 a first class in *literae humaniores* and a fellowship at Queen's College. Having been a lecturer in classics at Trinity from 1866, he was in 1871 elected under a special statute to a life fellowship there, and thenceforth took a leading part in the administration of the college, as bursar from 1887 and vice-president from 1894, remaining continuously in residence until his death. He would probably have been elected president in 1878 if laymen had then been eligible (he was a professed agnostic); in 1887, 1897, and 1907 he declined to accept the post.

In the university Raper soon acquired extensive though informal influence; he only once acted as an examiner, but he was a curator of the parks from 1885, of the botanic garden from 1887, and a visitor of the Ashmolean Museum from 1895 to 1908. He lectured mainly on favourite authors—Homer, Virgil, Aristophanes, and Tacitus—but he published nothing except articles in the *Journal of Philology* (1885) and the *Classical Review* (1913), a remarkable imitation of Walt Whitman in *Echoes from the Oxford Magazine* (1890), and a few brilliant versions in Latin verse in the *Nova anthologia Oxoniensis* of 1899. From 1907 it was Raper who supplied the Latin formulas required by the university's chancellor, Lord Curzon, of whom Raper had been a friend since Curzon's undergraduate days, and he managed to outdo Benjamin Jowett, another early friend, in a celebrated exchange (*Encyclopaedia of Oxford*, s.v. Gordouli).

From an early date Raper's wide acquaintance with influential Oxford men enabled him to recommend Trinity men of promise and others for tutorial, scholastic, and secretarial posts—it was usual for tutors in other colleges to advise their pupils to 'call on Mr Raper of Trinity and tell him I advised you to do so'. Eventually, finding himself with more patronage than he had candidates to recommend, and stimulated by the earlier success of Professor W. J. Lewis in establishing the Cambridge Scholastic Agency to place graduates in teaching posts, in 1892 he founded the Oxford University Appointments Committee (OUAC). This was the earliest agency for the placement of graduates set up in any British university by a representative body of dons; Cambridge followed suit in 1899. Raper was chairman of OUAC (renamed the Oxford University Careers Service in 1991) from 1892 to 1899, and a permanent member from 1908 until his death.

As an accomplished cricketer, rider, and skater, Raper was familiar with athletes as well as with reading men, and favoured making the services of OUAC available to women (1899); but he was best known, especially in his own college, as a genial and judicious host, a sagacious and witty counsellor—'silent and infinitely wise' according to John Buchan (*Memory Hold the Door*, 1940, 49)—and a sympathetic and, on the whole, sound disciplinarian; his bursarial notices to undergraduates of Trinity were lucid and entertaining.

Raper was not drawn into public life except in connection with the preservation of open spaces. Aided by his Colwall neighbour Stephen Ballard (1804–1890), he defended the rights both of the commoners and of the general public to the enjoyment of the Malvern hills. With the help of John Gent (1844–1927), his colleague in jurisprudence at Trinity, he obtained the Malvern Hills Conservation Act in 1884, by which he was named as a conservator; he was chairman of the conservators from 1884 to 1890. Raper himself gave 16 acres of land. In later life he lost local influence and became entangled in controversy and even litigation; but he was not unsupported, and in 1905 and later he conveyed some more land and manorial rights, which he had purchased to prevent encroachments and to control quarrying. He was named by Oxford University as its representative on the council of the National Trust from 1895, serving on an important subcommittee which considered the question of the protection of places or sites.

Raper was a small man, with straggling hair and a pointed beard. He was unmarried. As a young man he was somewhat of an invalid, but later enjoyed life fully, until he failed rather rapidly, and died suddenly in his college rooms on 15 July 1915. He was buried at Colwall.

H. E. D. Blakiston, *rev.* J. F. A. Mason

Sources *Oxford University Calendar* · T. Weston, *From appointments to careers: a history of the Oxford University Careers Service, 1892–1992* (1994) · P. Hurle, *The Malvern hills: a hundred years of conservation* (1984) · private information (2004) [P. Hurle] · Curzon, *The Times* (17 July 1915) · Curzon, *The Times* (20 July 1915) · *Malvern News* (24 July 1915) · *The Cheltonian*, 2nd ser., 41 (1915), 276–8 · *Oxford Magazine* (29 Oct 1915) · Earl of Ronaldshay [L. J. L. Dundas], *The life of Lord Curzon*, 1 (1928) · Earl of Ronaldshay [L. J. L. Dundas], *The life of Lord Curzon*, 3 (1928) [chap. 6] · L. Magnus, *Herbert Warren of Magdalen* (1932) · G. B. Grundy, *Fifty-five years at Oxford: an unconventional autobiography*, 2nd edn [1946] · inscription at Colwall · Oxford University appointments, Oxf. UA, Committee archives

Archives BL OIOC, letters to G. N. Curzon

Likenesses B. Hatton, oils, 1914, Trinity College, Oxford · G. P. Jacomb-Hood, chalk drawing, *c*.1916, Trinity College, Oxford · B. Hatton, oils, priv. coll. · G. P. Jacomb-Hood, portrait, priv. coll.; on loan to Oxford University Careers Service · bronze plaque, Malvern Museum, Worcestershire · memorial window, Trinity College, Oxford

Wealth at death £8458 3*s*. 3*d*.: probate, 13 Jan 1916, *CGPLA Eng. & Wales*

Raphael, Henry Lewis (1832–1899), merchant banker, was born in The Crescent, Minories, in the City of London, on 6 April 1832, the second of three sons of Lewis Raphael (1794–1856), merchant, and his wife, Rachael, *née* Mocatta, of the well-known family of bullion brokers. Henry, like his two brothers and a cousin, was trained in the family business of Raphael and Joseph, founded when his grandfather Raphael Raphael (1763–1845), a Sephardic Jew of Portuguese-French origin, moved from Amsterdam to London about 1787. Trade with Amsterdam and Hamburg evidently prospered during the difficult period of the French wars, 1793–1815, so that Raphael and his five sons had been able to move into banking, the bullion trade, and stockbroking in the 1820s and 1830s, trading as R. Raphael & Sons by 1842. Henry Lewis Raphael came to manhood in the years when London dominated international trade and finance and when the Raphael family business reached across Europe and beyond. On 7 March 1855 he married his cousin, Henrietta Raphael (*d*. 1899). There were five sons and four daughters.

The Raphaels' most important enterprise was probably Anglo-American finance, selling American railroad bonds and other shares through the agency of Louis von Hoffman & Co. of New York. The firm's traditional European business was, however, by no means eclipsed. In the 1860s H. L. Raphael and his younger brother George Charles (1835–1906) took some bold initiatives by launching out into the flotation of bonds for foreign governments, notably Denmark in 1864, Russia and Sweden in 1868, Hungary in 1871, Turkey in 1872, and Hungary again in 1873, taking business from the usual sponsors of such issues, Barings, Rothschilds, and Hambros. It is doubtful that these risky new areas were highly profitable, but H. L. Raphael greatly increased his firm's fortunes by successful speculation at the time of the Franco-Prussian War (1870–71). A branch was opened in Paris which played a leading role in selling bonds to pay off the French war indemnity.

Meanwhile international finance was changing rapidly after the transatlantic and other ocean cables allowed instant global communication. City of London enterprise created a whole new business called arbitrage, that is, buying and selling large blocks of shares by cable in response to small differences in prices that continually appeared between the major markets in London, Paris, and New York. A large part of arbitrage business was in American railroad shares, whose prices fluctuated widely. Raphaels was already among the leaders of railroad finance so it is not surprising that it took an early lead in arbitrage transactions. In the early 1880s Rothschilds enviously reported that Raphaels and its American agents never had less than a million pounds worth of American stocks being sold, and the arbitrage business was correspondingly large. In this decade and the next, South African diamonds and gold became big business for Raphaels, and it acquired a refinery at Limehouse to purify the precious metal before trans-shipment to Paris and other markets.

All this activity led to the accumulation of an extraordinarily large capital; in 1876, the date from which the partners' accounts survive, the capital was already just over £2 million and this rose to a peak of £2.9 million in 1882. Until 1914 there were no more than four or five merchants banks in the City with capital of more than £3 million, and the number of millionaires produced by the Raphael family was second only to the Rothschilds in Victorian Britain. H. L. Raphael left £1.53 million in 1899, while his elder brother Edward Lewis left £1.13 million in 1903, and his younger brother George £1.12 million in 1906. The Raphaels' membership of the élite of City of London financial houses is confirmed by intermarriage with other wealthy families; the family's pedigree reads like a roll-call of the most eminent European Jewish families of the day, as they became linked to the Warburgs (Hamburg bankers), Sir Julian Salomons (stockbroker), David Weill of Lazard Frères (French bankers), the Sassoons (Persian Jews eminent in the India trade), and the Melchiors (merchants in Hamburg and Copenhagen). Respected as a pillar of the stock exchange, Raphael was a keen follower of horse-racing and owned a house at Newmarket, Suffolk, where he died of coronary disease on 11 May 1899. Like many of this élite, the Raphael brothers were generous contributors to Jewish charities, but most of their donations were anonymously given and few details are known. Raphael's bequests included £20,000 to endow the Henrietta Ward at Guy's Hospital in memory of his wife, who had died a short time before.

S. D. CHAPMAN

Sources S. D. Chapman, *Raphael bicentenary, 1787–1987* (privately printed, London, 1987) · *Jewish Chronicle* (8 March 1912), 23 · *Jewish Chronicle* (12 May 1899) · *The Times* (12 May 1899), 10f · private information (2004) · d. cert.
Likenesses portrait, repro. in Chapman, *Raphael centenary*
Wealth at death £1,530,000

Raphael, Marco (*fl.* 1529–1534), Hebraist, was a Jewish convert to Christianity from Venice, where he was rewarded by the council of ten for inventing an improved brand of invisible ink. In 1529 he was recruited to the cause of Henry VIII's divorce by another Venetian, Francesco Giorgi (1466–1540), the leading Christian cabbalist of his day and one of Henry's most steadfast and active supporters. Henry's agents in Italy, led by Richard Croke, had been seeking a Jewish rabbi who could resolve contradictions between the books of Leviticus and Deuteronomy and thereby demonstrate that the king's marriage to Katherine of Aragon was irrevocably abhorrent to God's moral law on the grounds of her previous marriage to his late brother, Arthur. Two celebrated scholars, Rabbi

Elijah Menahem Halfan and Jacob Mantino, had withdrawn rather than antagonize Katherine's nephew, Emperor Charles V. Raphael was intended to take their place.

Raphael's opinion regarding the thorny question of biblical marriage was soon circulating in various drafts in the pro-Henry camp and in London. His task was complicated in the autumn of 1530 by the suspiciously timed marriage at Rome itself of a Sephardi Jewish man and his brother's widow. Towards the end of 1530 plans were in place to bring Raphael to England, and Charles V's agents in Rome were advising him to mobilize all of his available forces to prevent this. Nevertheless Raphael had reached London by 25 January 1531. He had two audiences with Henry VIII within the week and explained to the king that although in theory a Jewish man may marry his brother's widow, in practice this had been outlawed among the Ashkenazi Jews in the eleventh century. The Roman case involved Sephardim. Furthermore, Raphael helpfully pointed out that in exceptional circumstances Jews were allowed to take a second wife without divorcing the first, provided that the approval of 100 rabbis was obtained. Henry was said to have been displeased with this useless information, and Raphael gradually began to feel that his welcome was wearing thin, especially after making another fruitless stab at Talmudic interpretation in March.

On 29 April 1531 Charles V was informed by his ambassador at London that Raphael was hoping to be allowed to make his peace with the emperor. But all was not yet lost for him in England, where on 24 May 1532 he was granted a licence to import 600 tons of Gascon wine and Toulouse woad. No less significantly, Henry took Raphael with him to Calais when he met François I in October 1532, as part of a last attempt to arrange a fair hearing for his case before the pope.

The meeting at Calais was Raphael's swansong, however. All that remains of him in the records subsequently is a series of small bills, some from Calais, a payment of £20 to him in October 1533, and finally two references in lists of 'bills to be signed' among Cromwell's 'remembrances' for 1534. With that he disappears. He may have gone back to Venice—had he stayed on in England he would probably have taught Hebrew at one of the universities, and no trace of this survives. He may simply have died in 1534. In any case, by that time the Levitical argument had become a theological irrelevance. On 28 May 1533 Henry's marriage to Anne Boleyn was declared lawful, a little over three months before the birth of Princess Elizabeth. Marco Raphael was a witness to these great events that he had not helped to bring about, the sole survivor of the Jewish advocates of Henry VIII's divorce.

DAVID S. KATZ

Sources D. S. Katz, 'The Jewish advocates of Henry VIII's divorce', *The Jews in the history of England, 1485–1850* (1994)

Raphael, Ralph Alexander (1921–1998), organic chemist, was born on 1 January 1921 in Croydon, Surrey, the only son and eldest of four children of Jacob (Jack) Raphael (1889–1978), a master tailor, and his wife, Lily, *née* Woolf

(1892–1956). His father, whose family moved to Britain from Poland towards the end of the nineteenth century, was a moderately Orthodox Jew who found it difficult to stay in steady work during the depression, so Raphael's early schooling was disjointed, and included spells at schools in Leeds, Sunderland, and Dublin, as well as in London. His talent for science and mathematics having been discovered and nurtured at Tottenham county school (1936–9), he studied chemistry at Imperial College, graduating from the wartime two-year course in 1941 with first class honours and the Hofmann prize for practical chemistry. Under E. R. H. (Ewart) Jones's supervision he completed a brilliantly successful two-year PhD thesis, which fired his lifelong enthusiasm for the chemistry of acetylenes. In 1943 he was sent to May and Baker Ltd under wartime government direction to work on the newly discovered antibiotic penicillin. On 23 May 1944 he married Prudence Marguerite Anne Gaffikin (b. 1922), a violinist, and daughter of Colonel Dr P. J. Gaffikin, medical officer of health for Maidstone; they remained happily together for the rest of his life and had two children, Richard Anthony (Tony; b. 1945), later a research chemist, and Sonia Elizabeth (b. 1952), later a schoolteacher. Raphael turned away from religion entirely in 1941.

Raphael returned to Imperial College in 1946 as an ICI research fellow. His imaginative research on the applications of acetylenes in organic synthesis was recognized in 1948 by the award of the Meldola medal of the Royal Institute of Chemistry. He was appointed lecturer at the University of Glasgow in 1949, and then moved in 1954 to become the first professor of organic chemistry at Queen's University, Belfast, where he built up a successful new department and published an influential monograph, *Acetylenic Compounds in Organic Synthesis* (1955). He was called back to Glasgow in 1957 to be regius professor of chemistry, a post he held until moving to Cambridge in 1972.

Raphael's tenure in Glasgow saw the greatest blossoming of his scientific work, including pioneering syntheses of shikimic acid (an important intermediate in amino acid biosynthesis), queen bee substance (a key insect pheromone), and chrysanthemic acid (a component of natural insecticides). In recognition of his contributions he was elected a fellow of the Royal Society of Edinburgh in 1958 and of the Royal Society in 1962, and was awarded the Chemical Society's Tilden medal in 1960. He was a popular teacher and an inspiring research supervisor, his period at Glasgow producing a generation of outstanding organic chemists including both academics (including J. R. Maxwell FRS, R. Ramage FRS, A. I. Scott FRS, and W. Parker, who died prematurely) and pharmaceutical company executives (including P. Doyle and T. McKillop, both of ICI/Zeneca). He was also a highly effective collaborator, notably with Geoffrey Eglinton in devising applications for gas-liquid chromatography.

In 1972 Raphael was elected 1702 professor of organic chemistry at Cambridge, as successor to Lord Todd. This position carried with it the headship of the department of

organic, inorganic, and theoretical chemistry; the separate department of physical chemistry shared the same building and facilities, an arrangement which did not always lead to comfortable relationships between the two departments. At Cambridge, Raphael continued to produce a stream of innovative and elegant natural product syntheses, including virantmycin (an antiviral compound), aaptamine (an α-adrenoceptor blocker), and steganacin (an anti-leukaemic). He received the Pedler medal of the Chemical Society in 1973, its Ciba-Geigy award in 1975, and the Davy medal of the Royal Society in 1981, and was appointed CBE in 1982. He also received honorary doctorates from the universities of Stirling and East Anglia (both 1982), and from Queen's University, Belfast (1989). He became a fellow of Christ's College, Cambridge, in 1972, and was elected an honorary fellow on his retirement in 1988. Above all he valued his fellowship of Imperial College, awarded in 1991.

As head of department Raphael encouraged his younger staff to explore new and unconventional areas of science. He defined his success not in selfish terms of his own scientific or monetary triumphs, but through the collective achievements of his department, and he took great pleasure in the success of some of those he had appointed, particularly A. B. Holmes FRS, J. K. M. Sanders FRS, and C. Abell. His style did not sit easily with the accountancy-led world of the 1980s: he saw the university as publicly funded for the benefit of the country, and he gave his scientific advice freely. Within the department and elsewhere he was a popular and avuncular figure, always available for constructive advice or an amusing but relevant anecdote.

Although most of his research fell within the conventional boundaries of organic chemistry, Raphael's broader interests, particularly in music, were displayed in some of his more unusual research papers, and he collaborated with David Rubio (a Cambridge violin maker) to produce modern preparations that replicated some of the warm tones of the instruments of Stradivarius and the Cremona school. He retired in 1988, but retained a lively interest in chemistry, reading the latest papers enthusiastically until a few weeks before his death from ischaemic heart disease at Addenbrooke's Hospital, Cambridge, on 27 April 1998. His body was donated to the university's department of anatomy and then cremated, on 1 June 1999. He was survived by his wife and two children.

JEREMY SANDERS

Sources L. Crombie, *Memoirs FRS*, 46 (2000), 467–81 · *The Independent* (6 May 1998) · *The Guardian* (7 May 1998) · *The Times* (20 May 1998) · WWW · personal knowledge (2004) · private information (2004)
Likenesses W. Bird, photograph, 1963, RS · Alexander of Haifa, photograph, 1971, Technion-Israel Institute of Technology, Haifa, chemistry department; repro. in Crombie, *Memoirs FRS* · photograph, 1972?, U. Cam., department of chemistry · photograph, 1972?, Christ's College, Cambridge
Wealth at death £261,624: probate, 8 July 1998, *CGPLA Eng. & Wales*

Raphson, Joseph (*fl.* **1689–1712**), mathematician and writer, was possibly born in 1648, though this date, found in some standard biographies, must be regarded as speculative. No details of his early life have been found.

Since the middle of the sixteenth century, mathematicians had been able to solve analytically simple polynomial equations of a single variable up to the fourth order, usually known simply as quartic equations. More complicated equations were generally intractable. Mathematicians tried to resolve these using numerical methods, the standard but slow one being that of François Viète. In 1689 Raphson replaced the divisor in Viète's method by what is now called the first derivative or slope of the function in the equation to be solved, though he did so without reference to the calculus of either Newton or Leibniz. His formula was novel in that it could be used repeatedly, making the method iterative. He showed that on each step the number of correct decimal places of the solution doubles, which means that convergence to the solution is rapid. He published his work in 1690 in the form of a book, *Analysis aequationum universalis*.

On 27 November 1689 Edmond Halley proposed Raphson for fellowship of the Royal Society, and he was elected just three days later. On 4 December he was admitted and signed the charter book and a bond guaranteeing payment of dues, on which he described himself as being 'of London, Gent.'; this might indicate that he was a landowner, but no corroborating records have been found. These are the only known signatures, and like many other fellows he seems not to have taken the second very seriously—surviving records show payments only in 1692 and 1693. By 1708 he had been excused such, possibly because he was unable to attend the society's meetings.

In the summer of 1691 Halley and Raphson met Newton with the intention of publishing Newton's work on the quadrature (integration) of curves, though ultimately Newton published it himself. The following year a royal mandate issued on 30 March instructed the University of Cambridge to confer on Raphson the degree of MA, and he was admitted to Jesus College as a fellow-commoner on 31 May. It was customary to donate silver to the college in these circumstances, and his unnecessarily extravagant gift was a monteith weighing no less than 46 oz 10 dwt. He gave his address at this time as Middlesex.

Raphson was well educated, but no details of his schooling have been traced. He wrote up his own work consistently in Latin, even at a time when the use of the vernacular was becoming popular. His second, more learned, book was *De spatio reali*, published in 1697 as an annex to the second edition of the *Analysis*. An English translation of *Mathesis enucleata* by Johan Christoph Sturm appeared in 1700 under the abbreviated Latin form 'J.R. A.M. & R.S.S.', which is presumed to mean that Raphson was the translator. His translation of Ozanam's *Dictionnaire mathématique* appeared under his full surname in 1702, and in November he even took the trouble of advertising in the press that the publishers had added material that he wished to disclaim, and had misspelt his name.

The full extent of Raphson's scholarship became apparent with the publication in 1710 of the heavy-going *Demonstratio de Deo*, which shows that his knowledge even

extended to the Kabbalah, which together with his name suggests that he was probably of Jewish extraction and of an Irish immigrant family.

Roger Cotes reported in a letter dated 15 February 1711 that he met Raphson in the summer of 1709 and was surprised by his lack of interest in some of Newton's papers relevant to the writing of Raphson's *Historia fluxionum*. When this was published posthumously in 1715 it turned out to be a biased history of Newton's development of the differential calculus. No direct record of Raphson's death is known; conflicting circumstantial arguments place it in either 1715 or, more probably, late in 1712, the last year for which he was listed as belonging to the Royal Society.

Raphson's works continued to be published and reprinted after his death, and indeed his translation of Newton's *Arithmetica universalis* appeared for the first time as late as 1720. His method was formally related to Newton's fluxional calculus in 1740 by Simpson, and survives to this day in a form due to Lagrange (1797) but often attributed to Newton:

$$a \to a - f(a)/f'(a)$$

in which a is the iteratively estimated solution of the equation $f(a) = 0$ and $f'(a)$ is the slope of f at a. This is now commonly called the Newton–Raphson method and is very often the method of choice in computer programs, where its simple iterative structure and rapid convergence are both desirable advantages.

DAVID J. THOMAS

Sources D. J. Thomas and J. M. Smith, 'Joseph Raphson', *Notes and Records of the Royal Society*, 44 (1990), 151–67 · journal book (copy), 1689–1715, RS · B. P. Copenhaver, 'Jewish theologies of space in the scientific revolution: Henry More, Joseph Raphson, Isaac Newton and their predecessors', *Annals of Science*, 37 (1980), 489–548 · E. G. R. Taylor, *The mathematical practitioners of Tudor and Stuart England* (1954), 418 · *The correspondence of Isaac Newton*, ed. H. W. Turnbull and others, 5–7 (1975–7) · M. Hunter, *The Royal Society and its fellows, 1660–1700: the morphology of an early scientific institution* (1982) · *The correspondence of Isaac Newton*, ed. H. W. Turnbull and others, 2–3 (1960–61) · R. S. Westfall, *Never at rest: a biography of Isaac Newton* (1980) · D. Alexander, 'Newton's method: or is it?', *Focus*, 16/5 (1996), 32–3 · T. J. Ypma, 'Historical development of the Newton–Raphson method', *SIAM Review*, 37 (1995), 531–51 · N. Kollerstrom, 'Thomas Simpson and "Newton's method of approximation": an enduring myth', *BJHS*, 25 (1992), 347–54 · F. Cajori, 'Historical note on the Newton–Raphson method of approximation', *American Mathematical Monthly*, 18 (1911), 29–32 · CUL, department of manuscripts and university archives

Rapin de Thoyras [Rapin], **Paul de** (1661–1725), army officer and historian, was born in Castres, France, on 25 March 1661, the third of the six children of Jacques Rapin, sieur de Thoyras (1613–1685), an advocate, and Jeanne Pélisson (d. 1706). He came from a protestant Savoyard family who had emigrated to France in the reign of François I and settled in Languedoc. His father practised law in the chamber of the edict of Castres, and his mother was a daughter of a councillor in the same court. The young Rapin, reportedly a serious and studious child, was educated at the Huguenot academies of Puylaurens and Saumur. In 1679 he was received as an advocate, although in all his life he is said to have only pleaded one case. The same year the court of Castres, which had been set up as a

Paul de Rapin de Thoyras (1661–1725), by Jacob Houbraken, 1725
(after Jan Henrik Brandon)

result of the edict of Nantes, was abolished and the Rapin family moved to Toulouse.

In 1685 Rapin's father died, and the revocation of the edict of Nantes forced the family to flee Toulouse for the country. In March 1686 Rapin and his younger brother Salomon went to London, where the connections between his uncle Paul Pélisson and the French ambassador, Paul Barillon, secured a favourable welcome. Despite the best efforts of his uncle, the ambassador, and the ambassador's circle, Rapin resisted conversion to Catholicism, and as a result failed to gain advancement in the England of James II. In 1688 he went to the Netherlands where he enlisted in a company of French refugee volunteers at Utrecht commanded by his cousin, Daniel de Rapin. In November 1688 this company formed part of the army that landed with William of Orange at Torbay. For both British whigs and Huguenots, William was the focus of protestant resistance to French and English Catholicism, and Rapin's part in the battles of the revolution of 1688 did much to form his version of British history. He became an ensign in Lord Kingston's regiment of foot and was part of the force sent to Ireland under the duke of Schomberg. He fought at Carrickfergus and the Boyne, and was shot in the shoulder with a musket-ball in the unsuccessful assault on Limerick in August 1690. In June 1691 he took part in the capture of Athlone, and was stationed at Kinsale. Rapin later wrote that it was here, under the influence of the governor of Kinsale, James Waller,

that he first had the idea of writing a history of England, to explain to the other peoples of Europe the significance of the events he was taking part in.

In 1693, while still at Kinsale, Rapin was offered, at the recommendation of the marquis de Ruvigny, the post of governor to the eleven-year-old Lord Woodstock, the son of Hans Willem Bentinck, first earl of Portland. Rapin was described at this time as having 'un certain air du beau monde et ces manières nobles et aisées qu'on n'attrape qu'avec gens de qualité' (Trevor-Roper, 7). It was apparently at the urging of William III himself that Rapin accepted the post, and he spent the next thirteen years living in England and The Hague. In 1698, after the treaty of Ryswick, he accompanied Portland on an embassy to the court of Versailles. In 1699 he married Marie-Anne Testart (c.1674–1749), who was described as 'jeune, riche et surtout vertueuse' (ibid., 9); she came from a Huguenot family in St Quentin which had sought refuge in the Netherlands. In January 1700 Marie-Anne gave birth to Jeanne-Henriette (1700–1782), the first of twelve children, seven of whom survived infancy. But in 1701 the family life was disrupted, as Rapin was obliged to accompany the eighteen-year-old Lord Woodstock on his grand tour through Germany, Austria, and Italy—an experience which, Rapin's surviving letters in Nottingham University Library suggest, he found something of a trial.

The time Rapin spent at The Hague provided him with the company of distinguished Huguenot scholars and intellectuals. As a member of a literary club known as La Pléïade (later La Féauté), which met at Rapin's elegant house in The Hague, he regularly met Abel Rotolp, sieur de la Devèze, Henri Basnage de Beauval, Jacques Basnage, and Jean Rou (who gives an account of Rapin at this time in his *Mémoires*). Rapin wrote an unpublished poem, 'Satire on la société de la Haye', in 1706, and so was clearly nursing literary ambitions. In 1702 his pension of 1100 florins a year, granted him by William III, ceased upon the monarch's death. In 1704 his employment with the Portlands ended when Lord Woodstock married, moved to England, and became MP for Southampton. Rapin now had the freedom to pursue his historical studies, which he appears to have begun in 1705, although his circumstances now required a less expensive way of life, especially in the light of his ever-expanding family. In 1707 he moved to Wesel with his wife and children, a cheaper although less cosmopolitan and sophisticated alternative to The Hague.

Rapin's Huguenot connections, however, continued to support him. In 1704 Jean Leclerc (with whom Rapin had studied at Puylaurens) received the first volume of Thomas Rymer's *Foedera*, a collection of transcripts of British treaties, letters, and acts which Rymer had compiled, and was now sending for a review in Leclerc's *Bibliotèque choisie*. Leclerc reviewed the first volume but sent the subsequent ones to Rapin, whom he described as 'a gentleman of merit who is working on the history of England' (Trevor-Roper, 12). Rapin produced abstracts of these acts for Leclerc's publication, and by 1708 had completed the first eight volumes. By 1725 he had completed seventeen, and these abstracts were published in an English translation by Stephen Whateley as *Acta regia, or, An account of the treaties, letters and instruments between the monarchs of England and foreign powers, published in Mr Rymer's Foedera* (1726). This privileged access to historical material provided the source for Rapin's history. 'I am convinced', he wrote, 'that there is not one piece in the Foedera but what may be of use, especially to such as would write the History of England' (*Acta regia*, 104), and he was spurred on to a more ambitious history than he had hitherto envisaged.

In 1717 Rapin's first effort to formulate his vision of the pattern of British history came in his *Dissertation sur les whigs et les tories* (La Haye, 1717), in which he attempted to explain, for the benefit of continental Europeans, the British party system. The translation of the work into German, Dutch, Danish, Spanish, and English provides some indication of the work's accessibility and lucidity. But it was apparently at the instigation of an Englishman, Andrew Fountaine, that Rapin published the work, and in England it became a standard, if whig-slanted, elucidation of a post-revolution construction of the national past.

Rapin had let it be known in 1714 that he was working on a history of England, and by 1717 he had written at least the first two volumes covering the Anglo-Saxons to the reign of William the Conqueror; in 1722 he had reached the year 1640. After publishing extracts in Leclerc's *Bibliotèque germanique* and in *Bibliotèque ancienne et moderne*, Rapin published the first eight volumes of his *Histoire d'Angleterre* in The Hague in 1723. Two more volumes were published in 1725, taking the history down to the coronation of William and Mary. Rapin, however, did not live to see the full extent of his success as in 1725 he fell ill with a stomach condition and a fever. He died after a week's illness on 16 May 1725 in Wesel and was buried there. He was survived by his wife, six daughters, and one son, Jacques-Benjamin (1707–1763), who became a Prussian official. Details of Rapin's life were published first in an essay by his elder brother, Charles Rapin-Puginier (1658–1730), and later in the laudatory history of the Rapin family by Raoul de Cazenove, which reprints a great deal of Rapin's correspondence.

Rapin's contemporaries depicted him as 'naturally of a serious temper' ('Life of Rapin', no pagination), a man of culture, music, and reason, as well as adept in Italian, Spanish, English, Greek, and Latin. His stern features, with his robust and strong complexion, and his penetrating gaze, can be seen in his portrait, appended to numerous editions of the *History of England*, in which he rests his armoured arm on a pile of his own history books.

The subsequent history of Rapin's magnum opus in England is no less remarkable than his life. His text was politically suited to the times, and stylistically amenable to the British public. The *History* formulated the English past as an essential struggle between the 'prerogatives' of the crown and the 'privileges' of the people. When the two are in balance 'liberty' is maintained. The perfect system of government was parliamentary and constitutional, and had been established by the Saxons in England, who,

after their invasion in the fifth century, established a 'Wittenagemote', which Rapin depicts as an early form of parliament. All upheavals since that establishment were simply instances of the ongoing struggle to maintain this Saxon system, of which the revolution of 1688 was just the most recent example. Although intended for 'foreigners', the work simplified the system for the English market, and Rapin's eclectic style, veering between the painstaking elucidation of historical documents (for instance his essay on the Salic law) and the bloodthirsty sensationalism of a novelist, endeared him to London booksellers. The first translation, by Nicholas Tindal, appeared in fifteen volumes between 1725 and 1731, and was challenged by a translation by John Kelly (1732–6). The text was issued in all the possible forms that booksellers had at their disposal, including part-books, continuations by David Durand (1734–5), Thomas Lediard (1736 onwards), and Tindall (1744–5), and a schoolbook adapted from Rapin by John Lockman, *The History of England by Question and Answer* (1739). The wealth of romantic and gory stories in the original text made it an attractive option for illustration, and the first versions provided work for London's illustrators. George Vertue's *Heads of the Kings of England Proper for Rapin's History* (1736) fulfilled a Georgian taste for grangerization, while the elaborate decorations for the third edition (1743–7) were important forebears of the British 'history painting'. Artists such as Angelica Kauffman later cited Rapin as the source for their subjects.

Rapin's initial critics objected to the clear whig slant of the *History*, as in the case of the splenetic *Defence of English History Against the Misrepresentations of M. de Rapin-Thoyras* (1734), which criticized the history as anti-monarchical, anti-church, and 'the sweet singing of anarchy and levelling' (*Defence*, 8). Rapin's chief political champion was Lord Bolingbroke, who plundered the *History* for his own *Remarks on the History of England*, directed towards the political struggle against Robert Walpole. The wide distribution given to Rapin's text and ideas in the 1730s established the *History* as a classic, and continued versions were appearing until the 1780s. Rapin's hegemony in British historiography was ultimately usurped by David Hume, whose own *History of England* (1754–62) superseded Rapin's as the standard work. Hume later described the Frenchman as 'despicable' (*Letters*, 258), both in style and content, and ultimately it was the more literary, less politically engaged, philosophical tenor of Hume's *History* that was appreciated by the later Georgian readership. Nevertheless, Rapin's work remains a key milestone in British historiography, political thought, and bibliography, and its author as deserving of scholarly attention as his successors.   M. G. SULLIVAN

Sources H. Trevor-Roper, 'A Huguenot historian: Paul Rapin', *Huguenots in Britain and their French background, 1550–1800*, ed. I. Scouloudi (1987), 3–19 · 'Life of Rapin', P. de Rapin-Thoyras, *The history of England*, ed. and trans. N. Tindal, 1 (1725), vol. 1 · 'Some further particulars of Mons Rapin's life in a letter to —', P. de Rapin-Thoyras, *The history of England*, ed. and trans. N. Tindal, 1 (1732) · M. Raoul de Cazenove, *Rapin-Thoyras, sa famille, sa vie, et ses œuvres* (Paris, 1866) · *DNB* · *Mémoires inédits et opuscules de Jean Rou*, ed. F. Waddington, 2 (Paris, 1857) · P. de Rapin-Thoyras, letter to

Lord Raby, 2 Jan 1709, BL, Add. MS 31135, fols. 3–4 • P. de Rapin-Thoyras, letter to J. Robethon, May 1717, BL, Stowe MS 230, fols. 117–21 • *Defence of English history against the misrepresentations of M. de Rapin-Thoyras* (1734) • M. G. Sullivan, 'Historiography and visual culture in Britain, 1660–1783', PhD diss., U. Leeds, 1998 • *The letters of David Hume*, ed. J. Y. T. Greig, 1 (1932)

Archives BL, letters to duke of Portland and corresp., Egerton MS 1706 • U. Nott., letters to duke of Portland

Likenesses J. Houbraken, line engraving, 1725 (after J. H. Brandon), NPG [*see illus.*] • G. King, line engraving, 1732 (after J. Brandon), NPG • G. Vertue, line engraving, 1734, NPG; repro. in Rapin-Thoyras, *History of England*

Rapson, Edward James (1861–1937), Sanskritist, was born at Leicester on 12 May 1861, the son of Edward Rapson, who later opened a school at Ledbury and afterwards became vicar of West Bradley, Somerset. His mother was Eleanor McArdle from co. Dublin. He was educated at Hereford Cathedral school, where he formed a lifelong interest in music, and from there went up to St John's College, Cambridge, in 1879, being elected to a foundation scholarship in 1883. He was awarded a first class in the classical tripos of 1883 and in the Indian languages tripos (Sanskrit and comparative philology) of 1885, as well as winning the Brotherton prize for Sanskrit (1884) and the Hutchinson studentship (1885). He studied Sanskrit under E. B. Cowell. His first published work, *The Struggle between England and France for Supremacy in India* (1887), had gained for him the Le Bas prize in 1886, and in 1887 he was elected into a fellowship at his college, which he held until 1893.

In 1887 after a short period as assistant librarian under Sir Monier Monier-Williams at the newly founded Indian Institute at Oxford, Rapson was appointed assistant keeper in the department of coins and medals at the British Museum. The rich collections of the museum provided ample scope for Rapson's talents and industry, and he soon established himself as a leading authority on Indian numismatics. His two major publications in this field are *Indian Coins* (1898), which appeared as one of the volumes of J. G. Bühler's Grundriss der Indo-arischen Philologie und Altertumskunde, and the *Catalogue of the coins of the Andhra dynasty, the western Kṣatrapas, the Traikūṭaka dynasty, and the 'Bodhi' dynasty* (1908). The latter work is a masterpiece of reconstruction, and established for the first time some degree of clarity in a very obscure period of Indian history.

Rapson married on 8 April 1902 Ellen Daisy (*d.* 1921), daughter of William B. Allen, of West Bradley; they had no children. From 1903 to 1906 he occupied, concurrently with his post in the British Museum, the chair of Sanskrit in University College, London. He left the museum in 1906 on his election to the professorship of Sanskrit at Cambridge in succession to Cecil Bendall. A born teacher and never sparing of his own time and efforts, Rapson applied himself to his new duties with conspicuous energy and success. His duties as a teacher were by no means light, but they did not prevent him from continuing his literary and scholarly work. In 1914 appeared his *Ancient India from the Earliest Times to the First Century AD* which provided for the general reader an excellent summary of all that was then known about the early history and culture of India.

Two major works occupied his attention during his tenure of the professorship at Cambridge. In 1901 Aurel Stein had discovered in Chinese Turkestan a collection of ancient documents written in a variety of the Indian Kharosthi script. Rapson's preliminary decipherment appeared in 1905, and for many years, in conjunction with two French scholars, Auguste M. Boyer and Émile Senart, he worked on the task of editing the texts. The publication appeared in three parts between 1920 and 1929. His second important undertaking was editing the first two volumes of the *Cambridge History of India*. The first volume was published in 1922. Preparation of the second volume occupied him for the rest of his life, but the difficulties inherent in a subject where so few collaborators could be found prevented him from realizing the project.

As a scholar Rapson was distinguished by great thoroughness and strict adherence to scientific method. The same virtues characterized his teaching. He was elected a fellow of the British Academy in 1931. After holding his chair for thirty years he resigned it in 1936. A little over a year later, on 3 October 1937, he died suddenly, at St John's College, Cambridge. T. BURROW, *rev.* J. B. KATZ

Sources L. D. Barnett, 'Edward James Rapson, 1861–1937', *PBA*, 23 (1937), 526–37 • R. L. Turner, 'Professor E. J. Rapson', *Journal of the Royal Asiatic Society of Great Britain and Ireland* (1938), 639–43 • R. Burn, 'Professor E. J. Rapson', *Journal of the Royal Asiatic Society of Great Britain and Ireland* (1938), 639–43, esp. 642–3 • personal knowledge (1949) • Venn, *Alum. Cant.* • *CGPLA Eng. & Wales* (1937)

Archives CUL, corresp. | Bodl. Oxf., corresp. with Sir Aurel Stein

Likenesses W. Stoneman, photograph, 1932, NPG

Wealth at death £13,983 11s. 2d.: probate, 9 Nov 1937, *CGPLA Eng. & Wales*

Ras Prince Monolulu. *See* MacKay, Peter Carl (1881?–1965).

Rasbotham, Dorning (1730–1791), antiquary and playwright, was born at Manchester and baptized on 10 May 1730 at Cross Street Presbyterian Chapel, Manchester. The son of Peter Rasbotham and his wife, Hannah, daughter of John Dorning, of Birch House, Farnworth, in the parish of Dean, Lancashire, he was educated at the Manchester grammar school. On 24 July 1754 he married Sarah, eldest daughter of James Bayley, of Withington, near Manchester, granddaughter of Samuel Peploe, bishop of Chester. They had five children; a son, the Revd Dorning Rasbotham, became a fellow of Manchester collegiate church.

Rasbotham was chairman of the quarter sessions at Manchester for twenty-five years, and high sheriff of Lancashire in 1769. He made extensive collections for a history of Lancashire, and his manuscripts, partly written in Byrom's shorthand, proved of great use to Edward Baines when compiling his history of Lancashire. In 1774 Rasbotham wrote *Codrus, a Tragedy*, in five acts and in verse, which although refused by two London managers was successfully performed at Manchester in that year. He published it anonymously to test the public's reaction to this verdict. It was produced again at Manchester in 1778 for the benefit of Younger the actor, when Kemble, Lewis, and Mrs Siddons took part in the performance. In 1782 he printed *Verses originally intended to have been spoken at the breaking-up of the free grammar school in Manchester*. He is also thought to have written *A Dissuasive from Popular Rioting Directed Against Mechanical Manufacturing Improvements* (1779). Rasbotham died on 7 November 1791 and was buried at the parish church of Dean, where a mural tablet was placed to his memory, with an inscription by Thomas Barnes DD.   C. W. SUTTON, *rev.* J. A. MARCHAND

Sources E. Baines and W. R. Whatton, *The history of the county palatine and duchy of Lancaster*, 2 (1836), 42 · *IGI* · F. R. Raines, *The fellows of the collegiate church of Manchester*, ed. F. Renaud, 2, Chetham Society, new ser., 23 (1891), 294 · J. F. Smith, ed., *The admission register of the Manchester School, with some notices of the more distinguished scholars*, 1, Chetham Society, 69 (1866), 162, 189 · D. E. Baker, *Biographia dramatica, or, A companion to the playhouse*, rev. I. Reed, new edn, rev. S. Jones, 3 (1812), 111 · R. W. Procter, *Manchester in holiday dress* (1866), 68 · J. C. Scholes, *Bolton bibliography* (1886), 59

Likenesses H. Robinson, stipple and line engraving, pubd 1833 (after H. Pickering), BM, NPG · portrait, repro. in Baines and Whatton, *History*

Hastings Rashdall (1858–1924), by Walter Stoneman, 1918

Rashdall, Hastings (1858–1924), moral philosopher, theologian, and historian, was born at 34 St George's Road, Kensington, London, on 24 June 1858, the eldest child of the Revd John Rashdall (*d.* 1869?), incumbent of Eaton Chapel, Eaton Square, London, and afterwards (1864–9) of Dawlish, and of Emily, *née* Hankey (1831–1923), who came from a prominent Clapham evangelical family. Although he was to reject evangelicalism, Rashdall retained the moral seriousness of his upbringing and the combination of broad sympathy and firm churchmanship presented by his parents. John Rashdall was widely read and travelled, with many literary contacts; as a clergyman he worked closely with dissenters, an example which his son followed. At the same time he had an intense love of church order and worship, from which Hastings derived an appreciation of beautiful ceremonial, and of the liturgical proprieties. As a small child he preached sermons to his brother and sister in a night-gown with a red stocking for a hood. On his father's death the family moved to Cheltenham. Rashdall remained particularly close to his mother, an intellectually serious woman, with whom he talked and corresponded about theology and religious history, among many other things.

Early career In 1871 Rashdall went to Harrow School, to the house of the headmaster, Montagu Butler, whom he greatly admired and from whom he drew the initial inspiration for his liberal churchmanship. When later asked whom he considered his most distinguished pupil, Butler replied: 'It is not easy to say, but, if you press me, I think—Rashdall' (Matheson, 26). During his school holidays he visited art galleries and law courts, and developed a fascination for legal questions (indeed he later said that he would have liked to be a judge). In 1876 he became head of house and in 1877 head of school. In 1877 Rashdall won a scholarship to New College, Oxford, where he got a second both in classical moderations (1878) and in greats (1881). He was never a very accurate classicist, and was probably not helped in examinations by his appalling

handwriting. He had spent much of his time as an undergraduate working on history, and in 1879 won the Stanhope essay prize with an essay on John Hus. He twice failed to win a fellowship by examination, but won the chancellor's essay prize in 1883 for an essay on the universities of the middle ages. After teaching briefly at the recently founded Oxford high school he went in 1883 as a lecturer to St David's College, Lampeter (where he became a friend of T. F. Tout, then professor of history), and then to University College, Durham, between 1884 and 1888. In 1884 and 1886 he was ordained deacon and priest respectively. In 1888 he returned to Oxford as a fellow of Hertford College, to teach philosophy for *literae humaniores*. He remained there until 1895, although in 1894–5 he held the fellowship in combination with the chaplaincy (and tutorship in divinity) at Balliol, where he lived. In 1895 he was elected to a fellowship and tutorship in philosophy at New College, a post which he held for the next twenty-two years.

A legend for his absent-mindedness, untidy appearance, and lack of physical co-ordination, Rashdall was a much loved tutor, remembered for being fresh and interested during tutorials, and for taking his pupils for long argumentative walks or on reading parties, and for drawing out the socially awkward. A colleague recalled returning to his room to find all his chairs borrowed for one of Rashdall's fortnightly symposia on the philosophy of religion, which were occasions of great high spirits. His lectures attracted large audiences and provoked lively discussion. Even as an undergraduate he had been known as 'the Socrates of the Cornmarket': he believed in the challenge of critical exchange, whether in the lecture hall, in his study, in the park, or on street corners, and his fundamental seriousness of purpose was reinforced by an infectious sense of humour. A fairly short man, with a large round head and high brow, his thoughtful eyes under shaggy eyebrows were frequently filled with laughter.

Rashdall corresponded extensively with former pupils, and with many who read and used his writings as aids to teaching or stimuli to creative thought. A man of vehement opinions—'It is astonishing how I hate a Tory peer' (Joseph, 276)—and of great kindness—a tory peer was in the flesh quite safe with him—he was an influential teacher and critic, and in all that he did emphasized the importance of study as the prerequisite to action.

Works During this period Rashdall wrote, preached, lectured, and published over an extraordinary intellectual range. He never thought in compartments. He had the spirit and courage to take on research projects which would have daunted others (he habitually worked late into the night) and to champion unpopular causes and lines of argument, to the ultimate detriment of his career in the church. The central contours of his thought remained consistent throughout his life. His first major publication, the three-volume historical work *The Universities of Europe in the Middle Ages* (1895)—an expansion of his chancellor's prize essay—remains to this day a standard work. A volume of university sermons was published in 1898 as *Doctrine and Development*. *The Theory of Good and Evil* (1907) brought together and elaborated his lectures on moral philosophy. Both works incorporated distinctive and controversial arguments about the limitations of divine power. Both were widely read, and appreciated: Rashdall received many letters from laypeople and clergy thanking him for making it philosophically respectable to be a theist. He also published extensively in periodicals such as *Mind* and the *International Journal of Ethics*, as well as in the *English Historical Review* from its first number.

The historical perspective remained fundamental to Rashdall. His work on medieval universities focused on the twelfth and thirteenth centuries, significantly a period of revived incarnationalism and natural philosophy. The twelfth-century theologian Peter Abelard was a major inspiration, both in his stress on the exemplary aspects of the incarnation and the crucifixion, and in the attention which he paid to the context in which intellectual and theological positions were developed. Rashdall always stressed the importance of recognizing the existence of traditions, to which one should apply critical reason. He sharply attacked any philosophical approach which tried to present Christianity without reference to the historical person of Christ, and worked to demonstrate how the Christian tradition could be discussed in a modern intellectual context, and the implications of this for a successful moral philosophy. As a historian he pointed out the futility of looking for biblical proof texts to support particular social or moral positions, instead of realizing that the real meaning of an ethical formula can only be discovered from its context, which is a developing one. He was preoccupied with the fundamental nature of the relationship between philosophy and theology, and its bearing on moral understanding, and was concerned about how the philosophical trends of his day threatened to undermine the force of this relationship. His own philosophical position, which he called 'ideal utilitarianism' or 'empirical idealism', modified the extremes of both utilitarianism and idealism in an attempt to draw on the strengths of both Henry Sidgwick and T. H. Green. He

tried to trace a path between the relativism which could come from fashionable reference to the psychology of religious experience, and the forms of philosophical absolutism which seemed to lower the philosophical status of personality and to deny significance to history.

Rashdall's philosophical and theological concerns were always practical, and were always directed educationally. The full force of his invective was directed against facile polarization between the spiritual and the worldly, which could provide an excuse for failure to apply faith practically. He passionately believed that theology had to be reconstructed to be both metaphysically plausible and practically engaging. This project he pursued as a member of the Synthetic Society for philosophical and theological discussion, set up in 1896 (out of the Metaphysical Society) by Arthur Balfour, Wilfrid Ward, and Bishop E. S. Talbot to confront the challenge of agnosticism and to reinforce a working philosophy of religious belief. He pursued it more broadly in his work for the Workers' Educational Association, and in his lectures to university extension students and to Toynbee Hall in London. He was a founding member of the Christian Social Union from 1890, and from 1892 to 1910 was an editor of its organ, the *Economic Review*. He was among the most effective defenders of the rationale for such a body, set up to stimulate Christian reflection on ethics and economics, and to revive a commitment to Christian social ethics. He published influential articles, especially on the relationship between the individual, the church, and the state. In 1897 he was appointed preacher (for five years) at Lincoln's Inn. From its establishment in 1898 he was vice-president of the Churchmen's Union 'for the advancement of liberal religious thought', and took an active role in its work (which was recognized by his election as its president in 1923). He published frequently in the *Liberal Churchman* (later the *Modern Churchman*). A supporter of progressive movements in general (such as women's suffrage), he was a liberal in politics (although unionist by inclination: until 1906 he opposed home rule for Ireland, and he argued strongly against disestablishment of the Welsh church).

Marriage: later career In July 1905 Hastings Rashdall married Constance Makins, and they settled in 18 Longwall, Oxford, where they entertained generously. Theirs was a very close and happy marriage. In Oxford, Rashdall continued to be active on many fronts, and was called on to contribute to the debate on university reform. His proposals on how to enhance the career of the college tutor had an influence on the revised statutes of 1926. He also strongly supported granting degrees to women in Oxford. In 1909 Rashdall was appointed by the liberal bishop John Percival to a canonry at Hereford, and to share in running a (short-lived) experiment in reformed clerical education. He was installed in 1910, and for the next seven years was resident for five months of the year, retaining his fellowship (without the tutorship) at New College, where he spent the rest of each year. Rashdall was consistently committed to improving clerical training, and believed that the church would lose its influence in national life if it failed to prepare the clergy better for responding to the intellectual demands of the laity. He emphasized that such intellectual demands came just as much from working people as from the middle classes, and regarded the wide range of contexts in which he pursued his own preaching and teaching ministry in this light.

In 1913 Rashdall went with his wife to the United States to lecture in California and Ohio and to visit New York and Harvard. In 1915 he delivered the Bampton lectures in Oxford, published in 1919 as *The Idea of the Atonement in Christian Theology*, which drew on his lifelong engagement with Abelard's resolution of the relationship between the life and death of Christ in the work of redemption. The lectures were well received and reinforced the seriousness of his reputation as a theologian. Meanwhile, Rashdall hoped that the outbreak of war would focus the church more effectively on reforming itself and defining its role in national renewal. He continued to publish energetically, on the problem of evil, on the moral dilemmas associated with conscientious objection, on social and educational reform. He also yearned to find a way of getting personally involved in the war effort. He joined the volunteer corps in Oxford in 1915, and in 1917 finally obtained employment in the Admiralty intelligence department. In May 1917, under the aegis of the coalition government, he was appointed dean of Carlisle, and resigned the canonry and his fellowship at New College (he was elected to an honorary fellowship in 1920). He and Constance put enormous energy into their role in Carlisle. A notable feature of this was the bringing together of other city clergy and of nonconformist ministers in cathedral life and worship, which began during the last year of the war. Rashdall's consistent respect for nonconformity was rewarded when all the nonconformist ministers of Carlisle signed a letter of protest against allegations in 1921 that he had denied the divinity of Christ. These allegations caused Rashdall much distress, compounded by increasing problems of ill health. Long a sufferer from rheumatic pain, he was now diagnosed with cancer, and on 9 February 1924 he died at Worthing. He was buried on 13 February at Holywell cemetery in Oxford; his wife survived him. A memorial tablet was placed in New College cloister by the warden and fellows, and another was placed in the south aisle of Carlisle Cathedral by his wife, who also gave two bells to complete a peal to be rung annually on his birthday. An exhibition was founded by his friends for boys and girls from the diocese of Carlisle awarded scholarships or exhibitions at Oxford.

Reputation and legacy Rashdall's personal influence was deep and extensive, as was revealed by the appreciations of his life by major figures in liberal churchmanship, as well as by the tributes paid by much wider circles of people. The fertility of his published work was striking. Yet his reputation suffered something of the fate which he perceived to have befallen several of the medieval philosophical and theological thinkers whom he himself had studied and in whose ideas he had helped to revive interest. His intellectual position was an independent one, for he stood outside established camps and was not by temperament a systematizer. He said of himself: 'My position is very difficult. You see I am on the left wing of the Church and the right wing of the philosophers' (Matheson, 78). Historians of religious thought have taken some account of his liberal churchmanship. But philosophers have underplayed the persistence and vitality of the idealist tradition in the early twentieth century, and have ignored as leading nowhere the distinctively modified idealism which Rashdall developed. They have tended to take an unhistorical view, and to regard as insignificant what seemed in terms of later philosophical fashion to be outmoded. Although even in his own day Rashdall was a maverick, he was highly respected as such, and the issues with which he engaged were central ones. The challenge of reinforcing an intellectually satisfactory Christian moral and social philosophy continued to be real, and was one to which Rashdall was principally devoted. Only from the late 1980s have there been renewed flickers of interest in Rashdall among liberal intellectual churchpeople facing a new set of challenges to the sorts of approach to faith and reason which he advocated. JANE GARNETT

Sources P. E. Matheson, *The life of Hastings Rashdall, D.D.* (1928) · H. W. B. Joseph, *Oxford Magazine*, 42/12 (Feb 1924), 275–7 · H. D. A. Major, *Modern Churchman*, 13 (1923–4), 634–42 · P. J. Kirby, 'Dean Hastings Rashdall', *Modern Churchman* (Oct 1927), 481 8 · J. Garnett, 'Hastings Rashdall and the renewal of Christian social ethics, c.1890–1920', *Revival and religion since 1700: essays for John Walsh*, ed. J. Garnett and C. Matthew (1993), 279–316 · Rashdall corresp., New College, Oxford · Rashdall correspondence, Bodl. Oxf., MS Eng. lett. · M. Marsh, ed., *Hastings Rashdall: bibliography of the published writings* (1993) · D. Postle and M. Marsh, *Hastings Rashdall: dean of Carlisle, 1917–1924* (2000)

Archives Bodl. Oxf., corresp. and papers · Bodl. Oxf., journal · Bodl. Oxf., school diary · New College, Oxford, family corresp. · Pusey Oxf., sermons, lectures, and academic papers | Bodl. Oxf., letters to Percy Gardner · Bodl. Oxf., Ripon MSS · U. St Andr. L., letters to Canon A. L. Lilley

Likenesses W. Stoneman, photograph, 1918, NPG [*see illus.*] · O. Birley, portrait, repro. in Matheson, *Life of Hastings Rashdall* · portrait, repro. in Matheson, *Life of Hastings Rashdall*, frontispiece

Wealth at death £17,518 7s.: probate, 12 May 1924, *CGPLA Eng. & Wales*

Rashleigh, Philip (1729–1811), mineralogist and antiquary, was born on 28 December 1729 at Aldermanbury, London, the eldest son of Jonathan Rashleigh (1693–1764), a London merchant, and his wife, Mary, *née* Clayton. Rashleigh matriculated from New College, Oxford, in 1749 but left without taking a degree. Members of the family, owners of estates throughout Cornwall, had represented the borough of Fowey in parliament for generations. On the death of his father, Rashleigh was elected member for Fowey in 1765 and sat continuously, despite various contests and disputes, until retiring in 1802, by which time he had become the 'father' of the House of Commons. 'A thoroughly independent country gentleman, critical of general reform and of radicals'; only three speeches of his are reported, all of very minor importance (Namier, 3.348). 'His attendance was poor'; in 1796 he wrote, 'I have no inclination to fling away £50 on a journey to add one more to a majority' (Thorne, 5.9).

The expansion of tin and copper mining during his lifetime led to Rashleigh's interest in mineralogy. Initially through his own efforts, he amassed a significant mineral collection, but later added to it by exchange and purchase from British and European collectors and dealers. It was, and still remains, unrivalled for its content of Cornish specimens. The upper zones of the rich Cornwall deposits were being exploited when Rashleigh formed the collection and he obtained a tremendous variety of unusual and rare minerals, many of them known only from this region and several only from his specimens. He was ahead of his time in cataloguing the source and locality of the specimens. He attempted moderate scientific experiments and analysis, but as the science became more technical he declared, 'I think we shall Refine Mineralogy too much' (letter, 22 March 1789, Russell bequest, NHM); but he assisted in its development by providing material for others. In 1787 Rashleigh published the first volume of his *Specimens of British Minerals*, with the second volume appearing in 1802. In this he achieved his ambition to provide accurate coloured illustrations of minerals—the first successful attempt in Britain, which has also become bibliographically significant owing to its typography (Bethel). His knowledge of mineralogy led to his election as a fellow of the Royal Society in 1788. The threat of invasion by Napoleon made him consider giving up collecting and the increase in competition and prices reduced the number of acquisitions but he continued to make substantial purchases up to 1809.

Rashleigh had an interest in antiquities, particularly artefacts obtained from tin streamworks that related to the prehistory of Cornish mining and his collection once contained the late Saxon hoard of metalwork from Trewhiddle (later moved to the British Museum). He became a fellow of the Society of Antiquaries and published several papers in *Archaeologia*.

From 1756 Rashleigh virtually retired to Cornwall, and upon inheriting the estates he was forced to live modestly while he restored the family's position and by prudent management cleared the debts arising from his father's excesses. He managed the estate and finances of his several wards until they came of age. To settle the family's finances he exploited the family's involvement in local mining activities. Such financial difficulties had reduced his own marriage prospects but on 17 April 1782, at the age of fifty-two, he married his first cousin, Jane Pole (1720–1795).

Letters reveal that Rashleigh was often confined to the house, Menabilly, near Fowey, during the latter years of his life: 'My time of Life draws fast to an End and my Infirmities grow likewise' (10 July 1792, Russell bequest, NHM; 6 April 1804, Sowerby archive, NHM). However, he remained active until 1811, when he died at his home on 26 June 'without a single groan or Struggle' (Charles Rashleigh, Antony House Archives, CC/M/44), having made meticulous bequests to all his relatives, friends, and servants. He was buried at Tywardreath, Cornwall. Through his management the Rashleigh family was reinstated as one of the leaders in mining and agricultural reforms within the county and, his being childless, his estates passed to a nephew, William Rashleigh (1777–1855).

R. J. CLEEVELY

Sources V. M. Chesher, 'Some Cornish landowners 1690–1760: a social and economic study', deposited thesis, 1957, Bodl. Oxf. · R. D. Penhallurick, 'The mineral collection of the Royal Institution of Cornwall', *UK Journal of Mines and Minerals*, 18 (1997), 17–32 · A. Russell, 'Philip Rashleigh of Menabilly, Cornwall, and his mineral collection', *Journal of the Royal Institution of Cornwall*, new ser., 1 (1946–52), 96–118 · P. G. Embrey and R. F. Symes, *Minerals of Cornwall and Devon* (1987), 64–8 · R. W. Jones, 'Philip Rashleigh and his specimens of British minerals (1797 and 1802)', *Mineralogical Record*, 26/4 (1995), 77–84 · W. E. Wilson, 'The history of mineral collecting, 1530–1799', *Mineralogical Record*, 25/6 (1994), 71–4, 189 · L. B. Namier, 'Rashleigh, Philip', HoP, *Commons, 1754–90*, 3.347–8 · R. G. Thorne, 'Rashleigh, Philip', HoP, *Commons, 1790–1820*, 5.9–10 · D. Bethel, 'Mr Rashleigh's cabinet of minerals and William Martin's great primer', *Antiquarian Book Monthly*, 21 (1994), 20–21 · J. D. Enys, 'The Rashleigh collection of minerals', *Journal of the Royal Institution of Cornwall*, 15 (1901–2), 324–7 · A. W. G. Kingsbury, 'Some minerals of special interest in south-west England', *Present views of some aspects of the geology of Cornwall and Devon*, ed. K. F. G. Hosking and G. J. Shrimpton (1964), 247–65, esp. 252–3 · M. Cooper, ed., letters from Henry Heuland to Philip Rashleigh, Cornwall RO, MSS 1997 · R. D. Penhallurick, *Tin in antiquity: its mining and trade throughout the ancient world with particular reference to Cornwall* (1987) · parish register, St Mary the Virgin, Aldermanbury, London, 1/1/1730 [baptism] · *GM*, 1st ser., 54 (1784), 857 · *GM*, 1st ser., 65 (1795), 112 · parish records, St Breock, Cornwall RO, 25/3/1720 [Jane Pole, baptism] · R. J. Cleevely, 'The contributions of a trio of Cornish geologists to the development of 18th century mineralogy', *Transactions of the Royal Geological Society of Cornwall*, 22 (2000), 89–120 · R. J. Cleevely, 'Carew and Rashleigh—a cornish link during the "age of the curiosity collector": their association with Peter Pallas, "the Russian" German traveller–naturalist (1741–1811)', *Journal of the Royal Institution of Cornwall* (2002), 9–29

Archives Cornwall RO, mineralogical corresp. and papers · NHM, geological drawings and papers · Royal Institution of Cornwall, Truro, geological corresp. and papers · Royal Institution of Cornwall, Truro, mineral collection | Cornwall RO, letters to George Fox · Cornwall RO, letters to John Hawkins · NHM, earth sciences library, letters to John Hawkins · NHM, *Russell bequest*, letters to John Hawkins · NHM, Russell collection, mineral collection · NHM, letters to members of the Sowerby family · priv. coll., Carew, Pole and Butler family documents · W. Sussex RO, corresp. with John Hawkins · Warks. CRO, letters to Thomas Pennant

Likenesses H. J. Stubble, watercolour miniature, 1786, V&A · J. Opie, portrait, *c*.1795, County Museum, Truro; repro. in Russell, 'Philip Rashleigh', facing p. 2 · H. Bone, miniature, priv. coll.; repro. in Russell, 'Philip Rashleigh', facing p. 4 · photograph (after J. Opie), NHM, department of mineralogy

Raspe, Rudolf Erich (1737–1794), writer, was born at Hanover, the first child and only son of Christian Theophilus Raspe, an accountant in the Hanoverian department of mines and forests, and Luisa Catherina von Einem, the daughter of a Prussian landed family. He had two younger sisters, Dorothea Frederica and Catherina Maria Sophia. Nothing is known about Raspe's early schooling, but he and his family maintained close ties with the mining communities of Goslar and Clausthal in the Harz. Visiting often, they absorbed both the practical knowledge of the miners and the regional tradition of extravagant folklore.

In 1755, aged eighteen, Raspe entered the university at

Göttingen to study law, remaining for a year. Having become the tutor and companion of a young well-to-do Prussian named von Lüden he transferred to Leipzig, a centre of German rationalism. After three years there of living beyond his means Raspe returned to Göttingen for his master's degree; on graduation in 1760 he accepted a clerical position in the manuscript department of the Royal Library at Hanover. During a tenure of seven years, he cultivated masonic friends, explored the library's large collection of Leibniz papers, and began to publish.

The Lisbon earthquake of 1 November 1755, coincident with Raspe's first year at university, was for Europeans an intellectual as well as physical shock and did much to establish increasingly naturalistic interpretations of geological phenomena. For his part Raspe was led by the Lisbon catastrophe to rediscover the posthumous, almost forgotten *Lectures and Discourses of Earthquakes* (1705) by Robert Hooke, which had been written in 1668. In 1763 Raspe published in Latin, as a 191-page 'specimen' of a larger work—often promised but never to appear—*Specimen historiae naturalis globi terraquei* (*An Introduction to the Natural History of the Terrestrial Sphere*). In it he compiled an impressive catalogue of new islands and mountains that had emerged within historical times, summarized classical and more recent attempts to explain their formation, and gave special prominence (though not unqualified approval) to Hooke's theory, which emphasized the constructive power of earthquakes. In a blatant attempt to win British recognition for his accomplishments, Raspe dedicated his book to the Royal Society of London and its fellows. He was duly elected to membership in 1769. Raspe wrote three papers for the *Philosophical Transactions*, one each on fossil elephants (1769), German marble quarries (1770), and the origin of basalt (1771). He also published on geology and other topics in German periodicals, one of which he edited (1772).

In addition to his geological researches, Raspe attempted to gain a reputation as a man of letters. No literary works were of greater immediate interest at this time than the several attempts by James Macpherson to authenticate his supposed discoveries (in fact, forgeries) of 'ancient' epics by a fictitious Scottish poet named Ossian (*Fingal*, 1762; *Temora*, 1763). These spurious works enjoyed a tremendous vogue throughout Europe and were championed in Germany by Raspe in a five-part periodical essay (1763). In 1766 he twice reviewed, for another German periodical, Thomas Percy's *Reliques of Ancient English Poetry* (1765), which were authentic ballads and destined to become influential. That same year Raspe ventured on poetic creation himself with *Hermin und Gunilde*, an allegory in verse. This well-received attempt had been preceded in 1764 by two anonymous publications, one a poetic comedy and the other a celebration in verse of his sister's wedding. In 1765 he published an anonymous translation into German of a French comedy by Charles-Simon Favart. More important were Raspe's signed article on the manuscripts of Leibniz (1762) and his 1765 edition of six previously unknown essays by the great philosopher.

Though Raspe was becoming known as a man of letters, his standard of living required more money than the Royal Library was paying him. He found the patron he sought in General Count von Walmoden, the illegitimate but influential son of George II and the countess of Yarmouth. Having a very large collection of pictures and antique sculptures, the count invited Raspe to catalogue it. A 42-page listing of his was published in 1767. By then, however, a much better situation was available to Raspe, who accepted the curatorship of collections belonging to Frederick, the landgrave of Hesse-Cassel; with that position came the chair of antiquity at Kassel's university, the Collegium Carolinum, and a seat on the Hessian privy council as well.

On 27 March 1769, in attestation to the diligence for which he was known, Raspe presented to the landgrave a twelve-volume manuscript catalogue in which he had enumerated and described more than 15,000 coins, medals, and other curiosities. The finest of these objects, moreover, were now displayed in some innovative glass cases, transforming the previously cluttered Museum Fredericianum into one of the model collections of Europe. By now seriously in debt, Raspe took the occasion to request a modest increase in his salary—and was brusquely refused. That autumn, desperate for money, he began to pilfer and pawn some of the coins and medals entrusted to his care.

In 1770 Raspe visited Berlin, hoping to garner the Prussian king, Frederick II, as his next and more generous patron. In lieu of that employment he met and married, on 9 April 1771, Elizabeth Langens, the daughter of a wealthy Berlin doctor, with a useful and much needed dowry. Before she divorced him in 1780 they had two children, Friederich and Philippine Caroline. Raspe's wedding brought with it a token increase in his salary. However, Raspe's burden of indebtedness remained and, despite a growing literary reputation, he lived in constant fear that his thefts from the landgrave's collections would be discovered.

In September 1774 Raspe was appointed Hessian resident in Venice. Forced to leave Kassel and the keys to the landgrave's collections behind, he went immediately to Berlin and that October obtained a loan from his father-in-law equivalent to about half his debts, which were becoming known. But in his absence there had been an investigation, and on 15 November he was ordered back to Kassel for an accounting. Dawdling as long as he could, Raspe returned only late in February 1775, was exposed, lost everything he had, and to avoid imminent incarceration was obliged to flee Germany for ever. The warrant for his arrest described him as being of medium height, long-faced, and small-eyed with a prominent, beaky nose and red hair.

Raspe is next heard of in Holland, where he wrote former friends in Kassel two long, ineffectual letters of apology (both eventually published) before going on that August to Britain, a country he henceforth saw as his own. Ever resourceful and beyond the reach of German law, Raspe approached Lockyer Davis, the Royal Society's printer, in London and contracted with him to undertake a series of translations from German and Italian sources on behalf of English science. Though Raspe was expelled from the Royal Society on 7 December 1775, by reason of deficient character, his arrangement with Davis was maintained.

The first volume in the series was a translation of one that Raspe himself had published in German (1774): *An account of some German volcanos and their productions with a new hypothesis of the prismatic basaltes established upon facts* (1776). The second volume, by John James Ferber (praised in the first for the quality of his observations), was *Travels through Italy, in the years 1771 and 1772, described in a series of letters to Baron Born* (1776); and the third, logically enough, was Baron Inigo Born, *Travels through the Bannat of Temeswar, Transylvania, and Hungary, in the year 1770, described in a series of letters to prof. Ferber* (1777). By then, however, Davis was no longer the publisher. Other volumes were announced but did not appear.

In 1779 Raspe toured parts of England as the travelling companion of a Baron von Offenburg from Lithuania. Equipped with letters of introduction from influential friends who had not abandoned him, Raspe was admitted to a number of prestigious country houses. At Cambridge he discovered in the manuscript rooms of the university library a medieval treatise proving (*contra* Vasari) that artists preceding the Van Eycks had painted in oils. Having suggested the same thing in his *Anecdotes of Painting* (1762), Horace Walpole began to take an interest in Raspe—and was soon called upon to bail him out of debtors' prison. Raspe was served with Prussian divorce papers about the same time. Even so, he struggled on to complete *A Critical Essay on the Origins of Oil Painting* (1781), the costs of which were underwritten in part by Walpole. Though favourably reviewed, the book was highly opinionated, as monks, Vasari, and Raspe's former, now hopelessly alienated patron, the landgrave Frederick, were pilloried in turn.

Raspe next tried unsuccessfully to publish English translations of German literary works, well before German literature was fashionable in England. His first attempt, *Tabby in Elysium* (1781; original, 1757) by the obscure J. F. W. Zacharia, was a light verse mock epic of a cat's adventures in the underworld. Raspe's second attempt, Lessing's play *Nathan the Wise* (1781; original, 1779), derived from a more worthy source, but both translations were thoroughly pedestrian and deserved to fail, as they did. On 30 November 1781 Raspe proposed by advertisement in the *Monthly Review* a 'literary expedition to Egypt' led by himself to collect and decipher hieroglyphic inscriptions, but nothing came of it. Depressed and alone, he had lost all sense of direction.

A year later, after twelve months of obscurity, Raspe appeared at Cosgarne House, near Chacewater mine in Cornwall, the local headquarters of Boulton and Watt. He had been in Cornwall for some time, visiting mines, inspecting their machinery, and buying mineral specimens (but where he got the money is unclear). Raspe lived in Redruth for several years as an associate of the firm, eventually becoming its assay master. In October 1783 a

German periodical essay surely by him provided eyewitness accounts of the Cornish mining industry and its steam engines.

In June 1784 Raspe visited London and while there sat to James Tassie in Leicester Fields for a medallion portrait, the only one of him that exists. Seven years later Raspe published an extensive catalogue in two volumes of the 'Ancient and Modern Gems' cast by Tassie in paste from loaned originals. He listed and described almost 16,000 entries, together with a learned preface.

For all of Raspe's prodigious accomplishments as a compiler and translator—for all of his contributions to periodicals and the science of geology—he is now remembered primarily for a short *jeu d'esprit* chapbook of only forty-two pages called *Baron Munchausen's Narrative of his Marvellous Travels and Campaigns in Russia* (1786). Published anonymously, the work was not definitively identified as Raspe's until 1824, by which time it had been reprinted, expanded, illustrated, and translated in a vast number of editions; the editions continue to this day, and it has also been adapted for the cinema.

Though the greatest of all travel liars, Raspe's Munchausen was based on a real German original, Karl Friedrich Hieronymus, Freiherr von Münchausen (1720–1797), who during his youth had fought in Russia against the Turks. Years afterward, as a country squire at Bodenwerder, near Hameln, he regaled his guests (Raspe supposedly among them) with droll recitations of incredible personal adventures, adding straight-faced assurances of their veracity. Seventeen tales attributed to him were published in the German periodical *Vade Mecum für lustige Leute* between 1781 and 1783, some or all of which have been attributed to Raspe. The latter's five examples of the baron's stories, rendered into English in 1786, include Cornish mining slang and scenery. Later augmentations added topical allusions and adapted fantastic plots from earlier tellers.

In 1786 the Boulton and Watt assay office in Cornwall was closed, and Raspe returned to London, finding work in Tassie's shop as his catalogue moved to completion. He also translated Baron Born's treatise on the amalgamation of gold and silver ores (1791). From 1789 to 1790 Raspe was in Scotland, where he had been commissioned to make a mineralogical survey of the highlands. He visited the Hebrides and went as far north as Thurso. But his assurances of mineralogical richness seemed unlikely to some: he was accused of salting barren moors with specimens of Cornish ore, and was later caricatured as the dishonest Hermann Dousterswivel in Walter Scott's novel *The Antiquary* (1816).

After two more years of routine business and failing health in London (with excursions to Scotland, Wales, and Cornwall), Raspe visited Ireland in November 1793 to see a number of its mines. He died in 1794 at Muckross, near Killarney, of scarlet fever and was buried in the hillside graveyard of Killeaghy Chapel.   DENNIS R. DEAN

Sources J. Carswell, *The prospector: being the life and times of Rudolf Erich Raspe, 1737–1794* (1950) • R. E. Raspe, *Singular travels, campaigns and adventures of Baron Munchausen: with an introduction by John*

Carswell (1948) • R. Raspe, *Introduction to the natural history of the terrestrial sphere*, ed. and trans. A. N. Iversen and A. V. Carozzi (1970) • H. Garland and M. Garland, *The Oxford companion to German literature* (1997) • A. Geikie, *Annals of the Royal Society Club* (1917), 128–35
Archives RS, essays • U. Edin. L., essays | Birm. CA, letters to Matthew Boulton • Birmingham Assay Office, Matthew Boulton collection
Likenesses J. Tassie, paste medallion, 1784, Scot. NPG; repro. in Carswell, *The prospector*, frontispiece • J. H. Tischbein, portrait; now lost
Wealth at death very little: Carswell, *The prospector*

Rassam, Christian Anthony (1808–1872). *See under* Rassam, Hormuzd (1826–1910).

Rassam, Hormuzd (1826–1910), archaeologist and civil servant, was born in Mosul, Mesopotamia, then within the Ottoman empire, afterwards in northern Iraq. He was the youngest son and eighth child of Antun and Theresa Rassam, who were members of Mosul's Christian Chaldean community, his father being archdeacon of the uniate Chaldean church there. Originally the family were designers of muslins, once Mosul's staple product.

The family had British connections through the eldest son, **Christian Anthony** [*formerly* Isa Antun] **Rassam** (1808–1872), who after five years' training with the Church Missionary Society in Cairo became the society's Arabic translator in Malta in 1832. There he joined the Church of England and married on 1 January 1835 Matilda Badger (*d.* 1867), sister of the Revd George Badger, missionary and Arabist; three months later he joined Francis Chesney's Euphrates expedition as principal interpreter (1835–7), after which he accompanied W. F. Ainsworth on his two expeditions to Kurdistan and Asiatic Turkey (1837; 1838–40) before returning to Mosul, his home town, where he had already, as from December 1839, been appointed British vice-consul. There he had a Scottish business partner, A. H. Ross, from 1844 to 1848, and 'brought the Yezidis into the 19th century' (Guest, 67). He died in Mosul on 30 May 1872.

As a child Hormuzd Rassam spoke Arabic and two dialects of Syriac. An Anglophile since boyhood, he learned English with the help of Maria Badger, his brother's mother-in-law, who also converted him to protestantism. In 1842 he first met, in his brother Christian's house, Henry Layard, who was then *en route* for Constantinople from Persia, and would become Rassam's mentor and lifelong friend. Three years later, when Layard returned to Mosul to begin his excavations of the mounds of Nimrud and Kuyunjik, he engaged Rassam, who was then working as a clerk for his brother, as secretary, paymaster, and general factotum. Rassam remained with Layard throughout this expedition, which lasted from October 1845 to June 1847.

Rassam travelled with Layard to England in December 1847 and spent some months in Oxford preparing to enter Magdalen College, but abandoned this idea when his brother Christian, who was funding his stay in England, persuaded him to return to Mosul with Layard. They reached Mosul at the end of September 1849 and Rassam

Hormuzd Rassam (1826–1910), by Lock & Whitfield, pubd 1881

worked with Layard in Assyria and Babylonia, as well as paying short visits to Van and Syrian Khabur before both men returned to London in spring 1851. Christian Rassam was left in charge of further work at Kuyunjik in their absence.

In 1852, Layard having decided to enter politics, the British Museum appointed Hormuzd Rassam on a two-year contract to continue Layard's work under the nominal supervision of Henry Rawlinson, the British consul-general and resident in Baghdad. Rassam left London for Mosul in August 1852 to begin his career as an archaeologist in his own right; he remained in Mesopotamia until August 1854 when he returned to England. During this time he made some remarkable discoveries at both Nimrud and Kuyunjik, among them Ashurbanipal's north palace, and its lion-hunt sculptures and cuneiform texts.

On his visits to England, Rassam was well received as the friend and close associate of the now celebrated Layard. He got to know Pusey and other leaders of the Oxford Movement but fell out with them over his evangelism. In 1854 he was invited by James Outram (whom he had first met in 1852) to become Arabic interpreter in Aden, where Outram was political agent. The British Museum hoped that Rassam would return to Mesopotamia but he opted for Aden, where he received steady promotion, becoming second then first assistant political agent. His main work was with the Arab tribes and he was commended and rewarded by the government of India for his handling of them during the Indian mutiny. He also became a magistrate, and was responsible for the post office, the municipality, and the waterworks. During 1860 and 1861 Rassam spent over a year in Muscat during negotiations for a settlement over Zanzibar, whose sovereignty was disputed between the sultan of Muscat and his brother.

Rassam's responsibilities in both southern Arabia and the African coast opposite led to his selection in 1864 for the delicate and dangerous mission, carried out under the aegis of the Foreign Office, of delivering a letter from Queen Victoria to Emperor Theodore of Ethiopia. This was an attempt to secure the release of the British consul, Charles Duncan Cameron, and a number of Europeans, among them Henry Aaron Stern and other missionaries, some with families, who had been working for the London Mission to the Jews. All were held prisoner in the Ethiopian highlands.

Rassam landed at Massawa in the Sudan, which was then under Egyptian rule, on 23 July 1864 and, apart from a short visit to Cairo, remained there for over a year before receiving Theodore's permission to enter Ethiopia. Accompanied by Lieutenant W. F. Prideaux of the Bombay staff corps and Dr Henry Blanc of the Indian Medical Service, Rassam eventually left Massawa in October 1865 on the long and difficult trek to Theodore's camp at Damot, where on 28 January 1866 he delivered the queen's letter to the emperor. At first all seemed to go well; the prisoners were released and allowed to join Rassam, and were ready to leave for the coast with him in April when the unpredictable Theodore had the whole party, including Rassam, arrested. They were taken to the mountain fortress of Magdala where they were put in chains, and where they remained until April 1868 when they were saved by the arrival of Sir Robert Napier and his troops from India. Remarkably, despite incarceration, Rassam remained on relatively good terms with the emperor and was able to communicate via Massawa with Aden.

Rassam reached London on 22 June 1868. His detailed report on his mission to Ethiopia was published in December as a parliamentary paper, together with a letter to him from the foreign secretary, Lord Stanley, expressing the British government's:

> high sense of your conduct … you appear throughout to have acted for the best, and your prudence, discretion, and good management seem to have tended greatly to preserve the lives and thus to secure the ultimate release of the captives. ('Report')

He was also awarded £5000 as compensation for his four-year ordeal.

Before retiring on an India Office pension at the end of 1869 Rassam took leave, and on 8 June 1869 married Anne Eliza, daughter of Captain S. C. Price, formerly of the 72nd highlanders. He also had his two-volume *Narrative of the British Mission to Theodore, King of Abyssinia* published. There followed travels in the United Kingdom and the Near East before he settled in Middlesex, first at Twickenham and then at Isleworth.

On the death of George Smith of the British Museum in 1876, Rassam accepted the trustees' invitation to return to Mesopotamia, primarily to continue Smith's search for inscribed tablets, interest in Mesopotamian archaeology having been revived by Smith's decipherment of a fragment describing the biblical flood. Rassam reached Constantinople early in 1877, a few months ahead of his old friend Layard, Britain's new ambassador to the Porte. Layard was able to obtain for him two firmans permitting both the renewal of his earlier work and simultaneous excavations virtually anywhere in the provinces of Aleppo, Van, and Baghdad (modern Syria, eastern Turkey, and Iraq). However, before this he spent from July to December in Asiatic Turkey investigating for the Foreign Office the condition of the Christian minorities there. In January 1878 he reached Mosul at the start of four seasons' work for the British Museum, ending in July 1882. He was on his own without an assistant, artist, or camera. On returning to London at the end of both his first two seasons he resigned as he wished to remain at home but, as the museum was unable to find a replacement, dutifully agreed to carry on. Throughout this period Rassam concentrated on Babylonia but also initiated excavations in Assyria, Van, and Khabur, moving rapidly from one site to another after leaving a trusted overseer in charge. He made some exciting discoveries, among them the bronze gates of Shalmaneser II's Balawat palace and a cylinder fragment recording Cyrus's capture of Babylon. He also discovered Sippar (Abu Habbah), the biblical Sepharvaim, where he unearthed 60,000–70,000 inscribed tablets and fragments. In all it is estimated that Rassam added some 134,000 such tablets, including some bought from dealers in Baghdad, to the British Museum's collection. Sadly, Rassam was unable to find a publisher in England and his account of the four expeditions, *Asshur and the Land of Nimrud*, was not published until 1897, and then in New York.

Rassam was elected a fellow of the Royal Geographical Society in 1868 and became a British subject by naturalization on 14 October 1870. He had five daughters and one son. After 1882 he lived mostly in Brighton and Hove. There he wrote articles on Assyro-Babylonian exploration, the Christian sects of the Middle East, and current religious controversy in England. He ended his life in disappointment and relative obscurity. His reputation suffered both in his lifetime and afterwards from criticism of his archaeological methods. Undoubtedly, prejudices against his oriental origin told against him; he was hurt by press criticism of his performance in Ethiopia and by poor public recognition of his discoveries, some of the more important being attributed to others, and above all by stories emanating from Wallis Budge of the British Museum that he and his Chaldean relatives had been involved in the theft of antiquities. It was small comfort to win £50 damages against Budge in a libel action, which lasted five days in 1893. In this action he was strongly supported by Theophilus Pinches, then Britain's leading Assyriologist, and by Henry Layard, who had once described him as 'one of the honestest and most straight forward fellows I ever knew, and whose great services have never been acknowledged' (Waterfield, 478). In 1987, in tardy recognition of those services, the British Museum dedicated volume 7 of its catalogue of Babylonian tablets to his memory.

Rassam died at his home, 30 Westbourne Villas, Hove, on 15 September 1910 and was buried in a cemetery in Brighton. He was survived by his wife. The manuscript autobiography he left has since been lost.

DENIS WRIGHT

Sources DNB · H. Rassam, *Asshur and the land of Nimrud* (1897) · H. Rassam, *Narrative of the British mission to Theodore, king of Abyssinia*, 2 vols. (1869) · 'Report … respecting his mission to Abyssinia', *Parl. papers* (1868–9), 63.659, no. 4088 · M. T. Larsen, *The conquest of Assyria* (1997) · J. E. Reade, 'Hormuzd Rassam and his discoveries', *Iraq* [journal of British School of Archaeology in Iraq], 55 (1993) · J. E. Reade, introduction, in E. Leichty, *Catalogue of Babylonian tablets in the British Museum, 6: Tablets from Sippar 1* (1986) · G. Waterfield, *Layard of Nineveh* (1963) · A. Moorehead, *The Blue Nile* (1962) · A. H. Layard, *Nineveh and its remains*, 2 vols. (1849) · H. Blanc, *A narrative of captivity in Abyssinia* (1868) · H. A. Stern, *The captive missionaries* (1869) · C. R. Markham and W. F. Prideaux, *A history of the Abyssinian expedition* (1869) · *FO List* (1872) · *FO List* (1877) · *FO List* (1910) · *The Times* (17 Sept 1910) · C. J. Gadd, *The stones of Assyria* (1936) · J. S. Guest, *The Yezidis: a study in survival* (1987) · W. F. Ainsworth, *A personal narrative of the Euphrates expedition* (1888) · W. F. Ainsworth, *Travels and researches in Asia Minor, Mesopotamia, Chaldea and Armenia*, 2 vols. (1842) · F. R. Chesney, *Narrative of the Euphrates expedition* (1868) · R. J. Gavin, *Aden under British rule, 1839–1967* (1975)

Archives BL, corresp., mainly with Austen Layard, accounts, etc., Add. MSS 38977–39142, *passim* · BL OIOC, papers, mostly corresp. with Theodore II, King of Abyssinia, MS Eur. F 103 · Pembroke College, Oxford, letters, mainly to Sir Peter Renouf and Lady Renouf · PRO, Foreign Office papers

Likenesses A. A. Hunt, oils, exh. RA 1869, BM · F. C. Cooper?, two oil paintings, priv. coll.; repro. in J. E. Reade, 'Hormuzd Rassam and his discoveries' · I. L. Finkel, photograph (in middle age), BM · Lock & Whitfield, woodburytype photograph, NPG; repro. in T. Cooper, *Men of mark: a gallery of contemporary portraits*, 5 (1881) [*see illus.*] · photograph (in middle age), Hult. Arch.

Wealth at death £775 11s. 9d.: administration with will, 18 Nov 1910, CGPLA Eng. & Wales

Rastell, John (*c.*1475–1536), lawyer and printer, was the son of Thomas Rastell (*d.* 1505?); he was probably born in Coventry, though John Bale later claimed Rastell was a Londoner by birth. Rastell's father and grandfather both had civic and legal responsibilities in Coventry, and in 1489 Rastell was admitted to the city's Corpus Christi Guild (fourteen being the normal age for admission). The first instalment of his guild fee was paid by Joan Symonds, widow of a former mayor of Coventry, who acted as godmother to Rastell's daughter (probably named after her), and may well have been his aunt; in 1507 Rastell benefited significantly by her will.

Rastell acquired French and Latin, requisites for a legal career that was furthered at Middle Temple, London, where he was an 'utter' (outer) barrister by 1502, with Christopher St Germain of Coventry as a companion. (Anthony Wood's later claim that Rastell matriculated at Oxford conflates Rastell with a contemporary namesake.) Perhaps as early as 1497 Rastell married Elizabeth (1482–1537), daughter of Sir John *More and sister of Thomas *More; they had three children: Joan (who later married the playwright John Heywood), John (*b. c.*1497), and William *Rastell (*d.* 1565). By 1504, Rastell was residing in Coventry, where, in 1506 after an interim, he succeeded his father as coroner, an office that involved presiding over the court of statute merchants and acting as clerk of

recognizances of debts. About this time, Thomas More visited his sister and brother-in-law in Coventry.

Possibly discouraged by Coventry's economic decline and castigated for Lollard tendencies, Rastell resigned as the coroner in 1508, and by the following year he had taken his family to London, where he ran a successful legal practice for over twenty years; something is known of his involvement in chancery suits during 1529–32. From about 1509 he also seems to have begun to print and publish: initially where he was dwelling 'at the Fleet Bridge at the Abbot of Winchcombe's Place', then by 1515 near St Paul's (where his premises comprised a room for the press, a shop, and living quarters), and eventually from Michaelmas 1519 at Paul's Gate, Cheapside. Rastell's shop sign was a mermaid; one of his two printing devices included a merman and mermaid.

Perhaps the first book Rastell printed was a Thomas More translation, *The Lyfe of Iohan Picus* (with related material) (*c.*1509)—the unspecified author being Gianfrancesco Pico. Also of this early phase of Rastell's printing was his compilation of the statutes of Edward V and Richard III. He concentrated on producing law books, and over the years came increasingly to edit or write the books his press produced. Over his career his publication list came to comprise over fifty titles (a few he re-edited, some reprinted), including, in 800 folio leaves, the ambitious *La grande abbregement de la ley* (1514–16) by Anthony Fitzherbert—appointed Coventry's recorder in 1509—in three volumes and priced at 40s. (Only the first volume was printed by Rastell, his small press being utilized for humanistic texts of More's circle); its *Tabula*, compiled by Rastell, appeared in February 1517. Other publications (most, seemingly, from his own press) included a liturgy, of which only two leaves survive; works on literacy and astrology; *A C. Mery Talys* (*c.*1524–5), compiled if not written by Rastell, and apparently the earliest printing of the so-called 'Shakespeare's jest book'; and *The Pastyme of People* (1529–30). This last work, more familiarly known as 'Rastell's chronicle', was based by Rastell on Robert Fabyan's chronicle, its second part enhanced with eighteen full-page woodcut portrait effigies of English monarchs from William I to Richard III, thereby forming the first English printed portrait-book.

Some time between November 1519 and mid-1520 Rastell printed his *New Interlude and a Mery of the Nature of the .iiij. Elements*, a moral play that not only was apparently the first English printed work to define the New World as America but also, in its inclusion of a three-part song, 'Tyme to pas', with music, marked the first attempt anywhere in Europe to print a musical score. About 1525–7 he also provided music for the ballad 'A Wey Mornynge' on a printed broadside. Music printing normally required each page to be printed twice; however, Rastell's music type—cut for him probably in northern Europe—was specially cast, enabling him to be the first printer to print music in a single impression. Innovative, too, was his 1513 introduction from Rouen of small secretary-type for law books in French; the font, much worn, was still in service in 1528. A 1535 reference to a 'castynghowse' suggests that Rastell was able to cast at least some of his types in-house (Devereux, 29).

Rastell's move to London in 1508–9 may have been encouraged by Sir Edward Belknap, formerly of Coventry and then a privy councillor with court influence, as Belknap engaged Rastell in an organizational capacity during the 1512–14 French war. In January 1515 Rastell leased a country house and grounds at Monken Hadley, near High Barnet, where he cleared land and pursued gentlemanly recreations; Thomas Cromwell was among the guests. As master of wards, on 7 October 1515 Belknap also secured for Rastell lands and goods of the Lollard heretic Richard Hunne, on the understanding that, as ward of Hunne's two daughters, Rastell provided the crown with their dowries. Rastell defaulted in this, his American venture having failed, and in May 1523 Hunne's property was granted to another, though Rastell managed to retain possession until 1529, when he finally lost the lawsuit. Rastell was litigious by nature and was prone to financial misjudgements: he lost his estate at Monken Hadley in a court case in 1534, when he brought a suit against Dame Alice [see More, Alice], his mother-in-law, and Richard Staverton, his brother-in-law, for mismanaging his property during a forced absence in Ireland. That same year he was involved in a court case regarding his Paul's Gate premises.

Late in 1516 More's *Utopia* was printed in Louvain, and this may have inspired Rastell to undertake a commercial and explorative venture to 'this newe landys founde latley / Ben callyd America by cause only / Americus dyd furst then fynde', the object being to settle the land claimed for England in 1497, and to search for the north-west passage to Asia (*Four Elements*, lines 838–40). Royal letters of recommendation were granted to him and two London merchants, with a small loan, on 5 March 1517. The expedition starting late in the summer was assigned at least one royal ship and comprised at least four vessels with supplies. However, the venture proved a financial disaster. Rastell's ship, with the printer Thomas Bercula on board, reached Waterford, where the sailors abandoned him, and then sold his cargo in Bordeaux. As a result Rastell sojourned in Ireland from the summer of 1517 for some two years, taking the opportunity to write his *Four Elements*.

Belknap was also responsible for Rastell's involvement in the beautifying of the roof of the temporary royal pavilion at the Field of Cloth of Gold in 1520; in the same year and in the same capacity Rastell probably painted the roof of the Roundhouse in Calais. In 1522 Rastell wrote and choreographed the pageant performed in London at the king's meeting with the emperor; five years later he did the same for the opening entertainment, on 5 May 1527, at the theatre at Greenwich, a theatre which he had helped decorate. In August 1524 he served as 'trenchmaker' under Charles Brandon, duke of Suffolk, during the French campaign. In the same year he took a forty-year lease on an acre or so of land at Finsbury Fields, where he built a house and the earliest known permanent Tudor stage, at which he held public performances. (He later initiated a lawsuit against the theatrical manager, John Walton, over damage to stage properties.)

More was probably instrumental in returning Rastell in 1529 to the so-called Reformation Parliament for the Cornish borough of Dunheved, and Rastell was commissioned to print the statutes passed by the parliament's first session. Initially, Rastell opposed religious change: he had already published Christopher St Germain's neutral *Dialogus de fundamentis legum Angliae et de conscientia* (1528) and in 1529 he published More's *Dyaloge* concerning heresies, which was directed against the rising tide of Lutheranism in England. That year he spent some six months in France on government business, probably seeking support from the academics of Paris University for the king's divorce. In October 1530 he printed his own *New Boke of Purgatory*, backing More's *Dialogue*. A printed exchange with the young John Frith followed, with the resulting conversion of Rastell to the reformed faith marking the parting of the way with his brother-in-law. Rastell became an agent to Thomas Cromwell, and in 1533 was appointed to investigate legal fraud in London; that same year, he shared a lead-mining lease (which proved unsuccessful) in Dartmoor with Cromwell and others. In 1534 he served on a commission investigating lawlessness in Wales.

Rastell's printing and publishing apparently brought him a steady income until the early 1530s. Following his conversion in 1531, he began issuing protestant treatises: the business declined to the extent that a young servant of his, William Mayhewe, eventually took over its operation, and by summer 1533 half the shop was leased out to the bookseller John Gough, known for selling heretical publications. Sending a draft of his 'Book of the charge' to Cromwell, probably in 1534, Rastell petitioned for permission to print it as issued by the king for distribution to all judges and officials in legal courts, so they would learn the true faith. In spring 1535 he daily visited the Charterhouse seeking to convert its monks. Increasingly radical, he looked in vain to Cromwell for privileges to print and publish protestant tracts, including one on allowing priests to marry, while his type appears to have been used for the anonymously printed *Dyaloge betwene Clemente and Bernarde* (c.1532), opposed to convocation's taxation powers. Consistent with these views, Rastell himself denied clerical rights to tithe in 1535; he appeared before Cranmer and was committed to prison. He was still in custody on 20 April 1536, six days after parliament was dissolved, when he made his will, in which he named Henry VIII as one of his executors, as 'I am moste in daunger to the kings grace by bondes and oders of his comyn lawe' (Plomer, *Abstracts*, 5). Rastell died in poverty in the Tower about 25 June, a prime example of the turn of fortune's wheel in Tudor England.

CECIL H. CLOUGH

Sources A. J. Geritz and A. L. Laine, *John Rastell* (1983) • A. Harding, 'Rastell, John', HoP, *Commons, 1509–58*, 3.176–9 • A. W. Reed, *Early Tudor drama* (1926), 1–20, 187–233 • H. R. Plomer, 'John Rastell and his contemporaries', *Bibliographica*, 2 (1896), 437–51 • J. Rastell, *The four elements*, ed. R. Coleman (1971), 1–24 • *Three Rastell plays*, ed. R. Axton (1979), 1–27 • A. W. Pollard, 'Pleadings in *Rastell v. Walton*, a theatrical lawsuit, *temp.* Henry VIII', *An English garner: fifteenth century prose and verse* (1903), 305–21 • S. Anglo, 'Le champ du Drap d'Or', *Fêtes et cérémonies au temps de Charles Quint*, ed. J. Jacquot and

E. Konigson (1960), 113–34, esp. 130–31, 134 · S. Anglo, 'The imperial alliance and the entry of the emperor Charles V into London', *Guildhall Miscellany*, 2 (1960–68), 131–55 · A. Hyatt King, 'Rastell reunited', *Essays in honour of Victor Scholderer*, ed. D. E. Rhodes (1970), 213–18 · A. Hyatt King, 'The significance of John Rastell in early music printing', *The Library*, 5th ser., 26 (1971), 197–214 · C. H. Clough, 'The enigma of Richard III's woodcut portrait of 1529', *The Ricardian*, 11 (1997–9), 114–39 · C. Warner, '*A dyaloge betwene Clemente and Bernarde, c.*1532: a neglected tract belonging to the last period of John Rastell's career', *Sixteenth Century Journal*, 29 (1998), 55–65 · R. J. Roberts, 'John Rastell's inventory of 1538', *The Library*, 6th ser., 1 (1979), 34–42 · H. R. Plomer, *Abstracts from the wills of English printers and stationers from 1492 to 1630* (1903), 5–6 · A. J. Geritz, 'The marriage date of John Rastell and Elizabeth More', *Moreana*, 52 (1976), 23–4 · E. J. Devereux, *A bibliography of John Rastell* (1999) · Rymer, *Foedera*, 3rd edn, 6/1.131 · D. B. Quinn, 'Rastell, John', *DCB*, vol. 1 · A. J. Geritz, 'The relationship of brothers-in-law Thomas More and John Rastell', *Moreana*, 139–40 (1999), 35–48 · J. Parr, 'John Rastell's geographical knowledge of America', *Philological Quarterly*, 27 (1948), 229–40

Wealth at death had significant debts at death: will, Geritz and Laine, *John Rastell*, 21–22, 26 · Roberts, 'inventory', 34–42

Rastell, John (1530–1577), author and Jesuit, was born in Gloucester of a family prominent in local commerce and administration. He was admitted to Winchester College in 1543 and later attended New College, Oxford, graduating BA before his election as fellow in 1549, and proceeding MA on 26 June 1555. Rastell's career at Oxford ended in 1560, when he fled England for Louvain, joining other fellows of his college in exile for religion's sake.

Marking the period immediately preceding Rastell's flight was the so-called 'challenge sermon', preached at Paul's Cross in November 1559 and March 1560 by John Jewel, bishop of Salisbury, who attacked various Roman Catholic practices and beliefs as things unknown during the first six hundred years of Christianity. Before leaving England, Rastell wrote his *A Confutation of a Sermon, Prounounced by M. Juell, at Paules Crosse*. On account of the censorship of Roman Catholic authors in England, Rastell wrote (as he says in a preface) for 'one frind alone, to auoyde feare of foes' (Rastell, *Confutation*, sig. A2v). The book was published at Antwerp in November 1564, after Rastell had become a candidate in theology at Louvain.

Rastell's book was ignored by Jewel and other protestant controversialists, who concentrated their fire against Catholic doctors of divinity (especially Thomas Harding, another former Winchester and Oxford scholar). Nevertheless Rastell continued to publish books opposing Jewel. In January 1565 he issued a partly satirical challenge to Jewel, *A Copie of a Challenge*, originally the final section of his *A Confutation*. Two months later appeared Rastell's *A Replie Against an Answer (Falslie Intitled) In Defence of the Truth*, taking issue with a book by the Oxford protestant Thomas Cooper, who had in 1562 attacked an anonymous Catholic answer to Jewel. Like Jewel, Cooper never answered Rastell. Nevertheless Rastell continued his side of the book war, in early 1566 answering one of Jewel's responses to Harding with *A Treatise Intitled, Beware of M. Jewel*, in two books, followed in November 1566 by *The third booke, declaring by examples out of auncient councels, fathers, and later writers, that it is time to beware of M. Jewel*. Still failing to provoke any response, in 1567 Rastell published one more

controversial work, *A briefe shew of the false wares packt together in the named, apology of the Churche of England*, supporting Harding's *Confutation* (1565) of Jewel's *An Apologie, or, Answere in Defence of the Churche of Englande* (1564). Rastell's final effort too was disregarded by subsequent controversialists; not until 1579 was any notice taken of him, when William Fulke published 'A refutation of Maister John Rastels confutation', one part of a book bracketing answers to three Catholic writers. Fulke cites yet another work by Rastell, 'Rastels returne of untruths', which (Fulke says) was 'answered by M. Jewell', although neither book is extant or mentioned anywhere else.

Ordained a priest in 1566 Rastell later left the Spanish Netherlands for Rome, entering the Society of Jesus on 4 April 1568, three weeks after his younger brother Edward had also become a Jesuit novice there. Both brothers were posted to Bavaria in 1569, John to assist Peter Canisius at Dillingen in writing his book against the Magdeburg Centurists. Rastell served also at Augsburg and Halle; he was appointed vice-rector at Ingolstadt before May 1576 and died there on 5 June 1577.   DENNIS FLYNN

Sources T. M. McCoog, ed., *Monumenta Angliae*, 2: *English and Welsh Jesuits, catalogues, 1630–1640* (1992) · P. Milward, *Religious controversies of the Elizabethan age* (1977) · Foster, *Alum. Oxon.* · W. Fulke, *D. Heskins, D. Sanders, and M. Rastel, accounted (among their faction) three pillers and archpatriarches of the popish synagogue* (1579) · O. Braunsberger, *Beati Petri Canisii, Societatis Jesu, epistulae et acta*, 8 vols. (1896–1923), vols. 6–7 · T. H. Clancy, 'The first generation of Jesuits', *Archivum Historicum Societatis Iesu*, 57 (1988), 137–62 · *VCH Gloucestershire* · A. F. Leach, *A history of Winchester College* (1899) · Wood, *Ath. Oxon.*, new edn, 1.100

Rastell, William (1508–1565), printer and legal writer, was born in Coventry, a younger son of the printer and adventurer John *Rastell (c.1475–1536) and Elizabeth (1482–1537), sister of Sir Thomas *More. According to Wood, he went to Oxford University in 1525, aged about seventeen, though this seems unlikely since he was already working in his father's printing business. Rastell became a prominent member of Thomas More's circle. He set up his own press in 1529, and was More's principal publisher, venturing also into drama, for instance with John Heywood's *The Play of Love*. His main contribution as a law printer was the first edition of the register of writs (*Registrum omnium brevium*) in 1531; and he produced in 1534 an omnibus student handbook combining, in small print, the *Natura brevium*, the old and new tenures, the book for justices of the peace, *Novae narrationes*, *Returna brevium*, and *Carta feodi*, described in the preface as 'compacte into one volume, ryght studyously corrected'.

Rastell ceased printing in 1534, having by then turned to legal studies. Admitted to Lincoln's Inn in 1532, no doubt with More's support, he was called to the bar in 1539 and to the bench of the inn in 1546. He gave his first reading in the autumn of 1547 on the statute *Quia emptores* (1290). Soon after being elected as treasurer of the inn, in 1549, he quit the country on 21 December for religious reasons and remained in Louvain until the accession of Mary I. While in Louvain, in July 1553, his young wife, Winifred, the daughter of Sir Thomas More's adopted daughter, Mary Giggs, and the physician John *Clement, whom he had married in 1544, died of a fever. Rastell may have spent part of his time in exile composing the table to Fitzherbert's *Natura brevium*, which was included in the new edition of 1553 and all subsequent editions.

Rastell returned to England in 1553, and served for three years in parliament as member for Hindon, Ripon, and Canterbury respectively. In 1555, patronized by Cardinal Pole, he was created a serjeant-at-law, and the following year became standing counsel to the city of Canterbury. The Canterbury connection was William Roper, a fellow bencher of Lincoln's Inn, and his second patron as a serjeant, who was the husband of Sir Thomas More's daughter Margaret. According to Plowden, Rastell had a home in Kent. During the 1550s Rastell completed an edition of More's collected English works, which was published in 1557, with a dedication to the queen. It is a valuable resource, including material that would otherwise have been lost.

Rastell's appointment as a justice of the queen's bench on 27 October 1558, three weeks before the queen's death, was renewed the following month by Elizabeth I, but he was unable to reconcile himself to the new religious settlement and on 3 January 1562 he again fled to Louvain. An inventory of the books seized from his study in Serjeants' Inn included a selection of classical authors. Rastell lived in Louvain until his death on 27 August 1565, when he was buried in the church of St Pierre beside his wife, Winifred. During this second exile Rastell is said to have written a life of More. Only a fragment of it, mostly concerning John Fisher, has survived for certain; though a Latin account of More's condemnation ('Ordo condemnationis Mori') has also been attributed to him. Rastell had no children, and by his will (registered in Antwerp) left his property in North Mimms, Hertfordshire, and his gold locket with More's portrait, to his nephew, the Jesuit Ellis *Heywood.

Rastell made two significant contributions to legal literature, both of which were developments of his interest in reference materials which began when he was printing law books in his youth. Perhaps inspired by his father's *Magnum abbreviamentum statutorum Anglie* (1528), William Rastell published in 1557 a more ambitious *Collection of All the Statutes*, containing texts of all the public legislation still in force, abridged under alphabetical headings, with tables and catchwords. As in the 1528 abridgment, he left the old statutes in their original language, 'for feare of misse interpretation'. The *Collection* was such a valuable reference tool that it enjoyed an enormous success, and was reprinted at the end of almost every session of parliament until the 1620s, when it was overtaken by Pulton and the precursors of the *Statutes at Large*. Rastell's other compilation, the *Colleccion of Entrees*, was the best source of precedents of pleading and court-forms printed in the sixteenth century. It combined precedents from the manuscript collections of his grandfather Sir John *More (d. 1530), of Edward Stubbe (d. 1533), chief protonotary of the common pleas, whose son married Rastell's niece, and of John Lucas (d. 1525), secondary of the king's bench

under William Roper, adding a few of his own. The book was compiled in Louvain ('out of England, and lacking conference with learned men'), where the preface was written on 28 March 1564, and was published posthumously in 1566, with new editions in 1574, 1596, and 1670. Rastell also published a chronological *Table* of the monarchs of England (1558), reprinted several times down to the reign of Charles I.   J. H. BAKER

Sources HoP, *Commons, 1509–58*, 3.179–80 • A. W. Reed, 'The editor of Sir Thomas More's English works: William Rastell', *The Library*, 4th ser., 4 (1923–4), 25–49 • H. J. Graham, 'The Rastells and the printed English law books of the Renaissance', *Law Library Journal*, 47 (1954), 6–25 • J. H. Baker, 'The books of the common law', *The book in Britain*, 3 (1400–1557), ed. L. Hellinga and J. B. Trapp (1999), 411–32 • Baker, *Serjeants*, 170, 434, 533 • Wood, *Ath. Oxon.*, new edn, 1.343–5 • *Les commentaries, ou, Les reportes de Edmunde Plowden* (1571), fol. 164 • Sainty, *Judges*, 30 • J. H. Beale, *A bibliography of early English law books* (1926) • J. D. Cowley, *A bibliography of abridgments, digests, dictionaries and indexes of English law to the year 1800* (1932) • H. de Vocht, *Acta Thomae Mori* (1947) • Ro: Ba:, *The lyfe of Syr Thomas More, sometymes lord chancellor of England*, ed. E. V. Hitchcock and P. E. Hallett, EETS, 222 (1950), 219–52 • *Law Magazine*, 31 (1844), 57–60 [inventory of Rastell's goods, 1562]

Rastrick, John (1650–1727), Presbyterian minister, son of John Rastrige (*bap.* 1616?) and his wife, Afling, was born on 26 March 1650 at Heckington, Lincolnshire, where he was baptized the following day. His father was a yeoman and fellmonger. Rastrick was educated at Trinity College, Cambridge, where he matriculated on 5 June 1667, graduated BA in 1671, and proceeded MA in 1674. In 1672 he was curate at Wyberton, Lincolnshire. Ordained priest on 25 May 1673, he became in 1674 the conscientious vicar of Kirton, near Boston, Lincolnshire, where he showed himself a clergyman of puritan stamp. The parish, which included Kirton Holme and Skeldyke, was 'four to five Miles in Length', and the congregation 'large'; thus he felt 'a very sensible Concern' (Rastrick, *Account*, 3). Fearful of profaning the sacraments, he would not baptize illegitimate children until their parents demonstrated repentance; not all did so. Likewise he withheld communion from persons manifestly unprepared.

Eventually inquiries into Rastrick's practices led to his appearance, in April 1687, before the ecclesiastical court at Lincoln, charged with several irregularities, including not always wearing a surplice when required, and refusal to baptize. The court, however, disconcerted that day by James II's declaration of indulgence, required only a written defence forthwith; Rastrick supplied one, and heard no more. Nevertheless, uneasy with conformity, later that year, on 27 November, he took advantage of the declaration to resign his incumbency, intending to resume office in the church should its long-discontinued protestantization recommence. He preached as a nonconformist from February 1688. He recorded that 'The sober Dissenters' of Spalding invited him to become minister there, to counter 'the Quakers and Arminianiz'd Anabaptists ... [who] grew so much there they were like to carry all before them'; and he added that he had seen his role as to withstand this 'Sectarian Spirit': 'For were it not better to keep the people in a posture of Readiness to return to the Communion of the Church of England whensoever Providence should by a Reformation make way for it' (BL, Rastrick, *Account*, 1705, 38, marginalia). For himself, the failure of the comprehension schemes of William III's ecclesiastical commission was to make the chances of such a return seem hopeless. Rastrick ministered at Spalding for nine years from Lady day 1688, and then at Rotherham. From 1701 until his death he was Presbyterian pastor at Spinner Lane, King's Lynn, Norfolk, initially as colleague to Anthony Williamson. In the account of his nonconformity, which he wrote at the request of Edmund Calamy, first published in 1705, Rastrick stressed how he had 'a high Value, Honour and Reverence for able worthy Men of either Way', conformist or dissenter:

> Tho' I exceedingly disgusted some of the Dissenters thereby, as I had done some on the Church side before. So that I often thought and said, (as the state of things is in *England*) that I was neither fit for Church nor Meeting. But who can help it? (Rastrick, *Account*, 37)

Of the numerous children of Rastrick's marriages, only those who survived to be mentioned in his or his third wife's last wills (1725 and 1733 respectively) are listed here. Rastrick married on 25 June 1672 at Wyberton, where he was curate, Jane Wilson (d. 1684): their daughter Elizabeth became the wife of Edmund Burton of Wisbech (Norfolk RO, will of John Rastrick, 1725); the Rastricks' sons were John, a 'Stocking-weaver', 'now or late in Carolina' (ibid.), and Samuel, a London silk-dyer (ibid.). 'A narrative, or, An historicall account of the most materiall passages in the life of John Rastrick' (Huntington Library, HM 6131) portrays Rastrick's marriage to Jane and the depression from which she suffered. He married Mary Harrison (d. 1687×92), a widow, on 26 March 1685. On 1 September 1692 at Moulton, near Spalding, he married Elizabeth Horn (d. 1740), whose will shows she was a cousin and legatee of Lynn grammar school's distinguished master John Horn or Horne, son of the Arminian founder of Lynn's Presbyterian interest, John Horne (1614–1676). Their children included daughters and son, William (d. 1752), the Lynn preacher and savant (Norfolk RO, will of John Rastrick, 1725; will of Elizabeth Rastrick, 1733).

Rastrick was moderate and eirenic, a figure in the Baxterian tradition. At Kirton he redeemed, and restored to their owners, goods distrained in persecution from earnest Baptists. Through preaching during a vacancy in 1699 at Mill Hill Chapel, Leeds, he met the antiquary Ralph Thoresby, who noted that in religious discussions Rastrick stressed only 'the essentials of religion, wherein all are agreed' (*Diary*, 1.332). In 1714 Rastrick enunciated a middle way belief that two ostensibly opposed doctrines, namely of special election and of general grace available to all, must be held simultaneously (Rastrick, *Sermon*, 68). Yet, at Lynn, he experienced hostility. His congregation once included a party that angrily rejected the discipline he had carefully explained, and locked him out of the chapel (ibid., iv). A continuing hyper-Calvinistic faction maintained that the elect, sure of salvation, need not keep God's moral laws. About 1720 Rastrick digested his teaching, given at Lynn and elsewhere, against this modish antinomianism into a book-length manuscript, 'Plain and easy principles of Christian religion and obedience'. Acquired by William Richards (1749–1818), whose *History of Lynn* (1812) describes it (2.1058–62), it disappeared after Richards's executors ignored their duty to send the latter's manuscripts to Brown University, Rhode Island. Its appendix treated of a sub-Athanasian Christology apparently like that of James Peirce (1674?–1726), which Rastrick had come to favour after studies that the Salters' Hall clash over the Trinity (1719) had prompted him to make. The same appendix contained his theory concerning comets (which resembled that of Cotton Mather); these he considered former worlds, ablaze through divine judgment, their impenitent populations having rejected their respective saviours—Christ, in Rastrick's belief, was earth's saviour only. Rastrick's ode 'The Dissolution' portrays deserted earth's consumption by eschatological fire. Richards's recension in the *Gentleman's Magazine* (1st ser., 59, 1789, 1033–4) seems full; the version in his *History of Lynn* (2.1065–6) omits six lines; John Evans's in *Memoirs of … William Richards* (1819, 160–63), again full, is faulty, but he preserves another poem (p. 163). Other works Rastrick left in manuscript have been lost.

Indubitably Rastrick's mind was lively and cultivated. His will mentions his books, manuscripts, mathematical instruments, telescopes, double barometer, and 'picture done by Deconing' (De Koninck?)—he collected pictures. His intelligence, like his goodness, impressed Ralph Thoresby, to whom he sent archaeological information, coins, and astroites. His letter to Hans Sloane about the discovery of Roman coins at Fleet, near Spalding, a communication echoed in Edmund Gibson's later editions (1722, 1772) of William Camden's *Britannia*, appeared anonymously in the Royal Society's *Philosophical Transactions* (23, 1702, 1156–8); the same volume (pp. 1158–60) carried Thoresby's letter quoting, still unattributed, Rastrick's account of discoveries at Spalding (later amended by Thoresby, 32, 1723, 344–6).

William Rastrick's holograph *Index* (1734) records that John Rastrick died on 18 August 1727, aged seventy-seven (probably at his home in Spinner Lane, King's Lynn). He was buried on 21 August in Lynn's medieval St Nicholas's Chapel.   J. A. ODDY

Sources W. Richards, *The history of Lynn*, 2 vols. (1812), vol. 2 · Venn, *Alum. Cant.* · J. Rastrick, *An account of the nonconformity of John Rastrick* (1705) · J. Rastrick, marginalia in J. Rastrick, *An account of the nonconformity of John Rastrick* (1705), BL · J. Rastrick, *A sermon preach'd at the ordination of Mr Samuel Savage* (1714) · will, Norfolk RO, 82 Kirke · will, Norfolk RO, 289 Goats [Elizabeth Rastrick] · parish register, Heckington, St Andrew, 27 March 1650, Lincs. Arch. [baptism] · parish register, Moulton, All Saints', Lincs. Arch., 1 Sept 1642 [marriage] · D. H. Atkinson, *Ralph Thoresby, the topographer, his town and times*, 2 vols. (1885), 1.418–19 · *The diary of Ralph Thoresby*, ed. J. Hunter, 2 vols. (1830), 1.331–2 · J. Rastrick, three letters to Will Steevens, DWL, MS 24. 115, fols. 44–6 · W. Rastrick, 'Index eorum theologorum', 1734, King's Lynn Central Library · A. Gordon, ed., *Freedom after ejection: a review (1690–1692) of presbyterian and congregational nonconformity in England and Wales* (1917), 337 · 'Rastrick genealogy', King's Lynn Central Library · parish register, Wyberton, Lincs. Arch., 25 June 1672 [marriage] · parish register, Skirbeck, Lincs. Arch. [marriage], 26 March 1685 · 'A narrative, or, An historicall account of the most materiall passages in the life of John Rastrick', Hunt. L., HM 6131

Archives DWL, letters to Mr Will Steevens, Factor at Queen-Hithe, London: 14 Dec 1721, 1 Aug 1724, 21 July 1725, MSS 24.115, fols. 44–6 | DWL, letters to Mr Will Steevens, MSS 24.115, fols. 44–6

Wealth at death owned land, library, scientific instruments, and dwelling house; less than £30 p.a. income: will, Norfolk RO, Norwich, 82 Kirke; DWL, MS 24.115, fol. 46

Rastrick, John Urpeth (1780–1856), civil engineer, was born at Morpeth, Northumberland, on 26 January 1780, the eldest son of John Rastrick, engineer, mill wright, and pump and patent churn maker. At the age of fifteen he was apprenticed to his father, but about 1801 he entered the Ketley ironworks in Shropshire to gain experience in the use of cast iron for machinery. He remained there for approximately seven years before joining in partnership with John Hazeldine of Bridgnorth, to establish a mechanical engineering business. Rastrick took special charge of the iron foundry. During the partnership he continued to practise independently as a civil engineer. In 1814 he took out a patent for a steam engine (no. 3799), and soon engaged in experiments on traction for railways. In 1815–16 he built a cast-iron bridge, with 112 foot span, over the Wye at Chepstow. On the death of Hazeldine, about 1817, Rastrick became the managing partner in the firm of Bradley, Foster, Rastrick & Co., ironfounders and manufacturers of machinery at Stourbridge, Worcestershire. Rastrick himself took the principal engineering part in the design and construction of rolling mills, steam engines, and other large works. At this time he designed ironworks at Chillington, near Wolverhampton, and at Shut End, near Stourbridge.

In January 1825 Rastrick was sufficiently well known as an engineer to be engaged by the promoters of the Liverpool and Manchester Railway, along with George Stephenson and others, to visit collieries in the north of England, and report on their tramroads, and engines both locomotive and stationary. In the following April he was the first witness called before the parliamentary committee in support of the railway company, which was opposed by the canal companies. From that time onwards Rastrick was employed to support, in parliament, a large portion of the principal railway lines in the United Kingdom. In 1826 and 1827 he constructed a line about 16 miles long between Stratford upon Avon and Moreton in Marsh, the first line laid with Birkenshaw's patent wrought-iron rails. On 2 June 1829 he completed and opened the Shutt End Colliery Railway from Kingswinford to the Staffordshire and Worcestershire Canal, working it with a locomotive engine built under his own superintendence. This engine had three flues in the boiler, and, in economy, speed, and accuracy of workmanship, excelled any engine previously made.

Rastrick, as a manufacturer of locomotive engines himself (the most notable being the *Stourbridge Lion* shipped to New York in August 1829), played an important part in stimulating uncertainty among the directors of the Liverpool and Manchester Railway as to their choice of motive power. Until the late 1820s steam locomotives had been employed on short colliery lines, except for the Stockton and Darlington Railway, which opened in 1825. That company had experienced substantial problems with locomotive traction, and although they had been largely resolved by 1829, they were sufficient to give pause for thought on the part of a railway, which envisaged substantial light freight traffic. In November 1828, therefore, the Liverpool and Manchester directors commissioned Rastrick and his fellow engineer, James Walker of Limehouse, to assess the respective merits and capabilities of 'Fixed Engines and Locomotive Engines'. As part of their brief Rastrick and Walker inspected several operational railways, principally in the north-east of England, paying particular attention to the reliability and efficiency of the differing modes of traction. Their recommendations, submitted to the Liverpool and Manchester directors on 9 March 1829, proved to be inconclusive, both in respect of cost and efficiency. While the capital cost of installing a fixed engine system was relatively high compared with locomotive haulage, running costs would be lower. Steam locomotives may have been the subject of recent design improvements, which held out the prospect of greater efficiency in operation, but the existing technology of fixed engines would ensure safer and more reliable working of the line. Confronted by these qualifications, and prompted by those board members favourably disposed towards locomotives, the directors decided to offer a premium of £500 'for a Locomotive Engine, which shall be a decided improvement on those now in use, as respects the consumption of smoke, increased speed, adequate power, and moderate weight' (Carlson, 214). The resulting Rainhill trials were held early in October 1829. Rastrick was appointed as one of the judges, and on 6 October he and his colleagues decided in favour of George Stephenson's *Rocket*.

In 1830 Rastrick worked with Stephenson in surveying the line from Birmingham to join the Liverpool and Manchester Railway, afterwards called the Grand Junction. He also marked out a line from Manchester to Crewe, thereby paving the way for the Manchester and Cheshire Junction Railway project, which was brought forward in 1835, with Rastrick as the engineer. This line was opposed by a competing project called the South Union Railway, but after two years of parliamentary inquiry, the act was obtained for the original line. With Sir John Rennie, in 1837, Rastrick carried the direct Brighton line against several competing projects. Towards the close of that year he was appointed superintendent of the line, with responsibility for the Shoreham branch, and also for the heavy works, comprising the Merstham, Balcombe, and Clayton tunnels, and the Ouse Viaduct of thirty-seven arches at an elevation of 100 feet. These works were completed by the autumn of 1840. Rastrick later constructed extensions, which eventually were to form the series of lines known as the London, Brighton, and South Coast Railway.

Possessing a very resolute character, Rastrick was always a shrewd and cool witness before parliamentary committees. He was a member of the Institution of Civil Engineers from 1827, and a fellow of the Royal Society from 1837. With James Walker he published in 1829 *Report on the Comparative Merits of Locomotive and Fixed Engines as a Moving Power*. He retired from active work in 1847, and died at his residence, Sayes Court, near Chertsey, Surrey, on 1 November 1856; he was buried in the new cemetery at Brighton. Nothing is known about his wife, but a son, Henry, died at Woking on 1 November 1893.

G. C. BOASE, *rev.* M. W. KIRBY

Sources C. F. D. Marshall, *A history of railway locomotives down to the end of the year 1830* (1953) · R. E. Carlson, *The Liverpool and Manchester railway project, 1821–1823* (1969) · L. T. C. Rolt, *George and Robert Stephenson: the railway revolution* (1960) · *PICE*, 16 (1856–7), 128–33 · d. cert.
Archives LUL, corresp., diaries, notebooks, and papers · Shrops. RRC, Bridgnorth diary · UCL | Glamorgan RO, Cardiff, letters to Dowlais Iron Co. · LUL, letters of Stourbridge Iron Works · PRO, volume of drawings

Rastrick, William (*bap.* **1697**, *d.* **1752**), Presbyterian preacher, was baptized on 14 March 1697 at Spalding, Lincolnshire, a son of John *Rastrick (1650–1727), then a nonconformist minister in Rotherham, and his third wife, Elizabeth Horn (*d.* 1740). He was probably educated by his father, on whose death he succeeded as minister to King's Lynn's divided Presbyterian congregation, some of whom were combatively hyper-Calvinist. By disposition retiring, he eschewed ordination, although this meant exchanging, at communion times, with the minister at Wisbech, 13 miles away. Eventually the hyper-Calvinists seceded from his congregation, reportedly in 1744 to form an independent body that about 1777, after his death, became a Particular Baptist church, with William Richards (1749–1818) as minister. Richards, who arrived in Lynn in 1776, when William Rastrick's immediate successor, Anthony Mayhew, was in post, was friendly with Mayhew's own successor and son-in-law, William Warner, and portrays Rastrick sympathetically in his *History of Lynn* (1812). His character, says Richards, was virtuous, his interests scholarly; and because of his local pre-eminence in knowledge, 'especially the mathematics', 'his superior skill and judgement would accordingly be resorted to on such difficult occasions as required extraordinary scientific expertness or accuracy' (W. Richards, 2.1067).

By continuing a preacher, Rastrick had fulfilled the conditions of his father's complex will and so inherited John Rastrick's mathematical instruments, telescopes, and library. He sent the Royal Society's vice-president, Martin Folkes, who had local connections, his Latin report of displays during 1723–7 of the aurora borealis; this, 'Registrum observationum de lumine boreali per quadriennium', appeared in the *Philosophical Transactions*, 34 (1727), 255–6. Rastrick's plan of Lynn, *Ichnographia burgi perantiqui Lennae regis in agro Norfolciensi accurate delineata*, published in 1725 and dedicated to Sir Robert Walpole, Lynn's MP, is impressive and important. It includes his prospect of Lynn from the west and his drawings of Henry Bell's custom house (1685) and market cross (1710). 'Index eorum theologorum aliorumque … alphabetico ordine ac

secundum gradus suos dispositus', Rastrick's manuscript index of ejected ministers of 1662, used material from Edmund Calamy's *Account* of them, Calamy's *Continuation of the Account*, and from the *valor ecclesiasticus* (1535), and was employed in *The Nonconformist's Memorial* of Samuel Palmer, who had access to the copy Rastrick had presented to Calamy. A holograph of the 'Index', dated 1734, is in Lynn's central library.

Apparently never married, Rastrick lived in his father's house in Spinner Lane. He died in early August 1752, and was buried on 9 August in Lynn's St Nicholas's Chapel.

J. A. ODDY

Sources W. Richards, *History of Lynn*, 2 vols. (1812) · *DNB* · will, 1727, Norfolk RO, 82 Kirke (MF 96) [John Rastrick] · *Calamy rev.* · *The nonconformist's memorial … originally written by … Edmund Calamy*, ed. S. Palmer, [3rd edn], 1 (1802), preface · H. J. Hillen, *History of King's Lynn*, 2 vols. (1907) · parish register, St Nicholas's, King's Lynn, 23 Nov 1740 [burial; Elizabeth Rastrick] · parish register, St Nicholas's, King's Lynn, 9 Aug 1752 [burial] · P. Richards, *King's Lynn* (1990), 15, 42 · *IGI* · A. Gordon, ed., *Freedom after ejection: a review (1690–1692) of presbyterian and congregational nonconformity in England and Wales* (1917), 337 · baptismal register, St Mary and St Nicholas, Spalding
Archives King's Lynn Central Library, Norfolk, holograph MS of Rastrick's 'Index' | DWL, Samuel Say MSS, holograph letters · Lincs. Arch., holograph letters to Edmund Calamy, 2 Cragg 4/7, fols. 10–12, 13

Rasyn, Pernell of (*fl.* 1350). *See under* Women medical practitioners in England (*act. c.*1200–*c.*1475).

Ratcliffe, Henry (1808–1877), actuary and friendly society administrator, was born at Tyldesley, Lancashire, on 4 November 1808. Nothing is known about his origins, except that he had one brother. Henry spent his whole career with one friendly society, the Manchester Unity of Oddfellows, whose Chowbent division he joined in 1833. Ratcliffe became provincial grandmaster in 1836, and by 1848 was corresponding secretary of the whole order. He displayed great administrative ability, and played a key role in establishing the Manchester Unity, one of the largest friendly societies, on a sound actuarial basis. His most important contribution stemmed from his work on vital statistics, at the time a comparatively new study.

In 1850 Ratcliffe brought out his *Observations of the Rate of Mortality and Sickness Existing among Friendly Societies*, which at once became a standard authority. The monetary tables which were appended were thenceforth known as the Ratcliffe tables, and the data dealing with thirty-one trades proved of permanent value. They became the guiding light of every other order that adopted financial reforms. In 1852 Ratcliffe issued a supplement, giving further financial details, and recommending a quinquennial valuation of the assets and liabilities of all friendly societies—a suggestion which was adopted by government in 1870, when it put the activities of friendly societies on a statutory basis.

In 1862 Ratcliffe republished his actuarial tables, basing them on far wider calculations. In 1871 he undertook a special valuation of his own society. He was nominated a public valuer under the Friendly Societies Act of 1870. Ratcliffe, who was a widower and a congregationalist, died at the society's offices in Manchester on 25 May 1877. He was survived by a son, John, and was buried at Brooklands cemetery, near Sale, where the Manchester Unity erected a monument to his memory.

[ANON.], rev. ROBERT BROWN

Sources J. F. Wilkinson, *Mutual thrift* (1891) · J. F. Wilkinson, *The friendly society movement* (1886) · J. Spry, *The history of odd-fellowship* (1867) · C. Walford, *The insurance cyclopaedia*, 4 (1876) · Boase, *Mod. Eng. biog.* · d. cert. · *CGPLA Eng. & Wales* (1877)
Wealth at death £5000: resworn administration, Jan 1878, *CGPLA Eng. & Wales* (1877)

Ratcliffe [*née* Brerewood], **Jane** (*d.* 1638), exemplar of godly life, was the daughter of John Brerewood (*c.*1561–1599), citizen and skinner of Chester, and his wife, Mary Parrey (*d.* 1592), of Esciviock, Nanarth, Flintshire; Sir Robert *Brerewood (1588–1654) was her brother and Edward *Brerewood, the puritan professor of Gresham College, was her uncle. She married as his second wife a brewer, John Ratcliffe (*d.* 1633), whose first wife died in 1602 and who was twice mayor of Chester and sometime MP for the town. She took up a devoutly godly way of life under the influence of the Cheshire minister Nicholas Byfield—a client of her family—in the aftermath of her bereavement at the death at birth of her first child, possibly about 1610. Her spiritual life was memorialized after her own death by the Chester minister John Ley, another client of the Ratcliffes, in a funeral sermon published in London in 1640.

Following the conventions of puritan biography Ley offered 'some portraiture of her manifold graces' of entirely unextraordinary banality (Lake, 145). Jane Ratcliffe was renowned for her devotion to prayer and sermon, to which she brought a lively and acute intelligence. Her personal piety was placed firmly and obediently within the context of formal structures of the established church. Having been under threat of suspension from the sacrament for a while, she happily followed prescribed forms of public worship once she had satisfied herself, in counsel with the godly, that it was no sin to do so, setting aside her scruples about receiving the Lord's supper on her knees. She was stoical in the face of earthly challenges, temptations, and sufferings. She eschewed vanity, gossip, and shrewish pride, embracing humility, introspective soul-searching, and the mutual support of godly society. She showed at all times a loving obedience to her husband. Yet she also made the maximum use of that loophole in the stone wall of contemporary patriarchalism permitted by puritan ministers to the wives of men who were not as 'painful' as they were in their profession of the faith.

On the strength of Ley's efforts Jane Ratcliffe has been held up as offering 'a glimpse, if no more, of the ways in which women could and did take up and use a puritan style of godliness for their own, at least partially, emancipatory purposes' (Lake, 161). It is equally true that little or nothing would have been known about her spiritual life had it not served a purpose, at least partly polemical, for moderate puritans like Ley, seeking a means of reply to their Laudian critics, to publicize the moderation and conformability of insignificant figures like her. 'Mrs Ratcliffe

provided living (or only recently dead) proof that … an ardent but moderate puritan zeal was entirely compatible with a full and loyal membership of the national church' (ibid., 146). Ley also took the opportunity to reply to more radical puritans by denying the rumours that Mrs Ratcliffe regretted her decision to kneel to receive the sacrament, making it clear that, in his opinion, conformity in the matter did not compromise godly conviction. In reality, it was not the life so much as the exemplar of Jane Ratcliffe which was recruited to the task of edifying the living, offering an opportunity for an exhortation to godliness, and a confirmation of the godly experience. It also allowed her biographer to affirm his own place in the public sphere in an appealing, possibly even a profitable way. He certainly took the opportunity to dedicate his pamphlet to two of the most important godly patrons of the age, Brilliana, Lady Harley, and Alice, Lady Lucy, 'that I may professe mine owne gratitude, whereto your favours have much engaged mee' (Ley, foreword, sig. A3*v*).

The retrievable details of Mrs Ratcliffe's life, even such as can be gleaned from Ley's biography, are few and slight. Evidently she managed the family brewing business after her husband's death (with perhaps a predictable aversion to profit, and stoic indifference to the accidents and contingencies of the market place). She and Alderman Ratcliffe had at least two children who reached adulthood: John Ratcliffe joined the Long Parliament as MP for Chester in 1646, and a daughter married a citizen of London. Mistress Ratcliffe died in London on 17 August 1638 while visiting her daughter, and was buried there on 21 August.

SEAN KELSEY

Sources J. Ley, *A patterne of pietie, or, The religious life and death of that grave and gracious matron, Mrs. Jane Ratcliffe* (1640) · *Visitation of Cheshire, 1613*, Harleian Society, 59 · P. Lake, 'Feminine piety and personal potency: the "emancipation" of Mrs Jane Ratcliffe', *The Seventeenth Century*, 2 (1987), 143–65 · *Wills proved at Chester*, Lancashire and Cheshire RS, 4 (1881), 181

Ratcliffe [Radcliffe], **John, sixth Baron Fitzwalter** (1452–1496), rebel, of Attleborough, Norfolk, was nine years old when his father, John, was killed on 28 March 1461, the day before the battle of Towton. At three his mother, Elizabeth *Fitzwalter (1430–*c.*1485) [*see under* Fitzwalter family (*per. c.*1200–*c.*1500)], had been acquired as ward by his grandfather to secure the ennoblement of the Ratcliffes via the Fitzwalter barony. Although, in 1467, Lady Fitzwalter married John Dynham, who ultimately became Henry VII's lord treasurer, her first husband's death deprived the family of the status accruing from a successful baronial career. It is possible that, in the 1460s, Ratcliffe was brought up partly in Devon; but his first public duty was as JP in Norfolk during Henry VI's government of 1470–71.

The coincidence from which Ratcliffe's career sprang happened in Calais in 1476. He may already have been serving in Calais, for among Calais's officers was his uncle Robert. John led a retinue to fight in France in 1475, and, in that year or early 1476, married Margaret, the daughter of the lieutenant of Guînes Castle, Sir Richard Whetehill. The couple returned to England in the summer of 1476.

Through family friendship with the Pastons, Ratcliffe supplied William, Lord Hastings, lieutenant of Calais, with a cook, a talented man who had worked for both himself and his father-in-law. Instantly Ratcliffe was JP and MP for Norfolk, and afterwards assuredly powerful in Norfolk and East Anglia. Hastings's execution in 1483 ended his sense of secure political place. Ratcliffe quickly accommodated himself with the new king. On 6 July, three weeks after Hastings's death, he was a sewer (server of dishes) at Richard III's coronation, and by the end of the year associated with Richard's comptroller of the household. Yet he may have been dabbling treasonably with Henry Tudor. On Henry's accession Ratcliffe was showered with offices: steward and receiver of the honour of Richmond in Norfolk; steward of the duchy of Lancaster in Norfolk, Suffolk, and Cambridge; feodary in Norfolk and Suffolk; chief justice and warden of forests south of the Trent and then of all forests. Perhaps his stewardship of the household was reward for his commitment to Tudor before Bosworth; a commitment similar to his promise to Warbeck in 1493.

From 1485 to 1492 Fitzwalter played a key role in East Anglia; but almost all records show him in conflict with his neighbours: in the winter of 1484-5 he quarrelled with Sir Robert Chamberlain; as steward of the duchy of Lancaster he reprimanded the Pastons. In politics, and personally, he was duplicitous. In October 1485 he charged the servants of Elizabeth, countess of Surrey, with making treasonable remarks about the new king. Fitzwalter had already promised the earl of Oxford and Elizabeth that he would be a good lord to her and her imprisoned husband, Thomas Howard. The countess besought Fitzwalter's Paston friends to remind him of his promise, and expressed amazement at his behaviour; he was a near relation as well as neighbour. Two years later similarly disingenuous behaviour occurred before the battle of East Stoke. In April 1487 Fitzwalter was empowered to repair beacons and array troops in Norfolk and Essex; but in May the earl of Oxford was given wide-ranging powers to raise troops in East Anglia. Fitzwalter summoned several important gentry to Attleborough and told them that Oxford's commission was illegal, and that as steward of the household he had precedence: they should not march with Oxford. John Paston (he lied) was considering not marching with Oxford, and was in touch with the rebel Francis, Lord Lovell. Fitzwalter's lack of wealth may have contributed to his recklessness. In the late 1480s he forcibly took Normans Manor, Norfolk, from William Doget and his wife. When in 1492 he lost the case arising in the king's council, he relaunched it in the court of common pleas. This provoked Henry VII's angry intervention in Star Chamber. Fitzwalter's political ambition was doomed. The earl of Surrey had re-entered national politics and was about to be restored in East Anglia as equal in power with Oxford. Although Fitzwalter was still in local government between 1488 and 1491, he lost his stewardship of the duchy, and in 1490 he was judged to be in contempt of the king's council in Doget's case. He remained

on the bench in Essex until 1495; elsewhere he had lost his positions in the administration of East Anglia.

This failing career coincided with the Perkin Warbeck conspiracy. On 12 and 14 January 1493 Fitzwalter, with Sir Robert Clifford, decided to offer support to Margaret of Burgundy. Fitzwalter allegedly promised fifty men-at-arms to fight for Warbeck, wherever he landed. Members of Fitzwalter's family may have been drawn into the conspiracy: his uncle Robert, former porter of Calais, and his steward and cousin Thomas Cressener. He was also said to have sent to Warbeck three men who later took part in his landing at Deal in 1495. Despite maintaining an outward show of loyalty, notably at the creation of the king's son Henry as duke of York in December 1493, Fitzwalter was exposed when Sir Robert Clifford, who had fled to Flanders, returned to England in 1494. Fitzwalter was arrested and delivered to court, on 20 January 1495, by servants of the earl of Oxford. Unlike Sir William Stanley, Henry VII's chamberlain, Fitzwalter was not immediately executed. He was tried, on 23 February 1495, and then transported to Guînes, previously familiar to him and near his Whetehill brother-in-law, then comptroller of Calais. Fitzwalter, however, did not learn his lesson, and in the autumn of 1496 tried to escape from Guînes. By now England and Scotland were at war, with Warbeck as the cause. Fitzwalter's behaviour was not to be tolerated and he was executed that November, either at Guînes or at Calais; he was buried in the December following. The judgment might seem harsh, but it received a sort of vindication three years later, when a last pretender, Ralph Wilford, emerged in Fitzwalter's home territory of East Anglia to trouble the king's peace. IAN ARTHURSON

Sources GEC, *Peerage* · CPR, 1461–1509 · *The Paston letters, AD 1422–1509*, ed. J. Gairdner, new edn, 6 vols. (1904) · N. Davis, ed., *Paston letters and papers of the fifteenth century*, 2 vols. (1971–6) · F. P. Barnard, *Edward IV's French expedition of 1475: the leaders and their badges* (1925); repr. (1975) · W. G. Davis, 'Whetehill of Calais [pt 1]', *New England Historical and Genealogical Register*, 102 (1948), 241–53 · W. G. Davis, 'Whetehill of Calais [pt 2]', *New England Historical and Genealogical Register*, 103 (1949), 5–19 · A. F. Sutton and P. W. Hammond, eds., *The coronation of Richard III: the extant documents* (1983) · R. Virgoe, 'The recovery of the Howards in East Anglia, 1485–1529', *Wealth and power in Tudor England: essays presented to S. T. Bindoff*, ed. E. W. Ives, R. J. Knecht, and J. J. Scarisbrick (1978), 1–20 · T. B. Pugh, 'Henry VII and the English nobility', *The Tudor nobility*, ed. G. W. Bernard (1992), 49–110 · C. G. Bayne and W. H. Dunham, eds., *Select cases in the council of Henry VII*, SeldS, 75 (1958) · J. A. Guy, *The cardinal's court: the impact of Thomas Wolsey in star chamber* (1977) · I. Arthurson, *The Perkin Warbeck conspiracy, 1491–1499* (1994) · B. P. Wolffe, *The crown lands, 1461–1536* (1970), 144 · M. St C. Byrne, ed., *The Lisle letters*, 6 vols. (1981), vol. 4, p. 197 · GEC, *Peerage*, new edn, 5.486–7 · J. C. Wedgwood and A. D. Holt, *History of parliament*, 1: *Biographies of the members of the Commons house, 1439–1509* (1936) · A. H. Thomas and I. D. Thornley, eds., *The great chronicle of London* (1938)

Archives BL, extracts from no longer extant issue book of Henry VII, Add. MS 7099 · PRO, Henry VII issue books, E101, etc. · PRO, king's bench indictment, KB9

Wealth at death £647 9s. 10¼d.—lands yielding this amount: Wolffe, *The crown lands*, 144

Ratcliffe [Sicklemore], **John** (*d.* 1610), mariner and colonist, is a mysterious figure. His family name appears to have been Sicklemore; why he chose to call himself Ratcliffe remains a riddle. His patent abilities as a mariner and his evident willingness to gamble at speculative ventures most likely account for why officials in the Virginia Company of London named him a leader of their colonial enterprise in 1606. He commanded the pinnace *Discovery*, one of the three vessels that bore the original complement of adventurers to Jamestown in 1607, and he held a seat on the resident council of the colony.

Unbeknown to Ratcliffe and the others, the worst drought in more than seven centuries lay upon eastern Virginia in 1607, and it continued well into the 1610s. Arid weather made the usual heat and dryness of summers there intensely more unbearable for the colonists, who had little tolerance for such a climate. Drought also raised the salinity of the James River and the shallow aquifers around Jamestown, and it lessened available stocks of edibles that might be gleaned from the land or the natives. Those environmental conditions give an added poignancy to the accounts of George Percy, Edward Maria Wingfield, and others, which detailed the misery and privation that befell the struggling colony.

Death reduced numbers and dwindling supplies pinched stomachs. Constant bickering bespoke suspicions that Ratcliffe, his council colleagues, and the men all harboured for one another; contention also revealed a failure of leadership, especially that of the president, Wingfield. Ratcliffe soon fell in behind a majority of the resident council, who expelled the sickly, ever wary Wingfield in the summer of 1607 and made Ratcliffe president.

Ratcliffe retained the presidency for about a year. On his watch, the colony survived its first winter and welcomed two additional supplies of settlers and necessaries. Even so there was little cause for cheer because new colonists died off as fast as those they had intended to replace, whereas the colony lacked a means of sustaining itself and bringing profits to the company. Those difficulties were not wholly the fault of Ratcliffe, but a measure of responsibility was surely his, given that his talents for seamanship did not translate readily into skills for leading men on dry land. Indolence and a distrustful nature also got in his way. Like Wingfield before him, Ratcliffe gave too frequent ear to whispers of conspiracies, and, like Wingfield, he turned on the boisterous but effective Captain John Smith, who had helped him rise to his place. His own illness and a severe injury limited his effectiveness too. Such liabilities put an unsteady hand on the colony's tiller and bred continued talk of mutiny.

After the fact, John Smith hinted that mutiny finally brought Ratcliffe down in September 1608, when Smith himself became president of Virginia. Smith's allegation may have enlarged upon reality because councillors held the presidency only for a year, which was just about the length of time Ratcliffe had been in office. Whatever the truth, Ratcliffe, on Smith's orders, sailed for England in December 1608. Smith then warned company officials to keep him there because he was so fractious, but Ratcliffe returned the following August. He was one of the councillors who took charge after a gunpowder accident forced

his enemy Smith back to London in search of a cure for his wound.

Ratcliffe lived into 1610. While he was on a trading expedition a force of natives attacked his party and killed them all. He was buried in Virginia. It was another colonist, Ralph Hamor, who perhaps best summed up Ratcliffe's effect on Virginia: 'Capt: *Ratleife*', he noted, was not 'worthy remembring, but to his dishonor' (Hamor, 7). He may have been married, since one Dorothy Ratcliffe, whose husband had been dead for two years, married George Warburton in 1612. It is, however, unlikely that he was the Ratcliff who served as a captain of horse in the Netherlands and was captured at the battle of Mulheim in 1605, since the latter was back in Dutch pay by 1607.

WARREN M. BILLINGS

Sources *The complete works of Captain John Smith (1580–1631)*, ed. P. L. Barbour, 3 vols. (1986) · P. L. Barbour, ed., *The Jamestown voyages under the first charter, 1606–1609*, 2 vols., Hakluyt Society, 2nd ser., 136–7 (1969) · P. L. Barbour, *The three worlds of Captain John Smith* (1964) · W. M. Billings, *Jamestown and the founding of the nation* (1991) · D. W. Stahle and others, 'The lost colony and Jamestown droughts', *Science*, 280 (1998), 564–7 · R. Hamor, *A true discourse of the present state of Virginia* (1615)

Ratcliffe, John (1707–1776), book collector, was born at Bermondsey on 20 November 1707, the son of Thomas Ratcliffe, a victualler of the parish of St Mary Magdalen, Bermondsey, and his wife, Ann. He was baptized on 7 December at St Mary Magdalen. Little is known of his life, but an account derived mainly from T. F. Dibdin and printed in the *Gentleman's Magazine* in 1812, and later augmented by John Nichols in his *Literary Anecdotes*, claims that Ratcliffe's love of books was kindled by studying the leaves and scraps of books which, as a chandler, he purchased as waste paper, or which were brought into his Bermondsey shop for his use in wrapping cheese. These sources, too, paint a curious picture of him later in life: corpulent, with very thick legs, walking very slowly from his house in East Lane, Rotherhithe, to the Presbyterian chapel in Jamaica Road when Dr Roger Flexman was the minister there, wearing:

> a fine coat, either red or brown, with gold lace buttons, and a fine silk embroidered waistcoat, of scarlet with gold lace, and a large and well-powdered wig. With his hat in one hand and a gold-headed cane in the other, he marched royally along, and not unfrequently followed by a parcel of children, wondering who the stately man could be.

Ratcliffe evidently prospered in his trade; he married (though the identity of his wife is not known) and had two children, who both died young. He found himself able to indulge his passion for books, spending days at a time in the warehouses of booksellers, sending out for food at intervals. In his last thirty years he amassed in his house a formidable collection, which included some very rare items. On Thursday mornings he would show his latest acquisitions to other book and print collectors of the day, such as James West, Anthony Askew, and Topham Beauclerk.

Ratcliffe died early in 1776 and was buried on 3 February

in the great vault of the church of St Andrew by the Wardrobe, in the City of London, which also contained the bodies of his two children. His will, made in 1770, contained elaborate and detailed arrangements for his interment, and probate was granted in the prerogative court of Canterbury five days before his funeral. The will makes clear that he held leasehold property in Shoe Lane, off Fleet Street. His widow was well provided for, as were other relatives and friends—but, curiously, his library was not mentioned. The entire collection was sold by Christies on nine successive evenings, beginning on 27 May 1776. Entitled by the catalogue *Bibliotheca Ratcliffiana* and described as 'the elegant and truly valuable library of John Ratcliffe, Esq ... collected with great judgment and expence during the last thirty years of his life', the library was sold in 1675 lots, many of them comprising up to 100 items. It was particularly strong in the productions of early English printers and in books of the sixteenth century. At least 100 incunables are individually mentioned, including forty-eight Caxtons, twenty of which were acquired by George III. There were also many manuscripts including (lot no. 1674) Ratcliffe's own four-volume catalogue 'of the rare old black letter, and other curious and uncommon books'. Copies of the sale catalogue, with prices, exist in both the British Library and the Bodleian. They show that one of the highest-priced lots (no. 1373), at £9, was the dedication manuscript copy, made for Humfrey, duke of Gloucester, of the English verse translation of Palladius, *Opus agriculturae*, with, fixed to its upper cover, a painted enamel miniature purporting to be a portrait of Duke Humfrey's wife, Jacqueline of Hainault (Bodl. Oxf., MS Duke Humfrey d. 2). Ratcliffe's books, though now scattered, can often be identified by collation and other notes in his hand on the flyleaves.   DAVID VAISEY

Sources Nichols, *Lit. anecdotes*, 3.621–2, 8.456–7 • *GM*, 1st ser., 82/1 (1812), 55, 114 • *N&Q*, 4th ser., 1 (1868), 556 • *Bibliotheca Ratcliffiana: a catalogue of the library of John Ratcliffe* (1776) • W. Y. Fletcher, *English book collectors* (1902), 199–203 • *DNB* • parish register, Bermondsey, St Mary Magdalen, LMA, 7 Dec 1707 [baptism] • parish register, London, St Andrew by the Wardrobe, 3 Feb 1776, GL [burial] • will, PRO, PROB 11/1015, fols. 286v–287v

Ratcliffe, John Ashworth (1902–1987), physicist, was born on 12 December 1902 in Bacup, Lancashire, the elder son (there were no daughters) of Harry Heys Ratcliffe, partner in the stone-quarrying firm of Henry Heys & Co., and his wife, Beatrice Alice, daughter of Richard Ashworth, founder of the firm of Mitchell, Ashworth, Stansfield & Co., felt manufacturers. He attended Giggleswick School, where he acquired a real interest in mathematics and science, and particularly physics. In 1921 he went to Sidney Sussex College, Cambridge, on a scholarship and obtained first classes in both parts of the natural sciences tripos (1923 and 1924).

In June 1924 Ratcliffe started research on radio wave propagation under Edward Appleton. His interest in this subject came through hearing Appleton's lecture course 'Electrical oscillations and radio telegraphy'. In 1927 he was elected a fellow of Sidney Sussex College (honorary fellow, 1962) and appointed a university demonstrator in the Cavendish Laboratory. He was promoted to lecturer (1933) and to reader in physics (1947). He played a major part in the organization of the teaching in the Cavendish. He enjoyed lecturing and had the highest reputation for clarity of presentation. His books—such as *Sun, Earth and Radio* (1970) and *An Introduction to the Ionosphere and magnetosphere* (1972)—and his papers are models of clear exposition and many of his students would say that in the use of English for scientific explanations he surpassed all others.

Ratcliffe became head of a group in the Cavendish Laboratory known as the radio ionosphere research group. Upgoing radio waves can be reflected back to earth by ionized regions of the upper atmosphere, once known as the 'Heaviside layer' but later called the 'ionosphere'. Ratcliffe had helped with experiments by Appleton and M. A. F. Barnett that established the existence of the reflecting layers and his research group was now concerned with studying how the radio waves were reflected, and how the ionized layers were formed. This work continued until 1939.

During the Second World War Ratcliffe was a member of the Air Ministry research establishment, which was later known as the TRE (telecommunications research establishment). At first he was head of a group concerned with a new type of ground radar equipment, called CHL, for detecting low-flying aircraft that could be missed by the existing chain of radar stations. In September 1940 he moved to Petersham, Surrey, and there organized the AA Radio School, whose object was to train scientists to keep the anti-aircraft radars working on the gun sites, particularly those round London. In August 1941 he returned to TRE to become head of a new organization, later known as TRE Development Services, which tackled the problem of taking radar equipment that was new and untried and making it work in the field.

In 1945 Ratcliffe returned to the Cavendish Laboratory, where there were now better facilities. The work of the radio ionosphere group was resumed and expanded. Martin Ryle and some others from TRE joined the group and decided to follow up the discovery of radio emission from the sun, using techniques and skills derived from their work on radar. Thus the radio group divided into two sections, radio ionosphere under Ratcliffe and radio astronomy under Ryle, with Ratcliffe in overall charge. Both sections flourished and became internationally famous. Ratcliffe was elected a fellow of the Royal Society in 1951. It was through him, more than any other person, that the new subject ionospheric physics was launched as a major branch of science.

In 1960 Ratcliffe left Cambridge to take up the posts of director of radio research in the Department of Scientific and Industrial Research, and director of the Radio Research Station at Slough. The move gave him enlarged opportunities. Artificial satellites were then coming into use for studying the upper atmosphere and beyond it. This was part of the new subject of 'space physics'. In April 1965 the name of the station at Slough was changed to the Radio and Space Research Station.

Ratcliffe always carried a heavy load of administration. In Cambridge he served on numerous boards and committees. In 1954–5 he was a member of the council of the Royal Society and he served on several Royal Society committees. He was deeply interested in the advance of radio science as part of electrical engineering, and served on many committees of the Institution of Electrical Engineers, of which he was president in 1966–7. He accepted numerous other similar tasks. He retired in 1966 but remained active in many fields for another ten years. He was appointed OBE in 1947, CBE in 1959, and CB in 1965.

In 1930 Ratcliffe married Nora, daughter of Walter Disley, mill owner and manufacturer of blankets, of Waterfoot, Lancashire. They had two daughters, the younger of whom died in 1965. In 1937 they moved to a newly built house, 193 Huntingdon Road, Cambridge, which remained their home for most of the rest of his life. Nora's health declined and from about 1967 onwards Ratcliffe cared for her devotedly at home. She was moved to hospital in 1975 and died in 1977.

Ratcliffe was about 6 feet tall, with an upright stance and somewhat athletic appearance. He walked briskly and his speech, in conversation and in lecturing, was very clear, with a trace of a Lancashire accent. He had done some cross-country running and played fives and squash. From the age of seventy onwards he often joined groups of old schoolfriends for walking in the hills. He suffered from asthma, which curtailed his activities in later years, and died at home in Cambridge on 25 October 1987.

K. G. BUDDEN, rev.

Sources K. G. Budden, *Memoirs FRS*, 34 (1988), 671–711 · *The Independent* (12 Nov 1987) · *The Times* (28 Oct 1987) · personal knowledge (1996) · private information (1996) · *CGPLA Eng. & Wales* (1988) **Archives** CAC Cam., corresp. and papers | U. Edin. L., corresp. with Sir Edward Appleton **Likenesses** photograph, RS **Wealth at death** £640,336: probate, 17 May 1988, *CGPLA Eng. & Wales*

Ratcliffe, Sir Richard (*d.* 1485), royal councillor, was a younger son of Thomas Ratcliffe, esquire, of the Isle of Derwentwater (Cumberland), and his wife, Margaret, a daughter of Sir Thomas Parr of Kendal. By 1475 Ratcliffe was in the service of Richard, duke of Gloucester, perhaps through the Parr connection—one of his Parr uncles, Thomas, died in the duke's service at Barnet in 1471. Ratcliffe was active on the duke's behalf in co. Durham, and was his constable of Barnard Castle. He was a member of the ducal council by 1477. He served under the duke on the Scottish campaigns of 1480–2, and was knighted by him beside Berwick in 1481 and advanced to banneret in Scotland the following year.

Ratcliffe was one of Gloucester's trusted associates in the events leading up to his seizure of the throne in June 1483. Ratcliffe carried the duke's letters of 10 June requesting military help from the city of York against the queen's affinity, and was present when the northern forces mustered at Pontefract a fortnight later, apparently presiding over the execution of Rivers, Vaughan, and Grey, before accompanying the army south. Richard III made him a knight of his body and he was chosen a knight of the Garter early in the reign. In September 1484 he received a major grant of land (valued at 1000 marks) in the southwest, much of it once held by the Courtenay earls of Devon. He does not, however, appear to have taken on a significant role in the region, his interests remaining primarily northern. In the first year of the reign the prior of Durham commented on 'the great rule that he beareth under the king's grace in our country' (Pollard, 358). Ratcliffe succeeded his uncle, William Parr, as sheriff of Westmorland in August 1484. He was much involved in the negotiations for a truce with Scotland, and on the death of Humphrey, Lord Dacre, in May 1485, succeeded him as the king's deputy lieutenant on the west march. Ratcliffe was one of the king's closest councillors, and after the death of Queen Anne spoke out against the possibility of Richard's marrying his niece, Elizabeth of York, on the grounds that it would alienate the king's northern supporters. His influence over the king is shown by William Collingbourne's famous couplet:

> The Cat, the Rat and Lovell our dog
> Rule all England under the Hog.
> (Horrox, 222)

It was also recognized by William Wainflete, the bishop of Winchester, who made Ratcliffe constable of his castle of Taunton in March 1484.

Ratcliffe fought for Richard III at the battle of Bosworth on 22 August 1485 and was probably, as the Crowland continuator states, killed there. But there was evidently some initial confusion about his fate. The royal proclamation issued immediately after the battle named him among the dead, but the next day Henry VII ordered him to be arrested and brought before him. The government apparently still believed him to be at large on 24 September, when he headed the list of those excluded from pardon, but by then his family knew him to be dead, and already on 20 September the bishop of Dromore had been commissioned to veil his widow. Ratcliffe was attainted in Henry VII's first parliament.

Ratcliffe married Agnes (erroneously called Alice in the commission to veil her), daughter of Henry, Lord Scrope of Bolton, whose first husband, Christopher Boynton of Sedbury in Gilling, near Richmond in the North Riding of Yorkshire, had died in 1479. Agnes was dead by July 1509 when her eldest son from her first marriage, Henry Boynton, received a pardon as her executor. She had two children with Ratcliffe: a daughter, Isabel, who married Roger Lumley, and a son, Richard, who married Margaret Wilberfoss. Richard secured the reversal of his father's attainder in 1495, when he argued that as his father had been a younger son, with two older brothers still living, both of whom had several children, there was nothing to forfeit other than the grants made by Richard III, which had in any case been resumed.

ROSEMARY HORROX

Sources PRO · *RotP* · R. Horrox, *Richard III, a study of service*, Cambridge Studies in Medieval Life and Thought, 4th ser., 11 (1989) · A. J. Pollard, *North-eastern England during the Wars of the Roses: lay society, war and politics, 1450–1500* (1990) · L. C. Attreed, ed., *The York House books, 1461–1490*, 2 vols. (1991) · N. Pronay and J. Cox, eds., *The Crowland chronicle continuations, 1459–1486* (1986) · J. Anstis, ed., *The* register of the most noble order of the Garter, 2 vols. (1724) • [J. Raine], ed., *Testamenta Eboracensia*, 3, SurtS, 45 (1865) • [J. Raine], ed., *Testamenta Eboracensia*, 4, SurtS, 53 (1869) • M. A. Hicks, 'Dynastic change and northern society: the career of the fourth earl of Northumberland, 1470–89', *Northern History*, 14 (1978), 78–107

Wealth at death est. to be approximately £800 p.a.

Ratcliffe, Thomas (*d.* 1599), Church of England clergyman, was admitted as a pensioner to Peterhouse, Cambridge, on 10 January 1573; his matriculation in June that year was mistakenly registered under the forename Robert. He migrated to Trinity College, Cambridge, and graduated BA in 1578. On 20 October 1582 he was licensed to teach grammar in the diocese of Norwich. In 1585 he was elected a chaplain of St Saviour's, Southwark, where for a yearly salary of £13 13*s.* 8*d.* he took services and 'caterkised on the saboth day afternoon'. His *Short Summe of the Whole Catechisme* continued this work among 'the common people and children'. According to its preface, signed from Southwark, 22 October 1592, the book was intended 'to be diligently read in your houses, for hereby ye your selves, your children and servants, may profit more in the principal points of your salvation'. It was republished in 1619 and 1620. Ratcliffe died at Southwark on 6 February 1599 and was buried at St Saviour's. In his will, drawn up on 26 December 1598 and subsequently added to, Ratcliffe named his wife, Elizabeth, as his executor and residuary legatee. She had evidently been a widow when he married her, since he bequeathed £20 to 'Stephen Fitche, my wives sonne'. Other legacies went to a sister, two nieces, a cousin, and a brother-in-law, and Ratcliffe also remembered neighbours, servants, and three of his fellow clergymen, including 'Mr Harryson mynister of Saint Thomas hospitall', who received 'my best coate' (PRO, PROB 11/93, fol. 149r–v). STEPHEN WRIGHT

Sources Venn, *Alum. Cant.*, 1/3.414 • W. Thompson, *The history and antiquities of the Cathedral of St Saviour* (1906) • T. Ratcliffe, *Short summe of the whole catechisme* (1594?) • will, PRO, PROB 11/93, fol. 149r–v • T. A. Walker, *A biographical register of Peterhouse men*, 1 (1927)

Wealth at death approx. £50: will, PRO, PROB 11/93, fol. 149r–v

Ratcliffe, William Whitehead (1870–1955). *See under* Camden Town Group (*act.* 1911–1913).

Rathbone, (Philip St John) Basil (1892–1967), actor, was born on 13 June 1892 in Johannesburg, Transvaal republic, the son of British parents, Edgar Philip Rathbone (1856–1924), a mining engineer, and his wife, Anne Barbara George (1866–1917), a violinist. He had a younger brother and sister. He spent some years in the Transvaal before attending Repton School in Derbyshire (1906–10), where he was particularly interested in sport, debating, and music. He worked briefly for the Liverpool, London and Globe Insurance Company before joining the number two company of Frank Benson.

Rathbone's acting début, in April 1911, was as Hortensio in *The Taming of the Shrew* at the Theatre Royal, Ipswich. In 1913 he toured the United States with Benson, playing a number of lesser Shakespearian roles. Rathbone's London début was in July 1914 at the Savoy as Finch in *The Sin of David* by Stephen Phillips. On 13 October 1914, at St Luke's

(Philip St John) Basil Rathbone (1892–1967), by Bassano, 1920

Church, Battersea, he married Ethel Marian Forman (1887–1976), an actress. They had a son but divorced in 1925. Later in the year he played the Dauphin in *Henry V* at the Shaftesbury Theatre. During the First World War Rathbone served as a private in the London Scottish regiment before being commissioned and reaching the rank of captain in the Liverpool Scottish; he was awarded the Military Cross in 1918 for gaining information about the enemy. After the war he played major Shakespearian roles at the 1919 summer festival at Stratford upon Avon with the New Shakespeare Company. Subsequent West End roles included the title-role in *Peter Ibbetson* and Alfred de Musset in *Madame Sand* (both 1920), and the Prince of Wales in *Henry IV, Part 2* and Iago in *Othello* (both 1921).

In 1921 Rathbone made his first films, *The Fruitful Vine* and *The Innocent*, both for director Maurice Elvey, and in the following year made his New York stage début in *The Czarina*; the rest of his career was almost exclusively in the United States, alternating for some years between the theatre and films. On stage he appeared in *The Swan* by Ferenc Molnar (1923), *The Dark* (1925), *Judas* (1925), a play he co-authored, and *Julius Caesar* (1927). He also had screen roles in *Trouping with Ellen* (1924), *The Masked Bride* (1925), and *The Great Deception* (1926). On 18 April 1926, at the Dutch Reformed church, New York city, Rathbone married Ouida Bergère (1886–1974), a scenario writer. For many years in Hollywood they gave lavish parties, invitations to which were highly prized in film circles. They had one adopted daughter. Rathbone was tall, dark, and handsome with a fine profile, and with the arrival of 'talkies', as an actor with clear diction and a resonant, authoritative voice, his film career seemed assured. His first talkie was *The Last of Mrs Cheyney* (1929); the following year he played Van Dine's detective Philo Vance in *The Bishop Murder Case*. He continued stage appearances in the early 1930s, including an acclaimed performance in *Diplomacy* by B. C. Stephenson and C. Scott at the Prince's in London (1933), a nationwide tour in 1934 with Katharine Cornell in *The Barretts of Wimpole Street* by R. Besier, *Candida* by Bernard Shaw, and a memorable New York production of *Romeo and Juliet*. It was several years, however, before he really caught on with filmgoers. That changed in 1935 when he proved to be a great screen villain with notable performances as the Marquis St Evremonde in *A Tale of Two Cities*, Pontius Pilate in *The Last Days of Pompeii*, Captain Levasseur in *Captain Blood*, Karenin in *Anna Karenina*, and a memorable Mr Murdstone in *David Copperfield*. *Captain Blood* featured a thrilling swordfight with Errol Flynn, something he repeated when he played dastardly Sir Guy of Gisbourne in *The Adventures of Robin Hood* (1938). Rathbone's brilliant swordplay resulted from taking fencing lessons as a young man. This skill was again prominent when he fought Tyrone Power in *The Mark of Zorro* (1940). Also in the 1930s he portrayed shades of villainy or evil in *Love from a Stranger* (in Britain, 1937); as King Louis XI in *If I Were King* (1938), for which he was Oscar-nominated as best supporting actor; and as the *Son of Frankenstein* and Richard III in *Tower of London* (both 1939). His supporting role as Tybalt in *Romeo and Juliet* (1936) received an Oscar nomination; and he also appeared in a variety of dramatic co-starring roles of note (*The Garden of Allah*, 1936; *Tovarich*, 1937; *The Adventures of Marco Polo*, 1938; and *The Dawn Patrol*, 1938).

In 1939 Twentieth Century Fox cast Rathbone as Sherlock Holmes in *The Hound of the Baskervilles*; its success led to a sequel, *The Adventures of Sherlock Holmes*. Nigel Bruce supported in both as Dr Watson. Three years later the series resumed at Universal Studios. Rathbone and Bruce were reunited and twelve films followed in five years. Stories, now bearing little resemblance to Conan Doyle, were updated, usually to have Holmes battling the Nazis, and each film ended with a stirring, flag-waving speech by him. Towards the end of the series the quality was waning, but *The Scarlet Claw* (1944) was an excellent mystery, and 'Rathbone—smooth, cunning, seldom caught by surprise; and Bruce—talkative, bumbling, never close to understanding the situation at hand' (Maltin, 1242) never failed to entertain. They also played the duo on radio for six seasons, and in delightful unbilled cameos in *Crazy House* (1943).

Ironically Rathbone himself played Nazis in both *Paris Calling* (1941) and *Above Suspicion* (1943), but apart from *Frenchman's Creek* and *Bathing Beauty* (both 1944), had few good movie roles again. He had borne an uncanny resemblance to Holmes as originally illustrated; as he feared, typecasting seemed detrimental to his film career. Rathbone did, however, provide excellent narration to 'The Wind in the Willows' segment of Disney's animated *Adventures of Ichabod and Mr Toad* (1949), and enjoyably spoofed his earlier villainous persona in *Casanova's Big

Night (with Bob Hope, 1954) and *The Court Jester* (with Danny Kaye, 1956), and he was excellent as a nasty banker in John Ford's *The Last Hurrah* (1958). He did, though, return to the stage, on tour and then in New York, with *Obsession* (1946). Rathbone played Dr Sloper in *The Heiress* by A. Goetz on Broadway in 1947 (for which he received a Tony award) and then on tour. In 1950 he was cast as Sir Robert Morton in Terence Rattigan's *The Winslow Boy*. His last Broadway appearance was in *J. B.* (1959) and in 1960 he toured Australia as Paul Delville in *The Marriage-Go-Round*.

Rathbone was very busy on radio throughout the 1940s and 1950s. In 1951 he toured colleges giving dramatic readings, and he later made a number of recordings. Frequent television appearances included *Dr Jekyll and Mr Hyde* (1951) as well as the Emperor in *Aladdin* (1958) and Disraeli in *Victoria Regina* (1961). His autobiography, *In and Out of Character*, appeared in 1962, fortunately before the crop of poor films he made in the 1960s. After a good start to the decade with appearances in two Roger Corman films, *Tales of Terror* (1962) and *The Comedy of Terrors* (1963), the titles of his final films tell all: *Voyage to the Prehistoric Planet* (1965), *The Ghost in the Invisible Bikini* (1966), *Hillbillys in a Haunted House*, and, in Mexico, *Autopsy of a Ghost* (both 1967). Away from the acting, Rathbone loved dogs and books, boxing, baseball, and golf. A resident of New York city from about 1946, he died there at home of a heart attack on 21 July 1967. He was buried at Ferncliff cemetery, Hartsdale, New York.

ROBERT SHARP

Sources *DAB*, suppl. 8 · D. Shipman, *The great movie stars: the golden years* (1970) · E. Katz, *The international film encyclopedia* (1980) · Leonard Maltin's *2000 movie and video guide* (1999) · *The Times* (22 July 1967), 12h · www.basilrathbone.net, 10 Jan 2001 · C. Steinbrunner and N. Michaels, *The films of Sherlock Holmes* (New York, 1974)
Archives NYPL for the Performing Arts
Likenesses Bassano, photograph, 1920, NPG [*see illus.*] · photographs, 1925–65, Hult. Arch. · R. S. Sherriffs, caricature, ink and wash drawing, 1937, NPG · two photographs, Theatre Museum, London

Rathbone, Eleanor Florence (1872–1946), social reformer, was born on 12 May 1872 at 14 Princes Gardens, London, the tenth of eleven children of William *Rathbone (1819–1902), the last six of whom were born to his second wife, Emily Acheson Lyle (1832–1918).

Family and education William Rathbone, merchant and philanthropist, was a Liberal member of parliament from 1868 until 1895, and Eleanor's childhood years were divided between London and Greenbank, the family home in Liverpool, where successive generations of Rathbones had played a prominent role in civic life. Important Liberal politicians, reformers, and intellectuals were regular visitors in the Rathbone home, and Eleanor grew up with the understanding that public service was, in a sense, a dynastic obligation. Yet her childhood was also rather lonely. The eight Rathbone sons were sent away to boarding-schools, and since her half-sister and sister were considerably her elders, Eleanor found herself often alone. She grew into an introspective and serious girl, much attached to her loving but moralistic father and anxious for parental approbation.

Eleanor Florence Rathbone (1872–1946), by Sir James Gunn, 1933

Except for a year at Kensington Girls' School (1889–90), Eleanor's education was conducted at home. Years later she remarked that there were worse ways of educating girls than to let them roam freely through their fathers' libraries; certainly she preferred such solitary exploration to the social obligations of her first London season. In 1892 she began studying Greek with Janet Case, a recent student at Girton College, Cambridge, and—encouraged by Case and by Oliver Lodge, professor of physics at Liverpool University and a close family friend—broached to her parents the subject of attending Cambridge. Something of a family crisis ensued, for Emily Rathbone had other ambitions for her intelligent and attractive daughter, but with her father's support Eleanor was allowed to go to Somerville Hall, Oxford, in 1893, which was then only a hall of residence and had a less rigorously academic reputation than Girton. Yet Somerville declared itself a college one year later and provided her with an excellent education. The only Somerville student in her year to attempt 'greats', she studied philosophy with David Ritchie, Charles Cannan, and Edward Caird, and Roman history with Henry Pelham. A mediocre classicist and technically poorly trained, she nevertheless impressed her tutors with her powerful mind. They, in their turn, gave her the same grounding in idealist thought that influenced Toynbee, Beveridge, and other prominent social reformers.

Somerville also provided Eleanor with a community of like-minded friends and the intellectual freedom to work out her own views. Years later her fellow students recalled her intellectual seriousness, her addiction to smoking, her utter hopelessness at games—and also her feminism. Surrounded from childhood by strong-minded women and influenced by Quaker and Unitarian principles, Eleanor arrived at Somerville a self-identified feminist. With Margery Fry, Hilda Oakeley, and a few other young women, she participated in a discussion group, the Associated Prigs, which canvassed intellectual and social questions. Her studies, her interests, and her college friendships all confirmed her sense of election and obligation; when, after her final examinations, she was awarded second class honours, she felt she had let her college and her sex down. She left Somerville in 1896, uncertain how to use her philosophical training or express her commitment to feminism.

Eleanor returned to Liverpool rather than London, for her father had retired from parliament in 1895. She took over the secretaryship of the Liverpool Women's Suffrage Society and of the local branch of the Women's Industrial Council, but her return to the family home was not entirely easy. Her attempts to study were constantly interrupted by domestic plans; efforts to pick up journalistic work came to naught. Along with other socially concerned young women, she volunteered as a home visitor for the Liverpool Central Relief Society, taking a district and devising strategies to lift destitute families out of poverty. Although this work was painstaking and often frustrating, it gave her a sense of purpose and concentrated her mind; in reports summarizing efforts in her district she sought to understand not simply the personal failings that led to distress, but equally the wider causes of poverty. Her father, disappointed in his sons, encouraged these activities; as his health began to fail he came to rely on Eleanor to sustain his own philanthropic efforts. Encouraged by Charles Booth, father and daughter began a new investigation into Liverpool's system of dock labour. But early in 1902, with that work in embryo, William Rathbone died.

Eleanor, now thirty, found his death devastating. From girlhood her father had been her confidant and guide. Like so many eminent Victorians, she worked through her grief with her pen, writing an admiring but restrained account of her father's life (*William Rathbone: a Memoir*, 1905). Yet if her father's death was a great sorrow, it was also a liberation. Believing as he did in women's independence, William Rathbone had settled money on Eleanor before his death; in his will she received another substantial portion. Now a woman of some means, she had few domestic obligations. Her unmarried half-sister, Elsie, had always managed the Greenbank home; her mother, long since reconciled to Eleanor's unmarried state, was proud of her daughter's achievements. Moreover, as her father's last collaborator and his biographer, Eleanor established herself as his heir. She, rather than any of his many sons, continued the Rathbone philanthropic tradition.

Liverpool politics: social work and women's suffrage Over the next two decades, a period marked by the Second South African War and the death of her father on the one hand and the First World War and the death of her mother on the other, Eleanor Rathbone became the most prominent woman in Liverpool's public life. There was a dynastic element to her achievement, surely, for the name of Rathbone was one to be reckoned with in Liverpool politics. Yet if she drew on that tradition, she also in some ways broke with it: for example, to the distress of her male relations on the city council, she identified herself politically as an independent; both her vehement support for women's rights and her growing scepticism about the rationality of the market distanced her from her family's historic Liberalism. Her politics were thus shaped as much by her feminism as by her family inheritance; they were also increasingly linked to her own original economic thought. Rathbone's activities in these years are hard to disentangle, for her roles as a social reformer, social thinker, feminist, and practical politician fed off one another, together providing the foundation for her commanding role as the architect of a 'new feminism' after 1918.

Initially, social work took centre stage. In 1903 Rathbone began working with the Victoria Women's Settlement, which had opened in 1898 and was now entering a moment of expansion. In 1902 the settlement had appointed a dynamic new warden, Elizabeth *Macadam (1871–1948), a Scottish social worker who had trained at London's Women's University Settlement. Rathbone and Macadam probably met about the time of William's death, and the two became close friends and collaborators. Forthright where Eleanor was reserved, practical where Eleanor was abstracted, Macadam answered Rathbone's only half acknowledged need for friendship and a cause: over the next seventeen years the two used the settlement to anchor a growing local women's movement. They put the settlement on a solid financial footing, recruited some dozens of supporters and co-workers, established a training programme for social workers (a programme that was in 1910 brought under the umbrella of Liverpool University, which then appointed Macadam as a lecturer), and built up an array of social services for local women and children. Great believers in co-ordination between voluntary and public services, the two helped in 1909 to found the Liverpool Council of Voluntary Aid, an umbrella organization which gradually absorbed the work of many older philanthropic societies.

As the settlement's honorary secretary until 1915, Eleanor Rathbone took part in all aspects of this expansion. She paid special attention, however, to social investigation, scrutinizing successive facets of Liverpool's economy and social life with a critical and feminist eye. Her most ambitious study focused entirely on men: her *Report of an Inquiry into the Conditions of Dock Labour at the Liverpool Docks* (1904) laid bare the inefficiencies as well as the hardships of the casual labour system and catalysed later efforts at decasualization. Already in that study, however, she noted the devastating impact of erratic wages on dockers' wives; a later survey of household budgets (*How the Casual Labourer Lives*, 1909) further dramatized their predicament. Her earlier studies of women's employment opportunities in Liverpool, undertaken for the Liverpool Women's Industrial Council in the 1890s, had shown that married working-class women had little chance to earn: demand for their labour was low, and most were fully occupied with their children. But must these women be condemned to poverty and dependence? With Liverpool's working mothers as her point of reference, Rathbone began to think more systematically about the problem of the lack of 'fit' between a labour market and wage system geared to compensate individual (and usually male) effort and the needs of women and children. In 1912, in essays published in the feminist press, she raised the possibility of direct state provision for the cost of raising children, and in her political interventions she became bolder as well. Having marshalled the support of the seamen's union and the great shipping lines, she helped to work out an arrangement in 1912 whereby seamen could have a portion of their wages paid directly to their wives; in 1914, after subjecting Liverpool's poor-law unions to a blistering attack (*The Condition of Widows under the Poor Law in Liverpool*, 1913), she advocated state pensions for widows raising young children on their own.

Behind Rathbone's new activism lay more than intellectual conviction: feminist political successes also fuelled her optimism. From the 1890s Liverpool women had served as poor-law guardians and (later) as school governors; in 1906 they won the right to stand for election to the city council. Almost inevitably, the first woman to exercise that right was Rathbone herself: in 1909, in a campaign run largely from the settlement, she won election as an independent representing Granby ward, a seat she held without interruption (and usually unchallenged) until 1935. On the council she became an energetic advocate for municipal housing and for the corporation's women employees, but she also expressed her suffragist views. In 1911, still the council's lone woman member, she persuaded her colleagues to pass a resolution in favour of a women's suffrage bill then before parliament. As both a practical politician and an outspoken feminist, Rathbone's position was not always easy: in 1910 she faced criticism from Archibald Salvidge and other Conservative opponents for endorsing a socialist parliamentary candidate who supported women's suffrage; on the other hand, after 1906 she found her constitutionalist views challenged by a local militant movement loyal to the Pankhursts. She remained, however, both staunchly constitutionalist and progressive: under her leadership the Liverpool Women's Suffrage Society repeatedly condemned militancy while also building up grass-roots support in the towns and rural areas of Lancashire and north Wales. By 1912, with the militant movement in decline, she had become the president of a regional federation of some twenty-seven constitutionalist suffrage societies.

With her political acumen and independent base, Rathbone was an important asset for the national suffrage movement. She served uninterruptedly on the executive of the National Union of Women's Suffrage Societies (NUWSS) from 1896, wrote regularly for the *Common Cause*, its affiliated paper, and took part in numerous deputations. She was also involved in formulating political strategy, reaching out to progressives within the Liberal Party and opposing the policy, crafted in 1912 by Catherine Marshall and supported by Millicent Fawcett, of allying with the Labour Party in order to put pressure on the Liberals. Convinced that this tactic would strengthen the Conservative Party and ultimately harm the women's cause, Rathbone organized an internal opposition to it, only to have her actions denounced as disloyal. Hurt and shocked, she resigned from the NUWSS executive early in 1914, but that break, while painful, proved temporary. Although horrified by the outbreak of war, she had no doubts of Germany's guilt or of British women's duty to support their country. When the pacifist wing of the executive resigned *en masse* over the national union's relatively pro-war stance, Rathbone regained her position. From 1915 she was the dominant figure on the national union's executive and, effectively, Fawcett's successor-designate. She managed much of the negotiation over the suffrage issue when it re-emerged in 1916 and—in spite of many feminists' reservations—arranged for a successful amendment to the bill which extended the local franchise to the wives of male local government electors—a provision that increased the women's local government electorate fourfold.

The war also multiplied Rathbone's Liverpool involvements. At its outbreak Liverpool's mayor (and Eleanor's cousin), Herbert R. Rathbone, asked her and Macadam to organize assistance to soldiers' and sailors' wives. This proved to be a complex task, for the Liberal government had promised to pay 'separation allowances' to the families of volunteers, but had no machinery to cope with the half-million immediate claims. Philanthropic organizations were thus deputed to process applications and advance payment. In Liverpool, Rathbone pressed her settlement house allies into service, setting up several dozen local offices staffed by hundreds of voluntary workers. In time the war government transferred these functions to a new Ministry of Pensions, but Rathbone's Liverpool organization remained in operation, supplementing state payments, visiting wives and families, and becoming a model for family-based social work. At the end of the war she helped to create the Liverpool Personal Service Society to carry on such work and recruited Dorothy Keeling, a successful Bradford social worker, to run it.

Rathbone's wartime work convinced her of the need for activist women to become involved in state administration itself; more importantly, it suggested a model for addressing the problem of women's dependence that had troubled her for so long. Separation allowances, although far from generous, were proportional to the size of the family and were paid directly into the woman's hands—and Liverpool's poor wives and mothers, Rathbone discovered, usually had less trouble managing on such payments than on their husbands' pay. Already by 1916, then, Rathbone had begun to wonder whether separation allowances might not provide a model for a more comprehensive peacetime policy. In articles in the *Economic Journal* and *The Times* she laid out the intellectual case, and early in 1918, with six other collaborators (H. N. Brailsford, Kathleen Courtney, Mary Stocks, Maude Royden, Emile

Burns, and Elinor Burns), published a practical proposal (*Equal Pay and the Family*). One benefit of family endowment, she argued, was that it would make equal pay between men and women possible: with direct state support of children, the case for the (already fictive and inefficient) male family wage would disappear. This group, now renamed the Family Endowment Committee, began presenting their case to public bodies, government planning committees, and the press, and in the statist and reconstruction-obsessed years at the end of the war they received a hearing.

Home life: Elizabeth Macadam The war years consolidated Rathbone's Liverpool position and enhanced her national reputation, but they also posed a question about her future work. Although profoundly linked to Liverpool, by the end of the war she was travelling almost weekly to London; how, in the future, should she balance these demands? Personal crises sharpened this dilemma. Early in 1918 her mother, Emily, died, and the family home of Greenbank passed, as William had arranged, to her sister, Evie, and brother-in-law, Hugh Reynolds Rathbone, now effectively head of the family in Liverpool. Eleanor planned to share a house with Elsie, her elder half-sister, to whom she was very close, and hoped that Elizabeth Macadam would join them. At the end of the war, however, Macadam was offered the secretaryship of the new Joint Universities Council on Social Studies, whose headquarters were in London. Having just lost her mother, Eleanor thus faced the prospect of losing Elizabeth as well. This crisis made her acknowledge how important Elizabeth's love and support were for her; while she urged Elizabeth to pursue the career that would make her most happy, she promised, in essence, to follow her. In 1919 the two friends bought a house together in Romney Street, just off Smith Square and within an easy walk of parliament. Rathbone's Liverpool commitments remained substantial: she stayed on the city council, continued to lecture for the Liverpool School of Social Service, founded (and became president of) a new cross-party Liverpool Women's Citizens' Association, and made an unsuccessful bid for a parliamentary seat in the election of 1922. She kept a comfortable house in Liverpool—initially with Elsie and after her death alone—but with Elizabeth in London, Romney Street became her primary home. Cushioned by the fortune Elsie left to Eleanor on her death, Eleanor and Elizabeth lived comfortably together for the rest of Eleanor's life.

The nature of that relationship is difficult to recapture, especially since both women were concerned to protect their privacy and arranged that their mutual correspondence be burnt after their deaths. It is not likely to have been actively sexual, for Rathbone in particular was somewhat prudish, hostile to Freudianism and other theories elevating the importance of instinctual life, and prone to define sexual feeling as a troublesome male failing. Yet, for her, Macadam was much more than a friend and companion. Eleanor once told Elizabeth that she had allowed no one else inside 'the ring-fence of my personality' (Stocks, 181); only with Elizabeth did she feel fully herself, only with Elizabeth could she be completely uncon-strained. Rathbone took Macadam's advice on all aspects of her work, but she also relied on her practical and social skills, counting on Macadam to run their joint household and manage their schedules. Gradually, then, and espe-cially after Rathbone's election to parliament in 1929, Macadam's independent career gave way to her role as Eleanor's trusted deputy, emotional support, and, in a sense, 'political wife'. This shift in the relationship caused some tension, for Macadam was a strong-minded but sen-sitive woman, proud of her own accomplishments and quick to resent those who saw her only as Eleanor's com-panion. Yet Rathbone, for her part, never took Macadam for granted; although the more prominent, she was also the more dependent. In 1919 Eleanor had written to Eliza-beth that the prospect of a shared life dedicated to the work of social reform would bring her 'a happiness too great to seem possible' (letter, Rathbone papers); all the evidence is that it did so.

Feminist reforms and election as MP After her death Elea-nor Rathbone came to be remembered primarily for her successful campaign in support of family allowances, and indeed that cause figured prominently throughout her life. Yet such a characterization overlooks her central role in pre-war Liverpool politics; nor does it do justice either to the lasting importance of her economic thought or to the range of national causes on which she made a mark. After 1919 Rathbone took up five main political issues, those of the integration of women into political life, the development of state benefits for the family, the protec-tion of women in Britain's colonial empire, the defence of democratic political ideals in the face of the rise of fas-cism, and the rescue and reception of refugees from Francoist Spain and Nazi Germany. She became the dom-inant figure in the first two arenas, and played a signifi-cant, if less well-known, role in the last three. And in all five areas she exhibited a combination of progressive idealism and pragmatic political acumen that mark her out as one of the most accomplished public campaigners of the years between the wars.

Perhaps inevitably, feminism dominated Rathbone's thoughts after 1918. Millicent Fawcett's determination to step down as the leader of the constitutionalist suffrage federation, combined with the failure of all the women candidates (save Constance Markievicz, who did not take her seat) at the 'khaki' election, forced politically active women to think concretely about their aims and strat-egies. Rathbone knew what she wanted: as a political inde-pendent, she did not wish to see women simply absorbed into the established political parties; she was convinced that cross-party feminist activism remained essential to women's advancement. In 1919 she was elected to succeed Fawcett as president of the now renamed National Union of Societies for Equal Citizenship (NUSEC).

During the years of Rathbone's presidency the national union pursued several feminist reforms, among them an equalization of the franchise, equal guardianship of children, divorce-law reform, and widows' pensions. Par-liamentary and political activity remained the focus, and

with the aid of her close friend Eva Hubback, who served as parliamentary secretary, Rathbone turned the union into a very effective lobbying organization, skilled in drafting legislation, adept at finding parliamentary allies, and capable of drumming up waves of resolutions from branches and allied women's groups across the country. These efforts met with some real success: by 1929, when Rathbone stepped down as president, she could point to a number of measures—among them the introduction of widows' pensions in 1925 and the equal franchise legisla-tion of 1928—that had improved the lives of many mil-lions of women.

Yet for all NUSEC's legislative success, the twenties proved difficult years for feminism. Without the vote to campaign for, feminist organizations proved hard to sus-tain: younger women professed themselves uninterested, while veteran campaigners often devoted themselves to single-issue causes. Rathbone responded to this problem creatively but controversially, insisting that feminists not only demand all those rights and privileges hitherto mon-opolized by men (a project she tended to identify as 'the old feminism'), but also begin to adapt social institutions to reflect women's own values and work. 'At last we can stop looking at all our problems through men's eyes and discussing them in men's phraseology,' she told a divided NUSEC conference in 1925. 'We can demand what we want for women, not because it is what men have got, but because it is what women need to fulfil the potentialities of their own natures and to adjust themselves to the cir-cumstances of their own lives' (*Woman's Leader*, 13 March 1925, 52). Such was Rathbone's standing that she brought her organization with her: NUSEC added family allow-ances to its programme in 1925 and, even more controver-sially, moderated its uniformly hostile stand on protective legislation in 1927. Yet these victories came at a real cost, for the 'new feminist' agenda alienated many old sup-porters; after the vote on protective legislation in 1927, fully half the executive committee resigned. Already much diminished, NUSEC could not afford these losses; in the thirties, after setting up the townswomen's guilds as a successful offshoot, it subsided into a still smaller National Council for Equal Citizenship, restricting its activity to specific lobbying efforts.

If feminist organizations declined, however, some femi-nist politicians flourished, among them Rathbone. In 1929, at the urging of several friends at Liverpool and Man-chester universities, she agreed to stand as an independ-ent for the parliamentary seat of Combined English Uni-versities. To her surprise, she won the seat easily—and had little trouble holding it through three subsequent elections until her death. As MP for the Combined Univer-sities, a political independent, and a woman, she might be thought entirely marginal to the Commons, but she made the first two liabilities work in her favour, taking advan-tage of her intellectual standing and non-party status to speak on the basis of conscience alone. Even more import-ant, she made an impressive case for women MPs. True, she gave 'women's questions' special attention, and unlike many of her fellow women MPs did not hesitate to identify herself as a feminist. Yet she also followed colonial and foreign policy closely, and some of her very best speeches were on such questions as British policy towards Ethiopia or Home Office regulations on the admission of refugees. Always well prepared, pointed, and capable equally of espousing common sense arguments or of quoting Macaulay and Mill, she struck the *Manchester Guardian*'s parliamentary correspondent as having a 'masculine mind'—but it would be truer to say that she established the principle that the mind has no sex, and that women could speak with as much force and intelligence as men on matters of national importance. Skilled lobbyist as she was, Rathbone also mastered the ways of the house, learning how to extract meetings or concessions from ministers with the threat of a parliamentary question and buttonholing government spokesmen, who, Harold Nicolson recalled, used to dive into doorways to avoid her.

Family allowances The status and rights of women was thus always one of Rathbone's central concerns in the years after 1919, but that focus often shaded imperceptibly into a second area of activity. By the end of the war she had become convinced that only by disaggregating male wages and paying mothers directly for the work of reproduction could women achieve full citizenship, and she never changed her view. Throughout the twenties she built up the intellectual case for and a political coalition behind the ideal of family endowment. The founding document was her own comprehensive but impassioned study, *The disinherited family: a plea for direct provision for the costs of child maintenance through family allowances* (1924; rev. edn, 1927). Heralded by William Beveridge, Hugh Dalton, and other prominent economists as one of the most important modern treatises on distributive economics, Rathbone's book began with a cogent statistical proof of the lack of 'fit' between wages and family needs, proceeded to make the case for direct endowment of motherhood on moral, economic, humanitarian, and demographic grounds, and concluded with a thorough survey of the family allowance systems introduced on the continent and across the empire.

Widely reviewed, *The Disinherited Family* won a number of prominent converts, allowing Rathbone to set up a broader Family Endowment Society devoted to propagandizing the cause. From 1924 the society presented the case for family endowment to royal commissions and party committees, interested businessmen, and activist women. There were some victories: in 1925, with Beveridge's support, the royal commission on the coal industry recommended that a system of family allowances be set up to mitigate the effects of wage reductions for miners; in 1926 the Independent Labour Party made a system of state-funded family allowances the cornerstone of their expansionist platform, 'Socialism in our time'. Yet there were few practical experiments. Beveridge set up a family allowances programme at the London School of Economics; a few progressive employers introduced firm-based schemes; a few city councils introduced rent rebates for families with young children. But no major party came

out in favour of the policy: even the Labour Party, which looked likely to support it in the run-up to the general election of 1929, in the end bowed to trade-union fears of possible effects upon wage bargaining. And as the slump worsened in the early thirties, family endowment looked likely to be postponed for ever.

Yet Rathbone found a way to adjust even to these dismal circumstances. As she noted, in a period of downturn it was even more crucial to put the welfare of children first, and in 1934 she founded the Children's Minimum Campaign Committee to press for better social services—including free milk and school meals—for children in poverty. That men with large families could sometimes receive more from unemployment insurance and assistance (which included children's allowances) than they could earn as unskilled labourers also crystallized the argument for universal allowances. By the late thirties such planning advocates as the Next Five Years Group and the management research groups had taken a new interest in family endowment; populationist concerns brought such Conservatives as Leo Amery on board. By the spring of 1941 more than 150 MPs joined Rathbone in a petition urging the government to introduce a state scheme; one year later such a resolution passed the Commons. When William Beveridge worked out a comprehensive plan for social security during the Second World War, he made a universal system of children's allowances (for the second child and beyond) one of the assumptions of his plan. In the end the wartime government bowed to the inevitable and introduced a Family Allowances Bill, but only after serious pressure from Rathbone and the women's organizations would it contemplate making the payment directly to the mother. Rathbone, who was suffering from an injured leg, attended the bill's final stages in a wheelchair; characteristically, she was embarrassed and confused when the house rose to cheer her.

Women in the British empire Her desire to improve the status of mothers always lay at the heart of Rathbone's social policy efforts, and they motivated her ten-year excursion into colonial questions as well. In 1925 she had been appointed assessor, representing the international women's organizations, to the child welfare committee of the League of Nations. The Geneva conferences she attended drew her attention to the oppression of women and children in other parts of the world; increasingly, she saw feminism in an international and imperial frame. In 1927, when the American muckraker Katherine Mayo published *Mother India*, her tendentious exposé of the sexual subjection of Indian women and children, Rathbone sprang into action. At two NUSEC-sponsored conferences and in an early article she urged British women to take up the domestic subjection of colonized women. For the next eight years in parliamentary questions, articles, speeches, and a short book on the subject (*Child Marriage: an Indian Minotaur*, 1934) she argued for a robust campaign against child marriage by British authorities and Indian reformers alike.

Yet her foray into Indian questions proved difficult. Rathbone assumed that the British authorities in India could best act to stamp out child marriage: to her surprise, however, neither politically active Indian women nor the government of India shared her views. Progressive Indian women had been profoundly offended by Mayo's openly racist views and insisted that India's social problems should be addressed by Indians alone; the India Office and the government of India, for their part, were reluctant to undertake legislation likely to cause local unrest. After two years of fruitless parliamentary lobbying Rathbone changed tactics. From 1930 until 1935, when the Government of India Act finally passed, she worked indefatigably to increase Indian women's representation, both as electors and as legislators, in the new constitution. Once again her proposals drew criticism from some Indian feminists eager to maintain the principle of strictly equal qualifications for women and men, and her six-week trip to India in 1932 only partially dispelled their suspicions. Yet she pursued her goal with great skill, keeping in close touch with Indian progressives and feminists (even those with whom she disagreed), cultivating successive secretaries of state for India and their under-secretaries (she became close to Lord Lothian in particular), giving evidence to the round-table conference and its subcommittees, setting up a formidable British women's lobby to press her proposals, and arranging for the introduction of a raft of amendments during the bill's final stages. By 1935 many in Britain and India agreed about the need to improve women's political representation, but the form in which this was done—through a special wife's franchise and reserved women's seats—owed much to Rathbone's interventions.

Nor was India Rathbone's only colonial cause. In December 1929, in an act of remarkable political courage, she and the duchess of Atholl rose in the Commons to denounce the practice of clitoridectomy in some African territories and to ask whether some African women's situation did not resemble slavery. With Atholl and Josiah Wedgwood, she founded a small, cross-party committee for the protection of coloured women in the crown colonies, which gradually extracted some information about African women's social conditions from a reluctant Colonial Office. Rathbone also kept a watching brief on women's political rights across the colonies, speaking up to defend women's franchise in Bermuda and Palestine, and to argue for British women's right to retain their nationality on marriage. A visit to Palestine with Macadam in 1934 at the invitation of the Palestine Women's Equal Rights Association aroused an incipient Zionism. Impressed with Jewish settlers' educational and social institutions, and struck by the equal role accorded women, she told the association that, had she her life to live over again, she might choose to return as a Jew in Palestine.

Rathbone's colonial involvements, which dominated her life in the early thirties, were always principally feminist in aim: she wished to improve women's position in all Britain's imperial possessions. Yet her efforts brought about a subtle shift in her thought, for if she began by asserting British women's rights to protect colonized women, she ended by seeking to extend such women's own political rights. This shift strengthened her core democratic principles: to those who claimed that Indian or Arab women were too illiterate or backward to exercise political power Rathbone retorted—following Mill—that through such exercise women would grow in capacity and knowledge. Gradually, then, a fundamentally humanitarian approach gave way to an overtly political stance, positioning her well for the role she played as democratic tribune in the last decade of her life.

Anti-appeasement, rescue of refugees Rathbone took up that role early. In April 1933 she was already pointing to the danger posed to European democracies by the Nazi seizure of power and arguing against a policy of conciliation. In the following year, in parliament and on the executive of the League of Nations Union, she urged a vigorous defence of Ethiopia in the face of Italian aggression. Frustrated by the union's dilatory procedures and by the widespread public sentiment in favour of peace at almost any price, she tried allying with an assortment of groups—Lloyd George's Council of Action, the National Council for Civil Liberties—which she hoped might take a more robustly anti-fascist line. Usually, however, she worked with a few trusted friends, especially the duchess of Atholl, who shared her disgust at the policy of appeasement. In February 1937 she and Atholl met political leaders and intellectuals in Romania, Yugoslavia, and Czechoslovakia to urge them to resist German influence; in Britain as well Rathbone warned that fascist powers would be encouraged and not appeased by concessions. The democratic powers must defend the principles of the league, with force if necessary, she wrote in *War can be Averted*, published by the Left Book Club in early 1938. Yet, looking at the 'doubtful hesitating set of men' on the front bench (*Hansard 5C*, 343, 31 Jan 1939, 149), she felt anything but optimistic. Having predicted as early as 1936 that only a 'real National Government' led by Churchill and backed by Labour would effectively stand up to the fascist powers (Rathbone papers, XIV.3.34), in the wake of the Munich crisis she set up a cross-party parliamentary action group which helped to pave the way for Churchill's accession.

But it was the Spanish conflict that most absorbed Rathbone's energies in the late thirties. Although anything but a communist, she saw it in black and white terms: to her mind, a democratic republic was seeking to defend itself from precisely the same forces as had seized control in Italy and Germany. She could not, then, understand why the democratic powers refused to come to the republic's defence. Critical from the outset of the policy of non-intervention, Rathbone publicized information about German and Italian violations of the pact and bombarded the government with parliamentary questions (by the late thirties well over half of her questions were about this conflict). She also took on extensive extra-parliamentary commitments. At the end of 1936 she accepted the vice-chairmanship of a newly formed national joint committee for Spanish relief, which organized the evacuation, care, and eventual repatriation of some 4000 refugee children. With the duchess of Atholl, Ellen Wilkinson, and Dame Rachel Crowdy, she travelled to Spain in the spring of 1937—braving bombardment in Valencia—to review the situation of refugees and political prisoners for herself. Nothing she saw there diminished her enthusiasm for the republican cause, and as its fortunes worsened, she put herself at some political risk to try to get refugees out. By the spring of 1939, unable to mobilize either the Foreign or Home Office and with the republic all but defeated, she simply tried to charter a ship to run the blockade and remove from Valencia republican sympathizers sure to suffer Franco's vengeance.

Rathbone's Spanish adventures turned her into a refugee expert. She harangued and pleaded with a reluctant Home Office for more generous policies on entry and, when she found herself inundated by individual requests for aid, set up a parliamentary committee for refugees to take up such cases. As she saw it, having so singularly failed to defend Europe's vulnerable democracies, Britain was morally required to give shelter once those democracies had fallen. Late in 1938 she tried to secure entry for Czech and German socialists and Jews threatened by Nazi occupation of the Sudetenland; January 1939 found her in Prague, trying to make sure that such refugees were not simply—in compliance with Nazi wishes—shipped back to Germany. This was a strenuous life for a woman who was almost seventy, but she seems to have thrived on it: there is no suggestion before the 1940s that foreign travel, long hours, constant smoking, and sporadic sleep taxed her robust constitution.

With the outbreak of war Rathbone felt a measure of relief as well as horror: the expiation for appeasement was finally at hand. Certainly, she dreaded the loss of life and utterly rejected the idea that it should fall on young men alone. To the contrary, she insisted on women's duty to risk their lives and eagerly backed the campaign, run mostly by her fellow women MPs, to bring women into all (and even the most dangerous) of wartime occupations. Both she and Elizabeth filled out their voluntary service forms, Rathbone professing herself in excellent health, able to drive, and willing to do anything required. Both women refused to leave London during the blitz and simply moved round the corner to Tufton Court when Romney Street was destroyed by bombs in 1940. Rathbone had a busy war, reviving the family endowment campaign, helping to found the Citizens' Advice Bureau, entering into a much reported if ill-advised correspondence with Jawaharlal Nehru, and, especially, carrying on with her refugee work.

In June 1940, with an invasion of Britain possible, the Home Office interned some tens of thousands of 'enemy aliens'; to Rathbone's horror, these included socialist and Jewish refugees from Nazism—who remained, in Home Office eyes, German. Refugees interned in haste were released at leisure, and Rathbone and her allies found themselves locked in combat with Herbert Morrison and his under-secretaries both about policy and about individual cases. Her persistence and expertise made her at the same time respected and (in some cases) disliked by the officials and ministers whom she badgered almost daily.

So strained did her relations become with Morrison in particular that Rathbone, fearing that his hostility would jeopardize particular cases, began working through other MPs. Yet within the refugee community itself and among a loyal group of parliamentary and political co-workers she won a reputation for her almost saintly devotion and integrity. As always, much of her work was funded from her own pocket.

As news of Nazi mass murders made its way to Britain, Rathbone's parliamentary committee joined Jewish organizations in trying to frame some response. When Jan Karski reached England late in 1942 bringing word of extermination camps in Poland and the early use of gas, Rathbone was among those he contacted. For the next two years this issue almost blotted out all others. Together with Victor Gollancz, Victor Cazalet, and others, she founded a new organization, the National Committee for Rescue from Nazi Terror, to press the government to mount efforts to rescue those threatened with annihilation. A wide range of proposals—from underground work to pressure on neutrals and the satellite states and an actual offer to Hitler to take in all Jews from occupied lands—made their way from her committee to the Foreign and Home offices. Until 1944 at least its efforts met with very little response: officials adopted a dilatory, wait and see attitude and, to Rathbone's fury, tied the question up in leisurely international consultations. Repeatedly warned by officials that publicity might lead to retaliation against those she wished to help, she usually held her tongue; on a few occasions, though, she and her allies forced bitter Commons debates. Although Rathbone accepted that military efforts must come first, she could not understand the government's unwillingness even to contemplate attempts at rescue. As the death toll mounted, a sense of impotence occasionally overwhelmed her. Yet she never succumbed to despair or to talk of revenge: she was one of the few British politicians to denounce forthrightly the deportations of Germans at the end of the war and, together with Victor Gollancz, spearheaded a civilian effort to send foodstuffs to her former enemies in that dreadful post-war winter. She was caught up in this effort when she died suddenly of a stroke at her home, 26 Hampstead Lane, Highgate, Middlesex, on 2 January 1946. She was cremated and her name added to the family monument in the Smithfield Road cemetery, Liverpool.

Reputation and legacy A wave of tributes from parliamentary allies and humanitarians followed. A memorial lecture series was established at the civic universities and a home for refugee children built in Rathbone's memory in Israel. Over the next thirty years, however, she slipped out of the public mind. The university seat which she represented with such distinction was abolished soon after the war; moreover, given her political independence, no party could claim—and thus publicize—her achievements. Her name was associated with family allowances, but during the post-war economic boom these were allowed to stagnate and found few advocates.

In the 1970s, however, Rathbone's life and, more

importantly, her ideas won renewed attention. Economic downturn and the emergence of such lobbies as the Child Poverty Action Group put family allowances back on the political agenda, and with the rise of second-wave feminism the efforts of earlier women activists received another look. Sometimes that effort at recovery generated as much heat as light. The battles of the 1920s between 'new feminists' and 'equalitarians' were refought in the pages of academic journals in the 1980s, with Rathbone's ideas often caricatured or singled out for particular praise or blame. Gradually, though, scholars came to see British feminism's inter-war quarrels as part of a broader argument over citizenship and social rights played out in most western states in the wake of the First World War, and to appreciate the combination of pragmatism and analytical power Rathbone brought to that debate. Having spent many years among Liverpool's working-class families, she had the wit to recognize that mothers raising children were indeed working and the moral imagination to envisage a world in which such work might carry its own economic reward. She was, then, one of the first thinkers to move beyond an arid argument about whether women should seek equality or ask for the accommodation of difference and to recognize the profoundly gendered—to use twenty-first-century terminology—nature of labour markets, wage systems, and political structures. In her insistence that feminists pursue not only equal opportunities within that gendered system but equally the reconditioning of those structures to eradicate their masculine bias Rathbone anticipated much later feminist thinking and politics. Few have thought so creatively and at the same time so practically about what it would take to bring about a genuinely equal citizenship for women.

But the renewed interest in Rathbone's life and work came from a second direction as well. Throughout the 1970s and 1980s, as the official records on Indian policy, appeasement, the Spanish Civil War, and allied responses to the Holocaust began to open, scholars working in all these areas were surprised to find the figure of an indomitable middle-aged humanitarian constantly crossing their path. In her own day Rathbone's central role in many of the international and reform movements of the thirties and early forties escaped public notice, for she tended to work through sympathetic fellow MPs or cross-party lobbying groups and to use the threat of publicity to force reluctant ministers to hear her out. But those who worked with her closely found her (as Harold Nicolson recalled) to be a subtle tactician and an adept political operator; certainly no other backbench MP of this period can be credited with such a range of accomplishments. 'No Parliamentary career has been more useful and fruitful,' the *Manchester Guardian* insisted on her death (*Manchester Guardian*, 3 Jan 1946, 3), and as scholars bring to light her central role in humanitarian causes ranging from better child nutrition to Spanish relief, from family allowances to the release of interned aliens, this verdict seems justifiable.

Rathbone herself would have been bemused by this posthumous attention. Personally reticent and driven by conscience rather than ambition, she found public attention disconcerting and embarrassing. She could not be persuaded to accept an honour for her work in either the First World War or the Second (although she did accept honorary degrees from Durham, Liverpool, and Oxford) and, when a group of friends insisted on having her portrait painted in 1932, she was quite taken aback. 'I do not believe that I belong to the small class of persons who justify public portraits,' she protested in a letter; fifty years from now, she predicted, that portrait would languish forgotten in some dark corner or cupboard (Beveridge papers, II b, 31, London School of Economics). But here her predictive antennae proved faulty. James Gunn's portrait of Eleanor Rathbone was hung in the National Portrait Gallery, and her ideas and achievements continue to compel our attention. Brilliant, systematic, and pragmatic enough to translate visionary ideas into piecemeal reforms, she stands as both the most significant feminist thinker and the most effective woman politician of the first half of the twentieth century.   SUSAN PEDERSEN

Sources Rathbone papers, U. Lpool · *Hansard 5C* (1929–46) · M. D. Stocks, *Eleanor Rathbone: a biography* (1949) · *Common Cause* [later *Woman's Leader and the Common Cause*] (1909–31) · S. Pedersen, *Women's stake in democracy: Eleanor Rathbone's answer to Virginia Woolf* (Austin, Texas, 2000) · S. Pedersen, 'Rathbone and daughter: feminism and the father at the fin-de-siècle', *Journal of Victorian Culture*, 1/1 (Jan 1996) · S. Pedersen, 'Eleanor Rathbone, 1872–1946: the Victorian family under the daughter's eye', *After the Victorians*, ed. S. Pedersen and P. Mandler (1994) · B. Harrison, 'Constructive crusader: Eleanor Rathbone', *Prudent revolutionaries: portraits of British feminists between the wars* (1987) · J. Alberti, *Eleanor Rathbone* (1996) · Foreign and Home Office papers, PRO · BL OIOC · BLPES, Beveridge MSS · archives, Somerville College, Oxford · U. Birm., Oliver Lodge MSS · U. Warwick Mod. RC, Wilfred Roberts papers, MSS 308 · Lothian papers, NA Scot. · Katherine Mayo papers, Yale U. · Nancy Astor papers, U. Reading · S. Pedersen, *Family, dependence and the origins of the welfare state: Britain and France, 1914–1945* (1993) · J. Alberti, *Beyond suffrage: feminists in war and peace, 1914–1928* (1989) · B. Wasserstein, *Britain and the Jews of Europe, 1939–1945* (1979)

Archives Somerville College, Oxford · U. Lpool, corresp. and papers · Women's Library, London, papers | BL, corresp. with Lord Cecil, Add. MS 51141 · BL, corresp. with Society of Authors, Add. MS 56786 · BL OIOC, Indian Office papers · BL OIOC, corresp. with John Simon, MS Eur. F 77 · BLPES, corresp. with William Beveridge · Bodl. Oxf., corresp. with Gilbert Murray · CAC Cam., corresp. with A. V. Hill · JRL, letters to the *Manchester Guardian* · NA Scot., corresp. with Lord Lothian · PRO, Foreign and Home Office papers · U. Birm., Oliver Lodge papers · U. Reading, Astor papers · U. Warwick Mod. RC, Wilfred Roberts papers · Women's Library, London, corresp. relating to Indian women's affairs · Yale U., Katherine Mayo papers | FILM BFI NFTVA, documentary footage | SOUND BL NSA

Likenesses photograph, *c.*1909, U. Lpool, Rathbone Archives; repro. in Pedersen, 'Eleanor Rathbone' · J. Gunn, oils, 1933, NPG [*see illus.*]

Wealth at death £96,999: probate, 14 June 1946, *CGPLA Eng. & Wales*

Rathbone [*née* Reynolds]**, Hannah Mary** (1798–1878), writer, was born into a Quaker family at Ketley, near Wellington, Shropshire, on 5 July 1798, the fourth of seven children of Joseph Reynolds (*b.* 1768, *d.* after 1857), an ironmaster, who had married his own master's niece Deborah

Dearman (1770–1803). After their mother's death in child-birth the children were cared for by her sister Ann Dearman; Hannah Mary and her two sisters were educated at Mrs Herrick's school in Leicester. Hannah Mary Reynolds had been named after and was close to her father's half-sister Hannah Mary (1761–1839), who in 1786 had married the prominent Liverpool Quaker cotton merchant William *Rathbone (1757–1809). The familial connections were strong, and on 8 April 1817 the young Hannah Mary Reynolds married the Rathbones' second son, Richard (1788–1860). Nearly ten years older, he was now helping to run the family firm, and Hannah Mary initially felt isolated because of the long hours that her husband worked. The couple had three sons and three daughters, born over twenty years. The family lived first in Liverpool, and then outside the city.

Hannah Mary Rathbone was a talented artist. In the early 1830s she published drawings from Pinelli's etchings of Italian peasantry and contributed twenty paintings of birds to *The Poetry of Birds* (1833). Later she edited a poetry anthology on childhood: it featured many writers—including Wordsworth, Coleridge, Shelley, Hemans, 'L. E. L.', Scott, Tennyson, and Barrett—as well as Rathbone herself. It was published in 1840 as 'by a lady', and in 1841 with a preface over Rathbone's own name. In 1858 she would bring out a collection of her own original but indifferent poetry.

Mother–child relations were also central to Rathbone's most important publication, *The Diary of Lady Willoughby*. She had read many histories and memoirs of the civil war and adjacent periods, and in 1844 produced a diary—fictitious, but based on the life of Elizabeth, Lady Willoughby, whose husband had supported parliament and then the royalists during the civil war and its aftermath. This covered the period from 1635 to 1648; a second volume (1848) took the story into the 1660s. Rathbone's Lady Willoughby is characterized by her devotion to her mother, husband, and children, as well as to her (moderate Anglican) faith; she takes a humanitarian rather than a partisan approach to political and religious conflict. While her personality reflects her creator's strong family ties and Quaker outlook, Rathbone also skilfully shows Lady Willoughby self-censoring some potential criticism of others.

The 1844 *Diary* came out anonymously, and the publisher, Thomas Longman, presented it with seventeenth-century typeface and binding. Some assumed it was a genuine diary, others attributed it to Southey, Lord John Manners, or John Murray, but a preface to the third edition (1845) explained its fictitious nature. The *Diary* went into several editions, the last in 1873. It fostered a minor vogue for first-person historical narratives in contemporary typefaces, notably Anne Manning's 1850 account of Mary Powell (Milton's first wife), and Thackeray's *Henry Esmond* (1852).

Rathbone said in 1845 that she wrote for relaxation. In 1852 she produced a life and letters of her paternal grandfather, the philanthropist Richard *Reynolds (1735–1816),

partly as a respite from family troubles. Financial difficulties in the mid-1840s had forced a return to Liverpool, but this had also aggravated the always fragile health of both Rathbone and her eldest daughter. Meanwhile the Rathbones' son Basil's business failures and drinking caused anguish and shame to his parents. By late 1853 both the invalid daughter and the long-estranged Basil were dead. On the other hand, financial improvements, helped by the profits from the *Diary*, had enabled the family to buy a country property, Woodcote. Rathbone lost her husband in 1860, and later moved to Garston in Liverpool. She died at her home there, Ivy Lodge in Aigburth, aged seventy-nine, of paralysis aggravated by apoplexy, on 26 March 1878. JOANNE WILKES

Sources U. Lpool L., special collections and archives, Rathbone MSS, IV, VII, XV, XIX, XX, XXII [includes in typescript expanded version of *Old DNB* article on subject — XVB 3.9 (1)] · E. Greg, ed., *Reynolds–Rathbone diaries and letters, 1753–1839* (1905) · private information (1896)
Archives U. Lpool L., corresp. and papers
Likenesses G. Hargreaves, miniature, 1817, U. Lpool; repro. in Greg, ed., *Reynolds–Rathbone diaries and letters* · F. T. Goodall, oils, sketch, 1870, U. Lpool
Wealth at death under £8000: probate, 2 May 1878, *CGPLA Eng. & Wales*

Rathbone, John (*c*.1750–1807), painter, was born in Cheshire. Of his parents, nothing is known. He is thought to have been self-taught and spent his early years variously in Manchester, Preston, and Leeds. His landscapes at this time earned him a reputation as 'the Manchester Wilson'. In 1774 he submitted three of these to the Society of Arts exhibition at 30 John Street, Liverpool, the catalogue listing him as 'now at Preston'. He passed a brief period in Leeds in 1775 where a commission from a local merchant to paint the Turkish Arms on the contents of an export consignment tested Rathbone's resourcefulness and enterprise. He was settled in London by 1785, sending work to the Royal Academy that year from 78 Welbeck Street, Cavendish Square. His output proved to be considerable and between 1785 and 1806 he exhibited no fewer than forty-eight landscapes at the Royal Academy, showing a further two at the Society of Arts in London. He continued to travel extensively and through his paintings has become associated with areas such as the Lake District and Northumbria. He was often in the company of George Morland and J. C. Ibbetson, both of whom contributed figures to Rathbone's landscapes. For a short period he gave instruction to T. C. Hofland and Earl Harcourt is said to have received lessons from Rathbone too.

A number of his works are held in national public collections. There are three watercolour drawings by Rathbone in the British Museum and another in the Victoria and Albert Museum, London, and both the Walker Art Gallery and Royal Salford Museum have two oils each. Rathbone worked on panel, too, and an example is in Leeds City Art Gallery. Rathbone died in London in 1807. The painter Mary Rathbone (*fl.* 1795–1802) is thought to have been a relative, possibly his wife. TINA FISKE

Sources artist's file, archive material, Courtauld Inst., Witt Library · M. H. Grant, *A chronological history of the old English landscape*

painters, rev. edn, 8 vols. (1957–61) • E. R. Dibdin, 'Liverpool art and artists in the eighteenth century', *Walpole Society*, 6 (1917–18), 59–91 • J. Mayer, *Early exhibitions of arts in Liverpool* (1876) [privately printed] • Waterhouse, *18c painters* • Mallalieu, *Watercolour artists* • J. Hassell, *Memoirs of the life of … the late George Morland* (1806) • Graves, *RA exhibitors* • Bénézit, *Dict.* • A. Graves, *Art sales from early in the eighteenth century to early in the twentieth century*, 3 vols. (1918–21); repr. (1973) • J. Gould, *Biographical dictionary of painters, sculptors, engravers and architects*, new edn, 2 vols. (1839) • Bryan, *Painters* • R. N. James, *Painters and their works*, 3 vols. (1896–7) • Redgrave, *Artists* • S. Penketh, ed., *Concise illustrated catalogue of British paintings in the Walker Art Gallery and at Sudley* (1995) • L. Lambourne and J. Hamilton, eds., *British watercolours in the Victoria and Albert Museum* (1980) • L. Binyon, *Catalogue of drawings by British artists and artists of foreign origin working in Great Britain*, 4 vols. (1898–1907) • M. Strickland-Constable and others, eds., *Leeds City Art Galleries: concise catalogue* (1976) • Farington, *Diary*

Rathbone, William (1757–1809), merchant and philanthropist, the eldest son of William Rathbone (1726–1789) and his first wife, Rachel Rutter, was born at Liverpool. The family, originally sawyers from Gawsworth, Cheshire, migrated to Liverpool before 1730 to become timber merchants and ultimately shipbuilders and shipowners. By 1868 four generations of the family had been engaged in trade, having fulfilled a critical role in the commercial expansion of Liverpool as a port city. The vehicle for their entrepreneurial activities was the firm of William Rathbone & Sons, founded in Liverpool in 1746. During the succeeding fifty years the firm was to gain a notable place in the Liverpool merchant community as a result of its external trading connections with Europe, North America, and the West Indies. In 1784 it imported the first consignment (eight bales and three barrels) of raw cotton to be grown in the United States. Previously, virtually all cotton imports had come from the West Indies, and the new consignment was seized at the custom house as an evasion of the navigation laws on the grounds that cotton was not grown in North America. The importation of raw cotton proved to be a lucrative business both for the Rathbones and other Liverpool merchants in the heyday of expansion of the Lancashire cotton industry before 1850. Their links with North America remained dominant, although they maintained a diversity of trading interests. In addition to raw cotton, turpentine, tar, ashes, flour, and tobacco were imported from the USA, hides from South America, wool from Australia, mahogany and sugar from the West Indies, and oats, barley, and butter from Ireland.

Rathbone was a birthright member of the Society of Friends and received a Quaker education. Well read in the classics, eloquent and energetic, he complemented his business interests with strong adherence to public causes of a liberal nature, both local and national. On 17 August 1786 he married Hannah Mary (d. 1839), the only daughter of Richard *Reynolds (1735–1816); they had four sons and one daughter.

In 1792 Rathbone was prominent in efforts to avert the war with France, and in that year, and again in 1809, led a campaign against the monopoly of the East India Company. He also advocated freedom of trade with the United States and gave evidence before parliament on that subject. Equally controversially, he participated in the early anti-slavery movement and lent powerful support to his fellow Liverpudlian William Roscoe in calling for the abolition of the slave trade. In view of Liverpool's leading role in the trade, it was to Rathbone's credit that he was prepared to endure the censure of his fellow merchants.

In religious terms Rathbone was an early critic of some fundamental aspects of Quaker discipline. He objected especially to the disownment of Friends for mixed marriages and to the voluntary payment of tithes. He also argued in favour of wider latitude of behaviour in relation to Quaker doctrinal principles. Thus in 1792 he became a subscriber to the Unitarian Book Society of London, an action which produced a remonstrance (31 August 1793) from an Irish Friend, Job Scott. In the later 1790s Rathbone became embroiled in a doctrinal dispute emanating from Irish Friends, focusing on the infallibility of scripture. Abraham Shackleton took the side of heterodoxy, and the emergent controversy was fomented by Hannah Barnard (d. 1828) from New York. The heterodox party was then labelled the 'Barnard schism'. On 30 March 1804 Rathbone published a *Narrative* of the schism, 'correct in regard to documentary facts', for which action he was disowned by the Hardshaw (St Helens) monthly meeting at Manchester on 28 February 1805, on the grounds that he had expressed opinions contrary to Friends' doctrine on the immediate teaching of Christ and to the reverence due to the scriptures. Rathbone did not appeal against the decision, nor did he join any other religious body. He did, however, worship occasionally with the Unitarian congregation presided over by Robert Lewin at Benn's Garden, Liverpool. His close associate William Roscoe also attended the church.

Rathbone died at his residence, Greenbank, near Liverpool, on 11 February 1809 and was interred at the Quaker burial-ground in Liverpool. His commercial interests were inherited by his eldest son, also called **William Rathbone** (1787–1868), who inherited his father's philanthropic spirit in full measure and became eminent in Liverpool for his beneficence and altruism. Born in Liverpool on 17 June 1787, he was educated at a school in Hackney, Middlesex, under Thomas Belsham until 1803, when he proceeded to Oxford for private tuition by Theophilus Houlbroke. A unitarian by religious conviction, he maintained his Quaker connections until his marriage in 1812 to Elizabeth, the eldest child of Samuel *Greg and the sister of Robert Hyde Greg, Samuel Greg, and William Rathbone Greg. For marrying out of the Society of Friends he was disowned, but was later reinstated. He withdrew finally from the society in 1829.

Rathbone achieved public recognition in the 1820s as an advocate of Roman Catholic emancipation. Coincidentally he developed an interest in parliamentary and municipal reform. On 13 January 1836 a public presentation was made to him in recognition of his services in these respects, an event which led to his appointment as mayor of Liverpool the following year. As a local politician he took a keen interest in educational provision and was instrumental in securing the advantages of the corporation schools on terms satisfactory to all denominations.

In 1844 he presided at a meeting held in Liverpool to vindicate the actions of the Irish Roman Catholic lawyer Daniel O'Connell in favour of the abolition of the Anglo-Irish union inaugurated in 1801. Rathbone's interest in Irish affairs was further indicated in 1846-7, when he was placed in sole charge of the fund (c.£70,000 to £80,000) contributed by the New England states for the relief of suffering consequent on the Irish famine. In Quaker terms he was 'worldly' and, aside from his highly visible public career, possessed a taste for art.

Rathbone died at Greenbank on 1 February 1868 after an operation for calculus, and was buried in the borough cemetery. Joseph Blanco White had been his guest during his last days. A mural monument to his memory was placed in Renshaw Street Chapel, and a public statue was erected in Sefton Park, Liverpool. His wife, Elizabeth, died on 24 October 1882, aged ninety-two. Their eldest child, Elizabeth, married John Paget, a magistrate of London, in 1839, while their second daughter, Hannah Mary (1816–1872), married John Hamilton Thom on 2 January 1838. Their eldest son, William *Rathbone (1819–1902), was at one time MP for North Caernarvonshire.

ALEXANDER GORDON, rev. M. W. KIRBY

Sources E. A. Rathbone, *Records of the Rathbone family* (1913) · S. Marriner, *Rathbones of Liverpool* (1961) · S. Marriner, *The economic and social development of Merseyside* (1982) · F. E. Hyde, *Liverpool and the Mersey: an economic history of a port, 1700–1970* (1971) · J. R. Harris, ed., *Liverpool and Merseyside: essays in the economic and social history of the port and its hinterland* (1969)
Archives U. Lpool L., Sydney Jones Library, corresp. and papers
Likenesses E. Smith, line engraving (after J. Allen), BM, NPG · statue (William Rathbone jun.), Sefton Park, Liverpool
Wealth at death under £160,000—William Rathbone the younger: probate, 15 April 1868, *CGPLA Eng. & Wales*

Rathbone, William (1787–1868). *See under* Rathbone, William (1757–1809).

Rathbone, William (1819–1902), merchant and philanthropist, was born in Liverpool on 11 February 1819, the eldest son of William *Rathbone (1787–1868) [*see under* Rathbone, William (1757–1809)] and his wife, Elizabeth Rathbone, *née* Greg (1789/90–1882). After passing through schools at Gateacre, Cheam, and Everton he was apprenticed (1835–8) to Nicol, Duckworth & Co., Bombay merchants, in Liverpool. In October 1838 he went with Thomas Ashton (1818–1898), the father of Baron Ashton of Hyde, for a semester at the University of Heidelberg. From Heidelberg he toured Italy (1839), and on his return obtained a clerkship in the London firm of Baring Brothers. In April 1841 the senior partner, Joshua Bates, took him on a business tour to the United States; the impression of this visit and two later ones made him a committed free-trader.

At the end of 1841 Rathbone became a partner in his father's firm, Rathbone Brothers & Co., which was then at a low point in its fortunes; by 1842 its capital had fallen to £40,000. With his brother Samuel Greg Rathbone, who became a partner in 1847, he rebuilt the firm's position and diversified its operations, expanding the range of commodities handled, establishing branch houses in

William Rathbone (1819–1902), by unknown photographer, c.1889

China and an agency in New York, increasing its consignment business, and building up a fleet of clippers. Although William Rathbone withdrew from active management of the firm after his entry into parliament, just as it was reaching the height of its prosperity, his partners continued to rely on his advice, especially during financial crises in the 1880s and 1890s. On 6 September 1847 he married Lucretia Wainwright Gair, the eldest daughter of his former partner at Baring Brothers, Samuel Gair; the couple had four sons and one daughter.

Rathbone's high ideals of public duty were formed under the influences of his mother, Elizabeth Greg, the daughter of Samuel Greg of Quarry Bank and an authority on school management, and of John Hamilton Thom, minister of the Renshaw Street Unitarian Church in Liverpool, who had married his sister Hannah in 1838. Convinced that wealth was a 'trust', Rathbone determined at an early age to devote an ever-increasing proportion of his income to public objects. Three causes in particular absorbed his attention. First, he was closely concerned with the relief of poverty and the organization of philanthropic efforts in his native town. He worked as a collector for the District Provident Society from 1849, thus gaining some insight into the living conditions of the poor; he helped to raise and administer the £100,000 that Liverpool contributed to the Cotton Famine Relief Fund in 1862–3;

he served on the executive of the Liverpool Central Relief and Charity Organization Society; and he was a member of the Liverpool select vestry from 1867 until his death. In his best-known work, *Social duties: Considered in Reference to the Organisation of Effort in Works of Benevolence and Public Utility* (1867), he denounced 'the desultory nature of much of our charity', and argued that philanthropic efforts must both be better organized and serve to rebuild 'relations of personal kindness and friendly intercourse' between rich and poor. In 1871 and again in 1887 he persuaded the Local Government Board to investigate the system prevalent in Elberfeld and some German towns whereby volunteer almoners accepted responsibility for administering poor relief; while there was little national enthusiasm for this system, in the late 1880s he convinced the Liverpool Central Relief Society to set up district committees and enlist volunteer 'friendly visitors' to investigate and manage cases.

Rathbone had greater success in a second field of endeavour, the establishment of district nursing. His first experiment in this area arose out of personal tragedy—the death, on 27 May 1859, of his wife. Having witnessed the extent to which skilled nursing had eased her suffering, he engaged Mary Robinson, the nurse who had attended her, to work in the homes of the poor. Convinced of the extent of the need, and after consultation with Florence Nightingale, he established the Liverpool Training School and Home for Nurses, which began work on 1 July 1862. By the end of 1865 Liverpool had been divided into eighteen districts, each provided with nursing under the superintendence of ladies who made themselves responsible for expenses; for about a year Rathbone himself took the place of one of the superintendents during her absence. Rathbone also achieved the reform of nursing in the workhouses, by securing in 1865 the invaluable services of Agnes Elizabeth Jones (1832–1868). For three years he bore the entire expenses. His nursing reforms were extended to Birmingham and Manchester, and to London in 1874, when the National Association for Providing Trained Nurses was formed, with Rathbone as chairman of its subcommittee for organizing district nursing. In 1888–9 he was honorary secretary, and subsequently vice-president, of Queen Victoria's Jubilee Institute for Nurses, to which the queen had devoted £70,000 out of the women's offering. In his work with district nursing he was greatly assisted by his second wife, Emily Acheson Lyle (1832–1918), the daughter of Acheson Lyle of Londonderry (and a second cousin), whom he married on 6 February 1862, and with whom he had two daughters and four sons.

Rathbone also played a large part in efforts to improve educational provision. He helped to found the University College of Liverpool, which was opened in January 1882; with his two brothers he endowed the King Alfred chair of modern literature and English language; and he was president of the college from 1892. In addition he was very active in the movement for establishing the University College of North Wales (opened in October 1884), of which he was president from 1891. He was actively concerned in the Welsh Intermediate Education Act of 1889. Liverpool gave him the freedom of the city on 21 October 1891. In May 1895 he was made LLD by Victoria University.

The Rathbones were one of Liverpool's pre-eminent Liberal families: William's father and two brothers all served on the city council. His own political activity began in 1852, when he organized the Liberal election campaign in the north end of the city; subsequently he became chairman of the local party. Gladstone's election in 1865 for South Lancashire owed much to his energy. In November 1868 he was elected as one of the three members for Liverpool. Among other matters he took part in shaping the Bankruptcy Bill of 1869. He was especially interested in measures for local government, about which he published several essays, and in the licensing laws, opposing prohibition and demanding not more legislation but stricter administration. He sat for Liverpool until 1880, when, after declining to pledge to support the views of the Home Rule Association, he chose to stand aside in Liverpool and instead to contest South-West Lancashire. He was defeated, but was returned in the following November at a by-election for Caernarvonshire; he sat for the county until 1885, and from 1885 for North Caernarvonshire. He remained in the Gladstonian wing of the party, but refused to vote for the third reading of the Home Rule Bill in 1893. In 1895 Rathbone retired from parliament. He was deputy lieutenant for Lancashire.

Rathbone's contemporaries considered that 'straightforwardness and pertinacity, with entire unselfishness', were the essential features in his character. He lacked the bonhomie and humour of his father, but although his manner was dry, his actions witnessed to his deep humanity. His private correspondence reveals a man deeply devoted to his wife and full of anxious concern for the moral development of his children, several of whom sought to carry on his business, political, and philanthropic interests. His sons William Gair (1849–1919), Thomas Ashton (1856–1895), and Francis Warre (1875–1939) became partners in Rathbone Brothers; his daughter Elizabeth Lucretia (1851–1920) helped with the management of district nursing and became a poor-law guardian; another daughter, Emily Evelyn (1865–1954), and her husband, Hugh Reynolds Rathbone (1862–1940), were greatly concerned with the management of Liverpool University; his son Acheson Lyle (1868–1923) served on the city council. But it was his youngest daughter, Eleanor *Rathbone (1872–1946), who most resembled him in character, became his assistant and confidante after his retirement from parliament, wrote his biography after his death, and succeeded him as a municipal reformer and in parliament. The conventions of biography seek to isolate individual contributions, but many of Rathbone's projects were collaborative and much of his influence lay in his ability to inspire and organize broader efforts. He died at his home, Greenbank, Toxteth Park, Liverpool, on 6 March 1902, and was buried in Toxteth cemetery.

SUSAN PEDERSEN

Sources E. F. Rathbone, *William Rathbone: a memoir* (1905) · *The Times* (7 March 1902) · *Christian Life* (7 March 1902) · *Christian Life* (12

March 1902) · *Christian Life* (29 March 1902) · S. Marriner, *Rathbones of Liverpool, 1845–73* (1961) · M. Simey, *Charitable effort in Liverpool in the nineteenth century* (1951) · L. Nottingham, *Rathbone Brothers: from merchant to banker, 1742–1992* (1992) · G. Hardy, *William Rathbone and the early history of district nursing* (1981) · *DNB*

Archives Leics. RO, political and misc. letters received · U. Lpool L., Sydney Jones Library, corresp. and papers | Bishopsgate Institute, London, letters to George Howell · BL, memoranda and corresp. with W. E. Gladstone, Add. MSS 44402–44784 · BL, corresp. with Florence Nightingale · Bodl. Oxf., letters to Sir Henry Burdett · Lpool RO, letters from Florence Nightingale, with related papers · U. Wales, Bangor, Department of Manuscripts and Archives, letters from Florence Nightingale relating to Bangor typhoid epidemic of 1882

Likenesses Elliott & Fry, carte-de-visite, 1883, NPG · H. Bond, bust, 1889, Liverpool Reform Club · photograph, *c.*1889, NPG [*see illus.*] · C. J. Allen, bronze medallion, 1899, NPG · G. Frampton, bronze statue, *c.*1899, St John's Gardens, Liverpool · photograph, 1899, repro. in Rathbone, *William Rathbone* · C. J. Allen, bust, University College, Liverpool · W. Richmond, oils, Rathbone Bros. Offices, Liverpool · marble relief bust, Unitarian church, Ullet Road, Liverpool

Wealth at death £234,558 12*s.* 2*d.*: probate, 2 May 1902, *CGPLA Eng. & Wales*

Rathborne, Aaron (*b.* 1571/2), land surveyor and author, was possibly trained by the London mathematician and teacher John Goodwyn, but his origins are obscure. From 1605 he was surveying estates in Yorkshire, Cumberland, Durham, and Lincolnshire, and he was one of those employed in the Jacobean surveys of crown lands. He surveyed land in Suffolk in 1613.

Rathborne was lodging with Roger Burgis against Salisbury House Gate in the Strand, London, when he published *The Surveyor in Foure Bookes* (1616). This influential textbook addressed the practical everyday needs of surveyors more realistically than had been done hitherto. Rathborne placed surveying firmly among the mathematical sciences and the first two books of *The Surveyor* dealt with the elements of geometry, especially with those relevant to surveying. The third book described surveying instruments and their application. Rathborne was particularly concerned with the need to maintain professional standards and pointed out common errors in the use of the plane table (a popular surveying instrument), and suggested ways of overcoming them. He introduced a 'decimal chain'—a predecessor to the one devised by Edmund Gunter—in which each perch was subdivided into 100 parts, and discussed its employment in land measurement using geometrical methods. The title page to *The Surveyor* promoted the use of the altazimuth theodolite (an instrument that enabled simultaneous measurement of horizontal and vertical angles) but Rathborne treated it dismissively in the text, as a complicated instrument already well described. Instead, he recommended his azimuth theodolite or 'peractor' (an instrument for measuring horizontal angles) and a circumferentor (a type of surveying compass) for measuring large areas. The final book of *The Surveyor* followed earlier texts in discussing legal and manorial issues.

Two years after this publication Rathborne was granted

Aaron Rathborne (*b.* 1571/2), by Simon de Passe, 1616

a patent to make a map of the cities of London and Westminster, as well as maps of York, Bristol, Norwich, Canterbury, Bath, Oxford, Cambridge, and Windsor. The co-patentee was Roger Bruges (probably his landlord of 1616). Rathborne was consulted about estate business in Galtres Forest in the North Riding of Yorkshire in 1622. Neither his later activities nor his date of death are known.

SARAH BENDALL

Sources A. Rathborne, *The surveyor in foure bookes* (1616) · F. W. Steer and others, *Dictionary of land surveyors and local map-makers of Great Britain and Ireland, 1530–1850*, ed. P. Eden, 2nd edn, ed. S. Bendall, 2 vols. (1997) · J. A. Bennett, 'Geometry and surveying in early-seventeenth-century England', *Annals of Science*, 48 (1991), 345–54 · H. Lawrence, 'John Norden and his colleagues: surveyors of crown lands', *Cartographic Journal*, 22 (1985), 54–6 · J. A. Bennett, *The divided circle: a history of instruments for astronomy, navigation and surveying* (1987) · E. G. R. Taylor, *The mathematical practitioners of Tudor and Stuart England* (1954); repr. (1970) · Rymer, *Foedera*, 2nd edn · *Report on manuscripts in various collections*, 8 vols., HMC, 55 (1901–14), vol. 8 · *CSP dom., 1603–10* · J. A. Bennett and O. Brown, *The compleat surveyor* (1982) · R. W. Hoyle, '"Shearing the hog": the reform of the estates *c.* 1598–1640', *The estates of the English crown, 1558–1640*, ed. R. W. Hoyle (1992), 204–62 · T. S. Willan and E. W. Crossley, eds., *Three seventeenth-century Yorkshire surveys* (1941) · N. Yorks. CRO, ZBA 11/8/5/2

Archives N. Yorks. CRO, map · W. Yorks. AS, Leeds, Yorkshire Archaeological Society, map | BL, Add. MSS · BL, Lansdowne MSS

Likenesses S. de Passe, engraving, 1616, NPG [*see illus.*] · engraving, repro. in Rathbone, *Surveyor*

Rathborne, Wilson (1748–1831), naval officer, son of Richard Rathborne, a protestant clergyman, was born at Balnakil, near Loughrea, co. Galway, on 16 July 1748. In September 1763 he was entered as an able seaman in the *Niger*, with Sir Thomas Adams, on the Newfoundland station. As able seaman and midshipman he served for six years in the *Niger*. He then followed Adams to the *Boston*, and ten months later to the *Romney*, in which he returned to England in 1770. In 1773 he joined the sloop *Hunter* as able seaman, in which rating he continued for a year. He was then a midshipman for some months, and, seeing no prospect of promotion, accepted a warrant as master of the *Hunter*.

It was not until 1780 that Rathborne was allowed to return to England, and, having obtained an introduction to the earl of Sandwich, he passed his examination on 16 March; two days later he was promoted lieutenant of the *Bedford*, with Commodore Edmund Affleck. In the *Bedford* he was present in the actions off the Chesapeake on 16 March and 5 September 1781, at St Kitts in January, and in Admiral George Rodney's actions under the lee of Dominica on 9 and 12 April 1782. In the summer of 1783 the *Bedford* returned to England and was paid off. At the time of the armament of 1787 Rathborne was in the *Atlas*, carrying Sir Edmund Affleck's flag; afterwards he was appointed to the *Colossus*, one of the Channel Fleet, in which he remained until 1791. In December 1792 he was appointed to the *Captain*, in which he went to the Mediterranean in 1793, and took part in the occupation of Toulon, the reduction of Corsica, and the action of 14 March 1795, when he was severely wounded in the right arm, and lost his right eye. He was invalided for the recovery of his health, and on 9 November 1795 was promoted to the rank of commander.

In 1797 Rathborne had command of the *Good Design*, convoying the trade from Leith to the Elbe, or to Elsinore. In December 1799 he was appointed to the brig *Racoon*, which he commanded in the channel, the Mediterranean, and the West Indies. On 18 November 1802 he was promoted captain and posted to the *Santa Margarita*, He returned to England in 1803, and, in the *Santa Margarita*, was attached to the Channel Fleet. On 4 November 1805 he was in company with Sir Richard John Strachan when he fell in with the French ships which, under Dumanoir, had escaped from Trafalgar. Now, harassed by the frigates *Santa Margarita* and *Phoenix*, they were brought to action and all taken. Rathborne almost immediately afterwards received an appointment to the *Foudroyant*, to which he objected, and on Admiralty orders he was permitted to remain in the *Santa Margarita* until December 1807, when the ship, being quite worn out, was paid off. For the next two years Rathborne commanded the sea fencibles of the Essex coast, and from 1810 to 1813 he had charge of the impress service in the Tyne. In 1822 he was appointed superintendent of the ordinary at Chatham, a post which he held until 1825. He had married, in 1805, Cecilia Mary, a daughter of John French of Loughrea, co. Galway; the couple had three sons. His sister Hester was the mother of John Wilson Croker, the politician and writer. Rathborne retained a connection with Loughrea all his life, and may have had property there, as well as a house in Kensington, London. He died in the summer of 1831.

J. K. Laughton, *rev.* A. W. H. Pearsall

Sources J. Leyland, ed., *Dispatches and letters relating to the blockade of Brest, 1803–1805*, 2 vols., Navy RS, 14, 21 (1899–1902) · *The Croker papers: the correspondence and diaries of … John Wilson Croker*, ed. L. J. Jennings, 3 vols. (1884) · J. Ralfe, *The naval biography of Great Britain*, 4 vols. (1828) · J. Marshall, *Royal naval biography*, 2/2 (1825), 739–43 · PRO, ADM 1/2400–3, 51/466, 37/7446, 7489, 7870, 107/8, p.34 · *Navy List*

Archives PRO

Ratsey, Gamaliel (*d.* 1605), highwayman, was said to have been the son of Richard Ratsey, gentleman, of Market Deeping, Lincolnshire. Because relevant quarter session and assize records of the period have not survived his career is obscure. According to a contemporary biographer, writing in the *Life and Death of Gamaliel Ratsey* of 1605, Ratsey's first theft was of a bag containing £40 from an inn in Spalding. Arrested at Market Deeping, he was committed to gaol but escaped 'in his shirt'. This incident seems to have occurred in 1599 for the Market Deeping constables' accounts of that year mention the sum of 32*s*. 6*d*. 'laid out for caryinge Gamaliell Ratsey to Lincoln goale' (Market Deeping parish officers' accounts, 1570–1647, section D, fol. 13*v*). A period of military service followed. Ratsey may have received a pardon on condition of military service or have joined the army as a fugitive. However this may be, he is said to have gone to Ireland with the army of Robert Devereux, second earl of Essex, in 1599. He distinguished himself there, attaining the rank of sergeant in Captain Roger Langford's company of foot, stationed at Carrickfergus, and then, in 1603, returned to England with Charles Blount, eighth Lord Mountjoy. Thereafter, unable to settle to peaceful pursuits, he turned to highway robbery.

Nothing is known of Ratsey's exploits beyond what is alleged in contemporary pamphlet literature. However, he seems to have operated mainly in the east midlands, sometimes alone and sometimes in confederacy with two thieves named Henry Shorthose and George Snell. 'Shorthose' is often supposed to have been a nickname but, like Ratsey, this man is said to have hailed from Market Deeping, and bishops' transcripts and other records of the period do document the existence of a family of that name in the parish. The pamphlets depict Ratsey as bold, artful, generous to the poor, and possessed of a rough sense of humour. In one tale he bestows 40*s*. upon an old couple on the road to St Ives, declaring that he would 'favour and pitie them that are poore … for the rich can helpe themselves' (Atkins, sig. C3*v*); in another he robs two clothiers near Stamford and then knights them as Sir Walter Woolsack and Sir Samuel Sheepskin. A few of these stories, like that recounting his robbery of nine men on Helpston Heath, Northamptonshire, may be embroidered versions of genuine incidents, but most appear to be fictitious. The tale of Ratsey and the poor farmer appears in different guises in the literature of many famous outlaws, including Robin Hood and Dick Turpin.

Ratsey was convicted of highway robbery and sentenced to death at the Lent assizes for Bedfordshire in 1605 and executed in Bedford on 26 or 27 March 1605. He achieved a measure of contemporary fame. Two pamphlets appeared in the months following his execution. *The Life and Death of Gamaliel Ratsey, a Famous Thief of England*, was entered on the Stationers' register to John Trundell on 2 May 1605, and *Ratseis Ghost, or, The Second Part of his Madde Prankes and Robberies*, was printed by Valentine Syms and entered to John Hodges of St Paul's Churchyard on 31 May. Two ballads, of which no copies survive, were also entered at Stationers' Hall to Thomas Pavyer on 2 May 1605. Ratsey was the subject of two epigrams in Jacob Johnson's *Epigrammatum libellus* (1615). A number of other curious allusions to him occur in seventeenth-century literature. Ben Jonson, in *The Alchemist* (1610), speaks of 'a face, cut for thee, worse than Gamaliel Ratsey's' (Herford and Simpson, 5.298) and Thomas Randolph's *Hey for Honesty* (1651) carries this reference to an old painted lady: 'Take but the white-loam from this old mud-wall, And she will look worse than Gamaliel Ratsey' (*Poetical and Dramatic Works*, 2.470). It is speculated that these allusions may have been inspired by a grotesque mask worn by Ratsey during robberies to terrify his victims into submission. Gabriel Harvey's reference to Gamaliell Hobgoblin in *Pierces Supererogation* (1593), commonly explained in the same way, is, however, too early to be an allusion to Ratsey.

PHILIP SUGDEN

Sources S. H. Atkins, ed., *The life and death of Gamaliel Ratsey a famous thief, of England, executed at Bedford the 26th of March ... 1605* (1935) • H. B. Charlton, ed., *Ratseis ghost* (1932) • parish officers' accounts, Market Deeping, 1570–1647, Lincs. Arch., 10/1, section D, fols. 13v, 22 • Arber, *Regs. Stationers*, vol. 3 • *CSP Ire.*, 1601–3 • Ben Jonson, ed. C. H. Herford, P. Simpson, and E. M. Simpson, 11 vols. (1925–52), vol. 5 • *Poetical and dramatic works of Thomas Randolph*, ed. W. C. Hazlitt, 2 (1875) • *The works of Gabriel Harvey*, ed. A. B. Grosart, 2 (1884) • bishops' transcripts, Market Deeping, 1562–1600, Lincs. Arch. • *DNB* • S. Lee, *A life of William Shakespeare* (1916), 278–9 • J. O. Halliwell-Phillipps, *Outlines of the life of Shakespeare*, 1 (1887)

Rattee, James (1820–1855), woodcarver and mason, was born at Fundenhall, Norfolk. Of his parents, nothing is known. He was apprenticed to a carpenter and joiner of Norwich, named Ollett. He became interested in ecclesiastical art, frequenting the cathedral and other churches in the city and its neighbourhood; at his request his employer taught him carving, in which he soon demonstrated a remarkable skill. In 1842 he left Norwich and went into business as a woodcarver in Sidney Street, Cambridge. His talent was recognized by the Cambridge Camden Society which employed him on the famous restoration of Holy Sepulchre Church (the Round Church) in Cambridge (1841–3), under the direction of Anthony Salvin. The continuing patronage of members of the society enabled him to expand his business and in 1850 he established large-scale workshops, with steam-powered plant, on the Hills Road, Cambridge.

Rattee worked with A. W. N. Pugin in restoring the choir of Jesus College chapel (1846–9); some of the design work was carried out by Rattee and submitted to Pugin before execution. In the choir of Ely Cathedral, beginning *c.*1850, he carried out the designs of George Gilbert Scott, and his work on the oak screen, stalls, organ-case, and restored tomb of Bishop William de Luda (*d.* 1298) was of the highest quality. In 1852 he was sent abroad for his health and travelled in Belgium and Germany, studying the work of such medieval artists as Quinten Metsys (1466–1530). On his return he was commissioned to construct an elaborate new reredos at Ely Cathedral to Scott's design, incorporating carved alabaster and inlaid work. His work, on a more modest scale, is found in numerous churches in Cambridgeshire and across the country, with examples abroad as far away as Newfoundland Cathedral.

Rattee died at his house in Hills Road, Cambridge, on 29 March 1855, and was buried on 6 April in the cemetery in Mill Road. He had no children, but his widow, Caroline, kept an interest in his business which, renamed Rattee and Kett, continued under the direction of another Norfolk woodcarver, George Kett (1809–1872), and his descendants until it was sold in 1926.

G. C. BOASE, *rev.* CHRISTOPHER MARSDEN

Sources *The Builder*, 13 (1855), 190 • *The Ecclesiologist*, 16 (1855), 174 • *GM*, 2nd ser., 43 (1855), 539 • A. de Salvo, *Kett of Cambridge: an eminent Victorian and his family* (1993) • trade directories • *Cambridgeshire*, Pevsner (1970)

Rattenbury [*née* Wolfe], **Alma Victoria** (1897/8–1935), accused murderer, was born probably in Prince Rupert, British Columbia, Canada, the daughter of a goldmining prospector named Wolfe (who subsequently disappeared) and his wife, Elizabeth, reputedly a relative of W. G. Grace. After her mother's remarriage Alma took her stepfather's surname of Clarke. She was educated in Kamloops and Toronto. From an early age she showed musical talent and reputedly was a soloist with the Toronto Symphony Orchestra at the age of seventeen. Later she composed sentimental ballads under the name of Lozanne.

In 1914 Alma married Calendon Robert Radclyffe Dolling (1890?–1916), nephew of the earl of Caledon, an Anglo-Irishman. On the outbreak of the First World World he enlisted in the Royal Welch Fusiliers and she worked in the War Office. After his death in action she joined the Scottish Women's Hospital attached to the French Red Cross as a stretcher-bearer, during which time she was twice wounded and awarded the Croix de Guerre with star and palm. In peacetime she met Captain Thomas Compton Pakenham (1893–1957), a kinsman of the earl of Longford. In 1920 Alma was cited as a co-respondent in Pakenham's divorce and she married him in 1921. After separating from Pakenham and returning to Canada, Alma earned her living by giving music lessons and writing sentimental songs.

In Canada, Alma met Francis Mawson Rattenbury (1867–1935), who had established a successful architectural practice in Victoria and whose marriage was moribund. In 1925 Alma divorced Pakenham and was cited as co-respondent in Rattenbury's divorce. They married later that year, but the scandal of the divorce forced them to leave Victoria. A child, John, was born in 1928 and shortly afterwards they settled in Bournemouth at the Villa Madeira, 5 Manor Road. The marriage was happy but celibate after the birth of John. Alma, whose songs were sung by Richard Tauber and Frank Titterton as well as being broadcast by celebrated band leaders such as Ambrose, was in 1932 diagnosed with tuberculosis. Her moods became volatile, and her habits more intemperate.

In 1934 Rattenbury engaged as a chauffeur and handyman George Percy Stoner (b. 1916). Stoner and Alma soon became lovers, with Rattenbury acting as a *mari complaisant*. After his seduction, Stoner changed from being an unassuming youth to a self-asserting character. On 24 March 1935 the Rattenburys mooted a visit to Bridport. Stoner, when he heard of this proposal, became agitated lest conjugal relations be resumed. At 1.30 a.m. on 25 March the police were summoned to Villa Madeira; Rattenbury had been taken to Strathallen Nursing Home with head injuries, and foul play was suspected. They found Alma highly excited, incoherent, and intoxicated. She repeatedly declared that she had attacked her husband with a mallet.

Alma found herself in prison with no clear recollection of what had happened. She did not remember signing or reaffirming her confession but refused to reject it. In her infatuation with Stoner she assumed responsibility for what had happened. After Rattenbury's death on 28 March Stoner was arrested and admitted hitting Rattenbury with his mallet. On 29 March he and Alma were charged in the Bournemouth police court. The director of public prosecutions decided to proceed with the case against both the accused, each being a self-confessed murderer. He did not charge them with conspiracy, as there was no evidence of collusion. Each was to be charged individually with murder but in the same indictment, so that they were tried together. Alma was cajoled by Daphne Kingham, Pakenham's sister, into withdrawing her confession because it would haunt her two sons for all their lives. Mrs Kingham threatened that if Alma would not protect her children, she must not expect anyone to care for them if she was convicted. A few days before the trial Mrs Kingham brought Christopher Pakenham to see his mother and this broke Alma's resistance.

The joint trial, which opened on 27 May at the central criminal court before Sir Travers Humphreys, was the criminal sensation of the year. Alma was offered up to £3500 for her story, then a considerable sum, which she refused. Following a clear direction from the judge, the jury were out for less than an hour before acquitting Alma but convicting Stoner (31 May). Mrs Kingham took Alma away but the press besieged the flat. Her doctor took her to a nursing home pursued by journalists. Alma was physically and mentally ill. Her grief, misery, and shame for her children and Stoner were indescribable. On 4 June she bought a kitchen knife, took a train to Bournemouth, and on the Avon riverbank near Christchurch she drove the knife into her breast six times, three times penetrating her heart. She left scraps of paper, none containing a confession, the last of which said 'If I only thought it would help Stoner I would stay but it has been pointed out too vividly that I cannot help him—and that is my death sentence' (Napley, 211). When Stoner learned of her death, he wept.

Alma Rattenbury was buried on 8 June 1935 at St Peter's Church, Bournemouth. The conduct at her funeral was disgraceful: flowers were taken from her grave as souvenirs. At first flowers were also taken from the garden of Villa Madeira but others subsequently forced an entry and stole various objects, including children's toys, letters, and photographs. After hearing of Alma's death, Stoner made a statement to the effect that he was not guilty. His appeal was turned down but a petition was launched and Stoner was reprieved. He served seven years before being released to serve in the army during the Second World War. Several television dramas have since been based on the story and Terence Rattigan's *Cause célèbre* (1977) was based on the Stoner–Rattenbury murder trial.

ELIZABETH MURRAY

Sources Michael Havers, *Tragedy in three voices: the Rattenbury murder* (1980) · D. Napley, *Murder at the Villa Madeira: the Rattenbury case* (1988) · T. Reksten, *Rattenbury* (1978) · J. D. Casswell, *A lance for liberty* (1961) · F. T. Jesse, *The trial of Alma Victoria Rattenbury and George Percy Stoner* (1935) · *The Times* (28–30 May 1935) · *The Times* (10 June 1935) · *Bournemouth Evening Echo* (March–June 1935) · *Daily Mail* (28–31 May 1935) · *Daily Mail* (1 June 1935) · *Daily Mail* (10 June 1935) · *News of the World* (9 June 1935) · *Daily Express* (10 June 1935) · J. Mortimer, *Famous trials* (1984) · J. Agate, *Ego 2: being more of the autobiography of James Agate* (1936), 187–9 · CGPLA Eng. & Wales (1937) · d. cert.

Likenesses photographs, repro. in Napley, *Murder at the Villa Madeira*

Wealth at death £280 19s. 9d. in England: administration with will, 17 Nov 1937, CGPLA Eng. & Wales

Rattigan, Sir Terence Mervyn (1911–1977), playwright, was born on 9 June 1911 at Cornwall Gardens, Kensington, London, the second son of (William) Frank Rattigan (1878–1952) and his wife, Vera Houston (1885–1971). His father's diplomatic career reached its zenith in 1922 on his appointment as acting high commissioner in Constantinople; shortly afterwards he was suspended, ostensibly after a clash with the foreign secretary, Lord Curzon, but in fact because of his liaison with Princess Elizabeth of Romania and her subsequent abortion. This event cast a pall over Rattigan's adolescence and rocked the family's finances. Later Rattigan was to adopt a more relaxed attitude to his father's philandering, making it the subject of one of his minor comedies, *Who is Sylvia?* (1950).

In a talk on the BBC Home Service in 1949, Rattigan spoke of the thrill of his first trip to the theatre, to see *Cinderella*, in terms which indicate not merely its hold on his seven-year-old imagination but its lasting effect on his work: 'The character had completely captured the audience's imagination, and mine with it, as no inanimate object like a theme or an idea or a moral could ever do' (Wansell, 19). He developed his literary ambitions when he joined his elder brother Brian at Sandroyd preparatory school near Cobham in Surrey in 1920, billing his precocious efforts as by 'the famous playwrite and author T. M. Rattigan' (Wansell, 80; the M for Mervyn being his own affectation). His passion for the theatre grew so great that, as he later explained to his arch-critic, Kenneth Tynan, when offered a choice between a beating and giving up a part in the school play, he opted for the former.

Rattigan won the seventh entrance scholarship to Harrow School in 1925 and enjoyed a distinguished school career, winning the English literature prize and the Bourchier prize for modern history. He followed in his father's

Sir Terence Mervyn Rattigan (1911–1977), by Yousuf Karsh, 1954

footsteps by performing well in the cricket eleven. He honed his theatrical instincts by studying the work of Galsworthy, Barrie, and Shaw, and by writing his own short plays, including one at the behest of his French master, which received the now-celebrated assessment 'French execrable. Theatre sense first class' (Darlow and Hodson, 34). He also confirmed his own sexual tastes, nurtured in early fumblings at Sandroyd, by embarking, at the age of sixteen, on a serious affair with Geoffrey Gilbey, the racing correspondent of the *Daily Express*.

In 1930 Rattigan won a minor scholarship to Trinity College, Oxford, but his true alma mater turned out to be the Oxford University Dramatic Society (OUDS), where he met Frith Banbury and Peter Glenville, both to become distinguished directors of his post-war work; represented Treachery in a tableau of the Seven Deadly Sins opposite Angus Wilson's Buggery; and, most significantly, played a one-line part in John Gielgud's production of *Romeo and Juliet*, in which, as was then the custom, established West End actresses—here Peggy Ashcroft and Edith Evans—were imported to play the female roles. Gielgud was to prove a lifelong friend and inspiration to Rattigan. In 1934 they collaborated on a stage version of *A Tale of Two Cities* which, much to Rattigan's disappointment, was abandoned after an appeal by the veteran actor Sir John Martin-Harvey, who had been playing Sidney Carton on tour for forty-five years. Later Rattigan wrote two of his finest characters, the barnstorming barrister Sir Robert Morton in *The Winslow Boy* and the desiccated classicist Andrew Crocker-Harris in *The Browning Version*, for Gielgud (who declined both) and used the actor as a model for two

others, Arthur Gosport in *Harlequinade* and Major Pollock in *Separate Tables*.

Rattigan left Oxford in 1933 without taking his degree as a deliberate snub to his father, who was pushing him towards a diplomatic career. His own sights were set on the theatre and his time at Oxford had provided him with the material both for his first performed play, the aptly titled *First Episode*, and his first great success, *French Without Tears*. *First Episode*, which enjoyed a brief West End run in 1934, was based partly on his own unrequited passion for his friend and collaborator Philip Heimann, and partly on his observation of the devastating effect that Peggy Ashcroft had had on her undergraduate colleagues during the OUDS *Romeo and Juliet*. It marks the first appearance of the romantic triangle which was to figure throughout his work.

French Without Tears, which was based on his time at a 'crammers' near Wimereux in France in preparation for his intended diplomatic career, opened at the Criterion in November 1936, with a cast of young hopefuls, including Rex Harrison and Trevor Howard. Reviews were mixed, with W. A. Darlington in the *Daily Telegraph* declaring that 'the gift of real lightness is a rare one in the theatre and Terence Rattigan is a lucky young man to have it' (Wansell, 80), while James Agate in the *Sunday Times* carped that 'this is not a play. It is not anything. It is nothing. It is not witty. It has no plot. It is almost without characterisation' (Wansell, 80). And yet it made Rattigan's name, ran for over a thousand performances, and its soufflé-light charm has held the stage ever since.

Rattigan's next two plays, *Follow my Leader*, a comic spoof of Nazism, initially banned by the lord chamberlain for fear of offending German sensibilities, on which he collaborated with his Harrow and Oxford friend Tony Goldschmidt, and *After the Dance*, a portrait of the cynicism and disillusionment of the post-First World War generation, were not successes. But in 1942 *Flare Path*, a study of fighter pilots and their wives and lovers, based on his own wartime experience in the Royal Air Force, and written while on active service as a flight lieutenant, restored his reputation with critics and public alike. He followed this with *While the Sun Shines* (1943), a light-hearted comedy in a Wodehousian vein which so charmed the previously hostile Agate that he described Rattigan in the terms which Shaw had used of Wilde as 'playing with everything: with wit, with philosophy, with drama, with actors and audience, with the whole theatre' (Wansell, 136). *While the Sun Shines* went on to beat Rattigan's own record and run for 1154 performances in the West End.

After the minor comedy *Love in Idleness*, most notable for the stellar presence of the Lunts, Rattigan wrote *The Winslow Boy* (1946), about a family's attempt to clear the name of a boy falsely accused of stealing a postal order, which was loosely based on the case involving George Archer *Shee (1895–1914). He dedicated the play to 'Master Paul Channon', with whose father, Chips Channon, he was conducting a light-hearted affair. This was followed by *Playbill* (1948), a double bill comprising his masterpiece, *The Browning Version*, a study of a failed schoolmaster redeemed by an act of kindness, and *Harlequinade*, a portrait of a group of actors, which is now as dated as the theatre it celebrates. A rare failure in this decade of triumphs was *Adventure Story* (1949), a play about Alexander the Great, which Rattigan conceived in the strange belief that it was as necessary for an author to dramatize great historical figures as for an actor to attempt the classics. As with *Ross* (1960), his drama of Lawrence of Arabia, he reduced the protagonist to a Freudian case study and a subject which cried out for poetic treatment to middlebrow prose.

Rattigan returned to more familiar ground with his finest full-length play, *The Deep Blue Sea* (1952), an anatomy of a middle-class woman's passion for an airman who is both her junior and her emotional inferior, which was inspired by the suicide of his erstwhile lover Kenneth Morgan, and *Separate Tables* (1956), a poignant portrait of the emotional turmoil of a group of guests in a small private hotel. It was, by then, two decades since the success of *French Without Tears*, and Somerset Maugham's warning that a playwright could only expect to remain popular for twenty years was about to prove prophetic. The change of theatrical idiom brought about by *Waiting for Godot* (1955) and of theatrical taste brought about by *Look Back in Anger* (1956) were to topple Rattigan from his gilded perch.

Rattigan always championed the cause of the well-made play, provoking furious counterblasts from fellow dramatists James Bridie, Benn Levy, and Bernard Shaw, when in a 1950 *New Statesman* article he lauded the theatre of character over the theatre of ideas. But his most significant contribution to theatrical theory came in the preface to his second volume of *Collected Plays* (1953) with the creation of Aunt Edna, the personification of the 'nice, respectable, middle-class, middle-aged maiden lady', whom the theatre could not afford to offend. For many years Aunt Edna threatened to overshadow his subtler literary creations. Few playwrights have ever made a sharper rod for their own backs. To the Royal Court generation, Rattigan was regarded as providing genteel escapist fare for the middle classes, an impression confirmed by his first post-Osborne play, the feeble *Variations on a Theme* (1958), based partly on Margaret Leighton's relationship with Laurence Harvey, partly on his own experience of exploitative young men, and, largely, on Dumas's *La dame aux camélias*.

For most of the 1960s Rattigan devoted the bulk of his energies to film, a medium in which he had worked ever since 1936, when he became a contract writer for Warner Brothers. Many of his own plays were filmed: *French Without Tears*, *The Deep Blue Sea*, and *A Bequest to the Nation* proving unsuccessful, largely because of unsuitable casting, while *The Browning Version*, *Separate Tables*, and *The Prince and the Showgirl* have become classics. In the 1940s and 1950s he scripted many English films, often for the director Anthony Asquith and producer Anatole de Grunwald. But the Hollywood blockbusters of his later years, including *The VIPs*, *The Yellow Rolls Royce*, and the musical version of *Goodbye Mr Chips*, achieved more for his bank balance than for his art.

In the final years of his life Rattigan enjoyed something

of a renaissance. His achievements were officially honoured with a knighthood in 1971 (he had been appointed CBE in 1958). His last three plays were: *A Bequest to the Nation* (1970) about Nelson and Lady Hamilton; *In Praise of Love* (1973), inspired by Rex Harrison's discovery that his wife Kay Kendall was dying of leukaemia; and *Cause célèbre* (1977), a dramatization of the Alma Rattenbury case, which mixed his favourite ingredients of unequal passion and middle-class repression. All enjoyed moderate success, while several of his earlier plays had triumphant revivals. By the time of his death from cancer in Bermuda on 30 November 1977, it was clear that much of his work would endure, and indeed it has dated far less than that of Osborne, which was said to have rendered it obsolete. Rattigan was cremated in Canada, and his ashes buried at Kensal Green cemetery, London.

Rattigan has claims to being considered the finest writer of short plays in the language. With the exception of *The Deep Blue Sea*, his greatest works (*The Browning Version*; the second part of *Separate Tables*; the original version of *In Praise of Love*) are all in one act. They will survive because of their unflinching portrayal of the folly, passion, and desperation of the human heart. Although Sebastian Cruttwell in *In Praise of Love* rails against 'le vice anglais', defining it as 'our refusal to admit our emotions', it was this code of reticence which turned out to be Rattigan's trump card. It gave him an objectivity as well as a subject. When he attempted to deal directly with homosexuality, it proved to be either redundant, as in the proposed revisions of *Separate Tables* for Broadway, or prurient, as in *Man and Boy* (1960). Elsewhere, as fellow playwright David Rudkin put it, 'I think Rattigan is not at all the commercial, middlebrow dramatist his image suggests but someone peculiarly haunting and oblique who certainly speaks to me with resonance of existential bleakness and irresoluble carnal solitude' (Darlow and Hodson, 15).

MICHAEL ARDITTI

Sources G. Wansell, *Terence Rattigan: a biography* (1995) · M. Darlow and G. Hodson, *Terence Rattigan: the man and his work* (1979) · B. A. Young, *The Rattigan version* (1986) · CGPLA Eng. & Wales (1978)
Archives BL, corresp., literary MSS, and papers · NRA, corresp. and literary papers | Theatre Museum, London, corresp. with Christopher Fry
Likenesses T. Purvis, pastel drawing, 1940–49, NPG · T. Purvis, pencil drawing, 1940–49, NPG · B. Brandt, bromide print, before 1945, NPG · photographs, 1946–65, Hult. Arch. · Y. Karsh, bromide print, 1954, NPG [*see illus.*]
Wealth at death £160,754—in England and Wales: Bermudan probate sealed in England, 15 May 1978, CGPLA Eng. & Wales

Rattigan, Sir William Henry (1842–1904), jurist in India, was born at Delhi on 4 September 1842, the youngest son of Bartholomew Rattigan, who left his home, Athy, co. Kildare, at an early age and entered the ordnance department of the East India Company, and his wife, Sarah, *née* Abbott, of Deptford. Educated at the high school, Agra, Rattigan entered the 'uncovenanted' Bombay civil service in youth and was an extra assistant commissioner at Lahore in the Punjab, acting for a short time as judge of the small causes court at Delhi. Dissatisfied with his prospects he resigned, against his family's wishes, to study law. Enrolled as a pleader of the Punjab chief court on its establishment in 1866, he built up an extensive practice, first in partnership with Mr Scarlett, and then on his own account.

Rattigan was admitted a student of Lincoln's Inn on 3 November 1871, and was called to the bar there on 7 June 1873, also studying at King's College, London. He returned to Lahore where he speedily rose to be head of his profession. He was for many years government advocate, and in 1880, 1881, 1882, and 1886, for varying short periods acted as a judge of the chief court. In November 1886 he resigned his acting judgeship to continue his practice without interruption. A linguist of unusual ability, he mastered five European languages, several Indian vernaculars, and Persian. German he studied assiduously, and he translated as *Jural Relations* (1883) the second book of Savigny's work on modern Roman law. In 1885 he took the degree of DL, with first-class honours, at Göttingen.

In February 1887 Rattigan became vice-chancellor of Punjab University, then on the verge of bankruptcy. He succeeded in regenerating it and was reappointed biennially, retaining the vice-chancellorship until April 1895. He was made a DL of the university in January 1896, and LLD of Glasgow in 1901. In 1891 he accepted the presidentship of the Khalsa College committee, and by his energy and influence overcame dissension among the Sikhs, with the result that an institution for their higher education on a religious basis was established at Amritsar in 1897. When he retired from India in April 1900 the Sikh council appointed him life president, and on his death a memorial hospital was erected at the college (opened in 1906). He was an additional member of the viceroy's legislative council in 1892–3 and of the Punjab legislative council in 1898–9.

A self-made man, without advantages of family influence, Rattigan made substantial contributions to legal literature amid his professional and public labours. He published *Selected Cases in Hindu Law Decided by the Privy Council and the Superior Indian Courts* (2 vols., 1870–71), *The Hindu Law of Adoption* (1873), and *De jure personarum* (1873), and he collaborated with Charles Boulnois (1832–1912) of the Punjab chief court in *Notes on the Customary Law as Administered in the Punjab* (1878). His most important book, *A Digest of Civil and Customary Law of the Punjab* (1880), which reached a seventh edition (1909), was designed to classify material for a future codification, and rendered Rattigan a foremost authority on customary law in northern India. His other works were *The Science of Jurisprudence* (1888), which, chiefly intended for Indian students, reached a third edition (1899); *Private International Law* (1895); and a pamphlet on the international aspects of the case of the Netherlands South African Railway (1901). Rattigan was knighted in January 1895, made QC in May 1897, and elected bencher of his inn in June 1903.

Rattigan was married twice: first, on 21 December 1861 at Delhi to Teresa Matilda (*d.* 1876), daughter of Colonel A. C. B. Higgins CIE, examiner of accounts, public works department; and second at Melbourne—in a marriage that could not then legally have taken place in England—on 1 April 1878 to her sister Evelyn. By his first marriage he had two daughters and four sons, and by his second three sons.

Rattigan settled in England in 1900, and practised before the privy council. In the 1900 'khaki' general election he contested as a Liberal Unionist the largely mining constituency of North-Eastern Lanarkshire and was defeated by the Liberal candidate. However at a by-election there on 26 September 1901, with the anti-Unionist vote split between the Liberal candidate and Robert Smillie of the Scottish Workers' Representation Committee, Rattigan was elected on a minority of votes and sat until his death. Speaking rarely, and chiefly on Indian subjects, he was respected by all parties. He was killed in a motor accident at Langford near Biggleswade, Bedfordshire, on his way to Scotland, on 4 July 1904, and was buried in Kensal Green cemetery, London. He was survived by his second wife. A memorial window was placed in the chapel of Harrow School, where his sons were educated, and a tablet in Lahore Cathedral. F. H. BROWN, *rev.* ROGER T. STEARN

Sources *The Times* (5 July 1904) · *The Times* (6 July 1904) · *The Times* (7 July 1904) · *The Times* (11 July 1904) · *Punjab Magazine* (Feb 1895) · *Men of merit* (1900) · *The Biographer* (Nov 1901) · *Civil and Military Gazette* (7 July 1904) · *Civil and Military Gazette* (9 July 1904) · *Civil and Military Gazette* (22 July 1904) · *The Pioneer* (7 July 1904) · *Law Times* (9 July 1904) · private information (1912) [Lady Rattigan] · *WWW*, *1897–1915* · WWBMP, vol. 2 · F. W. S. Craig, *British parliamentary election results, 1885–1918* (1974) · W. P. Baildon, ed., *The records of the Honorable Society of Lincoln's Inn: admissions*, 2 (1896) · W. Menski, *Indian legal systems past and present* (1997) · R. K. Renford, *The non-official British in India to 1920* (1987)

Archives Bodl. Oxf., letters to Sir Aurel Stein

Wealth at death £12,466 2s. 6d.: probate, 20 Sept 1904, CGPLA Eng. & Wales

Rattray, John (1707–1771), golfer and physician, was born on 22 September 1707 at Craighall Castle, Blairgowrie, Perthshire, the second son of Thomas *Rattray (1684–1743), Scottish Episcopal bishop of Dunkeld, and Margaret (*c.*1690–1737), daughter of Thomas Galloway, second Baron Dunkeld. In 1728 he was apprenticed to John Semple, a practitioner surgeon in Edinburgh; he completed his apprenticeship in 1735. In 1740 he passed the four examining sessions of the Company of Surgeons of Edinburgh and was subsequently admitted a freeman surgeon. On 7 May 1742 he married his first wife, Christian, the daughter of George Main, an Edinburgh jeweller; the couple had three sons and three daughters. After her death he married Margaret, daughter of the politician and Jacobite sympathizer George Lockhart of Carnwath, with whom he had one daughter.

In addition to his medical studies Rattray was a keen and skilled sportsman. In 1731 he became a member of the Royal Company of Archers; he was four times winner of their silver bowl (1732, 1735, 1740, and 1742) and twice—in 1735 and 1744—received the company's highest award, the silver arrow. He was also the leading golfer at Leith links near Edinburgh, the setting for the first printed book devoted to golf, Thomas Mathison's *The Goff* (1743) in which he appears:

> Rattray for skill, and Corse for strength renowned,
> Stewart and Lesly beat the sandy ground.
> (Mathison, 4)

In the year after *The Goff*'s publication the regular players at Leith, including Rattray, moved to establish an annual golfing competition for a silver club presented by the city of Edinburgh, equivalent to the silver arrow donated to the Royal Company of Archers in 1709. The city corporation noted that the newly formed Company of Gentlemen Golfers had drawn up regulations for play, consisting of twelve generic articles or rules plus one specific to Leith links, which they approved in March 1744. In April Rattray was victorious in this first ever golf tournament and so earned the title 'captain of the goff' for winning the £15 silver club. Rattray, as captain, had the authority to settle disputes between fellow golfers and was responsible for superintending the course in the year of his captaincy. Debate surrounds the authorship of these regulations, which were signed by Rattray and which—on matters of order of play, outside interference, water hazards, holing out, making a stroke, and the stroke and distance penalty for the loss of a ball—remain an integral part of the modern game. Rattray's sole signature does not guarantee that he was wholly responsible for them, though his prominence within the company and Edinburgh society at large makes him the most likely candidate. Under these rules he went on to win the silver club for a second time in April 1745.

Rattray was prevented from defending his captaincy in the following year because of his role in the Jacobite rising of 1745 as a surgeon to Charles Edward Stuart, the Young Pretender. From a family long sympathetic to the Stuart cause, Rattray became involved with the Jacobite campaign in the aftermath of the victory at Prestonpans (September 1745). Summoned from his house at 1a South Foulis Close, Edinburgh, by Laurence Oliphant, sixth laird of Gask, Rattray rode to the battlefield with a fellow surgeon, George Lauder. From there he accompanied the Jacobite army into England (whether voluntarily or under coercion is unknown) and then followed the Young Pretender's forces as they retreated from Derby in the spring of 1746. Rattray surrendered to Cumberland's army following the defeat at Culloden. He was subsequently rearrested in Edinburgh in May and sent to London under house arrest before being released in 1747 as part of a general amnesty once he had signed an oath of obedience.

Having sworn his allegiance to the Hanoverian regime, Rattray returned to his life as an Edinburgh surgeon and golfer. In 1751 he won back the silver club and captaincy (his third and final victory), but did not compete in the following year. The last reference to him in the company's archives is 1759, the year in which he described himself as a 'cripple'. Bills for service to Lord Milton show that he continued to practise as a surgeon until at least 1766. He died at Leith Walk, Edinburgh, on 5 July 1771. As an episcopalian and a nonjuror his burial record has been erased from the Edinburgh register.

COLIN J. L. STRACHAN and JAN BARKER

Sources T. Mathison, *'The Goff': an heroi-comical poem* (1743) · 'Regulations for playing for the city's silver club', minutes, Edinburgh town council, 7 March 1744 · *Scots Magazine*, 6 (1744), 197 · *Records of the Royal College of Surgeons of Edinburgh* (1740) · J. Gilhooley, *A directory of Edinburgh in 1752* (1988) · K. G. Chapman, *The rules of the green: authority of the rules of golf* (Chicago, 1997) · A. J. Johnston and J. F. Johnston, *The chronicles of golf, 1457–1857* (Cleveland, 1993) · J. S. Lawson, *The original rules of golf* (1981) · O. M. Geddes, *A swing through time: golf in Scotland, 1457–1743* (1992) · M. M. Whittet, 'Medical resources of the 'Forty Five', *Transactions of the Gaelic Society of Inverness*, 44 (1961), 1–41 · W. A. Macnaughton, 'Medical heroes of the Forty Five', *Caledonian Medical Journal*, 3 (1897–9), 82–93, 155–62, 208–13 · NL Scot., Lockhart of Lee MSS · parish register, Edinburgh, 1742 [marriage to Christian Main] · NL Scot., Milton MSS

Archives Royal College of Surgeons, Edinburgh, records and book of intrants
Likenesses portrait; formerly at Craighall, Fife [now stolen]

Rattray, Robert Sutherland (1881–1938), colonial official and ethnographer, was born on 5 September 1881 in Bahr, Bengal, the fourth child of Arthur Rattray, Indian civil servant, and his wife, Mary Sutherland. A scion of distinguished Anglo-Indian families, he was sent home as a child to Gatehouse of Fleet in Scotland where, before his father's retirement from the Indian Civil Service, he and a sister were cared for by a great-aunt. After local schooling he attended Stirling high school but left to join the imperial yeomanry at the outbreak of the Second South African War in 1899. In December 1902 he joined the central African trading company, the African Lakes Corporation. Initially based in Blantyre, Nyasaland, he was soon sent 'up-country' to Lilongwe. While his leisure was dedicated to a lifetime devotion to game shooting, here Rattray began his serious study of what he initially called 'folklore', which he learned from local hunters whose languages he mastered. Much of this material appeared in his first publication, *Folklore, Stories and Songs in Chinyanja* (1907).

In 1906 Rattray joined the customs service of the west African colony of the Gold Coast. Taking advantage of a Colonial Office scheme, he enrolled in his first home leave as a student in anthropology at Exeter College, Oxford, where he studied with R. R. Marett, eventually securing a diploma in 1914, the degree of BSc in 1925, and that of DSc in 1929. During the same leave he joined Gray's Inn and began writing his law examinations before returning to his post in the eastern Gold Coast. In 1913 he was appointed assistant district commissioner in Ejura, in the northern region of Asante. A talented linguist, Rattray had already mastered the lingua franca of many of the labourers and traders in the northern Gold Coast. This led to his *Hausa Folklore* and his *Elementary Mole Grammar* of 1918. Now, in Asante, his interest turned to the culture of the dominant political force of the pre-colonial Gold Coast, a polity which, after a sequence of wars, had been finally defeated by the British in 1896. The first fruit of his study was *Ashanti Proverbs* (1916). Although the work bore the patronizing subtitle 'The primitive ethics of a savage people', what Rattray consciously displayed was both sophisticated and complex.

In 1914 Rattray married Constance Mary Stanley, with whom he returned to the Gold Coast as war broke out with Germany. Created a captain in the Gold Coast regiment—he used this title for the rest of his life—he saw action during the invasion of the German colony of Togoland; he was now asked to administer part of the conquered territory, though its Ewe-speaking population never attracted his ethnographic interest. During leave in 1915 he worked further on his law examinations, and he was called to the bar in 1918; in the same leave he learned to fly. In 1919 he was posted to the colonial capital, Accra, as assistant colonial secretary and clerk to the legislative assembly; this bored him. Relief came with his appointment as special commissioner and the first 'government anthropologist' in 1920, a post exclusively attached to the Asante region. Reflecting his academic training, his initial enquiries were focused on religion and kinship.

Although an employee of government, Rattray's research agenda was only slightly shaped by administrative imperatives. Thus the first results of his work were to be a general survey, *Ashanti* (1923), followed by *Religion and Art in Ashanti* (1927). The latter displays not only the command of ethnographic detail of the former but also a deep sympathy with the moral basis of Asante cosmology. In the same period he played a major part in organizing the much admired Gold Coast exhibits at the British Empire Exhibition of 1924. Rattray's work was becoming relevant to the administrative ambition to restore the Asante confederacy. His legal training and the current concerns of social anthropology rather than policy, however, led him to the collection of the material which was published in his *Ashanti Law and Constitution* (1929). Much of the colonial understanding of Asante which governed the eventual restoration of the confederacy in 1936 was drawn from this influential book. Taken together, his three major books on the Asante people constitute the most detailed ethnographic study of any African people in the inter-war period and retain their importance as primary sources for modern scholars.

Rattray was felt to be far too eccentric and temperamental to rise to higher levels of the administration; however, because of his growing reputation he was given the status and pay of a provincial commissioner but without the duties. His interest in the Asante seems to have declined and his final book on this polity, *Akan-Ashanti Folk-Tales* (1930), is basically raw, un-analysed data. He was now drawn to the northern Gold Coast, and his research here resulted in his *Tribes of the Ashanti Hinterland* (1932). An enthusiastic pilot, Rattray flew his biplane from London to Accra in 1928, shortly before retiring from the colonial service. On retirement he unsuccessfully pursued innumerable academic posts and research grants. His much respected empirical work had not been followed by theoretical publications; this and his age presumably conspired against an academic career, although he taught Hausa to colonial service staff in Cambridge in the mid-1930s. He

was to irritate the Colonial Office by writing articles hostile to the policy of indirect rule. Always delighted by evidence of African cultural self-assertion, he dedicated his romantic novel *The Leopard Princess* (1934) to Paul Robeson.

Rattray's private life is something of a mystery. His marriage failed, and he spent years unsuccessfully trying to divorce his wife. He was the father of a girl, the result of a liaison with a Frenchwoman during a leave period taken in France. He was killed in a gliding accident on 14 May 1938 at Farmoor, Oxfordshire. RICHARD RATHBONE

Sources N. Machin, *Government anthropologist: a life of R. S. Rattray*, ed. J. Eades (1998) · T. H. Von Laue, 'Anthropology and power: R. S. Rattray among the Ashanti', *African Affairs*, 75 (1976), 33–54 · A. F. Robertson, 'Anthropology and government in Ghana', *African Affairs*, 74 (1975), 51–9 · E. W. Smith, *Man: Monthly Record of Anthropological Science*, nos. 110–12 (July 1938), 107–8 · I. Wilks, *Asante in the 19th century: the structure and evolution of a political order*, 2nd edn (1989) · T. C. McCaskie, *State and society in pre-colonial Asante* (1995) · W. Tordoff, *Ashanti under the Prempehs, 1888–1935* (1965) · *CGPLA Eng. & Wales* (1938)

Archives Royal Anthropological Institute, London, MSS
Likenesses portrait, repro. in R. S. Rattray, *Religion and art in Ashanti* (1927), 29
Wealth at death £1980 15s. 9d.: resworn probate, 14 July 1938, *CGPLA Eng. & Wales*

Rattray, Sylvester (*fl.* 1650–1666), medical writer, a native of Forfarshire, Scotland, was probably descended from Sir Sylvester Rattray, of Rattray Castle, Perthshire, who in 1463 was one of the ambassadors sent to London to treat with Edward IV, and exerted great influence at the Scottish court. Rattray may have been the son of a later Sylvester Rattray who had two sons, David and Sylvester. The latter is said to have been 'bred to the church', and on the title-page of his *Prognosis medica* he is credited with a theological degree as well as with that of MD.

Rattray was author of *Aditus novus ad occultas sympathiae et antipathiae causas inveniendas: per principia philosphiae naturalis, ex fermentorum artificiosa anatomia hausta, patefactus* (1658), dedicated to Johannes Scotus. The *Aditus novus* was reprinted in *Theatrum sympatheticum variorum authorum de pulvere sympathetico* (1662). Rattray's second book, *Prognosis medica ad usum praxeos facili methodo digesta*, (1666) was dedicated to Dr John Wedderburn.

In May 1652 Rattray married at Cupar, Fife, 'Ingells, Kynggaskes daughter' (*Diary of Mr John Lamont*, 42). He had a son, Sylvester, a student of medicine at Glasgow in 1680. G. LE G. NORGATE, *rev.* PATRICK WALLIS

Sources *The diary of Mr John Lamont of Newton, 1649–1671*, ed. G. R. Kinloch, Maitland Club, 7 (1830) · W. Anderson, *The Scottish nation*, 3 vols. (1866–77) · Watt, *Bibl. Brit.*

Rattray, Thomas, of Craighall (1684–1743), Scottish Episcopal bishop of Dunkeld, was the eldest son of James Rattray (*d.* 1692), laird of Craighall, near Blairgowrie, Perthshire, and Elizabeth, daughter of Sir George Hay of Megginch. He succeeded as laird at his father's death on 13 July 1692. In 1713, when he was twenty-nine, Rattray sought baptism by immersion and confirmation from Bishop John Falconer, probably as the necessary canonical preliminary to ordination. By 1724 at least he was one of the clergy in the former diocese of Brechin. He married Margaret (c.1690–1737), daughter of Thomas Galloway, second Baron Dunkeld, and they had two sons, including the golfer and physician John *Rattray, and three daughters.

Rattray came to prominence in the Scottish Episcopal church as a theologian. In 1716 he assisted Bishop Nathaniel Spinckes in translating into Greek the English non-jurors' abortive proposal for a union between themselves and the Greek Orthodox church. In 1718 the English non-jurors appealed to the Scottish bishops for a ruling in their dispute over the use of ancient eucharistic ceremonies and prayers for the dead. The Scottish bishops offered only to mediate rather than to decide the issue and turned to Rattray as a recognized expert in the matter. He advised the occasional use of the opposite form by both parties, but this was unsatisfactory to both sides. The same controversy also divided the Scottish Episcopal church where it was further complicated by the usagers' support for the Scottish communion office, a liturgy derived from the Scottish prayer book of 1637.

In 1720 this growing division among episcopalians was deepened by disagreement over whether the episcopate should govern the church as a council of non-territorial bishops, or as diocesan bishops. The issue was inflamed in that year when Bishop John Fullarton accepted election to the diocese of Edinburgh. Diocesan episcopacy had been avoided by episcopalians since the revolution of 1688, the bishops governing their church collectively as a college. Fullarton's unilateral acceptance of a diocesan title was seen by the anti-usager bishops as a usurpation of the royal nomination of bishops which, as Jacobites, they accorded to the son of James Stuart, claimant to the British throne. The bishops managed to thrash out some agreement for the sake of their disorganized church by circulating a pastoral letter in February 1723 against the liturgical usages as ill-advised in the present predicament of their legally proscribed church. They also required the clergy to sign an agreement to that effect. Rattray responded in the tract *Some Remarks on the Circular Letter of the Edinburgh Bishops*. In this he set out his arguments for diocesan episcopacy as the only recognized form in the early church, asserting that a non-diocesan bishop could not claim authority over the clergy and laity within that district. In common with the usager party among the English nonjurors, he claimed that the usages were necessary for the celebration of the eucharist because their use in the early church pointed to their institution by Christ himself. Rattray also opposed the subscription required of the clergy as beyond the jurisdictions of non-diocesan bishops; as valuing peace more than truth; and as illegitimate because there was no authorized single form of liturgy and ceremonies in the Episcopal church.

After the death of Bishop Falconer in July 1723, Rattray became the leader as well as the theologian of the usager and diocesan party of Scottish Episcopalians. Consequently he was chosen by the majority usager clergy and laity of the diocese of Brechin to succeed Falconer. However, the college bishops' majority resulted in the appointment of their candidate, Robert Norrie, though Rattray lodged a long and learned protest against overturning the clergy's election. On Norrie's death in 1727 the usager party grew in strength among the bishops when the Brechin clergy repeated their election of Rattray. He was consecrated at Edinburgh on 4 June 1727 by Primus Arthur Millar, and bishops James Gadderar and Andrew Cant, despite protests from the college party. Rattray's elevation was one of a series of rival consecrations by both parties designed to augment their respective strengths.

As bishop of the diocese encompassing Angus, the Mearns, and Perthshire east of the River Tay, Rattray experienced the same divisions that he was partly responsible for among the bishops. Leading male managers of the congregation in Perth had become accustomed to controlling their church, regarding the clergy as paid employees who carried out their instructions. They opposed Rattray on the apparent grounds of an anti-usages position, but underlying the division was a conflict between attitudes to lay and ordained authority in which Rattray's high theology of ordained authority inevitably conflicted with the managers' desire for unimpeded control of the Perth congregation. Rattray initially sought to avoid conflict by being cautious about his episcopal authority, but in 1740 a schism occurred over the managers' unilateral appointment of a new incumbent, with the managers refusing Rattray's offer of a neutral referee. Consequently Rattray proceeded to the deposition of the incumbent, being unprepared to accept public flouting of his divine authority as bishop.

Rattray had already set out his theology of episcopacy as divinely instituted in his *Essay on the nature of the church, and a review of the elections of bishops in the primitive church* (1728), which became a standard theological work in episcopalian circles. The ability of determined laity to oppose Rattray ostensibly from an anti-usage position demonstrates that a concordat in 1731 between the two parties of bishops had not resolved episcopalian divisions. In that document the declining power of the collegers was evident in their agreement to divide Scotland into ten dioceses and in their acceptance of appointment to dioceses through the principle of election rather than royal nomination. Diocesan episcopacy having been achieved, the usages controversy was resolved in an agreed compromise to permit both the Scottish and English liturgies. Rattray relinquished his claim to be bishop of Brechin to the leading colleger bishop, John Ochterlonie, and was henceforth accepted as bishop of Dunkeld (1732). However, it did require a visit by Rattray to his old diocese to reconcile his supporters there to being governed by the leading colleger bishop.

After many years of bitter and conscientious division, rancour still continued among the bishops and their clerical and lay supporters. Rattray therefore proposed to Primus David Freebairn that an episcopal synod be held to reconcile the bishops' divisions. In 1738 the bishops, in Edinburgh for this proposed synod, divided along the usual lines over whether or not Bishop Gavin Dunbar could send a priest as his proxy, to which the collegers objected. Consequently the diocesans met separately and, as now they were the majority of the bishops, they proceeded to elect Rattray as primus in place of Freebairn. It meant that a younger and more vigorous man replaced an old and infirm one, but the partisan election only exacerbated the differences between the leaders of a dwindling church. This impasse was only solved by default with the death of Freebairn in 1739. Rattray then offered his resignation as primus, which was unacceptable to the bishops of his party who now virtually monopolized the episcopate.

As primus Rattray endeavoured to embody in his church the findings of his theological scholarship, and to develop a working structure for his disorganized church. However, he only had a free hand for this following the death of his able opponent Ochterlone in 1742. His scholarship and his authority were consistently behind the use of the Scottish communion office as against the eucharistic liturgy of the English Book of Common Prayer. His proposed code of canons formed the basis of the original code accepted after his death by the episcopal synod in 1743. But in a reversal of his earlier views as primus, Rattray objected to independent action by the clergy as, for example, in 1739 when the Edinburgh clergy maintained their rights against the episcopal synod in an election for their new bishop.

Most of Rattray's theological works were published posthumously, including his edition of *The Ancient Liturgy of the Church of Jerusalem* (1744). Rattray believed this liturgy to be so ancient that he was anxious for the Scottish communion office to conform to it. A liturgical adaptation along these lines was actually produced by Rattray, although probably only used in his private chapel on his estate at Craighall, Perthshire. It was published as an appendix in the 1748 edition. His liturgical work was more influential in shaping the definitive edition of the Scottish communion office of 1764. Another posthumous work was *Some particular instructions concerning the Christian covenant, and the mysteries by which it is transacted and maintained* (1748). These and other unpublished sermons and dissertations were published in 1860 by the high-church episcopalian theologian George Forbes through his private Pitsligo Press. Rattray died on 12 May 1743, probably in Edinburgh, aged sixty.   ROWAN STRONG

Sources DNB · *Rattray's works*, ed. G. H. Forbes (1860) · G. Grub, *An ecclesiastical history of Scotland*, 4 vols. (1861) · J. Skinner, *Ecclesiastical history of Scotland* (1788) · T. Stephen, *The history of the Church of Scotland*, 4 (1845) · R. Keith and J. Spottiswoode, *An historical catalogue of the Scottish bishops, down to the year 1688*, new edn, ed. M. Russel [M. Russell] (1824) · J. P. Lawson, *History of the Scottish Episcopal church* (1843) · H. R. Sefton, 'The Scottish bishops and Archbishop Arsenius', *The Orthodox churches and the West*, ed. D. Baker, SCH, 13 (1976), 239–46 · G. T. S. Farquhar, *The episcopal history of Perth, 1689–1894* (1894)
Archives NA Scot., Scottish Episcopal Church MSS

Rau, Sir Benegal Narsinga (1887–1953), judge and diplomatist, was born at Karkala, near Mangalore, in the Madras presidency, south India, on 26 February 1887, second of the four sons of Benegal Raghavendra Rao, a doctor in the Madras medical service, and his wife, Radha Bai (1864/5–1947). It was a remarkable family. Of his brothers,

B. Sanjiva Rao became a distinguished educationist, B. Rama Rao a governor of the Reserve Bank of India, and B. Shiva Rao the Delhi correspondent for the *Manchester Guardian* and a member of India's parliament. Narsinga Rau was educated at Kanara high school, Mangalore, and Presidency College, Madras, where he graduated in 1905 with a triple first in English, physics, and Sanskrit. In 1906 he took up a government scholarship to Trinity College, Cambridge, and on graduating as ninth wrangler in 1909 turned down a Trinity fellowship in favour of the Indian Civil Service. He returned home in November 1910 to a post as an assistant magistrate in Bengal.

In 1920 Rau was transferred to Assam. A witty and engaging man, he was popular with his fellow officers, not least for his talent at the quintessentially British pastimes of bridge, tennis, billiards, and golf. In 1925 he was appointed secretary to the provincial legislative department and legal remembrancer, and in 1933 was dispatched to London to argue Assam's case before the joint select committee on India's constitutional reforms. He was appointed CIE in 1934 and in 1935 was offered a judgeship on the Calcutta high court, but opted instead for the more challenging, if less remunerative, post of draftsman in the law department of the government of India. In just eighteen months he revised India's vast body of central and provincial statutes to bring them into line with the Government of India Act of 1935, thus enabling the new constitution to take effect, as scheduled, in 1937. Meanwhile Sir Maurice Gwyer, the first chief justice of the federal court in New Delhi, was anxious to get Rau as a colleague, but to qualify Rau had first to serve at least five years as a High Court judge, so in December 1938 he finally took up a seat on the Calcutta high court. He had been knighted the previous June. Ironically, such was the government's demand for Rau's skills that he never completed his five-year apprenticeship. At the government's request, he chaired an inquiry into disputed wages and conditions at the Great Indian Peninsula Railway Company, presided over a committee exploring the codification of Hindu law (1941), and headed the Indus waters commission (1942) charged with determining the equitable distribution of the Indus's liquid wealth among the provinces and states of western India.

In 1944, with the federal judgeship still beyond reach, Rau retired from the civil service and accepted the prime ministership of Kashmir, but the politics and intrigue of an Indian court were alien to the traditions of the civil service and, after eighteen difficult months, he resigned the post. The Calcutta high court beckoned again, but Rau let it be known that he wanted to share in the drafting of the laws for federation and the other big constitutional changes which lay ahead. In September 1945 Lord Wavell, who thought highly of his skills, set him to work in the reforms office on an Indo-British treaty to be implemented after independence.

In July 1946, with independence in sight but still of indistinct form, Rau was appointed constitutional adviser to the constituent assembly. It was an honorary appointment, taken on, he insisted, as 'a labour of love' (Rao, xxix). He was a popular choice. The leaders of the Indian National Congress respected his objectivity and silent patriotism, most recently in evidence when he had quietly assisted in the defence of the Indian National Army men who were tried for treason in 1945. But the leader of the Muslim League, M. A. Jinnah, was also friendly to Rau and valued his scrupulous constitutionalism. Amid India's plans for the future, Rau also found time to assist neighbouring Burma in drafting her constitution too.

After independence Jawaharlal Nehru, India's first prime minister, was keen to make the most of the man whom he described as 'the perfect civil servant' (*The Hindu*, 1 Dec 1953, 4) and in 1948 Rau was appointed a member of India's delegation to the United Nations general assembly. In 1950–51 he represented India on the Security Council, and was president of the council in June 1950 when North Korea crossed the 38th parallel and the UN recommended intervention to help South Korea. He was the architect of the first Asian–African bloc in the UN and, with his detailed knowledge of Kashmir, proved a worthy opponent of the Pakistanis. He was touted as a future secretary-general, but he was increasingly afflicted by stomach cancer. In December 1951 he was elected to the International Court of Justice at The Hague, but he was barely a year in the post when a recurrence of the cancer put him in a nursing home in Zürich. He died there on 29 November 1953. He was cremated on 1 December and his ashes returned to India.

Rau was one of the outstanding members of the Indian Civil Service, whose integrity and legal acumen won worldwide recognition. He was a suave, immaculately dressed man, of small build with refined features crowned, in later years, with luxuriant silver hair. Friends and colleagues remembered him as an elegant, even precious speaker, an intensely private man whose courtesy disguised a resolute and hard-headed pragmatism. He never married. In 1960 his brother Shiva brought together some of the many constitutional schemes which he had drafted in a book entitled *India's Constitution in the Making*.

S. GOPAL, *rev.* KATHERINE PRIOR

Sources B. S. Rao, 'A biographical sketch', in B. Rao, *India's constitution in the making*, 2nd edn (1963), xvii–xxxv · *The Times* (30 Nov 1953) · *The Times* (1 Dec 1953) · *The Times* (7 Dec 1953) · *The Hindu* (1 Dec 1953) · *The India Office and Burma Office List* (1940) · S. P. Sen, ed., *Dictionary of national biography*, 4 vols. (1972–4), vol. 3 [India] · *WWW* · private information (1971) · personal knowledge (1971) · *CGPLA Eng. & Wales* (1954)
Likenesses photograph, repro. in Rao, 'A biographical sketch', frontispiece
Wealth at death £1045 14*s.* 0*d.* in England: administration with will, 30 Oct 1954, *CGPLA Eng. & Wales*

Raue, Christian. *See* Ravis, Christian (1613–1677).

Rauzzini, Matteo (1754–1791). *See under* Rauzzini, Venanzio (1746–1810).

Rauzzini, Venanzio (1746–1810), singer and music teacher, was born in Camerino in the Roman Apennines on 18 December 1746 and studied singing and composition at Rome. During the carnival seasons in 1764–6 the handsome young castrato sang in intermezzos at the Teatro della Valle, taking female roles, for in Rome women were not allowed to appear on the public stage. He sang the title role in Pietro Guglielmi's opera *Sesostri* in the Ascension festival at Venice in 1766 and entered the service of the elector of Bavaria, who spent lavishly on opera at Munich. Rauzzini was permitted to sing in opera at Vienna and Venice in 1767 but otherwise remained in Munich, where Charles Burney found him 'a charming singer, a pleasing figure, and a good actor' as well as an excellent performer on the harpsichord and a skilful composer of comic operas and *opera seria* arias (Burney, *Present State*, 1.128). Rauzzini's brother **Matteo Rauzzini** (1754–1791), composer and singing teacher, was also in Munich; Matteo later worked in Venice and in Dublin, where he died. According to Michael Kelly, Venanzio Rauzzini was advised to leave Munich in 1772 after 'an exalted personage became deeply and hopelessly enamoured of him' (Kelly, 1.10) and he appeared in operas at Milan, Venice, Padua, and Turin. In Milan he created the role of Cecilio in Mozart's *Lucio Silla*, first performed in December 1772, and Mozart then composed the virtuoso solo motet *Exsultate, Jubilate* for him.

Rauzzini made his London début at the King's Theatre in November 1774 as Rinaldo in the pasticcio *Armida*, singing arias which he himself had composed. He sang with 'the disadvantage of a terrible cold' (*Early Journals and Letters of Fanny Burney*, 2.187), but 'his taste, fancy, and delicacy, together with his beautiful person and spirited and intelligent manner of acting, before the season was over, gained him general approbation' (Burney, *Hist. mus.*, 4.501). David Garrick, impressed by Rauzzini's acting in the title role of Antonio Sacchini's *Montezuma*, is said to have rushed backstage to embrace him. Rauzzini remained as primo uomo at the King's Theatre for three seasons and also composed for the company. His most successful opera, the two-act tragedy *Piramo e Tisbe*, had its première on 16 March 1775, with Rauzzini as Piramo, and was revived in three later seasons. His pastoral *L'ali d'amore* was produced in 1776 and 1777, with his pupil Nancy Storace as Cupido. Rauzzini also sang at concerts in aid of the Fund for the Support of Decayed Musicians and the Lock Hospital, at the Three Choirs meetings in 1775–7, and festivals at Oxford, Winchester, and Salisbury.

In autumn 1777 Rauzzini was replaced by Francesco Roncaglia as principal man at the opera, but he was in demand as a performer in private concerts and as a teacher of gifted amateur and professional singers. From autumn 1777 he worked with the violinist Franz Lamotte in three winter subscription series in Bath, at the Rotunda in Dublin (summer 1778), and in two spring subscription series in London. Lamotte, in debt, fled to the continent in summer 1780 leaving Rauzzini in financial difficulties for the next few years. In London in 1781–2 he sang at benefits for his pupil, the composer and pianist Jane Guest, and had his own concert series in spring 1781. That September and Christmas he took part as composer and singer in lavish entertainments given by the young William Beckford at Fonthill, Wiltshire. During the next few years he composed four operas, an act of a pasticcio, and ballet music for the King's Theatre. The 1781-2 season was marred by a dispute with his colleague Sacchini over the authorship of some opera arias. The company was in artistic and financial disarray and Rauzzini's last opera, *La vestale* (1 May 1787), had only two performances. After this he lived permanently in Bath, having been in sole charge of the concerts there since at least January 1781.

Rauzzini lived in a town house in Bath and in the summer at Perrymead Villa, Widcombe, overlooking the city. Haydn visited him there in August 1794 and composed the canon 'Turk was a Faithful Dog' as a gift for his host, taking the words from the garden memorial to Rauzzini's favourite dog. Rauzzini was acknowledged as 'the father of a new style in English singing, and a new race of singers' (*Monthly Mirror*, 1807, 232), teaching Elizabeth Billington, John Braham, Elizabeth Clendining, Charles Incledon, Rosemond Mountain, and Nancy Storace. In Dublin in 1778 he had given lessons to the tenor Michael Kelly and advised him to study in Italy; Kelly writes glowingly of Rauzzini's hospitality and the devotion of his pupils, telling of how Mrs Billington renounced profitable engagements to perform gratis at Bath. Rauzzini remained a prolific composer of instrumental pieces and vocal music in English and Italian. In 1808 he published *Twelve Solfeggi*, with an introduction 'To my Scholars' which is full of sound advice. He died at his home, 13 Gay Street, on 8 April 1810, while preparing for the Bath June music festival. Four days later the *Bath Chronicle* wrote:

> In private life few men were more esteemed; none more generally beloved. A polished suavity of manners, a mild and cheerful disposition, and a copious fund of general and polite information, rendered him an attractive and agreeable companion. … In Mr. Rauzzini, this city has sustained a public loss.

He was buried in Bath Abbey, where there is a memorial to him erected by 'his affectionate Pupils Anna Selina Storace and John Braham'.

OLIVE BALDWIN and THELMA WILSON

Sources G. W. Stone, ed., *The London stage, 1660–1800*, pt 4: 1747–1776 (1962) • C. B. Hogan, ed., *The London stage, 1660–1800*, pt 5: 1776–1800 (1968) • C. Sartori, *I libretti italiani a stampa dalle origini al 1800*, 7 vols. (Cuneo, 1990–94) • S. McVeigh, *Calendar of London concerts, 1750–1800* [unpublished computer database, Goldsmiths' College, London] • C. Burney, *The present state of music in Germany, the Netherlands and the United Provinces*, 1 (1773), 128 • Burney, *Hist. mus.*, vol. 4 • *The early journals and letters of Fanny Burney*, ed. L. E. Troide, 2: 1774–1777 (1990) • 'Memoirs of Signor Rauzzini', *Monthly Mirror*, new ser., 1 (1807), 227–33 • 'Biographical sketch of Mr Braham', *Monthly Mirror*, 16 (1803), 5–8 • M. Kelly, *Reminiscences*, 1 (1826) • *Music and theatre in Handel's world: the family papers of James Harris, 1732–1780*, ed. D. Burrows and R. Dunhill (2002) • *Bath Chronicle* (12 April 1810) • *GM*, 1st ser., 80 (1810), 397–8, 490 • R. Edgcumbe, *Musical reminiscences of an old amateur: chiefly respecting the Italian opera in England for fifty years, from 1773 to 1823*, 2nd edn (1827) • W. Bingley, *Musical biography*, 2 (1814), 315–19 • J. Britton, *The history and antiquities of Bath Abbey church* (1825) • *ABC dario musico* (privately printed, Bath, 1780) • D. Lysons and others, *Origin and progress of the meeting of the three choirs of Gloucester, Worcester and Hereford* (1895) • B. Boydell, *Rotunda music in eighteenth-century Dublin* (Dublin, 1992) • D. J. Reid, 'Some festival programmes of the eighteenth and nineteenth centuries [pts 1–2]', *Royal Musical Association Research Chronicle*, 5 (1965), 51–79; 6 (1966), 3–23 • C. Price, J. Milhous, and R. D. Hume, *Italian opera in late eighteenth-century London*, 1: *The King's Theatre, Haymarket, 1778–1791* (1995) • *The letters of Mozart and his family*, ed. and trans. E. Anderson, rev. S. Sadie and F. Smart, 3rd edn (1985) • H. C. Robbins Landon, *Haydn in England: 1791–1795* (1976), vol. 3 of *Haydn: chronicle and works* • Dotted Crotchet, 'Bath: its musical associations', *MT*, 49 (1908), 695–704 • S. Hodges, 'Venanzio Rauzzini', *Music Review*, 52 (1991), 12–30 • M. Sands, 'Venanzio Rauzzini—singer, composer, traveller', *MT*, 94 (1953), 15–19 • M. Sands, 'Rauzzini at Bath', *MT*, 94 (1953), 108–11 • L. Baillie and R. Balchin, eds., *The catalogue of printed music in the British Library to 1980*, 62 vols. (1981–7), vol. 47 • K. K. Hansell, 'Rauzzini, Matteo', *New Grove*, 2nd edn [Matteo Rauzzini]

Likenesses double portrait, engraving, 1775 (as Montezuma in *Montezuma*, with Catherine Schindlerin), BM, Harvard TC • engraving, 1775–6 (as Piramo in his opera *Piramo e Tisbe*; after Cossa), BM • J. Nixon, double portrait, wash drawing, 1796 (with Madame Mara), repro. in 'Mara, Gertrud', *New Grove* • R. Hancock, stipple, pubd 1800 (after J. Hutchison), BM • Landseer, medallion, 1801 (after de Loutherbourg) • S. Freeman, stipple, pubd 1807 (after W. M. Bennett), BM, NPG; repro. in *Monthly Mirror* (1807) • J. Hutchison, miniature, Victoria Art Gallery, Bath • J. Hutchison, oils, Victoria Art Gallery, Bath • medallion, BM • oils, Holburne Museum of Art, Bath

Wealth at death £2000—valuation of estate: grant of administration: M. Sands, 'Rauzzini at Bath', *MT*, 94 (1953), 108–11

Raven, Charles Earle (1885–1964), theologian, was born on 4 July 1885 in Paddington, London, the eldest of the three children of John Earle Raven, barrister, and his wife, Alice, daughter of Edward Comber, a Liverpool merchant. His younger brother was Edward Earle Raven who was chaplain of St John's College, Cambridge (1921–6), and dean from 1927 until his death in 1951. Charles Raven was educated at Uppingham School, in Fircroft House which was then under his uncle, the Revd Tancred Earle Raven. He won a classical scholarship to Gonville and Caius College, Cambridge, and obtained a first class in part one of the classical tripos in 1907, and a first with distinction in part two of the theological tripos in 1908, specializing in early Christian doctrine. In July 1906, while still an undergraduate, he became engaged to the master's niece, Margaret Ermyntrude Buchanan (Bee) Wollaston, whom he married in 1910. They had a son and three daughters. Raven started his career as assistant secretary for secondary education under the Liverpool city council (1908–9), where he was miserable; for the first time, however, he saw beyond his middle-class upbringing, to understand the meaning of fellowship and dedication, when he engaged in the work of a boys' club. In 1909 he was offered the position of lecturer in divinity, fellow, and dean of Emmanuel College, Cambridge, provided he would be ordained that December. The idea fitted his newly found sense of vocation, and he took up the post at the beginning of 1910. There he was instantly thrown into a tense college and university controversy as the master, William Chawner, had issued a pamphlet declaring that Christian orthodoxy was indefensible: Raven, *ex officio* at the centre of the ensuing storm, went through a time of intense anxiety.

After the outbreak of war, Raven was assistant master at

Tonbridge School, in 1915–17, and a front-line army chaplain in France during 1917–18, where he suffered slightly from being gassed. He returned to Emmanuel and, needing a home for his wife and four children, accepted the college living of Bletchingley, Surrey, where he was rector for four years, until he became residentiary canon of the new Liverpool Cathedral from 1924 to 1932. Raven was already well known for his oratory, and as early as 1920 he was appointed a chaplain to the king. Within the life of the travelling preacher he managed to write two important books. *Christian Socialism, 1848–1854* (1920) was the first to treat this important Victorian movement historically; he felt strong links with the ideals of Christian socialism, and was one of the chief organizers of the influential Conference on Christian Politics, Economics and Citizenship (Copec) in 1924: he was its joint secretary from 1920 to 1928, under the chairmanship of William Temple, who remained a lifelong friend. In 1923 he published *Apollinarianism*, a sober and fundamental study of a then neglected aspect of primitive Christian thought, which made his name in a different world, that of academic divinity, and gained him a Cambridge DD. In 1932 he was appointed regius professor of divinity at Cambridge. With the chair he held a canonry at Ely Cathedral (1932–40), a fellowship at Christ's College, and from 1939 to 1950 the mastership of Christ's.

As professor Raven had a full audience; he would lecture *extempore*, pacing with restless energy about the room. The lectures were not geared to undergraduates' needs to pass examinations, nor easy to summarize in the form of notes. The austere Cambridge tradition of linguistic knowledge and historical texts he regarded as excellent but far too narrow. He long argued for a wider syllabus, especially to include the place of theology in the modern world, and like many reformers he did not see the reform for which he had worked until after he had retired. But his own lectures took the great Christian themes one by one—God, Christ, Holy Spirit, creation, creed, future life, idea of the church—and tried to expound them in the context of a scientific world and contemporary social need. The thinkers to whom he loved to point were those who tried to marry faith with the reason and science of their own day: the Alexandrian fathers in the third century, or the Cambridge Platonists in the seventeenth. The difficulty, as in all his writing, lay in showing how the drastic reinterpretation which he called for would differ from the watering down of Christianity (as he thought it) in the work of scientific modernists such as Ernest William Barnes or James Bethune-Baker. He had a deeper sense of immediacy—even ecstasy—in religious experience, and a quicker perception of the numinous in nature, which he could more easily make men feel than himself analyse. A brilliant scholar, he had too large a heart to attain the detachment of the pure academic.

From boyhood Raven loved birds and insects and wild flowers, and as an adult he made himself expert in the history of the life-sciences. He wrote a happy little book, *In Praise of Birds* (1925), painted wild flowers and birds with exquisite precision, and was a pioneer of the photography of birds in flight. His desire to heal the breach between faith and reason turned slowly towards reconciling science and religion: he believed that the evolutionary process could be accounted for only in terms of the movement of spirit. He wrote and lectured more on the theme of science and religion than on any other subject: to him, science meant biology and evolution, and religion a humane and liberal interpretation of Christianity. The most ambitious of these efforts were the Gifford lectures at Edinburgh for 1951–2, published as *Natural Religion and Christian Theology* (1953). But his best books in the field were more modest endeavours to explain early English science: *John Ray, Naturalist* (1942) and *English Naturalists from Neckam to Ray* (1947—which won a James Tait Black prize) were notable contributions to the history of biology. As war approached in the late thirties, liberal divinity was assailed as too facile for the ills of the age. Raven vehemently denounced the swing against reason and the leaders of European intellectual reaction headed by Karl Barth. In his later years as professor he felt grief that young men seemed to be neglecting his type of liberal thought, and it came as a relief when the French Jesuit Teilhard de Chardin won posthumous celebrity for a proposal to reconcile evolution with faith along lines which were in substance those proposed by Raven himself three decades before. In 1962 Raven published the first English biography of de Chardin.

Meanwhile Raven met the course of the world head on over the question of pacifism. During the twenties he slowly came to adopt the position as faithful to the New Testament, and in 1932 he became chairman of the Fellowship of Reconciliation and two years later one of the sponsors of the Peace Pledge Union with the Revd H. R. L. (Dick) Sheppard; he delivered an impressive apologia in his Halley Stewart lectures of 1934, published as *Is War Obsolete?* (1935). This movement lost influence unsteadily from 1937 as the Nazi threat grew, but Raven was a man who committed his heart to a cause and did not waver, in spite of frustration and depression of spirit. At the outbreak of the Second World War in 1939 he therefore faced unpopularity and contempt, although he gave unfailing help to refugees in England, and at times even he could not quite be constant, as when he gave thanks in the college chapel for the victory at El Alamein. He would have liked high office in the Church of England, but so much controversy surrounded his name during the years when he was the right age that he was passed over. In 1947, however, Cambridge University unexpectedly summoned him to be vice-chancellor. His two years of office were difficult, with so many returned soldiers crowding two into a room; but Raven confounded prophets who predicted that so charismatic a man could not administer a great institution. As one who had long contended for the advancement of women (including their ordination) he had the special happiness of presiding over the belated but at last unopposed admission of women to full membership of the university, and of bringing the queen to an honorary degree as the first women graduated in 1948. In the same year he helped to choose J. C. Smuts as the university's new chancellor; they had been friends for many years.

On his retirement from both chair and mastership in 1950, Raven accepted the position of warden of Madingley Hall, which the university had just bought as a hostel. The hall needed a good secretary, not one of the principal orators of Europe who felt that it was 'a backwater' offering little scope for his talents; the result was not altogether happy, and he gave up the wardenship in 1954. However, Raven travelled, lectured, and preached more widely than ever after his retirement, visiting the United States several times, Australia and New Zealand (1950), Canada (1952), Russia (1954), and India in 1955–6. He spent much time in visiting schools, too, where he would both preach and talk informally to the boys, and it was said that his ministry to sixth-formers may have been the most influential of his career; he was also a popular figure on radio and television (once the wartime ban on his voice as a pacifist had been lifted), giving a new dimension to religious broadcasting. All his adult life he had been a great preacher and a natural leader of men: tall and spare, with chiselled features, brilliant eyes, a youthful appearance, dynamic energy, and a magical voice, he never spoke without riveting attention; yet he never outgrew a certain nervousness before preaching, and would privately rehearse like an actor in order to speak without notes. On religious subjects he felt passionately, and at his best he could communicate the fervour and agony which were a part of his being. With an evangelical gospel, he was simultaneously an intellectual and a classicist trying to integrate his own faith and that of his hearers into the honest apprehension of a scientific world—a quality which made him wanted as a lecturer and in pulpits everywhere. He retained the magnetic power of his oratory until the end of his life.

Raven was a trustee of the British Museum from 1950, a fellow of the British Academy from 1948, president of the Botanical Society of the British Isles in 1951–5, and fellow of the Linnean Society; and he received honorary degrees from many universities: the one he valued most was a doctorate of science from Manchester. He wrote many books besides those mentioned: the most important were his Hulsean and Noble lectures of 1926–7, combined as *The Creator Spirit* in 1927; *Jesus and the Gospel of Love* (1931); *Evolution and the Christian Concept of God* (1936); *Science, Religion and the Future* (1943, the published version of his Cambridge Open lectures); and *Good News of God* (1943).

Raven's first wife died in 1944—a shattering blow, only a year after his own serious illness. After her death his eldest daughter, Mary, presided at the lodge, until in 1954 he married Ethel, widow of John Moors, of Boston, Massachusetts, with whom he had worked closely in the pacifist cause. She was already eighty, and died on honeymoon within a fortnight of the marriage. In 1956 he married Hélène Jeanty (Ninette), a former worker in the Belgian resistance whose first husband had been shot by the Nazis; living partly in Cambridge and partly in Brussels, they dedicated themselves to a mission of reconciliation between students of different races. Raven died at his home, 10 Madingley Road, Cambridge, on 8 July 1964. His only son, John Earle Raven (d. 1980), became a fellow and dean of King's College, Cambridge, and an authority upon both ancient Greek philosophy and mountain plants.

OWEN CHADWICK, *rev.*

Sources C. E. Raven, *A wanderer's way* (1928) • C. E. Raven, *Musings and memories* (1931) • F. W. Dillistone, *Charles Raven* (1975) • I. T. Ramsey, 'Charles Earle Raven (1885–1964)', *PBA*, 51 (1965), 467–84 • *The Times* (10 July 1964) • H. J. Raven, *Without frontiers* (1960) • personal knowledge (1981) • *CGPLA Eng. & Wales* (1964)
Archives U. Warwick Mod. RC, corresp. with Victor Gollancz
Likenesses W. Stoneman, photograph, 1947, NPG • E. Nelson, oils, 1949, Christ's College, Cambridge • W. Stoneman, photograph, 1957, NPG; repro. in Ramsey, *PBA*, 51 (1965), facing p. 467 • A. Allard, oils, 1962, priv. coll.
Wealth at death £72,121: probate, 17 Sept 1964, *CGPLA Eng. & Wales*

Raven, John James (1833–1906), antiquary and campanologist, born on 25 June 1833 at Boston, Lincolnshire, was the eldest son of eight children of John Hardy Raven, of Huguenot descent, rector of Worlington, near Mildenhall, Suffolk, and his wife, Jane Augusta, daughter of John Richman, attorney, of Lymington, Hampshire. His younger brother, the Revd John Hardy Raven (1842–1911), was headmaster of Beccles School.

Educated at home, Raven entered St Catharine's College, Cambridge, on 18 October 1853, and migrated in December that year to Emmanuel College with an exhibition. A senior optime in the mathematical tripos of 1857, he proceeded MA in 1860 and DD in 1872. He married on 19 March 1860, at Mildenhall parish church, Suffolk, Fanny, youngest daughter of Robert Homer Harris of Botesdale; they had two daughters and seven sons, three of whom took holy orders.

In 1857 Raven was appointed second master of Sevenoaks grammar school, and was ordained curate of the parish church there. In 1859 he became headmaster of Bungay grammar school, an office always in the gift of Emmanuel College. He improved the school, and raised money for a new building, which was opened in 1863. From 1866 to 1885 he was headmaster of Great Yarmouth grammar school, where a tower commemorates his time. He served for some time as curate of the parish church in Great Yarmouth, and was from 1881 to 1885 vicar of St George's in that town. In 1885 he was presented by Emmanuel to the cure of Fressingfield and Withersdale, and in 1895 to Metfield, all in Suffolk. An honorary canon of Norwich from 1888, and rural dean of Hoxne from 1896, he was co-opted as a founder member of the county education committee in 1902.

Raven began his lifelong antiquarian studies by examining the bells of the churches near his home at Worlington, and was only twenty-one when he contributed to the Parkers' *Ecclesiastical History of Suffolk* in 1855. He served from 1881 until his death on the committee of the Norfolk and Norwich Archaeological Society, which he joined in 1871, was a vice-president of the Suffolk Institute of Archaeology, and was elected FSA on 23 April 1891. A keen bell ringer, and president of the Norwich Diocesan Association of Change Ringers, Raven was a leading writer on campanology among those then publishing county surveys. His *Church Bells of Cambridgeshire* (1869), *Church Bells of Suffolk* (1890), and *Bells of England* (1906) remain standard works of reference. He also published a popular *History of Suffolk* in 1895, which he fittingly claimed was 'a personal intercourse with all classes', and was a contributor to the Victoria county history of Suffolk.

Raven died at Fressingfield vicarage on 20 September 1906, and was buried in the churchyard there on 24 September. A reredos was erected to his memory and a lectern provided in the church. His fine library of county and bell literature was sold at Fressingfield in November 1906.

T. C. HUGHES, rev. J. M. BLATCHLY

Sources WWW · *The Athenaeum* (29 Sept 1906), 366–7 · *Emmanuel College Magazine*, 17 (1906–7) · private information (1912) · Venn, *Alum. Cant.* · *CGPLA Eng. & Wales* (1906) · parish register (marriage), Mildenhall parish church, Suffolk, 19 March 1860 · parish register (burial), Fressingfield church, Suffolk, 24 Sept 1906
Archives BL, corresp. and collections relating to church bells, Add. MSS 37426–37440 · Suffolk RO, Ipswich, diaries, MSS · Suffolk RO, Bury St Edmunds, notes and papers, incl. MS of *History of Suffolk*
Likenesses photograph, c.1900, repro. in *Norwich Diocesan Association of Ringers: 28th report* (1906) · A. L. Baldry, portrait, priv. coll.
Wealth at death £3577 13s. 2d.: probate, 8 Nov 1906, *CGPLA Eng. & Wales*

Raven, John Samuel (1829–1877), landscape painter, was born on 21 August 1829, probably in Preston, the son of the Revd Thomas Raven (c.1795–1868), the minister of Holy Trinity Church in Preston, and his wife, Susanna Horrocks; he was baptized at St John's, Preston, on 5 October 1829. Thomas Raven, who later lived in Torquay, was himself a painter, and produced watercolours of mountain and coastal subjects; he is represented by a group of six drawings of Welsh and Devon subjects which he presented to the Victoria and Albert Museum. It seems that the Raven family were financially independent, although it is not known how this fortune originated. According to J. S. Raven's obituary in *The Academy*, he was descended on his mother's side from the astronomer Jeremiah Horrocks.

John Samuel Raven seems to have had no other professional instruction beyond that which he received from his father and what he learned from looking at the works of earlier British landscape painters. According to the author of the introduction to the catalogue of the 1878 Burlington Fine Arts Club exhibition of Raven's paintings, Raven, as a young man, studied the work of John Crome and Constable; certainly his early paintings have a breadth of handling and harmonious balance of tone reminiscent of the Norwich school. Raven is also believed to have looked carefully at works by the Scottish painter the Revd John Thomson of Duddingston.

Although there is no indication of direct contact by Raven with artists such as Millais, Holman Hunt, or Ford Madox Brown, the influence of Pre-Raphaelitism is strongly felt in his landscape paintings of the 1850s. Works such as *Saint-Foin in Bloom* (exh. RA, 1859; priv. coll.) are characterized by extraordinary elaboration of detail, rich and intense colour, and poetic feeling. Admired by John Ruskin, it was perhaps *Saint-Foin in Bloom* that the author of the 1878 catalogue introduction had in mind when writing of him: 'he has attained a level, which is superior to any school or special method, and has shown a consummate skill in realising, by original means, effects which none but a poetical mind could have conceived' (*Collected Works of the Late John Samuel Raven*, 4). The artist's instinct towards meticulous detail crossed with intense mood was maintained at least until the end of the 1860s. The view at Dunkeld on the River Tay that he exhibited at the Royal Academy in 1869 (Perth Museum and Art Gallery) was looked on with favour by the reviewer of the *Art Journal*:

> J. S. Raven, an artist of much promise in years gone by, we had almost lost sight of … The study is most conscientious, and really, in these days, to come upon one remnant of the now wholly obsolete Pre-Raffaelitism of the past, is a delightful curiosity.   (*Art Journal*, 1869, 172)

During the early and mid-1850s Raven lived at St Leonards, Sussex. From 1856 he seems to have moved from place to place, sending paintings to exhibitions from addresses in Torquay (Lansdown Hall, where perhaps Thomas Raven was living in retirement), and Bedale in Yorkshire (where his brother, the Revd Milville Raven, was rector). On 15 June 1869 he married Margaret Sinclair, daughter of Peter Dunbar, an Indian army officer, and in that year he seems to have settled in London, living first at James Street, Westbourne Terrace, and then at Westbourne Park. In 1871 alpine and north Italian subjects by Raven appeared at exhibition, presumably the result of a honeymoon tour.

Raven was represented at the Royal Academy summer exhibitions most years from 1849 through to the year of his death. None the less, according to *The Academy*, he 'was one of the painters who had reason to think themselves other than handsomely treated by the Royal Academy'; the writer added, as a comment on the academy's well-known prejudice against progressive landscape painting, 'in this, indeed, he had plenty of landscapists to keep him company' (1877, 75). Raven worked chiefly in oils, but occasionally also in watercolour. He was not a prolific artist, and many of his recorded works, including *Midsummer Moonlight* (said by *The Academy* to be his finest painting), remain untraced.

Raven drowned while bathing at Harlech in north Wales on 13 July 1877. He left one son, and his widow later married the painter William Bright Morris; Raven's sister Kate had married the painter and designer Henry Holiday in 1864. A memorial exhibition of Raven's paintings and sketches was held at the Burlington Fine Arts Club in 1878.

CHRISTOPHER NEWALL

Sources *Collected works of the late John Samuel Raven* (1878) [exhibition catalogue, Burlington Fine Arts Club, London] · *The Times* (21 July 1877), 12 · *The Academy* (21 July 1877), 75 · 'Twilight in the wood', *Art Journal*, 36 (1874), 212 · *Art Journal*, 39 (1877), 309 · Bryan, *Painters* (1903–5) · IGI · m. cert. · d. cert. · *CGPLA Eng. & Wales* (1877)
Wealth at death under £7000: resworn administration, July 1878, *CGPLA Eng. & Wales*

Raven, Dame **Kathleen Annie** (1910–1999), nurse, was born on 9 November 1910 at Mountain View, Coniston, Lancashire, the only daughter of Frederick William Raven, director of a slate quarry, and his wife, Annie Williams Mason, who claimed descent from the potter Miles Mason. She grew up with three brothers in a Plymouth Brethren household. Kathleen was educated privately and at Ulverston grammar school. Nursing was not her original choice as a career, but she was influenced by her eldest brother, Ronald William Raven (1904–1991), who studied medicine at St Bartholomew's Hospital, London, and later became a distinguished surgeon. Kathleen followed him by training at Bart's, as a nurse and midwife. She was extremely close to Ronald and greatly distressed by his death in 1991. During the Second World War Kathleen, a young ward sister, remained at Bart's as one of the skeleton staff after most of the patients had been evacuated. In 'London, 1940', an article published in the *History of Nursing Society Journal* in 1990, she recalled standing on the hospital roof on 29 December 1940 and watching the city in flames, while St Paul's Cathedral stood as a beacon of hope. Her recollections were quoted by Sir Christopher Walford, lord mayor of London, in the speech of welcome preceding the Guildhall banquet of 6 May 1997 commemorating the fiftieth anniversary of the end of the war in Europe (CLRO, RDCB/21/1).

In 1949 Kathleen left Bart's, where she was an assistant matron, to become matron at the General Infirmary at Leeds. She knew of her very apt nickname, 'the Pocket Battleship', and was both amused and rather proud of it. She soon became a national figure, noted for her ability, her farsightedness for nursing, and her persuasive and forceful way of putting her arguments. Many senior nurses from overseas visited Leeds for advice. In 1957 she was appointed deputy to Dame Elizabeth Cockayne, chief nursing officer to the Ministry of Health, and she succeeded her famous predecessor in 1959. She married, on 12 December in the same year, John Thornton Ingram (1898/9–1972), professor of dermatology at Newcastle University. They were often separated by distance and the demands of work, but it was an extremely happy marriage, and those years were probably the peak of her influence on nursing. There were no children. Kathleen was devastated at his death following a short illness only six months after her retirement in 1972. She resumed her work with typical courage, but it remained the great sadness of her life. His full length painting dominated the sitting room of their lovely home in Burcott.

Kathleen Raven was appointed DBE in 1968 and was chief nursing officer for fourteen years, being responsible for some of the most important changes and developments in nursing. She was instrumental in setting up the Salmon committee on management of nursing and advocated the introduction of intensive care units and systems of progressive patient care following her experiences in the USA. She organized a hospital planning unit, studies on the ratio of nurses to patients, and many other initiatives. Perhaps the most important was the Briggs committee on nurse training, chaired by Professor Asa Briggs. In

Dame Kathleen Annie Raven (1910–1999), by unknown photographer, 1958

1963 she became officer (sister) of the order of St John. Already a vice-president of the Royal College of Nursing in 1986 she was elected a fellow in recognition of her leadership as chief nursing officer. She served as a civil service commissioner from 1972 to 1986, and was appointed chief nursing adviser to the Allied Medical Group, which involved her in hospitals under British management in Saudi Arabia, the Emirates, Iran, and Egypt. The Distressed Gentlefolk Association was another organization to which she devoted a great deal of time. She received the freedom of the City of London in 1986 and honorary doctorates from the universities of Leeds and Keele, and in 1981 was appointed honorary freewoman of the Worshipful Company of Barbers.

In her later years Kathleen Raven was critical of the concentration on academic learning in nurse education. She did not object to higher education for nurses, but felt that in moving their education into colleges and universities ward experience and close contact with patients would be lost, and nursing care suffer. Towards the end of her life she wished to set up a chair in clinical nursing in Leeds. She was less able to travel, so the relevant university officials met in her home, and a colleague took her place in the appointment of the first Raven professor in clinical nursing in 1997. She was delighted, and met the appointee at her home in Burcott. Kathleen was equally interested in general education, and served as a foundation governor of Aylesbury grammar school and member of council of Epsom College.

One task remained: to influence the training of the nurse and improvement in clinical practice. Kathleen Raven invited a number of eminent persons to form a group. She launched the first meeting in London, but it was also her last; without Kathleen's inspiration, and after a report was sent to the Department of Health, the group ended their work. In the meantime her health had deteriorated, and she entered the Acland Hospital, Oxford, where she died peacefully, firm in her Christian faith, on 19 April 1999. The funeral service was held on 27 April at St Paul's Church, Wingrave, Buckinghamshire, where she was buried in the same grave as her husband John. A memorial service was held in St Giles, Cripplegate, the following July. Her obituarist in *The Times* recalled her as 'a lively hostess who thought nothing of cooking lunch for 40 … a lively character, but always dignified' and noted her hobbies as painting and friendship.

SHEILA QUINN

Sources *The Guardian* (23 April 1999) · *Daily Telegraph* (23 April 1999) · L. Dobson, 'Dame Kathleen Raven', *The Independent* (21 April 1999) · *WW* (1998) · citation for fellowship, 1986, Royal College of Nursing Archives, Edinburgh · recording of lord mayor's speech, 6 May 1997, CLRO, RDCB/21/1 · *The Times* (21 April 1999), 25a–h · A. Lettin, 'Dame Kathleen Raven DBE, OST, FRCN, Hon D. Litt, Hon LLD, 1910–1999', *Annals of the Royal College of Surgeons of England*, 81 (1999), 218–19 [suppl.] · K. Raven, 'London, 1940', *History of Nursing Society Journal*, 3/3 (1990), 37–50 · K. Raven, 'War and peace', *International History of Nursing Journal*, 1/2 (1995), 53–74 · personal knowledge (2004) · private information (2004) · b. cert. · m. cert. · d. cert.

Likenesses photograph, 1958, repro. in *The Independent* · photograph, 1958, Hult. Arch. [*see illus.*] · photograph, 1959, repro. in *The Times* · photograph, 1960–1969?, repro. in *The Guardian* · photograph, 1968, repro. in *Daily Telegraph* · portraits, repro. in Lettin, 'Dame Kathleen Raven'

Wealth at death £1,712,392—gross; £1,701,608—net: probate, 24 Sept 1999, *CGPLA Eng. & Wales*

Ravenet, Simon François (1721–1774), engraver, was born in Paris and trained there with Jacques Philippe Le Bas. Little of his early work is known, but he must have been well respected at an early age, since he was among those chosen to engrave reproductions of Charles Le Brun's decorative paintings at Versailles for Jean-Baptiste Massé's *Grande galerie de Versailles* (1731–51); the engravers involved in this ambitious volume are described on the title-page as 'les meilleurs Maîtres du tems'. Engravers trained in the virtuoso techniques developed in seventeenth-century Paris were still unsurpassed in the mid-eighteenth century, and in 1743 when William Hogarth wanted to publish high-quality reproductions of his *Marriage à la mode* paintings he went out of his way to commission French engravers. Ravenet travelled to London to engrave the fourth and fifth of the series (the others were engraved by Bernard Baron and Gérard Scotin), and he appears to have settled into the émigré community, never returning to France.

In 1745–6 Richard Dalton employed Ravenet to engrave a series of large prints of classical sculpture in Italian collections and, with Jean Baptiste Claude Chatelain, to engrave a scene from book 6 of Milton's *Paradise Lost*. In 1752 he engraved the first of the large plates after John van Rymsdyck's drawings showing the dissection of a woman in an advanced stage of pregnancy for William Hunter's *Anatomy of the Human Gravid Uterus*, eventually published in 1774. In 1753 he engraved Benjamin Wilson's painting *David Garrick and Miss Bellamy as Romeo and Juliet*, which was sold by subscription, possibly at the painter's instigation.

The majority of Ravenet's work was produced for large-scale publishers: Robert Sayer, John and Paul Knapton, and, especially, John Boydell. In 1759 or 1760 Ravenet was working again with Hogarth on two illustrations after the artist for the second edition of Laurence Sterne's *Tristram Shandy* (vol. 1, 1760; vol. 4, 1761). Hogarth hoped that Ravenet would also engrave his controversial painting *Sigismunda Mourning over the Heart of Guiscardo*, but the subscription was stopped on 26 March 1761 after about three weeks, evidently because Ravenet was committed to a project for Boydell. He had already been employed by Boydell to engrave Andrea Casali's *Gunhilda* (priced at 7s. 6d.), one of five prints issued to subscribers in April 1761 after paintings at the first exhibition of the Society of Artists (the other four were engraved by William Woollett). In 1763 Boydell advertised for subscriptions to *A Collection of Prints, Engraved from the most Capital Paintings in England*. The series was published in three volumes from 1769 to 1773 under the title *Sculptura Britannica*, and its huge international success marked the beginning of the domination of the European art world by British print-publishers. Ravenet produced about a quarter of the prints in the first volume and most of those in the second.

Ravenet played a significant part in the London art institutions that were coming into being in the late eighteenth century, sitting on the committee of the Society of Artists in 1767 and in 1770 joining the Royal Academy as one of only six associate engravers. In 1772, after the artist's death, Ravenet engraved Hogarth's paintings of *The Pool of Bethesda* and *The Good Samaritan* at St Bartholomew's Hospital, London, working with Victor Marie Picot and Jean Marie Delattre, who were partners in a printselling business in St Martin's Lane. Picot was married to Ravenet's daughter Angelique. About this time Ravenet retired to Kentish Town, then a suburban village. He died there on 2 April 1774.

Ravenet's son, also Simon François Ravenet (1748–1814), followed in his father's footsteps as an engraver. It is possible that a number of small portraits and book illustrations signed 'Ravenet' may be his juvenile work rather than that of his father. He moved to Paris in the mid-1770s and studied under François Boucher. In 1779 he was appointed engraver to the duke of Parma, became director of the academy in Parma, and made a series of engravings of the paintings of Correggio in that city.

SHEILA O'CONNELL

Sources T. Clayton, *The English print, 1688–1802* (1997) · R. Paulson, *Hogarth's graphic works*, 3rd edn (1989) · D. Alexander, 'Ravenet, Simon François', *The dictionary of art*, ed. J. Turner (1996) · *DNB*
Likenesses S. F. Ravenet, line engraving, 1763 (after J. Zoffany), BM, NPG · J. Zoffany, oils, c.1770, priv. coll.

Ravenhill, Alice (1859–1954), educationist and promoter of the household science movement, was born on 31 March 1859 in Snaresbrook, Essex, the fourth of the seven children of John Ravenhill (1824–1894), naval architect and marine engineer, and his wife, Fanny Pocock (c.1831–1903), daughter of Thomas Pike Pocock and Martha Pike.

Like many women of the nineteenth century Ravenhill was thwarted in her intellectual ambitions by middle-class conventions which stressed 'accomplishments' rather than academic achievement. She was educated privately and at residential schools in Richmond and St John's Wood, but her father prohibited her from following her first ambitions to train as a nurse or attend the National Training School for Cookery. A holiday in Weymouth, however, sparked her interest in geology, and she later taught herself biology and physiology, surreptitiously dissecting snails, worms, and even an ox's eye in her bedroom. It was only after her father's financial collapse while Ravenhill was in her late twenties that she was able to pursue her interests in science and social welfare—interests which stemmed from an 'unquenchable search for knowledge and childhood yearning to help my fellow man to a happier and less-troubled existence' (Ravenhill, 45). Opting for the more respectable preventative health work, she enrolled in the National Health Society's year-long training course for county council hygiene lecturers—at the time the only such course open to women intending to work in public health. Two fellow students, Lucy Deane and Rose Squire, later became the first women sanitary inspectors and subsequently two of the first women factory inspectors. Ravenhill was also invited to interview for a sanitary inspection post upon finishing in 1892, but declined the offer, and instead found scope for her interests in researching and preparing reports on various health-related subjects. The first was an unofficial report about women in the fish-curing industry in conjunction with the royal commission on labour, written at the behest of her friend Edith Temple Orme. Ravenhill's developing career in public health was also aided by her friendship with Prince Leopold, whose estate in Wiltshire bordered that of her father, and Princess Christian, who introduced her to many leading social reformers and other public figures of the period. It was through this friendship that Ravenhill served, from 1894 to 1897, as secretary to the Royal British Nurses Association, one of Princess Christian's causes.

Ravenhill resigned this position in 1897 to work as a lecturer in public health law for the Co-operative Society and the Women's Co-operative Guild, beginning a long career in health education. In her first year she gave a series of over forty lectures in various manufacturing areas, after which she took a post under the West Riding county council (1899–1904), teaching a course which she had devised herself for teachers on the correlation of hygiene and health education with ordinary school subjects, and serving as an inspector of hygiene and domestic economy at various technical institutes and evening schools. In 1899 she was secretary of the school hygiene section at the Royal Sanitary Institute's congress at Southampton. The same year she represented the National Health Society at the International Congress of Women at Westminster, where she first met Michael Sadler, head of the special report department of the Board of Education, with whom she maintained a lifelong friendship.

It was while attending the congress of the Royal Sanitary Institute in Paris in 1900 that Ravenhill first became interested in American home economics education. The topic had been prominent in the Paris Exhibition of that year, although she noted that the idea of applying science to household matters, and offering the subject at university level, was regarded with great suspicion there. Ravenhill, however, was enthusiastic about the new discipline. She approached Michael Sadler about the need for a report on the American experience; Robert Morant, president of the Board of Education, gave her the commission. Ravenhill approached the Royal Sanitary Institute and the West Riding county council to help fund her trip, agreeing to submit separate reports on school sanitation and on home economics courses in American schools. Her research trip in the summer of 1901 ignited her enthusiasm for establishing a university home economics course in Britain. Arranged by Ellen H. Richards, one of the founders of the American Home Economics Association, Ravenhill's tour took her across the American north-east and midwest and into Canada, bringing her into contact with many prominent social reformers. In New York she attended the Third Lake Placid Conference (1901) of home economics educators, the forerunner of the American Home Economics Association. Ravenhill was so impressed with the American movement that she strongly considered returning to train there herself so that she could be a stronger advocate for the idea in Britain; Sadler dissuaded her, arguing that she could accomplish more by staying in England.

Ravenhill's reports for the Royal Sanitary Institute (1902), which elected her as its first woman fellow in 1904, and for the Board of Education (1905) received much press attention, and as a result Ravenhill was invited to join various committees relating to school hygiene and health. On some of these committees she was the only woman; other women were, as she noted, more involved in the suffrage movement at that time. Although not anti-suffrage by inclination, she had an aversion, in deference to her much admired elder sister Margaret, against being a 'platform woman'; and Ravenhill's commitment to promoting the scientific study of social problems outweighed any desire to become involved in suffrage organizations. Her membership on the school hygiene subcommittees of the Royal Sanitary Institute and the British Association had alerted her to the need for more attention to children's formative years and their nutritional requirements, and prompted her to undertake several research projects. Her investigations into the sleep requirements of elementary school children were presented before the International Congress on School Hygiene in London (1907) and published as *Some Characteristics and Requirements of Childhood* (1908). In 1906–7 she visited physical training colleges for women in England, Scotland, Denmark, and Sweden, accompanied by the surgeon Dame Mary Scharlieb, after which Ravenhill was sent by the English board of education as a temporary inspector to visit women's training colleges and report on methods of physical exercise. She later declined an offer from Robert Morant to become the second woman inspector of schools. Other studies included an investigation into moral education in elementary schools for a private commission established in 1907 (presided over by Lord Bryce and Michael Sadler) and a report for the Child Study Society on the play interests of elementary school children (1910). She also wrote several school textbooks on domestic and personal hygiene, as well as an edited volume (with Catherine Schiff), *Household Administration: its Place in the Higher Education of Women* (1911).

It was in this context of public interest in social welfare issues that Ravenhill became involved in a movement to develop a university course in home economics in Britain, an idea which had gained currency in the aftermath of the report of the interdepartmental committee on physical deterioration (1904) and its recommendation that girls should be given better domestic science instruction. A university-level course in 'home science' was seen as a way to provide teachers qualified to develop scientifically based domestic courses for secondary school girls, give home-related subjects such as domestic hygiene and food preparation a higher social status, and provide an option for university women wanting to take up positions in social welfare work which were then being opened to women. The idea found fertile ground at King's College for Women, London, where Ravenhill was lecturing in hygiene, among a number of women and men who were interested in the reform of higher education in order to make it more relevant to modern life, including: Lilian M. Faithfull, vice-principal of King's College for Women (1894–1907); her successor, Hilda D. Oakeley; Halford Mackinder, principal of the London School of Economics; Herbert Jackson, professor of organic chemistry at King's College; Sir Arthur Rucker, principal of the University of London (1901–8); and his wife, Thereza, Lady Rucker. Inaugurated in 1908, household and social science was established as a London BSc course in 1920 and led to the founding of King's College of Household and Social Science in 1928.

Ravenhill reluctantly agreed to her younger sister Edith's suggestion in 1910 that they accompany their brother Horace and his son to Canada, a decision which she took with 'great pain' as it meant giving up her work in England (Ravenhill, 170). The sojourn was intended to last only four years, but her return in 1914 was cancelled due to the outbreak of war in Europe, and she was never able to afford the return trip afterwards. Ravenhill at first threw her energies into the homestead at Shawnigan Lake on Vancouver Island, British Columbia, and into the local

community, but was soon disillusioned by the lack of public-spirited women and the sharp demarcation between the sexes in terms of activities and occupations. Again she found scope for her interests in American home economics education. She held annual visiting lectureships at Oregon State College at Corvallis, and was appointed in 1917 by the Ellen H. Richards Memorial Fund as the first international lecturer in home economics, undertaking a two-month tour through Texas and various midwestern states. She also served as director of home economics at Utah State Agricultural College, Logan, from 1917 to 1919. This she considered in hindsight to be one of the 'greatest and costly mistakes' of her life as a result of her experiences with the Mormon social system and a severe case of Spanish influenza which forced her resignation and effectively ended her career as a lecturer (ibid., 197). None the less her early research on American home economics had earned her great appreciation among the American pioneers, and she was made an honorary doctor of home economics by the American Home Economics Association during their jubilee in 1950.

Having moved to Victoria in 1919, Ravenhill became active in the Women's Institutes movement, and it was through a request to adapt native tribal designs onto hooked rugs that she began a three-year research project on the arts and crafts of native British Columbian tribes, culminating in the publication of *The Native Tribes of British Columbia* (1938), a school textbook, and *A Corner Stone of Canadian Culture* (1944), a handbook on native designs. For this work, as well as for her establishment of the Society for Native Columbian Indian Arts and Crafts in 1940 to help improve the self-esteem and economic independence of native Canadians, the University of British Columbia awarded her an honorary doctor of science degree in 1948.

Ravenhill never married: an engagement in 1882 to a young doctor was broken off by her parents shortly before the wedding due to a dispute over the settlement. Her younger sister Edith became her lifelong companion and housekeeper. Of average build and slight of figure, Ravenhill had excelled at music and dancing in her youth, but was always of somewhat indifferent health, suffering from a number of serious illnesses throughout her life which required long periods of convalescence and prevented her from pursuing her interests with the vigour she desired. A period of recuperation in Bournemouth following an attack of rheumatic fever in 1887 brought her into the care of a doctor who challenged her religious faith, and, although she never rejected Christianity, she later valued the experience for enabling her to question religious dogma and to weigh carefully the arguments on both sides of a vital question. Despite her achievements and her lifelong desire for knowledge, she always felt keenly the lack of academic training, and ascribed her successes to perseverance, a quick intuition, and self-application. She died in Victoria, British Columbia, on 27 May 1954.   NANCY L. BLAKESTAD

Sources A. Ravenhill, *Memoirs of an educational pioneer* (1951) • N. L. Blakestad, 'King's College of Household and Social Science and the household science movement in English higher education, *c.*1908–1939', DPhil diss., U. Oxf., 1994 • N. Marsh, *The history of Queen Elizabeth College: one hundred years of university education in Kensington* (1986) • N. L. Blakestad, 'King's College of Household and Social Science and the origins of dietetics education', *Nutrition in Britain: science, scientists, and politics in the twentieth century*, ed. D. F. Smith (1997), 75–98

Archives University of British Columbia Library, incl. university archives • Utah State University Library, Logan

Likenesses double portrait, photograph, 1917, repro. in Ravenhill, *Memoirs*, facing p. 212 • photograph, 1917 (as director of home economics), repro. in Ravenhill, *Memoirs*, facing p. 180 • photograph (as doctor of science), repro. in Ravenhill, *Memoirs*, frontispiece

Ravenhill, William Lionel Desmond (1919–1995), geographer and historian of cartography, was born on 30 December 1919 in Carmarthen, the son of George Ravenhill (*c.*1880–1967), a master plumber, and his wife, Elizabeth (1893–1993). He had a brother and a sister. Ravenhill won a scholarship to Queen Elizabeth Grammar School, Carmarthen, in 1930 and entered the University College of Wales, Aberystwyth, in 1938 to read geography. His academic studies were interrupted in 1940 by war service as a Royal Air Force fighter pilot in Malta, Italy, Yugoslavia, and Egypt. After demobilization, he completed his degree and took a diploma in education; he was then appointed to an assistant lectureship at the University College of the South West, later the University of Exeter (1948), and was subsequently promoted to lecturer (1951) and senior lecturer (1962). He became professor of human geography in 1969 and Reardon Smith professor of geography and head of department in 1971, which post he held until his retirement in 1983; he also served the university as dean of its faculty of social studies and deputy vice-chancellor.

Ravenhill inherited a department of geography which the university had allowed to languish in the 1960s—that decade of great expansion elsewhere in higher education. But he had a clear, long-term vision for the future of what he saw very much as his department. He devoted himself to its development, won a series of new posts in the 1970s, and appointed wisely—no fewer than eight of his then 'junior' colleagues (Ravenhill had a strictly hierarchical view of university departments and their personnel) later held professorial chairs. Always a very formal man, even somewhat austere and forbidding to the non-academic members of his department, Ravenhill delighted in the collegiality of the senior common room and lectured with the panache and sense of theatre so characteristic of university teachers of his generation.

Despite a long life in, and great affection for, the south-west of England, Ravenhill remained fiercely proud of his Welsh roots. It is thus no surprise that his earliest research concerned the Celtic origins of settlement. His MA thesis for the University of Wales (1951) analysed early settlement in Devon, and his doctoral thesis for the University of London (1957) investigated early settlement sites in Devon and Cornwall and their influence on the modern settlement pattern. His seminal contribution to the historical geography of south-west England is his analysis of the settlement patterns, agrarian economy, and rural society of eleventh-century Cornwall, published as 'Cornwall' in *The Domesday Geography of South-West England* (H. C. Darby and R. Welldon Finn, 1967). A series of articles in learned journals by Ravenhill in association with the archaeologist Lady Aileen Fox confirmed the academic reputation of this geographer among archaeologists. He was elected a fellow of the Society of Antiquaries of London and in 1989 was appointed president of the Devon Archaeological Society. In his retirement he was co-editor with Roger Kain of a *Historical Atlas of South-West England* (1999), a work which celebrates his lifelong commitment to the University of Exeter's regional mission.

Significant though these works on the historical geography and archaeology of the south-west are, Ravenhill's particular and lasting academic contribution was to pioneer the history of cartography in Devon and Cornwall. It was within the close-knit academic world of cartography and map history where humanistic scholarship is combined with scientific analysis that he felt academically most comfortable. His *Benjamin Donn: a Map of the County of Devon, 1765* (1965) was followed by *John Norden's Manuscript Maps of Cornwall and its Nine Hundreds* (1972) and (with Oliver Padel) *A Map of the County of Cornwall Newly Surveyed by Joel Gascoyne, 1699* (1991). These major studies are supported by numerous papers in local and national journals and more popular books such as *Christopher Saxton's 16th-Century Maps: the Counties of England and Wales* (1992). Leukaemia, fought with great stoicism over a number of years, took Ravenhill from this life before he could bring all the strands of his cartographic work together in a much-hoped-for monograph on the cartographic history of south-west England. He died in the Royal Devon and Exeter Hospital, Wonford, Exeter, on 9 October 1995, and was cremated on 16 October. His widow, Mary Rose, *née* Atkinson (b. 1928), whom he married on 5 August 1952, worked with him throughout his life, and following his death continued his work with publications on historical maps of the west country. They had no children.

ROGER J. P. KAIN

Sources R. J. P. Kain, *Imago Mundi*, 48 (1996), 212–15 [incl. bibliography] • R. Kain, 'William Ravenhill, FSA, 1919–1995', *GJ*, 162 (1996), 134 • *CGPLA Eng. & Wales* (1995) • personal knowledge (2004) • private information (2004)

Likenesses photograph, repro. in Kain, *Imago Mundi*, p. 212

Wealth at death £297,715: probate, 22 Nov 1995, *CGPLA Eng. & Wales*

Ravenscroft, Edward (*fl.* 1659–1697), playwright, was the sixth son of James Ravenscroft of High Holborn, and descended from the Ravenscrofts of Ravenscroft, Flintshire, where a kinsman was high sheriff (dedication of *The Anatomist*). While there is no extant evidence of his early education, he was admitted to the Inner Temple on 28 November 1659, and to the Middle Temple on 2 April 1667. There is no record of his attending or not attending learning exercises, or of being called to the bar (Hutchinson, 202). In 1671 he wrote his first play, having, according to its prologue, feigned two weeks of 'sickness'. Two years later, on 30 May 1673, his chamber was seized for arrears in rent

(C. T. Martin, ed., *Middle Temple Records: Minutes of Parliament, 1501–1703*, 1905, 3.1274).

The first known performance of Ravenscroft's *The Citizen Turned Gentleman*, sometimes performed as *Mamamouchi*, was produced on 4 July 1672 at Dorset Garden. It was published the same year with a dedication to Prince Rupert. The play was taken from Molière's *Le bourgeois gentilhomme*, which was performed in 1670. The character of Sir Simon Softhead was borrowed from Molière's *Monsieur de Pourceaugnac* (1669). *The Citizen* was a great success with an outstanding performance by the famous comedy actor James Nokes. It ran for nine consecutive days with full houses, was acted at least thirty times before 1675, and became a stock comedy for several decades. In the original prologue, Ravenscroft attacked John Dryden's sense of comedy, praising the audience for their discernment in disliking Dryden's *Assignation* (1672). The play ridiculed the pretensions of London's puritan 'cits' (a parody on citizens) during the Third Anglo-Dutch War when theatres were more dependent on them for patronage.

Ravenscroft's next play, *Careless Lovers*, performed in Lent 1673 and printed that year, also premiered at Dorset Garden. A genteel comedy with satire and farcical intrigue, it was written to expose marital servitude, portraying women as intellectually equal or superior. Careless, an 'atheist in love' who asks for everything and promises nothing, is eventually defeated by Hillaria, an attractive 'mad' woman with no rules of propriety who brings him to marry her by beating him in the game of wits. Ravenscroft continued the attack on Dryden in its prologue, accusing him of plagiarism (the play itself borrows and reworks a plot from Dryden's *Secret Love*).

The Wrangling Lovers, or, The Invisible Mistress, was acted at Dorset Garden in 1676 (its first known performance was 25 July) and was published in the same year. It proved a popular comedy of intrigue, bordering on farce. Ravenscroft displayed his versatility in producing *Scaramouch a Philosopher* (1677) at the Theatre Royal in May 1677, using the old *commedia dell'arte* in a Gypsy plot. Presented as an Italian play, it was based on Molière's *Le mariage forcé* (1664) and *Les fourberies de Scapin* (1671), and showed Ravenscroft's continued fascination with Molière's *Monsieur de Pourceaugnac*. According to the prologue the play was held up in production by actors who opposed French farce, which curtailed its success, although Thomas Otway's rival version of *Les fourberies*, *The Cheats of Scapin*, which reached the stage first (probably the previous November), might also have caused the delay.

Perhaps the problems with *Scaramouch* caused Ravenscroft to adopt a new mode later that year, when his historical tragicomedy *King Edgar and Alfreda* reached the stage (probably no later than October). (In the prologue Ravenscroft claimed that the play had been written 'at least Ten Years ago', but could not be staged until public tastes had changed; it is impossible to know whether this was the case.) Some critics complained that it had been plagiarized from William Shakespeare. His next play, staged at the end of 1677 and published in 1678, was *The English Lawyer*, an adaptation of George Ruggle's Latin comedy *Ignoramus* (1615).

Ravenscroft returned with a more contemporaneous play in the 1678–9 season with *Titus Andronicus, or, The Rape of Lavinia*, acted at the Theatre Royal. Derived from Shakespeare's original, it adapted the concept of rape as an invasion of the right of princes to the duke of Monmouth's exile into Holland in September 1679. Again accused of plagiarism, by Gerald Langbaine and others, Ravenscroft claimed to be putting 'right' Shakespeare's version. Where the play marked new ground, however, was in the rape scenes. Ravenscroft used the growing fashion for female actresses to display the human body in extreme forms.

The playwright built on shock values in his outrageous farce *The London Cuckolds*, first performed at Dorset Garden about November 1681, and published in the following year. The play focuses on three 'old puritan cheats' called 'cits' who brainwash their wives to stay home like pets or slaves in order to keep them out of trouble while the cits pursue their business in the city fearful of losing a deal. The husbands are mocked throughout the play as cuckolds, while some of their wives fall prey to young men's healthy appetites. All parts are one-dimensional, both sexes are ridiculed, and no morals are drawn. A romp replete with smutty dialogue and abundant consummations, it was so effective that *Cuckolds* became the stock comedy performed on lord mayor's day annually until 1752. There were twenty-five performances between 1685 and 1714, and eighty from 1714 to 1747. Revived in 1782 at its centenary, it was eventually banished.

The London Cuckolds was followed in May 1683 with the comedy *Dame Dobson, or, The Cunning Woman* (published in 1684), which Ravenscroft called his 'Recantation' play. Trying to reverse the wit and amorality of the former, he tried to placate the 'moral element' in his audiences with a 'sympathetic comedy' that highlighted civility (Hume, 60–63), as well as closing with an epilogue that attacked the whigs. The play failed. Ravenscroft produced no more plays for a decade. In September 1694 he brought to the Theatre Royal a comedy called *The Canterbury Guests, or, The Bargain Broken* (published in 1695), which was cobbled together with some scenes from earlier pieces of his own. It too 'met with only a very indifferent success' (Genest, *Eng. stage*, 2.517–18).

Ravenscroft's last successful play was his comedy or farce *The Anatomist, or, The Sham Doctor*, which was performed at Lincoln's Inn Fields in autumn 1696 and published the next year. Based on Noël le Breton de Hauteroche's popular play *Crispin médecin* (1680), it was a great success. The short farce was performed with Peter Motteux's musical extravaganza *The Loves of Mars and Venus*, with music by John Eccles and Gottfried Finger. Often given as an after piece, it had 131 performances between 1714 and 1747, and 165 between 1747 and 1779. While Ravenscroft regarded it as 'the most trivial' of his plays, its story-line of witty servants helping young men keep young women away from old dotards, spiced with bawdy and lively music, enabled it to appeal to all ages. Revised in 1743, having been compressed first into two acts and then into a single act, it was reproduced repeatedly until performed apparently for the last time in 1801.

Ravenscroft's last play, *The Italian Husband*, was a tragedy performed at Lincoln's Inn Fields in November 1697 and published in the next year. Based on Thomas Wright's *The Glory of God's Revenge Against Murther and Adultery* (1685), it was a defence of farce as a serious dramatic genre. The adultery plot did not work, and according to some contemporaries required too much compassion on the part of the audience (Kewes, 220).

While Ravenscroft's career extended over more than a quarter of a century, he seems to have died comparatively young. He is not known to have produced any play after 1697. Most of his plays were written for the Duke's Company, managed by Thomas Killigrew and Sir William Davenant. He had few if any superiors among his contemporaries in farce, and as a writer had considerable cleverness in adaptation, skill in construction, and an unusual fluency and ease in dialogue. His quarrel with Dryden obtained for him a greater posthumous notoriety than he deserved. But since he borrowed so freely from others, the vituperations of Laingbaine, Dibdin, and other critics that his plays are 'a series of thefts from beginning to end' (Dibdin, 4.204) have given him a press that has held the field in the absence of any critical edition of his work.   Louis A. Knafla

Sources T. Cibber, 'Ravenscroft', *The lives of the poets of Great Britain and Ireland*, 3 (1753) • Genest, *Eng. stage*, 1.232–6, 365–6, 2.122, 517–18, 4.59, 204 • C. Dibdin, *A complete history of the English stage*, 4 (1800) • G. Langbaine, *An account of the English dramatick poets* (1691) • [J. Mottley], *A compleat list of all the English dramatic poets*, pubd with T. Whincop, *Scanderbeg* (1747) • J. Hutchinson, ed., *Notable Middle Templars* (1902) • H. A. C. Sturgess, ed., *Register of admissions to the Honourable Society of the Middle Temple, from the fifteenth century to the year 1944*, 1 (1949) • R. D. Hume, *The rakish stage: studies in English drama, 1660–1800* (1983) • J. T. Harwood, *Critics, values, and Restoration comedy* (1982), xiii • B. R. Schneider jun., *The ethos of Restoration comedy* (1971) • D. P. Fisk, ed., *The Cambridge companion to English Restoration theatre* (2000) • P. Kewes, *Authorship and appropriation: writing for the stage in England, 1660–1710* (1998), 17–18, 81–2, 90, 121, 216, 220 • D. Hughes, *English drama, 1660–1700* (1996) • S. J. Owen, *Restoration theatre and crisis* (1996) • F. M. Kevenik, *British drama, 1660–1779: a critical history* (1995)

Ravenscroft, George (1632/3–1683), merchant and glass manufacturer, was baptized in April 1633 at Alconbury Weston, near Huntingdon, the fourth of the eleven children of James Ravenscroft (1595–1680), lawyer and merchant, and his wife, Mary Peck of Spixworth, near Norwich. His parents were Roman Catholics, 'church papists', who practised their faith privately while outwardly conforming to the Anglican rite. In June 1643 they clandestinely sent George and his elder brother, Thomas, to the English College at Douai in the Spanish Netherlands. George left in May 1651, abandoning his training for the priesthood. Little is definitely known of his activities during the next fifteen years. In October 1656 a 'George Ravenscraft, Anglus' matriculated at the University of Padua. Ravenscroft certainly lived for some years in Venice, trading with his brothers James and Francis on their father's behalf 'and brought home a considerable capital' (*CSP Venice*, 38.265).

By 1666 Ravenscroft was resident in London, importing glass, lace, and currants from Venice, and re-exporting goods to northern Europe. In 1670 or 1671 he married Hellen Appleby (*b. c.*1650), daughter of Thomas Appleby of Linton upon Ouse, near York, and his wife, Hellen; her maternal grandfather, the staunchly Catholic Sir Thomas Gascoigne, had become her guardian on her mother's early death and father's remarriage. With her Ravenscroft had three children.

Venice was the acknowledged centre of European glass making, but emigrant craftsmen had diffused its techniques across the continent. By the 1670s English glassware was of sufficiently good quality to reduce dramatically the demand for Venetian imports. To complement his increasingly vulnerable import business, in 1673 Ravenscroft established a glassworks at the Savoy, London, in conjunction with a Signor da Costa and other Italian glass makers. In March 1674, claiming to have 'attained to the art and manufacture of a particular sort of Cristaline Glasses resembling Rock Cristall', previously not made in England, Ravenscroft applied for a patent. Issued two months later, this gave him a seven year monopoly over 'the said manufacture of cristaline glasse for drinking glasses'. Simultaneously, he contracted to deliver his entire output to the London Glass Sellers' Company for three years. In October 1674 the company agreed to his establishing a second glasshouse for one year at Henley-on-Thames, possibly in connection with attempts to resolve early technical problems.

The reputation of Ravenscroft's new glassware was severely damaged by rapid 'crizzling' (innumerable fine cracks which made it grey and opaque). In June 1676 he certified that the problem had been resolved; in October he advertised that his new glasses would bear a raven's head seal 'for distinguishing them from the former fabrick', and offered a money-back guarantee. Sealed glasses surviving from this period contain a small quantity of lead oxide. Ravenscroft is commonly thought to have added the lead in order to remedy the crizzling, which had resulted from over-purified ingredients containing an excess of alkaline salts, in an attempt to imitate Venetian soda glass (Moody, 201–3, 207–8). Alternatively, he was possibly using lead oxide already in 1674, but insufficient to stabilize the glass: hence his claim to have produced a distinctively new type of glass, meriting a patent (MacLeod, 791–800; Watts, *Glass Circle*, 71–8).

It seems unlikely that a wealthy merchant of Ravenscroft's standing would have involved himself closely in the technical aspects of the invention and manufacture; more probably, he contributed the financial support and marketing network for Costa or another professional glass maker. Lead crystal proved to be the ideal medium for the sturdier, plainer designs of drinking glasses then becoming fashionable in England, but it may not have been immediately popular. Ravenscroft's enterprise was probably not a commercial success. In August 1678 he gave the Glass Sellers' Company six months' notice to terminate their agreement, and there is no further reference to his manufacture of drinking glasses, although he continued to produce plate glass until at least 1680. A former employee, Hawley Bishopp, resumed production at the Savoy in 1682, and within a decade lead crystal was widely made in England.

Ravenscroft died on 7 June 1683, from 'a palsy which seized him and continued strong upon him till his death' (Moody, 204). He was buried in the family vault in the church of St John the Baptist, Chipping Barnet, Hertfordshire, and was commemorated by a tablet. There is no known likeness. His will, made in February 1682, refers to several estates in Huntingdonshire and Monmouthshire, some recently inherited from his father and paternal uncle. It confirms a contemporary description of Ravenscroft as 'a greate moneyed man' (PRO, C5/543/74), his assets spread across trade, land, and manufacturing. His father, 'the great benefactor' of Barnet, commending in his will George's 'industry and good courses', recognized in him a responsible son and a shrewd businessman, the counsellor and mainstay of his family (PRO, PROB 11/365, fol. 113). CHRISTINE MACLEOD

Sources B. E. Moody, 'The life of George Ravenscroft', *Glass Technology*, 29 (1988), 198–210 · D. C. Watts, 'How did George Ravenscroft discover lead crystal?', *Glass Circle*, 2 (1975), 71–8 · C. MacLeod, 'Accident or design? George Ravenscroft's patent and the invention of lead crystal glass', *Technology and Culture*, 28 (1987), 776–803 · R. J. Charleston, 'George Ravenscroft: new light on the development of his "christalline glasses"', *Journal of Glass Studies*, 10 (1968), 156–67 · R. Rendel, 'Who was George Ravenscroft?', *Glass Circle*, 2 (1975), 65–9 · R. Rendel, 'The true identity of George Ravenscroft, glassman', *Recusant History*, 13 (1975–6), 101–5 · P. R. P. Knell, 'A seventeenth-century schismatic and his Catholic family', *London Recusant*, 1/2 (1971) · R. I. Walker, 'The Ravenscrofts, Barnet branch', *Barnet Local History Society Bulletin*, 2 (1982) · D. C. Watts, 'Why George Ravenscroft introduced lead oxide into crystal glass', *Glass Technology*, 31 (1990), 208–12 · E. H. Burton and T. L. Williams, eds., *The Douay College diaries, third, fourth and fifth, 1598–1654*, 2, Catholic RS, 11 (1911) · *CSP Venice* · H. F. Brown, ed., *Inglezi e Scozzesi all'Università di Padova, dall'anno 1618 sino al 1765* (1921) · Chancery Proceedings, PRO, (C5–C9) C5/543/74 · wills, PRO, PROB 11/365, 11/368, 11/373 · parish register, Alconbury Weston, Cambs. AS
Wealth at death presumably rich; estates at Alconbury, Huntingdonshire; in Monmouthshire two thirds of 'a considerable purchase of lands' under father's will (1680); over £2000 cash legacies; inherited major shares of father's and uncle's property in 1680–81: will, proved 30 June 1683, PRO, PROB 11/373 fol. 192; PRO, PROB 11/365, fol. 15 [James Ravenscroft?]; PRO, PROB 11/PROB 11/368, fol. 356 [John Ravenscroft]

Ravenscroft, Thomas (b. 1591/2), music theorist and composer, was quite probably one of the Flintshire Ravenscrofts: on a flyleaf of the copy of *A Briefe Discourse* (1614) that he presented to Sir John Egerton, whose mother was Elizabeth Ravenscroft of Bretton, the author described himself as 'the meanest of a name soe much honored by you'. The Hawarden parish register does not support the claim, made by Venn (3.424) and others, that Thomas was baptized on 13 June 1592, the son of Roger Ravenscroft, canon of Chester.

By 1598 Ravenscroft was a chorister at St Paul's Cathedral under Thomas Giles, and he was still there in 1600 when Edward Pearce became organist and master of the choristers. Ravenscroft was involved in the activities of the St Paul's company of child actors, which, like the children of the Chapel Royal, catered for more sophisticated audiences by including in their plays specially written songs performed by trained voices and instrumentalists. According to a marginal note in his *Briefe Discourse*, he graduated MusB from Cambridge at the age of fourteen: since a poem in this source gives his age at that point as twenty-two, it is likely he was the Thomas Rangcrofte of Pembroke College who so graduated on 21 June 1605. He was also a student at Gresham College, to whose 'most worthy and Grave Senators' he dedicated *A Briefe Discourse*.

In 1609 Ravenscroft published the first edition of *Pammelia*, the earliest English printed collection of rounds and catches, 'Art having reformed what pleasing tunes injurious time and ignorance had deformed' ('To the reader', *Pammelia*). Its 100 examples comprise settings of sacred texts, tavern songs, vendors' cries, sol-faing pieces, traditional ballads, and songs from the contemporary theatre. The contents of *Deuteromelia* (also 1609) were similarly 'made truely Musicall with Art by my *correction*', the aim being not only to entertain but to preserve, for 'pittie were it, such Mirth should be *forgotten* of us' ('To the reader', *Deuteromelia*). Among its fourteen 'Freemen's Songs' and seventeen catches are 'Hold thy peace, knave', sung in *Twelfth Night*, and 'Three blind mice'. *Melismata* (1611), dedicated to his kinsmen Thomas and William Ravenscroft, contains twenty-three settings of which nine are 'Citie' and 'Country' rounds; appropriate dramatic contexts have been suggested for a number of its songs.

Whereas the music of these collections is anonymous, of the songs appended to Ravenscroft's treatise *A Briefe Discourse* to illustrate his theoretical ideas, twelve are attributed to him, six others are by John Bennet, and two are by Edward Pearce. The work itself laments the contemporary abuse of mensuration signs, and advocates a return to medieval practice. The music includes play songs, madrigalian pieces, and a jig-like series of pieces in which Hodge Trillinde woos Malkyn in a broad west-country dialect. Ravenscroft may have maintained his youthful links with the theatre, for early in 1618 he witnessed the will of the actor Richard Cowley. From January 1618 to November 1622 he was music master at Christ's Hospital, where he was paid £10 annually 'to teach the children of this house pricksong'.

Ravenscroft's *The Whole Booke of Psalmes* (1621), to which he contributed fifty-five of its 105 settings, is one of the most important psalters of the period, though it contains much music from earlier publications. A number of his vocal and instrumental compositions, as well as a 'Treatise of musick', survive in manuscript. His part-writing often lacks fluency, and his powers of melodic and harmonic invention rarely achieve a consistently high level of inspiration. The date of Ravenscroft's death is unknown and no will has been traced. Presumably he was still alive in 1633 when the second edition of his psalter appeared. DAVID MATEER

Sources Cambridge University Grace Book 'E', CUL · CUL, MS Book of Supplicats · L. P. Austern, 'Thomas Ravenscroft: musical chronicler of an Elizabethan theater company', *Journal of the American Musicological Society*, 38 (1985), 238–63 · A. J. Sabol, 'Ravencroft's "Melismata" and the children of Paul's', *Renaissance News*, 12 (1959), 3–9 · A. J. Sabol, 'Two songs with accompaniment for an Elizabethan choirboy play', *Studies in the Renaissance*, 5 (1958), 145–59 · L. P. Austern, *Music in English children's drama of the later Renaissance* (1992) · H. N. Hillebrand, *The child actors*, 2 vols. (1926) · E. H. Fellowes, ed., *English madrigal verse, 1588–1632* (1920); 3rd edn F. W. Sternfeld and D. Greer, revs. (1967) [3rd edn 1967] · C. Monson, *Voices and viols in England, 1600–1650: the sources and the music* (1982) · M. Frost, *English and Scottish psalm and hymn tunes, c.1543–1677* (1953) · E. A. J. Honigmann and S. Brock, eds., *Playhouse wills, 1558–1642: an edition of wills by Shakespeare and his contemporaries in the London theatre* (1993) · W. E. B. Whittaker, 'Ravenscroft of Bretton and Broadlane in Hawarden', *Genealogical Magazine*, 3 (1903–4), 528–35 · E. II. Pearce, *Annals of Christ's Hospital*, another edn (1908) · W. J. Lawrence, 'Thomas Ravenscroft's theatrical associations', *Modern Language Review*, 19 (1924), 418–23 · R. Gair, *The Children of Paul's: the story of a theatre company, 1553–1608* (1982)
Archives CUL, Book of Supplicats · CUL, Grace Book 'E'

Ravensdale. For this title name see Curzon, (Mary) Irene, *suo jure* Baroness Ravensdale, and Baroness Ravensdale of Kedleston (1896–1966).

Ravenser, Richard (*d.* 1386), administrator, was one of a large family clan of royal servants who came from the parts of Yorkshire and Lincolnshire on either side of the Humber; its members included John Thoresby, archbishop of York (*d.* 1373), and John Waltham, bishop of Salisbury (*d.* 1395). Waltham was Thoresby's great-nephew, while Ravenser and Waltham's father were cousins. In 1343 Ravenser was attorney to Queen Philippa (*d.* 1369), and by October 1353 was described as a chancery clerk. He was keeper of the hanaper of chancery, an office to which he was appointed on 1 September 1357, and which he had vacated by 11 July 1359, and in 1363 he was promoted to the rank of greater clerk of chancery. Twice he was one of a commission who took charge of the great seal: in 1372 when the chancellor, Sir Robert Thorpe, was dying, and in 1377, during the last days of Edward III. Concurrently with his chancery duties he served three royal ladies: Queen Philippa, for whom he was attorney, receiver of rents and debts, and, from 1362 to 1367, treasurer; the queen mother, Isabella (*d.* 1358), for whom he performed similar duties and administered her goods after her death; and Princess Isabella (*d.* 1379), whose employment he had entered by 1364. In 1370 he founded a chantry at Beverley for the souls of Queen Isabella and Queen Philippa. Ravenser continued in chancery service until at least December 1384, and died between 17 May and 1 June 1386. He was buried in Lincoln Cathedral.

Ravenser's secular career was rewarded by ecclesiastical preferment; after 1349, when he was granted Anderby rectory, Lincolnshire, royal patronage brought him a succession of presentations. But he exchanged most of his benefices, showing a preference for those in Lincolnshire and south Yorkshire, an area to which he remained attached; he founded a hospital in Beverley, as well as a chantry there, three chantries in Lincolnshire, and, with relatives, gave generously to churches in Beverley and Hull. Notable appointments included the provostship of Beverley (1360–68) and the archdeaconry of Lincoln (from 1368 until his death). Ravenser was involved in controversy at both places. He inherited a claim, advanced by the previous holder, to exceptional powers of jurisdiction in the archdeaconry of Lincoln, and on appeal secured a ruling very favourable (though personal) to himself; one of the appeal judges was the previous archdeacon, William Wykeham (*d.* 1404). At Beverley he led the resistance to Archbishop Alexander Neville's proposed visitation in 1381, giving shelter at Lincoln to other rebels. For this Neville deprived him of his prebends in Beverley (St Martin's, from 1363) and York Minster (Knaresborough, from 1371). Though it cannot be computed with any accuracy Ravenser's wealth was considerable at the time of his death, and he maintained homes in Yorkshire, Lincoln, and London.

A. K. McHardy

Sources B. Wilkinson, *The chancery under Edward III* (1929) · A. H. Thompson, 'The registers of the archdeaconry of Richmond', *Yorkshire Archaeological Journal*, 25 (1918–20), 129–268, esp. 251–3 · *Memorials illustrative of the history of the county of Lincoln*, Royal Archaeological Institute, London (1850), 312–17 · Tout, *Admin. hist.* · *Fasti Angl., 1300–1541*, [Lincoln; Hereford; Salisbury; Monastic cathedrals; St Paul's, London; Northern province] · *Chancery records* · C. Morris, 'The Ravenser composition', *Lincolnshire Architectural and Archaeological Society Reports and Papers*, 10/1 (1963), 24–39 · R. K. Morris and E. Cambridge, 'Beverley Minster before the early 13th century', *Medieval art and architecture in the East Riding of Yorkshire*, ed. C. Wilson, British Archaeological Association Conference Transactions, 9 (1989) · *CEPR letters*, vols. 3–4 · W. H. Bliss, ed., *Calendar of entries in the papal registers relating to Great Britain and Ireland: petitions to the pope* (1896) · J. Hughes, *Pastors and visionaries: religion and secular life in late medieval Yorkshire* (1988)
Wealth at death wealthy; several hundred pounds

Ravenstein, Ernst Georg (1834–1913), geographer and cartographer, was born in Frankfurt am Main on 30 December 1834 into a family which had a long tradition of work in engraving and cartography. After studying at the Frankfurt Gymnasium and the Städelsches Kunstinstitut, he emigrated to London in 1852 and soon became a pupil of August Petermann before, in 1855, accepting a post as cartographer with the topographic department of the War Office. In 1858 his ties with England were strengthened when he married Ada Sarah Parry of Bromley, Kent, fifty years of marriage to whom he celebrated with the publication of *A Life's Work* (1908). He began to write in 1856, publishing a work on Russian exploration (in English) and travel guides and general geographical handbooks (in German). He developed his interest in sport: he published works on gymnastics and was a founder and the first president of the German Gymnastic Society (a post he held until 1871), as well as president of the London swimming club.

In 1872 Ravenstein retired from the War Office and, as he had declined the position of chief cartographer at the Royal Geographical Society after being refused permission to smoke on the premises, he had time to develop his own research interests. He continued to compile and publish maps, especially of Africa, many of which appeared in the publications of the Royal Geographical Society; he was an active member of the society, and, from 1894 to

Ernst Georg Ravenstein (1834–1913), by unknown photographer [detail]

1896, a member of council. He was also cartographic editor of the *Geographical Magazine*, a semi-official publication of the society. His relations with the society were not always smooth, notably when he was preparing his 'Map of eastern equatorial Africa', which took far longer than the society hoped, though its standard was exceptionally high. None the less, the society was his natural base, given his interest in both exploration and systematic geography. He was also on the council of the Royal Statistical Society and of the British Association for the Advancement of Science, and an active member of the International Geographical Union and several foreign learned societies. He lectured on physical geography at Bedford College in 1882–3, being styled 'professor', but apparently with little success. He developed his interest in discovery, plotting the course of African exploration in his maps and helping to supply meteorological instruments to African settlers and missionaries and publishing their observations. His interest in the history of discovery led to his translation of the account of Vasco da Gama's first voyage (1898). In particular he developed his ideas on demography, notably his laws of migration, and it is for these that he is chiefly remembered. His laws reflected his familiarity with German advances in statistical and thematic mapping, notably those of Petermann, and his wish to explain geographical phenomena after detailed empirical observation. This, and work such as his study of Celtic languages in the British Isles (1879) based on questionnaire data and his maps of religious denominations in Britain, used methods ahead of their time.

In 1902 Ravenstein was awarded the first Victoria gold medal of the Royal Geographical Society in recognition of his services to cartography and demography. In 1909 he was awarded an honorary doctorate from the University of Göttingen for his book on the Nuremberg geographer Martin Behaim (1908), a work which is still respected. He died on 13 March 1913 at Dr Schulze's Sanatorium at Hofheim in the Taunus Mountains in Germany. His dogged and loyal work for the Royal Geographical Society and his independent research were always of a high standard, but have not received the recognition they deserve in either England or Germany. Ravenstein was important in improving the standard of British cartography, and his work on migration has influenced demographers, sociologists, and economists, as well as geographers. His work has endured beyond that of many who achieved greater prominence in their lifetime. His 'Oarsman's and Angler's Map of the River Thames' (1893) was reprinted in 1991, and shows the rediscovery of the lighter side of his work.

ELIZABETH BAIGENT

Sources D. B. Grigg, 'Ernst Georg Ravenstein, 1834–1913', *Geographers: biobibliographical studies*, 1, ed. T. W. Freeman, M. Oughton, and P. Pinchemel (1977), 79–82 · D. B. Grigg, 'E. G. Ravenstein and the "laws of migration"', *Journal of Historical Geography*, 3 (1977), 41–54 · E. P., 'Ernst Georg Ravenstein', *GJ*, 41 (1913), 497–8 · J. S. Keltie, 'Thirty years' work of the Royal Geographical Society', *GJ*, 49 (1917), 350–76 · *Bulletin of the American Geographical Society*, 45 (1913), 453 · S. H. Bederman, 'The Royal Geographical Society, E. G. Ravenstein and *A map of eastern equatorial Africa*', *Imago Mundi*, 44 (1992), 106–19 · D. B. Grigg, 'The first new English geographer', *Geographical Magazine*, 46 (1973–4), 246–7 · *CGPLA Eng. & Wales* (1913)
Archives RGS
Likenesses photograph, repro. in Grigg, 'Ernst Georg Ravenstein, 1834–1913' · photograph, RGS [*see illus.*]
Wealth at death £825: resworn probate, 21 June 1913, *CGPLA Eng. & Wales*

Ravensworth. For this title name *see* Liddell, Henry, first Baron Ravensworth (*bap.* 1708, *d.* 1784); Liddell, Henry Thomas, first earl of Ravensworth (1797–1878).

Raverat [*née* Darwin], **Gwendolen Mary** [Gwen] (1885–1957), artist, the daughter of the astronomer Sir George Howard *Darwin (1845–1912) and his wife, Maud du Puy (1861–1947), of Philadelphia, was born on 26 August 1885 in Cambridge, where she spent her childhood, though she made periodic visits to Down House in Kent, the home of her paternal grandfather, Charles *Darwin (1809–1882). Her father was professor of astronomy and she had two uncles at Cambridge, while her mother's uncle by marriage was Sir Richard Jebb, professor of Greek.

By the age of ten Gwen Darwin was already drawing continuously from life and strongly wished to become an artist. In 1908 she went to the Slade School of Art, then under Frederick Brown and Henry Tonks, where she learned painting, but she taught herself wood-engraving. At Cambridge before the First World War she found herself a member of a group of talented young men and women, of whom the most prominent was Rupert Brooke. She fell in love with Jacques Pierre Raverat, a young French mathematical student from the Sorbonne who was continuing his studies at Emmanuel College, and persuaded him to become a painter and join her at the Slade. They were married in 1911.

Gwendolen Mary Raverat (1885–1957), self-portrait

At the outbreak of war the Raverats were living in Cambridgeshire, but in 1915 they went to Le Havre to be near his family. Jacques Pierre Raverat, by then suffering from disseminated sclerosis, tried to join the French army as an interpreter. He failed, and the couple returned to England and lived at Weston, near Baldock, Hertfordshire, where their two daughters were born. In 1920 they went again to France and lived at Vence, where Gwen Raverat nursed her husband through his long final illness, until his death in 1925. She then returned to England to live at the Old Rectory, at Harlton, near Cambridge. In 1941 she moved into rooms in Cambridge, and finally took the Old Granary at the end of the garden of her birthplace, Newnham Grange.

Everything that Gwen Raverat undertook was done with intelligence and skill—her graphic work for the Admiralty in the Second World War, as well as her theatre designs and paintings and drawings—but it was through wood-engraving that she was able to communicate her vision most fully. In her engraving she did not aim at decoration or use a strong decorative line, like her friend Eric Gill; nor was she a naturalist interested in the rendering of a bird's plumage or an animal's fur, like Thomas Bewick. Rather, she was a master of light, shade, and the interplay of textures, with a deceptively simple technique, and a bold sense of design.

Apart from illustrating *Spring Morning* (1915), a little paper-bound book of early poems by her lifelong friend and cousin Frances Cornford, Raverat's work until the 1930s consisted of single prints. These were widely exhibited, and gave her a standing among fellow artists and collectors. She was a founder member of the Society of Wood Engravers in 1920, and active on its committees, which met at her studio in Mecklenburgh Square, London. Margaret Pilkington reported in her diary (1931) how 'Gwen presided over the tea table like a beneficent deity'. After 1932, when the Cambridge University Press published her engravings for a second edition of *The Cambridge Book of Poetry for Children*, selected by Kenneth Grahame, her work was in continual demand from publishers. Her illustrations, including a few examples in colour, have the seriousness and vividness of the best Victorian work, and often a sharp sense of humour. Her last important work was the writing of *Period Piece* (1952), a perceptive account of her upbringing and family. She contributed art criticism to *Time and Tide* between 1928 and 1939, but, never having thought of herself as a writer, was amazed to find *Period Piece* a best-seller on both sides of the Atlantic.

After a stroke in 1951 Raverat could no longer engrave, but she continued to paint. She was short in stature, and in her last years became stout, and she looked like one of her own engravings of an ancient. 'You *are* an old monolith', Virginia Woolf once said to her. She enjoyed the company of the young, who gave her their respect and affection. She died in Cambridge on 11 February 1957. Her engravings can be seen in the Victoria and Albert Museum; the Fitzwilliam Museum, Cambridge; the Whitworth Art Gallery, Manchester; and the Ashmolean Museum, Oxford.

REYNOLDS STONE, *rev.* JAMES HAMILTON

Sources G. Raverat, *Period piece* (1952) • G. Raverat, *Wood engravings of Gwen Raverat*, new edn (1989) • C. Cornford, review of *The old mistress*, *Cambridge Review* (23 Jan 1960) • J. Hamilton, *Wood engraving and the woodcut in Britain, c.1890–1990* (1994) • M. Pilkington, diary, 1931, JRL • CGPLA Eng. & Wales (1957)
Archives CUL, legal corresp.; papers, incl. those of Jacques Pierre Raverat | BL, letters to F. C. Cornford, Add. MSS 58398–58399 • BL, corresp. with Macmillans, Add. MS 55233 • U. Sussex, corresp. with Virginia Woolf
Likenesses G. Raverat, self-portrait, priv. coll. [*see illus.*] • E. Vellacott, pencil drawing, Kettler's Yard, Cambridge
Wealth at death £49,361 17s. 7d.: probate, 17 April 1957, CGPLA Eng. & Wales

Raverty, Henry George (1825–1906), army officer and orientalist, born at Falmouth on 31 May 1825, was the son of Peter Raverty of co. Tyrone, a surgeon in the navy. His mother belonged to the family of Drown of Falmouth. Educated at Falmouth and Penzance, at fifteen or sixteen he resolved to become a soldier. The interest of Sir Charles Lemon secured him a cadetship, and he sailed for India. Appointed to the Welch fusiliers, he soon (in 1843) transferred to the 3rd Bombay native infantry. With his regiment he was present at the siege of Multan in 1848; he served in Gujarat and in the first frontier expedition in 1850 against tribes on the Swat border. Raverty held a civil appointment as assistant commissioner in the Punjab from 1852 to 1859. He was promoted major in 1863 and retired from the army the following year. He settled in England, first near Ottery St Mary, Devon, and afterwards at Grampound Road, Cornwall. In 1865 he married Fanny Vigurs, only daughter of Commander George Pooley RN; they had no children.

Raverty pursued until the end of his long life various oriental studies, which he had begun in India. Although he lacked academic training, he was gifted with scholarly instincts, and devoted himself to linguistic, historical, geographical, and ethnological study. In India he first learned Hindustani, Persian, Gujarati, and Marathi and for his knowledge of these languages gained the 'high proficiency' prize of 1000 rupees from his government. A *Thesaurus of English Hindustani Technical Terms* (1859) proved his linguistic aptitude in Hindustani. His transfer to the north-west frontier at Peshawar in 1849 had meanwhile directed his chief attention to the Pushtu or Afghan language, history, and ethnology. To the *Transactions* of the Geographical Society of Bombay, Raverty contributed in 1851 'An account of the city and province of Peshawar', illustrated with maps and sepia sketches. In order to acquire practical knowledge of the Pushtu tongue he had to collect, arrange, and systematize almost the whole of the needful grammatical and lexical material. In 1855 he published his *Grammar of the Pushto or Language of the Afghans*, which Dr Dorn, the eminent orientalist of St Petersburg, warmly commended. In 1860, besides a second and improved edition of the grammar (3rd edn, 1867), he published his monumental *Dictionary of the Pushto or Afghan Language* (2nd edn, 1867), and his admirable anthology of Pushtu prose and poetry entitled *Gulshan i Roh*. He was as well acquainted with Pushtu literature as with the spoken language. In 1862 there followed *Selections from the Poetry of the Afghans from the Sixteenth to the Nineteenth Century* in an English translation.

After leaving India Raverty published in 1871 a translation of *Aesop's Fables* into Pushtu, and in 1880 a *Pushtu Manual*. Between 1881 and 1888 he issued in four instalments his ponderous work *Notes on Afghanistan and Baluchistan*. This book was never generally available and remains little known except to specialists. Although it contains a great deal of useful geographical and ethnographic data, Raverty's lack of formal academic training is most evident in this volume. The 734-page work has no table of contents, no maps, and no bibliography; only a serviceable index saves it for research purposes. Sources quoted in the text are rarely identified in a satisfactory manner and one is frequently at a loss to know whether Raverty is quoting from a manuscript or speaking from his own knowledge.

Simultaneously Raverty was working at his translation of the *Tabakat-i-Nasiri* which was published in 1881. It is a rendering from Persian into English of Minhaj ibn Siraj's work on general history, with special reference to the Muslim dynasties of Asia, and particularly those of Ghur, Ghaznah, and Hindustan, AD 810–1260. By his critical remarks and copious illustrative notes derived from his wide reading of other eastern authors, Raverty vastly enhanced the historical value and completeness of Minhaj's work.

Other of Raverty's valuable studies appeared chiefly in the *Journal of the Asiatic Society*, Bengal. Among these papers were 'Remarks on the origin of the Afghan people' (1854); 'Notes on Kafiristan and the Siah-Posh Kafir tribes' (1858); 'On the language of the Siah-Posh Kafirs of Kafiristan' (1864); 'An account of Upper Kashghar and Chitral' (1864); 'Memoir of the author of the Tabakāt i Nāsirī' (1882); 'The Mihran of Sind and its tributaries—a geographical study' (1892); and 'Tibbat three hundred and sixty-five years ago' (1895). 'Muscovite proceedings on the Afghan frontier' was reprinted from the *United Service Gazette* in 1885.

Raverty died at his home, Florence Villa, Grampound Road, Cornwall, on 20 October 1906. His wife survived him. Raverty, whose frankness in controversy cost him many friends, received small recognition in his lifetime from his fellow countrymen, but his immense labours gave him a high reputation among foreign oriental scholars. At his death he had no fewer than seven important works either completed in manuscript or in preparation, among them 'A history of Herat and its dependencies and the annals of Khurāsān from the earliest down to modern times', based upon the works of eastern historians, which are treated with critical acumen; the six bulky quarto volumes of manuscript, the result of fifty years' research, are now at the India Office.

EDWARD EDWARDS, *rev.* SCHUYLER JONES

Sources *The Times* (26 Oct 1906) • C. E. Buckland, *Dictionary of Indian biography* (1906) • H. B., 'Major Henry George Raverty', *Journal of the Royal Asiatic Society of Great Britain and Ireland* (1907), 251–3 • private information (1912) [Fanny Vigurs Raverty, widow] • CGPLA *Eng. & Wales* (1907)
Wealth at death £153 6s. 9d.: probate, 31 Jan 1907, CGPLA *Eng. & Wales*

Ravilious, Eric William (1903–1942), artist and designer, was born at Acton, London, on 22 July 1903, the second son and youngest of three surviving children of Frank Ravilious, coach-builder and owner of a furniture and upholstery business, and his wife, Emma, daughter of William Ford, farmer, of Kingsbridge, Devon. His unusual name he claimed to be of Huguenot origin. His family moved to Eastbourne, Sussex, where his father started a business as a dealer in antiques and second-hand books.

Ravilious was educated at the Eastbourne Municipal Boys' School and the Eastbourne School of Art, and gained a scholarship in September 1922 to the Royal College of Art. He had a winning personality and was an accomplished games-player. A fellow student at Eastbourne, John Lake, wrote that even as a young man 'he always seemed to be slightly somewhere else, as if he lived a private life which did not completely coincide with material existence' (Binyon, 23). At the royal college he made firm friends with Edward Bawden. Both were in the school of design and belonged to a select group who learned wood-engraving under Paul Nash, whose dry watercolour style they emulated. Ravilious specialized in mural design for his final exam. He and Bawden used the resources of the Victoria and Albert Museum to good effect and also found sympathetic antecedents in the work of Francis Towne, J. S. Cotman, and Samuel Palmer. Ravilious left the college in 1925 with a travelling scholarship. He spent the summer in Florence but was not visibly affected by the experience. The talents of Bawden and Ravilious had been noticed even by 1924. Early in his career Ravilious enjoyed the patronage of Sir Geoffrey Fry, private secretary to the prime minister, Stanley Baldwin. He specialized in wood-engraving, his first book illustrations being for Martin Armstrong's novel *Desert* (1926). The folk-art quality of his earliest wood-engravings soon changed to a distinctive and controlled linear style, exploring architectural space and landscape laden with reverie and suggestion, populated by doll-like figures, and designed with a pattern of black and white. He illustrated private press editions for the Golden Cockerel Press, including *The Twelve Moneths* (1927) and *Twelfth Night* (1932). A set of zodiacal signs for the Lanston Monotype Corporation in 1929 indicated his ability in resurrecting the graphic quality of traditional symbolism. In 1938 he illustrated *The Natural History of Selborne*, by Gilbert White, for the Nonesuch Press. His wood-engravings became familiar to a wide public through their use by London Transport, Dent's Everyman's Library, and Wisden's *Cricketer's Almanac*. He made pictures of unusual shop fronts, drawn as lithographs in three colours, which were given a text by his friend the architectural critic J. M. Richards and published in 1939 as *High Street*.

Ravilious and Bawden shared the design and execution of murals in the refreshment room at Morley College, Lambeth, funded by Lord Duveen and opened early in 1930 after two years' work. Depicting scenes from Shakespeare and his contemporaries these were lighthearted but fine-tuned in their colour and drawing, and were an instant success. In 1972 Bawden recalled their collaboration thus:

> Elizabethan plays, Shakespeare, Olympian gods and goddesses, Punch and Judy, a Miracle play and a doll's house—Gosh! what a riot it was. Whatever beneficial influence Italy had had on Eric was now to some extent revealed, not by plagiarism, rather by his skill in organising space and in creating it for figures to be sent dancing and swinging in ballet movement across the walls. (*Eric Ravilious, 1903–1942*, exhibition catalogue)

The murals were destroyed by bombing. Ravilious painted others at the Midland Hotel, Morecambe, in 1933, now lost through water damage, and in the Pier Pavilion, Colwyn Bay, 1935, now also lost.

Throughout his life Ravilious painted watercolours, mostly of rural scenes, buildings, and machinery, and occasionally of interiors, to which he gave a quality of imaginative intensity. The technique that he and Bawden developed together became more refined, and Ravilious was the more delicate in atmosphere, touch, and colour. In 1930 he and Bawden rented part of Brick House, Great Bardfield, Essex, and spent holidays and weekends there, furnishing the house in a distinctive decorative style. Ravilious preferred the landscape of Sussex, however, and many of his paintings were done while staying with the artist Peggy Angus in her cottage, Furlongs, near Glynde. He was self-critical and destroyed much of his work but held one-man shows in London, at the Zwemmer Gallery

in 1934 and 1937, and at Arthur Tooth's Gallery in 1939. His favourite subjects included ships, railways, quarries and their machinery, quaysides, the interiors of greenhouses, and deserted downland with figures cut in the chalk. His work was admired by modernists for its abstract quality, while always remaining figurative.

Ravilious combined painting with design activity, working for the potters Josiah Wedgwood in the design of transfer patterns for use on existing shapes; he began with the 1937 coronation mug, a mixture of traditional symbolism (a royal arms simplified in silhouette) and almost abstract patterning based on fireworks, with loosely brushed colour recalling Staffordshire or Sunderland ware of the 1820s. He designed other commemorative pieces, notably the Boat Race bowl and goblet (1938) and three complete services: 'Persephone' (1936), 'Travel' (1938), and 'Garden' (1938). The most popular design, reissued several times, was 'Nursery china' (1937), usually described as 'Alphabet'. He designed a dining-room table and chairs of Regency inspiration for the firm of Dunbar Hay, as well as china and glass made by Stuart Crystal of Stourbridge; he was also involved in experimental textile pattern design with lithography for the Cotton Board in 1941, producing some specimens of a decorative child's handkerchief.

On 5 July 1930 Ravilious married Eileen Lucy (Tirzah; 1908–1951), daughter of Lieutenant-Colonel Frederick Scott Garwood, Royal Engineers, who had been a pupil of his at Eastbourne School of Art and was a fine wood-engraver. She also made marbled paper and, in later years, imaginative framed models of typical country village buildings. They had two sons and one daughter; having children made it difficult for her to work as an artist. They lived in Earls Court, then near the Thames in Hammersmith, and continued sharing Brick House before moving to Bank House, Castle Hedingham, Essex, in 1935. Ravilious was attractive to women in general and between 1934 and 1938 had an affair with the artist Helen Binyon, a fellow student from the Royal College of Art, who finally broke it off and remained friendly with Tirzah. Encouraged by the children she wrote a monograph on Ravilious which was published posthumously in 1983.

In December 1939 Ravilious was invited to serve as a war artist with the Admiralty and given the rank of captain in the Royal Marines. His talents were well matched to subjects involving sea, sky, ships, aircraft, and such unexpected occurrences as the quilted counterpane of a sick bay at Dundee (painting, Imperial War Museum, London) or the inside of Corporal Steddiford's mobile pigeon loft (painting, Whitworth Art Gallery, Manchester). He produced some of his best paintings in this role and also worked on a series of lithographs of submarines, intended for a book to promote the navy that was never brought to publication. At the end of August 1942 he flew to Iceland to paint the Norwegian squadron. He joined an air sea rescue flight from Kaldadarnes on 2 September, in order to observe it in action, but the plane went missing and no trace of it was ever found.

Ravilious's work contributed to a new style of representing England and Englishness, both topographically and in official commissions, such as the catalogue covers that he executed for the British pavilions at international exhibitions in Paris (1937) and New York (1939). His graphic, wiry style was influential in the design of the Festival of Britain in 1951 and has subsequently attracted a small but avid and increasing interest.

H. B. GRIMSDITCH, rev. ALAN POWERS

Sources H. Binyon, *Eric Ravilious: memoir of an artist* (1983) · P. R. Andrew, *Eric Ravilious, 1903–42: a reassessment of his life and work* (1986) [exhibition catalogue, Towner Art Gallery, Eastbourne] · J. M. Richards, *The wood engravings of Eric Ravilious* (1972), introduction · R. Harling, *Notes on the wood engravings of Eric Ravilious* (1945) · *Eric Ravilious, 1903–1942* (1972) [exhibition catalogue, The Minories, Colchester] · F. Constable, *The England of Eric Ravilious* (1982) · R. Dalrymple, *Ravilious and Wedgwood* (1986) · R. Y. Goodden, 'Eric Ravilious as a designer', *ArchR*, 94 (1943), 155–61 · A. Ullmann and others, *The wood engravings of Tirzah Garwood* (1987) · *CGPLA Eng. & Wales* (1943)

Archives IWM, MSS | Tate collection, letters to Lady Sempill

Likenesses N. Parkinson, photograph, 1937, priv. coll. · S. Chermayeff, photograph, pubd c.1938; lost · P. Dodd, portrait, priv. coll.

Wealth at death £276 10s. 2d.: administration with will, 7 Aug 1943, *CGPLA Eng. & Wales*

Ravis [*formerly* Raue], **Christian** [Christianus Ravius] (1613–1677), oriental and biblical scholar, was born on 25 January 1613 at Berlin, Brandenburg, the son of Johann Raue, deacon at the Nikolahs-Kirche, and his wife, Margarete Guericke. After attending the Berlin Gymnasium, in 1630 he entered Wittenberg University, where he studied oriental languages under Trostius (author of a Syriac lexicon and a Hebrew grammar), and graduated MA in 1633. From 1636 he visited the universities of Leipzig, Königsberg, and Rostock, and travelled in Denmark and Sweden, before going to Holland in 1637 to study Arabic under Golius. He there made the acquaintance of the eminent scholar G. J. Vossius and of Johann Elichmann, a physician interested in oriental languages.

In July 1638, supported by recommendations from these and the English ambassador William Boswell, Ravis (as his name became Anglicized) went to England, whence he wrote to Archbishop Ussher in Ireland, requesting support for proposed scholarly travels in the east. Ussher, acting through Samuel Hartlib, granted him an annual stipend of £24 in return for a promise to look for manuscripts that Ussher wanted. Ravis set out for Constantinople in 1639, travelling via Paris, where Hugo Grotius introduced him to Cardinal Richelieu, who, according to Ravis, tried to recruit him into his service. He also made the acquaintance of Mersenne and Desargues, and issued as Christianus Ravius (the name by which he was known in the continental scholarly world and which he himself adopted) his first publication, a pamphlet pompously entitled *Dissertatio mathematica proponens novum summumque totius matheseos inventum problemata omnia certa methodo inveniendi, & inventa solvendi*, which praised John Pell. Taking ship from Marseilles, Ravis reached Constantinople in July, almost destitute. But the Arabist Edward Pococke, who was living with the English

ambassador Sir Sackville Crowe, arranged for him to be taken into that household. He began to study Turkish and Arabic, and to collect manuscripts. In September he travelled to Smyrna with Edward Stringer, who had been appointed English consul there, but soon returned to Constantinople, where he remained until early 1641 when he embarked on a tour of Asia Minor in the company of Charles Cavendish, son of the earl of Devonshire.

A four-month voyage from Smyrna brought Ravis to London late in 1641. He carried with him some 300 manuscripts, mostly oriental, of which the most notable was an Arabic version of Apollonius' *Conics*. He also brought Nicolaus Petri, an Arabic-speaking Greek from Aleppo, whom he had persuaded to be his amanuensis. Nicolaus's Arabic letters to Pococke and Golius paint a vivid picture of Ravis's penury, duplicity, and vain attempts to find employment in England and later in Holland. Ravis petitioned parliament to set up a college for converting the Jews and oriental learning, with no result. He was given money by John Selden, but was forced to pledge or sell a number of his manuscripts to Sir Simonds D'Ewes, Richard Holdsworth, and others, and, despairing of finding employment in England, moved to the Netherlands. Ravis was in Leiden in March 1642, but had no greater success there or in Denmark. Subsequently he was permitted to give lectures (some of which he published) on oriental languages at Utrecht (1643–4) and Amsterdam (1645–6), and was rewarded with an occasional honorarium, but his requests for a permanent appointment, although supported by Vossius, were unsuccessful.

In June 1647 Ravis returned to England, ostensibly to redeem his manuscripts, but in fact encouraged by Hartlib with the prospect of a new post teaching oriental languages in London. This was established in July by the provincial presbyterian synod of London, centred on Sion College, and was probably subsidized by Thomas Adams and other wealthy citizens of London. Ravis began to lecture in August at London House; the content of his lectures, some of which were in English, may be surmised from his book, *A Generall Grammer for the Ebrew, Samaritan, Calde, Syriac, Arabic, and Ethiopic Tongue*, which went into several editions from 1648 to 1650, and was published with his *Discourse of the Orientall Tongues*, and a collection of letters from scholars. In this work he propounded his peculiar theory that these six languages are not merely related, but are in fact the same language (which may be called 'Arabic'). Among his pupils in London were Hanserd Knollys and Thomas Danson. However, the financial basis of this lectureship was shaky, and an appeal by the ministers of London to parliament for support (seconded by a personal appeal by Ravis to an influential parliamentarian, John Selden) was unsuccessful, so Ravis sought other prospects.

When it seemed likely that Pococke would lose his Arabic professorship at Oxford for royalist sympathies, Ravis aspired to replace him, but was warned off by Selden and Ussher. However, he had sufficient influence in the parliamentary committee supervising Oxford University that on 5 March 1649 he became one of those chosen to replace almost the whole body of fellows of Magdalen College. He was also made librarian of the college and Hebrew lecturer.

Ravis was soon (if not already) negotiating for a better post. Johannes Matthiae, bishop of Strängnäs, who was a friend of Hartlib and of Ravis's brother Johannes (professor at Rostock), persuaded Queen Kristina of Sweden (whose tutor he had been) to offer Ravis employment. In February 1650 he travelled to Sweden via Amsterdam, where he bought the Hebrew press of Menasseh ben Israel on behalf of Kristina. The queen appointed him professor of oriental languages at Uppsala University in November 1650. In 1651 he married Matthiae's niece, Christina Andreae. Nevertheless, his financial difficulties continued. He had left his books and manuscripts behind in England as pledges for his debts, but Selden redeemed them in 1652. In January 1654 Ravis was glad to accept £5 from the English ambassador Bulstrode Whitelocke, to whom he expressed regret for leaving England. He was quarrelling with the theological faculty, who resented his intrusion into their territory by publishing on biblical matters. In 1655 he was appointed royal librarian, moving to Stockholm in 1656. In 1659 King Karl Gustav reappointed him professor of oriental languages at Uppsala, where he remained until 1669. His quarrels with the theologians worsened, particularly after he began to propound his peculiar theories on biblical chronology. After leaving for Kiel in 1669, he published these as *Unica vera et infallibilis chronologia biblica* (1670), which met with almost universal derision. He devoted the rest of his life, and several publications, to defending this. While at Kiel he also (1669) published a bad Latin translation of part of the Arabic *Conics*, and a catalogue of his manuscripts which he was offering for sale. In 1672 the elector of Brandenburg appointed him professor of oriental languages and biblical chronology at the University of Frankfurt an der Oder, where he died of scurvy on 21 June 1677 and was buried in S. Marien-Kirche. He was survived by his wife (who died on 21 March 1678) and four children. Most of his manuscripts survived in Berlin, but his treasured Apollonius went to the Bodleian Library, Oxford.

Ravis was a facile linguist (his English writings are thoroughly idiomatic), but not a profound one. He strove for the original, but usually achieved only the bizarre. Except for the books he wrote in England, most of his numerous publications were issued by himself in minuscule editions, paid for by himself, and are extremely rare: of some only one copy, or none, is known. His acquaintance among European scholars was large, but his friends few: his assiduous flattery was offset by his boastfulness, extravagant promises of the unattainable, and duplicity—his amanuensis called him a 'treasury of lies' (Houtsma, 92).   G. J. TOOMER

Sources J. Moller, *Cimbria literata*, 2 (1744), 680–88 · G. J. Toomer, *Eastern wisedome and learning: the study of Arabic in seventeenth-century England* (1996), 83–4, 142–5, 150–52, 183–200, 238 · C. Annerstedt, *Uppsala Universitets historia*, 5 vols. (Uppsala, 1877–1914), vol. 1, pp. 330–31, 401; vol. 2/1, pp. 20, 30–39, 52–3, 85–90; vol. 2/2, pp. 113, 288–93; bihang 2/1 12, 32, 34–5, 43, 71; bihang 2/2 132 · Sheffield University, Hartlib MSS, 3/3/32–33, 4/2/22, 10/8/1, 15/6/7, 15/6/17/18, 15/6/24, 15/6/27–28, 23/2/9, 28/1/35, 31/5/3, 36/1/9–10, 37/125B, 37/127, 37/161, 41/1/93B, 47/12/1 · J. C. Becmanus, *Notitia Universitatis Francofurtanae* (1707), 71, 267–70 · M. T. Houtsma, *Uit de oostersche correspondentie van Th. Erpenius Jac. Golius en Lev. Warner* (1887), 80–106 · L. Twells and S. Burdy, *The lives of Dr Edward Pocock … Dr Zachary Pearce … Dr Thomas Newton … and of the Rev Philip Skelton*, 1 (1816), 60–61, 138–40, 219 · R. Parr, ed., *The life of the most reverend father in God, James Usher … with a collection of three hundred letters* (1686), nos. 60, 213, 252, 304–5, appxs 8–9 · W. D. Macray, *A register of the members of St Mary Magdalen College, Oxford*, 4 (1904), 78–84 · B. Whitelocke, *A journal of the Swedish embassy*, ed. C. Morton, rev. H. Reeve, new edn, 1 (1855), 281–2, 394 · Bodl. Oxf., MS Dep.d.69; MS Selden supra 108 fols. 23, 48 · Wood, *Ath. Oxon.*, new edn, 3.1130–33; 4.591 · C. Burmann, *Trajectum eruditum* (1738), 285–8 · J. A. Wijnne, ed., *Resolutiën genomen bij de vroedschap van Utrecht betreffende de illustre school en de akademie* (1888), 52–7 · G. W. Kernkamp, ed., *Acta et decreta senatus: vroedschapsresolutiën en andere bescheiden betreffende de Utrechtsche Akademie* (1936), 177–8, 193–4, 202 · P. C. Molhuysen, ed., *Bronnen tot de geschiedenis der Leidsche Universiteit*, 2 (The Hague, 1916), 220, 269 · P. Colomesius, ed., *Gerardi Joann. Vossii et clarorum virorum ad eum epistolae* (1690), 190–91, 195–6, 220–21, 320, 427–8 · [C. Ravius], *Specimen lexici Arabico-Persici-Latini* (1645) · O. A. Knoes, *Analecta epistolarum*, specimen 4 (1789), 68

Archives BL, unpublished treatise on Turkish language, autograph, Harley MS 3496, fols. 90–118 · Staatsbibliothek, Berlin, collected MSS

Likenesses line engraving, 1645, NPG; repro. in C. Ravis, *Generall grammer* (1650)

Ravis, Thomas (*b.* in or before **1560**, *d.* **1609**), bishop of London, was born at Malden, Surrey, probably the son of Thomas Ravis and his wife, Mary, daughter of Thomas Lisle of Reigate and widow of Robert Benson. Educated at Westminster School, he was elected to Christ Church, Oxford, on 6 July 1575. When the college at first refused him entry, alleging that Westminster scholars, though well grounded in grammar, were less proficient in logic than other candidates, Ravis wrote an appeal to Lord Burghley, whose patronage secured his admission. He duly graduated BA on 12 November 1578, and proceeded MA on 3 March 1582, and BD on 6 July 1589. He served as proctor in 1588 and vice-chancellor in 1596/7 and 1597/8. He had been ordained in 1582 and spent some years preaching in and around Oxford, but no benefice is recorded until he obtained the rectory of Merstham, Surrey, in 1591, and the London vicarage of All Hallows Barking by the Tower, on 27 December the same year (vacating in May 1598). On 20 February 1593 he was installed as canon of Westminster, a post he retained until 1607 (his successor being installed on 10 May). He served as chapter treasurer in 1593/4 and for three other yearly terms, and as steward in 1595/6.

After gaining the DD in 1595, Ravis was, on 19 June 1596, appointed to the deanery of Christ Church at the request of Lord Buckhurst, who, as chancellor of Oxford University, felt entitled to exercise the crown's patronage. Ravis's nomination was also supported by Sir Robert Cecil against a nominee of the earl of Essex. Ravis at once introduced unpopular reforms, replacing traditional commons allowances with cash payments. Dudley Carleton, reporting the dean's 'great tyranny', said that Ravis had the support of Archbishop Whitgift, and that some of the college had been sent before the privy council, others

Thomas Ravis (*b.* in or before 1560, *d.* 1609), by unknown artist, in or after 1607

imprisoned (*CSP dom.*, 1595–7, 361). Carleton was still at odds with the dean over his own income in 1603.

On 15 May 1598 Ravis was presented by the dean and chapter of Westminster to their prime living, the vicarage of Islip, Oxfordshire, to which he was instituted on 7 July. On 19 October that year he also became vicar of Wittenham Abbas, Berkshire. Before 11 October 1602 he had married Alice, later wife of Sir John Borlase, master of the ordnance of Ireland. He was suggested for the bishopric of Norwich by Whitgift in October 1602, but it was still as a dean that Ravis attended the Hampton Court conference in 1604. His notes were used by Bishop Barlow in his published account of the proceedings. Subsequently Ravis sat on the committee which translated the gospels, the Acts of the Apostles, and the book of Revelation for the Authorized Version of the Bible. He was also prolocutor of the lower house of the convocation of Canterbury in 1604, being confirmed as such on 23 March. On 30 May he claimed he had been maliciously subpoenaed by those whose real target was Bancroft; his accusers were themselves promptly arrested by the crown's officers. When in September 1604 it became known that Ravis was to be made bishop of Gloucester and might be allowed to retain his deanery *in commendam*, the canons of Christ Church protested strongly that their head of house ought to be permanently resident. Nevertheless on 15 February 1605 Ravis duly received licence to hold his deanery, canonry of Westminster, and livings of Islip and Wittenham along with his bishopric. He was consecrated on 17 March and, notwithstanding his dispensation, resigned the deanery

of Christ Church (to which a successor was appointed on 1 August 1605). He retained the canonry of Westminster: the prebendal house was a valuable perquisite for a bishop without an official London residence. On 24 March 1606 he preached the accession day sermon at Paul's Cross. His translation to bishop of London was anticipated (suit being made for his Islip living) on 10 April 1607, and came with election on 29 April and confirmation on 18 May.

In his successive episcopates Ravis was a diligent administrator; though an unreconstructed Calvinist, he was a scourge of nonconforming clergy. At Gloucester he won the respect of clerical and county society with his hospitality and careful ministry, at his primary visitation in 1605 reserving almost fifty cases for further consideration. Three nonconformist clergy were eventually ejected. He later rarely missed sessions of his consistory court, save in parliament time; he brought sanitation and other improvements to the episcopal residences, and at London personally examined ordinands and encouraged training for non-preaching clergy, sending at least a dozen to the archdeacons for this purpose. He continued to press for conformity, and reported the worst cases to the high commission. 'By the help of Jesu', he told Richard Rogers, 'I will not leave one preacher in my dioces that doth not subscribe' (Knappen, 31). Five lecturers were suspended, and as many beneficed clergy deprived.

Ravis's wife was the sole executor named in his will of 12 November 1609; the overseers were his brother-in-law, Thomas Edwardes LLD, and Nicholas Kempe. Ravis died on 14 November 1609, probably in London, and was buried in St Paul's Cathedral.   C. S. KNIGHTON

Sources *Old Westminsters*, vols. 1–2 · Foster, *Alum. Oxon.* · Wood, *Ath. Oxon.*, new edn, 2.849 · *N&Q*, 173 (1937), 384–5 · *Fasti Angl., 1541–1857*, [St Paul's, London], 2 · *Fasti Angl., 1541–1857*, [Ely], 78, 81 · *Fasti Angl., 1541–1857*, [Bristol], 41 · *CSP dom.*, 1595–7, 361; 1603–10, 2, 159, 196, 243 · *Calendar of the manuscripts of the most hon. the marquis of Salisbury*, 6, HMC, 9 (1895), 194–5, 197; 12 (1910), 437–8; 16 (1933), 309 · A. W. Pollard, ed., *Records of the English Bible: the documents relating to the translation and publication of the Bible in English, 1525–1611* (1911), 52 · R. G. Usher, *The reconstruction of the English church*, 2 vols. (1910), 1.347; 2.48 · D. Wilkins, ed., *Concilia Magnae Britanniae et Hiberniae*, 4 (1737), 379 · K. Fincham, ed., *Visitation articles and injunctions of the early Stuart church*, 1 (1994), 39 · W. Barlow, ed., *The summe and substance of the conference* (1604), sigs. A3v, B1 · J. Strype, *Annals of the Reformation and establishment of religion … during Queen Elizabeth's happy reign*, new edn, 2/1 (1824), 553–6 · *Two Elizabethan puritan diaries, by Richard Rogers and Samuel Ward*, ed. M. M. Knappen, SCH, 2 [1933], 31 · C. S. Knighton, ed., *Acts of the dean and chapter of Westminster*, 2 (1999), nos. 447, 456, 465, 494, 534, 539, 546 · *DNB*

Archives GL, MS 9531/14, fols. 104–47 · Glos. RO, episcopal registers, GDR 27A, fols. 287–321

Likenesses oils, in or after 1607, Christ Church Oxf. [*see illus.*] · oils, copy, Fulham Palace, London

Wealth at death see will, PRO, PROB 11/115, fols. 60v–61

Rawcliffe, Gordon Hindle (1910–1979), electrical engineer and university teacher, was born on 2 June 1910 at Sunny Bank, Sheffield, the elder son and first of three children of the Revd James Hindle Rawcliffe (1874–1920) of St Matthias's Church, Sheffield, the son of a Burnley grocer, and his wife, Mary Jane Thompson (1883–1940), the daughter of a Lytham hotelier. The family moved to Gloucester when Rawcliffe was two; his father died there eight years later. Rawcliffe was educated at King's School, Gloucester (1921–3), Hereford Cathedral school (1923–4), and St Edmund's School, Canterbury (1924–9). He then went as an exhibitioner to Keble College, Oxford; he first read mathematics, obtaining a second class in mathematical moderations (1930), then, under Richard V. Southwell, he read engineering science, achieving first-class honours in 1932.

His first professional appointment was with Metropolitan-Vickers Electrical Co. Ltd of Manchester, where he spent two years as a college apprentice and upwards of three as a design engineer. This comparatively short period in industry made him thoroughly familiar with electrical machinery and gave him opportunities for writing and debate; not least, it brought him into contact with men like E. S. Booth, Willis Jackson, and Frederic C. Williams. However, Rawcliffe was more interested in the science of engineering than in production processes, and in 1937 he accepted appointment as lecturer in electrical engineering in the University of Liverpool, whence in 1941 he moved to Aberdeen to take up the joint post of lecturer in charge of electrical engineering in the university and head of department in Robert Gordon's Technical College. Three years later the university awarded him the degree of DSc. In the same year he moved again, having been appointed at the early age of thirty-four to the chair of electrical engineering in the University of Bristol, where he was to remain until his retirement in 1975.

Rawcliffe began the major work for which he is remembered in 1955, when he started a systematic reconsideration of the polyphase winding of alternating current machinery, a reconsideration which involved questioning and ultimately changing some of the established dogma of the electrical world. Initially he concentrated on the induction motor, the simple, reliable machine which drives most of the world's industry, but which then had one unfortunate characteristic: it would run at only one speed. From Rawcliffe's studies emerged what he called the principle of pole amplitude modulation—PAM—which showed how by simple means current could be reversed in parts of motor windings, so changing the pole distribution and number, and with it the speed of rotation. The ramifications of this simple idea were many; Rawcliffe devoted to its development years of intense single-minded concentration and by the time of his death he and his collaborators (in particular W. Fong and A. R. W. Broadway) had filed some sixty patents worldwide and published numerous scientific papers, while the large-scale manufacture of PAM motors had already become common throughout the world.

Rawcliffe was the recipient of many honours. The Royal Society elected him fellow (1972) and Clifford Paterson lecturer (1977); to his MA (Oxon., 1937) and DSc (Aberdeen, 1944) were added honorary DTech (Loughborough, 1974) and honorary DSc (Bath, 1976). Keble College elected him to an honorary fellowship (1976). He became vice-president (1972–5) and honorary fellow (1978) of the Institution of Electrical Engineers. The Fellowship of Engineering elected him FEng (1976).

Rawcliffe was a vital character with an apparently inexhaustible store of restless energy; this was despite chronic ill health, especially bronchial asthma, which dogged him throughout his life and which was at times totally disabling. Because of his intense devotion to PAM, his scientific interests were perhaps narrow. His general interests ranged widely; education, languages (especially English, for he loved poetry), law, and music were all important to him. A former president and life member of the Oxford University Archaeological Society, he had a wide knowledge of church and cathedral origins and architecture. He was a most positive man: he liked bright colours and loud music, and saw most problems as a choice between clearly defined alternatives. He would make a rapid assessment and decision, giving his views bluntly and without equivocation.

Rawcliffe married first (1940) Stella Mary, daughter of Arthur Eustace Morgan, principal of McGill University, Montreal, and later of the Ministry of Labour, London; they had two daughters. Separation and divorce ended the marriage in 1952. In the same year he married Sheila Mary, daughter of Charles William Wicks, schoolmaster; they also had two daughters. Rawcliffe died of a heart attack following a bout of asthma on 3 September 1979 at his home, 28 Upper Belgrave Road, Clifton, Bristol.

RODERICK COLLAR, *rev.*

Sources A. R. Collar and A. R. W. Broadway, *Memoirs FRS*, 27 (1981), 479–503 · private information (2004) · personal knowledge (2004) · *CGPLA Eng. & Wales* (1979)
Archives Inst. EE, working papers and corresp. | ICL, corresp. with Lord Jackson
Wealth at death £58,829: probate, 7 Dec 1979, *CGPLA Eng. & Wales*

Rawdon, Christopher (1780–1858), businessman and benefactor of a fund for Unitarian ministers, was born at Halifax on 13 April 1780, the eldest son of Christopher and Sophia Rawdon. His father (*d.* 1822), the sixth in succession with this name, owned mills at Underbank, near Todmorden, Yorkshire. Rawdon was educated in Switzerland (1787–90) and at Mr Catlow's school at Mansfield, Nottinghamshire (*c.*1790–1793). In 1793 his father met a Portuguese gentleman at Falmouth, and, in order to improve their children's knowledge of foreign languages, they agreed to exchange sons for a year. The elder Rawdon dispatched home the following letter: 'Dear Wife,—Deliver to the bearer thy first-born. Christopher Rawdon'. His wife 'knew too well the decision of her husband's character to hesitate a moment in yielding obedience' (*Christian Reformer*, 1858, 738). After a year at Lisbon and further schooling at Mansfield (1794–7), Rawdon in 1797 became manager at Underbank. In 1807 he went to Portugal as representative of his father's firm, and held this position until 1823, when he settled in Liverpool. He married, on 23 October 1821, Charlotte (*b. c.*1796), daughter of Rawdon Briggs, banker, of Halifax, and his wife, Ann.

Rawdon was a successful man of business, a member of

the Liverpool town council for three years, and a borough and county magistrate. In politics he was an active Liberal, in religion an assertive Unitarian. The Dissenters' Chapels Act of 1844 finally established the right, after decades of litigation, of Unitarians to the possession of their old meeting-houses together with associated endowments. However, the act did not prevent the removal of Unitarians from the Lady Hewley Trust, and many ministers suffered financial hardship as a result. Rawdon therefore decided to create a new fund for the benefit of Unitarian ministers serving congregations in the north of England. The successful formation of the trust from the will of Robert Hibbert in 1853, which fostered the best entrants to the Unitarian ministry, prompted Rawdon and his brother James (1782–1855) to donate £1000, which was later doubled, towards the creation of a fund to aid poorer ministers. In the following year appeals in the press and elsewhere soon increased the total to nearly £19,000. This large sum was made into the Ministers' Stipend Augmentation Fund in 1856, in the control of trustees, to benefit Unitarian ministers serving congregations north of the River Trent. A pioneering venture at this time within dissent, the trust still continued to fulfil its original purpose some 150 years later.

Rawdon died at Elm House, Anfield, Liverpool, on 22 October 1858, and was buried at Toxteth Park Chapel, Liverpool. His obituary in the *Christian Reformer* stated, 'Many a poor minister, in his struggles and discouragements, will think in gratitude of him'.

ALEXANDER GORDON, rev. ALAN RUSTON

Sources *Christian Reformer, or, Unitarian Magazine and Review*, new ser., 14 (1858), 711–12, 737–46 · 'Minister's stipend augmentation fund', *Christian Reformer, or, Unitarian Magazine and Review*, new ser., 12 (1856), 570–74 · G. E. Evans, *A history of Renshaw Street Chapel* (1887), 161 · A. Ruston, 'Unitarian trust funds: the Hibbert and the Rawdon', *Transactions of the Unitarian Historical Society*, 17/3 (1985), 138–51 · H. McLachlan, *The Widows' Fund Association* (1937), 81–2 · *General Assembly of Unitarian and Free Christian Churches handbook* (1991), 38 · *The Inquirer* (30 Oct 1858), 698, 710 · V. Davis, *Ancient chapel of Toxteth Park* (1884), 55 · IGI
Likenesses marble relief bust, Unitarian church, Ullet Road, Liverpool
Wealth at death £6000: probate, 3 June 1859, *CGPLA Eng. & Wales*

Rawdon [née Hastings], **Elizabeth**, *suo jure* Baroness Botreaux, *suo jure* Baroness Hungerford, *suo jure* Baroness Moleyns, *suo jure* Baroness Hastings, and countess of Moira (1731–1808), literary patron and antiquary, was born at Donington Park, Leicestershire, on 23 March 1731, the eldest surviving daughter of the four sons and three daughters of Theophilus Hastings, ninth earl of Huntingdon (1696–1746), landowner, and his wife, Selina Shirley (1707–1791) [see Hastings, Selina], founder of the Countess of Huntingdon Connexion. She was educated at home. On 26 February 1752 she became the third wife of Sir John Rawdon, fourth baronet (1719/20–1793), of Moira, co. Down, who was created earl of Moira in 1762. She admitted that her inducement to marry had been the frustration at living 'a life of duty with my mother' (*Hastings MSS*,

3.79). In 1760, shortly after preaching at Moira, John Wesley wrote to her berating her for her loss of faith and for loving the worldly virtues of visiting and conversation. In later life she openly professed the most violent enmity to religion.

Lady Moira possessed a sharp intelligence tempered by intermittent bouts of depression and a sometimes strained relationship with her husband, who was described by Lady Mary Wortley Montagu as 'something of a poltroon and a common butt' (GEC, *Peerage*, 9.30). While she could seek emotional refuge in the upbringing of her six sons and five daughters, she also interested herself in Dublin's literary circles and the intellectual clique surrounding Bishop Thomas Percy at Dromore from 1782 to 1810. Moira House, Dublin, was described as 'the gathering place of people of genius' (*Annual Register*, 151). In the 1780s she befriended the young Maria Edgeworth and later edited extracts of Edgeworth's work. She was used by Maria three times as a model for the characters of Mrs Hungerford in *Patronage* (1812), Lady Oranmore in *The Absentee* (1813), and the countess of Annaly in *Ormond* (1817). Lady Moira was also a personal friend of Charlotte Brooke, author of the *Reliques of Irish Poetry* (1816), and aided her in compiling and translating sections of the work. She gave her patronage to Thomas Dermody, best known for his *Poems Moral and Descriptive* (1800), which was dedicated to the countess who had financed his early education. Within her social circle she was also a combatant on behalf of Mary Wollstonecraft, following attacks on *A Vindication of the Rights of Woman* (1792) by Dr Thomas O'Beirne, bishop of Meath, as Lady Mountcashell, the wife of Lady Moira's grandson and a former pupil of Wollstonecraft, perceived the criticisms to be a slight on her own family. Lady Moira also provided Thomas Romney Robinson, who penned *Juvenile Poems* (1807), with support and encouragement.

As an antiquarian Lady Moira was instrumental in encouraging her husband to become one of the founder members of the Royal Irish Academy and herself became the first woman to be published in *Archaeologia* in 1783 when she submitted a discourse concerning the remains of a human skeleton discovered on the Rawdon estate. In 1788 J. C. Walker admitted in his *Historical Essay on the Dress of the Ancient and Modern Irish* that few pages of the book could not 'boast some obligation to her ladyship' (Walker, preface).

Although Lady Moira generally expressed an antipathy to politics, she was an intimate of Henry Flood, the noted Irish patriot. In 1770 she hosted a fancy-dress ball to encourage the Irish linen industry. This was financed by the Irish government and attended by 600 of the country's nobility and gentry. Shortly after this a news sheet against the Augmentation Bill was announced on the Dublin streets as 'Lady Moira's answer to Dr Lucas', thus publicly identifying her with the patriot opposition. In 1772 she expressed public concern at the plight of the Hearts of Steel, an agrarian movement based in counties Down and Antrim formed to protest against high levies of county cess, and much later, in 1798, as Baroness Botreaux, Hungerford, Moleyns, Hastings of Hastings, and Hastings of Hungerford in her own right, she wrote to lords Camden and Castlereagh protesting against the government's methods of suppressing the United Irishmen. Her papers contain the material she compiled to supplement her son's speech in the Irish House of Lords on 19 February 1798 condemning the excesses of the army in Ireland. Lady Moira died aged seventy-seven on 11 April 1808 at Moira House and was buried at Moira.

ROSEMARY RICHEY

Sources GEC, *Peerage*, new edn, vols. 6, 9 · *Report on the manuscripts of the late Reginald Rawdon Hastings*, 4 vols., HMC, 78 (1928–47), vol. 3 · PRO NIre., Granard MSS, T 3765 [transcripts of MSS held at Castleforbes by the earl of Granard] · *Annual Register* (1808), 150–51 · *Walker's Hibernian Magazine* (May 1808) · *The letters of the Rev. John Wesley*, ed. J. Telford, 8 vols. (1931) · A. C. C. Gaussen, *Percy: prelate and poet* (1908) · preface, J. C. Walker, *An historical essay on the dress of the ancient and modern Irish* (1788) · D. Hempton and M. Hill, *Evangelical protestantism in Ulster society, 1740–1890* (1992)
Archives NA Scot., personal papers · NRA, priv. coll., corresp. and papers | Bodl. Oxf., Napier MSS · Hunt. L., Hastings MSS · NL Ire., letters to Denis Scully · PRO NIre., Granard MSS
Likenesses portrait (*The late countess of Moira*), NG Ire.; repro. in *Walker's Hibernian Magazine* (May 1808)
Wealth at death approx. £1200 p.a.: PRO NIre., private papers in Granard MSS

Rawdon, Sir George, first baronet (1604–1684), army officer and politician, was born in November 1604, the only son of Francis Rawdon (1581?–1668) of Rawdon Hall in the West Riding of Yorkshire and Dorothy (d. 1660), daughter of William Aldborough.

At the age of twenty-one George Rawdon became private secretary to Edward, Viscount Conway, secretary of state, and after Conway's death in 1631 he acted as secretary and agent to his son, also Edward, second Viscount Conway. Increasingly Rawdon was to reside on Conway's Ulster estates, particularly at Brookhill, near Lisburn, co. Antrim, leasing and purchasing Irish land on his own behalf. He proved an active agent, recruiting tenants from England for Conway's estates, engaging in legal activity, and drawing up plans for 'improvement', a recurrent theme in his career. An extensive correspondence he conducted with members of the Conway family has survived, covering several decades from the 1630s, and treating of all manner of aspects of life in east Ulster and beyond.

Rawdon married (probably in 1635) Ursula, daughter of Sir Francis Stafford of Portglenone, co. Antrim, and his wife, Anne (née Grogan), and widow of Francis Hill. She and their only child died the following year. In 1639 he was involved in enforcing the 'black oath' repudiating the national covenant upon the Scottish inhabitants of Ulster. He was returned for Belfast to the Irish parliament of 1640. He had held a captaincy in the Irish army since 1635, and with the outbreak of the 1641 rising he returned from London to assist in the assembly of local forces to counter the insurgents. His own residence, at Brookhill, was pillaged and burnt. He participated in successive campaigns, attaining the rank of major. In the aftermath of the cessation negotiated between Charles and the Catholic confederates in September 1643 his reports that Ulster officers

sought peace in England but war in Ireland, appear to have reflected his own views. Certainly he engaged in the renewed fighting in Ulster from 1644, and by 1647 was in London seeking additional support from parliament for the protestant forces in Ireland.

By the late 1640s tensions within the protestant camp in Ulster were high, and Rawdon won praise for his support of the English parliamentarian interest against the Scots in the province from parliament's commander, George Monck, with whom he was to sustain a friendship. He held a series of offices in Ulster in the 1650s including those of commissioner for confiscated lands, revenue commissioner, and JP and participated in schemes for ecclesiastical reform. He was elected for the combined counties of Antrim, Down, and Armagh to the 1659 protectorate parliament. He rebuilt Brookhill, consolidated his landholdings, especially around Moira, co. Down, and was rewarded by the state with further land grants. Like his neighbour Arthur Hill he combined service to the Commonwealth regimes with a departure from their religious preferences, the only point of contact being a common suspicion of presbyterianism. Instead, at Conway's request, he gave shelter to the future bishop, Jeremy Taylor, and remained in close contact with him after his elevation to the see of Down and Connor in 1661.

In the summer of 1659 Rawdon journeyed to Scotland to consult Monck on political developments. In the following spring he was elected to the Irish Convention for co. Antrim and, with the restoration of Charles II under way, travelled to London to represent the interests of the military in Ireland and subsequently the convention itself. He was elected in 1661 to the Irish parliament for Carlingford, and was appointed a privy councillor and a commissioner to execute the proposed land settlement. Following his own representations he was created a baronet on 20 May 1665. Retaining the confidence of the new government, he continued to oppose presbyterian activities in Ulster. Ongoing concerns about covenanter insurgency in Scotland lent force to his suspicions and his hostility to any policy of indulgence. As late as 1681 he remarked to Conway, concerning an application to build a presbyterian meeting-house, that it 'is near 50 years we have lived here in peace and I shall not willingly admit any such interruption in my days' (Bailie, 8).

Rawdon's lands, principally in co. Down, but also in counties Louth, Meath, and Dublin were confirmed to him, and further augmented, by the Restoration regime. He undertook additional purchases, and the construction of the co. Down market towns of Moira and Ballynahinch. He persisted with efforts in agricultural improvement and industrial diversification, both on his own property and as agent for Conway. Although not all his ventures proved successful, his efforts at road improvement won him contemporary praise as 'the Best High Way man in the kingdom' (Hill, 385). His energetic engagement was crucial to the rise of Lisburn as a commercial centre in south Antrim and the site of the new cathedral and a leading local school.

On 4 September 1654 Rawdon had married his second

wife, Dorothy Conway (d. 1676), eldest daughter of the second viscount, and his wife, Frances (née Popham), with whom he had seven sons and three daughters. He died on 18 August 1684 and was buried in Lisburn Cathedral ten days later. Only one of Rawdon's sons survived him, Sir Arthur Rawdon, second baronet, who was in turn grandfather of John Rawdon, fourth baronet and first earl of Moira.

George Rawdon's career draws together many of the strands of English settlement in seventeenth-century Ulster: the acquisition of land and the harnessing of resources in economic improvement, building, and the construction of an urban and communications network; the blending of military and civil office; and a commitment to the fortunes of the established church. In his case such aims were pursued with unusual energy and an interpretation of the 'English interest' which would allow for co-operation with the interregnum regimes, but also a hostility towards presbyterianism which caused him to remark, using the language of Daniel 8, that his 'troublesome neighbours' 'the Scots presbetry ... esteem me one of the horns against the Kirk' (*CSP Ire.*, 1647–60, 662).

R. M. ARMSTRONG

Sources M. Beckett, *Sir George Rawdon: a sketch of his life and times* (1935) • B. McGrath, 'A biographical dictionary of the membership of the Irish House of Commons, 1640–1641', PhD diss., University of Dublin, 1997 • *DNB* • GEC, *Baronetage* • R. Gillespie, 'George Rawdon's Lisburn', *Lisburn Historical Society Journal*, 8 (1991), 32–6 • *Report on the manuscripts of the late Reginald Rawdon Hastings*, 4 vols., HMC, 78 (1928–47), vol. 2 • R. Gillespie, *Colonial Ulster: the settlement of east Ulster, 1600–1641* (1985) • *CSP Ire.*, 1625–70 • W. D. Bailie, 'Sir George Rawdon: one of the horns against the kirk in the seventeenth century', *Bulletin of the Presbyterian Historical Society of Ireland*, 13 (1984), 1–9 • A. Clarke, *Prelude to Restoration in Ireland* (1999) • R. L. Greaves, *God's other children: protestant nonconformists and the emergence of denominational churches in Ireland* (1997) • E. Berwick, ed., *Rawdon papers* (1819) • G. Hill, *An historical account of the MacDonnells of Antrim* (1873) • J. Lodge, *The peerage of Ireland*, rev. M. Archdall, rev. edn, 7 vols. (1789)

Archives Hunt. L., Hastings MSS • PRO, state papers, Ireland, SP 63

Likenesses R. White, line engraving, BM, NPG • portrait, repro. in Bailie, 'Sir George Rawdon', 3

Rawdon, Marmaduke (bap. **1610**, d. **1669**), traveller and antiquary, was baptized at St Crux Church, York, on 17 March 1610, the youngest son of Laurence Rawdon (1568?–1626), a merchant and alderman of the city who was descended from a younger branch of the family of Rawdon, Yorkshire, and his wife, Margery Barton (1570?–1644) of Cawton in the same county. He almost certainly attended St Peter's Grammar School in York. On the death of his father in 1626 he was adopted by his uncle Marmaduke (later Sir Marmaduke) Rawdon, a prominent London wine merchant.

From 1627 Rawdon was stationed at Bordeaux, where he dealt with his uncle's business and those of other wine merchants. In 1631 he was entrusted with the management of his uncle's affairs on the island of Tenerife, and he lived in the Canary Islands, principally at La Laguna, Gran Canaria, with brief intervals, for over twenty years. During this period he supervised the English factory established on the island and engaged in trade on his own account; he also ascended the peak of Tenerife.

In 1656, in consequence of England's rupture with Spain, Rawdon returned to England, and during most of the remainder of his life lived with his cousin and namesake Marmaduke Rawdon of Hoddesdon, Hertfordshire. His biographer describes how in the early 1660s he passed some of his time 'att home, for the most part in his closet reading or writinge, beinge naturally inclind to studdie' (Davies, 92). He compiled a number of commonplace books, journals, and accounts, among them a genealogical memoir of the Rawdon family and a history of cathedrals. In 1712 Ralph Thoresby was permitted to inspect the collection, and extracts from some of the manuscripts are made use of in his *Ducatus Leodiensis* (1715).

According to his biographer, Rawdon was as inclined to action as he was to study, 'followinge booth with some earnestnesse' (Davies, 196). He undertook many journeys. These were largely within England, but in 1662, for instance, with his cousin, he visited the Low Countries, recording his observations of Flemish and Dutch churches, gardens, hospitals, and trade. Rawdon did not completely neglect his mercantile activities in later life, and in the mid-1660s he was admitted a member of the shortlived Canary Company, in which he invested £1500.

Rawdon died, unmarried, at Hoddesdon on 6 February 1669 and was buried, probably on 20 February, in the chancel of the church at Broxbourne. By his will he left to the corporation of York funds to enable the chief market place, the Pavement, to be enlarged, the gold 'poculum caritatis', or loving cup, and money to purchase the gold chain still worn at the close of the twentieth century by every lady mayoress of York.

NATASHA GLAISYER

Sources *The life of Marmaduke Rawdon of York*, ed. R. Davies, CS, old ser., 85 (1863) • *The diary of Ralph Thoresby*, ed. J. Hunter, 2 (1830) • R. Thoresby, *Ducatus Leodiensis, or, The topography of ... Leedes* (1715) • H. F. Killick, 'Memoirs of Sir Marmaduke Rawden', *Yorkshire Archaeological Journal*, 25 (1918–20), 315–30 • J. W. Stoye, *English travellers abroad, 1604–1667*, rev. edn (1989)

Archives BL, life of M. Rawdon, Add. MS 34206 • priv. coll., commonplace books

Likenesses R. White, line engraving, BM, NPG; repro. in *Engraved Brit. ports.*, 3 (1912), 547

Rawes, Henry Augustus (1826–1885), Roman Catholic priest and convert, was born at Easington, near Durham, on 11 December 1826 and educated at Houghton-le-Spring grammar school, of which his father, the Revd William Rawes (1764–1827), was sometime headmaster. On 26 March 1845 he was admitted as a sizar to Trinity College, Cambridge, where he graduated BA in 1849 and MA in 1852. After ordination in 1852 he became curate of St Bartholomew, Moor Lane, London, in June 1853, and warden of the House of Charity, Soho, in May 1854.

Rawes was received into the Roman Catholic church in March 1856, and the following year joined the Oblates of St Charles on the foundation of that congregation by H. E. Manning. After receiving Roman orders in November 1857 he had charge of the Notting Hill district, where he built the church of St Francis. In 1874 he was appointed prefect of studies in St Charles's College, the grammar school opened by Manning in North Kensington. Created DD by Pius IX in 1875, he was elected superior of the Oblate fathers in 1879. For twenty-eight years he was well known in London as a preacher and writer, and was the author of many devotional works and religious poems. He died at Brighton on 24 April 1885, and was buried at Mortlake Catholic cemetery, Surrey.

THOMPSON COOPER, rev. G. MARTIN MURPHY

Sources *The Tablet* (2 May 1885), 703 • Venn, *Alum. Cant.* • Boase, *Mod. Eng. biog.* • *Men of the time* (1884) • Gillow, *Lit. biog. hist.*

Rawghton, Emma (*fl.* 1422–1436), anchoress, is known primarily from the work of John Rous, a Warwickshire antiquary who was chaplain from 1444 to his death in 1491 at a hermitage known as Guy's Cliffe near Warwick which was under the patronage of the earls of Warwick. Between 1483 and 1485 Rous wrote the English version of his illustrated history of the earls of Warwick known as the Rous roll in which he describes the prophecies of Emma, a recluse of All Saints' Church in York. Another work connected with the earls of Warwick, *The Pageants of the Birth, Life and Death of Richard Beauchamp, Earl of Warwick*, written towards the end of the fifteenth century and commissioned in 1493, by Anne, the widow of Richard Neville, earl of Warwick and Salisbury (the Kingmaker), portrays in fifty-three pencil drawings episodes in the earl of Warwick's life, including a drawing celebrating two of Emma's prophecies.

In 1422 she claimed that Our Lady had showed her that the infant Henry VI ought to be crowned in France as well as England, and that no person was better fitted to be his guardian than Richard Beauchamp, earl of Warwick. Her advice may have been followed, for soon after Beauchamp became a member of the council that ruled for the child king. On 1 June 1428 he became the king's tutor, and three years later accompanied Henry VI to France for his coronation in Paris on 2 December 1431.

In the first year of Henry VI's reign Emma informed Beauchamp that she had had seven visions of the Virgin in a year and was told that if the earl founded a chantry in the chapel of the hermitage of Guy's Cliffe (so named by Thomas Beauchamp, Richard's grandfather, after the legendary tenth-century warrior, Sir Guy of Warwick), God would grant him a male heir. She also predicted that the chantry with the relics of Sir Guy (his alleged sword and hauberk which were in the family's possession) would become a centre of pilgrimage. In the first year of Henry VI's reign Richard Beauchamp obtained a licence to found a perpetual chantry in the chapel of Guy's Cliffe where two priests were to perform divine service for the souls of the king and the founders. Two years later on 22 March 1425 Beauchamp's son and heir was born. John Rous was chaplain in this chapel from 1444 and provided the information about its foundation. The chapel, restored in 1875, is hewn in rock and contains a statue of

Sir Guy of Warwick. Also surviving are a range of cells cut in the cliff.

Because such influential soldiers and courtiers as the earl of Warwick sought her advice on matters of politics and chivalry, Emma can be considered an English equivalent of her contemporary, Jeanne d'Arc. Her influence on the earl of Warwick, the king's tutor from 1428 to 1436, ensured that she indirectly exerted influence on the piety of the young king. Emma's visionary piety also left its mark on the religion of the female members of the Warwick family such as Anne, countess of Warwick, who commissioned *The Pageants of … Richard Beauchamp*, and the Kingmaker's daughter, Anne Neville, who owned a copy of the *Revelations of St Mechtild*.

Emma may have been just one of a group of intellectually distinguished anchoresses attached to York parish churches who were encouraged by the support of Adam Wigan, a Balliol scholar who was rector of St Saviour's from 1399 to 1433. Wigan left money to Emma and to two other anchoresses within York's walls and to three anchoresses within the diocese of York. He also influenced leading York merchants connected with St Saviour's to become patrons of recluses, such as John Bolton, who made a general bequest to York anchorites, and Richard Russel, who left Emma Rawghton 40s. Emma also received legacies from three other York citizens between 1430 and 1436.

Traces of Emma's two-storey cell possibly remain at the west end of the north aisle of All Saints' Church, North Street.

JONATHAN HUGHES

Sources A. K. Warren, *Anchorites and their patrons in medieval England* (1985) • R. M. Clay, *Hermits and anchorites of England* (1914) • *Thys rol was laburd and finished by Master John Rows of Warrewyk*, ed. W. Courthope (1859) • *The pageants of Richard Beauchamp, earl of Warwick*, ed. W. Proby (1908) • J. Hughes, *Pastors and visionaries: religion and secular life in late medieval Yorkshire* (1988)

Rawle, Francis (*c.*1660–1727), writer on trade and finance, was probably born in Plymouth, the son of Francis Rawle and his wife, Jane. He was descended from an old Cornish family of some wealth and standing, once settled near St Juliot on the north Cornish coast and later in the Plymouth region. Both father and son were Quakers, and were persecuted for their religious belief and imprisoned together at Exeter in 1683. On this account they obtained a grant from William Penn, left Plymouth in the *Desire*, and arrived at Philadelphia on 23 June 1686.

Rawle first settled on 2500 acres in New Plymouth, where he founded the society known as the Plymouth Friends. He married Martha, daughter of Robert Turner, an Irish merchant, in 1689; they had ten children. The family moved to Philadelphia, where Rawle's substance and talents, and wealth from his marriage, soon brought him to note. In early 1689 he became a justice of the peace and judge of the court of common pleas; under the charter of 1691 he was one of six aldermen of Philadelphia; and in 1692 he became deputy registrar of wills and in 1694 commissioner of property. He sat in the assembly between 1704 and 1709, and was appointed again from 1719 to 1726. As a member Rawle participated in most of the important committees of the house, including that dealing with currency issues.

It was for contributions to this field that Rawle is principally remembered. Pennsylvania, like other colonies at the time, faced a continual shortage of hard currency in the form of gold and silver coin due in part to laws forbidding the export of British coinage. Attempts by colonial governors to attract hard currency by raising its value had led Westminster to introduce paper money as the principal means of trade. In *Some Remedies Proposed for Restoring the Sunk Credit of the Province of Pennsylvania* (1721), Rawle called for the issue of a limited amount of paper money secured by land, and for its acceptance as full legal tender to prevent future depreciations of value. He was fully involved in the currency committee's drafting of the Paper Money Act (1723).

In two further works, *Ways and Means for the Inhabitants of Delaware to Become Rich* (1725) and *A Just Rebuke to a Dialogue betwixt Simon and Timothy* (1726), Rawle stressed the importance of achieving a favourable balance of trade, by stimulating exports and controlling imports through tariffs on such items as West Indian rum. Rawle died in Philadelphia on 5 March 1727.   C. A. HARRIS, *rev.* PHILIP CARTER

Sources S. Bruchey, 'Rawle, Francis', *ANB* · E. J. Rawle, *Records of the Rawle family* (1898)
Archives Hist. Soc. Penn.

Rawle, Richard (1812–1889),

bishop of Trinidad, born at Plymouth on 27 February 1812, was a son of Francis Rawle (1778–1854), an attorney at Liskeard, who on abandoning practice had settled at Plymouth; his mother, Amelia, *née* Millett, died on 6 October 1814. Rawle was educated at Plymouth new grammar school, and on 7 February 1831 was admitted pensioner of Trinity College, Cambridge, under the tutorship of William Whewell. On 19 April 1833 he obtained a scholarship at his college, and in 1835 he graduated BA, being third wrangler and fourth classic. He was elected minor fellow of Trinity College on 3 October 1836, and major fellow on 3 July 1838, in which year he proceeded MA and became sub-lector *tertius*; he acted as assistant tutor from 1836 to 1839. In 1839 he was ordained both deacon and priest, and accepted the rectory of Cheadle in Staffordshire. He resigned his post in 1847, though he returned to marry on 14 January 1851 at Cheadle parish church Susan Anne Blagg, daughter of John Michael Blagg, of Rosehill in that parish.

From 1847 to 1864 Rawle was principal of Codrington College in Barbados; about 1859 he declined the offer of the bishopric of Antigua. In 1864 he returned to England, and after refusing the offer of an honorary canonry in Ely Cathedral he acted as vicar of Tamworth, from 1869 to 1872. On 29 June 1872 he was consecrated in Lichfield Cathedral as bishop of Trinidad, where he worked with great energy until his resignation in 1888. His wife died on 1 March 1888 at Bournemouth, and was buried at Cheadle churchyard on 5 March. Rawle reaccepted the post of principal and professor of divinity at Codrington College, where he died on 10 May 1889; he was buried next day in the college burial-ground.

Rawle was the last male representative of the family of

Rawle owning the farmstead of Hennett and other property in the parish of St Juliot, on the north coast of Cornwall, and his generosity raised the income of the benefice, restored the church, and built new schools.

    W. P. COURTNEY, *rev.* H. C. G. MATTHEW

Sources G. Mather and C. J. Blagg, *Bishop Rawle* (1890) · Venn, *Alum. Cant.* · Boase & Courtney, *Bibl. Corn.* · G. C. Boase, *Collectanea Cornubiensia: a collection of biographical and topographical notes relating to the county of Cornwall* (1890)
Archives UCL, papers, incl. family papers | LPL, corresp. with A. C. Tait and related papers
Wealth at death £3114 15s. 10d.: probate, 29 July 1889, *CGPLA Eng. & Wales*

Rawle, Samuel (1775/6–1860),

engraver and draughtsman, was the son of George Rawle; his family came from Dunster in Somerset. By the age of seventeen he was apprenticed to Thomas Bonnors, an engraver of Gloucester, and in January 1796 was working in the London branch of his business, which was run by John Bonnors. A number of his plates appeared in the *European Magazine* and *Gentleman's Magazine*, and in 1801 his first landscape painting was exhibited at the Royal Academy; it was followed by another in 1806. He married Mary Purkess (1776–1860) on 28 April 1801 in St Pancras Old Church, and by 1815 they had had at least six children, who were listed by age in a return made to the Artists' Annuity Fund on 22 December 1836.

Rawle began a long association with important topographical works, producing illustrations on copper for such publications as E. W. Brayley's *Beauties of England* (1801–17), J. C. Murphy's *Arabian Antiquities of Spain* (1816), and James Hakewill's *Picturesque Tour of Italy* (1818–20); he also did two plates for T. D. Whittaker's *A History of Richmondshire* (1823) and others for J. P. Neale's *Views of the Seats of Noblemen* (1818–24). At this time he was living at 3 Tottenham Street, Tottenham Court Road, London. His best work was the five plates on steel engraved between May 1828 and November 1829 for William Brockedon's *Illustrations of the Passes of the Alps* and three plates for William Westall's *Great Britain Illustrated* (1830). The engravings in this latter work were under the direction of Edward Finden, for whom he undertook other work such as etching and finishing plates, receiving small payments.

Rawle also worked for Mr Parker on plates for William Pinnock's *Geography* (c.1830) and engraved for some of John Britton's works. His engravings were precise and well finished, but he seems to have had difficulty in adapting to steel, and it is possible that he later worked more as an architectural draughtsman to provide an income. Credits did not always appear on his engravings, and hence his contributions tend to be overlooked and are revealed only through other evidence, such as two notebooks, together with three letters, preserved in the St Bride Printing Library in London. These also show a son, who may be G. Rawle, apprenticed to his father, doing much of the preparatory work on plates. Samuel Rawle is known to have engraved several portraits, including those of Robert Burns, Sebastian Cabot (1824), and William Shakespeare. He probably retired about 1841, and is described in his will as a gentleman, although his death certificate proclaims him a landscape engraver. He died on 1 November 1860, after a prolonged bout of bronchitis, at his home, 19 Leverton Street, Kentish Town, London. His wife predeceased him by a few days, so his meagre property went to his other executor, George Dobrée.

B. HUNNISETT

Sources Redgrave, *Artists*, 349 · Graves, *Artists*, 1st edn · B. Hunnisett, *An illustrated dictionary of British steel engravers*, new edn (1989), 74 · notebooks and letters, St Bride Institute, London, St Bride Printing Library · d. cert. · will · *IGI* · *Engraved Brit. ports.* · W. Upcott, *A bibliographical account of the principal work relating to English topography*, 3 vols. (1818) · M. Holloway, ed., *Steel engravings in nineteenth century British topographical books: a bibliography* (1977), 171–8
Archives St Bride Institute, London, St Bride Printing Library
Wealth at death under £100: probate, 20 Nov 1860, *CGPLA Eng. & Wales*

Rawlet, John (*bap.* 1642, *d.* 1686), Church of England clergyman, was baptized at St Editha's Church, Tamworth, on the Warwickshire–Staffordshire border, on 27 March 1642, the son of William Rawlet (*d.* 1643) and his wife, Margery. His father was killed fighting in the civil war (probably as a parliamentarian soldier) in late 1643. From his mother Rawlet received a 'pious education' (Rawlet, 3). He probably attended Tamworth grammar school, where the presbyterian Samuel Shaw became master in 1656; when Shaw became curate of Moseley chapel in the parish of Bromsgrove, Worcestershire, in 1657 Rawlet followed him, perhaps continuing as his pupil. He was admitted sizar to Pembroke College, Cambridge, on 30 November 1658, matriculating on 1 December 1659. However, owing to poverty he did not graduate, though he was later created BD, on 23 June 1676 by royal mandate. The apparent coincidence of his withdrawal from Cambridge with the establishment of the Restoration settlement, his connections with presbyterian ministers before and after 1660, and the long period before he received Anglican ordination suggest that conscientious scruples as well as financial reasons may have terminated his Cambridge education.

After Cambridge Rawlet spent some time 'at my Cozen Woods alone' (Manuell, 'John Rawlett, BD', 3), probably his cousin John Wood, curate of the chapel of St Leonard's in the parish of Aston Clifton, Buckinghamshire. After some years he moved to London to serve as tutor and (although he had not apparently yet taken holy orders) chaplain in the household of John Pynsent, protonotary of the court of common pleas, in Bartlett's court in St Andrew's, Holborn. He was there at the time of the great plague of 1665; in the 'consolatory letter' which he wrote to his mother at this time he expressed his fear of dying from the pestilence. In 1667 Rawlet published *A Treatise of Sacramental Covenanting with Christ* (in the first edition anonymously under the initials M. M.); it had reached eight editions by 1736. Richard Baxter, who may have known Rawlet from his Moseley days, provided the preface, dated 6 September 1666, describing the book as 'high and excellent' in its aim 'to convince poor, impenitent,

unholy souls, of the absolute necessity of a speedy, resolute, faithful consent to the Covenant of Grace' (Keeble and Nuttall, 2.53).

Through the Pynsent connection Rawlet evidently preached at Hulcott in Buckinghamshire, where Pynsent's daughter Anne lived. In late 1669 or late 1670 Rawlet became curate of Dunton in the same county. In the spring of 1670 he was ordained and became curate of Wigan, Lancashire, a rectory held *in commendam* by the bishop of Chester, John Wilkins; he also acted for a short time as Wilkins's chaplain. Rawlet noted in a letter to Baxter concerning his move to Wigan, 'I table in a good honest family, with one Mr Herle, son to him [Charles Herle] who was sometime prolocutor of the [Westminster] Assembly'. He went on to describe how he was £20 poorer for his move, but was rewarded by having twenty times more people to preach to than at Hulcott and Dunton (Keeble and Nuttall, 2.89–90). John Tillotson suggested that Rawlet apply for the position of lecturer in Baxter's old parish of Kidderminster, Worcestershire, and Rawlet went as far as delivering a trial sermon in September 1671. But he concluded that his services were better employed in Wigan, where 'beside the too large parish with which I am in some sort charged, there are few holy daies but I am engagd to preach somewhere about us', for which he had Wilkins's 'free leave' (Keeble and Nuttall, 2.119). On 18 September the nonconformist minister Oliver Heywood heard one such sermon when Rawlet preached outside his parish at Bolton. In 1672 Rawlet published *An explication of the creed, the ten commandments and the Lord's Prayer*, like his first work a devotional work designed for the use of the poor.

From 1673 to 1682 Rawlet was minister of Kirkby Stephen, Westmorland. On 25 June 1679 he succeeded John Marsh in the lectureship of St Nicholas, Newcastle upon Tyne, and then was spoken of as 'a very pious and charitable man' (Longstaffe, 418). From early 1682 he was appointed to the newly restored chapel of St Ann's in the slum area of Sandgate, with responsibility for catechizing the children in the school that the council had established there. Evidently a popular minister, in March 1682 he declined the offer of Simon Digby, Lord Digby, of the vicarage of Coleshill in Warwickshire because the people of Newcastle 'so earnestly beset him with their intreaties, not to leave them', and instead he recommended Thomas Kettlewell to the vacancy (Bray, preface). Rawlet remained in Newcastle for the rest of his life. He was described as 'the happy instrument of gaining more souls to God, by his plain, pathetic and practical preaching, and by an uncommon exemplariness in life and conversation, than most others in the days he lived in' (Bray, sig. C). He continued his work of proselytizing the poor in print. In 1685 he published *A Dialogue betwixt Two Protestants, in Answer to a Popish Catechism*, and the following year *The Christian Monitor*, which went through many editions in the seventeenth and eighteenth centuries (seven alone in its first year) and was translated into French and Welsh. The twentieth edition, published in 1696, claimed that 95,000 copies had by then been sold. Rawlet hoped that it would be 'scattered abroad upon pedlars stalls and thence come into the hands of the common people' (Green, 357), and while it was normally sold at 3*d*., it was also offered in job lots of 100 copies for £1 to the charitably disposed to give away.

When close to death, on 25 September 1686 Rawlet went through the ceremony of marriage with Anne (1650/51–1703), the daughter of Thomas Butler, a merchant of Newcastle who had been sheriff there in 1652. The marriage took place at her request, and they had apparently 'been some time in love together' (Longstaffe, 54). He died in Newcastle three days later, on 28 September 1686, and was buried on 30 September at St Nicholas's. In his will he left landed property in Tamworth, yielding an annual income of just over £23, and his library of over 900 books to his native town, in the hope of benefiting its school and inhabitants. CAROLINE L. LEACHMAN

Sources T. Bray, 'A brief account of the life of the Reverend Mr John Rawlet', in G. Carleton and T. Bray, *Two select and exemplary lives, of two parochial ministers* (1728) [incl. J. Rawlet, 'Letter to his mother, written on the oaccasion of his apprehension of dying by the great plague 1665'] • M. Manuell, 'John Rawlett, BD (1642–1686: church of England clergyman, devotional writer, preacher and minor poet', 1982, Oxford University Press, Oxford DNB archives • Venn, *Alum. Cant.* • *Memoirs of the life of Mr Ambrose Barnes*, ed. [W. H. D. Longstaffe], SurtS, 50 (1867), 54, 418, 429–30 • *The Rev. Oliver Heywood … his autobiography, diaries, anecdote and event books*, ed. J. H. Turner, 1 (1881), 282 • Wood, *Ath. Oxon.*, new edn, 4.584 • *Calendar of the correspondence of Richard Baxter*, ed. N. H. Keeble and G. F. Nuttall, 2 (1991) • I. Green, *Print and protestantism in early modern England* (2000) • M. Manuell, 'My very agreeable friend Mr John Rawlet', 1982, Tamworth Central Library and the Rawlett School, Tamworth

Likenesses R. White, line engraving, BM, NPG; repro. in *Poetick miscellanies of Mr. John Rawlet* (1687) • portrait, Tamworth town hall, Staffordshire

Rawley, William (*c*.1588–1667), Church of England clergyman and literary editor, was born in Norwich, of unknown parentage. On 22 January 1600 he was admitted Bible clerk of Corpus Christi College, Cambridge, where he was tutored by a Mr Chapman, and, after graduating BA in 1605 and MA in 1608, was elected fellow and tutor on 19 March 1610. Ordained at Peterborough on 18 April 1611, on 10 December 1612 he was instituted by the university to St Michael's in Bowthorpe, Norfolk, a post he held until his death, the church being 'neglected and laid in decay, without any Service, it being esteemed as a Sine-Cure' (Blomefield, 1.638). He proceeded BD in 1615. His fellowship was briefly suspended in April 1616, after he protested against the enforced appointment of the master's son as fellow.

By this time Rawley was chaplain and 'amanuensis, or daily instrument' to Sir Francis Bacon (Bacon, *Opuscula*, (a) 2r), aiding him in preparing texts for publication; Bacon's influence caused Corpus Christi to give Rawley the Cambridgeshire rectory of All Saints, Landbeach, in 1616. After his fall in 1621 Bacon recommended Rawley, who that year proceeded DD, to his successor as lord keeper, John Williams, but Rawley remained with Bacon. In *A Sermon of Meekenesse, Preached at the Spittle upon Easter Tuesday* (1623), he claimed that 'whatsoever is any way eminent either in

my Estate, or Name, I am ready to ascribe it to your Lordship, from whence I have received it' (A2r–v). After Bacon's death Rawley devoted his life to creating an unblemished portrait of his master, compiling a volume of commemorative verse, and editing, translating, and publishing selections of his work, culminating in the *Resuscitatio* (1657) and *Opuscula varia posthuma* (1658), which contained (in English and Latin respectively) his hagiographical but highly influential life of Bacon. His editorial endeavours led to correspondence with intellectuals including John Selden, Isaac Gruter, and Elie Diodati.

During much of this period Rawley served as chaplain to Charles I, and attracted the patronage of Elizabeth of Bohemia. He returned to Landbeach in 1638, and married Barbara Weld, widow, daughter of a former Cambridge alderman, John Wicksted; they had two children, Mary, who died in infancy, and William. During the civil war Rawley encountered dissent within his flock, perhaps on political grounds: in 1644 twelve Landbeach men petitioned at Cambridge against him, and in 1652 he leased the rectory, presumably leaving the village.

At the Restoration Rawley was appointed chaplain to Charles II. In 1661 he was elected to convocation as proctor of clergy for the Ely diocese, and subscribed the revised Book of Common Prayer. His son, who had graduated BA from Corpus Christi College, Cambridge, in 1660 and been elected a fellow there in 1663, forfeited his fellowship in 1666 by failing to take deacon's orders, but the king intervened to persuade Corpus Christi 'to suffer William Rawley still to employ his fellowship there' (*CSP dom.*, 1665–6, 386). However, William the younger, Barbara Rawley, and several servants of the family died of the plague the same year. Rawley himself died at Landbeach on 18 June 1667, and was buried in his church there. Beneficiaries of his will, drawn up on 12 January 1667, included his brother, Alderman Rawley of Norwich, numerous nieces and nephews, his stepsons Wicksted, Martin, John, and Matthew Weld, and Corpus Christi College, which received several of his books. ALAN STEWART

Sources G. Rees, 'Introduction', in F. Bacon, *The instauratio magna: last writings*, ed. G. Rees (2000) • R. Masters, *The history of the College of Corpus Christi and the B. Virgin Mary … in the University of Cambridge* (1753) • F. Blomefield and C. Parkin, *An essay towards a topographical history of the county of Norfolk*, 5 vols. (1739–75), vol. 1 • W. K. Clay, *History of the parish of Landbeach in the county of Cambridge* (1861) • *CSP dom.*, 1633–4; 1665–6 • F. Bacon, *Opuscula varia posthuma* (1658) • *The letters and life of Francis Bacon*, ed. J. Spedding, 7 vols. (1861–74) • L. Jardine and A. Stewart, *Hostage to fortune: the troubled life of Francis Bacon, 1561–1626* (1998) • H. P. Stokes, *Corpus Christi* (1898) • will, PRO, PROB 11/324, sig. 97 • Venn, *Alum. Cant.* • DNB

Archives LPL, commonplace book

Wealth at death see will, PRO, PROB 11/324, sig. 97

Rawlin, Richard (1686/7–1757), Independent minister, was probably the son of Richard Rawlin, the dissenting minister at Linton, Cambridgeshire, and subsequently at St Neot's, Huntingdonshire, and Stroud, Gloucestershire. He received his ministerial training at the small private academy run by William Payne at Saffron Walden. After completing his studies there he was appointed domestic chaplain to the family of Andrew Warner of Badmondisfield, Suffolk, where he also ministered to a congregation meeting in a registered barn on Warner's estate. In 1716 he accepted the invitation to become pastor of the Independent meeting at Bishop's Stortford, Hertfordshire, commencing his ministry there on 5 November. He was a popular preacher and has been described by Walter Wilson as 'a judicious, practical and experimental devine; a serious, affectionate and solid preacher' (Wilson, 2.456). According to the Evans List he had a congregation of 600 hearers and 40 county voters. He remained at Bishop's Stortford until 1730 when he succeeded Thomas Tingey as minister at the Independent meeting in Fetter Lane, London.

Rawlin continued as minister at Fetter Lane for the remainder of his life. After he had been there for two years a new and larger meeting-house was built for him on the opposite side of the street. The congregation continued to grow and a succession of ministers was engaged to assist Rawlin. The first was John Farmer, followed by Edward Hitchen and finally Edward Hickman. In 1738 Rawlin was chosen to succeed Robert Bragge as one of the six Merchants lecturers at Pinners' Hall. His first contribution was a series of seven sermons on the doctrine of justification. These were subsequently published under the title *Christ the Righteousness of the People* (1741), which ran to several editions. However, this was one of only two published works by Rawlin, the other being an address delivered at the ordination of Thomas Gibbons at Haberdashers' Hall in 1743.

Rawlin died in St John's Square, London, on 15 December 1757 and was buried in the same vault in Bunhill Fields as his wife (1693–1749), a daughter of Joseph Brooksbank of Hackney, who had died in 1749. His funeral sermon was preached by John Guyse at the chapel in New Broad Street.   Alexander Gordon, *rev.* M. J. Mercer

Sources W. Wilson, *The history and antiquities of the dissenting churches and meeting houses in London, Westminster and Southwark*, 4 vols. (1808–14), vol. 3 · W. Urwick, *Nonconformity in Hertfordshire* (1884) · J. Browne, *A history of Congregationalism and memorials of the churches in Norfolk and Suffolk* (1877) · Surman, index of nonconformist ministers, DWL · J. A. Jones, ed., *Bunhill memorials* (1849) · *GM*, 1st ser., 19 (1749) · *GM*, 1st ser., 27 (1757), 578 · J. Evans, 'List of dissenting congregations and ministers in England and Wales, 1715–1729', DWL, MS 38.4

Archives DWL, New College archives, sermons

Rawling, Cecil Godfrey (1870–1917), army officer and explorer, was born at Stoke, Devonport, on 16 February 1870, the second son of Samuel Bartlett Rawling, of Stoke, and his wife, Ada Bathe Withers, of Purton, Wiltshire. He was educated at Clifton College, Bristol.

Rawling entered the army through the militia and was commissioned on 10 October 1891 a second lieutenant in the Somerset light infantry. He was promoted lieutenant on 1 February 1896 and spent most of his service in India, where his love of hunting took him on leave into and across the Himalayan mountains. In 1902 he crossed the Lanak-la Pass into Tibet as a preliminary reconnaissance for a more ambitious expedition. Rawling, accompanied by Lieutenant A. J. G. Hargreaves, retraced his steps the next year and crossed the same pass on an unofficial

exploration mission. Over the next nine months his party explored and mapped approximately 38,000 miles of hitherto unsurveyed country in western Tibet and Rudok, an achievement for which they later received the thanks of the government of India.

Rawling was employed in 1904 with the Lhasa mission. When Sir Francis Younghusband, the British commissioner, returned from Lhasa to Gyantse he selected Rawling to lead the very important exploration of the upper Tsanpo River (the Brahmaputra) in 1904–5. This was recognized as a potentially hazardous undertaking since the Tibetans were thought to be hostile and the return journey to Simla would have to be made in the middle of winter. Rawling's small detachment left the main party at Gyantse, and travelled west along the north of Nepal, through Gartok, and then on to Simla; during its journey the party clearly identified Mount Everest, for the first time from the north. He briefly returned to England, and then in 1909 was made a CIE and was appointed a surveyor to the Ornithologists' Union's scientific expedition in Dutch New Guinea, of which he later took successful command when its leader was invalided. He mapped a large area of this hitherto unknown country and was the first European to encounter the Tapiro pygmies. For his services Rawling received the thanks of the Dutch government. Rawling was also rewarded by the Royal Geographical Society with the Murchison bequest (1909) and the patrons' gold medal (1917). In 1911 he returned to his regiment and on 27 November 1913 he was promoted major.

Following the outbreak of the First World War Rawling, promoted temporary lieutenant-colonel on 11 August 1914, raised and trained the 6th (service) battalion of the Somerset light infantry. He subsequently commanded this unit in France with the rank of colonel. Rawling fought at Hooge in July–August 1915, served during the winter of 1915–16 in the Ypres salient, and then took part in the battle of the Somme, including the capture of Fricourt, Mametz Wood, and Gueudecourt after fierce fighting. He was created CMG and in July 1916 was promoted brigadier-general. During the summer of 1917 he participated in fighting on the Hindenburg line, and later he was at Passchendaele in command of the 62nd infantry brigade, and was awarded the DSO. On 28 October 1917 Rawling was killed, at the age of forty-seven, outside his brigade headquarters at Hooge by a stray shell. He was buried at the Huts cemetery, near Ypres, in Belgium.

    T. R. Moreman

Sources [C. E. Rawling], 'Brigadier-General C. G. Rawling', *GJ*, 50 (1917), 464–6 · *Army List* · *DNB* · C. G. Rawling, *The great plateau: being an account of exploration in central Tibet, 1903, and the Gartok expedition, 1904–1905* (1905) · C. G. Rawling, *The land of the New Guinea pygmies. An account of the story of a pioneer journey of exploration into the heart of New Guinea* (1913) · E. Wyrall, *The history of the Somerset light infantry Prince Albert's, 1914–1919* (1927) · J. E. Edmonds, ed., *Military operations, France and Belgium*, 14 vols., History of the Great War (1922–48) · P. Fleming, *Bayonets to Lhasa*, another edn (1985) · *CGPLA Eng. & Wales* (1918)

Archives RGS, corresp. and papers relating to north India and New Guinea

Wealth at death £4493 18s. 2d.: probate, 14 March 1918, *CGPLA Eng. & Wales*

Rawlings, Sir (Henry) Bernard Hughes (1889–1962), naval officer, was born at Downes, St Erth, Cornwall, on 21 May 1889, the son of William John Rawlings, accountant, and his wife, Marion Florence Hughes. He entered HMS *Britannia* as a cadet in 1904, and first went to sea in HMS *Goliath* in 1905. Soon after the outbreak of the First World War he was put in command of torpedo boat no. 11 in the Nore flotilla. In 1915 he specialized in torpedoes at HMS *Vernon* and for the rest of the war was afloat as torpedo officer in *Antrim*, *Undaunted*, and *Coventry*.

In 1919 Rawlings was appointed naval liaison officer with the British military mission to Poland, a duty which earned him the OBE in 1920. On return to Britain he was appointed to the cruiser *Diomede*. He married Eva Loveday, the daughter of William Hastings Beaumont, of Esher, in 1922. They had two sons and one daughter. In June 1923 he was promoted to commander. Staff appointments to the torpedo school and HMS *Nelson* were followed by two and a half years as executive officer of the battleship *Emperor of India*.

Promoted to captain from this appointment in December 1930, Rawlings then served in command at sea in the Mediterranean for over three years: in the *Active* as divisional leader in the third destroyer flotilla and then in the cruisers *Curacoa* and *Delhi*. After a year at the Imperial Defence College in 1935 he was appointed naval attaché at Tokyo, a post he held for three years amid increasing restrictions and frustrations that greatly inhibited accurate reporting of Japanese capabilities and intentions.

Rawlings was appointed to command the battleship *Valiant* on the outbreak of the Second World War. Here he was remembered by several officers who subsequently achieved the highest ranks as an exemplary captain, cheerful, alert, always human and humorous, ready to listen to constructive suggestions from whatever quarter. He was permanently on the bridge at sea, clad generally in a duffel coat and seagoing uniform over pyjamas, with a battered uniform cap or steel helmet according to the situation. At action stations he conned the ship himself, stationing a sharp-eyed midshipman to observe attacking dive-bombers, so that he could order hard-a-starboard or hard-a-port at the moment of bomb release and thus dodge the bombs.

In 1940 Rawlings, first as acting rear-admiral and then in the substantive rank, commanded the 1st battle squadron in the Mediterranean and then the 7th cruiser squadron. It was nominally in this capacity that he was in charge of the covering force in the battle for Crete. Here British naval forces, heavily attacked by shore-based German aircraft and with virtually no air cover of their own, suffered serious losses. Rawlings's leadership ensured that the depleted forces remained in action and evacuated a large part of the British land force. He was mentioned in dispatches for this outstanding service.

Spells at the Admiralty and as flag officer, west Africa, were followed in 1943 by appointment as flag officer, Levant and eastern Mediterranean. Here Rawlings supervised Aegean operations in one of the more piratical

Sir (Henry) Bernard Hughes Rawlings (1889–1962), by Walter Stoneman, 1942

phases of the war. This was not entirely to his taste—he disliked 'private navies'—but he gave its practitioners full scope. By now a vice-admiral, he was created KCB in the 1944 birthday honours.

Towards the end of 1944 Rawlings was appointed flag officer, second in command, British Pacific Fleet. This was to test his professional skill in the most comprehensive way. The force, though large and powerful by British standards, was numerically much smaller than the massive American effort on station and, more importantly, far less experienced and well equipped for the aircraft-carrier operations that formed the bulk of its work.

Rawlings came through this test triumphantly. He was himself always ready to learn from his American colleagues, particularly in the fields of carrier operations, battle formations, and underway replenishment, and his wise leadership and management ensured that ships' companies, many of them war-weary and anxious to return home, remained in the best possible heart. He was highly respected by the American authorities and the utmost help to his commander-in-chief, Sir Bruce Fraser. The forces under his command were by no means unscathed even in this final phase of the war: in operations to neutralize Sakishima Gunto during the Okinawa campaign, his ships were hit on many occasions by Japanese kamikaze suicide bombers. British carriers, with armoured flight decks, proved particularly robust in the face of these attacks.

Rawlings, created KBE for his services in the Far East and promoted to GBE in 1946, retired at his own request in that year. He was deputy lieutenant for Cornwall and was high sheriff of the county in 1950. He died on 30 September 1962 at his home, Clerkenwater, Helland, Bodmin, Cornwall, and was survived by his wife.

RICHARD HILL

Sources *The Times* (2 Oct 1962) • *WWW* • *Navy List* (1905–45) • S. W. Roskill, *The war at sea, 1939–1945*, 3 vols. in 4 (1954–61) • b. cert. • d. cert. • *CGPLA Eng. & Wales* (1963) • private information (2004) **Archives** FILM BFI NFTVA, news footage • IWM FVA, actuality footage • IWM FVA, news footage | SOUND IWM SA, oral history interview **Likenesses** W. Stoneman, photograph, 1942, NPG [*see illus.*] • O. Birley, oils, *c.*1948, Royal Naval Staff College, Greenwich **Wealth at death** £17,027 14*s.*: probate, 10 June 1963, *CGPLA Eng. & Wales*

Rawlings, Margaret Lilian [*married name* Margaret Lilian Barlow, Lady Barlow] **(1906–1996)**, actress, was born on 5 June 1906 in Osaka, Japan, the daughter of the Revd George William Rawlings, a missionary and the headmaster of an English school, and his wife, Lilian, *née* Boddington. She was educated at a local French convent, at Oxford High School for Girls, and at Lady Margaret Hall, Oxford, where she read French. Refused permission to act with John Masefield's amateur group, she left after a year and joined the Charles Macdona Players in 1927 in their touring repertory of plays by Shaw. On 3 July of that year she married the actor Gabriel Toyne (1905–1963). She made her London début for the Venturers as Louise in *Jordan* (1928) at the Strand Theatre and made her film début in *The Woman he Scorned* (1929), before touring North America (1929–30) with Maurice Colbourne's company. Having appeared in Paris in *On the Spot* (1930) and in New York in *Masque* (1931), she scored successes in London as Bianca Capello in Bax's *The Venetian* at the Little Theatre and as Wilde's *Salome* at the Gate (both 1931); in the latter she performed an erotic dance of the seven veils. In 1932 she toured Australasia, chiefly as Elizabeth Barrett Browning in *The Barretts of Wimpole Street*.

Rawlings was no typical 1930s heroine, a fragile blonde with a light voice; she had an 'instinctive unstrained emotion and … black velvet voice' (*The Times*, 4 June 1996) of great range and timbre to accompany her sultry, dark good looks. She received good notices as Mary Fritton in *This Side Idolatry* (1933) at the Lyric and as Liza Kingdom in *The Old Folks at Home* (1934) at the Queen's, but roles as Josephine in *Napoleon* and Jean in *The Greeks had a Word for it* (both 1934) were less challenging. She rejoined the Macdona Players in 1935 for more Shaw, as Eliza Doolittle in *Pygmalion* and as Ann Whitefield in *Man and Superman* at the Cambridge Theatre. Then came a notable success at the Ethel Barrymore Theatre, New York (1935), and also at the Gate (1936), as Katie O'Shea in *Parnell*. Following its banning, Rawlings herself partly rewrote the text for its restaging at the New Theatre. Before it transferred she had the bizarre experience of playing Charmian in *Antony and Cleopatra*, also at the New. The Russian-American Eugenie Leontovich as Cleopatra was no tragic actress and no verse speaker, and on Cleopatra's death the clarity and tonal quality of Rawlings's lament made it clear to a suddenly alert audience who should have played the queen. Her star as a leading tragic actress was rising, and more successes followed—as Lady Macbeth for the Oxford University Dramatic Society and as Helen in *The Trojan Women* at the Adelphi (both 1937). Then came a major triumph, as Karen Selby in *The Flashing Stream* (1938) at the Lyric, which

Margaret Lilian Rawlings (1906–1996), by Dorothy Wilding, 1933

Charles Morgan, novelist and drama critic of *The Times*, with whom she was in love, had written for her as his first play. It was equally successful at the Biltmore, New York, in the following April. After several more roles, especially in comedy, including Eliza Doolittle again (1939) and Mrs Dearth in Gielgud's revival of *Dear Brutus* (1941), she disappeared from the stage for some years. She had divorced in 1938, and on 14 February 1942 she married Robert Barlow (1891–1976), founder of the Metal Box Company; he was knighted in 1943. They had a daughter.

Rawlings returned to the stage as Gwendolen Fairfax in *The Importance of being Earnest* (1946), a royal command performance, and in two productions by Robert Helpmann, as Titania in Purcell's masque *The Fairy Queen* (1946), seeming oddly uncomfortable, and as an unforgettable Vittoria Corombona in Webster's *The White Devil* (1947) at the Duchess, where 'she astonished audiences and critics with her voluptuous vigour' (*Daily Telegraph*, 5 June 1996). Also in 1947 she played Gertrude to John Byron's Hamlet on television. More successful roles followed: an 'unremittingly intense' Lady Macbeth (1950) at the Arts Theatre; Zabrina to Donald Wolfit's Tamburlaine (1951) at the Old Vic; Lysistrata in Shaw's *The Apple Cart* (1953) at the Haymarket; in *The Winter's Tale* and *The Merry Wives of Windsor* (1955–6) at the Old Vic; Sappho at the Edinburgh festival (1961); Ella Rentheim in Ibsen's *John Gabriel Bjorkman* (1963) at the Duchess; and Jocasta in *Oedipus the King* in Nottingham (1964). She also played a favourite role, Racine's *Phèdre* (1957–8), at the Theatre in the Round and on tour, but had greater success with her own translation of it (subsequently published) at the Arts Theatre in Cambridge (1963). And she reprised her Gertrude in *Hamlet* at the Ludlow festival (1965).

In the early 1970s Rawlings virtually retired from the stage to nurse her husband, but she returned in 1979 in perhaps her most remarkable dramatic achievement, winning enthusiastic reviews. In the long part of *Empress*

Eugénie, Jason Lindsey's one-woman show about the extravagant wife of Emperor Napoleon III, 'a performance rich in variety of mood, pace, inflexion and salty humour' (*The Independent*, 4 June 1996), between 1979 and 1983 she appeared thrice in London, in several English theatres, in Scotland and Ireland, and in Germany and America. And she played in *Lord Arthur Savile's Crime* (1980) at the Malvern festival and on tour, and in *Uncle Vanya* (1982) at the Haymarket.

Rawlings's few films included *Roman Holiday* (1953), *Hands of the Ripper* (1971), and Carol Reed's *Follow me* (1972). She also played the mother of Dr Jekyll (Michael Caine) in the television film *Jekyll & Hyde* (1990). Her last appearance was in the documentary *The Tales of Helpmann* (1990); she had helped to foster Helpmann's career since seeing him in Australia in 1932. In her later years Rawlings appeared frequently on television and radio, particularly with poetry recitals, on radio. She was a founder member of Equity, and served on its council for thirty years and as vice-president in 1973–4 and 1975–6. Away from acting she pursued a great interest in poetry and in the preservation of the countryside. She died of bronchopneumonia at her home, Rocketer, Rocky Lane, Wendover, near Aylesbury, on 19 May 1996, survived by her daughter.

ROBERT SHARP

Sources WW · *The Times* (4 June 1996) · *The Independent* (4 June 1996) · *Daily Telegraph* (5 June 1996), 29 · *The Guardian* (5 June 1996), 15 · I. Herbert, ed., *Who's who in the theatre*, 17th edn, 2 vols. (1981) · m. certs. · d. cert.
Likenesses photograph, 1931, Hult. Arch. · D. Wilding, photograph, 1933, NPG [*see illus.*] · P. Annigoni, portrait, repro. in *Daily Telegraph* · photograph, repro. in *The Times*

Rawlings, Robert (1742–1816). *See under* Rawlings, Thomas (*c.*1703–1767).

Rawlings [Rawlins], **Thomas** (*c.*1703–1767), musician and music copyist, was born 'about the year 1703' according to information supplied by his grandson to John Sainsbury for his *Dictionary of Musicians* of 1824. It has been suggested that he may have been the son of the instrument maker and seller Mickepher Rawlings (or Rawlins), although no son named Thomas has been traced. He may, instead, have been the Thomas Rawlins, son of John and Martha Rawlins, who was baptized on 17 October 1703 at St Andrew's, Holborn, London.

According to his grandson, Rawlings was a 'scholar of the celebrated Dr [John Christopher] Pepusch', to whom he referred on at least one occasion as 'my Mastr' (Hunt. L., Stowe MS 87, p. 91), and it is likely that he was formally apprenticed to that renowned composer, antiquary, and teacher of music. Rawlings was employed by James Brydges, first duke of Chandos, from Michaelmas 1719 to some time in 1721 as a second violinist in an ensemble directed by Pepusch; his quarterly salary was £7 10s. He continued to work with his teacher in the 1720s at John Rich's theatre in Lincoln's Inn Fields, where Pepusch was music director. Rawlings was a member of the band there by 5 November 1724 and appeared on the theatre's free list in succeeding years, on 19 November 1728 with both his sister and his wife, Elizabeth. No details are known of his wife's background, nor of the date or place of their marriage. In August 1737 he wrote that 'All my little family has been ill' (Rawlings to J. Harris, 13 Aug 1737, Hants. RO, 9M73/G557/1), implying that he had at least two children. These presumably included William, born to Thomas and Elizabeth Rawlins and baptized on 26 August 1732 at St Edmund King and Martyr in Lombard Street, and Ann, who as a married woman was left a bequest of £20 by her godmother, her father's patroness Anne Temple (*née* Halsey), Lady Cobham. The birth of another son named William to Thomas and Elizabeth Rawlins, baptized on 24 November 1738 at St Michael Cornhill, may indicate that the elder William had died. Birth records have not been traced for Thomas Rawlings's son Robert [*see below*], who became a professional musician.

In the 1720s Thomas Rawlings apparently formed a connection with the composer George Frideric Handel, whom he may previously have encountered at Cannons; according to his grandson, he 'performed at almost all Handel's oratorios, operas, &c.' (Rawlings, 2.339). Records of these ensembles are almost completely lacking, but he was listed as a violist in the orchestra for the Foundling Hospital performance of *Messiah* in May 1754. By 1737 he had become music master to Handel's staunch supporter Lady Cobham, the wife of the distinguished general and politician Richard Temple, Viscount Cobham, and he was in August that year resident at the Cobham seat of Stowe, Buckinghamshire. In her will, dated 28 October 1759, Lady Cobham left 'to Mr Rawlins my old harpsicord that is at Stoke [*sic*] and all my Musick Books' (Hunt. L., Stowe Temple MS 16 (12)). Rawlings was also connected with another of Handel's patrons, William Freeman of Hamels, Hertfordshire, who died in 1750 leaving to 'Mr. Thomas Rawlins Musician all my musick' (Matthews, 'The organ').

Rawlings augmented his income as a performer and teacher by working as a music copyist. From correspondence with James Harris of Salisbury and his circle, it is clear that Rawlings was prepared to provide copies of Handel's music at a rate lower than that charged by the composer's principal copyist, John Christopher Smith the elder, and that he copied works from Lady Cobham's collection at Stowe and from material provided by Handel's librettist Charles Jennens.

Rawlings moved to Rich's new theatre in Covent Garden in 1732, and on the one surviving list of theatre musicians dated 22 September 1760 his daily salary was noted as 3s. 4d. He received regular benefit nights at Covent Garden from 1738 to 1766. Rawlings was admitted to the king's musick on 17 January 1736, although he may have been serving as a deputy for some time before that, since payments to him can be traced from the previous year; his annual salary was £40. The mistaken assertion that Rawlings entered the Chapel Royal as a singer in 1737 may derive from the confusion of him with the singer and violinist Peter Randall. On 28 August 1739 Rawlings was one of the original subscribers, together with Handel and Pepusch, to the Fund for Decayed Musicians, later called the Royal Society of Musicians.

According to William H. Husk in the first edition of *Grove's Dictionary of Music and Musicians*, Rawlings was appointed organist at Chelsea Hospital on 14 March 1753. In 1763 *Mortimer's Directory* listed him as a member of the king's band living in Great Russell Street, Bloomsbury. He was replaced in that ensemble on 10 April 1767, and his son William was granted administration of his estate on 6 June 1767. At the time of his death, which occurred in London, Thomas Rawlings was a widower still living in the parish of St George, Bloomsbury.

Thomas Rawlings's son **Robert Rawlings** (1742–1816) followed in his father's footsteps. According to information supplied to Sainsbury by Robert's own son, he was born in London in 1742 and studied music with his father and with the 'old Italian' and 'very celebrated theorist' (Rawlings, 2.339) Barsanti (presumably the composer Francesco Barsanti). He may also have had an early appointment as organist of Chelsea College. At the age of seventeen he was appointed musical page to Prince Edward Augustus, duke of York, with whom he travelled on the continent until the latter's death in 1767. He returned to London, having already become a member of the Royal Society of Musicians on 1 May 1763. According to his son, he was personally appointed by George III as a violinist in the king's musick; the appointment took place on 5 January 1773. He was also, according to his son, appointed to Queen Charlotte's private band. About this time he married his wife, Jane, about whom no details are known beyond her name, revealed by the parish register at the baptism of their son Thomas Augustus Rawlings [*see below*].

By 1783 Robert Rawlings was playing in the orchestra at the King's Theatre in the Haymarket, and in 1784 he was presumably the 'Mr Rawlins' who played second violin in the orchestra for the Handel commemoration. He may also have been the Rawlings listed among the second violins at the King's Theatre and the Pantheon in 1791, and he certainly played for the oratorio season at Covent Garden Theatre in March of that year. In May 1792 he played the violin in the annual benefit concerts at St Paul's Cathedral for the Royal Society of Musicians.

Doane's *Directory* of 1794 listed Robert Rawlings as residing at 15 Paddington Street in the parish of Marylebone and as participating in the king's musick and the Professional Concerts. He continued to play at the benefit concerts for the Royal Society of Musicians at least until 1806. He was replaced in the king's musick on 3 October 1816 and died seven days later; his wife had died before him. The administration of his estate was granted to his son Thomas Augustus Rawlings on 14 January 1817.

Thomas Augustus Rawlings (1774–1849) was born on 18 November 1774 and baptized on 8 December 1774 at St George's, Bloomsbury, the son of Robert Rawlings and his wife, Jane. According to the information he supplied to John Sainsbury, he studied music with his father and for seven years, beginning at the age of thirteen, with the Austrian theorist Joseph Diettenhofer, who settled in London in 1780. As a young man he had some of his works performed at the Professional Concerts and met Franz Joseph Haydn on one of the aged composer's visits to London. By his own account, Thomas Augustus performed as a violinist and cellist for all the London concert organizations, including the opera and the Concerts of Ancient Music. He may also have been the Thomas 'Rawley' who was listed as a member of the king's musick in 1793. On 2 November 1800 his father recommended him for membership in the Royal Society of Musicians, attesting that he 'Plays on the Violin, Tenor & Violoncello & pianoforte' (Matthews, *Royal Society*, 120). He performed at the annual benefit concerts for the Royal Society of Musicians in St Paul's Cathedral in 1811 and 1812.

In the 1790s Rawlings published a number of instrumental works, including a set of three piano sonatas and a concerto for piano, flute, and strings, as well as a *Cantata on the Death of the Late Unfortunate Marie Antoinette, Queen of France*. After 1800 he published mostly songs and smaller piano pieces. A detailed list of his works is given by Sainsbury.

On 11 August 1821 Thomas Augustus Rawlings married Mary Hughes (1787/8–1848) at St Martin-in-the-Fields, and in 1839 he testified to the Royal Society of Musicians that he then had no children under the age of fourteen. He was one of the 100 significant British musicians who responded to Sainsbury's requests for their biographies in 1823, providing valuable information about his father and grandfather. François-Joseph Fétis, another music historian, reported meeting him in London in 1829. His career must have declined subsequently, as in 1838 he began receiving assistance from the Royal Society of Musicians. By the terms of his will, dated 24 November 1840, he left a house at 4 Exeter Row, Fulham, to his wife. He was then living at 20 Paul Street, Portman Market. His wife died at 31 Exeter Street, Lisson Grove, on 22 January 1848 aged sixty; the Royal Society of Musicians provided £8 19s. for her funeral. Rawlings died of dropsy at the same address on 19 January 1849. His will was proved on 30 January 1849, and administration was granted to his executor Susanna Roberts, the widow of William Roberts.

A James Henry Rawlins, who may have been a relation, was recommended for membership in the Royal Society of Musicians on 2 December 1781, his reference asserting that he had served a musical apprenticeship, played the violin, viola, and clarinet, was married, and was then twenty-four years of age. Presumably he was the James Henry Rawlins who had married Mary Mann at St George's, Hanover Square, on 10 December 1776. He was accepted into the society on 3 February 1782. Doane's *Musical Directory* of 1794 lists him as a cellist living at 15 Paddington Street, which was also the address of Robert Rawlings, and credits him with membership in the queen's band and the orchestra for the Handel commemorations in Westminster Abbey (although he is not named as a cellist in Burney's list of participants in 1784). He took part in the benefit concerts for the Royal Society of Musicians in May 1794.

On 7 December 1794 James Henry Rawlins petitioned the Royal Society of Musicians for assistance, stating that he was then the father of one son and five daughters. He continued to receive aid until his death in 1807, and on 6 September 1807 the society gave £8 for his funeral. His widow was given a monthly pension of £2 12s. 6d. until her death, and on 3 July 1819 the society granted £8 for her funeral.   GRAYDON BEEKS

Sources [J. S. Sainsbury], ed., *A dictionary of musicians*, 2 vols. (1825); repr. (New York, 1966) · W. H. Husk, 'Rawlings [Rawlins] family', Grove, *Dict. mus.* (1878–90) · Highfill, Burnim & Langhans, *BDA* · Cannons receipt book for wages, 1718–21, Hunt. L., Stowe MS 87 · will, 28 Oct 1759, Hunt. L., Stowe Temple MS 16 (12) [Anne Temple (*née* Halsey), Lady Cobham] · administration, 6 June 1767, PRO, PROB 6/143, fol. 232v [Thomas Rawlings] · administration, 14 Jan 1817, LMA, DL/C/383/Robert Rawlings/1817/January · will, 24 Nov 1840, and notice of probate of his estate, 30 Jan 1849, LMA, DL/C/409/Thomas Augustus Rawlings/1849/January · *Music and theatre in Handel's world: the family papers of James Harris, 1732–1780*, ed. D. Burrows and R. Dunhill (2002) · private information (2004) [D. Burrows] · B. Matthews, 'The organ in the Oxford Music Room', *The Organ* (Jan 1980), 98 · *IGI* · P. Platt, 'Rawlings [Rawlins]', *New Grove*, 2nd edn · B. Matthews, ed., *The Royal Society of Musicians of Great Britain: list of members, 1738–1984* (1985) · *Mortimer's Directory* (1763)
Archives Hants. RO, corresp. with J. Harris · U. Glas., letter to J. Sainsbury [Thomas Augustus Rawlings]
Wealth at death £1500—Robert Rawlings

Rawlings, Thomas Augustus (1774–1849). *See under* Rawlings, Thomas (*c.*1703–1767).

Rawlins, Richard (*c.*1460–1536), college head and bishop of St David's, was elected bachelor of Merton College in 1480. In 1484 he incepted MA and became a fellow, subsequently serving as the college's almoner, dean, and (in 1492) king of the beans, master of the Christmas revels. He was admitted BTh in 1493 and had his doctorate by 1495. On 1 March 1488 Rawlins was ordained acolyte to the title of his fellowship in the chapel of Durham College, the Oxford house of the Benedictines of Durham Priory; he became deacon on 19 December 1489 and was priested on 6 March 1490. He then embarked on a lucrative clerical career centred on London and the court. Admitted rector of St Mary Woolnoth in 1494, Rawlins became a canon of St Paul's (with the prebend of Willesdon) in 1499 and vicar of Hendon in 1504. He collected several further benefices, including canonries both of Howden, Yorkshire (presented 1506), and St George's Chapel, Windsor (appointed 1508). As chaplain to the king, Rawlins attended Henry VII's funeral and distributed several hundred pounds' worth of alms. He preached at the funeral of the infant Prince Henry in 1511, and was among those who received 20s. for preaching in 1521; his fellow royal chaplain and immediate successor as warden of Merton, Rowland Philipps, appears as vicar of Croydon in the same list.

On 17 February 1509 Rawlins was admitted warden of Merton, his return to college celebrated with a service in chapel, a play in the hall, and drinking and part songs. Judging by the theologically conservative standards of Richard Fitzjames, warden between 1483 and 1507, Richard Rawlins was a cautious reformer. But he maintained good relations with Fitzjames, by now bishop of London, lending him two censers and other plate from his own

household in 1516. Rawlins's impact as warden is best measured by the college fabric. He presented a 1505 Venetian edition of Euclid's *Elementa* to the library, and constructed the bridge from the hall to the sacristy tower which still bears his punning rebus, the letters 'RAW' with some lines carved beneath. New heraldic windows were installed in the hall on Richard Nele's benefaction in 1517; one of these 'glasyngs', the arms of the see of Rochester impaling those invented for Walter de Merton, survives in the chapel. The following year Katherine of Aragon visited the college during her pilgrimage to the shrine of St Frideswide, prompting a rather gushing speech from Rawlins comparing the queen to Juno and Minerva. He was well known to the king, accompanying Henry VIII to France in 1513 and again in 1520. Perhaps this familiarity provoked envy among the fellows; certainly they resented his periods of absence from college. In winter 1520–21 Rawlins was accused of misappropriating revenues and alienating land. He had evidently struck a private deal with Bishop Richard Fox of Winchester, whose new foundation of Corpus Christi was arising on Merton property next to the college in return for an annual rent of £4 6s. 8d. (a sum still paid to Merton each Lady day). Rawlins also, the fellows added peevishly, kept three unauthorized horses in his stables. The warden blustered, refused to co-operate with the archbishop's commissary who had been sent to investigate, and was finally deposed by Warham in his capacity as the college visitor on 19 September 1521.

His Oxford career over, Rawlins was forced to look further afield for a position of equivalent rank. He found it in St David's, the largest of the Welsh sees: its cathedral housed the shrine of the national saint and drew in many pilgrims. Rawlins was consecrated bishop of St David's at Lambeth on 26 April 1523. He was now in advancing years, and any earlier interest in the cause of reform had deserted him. Although Rawlins took the 1534 oath renouncing papal jurisdiction, he resented the imposition of the evangelical zealot William Barlow as prior of Haverfordwest that same summer. Bishop Rawlins's resistance to the protestant prior's anti-papal good news goaded Barlow into a general denunciation of the 'enormous vices, fraudulent exactions, misordered living and heathen idolatry' of the diocese (Williams, 64). Worse was to come in 1535, when Cromwell appointed Barlow as suffragan bishop. Rawlins found himself forced to define his opinion on the fate of souls: while 'not minding to revive again a popish purgatory' of candles and paternosters before altars, he restated his belief that it was meet to pray for the souls of the dead (*LP Henry VIII*, 10, no. 225). The final indignity came after Rawlins's death on 15 February 1536: William Barlow was his successor at St David's.

The British Library catalogue attributes one letter to Richard Rawlins. Addressed to Warham and dated 14 June 1527, it refers approvingly to the archbishop's recent campaign to buy up 'all the bokes of the newe testamente translated into Englisshe and prynted beyonde the see' (*BL cat.*), principally William Tyndale's 1526 Worms edition, in order to destroy them. The writer, certainly a bishop, subscribed 10 marks to offset Warham's expenses of £66 9s. 4d. and sent a note of congratulation: 'Surely in myn opynion you have done therin a graciouse and a blessed dede and god I doubt not shall highly rewarde you therfore' (BL, Cotton Vitellius B.ix., fol. 131). The signature is indistinct, but bears similarities to that of Richard Nix, bishop of Norwich (d. 1535). Nix was a staunch opponent of Lollardy; the source of the letter (Hoxne in north Suffolk, where Nix had his palace and from which he addressed most of his correspondence in his last years) confirms that he, and not Rawlins, was Warham's correspondent.   J. P. D. COOPER

Sources Emden, Oxf., 3.1551–2 · Wood, Ath. Oxon., new edn, 2.743–4 · LP Henry VIII · BL, MS Cotton Vitellius B.ix., fol. 131 · BL, Lansdowne MS 979, fol. 116 · G. H. Martin and J. R. L. Highfield, A history of Merton College (1997) · G. Williams, Wales and the Reformation (1997) · A. Bott, 'The coats of arms of Walter de Merton and his college', Postmaster and the Merton Record (1997), 73–9 · Hist. U. Oxf. 3: Colleg. univ., 491, 496 · D. MacCulloch, Suffolk and the Tudors: politics and religion in an English county, 1500–1600 (1986), 49

Rawlins, Thomas (c.1620–1670), engraver, medallist, and playwright, is of unknown origin. Best known for his skills and services as an engraver, he initially made his name as a playwright in 1640 when he published The Rebellion, a tragedy set in Seville, which he dedicated to Robert Ducie of Aston, Staffordshire, a relative. The title was to prove prophetic, since it was during the 'great rebellion' that he achieved prominence as an engraver and medallist. This occupation commanded his full attention, and it is not known when the two comedies published after his death were written. Tom Essence, or, The Modish Life was licensed to be performed at Dorset Gardens on 4 November 1676 and printed in 1677, and Tunbridge Wells, or, A Day's Courtship was printed in 1678. A series of poems entitled Calanthe of 1648, signed 'T.R.', are attributed to him, and he also wrote verses to introduce Nathaniel Richards's Messallina and Richard Lovelace's Lucasta.

Rawlins is believed to have served as an apprentice goldsmith and gem-engraver in London before taking employment at the royal mint working under Nicholas Briot, the renowned French engraver and medallist who went to England in 1626. His earliest known work is a medal of William Wade of 1641. At the commencement of the civil war the Tower mint came under the control of parliament. The king initially settled at Shrewsbury and, anxious to establish a mint, ordered Thomas Bushell to come up from Aberystwyth with all dies, puncheons, and machinery from that mint, which had been established in 1637 as a satellite to the Tower to coin the Welsh silver. After three months Charles I moved to Oxford, to which place members of the Tower mint loyal to him repaired: Thomas Rawlins was one and Sir William Parkhurst, warden of the mint, was another. On 3 January 1643 the equipment from Shrewsbury arrived at Oxford, where Rawlins was to do his best work. Plate, both gold and silver, was ordered in or voluntarily supplied by the king's adherents to be melted for coining. To accomplish this as expeditiously as possible, the largest denominations hitherto

current in both gold and silver were struck. These were the gold triple unite (a £3 piece) and the silver pound and half-pound pieces, all of which had initially been produced at Shrewsbury by Bushell.

Rawlins was appointed graver of seals, stamps, and medals at Oxford in 1643. While he was responsible for all denominations, his best works were the pound and crown of 1644, the former showing the king riding a spirited horse over arms and armour and his declaration in a cartouche on the reverse with the date below, and the latter showing the king riding over a view of the city of Oxford, the declaration within scrolls, the date in script, and 'OXON' below. This fine piece, comparable to continental city thalers, has become known as the 'celebrated Oxford crown'. Rawlins was appointed chief engraver at the Tower and elsewhere in 1645.

Rawlins also produced medals and badges at Oxford, significant being the gold Shrewsbury medal commissioned on 23 January 1643 for award to a select few who had afforded considerable support to the king while he was there. The obverse depicted the conjoined busts of Charles I and Charles, prince of Wales, and was used again to produce the 'forlorn hope badge', which was commissioned on 18 May 1643, taking the form of a uniface silver cliché with holes pierced near its edge to enable it to be stitched to the tunics of all who served in that body. By a commission of 1 June 1643 it finally formed the obverses of the gold medals awarded to Captain Sir John Smith and Lieutenant Sir Robert Welch for their retrieval of the royal standard at Edgehill: the reverses were named to the recipients. Rawlins produced a medal for the reunion of the king and queen at Kineton on 13 July 1643 and the 'peace or war medal', showing an olive branch and sword crossed, on the fall of Bristol to Prince Rupert on 26 July. In 1644 he produced a portrait medal of Sir William Parkhurst, showing him holding one of Rawlins's civil war badges. Rawlins produced a series of badges which were cast and chased and may have been awarded for acts of valour or merely made for wear by the king's supporters.

Oxford surrendered on 24 June 1646. Little is known of Rawlins's movements during the next year or so, but he surfaced to produce badges and medals in memory of Charles I. It seems he then went to France, but he did return to England and is known to have been imprisoned for debt. At the Restoration he was restored as chief engraver, with appropriate lodgings, and produced a medal for the coronation. Thomas Simon, however, was responsible for the great seal and the hammered coinage of the first two years and was himself eclipsed by John Roettier, who was responsible for the milled coinage introduced in 1662 and most of the subsequent medals. Rawlins's incarceration for debt is thus perhaps explained by a seeming lack of employment during the interregnum.

Little is known of Rawlins's private life other than that he married Dorothea Narbona. He died in 1670, presumably in London. His signature was variously 'T. Rawlins', 'T.R.', or 'R.'. The last has caused confusion because it was also the signature of David Ramage, an engraver to the Commonwealth, who produced a number of farthing tokens and was known as the farthing maker.

MICHAEL SHARP

Sources L. Forrer, *Biographical dictionary of medallists*, 8 vols. (1904–30) • E. Hawkins, *Medallic illustrations of the history of Great Britain and Ireland*, 2 vols. (1885) • H. Farquhar, 'The Shrewsbury medal', *British Numismatic Journal*, 18 (1925–6), 125–34 • E. Besly, *Coins and medals of the English Civil War* (1990) • *DNB* • E. Besly, '"To reward their deservings": the badge for the forlorn hope', *The Medal*, 19 (1991), 20–27
Archives Bodl. Oxf., literary corresp.

Rawlinson, Alfred Edward John [Jack] (1884–1960), bishop of Derby and theologian, was born at Park Road, Newton-le-Willows, Lancashire, on 17 July 1884, the first son of Alfred John Rawlinson (b. 1865), accountant, and his second wife, Anna Margaret Marshall of Sekondi, Gold Coast. After education at Dulwich College, in 1900–03, he became an exhibitioner and later scholar at Corpus Christi College, Oxford. Although his parents were Congregationalists he adopted a non-dogmatic Anglo-Catholicism at Oxford. After graduating with a first in mods and Greats in 1907, he won the Liddon and Denyer and Johnson scholarships, achieving a first in theology in 1908. He trained at Cuddesdon and was ordained to a tutorship at Keble in 1909, where he contributed to the controversial volume *Foundations* (1912). In 1913 he became lecturer in theology, and from 1914 to 1929 was student and tutor, at Christ Church. He was a popular tutor, visited by students with religious doubts who 'soon discovered that their … uncertainties were but a drop in the bucket compared with his, and departed much reassured' (H. Chadwick, 446). He was chaplain to the forces during 1915–17, becoming priest-in-charge of St John's, Wilton Road, London (1917–18). In 1919 he married Mildred Ansley Ellis ('Cuckoo'), daughter of the Revd Ansley Ellis, a missionary with the Society for the Propagation of the Gospel.

During the 1920s Rawlinson gave the Paddock lectures, published as *Authority and Freedom*, in New York (1923), contributed to *Essays Catholic and Critical* (1926), and edited *Essays on the Trinity and the Incarnation* (1928). He was well versed in German theology, assessing both Catholic modernism and liberal protestantism in his Bampton lectures, *The New Testament Doctrine of Christ* (1926). In 1925 he published his widely read textual commentary on St Mark, one of the first 'form-critical' works in English. He took part in the Anglo-German theological conferences at Canterbury (1925), Wartburg (1928), and Chichester (1931), and continued to write on the authority of the church. He was much in demand as a lecturer and preacher, becoming select preacher at both Oxford (1923–5, 1941–2) and Cambridge (1924, 1928, 1937). He was awarded DDs at Oxford (1925) and Durham (1931), and served on the archbishops' doctrine commission from 1922. Nevertheless, he failed to secure both the Oxford Lady Margaret chair in 1927 (losing by two votes to his friend N. P. Williams) and the regius chair in 1943.

In 1929 Rawlinson became archdeacon of Auckland and canon of Durham under Hensley Henson, who found him 'able and amiable' (Henson, 2.250). Rawlinson's brand of liberal Catholicism, which denied any claim to absolute truth, made him a natural ecumenist, and in 1934 he helped establish ecumenical relations with the Finnish church. In 1936 he became second bishop of Derby, one of the few theologians on the bench. According to Michael Ramsey, 'If you walked from Humber to Severn and dodged Derby, you would not find a bishop who could read or write' (O. Chadwick, 76). His primary charge called for increased clergy discipline, which helped make him unpopular in the diocese. He seldom visited rural parishes and often dealt with pastoral matters in a heavy-handed fashion. He continued to play a leading role in ecumenical discussions with the free churches and the Church of Scotland, staunchly defended the Church of South India scheme, and was an official delegate to the Russian Orthodox church in 1956. He was a frequent speaker in the House of Lords, where, although maintaining conservative attitudes on moral issues, he was outspoken on social issues. He retired on 11 April 1959, dying at St Bartholomew's Hospital, London, on 17 July 1960. His ashes were interred at Derby Cathedral on 17 September.

Throughout his life Rawlinson remained a scholar, displaying an aloofness and shyness which made him unsuited to episcopal life. He was a man of contradictions: although he taught a liberal theology of authority he exercised episcopal authoritarianism; although he stressed religious experience, he was 'without an ounce of mysticism' (Dell, 154). A man of small stature, he was often overshadowed by his wife, an extrovert and dominant personality. Potentially one of the leading theologians of his generation, he was not served well by either his church or university.

MARK D. CHAPMAN

Sources R. Dell, *John Rawlinson: honest thinker* (1998) • *The Times* (20 July 1960) • *Church Times* (22 July 1960) • *Derby Diocesan Leaflet* (Sept 1960) • R. D. Whitehorn, recollections, *The Times* (20 July 1960) • Canon Busby, recollections, *The Times* (22 July 1960) • P. S. Richards, recollections, *Pelican Record*, 33 (1959–61), 90 • P. A. Hunt, *Corpus Christi College biographical register*, ed. N. A. Flanagan (1988) • H. H. Henson, *Retrospect of an unimportant life*, 3 vols. (1942–50) • H. Chadwick, *Theology*, 65 (1962), 446 • O. Chadwick, *Michael Ramsey: a life* (1991) • E. Carpenter, *Archbishop Fisher: his life and times* (1991) • J. K. Mozley, *Some tendencies in British theology* (1951) • A. M. Ramsey, *From Gore to Temple* (1960) • *The Anglican community in Christendom* (1960) [bibliography] • M. D. Chapman, 'Rawlinson, Alfred Edward John', *Biographisch-Bibliographisches Kirchenlexikon*, 6 (1993), 1426–9 • *CGPLA Eng. & Wales* (1960)
Archives Derby Cathedral, Rawlinson Library, papers | Dulwich College, London, archives
Likenesses photographs, Derby Cathedral, Rawlinson Library • portrait, Derby Cathedral Song School
Wealth at death £12,533 8s. 7d.: probate, 3 Oct 1960, *CGPLA Eng. & Wales*

Rawlinson, Christopher (1677–1733), antiquary, was born at Springfield, Essex, on 13 June 1677, the second son of Curwen Rawlinson (1641–1689), landowner and MP, of Carke Hall in Cartmel, Lancashire, and his wife, Elizabeth (d. 1691), daughter of Nicholas *Monck, bishop of Hereford. He matriculated from Queen's College, Oxford, on 14 June 1695; there he was one of the group of Anglo-Saxon scholars who worked with Edward Thwaites, fellow of the college. He published in 1698 an edition of King Alfred's translation of Boethius, *De consolationis philosophiæ*, from a transcript made by Francis Junius (Bodl. Oxf., MS Junius 12); this was printed at Oxford University Press with the Junian types. Thwaites dedicated his *Grammatica Anglo-Saxonica ex Hickesiano thesauro excerpta* to Rawlinson in 1711.

Rawlinson, having inherited his father's estates, died unmarried and intestate in Holborn Row, London, on 8 January 1733; he was buried in the abbey church of St Albans, Hertfordshire, on 31 January. His landed estates passed to the children of his father's sisters Anne and Katherine. The furniture of Carke Hall was sold by auction and his manuscripts were disposed of in bundles and bought for pence by the villagers. Rawlinson had made valuable collections for the history of Lancashire, Westmorland, and Cumberland, none of which appear to have survived. Sir Daniel Fleming had however copied extracts from the portion relating to Westmorland, and these extracts, in the collection of manuscripts at Rydal Hall, were used by Joseph Nicolson and R. Burn in their *History and Antiquities of the Counties of Westmorland and Cumberland* (1777). W. W. WROTH, *rev.* MARY CLAPINSON

Sources J. Stockdale, *Annales Caermoelenses, or, Annals of Cartmel* (1872), 457–60 · T. D. Whitaker, *An history of the original parish of Whalley*, rev. J. G. Nichols and P. A. Lyons, 4th edn, 2 (1876), 591 · J. Nicolson and R. Burn, *The history and antiquities of the counties of Westmorland and Cumberland*, 1 (1777) · E. Baines and W. R. Whatton, *The history of the county palatine and duchy of Lancaster*, rev. edn, ed. J. Harland and B. Herford, 2 (1870), 668 · Nichols, *Lit. anecdotes*, 4.146 · *GM*, 1st ser., 3 (1733), 45 · Foster, *Alum. Oxon.*

Likenesses J. Smith, mezzotint, 1701 (after A. Grace), BM, NPG · J. Nutting, engraving, Bodl. Oxf.

Rawlinson, Sir Christopher (1806–1888), judge in India, was born at Combe, Hampshire, on 10 July 1806, the second son of John Rawlinson (1777/8–1847), of the Middle Temple and Combe and Alresford, Hampshire, police magistrate at Marylebone, Middlesex, and his wife, Felicia, *née* Watson. He was educated at Charterhouse School, London (January 1819 to December 1823) and at Trinity College, Cambridge (matriculated 1824, BA 1828, MA 1831). Admitted at the Middle Temple on 28 March 1828 and called to the bar on 25 November 1831, he joined the western circuit in 1832, and was recorder of Portsmouth from 1840 to 1847. On 27 May 1847 he married Georgina Maria, younger daughter of Alexander Radclyffe Sidebottom, barrister; they had three sons and one daughter.

Rawlinson was recorder of Prince of Wales Island, Singapore, and Malacca from March 1847 to April 1850. On 24 February 1847 he was knighted. From April 1850 he was chief justice of the supreme court of judicature at Madras until he retired in 1859. In his charge to the grand jury on 5 January 1859 he expressed his belief that great benefits would accrue from the recent transfer of the government of India from the East India Company to the crown, and denied the assertion then commonly made by British officials in India, that no materials for self-government existed there. On 9 February 1859 he was presented with a farewell address by the Indian community of Madras at an

entertainment at which the governor, Lord Harris, was present.

Rawlinson published *The Municipal Corporation Act 5 & 6 Will. IV c. 76* (1842 and later editions). He died at his home, 33 Eaton Square, London, on 28 March 1888.

Rawlinson's eldest son, Christopher Rawlinson (1850–1916), was born in London on 13 March 1850, educated at Winchester College and Trinity College, Cambridge (BA 1871, MA 1874), admitted at the Inner Temple on 9 April 1870, and called to the bar on 26 January 1874. He was on the western circuit, became a revising barrister in 1883, and died on 2 September 1916. The second son, Albemarle Alexander Rawlinson (1853–1930), was born in Madras on 27 September 1853 and educated at Winchester. He was admitted at Trinity College, Cambridge, in 1872, but left for the 18th hussars (sub-lieutenant 1874, major 1883) and served in the Second Anglo-Afghan War. He died on 25 September 1930 at Shiplake, Oxfordshire.

The youngest son, John Frederick Peel Rawlinson (1860–1926), was born at Airsford on 21 December 1860 and educated at Eton College and Trinity Hall, Cambridge (LLB 1883, LLM 1887, honorary LLD 1920). He was an association football blue and played for England in 1882. He was admitted at the Inner Temple on 18 June 1881 and called to the bar on 25 June 1884; he was appointed QC in 1897, bencher in 1907. He represented the Treasury in the inquiry after the Jameson raid. He was recorder of Cambridge from 1906 to 1926, and Conservative MP for Cambridge University from 1906 until his death, unmarried, on 14 January 1926.

STEPHEN WHEELER, *rev.* ROGER T. STEARN

Sources *The Times* (2 April 1888) · *Madras Standard* (10 Jan 1859) · Venn, *Alum. Cant.* · [R. L. Arrowsmith], ed., *Charterhouse register, June 1769–May 1872* (1964) · H. A. C. Sturgess, ed., *Register of admissions to the Honourable Society of the Middle Temple, from the fifteenth century to the year 1944*, 2 (1949) · J. Hutchinson, ed., *A catalogue of notable Middle Templars: with brief biographical notices* (1902) · Boase, *Mod. Eng. biog.* · *WWW, 1916–28* · *WWBMP*, vol. 3 · J. Foster, *Men-at-the-bar: a biographical hand-list of the members of the various inns of court*, 2nd edn (1885)

Wealth at death £147,301 7s. 4d.: probate, 27 April 1888, CGPLA Eng. & Wales

Rawlinson, George (1812–1902), historian and Church of England clergyman, born on 23 November 1812 at Chadlington, Oxfordshire, was the third son of Abram Tyzack Rawlinson (1777–1845), a landowner and racehorse breeder, and his wife, Eliza Eudocia Albinia (d. 1863), daughter of Henry Creswicke of Morton, Worcester. Sir Henry Creswicke *Rawlinson, first baronet, was his brother. Educated at Swansea grammar school and at Ealing School, he matriculated in 1834 at Trinity College, Oxford, as a commoner, and in 1838 took a first class in the final school of classics, graduating BA in that year and proceeding MA in 1841. He played for Oxford in the cricket match with Cambridge in 1836 and was president of the Oxford Union Society in 1840. He was elected fellow of Exeter College in 1840 and tutor in 1841. In 1841 and 1842 he was ordained deacon and priest, and gained the Denyer prize for a theological essay twice—in 1842 and 1843. He vacated his fellowship and tutorship on his marriage (6

July 1846) to Louisa Wildman, daughter of Sir Robert Alexander *Chermside. They had four sons and five daughters.

Rawlinson remained prominent in university affairs. He was one of the first moderators (1852–4) in the newly organized intermediate examination of classical moderations and was an examiner in *literae humaniores* (Greats) in 1854, 1856, and 1867. He was interested in the relations between the university and the city, serving as a poor-law guardian from 1860 to 1863, and was a founder member of the Oxford Political Economy Club. He was particularly active on the committee of the Oxford Tutors' Association, which was revived in 1852 following the report of the royal commission on the university. Resisting the commissioners' proposals for strengthening the professoriate on German lines, the association defended the college system and tutorial teaching. On 20 December 1853, together with W. C. Lake, he put the views of the association to Gladstone in person, and thus had an important influence in shaping the Oxford University Act of 1854. Gladstone's interest in Rawlinson, with whom he frequently corresponded, was said to date from this interview.

During the 1850s Rawlinson prepared his best-known work, an English translation of *The History of Herodotus* (4 vols., 1858–60), which was dedicated to Gladstone. The annotations, in which he was assisted by his brother and Sir J. Gardner Wilkinson, who produced important supplementary essays, drew upon advances in Egyptology and Assyriology. The work reached a third edition in 1875 and was reprinted in Everyman's Library (1910). At the same time he was the champion of a learned orthodoxy in theology. His Bampton lectures in 1859, published as *The Historical Evidences of the Truth of the Scripture Records Stated Anew* (1859; 2nd edn, 1860), which defended the scriptures against the findings of modern criticism, received a critical review by Rowland Williams (*Westminster Review*, July 1860). He also contributed an article, 'On the genuineness and authenticity of the Pentateuch', to *Aids to Faith* (1861), the high-church counterblast to the liberal *Essays and Reviews*. His orthodox churchmanship was a factor in his election by Oxford's largely clerical convocation to the Camden chair of ancient history in October 1861.

As professor Rawlinson was a prolific author of scholarly summaries of the results of research and archaeological excavations in the Middle East, which remained standard during his lifetime. His *Five Great Monarchies of the Ancient Eastern World* (4 vols., 1862–7; 2nd edn, 3 vols., 1871) surveyed what was then known of the histories of Chaldea, Assyria, Babylonia, Media, and Persia. It was followed by similar works on Parthia (1873), the Sassanid empire (1876), ancient Egypt (1881), and Phoenicia (1889). He used archaeological evidence to support orthodox scriptural interpretation, contributing the essay 'The alleged historical difficulties of the Old and New Testaments' for the volume of *Modern Scepticism* (1871), produced by the Christian Evidence Society. As a biblical commentator and expositor he wrote on several Old Testament books for the Speaker's Commentary edited by F. C. Cook (1871–88) and for the Old Testament commentary edited by C. J. Ellicott (1884–92).

In 1872, on Gladstone's recommendations, Rawlinson was made a canon of Canterbury, where he lived until his death, though he retained his Oxford chair (which carried, until 1882, the comparatively small stipend of £140 a year). His connections with the university were much reduced and he played little part in the creation of a major school of ancient history at Oxford in the latter part of the century, which was largely the work of college tutors. Ironically, in view of his earlier advocacy of tutorial interests, he complained to the 1877 statutory commission that as professor he was virtually excluded from undergraduate teaching and examining. In 1885 no students attended his termly courses, and he stated that he regarded his main contribution to his discipline as writing books. For their part tutors circulated tales of his unwillingness to attract students; one story had it that after advertising a course of lectures outside the area in which undergraduates needed to study for their examinations, he would peer out from his window in the King's Arms Hotel, where he stayed on his rare visits to the university, to check that no auditors had come to hear his first lecture and then promptly leave the city until the start of the next term (Jones, 190). He eventually resigned the Camden chair in 1889.

At Canterbury, also, Rawlinson's position was questioned, as canons were increasingly expected to assume diocesan and parochial duties. At the 1889 visitation he defended his academic role within the cathedral, listing the numerous theological books he had published during his tenure of the canonry, and pointed out that at the time of his appointment it was intended that he should devote his time to literary work. He suffered from an indistinctiveness of speech, which made him a poor preacher. In 1888 the cathedral chapter presented him to the wealthy living of All Hallows, Lombard Street; he later made valuable gifts to the cathedral. The last of his many published works was a life of his brother (1898). He was a fellow of the Royal Geographical Society, and a corresponding member of the Royal Academy of Turin and the American Philosophical Society. Rawlinson died at his home in the precincts, Canterbury, on 6 October 1902, his health having given way two years earlier. He was buried in Holywell cemetery, Oxford.

RONALD BAYNE, *rev.* M. C. CURTHOYS

Sources *The Times* (7 Oct 1902) · *The Athenaeum* (11 Oct 1902), 486 · *Men and women of the time* (1899) · Burke, *Peerage* · W. R. Ward, *Victorian Oxford* (1965) · H. S. Jones, 'The foundation and history of the Camden chair', *Oxoniensia*, 8–9 (1943–4), 169–92 · P. Collinson, P. N. Ramsay, and M. Sparks, eds., *A history of Canterbury Cathedral* (1995) · O. Murray, 'The beginnings of Greats, 1800–1872: ancient history', *Hist. U. Oxf. 6: 19th-cent. Oxf.*, 520–42 · Gladstone, *Diaries*
Archives BL, corresp. with W. E. Gladstone, Add. MS 44282 · Bodl. Oxf., corresp. (incl. some copies) with Sir J. G. Wilkinson and papers relating to his edition of Herodotus' *Histories*
Likenesses J. W. Forster, oils, 1897, Trinity College, Oxford
Wealth at death £8675 7s.: probate, 29 Oct 1902, CGPLA Eng. & Wales

Rawlinson, Sir **Henry Creswicke**, first baronet (1810–1895), Assyriologist and diplomatist, was born at Chadlington, Oxfordshire, on 11 April 1810 into a north Lancashire family. He was the second son of Abram Tyzack Rawlinson, a breeder of racehorses, who married Eliza Eudocia Albinia Creswicke, of Gloucestershire, and settled in Chadlington in 1805. Educated at Wrington in Somerset and at a well-reputed school in Ealing, Rawlinson was entered for the East India Company's service and set out for India in 1827, sailing in the company of Sir John Malcolm, the well-known diplomatist and oriental scholar whose influence on him was profound. He outdistanced all his contemporaries in the acquisition of Persian and Indian vernacular languages. He received early promotion and was recognized as a smart officer, an outstanding horseman, and an exceptional linguist. From 1833 to 1839 with others he was engaged in reorganizing the Persian army. During this time he undertook tours in Susiana and Persian Kurdistan, for which explorations he was awarded the gold medal of the Royal Geographical Society in 1839. He returned to India and was appointed assistant to Sir W. Macnaughton in Afghanistan, where he saw much action and fought with distinction in 1842 at Kandahar, where he had become political agent for lower Afghanistan. These operations marked the successful end of his military career.

In 1843 Rawlinson was appointed political agent of the East India Company in Turkish Arabia and a year later also consul in Baghdad. His account of the cuneiform inscriptions of Bisitun was published in the *Journal of the Royal Asiatic Society* in 1846, after a close and difficult examination of the site, which he had first inspected in 1836. He was elected a member of the society in 1847, and contributed many papers to its journals and addressed many of its meetings on different subjects of historical and literary importance. He was director of the society from 1862 until his death, and president from 1878 to 1881. He was also a long-time member and president of the Royal Geographical Society, and a contributor to its journal. Moreover, his brother George *Rawlinson acknowledges in his *History of Herodotus* (the first volume of which was published in 1858) that 'Sir Henry exercised a general supervision over the Oriental portion of the work', which was crucial to its success. It was said of him: 'Few have left such a roll of continuous literary activity', particularly when he was a man of action rather than of the study. He was promoted to the post of consul-general in 1851 in Baghdad and was involved with Sir Henry Layard in his Assyrian excavations; when he came home in 1856 he was made a KCB.

Rawlinson is often referred to as the decipherer of cuneiform Akkadian, but this owes much to the adulatory biography published after his death by his scholar brother, George, and to his friendship with Sir Wallis Budge. In fact Rawlinson, though a fine scholar in Persian and Indian languages, was not well equipped to do so since he had no training in Semitic languages nor had he followed the decipherment of Egyptian hieroglyphs. He made copies of the old Persian rock inscription at Bisitun in 1836–7, but the similar inscriptions from Persepolis had already been deciphered in part in 1805 by Grotefend, whose work became available in English in 1833. Rawlinson's copy from Bisitun with an edition was published in 1847, by which time Edward *Hincks, a poor clergyman in co. Down eighteen years his senior, had already solved the main problems in the old Persian script. The two men were rivals in deciphering Akkadian cuneiform, both the language and the script. Rawlinson made a copy of the Akkadian version from the Bisitun trilingual inscription in 1847 and published it in 1852, but was hindered by treating the signs as alphabetic, while Hincks had already discovered their syllabic and logographic functions, thanks partly to his familiarity with Egyptian, and partly to his understanding of Semitic grammar. Layard, excavator of Nineveh, shared his finds with both scholars, and Rawlinson was put in charge of excavations when Hormuzd Rassam took over as field director. Rawlinson entered the competition organized at the Royal Asiatic Society in 1857 to submit a sealed translation of an Assyrian inscription, as did Hincks, Fox Talbot, and Jules Oppert. The four results were sufficiently alike to show that basic decipherment had genuinely been achieved. Rawlinson actively suppressed Hincks's work on Akkadian inscriptions in the British Museum, where he had a powerful ally in Budge. His disparagement of Assyrian art and architecture, his treatment of Rassam as an inferior and a foreigner, and his failure to deliver the results of his work to Layard eventually caused Layard to prefer Hincks, whom Rawlinson unjustifiably called 'an unscrupulous poacher'. Rawlinson was anxious to prove his own priority in discoveries, and claimed credit for others' work on several occasions: the five great volumes *The Cuneiform Inscriptions of Western Asia*, published under his name between 1861 and 1884, were in fact mainly the work of Edwin Norris, George Smith, and Theophilus Pinches.

Rawlinson was returned on 4 February 1858 as conservative MP for Reigate, and was member for Frome from 1865 to 1868. On 12 September 1858 he became a member of the newly created Council of India but resigned on being appointed minister to Persia with the rank of major-general. His uncompromising attitude towards Russia led to his resignation the following year, though he attended the shah, Nasir al-Din, during his visits to England in 1873 and 1889, and maintained good relations with him. His publication of *England and Russia in the East* (1875) stirred controversy with its outspokenness. He served as a trustee of the British Museum from 1876 to 1895. He was a commissioner for the Paris Universal Exhibition of 1878 and the Indian and Colonial Exhibition of 1886. He was president of the London Oriental Congress in 1874. He received many academic awards in this country and abroad. He was given the grand cross of the Bath on 23 July 1889, and created a baronet on 6 February 1891 on Lord Salisbury's recognition of 'his distinguished service to the state, stretching over a long series of years'.

On 2 September 1862 Rawlinson married Louisa Caroline (d. 1889), daughter of Henry Seymour of Knoyle, Wiltshire; they had two sons, of whom Henry Seymour *Rawlinson succeeded to the baronetcy. Rawlinson died on 5

March 1895 at his London home, 21 Charles Street, Berkeley Square. Among contemporaries, he enjoyed a fine reputation and though to some he seemed imperious in manner, others found his company 'delightful and profitable', and convivial without pretension. His undoubted energy, wealth, scholarship in languages, and high social standing promoted public interest in Assyriology, and gives reason for Budge, in *The Rise and Progress of Assyriology* (1925), to call him 'the father of Assyriology'.

R. W. Ferrier and Stephanie Dalley

Sources G. Rawlinson, *Memoir of Major-General Sir Henry Creswicke Rawlinson* (1898) · R. Crust, 'Sir Henry Rawlinson', *Journal of the Royal Asiatic Society* (July 1895), 681–90 · E. A. W. Budge, *The rise and progress of Assyriology* (1925) · G. Waterfield, *Layard of Nineveh* (1963) · J. Wiesehafer, *Ancient Persia* (1996) · C. B. E. Walker, 'Cuneiform', *Reading the past*, ed. J. T. Hooker (1990), 56–62 · R. Borger, *Handbuch der Keilschrift literatur I* (1967) · M. T. Larsen, *The conquest of Assyria* (1994) · P. T. Daniels, 'Edward Hincks's decipherment of Mesopotamian cuneiform', *The Edward Hincks bicentenary lectures*, ed. K. J. Cathcart (1994), 30–35 · *DNB*

Archives BL, corresp. and notebooks, Add. MSS 47619–47662 · RGS, corresp. and MSS · Royal Asiatic Society, London, corresp., journals, and MSS | BL, corresp. with Sir Austen Layard, Add. MSS 38976–39120, *passim* | BL OIOC, letters to H. H. Wilson, MS Eur. E. 301 · Bodl. Oxf., corresp. with Lord Kimberley · Hove Central Library, Sussex, letters to Viscount Wolseley · NA Scot., corresp. with Sir Charles Murray · NAM, letters to Earl Roberts · PRO, corresp. with Sir Arthur Nicholson, PRO 30/81

Likenesses R. C. Lucas, medallion, wax, 1850, NPG · S. Cousins, print, mezzotint, 1860 (after H. W. Phillips), NPG · Erns and Edwards, photograph, 1864, NPG · F. Holl, portrait, oils, 1881, Corsham Court, Wiltshire · Lock and Whitfield, photograph, 1882, NPG · Spy [L. Ward], caricature, watercolour, repro. in *VF* (12 July 1873) · engraving (after H. W. Phillips), Royal Asiatic Society, London · photograph, NPG · print, wood-engraving (after photograph by Elliott and Fry), repro. in *ILN* (12 July 1873)

Wealth at death £18,693 3s. 4d.: probate, 3 May 1895, *CGPLA Eng. & Wales*

Rawlinson, Henry Seymour, Baron Rawlinson (1864–1925), army officer, was the elder son of Sir Henry Creswicke *Rawlinson, first baronet (1810–1895), and his wife, Louisa (*d.* 1889), daughter of Henry Seymour. Rawlinson was born at Trent Manor, Dorset, on 20 February 1864, and educated at Eton College. His enthusiasm for sports secured him a comfortable passage through school. His father, a notable Assyriologist, saw military service in India, and formed a strong association with Frederick Roberts, subsequently commander-in-chief in India. This association was to assist the younger Rawlinson in his service career. Rawlinson entered the Royal Military College, Sandhurst, just before turning nineteen and soon thereafter served in India and Burma. In 1889, owing to the illness (soon followed by the death) of his mother, he returned to England, where he undertook the care of his ageing father, to whom he was much attached, and whom he succeeded in the baronetcy in 1895. On 6 November 1890 he married Meredith Sophia Frances (*d.* 1951), daughter of Coleridge John Kennard of Hampshire. The marriage endured for the rest of his life. There were no children.

Early career In 1893 Rawlinson entered the Staff College, Camberley, where he profited greatly from the teaching

Henry Seymour Rawlinson, Baron Rawlinson (1864–1925), by H. Walter Barnett

skills and engaging personality of the military historian G. F. R. Henderson. Although India at this time remained the centre of Britain's military concerns, Henderson also took his students through events more appropriate to the coming European struggle: the American Civil War and the Prussian campaign against France in 1870–71. The latter inspired Rawlinson to tour the battlefields of the Franco-Prussian war, and to visit the military establishments of Germany and France. He drew useful conclusions. For example, he noted that the German army did not keep its various elements—infantry, artillery, cavalry—in watertight units but got them working together. He regretted that in the British army, by comparison, 'It is no one's business to pool experience' (diary, CAC Cam., Rawlinson MSS).

In 1895 Rawlinson went to Aldershot with the rank of brigade major, and established a reputation as a promising staff officer. In January 1898, by chance or good management, he found himself in Cairo (where his wife had been directed for her health) just as General Kitchener was mounting his expedition against Khartoum. Needing a staff officer to manage the influx of troops, Kitchener turned to Rawlinson, who consequently secured for the first time a responsible position during a major military episode. Kitchener habitually operated with a less than sufficient staff, so that Rawlinson was soon fully engaged in transferring fresh arrivals to the front and coalescing them into a division. Kitchener was suitably impressed.

The Second South African War A year later Britain entered its largest and most testing colonial war: the Second South African War. Rawlinson soon took up a staff appointment there, and in short order found himself besieged in Ladysmith. He rapidly formed a favourable opinion of the Boers' skill with artillery, contrasting this with British gunners who 'think too much of their horses and not enough of their guns' (diary, CAC Cam., Rawlinson MSS). His developing awareness of the importance of artillery had a practical consequence. Before the Boer trap closed on Ladysmith, Rawlinson managed to bring in some long-range naval guns which proved serviceable in the subsequent siege.

Ladysmith was relieved early in March 1900. By then Rawlinson's long-term benefactor, Lord Roberts, had taken command in South Africa, with Kitchener as his chief of staff. Rawlinson was appointed to their staff and invited to live in Roberts's house: 'so I have kept up my practice of falling on my feet' (diary, CAC Cam., Rawlinson MSS). He was soon forging a coherent force out of the dispersed and diverse bodies of troops which were to accomplish the advance on Pretoria, thereby gaining experience in expanding a peacetime army into the much larger force required by war.

Roberts returned to Britain in November 1900, assuming that the Second South African War was as good as over. Rawlinson went with him. But the Boers resorted to an effective form of guerrilla warfare, and Rawlinson forthwith returned to join Kitchener. After performing much the same staff duties as before, he managed to persuade Kitchener to give him a command in the field. The ensuing brief periods of action seemed to him pretty enjoyable, even though once he became—if only for a matter of minutes—the prisoner of two Boers who had shot his horse from under him.

Rawlinson emerged from this spell with a reputation as an efficient commander in the field. Kitchener, he related on 2 January 1902, 'has been very nice to me and very complimentary' (diary, CAC Cam., Rawlinson MSS). Rawlinson was next placed in command of a big column to hunt the Boers in the Orange River Colony ('I am going up in the world'), and when the enemy there surrendered he was transferred to the western Transvaal, where he participated in the last Boer defeats of the war. Rawlinson noted that, between his taking up command on 1 April 1901 and the Boer capitulation in May 1902, his forces had marched 5211 miles, taken 1376 prisoners and 3 guns, and inflicted on the Boers 64 killed and 87 wounded, while the British had sustained casualties of 12 killed and 42 wounded. In terms of the large distances travelled and the small number of losses suffered by both sides, this was a very different war from the next in which he would participate.

On his return to Britain in 1902, Rawlinson was first assigned to the newly created department of education at the War Office, then appointed commandant of the Staff College; after that he was given command of an infantry brigade at Aldershot. He was then promoted to the rank of major-general and for four years commanded a division on Salisbury Plain. He travelled much, including a visit to the Sambre valley, where German railway building towards the Belgian frontier suggested ominous developments. All the time Rawlinson was seeking to divine the lessons to be learned from recent wars and changes in military technology. So in reflecting on the Russo-Japanese war of 1904–5 he noted the importance attached by the Japanese army to the employment of engineers, and their superior use of machine-guns in support of infantry.

Rawlinson did not always draw appropriate conclusions. He exaggerated the importance of morale on the battlefield as against weaponry, and he failed to recognize the potency of trench defences in slowing Japanese operations against the Russians. But, overall, when war came to Europe in 1914 he seemed well equipped to exercise command in battle.

The outbreak of the First World War As chance had it, on 1 August 1914 Rawlinson was not employed. Having recently handed over command of his division, he was on half pay and unoccupied. Britain's declaration of war on Germany on 4 August changed that, but not initially to his satisfaction. Instead of a command in the field, he was appointed director of recruiting at the War Office, renewing acquaintance with Kitchener (just appointed secretary of state for war) and drawing the same conclusions as his chief about the probable lengthy duration of the war.

Rawlinson soon made the transition to the battlefield. Briefly he replaced the injured commander of 4th division on the Aisne and caught a glimpse of the stalemated trench warfare already developing in France. Then, at the beginning of October 1914, he was given charge of an infantry and a cavalry division intended to assist the Belgians in the defence of Antwerp. In the event, Antwerp was doomed by the time he arrived, and his force was withdrawn to west Belgium to join the main British expeditionary force (BEF). Rawlinson was given command of the 4th corps, consisting of two infantry divisions, which took up position at Ypres on 14 October. There the Germans, seeking to strike towards the port of Calais, fell upon it, in what became the first battle of Ypres.

Rawlinson extricated his force from a potentially dangerous situation with skill, but in so doing aroused the displeasure of the commander-in-chief, Sir John French, who had expected him to show more aggression. It was the start of strained relations which would continue until, late in 1915, French was replaced.

1915: Neuve Chapelle to Loos Rawlinson was to participate in some of the key battles fought by the BEF in 1915, as a corps commander serving in Douglas Haig's First Army in a low-lying (and damp) part of Flanders. In March Haig directed him to devise a plan for seizing the village of Neuve Chapelle and proceeding on to the Aubers Ridge: the first set-piece attack against an entrenched position by the British army in this war. Rawlinson, from the outset, identified artillery predominance as vital to success, even against the single trench line which at the time was the norm. And he directed his attention just to the capture of this line and the village of Neuve Chapelle, notwithstanding Haig's directive that he should aim to press on to Aubers Ridge and open the way for cavalry exploitation.

The opening phase of the attack on 10 March 1915 was markedly successful, thanks to Rawlinson's well-calculated concentration of artillery. But then his forces passed beyond the support of the guns and were stopped by a hail of fire from German strongpoints. Renewed endeavours on the two days following achieved nothing, and the operation petered out. In the aftermath, Rawlinson blamed one of his divisional commanders for failing to press home the initial success, and called for his removal. It then transpired that any blame rested with Rawlinson. His conduct further stimulated French's antipathy towards him, and only the intervention of Haig saved him from demotion. That established a pattern. Rawlinson hereafter was dependent for advancement on Haig's goodwill.

Rawlinson derived clear lessons from Neuve Chapelle. Success against trench defences depended on artillery superiority. Cavalry had no part to play in such endeavours. And a limited advance ('bite and hold') was the most that could be hoped for. However, such insights did not inform all his subsequent actions. When called on to deliver a further attack on Aubers Ridge on 8 May, he deemed the guns 'well registered and we have enough' (diary, CAC Cam., Rawlinson MSS). Yet by Neuve Chapelle standards he clearly did not have enough, and the result was a costly fiasco. By contrast, when he attacked at Givenchy a month later, with similar results, he realized in advance that his artillery was insufficient.

Late in September 1915 Rawlinson was involved in the much larger operation at Loos. The available gunnery was recognized on all sides to be inadequate (only pressure from Kitchener, citing the needs of Britain's allies, caused the attack to be undertaken), but poison gas was employed in the hope of making good the deficiency in shells. Rawlinson's expectations ranged from the muted to the fairly optimistic. In the event, his forces overran their first objectives, but were then halted by an unimpaired second line of German defences. The only reserves available for the operation arrived late, having been kept under French's personal command. This hardly mattered. In the absence of adequate artillery support, the reserves had little chance of improving the situation whenever they appeared. But Rawlinson concluded otherwise. He took the view that only French's misuse of the reserves had denied him a considerable success. And, in company with others (including Haig), he conveyed this view to important people in London. In December 1915 French was replaced by Haig as commander-in-chief.

1916: The Somme The change soon led to Rawlinson's advancement. Initially he was given temporary command of First Army. Then, in January 1916, Haig called into being a new Fourth Army, largely made up of recruits raised and trained since the outbreak of war. Haig not only appointed Rawlinson to its command but assigned to it the principal role in Britain's major campaign for 1916: a large offensive astride the River Somme.

In his planning for this endeavour, Rawlinson straightaway stressed the primacy of artillery, disregarded the cavalry, and devised an operation that was essentially bite and hold. He proposed a bombardment lasting for several days to a depth of just 1 to 2000 yards. Thereby he would overwhelm and occupy the German first line. Then the artillery would move forward and the process be repeated against the second line. Haig was not impressed. In the first phase of planning, he proposed a scheme to capture the German second line at an early stage of the attack and to advance southwards along it so as to aid the French, who would be carrying out the major part of the offensive astride the Somme. Later, as it became clear that German operations at Verdun would force the French to play only a minor role on the Somme, Haig demanded of Rawlinson a new plan for overwhelming all three German defensive positions at the outset so as to open the way for cavalry exploitation.

Although clearly uneasy about this major extension of his first-stage objectives, Rawlinson did not protest. The most he felt able to do was persuade Haig to forgo the hurricane bombardment he favoured, although without bluntly telling his chief that his forces did not possess sufficient guns to dispatch the available shells except over an extended period. But he capitulated to Haig's insistence that the limited quantity of shells at their disposal should be spread to the depth of the entire German defensive system. The result was predictable. The preliminary bombardment had neither the weight nor the volume to eliminate the successive lines of enemy trenches. So when Rawlinson's forces went over the top on 1 July 1916, they suffered casualties unprecedented in British military history, and made no advance on two-thirds of the front attacked.

The campaign was not abandoned. Britain's New Army had spent two years training and accumulating munitions for this operation. France needed Britain's aid to relieve the terrible pressure being exerted by the Germans at Verdun. And early setback did not diminish Haig's conviction that, in time, he could still accomplish the sweeping advance promised for the first day.

Rawlinson's performance during the ensuing four and a half months, until rain and mud and diminishing manpower forced the British command to halt, was decidedly mixed. On some occasions, such as 14 July and 25 September, he employed large quantities of artillery against limited sectors and achieved moderate, and not too costly, advance. More often he allowed small units unsynchronized with one another to deliver piecemeal attacks which attracted disproportionately heavy resistance. Thereby he sustained severe casualties and made only trivial gains of ground. And although he sometimes acknowledged that such operations were not rewarding and were even being delivered in the wrong sectors, he persisted in these operations. He welcomed the appearance of the tank, which first saw battle in his large offensive of 15 September, but by rendering his artillery subordinate to the tanks he ensured that neither tanks nor infantry would achieve much. Overall, between the start of July and the middle of

November 1916, Rawlinson's operations inflicted substantial casualties on the enemy but brought even greater losses to his own army and advanced his line a bare 4 miles without strategic gain. The cost to the British army was 400,000 casualties.

1917: Sidelined Perhaps strangely, Rawlinson emerged from the Somme campaign a figure of note. He was promoted to full general, and written up favourably in the press. But his eminence was insubstantial. Lloyd George, who became Britain's prime minister in December 1916, had spoken of him disparagingly even before the Somme campaign began. And his conduct during that long endeavour had sometimes displeased his commander-in-chief. Haig had told him bluntly on 24 August that 'something is wanting in the methods employed', and had delivered him a lecture on the appropriate conduct of an army commander (general headquarters to Fourth Army, OAD 123, 24 Aug 1916, Fourth Army MSS).

So in 1917 Rawlinson found himself directing no large operations, and was soon writing of the Cinderella role assigned to his forces. In March and early April, as the enemy in his sector fell back to powerful defended positions (the Hindenburg line), he followed up cautiously, more convinced of the dangers of being counter-attacked in the open than he was eager to seize hypothetical opportunities. In May, after believing himself assured that he would direct Britain's next big offensive, he was (as he confided to his diary) 'very much disgusted and disappointed' to learn that he had been passed over. Although there would indeed be another great offensive, in the second half of 1917, the most that Rawlinson was asked to command was a subsidiary operation that would be delivered from the sea in conjunction with an advance along the Belgian coast once the main attack had made considerable progress.

The Ypres offensive never achieved this sort of success, so the proposed coastal operation remained a pipe dream. For Rawlinson the resulting inactivity was galling. 'I do not find much to occupy my time', he lamented in September; and, in October, 'I find it hard to get through the day'. Early in November he was belatedly placed in charge of the dying phase of the Ypres operation. Then, in February 1918, he was assigned to a different role. He was appointed British representative on the executive war board of what was euphemistically called the supreme war council, a body set up by Lloyd George to diminish Haig's role in military decision making. By nominating Rawlinson, Haig intended to ensure that little diminution would take place.

1918: Offensive and counter-offensive After a month Rawlinson was rescued from this unrewarding activity by dramatic events on the battlefield. On 21 March 1918 the Germans launched a massive, and initially successful, offensive against an undermanned British sector on the Somme. 'Not good days on the battlefront', Rawlinson noted in his diary. They proved, nevertheless, to be useful days for Rawlinson. On 28 March he was summoned to take command in the area of the setback. The situation awaiting him seemed perilous. His forces were drained in manpower, and few reinforcements were readily available. But the position was not beyond hope. The German advance had sustained heavy casualties and had outrun its artillery support. And in order to regain momentum, the German command decided to strike elsewhere, with only spasmodic efforts in Rawlinson's sector. By mid-year, with reinforcements and large quantities of weaponry to hand, and with raids by his Australian forces alerting him to the indifferent quality of the defences and troops opposing him, Rawlinson drew an important conclusion. The situation was hopeful for a counter-offensive with limited objectives. A trial run was carried out at Hamel on 4 July and yielded encouraging results. So in the next few weeks the Canadian and Australian corps and the British 3rd corps were concentrated near Amiens, and large supplies of weaponry brought in amid great secrecy. By employing, with all the skill now at his disposal, devastating amounts of artillery in combination with machine-guns and mortars and tanks and aircraft, he might, at tolerable cost in the lives of his troops, suppress enemy trenches and big guns long enough to get his forces forward at least to the distance that his artillery could bombard.

On 8 August 1918, outside Amiens, Rawlinson's forces attacked on a 19,000 yard front. By the end of the day, for moderate losses, they had overrun the main defended positions and eliminated six enemy divisions. The assault continued for three more days, but with steadily diminishing results. Rawlinson was then persuaded by his corps commanders that the operation should be halted. He succeeded in pressing this judgement on Haig. At last, and in marked contrast to the enemy's conduct so far that year, a measure of realism was prevailing in Britain's higher military circles.

On 23 August, after his artillery had moved forward, Rawlinson attacked again, once more driving the enemy from their defended positions. From then to 3 September his forces made limited advances daily. The German high command (much against its will) was obliged to withdraw to its 1917 stronghold, the Hindenburg line. Rawlinson's forces attacked these seemingly impregnable entrenchments in two operations. On 18 September they captured the ridge overlooking the main line, thereby securing artillery domination. Then on 29 September, after a truly massive bombardment, they pressed right through the Hindenburg positions. It was the British army's most distinguished operation of the war. By this stage Rawlinson was trusting to the expertise of a myriad of subordinate commanders, rather than dominating events himself. Yet he still had a role to play, for example by extending the length of front attacked on 29 September and so incorporating the area where the decisive advance was made.

Post-war career With this triumph and with the accelerating advance of the other British armies, along with the French and the Americans, Germany's capitulation could only be weeks away. It came on 11 November 1918. Rawlinson did not pass into retirement. In mid-1919, simultaneous with being created Baron Rawlinson of Trent and receiving a grant of £30,000 from a grateful parliament, he was sent to north Russia to evacuate British troops engaged (unavailingly) in aiding anti-Bolshevik forces. Back in Britain in November, he took over the Aldershot command. Then in August 1920, in fulfilment of a long-standing ambition, he was appointed commander-in-chief in India.

This was a difficult time in India, with the demands for self-government gaining momentum. Rawlinson, nevertheless, experienced a relatively successful occupancy. He decentralized the army headquarters. He ended a long controversy by establishing his post as the sole source of military advice to the Indian government. He countered the onset of economic stringency by reducing the military budget and the size of the Indian army while improving equipment and not harming efficiency. Although proving less than welcoming to the demand for full Indianization of his forces, he conceded enough to avoid severe confrontation. And by construction of roads and the establishment of military stations, he advanced military control into disaffected parts of the north-west frontier.

By early 1925 Rawlinson deemed his role in India fulfilled. He intended to return to London, but on 24 March 1925, while only sixty-one years of age and in seeming good health, he was taken ill following games of polo and cricket. Four days later, in Delhi, after an operation, apparently for appendicitis, he died. His remains were returned to England and interred at his home at Trent, Dorset, on 30 April. Since then Rawlinson has been largely forgotten. His private life lacked drama, and his diaries, when published, proved wanting in extreme malice. As regards his career, military rule in the British empire has ceased to attract attention. And although interest in the First World War continues unabated, the part played by army commanders is usually disregarded or judged adversely. At least as concerns Rawlinson's operations in 1918, this may seem less than just.

ROBIN PRIOR and TREVOR WILSON

Sources R. Prior and T. Wilson, *Command on the western front: the military career of Sir Henry Rawlinson, 1914–1918* (1992) • F. Maurice, *The life of General Lord Rawlinson of Trent* (1928) • J. F. Maurice and M. H. Grant, eds., *History of the war in South Africa, 1899–1902*, 4 vols. (1906–10) • J. E. Edmonds, ed., *Military operations, France and Belgium*, 14 vols., History of the Great War (1922–48) • CAC Cam., Rawlinson MSS • NAM, Rawlinson MSS • IWM, Fourth Army papers • *The Times* (28 March 1925) • *DNB* • *CGPLA Eng. & Wales* (1925)
Archives CAC Cam., diaries and papers • NAM, diaries and papers • NAM, papers relating to Sudan and South Africa | BL OIOC, corresp. with seventh earl of Derby, MS Eur. D 605 • Durham RO, corresp. with Lord Londonderry • IWM, Fourth Army MSS • IWM, corresp. with Sir Henry Wilson • King's Lond., Liddell Hart C., corresp. with Sir F. B. Maurice • Lpool RO, corresp. with seventh earl of Derby • NAM, letters to Lord Roberts • PRO, corresp. with Lord Kitchener, PRO 30/57; WO 159 | FILM BFI NFTVA, news footage • IWM FVA, actuality footage • IWM FVA, documentary footage | SOUND IWM SA, oral history interview
Likenesses I. Sheldon-Williams, pencil and watercolour drawing, 1900, NPG • F. Dodd, charcoal and watercolour drawing, 1917, IWM • W. Orpen, oils, 1918, IWM • W. Stoneman, photograph, 1918, NPG • J. S. Sargent, oils, c.1919–1922, NPG • O. Birley, oils, 1920–23, Staff College, Camberley • J. S. Sargent, group portrait, oils, 1922 (*General officers of World War I*), NPG • H. W. Barnett, photograph, NPG [*see illus.*]
Wealth at death £4042 8s. 7d.: resworn probate, 16 May 1925, CGPLA Eng. & Wales

Rawlinson, John (1576–1631), Church of England clergyman and college head, was the son of Robert Rawlinson, merchant tailor of London. Admitted to Merchant Taylors' School in 1585, and as a scholar to St John's College, Oxford, on 28 June 1591, he matriculated on 15 October, aged fifteen, graduated BA on 5 July 1595, and proceeded MA on 21 May 1599. He was a college lecturer in 1599 and the following year became master of Reading School. He contributed verses to William Vaughan's *The Golden-Grove Moralized* (1600), and left other poems (BL, Royal MS 12.A.LXIV, fol. 24) composed at St John's, where he was elected a fellow on 12 November 1605.

Rawlinson's sermon at Paul's Cross on Rogation Sunday, 5 May 1605, was published as *The Foure Summons of the Shulamite* (1606). Although not licensed to preach until 26 February 1606 he quickly gained a reputation as a fluent, florid, and edifying preacher, together with powerful patronage and lucrative preferment. Through Archbishop Richard Bancroft he was rector of Taplow, Buckinghamshire, from 1606 to 1610 and, having proceeded DD on 1 June 1608, vicar of Asheldam, Essex, and canon of New Sarum from 1609. The provost and fellows of Queen's College, Oxford, elected him principal of St Edmund Hall on 1 May 1610; he resigned his fellowship at St John's on 13 December with a gratuity of £10. Soon after he married, and his daughter Joyce was born within a few years; it is not known whether the Catherine named in his will was his first or a later wife. Certainly by 1611, and probably before 1609, when he dedicated his *Fishermen Fishers of Men* (preached at the Mercers' Chapel) to Sir John Egerton, Rawlinson was chaplain to Thomas Egerton, Lord Ellesmere. As chancellor of the university and a favourer of Calvinism, Ellesmere supported Rawlinson's candidature in 1611 for the presidency of St John's, the latter having nailed his anti-Catholic colours to the mast the previous year with *The Romish Judas* (1611), preached at the university church on 5 November. Narrowly defeated by William Laud, Rawlinson appealed unsuccessfully first to the college visitor and then to the king, but he retained the backing of the Egertons. In dedicating to Ellesmere his *Mercy to a Beast* (1612), 'an egg of your own laying', he acknowledged his long-standing gratitude. He acquired the rectories of Selsey, Sussex, in 1613 and Whitchurch, Shropshire, in 1614, and in time royal favour was also forthcoming. *Vivat rex* (1619), delivered at Paul's Cross on 24 March 1615, the twelfth anniversary of James's accession, stressed that the king must 'voluntarily submit his will to the direction of the law', but does not seem to have caused offence. James admitted Rawlinson to the prebend of Netherbury in Ecclesia at Salisbury and by 1619 he was a royal chaplain. *The Dove-Like Soule*, preached before Prince Charles on 19 February 1619, was one of his four Lenten sermons at Whitehall published in *Quadriga salutis* (1625).

Despite his manifold commitments elsewhere Oxford remained Rawlinson's base. His *Unmasking of the Hypocrite*

(1616) was preached at the university church. In 1623 he was among those before whom Gabriel Bridges was summoned for preaching a university sermon against absolute predestination. Two daughters, Elizabeth and Dorothy, were buried respectively in 1624 and 1629 at St Peter-in-the-East, adjacent to St Edmund Hall. In the interim Rawlinson built a new house on the High Street nearby. On 26 December 1627 William Juxon, now president of St John's, wrote elliptically to Rawlinson's erstwhile rival William Laud, now bishop of London, reporting the fact. In the course of conversation Rawlinson had suggested to Juxon several new ecclesiastical appointments, including Juxon's to the see of Worcester and his own to the see of Oxford 'for which his new house was well fitted'. Juxon 'trouble[d] the Bishop with these particulars that he may read the good conceit we have of ourselves at Oxford' (*CSP dom.*, *1627–8*, 479).

Rawlinson's daughter Joyce married Richard Alport at Whitchurch on 23 January 1630 or 1631. On 29 January 1631 Rawlinson drew up his will in the presence of Alport, leaving his Oxford house and property at Cassington, Oxfordshire, and Limbury, Dorset, to his wife, Catherine, during her widowhood, with reversion to Richard and Joyce, who also received property at Whitchurch and all her father's books. Bequests were also made to Rawlinson's sister Elizabeth Heale and her children, and to St Edmund Hall and St John's. The overseers were Rawlinson's 'sister-in-law' Ellen Alport and Richard Zouche, principal of St Alban Hall. Rawlinson died on 3 February 1631, and was buried at Whitchurch on 10 February.

LOUIS A. KNAFLA

Sources C. J. Robinson, ed., *A register of the scholars admitted into Merchant Taylors' School, from AD 1562 to 1874*, 1 (1882), 29 · Wood, *Ath. Oxon.*, 1st edn, 1.475–6 · Foster, *Alum. Oxon.*, *1500–1714*, vol. 3 · W. H. Stevenson and H. E. Salter, *The early history of St John's College, Oxford*, OHS, new ser., 1 (1939), 369 · R. Newcourt, *Repertorium ecclesiasticum parochiale Londinense*, 2 (1710), 17, 282 · M. McClure, *The Paul's Cross sermons, 1534–1642* (1958), 160, 235 · will, PRO, PROB 11/160, fol. 47 · *Fasti Angl.* (Hardy), 3.594 · A. Wood, *The history and antiquities of the University of Oxford*, ed. J. Gutch, 1 (1792), 540 · BL, Lansdowne MS 984, fol. 164 [biographical note] · BL, Lansdowne MS 984, fol. 109 [memoir] · *CSP dom.*, *1627–8*, 428, 479 · F. Madan, *The early Oxford press: a bibliography of printing and publishing in Oxford, 1468–1640*, OHS, 29 (1895), vol. 1 of *Oxford books: a bibliography of printed works* (1895–1931) · IGI [Whitchurch parish register] · N. Tyacke, *Anti-Calvinists: the rise of English Arminianism, c.1590–1640* (1987), 68

Wealth at death see will, PRO, PROB 11/160, fol. 47

Rawlinson, Richard (1690–1755), topographer and bishop of the nonjuring Church of England, was born on 3 January 1690 at his father's house in the Old Bailey, St Sepulchre's, London, eighth of the fifteen children of Sir Thomas *Rawlinson (*bap.* 1647, *d.* 1708), vintner and lord mayor of London, and his wife, Mary Taylor (1661/2–1725). He was educated at St Paul's School, probably from 1697, at Eton College from 1702, and at St John's College, Oxford, whence he matriculated in 1708, graduating BA in 1711 and proceeding MA in 1713. His early interest in topography is demonstrated by his compiling while at Eton a historical account of the places on the road between Eton and London. He early acquired from his older brother Thomas *Rawlinson (1681–1725) an enthusiasm for book

Richard Rawlinson (1690–1755), by William Smith (after George Vertue)

collecting and while a student he began to collect editions of the classics, books on English history, topography, and drama. His enthusiasm for antiquarian studies was encouraged at Oxford where he came under the influence of the second generation of Anglo-Saxon scholars and where the collections Anthony Wood had made the previous century for the history of Oxford and Oxford men made a lasting impression. He consulted manuscripts at the Ashmolean Museum from 1710 and at the Bodleian Library from 1711. In the latter year he published a *Life of Anthony Wood*, whose interests in topography and biography he was already emulating, travelling out of Oxford as an undergraduate to copy monumental inscriptions in neighbouring parish churches.

After 1711 Rawlinson began to share his brother Thomas's rooms in the Middle Temple, then followed him to Gray's Inn. The young antiquary developed 'a gift for editing other men's work and acted as foster-parent to many orphaned books' (Ward and Waller, 351). Many of the antiquarian books published by Edmund Curll were seen through the press by Rawlinson, among them Tristram Risdon's *Survey of Devon* (1714), Elias Ashmole's *Antiquities of Berkshire* (1719), John Aubrey's *Natural History and Antiquities of the County of Surrey* (1719), and accounts of the cathedrals of Hereford, Worcester, Lichfield, and Rochester all in 1717, and of Salisbury and Bath in 1719. In 1720 there appeared *The English topographer, or, An historical account of all the pieces that have been written relating to the natural history or topographical description of any part of England*. Considered by John Nichols as Rawlinson's principal work, it provided the pattern for Richard Gough's *Anecdotes of British Topography* (1768 and 1780).

In the summer of 1712 Rawlinson began his extensive journeys throughout England, during which he made antiquarian notes and copied monumental inscriptions. In 1718 he visited, in the company of Edmund Curll, most of the parishes of Oxfordshire, with the intention of compiling a history of the county, which was to include Anthony Wood's history of the city of Oxford. The plan never materialized, but the collections were preserved and, like so many of his antiquarian papers, survive in the Bodleian Library. In 1713 he became a governor of Bridewell and Bethlem hospitals in London and was in 1714 elected a fellow of the Royal Society. Rawlinson was, like his father, a staunch Jacobite and nonjuror. He was ordained deacon and priest in the nonjuring Church of England by Jeremy Collier in 1716, and, though he sought to keep his ordination secret, was active ministering among the nonjurors.

After travelling extensively in England, Rawlinson was keen to go abroad, to study foreign languages, to meet continental scholars, and to add to his collections. As a nonjuror in a church which was becoming increasingly divided over its liturgical practices, he was interested to see for himself foreign liturgical traditions. As a Jacobite he wished above all else to visit the court of James Stuart, the Pretender, at Rome. In 1719 he travelled in France and the Netherlands, and was enrolled as a student at the universities of Utrecht and Leiden. Oxford created him DCL the same year. In 1720 he began his tour of the continent, visiting the Netherlands, France, Germany, Italy, Sicily, and Malta; he matriculated at Padua University in 1722 and spent many months resident in Rome. He kept a diary of his tour, which survives among his manuscripts in the Bodleian Library (MS Rawlinson D. 1179–87).

Rawlinson decided to return to England on receiving news of the death of his banker, a long-time family friend whose executor he was, and at Genoa he read a newspaper account of the death of his brother Thomas. During Rawlinson's absence abroad Thomas had neglected his estates, accumulated huge debts in the course of adding to his collections of books, manuscripts, and prints, married unwisely, and finally disinherited his siblings by breaking the entail on the family estates and settling an allowance on his widow. It was his brother's unenviable task to reach a settlement with Thomas's widow, to set the management of the estates in order, to sell Thomas's vast collections, and to pay off his creditors. The arrangements for the auctions dominated Rawlinson's life for seven years from 1726, but the proceeds of the sales were much smaller than anticipated, and he was not free of debt until 1748. These financial difficulties forced him to live frugally and prevented him from travelling, from publishing or collecting on the scale he desired, and even from visiting Oxford for many years.

Rawlinson settled in London in 1726, first at his old rooms in Gray's Inn, then from 1734 at the apartments that were formerly his brother's in London House, Aldersgate Street. He was admitted a fellow of the Society of Antiquaries in 1727 and about this time became a freemason. By 1732 he was master of the lodge in Ludgate Street, warden of another, and member of two more. He was grand steward in 1734. He briefly returned to editing and publishing, with a *History of Sir John Perrott* (1728) and his own translation of Du Fresnoy, *New Method of Studying History* (1728). Both attracted more criticism than praise and thereafter Rawlinson confined himself to the publication of private reprints and facsimiles.

In 1728 Rawlinson was consecrated bishop by bishops Gandy, Doughty, and Blackbourne. With them he signed a declaration against the rituals advocated by Collier, among other 'usagers', and in favour of the continued use of the liturgy of the Church of England. He was party to the negotiations which culminated in the reunion of 1732, but the communion service remained a matter of controversy and the rift in the ranks of the nonjurors was only partially healed. Of lasting significance, however, was Rawlinson's role in preserving the records of the nonjurors, many of whose letters, sermons, and other papers survive in his manuscript collections at the Bodleian. He was tireless in his researches into the history of the nonjurors and sent out biographical questionnaires to all known nonjuring clergy and academics, arranging and binding the returns for safekeeping. Rawlinson's nonjuring and Jacobite loyalties never wavered. They eventually led to his falling out with colleagues in the Royal Society and then the Society of Antiquaries. His interest in antiquities and in early English history was stimulated, as it was in other nonjuring scholars, by his desiré to find precedents and tradition to justify their position. The nonjurors' emphasis on the importance of Anglo-Saxon studies probably influenced Rawlinson's endowment of a lecturer or professor in Anglo-Saxon at Oxford.

With the deaths of Thomas Hearne and Thomas Tanner in 1735, Rawlinson regarded the study of antiquity as at a low ebb, but this only increased his own determination to 'provide for posterity without regard to this ungrateful age' (Bodl. Oxf., MS Ballard 2, fol. 48v) by collecting books, manuscripts, and historical materials. In particular he devoted much of his last twenty years to collecting biographical information about living or recently deceased Oxford men, in continuation of Anthony Wood's *Athenae Oxonienses*. Thomas Tanner, who had inherited Wood's own collections on Oxford writers of 1500 to 1690, had published a supplementary volume in 1721. Rawlinson preferred merely to collect materials from 1690 to his own day, and to leave them to the Bodleian for a future editor to digest and publish. This project prompted his return to Oxford, made him many friends, and strengthened the ties between him and his 'dearest Oxford'.

Rawlinson took as his episcopal motto 'I collect and I preserve', words which accurately reflect his consuming passion, the love of collecting inspired by his conviction that materials must be acquired and preserved for future generations. Before he went abroad in 1719 his collections were small, but in the course of his travels he acquired not only books and manuscripts but also coins, medals, seals, and miscellaneous curiosities. It was a severe disappointment on his return to learn that he was not to inherit his brother Thomas's magnificent library and a bitter task to oversee its dispersal in a series of eleven sales. His meticulous records, compiled to satisfy the scrutiny of his sister-in-law's new husband, John Tabor, provide interesting insights into the mechanics of eighteenth-century book auctions. Prevented by his agreement with Tabor from simply withholding from sale those items which he wished to own, Rawlinson had to match the highest bid at auction. He nevertheless acquired considerable numbers of his brother's books and manuscripts.

Rawlinson's move to London House in 1734 marked the resumption of his collecting, particularly of manuscripts, on a grander scale. He frequented auction rooms and booksellers' premises and bought widely in all periods. His collections include many early charters, several monastic cartularies, hundreds of medieval liturgical, biblical, and classical manuscripts, an important group of medieval Irish manuscripts including the famous 'annals of Inisfallen', a series of some 250 poetical miscellanies mainly of the seventeenth century, over 100 volumes of seventeenth- and eighteenth-century literary and scholarly correspondence, and a wide range of manuscripts relating to topography, history and biography, heraldry and genealogy, theology, law, and medicine.

Rawlinson did not confine himself to the traditional means of purchasing manuscripts through auctioneers and booksellers. He vastly increased his collections by seeking papers of historical interest which had been sold for scrap, scouring grocers' and chandlers' shops, and purchasing by weight important seventeenth-century archives. He also developed unrivalled skill in locating papers which had strayed and were thought to have been lost—most notably the state papers of John Thurloe and the Admiralty papers of Samuel Pepys. He systematically sorted all the collections he bought as discarded bundles of loose papers and had them bound into volumes to reduce the risk of their being unwittingly or carelessly thrown away a second time.

Although increasingly convinced that his contemporaries did not value these materials as they ought, Rawlinson was always generous both in lending items from his collection to scholars who expressed an interest in their contents and in presenting them to institutions which could be relied on to preserve them. From the 1730s his gifts of books and portraits to the Bodleian Library became almost an annual event. As the fame of his collections grew, and he never married, speculation about their eventual fate became a matter for public discussion. Rawlinson's own loyalties were divided between the two institutions which seemed still to encourage the study of history and antiquities, the Society of Antiquaries and the University of Oxford, and his first will left part of his collections to each. Humphrey Owen, Bodley's librarian from 1747, was assiduous in his proper acknowledgement of Rawlinson's gifts already received and in offering space in the refurbished picture gallery for some of the bulkier items in his collections. Then the society, having elected

him vice-president in 1753, in 1754 removed him from the council on account of his Jacobite loyalties, and Rawlinson revoked his bequest to the antiquaries.

Rawlinson's health was already failing by then and he died on 6 April 1755 at Islington. Following his instructions his body was buried in St Giles' Church in Oxford and his heart in the chapel of St John's College, on 14 April. To the Bodleian, that 'sanctuary for use and curiosity' as he described it (Bodl. Oxf., MS Rawl. lett. 31, fol. 444), he bequeathed all his manuscripts, charters and seals, and a selection of his printed books. To St John's he bequeathed the bulk of his landed property, some of his books, and his coins and medals. In addition to his earlier endowment of a chair in Anglo-Saxon at Oxford, he made provision for the salary of the keeper of the Ashmolean Museum.

Rawlinson's political and religious views were at odds with the majority of his contemporaries, many of whom judged him only as a stubborn nonjuror and Jacobite. The intensity of the dislike his principles engendered is illustrated in the abusive attack on his character published in the *Evening Advertiser* of 19 November 1754, which labelled him a misanthrope, 'an opposer of our established religion' and 'abuser of the present government', one who pretended to be an antiquarian 'out of sheer hatred to the present generation' (Nichols, *Lit. anecdotes*, 9.617–19). Those who shared his enthusiasm for antiquity and his scholarly interest in preserving historical materials for the future acknowledged him as a generous patron who did all in his power to assist scholarly antiquarian enterprises. He was one of the greatest collectors of the eighteenth century and his lasting monument is the vast accumulation of 5000 manuscripts which have furnished material for all manner of historical, theological, and literary studies since they came to rest in the Bodleian in 1756.

MARY CLAPINSON

Sources B. J. Enright, 'Richard Rawlinson: collector, antiquary, and topographer', DPhil diss., U. Oxf., 1956 · G. R. Tashjian, D. R. Tashjian, and B. J. Enright, *Richard Rawlinson: a tercentenary memorial* (1990) · H. Broxap, *The later nonjurors* (1924) · I. Philip, *The Bodleian Library in the seventeenth and eighteenth centuries* (1983) · W. D. Macray, *Annals of the Bodleian Library, Oxford*, 2nd edn (1890) · Nichols, *Lit. anecdotes*, 5.489–98; 9.617–19 · *From Steele and Addison to Pope and Swift* (1912), vol. 9 of *The Cambridge history of English literature*, ed. A. W. Ward and A. R. Waller (1907–27) · *DNB*

Archives Bodl. Oxf., corresp., collections, and papers · Bodl. RH, diary of travels in Malta · St John's College, Oxford, papers | BL, letters to Thomas Birch, Add. MSS 4291, 4317, 4444, *passim* · Bodl. Oxf., letters to G. Ballard · Bodl. Oxf., letters to Thomas Hearne · Bodl. Oxf., letters to Thomas Rawlinson

Likenesses W. Smith, mezzotint (after G. Vertue), BM, NPG [*see illus.*] · M. Vandergucht, line engraving, BM, NPG · oils; known to be in Bodl. Oxf. in 1759 · pencil drawing, St John's College, Oxford · stipple (after a painting in Bodl. Oxf.), NPG; repro. in Macray, *Annals*, facing p. 231

Wealth at death bequeathed papers, charters and seals, and a selection of his printed books to Bodleian Library; bequeathed bulk of landed property to St John's College, Oxford; made provision for salary for keeper of Ashmolean Museum, Oxford

Rawlinson, Sir Robert (1810–1898), civil engineer, was born at Bristol on 28 February 1810, the son of Thomas Rawlinson, a builder, of Chorley, Lancashire, and his wife,

Grace Ellice of Exeter. He was educated at Lancaster, where his father moved shortly after his birth, and for a time assisted his father in his business as a builder, contractor, and millwright. He married in 1831 Ruth, daughter of Thomas Swallow of Lockwood, Yorkshire, and in the same year joined the civil engineering contractor Jesse Hartley, where he remained until 1836, working mainly on dock and harbour construction. He then worked under Robert Stephenson on the building of the London and Birmingham Railway.

In 1840 Rawlinson returned to Liverpool, becoming assistant surveyor to the corporation, and from 1843 to 1847 was employed as chief engineer under the Bridgewater trust. During this period, means of improving Liverpool's water supply were under discussion, and he advocated the utilization of Bala Lake in Wales as a reservoir for the city. A form of Rawlinson's scheme was eventually realized in the 1890s.

In 1848 Rawlinson was appointed a government public health inspector under the Public Health Act and later became head of the department. It was, however, through his dedicated and technically innovative work as head of the sanitary commission which was sent out by the government to the Crimea to investigate the sanitary conditions of the British army at Sevastopol that the foundations of Rawlinson's most important and enduring work in the field of public health and sanitation were laid. On his return from the Crimea Rawlinson took up his duties as chief engineering inspector under the Local Government Board, and prepared and published some highly influential guidelines for improved town sewerage and domestic drainage systems, intended for the engineers and surveyors to local boards, which contributed greatly to the development of urban sanitation for the rest of the nineteenth century.

In 1863 Rawlinson served as a member of the army sanitary committee. In April of that year, during the cotton famine in Lancashire, he was sent by Lord Palmerston, the prime minister, to organize relief works for the thousands of men and women thrown idle by the stoppage of the cotton supply from America owing to the civil war. The works he then started occupied his attention until 1869. In 1865 and in 1868 he was chairman of the commissions appointed to inquire into the best means of preventing industrial river pollution; and in 1876 he served on another commission considering town sewerage. In 1884 he was president of the congress of the Sanitary Institute of Great Britain held at Dublin, and published the address he delivered in that capacity.

For his many valuable services in connection with public health and sanitation Rawlinson was knighted on 24 July 1883, and in January 1888 he was made KCB. In that year he retired from the office which he had held for forty years as chief engineering inspector to the Local Government Board. He was elected a member of the Institution of Civil Engineers in March 1848; he served on its council for many years and became president in May 1894 when he was eighty-four. His presidential address was published in the same year. He died at his home, Lancaster Lodge, 11 The Boltons, South Kensington, on 31 May 1898, and was buried in Brompton cemetery on 4 June.

T. H. BEARE, rev. RALPH HARRINGTON

Sources The Times (2 June 1898), 6b • The Times (6 June 1898), 8c • PICE, 134 (1897–8), 386–91 • G. M. Binnie, Early Victorian water engineers (1981) • A. W. Kinglake, The invasion of the Crimea, 8 vols. (1863–87) • M. Chrimes, Civil engineering, 1839–1889: a photographic history (1991) • d. cert.
Archives Lpool RO, corresp. and papers relating to St George's Hall, Liverpool | BL, corresp. with Florence Nightingale, Add. MS 45769 • UCL, corresp. with Edmund Chadwick
Likenesses R. Fenton, double portrait, photograph, 1855 (with Dr John Sutherland), U. Texas, Gernsheim collection • prints, c.1855, NPG • R. Fenton, photograph, 1856, Inst. CE • P. Morris, oils, 1892, Inst. CE • T. O. Barlow, mezzotint (after P. Westcott), NPG • T. Fall and H. Mendelssohn, cabinet photographs, NPG • P. Westcott, mixed engraving (after T. O. Barlow), NPG
Wealth at death £83,750 12s. 11d.: probate, 27 June 1898, CGPLA Eng. & Wales

Rawlinson, Sir Thomas (bap. 1647, d. 1708), local politician, was baptized in the parish of St Dionis Backchurch, London, on 1 April 1647, the second son of Daniel Rawlinson (1614–1679), and his wife, Margaret Pever (d. 1666). His father was a London vintner who kept The Mitre tavern in Fenchurch Street. Young Rawlinson followed his father's business; he was admitted a freeman of the Vintners' Company on 12 October 1670, and emulating his father, later served as master, in 1687 and in 1696. In 1680 he married Mary (1661/2–1725), eldest daughter of Richard Taylor of Turnham Green, who kept The Devil tavern by the Temple. They had fifteen children, among them Thomas *Rawlinson (1681–1725), a noted book collector, and Richard *Rawlinson (1690–1755), antiquarian and likewise a noted collector of manuscripts and books. Shortly after marriage, the couple moved to the Old Bailey, which remained the principal family residence for the rest of Rawlinson's life.

Rawlinson first entered public life as a common councillor for Farringdon Without in 1683, and two years later was a juror in the tory-orchestrated trial of Henry Cornish. Under James II Rawlinson emerged as an important figure in the capital, both in political and business circles. In 1685 he gained election to the committee of the East India Company, on which he served to 1689, at which time he held £3750 stock. He later held a seat on the board in 1690–92, 1693–8, and 1700–07, and was a manager of the united East India trade in 1703–5. His tory loyalties were rewarded with appointment to the aldermanic bench in April 1686, and further honours duly followed. On 6 August 1686 he was knighted at Windsor, and in the following month was appointed sheriff of London and Middlesex by the king. However, he was removed as alderman in September 1687, presumably for giving less than wholehearted backing for the king's controversial religious policies. Despite this personal setback he remained loyal to the throne, and at the height of the revolution of 1688 defied the City whigs when they moved to send a laudatory address to William, prince of Orange, proposing instead that thanks be sent to James II for his return to London.

Although reviled by the whigs for his association with the discredited Stuart regime, Rawlinson proved a loyal subject under William, whom he later described as 'a gracious King' (Rawlinson letters 63, fol. 10v). He served as a common councillor in 1688–9, made two substantial loans to the government, and was appointed a colonel of the City's newly raised auxiliary forces during the invasion scare of July 1690. He regained a seat on the aldermanic bench in December 1696, and in the same year was appointed a commissioner for the abortive land bank. Under Anne, his civic honours multiplied, he being appointed a colonel of the White regiment on 21 June 1705. Three months later he became president of Bridewell and Bethlem hospitals, and the following Michaelmas day was chosen lord mayor. During his mayoralty the City celebrated Marlborough's victories in Flanders, and at Rawlinson's request, the queen presented the trophies and colours taken at Ramillies and other engagements to be hung in the Guildhall. His surviving papers reflect the meticulous care with which he performed his public duties, and he was later celebrated for being 'easy and sedate' (Rawlinson MSS, D862, fols. 90–91) in the mayoral chair.

Rawlinson died on 9 November 1708 at his house in the Old Bailey, and was buried on 18 November in the church of St Dionis, in the tomb of his father. His will, dated 20 January 1700, suggests a considerable personal fortune, listing properties in Warwickshire, London, Essex, and Lancashire. His widow twice remarried, and was buried in St Dionis Backchurch on 1 March 1725.

Rawlinson's kinsman, **Sir Thomas Rawlinson** (c.1710–1769), also served as lord mayor of London. He was son of the Revd Robert Rawlinson (1680–1747) of Charlwood, Surrey, and his wife, Margaret Ray (b. 1677). His grandfather Daniel Rawlinson was the first Sir Thomas Rawlinson's first cousin. By 1735 he had married his first cousin Dorothea (1704–1743), daughter of the Revd Richard Ray of Haughley, Suffolk; he soon established himself as one of the City's most prominent grocers. He was elected a common councillor in 1741–4, alderman of Broad Street ward in 1746, and sheriff of London and Middlesex two years later. He rose rapidly within the Grocers' Company, and in 1746–7 served the office of master. On the death, on 27 November 1753, of lord mayor Edward Ironside, Rawlinson took the chair for the remainder of the year. He was knighted in 1760, was colonel of the Red regiment of trained bands from 1762 to his death, and was a prominent member of the Honourable Artillery Company, to which he presented in 1763 a 'sheet of red colours'. He was elected vice-president of the company in July 1766 and held the presidency of St Bartholomew's Hospital from 1767 to his death. He lived latterly at his estate of Stowlangtoft Hall in Suffolk, which he bought in 1760, but died at his house in Fenchurch Street, London, on 3 December 1769, his body being returned to Suffolk for burial at Haughley. His son, Sir Walter Rawlinson, inherited his Suffolk estates and married Mary, daughter of Sir Robert Ladbroke, lord mayor of London; they had no children. Walter Rawlinson became a partner in the banking firm of

Ladbroke, Robinson, and Parker. He was elected alderman of Dowgate in 1773, and resigned in 1777. He was also president of Bridewell and Bethlem hospitals in 1773–7, was knighted in 1774, and represented Queenborough in parliament from 1774 to 1784, and Huntingdon from 1784 to 1790. He died at Devonshire Place, London, on 13 March 1805. CHARLES WELCH, rev. PERRY GAUCI

Sources Bodl. Oxf., MS Rawl. D. 862 · Bodl. Oxf., MS Rawl. letters 63 · J. L. Chester and G. J. Armytage, eds., *Allegations for marriage licences issued from the faculty office of the archbishop of Canterbury at London, 1543 to 1869*, Harleian Society, 24 (1886), 151 · J. Le Neve, *Monumenta Anglicana*, 5: 1700–15 (1719), 163 · *Le Neve's Pedigrees of the knights*, ed. G. W. Marshall, Harleian Society, 8 (1873), 405–6 · A. Crawford, *A history of the Vintners' Company* (1977), 180, 192–3 · N. Luttrell, *A brief historical relation of state affairs from September 1678 to April 1714*, 6 vols. (1857) · A. B. Beaven, ed., *The aldermen of the City of London, temp. Henry III–[1912]*, 2 vols. (1908–13), vol. 2, p. 129 · J. L. Chester, ed., *The reiester booke of Saynte De'nis Backchurch parishe ... begynnynge ... 1538*, Harleian Society, register section, 3 (1878), 277 · A. Davies, *Dictionary of British portraiture*, 1 (1979), 115 · J. R. Woodhead, *The rulers of London, 1660–1689* (1965), 135 · will, 1708, PRO, PROB 11/506/18 · *Miscellanea Genealogica et Heraldica*, 4th ser., 1 (1904–5), 17–19 [Thomas Rawlinson] · GL, MS 11597 [Thomas Rawlinson] · BL, Add. MS 19146, fol. 110v [Thomas Rawlinson] · will, 1769, Prerogative Court of Canterbury, reel 953/433 (Bogg) [Thomas Rawlinson (c.1710–1769)] · *London Directory* (1736); (1749); (1755); (1758); (1763) [Sir Thomas Rawlinson (c.1710–1769)] · GM, 1st ser., 39 (1769), 608 [Thomas Rawlinson] · G. A. Raikes, *The history of the Honourable Artillery Company*, 2 vols. (1878), 10, 13 [Sir Thomas Rawlinson (c.1710–1769)]

Archives Bodl. Oxf., letter-book

Likenesses oils, 1687, Vintners' Hall, London · G. Vertue, line engraving, 1719 (after G. Kneller), BM, NPG · G. Kneller, oils, Bridewell Royal Hospital, Witley, Surrey

Wealth at death very wealthy; lands in four counties; £12,000 East India stock: will, PRO, PROB 11/506/18 · very rich—Sir Thomas Rawlinson

Rawlinson, Thomas (1681–1725), book collector, was born on 25 March 1681 in the Old Bailey in the parish of St Sepulchre, London, the eldest son of Sir Thomas *Rawlinson (bap. 1647, d. 1708), vintner and later lord mayor of London, and Mary (1661/2–1725), the eldest daughter of Richard Taylor of Turnham Green, Middlesex. His brother, the nonjuror antiquary and collector Richard *Rawlinson (1690–1755), was the fourth son. Thomas was educated at Mr Day's school in Cheam, Surrey, and at Eton College until 1698. While still at Eton he was admitted a member of the Middle Temple in January 1696 or 1697. He matriculated from St John's College, Oxford, on 25 February 1699 and stayed until December 1701, but did not take a degree. After a tour through England and the Low Countries he returned to study municipal law at the Middle Temple. On 19 May 1705 he was called to the bar and the next year he was appointed a governor of Bridewell and Bethlem hospitals, of which his father became president soon after. He was made governor of St Bartholomew's Hospital on 7 July 1712. His inclination to practise law was minimal. It had been his passion for some time to collect books and manuscripts (he received an annuity for books from his grandfather Richard Taylor) and he pursued this occupation almost exclusively after inheriting his father's estates, becoming the 'Leviathan of book-collectors during nearly the first thirty years of the eighteenth century' (Dibdin, 458).

Rawlinson collected both at home and abroad, mainly in the Netherlands and Flanders, operating within a wide circle of antiquaries and collectors. He later fell out with rival collectors Edward Harley and John Murray, but worked closely with John Bagford, Thomas Hearne, Michael Maittaire, and Richard Mead. In 1712 Bishop William Nicolson asked him for corrections for a new edition of his *English Historical Library* (1714), and Maittaire acknowledged his assistance in his edition of Juvenal (1716). Joseph Ames and Maittaire owed much to Rawlinson's collections for their studies of early printing. Rawlinson also had a formative influence on the collecting and antiquarianism of his younger brother Richard. In 1717 he joined Hearne in a tour of Berkshire, and the next year both Rawlinsons undertook a perambulation of Oxfordshire for Richard's proposed antiquarian history of that county. Richard's *English Topographer* (1720) is largely a catalogue of Thomas's topographical materials. In 1713 Thomas became a member of the Royal Society and in 1724 of the Society of Antiquaries.

Rawlinson had a close relationship with the Oxford antiquary Thomas Hearne. They shared a love of antiquarian study and collecting and, as nonjurors and Jacobites, a deep-seated disaffection with the age they lived in. Both had outspoken and acrid temperaments: 'This Age (says my Friend) wants Monitors to Goodness, God knows; nay, ev'n severe ones, to scare th^m out of ill Practises. I do my part in speaking; You, whose Pen is happier, by your Immortal Writings' (*Remarks*, 7.178). They corresponded regularly, though unfortunately most of Rawlinson's letters to Hearne are not extant. Rawlinson almost every month sent boxes filled with books, manuscripts, and fragments for Hearne to evaluate. Hearne copied parts of Rawlinson's notebooks into his diaries and thus preserved some impression of Rawlinson as a bibliographer. Hearne much appreciated Rawlinson's classical, antiquarian, and bibliographical knowledge, and depended to an important extent on his information and judgements.

Rawlinson attached great importance to Hearne's scholarly output, and acted as one of his agents, finding new subscribers, distributing books in his London circles, and advising his friend on his publishing projects. He provided Hearne with critical comments and materials for his edition of Leland's *Itinerary* (1710–12), and with the manuscript for *Beverly* (1716). He was closely involved with the preparations and production processes of the editions of Camden's *Annals of Queen Elizabeth* (1717) and William of Newburgh's *Chronicle* (1719). On a personal level he repeatedly offered Hearne a place in London to help solve his friend's political problems at Oxford. Hearne dedicated the preface of his edition of John Rouse (1716) to Rawlinson. His diary entry for 4 September 1725 is a warm and appreciative biographical account of his friend.

In 1716 Rawlinson moved from London's Gray's Inn, where his chambers could no longer accommodate his collections and where he was forced to sleep in the passage, to the roomier London House in Aldersgate Street.

Rawlinson's collecting activities were so intense that he accumulated vast debts and was forced to sell parts of his collections. He had neglected the administration of the Rawlinson estates, and, if information from William Oldisworth to Hearne can be relied upon, a late attempt to remedy his financial problems through investing in the disastrous South Sea stock only aggravated the situation. Six sales took place between 4 December 1721 and Rawlinson's death.

On 22 September 1724 Rawlinson married his servant Amy Frewin, formerly a servant in an Aldersgate Street coffee house. The marriage appears to have embarrassed his family, angered his creditors, and, according to Richard's account of his brother, led to 'the hastening of his own death' (Bodl. Oxf., MS Rawl. J 4° 4, fols. 148–50). It also caused friends to speculate about his wife's character and questionable reputation. Rawlinson was much plagued by the creditors, and under the increasing pressure his health deteriorated fast. Hearne reflected that the booksellers should be more lenient and should in fact erect a statue to him, as Rawlinson had furthered their trade by driving up the prices of books through his frequent and high bidding. He died on 6 August 1725 in London House, and was buried on 12 August in the parish of St Botolph, Aldersgate.

After Thomas's death his brother Richard returned from his travels in Europe. Under the terms of their father's will the entailed estates now devolved upon him. Thomas's will, however, complicated matters, as he had made over the family property to a nonjuror friend as his executor to hold in trust for his widow and possible heirs (there were no children). In order to secure the administration of the Rawlinson estates, Richard challenged the validity of the will. Forced to settle Thomas's debts and sell the entire collection, he organized eleven further auction sales in seven years. Nevertheless he was able to buy (and later retrieve) a great part of Thomas's books and manuscripts himself. What Richard thus salvaged finally came to the Bodleian Library, Oxford, in his great bequest to that institution and to the nation. Among other prominent purchasers at the sales were Lord Coleraine, Edward Harley, and James West.

The auction sales of Rawlinson's collections of books and manuscripts took place at St Paul's Coffee House, Bedford Coffee House, and London House, between 4 December 1721 and 4 March 1734, the last being the sale of the manuscripts. His paintings were sold separately in April 1734; his prints may have been sold individually or retained by Richard. Thus there were seventeen sales in total, each auction lasting on average twenty days; the auctioneers were Charles Davis and Thomas Ballard, the latter assisted by Anthony Barker. The Bodleian holds copies of all the sale catalogues, annotated with the prices realized and a few of the buyers' names. According to De Ricci it was 'the largest library as yet sold in England and, with the Heber library, the largest sold to the present day' and comprised over 200,000 volumes (De Ricci, 45); Enright quotes 50,000 volumes and over 1000 manuscripts for the later sales (Enright, 'Later auction sales',

113). Among them were invaluable manuscripts and incunabula (his noteworthy collection of Caxtons), and choice Elzevier and Aldine editions of the classics, many with Rawlinson's characteristic collation mark, 'C&P' (collated and perfect). Prices at the sales were disappointingly low. This has been attributed to such factors as the sale arrangements, the great number of books released onto the market, the position and role of the booksellers, the condition of the items (often bad or imperfect), and the sales of other important collections in those years.

The value and 'omnigenous' character of Rawlinson's collections, often praised by Hearne in his publications, long remained difficult to appreciate because of their sheer size and lack of organization (despite the sale catalogues compiled by Thomas) and the subsequent dispersal of the library. Rawlinson's reputation as an antiquarian collector also suffered because of the general lack of appreciation for the work of antiquaries, bibliographers, and collectors in the Augustan age. Well known is Joseph Addison's satirical description of Tom Folio in *The Tatler* (no. 158, 1710), which was reputedly a portrait of Thomas Rawlinson. Hearne robustly countered this view in his affectionate account of his friend:

> Some gave out, & published it, too, in printed Papers, that Mr Rawlinson understood the Editions and Title-pages of Books only, without any other Skill in them, and thereupon they stiled him *Tom Folio*. But these were only Buffoons, and persons of very shallow Learning. 'Tis certain that Mr Rawlinson understood the Editions and Titles of Books better than any Man I ever knew (for he had a very great Memory), but then, besides this, he was a great Reader, and had read abundance of the best writers ancient and modern throughout, and was intirely master of the Learning contain'd in them. (*Remarks*, 9.20)

THEODOR HARMSEN

Sources Richard Rawlinson's biographical account of Thomas Rawlinson, and related papers, Bodl. Oxf., MS Rawl. J 4°4, fols. 147–55 · Bodl. Oxf., MSS Rawlinson K (Hearne–Smith) · *Remarks and collections of Thomas Hearne*, ed. C. E. Doble and others, 11 vols., OHS, 2, 7, 13, 34, 42–3, 48, 50, 65, 67, 72 (1885–1921) · B. J. Enright, 'Richard Rawlinson: collector, antiquary, and topographer', DPhil diss., U. Oxf., 1956 · B. J. Enright, 'The later auction sales of Thomas Rawlinson's library, 1727–34', *The Library*, 5th ser., 11 (1956), 23–40, 103–113 · W. Y. Fletcher, 'The Rawlinsons and their collections', *Transactions of the Bibliographical Society*, 5 (1898–9), 67–86 · T. H. B. M. Harmsen, *Antiquarianism in the Augustan age: Thomas Hearne, 1678–1735* (2000) · B. J. Enright, 'Rawlinson's proposed history of Oxfordshire', *Oxoniensia*, 16 (1951), 57–78 · B. J. Enright, '"I collect and I preserve": Richard Rawlinson, 1690–1755, and eighteenth-century book collecting: portrait of a bibliophile, XXVIII', *Book Collector*, 39 (1990), 27–54 · B. J. Enright, 'Rawlinson and the chandlers', *Bodleian Library Record*, 4 (1952–3), 216–27 · F. Madan and others, *A summary catalogue of Western manuscripts in the Bodleian Library at Oxford*, 7 vols. (1895–1953) · R. W. Hunt, 'The cataloguing of the Rawlinson manuscripts, 1771–1844', *Bodleian Library Record*, 2 (1941–9), 190–95 · G. R. Tashjian, D. R. Tashjian, and B. J. Enright, *Richard Rawlinson: a tercentenary memorial* (1990) · *A literary antiquary: memoir of William Oldys ... together with his diary*, ed. J. Yeowell (1862), 101 · W. D. Macray, *Catalogus codicum ... Ricardi Rawlinson*, 5 vols. (1862–1900) · S. De Ricci, *English collectors of books and manuscripts* (1930), 45–6 · M. Clapinson and T. D. Rogers, *Summary catalogue of post-medieval manuscripts in the Bodleian Library, Oxford* (1991) · T. F. Dibdin, *Bibliomania, or, Book madness: a bibliographical romance*, 2nd edn, [2 vols.] (1811), 343–6 · W. Y. Fletcher, *English book collectors* (1902), 176–83, 186–95 · W. D. Macray, *Annals of the Bodleian Library, Oxford*, 2nd edn (1890); facs. edn (1984), 232, 234, 242, 250, 264 · Foster, *Alum. Oxon.* · A. Chalmers, ed., *The general biographical dictionary*, new edn, 26 (1816), 67–9 · Nichols, *Lit. anecdotes*, 5.489–98, 704 · S. Gibson and M. A. Gibson, 'An index to Rawlinson's collections (*circa*1700–50) for a new edition of Wood's *Athenae Oxonienses*', *Oxford Bibliographical Society, Proceedings and Papers*, 1 (1922–6), 65–95
Archives Bodl. Oxf., letters, corresp. · St John's College, Oxford, muniments and account book, MS 268 | BL, Add. MSS, Harley MSS, Sloane MSS · Bodl. Oxf., MSS Hearne, diaries
Wealth at death left Heathcot estate in Warwickshire to wife; land in Warwickshire, Norfolk, Lancashire, etc.; had inherited father's and mother's estates; unclear how much remained; approx. £10,000 in debt: will, PRO, PROB 11/163, sig. 22; PRO, PROB 11/612; Enright, 'Later auction sales'; *Remarks*, ed. Doble and others, vol. 9, pp. 23–4; Tashjian, Tashjian, and Enright, eds. *Richard Rawlinson*

Rawlinson, Sir Thomas (*c.*1710–1769). *See under* Rawlinson, Sir Thomas (*bap.* 1647, *d.* 1708).

Rawlinson, Sir William (1640–1703), lawyer, was born on 16 June 1640 at Graythwaite, Lancashire, the second son of William Rawlinson (1606–1680) of Graythwaite and Rusland Hall, Lancashire, and his wife, Elizabeth (*d.* 1683), daughter of Anthony Sawrey of Plumpton, Lancashire. Rawlinson attended Hawkshead School, run by a Mr Bordley. On 13 April 1655 he was admitted to Christ's College, Cambridge, and on 20 February 1657 he was admitted to Gray's Inn. Rawlinson was called to the bar in 1667, where he emerged as a regular pleader in chancery cases, being the third most frequent pleader in 1680.

In April 1686 Rawlinson was made a serjeant-at-law, being sponsored by Laurence Hyde, first earl of Rochester, and Sir John Trevor. Following the revolution he was named on 1 March 1689 as one of three commissioners of the great seal, and knighted on the 5th. When Sir John Maynard (his wife's grandfather) was removed as a commissioner of the great seal in May 1690 and Sir Anthony Keck resigned, Rawlinson was continued in post along with two new appointees, Sir John Trevor and Sir George Hutchins. In November 1690 Rawlinson appeared before the House of Lords to oppose a bill regulating the court of chancery. He continued as a commissioner until Sir John Somers was made lord keeper in March 1693. Somers was instrumental in denying Rawlinson promotion to be chief baron of the exchequer, arguing that his inexperience in the 'course of the exchequer' (Sachse, 93) rendered him unfit for the office. Instead the incumbent, Sir Robert Atkyns, remained in post, and by late March Rawlinson had resumed his private practice in chancery. In February 1694 he appeared before the Lords in the high-profile *Montagu v. Bath* case. On 8 March that year Rawlinson appeared before a committee of the Lords considering the bill for settling the estate of Sir John Maynard, and he appears to have secured a clause on his wife's behalf. In May 1695 Sir John Lowther of Lowther, second baronet, the future Viscount Lonsdale, was promoting Rawlinson to succeed Atkyns as chief baron, but again to no avail. In April 1697 Rawlinson again appeared before the Lords as counsel in the *Montagu v. Bath* case, and in October 1697 he appeared as counsel when the duke of Devonshire and the marquess of Normanby went to chancery over the purchase of Berkeley House.

Rawlinson died in Hendon of apoplexy on 11 May 1703 and was buried in the church at Hendon, where he had purchased the old mansion owned by the Whichcotes in Brent Street. He was survived by his second wife, Jane (d. 1712), daughter of Edward Noseworthy of Devon and his wife, Honora, daughter of Sir John Maynard. He had two daughters by his first wife (whose identity is unknown): Anne, who predeceased her father and who in 1694 married John Aislabie; and Elizabeth, who married in 1687 William Lowther, a barrister of the Middle Temple and the son of Sir John Lowther of Lowther, first baronet, by his second wife, and, secondly, in 1702 Giles Earle, son of Sir Thomas Earle, MP and mayor of Bristol.

STUART HANDLEY

Sources Baker, *Serjeants* · J. Foster, ed., *Pedigrees of the county families of England*, 1: *Lancashire* (1873) · Venn, *Alum. Cant.* · J. Foster, *The register of admissions to Gray's Inn, 1521–1889, together with the register of marriages in Gray's Inn chapel, 1695–1754* (privately printed, London, 1889), 281 · will, PRO, PROB 11/469, fols. 277r–282v · *The manuscripts of the House of Lords*, 4 vols., HMC, 17 (1887–94), vols. 1, 3 · *The manuscripts of the House of Lords*, new ser., 12 vols. (1900–77), vols. 1–2 · *The manuscripts of the earl of Lonsdale*, HMC, 33 (1893), 104–6 · Burke, *Gen. GB* (1886), 1531 · N. Luttrell, *A brief historical relation of state affairs from September 1678 to April 1714*, 6 vols. (1857), vols. 1–4 · W. L. Sachse, *Lord Somers: a political portrait* (1975), 93 · D. Lemmings, *Gentlemen and barristers: the inns of court and the English bar, 1680–1730* (1990), 288 · *The life and times of Anthony Wood*, ed. A. Clark, 3, OHS, 26 (1894), 419 · J. Le Neve, *Monumenta Anglicana, 1700–15* (1717), 72 · *DNB*
Likenesses portrait, Harvard U., law school

Rawlinson, William George (1840–1928), art historian and collector, was born on 23 December 1840 in Silver Street, Taunton, Somerset, the only son of William Rawlinson, who owned a silk mill there, and his wife, Harriet Jeboult. Nothing is known of his education; about 1865 young Rawlinson joined a London silk firm, James Pearsall & Co., which handled the produce of the mill at Taunton. Later, as a partner in that business, he helped to create the English embroidery-silk trade, until then a German monopoly. In conjunction with Sir Thomas Wardle of Leek he reintroduced old methods of dyeing silk with the natural dyes of the East. On 26 September 1867 he married Mary Margherita (b. 1847/8), daughter of the Revd Alexander Cridland, incumbent of Hensall-cum-Heck, Snaith, Yorkshire; they had one son and three daughters. He retired from business in 1908.

Rawlinson is chiefly remembered for his scholarly publications on the engraved work of J. M. W. Turner, of whose drawings and prints he was an assiduous collector. In 1878 he published *Turner's 'Liber Studiorum': a Description and a Catalogue*, which he described in the preface as 'mainly compiled—a labour of love indeed—in such intervals as I have been able to snatch from City work' (Rawlinson, *Turner's Liber Studiorum*, vii). Based on the pioneering catalogue of the Burlington Fine Arts Club 1872 *Liber* exhibition, and much influenced by the writings of John Ruskin, this was the essential guide for all students and collectors of *Liber* prints. A second, much revised, edition

appeared in 1906, and was only superseded in 1924 by the more exhaustive catalogue of A. J. Finberg.

However, Rawlinson's other major Turner publication, the two-volume *Engraved Work of J. M. W. Turner* (1908–13), remains the only extensive catalogue of the nearly 900 prints, in addition to the *Liber Studiorum*, by and after Turner. The researches that led to these invaluable catalogues were based on Rawlinson's own collection. His collecting of the artist's watercolours is reflected in his contributions to a special number of *The Studio* on Turner's watercolours published in 1909. His choice collection of Turner watercolours was sold in 1917 to R. A. Tatton, after whose death it was dispersed at Christies on 14 December 1928. Rawlinson's collection of *Liber* proofs, of which he had issued a privately printed catalogue in 1887 (with a revised edition in 1912), was sold later in that year to Francis Bullard, of Boston, Massachusetts, and formed part of that collector's great bequest to the Boston Museum of Fine Arts in 1913. Rawlinson's unrivalled collection of other Turner engravings was bought, as a whole, in 1919 by S. L. Courtauld, and is now in the Yale Center for British Art, New Haven. Late in his career as a collector Rawlinson also became interested in coloured aquatints of the early nineteenth century and in blue and white Chinese porcelain.

For many years until he left it in 1919, subsequently taking a flat in Chelsea, Rawlinson's house on Campden Hill was the centre of a large circle of friends, especially writers and artists. He died at his home, 26 Cadogan Court, Draycott Avenue, Chelsea, on 13 May 1928.

LUKE HERRMANN

Sources *The Times* (15 May 1928) · b. cert. · m. cert. · d. cert. · *DNB* · W. G. Rawlinson, preface, *Turner's Liber Studiorum: a description and a catalogue* (1878), v–vii; 2nd edn (1906), v–vi · W. G. Rawlinson, *The engraved work of J. M. W. Turner*, 1 (1908), vii–viii · *CGPLA Eng. & Wales* (1928)
Wealth at death £143,106 17s. 2d.: resworn probate, 26 July 1928, *CGPLA Eng. & Wales*

Rawly (d. 1589). *See under* American Indians in England (*act.* c.1500–1609).

Rawnsley, Hardwicke Drummond (1851–1920), Church of England clergyman and conservationist, was born on 18 September 1851 at the rectory, Shiplake, Oxfordshire, the fourth of ten children of the Revd Robert Drummond Burrell Rawnsley (1817–1882), rector of Shiplake, and his wife, Catherine Ann (1818–1892), the daughter of Sir William Franklin and the niece of the Arctic explorer Sir John Franklin. Educated at Uppingham School (1862–70) under the headmastership of Edward Thring, where he gained a scholarship and won prizes for athletics and literature, Rawnsley went up to Balliol College, Oxford, in 1870. Here he distinguished himself in athletics and rowing, and gained a third class in natural science in 1874. Under the tutelage of John Ruskin he joined the 'Hinksey roadmenders', and through Ruskin was introduced to Octavia Hill.

After taking his MA Rawnsley was ordained deacon in 1875, and became the first chaplain of Clifton College mission. His success in winning the confidence of the people in one of Bristol's poorest areas, through his unconventional approach to the priestly ministry, paradoxically led to his dismissal. In 1877 he was ordained priest and in 1878 took up his ministry in Wray on Windermere. On 29 January 1878 he married Edith Fletcher (d. 1916) of Croft, Ambleside. They had one son, Noel, who, because of his parents' numerous activities and love of travel, suffered a somewhat solitary childhood.

Having elicited the support of Ruskin, Octavia Hill, and Sir Robert Hunter, solicitor to the Commons Preservation Society, in 1883 Rawnsley successfully spearheaded the campaign to prevent the construction of slate railways from the quarries above Buttermere, which would have ruined the unspoilt valleys of Newlands and Ennerdale. This, the first of his numerous campaigns to protect the region, hastened the foundation of the Lake District Defence Society. In 1883 he was appointed vicar of Crosthwaite and rural dean of Keswick, where, with the help of his artistically gifted wife, Edith, in November 1884 he founded the Keswick School of Industrial Arts to provide employment and craft training for local people. Rawnsley's interest in education for life led him to take a large part in the foundation of Keswick high school, which opened in October 1898, one of the first co-educational secondary schools in the country, of which he was a benefactor. Here he encouraged the introduction of a broad curriculum, including music, dance, drawing, carpentry, gymnastics, and gardening.

From 1888 Rawnsley served on the new Cumberland county council, opposing the construction of roads over lakeland passes, reducing mining pollution, and organizing the proper signposting of footpaths. His persistence and single-minded determination made him some enemies; his opposition to the granting of new liquor licences offended vested interests and lost him re-election in 1895. Undeterred from his reforming zeal, he went on in later years to inveigh against pornography and against screen violence in the cinema. In 1893 he was appointed canon of Carlisle Cathedral. Five years later he reluctantly declined the bishopric of Madagascar, feeling that he had already committed himself too deeply to the causes of conservation in the Lake District and, more recently, on a national scale. Refining ideas which Ruskin had been the first to promulgate, Sir Robert Hunter, Octavia Hill, and Rawnsley met in the offices of the Commons Preservation Society on 16 November 1893. The result of this meeting was the foundation of the organization which, eight months later, was officially inaugurated under the presidency of Hugh Lupus Grosvenor, first duke of Westminster, as the National Trust for Places of Historic Interest or Natural Beauty. Rawnsley, honorary secretary until his death, oversaw the acquisition of large areas of countryside, particularly in the Lake District and the west country.

An inveterate traveller, in 1896 Rawnsley was sent as a newspaper correspondent to cover the coronation of the tsar in Moscow, and three years later he toured the eastern states of the USA as ambassador for the National Trust. He had previously made visits to the Holy Land and to Egypt

to see the excavations of Sir Flinders Petrie and had undertaken several walking and painting tours in the Alps with his wife.

In 1912 Rawnsley was appointed honorary chaplain to George V, for whose coronation he had organized the national bonfire celebrations—having previously masterminded the bonfires for Queen Victoria's jubilees. In 1918 he chaired a war memorials committee and organized nationwide pyrotechnic displays in celebration of the armistice.

Rawnsley's friendship with the Potter family led eventually to the acquisition by the National Trust of Lake District farms and more than 4000 acres of land given during her lifetime and bequeathed at her death by Beatrix Potter (Heelis). Rawnsley had encouraged Beatrix Potter in her literary aspirations and had been instrumental in helping her to achieve publication of her first books, though Warne's did not accept the verse version of 'Peter Rabbit' which he had composed in the belief that in that form it might prove more acceptable to a publisher. In addition to innumerable pamphlets and articles, children's songs and hymns, Rawnsley published more than forty books, many of them about the life, history, and literary associations of the Lake District, and, as a minor lake poet, a vast output of verse, principally in the form of sonnets.

Rawnsley was impulsive, eloquent, irascible, and of a mercurial temperament, with a stocky figure, piercing blue eyes, and bristling beard. Though described by one parishioner as 'the most active volcano in Europe', he was none the less a charming and entertaining host, and, in spite of his heavy commitments nationwide, still found time for the pastoral care of his flock. An acute and sensitive observer of the natural world, a legacy of his schooldays under Thring, he had a profound reverence for the work and philosophy of Wordsworth, which coloured his view of the preservation of lakeland. A family connection with Alfred, Lord Tennyson led to the production by embroiderers of the Keswick School of Industrial Arts of the pall for the poet's coffin at Westminster Abbey.

Rawnsley's wife died in December 1916, and on 1 June 1918 he married his secretary, Eleanor Foster, the daughter of William Frederick Simpson of Grasmere. There were no children of this second marriage. Rawnsley retired from the ministry due to ill health in 1917, to live at Allan Bank, Grasmere, the former home of Wordsworth, where he died on 28 May 1920. He was buried on 1 June in Crosthwaite parish churchyard. Friars Crag, Derwentwater, was purchased by public subscription and given to the National Trust in his memory in 1922.

GRAHAM MURPHY

Sources E. F. Rawnsley, *Canon Rawnsley* (1923) · G. Murphy, *Founders of the National Trust* (1987) · *West Cumberland Times* (2 June 1920) · *Cumberland News* (22 Sept 1951) · private information (2004)
Archives Cumbria AS, Kendal, personal corresp. and papers · Cumbria AS, Kendal, corresp., papers, and sermons · priv. coll. | Balliol Oxf., corresp. with A. L. Smith · Cumbria AS, Kendal, corresp. with John Ruskin · NL Scot., corresp. with Blackwoods and poems · Surrey HC, corresp. with Sir Robert Hunter and others

Likenesses four photographs, 1862–1918, repro. in Rawnsley, *Canon Rawnsley* · R. Potter, double portrait, photograph, 1885, priv. coll. · R. Potter, group portrait, photograph, 1885, priv. coll. · F. Yates, pastel drawing, 1915, National Trust Library · F. Yates, two pastel drawings, 1915, priv. coll. · photograph, repro. in F. A. Benjamin, *The Ruskin linen industry of Keswick*, 6 (privately printed, Beckermet, Cumbria, 1974), 6

Wealth at death £60,511 8s. 9d.: probate, 21 Sept 1920, *CGPLA Eng. & Wales*

Rawson, George (1807–1889), hymn writer, was born in Park Square, Leeds, on 5 June 1807 into a Congregationalist family. Educated at Clunie's School, Manchester, he was articled to a firm of Leeds solicitors, and ultimately practised for himself. Retiring from business, he went to Clifton, Bristol, where he attended Highbury Chapel. He died at Clifton on 25 March 1889.

Rawson was an active Congregationalist layman and hymn writer. His earliest verses appeared anonymously, under the signature of a Leeds Layman, because he refused to allow his name to be appended to his hymns. In 1853 he assisted the Congregationalist ministers of Leeds in compiling the *Leeds Hymn-Book*, to which he contributed six hymns. He wrote twenty-seven compositions for the *Psalms and Hymns for the Use of the Baptist Denomination* (1858). He also published two notable collections of his own verses: *Hymns, Verses and Chants* (1876) and *Songs of Spiritual Thought* (1885). His best-known hymns are 'By Christ redeemed', 'Father in high heaven dwelling', and 'We limit not the truth of God'.

J. C. HADDEN, rev. LEON LITVACK

Sources J. Julian, ed., *A dictionary of hymnology*, rev. edn (1907); repr. in 2 vols. (1915) · J. I. Jones and others, *The Baptist hymn book companion*, ed. H. Martin (1962) · K. L. Parry, ed., *Companion to 'Congregational praise'* (1953) · E. Routley, *An English-speaking hymnal guide* (1979) · J. Brownlie, *The hymns and hymn writers of the church hymnary* (1911) · *Leeds Mercury* (30 March 1889) · J. Miller, *Singers and songs of the church* (1869) · K. L. Parry, 'The hymn writers of Bristol', *Hymn Society of Great Britain and Ireland Occasional Paper*, 4 (Oct 1946)

Archives UCL, letters to Henry Brougham and Lord Brougham

Rawson, Sir Harry Holdsworth (1843–1910), naval officer, second son of Christopher Rawson of Woolwich, JP for Surrey, and his wife, Frances Emily Wright, was born at Walton on the Hill, Lancashire, on 5 November 1843. He was at Marlborough College from February 1854 to Christmas 1855. Rawson entered the navy on 9 April 1857, and was appointed to the *Calcutta*, flagship of Sir Michael Seymour, on the China station. He served through the Second Opium War, being present in the *Calcutta*'s launch at the capture of the Taku (Dagu) forts in 1858, and in 1860 he was landed as aide-de-camp to Captain R. Dew of the *Encounter*, with whom he was present at the second capture of the Taku forts, at the battle of Palikiao (Baliqiao), and at the taking of Peking (Beijing).

Rawson saw much active service against the Chinese rebels; for the capture of Ningpo (Ningbo), which he afterwards held for three months against the rebels with 1300 Chinese under his command, and for Fungwha (Fenghua), where he was severely wounded, he was mentioned in dispatches. He was also thanked on the quarter-deck for jumping overboard at night in the Shanghai River to save

life. Rawson was promoted sub-lieutenant on 9 April 1863, and lieutenant a month later. In the same year he was one of the officers who took out to Japan the gunboat *Empress*, a present from Queen Victoria to the emperor and the first ship of the modern Japanese navy. Rawson then qualified as a gunnery lieutenant, and after serving a commission as first lieutenant of the *Bellerophon* in the channel, was appointed in January 1870 to the Royal yacht, on which on 7 September 1871 he was promoted commander. In August 1871 he gained the silver medal of the Royal Humane Society for saving life at Antwerp. He married on 19 October 1871 Florence Alice Stewart, daughter of John Ralph Shaw of Arrowe Park, Cheshire; they had five children.

As commander Rawson served two commissions in the *Hercules*, in the channel, and in the Mediterranean, and on 4 June 1877 he was promoted captain. In the November following he was appointed to the *Minotaur*, as flag captain to Lord John Hay, commanding the channel squadron; and, after going to the Mediterranean in 1878, he received the thanks of the Admiralty for a report on the capabilities of defence of the Suez Canal. He hoisted the British flag at Nicosia, Cyprus, and was for a month commandant there. Following this service he was again flag captain in the channel squadron, this time until March 1882, and he was then appointed to the troopship *Thalia* for the Egyptian campaign, during which he served as principal transport officer. He was awarded the third class of the Osmanieh, and the CB. From February 1883 to September 1885 he was flag captain to Lord John Hay, at that time commander-in-chief in the Mediterranean, and in October 1885 he became captain of the steam reserve at Devonport, where he remained until 1889. He was a member of the signal committee of 1886, was captain of the battleship *Benbow* in the Mediterranean from 1889 to 1891, and became an aide-de-camp to Queen Victoria in August 1890, a position he held until promoted to flag rank on 14 February 1892.

Rawson was a member of the international code signals committee from 1892 to 1895; in 1893 he was one of the umpires for the naval manoeuvres, and in May 1895 he was appointed commander-in-chief on the Cape of Good Hope and west coast of Africa station, with his flag in the cruiser *St George*. He held this command until May 1898, and during it organized and carried out two expeditions. In August 1895 he landed at Mombasa the naval brigade which, with a force of askaris, captured Mweli (some 15 miles from the coast), the stronghold of Mbarak bin Rachid, a Mazaria chief. In August 1896, following the unexpected death of Sultan Hamed bin Thwain, part of Rawson's squadron bombarded the palace at Zanzibar and deposed the claimant, Seyyid Khalid. Rawson received the Brilliant Star of Zanzibar, first class, in acknowledgement from the sultan; his action was officially approved, and he received the thanks of the Admiralty. In February 1897 he landed in command of a naval brigade from his squadron, with which, together with a force of Hausa, he advanced to Benin city to punish the massacre in January of British political officers, led by J. R. Phillips, the acting consul-general. In March Benin was captured and looted, then accidentally burnt. Rawson was created KCB in May 1897. On 19 March 1898 he was promoted vice-admiral.

Rawson commanded the channel squadron from December 1898 to April 1901, after which he was appointed president of the committee which investigated the structural strength of torpedo-boat destroyers. This was his last naval service. In January 1902 he was appointed governor of New South Wales, 'a post for which his tact, kindliness, and good sense were sturdy qualifications.' Lady Rawson died in the Red Sea on 3 December 1905, while on passage to Australia. Despite this personal tragedy Sir Harry was a successful and popular governor, and in 1908 his term of office was extended by one year to May 1909. He was promoted admiral on 12 August 1903, and retired on 3 November 1908; he was made a GCB in June 1906 and a GCMG in November 1909. He died at 3 Devonshire Terrace, Marylebone, London, following an operation for appendicitis, on 3 November 1910, and was buried at Bracknell parish church on 8 November, a memorial service being held at St Margaret's, Westminster.

L. G. C. Laughton, rev. Andrew Lambert

Sources G. Rawson, *Admiral Sir Harry Rawson* (1914) · W. L. Clowes, *The Royal Navy: a history from the earliest times to the present*, 7 vols. (1897–1903), vol. 7 · K. Ingham, *A history of East Africa* (1962) · CGPLA *Eng. & Wales* (1908)

Archives NL Aus., corresp. with Alfred Deakin

Likenesses Spy [L. Ward], chromolithograph caricature, NPG; repro. in *VF* (25 April 1901) · portrait, repro. in Rawson, *Admiral Sir Harry Rawson*

Wealth at death £16,428 1s. 11d.: resworn probate, 17 Dec 1910, CGPLA *Eng. & Wales*

Rawson, John, Viscount Clontarff (1470?–1547?), prior of the hospital of St John of Jerusalem in Ireland and administrator, was descended from a family long established at Water Fryston in Yorkshire. His father, Richard Rawson, was an alderman of London in 1476–7, senior warden of the Mercers' Company from 1478 to 1483, and sometime sheriff of London. His mother was Isabella Craford (d. 1497). His brother Richard (d. 1543) was chaplain to Henry VIII and archdeacon of Essex. John was the eldest son, and in 1492 was admitted free of the Mercers' Company. However, he joined the order of the knights of St John before 1497. In 1510 he was dispatched to Rome on a mission representing his order and *en route* was received by the doge at Venice. The following year he was appointed prior of the hospital of St John of Jerusalem at Kilmainham, Dublin. This office carried with it the headship of the order in Ireland and a seat in the Irish house of peers. At that time, Rawson was sworn a member of the privy council. He also held the preceptories of Quenington, Gloucestershire, and Swinfield.

In 1515 Rawson and the earl of Kildare dined with the king at Greenwich, and in that year he was commended by Fabrizio del Carretto, grand master of the order, for his good management at Kilmainham. In 1517 he was appointed treasurer of Ireland. The following year he was summoned to the defence of Rhodes, then besieged by the Ottomans. In 1519 he obtained a licence from the king to travel abroad for three years but he apparently did not leave England since his licence was revoked and he was obliged to return to Ireland in July 1520 with Lord Lieutenant Surrey. Further to Cardinal Wolsey's representations on his behalf, Rawson was appointed treasurer in February 1522. He remained in Ireland until March of that year and then appears to have travelled to Rhodes, as his name features at the head of the list of English knights reviewed there by the grand master, Philippe Villiers de l'Isle Adam in 1522. Following the surrender of Rhodes on 20 December 1522 Rawson returned to Ireland. In 1525 he again received a licence to travel abroad for three years and to retain his benefices and revenues in his absence. In June 1527 he accompanied Villiers de l'Isle Adam to Corneto in Italy and that same month he was appointed turcopolier or commander of the turcopoles or light infantry of the order. This office carried with it the headship of the English *langue* of the order and responsibility for the coastal defences of Malta.

In September 1528 Henry VIII reappointed Rawson treasurer of Ireland and in 1529 he served as undertreasurer. From September 1529 to August 1530 Rawson was a member of the secret council of Ireland which served as deputy lieutenant to Henry Fitzroy, duke of Richmond. In 1532 he travelled to England for consultations with the king and he also participated in the proceedings against Sir William Skeffington. He remained loyal to the crown during the Kildare rebellion. During the revolt his property was plundered by the insurgents and he was present at the surrender of Old Ross Castle in Wexford. In August 1534 he was at St David's in Wales, *en route* to inform Henry VIII of recent events in Ireland, but was unable to travel to the court as he was 'much diseased with the palsy, and may not well endure to ride' (*State Papers, Henry VIII*, vol. 2, pt 3, p. 201). In September 1535 Sir William Brabazon recommended Rawson to Cromwell as a suitable candidate for the lord chancellorship, but his advice was ignored.

By 1538 Rawson was elderly and very feeble. However, he was sufficiently active to arouse the animosity of George Browne, archbishop of Dublin, who termed him 'the pecuniose prior of Kilmainham'. He was also still shrewd enough to anticipate the monastic suppression campaign by leasing parcels of the property of Kilmainham Priory at low rates, particularly to family members. In September 1540 Lord Deputy St Leger and the Irish council requested that Rawson be elevated to the honour of Viscount Clontarff. After prolonged negotiations he surrendered the priory of Kilmainham on 22 November 1540 and subsequently received a pension of 500 marks. In December of the same year he was granted an annuity of 200 marks for life, payable out of the dissolved possessions of the order's property in Gloucestershire. On 20 June 1541 he was created Viscount Clontarff for life and was granted an annual fee of £10. He assumed the arms of his maternal family. In 1542 he is said to have been unlikely to live much longer, 'not well able to live … being now in manner impotent' (*State Papers, Henry VIII*, vol. 3, pt 3, p. 438). Yet he continued to attend council sessions until

1543. The date of his death is uncertain. He is thought to have died in 1547 when Oswald Massingberd was appointed grand master to succeed him as titular prior of Kilmainham. Some peerages state that he died in 1560 but his age makes this improbable. He had at least one natural child: a daughter named Katherine who married Rowland, son of Patrick White, baron of the Irish exchequer, and it has been suggested that the Sir John Rawson who frequently appears in Irish records during Elizabeth's reign may have been his son. Upon Clontarff's death the peerage became extinct.   MARY ANN LYONS

Sources J. S. Brewer and W. Bullen, eds., *Calendar of the Carew manuscripts*, 1: *1515–1574*, PRO (1867), 24, 27, 51, 57–8, 65–6, 122, 124, 126, 171 · *LP Henry VIII*, 2/1, no. 1359; 2/2, no. 3611; 4/1, no. 1294; 4/3, nos. 5903, 6097; 5, no. 1715; 7, no. 1045; 13/1, no. 641; 13/2, nos. 937, 1027, 1032; 14/1, no. 302; 15, nos. 82, 328, 912; 16, nos. 42, 57, 70, 77, 1119, 1284; 17, nos. 367, 491, 688, 881; 18/1, no. 553 · *State papers published under … Henry VIII*, 11 vols. (1830–52), vol. 2, pt 3, nos. 143–4, 150, 164, 166, 201–2, 212, 252, 279; vol. 2, pt 3, nos. 41, 51, 62, 93, 94, 108, 238, 246, 276, 302, 305, 321–2, 336, 340–41, 381, 396, 409, 421, 433, 445, 470; vol. 3, pt 3, nos. 9, 108, 111, 121, 179, 189, 225, 238–9, 244–5, 271, 294, 296, 307, 310, 317, 391, 400, 411, 438 · *CSP Ire.*, 1509–73, 2, 4, 8, 12, 19, 47, 50, 55, 62, 76 · M. C. Griffith, ed., *Calendar of inquisitions formerly in the office of the chief remembrancer of the exchequer*, IMC (1991), 7, 28, 87, 89–91, 93–4, 104–5, 110–11 · J. Morrin, ed., *Calendar of the patent and close rolls of chancery in Ireland, of the reigns of Henry VIII, Edward VI, Mary, and Elizabeth*, 1 (1861), 19, 53, 57, 194–5, 493 · 'Calendar of fiants, Henry VIII to Elizabeth', *Report of the deputy keeper of the public records in Ireland*, 7–22 (1875–90), appxs; repr. in *The Irish fiants of the Tudor sovereigns*, 4 vols. (1994) · N. B. White, ed., *Extents of Irish monastic possessions, 1540–41*, IMC (1943), 84, 86, 91 · G. Mac Niocaill, ed., *Crown surveys of lands, 1540–41, with the Kildare rental begun in 1518*, IMC (1992), 241–2, 261 · C. McNeill, ed., *Registrum de Kilmainham: register of chapter acts of the Hospital of Saint John of Jerusalem in Ireland, 1326–1339*, IMC (1932) · R. Lascelles, ed., *Liber munerum publicorum Hiberniae … or, The establishments of Ireland*, 2 vols. [1824–30], pt 3, p. 52 · J. Lodge, *The peerage of Ireland*, rev. M. Archdall, rev. edn, 3 (1789), 191 · GEC, *Peerage*, new edn · J. L. J. Hughes, ed., *Patentee officers in Ireland, 1173–1826, including high sheriffs, 1661–1816 and 1761–1816*, IMC (1960), 110 · J. Haydn, *The book of dignities: containing rolls of the official personages of the British empire* (1851) · T. W. Moody and others, eds., *A new history of Ireland*, 2: *Medieval Ireland, 1169–1534* (1987); repr. with corrections (1993), 655, 658, 671, 676, 678, 681–3, 774; 9: *Maps, genealogies, lists: a companion to Irish history, part 2* (1984), 480 · B. Bradshaw, *The dissolution of the religious orders in Ireland under Henry VIII* (1974), 28–9, 89, 122–3 · S. G. Ellis, *Ireland in the age of the Tudors* (1998), 34, 113, 115, 130, 132, 212–13, 367, 371 · Abbé Vertot, *History of the knights of Malta*, 1 (1786), 244–6

Rawson, Sir William. *See* Adams, Sir William (1783–1827).

Rawsthorne, Alan (1905–1971), composer, was born on 2 May 1905 at Deardengate House, Haslingden, Lancashire, the younger child and only son of Hubert Rawsthorne (1868–1943) and his wife, Janet Bridge (1877/8–1927). His father, a qualified doctor, came from a middle-class landowning family, and the young Rawsthorne's early years were spent amid beautiful rolling Lancashire moorland. He suffered much ill health as a child, his education being from private tutors apart from brief spells at schools in Southport. In his early years he evinced both musical and literary talent, but his parents at first opposed his wish to

Alan Rawsthorne (1905–1971), by Sir Cecil Beaton, pubd 1948

become a musician, and it was not until 1925, after abortive periods of studying dentistry and architecture at Liverpool University, that he was able to enter the Royal Manchester College of Music, where he studied the piano with Frank Merrick and the cello with Carl Fuchs. The Rawsthornes, including Alan's elder sister, Barbara, were an extraordinarily close-knit and affectionate family, giving the two children a secure and caring background, and his mother's death in 1927 at the age of forty-nine was a severe blow.

After leaving college in 1929, Rawsthorne continued his piano studies with Egon Petri, first in Zakopane, Poland, and later, briefly, in Berlin. During 1932–4 he provided the music for the school of dance and mime at Dartington Hall, Devon, composing, playing the piano, and teaching there. On leaving Dartington, he moved to London and concentrated on composition. In 1934 he married the violinist Jessie May Hinchliffe (1908–1989), who had been a fellow student at Manchester and was now in the BBC Symphony Orchestra. After some chamber works had made local impact, Rawsthorne's first international breakthrough came with his *Bagatelles* for piano, *Theme and Variations* for two violins (both 1938), and *Symphonic Studies* for orchestra (1939); the latter two were performed at festivals of the International Society for Contemporary Music in London and Warsaw respectively, and the *Bagatelles* in Oslo. By the outbreak of the Second World War in 1939, Rawsthorne's left-wing political affiliations and pacifist beliefs were deeply established, but he nevertheless felt impelled to join the armed forces in order to fight the racism of the Nazi regime.

Rawsthorne's pre-war works were greeted by British

critics as representing the influence of continental European trends, with their emphasis on contrapuntal techniques, freely and quickly moving tonality, and a highly chromatic style. The alertness, sensitivity, and underlying passion of his music were retained through the war years, during which he managed to complete the full orchestral version of his first piano concerto (1942) and the overture *Street Corner* (1944–5), both works achieving immediate success and sustained popularity. (The concerto's finale was encored at its Viennese première in 1950 in response to a great ovation.) The fantasy overture *Cortèges* (1945) is an especially dazzling display of contrapuntal wizardry. During the early war years Rawsthorne had sketched what became his first violin concerto (finally completed in 1947), but the sketches were lost when his flat in Bristol was bombed, and other works were also destroyed, notably *Kubla Khan*, a cantata for tenor, chorus, and orchestra of strings and percussion.

Following the war Rawsthorne became steadily productive across a range of mostly instrumental genres. He produced a fine *Concerto for String Orchestra* in 1949, his first symphony in 1950, and his greatest popular success, the second piano concerto, for the Festival of Britain in 1951, when it was first performed by Clifford Curzon, who recorded it. Curzon played it in numerous countries with conductors such as Sir John Barbirolli, Sir Thomas Beecham, Eduard van Beinum, Sergiu Celibidache, and Josef Krips. Other outstanding instrumental pieces from this period include a sonata for cello and piano and a sonatina for piano (both 1949), as well as the intense and passionate quartet for clarinet and strings of 1948. In these works, an added degree of romantic warmth seemed to be entering his music, though the magnificent second string quartet of 1954 combined this with exceptional economy of material. Parallel to this output was an increasingly important succession of major film scores, including *The Captive Heart* (1946), *Uncle Silas* (1947), *Pandora and the Flying Dutchman* (1950), and *The Cruel Sea* (1952): Rawsthorne became an outstanding practitioner of this art, and often greatly enhanced the dramatic or emotional impact of his films.

During the mid-1950s, however, Rawsthorne's concert music was less consistently inspired, and it seemed that his mannerisms were constricting his imaginative fluency. In 1953 he moved to a remote Essex village, Little Sampford, leaving behind his somewhat bohemian existence in London and, as he himself said, giving himself an 'escape to reality'. This return to the peace and tranquillity of the countryside gave him a new lease of creative life. The year after his divorce from Jessie in 1954, he married the painter Isabel Agnes Lambert, née Nicholas (1912–1992), the widow of one of Rawsthorne's closest friends and colleagues, Constant Lambert, and previously the wife of the journalist Sefton Delmer. Rawsthorne's second marriage was one of immense happiness, and it is significant that he and his new wife remained on terms of great friendship with his former wife. Isabel Lambert designed the décor of *Madame Chrysanthème* (Royal Opera House,

Covent Garden, London, 1955), Rawsthorne's only stage work.

In 1958, writing his sonata for violin and piano for Joseph Szigeti, Rawsthorne embarked on a final period of intense creativity, foreshadowed by the remarkable second violin concerto of 1956, whose disastrous première distracted attention from its great qualities and significant developments in style and technique. The violin sonata, a remarkably unified and resourceful work even for him, showed how he could integrate new elements into his familiar manner, and he continued to expand his technical and imaginative horizons over the next decade. The second symphony (*Pastoral Symphony*, 1959), with its soprano soloist in the reflective finale, shows an unexpected *rapprochement* to an English pastoral tradition that had always seemed inimical to him, without in any way diluting the individuality of his own musical personality, and in several works he made an equally successful linkage with Schoenbergian techniques, as in the quintet for piano and winds (1963). Perhaps his most striking and profound utterances from this period are the suite (really more of an oratorio) for soprano, chorus, and orchestra, *Carmen vitale* (1963), in which he uses medieval texts to make a personal statement of enormous power and demonstrates a remarkable insight into the medieval mind, and his third symphony (1964), music of passionate commitment in which he uses a twelve-note row in a distinctive and personal way to resolve cathartically the conflicts of earlier symphonic works.

In his last few years Rawsthorne's creative energies dimmed, but at the last, with his unfinished *Elegy* for guitar (1971), completed by its dedicatee Julian Bream, he proved still capable of the utmost delicacy and depth of thought, the passion beneath the surface of the music being as fresh and vivid as ever. He received increasing official recognition: he was made a CBE in 1961 and an honorary fellow of Downing College, Cambridge, in 1969, and received honorary doctorates from the universities of Belfast and Liverpool (1969) and Essex (1971). Rawsthorne was a most cultivated and charming man, whose precise use of language was particularly effective in expressing his dry wit. He was a courteous and gentle companion, and a writer of exceptional authority: his famous article on Chopin's ballades, fantasy, and scherzos (in *Frédéric Chopin*, ed. A. Walker, 1965) remains an exceptional contribution to Chopin scholarship. After his death in Addenbrooke's Hospital, Cambridge, from pneumonia complicated by a haemorrhage on 24 July 1971, and subsequent burial at Thaxted parish church, Essex, a number of works retained a hold on the repertory, and towards the end of the 1980s there was a marked increase in performances and recordings. Rawsthorne's music is wider-ranging than has been acknowledged. Its wit and delicacy, as well as strong intelligence, have always been recognized, but only recently has the range of its power and depth begun to be properly appreciated. He made a unique, and one must believe enduring, contribution to British musical life.   JOHN MCCABE

Sources J. McCabe, *Alan Rawsthorne: portrait of a composer* (1999) · personal knowledge (2004) · private information (2004) · Royal Northern College of Music, Manchester, Rawsthorne archives · Oxford University Press, Rawsthorne archives · *CGPLA Eng. & Wales* (1972)

Archives Oxford University Press, archive files · Royal Northern College of Music, Manchester, papers | FILM BFI NFTVA · BL NSA | SOUND BBC WAC · BFI NFTVA · BL NSA, documentary recordings · BL NSA, oral history interviews · BL NSA, performance recordings · BL NSA, 'The piano music of Alan Rawsthorne', 6 April 1966, 1CO R0000597 B22 · BL NSA, 'Rawsthorne at 60', M365R TRK2 · BL NSA, recorded lecture · BL NSA, *Talking about music*, 70, 1LP015167552 BD1 BBC TRANSC · British Music Information Centre, London

Likenesses C. Beaton, photograph, pubd 1948, NPG [*see illus.*] · J. Pannett, chalk drawing, *c*.1957–1958, NPG · R. Noakes, bronze cast of bust, 1965, NPG · I. Lambert, mixed media on canvas, 1966, repro. in *Isabel Rawsthorne, 1912–1992: paintings, drawings and designs* (1997–8) [exhibition catalogue, Mercer Art Gallery, Harrogate, and October Gallery, London] · I. Lambert, oils, 1966, NPG · I. Lambert, mixed media on canvas, 1967, repro. in S. Doyle, *Isabel Rawsthorne, 1912–1992: paintings, drawings and designs* (1997) [exhibition catalogue, Harrogate and London, 1 Nov 1997–1 Feb 1998] · R. Noakes, plaster cast of death mask, 1971, NPG · J. Blake, photographs, priv. coll. · D. Glass, photographs, priv. coll.

Wealth at death £17,085: administration with will, 6 Jan 1972, *CGPLA Eng. & Wales*

Ray. *See also* Rae, Wray.

Ray, Benjamin (1703/4–1760), antiquary and Church of England clergyman, was born in Spalding, Lincolnshire, the son of Joseph Ray, merchant, and his wife, who died early in 1736. He was educated at Spalding grammar school under Timothy Neve, and proceeded to St John's College, Cambridge, where he was admitted a pensioner on 10 October 1721, aged seventeen; he graduated BA in 1725 and MA in 1730. Having left the university he took holy orders and was made perpetual curate of Cowbit and Surfleet, Lincolnshire. From 1723 to 1736 he was master of the grammar school at Sleaford, where he also held a curacy.

In September 1723 Ray was elected a member of the well-known Spalding Gentlemen's Society, in whose foundation his former teacher Neve and his kinsman Maurice Johnson played a prominent part. Ray was secretary in 1735, and afterwards vice-president, and William Stukeley recorded that he exhibited many objects of antiquarian interest at the society's meetings. He composed several unpublished essays, including papers, which he sent to his friend and fellow antiquary Samuel Pegge, on Virgil's fourth eclogue and the ancient numismatic and epigraphic evidence for the coming of the Messiah. Out of these grew a paper delivered to the Spalding Gentlemen's Society entitled 'The truth of the Christian religion demonstrated from the report propagated throughout the gentile world about the birth of Christ, that a Messiah was expected, and from the authority of heathen writers, and from the coins of the Roman emperors'. Some of Ray's notes on specific ancient coins appeared in the *Gentleman's Magazine*. To the Royal Society he sent an 'Account of a waterspout raised upon land in Lincolnshire', of which an abstract was published in 1751. He also composed an unpublished account of the Lincolnshire fens, though his

native loyalty to that region was not undiluted by resentment, as he held its climate in part responsible for his poor health and the lack of visitors.

Apart from dabbling in poetry (a sample entitled 'Manners: a Satyr' survives among his letters to Pegge in the Bodleian Library) Ray also had a penchant for cataloguing and listing. In 1735–6 he composed 'A catalogue of the Italian princes and their palaces, & of the Italian painters and their celebrated performances', which survives in manuscript in the library of Spalding Gentlemen's Society, and also produced 'Catalogue of household goods removed out of the Presence Chamber, 26 Chas. II, Dec. 14, 1668'. In 1743, after a visit to Houghton Hall, the earl of Orford's house, he felt moved to send Mrs Pegge a lengthy description of the house and the more prominent works of art in it.

Ray never married, although he had been deeply attached to an unknown party in the 1730s, describing her as 'adeo modesta, adeo venusta, ut nihil supra' (Bodl. Oxf., MS Eng. lett. d. 46, fol. 183). She, however, had at length rejected him, partly it seems on the grounds that his living of £80 a year was no better than a porter's wages. This rankled for some years. Repeated approaches to superiors in the hope of gaining richer preferment outside the fens elicited warm compliments on his abilities but no success. His letters to Pegge, many of them entirely antiquarian in content, support the assessment of him in Chalmers's *Biographical Dictionary* as a 'most ingenious and worthy man, possessed of good learning, but ignorant of the world, indolent and thoughtless, and often very absent' (Chalmers, 26.73). As an example of the last characteristic Pegge cited the occasion when Ray had jotted down a recipe for punch on one of the pages of the sermon that he was composing for the following Sunday; in delivering the sermon he got halfway through the recipe before realizing what he was saying. He died at Spalding on 26 August 1760.

C. E. A. CHEESMAN

Sources Nichols, *Lit. anecdotes*, 6.97, 107 · Nichols, *Illustrations*, 8.548 · *The Gentleman's Society at Spalding: its origin and progress* (1851), 47 · *The family memoirs of the Rev. William Stukeley*, ed. W. C. Lukis, 3, SurtS, 80 (1887) · Venn, *Alum. Cant.* · B. Ray, letters and essays, Bodl. Oxf., MS Eng. lett. d. 46, fols. 171–466 · R. F. Scott, ed., *Admissions to the College of St John the Evangelist in the University of Cambridge*, 3: *July 1715 – November 1767* (1903) · *GM*, 1st ser., 30 (1760), 443 · A. Chalmers, ed., *The general biographical dictionary*, new edn, 26 (1816), 73–4 · *DNB*

Archives Bodl. Oxf., letters to S. Pegge and essays

Ray, Edward Rivers [Ted] (1877–1943), golfer, was born at Marais, Grouville, Jersey, on 6 April 1877, the son of Stephen Ray, a mariner who captained an oyster trawler, and his wife, Mary Ann Arm. In common with the other boys of the village of Grouville (from where also came Harry Vardon), he swung a makeshift golf club from a very early age. Ray's own first club was made by his father and was unusual, even by Grouville standards, in using, for the head, a wooden pin of the kind used by Jersey fishermen for mending nets. The shaft was a simple thorn stick. With this and other home-made implements Ray and his fellow villagers practised obsessively, when not caddying, on the

Edward Rivers [Ted] **Ray** (1877–1943), by unknown photographer, 1935

of which they won all but one. In the US open championship at the Country Club, Brookline, both Ray and Vardon shared the lead at the end of four rounds with the young Boston amateur Francis Ouimet, but the following day, in perhaps the most famous play-off in the history of golf, the unknown American Ouimet saw off his two illustrious British rivals. Play-offs had not been kind to Ray: in 1912 he lost both the German and Belgian opens in this way.

On returning to the USA in 1920, Ray once again found himself in close competition with Harry Vardon for the open title, and in a raging storm became one of only three Britons to date (Vardon and Tony Jacklin were the others) to win open championships on both sides of the Atlantic. At forty-three Ray was then also the oldest winner of the American title, until overtaken by Raymond Floyd in 1986. In the open championship itself, Ray had an excellent record: he finished in the first six on seven occasions apart from his solitary triumph, and came second by one stroke to Jim Barnes at Prestwick in 1925. He played his last open at Prince's, Sandwich, in 1932, aged fifty-five, and his last tournament victory came in the Hertfordshire open in 1935. Like almost all the great professional champions of his era, Ray also held a club position and, having succeeded Harry Vardon as professional at Ganton, Yorkshire, in 1904, he moved south in 1912 and for much of his career was attached to the Oxhey Park Golf Club at Watford Heath, north of London.

In 1926 Ray was appointed captain of a British Isles team which played an American team at Wentworth in what was a precursor of the Ryder cup. He also played three times in the Ryder cup itself, on the first occasion as replacement captain when Abe Mitchell was struck down with appendicitis on the way to catch the boat at Southampton.

Ray was a founder member of the Professional Golfers' Association (PGA), established in 1901 to protect and promote the interests of golf professionals. In later years he took an active role on the executive and it was Ray who persuaded the earl of Wilton to donate £500 to the PGA coffers when the organization faced a financial crisis immediately after the First World War. The executive committee minutes of the PGA show that Ray proposed a way of determining how many qualifying places for the open should stem from each qualifying section. He also seconded a motion in 1927 that those clubs that held gate-money tournaments should donate a proportion of the profits to the PGA benevolent fund. He was the major shareholder and a foundation director of the Professional Golfers' Co-operative Association, established in January 1921. The idea behind this successful enterprise was to buy golf equipment in bulk at discounted prices from the manufacturers and sell on to individual club professionals so that they could compete with the sports stores. Ray was a man of fierce integrity. When, in 1925, he was accused of leaking confidential information from executive committee meetings, he not only satisfied his colleagues that he had refused to answer questions from the press, but also insisted that an inquiry be held.

A huge, lumbering man with enormous hands, Ray was

links at Grouville, and this was to prove, as Ray confessed years later in his book *Inland Golf* (1912), invaluable training for his future career. His golfing enthusiasm was encouraged by George Boomer, the headmaster of La Moye School, which he attended.

Ray turned professional in 1894, aged seventeen, and was employed as a club-maker at the Royal Jersey Golf Club before working briefly as professional to a small club outside St Malo. He played in the open championship at Sandwich in 1899, and became the professional at Churston Golf Club in Devon, where he met his wife, Edith Hooper. His first major success came in 1903, when he was runner-up in the *News of the World* match play championship to James Braid, an outcome that was repeated in 1911. In 1912 he lost again in the final, this time to fellow islander Harry Vardon, but gained ample compensation by winning the open championship at Muirfield in the same year, where his winning score of 295 equalled the championship record set by J. H. Taylor three years previously. His book *Inland Golf*, with suggestions on the techniques necessary for inland (as distinct from links), courses appeared shortly after his open victory.

In 1913 Ray and Vardon toured North America under the sponsorship of Lord Northcliffe, proprietor of the *Daily Mail*. They travelled 35,000 miles in three months, and played forty-one well-paid exhibition four-ball matches, outgoing and ebullient, always prepared to voice his opinion, but with a relaxed attitude to life and golf. Once, when teaching, he was asked by a young pupil how the latter could gain more distance: 'hit it a bloody sight harder, mate!' was Ray's legendary response. Ray himself was always a powerful player who often finished off-balance after some of his long shots. He pioneered the high-flying approach, favouring the niblick (akin to a number nine iron) for shots to the flag. Surprisingly for such a big man, he was an excellent putter, with a delicate stroke around the greens. This touch served him well at lawn bowls, another sport at which he excelled. Most pictures of him in action show the buttoned-up jacket (even in the August heat of the central United States), trilby hat, and, very often, a characteristic pipe clenched between his teeth. He died at the Peace Memorial Hospital, Watford, on 26 August 1943. WRAY VAMPLEW

Sources P. N. Lewis, *The dawn of professional golf* (1995) · F. L. M. Corbet and others, *A biographical dictionary of Jersey*, [2] (1998) · minutes of the Professional Golfers' Association, Professional Golfers' Association, The Belfry, Sutton Coldfield · D. Stirk, *Golf history and tradition* (1998) · B. Ferrier and G. Hart, eds., *The Johnnie Walker encyclopedia of golf* (1994) · T. Barrett, *The Daily Telegraph golf chronicle* (1994) · R. Green, *The illustrated encyclopaedia of golf* (1994) · b. cert. · E. Ray, *Inland golf* (1913) · *CGPLA Eng. & Wales* (1944)
Archives Professional Golfers' Association, The Belfry, Sutton Coldfield | FILM BFI NFTVA, news footage
Likenesses photograph, 1935, Empics Sports Photo Agency, Nottingham [*see illus.*] · photograph, repro. in H. Cotton, *This game of golf* (1948) · photograph, repro. in Lewis, *Dawn of professional golf* · photograph, repro. in Stirk, *Golf history* · photograph, repro. in Ferrier and Hart, *Johnnie Walker encyclopaedia* · photograph, repro. in Barrett, *Daily Telegraph golf chronicle* · photograph, repro. in Green, *Illustrated encyclopaedia* · statuette, Royal and Ancient Golf Club, St Andrews, Fife
Wealth at death £25,671 5s. 6d.: probate, 1 March 1944, *CGPLA Eng. & Wales*

Ray, Gabrielle [*real name* Gabrielle Elizabeth Clifford Cook] (1883–1973), actress, was born at Bamford Grange, Cheadle, Stockport, on 28 April 1883, the daughter of an iron merchant, William Austin Cook, and his wife, Annie, *née* Holden. She made her first stage appearances as a child. In 1893 she took the part of Eveleen in John Hollingshead's short-lived operaticized version of *The Green Bushes*, *Miami*, in the West End. She also danced in Paul Valentine's Blackpool ballet and appeared as a winsome cupid in *Little Red Riding Hood* at Richmond before graduating to almost adult roles in the touring companies of *The Belle of New York* and *The Casino Girl*. While still in her teens she was taken to London by the George Edwardes organization to understudy Gertie Millar in *The Toreador* at the Gaiety Theatre. Having been promoted to the small but visible role as a suggestible ministerial secretary, Thisbe, in the next Gaiety musical, *The Orchid* (1903), she moved across to the Prince of Wales Theatre to take over the number three female role in *Lady Madcap*, in which she performed the latest Parisian dance craze, La Maxixe, with Dorothy Craske. By the time of the production of *The Little Cherub* (1906, in which she played the part of Lady Dorothy Congress) Gabs had become one of the most popular picture-postcard beauties of the day, and her role in that

Gabrielle Ray (1883–1973), by Bassano, 1910

piece—teamed with Zena Dare and Lily Elsie as the picturesque supporting daughters to the chief comedian—reflected her new status. She had good supporting roles in *See See* (1906, So-Hie) and *Les merveilleuses* (1906, Eglé) and headed the grisettes as the heels-upping Frou-Frou in *The Merry Widow* (1907) before Edwardes cast her up a notch, in a full-scale song-and-dance (and even almost acting) part as the perky Daisy in *The Dollar Princess* (1909). Miss Ray went on to appear alongside Phyllis Dare and Olive May in the Gaiety Theatre's *Peggy* (1911, Polly Polino), but then took her leave of the stage to marry the almost aristocratic Eric Raymond Loder (1888–1966). The marriage was celebrated at St Edward's Roman Catholic Church, Windsor, on 1 March 1912, but it was not successful. Gabs returned to the stage four years later, attempting to pick up where she had left off, and appeared in Edwardes's production of *Betty* (1916, Estelle) and in revue at the Hippodrome, but her moment of stamped and franked fame had passed, and her career soon faded away into variety and pantomime appearances and then into a long real retirement. She died on 21 May 1973 at Holloway Sanatorium, Egham, Surrey. KURT GÄNZL

Sources K. Gänzl, *The encyclopedia of the musical theatre*, 2 vols. (1994) · K. Gänzl, *The British musical theatre*, 2 vols. (1986) · *The Era* (1893–1918) · b. cert. · m. cert. · d. cert. · J. Parker, ed., *Who's who in the theatre*, 6th edn (1930) · Burke, *Peerage* (1967)
Likenesses Bassano, photograph, 1910, NPG [*see illus.*]

Ray, James (*fl.* 1745–1746), chronicler, was a native of Whitehaven in Cumberland. On the advance from Edinburgh of the Jacobite army under Charles Edward Stuart in the autumn of 1745, Ray marched with others from his town to join the royal garrison at Carlisle. The surrender of Carlisle to the Jacobites prior to his arrival led Ray then to follow the Jacobite advance to Derby as closely as he was able. All the information he obtained concerning them he reported to the duke of Cumberland, whose forces he met at Stafford on 5 January 1746. He continued with the duke's army until the final victory at Culloden in April. In the same year he published a 32-page pamphlet, *The Acts of the Rebels, Written by an Egyptian* (2nd edn, 1746). About the same date he published *A Complete History of the Rebellion in 1745*, which passed through nine editions by 1760. It remains a useful account of the campaign and of the state of feeling in England at this time.

ALBERT NICHOLSON, *rev.* EIRWEN E. C. NICHOLSON

Sources J. Ray, *The acts of the rebels, written by an Egyptian*, 2nd edn (1746) · J. Ray, *A complete history of the rebellion in 1745* (1746)
Likenesses engraving, repro. in Ray, *Complete history of the rebellion in 1745*

John Ray (1627–1705), by unknown artist, after 1680

Ray [*formerly* Wray], **John** (1627–1705), naturalist and theologian, was born at Black Notley, near Braintree, Essex, on 29 November 1627, the third child of Roger Wray (*bap.* 1594, *d.* 1655), a blacksmith, and his wife, Elizabeth (*c.*1600–1679), who was noted for her piety and her knowledge of medicinal herbs. Until 1670 he spelled his surname with an initial W, which he dropped in order to facilitate the Latinizing of his name.

Early years, writings, and travels Wray was sent to the grammar school at Braintree, and entered Trinity College, Cambridge, on 12 May 1644. On 28 June he moved to St Catharine's College, where he became the pupil of Daniel Duckfield. Following the death of his tutor and the expulsion of the master, Ralph Brownrig, Wray transferred to Trinity, where he became a sizar on 21 November 1646 under the tuition of James Duport. Wray took his BA degree in 1647/8, and on 8 September 1649 was elected to a minor fellowship. He held a succession of college positions thereafter, being elected Greek lecturer in 1651 (the year in which he graduated MA) and 1656, mathematical lecturer in 1653, humanities lecturer in 1655, praelector in 1657, junior dean in 1658, and college steward in 1659 and 1660. With Duport, Wray had honed his skill in Latin and Greek, and perhaps also Hebrew. He composed several Latin poems, including contributions to collections published in honour of Cromwell (1654) and Charles II (1660). In addition to college lectures and exercises, he also preached at Trinity and in Great St Mary's, including, in 1659, the funeral sermons of John Arrowsmith, master of Trinity, and John Nidd, a senior fellow. With Nidd and others Wray began to develop interests in natural philosophy during the 1650s, in particular through the study of embryology and chemistry. At this time Wray took pupils of his own, among them Philip Skippon and Timothy Burrell. He also came into contact with two fellow-commoners with similar interests, Francis Willughby, another pupil of Duport, and Peter Courthope.

Between 1650 and 1658 Trinity suspended the normal requirement that its fellows should take orders, but by January 1659 Wray was actively considering his position. He was offered the living of Cheadle in 1659, and in 1661 that of Kirkby Lonsdale. He complained to Courthope on 26 September 1660 that 'they have brought all things heer as they were [in] 1641', and asserted that 'I am long since come to two resolutions, 1. No promise of conformity 2. No orders rebus sic stantibus [as things stand]' (Ray to Courthope, 26 Sept 1660, E. Sussex RO, MS Danny 346). Yet the determination of his college to keep him persuaded Wray, and he was ordained by Robert Sanderson, bishop of Lincoln, in his chapel at the Barbican on 23 December 1660. Wray's personal piety was never in question, indeed it contributed to the sense of the duties of a priest which informed his later writings in natural theology, and which, at this time, led him to consider taking up a country living. However, several of his friends leaned towards nonconformity, and Wray himself had hopes for a more comprehensive settlement of the church than that achieved after the Restoration. Moreover, he was 'so nicely scrupulous about oaths' (Dale, Bodl. Oxf., MS Rawl. Essex 21, fol. 379*r*), that he felt unable to accept the terms of the abjuration of the solemn league and covenant required by the Act of Uniformity. On 24 August 1662 he thus forfeited his fellowship at Trinity, although he remained a loyal member of the Church of England. Wray cast himself 'upon Providence & good friends', resolving that 'Liberty is a sweet thing' (Ray to Courthope, 13 Aug 1662, E. Sussex RO, MS Danny 358). The prospect of support from Courthope, Willughby, or Skippon may have been one reason for Wray's decisions. The main explanation was, however, his determination to travel in pursuit of natural philosophical observations, in particular botanical specimens.

Wray had kept a small garden at Trinity in which he

planted specimens that he had collected or which his friends had sent to him, and where he was able to investigate the differences between specific varieties of plants and trees. His activity as a cultivator reflected his broader interest in the recording and collection of plant types and specimens, which had been stimulated by rides and walks taken in his youth. He had already acquired considerable familiarity with the existing English botanical literature and its limitations, and was struck by the absence of anyone who was proficient in the subject at the university. He thus decided in the early 1650s to embark on a catalogue of all the plants that he had found during his long walks in the countryside around Cambridge. He received encouragement from Nidd, Willughby, and Courthope, as well as assistance from John Worthington, master of Jesus College, who procured a manuscript of Joachim Jungius's as yet unpublished 'Isagoge phytoscopica' for him from Samuel Hartlib. His *Catalogus plantarum circa Cantabrigiam nascentium* (1660) described 558 species of native plant which he had recognized, as well as the crops growing in Cambridgeshire. An appendix was published in 1663. The catalogue was arranged alphabetically, with the titles used by Gerard, Parkinson, and Jean and Gaspard Bauhin also included. The circumstances and uses of the plants were described and the English names of their locations given. Wray added natural philosophical observations, for example concerning the behaviour of caterpillars, at appropriate points, and an index allowed the English reader to identify plants by their common names. The *Catalogus* demonstrated the meticulous nature of his approach to botany. It identified several new plants but reconciled many descriptions to avoid the unnecessary multiplication of species. Compared with his descriptions of flowering plants, however, those of trees, shrubs, and grasses were less satisfactory. Moreover, the catalogue contained only a very brief outline of the structure and classification of plants, which drew heavily on the work of Jean Bauhin, although its preface expressed the hope that similar studies might be undertaken in other localities, allowing the eventual composition of a complete 'Phytologia Britannica'.

On 9 August 1658 Wray had embarked on his first botanizing itinerary outside Cambridgeshire, riding to Northampton and then on to Warwick before journeying through the Peaks and into north Wales, returning to Cambridge on 18 September via Shrewsbury, Worcester, and Gloucester. On this tour he had collected botanical, natural philosophical, and topographical observations. By February 1660 his plans to undertake a new catalogue of all English plants led him to write to friends across the country asking for their assistance and to contemplate further itineraries of his own. That year he and Willughby embarked on a northern tour, probably taking in parts of Yorkshire, Cumberland, Westmorland, and the Isle of Man. In July the following year Wray set out on a further journey, this time in the company of Skippon. Much of this trip was devoted to visiting places of antiquarian interest in Lincolnshire, the north-east, and Yorkshire, but he also made observations of plants and sea creatures.

On 16 August he entered Scotland, travelling on to Edinburgh and Glasgow, before returning via Carlisle. In spring 1662 he spent some time in Sussex as Courthope's guest, returning via London where he inspected Robert Morison's work in St James's Park. In the months immediately preceding the end of his fellowship, Wray undertook his most ambitious itinerary yet, this time in the company of both Willughby and Skippon.

Travels and collaboration with Francis Willughby Setting out from Middleton Hall in Tamworth, the seat of the Willughbys, the three men travelled through the midlands into north Wales and continued on to Anglesey, and thence to Snowdonia, before turning south along the Welsh coast. On the way they described antiquities, local customs and legends, recorded plants, and observed fishes and birds, notably the puffins of Prestholm. Once they returned to England, Willughby split from the party, but Wray and Skippon went on together as far as Land's End before returning to London by way of Stonehenge. After a brief stay in Essex, Wray returned to Cambridge at the end of August to settle his affairs. Thereafter he stayed with friends, from October serving as a tutor in the household of Thomas Bacon at Friston Hall, near Saxmundham in Suffolk.

On 18 April 1663 Wray, Willughby, Skippon, and Nathaniel Bacon sailed from Dover for the continent. At Willughby's instigation they had planned a tour which would allow Wray to collect and catalogue plants that were not native to England and Willughby to observe birds, beasts, fishes, and insects. From Calais they travelled into Flanders and the Netherlands, then up the Rhine, and across southern Germany to Munich and Vienna, before heading by coach for Venice. After spending the winter in Padua, where Wray attended the anatomy lectures of Pietro Marchetti, they toured northern Italy. Travelling by Milan and Turin, they took a boat from Genoa along the coast to Lucca, Pisa, Leghorn, and, finally, Naples. There Wray and Skippon parted from Bacon and Willughby (who later travelled to Spain on his own) and went on together to Sicily and Malta, later returning by sea to Leghorn and thence to Florence. On 1 September 1664 they set out for Rome, where, in December, Wray made observations of the comet (published in the *Philosophical Transactions*, 1707). With Skippon he left Rome on 24 January 1665, returned to Venice, and then entered Switzerland via the lower Engadine. They eventually reached Geneva on 20 April and spent the summer there, botanizing in the mountains nearby. In late July they entered France, travelling to Montpellier where they remained for some time, and in the autumn and winter exploring southern France. On 1 February 1666 all English visitors were ordered to leave France within three months. Wray and Skippon headed north to Lyons and then stayed for a while in Paris where they met a number of prominent botanists. Wray embarked for England from Calais on 1 April 1666.

After his return Wray spent his time either in Essex or with his friends in Sussex, and also visited Cambridge. He conducted a programme of reading in natural philosophy, passing most of the winter with Willughby at Middleton before travelling with him to the west of England in summer 1667. On 7 November Wray was elected a fellow of the Royal Society, having been proposed by John Wilkins. Later that month Wray went to stay with Burrell in Sussex; he remained there until the spring, when he set out to travel between the homes of various friends and in the process traversed north Yorkshire and Westmorland, where he located several new species of plants. He wintered again at Middleton, conducting experiments of the rise of sap in trees and making observations of snails and of spiders' threads. In April 1669 Wray and Willughby visited Wilkins near Chester, and the former dissected a porpoise which had been caught by some fishermen. These activities were later written up and communicated to the Royal Society and accounts of them were published in the *Philosophical Transactions*. Until Willughby's premature death on 3 July 1672 Ray (as he now called himself) and his friend worked together for much of the time at Middleton on their respective projects in natural history. In July 1671, however, Ray was absent for a time on a further simpling tour with Thomas Willisel in the north of England.

Ray's travels had established the basis for his collaboration with Willughby, the fruits of which occupied him for much of the rest of his life. They provided information on birds, fishes, and insects, initially intended for use by Willughby, but later written up by Ray. They also generated evidence about antiquities, customs, and language, which Ray shared with Willughby and deployed himself in the *Collection of English Proverbs* (1670; rev. 1678) and the *Collection of English Words* (1674; rev. 1691). The *Observations Topographical, Moral, and Physiological* (1673) which Ray published of his and Willughby's continental journeys contained extensive discussions of these topics, as well as interventions in contemporary natural philosophical debates, such as that about fossil shells generated by Steno's *Prodromus* (1669). Furthermore, Ray's journeys had allowed him to expand his knowledge of plants, and build up a formidable collection of specimens.

Later writings on plants In 1666 Wilkins sought the collaboration of Ray and Willughby in drawing up the tables of plants and animals to be published in the *Essay towards a Real Character* (1668). This work, which took Ray a mere three weeks and which was harshly criticized by Morison, improved on the classifications given in Christopher Merret's *Pinax* but was limited by the need to conform to the existing schemes laid down by Wilkins. For a time Ray was occupied with an abortive Latin translation of the *Essay* but by 1670 he was ready to publish his *Catalogus plantarum Angliae*, which he dedicated to Willughby. A second edition was published in 1677, and an appendix of newly observed plants by 'John Ray and his friends', *Fasciculus stirpium Britannicarum* (1688), printed when Ray was unable to persuade the booksellers who held the copyright to issue a third edition. Ray's work was notable not only for its thoroughness but also for the extensive medical and pharmacological notes which accompanied the descriptions of plants. The preface to the volume made

clear Ray's conviction that the divine creation of plants implied a purpose to their existence, which might be discovered by putting them to use. Ray's work on classification and on the nature of plant species was continued in the 'Catalogue of plants not native of England' which he appended to the *Observations* and articulated more fully in the *Methodus plantarum nova* (1682).

This work rejected classifications based on localities or properties in favour of ones based on the structure of plants, drawing on Ray's own studies of seeds and the specific differences of plants (sent to the Royal Society on 30 November 1674) and on the discoveries of Marcello Malpighi. It also developed the views of a paper on the number of plants which Ray had composed for communication to the Royal Society, probably in 1674, but which was never sent. This made clear Ray's belief in the importance of essential, rather than accidental, characteristics in identifying a species, and his conviction that all local species were likely to be preserved by providence somewhere in the world. Ray anticipated Malpighi in making a distinction between monocotyledons and dicotyledons, and he later developed his observations of the invariability of the seed vessels of plants into the basis for his system of classification. In this he followed both Morison and Andrea Cesalpino, although he also asserted the importance of the form of the petals and calyx, and the arrangement of the plant's leaves, and was indebted to Jungius for his treatment of flowers. Ray's attempts at classification were, however, marred by his retention of a primary division of plants into herbs, shrubs, and trees, despite an awareness of the difficulties associated with it. His treatment of shrubs and trees remained less satisfactory than that of herbs. Even there, Ray's ignorance of marine and exotic plants led him into frequent errors.

The culmination of Ray's career as a botanist came with the publication of his *Historia plantarum*, whose two folio volumes appeared in 1686 and 1688, with a further supplementary volume eventually being published, after abortive attempts to raise subscriptions, in 1704. The first two volumes described approximately 6100 species of plant, many of which Ray had seen or had had described for him by his botanical correspondents, who now included Samuel Dale, Tancred Robinson, and Hans Sloane; the third volume was more of a compilation, detailing a further 10,000 species, largely on the evidence of printed sources. Despite the excellence of his contacts, Ray's work was hampered by increasing old age and infirmity, which in particular prevented him from visiting the gardens being cultivated at Oxford and Chelsea which might have allowed him to observe many exotic plants at first hand. Despite its ambitions to completeness Ray's herbal lacked illustrations, in part due to scruples about the potential inaccuracy of woodcuts, but mainly because of anxieties about their cost.

In 1690 Ray published *Synopsis methodica stirpium Britannicarum*, of which a second edition appeared in 1696, and a third, expanded by Johann Jakob Dillenius, in 1724. This work followed the classificatory system of Ray's *Methodus*. With Sloane's encouragement Ray produced an edition of Leonhart Rauwolf's travels (1693); he drew up all but one of the English county lists of plants for Edmund Gibson's edition of Camden's *Britannia* (1695); and, with the support of the Royal Society, he issued a further catalogue of European plants (*Stirpium Europaearum extra Britannias nascentium sylloge*) in 1694. This included a defence of his own method of classification against that of Rivinus (A. Q. Bachmann), which was based on differences in the shape of the flower. An exchange of letters with Rivinus appeared in the second edition of the *Synopsis*, where Ray referred to the writings of Joseph Pitton de Tournefort, also criticized in his *Dissertatio brevis* (1696). Ray took the work of both Rivinus and Tournefort into account in the composition of *Methodus plantarum emendata* (1703), which revised his classifications and introduced divisions between flowering and non-flowering plants.

Marriage and work on Willughby's intellectual legacy
Willughby's death in 1672 deprived Ray of both a collaborator and a patron but provided him with an annuity of £60, and hence a measure of financial independence. Ray also acquired fresh obligations as an executor of Willughby's will, charged with the care of his two young sons and the publication of his incomplete works in natural history. For three and a half years Ray lived at Middleton, and helped to educate the children. With this end in mind he published *Dictionariolum trilingue* (1675), later reissued as *Nomenclator classicus*, which went through four editions by the time of his death. More demanding work was required to turn Willughby's observations, notes, and descriptions into coherent treatises. Initially Ray embarked on revising Willughby's *Ornithology*, writing up its author's notes into proper descriptions, collating authorities, and imposing a method of classification which might make sense of the whole. Ray's descriptions gave detailed accounts of plumage, and his classification drew on the divisions according to habit in the tables which Willughby had provided for Wilkins, developing them by concentrating on structural and anatomical differences, for example in beaks or claws, which could be observed between species. In all Ray and Willughby described more than 230 species which they had themselves observed. The work was published in Latin in 1676, with illustrations paid for by Willughby's widow, Emma. These were largely re-engraved from other books and Ray found many of them unsatisfactory; nevertheless he reissued the *Ornithology* in English in 1678, with additional descriptions of seabirds and discussions of falconry and fowling.

On 5 June 1673 Ray married Margaret Oakeley (*c.*1653–*c.*1727), daughter of John Oakeley of Launton, near Bicester in Oxfordshire, and a member of the household at Middleton. The couple left Middleton during the winter of 1675–6, moving initially to Coleshill, and then settling at Sutton Coldfield in April 1676. By this time Willughby's mother had died and his widow had married Sir Josiah Child, bt, in the process quitting Middleton with her children, who were finally removed from Ray's charge by order of the lord chancellor in 1677. Ray's relations with Emma Child worsened over the next few years, in which she declined to assist with the costs of Ray's edition of her late

husband's work on fishes and quarrelled over the administration of the trust resulting from his will. Ray refused to act as a cipher to enable her to manage the trust 'more securely & unaccountably then if you had been appointed Sole Executrix' (Ray to Lady Child, 6 Sept 1680, Nottingham University, MS Mi E4/32). Unable any longer to fulfil his duties to Willughby's children, and deprived of the library at Middleton, Ray initially considered going abroad as a tutor, but instead moved back to Essex where he lodged at first in Faulkbourne Hall, near Witham, as a guest of Edward Bullock. In autumn 1677 he turned down the offer of the secretaryship of the Royal Society, in a letter to John Aubrey the following March giving as his reasons 'the consciousness of my inability to manage it, but chiefly its inconsistency w[i]th my profession' (*Further Correspondence*, 159). The death of his mother on 15 March 1679 allowed Ray and his wife to move back to Black Notley, and to settle in the family house at Dewlands, where they lived for the rest of their lives. They had four daughters, Margaret and Mary (*b.* 1684), Catharine (*b.* 1687), and Jane (*b.* 1689), all of whom later assisted their father in the collection of insects during the 1690s. Ray felt Mary's death from jaundice in January 1698 as 'a sore blow', writing to Edward Lhwyd on 12 March 1697 that she 'was very ingenious, & helpfull to me, & upon that account the more dear too' (ibid., 268).

During the later 1670s and the early 1680s Ray was extensively engaged in the revision of Willughby's notes for a natural history of fishes. He began in earnest in December 1674, starting to gather further information from books, notably the works of Gesner and Rondelet, and from his friends. The resulting *Historia piscium* (1686), which was largely Ray's own work, was finished some time before 1685, when Tancred Robinson brought it to the attention of the Royal Society. At the urging of Robert Plot, the society decided to commission new, engraved plates for the work, to be paid for by subscription, and to pay the costs of having it printed by the Oxford University Press. Samuel Pepys, the society's president, subscribed £50, which financed seventy-nine of the 187 plates. The expense so strained the resources of the society that it was forced for some time to pay its officers in multiple copies of the work. Even so enough of the 500 copies of the first edition remained unsold for it to be reissued only as late as 1743. The book was perhaps more of a success intellectually than financially. Ray was respectful towards Aristotle's classification of fishes, making further distinctions himself principally on the basis of fin structure, but again eschewing the unnecessary multiplication of species. He rejected the view common among his contemporaries that molluscs and other invertebrates should be classified as fish, but nevertheless continued to number cetaceans in that category.

On 18 April 1684 Robinson had prompted Ray to embark on 'a general history of nature' (*Correspondence*, 141), and during the early 1690s Ray worked on synopses of his treatments of quadrupeds and snakes (published in 1693) and of birds and fishes (largely completed by 1694, but not published until 1713). The first of these drew extensively on Willughby's work, his own observations, and the work of contemporary anatomists, notably in Paris. It rejected elements of Aristotle's system of classification and attacked the Cartesian theory of the beast machine. Ray agreed with the work of Francesco Redi in rejecting spontaneous generation. Inclining towards an ovist position, he was sceptical about some of the conclusions of the microscopist Antoni van Leeuwenhoek concerning spermatozoa, and also articulated his acceptance of the role of a plastic spirit in forming animals according to the divine plan. In this he followed the teachings of Ralph Cudworth and others of the Cambridge Platonists.

The last years of Ray's life were devoted to preparing a *Methodus* (1705) and *Historia* (left unfinished at his death, but published in 1710) of insects. Ray's work, which again drew on his collaboration with Willughby for its inspiration, was notable for its close observation of the various stages of an insect's life, and for its identification of many British species of butterflies. The activity of insects was prominent in Ray's consciousness for a different reason for most of the last eighteen years of his life. Ray suffered from chronic ill health during this period, in particular from incurable ulcers on his legs which, he reported in a letter to Sloane, he took 'to proceed from invisible insects' and from tumours 'which may be the nests of these insects (like ant-hills), they seeming to be gregarious' (*Correspondence*, 343). Whatever the cause of his infirmity, Ray was lame and in great discomfort much of the time. He died at Dewlands on 17 January 1705.

Natural theology and reputation During much of the 1690s Ray was engaged in correspondence with Edward Lhwyd and others about the nature of fossils. In general he was inclined to accept that they were the remains of once-living creatures, and he also suggested that their current distribution might owe something to observable changes in the nature of the surface of the earth. He qualified these opinions, however, by stressing that the fossils which had so far been discovered were not unlike known plants and animals, and that their burial might owe something to the action of the biblical flood, as well as to natural effects. He argued that those remains which seemed to be unfamiliar might represent species of which the surviving representatives had not yet been discovered. Although fossils were mentioned in the preface to his *Synopsis* (1690), his fullest treatment of them was in *Miscellaneous Discourses Concerning the Dissolution and Changes of the World* (1692). This was reworked and expanded as *Three Physico-Theological Discourses* (1693). Ray completed further revisions early in 1704, but the publication of a third edition was delayed until 1713 by the death of his bookseller, Samuel Smith. The work was also translated into Dutch (1694, 1783) and German (1698, 1732). In it Ray revisited lectures which he had delivered at Great St Mary's some thirty years earlier on the text of 2 Peter 3: 11. The publications of Thomas Burnet had rendered their subjects current, and Ray used them to provide a framework for his own discussion of creation, the deluge, and the future dissolution of the world.

In 1691 Ray had published another work which drew on the preaching of his Cambridge years, *The Wisdom of God Manifested in the Works of the Creation*. Three further editions appeared in his lifetime, and many more thereafter, and the book was also translated into French (1714) and German (1717). Basing himself on sermons he had delivered in the chapel of Trinity College, Ray produced a coherent natural theology in which the evidence of the heavens, geology, botany, zoology, and human anatomy suggested the providential action of a benevolent deity who was responsible for the creation of all things. He was critical of those ancient and modern authors, including Aristotle and Descartes, whose work appeared to give succour to atheists or deists.

Both *The Wisdom of God* and the *Miscellaneous Discourses* testified to Ray's skill in constructing an account of nature which remained compatible with orthodox interpretations of scripture. Although they were the most complete statements of his natural theology, Ray had referred to the theological benefits of contemplating the glories of creation many years before, for example in the preface to Willughby's *Ornithology*. Similar sentiments are also expressed in the preface to his own *Synopsis*, which also made clear his sense of relief following the revolution of 1688. As a result of the changed political and religious circumstances of the 1690s, exemplified by Archbishop Tillotson's offer of ecclesiastical preferment for him in 1691, Ray felt himself free to publish on matters of religion, and compelled to do so by the nature of contemporary debate. At the instigation of Edmund Elys, he composed the devotional *A Persuasive to a Holy Life* (1700). He had always believed that 'Divinity is my Profession' (*Further Correspondence*, 163), and argued that 'I know of no occupation which is more worthy or more delightful for a free man than to contemplate the beauteous works of Nature and to honour the infinite wisdom and goodness of God the Creator' (*Ray's Flora*, 26).

After Ray's death his widow complained to Sloane of her straitened circumstances, estimating that she had been left only £40 p.a. to support her family (Margaret Ray to Sloane, 19 Nov 1706, BL, MS Sloane 4040, fol. 255). Ray bequeathed his papers to Dale, from whom many of them eventually passed to William Derham who published an edition of Ray's correspondence in 1718 as *Philosophical Letters*. Ray gave instructions that he should be buried privately in the churchyard at Black Notley, asking that his corpse be 'nailed up that none might see him' (Dale, Bodl. Oxf., MS Rawl. Essex 21, fol. 380v). His friends erected a monument over the tomb. Ray's library was sold at auction in March 1708, making up nearly 1300 lots. His writings in natural theology proved influential throughout the eighteenth century, and were echoed in the work of William Paley. Despite this, it was as a botanist that Ray achieved most lasting fame. Linnaeus was so aware of his stature that he misrepresented his views in order to cite him as a fellow proponent of classification by a single variable. He also followed Plumier in naming a genus of yams after Ray. In the twentieth century Ray's most effective biographer, Charles Raven, co-opted him in an attempt to heal the perceived breach between science and religion, deploying the concept of organic design to suggest the unfolding of divine purpose through evolution.

SCOTT MANDELBROTE

Sources C. E. Raven, *John Ray, naturalist: his life and works*, 2nd edn (1950) · G. Keynes, *John Ray: a bibliography* (1951) · E. Lankester, ed., *Memorials of John Ray* (1846) · *The correspondence of John Ray*, ed. E. Lankester, Ray Society, 14 (1848) · *Further correspondence of John Ray*, ed. R. W. T. Gunther, Ray Society, 114 (1928) · *Philosophical letters: between the late learned Mr Ray and several of his ingenious correspondents*, ed. W. Derham (1718) · E. Sussex RO, Danny archives, MSS 344–364 · S. Dale, 'Life of Ray', Bodl. Oxf., MS Rawl. Essex 21, fols. 371r–380v · *Ray's flora of Cambridgeshire*, ed. and trans. A. H. Ewen and C. T. Prime (1975) · U. Nott., MS Mi E4/29–32 · BL, MS Sloane 4040, fol. 255 · Trinity Cam., nos. 17–24

Archives BL, corresp. and papers, Sloane MSS 3322–4100, *passim* · NHM, parts of *Hortus siccus* · U. Nott., plants preserved by him in a copy of *Historia plantarum*, MSS Mi LM 17–21 · U. Nott. L., papers | BL, letters to James Petiver, Sloane MSS 4063–4067 · BL, letters to Sir Hans Sloane, Add. MSS 4036–4060 · Bodl. Oxf., letters to John Aubrey · Bodl. Oxf., letters to Edward Lhwyd · E. Sussex RO, letters to Peter Courthope · NHM, corresp. with Martin Lister · NHM, corresp. with Sir Tancred Robinson · RS, letters to Royal Society · Trinity Cam., letters to Timothy Burrell · U. Nott., Middleton of Wollaton collection, letters

Likenesses W. Faithorne, pastels, after 1680, BM · oils, after 1680, NPG [*see illus.*] · attrib. G. D. Gaab, bronze medal, 1705, NPG · T. Hudson, oils, 1747, Trinity Cam.; replica, St Catharine's College, Cambridge · L. F. Roubiliac, marble bust, 1751, Trinity Cam. · A. de Blois, engraving (after W. Faithorne) · W. Elder, line engraving (after W. Faithorne), BM, NPG; repro. in J. Ray, *Synopsis methodica animalium* (1693) · T. A. Prior, group portrait, etching and line engraving (after P. Lely and J. Closterman?), NG Ire. · G. Vertue, engraving (after W. Faithorne), repro. in J. Ray, *Three physico-theological discourses* (1713) · cast (after L. F. Roubiliac), U. Cam., department of zoology · statue, Braintree, Essex

Wealth at death over £200—generating £40 p.a. for his heirs: Raven, *John Ray*, 481

Ray, Martha (1742?–1779), singer and murder victim, was

born near Covent Garden, London, probably in 1742, though some sources suggest 1745. When she was about fourteen her father, a stay maker, apprenticed her for five years to Mrs Sarah Silver, a maker of mantuas (cloaks) in Clerkenwell. At some point between 1760 and 1762 John *Montagu, fourth earl of Sandwich (1718–1792), made her acquaintance through a procurer, said to be Mrs Harding, and paid Martha's father £400 for 'the purchase of his daughter's honour', as it was put at the time of her death (*Westminster Magazine*, April 1779, 7.171), and £30 p.a. thereafter to her mother. Sandwich and his wife, Dorothy Fane, had been separated at least since 1755; she experienced serious mental disorder and became a ward of the state in 1767. He and Ray had nine children, five of whom survived to adulthood, including the literary figure Basil *Montagu.

Ray and Sandwich lived in large part as husband and wife for about eighteen years. While he was known to keep a distance between her and aristocratic ladies, she served as hostess at his estate, Hinchingbrooke House, near Huntingdon, and accompanied him to London, to public engagements, and on trips to naval events. However, the earl refused her entreaties to make a settlement

Martha Ray (1742?–1779), by Nathaniel Dance, 1777

upon her because he wanted to live more expensively than his modest means could permit. Ray clearly contemplated leaving him, either to marry or to make a career as an opera singer. The musician Joseph Cradock reports discussing with her an attractive offer tendered her by the King's Theatre towards the end of her life.

Through her relationship with Sandwich, Ray received the full education appropriate to a woman of social standing. Musically she was trained by two of the most important figures of the time, the composer Felice Giardini and the conductor Joah Bates, and came to be regarded as one of the best singers of her time. She took a unique path by performing almost exclusively at Sandwich's estate or in churches in the area, seemingly never in public concerts or the theatre. The earl's concerts, especially those held during Christmas week, were performed by the best of London's musicians and drew hundreds of guests, including the powerful musical intelligentsia. Known chiefly for singing music by G. F. Handel, Ray played an important role in the process by which his oratorios, odes, and masques became established as permanent and, indeed, canonic repertory, accomplished on a scale seen for no other deceased composer before that time. Sandwich was the main leader of the movement for 'ancient music', founding the Catch Club (1761) and the Concert of Antient Music (1776). For her part Ray established the most prominent interpretation of Iphis's famous aria 'Brighter scenes I seek above', from the oratorio *Jephtha*, and her repertory included a wide range of Italian and British music.

Ray also participated in Sandwich's political career by

dint of her being accused of colluding in his alleged corruption. As first lord of the Admiralty and one of the chief advisers to George III, he was attacked for handing out political and financial favours, especially in the naval dockyards, and it was claimed that Ray had made deals for him. Historians have since that time largely cleared the earl of these accusations.

In 1771 Ray met James *Hackman when he visited Hinchingbrooke as one of the many army officers whom Sandwich invited to the estate. The two were observed together by the Tahitian prince Omai, and details of that encounter were reported to the earl; it is likely that Ray seriously considered leaving Sandwich for Hackman, since she approached Joseph Cradock to discuss the question of a settlement shortly thereafter. She did, however, distance herself from Hackman, who subsequently left the army and was ordained deacon in February 1779. His continued passion for Ray led him into what later came to be called stalking. On 7 April 1779 Ray was followed by Hackman to Covent Garden Theatre, where she was attending a performance of Isaac Bickerstaff's *Love in a Village*. There she was seen talking with Lord Coleraine, whom a distraught Hackman suspected of being her new lover. On leaving the theatre she was approached by Hackman, who killed her with a gunshot to the head. Hackman then failed to take his own life in the same manner before being arrested and taken, along with Ray's body, to the Shakespeare tavern on St James Street. She was buried on 14 April in the chancel of the parish church at Elstree, Hertfordshire, and her body was later moved to the cemetery there.

In the ensuing press debate opinions were sharply divided over the murder, though Hackman probably drew more sympathy than Ray. Two publications, both entitled *Case and Memoirs of the Late Rev. Mr James Hackman*, argued the case from opposite perspectives, claiming either Ray's wilful duplicity or Hackman's determination to seek revenge. In 1780 the young Herbert Croft published an epistolary novel, *Love and Madness*, based on letters that he claimed were composed by the two protagonists. Unfortunately for Hackman the court had by then rejected Croft's strong suggestion of insanity and sentenced him to be hanged for murder on 19 April 1779.

WILLIAM WEBER

Sources *The case and memoirs of the late Rev. Mr James Hackman* (1779) · *The case and memoirs of Miss Martha Reay*, 2nd edn (1779) · H. Croft, *Love and madness* (1780) · J. Cradock, *Literary and miscellaneous memoirs*, ed. J. B. Nichols, 4 vols. (1828) · H. Walpole, *Letters* · *Thraliana: the diary of Mrs. Hester Lynch Thrale (later Mrs. Piozzi)*, 1776–1809, ed. K. C. Balderston, 2nd edn, 2 vols. (1951) · J. H. Jesse, *Memoirs of the life and reign of King George the Third*, 2nd edn, 3 vols. (1867) · N. A. M. Rodger, *The insatiable earl: a life of John Montagu, fourth earl of Sandwich* (1993) · M. E. Novak, 'Suicide, murder and sensibility: the case of Sir Herbert Croft's *Love and madness*', *Passionate encounters in a time of sensibility*, ed. M. E. Novak and A. Mellor (2000)
Archives NMM, letters to J. Montagu, earl of Sandwich
Likenesses oils, 1770–75, Gov. Art Coll. · N. Dance, portrait, 1777; Christies, 11 April 1997, lot 13 [*see illus.*] · V. Green, mezzotint, pubd 1779 (after N. Dance), BM, NPG · line engraving, pubd 1779, BM, NPG

Ray, Robin [*real name* Robin Olden] (1934–1998), broadcaster, was born at 630 Fulham Road, Fulham, London, elder of the two sons of Charles Olden (1909–1977), better known as the comedian Ted *Ray, and his wife, Dorothy Sybil Stevens, a dancer. He was educated at Highgate School (May 1947 to March 1950)—he wanted to become a concert pianist but realized he was not good enough—and at the Royal Academy of Dramatic Art, and did national service as a Royal Army Service Corps officer (second lieutenant, 5 December 1953). At school and in the army he used his real name, Olden, but he subsequently used as his professional name Robin Ray and became generally known by it: he omitted 'Olden' from his *Who's Who* entry. His television début was in 1956 in an ITV crime play, *The Guv'nor*, and his London stage début was in 1960 in *The Changeling* at the Royal Court Theatre. Following further acting, he was chief technical instructor at the Royal Academy of Dramatic Art (1961–5), but resigned over internal politics in support of the principal, John Fernald, then was associate director of the Meadowbrook Theater, Detroit (1965–6). He married on 25 January 1960 Susan Myra Ann Stranks (*b.* 1938/9), actress and later children's television presenter; they had one son.

Urbane, stylish, with boyish if then unfashionable good looks and an enthusiasm for and extensive knowledge of classical music—and since childhood an avid record-collector—Ray enjoyed from 1965 a successful and varied career in BBC and commercial radio and television broadcasting, as a writer, producer, and presenter. Programmes in which he was involved included *Face the Music*, *Call my Bluff*, *The Movie Quiz*, and *Cabbages and Kings*. He was musical adviser to the commercial radio station Classic FM, and its artistic director (1988–91), compiling for it a music database. He continued to act intermittently, and he wrote or devised and presented several shows including *Tomfoolery* (1980), *Café Puccini* (1986, with Andrew Lloyd Webber), and *Let's Do It* (1994). In 1977 he was a member of the Booker prize panel, and he was *Punch* drama critic (1986–7). He compiled several books including *Robin Ray's Music Quiz* (1978). After a short illness he died in Martlets Hospice, Wayfield Avenue, Hove, Sussex, on 29 November 1998 from lung cancer and was privately cremated on 3 December. His wife, Susan, survived him.　　ROGER T. STEARN

Sources *The Times* (30 Nov 1998) · *Daily Telegraph* (30 Nov 1998) · *The Guardian* (30 Nov 1998) · *The Independent* (30 Nov 1998) · *The Scotsman* (30 Nov 1998) · WWW · P. Hughes and I. F. Davies, eds., *Highgate School registers, 1833–1964* (1965) · *Army List* (Dec 1954) · b. cert. · m. cert. · d. cert.
Likenesses photograph, 1960 (with Susan Stranks), repro. in *Daily Telegraph* · photograph, 1972, repro. in *The Independent* · photograph, 1986, repro. in *The Times* · photograph, repro. in *The Guardian* · photograph, repro. in *The Scotsman*
Wealth at death £335,582, gross; £325,312, net: probate, 8 Jan 1999, CGPLA Eng. & Wales

Ray, Sidney Herbert (1858–1939), schoolteacher and linguist, was born on 28 May 1858 at 1 Ashford Street, Hoxton Old Town, London, the son of Septimus Ray, omnibus conductor, and his wife, Louisa Mary Ann Wort. He attended the British School at Abbey Street, Bethnal Green, until the age of fourteen. He spent two years working in city offices and then, in 1874, became a pupil-teacher in the boys' department of the Olga Street School in Bethnal Green. After a one-year (1880–81) teacher training course at St Mark's College, Chelsea, he returned to the Olga Street School and in January 1882 the London school board appointed him assistant master. He remained at the school until his retirement on 10 May 1928.

Ray's social and educational background was not that commonly associated with someone who establishes a significant scholarly career, yet he became the foremost expert on south Pacific languages in the first half of the twentieth century. In his teenage years, he developed a fascination with languages. Mostly on his own initiative, he studied French, German, Sanskrit, and briefly, Bantu.

In the early 1880s, Ray began an extended association with Robert Henry Codrington, vicar of Wadhurst, Sussex. Codrington had served as an Anglican missionary in New Guinea and was considered an authority on south Pacific languages. Inspired by Codrington, Ray began the study of Melanesian languages upon which his reputation as a linguist came to be based. It was Codrington who arranged for Ray to read, in 1886, his first scholarly paper before the congress of orientalists in London. Over the next fifty years he published dozens of articles and books in which he classified various New Guinea languages. His notable works included *The Languages of British New Guinea* (1894), *A Comparative Study of the Melanesian Island Languages* (1926), and (with E. B. Riley) *A Grammar of the Kiwai Language* (1933).

A major turning point in Ray's career occurred in the early 1890s when Codrington recommended him to A. C. Haddon, a prominent Australian anthropologist and linguist, who was preparing vocabularies he had gathered in the Torres Strait. Ray helped edit the vocabularies for publication and his work so impressed Haddon that in 1898 he invited Ray to join his Cambridge anthropological expedition to the Fly River delta area of New Guinea. This one-year Cambridge expedition was the only experience Ray had in the south Pacific. He spent most of his time on Kiwai Island where he received much support from the Revd James Chalmers, a noted missionary and anthropologist. The information Ray acquired on this expedition led to a prodigious output of linguistic scholarship beginning with volume 3 (1907) of the Cambridge expedition reports.

Ray's work represented the trends in linguistic studies at the time. He concerned himself with preparing grammars, vocabularies, and dictionaries. He also attempted to explain the origins of south Pacific languages. He proved that indigenous Papuan languages spoken on the southern coast of New Guinea differed markedly from immigrant Melanesian languages. He also contended that Indonesian, Melanesian, and Polynesian languages had common origins. Ray's vocabularies and dictionaries, especially for the Kiwai language of the south Fly River area, have remained useful, but the methodology for much of his work fell out of fashion with linguists in the second half of the twentieth century.

Ray was physically slight and frequently unwell. His persistence in the excruciatingly tedious mental labour required to complete his work astounded colleagues. The volume of his publications was made all the more remarkable from the fact that, except for 1898–9, he received no reprieve from the routine demands of his school position. He was in constant financial difficulties and his first wife, Eliza Rebecca Byrne (*b*. 1862), whom he married on 31 May 1887, was an invalid much of the time. She did, however, give considerable encouragement to her husband's work. They had no children. Following the death of his first wife Ray married, on 17 June 1933, Ethel Vergard (*b*. 1882), a much younger woman he had known for many years.

Although he was never offered a university appointment, Ray did earn numerous honours. Through the intervention of A. C. Haddon, he received an honorary MA from Cambridge University in 1907. In 1910, recognizing his assistance in the translation of scripture, the British and Foreign Bible Society made him an honorary life governor. The Royal Anthropological Institute, of which he had been a fellow since 1888, selected him as vice-president in 1919; and in 1927, again with the strong recommendation of Haddon, Ray was granted a much needed pension from the civil list. Not always in good health in his later years, he none the less continued his scholarship through the 1930s. His final publication appeared in 1938 just a few months before his death on 1 January 1939 at Southend Municipal Hospital, Rochford, Essex.

RONALD K. HUCH

Sources *The Times* (4 Jan 1939) · A. C. Haddon, *Man*, 39 (1939), 58–61 · *WWW* · b. cert. · m. certs. · d. cert. · A. Shnukal, 'At the Australian-Papuan linguistic boundary: Sidney Ray's classification of Torres Strait languages', *Cambridge and the Torres Strait: centenary essays on the 1898 anthropological expedition*, ed. A. Herle and S. Rouse (1998), 181–200 · S. Wurm, *Papuan languages of Oceania* (1982)
Archives SOAS, papers relating to the languages and ethnology of the Pacific islands | BLPES, letters to C. G. Seligman mainly relating to Hamitic peoples
Likenesses portrait, repro. in Haddon, *Man*
Wealth at death £1758 6s. 9d.: probate, 17 Feb 1939, *CGPLA Eng. & Wales*

Ray, Ted [*real name* Charles Olden] (1909–1977), comedian, was born in Wigan on 21 November 1909, the son of Charles Olden, comic singer and mimic, who used the stage name Charlie Alden, and Margaret Ellen Kenyon, of Oldham. Two previous babies had died in extreme infancy and he had one younger sister, Lena. Bred in Lancashire and educated at Anfield council school and the Liverpool collegiate school, he initially nursed some notions of being a professional footballer, as well as exhibiting the theatrical ambitions which soon predominated.

In the mid-1920s Olden joined up with a friend to form a musical act, Wardle and Olden. In 1927 he turned solo, playing his violin as Hugh Neek (Unique) and then as Nedlo (Olden reversed) the Gypsy Fiddler. Gradually he dropped the Gypsy character and added jokes to his act, as he progressed in revue, music-hall, and cine-variety, making a good first impression in London in 1930. The leading agent George Barclay agreed to represent him if he changed his billing, and thus he adopted the name of the

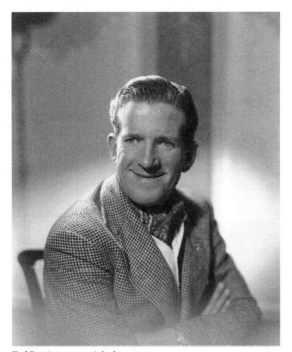

Ted Ray (1909–1977), by Lenare, 1949

British winner of the 1920 American Open golf championship—Ted Ray. Like his contemporaries Vic Oliver and Jimmy Wheeler (or like Bennett and Williams on their phono-fiddles), Ray used his violin as a prop and pointer to the humour, so that his bill matter, 'Fiddling and fooling', was very apt, although, in later years, he used the instrument only occasionally. At a time when music-hall comedians opted for grotesque garb and make-up, or else, at the other extreme, chose the West End uniform of the dinner jacket, Ray decided to rely on the more casual lounge suit, going on stage as if he had, in his own words, 'walked in from the street'. That everyday demeanour, topped off by a rapid-fire, pertinent delivery, with its insinuation of a transatlantic twang, sought a 'big laugh' every seven seconds. His first appearance at the London Palladium in 1932 was a major professional signpost and he initially broadcast on the radio in 1939, but plans for a mainline radio series had to be abandoned on the outbreak of the Second World War, during which his profile was relatively low as a troops' entertainer. In the post-war years he established himself as a successful support act at the Palladium in the days when American stars such as Danny Kaye were triumphant, and after accomplished contributions to the royal command variety shows of 1948 and 1949 he found widespread fame as a radio star.

Beginning in 1949, *Ray's a Laugh* became a long-running and highly popular radio series for twelve years. Shrewdly set neither in lavish nor impoverished location—the usual music-hall placements—but in somewhat featureless suburbia, the programme was a precursor of the television sitcom. Ray's style, matching a middle-class ordinariness with slick commentary, was ideally suited to the genre, and the target was seventy laughs in a half-hour show. The Australian actress Kitty Bluett played his wife, and there was lively assistance from, among others, Fred Yule, Kenneth Connor, Graham Stark, the musical duo Bob and Alf Pearson, and Peter Sellars in varied roles. The mundane triteness of domestic incident was tricked out with memorable catch-phrases—'it was agony, Ivy'—and absurd personages—the gangster Al K. Traz and the Russian Serge Suit—reminiscent of Tommy Handley's *ITMA*. George, the Man with a Conscience, was an interesting embodiment of Ray's invincibly cheerful average man: 'the pub humorist relaxing with his friends' was how *The Times* (9 November 1977) described his approach. Ray's irrepressible wisecracking, principally based on copious memory and nimble recall rather than spontaneity of wit, was much in demand on other radio programmes, such as *Calling All Forces*, *Joker's Wild*, and *Does the Team Think?*. He also made several minor film appearances, starred in the 1955 *Ted Ray Show* on television, was for some time master of ceremonies of the Granada TV quiz, *Spot the Tune*, made an excellent contribution reading on the children's storytime series *Jackanory*, and with Kay Walsh made a splendid fist of filming Noël Coward's *Red Peppers* playlet. However, it is as a radio comedian—his great success coming after a quarter century in the business—that he was most affectionately remembered.

Ray married Dorothy Sybil Stevens, dancer, at Croydon register office on 11 July 1933. They first lived in Mitcham, Surrey, before settling at Broad Walk, Winchmore Hill, north London. Their sons, Robin *Ray (1934–1998) and Andrew Ray (b. 1939), borrowing from different sides of their heritage, developed careers in music and acting respectively. Affable, sociable, golf-playing, Ted Ray enjoyed the affluence of his later career, being one of the first of the traditional school of comics to adopt a rather high suburban lifestyle. He had a very serious car accident in 1975 and was convicted of dangerous driving while under the influence of alcohol. Although he apparently recovered, when he returned to Highlands Hospital, Enfield, for further treatment, he died suddenly on 8 November 1977, a little before his sixty-eighth birthday; the subsequent inquest recorded the cause as heart failure.

ERIC MIDWINTER

Sources T. Ray, *Raising the laughs* (1952) · R. Busby, *British music hall: an illustrated who's who from 1850 to the present day* (1976) · Theatre Museum collections, London · *The Times* (9 Nov 1977)
Archives FILM BFI NFTVA, performance footage | SOUND BBC WAC, performance footage · BL NSA, 'Ted Ray: it's a funny old business', 1977, B7380/03 · BL NSA, documentary recordings · BL NSA, performance recordings
Likenesses Lenare, photograph, 1949, NPG [see illus.] · photographs, Theatre Museum, London · photographs, Trinity College of Music, London, Mander and Mitchenson Theatre Collection · photographs, Hult. Arch.
Wealth at death £192,199: probate, 24 Nov 1977, *CGPLA Eng. & Wales*

Ray, Thomas Mathew (1801–1881), political organizer, was born in Dublin, the eldest son of Mathew Ray, a master cooper, and his wife, Sarah Carton. Brought up a Catholic, he received a classical education at Dublin schools. In 1842 Ray was admitted to both the King's Inns, Dublin, and

Gray's Inn, London, but there is no record of him practising at the bar. Similarly, in 1843 he became a student at Trinity College, Dublin, but never graduated.

Ray worked as a scrivener before becoming secretary of the National Trades Political Union in 1832 and the Trades Union election committee. He was active in registering voters for Daniel O'Connell's return for Dublin in the 1832 election. In 1835 Ray published *A List of the Constituency of Dublin*. Appointed an official of O'Connell's General Association of Ireland of 1836, his stipend was continued by O'Connell when he dissolved the association in 1837. Ray was the linchpin of O'Connell's new Precursor Society in 1838. Detained elsewhere, O'Connell told Ray, 'you must prepare and have everything ready to commence operations on my arrival in Dublin'. Ray was told to establish a committee by attending parish meetings (*Limerick Standard*, 19 Oct 1838). Such remote control through Ray also characterized the celebrated Repeal Association set up by O'Connell in 1840. Ray happily undertook the details of party management, printing and distributing addresses, campaigning in the country, handling donations and the O'Connell rent, enrolling members, and furnishing the necessary returns. O'Connell even charged Ray with ordering his suits (*Correspondence of Daniel O'Connell*, 6.369).

Ray's letters to O'Connell sometimes bordered on the obsequious: 'Pardon me, my dear Liberator, for I fear in my anxiety I may trespass more than needful on your time' (*Correspondence of Daniel O'Connell*, 8.38). One of Ray's sons was christened O'Connell. Nevertheless, behind such deference Ray exercised very considerable influence. For his part, O'Connell had 'unlimited confidence' in Ray (ibid., 7.68). Advising his son John in 1840, O'Connell declared: 'Give your best support to Ray who is just the best man in his station I ever met with, beyond comparison the best' (ibid., 8.38). The 'Liberator' was aware that Ray's health was brittle and that he was beset by the problems of a large family. O'Connell told his son to shield Ray tactfully from a jealous opponent (ibid., 6.360). Publicly, O'Connell declared him 'a RAY to illumine the dark pages of our country's wrongs (cheering)' (*Limerick Reporter*). Ray's daughter Mary sometimes acted as O'Connell's personal secretary and was lauded by the 'Liberator' as the first female Repealer (*Freeman's Journal*, 5 Jan 1841).

In late 1844 the Peel government placed O'Connell and his lieutenants, including Ray, on trial for sedition, arising out of a series of 'monster' repeal meetings in the previous year. Ray's counsel, J. Hatchell QC, maintained that it was 'a monstrous thing to include Mr. Ray in this indictment'. As the paid organizer, working for the support of his family, he had attended only two meetings as a spectator. Ray's indictment deliberately precluded his citation, with the books of the Repeal Association, as a defence witness (Shaw, 335). The jury, containing no Catholics, found against Ray, who was sentenced to nine months' imprisonment and a fine of £50. Ray was comfortably incarcerated in the Richmond bridewell with O'Connell and other leaders from 30 May to 6 September, when the House of Lords acquitted all the accused.

In 1845 and 1846 O'Connell was increasingly challenged within the Repeal Association by William Smith O'Brien and the Young Irelanders. Ray strongly opposed the dissidents, rejecting *The Nation*'s defence of a healthy difference of opinion (*The Nation*). As the chief promoter of repeal reading rooms, Ray was glad to see *The Nation* barred from them. When the Young Irelanders withdrew in opposition to O'Connell's condemnation of all violence in achieving reform, Ray dispatched sharp letters of exclusion. The Young Irelanders retaliated by demanding the removal of paid officials from repeal committee decisions.

Heart-broken by O'Connell's death in May 1847, Ray blamed Young Ireland: O'Connell's 'balmy nature could not endure the sting of ingratitude' (NL Ire., MS 22,482). He continued as Repeal Association secretary under John O'Connell. Like John O'Connell, whom he persuaded to delay his rejection, Ray remained aloof from the Irish League, intended to reunite Young Irelanders and repealers in July 1848. The unsuccessful rising by Smith O'Brien later that month ended negotiations. When John O'Connell tried to revive the Repeal Association in October 1849, Ray subscribed but remained inactive before the association's final collapse in 1850.

Ray's last years were spent mainly in the office of deeds, of which he was assistant registrar, 1865–80. He was interested in the secretaryship of the Home Government Association in the early 1870s, but was politely rejected. He died at 5 Leinster Road, Rathmines, Dublin, on 5 January 1881 and was buried at Glasnevin cemetery two days later, mourned by his son, T. M. Ray junior. His wife, Mary, predeceased him in 1851, dying at the age of forty-nine. Their marriage was marred by the death of three children in infancy: Kate and Emma in 1839 and Jane in 1844.

Ray was responsible for many repeal reports. His most important publication was the *Report on the Irish Coercion Bill, the causes of discontent in Ireland, condition of the people, comparative criminality with England, remedial measures* (1846). According to Fergus O'Ferrall, the Repeal Association was the most sophisticated of O'Connell's organizations and 'Ray had it organised as a model of efficiency in different departments and committees' (O'Ferrall, 116).

RICHARD P. DAVIS

Sources *The correspondence of Daniel O'Connell*, ed. M. R. O'Connell, 5–8, IMC (1977–80) · H. S. Shaw, *Shaw's authenticated report of the Irish state trials, 1844* (1844) · E. Keane, P. Beryl Phair, and T. U. Sadleir, eds., *King's Inns admission papers, 1607–1867*, IMC (1982) · *The Nation* (23 May 1846) · *Freeman's Journal* [Dublin] (1832–49), (1851), (1881) · *Limerick Reporter* (16 June 1843) · *Limerick Standard* (19 Oct 1838) · O. MacDonagh, *The emancipist: Daniel O'Connell, 1830–47* (1989) · F. O'Ferrall, *Daniel O'Connell* (1981) · R. Davis, *The Young Ireland movement* (1987) · *Dublin Evening Mail* (7 Jan 1881)
Archives NL Ire. | King's Inns, Dublin, records · NL Ire., O'Connell MSS
Likenesses W. J. Linton, group portrait, woodcut, 1844 (*The state trial portraits*; after H. Anelay), BM · sketch, 1844 (*Capi e promotori della quistione Irlandese*; after Italian lithograph), repro. in C. G. Duffy, *Young Ireland: a fragment of Irish history, 1840–4*, 1 (1896), facing p. 63 · group portrait, wood-engraving (*The traversers*), NPG; repro. in *ILN* (25 Nov 1843)

Rayleigh. For this title name *see* Strutt, John William, third Baron Rayleigh (1842–1919); Strutt, Robert John, fourth Baron Rayleigh (1875–1947).

Rayman, Jacob (*b.* in or before **1596**, *d.* in or after **1658**), violin maker, was probably born in Faulenbach in Fussen, a town in the Tyrol well known for its lute makers, who had established instrument-making workshops throughout Europe. At an unknown date he left Faulenbach, possibly travelling via Brabant in the Spanish Netherlands, for England, where he is the earliest recorded maker of violins whose instruments survive into the twenty-first century. Sophere Rayman, widow and surgeon—stated to have been born in 's-Hertogenbosch, Brabant, and listed on 16 September 1618 as a stranger living in Blackman Street in the parish of Newington, Surrey—was probably a close relative; she married Nicholas Haynes at St Gregory by Paul in 1626. The earliest violin label bearing Rayman's name is reported to have been dated 1630, with the maker's address given as Bell Yard, Southwark, while the earliest surviving example, dated 1641, comes from Blackman Street, Long Southwark. Jacob Rayman's son, also Jacob, was baptized on 27 November 1642 at St Saviour, Southwark, and Rayman seems to have remained at Bell Yard or Blackman Street until at least 1658. Rayman was not associated with viol making, which was the principal occupation of stringed instrument makers in London at this date. Also in Southwark at this period was the distinguished English viol maker, Henry Jaye, and although no specific address is known for him, it is likely that the two men would have been at least aware of each other's work. Nothing is known of Rayman after 1658, although his son is supposed to have been working as a violin maker in 1691.

Modern interest in Rayman's work has mainly focused on the catalogue of the sale of the collection of Thomas Britton in 1714 (published in John Hawkins's *General History of the Science and Practice of Music* in 1776), which included four separate lots described as 'an extraordinary Rayman', offered for sale with examples of all the leading London makers of the time. James Fleming noted in *The Fiddle Fancier's Guide* (1883) that Rayman's instruments were 'neither scarce nor dear'. They continued to appear with some regularity in nineteenth-century saleroom catalogues, but very few examples have been identified today. This is possibly because their similarity to highly prized Brescian work and that of other better known Fussen trained makers has led to much misattribution and deliberate relabelling over the centuries. A further difficulty is the irregular size of his violins, one small and one over-large pattern, much like the Brescian instruments with which they are often compared. This may have made them awkward for professional musicians of the nineteenth century, and less likely to be conserved. Hawkins also stated that Rayman was particularly prized for his tenors (violas), and two recorded examples are interestingly decorated with an intriguing carved design around the scroll reminiscent of Celtic strapwork. His instruments also frequently bear ornate purfling motifs,

fashioned from inlaid strips of dyed hardwood, augmented with pokerwork similar in style to contemporary instruments made from the Netherlands to southern Germany. A small unlabelled violin attributed to Rayman has a Tudor rose surmounted by a crown inlaid in the centre of the back in this manner. A bass violin (or cello), which has a viol-like carved head in place of a scroll, has also been tentatively identified. The general form of Rayman's instruments is distinctively elongated with rather straight centre bouts and extended soundholes. The workmanship is however irregular and quickly executed.

Rayman's influence on subsequent early English violin makers such as William Baker of Oxford and Thomas Urquhart is clearly evident, but by the end of the seventeenth century the leading makers in London, among them Robert Cuthbert and Ralph Agutter had turned to more sophisticated Italian models and a more refined style.   A. F. POLLARD, *rev.* JOHN DILWORTH

Sources R. Bletschacher, *Die Lautern und Geigenmacher des Fussener Landes* (1978) · J. Hawkins, *A general history of the science and practice of music*, 5 vols. (1776) · AM Oxf., Hill Archive · Geigenbau Machold, Zürich, Hill Photographic Archive · parish register, Southwark, St Saviour, 27 Nov 1642, LMA, X097/284 [baptism] · PRO, SP 14/99 · J. M. Fleming, *The fiddle fancier's guide* (1892)

Archives AM Oxf., Hill Archive (W. E. Hill and sons) · Geigenbau Machold, Zürich, Hill Photographic Archive

Raymond le Gros. *See* Fitzgerald, Raymond fitz William (*d.* 1189x92).

Raymond, Anthony (1675–1726), Church of Ireland clergyman and Irish language scholar, was born at Ballyloughrane, near Listowel, co. Kerry, the second son of Anthony Raymond and his wife, Ann (*née* Taylor). The father was the second of the family to hold land in co. Kerry and he combined the post of sheriff of Kerry with that of steward to two powerful landowners, Sir William Fenton and Lord Kingston. The younger Anthony entered Trinity College, Dublin, as a pensioner in 1692, having received his previous schooling from a Mr Jones in Cobh, co. Cork. He was elected scholar in 1693, probably the year his father died, and was awarded the degrees of BA in 1695 and MA in 1699. Later in that year he was elected junior fellow, and when a Mr Dennis retired as the lecturer in physic his place was taken by Raymond. For some of the period between 1699 and 1703 he was appointed junior dean. He was ordained as a priest of the Church of Ireland in Cork in September 1699 and succeeded John Stearne to the vicarage of Trim, co. Meath, in 1705. He continued his studies and in 1707 he was awarded the degree of LLD and in July 1719 that of doctor of divinity.

It was in the context of his role as a country parson that Raymond probably met Jonathan Swift, as the latter's country parish of Laracor was only about 2 miles from the town of Trim. Swift's lady friends Esther Johnson (Stella) and Rebecca Dingley often stayed at the vicarage in Trim while Swift himself lodged in his little glebe house nearby. They all often ate meals together, drank wine, and played cards. Raymond married after taking up his post in Trim. His wife was named Elizabeth and the fact that one of his children was called Gybson suggests that this (or

Gibson) may have been her surname. Raymond features fairly often in Swift's *Journal to Stella* written from London between the years 1710 and 1713. Raymond was in London organizing some financial arrangements for part of this period and attempted to visit Swift often, sometimes to be rudely rebuffed. When he returned to Ireland the social relationship between them continued despite the fact that it was strained by Raymond's prodigal attitude to money. He entered into several complicated agreements with Stella and the dean which greatly annoyed Swift. Despite this Swift bought the 'impropriate tyths of the parish and rectory of Effernock' from Raymond in 1718 for £250 and was happy for his fellow cleric to be responsible for their collection.

Raymond must have been aware of a bilingual society as he grew up in co. Kerry and Cork, and he was part of the establishment of Trinity College, Dublin, when Edward Lhuyd, the great Celtic scholar, visited Ireland; but he states that his first major contact with the language was when he became vicar of Trim and discovered that three-quarters of his potential parishioners were monoglot Irish speakers. Raymond says that he not only learned the language well enough to carry out his duties as a priest in it, but that he also spent time and resources studying the ancient historical remains in the manuscripts that were to be found. This is how he met the Irish scribes, and for nearly twenty years the study of Irish was his obsession.

Raymond served as patron to a number of the scholars associated with the Dublin circle of the Ó Neachtains, namely Dermot O'Connor, Stephen Rice, Hugh McCurtin, and Tadhg Ó Neachtain. He bought manuscripts in their possession and paid them to translate and elucidate the material. In 1719 he embarked on a scheme to publish a corrected version of Geoffrey Keating's history of Ireland. In order to correct it he borrowed the *Book of Ballymote*, a fourteenth-century compendium of history and literature in Irish, from Trinity College Library in October 1719 and this started great copying activity among the scribes. His plan to publish a history was thwarted when one of his erstwhile helpers, Dermot O'Connor, went to London and succeeded in publishing a translation of Keating's work (*The General History of Ireland*, 1723). The rest of Raymond's life was spent in trying to salvage his history and his reputation. He nearly succeeded in 1725, as his brother, William, a merchant in Bristol, on his deathbed made his fortune over to Anthony; this enabled him to publish *A Short Preliminary Discourse to the History of Ireland* and to lobby on behalf of his longer work. This was the subject of the only surviving letter between Swift and Raymond, the dean encouraging him to repay his debts rather than continue with his publishing venture. Raymond seemingly ignored him, but died in London early in 1726 before he could finalize arrangements for the publication of his history of Ireland.   ALAN HARRISON

Sources A. Harrison, *The dean's friend: Anthony Raymond, 1675–1726, Jonathan Swift, and the Irish language* (1999) · Royal Irish Acad., MSS 24 G11–24 G14 · A. Harrison, *Ag cruinniú meala: Anthony Raymond (1675–1726)* (Baile Átha Cliath, 1988) · H. Cotton, *Fasti ecclesiae Hibernicae*, 6 vols. (1845–78); 2nd edn, 1 (1851) · J. Swift, *Journal to Stella*, ed. H. Williams, 2 vols. (1948) · *The account books of Jonathan Swift*, ed. P. V. Thompson and D. J. Thompson (1984) · *The correspondence of Jonathan Swift*, ed. H. Williams, 5 vols. (1963–5) · *Letter from Dr Raymond to my lord Inchiquin* (1723) · [A. Raymond], *An account of Dr Keting's history of Ireland, etc.* (1723) · A. Raymond, *A short preliminary discourse to the history of Ireland* (1725) · W. Nicolson, *The Irish historical library* (1724) · V. de Burgh and [T. O'Sullivan], *The memoirs of the right honourable the marquis of Clanricarde … to which is prefix'd a Dissertation* (1722) · *Remarks and collections of Thomas Hearne*, ed. C. E. Doble and others, 9, OHS, 65 (1914), 110–11 · B. Cunningham, *The world of Geoffrey Keating: history, myth and religion in seventeenth-century Ireland* (2000)
Archives BL, MSS · NL Ire., MSS · Royal Irish Acad., MSS · TCD

Raymond, Ernest (1888–1974), novelist, was born on 31 December 1888 at Argentières in the Haute Savoie, France. His parents were married to other partners. To give the child the semblance of legitimacy, he was baptized as the son of William and Florence Bell Raymond of Paris. Raymond's true father was Captain, later Major-General, George Frederic Blake of the Royal Marines (1836–1904). His mother was Ida Wilkinson, *née* Calder (1846–1918). Ernest Raymond was brought to England in 1891 and raised in London believing his mother was his aunt. Responsibility for bringing up the child was given to Emily Calder, Ida's younger sister, who was strict and narrow-minded. The general lodged with them until 1901, when his estranged wife died. Known affectionately as Dum, he was kindly, amusing, and generous. He then moved away and married Lilian McKellar. The one other permanent member of the unconventional *ménage* was Dorothy Makepeace. She was Raymond's elder half-sister, and though not acknowledged as such was the daughter of Emily and the general. Despite the unusual circumstances, Raymond's childhood was comparatively untroubled and happy. He discovered the complexities of his parentage in early manhood.

Raymond was educated at Colet Court preparatory school, Hammersmith, 1898–1901, and St Paul's School, London, 1901–5. Dum's death and a consequent lack of funds meant that Raymond spent his last year of education at a cheap boarding-school where he was restless and unhappy. At seventeen he left to become a clerk for the Army and Navy Stores. He had formed an abiding ambition to be a writer, but was persuaded to enter the teaching profession. From 1908 to 1911 he taught classics at Glengorse School, Eastbourne, then from 1911 to 1912 at St Christopher's, Bath. At Bath Raymond caught 'the splendid fever of Anglo-Catholicity' from a friend. (Raymond, *The Story of my Days*, 114.) He proceeded to Chichester Theological College, where he graduated first in his class, and then took a first-class degree preliminary to holy orders at Durham University in 1914. He was priested on Trinity Sunday 1915.

At the outbreak of the First World War, Raymond immediately applied to the chaplain-general for service overseas with the army. He served as chaplain to the 10th Manchester regiment (1915–17), to the 9th Worcestershire regiment (1917 and 1919), to the East Lancashire territorials in Gallipoli in August 1915, and on five other fronts: Sinai, France and Belgium, Mesopotamia, Persia, and Russia. No other campaign for him proved half so memorable, poignant, or glamorous as Gallipoli. 'In the secret places of his heart' he retained unsullied his patriotic idealism (Raymond, *The Story of my Days*, 131). In 1917 Raymond witnessed the dreadful slaughter at the Ypres salient, but on the whole his campaigning experience was comparatively comfortable and safe. During the war Raymond composed a religious work, 'God's wheat'. The manuscript was lost when the ship bearing it to England was torpedoed. The project was never resurrected.

Demobilized in 1919, Raymond returned to England and took up a curacy in the busy, prosperous parish of Brighton. In 1921 he married Zoe Irene Maude Doucett; they had two children. In 1922 Raymond published *Tell England: a Study in a Generation*. As a schoolmaster Raymond had begun a novel about his schooldays. While in Gallipoli he first realized that he might incorporate the material in a more ambitious work about young men who were called to fight and to die for England. This notion grew to become his first and most famous novel. Rejected by thirteen publishers *Tell England* was finally published by Cassell and reprinted twenty times in its first two years; it was still in print fifty years and forty impressions later. The reading public, anxious to be reassured that the sacrifice of a generation had been worth while, approved the novel's elegiac quality, its sentimentality, the mixture of patriotism and piety, the celebration of sacrifice, and not least the unquestioning acceptance by the protagonists of their destiny. The critics were hopelessly divided. It was acclaimed as an epic, and also condemned as commonplace, illiterate, and nauseating. It was made into a very successful film by Anthony Asquith in 1931. The book's success cast a long shadow over Raymond's other work. He was constantly reminded that nothing he wrote would ever match the amazing success of his first novel, while as a writer he was condemned for years to be labelled as a popular sentimentalist.

With Raymond's career as a writer spectacularly launched, each subsequent year produced a new novel. *Rossenal* (1922) recounted the experiences of a schoolmaster, *Damascus Gate* (1923) the tribulations of an aspiring novelist, and *Wanderlight* (1924) the agonies of conscience suffered by a young ordinand who withdraws from the priesthood. Throughout his training as deacon and priest Raymond retained his absolute devotion and loyalty to Anglo-Catholicism. As doubts began to grow, however, he realized he had been naïve and uncritical. Insupportable misery now replaced joyous belief and in 1923 he decided he must quit holy orders. Though his belief in God the creator remained inviolate, he found it impossible to accept the Trinity. During forty years of anguished self-exile, he never abandoned his love for the church, and when the church declared partial agnosticism to be admissible, he returned immediately.

From 1925 Raymond was a full-time writer producing novels of varying quality. His most successful book was a collection of essays, *Through Literature to Life* (1928), reprinted four times before the end of the year. On the strength of it he took part in a conference on literature and leisure in Vancouver in April 1929. In Toronto he started a two-year love affair with Hazel Reid Marsh. In 1929 he published *A Family that Was* (1929), the first novel in a three-volume family saga, the other volumes of which were *Mary Leith* (1931) and *The Jesting Army* (1930); they were published in one volume as *Once in England* (1932). In 1929 he turned his hand to drama; his play *The Berg*, based on the sinking of the *Titanic*, had a short run in the West End and was adapted for screen as *Atlantic*.

In 1933 Raymond was made president of the PEN Club (he had been one of its first members in 1922). At a PEN meeting in 1935 he met the novelist Diana Joan Young (*b. c.*1916), whom he married in 1940 after his divorce from his first wife in 1939. In 1935 *We, the Accused* was a considerable critical as well as commercial success, surprising many reviewers by its gritty realism. It won the Book Guild medal in 1935. It combined the story of a murder with informed criticism of the legal system. This novel was the first of a series of sixteen known collectively as *A London Gallery*.

During the Second World War, Raymond was an air raid warden and a member of the Home Guard in 1940. He produced a number of novels during the war, including *The Last to Rest* (1941) and *The Corporal of the Guard* (1943). With his son Patrick, Raymond wrote *Back to Humanity* (1945), an impassioned call for a return to human values after the alienation of war. Raymond wrote more than forty novels. The last, *A Georgian Love Story* (1971) satisfied his considerable and loyal readership. He also wrote biographical studies of Keats, Shelley, the Brontë family, and St Francis (on the strength of the last book he was made a knight officer in the order of merit of the Italian republic). Raymond's considerable contribution to popular literature was belatedly acknowledged by his appointment as OBE in 1972. He was made president of the Dickens Fellowship in 1971, and he campaigned to have Coleridge's remains reinterred in St Michael's, Highgate, London. He lived in Hampstead for thirty-five years and was on Hampstead council's libraries committee, and in 1961 served as a Liberal councillor. In 1966 he visited Israel in an effort to restore his lost faith; an account of this appears in *The Bethany Road* (1967).

Raymond died on 14 May 1974 at his home, 22 The Pryors, East Heath Road, Hampstead, London, of uraemia and an enlarged prostate; he was buried in Hampstead cemetery. His wife Diana survived him.

Raymond was a fluent, compelling story-teller. His novels are illuminated by his deep affection for the north of England and, above all, for London, where he lived for most of his life. There was a strong didactic streak in Raymond and his stories allowed him to examine social and religious themes with his own radical ideals and ideas. This was done without apology and with uncompromising moral earnestness. This, combined with his reputation for sentimentality, perhaps explains his fall from critical favour.   A. J. A. MORRIS

Sources E. Raymond, *The story of my days: an autobiography, 1888–1922* (1968) • *The Times* (16 May 1974) • *WW* • E. Raymond, *Please you, draw near: autobiography, 1922–1968* (1969) • S. Hynes, *A war imagined:*

the First World War and English culture (1990) • P. Parker, *The old lie: the Great War and the public school ethos* (1987) • *Hampstead and Highgate Express* (17 May 1974)

Archives BL, corresp. with Society of Authors, MSS 63319–63320 • Royal Society of Literature, London, letters to the Royal Society of Literature • University of Bristol, corresp. and statements relating to trial of *Lady Chatterley's Lover* • Wilson Library, Chapel Hill, University of North Carolina, A. P. Watt company records

Likenesses J. Bridie, pencil caricature, 1919, repro. in Raymond, *Story of my days* • group portraits, photographs (with his family), repro. in Raymond, *Story of my days*

Wealth at death £38,622: probate, 24 Jan 1975, *CGPLA Eng. & Wales*

Raymond, Henry J. *See* Worth, Adam (c.1844–1902).

Raymond, Robert, first Baron Raymond (1673–1733), judge, was born on 20 December 1673 in London, the only son of Sir Thomas *Raymond (1626/7–1683), judge, and his wife, Anne (1633–1715), daughter of Sir Edward Fishe, baronet, of Southill, Bedfordshire. At his father's request he was formally admitted to Gray's Inn at the age of nine, in 1682; he subsequently attended school at Eton College and became a pensioner of Christ's College, Cambridge, in 1689. Despite the early start to his legal career he was not called to the bar until November 1697, and his early entry into business suggests the fruits of sustained and conscientious study. Indeed, his common-law reports begin in 1694, and in Michaelmas 1698 he reported his own argument for the defendant in *Pullein* v. *Benson* (1698), an action of debt on a bond. The extent of his early success is evidenced by his retention as junior counsel for the crown in the 1702 trial of Richard Hathaway, a Southwark blacksmith's apprentice who had been exposed for a malicious prosecution of witchcraft. In April 1704 he appeared for the defence in the trial for high treason of the Scot David Lindsay, who was indicted under a statute enacted after the peace of Ryswick which was designed to minimize the threat of Jacobites returning from France. Although Lindsay was convicted, Raymond made an ambitious and learned argument to the effect that *pace Calvin's case* (*State trials*, 14.1007–15) as a Scot he was not within the scope of an act passed by the English parliament which referred to English subjects. Two years later he opened for the prosecution in the trial of Robert (Beau) Fielding, who was indicted for bigamy, having married the notorious Barbara Villiers, duchess of Cleveland, while his first wife was still alive.

Raymond's standing as a rising barrister was confirmed by his appearance in 1709 before the House of Lords against the Naturalization Bill, on behalf of the City of London, but there is little evidence of any early political commitment on his part. Certainly in December of the same year he was retained as one of the counsel for the defence of Dr Henry Sacheverell, but in the event he was not prepared to countenance Sacheverell's provocative high toryism, and in January 1710 he and Serjeant John Pratt returned their fees after reading their client's intemperate 'Answer' to the articles of impeachment. Nevertheless, on 13 May he was named solicitor-general in succession to Robert Eyre, and at the October general election he

was brought into parliament for Bishop's Castle in Shropshire on the nomination of Robert Harley. Raymond was subsequently knighted and voted with the tory administration during the last years of Queen Anne, being returned again for Bishop's Castle by Harley in 1713; but although he was not especially active in parliament, at the accession of George I he was replaced as solicitor-general on the recommendation of Lord Cowper.

After the 1715 election, having been elected on the tory interest for Yarmouth in the Isle of Wight, Raymond spoke on behalf of the tory opposition and defended his former patron Oxford against the charge of treason brought against him under articles of impeachment. Although he was unseated by petition on 12 April 1717, the delivery of a major speech against the Septennial Bill in 1716 suggests Raymond had established his parliamentary voice. He was sufficiently important to attract an offer of a seat from the whig government, and pliable enough to accept, returning to the Commons as MP for Ludlow in 1719, and being elected for Helston at the general election of 1722. Indeed, Raymond was one of the leading barristers in chancery and the House of Lords during 1720, and became attorney-general on 9 May 1720. In that capacity he conducted the proceedings arising out of the Atterbury plot, including the prosecution of Christopher Layer in king's bench at the end of 1722, but in parliament his previous tory affiliation was an embarrassment when it came to promoting the bill of pains and penalties against his former ally Atterbury, and he retired to a puisne judgeship in king's bench at the beginning of January 1724.

Despite his former toryism and limited parliamentary usefulness, Raymond clearly enjoyed the confidence of the Walpolian regime. In 1725 he was named one of the lords commissioners who had custody of the great seal for six months between the resignation of Lord Chancellor Macclesfield and the appointment of Lord Chancellor King, and on the death of Sir John Pratt he was advanced to be lord chief justice of king's bench (2 March 1725). He presided there for eight years, and evidently gave satisfaction, being reappointed on the accession of George II and raised to the peerage in 1731 as first Baron Raymond of Abbots Langley, Hertfordshire. As lord chief justice he is remembered for elaborate and very learned judgments which applied the common law carefully and conservatively. Certainly he helped to develop the law's distinction between murder and manslaughter. In 1727, giving judgment on a special verdict found against Major John Oneby for killing a man after a gambling argument, Raymond determined that an 'act of deliberation' on the part of the protagonist which occurred after the first quarrel showed that he was not deprived of his reason and therefore was guilty of murder. And two years later in *R.* v. *John Huggins* (*State trials*, 17.370–82), which arose out of the parliamentary inquiry into the condition of the prisons (Huggins was warden of the Fleet prison), he held that an officer could not be held criminally responsible for the acts of his deputy in the absence of his express consent, and Huggins was therefore not guilty of murdering an inmate who had died after ill treatment. He also had some impact on the law of libel, establishing the principle in *R. v. Curl* (1728) that publication of an obscene book is punishable as a libel at common law, if it 'tends to disturb the civil order of society', and temporarily shoring up the orthodox defences of government against criticism of the press in the important case of *R. v. Francklin* (1728), where the publisher of *The Craftsman* was indicted for criticizing the ministry's foreign policy. On this occasion Raymond reaffirmed the seventeenth-century principle that the jury were judges only of the defendant's responsibility for the publication and of its application to the king's ministers, and it was an issue of law for the court to determine whether the words were libellous. He also insisted that in seditious libel the truth of the matter alleged was no defence: 'it is not material whether the facts charged in a libel be true or false, if the prosecution is by indictment or information' (*State trials*, 17.658–9). This was the position later followed by Lord Mansfield.

Raymond was manifestly dedicated to the common law: near the end of his life he spoke in the Lords against the bill for recording legal proceedings in English; he also told his fellow peers that as a judge he would commit any one of them who claimed privileged immunity from giving evidence on oath. His reports continued to within a year of his death. He had married Anne (d. 1721), daughter of his colleague Sir Edward Northey, attorney-general when he was solicitor-general, and when he died at his London home at Red Lion Square on 18 March 1733 he left his estate of Langley Bury, at Abbots Langley in Hertfordshire, to their only son, Robert. He was buried at Abbots Langley church. His reports were published in 1743 and reached a fifth edition in 1832.   DAVID LEMMINGS

Sources *State trials*, 14.639–90, 1007– 15.1329–32; 17.30–57, 153–60, 370–82, 626–76 • HoP, *Commons*, 1715–54, 1.212, 257, 311; 2.379–80 • ER, vol. 91, 1 Lord Raymond; vol. 92, 2 Lord Raymond; also *R. v. Curl*, 2 Strange 788, 93 ER 849 • Cobbett, *Parl. hist.*, 7.73, 335–9; 8.39, 861 • G. Holmes, *The trial of Doctor Sacheverell* (1973), 105, 107 • *Manuscripts of the earl of Egmont: diary of Viscount Percival, afterwards first earl of Egmont*, 3 vols., HMC, 63 (1920–23), vol. 1, p. 277 • D. Lemmings, *Gentlemen and barristers: the inns of court and the English bar, 1680–1730* (1990) • E. Foss, *Biographia juridica: a biographical dictionary of the judges of England ... 1066–1870* (1870) • *DNB* • 'Raymond, Sir Robert', HoP, *Commons*, 1690–1715 [draft] • Sainty, *King's counsel* • Sainty, *Judges* • Venn, *Alum. Cant.* • GEC, *Peerage*
Archives Gray's Inn, London, commonplace books and notebooks • Kingston Museum and Heritage Service, legal opinion by him
Likenesses H. Cheere, marble bust, *c*.1732, V&A • H. Cheere, tomb effigy on monument, *c*.1732, St Lawrence Church, Abbots Langley, Hertfordshire • J. Simon, mezzotint (after I. Maubert), BM, NPG • attrib. J. Vanderbank, oils, Bodl. Oxf. • G. Vertue, line engraving (after J. Richardson), BM, NPG • oils, Gray's Inn, London

Raymond, Sir Thomas (1626/7–1683), judge, was the son of Robert Raymond (*c*.1583–1636), rector of Bures, Suffolk, and probably his second wife, Margaret, probably Margaret Harding, whom a Robert Raymond married in 1622. His father, having made clear his wish that Raymond be sent to the university, made provision for this in his will and appointed his wife, Margaret, executor. Raymond was duly educated at the school at Bishop's Stortford and then entered Christ's College, Cambridge, on 5 April 1643, aged

sixteen, and graduated BA in 1646. Meanwhile he had entered Gray's Inn on 6 February 1645, and was called to the bar on 11 February 1651. By December 1673, when his son Robert *Raymond was born, he had married Anne (1633–1715), daughter of Sir Edward Fishe, second baronet, of Southill, Bedfordshire. They also had two daughters who died in infancy. Raymond was created serjeant-at-law in October 1677, one of his sponsors being the earl of Danby. Elevation to the bench, as a baron of exchequer on 1 May 1679, was followed by a knighthood on 26 June. He was transferred to common pleas on 7 February 1680 and to the king's bench on 24 April 1680.

Raymond sat with Scroggs at Westminster during the trials of Elizabeth Cellier and Roger Palmer, earl of Castlemaine, and as an assessor to the House of Lords at the trial of Lord Stafford. He concurred with Chief Justice Sir Francis Pemberton in overruling, on 11 May 1681, the plea to the jurisdiction of the king's bench set up by Edward Fitzharris, and with Chief Justice Sir Francis North in passing sentence on 18 August the same year on Stephen College. He also concurred in the judgment on the *quo warranto* against the corporation of London in June 1683.

By this date Raymond must have been ill, because it was reported on 21 June 1683 that he was 'on the mending hand' (*Third Report*, HMC, 246). However, he died on 14 July, while on circuit. He was buried in Downham church, in which parish was situated his seat, Tremnall Park. To Roger North he was 'a mild, passive man, who had neither dexterity nor spirit to oppose a popular rage' (North, 1.131), such as accusations of witchcraft. Raymond left in manuscript a valuable collection of reports first printed in 1696 under the title *Reports of divers special cases adjudged in the courts of king's bench, common pleas, and exchequer in the reign of King Charles II*. A second edition appeared in 1743, with further editions in 1793 and 1803.

STUART HANDLEY

Sources Venn, *Alum. Cant.* • Sainty, *Judges*, 34, 78, 126 • Baker, *Serjeants*, 447, 533 • will, PRO, PROB 11/373, sig. 88 • will, PRO, PROB 11/546, sig. 99 • will, PRO, PROB 11/173, sig. 12 • J. Foster, *The register of admissions to Gray's Inn, 1521–1889, together with the register of marriages in Gray's Inn chapel, 1695–1754* (privately printed, London, 1889), 1.239 • J. E. Cussans, *History of Hertfordshire*, 3/2 (1881), 96 • R. North, *The lives of ... Francis North ... Dudley North ... and ... John North*, ed. A. Jessopp, 3 vols. (1890), 31 • G. W. Keeton, *Lord Chancellor Jeffreys and the Stuart cause* (1965), 196, 205, 208 • N. Luttrell, *A brief historical relation of state affairs from September 1678 to April 1714*, 1 (1857), 82, 117 • J. L. Chester and J. Foster, eds., *London marriage licences, 1521–1869* (1887), 1117 • Foss, *Judges*, 7.158–9 • *State trials*, 7.1048, 1104, 1528; 8.564, 1264 • *DNB*
Archives priv. coll., commonplace books
Likenesses oils, Gray's Inn, London

Raynald [Raynalde], **Thomas** (*fl.* 1539–1552?), physician and printer, was active as a printer from 1539. He used printing material that had previously belonged to the Southwark printer Peter Treveris. A deposition by three of his former servants on 20 August 1540, which noted that Raynald was recently resident at Hallywell near Finsbury, listed a number of books and engraved plates then in his possession, including an anatomical print 'graven in copper the one the man the other woman with their Intrayles thereto belonging' (Plomer, 21). *STC* suggests that his earliest printed work may have been an edition of Colet's *Accidence*, probably printed in 1539. In 1540 he published *The Byrth of Mankynde*, a translation of Eucharius Roesslin's midwifery manual and the first such text published in English; it was also the first work in England to include copper engravings. A revised edition 'corrected and augmented' by Raynald, who described himself as a physician, was published in 1545. In the prologue to the women readers he claimed that the book was being read out loud at confinements 'before the mydwife, and the rest of the wemen then beyng present' and the listeners were pleased 'to here the booke red by sum other, or els (such as could) to read it them selfes' (Eccles, 12). The work became the standard midwifery text, going through a total of thirteen editions before it was superseded in the 1650s. Raynald also translated a chemical treatise by Vesalius as *A Compendious Declaration of the Excellent Vertues of a Certain Lateli Inventid Oile*, which was published in Venice in 1551.

A namesake, and possibly a son, **Thomas Raynald** (*fl.* 1542–1552) was an apprentice of the London printer and member of the Drapers' Company, Thomas Petyt, between 1542 and his freedom as Thomas Reynolds in 1548. Distinguishing the works of the two men is not straightforward, although it seems that the presumably younger man may have been responsible for a number of religious and theological publications between 1548 and 1552, including works by John Bale, Thomas Becon, Erasmus, John Mardeley, William Tyndale, and Zwingli as well as an edition of the Matthew Bible in 1549. If so, he was based first in the parish of St Andrew by the Wardrobe from 1548 to 1549, and at the sign of the Star in St Paul's Churchyard from 1549 to 1551. It is not clear which of the two printers published the 1552 edition of *The Byrth of Mankynde*. No further biographical details are known about either man. I. GADD

Sources *STC, 1475–1640* · E. G. Duff, *A century of the English book trade* (1905) · private information (2004) [P. W. M. Blayney] · H. R. Plomer, 'Notices of English stationers in the archives of the City of London', *Transactions of the Bibliographical Society*, 6 (1901), 13–27 · L. Hellinga, 'Printing', *The Cambridge history of the book in Britain*, ed. L. Hellinga and J. B. Trapp, 3: *1400–1557* (1999), 65–108 · C. Webster, 'Alchemical and Paracelsian medicine', in C. Webster, *Health, medicine and mortality in the sixteenth century* (1979), 301–34 · A. Eccles, *Obstetrics and gynaecology in Tudor and Stuart England* (1982)

Raynald, Thomas (*fl.* **1542–1552**). *See under* Raynald, Thomas (*fl.* 1539–1552?).

Raynalde, Thomas. *See* Raynald, Thomas (*fl.* 1539–1552?).

Rayner, Ann Ingram (1825/6–1855). *See under* Rayner, Samuel (1806–1879).

Rayner, Derek George, Baron Rayner (1926–1998), businessman and civil servant, was born at 47 Waterloo Road, Norwich, on 30 March 1926, the son of George William Rayner, a shoe finisher, and his wife, Hilda Jane, *née* Rant. He had a comfortable upbringing and was educated at the City College, Norwich, before going to Selwyn College,

Derek George Rayner, Baron Rayner (1926–1998), by Peter Dunne, 1983

Cambridge, where he read theology. His initial intention was to enter holy orders, but he decided against this and after a national service commission in the RAF (1946–8) he started a career as the manager of a small 'fancy goods' retail business in Norwich. The failure of this venture, due mainly to a lack of capital, marked the start of his career at Marks and Spencer where he became a trainee manager in 1953. It was during his time as a trainee at the Oxford Street store that his talents were first recognized by the chairman, Marcus Sieff. Well educated and tall, Rayner most probably stood out from the average shop assistant, and Sieff was impressed by his knowledge of food retailing. He was quickly transferred to the organization's head office at Baker Street where he worked mainly in the food business.

In 1967 Rayner joined the management board. He was first and foremost a retailer and took an expert interest in the design, quality, and value-for-money aspects of Marks and Spencer. His business talents and transparent integrity were also recognized outside of retailing, and in 1970 the prime minister, Edward Heath, seconded Rayner into government service. He was placed in the defence procurement agency within the Ministry of Defence, where he became chief executive in 1971. Knighted in 1973, he returned to Marks and Spencer as a joint managing director, but the period up to 1983 was marked by a division of his time between the retail trade and government work. When Margaret Thatcher formed her first government in 1979 she also called upon Rayner to bring the cost-control techniques of Marks and Spencer into the civil service. Although he was well attuned to Thatcher's way of thinking, he always resisted suggestions that he was concerned only with cutting costs. Nevertheless his so-called efficiency unit did make large savings, and across some 135 government departments an estimated 10,000 jobs were cut. There were successes, most notably the simplification of the unemployment benefit system, but on the whole he failed to produce radical reforms. There were also more lasting criticisms, such as those relating to his attempts to cut costs at the central statistical office, which many believed led to a loss of reliable official statistics.

In 1983 Rayner received a life peerage, becoming Baron

Rayner of Crowborough, and returned to the full-time post of chief executive at Marks and Spencer, taking over as chairman from Lord Sieff in the following year. He was the first head of the company to be neither a family member nor Jewish, and it is to the credit of the Sieff family that they recognized his strong talents. During the early 1980s the company was starting to feel the pressure from new competitors in the high street and beginning to lose its supremacy. Rayner set about modernizing Marks and Spencer with a series of broad-ranging strategies all tied to new approaches, while retaining the company's traditions. Some have argued that he was not so much a breath of fresh air in the company as a force-nine gale. He was autocratic in his management style and had little tolerance for long discussions at business meetings. He led strategic developments overseas and took Marks and Spencer to the United States through the takeover of the Brook Brothers menswear chain. This was the start of a global strategy that saw the company expand into the Middle and Far East as well as continental Europe. The internationalization process did bring problems, especially in North America, where the company had to close stores in Canada, while operations in the USA proved too expensive, and yielded poor returns. A second of Rayner's reforms involved moving into 'out of town' sites, the first at the Metro-Centre at Gateshead. This marked a break with the high street tradition, but opened up important new opportunities. Other successful experiments involved the introduction of financial services for customers, alongside the St Michael chargecard and new lines of merchandise, including household goods and furniture. Of equal importance was Rayner's introduction of improved financial controls and the increased use of information technology throughout the company. These innovations restored the fortunes of the company and made it one of the most successful retailers in the world during the 1990s. Despite his efforts the North American operations did not go well. However, under Rayner's chairmanship, the company doubled its sales and pre-tax profits. He retired as chairman in 1991.

Rayner was a complex man, possessing a curious mixture of assurance, toughness, shyness, and a degree of sensitivity. This complexity was reflected in his beliefs, since he claimed that the study of theology as a student had stopped him believing. However, he had a lifelong striving for a sense of purpose, which involved a constant questioning of his life. This did not produce an introverted character, but rather someone with ambition, drive, and a love of the good things in life. He was a genial man of considerable charm. He found happiness and relaxation in good food, travel, and gardening. After his retirement from Marks and Spencer he became a keen gardener at his home in Crowborough, Sussex. His main joy was in classical music, especially Bach and Haydn, and choral music. In spite of his busy life, he found time to be president of St Bartholomew's Hospital Medical College, trustee of the Royal Botanic Gardens, Kew, and chairman of the Coronary Artery Disease Research Association.

Rayner never married, though he did strike up some long-standing intimate friendships. He died at Ashford Hospital, Stanwell, Surrey, on 26 June 1998.

GARETH SHAW

Sources J. Bevan, *The rise and fall of Marks and Spencer* (2001) • M. Sieff, *Don't ask the price: the memoirs of the president of Marks and Spencer* (1987) • A. Brummer, *The Guardian* (30 June 1998), 18 a–e • G. Bull, *The Independent* (2 July 1998), 6 a–b • *The Times* (30 June 1998), 23 a–f • *Daily Telegraph* (30 June 1998) • WWW • b. cert. • d. cert.
Likenesses P. Dunne, photograph, 1983, News International Syndication, London [*see illus.*] • photograph, repro. in *Daily Telegraph*

Rayner, Lionel Benjamin (1787–1855), actor, was born in Heckmondwike, in the West Riding of Yorkshire, on 10 October 1787. His father was a farmer and cloth manufacturer, and died before Rayner was seven years old. Not much is known of his early life except that a performance of *Speed the Plough* and *The Naval Pillar* at Leeds inspired him to take an interest in the theatre. At the age of nineteen he joined Crisp's company at Cheadle, Staffordshire, where he opened as Clodpole in the farce *Barnaby Buttle* and later played Jeremy Diddler in James Kenney's farce *Raising the Wind*.

Frustrated by his manager, who took many of the light-comedy parts which he sought for himself, Rayner then joined another company at Stone, also in Staffordshire, with which he remained for three years. He played with it at Stratford upon Avon, became as well known for his singing as for his acting, and by his performance of Solomon Lob in *Love Laughs at Locksmiths* raised his position and his salary. He appeared in Manchester as Robin Roughhead in *Fortune's Frolic*, and then joined the Nottingham company. While in this part of the country he married, at Shrewsbury on 25 December 1812, Margaret Remington, the daughter of the proprietor of the York circuit; they had one son. In the Nottingham company Rayner played Zekiel Homespun in Coleman's *The Heir-at-Law* to the Dr Pangloss of Bannister, who recommended him to the manager of the Haymarket Theatre. He consequently made his first appearance in London at the Haymarket, in June 1814, as Frank Oatland in Thomas Morton's *A Cure for the Heartache*. He went on to play other characters with great success, such as Sam in *Raising the Wind* and Stephen Harrowby in Coleman's *The Poor Gentleman*, and was given the opportunity to perform at Brighton, under the management of Trotter. Rayner was devoted to Shakespeare and instituted a celebration of the anniversary of his birth in Sunderland in 1817, which was presided over by his friend Stephen Kemble.

Around 1820 Rayner became a member of the York company and established a reputation for playing rustic characters in low comedy. He also visited Stamford, King's Lynn, Louth, Manchester, and Huntingdon. At Birmingham he became great friends with John Emery. At the end of 1822 he received an offer from R. W. Elliston to appear at Drury Lane as Dandie Dinmont in *Guy Mannering*. This was the only part he played at that house, however, as Elliston did not seem to want him for any other character. He was forced to retire to King's Lynn, until Arnold, the proprietor of the English Opera House (later the Lyceum), engaged him to play the part of Fixture in Morton's *A Roland for an Oliver* in July 1823. Emery's death in 1822 gave Rayner the chance to step into the latter's shoes and perform his celebrated role of Giles in *The Miller's Maid*. As a result of his success Charles Kemble engaged him at Covent Garden Theatre for three years, and he opened there in October 1823 as Tyke in Morton's *The School of Reform*. Other parts he went on to play include Sam Sharpset in Morton's *The Slave*, Pan in *Midas*, Friar Tuck in *Ivanhoe*, and Caliban in *The Tempest* (1825).

About 1831 Rayner purchased the lease of Burford's Panorama and proceeded to build on its site the Strand Theatre, initially naming it Rayner's New Subscription Theatre in the Strand. But faced with the opposition of the patent houses, and unable to obtain the lord chamberlain's licence to run the theatre, he was obliged to close it down within a few months. He then worked in the provinces, and achieved great success particularly as Lubin in the domestic drama *Love's Frailties*, written for him by J. J. Stafford and tailored to his strengths as an actor. The Strand Theatre had to be leased out to a Miss Kelly, but Rayner did not stop campaigning exhaustively for a lease until at last it was granted in 1836. However, the long struggle left him financially almost ruined, so that he was unable to continue as a theatrical manager. He resorted to writing for sporting newspapers and magazines, having been long interested in horse-racing. He also tried his hand at poetry. While engaged at Covent Garden he had had the prudence to subscribe to its Theatrical Fund, so on reaching the age of sixty he was able to claim from it an annuity, which supplemented his income from journalism. Some time after this he married again. He died on 24 September 1855, at his home, 17 Acton Street, Gray's Inn Road, London, from a disease of the throat which prevented him from swallowing. He was buried on 1 October 1855, in the old burial-ground at Camberwell, near his only son.

Rayner was 5 feet 8 inches in height, stout, with a dark complexion and hazel eyes. He was a good serio-comic actor whose gift for impromptu speech and talent for comic singing were perhaps his chief attractions.

JOSEPH KNIGHT, *rev.* NILANJANA BANERJI

Sources *The biography of the British stage, being correct narratives of the lives of all the principal actors and actresses* (1824) • *Oxberry's Dramatic Biography*, 2/25 (1825) • *The Era* (30 Sept 1855) • Hall, *Dramatic ports.* • Genest, *Eng. stage*

Likenesses portrait, repro. in *Oxberry's Dramatic Biography* • portrait, repro. in *The Drama* (1824) • portrait, repro. in *Mirror of the Stage* (20 Oct 1823) • prints, BM, NPG • prints, Harvard TC

Rayner, Louise Ingram (1832–1924). *See under* Rayner, Samuel (1806–1879).

Rayner, Samuel (1806–1879), watercolour painter and lithographer, was born on 15 April 1806 in Colnbrook in Buckinghamshire, the third of the five children of Samuel (*d.* 1817) and Margaret Rayner. In 1812 Rayner's parents moved to London, where they established an ironmonger's business at 7 Blandford Street, Portman Square, Marylebone. His grandfather Thomas Rayner was probably himself an artist and may have helped to teach the young Sam, as he was known, to draw. In 1821, at the age of

fifteen, Rayner had a picture of Malmesbury Abbey accepted for exhibition at the Royal Academy. By this time he was studying architectural draughtsmanship in the studio of John Britton, where he became a close friend of a fellow student, George Cattermole.

On 2 October 1823, after an elopement, Rayner married Ann Manser (1802–1890), the daughter of William Manser, a London publisher, who was herself an artist and engraver in black marble. They settled at 11 Blandford Street, and in 1827 they exhibited together two drawings of Westminster Abbey at the Royal Academy (a catalogue entry—'S. A. Rayner'—has resulted in mistaken references to Samuel A. Rayner). After receiving an inheritance from his grandfather and 'a VERY handsome order' from the sixth duke of Devonshire at Chatsworth, Rayner moved to Museum Parade, Matlock Bath, where he started business as publisher and printer. *Rayner's Sketches of Derbyshire Scenery Part 1*, lithographed by J. D. Harding, was published in 1830, and his *History and Antiquities of Haddon Hall* six years later, after Rayner had moved his business to 17 Friar Gate, Derby. He also opened the Cornmarket Gallery, which dealt in the family's pictures until the 1920s. Works by Rayner from this period include *The Derby Mechanics' Institute Exhibition, 1839* (Derby Museum and Art Gallery) and *Drawing Room in a Town House* (V&A).

Rayner's family were Baptists, but in 1835 he, his wife, and children joined the Irvingite Catholic Apostolic church. The failure of an illustrated publication entitled *The History, Antiquities and Topography of the Town of Derby* (only three out of twenty-four projected parts appeared) may have induced Rayner to return to London in 1842. In 1844 he and his family moved to 15 Berners Street which was to be the family home for sixteen years.

In February 1845 Rayner was elected an associate of the Society of Painters in Water Colours, exhibiting twenty-nine drawings with the society between 1845 and 1850. Most of his drawings were architectural studies of abbeys and scenic buildings—including six of Haddon Hall—and were sold at between 10 and 35 guineas. His monogram was 'SR' usually with a date. J. L. Roget commented of Rayner, perhaps unfairly, that 'his studies were cleverly handled and agreeable in colour, but obviously based upon the manner of George Cattermole, whose work they sometimes resemble so closely they may easily be taken for his' (Roget, 2.299). As well as making sketching trips around Britain, Rayner also travelled to France and Italy; some of his pictures were exhibited in Rome in 1839.

In 1851 Rayner became involved in an action in the court of queen's bench which related to a promissory note, which he had endorsed, drawn by William Manser for £2000, in favour of his daughter Ann (Nancy) Rayner [*see below*]. Manser pleaded that his signature was a forgery but the jury decided against him (which presumably obliged him to honour the bill). The case brought severe strain upon the family and seems to have resulted in the temporary separation of Rayner from his wife, who had appeared as witness for her father. Rayner was also expelled by unanimous vote from the Society of Painters in Water Colours. The Rayner family were eventually reunited, and lived in Brighton from 1859 until 1864 when they returned to London.

By nature, Rayner was a kindly but impulsive man: on one occasion, according to family tradition, he was offered less for a picture by a client than he was asking, and responded that if that was all the picture was worth to him, he was not to have it, promptly putting his foot through it. A drawing by Nancy Rayner of about 1840 shows her father with strong features, an open, fresh face, and thick black hair which, in subsequent photographs, turned white. Rayner died in Windsor on 19 August 1879.

Between 1821 and 1872 Rayner had exhibited twenty drawings at the Royal Academy, four at the British Institution, and nineteen at Suffolk Street. The British Museum, the Victoria and Albert Museum, and the Sheffield, Derby, and Stoke-on-Trent art galleries have collections of his work. Rayner's son, Richard Manser (1834–1908), and five daughters—Nancy, Rhoda, known as Rose (1828–1921), Frances (1834–c.1890), Louise [see below], and Margaret (1837–1920)—all became professional artists. The eldest daughter, **Ann Ingram** [Nancy] **Rayner** (1825/6–1855), watercolour painter, was born at 11 Blandford Street, London. Her drawing was influenced by Octavius Oakley who worked at the Cornmarket Gallery in Derby. In 1850 she was elected an associate of the Society of Painters in Water Colours; she exhibited thirteen pictures there, and showed three times at the Royal Academy. Her drawings were mostly interiors, including two of Knole in 1852, and rustic figures, and were sold for between 15 and 20 guineas. Nancy Rayner died from consumption at 15 Berners Street, London, on 14 August 1855, at the age of twenty-nine. The society voted £20 for the relief of her surviving sisters.

Louise Ingram Rayner (1832–1924), watercolour painter, was born in Museum Parade, Matlock Bath, on 21 June 1832. From 1852 to 1860 she exhibited oils at the Royal Academy, the first of which was entitled *The Interior of Haddon Chapel, Derbyshire*. In 1860, however, she began to exhibit with the Society of Women Artists and her subsequent work was in watercolour. Most of her drawings are street scenes which, although invariably populated, show considerable truth to nature. From 1870 she lived at Chester; she moved to Tunbridge Wells around 1910 and finally to 60 Southwater Road, St Leonards, where she died on 8 October 1924. She was a prolific artist; the Russell-Cotes Art Gallery, Bournemouth, and the Grosvenor Museum, Chester, hold examples of her work.

SIMON FENWICK

Sources private information (2004) [family] · J. L. Roget, *A history of the 'Old Water-Colour' Society*, 2 vols. (1891) · M. Bills, 'Louise Rayner, picturesque scenes of living architecture', *Antique Collecting*, 32/8 (Feb 1998), 27–32 · Bankside Gallery, London, Royal Watercolour Society MSS · d. cert. [Samuel Rayner] · d. cert. [Louise Rayner] · d. cert. [Nancy Rayner] · E. C. Clayton, *English female artists*, 2 vols. (1876)
Archives NRA, priv. coll., family MSS
Likenesses N. Rayner, self-portrait, c.1839 (Nancy Rayner), priv. coll. · N. Rayner, watercolour, c.1840, priv. coll. · N. Rayner, portrait, c.1847 (Louise Rayner), priv. coll. · photograph, 1865, priv. coll. · photograph, 1878, priv. coll.

Rayner [Reyner], **William** (*b.* 1565/6), Roman Catholic priest, was born in the diocese of Lincoln, the son of John and Ellen Rayner. He entered the English College, Rome, aged twenty, on 24 October 1586, where he was ordained priest, and then transferred to the English College, Valladolid, on 1 September 1591, where he completed his theological studies. On 15 September 1592 he left to undertake missionary work in England.

Later Rayner joined his cousin, Richard *Smith, future bishop of Chalcedon, and other learned clergy, who, on 26 October 1611, set up a college of writers in Paris called the Collège d'Arras (so called because the house belonged to the abbot of St Vaast, Arras, to whom they had been recommended by the English Benedictines of Douai). The enterprise was a counterblast to Chelsea College, founded by James I in 1609 to defend the reformed faith. Rayner's own contribution was as a Latin translator, first of James Anderton's (alias John Brerely) *The Protestants' Apology for the Roman Church*, published in Paris in 1615, then of Thomas Stapleton's *Fortress of Faith*, published in the same city in 1619, and finally Rayner participated in a collaborative translation into Latin of Stapleton's complete works (Paris, 1620). In 1615 he became a doctor of divinity at the Sorbonne. The date of his death is unknown.

DAVID DANIEL REES

Sources W. Kelly, ed., *Liber ruber venerabilis collegii Anglorum de urbe*, 1, Catholic RS, 37 (1940) · G. Anstruther, *The seminary priests*, 1 (1969) · E. Henson, ed., *The registers of the English College at Valladolid, 1589–1862*, Catholic RS, 30 (1930) · *Dodd's Church history of England*, ed. M. A. Tierney, 5 vols. (1839–43), vol. 5 · H. Foley, ed., *Records of the English province of the Society of Jesus*, 6 (1880) · A. F. Allison, 'Who was John Brereley? The identity of a seventeenth-century controversialist', *Recusant History*, 16 (1982–3), 17–41 · Gillow, *Lit. biog. hist.*, vol. 5 · P. Guilday, *The English Catholic refugees on the continent, 1558–1795* (1914)
Archives Southwark Archdiocesan archives, Tierney papers

Rayner, William (*bap.* 1699, *d.* 1761), printer and bookseller, the son of Christopher Rayner, mariner, and his wife, Anne, was baptized at the church of St Giles Cripplegate on 4 October 1699. In 1714 he was apprenticed to the City printer Anne Motte and in 1719 he was turned over to John Millet, a printer whose output consisted mainly of ballads, broadsides, and chapbooks. Rayner was later said to have married before completing the final two years of his term and he certainly did not become free of the Stationers' Company until 1737. However, unless he married outside London, the registers do not seem to corroborate the suggested timing. In 1724 a William Rayner married an Elizabeth Bray at St Martin-in-the-Fields and the elusive E. Rayner, the wife of William who worked in his shops and appeared on an increasing number of imprints identified only by an initial, was perhaps this Elizabeth. The careers of William Rayner and a fellow printer/publisher, Robert *Walker, followed a very similar trajectory and there were probably some ill-defined commercial links between them during the 1720s and 1730s as they came to dominate areas of the trade in cheap print. Both Rayner and Walker set up as pamphlet sellers and in 1728 they appeared jointly on the imprint of a virulent anti-Walpole pamphlet. *The Dunghill and the Oak* was printed for Walker and 'W. R.' and the publication of this form of occasional political material became characteristic of the initial phase of Rayner's and Walker's careers in publishing. At the end of 1729 both were independently implicated in the publication of pamphlets which hinted at Jacobite sympathies, although neither was prosecuted. By the early 1730s Rayner was running the New Pamphlet Shop next door to the George Tavern at Charing Cross, with the help of his wife and a female servant. The publications issued from this address were numerous and varied, but while E. Rayner appeared mainly on the imprint of light, non-controversial material, William Rayner himself moved into areas of commercial and political conflict. He was soon identified in print as a 'notorious Paper Pyrate', freely publishing versions of other people's work, including Henry Fielding, while he continued to cash in on the popularity of attacks on the government. Like Walker, Rayner contracted out at least part of his printing to other members of the trade, but by 1733 he had his own office in Marigold Court near the Exeter Exchange in the Strand. The link between the two publishers was given a concrete form in 1731 when Rayner's name appeared on an affidavit, printed in the *Daily Journal*, supporting Walker in his disclaimer of responsibility for the content of a libellous pamphlet.

The next phase in Rayner's erratic career was precipitated by a political prosecution. In 1731 a collection of leading essays published in *The Craftsman*, the main vehicle for opposition attacks on Walpole's government, was published in seven volumes. Each volume had an allegorical frontispiece and the popularity of the material provided Rayner with an opportunity to combine his piratical and political interests by reprinting the frontispieces on a single sheet under the title *Robin's Reign, or, Seven's the Main*. The official response to this was slow but it may have been the reprinting of the broadside under a modified title, combined with the presentment of this and related material by the Middlesex grand jury, that triggered the legal action. Robert Walker was among those arrested but the weight of the proceedings fell on Rayner. After a period on the run he was arrested, imprisoned, and brought to trial in 1733. His defence hinged on some implausible technicalities and was accompanied by a plea of poverty. If his debts were taken into account, it was claimed, and his wearing apparel excluded, he would not to be worth £5. The sentence took some account of this. He was fined £50 rather than the usual £100, sentenced to two years in prison, and ordered to find security for his good behaviour for seven years.

By September 1733 Rayner was in the king's bench prison in Southwark. Like the Fleet prison on the north bank of the Thames, the king's bench was surrounded by a network of streets and alleys in which the prisoners, mainly debtors, could obtain the right to work at their respective trades. On obtaining the 'Rules', Rayner's activities as a publisher continued unabated and he moved rapidly into new areas of cheap print centred on newspapers and the serial publication of works in parts. Among the first of his hybrid serials was *The Compleat Historian, or, The*

Oxford Penny-Post, advertised in September 1733. It was sold 'for the Benefit of William Rayner, Prisoner in the King's Bench' and was printed at his office in Marygold Court. The characteristically mixed content printed on three folio sheets and selling at 2*d*. included a combination of news, state trials, and a history of Scotland. It was to be published every Monday, Wednesday, and Friday. By September 1734 Rayner had opened a printing office in Bird Cage Alley in Southwark, next door to the Horse and Groom alehouse, where he employed, among others, the politically compromised compositor Doctor Gaylard.

Rayner's output, like that of Walker with which it overlaps, has a variety of confusing features compounded by deliberate attempts to conceal or mislead. The volume of material he produced was considerable and his premises seem to have become the focus for a network of book-trade outsiders, printers, engravers, and authors who provided the workforce on which his activities were based. Walker moved progressively away from the London market; Rayner, partly by force of circumstances, focused on the metropolis. In 1734 he was distantly involved in the Shakespeare piracies which preoccupied Robert Walker but while the volume of his cheap, serial output was increasing and his conflicts with members of the respectable London trade continued unabated, the scale of his business and the state of his personal circumstances remain hard to identify. In 1735 he was negotiating with Robert Bloomfield in Norfolk over the sale of a second-hand press, while the following year the bizarre plot to explode a parcel of leaflets in parliament was hatched in his immediate neighbourhood by the nonjuror Robert Nixon. This was more Gaylard's business but at the time he was still working for Rayner.

The stages by which William Rayner moved out of the king's bench and the causes of his long-term residence within the rules are equally obscure. In 1737 he became free of the Stationers' Company but remained within the prison. It may have provided a convenient base for his aggressive excursions into the market for print. In 1738, taking advantage of the split in the management of *The Craftsman*, which remained in print, Rayner began to orchestrate the publication of the *Original Craftsman* in head-on competition. Production was organized in association with the printer John Standen, who moved to the Old Bailey to facilitate publication. Rayner hired two of the floating population of hackney writers, Dennis de Coetlogon and Norton Defoe, to provide regular copy and seems to have monitored the printing though his name was entirely absent from the paper itself. His real position only emerged when official action was taken against the paper and Standen, Gaylard, and both authors were arrested and subjected to close examination. Whatever the outcome, Rayner, in the security of the king's bench, seems to have remained untouched. In May 1739 he set about disposing of a large quantity of stock consisting mainly of part works and copperplate-engravings. His position outside the charmed circles of the respectable trade probably forced him to deal directly with the public through the unusual device of a subscription sale, for which he issued 8000 tickets at 2s. 6d. each. In July he obtained his freedom of the City of London and the following year moved from Southwark to a new printing office in Wine Office Court in the ward of Farringdon Without. As usual, his personal circumstances are obscure. In a petition for release at the beginning of 1740 he claimed to be utterly unable to pay the money required from his original sentence.

This marked the beginning of the third phase in Rayner's career in the print trade. His output was still based on newspapers and part works although the controversial elements of his business were apparently in decline. His successful tri-weekly paper which had first appeared in 1736 as *Rayner's Morning Advertiser* continued in print under a variety of modified titles into 1743, while the annotated versions of the Bible which had provided one of his staples during the 1730s also remained an element in his output during the next decade. The indications are that Rayner was becoming respectable. In 1744 he took over two apprentices from John Standen and so became directly associated with the Stationers' Company whose members' interests he had been attempting to undermine for years. Walker remained combative and unassimilated by the respectable trade. Rayner may have joined it. The reason seems to lie partly in the change to his personal circumstances caused by a fortunate second marriage. In 1741 Sir John Dineley-Goodere was murdered by pirates who had been hired by his brother. Meanwhile, in the mid-1730s, Sir John's wife, Mary, had been imprisoned in the king's bench where she may have met Rayner. In 1743, according to John Nichols, they married and Rayner acquired the murdered husband's property, including the manor of Charlton in Worcestershire. Support for this account appeared in Rayner's will of 1761, where he described himself as formerly of Charlton in the county of Worcester. In May 1744 he was granted a licence under letters patent to the sole right to print and publish *A Family Bible, or, The Old and New Testament Explained by Way of Question and Answer* by William Friend, but already his direct engagement with the book trade was fading. For the rest of his life he held shares in various copies but there are no indications that he was subsequently involved in either the production or distribution of print. There is also some suggestion that he may have had a continuing interest in medicines. During the late 1730s, in tandem with Walker in Fleet Lane, he sold Daffy's Elixir and other medical specifics from his warehouse in Southwark. Under the terms of his will, George West, apothecary of Derby Street, Westminster, was appointed executor to oversee the sale of his property, while in the single year 1760 an entry in the land tax assessment for Fleet Lane identified a William Rayner. It seems possible that even at this late stage a link existed with Dr Walker as he now called himself. Some time in the mid-1740s Rayner may have moved to Charlton, though Nichols claimed that he alienated the property soon after he had acquired it. By the time he came to make his will in 1761 he was living on a copyhold estate in the prosperous London suburb of Hammersmith.

In his brief published comments, John Nichols implicated Rayner in a piece of sharp practice that may have occurred shortly before his death. The City printer Elizabeth Nunneley was said to have bequeathed a substantial property to her nephew and niece 'of which they were deprived by the chicanery of … their guardian' (Nichols, *Lit. anecdotes*, 8.447) identified by Nichols as the printer William Rayner. The date of Mrs Nunneley's death cannot have occurred much before 1760 and it was only in a correction to an earlier statement that Rayner's name was substituted for Baynes. However, Nichols identified Mrs Nunneley as publisher of the *St. James's Evening Post* and in 1761 Rayner held a 1/20 share in this paper as well as in its partner publication, *Read's Weekly Journal and London Spy*. Direct evidence is lacking, but it was the sort of action that a self-interested businessman of Rayner's type might have been ready to undertake.

Under Rayner's will, drawn up on 21 May 1761, he bequeathed his property to his third wife, Anne, of whom further details are unknown. There was no mention of children by this or any other marriage. His financial position appears to have been stable and the valuation of his stock made at the beginning of 1761 indicated his ownership of some useful properties. *Smith's Bible*, which Rayner had first issued in parts during the 1730s, was valued at £350. This, in combination with his interest in the Hammersmith estate and other accumulated assets, may have justified the use of the respectable title of esquire in the probate record. Rayner died not long after making his will, which was proved on 6 November 1761.

MICHAEL HARRIS

Sources M. Harris, *London newspapers in the age of Walpole* (1987) · M. Harris, 'Paper pirates: the alternative book trade in mid-eighteenth century London', *Fakes and frauds*, ed. R. Myers and M. Harris (1989), 47–69 · D. F. McKenzie, ed., *Stationers' Company apprentices*, [3]: *1701–1800* (1978) · Nichols, *Lit. anecdotes* · *The tryal of William Rayner* (1733) · Newspapers, BL, Burney collection · R. M. Wiles, *Serial publication in England before 1750* (1957) · H. R. Plomer and others, *A dictionary of the printers and booksellers who were at work in England, Scotland, and Ireland from 1726 to 1775* (1932) · *Boyd's miscellaneous marriage index*, ed. Society of Genealogists, 2nd ser. · *Boyd's London burials* · *IGI* · *ESTC*
Archives BL, literary assignments, Add. MS 33054 · PRO, examinations, TS 11/1027/43

Raynes, Richard Elliott [*name in religion* Raymond] (**1903–1958**), Church of England clergyman and religious superior, was born at 46 Avonmore Road, West Kensington, on 6 February 1903, the youngest of the four sons (and one daughter) of the Revd Herbert Alfred Raynes (1862–1933), at that time home superintendent of the British and Foreign Bible Society, and his wife, Sarah Alice Sargent (b. 1862/3). He was thus brought up in an evangelical Anglican family (to which he always recognized his debt); but from an early age, originally under the influence of an elder brother who was killed early in the First World War, he was attracted to Anglo-Catholicism. He won scholarships to St Paul's School, and to Pembroke College, Oxford, where he rowed for the college and was elected president of the junior common room, but obtained only third-class honours in Greats. Among his undergraduate friends was the future Dom Gregory Dix. After a year at Westcott House, Cambridge, he was ordained in 1926 to a title at Holy Trinity, Bury. He left the parish in 1930 to join the Anglican Community of the Resurrection at Mirfield, and was professed in it in 1932.

In 1933 his community sent Raynes to South Africa. He spent his first two years there teaching, in St John's College, Johannesburg, a public school for white boys for which the community was at that time responsible. But when it decided to withdraw from it in order to concentrate on its work with Africans, Raynes was invited to take over responsibility for the township of Sophiatown. Here, in partnership with Dorothy Maud, daughter of an English bishop, who had already done pioneer work in the area, he established over the next eight years the set-up so vividly, and poignantly, described by his successor, Trevor Huddleston, in *Naught for your Comfort*. It was in this setting that Raynes reached his full stature as a person: he had courage, spiritual authority, an immense capacity for work and for taking pains with people, and in the public authorities of Johannesburg a legitimate target for his latent anger and aggression—and his humour. He also developed a habitual disregard for his health: food never interested him, and sleep constantly took second place to work or prayer. He tended to keep going on strong tea and cigarettes. The eventual consequence was major surgery for a perforated ulcer in 1941: a pattern that was to repeat itself at intervals for the rest of his life.

In 1943 Raynes was elected superior of his community, and returned to England to set his mark upon it. Its original ethos had been academic, gentlemanly, and Tractarian in its restraint; Raynes's fuller-blooded and more demotic version of Anglo-Catholicism owed more to current Roman Catholic teaching and practice—soon to be transformed, ironically, in the church of its derivation by the reforms of the Second Vatican Council. The new emphasis carried probably a majority of the brethren with it, and certainly attracted recruits, more than at any other time in the community's history. It was accompanied by an intensified emphasis on mission, with its superior leading from in front both in organized campaigns in parishes and universities and in informal house parties arranged through lay friends. The impression that he made, both from the pulpit and in one-to-one encounters, was of a man speaking with authority, compelling an often reluctant attention.

It has been said of such persons that 'their importance is not in their rightness or balance but in the depth at which they disturb you' (Williams, 17). There was certainly an austerity about Raynes which some found frightening and even fanatical, including, at his first introduction, Archbishop Michael Ramsey, who on closer acquaintance came to recognize his 'gentleness, humility and practical wisdom' (letter to N. Mosley, Mirfield deposit, Borth. Inst.).

The most controversial episode of Raynes's life was unquestionably his decision in 1956 to recall Trevor Huddleston from South Africa. His choice of Huddleston to succeed him at Sophiatown had been his first act as superior and he had been consistently supportive of him. Raynes had never shirked confrontation, and to have bowed to political or ecclesiastical pressure, as some insinuated, would have been entirely out of character. There was indeed a danger that if Huddleston, a diabetic, was arrested, as was looking increasingly likely, the opportunity could be taken to withhold medication from him. But it is doubtful whether Raynes would have thought it right to give absolute protection to Huddleston's life at a time when his African associates were freely risking theirs. The remaining possible answer concerns Raynes's priorities as superior and his convictions about the nature of monastic commitment. If he had sensed that Huddleston's growing identification with the political aspirations of Africans, with all the exposure to publicity that went with it, could ultimately, if unchecked, lead him away from that commitment (and there is at least one piece of evidence that he had), there is no uncertainty about what his reaction would have been. For him church (and all thereby implied) could only come first.

In January 1958, already a very sick man, Raynes was voted out of office. He continued to fulfil preaching engagements; but in the course of one of them he suffered a coronary thrombosis. He died at the Royal Sussex County Hospital, Brighton, on 12 June 1958, and his funeral at Mirfield on 17 June was followed by burial in the cemetery of the community.   H. BENEDICT GREEN

Sources N. Mosley, *The life of Raymond Raynes* (1961) · A. Wilkinson, *The Community of the Resurrection: a centenary history* (1992) · T. Huddleston, *Naught for your comfort* (1956) · R. Denniston, *Trevor Huddleston: a life* (1999) · H. Ellis, T. Huddleston, and G. K. A. Bell, 'Raymond Raynes', *Community of the Resurrection Quarterly*, 223 (1958), 2–12 · R. Williams, '"The landscape became exact": reflections on Raymond Raynes', *Community of the Resurrection Quarterly*, 322 (1983), 15–17 · correspondence, Borth. Inst., Mirfield deposit [incl. letter, autograph, n.d., from A. M. Ramsey to N. Mosley] · private information (2004) · d. cert. [Herbert Alfred Raynes] · m. cert. [Herbert Alfred Raynes and Sarah Alice Sargent]
Archives Borth. Inst., Mirfield deposit, corresp. | Bodl. RH, corresp. relating to Trevor Huddleston and Africa Bureau
Likenesses photographs, Community of the Resurrection, Mirfield

Raynor, Geoffrey Vincent (1913–1983), metallurgist, was born in Nottingham on 2 October 1913, the youngest of the three sons (the second died in infancy and there were no daughters), of Alfred Ernest Raynor (*d.* 1927), a lace dressers' manager, and his wife, Florence Lottie Campion. His family encouraged his early academic studies and in 1925 he won a scholarship to Nottingham high school. There he developed into an outstanding scholar with special abilities in chemistry and science in general, and excelled in sport. Music always occupied a central place in his family life; from choral singing and piano this interest later extended into ballet, orchestral performances, and opera. The death of his father in 1927 led to serious difficulties for the family and there were pressures upon him to take a 'safe job'. Advice from his mentors prevailed and in 1931 he won a Nottingham county major scholarship which enabled him to enter Keble College, Oxford, in October 1932.

Raynor's undergraduate years coincided with a remarkable flowering of inorganic and organic chemistry at Oxford and he benefited greatly from the guidance of his tutors, F. M. Brewer and G. D. Parkes. He read for the final honour school of natural sciences, taking part one in 1935, and, most significantly, electing to undertake his part two research with the group led by Professor William Hume-Rothery. In 1936 he gained a first-class honours degree.

As a research student Raynor developed a close and fruitful working relationship with Hume-Rothery that influenced his entire career in the science of physical metallurgy. Raynor's special interest lay in establishing the influences of atomic size and electronic factors upon the constitution of copper- and magnesium-based alloys and upon the formation of intermediate phases. To his regret the demands of research interfered with opportunities for serious rowing which, in 1934, had led to him rowing in the university trial eights. Having made his individual mark in the well-known Hume-Rothery and Raynor research group he gained his DPhil in 1939. During the Second World War, Raynor directed alloy chemistry research at Oxford on behalf of the Ministry of Supply and Ministry of Aircraft Production, supplementing his income by acting as a university demonstrator in inorganic chemistry. This classified research prevented him from joining the army. In 1943 he married Emily Jean, daughter of Dr George Frederick Brockless, musician. They had three sons.

In 1945 pressing economic circumstances made Raynor decide to leave Oxford and to accept an ICI research fellowship in the department of metallurgy of the University of Birmingham where research effort focused upon two areas: mechanical properties under the direction of A. H. Cottrell and alloy research under Raynor. Promotion was rapid. Raynor became reader in theoretical metallurgy in 1947, professor of metal physics (1949–54), professor of physical metallurgy (1954–5), Feeney professor of physical metallurgy (1955–69), and head of department in 1955. An Oxford degree of DSc was awarded in 1948. His exceptional success in research inevitably drew him into the administrative complexities of university life. From 1966 to 1969 he was dean, faculty of science and engineering. During this period the faculty was expanding and changing greatly; in the metallurgical field it was notable for the installation of one of the first million-volt transmission electron microscopes in Britain. In 1969 a school of metallurgy was formed, combining the previously separate disciplines of physical and industrial metallurgy. In the same year Raynor became deputy principal of the university. Unfortunately his four years of office coincided with the aftermath of the 1968 student revolt; his role as chairman of the academic appointments committee was particularly wearing and difficult. In retrospect it was widely recognized that, despite provocation and some unwarranted vilification, he always acted in a courageous and steadfast manner in accordance with the best long-term interests of the university.

After relinquishing the deputy principalship, partly for reasons of ill health, Raynor, stimulated by a concurrent worldwide resurgence of interest, turned to the critical evaluation and annotation of published phase diagrams and the construction of a systematic corpus of information on the alloying characteristics of a range of metals, work he continued until his death. It was therefore a natural and personally satisfying step for him to become chairman of the important alloy phase diagram data committee of the Metals Society (1976) and to join the international council of the Data Program for Alloy Phase Diagrams which operated under the aegis of the American Society for Metals and the US Bureau of Standards. Raynor had acquired a considerable reputation in his chosen field of metallurgical research and was able to accept many professorships overseas, visiting the universities of Chicago (1951–2), Ohio State (1962), Witwatersrand (1974), New South Wales (1975), and Queen's University, Ontario (1979). Travel, particularly by sea, always held a deep appeal for him.

Raynor's numerous research papers and scientific articles exhibit a distinctive style combining elegance with economy of words. Two of his books, *The Structure of Metals and Alloys* (1944, 1954, 1962), which he wrote with Hume-Rothery, and *An Introduction to the Electron Theory of Metals* (1947, 1988) became classic metallurgical texts. He also wrote *The Physical Metallurgy of Magnesium and its Alloys* (1959), contributed to the *Encyclopaedia Britannica* (1949), and shortly before his death completed with V. G. Rivlin a book on *Phase Equilibria of Iron Ternary Alloys* (1988). Teaching had a special place in Raynor's professional life and his lectures, with their intensive and often novel style, were highly regarded by undergraduate students, many of whom joined his research group. These presentations of the latest ideas in alloy research were characterized by precision and a sense of urgency. He was gentle, kind-natured and considerate.

Prestigious scientific awards to Raynor included the Beilby memorial award of the Royal Institute of Chemistry and the Institute of Metals (1947), the Rosenhain medal of the Institute of Metals (1951), the Heyn medal of the Deutsche Gesellschaft für Metallkunde (1956), and the Hume-Rothery prize of the Metals Society (1981). Election as FRS (1959) was soon followed by election to the fellowship of the New York Academy of Sciences (1961). Raynor derived special pleasure from his honorary fellowship (1972) at Keble, his old Oxford college, and from the award of a Leverhulme emeritus fellowship (1981). He was simultaneously a fellow of the institutes of physics, of chemistry, and of metallurgists, and he contributed significantly to the national development of metallurgy by serving as vice-president of the Institute of Metals (1953–6) and the Institution of Metallurgists (1963–6, 1977–80), and as president of the Birmingham Metallurgical Society (1965–6). Raynor died on 20 October 1983 in Birmingham.

R. E. SMALLMAN, *rev.*

Sources A. Cottrell, *Memoirs FRS*, 30 (1984), 547–63 · R. E. Small-man, *Metals Society World* (Jan 1984) · personal knowledge (1990) · *The Times* (25 Oct 1983), 14g · *CGPLA Eng. & Wales* (1983)
Likenesses photograph, repro. in Cottrell, *Memoirs FRS*
Wealth at death £66,564: probate, 20 Dec 1983, *CGPLA Eng. & Wales*

Rea [*née* Bevan], **Betty Marion** (1904–1965), sculptor, was born on 6 August 1904 in London at 17 Kensington Garden Terrace, Paddington, the daughter of Arthur Bevan (*d.* 1952), a general medical practitioner of Welsh descent, and Amy Bevan, *née* Barnardo (*d.* 1947), a nurse and niece of Dr Thomas John Barnardo, the founder of homes for destitute children.

After being educated at Downe House School in Kent, Bevan studied art at Regent Street Polytechnic in London. From 1924 to 1927 she studied sculpture at the Royal College of Art. Rea's early carvings show the influence of Henry Moore, then a student teacher who became a good friend. On 13 April 1926 she married James Russell Rea (1902–1954), then a law student. Their two sons, Nicholas and Julian, were born in 1928 and 1931.

In the 1930s, partly influenced by her friendship with Professor J. D. S. Bernal, Rea became a passionately committed socialist and anti-fascist. She was deeply involved in a number of political and cultural organizations devoted to these causes. She was one of the earliest members of the Artists' International Association (AIA) and made important contributions to its development. While acting as AIA secretary between 1934 and 1936, she edited a book of polemical essays, *Five on Revolutionary Art*, for which she also wrote the foreword. Through the AIA, Rea met the painter Nancy Mayhew (Nan) *Youngman (1906–1995), who became her lifelong companion. Rea and Youngman shared interests in various organizations. Rea was involved in the Hogarth Group of Communist Party Artists; she was also chairman of the Arts Peace Campaign and was active on the Artists' Refugee Committee and the Peace Publicity Bureau. At the Paris World Fair in 1937 she worked with other artists on a mural for the unofficial peace pavilion. A unique contribution to the anti-fascist cause was the fist Rea modelled for the finial on the International Brigades' British section banner used in the Spanish Civil War.

In 1940, with the evacuation of the school at which she taught, Youngman left London and set up home with Rea in a caravan in the grounds of Hinchingbrook Castle, Huntingdon. Rea was divorced from her husband in 1942. Besides raising her own sons and also caring for three young children of a friend who had died in the war, Rea taught painting and modelling to young evacuees. In 1945 they moved their extended family to Papermills in Cambridge. This provided Rea with the opportunity of returning to making sculpture—at that time, mainly terracotta figures. Alongside her political work Rea was fervently committed to expanding and developing art education; this was reflected in her work at Homerton College, where she taught from 1949 to 1964, and in the active role she took in the Society for Education through Art.

One of the most significant events with which Rea was involved in the 1950s was the exhibition 'Looking at people' which she co-organized with Carel Weight and Paul Hogarth with the specific intent of widening access to the arts. This highly popular exhibition of realist art was staged in 1955 at the Whitworth Art Gallery in Manchester. An expanded version of the show, featuring the work of eight artists including Rea, travelled to the Pushkin Museum in Moscow in 1957. It was reputed to be the first exhibition of British contemporary art in Russia since 1917. Rea's work appealed to Soviet critics and, in 1960, *Girls in a Wind* (resin; Bretton Hall University College Collection, Wakefield) was singled out in an article surveying modern British art in *Iskusstvo* (vol. 2, 1960), the official journal of the Union of Soviet Artists.

Rea's sculpture was always based on the human figure. Its narrative style had much in sympathy with mid-1950s English 'social realism' but it had none of the didacticism of Soviet socialist realism. Her work in baked terracotta, or later modelled in clay for casting in ciment fondu, bronze, and resin, had a singularly personal character and demonstrated an acute sensitivity to movement and balance. She had a particular facility in expressing the diverse emotions, activities, and grace of youth, as can be seen in *Stretching Figure* (bronze resin, 1959; Herbert Art Gallery and Museum, Coventry).

In the later 1950s Rea's sculpture gained increasing acknowledgement and she was invited to exhibit in various group shows such as 'Three humanist sculptors' at the Zwemmer Gallery, London, in 1960. She was a regular exhibitor at the Royal Academy and with the Cambridge Society of Painters and Sculptors. Her sculpture was acquired for various public collections, including a number of colleges and education authorities such as those in Coventry and the West Riding of Yorkshire. In the last year of her life she obtained two major commissions: a half life-size figure group for Hockerill College, Bishop's Stortford, and a full life-size group for a new swimming pool being built in Cambridge. The latter, with reference to Rea's maquette, was completed posthumously by the sculptor John Mills, after Rea suffered a fatal cerebral haemorrhage and died in Addenbrooke's Hospital, Cambridge, on 2 April 1965. She was cremated at Bar Hill crematorium in Cambridge.

Rea has been described as an indefatigable woman who enthused those around her with energy and vivacity. Her important contributions to a range of cultural organizations, events, and developments were underpinned by a selfless consideration for broader social and political concerns. Like many women of her generation Rea faced a number of obstacles in combining the pursuit of a successful career as a sculptor with caring for an extended family. Initially, the critical reception of Rea's figurative sculpture was cool. In the cold war period it was equated with realism when such an idiom was viewed as not only politically suspect but also distinctly unfashionable. However, the narrow-minded genealogy of modernist art history has been dismantled, and a more pluralistic view now embraces the diversity of sculpture produced in the twentieth century, enabling Rea's kind of figurative humanist sculpture to be revalued. In the catalogue for a retrospective memorial exhibition held at the Zwemmer Gallery in 1965, friend and supporter Bryan Robertson eloquently described Rea as a 'perceptive and highly intelligent imaginative poet of everyday life' (*Betty Rea, 1904–1965*, no pagination).   GILLIAN WHITELEY

Sources private information (2004) [family] · family papers, priv. coll. · *Betty Rea, 1904–1965* (1965) [exhibition catalogue, Zwemmer Gallery, London] · K. Deepwell, *Ten decades: careers of ten women artists born 1897–1906* (1992) [exhibition catalogue, Norwich Gallery, Norfolk Institute of Art and Design, 30 March 1992 – 16 May 1992] · *Three humanist sculptors* (1960) [exhibition catalogue, Zwemmer Gallery, London] · D. D. Egbert, *Social radicalism and the arts—western Europe—a cultural history from the French Revolution to 1968* (1970) · L. Morris and R. Radford, *The story of the Artists International Association, 1933–1953* (1983) · D. Buckman, *Dictionary of artists in Britain since 1945* (1998) · P. Dunford, *A biographical dictionary of women artists in Europe and America since 1850* (1990) · b. cert. · m. cert. · d. cert.
Likenesses photograph, repro. in Deepwell, *Ten decades*
Wealth at death £5689: probate, 7 July 1965, *CGPLA Eng. & Wales*

Rea, John (d. 1681), nursery gardener, lived with his daughter, Minerva, and her husband, Samuel Gilbert, author of the *Florist's vademecum* (1682), at Kinlet, Shropshire, near Bewdley, Worcestershire. Rea describes the place in his *Flora* (1676) as 'a rural district where it was my unhappiness to plant my stock'. He was said to have had the largest collection of tulips in England and it was he who introduced *Corylus colurna* in 1665. Rea planned the gardens at Gerard's Bromley, Staffordshire, the seat of Charles, fourth Baron Gerard.

Rea published *Flora, seu, De florum cultura*, with a second engraved title-page, *Flora, Ceres, and Pomona*, in 1665 (3rd edn 1702); the work was dedicated to Sir Thomas Hanmer and members of his family, and to Baron Gerard's son. This was intended as a revision of John Parkinson's *Paradisi in sole paradisus terrestris* (1629), and includes designs for gardens, and many pages on fruit and tulips.

Rea died at Kinlet in November 1681, leaving his holding to his daughter.

G. S. BOULGER, *rev.* ANNE PIMLOTT BAKER

Sources M. Hadfield, *A history of British gardening*, 3rd edn (1979), 114–22 · 'Early writers on English gardening, no. 10: Rev. Samuel Gilbert', *Journal of Horticulture, Cottage Gardener and Country Gentleman*, 30 (1876), 172–3 · Desmond, *Botanists* · *The Garden*, 76 (1912), 643, 652

Reach, Angus Bethune (1821–1856), journalist, was born at Inverness on 23 January 1821, the son of Roderick Reach (d. 1853), a solicitor, and his wife, Ann, *née* Bethune. He was educated at the Inverness Royal Academy and then at Edinburgh University, where he contributed literary articles to the *Inverness Courier*, which his father had formerly owned.

In 1842 the family moved to London, where Charles Mackay, then sub-editor of the *Morning Chronicle*, found work for Reach as a reporter at the central criminal court and afterwards in the House of Commons gallery. In 1848 he contributed to the *Morning Chronicle* most of a series of articles entitled 'Labour and the poor', which Fox Bourne described as 'an unparalleled exploit in journalism' (Fox

Bourne, 2.154). They helped inspire Henry Mayhew's *London Labour and the London Poor* (1851, 1862), which also began life as a series of articles in the *Morning Chronicle*.

Besides the *Morning Chronicle*, Reach wrote for the *New Monthly Magazine* (January–October 1845), *Bentley's Miscellany* (February 1853 – October 1854), *Chambers's Journal*, *The Era*, and the *Sunday Times*. He was associated with two short-lived imitations of *Punch*, Henry and James Vizetelly's the *Puppet Show* (1848) (on which his leading colleagues were Henry Sutherland Edwards and James Hannay) and the *Man in the Moon* (1847–9), which he edited in collaboration with Albert Smith and which for a time threatened to rival *Punch* itself. He joined the staff of *Punch* in 1849. His pioneering gossip column in the *Illustrated London News* (1850–51), 'Town talk and table talk', was the forerunner of the paper's famous column 'Echoes of the week', edited for many years by George Augustus Sala. Between 1847 and 1850 he published several short humorous monographs, including four 'natural histories' of society in the style of Albert Smith's 'physiologies', and *A Romance of a Mince Pie* (1850), which was illustrated by Phiz. A sensational romance, *Clement Lorimer, or, The Book with the Iron Clasps*, with twelve etchings by Cruikshank, was published in monthly parts in 1848–9, in a single volume in 1849, and as a two-volume novel, *Leonard Lindsay, or, The Story of a Buccaneer*, in 1850. As a 'special commissioner' he wrote a much admired series of letters to the *Morning Chronicle* on the vineyards of France, republished in book form as *Claret and Olives* in 1852, and also reported on the manufacturing and coal-mining districts of the north of England. For more than ten years he was a musical, theatrical, and art critic, as well as principal book reviewer, for the *Morning Chronicle*. In addition he was London correspondent of the *Glasgow Citizen* and, after his father's death in 1853, of the *Inverness Courier*, a role in which first Shirley Brooks and then Edmund Yates succeeded him. He wrote many dramatic farces, of which only one, *Jenny Lind at Last, or, The Swedish Nightingale* (1847), appears to have been published.

Early in 1855 Reach was incapacitated by what Edmund Yates described as 'an attack of softening of the brain' (Yates, 1.270). Shirley Brooks obtained grants for him of £50 and £100 from the Royal Literary Fund and the Royal Bounty Fund respectively. On 31 March 1855 members of the Fielding Club led by Albert Smith and Yates staged a benefit pantomime at the Olympic Theatre to raise money for him and his wife: the audience included Dickens and Thackeray, and a repeat performance was given at Drury Lane Theatre before the queen, the prince consort, and the prince of Wales. For a year before his death Shirley Brooks carried out Reach's work for the *Morning Chronicle* and the *Inverness Courier*, handing the proceeds to Reach's wife.

Reach died at Camberwell Green, London, on 25 November 1856 and was buried in Norwood cemetery. Sala spoke of his 'brilliant talents', to which 'not half enough justice' was done in the forty years after his death, and described him as 'one of the most laborious and prolific writers' he had ever met with. But Reach still found time for late-night revelry with Sala and his bohemian circle at the Café de l'Europe in the Haymarket (*Life and Adventures*, 164–5), and it can probably be assumed that drink contributed as much as overwork to his early death. Yates remembered him as 'an earnest-faced long-haired young man' (Yates, 1.216). His name was pronounced as a disyllable: Re-ach.

P. D. EDWARDS

Sources E. Yates, *Recollections and experiences*, 2 vols. (1884) · *The life and adventures of George Augustus Sala*, 2 vols. (1895); repr. in 1 vol. (1896) · N. Cross, *The common writer: life in nineteenth-century Grub Street* (1985) · C. Mackay, *Forty years' recollections of life, literature and public affairs, from 1830–1870*, 2 vols. (1877) · H. R. Fox Bourne, *English newspapers: chapters in the history of journalism*, 2 vols. (1887) · M. H. Spielmann, *The history of 'Punch'* (1895) · b. cert. · d. cert. · DNB

Read. *See also* Reade, Rede, Reed, Reid.

Read, Alfred [Al] (1909–1987), comedian, was born at 11 Kipling Street, Salford, Lancashire, on 3 March 1909, the second of the six children of William Henry (Herbert) Read and his wife, Elizabeth Fielding. He spent the first six years of his life in 'a two up, two down in Kipling Street, Salford' (Read, 17). His father and uncles had been in the meat processing business but went bankrupt. Eventually their fortunes recovered, the debts were paid off, the business was relaunched, and the family moved to Sedgely Park when Al was six. He was educated at St John's infants school, Sedgely Park, and North Manchester preparatory grammar school, leaving at fifteen to join the family firm of E. and H. Read Ltd as a salesman. He was such a success that he was a director by the age of twenty-three and eventually, when his father retired, took over the running of the business. On 18 April 1938 he married Joyce (*b.* 1910/11), daughter of Fred Entwistle, town clerk. There were two sons and a daughter from that marriage, which ended in divorce in 1970. During the Second World War Read developed a new canned meal, Frax Fratters, which immediately became the butt of comedians' jokes. He also served in the Prestwich Home Guard.

Read's salesman patter had incorporated anecdotes, jokes, and accents; he developed this into an act, which he called 'Pictures from Life', and began to perform as an amateur in theatres and holiday camps and in after-dinner speeches. As a monologist he was in an established comic tradition already mastered by Robb Wilton and Norman Evans. One of his performances caught the attention of the BBC light entertainment producer Bowker Andrews, who signed him up for radio. He made his début on radio in *Variety Fanfare* in 1950. He was an immediate success and soon had his own show, *Such is Life*, which was to run in various guises for twenty years. It brought him the 'most promising comedy show' award at the 1951 *Daily Mail* radio awards and an invitation to perform for the royal family at Windsor. From radio he moved to the variety stage, topping the bill at Blackpool and the London Palladium. His catch-phrases, 'You'll be lucky' and 'Right, monkey', swept the nation. Read did summer seasons and pantomime and in 1954 opened at the Adelphi Theatre in London's West End in a revue, *You'll Be Lucky*, which ran for twelve months. He returned to the Adelphi in 1956 with another revue, *Such is Life*.

In the 1960s Read sold the family business and moved reluctantly and belatedly into television, but he did not like it and his style was anyway quintessentially radio. He abandoned television and retreated to the northern club circuit, playing his last Blackpool summer show in 1970. When his first marriage ended he married, on 13 June 1970, a model, Elizabeth Ann Read (*b.* 1937/8), a divorcee (whose former husband was also named Read) and daughter of Frederick Howard Allen, an architect. From then on he divided his time between Spain, where he had built a house near Almeria, and Yorkshire, where he had a cottage near Leyburn in the dales. In 1976 the BBC discovered that it had wiped all the tapes of his radio shows and he was persuaded to re-record his classic routines, which were subsequently issued on audio cassette. In 1985 he published an autobiography, *It's All in the Book*.

Read was a master of the monologue and radio was his ideal medium. In his show he did all the voices, including the dog. There were no costumes, wigs, or disguises—it was pure vocal comedy. Working with experienced scriptwriter Ronnie Taylor he had converted his ideas and anecdotes into perfectly honed and timed scripts, based on Read's total mastery of the vocal patterns, preoccupations, values, and mores of his northern audience. The laughter of recognition from the audience is continually in evidence in recordings of his shows. The nagging wife 'from the kitchen', the embarrassingly forthright and questioning child ('Dad, Dad, what's that man doing, Dad?'), the know-all from next door ('You'll be lucky, I say, you'll be lucky'), and a gormless phone-user ('Just, just, just a minute') were regular features, as were send-ups of institutions, the police force, the Post Office, hospitals, and garages. His classic sketches were 'The Decorator', 'The Gardener', 'The Football Match', and 'The Chip Shop'.

Read's signature tune, 'Such is life', which he wrote with Ronnie Taylor:

> Such is life,
> life is what you make it,
> Show 'em you can take it on the chin

was in the optimistic, never-say-die vein of fellow northern comedians such as Gracie Fields and George Formby. Audiences related to his routines because they were truthful and based on precise observation of reality. Read wrote:

> The comedy had grown up with me and reflected my own
> personal experience … I never tried to make people laugh,
> and there were never any 'gags' as such in my routines … All
> the story lines were culled from the small embarrassments
> and frustrations of everyday life … the tittle tattle that
> makes the world of ordinary folk go round; the exchange of
> rumours and confidences in small confined places—in the
> corner shop, on top of the bus.   (Read, 68–71)

Offstage Al Read was known for his sartorial elegance, a cultured voice, and a love of horses and riding. He died on 9 September 1987 in Rutson Hospital at Northallerton following a stroke. His wife survived him.

JEFFREY RICHARDS

Sources A. Read, *It's all in the book* (1985) · E. C. Midwinter, *Make 'em laugh: famous comedians and their worlds* (1979) · B. Band, *Blackpool's*

comedy greats (1995) · J. Richards, *Stars in our eyes* (1994) · *The Times* (11 Sept 1987) · b. cert. · m. certs. · d. cert.
Archives SOUND BL NSA, documentary recordings · BL NSA, performance recordings
Likenesses photograph, *c.*1952, Hult. Arch. · Baron, photograph, *c.*1960, Hult. Arch.

Read, Sir Alfred Henry (1871–1955), shipowner, was born at 10 Georges Road, West Derby Road, Liverpool on 18 July 1871, the son of Colonel Alfred Read of Chester, a partner in the coastal shipping firm of F. H. Powell & Co., and his wife, Emily Blanche, *née* Musgrave. He was educated at Liverpool College, and then in Switzerland and Paris, before being apprenticed to the Glasgow-based Anchor Line with services on the north Atlantic and to India. In 1893 at the age of twenty-two he joined the family firm, which then owned four small steamers. He gradually persuaded his partners to acquire more ships and Powells owned nine by the turn of the century. Read began to give all the ships names ending in 'Coast', and like other owners transferred some to single-ship companies to spread his risk.

From the beginning of his career Read was keenly concerned to improve accommodation for crews on his ships, and also to ensure that new recruits were well trained, playing an active role in the management of the Lancashire and National Sea Training Home. He was twice married, first to Jean Charlotte (*d.* 1919), daughter of Hugh Frederick Macneal, on 11 April 1918, then on 25 September 1920 to Elena, daughter of Henry Fisher and widow of Charles Vincent.

By the turn of the century Alfred Read was a prominent shipowner in Liverpool, and was elected to the Mersey Docks and Harbour Board, on which he served until 1920, and he was chairman of the Liverpool Steam Ship Owners' Association in 1912. In that year Powells acquired the competing coastal business of John Bacon Ltd, and in 1913 merged with Samuel Hough Ltd to form Powell Bacon and Hough Lines, with a combined fleet of twenty-two ships. Freight rates rose during the First World War, and the coastal trades experienced serious competition from the railway companies, whose rates were kept artificially low by the government. Because most coasters were too small to be requisitioned for military service, coastal shipping was not controlled until 1917, when Read was appointed director of home trade services at the Ministry of Shipping. His contribution to the organization of coastal services during the unrestricted U-boat campaign and his commitment to training young seafarers were recognized with a knighthood in 1919.

Powell Bacon and Hough Lines was sold in 1917 to the fast-expanding Royal Mail group of Sir Owen Cosby Philipps, who merged it with the British and Irish Steam Packet Company to form Coast Lines Ltd, with Read as managing director. The new company, designed to provide connections to the group's worldwide liner services, purchased six more coastal shipping concerns in 1919, including the City of Dublin Steam Packet Company and the Belfast Steamship Company. Other acquisitions followed—the Glasgow-based G. & J. Burns (in which Sir George Burns was the key figure) in 1920; the London Welsh Steamship Company in 1923; British Motorship Company in 1925, and Dundalk and Newry Steam Packet Company in 1926. By the late 1920s it was the largest coastal shipping company in the United Kingdom, and although part of the Royal Mail group it was effectively controlled by Read. An autocratic figure, he directed the greatly expanded group with paternalistic despotism, frequently visiting offices 'without warning to the staff [to see] how the work was being done' (*The Times* 10 March 1955). His unrivalled knowledge of the United Kingdom's coastal trades rapidly made Coast Lines the dominant force in the industry.

When the Royal Mail group collapsed in 1930, he quickly took action to save Coast Lines by taking independent advice from the distinguished accountant Sir John Mann. The complexity of restructuring the group made a stock market floatation impossible until 1934, and then only by the government of the Republic of Ireland agreeing to purchase all the Irish business. Read was managing director of the new firm until 1946, and finally retired as chairman in 1950. He also served as a member of the Port of London Authority from 1934 to 1941. He was a founder member of the Institute of Transport in 1919, acting as vice-president (1927–30) and president (1936–7).

Widely regarded as the doyen of coastal shipping, Read was a private man and typical of the new generation of managers who characterized British trade and industry in the first half of the twentieth century. One of his interests was hunting, and he served as joint master of the Avon Vale foxhounds in the west country. Sir Alfred died on 8 March 1955 at the British Hospital, Lisbon, Portugal. He was survived by his second wife.   MICHAEL S. MOSS

Sources *The Times* (10 March 1955), 10e · *Shipbuilding and Shipping Record* (1895–1955) · E. Green and M. Moss, *A business of national importance: the Royal Mail shipping group, 1902–1937* (1982) · C. E. Fayle, *The war and the shipping industry* (1927) · *Burke's Who's who in sport* (1922) · *Lancashire: biographies, rolls of honour* (1917) · d. cert. · b. cert. · CGPLA Eng. & Wales (1955) · *Shipbuilding and Shipping Record* (17 March 1955)
Likenesses portrait, repro. in *Shipbuilding and Shipping Record* (17 March 1955)
Wealth at death £27,216 19s. 0d.: probate, 5 Sept 1955, CGPLA Eng. & Wales

Read, Charles (1715–1774), politician in America, was born on 1 February 1715 at the corner of Front and High streets, Philadelphia, Pennsylvania, the eldest child of Charles Read (1686–1737), a merchant of Cornish parentage, and Anne Bond (*d.* 1731). His father served as Philadelphia's mayor and Pennsylvania councillor. Read was an Anglican and acquired a classical education at a small Philadelphia academy. He travelled to London in 1733, where he met Sir Charles *Wager, a privy councillor related to his mother. Appointed a navy midshipman through Wager's patronage, Read embarked for the Caribbean, where he met and married on 11 April 1737 Alice Thibou (1719–1769), daughter of Antigua's chief justice. They had at least two sons who reached adulthood. He sold his commission later in 1737, and returned home to Philadelphia just after his father died deeply in debt.

'No man knew so well as he how to riggle himself into

office', wrote fellow politician Aaron Leaming about Read, 'nor keep it so long, nor make so much of it' (Woodward, 405). Read relocated to nearby Burlington, New Jersey, where he bought a county clerkship in 1739; again with Wager's intercession, he became customs collector for Burlington's harbour. New Jersey governor Lewis Morris, another of Wager's protégés, commissioned Read as the circuit court's clerk in 1740 and as provincial secretary, scribe for the governor and his council, in 1743.

Read's salaries and fees provided investment capital for land speculation and smelting bog ore. He ultimately acquired over 35,000 acres of land, and built four iron-works, which later manufactured large stocks of munitions for American revolutionaries. He mastered the law quickly while clerking at court, and then established a thriving legal practice. He also developed two flourishing plantations of 305 acres and 492 acres as country seats.

Read first acquired a high political office in 1749, when he was appointed an associate justice on the supreme court. He was elected as assemblyman from Burlington in 1751 and immediately became the assembly's speaker. During the Seven Years' War he commanded Burlington county's militia with the rank of colonel, and helped to negotiate three treaties with the American Indians. The governor appointed him to his council's circle in 1761.

Read influenced the assembly to an unprecedented degree. 'From 1747 to 1771, he had the almost absolute rule of Governor, Council & Assembly', wrote Leaming. 'I have known the Governor & Council to do things against their inclination to please him & the Assembly have often done so', he added. 'During that time he took the whole disposal of all offices. He little considered the merits of the person he preferred; the sole object was whether it suited his party principles' (Woodward, 405).

By 1769 collapsing land prices left Read owing more on his lands than he could profitably earn from them, while ill health steadily sapped his vigour. Increasingly 'of unsettled mind' (Woodward, 406), he left furtively for Antigua in 1773 to claim his deceased wife's inheritance. Unable to settle her estate or honour his debts, he opened a modest store at Martinsburg, North Carolina—a backwater hamlet beyond reach of his New Jersey creditors. After a meteoric career infused with raw energy, opportunism, and panache, Read died there on 27 December 1774, a fugitive from debtors' prison.

THOMAS L. PURVIS

Sources C. R. Woodward, *Ploughs and politicks: Charles Read of New Jersey and his notes on agriculture, 1715–1774* (1941) • T. L. Purvis, *Proprietors, patronage, and paper money: legislative politics in New Jersey, 1703–1776* (1986) • C. R. Hildeburn, ed., *Baptisms and burials from the records of Christ Church, Philadelphia, 1709–1760* (1893) • W. W. Hinshaw, ed., *Encyclopedia of Quaker genealogy*, 7 vols. (1938)
Wealth at death heavily in debt; trying to avoid forced sale of assets

Read, Charles Anderson (1841–1878), writer, was born on 10 November 1841 at Kilsella House, near Sligo, the son of a gentleman who became a schoolmaster of Hilltown, near Newry. Charles was destined for the church, but family misfortunes led him to be apprenticed to a merchant of Rathfriland. He continued to study Latin and, with his mother, Irish, and at thirteen contributed to local journals. He subsequently became partner in and eventually proprietor of the firm, but it failed about 1863. Read, who had married Rebekah Harriette in 1862, obtained an appointment in the London publishing office of James Henderson. To Henderson's *Our Young Folks' Weekly Journal* he contributed from the first number in 1871 sketches, poems, and stories from the classics and nine successful serial stories, two of which, *Aileen Aroon* (1867) and *Savourneen Dheelish* (1867), were published separately. He also wrote for the *Dublin University Magazine* and produced some passable verse. Read suffered from consumption, and a voyage to Australia in 1873 was beneficial. His deep interest in Irish literature led to his best-known work, *The Cabinet of Irish Literature* (4 vols., 1876–80), which comprises selections from the writings of the most prominent Irish authors, from the earliest times to the date of publication. The fourth volume was completed by T. P. O'Connor. Read died prematurely on 23 January 1878 at his home, Ingoldsby Villa, Bensham Manor Road, Thornton Heath, Surrey. He was survived by his wife.

D. J. O'DONOGHUE, *rev.* JOHN D. HAIGH

Sources C. A. Read, *The cabinet of Irish literature: selections from the works of the chief poets, orators and prose writers of Ireland*, 4 (1880) [completed by T. P. O'Connor, incl. biographical sketch of Read] • D. J. O'Donoghue, *The poets of Ireland: a biographical dictionary with bibliographical particulars*, 1 vol. in 3 pts (1892–3) • *BL cat.* • Boase, *Mod. Eng. biog.* • Ward, *Men of the reign* • d. cert. • *CGPLA Eng. & Wales* (1878)
Likenesses portrait, repro. in *Our Young Folks' Weekly Journal* (19 Dec 1874) • portrait, repro. in *Our Young Folks' Weekly Journal* (9 Feb 1878)
Wealth at death under £600: probate, 26 April 1878, *CGPLA Eng. & Wales*

Read, Clare Sewell (1826–1905), agriculturist and politician, the eldest son of George Read of Barton Bendish Hall, Norfolk, and Sarah Ann, daughter of Clare Sewell, was born at Ketteringham on 6 November 1826. His ancestors had been tenant farmers in Norfolk since the end of the sixteenth century. He was educated privately at King's Lynn and from the age of fifteen until he was twenty learned practical agriculture on his father's farm. Before he was twenty-one he was managing the large farm of Kilpaison in Pembrokeshire, and was afterwards resident agent on the earl of Macclesfield's Oxfordshire estates. On returning to Norfolk in 1854, he took his father's farm at Plumstead, near Norwich, until 1865, when he succeeded a relative at Honingham Thorpe, and farmed about 800 acres there until Michaelmas 1896. In 1859 he married Sarah Maria, only daughter of J. Watson, former sheriff of Norwich; they had four daughters.

Read represented East Norfolk as a Conservative from July 1865 until the Reform Act of 1867, when Norfolk was divided into three constituencies. He sat for South Norfolk from 1868 to 1880, losing at the general election by one vote. He then declined to stand for North Lincolnshire and for Cambridgeshire, but in February 1884 was returned unopposed for West Norfolk; he retired from that seat in 1885, and in July 1886 unsuccessfully contested Norwich.

Read was an old-fashioned high-churchman who expressed the need for caution on the question of further extension of the parliamentary franchise. His object in entering parliament, however, was to represent the interests of farmers, especially tenant farmers, and in his speeches he confined himself to agricultural issues on which he was recognized as a distinguished authority. He commanded the attention of the house, and Gladstone made a point of listening to him and of himself referring to Read's views. In his first speech in parliament, in 1866, in support of Sir Fitzroy Kelly's motion for the repeal of the malt tax, Read suggested, as an alternative, a beer tax of 1d. per gallon on all beer that was sold; he also proposed that a licence should be paid by private brewers, and that all cottagers should be free to brew their own beer—a concession later granted. He strenuously supported and promoted all the acts of parliament passed for the suppression of cattle plague and all other imported diseases among livestock; advocated the inalienable right of the occupier of the land to destroy ground game; persistently contended for the compulsory payment by landowners for tenant farmers' improvements to the land; argued that all property, and not land and buildings alone, should contribute to local as well as national taxes; and in 1876 carried a unanimous resolution in the House of Commons in favour of representative county boards.

In 1865 Read served on the cattle plague commission, and for twenty years sat on almost every agricultural committee of the House of Commons. In February 1874 he was appointed by Disraeli parliamentary secretary to the Local Government Board, but resigned in January 1876, when the government refused to extend the Cattle Diseases Act to Ireland. This, however, soon afterwards became law. On resigning his government appointment, he was presented by the farmers of England with a silver salver and a purse of £5500 at a dinner given at the Cannon Street Hotel on 2 May 1876. When the duke of Richmond's royal commission on agriculture was appointed in June 1879, Read and Albert Pell were made assistant commissioners to visit the United States and Canada to inquire into and report on the conditions of agriculture there, particularly as related to the production of wheat for export to Europe. They were away six months and travelled 16,000 miles.

In 1848 Read won the Royal Agricultural Society's prize with an essay on the farming of south Wales, and in 1854 and 1856 obtained the society's prizes for similar reports on Oxfordshire and Buckinghamshire. He contributed numerous other papers to the Royal Agricultural Society's *Journal*, and acted frequently as judge at the Royal, Smithfield, Bath and West of England, and other agricultural shows. He also wrote on Norfolk agriculture for the fourth edition of White's *History, Gazetteer and Directory* of that county (1883). In January 1866 he joined the Farmers' Club (founded in 1842), and was an active member until his death, frequently reading papers at meetings, serving on the committee, and acting as chairman for two years, once in 1868 and again in 1892 (the club's jubilee year). He was a member of the council of the central chamber of agriculture (of which he was chairman in 1869) and of the Smithfield Club. He also served as a Norfolk magistrate.

When his intention to give up farming in Norfolk was made known, a county committee organized a fund for presenting Read with his portrait. In his later years he lived in London at 91 Kensington Gardens Square, where he died on 21 August 1905, but he was buried in his native soil at Barton Bendish.

Read was excellent company and a well-known and genial figure in farming circles. He was fond of the country, and particularly of shooting, and was said to detest town life and late hours. With his practical experience of farming and of land management he was one of the first members of parliament to speak with authority on agricultural matters, although his own background was more that of the squirearchy than of the ordinary farmers.

ERNEST CLARKE, *rev.* G. E. MINGAY

Sources *The Times* (23 Aug 1905) · *The Times* (28 Aug 1905) · *The Morning Post* (23 Aug 1905) · *Mark Lane Express* (18 Aug 1905) · C. A. M. Press, *Norfolk notabilities: a portrait gallery* (1893) · *WWW*
Archives Bodl. Oxf., letters to Benjamin Disraeli · Bodl. Oxf., Hughenden MSS
Likenesses J. B. Hunt, stipple, pubd 1868 (after photograph by C. Hunt), NPG · J. J. Shannon, oils, 1897, Castle Museum, Norwich · Ape [C. Pellegrini], watercolour study, NPG; repro. in *VF* (5 June 1875) · lithographs, repro. in F. Johnson, ed., *A catalogue of engraved Norfolk and Norwich portraits* (1911), 134 · photograph, repro. in L. L. Wilson, ed., *The Imperial gallery of portraiture and biographical encyclopaedia* (1902), 129
Wealth at death £21,757 16s. 5d.: probate, 30 Oct 1905, *CGPLA Eng. & Wales*

Read, David Charles (1790–1851), etcher and painter, was born at Boldre, near Lymington, Hampshire, on 1 March 1790. He went to London at an early age and was apprenticed to the engraver John Scott; but, his health suffering, he returned to the country, and there produced woodcuts for several works, including an edition of *The Pilgrim's Progress* published by William Sharp at Romsey (1816–17). In January 1820 he settled at Salisbury, where he continued to reside in the close until 1845, building a successful, though unremunerative, practice as a drawing-master. Read showed only one work at the Royal Academy, a landscape in oil, in 1823; this was followed by seven works at the British Institution and six more at the Suffolk Street gallery of the Society of British Artists before he ceased exhibiting in 1840. During this period he spent his spare time sketching in pencil, watercolours, and oils, working chiefly in the open air, and he prided himself on the fidelity with which he rendered weather and atmospheric effects.

Read made his first experiments in etching in 1826, and the works for which he is now best remembered were first published in 1828. He was a rapid draughtsman, and between that date and 1844 he produced 237 plates, mainly after his own works. Sixteen of them were portraits, including two of Goethe, and one of Handel, after Hogarth; the remainder were landscapes, many of views around Salisbury. Their merit is very unequal, however. At their best they recall the work of Rembrandt, especially in their extensive use of drypoint—unusual with English artists of this date. But in others the drawing is often faulty, and a black and harsh effect is produced by the mechanical cross-hatching of the shadows and an excess of roulette work. Read was scrupulous in his attention to the technical production of his work. Thus, although he sent his earliest plates to be printed in London, he soon obtained a press and pulled all the impressions himself. Moreover, he was careful not to print impressions from plates which showed signs of wear; he destroyed sixty-three of his plates in 1845, and the rest were cancelled by his family after his death.

Read published six series of etchings between 1829 and 1845. These include thirty-one views of *Wiltshire Scenery* (1837), a set of twenty-three *Etchings from Nature Designed to Illustrate a Few of the Leading Features of English Scenery* (1845), and a series of thirteen views of *Lake Scenery* (1840). Although he complained about the lack of attention his etchings attracted, Read was flattered to note the appreciation of Goethe and Mendelssohn, and he gained the support of a number of patrons. These included Chambers Hall, whose collection of his prints is now at the Ashmolean Museum, Oxford, and the first earl of Ellesmere. Read himself presented the British Museum with two volumes containing 168 of his etchings.

On leaving Salisbury in 1845 Read spent more than a year in Italy, and on his return he devoted himself to painting in oils, producing some of his best works for Dr Coope between 1846 and 1849. His health became seriously impaired towards the end of 1849, and he died, unmarried, at his home, 24 Bedford Place, Kensington, London, on 28 May 1851.

CAMPBELL DODGSON, *rev.* GREG SMITH

Sources R. W. Read, 'Manuscript memoir and catalogue of the etchings of David Charles Read', BM, department of prints and drawings · M. H. Grant, *A dictionary of British etchers* (1952)
Archives BM, MS memoir
Likenesses R. C. Lucas, plaster bust, 1840, AM Oxf. · D. C. Read, etching (after watercolour by J. Linnell, 1819)

Read, George (1733–1798), politician and lawyer, was born on 18 September 1733 in Cecil county, Maryland, the eldest of the seven children of John Read (1688–1756), planter, and his wife, Mary Howell (1711–1784). John Read was born in Dublin of an English family of comfortable means. Disheartened by the death of his fiancée he set off for Maryland with sufficient resources to buy property in Cecil county and neighbouring New Castle county, one of the lower counties of Pennsylvania, the future state of Delaware. Here he met and married the Welsh-born Mary Howell, who had come to New Castle as a child with her parents.

George Read attended an academy (1743–6) at New London, Pennsylvania, newly established by the Revd Francis Alison, and then read law (1747–53) with John Moland in Philadelphia, where a fellow student, John Dickinson, became his lifelong friend. Soon after admission to the bar in Philadelphia in 1753, Read moved to New Castle, though he also practised in several adjoining counties. In 1763 he married Gertrude, *née* Ross (d. 1802), widow of Thomas Till, and daughter of the rector of Immanuel,

New Castle's Anglican church, where Read was a communicant; they had three sons and a daughter.

The same year marked Read's appointment as attorney-general of the lower counties, a post he resigned only in 1774, probably in consequence of his increasing involvement in the political disputes with Britain. He was elected to the colonial assembly in 1765 and again in 1768, when he began a long service in the legislature that lasted, one year excepted, until 1788. As protests against parliamentary taxation magnified, Read became a prominent member of various supporting committees until in 1776 he was chosen president of a constitutional convention creating a state government for Delaware. Meanwhile, in 1774 he had begun service as a Delaware delegate to the continental congress. When the congress debated independence in July 1776, Read, like his friend Dickinson, opposed the measure, thinking it too precipitate. But after passage of the Declaration of Independence, Read, unlike Dickinson, signed the document. Significantly, Read was re-elected to congress in the autumn, whereas two Delaware delegates who supported independence were not.

As leader of the moderate party in Delaware during the revolution, Read helped keep Delaware in harmony with neighbouring states, while seeking to calm civil strife and, eventually, to reintroduce neutrals and loyalists, who were numerous, into political life. Although condemned by radical revolutionaries, his vision prevailed. Under his leadership Delaware made an exceptionally smooth transition from colony to state.

After the first elected president of Delaware was seized by the British, Read served briefly, in 1777–8, as acting president. In 1782 he accepted an appointment by congress to its court of appeals for admiralty cases, and he demonstrated his interest in strengthening the national government by attending a convention at Annapolis in 1786 for that purpose, as well as the constitutional convention at Philadelphia in 1787. In his instructions for the Delaware delegation to the latter convention Read included a demand that the delegates insist each state retain an equal vote in any new government. Subsequently, when Virginia delegates proposed proportional representation, Read objected that Delaware's representatives were not empowered to consider such an arrangement and the subject was postponed. But when a compromise granted Delaware equality only in the senate, Read was satisfied.

Delaware approved Read's course when on 7 December 1787 it became the first state to ratify the new constitution. Read was chosen as one of his state's first two senators in 1788 and was re-elected unanimously in 1790. As a strong nationalist he supported Alexander Hamilton's proposals for the course of government until 1793, when he resigned to become chief justice of Delaware under a new state constitution. He was chosen by the legislature to collect and edit the laws of Delaware, which appeared in a two-volume edition in 1797. He died in New Castle on 21 September 1798 and was buried in the yard of Immanuel church; he was survived by his wife.

Among the Reads' contemporaries, two near relatives

played significant roles in politics: Gunning Bedford sen., George's sister's husband, was governor of Delaware (1796–7), and Gertrude's brother George Ross as a Pennsylvania delegate was a fellow signer of the Declaration of Independence. The Reads' home, on the river-front in New Castle, burned down in 1824; its site was preserved in the garden of the home of their son George Read jun.

JOHN A. MUNROE

Sources J. A. Munroe, 'Read, George', *ANB* · W. T. Read, *Life and correspondence of George Read, a signer of the Declaration of Independence* (1870) · J. A. Munroe, *Federalist Delaware, 1775–1815* (1954) · D. T. Boughner, *George Read and the founding of the Delaware state, 1781–1798* (1968) · [J. Tilton], *The biographical history of Dionysius, tyrant of Delaware. By Timoleon* (Philadelphia, 1788); repr. with notes by T. Rodney, ed. J. A. Munroe (Newark, 1958) · J. A. Munroe, 'The Philadelawareans: a study in the relations between Philadelphia and Delaware in the late 18th century', *Penna Magazine of History and Biography*, 69 (1945), 128–49 · J. M. Coleman, *Thomas McKean* (1975) · H. P. Read, *Rossiana: papers relating to the ... Ross* [and] *Read* [*families*] (1908) · R. A. Martin, *A history of Delaware through its governors, 1776–1984* (1984) · J. T. Scharf, *History of Delaware*, 2 vols. (1888), 1.186–202 · H. B. Hancock, *Liberty and independence: the Delaware state during the revolution* (1976)

Archives Hist. Soc. Penn., family MSS · L. Cong., family MSS | Historical Society of Delaware, Wilmington, Richard S. Rodney MSS

Likenesses R. E. Pine, portrait, 1784–92, Smithsonian Institution, Washington, DC, National Portrait Gallery · T. Sully, portrait, 1808 (posthumous), Independence National Historic Park, Philadelphia; copy, 1808 · R. E. Pine, portrait, priv. coll. · S. Sartain, engraving (after T. Sully), repro. in Read, *Life and correspondence*, frontispiece

Read, Grantly Dick- (1890–1959), obstetrician and promoter of natural childbirth, was born at Beccles, Suffolk, on 26 January 1890, the son of Robert John Read (1851–1920), a flour miller of Norwich, and his wife, Frances (Fanny) Maria Sayer (1855–1942), of the White House, Thurlton, Norfolk, which had been in the family since 1704. Dick-Read (the hyphen was assumed in 1958) was the sixth of seven children and the second of three brothers. An unexceptional student but a good athlete, Read went from Bishop's Stortford College to St John's College, Cambridge. After obtaining a third class in part one of the natural sciences tripos in 1911 he became a clinical medical student at the London Hospital, where he came under the influence of Eardley Holland, one of the outstanding obstetricians and gynaecologists of his day. He also worked under the neurologist Sir Henry Head, whose research into pain influenced Read.

Less than a year after Read's arrival at the London Hospital he began treating the sick in some of the poorest areas of London. On one such visit he entered a small, damp, and poorly lit room in Whitechapel and delivered a woman of her first child. He recounted this event in his unpublished autobiography:

> As the baby's head made its appearance at the outlet of the birth canal and the dilatation of the passage was at a stage where I felt there should be discomfort and pain, I tried to persuade my patient to let me put the mask over her face so that she could inhale some chloroform. But the girl refused the mask, saying that she had no need of this help.

Later, as he was preparing to leave, he asked the woman

why she refused assistance and she responded: 'It didn't hurt. It wasn't meant to, was it Doctor?' (Dick-Read, 2.20–21). This became his favourite story. It was also a turning point in his medical career, and although he came to influence women around the world he remained on the fringe of the medical profession.

Read qualified in 1914 and immediately joined the Royal Army Medical Corps. While serving in Gallipoli he was badly injured and after recuperation served out the war in France. At the end of the First World War he returned to Cambridge University to assume a research post, and for a brief time he was demonstrator in pathology. He received his MD from Cambridge in 1920 and then spent a short time in private practice in Eastbourne before moving his practice to Woking with consulting-rooms in Harley Street, London. In 1921 he married Dorothea (Thea) Cannon (1899–1978), daughter of Neville Cannon, flour miller, of Bexley, Kent; they had two sons and two daughters.

Read's first book, *Natural Childbirth*, was published in 1933. But his most famous and popular book was *Revelation of Childbirth* published in 1942. It was published in the United States as *Childbirth without Fear* in 1944. He wrote at least eight books and more than forty articles in support of the fear–tension–pain theory, and his books were translated into Dutch, Danish, German, Swedish, Italian, French, Afrikaans, Norwegian, Portuguese, and Spanish. As a result, from 1933 until his death in 1959 he received an avalanche of correspondence from women in Britain and the United States, as well as from the European countries, South America, and South Africa, suggesting that his ideas had worldwide influence on how women were having babies. In these works Read introduced the concept that relaxation at the onset of labour was the most effective means of experiencing a conscious, joyful, childbirth in 95–7 per cent of cases. He wrote that informing and educating women on what was happening to their bodies during pregnancy and labour would enable them to relax. Relaxation, he contended, would eliminate the fear and the tension brought on by lack of knowledge. As a result, if a woman felt pain it would not be significant enough to require drugs.

Read wanted to become a member of the Royal College of Obstetricians and Gynaecologists but refused to sit for the required examination. However, the college offered him an opportunity to open a clinic in London in which he could put his natural childbirth theories into practice. He was offered a building suitable for delivering pregnant women and for teaching his methods of natural childbirth. Dissatisfied with the condition of the premises and their location in an area away from the major London hospitals, he turned down the offer and accused the Royal College of Obstetricians and Gynaecologists of professional jealousy. Read had an obstinate professional attitude, which contributed to his being an outcast among his peers. This led him to popularize his childbirth theories by appealing directly to the public and further alienating himself from the medical establishment. His former teacher and mentor, Sir Eardley Holland, brought this to his attention in a letter in 1949:

I would urge you, though, with respect, to take more thought to win the sympathies of the Profession as distinct from the Public, and give more time and take more trouble in doing so. … you seem to have alienated the sympathies of the … Gynaecological world. Have you even considered that you yourself may be to some extent to blame for that—sad state of affairs? You have sometimes tried even me very severely! (E. Holland to G. D. Read, 8 Jan 1949, Wellcome L., PP/GDR/D.150)

There is no indication that Read took this advice. In fact, his longed-for recognition in his own country and public honours from his peers and colleagues continued to elude him.

In 1948 Read moved his practice to South Africa. After a lengthy legal battle with the government over his licence to practise medicine he attached himself to a hospital on the outskirts of Johannesburg, the Marymount Maternity Hospital, run by Dominican nuns. Four years after arriving in South Africa he obtained a divorce from his first wife, and married in 1952 Jessica Beatrice Bennett, daughter of Leigh Cosart Winters, a businessman; he adopted her two sons.

In 1954 Read concluded that his work in South Africa had been completed, and, with his family, set out on a safari. His aim was to observe non-Westernized African women giving birth in their natural environment. At the end of this journey, which covered 6000 miles, he was totally satisfied that what he had said all along was true: Western civilization was responsible for the destruction of normal, natural childbirth.

On returning to England in 1954 Read was no longer in practice but maintained a high public profile through his worldwide lectures. He considered one of the greatest moments of his later life to be in 1956, when the pope granted him an audience and presented him with the silver papal medal for his work on natural childbirth. Also in 1956 his long-playing record of a woman experiencing natural childbirth was released and the film he made of four women giving birth naturally before he left South Africa was shown on BBC television in 1957. In 1957 and 1958 he engaged in a strenuous and lengthy lecture tour in the United States. Dick-Read died after a short illness at his home, Heronby, Beech Road, Wroxham, Norfolk, on 11 June 1959, and was buried at Eaton cemetery, Norwich, following a funeral service at St Andrew's Church, Eaton. A memorial service was held at St Martin-in-the-Fields, London, on 8 July 1959. He was survived by his wife.

MARY ALVEY THOMAS

Sources private information (2004) · A. N. Thomas, *Doctor Courageous: the story of Dr Grantly Dick Read* [1957] · G. Dick-Read, 'Autobiography', Wellcome L. · Wellcome L., Grantly Dick-Read MSS · M. Thomas, *Post-war mothers: childbirth letters to Grantly Dick-Read* (1997) · *DNB* · *CGPLA Eng. & Wales* (1959)
Archives Wellcome L., corresp. and papers | FILM BFI NFTVA
Likenesses photograph, repro. in Thomas, *Doctor Courageous* · photographs, Wellcome L.
Wealth at death £34,155 10s. 10d.: probate, 25 Sept 1959, *CGPLA Eng. & Wales*

Read, Sir Herbert Edward (1893–1968), poet, literary critic, and writer on art, was born on 4 December 1893 at Muscoates Grange, near Kirkby Moorside, in the North Riding of Yorkshire, the eldest of the four children of Herbert Edward Read (1868–1903), tenant farmer, and of Eliza (1867–1914), daughter of William Strickland, also a Kirkby Moorside tenant farmer, and his wife, Sarah. Read gives a dream-like account of his early childhood in the Vale of Pickering in his vivid autobiographical essay *The Innocent Eye* (1933).

Read's father, 'a man of austere habits and general uprightness' (Read, *Annals*, 31), died of fever following a hunting accident in February 1903. Read and his brother William were sent to board at the spartan Crossley and Porter Orphan Home and School in Halifax, from which Read emerged a precocious Disraelian Conservative. He worked, unhappily, from 1909 to 1912 as a clerk at the Skyrac and Morley Savings Bank in Leeds, but he continued his schooling at evening classes, matriculating in 1911. In 1912, aged nineteen, on the strength of a legacy held in trust by an uncle, Read enrolled at Leeds University, where he studied law and economics. That same year he joined the Leeds Arts Club, home to a northern avant-garde that promoted Nietzsche, theosophy, women's rights, various strands of ethical socialism, and, during the time of Read's membership, modernism in the visual arts. In this setting the markedly dichotomous nature of Read's personality, simultaneously coolly rational and intensely romantic, intellectual and instinctive, began to emerge.

Read formed important friendships with the painter Jacob Kramer and with Frank Rutter, the curator of Leeds City Art Gallery. He gained access to the collection of advanced European art, including work by Gauguin, Kandinsky, and Klee, being formed by the vice-chancellor of Leeds University, Michael Sadler. Read embarked on an eclectic course of extra-curricular study with Nietzsche as his 'real teacher' (Read, *Annals*, 86). In 1912 he lost his religious faith in favour of political beliefs shaped through reading John Ruskin, William Morris, Peter Kropotkin, and Georges Sorel. The stimulation he experienced during his course of hard-won self-education left him with a distrust of formally trained minds schooled in classics at Oxford or Cambridge. He knew Latin but no Greek and taught himself French, German, and Italian in order to read poetry.

In 1915 Read was commissioned as a second lieutenant in a battalion of the Yorkshire regiment, the Green Howards. He found his fellow officers, mostly masters and senior boys from Eton and other public schools, less sympathetic than the private soldiers under his command. As he experienced the horror of trench warfare, he discovered that 'men of imagination' like himself were 'the men of courage' (Read, *Annals*, 147). He drew and painted in a vorticist manner and his intense analytical letters from the western battlefront were addressed to a fiercely intelligent Leeds science student, Evelyn May Roff (1894–1972), whom he married on 7 August 1919; they had one son. Read left the army a captain, a convinced pacifist, a war poet, and a youthful war hero who had been awarded the Military Cross (1917) and the DSO (1918).

In 1919 Read joined the civil service, working first in the Ministry of Labour, then at the Treasury, and in 1921 becoming private secretary to the controller of establishments. But his career as a modern poet and literary critic was already well under way. During the course of the war, in snatched opportunities on leave, Read met the key figures in London's literary and artistic modern movement. With Frank Rutter he founded the journal *Art & Letters* (1917–20). In 1917 he met and impressed T. S. Eliot and in the autumn of 1918 he came to know the Sitwells, Ezra Pound, Wyndham Lewis, Richard Aldington, and Ford Madox Ford. He learned his skills as an essayist under the tutelage of A. R. Orage, editor of the *New Age*, and in 1921 took over Orage's 'Readers and writers' column in that journal.

Read always saw himself primarily as a poet, and his verse was much admired in his lifetime. *Songs of Chaos* (1917) was strongly influenced by William Blake and Ralph Hodgson. His subsequent wartime publications, *Naked Warriors* (1919) and *Eclogues* (1919), were cooler in tone, in the spirit of the imagist poetry of T. E. Hulme and Ezra Pound. War poems like *Liedholz* (1919) had memorable directness but Read's thoroughly decent humanist poetic voice was ultimately ill-served by tight diction and unrelenting emotional logic. However, *Vocal Avowals* (1962), a late series of short poems, was truly experimental, coming close to pure sound, untrammelled by verifiable meaning.

From 1923 Read contributed regularly to T. S. Eliot's journal *The Criterion* (founded 1922). For Read, Eliot was 'rather like a gloomy priest presiding over my affections and spontaneity' (King, 77). In turn Eliot disliked Read's use of psychoanalytic theory, the results of which were probing if highly subjective. For example, in his fine Clark lectures, delivered at Trinity College, Cambridge, and published as *Wordsworth* (1930), Read's description of the Lakeland poet's character as at once cold and passionate comes close to self-analysis. Read's unswerving commitment to literature was given further practical form when in 1937 he became literary adviser to the publishers Heinemann and Routledge and Kegan Paul. He worked with the latter until 1961, ending up as director. At Routledge's Read was able to give generous support to younger poets such as Sidney Keyes, John Heath Stubbs, and Henry Treece.

In 1922 Read left the civil service for a more congenial post as curator in the department of ceramics and glass in the Victoria and Albert Museum, subsequently becoming the director's assistant. He turned his attention to the applied arts. In *English Pottery* (1924), written with Bernard Rackham, Read went beyond classification to discuss national identity and to establish modernist standards of judgement that gave a context for the new art of studio pottery. In 1929 he was invited to contribute 'Weekly notes on art' to *The Listener*, short essays which were the basis of his brilliantly compressed primer *The Meaning of Art* (1931). The foundations for his approach had been laid when he edited T. E. Hulme's *Speculations* (1924), leading him to translate Wilhelm Worringer's *Formprobleme der Gotik* (1912) as *Form in Gothic* (1927). Worringer distinguished between empathetic art, expressing a confidence in the external world, and abstraction, reflecting human alienation and insecurity, thus providing Read with a reasoned justification for the artistic relativism already espoused by Roger Fry.

In 1931 Read took up the Watson Gordon professorship in fine art at the University of Edinburgh. Intellectually this brief academic interlude proved disappointing; Read resigned for personal reasons in 1933, becoming editor of the *Burlington Magazine* (1933–9). By 1929 his marriage to Evelyn Roff was failing, and in 1933 he left Edinburgh and his professorship precipitately with a young musician, Margaret Ludwig [*see below*]. They married on 12 February 1936 following Read's divorce, having already settled in Hampstead, London. There, during the happiest period of his life, Read wrote his only novel, *The Green Child* (1935), part adventure story, part contribution to utopian literature. Read's subsequent independence of institutions, particularly academic ones, helped give his thought and writing its daring breadth. But money was always a problem. Alimony paid to his first wife; three further sons and a daughter, all sent at his second wife's behest to Catholic boarding-schools; and in 1949 the purchase of Stonegrave House (a substantial old rectory near his Yorkshire birthplace) condemned Read to a ceaseless round of writing and lecturing, particularly after the Second World War.

Nowhere was Read's independence more marked than in his politics. He was an early critic of Nazi rule in Germany. He rejected Soviet communism and in 1937 he declared himself an anarchist, a decision that brought him moral peace, especially during the cold war. He was associated with the Freedom Press and when four fellow anarchists were arrested in 1945 for possessing and distributing seditious literature he spoke out against the 'fascist plutocracy' of post-war government (Read, *Freedom*, 5). He publicly defended a set of principled political values until the end of his life, joining sit-down protests against nuclear war in 1961, deploring the Vietnam War, and refusing to visit Spain under Franco.

Read personified the responsible, artistically minded intellectual in a democratic age. His sensitive, reticent features were recorded by many artists, including a fine drawing by Jacob Kramer (1914), a witty collage by Kurt Schwitters (1944–7), and Barbara Hepworth's haunting *The Poet Reading to his Children* (1948), variously showing his strength of character, his sense of fun, and his sweetness of nature. A memorable photograph of the 1940s shows a watchful, smiling Read in a tweed suit, a bow tie, and an anarchist's beret, and holding croquet mallets and hoops.

There were contradictions in Read's anarchism; but it was his second wife who persuaded Read, incongruously, to accept a knighthood for services to literature in 1953. To an extent her ebullient, dominant nature complemented his reserve. The daughter of a shipping broker, Charles Frederick Ludwig, and his wife, Helene Meid, **Margaret Read** (1905–1996) was born at 78 Beaconsfield Place, Aberdeen, on 27 March 1905. She was educated at Aberdeen high school before studying music at Edinburgh University under Donald Tovey. She continued her musical education at Cologne before being appointed to a lectureship in the music department at Edinburgh University, where she first met her husband. Ludo, as she was known to her friends, was a gifted viola player; her ambitions to become a composer were sacrificed for her husband. In post-war Yorkshire she revived the Hovingham Musical Festival and made Stonegrave House an unofficial cultural centre in north Yorkshire. It was a marriage of opposites. In particular her ardent Catholicism clashed with Read's liberal agnosticism. But she inspired Read's finest personal writing, *The Innocent Eye*, and the marriage was blessed by 'physical affinity and mutual respect' (King, 150). She died in the Convent of St Nicholas in London on 10 March 1996.

It would be difficult to overestimate Read's importance as an interpreter of continental art and as a supporter of advanced British work in the inter-war period. His contact with German theorists and his awareness of expressive central European and Scandinavian modernism as well as of the school of Paris greatly enriched his polemical *Art Now* (1933). In *Art and Industry* (1934) Read went on to suggest a practical role for the abstract artist—one he had already hinted at in his editorship of the book *Unit One* (1934)—as a designer for mass production. In design and content *Art and Industry* combined the Bauhaus principles of Walter Gropius and Laszlo Moholy-Nagy with a historicist sensibility that enabled Read, for instance, to juxtapose eighteenth-century British silver with modern movement metalwork.

In the early 1930s Read was a tireless supporter and friend of Barbara Hepworth, Henry Moore, and Ben Nicholson, but in 1936 his dialogic and generous mind and his psychoanalytical interests led him to endorse and write the catalogue introduction for the International Surrealist Exhibition held at the New Burlington Galleries, London. This was in part to take up a political position in which surrealism stood for individual freedom against the rising tide of fascism in Europe. Similarly liberal ideals informed two further books, *Art and Society* (1937) and *Education through Art* (1943), and his support for the Society for Education through Art and the 'Pictures for Schools' exhibitions begun in 1947. As director of the Design Research Unit (1943–5) he sought to involve artists with industry.

After the Second World War Read served on numerous committees. Characteristically, he would sit silently, and suddenly make a quiet remark that would settle the matter. He lectured internationally and wrote influential syntheses such as *A Concise History of Modern Painting* (1959) and *A Concise History of Modern Sculpture* (1964). He shaped the British art world of the 1950s, supporting individuals, helping set up the Gregory fellowships for poetry, art, and music at Leeds University, co-founding the Institute of Contemporary Art with Roland Penrose in 1947, and selecting a new post-war generation of British sculptors for the British Pavilion at the Venice Biennale of 1952. But with time he became less receptive to innovation. He found pop art tedious and in 1966 objected to the purchase of Roy Lichtenstein's *Whaam!* by the Tate Gallery. In 1964 a malignant tumour was removed from his tongue; however, his programme of work continued relentlessly. In January 1968 Read spoke at the International Cultural Congress at Havana, Cuba; in March he endured the last among a series of painful operations. He died in his sleep at Stonegrave House on 12 June 1968 and was buried three days later at St Gregory's Minster, Kirkdale, the church where he had worshipped as a small boy.

TANYA HARROD

Sources H. Read, *Annals of innocence and experience* (1940) · B. Read and D. Thistlewood, eds., *Herbert Read: a British vision of world art* (1993) · J. King, *The last modern: a life of Herbert Read* (1990) · G. Woodcock, *Herbert Read: the stream and the source* (1972) · D. Thistlewood, *Herbert Read: formlessness and form: an introduction to his aesthetics* (1984) · D. Goodway, ed., *Herbert Read reassessed* (1998) · *A tribute to Herbert Read, 1893–68* (1975) [exhibition catalogue, Manor House, Ilkley, 25 May – 22 June 1975] · R. Kinross, 'Herbert Read's art and industry: a history', *Journal of Design History*, 1/1 (1988) · *The Times* (5 March 1996) · B. Taylor, *Burlington Magazine*, 110 (Aug 1968) · L. Adeane, 'To the crystal city', BM, Add. MS 71198 [life of Herbert Read] · H. Read, *Freedom: is it a crime?* (1945) · m. certs. · d. cert. · b. cert. [Margaret Ludwig]

Archives NRA, corresp. and literary papers · University of Toronto, corresp. and papers · University of Victoria, British Columbia, archive | CAC Cam., corresp. with Monty Belgion · Lpool RO, corresp. with James Hanley · McMaster University, Hamilton, Ontario, William Ready division of archives and research collections, corresp. with Lord Russell and Lady Russell · Tate collection, corresp. with Lord Clark · Tate collection, letters to Margaret Nash · Tate collection, letters to Lady Norton · Tate collection, corresp. relating to *Unit one* · U. Reading L., letters to George Bell & Sons · V&A NAL, letters to E. Finlay · Yale U., Beinecke L., letters to Naum Gabo and his wife | SOUND BL NSA, performance recordings

Likenesses J. Kramer, drawing, c.1914, priv. coll. · H. Coster, photographs, 1934, NPG · F. Man, photograph, 1940, NPG · K. Schwitters, collage, 1944–7, priv. coll. · photograph, c.1945, Hult. Arch. · B. Hepworth, group portrait, oil and pencil, 1948 (*The poet reading to his children*), Leeds City Art Gallery · photograph, 1949, Hult. Arch. · P. Heron, oils, 1950, NPG · group photograph, 1950, Hult. Arch. · photograph, c.1950, Hult. Arch. · V. Richards, photograph, 1950–59, repro. in Goodway, ed., *Herbert Read* · B. Kneale, oils, 1958, York City Art Gallery · K. Appel, oils, 1962, Montreal Museum of Fine Art, Canada · F. Topolski, drawing, 1962, Royal Collection · M. Gerson, photograph, 1965, NPG · W. Bird, photograph, 1966, NPG · T. Halloway, drawing, repro. in *TLS* (22 Oct 1938) · F. Topolski, portrait, NPG · photograph, NPG · photograph, repro. in *The Times* (8 Dec 1973) · photograph, repro. in *The Times* (13 June 1968) · photographs, Hult. Arch.

Wealth at death £15,266: probate, 24 July 1968, CGPLA Eng. & Wales

Read, Herbert Harold (1889–1970), geologist, was born on 17 December 1889, at Whitstable, Kent, the third of four children of Herbert Read, dairy farmer, and his wife, Caroline Mary, *née* Kearn. He was descended from a long line of small farmers in east Kent, and Whitstable was to remain his family home. He was educated, with a scholarship, at Simon Langton School, Canterbury, where he became head boy, and then from 1908, at the Royal College of Science, London, where he graduated with first-class honours in 1911. After three years on the staff, during which time he gained an MSc, Read joined the Geological Survey of Great Britain. By then he had begun the revision of the already well-established *Rutley's Elements of Mineralogy*, a task he continued through eight successive editions until shortly before his death.

Read's career with the geological survey was interrupted by the First World War, in which he served with the Royal Fusiliers in the Mediterranean and France. He was invalided out in 1917 with the rank of corporal, his discharge papers recording him as 'sober and industrious and suitable for a minor post of trust'! He was still a patient in hospital in Sheffield when, on 21 June 1917, he married Edith Browning (*b.* 1889/90), daughter of Frederick Thomas Browning, coal merchant.

When he returned to the geological survey, Read was assigned to a mapping project in north-east Scotland, his director arguing that a diet of fresh fish in the fishing villages of Banffshire would improve his health. Read's health did improve, and the posting also initiated one of the most fruitful geological research projects of that era. Beginning in Banffshire, his geological studies later extended into Sutherland and thence to Unst, the most northerly of the Shetland Islands, the resulting maps and memoirs including the classic *The Geology of Central Sutherland* (1931).

In 1931 Read was appointed to the chair of geology in the University of Liverpool from where, in 1939, he moved to Imperial College, London, holding the chair of geology there until his retirement in 1955. In both universities he established a strong research tradition, recruiting some of the most able students of his day. Indeed, several of the research projects that he early initiated continued long after his death, particularly those dealing with the metamorphic and migmatitic rocks of northern Scotland and Shetland, and also the granites of Donegal, Ireland. The thrust of his research concerned the nature of regional metamorphism and its variations. Above all, he was concerned with the interrelationship between metamorphic rocks and granites, and the very nature of granite itself.

Read's views were highly influential, not least because he was an enthusiastic teacher, a highly accomplished lecturer, and a master of lucid prose. Although never averse to the introduction of new laboratory-based techniques he retained a certain scepticism concerning the overenthusiastic application of the early experimental results to complex geological phenomena and enjoyed his reputation as one of the most effective of disputants in some of the central debates of his time. The series of challenging addresses that he gave while presiding successively over the British Association, section C (1939), the Geologists' Association (1942–4), the Geological Society of London (1947–8), and as a keynote speaker at international conferences, were reprinted in book form as *The Granite Controversy* (1957), which remains a geological classic. He is said to have composed the elements of these important essays while on firewatching duties on the roof of Imperial College during the Second World War. A crowning achievement was his presidency, in 1948, of the eighteenth International Geological Congress in London.

Long after his retirement, Read's geological hammer continued to resound in the field, particularly in Donegal,

and from his pen flowed further important contributions which included three popular textbooks, two of which were written in conjunction with Janet Watson. Read received many honours including election to the Norwegian, French, and Belgian academies. He had been elected a fellow of the Royal Society in 1939 and in 1963 he received the Royal medal. He was also awarded the Bigsby, Wollaston, Penrose, and Steinmann medals, the principal awards of the geological societies of London, the United States, and Germany. Other honours included honorary doctorates of Columbia University (1954) and Dublin (1956), and honorary membership of the Royal Irish Academy. He came to be revered as an elder statesman, both in geological circles and at Imperial College, where he was successively dean of the Royal School of Mines (1943–5), pro-rector (1952–5), and acting head of the college (1954–5).

A plain-speaking and modest man, Read nevertheless viewed life with acuity, being fully awake to its vagaries. He was deeply religious, and during his many years of residence in his native Whitstable took an active part in the work of the parish. He died at his home, 35 Millstrood Road, Whitstable, on 29 March 1970, survived by his wife, Edith, and their only daughter, Marguerite.

W. S. PITCHER

Sources J. Sutton, *Memoirs FRS*, 16 (1970), 479–97 · D. Williams, 'Herbert Harold Read: an appreciation', *Proceedings of the Geologists' Association*, 81 (1970) · H. H. Read, *The granite controversy: geological addresses illustrating the evolution of a disputant* (1957) · personal knowledge (2004) · m. cert. · P. A. Sabine, *Year book*, RSE (1971–2), 1–3
Likenesses portrait, repro. in Williams, 'Herbert Harold Read', pl. 12, facing p. 405
Wealth at death £9111: probate, 19 June 1970, *CGPLA Eng. & Wales*

Read, Sir Herbert James (1863–1949), civil servant and colonial governor, was born at Honiton, Devon, on 17 March 1863, the second son of Charles Read, proprietor of a drapery store, and his wife, Mary Ann Avery. Read was educated at Allhallows School, Honiton, and at Brasenose College, Oxford, where he was an exhibitioner and gained a first in mathematics in 1884. He was also a good classical scholar, and his knowledge of the history of London in recent times was encyclopaedic.

Read entered the civil service as a higher division clerk at the War Office in 1887. In 1889 he was transferred to the Colonial Office where he remained until retirement. As a civil servant Read linked the Colonial Office to the world of science, championing—from within Whitehall—the practical application of scientific innovation for the benefit of those living and working in the empire, a generation before 'development and welfare' became serious official concerns. Throughout his career his work was mainly concerned with Britain's tropical African empire. In the colonial secretary, Joseph Chamberlain, who selected him as his assistant private secretary in 1896–8, Read found an appreciative and congenial chief. In turn, Read 'stimulated his chief's interest in tropical medicine', ensuring Chamberlain's 'desire to innovate was well fed, and that Colonial Office inertia was circumvented' (Kubicek,

Administration of Imperialism, 20, 142). He played a vital role in the early twentieth-century drive against tropical diseases, and matched scientific and technical advances with official support for their application throughout the empire.

Read was exceptional among his official colleagues, most of whom were graduates in the arts, in his quick recognition of the importance of scientific research in the future administration and development of tropical dependencies. He was largely instrumental in stimulating official interest in organizations concerned with tropical medicine and agriculture and in establishing contacts between his department and scientific institutions, some of which, such as the London School of Hygiene and Tropical Medicine and the Commonwealth institutes of entomology and mycology, owe their inception largely to him. The early investigation of trypanosomiasis in Uganda was directly due to his influence.

Read's promotion within the Colonial Office was rapid: he rose to be head, in turn, of both the east and west African departments. In 1911–12 he visited east Africa at a time when overseas visits by Colonial Office officials were rare. In 1916 he was appointed an assistant under-secretary of state with supervision over the two African departments. He became a prominent member of several committees which were greatly indebted to him for their achievements. This was due to his 'veritable genius for committee work, not only setting them up, but for seeing there was work for them to do and that they got on with it' (Mason-Bahr, 128).

Read was chairman of the colonial survey committee in 1905–24, of the colonial advisory medical and sanitary committee in 1909–24, of the committee on staffing of the agriculture departments in the colonies in 1919, and of the Bureau of Hygiene and Tropical Diseases in 1908–24. He served as British delegate to several international conferences, including the African liquor conference, Brussels, 1895, the commission on the Anglo-German frontier in east Africa, Berlin, 1905, the sleeping sickness conference, London, 1907–8, and the African arms traffic conference, Brussels, 1908. He was senior member of the Colonial Office delegacy to the Paris peace conference in 1919. Read went overseas as governor of Mauritius from 1925 to 1930 for the final phase of his official career. He was a vigorous governor, but his tour was hampered by the depression in the sugar industry on which the island depended, and by the death of his son there. He is remembered in Mauritius more for his good intentions than for his concrete achievements.

In retirement Read resumed the activities in keeping with his aptitudes, serving on a large number of committees concerned not only with scientific research but with social welfare, an interest to which he was now able to devote more time. He was an active member of the Reform Club, a fellow of the Royal Astronomical Society, and an honorary fellow of the Society for the Preservation of the Fauna of the Empire. He was a long-standing member of the committee of the Imperial Cancer Research Fund, a crown trustee of the London Parochial Charities,

chairman of the Corona Club, and Colonial Office representative on the governing body of Imperial College, and later chairman of its executive committee. He was a member of the court of the London School of Hygiene and Tropical Medicine, Colonial Office representative on the governing body of the Seamen's Hospital Society, and Colonial Office representative on the council of the Liverpool School of Tropical Medicine, and later honorary vice-president of the school. These latter positions provided the institutions with a Colonial Office link.

Tall, stooping, and superficially shy, Read had a lovable nature and ready sense of humour, and was effusive and genial in private. He endeared himself to his junior colleagues—particularly by his habit of retreating before them during discussion conducted standing up—and enjoyed a happy domestic life. He married in 1905 Violet Kate (*d.* 1951), daughter of Major Duncan Maclachlan, 90th regiment; they had one son and one daughter.

Read was appointed CMG in 1907, promoted KCMG in 1918 and GCMG in 1935, and appointed CB in 1914; he became a commander of the order of the crown of Belgium in 1919. He died at the Clarence Nursing Home, Tunbridge Wells, on 16 October 1949.

E. W. Evans, *rev.* Ashley Jackson

Sources *The Times* (18 Oct 1949) • P. Mason-Bahr, *History of the School of Tropical Medicine in London, 1899–1949* (1956), 127–8 • R. V. Kubicek, *The administration of imperialism: Joseph Chamberlain at the colonial office* (1969), p. 20 and chap. 7 • R. V. Kubicek, 'Joseph Chamberlain and the colonial office: a study in imperial administration', PhD diss., Duke U., 1965, 44–5 • *WWW, 1941–50* • C. Parkinson, *The colonial office from within* [1947], 48–9, 64 • R. D. Furse, *Aucuparius: recollections of a recruiting officer* (1962), 69, 70, 123, 137, 140 • P. J. Barnwell and A. Toussaint, *A short history of Mauritius* (1949), chap. 21 • C. Jeffries, *The colonial office* (1956), 18 • *CGPLA Eng. & Wales* (1950) • private information (1959) • personal knowledge (1959) • P. J. Barnwell, *Dictionnaire de biographie Mauricienne / The dictionary of Mauritian biography*
Likenesses W. Stoneman, photographs, 1920–31, NPG
Wealth at death £14,363 16s.: probate, 27 Jan 1950, *CGPLA Eng. & Wales*

Read, Sir (Charles) Hercules (1857–1929), museum curator, was born at Gillingham, Kent, on 6 July 1857, the third son of John Finsbury Read and his wife, Catherine, daughter of Hercules Angus, of Shetland. His father was a colour sergeant. He was apparently educated privately, and went to work at the South Kensington Museum at the age of sixteen or seventeen, but in 1874 was employed privately by A. W. Franks to act as his clerk and to assist in registering the ethnographical collections which Henry Christy had bequeathed to the British Museum in 1865. In 1880 Read was appointed assistant in the department of British and medieval antiquities and ethnography, of which he became keeper in succession to Franks in 1896. He retired in 1921.

Read is an enigma; good-looking and socially accomplished, he clearly had a chip on his shoulder concerning his lack of university education. He owed everything to Franks, with whom he travelled and through whom he became acquainted with many of the leading antiquaries of his day. Franks encouraged his career, made him secretary of the Society of Antiquaries in 1892, and ultimately made him the chief executor of his remarkable bequest to the museum (a difficult job, which Read took seriously). Kipling described Read as 'externally … very handsome, but his professional soul was black, even for that of a Curator …' (Kipling, 84–5), while his obituaries hint at an uneasy manner and shallow scholarship. He was deeply resentful that he did not succeed Maunde Thompson as principal librarian of the museum in 1909 and this is perhaps the 'unhappiness' mentioned by his obituarists. His successor, the gentle O. M. Dalton, wrote of him, 'he had a militant side to his nature, and what may be described as his imperfect sympathies were neither concealed nor readily abandoned' (Dalton, 529). He could be tough as an administrator, often for the right reasons, but attempts to humanize him sound stilted. One colleague, however, wrote more warmly that:

> His geniality and talent as a raconteur often enlivened the little marble-topped table round which his staff used to foregather with ritual punctuality at 4 p.m., and where the more entertaining experiences of museum life were interchanged in a social atmosphere. (Braunholtz, 112)

Read was, in effect, the first professional ethnographer in the British Museum, in which role he must have been trained by Franks; but like all members of staff at the time he had to range very widely in covering the department's collections, from Africa to Greenland and from America to Japan. His breadth of knowledge is agreed by all; but his knowledge was not deep. He was successful in acquiring material for the museum and was one of the founders of the Friends of the British Museum (one of the elements which later fused into the National Art Collections Fund). He wrote no major book, but he contributed many articles to professional journals and encouraged his staff to publish catalogues; he also initiated the series of popular departmental guides which are still useful works of reference. Rather surprisingly he was elected to the British Academy in 1913.

Read was a public man and an impressive speaker; he was twice president of the Society of Antiquaries of London (his predecessor Lord Lubbock, who was chancellor of St Andrews, obtained for him an honorary degree). As was then normal his presidency of the Society of Antiquaries led to his knighthood in 1912. He was president of section H of the British Association for the Advancement of Science, twice president of the Anthropological Institute, and a member of the Burlington Fine Arts Club. He had a broad range of acquaintanceship, none perhaps more important than his friendship with the American collector J. Pierpont Morgan, with whom he occasionally travelled. It was probably through Morgan that he was offered a post—reluctantly rejected—in the USA. Read married on 17 August 1880 Helen May, elder daughter of Frederick George Smith of Chelsea; they had two daughters. He died after a long illness at the Grand Hotel Excelsior, New Casino, Rapallo, Italy, on 11 February 1929.

DAVID M. WILSON

Sources DNB · O. M. Dalton, 'Sir Hercules Read, 1857–1929', PBA, 15 (1929), 519–35 · R. Kipling, Something of myself and other autobiographical writings, ed. T. Pinney (1991) · H. J. Braunholtz, 'History of ethnography in the museum, 1753–1938, pt 2', British Museum Quarterly, 18 (1953), 109–20 · J. Evans, A history of the Society of Antiquaries (1956) · M. Caygill and J. Cherry, eds., A. W. Franks: nineteenth-century collecting and the British Museum (1997) · m. cert. · CGPLA Eng. & Wales (1929)

Archives BM | Bodl. Oxf., corresp. with J. L. Myers · Bodl. Oxf., corresp. with Sir Aurel Stein · Salisbury and South Wiltshire Museum, letters to A. H. L. F. Pitt-Rivers · W. Yorks. AS, Bradford, letters to W. P. Baildon

Likenesses S. Lucas, drawing, 1912 · W. Stoneman, photograph, 1919, NPG · A. John, oils, 1921, Athenaeum, London

Wealth at death £64,448 13s. 1d.: resworn probate, 13 March 1929, CGPLA Eng. & Wales

Read, James (1777–1852), missionary in Cape Colony and political activist, was born on 3 December 1777, in Abridge, Essex, the son of Joseph and Susannah Read. A carpenter of little education, by early manhood he was a member of the Hackney church of the Anglican evangelical John Eyre. In November 1798 he set sail for the south seas under the aegis of the London Missionary Society (LMS). The LMS vessel was captured by the French off Brazil, and it was a year before Read could return to London, after vicissitudes which included stays in Montevideo and Lisbon. Undeterred, he next set sail for the Cape Colony, and arrived in Cape Town in September 1800.

The then British governor, Dundas, feared that evangelicals would further destabilize the war-torn eastern frontier of this recently acquired colony. He therefore refused Read permission to join his elderly Dutch colleague, the strong-willed, unconventional Johannes Theodorus van der Kemp, in his mission to the Xhosa of Ngqika beyond the colony. Read evangelized British soldiers instead, until 1801, when van der Kemp abandoned the Xhosa mission and the two missionaries met in Graaff-Reinet, a small settlement in the north-east of the colony, plunged into conflict between Africans and white farmers. There Read began his lifelong work among the Khoi-Khoi, once seminomadic cattle herders but now devastated by colonialism.

Despite violent settler resistance Read and van der Kemp ministered to a group of about 700 Khoi-Khoi refugees who had fled from frontier warfare. In August 1801 the two briefly visited Ngqika. In 1802 they led a small group of Khoi-Khoi to Botha's Farm, Algoa Bay. After an attack by other Khoi-Khoi who saw this group as having sold out, the community moved to Fort Frederick during the 1802 British withdrawal. In 1803 the incoming Batavian regime allotted new land for what would become Bethelsdorp, the first permanent African mission station of the LMS. On 20 June 1803 Read married Elizabeth Valentyn (1779–1849), a Khoi-Khoi convert. The couple had four surviving daughters and three sons, including James Read junior (1811–1894). In 1805 van der Kemp ordained Read after the congregation 'called' him as minister.

Emotional religious conversions occurred at Bethelsdorp at a time of great stress for the Khoi-Khoi and other groups, including former slaves. The station earned intense colonial opprobrium in the 1800s and 1810s, in large part because landless labourers used residence there to escape *de facto* forced labour on white farms. Laziness and sexual debauchery were said to be rampant, and the missionaries were accused in colonial circles of living like the Khoi-Khoi instead of 'raising' them up. There was also conflict over Khoi-Khoi obligations to carry out public work, and over conditions in the Khoi-Khoi regiment in Cape Town. In 1805 Read and van der Kemp were detained at the Cape by Governor Janssens, a Batavian. The incoming British permitted the pair to return in 1806. Read and van der Kemp continued to complain about settler violence against the Khoi-Khoi; in 1808 Read published a vivid account in the *Transactions of the London Missionary Society*. In the wake of high-level official comment, which may have pushed the government to establish district circuit courts in 1811, a series of court cases in 1812 lodged by Read and certain Khoi-Khoi plaintiffs threw the eastern Cape into turmoil; the judges' report may have concealed the truth, but the so-called 'black circuit' remained a significant Afrikaner grievance against the British.

In 1811 van der Kemp died, and Read became the LMS African superintendent. In 1816 he helped to revive a mission to the Xhosa and then led a large team of men and women from Bethelsdorp to found a mission beyond the colony to the southern Tswana Tlhaping. In 1817, however, dissatisfied LMS missionaries at the Cape accused Read and several others of sexual immorality and political insubordination, revealing that Read had had an illegitimate son with Sabina Pretorius, a Khoi convert. LMS directors dispatched two investigators, one of whom, John Philip (1775–1851), replaced Read as superintendent. Read was removed from Dithakong in 1820 and compelled to make a public confession at Bethelsdorp. He and his wife continued to work at Bethelsdorp, under James Kitchingman's headship.

Shortly after his return Read again earned official sanction after lodging accusations before the incoming acting governor, Sir Rufane Donkin, about maltreatment of the Khoi-Khoi. Although Donkin found the accusations malicious, in 1821 John Philip examined evidence which substantiated Read's claims and triggered his own campaign for race-blind legislation in southern Africa. The role of the work of Philip and Read in the 1828 passage of ordinance 50, which *inter alia* removed racial distinctions from Cape law, has been disputed; the LMS certainly took the credit, however, earning both loyalty and scorn as a result.

In 1829 a settlement of 'free' Khoi-Khoi was established on recently conquered land at Kat River as a buffer between settlers and Xhosa. Members of this community called Read as their minister. Read helped relay Khoi-Khoi protests against the Cape Colony's restoration of vagrancy legislation in 1834 after the abolition of slavery, and the authorities in London then overturned the legislation. When frontier warfare began again in 1834–5, Read channelled Xhosa complaints to Philip, who, through Thomas Fowell Buxton, had indirect influence with the Colonial Office. Meanwhile, Governor D'Urban banished the Reads from Kat River; Read blamed the governor for the death of his seventeen-year-old daughter during the move. In 1836–7 Read, Philip, James Read junior, Andries Stoffels, and Dyani Tshatshu travelled to London to testify

before the House of Commons select committee on Aborigines—a committee engineered by Fowell Buxton in part to publicize south African issues. D'Urban was recalled, and land was returned to the Xhosa, but Read returned to Africa in February 1838 to find himself one of the most hated men in the colony.

Kat River Khoi-Khoi ran important missions, co-ordinated by Read, among neighbouring African communities, including San and Thembu groups. Read argued throughout for an African clergy and for congregational autonomy in the choice of ministers, including the right to dismiss white missionaries. By the 1840s the majority of other LMS missionaries were infuriated by what they saw as Read's attempts to undermine their authority with local peoples. Tensions culminated in the mid-1840s when a large faction of the LMS, spearheaded by Henry Calderwood, tried unsuccessfully to oust Read, confirming the latter's growing isolation.

In 1846 frontier warfare erupted again. Kat River settlers, including Read and his sons, supported the colonial side, but the community was none the less subject to colonial abuse and was not recompensed for losses; thereafter it was maladministered, and harshly. It continued to bear the brunt of racially discriminatory economic policies as British settlers gained more political power. In 1851 many Khoi-Khoi, including a large minority of Kat River inhabitants, and other members of what was coming to be called the 'coloured' community, joined the Xhosa side during further frontier warfare as a consequence of their treatment by the colonial administration and the settlers. Read and his son James desperately tried to prevent the rebellion but were told by rebels that Read's 'writing to London' was no longer effective. In the disastrous aftermath of the failed rebellion, the government encouraged the purchase of much of Kat River by white land speculators. The elderly Khoi-Khoi *veldcornet* Andries Botha was condemned to death (though the sentence was later commuted) in a trial which was widely seen as a judgment on the entire Kat River Khoi-Khoi community, and particularly on James Read.

Read died at Eland's Post at the Kat River settlement, deeply depressed, on 8 May 1852, on the same day that Botha's death sentence was announced. He was buried locally, at Philipton. Caught between colonial ambiguities and convinced of his own failure, he probably had a greater impact in a variety of ways than most other missionaries of his generation.

ELIZABETH ELBOURNE

Sources D. Williams, 'Read, James', *DSAB* · South Africa: incoming correspondence, 1800–52, SOAS, Archives of the Council for World Mission (incorporating the London Missionary Society), box 27/2/C · B. Le Cordeur and C. Saunders, eds., *The Kitchingman papers: missionary letters and journals, 1817–1848, from the Brenthurst collection*, Johannesburg (1976) · G. M. Theal, ed., *Records of the Cape Colony*, 36 vols. (1897–1905) · J. Read, *The Kat river settlement in 1851* (1852) · 'Select committee on aborigines in British settlements', *Parl. papers* (1836), vol. 7, no. 538 · 'Select committee on aborigines', *Parl. papers* (1837), 7.238, no. 425 · I. H. Enklaar, *Life and work of Dr. J. Th. van der Kemp, 1747–1811: missionary pioneer and protagonist of racial equality in South Africa* (1988) · C. Saunders, 'James Read:

towards a reassessment', *The societies of southern Africa in the 19th and 20th centuries*, 7 (1976), 19–25 • A. Ross, *John Philip, 1775–1851: missions, race and politics in South Africa* (1986) • Memorial from Philipton settlers, 1834, Cape Archives, A50 • Cape Archives, Bethelsdorp MSS, private accessions 559 and 768 • D. I. Stuart, '"Of savages and heroes": discourses of race, nation and gender in the evangelical missions to southern Africa in the early nineteenth century', PhD diss., U. Lond., Institute of Commonwealth Studies, 1994 • E. Elbourne, 'Early Khoisan uses of mission Christianity', *Missions and Christianity in South African history*, ed. H. Bredekamp and R. Ross (1995)

Archives Brenthurst Library, Johannesburg, Kitchingman MSS • SOAS, Council for World Mission archives • Cape Town, South Africa, government MSS

Likenesses H. Room, group portrait, oils, *c.*1837 (before the House of Commons select committee on aborigines); formerly at Livingstone House, London • S. W. Fenning, group portrait, watercolour sketch, 1842, repro. in Le Cordeur and Saunders, eds., *Kitchingman papers* • R. Woodman, engraving, 1844 (after H. Room), repro. in Le Cordeur and Saunders, eds., *Kitchingman papers* • engraving (after portrait by E. B. Morris), repro. in *Evangelical Magazine* (July 1839), facing p. 313

Wealth at death presumed very little. London Missionary Society archives, letter from James Read jun. to London Missionary Society directors, 1852

Read, John (*fl.* 1588), surgeon, is presumed to have been a native of Gloucestershire. He was apparently in practice in Gloucester in 1587, since he describes his involvement in the prosecution of a Flemish quack in that year, although 'the matter was excused by way of charitie to be good to straungers'. Read probably came to London later that year. He was licensed by the archbishop of Canterbury on 6 January 1588, and on 24 June that same year was licensed to marry Cicely, daughter of John *Banister, lecturer in anatomy to the London Company of Barber–Surgeons. Banister had been admitted to the company as a foreign brother in 1572, but Read never joined, although he was on friendly terms with some of its leading members. He was one of a group of late sixteenth-century London surgeons, including Banister, William Clowes, and Thomas Gale, who endeavoured to raise the status of their profession. His principal claim to fame is his *A most excellent and compendious method of curing woundes in the head, and in other partes of the body*, published in 1588 but evidently completed in the preceding year; it was entered in the Stationers' register on 10 November 1587. It is for the most part a translation of *De recta curandorum vulnerum ratione* by Franciscus Arcaeus, but also includes John Arderne's *Treatise of the Fistula*, as well as an English version of the Hippocratic oath, various miscellaneous pieces, and substantial interpolations by Read. The dedication, addressed to Banister, Clowes, and William Pickering, described as 'my very good and loving friends', reiterates Read's beliefs 'that all chirurgians ought to be seene in phisicke [examined in medicine]: and that the barbors crafte ought to be a distinct mistery from chirurgery'. The latter of these desiderata came to pass in 1745 when the barbers and surgeons became separate companies, and the former in 1868 when the royal colleges of Physicians and Surgeons introduced reciprocal representation on their examining boards, followed in 1884 by the establishment of the conjoint examining board. Read further stresses his belief in

the unity of medicine and surgery in a six-page poem entitled 'A Complaint of the Abuse of the Noble Arte of Chirurgerie'. The other theme running through Read's work is his opposition to the activities of quacks, and he refers several times to the earlier writings of John Hall of Maidstone on this subject.   JOHN SYMONS

Sources *DNB* • J. Read, *A most … compendious method of curing woundes* (1588) • D'A. Power, 'John Banester', *British Journal of Surgery*, 5 (1917–18), 8–16 • D'A. Power, 'The education of a surgeon under Thomas Vicary', *British Journal of Surgery*, 8 (1920–21), 240–58 • A. W. J. Haggis, 'Register of episcopal medical licences' (typescript), Wellcome L., Western MSS 5334–5340, 5338 P–R • J. L. Chester and G. J. Armytage, eds., *Allegations for marriage licences issued by the bishop of London*, 1, Harleian Society, 25 (1887) • private information (2004) [I. G. Murray, archivist, Worshipful Company of Barbers]

Read, John (1884–1963), organic chemist, was born in Maiden Newton, Dorset, on 17 February 1884, in his father's seventieth year, the younger of two children of John Read, yeoman farmer, and his wife, Bessie Gatcombe. Apart from his sister, Read also had five older half-brothers and six older half-sisters. Both his parents were descended from a long line of farmers, and he was the first member of the family not to become a farmer.

Read was identified early as a clever boy at the village school at Sparkford, and proceeded after only three years to Sexey's School, Bruton, at the top of the county junior scholarship list; he left there in 1901 as head boy with a senior Somerset county scholarship of £60 per annum. He then spent four years at Finsbury Technical College, London, where he attended courses in both science and engineering before obtaining the college's diploma and chemistry prize in 1904, and becoming for a short time a college demonstrator in the department of chemistry. He was then awarded a London county council senior scholarship which enabled him to leave London, which he disliked, for the University of Zürich, to study for a doctorate under Professor Alfred Werner, then in the prime of his scientific life.

It is clear from his writings that Read enjoyed Zürich University. Not only did he find the scientific scene stimulating and rewarding, but he was able to develop his interest and proficiency in foreign languages, an interest which he maintained throughout his life. Although not directly involved in Werner's renowned research on the stereochemistry of inorganic complexes—that is, a study of the consequences of the three-dimensional structure of molecules containing metallic ions—he was greatly influenced by the stereochemical concepts being widely discussed. Consequently, after a successful defence of his PhD thesis in 1907, two years after his arrival in Zürich, Read decided to spend the remaining year of his scholarship at the Municipal School of Technology in Manchester, working with W. J. Pope, who had earned an international reputation for his studies of the stereochemistry of organic compounds (those based on carbon). Read's decision was important in determining his career, because in 1908 Pope was appointed to the chair of chemistry at Cambridge, and took Read with him as his assistant. Read became a member of Emmanuel College with the status of advanced student. In 1912 he was granted an MA.

For the next eight years Read was committed to his chemistry and made significant discoveries in the field of organic stereochemistry. His dedication is illustrated by the story of his synthesis of methyl ethyl selenide, which not only has one of the most offensive smells known, but can be detected at remarkably low concentrations. In view of this Read felt it wise to synthesize the substance in the open air on the roof of his laboratory; unfortunately his efforts coincided with a number of garden parties held to celebrate the Darwin centenary, and the subsequent furore forced Read into the fens to complete his work. There he noted that both insects and cows were attracted by the smell: 'Their whole behaviour indicated that they felt they were missing something really good'.

A major change occurred in 1916 when Read, at the age of thirty-two, was appointed to the chair of organic chemistry in Sydney, Australia. After a long and anxious voyage he arrived to find that he was required to give his first lecture that very day. The problems facing him were now very different. Large classes, the design and supervision of the construction of a new chemistry building, and the administration of the department all combined to reduce the time available for research. Nevertheless, Read initiated and pursued what came to be recognized as a significant investigation of the structure (and stereochemistry) of a series of organic materials which he isolated from Australian flora. These studies were all the more commendable because Read had very little research assistance.

While in Australia, in 1916 Read married Ida, daughter of Arthur Suddards, of Bradford, Yorkshire; they had two sons. Read was very happy in Sydney and his decision in 1923 to accept an invitation to succeed Robert Robinson in the Purdie chair of chemistry at St Andrews was not an easy one. The department there, first under Thomas Purdie, with his foresight in recognizing the importance of research in the context of university chemistry, and then under his outstanding pupil J. C. Irvine, had a reputation which had been enhanced by Robinson, despite his short stay (1921–2). Read soon settled down in the St Andrews atmosphere of scholarship and went on to produce a steady stream of original papers as well as a very successful series of textbooks; his *A Direct Entry to Organic Chemistry* (1948) ran to many editions and Read received, in 1949, the Premio Europeo-Cortina, a prize of 1 million lire for the best popular work in the field of physical science published in Europe in the preceding five years.

Read had always been interested in history; he said that, given a choice and free from the pressures of a science-orientated school, he would have specialized in history or languages, rather than science. Once at St Andrews he devoted more time to these interests, building up and writing about an extraordinarily important collection of manuscripts, books, and engravings relating to the history of science, and to alchemy. One notable outcome was his *Humour and Humanism in Chemistry* (1947). His interest in the dialects of Somerset and Dorset also found expression

in a series of plays and *The Farmer's Joy* (1949). His wide distinction is summarized by the citation of Read as 'one of the most versatile of Scientists as well known for his literary accomplishments as for his researches in organic chemistry', on his receiving the Dexter award for services to the history of chemistry, from the American Chemical Society (1959).

Read remained in St Andrews for almost forty years. He was widely acclaimed during his lifetime and was elected FRS in 1935, having gained his ScD at Cambridge in 1934. He was most proud, however, of the esteem in which he was held by his pupils. He was an excellent teacher and kindly man, who appeared untouched by the hurly-burly of modern chemical life.

Read died at his home, 1 Donaldson Gardens, St Andrews, on 21 January 1963, just one month short of his seventy-ninth birthday. He was survived by his wife.

JOHN CADOGAN, *rev.*

Sources E. L. Hirst, *Memoirs FRS*, 9 (1963), 237–60 · J. Read, *Humour and humanism in chemistry* (1947) · private information (1981) · *CGPLA Eng. & Wales* (1963)
Archives U. St Andr. L., scrapbook
Likenesses W. Stoneman, black and white photograph, 1946, RS · black and white polyfoto portrait, 1948, RS
Wealth at death £29,626 6s.: confirmation, 28 May 1963, *CCI*

Read, Katharine (1723–1778), portrait painter, was born on 3 February 1723 in Dundee, Forfarshire, the daughter of Alexander Read of Turfbeg, a Dundee merchant, and his wife, Elizabeth, *née* Wedderburn (1699–1756), daughter of Sir John Wedderburn, baronet. The family's strong Jacobite connections and the ensuing failure of the 1745 rising may have been a contributing factor in the decision to send her to Paris in 1745 to study crayon painting under Maurice-Quentin de La Tour. She remained in Paris until 1751, when she moved to Rome with the financial support of her brother, Captain Alexander Read. Her chaperone was the Abbé Peter Grant, the Roman agent for the Catholic church in Scotland. It was through the Abbé Grant's connections that she was able to establish a clientele from the Italian aristocracy and the transient British expatriate community who were in Rome on the grand tour. She was hopeful that her stay in Rome would enable her to establish herself as a professional artist in Britain, stating in a letter of 1752 to her brother, 'I have staid one year in Rome for Improvement, I must certainly stay in it another for Name, and then you'll see I'll top it with the best of them' (K. Read to A. Read, 6 Jan 1752, priv. coll.).

Read returned to Britain and set up her studio in London in 1753, establishing a reputation as one of the most fashionable portrait painters in crayon which she sustained for over twenty years. Inevitably she was compared to her male counterparts, as one critic stated: 'After *Cotes*, our best painter in crayons, (and perhaps the only good one) is Miss Read. She likewise paints very well in oil. Her pencilling is free and easy, and her colouring has a great deal of truth' (*Observations on the Pictures now in Exhibition at the Royal Academy, Spring Gardens, and Mr Christie's*, 1771, 6). She painted members of the royal family, including *A Portrait of her Majesty* [Queen Charlotte] *with the Prince of Wales* (exh.

Free Society of Artists, 1763) and *The Two Young Princes of Wales* (exh. Free Society of Artists, 1765) which depicts the prince of Wales with his brother, Frederick. An example of her oil painting is *The Countess of Sussex* (Ranger's House, Greenwich, London). An indication of the prices paid for her work is revealed in a letter of 1772: 12 guineas for a Madonna; 20 guineas for a portrait in crayon; 35 guineas for a half-length portrait in oils (Read to Lord (?), 17 Feb 1772, priv. coll.). She also appears to have had connections with literary circles, painting the actor David Garrick and executing two portraits of his wife, Eva Maria Garrick (Victoria and Albert Museum, London).

Katharine Read remained unmarried and lived for some years with her niece, Helena Beatson. Beatson demonstrated much artistic talent, a fact noted by Frances Burney on one of her visits to Read's studio (*Early Diary*, 284). In February 1777 Read, accompanied by her niece, travelled to India in the hope of establishing a practice for herself in Madras. In October 1777 Helena Beatson married Sir Charles Oakley, bt, governor of Madras. With her health failing, Read set sail for the Cape in 1778, and *en route* died on a Dutch ship on 15 December 1778; she was buried at sea. Her will of 1777, revised on 29 January 1778, details her substantial assets, accrued through her earnings as a professional crayon painter.

F. M. O'DONOGHUE, rev. DORCAS TAYLOR

Sources V. Manners, 'Catherine Read: the "English Rosalba"', *The Connoisseur*, 88 (1931), 376–86 · A. F. Steuart, 'Miss Katherine Read, court paintress', *SHR*, 2 (1904–5), 38–46 · W. Foster, 'British artists in India, 1760–1820', *Walpole Society*, 19 (1930–31), 1–88 · M. Archer, *India and British portraiture, 1770–1825* (1979) · E. Edwards, *Anecdotes of painters* (1808); facs. edn (1970) · *The early diary of Frances Burney, 1768–1778*, ed. A. R. Ellis, 2 vols. (1889) · J. Ingamells, ed., *A dictionary of British and Irish travellers in Italy, 1701–1800* (1997) · correspondence, priv. coll. · A. D. O. Wedderburn, *The Wedderburn book*, 1 (privately printed, 1898) · exhibition catalogues (1760–78) [Society of Artists] · exhibition catalogues (1761–78) [Free Society of Artists] · M. Morgan, 'Katherine Read: a woman painter in Romney's London', *Transactions of the Romney Society*, 4 (1999), 12–17

Archives NRA, priv. coll., corresp.

Likenesses R. Carriera, portrait, 1774? · K. Read, self-portrait, repro. in Manners, 'Catherine Read: the "English Rosalba"'

Wealth at death approx. £20,000: will, 29 Jan 1778, PRO

Read, Margaret, Lady Read (1905–1996). *See under* Read, Sir Herbert Edward (1893–1968).

Read, Margaret Helen (1889–1991), social anthropologist and colonial educationist, was born at Battersea Rise, south London, on 5 August 1889. She was the first of two children (including a son born in 1892) of Mabyn Read (1854–1936), a doctor and later the first medical officer of health in the town of Worcester, and Isabel Lawford (1863–1904). She was educated at Roedean School and later at Newnham College, Cambridge, where she studied history for three years (1908–11)—at a time when women were not awarded degrees at Cambridge—followed by a one-year diploma in geography. She never married though in later life confided to her half-brother's wife that she had once been engaged but that her husband-to-be died in the First World War. During that war she lived in London, but in 1919 she went to India to stay with her brother, a civil engineer, who spent most of his adult working life there. In later years she was guardian to his two children when they returned to England for educational reasons.

In the early 1920s Read acquired a lifelong interest in social anthropology by studying the women and children left behind in India by Indian migrant workers. This research, published in 1931 as *Indian Peasant Uprooted: a Study of the Human Machine*, was highly original for its time. In 1930 Read enrolled at the London School of Economics to study for a PhD in anthropology under Malinowski, the leading proponent of 'functionalism'. She was subsequently awarded a research fellowship by the International African Institute to study the effects of migratory labour on village life in Nyasaland. This work was later published as *The Ngoni of Nyasaland* (1956) and *Children of their Fathers: Growing up amongst the Nyoni of Nyasaland* (1959), both of which were subsequently reprinted. The latter is probably the most widely read of her published work today.

In the late 1930s Read so impressed Sir Fred Clarke, then director of the London Institute of Education, with her occasional lectures on the problems of culture clash in the colonial setting that he appointed her temporary head of the colonial department in 1940. Within a short time she was a close confidant of Christopher Cox, the educational adviser to the Colonial Office, and Arthur Creech Jones, later colonial secretary in Attlee's post-war Labour government. During the Second World War she played a key role in promoting the concept of mass or non-formal education, later called community development, as a central aspect of colonial education policy. In 1943 she started a long association with the Colonial Office advisory committee on education in the colonies which lasted until 1955. In June 1943 she was appointed a member of the Elliot commission, which examined the future of university education in west Africa.

Read's work for the Colonial Office continued unabated after 1945. She was a British delegate to UNESCO general conferences in Paris in 1946 and Mexico City in 1947, and a founding member of the Social Science Research Council and the advisory committee on colonial colleges of arts, science and technology. In 1947 she and Freda Gwilliam, the woman educational adviser (sic) to the Colonial Office, visited Northern Rhodesia and Nyasaland and reported on the education of women and girls. In 1950 she figured prominently in top-level Colonial Office discussions to decide how best to head off a Conservative call for a commission to reassess colonial education policy. She was also a leading speaker at the subsequent colonial education conference held at Cambridge in 1952.

In 1945 Read became permanent head of the colonial department at the Institute of Education, with the status of reader. Four years later she was appointed professor of education 'with special reference to colonial areas' and appointed CBE for her services to colonial education. On several occasions in the 1950s she was a visiting professor at American universities and did much to promote closer Anglo-American ties in education. In 1955 she published

Education and Social Change in Tropical Areas, a text which remained popular in American universities long after it was superseded in her homeland.

After retiring from the Institute of Education, Read reverted to her original role as a social anthropologist and spent a further fifteen productive years travelling widely as a United Nations consultant on health education, nursing, and community development. In 1966 she wrote a further book, *Culture, health and disease: social and cultural influences on health programmes in developing countries*.

One of the first British academics to combine the concerns of anthropology with those of education, Read is best remembered for her contribution to colonial education in the broadest sense. During the 1940s British colonial education policy had to be thought out afresh and put across to colonial peoples who were experiencing rapid socio-economic change, Read played a leading role in this. Her deep respect for indigenous cultures and the need to understand and protect them in the transition to modernity was a revelation to many of her students brought up to believe that progress lay in slavishly imitating western models.

Margaret Read's *Times* obituary mentioned her personal reticence and modesty as possible reasons why she had not yet received her due in the history of anthropology. By contrast, contemporaries who knew her in her prime as a professor at the Institute of Education recall a somewhat awesome figure who commanded enormous respect from staff and students alike. The director was known to refer to her privately as 'the battleaxe' when she had the bit between her teeth. Her nephew and niece likewise recall her as a loving aunt but equally a formidable adversary when roused. She died peacefully in a nursing home, Meadbank, 12 Parkgate Road, Battersea, near her longtime home in Paradise Walk, Chelsea, on 19 May 1991, aged 101.   CLIVE WHITEHEAD

Sources M. Read file, U. Lond., Institute of Education · C. Whitehead, 'Not wanted on the voyage', *Occasional Papers No. 11* [U. London, Institute of Education] (March 1988) · M. Read, 'Poverty, pollution and family life in a Victorian cathedral city', U. Lond., Institute of Education, Margaret Read MSS · C. Whitehead, 'When the bush takes fire', *Non-formal and non-governmental approaches*, ed. C. Modgil and S. Modgil (1997), vol. 4 of *Education and development: tradition and innovation* · PRO, Sir Christopher Cox papers, CO 1045 [especially CO 1045/304 for corresp. between Cox and Read] · U. Lond., Institute of Education, Margaret Read MSS · PRO, advisory committee on education in the colonies papers, CO 987 · annual reports, colonial department, U. Lond., Institute of Education · BLPES, Read MSS · private information (2004) · d. cert.
Archives BLPES, papers relating to Ngoni of Malawi · London School of Economics, MSS · Royal Anthropological Institute, London, reports · U. Lond., Institute of Education, corresp. and papers | Bodl. RH, corresp. with M. Perham · PRO, Sir Christopher Cox papers, CO 1045
Likenesses black and white photographs, U. Lond., Institute of Education, Margaret Read MSS
Wealth at death £265,191: probate, 19 Aug 1991, *CGPLA Eng. & Wales*

Read, Mary (*c*.1695–1721), pirate, was born in England, according to the account of her early life in Captain Charles Johnson's *History of the … Pyrates*. Her mother had married a sailor named Read and had a son, but the sailor disappeared, leaving her on her own. She had an affair and became pregnant again. To conceal her condition she left her husband's relatives and went to stay with friends in the country, where she gave birth to Mary Read. Some time later the son died and she decided to pass her daughter off as her son and to ask her wealthy mother-in-law for financial assistance. Mary was dressed as a boy and the mother-in-law agreed to provide a crown a week towards the child's maintenance. When the old woman died Mary was thirteen, and was sent to work as a foot-boy for a French lady. However, she tired of this menial life and, 'growing strong and having also a roving mind' (Johnson, 119), she went across to Flanders and joined a foot regiment as a cadet. She fought in several engagements and then fell in love with a handsome young Flemish soldier in her regiment. She revealed to him that she was a woman and they subsequently married, left the army, and set themselves up as proprietors of the Three Horse Shoes, an eating-house near Breda. Her husband died soon after this and Mary decided to assume men's clothing again and seek her fortune elsewhere.

After a brief spell in the army Mary Read boarded a ship and sailed to the West Indies. Her ship was captured by English pirates and she was persuaded to join their crew. In September 1717 a proclamation was issued in the name of George I that declared that any pirates who surrendered themselves should be pardoned. The crew of Mary's ship decided to take advantage of the pardon and made their way to Nassau, in the Bahamas. There Mary met up with a group of pirates led by Captain John Rackam, otherwise known as Calico Jack. One of the members of his crew was Anne Bonny, who, like Mary Read, was dressed as a man. Anne Bonny took such a liking to the handsome Mary Read that she let her know that she was a woman and was greatly disappointed when Mary admitted that she too was a woman. Considering how few women went to sea at that period it is extraordinary that two female pirates should have ended up on the same ship, but their subsequent pirating exploits are borne out by a number of documents. These include the transcript of their trial in Jamaica and a proclamation that was issued by Captain Woodes Rogers, the governor of the Bahamas, on 5 September 1720, in which he announced that John Rackam, several men, 'and two Women, by name Ann Fulford alias Bonny, & Mary Read' had stolen a 12 ton sloop from the harbour at Providence, had committed robbery and piracy, and 'are hereby proclaimed Pirates and Enemies to the Crown of Great Britain' (*Boston Gazette*). Towards the end of October 1720 Calico Jack and his crew were intercepted off the coast of Jamaica by an armed merchant ship. After a brief fight in which the two women put up a spirited resistance the pirates were captured and taken ashore to Spanish Town for trial. Rackam and the men were found guilty and hanged. A separate trial of the women took place on 28 November, and they too were found guilty of piracy and condemned to death. However, 'the prisoners informed the Court that they were both quick with child and prayed that execution of sentence might be stayed' (*Tryals of Captain John Rackam*, 19). When examined they both proved to be pregnant and thus escaped the death penalty. Mary Read died a few months later, in prison; the parish registers of the Jamaican district of St Catherine record that she was buried on 28 April 1721.   DAVID CORDINGLY

Sources C. Johnson, *A general history of the robberies and murders of the most notorious pyrates* (1724) · *The tryals of Captain John Rackam and other pirates*, transcript of trial, printed in Jamaica by Robert Baldwin, 1721, PRO, CO.137/14 · *Boston Gazette* (10–17 Oct 1720) · D. Cordingly, *Life among the pirates: the romance and the reality* (1995) · M. Rediker, 'Liberty beneath the Jolly Roger', *Iron men and wooden women*, ed. M. Creighton and L. Norling (1996) · parish register, Jamaica, St Catherine [burial]
Likenesses engravings (Mary Read and Anne Bonny), repro. in Johnson, *A general history*

Read, Nicholas (*c*.1733–1787), sculptor, was a pupil at the St Martin's Lane Academy, London. He was then apprenticed to François Roubiliac, who is said to have accepted him following entreaties from Read's father, despite his declared wish not to take apprentices. According to his obituary, Read finished one of Roubiliac's busts in his master's absence and on his return the sculptor was so delighted that 'they continued inseparable friends ever after and all distinction was lost in the affection he bore him' (*GM*, 1st ser., 57, 1787, 644). While this anecdote may be a variant of a familiar type, it seems to indicate rightly the important place that Read had within Roubiliac's small studio. In 1750 George Vertue mentioned a 'young man, an apprentice of Mr. Rubbilac' (with the name Nicholas added in the margin), and noted with approval a drawing of an academy figure which 'shows great skill & fire & spirit extraordinary' (Vertue, *Note books*, 3.152). Read's abilities as a carver were evidently valued by Roubiliac, and he was reported to have carved the skeletal Death on the monument to Joseph and Elizabeth Nightingale (commissioned 1758; erected 1761; Westminster Abbey), the most dramatic figure in one of Roubiliac's most celebrated works. After Roubiliac's death Read announced in January 1762 that, as 'a Person who for sixteen years past has studied under him, and executed a great Part of his most capital Works' he 'means to succeed him' (H. Walpole, 'Book of materials', I, 154, MS Lewis Walpole Library, Yale University, Farmington, Connecticut). This bid to continue the workshop did not succeed, for in March he was advertising casts from Roubiliac's 'Moulds for Busts', stating that 'these Moulds will shortly be disposed of by publick Auction' (ibid.).

Read executed (and signed) the monument to Francis Hooper in Trinity College, Cambridge, with its bust by Roubiliac, and is likely to have played a major role in the completion of some of the sculptor's later small monuments, such as those to Lucretia Betenson (*d*. 1758; Wrotham, Kent) and John Wale (*d*. 1761; Earl's Colne, Essex). But Read's activity as an independent sculptor following Roubiliac's death failed to live up to his early promise, though he was certainly not lacking in ambition. In the early 1760s his talent was recognized by the Society of Arts, which awarded him two of the largest premiums given for sculpture, the first of 100 guineas for a 'life-sized figure in marble of Actaeon and his dog' in 1762 and the second for £147 for a 'Diana by a Rock' two years later (Dossie, 440). From about this date until 1780 Read was a frequent exhibitor at both the Society of Artists and the Free Society. During the 1760s he received commissions for a number of small monuments, such as those to James Kendal (West Horsely, Sussex), incorporating motifs used earlier in Roubiliac's workshop. He also enjoyed some success in attracting those patrons who admired the dramatic narrative qualities of his master's later work. The monument to the merchant Nicholas Magens (*d*. 1764) at Brightlingsea, Essex (described in the *Ipswich Journal* for 8 November 1766), combines elements from Roubiliac's Warren, Hargrave, and Argyll monuments, albeit in an undisciplined way. A rather less elaborate but still dramatic monument at Probus, Cornwall, to Thomas Hawkins (*d*. 1766), with mourning widow and descending angel, may also be attributed to him. His best-known work, however, is the vast machine high on the south aisle in Westminster Abbey commemorating Admiral Tyrell (*d* 1766). This represents the almost naked figure of the admiral being summoned from the deep at the last trump in an illusionistic scene involving billowing waves, the admiral's ship, allegorical figures, and much else. Described in the 1783 guide to the abbey as a 'magnificent monument', it was already being ridiculed in the same year not only for its 'pancake' clouds but also for the way it combined so many disparate elements 'that we are no more tempted to dream of symmetry and arrangement at the view, than we should be at the sight of a broker's-shop in Moorside' (Ralph, 11–12). It was partially demolished in the later nineteenth century.

In 1779 Read unsuccessfully submitted a design for the monument to Lord Chatham, a commission given to John Bacon. He died on 11 July 1787, having been 'totally deprived of reason a short time before his death' (*GM*, 1st ser., 57, 1787, 644). A posthumous sale included plaster casts of busts, reliefs, and 'a small monument complete' (Gunnis, 318). Read was described by J. T. Smith as 'a conceited spark who used to annoy the great sculptor'. His larger monuments strive for the drama of his master's work but lack their intelligence; they are distinguished by their fine passages of carving, even if they are uncontrolled in their design. Rather than adapting Roubiliac's handling of the surfaces of marble sculpture to a new neoclassical aesthetic, as did Wilton and Bacon, Read continued to rework in an exaggerated way the scenic effects of his teacher, to the detriment of his own reputation.

                                                   MALCOLM BAKER

Sources Vertue, *Note books*, 3.152 · *GM*, 1st ser., 57 (1787), 644 · R. Dossie, *Memoirs of agriculture and other oeconomical arts* (1782), 440 · D. Bindman and M. Baker, *Roubiliac and the eighteenth-century monument: sculpture as theatre* (1995), 97, 183–4, 221, 265, 349, 354–5, 357–8 · K. A. Esdaile, *The life and works of Louis François Roubiliac* (1928), 213–17 · R. Gunnis, *Dictionary of British sculptors, 1660–1851* (1953); new edn (1968) · M. Whinney, *Sculpture in Britain, 1530 to 1830*, rev. J. Physick, 2nd edn (1988), 272–3, 400, 456, 461 · E. Hardcastle [W. H. Pyne], *Somerset House gazette and literary museum*, 2 vols. (1824), 396 · J. Ralph, *A critical review of the publick buildings, statues and ornaments in and about London and Westminster* (1783)

Read, Richard (1745?–1790?), engraver, of unknown origins, was a pupil of the London engraver James Caldwell when in 1771 he gained a premium of the Society for the Encouragement of Arts, Manufactures, and Commerce for his drawing. He gave his address as Birmingham in 1777, when he exhibited the mezzotinto print *A Storm* with the Society of Artists. This, his most ambitious plate, reproduced *Perdita Found by an Old Shepherd and a Clown*, a scene from *The Winter's Tale* after Paul Sandby, and was published by Valentine Green, another artist from the west midlands. Read did not engrave many prints of consequence, and his principal employment may have been in some other aspect of design. Dodd's verdict that 'he became a slovenly practitioner both in the chalk style and in mezzotint and eventually abandoned his practice to become a dealer and printer of some of Bartolozzi's worn out plates' is hardly unfair (Dodd, fol. 35). Read is thought to have died in 1790.

TIMOTHY CLAYTON and ANITA MCCONNELL

Sources T. Dodd, 'Memoirs of English engravers', BL, Add. MS 33404, fol. 35 · Redgrave, *Artists* · *Premiums offered by the society instituted at London for the encouragement of arts, manufactures and commerce*, Society for the Encouragement of Arts, Manufactures and Commerce, London (1778) · Graves, *Soc. Artists* · J. C. Smith, *British mezzotinto portraits*, 4 vols. in 5 (1878–84)

Read, Samuel (1817/18–1883), watercolour painter, was born at Needham Market, Suffolk. He began to train as a lawyer in the office of the town clerk of Ipswich, before becoming an architect's assistant. In 1841, abandoning both professions, he went to London to learn wood-engraving with Josiah W. Whymper; he also studied with W. C. Smith, the watercolour painter. He first exhibited at the Royal Academy in 1843, showing a drawing, *The Vestibule of the Painted Hall, Greenwich*, and he continued to exhibit there annually until 1857. By 1872 he had exhibited eighteen architectural drawings there, mainly interiors of English and Belgian churches, including several in Antwerp. He was the illustrator of several books, the first of which seems to have been *Zoological Studies*, published by the SPCK in 1844. In the same year he also began to do sketches for the *Illustrated London News*: his contributions to this paper included illustrations for stories and a series of large views of English cathedrals. In 1853 he was sent to Constantinople and the Black Sea, just before the outbreak of the Crimean War, as the first special artist for the *Illustrated London News*. In the 1860s architectural sketches from his travels in Europe appeared in the paper; some were republished as *Leaves from a Sketchbook* (1875).

Read was elected an associate of the Society of Painters in Water Colours (the Old Watercolour Society) in 1857, and a member in 1880. He contributed to every exhibition from 1857 onward, showing 210 paintings in all. In the 1870s he painted some landscapes, especially Scottish and Irish coastal views, but these were less successful than his European church interiors. On his way back from a sketching trip on the continent, he narrowly escaped death in the Staplehurst railway disaster of 9 June 1865: part of the train from Folkestone to London rolled off the embankment into a river, and the artist was trapped underwater. Charles Dickens was also a passenger on this train.

Read married a daughter of Robert Carruthers, the proprietor and editor of the *Inverness Courier*; the couple had one son and one daughter. During the later years of his life he lived at Parkside, in Bromley, Kent; he was unofficially retained in old age as art editor of the *Illustrated London News*. He died on 6 May 1883 at Fort Cottage, Sidmouth, Devon, following a stroke. The Victoria and Albert Museum, London, has seven of his watercolours, including *The Corridor, the Brewer's Hall, Antwerp* (1860), and the British Museum has several engraved proofs by the Dalziel brothers of his drawings. A characteristic drawing of Read's shows a cathedral, church, or castle, possibly ruined and covered in thick undergrowth, and 'delightfully dank and gloomy' (Houfe, 273).

ANNE PIMLOTT BAKER

Sources *ILN* (19 May 1883) · J. L. Roget, *A history of the 'Old Water-Colour' Society*, 2 (1891), 413–16 · Mallalieu, *Watercolour artists*, vols. 1–2 · R. K. Engen, *Dictionary of Victorian wood engravers* (1985) · S. Houfe, *The dictionary of 19th century British book illustrators and caricaturists*, rev. edn (1996) · Wood, *Vic. painters*, 3rd edn · Boase, *Mod. Eng. biog.* · J. Hatton, *Journalistic London* (1882) · Graves, *RA exhibitors* · L. Lambourne and J. Hamilton, eds., *British watercolours in the Victoria and Albert Museum* (1980) · DNB · *CGPLA Eng. & Wales* (1883)

Archives Suffolk RO, Ipswich, corresp. and papers

Likenesses Cundall, Downes & Co., carte-de-visite, NPG · engraving (after photograph by W. Cobb), repro. in Hatton, *Journalistic London* · group portrait, wood-engraving (*Our artists—past and present*), BM, NPG; repro. in *ILN* (14 May 1892) · wood-engraving (after photograph by R. Cade), NPG; repro. in *ILN* (19 May 1883)

Wealth at death £9173 19s. 10d.: probate, 24 May 1883, *CGPLA Eng. & Wales*

Read, Thomas. See Reade, Thomas (1606/7–1669).

Read, Walter William (1855–1907), cricketer, son of Robert Read and Elizabeth Jane, *née* Allwork, was born in West Street, Reigate, Surrey, on 23 November 1855. He was educated at the Reigate Priory School, of which his father was headmaster. For Reigate Priory club, at the age of thirteen, he scored 78 not out against Tonbridge. In 1873 he was introduced to Charles William Alcock, the secretary of Surrey County Cricket Club, and he played for the county from that date until 1897. He played an important part in Surrey's success in winning the county championship in every year except one between 1887 and 1895. He made 366 appearances and when at his best, in the late 1880s, he scored in successive matches in June 1887 against Lancashire and against Cambridge University 247 and 244 not out respectively, and, in the following year, 338 against Oxford University.

Read played on twenty-three occasions for the Gentlemen against the Players (1877–95), making 159 at the Oval in 1885. He also made seventeen appearances for England against Australia (1882–93), his most memorable performance being in 1884. Despite the fact that he was top of his county averages, his captain, Lord Harris, put him in to bat at number ten. Read responded with 117 runs, which over a century later was still the highest score to have been made by an England number ten. Two of his tests were in

Australia, where two sides visited in 1887–8. On that occasion Read captained an England eleven drawn from both visiting sides. He led England to victory, as he did in South Africa at Cape Town in March 1892.

In his career Read scored 22,349 runs and made thirty-eight centuries. Of strong physique, he was a punishing front-foot player and a very safe fielder, especially at point. From being a fast right-arm bowler, he became a slow left-arm 'lob' or underarm bowler. Like W. G. Grace, he provides an outstanding example of an amateur of his day being rewarded financially as if he were a professional. After assisting in his father's school, he was assistant secretary of Surrey County Cricket Club (1881–97) at a salary of £100 per annum. The county records give little indication of his doing very much work in the post. Surrey regularly gave him a bonus of £100 a season and they awarded him match expenses of 4 guineas. A testimonial raised £800 and he was twice given an *ex gratia* payment of £250. A partnership in an auctioneering and surveying firm in the City of London also assisted his finances.

John Shuter, Read's county captain, in an introduction to the latter's *Annals of Cricket* (1896), called him a model cricketer, modest and unassuming. The book itself is a secondary source on the game, drawing heavily on such authorities as James Pycroft. Read, a married man with three sons and a daughter, died on 6 January 1907 at 5 Colworth Road, off Bingham Road, Addiscombe Park, Croydon, and was buried at Shirley cemetery.

GERALD M. D. HOWAT

Sources H. A. Tate, *Cricket* (31 Jan 1907) • *Wisden* (1907) • *Wisden* (1908) • A. Haygarth, *Marylebone club cricket scores and biographies*, 12 (1879) • A. Haygarth, *Arthur Haygarth's cricket scores and biographies*, 14 (1895) • *Cricket* (19 April 1883) • *Cricket* (23 May 1895) • *Cricket* (29 June 1905) • W. W. Read, *Annals of cricket* (1896) • R. Daft, *Kings of cricket* (1893) • R. Sissons, *The players* (1988) • b. cert. • d. cert.
Likenesses R. P. Staples, painting, *c.*1887, priv. coll. • Hawkins of Brighton, photograph, 1890, repro. in *Cricket* (21 Aug 1890) • G. H. Barrable, painting; exh. Goupil Gallery, London, 1887 • V. Brooks, cartoon, repro. in *VF* (1888) • Lib [L. Prosperi], chromolithograph caricature, NPG; repro. in *VF* (28 July 1888) • Thiele & Co., photograph, repro. in Tate, *Cricket* • cartoon, repro. in *Punch* (13 Aug 1887)

Read, Sir William (*d.* 1715), itinerant oculist, was the son of an illiterate shoemaker in Halesworth, Suffolk. He was a man of little education, who flamboyantly advertised his medical and surgical skill, becoming the object of both high honours and considerable lampooning. Through self-promotion and the publication of handbills he established a well-placed London clientele, eventually becoming very wealthy and mixing in the very best London society. By 1694 he was living and practising in the York Buildings, the Strand (later moving to Durham Yard in the Strand), and between 1689 and 1693 he claimed to have performed many cures in provincial towns, including Oxford, where he said he restored thirty blind people to sight by couching. According to one handbill, he offered to treat gratis all wounded soldiers after the battle of Malplaquet (1709), provided their officers certified their participation in the battle. In 1705 Read was rewarded with an appointment as oculist to Queen Anne, and a knighthood

Sir William Read (*d.* 1715), by William Faithorne the younger

for treating seamen and soldiers gratis. In the same year an anonymous poem celebrating his skills and magnanimity appeared, entitled 'The Oculist, a Poem Address't to Sir W. Read'.

It is difficult to assess the validity of Read's claims, though many in his day considered him a fraud. Some said that he was illiterate, although he published a book and a number of handbills. It is certain that he did extensively plagiarize earlier writings, even to the point of repeating detailed case histories. This is evident in his book published about 1705, which circulated under two titles, *A Treatise on the Eye* and *A Short but Exact Account of All the Diseases Incident to the Eyes*. The first part of the book is an unacknowledged reprint (with a few spelling changes) of the *Breviary of the Eyes*, written by Richard Banister in 1621. Every detail of every case history recorded by Banister is repeated by Read as if the patients were his own. Read did omit, however, the chapter by Banister titled 'Of proud quacksalving montebanks, that would undertake all cures and performe few', perhaps because it too closely described his own practices. The second part of Read's book was a reprint (again unacknowledged) of the English translation of *Traité des maladies de l'oeil qui sont en nombre de cent treize* by Jacques Guillemeau, originally published in 1585. Only the final third of Read's book appears to be his own composition, and it is a forty-page discourse promoting his manual dexterity and his styptic water.

It is evident that, in addition to practising as an oculist, Read also sold various ointments, purges, and styptic waters during his travels throughout the country. A number of his flamboyant advertisements are preserved, including 'Post nubila Phoebus, nihil absque Deo' issued about 1695 (concerned with his remarkable cures of blind people in Oxford, Windsor, Bath, and elsewhere, and with other conditions, such as breast cancer, cured by styptic water) and 'Read's true and faithful experiments, lovingly communicated for the good of his countrymen, being a catalogue of those medicaments he sold off his stages during the time of his eighteen years travelling in England, Scotland, Ireland, and many foreign kingdoms', printed about 1705. These self-promoting handbills were cleverly satirized in a political broadsheet of 1710 entitled *Dr. Sacheverel turn'd oculist, or, Sir W—m R—d's lamentation for the loss of his business*. Read was also lampooned in *The Spectator* (no. 547), along with some other oculists and quacks of his day.

In London Read appears to have been considered by some to be skilful, despite his humble origins, irregular education, and boastful advertising. His lavish entertainment of guests prompted Jonathan Swift to write to Stella (5 April 1711):

> Henley would fain engage me to go with Steele, Rowe, &c., to an invitation at Sir William Read's; surely you have heard of him; he has been a mountebank, and is the queen's oculist. He makes admirable punch, and treats you in golden vessells. (*Journal to Stella*, 1984, 155)

Read died in Rochester, Kent, on 24 May 1715 and was buried there in the churchyard of St Nicholas. It is said that his widow, Augustina Read, continued his business in Durham Yard, presumably selling his various proprietary potions. Available evidence suggests that Sir William was a more effective self-promoter and plagiarist than he was an oculist.   EMILIE SAVAGE-SMITH

Sources *Le Neve's Pedigrees of the knights*, ed. G. W. Marshall, Harleian Society, 8 (1873), 490–91 · R. R. James, ed., *Studies in the history of ophthalmology in England prior to the year 1800* (1933), 122–9 · L. S. King, *The medical world of the eighteenth century* (1958), 47–50 · 'Some famous quacks: V., Sir William Read', *The Practitioner*, 78 (1907), 416–21 · PRO, A Prob 6/91, fol. 71 (146)*r*. · *Dr. Sacheverel turn'd oculist* (1710) [copy at BL] · 'Post nubila Phoebus, nihil absque Deo' [handbill; copy at BL] · W. Read, 'Read's true and faithful experiments' (*c*.1705) · 'The Oculist: a poem address't to Sir W. Read' (1705) [copy at BL] · G. Everitt, *Doctors and doctors: some curious chapters in medical history and quackery* (1888), 254–5 · W. Musgrave, *Obituary prior to 1800*, ed. G. J. Armytage, 5, Harleian Society, 48 (1901), 121 · *DNB*
Likenesses M. Burghers, engraving · W. Faithorne the younger, mezzotint, BM, RCPL, Wellcome L. [*see illus.*] · R. Grave, engraving (after W. Faithorne), Wellcome L.

Read, William [*pseud.* Eustace] (1795?–1866), poet, was born in co. Down, and at an early age became a contributor of poems to the first numbers of the *Literary Gazette*, under the pseudonym of Eustace. Read particularly impressed the then editor of the journal, William Jerdan, and went on to have a reasonably successful career as a poet. In 1818 he published at Belfast a lament on the death of Princess Charlotte, and a well-received volume, *The Hill of Caves and other Poems*. He followed this first success with a second volume three years later, containing poems on a variety of themes ranging from a vigorous denunciation of gambling to the beauty of the palace at Versailles. Read

published one final volume of poetry in 1859, *Sketches from Dover Castle* which again featured both descriptive sketches and narrative poems. In the second half of his life, Read resided at Tullychin, co. Down, and was more concerned with military discipline than poetic metre, rising to the rank of lieutenant-colonel in charge of the North Down Rifles. He died on 26 December 1866.

D. J. O'DONOGHUE, rev. JASON EDWARDS

Sources D. J. O'Donoghue, *The poets of Ireland: a biographical dictionary with bibliographical particulars*, 1 vol. in 3 pts (1892–3), 211 · W. Jerdan, *The autobiography of William Jerdan: with his literary, political, and social reminiscences and correspondence during the last fifty years*, 4 vols. (1852–3), vol. 2, p. 81; vol. 3, p. 277

Reade, Brian Edmund (1913–1989), art historian and critic, was born on 13 January 1913 at Holwood, 42 Trumlands Road, St Marychurch, Torquay, Devon, the second child and only son of Thomas Glover Reade (1870–1952) and Susan Mary (1873–1960), daughter of the Hon. William King of Queensland, Australia. T. G. Reade, a painter, was for many years art master at Torquay grammar school; his teaching was regarded by informed opinion as the best of its kind, and his art classes were used as a model by the Board of Education in its 1924 report on art teaching in England.

The young Reade was sent to Montpelier, a preparatory school at Paignton, and to Clifton College, where his unconventional manners and his habit of walking about Bristol in carpet slippers did not endear him to dull teachers. During term his great pleasure was to quarter the medieval streets of the city (which were out of bounds to pupils at the school), making himself familiar with the workshops of glass-blowers and wax candle makers; during the holidays he explored the cliffs and beaches of Petitor, Babbacombe, and Anstey's Cove, collecting natural history specimens in a matchbox. Precocious and imaginative, Reade as a boy was already recognizable as the man he became: independent, single-minded, intellectually curious into out-of-the-way knowledge, and intent on conducting original research.

In 1931 Reade went up to King's College, Cambridge, to read history under Sir John Clapham. He obtained a first class in part two of the history tripos and was awarded a studentship by the college to research the lost and dispersed art collections of Charles I. He travelled widely in Germany, Italy, Austria, Yugoslavia, and Turkey in search first of baroque and then of Byzantine art and architecture, about both of which he was passionately knowledgeable. In 1936 he abandoned his research because the subject was too large for a single scholar to master, and took a post in the department of prints and drawings at the Victoria and Albert Museum. He regarded the accepted English taste of the day, as represented by the Bloomsbury group, as narrow and provincial; his own enthusiasm was for the work of Klee, Picasso, Rouault, Ernst, and the German expressionists.

When the Second World War broke out, Reade worked at the War Office and was later seconded as a photographic interpreter to an intelligence unit working with the allied forces headquarters in Europe. On 24 April 1941 he married Margaret Tennant (b. 1916), daughter of his godfather Edmund Ware, and herself a talented artist in enamels and lithography who had studied at the Slade School. They had one son, Alban.

After the war Reade returned to the museum and began to publish the results of his researches. *Edward Lear's Parrots* (1949), a short, authoritative study of the subject, was followed by *The Dominance of Spain* (1951), a history of Spanish costume in the sixteenth century, and *Regency Antiques* (1953), which was notable for its author's rediscovery of George Bullock, a forgotten cabinet-maker whose work he described and made famous. Later his work on the Enthoven collection, core of a national archive of ballet design, was to bear fruit as *Ballet Designs and Illustrations* (1967). In the meantime he began to make a reputation as an organizer of exhibitions, among them the Edward Lear exhibition for the Arts Council (1958), the art nouveau and Alphonse Mucha show at the Victoria and Albert Museum (1963), and the Beardsley exhibition there (1966), which became legendary: it was the most successful and influential exhibition of its kind ever mounted by the museum and it captured the imagination of the thousands of visitors who flocked to see it. Reade's catalogue, a model of precise and learned commentary, has been the foundation of all subsequent work on Beardsley and established Reade as the doyen of Beardsley studies. His own large illustrated monograph, *Aubrey Beardsley* (1967), removed the artist from his position as the subject of an esoteric cult and gave him finally the status of a great master of design. The exhibition went to New York and Los Angeles, and Reade was offered several museum directorships in America, all of which he refused on the grounds that he wished to retain his independence.

Sexual Heretics (1970), a substantial by-product of Reade's enthusiasm for the 1890s, was an anthology of late nineteenth-century homosexual prose and verse with a long scholarly introduction. In 1971 he published a volume of his own poems, *Eye of a Needle*, and in 1987 a revised edition of his monograph on Beardsley. Reade was appointed deputy keeper in the department of prints and drawings in 1958; he retired in 1973. His last exhibition (1972) was on Louis Wain, an unusual artist in whom Reade had been interested for twenty-five years. The manuscript of Reade's biography of Wain, which was based on documentary material that included the private diaries of the alienists who treated Wain in his last years, was lost in the post and has never been found.

After his retirement Reade acted as adviser to several more Beardsley exhibitions around the world and wrote his last word on the subject, *Beardsley Re-Mounted* (1989). In 1977 he succeeded Henry Williamson as president of the Eighteen-Nineties Society.

A friend who knew him in his fifties described Reade as formidable in mind and appearance. He was tall, slender, and aquiline, with a fine voice and a perfectionist sensibility. He was often silent in company. His colleagues at the museum were used to finding him on the floor of his office, sunk in meditation among piles of paper, hidden in swirling clouds of smoke from the elegant oval Turkish cigarettes he liked.

Not long after his retirement Reade and his wife moved back to St Marychurch, to the house he had inherited from his father. His last years were marred by a mysterious disease resembling multiple sclerosis, which was never satisfactorily diagnosed. He lost the use of his legs and was confined to a wheelchair, but continued to enjoy talking to the young scholars and researchers who came constantly to seek his help and advice. He also endured periods of bitter frustration and depression. He died at home on 1 November 1989, leaving four volumes of unpublished memoirs and stories; he was survived by his wife and their only son. His remains were cremated on 10 November at Torquay.   GUTALA KRISHNAMURTI

Sources *The Independent* (9 Nov 1989) · *Daily Telegraph* (17 Nov 1989) · *The Times* (10 Nov 1989) · *Annual Report of the Council* [King's College, Cambridge] (1990) · personal knowledge (2004) · private information (2004) · b. cert. · m. cert. · d. cert.
Archives priv. coll.
Likenesses L. Lancaster, drawing · M. Reade, drawing
Wealth at death £408,286: probate, 5 April 1990, *CGPLA Eng. & Wales*

Reade, Charles (1814–1884), novelist and playwright, was born on 8 June 1814 at Ipsden House, Oxfordshire, the seventh son and tenth and youngest surviving child of John Reade (d. 1849) and his wife, Anna Maria (d. 1862), eldest daughter of Major John Scott (later Scott-*Waring) MP, a former associate of Warren Hastings in India. Reade's mother, a devout evangelical, was a friend of Samuel Wilberforce, G. S. Faber, and other leading low-church clergymen and public figures. Charles was her favourite child and many of his most distinctive qualities as a writer, including his crusading humanitarian zeal, his dogmatism, and blind conviction of his own rightness, and even his brusque prose style, have been plausibly attributed to her influence. His father, a tory squire of the old school, had little in common with his wife and youngest son. Reade professed to believe that the best of his Reade blood came from a great-grandmother who was the daughter of a village blacksmith.

Early years, 1814–1850 As a small boy Reade depended for emotional support on his mother and an elder sister, Julia, rather than on his father. Julia, who may have been the model for Julia Dodd in his novel *Hard Cash*, married when he was nine, and he was sent to a private school at Rose Hill, Iffley, run by the Revd John Slatter. Reade nicknamed Slatter Scourger, but other old boys of the school denied that he was a ferocious disciplinarian, a possible prototype of the sadistic gaoler Hawes in *It is Never too Late to Mend*. After four years at Rose Hill, Reade spent two happier years (1827–9) at Staines Lodge, a private school in Staines conducted by a curate named Hearn. He then studied with a crammer, a Mr Durham. His mother wished him to go to Oxford, expecting that he would enter the church after graduation, and in 1831 he won a demyship at Magdalen College with an essay on ambition and virtue. In 1835, according to the memoir by his son and elder brother, a college fellowship reserved for men born in

Oxfordshire fell vacant unexpectedly, spurring him to sit for his final examinations after only three weeks' preparation (Reade and Reade, 1.143). Although a third-class degree—in Greats—was the best he could manage in the circumstances, he was elected probationary fellow on 22 July 1835, Vinerian scholar on 1 December 1835, and fellow of Magdalen in the summer of 1836. His choice as fellow was challenged by a man with a better degree, and his parents and their friends were said to have secured him the Vinerian scholarship by bringing in MAs from miles around to vote for him. He remained a fellow of Magdalen for the rest of his life, serving as junior dean of arts in 1841 and 1843, bursar in 1844 and 1849, vice-president in 1851, and junior bursar in 1859. Once he had taken his MA degree (on 26 April 1838) his fellowship did not require him to reside in Oxford, but in the years of his fame, and particularly in the early 1860s, he did much of his writing in his rooms at Magdalen, using them as a retreat. His tenure of the fellowship was contingent on his remaining unmarried, a stipulation he complained of bitterly but continued to put up with, even when he was earning thousands a year as a writer and would hardly have missed the annual stipend of £250 (which may eventually have risen to £600).

As an undergraduate Reade laid the foundations of his lifelong reputation for eccentricity and nonconformity. He wore his hair unfashionably long, dressed colourfully, devoted all his time to reading, and abstained totally from alcohol and tobacco—as he was to do throughout his life. He was tall and burly, with a tiny head and ungainly gait (Elwin, 38). There is nothing to indicate that he ever intended to fall in with his mother's wishes and become ordained. His subsequent life and literary career leave no doubt that he would have found it impossible to submit to the discipline and decorum of the church and to subscribe to all of its teachings, especially those relating to sex. Both his fellowship and his Vinerian scholarship were lay awards, intended to enable him to read law (although later, in 1837 or 1838, he may also briefly have tried medicine, in Edinburgh). While he never actually practised law, litigation became one of his fiercest passions, and his legal training must also have played a significant part in developing the ostentatious reliance on 'facts', documentary evidence presented in the style of a courtroom advocate, which became the trade mark of his novels and plays 'with a purpose'. After being entered at Lincoln's Inn on 20 November 1835, he first read in chambers with Samuel Warren, the novelist, soon to score a hit with his novel *Ten Thousand a Year*, which Reade greatly admired and perhaps tried to imitate in some of his own fiction. Subsequently, from 1838 to 1842, he read with another barrister, Matthew Fortescue. On 17 February 1842, immediately after being called to the bar, he was elected to a Vinerian fellowship worth £80 a year which he thereafter held in conjunction with his college fellowship. He proceeded to the degree of DCL on 1 July 1847.

From the time he began reading with Fortescue, if not earlier, Reade lived in Soho, near Leicester Square, and pursued a mildly Bohemian existence, eating in out-of-the-way taverns and haunting the theatres. He was elected to the Garrick Club, of which he became a stalwart, on 14 December 1839. In the summer of 1839 he made his first trip abroad, to France and Switzerland. After his return he for the next few years 'oscillated between London, Ipsden, and Scotland' (Reade and Reade, 1.237). In London he collected, repaired, and traded in Cremona violins, about

Charles Reade (1814–1884),
attrib. Charles Mercier, *c.*1870

which he later published four learned articles in the *Pall Mall Gazette* (19–31 August 1872). At Ipsden he hunted and shot, played cricket, or boated and fished. In Scotland, where his elder brother William married and settled in 1837, he acquired a herring fishery (which proved unprofitable); more momentously, he fell in love with a pretty young woman, the prototype of his fictional heroine Christie Johnstone, and probably contracted a Scottish (common-law) marriage with her. If Reade's mother found out about the relationship, it can be assumed that she strongly opposed it, just as the mother of Christie's lover opposed his. But Reade continued to live with the young woman, when he could, from 1838 or 1839 until 1848, when she died giving birth to their son. The boy was called Charles Liston, presumably taking his mother's surname; he was passed off as Reade's godson until just before Reade's death, when he took the name Charles Liston Reade and was declared Reade's heir and literary executor.

Rise to fame, 1851–1870 According to Reade he 'began to make notes with a view to writing fiction' in 1835 (Reade and Reade, 2.159). However, his first published novel, *Peg Woffington*, did not appear until December 1852, when he was thirty-eight, and he was forty-two by the time he achieved his first great success as a novelist with *It is Never too Late to Mend* (1856). At the outset he had tried to make his mark as dramatist rather than novelist, producing no fewer than five plays that were staged in London in 1851–2 and several others that remained unacted. Most were translations or 'adaptations' from the French, including the first of his plays to be performed, *The Ladies' Battle* (Olympic Theatre, 7 May 1851), which was adapted from a play by Scribe and Legouvé that he had seen during one of his many visits to Paris as a dealer in violins. His first three novels were all initially written as plays and then turned into novels. *Christie Johnstone* (1853), which he said he wrote in 1849 or 1850, never saw the light of day in its dramatic form, but *It is Never too Late to Mend* was based on one successful play, *Gold*, which had opened at Drury Lane on 10 January 1853, and was later turned into another, *It's Never too Late to Mend* (Princess's Theatre, 4 October 1865). *Peg Woffington* was based on the highly popular sentimental comedy *Masks and Faces* (Haymarket Theatre, 20 November 1852), which Reade wrote in collaboration with his friend Tom Taylor, already an established dramatist; the collaboration proved difficult and Taylor completed the final draft on his own, Reade having withdrawn to Malvern to undergo a course of hydropathic treatment for his nerves. Dedicated to Taylor and published less than a month after *Masks and Faces* opened, *Peg Woffington* dealt with the same subject and appropriated much of Taylor's dialogue without his permission. This was one of the first and most notorious manifestations of what Edmund Yates described as Reade's 'odd notions of literary *meum* and *tuum*' (Yates, 2.164). Previously, like other English dramatists at the time, Reade had shown no compunction about adapting or translating French plays without permission; in *The Eighth Commandment* (1860), the impassioned plea for the sanctity of 'literary property' which he claimed

cost him £1000 to publish, he made out that he ceased doing so as soon as the International Copyright Act of 1851 came into force, but the facts suggest otherwise. Besides further adaptations from the French—including some for which he really did obtain the authors' permission—his early plays included a dramatized version of *Peregrine Pickle*. This opened in November 1854 at St James's Theatre, which he had leased for the season of 1854–5, installing his friend the actress Laura Seymour as manager.

Reade boasted that all his major novels—*It is Never too Late to Mend*, *The Cloister and the Hearth* (1861), *Hard Cash* (1863), *Griffith Gaunt* (1866), and *Put yourself in his Place* (1870)—were written on a scientific 'Baconian' system of induction from documented 'facts'. The subtitle 'A matter-of-fact romance' which he used for *It is Never too Late to Mend*, *Hard Cash*, and several of his shorter fictions reflects this aspiration to a documentary adherence to the 'truth', especially in the treatment of social problems. His principal source of facts was newspaper cuttings, which he began collecting in 1848 and continued to accumulate in hundreds of notebooks throughout his writing career. But he also drew unashamedly, often verbatim and at length, on facts set out in other people's books. In *It is Never too Late to Mend*, for example, the materials for his famously graphic exposure of the sadistic torture of prisoners, including the psychological torments caused by the 'silent and solitary' system in vogue at the time, were drawn partly from his own on-the-spot research at Durham, Oxford, and Reading gaols, partly from newspaper articles—including an opportune report of brutalities at Birmingham gaol in *The Times* (12 September 1853), but quite largely from a book by Hepworth Dixon, *The London Prisons* (1850). Some of the most admired details of the gold-digging scenes in the same novel were taken from William Howitt's *Land, Labour, and Gold, or, Two Years in Victoria*, and from other books. (Reade himself suffered from seasickness and never travelled further abroad than continental Europe.) He claimed to have toiled through eight volumes for the portrayal of Isaac Levi in *It is Never too Late to Mend*, but according to Wayne Burns (p. 143) Levi is virtually the same in the novel as he had been in the play *Gold*, written before this copious research was undertaken. For *A Good Fight* (1859), the short novel which grew into *The Cloister and the Hearth*, Reade said that he read seventy-nine books; while for *The Cloister and the Hearth* itself he filled three 'gigantic cards' with notes about hermits, and for *Hard Cash* no fewer than forty notecards containing 107,000 words. In the eyes of many reviewers the authenticity Reade laid claim to, especially when exposing social evils, was largely vitiated by his sensationalism and melodrama, which he defiantly defended, and which made it a simple matter for him to turn his novels into plays and his plays into novels. Several of his novels, particularly *Hard Cash*, *Griffith Gaunt*, and *A Terrible Temptation* (1871), also transgressed Victorian notions of sexual propriety. When *Hard Cash* (or *Very Hard Cash* as it was initially titled) reached the end of its serial run in *All the Year Round* (26 December 1863), Dickens took the extraordinary step of inserting a signed note after the final instalment effectively dissociating himself, as editor, from its 'statements and opinions', and although professing a high regard for Reade he privately considered some of the sexual episodes in *Griffith Gaunt* 'extremely coarse and disagreeable' (Burns, 261). But Reade's gift for rapid, exciting narrative, lively dialogue, and vivid, often horrific description ensured his popularity. For *Hard Cash* and *Griffith Gaunt*, the two novels that immediately followed his most acclaimed work, *The Cloister and the Hearth*, Reade probably received total rates of payment unequalled at the time by any other novelist except Dickens, George Eliot, and Wilkie Collins. He became proverbial for his vigilance and bargaining skills in his dealings with his publishers. The sales of his novels in their initial multi-volume form suffered from a virtual boycott by Mudie's Library, which rejected several of them on the grounds of indecency, but he compensated by obtaining large prices for the serial rights and for the cheaper, one-volume editions, particularly those issued in America where he was the first major English novelist to negotiate directly with publishers.

Reade's personal life during the years of his rise to fame and prosperity is not well documented. His passion for the theatre, dating back at least to his days as a law student, evidently had much to do with his attraction to actresses. One such was the acclaimed comic actress Mary-Anne (Fanny) Stirling, under whose management his first play was produced in 1851, who later appeared in it herself, and who spent a week with him at Oxford before being driven away, it was said, by his mother (Burns, 38–9); as she was already married Reade's fellowship cannot have been seriously at risk. A few years later, in 1853, he fell in love with another married actress, Laura Seymour; they began living together then or soon after and continued to do so until Seymour's death in 1879. Though known as Reade's 'housekeeper' she went on practising her profession until the onset of her terminal illness.

Later years, 1870–1884 Reade's literary career reached and passed its zenith about 1870. The year before, he and Laura Seymour had moved into a red-brick mansion at 2 Albert Gate, Knightsbridge, beside Hyde Park. In addition to the leasehold of this house he owned three freehold properties in the Brompton Road. All were purchased, presumably, with the huge proceeds of his novels *Hard Cash* and *Griffith Gaunt* and his play *It's Never too Late to Mend*, his first for eight years, which had its London opening at the Princess's Theatre on 4 October 1865, enjoyed a long run there, and was frequently revived afterwards. Reade and Seymour had previously resided first at 193 Piccadilly, and later, from 1856 to 1868, at 6 Bolton Row, Mayfair. In his new house Reade had a spacious writing-room overlooking the park and ample accommodation for a variety of animals, including at one time a 'small antelope or gazelle' (Maxwell, 324). *Put yourself in his Place*, the last three-volume novel written on Reade's 'great system' of laborious fact-gathering, was published in June 1870. It sold well and was received kindly by the reviewers because of its lurid exposure of outrages allegedly committed by trade unions. Subsequently, however, both the quality of his fiction and the lump-sum payments he received for it began to fall away. *A Terrible Temptation* (1871) achieved a modest *succès de scandale* after being savagely attacked for its 'indelicacy', and the novelette *The Wandering Heir* (1873) successfully cashed in on the excitement generated by the Tichborne claimant. But neither these nor any of the other five novels he produced in the 1870s and 1880s did anything to enhance his critical standing. His greatest hit was scored with a play, *Drink* (Princess's Theatre, 2 June 1879), adapted from Zola's *L'assomoire*. Some of his earlier plays were also revived with considerable success, for example *Masks and Faces*, with Squire and Marie Bancroft, in 1875, and with other actors in 1881 and 1883; *It's Never too Late to Mend*, with Ellen Terry in 1874, and with other actors in 1878 and 1881; and *The Courier of Lyons* (1854), revised as *The Lyons Mail*, with Henry Irving in 1877. But other theatrical ventures cost him dearly. In 1867 both *Dora* (Adelphi, 1 June), with Kate Terry, and *The Double Marriage* (Queen's, 24 October), with Ellen Terry, had failed miserably and no theatre would stage his dramatic adaptation of *Griffith Gaunt*. And in 1870 he was said to have lost £5000 when he staged *Free Labour*, adapted from *Put yourself in his Place*, at the Adelphi Theatre (28 May) under his own management, and subsequently at the National Standard Theatre and in the provinces. He was more successful with his stage version of *The Wandering Heir*, first performed in London at the Queen's Theatre, under Laura Seymour's management, on 15 November 1873; Ellen Terry began appearing in it on 28 February 1874 and remained with Reade's and Seymour's company when the play was subsequently transferred to Astley's Amphitheatre, then toured the provinces in repertory with several of Reade's other plays. Reade seems to have been infatuated with Terry, on stage at least.

Reade continued to indulge his propensity for litigation, almost regardless of the cost. With a few exceptions, including his earliest recourse to the courts, in March 1857, when he had unsuccessfully sued the publisher Richard Bentley for issuing a cheap edition of *Christie Johnstone* without his permission, he frequently acted on flimsy, if not vexatious grounds. One of his greatest victories, in a libel case against a New York paper which had branded *Griffith Gaunt* indecent—a charge Reade had responded to in a pamphlet entitled *The Prurient Prude*—returned him only a derisory six cents' damages. He did better later when similar complaints were made against *A Terrible Temptation*, suing and winning £200 damages from a 'cabal' of reviewers whom he branded 'the Licensed Victuallers', because they consorted in clubs and pubs where they learned 'the art of naughty interpretation and distortion of honest words' (Elwin, 240).

Allegations of plagiarism continued to dog Reade, the best-remembered of them arising from *Shilly-Shally*, his unauthorized dramatization of Anthony Trollope's novel *Ralph the Heir*, first performed at the Gaiety Theatre on 1 April 1872. Trollope protested angrily and publicly, and for several years afterwards he and Reade did not speak to each other even when playing whist or cribbage together at the Garrick Club. Closer friends like Tom Taylor were more forgiving, not doubting the sincerity of Reade's long campaign for the protection of literary and dramatic copyright in spite of his apparent double standards. At various stages of his career he waged many other campaigns with equal vehemence, and often with an almost laughable one-sidedness. Among the causes he took up were animal welfare and ambidexterity—which he believed all children should be taught. His favourite targets included the incompetence and obfuscations of the medical and legal professions and the institutionalized cruelties practised in prisons and lunatic asylums. He propagated his messages, indiscriminately, in novels, plays, pamphlets, and journal articles, once even employing a fifteenth-century soldier as his mouthpiece for a diatribe against the dangerous and ridiculous practices of the Victorian medical profession (*The Cloister and the Hearth*, chap. 26). His representations of the punitive tortures inflicted on inmates of prisons and lunatic asylums, which reached a blood-curdling climax in the play *It's Never too Late to Mend*, set a new standard of gruesome naturalism for the mid-Victorian period and reveal a vicarious sadism also evident, in a milder form, in many of the other scenes of violence in his novels and plays. For all his polemical combativeness and rhetorical violence, however, Reade seems to have been a soft-spoken man in private, and most of his contemporaries were perhaps more amused than affronted by his public pugnacity and conceit, viewing them, along with his odd physique and unconventional dress, as manifestations of an eccentric individualism that valuably enriched and enlivened the literary scene. Few would have dissented from Justin McCarthy's judgement that Reade:

> had a fine and noble nature under all his defects of temper and his inordinate self-esteem. No man was more chivalrous to stand by a cause which he believed to be just, or a friend whom he believed to be injured   (McCarthy, 1.419)

Convinced of his own genius, Reade made no secret of his scant regard for distinguished rival novelists such as George Eliot. He privately ranked *A Good Fight* above *A Tale of Two Cities*—even though he thought Dickens 'the greatest genius of the century' (Elwin, 191). A hundred years after his death his novels were all out of print. Opinions about his literary stature differed widely during his lifetime, but then and for a while afterwards *The Cloister and the Hearth*, with its endless succession of boisterous adventures in a sketchily picturesque medieval setting, and its topical theme of the evils of clerical celibacy, was regarded by some leading critics as perhaps the greatest historical novel in English.

Reade moved to 3 Blomfield Villas, Uxbridge Road, London, in 1881 and died there, after a long illness, on 11 April 1884, Good Friday. He was buried in Willesden old churchyard, alongside Laura Seymour and her husband, on 15 April. In his last years he was ostensibly 'converted' by a Presbyterian minister, Charles Graham.

P. D. EDWARDS

Sources M. Elwin, *Charles Reade: a biography* (1931) · W. Burns, *Charles Reade: a study in Victorian authorship* (1961) · Charles L. Reade and Compton Reade, *Charles Reade, dramatist, novelist, journalist: a memoir compiled chiefly from his literary remains*, 2 vols. (1887) · W. B. Maxwell, *Time gathered* (1938) · J. McCarthy, *Reminiscences*, 2 vols. (1899) · E. Yates, *Recollections and experiences*, 2 vols. (1884) · E. E. Smith, *Charles Reade* (1976) · J. A. Sutherland, *Victorian novelists and publishers* (1976)

Archives Bodl. Oxf., commonplace book · L. Cong., papers · London Library, commonplace books and MSS · Magd. Oxf., papers relating to lay fellowship case at Magdalen College, Oxford · NYPL, papers · Princeton University Library, corresp. · Princeton University Library, Parrish collection · Princeton University, commonplace book · Yale U. | BL, letters to Royal Literary Fund, loan 96 · Hunt. L., corresp., incl. much with J. T. Fields, and literary MSS · Morgan L., Harper's papers

Likenesses R. Lehmann, crayon drawing, 1869, BM · H. N. O'Neil, group portrait, oils, 1869 (*The billiard room of the Garrick Club*), Garr. Club · attrib. C. Mercier, oils, *c*.1870, NPG [*see illus.*] · P. Fitzgerald, bronze bust, Magd. Oxf. · P. Fitzgerald, bronzed plaster bust, NPG · caricature, woodcut, BM · portraits, repro. in Elwin, *Charles Reade* · prints, Harvard TC · stipple and line engraving, BM, NPG

Wealth at death £12,723 3s. 0d.: resworn probate, Aug 1884, CGPLA Eng. & Wales

Reade, Edward Anderdon (1807–1886), administrator in India, born at Ipsden, Oxfordshire, on 15 March 1807, was the fifth son of John Reade of Ipsden and his wife, Anna Maria, daughter of Major Scott-Waring, MP for Stockbridge. His youngest brother was Charles *Reade (1814–1884), the novelist. His four elder brothers, like himself, joined the East India Company's service. The eldest, John Thurlow (1797–1827), went to Bengal in 1816, and, attached to the revenue department, helped to frame the famous regulation VII of 1822, the basis of the periodical revision of land revenue settlements in the North-Western Provinces. He died in 1827, shortly after his appointment as the magistrate of Saharanpur.

Educated at the prebendary school at Chichester, Edward was nominated in 1823 to a writership in the East India Company's service, and studied at the East India College, Haileybury, where he distinguished himself as a linguist. Initially delayed by ill health, in June 1829 he was made assistant to the magistrate and collector of Gorakhpur district. Promotion and transfer to Cawnpore followed in 1832, where, to the government's satisfaction, he introduced the cultivation of the opium poppy to the district. In 1835 he returned to Gorakhpur as the magistrate and in 1841 completed the settlement of that district. In 1846 he was made commissioner of the Benares division, a post which he held until his further promotion in 1853 to the Sudder board of revenue, based in Agra.

Wherever he served, Reade cultivated good relations with the local gentry and respected their social pretensions. In the 1830s and 1840s such an affinity with the propertied classes was out of step with the revenue policy of the government of the North-Western Provinces, which aimed to circumvent landlord interests and make settlements directly with the peasant cultivators. After the 1857 uprising, however, Reade's inclination to patronize 'respectable native gentlemen' became the norm for a government chastened by the social upheaval its policies had apparently unleashed. He was in many ways the archetypal district officer: self-sufficient, plain-speaking, and somewhat opinionated. He privileged local knowledge far above provincial perspectives and often criticized his seniors for the abstraction of their political designs. He prided himself on his refusal to mystify Indian traditions as inscrutably exotic, disparaging as 'nervous' or 'excitable' those of his fellow officers who did.

At the outbreak of the uprising in 1857 Reade was in Agra as the senior member of the board of revenue, with John Russell Colvin as the lieutenant-governor of the North-Western Provinces. Reade knew Colvin well and considered him a timid man; his administration during the crisis, Reade thought, swung perilously between battle-shyness and imprudent bravado. Unlike Colvin, Reade did not fear widespread rebellion around Agra and he was confident that local merchants and landlords would side openly with the British if only given sufficient encouragement. He was furious, therefore, when Colvin ordered a forced loan from the city's bankers, which ruptured his own delicate negotiations with them for a voluntary loan, and he fumed at the siege mentality of the local military authorities, which, in early July 1857, saw European soldiers holed up in the Agra Fort while straggling bands of mutineers plundered the European station at will. He broke openly with Colvin over the fate of the government's papers and against his orders personally arranged for the conveyance of the huge bulk of the revenue records to the safety of the fort—an act of foresight which later won him favourable mention in a dispatch to the secretary of state. Colvin died on 9 September, whereupon Reade took temporary charge of the government and grasped the opportunity to curb the European instinct for indiscriminate revenge with relief. In May 1858 Lord Canning appointed him as one of the special commissioners to try rebels because, as Reade himself put it, the 'Sudder Judges … passed sentences of death so continually'. He repeatedly urged on government the loyalty of the propertied classes and subsequently received grateful testimonials from the bankers and merchants of several towns.

Reade's last official act at Agra was to read the proclamation transferring the government of India from the East India Company to the crown. In April 1860 he retired and returned to his ancestral home in Oxfordshire. He was made a Companion of the Bath and a magistrate for Oxfordshire and Berkshire. For twenty years he was chairman of the county bench at Wallingford. In retirement his appreciation of locality, always in evidence in India, flourished. He presented the Bodleian Library with several essays on local topography, along with court rolls, deeds, and copiously annotated transcripts of the Ipsden parish registers. He maintained an affectionate correspondence with the maharaja of Benares, Ishri Prasad Narayan Singh, who had looked upon Reade as a friend and adviser since his days as the commissioner of Benares. In 1863 the maharaja established a public well for the villagers of Stoke Row, a hamlet on the upper portion of the Ipsden estate. In charge of the well's construction, Reade was wryly amused that an Indian prince should thus give a lesson in charity to the English gentry.

Reade had married on 7 April 1838 Eliza, the youngest daughter of Richard Nossiter Burnard of Crewkerne and Colyford in Somerset. Five of their ten children survived him. He died at his home, Well Place House, Ipsden, on 12 February 1886, and was buried in Ipsden churchyard.

KATHERINE PRIOR

Sources BL OIOC, Reade MSS · Burke, *Gen. GB* (1972) · F. C. Danvers and others, *Memorials of old Haileybury College* (1894), 373, 617 · E. A. Reade, *Contributions to the 'Benares Recorder' in* 1852 (1858)

Archives BL OIOC, corresp. and papers, MSS Eur. B 52, D 279, E 116–117, 123–124, F 45 · Bodl. Oxf., autobiography, diaries, and Oxon. local history papers; copy of Richard Skirmer's *Antiquities of Wallingford* with MS notes and additions by Reade | LPL, letters to C. P. Golightly

Wealth at death £846 11s. 10d.: administration with will, 16 Dec 1886, *CGPLA Eng. & Wales*

Reade, John Edmund (1800–1870), poet and novelist, was born at Broadwell, Gloucestershire, the son of Thomas Reade (1762–1837) of Barton Manor, Berkshire, and his wife, Catherine (d. 1830), daughter of Sir John Hill. His grandfather Sir John Reade (1721–1773) was fifth baronet. Reade was educated at a school at Doulting Sheepslate, near Shepton Mallet. His first work, a collection of poems entitled *The Broken Heart*, was published in 1825. From that time until the close of his life he devoted himself to writing, and developed a remarkable capacity for imitation that often verged on plagiarism. Byron was his chief model, but his poems and plays are full of sentiments and phrases taken undisguisedly from the best-known writings of Scott, Wordsworth, Ben Jonson, and others. His ablest work, *Cain the Wanderer*, was published in 1829, and it obtained for its author an introduction to Coleridge and a eulogy from Goethe. Although Reade claimed to have made a sketch of a 'Cain' while still a boy, the work is redolent of Byron's play. In 1838, after a long stay in the south of Europe, he published *Italy: a Poem*, which while huge was shortened through the editing of Leigh Hunt and others. It bears a close resemblance to *Childe Harold*, reproducing even the dying gladiator.

Altogether Reade published nine volumes of poetry, mostly on sacred subjects, together with successively enlarged collected editions, beginning in 1852. To these were added five verse dramas, three novels, and a book of travels, *Prose from the South* (1849). His early poetry shared with the painter John Martin a histrionic attraction to biblical catastrophe, and was dismissed by Thomas Lister as theatrical 'clap-trap' in the *Edinburgh Review* (Lister, 109). Thirty years later *Wait and Hope* was included in H. L. Mansell's *Quarterly Review* survey of 'sensation novels', along with the works of Braddon and Collins, only to be found a 'very dull tale' full of 'insufferably tedious conversations' (*QR*, 113, 1863, 501). Reade was perceived as an inept sycophant by some other poets; his Bath acquaintance W. S. Landor savaged *A Record of the Pyramids* in 1842, especially the lengthy preface, full of 'unwearied flatteries' and 'piteous complaints', and he concluded that 'we would rather that a friend of ours should have written the three worst pages of Mrs. Hemans' than the nine thousand lines of *A Record* (*Blackwood*, 114). Macready claimed in 1839 that Reade, a 'ludicrously wretched fellow' attempted 'to *bribe* me by a promise of dedicating his miserable play to me, to act it'. The Drury Lane manager was also annoyed that the manuscript was a palimpsest of previous attempts at dedication (*Diaries of William Charles Macready*, 1.498). Despite the contempt of the literary world, Reade's works did have an audience, chiefly among the religious.

Most of Reade's life was spent in Bath and the west of England, but he was in the habit of making long journeys to central and southern Europe. He married his cousin, Maria Louisa, elder daughter of George Compton Reade, on 1 October 1847; they had a daughter, Agnes Coralie. Reade died of heart disease on 17 September 1870 at Budleigh Salterton, Devon.

E. I. CARLYLE, *rev.* D. E. LATANÉ, JR.

Sources DNB · Burke, *Peerage* · T. Powell, *The living authors of England* (1849) · [W. S. Landor], 'A record of the pyramids', *Blackwood*, 52 (1842), 113–19 · J. E. Reade, 'Dialogue between the author and a friend', *Can the wanderer; A vision of heaven; Darkness; and other poems* (1829) · J. E. Reade, *Prose from the south: comprising personal observations during a tour through Switzerland, Italy and Naples* (1849) · D. Patrick, ed., *Chambers's Cyclopedia of English literature*, new edn, 3 vols. (1901–3), vol. 3, p. 267 · T. H. Lister, 'Reade's poems', *EdinR*, 53 (1831), 105–19 · Ward, *Men of the reign* · Allibone, *Dict.* · *The diaries of William Charles Macready, 1833–1851*, ed. W. Toynbee, 2 vols. (1912)

Archives BL, letters to Royal Literary Fund, loan 96 · Sheff. Arch., letters | Bodl. Oxf., letters to Isaac Disraeli · Bodl. Oxf., letters to Miss Pigott · NL Scot., letters to Blackwoods · Trinity Cam., letters to Lord Houghton

Reade, Joseph Bancroft (1801–1870), microscopist and experimenter in photography, was born on 5 April 1801 at Kirkgate, Leeds, Yorkshire, the eldest of six sons and two daughters of Thomas Shaw Bancroft Reade (1776–1841) and his wife, Sarah (*d.* 1825), daughter of Richard Paley. His father was a merchant who was active in the British and Foreign Bible Society and author of several Christian pamphlets, and his mother was related to the natural theologian William Paley. He was educated at Leeds grammar school, and also had private tuition at Hull, before entering Trinity College, Cambridge, in 1821, from where he migrated to Gonville and Caius College in the following year. Immediately after graduating BA in 1825, he was ordained deacon as curate of Kegworth, Leicestershire. In the same year, on 25 July at St Paul's Cray, Kent, he married Charlotte Dorothy Farish (1796–1882), niece of Professor William Farish of Cambridge. They had three children, the longest-lived of whom, a daughter, died when she was twenty-one. In 1826 Reade took holy orders, and in 1828 proceeded MA.

From 1829 to 1832 he was curate at Halifax parish church, where began a lifetime friendship with an amateur meteorologist, John Waterhouse, remembered by photographers as inventor of 'Waterhouse stops'. After a part-time curacy at Harrow Weald from 1832 to 1834, Reade became proprietor of a school at Peckham, southeast of London. In December 1839, under the patronage of Dr John Lee of Hartwell, Buckinghamshire, and the Royal Astronomical Society (who owned the right of appointment), he became vicar of Stone, Buckinghamshire. At the vicarage a small school for about twenty pupils was established and an observatory was built in the garden. After

twenty years at Stone, by invitation of Lady Franklin Russell who lived at nearby Chequers, he became vicar of Ellesborough, Buckinghamshire, from 1859 to 1863, and from then until his death rector of Bishopsbourne, near Canterbury.

Reade's first scientific paper, 'Observations and experiments on the solar rays that occasion heat', was read at the Royal Society in December 1836 (*Proceedings* 3, 1830–37, 457; and manuscript at RS, AP.20. 14). In this paper he proposed the use of two convex lenses adjusted to condense sunlight onto a microscope specimen while defocusing the harmful rays of heat. He was greatly interested in the design of optical devices of the microscope, devising a hemispherical condenser, commonly known as 'Reade's kettledrum' (1861), and an equilateral prism (1869).

In several of his earliest papers Reade combined his optical interests with his love of chemistry by carrying out micro-incineration experiments on botanical specimens. His 'Observations of some new organic remains in the flint of chalk', published in November 1838 in *Annals of Natural History*, contains the first microscopic illustrations (from drawings) of microfossils, then named xanthidia, that more than a century later finally became identified as planktonic dinoflagellate cysts (important in identification of geological strata relating to petroleum). A wide-ranging interest in the chemistry of metal salts led in 1846 to his obtaining a patent for inks.

Reade described his small observatory and telescope at Stone in the *Monthly Notices of the Royal Astronomical Society* in 1853. His astronomical interests were strongly influenced by his association with Lee and the Meteorological Society at Hartwell House a few miles from Stone. However, his publications in this field are not extensive. Between 1844 and 1850 he contributed a series of observations of comets to the Royal Astronomical Society. He also designed a 'solid eyepiece', which received a medal at the exhibition of 1851.

Reade conducted some early experiments in photography, and he is noticed in the histories of photography. It has sometimes been suggested that he may have used photographic preparations of silver salts with oak-galls (gallic acid) and fixation with hyposulphite in 1836 or 1837. However, letters written by him early in 1839 provide evidence that he did not carry out such experiments before that year, and that his use of hyposulphite for fixing photographs followed Sir John Herschel's paper on photography read at the Royal Society on 14 March 1839. At the end of that month Reade used an infusion of nutgalls to make photographic paper more sensitive. This, together with the influence of Herschel, led to the discovery by W. H. F. Talbot that gallic acid developed the latent image. His early use of gallic acid led to the appearance of Reade (but not of Herschel) in 1854 as a defence witness in a lawsuit, *Talbot v. Laroche*, relating to Talbot's calotype patent, and his part in this case brought him attention in the photographic world during the rest of his life. He joined the Photographic Society in 1855 and as vice-president in the late 1860s often chaired its meetings.

Reade was a life member of the British Association from

its beginning in 1831, and was elected a fellow of the Royal Society in 1838. In 1839 he was a founding member of the Microscopical Society, in which he was especially active during his last years and of which he was president at the time of his death. The Revd Reade suffered from cancer during his last months and died from jaundice at his home, the rectory, Bishopsbourne, on 12 December 1870. He was buried four days later at St Mary's Church, Bishopsbourne. R. D. Wood

Sources A. L. Reade, 'Pedigree XXV: Reade of Leeds, etc.', *The Reades of Blackwood Hill in the parish of Horton, Staffordshire: a record of their descendants* (privately printed, London, 1906), 85–102 · R. D. Wood, 'J. B. Reade and the early history of photography', *Annals of Science*, 27 (1971), 13–83 · R. D. Wood, 'J. B. Reade's early photographic experiments', *British Journal of Photography* (28 July 1972) · J. Millar, *Monthly Microscopical Journal*, 5 (1871), 92–6 · R. D. Wood, 'Straightening the record on Reade', *British Journal of Photography* (3 July 1996) · R. D. Wood, 'Latent developments with gallic acid, 1839', *Journal of Photographic Science*, 28 (1980), 36–42 · C. H. Oakden, 'Joseph Bancroft Reade: his contributions to microscopical science', *Journal of the Royal Microscopical Society* (1926), 181–92 · C. H. Oakden, 'The photographic work of the Rev. Joseph Bancroft Reade', *British Journal of Photography* (27 July–3 Aug 1928), 435–5, 466–7 · A. Major, 'Bishopsbourne's eminent (but forgotten) Victorian: the Rev. Joseph Bancroft Reade', *Bygone Kent* (March 1989), 171–7 · RS · *Kentish Gazette* (20 Dec 1870), 5 · J. Venn and others, eds., *Biographical history of Gonville and Caius College*, 2: 1713–1897 (1898) · R. D. Wood, 'Rev. J. B. Reade FRS (1801–1870): a bibliography part 1, works written by Reade', RS, R63128
Archives National Museum of Photography, Film and Television, Bradford, Royal Photographic Society collection · priv. coll. · RS | AM Oxf., Hope collection · Bucks. RLSS, John Lee MSS · Wellcome L., Henry Lee collection, Western MS 5392
Likenesses Clarkington, photograph, 1860–69, PRO, Stationers' Hall Copyright Office, COPY 1/16, fol.1042 · Maull & Polyblank, photograph, 1860–69, National Museum of Photography, Bradford, Science Museum photographic collection · G. C. Wallich, two photographs, 1860–69, MHS Oxf., Royal Microscopical Society collection · photograph, 1860–69, Royal Institution of Great Britain, London · three photographs, RS
Wealth at death under £800: resworn probate, 7 Feb 1871, *CGPLA Eng. & Wales*

Reade, Robert. *See* Rede, Robert (d. 1415).

Reade [Read], **Thomas** (1606/7–1669), royalist army officer and civil lawyer, was born at Linkenholt, Hampshire, the second son of Robert Reade (d. 1626?) and his second wife, Mildred (d. 1630/31), sister of Sir Francis *Windebank, Charles I's secretary of state from 1632 to 1640. Thomas was schooled in Hampshire before in 1624, at the king's request, he was awarded a scholarship at New College, Oxford, where he was elected a fellow two years later. Despite his appointment Reade was a recalcitrant student, causing his uncle and the college warden concern both over his feckless behaviour and his religious conformity. After his mother's death (her will is dated 15 August 1630), and the receipt of his inheritance, Reade turned to civil law and graduated BCL on 11 October 1631. Windebank sent his son, John, from Winchester to New College in 1634, to be under Reade's tuition. The warden, Robert Pink, promised to keep a watchful eye over both of them: Reade, he commented, 'is very able and to spare' (*CSP dom.*, 1634–5, 230). As late as 1636 Reade had reason to confess to Windebank that, 'Evil fate has made him appear Rash and

ungrateful' (*CSP dom.*, 1636–7, 550). Reade corresponded with his uncle, chiefly in Latin, primarily about John's progress and welfare, until 1638, the year in which John graduated and Reade proceeded DCL.

When the civil war broke out in 1642 Reade proved himself a zealous royalist. He enlisted at Oxford under Captain William Holland, son of Thomas Holland, the regius professor of divinity at Oxford. With a few other doctors and many undergraduates he was drilled in 'the parke' of New College and at Christ Church, probably as a pikeman. Reade was appointed to provide for the maintenance of the kings' troop in Oxford, and was ordered to disburse the sum of £5 in the provision of bows and arrows. He was among about 100 other university men who left Oxford on 10 September 1642 attempting to serve as volunteers with Sir John Byron's troops. At Chipping Norton they were waylaid by a troop of horse under John Fiennes, son of Lord Saye and Sele, but Reade escaped to Worcester.

Reade returned to Oxford before 1643, and was admitted, by the king's mandate of 16 October 1643, principal of Magdalen Hall, replacing the parliamentarian Thomas Wilkinson who had already left the university. When Oxford surrendered to parliament in 1646 Wilkinson was restored. A warrant was issued on 7 July 1648 for Reade to be apprehended and brought with his papers and writings before the committee of both houses of parliament; another was issued in February 1649. Reade had gone to Paris before the first warrant was issued. He was received into the Catholic church and entered Douai College, where he took the oath of the profession of faith on 14 May 1648 and that of the alumni on 29 March 1649. He probably entered the Carthusian monastery of Nieuwpoort for some time with the intention of joining the order, but does not seem to have been ordained priest. He wrote in a reply to Edward Boughen's *Account of the Roman Church* (1653) in defence of Catholicism. His work was printed in Paris in 1659 under the initials R. T., but no copy seems extant.

At the Restoration, Reade returned to London, where he was quietly or clandestinely admitted into the college of advocates on 8 May 1661 'to obtain a bare livelihood' and allowed to live in Doctors' Commons (Wood, *Ath. Oxon.*, 3.831). He was appointed surrogate to Sir William, judge of the prerogative court of Canterbury. Early in March 1669 he died, aged sixty-two, in poverty at Exeter House on the Strand, where Doctors' Commons had moved after the great fire in 1666. On 7 March he made his deathbed dispositions, 'his speech not being Cleare, and he being slowe of utterance', leaving all that he had to his brother Robert in Paris, 'whose purse was open to him and … he could not have subsisted without him' (will, PRO, PROB 11/330, fol. 154r). Anthony Wood presumed that Thomas Reade was buried in the church attached to the Savoy Hospital, the parish in which Exeter House lay. Robert Reade was for a time secretary to Sir Francis Windebank.

Charlotte Fell-Smith, *rev.* S. L. Sadler

Sources B. P. Levack, *The civil lawyers in England, 1603–1641* (1973) · Gillow, *Lit. biog. hist.*, 5.399 · Wood, *Ath. Oxon.*, new edn, 3.831–2 · Foster, *Alum. Oxon.* · *CSP dom.*, 1623–38; 1648–9 · Wood, *Ath. Oxon.*:

Fasti · will, PRO, PROB 11/330, sig. 76 · A. Wood, *The history and antiquities of the University of Oxford*, ed. J. Gutch, 2 vols. in 3 pts (1792–6) · M. A. E. Green, ed., *Calendar of the proceedings of the committee for advance of money, 1642–1656*, 3 vols., PRO (1888) · Thomason Tracts

Archives BL, letter-book, Add. MS 38597

Wealth at death died in poverty; some pieces of gold and gold rings: Wood, *Ath. Oxon.*, 3 (1817) 831; will, PRO, PROB 11/330, sig. 76

Reade, Thomas Mellard (1832–1909), architect and geologist, was born on 27 May 1832 at 31 Mill Street, Toxteth Park, Liverpool, where his father, William James Reade (1794–1867), ran a small private school. The Reade family, formerly Staffordshire yeomen, included Joseph Bancroft *Reade and Sir Thomas Reade, deputy adjutant-general at St Helena during Napoleon's captivity. Reade's mother was Mary Mellard (1790–1866) of Newcastle under Lyme, who was aunt to the novelist Dinah Maria Mulock [see Craik, Dinah Maria].

Reade was educated in private schools before beginning work at the age of twelve in the offices of Edward Eyes & Sons, architects and surveyors in Liverpool. In 1853 he became a draughtsman for the London and North Western Railway Company, initially based in Warrington, subsequently in Liverpool. In 1860 he successfully set up in private practice as architect and civil engineer, working in and around Liverpool. He laid out the Blundellsands estate in 1865 and, from 1868 onwards, lived there in a house he had himself designed. On 19 May 1866 he married Emma Eliza Taylor, *née* Fox (d. 1895), the widow of his longstanding friend Alfred Taylor. They had three sons and a daughter. Reade became architect to the Liverpool school board in 1870 and thereafter designed most of their school buildings, until 1902 when the board was taken over by the city council. In 1890, while president of the Liverpool Architectural Society, he helped to found the school of architecture at University College, Liverpool.

As a result of his engineering work, Reade became interested in geology. He joined the Liverpool Geological Society in 1870 and subsequently published almost 200 scientific papers. Much of his early work concerned the local glacial and post-glacial deposits; it remains of great value since many of the sites and sections described are now built over and inaccessible for study.

In 1873, when the proposal to build a rail tunnel under the Mersey was being considered, Reade predicted the existence of a deep buried channel beneath the river. When the project was approved, the engineers prudently modified their plans so that the tunnel ran through bedrock below the supposed channel. Reade later had the satisfaction of visiting the tunnel works and seeing the bottom of the channel he had predicted in the roof overhead. However, some of Reade's other scientific work was less successful, including an attempt to estimate the age of the earth from the amount of lime carried in solution by rivers. In 1886 he published *The Origin of the Mountain Ranges* which was well received by his contemporaries. However, Reade's theories therein have not stood the test of time and are now of only historic interest. What is still of interest is an unusual geological memorial. In 1898

Reade persuaded Crosby district council to excavate an 18 ton erratic boulder from the glacial clays being worked in a local quarry. The boulder, which consisted of white gypsum, was then placed on public display. Now somewhat weatherworn, it still stands in Coronation Park, Great Crosby.

An illness in early childhood severely impaired Reade's hearing and the resulting deafness became increasingly pronounced in middle age. Consequently he found large meetings difficult to follow and rarely attended them. Nevertheless he became a fellow of the Geological Society of London in 1872 and was awarded its Murchison medal in 1896. He was president of the Liverpool Geological Society three times, president of the Liverpool Architectural Society, a fellow of the Royal Institute of British Architects, and an associate member of the Institution of Civil Engineers. Reade died at his home, Park Corner, Blundellsands, on 26 May 1909; he was buried at Sefton, Lancashire.

GEOFFREY TRESISE

Sources W. Hewitt, *The Liverpool Geological Society: a retrospect of fifty years' existence and work* (1910) · A. L. Reade, *The Reades of Blackwood Hill in the parish of Horton, Staffordshire: a record of their descendants* (privately printed, London, 1906) · 'Thomas Mellard Reade', *Geological Magazine*, new ser., 5th decade, 6 (1909), 333–6 · A. L. Reade, *The Mellards and their descendants ... with memoirs of Dinah Maria Mulock and Thomas Mellard Reade* (privately printed, London, 1915) · W. Hewitt, President's address, *Proceedings of the Liverpool Geological Society*, 11 (1910), 1–4 · A. L. Reade, *A family newsletter* (1930) · *CGPLA Eng. & Wales* (1919) · *Dir. Brit. archs.*, 1st edn, 756

Archives U. Lpool L., Sydney Jones Library, scientific corresp.

Likenesses photograph, National Museums and Galleries on Merseyside, Liverpool, Liverpool Geological Society, archives

Wealth at death £8717 1s. 2d.: probate, 2 July 1909, *CGPLA Eng. & Wales*

Reade [Kynnerd], **Sir William** (d. 1604), soldier, was most likely the illegitimate son of one Kynnerd of Worcester. Nothing is known of his early years, but he was probably recruited as a military client of John Dudley, duke of Northumberland, which would explain his continued association with the Dudley clientele. This may have been reinforced by the Worcestershire connection. He may have served Henry VIII too. Sir John Norris called him 'K[ing] H[enry] the 8['s] man' (*Household Accounts*, 349).

Reade probably started his career as a private soldier in the Calais garrison during the early 1540s. He was among the emerging professionals in England trained in the newest methods of siege warfare, fortification, and firearm use. In 1547 he became lieutenant of Wark Castle during Edward Seymour, duke of Somerset's, invasion of Scotland. He was a captain in the Berwick garrison from 1555 and captain of Holy and Farne Islands from 1555 until 1604. In 1562 Reade was a captain of the expeditionary force sent to Normandy under Ambrose Dudley, earl of Warwick. His good service during the siege of Le Havre in 1563 was such that Thomas Churchyard, writing in 1579, declared that Reade was 'a manne so worthie of memorie, and garnished with knowledge and courage, that he not onely merites to bee spoken of, but likewise deserveth to be honoured in Marshall causes, and exercises of warre'

(Churchyard, sig. Gjv). His grant of lands in Northumberland and Holy Island was originally connected with his service in France in 1562–3.

Reade was arrested during the northern uprising of 1569, under suspicion of treason, because of his earlier service under Sir Henry Percy and Thomas Howard, fourth duke of Norfolk. However, faithful service to the crown was always his prime motivation and proved his salvation. He was released in time to help defeat Leonard Dacre's followers at the battle of Naworth. In 1572 a Captain Read commanded one of three companies of English volunteers raised on behalf of Lumey de la Marck after his famous capture of Den Brielle. Some financial records relating to Read's company also survive in the Dutch archives, which indicate that he had returned to England by the late summer. If this was William Reade, then he was soon back on border business; he was one of the captains during Sir William Drury's successful siege of Edinburgh Castle in 1573, when English military technology and tactics greatly assisted the king's party in the civil war. He rose to the rank of sergeant-major with Robert Dudley, earl of Leicester, in the Netherlands in 1586 and commanded the infantry at the relief of Sluys the following year. Leicester, who valued his services very highly, knighted him in 1586. However, not everyone shared Leicester's views. Norris was dismissive of those he regarded as long-standing Dudley cronies but this may reflect his continued feud with the earl, who, conscious of such criticism, defended 'old Read' as 'worth [his] weight in pearl' (Correspondence, 417). Reade returned to Fenham, Holy Island, Northumberland, the old monastic manor house that he had leased from Elizabeth I in 1564.

Reade was wealthy enough and important enough in his locality to be appointed JP for Northumberland from 1577 and for co. Durham from 1583. He was named of the quorum for both commissions in 1593. His protestant beliefs reinforced his status as a member of Leicester's military clientele and he was well read and cultured, possessing various religious books, chronicles, and histories, including Holinshed. He was elected MP for Northumberland in 1593. Later he was visited by James VI and I, and was 'so comforted with the presence and gracious speeches of the King, that his spirits seemed so powerful within him, as he boasted himselfe to feele the warmth of youth stirre in his frost-nipt bloud' (J. Nichols, ed., The Progresses of King James I, 1828, 1.67). An inventory taken of Reade's household goods (worth £447 16s. 4d.) gives an interesting view of the house of a man of his class at the beginning of the seventeenth century. He was married three times. First, to Elizabeth (d. 1585), then to Mary (d. 1595), and finally to Elizabeth (d. after 1604), widow of Charles Towers of Holy Island. Nothing is known of their parentage. He had no known children of these marriages but did have two illegitimate children with two separate women, William Reade, who succeeded to his lands, and Charity Reade, daughter of a woman whose surname was Bell. Reade died of old age on 6 June 1604 on Holy Island, and was buried that day in the church there.

M. M. NORRIS

Sources [H. M. Wood], ed., *Wills and inventories from the registry at Durham*, 4, SurtS, 142 (1929), 2–3 · HoP, *Commons, 1558–1603* · J. Raine, *The history and antiquities of north Durham* (1852) · J. Bain, ed., *The border papers: calendar of letters and papers relating to the affairs of the borders of England and Scotland*, 2 vols. (1894–6) · CSP dom., addenda, 1547–1625 · CSP Scot., 1547–74; 1588–95; 1597–1603 · CPR, 1554–5 · T. Churchyard, *A generall rehearsall of warres* (1579) · J. Bruce, ed., *Correspondence of Robert Dudley, earl of Leycester*, CS, 27 (1844) · M. C. Fissel, *English warfare, 1511–1642* (2001) · S. Adams, ed., *Household accounts and disbursement books of Robert Dudley, earl of Leicester, 1558–1561, 1584–1586*, CS, 6 (1995)
Archives BL, MSS · PRO, MSS
Wealth at death £447 16s. 4d. in possessions: Raine, *History and antiquities*, 178

Reade, William Winwood (1838–1875), traveller, novelist, and controversialist, the eldest son of William Barrington Reade (1803–1881) and Elizabeth Reade (1810–1895) (daughter of Captain John Murray RN), of Ipsden House, Oxfordshire, was born at St Finan, near Crieff, Perthshire, on 26 December 1838. He was educated at Hyde House, Winchester, and for a brief period at Magdalen Hall, Oxford, although he left the university without a degree. His early attempts to master the art of fiction, in emulation of the literary success of his uncle Charles *Reade, whom he adored, met with disappointment. Both *Charlotte and Myra* (1859) and *Liberty Hall, Oxon* (1860) received very poor reviews. His scepticism about established Christianity found romantic expression in *The Veil of Isis, or, The Mysteries of the Druids*, published in 1861. In the same year he embarked on a tour of west Africa, which resulted in the publication of *Savage Africa* (1863), a miscellany of observations on the people and wildlife of that region, in which he paid particular attention to arguments then current about the character of gorillas and the existence of cannibalism. This work was essentially that of a dilettante, a romantic tourist who represented himself as a *flâneur* rather than a man of science.

On his return to England, in 1863, Reade read papers on his travels to a range of scientific societies, notably the newly formed Anthropological Society, with which he was to be associated for the next few years. In 1865 he became embroiled in a controversy over his views on the futility of Christian missions and the necessity of polygamy in west Africa, during which the explorer Richard Burton came to his defence. Seeking to broaden his knowledge of science and medicine, he entered as a student at St Mary's Hospital, London, in 1865, and in 1866 volunteered his services at a cholera hospital in Southampton. During this period he also visited North America and contributed to several literary and scientific periodicals published there. His ambition to follow in the footsteps of more famous African travellers was realized in 1868 when, with the aid of the Royal Geographical Society and Andrew Swanzy, a British trader, he undertook a second journey to west Africa. His attempt to explore the Asante kingdom having failed, he was encouraged by Sir Arthur Kennedy, governor of the British West African settlements, to undertake a journey from Sierra Leone to the upper Niger, including a visit to the goldmines of Bouré, a region not previously visited by Europeans. The fruits of this journey were to form the material for a large part of *The African Sketch Book*, an extraordinary medley of romantic fiction, popular anthropology, and travel narrative, published in 1873. In the same year he returned for the last time to west Africa, as the *Times* correspondent on the Second Anglo-Asante war, a conflict also covered by Henry Morton Stanley and G. A. Henty.

Reade's lasting reputation as a writer rests not on his novels, nor on his travel writing, but on a single epic work, *The Martyrdom of Man*, first published in 1872. This book, which has been described as a 'bible for secularists', defies easy categorization. According to Reade, his original intention was to restore Africa to a central place in world history through a consideration of such themes as the role of Islam, the history of the slave trade, and the evolution of mankind—an ambition shared by subsequent writers such as W. E. B. Du Bois. The book which actually emerged is a somewhat romantic study in universal history, treating the evolution of civilizations in the Mediterranean and the Near East in terms of the impact of war, religion, liberty, and the intellect on human life. Reade's militant agnosticism is manifest in his provocative account of the role of science in the modern world, in which Christianity itself is dismissed as the product of a passing age of superstition. Such sentiments were too radical for the orthodox press, as well as for many of his friends and family. Yet, despite unfavourable reviews, the book was to sell extremely well, especially after the publication of a cheap edition by the Rationalist Press Association in 1924.

Reade's final work, *The Outcast*, a reputedly autobiographical novel, was completed shortly before his death, in the house of Humphry Sandwith, at Church Street, Wimbledon, on 24 April 1875. He was buried in St Mary's Church, Ipsden, where a window is dedicated to his memory and to that of his brother, Malcolm. His uncle Charles Reade penned an epitaph shortly after his death which reveals as much about his time as it does about his life:

> The writer thus cut off in his prime entered life with excellent prospects; he was heir to considerable estates, and gifted with genius. But he did not live long enough to inherit the one or to mature the other. His whole public career embraced but fifteen years; yet in another fifteen he would probably have won a great name, and cured himself, as many thinking men have done, of certain obnoxious opinions which laid him open to reasonable censure. (*Daily Telegraph*)

FELIX DRIVER

Sources F. Driver, 'Becoming an explorer: the martyrdom of Winwood Reade', *Geography militant: cultures of exploration and empire* (2001), chap. 5 · Foster, *Alum. Oxon.* · *Daily Telegraph* (27 April 1875), 5 · C. Reade, *A record of the Redes* (1899) · J. D. Hargreaves, 'Winwood Reade and the discovery of Africa', *African Affairs*, 56 (1957), 306–16 · I. Burton, *The life of Captain Sir Richard F. Burton*, 2 vols. (1893) · W. S. Smith, *The London heretics, 1870–1914* (1967)
Archives RGS | Bodl. Oxf., letters to Lady Lytton · CUL, Darwin corresp. · Unilever House, London, United Africa Company archive, corresp. with Swanzy · W. Sussex RO, letters to F. A. Maxse [copies]
Likenesses photograph, Wilts. & Swindon RO · portrait (after photograph), repro. in W. Reade, *The martyrdom of man* (1934)
Wealth at death under £600: administration, 14 May 1875, *CGPLA Eng. & Wales*

Reader, William (*d. c.*1680), portrait painter, was the son of a Maidstone clergyman. After studying under Gerard Soest, he was supported and patronized by a nobleman in the west of England (perhaps the earl of Aylesford; in 1937 a number of Reader's portraits appeared in the Aylesford sale). His portrait of the composer John Blow was engraved by T. Beckett. A portrait by Reader of Robert Plot is in the Ashmolean Museum, Oxford. There may also be as yet undiscovered portraits by him, under the names of more eminent artists. He is described by Waterhouse as 'a clumsy portraitist of some character' (Waterhouse, 223). Vertue noted that Reader died impoverished about 1680 as an inmate of the Charterhouse (Vertue, *Note books*, 4.83).

L. H. CUST, *rev.* SUSAN COOPER MORGAN

Sources E. Waterhouse, *Painting in Britain, 1530–1790*, 4th edn (1978) · E. K. Waterhouse, *The dictionary of British 16th and 17th century painters* (1988) · Bénézit, *Dict.*, 4th edn · Redgrave, *Artists* · H. Walpole, *Anecdotes of painting in England: with some account of the principal artists*, ed. R. N. Wornum, new edn, 3 vols. (1849); repr. (1862) · Bryan, *Painters* (1886–9) · Vertue, *Note books*, 4.83
Archives Courtauld Inst., Witt Library, cuttings, photographs, sale catalogues

Reader, William (1782–1852), newspaper proprietor and topographer, was born on 28 December 1782 at High Cross, near Rowington, Warwickshire, one of eleven children of William Reader (1752–1808), farmer, and his wife, Mary, *née* White (1758–1837). The young William was adopted *c.*1785 by his great-uncle the antiquarian James Kettle, minister of the Presbyterian chapel at Warwick, and his wife, Martha. After an education at the academy of the Revd John Kendall, vicar of Budbrooke, William was in 1797 apprenticed to Noah Rollason, printer–proprietor of the *Coventry Mercury*. He was made a partner in 1808, and became sole proprietor on Rollason's death in 1813. In 1815 he married Elizabeth Hadley (*d.* 1870), with whom he had seven children. Admitted to the freedom of the city of Coventry in 1804, he played an active part in civic affairs, and rose in 1823 to the office of chamberlain.

Reader's business, in difficulties by the 1820s, failed in 1833. Forced to sell much of his property, he moved in 1835 to Birmingham, where not only did his financial position deteriorate further but also he suffered the loss of two of his daughters; a third daughter had earlier died in Coventry. In 1837 he settled in Shoreditch, London. His fortunes never rallied, but he managed sporadically to continue collecting for his projected history of Coventry. In 1844 one of his sons died. Reader himself died on 3 October 1852 at 42 Maria Street, Shoreditch, and was buried at St John's Church, Hoxton. He was survived by his wife and by only two sons.

An intense interest in his adopted city led Reader to amass material relating to Coventry's history, some of which formed the basis of articles in his newspaper and in the *Gentleman's Magazine*, to which he contributed until his death. His most successful work, *The History and Antiquities of the City of Coventry* (1810), was a popular history and guidebook which ran to several editions. He produced several other works devoted to Coventry and, like many antiquaries of the period, collected assiduously for a major work which he never quite completed: the draft of a greatly expanded history of Coventry survives in the Bodleian Library, Oxford.

Reader belonged to a generation of antiquaries which differed from its seventeenth- and eighteenth-century predecessors in having an urban and commercial, rather than a gentry, background, and correspondingly wider concerns. Hence its new-fashioned interest in the history of towns, in providing guidebooks for a new, travelling, public, and in addressing a more popular market generally. Reader's collections relied heavily on printed sources, but in making use of his official position to search corporation records he made an original contribution in particular to Coventry's institutional and topographical history. While he played a part in advancing the scope of antiquarian studies, his work nevertheless was imbued with a very traditionalist political and religious sensitivity. His newspaper adopted a decidedly conservative stance, as did some of his pamphlets; the same convictions pervaded, in a less obtrusive form, his historical collections. Some of Reader's collections housed in Coventry's central library were destroyed by bombing during the Second World War; others survive in the Bodleian Library.   CHRISTOPHER DAY

Sources GM, 2nd ser., 38 (1852), 649–52 · DNB · M. H. M. Hulton, 'William Reader, printer and antiquary', Warwickshire History, 4/5 (1980), 175–88 · B. J. Ronchetti, 'Antiquarian scholarship in Warwickshire, 1800–1860', MA diss., U. Birm., 1952 · parish register, Rowington, Warwickshire, 19 Nov 1782 [marriage] · parish register, Rowington, Warwickshire, 7 Jan 1783 [baptism]

Archives Bodl. Oxf., MSS collections for the history of Coventry

Reader, William Joseph [Bill] (1920–1990), business historian, was born on 20 November 1920 at 16 Queens Road, Weston-super-Mare, Somerset, the only child of Kenneth Joseph Reader, a poultry farmer, and his wife, Ethel, née Till. His parents separated when he was a child and he did not meet his father again until he was an adult. Brought up in Weston by his mother, a strong-minded and successful hotelier, Bill was educated first at Westgate preparatory school and then at Taunton School. It was at Taunton that his history master, J. F. Elam, nurtured a keen interest in history, and this provided both a professional and a personal mainspring throughout Bill Reader's life. In October 1939 he went up as a scholar to Jesus College, Cambridge, to read history. In 1940 he joined the Royal Corps of Signals believing, mistakenly as he soon found out and later wrote, that life in the signals would be 'less mathematical than gunnery and more comfortable than the infantry' (Shaw, 428). After a lengthy training in electrical theory and other technical matters he was sent to India, where he was also obliged to learn to ride a horse—skills he thankfully forgot when he returned to civilian life. He did, however, develop what became an abiding interest in aspects of military history, some of which he explored in his last published book: At Duty's Call (1988).

Demobilized from the army Reader returned to Cambridge, where he completed his degree in 1947. Charles Wilson, his tutor at Jesus (later professor of modern history at Cambridge), invited Reader to be his research assistant on a newly commissioned history of Unilever. At that time business history was neither an academic nor a scholarly discipline, being practised largely as 'an heroic mythology on the one hand and a kind of economic Crime Club on the other' (Wilson, v). Wilson's two-volume history of Unilever, published in 1954, a pioneering model for business histories, acknowledged the contribution to the project made by Reader's imaginative insight.

For the next fifteen years Reader worked for Unilever in market research, advertising, and public relations, including drafting the chairman's speeches. At the same time he began to write business history and, expanding his interests, he wrote a very successful illustrated social history: Life in Victorian England (1964). In this he was much encouraged by his wife, Ann, née Maffet, whom he had married in 1950 (about which time she was qualifying as a doctor). In 1964 Reader left Unilever to become a freelance historian, with commissions to write a biography of Lord Weir and a history of Imperial Chemical Industries (ICI), then one of the UK's largest and most significant companies. His two-volume history of ICI (published by Oxford University Press in 1970 and 1975) was a major contribution to business history, recognized by the award in 1972 of a PhD degree by Cambridge University for his publications.

Through the 1970s and the 1980s Reader continued to write and publish commissioned histories which exemplified scholarship, good writing, and an understanding of social and economic history. His books embodied his understanding of business and business people and his view of large corporations:

> One is looking at power politics in an economic landscape. Businessmen are often driven by motives which are by no means commercial. They seek power. They engage in rivalry … in business history, as in political history, we are concerned with the interplay between men and events, and it is equally important to understand both. (Reader, 'Personality', 108)

Reader's academic connections were strong, including as they did links with Cambridge, the London School of Economics (LSE), and colleges across the Atlantic. He was visiting professor at the University of Delaware in 1973 and 1976. He worked to raise money for the establishment, in 1979, of the Business History Unit at the LSE, where he was Texaco fellow in 1979–80. He was a member of the unit's academic management committee from its establishment until his death, advising on such major projects as the Dictionary of Business Biography and the commissioned histories—of Glaxo, for example–undertaken by the unit. The encouragement and support he gave to young business historians was always sustaining and generous. To them he communicated his high standards of scholarship and professionalism, and with them he shared his knowledge generously.

Reader was an excellent interviewer: unobtrusive and percipient, he drew out full and frank information from interviewees. He used this technique effectively with senior management in the companies whose histories he was writing, and for some, such as ICI, he continued to interview directors when they retired, creating an oral archive. He also interviewed a number of distinguished City figures for the National Sound Archive's National Life Story Collection. In the two years before he died he was working on a history of Unilever's last thirty years, to be extensively based on oral history. In the early 1980s he and his wife had moved from north London to live in Cambridge, where they much enjoyed entertaining friends and colleagues, sharing their love of good food and wine. Reader's commitment to complete work he had undertaken meant that until a few days before his death he was continuing to work on the Unilever project. Bill Reader died at his home, 46 Gough Way, Cambridge, on 5 June 1990, and was buried in Cambridge. He was survived by his wife and their two sons.   JUDY SLINN

Sources C. Shaw, 'W. J. Reader (1920–1990): an appreciation', *Annali di Storia dell' Impresa*, 7 (1991), 427–38 • *The Independent* (20 June 1990) • *The Times* (2 July 1990) • Jesus College, Cambridge [obit.] • W. J. Reader, 'Personality, strategy and structure: some consequences of strong minds', *Management strategy and business development: an historical and comparative study*, ed. L. Hannah (1976) • C. Wilson, *The history of Unilever: a study in economic growth and social change*, 1 (1954) • b. cert. • d. cert.
Archives Jesus College, Cambridge, working papers | SOUND BL NSA [as interviewer]
Wealth at death £179,825: probate, 9 July 1990, *CGPLA Eng. & Wales*

Reading. For this title name *see* Isaacs, Rufus Daniel, first marquess of Reading (1860–1935); Isaacs, Stella, marchioness of Reading and Baroness Swanborough (1894–1971).

Reading, Burnet (1749/50–1838), engraver and draughtsman, was born in Colchester of unknown parents. By 1770 he was working in London, producing engraved portraits for booksellers. Some of his portraits were printed in red, according to the fashion of the time, and he often worked in stipple. All his portraits are lively and bold in their style. His subjects tend to be contemporary celebrities, from the actor David Garrick to the painter Benjamin West and the socialite Emma Hamilton. He produced a set of six portraits of members of the Royal Academy from drawings by Peter Falconet. Many of his portraits appeared in Bell's *British Theatre* (1776–86) and the *European Magazine* (1783–93). Reading's love of theatrical subjects in particular is reflected in the fact that he executed a series of twelve etchings from drawings by Mortimer, *Characters to Illustrate Shakespeare*, published by T. and H. Rodd, and produced some of the plates to Boydell's *Shakespeare*. He also engraved various portraits of politicians and historical figures. In 1783 he produced a set of portraits of members of the American congress, and he was responsible for many of the portraits in Granger's *History of England* (1820 and 1822), including that of Oliver Cromwell. Other engravings included *Lavinia and her Mother*, after W. Bigg, and *Charlotte at the Tomb of Wether*, which was executed after his own design. The British Museum holds a collection of sixty-two examples of his portrait engravings, one of which is a self-portrait.

Reading was employed as drawing- and riding-master by the earl of Pomfret at Windsor, although there is no evidence as to when he held this position. A portrait of him was etched by Samuel De Wilde in 1798. This shows him as a young man, wearing a broad-brimmed hat. He sits in a chair, leaning one arm on the back of the chair; his flamboyant pose and direct gaze are an indication of his confidence and hint at a slight arrogance in his character. His last engravings were published in 1822; he died in north London late in 1838 and was buried at St Paul's, Covent Garden.   ELEANOR TOLLFREE

Sources Redgrave, *Artists*, 2nd edn, 350 • *Engraved Brit. ports.*, 3.551; 6.667–8 • Dodd's memoirs of English engravers, BL, Add. MS 33404 • parish register, St Paul's, Covent Garden, City Westm. AC [burial]
Likenesses S. De Wilde, engraving, 1798, BM, NPG • B. Reading, self-portrait, engraving, BM

Reading, John (d. 1346), theologian and Franciscan friar, is first recorded on 20 September 1292, when, already a friar, he was ordained subdeacon. He became a deacon two years later. He was trained at the Franciscan school at Oxford, becoming its forty-fifth lector about 1319, and holding that office for two years. By August 1321 he was DTh. At about this time he went to Avignon, where he revised his commentary on the first book of Peter Lombard's *Sentences*, and where he was one of the theologians whom John XXII consulted before he issued his decretal 'Antiquae concertationi' on 1 December 1323. He appears to have remained at Avignon, since he is reported to have died and been buried there in 1346.

John Reading was one of Duns Scotus's most loyal and dedicated defenders, particularly against the criticisms of William Ockham. Surprisingly, however, in *quaestio* 3 of the prologue to Ockham's *Commentary on Book 1 of the 'Sentences'* Reading appears as one of the sources for Ockham, who quotes him verbatim, picking pieces here and there from *quaestio* 2 of Reading's prologue to his *Commentary on Lombard's 'Sentences'*. In short, it seems necessary to postulate that John made two commentaries on Lombard's *Sentences*—an earlier one, which was a source for Ockham's *Sentences*, and another and later one, criticizing the same work of Ockham. Yet, despite such a postulate, both commentaries had large portions verbally in common, since the text that survives and serves as Ockham's source is the same as the later, and sole surviving, text that provides a Scotistic response to Ockham.

The fact that he became lector at Oxford about 1319, rather than providing a probable date for a sole *Commentary on the 'Sentences'* by Reading, indicates that he had already, as a bachelor of the *Sentences*, commented earlier on Lombard's work. Unlike earlier, more independent, associates of Duns Scotus—Robert Cowton, William of Nottingham, and William of Alnwick—Reading was, from the evidence of his writings, like Walter Chatton, among the more devoted followers of Scotus, for whom Ockham was in competition with Scotus for the leadership of the Franciscan school.

A look at particular questions shows this fervent devotion to Scotus's positions. The postulate of an intelligible impressed species was attacked by many authors as putting an intermediary between the object known and the knower that interfered with the direct knowledge of things. Scotus defended its existence, particularly against Henri de Gand and Godefroi de Fontaines. His arguments were attacked by Ockham and by another Franciscan master, Richard Drayton. Reading defended Scotus against these Franciscan authors and the tradition which supported them. Yet it would be wrong to think that Reading follows Scotus after the manner of a one-book man. In his discussion of finality, he is influenced by Robert Cowton, and even by Pierre Aureole, with whom he finally disagrees. Nor should his frequent conflicts with Ockham be seen as judgements of absolute opposition. Ockham's *Disputed Question 'De fine'* shows that he has accepted Reading's position with respect.

Regrettably, the only surviving copy of Reading's *Commentary on the 'Sentences'*, found in Florence, Biblioteca Nazionale, cod. Conv. soppr. D. IV. 95, ends with distinction 6 of book 1. Nevertheless, the manuscript offers a wealth of information about various authors and opinions of his day, and also represents an important chapter in the development of the Scotistic school. As far as Reading himself is concerned, it is possible to say that on the scientific character of theology he disagreed with Thomas Aquinas, and did so on the basis of his agreement with Duns Scotus, that it is impossible to have faith and science concerning the same object. The theologian who receives his principles on faith from God, cannot then claim to have science or scientific knowledge concerning the conclusions he deduces from premises that have faith as their warrant. Likewise, in opposition to two of Scotus's main opponents, Gand and Conington, Reading attempted to establish that there were proper boundaries for certain sciences, and warned that the jurisdiction of theology should not overextend itself into the autonomous domains of those sciences. Finally, the surviving texts show that Reading's main concerns in regard to causality were to clarify the Scotistic notions involved in proving the existence and unicity of God, and to defend these positions against the attacks of William Alnwick, Pierre Aureole, and Ockham.   S. F. BROWN

Sources E. Longpré, 'Jean de Reading et le B. Jean Duns Scot', *La France Franciscaine*, 7 (1924), 99–109 • R. Schönberger and B. Kible, *Repertorium edierter Texte des Mittelalters* (Berlin, 1994), nn. 14589–94 • S. F. Brown, 'Sources for Ockham's prologue to the *Sentences* [pt 1]', *Franciscan Studies*, new ser., 26 (1966), 36–65 • 'Quaestio Ioannis de Reading de necessitate specierum intelligibilium: defensio doctrinae Scoti', ed. G. Gál, *Franciscan Studies*, new ser., 29 (1969), 66–156 • G. J. Etzkorn, 'John of Reading on the existence and unicity of God, efficient and final causality', *Franciscan Studies*, new ser., 41 (1981), 125–221 • S. J. Livesey, *Theology and science in the fourteenth century: three questions on the unity and subalternation of the sciences from John of Reading's commentary on the 'Sentences'* (1989) • J. Percan, *Teologia come 'scienza pratica' secondo Giovanni de Reading*, Spicilegium Bonaventurianum, 26 (1986) • Emden, *Oxf.*, 3.1554 • *Fratris Thomae vulgo dicti de Eccleston tractatus de adventu Fratrum Minorum in Angliam*, ed. A. G. Little (1951)

Reading, John (*d.* 1368/9), Benedictine monk and historian, was a monk of Westminster Abbey by 1339/40 and had been priested by 1341/2, when he sang his first mass. He is recorded as *custos ordinis* of the abbey in 1349, and from 1350 to 1353 he held the office of infirmarer. His death is recorded in the abbey's infirmary roll for 1368/9. He wrote a continuation of the *Flores historiarum*, the St Albans chronicle acquired by Westminster Abbey in 1265 and thereafter augmented by a series of independent narratives. Reading's continuation covers the period 1346–67, though it was not begun until 1366 and the chronology of some of its earlier sections is distinctly confused. Down to 1356 the account of Edward III's French wars is dependent on the chronicle of Robert of Avesbury; Reading also drew on the continuation of the *Polychronicon* of Ranulf Higden. After 1356, however, the account appears to be independent, or at least to draw on sources now lost. Reading provides one of the most detailed accounts of English history in the 1360s, a period otherwise largely devoid of good historical writing.

Reading apologized for his lack of learning; certainly, the work has little literary merit and the Latin is sometimes ungrammatical. On the other hand, it represents a very interesting catalogue of information drawn together by a well-informed man living in close proximity to the centres of political power in Westminster and London. The chronicle includes a good deal of material on the internal history of Westminster Abbey: for example, Reading blamed the financial problems of the abbey in the mid-fourteenth century on the extravagance of Abbot Simon Bircheston (1344–9), and recounted the visit of Edward III to the abbey church on the eve of his departure for France in 1359. However, the chronicle is much more than a set of monastic annals, and provides information and commentary on the black death and its socio-economic consequences, various items of parliamentary legislation from the Statute of Labourers (1351) to the abolition of 'Peter's pence' (1365), the contemporary tensions between the black monks and the friars, and the ratification of the treaty of Calais (1360) in the parliament of 1361. Reading was highly critical of the mores of the age, and regarded the plague as God's vengeance on an unworthy people; he also contributed to the contemporary debate on the laziness and wilfulness of the labouring classes. His moralizing is typical of the reactionary attitudes of the upper classes—and particularly of the monastic orders—during the period of turmoil that followed the black death.

John Reading's chronicle survives in only one medieval manuscript (BL, Cotton MS Cleopatra A.xvi). However, a number of later chronicles (various continuations of the *Polychronicon* and the chronicle of Adam Murimuth, and especially the St Albans *Historia Anglicana* and the continuation of the English *Brut* chronicle) borrowed extensively and sometimes transcribed or translated directly from Reading; this indicates that other manuscripts of the latter's text must have circulated in the later fourteenth and fifteenth centuries. Slight variations and a greater degree of accuracy in certain of the relevant passages in the *Historia Anglicana* and the *Brut* also suggest that the surviving manuscript is a slightly inferior transcription of Reading's lost original.   W. M. ORMROD

Sources *Chronica Johannis de Reading et anonymi Cantuariensis, 1346–1367*, ed. J. Tait (1914) • A. Gransden, *Historical writing in England*, 2 (1982) • J. Taylor, *English historical literature in the fourteenth century* (1987) • B. Harvey, *Westminster Abbey and its estates in the middle ages* (1977)

Reading, John (1587/8–1667), Church of England clergyman and religious controversialist, was born in Buckinghamshire of 'sufficient parents' (Wood, *Ath. Oxon.*, 3.794). He matriculated from Magdalen Hall, Oxford, on 4 May 1604, aged sixteen, graduated BA on 17 October 1607, and proceeded MA from St Mary Hall on 22 June 1610. In February 1612 he was ordained deacon by the bishop of Oxford and on 19 June 1614 he was made a priest. About the same time he became chaplain to Edward la Zouche, Lord Zouche, from July 1615 warden of the Cinque Ports and governor of Dover Castle. He moved to Dover, where on 2 December 1616 he was made minister of St Mary the Virgin at the request of the parishioners who were, according to Wood, 'very much taken with his preaching' (Wood, *Ath. Oxon.*, 3.794). In 1621 he described this congregation as 'zealous' (*Old Mans Staff*, sig. A2r). Some time after 1625 he seems to have been appointed chaplain-in-ordinary to Charles I and to have received a BD from one of the universities. By 1627 he had married: a son, William, was baptized at St Mary's on 14 December that year.

In the 1620s and 1630s Reading published a number of pamphlets based on sermons that he had given at St Mary's. *A Faire Warning* (1621), dedicated to Lucy Russell, countess of Bedford, indicates that he had recently recovered from a serious illness. *The Old Mans Staff* (1621), a meditation on 'the dignitie belonging to the aged', was dedicated to Lord Zouche. On election day 1626 he preached a sermon which argued that the 'late visitations' of God were the punishment for the 'cursed libertie of sinning' (*Moses and Jethro*, 1626, sig. A2r–v). *Davids Soliloquie* (1627), dedicated to Lady Sara Hastings, a member of his congregation, seems to suggest that he had been (and perhaps still was) plagued with melancholy—it is possible that this is the illness to which he referred in *A Faire Warning*. On 21 September 1637 he preached the funeral sermon of Alice Percivall, the wife of his friend Anthony Percivall, controller of customs for Kent, later published as *Characters of True Blessednesse* (1638). In 1638 he questioned a suspected Catholic priest who had arrived in Dover from Flanders, and in the following year he informed Archbishop William Laud about a freemason who had 'spread sundry opinions repugnant to the doctrine of the Church of England' (*CSP dom.*, 1638–9, 156; 1639–40, 80–81).

Reading, a 'severe Calvinist', was a good preacher 'very much resorted to for his frequent and edifying sermons, and held in great esteem by the neighbourhood, especially by the puritanical party' (Wood, *Ath. Oxon.*, 3.794). During the early 1640s, however, he preached forcefully against rebellion and in favour of the king. On 23 August 1641 he delivered an assize sermon at Maidstone in Kent, published as *A Sermon Delivered* (1642), which condemned

the 'state-threatening schismaticks' and took as its motto Romans 16:17, 'I beseech you brethren, marke them who cause divisions and offences, contrary to the doctrine ye have learned, and avoid them' (pp. 1, 4). The address seems to have caused offence to many of those who heard it and Reading subsequently claimed that his only desire had been to 'perswade to an holy unity in Christ'. He dedicated this pamphlet to the royalists Sir Thomas Mallet and Sir Edward Dering, and added his 'hearty prayers for the good successe of … [their] … prudent endeavours' in the Commons (sig. A3v, A4r).

In April 1642 Reading's 'study of books' was plundered by the Kent militia and in November of the same year he was 'taken violently by soldiers out of his study … and sent to prison and banishment for a year and seven months' (Wood, *Ath. Oxon.*). He may have been imprisoned in the Tower during this period. On 27 January 1643 the king wrote to Archbishop Laud asking him to bestow the parsonage of Chartham, Kent, upon Reading 'now beneficed at Dover but deprived of his small livelihood by the perverse disposition of some of his turbulent parishioners' (*CSP dom.*, 1641–3, 440). The Commons blocked this appointment and, at the same time, passed an ordinance sequestering Laud's temporalities. Reading was then appointed to a prebend in Canterbury Cathedral, but does not seem to have taken possession of this office. His *A Grain of Incense*, which George Thomason bought on 8 April 1643, called for God's blessing upon the king and asked him to grant 'an happy Understanding and Accord' between the king and 'His great Counsell the Parliament' (sig. A3v–4r). Reading's *Evening Sacrifice or Prayer*, which Thomason bought on 5 August 1643, called for God's blessing on the royal family but did not make any mention of parliament.

In July 1644 Sir William Brockman presented Reading to the parsonage of Cheriton, Kent, and about the same time he was appointed by the assembly of divines to be one of the nine clergymen to write annotations on the New Testament. At some point in late 1644 or early 1645 the authorities discovered a royalist plot to seize Dover Castle, and Reading was 'inhumanely seized on in a cold winter night in his house' (Wood, *Ath. Oxon.*). He was held overnight in Dover Castle and then consigned to Leeds Castle where he wrote *A Guide to the Holy City*, which was published in 1651. On 8 January 1647 he was a prisoner in the Fleet. The parliamentary committee for Kent ordered his release at an unspecified date, and although his personal goods were returned to him his livings were sequestered. However, despite the refusal of the committee for plundered ministers on 24 August 1647 to entertain his petition to be restored, his son William claimed in an exchequer deposition of 1652 that Reading was rector of Cheriton and had been for eight years.

Donald Wing attributes *Little Benjamin, or, Truth Discovering Error* (1649) to Reading, but this is unlikely because *Little Benjamin* is a forceful defence of the regicide. Wing's attribution of *The Ranters Ranting* (1650) to Reading is more convincing, however. On 10 March 1650 he publicly debated with an Anabaptist named Samuel Fisher in

Folkestone, Kent, concerning the right of Christians to 'preach the gospel without ecclesiastical ordination, or contrary to the commands of the civil magistrate' (Wood, *Ath. Oxon.*). Fisher argued for the motion and apparently took most of his arguments from Jeremy Taylor's *Liberty of Prophesying*. This experience led Reading to pen *An Antidote Against Anabaptism* (1654), an attack on the 'curiously impartial' (*DNB*) section of Taylor's book which examined the opinions of the Anabaptists on infant baptism. Reading published an enlarged edition of *An Antidote* under the title *Anabaptism Routed* in 1655: both editions were dedicated to Sir William Brockman and his wife, Anne.

On 24 May 1660 Reading made a short speech and presented Charles II with a 'large Bible with gold clasps' in the name of the corporation of Dover upon the king's return to England. Soon after he was restored to his prebend of Canterbury and the rectory of Chartham. He was restored to Cheriton on 18 July 1660, but resigned this living at an unknown date before August 1662. In October 1660 the king wrote to Oxford University requesting that Reading be awarded a DD. In 1660 he wrote *Christmas Revived*, a defence of 'the observation of a day in memorie of [the birth of] our Saviour' (p. 1), and three years later he published *A Sermon Lately Delivered* in Canterbury Cathedral in defence of 'Church-Musick'. He died on 26 October 1667 and was buried four days later in the chancel of Chartham parish church. Anthony Wood provides interesting details of a number of manuscripts written by Reading but never published. JASON MᶜELLIGOTT

Sources Walker rev., 224 · Foster, *Alum. Oxon.* · Wood, *Ath. Oxon.*, new edn, 3.794–7 · *CSP dom.*, 1635–67 · *STC, 1475–1640* · *Sixth report*, HMC, 5 (1877–8), 152 · *IGI* [St Mary the Virgin, Dover parish register]
Archives BL, Egerton MS 2584, fol. 305; Lansdowne MS 986, fol. 70; Add. MS 18671, fol. 184

Reading, John (*c.*1645–1692), musician and composer, of unknown parentage, is listed among the choristers of St Paul's Cathedral in 1661, and it is likely that it was he who became a junior vicar-choral in 1667 (10 October) and poor clerk (28 November) at Lincoln Cathedral. He became master of the choristers there in 1670 but in 1675 moved to Chichester Cathedral, where he was appointed organist and master of the choristers on 4 January, with the additional emolument of a Sherburne clerkship. On 25 March 1675 he applied for a licence to marry Ann Micklethwayte of Lincoln, from which it appears that he was a widower of about thirty.

Less than a year after his appointment to Chichester, Reading succeeded Randolph Jewett at Winchester Cathedral, becoming organist, lay clerk, and master of the choristers on 25 November 1675. On 9 September 1678 he was admonished for giving 'undue and over severe correction to some of the Choristers' and told 'to take greater care and diligence in the improvement of the Choristers in Musick than hitherto he hath done' (Matthews, *Organs and Organists*, 22). This may have hastened his departure to Winchester College, where he appears as organist between 1681 and 1692. During his time there the organ was rebuilt by Renatus Harris (1683–5), and his stipend as

organist was considerably increased from £5 to £50 a year.

Reading was the composer of the Winchester College song *Dulce domum* and the college Latin graces (see Philip Hayes, *Harmonia Wiccamica*, 1780). The survival of his church music is rather patchy. There are remains of an anthem and burial service at Chichester, and the top and bottom parts of several anthems by him in an organ book (partly autograph) originally from Winchester and now at the University of California, Berkeley. The latter's anthems are not in such a condition as to enable a fair estimate of them to be made, apart from an agreeable setting of the responses and litany. Quite a number of his songs came out in popular miscellanies such as Playford's *Choice Ayres and Songs* (1681) and some instrumental pieces were also published. Reading died in Winchester in 1692.

Reading was one of three musicians of that name active in the late seventeenth and early eighteenth centuries. John *Reading (*c.*1685–1764), organist and composer (and from 1702 to 1708 like his namesake master of the choristers at Lincoln Cathedral), was probably his son or nephew. The third John Reading, a bass singer, seems to have sung in James II's Catholic chapel and gone on to perform in a number of Purcell's works. IAN SPINK

Sources A. Ashbee and D. Lasocki, eds., *A biographical dictionary of English court musicians, 1485–1714*, 2 (1998), 948–9 · H. W. Shaw, *The succession of organists of the Chapel Royal and the cathedrals of England and Wales from c.1538* (1991), 76–7, 160, 298 · B. Matthews, *The music of Winchester Cathedral* (1964), 22 · B. Matthews, *The organs and organists of Winchester Cathedral*, 3rd edn (1975)

Reading, John (*c.*1685–1764), organist and composer, was perhaps the son of the John Reading (*d.* 1692) who was master of the choristers at Lincoln (*c.*1670–1675) before becoming organist at Winchester, first at the cathedral (1675–81) and then at the college (1681–92). But there were other musical Readings in London who might also have been the boy's father: Balthazar, bass in the Chapel Royal, Valentine, a string player in the private musick (both *fl.* 1685–8), and another John (*fl.* 1684–1717), a bass theatre singer. The younger John Reading was a choirboy in the Chapel Royal and a pupil of John Blow; warrants at his dismissal are dated 22 December 1699. Although not officially appointed because of difficulties with his predecessor, he was organist at Dulwich College between March 1700 and 26 September 1702 and retained a close and friendly association with the college all his life. From 21 November 1702 he served as a junior vicar and poor clerk at Lincoln Cathedral, becoming master of the children there on 5 October 1703. No further mention of him at Lincoln occurs after 1705.

On 13 April 1703 John Reading of St Margaret's, Lincoln, married Ann Corbet of St Andrew's, Holborn, at St Mary Magdalen, Old Fish Street, London. On 1 December 1707 he witnessed the death of Jeremiah Clarke, who shot himself in his house in St Paul's Churchyard; Sir John Hawkins records that Reading 'was passing by at the instant the pistol went off, and entering the house found his friend in the agonies of death.' He was elected as organist at St John's, Hackney, on 28 January 1708. In 1718 questions were raised about his absence from his post, and on 12 December 1719 he was threatened with dismissal, having been reprimanded concerning

> irregularities relating to the execution of his Office as Organist of this Parish, and particularly for playing the Voluntary too long, and using persistently too light, Airy and Jyggy Tunes, no ways proper to raise the Devotion Suitable for a Releigous Assembly. (LMA, P79/JNI/140)

Having promised 'to amend' (ibid.) at a hearing on 19 April 1720, he continued serving at St John's until 4 April 1727, when he was ordered 'to provide himself with another place' (LMA, P79/JNI/141, fol. 63r) within three months.

In 1719 he became the first teacher of John Stanley. During his time at St John's he had published *A Book of New Songs* (after the Italian Manner) (c.1710), when he was living at Arundel Street, Strand, and *A Book of New Anthems* (c.1715), by which time he had moved to 'Swan passage in Orrange Street near Red-Lyon Square in Holborne' (*A Book of New Anthems*, title-page). In his early years he was an enthusiast for the Italian style and hoped that his *Book of New Songs* would 'incite our Great masters to improve the Design to such perfection that our English Composers might be inspired with the utmost delicacy of a *Roman Genius*' (*A Book of New Songs*, preface). The *Book of New Anthems* comprises six multi-movement works in modern style, employing solo voices and incorporating elaborate instrumental interludes. The reprimand received by Reading for his 'light, Airy and Jyggy Tunes' is at odds with his keyboard music, sober in nature and skilfully written. His organ voluntaries helped set the pattern for later composers like Stanley, with a slow opening movement followed by a brisk or fugal one. Reading was not only a composer but also an assiduous compiler of collections of keyboard music and of songs. Seventeen manuscript volumes of these collections survive, some very large, most of which Reading bequeathed to Dulwich College. They include some of the most important sources for English organ music of the period.

On 30 June 1727 Reading became organist at St Mary Woolnoth with St Mary Woolchurch, with an annual fee of £20 (which dropped to £12 in 1758), and on 9 April 1731 he added the position of organist at St Dunstan-in-the-West (fee £21 p.a.); he held both places until his death. He was a founder member of the Royal Society of Musicians in August 1739. Reading died on 2 September 1764, aged eighty-seven according to the *Gentleman's Magazine*, but this seems about ten years too old for his service as choirboy in the Chapel Royal. ANDREW ASHBEE

Sources GM, 1st ser., 34 (1764), 450 · J. Hawkins, *A general history of the science and practice of music*, new edn, 3 vols. (1853); repr. in 2 vols. (1963) · R. Simpson, *Memorials of St John at Hackney*, 3 pts (1881–2), pt 3 · F. B. Bickley, ed., *Catalogue of the manuscripts and muniments of Alleyn's College of God's Gift at Dulwich: second series* (1903) · D. Dawe, *Organists of the City of London, 1660–1860* (1983) · A. Ashbee, ed., *Records of English court music*, 2 (1987); 5 (1991) · J. Harley, *British harpsichord music*, 2 vols. (1992); (1994) · D. Burshell, '"The psalms set full for the organ" by John Reading', *Journal of the British Institute of Organ Studies*, 16 (1992), 14–28 · I. Spink, *Restoration cathedral music, 1660–1714* (1995) · S. Jeans and H. D. Johnstone, 'Reading, John (iii)', *New Grove*, 2nd edn
Likenesses portrait, Dulwich Picture Gallery, London

Reading, Robert (*d.* 1317), Benedictine monk and historian, of Westminster Abbey, wrote part of his house's continuation of the *Flores historiarum* of Matthew Paris. Reading is mentioned in the infirmarer's accounts in 1294 and 1298, in the list of monks imprisoned on suspicion of robbing the king's treasury in 1303, in the Westminster treasurer's accounts for undertaking a journey to York in the same year, and as one of the monks protesting at the deprivation of Prior Hadham in 1307. The almoner's accounts for 1317 mention his death in that year. According to a note in the Chetham's Library manuscript version of the Westminster *Flores*, inserted at 1326, this was the point at which both his chronicle and his life ended; but the note, which must have been written after 1347, cannot be relied upon for strict accuracy on the portion of the chronicle to be attributed to Reading, even though it provides evidence that he wrote some of it. Most probably, like his fellow monk John Bever, who seems to have composed the section ending in 1307, Reading was one of a group of annalists engaged in recording contemporary events, and the evidence of the almoner's account must be preferred to that of a much later note in the *Flores*. As one of the chroniclers of Edward II's reign he adopts, like his predecessor, a rhetorical and homiletic style, and does not hide his disappointment with the policy and achievements of the king, his contempt for Edward's stratagems to avoid taking the advice of his nobility, and his loathing for Piers Gaveston, whose murder in 1312 he describes as a just proceeding. His lively prejudice against the Dominican friars allowed him to include a pamphlet circulated in London against them. As he cannot be credited with the annals for 1317–26, he cannot have been writing at the behest of Queen Isabella and Roger Mortimer as has been suggested, but he and his successor as annalist agree in their low view of Edward II. He maintained the Westminster tradition of monastic chronicle writing in a period when many other abbeys seem to have diminished or abandoned their keeping of independent annals, and his part of the *Flores* was circulated with the rest to other monastic houses in place of the latter's own efforts.

JEREMY CATTO

Sources 'Flores historiarum', Chetham's Library, Manchester, MS 9712 · infirmarer's accounts, 1294, 1298, Westminster Abbey Muniments · treasurer's accounts, 1303, Westminster Abbey Muniments · almoner's accounts, 1317, Westminster Abbey Muniments · B. F. Harvey, ed., *Documents illustrating the rule of Walter de Wenlok abbot of Westminster, 1283–1307*, CS, 4th ser., 2 (1965), 95–6 · CPR, 1301–7, 195 · H. R. Luard, ed., *Flores historiarum*, 3 vols., Rolls Series, 95 (1890) · E. H. Pearce, *The monks of Westminster* (1916) · T. F. Tout, 'The Westminster Chronicle attributed to Robert of Reading', *EngHR*, 31 (1916), 450–64 · A. Gransden, 'The continuations of the *Flores historiarum* from 1265 to 1327', *Mediaeval Studies*, 36 (1974), 472–92 · A. Gransden, *Historical writing in England*, 1 (1974) · A. Gransden, *Historical writing in England*, 2 (1982) · J. Taylor, *English historical literature in the fourteenth century* (1987)
Archives Chetham's Library, Manchester, MS 9712

Reading, William (1674–1744), librarian, was born on 17 September 1674 at Swin in the parish of Wombourne, Staffordshire, the son of William and Joan Redding. He describes his father as 'a refiner of iron'. He was educated at Halesowen School by Josiah Read and Robert Durant. He matriculated from University College, Oxford, on 1 June 1693, graduated BA in 1697, and proceeded MA from St Mary Hall on 28 June 1703. He was ordained deacon on 19 September 1697 and priest, by Henry Compton, bishop of London, on 21 December 1707.

Reading's appointment as library keeper at Sion College, London Wall, on 15 November 1708, upon the recommendation of Bishop Compton, may well have been connected with the conferment of legal deposit status on the library, as this was currently being discussed by parliament, and became law under the Act for the Encouragement of Learning on 10 April 1710. The act, as the other libraries of deposit discovered, was not wholly effective in securing deposit by the Stationers of the kind of book that the libraries required. Reading's librarianship, however, saw a substantial increase in the stock and use of the library. In addition to deposited books, there were large gifts or bequests of books from Bishop Compton (1707 and 1713–14), Mrs Eleanor James (1711), Edward Waple (1712), and Francis Bugg (1717?). Having brought the vellum book of benefactors up to date, Reading submitted to the college court a proposal for settling the library and putting it in good order (5 September 1720). He was able to extend the shelving of the library, so that it could be arranged in a classified order with space for accessions, and to remove the chains from the books. These improvements are apparent in the *Bibliothecae cleri Londinensis in Collegio Sionensi catalogus*, a volume in folio which Reading brought out in 1724. The first part, printed by John Watts, the best printer of his day, is in classified shelf order, with detailed entries which include the printer's name and the name of the benefactor (when this was known to the cataloguer). The second part is an index by author and subject, and the third a history of the library (in English). Modelled on the 1693 catalogue of Charles Maurice Le Tellier's collection, Reading's elaborate catalogue was highly valued for its classifications at a time when very few English libraries boasted published catalogues.

Reading had married by 1714, when his eldest son, Thomas Granger Reading, was born to his wife, Catherine (*d.* 1730). The births of six children are recorded in the registers of St Alfege's Church. The family lived in a house adjoining the college, and his wife and later his eldest son assisted Reading in the library. Catherine Reading died in 1730 and was buried in the church on 28 August.

Reading held lectureships in several London churches, including St Alfege, St Michael, Crooked Lane, and Christchurch, Newgate Street; in the dedications to Archbishop William Wake of his volumes of sermons he nevertheless displayed some disappointment at the lack of preferment in the church. The office of clerk or register of the college, and that of librarian, had been split at the time of his appointment; they were reunited in 1724, and the additional burden that fell upon Reading is clear from the minutes of the college court.

In addition to the achievement of the 1724 catalogue, Reading published an edition of the ecclesiastical historians—Eusebius, Socrates, Sozomen, and others—in three

volumes at Cambridge in 1720. Three volumes of sermons were published in his lifetime, and they were collected as *One Hundred and Sixteen Sermons* in 1755.

Reading continued to write the minutes of the court until 17 April 1744. He died on 10 December 1744. In his will he left bequests of £20 apiece to his younger children, and £30 to the eldest child, Thomas. He asked to be buried in the porch of St Alfege's Church near the grave of his wife, Catherine. Thomas Reading evidently hoped to succeed his father as librarian, but an improvement in the finances of the college enabled the court to appoint William Brakenridge as principal librarian, while Thomas Reading was continued as assistant register or clerk. He did, however, remain in the house his father had occupied.

William Reading left at his death a reputation for his plain and honest manner of life and preaching, according to the *Gentleman's Magazine* (1st ser., 14, 1744, 676). The catalogue of 1724 also shows how ably he had built upon the library's status as one of deposit, augmented by important benefactions, to become one of London's richest and most accessible resources for scholarship.

R. JULIAN ROBERTS

Sources E. H. Pearce, *Sion College and Library* (1913) · Bodl. Oxf., MS Rawl. J, fol. 4, fol. 265 · St Alfege's registers, GL, MSS 5746/1–2 · court minute books of Sion College, GL · private information (2004) [Douglas Johnson, Staffordshire RS] · *DNB* · will, PRO, PROB 11/741, fols. 59r–60v
Archives GL, court minute books of Sion College
Wealth at death bequests to five children of £20 and to a sixth (the eldest and executor) suggest he didn't have much: will, PRO, PROB 11/741, fols. 59r–60v

Ready, William James Durant (1823–1873), marine painter, was born on 11 May 1823 in London, the son of a customs clerk. He taught himself painting, before moving to the United States for five years. He painted in oils and watercolours, mainly scenes of the south coast of England. Ready did not exhibit any paintings until 1861, when a watercolour, *View on the Thames*, was shown at the Suffolk Street Gallery in London. He exhibited three paintings at the British Institution—*Gorlestone Pier, Suffolk* in 1861, *Dirty Weather Clearing off* in 1862, *Coast Scene Near Harwich* in 1865, and two at the Royal Academy in 1867. His pictures are usually signed W. F. R., but the Royal Academy paintings are signed W. F. Durant. The painter David Roberts is said to have admired his work. He died in Brighton, Sussex, on 29 November 1873.

ANNE PIMLOTT BAKER

Sources E. H. H. Archibald, *Dictionary of sea painters* (1980), 160 · Wood, *Vic. painters*, 3rd edn · J. Johnson, ed., *Works exhibited at the Royal Society of British Artists, 1824–1893, and the New English Art Club, 1888–1917*, 2 vols. (1975), 388 · Boase, *Mod. Eng. biog.* · Graves, *RA exhibitors*

Reaney [*née* Edis], **Isabella Emily Thomasa** [Isabel] (1847–1929), preacher and social activist, was born on 15 July 1847 in Huntingdon, the sixth of seven children of Robert Edis and his wife, Emma Ekin. Her father was a literary bookseller and a well-known man in the town. One of her brothers, Dr Arthur Wellesley Edis (1840–1893), was to become a noted specialist in the treatment of women's illnesses. She was to work closely with him in campaigns for reducing the hours and improving the working conditions of shop-girls. Another brother, Robert William Edis (1839–1927), was an architect especially concerned with interior decoration, 'healthy furniture', and sanitary improvements in houses. Isabel Edis was educated at a boarding-school. In her teens she began to work among the poor of Huntingdon, reading and teaching from the Bible. She instituted a cottage service, which soon became so crowded that it was transferred to a large classroom belonging to the local Congregationalists. Eventually attendances were so large that the services were moved to the Institution Hall of Huntingdon, where they attracted the attention of the bishop of the diocese. He criticized Isabel Edis for disturbing the regular order of the church. However, on hearing her reply—that her authority was higher than that of bishops and archbishops, and so she must speak, but that if her work was likely to injure the church she would withdraw from it—the bishop seems to have allowed her to carry on, with his blessing. She continued to hold services there until her marriage on 4 March 1873 to the Revd George Sale Reaney (1838–1901), a prominent Congregational minister in Warrington. She moved her activities there, and conducted Sunday afternoon services in the public hall. Her husband's health having broken down from overwork, in 1876 they moved to a smaller church in Reading, Berkshire, for six years, and then (in 1882) to the East End of London, where he took charge of Stepney meeting-house.

In the East End, Isabel Reaney continued to work among the poor, and also, in emergencies, took her husband's place at meeting, although remaining herself a staunch member of the Church of England. On one occasion she conducted a special service in the City Temple for Dr Joseph Parker. While living at Stepney she worked with Henrietta Barnett to set up a Children's Country Holiday Fund, and she herself established a home for convalescents at Folkestone. When her husband left London to take charge of Dr Parker's former church, Cavendish Street Chapel, in Manchester, she founded a similar home at Blackpool (by 1894 capable of accommodating 130 people), and was a significant figure in the promotion of Blackpool as a winter health resort. In 1890 George Sale Reaney left Congregationalism for the Church of England, disillusioned with what he felt to be the excessive individualism of the Congregational ideal and attracted by the national idea, as propounded by F. D. Maurice (1805–1872) and Samuel Barnett (1844–1913). His wife's example was scarcely less important. He was always totally supportive of her public work, having written in 1886 a memorable riposte to an attack on women preachers, in which he began by observing that: 'It is always a rather difficult task for men to discuss the true sphere of women. ... The truest conception of womanhood can only be possessed by women' (G. S. Reaney, 'Preaching women', 844–5). He served as a curate at Riverhead, Kent (1890–91), and at Bickley, in the same county (1891–3), and in 1893 was appointed vicar of Greenwich, where Isabel Reaney was able to return to the sort of work which she had done

in Stepney. She supported the Women's Convalescent Home Association to establish homes providing a fortnight's rest for women employed in factories, warehouses, workshops, and offices, and for the wives and daughters of London workmen. In 1894 she played an important part in getting the baths at the London People's Palace opened in the evenings (on Tuesdays they were opened from 6 a.m. to 10 p.m.) for the use of ladies in business. She and her husband held Sunday afternoon services for the people at Good Duke Humphrey's Hall (a temperance restaurant of which Isabel Reaney was the honorary director): G. S. Reaney held the service on the first Sunday of the month for men only, Isabel Reaney conducting all the rest, for men and women. On Thursday nights she organized magic lantern lectures and, on Saturday nights, popular concerts and entertainments.

From the time when they moved to Stepney, Isabel Reaney became a great campaigner on behalf of tramcar drivers. Feeling the poverty of 'mittens and tracts' as a means of expressing sympathy with their terrible working conditions, she qualified as a shareholder in several metropolitan companies so that she could press their cause more effectively. In 1885 she got Samuel Smith MP to put a question to the home secretary in the Commons about the long hours worked. She also attended a shareholders' meeting of the North Metropolitan Tramways Company, where 70 shareholders out of about 4000 were present. To the sound of shuffling feet and hissing she urged the injustices of the drivers' working conditions. Gaining only six supporters, she proceeded to launch a campaign, canvassing shareholders by pamphlet and mobilizing the press. By the next half-yearly meeting (February 1886) she had a considerable body of support, and, even though her motion was defeated, the chairman reluctantly promised to do something. The press meanwhile drew public attention to conditions in Liverpool, Glasgow, Bristol, and Leicester—even in Melbourne and Sydney; and under the Revd F. Barclay and others a new union was established in south London. In a powerful article in the *Contemporary Review* (56, 1889, 649–58), 'Slave-driving by public companies', which culminated in a quotation from Mazzini, Isabel Reaney underlined the status of tramway and railway companies as public companies. Since they were under parliamentary sanction, state intervention was justified to ensure that they were run properly. She even urged the advantages of the municipalization of tramways and of the nationalization of railways.

Isabel Reaney was a prominent temperance activist throughout her life, and wrote innumerable temperance stories. Her three-decker novel, *Dr Grey's Patient*, published in 1893 as part of the Story Book Series, was much more than a temperance tract: it was well paced and compelling, and provoked much discussion. She also published advice manuals for girls and boys (between 1879 and 1882) and a book of devotional texts for the use of girls' schools and colleges, relating religion to everyday life. In *English Girls: their Place and Power* (1879) she cited John Ruskin

(1819–1900) on the need for girls at home to develop a sense of will and drive, including reading for a purpose. She supported higher education for women, but felt that it needed to embrace every aspect of womanhood, training heart and hand as well as head. In February 1892 she founded a popular monthly magazine, *Our Mothers and Daughters*, which she edited until July 1896 (the magazine continued, becoming a weekly in mid-1897, until October 1898). It cost 1*d.* and 20,000 copies of the first issue were printed. It was offered to secretaries of YWCAs, mothers' meetings, and Girls' Guilds at a reduced price (and back numbers were subsequently offered free to boost circulation). It was aimed at 'tired mothers and busy daughters', and contained a mixture of reports on women's activities, home remedies, recipes, serialized stories, Sunday talks for the use of mothers and Sunday school teachers, and articles by famous guest writers. The tone was very firmly set by Isabel Reaney's strong editorials, and many of the series—for example, 'The duty of girls in regard to self-education'—were written by her. In issue 4 she poured scorn on well-off women who denied the need for women's rights, and she continually urged women to exercise their influence and not to be afraid to campaign publicly against wrongdoing. In her editorial for the eighth issue she commented:

> Mothers are to be commended for impressing upon their daughters the fact that marriage is not the end of a girl's life. … No girl with a fair amount of ability, courage and enterprise, need ever marry 'for the sake of a home'. She may establish a home for herself. (*Our Mothers and Daughters*, 1/8, 1892, 133)

She publicized the achievements of professional women and commended new career opportunities, citing one woman who had set herself up as 'accountant and auditor' for a large household, charging a sum equivalent to a lawyer's fee for an hour's work. She noted with approval that in America women commercial travellers were being employed in trades concerning exclusively women and children. She urged the need for more women factory inspectors, feeling that women were likely to be tougher on employers of female workforces. She urged women to refuse to buy cheap underclothes, undoubtedly produced by sweated labour, and called for an early shopping pledge (not to shop after 8 p.m.). She publicized the demonstration in a northern town of domestic servants demanding shorter hours and a weekly half-holiday. She commended vegetarianism, supported dress reform, opposed the use of birds in millinery, advertised the Royal Society for the Protection of Birds, and offered up a paean of praise to the bicycle as part of her promotion of physical exercise for women. She wrote for women whose principal role was to be in the home (and for whom she offered advice in reducing the time spent on domestic duties) as well as for those who were to be doing paid work. She saw no fundamental distinction in that each was to exercise usefulness beyond the minimum requirements of her job. She herself carved out a career which transcended the conventions of her position, and gained widespread respect for so doing.

In 1894 Isabel Reaney achieved the distinction of having her profile published in the magazine *Men and Women of the Day* (7/74, 1894). The photograph which accompanied it showed a handsome, slim woman with dark, wavy hair and a face, with the crinkles of one who smiled a lot, at once clear-eyed, intelligent, and energetic. Isabel Reaney outlived her husband, whose *Occasional Papers, Serious and Otherwise* (1902) she edited. She continued to publish on her established themes: *Temperance Sketches from Life* appeared in 1911, and *Daisy Snowflake's Secret* in 1913, for example. She died at her home, 26 The College, Bromley, Kent, on 19 June 1929.   JANE GARNETT

Sources *Men and Women of the Day*, 7 (1894), 11–12 • Mrs G. S. Reaney, 'Slave-driving by public companies', *Contemporary Review*, 56 (1889), 649–58 • *Our Mothers and Daughters* (1892–6) • I. Reaney, *English girls: their place and power* (1879) • G. S. Reaney, 'Preaching women', *The Congregationalist*, 15 (1886), 844–9 • D. Bank and others, eds., *British biographical archive* (1984–98) [microfiche; with index, 2nd edn, 1998] • *WW* [Robert William Edis] • b. cert. • m. cert. • W. Sinclair, introduction, in G. S. Reaney, *Occasional papers, serious and otherwise*, ed. I. Reaney (1902), xi–xvi • *CGPLA Eng. & Wales* (1929)
Likenesses photograph, repro. in *Men and Women of the Day*, 7 (1894)
Wealth at death £615 2*s.* 7*d.*: probate, July 1929, *CGPLA Eng. & Wales*

Reay. For this title name *see* Mackay, Donald, first Lord Reay (1591–1649); Mackay, John, second Lord Reay (*c.*1612–1680) [*see under* Mackay, Donald, first Lord Reay (1591–1649)]; Mackay, Donald James, eleventh Lord Reay and Baron Reay (1839–1921).

Reay, Stephen [*pseud.* Pileus Quadratus] (1782–1861), orientalist, only son of the Revd John Reay, born at Montrose, Forfarshire, on 29 March 1782, studied at the University of Edinburgh under the philosopher Dugald Stewart, and graduated in 1802. After ordination in 1806, he was licensed to several curacies, but later in life he resumed his studies at Oxford, where he matriculated in 1814 at St Alban's Hall, graduating BA in 1817, MA in 1823, and BD in 1841, and becoming for some time vice-principal of his hall. In 1828 he was appointed sub-librarian of the Bodleian Library, where he had charge of the oriental books, particularly Hebrew volumes. He retired on a pension in 1860. He had been in poor health since at least 1855 and unable to carry out his duties effectively alone. In 1840 he was made Laudian professor of Arabic at Oxford and held this office until his death at Oxford on 20 January 1861.

Though contemporary writers paid high tributes to his learning and scholarship, Reay published only three works: a pamphlet entitled *Observations on the defence of the Church Missionary Society against the objections of the archdeacon of Bath* (1818) under the pseudonym of Pileus Quadratus; *Narratio de Josepho e sacro codice* (1822); and lastly *Textus Hebraicus* (1840). He is also referred to in the *Scripturae linguaque phoeniciae monumenta* (2 vols., 1837) of Wilhelm Gesenius, who obtained from Reay copies of the Phoenician inscription at Oxford.

Reay was in build tall, spare, and handsome, if bowed as

his health deteriorated. In character he was mild and ineffectual, although remembered by colleagues with affection for his habits of pottering around the library in search of his spectacles and hovering over hot-air gratings in search of warmth.

D. S. MARGOLIOUTH, *rev.* ELIZABETH BAIGENT

Sources *GM*, 3rd ser., 10 (1861), 347 • *CGPLA Eng. & Wales* (1861) • Foster, *Alum. Oxon.* • Allibone, *Dict.* • W. D. Macray, *Annals of the Bodleian Library, Oxford*, 2nd edn (1890) • H. H. E. Craster, *History of the Bodleian Library, 1845–1945* (1952)

Wealth at death £8000: probate, 7 Aug 1861, *CGPLA Eng. & Wales*

Rebecca, Biagio (1734/5–1808), painter, was born at Osimo in the marches of Ancona, Italy. Of his parents, nothing is known. He studied at the Accademia di San Luca, Rome, and while there he met the painter Benjamin West, who remained his lifelong friend. Rebecca went to England in 1761 with the portraitist James George, with whom he was in partnership for a short time. On 31 January 1769 he was one of the first students to enter Royal Academy Schools and was elected an associate of the Royal Academy in 1771; he exhibited history paintings there for only two years, his historical subjects being of little merit. He painted portraits, for example six whole lengths of Sir John Griffin Griffin's ancestors (1774; Audley End, Essex). He was commissioned to produce watercolour cartoons for painted glass in the chapels at Audley End and New College, Oxford (the latter are now in the City of York Art Gallery), and he was one of the artists who worked on the decoration of the new rooms at Somerset House. Edward Croft-Murray noted that Rebecca subscribed to George Richardson's *A Book of Ceilings, Composed in the Style of the Antique Grotesque* (1776), and designed the admission ticket for the first performance of the Handel Commemoration in Westminster Abbey on 26 May 1784 (Croft-Murray, 258). He also contributed illustrations for John Bell's *The Poets of Great Britain Complete from Chaucer to Churchill* (1779–88).

Rebecca was especially skilled in decorative painting and became one of the most prolific and talented of the Adam school, working not only for the Adam brothers but also for James and Samuel Wyatt and Henry Holland. He gained a considerable reputation for his grotesque painting (at Heaton Hall, Lancashire, and Lansdowne House, now in the Philadelphia Museum of Art), and feigned bas-reliefs (at Harewood House, Yorkshire, and Kedleston Hall, Derbyshire). With West he was employed at Windsor Castle, where the royal family were much amused by his eccentricities, such as painting a silver coin, placing it in one of the rooms, and laughing 'to exhaustion' at a courtier running to pick it up (Thornbury, 2.2). Reports on Rebecca's character vary from 'infinite belief in himself and infinite contempt for everyone else' (ibid., 2.2–3) to 'simplicity of manners and a humane disposition' (*The Examiner*, 28 Feb 1808, 141–2).

Reduced to poverty during his last years, Rebecca obtained a pension from the Royal Academy and died at his lodgings in Oxford Street, London, on 22 February 1808. Joseph Farington noted in his diary that West's account of him would appear in *The Examiner*, where it was reported that 'he was handsomely buried at the direction

of Mr West, and at the expense of the Royal Academy in St. Pancras churchyard' (Farington, *Diary*, 9.3230, 27 Feb 1808). His son, John Biagio Rebecca (*d.* 1847) was an architect.

MALISE FORBES ADAM

Sources E. Croft-Murray, *Decorative painting in England, 1537–1837*, 2 (1970), 258 • R. J. B. Walker, *Audley End: catalogue of pictures in the state rooms*, 4th edn (1973) • G. W. Thornbury, *British art from Hogarth to Turner*, 2 vols. (1861), 2.20 • J. E. Hodgson and F. A. Eaton, *The Royal Academy and its members, 1768–1830* (1905), 245 • Farington, *Diary*, 1.135; 9.3229–30; 15.5286; vols. 3, 6–7, *passim* • *DNB* • *The Examiner* (28 Feb 1808), 141–2 • W. Sandby, *The history of the Royal Academy of Arts*, 1 (1862), 239 • Colvin, *Archs.* • S. C. Hutchison, 'The Royal Academy Schools, 1768–1830', *Walpole Society*, 38 (1960–62), 123–91, esp. 132

Wealth at death impoverished; received a pension from the RA for last three years of life

Reckitt, Sir James, first baronet (1833–1924), businessman and philanthropist, was born on 14 November 1833 in Nottingham, the sixth of seven children of Isaac Reckitt (1792–1862), miller and corn factor, and his wife, Anne (*d.* 1874), daughter of Charles and Elizabeth Coleby of Hempstead, Norfolk. His formal education was at Packer's academy in Nottingham and the Society of Friends' Ackworth School, near Pontefract. In 1848 he joined his father's starch and blue business, which had been acquired in 1840, as a travelling salesman. After Isaac's death in 1862 James and two of his brothers carried on their father's business as a partnership. On 12 October 1865 he married Kathleen (*d.* 1923), daughter of Robert Saunders, agent; they had two sons.

Between 1879, when the business was incorporated as Reckitt & Sons Ltd, and 1917, Reckitt and his elder brother, Francis, were alternate chairmen; James was sole chairman between 1917 and 1924. Through innovative marketing, which included branding and heavy advertising, the production and sale of starch, blue, and boot and metal polish proved an international success. In 1888 the business became a private joint-stock company, and in 1899 it was reconstructed to form a new public company. Its capitalization was then £1.7 million, though it was still owned mainly by the family. By 1914 it had become a multinational manufacturing company employing more than 5000 people.

During the 1890s Reckitt entered into negotiations with J. and J. Colman of Norwich, a competitor in the starch and blue trades. With a view to diversification, he proposed that Reckitt and Colman should become joint buyers of Keen Robinson, a successful mustard, spice, and cereal foods manufacturer, but support from the Colmans was not forthcoming. None the less, perceived common interests in limiting competition brought Reckitt and Colman together in 1913, when the two companies combined to form a joint exports committee, the first of several. This policy culminated, in 1938, in the formation of Reckitt and Colman Ltd, representing a merger of the trading interests of the two companies; Philip Reckitt, Sir James's younger son, was the first chairman.

Sir James and Philip were active in the provision of welfare and environmental improvements affecting employees and others. In 1905–6 the company appointed full-time welfare workers for female and male employees; medical services for all Reckitt workers were introduced in 1907. A day continuation school for girls was established in 1910, and for boys in 1919. A non-contributory pension fund was set up in 1890. A major investment in the garden village, a private freehold estate consisting of 600 dwellings, was undertaken by a development company, The Garden Village (Hull) Ltd, set up by Reckitt and his fellow directors; two-thirds of the £150,000 capital was provided by the company, while during his lifetime Reckitt waived £50,000 in dividends to benefit the village. His objective was to create an environment within easy reach of the factory yet comprising high-quality houses at low rentals, with gardens and services. A recreation ground and hall were added after the village opened in 1907.

In the wider community Reckitt was elected to Hull's first school board in 1870, was a supporter and benefactor of the Newland Homes for seamen's orphans, and established the James Reckitt Home for girls, opened in 1905. As a member of the board of management of Hull Infirmary, chairman of the finance and house committees, and chairman of the management board in 1900, he secured a charter of incorporation, led a successful appeal to build a major extension to the hospital, and financed the building of the Withernsea Consumptive Sanatorium and an annexe for the Hull Nursing Association. In 1891 he built and endowed a library for public use in order to prove that it could be financed on a penny rate. His last major philanthropic enterprise was the setting up of the Sir James Reckitt Trust devoted to those charitable purposes approved of by Quakers and to the benefit mainly of the local population.

Reckitt was created a baronet in 1894 in recognition, in part, of public service but also in acknowledgement of Reckitt's political role in the East Riding. He was a county councillor, deputy lieutenant and JP, and from 1873 an effective chairman of the Hull Liberal Party. He received the freedom of Hull in 1908. He died at his home, Swanland Manor, Swanland, near Hull, on 18 March 1924; his estate was valued at £487,152.

Sir Philip Bealby Reckitt, third baronet (1873–1944), was born at Hessle, near Hull, on 1 January 1873, the second son of James Reckitt. He was educated at Oliver's Mount School, Scarborough, and King's College, Cambridge, where he read natural sciences. He joined Reckitts in 1898, became a director in 1904, and as chairman of the company's works council assumed responsibility for welfare policy. On 19 April 1900 he married Hilda, daughter of Frederick Brent Grotrian. She died in 1935. Despite ill health he became company chairman in 1930 and was chairman of Reckitt and Colman Ltd from 1938 until his death in 1944. He was a JP for the North and East Ridings, and also the first chairman of the City of Hull Conservative Association. For twenty years he was president of the Hull Institute for the Blind and of the Deaf and Dumb Institute. As treasurer of the Royal Infirmary between 1911 and 1932 he was instrumental in financing expansion. His donations to local institutions also included the new Hull

University College, founded in 1928 by Thomas Ferens, then chairman of Reckitt & Sons Ltd. In 1918 Reckitt was appointed OBE for his services as commandant of the military hospital set up in the firm's social hall. He succeeded his brother, Harold, as baronet in 1930. On 28 April 1939 he married Margarida Elizabeth Bishop (*née* Barrington), a widow. Shortly before his death an endowment of £20,000 launched the Philip Reckitt Educational Trust for the purpose of encouraging employees to travel and study abroad. He died at his home, Little Green, Compton, near Chichester, on 17 November 1944.   Roy Church

Sources B. N. Reckitt, *The history of Reckitt and Sons Ltd* (1951) • D. Chapman-Huston, *Sir James Reckitt: a memoir* (1927) • *The Times* (20 March 1923) • *Ours* (April 1924) • *Hull Daily Mail* (18 Nov 1944) [Philip Reckitt] • *Ours* (Dec 1944) [Philip Reckitt] • d. cert. [Philip Reckitt]
Archives Reckitt and Colman Products Ltd, Hull
Wealth at death £487,152 9s. 2d.: resworn probate, 10 June 1924, *CGPLA Eng. & Wales* • £680,790 7s. 9d.—Philip Reckitt: probate, 15 May 1945, *CGPLA Eng. & Wales*

Reckitt, Maurice Benington (1888–1980), writer and Christian sociologist, was born in Beverley, East Riding of Yorkshire, on 19 June 1888, the eldest of the three children and elder son of Arthur Benington Reckitt and his wife, Helen Annie Thomas. His parents' influence on his character was both creditable and corrosive. Arthur Reckitt, a director of Reckitt's of Hull (producer of Reckitt's Blue) ensured that there was always an income (and later a fortune) without his son having to work for it. But his suicide in 1927 bequeathed to Maurice Reckitt a deep emotional fear of himself. His mother, nurtured in the Catholic tradition of the Church of England, gave her son the foundation of a firm faith. The too-distant father was more than complemented by an over-protective and possessive mother. Her doting fondness fostered her son's vanity which later sometimes led to a morbid egotism.

Delicate health in boyhood deprived Reckitt of formal education and prevented him serving in the First World War, but a procession of private tutors enabled him to reach St John's College, Oxford, in 1907. He gained a second class in modern history in 1911. Ernest Barker kindled in him an abiding interest in the nature and significance of medieval order. Other educators at this and later stages of his life were H. A. L. Fisher, G. K. Chesterton, A. R. Orage, J. N. Figgis, P. E. T. Widdrington, and V. A. Demant.

For two years only Reckitt earned his living as a schoolmaster at Ipswich grammar school. 'A meteor flashed across our sky', was the headmaster's comment. Returning to Oxford in 1913 Reckitt intended writing a thesis but he was diverted by other claims and interests. An unlikely friendship developed between Reckitt and G. D. H. Cole. Although an unapproachable cold atheist, and at root an anarchist, Cole joined forces with Reckitt, the clubbable, romantic medievalist, archetypal bourgeois, and unswerving Anglican with a dogmatic faith, to found the National Guilds League in 1915. Its aim was to promote the abolition of the wage system and the establishment of self-government in industry through a structure of national guilds working in conjunction with the state. Reckitt's interest in the restoration of medieval guilds waned when the guild movement began to split in 1920. He became a prominent member of the Church Socialist League and editor of its journal, *Church Socialist* (1915–19) and in 1923 chairman of the new League of the Kingdom of God. This developed as a reaction against the politicization of the church's social teaching and the adulation of communism by some of his friends. If Reckitt hated anything it was Soviet communism, which he saw as atheist, autocratic, ruthless, and materialist. This caused many strains in his relationships, not least with his sister, Eva Collet Reckitt (the founder of Collet's Bookshop—known as the 'Bomb Shop'). If Reckitt's conviction was always socialist his commitment was to 'earth and altar', to church social action rather than political action.

Reckitt's vocation was to be available. He spent a lifetime co-ordinating and leavening the thinking of small groups together with such people as T. S. Eliot, Dorothy L. Sayers, T. M. Heron, Philip Mairet, and many priests. He spoke at most of the major church conferences of his time, and was a good organizer. Though voluble and loquacious he always expressed an independent judgement: the dullest committee was enlivened and shaken by the friendly lash of his tongue. He was a member of the church assembly, the British Council of Churches, and many other bodies. He chaired committees, some of which produced significant reports such as *Gambling: an Ethical Discussion* (1950).

Above all Reckitt was a writer and Christian sociologist. His literary output was prodigious. Books, pamphlets, essays, articles, and reviews flowed from his pen. He was a contributor and reviewer for Orage's *New Age*, a member of the editorial board of *G. K.'s Weekly*, and an editorial writer for the *New English Weekly*. Among his books, *Faith and Society* (1932) was a seminal work and his Scott Holland memorial lectures of 1946, *Maurice to Temple* (1947), describing a century of the social movement in the Church of England, are of permanent value. He most enjoyed collaborating with others in producing books, the most notable being *Prospect for Christendom* (1945), which he edited.

Perhaps Reckitt's abiding legacy is *Christendom*, a quarterly journal of Christian sociology which he edited from 1931 to 1950. Together with the annual summer school of sociology at Oxford it shone like a beacon for those churchmen who felt despondent, disillusioned, and discontented. Spirited thinkers and debaters wrote in *Christendom* and spoke at the summer schools. The Christendom group stood for autochthonous thought and activity and was once denounced as 'the rudest group in the Church of England' (private information). Reckitt himself eschewed social scientists and scientific economics and bypassed sociological evidence. Reckitt was one of the best-known names in the church, which he maintained had three functions: to worship God, to bind up the wounds of the world, and to prophesy. He endeavoured to live according to the spirit of a phrase of G. K. Chesterton's which he often quoted: 'One must somehow learn to love the world without trusting it.' (private information).

Reckitt had some irritating quirks of character. He was fastidious about what he ate and when he ate it. His handwriting was notoriously illegible. Towards the end of his life he was much given to introspection and anxiety about whether he would get through the needle's eye. On 25 November 1920 he married Evelyn Aimée (1890/91–1968), daughter of Arthur Douglas Peppercorn, artist. She was a professional violinist (Aimée Carvel). She shared many of her husband's recreational pursuits but not his faith. They had no children.

Reckitt's recreations were pursued with verve and vigour. He was a ballroom dancer of distinction, a writer of revues and ballades, and a patron of the theatre. Chiefly he played 'the noble game' of croquet and was president of the Croquet Association from 1967 until 1975. He played in every Brighton August tournament for sixty years and represented Surrey on forty occasions. The Christendom Trust was established in 1968 and an M. B. Reckitt research fellowship was established at the University of Sussex. Reckitt died on 11 January 1980 at Rochampton, London.

J. S. PEART-BINNS, rev.

Sources M. B. Reckitt, *As it happened: an autobiography* (1941) • V. A. Demant, *Maurice B. Reckitt: a record of vocation and versatility* (1978) • *The Times* (14 Jan 1980) • private information (1986) • *CGPLA Eng. & Wales* (1980) • J. S. Peart-Binns, *Maurice B. Reckitt: a life* (1988)
Archives Nuffield Oxf., papers incl. some poems • U. Sussex, corresp. and papers incl. literary MSS • University of Bradford, J. B. Priestley Library, MSS
Likenesses M. Noakes, portrait (aged eighty), U. Sussex, Meeting House • M. Noakes, portrait (aged ninety), repro. in Peart-Binns, *Maurice B. Reckitt*, jacket
Wealth at death £164,437: probate, 1 Feb 1980, *CGPLA Eng. & Wales*

Reckitt, Sir Philip Bealby, third baronet (1873–1944). See under Reckitt, Sir James, first baronet (1833–1924).

Recorde, Robert (*c.*1512–1558), mathematician, was the second son of Thomas Recorde of Tenby, Pembrokeshire, and Rose, daughter of Thomas Johns of Machynlleth in Montgomeryshire. Little is known about Recorde's personal life and there is no evidence that he married or had children. A portrait formerly identified as of Recorde is now considered to be Flemish and was found on cleaning to depict a seventeenth-century sitter (Cassels, 59–61).

Recorde studied at Oxford; he graduated BA in 1531 and became a fellow of All Souls in that year. He is reported to have taught mathematics at Oxford and must also have begun the study of medicine there. However, he vacated his fellowship in 1535, and at an unknown date moved to Cambridge where he received an MD in 1545. Recorde was presumably pursuing a career as a physician at this time, and his only non-mathematical publication, *The Urinal of Physick*, appeared in 1547. The book was dedicated to the warden and Company of Surgeons in London and the dedication shows that Recorde was based in London by 1547. The text is a short compendium on the traditional topic of diagnosis from urine; it was evidently popular and was frequently reprinted, the last edition apparently issued under the title *The Judgement of Urines* in 1679.

Recorde's only other medical writing, an unpublished work on anatomy, has been lost.

Active as a technical adviser in the last decade of his life, Recorde was consulted on questions of navigation and dedicated his *Whetstone of Witte* (1557) to the Muscovy Company. However, his promise to publish a text on navigation remained unfulfilled. He also advised on a voyage in search of the north-west passage, presumably in the 1550s.

Recorde's most prominent service was to the crown as a mint administrator. Shortly after the accession of Edward VI he was appointed as one of the commissioners to investigate the running of the Bristol mint, which had been reopened in 1546. As a result of the commission, the under-treasurer, William Sharington, was sent to the Tower and Recorde was appointed comptroller of the Bristol mint in January 1549. He was also appointed comptroller of a new mint at Durham House in the Strand. Recorde was placed fully in charge of the Bristol mint in June 1549 but the mint was closed in October and he was confined to court for sixty days after supporting Protector Somerset against Edward VI, and refusing to divert money to Lord John Russell and Sir William Herbert (later earl of Pembroke).

Recorde was nevertheless appointed surveyor of the mines and moneys in Ireland in 1551 and placed in charge of both the Dublin mint and a project to develop silver mines at Wexford. The silver mines failed technically and financially and Recorde was recalled in 1553, having also clashed with the earl of Pembroke over the running of the mint. In 1556 Recorde brought a suit of malfeasance against Pembroke, who in return sued for libel in October of that year. After the hearing in January 1557 Pembroke was awarded £1000 in damages, and Recorde was subsequently committed to the king's bench prison, presumably for debt. Recorde's will was written in the king's bench prison, where he died. It was proved on 18 June 1558. Ironically, in 1570 his estate was paid about £1000 in belated recompense for his services in Ireland.

Recorde had a reputation for wide learning among scholarly contemporaries. He was a student of Greek and Old English and also concerned himself with British history; he had a hand in the 1559 edition of Fabyan's *Chronicle* and made at least one addition to it. His intellectual range is indicated by a list of works announced in 1551:

> Of the peregrination of man, and the original of all nations, The state of times and mutations of realms, The image of a perfect commonwealth, with diverse other works in natural sciences, Of the wonderful works and effects in beasts, plants and minerals.   (R. Recorde, *The Pathway to Knowledge*, 1551, sig. a4*r*)

Recorde also collected manuscripts and his library was used by bibliophiles such as John Bale. Recorde did not shrink from the religious and political issues of the day. Bale mentions that Recorde had composed tracts 'De auriculari confessione' and 'De negotio Eucharistae', and in late 1550 or early 1551 he testified as a prosecution witness in the trial of Bishop Gardiner. His testimony suggests not only that he was a committed protestant but

emphasizes that he was a familiar figure at court; in addition, Recorde says that he was then thirty-eight or thereabouts, providing the most direct evidence for his year of birth.

However, despite this wide range of activity, Recorde is primarily remembered for his mathematical texts. His first publication was his most basic and popular, *The Grounde of Artes* (1543), an elementary introduction to arithmetic written in dialogue form. After several reissues, the book was enlarged in 1552 with a new dedication to Edward VI which draws on Recorde's mint experience. Though referring to inadequacies in mint standards, he deferred such matters (presumably the debasement of the coinage) to further writings which would need crown approval. After Recorde's death the *Grounde* was edited first by John Dee and then by a string of successors, passing through at least forty-five editions up to 1699.

Recorde had given considerable and independent thought to questions of didactic exposition and his subsequent mathematical works were issued in the sequence he considered appropriate for teaching. After arithmetic came geometry in the two books of *The Pathway to Knowledge* (1551; reissued 1574 and 1602). Recorde was conscious that he was here treating a subject never before published in English, and dedicated the work to Edward VI. As printed, the *Pathway* was, like *The Grounde of Artes*, an introductory text, in this case simplifying and rearranging the first four books of Euclid's *Elements*. However, Recorde had intended that there should be two further books leading on from elementary geometry to practical matters such as surveying and map-making. These were not published and neither were other planned works advertised in the *Pathway* on instruments such as geometrical quadrants, the astronomer's staff, sundials, and an unidentified surveying instrument. Some of this material was no doubt incorporated in a lost text, *The Gate of Knowledge*, which Recorde later referred to as an account of practical geometry and measurement by the quadrant.

Equipped with the rudiments of geometry the mathematical student could pass on in an orderly and methodical progression from the *Pathway* to *The Castle of Knowledge* (1556; reissued 1596). Recorde dedicated this astronomical textbook on the sphere to Queen Mary and also included a Latin address to Cardinal Pole. The text itself drew on and critically reviewed a wide range of Greek and Latin sources from antiquity to the Renaissance, as well as offering instructions on the actual construction of an armillary sphere. Though beyond the scope of his elementary treatment, Recorde made a subtly favourable reference to Copernicus, having the master in the dialogue caution his pupil against an over-hasty dismissal of the seeming absurdity of a moving earth. Such sophisticated and controversial issues of astronomy and cosmology were perhaps intended for another projected but unpublished work, *The Treasure of Knowledge*.

Although abandoning the previous practice of naming his books as a sequence, Recorde's final publication did develop his didactic scheme. *The Whetstone of Witte* (1557) supplemented *The Grounde of Artes* by providing a more advanced treatment of arithmetic as well as some algebra. The work, based principally on German cossist authors such as Johann Scheubel and Michael Stifel, introduced the '+' and '−' signs for the first time in England. Recorde's own contribution to notation was the '=' sign still used today, devised to avoid the tedious repetition of the words 'is equal to' and chosen because he could imagine nothing more equal than two parallel lines of the same length.

Recorde's works were intended as an accessible and readable introduction to mathematics, rather than a repository of elevated or novel results. His preferred dialogue form and choice of the vernacular were meant to render a previously forbidding subject familiar to all, especially those unskilful in Latin. His concern with pedagogical order and his own experience of teaching led him to emphasize the presentation of propositions over the proof of their validity; he believed that students could more readily grasp the subject if the exposition of results was separated from demonstration.

Not all of Recorde's innovations were successful. For example, his efforts to replace Latin terminology with vernacular mathematical terms, such as 'cinkeangle' for pentagon and 'siseangle' for hexagon, were not generally adopted. However, his texts became the undoubted starting point for the vernacular tradition of mathematics in England and there are many references to their importance in the formation of succeeding generations of mathematicians and mathematical practitioners. Although his published mathematical works were largely limited to arithmetic, geometry, and spherical astronomy, his complete programme of publication promoted the idea of the mathematical sciences as a much broader field encompassing practical arts such as surveying and navigation.

STEPHEN JOHNSTON

Sources J. B. Easton, 'Recorde, Robert', *DSB* · Emden, *Oxf.* · J. Venn, ed., *Grace book Δ* (1910) · G. Howson, *A history of mathematics education in England* (1982), chap. 1 · F. R. Johnson and S. V. Larkey, 'Robert Recorde's mathematical teaching and the anti-Aristotelian movement', *Huntington Library Bulletin*, 7 (1935), 59–87 · J. Williams, 'Mathematics and the alloying of coinage, 1202–1700 [pt 1]', *Annals of Science*, 52 (1995), 213–63 · E. Kaplan, 'Robert Recorde, *c.*1510–1558: studies in the life and work of a Tudor scientist', PhD diss., New York University, 1960 · *The acts and monuments of John Foxe*, ed. J. Pratt, [new edn], 6 (1877), 155–6 · E. G. R. Taylor, *Tudor geography, 1485–1583* (1930), 94 · Bale, *Index* · *Heraldic visitations of Wales and part of the marches … by Lewys Dwnn*, ed. S. R. Meyrick, 1 (1846), 68–9 · R. Fabyan, *The new chronicles of England and France*, ed. H. Ellis, new edn (1811), 19 · will, PRO, PROB 11/40 sig 29 · J. W. S. Cassels, 'Is this a Recorde?', *Mathematical Gazette*, 60 (1976), 59–61

Red Piers. *See* Butler, Piers, first earl of Ossory and eighth earl of Ormond (*b.* in or after 1467, *d.* 1539).

Redcliffe-Maud. For this title name *see* Maud, (Margaret) Jean Hay, Lady Redcliffe-Maud (1904–1993) [*see under* Maud, John Primatt Redcliffe, Baron Redcliffe-Maud (1906–1982)]; Maud, John Primatt Redcliffe, Baron Redcliffe-Maud (1906–1982).

Reddie, Cecil (1858–1932), educationist, was born on 10 October 1858 in Colehill Lodge, Fulham, London, the sixth of ten children of James Reddie, Admiralty civil servant

from Kinross farming stock, and his wife, Caroline Susannah, daughter of Daniel Burton Scott of Ingham, Norfolk. He spent four years as a day boy at Godolphin School in London, but after his parents' death and the children's dispersal throughout Britain he was a day pupil at Birkenhead School in 1871–2, and a boarder at Fettes College, Edinburgh, from 1872 to 1878. At Edinburgh University, in 1878–82, he read in succession medicine and science, and after two years at Göttingen University took a doctorate in chemistry in 1884. He returned to Fettes to teach science, moving thence to Clifton College, Bristol, in April 1887; after a breakdown he left Clifton in April 1888. In October 1889 he helped to open Abbotsholme, a private school in Derbyshire, and he made the school his life's work, until retirement in 1927.

Reddie was unhappy in the traditional boarding-school. As a pupil he was bored by the classical curriculum and by competitive games; agonizing over his homosexual nature, he craved emotional guidance. Ideas for school reform came to him as a young teacher, his mentors including his Fettes colleague Clement Charles Cotterill, the Scottish polymath Patrick Geddes, and the romantic socialist Edward Carpenter. They were Ruskinians, and Abbotsholme was inspired by Ruskin's disdain for the competitive society, and his wish to replace undue bookishness with 'learning by doing' so as to foster co-operativeness. Other influences on Reddie were Whitman's vision of the 'love of comrades', or guiltless affection between men, and Thoreau's endorsement of rural life as more 'natural' than the town. In 1888–9 Reddie lived with Carpenter, and planned the 'new school' with his circle, the Fellowship of the New Life. Abbotsholme, the first modern progressive school, began as a joint venture, but after friction Reddie soon bought the others out with borrowed money.

The Abbotsholme regime stressed practical work on the school estate. Although Reddie was a very directive headmaster, pupils were given unusual freedom to roam the countryside, while their responsibilities stretched as far as the stitching of cuts by 'boy surgeons'. Progressive parents were attracted by its ingenious combination of Ruskinian 'helpfulness' with public-school authoritarianism, its sympathetic atmosphere and sensitive sex instruction, its eclectic Christianity with chapel readings from Confucius and Emerson, its Jaeger uniform, and its cult of fresh air. Some of the sixty pupils present in 1900 came from the empire and continental Europe. Abbotsholme was a model for similar foundations in France and Germany. Yet growth was discouraged by the lack of concern for specialist teaching and external examinations. Reddie liked boys to be spirited but saw adult disagreement as a threat; he chose yes-men as assistants and they were often poor teachers. His contradictory temperament, subject to intense drives that were inadequately sublimated, led to tangled emotional storms. In 1906 numbers dropped to thirty and the school never fully recovered. Isolated in Abbotsholme, Reddie abandoned his flirtation with romantic socialism and developed his authoritarian strain, an inconsistency for an apostle of co-operativeness; he saw the German state as the model that Britain should follow to defeat commercial competition. During the First World War, an old boy recalled, 'only Germany was extolled, although … German bullets were tearing Old Abbotsholmians to death' (*Fifty Years of Abbotsholme*, 38). Numbers fell again, and when Reddie transferred Abbotsholme to a group of old boys in 1927, only two pupils were left; yet the school's achievements since then have been based on the progressive tradition he initiated. Reddie retired to 1 High Oaks Road, Welwyn Garden City, and died in St Bartholomew's Hospital, London, on 6 February 1932. He was buried in the grounds of Abbotsholme.   PETER SEARBY

Sources P. Searby, 'The new school and the new life: Cecil Reddie (1858–1932) and the early years of Abbotsholme School', *History of Education*, 18 (1989) · B. M. Ward, *Reddie of Abbotsholme* (1934) · C. Reddie, *Abbotsholme* (1900) · *Fifty years of Abbotsholme* (1939) · W. A. C. Stewart, *The educational innovators*, 2: *Progressive schools, 1881–1967* (1968)
Archives Abbotsholme School, Derbyshire, archives · NRA, corresp., diaries, sermons | University of Strathclyde, Glasgow, letters to Sir Patrick Geddes
Wealth at death £6290 6s. 8d.: probate, 6 May 1932, *CGPLA Eng. & Wales*

Reddie, James (1775–1852), jurist, was born on 25 November 1775 at Dysart, Fife, the third son of John Reddie (1731–1827), merchant in Dysart and later in Edinburgh, and May Burd (*b.* 1744). He was educated at Edinburgh high school before matriculating in the University of Edinburgh in 1790. He studied arts and law in Edinburgh until 1795; he then matriculated in the University of Glasgow, where he studied law with John Millar, then at the height of his fame as a teacher. Reddie again matriculated in law in Edinburgh in the autumn of 1796 to prepare for his admission to the Faculty of Advocates on 11 July 1797. Reddie was closely connected to those at the *Edinburgh Review* with whom he had been associated in the Academy of Physics between 1797 and 1800. He remained a close friend of Francis Horner and maintained his links with Henry Brougham and Francis Jeffrey throughout his life.

Although Reddie seemed set for a successful career at the bar, perhaps because of health problems he accepted in 1804 the offices of town clerk of Glasgow, assessor of the magistrates, and judge in the burgh court. Until a resident sheriff was appointed in Glasgow in 1822, he was involved in much commercial litigation. Reddie soon seems to have regretted this choice of career, and to have hoped for a chair in a university or appointment as a commissary or Admiralty judge. His short period of practice at the bar prevented the fulfilment of either of these last two prospects, but he was appointed a judge admiral-depute in 1805. He drew up a form of process for the burgh court which attracted the attention and approval of Jeremy Bentham.

On 13 August 1804 Reddie married Charlotte Marion Campbell (1782–1834), daughter of James Campbell, saddler in Glasgow. Five sons, including John Reddie (1805–1851), admitted as an advocate on 27 June 1826, and a number of daughters, were born to the marriage. John Reddie (like three of his brothers) was educated at the University

of Glasgow, matriculating in 1820, before studying law at Göttingen under Gustav Hugo from 1823 to 1825 and writing a doctoral thesis, *De edictis praetorum specimen primum* (1825). He drew on his experience of Roman law in Germany and of the German historical school in writing *Historical Notices of the Roman Law and of the Recent Progress of its Study in Germany* (1826), and *A letter to the lord high chancellor of Great Britain on the expediency of the proposal to form a new civil code for England* (1828). After a chequered legal career in the colonies he died young, as first judge of the Calcutta court of small causes, on 28 November 1851.

From 1803 onwards, James Reddie had been planning works and lectures on international and maritime law. These plans came to fruition only late in his life, under the stimulus of legal scholarship in Germany; Reddie saw the work of men such as Hugo and F. C. von Savigny as continuing the pursuits of the great legal scholars of the Scottish Enlightenment, and his own researches resulted in *Inquiries, Elementary and Historical, on the Science of Law* (1840, 2nd edn 1847), *An Historical View of the Law of Maritime Commerce* (1841), *Inquiries into International Law* (1842, 2nd edn 1851), and *Researches, Historical and Critical, in Maritime International Law* (2 vols., 1844–5). He also published a number of papers in the *Law Journal*. In these works Reddie demonstrated not only a familiarity with the new European scholarship but also the ideals he had inherited from the scientific legal thought of the Scottish Enlightenment. He died a widower on 5 April 1852, at 12 Blythswood Square, Glasgow.   JOHN W. CAIRNS

Sources H. Brougham, 'James Reddie, LLD', *Law Review*, 17 (1852–3), 63–9 · NL Scot., MS 3704 · D. Walsh, *Account of the life and writings of Thomas Brown* (1825) · W. I. Addison, ed., *The matriculation albums of the University of Glasgow from 1728 to 1858* (1913) · matriculation albums, U. Edin. L., special collections division, university archives · U. Glas., Archives and Business Records Centre, archives, no. 26680 · parish registers, NA Scot. · F. J. Grant, ed., *The Faculty of Advocates in Scotland, 1532–1943*, Scottish RS, 145 (1944)
Archives NL Scot., corresp.
Wealth at death £5950 7s. 3d.: inventory, 1853, Scotland

Redding, Cyrus (1785–1870), journalist, was born in Cornwall, probably at Truro, on 2 February 1785, the son of Robert Redding (1755–1807), a Baptist minister at Falmouth and later Truro, and his wife, Joanna, *née* Hornblower. Cyrus was educated mainly at home by his wealthy father, and had some juvenile verses printed at his own expense. His earliest recollections included seeing John Wesley preach from a stack of Norway timber on Falmouth quay. One of his youthful companions was Henry Martyn, the missionary. For a time he seems to have attended the classes at Truro grammar school. He settled in London about 1806, took rooms in Gough Square, dined frequently at the Cheshire Cheese, and settled down to a life of continuous industry as a journalist. For a time he served on the staff of *The Pilot*, founded in 1807 to cover East Indian questions, but in 1808 he returned to the west of England and edited the weekly *Plymouth Chronicle*. In June 1810 he started and edited the *West Briton and Cornwall Advertiser*. He married at Kenwyn, near Truro, on 8 May 1812, Julia Ann Moyle of Chacewater, who survived him along with their two daughters, one of whom eventually married and settled in San Francisco.

In 1814 Redding went to Paris, where from 1815 to 1818, from 18 rue Vivienne, he edited *Galignani's Messenger*. In 1815 he also wrote the Paris correspondence for the London *Examiner* and was 'proud to be able to share' with his fellow countrymen what has been described as 'the greatest ever scoop: the defeat of Napoleon by Wellington at Waterloo in June 1815' (Griffiths, 480). During 1818–19 he travelled in France and acquired information which proved of service in his *History of Wines* (see below). From 1821 to 1830 he was working editor of the *New Monthly Magazine*, started, under the nominal editorship of the poet Thomas Campbell (1777–1844), to rival *The Monthly* of Sir Richard Phillips Redding. Also a contributor of numerous articles, Cyrus Redding was indefatigable in the management of the magazine, Campbell being a mere figurehead, and for ten years, according to Coventry Patmore (1823–1896), 'the public got a better magazine for the money than they had ever obtained before'. From 1831 to 1833 Redding edited, again in conjunction with Campbell, *The Metropolitan*, a monthly journal of literature, science, and art, and on its failure to realize expectations he recruited the ranks of provincial editors, directing in succession the *Bath Guardian* (1834–5) and the *Staffordshire Examiner* (1836–40). In 1841 he started in succession two abortive ventures, the *English Journal* and the *London Journal*.

From 1841 Redding devoted himself more exclusively to books, his versatility and industry being alike remarkable. His most influential work was his *History and Description of Modern Wines* (1833, with later editions in 1836, 1851, and 1860); the text was based on careful personal observation and gleanings from many sources, including the treatise of 1787 by John Croft of York. By advocating the reduction of the duties on French wines, Redding's work did much to educate public opinion on this subject and to prepare the way for the rectification of the tariff in 1860, and it was superseded by J. L. W. Thudichum's *Treatise on Wines* only in 1894. Christopher North emphatically praised Redding's *Gabrielle: a Tale of the Swiss Mountains* (1829), and his *Shipwrecks and Disasters at Sea* (1833), aimed at younger readers, was a best-seller. Redding produced *An Illustrated Itinerary of the County of Cornwall* (1842), intended as part of a series of county histories, of which only one further volume, on Lancashire, appeared; and he wrote or edited numerous other works of biography, reminiscence, and fiction, in poetry and prose, as well as several travel books. The contemporary reception of his prolific output was mixed: his *Literary Reminiscences* of his collaborator Thomas Campbell (1860) was, for example, well reviewed, but *All's Well that Ends Well, a Simple Story* (1862) was described as 'three dry, prosing, stupid volumes' (Allibone, *Dict.*).

In politics Redding was a staunch and consistent upholder of the tradition of Charles James Fox. His services to the whig party were numerous and confidential, but his sole reward was a modest civil-list pension 'in consideration of his labours in the field of political and other literature, extending over more than half a century', which he accepted in 1863 (Allibone, *Dict.*). During his long life he came into contact with many notable figures. Besides Thomas Campbell he was friends with William Beckford, of whom he wrote a memoir in 1859, and John Wilson, acting editor of *Blackwood's Magazine* from 1817 to his death in 1854. In his rambling three-volume autobiography, entitled *Fifty Years' Recollections, Literary and Personal, with Observations on Men and Things* (1858), he also talks of his friendship with Daniel O'Connell, Mme de Stael, J. W. M. Turner, and August von Schlegel (1767–1845), professor of literature at Bonn and the greatest literary critic produced by the German romantic movement.

Redding outlived most of his generation, and died, half-forgotten, at his home in Hill Road, St John's Wood, London, on 28 May 1870. He was buried at Willesden cemetery on 3 June.   THOMAS SECCOMBE, *rev.* RAY BOSTON

Sources D. Griffiths, ed., *The encyclopedia of the British press, 1422–1992* (1992), 480 • C. Redding, *Fifty years' recollections, literary and personal*, 2nd edn, 3 vols. (1858) • C. Redding, *Personal reminiscences of eminent men*, 3 vols. (1867) • H. R. Fox Bourne, *English newspapers: chapters in the history of journalism*, 1 (1887), 366 • A. Andrews, *The history of British journalism*, 2 (1859), 68–9 • *ILN* (11 June 1870) • *The Athenaeum* (4 June 1870), 742 • *The Athenaeum* (11 June 1870), 775 • *Morning Post* (2 June 1870) • *St James's Magazine*, new ser., 5 (1870), 444–8 • BL, Add. MSS 28512, fols. 17–18 [*Griffin's contemporary biography*] • Boase, *Mod. Eng. biog.* • Allibone, *Dict.* • IGI

Archives Bodl. Oxf., MS memoirs of William Beckford | Cornwall RO, letters to M. P. Moyle

Reddish, Samuel (1735–1785), actor and theatre manager, was born in Frome, Somerset, the son of a tradesman. He was educated at Frome grammar school and apprenticed, at the age of fifteen, to a surgeon in Plymouth. For facts about his early life we have generally to rely on his own account, rewritten and glossed as 'Memoirs of Mr Reddish' in the *Covent Garden Magazine* of 1773. It recounts that he ran away to join a Norwich company, playing small roles for a salary of 15s. per week. After two years he was employed by Henry Woodward for the Crow Street Theatre, Dublin, and appeared as Lord Townley in Sir John Vanbrugh's *The Provoked Husband*, a part he made his own, in October 1759. He took the part of Pierre in Thomas Otway's *Venice Preserv'd* at Edinburgh the following year. By November 1761 he was at the Smock Alley Theatre, Dublin. For the next five years he circulated between Norwich, Cork, and the Theatre Royal, Edinburgh, where he played Captain Macheath in John Gay's *The Beggar's Opera* in July 1764. The following season he returned to Smock Alley with a Mrs Reddish, possibly Polly Hart (d. 1799), an actress who had played briefly at Drury Lane. The *Covent Garden* account drily notes that Polly had 'an annuity of 200 l. settled on her for *former services*, which gave every spur to his assiduity'. Undoubtedly Reddish's financial affairs were in a state of some disarray by 1766. The *Covent Garden Magazine* enjoys the story of his bid to stave off his Irish creditors with promises of income from his benefit night. He even persuaded some to purchase tickets for his *Richard III*, but their tickets were refused at the door, and by the morning Reddish was on his way to England with the receipts.

Samuel and Polly next appear at the Orchard Theatre, Bath, for the 1766–7 season and at the new theatre in Bristol. Reddish was to take on the running of the Bristol theatre in 1770 with Clarke, Dodd, and William Parsons, and he managed it single-handedly from 1774 to 1776. However, Bristol was not the focus of his performance activity. He had finally won himself a place in Garrick's Drury Lane company, and he made his début, as Lord Townley, on 18 September 1767. Hopkins, the prompter, thought him 'but an indifferent figure—will be useful'. Indeed, Reddish was useful that season tackling a series of young sentimental heroes and noblemen, including Lord Falbridge in George Colman's *The English Merchant*, Posthumus in *Cymbeline*, George Barnwell in George Lillo's *The London Merchant*, Moneses in Nicholas Rowe's *Tamerlane*, Fainall in William Congreve's *The Way of the World*, Macduff to Garrick's Macbeth, and Edgar in *King Lear*. He was offered the title role in Nathaniel Lee's *Theodosius*, and he originated the role of Frederick Melmoth in William Kenrick's *The Widowed Wife* and Lord Winworth in Hugh Kelly's *False Delicacy*. Throughout his career at Drury Lane, Reddish was entrusted with leading roles in new comedies, such as Frampton in Elizabeth Griffith's *The School for Rakes*, Belville in Kelly's *The School for Wives*, and Sir John Dormer in his *A Word to the Wise*, as well as in roles in Alexander Dow's tragedies: Zemouca in *Zingis* and Menes in *Sethona*. He even turned his hand to producing, and adapted a musical spectacle, *The Heroine of the Cave*, with Henry Jones and Paul Hiffernan. In all, Reddish played winter seasons at Drury Lane for ten years, where his weekly earnings increased year on year from £8 in the 1773 season to £12 per week during his final season, 1776–7, under Sheridan. Reddish also had income from his summers as actor–manager at Bristol.

Polly Hart Reddish performed at Drury Lane during the 1771–2 season, but by the end of that year she had been replaced as Mrs Reddish by Mary Ann Canning (c.1747–1827), although the couple did not marry. Mary Ann's aspirations to act were unhindered by talent. Undeterred by regular hissings, Samuel championed her and insisted on lead roles for her at Bristol. She was the unhappy butt of Hannah More's quip in a letter to Garrick on 28 July 1777: 'This is the second or third wife he has produced at Bristol: in a short time we have had a whole bunch of Reddishes, and all remarkably unpungent' (Highfill, Burnim & Langhans, *BDA*).

Critical response to Reddish himself was equivocal. The *Dramatic Censor* (1770) thought that as Macduff he demonstrated 'superior strength and beauty: his feelings are manly, yet tender; spirited without excess' (Gentleman, 1.111). However, his playing of more passionate characters was hampered by his weak voice. The same critic thought him 'deficient in powers for the most impassioned speeches' of Alonzo in Aphra Behn's *The Revenge*, and with 'nothing of the requisite volubility' required to play Young Belmont in Moore's *The Foundling* (Gentleman,

2.332, 220). An even-handed assessment of his ability perhaps comes in Frederick Pilon's *The Drama: a Poem* (1775):

> Reddish wants pow'r, th'emotions strong to raise,
> But his attention gains, and merits praise;
> Tho' voice and feeling small assistance lend,
> He oft has pleas'd, and seldom does offend.

By 1774 Reddish was beginning to show signs of the mental disorder which was to dog the rest of his life. In April 1775 Hopkins noted that: '*Matilda* was advertis'd for this Night, but Mr Reddish came Yesterday as Mad as a March Hare … & behav'd like a Man in Despair' (Highfill, Burnim & Langhans, *BDA*). During the summer at Bristol, William Parsons wrote to Garrick that Reddish had been unable to perform at all: 'His countenance undergoes the most sudden alterations. His memory fails him' (ibid.). These temporary lapses of memory and alterations became apparent to audiences by November 1776, and he was booed off as Vainlove in Congreve's *The Old Batchelor*. Sheridan did not renew his contract to play at Drury Lane the following year, and 1777 was also his last season at Bristol.

After a disastrous benefit night, he sold his share and played a final season at the Crow Street Theatre, Dublin. He appeared twice more in London, as Hamlet in a one-off performance at Covent Garden in October 1778, and then when he elected to reprise Posthumus in a benefit at Covent Garden on 5 May 1779. John Ireland recounts that Reddish arrived at the theatre under the impression he was to play Romeo. 'The instant he came in sight of the audience his recollection seemed to return … it was only the stage that had the power to unsettle this delusion' (Highfill, Burnim & Langhans, *BDA*).

Reddish's delicate financial affairs were in ruins by the end of his life, and he applied for assistance to the Drury Lane Actors' Fund in 1778 for the support of his three surviving children by Mary Ann Canning. He disappeared from view over the next few years, but he was confined at some point to York Asylum, where he died on 13 December 1785.   J. MILLING

Sources Highfill, Burnim & Langhans, *BDA* · 'Memoirs of Mr Reddish', *Covent Garden Magazine* (1773) · F. Gentleman, *The dramatic censor, or, Critical companion*, 2 vols. (1770) · F. Pilon, *The drama: a poem* (1775) · J. Boaden, *Memoirs of the life of John Philip Kemble*, 2 vols. (1825)
Likenesses V. Green, engraving, 1771 (after R. E. Pine) · G. Grignion, engraving, 1775 (after T. Parkinson), repro. in J. Bell, ed., *Bell's edition of Shakespeare's plays*, 9 vols. (1773–4) · J. M. Delatre, engraving, 1776 (after J. J. Barralet), repro. in *The New English theatre*, 12 vols. (1776–7) · J. Thornthwaite, engraving, 1776 (after J. Roberts), repro. in J. Bell, *Bell's British theatre* · T. Parkinson, oils, 1778?, Garr. Club · J. J. Barralet, pen-and-ink drawing, Folger · T. Parkinson, ink and watercolour drawing, BM · T. Parkinson, watercolour, BM · J. Roberts, watercolour, BM · theatrical prints, BM, NPG
Wealth at death nil (supported by Drury Lane Actors' Fund): Folger, 1778 entry, James Winston's transcriptions; Highfill, Burnim & Langhans, *BDA*

Reddish, Sarah (1850–1928), co-operative movement activist and suffragist, was born into a working-class family in Bolton. She started work as a child, leaving school at the age of eleven. Her first job was at home winding silk for her mother and her neighbours to weave on handlooms. She then went to work in a cotton mill where her responsibilities included giving first aid to women who had suffered from the frequent machine accidents.

Sarah Reddish joined the co-operative society in 1879 and became a respected figure in the local and the national hierarchy. In 1886 she became president of the Bolton Women's Co-operative Guild, a post she held for the next fifteen years. In 1889 she was first elected to the guild's central committee and in 1897 was its national president. For two years from 1893 she was appointed as a regional organizer for the Women's Co-operative Guild in the north of England and succeeded in increasing membership throughout the region. Through her the guild became a meeting-place where suffrage speakers were always sure of a sympathetic audience. She was also involved in the guild campaign to improve the wages of female co-operative employees.

In the late 1890s Sarah Reddish developed her public-speaking skills travelling around the north of England with a small group of women in a caravan holding public meetings on the value of socialism. In 1899 she was appointed a part-time organizer for the Women's Trade Union League which was concerned with providing support for women workers.

Sarah Reddish was an active supporter of the suffrage movement, and she was closely involved in the 1900–01 campaign to petition women factory workers in support of women's suffrage. When a group of women presented the resulting petition to Westminster, Sarah Reddish, as the most senior and influential woman present, introduced the deputation. The campaign was judged to be so successful it was decided that the wool workers in Yorkshire and the cotton and silk workers of north Cheshire should also be petitioned on this subject. It was partly due to pressure from Sarah Reddish that the Women's Cooperative Guild voted at its annual conference in 1904 to support the latest franchise bill.

A number of suffrage organizations made use of Sarah Reddish's skills as an organizer and public speaker. Between 1903 and 1905 she acted as an organizer for the North of England Society for Women's Suffrage but resigned in 1905 in disagreement over tactics to secure the aim of women's suffrage. In 1903 she was a founder member, and later treasurer, of the Lancashire and Cheshire Women Textile and Other Workers Representation Committee formed to select a suitable parliamentary candidate who would fight for the enfranchisement of women workers. On occasions she was also employed as a salaried organizer for the National Union of Women's Suffrage Societies in London. She was a member of the Manchester and Salford women's trade and labour council and the National Industrial and Professional Women's Suffrage Society. Sarah Reddish felt that it was vital for women to stand for local elections, as this would strengthen their claim for the parliamentary franchise, a view she put forward when she wrote Women and County Borough Councils: a Claim for Eligibility (1903). She herself served on the committee of the Bolton Association for the Return of Women as Poor Law Guardians from its establishment in 1897

although, because of other commitments, she did not stand for election herself until 1905. Once elected, however, she remained a poor-law guardian until 1921, when she was over seventy years old. In 1898 she was one of the successful candidates in the Bolton school board elections and in 1919 she organized the Bolton Women's Citizens Associations. In 1911 she was made president of the Manchester and Salford Women's Trade Society. She was forced by illness, however, to give up her many public campaigns. Sarah Reddish died at Townleys Hospital, Farnworth, Lancashire, on 19 February 1928.

SERENA KELLY

Sources J. Liddington and J. Norris, *One hand tied behind us: the rise of the women's suffrage movement* (1978) · O. Banks, *The biographical dictionary of British feminists*, 1 (1985) · d. cert.
Likenesses photograph, repro. in Liddington and Norris, *One hand tied behind us*
Wealth at death £1403 10s. 7d.: probate, 12 April 1928, CGPLA Eng. & Wales

Rede, Leman Thomas Tertius (1799–1832), writer, was the son of Leman Thomas Rede of Suffolk, a student of the Inner Temple and a friend of George Canning's father. He was a newspaper hack, a minor translator, and a writer on various subjects including law. He was obliged by debts to leave England for Hamburg, and died there in December 1810, whereupon his widow, with five children, returned to England.

Leman Thomas Tertius Rede was, like his father, bred to the law, but inherited his father's improvidence, and took to the stage and teaching elocution. In 1824 he married Catherine Elizabeth Oxberry, *née* Hewitt, the widow of the actor William Oxberry. He and his brother William Leman *Rede were known in London life as 'the inseparables'. Both possessed literary talent and varied conversational powers, and both were always in want of money. Leman published a book called *The Art of Money Getting*. He performed 'divers melodramatic characters in the provinces' and in London. His last appearance on the stage took place at Sadler's Wells Theatre a fortnight before his death. He died on 12 December 1832, and was buried in Clerkenwell cemetery. His brother was buried in the same grave in 1847.

Of Rede's various writings, his manual of acting, *The Road to the Stage, or, The Performer's Preceptor* (1827), of interest to the theatre historian, and his edition, together with his brother, of *Oxberry's Dramatic Biography* (5 vols., 1825–6) are noteworthy.

W. P. COURTNEY, *rev.* KLAUS STIERSTORFER

Sources *GM*, 1st ser., 102/2 (1832), 581 · *N&Q*, 6th ser., 10 (1884), 408 · 'Oxberry, William', *DNB*
Archives Yale U., Beinecke L., unpublished anecdotes

Rede, Mary Leman. See Gillies, Mary Leman (*b. c.*1800, *d.* in or after 1851).

Rede, Sir Richard (1510/11–1575). See under Rede, Sir Robert (*d.* 1519).

Rede [Reade], **Robert** (*d.* 1415), bishop of Chichester, was a Dominican friar, probably of the house at Langley, Hertfordshire, much favoured by Richard II, to which the bishop would make extensive bequests. The house at Hereford was also singled out particularly in the bishop's will, but so too on a smaller scale were many other houses, perhaps suggesting that Rede achieved an office embracing the whole province of the order at some time. His brother, William, was in turn archdeacon, chancellor, and treasurer of Chichester, all in his own gift. One Thomas Rede had a small bequest. Of most interest, he identified his distinguished predecessor at Chichester, Bishop William *Rede, as a kinsman, and asked to be buried at his feet.

Rede was a doctor of theology. It is not known where he studied, even though Bishop William had made such a mark at Merton College, Oxford. He also had collections of civil- and canon-law books. His public career is very obscure, but possibly he had a longer and closer connection with Richard II's court than is apparent. On 9 September 1394, for example, he was papally provided to the see of Lismore and Waterford, and accompanied Richard II on his expedition to Ireland in that year. On 26 January 1396 he was translated at the king's request to the see of Carlisle, overriding the election of William Strickland; he obtained the temporalities on 30 March, with retrospective effect from the beginning of the vacancy, usually a sign of personal royal favour. However, on 5 October 1396 he was translated once more, to Chichester, with the temporalities restored on 6 March. This was a somewhat wealthier see, and if Rede did also have some personal affection for it through his predecessor, the move is understandable. He certainly managed to spend long periods of time there, even though he was a frequent attender at Richard II's court, and on the council of regency the king left behind when he went to Ireland again in 1399.

The revolution of September 1399 did not incite the public and popular animosity against Rede that it did against other ecclesiastical associates of the late king, but it made him an entirely resident diocesan, mainly at Amberley and Drungewick. In April 1400 Archbishop Arundel reproached him sharply for having ceased to wear a friar's habit. Rede apologized. In January 1401 he sent proctors to convocation, pleading serious ill health and other obstacles. He attended parliaments fairly regularly in the following years, but had no active role in government. He was on bad terms with the cathedral chapter, upon whom he imposed critical visitations as often as canon law allowed, but such friction was not unusual at Chichester. From November 1412 Rede was entirely at Aldingbourne, perhaps in declining health. He made his will on 10 August 1414 and died the following year, before 21 June, having asked to be buried before the altar in the choir of the cathedral, at the feet of Bishop William Rede.   R. G. DAVIES

Sources R. G. Davies, 'The episcopate in England and Wales, 1375–1443', PhD diss., University of Manchester, 1974, 3.ccxxvi–ccxxvii · *The episcopal register of Robert Rede*, ed. C. Deedes, 2 vols., Sussex RS, 8, 11 (1908–10) · E. F. Jacob, ed., *The register of Henry Chichele, archbishop of Canterbury, 1414–1443*, 2, CYS, 42 (1937), 37–41 [will] · *RotP*, vol. 3 · N. H. Nicolas, ed., *Proceedings and ordinances of the privy council of England*, 7 vols., RC, 26 (1834–7), vols. 1–2 · *Johannis de Trokelowe et Henrici de Blaneforde … chronica et annales*, ed. H. T. Riley, pt 3 of *Chronica monasterii S. Albani*, Rolls Series, 28 (1866) · *Chancery records*

Rede, Sir Robert (*d.* 1519), judge, was the son of William Rede of Wrangle in Lincolnshire, a Calais merchant, and his wife, Joan. He was admitted to Lincoln's Inn in 1467, and his name occurs in reported cases from 1481, the year of his first reading. He may have been previously at Clement's Inn, which sued a Robert Rede for dues in 1482. The Lincoln's Inn connection explains Rede's settlement in Kent. John Alfegh or Alphay, who built Bore Place in Chiddingstone, was ten years senior to Rede in the inn. Rede married Alfegh's daughter Margaret in the 1470s, and acquired lands in Hoo under the provisions of the marriage settlement; Bore Place came to Margaret and Robert in tail under the terms of Alfegh's will in 1489.

By 1486 Rede was sufficiently advanced in his profession to take the coif. Within a year of his being taken into the crown's service as a king's serjeant in 1494, he was made a justice of the king's bench; he sat there (under Sir John Fyneux) for more than ten years and was knighted in 1501. In 1506 he was translated to the common pleas as chief justice, for which promotion he reputedly paid 400 marks, and he presided over that court until his death on 7 or 8 January 1519. A long hiatus in the year-books between 1506 and 1520 renders Rede less prominent in legal history than his length of service might warrant, though the coincidence is probably no reflection on him; a few of his judicial opinions are preserved in the reports of Caryll (his son-in-law) and Spelman.

Rede's eldest son, Edmund, died in 1501. Another son, John (who joined the Inner Temple and practised briefly), and his daughter Mary Barantyne, also predeceased him. The fee income of the common pleas provided some support for Rede's other three daughters. Jane married John Caryll (*d.* 1523), who was third protonotary of the court before taking the coif in 1510. Bridget married Thomas Willoughby (*d.* 1545) of Lincoln's Inn, who enjoyed the profitable filazership of London and Middlesex for four years under Rede (1513–16), but who made his career at the bar and in 1537 became a judge of the same court; Bridget was left Bore Place in her father's will. Dorothy married Edward Wotton (*d.* 1551) of Lincoln's Inn, who was filazer for Suffolk from 1513, and for London from 1517. Dorothy was left a house in St Sepulchre's parish by Newgate, where Rede had lived when in London, and which had belonged to Chief Justice Bryan. Shortly before his death, Rede was able to make an appointment to the lucrative position of chief protonotary, and chose Edward Stubbe of Lincoln's Inn, formerly filazer for Kent.

Rede made many benefactions for the good of his soul, and was a lay brother of several religious fraternities. As early as 1503, he founded a chapel at Waltham Holy Cross for a chantry called 'Rede's Mass the Justice'. In 1516 he built the north chapel of Chiddingstone church 'to the honour of God and St Catharine', and in 1517 he endowed a perpetual chantry there, giving the patronage to the prior of the London Charterhouse. He asked to be buried in the latter, where he had endowed another perpetual chantry, though the only Rede inscription recorded there was for Sir Bartholomew Rede (d. 1505), lord mayor of London. His will contains numerous bequests to religious houses, hospitals, and colleges, in return for prayers and masses. But the benefaction for which he is principally remembered was arranged posthumously in 1524 by his executors, who included the master of Jesus College, Cambridge. The foundation provided for an annual stipend of £4 to support three lectureships in the 'Common Schooles' in Cambridge, one in the humanities, the second in logic, and the third in natural or moral philosophy. These lectures had been provided since the 1480s without endowment, but were now secured through Jesus College as trustee. By custom the lecturers came to be elected on the eve of St Barnabas (11 June), and were known as the 'Barnaby lecturers'. Since 1858 the fund has supported a single annual lecture by a person of eminence, still known as the Rede lecture.

Sir Richard Rede (1510/11–1575), civil lawyer, came from a different family of Redes settled at Nether Wallop in Hampshire. He went up from Winchester College to New College, Oxford, in 1528. During his ten years as a fellow of New College, from 1530 to 1540, he read law and graduated BCL in 1537. On becoming DCL in 1540 he left Oxford and was admitted to Doctors' Commons. Besides the usual ecclesiastical and admiralty business of a practising civilian, he became a master in chancery in 1546 and a master of requests in 1553, serving also briefly in Ireland as lord chancellor from 1546 to 1548; he was knighted in the 1540s. During the reign of Edward VI he participated in the trials of bishops Heath, Day, Tunstall, and Bonner. His wife, Anne, was the daughter of Dr John Tregonwell, judge of the admiralty. Rede died at Redbourn, Hertfordshire, on 11 July 1575. He left to New College all the law books at his house in Chancery Lane, and many of them are still in the college library. J. H. BAKER

Sources E. W. Ives, *The common lawyers of pre-Reformation England* (1983), 474–5 • *The reports of Sir John Spelman*, ed. J. H. Baker, 2, SeldS, 94 (1978), 358, 371–2, 386 • Baker, *Serjeants* • Sainty, *Judges* • Emden, *Cam.*, 475, 481 • D. R. Leader, 'Professorships and academic reform at Cambridge, 1488–1520', *Sixteenth Century Journal*, 14 (1983), 215–27, 215, 222–4 • J. W. Clark, *Endowments of the University of Cambridge* (1904), 261–268 • G. D. Squibb, *Doctors' Commons: a history of the College of Advocates and Doctors of Law* (1977), 48 • J. Weever, *Antient funeral monuments*, ed. W. Tooke (1767), 120 • T. Madox, *Formulare Anglicanum* (1702), 338–340 • A. Hussey, ed., *Kent chantries*, Kent Records, 12 (1936), 101–5 • C. R. Councer, *Lost glass from Kent churches*, Kent Records, 22 (1980), 30–31 • *CIPM, Henry VII*, 1, no. 530 • will of John Alfegh, PRO, PROB 11/8, sig. 18 • statutes of Chiddingstone chantry, PRO, Augmentation Office, miscellaneous books, E 315/50 • PRO, plea rolls of the court of common pleas, CP 40 [several references] • R. R. Sharpe, ed., *Calendar of wills proved and enrolled in the court of husting, London, AD 1258 – AD 1688*, 2 (1890), 614 • will, PRO, PROB 11/19, sig. 13

Rede, William (c.1315–1385), bishop of Chichester, theologian, and astronomer, was a native of the diocese of Exeter, although he was linked with the county of Kent through the patronage of Nicholas Sandwich. Rede's will states that Sandwich, who was lord of Bilsington and Folkestone, cared for or educated him (*educavit*) from boyhood to maturity, but it is not known how they met. A note by Robert Walter, Rede's secretary, intimates that he was studying at Oxford at least as early as 1337, but the only firm information as to his education comes from the records of Merton College, where he was a fellow by 1344, still so in 1357, second bursar in 1352–3, and sub-warden in 1353–4. At some time before 1362 he became doctor of theology. His origins in a district associated with Exeter College, Oxford, and his gifts to that college, have led to otherwise unsupported claims that he was a fellow there, but the evidence is slender, and there is no entry in the rector's rolls to suggest that he was ever a fellow of that college.

Rede was given recommendations (letters dimissory) in 1354 by the bishop of Exeter and was ordained successively subdeacon, deacon, and priest, on the title of Merton College, in the diocese of Rochester, Kent, in 1356. He enjoyed a succession of ecclesiastical appointments, including those of archdeacon of Rochester (1359) and provost of Wingham, Kent (1363), which he vacated on his promotion to bishop of Chichester by papal provision on 11 October 1368; the temporalities were restored on 4 June 1369. He was consecrated by the pope at Avignon on 2 September 1369—he spoke in his will of Pope Urban V (r. 1362–70) as his *promotor*—and he occupied this see until his death.

Rede was active in public life: he lent money to the king, he built a castle on his manor at Amberley, and he was a trier of petitions in various parliaments from 1369 to 1380. But although he made collections of provincial constitutions and of documents concerning his see, no register survives to shed light on the day-to-day administration of his diocese, and he is best remembered as a scholar and scientist. His collection of some 370 books must have been one of the largest privately owned libraries in the country, and was greater than that of any Oxford college. It was rich in theology, natural philosophy, astronomy, and astrology. By his will, proved on 9 November 1385, he left 250 books to various Oxford colleges—including 100 to Merton—of which at least 58 survive. Many of them show Rede's marked scientific interests, but one of the most important reflects Mertonian theological concerns: copied for Rede and paid for by money given by Sandwich, it contains Thomas Bradwardine's *De causa Dei* and Thomas Buckingham's *Quaestiones*, searching for a compromise between the errors of Pelagius, Cicero, and Scotus on the problem of human freedom of action. Rede not only provided handsomely for the contents of Merton College Library, but at some time in the period 1373–8 he also provided much, perhaps most, of the money to build what amounts to the main shell of the college library in what is now called Mob Quad, and money for library fittings. The bishop's portrait was at some stage placed in the library, for John Leland reported having seen it and an inscription saying that Rede caused the library to be built.

By his will Rede bequeathed or confirmed numerous other gifts of money, books, chalices, and plate, but to Merton he also left an important gift of scientific instruments. One of his own astrolabes had been bequeathed to him by his somewhat older contemporary Simon Bredon (d. 1372), a former fellow of Merton who had for a time been prebendary and canon of Wingham. Rede's own will is less specific than Bredon's in respect of his astronomical instruments, but among his gifts to the college made in his lifetime (probably in 1374) were the following: an albion (an instrument designed by Richard Wallingford, d. 1336), an equatorium (by which, as by the albion, planetary positions could be calculated), a quadrant, a chilindrum (a type of sundial), a celestial sphere and an armillary sphere, a sea chart and a constellation chart. One or two of these can perhaps be identified with instruments still extant in the college, notably the equatorium. A college list of 1452 mentions also what was probably an observing instrument (*triangulum*, possibly a triquetrum) in a box inscribed with Rede's name.

This cornucopia of fourteenth-century science reflected more than the largesse of a relatively wealthy bishop. It represented Rede's own interests and expertise. His name was known in astronomical circles throughout England, and even abroad, for an edition he drew up, around 1340, of the astronomical tables known as the Alfonsine. These tables, which continued a long tradition going back through Islamic astronomy to Claudius Ptolemy (second-century Alexandria) and beyond, were produced under the patronage of Alfonso X of León and Castile between 1263 and 1272. Versions of the tables, much modified in Paris, were circulating in England by the 1330s. Rede's modification of them—he adapted them to the longitude of Oxford, and in other slight respects—was not especially remarkable from an astronomical point of view, but a simple set of canons he wrote to facilitate their use was to be much copied. In 1348 a superior version was issued, possibly by William Batecombe, but Rede's tables long continued to have their adherents. Their popularity can be partly explained by the fact that they were intuitively slightly easier to grasp than their Parisian models, and also by the fact of Oxford's being the most important centre of astronomical education in England at the time. They supplied an important need, namely, a basis for astrological calculation. Rede's astrological motives are made plain by two surviving examples of his work, one a set of prognostications based on an eclipse of the moon and a conjunction of Saturn, Jupiter, and Mars in 1345, the other a set of calculations done in 1357 for a conjunction of Jupiter and Saturn that was due to take place no less than eight years hence (October 1365). In the first case he performed the calculations, while the prognostication proper was done by his Merton colleague John Ashenden (d. 1368).

Among Rede's pupils in astronomy was Reginald Lambourne, fellow of Merton in 1353 and still in 1357, who left to become a Benedictine monk. Shortly after Rede was elevated to the see of Chichester, Lambourne sent him an astrological prognostication of the weather covering the years up to 1374, which is one of several tracts collected together by Rede and bound together in what is now Bodl. Oxf., MS Digby 176. This is one of three volumes left by Rede for the use of his kin, and is the single most useful source for his scientific interests. Its table of contents is in

the hand of Robert Walter, his secretary. Nicholas Sandwich supplied part, and other parts came from the executors of Thomas Bradwardine (d. 1349) and Richard Campsall (d. 1360). The earliest work of Rede's to which a reasonably precise date can be attached, a solar almanac, or set of tables of the sun's position for the years 1341–4 inclusive, is included in the volume. According to Robert Walter it was prepared in 1337, probably on the basis of his more comprehensive Alfonsine tables, which can therefore be roughly assigned to the period 1337–40—the latter a date used as a standard of reference (*radix*) in them. Since he is likely to have studied astronomy for five or six years before being competent to do this kind of work, he was of the order of seventy years old when he died on 18 August 1385 at Selsey, Sussex. He was buried in the chancel before the high altar of Selsey church, in his own diocese.

J. D. NORTH

Sources Emden, *Oxf.* · J. D. North, 'The Alfonsine tables in England', *Stars, minds and fate: essays in ancient and medieval cosmology* (1989), 327–59 · F. M. Powicke, *The medieval books of Merton College* (1931) · J. R. L. Highfield, 'The relations between the church and the English crown during the pontificates of Clement V and John XXII, 1305–1334', DPhil diss., U. Oxf., 1951, 446–71 · *Richard of Wallingford: an edition of his writings*, ed. and trans. J. D. North, 3 vols. (1976), vol. 3, appx 15 [Lat. orig., with parallel Eng. trans.] · K. V. Snedegar, 'John Ashenden and the Scientia Astrorum Mertonensis', DPhil diss., U. Oxf., 1988, 55–9 · G. A. Clarkson, 'Notes on Amberley, its castle, church, &c', *Sussex Archaeological Collections*, 17 (1865), 194–7
Archives Bodl. Oxf., MS Digby 176
Wealth at death considerable: will, 9 Nov 1385, Powicke, *The medieval books*, 87–91

Rede, William Leman (1802–1847), actor and playwright, was born in Hamburg on 31 January 1802, one of the five children of Leman Thomas Rede, attorney and author, who had fled to Germany in 1799, to escape English creditors. After his early death there in October 1810, his widow (probably called Ann, *née* Bullen) and family returned to London. As a youngster Rede developed a fascination with pugilism and even thought of making it a career; but the amateur stage exerted a stronger fascination than both it and the legal career that he initially entered with a view to articles. He eventually followed his elder brother Leman Thomas *Rede jun. (1799–1832) into the professional theatre, where they became known as 'the Inseparables'. His marriage in London to Frances Lucy Mellor (1804/5–1824), sister to an actor at Sadler's Wells, on 26 February 1821 (which produced three children, all of whom died young) preceded his first stage appearance in 1823, as Young Marlowe in *She Stoops to Conquer* at Margate. After Frances's death aged nineteen in 1824, Rede took to the road as an itinerant player, acting in barns and on other makeshift stages. He was for a time at Bristol and then at the lowly West London (or Tottenham Street) Theatre between about 1825 and 1828, after which he resumed his provincial career, but this time as a leading actor, on the York, Liverpool, Edinburgh, and Richmond circuits.

From 1832 Rede settled in London, where he began writing plays and became involved, possibly as a founder member, with the newly constituted Dramatic Authors' Society. Rede wrote exclusively for the minor theatres at that juncture when they were fighting for their existence against the patent houses' attempts to perpetuate their theatrical monopoly. He was associated with the early history of the Strand, then known as the New Strand Subscription Theatre because, since it was run in defiance of the lord chamberlain, tickets could not be openly sold. For the début there of the Yorkshire comedian Lionel Benjamin Rayner, Rede wrote the burlesque *Professionals Puzzled, or, Struggles at Starting* (26 January 1832), which hit at the wrangles surrounding the theatre's opening. Rede's popular success, *The Rake's Progress* (City, 1832), was his first drama to be printed. He worked energetically but with little discipline: it is said that nothing of this play was written down until revised for publication by John Duncombe. Probably in February 1832 Rede remarried, his bride being the actress Sarah Cooke, daughter of John Cooke, a bass singer at Drury Lane.

Rede enjoyed better success as a minor theatre playwright than as an actor, although he continued playing at the Pavilion, Olympic, Surrey, and elsewhere except for an enforced sabbatical from 1834 to 1838 because of an accident. He wrote for the Queen's, English Opera House (including *The Gaberlunzie Man*, 'a Scottish operatic drama', 1836), and the Adelphi (where his burlesque of Dickens was staged as *The Peregrinations of Pickwick, or, Boz-i-a-n-a*, 1837). His most successful partnership was with the Vestris management at the Olympic. In his burletta *The Old Stager and the New* (1835), written expressly for the theatre's seasoned comedian John Liston to introduce the new recruit Charles James Mathews, the former was shown as a traditional kind of coachman and the latter as his son cocking a snook at the old ways. One of Rede's best pieces (described by the reviewer in *The Times* as 'more original, and infinitely more comical' than any of the other pieces on the bill that evening), it combined sharp dialogue with a vividly realized situation which accented the analogy between the forward-looking strategy of Olympic productions and the old-fashioned techniques of the patent houses. Rede's relationship with the Olympic continued after Vestris's departure with such successes as *Sixteen-String Jack* (1841), *Life's a Lottery* (1842), *Our Village* (1843), and *The Boyhood of Bacchus* (1845), probably Rede's last play. His melodrama *The Old House of West Street* was withdrawn from the licensing process in 1844 on advice from the lord chamberlain's examiner of plays because of its excessive violence.

Rede had considerable insider knowledge as actor and dramatist. He may have contributed to the supplementary volumes of *Oxberry's Dramatic Biography*, with which his brother was involved from 1825; and in 1836, after the latter's death, he edited an augmented edition of Leman Thomas Rede's handbook *The Road to the Stage* (originally published in 1827), which had proved an indispensable manual for would-be actors and playwrights.

Rede was active on several fronts. There was at least one novel, *The Wedded Wanderer, or, The Soldier's Fate* (1827), and a 'satirical romance' on George IV entitled *The Royal Rake, and the Adventures of Alfred Chesterton* (privately printed, 1842, and serialized in the *Sunday Times*, 1846). Between 1834 and 1838 Rede contributed to the *New Monthly Magazine*, notably on Edmund Kean (1834) and the anecdotal reminiscences of 'a [fictionalized] stage veteran' (1834-7). In 1842 he started a rival magazine to *Punch*, inevitably perhaps called *Judy*, but it failed after only two issues. At his death Rede was in the midst of another novel, *The Man in Possession*, again being serialized in the *Sunday Times*.

Perpetually impecunious (a family failing, it seems), Rede was ever cheerful, witty, gregarious, a loyal friend and willing performer at benefits. A contemporary asserted that he 'bequeathed little to sustain his memory with posterity', preferring instead to scatter 'his good things to the winds in the intercourse of fellowship' ('Recollections', 109). By habit an early riser, athletic, and a plain liver shunning tobacco and snuff, Rede unexpectedly died from apoplexy at home in Southampton Street, Strand, London, on 3 April 1847, aged forty-five, leaving a widow and ten-year-old son. He was buried in Clerkenwell cemetery on 11 April, in the same grave as his beloved brother.

JOHN RUSSELL STEPHENS

Sources 'Recollections of Leman Rede', *New Monthly Magazine*, new ser., 80 (1847), 102-9 · *GM*, 2nd ser., 27 (1847), 666 · *The Era* (11 April 1847) · review, *The Times* (8 Dec 1835), 5 · J. Davis, *John Liston: comedian* (1985) · *Wellesley index* · A. Nicoll, *Late eighteenth century drama, 1750-1800*, 2nd edn (1952), vol. 3 of *A history of English drama, 1660-1900* (1952-9) · J. Shattock, ed., *The Cambridge bibliography of English literature*, 3rd edn, 4 (1999) · J. R. Stephens, *The censorship of English drama, 1824-1901* (1980) · *IGI* [parish records, St James's, Westminster, and St Dunstan's in the West, London] · Hall, *Dramatic ports.*, vol. 3
Archives Yale U., unpublished anecdotes | BL, licensing copies of plays, Add. MSS 42922-43018 · BL, letters to Royal Literary Fund, loan 96
Likenesses print, 1841 · vignette (as Tom Rakewell in *The rake's progress*)

Redesdale. For this title name *see* Mitford, John Freeman-, first Baron Redesdale (1748-1830); Mitford, John Thomas Freeman-, first earl of Redesdale (1805-1886); Mitford, Algernon Bertram Freeman-, first Baron Redesdale (1837-1916).

Redesdale, Robin of. See Robin of Redesdale (*fl.* 1469).

Redfearn, Anne (*d.* 1612). *See under* Pendle witches (*act.* 1612).

Redfern, James Frank (*bap.* 1837, *d.* 1876), sculptor, was born at Hartington, Derbyshire, where he was baptized on 22 January 1837, the son of William Redfern (*d. c.*1843) and his wife, Mary. A number of contemporary accounts describe how as a boy he showed a taste for drawing and carving. The Revd Winger, vicar of Hartington, encouraged Redfern's artistic endeavours. At his suggestion Redfern carved a group of a warrior and a dead horse in alabaster, which was brought to the attention of the politician Alexander James Beresford Hope, on whose estate Redfern was born. Hope sent Redfern to study art in London, possibly under J. R. Clayton, and in Paris, at the atelier of Charles Gleyre. On 29 August 1867 Redfern married Clara Margaret (*bap.* 1843), daughter of Edward Allen.

Between 1859 and 1876 Redfern was a regular exhibitor at the Royal Academy. Many of his works were of religious subjects, the earliest being *Cain and Abel* (exh. RA, 1859) and a *Holy Family* (exh. RA, 1861). However, he also exhibited a number of portrait busts including Hugh Beresford Hope (exh. RA, 1866) and G. Wingfield Digby (exh. RA, 1867), a statue of Lord Macaulay (exh. RA, 1863), and a mythological work entitled *A Nymph of Diana and Cupid* (exh. RA, 1864). Redfern worked for the architect George Gilbert Scott on a number of occasions. He provided four statues of Virtues for the Albert Memorial, in Kensington Gardens (the model for the figure of Fortitude was shown at the Royal Academy in 1869) and executed sculptures for a number of Scott's cathedral restorations. These include the statues on the west front of Salisbury Cathedral (1866–70); statues of the apostles in the Octagon at Ely (1875); the statues in the south porch (c.1870), the figure groups for the reredos (unveiled in 1873), and the figures for the sedilia (1872) at Gloucester; and a statue of *Our Lord in Majesty* in the chapter house at Westminster Abbey. A. J. Beresford Hope's contacts in the Anglo-Catholic movement may have assisted Redfern in obtaining commissions for church decoration. He provided reredos sculptures for two church restorations undertaken by the Cambridge Camden Society: Christ Church, Kilndown, Kent (1869–70) and St Andrew's, Wells Street (1862–85, the reredos was re-erected at Kingsbury in 1933). Redfern also worked for the architectural firms of Bodley and Garner and G. E. Street, which were particularly favoured among ecclesiological circles. For Bodley and Garner he executed some of the figure carving for the church of Holy Angels, Hoar Cross, Staffordshire (c.1873–6). Redfern's statues for the north porch of Bristol Cathedral, restored by Street, caused considerable controversy. The figures were regarded by many as tending towards Romanism and Redfern was accused of copying a statue of St Gregory from another, Roman Catholic, church. This charge he vigorously denied. Redfern died at Clifton House, South End Green, Hampstead, on 13 June 1876, and was survived by his wife. George Gilbert Scott wrote:

> I had thought him a successful man, but it turns out that his spirits were broken by pecuniary distress, and that he had fallen into the hands of cruel usurers, who made his life a torment to him, and so undermined his health that he fell victim to some, otherwise slight, attack of indisposition. (Scott, 306–7)

EMMA HARDY

Sources *Art Journal*, 38 (1876), 276 · *The Builder*, 34 (1876), 600 · *Building News* (23 June 1876) · Redgrave, *Artists* · G. G. Scott, *Personal and professional recollections* (1879) · Graves, *RA exhibitors* · B. Read, *Victorian sculpture* (1982) · *The Post Office London directory* · *The architect's, engineer's, and building-trades' directory* (1868) · A. E. Street, *Memoir of George Edmund Street* (1888) · *The Builder*, 18–34 (1860–76) · *Building News* (1867–76) · d. cert. · *CGPLA Eng. & Wales* (1876) · IGI
Wealth at death under £800: probate, 30 June 1876, *CGPLA Eng. & Wales*

Redfern, William (1774/5?–1833), convict surgeon and pastoralist in Australia, had relatives in Londonderry, Wiltshire, and possibly Canada, but details are unknown. He acquired the diploma of the London Company of Surgeons in January 1797 and immediately joined HMS *Standard* as surgeon's first mate. Later that year he provided medical care and probably moral support to the mutineers at the Nore. He was convicted of mutiny but his death sentence was commuted to life imprisonment perhaps because of his professional association with the sailors and because of his youth and inexperience. Transported to New South Wales in 1801, he was sent to the penal settlement on Norfolk Island as assistant to the surgeon. Diligent work led to a free pardon in 1803, but he also acquired property, livestock, and probably a convict mistress before his transfer to Sydney in 1808.

Having been appointed assistant colonial surgeon, Redfern, aided by an apprentice, every morning saw all the inpatients at the hospital, as well as convict outpatients, and also supervised the dispensing of medicines and stores. Possibly at times to the detriment of his hospital responsibilities, he developed an extensive private practice, gaining the respect of colleagues and the confidence of patients of all classes. He remained socially unacceptable to the 'exclusivist' civil and military officers despite his acceptance by Governor and Mrs Macquarie as 'our friend and family physician'—a rejection perhaps accounting for a reputedly brusque bedside manner.

Following the arrival of three 'sickly' convict transports in 1814, Lachlan Macquarie directed Redfern to investigate. His report comprehensively exposed all aspects of convict maltreatment and mismanagement occurring during transportation. His recommendations for shipboard hygiene and medical care reflected the best naval practice of the period, but his most perceptive, and influential, suggestion was that only experienced naval surgeons should be employed on transports and they should have absolute authority over convict management. Its speedy adoption by the transport commissioners led to a marked decline in convict morbidity and mortality.

In 1810 Redfern reintroduced Jennerian vaccination to all parts of the colony, and from about this period onwards he supported various philanthropic and charitable organizations financially and professionally. A foundation shareholder and director of the colony's first bank, established in 1817, he survived criticism of using his position to personal advantage in a protracted controversy.

On 4 March 1811 Redfern married Sarah Wills at St Philip's Anglican church. Instead of developing a grant in what is now the Sydney suburb of Redfern, he developed grants at his property Campbellfield, in the Airds district, as a farm for sheep, cattle, and a variety of crops. Aided by John Grant, his one-time assigned servant, he gradually acquired large holdings west of the Blue Mountains, extending as far as the Lachlan River.

By the 1820s emancipists were making major contributions to the colony's economy and development. They were shocked by legal decisions in London and Sydney that civil and property rights were not restored by a colonial pardon. In 1821 Redfern became one of two emancipists deputed to present a petition to king and parliament. He had already suffered a severe blow to his pride and professional aspirations when Earl Bathurst rejected his appointment as principal surgeon in 1818, a position previously promised to him by Macquarie. Outraged, Redfern resigned and an embarrassed Macquarie appointed him a magistrate. J. T. Bigge, commissioned by Bathurst to report on the state of the colony and fundamentally antipathetic to the emancipist cause, objected to this elevation of an ex-convict. Macquarie obstinately persisted but Bathurst ultimately revoked the appointment. Meanwhile, Redfern had clashed with Bigge when he appeared to give evidence. He subsequently wrote, angrily refusing to appear again, accusing Bigge of arrogance and bias. It is to Bigge's credit that his reports commend Redfern's professional and farming attainments, although he deprecated his 'irritability or rather a violence of temper towards his inferiors and superiors' (Bigge, *Report of the Commission*, 86). In effect, Redfern personified the conflict between Bigge and Macquarie on the emancipist issue.

Unsettled, Redfern sold stock and property and took his elder son, William Lachlan (*b*. 1819) to Edinburgh, leaving his wife and younger son, Joseph Foveaux (*b*. 1823), at Campbellfield. As on his previous visit in 1822, he enrolled at Edinburgh University in 1829 and 1830, but Mrs Macquarie, who visited him, stated that he was behaving extravagantly and keeping poor company, and had deteriorated mentally and physically. He died in Edinburgh on 17 July 1833 and was buried there at the new Calton cemetery on 23 July. His will essentially left extensive property to his surviving son (Joseph died in 1830) with certain interests for his wife; a codicil in 1828 made some provision for two sisters and the children of one of them.

Redfern was keenly perceptive of injustice, probably a factor in his transportation, and to his involvement in other controversies. Despite his irascible nature he made an invaluable contribution to both the medical and the pastoral development of the colony while also contributing politically to the advancement of the emancipist cause. A play about Redfern's life, *The Emancipist*, by John Macquarie Antill and Rose Antill, was published in 1936.

BRYAN GANDEVIA

Sources R. N. Pescott, 'Emancipist and autocrat: Dr William Redfern and his relationship with Governor Macquarie in the society of New South Wales', MA (Qual.) diss., Australian National University, 1970 · E. Ford, 'The life and work of William Redfern', *Bulletin of the Post-Graduate Committee in Medicine* [University of Sydney], 9 (1953–4), 1–36 · Mitchell L., NSW, Bigge Transcripts · Mitchell L., NSW, Redfern MSS · Mitchell L., NSW, Wentworth MSS · Royal Australian College of Physicians, Sydney, History of Medicine Library, Redfern file · private information · J. Ritchie, *The evidence to the Bigge reports*, 2 vols. (1971) · J. F. Watson, *The history of Sydney Hospital from 1811 to 1911* (1911) · N. J. Dunlop, 'William Redfern, the first Australian medical graduate, and his times', *Royal Australian Historical Society Journal and Proceedings*, 14 (1928), 57–105, 299 · J. Grant, 'Providence: the life and times of John Grant (1792–1866)', Sturt University, Bathurst · [F. Watson], ed., *Historical records of Australia*, 4 ser. in 32 vols. (1914–25) · burial records, new Calton burial-ground, Edinburgh · RCS Eng., archives · J. T. Bigge, *Report of the commissioner of inquiry into the state of the colony of New South Wales* [1822]

Archives Mitchell L., NSW | Mitchell L., NSW, Wentworth MSS and Bigge transcripts

Likenesses G. M. Mather, watercolour miniature, 1832, priv. coll.

Wealth at death £582 minor assets in Edinburgh; plus approx. 6000 acres at Airds (Campbellfield); approx. 12,000 acres west of Blue Mountains; also two building blocks in Geelong, Port Phillip (Victoria): will; Grant, 'Providence'

Redford, George (1785–1860), Congregational minister, was born on 27 September 1785 in Oxford Street, London, son of a deacon of the Chapel Street Church, Soho, who was later minister of the Independent church in Windsor, Berkshire, and his wife, who was of Huguenot descent. He was educated at Hoxton Academy, and matriculated at the University of Glasgow in 1808, graduating MA in 1811. He was ordained to the Congregational ministry in 1809, and became minister at Uxbridge in 1812. There he started the *Congregational Magazine* in 1819, remaining one of the editors for some years. He also, with Thomas Harry Riches, published *The History of the Ancient Town and Borough of Uxbridge* (1818). In June 1826 he succeeded Dr Robert Vaughan as minister of Angel Street Chapel, Worcester. By then he was married, with seven children.

Redford was present at the meeting on 10 May 1831 which went on, three days later, to form the Congregational Union of England and Wales, and he drafted the declaration of faith and order, which was adopted in 1833. He became chairman of the union in 1834, and successfully urged the creation, in 1836, of a Colonial Missionary Society as part of the union. His Congregational lectures in 1837 were later published as *Holy scripture verified, or, The divine authority of the Bible confirmed by an appeal to facts of science, history, and human consciousness* (1837). He also pressed, in 1839, for the Home Missionary Society to extend its activities from preaching the gospel to setting up new churches.

In 1845 Redford read a paper, 'The literature of our denomination', a survey of the attitude of the Independent churches to learning. He urged the formation of a literature committee to prepare a cheap supply of reading matter and to encourage better literature. He himself published a number of works, including *A Defence of Extempore Prayer* (1816), *The Church of England Indefensible from the Holy Scriptures* (1833), *The Great Change: a Treatise on Conversion* (1843), and *Body and Soul, or, Life, Mind, and Matter* (1847). He was a contributor to the *British Quarterly Review*, founded in 1845, and other journals, and he edited, with John Leifchild, *The Evangelist*, a monthly magazine, from May 1837 to June 1839.

Redford was made an LLD by the University of Glasgow in 1834, and was later awarded a DD by Amherst College, Massachusetts. His wife died about 1855, and in 1856 he resigned from his ministry at Worcester because of poor health, retiring to Edgbaston, Birmingham, to be near his friend John Angell James. He died at his home in Monument Lane, Edgbaston, on 20 May 1860, and was buried at Worcester on 29 May.

THOMPSON COOPER, *rev.* ANNE PIMLOTT BAKER

Sources A. Peel, *These hundred years: a history of the Congregational Union of England and Wales, 1831–1931* (1931) · *Congregational Year Book* (1861), 230–33 · *The Nonconformist* (30 May 1860), 438 · *Berrow's Worcester Journal* (25 May 1860)

Likenesses photograph, repro. in Peel, *These hundred years*, facing p. 16

Wealth at death under £3000: probate, 7 June 1860, *CGPLA Eng. & Wales*

Redford, Sir Henry. *See* Retford, Sir Henry (*c*.1354–1409).

Redford, John (*c*.1500–1547), composer, is of unknown parentage and date of birth. Since many of his musical and literary associates, as well as his brother Henry, lived well into the later sixteenth century, however, it may be conjectured that he was born about 1500. He was one of the earliest English composers of organ music, and also a writer of plays and poems. In 1534 he signed, as one of the six vicars-choral of St Paul's Cathedral in London, the acknowledgement of the royal supremacy. It was probably in that year, on the death of Thomas Hickman, that he became almoner and master of the choristers; certainly in 1542 he was a resident of the parish of St Gregory, in which parish lay the almoner's house in St Paul's Churchyard. He was assessed for £20 in the lay subsidy roll for 1547. Redford's will was made on 7 October 1547 and proved on 29 November. It included bequests to his brothers William and Henry, and to his sister Margaret Cox; his executor and residuary legatee was Sebastian Westcote, who succeeded him as almoner. Margaret died in 1558, having appointed Westcote as her own executor; Westcote himself and Henry died within a short time of each other in 1582.

Redford's literary circle may be deduced from the contents of BL, Add. MS 15233; apart from Redford's own morality play, *Wyt and Science*, a fragment of another play and some poems by him, it includes poems by John Heywood (probably the vicar-choral of St Paul's of that name, in office from *c*.1530 to 1574), Thomas Prideaux, Miles Huggard, John Thorne, and 'Master Knight'. Thorne was probably the musician who became organist of York Minster, and Knight possibly Thomas Knight, a composer represented, along with Redford, by musical works in BL, Add. MSS 17802–17805. Several of these men, like Westcote, were to remain Catholic on Elizabeth's accession. *Wyt and Science* was presumably written for the choristers of St Paul's, who certainly performed plays under Westcote. It includes three songs, written out separately in the manuscript, but without music. Although critical reaction to Redford's literary work has been muted, the play has been edited three times since the nineteenth century.

It is, however, as a composer of organ music that Redford especially deserves to be remembered. The organ had long played a part in church services, acting as a substitute for the voices in alternate verses of hymns and in a similar way in other parts of the liturgy. Originally this had been done by extemporization on the appropriate plainsong. Redford was among the first in England to write down such pieces, whereby the potential of the form was greatly enhanced. All his known organ compositions—over forty of them—are of this kind, ranging from short 'verses' to quite lengthy compositions. He may also have written some of the many similar anonymous works that survive.

The only manuscript of Redford's organ music compiled for liturgical use is the earliest section of BL, Add. MS 29996, copied by a provincial organist in the late 1540s. About two-fifths of the pieces in this manuscript are definitely by Redford. Other manuscripts are non-liturgical compilations or fragments. The earliest of these is a separate booklet bound with the literary material of BL, Add. MS 15233: its surviving portion is devoted entirely to Redford's organ music. Another important source is the Mulliner book (BL, Add. MS 30513), copied by Thomas Mulliner. Later manuscripts contain less of his music, but there is at least one seventeenth-century copy of an isolated piece, its liturgical function no longer understood. The preservation of Redford's organ music owes much to the interest of Thomas Tomkins and his son Nathaniel, both of whom owned BL, Add. MS 29996.

There are also two genuine vocal works by Redford, both liturgical. While the original purpose of his music was lost sight of after Mary's reign, the memory of his art was preserved through later copies and in literary allusions. Thomas Tusser relates having been a chorister under Redford, whose skill he warmly praises ('the like nowhere / For cunning such, and virtue much'), while Thomas Morley mentions Redford as one skilled in 'breaking the plainsong' (ornamenting it in a polyphonic composition). The true significance of his organ music was not rediscovered until the second half of the twentieth century.   JOHN CALDWELL

Sources A. Brown and D. Stevens, 'Redford, John', Grove, *Dict. mus.* (1954), 7.79–82 · D. Stevens, *The Mulliner Book: a commentary* (1952) · F. L. Harrison, *Music in medieval Britain* (1958), 13, 360–61, 386–8, 410 · J. Caldwell, *English keyboard music before the nineteenth century* (1973), 26–30 · H. W. Shaw, *The succession of organists of the Chapel Royal and the cathedrals of England and Wales from c.1538* (1991), 171 · BL, Add. MSS 15233, 17802–17805, 29996, 30513 · Bodl. Oxf., MS Tenbury 389 · Christ Church Oxf., Mus. MSS 371, 1034A, 979–983 · T. Tusser, *A hundreth good pointes of husbandrie* (1557) · T. Morley, *A plaine and easie introduction to practicall musicke* (1597), 96 · J. Redford, *The moral play of wit and science, and early poetical miscellanies*, ed. J. O. Halliwell (1848) · P. Happé, ed., *Tudor interludes* (1972) · D. Stevens, ed., *The Mulliner book*, Musica Britannica, 1 (1951) · J. Caldwell, ed., *Early Tudor organ music, 1: Music for the office*, Early English Church Music, 6 (1966) · D. Stevens, ed., *Early Tudor organ music, 2: Music for the mass*, Early English Church Music, 10 (1969) · W. H. G. Flood, *Early Tudor composers* (1925), 95–9 · C. F. Pfatteicher, *John Redford* (1934) · C. F. Pfatteicher, *The organ works of John Redford* (1934) · T. W. Craik, *The Tudor interlude: stage, costume, and acting* (1958) · will, PRO, PROB 11/31, sig. 50
Wealth at death approx. £20—assessed in lay subsidy roll (1547): Brown and Stevens, 'Redford, John', 7.80

Redgrave, Alexander (1818–1894), factory inspector, was born on 9 June 1818 in King's Road, Belgravia, London, one of the two children of William Redgrave, a manufacturer of wire fencing, and his second wife, Margaret, the widow of a Captain Ogilvie of Banffshire. Among his seven half-brothers and sisters were Samuel *Redgrave, civil servant and writer on art, and Richard *Redgrave, the subject and landscape painter.

Redgrave's early life was spent in straitened circumstances owing to his father's lack of business success. In February 1834, after attending a local day school, he entered the criminal registry department of the Home Office as an 'extra clerk'. In so doing he joined his half-brother Samuel, who was then assistant keeper of the criminal register. He took over as assistant keeper, at a salary of £120 p.a. when Samuel relinquished the position in October 1841. In December 1844 he was appointed clerk in the factory office at an annual salary of £150, rising to £400. He became sub-inspector of factories in September 1847 and a full inspector in May 1852, at which time his salary was £1150 p.a. Redgrave remained a factory inspector until his retirement in September 1891, by which time he had spent more than fifty-seven years as a civil servant, nearly forty-seven of them in the factory department. Between 1861 and 1878 he was, with Robert Baker, joint chief inspector of factories; for the final thirteen years of his career he was chief inspector.

Redgrave and Baker despised each other. This mutual animosity probably arose out of Baker's sense of grievance when Redgrave gained full inspector status before him, notwithstanding his comparative youth, lack of experience of factory conditions, and short service as a sub-inspector. Under their joint control the factory inspectorate was riven with discord. The two men seldom met to discuss or co-ordinate policy and their joint reports were perfunctory documents. In 1868 a Home Office inquiry resulted in both inspectors' being censured. However, 'great quarrelling and disorganization in the office' continued. Under these circumstances there arose major differences in the administration of the Factory Acts in their respective districts, Redgrave being significantly less 'prosecution-minded' than his colleague.

Under Redgrave's leadership the factory department's approach to enforcement was characterized by strong emphasis on conciliation and persuasion, with prosecution being employed as a weapon only of last resort, which was confined to the worst and clearest cases. Though given to complacency, Redgrave was a keen observer of factory conditions and a capable administrator. Some trade unionists regarded him as a 'masters' man', but he did much to encourage regulation of the 'dangerous trades', and also to establish an efficient administrative structure for the inspectorate. Redgrave was the first factory inspector to have no personal fortune or private income, and the first career bureaucrat to serve in the inspectorate. Of lower social status than the earliest appointees, his swift promotion suggests that he was highly regarded within the civil service and also that he had, as Baker alleged, a political patron.

In 1851 Redgrave played a part in organizing visits by working men to the International Exhibition at Hyde Park. He was the author of *The Progress of Nations* (1872) and *The Factory and Workshop Act* (1878), a fifth edition of which appeared in 1893. A fellow of the Royal Statistical Society from 1856, Redgrave was made a companion of the Bath in 1877.

Redgrave married Mary Ann Hodgkinson on 4 January 1845. They had three sons, the eldest of whom, Jasper Alexander, was appointed to the factory inspectorate in 1872, having previously acted as his father's clerk and private secretary. Throughout his life Redgrave resided in

London. He died at 23 Pembroke Gardens, Kensington, on 6 December 1894 and was buried at Kensal Green cemetery on 12 December. His wife predeceased him, in 1883.

P. W. J. BARTRIP

Sources Boase, *Mod. Eng. biog.* · *The Times* (8 Dec 1894) · *The Graphic* (26 Sept 1891) · P. W. J. Bartrip and P. T. Fenn, 'The evolution of regulatory style in the nineteenth century British factory inspectorate', *Journal of Law and Society*, 10 (1983), 201–22 · B. Martin, The development of the factory offce up to 1878 · PRO, H 045, H 082, H 087, LAB 15, T 13
Archives PRO, Home Office records
Likenesses photograph, repro. in *The Graphic*, 356
Wealth at death £5711 12s. 1d.: probate, May 1895, CGPLA Eng. & Wales

Redgrave, Sir Michael Scudamore (1908–1985), actor, was born on 20 March 1908 in theatrical lodgings at St Michael's Hill, Bristol, the only child of George Ellsworthy (Roy) Redgrave, actor, a specialist in melodrama, and his second wife, Margaret (Daisy) Scudamore (1884–1958), actress, daughter of Fortunatus Augustin Scudamore, dramatist. Sixteen months after his birth his mother took him for a short time to Australia where his father was acting. Three years later his parents were divorced. In 1922 his mother, who looked after him, married J. P. Anderson, who had formerly been employed by the Ceylon and Eastern Agency in Ceylon. They had a daughter, Peggy, a half-sister to Michael.

Michael Redgrave went to Clifton College, Bristol, where he became a competent schoolboy player in male and female parts. His Macbeth, at seventeen, made his mother, who had been opposed to this, think twice about him becoming a professional actor. In 1927 he went to Magdalene College, Cambridge, to study medieval and modern languages, and English. He undertook much undergraduate acting and wrote for and edited university magazines before graduating in 1931. He then went to Cranleigh School, Surrey, as modern languages master. Here, in effect, he was an actor–manager, doing six productions and playing, among other parts, Samson Agonistes, Hamlet, and Lear; moreover he was given work in the semi-professional Guildford repertory company, which was glad to have a recruit so accomplished and personable: he was 6 feet 3 inches tall and strikingly handsome. Confidently he resigned from Cranleigh and got an audition from Lilian Baylis of the Old Vic, who offered him a contract at £3 a week. Before accepting, he had an interview with William Armstrong, the director of Liverpool Playhouse, who persuaded him to go there; between 1934 and 1936 he had a wide variety of parts in the most sympathetic circumstances.

More important to him, Redgrave fell in love with Rachel Kempson (1910–2003) when they acted together in John Van Druten's *The Flowers of the Forest*; two years younger than he, she was the daughter of Eric William Edward Kempson, headmaster of the Royal Naval College at Dartmouth. They were married in the college chapel on 18 July 1935 and for another year remained at Liverpool. It was then that Tyrone Guthrie, who was becoming one of the principal directors of his time, invited them for a season at the Old Vic where in September 1936 they

Sir Michael Scudamore Redgrave (1908–1985), by Howard Coster, 1936

opened as Ferdinand of Navarre and the Princess of France in *Love's Labour's Lost*. In 1936–7 Redgrave was Horner in *The Country Wife* (with the American actress Ruth Gordon) and, to his delight, Orlando in *As You Like It* to the Rosalind of Edith Evans, then forty-eight but, with her unerring sense of comedy, ready for the adventure. At once they were attracted to each other, an association they sustained during the Old Vic run and a transference for three months to what was then the New Theatre. Before then Redgrave had another rich experience, Laertes to Laurence Olivier's vigorous Hamlet. A daughter, Vanessa, was born to Redgrave and Rachel in January 1937. They later had a son, Corin Redgrave (b. 1939), and another daughter, Lynn Redgrave (b. 1943). All three became well-known actors. His son later wrote a book about his father, in which he revealed that despite his marriage, Redgrave had a number of homosexual relationships in his later life. Corin Redgrave commented that 'My father was bisexual. He wanted to write about it but never managed to' (C. Redgrave, 4).

Even after so brief a time in London, it was clear that Redgrave would be an important player; recognizing this, John Gielgud gave him several parts (including Tusenbach in *Three Sisters*) in a season at the Queen's Theatre (1937–8). Work came easily. When he played, surprisingly, Sir Andrew Aguecheek during a production of *Twelfth Night* in the West End in 1938, the drama critic James Agate called him 'a giddy, witty maypole'. At the Westminster Theatre

in 1939 he was the first Harry Monchensey in T. S. Eliot's *The Family Reunion*, and he had also, inevitably but reluctantly, gone into films: Alfred Hitchcock cast him in *The Lady Vanishes* (1939). With the outbreak of war he had to abandon an Old Vic opportunity; instead, during 1940, he acted and sang Macheath in *The Beggar's Opera* at the Haymarket Theatre; later, at a small Kensington theatre and in the West End, he appeared most sensitively as the idealistic recluse of Robert Ardrey's *Thunder Rock*.

Redgrave's call-up papers reached him in June 1941 as he was in the middle of making a film and he found himself, as an ordinary seaman, training in devastated Plymouth. Discharged after a year for medical reasons, he returned to the stage in a sequence of plays, some as successful as Turgenev's *A Month in the Country* (he was Rakitin in 1943) and an American melodrama, *Uncle Harry* (1944), in which he acted with exciting nervous power. Curiously in 1947 he appeared to be out of key in an elaborate production of *Macbeth*. Another good spell was coming: first, the relentless tragedy of Strindberg's *The Father* (1948–9), then a long season with the Old Vic Company at the New Theatre (its final period before going back to Waterloo Road). Redgrave ended with Hamlet (1950), a performance which lacked only the final quality of excitement: as a disciple of Konstantin Stanislavsky he was apt to concentrate upon a close dissection of the text. From that he went to Stratford upon Avon for a pair of remarkable performances, an intellectually searching Richard II (1951) in which he did not disguise the man's sexual ambiguity, and a Hotspur, grandly direct, with a precise Northumbrian accent. That summer he also played Prospero and the *Henry V* Chorus. In 1952, at the St James's, he was admirable in *Winter Journey*, Clifford Odets's American drama, though at the time there were awkward differences of opinion with a fellow actor. A good company man, Redgrave never hesitated to speak his mind. Meanwhile he gave an excellent performance as the schoolmaster in the film *The Browning Version* (1951).

During another Stratford year (1953) Redgrave had to perform the unnerving trinity of Shylock, Lear, and the Antony of *Antony and Cleopatra*. As the triumvir at sunset he reached his Shakespearian height—Peggy Ashcroft was Cleopatra—and the play had a London season at the Princes. Films, such as *The Dam Busters* (1954), continued to occupy much of his time. He returned in 1958 to Stratford—his last appearance there—and again, at fifty, acted as Hamlet, a performance mature and deeply considered. Appointed CBE in 1952, he was knighted in 1959. His final major work in the theatre was at the Chichester festival of 1962 (as Uncle Vanya) and at the opening of the National Theatre in 1963, in the Old Vic, when he was an authoritative Claudius to the Hamlet of Peter O'Toole. The next year (1964) he was Solness in Ibsen's *The Master Builder*.

At the opening of the Yvonne Arnaud Theatre, Guildford, in May 1965, Redgrave returned to *A Month in the Country*, which also had a West End showing. He had become a prodigiously popular film star in such productions as *Kipps* (1941) in which he played the title part, *The Way to the Stars* (1945), *The Importance of being Earnest* (1952), and *The*

Quiet American (1957); one of his last roles was General Wilson in *Oh what a lovely war* in 1969. Illness was developing: he had Parkinson's disease and he kept to readings, on various international tours, during the ebb of his career. His last appearance was in Simon Gray's *Close of Play* (National, 1979), a practically silent part during which he sat in a wheelchair for most of the play. Sir Michael Redgrave died on 21 March 1985 in a nursing home at Denham, Buckinghamshire. He was cremated at Mortlake crematorium, London, on 26 March, and a memorial service was held at St Paul's, Covent Garden, London (the actors' church) on 18 July. His wife survived him.

Redgrave's publications include *The Actor's Ways and Means* (1953) and *Mask or Face* (1958), and a version of *The Aspern Papers* by Henry James, in which he acted, as 'H. J.', at the Queen's in 1959. He published in 1983 an autobiography, *In my Mind's Eye*.   J. C. TREWIN, *rev.*

Sources M. Redgrave, *In my mind's eye* (1983) · R. Kempson, *A family and its fortunes* (1986) · C. Redgrave, *Michael Redgrave, my father* (1995) · *The Times* (22 March 1985) · *The Times* (27 March 1985) · *The Times* (19 July 1985) · I. Herbert, ed., *Who's who in the theatre*, 16th edn (1977) · G. Rowell, *The Old Vic theatre: a history* (1992) · m. cert. · personal knowledge (1990)
Archives Theatre Museum, London, personal and family corresp., diaries, notebooks, and papers | King's AC Cam., letters and postcards to G. H. W. Rylands · U. Reading L., corresp. with Edward Thompson of Heinemann | FILM BFI NFTVA, *Omnibus*, BBC 1, 13 July 1997 · BFI NFTVA, documentary footage · BFI NFTVA, performance footage | SOUND BL NSA, documentary recordings · BL NSA, oral history recordings · BL NSA, performance recordings
Likenesses H. Coster, photograph, 1936, NPG [*see illus.*] · photographs, *c.*1937–1971, Hult. Arch. · Y. Karsh, bromide print, 1954, NPG
Wealth at death £111,244: probate, 16 Sept 1985, *CGPLA Eng. & Wales*

Redgrave, Richard (1804–1888), painter and arts administrator, was born on 30 April 1804 at 2 Belgrave Terrace, London, the second son of William Redgrave (1775–1845), a manufacturer, and his wife, Mary (*d. c.*1814), and the younger brother of the art historian Samuel *Redgrave (1802–1876). Educated at home and at a school in Chelsea, Redgrave began work as a clerk and draughtsman in his father's factory, which produced wire fencing. Here he developed an aversion to business, a determination to become an artist, and a sympathy for the working poor which would manifest itself later in the subjects of his most important paintings. In 1825 his landscape *The River Brent, Near Hanwell* was accepted for exhibition at the Royal Academy; in the following year he entered the Royal Academy Schools at the late age of twenty-two. Thereafter his works (oils and watercolours) were exhibited regularly at the Royal Academy, the British Institution, and the Society of British Artists. He was a founding and life-long member of the Etching Club from 1837.

In the early years Redgrave supported himself by teaching drawing during the day while studying at night in the academy schools. In 1836 he achieved his first popular success at the British Institution with a humorous scene from Jonathan Swift's *Gulliver's Travels*, entitled *Gulliver Exhibited to the Brobdingnag Farmer* (exh. 1836; V&A). Paintings

Richard Redgrave (1804–1888), self-portrait

inspired by British literature remained an important staple in his career. Addison, Bunyan, Chaucer, Crabbe, Goldsmith (*Olivia's Return to her Parents*, exh. RA, 1839; ex Sothebys, New York, 17 February 1986), Johnson (*The Reduced Gentleman's Daughter*, exh. RA, 1840; V&A), Shakespeare (*Ophelia*, exh. RA, 1843; V&A), and Spenser, among other authors, were plumbed for material. Historical subjects treated as everyday scenes also contributed to his *œuvre*. Redgrave was elected an associate at the academy in 1840 and RA in 1851. This professional success allowed him to marry Rose Margaret Bacon (1811–1899) on 30 May 1843. A son and two daughters were born soon afterwards. It was in the 1840s that Redgrave produced his most memorable paintings, 'lessons of philanthropic appeal on behalf of the oppressed and miserable' (Dafforne, 205), especially poignant scenes of poor working women.

In 1843 Redgrave exhibited *Going to Service* (priv. coll.) and *The Poor Teacher*. Both feature attractive young women forced by poverty into employment outside the security of their own homes, a perilous prospect in the Victorian age. Both embody Redgrave's self-proclaimed goal of 'calling attention to the trials and struggles of the poor and the oppressed' ('Autobiography of Richard Redgrave', 49). *The Poor Teacher* was a great success and Redgrave made several versions, including one for his most important patron, John Sheepshanks, entitled *The Governess*, of 1844 (exh. RA, 1845; V&A). The reviewer for the *Art Union* found it 'an appeal on behalf of a class that demands our best sympathies, it is, in fact, a painted sermon—a large and valuable contribution to the cause of humanity' (*Art Union*, 180). Such scenes culminated with *The Sempstress*, of 1844 (exh. RA, 1844), inspired by Thomas Hood's poem *The Song of the Shirt* (1843), which plaintively decried the condition of urban needlewomen. As was true of his earlier paintings, carefully selected details enrich the narrative and speak of the woman's dismal plight. By focusing on one idealized, saintly needlewoman (rather than upon a more realistic crowd of unkempt, disgruntled workers), Redgrave could more easily elicit sympathy for this working-class martyr from the middle- and upper-class viewing public. This was also his goal in *The Outcast*, of 1851 (exh. RA, 1851; Royal Academy of Arts), a scene which addresses the modern moral subject of 'the fallen woman' (one of the first paintings to do so). This was Redgrave's RA diploma work, following his election to full membership in 1851, and it reflects his desire to be identified professionally with subjects treating modern moral and social issues. Surprisingly, Redgrave turned away from such themes in his later career, focusing instead on landscape subjects—with the exception of *The Emigrants' Last Sight of Home*, of 1858 (exh. RA, 1859; Tate collection), which, while depicting the timely social theme of emigration which surged in the 1840s and 1850s, features a stunning Surrey landscape as backdrop for a family of emigrants bravely bidding goodbye to their village. By the 1850s landscape subjects began to dominate his output, often inspired by the countryside near his summer house in Abinger, Surrey. These naturalistic landscapes of wooded glens, mossy rocks, and meandering streams (for example, *The Woodland Mirror*, exh. RA, 1851), were painted with highly detailed, microscopic detail, not unlike Pre-Raphaelite works, though Redgrave's earliest efforts pre-date their examples. His more conventional landscapes were characterized by an intentionally 'romantic' quality emphasized by the lines of poetry that he often attached to them.

Redgrave's productivity as a painter decreased in the last decades of his life as he assumed the new and influential roles of arts administrator and author. Along with Henry Cole, Redgrave became the driving force behind the reform of art education in Great Britain. He held several positions in the Government School of Design (later the Royal College of Art): botanical teacher (1847), headmaster (1848), art superintendent (1852), and in 1857 he became inspector–general for art, in which capacity he developed a national curriculum for art instruction. The School of Design was founded in the 1830s to train craftsmen to improve British industrial design, always a keen interest of Redgrave's. In the late 1840s he contributed designs for 'Felix Summerly's art manufactures', Cole's scheme to engage professional artists in the design of manufactured objects; later he produced the impressive design for the duke of Wellington's funeral carriage (1852). Redgrave and Cole supervised the new South Kensington Museum (now the Victoria and Albert Museum), for which Redgrave designed the innovative art gallery to house John Sheepshanks's extensive collection of British art, given to the state in 1857. He, Cole, and Sheepshanks all held liberal views and wished to make the museum accessible to the working class with generous evening and weekend opening hours.

In response to Redgrave's exceptional administrative skill, more tasks were heaped upon him. He organized the British art section for both the Universal Exhibition in Paris in 1855 (for which he received the cross of the French Légion d'honneur) and for the International Exhibition in London in 1862. In 1857 he was appointed surveyor of the queen's pictures, a position he held with great distinction until 1880, during which time he produced a meticulous thirty-four-volume manuscript catalogue of the paintings in the Royal Collection, notable for its commentary on conservation. On his retirement he was created a CB. Redgrave published various texts on art and design, and also wrote with his brother Samuel a valuable history of British art which remains a standard authority, *A Century of Painters of the English School* (1866), in which he expressed national pride in the development of an English school of art.

Redgrave died at home at 27 Hyde Park Gate, Kensington, London, on 14 December 1888 after suffering for years from increasing blindness and physical debility. His funeral service was held on 18 December at St Mary Abbot's, Kensington, followed by burial in Brompton cemetery. The breadth and depth of his achievements as an artist and civil servant make him an excellent example of the energetic spirit and productivity of the Victorian age.

KATHRYN MOORE HELENIAK

Sources F. M. Redgrave, *Richard Redgrave, C.B., R.A.: a memoir compiled from his diary* (1891) · 'The autobiography of Richard Redgrave, ARA', *Art Journal*, 12 (1850), 48–9 · J. Dafforne, 'British artists: their style and character, no. 65, Richard Redgrave', *Art Journal*, 19 (1859), 205–7 · S. P. Casteras and R. Parkinson, eds., *Richard Redgrave, 1804–1888* (1988) · F. G. Stephens, 'Richard Redgrave C.B. hon retired R.A.', *Artists at home* (New York, 1984), 35–8 · R. Redgrave, *On the gift of the Sheepshanks collection with a view to the formation of a national gallery of British art* (1857) · *DNB* · L. Lamborne, 'Richard Redgrave RA: artist and administrator', *V&A Album*, 2 (1983), 115–20 · J. F. Codell, 'Righting the Victorian artist: the Redgraves' *A century of painters of the English school*, and the serialization of art history', *Oxford Art Journal*, 23/2 (2000), 95–120 · K. M. Heleniak, 'Victorian collections and British nationalism', *Journal of the History of Collections*, 12 (2000), 91–107 · F. Collard, 'Richard Redgrave and the Summerly art-manufactures', *Burlington Magazine*, 136 (1994), 314–6 · J. Physick, *The Victoria and Albert Museum: the history of its building* (1982) · L. Ettlinger, 'The duke of Wellington's funeral car', *Journal of the Warburg and Courtauld Institutes*, 3 (1939–40), 154–9 · Graves, *Brit. Inst.* · Graves, *RA exhibitors* · J. Johnson, ed., *Works exhibited at the Royal Society of British Artists, 1824–1893, and the New English Art Club, 1888–1917*, 2 vols. (1975) · *Art Union*, 7 (1845), 180 · *The Times* (8 May 1844), 7 · m. cert. · d. cert.

Archives V&A, family corresp.; letters | V&A, corresp. with H. Cole

Likenesses R. Redgrave, self-portrait, oils, c.1827, Yale U. CBA · F. Grant, pencil and brown wash, 1872, NPG · A. S. Cope, oils, 1884, Aberdeen Art Gallery · G. Ledward, marble bust, 1915–16 (after terracotta by R. A. Ledward, 1881), V&A · Elliott & Fry, carte-de-visite, NPG · Lock & Whitfield, woodburytype, NPG; repro. in T. Cooper, *Men of mark: a gallery of contemporary portraits* (1878) · J. P. Mayall, photogravure (as an elderly man), repro. in Stephens, 'Richard Redgrave', facing p. 38 · R. Redgrave, self-portrait, oils, NPG [see illus.] · woodcut, BM; repro. in 'Autobiography of Richard Redgrave', *Art Journal*, 12 (1850)

Wealth at death £42,769 14s. 9d.: probate, 1 Feb 1889, CGPLA Eng. & Wales

Redgrave, Samuel (1802–1876), art historian and civil servant, was born at 9 Upper Eaton Street, Pimlico, London, on 3 October 1802, the eldest son of William Redgrave

(1775–1845), a manufacturer, and his wife, Mary (d. c.1814), and brother of Richard *Redgrave (1804–1888). He was educated at home and at a school in Chelsea; as a youth he studied watercolour and architectural drawing with John Powell. In 1833 he was admitted to the Royal Academy Schools as an architectural student for ten years. He was a member of the Etching Club from its foundation in 1837, serving as secretary from 1842 until his death. From the late 1840s he was an active member of the Society of Arts; he served on many committees and held the offices of treasurer and vice-president.

Although art and architecture were his first love, Redgrave's income derived from his work at the Home Office where he began as a clerk in 1818 at the age of fifteen and rose over the decades to positions of importance. In 1838 he became assistant secretary to Lord John Russell who was colonial secretary; in 1839 he was appointed the secretary to the constabulary force commission; from 1839 to 1845 he was private secretary to Fox Maule, under-secretary at the Home Office. As keeper of the criminal register Redgrave also gathered criminal statistics and was made a life member of the Statistical Society. From 1852 until 1855 he was private secretary to Henry Fitzroy, under-secretary in the Home department. At this time he wrote two valuable treatises: *Some account of the powers, authorities, and duties of her majesty's principal secretary of state for the Home department* (1852) and *Murray's Handbook of Church and State* (1852; rev. edn, 1855).

Following his retirement in 1860, Redgrave belatedly devoted himself to art as both curator and art historian. He organized numerous exhibitions at the South Kensington Museum and at the Royal Academy of Arts, and helped with the international exhibitions in London (1862) and Paris (1867). However, his most valuable contribution to art history was as the author of two valuable texts on British painting, particularly with regard to minor artists: *A Century of Painters of the English School* (1866; later editions of 1890 and 1947 titled *A Century of British Painters*), co-authored with his brother Richard Redgrave; and *A dictionary of artists of the English school: painters, sculptors, architects, engravers and ornamentists; with notices of their lives and work* (1874; rev. edns, 1878, 1970). These biographically based accounts remain both accessible and authoritative introductions to the history of British art. His *Descriptive catalogue of the historical collection of British paintings in watercolours in the South Kensington Museum*, whose informative preface outlined the history of the British watercolour, appeared posthumously in 1877.

Redgrave's productive public life must have helped alleviate the sorrow in his private life. He married Amelia Ann Sarah, daughter of William Orlebar, a solicitor, at St George's Church, London, on 23 July 1839. She died in 1845; two daughters, Mary Ann (1841–1859) and Alice (1842–1856), also predeceased him. He died at his home, 17 Hyde Park Gate South, Kensington, London, on 20 March 1876, after a long illness, and was buried in the churchyard of Holy Trinity, Brompton, London.

KATHRYN MOORE HELENIAK

Sources E. Bonython, 'Richard and Samuel Redgrave and their family', *Richard Redgrave, 1804–1888*, ed. S. P. Casteras and R. Parkinson (1988), 1–8 • Redgrave, *Artists*, 2nd edn, vii–xi • DNB • F. M. Redgrave, *Richard Redgrave, C.B., R.A.: a memoir* (1891) • *Athenaeum*, 1 (1876), 435 • J. F. Codell, 'Righting the Victorian artist: the Redgraves' *A century of painters of the English school*, and the serialization of art history', *Oxford Art Journal*, 23/2 (2000), 95–120 • *Catalogue of the valuable collection of pictures, drawings, miniatures and other objects of art formed by that well-known connoisseur, S. Redgrave, esq.* (1877) [sale catalogue, Christies, 23–4 March 1877] • m. cert. • d. cert.

Archives UCL, corresp. with E. Chadwick

Wealth at death under £14,000: probate, 4 May 1876, CGPLA Eng. & Wales

Redhead, Brian Leonard (1929–1994), broadcaster and journalist, was born on 28 December 1929 at Princess Mary Maternity Hospital, Newcastle upon Tyne, the only child of Ernest Leonard Redhead, a silk screen printer and advertising agent, and his wife, Janet Crossley, née Fairley. Precocious and, as he later admitted, 'cocky' (Redhead, *Desert Island Discs*, BBC Radio 4, 6 July 1986), Redhead won a scholarship to Newcastle's Royal Grammar School, played the clarinet on *Children's Hour* and, following national service and a stint on the Whitley Bay *Seaside Chronicle*, went to Downing College, Cambridge, where he took a first in part one of the history tripos but only a second in part two. Much of his subsequent work, and his civic activity, reflected continuing awareness of the importance of the past: 'Journalism should be seen, and heard, as the first attempt at writing history', he wrote (Redhead, *The Best of 'From our Own Correspondent'* 4).

Redhead joined the staff of the *Manchester Guardian* in 1954, rising quickly through the ranks. In the same year, on 19 June, he married Jean (generally known as Jenni) Salmon (b. c.1930), a teacher and fellow Geordie. They had two sons, Stephen and James, and then twins, Annabel (Abby) and William. After making his mark as an innovative and energetic features editor, in 1965 Redhead was appointed northern editor of what was by now The Guardian. Four years later he was made editor of its sister paper, the *Manchester Evening News*, but the ultimate prize of editing The Guardian eluded him. He applied when the post fell vacant in 1975 but was beaten by Peter Preston. A few months later he left the company, saying he had been sacked; others felt he had walked out in a fit of pique. One problem was that he had been absent too often, his good looks, lilting voice, unassailable self-confidence, and enviable fluency making him much in demand as a broadcaster. This had started in the late 1950s, when he regularly hosted BBC's weekly Manchester-based television show *Points North*. He resigned from The Guardian in the early 1960s to join BBC's popular television programme *Tonight* (moving with his family briefly to London) but was back on The Guardian within a year. He chaired Radio 4's talk series *A Word In Edgeways* for more than twenty years.

It was this natural broadcasting talent that resulted in an invitation to co-present Radio 4's breakfast programme, *Today*, in succession to Robert Robinson. He signed for an initial three months but stayed for eighteen

Brian Leonard Redhead (1929–1994), by Nils Jorgensen, 1992

years, taking a London flat in the Barbican but maintaining the family home in Rainow, outside Macclesfield. He brought to the programme verbal dexterity, political acumen, and Pennine folksiness. For ten years he and John Timpson, the other main presenter, formed the greatest double act ever to accompany the British breakfast. They complemented one another perfectly: tenor and baritone, town and country, north and south and (many felt) left and right, though in truth their politics were more complex than that. True, Redhead irritated the tory faithful with his frequent anti-Conservative jibes, clashing on air with Nigel Lawson (1987) and Peter Lilley (1991) over his alleged support for Labour. But he was also a staunch defender of Britain's constitutional monarchy, described himself as a 'wet' (Donovan, *All Our Todays*, 99), sent all his children to a fee-paying school (Cheadle Hulme), and had a lucrative sideline making corporate videos. Lady Thatcher, who during his era gave *Today* a unique imprimatur by telephoning it direct from 10 Downing Street, paid tribute to him on air after his death. Having spent so many hours in the studio in the presence of Redhead's shaggy beard and elfin twinkle, it was Timpson who came up with the best physical description of his partner: 'I always felt he would look most at home sitting with a fishing rod beside a garden pond with a little curly hat with a pom-pom on top. He was everybody's idea of a lovable garden gnome' (Donovan, *All Our Todays*, 59).

Redhead had a sharp rather than a deep mind, but he found himself setting out on a long spiritual journey after his youngest son was killed in a road accident in France in 1982 at the age of eighteen. The tragedy drew him towards the Church of England and he was confirmed seven months later, going on to 'read the Bible from cover to cover' (Donovan, *All Our Todays*, 78), and to make an epic Radio 4 series about it entitled *The Good Book*. When it was broadcast in 1986 he wrote: 'The whole point of a pilgrimage is not the distance covered but the act of identifying yourself with a purpose larger than your own' (Redhead, *Personal Perspectives*, 34).

One of the many causes for which Redhead campaigned and raised funds was the hospice movement, which he described as 'the best thing that has happened in this country since the Second World War' (Redhead, *Personal Perspectives*, 30). Sadly, he was not able to spend his own last days in one. Having in 1993 arranged to leave *Today* the following year to concentrate on his chancellorship of Manchester University, his lay work in the church, and a new Radio 4 series, he was admitted to hospital in December for a hip operation. Found to have a ruptured appendix discharging toxins into his body, he died of acute kidney failure and blood poisoning in Macclesfield District General Hospital on 23 January 1994. After a funeral service in Rainow parish church he was cremated at Macclesfield crematorium on 28 January, and his ashes were scattered behind his home. He was survived by his wife, Jenni, and by their two elder sons, and their daughter.

Redhead was a professional northerner who became a national voice. There was much national sadness when he died at the early age of sixty-four. Cheeky, opinionated, and often politically provocative, he had made *Today* the one programme no member of the decision-making classes could afford to miss. Insufferably bumptious for some of his colleagues, irrepressibly cheerful for most of his listeners, Redhead it was who first noted that *Today* was where people came to 'drop a word in the nation's ear' (*Evening Standard*, 3 July 1978). The archbishop of Canterbury wrote to the programme after his death: 'The loss of such a brilliant and warm personality must leave you all feeling bereft and very sad' (private information). One listener from Stoke-on-Trent spoke for many others when she said that for eighteen years Redhead had for her been 'a friend, brother, and teacher' (Donovan, *All Our Todays*, 111).   PAUL DONOVAN

Sources P. Donovan, *All our todays: forty years of Radio 4's 'Today' programme* (1997) · B. Redhead, *Personal perspectives* (1994) · *The Times* (24 Jan 1994) · *The Guardian* (24 Jan 1994) · *The Independent* (24 Jan 1994) · b. cert. · m. cert. · d. cert. · P. Donovan, *The radio companion* (1991) · *The Times* (24 Jan 1994) · B. Redhead, *Desert island discs*, transcript, 6 July 1986, BBC Radio 4 · B. Redhead, foreword, *The best of 'From our own correspondent'*, ed. G. Spink, 4 (1993), ix · *Cambridge University Calendar* · private information (2004) [Revd Leslie Lewis, Rainow, 5 March 1999] · *Today*, BL NSA, BBC sound archive

Archives FILM BFI NFTVA, *Books by my bedside*, Thames Television, 20 Sept 1990 · BFI NFTVA, current affairs footage | SOUND BBC WAC · BL NSA, documentary recording · BL NSA, performance recording

Likenesses photograph, 1978, Hult. Arch. · group portrait, photograph, 1986, BBC · N. Jorgensen, photograph, 1992, Rex Features Ltd, London [*see illus.*] · photograph, repro. in *The Times* · photograph, repro. in *The Guardian* · photograph, repro. in *The Independent* · photographs, repro. in Donovan, *All our todays* · photographs, repro. in Redhead, *Personal perspectives*

Wealth at death £682,980: probate, 15 June 1994, *CGPLA Eng. & Wales*

Redhouse, Sir James William (1811–1892), lexicographer of Turkish, born, possibly in Surrey, on 30 December 1811, was the eldest son of James Redhouse and his wife, Elizabeth Saunders. Left fatherless at five, he entered Christ's Hospital, London, in 1819 but was expelled in 1826, after a truancy of six days. Within Christ's Hospital, the mathematical school of which Redhouse had been a pupil prepared boys for maritime careers. Redhouse probably studied mathematics through trigonometry, navigation, technical drawing, and some Latin. He had no further formal education. This curriculum helps explain certain stages of his career and the prominence of technical terminology in his dictionaries.

Redhouse later gave out that he had finished the mathematical school, travelled in the Mediterranean, and been offered a post as a draughtsman in Constantinople. By about 1828 he was a teacher at the Ottoman naval academy, having 'run away from a merchantship in the harbour, on board of which he was a cabin-boy, and then apostatized to avoid being retaken' (Slade, new edn, 1854, 56). No other source says that Redhouse ever converted to Islam. Slade must be wrong about that, but his account suggests how Redhouse made his way into Ottoman service, where he remained, on and off, from 1826 until 1853.

When Redhouse reached Constantinople military reform was of desperate urgency. With the Greek revolution ongoing, the Ottomans dependent on their overmighty Egyptian vassal Mehmet Ali to repress it, and the European powers provoked by his victories, the Constantinople government had in June 1826 finally abolished its janizary infantry, which had failed in Greece. Having jumped ship in Constantinople, Redhouse unwittingly landed in a situation where the Ottomans were trying to build a new army from zero with a war going on. Exactly how Redhouse gained the attention of influential Ottomans he later chose not to divulge. His education and experience at sea, both limited, must have helped. However, he could not have been very useful without much language study. He later asserted that he learned Turkish, acquired the knowledge of Persian and Arabic needed for Ottoman Turkish, mastered French and Italian, and started modern Greek and German within a few years of reaching Constantinople. Simultaneously, he served in the military and naval academies, war office, and the translation office of the Sublime Porte (the grand vizier's headquarters, in which the foreign ministry was located).

Redhouse's path is not easily followed during his early years in Ottoman service. In 1830 he travelled to southern Russia for obscure reasons, returning to Constantinople in 1833. By 1834 he was in London, serving the Ottoman ambassadors, partly by supervising Ottoman military students in England. He returned to Constantinople in 1838 on assignment from the ambassador in London. In 1836 he had married Jane Carruthers (d. 1887), daughter of Thomas Slade of Deptford and Liverpool; she left England

with him. In Constantinople, Redhouse returned to the translation office at the Porte. During the Ottoman–Egyptian crisis of 1839–41 he became translator for the navy. From 1839 he was repeatedly mentioned as confidential medium of communication between the Ottomans and the British embassy.

During the Syrian campaign of 1840–41 against Mehmet Ali, Redhouse served as liaison between the Ottoman and European naval forces and the Ottoman authorities on land, receiving the Ottoman decoration Nişan-i Iftihar in brilliants in return. After returning to the translation office of the Porte, Redhouse passed temporarily into British service as secretary-interpreter at the Ottoman–Iranian border negotiations, jointly mediated by Britain and Russia at Erzurum in eastern Anatolia (1843–7). He recorded the negotiations in French and drafted the Turkish, Persian, and French texts of the treaty, receiving the Persian order of the Lion and Sun (Shîr-u-Khurshîd) for his services. Returning to Constantinople and the translation office in 1847, Redhouse became a member of the Imperial Academy of Arts and Sciences (Encümen-i Daniş) in 1850.

By then Redhouse had produced his first linguistic publications. The *Müntahabat-i Lügat-i Osmaniye*, containing Ottoman definitions of widely used Arabic and Persian words, was finished in 1842 and published anonymously in 1852. Long used in Ottoman schools, it was often republished, after 1872 under Redhouse's name. Reflecting Redhouse's non-academic route to mastery of Turkish, his *Grammaire raisonnée de la langue ottomane* (1846) described Turkish vowel harmony at a time when school-trained authors, less adept in the spoken language, often still could not.

On the eve of the Crimean War health problems led Redhouse to return to London, where he took the post of oriental translator to the Foreign Office, worth £400 a year. The secretaryship of the Royal Asiatic Society yielded another £90 a year from 1861 to 1864. Foreign Secretary Lord Clarendon rejected appeals for a pension on the ground that Redhouse had performed most of his service for the Ottomans. Redhouse did receive an Ottoman pension, worth £240 a year in 1860, which was doubled in 1869.

In England, Redhouse found opportunities in publishing. In response to the Crimean War, he brought out a pocket manual of colloquial Ottoman and a small dictionary. The British and Foreign Bible Society commissioned a Bible translation but grew dissatisfied with Redhouse's work, citing his ignorance of Greek and Hebrew. His name became lastingly linked with missionaries, however, thanks to an American-backed effort to spread knowledge of English. His first big contribution to this project was a *Lexicon of English and Turkish* (1861), intended for Turkish-speakers. He received £600 for this work. Its success financed a revised edition (1877) and a commission for Redhouse to prepare a Turkish–English dictionary for £500. The result was the *Turkish and English Lexicon* (1890), often reprinted, and at the close of the twentieth century still considered the most complete Ottoman dictionary ever published. Despite radical change in the language since the fall of the empire, American missionary interests continued to publish, through their Redhouse Press in Constantinople, widely used dictionaries adapted from Redhouse's, whose name they still bear.

In his later years Redhouse produced other miscellaneous publications and attempted dictionaries of grander scope. From 1864 to 1885 he laboured on a dictionary in Turkish, intended to include all Ottoman words, whether of Turkish, Arabic, Persian, or European origin. Simultaneously, he began a comparable Ottoman–English work. He abandoned both in 1885, sending the Ottoman manuscript to Constantinople, where its whereabouts are unknown, and the Ottoman–English manuscript to the British Museum.

Age brought him recognition. Cambridge University awarded Redhouse an honorary LittD (1884). Presumably for services in diplomacy rather than lexicography, Redhouse was made a CMG in 1885 and KCMG in 1888. Widowed in 1887, Redhouse married in 1888 Eliza Colquhoun, daughter of Sir Patrick *Colquhoun (1815–1891), whom Redhouse had met in Constantinople, and who left some £12,000 to Eliza, so freeing Redhouse's last days from financial worry. Redhouse died on 2 January 1892 at his home, 14 Kilburn Priory, London; he was buried in Brookwood cemetery. Lady Redhouse died in 1923, leaving Christ's Hospital £2000 to endow a Colquhoun-Redhouse scholarship for university study.

Redhouse was an orphan who had no children and left little personal correspondence, and his personality is hard to discern. His roles, in both Ottoman–British relations and lexicography, perhaps schooled him in self-effacement. Risen from cabin boy to KCMG, Redhouse guarded his image, as, for example, when he pasted a photograph of himself with his decorations, together with his entry from Debrett's *Peerage*, into the unfinished dictionary that he presented to the British Museum. Not hesitant to express controversial views in letters and occasional publications, Redhouse was a passionate Turkophile at a time when few were so in England. Consciously a pioneer in Turkish lexicography, he was a true mediator between cultures. No one ever did more to enable Turkish-speakers to learn English, or English-speakers to learn Turkish.   CARTER VAUGHN FINDLEY

Sources C. V. Findley, 'Sir James W. Redhouse (1811–1892): the making of a perfect orientalist?', *Journal of the American Oriental Society*, 99 (1979), 573–600 · K. Karpat, 'Letters of I. W. Redhouse to the British foreign ministry', *International Journal of Turkish Studies*, 1 (1979–80), 120–28 · 'James William Redhouse, K.C.L.S.', *New Monthly Magazine*, 4th ser., 2 (1880), 662–9 · A. Slade, *Records of travels in Turkey, Greece, etc.* (1832) · GL, MS 12811/17, fol. 294 · W. F. Williams, 'Memo of the services of Mr. Redhouse in Turkey', *c*.18 March 1857, PRO, FO 78/1325 · H. Bowen, *British contributions to Turkish studies* (1945), 44–7 · *The Times* (4 Jan 1892) · *New Monthly Magazine*, 4th ser., 2 (1880), facing p. 658 · will of Eliza Colquhoun Redhouse, 1923
Archives BM, MSS · LMA, papers, mainly relating to his Turkish lexicon | BL, letters to Sir Austen Henry Layard, Add. MSS 38988–39106 · CUL, corresp. with E. J. W. Gibb and E. B. Cowell · NA Scot., letters to Sir Charles Augustus Murray · PRO, letters to Sir Charles Augustus Murray, FO 78 · U. Durham L., letters to Viscount Ponsonby
Likenesses photograph, BM, Or. MS 2959, vol. 1, facing title page
Wealth at death £3096 7*s*. 1*d*.: probate, 29 Feb 1892, *CGPLA Eng. & Wales*

Redington, Sir Thomas Nicholas (1815–1862), politician, only son of Christopher Redington (1780–1825), a captain in the army, and his wife, Frances, only daughter of Henry Dowell of Cadiz, was born at Kilcornan, Oranmore, co. Galway, on 2 October 1815. He was educated at Oscott College and at Christ's College, Cambridge, where he was in residence for ten terms but did not graduate, since Cambridge degrees were still closed to non-Anglicans. He was MP for Dundalk from 1837 to 1846, standing as a Liberal, though he voted against repeal of the corn laws. He married on 30 August 1842 Anna Eliza Mary, eldest daughter and coheir of John Hyacinth Talbot, MP, of Talbot Hall, co. Wexford.

On 11 July 1846 Redington was appointed undersecretary of state for Ireland, in 1847 a commissioner of national education, and *ex officio* an Irish poor-law commissioner. As a member of Sir John Burgoyne's relief commission in 1847 he rendered much active service during the famine, and in consequence of his services he was on 28 August 1849 nominated a knight commander of the civil division of the Bath, soon after Queen Victoria's first visit to Ireland. He served as secretary to the Board of Control from December 1852 to 1856, when he accepted the post of commissioner of inquiry respecting lunatic asylums in Ireland. He lived at Kilcornan House, but he died in London on 11 October 1862.

Redington's eldest son, Christopher Thomas Talbot Redington (1847–1899), a landowner in Galway and Wexford, was a member of the piers and roads commission (1885), the poor-relief inquiry commission (1886), the mining royalties commission (1889–93), and the evicted tenants commission (1892–3). He was a commissioner of national education (1886) and vice-chancellor of the Royal University of Ireland.   G. C. BOASE, rev. DAVID HUDDLESTON

Sources GM, 3rd ser., 13 (1862), 636 · *Dod's Peerage* (1862), 180 · Burke, *Gen. GB* · *Men of the time* (1862), 648 · WWBMP · C. Kinealy, *This great calamity: the Irish famine, 1845–52* (1994) · D. H. Akenson, *The Irish education experiment: the national system of education in the nineteenth century* (1970)
Archives Bodl. Oxf., letters to Lord Clarendon · Borth. Inst., corresp. with Sir Charles Wood
Wealth at death £10,000: probate, 20 Nov 1862, *CGPLA Ire.*

Redlich, Hans Ferdinand (1903–1968), musicologist, was born on 11 February 1903 in Vienna, the only son of Professor Joseph Redlich and his wife, Alix Leo Simon. He was educated at the Schotten Gymnasium in Vienna, and after studying the piano with Paul Weingarten, theory with Hugo Kauder, and composition with Carl Orff he entered the University of Vienna in 1921. He also studied in Munich. He pursued a career as an opera conductor in the 1920s, as assistant conductor at the Charlottenburg opera house in Berlin from 1924 to 1925 and as conductor at the Stadttheater in Mainz from 1925 to 1929. In 1930 he married Elise Gerlach (*d*. 1959). It may have been the influence of Carl Orff, who was working on Monteverdi in Munich in the 1920s and who produced realizations of several scores, including a new realization of *Orfeo* in 1923, that led Redlich to write a thesis on the madrigals of Monteverdi for his doctorate at the University of Frankfurt am Main, awarded in 1931. This was published in book form in 1932.

Redlich moved to England in 1939 and took British nationality in 1947. He was involved in the Morley College concerts during and after the war, and in 1948 the college choir and orchestra gave the first London performance of Monteverdi's *The Coronation of Poppea*, a concert performance using the score prepared by Redlich, who played the harpsichord accompaniment. From 1942 to 1955 he was a very popular extramural lecturer for the universities of Cambridge and Birmingham, before his appointment in 1955 as lecturer in the history of music at the University of Edinburgh. In 1962 he moved to the chair of music at the University of Manchester.

Redlich wrote in German and in English on Monteverdi, including *Monteverdi: Leben und Werk* (1949), translated into English in 1952, a work that played an important part in the revival of interest in the composer, and he published an edition of the Monteverdi *Vespers* in Vienna in 1949. He also wrote about late nineteenth- and early twentieth-century Austrian music: his books included *Bruckner and Mahler* (1955) and *Alban Berg: the Man and his Music* (1957). He wrote about Wagner's operas, with books on *Tristan and Isolde* (1945), *Lohengrin* (1949), and *Parsifal* (1951). He produced editions of Handel's early works composed in Halle and his twelve concerti grossi, op. 6; his editions of the 'Water Music' and 'Music for the Royal Fireworks', published in 1962, gave English audiences their first opportunity to hear these as originally scored rather than the modern arrangements, as orchestral suites, by Hamilton Harty. He was engaged on a new critical edition of Handel when he died. He was also general editor of the Eulenburg miniature scores, and in 1968 contributed the chapter on early baroque church music to volume 4 of the *New Oxford History of Music*. In his Percival lecture, 'The meaning and the aims of musicology', to the Manchester Literary and Philosophical Society in 1963, he made a plea for greater importance to be attached to the study of the history of music in British universities.

Redlich married again in 1961; his second wife was Erika Burger. In 1967 he was awarded an honorary DMus by the University of Edinburgh. He died on 27 November 1968 at his home, 1 Morville Road, Manchester, and was cremated in Manchester two days later.   ANNE PIMLOTT BAKER

Sources *New Grove*, 2nd edn · *The Times* (28 Nov 1968) · *WW*

Redlich, Josef (1869–1936), scholar and politician, was born on 18 June 1869 at Göding (Hodonin), Moravia, the second of five children and younger son of Adolf Redlich (1839–1896), sugar manufacturer, and his wife, Rosa Fanto (d. 1908). Coming from a German-Jewish family background in a rural Slav area, he was sent to Vienna in 1878 to attend the Akademisches Gymnasium, one of the leading secondary schools, from which he graduated in 1886.

From 1886 to 1891 he studied law, political science, and history at the universities of Vienna, Leipzig, and Tübingen. During this period he visited England for the first time. He was awarded a doctorate in law at the University of Vienna in 1891.

After two years of administrative work at the office of the governor of Moravia, Redlich returned to Vienna to engage in scholarly research. He visited England frequently in the following years, winning the friendship of such men as F. W. Maitland, A. W. Dicey, James Bryce, R. W. Seton-Watson, and F. W. Hirst, and was deeply influenced by the political programme of the Fabian Society. In 1893 he participated in organizing a Fabian Society in Vienna and became co-founder of the weekly *Die Zeit* (later turned into an influential liberal daily), to which he contributed articles dealing with legal, administrative, and political topics. In 1897 he was baptized as a protestant before marrying Alice, daughter of Konsul Gustav Simon from Königsberg, with whom he had a son, Hans Ferdinand *Redlich, who became a renowned musicologist.

Entering a career as a scholar, Redlich was led by the study of Rudolf Gneist's works on English administrative and constitutional history to undertake intensive research in English administrative law. This resulted in a two-volume study, *Local Government in England*, first published in German at Vienna in 1901 and translated and edited by his friend Hirst in 1903. Based on the thesis that the English system of local administration represented the direct influence of the political and social ideas of democracy on the organization and function of government, the book established his reputation as a scholar and led to his being recognized as a leading authority on English political science. It gained him the appointment as *Privatdozent für Staats- und Verwaltungsrecht* at the University of Vienna in 1901.

Redlich's next book, *Recht und Technik des englischen Parlamentarismus* (1905) was translated into English and published in three volumes as *The Procedure of the House of Commons* (1908). It became the standard and authoritative handbook for parliamentary procedure in England. Courtenay Ilbert, clerk of the House of Commons, who wrote an introduction to the translation, described the work as indispensable not only for the scholar but even more for the routine activities of the members of parliament. In 1910 Redlich demonstrated in his third book, *Das Wesen der österreichischen Kommunalverfassung*, his insight into the complicated administrative system of his fatherland.

Redlich's scholarly activities were made possible by the family agreement, which had made his beloved elder brother Fritz the manager of the factory and financial holdings of the family, while Josef was guaranteed a regular income from the family property. By this arrangement he could lead a carefree life which enabled him to buy a spacious Biedermeier-style villa in the fashionable Döbling district in Vienna even during his years as unpaid *Privatdozent*. In 1906 he entered politics, being elected to the Moravian diet as representative of his native town, Göding. He was elected representative to the lower house of parliament in 1907, joining the Deutscher Nationalverband. In 1908 he was appointed professor of constitutional and administrative law at the Technical University of Vienna. While he was successful during these years as a scholar and in politics, his marriage broke down and in 1908 he divorced his unfaithful wife.

The diaries which Redlich kept during the years 1908 to 1919 show how he managed to combine political engagement, scholarly activities, and a busy social life. An ebullient manner combined with his scintillating wit and brilliant conversation made him a well-liked guest in aristocratic circles as well as a close friend of leading artists and writers such as Gustav Mahler, Hermann Bahr, and Hugo von Hofmannsthal. A passionate letter writer, his correspondence with Bahr and von Hofmannsthal, along with Austrian statesmen and diplomatists, as well as with leading scholars in England and the USA is a highly valuable source for the political, social, and cultural history of the first twenty years of the twentieth century. Redlich's position in parliament was that of an outsider who was admired for his eloquent speeches, but viewed with suspicion for his nonconformist tendencies, such as maintaining contact with representatives from other parties and with representatives from non-German nationalities. He had a close relationship to T. G. Masaryk who, born in Göding on the Redlich property, was rumoured to be more than just a friend to the family.

Redlich's scholarly reputation as an expert in Anglo-Saxon law brought him invitations to lecture in the USA. In 1910 he was invited to Harvard University as Godkin lecturer and later travelled to the United States as guest speaker at various universities. During 1913–14 he taught comparative law at the James Schouler Foundation of the Johns Hopkins University. Invited by the Carnegie Foundation for the Advancement of Teaching to study the methods of legal studies in the USA, he published in 1914 *The Common Law and the Case Method in American University Law Schools*, which gained him admiration from the American scholarly establishment.

As an expert on administrative law Redlich was appointed head of a committee to reform and streamline the Austrian bureaucracy. His close contacts with the foreign minister, Aehrenthal, and friendship with several of the younger diplomatists in the Austro-Hungarian foreign service also led to various assignments in Balkan affairs. Redlich supported the position of the Austro-Hungarian and the German governments at the outbreak of the First World War, but he slowly became critical of German imperialism and war policy, breaking with his party of German nationalists in parliament. In July 1917 Emperor Charles briefly considered appointing him prime minister, and he was appointed minister of finance in the last cabinet of the Habsburg monarchy in October–November 1918. In that depressing period Redlich found consolation in private fulfilments. At the home of his brother he met Gertrude Flaschar (1900–1976), daughter of a Styrian lawyer; they married on 10 August 1919 and had two daughters, Lore, born in 1920 and Rosemary, born in 1922.

After the collapse of the Habsburg monarchy Redlich withdrew from politics, though the republican government tried in 1921 to exploit his transatlantic reputation by sending him as an unofficial envoy to the USA in order to raise a loan to avert national bankruptcy. This journey brought no positive results for the Austrian government but led to the re-establishment of Redlich's contact with American universities. Redlich resumed the life of a savant, spreading his interests as well as his activities over two continents: during the war years Redlich had already begun a monumental study, *Das österreichische Staats- und Reichsproblem*, a history of administrative and constitutional changes in Austria from Empress Maria Theresa to Emperor Franz Josef, and it was published in two volumes, in 1920 and 1926. On an assignment for the Carnegie Foundation on War and Peace he prepared a small book, *Austrian War Government* (1929). In 1922 he was invited as Lowell lecturer at Boston to speak on problems of national self-determination at the Institute of Politics in Williamstown, Massachusetts. In 1926 he became professor of comparative public law at Harvard law school, being appointed to the Charles Stebbins Fairchild chair three years later. While living in the USA he wrote a biography of Emperor Franz Josef, published simultaneously in English and German (1929). Having been elected in 1929 deputy judge to the Permanent Court of International Justice at The Hague he returned to Austrian politics in 1931, when Karl Buresch invited him to join his government as minister of finance, hoping that Redlich's international reputation might be of help in solving the financial crisis of the republic. Once again Redlich's government engagement was of short duration for he resigned after four months, returning to his academic position in the USA. In 1934, when his physical health began to fail, he resigned his professorship at Harvard and returned to Vienna, where he died on 11 November 1936. He was buried in the Döblinger cemetery, Vienna.   FRITZ FELLNER

Sources papers of Josef Redlich, priv. coll. · *Schicksaljahre Österreichs, 1908–1919: das politische Tagebuch Josef Redlichs*, ed. F. Fellner, 2 vols. (1953–4) · *Hugo von Hofmannsthal–Josef Redlich: Briefwechsel*, ed. H. Fussgänger (1971) · *Dichter und Gelehrter: Hermann Bahr und Josef Redlich in ihren Briefen, 1896–1934*, ed. F. Fellner (Salzburg, 1980)

Archives priv. coll., private papers including corresp., diaries, manuscripts, fragments of memoirs, personal documents, photographs

Likenesses photographs, priv. coll. · photographs, repro. in *Schicksaljahre Österreichs*, ed. Fellner · photographs, repro. in *Hugo von Hofmannsthal–Josef Redlich: Briefwechsel*, ed. Fussgänger · photographs, repro. in *Dichter und Gelehrter*, ed. Fellner

Redman, Henry (d. **1528**), master mason, was the son of Thomas Redman (d. 1516), a mason, and, presumably, of his wife in 1516, Alice. Henry's will of 1 July 1528 reveals him to be of the family of 'Reedmans' living 'besyde our Lady of Reedbone', a chapel in the parish of Bury near Ramsey in Huntingdonshire. Henry's father was a working mason at Westminster Abbey from 1490 until 1505, when he became the abbey's master mason. He held this post until his death in 1516, when he was succeeded by Henry. In 1495–7 Redman was working on the completion of the nave of Westminster Abbey, at the same rate of pay as his father. He is next documented in 1501–4 carrying out a contract for building the Observant Franciscan friary founded by Henry VII beside his newly reconstructed palace of Richmond. Redman's fellow contractors were Henry Binks, master of the London Carpenters' Company, and Robert Nevill, a brickmaker and bricklayer.

In his capacity as master mason of Westminster Abbey, Henry Redman continued the building of the nave and rebuilt the chancel of St Margaret's Church from 1516 to 1523. It is highly likely that he was also responsible for the sumptuous chantry chapel built by Abbot Islip on the north side of the presbytery during the early 1520s. In 1516, along with the master mason William Vertue and the master carpenter Humphrey Coke, Redman drew up the designs for the west cloister range and gatehouse (Lupton's Tower) at Eton College. In the meantime he had been put in charge of Cardinal Wolsey's two main building projects, York Place (later Whitehall Palace) and Hampton Court, begun in 1514 and 1515 respectively. By 1525 he had become joint master mason with John Lebons for Wolsey's third great project, Cardinal College (now Christ Church), Oxford. The simultaneous employment of two master masons is unusual in the late medieval and early modern periods in England, but it is a feature of many of the largest and most rapidly prosecuted early Tudor royal works. It was probably intended to insure against the disruption which the sudden demise of a master mason would normally cause, and it may well be significant that the plague was especially virulent during these years. Lebons seems to have been the more active of the college's two master masons until the work was halted by Wolsey's fall in 1529.

For Henry VIII, Redman built in 1516–19 two towers for viewing jousts in the tiltyard of Greenwich Palace. On 12 September 1519 he became king's chief mason, jointly with William Vertue, and on 19 July 1520 he was appointed chief mason at Windsor Castle, evidently a sinecure. The fact that when Redman died on 10 July 1528 Henry VIII said that he was 'sorry' indicates that the king had good cause to regret the loss of his master mason, the implication being that Redman was very competent and had done considerably more royal work than is revealed by the extant documentation. Redman typifies the architects employed by Wolsey and by Henry VIII during the earlier part of his reign in that his work was stylistically heavily dependent on the principal buildings erected for Henry VII. His work at York Place and Hampton Court, in brick with stone dressings, has the same informality of composition and simplicity of detailing as the north range of Greenwich Palace by Robert Vertue (begun 1500), and the only technically and aesthetically complex work attributable to Redman, the Islip chantry chapel, reiterates with minimal variation much of the rich and novel ornamental vocabulary of the nearby lady chapel (Henry VII's Chapel), designed by Robert Janyns and begun in 1503.

A damaged and incomplete brass showing two unnamed daughters survives (in the Museum of London) from an otherwise lost monument erected to Redman and his wife, Joan, in the chapel of St Lawrence, Brentford,

Middlesex. The original site of the monument, on the north side of the sanctuary, was the most prestigious available for any tomb, and was no doubt granted because Henry and Joan had given lands which doubled the income of the chapel's priest. That the trustees of this endowment were Master John Spelman, the future king's bench judge, and his wife and son, is valuable evidence of the connections and social standing of a royal master mason early in Henry VIII's reign.

CHRISTOPHER WILSON

Sources J. Harvey and A. Oswald, *English mediaeval architects: a biographical dictionary down to 1550*, 2nd edn (1984) · H. M. Colvin and others, eds., *The history of the king's works*, 6 vols. (1963–82), vol. 3, pp. 26–7, 189, 195, 214, 304, 408, 415; vol. 4, pp.101, 305 · T. Faulkner, *The history and antiquities of Brentford, Ealing and Chiswick* (1845) · H. K. Cameron, 'The brasses of Middlesex, II', *Transactions of the London and Middlesex Archaeological Society*, new ser., 11 (1954), 48–57 · will

Redman, John (1499–1551), theologian and college head, is thought to have been a younger son of William Redman (d. 1536), a landowner of Twisleton, Yorkshire, and Urswick, Lancashire, and Margaret, daughter of Sir Thomas Tunstall and his wife, Alice. Influenced by his mother's half-brother, Bishop Cuthbert *Tunstal, Redman studied initially at Oxford, then at St John's College, Cambridge, where he graduated BA in 1526, and finally at Paris, proceeding MA in 1528. In 1530 his degree was incorporated at Cambridge, and he was made fellow of St John's College on 3 November. He became rector of Redmarshall, Durham, on 17 August 1533, and Tunstall ordained him subdeacon on 20 September following. Although Redman quickly established himself as a leading classicist, he moved on to theology, receiving his BTh in 1534 and DTh in 1537. In 1537 he acted as public orator and was Lady Margaret professor by 1538 (possibly from 1536). Informed by his exacting scholarship, Redman was noted for both his consistent practice of a godly life and his sermons which excelled at helping his hearers do likewise.

This pragmatic, patristic emphasis on Christian living was the hallmark of Redman's theology. In 1540 he was appointed to a commission charged with settling doctrinal disputes. He accepted the royal supremacy, but maintained a spirited defence of traditional Catholic doctrine as expounded by humanist scholarship, culminating in the manuscript on justification and good works that he presented to Henry VIII in 1543. *De justificatione* argued from scripture for an intrinsic change to holiness brought about by personal choice in co-operation with divine grace. With Redman serving on what seems to have been a six-member subcommittee delegated to write a new formulary, these cardinal Catholic principles were incorporated into *A Necessary Doctrine and Erudition for any Christian Man* when published later in 1543.

Theologically compatible with the king, Redman became a royal chaplain and was a member of the convocation that declared Henry's marriage of Anne of Cleves invalid on 9 July 1540. In the same year he was appointed a canon of Westminster, and made archdeacon of Stafford. By 1542 he had vacated his Lady Margaret professorship and was both the archdeacon of Taunton with its annexed prebend of Milverton I and the new warden of the King's Hall, Cambridge. He was also appointed to a committee of convocation responsible for preparing a new translation of the Bible, although the work was to be abandoned. On 20 June 1544 he received the rectory of Sedgefield; he had resigned Redmarshall by 18 August. On 16 January 1546 Redman was appointed, along with Parker and May, as a commissioner to survey the property of Cambridge colleges, reporting back the next month. In the summer he was also part of a delegation that convinced Nicholas Shaxton to subscribe to the six articles, and on 19 December 1546 he was made first master of Trinity College, Cambridge.

Redman served the protestant regime of Edward VI as best he could. On 19 April 1547 he was appointed to help to settle the divorce case of William Parr (renewed on 7 May), and in December he provided convocation with his written opinion that scripture permitted clergy to marry once during their lifetime. On 4 March 1548 he preached before the king a sermon said to affirm Christ's real presence in the sacrament, while in September he was part of the Windsor Commission which helped prepare the new prayer book. From 12 April 1549 he served on the commission charged with suppressing Anabaptists and enforcing conformity to the new liturgy (renewed on 18 January 1551). Redman resigned as archdeacon of Stafford in 1547 but became rector of Calverton, Buckinghamshire, on 8 April 1548. Along with Nicholas Wilford, he acted as patron under a grant from Henry VIII to appoint William Bell as rector of Middleton in Teesdale on 20 July 1549. By the following January Redman had resigned Calverton. On 29 May 1550 he even subscribed to the Book of Homilies, with its clear teaching of justification by faith, when allowed to understand three troublesome sentences according to his own interpretation. Even-handed, Redman gave on 31 January 1551 a supportive deposition in Stephen Gardiner's trial, while on 2 March he preached a complimentary sermon at Bucer's funeral. Near the end of his life, however, Redman expressed his deep disappointment with the Edwardian church in a manuscript entitled 'The complaint of grace'. While acknowledging medieval errors such as the imperial papacy and hypocrisy among the religious orders, he accused his contemporaries of being even worse in their unteachableness, spiritual laziness, and greed.

On 2 November 1551, as Redman grew close to death of consumption, he discussed his views on the contentious religious issues of the day with colleagues from Westminster and Cambridge, an account of which was printed at London on 12 December as *A Reporte of Master Doctor Redmans Answeres*. Redman was said to have died a good protestant on both justification by faith and Christ's presence in the eucharist. The Marian regime countered by publishing Redman's manuscripts, Cuthbert Tunstall preparing *De justificatione opus* (Antwerp, 1555) and Thomas Smyth *A Compendious Treatise called the Complaint of Grace* (London, 1556?)—albeit minus the anti-papal section which William Crashaw later restored (London, 1609). In the light of the fuller texts printed by Foxe, it would seem that Redman died as he had lived, an Erasmian theologian. His long-standing commitment to Christian moralism prevented him from accepting justification by faith alone, while his patristic scholarship led him to reject transubstantiation, leaving him committed to a real, but ambiguously spiritual, presence. He was buried in the north transept of Westminster Abbey. Although his grave is no longer marked, his epitaph is recorded in Camden and dated 4 November 1551. ASHLEY NULL

Sources 'Liber procuratorum nationis Alemanniae, 1521–1552', Bibliothèque de la Sorbonne (Archives de l'ancienne Université de Paris), Register 15, fols. 141r–145v · 'Liber receptorum nationis Alemanniae, 1494–1530', Bibliothèque de la Sorbonne (Archives de l'ancienne Université de Paris), Register 91, fols. 249v–250r · voting record, convocation debate on clerical marriage, 1547, CCC Cam., MS 114A, pp. [398]–[400] · description of Shaxton's subscription to the Six Articles from Bonner's register, GL, MS 9531/12 (pt I), fols. 108–109r · Redman's answers to the 1540 theological questionnaire, LPL, MS 1108, fols. 110–113r · a record of Redman's subscription to the Book of Homilies, PRO, SP 10/7, no. 23 · *The whole works of Roger Ascham*, ed. J. A. Giles (1865), 1.37–46, 293–6; 3.142 · M. Bateson, ed., *Grace book B*, 2 (1905), 131, 155–6, 187, 203 · [W. Camden], *Reges, reginae, nobiles* (1600), sigs. [I4]r–K[1]v · J. Foxe, *Actes and monuments* (1563), 794, 854, 867–74, 1308 · *Literary remains of King Edward the Sixth*, ed. J. G. Nichols, 2 vols., Roxburghe Club, 75 (1857); repr. [1963] · H. Robinson, ed. and trans., *Original letters relative to the English Reformation*, 1, Parker Society, [26] (1846), 150–52 · *Documents relating to the university and colleges of Cambridge*, 1 (1852), 105–294 · *CPR, 1547–8*, 137, 261; *1548–9*, 406; *1549–51*, 347 · *Fasti Angl.* (Hardy), 3.613–15, 653–5 · *Fasti Angl., 1541–1857*, [Bath and Wells], 16 · *Fasti Angl., 1541–1857*, [Ely], 72 · *Fasti Angl., 1300–1541*, [Coventry], 20 · G. Lipscomb, *The history and antiquities of the county of Buckingham*, 4 vols. (1831–47), vol. 4, pp. 84–8 · Venn, *Alum. Cant.* · Cooper, *Ath. Cantab.*, vol. 1 · F. A. Gasquet and E. Bishop, *Edward VI and the Book of Common Prayer* (1928) · W. Greenwood, *The Redmans of Levens and Harewood* (1905) · R. Rex, *Henry VIII and the English Reformation* (1993) · F. Procter and W. H. Frere, *A new history of the Book of Common Prayer* (1949) · C. Sturge, *Cuthbert Tunstal: churchman, scholar, statesman, administrator* (1938) · Emden, *Oxf.*, vol. 4 · will, PRO, PROB 11/40, fol. 21v · C. S. Knighton, ed., *Acts of the dean and chapter of Westminster*, 1 (1997), nos. 11, 26 · *The registers of Cuthbert Tunstall … and James Pilkington*, ed. G. Hinde, SurtS, 161 (1952) · R. Rex, 'Lady Margaret Beaufort and her professorships: 1502–1559', in P. Collinson, R. Rex, and G. Stanton, *Lady Margaret Beaufort and her professors of divinity at Cambridge, 1502–1649* (2003)

Redman [Redmayne], **Sir Richard** (d. 1426), soldier, administrator, and speaker of the House of Commons, was the son of Sir Matthew Redman of Levens, Westmorland, and his first wife, Lucy. The Redman family had been prominent in north-west England since the mid-twelfth century, usually as soldiers, and Sir Matthew fought in both Scotland and France. Richard Redman, who had been knighted by 1376, also began his career as a soldier, in campaigns on the continent *c*.1380. A king's knight by 1388, he survived the purge of that year, to be appointed sheriff of Cumberland in November 1389, and to be retained by the king with an annual fee of 40 marks. Appointed sheriff of Cumberland three more times during the following decade (in 1393, 1396, and 1398), Redman accompanied Richard II to Ireland in 1394, and again in 1399, while in 1397 he became master of the king's horse. But although he lost his shrievalty at the usurpation of Henry IV, he survived that revolution otherwise unscathed. This may have been because he also had Lancastrian connections, having received a yearly fee from John of Gaunt, duke of Lancaster. His second marriage, to Elizabeth (1364–1417), daughter and coheir of William, Lord Aldeburgh, which brought him lands in Yorkshire, enhanced Redman's potential usefulness to the crown in the north. In 1410 he went on two embassies to Scotland, and he was twice more appointed sheriff of Cumberland (1401 and 1411), and also twice sheriff of Yorkshire (1403 and 1415). He continued to be retained by the king, who supported Redman in his efforts to secure the estates of his wife's first husband, Sir Brian Stapleton, to the effective disinheritance of Stapleton's heir. Redman, for his part, was consistently loyal to Henry IV. In 1406 he was elected a member of parliament for Yorkshire, and was returned for that constituency on four more occasions, in 1414, 1415, and 1421. The apogee of his parliamentary career came in November 1415, when he was chosen speaker of the Commons. Held immediately after the battle of Agincourt, the session was an easy one; the necessary supplies were soon granted, and parliament was quickly dissolved. In 1417 Henry V excused Redman from further office holding, though he acted for a while as a councillor to John, duke of Bedford. Predeceased by two of his sons, he made provision for the descent of his estates to his grandson, another Richard. He died on 22 March 1426, and was buried in the church of the Blackfriars, York.   HENRY SUMMERSON

Sources HoP, *Commons* · C. Given-Wilson, *The royal household and the king's affinity: service, politics and finance in England, 1360–1413* (1986)
Likenesses effigy, Harewood parish church, Yorkshire

Redman, Richard (d. 1505), abbot of Shap and bishop of Ely, was probably the son of Richard Redman of Bossall, one of a leading Westmorland family whose most important member, Sir Richard *Redman (d. 1426) of Levens, was speaker of the Commons in 1415. Nothing is known of the youngest Richard Redman's upbringing or education, and there is no evidence that he attended university. It was probably due to family influence that he became abbot of the Premonstratensian house of Shap, Westmorland, in 1458. In the following year, with the support of the abbey's patron, John, Lord Clifford, he became the abbot of Prémontré's visitor-general in the British Isles, though only after a lengthy contest, lasting until 1466, with the previous visitor. Confirmed in office by the pope on 2 January 1468, Redman held until death a position that made him the effective head of his order in England and Wales. The Redman family had links with the Nevilles of Middleham, and after 1471 moved into the affinity of Richard of Gloucester. This connection may account for Richard Redman's being appointed bishop of St Asaph on 13 October 1471. Papal provision followed on 17 August 1472, together with licence to retain the abbacy of Shap *in commendam*, such was the poverty of the see.

In 1473 and 1474 Redman was appointed to commissions to negotiate with the Scots, but his role in government in these years was limited. He spent some time in his diocese, where he carried out substantial repairs to his cathedral—as late as 1720 his arms could still be seen, 'fixed in divers parts of the Church' (*Willis' Survey*, 1.87). But he was principally active as the visitor of his order, conducting six nationwide visitations between 1478 and 1500. Methodical inspections of up to thirty-two houses, they were carefully planned in advance to last for several months, taking Redman from one end of the country to the other. His register (Bodl. Oxf., MS Ashmole 1519) shows him to have been a most conscientious visitor, and a martinet towards monks convicted of apostasy, narrowly construed as leaving the monastery without permission. It also records that he started his visitations of 1478 and 1488 in his diocese, but intended to end them in the north. It is likely that he spent more time at Shap than at St Asaph. In 1473 he acted as arbiter at Penrith in a dispute between two Westmorland landowners, and in 1481 witnessed a grant of land in Bampton, also in Westmorland.

After Richard of Gloucester's usurpation in 1483, Redman became more prominent in public affairs. He bore the patten at Richard III's coronation, and may have acted for the aged Archbishop Bourchier in presenting the new king to his people. His kinsman Edward Redman became sheriff of Somerset and Dorset, and an important representative of the government in the south-west, and Redman was probably active with him—on 24 February 1484 the receiver in the west was ordered to pay him 500 marks per annum during pleasure. In September 1484 he attended the important negotiations with the Scots conducted at Nottingham, and he accompanied the king back to Westminster afterwards. When Richard III was overthrown, Redman retired to Shap, being recorded there on 6 December 1485. He was not summoned to the first parliament of Henry VII's reign, and only received a pardon on 22 February 1486. The new regime may have held him in some suspicion, for on 9 January 1488 the pope ordered Archbishop Morton and three other bishops to act against Redman for conduct contrary to the peace and tranquillity of the realm. This may have been a case of guilt by association, for Redman had been at Shap in March 1487, at a time when there were stirrings of discontent against Henry VII's government in the north-west, subsequently given focus by the earl of Lincoln's landing in Furness in early June. As it was, Redman was soon cleared, on 24 April 1488 being himself licensed by Morton to absolve Premonstratensians and others involved in disorders. In the summer of that year he held his first nationwide monastic visitation since 1482.

Now no longer under suspicion, Redman was appointed several times between 1488 and 1494 to treat with the Scots for extensions of truces or settlements of border disputes. In 1489 he was a trier of petitions in parliament, and served at least intermittently as a royal councillor from that year onwards. In November 1494 he was present when Prince Henry was made duke of York. It was presumably for such services as these that, perhaps rather surprisingly, Redman was translated to the see of Exeter by papal provision on 6 November 1495, the temporalities being restored on 7 January following. Although he occasionally resided, he usually seems to have administered his diocese through vicars-general. He remained abbot of Shap and Premonstratensian visitor, and was probably most often in his monastery when he was not on the road. His visitation of 1500 began and ended at Shap, though he expected to spend the months between late May and early September in his diocese of Exeter. His planning to spend three days with the king at Basingstoke during his return journey shows that Redman had retained contacts with the court. In 1501 he was present at the reception of Katherine of Aragon on her arrival in England.

On 27 March 1501 Redman celebrated orders at Barnard Castle on behalf of the powerful Richard Fox, bishop of Durham. It may have been through the latter's favour that on 26 May the pope translated Redman to the wealthy see of Ely. The temporalities were restored on 26 September. In September and October 1503 he planned a visitation of Premonstratensian houses in the diocese of Lincoln alone, and in May 1504 was in the bishop's palace at Ely, suggesting that restricted mobility was confining him to central and southern England. He died at Ely House, Holborn, Middlesex, on 24 or 25 August 1505. In his will, dated 18 August, Redman bequeathed his body for burial in his cathedral, in a sumptuous tomb surmounted by his effigy on the north side of the choir. But his heart clearly remained in the north. He left 100 marks to the fabric of Ely Cathedral, and made bequests to its monks and to several other religious houses in his small diocese. But the residue of all his goods, whether livestock, household stuff, plate, or money, he left to his monastery of Shap, 'which now I rule' (PRO, PROB 11/14, fol. 301).

RICHARD K. ROSE

Sources *Chancery records* · F. A. Gasquet, ed., *Collectanea Anglo-Premonstratensia*, 3 vols., CS, 3rd ser., 6, 10, 12 (1904–6) · Bodl. Oxf., MS Ashmole 1519 · R. Horrox and P. W. Hammond, eds., *British Library Harleian manuscript 433*, 4 vols. (1979–83) · A. F. Sutton and P. W. Hammond, eds., *The coronation of Richard III: the extant documents* (1983) · J. Gairdner, ed., *Letters and papers illustrative of the reigns of Richard III and Henry VII*, 2 vols., Rolls Series, 24 (1861–3) · Rymer, *Foedera*, vols. 11–13 · *RotP*, vol. 6 · *RotS*, vol. 2 · *CEPR letters*, 12.329; 13.316 · C. G. Bayne and W. H. Dunham, eds., *Select cases in the council of Henry VII*, SeldS, 75 (1958) · Prerogative court of Canterbury, wills, PRO, PROB 11/14, fol. 301 · F. W. Ragg, 'Two documents relating to Shap Abbey', *Transactions of the Cumberland and Westmorland Antiquarian and Archaeological Society*, new ser., 9 (1908–9), 271–81 · F. W. Ragg, 'Cliburn Hervy and Cliburn Tailbois, pt 2', *Transactions of the Cumberland and Westmorland Antiquarian and Archaeological Society*, new ser., 28 (1927–8), 179–272 · *Willis' survey of St Asaph, considerably enlarged and brought down to the present time*, ed. E. Edwards, 2 vols. (1801) · J. S. Roskell, 'Sir Richard Redmayne of Levens', *Parliaments and politics in late medieval England*, 3 (1983), 205–36 · *VCH Cambridgeshire and the Isle of Ely*, vol. 4 · J. A. F. Thomson, *The early Tudor church and society, 1485–1529* (1993) · H. M. Colvin, *The white canons in England* (1951) · D. Knowles [M. C. Knowles], *The religious orders in England*, 3 (1959) · F. D. Logan, *Runaway religious in medieval England, c.1240–1540*, Cambridge Studies in Medieval Life and Thought, 4th ser., 32 (1996) · *Fasti Angl., 1300–1541*, [Welsh dioceses], 39 · *Fasti Angl., 1300–1541*, [Exeter], 3 · *Fasti Angl., 1300–1541*, [Monastic cathedrals], 15 · J. A. Gribbin, *The Premonstratensian order in late medieval England* (2001)
Archives Bodl. Oxf., register, Ashmole MS 1519
Likenesses tomb effigy, Ely Cathedral

Redman, Robert (*d.* 1540), printer, first comes to notice in a record of a fine paid for selling foreign books in 1521 when his freedom is described, as in his will: 'Stacioner and Freman of London' (PRO, PROB 11/28, fol. 117*r*). He was assessed in the Middlesex lay subsidy of 1523/4 for £10 in the parish of St Clement Danes. The London stationer John Redman, who printed editions for him in 1534 and 1539, may have been a relation. Robert Redman operated his business from a number of carefully chosen premises. He began printing as well as selling books in 1525 at the sign of the George in St Clement's, outside Temple Bar. He was in the main a printer of law books, and adopted the same sign as his main competitor in this trade, Richard Pynson, the king's printer at the sign of the George in nearby Fleet Street. In 1527 Redman moved his own shop to Fleet Street, under the same sign, only 100 yards from Pynson. When Pynson died in 1530, Redman moved his business to Pynson's old shop.

Redman was a prolific printer: 203 editions were printed for or by him between 1523 and 1540. He printed vernacular devotional manuals and other popular texts, such as herbals and saints' lives. Legal texts, however, comprised more than 60 per cent of his output. His use of Pynson's signs, and later devices, and printing material, were one way that he secured access to the legal book market, which was monopolized by the king's printers. In the 1520s Redman had issued editions of the Magna Carta, Thomas Littleton's *Tenures*, and yearbooks in direct competition with Pynson. This, and his encroachment upon his competitor's sign and shop, led Pynson to call him 'Rob. Redman, sed verius Rudeman' in his own 1520s editions of the *Tenures*. In the 1530s Redman continued to compete with Pynson's successor as king's printer, Thomas Berthelet, by issuing further editions of the *Tenures*, as well as Christopher St German's *Division betwene the Spirytualtie and Temporaltie*, the *Natura brevium*, and law books by Anthony Fitzherbert, for which Berthelet apparently held privileges. It was perhaps at Berthelet's instigation that Redman was brought before the privy council on 15 May 1533 and bound over for 500 marks not to sell St German's work, or any other books privileged by the king.

Redman was perhaps sympathetic to religious reform. He may have used a Wycliffite translation for parts of his *Prayers of the Byble* (1535, STC 20200.3), one of the earliest books of English scripture. He certainly printed William Hardy's Lollard *Lanterne of Lyght* in 1535, and reformist material by John Frith in 1534. Redman's name appears in relation to an English primer in correspondence between Thomas Cromwell and Thomas Cranmer in 1537; a year earlier he printed a translation of a text by Erasmus that the reformist author Richard Taverner dedicated to Cromwell. In the latter year he was also commissioned to print a translation by another reformer, Tristram Revel, for presentation to Anne Boleyn, but the author was brought before the council and the edition cancelled. In 1541 the printer Robert Bankes was brought before the council accused of producing ballads by Thomas Smyth attacking Cromwell, and responses by William Gray accusing Smyth of popery. Bankes claimed that the broadsides had false imprints and had in fact been printed by Richard Grafton and Redman, who was by then dead; Grafton admitted the charge and was imprisoned.

Redman died at some point between 21 October 1540, when he drew up his will, and 4 November 1540, when it was proved. Among his beneficiaries was Henry Smith, his son-in-law and a fellow printer of law books. He left the main part of his business to his widow. His first wife, whose name is unknown, died in 1537. His second became the first English woman to print books under her maiden name, **Elisabeth Pickering** (c.1510–1562), although by the time of her marriage to Redman she had already been married to a man named Jackson, with whom she had two daughters, Lucy and Elizabeth. In the nine months or so after Redman's death, Elisabeth printed at least thirteen editions that survive, eleven bearing her name. All her editions were from earlier Redman prints, mostly medical tracts and law books. She married again in 1541, about which time she sold her business to William Middleton. Elisabeth's new husband was William Cholmeley (d. in or before 1546), a gentleman of Lincoln's Inn. Like Redman, Cholmeley mentions Henry Smith in his will, which was proved in April 1546. Alice Redman, later Alice Hilton, a daughter of Elisabeth and Redman, as well as Lucy and Elizabeth Jackson, are mentioned. Another daughter of Elisabeth and Redman, Mildred Hanbury, in disgrace after marrying under age, is not mentioned. William Cholmeley was freed as a member of the Stationers shortly before he and Elisabeth married. He may, at her instigation, have assisted with the unsuccessful 1542 charter of incorporation of that company. Following Cholmeley's death, Elisabeth married William's relative, Ranulph Cholmeley (d. 1563), who, from 1554, was the recorder of London, and sometime counsel to the Stationers'. Ranulph was probably the author of the Stationers' successful charter of incorporation of 1556. It is likely that Elisabeth's own interest in the book trade is linked to the important role her last two husbands played in the Stationers' incorporation. Elisabeth died in October 1562, when the administration of her previous husbands' goods was granted to Ranulph Cholmeley. She was buried in St Dunstan-in-the-West Church; Ranulph was buried next to her when he died in late April 1563. His will, proved in May, gives some indication of Elisabeth's circle about the time of her death: among those named are William Roper, the printer Richard Tottell, and no fewer than three former lord mayors of London: Thomas Leigh, Thomas Offley, and William Chester. Her funeral service was held at St Margaret Lothbury and her body then carried for burial in St Dunstan-in-the-West, where her last husband was buried six months later. ALEXANDRA GILLESPIE

Sources STC, 1475–1640 · LP Henry VIII, 6.480; 10.371; 13/2.986; 16.422–4 · E. G. Duff, A century of the English book trade (1905) · J. C. Warner, Henry VIII's divorce: literature and politics of the printing press (1998), 83–4 · H. S. Bennett, English books and readers, 1475–1557 (1969), 63, 77–82, 85, 196, 210, 223, 237 · The diary of Henry Machyn, citizen and merchant-taylor of London, from AD 1550 to AD 1563, ed. J. G. Nichols, CS, 42 (1848) · private information (2004) [B. Kreps] · will, PRO, PROB 11/28, sig. 15 · P. Blayney, The Stationers' Company before the charter, 1403–1557 (2003) · will, PRO, PROB 11/31, sig. 7 [W. Cholmeley] · fine book, CLRO, Ex-GL MS 87, fol. 27r · Middlesex lay subsidy 1523/4, PRO, E 179/238/98 · will, PRO, PROB 11/46, sig. 23 [R. Cholmeley] · administration, PRO, PROB 6/1, fol. 52v [R. Cholmeley] · administration, PRO, PROB 6/3, fol. 171v [A. Hilton] · R. Lemon, Catalogue of a collection of printed broadsides … of the Society of Antiquaries in London (1866) · C. Butterworth, 'Robert Redman's Prayers of the Byble', The Library, 5th ser., 3 (1948–9), 279–86 · State papers published under … Henry VIII, 11 vols. (1830–52), 1.559 · A. Hudson, '"No newe thyng": the printing of medieval texts in the early Reformation period', Lollards and their books (1985), 227–48 · J. H. Baker, 'The books of the common law', The Cambridge history of the book in Britain, ed. L. Hellinga and J. B. Trapp, 3: 1400–1557 (1999), 411–32 · St Dunstan-in-the-West, churchwardens' accounts, GL, MS 2968/1 · M. W. Driver, 'Women printers and the page, 1477–1541', Gutenberg Jahrbuch (1998), 139–53 · DNB

Redman, Roderick Oliver (1905–1975), astronomer, was born on 17 July 1905 at Rodborough, near Stroud, Gloucestershire, the eldest child and only son of Roderick George Redman, an outfitter, and his wife, Elizabeth Miriam Stone. He attended Marling School in Stroud, where the headmaster recognized the boy's outstanding aptitude for mathematics and advised his parents to enter him for Cambridge. At the age of seventeen he gained an open scholarship in physics and mathematics at St John's College.

Redman went up to Cambridge in 1923 and graduated with distinction in the mathematical tripos three years later. As a research student he started work under Arthur Eddington on a study of the parallaxes and motions of stars. Having published a theoretical paper in 1927, Redman decided to acquire observational data on radial velocities using the 72 inch reflector of the Dominion Observatory at Victoria, British Columbia. He worked there for three years with a travelling fellowship, gaining his PhD from Cambridge in 1930, and remained there as assistant astronomer. He returned to Cambridge in 1931 on being appointed assistant director of the solar physics observatory under F. J. M. Stratton. He was elected a fellow of St John's College a year later.

The first problem tackled by Redman at Cambridge was the photographic photometry of the solar spectrum. Using the observatory's large Littrow spectrograph, he found that the observed line profiles were strongly affected by scattered light. To remedy this he replaced the usual colour filters in the solar beam by a low-dispersion monochromator of his own design. The result was a reduction of the central intensities of strong lines from 10 to 2 per cent of the intensity of the continuous spectrum. Still in the field of photographic photometry, Redman also achieved remarkably good results on elliptical galaxies observed with an old 36 inch reflector.

He married a Canadian, Annie Kathleen Bancroft, in Victoria on 15 June 1935. They had four children, three sons and a daughter, all of whom became Cambridge graduates.

In 1938 Redman resigned his post to become chief assistant to H. Knox-Shaw at the Radcliffe Observatory in Pretoria, South Africa. A 74 inch telescope which would be the largest telescope in the southern hemisphere was being constructed by the firm of Grubb Parsons of Newcastle upon Tyne for this observatory. Having supervised the construction of the telescope and of its Cassegrain spectrograph, Redman moved to South Africa in February 1939. The mirror of the telescope, in need of refiguring, was yet to be delivered. When the Second World War broke out in September 1939 the Radcliffe Observatory was still without the mirror. Redman, disappointed but not despairing, started work on stellar photographic photometry with the finder telescope and a 12 inch mirror bolted onto the 74 inch tube. Using the Fabry method of measuring extra-focal images he was able to achieve standard errors in stellar photometry of as low as .01 magnitude. He also completed a substantial photometric programme in co-operation with the Cape observatory.

In 1946 Redman was elected a fellow of the Royal Society, and in the following year he was called back to Cambridge as professor of astrophysics and director of the combined university and solar physics observatories. His immediate task was one of modernization. He started by creating a well-equipped and well-staffed workshop, which began its operations in 1951. Old instruments were discarded. The solar installation, formerly the McClean instrument, was re-equipped in 1953 with quartz mirrors, a 12 inch object glass, and a new Littrow spectrograph with a fine diffraction grating ruled by Babcock. The early 1950s saw also the provision of two new stellar instruments, both constructed by Grubb Parsons, a Schmidt camera of 17 inches aperture and a 36 inch reflector used for some pioneering narrow-band multichannel photometry. Redman observed both the 1952 and 1954 eclipses, the first from Khartoum in the Sudan, the second from an island off the coast of Sweden, and obtained spectra of the chromosphere of outstanding quality.

Redman's later years, including those after his formal retirement in 1970, were taken up largely with the reorganization on a national basis of British astronomy. Following the creation of the Science Research Council in 1965 he became an important member of many of its advisory bodies. He gave particularly strong support to the 150 inch Anglo-Australian telescope project, which involved him in several visits to Australia. He also took part in the planning of the northern hemisphere observatory and was chairman of the committee of the Royal Observatory, Edinburgh. He served the Royal Astronomical Society for many years, on its council and as its president between 1959 and 1961. He was also on the council of the Royal Society from 1953 to 1954. He was president of the commission on solar eclipses of the International Astronomical Union between 1955 and 1961.

Redman was greatly valued on committees for his ability to give disinterested advice based on his vast practical experience. He had the reputation in scientific circles of being a pessimist, but this was simply a manifestation of his perfectionism. Among his colleagues, as in private life, he was averse to all publicity or ostentation, unassuming, charming, and with an infectious laugh. He was sustained in his busy existence by a happy family life. He died in Addenbrooke's Hospital, Cambridge, on 6 March 1975.

HERMANN A. BRÜCK

Sources R. F. Griffin and R. Woolley, *Memoirs FRS*, 22 (1976), 335–57 · D. E. Blackwell and D. W. Dewhirst, *Quarterly Journal of the Royal Astronomical Society*, 17 (1976), 80–86 · personal knowledge (2004) · d. cert.

Archives CUL, papers · CUL, research notebooks, corresp., reports

Likenesses photograph, 1946, RS; repro. in *Memoirs FRS* · photograph, 1959, RAS; repro. in *Quarterly Journal of the Royal Astronomical Society*, 2 (1961)

Wealth at death £46,296: probate, 25 April 1975, *CGPLA Eng. & Wales*

Redman, William (*c*.1541–1602), bishop of Norwich, was the only son of John Redman, gentleman, of Great Shelford, Cambridgeshire (*d*. 1558), and Margaret (*née* Maye) who died as the wife of Christopher Torrell, also of Great Shelford, in 1570. He entered Trinity College, Cambridge, in 1558, where he was soon elected a scholar and, in due course, fellow. He graduated BA in 1563, proceeded MA in 1566, and BTh as a senior fellow in 1573; he remembered his college with a bequest of 100 marks towards wainscote for the library. He must temporarily have given up his fellowship during a first marriage to Elizabeth Hanchett, whom he married at Great Shelford on 16 June 1566. In July 1571 he was presented to the rectory of Ovington, Essex, by Anne, dowager Lady Maltravers. This he resigned on taking Toppesfield the following March. In 1576 he was appointed archdeacon of Canterbury by Archbishop Edmund Grindal. Two years later, by then DTh, he was presented to the rectory of Upper Hardres, Kent, and resigned Toppesfield. He also held the living of Bishopsbourne, in which he was succeeded by Richard Hooker in 1594.

About 1578 Redman married Isabel (*d*. 1613), daughter of Nicholas Calverley of Christchurch, Newgate Street, in London. Two infants of the marriage were buried at Christ Church, Canterbury. However, three sons and three daughters survived their father, all unmarried at his death. From 1576 Redman's preferments came from the queen on the recommendation of Archbishop Grindal, whose chaplain and eventual executor he was; Grindal left him a riding horse. When John Whitgift became archbishop in 1583 Redman was appointed one of his chaplains. In 1584 and in 1586 he was prolocutor of the lower house of convocation, and late in 1589 a canon of Canterbury. He was elected bishop of Norwich on 17 December 1594 and consecrated on 10 January following, the first of Whitgift's chaplains to become a bishop.

At the 1597 visitation of the diocese, Redman's principal official seems to have been properly searching and impartial in his inquiries, carrying them out in the efficient tradition of Elizabethan administration. Redman evidently followed Whitgift's policy of encouraging the rite of confirmation. He also insisted on the full observance of Lent throughout his diocese, and in 1596 expressed approval when the magistrates of Bury St Edmunds called for an extraordinary public fast. After fewer than eight years as bishop he died at his palace in Norwich on 25 September 1602, and was buried under a plain slab opposite the pulpit in his cathedral choir, but not until 2 December. This delay allowed William Camden, Clarenceux king of arms, to devise a grand ceremonial, in which the coffin was dwarfed by a standing hearse decked with heraldic banners, shields, and mitres. Redman's far from ascetic choice of arms in 1595 was a cross between four ermine cushions with gold tassels. He may not have been a particularly skilful manager of his finances. Allowed three years to pay his first fruits, he complained when he arrived in his diocese that his demesnes had been run down by his predecessor, Edmund Scambler. In the late 1590s he took action to prevent the loss of episcopal estates claimed for the crown as 'concealments' on a legal technicality, and obtained the protection of an act of parliament for them. But he maintained a large and costly household—in one year he spent nearly £300 out of an income of nearly £1000 on maintaining it—and subsequently died in debt. His successor, John Jegon, claimed £194 from Redman's estate for repairs needed to the palace, and found the deeds relating to the diocesan temporalities in such disarray that he brought in Anthony Harison to sort them, and the finances, out.

A loyal and moderate churchman, Redman seems to have avoided conflict during his smooth climb almost to the top of the church hierarchy. Writing to Sir Dudley Carleton, John Chamberlain, a contemporary of Redman's at Trinity, implied as much by describing him as 'one of the wisest of his coat' (CSP dom., 1601–3, 249). Isabel Redman died on 7 December 1613 and was buried six days later at Great Shelford with her husband's parents, making it possible for her son, another William Redman, to erect a mural monument there to three generations of his family, including his father the bishop.

J. M. BLATCHLY

Sources F. Blomefield and C. Parkin, *An essay towards a topographical history of the county of Norfolk*, [2nd edn], 11 vols. (1805–10), 561 · T. Browne, *Repertorium* (1712), 16 and pl. facing · *Miscellanea genealogica et heraldica*, new ser., 4, 156 [Pedigree of Redman of Great Shelford] · J. F. Williams, ed., *Diocese of Norwich, Bishop Redman's visitation, 1597*, Norfolk RS, 18 (1946) · memorial, Great Shelford church, Cambridgeshire · F. Heal, *Of prelates and princes: a study of the economic and social position of the Tudor episcopate* (1980) · J. Berlatsky, 'The Elizabethan episcopate: patterns of life and expenditure', *Princes and paupers in the English church, 1500–1800*, ed. R. O'Day and F. Heal (1981), 111–27 · D. MacCulloch, *Suffolk and the Tudors: politics and religion in an English county, 1500–1600* (1986) · Venn, *Alum. Cant.*, 1/3.436 · PRO, PROB 6/6, fol. 133v

Wealth at death see administration, PRO, PROB, 6/6, fol. 133v

Redmayne, Martin, first baronet and Baron Redmayne (1910–1983), politician, was born in Nottingham on 16 November 1910, the second son and third child in the family of three sons and three daughters of Leonard Redmayne (1877–1952), civil engineer and farmer, and his wife, Mildred (d. 1955), daughter of Edward Jackson. He was educated at Radley College and worked in the family sports business in Nottingham both before and after the Second World War when he was managing director. He married on 6 May 1932 Anne (d. 1982), daughter of John Griffiths, coal miner. They had one son. During the war he served with the Sherwood Foresters, commanding the 14th battalion in the Italian campaign and later forming and commanding the 66th infantry brigade. He was appointed to the DSO in 1944. He was Conservative MP for the Rushcliffe division of Nottinghamshire from 1950 until the general election of 1966. He was also a JP for Nottingham (1946–66).

Redmayne's unusual political career was spent almost entirely in the Conservative whips' office in a period when the party formed the government from October 1951 to October 1964. With his distinguished war record, it was no surprise to find him in the whips' office by 1951 nor, when he became chief whip in 1959, that he should run it like a military headquarters and, off duty, like an officers' mess. He was sworn of the privy council in 1959.

Redmayne was a shy and reserved man, appearing aloof and even severe to some who served under him. However, he was generally regarded as courteous, loyal, fair, and immensely conscientious in his attention to detail. It came quite naturally to him both to obey commands without question and to expect his orders to be similarly obeyed. He therefore ran an efficient whips' office, though not a particularly imaginative one. He might have flourished as chief whip at a relatively uneventful time but 1959 to 1964 was not such a period. Redmayne had courage, stoicism, and durability but he lacked the intuitive 'feel' for a crisis and the vision to handle it successfully.

Redmayne has been criticized for not being sufficiently quick to perceive the various serious problems which arose within the Conservative Party during the period 1959–64 and which adversely affected both the prime minister personally and the government. Nor was he sufficiently influential with Harold Macmillan to be able to alert him in time or to exercise what might be called the 'higher loyalty': putting at his leader's disposal not only his best efforts in carrying out the leader's instructions, but also any intuitive doubts as to the wisdom of what the leader was doing.

Thus Redmayne has been criticized for allowing 'the night of the long knives' in summer 1962 to happen, for failing to alert Macmillan much earlier to the dangers of the Profumo affair, and, more important politically, for his part in handling the succession to Macmillan. It is generally agreed that the open leadership battle at the Conservative Party conference at Blackpool in October 1963 was an avoidable blunder and that, if the succession had been decided calmly in London in the normal manner after the conference was over, the Conservatives might well have won the general election of October 1964.

However, Redmayne would have been a most remarkable person to influence all those situations successfully. Indeed he would have deserved—like Edward Heath, his predecessor as chief whip, and William Whitelaw, his successor—to have gone much further in politics.

After the Conservative defeat in the general election of 1964, Redmayne was made a baronet and was successively shadow postmaster-general and Conservative spokesman on agriculture and transport. After losing his seat in 1966 he was created a life peer and served in his later years as deputy chairman of the House of Fraser, a director of Boots, and chairman of the Retail Consortium.

In his limited leisure, in addition to some golfing and

fishing, Redmayne was an enthusiastic watercolour painter. He died at King Edward VII Hospital, London, on 28 April 1983. His son, Nicholas John Redmayne (*b.* 1938) succeeded to the baronetcy. MICHAEL FRASER, *rev.*

Sources private information (1990) · personal knowledge (1990) · *The Times* (30 April 1963) · J. Ramsden, *The winds of change: Macmillan to Heath, 1957–1975* (1996) · Burke, *Peerage* (2000) · *CGPLA Eng. & Wales* (1983)

Archives Bodl. Oxf., papers |SOUND BL NSA, documentary recordings

Wealth at death £129,913: probate, 28 June 1983, *CGPLA Eng. & Wales*

Redmayne, Sir Richard Augustine Studdert (1865–1955), mining engineer, was born at South Dene, Low Fell, co. Durham, on 22 July 1865, the fourth son of John Marriner Redmayne, alkali manufacturer, and his wife, Jane Anna Fitzgerald Studdert. Educated privately and at the Durham College of Science, Newcastle upon Tyne, he became an articled apprentice of William Armstrong, a prominent north-country mining engineer, and was trained at Hetton Collieries, co. Durham. There he rose to be an under-manager, before leaving for South Africa in 1891, where he spent two years managing collieries and making reports and surveys on mining properties in Natal. He returned to England in 1894, and became the resident manager at Seaton Delaval Collieries, Northumberland. In 1898 he married Edith Rose (*d.* 1942), daughter of Thomas Picton Richards, shipowner, of Swansea; they had one son, John, and two daughters.

In 1902 Redmayne was appointed professor of mining at the newly created University of Birmingham. The mining industry at that time laid less stress on university education than on apprenticeship or practical experience, supplemented by education at local technical colleges. Redmayne studied the methods followed by advanced mining schools in North America, where in laboratory, classroom, and field, the conditions were simulated in which the student would later work professionally. With these in mind, Redmayne organized a mining department which, for the first time in Britain, included an ore-dressing laboratory and a model underground coalmine, where practical problems could be studied. His pioneer work greatly encouraged higher education and training for mining engineers.

Redmayne served as a mining expert on a number of official inquiries into the organization and safety procedures of the coal industry. In 1906 he was a member of the committee which inquired into the economic effect of an eight-hour working day for coalminers. Following the committee's recommendation, the government introduced the Eight Hour Act. In 1908 Redmayne became chairman of the royal commission appointed to study the causes and prevention of accidents in mines arising from falls of ground, underground transport, and in shafts: its main recommendations were subsequently incorporated in legislation. In the same year Redmayne was appointed a commissioner to inquire into a disaster at Hamstead colliery and between 1908 and 1913 he conducted similar

Sir Richard Augustine Studdert Redmayne (1865–1955), by Dorothy Vicaji

inquiries at Maypole, West Stanley, Wellington, Hulton, Cadeby, and Senghenydd collieries into disasters which caused a loss of 1250 lives. He was knighted in 1914.

Redmayne resigned his professorship in 1908 to join the Home Office as the first chief inspector of mines in Britain. His primary responsibility was for safety in the mining industry, and involved supervising the work of district inspectors of mines, advising the secretary of state on mining matters, conducting inquiries into accidents in mines, and editing the annual report on mines and quarries. One of his most notable contributions as chief inspector was his work with Sir Malcolm Delevingne on the framing of the comprehensive Coal Mines Act of 1911 which enforced higher standards of safety in mines. From 1917 to 1919 he was chief technical adviser to the controller of coalmines, and in 1919 he acted as assessor to Sir John Sankey, chairman of the royal commission on coalmines.

In 1919 Redmayne resigned from his post as chief inspector in order to devote himself to the work of the Imperial Mineral Resources Bureau (amalgamated in 1925 with the Imperial Institute), of which he was chairman from 1918 until 1935, and to practise as a consulting engineer. Chairman of the board for mining examinations from its inception in 1912 until 1950, he also became, in 1922, the first president of the Institution of Professional Civil Servants, an office to which he was re-elected annually until his death. He played an active part in the work of professional engineering institutions, and was elected honorary member of the Institution of Mining Engineers in 1909, president of the Institution of Mining and Metallurgy in 1916, and president of the Institution of Civil Engineers in 1934–5. During the 1930s Redmayne held a number of senior non-executive appointments. He was the independent chairman of the national conciliation board on road motor haulage (1934–8), and also acted as chairman of the road haulage wages board from 1938 until 1941.

An able administrator and speaker, a man of fine presence, tact, and charm, Redmayne also enjoyed the confidence of the miners with whom his work brought him into contact. Possessing a keen sense of humour, he was a superb teller of stories in the Tyneside dialect. He also made numerous contributions to professional and technical journals and was the author of several authoritative books on mining. He was the co-author of *Colliery Working and Management*, first published in 1896, which became a standard work; and also of *Modern Practice in Mining* (5 vols., 1908–32). His autobiography, *Men, Mines and Memories* (1942), throws interesting light on little-known aspects of British industrial life. He died, aged ninety, at his home, Lodge Farm, Little Hadham, Hertfordshire, on 27 December 1955.   ANDREW BRYAN, *rev.* ROBERT BROWN

Sources R. A. S. Redmayne, *Men, mines and memories* (1942) · R. Church, A. Hall, and J. Kanefsky, *Victorian pre-eminence: 1830–1913* (1986), vol. 3 of *The history of the British coal industry* (1984–93) · B. Supple, *The political economy of decline: 1913–1946* (1987), vol. 4 of *The history of the British coal industry* (1984–93) · *The Times* (29 Dec 1955) · personal knowledge (1971) · 'Royal commission on mines', *Parl. papers* (1909), 34.1111, Cd 4821 · d. cert.
Likenesses W. Stoneman, photograph, 1917, NPG · W. Stoneman, photograph, 1943, NPG · D. Vicaji, oils, Inst. CE [*see illus.*]
Wealth at death £16,393 18s. 11d.: probate, 20 April 1956, CGPLA Eng. & Wales

Redmond, John Edward (1856–1918), politician, was born on 1 September 1856 at Ballytrent House, co. Wexford, an old family mansion. He was the elder son of William Archer Redmond MP (d. 1880) and his wife, Mary, daughter of Major Hoey of Hoeyfield, co. Wicklow. Of his sisters, one (who died young) became a nun of the order of Marie Réparatrice and the other married L. G. Howard, an Englishman in New South Wales. The Redmonds were an established Catholic gentry family in the county and had long been associated with Wexford town. One of the family became member for Wexford in 1859 and on his death in 1872 was succeeded by his nephew Redmond's father, a supporter of the home-rule policy of Isaac Butt.

Family influences and early career Redmond's family heritage was rather more complex than that of most of his colleagues in the nationalist political class. His mother came from a protestant and unionist family and, though she converted to Catholicism on marriage, she never converted to nationalism. His uncle General John Patrick Redmond, who had inherited the family estate, was created CB for his role during the Indian mutiny; he disliked his nephew's involvement in agrarian nationalism of the

John Edward Redmond (1856–1918), by Henry Jones Thaddeus, 1901

1880s. John Redmond liked to boast of his family's involvement in the 1798 rising in co. Wexford: a 'Miss Redmond' had ridden to the support of the rebels, and a moderate Father Redmond was hanged by the yeomanry, as was a maternal ancestor, William Kearney. But another ancestor, William Redmond, had been on the yeoman side and John Redmond's nationalist colleague John Dillon privately insisted that the Redmonds of the 1790s had been prosperous drapers who were even more conservative than their protestant neighbours.

From 1868 to 1874 Redmond and his brother Willie were educated by the Jesuits at Clongowes Wood, co. Kildare, where John was regarded as the best speaker in the college debating society and performed the lead in school plays. After leaving Clongowes, he entered Trinity College, Dublin, but left in 1876 to live with his father in London, with a view to becoming a barrister. He acted as his father's assistant at Westminster; even at this stage, politics was more of a fascination than law. Redmond's father inclined to the conservative nationalism of Isaac Butt, but in 1877—in a gesture which reflects above all the sentimentalism which surrounded the Fenians a decade after their spectacularly unsuccessful rising—he took his two sons to the reception in a London hotel to mark the release of a celebrated Fenian prisoner, Michael Davitt. This seems to have been John Redmond's first recorded political act. In 1880 he took up a paid clerkship in the House of Commons; though there is a suggestion of familial pressure in the opposite direction, he increasingly identified his fortunes with those of C. S. Parnell, a noted 'obstructionist' in the House of Commons and president of the Land League movement founded in 1879.

Politics in the 1880s In the spring of 1879 Redmond attended with Parnell the meeting at Enniscorthy, when the supporters of the then representative for Wexford County, The O'Clery, attacked Parnell's platform. After Redmond was knocked down by the crowd, Parnell commented drily 'well, you have shed your blood for me at all events' (Bew, *John Redmond*, 8). When his father died later in 1880, Redmond sought Parnell's support as the natural replacement as the MP for Wexford. Parnell, however, insisted that his then secretary, Tim Healy, was the better candidate. Reluctantly swallowing his disappointment, early in the next year Redmond was to become the official candidate for New Ross in a by-election, and was returned unopposed. On election (31 January 1881) he rushed straight away to the House of Commons, where there were stormy scenes following the arrest of Michael Davitt, by then a Land League leader. The next day Redmond took his seat, made his maiden speech, and was expelled from the House of Commons all on the same evening.

The Land League conflict now entered a very turbulent phase; unlike most of the other Parnellite lieutenants, Redmond managed to stay out of gaol. This, in part, reflected Wexford's relatively low-key involvement in agrarian disturbance. Even the beleaguered Irish government regarded him as decent and moderate. In early 1882, by luck in the ballot, he won first place for a bill to amend the Land Act of 1881; his bill became the focus of attempts to reach a compromise between the Land League and the government and played a part in the events leading to the Kilmainham 'treaty' of 1882.

In early 1882 Redmond and his brother Willie were sent to Australia on a fund-raising mission; despite bad publicity resulting from the Phoenix Park murders, the trip was a success, both in political and personal terms. Not without arousing local jealousy—expressed in a fist fight on the eve of the wedding—he and his brother married into the prosperous Daltons, an Irish-Australian family, with Redmond marrying Johanna Dalton in September 1883. She died in early 1889, having borne Redmond three children; but it was a happy, if short-lived, marriage. Although he was to use more extreme language on American trips in 1884, 1886, and 1904, the Australian trip had an enduring moderating effect on Redmond's political outlook: in part, because as William O'Brien noted in 1886, he found his contacts with Irish-American extremism daunting. Impressed by the success of Irish Australians such as the Daltons, he now embraced an Irish version of Liberal Imperialism; he was always anxious, for example, to retain Irish representation at Westminster even after the implementation of home rule. During the debate which followed Gladstone's conversion to home rule in 1886, he declared:

> As a Nationalist, I do not regard as entirely palatable the idea that forever and a day Ireland's voice should be excluded from the councils of an empire which the genius and valour

of her sons have done so much to build up and of which she is to remain.   (D. Gwynn, 55)

In 1888, following an unusually strong and conceivably intimidatory speech, Redmond received five weeks' imprisonment with hard labour. Having belatedly qualified as a barrister (he was called to the Irish bar in Michaelmas 1887), he now busied himself with agrarian cases; he was involved in an appeal in such a case to the Clonmel county court judge in November 1890, when he heard of the news of Parnell's decision not to contest the O'Shea divorce petition. As he immediately told a journalist friend: 'I don't know what you will do but I'll stick to Parnell' (*Freeman's Journal*, 9 March 1918). This he did, despite his very conventional Catholic religious views, though some detected a wavering when he did not attend—as advertised—Parnell's last public meetings. Following Parnell's death, and by now the undisputed leader of Parnellism, he resigned the Wexford seat which had been his since the Redistribution Act of 1885, and stood unsuccessfully for Cork, which Parnell had represented. He did, however, win a seat in Waterford a few months later, on 23 December 1891.

Leader of the Parnellites and party reunion As leader of the small Parnellite minority of MPs, Redmond pushed policy in a novel conciliatory direction—though hints of his approach can be found in Parnell's increasingly moderate speeches of 1890–91. He also dropped all interest in agrarian radicalism and, unlike the mainstream nationalists, worked alongside Unionists in the recess committee of 1895 which led to the establishment in 1899 of the department of agriculture. After the democratization of Irish local government in 1898, he argued that Parnellite voters should use some of their electoral clout to return public-spirited non-nationalists—the 'policy of toleration', as it was known. In 1899 Redmond married his second wife, Ada Beesley, an English protestant who later converted to Catholicism (but only after his death).

In 1900 the split in parliamentary nationalism was healed. Redmond was elected chairman of the new party but he was never granted the authority and prestige of true leadership by powerful colleagues such as John Dillon, William O'Brien, Tim Healy, and Joe Devlin. Leadership was at best a balancing act; following the amicable land conference of 1903, involving landlord and tenant leaders, the benign and imaginative Wyndham Land Act of 1903 was passed. Redmond, in tune with his characteristic themes of the 1890s, was inclined to see a great opportunity for a new strategy of conciliation of those in Ireland who were traditionally suspicious of nationalist objectives. Dillon in his famous 'Swinford revolt' blocked any such move; William O'Brien urged Redmond to follow his own deepest convictions but, fearing another split, he quietly endured Dillon's diktat. He was also weakened at that moment by the general bad publicity arising out of the price he had originally sought for the sale of the family estate inherited from General Redmond: it seems also that General Redmond had so arranged his will that the inheritance was financially and politically a burden.

Home rule and the Liberals The Liberal landslide of 1906 gave an increasingly rotund Redmond renewed opportunities for working with, rather than against, the grain of government policy. He was privately keen to accept the scheme of devolution offered in 1907, but a convention of his party insisted that only the full measure of Gladstonian home rule was acceptable. Redmond also had to accept with great reluctance the revival of agrarian radicalism in the ranch war of 1916–10 but help was at hand. The closely fought general elections of 1910, combined with the destruction of the veto power of the House of Lords, gave him the balance of power at Westminster and thus the ability to pursue a Dublin parliament more seriously. In February 1912 the third Home Rule Bill was introduced; Redmond had at last become a nationalist hero of Parnellite stature. But like many of his colleagues in the nationalist leadership, he knew little of Ulster and the intensity of Unionist sentiment there. Protracted attempts to broker a compromise with the Unionist leader, Sir Edward Carson—with whom he had always had good personal relations, based on shared experiences at Trinity College, Dublin, and the Irish bar—eventually failed at the Buckingham Palace conference of July 1914. Many feared that Ireland was drifting towards massive civil strife as Unionist and nationalist volunteers drilled openly and armed; but the First World War intervened. Redmond reacted in a precisely calculated fashion when, in exchange for prime minister H. H. Asquith's commitment to place the Home Rule Bill on the statute book (and to make some later provision for Ulster), he supported the British war effort. His reasons were complex; he had a niece who was a nun in Belgium and this led him to sympathize profoundly with the anti-German cause. He also hoped that common sacrifice by Irish nationalists and Unionists would bring them closer together; even if not, Irish nationalists could not afford to allow the Ulster Unionists to cash the benefits of being the only 'loyal' faction in Ireland. Nevertheless, following his declaration of a pro-British policy at Woodenbridge, the Irish Nationalist Volunteers split; a large majority, calling themselves 'national volunteers' supported him but a vocal and increasingly influential minority, the Irish Volunteers, broke away and provided the cadre for the Easter rising of 1916. Until Easter 1916—judged by the steady, if decidedly unspectacular, electoral success of the Irish Parliamentary Party in every contested Irish by-election—he held the support of a majority of nationalists for this approach. He felt strong enough to turn down the offer of a cabinet place in 1915, even though this would have given him greater opportunity to influence the War Office, which he felt was guilty of insensitivity in important matters of Irish military symbolism. It would also have 'balanced' Sir Edward Carson's appointment to the war cabinet. Redmond flew the union flag alongside the green flag at Augavanagh; and he was the first to sing the national anthem at Westminster social gatherings while some of his fellow countrymen looked on in disbelief.

The Easter rising, 1916, and its aftermath Despite friendly warnings from Bonar Law and others, Redmond had not expected the Easter rising and certainly felt that the execution of the inner core of its radical nationalist leaders was just. Later in 1916, and finally and most gallantly at the 1917 Irish convention representative of the principal political interests in the country, he made desperate efforts to broker a new compromise with Irish unionism but, as public opinion in nationalist Ireland turned decisively against his party, these efforts had little chance of success; Unionists clearly perceived that he could no longer deliver on his side of any bargain. A series of blows fell that were political but with a bitter personal element. His brother Willie died gallantly at the front, but in July 1917 his seat in East Clare was won by Eamon de Valera, the most senior surviving commandant of the Easter insurgents. In September de Valera's campaign organizer, Thomas Ashe, died on hunger strike; Redmond's son-in-law Max Green was chairman of the general prisoners' board and involved in key decisions concerning the Ashe case. Inevitably, Max Green became the object of much caustic nationalist comment. Redmond himself was assaulted in the street by a crowd of young Dublin Sinn Féin supporters, including C. S. 'Tod' Andrews, one of the most single-minded (some would say narrow-minded) apparatchiks of the approaching new revolutionary order.

Redmond had a conciliatory agenda—'a plea for concord between the two races that providence has designed should work as neighbours together'—as he expressed it in his final words in parliament. But this agenda often remained hidden as he was forced to pursue the twin objectives of survival and party unity. As Warre B. Wells, one of his biographers, explained:

> In retrospect, one sees the dominant purpose of his political life as a recurrent *motif* of gathering force: the Recess Committee, the Land Conference, the Convention, that last chance of recovering the lost and misused opportunity which the war created—in these episodes most unmistakably the purpose grows and broadens.　(Wells, 204)

But 'in retrospect' is the key phrase here; Redmond's public purposes were often unclear; for every moderate speech there was a militant counterpart. Above all, during the Ulster crisis, he seems to have accepted the concept of a (non-time limited) county opt-out from the home-rule scheme, but failed to give it real political expression until it was too late. There is an Irish nationalist view that he was 'let down by everyone', in particular the Ulster Unionists, the British tories, and both the British government (especially Lloyd George) and the War Office during the war. But this is to ignore the well-advertised convictions of the Ulster Unionists, the relative indeterminacy of view among the British tories on the eve of the home-rule crisis, and the priorities of the British war machine, locked as it was in a life or death struggle with imperial Germany. Redmond, it should not be forgotten, was supremely confident and optimistic on the eve of the Easter rising; it was the insurrection which destroyed his plans, as he himself always acknowledged. He was allowed one posthumous victory of note: his son Captain William Archer Redmond retained his Waterford seat in 1918, despite the Sinn Féin landslide, in part because of his father's excellent record as a local member. Indeed, the family's strong political influence survived in Waterford well into the 1930s, as a reminder of a more cosmopolitan and relaxed form of nationalist politics in which an Irish parliament existed for democratic reasons, not to fulfil some intense racial and cultural agenda handed down by history.

Aloof, often a recluse at Parnell's old shooting lodge when in Ireland, Redmond had a distinctive Irish political temperament that can be detected in an elegant phrase by Alexander Sullivan: 'He was slow, cautious, cynical, with a prejudice in favour of truth that was almost English' (p. 137). His health was permanently affected by an accident in 1912. By mid-1917 he was visibly in decline; an operation in March 1918 to remove an intestinal obstruction followed, after which he at first made good progress but then suffered heart failure. He died a few hours later in a London nursing home at 8 York Place on 6 March 1918. After a funeral mass in Westminster Cathedral his remains were interred in a family vault in Wexford city.   PAUL BEW

Sources D. Gwynn, *The life of John Redmond* (1932) • S. Gwynn, *John Redmond's last years* (1919) • W. B. Wells, *John Redmond* (1910) • P. Bew, *Conflict and conciliation in Ireland, 1880–1910* (1987) • P. Bew, *Ideology and the Irish question* (1994) • P. Bew, *John Redmond* (1996) • A. M. Sullivan, *Old Ireland* (1927) • R. B. O'Brien, ed., *Home rule: speeches of John Redmond* (1910) • W. O'Brien, *Evening memories* (1920) • *Freeman's Journal* [Dublin] (9 March 1918)
Archives NL Ire., corresp. and papers | Bodl. Oxf., corresp. with H. H. Asquith • FM Cam., letters to W. S. Blunt • HLRO, corresp. with Andrew Bonar Law • HLRO, letters to David Lloyd George • HLRO, corresp. with Herbert Samuel • NL Ire., Harrington MSS • Plunkett Foundation, Long Hanborough, Oxfordshire, corresp. with Sir Horace Plunkett • Sheff. Arch., letters to Sir Robert Hadfield • TCD, Davitt MSS • TCD, corresp. with John Dillon | FILM BFI NFTVA, documentary footage; propaganda footage (Hepworth Manufacturing Company)
Likenesses H. J. Thaddeus, portrait, 1901, NG Ire. [*see illus.*] • G. C. Beresford, photograph, 1902, NPG • H. Speed, sanguine drawing, 1907, NPG • F. W. Doyle-Jones, bronze bust, 1910, Palace of Westminster, London • J. G. Day, etching, NPG • F. C. Gould, caricature, sketch, NPG • S. P. Hall, pencil drawings, NG Ire. • F. D. Jones, bust, House of Commons, London; copy, NG Ire. • T. H. Jones, portrait, NG Ire. • J. Lavery, oils, Hugh Lane Gallery of Modern Art, Dublin • B. Partridge, pen-and-ink caricature, NPG; repro. in *Punch* (6 May 1903) • B. Partridge, pen-and-ink caricature, NPG; repro. in *Punch* (5 April 1911) • Spy [L. Ward], caricature, watercolour study, repro. in *VF* (7 July 1904) • Spy [L. Ward], repro. in *VF* (12 Nov 1892) • B. Stone, photographs, NPG • cartoon, repro. in *Punch* (1 May 1912)
Wealth at death £1877 16s. 9d.: Irish probate sealed in London, 22 April 1918, CGPLA Eng. & Wales

Redmond, Thomas (*c.*1745–1785), miniature painter, was the son of a clergyman at Brecon and was apprenticed to a house painter at Bristol. Redmond is occasionally referred to as Redman in some dictionaries of artists. He moved to London and studied for a short time at the St Martin's Lane Academy. He lived in Soho from 1762 to 1766 but afterwards he settled at Bath, where he continued to practise with success as a miniature painter until his death; from 1782 to 1784 he lived in Church Street. In 1762 he began to exhibit with the Society of Artists; and contributed six portraits in all to their exhibitions, thirteen to those of the Free Society of Artists, and eleven to the exhibitions of the Royal Academy. Redmond also painted pictures and made small crayon portraits, which he signed TR in cursive capitals. A miniature of a clergyman by Redmond is in the Victoria and Albert Museum, London.

Redmond died a widower, about forty years old, in the latter part of 1785, leaving three sons, who were taken into the care of Mr Coward, mayor of Bath in 1782, and a relative of the three children.

CAMPBELL DODGSON, rev. ANNETTE PEACH

Sources D. Foskett, *Miniatures: dictionary and guide* (1987) • E. Edwards, *Anecdotes of painters* (1808); facs. edn (1970)

Redmond, William Archer (1886–1932), politician, was born in Waterford on 1 January 1886, only son of John Edward *Redmond (d. 1918), MP and subsequently chairman of the Irish party, and Johanna, daughter of James Dalton, of New South Wales. Redmond was from a co. Wexford Catholic gentry family which had played a considerable role in local and national political life: his father, uncle, and grandfather had all sat in the House of Commons and his parents had met and married during his father's fund-raising tour to Australia and New Zealand on behalf of the Irish party in 1883. He was educated at Clongowes Wood College and Trinity College, Dublin, and was called to the Irish bar in 1910 and English bar at Gray's Inn in 1921.

Redmond early sought a place on the political stage, making his first political speech in Belfast in 1910 and narrowly defeating a Unionist opponent to win East Tyrone at the general election of December 1910. When the First World War broke out John Redmond was at the forefront in urging Irishmen to join up. Young William Archer Redmond followed this advice but to his father's chagrin he was refused a commission in the 16th (Irish) division in February 1915 by General Sir Lawrence Parsons, who regarded him as a 'perfectly poisonous bounder' (quoted in T. Denman, *Ireland's Unknown Soldiers: the 16th (Irish) Division in the Great War*, Dublin, 1992, 199). Therefore Redmond enlisted in the Royal Dublin Fusiliers and received a commission later, on transferring to the Irish Guards. In 1917 he was mentioned in dispatches and was awarded the DSO after holding a strategic outpost in the face of great odds, with a handful of Irish troops.

Upon the death of his father in March 1918 Redmond resigned his seat at East Tyrone and, wearing his military uniform, won the by-election for his father's seat, Waterford City, in a rough contest with Sinn Féin. At the ensuing general election on 14 December 1918 he retained the seat, scoring the only triumph for the Irish party outside Ulster. He held the seat until the southern Irish representation in the Westminster House of Commons was abolished in October 1922 with the establishment of the Irish Free State. He did not stand for Dáil Éireann in 1922 as 'this is not the time to stir up strife' (Laffan, 339), but was returned as an independent TD for co. Waterford at the general election on 27 August 1923, into which his former constituency had been merged. In each subsequent election he topped the poll, and retained the seat until his death. In the Dáil he represented what was left of his father's constitutional nationalist movement, famously objecting in 1923 to the department of external affairs as a propaganda agency for the governing party. Perhaps his most significant incursion into political life came in 1926 when he took the lead in establishing the National League and National League party. This was made up in part from the remnants of his father's organization, though Redmond emphasized that it was not merely the resurrection of the old Irish party but a new political association. It came together on 10 June 1926 and issued a manifesto on 8 September, with the party being launched four days later. The league was founded on the basis of a need for an opposition that unreservedly accepted the treaty and the constitution and which stood for sound finance and 'the closest economy in public expenditure' (Gallagher, 100). Redmond himself was strongly in favour of free trade. At the first annual conference he defined the aims of the movement as the peaceful unification of the island, improvement of the economy, reduced taxation, and the abolition of compulsory Irish language in schools (this last tenet caused some unease among supporters). But Redmond had little enthusiasm for organizational labour and was selective in his attendance of meetings around the country. Urban tenants were perceived as key constituents of the party, and on 17 November 1926 Redmond introduced a bill to give them greater rights; it gained a second reading on 26 January 1927 but foundered when opposed by the government.

Under Redmond's leadership the party garnered 7 per cent of the first preference votes under proportional representation at the general election on 9 June 1927, returning eight members to the Dáil. Internal differences soon surfaced, however, coming to a head on a no confidence vote in the government of William T. Cosgrave. In the event of the motion's success a coalition cabinet was to be formed with Redmond taking the portfolio of external affairs, but the mysterious absence of one member of his party led to the government narrowly surviving the no confidence vote. Thereafter the party rapidly disintegrated; at the general election on 15 September 1927 Redmond was one of only two candidates elected, and in January 1931 the party was dissolved. On 26 November Redmond joined Cumann na nGaedheal, and issued an earnest appeal to all followers of the old parliamentary party to follow his lead. He also toured the west of Ireland with Cosgrave and campaigned vigorously across the country during the 1932 general election, at which Eamon de Valera's Fianna Fáil was victorious.

Redmond had been active at the bar since 1922 and had a substantial practice on the south-east circuit in Ireland. Additionally he took a large interest in the affairs of ex-servicemen, promoting their interests and claims. He was a prominent member of the Irish council of the British Legion, and was also one of the free state representatives on the general council in London. On 18 November 1930 he married Bridget Mary Mallick (1905–1952) of Newbridge, co. Kildare, elder daughter of John Mallick, a well-known figure in hunting and sporting circles in the county. Redmond himself was an enthusiast for the turf, known as a very good shot and all-round sportsman. The final two years of his life were clouded by a car crash in which a cyclist died; he was charged with manslaughter but acquitted. Redmond died suddenly while attending the funeral of an old Irish party loyalist in Waterford on 17 April 1932. He had suffered from epilepsy as a boy and was vulnerable to heart failure. After a funeral mass in Waterford Cathedral on 19 April he was interred in the family vault at St John's Church, Wexford. His widow was returned for Waterford in the Dáil at the first general election after his death (24 January 1933), retaining it until her death in 1952.   ALAN O'DAY

Sources J. A. Gaughan, *A political odyssey* (1983) · M. Gallagher, *Political parties in the Republic of Ireland* (1985) · D. Gwynn, *Life of John Redmond* (1932) · *Irish Times* (18–21 April 1932) · *Irish Independent* (18 April 1932) · M. Laffan, *The resurrection of Ireland* (1999) · P. Keatinge, *The formulation of Irish foreign policy* (1973) · *WWW* · *The Times* (18–19 April 1932) · D. Fitzpatrick, *The two Irelands, 1912–1939* (1998) · *Dod's Peerage* (1920) · m. cert.
Archives NL Ire., papers | TCD, J. Dillam MSS
Likenesses portrait, repro. in *Irish Independent*

Redmond, William Hoey Kearney [Willie] (1861–1917), Irish nationalist, second son of William Archer Redmond (1825–1880), and the younger brother of John Edward *Redmond, was born in Grassendale, Liverpool, on 13 April 1861. He came from a Catholic family associated with co. Wexford for centuries. His father sat in parliament for the Home Rule Party from 1872 to 1880. His mother, Mary Hoey, of protestant stock, was from co. Wicklow. He had two sisters. He grew up at Ballytrent, at the south-eastern tip of co. Wexford. He was educated at Carlow College (1871–2) and Clongowes Wood College (1873–6).

After leaving Clongowes, Redmond served in the merchant marine. He then took a second lieutenancy in the Wexford militia in December 1879 (becoming lieutenant in October 1880), and contemplated a regular army career. But he resigned from the militia to join the Land League agitation. He was arrested in February 1882 in possession of seditious literature and sentenced to three months' imprisonment. At Kilmainham he shared a cell with Charles Stewart Parnell, to whom his political loyalty never wavered. He went to the United States in June 1882 with Michael Davitt to collect funds for the Land League. In February 1883 he arrived with his brother in Australia, with which he developed close links. Here he met Eleanor Mary Dalton (d. 1947), eldest daughter of James Dalton, of Orange, New South Wales (he married her in London in February 1886); her aunt, James Dalton's half-sister, Johanna, married John Redmond in September 1883. The Redmonds collected £15,000 for the Irish National League, and then travelled to the United States and collected £15,000 more. In his absence, in July 1883, he was elected MP for Wexford, his father's old constituency.

Willie Redmond sat as an MP until his death, representing Wexford (1883–5), North Fermanagh (1885–92), and East Clare (1892–1917). He was a frequent speaker in the Commons, but the ardour of his speeches often exceeded their intellectual coherence. He was ejected several times from the house for his excesses and involved in several violent confrontations with Unionist MPs. He remained

William Hoey Kearney Redmond (1861–1917), by James Russell
& Sons, *c.*1915

popular, even with his political opponents. He was even
less restrained on Irish platforms and there often spoke of
violent insurrection (when the time was ripe). Yet he
remained a constitutionalist at heart. He was imprisoned
for three months in September 1888 for helping to resist
an eviction. When the Irish party split in 1890 he supported Parnell completely. His only child, a boy aged five,
died early in 1891; he had no more children. After Parnell's
death in October 1891, under stress of emotion, he lost all
sense of political direction for a time. One of the most
devout Catholics in the Irish party, he was deeply grieved
by the opposition of that church to Parnell. In 1891 he was
called to the Irish bar, but never practised.

Redmond joined with younger nationalists, such as
Arthur Griffith and Maud Gonne, to oppose the Second
South African War. He was co-treasurer to the Irish Transvaal committee. He was imprisoned again in November
1902 for inflammatory speeches. He made numerous
visits to Irish communities worldwide, and wrote two
books on his Australian journeys: *A Shooting Trip to the Australian Bush* (1898) and *Through the New Commonwealth*
(1906). The dominion status enjoyed by Canada and Australia influenced his conception of eventual Irish home
rule. A strict teetotaller but inveterate smoker, he devoted
much time to encouraging tobacco growing in Ireland.

Willie Redmond will be remembered for his part in the
First World War. He threw himself behind his brother's

support for the war. Although fifty-four, he enlisted as a
captain in the 6th Royal Irish regiment of the 16th (Irish)
division, largely composed of nationalists. He went overseas in December 1915, and commanded B company of his
battalion for six months. He wrote several newspaper articles (published posthumously in 1917 as *Trench Pictures
from France*). The Easter rising of 1916 shook him, and he
seems to have realized that the tide was now turning away
from constitutional nationalism. His health broken, he
was transferred to a staff post. He was promoted major in
July 1916. When on leave he spoke in the Commons, most
famously in March 1917, when he defended Irish involvement in the war and asked for immediate home rule. He
believed that by serving together in the trenches the
Unionist and nationalist traditions could be reconciled
after the war.

Redmond got permission to join his battalion for the
attack on Wytschaete on 7 June 1917. Wounded, apparently lightly, he died that day at Dranoutre, Belgium, in
the field hospital of the Unionist 36th (Ulster) division,
which attacked alongside his unit. His death caused grief
worldwide. He was buried the next day in the garden of
the convent at Locre in Belgium. The grave, symbolic perhaps in its isolation, is still there today. Commemorations
at Loker (organized by local people) took place in 1967 and
1997. In Wexford there is a bust of him in a local park. His
Irish home, Glenbrook, Delgany, co. Wicklow, still stands.
His wife survived him.

Willie Redmond was very different from his brother:
open-hearted, volatile, pugnacious, and garrulous. Until
the war rapidly aged him he had a perennially youthful
(albeit well-rounded) aspect. He was more radical than his
brother on many social issues, such as female suffrage. He
seems now the most representative figure of the thousands of Irish nationalists who served with the British forces in 1914–18. The East Clare constituency left vacant by
his death was, tellingly, won by Eamon de Valera of Sinn
Féin.   TERENCE DENMAN

Sources T. Denman, *A lonely grave: the life and death of William Red-
mond* (1995) · *DNB* · S. Gwynn, *John Redmond's last years* (1919) · *Major
William Redmond* (1917) · W. H. K. Redmond, *Trench pictures from
France* (1917) [with biographical notice] · *CGPLA Éire* (1917) · private
information (2004) [M. Green] · War Office records, 1917
Archives priv. coll. | FILM IWM FVA, actuality footage
Likenesses S. P. Hall, group portrait, pencil drawing, *c.*1888–1889
(*Parnell commission*), NPG · F. Pegram, pencil drawing, *c.*1888–1889,
V&A · J. Russell & Sons, photograph, *c.*1915, NPG [*see illus.*] · S. P.
Hall, pencil drawings, NG Ire. · photographs, NPG; repro. in
Denman, *Lonely grave*
Wealth at death £4018 2*s.* 9*d.*: administration, 6 Sept 1917, *CGPLA
Ire.* · £3819 2*s.* 2*d.*—effects in England: administration with will, 15
Sept 1917, *CGPLA Ire.*

Redpath, Anne (1895–1965), painter, the second child of
Thomas Brown Redpath (1863–1933), a tweed pattern
weaver, and his wife, Agnes Milne, was born at 89 Scott
Street, in the mill town of Galashiels, Selkirkshire, on 29
March 1895. Thomas Redpath's four children were given a
strictly nonconformist upbringing. As the daughter of a
tweed designer, Anne Redpath gained an early understanding of colour and texture. Years later describing the

Anne Redpath (1895–1965), self-portrait, c.1958–60

weaver's technique of colour flecking used for scumbling she explained: 'I do with a spot of red or yellow in a harmony of grey, what my father did in his tweed' (*Anne Redpath*, 1). She attended Hawick high school (1901–13) and in 1913 enrolled at Edinburgh College of Art. Parental permission for this course was granted with the proviso that she should concurrently train as an art teacher at Moray House, Edinburgh, where she qualified in 1917. Instruction at Edinburgh College of Art was rigorous and academic; among her tutors were Henry Linlott, Robert Burns, and D. M. Sutherland. Anne Redpath gained her diploma in 1917 and after a postgraduate year was awarded a travelling scholarship which, in 1919, enabled her to visit Brussels, Bruges, Paris, Florence, and Siena. She returned profoundly impressed by the works of the Sienese primitives.

On 21 September 1920 Anne Redpath married at Teviothead church James Beattie Michie (1891–1958), a young architect about to take up an appointment with the Imperial War Graves Commission in northern France. The house at St Martin, Pas-de-Calais, where their first two sons were born, was large and their finances strained. It was then that Anne Redpath began to decorate simple furniture with bright flowers, birds, and garlands, which later featured in her still-life paintings. Her family was her primary concern but by 1921 she had produced sufficient work, mainly watercolours in muted tones, for an exhibition at St Omer. Some years later James Michie became architect to a millionaire in the south of France. A third son was born and the family lived in idyllic surroundings at St Raphael and St Jean, Cap Ferrat. Anne Redpath's painting output was sparse but she maintained artistic contacts. The painter William Mactaggart who had been a fellow student at Edinburgh was a frequent visitor. In 1928 she exhibited at the casino at St Raphael.

In 1934 James Michie's employer lost his fortune. Anne Redpath and her sons returned to Hawick and James Michie found work in London. Soon after her return she began to show at the Royal Scottish Academy and in many group exhibitions. Many of her paintings at that time were competent landscapes of views around Hawick often recorded in her 'Notes from Nature' sketchbooks and painted in her studio. But it was in a domestic setting that her highly individual viewpoint expressed her affection for familiar household objects. Cups, jugs, teapots, and flowers disconcertingly displayed on a tilting table-top became characteristic of her style. The pure and effortless quality of her painting, particularly in the handling of white, could make a collection of flowers lyrical, almost ethereal. Early in the 1940s Redpath created one of her most significant works, *The Indian Rug* ('Red Slippers'; Scottish National Gallery of Modern Art, Edinburgh). This painting signalled a release of ideas long held in reserve and presaged a new and liberated approach. The placing of a vivid red chair, comfortable slippers, and folk-art rug clearly defined on a black background and formalized into a flat surface pattern demonstrates her mastery of structure. The boldly painted *Still Life with Orange Chair* (1944; priv. coll.) also exemplifies a sense of continuity with the Scottish colourists Francis Cadell and Samuel Peploe.

From 1944 to 1947 Redpath was president of the Scottish Society of Women Artists. She became an associate of the Royal Scottish Academy in 1947 and in 1952 was the first woman painter to be elected academician. Critical acclaim for her exhibition at the Scottish Gallery in 1950 brought public recognition for the distinction of her work but Redpath's vision was never static; she was responsive to post-war art movements and like Matisse, whom she admired, pursued her own rigorous path.

A journey to remote northern Spain in 1951 called for new strengths in Redpath's work. Her style radically altered becoming more emotive and her palette sombre reflecting the stark landscape and poverty of the hill villages as in *Rain in Spain-Ubeda* (1951; Scottish National Gallery of Modern Art, Edinburgh). Subsequent visits to Corsica, Brittany, and the Canary Islands released fresh colour harmonies; rich chestnut browns, purples, and rare pinks surged from her brush. The resultant landscapes, painted with new urgency and expressionist fervour, were enthusiastically received at the Scottish Gallery's 1960 Edinburgh festival exhibition.

In 1955 Anne Redpath became an OBE and was also granted an honorary LLD by Edinburgh University. The following year she attended a comprehensive exhibition of her work in the four main galleries of the Royal West of England Academy in Bristol. She became an academician of that society in 1959 and an associate of the Royal Academy in 1960. Redpath paintings were acquired by the Tate Gallery and many public collections. In her lifetime there were frequent exhibitions in Britain; she enjoyed the ensuing celebrity, wearing spectacular hats and designer clothes and talking with animation at convivial gatherings. On one occasion she discussed volubly with Chagall in fluent French the joys of being 'an old peasant' (Bourne, 54). This light-hearted acceptance of fame contrasts with her solemn self-portrait in the Scottish National Portrait Gallery, Edinburgh (another is in the Glasgow Art Gallery and Museum) which indicates her steady contemplative nature. She was deeply interested in world affairs from which she felt that art should not be isolated. Many guests remember evenings spent in her colourful room among bright pictures and painted furniture discussing art, politics, and social justice. Her generous spirit and engagement with humanity give even her lesser works a life-enhancing quality. The mature paintings of golden baroque altars and richly glowing church interiors in Lisbon and Venice painted in her last years are considered by many to be her finest achievements. Earlier heart attacks had brought grave health warnings but, undaunted, Anne Redpath's determination to develop her work never faltered. Such inspired commitment and sustained vitality have ensured her an enduring place in the history of twentieth-century Scottish painting. Following a fall in her Edinburgh home, 7 London Street, Anne Redpath died on 7 January 1965 at 19 Drumsheugh Gardens, Edinburgh, and was cremated on 9 January at Warriston crematorium, Edinburgh. Her work is represented in public collections in Aberdeen, Edinburgh, Glasgow, Hull, Manchester, Newcastle upon Tyne, and Preston, as well as in London and several Commonwealth galleries.   RUTH JONES

Sources G. Bruce, *Anne Redpath* (1974) · P. Bourne, *Anne Redpath 1895–1965: her life and work* (1989) · *Anne Redpath, 1895–1965: all the works in the collection*, no. 1 (1975) [exhibition catalogue, National Gallery of Modern Art, Edinburgh, Oct 1975] · L. Errington, *Anne Redpath* (1995) [exhibition catalogue, Aberdeen Art Gallery, 25 Nov 1995–27 Jan 1996] · T. Mullaly, ed., *Anne Redpath ... a memorial exhibition* (1965) [exhibition catalogue, Edinburgh, Nov 1965] · P. Long, *Anne Redpath 1895–1965* (1996) [exhibition catalogue, Scottish National Gallery of Modern Art, Edinburgh, 2 Nov 1996 – 19 Jan 1997] · *DNB* · private information (2004) [David Michie (son)] · b. cert. · m. cert. · d. cert. · *The Times* (4 Jan 1965)
Archives Royal Scot. Acad., works and MSS · Scottish National Gallery of Modern Art Archive, works and MSS | FILM BBC film shown in 'Counterpoint', 31 January 1961, directed by George Bruce; transcript in Bourne, *Anne Redpath*, 87
Likenesses L. Muszynski, oils, 1948, NPG · R. Philipson, group portrait, oils, *c*.1952 (*Gathering at 7 London Street*), Scot. NPG · A. Redpath, self-portrait, chalk drawing, *c*.1958–1960, Scot. NPG [*see illus.*] · A. Redpath, self-portrait, chalk drawing, *c*.1958–1960, Art Gallery and Museum, Glasgow · S. Beadle, chalk drawing, 1963, Scot. NPG · A. Redpath, self-portrait, priv. coll. · photograph, repro. in *The Times*
Wealth at death £34,253 9s.: confirmation, 30 April 1965, NA Scot., SC 70/1/1586/710

Redpath, Henry Adeney (1848–1908), biblical and linguistic scholar, was born at Sydenham, Kent, on 19 June 1848, the eldest son of Henry Syme Redpath, solicitor, of Sydenham, and his wife, Harriet Adeney, of Islington. In 1857 he entered Merchant Taylors' School, London, and in 1867 he won a scholarship to Queen's College, Oxford. He was awarded a second class in classical moderations in 1869 and a third class in *literae humaniores* in 1871; he graduated

BA in 1871, MA in 1874, and DLitt in 1901. Ordained deacon in 1872 and priest in 1874, Redpath, after being curate of Southam, near Rugby, and then of Luddesdown, near Gravesend, was successively vicar of Wolvercote, near Oxford (1880–83) and rector of Holwell, Sherborne (1883–90). On 5 October 1886, at Marsh Caundle, Dorset, he married Catherine Helen, daughter of Henry Peter Auber of Marsh Court, Sherborne. They had one son before her death at Shottermill, Surrey, on 26 August 1898.

Redpath served as vicar of Sparsholt with Kingston Lisle, near Wantage, from 1890 to 1898, when he exchanged this job to become rector of St Dunstan-in-the-East, in the City of London. He was also sub-warden of the Society of Sacred Study in the diocese of London, and examining chaplain to the bishop of London from 1905 to 1908. Redpath, who had learned Hebrew at Merchant Taylors' School, specialized while a country parson in the Greek of the Septuagint, completing and publishing a work which the theologian and religious historian Edwin Hatch had left unfinished: *A Concordance to the Septuagint and other Greek Translations of the Old Testament* (3 vols., 1892–1906). The work found recognition both in England and in Europe. Redpath was Grinfield lecturer on the Septuagint at Oxford from 1901 to 1905, and shortly before his death he designed a *Dictionary of Patristic Greek*.

Redpath's biblical scholarship was conservative. He was reactionary in his opposition to the critical approach to the Old Testament, arguing in *Modern Criticism and the Book of Genesis* (1905), published by the Society for Promoting Christian Knowledge, that Genesis was not of a composite structure. A work which was much more favourably received was his painstaking *Westminster Commentary* on Ezekiel, with introduction and notes (1907). He also contributed to James Hastings's *Dictionary of the Bible* (4 vols., 1904) and to the *Illustrated Bible Dictionary*. Redpath died at 35 Kirkdale, Sydenham, on 24 September 1908, and was buried at Shottermill, Surrey.

E. H. PEARCE, *rev.* JOANNA HAWKE

Sources *The Times* (25 Sept 1908) · *Guardian* (30 Sept 1908) · *Guardian* (7 Oct 1908) · private information (1912) · A. Deissmann, *The philology of the Greek Bible* (1908), 69–78
Wealth at death £4198 13s. 7d.: probate, 26 Oct 1908, CGPLA Eng. & Wales

Redpath, Leopold (b. 1816?, d. in or after 1868), swindler, was probably born in 1816 (1813 by another account), and was the son of James Redpath, a poor man. When young he worked as a clerk. On 23 February 1840 (pretentiously describing himself as a merchant and his father as a gentleman) he married a lady's companion, Jessie, daughter of Thomas Sherman, whom he dubiously registered as a major of the Royal Marines. He set up as a shipbroker in Lime Street, in the City of London, but went bankrupt in 1840 with liabilities of £5000 as the result of overreaching himself with a showy house and furnishings at Blackheath. In 1846 he became a clerk of the Great Northern Railway Company, and was promoted to registrar in 1854 at an annual salary of £250. Recognizing that once stock had been entered on a company's books, it was almost as negotiable as cash, Redpath in 1848 began to transfer stock to his own name and then sell it through his stockbroker. He also falsified coupons to increase the value of his stock and forged share transfers to fictitious names. Stock worth the huge sum of £220,000 was fraudulently issued. Attributing his prosperity to successful investments, Redpath took a smart London house (27 Chester Terrace, Regent's Park) and entertained lavishly; later there was a second house at Weybridge. He posed as an affable philanthropist and enjoyed the applause that accompanied his charities.

The discovery in September 1856 of the share-register frauds of William Robson agitated many rentiers, and a special investigation of the Great Northern Railway accounts was instituted in November 1856, for its directors had known since 1854 that they were paying a larger sum in dividends than could be accounted for. Redpath was detained after an abortive flight to Paris, and stood trial on 16 January 1857. He was sentenced to transportation for life and reached the penal settlement in Western Australia in October 1858. After receiving a ticket-of-leave in June 1861 he outraged local feeling in Australia by his unrepentant manner. His case was often cited as an example of undue leniency in the convict system, and in 1864 he was returned to prison for twelve months for insolence to a clergyman called Bostock, president of the Working Men's Association in Fremantle. He received a conditional pardon in Western Australia on 7 February 1868, and was apparently alive on 16 March, the date of the final dividend meeting of his British creditors.

RICHARD DAVENPORT-HINES

Sources D. M. Evans, *Facts, failures, and frauds: revelations financial, mercantile, criminal* (1859) · A. J. Wrottesley, *The Great Northern railway*, 1 (1979), 105–12 · *Perth Inquirer* (28 Sept 1864) · *The Times* (22 April 1840) · *The Times* (2 May 1840) · *The Times* (4 June 1840) · *The Times* (16 Jan 1857) · *The Times* (17 Jan 1857) · *The Times* (19 Jan 1857) · *The Times* (17 Jan 1865) · G. Robb, *White collar crime in modern England* (1992) · R. Erickson, ed., *Dictionary of Western Australians, 1829–1914*, 5 vols. (1979–86) · m. cert.

Redpath, Peter (1821–1894), merchant and benefactor, son of John Redpath and Janet McPhee, was born at Montreal on 1 August 1821. His family was of Scottish lineage, and settled in Canada at the beginning of the century. He was educated at St Paul's School, Montreal, and was then sent to be trained for business in Manchester. After returning to Montreal, he entered first the firm of Dougall, Redpath & Co., and later his father's sugar refinery, which became John Redpath & Son. He married, on 16 October 1847, Grace, daughter of William Wood of Bowden, Manchester. They had no children.

In 1866 Redpath left the family firm to become a director of the Bank of Montreal, and soon afterwards of the Montreal Rolling Mills, the Montreal Telegraph Company, several mining companies, and the Intercolonial Coal Company; he thus identified himself with the encouragement of important Canadian industries, but he took special interest in the development of the Northwest Territories

with particular reference to their coal reserves. In 1879 he resigned most of his directorates and settled in England, making frequent visits to Canada. In 1882 he still further limited his connection with business, thenceforth remaining only on the London board of the Bank of Montreal. He found occupation, however, for he became a member of the Middle Temple, was on the council of the Royal Colonial Institute from June 1886 until his death, and took an active interest in the establishment of the Imperial Institute.

Redpath is remembered for a series of munificent donations to McGill University at Montreal. He endowed the Peter Redpath chair of natural philosophy in 1871. In 1880 he established and funded the Redpath Museum as a centre for the study of geology, mineralogy, palaeontology, zoology, and botany; its formal opening in 1882 has been described as 'a landmark in Canadian scientific history' ('Dawson', *DCB*). In 1891 he also provided, at a cost of some £75,000, a library for the use of students in arts, science, medicine, and law; he spent much time in examining libraries in England and on the continent, and the Redpath Library was arranged on his own plans, with the result that it afforded, at the time, more accommodation for its size than any other similar building. It was opened on 31 October 1893 by Lord Aberdeen. He also gave the library some 3000 volumes on history. And at the college he instituted various prizes and medals. Besides encouraging liberal education Redpath was a generous subscriber to works more strictly charitable, and was for some years president of the Montreal General Hospital. He died on 1 February 1894, at his residence, the Manor House, Chislehurst, Kent. He was survived by his wife.

C. A. HARRIS, *rev.* ROBERT BROWN

Sources G. Tulchinsky, 'Redpath, John', *DCB*, vol. 9 · P. R. Eakins and J. S. Eakins, 'Dawson, Sir John William', *DCB*, vol. 12 · *The Globe* [Toronto] (3 Feb 1894) · *The Times* (3 Feb 1894) · Boase, *Mod. Eng. biog.*

Wealth at death £5864 8s. 3d.: probate, 18 April 1894, *CGPLA Eng. & Wales*

Redvers family (*per.* 1084–1293). For information on the family *see* Revières, Baldwin de (*c.*1095–1155).

Redwald. See Rædwald (*d.* 616x27).

Redwood, Abraham (1709–1788), philanthropist and merchant in America, was born on 15 April 1709 in Antigua, the third of the six children of Abraham Redwood (1665–1729), sea captain and plantation owner, and his wife, Mehetable (*c.*1676–1715), daughter of Jonas and Mary Langford of Antigua. Though he had a successful career as a merchant Redwood is remembered primarily for giving the large sum of £500 to purchase a starting collection of books for a library in Newport, Rhode Island, that was subsequently named after him. Housed in a neo-classical, temple-style building designed by the famed architect Peter Harrison, the Redwood Library Company's entire initial collection—1338 volumes at its opening in 1750—

had been purchased with Redwood's donation. Known as a proprietary library because patrons subscribed a specified sum to be a member of the company, the Redwood Library was also open to non-members, who could borrow books for a fee. It thus became New England's first quasi-public library and the third of its type in the American colonies, joining the library companies of Philadelphia and Darby, Pennsylvania.

Redwood's philanthropy flowed from a love of the arts and sciences that he developed as a gentleman of economic substance in cosmopolitan Newport. Brought to New England at the age of three by his parents, who sought a more comfortable and refined life than the one afforded by the isolation of a West Indian sugar plantation, Redwood, aged eleven, spent six months in Philadelphia at a Quaker school before joining his wealthy father in business in Newport. He became his father's partner and primary heir after his two elder brothers died in their youth. The Redwood family holdings included its Antigua plantation, Cassada Garden, and a coastal shipping business that specialized in sending New England timber and fish to the Caribbean in exchange for cash and molasses. In the 1730s and 1740s Redwood extended his merchant activities into the slave trade and became one of the major slave merchants of Newport, which was rapidly becoming infamous in the rest of New England for its unsavoury involvement in transporting human cargoes. Without a doubt the slave trade provided Redwood with the enormous profits that allowed him to become, as he was described at his death, 'the greatest public and private benefactor on Rhode Island' (Mason, 260). In addition to his gift to Newport's library Redwood made major contributions to the College of Rhode Island (Brown University) and to a school in Newport for the education of Quakers.

Much of Redwood's life abounded in seeming paradox. A Quaker and pacifist, on 8 February 1727 he married Martha Coggeshall (1709–1760), also a Quaker from Newport, outside the auspices of the Quaker meeting, owing to his father's disapproval of the union, and was severely reprimanded for doing so. Apparently devoted to his wife, with whom he had six children, Redwood was also renowned for his carousing behaviour. He became one of the leading lights in sophisticated Newport's famed Society for the Promotion of Knowledge and Virtue or, as it was more commonly known, the Philosophical Club. Dominated by Newport's Anglican upper class, Redwood's intellectual circle disdained his Quaker co-religionists. Though an ostentatious man who lived in splendour as a grandee he had little interest in political power. After being rewarded with a seat on the governor's council in 1747, in return for his support of the victorious Governor William Greene, he seldom attended council meetings and preferred to spend his spare time tending the garden of his country estate (Newport was famous for its gardens and Redwood's was the most famous on the island). And late in his life, after giving more money to charity than anyone else in New England, he refused to free his slaves, as demanded of him by the local Quaker

meeting, which therefore 'disown[ed] him' in 1775 (Bolhouse, 8). If others saw conflict among these three areas of activity Redwood either did not or was not unduly bothered by them. He withdrew from most of his merchant business in the 1760s but he continued to invest in other men's slave-trading voyages and continued to buy more slaves for his plantation in Antigua.

Like most Newporters, Redwood experienced financial losses and hardship during the American War of Independence, when Newport was shelled and occupied by British troops. Forced to flee to inland safety for several years he returned to Newport after the war and died there on 8 March 1788; he was buried in Coddington cemetery.

BRUCE C. DANIELS

Sources G. E. Bolhouse, 'Abraham Redwood: reluctant Quaker, philanthropist, botanist', *Redwood papers: a bicentennial collection*, ed. L. Dexter and A. Pryce-Jones (1976) · A. J. Worrall, 'Redwood, Abraham', *ANB* · E. F. Crane, *A dependent people: Newport, Rhode Island in the revolutionary era* (1985) · M. McCorison, ed., *The 1764 catalog of the Redwood Library Company at Newport, Rhode Island* (1965) · S. V. James, *Colonial Rhode Island: a history* (1975) · G. C. Mason, *Reminiscences of Newport* (1884) · B. Lippencott, 'Genealogy notes', unpublished file, Newport Historical Society, Rhode Island
Archives Newport Historical Society, Rhode Island, MS · Newport Historical Society, Rhode Island, papers · Rhode Island Historical Society, Providence, letters
Likenesses S. King, oils, *c*.1780, Redwood Library, Newport, Rhode Island
Wealth at death wealthy; owned Cassada plantation, Antigua; sumptuous home in Newport, Rhode Island; country estate in Portsmouth, Rhode Island; property in Mendon, Massachusetts; also business investments: will, repr. in Bolhouse, 'Abraham Redwood', 10–11

Redwood, Sir (Thomas) Boverton, first baronet (1846–1919), petroleum consultant, was born in London on 26 April 1846, the eldest in the family of six sons and two daughters of Theophilus Redwood (1806–1892) and his wife, Charlotte Elizabeth (*d*. 1868), daughter of Thomas Newborn Robert *Morson [see under Morson, Thomas], who owned a London pharmaceutical firm. After education at University College School, London (*c*.1857–1862), he worked in the laboratory of his father, a professor in the School of Pharmacy of the Pharmaceutical Society of Great Britain and editor of the *Pharmaceutical Journal*. His future in pharmacy seemed to be determined; then in 1869 he abruptly changed direction by becoming secretary of the Petroleum Association, where he developed his expertise as an analytical chemist. Four years later he married Mary Elizabeth (*d*. 1937), daughter of Frederick Letchford; they had two daughters and a son who died in 1911.

Redwood made his reputation in undertaking technical enquiries, for example, to devise a reliable method of testing the flashpoint of combustible oil products. He invented the viscometer in 1886 to measure the fluidity of oil. He was soon in constant demand as an expert both on select committees to do with safety legislation and on inquiries into oil explosions and other accidents. He became technical adviser to the corporation of the City of London and to the Port of London Authority, and was an

Sir (Thomas) Boverton Redwood, first baronet (1846–1919), by Mayall & Co., pubd 1913

potential value of the oil deposits. During the same period, Weetman Pearson (later Lord Cowdray) likewise made use of Redwood for a survey of the large areas in Mexico over which he had oil prospecting rights.

From 1911 onwards Winston Churchill as first lord of the Admiralty was determined to change the fuel used in warships from coal to oil. This led to the establishment in 1912 of a royal commission on fuel and engines, of which Redwood was a member: it investigated the whole question of oil for the navy, and led to the government's purchase of a majority share in Anglo-Persian. During the First World War, Redwood's professional expertise was much in demand, most notably when he was petroleum adviser to the Ministry of Munitions. In 1917 he was appointed director of technical investigations in the newly set up petroleum executive, and was in charge of the technical problems of oil production and research. The strain of this unremitting toil throughout the war was undoubtedly responsible for his death in London on 4 June 1919. He was survived by his wife.

Redwood was the first (and only) petroleum consultant of his kind. He not only helped to devise an oil strategy for Britain but also educated non-expert officials and businessmen alike in the technicalities of oil.

T. A. B. CORLEY

Sources G. Jones and F. Goodall, 'Redwood, Sir Thomas Boverton', *DBB* · G. Jones, *The state and the emergence of the British oil industry* (1981) · R. W. Ferrier, *The history of the British Petroleum Company*, 1: *The developing years, 1901–1932* (1982) · T. A. B. Corley, *A history of the Burmah Oil Company*, 1: *1886–1924* (1983) · *Journal of the Institution of Petroleum Technology* (July 1919) · *Nature*, 103 (1919), 287–8 · *Quarterly Journal of the Geological Society*, 55 (1919) · *The Times* (5 June 1919) · Burke, *Peerage* · A. Beeby-Thompson, *Oil pioneer* (1961) · R. D. Q. Henriques, *Marcus Samuel: first Viscount Bearsted and founder of the Shell Trading and Transport Company* (*c*.1960) · *WWW* · PRO, ADM 116/1208/9
Archives Burmah Castrol plc, Swindon · U. Warwick Mod. RC, BPC archives | CAC Cam., letters to Lord Fisher
Likenesses Mayall & Co., photograph, pubd 1913, NPG [*see illus.*] · Spy [L. Ward], cartoon, Institute of Petroleum, London · photographs, British Petroleum Co. plc · photographs, Burmah Oil
Wealth at death £165,013 14s. 5d.: probate, 15 Aug 1919, CGPLA Eng. & Wales

honorary adviser to a number of government departments, including the Home Office and the Admiralty. He was knighted in 1905 and was created a baronet in 1911.

Tall and of impressive presence, with heavy jutting eyebrows and a strong profile, Redwood was always immaculately turned out, with an orchid in his buttonhole. Those whom he advised were much taken with his charm and with the easy way in which he was able to put over complex facts and issues. The less charitable noted his affected and deliberate manner of speaking and his provincial accent, and the vanity that gave him pleasure when mistaken for the actor Sir Henry Irving.

Redwood's regular travels to oilfields in many parts of the world, notably the United States, Russia, and India, gave him a uniquely global view of oil affairs. In 1893 he became a part-time consultant to the Burmah Oil Company, a post he held for life. When in 1905 the Admiralty sought a British purchaser for the oil concession in Persia held by William Knox D'Arcy, who had so far failed to discover the extensive oil reserves there, it is almost certain that Redwood suggested Burmah Oil, which bought the concession. After three years, oil was finally discovered in Persia by George Bernard Reynolds; and when in 1909 the Anglo-Persian Oil Company (later British Petroleum) was registered, the prospectus cited Redwood's report on the

Rée, Harry Alfred (1914–1991), resistance fighter and educationist, was born on 15 October 1914 at 15 Mauldeth Road, Withington, Manchester, the youngest of eight children of Alfred Rée, chemical manufacturer, and his wife, Lavinia Elizabeth, *née* Dimmick. One of his grandfathers had migrated from Germany in the 1870s and his mother was French. He spoke fluent French, though with a marked north-country accent which later obliged his fellow resistance fighters in the Second World War to pass him off as a visiting cousin from Alsace. He was educated at Shrewsbury School and St John's College, Cambridge, where he read modern languages and economics and met Henry Morris, Cambridgeshire's visionary chief education officer, who converted him to community education. He began his career as a teacher in 1937 at Penge grammar school, London—a lively, idealistic, civilized, and not untypical young grammar-school master of that time. A

Harry Alfred Rée (1914–1991), by unknown photographer

former pupil remembered him as 'full of high spirits, sharp iconoclastic informality, and kindliness' (*The Independent*, 8 June 1991).

Then came the Second World War. Rée began the war as a conscientious objector. But Hitler's invasion of the Low Countries and of Norway changed his mind and he joined the army, initially as a gunner. He joined the independent French (F) section of the special operations executive (SOE) in 1942. Early in 1943 he married Hetty Vine (*d.* 1961); shortly afterwards he was dropped out of a Lysander to join the Maquis. From his landing his exploits read as if lifted from *The Magnet* or Bulldog Drummond: a near-capture on landing; escape from Burgundy just before the Gestapo arrested the leaders of the 'Acrobat' circuit; numerous acts of sabotage in the foothills of the Jura Mountains; a bold approach to one of the Peugeot brothers offering internal sabotage to the tank factory near Montbéliard in exchange for a promise by the RAF not to bomb it; and a hand-to-hand struggle with a German security sergeant from which he escaped to Switzerland in November 1943, badly wounded, to send a telegram to his wife saying 'Skiing here marvellous'. He never lost his admiration for the French peasants and workers who protected him, fought by his side, and saved his life. For his exploits he was awarded the DSO and the Croix de Guerre. The birth of his daughter was announced to him

in code by the BBC while he was in France; two sons followed.

After the war Rée returned to schoolteaching, at Bradford grammar school. While there he made a film, *School for Danger*, and broadcast for the BBC's *Children's Hour*. In 1951 he was appointed as the relatively young headmaster of Watford grammar school. For a while he remained an enthusiast for the grammar school, seeing it as the successor to the public school and writing *The Essential Grammar School* (1956) as a lively exposition of his ideas and beliefs.

In 1961 Rée was appointed professor of education at the University of York, then being planned under the leadership of Eric James, the founding vice-chancellor. Rée later came to believe that his acceptance of the chair was a mistake, though one mitigated somewhat by his appointment as provost of Derwent College. While at York he underwent another ideological transformation, from champion of the grammar school to fervent supporter of the comprehensive school. From this new vision of learning he never afterwards wavered. As a devoted member of the York education committee he advocated a comprehensive solution for the city. His move to York in 1961 coincided with the death of his first wife, Hetty, but he again found happiness, with Petronella Ann (Peta) Garrett (*b.* 1929/30), teacher of typewriting, and daughter of Brigadier-General Osmond Luxmoore Jones, army officer; they married on 23 March 1966.

As a believer in planned demotion before retirement, Rée resigned his chair at York in 1974 and determinedly descended the upward escalator to teach modern languages at Woodbury Down, a London comprehensive. The move was no momentary gesture but a characteristic and sustained defiance of conventional hierarchy which lasted until his retirement in 1979. He finally settled in the Yorkshire dales at Colt Park, in Ribblesdale, in a large stone-built farmhouse at a remote spot among the limestone scenery of the upper Ribble valley, whence he tramped the vast surrounding wilderness and where he was visited by his many friends, to be entertained to delicious French food and enlivening conversation. All this was interspersed with frequent forays to London, Coventry, France, and beyond. In retirement he was closely involved with the Community Education Development Centre, editing its journal, *Network*. He had already published a biography of Henry Morris, *Educator Extraordinary*, in 1973, and a selection of Morris's writings and speeches, *The Henry Morris Collection* (1984).

Rée was forever arriving somewhere and always eager to listen to the latest news. Somewhere on his travels he left behind the conventional religion of his childhood. But he retained and developed a deep spirituality, disguised by frequent laughter and punctuated by an irreverence towards the pomposities of this world. He was a hugely refreshing inspiration for children of all ages and one of the best loved men of his generation. He died at his home, Colt Park, Ribblehead, of heart failure, on 17 May 1991, and was survived by his second wife, Peta, and the three children of his first marriage.   A. H. HALSEY

Sources *The Independent* (21 May 1991) · *The Independent* (25 May 1991) · *The Independent* (8 June 1991) · *The Times* (22 May 1991) · personal knowledge (2004) · b. cert. · m. cert. · d. cert.
Archives U. Lond., Institute of Education, corresp. and papers |FILM 'School for danger', *Children's hour*, BBC, (1946x49)? |SOUND *Children's hour*, BBC, (1946x9) [broadcasts from Manchester?]
Likenesses C. Forbes, photograph, repro. in *The Independent* (21 May 1991) · photograph, News International Syndication, London [*see illus.*]
Wealth at death £250,293: probate, 5 Aug 1991, *CGPLA Eng. & Wales*

Reece, Sir Gerald (1897–1985), colonial administrator, was born on 10 January 1897 in Christchurch, New Zealand, the only son and second child of Edward Mackintosh Reece and his wife, Rose Emily Shaw, of Birmingham. His grandfather had an ironmongery business and cattle farm in New Zealand, as well as a plantation in Fiji. Educated at Rugby School, he was commissioned into the Sherwood Foresters in 1915, and saw active service in France and Belgium. After the war he qualified as a solicitor, and practised in London from 1921 to 1925, also serving as a territorial in the London Scottish regiment.

Reece joined the Kenya administration in 1925, and was posted as a district officer to West Suk, in the Turkana district. In 1928 he was appointed district commissioner in Mandera, in the northern frontier district, an area of 100,000 square miles of semi-desert covered with thorny scrub between the frontiers of Ethiopia and Italian Somaliland. There were no European settlers and it was sparsely populated by pastoral nomadic peoples, the camel-owning Somali and the cattle-herding Boran. It was a closed district and special permits were required to enter the area: this was an attempt to check the south-westerly drive of the Somali, which threatened the European-settled highlands to the south. The district commissioners spent much of their time travelling on foot among the scattered tribesmen, settling disputes, collecting taxes, and improving grazing and water supplies, but the key issue was the control of grazing. In Mandera, Reece trained a tribal police force known as Dubas after their red turbans, recruited from the leading families, and responsible only to the district commissioner. An élite force, the Dubas were independent of the Kenya police, whom Reece regarded as unreliable. The Dubas were later introduced into the other frontier districts. As district commissioner in Moyale from 1932, Reece was seconded to the Foreign Office in 1934 as British consul for southern Ethiopia, at Mega, where he had to cope with the refugees who poured over the mountains after the Italian invasion of Ethiopia in 1935. He was appointed district commissioner in Marsabit in 1936.

Since 1934 the officer in charge of the northern frontier district had been Vincent Glenday, who was district commissioner in Turkana when Reece first arrived in Kenya. Glenday expected his junior officers to remain unmarried until they had done at least two tours of duty, and it was not until 20 March 1936 that Reece married Alys Isabel Wingfield (*b.* 1912/13), daughter of Horace Ernest Humphrey Tracy of Bury St Edmunds, a retired RAF squadron

Sir Gerald Reece (1897–1985), by Elliott & Fry, 1948

leader, and sister of the writer Honor Tracy; they had two sons and two daughters. Alys Reece later wrote an account of their life in Kenya, *To my Wife: Fifty Camels* (1963).

While Glenday was on leave in 1938, Reece acted as officer in charge at Isiolo, headquarters of the northern frontier district; and when Glenday left Kenya to become governor of the Somaliland protectorate in 1939, Reece was appointed in his place. Very similar in outlook to Glenday, Reece loved the tough frontier life, and wrote that the northern frontier district was where 'real life' was to be found: 'there was something genuine and real about it all … those of us who'd had hard lives in the war found a certain peace in the solitude of the desert' (Allen, 96). He was very demanding, expecting his officers to work long hours, and to spend at least half of each month on foot safari. He was a stickler for detail, and bombarded his young officers with detailed orders and circulars. Reece was admired and respected by all, and inspired great affection in many, even among the Goan clerks serving in remote districts, to whose welfare he paid great attention. He came to be universally known as Uncle. A man of many interests, he was especially fond of the poetry of R. L. Stevenson. Reece was made an OBE in 1937 and a CBE in 1943.

When Italian forces invaded Kenya in June 1940, the British abandoned the frontier area, including Mandera and Moyale, but when the Italians were pushed out of Italian east Africa and Haile Selassie was restored to the throne of Ethiopia in 1941, Reece argued the case for establishing a British military administration in Borana, in southern Ethiopia. When the occupied enemy territory administration took over in 1941, he was appointed senior political officer for the Borana province, in addition to his position in the northern frontier district. He faced the task of trying to keep the peace among warring tribesmen armed with rifles, and he managed to extract compensation from them for years of raids south of the border with Kenya. He moved his wife and family from Isiolo to Marsabit, and often did not see them for months on end. In 1942 the Ethiopians took over from the occupied enemy territory administration, but the raids from Borana into the northern frontier district continued until the end of 1943. After the war Reece was appointed the first provincial commissioner of the new Northern Province, which was expanded in 1947 to include Turkana. He faced the problem of the increasing political activity of the Somali Youth League. Formed in 1943 in the former Italian Somaliland as the Somali Youth Club, it aimed to unite all Somali in an independent Somalia. Reece banned the movement in Garissa as subversive, and later extended the ban to the whole province in 1948.

Reece left Kenya in 1948 to become the first post-war governor of the Somaliland protectorate and military administrator of the Haud and reserved areas along the Ethiopian border. Since 1941, a British military administration had controlled British Somaliland, the former Italian Somaliland, and the Ogaden area of Ethiopia. However, the Bevin Plan of 1946, proposing the formation of a united Somali state under the trusteeship of the United Nations, was rejected, and Somalia was divided again, with Ogaden handed back to Ethiopia in 1948, Italian Somaliland placed under United Nations trusteeship administered by Italy, while British Somaliland reverted to protectorate status. Under Reece's governorship, the civil administration was restored, the Somalization of the civil service and the police began, in preparation for independence, although no date had been set, and he devoted himself to educational and economic development. A trade school opened in Hargeisa in 1952, and the first government school for girls and the first secondary school for boys in 1953, while water storage basins were excavated along the southern boundary of the protectorate. He also managed to get funds from the Colonial Office to build a road over the Daloh Pass, from Erigavo in the mountains down a 7000 ft escarpment to Mait on the coast of the Gulf of Aden, which he opened himself in 1953. Despite the bias of the British government towards the Ethiopians, Reece had grown to respect the Somali, and he was remembered long after his retirement. He was bitterly disappointed when the Foreign Office decided to return the Somali grazing areas of the Haud and reserved areas to Ethiopian control according to the treaty of 1897, and he decided to retire in 1953, rather than have to implement this decision. He was made a KCMG in 1950.

Reece settled in East Lothian, Scotland, and in his retirement he worked for prison reform as Scottish chairman of the Howard League for Penal Reform from 1961 to 1973, and chairman of the managers of Loaningdale Approved School from 1968 to 1976. He continued to take an interest in Somali affairs, and in the 1960s argued the case for the secession of the Somali part of the Northern Province of Kenya to Somalia. He was patron of the Anglo-Somali Society from 1978. He also took part in local affairs, serving as honorary sheriff of East Lothian from 1962 to 1973, and as deputy lieutenant in 1971. Reece died on 14 October 1985 in Roodlands Hospital, Haddington, East Lothian.

ANNE PIMLOTT BAKER

Sources C. C. Trench, *Men who ruled Kenya: the Kenya administration, 1892–1963* (1993) · C. C. Trench, *The desert's dusty face* (1964) · N. Farson, *Last chance in Africa* (1949), chaps. 21–5, pp. 267–357 · I. M. Lewis, *A modern history of Somalia*, rev. edn (1988) · A. Reece, *To my wife: fifty camels* (1963) · G. Reece, 'The northern frontier district of Kenya', *Geographical Magazine*, 36 (1963–4), 698–709 · I. M. Lewis, 'The problem of the northern frontier district of Kenya', *Race*, 5 (1963), 48–60 · I. M. Lewis, 'Modern political movements in Somaliland', *Africa*, 28/3 (1958), 244–61, 1 and 2; 28/4 (1958), 344–64 · *The Times* (18 Oct 1985) · WW · C. Allen, *Tales from the dark continent* (1977), 95–107 · private information (2004) · m. cert.
Archives Bodl. RH, Kenya National Archives, provincial and district annual reports and record books, handing over reports, corresp., station diaries, and civil and military reports by administration officers [microfilms]
Likenesses Elliott & Fry, photograph, 1948, NPG [*see illus.*] · photograph, repro. in Reece, *To my wife*, facing p. 208
Wealth at death £21,832.80: confirmation, 26 Nov 1985, *CCI*

Reece, Richard (1775–1831), physician, was the third and youngest son of William Reece (d. 1781), vicar of Bosbury, rector of Coddington, and curate of Colwall in Herefordshire, and his wife, Elizabeth Anna Mackafee, of Battleborough, Somerset. At the age of twenty Reece became resident surgeon at the Hereford Infirmary. He became a member of the Company of Surgeons in 1796, and from 1797 to 1808 he practised in Chepstow and Cardiff. The Royal Humane Society in 1799 awarded him its silver medal 'for his medical services in the cause of humanity *vitam ob restitutam*', and he afterwards became one of the society's medical assistants. He was living in London in 1812, and he subsequently graduated MD, but it is not known from which university. He developed a considerable practice in London, and was consulted by Joanna Southcott, then aged sixty-four, as to the possibility of her supernatural pregnancy. He seems to have given a guarded diagnosis, which he had an opportunity to state with greater certainty when he assisted at her autopsy after her death on 27 December 1814.

Reece led an active life, and, in addition to his practice, studied chemistry and botany. His knowledge of the medicinal properties of plants enabled him to introduce several new drugs into general use. He was married to Kitty Blackborow, a daughter of Judge Blackborow.

Reece's publications include: *The medical guide, for the use of the clergy, heads of families, and practitioners in medicine and surgery* (1802); *Observations on the Anti-Phthisical Properties of Lichen Islandicus, or Iceland Moss* (1803); *Letters Addressed to Mic. G. Prendergast on the Present State of Medicine in Great Britain* (1810); *The Chemical Guide* (1814); and *Statement of the last illness and death of Mrs. [Joanna] Southcott, with the appearances on dissection* (1815).

Reece died in Bolton Row, London, on 26 September 1831, and was buried in St George's burial-ground, Bayswater Road, London.

D'A. POWER, *rev.* MICHAEL BEVAN

Sources *GM*, 1st ser., 101/2 (1831), 473 · private information (1896)
Likenesses R. Bull, stipple, 1813 (after his earlier work by R. Bull), Wellcome L. · R. Bull, miniature, oils, priv. coll.

Reece, Robert (1838–1891), playwright, was born on the island of Barbados in the West Indies on 2 May 1838, the son of Robert Reece (1808–1874), a barrister of the Inner Temple. Robert Reece the younger matriculated from Balliol College, Oxford, on 28 January 1857, and graduated BA in 1860 and MA in 1864. He was admitted a student at the Inner Temple in 1860, but was not called to the bar. For a short time he was a medical student; then, between 1861 and 1863, he was an extra clerk in the office of the ecclesiastical commissioners, and from 1864 to 1868 an extra temporary clerk to the emigration commissioners. On 7 March 1867 he married Mary Arnold Chipperfield.

Meanwhile Reece wrote comic pieces for the stage with some success. He was industrious and facile with rhymes. His first effort was the libretto of an operetta, *Castle Grim* (music by G. Allen), produced at the Royalty Theatre on 2 September 1865, and which the critic Edward Leman Blanchard described as a 'very grim affair' (Scott and Howard, 1.314). Between 1865 and 1882 Reece contributed many burlesques to London theatres such as the Globe, the Olympic, the Vaudeville, the Strand, and the Gaiety. His plays included *Prometheus* (23 December 1865), which was reprinted as volume 68 of Lacy's *Acting Editions of Plays*, and *Little Robin Hood: a Burlesque*, which was first performed on 18 April 1871, and revived at the Gaiety Theatre in 1882. His work for this latter theatre was particularly prolific: between 14 September 1872 and 8 April 1884 he produced fourteen plays for performance there, including what was probably his best-known work, *Forty Thieves* (23 December 1880), and *Valentine and Orson* (23 December 1882; printed 1882). He collaborated with Henry Brougham Farnie, on fifteen pieces, and occasionally joined other dramatic writers working on like lines to his own. William Archer noted in *English Dramatists of To-Day* (1882) that Reece's main skill was dialogue; unfortunately 'it was his fate to come to the front in the dramatic world just as the rage for burlesque was at its height', meaning for Archer that Reece's 'undoubted wit and ability' were largely expended on 'hack-work' (Archer, 292, 289). Reece died at 10 Cantlowes Road, Camden Square, London, on 8 July 1891, and was buried in Kensal Green cemetery. Although the recorded cause of death was 'spinal myelitis' and 'apoplexy', contemporaries felt that his death may well have been hastened by the loss of most of his property in unfortunate investments in the West Indies.

G. C. BOASE, *rev.* MEGAN A. STEPHAN

Sources W. Archer, *English dramatists of to-day* (1882), 289–93 · Boase, *Mod. Eng. biog.*, vol. 3 · *ILN* (18 July 1891), 71 · *The life and reminiscences of E. L. Blanchard, with notes from the diary of Wm. Blanchard*, ed. C. W. Scott and C. Howard, 2 vols. (1891) · C. Scott, 'Biographical

introduction', in J. Morton, *Plays for home performance* (1889), xi · Foster, *Alum. Oxon.* · d. cert.
Likenesses R. T., wood-engraving, NPG; repro. in *ILN* (18 July 1891) · portrait, repro. in *Illustrated Sporting and Dramatic News* (1881), 357 · portrait, repro. in *Saturday Programme* (25 Oct 1876), 3–4 · portrait, repro. in *Figaro* (18 July 1891), 14
Wealth at death £66 6s. 6d.: administration with will, 13 Feb 1892, *CGPLA Eng. & Wales*

Reed. *See also* Read, Reade, Rede, Reid.

Reed, Alfred German (1847–1895). *See under* Reed, (Thomas) German (1817–1888).

Reed, Andrew (1787–1862), philanthropist and Congregational minister, born at Beaumont House, Butcher Row, St Clement Danes, London, on 27 November 1787, was the fourth son of Andrew Reed, watchmaker, and his wife, Mary Ann Mullen, who before her marriage taught a school in Little Britain. The father moved as a young man to London from Maiden Newton in Dorset. He belonged to the Independents, and acted as lay evangelist and preacher to the end of his life. The family was 'suffused with evangelical religiosity' (Helmstadter, 12). Young Andrew was privately educated. Aged sixteen, he joined the congregational church in New Road, Whitechapel. Brought up to work in his father's business, he soon found it uncongenial, and on the advice of the Revd Matthew Wilks of the Tabernacle, Moorfields, entered Hackney College as a theological student under the Revd George Collison in 1807. He was ordained to the ministry on his twenty-fourth birthday, November 1811, as pastor of the New Road chapel. It is said that Reed courted a wealthy widow, Mary Cave, who died in 1814, leaving him £1000 (Helmstadter, 18).

In 1816 Reed married Elizabeth (Eliza), eldest daughter of Jasper Thomas Holmes, a wealthy City merchant retired to Reading. Elizabeth probably brought a substantial sum to the marriage. Reed's autobiographical novel, *No Fiction: a Narrative Founded on Facts* (2 vols., 1819), contained an unflattering portrait of his friend Francis Barnett which led to a prolonged quarrel and a hostile depiction of Reed in Barnett's *Memoirs … the Lefevre of 'No fiction': and a review of that work, with letters and authentic documents* (1823). After seventeen years' effective service at New Road he set about building a larger chapel; called Wycliffe Chapel, and seating 2000, it opened on 21 June 1831. He was its minister until November 1861. In 1834 Reed was sent by the Congregational Union of England and Wales as a deputation with the Revd J. Matheson to the congregational churches of America, in order to promote peace and friendship between the two communities. Yale University conferred upon him the honorary degree of DD, and he returned home after an absence of eight months. With Matheson he published *A Narrative of the Visit* (2 vols., 1834).

In addition to this energetic ministry Reed became one of the leading and most effective philanthropists of his day, benefiting his contemporaries through the asylums he built and his family through the status and contacts he gained. He created five major charities, without using his own money or that of his wife. In 1813 he opened the London Orphan Asylum, financed by members of his congregation and by City merchants encouraged by the support for Reed given by the duke of Kent. This fund-raising formula—the systematic combination of City merchants and royalty—was innovatory, and especially so in nonconformist circles. The orphanage cost £25,000, and its permanent building was opened in 1825 in Clapton by the duke of Cambridge. In 1827 Reed founded the Infant Orphan Asylum for orphans under seven years of age. He gained support from the dukes of Gloucester and Clarence and from the duchess of Kent. This orphanage, first at Hackney Road, expanded and in June 1841 Prince Albert laid the foundation stone of a new building at Wanstead. The governors insisted on the Church of England catechism's being used in the orphanage, and Reed resigned from the board, though still supporting the charity financially. He always favoured non-denominational philanthropy. In 1844 he founded in Richmond, as an alternative, the Asylum for Fatherless Children, which, via temporary premises in Hackney, and then Stamford Hill, became Reedham Asylum (named for Reed) at Coulsdon, near Croydon. In 1847 Reed began the Asylum for Idiots, which eventually settled at Earlswood, Surrey, with a branch at Essex Hall, Colchester. This was a progressive and highly regarded institution. His last major project was the Royal Hospital for Incurables, instituted in 1854. He raised almost £130,000 for his asylums.

With a substantial salary from his successful church Reed was able to build himself a house at Cambridge Heath, Hackney. His five children prospered. One of his two daughters, Elizabeth, married Thomas Spalding, the stationer, and the third of his five sons, Charles *Reed, was a prominent businessman and educationist. Charles and the first son, Andrew, compiled the *Memoirs* of their father (1883) which have much contemporary material, including extracts from his journal, the original of which is lost. In addition to *No Fiction* Reed published a memoir of his sister Martha (1821) and various evangelical works, including *Eminent Piety Essential to Eminent Usefulness* (1842); his sermons delivered on special occasions were collected in 1861. Reed also composed hymns and published a hymnbook (1841). He rarely ventured into politics, though he was, like almost all congregationalists, a Liberal; but in 1843–4 he chaired the committee of dissenters opposing the educational clauses of Sir James Graham's Factory Act. Reed resigned the pastorate of Wycliffe Chapel on the celebration of his jubilee in November 1861, and died at his house at Cambridge Heath, Hackney, London, on Tuesday 25 February 1862. **H. C. G. MATTHEW**

Sources A. Reed and C. Reed, eds., *Memoirs of the life and philanthropic labours of Andrew Reed, D.D. with selections from his journals* (1863) · D. M. Lewis, ed., *The Blackwell dictionary of evangelical biography, 1730–1860*, 2 vols. (1995) · R. J. Helmstadter, 'The Reverend Andrew Reed', in R. W. Davis and R. J. Helmstadter, *Religion and irreligion in Victorian society* (1992), 7–28 · K. Hensman, *Evangelists in action* (1862) · F. Prochaska, *Royal bounty: the making of a welfare monarchy* (1995) · F. Prochaska, *The voluntary impulse* (1988) · DNB

Likenesses G. Paten, oils, 1838, London Orphan Asylum, Clapton; at London Orphan Asylum, Clapton, in 1896 · J. Parker, line engraving (after Wildman), BM, NPG · D. J. Pound, stipple and line engraving (after photograph by Mayall), NPG · photograph, NPG

Wealth at death under £12,000: probate, 8 April 1862, *CGPLA Eng. & Wales*

Reed, Sir Andrew (1837–1914), police officer, was born in Galway town, Ireland, on 26 September 1837, the only son and third of the four children (the others of whom died in childhood or adolescence) of John Reed, land agent, and his wife, Mary, daughter of John Adamson of Moate, co. Westmeath. His mother died when he was three and in 1847 his father remarried. He was brought up partly by his father's family, many of whom were Roman Catholics, and for a time was fostered among Irish-speaking peasants. He attended dame-school and Erasmus Smith's school in Galway, and at sixteen he was earning his living as a tutor. In 1856 he won a science scholarship, which enabled him to enter Queen's College, Galway, from which he obtained an LLB.

In 1859 Reed passed the examination for entry into the Royal Irish Constabulary (RIC) as an officer cadet and went to Dublin to train at the force's depot in Phoenix Park. After four months he was appointed a sub-inspector in north co. Tipperary. But his district was rather too quiet for his taste and in 1862 he obtained a transfer to co. Donegal. The rugged west coast of Donegal was a favourite haunt of illicit distillers and he spent an adventurous four years in pursuit of them. In 1866 he was transferred to co. Kilkenny and then in 1867 to Belfast. In the latter year he married Elizabeth Mary (d. 1913), only daughter of Hamilton Lyster of Croghan House, near Birr, King's county. They had one son and three daughters.

Reed's stay in Belfast was brief, for, late in 1868, he was invited by Colonel John Stewart Wood, the inspector-general of the RIC, to become his private secretary in Dublin. He filled this position for eleven years, first under Wood, and then from 1876 under his successor, Lieutenant-Colonel George Hillier. During these years he found time to study law and, when in 1873 he was called to the Irish bar, he contemplated retiring from the RIC to practise law. But Wood dissuaded him. At Wood's request, Reed also substantially revised the RIC manual, first issued in 1866, and produced his own *Irish Constable's Guide*, which was to become the Irish policeman's bible. In 1874, prompted by his commitment to temperance, he published what became a standard text on *The Liquor Licensing Laws of Ireland*.

In 1879 Reed passed the examination for county inspector and was appointed to Donegal, with his headquarters in Letterkenny. This gave him 'the greatest delight', he later wrote, as he was tired of the job of clerk and 'longed … for the pleasant outdoor life, and the variety in work, of an Irish police officer' (Reed, 3). But, with the spread of the land war to Donegal in 1880, he found himself with the far from agreeable duty of providing police protection at numerous evictions. As the land agitation escalated he was recalled to Dublin in June 1881 and put in charge of the RIC's crime division, with the task of combating politically inspired crime. He was thus closely involved in investigating many of the controversial crimes of the period. By his own reckoning, from June 1881 to November 1882, he was only absent from his office for one day. When Hillier's health broke down in 1882 owing to the strain of work, he was appointed assistant inspector-general, and in 1884 he became one of the country's four new divisional magistrates, based in Athlone.

In August 1885 Reed was offered the inspector-generalship of the RIC. He was initially reluctant to accept, fearing charges of anti-Catholic bias because his appointment would leapfrog the claims of seniority of the Catholic deputy inspector-general. He agreed, however, when told that an outsider would be sought if he refused the appointment. He served in the position until his retirement in August 1900, the year he was appointed CVO. He was knighted in 1889 and appointed KCB in 1897.

Although these years were not as difficult as those of the land war, the so-called Plan of Campaign, directed against selected landlords between 1886 and 1891, produced a number of serious clashes between the RIC and protesting tenants. Reed also took personal charge of the RIC in Belfast during the riots of August and September 1886, the worst of the century, which he later described as the 'most arduous' duty of his whole police career.

Reed was the only inspector-general without a military background; the only one to rise through the ranks from a cadetship; and the only one with academic and legal training. He thus placed less emphasis on military drill and the use of firearms and more on the mastering of the legal and technical aspects of police duties. His attempts to turn RIC men from soldiers into policemen may have been appropriate in the largely peaceful Ireland of the mid- and late 1890s, but when the RIC was called upon in 1919 to resume its military character in order to defeat the IRA, it proved unequal to the task.

Reed died at his home 5 Dartmouth Road, Dublin, on 7 November 1914, having spent much of his retirement travelling in Europe and America. His son Captain Hamilton Lyster Reed, of the Royal Artillery, won the VC at the battle of Colenso in 1899.   ELIZABETH MALCOLM

Sources A. Reed, 'Recollections of my life', priv. coll. · private information (1996)
Archives priv. coll.
Likenesses photograph, 1900, repro. in R. J. K. Sinclair and F. J. M. Scully, eds., *Arresting memories: captured moments in constabulary life* (1982), pl. 26 · portrait, priv. coll.
Wealth at death £1857 5s. 9d.: Irish probate sealed in London, 14 Dec 1914, CGPLA Ire. · £7665 19s. 3d.: probate, 24 Nov 1914, CGPLA Ire.

Reed, Austin Leonard (1873–1954), tailor and retailer, was born on 6 September 1873, at 12 Howard Street, Reading, Berkshire, the eldest son of William Bilkey Reed, hosier and hatter in Reading, and his wife, Emma Florence Bowler.

After education at Reading School and some experience working in his father's shop, Reed joined the staff of a firm of hosiers in Ludgate Hill, London, as a clerk. In 1893 he went to the United States, where he worked in Wannamaker's General Store in Philadelphia, and with Hackett, Carhart & Co., clothiers of New York, and Lincoln Bartlett, menswear importers in Chicago. He went back to Britain in 1896 with the ambition of founding a store inspired by those in America, which could provide the expanding ranks of new white-collar city workers with the latest in modern men's clothing. On 7 July 1900 Reed opened a new branch of the family shop under his own name in Fenchurch Street, London. This was followed by the opening of a second City store in 1905, by which time Reed's father had retired, selling the Reading business and leaving his son in control of a thriving London concern.

From the beginning Reed worked on clear principles. High-quality but unpretentious merchandise was to be presented through honest promotion with prices plainly marked and close attention paid to customer service. Much effort was devoted to originality in window display and shop fittings, and from the first advertising played an important part in the expansion of the business. Traditional press publicity was dropped by 1907 in favour of poster campaigns and a concentration on direct mailing, adapted to the particular requirements of individual clients. By 1908 there were three shops in the City and in 1911 the first West End branch was opened in Regent Street. In 1913 Reed made his first excursion into the provinces, in Birmingham. Manchester followed the next year and by 1930 most of the major cities in England were served, as well as Glasgow and Belfast. In 1929 a shop was opened aboard the liner *Aquitania*, and two were later opened on both the *Queen Mary* and the first *Queen Elizabeth*.

In 1910 the concern had become a private company and in 1920 Austin Reed Ltd offered their shares to the public on the stock exchange in an attempt to provide capital for continued growth. Although the post-war slump in the economy limited the take-up of shares, Reed put his faith in increased expansion, and, following careful customer research and a further trip to America, he implemented his plan to provide what he called 'a Savile Row suit for the middle-class man' at a price he could afford. He deplored what he saw as the decline in British taste and, in competition with the democratizing trends of 'made to measure' tailoring chains such as Burtons and Hepworths, offered a range of 'New Tailoring' from 1925. It was distinctive through its good workmanship, wide variety of fittings, and heightened sense of fashionableness.

The new Regent Street shop, opened in 1926, provided a worthy setting for Reed's ideas. Nash's Regent Street was in process of demolition and Reed was lucky to obtain a place in the Quadrant at the lower end designed by Sir Reginald Blomfield. There the firm was able to provide every modern facility. Reed was a founder member of the Regent Street Association and its chairman in 1927. He was also a founder member of the National Association of Outfitters, president of the City of London Trade Association, a council member of the Multiple Shops Federation, and master of the Glovers' Company.

Through the 1920s and 1930s Reed ensured that the

company retained its reputation for innovation, employing modernist designers including Tom Purvis and Fougasse, who lent a contemporary identity to promotional material. Employees also experimented with publishing *Modern Man*, a fashion magazine for men, and directed their energies towards niche marketing, supplying the clothing needs of Britain's colonial administrators in particular. On the outbreak of war in 1939, Reed deferred plans to retire. The provision of officers' military uniforms occupied the business until demobilization, and the return to civilian dress provided new challenges from 1945. Reed finally retired from the chairmanship in 1948.

Austin Reed was not only a highly skilled businessman, but won wide regard and friendship by his ideals of simplicity, sincerity, and a service devoted to good distribution with fair dealing and avoidance of exploitation. He combined these with a flair for forward-looking retail methods which reflected and encouraged the concurrent modernization of British menswear. He was an active Congregationalist and was deeply influenced by Frank Buchman, founder of the Moral Re-Armament movement, whom he met in 1933.

On 10 March 1902 Reed married Emily (*d.* 1953), daughter of Alfred Wilson, a Reading butcher; they had two sons and four daughters. The younger son was killed as a fighter pilot in north Africa during the war. The elder son, Douglas, became vice-chairman of the firm in 1953. Austin Reed died at his home, Garden Reach, Camp Road, Bulstrode Park, Gerrards Cross, on 5 May 1954.

CHRISTOPHER BREWARD

Sources B. Ritchie, *A touch of class: the story of Austin Reed* (1990) · *Fine and fifty* (1950) · *DNB* · *CGPLA Eng. & Wales* (1954) · d. cert. · b. cert.
Archives Austin Reed Company, London, archive
Likenesses F. May, caricature, gouache drawing, 1927?, NPG · J. Gunn, oils, priv. coll.; copy, Austin Reed, Regent Street, London
Wealth at death £108,663 0s. 11d.: probate, 17 July 1954, *CGPLA Eng. & Wales*

Reed, Sir Carol (1906–1976), film director, was born on 30 December 1906, at Daisyfield, West Hill, Wandsworth, London, the fourth son of the actor–manager Sir Herbert Beerbohm *Tree (1852–1917) and (Beatrice) May Reed, formerly Pinney, the daughter of a clergyman. Tree was already married, with three daughters, but he maintained a second household with May Pinney, who had changed her name to Reed in 1904, and their relationship continued until his death in 1917. Carol Reed was educated at the Grey Coat School in Putney and at King's School, Canterbury.

Early directing career In 1923 Reed went to America to join his brother Guy, who was working on a farm in Massachusetts. After six months he returned to England, determined to be an actor. His first appearance was as Constantine, a minor character in Sir Howard de Walden's *Heraclitus* at the Holborn Empire in 1924. Reed was a keen and conscientious actor, and over the next three years he worked with a number of different companies, but he found himself increasingly involved with production.

Sir Carol Reed (1906–1976), by Anthony Buckley, 1938

After acting in Edgar Wallace's *The Terror* in 1927, he began directing Wallace's prolific output of plays.

Wallace was chairman of the British Lion Film Corporation and he asked Reed to assist him in directing film versions of his novels and plays. Their fruitful relationship was terminated by Wallace's sudden death in Hollywood in February 1932. Reed continued working as a stage director, putting on a season of Shakespeare plays at the Open Air Theatre in Regent's Park, but in 1933 the theatrical impresario Basil Dean invited him to join Associated Talking Pictures, a film company he had set up with studios at Ealing, to make film versions of plays. After working as dialogue coach and assistant director on a number of films, and co-directing *It Happened in Paris* with Robert Wyler, Reed was given the task of directing *Midshipman Easy* in 1935.

Reed's competence, ingenuity, and thoroughness marked him out as a director of distinction. Graham Greene, often caustic in his film column in *The Spectator*, welcomed Reed as having 'more sense of the cinema than most veteran British directors' (Wapshott, 103), and on the release of Reed's next film, an adaptation of J. B. Priestley's *Laburnum Grove* (1936), Greene exclaimed that 'Here at last is an English film one can unreservedly praise', and forecast that 'Mr Reed, when he gets the right script, will prove far more than efficient' (ibid., 105). This opportunity came seven films later with *The Stars Look Down* (1939), an ambitious adaptation of A. J. Cronin's novel. Reed had already proved his affinity for realist subjects with *Bank Holiday* (1937), and here he had a much larger budget to explore the miserable conditions endured by Britain's coalminers. However, Reed disclaimed any socialist sympathies and expressed the view that, if the film was a powerful plea for nationalization of the mines, he could just as willingly have made a film arguing the opposite case.

During the early part of the Second World War, Reed worked at the Gainsborough–Gaumont-British studio in Shepherd's Bush. After *Night Train to Munich* (1940), a comedy thriller in the mould of Hitchcock's *The Lady Vanishes* (1938), and *The Girl in the News* (1941), he made two bigger-budget films financed by Twentieth Century Fox: *Kipps* (1941) and *The Young Mr Pitt* (1942). In 1940 he met and fell in love with Dorothy Isobel Cox (1906–1964) [*see* Wynyard, Diana], who plays Helen Walsingham in *Kipps*, and on 3 February 1943 they married. Reed had joined the army kinematograph unit in 1942 and he made a forty-minute film, *The New Lot* (1942), with a script by Eric Ambler and Peter Ustinov, that showed how a bunch of raw recruits were turned into an effective fighting force. This led to *The Way Ahead* (1944), a full-length feature film on the same subject. Reed was then chosen to work with the American writer and director Garson Kanin on a newsreel compilation film that would chart the progress of the allied armies from D-day to final victory. General Eisenhower had ensured that hundreds of cameramen accompanied the invading troops and Reed and Kanin were presented with about 10 million feet of film to edit. The resulting film, *The True Glory* (1945), was praised for capturing the team work and everyday heroism of the allied forces, and it won a special Academy award for distinctive achievement in documentary production.

Finest films Although Reed was never affiliated to the British documentary-film movement his films, such as *Bank Holiday*, *The Stars Look Down*, *The Way Ahead*, and *The True Glory*, were seen as important landmarks in British realist cinema. His first post-war film, *Odd Man Out* (1947), a gloomy, expressionist drama about the last twenty-four hours of a wounded IRA gunman, was very different. Andrew Sarris argues that, with 'its aura of the past, of lost causes and romantic love and the mystic intensity of death', *Odd Man Out* marked a 'peak of romantic intensity which Reed was never to scale again' (Sarris, 'First of the realists', 32). After the film was released Reed severed his links with the Rank Organisation, which had financed *The Way Ahead* and *Odd Man Out*, and joined Alexander Korda's London Films. In July 1947 Reed and Diana Wynyard divorced, and in January 1948 he married Penelope Pelissier, *née* Dudley Ward (1918–1982), an actress who had appeared briefly in *The Way Ahead* and had also starred in two films directed by Anthony Asquith, *The Demi-Paradise* (1943) and *English without Tears* (1944). Reed and his second wife had a son, Max.

Korda introduced Reed to Graham Greene and persuaded them to collaborate on turning Greene's short story *The Basement Room* into a feature film. Retitled *The Fallen Idol* (1948), this well-observed story of a boy's relationship with his parents' butler, who he mistakenly thinks has murdered his ferocious wife, seemed to mark Reed's return to the realist mainstream of British cinemas. But Greene and Reed's next collaboration, *The Third Man* (1949), was radically different—a European thriller with an international cast but a British viewpoint and a distinctive directorial style. Reed resisted pressure—particularly from David Selznick, one of his executive producers—to make changes which would have made the film more conventional: he held out against a happy ending, jettisoned an orchestral score in favour of Anton Karas's haunting zither music, persuaded Orson Welles to appear as Harry Lime, allowed Robert *Krasker full rein for his experimental cinematography, and drew wonderfully resonant performances from his cast. *The Third Man* is Reed's one undisputed masterpiece. Lindsay Anderson asserts that 'it comes nearest in all Reed's work to a kind of personal poetry of disillusion, estrangement and loss' (Anderson). But it was a personal poetry which never again found full expression, and Reed was unable to live up to the expectations that the film aroused. *Outcast of the Islands* (1952), for example, was seen as a worthy attempt to adapt Joseph Conrad's difficult novel, but was none the less a disappointment. Subsequent attempts to rehabilitate the film have foundered on the unsympathetic nature of the protagonist (despite a fine performance by Trevor Howard) and the inauthenticity of white actors playing native tribesmen. The film met with a disappointing critical reception. Nevertheless, Reed's stature was such that a knighthood was bestowed on him in 1952.

Reed's next film, *The Man Between* (1954) was set in the divided city of Berlin. Inevitably it was compared with *The Third Man* (particularly in view of the title change from *Susanne in Berlin*) and the comparisons were uniformly unfavourable. In contrast to the fruitful collaboration Reed had enjoyed with Graham Greene, he had found it difficult to work with Harry Kurnitz, the Hollywood writer brought in to adapt the novel on which the script was based, and the film began production with problems still unresolved. This put budgetary pressures on Reed that strained his normally amicable relations with Korda. The resulting film is no masterpiece, but there are typical Reed motifs such as 'the villain's snow-encrusted car, which like some frightening primordial monster, stalks the unsuspecting Suzanne and finally swallows her up' (Moss, 209). The film is also a visually striking evocation of divided, war-battered Berlin.

Later films Reed's last film for Korda, *A Kid for Two Farthings* (1955), has an improbably Mayfair-accented six-year-old causing miracles to occur in a cosy Jewish East End community. It is enjoyably bizarre but not what one would expect from a major director, and it indicates Reed's difficulty in finding a sufficiently rich vein to work in the British film industry—a difficulty shared by other significant directors such as Michael Powell. Reed had visited Hollywood in 1937 and would have been welcomed there any time after 1940, when *The Stars Look Down* established his reputation as a talented and original director. He had chosen to stay in England but by the mid-1950s the monolithic Hollywood studio system was breaking up and increasing numbers of American films were being made on location in Europe. Reed accepted an offer from the independent production company Hill-Hecht-Lancaster to make *Trapeze*, a big-budget film to be shot in the Cirque d'Hiver in Paris. It was a good subject for Reed, who was fascinated by animals, loved actors and backstage life, and had a talent for inventive composition (the film was to be shot in colour using the new Cinemascope process) and *Trapeze* (1956) emerged as a visually stunning and highly enjoyable film. Though it did little for Reed's critical reputation it was hugely popular with audiences and opened the door to a successful career in Hollywood.

Several projects were mooted for Reed's next project, but unfortunately the one he chose, *The Key* (1958)—an intriguing Second World War melodrama, made in England but with American money and an international cast—confused both critics and audiences and fared badly. He turned back to Graham Greene for *Our Man in Havana* (1960), but even here, with a strong cast, a good script, and an interesting setting (the film was shot in Cuba shortly after Fidel Castro's revolution) Reed seemed unable to recapture the magic of his earlier films.

In Britain, Reed felt out of tune with the new wave of working-class realist films made by young directors such as Tony Richardson, Karel Reisz, John Schlesinger, and Lindsay Anderson. He ostentatiously ignored Anderson when introduced to him and complained to the press that cinemagoers didn't want 'to look for an hour or two at a kitchen sink, a one-set movie, the greasy dishes and the mental and moral miasma of certain elements in society' (Murphy, 26). This was regrettable: one of Richardson's few ventures into film criticism had been in defence of Reed ('The metteur en scène', *Sight and Sound*, Oct–Dec 1954, 62–6), and Reed might have served as a mentor to this new generation, just as Jean Renoir had to the directors of the French *nouvelle vague*. Instead, Reed took up a lucrative offer to direct a re-make of *The Mutiny on the Bounty* for MGM. After a protracted struggle with the egotistical demands of Marlon Brando, he resigned from the production. His next film, *The Running Man* (1963), though it starred Laurence Harvey from *Room at the Top* (1958) and Alan Bates from *A Kind of Loving* (1962), could not have been more different from the 'kitchen-sink' films Reed despised. It was made in colour, shot mainly in Spain, and was a dark, cynical comedy. It was not well received, and although he was given another stab at a Hollywood epic— Twentieth Century Fox's *The Agony and the Ecstasy* (1965) with Charlton Heston as Michelangelo—by the late 1960s Reed's career seemed to be drawing to a close. It was therefore against the wishes of John Woolf's American backers, Columbia, that he asked Reed to undertake the daunting task of bringing Lionel Bart's musical *Oliver!* to the screen. Woolf had launched the British new wave with *Room at the Top*, but he had also collaborated with Korda in the 1950s and had considerable respect for Reed's talents. His faith was fully justified. *Oliver!* (1968) was a box office success and it drew praise from the New York film critic Pauline Kael, who applauded 'the commercial heroism of a director who can steer a huge production and keep his sanity and perspective and decent human feelings as beautifully

intact as they are in *Oliver!*' (Kael, 204). Reed won the Academy award for best director. He could have retired at this point, as he had made enough money not to have to work again. But films were his life, and his Oscar success gave him virtual *carte blanche* to make what he liked. He proceeded to squander his blank cheque on an extravagant, heavy-handed comedy, *The Last Warrior* (1969), that was considered so bad by its backers, Warner Brothers, that it was given only a limited release despite its big budget, and it was universally condemned by film critics. Reed failed to redeem himself with the irritatingly flimsy *Follow me* (1970). These were to be his last films. He died at his home, 213 King's Road, Chelsea, on 25 April 1976, and was buried at Gunnersbury cemetery.

Posthumous reputation Reed never suffered the critical neglect endured by his contemporaries Michael Powell and Emeric Pressburger. In 1974 Michael Voigt published the long appreciative essay 'Sir Carol Reed: pictures of innocence', and in 1978 Brenda Davies organized a retrospective of Reed's films at the National Film Theatre and also edited a collection of essays and interviews for the British Film Institute. A scholarly American monograph on Reed and his films and a painstaking biography followed. Despite this, Reed has failed to maintain his status as an internationally significant director. In an otherwise appreciative essay on Reed, Lindsay Anderson, another director whose career as a film director ended disappointingly, posed the question: 'Can you be an artist of distinction if you don't care what you make films about, or never manage to find your subject, or perhaps never find yourself?' (Anderson). When asked what he thought of the auteur theory, Reed responded: 'I don't think a director should stand out. The audience should be unconscious that the damned thing's been directed at all', and he argued that 'a director who knows how to put a film together' does not 'need to impose his ideas on the world' (Davis, 10, 12). This meticulous neutrality allowed him to make films on a range of controversial topics—the plight of Britain's coalminers in the inter-war years, a compassionate portrait of an IRA gunman, dealings in contaminated penicillin in war-ravaged Vienna, a white man's sexual passion for a native girl, a film set in Berlin that eschews cold-war rhetoric—without moralizing or pushing through a narrowly personal point of view. The fact that millions of people might have enjoyed *The Way Ahead* (one of the most resonant and influential British films of the Second World War), *The Third Man*, *Trapeze*, and *Oliver!* without realizing that they were directed by the same person does not make them any less significant as films.

Reed's career ended disappointingly, but perhaps it is appropriate to recall his refusal to impose happy endings on his films, insisting that 'A picture should end as it has to. I don't think anything in life ends right' (Davis, 16). Carol Reed, a shy and private man, is less accessible as an object of study than ebullient self-promoters such as Michael Powell and Alfred Hitchcock, but as a craftsman who has left a significant legacy of films he commands considerable respect.　　　　ROBERT MURPHY

Sources P. Kael, *Going steady* (1970) • R. Murphy, *Sixties British cinema* (1992) • N. Wapshott, *The man between: a biography of Carol Reed* (1990) • R. F. Moss, *The films of Carol Reed* (1987) • B. Davis, ed., *Carol Reed* (1978) • M. Voigt, 'Pictures of innocence: Sir Carol Reed', *Focus on Film*, 17 (spring 1974), 17–38 • G. D. Philips, 'Carol Reed', *Films in Review*, 30/4 (July–Aug 1994), 389–95 • M. Fawcett, 'Sir Carol Reed', *Films in Review*, 10/3 (March 1959), 134–41 • A. Sarris, 'First of the realists', *Films and Filming* (Sept 1957) • A. Sarris, 'The stylist goes to Hollywood', *Films and Filming* (Oct 1957), 9, 10, 32 • L. Anderson, review of N. Wapshott, *The man between*, *Independent on Sunday* (30 Sept 1990) • *CGPLA Eng. & Wales* (1976)
Archives BFI, collection, papers and cuttings | SOUND BL NSA, performance recording
Likenesses A. Buckley, photograph, 1938, NPG [*see illus.*] • photographs, 1943–68, Hult. Arch.
Wealth at death £10,113: probate, 4 June 1976, *CGPLA Eng. & Wales*

Reed, Sir Charles (1819–1881), educationist, third son in the family of five sons and two daughters of Andrew *Reed, the philanthropist, and his wife, Eliza Holmes, was born at a farmhouse near Sonning in Berkshire on 20 June 1819, and was educated, successively, at Madras House, Hackney, under John Allen (1771–1839); at the Hackney grammar school; and at Silcoates School, near Wakefield in Yorkshire. As a youth he was admitted a professed member of his father's Congregationalist church, and for a time had thoughts of becoming a minister of the gospel. After attending lectures at University College, London, he was apprenticed in December 1836 to a firm of woollen manufacturers at Leeds. In 1839, with his friend Thomas Edward Plint, he started and edited a magazine called the *Leeds Repository*. He was active in civic institutions, being secretary of the Leeds Sunday School Union and the Leeds Literary Institution. A Liberal and free-trader, he supported Lord Morpeth's candidature for the West Riding in 1841. He took a voluntaryist position in educational controversies, acting as secretary to a London committee opposing Sir James Graham's Factory Education Bill in 1843. On 22 May 1844 he married Margaret (d. 1891), youngest daughter of Edward *Baines (1774–1848), MP for Leeds.

In 1842, in conjunction with W. Tyler, Reed founded at Bolt Court, Fleet Street, London, the firm of Tyler and Reed, printers. In 1849 he left Tyler to continue the same trade with Benjamin Pardon of Hatton Garden. The firm afterwards moved to Lovell's Court, Paternoster Row. In 1861, when Reed's friend Alderman Robert Besley retired from the typefounding business, he took advantage of the new opening and set up a typefounding factory in Fann Street, City of London. The enterprise proved highly successful and, as Sir Charles Reed & Sons Ltd, became a flourishing concern.

In London, Reed continued his early interest in popular education. In 1844 he joined the Sunday School Union in London, and subsequently inspected numerous schools connected with the association in large towns. In 1851 he won a first prize offered by the London union for an essay on *The Infant Class in the Sunday School*, and he published many new-year addresses on the education of the poor.

Those called respectively *Diamonds in the Dust* (1866) and *The Teacher's Keys* (1872) had a wide circulation. He supported the foundation, by the Congregational board of education, of Homerton College for training teachers. In politics, he was on the committee of the Protestant Dissenting Deputies from 1847, and supported the movement for disestablishing the Anglican church. During the 1847 general election he organized the publication of a weekly paper, the *Nonconformist Elector*.

In 1855 Reed became a member of the common council for the ward of Farringdon Within, and actively aided in developing the Guildhall Library, under the Public Libraries Act, and the City of London School. He also interested himself in the preservation of Bunhill Fields burial-ground and in the administration of the Irish Society's estates in Ulster, which he visited officially. He was one of George Peabody's British executors in 1869, and helped to carry out his philanthropic designs.

On 17 November 1868 Reed was returned to parliament as the first of two representatives for Hackney, after a contest between five Liberal candidates. By then his earlier radicalism had mellowed. He made his maiden speech on introducing a bill for exempting Sunday and ragged schools from poor rates, a measure which was carried into law. In 1870 he took a prominent part in the debates on the Elementary Education Bill, his stand in support of the bill marking a break from his earlier position. He advocated Bible instruction without sectarian teaching. On 6 February 1874 he was re-elected for Hackney, but, through a technical informality on the part of the returning officer, he was unseated on petition (14 April 1874), and, declining to be nominated again, suggested the selection of Henry Fawcett as candidate in his stead.

Out of parliament, Reed concentrated on his work for the London school board. He was elected member for Hackney to the first board on 27 November 1870, and in December he became the vice-chairman, and chairman of the works committee. On 10 December 1873 he was chosen chairman of the board in succession to Lord Lawrence, and held the position until his death. He worked to uphold the religious compromise which the 1870 act embodied, and defended Bible teaching in schools. As chairman he delivered and published seven valuable annual statements. Latterly he resisted pressure to abolish fees.

Reed visited America in 1873, and on his return was created a doctor of laws by Yale University. On 21 February 1874 he was knighted on Gladstone's recommendation by the queen at Windsor Castle. Throughout life he had antiquarian interests. In 1849 he was elected a fellow of the Society of Antiquaries, and he assiduously collected keys and autograph letters. In 1861 he exposed as forgeries a collection of 'pilgrims' signs' said to have been found by workmen when excavating Shadwell Dock. In 1861 he assisted H. T. Riley in translating the *Liber albus*, the *White Book of the City of London*, published in the Rolls Series. For many years he contributed to *Notes and Queries*. He was author, with his brother Andrew, of *Memoirs* of the life of their father (1863), and he also took an active part in the direction of the Religious Tract, the British and Foreign Bible, and the London Missionary societies.

Reed entered parliament again when he was elected Liberal MP for St Ives (5 April 1880). He voted against his party in the Bradlaugh debates, deploring Bradlaugh's atheism. Worn down by contention on the London school board and the strain of all-night sittings during the Irish party's campaign of obstruction, he died at his home Earlsmead, Page Green, Tottenham, Middlesex, on 25 March 1881, and was buried in Abney Park cemetery.

Reed had four sons and four daughters, including Talbot Baines *Reed and Eliot Pye Smith Reed who became chairman of Sir Charles Reed & Sons Ltd in 1890. The eldest son, **Charles Edward Baines Reed** (1845–1884), secretary of the British and Foreign Bible Society, was born in New Broad Street, City of London, on 24 July 1845. He entered the City of London School in 1857, and proceeded to Trinity College, Cambridge, in 1864, where he gained a foundation scholarship, and graduated BA in 1868 in the first class of the classical tripos, and MA in 1871. After further theological study at New College, London, he became minister of Common Close Congregational Chapel at Warminster, Wiltshire, in 1871. In 1874 he was appointed one of the secretaries of the British and Foreign Bible Society and proved to be admirably fitted for that post. He wrote *The Companions of Our Lord* (1872) and a memoir of his father in 1883. He was accidentally killed while visiting Switzerland by a fall over a precipice near the Morteratsch glacier at Pontresina on 29 July 1884. He left a widow, Alice Elizabeth Reed, and at least one son.

G. C. BOASE, *rev.* M. C. CURTHOYS

Sources C. E. B. Reed, *Memoir of Sir Charles Reed* (1883) · [G. J. Stevenson], *Sir Charles Reed, chairman of the London School Board: a life sketch* (1884) · *Daily News* (26 March 1881), 5 · *ILN* (20 Dec 1873), 609–10 · *ILN* (2 April 1881), 329 · *The Graphic* (14 Feb 1874), 146, 148 · *Biograph and Review*, 4 (1880), 288–92 · J. P. Parry, *Democracy and religion* (1986) · Boase, *Mod. Eng. biog.* [Charles Edward Baines Reed] · Venn, *Alum. Cant.* [Charles Edward Baines Reed] · *Congregational Year Book* (1885), 219–21 [Charles Edward Baines Reed] · *CGPLA Eng. & Wales* (1881) · *CGPLA Eng. & Wales* (1884) [Charles Edward Baines Reed]

Likenesses portrait, 1876; at Hackney Town Hall in 1883 · O. Ford, marble bust, after 1881 · Lock & Whitfield, woodburytype photograph, NPG; repro. in T. Cooper, *Men of mark: a gallery of contemporary portraits* (1880) · London Stereoscopic Co., carte-de-visite, NPG · G. J. Stodart, stipple, NPG; repro. in Reed, *Memoir*, frontispiece · chromolithograph, NPG · photograph, repro. in Stevenson, *Sir Charles Reed: a life sketch* (c.1880) · wood-engraving, NPG; repro. in *ILN* (2 April 1881), 329 · wood-engraving, NPG; repro. in *ILN* (20 Dec 1873)

Wealth at death under £70,000: resworn probate, Aug 1881, *CGPLA Eng. & Wales* · £13,592 11s. 3d.—Charles Edward Baines Reed: probate, 19 Aug 1884, *CGPLA Eng. & Wales*

Reed, Charles Edward Baines (1845–1884). *See under* Reed, Sir Charles (1819–1881).

Reed, Sir Edward James (1830–1906), naval architect, was born at Sheerness on 20 September 1830, the son of John Reed. He became an apprentice at Sheerness Dockyard

Sir Edward James Reed (1830–1906), by London Stereoscopic Co.

where his outstanding ability led to selection in 1849 for the Central School of Mathematics and Naval Architecture at Portsmouth, which had opened the previous year with Dr Joseph Wooley as principal. There were nine students in his year, several of whom were to become his assistants in later years. In 1851 he married Rosetta Barnaby, sister of Nathaniel *Barnaby, a fellow student, and eldest daughter of Nathaniel Barnaby of Sheerness. Reed graduated in 1852, and was appointed a supernumerary draughtsman, working in the mould loft at Sheerness. Although this was a normal first appointment Reed found the work frustrating and lacking in responsibility, and even his first book of poetry, *Corona and other Poems* (1857), failed to satisfy his creative instincts. It is said that he regarded compulsory service in the militia as the last straw.

In 1853 Reed accepted the post of editor of the *Mechanic's Magazine*, an influential journal widely read among the rising number of engineers and technicians. The following year he offered the Admiralty a design for an armoured frigate but the concept was ahead of its time and, engaged in war with Russia, the Admiralty saw no requirement for such a ship. At the end of 1859 Scott Russell called a meeting which led to the formation of the Institution of Naval Architects, and at the first meeting in January 1860 Reed was appointed secretary and editor of the *Transactions*.

Early responsibility In 1861 Reed sent a design to the Admiralty for an armoured corvette, acknowledging the help of his brother-in-law. In the following year he proposed a scheme for converting wooden sloops into armoured ships and was invited to develop these ideas within the Admiralty. He also produced, with assistance from Barnaby, designs for larger ships for which he was later to receive an *ex gratia* payment of £5000 from the Admiralty. When Isaac Watts retired in 1863 the first lord (the duke of Somerset) invited Reed to become the chief constructor. This appointment was criticized in parliament on the grounds of Reed's lack of experience but he defended himself vigorously, and to such an extent that he was forced to apologize.

As more and more powerful guns became available, ships required thicker protective armour, but the weight of armour meant that the area to be protected had to be reduced. Reed tackled this in two ways: he concentrated the armour in a shallow waterline belt with a short armoured battery amidships; and he made his ships relatively shorter. The length of the ship was determined by the number of guns carried and his short ship was possible only because fewer of the new, bigger guns were required. There was a considerable power penalty for the shorter ship but the overall cost was less. Particularly after the battle of Lissa (1866) there was emphasis on end-on attack, including ramming. Reed developed a number of features such as movable bulwarks and recessed gunports, which were not entirely satisfactory, to enable guns in his central battery to fire parallel to the keel. In the *Bellerophon*, and other earlier ships, a lightly protected battery was arranged in the bow. Reed and Barnaby saved further weight in the *Bellerophon* by a lighter structure, better aligned to the loading. This system, known as the 'bracket frame' system, was also easier to build and had been little changed in principle when the long reign of the battleship ended in the Second World War.

In 1865 Reed was given permission to design the *Fatikh* for Turkey, later sold to Germany, which was to influence the double deck height battery in the British *Audacious* class, designed with a shallow draught for overseas service. This class introduced further weight-saving measures, mainly ones concerned with reducing the thickness of the structure away from amidships. Reed also intended to take account of William Froude's early work on rolling in waves by reducing the metacentric height. It appears that his reduction in stability was too much and the class required a considerable amount of ballast. Once this was installed they proved successful and well-liked ships.

Revolution in ship design Under Reed there was a complete revolution in the way ships were designed; rules of thumb gave way to calculations based on theoretically sound principles and careful experiment. He encouraged work on stability by Barnes and others of his staff; with the assistance of White, Reed himself developed a method of calculating loading on a ship at sea which led to a rational structural design method. Both of these advances depended on the accurate estimate of the weights of a new ship. Having adopted Froude's early work on rolling,

he encouraged Froude's later work on the use of models to improve hull forms and to estimate power requirements. It was Reed who persuaded the Admiralty to pay for Froude to build the first ship model test tank at Torquay which began to operate in 1872.

Reed was always interested in technical education, and strongly supported the establishment of the Royal School of Naval Architecture and Marine Engineering at South Kensington in 1864. This school was transferred to the Royal Naval College, Greenwich, in 1872 and moved to University College, London, in 1967. He contributed to the work of the school and helped to progress the careers of its graduates. From 1872 to 1875 he was proprietor and editor of *Naval Science*, an influential technical quarterly, and contributed many articles himself.

Outstanding team leader This era shows Reed at his best, initiating work himself, encouraging his staff—he was far more willing to give credit to his assistants than most men of his age—and also adopting and supporting work from outside. Less obvious, these new procedures marked the change from the individual designer to the leader of a team. Reed owed much to the wise guidance of the controller, Spencer Robinson.

Reed developed the centre battery ship with full sailing rig in a number of successful designs such as that of the *Hercules* and the *Sultan*. In 1866 the government of the colony of Victoria asked the Admiralty to design a low freeboard coastal defence turret ship based on Ericsson's *Monitor*. Though Reed was impressed by many features of Ericsson's ship he thought the low freeboard unsafe, and in developing the design of *Cerberus* he added an armoured breastwork which raised the turrets and provided protected access and ventilation for the low main hull. The remains of *Cerberus* may be seen today in the outskirts of Melbourne. He designed similar ships for India and for the Royal Navy, culminating in 1869 with the design of the much larger *Devastation* for the Royal Navy. She was the first battleship for the navy designed without sailing rig and her style may be seen as the prototype for all later battleships. Her two main turrets were mounted high up on the breastwork at each end, and this gave them wide arcs of fire. Her sister, *Thunderer*, introduced hydraulic loading for her 12 inch muzzle loaders. The low freeboard of the main hull made these vessels poor seaboats, and they lost speed rapidly in a head sea.

Quarrels and controversies In the meantime Captain Coles, the designer of the turret gun mounting, was agitating for a low-freeboard, fully-rigged sailing battleship. Reed and many seamen felt that the combination of sails and low freeboard was unsafe and after a searching inquiry in 1865 the Admiralty decided to build a rigged turret ship but with a considerable freeboard. Reed designed the *Monarch* on this basis but though she had a long career and was liked in the service, Reed felt that she offered no advantage over a centre battery ship. Coles, too, was unhappy and eventually persuaded the first lord (Somerset) to agree to a ship of his concept. The design work was carried out by Lairds but the design revolution described above had not reached Birkenhead and the company greatly underestimated the weight of such a ship while its estimate of the height of the centre of gravity was an inaccurate guess.

Reed and Spencer Robinson gave specific warnings of the dangers of the proposed ship but the first lord (Packington) ordered the *Captain* to be built by Lairds who were entirely responsible for her. Technical evidence of serious problems accumulated during her building and she completed grossly overweight, floating 22 inches deeper than intended; this further reduced her already inadequate freeboard to 6 feet 7 inches. She performed well on her first two voyages but prior to the third an inclining experiment was carried out to measure her stability. It was found to be perfectly adequate for small angles of heel but disappeared at larger angles. The theory of large angle stability was known from Attwood's work in the late eighteenth century but the solution of the equations was too difficult until one of Reed's assistants, Barnes, developed a practical method in the late 1860s, the *Captain* being only the second ship to which it was applied.

Unfortunately the *Captain* had sailed on her third voyage before Barnes completed his calculations on the vessel, which showed her to be unsafe at over 20 degrees heel. This result was confirmed when she capsized on 6 September 1870 with the loss of nearly 500 men, including Coles. By this time Reed had already resigned, tired of quarrels with ministers over *Captain* and other technical issues, though the prolonged argument over his salary in 1869–70 may have contributed to his decision. He joined Whitworth briefly but in 1871 he became chairman of Earle's shipyard in Hull while at the same time launching his own naval architecture consultancy in London.

Later years Reed designed ships for other countries, including Germany, Brazil, and Chile. One of these, a turret ship generally similar to the *Monarch*, was purchased for the Royal Navy as the *Neptune*. Though these ships were reasonably successful they lacked the originality of his earlier work, confirming that Reed was a brilliant team leader, working best with guidance from above and support from his staff. His last major design was for two Chilean battleships which were bought for the Royal Navy as the *Swiftsure* and the *Triumph*. His paper on their design to the Institution of Naval Architects drew strong criticism: they were seen as a mere copy of White's big cruisers.

Reed wrote clearly and both his technical papers and his more popular works were easily understood. His most important technical works were his Royal Society paper on structural design in 1866 and that on stability of low freeboard sailing ships to the Institution of Naval Architects in 1868. *Our Ironclad Ships* (1869) was a more popular, though technically correct, justification of his design work. *Shipbuilding in Iron and Steel* was a very readable textbook on the subject. There were other books and papers on warships, two on travels in Russia and Japan, a novel, and a second book of poems. He wrote frequent letters to *The Times* and various journals on a range of topics, the majority of these being criticisms of Admiralty design policy. In particular he advocated armour belts from end to end, seeing subdivision as inadequate protection even though some of the last designs while he was chief constructor incorporated this feature.

As a result of one such campaign of criticism a well qualified committee was set up in 1878 to examine the design of the *Inflexible*, their report dismissing Reed's fears. In 1889 he was to criticize White's design for the *Royal Sovereign*. White was permitted to present a very detailed paper to the Institution of Naval Architects and in a very long and heated debate fully justified his work with firm evidence to rebut all Reed's allegations.

Reed unsuccessfully contested Hull in 1873 but was elected MP for Pembroke district in 1874. From 1880 to 1895 and from 1900 to 1906 he represented Cardiff district, serving briefly as a lord of the Treasury in 1886. He was a Liberal until March 1905 when he joined the Liberal Unionists. For many years he was a JP in Glamorgan. He served on several parliamentary committees including the Load Line committee of 1884 and the Manning committee of 1894, both of which made important contributions to merchant ship safety. He was the commissioner for the investigation into the capsize of the *Daphne* on launching with the loss of 124 lives. He advocated the construction of a tubular railway across the bed of the English Channel as an alternative to Sir Edward Watkin's tunnel scheme.

Reed was a strong supporter of the Institution of Naval Architects and was elected to council following his resignation as secretary in 1863; he became vice-president in 1865 and honorary vice-president in 1905, a position in which he served until his death. He presented a number of papers and took an active part in many discussions. Reed was active in other institutions and was a member of council of the Institution of Civil Engineers from 1865 to 1896. He was elected FRS in 1876, created CB in 1868 (advanced to KCB in 1880), and awarded decorations by Russia, Austria, Turkey, and Japan.

A son, Edward Tennyson *Reed, was born in 1860 and later became an artist for *Punch*. In later years his daughter, Emily Sarah, who had a strong mechanical bent, acted as his secretary. She was to persuade Eustace Tennyson-D'Eyncourt to become a naval architect. Reed died at 65 Savoy Court, the Strand, London, on 30 November 1906, and was buried at Putney Vale cemetery.

DAVID K. BROWN

Sources DNB · *Transactions of the Institution of Naval Architects*, 49 (1907) · O. Parkes, *British battleships, 'Warrior' 1860 to 'Vanguard' 1950: a history of design, construction, and armament* [1957] · D. K. Brown, *Warrior to Dreadnought: warship development, 1860–1905* (1997) · *Parl. papers* · Kelly, *Handbk* (1893) · *WWW, 1897–1915* · *WWBMP*, vol. 2 · *CGPLA Eng. & Wales* (1907)
Archives BL, corresp. with W. E. Gladstone, Add. MSS 44494–44515, *passim* · Bodl. Oxf., corresp. with Sir William Harcourt
Likenesses G. Frampton, memorial relief, exh. RA 1917, town hall, Cardiff · Ape [C. Pellegrini], caricature, chromolithograph, NPG; repro. in *VF* (20 March 1875) · London Stereoscopic Co., photograph, NPG [*see illus.*] · W. H. Mote, stipple (after photograph), BM · B. Stone, photograph, NPG · portrait, repro. in *Transactions of the Institution of Naval Architects* · wood-engraving (after photograph by John and Charles Watkins), NPG; repro. in *ILN* (16 Jan 1866)

Wealth at death £19,022 19s. 7d.: resworn probate, 21 Feb 1907, *CGPLA Eng. & Wales*

Reed, Edward Tennyson (1860–1933), cartoonist and caricaturist, was born on 27 March 1860, at Greenwich, London, the only son of the naval architect Sir Edward James *Reed (1830–1906) and his wife, Rosetta, eldest daughter of Nathaniel Barnaby of Sheerness, Kent, and sister of the naval architect Sir Nathaniel Barnaby. He was educated at Harrow School and at the age of twenty had visited Egypt, China, and Japan. As a young man he spent time at the House of Commons sketching politicians in action. In March 1890 he became a permanent member of the staff of *Punch*, having been recommended by his friend and fellow cartoonist Linley Sambourne. He had very little early training as a draughtsman, but he conceived the idea of applying a burlesque of prehistoric life to contemporary events and persons and called the series Prehistoric Peeps. Thus *A Quiet Game of Whist in Early Times* demonstrates the inconvenience caused to card-playing cave dwellers by the presence of the stegosaurus, the triceratops, and the pterodactyl. The drawings, which were executed in a spirit of broad and riotous comedy, became fashionable, and no doubt the fact that the Natural History Museum at South Kensington had not been open long enough for the skeletons of ancient monsters to lose the charm of novelty, greatly added to their appeal. It is certain that scientific lecturers bore witness at the time to their probable verisimilitude, and that schools applied for the use of Reed's pictures as instructional magic-lantern-slides. For many years he used palaeontology, archaeology, and heraldry as the basis of his humour.

In 1891 Reed married Beatrice, daughter of William Bullen of Earlsfield; they had a son and a daughter. He succeeded Harry Furniss in 1894 as the illustrator of *Punch's* parliamentary pages under the title Essence of Parliament, a post which he held for eighteen years. His style was similar to that of his rival Sir Francis Carruthers Gould in the *Westminster Gazette*. He captured the likenesses of politicians with the soft shading of a pencil. He was a popular after-dinner speaker and lecturer, and his cartoons were purchased by politicians. George V visited his exhibition at the Dudley Gallery in Piccadilly and purchased two cartoons. Many of his drawings were published in collections, notably *Mr. Punch's Prehistoric Peeps* (1896), *Mr. Punch's Animal Land* (1898), *Mr. Punch's Book of Arms* (1899), and *The Tablets of Azit-Tigleth-Miphansi the Scribe* (1900), the last-named (as the portentous paronomasia implies) being a mock-historical record of current politics illustrated in the Assyrian monumental manner.

Reed left the staff of *Punch* in 1912 and subsequently drew for *The Bystander*, the *Passing Show*, the *Sunday Times*, *Pall Mall Gazette*, *Sunday Evening Telegraph*, and the *Evening Standard*. He died in London on 12 July 1933 after a long illness. E. V. KNOX, *rev.* JANE NEWTON

Sources personal knowledge (1949) • S. Leslie, ed., *Edward Tennyson Reed, 1860–1933* [1957] • J. A. Hammerton, *Humorists of the pencil* (1905) • D. Wootton, *The illustrators: the British art of illustration, 1780–*1996 (1996) [exhibition catalogue, Chris Beetles Ltd, London] • S. Houfe, *The dictionary of British book illustrators and caricaturists, 1800–1914* (1978) • R. G. G. Price, *A history of Punch* (1957) • M. Bryant and S. Heneage, eds., *Dictionary of British cartoonists and caricaturists, 1730–1980* (1994) • *The Studio* [special issue, *Modern pen drawings: European and American*, ed. C. Holme] (1900–01), 23 • B. Peppin and L. Micklethwaite, *Dictionary of British book illustrators: the twentieth century* (1983) • *Punch*, 185 (1933), 74

Reed [née de Berdt], **Esther** (1746–1780), revolutionary leader in America, was born on 22 October 1746 in London, to Dennys de Berdt (1694–1770), a prosperous merchant, and his wife, Martha, née Symons. The de Berdts were devout Independents descended from Flemish Huguenot exiles. Dennys de Berdt was a successful Anglo-colonial merchant and served as an agent for Massachusetts and Delaware (1766–70), whereupon he aided in the repeal of the Stamp Act (1765), an attempt by parliament to tax internal American trade directly. Esther, known as Hetta or Hettie to family and friends, and her brother, Dennis, grew up in Artillery Court, near the houses of parliament, and spent summers in Enfield, outside London. Although not formally educated, Esther was schooled in the evangelical tradition, with a taste for the sentimental. She attended the theatre at the height of Garrick's celebrity and read 'Hervey's *Mediations*, Watts, Shentone, and Young's *Night Thoughts*' (Reed, 23). Her grandson, William Bradford Reed, described her as 'slight of frame, with light hair, and fair complexion, and an air of sprightly intelligence and refinement' (ibid.).

Esther met Joseph *Reed (1741–1785), a lawyer from Trenton, New Jersey, who studied law in the Middle Temple, London, from 1763 to 1765, while also representing his father's business affairs to the De Berdt firm. Upon his departure and despite her father's disapproval of Reed's dubious financial prospects, Esther and Joseph maintained a five-year correspondence. They were married at St Luke's Church in Kentish Town, London, on 31 May 1770. The couple had originally planned to stay in London, but her father's death seven weeks prior compromised the family's finances. The Reeds, along with Esther's mother, arrived in Trenton in October and then settled in Philadelphia, where Reed's law practice soon flourished. Esther and Joseph had six children: Martha; Joseph (1772–1846); Esther; Theodosia, who died in infancy of smallpox in 1778; Dennis de Berdt; and George Washington (*b.* 1780).

Throughout their marriage the Reeds became increasingly involved in revolutionary politics. Joseph was elected president of Pennsylvania's second provincial congress in 1775 and served as president of the supreme executive council of Pennsylvania (1778–81). Esther was Pennsylvania's 'first lady', a role in which she excelled, according to continental congressman Silas Deane, who described her as 'a Daughter of Liberty, zealously affected in a Good cause', who possessed 'a most elegant figure and countenance' (*Correspondence*, 2.185). While her husband served as an adjutant-general to George Washington in the continental army, Esther took up the patriot cause with great vigour. On 22 July 1775 she wrote from Philadelphia to her brother:

> every heart and every hand almost, is warm and active in the cause: certainly, my dear brother, it is a glorious one. You see every person willing to sacrifice his private interest in this glorious contest. Virtue, honour, unanimity, bravery,—all conspire to carry it on, and sure it has at least a chance to be victorious. I believe it *will*, at last, whatever difficulties and discouragements it may meet with at first. (Reed, 219)

Esther de Berdt Reed played a central role as a wartime organizer and activist. She spearheaded the Daughters of Liberty and became president of the Ladies Association. Her most galvanizing action was her wartime petition, *The Sentiments of an American Woman*, published as a broadside on 10 January 1780. Reed cited biblical and secular leaders—Deborah, Judith, Esther, Joan of Arc, and 'the Elizabeths, the Maries, the Catharines, who have extended the empire of liberty'—as role models, and thereby countered criticism that such civic involvement constituted 'unladylike behavior'. The petition closed with this call: 'Let us not lose a moment; let us be engaged to offer the homage of our gratitude at the altar of military valour … receive with a free hand our offering, the purest which can be presented to your virtue'. Three days after its publication thirty-six women met to implement Reed's plan to present gifts to the soldiers. The group grew to thirty-nine and included prominent Philadelphians Sarah Franklin Bache (daughter of Benjamin Franklin), Julia Stockton Rush, Alice Lee Shippen, and Sally McKean, and garnered the support from Virginia of Martha Walyes Jefferson. Contributions were accepted in any amount and grew to 1645 donations, ranging from that of the marquise de Lafayette, who gave 100 guineas, to an 'African woman', Phillis, perhaps the poet Phillis Wheatley, who contributed 7s. 6d. By 4 July 1780 the women had raised 300,766 paper dollars by canvassing the neighbourhoods door-to-door in an unprecedented campaign. Similar plans were adopted in six other states. Their initial intention was to provide each soldier $2 of supplemental pay, but General Washington rejected this plan, as it underscored the soldiers' poor wages and potentially encouraged squandering funds on drink and gambling. Instead, he suggested that the money be deposited in the national bank. Esther Reed stood firm, and, after an exchange of letters with Washington, a compromise was reached whereby the money was deposited in a special account to purchase linen and other supplies for shirt making. In all, the women made 2200 shirts, with each sewer's name emblazoned on each one.

Unfortunately the project was completed without its original benefactor, for on 18 September 1780 Esther succumbed to dysentery during an epidemic, in Philadelphia, at the age of thirty-three. Sarah Franklin Bache carried the relief work to completion. Esther de Berdt Reed was buried at Philadelphia's Second Presbyterian Church, and in 1868 her remains, along with Joseph Reed's, were moved to Laurel Hill cemetery in Philadelphia.

SUSAN CLAIR IMBARRATO

Sources S. M. Harris, ed., 'Esther De Berdt Reed', *American women writers to 1800* (1996), 255–6 • L. Kerber, *Women of the republic: intellect and ideology in revolutionary America* (1980) • W. B. Reed, *The life of Esther De Berdt* (1853) [repr. 1971] • M. B. Norton, *Liberty's daughters: the revolutionary experience of American women, 1750–1800* (1980) • J. F. Roche, 'Esther De Berdt Reed', *Notable American women 1607–1950: a biographical dictionary*, ed. E. T. James (1971), 3.123–4 • H. M. Ward, 'Reed, Esther De Berdt', *ANB* • 'Joseph Reed', *Appleton's cyclopaedia of American biography*, ed. J. G. Wilson and J. Fiske, 5 (1888), 208–10 • R. J. Allison, ed., *American eras: the revolutionary era, 1754–83*, 2 (1987) • *Correspondence of Silas Deane* (Hartford, CN, 1870), 185 • L. Diamant, ed., *Revolutionary women in the war for American independence: a one-volume revised edition of Elizabeth Ellet's 1848 landmark series* (1998) • M. S. Benson, *Women in eighteenth-century America: a study of opinion and social usage* (1935) • C. E. Claghorn, 'Esther De Berdt Reed', *Women patriots of the American Revolution: a biographical dictionary* (1991), 160–61 • R. B. Moynihan, C. Russet, and L. Crumpacker, *Second to none: a documentary history of American women*, 1 (1993) • C. Zilboorg, *Women's firsts* (1997) • *Pennsylvania Gazette and Weekly Advertiser* (27 Sept 1780)

Archives New York Historical Society, letters, Reed papers, vols. 2–8 • New York Historical Society, subscription lots for Philadelphia women's relief committee, Reed papers, vol. 7 | New York Historical Society, corresp. with J. Reed during engagement, Reed papers, vol. 1

Likenesses C. W. Peale, oils, 1785, priv. coll.

Reed, (Thomas) German (1817–1888), musician and actor, the son of Thomas Reed, a musician, and his wife, Frances German, was born in Bristol on 27 June 1817. At the age of ten he began a career that lasted more than forty years by appearing as a musical performer at the Bath concerts and Bath Theatre. He next went to the Haymarket Theatre, London, to play the piano, sing, and act under the direction of his father, who had become conductor there. After this Reed was also an organist, his father's deputy bandleader at the Garrick Theatre, a teacher, chapel master, music director at the Haymarket, and conductor at the Olympic Theatre and, in 1852, of Priscilla Horton's summer operatic season at Sadler's Wells. He was a member of the Society of British Musicians.

On 24 March 1844 German Reed (he had ceased to use his first name) married Priscilla Horton [**Priscilla Reed** (1818–1895)], a singer and actress, whose fame outshone his. The daughter of Thomas Horton and Barbara Westwater of Perth, she was born in Birmingham on 1 January 1818. When she was ten she played a Gypsy girl in *Guy Mannering* at London's Surrey Theatre, and she made her Covent Garden début as Mealy Moth in *Harlequin Pat and Bat* on 26 December 1830. In 1834 she was a member of the Victoria Theatre company, 'a pretty little person', as Princess Victoria called her, when she played Julia in a musical version of *Guy Mannering* (Rowell, 27). She also appeared as Romeo, as Desdemona, as Oscar in *Gustavus the Third*, and as Kate in Sheridan Knowles's rewritten *The Blind Beggar of Bethnal Green*. By 1837 she had joined W. C. Macready's company at Covent Garden, and took the parts of Mopsa (*The Winter's Tale*), the Boy (*Henry V*), and Lear's Fool, whom Macready reinstated after some 150 years of Nahum Tate's version being standard. In 1838 she sang and flew as Ariel in Macready's restoration of Shakespeare's own version of *The Tempest*, hitherto played in the Dryden–Davenant adaptation. While a member of Benjamin Webster's company at the Haymarket Theatre, Priscilla Horton was a touching Ophelia to Macready's Hamlet, approaching 'very nearly to the wild pathos of the original in one scene, and …

(Thomas) German Reed (1817–1888), by Squires

touching and beautiful in all', according to *The Athenaeum* (21 March 1840, 238). With Macready at Drury Lane, she created the role of Georgina Vesey (8 December 1840) in Bulwer-Lytton's satirical comedy *Money*; in 1842 she sang Acis in Handel's *Acis and Galatea*, and at Easter 1843 created Myrtina/Fortunio, the girl-boy of J. R. Planché's *Fortunio and his Seven Gifted Servants*. Thereafter she performed in Planché's fairy-tale extravaganzas and revues until 1847. Her personality here was cheerful and jaunty, while her voice had developed into an admirable contralto. After her marriage in 1844 she continued to act professionally, and in 1851 she appeared as Hecate in Macready's farewell *Macbeth*.

In 1854 German and Priscilla Reed embarked on a successful provincial tour as an 'entertainment', he playing the piano, she imitating vocalists and their styles. They took their show to London in 1855, first to St Martin's Hall, then, on 4 February 1856 and for seventeen years thereafter, to the Gallery of Illustration, Regent Street. First known as 'Miss P. Horton's Illustrative Gatherings', these performances became known as 'Mr and Mrs German Reed's Entertainment', and the programmes were composed of music and impersonations. Their last move was to St George's Hall in 1874. At the Gallery, German Reed became what the *Illustrated London News* called him in its obituary (7 April 1888): a public benefactor 'in providing a special form of refined amusement, which somehow

proved acceptable to a class of good people not accustomed to frequent the ordinary London Theatres'.

In 1860 the Reeds were joined by John Parry, a former concert singer and entertainer, whose métier was mimicry, and their playbills settled into a format, which continued even after Parry retired in 1869: a musical monologue to piano accompaniment by Parry or his massive, satirical replacement, Corney Grain, preceded and/or followed by a musical piece, later two, often farcical, often a pocket operetta. In these the Reeds and their associates generally played multiple roles, and their authors had to write dialogue covering the absence of an off-stage character or characters who were doing a quick change into someone else. For instance, in F. C. Burnand's *Inquire within*, German Reed played a deaf flute player, a speech-making deputy lieutenant, a naval lover, and a fussy elderly solicitor, while Mrs Reed quadrupled as a Scottish housekeeper, a flirting spinster, a busybody, and the deputy lieutenant's wife. Parry was a stingy baronet and a big boy in a short jacket (*The Era*, 26 July 1868). At the Gallery these plays were called 'illustrations', acts were 'parts', and roles were referred to as 'assumptions', thus ensuring respectability. The accompaniment of piano, harmonium, and at times a harp also emphasized the presumably untheatrical nature of the entertainment.

The Reeds' repertory included, especially in the 1860s and early 1870s, works by some of the most popular comic writers of the day, notably Shirley Brooks (*Our Card Basket*, 1861), William Brough (*A Peculiar Family*, 1865), Tom Robertson (*A Dream in Venice*, 1867), Arthur Sketchley (*Near Relations*, 1871), J. R. Planché (*King Christmas: a Fancy-Full Morality*, 1871), and F. C. Burnand (*Very Catching*, 1872, and *Old China*, 1875, among others). W. S. Gilbert wrote six very amusing pieces for the Reeds, the second of which, *Ages Ago* (22 November 1869), with music by Frederic Clay, was the Gallery of Illustration's longest-running and most often revived production, even more successful than Burnand and Arthur Sullivan's *Cox and Box* (1867). Other musicians included Alfred Cellier and J. L. Molloy, while Reed, proficient in adapting tunes or composing original scores, set many of the Gallery's pieces himself. He also engaged the best scenic artists available, including Grieve, Telbin, and John O'Connor. If Reed's nomenclature attracted the almost rigidly righteous, the excellent quality of cast, text, music, and settings and the careful rehearsals attracted more sophisticated playgoers. The permanent company, beginning in 1869, included the soprano Fanny Holland and the tenor Arthur Cecil (Blunt), both of whom later played on the larger professional stage. Fanny Holland's replacement, Leonora Braham, went on to create leading soprano roles in several Gilbert and Sullivan operas at the Savoy Theatre. Eventually, having married Arthur Law, the author of nineteen pieces for Reed, Miss Holland returned to undertake the sort of roles Priscilla Reed played. Cecil acted in Shakespeare and Pinero, composed the libretto for a Savoy curtain-raiser, and for a time co-managed the Court Theatre with John Clayton.

In 1863 Reed decided to experiment with what he called *opera di camera*, an opera so simply constructed that it could be staged in a drawing-room with only a piano accompaniment. Choosing a much simplified version of *L'elisir d'amore*, with new music by G. A. Macfarren and with Dr Dulcamara feminized to a Gypsy girl, Reed renamed the resulting opera *Jessy Lea*. Neither he nor his wife played in it, and it was not a success. Nor was the comic opera season he mounted four years later at St George's Hall with a large chorus and orchestra and a repertory which included Burnand and Sullivan's *The Contrabandista*, Gay's *The Beggar's Opera*, and William Brough's adaptation of Halévy and Offenbach's *Ba-ta-clan*, retitled *Ching-chow-hi*. Thereafter Reed contented himself with the smaller scope of the Gallery of Illustration, no programme of which, he boasted, had ever failed. The reason, he said, was the fact that the Reeds had always worked for a principle, not only for a profit, and had tried to establish a dramatic entertainment to 'meet the tastes of the most scrupulous' (*The Era*, 3 Aug 1873).

After a fall while hunting, Reed retired from the stage in 1871 and was replaced in comic roles by his son **Alfred German Reed** (1847–1895). Alfred had been apprenticed to an engineering firm, John Pett & Sons of Greenwich, but had begun to play small parts at the Theatre Royal, Manchester. From 1877 to 1895 he managed the 'entertainment' in partnership with Corney Grain, although Mrs Reed continued to act until 1878 or 1879. Under Alfred Reed the tradition of excellent acting was maintained, and he introduced stringed instruments in 1894 to replace the piano and organ. German Reed died on 21 March 1888 at his home, St Croix, Upper East Sheen, Surrey, and was buried in Mortlake cemetery. Priscilla Reed, Alfred Reed, and Corney Grain died within an eight-day period during the 1895 influenza epidemic, she on 18 March at High Elms, the house of her son-in-law Edward Mitchell, at Bexleyheath, Kent, Alfred on 10 March at 13 Fernshaw Road, Chelsea. He was buried in Brompton cemetery, leaving a son, Walter German Reed. Corney Grain died on 16 March. *The Athenaeum* reported (8 June 1895) that Henry Reed, another member of the family, would attempt to continue the German Reed entertainment, and Rutland Barrington, a mainstay of Gilbert and Sullivan opera, opened the next season with a revival of Gilbert's *Happy Arcadia*. Although the new company made the usual autumn tour, it did not draw large audiences. As Barrington put it, the glamour had departed.

JANE W. STEDMAN

Sources *Gilbert before Sullivan: six comic plays by W. S. Gilbert*, ed. J. W. Stedman (Chicago, 1967), 1–51 • D. Williamson, *The German Reeds and Corney Grain: records and reminiscences* (1895) • F. C. Burnand, *Records and reminiscences, personal and general*, 2 (1904), 330–42 • *ILN* (7 April 1888) • 'The last of the Gallery [of] Illustration', *The Era* (3 Aug 1873), 11 • *The Era* (26 July 1868), 12 • *The journal of William Charles Macready*, ed. J. C. Trewin (1967) • *The Athenaeum* (21 March 1840), 238 • 'Occasional notes', *Pall Mall Gazette* (13 March 1895), 2 • G. Rowell, *The Old Vic Theatre: a history* (1993), 27–8, 31 • R. Barrington, *Rutland Barrington by himself* (1908), 102–4 • *Corney Grain: by himself* (1888), chap. 2 • *The Athenaeum* (8 June 1895), 748 • *DNB* • *CGPLA Eng. & Wales* (1895) [Alfred German Reed] • d. cert. [Alfred German Reed]

Likenesses W. S. Gilbert, sketch (Alfred German Reed; as Uncle Cassandre in *Eyes and no eyes*), Morgan L., Gilbert and Sullivan Collection • Squires, photograph, NPG [*see illus.*] • R. Taylor, print (after photograph by J. Watkins), BM, NPG; repro. in *ILN* • engraving (Priscilla Horton Reed), repro. in Stedman, ed., *Gilbert before Sullivan* • engraving (Priscilla Horton Reed), repro. in Williamson, *The German Reeds and Corney Grain* • oils (Priscilla Horton Reed as Ariel), Royal Shakespeare Theatre, Stratford upon Avon • photograph, repro. in Stedman, ed., *Gilbert before Sullivan* • photograph, repro. in Williamson, *The German Reeds and Corney Grain* • photograph (Alfred German Reed), repro. in Stedman, ed., *Gilbert before Sullivan* • photograph (Alfred German Reed), repro. in Williamson, *The German Reeds and Corney Grain* • portrait (Priscilla Horton Reed), repro. in J. R. Planché, *Extravaganzas* (1879), vol. 3 • portrait (Priscilla Horton Reed), repro. in *Cassell's Saturday Journal* (13 July 1894) • portrait (Priscilla Horton Reed; in *Sensation novel*), Morgan L., Gilbert and Sullivan collection • portraits, music covers and posters, Theatre Museum, London • portraits, music covers and posters (Priscilla Horton Reed), Theatre Museum, London • woodcut (after photograph by J. Watkins), Harvard TC

Wealth at death £2000 19s. 5d.: probate, 26 May 1888, *CGPLA Eng. & Wales* • £612 12s. 3d.—Priscilla Horton Reed: probate, 25 April 1895, *CGPLA Eng. & Wales* • £5743 15s. 8d.—Alfred German Reed: probate, 7 May 1895, *CGPLA Eng. & Wales*

Reed, Henry (1914–1986), poet and playwright, was born in Birmingham on 22 February 1914, the elder child and only son of Henry Reed, master bricklayer and foreman at Nocks Brickworks, and his wife, Mary Ann Ball. He was educated at King Edward VI Grammar School, Aston, Birmingham, where he specialized in classics. Since Greek was not taught, he taught himself, and went on to win the Temperley Latin prize and a scholarship to Birmingham University, gaining a first-class degree (1934) and an MA for a thesis on the novels of Thomas Hardy (1936).

Like many other writers of the 1930s, Reed tried teaching and, again like most of them, hated it and left to make his way as a freelance writer and critic. In 1941 he was conscripted into the Royal Army Ordnance Corps, in which he served—'or rather *studied*', as he preferred to put it—until 1942 when, following a serious bout of pneumonia and a prolonged convalescence, he was transferred to the Government Code and Cypher School at Bletchley. At first employed as a cryptanalyst in the Italian section, he was subsequently moved to the Japanese section, where he learned the language and worked as a translator. In the evenings he wrote much of his first radio play, *Moby Dick* (1947), and many of the poems later to be published in *A Map of Verona* (1946).

The most famous of these—indeed, the most famous English poem to emerge from the Second World War—derived from Reed's experience of basic training in the ordnance corps. A brilliant mimic, he would entertain his friends with a comic imitation of a sergeant instructing his recruits. After a few performances, he noticed that the words of the weapon-training instructor, couched in the style of the military manual, fell into certain rhythmic patterns which fascinated him and eventually provided the structure of 'Naming of Parts'. In this and two subsequent 'Lessons of the War', the military voice is wittily counterpointed by the inner voice—more civilized and still civilian—of a listening recruit with his mind on other matters. At approximately the same point in each of the first four stanzas, the recruit's attention wanders from the instructor's lesson in the unnatural art of handling a lethal weapon, back to the natural world: branches, blossom, Edenic life as opposed to death. The dialectical opposition of two voices, two views of a landscape associated with sexual desire, is a strategy refined in two remarkable poems of Reed's middle years: 'The Changeling', a brilliantly condensed (and disguised) autobiography, and 'The Auction Sale', a Forsterian or Hardyesque short story. Both deal with the loss of Eden, for which Reed, an unmarried, unhappy homosexual, would continue to search in vain. He came to associate the Great Good Place with Italy, the setting of some of his later poems, such of his radio plays as *Return to Naples* and *The Streets of Pompeii* (published 1971), and two fine verse plays about another poet whose work he was translating and with whom he identified strongly, Giacomo Leopardi.

In the mid-1950s Reed made a major liberating decision: he abandoned a projected biography of Hardy, which for years had burdened him with guilt like the Ancient Mariner's albatross. That failed quest, perhaps related to the failure of his earlier quest for lasting love, played out a dominant theme of his radio plays: from failure as a biographer, he turned to triumphant success in a radio play about a nervous young biographer, Herbert Reeve, engaged on just such a quest as he had himself abandoned. Reed's hero (whose name owes something to that of Herbert Read, the poet and critic, with whom he was tired of being confused) assembles a mass of conflicting testimony about his author, the novelist Richard Shewin. His witnesses include a waspish brother, his wife, two spinsters of uncertain virtue, and (the finest comic role he was to create for radio) the twelve-tone female composer Hilda Tablet. The success of *A Very Great Man Indeed* (1953) prompted six sequels, the best of them *The Private Life of Hilda Tablet* (1954), in which Reeve is browbeaten into switching the subject of his biography from the dumb dead to the exuberantly vocal living female composer.

The modest income that Reed's work for radio brought him he supplemented with the still more modest rewards of book reviewing and translation. The reviewing was to result in a British Council booklet, *The Novel since 1939* (1946), and his published translations include Ugo Betti's *Three Plays* (1956) and *Crime on Goat Island* (1960), Honoré de Balzac's *Le père Goriot* (1962) and *Eugénie Grandet* (1964), and Natalia Ginzburg's *The Advertisement* (1969). Several of his translations found their way into the theatre, and in the autumn of 1955 there were London premières of no fewer than three.

Reed's greatest imaginative investment, however, was in his poems, but as a perfectionist he could not bring himself to release what he must have recognized would be his last book until it was as good as he could make it— and it never was. Only with the posthumous publication of his *Collected Poems* (1991) would he take his rightful place 'among the English poets'. In his last years he became increasingly incapacitated and reclusive, but devoted friends never ceased to visit him in the London flat he continued to occupy in Upper Montagu Street, Marylebone,

thanks to the generosity of a long-suffering landlady, until, removed to St Charles Hospital, Kensington, he died on 8 December 1986. JON STALLWORTHY, *rev.*

Sources H. Reed, *The lessons of the war* (1970) · H. Reed, *The streets of Pompeii and other plays for radio* (1971) · H. Reed, *Hilda Tablet and others: four pieces for radio* (1971) · *Collected poems: Henry Reed*, ed. J. Stallworthy (1991) · *The Independent* (11 Dec 1986) · *The Times* (9 Dec 1986)

Archives Bodl. Oxf. · U. Birm., corresp. and literary papers · U. Reading | BBC WAC, corresp. with staff of BBC · BL, corresp. with Sir Sydney Cockerell, Add. MS 52745 · U. Durham L., letters to William Plomer · U. Sussex, letter to Kingsley Martin | SOUND BL NSA

Likenesses photograph, U. Birm.

Wealth at death under £40,000: probate, 23 March 1987, *CGPLA Eng. & Wales*

Reed, Isaac (1742–1807), literary editor and book collector, was born on 1 January 1742 at Stewart Street, near the Old Artillery Ground, London, the son of Isaac Reed (*d.* 1757), a baker, and his wife, Margaret, *née* Adamson (*d.* 1788). His father, whose shop was in Fleet Street, was a man of intelligence and inspired his son with a love of reading. Because of his delicate constitution, the young Isaac was kept at home for some years and then sent to a private school at Streatham. In 1757, the year of his father's death, he became an articled clerk to Messrs Perrot and Hodgson, a firm of London solicitors. On the expiry of his articles he assisted a Lincoln's Inn conveyancer named Hoskins, but at the end of a year set up for himself as a conveyancer in chambers at Gray's Inn. He soon moved to Staple's Inn, where he secured a good practice, but he was never satisfied with the profession of law.

From boyhood Reed had studied literature and archaeology, and throughout his life he devoted his leisure to literary research. He collected a large and valuable library in his rooms at Staple's Inn, and there welcomed many colleagues, with whom he freely shared his books and his personal knowledge. He sent notes to Samuel Johnson in 1781 when the latter was preparing his *Lives of the Poets*, and James Boswell declared Reed's extensive and accurate knowledge of English literature and history to be 'wonderful'. John Nichols, whom Reed often accompanied in walks about Enfield, owed much to his suggestions when preparing his collection of William King's works and the supplement to Jonathan Swift's works (vol. 24) in 1776, his *Biographical and Literary Anecdotes of William Bowyer* in 1782, and his *History of Leicestershire* in 1795. Reed corresponded with Horace Walpole and Bishop Thomas Percy, but his most intimate friends were Richard Farmer, master of Emmanuel College, Cambridge, with whom he spent a month each autumn, and George Steevens, whose ill temper he had the unique distinction of never having provoked. He also knew James Bindley, the painters George Romney and William Hayley, Edmund Malone, John Philip Kemble, Henry John Todd, the editor of Milton, and Ralph Heathcote, with whom he visited the Netherlands in 1777. Most of these were members of the Unincreasable Club which met at the Queen's Head, Holborn, and of which Reed was founder and for which he acted as president for many years. He was also a frequent guest at the literary parties of the publisher Charles Dilly, and was elected fellow of the Society of Antiquaries on Richard Gough's recommendation on 12 June 1777.

Reed wrote little in his own name, being of a retiring disposition. His vocation was mainly that of commentator or editor, and almost all his publications were issued anonymously. He would prefer, he wrote in 1778, to stand in the pillory rather than put his name to a book. He kept an annual diary from 1762 to 1804 in which he listed his activities, including visits, dinners, and entertainments (published as *Isaac Reed Diaries, 1762–1804*, ed. Claude E. Jones, 1946). In 1768 he collected the poetical works of Lady Mary Wortley Montagu. He also edited *A complete collection of the Cambridge prize poems, from their institution in 1750 till the present time* (1773) and *The Repository: a Select Collection of Fugitive Pieces of Wit and Humour* (4 vols., 1777–83). In 1778 he printed a few copies of Thomas Middleton's *Witch* for his friends, and edited the sixth volume of Edward Young's *Works*. In 1777 he edited *Historical Memoirs of Dr William Dodd* (which have sometimes been attributed in error to John Duncombe), and Dodd's *Thoughts in Prison*. Reed compiled the biographical notes for both Ralph Dodsley's and George Pearch's collections of poems (published respectively in 1782 and 1783).

Reed's knowledge of literary history, combined with the resources of his extensive library, made his editorial involvement a necessity for many authors. John Nichols wrote of Reed that:

> for the last 30 years, there has scarcely appeared any literary work in this country, of the least consequence, that required minute and extensive research, which had not the advantage of his liberal assistance, as the grateful prefaces of a variety of writers have abundantly testified. (*GM*, 1st ser., 77, 80)

He himself acknowledged Reed's assistance with his *Progresses and Public Processions of Queen Elizabeth* (vols. 1–2, 1788, vol. 3, 1807) and the *History of Leicestershire* (1795). Among the others who expressed appreciation for Reed's advice and contributions were: Thomas Evans, *Old Ballads* (1777); Andrew Kippis, *Biographia Britannica* (1778–93); Richard Gough, *British Topography* (1780); Treadway Nash, editor of Samuel Butler, *Hudibras* (1791); Daniel Lysons, *Environs of London*, vol. 2 (1795); Stephen Jones, *New Biographical Dictionary* (1799); Henry John Todd, *Poetical Works of John Milton* (1801) and *Works of Edmund Spenser* (1805); Thomas Park, editor of Horace Walpole, *Catalogue of Royal and Noble Authors* (1806); and William Beloe, *Anecdotes of Literature and Scarce Books* (6 vols., 1805).

From 1773 to 1780 Reed contributed biographical articles to the *Westminster Magazine* and wrote for the *Gentleman's Magazine* and the *European Magazine*. Of the latter he was proprietor, and though he denied in 1800 that he was the editor, he was *de facto* editor from November 1782 until his death in 1807 (Sherbo, 'Isaac Reed and the European Magazine', 210).

Reed gradually concentrated his attention on the drama. In 1782 he published *Biographia dramatica*, a useful expansion of David Erskine Baker's *Companion to the Playhouse*; it was re-edited by Stephen Jones in 1812. A similar venture, 'Notitia dramatica', a chronicle of English theatrical history from November 1734 to 31 December 1785, remains in manuscript in the British Library (Add. MSS 25390–25392). It was mainly compiled from the *Public Advertiser*, a file of which was lent to the compiler by the publisher Henry Sampson Woodfall. In 1780 Reed prepared a new edition of Robert Dodsley's *Old Plays* in twelve volumes.

Subsequently his friends, Richard Farmer and George Steevens, urged Reed to re-edit the variorum edition of Shakespeare known as Johnson and Steevens's edition, which had originally appeared in 1773. Reed agreed, and the work was published in ten volumes in 1785. Reed had performed his task conscientiously, but added little of importance to the results of his predecessors, and Joseph Ritson sneered at his textual criticism (but not at Reed himself), in *The Quip Modest* (1788). When another issue of the work was called for, Steevens resumed as editor, but corrected all the proof-sheets through the night in Reed's chambers, and benefited largely by Reed's suggestions. This edition was completed in fifteen volumes in 1793. In 1800 Steevens died, leaving Reed his corrected copy of Shakespeare and 200 guineas. In 1803 Reed produced an elaborately revised version, in twenty-one volumes, which is generally known as the first variorum, Reed receiving £300 for his services.

Reed died, after many years of suffering, from a paralytic affection at Staple's Inn on 5 January 1807, and was buried on 13 January at Amwell, where he had a country residence. A slab in the church there bears an unusual rhyming inscription, warning the passer-by that he must die, though he read until his eyes ache. Reed's will, with twelve codicils, was printed in the *Monthly Mirror* (1807, 130). His large library—which was especially rich in English dramatic and poetical literature and in pamphlets—was sold by auction in London in November and December 1807; the sale lasted thirty-nine days, and the 8957 lots brought £4125 13*s*.

SIDNEY LEE, rev. RICHARD W. CLEMENT

Sources *Isaac Reed diaries, 1762–1804*, ed. Claude E. Jones (1946) · A. Sherbo, *Isaac Reed, editorial factotum* (1989) · J. N. [J. Nichols], 'Biographical memoirs of the late Isaac Reed, esq.', *GM*, 1st ser., 77 (1807), 80–82 · J. B. [J. Bindley], 'An account of Isaac Reed', *European Magazine and London Review*, 51 (1807), 83–6 · *Bibliotheca Reediana: a catalogue of the … library of the late Isaac Reed* (1807) [sale catalogue, King and Lochee, London, Nov–Dec 1807] · *Monthly Mirror* (1 Feb 1807), 140–44 [Reed's will] · A. Sherbo, 'Isaac Reed and the European Magazine', *Studies in Bibliography*, 37 (1984), 210–27 · IGI

Archives BL, 'Notitia Dramatica', Add. MSS 25390–25392 · Bodl. Oxf., corresp. · Emmanuel College, Cambridge, diaries of visits to Cambridge · Folger | BL, letters to William Julius Mickle, RP269 [copies] · Yale U., Beinecke L., letters to William Julius Mickle

Likenesses G. Romney, portrait, 1796, BL, Add. MS 32348, fol. 69 · engraving, 1807 (after Romney), BL, Add. MS 38728, fol. 62v; repro. in *Bibliotheca Reediana* (1807) · S. Freeman, stipple (after G. Romney), BM, NPG; repro. in *Monthly Mirror* · C. Knight, stipple (after S. Harding), BM, NPG; repro. in S. Harding, *Shakespeare illustrated* (1793)

Reed, Joseph (1723–1787), playwright and poet, was born the second son to a self-employed rope maker, John Reed, in March 1723 in Stockton-on-Tees, co. Durham, and was baptized at the High Street Presbyterian Church, Stockton, on 9 April 1723. Following an inconsistent and largely informal education, Reed assumed the family business and ran it with vigour and expertise in Stockton as well as in London until his death. On 24 December 1750 Reed married Sarah Watson at Middlesbrough; they had three children. He began his literary career as a driven hobbyist whose self-assessment as an 'amateur' writer never changed, despite the publication of several of his works in a variety of genres and the success of numerous dramatic productions.

Reed's first professional literary work was the poem 'in imitation of the Scottish dialect, on the death of Mr Pope', that appeared in *Gentleman's Magazine* in August 1744. Shortly thereafter his farce *The Superannuated Gallant* appeared in print but failed to result in a live performance. On 6 July 1758 Colley Cibber's son, Theophilus, produced Reed's five-act tragedy *Madrigal and Trulletta* at Covent Garden. The failure of the play, resulting from both poor management and immature writing, led to Reed's publishing the argumentative pamphlet *A Sop in the Pan for a Physical Critick* (1759) in response to Smollett's caustic assessment of the play in the *Critical Review*. Reed soon developed a penchant for publicly rebutting negative criticism and innuendo as well as for expressing his political opinions. For example, he contributed to the *Monitor*, a journal committed to the earl of Bute's administration, and wrote the tract *A rope's end for hempen monopolists, or, A dialogue between a broker, a rope maker, and the ghost of Jonas Hanway* (1786) that criticized those companies or individuals attempting to control the hemp market. Reed also published a defence of David Garrick in the *Morning Chronicle* against the libellous claims of William Kenrick, author of *Love in the Suds*.

In addition to these works, Reed wrote four plays between 1761 and 1776, including his two most notable pieces, the two-act farce *The Register Office* in 1761, and the comic opera *Tom Jones* in 1769. Both of these pieces benefited significantly from his personal relationship with Henry Fielding. In the case of *The Register Office*, produced at Drury Lane on 23 April 1761, the plot of the play derived from Fielding's political effort to organize an employment office for the City of London that would establish a list of people and qualifications which would be available to prospective employers. The farce juxtaposes the inherent value of such a system with the corruptibility of the individual by relating the tale of the master of the office who abuses the system with false advertising and register 'stuffing', but who ultimately pays a price for his deceitful actions. Although the pointed humour of the piece led to Reed having altercations with the censor, the initial production of *The Register Office* piqued the interest of the public, and the play quickly became a standard theatrical afterpiece, as it was 'appended to many a main piece after 1761' (Van Lennep, 4.78).

In addition to the scandalous political content of *The Register Office*, inferences of plagiarism dogged the whole production, and the character of Mrs Snarewell in particular, and clearly contributed to the intrigue surrounding the play. The said Mrs Snarewell appeared to bear many similarities to Mrs Cole of Samuel Foote's piece *The Minor*; indeed, the 'coincidences' were so numerous and profound that Reed actually attached a repudiation of the charge of plagiarism on the grounds that Foote was in possession of the original manuscript of *The Register Office* a full two years before the staging of *The Minor* because Reed had submitted the drama to Foote with the hope of acquiring his support for a production. None the less, when the play was revived at Drury Lane on 12 February 1768, Reed introduced a new character, Mrs Doggerel, in an apparent attempt to ease the association with Foote.

Reed's other celebrated work that profited from a connection with the great Fielding was *Tom Jones*: a comedic, operatic presentation of the novel of the same name that premièred at Covent Garden and enjoyed another thirteen performances. Fielding encouraged Reed to construct the adaptation and was quite vocal in praising Reed's work and celebrating the achievements of the piece.

In addition to these two extraordinarily successful dramas, Reed wrote the following plays: the aforementioned *Madrigal and Trulletta*; *The Imposters, or, A Cure for Credulity*, adapted from Gil Blas and produced on 17 March 1776; and, finally, the tragedy *Dido* (1767) which was posthumously revived as *The Queen of Carthage* on 28 April 1797. Most of these productions were nondescript and in no way approached the successes of *The Register Office* and *Tom Jones*; *Dido* is notable, however, if only for its marking Reed's collaboration with Garrick and the controversy surrounding its revival. *Dido* premièred as a benefit for Charles Holland on 28 March 1767 at Drury Lane and contained a prologue written by Garrick; apparently Reed was disappointed that *Dido* was not revived and, in 1787, he publicly attacked Thomas Linley, the manager of Drury Lane, in *The Retort Courteous, or, A Candid Appeal*, for failing to stage the play. Trouble followed *Dido* for some time as Reed's friend Joseph Ritson prepared it for press in 1792, but it was not printed and distributed until 1808. Unfortunately, no copies of this printing exist as they all perished in a fire at Nichols's printing office before distribution and the work was never reprinted.

While Reed's most notable literary achievements are linked to one of the eighteenth century's greatest authors and are consequently overshadowed by the extraordinary accomplishments of Fielding, Reed wrote well in a variety of genres, for various media, to substantial critical and public acclaim. He died of natural causes on 15 August 1787 at his home in Sun Tavern Fields, London, and was interred at Bunhill Fields. His wife survived him.

L. LYNNETTE ECKERSLEY

Sources W. Van Lennep and others, eds., *The London stage, 1660–1800*, 5 pts in 11 vols. (1960–68) • *GM*, 1st ser., 57 (1787), 745 • Highfill, Burnim & Langhans, *BDA* • R. D. Hume, ed., *The London theatre world, 1660–1800* (1980) • A. London, 'Controlling the text: women in *Tom Jones*', *Critical essays on Henry Fielding*, ed. A. J. Rivero (1998), 131–40 • A. J. Rivero, *The plays of Henry Fielding: a critical study of his dramatic career* (Charlottesville, Virginia, 1989) • A. J. Rivero, ed., *Critical essays on Henry Fielding* (1998) • E. Rothstein, 'Virtues of authority in *Tom Jones*', *Critical essays on Henry Fielding*, ed. A. J. Rivero (1998), 141–

63 · P. Sawyer, 'Garrick, Joseph Reed, and *Dido*', *Restoration and eighteenth-century theatre research*, 6/2 (1967), 44–50 · *IGI* · *DNB*
Archives Folger · Hunt. L.

Reed, Joseph (1741–1785), politician and revolutionary army officer in America, was born on 27 August 1741 in Trenton, New Jersey, the third of eight children of Andrew Reed (*d*. 1769) and the eldest of Andrew's second wife, Theodosia Bowes (*d*. 1753). Andrew was a merchant, forge owner, and local official; Theodosia's father was a prosperous lawyer and landowner. Joseph received his education at Philadelphia Academy (1751–3), at the College of New Jersey (BA, 1757; MA, 1760), as clerk to a prominent lawyer, Richard Stockton (1758–63), and at the Middle Temple (1763–5). In 1765 Reed opened a successful law office in Trenton. He married Esther De Bert (1746–1780) [*see* Reed, Esther], daughter of the colonial agent Dennys De Bert, in London on 31 May 1770. The couple returned to Philadelphia, where Reed was ranked the most prominent lawyer.

Reed began his political career in December 1773 by corresponding with the earl of Dartmouth about possible reconciliation of imperial differences, but to no avail. He served in the first provincial congress of July 1774, presided over the second in early 1775, and chaired the Philadelphia committee of observation of 1774–5. Newly appointed general George Washington, impressed by Reed's activism and ability, appointed him as secretary. Reed served ably, becoming Washington's confidant, until leaving the army in October 1775 to rejoin his family.

Reed's political career continued when Philadelphia elected him to the assembly in January 1776. He opposed the pro-independence group's effort to set aside the colonial assembly and erect a new government for Pennsylvania. Reed by March 1776 admitted the inevitability of independence, but hoped it might be delayed pending further reconciliation efforts. In June 1776 he helped draft Pennsylvania's revised instructions, permitting a vote for independence, to its continental congress delegates.

That same month, at Washington's behest, Reed accepted appointment as adjutant-general of the continental army. Washington often assigned Reed to reconnoitring duties, which he carried out ably. He resigned in January 1777, but served as volunteer aide when General Howe moved against Philadelphia the same year. When elected to congress in January 1778, Reed was immediately appointed to the committee to confer with Washington at Valley Forge and White Plains. Reed also served as volunteer aide at the battle of Monmouth in June 1778.

Reed returned to Pennsylvania politics in September 1778 as assistant attorney-general for the prosecution of disaffected persons. He showed that though he had not approved the Pennsylvania constitution wholeheartedly, he was strongly anti-loyalist. His Presbyterian affiliation also helped him politically. The next month he won election to the supreme executive council of the state as one of the constitutionalists, the dominant party, and in

December became president of the council. Reed was anxious for 'coalition' with those opposed to the Pennsylvania constitution. He advocated gradually abolishing slavery (he held slave house-servants), putting the College of Philadelphia under state control, and providing backing for the large paper-money issues of the state. He showed little sympathy for lower-class action against merchants, and helped to disperse the mob that besieged James Wilson's house in October 1779. In January 1781 he bravely negotiated directly with the Pennsylvania line mutiny-leaders and got them to disperse in exchange for supplies, pay, and ending of enlistments.

The opponents of the constitution gained strength in Philadelphia after 1781, and Reed failed to return to elective office. When the constitutionalists returned to power in 1784 they elected Reed as congress delegate. But now he was severely ill of a paralytic sickness, which appeared in 1783, and died in Philadelphia on 5 March 1785. He was buried on 9 March at the Second Presbyterian Church, Philadelphia.

As a leader Reed succeeded because he was very intelligent, could offer good advice, could grasp what needed to be done in critical situations, and remained resolute in carrying out his plans. He is rightly seen as a 'moderate'—determined to resist British oppression, cautious about independence, opposed to overturning Pennsylvania's colonial government, favouring some radical policies but protecting upper-class interests as well. His sense of political balance made him successful and popular.

B<small>ENJAMIN</small> H. N<small>EWCOMB</small>

Sources J. F. Roche, *Joseph Reed: a moderate in the American Revolution* (1957) · G. Rowe, 'Reed, Joseph', *ANB* · W. B. Reed, *Life and correspondence of Joseph Reed*, 2 vols. (1847) · R. A. Ryerson, *The revolution is now begun: the radical committees of Philadelphia* (1978) · J. T. Flexner, *George Washington in the American Revolution, 1775–1783* (1968) · S. Rosswurm, *Arms, country, and class: the Philadelphia militia and the 'lower sort' during the American revolution, 1775–1783* (1987) · R. L. Brunhouse, *The counter-revolution in Pennsylvania, 1776–1790* (1942) · J. S. Foster, *In pursuit of equal liberty: George Bryan and the revolution in Pennsylvania* (1994) · G. S. Rowe, *Thomas McKean: the shaping of an American republicanism* (1978) · M. E. Flower, *John Dickinson: conservative revolutionary* (1983)
Archives New York Historical Society, MSS | Hist. Soc. Penn., John Cadwalader MSS · Hist. Soc. Penn., Frank M. Etting collection · NYPL, Bancroft MSS
Likenesses C. W. Peale, oils, Independence National Historical Park Collection

Reed, Joseph Charles (1822–1877), watercolour painter, was elected an associate of the New Society of Painters in Water Colours (later the Institute of Painters in Water Colours) in 1860 and a member in 1866. Between 1860 and 1877 he exhibited 186 paintings with the society, many of which sold at high prices. He also exhibited one landscape, *The Llugwy Near its Source*, at the Royal Academy in 1874, and three Welsh scenes at the Society of British Artists in Suffolk Street, London, in 1860. Reed died, unmarried, on 27 October 1877 at his home, 78 Charlotte Street, Fitzroy Square, London.

C<small>AMPBELL</small> D<small>ODGSON</small>, *rev.* A<small>NNE</small> P<small>IMLOTT</small> B<small>AKER</small>

Sources Mallalieu, *Watercolour artists*, vols. 1–2 · Wood, *Vic. painters*, 3rd edn · J. Johnson, ed., *Works exhibited at the Royal Society of*

British Artists, 1824–1893, and the New English Art Club, 1888–1917, 2 vols. (1975) • Graves, *RA exhibitors* • Boase, *Mod. Eng. biog.* • d. cert. • *CGPLA Eng. & Wales* (1877)

Wealth at death under £300: administration, 10 Nov 1877, *CGPLA Eng. & Wales*

Reed, Priscilla (1818–1895). *See under* Reed, (Thomas) German (1817–1888).

Reed, Sir (Herbert) Stanley (1872–1969), newspaper editor and politician, was born in the Ashley district of Bristol on 28 January 1872, the son of William Reed, a grocer of Fremantle Villa, Bristol, and his wife, Amelia Whitney. He was educated privately, became a journalist, and in 1897 joined the staff of the *Times of India* in Bombay, then under the editorship of Thomas Bennett. As a young bachelor Reed entered fully into the lively social life of Bombay at the turn of the century, enjoying sailing, riding, and hunting over the dry rice fields of the surrounding countryside; he was eventually to become an enthusiastic member of the Bombay light horse and to command that volunteer body with the rank of lieutenant-colonel. In 1901 he married Lilian (*d.* 1947), daughter of John Humphrey. They had no children. She fully shared his interest in India, where they spent much of their married life and made many friends.

From the time of his arrival in India, Reed was keen to travel and see as much of the country as possible, and in 1900 he broke new ground for his newspaper with an extensive tour of famine-affected areas. He sent reports of what he had seen in the countryside not only to his own newspaper but also to the *Daily Chronicle*, as its special correspondent. In his book *The India I Knew*, published in 1952, Reed described how he invaded the placid leader writing sanctum of Bennett with this revolutionary suggestion:

> I am doing little or nothing here. Yet the city is ravaged by plague. Poona is deserted. … The Black Death has swept over Sholapur, Surat and Ahmedabad. … The embers of the famine are slowly dying and we have nothing about these great happenings.

That was the start of travels which ranged over the length and breadth of India. Reed accompanied George V and Queen Mary when, as prince and princess of Wales, they toured India in 1905. His dispatches were republished in book form in 1906, with a preface by Sir Walter Lawrence, who abandoned his intention of writing an official record of the royal visit when he found that Reed had virtually done the job for him. During these travels Reed acquired the profound knowledge and sympathetic understanding of the Indian people which were later to stamp his writing as an editor and his speeches as a British parliamentarian.

Reed was appointed editor of the *Times of India* in 1907, and under his control the newspaper became not only one of the two most influential journals in India (the other was *The Statesman*, based in Calcutta on the other side of the subcontinent), but in its general conduct and appearance able to challenge comparison with any English daily. Under the editorship of his predecessor, Lovat Fraser, the status of the *Times of India* had been raised from that of a respectable provincial newspaper into an Indian organ of opinion which Lord Curzon of Kedleston described as the leading paper of Asia. Reed saw that it lacked two things: a sensible selling price and a comprehensive foreign news service. He persuaded its proprietors to drop its selling price from 4*d.* to 1*d.* This led to a fourfold rise in circulation in three days, and Reed went on to play an influential role in the Imperial Press Conference in 1909, where the case for cheap telegraphic rates between the countries of the empire was pressed.

In the First World War, Reed was director of publicity to the government of India, and towards its end he was called upon to counsel on the functions and organization of the central publicity board, of which he became vice-president (1918). This was a belated attempt to improve the understanding of the people of India about a war to which they had been committed four years earlier by Lord Hardinge of Penshurst, then the viceroy. Reed had, in the columns of his newspaper, written very critically about the military disaster in Mesopotamia and was in consequence not universally popular at government headquarters in Simla, but he pressed through a number of reforms aimed at helping the press and some sections of the public to understand how and why the war was being fought. The isolation of the government of India from public opinion at that time, Reed wrote many years later, was almost inconceivable. In 1919 he was created KBE, having been knighted in 1916.

Reed retired from India in 1923, having founded the *Indian Year Book* in the previous year, but continued to write for his paper from London for many years. With Patrick Cadell he wrote *India: the New Phase* (1928), which presented a lucid summary of the Montagu–Chelmsford reforms introduced by the Government of India Act of 1919. He quickly became involved in British politics and in 1929 unsuccessfully contested the Stourbridge constituency in Worcestershire as a conservative; but in 1938 he fought and won a by-election in the Aylesbury division of Buckinghamshire. The first suggestion that he should stand for parliament had come from the Labour Party secretary, Arthur Henderson, when they were both members of the British delegation to the League of Nations in 1924. Reed had certain natural affiliations with the Labour Party but he professed himself unable to swallow nationalization and the capital levy, and it was finally his old Indian guru, Sir Walter Lawrence, who persuaded him to enter the lists on the tory side. He contributed many useful speeches to the House of Commons on Indian questions and on a variety of other topics and, if his independence of mind did not always endear him to the whips, his well studied briefs ensured him an attentive audience. He and Alan Herbert jointly presented a private member's bill to amend the law of defamation; this ended in the appointment of a committee presided over by Lord Porter, which for a variety of reasons could not report until 1948. It was, however, on Indian subjects that Reed spoke most frequently, and his support for Indian independence after the war was tempered with regret that Britain had taken so long to complete a process which, he reminded the house, had begun in 1917. He retired from politics in 1950 and lived on in London until he died in Westminster Hospital on 17 January 1969.   EVAN CHARLTON, *rev.*

Sources *The Times* (18 Jan 1969) · *The Times* (23 Jan 1969) · H. S. Reed, *The India I knew, 1897–1947* (1952) · *CGPLA Eng. & Wales* (1969)
Archives News Int. RO, papers
Likenesses W. Stoneman, two photographs, 1930–47, NPG
Wealth at death £343,264: probate, 24 Feb 1969, *CGPLA Eng. & Wales*

Reed, Talbot Baines (1852–1893), children's writer and printer, was born on 3 April 1852 at St Thomas's Square, Hackney, Middlesex, the third of the five sons of Sir Charles *Reed (1819–1881), Liberal MP for Hackney and chairman of the London school board, and his wife Margaret (*d.* 1891), daughter of Edward *Baines (1774–1848), MP for Leeds. The family was staunchly Liberal in politics and committedly Christian, being devout Congregationalists. Talbot's grandfather Andrew *Reed (1787–1862) was a Congregationalist minister, a hymn writer of distinction, and the founder of orphanages, asylums, and hospitals for incurables. Talbot's eldest brother, Charles Edward Baines *Reed (1845–1884) [*see under* Reed, Sir Charles], was also a Congregationalist minister and secretary of the British and Foreign Bible Society. Talbot, familiarly known as Tib or Tibbie, shared the political and religious beliefs of his family to the full. He attended Priory House School, Clapton, and from 1864 to 1868 the City of London School, where he was remembered as a first-rate sportsman.

Reed grew up to become the best kind of Victorian, a man of high principle, enormous industry, strong social conscience, and a robust sense of humour. His friend John Sime called him 'the very ideal of a chivalrous English gentleman' and a schoolfellow dubbed him 'a true follower of Christ', adding that 'the simple, cheerful Puritanism in which he had been brought up was eminently suited to his simple, manly character and disposition'. In many respects he resembled Thomas Hughes, author of *Tom Brown's Schooldays*, whose successor he became in the formulation of the public-school story.

Reed was a devoted family man. He married on 15 June 1876 Elizabeth Jane, third daughter of Samuel MacCurdy *Greer (1809–1880), the former MP for Londonderry County and later a county court judge. They had four children, two sons and two daughters. Reed always loved Ireland, visiting it regularly and setting two of his later novels (*Sir Ludar* and *Kilgorman*) there. He was also a keen all-round sportsman, both a member of the London rifle brigade and a strong swimmer (he won the Royal Humane Society medal at 17 for having saved a cousin from drowning). He was a selfless worker for others: a deacon of the Congregationalist church and a strong supporter of philanthropic enterprises.

On leaving school, Reed joined the family typefounding business, Sir Charles Reed & Sons Ltd, rising eventually to be managing director. He loved the work and developed such a fascination for the history of typefounding that he

Talbot Baines Reed (1852–1893), by unknown engraver, pubd 1893 (after London Stereoscopic Co.)

devoted ten years to researching what became the standard history of the subject, *History of old English letter foundries with notes historical and bibliographical on the rise and progress of English typography* (1887). He also completed the unfinished *Pentateuch of Printing* by William Blades. He was a fellow of the Society of Antiquaries and a founder member and first secretary of the Bibliographical Society in 1892. He wrote a regular weekly column for the *Leeds Mercury*, a newspaper owned by his cousin Edward Baines.

Reed's enduring legacy lies in his books for boys. Most of these originated as serials written for the *Boy's Own Paper*, the influential magazine popularly known as the *BOP*, which was produced by the Religious Tract Society and aimed to provide wholesome reading for boys. The Reed family was closely involved with the society. Sir Charles was a member from 1864 until his death, and the Revd Charles Edward Reed, Talbot's brother, was a member of the committee set up to launch the *BOP*. Reed, who had already written articles for boys for the magazine *Morning of Life*, was recruited by the *BOP*'s first editor, George Andrew Hutchison. His article 'My First Football Match' by An Old Boy appeared on the front page of the *Boy's Own Paper* when it was launched on 18 January 1879. After he had produced a number of short stories, Hutchison persuaded him to try a full-length serial and Reed wrote *The Adventures of a Three Guinea Watch*, which the *BOP* ran in 1880–81 and which was subsequently issued as a book. Thereafter Reed confined himself to serials, all of which were subsequently issued as books, with the copyrights donated to the Religious Tract Society. There were thirteen in all, with two collections of short stories published posthumously. The 'new Talbot Baines Reed' became a major attraction of the *BOP* and many of the books were to remain continuously in print until the 1950s. Most of them were school stories. The best-loved of them were *The Fifth Form at St Dominic's* (1887), *The Willoughby Captains* (1887), *The Cock-House at Fellsgarth* (1893), and *Tom, Dick and Harry* (1894). He also wrote two historical novels, *Sir Ludar* (1889) and *Kilgorman* (1895), but it was the school stories that earned him the devotion of generations of boy readers. Vivid and readable, they represented a fusion of the twin traditions of the school story, the moralistic established by Dean Farrar in *Eric* and the athletic established by Thomas Hughes in *Tom Brown's Schooldays*. Reed's was a formula that many other writers were to follow. His success can be partly explained by his own eternally boyish spirit. G. A. Hutchison wrote of him: 'He was to the last a real boy among boys—never seemingly so happy as when thinking or planning for the lads or actually in their company' (Hutchison).

However, Reed's workaholic regime undermined his constitution. He contracted consumption and died at the age of forty-one at his home in Hampstead Lane, Highgate, Middlesex, on 28 November 1893. His wife survived him. He was buried next to his father and grandfather at Abney Park cemetery on 2 December 1893. He was widely mourned.   JEFFREY RICHARDS

Sources S. Morison, *Talbot Baines Reed: author, bibliographer, typefounder* (1960) · G. A. Hutchison, 'Introductory sketch', in T. B. Reed, *A book of short stories* (1901), 9–26 · J. Sime, 'In memoriam — Talbot Baines Reed', in T. B. Reed, *Kilgorman: a story of Ireland in 1798* (1906), vii–xxiv · J. Richards, *Happiest days* (1988) · J. Cox, *Take a cold tub sir! the story of the Boy's Own Paper* (1982) · P. Dunae, 'The Boy's Own Paper: origins and editorial policy', *Private Library*, 9 (1976), 123–58 · *DNB* · *The Times* (1 Dec 1893) · F. J. Harvey Darton, *Children's books in England: five centuries of social life* (1932)
Archives Birm. CA, letters
Likenesses engraving, pubd 1893 (after London Stereoscopic Co.), NPG [*see illus.*] · engraving (after photograph), repro. in *Boy's Own Paper* (2 Oct 1880)
Wealth at death £21,326 14*s.* 6*d.*: resworn probate, July 1894, *CGPLA Eng. & Wales* (1893)

Reed, Sir Thomas (1796–1883), army officer, was born on 11 September 1796 in Dublin, son of Thomas Reed of Dublin, and Eliza, daughter of Colonel Sir Francis James Buchanan. Educated at the Royal Military College, Sandhurst, he entered the army as cornet in the 12th light dragoons on 26 August 1813, and became lieutenant on 2 May 1815. He was present with his regiment at Waterloo, when it was commanded by Colonel Frederic Cavendish Ponsonby. On 19 February 1824 he was promoted captain, and on 7 October 1824 obtained a company in the 53rd foot, in which he became major on 15 June 1826. On 11 August 1829 he was promoted to a half pay lieutenant-colonelcy, and on 30 May 1834 he became lieutenant-colonel of the 62nd foot, a position he held for eighteen years. On 8 January 1835 he married Elizabeth Jane, daughter of John Clayton of Enfield Old Park, Middlesex. Reed was made brevet colonel on 23 November 1841, and in 1842 aide-de-camp to the queen. In 1844 he was made a CB.

When the First Anglo-Sikh War broke out Reed's regiment was part of the force under Sir John Hunter Littler which held Ferozepore, and at the battle of Ferozeshahr (22 December 1845) Reed commanded a brigade (including his own regiment) of Littler's division. His brigade was ordered to attack the strongest part of the Sikh entrenchments, where there was a large number of heavy guns firing grape and canister. The attack was unsuccessful, and Littler, in his report, said that the 62nd gave way to panic. This caused great resentment, for the regiment had lost seventeen officers and 185 men, and Reed stated that they retired by his orders, because he saw that they were

exposed to destructive fire and could not move forward. The commander-in-chief, Sir Hugh Gough, soon afterwards assured the regiment that he approved its conduct at Ferozeshahr. Reed, whom Littler described in his report as zealous and indefatigable, was slightly wounded in the battle.

On 2 April 1852 Reed went on half pay, and was employed as colonel on the staff at Birmingham. He was promoted major-general on 20 June 1854, and in 1855 went to command the troops in Ceylon. In 1856 he was transferred to a division of the Madras army, and soon afterwards to the command of the troops in the Punjab. He was in this position when the Indian mutiny broke out in 1857; and on General Anson's death (27 May) he became provisional commander-in-chief, as the senior officer in the Bengal presidency, until Sir Patrick Grant arrived at Calcutta (17 June). Illness prevented his taking part in military actions. Reed's letters to Sir John Lawrence during the early part of the siege of Delhi, according to J. W. Kaye, showed clear good sense. He made two excellent appointments which showed his judgement of men: Neville Chamberlain as adjutant-general and John Nicholson (1821–1857) as commander of the movable column. In the council of war on 15 June he gave his opinion—shared by Colonel Archdale Wilson and Sir Henry Barnard—in favour of waiting for reinforcements before risking an assault.

On Barnard's death (5 July), Reed assumed command of the field force; but the exertions and anxieties of that position were too much for him, and on 17 July he reported to the governor-general that his shattered health compelled his medical officers to urge his going to the hills, and that accordingly he was going to Simla. He selected Wilson as his successor, and gave him the rank of brigadier-general, as he was not senior officer. The situation, as described by Wilson—with the British force heavily outnumbered and losing casualties to repeated enemy attacks, and the enemy well equipped and strongly entrenched—was such that Reed had strong reasons for hesitating to adopt the proposals for an immediate assault which had been made by the chief engineer, Richard Baird Smith, in the early part of July.

Reed saw no further service in the field. He was given the colonelcy of the 44th foot on 2 August 1858, became lieutenant-general on 4 May 1860, and general on 1 January 1868. On 1 October 1877 he was placed on the retired list. He had been made KCB on 28 March 1865, and GCB on 29 May 1875. He died at his home, Baddesley Manor, Romsey, Hampshire, on 24 July 1883, and was survived by his wife.   E. M. LLOYD, rev. JAMES LUNT

Sources *The Times* (28 July 1883) · *Despatches of … Lord Hardinge … Lord Gough and other documents* (Oliver and Ackerman) (1846) · J. W. Kaye, *A history of the Sepoy War in India, 1857–1858*, 2nd edn, 3 vols. (1876) · G. W. Forrest, ed., *Selections from the letters, despatches and other state papers preserved in the military department of the government of India, 1857–1858*, 4 vols. (1893–1912) · J. W. Kaye and G. B. Malleson, *Kaye's and Malleson's History of the Indian mutiny of 1857–8*, new edn, 6 vols. (1897–8) · H. C. B. Cook, *The Sikh wars: the British army in the Punjab, 1845–1849* (1975) · *The military memoirs of Lt-Gen Sir Joseph Thackwell*, ed. N. C. Wylly (1908) · G. W. Forrest, *Life of Field-Marshal*

Sir Neville Chamberlain (1909) • Fortescue, *Brit. army*, vol. 13 • R. G. Burton, *The First and Second Sikh wars* (1911) • G. B. O'Connor, *Historical records of the Wiltshire regiment* (1885) • Boase, *Mod. Eng. biog.* • Kelly, *Handbk* (1879) • Burke, *Peerage* (1879)

Wealth at death £14,819 10s.: probate, 26 Nov 1883, *CGPLA Eng. & Wales*

Reed, William Henry [Billy] (1876–1942), violinist and composer, was born on 29 July 1875 at Christ Church Street, Frome, Somerset, the son of Francis John Reed, an Inland Revenue officer, and his wife, Emma Mary Warren. He was educated privately, and studied the violin with Emile Sauret and composition with Ebenezer Prout at the Royal Academy of Music. On 9 April 1902 he married Harriet Eveline (*b*. 1876/7), daughter of Arthur Dreyfus, a broker. Reed joined the Queen's Hall Orchestra, and when the London Symphony Orchestra (LSO) was formed in 1904 he was one of many players who left to join the new orchestra, under its principal conductor Hans Richter. In 1912 he became leader, a position he held until 1935. With Arthur Nikisch as conductor, the LSO was the first British orchestra to visit the United States and Canada. When Reed resigned as leader in 1935 he was invited to become chairman of the LSO board.

Reed was associated with the Three Choirs festival from 1902, when he first played in the orchestra; in 1910 he became leader of the Festival Orchestra, continuing to lead it until 1938, the last festival before the war. Through the festival he became a close friend of Sir Edward Elgar, and when Elgar was working on his violin concerto, op. 61, in 1910, he called on Reed to help with the arrangement of the passage work, the bowings, and the fingerings, and to play new passages as he wrote them, so that he could get them down exactly as he wished them to be played. In August 1910 Reed was asked by Elgar to play the whole concerto to a group of friends before the Gloucester festival, with the composer at the piano, and when the concerto had its first public performance in November 1910 with Fritz Kreisler as the soloist, and the Royal Philharmonic Orchestra, Reed played in the orchestra. After the composer's death, Reed published an article, 'Elgar's violin concerto', in *Music and Letters* (16, 1935). As an indication of his friendship, in 1914 Elgar dedicated *Sospiri*, op. 70, for strings, harp, and organ, to 'W. H. Reed'. Elgar continued to seek Reed's help when writing violin music, and in 1918 Reed helped with the violin sonata, op. 82, and gave its first public performance with Landon Ronald at the Aeolian Hall. As second violin of the British String Quartet he took part in the first performances of Elgar's string quartet, op. 83, and piano quintet, op. 84, in 1919, and he was a member of the string quartet that played at the funeral of Alice, Lady Elgar, on 10 April 1920. Reed also took part in the recording of some of Elgar's works, including the first recordings of *Falstaff* (op. 68) in 1929, and the *Nursery Suite*, in both of which he played the solo violin part with the LSO. After the BBC commissioned Elgar to write a third symphony in 1932, he worked closely with Reed until his own final illness, when he asked Reed, a few months before his death in 1934, to promise not to let anyone 'tinker' with the unfinished symphony after

his death. Despite this, and despite the assurances given by the BBC to Elgar's daughter, who had handed the manuscripts over to the BBC for safe keeping, that none of them would be published in whole or in part, Reed reproduced forty pages of the sketches for the symphony in facsimile, together with a detailed commentary based on his discussions with the composer, in *Elgar as I Knew Him* (1936). On the basis of these the symphony was reconstructed and completed by Anthony Payne in 1997 to great acclaim. Reed also wrote a biography of Elgar in the Master Musicians series, which was published in 1939.

Reed was a prolific composer himself, and many of his orchestral works were first performed at the Three Choirs Festival from 1904 onwards, when his orchestral fantasia, *Scenes from the Ballet*, was played at the Gloucester festival. His most popular works were *Will o' the Wisp* (Gloucester 1913), *Lincoln Imp* (Hereford 1921), and *Aesop's Fables* (Hereford 1924), and other works included the scherzo fantastique *Caliban* (Gloucester 1907), *Variations for Strings* (Worcester 1911), the rhapsody for viola and orchestra (Hereford 1927), the *Symphony for Strings* (Gloucester 1934), and the overture *Merry Andrew* (composed for the cancelled 1939 festival and first performed at Hereford in 1946). Reed taught the violin at the Royal College of Music, where he had many devoted pupils. He also conducted several amateur orchestras, including the Croydon Symphony Orchestra, which he helped to found in 1920 as the Croydon String Players Club, and when the Croydon Philharmonic Society organized an Elgar festival in 1935 Reed performed the violin concerto.

In 1939 the archbishop of Canterbury conferred on Reed the honorary degree of MusD. Reed died of heart failure on 2 July 1942 at St Joseph's College, Dumfries, while examining candidates for the Associated Board. The strings of the London Symphony Orchestra played at his memorial service in Croydon parish church on 18 July 1942, and his ashes were buried in Worcester Cathedral, near the Elgar memorial window, on 15 October 1942.

ANNE PIMLOTT BAKER

Sources H. Foss and N. Goodwin, *London Symphony: portrait of an orchestra* (1954) • W. H. Reed, *Elgar as I knew him* (1936) • H. Watkins Shaw, *The Three Choirs Festival* (1954) • *The Times* (4 July 1942) • *New Grove*, 2nd edn • *WW* • b. cert. • m. cert.

Likenesses E. Hall, photograph (with Elgar), repro. in Reed, *Elgar*, 142 • group portrait, photograph, repro. in Foss and Goodwin, *London Symphony*, facing p. 144

Wealth at death £9880 13s. 9d.: probate, 4 Dec 1942, *CGPLA Eng. & Wales*

Reed, Wilmot (*d*. 1692). See under Salem witches and their accusers (*act*. 1692).

Reede. For this title name *see* Reede van Renswouden, Johan van, Baron Reede (1593–1682).

Reede van Renswouden, Johan van [John de Reede], Baron Reede (1593–1682), diplomat and politician, was born in Utrecht, Netherlands, the third son of Gerard van Reede (*c*.1562–1612) and Mechteld Peunis (*c*.1560–1615). On 16 June 1616, against the wishes of her parents, he married Jacoba van Eeden (1595–1671) by special permission of the Utrecht city government; they had eight children. On 27

November 1611 van Reede had been appointed canon in Utrecht Cathedral, and in June 1620 he became dean. He acquired the title and lands of Renswoude in 1623, and in 1639 ordered the construction there of a new church, which was probably designed by the Dutch classicist architect Jacob van Campen. He got considerable financial help for this project from the states of Utrecht, the cathedral chapter, Frederick Hendrik, prince of Orange, and possibly Frederick and Elizabeth, the exiled king and queen of Bohemia. Over the entrance the coat of arms of Johan van Reede and his wife are displayed, and a plate shows the distinguished order of the Elephant, given to him by the Danish king. In 1654 he had the ruins of the medieval house in Renswoude replaced with a castle.

As a deputy of Utrecht in the states general, van Reede undertook several diplomatic missions. In January 1644—together with Willem Boreel, pensionary of Amsterdam—he was sent to England as ambassador-extraordinary of the states general to negotiate between King Charles I and the English parliament. The Dutch delegation was met in Gravesend by Sir Oliver Fleming, master of ceremonies of the parliament, and in Greenwich the earl of Denbigh on behalf of the Lords, and Sir Henry Mildmay and Walter Strickland on behalf of the Commons, escorted the ambassadors to London, where they were greeted with cannon shots fired from the River Thames, an honour until then only bestowed upon royal ambassadors. However, Boreel and van Reede chose not to lodge in the house provided for them by parliament and did not formally request an audience with both houses. Instead, they approached individual members, but were told that no negotiations were possible until the king had officially acknowledged parliament.

In February the delegation travelled on to Oxford to meet Charles I. It soon became evident that the king would not meet parliament's demands, although he agreed to participate in future discussions. By mid-March they were back in London. However, rumours of the embassy's royalist sympathies circulated among members of the houses, greatly troubling the negotiations. More importantly the 'war faction' within parliament had gathered force, and audiences were delayed and put off, while letters from the delegates stayed unanswered: 'In the government of Parliament lies the ruin of our State', van Reede concluded in a letter to Constantijn Huygens, the prince of Orange's secretary, in November 1644 (*Briefwisseling*, 4.95). In their farewell speech to the Lords and Commons in April 1645, as well as in their subsequent meetings with the states general after their return to the Netherlands in May, they blamed parliament for the failure of the negotiations. On 24 March van Reede had been created by Charles I Baron Reede; a medal engraved by Thomas Simon in 1645 and a portrait designed by Wenceslaus Hollar (1650) commemorate this event.

In September 1652 Reede directly offered his services to Charles II. He corresponded in 1655 with Secretary Edward Nicholas on political matters and in 1656 on the appointment of his son Hendrik to the post of Dutch ambassador to Spain. He was president of the states of Utrecht between 1652 and 1671, and resumed the position in 1674. He died in The Hague on 7 February 1682.

MARIKA KEBLUSEK

Sources *Nieuw Nederlandsch biografisch woordenboek* (1911–37), vol. 3, cols. 1037–8 · S. Groenveld, *Verlopend getij: de Nederlandse republiek en de Engelse burgeroorlog, 1640–1646* (Dieren, 1984) · G. van Loon, *Beschryving der Nederlandsche historipenningen*, 2 (The Hague, 1726), 282; 3 (1728), 131 · E. Wolleswinkel, *Renswoude: geschiedenis en architectuur* (Zeist, 1998) · J. Heringa, *Eer en hoogheid van de staat* (Groningen, 1961), 92, 94, 142, 161, 321, 349 · *De briefwisseling van Constantijn Huygens*, ed. J. A. Worp (The Hague, 1911–17), vols. 3–5 · O. Schutte, ed., *Repertorium der Nederlandse vertegenwoordigers residerende in het buitenland, 1584–1810* (The Hague, 1976) · *Poincten van consideratien … uyt het rapport van … Boreel, ende Renswoude* (1645) · L. van Aitzema, *Saken van staet en oorlogh*, 2 (The Hague, 1669), 983 · papers and documents relating to embassy, 1644–5, Nationaal Archief, The Hague · BL, Add. MS 17677 R, fols. 246–69 · GEC, *Peerage*
Archives Nationaal Archief, The Hague, states-general archives
Likenesses P. Moreelse, oils, 1619, priv. coll. · C. van Simons, engraving on coin, 1645, repro. in Loon, *Beschryving*, 283 · W. Hollar, engraving, 1650, BM · W. Hollar, etching, 1650, NPG · portrait, 1673, Centraal Museum, Utrecht
Wealth at death estate of Renswoude

Rees. *See also* Reece, Rhees, Rhys.

Rees, Abraham (1743–1825), Presbyterian minister and encyclopaedist, was born at the Old Independent Chapel House at Llanbrynmair, Montgomeryshire, the second son of Lewis Rees (1710–1800), Independent minister, and his wife, Esther Penry. The family moved in 1759, when his father became Independent minister at Mynyddbach, Glamorgan.

After early education at Llanfyllin, Montgomeryshire, and attending a grammar school in Carmarthen, Abraham in 1759 began his education for the ministry at Coward's academy in Wellclose Square, London, under David Jennings. In 1762, before he had completed his studies, he was appointed assistant tutor in mathematics and natural philosophy at the academy. He taught mathematics, statics, hydrostatics, optics, spherical geometry, and the use of applied mathematics in navigation, geography, and astronomy. Following the academy's move to Hoxton in 1762, after Jennings's death, Rees became resident tutor, a position he held until 1785. From 1786 to 1796 he was tutor in Hebrew and mathematics at New College, Hackney, established by rational dissenters in London.

Rees's first ministerial post was to preach once a fortnight to the Independent congregation at Clapham as assistant to Philip Furneaux. In July 1768 he succeeded Henry Read as pastor to the Presbyterian congregation in St Thomas's, Southwark. From 1773 he shared the Sunday evening lecture at Salters' Hall and was one of the Tuesday morning lecturers there until 1795. He moved to become pastor of the Old Jewry congregation in 1783, and continued there until his death. A new meeting-house was built for him in Jewin Street and opened on 10 December 1809.

Rees was elected a trustee of Dr Williams's foundation

Abraham Rees (1743–1825), by John Opie, exh. RA 1796

in 1774 and secretary to the Presbyterian Board in 1778; he held both offices until his death. He received the degree of DD from Edinburgh University on 31 January 1775. A dedicated tutor, Rees was an examiner of students at Carmarthen Academy, where he travelled every three years, and in 1806 he was appointed distributor of the English *regium donum*, the parliamentary fund for indigent dissenting ministers and their widows. He was deputed to present the address of loyalty on behalf of the three denominations (Baptists, Independents, and Presbyterians) of ministers residing in London on the accessions of both George III and George IV. On the earlier occasion Lord Halifax, lord-in-waiting, expressed the opinion that had Rees not been a dissenter, his loyalty might have been personally rewarded.

Rees was a popular preacher, having a majestic presence and deep, sonorous voice. Four volumes of *Practical Sermons* were published between 1812 and 1821, which Rees valued more than any other of his works. 'Untinctured by enthusiasm, and undebased by illiberality' (Evans, 8), his sermons typified his clear, logical reasoning and tolerance towards other denominations. He retained his father's concern for the interests of Welsh nonconformity and was the administrator for private donations to poor congregations in Wales. His theology bore a mediating and transitional character and he believed in universal restoration. Though 'owning no human authority in religion' (Aspland, 37), Rees inclined towards the doctrines of Richard Price and shared his Arian views of the Trinity.

Rees's great interest in mathematics and the physical sciences led him to re-edit Ephraim Chambers's *Cyclopaedia*, originally published in 1728, for its publishers, Longmans. Rees's new edition appeared in 1778 in one folio volume. He augmented it with new material and published a four-volume edition in 1781–6 (reprinted 1788–9). He was rewarded for his work by being elected a fellow of the Royal Society in 1786. He subsequently was elected to the Linnean Society, the American Philosophical Society, and the Royal Society of Literature. The success of his edition of Chambers led Thomas Longman to invite Rees to edit a similar but much more comprehensive publication. This was *The New Cyclopaedia, or, Universal Dictionary of the Arts and Sciences*, more commonly known as Rees's *Cyclopaedia*. The first half-volume was published on 2 January 1802, and succeeding parts, in alphabetical order, appeared at fairly regular intervals; the work was completed with the issuing of six half-volumes of plates in August 1820. The work extended to thirty-nine volumes of text, five volumes of plates, and an atlas. It sold for £85, but was reputed to have cost Longmans nearly £300,000. The *Cyclopaedia* contains around 39 million words; over 500 articles each exceeded 10,000 words. On the completion of his task Longmans gave Rees a gratuity of 300 guineas. A pirated edition was published in America in 1806–22 by Samuel Bradford of Philadelphia, and was expanded with specifically American material to reach forty-two volumes of text and six volumes of plates.

Rees had considerable assistance from about 100 contributors, most of whom were nonconformists of various persuasions. They were eminent specialists in their respective fields, proficient in the sciences, technology, manufacturing, agriculture, banking, and transportation, as well as the arts and humanities. A number were members of the teaching staffs of the Royal Military Academy and the East India Company's Addiscombe College. Other contributors were working journalists who wrote for scientific, medical, and technical periodicals of the time. Several of the contributors were active in radical politics; one was gaoled for sedition and another indicted for treason. At the time of its publication, when philosophical radicalism was so suspect in Britain, aspects of the *Cyclopaedia* were thought to be subversive and attracted the hostility of the loyalist press. The editor and authors went to great pains to emphasize their Englishness, to the extent of Anglicizing many French words. The French kings Louis appear under the heading Lewis, for example.

Rees's *Cyclopaedia* has been superseded by more modern works, but has also been ignored by scholarship. It has, however, been cherished by specialists in the history of science and technology of the period. For the modern reader it is an incomparable manual for all facets of Regency endeavour, since it reflects the scope of knowledge, particularly scientific and technical, during the British Enlightenment. It is particularly valuable for the early phase of the industrial revolution.

Rees was married, but nothing is known about his wife, who predeceased him. They had three sons and a daughter, who was the first wife of the Unitarian minister John

*Jones (c.1766–1827) and died in 1815. One of his sons, Nathaniel Penry Rees, died on 8 July 1802 on a voyage from Bengal to St Helena. His two other sons predeceased him, but he is known to have been survived by grandchildren.

The inventor Joseph Chessborough Dyer, who greatly admired Rees as a scholar and as a man, gave a full description of him in his unpublished memoirs: 'Dr Rees was of a middle stature, rather stout and inclined to corpulency, an open and genial expression of countenance, giving the idea of a jovial country squire, rather than of a great scholar and profound philosopher' (Chessborough Dyer, memoirs). Rees died at his residence in Artillery Place, Finsbury, on 9 June 1825, and was buried in Bunhill Fields on 18 June. His pallbearers represented the three denominations. At Rees's request, Robert Aspland preached the funeral sermon on Sunday the 19th and Thomas Rees (no relation) gave the address, both of whom were Unitarian. Rees's significance is best summarized by Aspland: 'Our reverend friend was Protestant Dissenter from full and growing conviction. No man ever did more in the same space of time … for the promotion of our principles and of our credit in the eyes of the world' (Aspland, 36).

A. P. WOOLRICH

Sources DNB · DWB · H. McLachlan, *Unitarian movement in the religious life of England and its contribution to thought and learning* (1934) · J. Z. Fullmer, 'Proposal for the creation of 'The readers guide to Rees's *Cyclopedia*'', 1986 [privately circulated document] · A. P. Woolrich, 'John Farey, jr, technical author and draughtsman: his contribution to Rees's *Cyclopaedia*', *Industrial Archaeology Review*, 20 (1998), 49–68 · J. Chessborough Dyer, MS of his memoirs, 1868, Mass. Hist. Soc. · W. Wilson, *The history and antiquities of the dissenting churches and meeting houses in London, Westminster and Southwark*, 4 vols. (1808–14), vol. 2, pp. 398–400 · R. Aspland, *Funeral sermon* (1825) · J. Evans, 'Memoir of Abraham Rees, D.D., F.R.S., F.L.S., &c.', *Christian Moderator*, 1/1 (1826), 4–9 · *London Christian Instructor, or, Congregational Magazine*, new ser., 1 (1825), 447–8 · *Monthly Repository*, 20 (1825), 372–3

Archives DWL, sermons in shorthand | U. Reading, Longmans Archives, letters

Likenesses J. Sayers, caricature, etching, pubd 1790, BM, NPG · W. Daniell, etching, 1794 (after G. Dance), NPG · J. Opie, oils, exh. RA 1796, DWL [*see illus.*] · W. Holl, engraving (after J. Opie), repro. in A. Rees, *Cyclopaedia*, 1 (1819) · J. Lonsdale, oils, NPG · Thompson, engraving (after J. Opie), repro. in Wilson, *History and antiquities*, vol. 2, facing p. 400 · mezzotint (after J. Opie), NPG

Rees, Alwyn David (1911–1974), social anthropologist and Welsh nationalist, was born at Llanarel, Coalbrook, Gorseinon, Glamorgan, on 27 March 1911, the son of Theophilus Rees, a winder at the Mynydd colliery in Gorseinon, and his wife, Mary, *née* Davies. Alwyn was the eldest of their four children, all of whom became involved in the world of education. He attended the primary school at Penyrheol and later the county school in Gowerton. In October 1930 he went to the University College of Wales, Aberystwyth, where he gained first-class honours in geography and anthropology. In 1934 he qualified for the diploma in education and the Board of Education teachers' certificate, but through the award of a Sir John Williams studentship he was able to research in 'Welsh literature', though the actual research was oriented more towards historical geography and anthropology. He gained his MA

in 1937 with a study of some of the survivals of pagan elements in early Celtic Christianity.

In 1936 Rees was appointed a tutor in the extramural department at Aberystwyth and worked in that position throughout the war years until 1946. On 8 June 1940 he married Myfanwy Elizabeth Howells (b. 1912/13), daughter of Albert Burgess Howells, a mechanic. She was from Ceri, Newtown, and they had met while he was tutor in residence in Montgomeryshire. As well as organizing adult-education classes in the area with the needs of service personnel in mind, he undertook extensive fieldwork in Llanfihangel-yng-Ngwynfa in north Montgomeryshire for a case study in social anthropology which was published by the University of Wales Press in 1950 as *Life in a Welsh Countryside*. This innovative and seminal work has been widely acclaimed as the beginning of 'community' studies in Britain. It was a study which engaged him both intellectually and emotionally, for he saw the values of traditional rural society as a challenge to those who pondered social change. Social change or rather social decline was the subject of his first book, written in 1943, *Adfeilion*, a social commentary on a world at war, for a popular series written by established and up-and-coming Welsh-language writers and thinkers. In 1946 he was appointed a lecturer in his old department of geography and anthropology, where he taught undergraduate courses on 'ancient civilizations' and 'social anthropology', and a specialized third-year course on the 'social anthropology of modern communities'.

This brief but crucial period in Rees's intellectual development came to an end in 1949, when he successfully applied for the post of director of extramural studies at Aberystwyth. The gain of the department of extramural studies was a loss to the academic study of Welsh rural communities. His creative output after the second edition of *Life in a Welsh Countryside* in 1951 was slight and dried up completely between 1954 and 1960, when he co-edited *Welsh Rural Communities*. His department, however, was flourishing. In 1955 the area covered by Aberystwyth's extramural department had a fuller provision of adult-education classes in relation to population than any other extramural area in the British Isles. He was also occupied with his brother, Brinley, in writing *Celtic Heritage*, which was published in 1961.

Some time during the late 1950s Rees became converted from a left-of-centre Liberal to the cause of Welsh nationalism. The Welsh language took on a new political and ideological significance in Welsh politics and no-one advocated the cause more skilfully than Rees. In defending the federal nature of the University of Wales he was able to articulate his new passion. In 1960 a commission was established to consider the future of the University of Wales. He regarded the university as one of the main institutions to serve the people of Wales, and led a masterly and successful campaign to persuade the graduates of the university to reject its break-up into its constituent parts.

In February 1966 Rees took over the editorship of the literary magazine *Barn* which soon established his wider reputation beyond the academic sphere. Under his editorship *Barn* became an active force in Welsh radical politics. In its pages he fulminated against representatives of English legal and political authority in Wales, and employed his acidic wit to represent minorities against majorities. He attacked the census and the tyranny of numbers which it promoted, criticized those who opposed the wider use of Welsh because of cost, and advocated the case against university expansion, on the grounds of retention of Welsh identity. He promoted the notion of a Welsh-speaking college in the Old College in Aberystwyth and effectively halted the Aberystwyth plans for expansion. As a radical cultural nationalist, he made the Welsh language central to his view of Welsh nationalism. The best service a non-Welsh-speaking nationalist could do, he argued, was not to dream of a socialist paradise but to learn the language. He had been unwell since 1973, but he was at his desk in the extramural department at Marine Terrace, Aberystwyth, when he died of a heart attack on 6 December 1974. The January 1975 edition of *Barn* contained tributes from colleagues and co-workers, including the principal of the University College of Wales, Aberystwyth, and the chairman of the Welsh Language Society.

HYWEL MEILYR DAVIES

Sources R. M. Jones, *Ym marn Alwyn D. Rees* (1976) · *Barn* (Jan 1975) · D. Rees, *Life in a Welsh countryside: a social study of Llanfihangel yng Ngwynfa* (1996) [foreword by H. Carter] · b. cert. · m. cert. · *CGPLA Eng. & Wales* (1975)
Archives NL Wales, corresp. and papers · U. Wales, Aberystwyth
Likenesses photograph, repro. in Jones, *Ym marn Alwyn D. Rees* · photograph, repro. in A. D. Rees, *Adfeilion* (1943)
Wealth at death £20,625: probate, 13 Feb 1975, *CGPLA Eng. & Wales*

Rees, David [*called* y Cynhyrfwr] (**1801–1869**), Congregational minister and journal editor, son of Bernard and Anna Rees, was born on 14 November 1801 at Gelli Lwyd in the parish of Tre-lech, Carmarthenshire. Having resolved to enter the Independent ministry, he attended for a short time the grammar schools at Haverfordwest, Carmarthen, and Newtown, and in 1825 was admitted to the Independent college at Newtown. On 15 July 1829 he was ordained minister of Capel Als, Llanelli, in his native county, a position he held until his death.

In August 1835 the Independent ministers of south Wales, dissatisfied with the political tone of *Yr Efangylydd*, a monthly journal circulating widely among them, started *Y Diwygiwr* ('The reformer'), with Rees as its editor. He also established a printing office at Llanelli. In this position he wielded great influence in south Wales for thirty years, advocating vigorously a wide range of political causes, including the abolition of church rates, the repeal of the corn laws, electoral reform, and disestablishment. An admirer of the Irishman Daniel O'Connell, he became known as y Cynhyrfwr ('the agitator') and he brought a radical influence to bear on the nonconformity of his day. Unlike many of his fellow ministers, he was an advocate of state aid for elementary instruction, and did much to reconcile the dissenters of south Wales to the principle. A keen advocate of the temperance movement, he edited

and published two short-lived temperance periodicals between 1838 and 1841. He also founded *Tywysydd yr Ieuainc* ('Guide for young people'), a monthly children's periodical in 1837, and his press issued a substantial number of books and pamphlets, mainly on religious subjects. He took a prominent part in the public life of Llanelli, and founded three Congregationalist churches in the town.

Rees was married twice; his first wife was Sarah, the daughter of John Roberts, whom he married on 9 January 1832. They had a daughter and four sons, the two youngest of whom were drowned while bathing in the sea at Llanelli in 1851. Sarah Rees died on 8 July 1857, and Rees married a widow, Margaret Phillips (*née* Lloyd) of Fountain Hall, Carmarthen, on 17 November 1858. They had no children. Rees resigned his editorship in 1869 and died on 31 March 1869 at his home, Goring Villa, Llanelli. He was buried in Llanelli public cemetery on 5 April. His second wife survived him, dying on 11 October 1875.

J. E. LLOYD, *rev.* HUW WALTERS

Sources Iorwerth Jones, *David Rees, y Cynhyrfwr* (1971) · Thomas Davies, *Bywyd ac ysgrifeniadau y diweddar Barch. D. Rees, Llanelli* (1871) · *Y Tyst* (9 April 1869) · *Y Tyst* (5 Nov 1875) · *Congregational Year Book* (1870), 317–18 · *CGPLA Eng. & Wales* (1869)
Archives NL Wales, sermons
Likenesses J. Thomas, photograph, *c.*1865, NL Wales, John Thomas 'Cambrian Gallery' collection · J. Cochran, stipple (after W. Cush), repro. in Jones, *David Rees*
Wealth at death under £1500: probate, 10 May 1869, *CGPLA Eng. & Wales*

Rees, David James [Dai] (**1913–1983**), golfer, was born on 31 March 1913 in the village of Ffontigari y Barri, Glamorgan, the son of David Evans Rees (*d.* 1959), greenkeeper at Barry golf club, and his wife, Louisa Alice Trow. He attended St Athan primary school at Gileston, then Jenner Park School in Barry, where he played football and gained a Welsh schools trial. Not until he was twelve did he become dedicated to golf, when his family had moved to Aberdâr and Dai became a pupil at Aber-nant School.

The young Dai Rees was brought up in a golfing environment, as his father was professional successively at The Leys and Brynhill, both small Welsh clubs. Nevertheless his early golfing education came from a Leys club member, R. J. Middle. At the age of five Rees played a downhill hole of 300 yards in just five strokes, holing his approach shot. In February 1929, aged fifteen, he turned professional, working as assistant to his father, when his entry to the Welsh boys' championship was rejected on the grounds that he had earned money as a caddy.

In 1934 Rees secured an assistantship at Surbiton and in 1935 and 1936 he won the British assistants' championship. Non-selection for the 1935 Ryder cup tempted him to emigrate to South Africa, but he was dissuaded by the lack of tournaments there. In spring 1939 he married Eunice Thomas, about the same time that he moved as professional to Hindhead. He left that club in 1946, feeling that the atmosphere had become rather stuffy and snobbish, and moved to become the professional at South Hertfordshire, Totteridge, where he remained for over twenty years, before turning to golf clinics and journalism. During the Second World War he enlisted in the RAF, hoping

David James [Dai] **Rees** (1913–1983), by unknown photographer, *c*.1950

to become a pilot, but he was, like many professional sportsmen, selected to be a physical training instructor. Eventually, however, he became a driver, and served in the Middle East.

Rees made his début in the Ryder cup in 1937 when, as the Professional Golfers' Association (PGA) match play champion, he was an automatic choice. He made an auspicious start by beating Byron Nelson in the singles. This was the first of a record-breaking ten appearances, three of them as team captain, including the famous match of 1957 at Lindrick, where the British team finally regained the trophy after twenty-four years. He was also non-playing captain in 1967. His Ryder cup singles record of five wins from ten games was strong at a time when the British Isles usually lost. After the Lindrick triumph Rees was voted BBC sports personality of the year and made a CBE in the new year's honours list.

A non-smoker and virtual teetotaller, Rees kept himself fit and believed that strength was important to a golfer. He developed this in his legs by walking and cycling in the hilly terrain of the Welsh countryside as well as, in his teenage years, working during the winter at Aberdâr golf club loading barrows with rocks, earth, and turf and trundling them for miles along the fairways. He also felt that being Welsh and of small stature gave him the need to prove himself. Never a long hitter, he was a confident putter and a very gritty, competitive match play golfer— something he attributed to an individualistic childhood in which he spent much time on his own. A perfectionist, Rees was often dissatisfied with his own game or with the

course, his caddy, the gallery, and any number of extraneous agencies beyond the match in hand. But as he said when asked to consider the difference between Welsh golfers and others, 'Remember we are Celtic, and Celts sometimes blow their tops. But you'll never find a Welsh golfer with ulcers!' (Houghton, 118).

Rees was elected to the executive committee of the PGA in 1946 and served on its trade subcommittee from its inception in 1947. However, by 1950 he had left the executive. Although a supporter of the PGA, he, like many other tournament professionals, felt that the executive was prejudiced towards the interests of the club professional. Rees was among the group who lobbied for an improved tournament structure in the late 1950s. In 1960 he led another challenge to the PGA hierarchy by delivering a players' manifesto that demanded more diversification in its list of sponsors.

Rees's tournament record included victories at both ends of the age spectrum, the assistants' championship in 1935 and the seniors' title in 1966. In between he won the British PGA match play four times (1936, 1938, 1949, and 1950) and lost in the final in 1955, 1967, and 1969, the last when aged fifty-six. The open itself always eluded him, although he finished runner-up to three great golfers: Ben Hogan, in 1953; Peter Thomson, in 1954; and Arnold Palmer, in 1961. In 1959, to the delight of his father, he won his first tournament in Wales, the British closed PGA championship. His last title was the South of England PGA in 1975; in the following year he became an honorary member of the Royal and Ancient Golf Club of St Andrews. He wrote five books on the game, *Golf my Way* (1951), *Dai Rees on Golf* (1959), *The Key to Golf* (1961), *Golf Today* (1962), and *Thirty Years of Championship Golf* (1968). He died at Barnet General Hospital, Barnet, on 15 November 1983.

WRAY VAMPLEW

Sources D. Rees, *Thirty years of championship golf* (1968) · D. Rees, *Dai Rees on golf* (1959) · minutes of the Professional Golfers' Association, Professional Golfers' Association, The Belfry, Sutton Coldfield · P. Alliss, *Who's who of golf* (1983) · B. Ferrier and G. Hart, eds., *The Johnnie Walker encyclopedia of golf* (1994) · G. W. Houghton, *Golf addict invades Wales: the account of a crusade* (1969) · b. cert. · d. cert.
Archives Professional Golfers' Association, The Belfry, Sutton Coldfield | FILM BFI NFTVA, news footage
Likenesses photographs, 1936–71, Hult. Arch. [*see illus.*] · photographs, repro. in Rees, *Thirty years*
Wealth at death £22,097: probate, 27 Jan 1984, CGPLA Eng. & Wales

Rees [*née* Jones], **Dame Dorothy Mary** (1898–1987), politician, was born on 29 July 1898 at 6 Newland Street, Barry, Glamorgan, the daughter of Henry Jones, a dock labourer, and his wife, Catherine Owens. Welsh-speaking and nonconformist in religion, she was educated at Holton School before winning a scholarship to Barry county school, proceeding to qualify as a teacher at the Glamorgan Training College. She taught for eight years, in Neath, Caerphilly, and Barry, before marrying David Rees, a sailor (later channel pilot) who had been awarded the Conspicuous Gallantry Medal for bravery during the First World War. He died, aged forty, in November 1938; there were no children.

Dorothy Rees joined the Labour Party in 1922. She was a founder (later secretary) of the Barry Fabian Society, and a member of the National Union of Teachers. In 1933, standing as the Labour candidate, she narrowly failed to unseat the sitting Conservative in the Cadoxton ward of Barry urban district council. In 1934 she defeated the sitting independent member in the Barry docks division of Glamorgan county council, and was immediately elected to its aldermanic bench. She was only the second female county councillor in Glamorgan, working closely with her predecessor, labour alderman Rose Davies of Aberdâr. Nevertheless she later wrote warmly of the welcome she received from the male councillors, particularly those representing mining areas (Rees, 21–5). In 1936 she was also elected to the Barry urban district council for the Holton ward. In 1940 she resigned from both councils to take a full-time post as liaison officer with the Ministry of Food, leaving this in 1945 to act as the Labour Party's agent and organizer in the Llandaff and Barry constituency (won by A. L. Ungoed-Thomas for Labour in that year's general election). She was co-opted back onto the aldermanic bench of the Barry borough council in 1946 (resigning in 1949) and was re-elected to the Glamorgan county council in the same year (also to the aldermanic bench).

The sitting member having declared his intention of seeking another seat, Rees, by this time honorary secretary of the Barry divisional Labour Party, was selected in 1949 as Labour prospective parliamentary candidate for the newly redrawn constituency of Barry. In the general election of 1950 she won a majority of 1025 votes over Conservative and Liberal opponents, becoming one of the first two women Labour MPs elected in Wales (with Eirene White in East Flint). Rees was in parliament for too short a time to have had much impact; her two speeches there dealt with the housing shortage and with the need for more technical education in Wales. She nevertheless did valuable work as parliamentary private secretary to Edith Summerskill at the Ministry of National Insurance. In the 1951 general election she lost her seat by 1649 votes to her Conservative opponent.

Rees's main contribution to public life, beyond her importance as the first female Labour MP in industrial south Wales, was in local government. She continued to serve on the Glamorgan county council, becoming its vice-chairman in 1963 and its chairman in 1964. She took particular interest in education (especially that of girls), health, and housing. She was a member of the Joint Education Committee for Wales, served on the Welsh Teaching Hospitals Board and on the National Insurance Advisory Committee, and was chairman of the Morgannwg Hospital management committee. Between 1964 and 1967 she was a member of the Central Training Council in Child Care and in 1965 she was appointed to the Welsh Economic Council. As a magistrate she served on the Dinas Powys bench, and she chaired the executive committee organizing the 1968 royal national eisteddfod in Barry.

Rees was made the first female honorary freeman of Barry in 1956, was appointed CBE in 1964, and was made a DBE in 1975, after her retirement from public life. She died on 20 August 1987 at her home, Mor-Hafren, 341 Barry Road, Barry. A talented organizer and administrator and an able debater, Dorothy Rees impressed political colleagues and opponents alike with her ability, charm, and dignity, and inspired great affection and admiration from many of her townspeople (Beddoe, 6–7, 156; Stead, 'Barry since 1939', 455–6).　　　　Chris Williams

Sources P. Stead, 'Barry since 1939: war-time prosperity and post-war uncertainty', *Barry: the centenary book*, ed. D. Moore, 2nd edn (1985), 429–81 · D. Beddoe, *Out of the shadows: a history of women in twentieth-century Wales* (2000) · N. Evans and D. Jones, '"To help forward the great work of humanity": women in the labour party in Wales', *The labour party in Wales, 1900–2000*, ed. D. Tanner, C. Williams, and D. Hopkin (2000), 215–40 · D. Rees, 'County Alderman Mrs Dorothy Rees of Barry, CBE JP', *Reminiscences of the Glamorgan county council* (1974), 21–5 · *Barry and District News* (1933–87) · *Barry and District News* (27 Aug 1987) · *Barry Herald* (1933–51) · *Western Mail* [Cardiff] (22 Aug 1987) · b. cert. · d. cert.

Likenesses photograph, repro. in *Barry and District News* (16 Feb 1950) · photograph, repro. in *Barry and District News* (10 April 1936) · photograph, repro. in *Barry and District News* (2 April 1964) · photograph, repro. in *Barry and District News* (2 Jan 1975) · photograph, repro. in *Western Mail* · photograph, repro. in *Barry Herald* (2 March 1934) · photographs, repro. in Stead, 'The town that had come of age', *Barry: the centenary book*, ed. Moore

Wealth at death under £70,000: probate, 14 Sept 1987, *CGPLA Eng. & Wales*

Rees, George (1776–1846), physician, was born in Pembrokeshire, where his father was a clergyman. He received his medical education in London at the united hospitals of St Thomas's and Guy's, also attending some lectures at St Bartholomew's, where he became a member of the students' medical and physical society.

Rees was house surgeon at the Lock Hospital, London, and having graduated MD at Glasgow on 28 May 1801 he began practice at 2 Soho Square, where he gave a course of twelve lectures on venereal diseases. These were published in 1802 as *A Treatise on the Primary Symptoms of Lues venerea*. In 1805 he published *Observations on Diseases of the Uterus*, dedicated to Andrew Thynne, sometime lecturer on the subject at St Bartholomew's Hospital. On 11 April 1808 Rees was admitted a licentiate of the Royal College of Physicians. In 1810 he published *Practical Observations on Disorders of the Stomach*, which contains a clearly described case of cirrhosis of the liver due to alcohol, one of the first examples of a distinction then being made within the group of diseases known as 'scirrhus' of the liver. In 1813 Rees published *A Practical Treatise on Haemoptysis*, in which he advised treatment by emetics; but neither this nor his other works contain original observations of much value.

Rees next moved to Finsbury Square, London, and established a private lunatic asylum, Pembroke House, at Hackney. He then spent some time as medical superintendent of the lunatic asylum at Bodmin, Cornwall. Rees returned to London and lived in Euston Square, where he died on 7 December 1846.

Norman Moore, rev. Patrick Wallis

Sources Munk, *Roll* · *GM*, 2nd ser., 27 (1847) · P. J. Wallis and R. V. Wallis, *Eighteenth century medics*, 2nd edn (1988)

Rees, George Owen (1813–1889), physician, was born at Smyrna, Turkey, in November 1813, the second child of Josiah Rees, a Levantine merchant and British consul at Smyrna of Welsh descent, and his Italian wife. His uncle Thomas Rees (1777–1864) was a partner in Longmans, the publishers. When Josiah Rees's business failed he moved to London where Rees attended a private school in Clapham. He entered Guy's Hospital in 1829 as a pupil of the apothecary Richard Stocker; his ability in chemical analysis was noted by Richard Bright and from 1833 he joined Bright's team of pupils and young physicians investigating albuminuria.

With Bright, Rees conducted chemical and microscopical analyses of blood and urine in kidney diseases and identified urea in the blood serum of diabetics. His first book, *On the Analysis of the Blood and Urine in Health and Disease*, was published in 1836.

Rees then studied in Paris and at the University of Glasgow, graduating MD on 27 April 1837. He began medical practice at the family home in Guilford Street, Russell Square, but his interests lay in chemical and physiological studies. He contributed to a report on the analysis of human glands following the British Association meeting of 1837 and also proposed a new method of extracting sugar crystals from diabetic blood serum. He investigated the chemical composition of chyle, lymph, and blood for Samuel Lane's articles in Todd's *Cyclopaedia of Anatomy and Physiology* and later contributed articles in his own name. Many of these became accepted standards in nineteenth-century medicine. In 1841 Rees and Lane published their important observations on the shape and structure of blood corpuscles, including the effects of saline and other solutions. Rees noted that the red corpuscles remained unchanged in a salt solution with the same specific gravity as blood serum. Two years later he made quantitative analyses of blood serum, urine, and the fluids of the ventricles of the brain, pleura, and peritoneum for G. H. Barlow's account of Bright's work on albuminuria.

Continuing his studies of chyle and blood and encouraged by his friend P. M. Roget, Rees presented a paper to the Royal Society on the contents of the human thoracic duct, using fluid taken from the body of an executed criminal one hour after death. He also observed that the numbers of fat globules in the chyle of herbivores and carnivores were similar and suggested that during respiration fatty matter reacted with nitrogen as well as oxygen, producing albumin which took part in nutrition.

In 1842 Rees was appointed physician to the Northern Dispensary and he became assistant physician to Guy's Hospital in the following year. His studies on the blood and animal chemistry led to his election to the fellowship of the Royal Society in February 1843 and in the same year Sir Benjamin Brodie secured his appointment as physician to the new Pentonville prison. In 1844 he was elected a fellow of the Royal College of Physicians where he was later censor (1852–3) and senior censor (1863–4), and in the years between 1845 and 1869 he was elected to deliver many of the most prestigious medical lectures. Reported

in the medical press, his views were widely known. Physicians received his clinical chemistry with polite interest but little enthusiasm, though chemists respected him and he was a founder member of the Chemical Society of London in 1841.

Rees was one of the first to study the chemistry of the urine and his work in this and other branches of animal chemistry ensure his place in the history of medicine. In 1850 he published a practical treatise *On the nature and treatment of disorders of the kidney connected with albuminous urine* (*morbus Brightii*) and in 1851 his Lettsomian lectures at the Medical Society of London were also on the pathology of the urine. Rees's analytical work was often used in evidence by his colleague Alfred Swaine Taylor, with whom he was brought to public notice in 1856 at the famous trial of William Palmer, the Rugeley poisoner. In 1856 Rees was made physician at Guy's and appointed lecturer on the practice of medicine; he held both posts until his retirement on 26 February 1873. He was consultant physician to Guy's until his death.

Although slight in stature Rees had a hearty laugh, a genial voice, and convivial manner. Always courteous, he was generally well liked, but he had a sharp tongue when annoyed. Fastidious in person and dress, he was appalled by the squalid environment of many of his hospital patients and disgusted by the unpleasant smells of the post-mortem room. He had a love of good company, and many friends. He read widely in French, German, and Italian and he was a witty after dinner speaker. His private practice was fashionable, including many prominent people among whom rheumatism, gout, and calculous diseases were common. In 1849 he published a short tract on the use of lemon juice for the relief of rheumatism and gout, a remedy which he employed liberally.

Rees never married; for many years he lived with and supported his mother, two sisters, and a brother. Late in life he became physician to Queen Charlotte's Lying-in Hospital and in December 1882 he was appointed physician-extraordinary to the queen. In 1886 he suffered a paralytic stroke from which he never fully recovered; he died on 27 May 1889, at Mayfield, Station Road, Watford, following a second cerebral haemorrhage. He was buried in Abney Park cemetery, London.   N. G. COLEY

Sources S. Wilks, *Guy's Hospital Reports*, 3rd ser., 31 (1889), xxiii–xxxiii · *BMJ* (15 June 1889), 1383 · *The Lancet* (22 June 1889), 1282–3 · S. Wilks and G. T. Bettany, *A biographical history of Guy's Hospital* (1892) · S. W. [S. Wilks], *PRS*, 46 (1889), xi–xiii · N. G. Coley, 'George Owen Rees (1813–89): pioneer of medical chemistry', *Medical History*, 30 (1986), 173–90 · Munk, *Roll*, 4.38 · *The Times* (5 June 1889) · Boase, *Mod. Eng. biog.*
Likenesses S. Buck, oils, *c.*1840–1850, RCP Lond. · photograph, Guy's Hospital, London
Wealth at death £2530 0s. 2d.: probate, 26 June 1889, *CGPLA Eng. & Wales*

Rees, (Morgan) Goronwy (1909–1979), writer and university principal, was born on 29 November 1909 at Aberystwyth. He was the younger son and youngest of four children of the Revd Richard Jenkyn Rees (1868–1963), Calvinistic Methodist minister and graduate of both Aberystwyth and Mansfield College, Oxford, and his wife, Apphia Mary

James (*d.* 1931), the daughter of a Cardiganshire tenant farmer. The family was Welsh-speaking and its tone sombre. In 1921, when Rees was only eleven, his father was unexpectedly caught up in a massive political controversy, when he clashed with his chapel congregation following his support of a Lloyd George Liberal in opposition to an Asquithian in the Cardiganshire by-election. The family had to leave Aberystwyth in 1923 and moved to Roath in Cardiff. Rees was educated at Cardiff High School for Boys (1923–8) and then gained a scholarship to New College, Oxford. He took first-class honours in philosophy, politics, and economics in 1931 and was then elected to a prize fellowship at All Souls, the first Welshman so nominated. In that year he published the first of three novels, *The Summer Flood*, based on south Wales.

Rees then did some desultory research in Berlin and also played a minor role in a German film, impersonating a highland officer. Returning to England, he became a leader writer on the *Manchester Guardian* (1932–5) and then assistant editor of *The Spectator*. His second novel, *A Bridge to Divide them*, also about south Wales, appeared in 1937. At this time he enjoyed a colourful social life in literary and academic circles, and had vivid relationships with, among others, Shiela Grant Duff, Elizabeth Bowen, and Rosamond Lehmann. He also began in 1934 a fateful friendship with Guy Burgess that was profoundly to affect the rest of his life. Burgess told him in 1937 that he was an agent for the Comintern; many were later to allege that Rees, very sympathetic to communism in the thirties, was an agent or even a double agent himself.

However, when the war began Rees renounced communism and, already in the Territorial Army (Royal Artillery), mobilized as a gunner in the 90th field regiment. He took an officer's course at Sandhurst and was commissioned in the Royal Welch Fusiliers. He had an active war, serving in the raid on Dieppe, operating on the staff of General Sir Bernard Montgomery, and working as a colonel in the Allied Control Commission in Germany at the end of the war. On 20 December 1940 he had married Margaret (Margie) Ewing (1921–1976), the daughter of Thomas Tuckness Morris, underwriter, of Liverpool. They were to have five children, two girls and three boys. The marriage was a strong and successful one, and Rees's wife was a tower of refuge in the many crises that later beset his career.

In the post-war years, Rees became a director of Pontifex, general engineers and coppersmiths, the family firm of a friend, the novelist Henry Yorke. In 1950 he published his most successful novel, *Where No Wounds Were*. He returned to All Souls in 1951 and served successfully as the bursar of its considerable estates. Then in 1953, at the invitation of its president, Thomas Jones, Rees returned unexpectedly to Aberystwyth to become principal of the University College of Wales. This proved to be a catastrophe. Rees made a strong impression initially and a memorable principal's inaugural lecture recalled Mark Pattison in insisting that universities should mould character and culture: 'The result of learning is not a book but a man'. However, his unconventional social behaviour offended local sensibilities, while his English wife was never happy in so small and Welsh a town.

Rees's past relationship with Guy Burgess continued to haunt him. He had worked for MI6 after the war and in 1951 informed them of Burgess's record as a spy when Burgess and Maclean defected to Moscow; later he was to reveal Sir Anthony Blunt as 'the fourth man'. Visitors to the principal's residence, Plas Penglais, were startled to discover that the principal's dog was named Burgess. Disaster struck when, partly through need for money, Rees published in *The People* newspaper in 1956 a series of sensationalist articles about Burgess's activities and lifestyle. The college was scandalized and a commission of inquiry under Lord Willink severely criticized Rees's behaviour. Although a majority of the Aberystwyth council felt that no action need be taken after the commission's report, Rees decided to resign as principal in 1957. Meanwhile some colleagues in Oxford and Cambridge condemned him for disloyalty to his friends.

Rees then suffered a run of extreme bad luck. Shortly after leaving Aberystwyth, he was knocked down and almost killed in a car accident, while a venture into the building trade nearly ruined him financially. However, he found a niche for himself in writing and journalism. Under the *nom de plume* R he wrote a monthly column for *Encounter*, marked by a strongly anti-communist tone. He also wrote a series of relatively lucrative works, *The Multi-Millionaires* (1961); a historical guide, *The Rhine* (1967); *St Michael*, a history of Marks and Spencer (1969); and *The Great Slump* (1970). What established him as an unusually gifted writer, however, were two remarkable works of autobiography. *A Bundle of Sensations* (1960), whose title refers to Hume's theory of the self, was a series of incisive sketches of episodes in his life down to the 1950s. *A Chapter of Accidents* (1972) was a brilliant autobiography which revealed both the nuances of his complicated relationship with Burgess and his bitterness towards Aberystwyth. He also appeared successfully in the BBC television series *The Brains Trust*.

Rees's later years were difficult ones, with money and health problems and the death of his wife in 1976 after a long illness. The earlier crises of his life were recalled in works by Andrew Boyle and others which reflected on his contacts with Burgess, Blunt, and other spies. After his death it was alleged that he was a Soviet agent as they were, but his daughter's biography in 1994 concluded that his activities in this area were low-level and very short-lived. The truth is almost impenetrable. He died of cancer in Charing Cross Hospital, London, on 12 December 1979 and was cremated at Mortlake cemetery.

Goronwy Rees was a strikingly handsome, charming, intellectually gifted man. He had a graceful literary style and a remarkable command of languages. In Oxford in the thirties he was an attractive figure—amusing, unconventional, with a beguiling air of being the Celtic outsider, and yet later the charm could seem a professional artifice. His two works of autobiography established him as a writer of brilliance. Yet his career was disappointing and his talents remained unfulfilled, as he never really established his credentials either as a scholar or as a novelist. His tortuous relationship with Burgess confirmed for some Rees's unreliability as a witness and as a friend. His principalship at Aberystwyth revealed an astonishing lack of judgement for a public figure, however culpable his more puritanical critics there. Alone of recent principals, his portrait was not painted. He won many admirers, male and female, but made as many enemies. He will remain an intriguing figure in the world of Anglo-Welsh letters but it is his still mysterious connection with espionage and security in the cold war years for which he will be most remembered.   KENNETH O. MORGAN

Sources G. Rees, *A bundle of sensations* (1960) · G. Rees, *A chapter of accidents* (1972) · J. Rees, *Looking for Mr Nobody* (1994) · A. Boyle, *The climate of treason: five who spied for Russia* (1979) · archive records, U. Wales, Aberystwyth · E. L. Ellis, *The University College of Wales, Aberystwyth, 1872–1972* (1972) · T. Bower, *The perfect English spy* (1995) · S. Grant Duff, *The parting of ways: a personal account of the thirties* (1982) · NL Wales, Thomas Jones papers · personal knowledge (2004) · BBC (Wales) video material · G. Rees' inaugural lecture, priv. coll. · private information (2004) [Lord Jay of Battersea; R. Cobb; S. Balsom] · m. cert.
Archives NL Scot., transcript history of Dalgety Ltd | NL Scot., corresp. with Lord Tweedsmuir · NL Wales, corresp. with Emyn Humphreys · NL Wales, Thomas Jones MSS · U. Wales, Aberystwyth, archives |FILM BBC (Wales) |SOUND BBC (Wales)

Rees, (Florence) Gwendolen (1906–1994), parasitologist, was born on 3 July 1906 in Abercynon, Glamorgan, the younger daughter of Ebenezer Rees (1865–1948), superintendent of police in the Glamorgan constabulary, and his wife (Elizabeth) Agnes, *née* Jones (1877–1921). After a brief period of residence in Llandaff, near Cardiff, in 1912 the family settled at 4 Elm Grove, Aberdâr. Rees's father ('Super Rees') was a respected local figure who required his daughters to adhere to the highest standards of self-discipline, dress, and behaviour. Her mother, who had taken a diploma in dairying at the University of Reading, died when Gwen was only fourteen years old. Her sister, Iris Mary, who was her senior by two and a half years, remained in Aberdâr until her marriage to the Revd Maldwyn Humphries.

Rees was educated at the Park council school, Aberdâr, from 1912 to 1918, and at Aberdâr girls' grammar school, from 1918 to 1924. She obtained her higher school certificate with distinction in botany and zoology, and was awarded two prize scholarships and a grant, which together enabled her in October 1924 to enter the University College of South Wales and Monmouthshire, Cardiff, to study zoology. She was highly disciplined and painstaking in all that she did, and although primarily committed to her academic studies she also enjoyed music (she had learned to play the piano and violin), visits to the theatre, and sporting pastimes, including hockey, tennis, gymnastics, and horse-riding. Her decision to specialize in parasitology was taken at the start of her final year. She graduated in 1927 with an upper second-class degree. The following year was spent in a course of professional training that qualified her for a certificate of education, but in 1928 a scholarship from her university hall of residence enabled her to return to the department of zoology as a graduate student.

There was at that time considerable local concern regarding the high incidence of liver fluke disease in flocks of sheep in south Wales, and Rees attached herself to a small team investigating the distribution of the snails that served as intermediate hosts of the infectious larval trematodes. Total dedication and a prodigious work rate enabled her to complete her PhD studies in a mere eighteen months. In this period she examined more than 5000 snails from over a hundred localities and found that some 13 per cent were infected. Ten distinct larval trematodes were discovered, of which three proved to be new species. Her PhD thesis was illustrated with over fifty plates of meticulously accurate drawings, remarkable in their clarity and representation of forms and structures. This exceptional artistry in illustration was to become characteristic of all of her future published works.

The examiner of Rees's thesis was so impressed by its quality that he brought her to the attention of Douglas Laurie, professor of zoology at the University College of Wales, Aberystwyth, who in 1930 appointed her to an assistant lectureship in his department. She remained in Aberystwyth for the rest of her life, becoming senior lecturer (1946–66), reader (1966–71), professor (1971–3), and thereafter professor emeritus. In this seaside location she displayed a particular interest in trematodes (flukes) that infected molluscs and fish but she also contributed greatly to knowledge of cestodes (tapeworms). Besides marine and freshwater fish she examined numerous other hosts, including insects, amphibians, reptiles, and mammals. Particularly influential was the distinction that she drew between infestation and disease, with the latter in her view stemming from 'occasional maladjustment between the parasite and host' (Morris, 456). At various times she worked for short periods in Ghana and Bermuda. She was a founding member of the British Society for Parasitology and served as its president from 1972 to 1974. She was also chairman of the editorial board of the journal *Parasitology* (1970–81). She was elected fellow of the Royal Society in 1971 (the first woman working in Wales to be so honoured). Her lifetime contributions to the advancement of her discipline were recognized by the award to her in 1990 of the Linnean medal for zoology.

For all her accomplishments Rees remained a genuinely modest person, 'friendly, courteous and scholarly' (*The Times*). By her teaching she inspired generations of prospective parasitologists, and through her wide-ranging and definitive researches she greatly advanced the development of helminthology in Britain. The quest for perfection that was so evident in her academic work also motivated her personal life. She was noted for her style and elegance, illustrated in *Vogue* magazine in a 1975 article devoted to some of Britain's most influential women. However, she lived simply and privately, enjoying the friendship of past students and colleagues until, after a short confinement in Bronglais Hospital, Aberystwyth, she died there, quietly, on 4 October 1994. She never married.   J. GARETH MORRIS

Sources personal record, RS · G. Morris, *Memoirs FRS*, 43 (1997), 445–59 · H. Williams, 'Gwendolen Rees FRS: fifty-six years (1930 to date) in research', *Parasitology*, 92 (1986), 483–98 · M. Beverley-Burton, 'Gwendolen Rees FRS', *International Journal for Parasitology*, 25 (1995), 1145–8 · *The Independent* (20 Oct 1994) · *The Times* (28 Oct 1994) · H. Williams, 'Gwendolen Rees DSc, FRS: a biographical sketch', *Journal of Parasitology*, 72 (1986), 3–8 · V. Southgate, 'Memories of Professor F. Gwendolen Rees FRS', *Journal of Parasitology*, 72 (1986), 9 · personal knowledge (2004) · private information (2004) · d. cert. · *CGPLA Eng. & Wales* (1995)
Archives NMG Wales, Harford Williams collection, papers and drawings
Likenesses two photographs, 1928–30, repro. in Beverley-Burton, 'Gwendolen Rees FRS' · photograph, RS; repro. in Morris, *Memoirs FRS*
Wealth at death £344,137: probate, 21 July 1995, *CGPLA Eng. & Wales*

Rees, Henry

Rees, Henry (1798–1869), Calvinistic Methodist minister, eldest son of David Rees of Chwibren Isaf in the parish of Llansannan, Denbighshire, and Anne, *née* Williams, of Cefn Fforest, was born on 15 February 1798. William *Rees (1802–1883) was his brother. His father, who moved in a short time to Rhydloyw and from there to Cae-du in the same district, was a lay officer of the Calvinistic Methodist connexion, and Henry showed at an early age a deep interest in religious work. In May 1816 he left home to take employment on a farm near Betws Abergele, and while in this district, in the spring of 1819, began to preach. Resolving to devote himself to the Calvinistic Methodist ministry, he came home to Cae-du in May, and was then tutored for two years by Thomas Lloyd of Abergele.

It was not the practice of the ministers of his connexion at this time to depend wholly on the ministry for support, and accordingly, in 1821, Rees went to Shrewsbury to learn bookbinding. In the following year he accepted the charge of the Calvinistic Methodist church there in return for his maintenance. He was ordained to the full work of the ministry at Bala on 13 June 1827, and on 20 October 1830 married Mary Roberts (d. 1879) of Shrewsbury. During his stay in Shrewsbury Rees rapidly won a position as one of the foremost preachers of his connexion, and from this time until his death was a regular preacher at the great meetings of the North Wales Association. At the end of 1836 he accepted the superintendence of the Calvinistic Methodist churches in Liverpool, where he spent the rest of his life. He died on 18 February 1869 at Benarth, near Conwy, his son-in-law's house, and was buried in Llandysilio churchyard, near Menai Bridge. He left one daughter, Anne, who married Richard Davies of Treborth, Liberal MP for Anglesey (1868–86).

Rees devoted himself to the two duties of preaching and connexional administration. After the death of John Elias in 1841 he was for a quarter of a century the recognized leader of the Calvinistic Methodists of north Wales, and had the largest share in forming the policy of the northern association, serving as moderator in 1855 and 1867. He was elected first moderator of the general assembly of the connexion in 1864. His opposition to the 1843 royal commission on education in Wales helped to promote the development of political radicalism among the Calvinistic Methodists. As a preacher he had scarcely a rival in the denomination, his sermons being precise but forceful. He distrusted rhetorical effect. A selection of his sermons was published at Holywell in three volumes (1872, 1875, 1881).

J. E. LLOYD, *rev.* MARTIN WELLINGS

Sources DWB · E. ap N. Roberts, 'Rees, Henry', *The Blackwell dictionary of evangelical biography, 1730–1860*, ed. D. M. Lewis (1995)
Archives NL Wales, corresp. and papers; corresp., family letters, papers, and sermons | NL Wales, letters to Lewis Edwards · NL Wales, letters to Owen Thomas, etc.
Likenesses Schenck and McFarlane, lithograph (after photograph), BM · portrait, repro. in A. M. Davies, *Life and letters of Henry Rees* (1904)
Wealth at death under £8000: probate, 8 April 1869, *CGPLA Eng. & Wales*

Rees, John Rawlings

Rees, John Rawlings (1890–1969), psychiatrist, was born on 25 June 1890 at 9 The Crescent, King Street, Leicester, the fourth of seven children of Robert Montgomery Rees, a Wesleyan Methodist minister, and his wife, Catherine Millar Tait. A secure childhood in a religious household led Rees to consider becoming a missionary but instead he trained in medicine. Rees was educated at Leeds and Bradford grammar schools, King's College, Cambridge, and the London Hospital, qualifying LRCP, MRCS, in 1914, and MB BChir in 1915. At the outset of war he joined the Friends' Ambulance Unit and saw immediate service in France for which he was awarded the 1914 medal. He transferred to the Royal Army Medical Corps and served at the Somme where he saw soldiers executed for desertion having, in his opinion, suffered nervous breakdown. Later he served in Mesopotamia and India and wrote that he grew up emotionally through his military experience which had also prepared him for his career in army psychiatry in the Second World War, when he saw to it that psychiatric casualties were appropriately diagnosed and properly treated.

Though attracted to public health (he was awarded the DPH by the University of Cambridge in 1920), chance brought Rees to psychological medicine by meeting Hugh Crichton-Miller, a pioneer psychotherapist, founder of Bowden House, a clinic for the early treatment of psychiatric disorder, and later the founder of the Tavistock Clinic. At Bowden House he met Dr Mary (Molly) Isabel (1887–1954), daughter of Charles Robert Hemmingway, a railway contractor. They married on 15 December 1921, and later had one daughter.

In 1932 Crichton-Miller abruptly resigned from the Tavistock Clinic, hurt by criticism of his methods and was succeeded by Rees as director. Under Rees's directorship much energy was liberated; he recruited talented therapists and by 1939 the Tavistock was the major centre of psychodynamic psychiatry in the United Kingdom. Training in psychiatric social work and child guidance work was pioneered there. Rees's own analysis was with Maurice Nicoll but he did not join the British Psychoanalytic Society.

Rees, in contrast to Crichton-Miller, who was an aristocrat in temperament, was a much more natural democrat. Though he shared with Crichton-Miller the background of being a son of the manse and possessing strong Christian values (the Tavistock was derisively termed 'the parson's clinic' by Professor Edward Maypother of its rival, the Maudsley Hospital), Rees did not share his zeal for discovering bodily causes of mental illness such as focal sepsis or endocrine disorders:

> If Crichton-Miller was a Don Quixote with a very high aim, J. R. Rees was the necessary complement as his Sancho Panza, mundane, much more down-to-earth, practical organising and executive person who actually made the Tavistock Clinic function as a living institution.   (Dicks, 59)

Rees had an almost missionary zeal to promote not only the Tavistock Clinic, but the spread of knowledge of and the techniques of psychotherapy and mental health into wider fields. This he achieved in British army psychiatry and then found his apogee in the World Federation of Mental Health. What he achieved for the Tavistock was one phase of the career of someone who was described as 'this natural unself-conscious leader and originator' (Dicks, 296).

To his surprise, Rees was invited in 1939 to take command of British army psychiatry at home, where he initially found that he was the only psychiatrist available. He quickly assembled a team, mostly from colleagues at the Tavistock Clinic, several of whom had also served in the First World War. Their collective experience gained psychiatrists respect from serving officers and opened the way for them to be both acceptable and influential throughout the war. By 1945 there were 300 trained psychiatrists in the army and significant work was done in personnel selection, the study of morale breakdown and maintenance, and the psychiatric rehabilitation of neurotic soldiers and of returning prisoners of war. Under his direction army psychiatry became efficient and humane. The education and training of mentally handicapped soldiers was a major innovation which led the way in postwar developments. He finished the war with the rank of brigadier.

After succeeding Crichton-Miller, Rees had greatly fostered the growth of the Tavistock Clinic but the position altered greatly after the Second World War. The Tavistock itself was a changed place: a younger generation had experienced power and influence in the armed forces and were enthusiastic to acquire and use psychoanalytic knowledge. Rees, however, was not in tune with this enthusiasm. He felt pressured by the power of the younger generation to give up his position as director, which he did in 1947. So began the third phase of his career. Rees became a leading figure in the movement to maintain and develop wartime co-operation among psychiatrists, to build on what had been learned and his mission became to research and to treat mental illness in its social roots. After organizing the first Mental Health Congress in London in 1948, he was highly influential in the formation soon afterwards of the World Federation for Mental Health, of which he was president for one year, subsequently director for many years. Indefatigable, diplomatic, his activities widely recognized, he became honorary president after retirement. The federation brought modern psychiatry to developing countries, trained their personnel, and stimulated research. His modest apartment at 116 Bickenhall Mansions, Baker Street, London, was at the heart of this new movement, a welcoming place for colleagues worldwide. At one point when the treasurer of the World Federation for Mental Health had to declare the treasury empty he produced a shilling from his pocket to secure its future.

Rees was able to acknowledge that he was not in the top rank of psychiatrists or psychotherapists. His influence derived from his dedication, and his ability to assemble, to work with teams, and to encourage individual development. His tolerant, genial personality and democratic style of leadership was significant in the great expansion of the Tavistock Clinic in the 1930s, to army psychiatry in the Second World War, and in the World Federation of Mental Health. The great influence of the Tavistock Clinic in the professionalization of work in the field of mental health and illness has been analysed by Nikolas Rose in *The Psychological Complex* (1985) and *Governing the Soul* (1990).

Among Rees's writings the most personal is *Reflections* (1966) published at his retirement by the United States committee of the World Federation for Mental Health. His wartime experience is described in *The Shaping of Psychiatry by War* (1945) and in *The Case of Rudolph Hess* (1947). He became a member of the Royal College of Physicians in 1936, a fellow in 1944, and was made CBE in 1946. Rees died on 11 April 1969 at his home, 116 Bickenhall Mansions, Baker Street, London.   MALCOLM PINES

Sources *The Lancet* (19 April 1969) · *BMJ* (26 April 1969), 253 · J. R. Rees, *Reflections* (1966) · J. R. Rees, *Mary Hemmingway Rees: a memoir* (privately printed, 1967) · H. V. Dicks, *Fifty years of the Tavistock Clinic* (1970) · N. Rose, *Governing the soul* (1990) · b. cert. · m. cert. · d. cert. · *Medical Directory*
Archives Tavistock Clinic Library, 120 Belsize Park, London
Wealth at death £19,343: probate, 17 July 1969, *CGPLA Eng. & Wales*

Rees, Josiah (1744–1804), Unitarian minister and journal editor, was born on 2 October 1744 at Clun-pentan in the parish of Llanfair-ar-y-bryn, near Llandovery, Carmarthenshire, the son of Owen Rees (1716–1768), and his wife, Mary Howell (1718–1818). His father, who was ordained minister to a congregation of protestant dissenters at Pentre-tŷ-gwyn in March 1741, was the first nonconformist minister to be ordained in the parish of Aberdâr in 1751.

Rees received his early education at the grammar school of Solomon Harries in Swansea, and then proceeded to the Presbyterian college at Carmarthen in 1762, where his lifelong friend the Revd David Davies of Castellhywel was among his fellow students. He became minister-elect of Gellionnen church in the parish of Llan-giwg, Glamorgan, in 1763 but continued his studies at Carmarthen until he was ordained minister at Gellionnen on 6 August 1767. He also kept a school at his home, Gelli-gron, until about 1785. In the same year he declined the principalship of the Carmarthen Presbyterian college, when it moved to Swansea, but he consented to deliver a series of lectures on divinity there.

Rees led his congregation through various stages of Arminianism to Arianism, and eventually to Unitarianism, and his church, which was rebuilt and enlarged in 1801, became an important centre for the Unitarians of south Wales. On 8 October 1802 it was the chosen venue for a meeting to discuss proposals for the establishment of the South Wales Unitarian Association, and Rees was the preacher at the association's first public assembly at Cefncoedycymer, Merthyr Tudful, on 26 June 1803.

Rees married twice: first, Catherine (*d*. 1768), daughter of Evan David Howell; and second, Mary (1747–1829), daughter of Thomas Jones of Pen-y-glôg, Carmarthen. Ten children were born of the second marriage, among whom were Owen *Rees (1770–1837) [*see under* Rees, Thomas], who became a partner in the publishing firm of Longman in 1794, and Thomas *Rees (1777–1864), Unitarian minister and historical writer.

Rees was acquainted with collections of Welsh manuscripts and their owners in Glamorgan, and his friendship with these antiquaries induced him to launch a Welsh magazine entitled *Trysorfa Gwybodaeth, neu, Eurgrawn Cymraeg* ('Treasury of knowledge, or, Welsh magazine') in 1770. If we except *Tlysau yr hen oesoedd* ('Gems of past ages'), established in 1735 by Lewis Morris (1701–1765), of which one number only appeared, *Trysorfa Gwybodaeth* was the first successful periodical publication in Welsh. Rees was probably assisted in the venture by the Revd Peter Williams (1723–1796) and the printer–poet Evan Thomas (1733–1814). Fifteen fortnightly issues were printed by John Ross at Carmarthen between March and September 1770. Each number comprised four separately paginated sections: eight pages of Welsh history (the text of *Brut y tywysogyon*), eight pages of miscellaneous essays, eight pages of verse, and eight pages of home and foreign news. At the end of the year purchasers were expected to bind up the magazine into four separate volumes. Although the contents were varied and interesting the Welsh-reading public was unready for such an ambitious project, and after incurring debts of over £100 Rees was compelled to bring the periodical to an end.

Rees also translated several works into Welsh, among which the most important are *Catecism, neu, Egwyddorion crefydd* ('A catechism, or, The principles of religion') by Henry Read (1770) and *Hunan-adnabyddiaeth* ('Self-knowledge') by John Mason (1771). In 1804 he wrote a tract, a copy of which has not survived but which evoked the Revd Joseph Harris (Gomer; 1773–1825) to reply in his *Bwyall Crist yng nghoed Anghrist* ('The axe of Christ in the forest of Antichrist') in the same year. Rees died on 20 September 1804 at Gelli-gron, Llan-giwg, Glamorgan, and was buried in Gellionnen cemetery.   HUW WALTERS

Sources G. J. Williams, *Traddodiad llenyddol Morgannwg* (1948), 309–15 · G. J. Williams, 'Trysorfa gwybodaeth (1770)', *Iolo Morganwg* (1956), 161–5 · G. J. Williams, 'Josiah Rees a'r *Eurgrawn Cymraeg* (1770)', *Llên Cymru*, 3 (1954), 119 · G. M. Roberts, *Bywyd a gwaith Peter Williams* (1943), 176–84 · W. J. Phillips, 'Gweinidogaeth Josiah Rees', *Yr Ymofynnydd*, 62 (Oct 1962), 165–7 · W. J. Phillips, 'Gweinidogaeth Josiah Rees', *Yr Ymofynnydd*, 62 (Nov 1962), 177–9 · E. Rees, ed., *Libri Walliae: a catalogue of Welsh books and books printed in Wales, 1546–1820*, 2 vols. (1987) · 'Dyddlyfr Morgan Williams', NL Wales, MS 14916A ['The diary of Morgan Williams'] · Richard Rees, Alltycham, Pontardawe, album, NL Wales, MS 11138D · W. J. Phillips, 'Iolo Morganwg and the Rees family of Gelligron', *National Library of Wales Journal*, 14 (1965–6), 227–36 · D. E. Walters, 'Hen Emynwyr: Josiah Rees, Gellionnen, 1744–1804', *Y Tyst* (1 Nov 1954) · D. E. Walters, 'Hen Emynwyr: Josiah Rees, Gellionnen, 1744–1804', *Y Tyst* (8 Nov 1954) · D. Evans, *Welsh Unitarians as schoolmasters* [1945] · T. O. Williams, *Undodiaeth a rhyddid meddwl* (1962)
Archives NL Wales, Richard Rees MS
Likenesses pencil drawing, NL Wales, MS 11138D, 21

Rees, Lionel Wilmot Brabazon (1884–1955), air force officer, was born at 5 Castle Street, Caernarfon, on 31 July 1884, son of Charles Herbert Rees (*d*. 1930), a solicitor and honorary colonel of the 3rd volunteer battalion the Royal Welch Fusiliers, and his wife, Leonora Maria, daughter of Smith William Davids from Caernarfon. Rees's early years were spent at Plas Llanwnda in Castle Street. Educated at Elms preparatory school, Colwall, and Eastbourne College, he entered the Royal Military Academy, Woolwich, on 29 January 1902, where he secured the Tombs memorial prize. Commissioned second lieutenant in the Royal Artillery on 23 December 1903, he joined the Royal Garrison Artillery at Gibraltar, where he advanced to lieutenant on 23 December 1906. From 1908 he was in Sierra Leone, on 21 May 1913 being seconded to the Southern Nigeria regiment.

During leave, Rees at his own expense took flying lessons at the Bristol School, Larkhill, gaining Royal Aero Club certificate no. 392 after one week on 7 January 1913. Attached to the Royal Flying Corps on 10 August 1914 and promoted captain on 30 October 1914 while instructing at the Central Flying School, he went on to command 7 squadron at Netheravon and, from 14 February 1915, 11 squadron. Landing near Amiens on 25 July 1915, the squadron's pilots found their commanding officer, who had flown ahead, in overalls repairing his machine damaged in combat the previous day. During the ensuing three months, Rees shot down three enemy aircraft, damaged several others, was mentioned in dispatches, and was awarded the MC 'for conspicuous gallantry and skill on several occasions … notably on 21st Sept 1915' (*London Gazette*, 29 Oct 1915). While commanding the Central Flying School, Upavon, he advanced to temporary major on 28 November 1915.

Back in France leading 32 squadron, Rees repeatedly flew sorties over enemy lines and also wrote a pamphlet *Fighting in the Air*, a comprehensive analysis of equipment, machines, and tactics in current use. On 5 August 1916 he was awarded the VC 'for conspicuous gallantry and devotion to duty' (*London Gazette*) on 1 July 1916, when he received a thigh-wound that left him with a lifelong limp. Patrolling alone, near Double Crassieurs, he initially mistook seven German machines for returning British bombers, then attacked to drive them all back over their own trenches despite his painful wound and severe damage to his aircraft.

After convalescence Rees accompanied a War Office mission to the USA, advancing to temporary lieutenant-colonel on 1 May 1917. When he was in charge of the School of Aerial Fighting at Turnberry in Scotland, a series of crashes undermined the confidence of staff and pupils in the Sopwith Camel, so Rees promptly performed aerobatics at 500 feet. He became a substantive major on 4 April 1918 and brevet lieutenant-colonel on 3 June 1918. He appeared in the newly formed Royal Air Force from 1 April 1918 as a temporary lieutenant-colonel, and on 2 November 1918 was appointed OBE and awarded the AFC. In 1919 Rees secured second place in the Gordon-Shephard memorial prize essay competition. On 15 January 1920 he was presented with a sword of honour and the freedom of the borough of Caernarfon. He took command of the flying wing at the RAF College, Cranwell, on 21 June 1920 and became assistant commandant there on 26 March 1923. Rees was promoted group captain, appointed deputy director of the directorate of training at the Air Ministry, and made additional air aide-de-camp to the king on 1 January 1925.

Posted to RAF Transjordan at Amman on 6 May 1926, Rees assumed command of RAF Transjordan and Palestine on 1 October 1926. He took charge of the RAF depot at Uxbridge on 9 April 1929, 21 group at West Drayton on 16 December 1929. He retired from the RAF on 1 August 1931.

In 1933 Rees sailed his 34 foot ketch single-handed from Porth-yr-aur to the Bahamas, for which he received the Cruising Club of America's blue water medal, and settled at Nassau. He returned to the active list as a wing commander on 21 January 1941 and served until 1942 in Africa. On 12 August 1947 he married, at Andros, Sylvia Williams, who was of west African descent, the eighteen-year-old daughter of Alexander and Mary Williams. They set up home at Mangrove Cay, and had two sons and a daughter (Williams, 252–5).

Rees was reputedly an excellent shot, able to hit with either hand a business card held by a colleague at 25 yards. His air gunner during the First World War, Flight Sergeant J. M. Hargreaves, described him as 'a gentleman, a real gentleman, a rare species' (Bowyer, 67). Sir Harry Luke, who served with him in the Near East, thought Rees a 'rare and strange personality … solitary'. Nevertheless, although reserved, his 'highly original characteristics failed to endear him to his immediate superior in Egypt'. Privately, his 'unselfish and generous instincts were matched by the monastic austerity of his private life' (The Times, 4 Oct 1955). In Transjordan, and possibly at other times, relying on personal wealth he unobtrusively donated his pay to RAF charities. Rees was also a keen amateur archaeologist with 'an uncanny knowledge' of the desert. He died of leukaemia at the Princess Margaret Hospital, Nassau, on 28 September 1955, and was survived by his wife. Memorials to him were placed in Nassau war cemetery, where he was buried, and St George's royal garrison church, Woolwich.   JOHN SWEETMAN

Sources Army List · Air Force List · C. Bowyer, For valour: the air VCs (1978) · The register of the Victoria cross (1981) · O'M. Creagh and E. M. Humphris, The V.C. and D.S.O., 1 [1920] · R. Stewart, ed., The Victoria Cross (1916) · P. Cooksley, The air VCs (1996) · WWW, 1951–60 · The Times (29 Sept 1955) · The Times (4 Oct 1955) · W. A. Williams, Against the odds: the life of Group Captain Lionel Rees VC, OBE, MC, AFC (1989) · G. H. Lewis, Wings over the Somme, 1916–1918 (1976) · b. cert.

Archives SOUND IWM SA, oral history interview
Likenesses photographs, 1903–42, repro. in Williams, Against the odds · N. Arnold, portraits, IWM · C. Dobson, portrait, IWM · photographs, repro. in Bowyer, For valour, facing pp. 70, 162

Rees, Owen (1770–1837). See under Rees, Thomas (1777–1864).

Rees, Rice (1804–1839), historian, son of David and Sarah Rees, was born at Ton in the parish of Llandingad, Carmarthenshire, on 31 March 1804. From 1819 he was educated at Lampeter grammar school. He matriculated at Oxford, from Jesus College, in May 1822. He graduated BA in 1826, MA in 1828, and BD in 1837. From 1825 to 1828 he was a scholar of his college, and in the latter year he was elected fellow. In March 1827 St David's College, Lampeter, was opened; Rees's tutor in Oxford became principal, and Rees was appointed professor of Welsh, tutor, and librarian. He was ordained deacon in the same year and priest in 1828. In 1832 he became rector of Llanddewi Felffre, Pembrokeshire, and in October 1838 he was appointed domestic chaplain to Bishop J. B. Jenkinson. He had already been entrusted with the responsibility of examining candidates for holy orders, in Welsh. He was also a member of the committee appointed to produce a revised edition of the Welsh Book of Common Prayer.

While Rees was still a pupil at Lampeter grammar school, his interest in Welsh history and culture had been awakened by John Howell (Ioan Glan Dryfroedd). As rector of Llanddewi Felffre, he devoted himself to Welsh studies. In August 1835 he won the prize offered at the Carmarthen eisteddfod for the best account of the early founders of Welsh churches. The prize composition was expanded into the full and luminous Essay on the Welsh Saints published in 1836, an authority for the early history of the Welsh church.

Rees died suddenly, probably of overwork, on 20 May 1839, at Newbridge-on-Wye, Brecknockshire, while travelling from Casgob to Lampeter, and was buried in Llandingad churchyard. At the time of his death he was working on an edition of the Liber Landavensis, which was completed unsatisfactorily by his uncle, William Jenkins *Rees, in 1853, and also on a new edition of Rhys Prichard's Canwyll y Cymry, which was finished in 1841 by his brother, William Rees, a publisher in Llandovery.

J. E. LLOYD, rev. NILANJANA BANERJI

Sources DWB · Foster, Alum. Oxon. · R. Williams, Enwogion Cymru: a biographical dictionary of eminent Welshmen (1852) · R. Rees, An essay on the Welsh saints (1836), preface · R. Prichard, Canwyll y Cymry, 1867 edn (1672), 60

Rees, Rosemary Theresa. See Du Cros, Rosemary Theresa, Lady Du Cros (1901–1994).

Rees, Sarah Jane [pseud. Cranogwen] (1839–1916), sailor, schoolmistress, and poet, was born on 9 January 1839 at Dolgoy Fach, a cottage some 2½ miles from the coastal village of Llangrannog on Cardigan Bay, from which she took her bardic name, Cranogwen. She was the youngest of three children of Captain John Rees (1807–1893) and his wife, Frances (1803–1884).

Cranogwen was passionately devoted to education

Sarah Jane Rees [Cranogwen] (**1839–1916**), by John Thomas

throughout her life. Her own schooling began in the small village school at Pontgarreg, run by the old, but highly regarded, Hugh Davies. When she left school her parents planned that she should take up an apprenticeship as a dressmaker in Cardigan. This was not at all to her liking, and instead she insisted on accompanying her father to sea. She spent two years as a sailor aboard her father's ketch, which travelled between the ports of Wales, England, and France, and carried cargoes of coal and household goods. Then she resumed her education, attending 'higher schools' in Newquay (where she studied navigation), Pont-siân, and Cardigan. She studied at a nautical school in London, where she gained her master's certificate, a qualification allowing her to command a ship in any part of the world. At some point she also studied English literature at Blackburne House in Liverpool.

A tall, dark, striking woman, strong-willed and supremely confident, but possessed of a delightful sense of humour, Cranogwen was, without doubt, the most outstanding Welsh woman of the nineteenth century. Cranogwen broke new ground for women in many fields and appears never to have been constrained by the English ideal of the 'perfect lady', a model of femininity which could, at best, have limited application in the different economic circumstances of Wales. She was to lead a very public life, lecturing to wide audiences and preaching in chapels, and she became something of a national institution in her own lifetime. She appeared to live life according to the principle that there was nothing that she could

not do, and for much of her life she enjoyed the support of her close friend, Jane Thomas.

Following her time at sea and her continued education, Cranogwen returned to Llangrannog, where from 1860 to 1866 she ran the old school at Pontgarreg, which she herself had attended. Despite objections raised by the governors of this British School at the appointment of a 21-year-old woman, Cranogwen, as ever, prevailed. Here she taught navigation and seamanship to the young men of the district, as well as providing children with their elementary education.

During her years as a schoolmistress Cranogwen turned her attention to writing poetry. She competed successfully at various local eisteddfods and in 1865 she entered, for the first time, the national eisteddfod, held that year in Aberystwyth. She won. She was the first woman to do so and became famous overnight. With her winning poem, 'Y fodrwy briodasol', a moving account of a married woman's lot, she beat the leading bards of the day, Islwyn and Ceiriog. She went on to further successes at the national eisteddfod in Chester the following year and later won chairs at eisteddfods in Caerphilly and Aberaeron, where she won in 1873 with her long poem in free verse on the wreck of the north fleet, 'Drylliad y north fleet'. Her poetry was very popular and she wrote on a broad range of themes, such as nature, her love of Wales, her Christian faith, the evils of drink, storms and shipwrecks, and her everyday experiences, including the trials of missing a train. A collection of some forty of her poems, *Caniadau Cranogwen*, was published about 1870.

In 1866 Cranogwen gave up the school at Pontgarreg to concentrate on a new career as a lecturer and preacher. She travelled extensively throughout Wales and made two American lecture tours (1869 and 1888). Despite vocal opposition from some quarters to a woman speaking from a public platform Cranogwen, with her powerful voice, vivid use of language, and appreciation of the use of the dramatic pause, was a very popular lecturer. She was a deeply religious woman and, like many of her contemporaries, was influenced by the religious and temperance revival of 1859. She felt a vocation to preach the word of God, but the pulpit was viewed as a far cry from the lecture platform and Cranogwen suffered much highly personal abuse, which dented her confidence and led to bouts of depression. But in this, as in other spheres, she was a ground-breaker, and she gained the support of Thomas Levi, a prominent nonconformist leader.

In 1879 Cranogwen became the first woman ever to edit a Welsh-language women's magazine, when she brought out *Y Frythones*, which she edited until 1889. An attractive, illustrated publication with stories, poems, features, and a problem page, the magazine was aimed primarily at working-class young women. Cranogwen contributed a great deal to its contents and provided a platform for other Welsh women writers. The magazine advocated secondary and higher education for women, the virtues of temperance, and the extension of opportunities by which women might earn independent and respectable livings. Although the question of women's suffrage did not figure prominently in *Y Frythones*, those articles which did address the issue were firmly in favour. Cranogwen herself, though not known to have been a member of any suffrage organization, seems to have believed that it would be just a matter of time before women were enfranchised and that this would mark an important step on the road to women gaining full legal rights.

Temperance had always been an issue close to Cranogwen's heart and in 1901 she founded Undeb Dirwestol Merched y De (South Wales women's temperance union). By the time of her death in 1916 there were some 140 branches throughout south Wales. She did not live to see her dream of a house for young women who had appeared in court on charges of drunkenness 'and associated evils', but a fund was raised after her death and Llety Cranogwen was opened as a memorial to her by the Rhondda branch in 1922. Cranogwen died at the home of her niece, 50 Wood Street, Cilfynydd, Pontypridd, on 27 June 1916, and was buried alongside her parents in the churchyard of St Carannog's Church, Llangrannog.

DEIRDRE BEDDOE

Sources D. G. Jones, *Cofiant Cranogwen* (1932) · C. Lloyd-Morgan, 'From temperance to suffrage?', *Our mother's land: chapters in Welsh women's history, 1830–1939*, ed. A. V. John (1991), 135–58 · S. R. Williams, 'The true "Cymraes": images of women in women's nineteenth century Welsh periodicals', *Our mother's land: chapters in Welsh women's history, 1830–1939*, ed. A. V. John (1991), 69–91 · *Y Frythones* (1879–89) · 'Cranogwen dead', *Western Mail* [Cardiff] (28 June 1916) · *Cardiff Times* (1 July 1916) · C. Lloyd-Morgan, 'Cranogwen a barddoniaeth merched yn y Gymraeg', *Barddas*, 211 (Nov 1994) · G. Jones, *Cranogwen: Portread Newydd, Gerallt Jones* (1981) · d. cert. · private information (2004) · *CGPLA Eng. & Wales* (1916)
Archives NL Wales, papurau Undeb Dirwestol Merched y De (South Wales women's temperance union papers)
Likenesses photograph, *c*.1885, Cardiff Central Library · J. Thomas, photograph, *c*.1910, NL Wales · B. Owen, photograph, NL Wales · J. Thomas, photograph, NL Wales [*see illus.*] · photograph, NL Wales
Wealth at death £530 5*s*. 1*d*.: probate, 19 Dec 1916, *CGPLA Eng. & Wales*

Rees, Thomas (1777–1864), Unitarian minister and writer on theological history, was born at Gelli-gron, Glamorgan, a younger son of Josiah *Rees (1744–1804), dissenting minister at Gellionnen. He was apprenticed to a bookseller, but Abraham Rees (to whom he was not related) encouraged him to enter the ministry, and accordingly he studied at the Presbyterian college, Carmarthen, from 1799 to 1802. In 1802–3 he preached at Cirencester, in 1803–5 at Ipswich, and in 1805–6 at Gellionnen. In 1807 he became afternoon preacher at Newington Green Chapel, Middlesex, of which he had sole charge from 1808 to 1813, when he moved to St Thomas's Chapel, Southwark, which was closed in 1822. On 12 October 1823 a new chapel was opened in Stamford Street, Blackfriars, built from the proceeds of the sale of St Thomas's and of the chapel in Prince's Street, Westminster. Rees ministered to the merged congregations until 1831, when he ceased to hold a regular charge.

Rees was a man of varied attainments and an ardent Unitarian. He was a fellow of the Society of Arts, and received the degree of LLD from the University of Aberdeen in May 1818. He was made a trustee of Dr Williams's foundation in 1809 and a member of the Presbyterian Board in 1813, serving as its secretary from 1825; for a time he was also secretary of the Unitarian Society.

In 1828 Rees became secretary of the London union of ministers of the 'three denominations'—Presbyterians, Congregationalists, and Baptists—but in 1835 the newly confident and numerically superior orthodox terminated his appointment, reflecting a determination to deny the precedence assumed by Unitarians, who claimed to represent the English Presbyterians, once the largest of dissenting denominations but which congregational splits or theological evolution had deprived of all but nominal existence. Resenting the action, the Unitarians seceded from the union and obtained the separate privilege of presenting addresses to the throne. No personal disrespect had been intended to Rees, and in 1837 the three denominations nominated him for appointment as principal receiver of the English *regium donum*—a government grant to English dissenting ministers and their widows, of which Rees had published a brief history in 1834.

Rees had no equal in his time as an authority on the history of anti-trinitarian opinion, especially during the sixteenth century. He made a remarkable collection of the literature on this theme—which his misfortunes forced him to sell—and, excepting Hungarian and Polish, he was at home in all the languages necessary for access to original sources. His breadth of treatment gave his topic more than sectarian interest. He published a number of articles in the *Monthly Repository* and the *Christian Reformer*, and his translation of the Racovian catechism, with a preliminary sketch of the history of Polish Unitarianism (1818), was crucial in advancing English awareness of the long history of Unitarianism in eastern Europe. His intention, announced as early as 1833, to publish a comprehensive work on the subject was never fulfilled; in some sense he was forestalled by the *Anti-Trinitarian Biography* (1850), compiled by Robert Wallace. Nor did his promised memoir of Abraham Rees appear. In Dr Williams's Library is Rees's manuscript 'The anti-papal reformers of Italy in the sixteenth century, with a glance at their forerunners, the sectaries of the Middle Ages', in six quarto volumes, as well as a manuscript translation, with notes, of Orelli's life of Laelius Socinus, the Italian heresiarch. To him has been assigned, evidently in error, *A New System of Stenography* (1795), by 'Thomas Rees, stenographer'.

In 1853 Rees resigned all his posts and left England for Spain, being unable to meet charges in regard to trust funds in his keeping; ultimately he made full restitution. He died in obscurity in Brighton, of 'natural decay', on 1 August 1864. His wife, Elizabeth *née* Jacks, had died at Hythe on 20 August 1856; there were no children.

Thomas Rees's eldest brother, **Owen Rees** (1770–1837), was born at Gelli-gron and became a bookseller in Bristol. He then moved to London, where he was taken into partnership by Thomas Norton Longman, the publisher. He was a close friend of the poet Thomas Moore (1779–1852).

Early in 1837 he retired from business to the estate at Gelligron, which he had done much to improve, and died there, unmarried, on 5 September 1837.

ALEXANDER GORDON, rev. R. K. WEBB

Sources DNB · G. E. Evans, *Vestiges of protestant dissent* (1897) · *The Standard*; repr. in *The Times* (12 Sept 1837) [Owen Rees] · *The Times* (12 Sept 1837) [Owen Rees] · H. C. Robinson, diary, 31 March 1853, DWL · Presbyterian Board minutes, 4 April 1853, DWL · Presbyterian Board minutes, 4 Feb 1954, DWL · Presbyterian Board minutes, 6 March 1954, DWL
Archives BL, letters to J. Hunter, Add. MS 24874 · LUL, letters to Society for the Diffusion of Useful Knowledge
Likenesses photograph, DWL, trustees album

Rees, Thomas (1815–1885), Congregational minister and historian, son of Thomas Rees and his wife, Hannah William, was born at Pen Pontbren in the parish of Llanfynydd, Carmarthenshire, on 13 December 1815. He was brought up by his mother's family at Banc-y-fer, Llangathen, and helped his grandfather, Dafydd William, in his work as a basket maker. He joined the Independent church at Capel Isaac, and began to preach in March 1832. In 1835 he found employment in the colliery at Llwydcoed, Aberdâr; but, after a serious illness, he set up a small school and assisted the Revd Joseph Harrison at Ebenezer Chapel. In 1836 he moved to Craig-y-bargod, Merthyr Tudful, and took charge of a small school. Soon he was invited to take charge of the Independent church at Craig-y-bargod, where he was ordained on 15 September 1836. He married Jane Williams (d. 1876) of Pant Ffawyddog, Bedwellte, on 25 August 1838 and opened a shop at Pont Aberbargoed. However, the business failed and Rees spent a week or so in Cardiff prison as a debtor. In August 1840 he became pastor of Ebenezer Chapel, Aberdâr, continuing his work at Craig-y-bargod until 1841. He moved to Siloa Chapel, Llanelli, in March 1842, then to Cendl (Beaufort), Monmouthshire, in June 1849. In April 1862 he moved to Ebenezer Chapel, Swansea. In 1862 Marietta College, Ohio, conferred upon him the degree of DD. He was twice (1873, 1875) chairman of the Union of Welsh Independents and in 1884 he was elected chairman of the Congregational Union of England and Wales, a position he did not live to fill.

Although highly esteemed as a preacher and hymn writer, Rees was more widely known for his biblical commentaries. He was one of the founders of *Yr Adolygydd*, the first Welsh Independent quarterly. However, he is most noted for his historical writing, particularly on the history of nonconformity and Independency in Wales. His *History of Protestant Nonconformity in Wales* (1861; 2nd edn, 1883) prepared the ground for his history of Welsh Independent churches, *Hanes eglwysi Annibynol Cymru*, on which he worked with John Thomas (1821–1892). Publication began in 1870, and by 1875 four volumes had been completed. The fifth was finished by Thomas in 1891. Although Rees has been severely and fairly criticized for his evident denominational prejudice, his enthusiasm for sources was praiseworthy. He was willing to travel miles to consult books and manuscripts (including the 'church books'

of older dissenting churches) and to collect local traditions. He was an inaccurate transcriber of documents and frequently resorted to abridgement, but *Hanes eglwysi Annibynol Cymru* remains an important source for the history of Welsh denominationalism.

Rees died on 29 April 1885 at his home in Calvert Terrace, Swansea, and was buried at the nearby Sketty cemetery on 5 May.

J. E. LLOYD, rev. MARI A. WILLIAMS

Sources J. Thomas, *Cofiant y Parch. T. Rees* (1888) · DWB · CGPLA Eng. & Wales (1885)
Archives NL Wales, corresp., diaries, notebooks, etc. | NL Wales, J. Dyfnallt Owen MSS · NL Wales, John Williams MSS
Likenesses J. Cochran, engraving, NL Wales · J. Cochran, stipple, BM; repro. in *Evangelical Magazine* · Rees, portrait (after photograph), repro. in *The Congregationalist* (11 July 1882) · J. Thomas, photograph, NL Wales · engraving, repro. in Thomas, *Cofiant y Parch. T. Rees* · line, repro. in *Trysorfa'r Plant* (July 1885) · lithograph, NL Wales
Wealth at death £846 5s. 1d.: probate, 8 Aug 1885, CGPLA Eng. & Wales

Rees, Thomas Percy (1899–1963), psychiatrist, was born in Bwlch, Carmarthenshire, on 16 March 1899, the son of Thomas Rees, a farmer, and his wife, Elizabeth, *née* Davies, also from a farming family. After leaving school he served in the machine-gun corps during the First World War. He was then a medical student at the Welsh National School of Medicine, followed by clinical training at St Bartholomew's Hospital, London. He obtained the conjoint qualification in 1923 and graduated MB in the University of Wales two years later, having previously taken a BSc. He obtained the MRCP in 1926.

Rees first intended to undertake academic research in psychiatry, but instead he decided upon mental hospital work. From Napsbury Hospital he went in 1927 to Croydon Borough Mental Hospital (later Warlingham Park Hospital) as deputy physician superintendent. In 1935 he became superintendent, and his first act was to throw open the iron gates at the hospital entrance, after which they were never shut again. Over the next few years all ward doors were unlocked during the day, while nearly all restraint and isolation of patients were abolished.

> For Rees, however, the 'open door' policy did not consist in a mere unlocking of doors; it implied a general attitude of enthusiasm, activism, fresh-mindedness, permissiveness and general friendliness, which exerted their beneficent effects not only in his own institution but in widening circles both in his own country and elsewhere. (MacKeith, 311)

Among psychiatrists in other hospitals there was then a good deal of doubt that such a policy could be safe—even frank incredulity that the ward doors were really unlocked. However:

> He would recall how, when he first went to the hospital, a long row of actively suicidal patients sat unemployed all day long behind a heavy table in the refractory ward with a male nurse at either end. This sight seems to have made a deep impression on him. (ibid.)

Some of the male nursing staff were resistant to his innovations, and Rees did not hesitate to dismiss some on that account. Patients then had greater freedom of movement than was usual in mental hospitals of the time. According to E. H. Hare:

Although he was inclined to attribute the origins of the new enlightenment in mental hospitals to the introduction of a useful treatment for general paralysis of the insane, Rees had little faith in the efficacy of physical treatment for most mental illness. Patients come to mental hospitals, he used to say, to learn to live with other people. (*The Lancet*, 1331)

Yet he gave freedom to his medical staff to pursue their clinical interests, and pioneering work was done at War-lingham Park with insulin coma therapy, electroconvul-sive therapy, prefrontal leucotomy, and the treatment of alcoholism; the first specialized alcoholism unit in Britain was established there by Dr Max Glatt in 1953. Rees also became consultant psychiatrist to Croydon General Hos-pital and the Croydon Child Guidance Clinic. In 1939 he was a member of the Feversham committee on voluntary mental health organizations, and subsequently became consultant to the National Association for Mental Health and to the London Marriage Guidance Council. He devoted much effort to health education, among both his hospital staff and people of all kinds in the community in Croydon and more widely—being especially skilful in explaining psychiatric problems to lay people.

Following the inauguration of the National Health Ser-vice (NHS) in 1948 Rees became a member of the South-West Metropolitan Regional Hospital Board, and was appointed OBE in 1949. He was adviser in mental health to the World Health Organization, and in that capacity was a member of an expert committee which produced an influ-ential report on the future of psychiatric hospitals in 1953. It was said that the ideal hospital described there was actu-ally an account of Warlingham Park. This report was fairly negative on the relationship of psychiatry to general hospitals—a view which Rees held fairly strongly himself. This emerged in 'Back to moral treatment and community care' (*Journal of Mental Science*, 1956), the published version of his presidential address to the Royal Medico-Psychological Association and one of the very few papers that he wrote. Nor did he participate in systematic research.

One of Rees's most significant activities was member-ship of the royal commission on the law relating to men-tal illness and mental deficiency, 1954–7. Its report was largely embodied in the Mental Health Act of 1959, which revolutionized the legal and administrative basis of men-tal health care; it also provided an ideology of moving the emphasis of treatment and care into the community—a process which remained slow and uneven due to financial limitations. Rees provided the main psychiatric influence within the commission.

In 1956, the year of his presidency of the Royal Medico-Psychological Association, Rees retired from the NHS and entered private practice in Harley Street. Congratulating him on his presidential address Dr Tom Main said that:

whilst his work was based on the solid foundations of all that was best in past traditions of mental hospital work, he had not been content merely to follow established custom, but had made his own personal contribution by adventurously adopting the concept of the hospital as a therapeutic community. (*Journal of Mental Science*, 24)

In the same year the county borough of Croydon acknow-ledged his service to the local community by awarding him the freedom of the borough, and the Royal College of Physicians made him a fellow (thirty years after his mem-bership).

T. P., as he was universally known (distinguishing him from both J. R. and Linford Rees, who were equally well-known psychiatrists of the time), had a Welsh fluency of speech and conversational wit. He also had great energy and a personality which tended to dominate any group in which he was a member. He was acknowledged to be a highly influential figure in mental health care, but this influence was almost wholly administrative and institu-tional. His belief in the positive power of leadership was to become unpopular in the more egalitarian 1960s and the position of physician superintendent—which he regarded as essential to the leadership role—would then disappear in England and Wales. Indeed, the mental hosp-itals themselves would largely be gone by the end of the century.

Opinions of Rees as a person vary. His successor, Stephen MacKeith, believed he had 'high intelligence, flexible thinking and an intuitive flair for the manage-ment of men and women' (MacKeith, 311–12). For Denis Martin, 'his authority was never oppressive … he was a chief who encouraged ideas and initiative, and gave his staff the freedom to work out any changes in the hospital which he thought might prove valuable' (*The Lancet*, 1331). The anonymous obituarist of Munk's *Roll*, however, states that Rees, 'did not always endear himself to his col-leagues; he could be dogmatic, and obstinate, give an impression of arrogance and seem to be too interested in his own ideas to listen carefully to another point of view' (Munk, *Roll*, 345). Some of his hospital staff described him as a pocket dictator, because of his style of decision mak-ing, but on the other hand, his office door was always open and he maintained that everyone had access to him there.

Rees was fortunate in his time and place in that they pro-vided an ideal milieu for the positive exercise of his par-ticular gifts. He was rightly critical of university teaching departments who did not concern themselves with the problem of the chronic patient. In 1932 he married Adel-ine Isabel, daughter of F. J. Stephens of the ink manufac-turing family; they had one daughter and three sons. Rees died in the Westminster Hospital, London, on 2 June 1963. He was survived by his wife. HUGH FREEMAN

Sources Munk, *Roll*, 344–5 · S. MacKeith, *American Journal of Psy-chiatry*, 20 (1963), 311–12 · *The Lancet* (15 June 1963), 1331–2 · *Journal of Mental Science*, 103 (1956), 24 · b. cert. · d. cert. · CGPLA Eng. & Wales (1963)
Likenesses portrait, repro. in *The Lancet*, 1331
Wealth at death £36,709 8s.: probate, 31 July 1963, CGPLA Eng. & Wales

Rees, Walter Enoch (1863–1949), rugby administrator, was born at 6 East Side of London Road, Neath, Glamor-gan, on 13 April 1863, the second of the six children of Joseph Cook Rees (1833–1883), builder and contractor, and his wife, Margaret, *née* Howell (1837–1930). After schooling in Neath and Barnstaple he entered the family business in Neath and on 18 September 1898 married Elizabeth Leith Peters (1872–1944), the youngest daughter of George Peters of Aberdeen. Their only child, Walter Douglas Rees, was born on 28 June 1901.

Rees served on the Welsh Rugby Union (WRU) for fifty-nine years. A freemason, a Conservative, and an Anglican, he was hardly typical of most of the players who came under his jurisdiction. His career in rugby administration began in 1888, when he became secretary and treasurer of Neath rugby club and promptly improved both its fixture list and its finances. He served in this dual capacity for only two years, since in 1889 he was elected on the match (that is, general) committee of the WRU. Unlike most sports administrators of that era he was not a former player himself, but his astuteness and attention to detail caught the eye. He was first proposed for the secretaryship of the union in 1891 and secured it in 1896. He went on to become the longest-serving secretary of any of the rugby unions, holding his post almost until his death.

When Rees took office the WRU numbered thirty-seven member clubs and international match receipts totalled £1000; by the time he resigned in 1948 the corresponding figures were 104 clubs and £9000. The first salaried official of the WRU, he brought a new professionalism to the running of its affairs and turned its lack of any proper office accommodation (a defect rectified only in 1956) to his own advantage. He ran Welsh rugby virtually single-handedly from his house, Norwood, Victoria Gardens, Neath, and became a national figure through being associated with the golden era of Welsh rugby, between 1900 and 1911, when the Welsh fifteen won six triple crowns and achieved a historic victory (in 1905) over the otherwise undefeated New Zealand All Blacks. He represented Wales on the International Rugby Board from 1896 to 1900, and in 1910 accompanied the British Isles rugby touring team to South Africa as assistant manager. Widely regarded, in the inter-war period in particular, as high-handed and dictatorial, for instance in his strict insistence on the letter of the law in reimbursing the travel expenses of working-class players while allowing 'varsity' men much greater latitude, his ritual pre-match perambulation of the touchline with the chief constable on international days was the occasion for much banter from the crowd, not all of it friendly. He acquired a reputation for being a law unto himself in the execution of WRU business, and the little black pocket-book in which he noted the names of those he privileged with international match tickets acquired wide notoriety.

Rees was elected to Neath town council in 1900, became the town's mayor in 1905, and a JP in 1918. He continued on the local authority until 1919, serving on all the major committees. He was never narrowly sectarian in his sporting interests: in September 1893 he chaired the founding meeting of Neath association football club. But it was his renown in rugby affairs, coupled with his experience of local government, that led to his appointment in 1916 as recruiting officer for Neath and district. In recognition of his services the War Office conferred on him the rank of

captain, which further confirmed his autocratic tendencies.

Captain Rees, as he liked to be known, clung tenaciously to the secretaryship of the WRU into the post-1945 era, but in a new bureaucratic and democratic world the former doyen of rugby administrators increasingly appeared to be an outmoded survivor from a bygone era. On 19 March 1948 he at last tendered his resignation, with effect from 30 June. He died on 6 June 1949 in Bridgend and District Hospital and was interred three days later in Llantwit Major in the Vale of Glamorgan.   GARETH WILLIAMS

Sources D. Smith and G. Williams, *Fields of praise: the official history of the Welsh Rugby Union, 1881–1981* · *Neath Guardian* (10 June 1949) · *Western Mail* [Cardiff] (7 June 1949) · J. B. G. Thomas, *Rugger in the blood* (1985) · *Playfair Welsh Rugby Annual* (1949–50) · J. A. Jenkins, *South Wales and Monmouthshire at the opening of the twentieth century: contemporary biographies*, ed. W. T. Pike (1907); facs. edn as *A dictionary of Edwardian biography: South Wales and Monmouthshire* (1986) · *Slater's commercial dictionary* (1868)
Likenesses photograph, repro. in J. B. G. Thomas, *The illustrated history of Welsh rugby* (1980), 182
Wealth at death £10,600 18s. 10d.: probate, 23 July 1949, *CGPLA Eng. & Wales*

Rees, William [*pseud*. Gwilym Hiraethog] (1802–1883), Congregational minister and writer, was born on 8 November 1802 at a farmhouse called Chwibren-isaf, near Llansannan, Denbighshire. The village lies at the foot of a mountain known as Hiraethog, from which Rees took his bardic name. He was the second son of David Rees, a farmer, and his wife, Anne. Henry *Rees was his elder brother.

At the age of three William lost the sight of his right eye by smallpox. He received very little formal education and only attended the village school kept by John Jones at Llansannan, during the winter months. From an early age he was employed as a shepherd, but he continued to study in his leisure time. At the age of twenty he devoted himself to Welsh poetry, and under the guidance of Robert ap Dafydd of Cilfach Lwyd, he mastered the rules of Welsh strict-metre poetry, and began writing his own poems. At the Brecon eisteddfod in 1826 he was awarded first prize for a *cywydd* on the battle of Trafalgar, and at the Denbigh eisteddfod two years later another prize-winning *cywydd* secured his reputation as a poet of note.

Although Rees's parents had brought him up as a Calvinistic Methodist, he joined the Independents in 1828. A dispute within the local Methodist church following the expulsion of a member, had led to the departure of a handful of the congregation, including Rees. The subsequent establishment of an Independent cause in Llansannan proved a turning point in his career. In 1829 he began to preach, and in 1831 he became pastor of the small Congregational church at Mostyn, Flintshire, where he was ordained on 20 April 1832. In February 1837 he removed to Swan Lane, Denbigh, where he established himself as a popular Welsh preacher. In May 1843 he succeeded his close friend William Williams of Wern (1781–1840) at the Tabernacle Church, Great Crosshall Street,

Liverpool. In 1853 he moved, with part of his congregation, to Salem Chapel, Brownlow Hill, and in 1867 this chapel was elaborately rebuilt in Grove Street.

Rees held ministerial office in Liverpool for thirty-two years, during which he played a leading role in political and educational movements in the city. But he exercised a still more powerful influence on the politics, poetry, and literature of Wales. His eloquence made him one of the greatest Welsh preachers and popular lecturers of his time. In politics he was a staunch Liberal and in 1843 he established, with John Jones, of Castle Street, Liverpool, the first successful Welsh Liberal newspaper, *Yr Amserau*, which he edited until 1853. Its success was largely due to the series of letters written by him in the dialect of his home county under the cognomen of Yr Hen Ffarmwr (the Old Farmer). The letters dealt with current political and religious issues, such as the corn laws and education. Although inspired by English radicalism, the ideas espoused in *Yr Amserau* (amalgamated in 1859 with *Y Faner*) contributed greatly towards the awakening of a distinctly Welsh, radical movement, providing an important mouthpiece for the exponents of Liberal politics. Rees was a great supporter of Italian and Hungarian nationalist causes and corresponded for some time with Mazzini. He also strongly advocated the abolition of slavery in his book, *Aelwyd f'ewythr Robert* (1853). As a prominent public orator and lecturer, he was frequently given the opportunity to speak publicly on a wide range of political, religious, literary, and scientific subjects. Rees's literary versatility was remarkable: in prose he appeared as biographer, novelist, journalist, religious writer, and dramatist. As a poet and hymn writer his works were voluminous: several collections, in both free and strict metre, were published. His longest poetic publication was an epic poem, called *Emmanuel*, published in two volumes (1861, 1867). His religious works include a catechism, *Y cyfarwyddwr* (1833), and several expositions and commentaries. The extent of his reputation was displayed in 1866, when both Marietta University, Ohio, and Amherst College, Massachusetts, honoured him with DD degrees.

Rees married Ann Edwards of Waunddeilen, Nantglyn, in 1823; she died in February 1874 and the following year Rees retired from the ministry and settled with one of his daughters at Chester. Active to the last he continued to write and, on occasion, preach. He was awarded the first medal of the Honourable Society of Cymmrodorion in 1882, but he did not live to receive it formally. He died on 8 November 1883 at Chester, and was buried in Smithdown Road cemetery, Liverpool, on 13 November.

R. A. JOHNSON, *rev.* MARI A. WILLIAMS

Sources E. Rees, *Memoir of William Rees 'Hiraethog'*, ed. H. E. Lewis (1915) · T. Roberts and D. Roberts, *Cofiant y Parch. W. Rees* (1893) · T. Rees and J. Thomas, *Hanes eglwysi annibynol Cymru*, 5 (1891) · *DWB* · D. Adams, 'The Revd W. Rees', *Welsh religious leaders in the Victorian era*, ed. J. Vyrnwy Morgan (1905) · T. E. Davies, *Cyfraniad William Rees (Gwilym Hiraethog) i Fywyd a Llen ei Gyfnod*, MA diss., U. Wales, 1931 · Cadran, 'Hiraethog', *Y Geninen*, 25 (1907), 263–6 · *Y Gwyddoniadur*, 2nd edn (1896) · *CGPLA Eng. & Wales* (1884)
Archives NL Wales, letters and papers · U. Lpool L., Sydney Jones Library, notebooks | NL Wales, Daniel MSS · NL Wales, letters to Lewis Edwards · NL Wales, W. J. Gruffydd MSS · NL Wales, NLW MSS · NL Wales, letters to Ebenezer Thomas
Likenesses H. Hughes, lithograph, 1847, NL Wales · McFarlane & Erskine, etching, *c*.1875, NL Wales · J. D. Mercier, oils, 1877, U. Wales, Aberystwyth · J. Cochran, engraving (after photograph), NL Wales · Hill, engraving (after photograph), NL Wales · G. J. Stoddart, engraving (after photograph by G. W. Webster), NL Wales · J. Thomas, photograph, NL Wales · W. Williams, portrait, NL Wales · photograph, repro. in Vyrnwy Morgan, ed., *Welsh religious leaders* · portraits, repro. in Rees, *Memoir of William Rees 'Hiraethog'*
Wealth at death £3597 11*s.* 4*d.*: administration, 22 Feb 1884, *CGPLA Eng. & Wales*

Rees, William Jenkins (1772–1855), Church of England clergyman and antiquary, son of Rees Rees of Tonn, Llandovery, Carmarthenshire, was born in that parish on 10 January 1772. He was educated at a school held in the church of Llanfair-ar-y-bryn, Llandovery, and at Carmarthen grammar school from 1789. On 12 April 1791 he matriculated at Oxford from Wadham College, where he graduated BA in 1795 and proceeded MA in 1797. Ordained in 1796, he first held the curacy of Stoke Edith and West Hide, Herefordshire. From 1806 he was rector of Cascob, Radnorshire, where he spent the rest of his life. He was also vicar of Heyop, near Knighton. In 1820 he was made a prebendary of Christ College, Brecon, and in 1840 a fellow of the Society of Antiquaries.

In 1803 Rees published *A Short and Practical Account of the Principal Doctrines of Christianity*, which was followed in 1809 by an essay on *Clerical Elocution*, and in 1811 by a tract on pastoral work. He was more significant, however, as a leading figure in the Welsh cultural revival: he was an enthusiastic and hard-working member of a group of Anglican clergymen, later to be called the 'Old Literary Clerics', who fostered Welsh culture during the years 1818–58, and who transformed the eisteddfod from a gathering of poets into a national festival of arts. Rees's main contribution was as one of the editors of the Welsh Manuscripts Society. The preparation of the society's edition of the *Liber Landavensis*, initially entrusted to his nephew Rice Rees (1804–1839), was completed by Rees after his nephew's death and published in 1840. In 1853 Rees also edited for the society their collection of *The Lives of the Cambro-British Saints* (text and English translation). However, his enthusiasm was not matched by his scholarship: both works were criticized by later nineteenth-century scholars. Rees died unmarried on 18 January 1855 at Cascob, and was buried there on 23 January.

J. E. LLOYD, *rev.* BETI JONES

Sources M. Ellis, 'W. J. Rees: a portrait', *Transactions of the Radnorshire Society*, 39–42 (1969–72) · *DWB* · *GM*, 2nd ser., 43 (1855), 317 · Foster, *Alum. Oxon.*
Archives Cardiff City Library, corresp. and papers · Cardiff City Library, Tonn MSS · NL Wales, corresp. and papers | NL Wales, letters to J. M. Traherne · S. Antiquaries, Lond., letters to Thomas Wakeman
Likenesses H. Hughes, oils, NMG Wales · R. Woodman, engraving (after H. Hughes), NL Wales

Reese, (John) Terence (1913–1996), bridge player and writer, was born on 28 August 1913 in the High Street, Epsom, Surrey, the son of John Reese, baker and confectioner, and his wife, Annie Maria Riddington, *née*

Hutchings. His parents had met when 'first gentleman' and 'first lady' at a whist drive. He first played bridge at the age of seven, during a family holiday in Dorset. Finding thirteen cards rather a handful, he would dismount from his chair and sort his cards behind a cushion. He was educated at Bilton Grange preparatory school, then at Bradfield College, where he gained his colours at football and cricket. Very much an all-rounder, he won the top classical scholarship to New College, Oxford, and it was there that he first played bridge seriously. In the inaugural inter-varsity match he captained the Oxford team, defeating a Cambridge side led by Iain Macleod, the future chancellor of the exchequer. Unknown to the college authorities, Reese subsidized his lifestyle by running a book at nearby greyhound tracks. After leaving Oxford with a third-class degree in *literae humaniores* in 1935 he worked briefly at Harrods before becoming a full-time professional bridge player and writer. With four leading players of the day—Macleod, Jack Marx, Maurice Harrison-Gray, and Skid Simon—Reese invented the Acol bidding system. Still used by most British players, it embraced a variable no-trump, openings of one spade and one heart on a four-card suit, and intermediate two-bids. Joining forces with Hubert Phillips and Harold Franklin in 1936, he hosted early radio and television bridge programmes.

The tall, balding Reese soon became the dominant figure in the tournament world. He formed a famous partnership with Boris Schapiro, winning the gold cup eight times and the master pairs seven times. Reese was a masterful card player but conservative in the auction; Schapiro was more flamboyant, choosing bids and plays likely to provoke the opponents into error. They were the anchor pair in British teams that won the European championship in 1948, 1949, 1954, and 1963. In 1955 came his supreme achievement, winning the world championship in New York. In 1961 he won the World Par Olympiad (where the hands are pre-set by an expert panel), and in 1962 added the World Pairs Olympiad. His supreme technique, and the consistency of his results, led many to rank him as the world's finest player.

The 1965 world championships in Buenos Aires witnessed the biggest scandal ever to hit the world of bridge. Reese and Schapiro were accused of exchanging illicit information during the bidding—signalling how many hearts they held by varying their finger positions. The World Bridge Federation judged them to be guilty. The verdict was not accepted in Britain and a full tribunal, headed by Sir John Foster and Lord Bourne, sat intermittently for many months. The visual evidence of finger signalling seemed convincing, but a detailed analysis of the subsequent bids and plays offered no evidence whatsoever that the pair had benefited from the information supposedly gained. Reese and Schapiro were eventually acquitted—a verdict rejected by the World Bridge Federation.

Reese achieved his greatest fame as a writer. Editor of the *British Bridge World* magazine from 1955 to 1962, he became the game's most prolific author, producing over ninety titles. He combined exceptional insight into the game with a mastery of the English language. His famous classics, *Reese on Play* (1948) and *The Expert Game* (1958), dealt with areas of the game that players today still find difficult. He was also bridge correspondent for *The Observer*, the *Evening News* (later the *Evening Standard*) and *The Lady*. He made many lifelong friends but not everyone appreciated the way in which he expressed his opinions so openly. His terse book reviews were legendary. He dismissed one new work with: 'This writer knows little about bridge, even less about punctuation.' A book entitled *Twelve Lessons on Bridge* was treated to: 'The author should hasten to take them!' When asked whether he received many letters from readers of his columns, Reese replied: 'They're not to be encouraged at any cost. I just return the letter with the odd "yes" or "no" scribbled on it. I rarely receive a second letter from the same source.'

Reese married Alwyn Sherrington (*b*. 1939/40), a computer trainer's registrar and daughter of Richard Sherrington, builder, on 23 January 1970, and for many years they lived in Woods Mews, off Park Lane in central London. They then moved to a fine Edwardian apartment overlooking the seafront in Hove. At the age of eighty-three, now very deaf, Reese attended the Macallan International Pairs in London. 'Why on earth did he hold on to the diamonds?' he exclaimed loudly, after a world champion had misdefended a hand. 'It was obvious to keep the clubs.' Two days later, on 29 January 1996, he died at his home, Flat 5, 23 Adelaide Crescent, Hove, Sussex, of aspirin poisoning. An inquest held on 14 February returned a verdict of accidental death. He was survived by his wife.   DAVID BIRD

Sources T. Reese, *Bridge at the top* (1977) · *The Guardian* (1 Feb 1996) · personal knowledge (2004) · private information (2004) · b. cert. · m. cert. · d. cert.
Likenesses photograph, repro. in *The Times* (31 Jan 1996) · photograph, repro. in *The Guardian* · photograph, repro. in *The Independent* (1 Feb 1996)

Reeve, Clara (1729–1807), novelist and poet, was born at Ipswich on 23 January 1729, the eldest daughter of William Reeve (*d*. 1755), rector of Freston and of Kerton, Suffolk, and perpetual curate of St Nicholas, Ipswich. Her mother, Hannah, was a daughter of William Smithies, goldsmith and jeweller to George I.

Family and early years There were eight children of the marriage. One son, Samuel, became vice-admiral of the white; another, Thomas, became rector of Brockley, Suffolk, and master of Bungay grammar school. The Reeve family had long been residents of Ipswich, where, Clara told a friend, 'my family have resided several Centuries, & been free Burgesses ever since the first Charter' (letter to Walker, October 1804). Her paternal grandfather, Thomas Reeve, was rector of St Mary Stoke there. Clara wrote of her father, 'from him I have learned all that I know; he was my oracle' (undated letter quoted in W. Scott, *Lives of the Novelists*, n.d., 204). She described him as 'an old Whig', and when she was still young he had her read to him after supper from newspaper reports of the parliamentary debates and made her study favourite works of eighteenth-century classical republicans. These included Greek and

Roman histories, Plutarch's *Lives*, an English translation of Rapin de Thoyras's history of England, and *Cato's Letters* (1720–23) by John Trenchard and Thomas Gordon.

At William Reeve's death on 13 September 1755 his widow moved with Clara and two other daughters to Colchester; later the sisters moved to Ipswich. At about this time Reeve took up conchology, which she pursued avidly for many years. Thirty years later, when she received a large addition to her shell collection from Thomas Percy, she told him that she followed the system and principles of Emanuel Mendes da Costa (Bodl. Oxf., Percy MS c. 3, fols. 32–3), who promoted the science as a rational pursuit inducing admiration of the divine hand in nature. One sister married, two remained unmarried, and at some point Reeve took lodgings of her own at Ipswich, and turned to writing to support herself, disapproved of by her family. By the 1790s she was living in Car Street, in what she described as a 'cottage' (letter to Walker, 29 April 1790).

Early works and The Old English Baron Reeve's first book, *Original Poems on Several Occasions*, 'By C. R.' (1769), was published by subscription. Most of the approximately 500 subscribers came from around East Anglia; about half were women and the rest mostly clergy and military men, with a sprinkling of titled people. The book reveals Reeve's devotion to music, which she treats as a philosophical inquiry rather than the more usual genteel feminine avocation. One poem, 'To my friend, Mrs.—', on her holding an argument in favour of the natural equality of both the sexes', comments on the plight of talented, intellectual women with small means. Reeve denies that men and women are born equals, but acknowledges exceptions such as Katherine Philips, Elizabeth Carter, and Charlotte Lennox.

Reeve next published, anonymously, *The Phoenix, or, The History of Polyarchus and Argenis* (4 vols., 1772), an English version of John Barclay's *Argenis* (1621), a Latin prose allegory of religious and political conflicts in France under Henri IV which in 1772 could be applied to recent polarization of English politics over 'Wilkes and Liberty'. Reeve remarks,

> Since England is become a nation of politicians, and men of all ranks and degrees believe themselves capable of investigating the art of government, and since women have written with success upon the subject, the editor has thought herself at liberty to aim a blow at popular error, from behind Barclay.

The work also suggests that 'romance', a genre associated with women, can contribute to civil society, as one character encourages another to proceed with writing a 'stately fable' on public affairs to instruct the public and thereby improve the 'commonwealth' (*The Phoenix*, 2.45–6).

Reeve took this advice herself with her next and best-known work, published anonymously at Colchester in 1777 as *The Champion of Virtue*. She then received £10 from the London firm of Dilly, who republished it a year later, with her name on the title-page, as *The Old English Baron: a Gothic Story*, though she retained the copyright (letter to Walker, 25 April 1791). The text was supposedly revised by her friend Martha Bridgen, daughter of Samuel Richardson; in fact, most changes merely correct the carelessly printed Colchester edition. The preface to *The Old English Baron* describes it as 'the literary offspring' of Horace Walpole's *The Castle of Otranto* (1765), similarly designed 'to unite the most attractive and interesting circumstances of the ancient Romance and modern Novel' while assuming 'a character and manner of its own, that differs from both; it is distinguished by the appellation of a Gothic Story, being a picture of Gothic [i.e., medieval] times and manners'. The story, like many of the time, concerns usurpation unmasked and legitimate succession restored by a hero resembling an idealized mid-eighteenth-century gentrified professional man. This fable continued to speak to the largely professional middle-class reading public. An eighth edition appeared in 1807, Anna Letitia Barbauld included it in her *British Novelists* (1810), and there were many further reprints throughout the century, when it was often paired with Walpole's *Otranto*.

Reeve's next novel, *The Two Mentors: a Modern Story* (2 vols., 1783), turns from medieval to contemporary life in order 'to recommend and promote the social and domestic Virtues' (preface). A series of letters recounts the genteel young protagonist's encounter with and triumph over a decadent courtly social world, while advised by two different mentors, one worldly and the other moral, with an inset autobiography of a middle-class clerk and his family. At the time, novels were commonly denigrated as inartistic and corrupting, and Reeve herself later told Walker that 'Romances & Novels are the most saleable of anything, & therefore I have used my pen in that way, tho' I have wished to employ it to better purpose' (letter of 29 April 1790). Nevertheless, she defended the form's public utility in her next work, *The progress of romance, through times, countries, and manners; with remarks on the good and bad effects of it, on them respectively; in a course of evening conversations* (1785), also published at Colchester. She later told Walker that 'it has been the most unfortunate of any of my publications, altho it has cost me more time and labour than any other, and in my estimation it is of more value than all the rest' (ibid.). It comprises a polemical preface, the 'Progress of romance', and a short prose fiction, 'The History of Charoba, queen of Ægypt', adapted from a French version of an Arabic story. The preface presents romance as the 'polite', or culturally polished and socially polishing literature of all ages and cultures. The 'Progress of romance', in twelve dialogues, argues that 'romance' is as important culturally as classical epic and surveys the form from ancient times to the recent past. In 'The History of Charoba' the daughter of the despotic pharaoh Totis resists all attempts by foreign male rulers to master her and her country, and so establishes an age of peace and prosperity. The book did not sell: of a thousand copies printed, Reeve in 1790 still had between three and four hundred copies 'upon my hands' and attributed this 'ill success' to the reluctance of London booksellers to promote a work published in the provinces (letter to Walker, 29 April 1790). She kept a copy interleaved with additions for a new edition, but in 1791 sent it to Walker to do with as he wished.

Reeve then took up a couple of novels already in hand. What she called a 'ghost story', 'Castle Connor: an Irish story', was completed in 1787 but lost in transit on the Ipswich to London coach. *The Exiles; or, Memoirs of the Count de Cronstadt* (3 vols., 1788) was to have been co-written with an unnamed gentleman, but she completed it alone (preface). The *Gentleman's Magazine* claimed that 'the principal incidents … are borrowed from' a novel by François Thomas de Baculard d'Arnaud (*GM*, 77, 1807, p. 1233); there is a general resemblance between Reeve's story of Cronstadt and Jacquelina, and 'Liebman: anecdote allemande' in Arnaud's *Épreuves du sentiment* (1772–81). *The Exiles* is an epistolary novel with inset 'memoirs' by the three main characters, but dominated by Cronstadt's story of his courtship of and secret marriage to an illiterate but virtuous country girl.

After some difficulties with her publisher, T. Hookham, Reeve published *The School for Widows: a Novel* (1791), which she described as 'a lighter work, written for the circulating library, sprinkled however, with moral inferences', and published in three volumes 'against my will', for 'I think two neat Volumes, are better than three Grubstreet ones' (letter to Walker, 12 April 1791). The novel criticizes the fashionable culture of sensibility then embraced by some political extremists, but also maintains the reformist classical republicanism learnt from her father, and develops an increasingly religious emphasis. The 'school' of the title is adversity, which teaches women, in particular, unique skills and knowledge useful in private and local life but ignored by male-dominated learned culture. The novel combines letters, dialogue, and narration to represent common life from women's perspective.

Politics and reform At first Reeve welcomed the French Revolution, reading 'nothing but Politics', including Burke's *Reflections* and 'all the answers to it'. She told Walker that 'I am a friend to liberty, and the security of property, and the rights of man' (letter to Walker, 12 April 1791) and attributed this view to her father's instruction:

> I had read the Greek and Roman Histories, and Plutarch's lives when quite a child, from them I imbibed principles that can never be shaken. … A love of liberty, a hatred of Tyranny, an affection to the whole race of mankind, a wish to support their rights and properties.   (ibid.)

She started a historical novel designed to intervene in the revolution debate, telling Walker, 'In my Gothic Story my principles will appear, it will speak to men, to citizens, to Princes, & to the People'. She assured Walker, 'I have not falsified historical facts, persons, or characters, but have given them under the seal of truth' and, aware of the growing animosity in public debate, she confessed, 'I shall risk my reputation upon it [and] it will probably be my *Vale* to the public' (letter to Walker, 25 April 1791).

Meanwhile Reeve joined those women proposing social improvement through educational reform, with *Plans of education; with remarks on the systems of other writers; in a series of letters between Mrs. Darnford and her friends* (1792). It echoes the classical republican idea of a patriot king and calls for national regeneration amid the crisis precipitated by the French Revolution:

> The Revolution in France will be a standing lesson to Princes and to People of all countries; it is a warning to Kings, how they oppress and impoverish their people; it warns them to reform the errors and corruptions of their governments, and to prevent the necessity of a revolution.   (p. 214)

The book envisages a major role for women in this public task, joining a tradition of such works from Mary Astell's *A Serious Proposal to the Ladies* (1694) through Sarah Scott's *Description of Millenium Hall* (1762) to Catharine Macaulay Graham's *Letters on Education* (1790) and Mary Wollstonecraft's *Vindication of the Rights of Woman* (1792). Reeve's design is socially and politically more conservative than Macaulay Graham's or Wollstonecraft's, however, calling for discipline, order, and hierarchy in line with such counter-revolutionary women writers as Hannah More. Encouraged by her friends, Reeve had several copies bound and presented 'to the great Ladies', perhaps literary patrons such as Elizabeth Montagu, but confessed that 'I am not very sanguine in my expectations' (letter to Walker, 1 Dec 1792).

Reeve deplored the increasing violence of the French Revolution because it would discredit classical republicanism, complaining to Walker,

> My politics are all overthrown[.] France has ruined herself and hurt all the other countries of Europe. … She has strengthened the hands of the enemies of liberty, who will now boldly assert, that mankind are not to be trusted with it.

She acknowledged that 'Both parties have a mixture of right and wrong, of truth & falsehood', but asserted that 'it is the business of wise & honest men to discriminate them, and show the fallacy on both sides' (letter of 7 Sept 1792). She tried to do so with her 'Gothic story', *Memoirs of Sir Roger de Clarendon, the natural son of Edward prince of Wales, commonly called the Black Prince; with anecdotes of many other eminent persons of the fourteenth century* (3 vols., 1793). The preface praises Plutarch's classical republican project of recommending public virtue to his own time through lives of figures from the past, and sets this against the 'English Jacobins':

> The new philosophy of the present day avows a levelling principle, and declares that a state of anarchy is more beautiful than that of order and regularity. There is nothing more likely to convince mankind of the errors of these men, than to set before them examples of good government, and warnings of the mischievous consequences of their own principles.   (pp. xvi–xvii)

The novel awkwardly alternates a story of parallel courtships with the memoirs of Sir Roger de Clarendon, including many episodes from history, and closes with a polemical essay on the current situation.

Reeve tried to get the Dublin publisher Archer to republish some of her work, if not contrary to copyright law; otherwise, she told Walker, 'I would rather finish one of my beginnings, of which I have many by me, and send it to Dublin to seek its fortune …' (letter of 25 April 1791). She had more problems with her London publisher and asked

Walker to intervene, explaining that 'Men of this profession are inclined to treat our sex en Cavalier, but to a gentleman they will behave in a different manner' (letter of 21 Sept 1792). She continued to follow the 'paper war' on the revolution and found that the shooting war was filling Ipswich with armed forces and driving up prices. She confessed to Walker, 'I am frightened at the prospect before me, and have thought of putting off my house, and going to board in a family, where I might be under protection in case of dangers of every kind' (ibid.). In the mid-1790s she may have published at least one anonymous political pamphlet, and in 1799 she published her last full-length novel, *Destination, or, Memoirs of a Private Family* (3 vols.). It recounts the lives of several interconnected gentry and upper middle-class families, extending from England to colonial India; the 'destination' of the title is pursuit of a profession. Again the story is told through a combination of narrative, dialogue, and letters, and matter and method resemble those of Jane Austen. Reeve's aim, as before, is moral and didactic as well as patriotic: the narrator declares in closing:

> It is the duty of parents and guardians to study the genius and disposition of all those who are committed to their charge, and to put them into a situation that will employ them to their own advantage, and to the good of the public. (vol. 3, p. 207)

Education for the national good was also the aim of Reeve's last-known published work, *Edwin, King of Northumberland: a Story of the Seventh Century* (1802). It is a historical fiction for youth, a genre with a rapidly increasing market. In the prefatory dialogue, Preceptor tells Pupil,

> It is a mark of a well-disposed mind, to believe that your own country is the best and happiest of all others; to be well instructed in the history of it; to know the advantages it possesses; the climate, the soil, the produce; you ought also to know the commerce, the agriculture, and the resources it contains within itself; and more specially the great men it has produced, for this will give you the greatest respect for it, and the true *amor patria*. (p. v)

The passage echoes one in Reeve's *Memoirs of Sir Roger de Clarendon*, and the story recounts the historical contention for the throne of the seventh-century Anglo-Saxon kingdom of Northumberland amid conflict between other kingdoms for domination of England. Readers of the time could readily find a parallel to the situation of Great Britain in 1802, divided internally by social conflict amid a long struggle against external foes.

By now Reeve was weary of a lifetime's struggle in the public interest. In October 1804 she declined Walker's request for a new edition of *The Progress of Romance*, declaring, 'I have written 21 Volumes, beside pamphlets' but 'after seventy years of age, an old woman is good for little, writing for the press is out of question' (letter to Walker). She admitted that she had 'several drawers full of matter' which she could not decide whether to preserve or burn but, referring to the proverb that a prophet is not respected in her own country, thought it would 'all go to the flames'. She told another friend, 'I have been all my life

straitened in my circumstances, and used my pen to support a scanty establishment; yet, to the best of my knowledge, I have drawn it on the side of truth, virtue and morality' (Barbauld, iii). She continued to read, having what she called 'a tolerable collection of books', and told Walker, 'I ought to be thankful that I can read at all for that is a part of my daily bread' (letters). She also told Walker that her three sisters 'keep much company, I very little. I have renounced cards, and that leaves me in quiet' (letter of October 1804). She died on 3 December 1807 at Ipswich, and was buried there, in the churchyard of St Stephen's. Ironically, she had a brief posthumous celebrity thanks to a moralistic novel entitled *Fatherless Fanny* (1819), attributed to her and reprinted into the 1830s, but unlikely to be hers.

GARY KELLY

Sources A. L. Barbauld, 'Clara Reeve', *The British novelists*, ed. A. L. Barbauld (1810), 22, i–iii · C. Reeve, letters to Joseph Cooper Walker, TCD, MS 1461 · W. Scott, 'Prefatory memoir to Clara Reeve', *Ballantyne's novelist's library*, ed. W. Scott, 5 (1823), lxxix–lxxxvii · E. Napier, 'Clara Reeve', *British novelists, 1660–1800, ed. M. C. Battestin, DLitB, 39/2 (1985)*

Archives TCD, Joseph Cooper Walker MSS, letters

Likenesses T. Blood, stipple, BM, NPG; repro. in *La Belle Assemblée* (1824) · A. H. Tourrier, portrait, repro. in C. Reeve and H. Walpole, *The old English baron also The castle of Otronto* (1883)

Reeve, Sir Edmund (c.1589–1647), judge, was born at Felthorpe, Norfolk, one of at least four sons and five children of Christopher Reeve of Aylsham and Felthorpe, attorney, and his wife, Martha, daughter of Edward Grimston of Oxborough. Having been admitted to Gonville and Caius College, Cambridge, on 30 September 1605, he then proceeded to Barnard's Inn and entered Gray's Inn on 8 August 1607. He was called to the bar in 1611. At an unknown date he married Mary Corie of Brampton, Norfolk.

For some time Reeve resided in Norwich where in 1624, with his 'brother-in-law' and contemporary at Barnard's and Gray's inns, Francis *Bacon (c.1587–1657), he gave money for the repair of the font at St Gregory's Church. He became recorder of Great Yarmouth in 1629, steward of Norwich in 1631, and a JP for Norfolk. Elected a bencher and reader at Gray's Inn in 1632, he was made serjeant-at-law on 20 May 1636 and a justice of the common pleas on 24 March 1639, following the death of Richard Hutton. Later that year, on 12 October, he was knighted by the king at Whitehall. By this time he had bought from Sir Edmund Bedingfield the manor of Stratton St Mary, Norfolk, which became his home.

Reeve's adherence to the Long Parliament is well documented. At the summer assize in 1640 he refused to proceed upon an indictment of one of the Lambeth rioters, and in July 1640 he refused the king's request to have the captured John Bastwick indicted for treason without the sanction of parliament and the other judges. At the end of 1642 he was one of only three common-law judges still sitting at Westminster in defiance of the king's will, Francis Bacon being newly appointed in king's bench, and Baron Trevor continuing in exchequer. Reeve's continuation on the bench became a condition in parliamentary overtures to the king in early 1643, and enabled the Long Parliament to maintain a semblance of regularity in the administration of justice even though war and lack of personnel disrupted the assizes. Reeve, like his brother John (d. 1657), rector of Stratton St Mary, took the covenant; his response to a royal proclamation commanding him to adjourn his court to Oxford in Michaelmas 1643 was to order the arrest of the messenger, who was subsequently condemned and executed as a spy.

After the resumption of regular circuits in 1646, Reeve served, as he had before the civil war, on the home and midland assize circuits. He died on 27 March 1647 and was buried, as he had wished, at Stratton St Mary church. In his will, dated 8 January that year, he left his widow and executor, Dame Mary, a life interest in lands in Norfolk and Suffolk, some of which were in a trust administered by Bacon and by Reeve's nephew, Nicholas Carre of Norwich. Having apparently no children but considerable wealth, Reeve provided generously for other relatives, including his brothers Thomas and John, and the younger children of Thomas and Augustine (another brother). He left the greatest share of his estates to his nephews Thomas (son of Thomas) and Christopher (son of John), and to his great-nieces Barbara and Margaret Carre, whom he designated as their future wives. Reeve had been, observed Clarendon, 'a man of a good reputation for learning and integrity, … who in good times would have been a good judge' (Clarendon, Hist. rebellion, 2.241).

D. A. ORR

Sources J. Foster, *The register of admissions to Gray's Inn, 1521–1889, together with the register of marriages in Gray's Inn chapel, 1695–1754* (privately printed, London, 1889) · W. R. Prest, *The rise of the barristers: a social history of the English bar, 1590–1640*, 2nd edn (1991), 387 · will, PRO, PROB 11/199, fols. 382v–385r · F. Blomefield and C. Parkin, *An essay towards a topographical history of the county of Norfolk*, [2nd edn], 11 vols. (1805–10), vol. 4, p. 274; vol. 5, pp. 190, 192 · Clarendon, *Hist. rebellion*, 2.241–4, 442; 3.252 · J. S. Cockburn, *A history of English assizes, 1558–1714* (1972), 219–45, 273–4 · Foss, *Judges*, 6.357–8 · S. F. Black, 'The courts and judges of Westminster Hall during the great rebellion, 1640–1660', *Journal of Legal History*, 7 (1986), 23–52 · J. S. Hart, *Justice upon petition: the House of Lords and the reformation of justice, 1621–1675* (1991), 175–217 · H. Phillips, *The grandeur of the law* (1684), 87 · S. R. Gardiner, ed., *Constitutional documents of the puritan revolution, 1625–1660*, 3rd edn (1906), 265

Reeve [Rive], **Edmund** (d. 1660), linguistic scholar and Church of England clergyman, may have come from East Anglia (where the family name was well known) or had an early connection with Cambridge. In later life he acknowledged that 'the first instrument which Godd used for to instruct me in the catholicke faith' was John Overall, professor of theology and master of St Catharine's College, Cambridge, about the turn of the sixteenth century and later bishop of Norwich (E. Reeve, *The Communion Booke Catechisme Expounded*, 1635, sig. B3), although it is not clear whether or when they were personally acquainted. Reeve was clearly well educated: by 1609 he was living in London and teaching Latin, Greek, and other biblical languages.

In 1614 Reeve issued the first of his many publications, a Latin commentary on the canticles. This was followed by several linguistic manuals: *An Heptaglotterie* (1617–18); *Ten Grammaticall Chapters* (1620), in which he revealed he was

living near Christ Church; *Twelve Rules Instructing to the Art of Latine* (1620), in which he was described as a teacher of Hebrew; *A Brief Treatise of the Necessity of Knowledge of the Principall Languages* (1621); and *Dialogues Concerning the most Usefull Words of the Latine Tounge* (1623), a part translation from the Latin *Discorsi* of Johannes Posselius. At the back of this work he drew attention to the fact that he 'had now above fourteene yeeres experiment in this honourable Cittie', claiming that through his instruction, 'many hundreds have beene suficiently enabled … to attaine unto their desired knowledge in the Language, which to learn they enterprized' (p. 74).

In 1627 Reeve gained the degree of BD from Cambridge. On 30 October in the same year he was presented by Humphrey Bradbourne to the vicarage of Hayes, Middlesex, to be held with the chapelry of Norwood. Here, if not before, he was an ardent advocate of the ecclesiastical policies pursued by William Laud and others. His anti-puritan writings defended divine-right episcopacy and the priesthood, clerical surplices, and ceremonies including the highly controversial altar policy. 'Let all things be done decently and in order' he asserted in his *Christian Divinitie Contained in the Divine Service of the Church of England* (1631), a celebration of uniformity dedicated to Charles I. His theological position is best defined as Arminian, given his writings against absolute predestination and for the efficacy of baptismal and liturgical sacraments. His *Communion Booke Catechisme* (1635) acknowledged the inspiration of leading clergy linked to Arminianism, not only Overall but also John Buckeridge, late bishop of Ely, 'that renowned and profoundly understanding prelate' from whom he received 'further light in the great Mysterie of godlinesse' (sig. B3). The dedication to Robert Wright, bishop of Coventry and Lichfield, apparently his chief current patron, revealed his high view of the role of bishops. William Prynne in *A Quenche Coale* (1637) attacked Reeve's brand of divinity, labelling him as 'this ridiculous Ignoranum'.

By late 1644 Reeve had been sequestered from Hayes and replaced by Joshua Kirby. He seems to have returned to language teaching in London. His *A Way unto True Christian Unitie* (1648) was dedicated from his lodging in Old Bailey to his neighbour, the physician John Bathurst. *An Introduction into the Greek Tongue* (1650) saw him back on familiar ground, but his final work, *The New Jerusalem* (1652), preached on 14 August 1651 to the Society of Astronomers, 'against whose Profession some divines have inveighed' (sig. A2r), took a new turn in its defence of the compatibility of astronomy and Christianity. Reeve died in 1660 without regaining his benefice. PETER DAVID YORKE

Sources N. Tyacke, *Anti-Calvinists: the rise of English Arminianism, c.1590–1640* (1987) · Venn, *Alum. Cant.* · G. Hennessy, *Novum repertorium ecclesiasticum parochiale Londinense, or, London diocesan clergy succession from the earliest time to the year 1898* (1898), 209 · *Walker rev.*, 261

Reeve, Henry (1780–1814), physician, was born in September 1780 at Hadleigh, Suffolk, the second son of Abraham Reeve and Elizabeth Wallace, eldest daughter of Dr Wallace, rector of Messing, Essex. At the age of nine he went to school at Dedham, Essex, where he excelled in Latin and developed his interest in natural history. After leaving school in 1796 Reeve spent four years studying under the Norwich surgeon Philip Meadows Martineau, uncle of Harriet Martineau, before matriculating at Edinburgh University in 1800.

At Edinburgh, Reeve took a prominent part in the undergraduate life of the medical school and served as one of the four presidents of the Royal Medical Society in his second year, 1801–2. However, his interests extended beyond medicine. Edinburgh at the time was a lively intellectual melting pot, attracting an unusually rich influx of talent. Among Reeve's fellow students were Sydney Smith, Henry Brougham, Francis Horner, and Francis Jeffrey. Reeve mixed in this company, both in the University Speculative Society and in the discussions leading to the founding of the *Edinburgh Review* in 1802. Reeve's article on P. Pinel's *Traité sur l'aliénation mentale* (*Edinburgh Review*, 2, 1802, 160–72) showed the germ of his interest in cretinism, a subject to which he would later return.

Reeve graduated MD at Edinburgh in June 1803. Like many of his contemporaries he left Edinburgh to complete his medical training in London. With his friend Thomas Bateman he attended Robert Willan's practice at the Public Dispensary in Carey Street, a leading centre of clinical instruction. In December 1803 Reeve was elected a fellow of the Medical Society of London, and he attended its meetings regularly until April 1805. In that year he joined Bateman and Andrew Duncan the younger in launching the quarterly *Edinburgh Medical and Surgical Journal*, to which he was a frequent, if usually anonymous, contributor, until ill health intervened.

In April 1805 Reeve embarked on the central adventure of his life, a year-long continental tour, initially in company with a fellow physician, the Swiss-born Jean-Jacques de Roches, who was returning home. War with Napoleonic France dictated a circuitous route to Switzerland, through eastern Germany. The two travellers found the German medical intelligentsia immersed in the controversies surrounding the natural philosophy of F. W. J. von Schelling, and obsessed with the theories of the phrenologist F. J. Gall. In the end his exposure to German philosophy left Reeve unimpressed; he dismissed 'these theories … not founded upon any newly discovered facts, but … merely the result of premature metaphysical generalizations' ('On the present state', 72).

After parting from Roches, Reeve travelled through rural Switzerland and Bavaria before reaching Vienna on 30 September 1805 and finding himself marooned by the developing European crisis as Napoleon's forces advanced on Austria. He witnessed the scenes which followed the battle of Austerlitz; he saw Napoleon at Schönbrunn, met Haydn, and attended a performance of *Fidelio* conducted by Beethoven. During his extended stay he studied German and conducted experiments on hibernation with the hamster, hedgehogs, and marmots kept at his lodgings for the purpose. He left Vienna in early February 1806 and travelled to Berlin via Prague and Dresden before embarking from Hamburg in April. At every opportunity Reeve

introduced himself to leading medical and scientific figures—J. C. Reil at Halle, G. Procháska in Vienna, M. H. Klaproth and A. von Humboldt in Berlin—and inspected hospitals, asylums, medical schools, and anatomical museums.

The results of Reeve's continental investigations were published in the *Edinburgh Medical and Surgical Journal*, which printed accounts in 1806–7 of the medical topography of Berlin and of the general hospital and medical school in Vienna (*EMSJ*, 2, 1806, 376–80, 491–6; 3, 1807, 122–5), and of the baths at Leuk, Switzerland (vol. 3, 1807, 150–54). In 1808 Reeve contributed an article on the state of medical science in Germany ('On the present state', 69–73). His continental tour also furnished material for his paper on cretinism, read to the Royal Society in 1808 (*Philosophical Transactions*, 98, 1808, 111–19), and for his *Essay on the Torpidity of Animals* (1809), where Reeve developed the theme of his MD dissertation. Although Sydney Smith claimed that Reeve would do himself 'more real good by superintending one woman of quality in London, than by drinking tea with all the German professors that ever existed' (Holland, vol. 2, letter no. 16), Reeve performed the valuable service of maintaining channels of communication for a Britain temporarily deprived of regular contacts with the continent.

On his return Reeve settled in Norwich. In 1807 he married Susan Taylor (1788–1853), eldest daughter of John *Taylor (1750–1826), the Unitarian hymn writer, and his wife, Susanna (1755–1823), and sister of Richard *Taylor (1781–1858), Edward *Taylor (1784–1863), Philip *Taylor (1786–1870), and Sarah *Austin (1793–1867). Of Reeve's three children only the youngest, Henry *Reeve (1813–1895), later editor of the *Edinburgh Review*, survived infancy. Also in 1807 Reeve was admitted an extra-licentiate of the Royal College of Physicians. Apart from his successful private practice he served as physician to the Norfolk Public Dispensary, and from 1808 was physician to the Norfolk and Norwich Hospital and the Bethel Hospital for Lunatics. He was active in promoting the Norwich Philosophical Society and in founding a non-denominational charity school in the city. But Reeve's health was soon undermined by the onset of an unknown disease in the winter of 1811–12, from which he eventually died on 27 September 1814, at his parents' home at Hadleigh. A memorial was raised in the Octagon Unitarian chapel, Norwich, by his widow.

Reeve was described as 'open, generous, lively, simple and affectionate' (*Edinburgh Medical and Surgical Journal*, 11, 1815, 262). His continental journal is that of a witty and sceptical observer who, while harbouring the instincts of a patriotic Englishman, revealed none the less an open and enquiring mind.   RICHARD ASPIN

Sources [T. Bateman], 'Biographical memoir of the late Henry Reeve', *Edinburgh Medical and Surgical Journal*, 11 (1815), 249–63 · H. Reeve, *Journal of a residence at Vienna and Berlin in the eventful winter 1805–6* (1877) · Lady Holland, *A memoir of the Reverend Sydney Smith … with a selection from his letters*, ed. Mrs Austin, 2 vols. (1855) · J. Gray, *History of the Royal Medical Society, 1737–1937*, ed. D. Guthrie (1952) · J. A. Ross, *Three generations of Englishwomen: memoirs and correspondence of Mrs John Taylor, Mrs Sarah Austin and Lady Duff Gordon*, 2 vols.

(1888) · [H. Reeve], 'On the present state of medical science in Germany', *Edinburgh Medical and Surgical Journal*, 4 (1808), 69–73 · Munk, *Roll* · [H. Reeve], 'Some account of the "medical topography of Berlin", with a list of diseases at the public hospital in that place', *Edinburgh Medical and Surgical Journal*, 2 (1806), 376–80 · [H. Reeve], 'Some account of the General Hospital and medical school at Vienna', *Edinburgh Medical and Surgical Journal*, 2 (1806), 491–6
Archives Wellcome L., continental travel journal

Henry Reeve (1813–1895), by unknown engraver (after Elizabeth Rigby, later Lady Eastlake, 1845)

Reeve, Henry (1813–1895), translator and magazine editor, was born at Norwich on 9 September 1813, the youngest of the three children of Henry *Reeve (1780–1814), physician, and his wife, Susan (1788–1853), daughter of the Unitarian hymn writer John *Taylor (1750–1826) and sister of the celebrated Sarah *Austin (1793–1867). Anna Barbauld and Maria Edgeworth were among the family's distinguished circle of acquaintance.

Susan Reeve, widowed in 1814, lost two older children in 1814 and 1815 and was left at the age of twenty-seven with an income of £500 a year to bring up her surviving child. Despite such modest means, Henry benefited from the excellent education available to the provincial élite in Norwich at the time: Mr Drummond's day school, Norwich School under Edward Valpy, and various local tutors provided a solid grounding in the classics. Reeve finished his education as a student of *belles-lettres* at the Auditoire in Geneva, where he came into contact with leading figures of the European intelligentsia, including the Polish exiles Krasinski and Mickiewicz, and established his habit of forming lasting friendships with the eminent in many walks of life and letters.

Early in his career Reeve learned to make judicious use of such contacts as came his way. Counting the Opies and Austins among his kin, he was able in the 1830s to gain access to artistic and political circles in London, meeting such notables as Carlyle and Thackeray, Godwin and Kemble. Youthful European travels and residence in Paris in 1832 enabled him to enlarge his artistic acquaintance to include Hugo, de Vigny, Balzac, Kenelm Digby, and Liszt. Slipping effortlessly into a career in letters, in his early twenties he consolidated his professional network, combining an extensive European tour with networking and journalism for the *British and Foreign Review*, and with a commission from his uncle John Austin (1790–1859), a member of the criminal law commission, to report on the French criminal justice system. At twenty-two he embarked on a translation of his friend Alexis de Tocqueville's *De la démocratie en Amérique* (published in 1835 and 1840). Reeve's edition remained the basis of the standard English-language version of this influential work until well into the twentieth century.

In 1835 an introduction to Lord Lansdowne led to Reeve's appointment, on the basis of his comparative legal studies, to the lucrative post of clerk of appeals to the judicial committee of the privy council, a body responsible for adjudicating colonial appeals based on foreign law. He was promoted to registrar in the same office in 1843.

Meanwhile Reeve continued to pursue a literary career, privately publishing a modest volume of poems, *Graphidae, or, Characteristics of Painters*, in 1838 for circulation among friends. Sharing, from 1838 to 1841, a lively bachelor establishment in Grosvenor Place with his friend Henry Fothergill Chorley, Reeve could boast Prince Louis Napoleon, Count D'Orsay, the Carlyles, Austins, and Thackeray among a glittering array of familiar guests. In 1840 Reeve joined *The Times* as leader writer and foreign correspondent. Despite the nickname Il Pomposo conferred on him by the editor Delane, Reeve was highly respected in this role: his intimacy with politicians and statesmen such as Guizot, de Tocqueville, Cousin, Clarendon, and Thiers, as well as his access to the privy council, qualified him to gauge, and to some degree influence, the tenor of foreign policy during such tense times as the Middle Eastern crisis of 1840. However, in this instance the experience of having his tactful interventions superseded by Lord Palmerston's robust military response left him with a more cautious opinion of his own influence and insight. His intimate, if not always confidential, relations with Guizot in particular enabled him to contribute to *The Times*'s influential articles on the duc de Bordeaux (1842), Pritchard's expulsion from Tahiti (1844), and the Spanish marriages (1846). The same instinct for friendship and diplomacy, combined with his reputation for discretion, rendered him a useful channel of communication between mainland governments and successive whig ministries for the remainder of his career.

Reeve married Hope Richardson (1815–1842) on 28 December 1841. She gave birth to a daughter, also named Hope, on 27 October 1842, but died on 27 November of the same year following complications associated with childbearing. On 21 August 1851 he married Christine Georgina Jane, *née* Gollop, an author in her own right who wrote a *Manual of Domestic Economy* which went into several editions in the 1880s. She also published and provided an introduction to *Sermons for Children* (1883), a translation of the original by Auguste Decoppet.

Although he continued to contribute letters to *The Times* under the pseudonym Senex, Reeve resigned from its staff in 1855, taking over the editorship of the *Edinburgh Review*. He continued in this role until his death, contributing copious articles of his own on cultural and political affairs, and maintaining the *Edinburgh*'s reputation as a highly respected organ of liberal thought. As an editor, Reeve insisted on the anonymity of his contributors long after the convention had fallen into disuse among rival periodicals. Indeed his mania for independence and impartiality extended to printing harsh reviews of works by friends, and of publications by Longman, his employer. Nevertheless, there is evidence that Lord Clarendon would sometimes 'borrow' from Reeve the proof sheets of a forthcoming *Edinburgh* article in order to prepare for a debate in the Lords; conversely Reeve would occasionally allow the *Edinburgh Review* to act as mouthpiece for Clarendon's views (as, for example, when the latter channelled through Reeve his objections to Kinglake's *Invasion of the Crimea* in 1863).

In 1865, when seriously ill, Charles Greville had expressed his wish to leave his monumental ninety-volume journal in Reeve's hands, and to Reeve's discretion. After the death of Henry Greville in 1872, Reeve determined to publish significant portions of the Greville *Memoirs*. The first part appeared in 1874, 8000 copies selling within six months despite, or because of, disparaging reviews and a hostile motion on the subject in the House of Commons. Its publication was said, furthermore, to have offended the queen, who sensed in it insults to her family and to the monarchy. The incident may have contributed to Reeve's not being appointed KCB.

Reeve's election in 1861 to The Club, the exclusive literary dining society founded by Johnson and Reynolds a century earlier, would henceforth provide a key ingredient to his already active and cosmopolitan social life. In the 1870s he built Foxholes, a handsome house in Southbourne near Bournemouth commanding panoramic sea views, and here subsequently passed such parts of the year as were free from privy council and other London duties. In 1871 he was appointed companion of the Bath.

Although a severe illness in 1880 somewhat curtailed his social life and travel, Reeve remained active in literary life and maintained his prolific correspondence with the great figures of European politics and culture. In 1887 Reeve resigned his registrarship of the privy council—a post he had held for fifty years. However he continued as literary adviser to the publisher Longman and as editor of the *Edinburgh* until his death on 21 October 1895 at Foxholes. He was buried at Brookwood cemetery, Woking, on 24 October, and was survived by his second wife.

As his obituarists and biographer agreed, Reeve's influence on Victorian political and cultural life, and on international relations in particular, was diffuse and pervasive, and for that reason difficult to evaluate. For the most part it consisted in his role as confidential mediator for the great and powerful, rather than in direct influence over events. Although Reeve was clearly a power broker of some magnitude, especially during his years at *The Times*, there is evidence that the aristocratic friendships upon which his prestige and influence were based were not necessarily reciprocated. As Tom Morley observed, Greville, one of Reeve's most significant patrons, 'never forgot Reeve's "humble position, his obscurity, his apparent

nothingness" and confided to Clarendon that "R. would tomber de son haut" if he knew what was being written about him by those whose company he so valued.' (T. Morley, '"The arcane of that great machine": politicians and *The Times* in the late 1940s', *History*, 73/237, February 1988, 49). In book form his output was mainly as a translator, editor, and popularizer, though in 1872 he published reprints of twelve of his own *Edinburgh* articles as *Royal and Republican France*.

In 1878 Reeve contributed a short volume on *Petrarch* to Margaret Oliphant's Foreign Classics series. The story of the poet's humble origins, judicious use of powerful patrons, and attainment of long-lasting honour and influence at a time when other, perhaps greater figures were subject to violently shifting political fortunes, had many echoes of Reeve's own. TREV LYNN BROUGHTON

Sources J. Knox Laughton, *Memoirs of the life and correspondence of Henry Reeve, C.B., D.C.L.*, 2 vols. (1898) • A. H. Johnson, ed., *The letters of Charles Greville and Henry Reeve, 1836–65* (1924) • H. Reeve, ed., *Journal of a residence at Vienna and Berlin in the eventful winter 1805–6 by the late Henry Reeve MD* (1877) • P. M. Tyler, *The letters of Philip Meadows Taylor to Henry Reeve*, ed. P. Cadell (1947) • O. Woods and J. Bishop, *The story of The Times* (1985) • 'Henry Reeve, CB, FSA, DCL', *EdinR*, 183 (1896), 267–71 • *Wellesley index*, 1.420–21 • [H. Reeve], *Graphidae, or, Characteristics of painters* (1838) • [C. G. J. Reeve], *Cookery and housekeeping: a manual of domestic economy for large and small families*, 3rd edn (1882)
Archives Rutgers University, New Jersey, corresp. • University of Toronto, corresp. | All Souls Oxf., corresp. with A. de Tocqueville • BL, corresp. with Lord Aberdeen, Add. MS 43245 • BL, corresp. with Lord Carnarvon, Add. MS 60778 • BL, corresp. with W. E. Gladstone, Add. MSS 44286–44783, *passim* • BL, corresp. with C. C. Fulke Greville, Add. MSS 41184–41185 • BL, letters to A. S. Layard, Add. MSS 38981–39100, *passim* • BL OIOC, letters to M. G. Duff, MSS Eur F 234 • King's Cam., letters to O. Browning • LPL, corresp. with A. C. Tait • NL Scot., corresp. with Blackwoods • NL Wales, letters to G. Cornewall Lewis • priv. coll. (NRA), letters to S. H. Walpole • PRO, letters to second Earl Granville, 30/29 • U. St Andr., corresp. with J. D. Forbes.
Likenesses Count D'Orsay, portrait • Lady Eastlake, portrait, repro. in Knox Laughton, *Memoirs of the life and correspondence of Henry Reeve*, 1 • engraving (after E. Rigby, 1845), NPG [*see illus.*] • photograph (as an older man), repro. in Knox Laughton, *Memoirs of the life and correspondence of Henry Reeve*, 2
Wealth at death £28,668 8s. 11d.: resworn probate, June 1896, CGPLA Eng. & Wales

Reeve, John (1608–1658), co-founder of the Muggletonians, was born in Wiltshire, the second son of Walter Reeve. His father, described as 'clerk to a deputy of Ireland', was of a good family that had fallen into decay. John and his older brother, William, were apprenticed in London as tailors. They had a cousin, Lodowicke *Muggleton, who became journeyman to William Reeve in 1631. There is, however, no evidence of a close association between John Reeve and Muggleton until 1651. From that date until Reeve's death in 1658 the two became co-founders of a religious sect (later known as the Muggletonians) which lasted until the twentieth century, as became known by the chance recovery of their archive in 1974. The last Muggletonian (so it is believed), Philip Noakes, a Kent fruit farmer, was the last custodian of the archive, which is now housed in the British Library (Add. MSS 60168–60256).

Reeve and Muggleton may have been co-founders, but they were not equals in Reeve's lifetime. It was Reeve to whom God spoke on three successive February mornings in 1652, and who was told by Him that he was God's 'last messenger' and that Muggleton was to be Reeve's 'mouth'. They were the two last witnesses prophesied in the book of Revelation (chapter 11). Henceforth their writings were published jointly. There are letters which have survived from Reeve alone, but they are not numerous. In one of these he wrote to a correspondent in 1656 of his preference for face-to-face encounters over letter-writing (Reeve and Muggleton, *Stream from the Tree of Life*, 66). This makes for a telling contrast with Muggleton, who proved to be a prolific letter-writer after Reeve's death. Significantly, no letters from Muggleton alone have survived from the period when Reeve was alive. When Reeve described his period of confinement in Newgate prison to another correspondent, he acknowledged that his ordeal was shared with 'one more with me upon the same account' (Reeve, 70). The impersonality of the reference to his cousin is slighting.

After Reeve's death, there was a dramatic reversal. Muggleton, in printed works as well as letters, presented his version of Reeve's contribution. The effect was subtly to downplay it. Reeve may have consulted God, but the real breakthrough was earlier. In April 1651 Muggleton had the important spiritual enlightenment. This prompted Reeve to daily visits to his cousin, badgering him with requests for his spiritual secrets. Reeve was the supplicant until that time in 1652 when God selected him for direct contact, and they then became jointly the last witnesses. Those claims come from Muggleton's posthumous memoirs, *The Acts of the Witnesses* (1699), as does much of the incidental information about Reeve's background. The suspicion that history has been rewritten is only reinforced by the dedicatory epistle to the work by the Muggletonian to whom Muggleton had entrusted his manuscript, Thomas Tomkinson. Tomkinson is at pains to stress the equality of the commission given to them by God, and that there could be no salvation to those who reject Muggleton 'altho' they pretend to own John Reeve' (Muggleton, 27).

Why should some followers pretend to own John Reeve in 1699 against Muggleton? Throughout the long history of a small sect there were recurrent rebellions of 'Reevonians' against what was perceived as an appropriation of Reeve's doctrines by Muggleton. What substance was there in such beliefs? The first charge of God's commission was that the witnesses should bless believers and curse sceptics: this practice began in 1652 and continued right through to the nineteenth century. When Reeve came round to tell Muggleton of his first contact with God, the first beneficiary (according to Muggleton) was Muggleton's own daughter Sarah. She was coming down the stairs to witness their meeting, and was surprised to find Reeve blessing her. He had always preferred her younger sister. Reeve (in their joint names) developed six articles of belief for their followers. They were in turn: the knowledge of the nature of God (He *was* the Man Jesus:

this was a Unitarian creed), of the nature of the Devil (a projection of men's fears), of the nature of heaven (6 miles up in the sky), of the nature of hell (within one's self), of the nature of angels, and of the mortality of the soul (in an earlier formulation it had been the creation and fall of Adam, but Reeve had published his own mortalist beliefs before his death). Muggleton added glosses on them after 1658, but never fundamentally deviated from any of them. Similarly he accepted the belief (also expounded earlier in joint publications) of the presence of two seeds in any person: faith (good) and reason (bad). There was only one difference between the two of them, but that was crucial. Muggleton asserted that God took no 'immediate notice' of his creatures. Reeve had believed the opposite, but Muggleton had educated him out of his error before his death. No record has survived of that alleged debate, or of its happy resolution. Again the source is Muggleton, and later generations challenged its authenticity. Yet Muggleton's success in imposing his quietist beliefs (acceptable to deists later) upon the movement may have been indeed crucial in its survival beyond the Restoration.

For the earlier confrontational period we have two main sources: Reeve's account (as always, in their joint names), *A Transcendent Spirituall Treatise* (1652), as well as Muggleton's posthumous autobiography. The prophets made their initial mark by their success in cursing. John Robins and another rival prophet, John Tany, were the first to be damned. A man named Penson struck blows at Muggleton, only to die ten days later. At a tavern frequented by Ranters, Reeve put his head on the ground for an enemy to trample upon. The infidel's foot was arrested in flight. A cynical Captain Stasy invited the prophets to dinner with a divine called Gostlin. The dinner ended predictably enough for the clergyman with a curse on his head. Since, according to Muggleton, the captain was 'a great Enemy to the Clergy', he was well satisfied with the outcome. Less so were Muggleton and Reeve, who began six months in Newgate (from September 1653 to April 1654), where they were subjected to much ill treatment by fellow prisoners.

It is doubtful whether Reeve ever fully recovered from that ordeal. Trying to avoid rearrest in Gravesend in 1656, he caught a chill which developed into a consumption. For two years he survived in straitened conditions. The letters that survive from the period are mostly begging ones. His wife, whose name is now lost, died on 29 March 1656, and he lodged with three sisters at a seamstress's shop in Bishopsgate Street, London. Ann Adams (later Cakebread) was 'his handmaid to guide him to other friends' houses'. He died at the end of July 1658 and asked one of the sisters to 'close up mine eyes, lest mine enemies say I died a staring prophet'. He was buried in Bethlehem new churchyard, near the present Liverpool Street railway station.

Muggleton may have been anxious to assert his own position, but revision by him, even so, had its limits. There was, it is true, an occasional asperity—for instance, in his comment on the tendency of those who had been blessed by Reeve not to come up to scratch after his death. Yet his

REEVE, JOHN 342

own authority also derived in the final analysis from Reeve's initial commission from God. He was therefore at pains, in later letters, to clear Reeve of having been immoral (a confusion with his Ranter brother, William), or of having been a sponger (his wife and children had supported him). He also showed a touching concern in 1683 that Ann Cakebread, now widowed, should not be thrown onto the parish with her children. He recalled her services to John Reeve, and arranged for a secret collection on her behalf, to which he contributed (Reeve and Muggleton, *Volume of Spiritual Epistles*, 529). Muggleton's most striking distancing of himself from Reeve was in his amendments of 1661 to Reeve's *Divine Looking Glass* of 1656. There were recurrent arguments about the status of the two editions throughout the later history of the movement. At one level it could be represented (and was) as a prudent Restoration tidying-up of earlier over-fulsome tributes to Oliver Cromwell; at another level it could be seen as part of that same process as the denial of God's 'immediate notice', by which one of the 'world turned upside down' sects of the 1650s adapted, and survived, into a very different political climate after the Restoration. Those who thought the latter, and regretted it, found their hero in the dead John Reeve.

WILLIAM LAMONT

Sources BL, Muggletonian MSS, Add. MSS 60168–60256 · *The works of John Reeve and Lodowicke Muggleton*, ed. J. Frost and I. Frost, 3 vols. (1832) · L. Muggleton, *The acts of the witnesses*, ed. T. L. Underwood (1999) · C. Hill, B. Reay, and W. Lamont, *The world of the Muggletonians* (1983) · E. P. Thompson, *Witness against the beast* (1993) · W. Lamont, *Puritanism and historical controversy* (1996) · A. Gordon, *The origins of the Muggletonians* (1869) · A. Gordon, *Ancient and modern Muggletonians* (1870) · J. Reeve and L. Muggleton, *A volume of spiritual epistles*, ed. A. Delamaine (1755) · J. Reeve, *Sacred remains*, ed. J. Frost (1856) · J. Reeve and L. Muggleton, *A stream from the tree of life*, ed. J. Peat (1758) · J. Reeve and L. Muggleton, *Supplement to the book of letters*, ed. J. Frost and I. Frost (1831)
Archives BL, corresp. and papers, Add. MSS 60168–60256 [mainly copies]
Wealth at death dependent on charity at end of life: Reeve and Muggleton, *A volume of spiritual epistles*, iii, 114

Reeve, John (1799–1838), actor, the son of Thomas Reeve, a hosier and common councillor, was born at his father's shop on Ludgate Hill, London, on 2 February 1799. His uncles were the composer William Reeve and Alderman Robert Waithman MP. At a school at Winchmore Hill, near Enfield, kept by a Mr Thompson, he had for companion Frederick Yates (1797–1842), the actor, a sharer with him in some juvenile escapades. Reeve began work at the age of fourteen behind his father's counter, where he remained for two years. Then, on his father's retirement, he was placed with a firm of wholesale hosiers named Nevill or Neville in Maiden Lane, Wood Street, Cheapside. After staying there for three years, he left, in consequence of complaints from the neighbours about his nocturnal declamations and singing on the roof of the premises. He then became a clerk in Gosling's Bank, Fleet Street, and, like other clerks, subscribed 3s. 6d. a week in order to hire Pym's Theatre, Wilson Street, Gray's Inn Road, once a fortnight. His first appearance was as the waiter at a gambling house in Thomas Morton's *Town and Country*; in this he had

to speak the monosyllable 'No', for which, in nervousness, he substituted 'Yes'. Once, in the off-season at the Haymarket, he played the First Gravedigger in *Hamlet*.

Finding himself condemned to obscure parts by his companions at Pym's Theatre, Reeve took the house on his own account for £10, printed his own bills, and selected his own company. On this occasion he played Othello (his friend the composer George Herbert Bonaparte Rodwel being Roderigo) and Sylvester Daggerwood in a farce so named extracted from Colman's *New Hay at the Old Market*. In the latter character he gave imitations of actors, which met with such success that he repeated *Sylvester Daggerwood* on 8 June 1819 at Drury Lane, for the benefit of Mr Rodwell, senior, the box-keeper at the theatre, and then played it for a few nights at the Haymarket. He was then offered an engagement by Arnold at the Lyceum, and he appeared there in July 1819 as Harry Elias in a piece called *One, Two, Three, Four, Five by Advertisement*, a role in which, once again, imitations were called for. He then resigned his situation in the bank and adopted the stage as his occupation.

At the Lyceum Reeve played, for his benefit, two other characters—Pedrillo and Crack—without winning from the press any recognition except as a mimic. His friend Rodwell, in conjunction with Willis Jones, took the Sans-Pareil Theatre in the Strand and opened it on 18 October 1819 as the Adelphi. Reeve appeared there as Squire Rattlepate in Moncrieff's burletta *The Green Dragon, or, I've quite Forgot* and Lord Grizzle in the burlesque of *Tom Thumb*. But, feeling himself deficient in experience, he joined the elder Macready's company in Bristol, where, as well as at Cheltenham, he played Falstaff, Autolycus, and other characters. At Bristol, in 1821, he married a Miss Aylett, the daughter of an upholsterer in Finsbury, and a dancer in Macready's company. She died at Swansea the following year while giving birth to their son, who was also named John Reeve and who later became a burlesque actor. Reeve soon married again, and he and his second wife, whose maiden name is not known, eventually had two daughters.

Reeve soon returned to the Adelphi, where he succeeded Watkins Burroughs as Jerry Hawthorn in Moncrieff's adaptation from Pierce Egan's *Tom and Jerry, or, Life in London*. At the close of the season in 1823, in association with Wilkinson, he gave at the Adelphi an entertainment called *Trifles Light as Air*, and spoke or acted a monopologue called *Bachelor's Torments*. On the departure of Wilkinson he continued the entertainment alone. He imitated Kean successfully in *Quadrupeds* and played in a drama called *Killigrew*. Thereafter he performed at the Surrey and the Cobourg, rising high in public estimation. Ollapod in *The Poor Gentleman*, Bob Acres in *The Rivals*, and numerous similar roles established his position in comedy, and he was compared with John Edwin. He opened the Haymarket season in June 1827 with *Paul Pry*, and in 1828 he reappeared as Figaro and played the parts of Don Ferolo in *The Critic* and Tony Lumpkin in *She Stoops to Conquer*. The following year he added to his repertory varied roles, from Pierre in *The Rencountre* to John Bates in *Procrastination*. In 1830 he acted his last season at the Haymarket. Having quarrelled with the management over their terms, he transferred to the Adelphi, and in October 1830 appeared as Magog in Buckstone's *Wreck Ashore*. He then went to Covent Garden, where he added nothing to his reputation, and is said, indeed, to have 'signally failed'.

It was with the Adelphi that Reeve's principal original triumphs were associated. Here he played in a burlesque of *Cupid*, was in January 1833 Sancho Panza in *Don Quixote*, and acted in Hall's *Grace Huntley* and other pieces. After performing for two years at the Queen's he went, in 1835, to America, where he gained much money but little reputation. He returned, at a salary of £40 a week, to the Adelphi, then under the management of Yates, and reappeared there in a piece entitled *Novelty*; it was little more than a framework for his American adventures, particulars of which he sang or declaimed. In 1837 he played Sam Weller in *The Peregrinations of Pickwick* and was seen in a few other characters.

From an early date Reeve had been given to excess in drinking, and was consequently frequently imperfect in his part. This may account for the paucity of the original characters assigned him at the Haymarket and Covent Garden. It is said that during his American tour he was not once perfect in any stock comedy, and during 1836, when he was to have played at the Surrey the principal part in a drama called *The Skeleton Witness*, even at the final rehearsal he knew no word of his part. Reeve's last appearance was at the Surrey in 1837, with a portion of the Adelphi company. In a performance of a part he had chosen in a new drama, *The Wandering Tribe*, he was conspicuously imperfect. While returning from the theatre after the second representation, he broke a blood vessel. A fatal illness ensued, and although his reappearance at the Adelphi was promised in October, Reeve died at his house, 46 Brompton Row, on 24 January 1838, and was buried in Brompton churchyard.

Very different opinions are recorded concerning Reeve's merits. Hazlitt said that he was disappointed with his imitations, which were not so good as those of Mathews. His biographer, Douglas Bannister, was at no pains to disguise his ill opinion of Reeve either. However, Reeve was a great favourite with the public, and, in spite of their knowledge of his infirmities, managers were compelled to engage him. He was 5 feet 10 inches in height, dark in complexion, and had great flexibility of feature and limb. Though a bulky man, he walked and danced with the appearance of great lightness. His singing voice was a baritone with a sweet falsetto.

JOSEPH KNIGHT, rev. NILANJANA BANERJI

Sources B. N. Webster, ed., *The acting national drama*, 1 (1837) · *The biography of the British stage, being correct narratives of the lives of all the principal actors and actresses* (1824) · *Era Almanack and Annual* (1877) · *Oxberry's Dramatic Biography*, new ser., 1/11 (1827), 181–92 · T. A. Brown, *History of the American stage* (1870) · Hall, *Dramatic ports.* · E. Stirling, *Old Drury Lane*, 2 vols. (1881) · D. Bannister, *Life of Reeve* (1838) · Genest, *Eng. stage* · H. B. Wheatley and P. Cunningham, *London past and present*, 3 vols. (1891) · P. Cunningham, *A handbook for London: past and present*, 2 vols. (1849) · H. B. Baker, *The London stage: its history and traditions from 1576 to 1888*, 2 vols. (1889)

Likenesses C. Ambrose, oils, Garr. Club · J. Northcote, oils (as Henry Alias in *One, two, three, four, five*), Art Gallery and Museum, Brighton · Wageman, portrait, repro. in Bannister, *Life of Reeve* · forty prints, Harvard TC · portrait, repro. in *Mirror of the stage* (1823) · portrait, repro. in *Theatrical Register* (8 Oct 1838) · portrait, repro. in *Oxberry's Dramatic Biography* · portrait, repro. in Oxberry, *New English drama* (1823) · portrait, repro. in Cumberland, *British theatre* (1829) · portrait, repro. in S. Coyne, *The queer subject* · prints, BM, NPG

Reeve, Joseph (1733–1820), biblical scholar and Jesuit, was born on 11 May 1733, one of at least three sons of Richard Reeve of Island Hill in the parish of Studley, Warwickshire, and his wife, Anne Haskey. In his fourteenth year he was sent to the college of the English Jesuits at St Omer; on 7 September 1752 he entered the novitiate of the society at Watten, and he was professed of the four vows on 2 February 1770. He taught humanities at St Omer and at Bruges for eight years. Being ordained priest, he defended the whole course of theology at Liège in Lent 1767, and then he assisted the Benedictine nuns at Ypres for some months. In August 1767 he was sent to Ugbrooke Park as chaplain to Lord Clifford, and he remained there until his death on 2 May 1820.

Reeve was the author of a number of works in verse and prose. He wrote an account of the expulsion of the English Jesuits from their college at St Omer, parts of which were used by H. Foley in his history of the English Jesuits. *Ugbrooke Park: a Poem* appeared in 1776. A work entitled *The History of the Holy Bible* (1780) was also published in a completely recast edition two years later. *Practical Discourses on the Perfections and Wonderful Works of God* (1788) was reprinted in 1793, together with a second volume, entitled *Practical Discourses upon the Divinity and Wonderful Works of Jesus Christ* (1793). His other works included *A View of the Oath Tendered by the Legislature to the Roman Catholics of England* (1790). This was answered in *An Argumentative Letter* by William Pilling, a Franciscan friar. A volume of his English and Latin poetry went through at least two editions by 1794. This included a translation of Joseph Addison's 'Cato' in Latin verse and an eclogue, 'S. Catharina de morte triumphans'. Reeve's last major work was *A short view of the history of the Christian church, from its first establishment to the present century*, which was first published in Exeter in three volumes in 1802–3. It was republished in 1820 and 1860. Many of Reeve's letters and manuscripts were preserved in the archives of the English province of the Society of Jesus.

THOMPSON COOPER, rev. ROBERT BROWN

Sources Gillow, *Lit. biog. hist.* · G. Holt, *The English Jesuits, 1650–1829: a biographical dictionary*, Catholic RS, 70 (1984) · H. Foley, ed., *Records of the English province of the Society of Jesus*, 7 vols. in 8 (1875–83) · G. Oliver, *Collections illustrating the history of the Catholic religion in the counties of Cornwall, Devon, Dorset, Somerset, Wilts, and Gloucester* (1857) · G. Oliver, *Collections towards illustrating the biography of the Scotch, English and Irish members of the Society of Jesus* (1835)

Reeve, Lovell Augustus (1814–1865), conchologist and publisher, was born at Ludgate Hill, London, on 19 April 1814, the son of Thomas Reeve, draper and mercer, and his wife, Fanny Lovell. After attending school at Stockwell he was apprenticed at the age of thirteen to a Mr Graham, a grocer of Ludgate Hill. The chance visit of a sailor to the family shop with a calico handkerchief full of cowry shells, which he purchased for a few pence, led to Reeve's becoming a lifelong student of conchology. In 1833 he attended the meeting of the British Association at Cambridge where he acted as conchologist to the natural history section on its excursion into the fens between Cambridge and Ely.

His apprenticeship over, Reeve visited Paris where he read a paper on the classification of the Mollusca before the French Academy of Sciences. He returned to London and began work on his first book, *Conchologia systematica* (2 vols., 1841–2). The publication costs, however, used up all the moneys left to him by his father and compelled him to make a fresh start in life. An opportunity to make some money came from his purchase, at Rotterdam, of a large collection of shells amassed by the Dutch governor-general of the Moluccas, General Ryder. Its profitable sale enabled Reeve to open a shop in King William Street, Strand, where he established himself as a dealer in natural objects and as a publisher specializing in natural history books.

About 1848 Reeve moved his business to 5 Henrietta Street, Covent Garden, the address which also became his home from 1864. As a publisher he dealt with eminent scientists such as the botanist William Jackson Hooker, the geologist Charles Lyell, and the traveller–naturalist Alfred Russel Wallace. He did not always enjoy the confidence of his authors, however, for some of them regarded him as a bad businessman who was often parsimonious and who tended to over-commit himself with his publishing projects. He was elected a fellow of the Linnean Society (1846) and of the Geological Society (1853), but, despite being sponsored by Charles Darwin, was unsuccessful in his attempt (1849) to become a fellow of the Royal Society. This was possibly because Reeve was in the publishing trade. A handsome man, reportedly fresh featured with full lips and kindly eyes, he married, on 12 October 1837, Eliza Baker, a relative of his former master, Mr Graham; after her death he married, on 9 January 1854, Martha Reeve (possibly the author of *Edible British Molluscs* (1867) under the pen name M. S. Lovell).

Reeve was a competent photographer and edited and published the *Stereoscopic Magazine* from 1858. He also issued several sets of stereoscopic pictures. His most substantial contribution, however, was to the literature of conchology. Among his works was the Mollusca section of *The Zoology of the Voyage of HMS Samarang* (1848–50), written in collaboration with Arthur Adams. In this, and in his *Elements of Conchology* (1846–60) and *The Land and Freshwater Mollusks Indigenous to, or Naturalized in the British Isles* (1863), he often discusses and illustrates living molluscs as well as their shells.

Very different in character was Reeve's *Conchologia iconica, or, Illustrations of the Shells of Molluscous Animals*, begun in 1843 and finally published in 1878. His close friendship with the London-based collector Hugh Cuming

gave him access to an unrivalled shell collection, so he embarked on an ambitious plan to publish a series of monographs describing and illustrating the molluscan shells of the world. He prepared the descriptions and George Brettingham Sowerby (1812–1884) provided the accompanying lithographs (and continued the work after Reeve's death). The twenty-volume work contains 281 monographs and has 2727 hand-coloured plates. It illustrates most of the two thousand or so species described by Reeve himself as new to science and those described up to his own time by others. As for all his books, he wrote it for the benefit of shell collectors rather than for discerning scientists and so he and his book came under critical scrutiny. John Edward Gray of the British Museum, for instance, considered him guilty of a tendency to describe as species new to science forms of well-known species. Nevertheless, the *Conchologia iconica*, Reeve's magnum opus and lasting memorial, remains a valuable record of descriptive conchology in the middle years of the nineteenth century. Reeve died at his home in Henrietta Street on 18 November 1865. His wife, Martha, survived him.

S. PETER DANCE

Sources J. C. Melvill, 'Lovell Reeve: a brief sketch of his life and career', *Journal of Conchology*, 9 (1900), 344–57 • S. P. Dance, *A history of shell collecting*, rev. edn (1986) • E. Walford, 'Lovell Reeve', in E. Edwards, *Portraits of men of eminence in literature, science, and art, with biographical memoirs*, 4, ed. E. Walford (1866), 85–8 • *Proceedings of the Linnean Society of London* (1865–6), 83 • m. cert. • CGPLA Eng. & Wales (1866) • J. H. Price, 'Goody two-shoes or a monument to industry? Aspects of the *Phycologia Britannica* of William Henry Harvey (1811 to 1866)', *Bulletin of the British Museum (Natural History)* [Historical Series], 16 (1988), 87–216

Archives RBG Kew | NHM, corresp. with Sir Richard Owen and William Cliff

Likenesses H. Watkins, photograph, c.1860, repro. in Dance, *History of shell collecting*, pl. 26 • T. H. Maguire, lithograph, BM, NPG; repro. in T. H. Maguire, *Portraits of honorary members of the Ipswich Museum* (1852) • photograph, repro. in Melvill, 'Lovell Reeve', 344

Wealth at death under £3000: probate, 14 Sept 1866, CGPLA Eng. & Wales

Reeve, Richard (d. 1666), maker of optical instruments, was of obscure origin, but in the records of a London court case of 1664 he was described as a gentleman (rather than an artisan or a freeman of a City guild company) with landed relatives in Burghfield, Berkshire. His skill in the polite art of turning on the lathe and a facility for working optical glass led to him playing a central role in a concerted programme to improve the image quality in refracting telescopes and microscopes.

The first mention of Reeve's optical work is in 1639, in a letter from a correspondent of Samuel Hartlib. Between 1641 and 1643 Reeve was associated with the circle of Charles Cavendish, working with the mathematician John Pell in the ambitious (and ultimately fruitless) task of grinding lenses with the idealized hyperbolic sections recommended by René Descartes. The reported achievements of the German optician Johann Wiesel prompted further work, notably under the patronage of the courtier Sir Paul Neile. Reeve constructed telescopes of increasing focal length and magnification for Neile, including several for the observatory established in 1650 by Seth Ward at Wadham College, Oxford. This was the focus for a group of royalist astronomers and natural philosophers during the interregnum, centred on Ward, Dr John Wilkins, Robert Boyle, and his assistant and protégé Robert Hooke, and including Neile's son William and the young Christopher Wren. By 1652 Reeve was well established as a telescope maker in London and was described by the diarist John Evelyn as 'that admirable Artiste Reeves famous for Perspectives, & turning curiosities in Ivorie' (Evelyn, 64). In the same year Reeve developed an improved form of compound microscope which was marketed commercially. Reeve microscopes were used by Wren for his pioneering illustrations of microscopic objects, some of which were presented to Charles II in 1661. Hooke was closely involved with this project which came to published fruition as his *Micrographia* of 1664 and formed a valuable advertisement for Reeve's instruments.

By 1656 Reeve had produced the first of a series of successful 36 feet long telescopes, for Neile's house at White Waltham, Berkshire. There it was used by Wren for his important work on the structure of Saturn's rings before being transferred to Gresham College, London, for Wren's use after his appointment as Gresham professor of astronomy in 1657. The telescope attracted the interest of Charles II, to whom it was demonstrated in 1660, and for a time it was relocated at Whitehall Palace before being remounted in 1664 by Hooke at Gresham, where he became professor of geometry. A further Reeve telescope of this size was presented by Charles as a diplomatic gift to his brother-in-law Philippe, duke of Orléans, brother of Louis XIV. With the encouragement of Hooke, Reeve developed telescopes of 60 feet in length during the period 1662–5, and one was purchased by Boyle for Hooke's use at Gresham. More typical of Reeve's fashionable trade was the construction of smaller terrestrial telescopes such as the 4 foot instrument purchased by William, first duke of Bedford, in 1661, probably in anticipation of the transit of Mercury that year. A list of Reeve's prices for instruments is included in correspondence of 1660 with the microscopist Henry Power in the British Library.

Reeve's first marriage is tentatively identified with that recorded at St Martin-in-the-Fields on 5 October 1624 between Richard Reeve and Margeria Alexander. The baptisms of two children are known: in 1626 or 1627 that of a daughter, Elizabeth, and in 1630 that of a son, Richard, who equates with the Richard who succeeded Reeve in business at his death. Reeve subsequently married Alice Groves in St Paul's, Covent Garden, in 1659. She died from accidental domestic injuries received in 1664 and Reeve was indicted for manslaughter. He was able to secure a royal pardon in 1665 but at considerable expense.

Reeve may be identified with the Richard Reeve who died in January 1666 in Hampstead, and was buried at St Paul's, Covent Garden, leaving the remaining lease of his house in Henrietta Street, Covent Garden, to his then wife, Dorothy, in a will contested by his cousin. The lease was originally taken out by Reeve in 1633 and Dorothy Reeve is recorded as the occupant for 1667 and 1668. The Reeve business was at the west end of Longacre, trading at the Blue Blanket 1656–73 (and perhaps earlier at Cross Lane, Longacre, 1643–51). The younger Reeve, who was recorded in Samuel Pepys's diary, was not as successful as his father and soon lost the approbation of Hooke and the Royal Society. They came to favour Christopher Cock, an optical instrument maker who may earlier have worked under the elder Reeve and is associated with a commission undertaken by Reeve for the mathematician James Gregory in 1663. In 1675 a Richard Reeve, gentleman, who may be identical with the younger Reeve, obtained a patent for a type of reflector lamp for street lighting, but his later circumstances are unknown.

A. D. C. SIMPSON

Sources A. D. C. Simpson, 'Robert Hooke and practical optics: technical support at a scientific frontier', *Robert Hooke: new studies* [London 1989], ed. M. Hunter and S. Schaffer (1989), 33–61 · A. D. C. Simpson, 'Richard Reeve—the "English Campani"—and the origins of the London telescope-making tradition', *Vistas in Astronomy*, 28 (1985), 357–65 · I. Keil, 'Technology transfer and scientific specialization: Johann Wiesel, optician of Augsburg, and the Hartlib circle', *Samuel Hartlib and universal reformation: studies in intellectual communication*, ed. M. Greengrass, M. Leslie, and T. Raylor (1994), 268–78 · *DNB* · Evelyn, *Diary*, 3.64 · R. T. Gunther, *Early science in Oxford*, 6: *The life and work of Robert Hooke* (1930), 206, 218 · parish record (marriage), St Martin-in-the-Fields, 5 Oct 1624 · parish record (marriage), St Paul's, Covent Garden, 21 June 1659 · parish record (burial), St Paul's, Covent Garden, 15 Oct 1664 [Alice Reeve] · parish record (burial), St Paul's, Covent Garden, 30 Jan 1666 · Bedford estates archives, accounts of George Callop, receiver of revenues of William, earl of Bedford 1661–1662 · BL, correspondence of Reeve and Henry Power, BL MS 1326 · trial records of Reeve, LMA [Newgate gaol delivery register and book, MJ/GBR 6 and MJ/GBB/119–122; Middlesex session rolls, MJ/SR 1297] · poor rate ledgers and overseers' accounts, St Paul's, Covent Garden, and St Martin-in-the-Fields, City Westm. AC · PRO, patent documents, 1675, PRO state papers SP 29/373, no 200, and home office warrant Book 1, SP 44/334, 84 · extension lease of Henrietta Street property to Richard Reeve, 1667–88, LMA, Bedford estate papers, Covent Garden, E/BER/CG/L73/4

Reeve, Richard [*name in religion* Wilfrid] (1642–1693), Benedictine monk, was the son of William Reeve, *plebeius*, and was born in the parish of the Holy Trinity, Gloucester, on 22 June 1642. An attack of palsy 'when he was a quarter old' made him incurably lame on his left side, and in consequence he was 'bred up to learning'. He was educated in the school of St Mary-le-Crypt, Gloucester, where he spent four years, and afterwards he was removed to the school belonging to the cathedral church. He matriculated at Oxford, as a servitor of Trinity College, on 19 July 1661, and was appointed one of the Lord John Craven's exhibitioners. He graduated BA on 18 December 1665, joined the Roman Catholic church in 1667, at George Napier's chapel in Holywell, where he received communion, and was made usher of the school adjoining Magdalen College in 1668. On 9 July that year he commenced MA as a member of Magdalen College. He was appointed master of the school in 1670, and resigned that post on 21 December 1673 after having received a warning from the president that he would be ejected unless he gave in his adhesion to the Anglican church. This resulted from his part in the conversion of Walter Harris, the later physician, 'who had a Worm in his Pate' and was impressed by Reeve's discourses and example. 'He knew he [Reeve] had no manner of temporal motive to quit his All for Religion's sake, besides the preservation of a good Conscience' (Wood, *Ath. Oxon.*, 2.993–4).

During 1673 Reeve assisted Dr John Fell in translating and transcribing into Latin Anthony Wood's *History and Antiquities of the University of Oxford*. Reeve was a friend of Wood and acquired Catholic books and manuscripts for him, though his attempt to convert Wood to Catholicism failed. In August 1674 Reeve went to Douai, where he lived some time privately as a convictor in the priory of St Gregory, belonging to the English Benedictines, where he continued to help Wood with his enquiries. In 1675 he became a monk, assuming in religion the name Wilfrid, but, on account of his lameness, he never took holy orders. For ten years he was engaged in instructing English youths at St Gregory's in classics, poetry, rhetoric, and Greek. As a monk his declamatory skills were employed in the composition of encomiastic Latin verses which were recited on festivals and commemorations. He is, however, especially remembered for his painstaking and strenuous labour in copying, between 1677 and 1681, the mystical writings of the English Benedictine, Augustine Baker. Seventeen copies are still extant. He acquainted Wood with Baker's life and thought, as well as with an abridgement of the English medieval treatise, 'Cloud of unknowing'. His Stuart sympathies brought him some notoriety in the Popish Plot in 1678. From 1685 he spent two years teaching in the English Benedictine priory at La Celle in the diocese of Meaux. The contemporary English Benedictine annalist, Dom Benet Weldon, states that Bossuet took great satisfaction in his company, and made very great account of him.

Reeve was recalled to England in 1688 to be reinstated, by the authority of James II, as master of Magdalen College School, but, owing to the unsettled state of affairs at Oxford, he declined the appointment, and was by royal mandate nominated master of the Blue Coat School at Gloucester, where he was to instruct 'popish youths'. On the outbreak of the revolution he sought an asylum at Bourton on the Water in the house of Charles Trinder, the Roman Catholic recorder of Gloucester, but he was apprehended on 12 December 1688 as a priest and Jesuit, and brought back to that city. He was set at liberty on 10 August 1689, and afterwards lived successively at Bourton on the Water, at Kiddington, Oxfordshire, where he lodged with his former pupil Sir Charles Browne, at Oxford, and at Berkeley Street, Piccadilly, London, where he died on 31 October 1693. He was buried in the church of St Martin-in-the-Fields.

Wood, who knew Reeve well, says:

> he was accounted a perfect philologist, admirably well versed in all classical learning, and a good Grecian; and had been so sedulous in his profession of pædagogy that he had educated sixty ministers of the church of England, and about forty Roman priests. (*Life and Times*)

Reeve shared the imaginative views about teaching, then current at Magdalen College School, which inculcated a child-centred approach and a preference for the vernacular in the teaching of the classics, which were unusual for that time. Such preferences are reflected in his correspondence with John Shipman, vicar of Fairford, between 1669 and 1671. 'Mr. Reeves the best grammarian in the world', was what one pupil scrawled on his book (R. S. Stanier, *Magdalen School, Oxford*, 1940, 105).

THOMPSON COOPER, *rev.* GEOFFREY SCOTT

Sources Gillow, *Lit. biog. hist.*, 5.403–4 · Wood, *Ath. Oxon.*, 2nd edn, 2.531, 905–6, 993–4 · *The life and times of Anthony Wood*, ed. A. Clark, 2, OHS, 21 (1892), 253, 289 · J. McCann and H. Connolly, eds., *Memorials of Father Augustine Baker and other documents relating to the English Benedictines*, Catholic RS, 33 (1933) · D. Lunn, *The English Benedictines, 1540–1688* (1980) · H. Wansbrough and A. Marett-Crosby, eds., *Benedictines in Oxford* (1997) · clothing and profession books, St Gregory's, Douai, Downside Abbey, Somerset · B. Weldon, 'Memorials', Douai Abbey, Woolhampton, Berkshire, English Benedictine Congregation Archives · A. Allanson, *Biography of the English Benedictines* (1999)

Archives Douai Abbey, Woolhampton, Berkshire, Weldon, 'Memorials' | Bodl. Oxf., Rawl. MSS D 191, D 973 · Colwich Abbey, Stafford, Baker MSS · Downside Abbey, near Bath, Baker MSS

Reeve, Thomas (1593/4–1672), Church of England clergyman, was born in Langley, Norfolk, the son of Thomas Reeve, husbandman and gentleman. He attended a school run by a Mr Matchet at Moulton, and was admitted a sizar of Gonville and Caius College, Cambridge, on 30 June 1610, aged sixteen. He was a college scholar between 1610 and 1614, and graduated BA in 1614. On 19 June that year he was ordained priest at Norwich. He proceeded MA in 1617. Little is known of him over the next twenty-five years, and he seems to have been sometimes confused with Thomas Reeve who graduated BA from Caius in 1604, was ordained at Lincoln in 1609, and was rector of Upwell, Norfolk, from 1625 until his death in 1651. However, it is more likely to have been the Langley man who delivered on 19 October 1623, as preacher at Great Yarmouth, a sermon published as *Mephibosheths Hearts-Ioy* (1624), celebrating Prince Charles's return from Spain. He proceeded BD in 1624 and became rector of the Norfolk parishes of Aldborough and Colby in 1628. His younger brother Michael, who had followed him to Caius in 1621, also became a clergyman in Norfolk. The following year, as minister of 'Coleby', he preached a 5 November commemoratory sermon in Norwich Cathedral, published as *The Churches Hazard* (1632).

Reeve was imprisoned by the House of Commons in November 1642 for maligning and deriding the proceedings of parliament. He was ejected from his livings in August 1644 on the grounds that he had observed Bishop Matthew Wren's *Injunctions*; had been absent from his parishes for the past 12 months; had paid no parliamentary assessments, and had discouraged others from doing so, and had not taken the covenant. He was married with six children, and his wife, Mary (about whom nothing else is known), was granted fifths from both his sequestered livings.

In 1647 Reeve preached the funeral sermon of his friend the sequestrated royalist clergyman Ephraim Udall, published as *Lazarus his Rest* (1647). In 1652 the sequestration upon his personal estate, which had been valued at £24 15s., was lifted because, although there was proof of his disaffection to the regime, there was none of his active delinquency. During the 1650s he delivered 'certain Sermons, within the City of London' and may have performed services at St Dunstan's. In 1657 he was living at 'the Bunch of Grapes in Chancery-lane, near Lincolns-Inne'. In that year he dedicated his *God's Plea for Nineveh, or, London's Precedent for Mercy* to his 'Honoured Friend' Thomas Rich, 'a very eminent Citizen of London' (*CSP dom.*, 1655, 95; T. Reeve, *God's Plea for Nineveh*, 1657, title-page, sig. A2r).

After the Restoration, Reeve was awarded a DD and presented to the parish of Fulbourn St Vigors, Cambridgeshire, by the Broad Seal, an appointment which led to a dispute with John Masterson, who claimed that he had been presented to the parish by Charles I. Reeve preached on 15 November 1660 at Waltham Abbey, Essex, the funeral sermon for James Hay, second earl of Carlisle; by the time it was published as *A Cedars Sad and Solemn Fall* (1661), if not before, he was chaplain to Carlisle's widow, Margaret (*née* Russell), and from that year was preacher at the abbey. Reeve dedicated two collections of sermons, *England's Restitution* (1661) and *England's Beauty* (1661), to Charles II; *A Dead Man Speaking, or, The Famous Memory of King Charles the I* (1661) to James, duke of York; and a sermon entitled *England's Backwardnesse, or, A Lingring Party in Bringing back a Lawful King* (1662) to Thomas Wriothesley, earl of Southampton. He died at Waltham Abbey in 1672 and was buried at West Waltham, Essex, in February. Shortened versions of his 1657 pamphlet *God's Plea for Nineveh* were published posthumously as *Mr Reeves his Alarm to London* (1678), *London's Remembrancer* (1683) and *Prophetick Admonitions to the City of London* (1694).

JASON MᶜELLIGOTT

Sources Walker rev., 272 • Venn, *Alum. Cant.* • *CSP dom.*, 1640–72 • J. Caius, *The annals of Gonville and Caius College*, ed. J. Venn (1904) • R. Newcourt, *Repertorium ecclesiasticum parochiale Londinense*, 2 vols. (1708–10)
Archives BL, Add. MS 5879, fol. 39b

Reeve, Sir Thomas (1672/3–1737), judge, was the son of Richard Reeve, of New Windsor, Berkshire, who erected four almshouses in the parish in 1688. Admitted to Trinity College, Oxford, at the age of fifteen in 1688, and to the Inner Temple in 1690, Reeve was called to the bar in 1698. In 1713 he migrated to the Middle Temple, where he was called to the bench in 1720 and served as treasurer in 1728. In 1717 he was appointed king's counsel, and in 1722 succeeded Alexander Denton as attorney-general of the duchy of Lancaster. He had by this time a very busy practice in the king's bench, and an analysis of the crown-side business of that court in 1720 shows him engaged in more cases than any other barrister. He held both offices until his appointment as a puisne justice of the common pleas in 1733, whereupon he was created a serjeant pro forma.

Soon after the death of Chief Justice Eyre in December 1735 it was rumoured that Reeve was to succeed him, and he was supported by the duke of Somerset, though the office was also sought by Denton and the patent was not

Sir Thomas Reeve (1672/3–1737), by Jacopo Amigoni, 1736

sealed until 26 January 1736, when Reeve was also knighted. Denton had been passed over partly on health grounds, but as fate would have it Reeve survived for less than a year. He died on 19 January 1737 at his chambers in Pump Court, Middle Temple, and was buried in Temple Church, London, on 28 January. A monument surmounted by a bust in robes was placed in the church at New Windsor.

Reeve was known as a patron of the literary men of his day, and several verses were published in his honour. He was the author of some instructions concerning the study of the law, addressed to his nephew, which Hargrave printed in 1792. He was married to Annabella Topham; they had no children. Her brother was Richard Topham, of New Windsor, keeper of the records in the Tower, as an executor of whose will Reeve presented to Eton College a collection of drawings after the antique. He resided both at Eton and in Gey's House at Maidenhead. His wealth was considerable, and it is said that in old age he was vainly courted by Lord Sydney Beauclerk in the hope of a legacy. His estate included over £22,000 in personal property, besides his real property in Berkshire and London, which included a moiety of the playhouse in Lincoln's Inn Fields.

J. H. BAKER

Sources Foster, *Alum. Oxon.* • Baker, *Serjeants* • Sainty, *King's counsel* • Sainty, *Judges* • BL, Yorke correspondence, Add. MS 35585, fols. 305–14 • Inner Temple, London • H. A. C. Sturgess, ed., *Register of admissions to the Honourable Society of the Middle Temple, from the fifteenth century to the year 1944*, 3 vols. (1949) • D. Lemmings, *Gentlemen and barristers: the inns of court and the English bar, 1680–1730* (1990), 269 • D. Lemmings, *Professors of law* (2000) • Foss, *Judges* • *Register of burials at the Temple Church, 1628–1853* (1905), 47 [with introduction by H. G. Woods] • G. Lipscomb, *The history and antiquities of the*

county of Buckingham, 4 vols. (1831–47), vol. 4, p. 492 • R. Somerville, *Office holders in the duchy and county palatine of Lancaster* (1972) • W. Musgrave, *Obituary prior to 1800*, ed. G. J. Armytage, 1, Harleian Society, 44 (1899)
Likenesses J. Amigoni, oils, 1736, Graves Art Gallery, Sheffield [*see illus.*] • B. Baron, line engraving, 1736 (after J. Amigoni), BM, NPG • G. Bockman, mezzotint (after oils by J. Amigoni), BM, NPG • bust on monument, New Windsor, Berkshire
Wealth at death over £22,000—in personal property and real estate: Foss, *Judges*; *Windsor*

Reeve, William (1757–1815), actor and composer, was born in London and was apprenticed to a law stationer in Chancery Lane, where a fellow clerk was Joseph Munden, later a comedian. Keen to become a musician, Reeve gave up business to study with Richardson, organist of St James's, Piccadilly. In 1781 he took up a position as organist at Totnes, Devon, but he resigned his post two years later to become a composer to Astley's Amphitheatre.

In 1787 Reeve was engaged by John Palmer at the Royalty Theatre to compose music for the variety of short operas, ballets, and burlettas performed there, one of which, *The Deserter of Naples*, to a libretto by Carlo Antonio Delpini, was successful enough to be performed at Drury Lane in 1788. At about this time Reeve was first given walk-on parts at Covent Garden. One of his more successful acting parts was as the Knifegrinder at the Haymarket in George Colman's successful play *Ut pictura poesis, or, The Enraged Musician*. By 1789 he had a tripartite role at Covent Garden—as composer, singer, and actor—although he did not continue to act for many more years or with much distinction.

Reeve's composing career was given an unexpected boost in 1791; William Shield resigned from Covent Garden, leaving a pantomime, *Oscar and Malvina*, unfinished. Reeve completed the piece, and its success secured his place as the composer of many of the Covent Garden operas and pantomimes over a period of fifteen years. During this time he earned a reputation for unashamedly borrowing and adapting the music of other composers, adding these works to his own compositions to create simple, memorable tunes for populist productions. Indeed, Charles Dibdin wryly observed that 'The music of every piece composed during the [1803] season was composed by Mr Reeve' (Highfill, Burnim & Langhans, *BDA*).

By 1808 Reeve was writing nearly all of the music for Sadler's Wells Theatre, having acquired an eighth share in the company in 1802. He continued to produce music at Dibdin's request until his death. Although most of his work was written for Covent Garden and later for Sadler's Wells, he also worked for Astley's, the Royalty, the Haymarket, the Royal Circus, Drury Lane, and the Lyceum. Despite his exceptionally large musical output, his music was always considered to be rather more workmanlike than inspired. Dibdin's observation was not intended as a compliment, and later commentators are even more unkind; in 1986 Roger Fiske wrote that 'Reeve's pantomimes, ballets, and afterpieces have abysmal music' (Fiske, 576).

It seems likely that the Mrs Reeve who acted and sang at Astley's Amphitheatre in the 1780s was William Reeve's wife. They had two children, George, who also composed at Sadler's Wells, and Charlotte, an actress. According to the *Dictionary of National Biography*, Reeve earned a 'comfortable independence', and he was considered kind and honest by Dibdin. He was admitted to the Royal Society of Musicians on 4 March 1787.

Reeve died on 22 June 1815 at his home in Marchmont Street, Russell Square, London, the administration of his estate being granted to Charlotte Reeve on 23 August of that year. Victoria Halliwell

Sources Highfill, Burnim & Langhans, *BDA* • [J. S. Sainsbury], ed., *A dictionary of musicians*, 2 vols. (1825) • *DNB* • R. Fiske, *English theatre music in the eighteenth century*, 2nd edn (1986) • C. B. Hogan, ed., *The London stage, 1660–1800*, pt 5: *1776–1800* (1968)
Likenesses J. Hopwood, stipple (after E. Smith), BM, NPG; repro. in *The cabinet* (1807)

Reeves, (Richard) Ambrose (1899–1980), bishop of Johannesburg, was born on 6 December 1899 at 71 College Road, Heigham, Norwich, the son of Richard Reeves, a chemist's manager, and his wife, Clarissa Lydamore. His father died when Ambrose was six. He went to Great Yarmouth grammar school in 1912, from where he joined the West Kent regiment in 1917. Poor eyesight prevented him from seeing active service in France, but the experience of being a private soldier in the First World War was decisive for his growing Christian commitment and involvement in industrial and secular affairs. In 1921 he entered Sidney Sussex College, Cambridge, to read history and moral science. He graduated in 1924 (proceeding to the MA in 1943), and became an Anglican ordinand at the College of the Resurrection at Mirfield, near Huddersfield, in the West Riding of Yorkshire, run by the Community of the Resurrection. Reeves combined a Catholic spirituality with a strong ecumenical and social vision. He was ordained deacon in 1926, after which he studied at the General Theological Seminary in New York. Priested in 1927, he served as curate at St Albans, Golders Green, while working for the Student Christian Movement (SCM) in London. On 28 April 1931 he married Ada Margaret van Ryssen (*b.* 1902/3). They had two daughters and two sons, one of whom was drowned in a bathing accident in 1959, while the family was in South Africa.

From 1931 to 1935 Reeves served as rector of St Margaret's, Leven, in Fife. His work with SCM had given him important insights into the churches in Europe, including the Orthodox communities of eastern Europe, and from 1935 to 1937 he was employed by the World Student Christian Federation in Geneva. Convinced that he needed to return to parish life, he became vicar of St James's, Haydock, in the Liverpool diocese (1937–42), before being appointed vicar of St Nicholas's, the parish church of Liverpool (1942–9), which had been destroyed by enemy bombing in 1941. Liverpool proved a good place for Reeves to exercise his strong commitment to industrial mission. In 1945 he played a key role as mediator in the Liverpool dock strike. His ability both to articulate strongly the basic grievances of the dockers, and successfully to work towards a settlement acceptable to both sides, brought him wide acclaim, and led to his consideration by the synod of the diocese of Johannesburg as its bishop. Bishop George Bell (like Reeves involved in the newly inaugurated World Council of Churches) urged him to think seriously about a call to 'the second most important See in the Anglican communion' (Peart-Binns, 64). Reeves was elected, consecrated bishop in Cape Town on 12 June, and enthroned in Johannesburg on 24 June 1949.

The Johannesburg diocese was in the industrial heartland of South Africa, and included the goldmines of the Rand. The Anglican church had important work both in the black community and in the white, the members of which were largely of British descent. When Reeves took up office, the National Party had just come to power in South Africa and was beginning to formulate and implement its policies of radical racial 'separate development'. From the first, Reeves was critical of apartheid, both as a philosophy and in its inhuman implementation. It was, he said, 'an insult to human dignity'. Reeves was keenly aware not only of the theological unacceptability of apartheid, but of its destructive effects on economic and industrial relations, and of the use of power and coercion. The effect of the pass laws was to 'reduce the bargaining position of African workers by forcing them into a convenient labour pool', as well as placing enormous strains on family life (LPL, Canon Collins papers, MS 3297).

In 1953 Reeves, alone among the South African bishops (like him largely English born and educated), decided he could not in conscience conform to the regulations of the Bantu Education Act which required that church schools submit to government control and teach the new culturally restricted and regressive curriculum. He preferred to see the diocesan schools close rather than submit to such directives. Unfortunately, his attempt to establish alternative 'Church family centres' lacked the resources to become effective. His perceived intransigence made him unpopular with fellow bishops who had opted for compromise. Already in 1951 the Reeves's home had been the subject of an arson attack. His attempt to help finance a radical Afrikaans trades union newspaper, *Saamtrak*, infuriated the National Party establishment, and Reeves's links with Canon John Collins and anti-apartheid activists in London made him extremely unpopular with many sections of white South African society. Reeves and Collins were instrumental from 1956 in establishing a fund to pay the legal costs of the treason trial involving Nelson Mandela and Oliver Tambo (an Anglican whom Reeves had considered putting forward to ordination) and other leaders of the African National Congress.

On 21 March 1960 the Sharpeville massacre took place. A demonstration against the pass laws at Sharpeville, a township of Vereeniging, was fired upon by the police: 69 people were killed, 180 injured. Sharpeville was in the Johannesburg diocese. Reeves rushed to the hospital and talked to the injured. Convinced that he must tell the world what had happened and that he might be arrested, he decided to slip out of the country. He arrived in Swaziland and from there flew to London (where, later in the year, he published *Shooting at Sharpeville: the Agony of South Africa*).

'Almost certainly Reeves' flight … was a major error of judgement which gravely weakened his moral authority and from which he never really recovered' (Hastings, 144). It made him *persona non grata* in South Africa; and it removed him from a position where he could influence developments in that country. It was also certainly an embarrassment to the Church of England. Harold Macmillan, the prime minister, was reluctant to appoint Reeves as a bishop in England for fear of further alienating the South African government (which was about to leave the Commonwealth). Important figures within the Church of England were antagonized by Reeves's overtly political involvement. Even a suggestion that he should head the church's board of social responsibility was opposed on the grounds that it might alienate powerful sections of British business.

Reeves decided to return to Johannesburg in September 1960—only to be deported immediately. He then felt obliged to resign, but offers of a job in England were extremely limited. In 1962, his chances of promotion to the English hierarchy effectively dead, he accepted the office of general secretary of the SCM. Another book by him, *South Africa, Yesterday and Tomorrow: the Challenge to Christians*, appeared in 1962. In 1966 he became priest in charge of St Michael's Church in Lewes (becoming rector there in 1968). He retired in 1972 and died on 23 December 1980 at Whitefriars, Church Street, Shoreham by Sea, Sussex. Reeves's commitment to Christian socialism, his willingness to involve himself with political activists and to take part in the detailed planning of political action in the secular arena, distinguished him as bishop. Such overt commitment was troublesome to leaders of the establishment in South Africa and in Britain, but has given him a very high reputation among black South Africans, as one who sacrificed himself unstintingly in the struggle for justice and freedom in South Africa. KEVIN WARD

Sources J. Peart-Binns, *Ambrose Reeves* (1973) · A. Hastings, *A history of African Christianity, 1950–75* (1979) · LPL, Fisher papers · b. cert. · m. cert.
Archives LPL, Canon Collins papers, MS 3294 · LPL, Fisher papers · University of the Witwatersrand, Johannesburg, Church of the Province of South Africa Central Records Library
Likenesses photographs, repro. in Peart-Binn, *Ambrose Reeves*

Reeves, Cecilia Grace Hunt. *See* Gillie, Cecilia Grace Hunt (1907–1996).

Reeves, Charles (1815–1866), architect, was born at Fordingbridge, Hampshire, and baptized on 8 April 1816 at Bishop's Waltham, Hampshire, the son of Charles Reeves and his wife, Sarah. He studied under Thomas Loader of Romsey and Richard Suter and Annesley Voysey of London. In 1843 he was appointed architect and surveyor to the Metropolitan Police, for whom he designed and superintended forty-four new police stations, some with police courts attached (for example, at Westminster, opened 1846). In 1847 he also became architect to the national network of county courts established in the previous year, and subsequently constructed or adapted sixty-four new court buildings across the country. Drawings for twenty-six of these survive in the Public Record Office. Reeves was awarded a medal for his services to the 1851 and 1862 exhibitions. He also maintained a practice at 102 Guilford Street, London, with Henry Annesley Voysey as his partner from 1847 until 1852, and Lewis G. Butcher from 1853 onwards. Private commissions included Coalbrookdale church, Staffordshire (1850–54); Shad Thames flour mills; and the Church Missionary Society's children's home, Highbury Grove (opened 1853). Reeves's preferred style was a heavy, somewhat builderly, version of Italianate; his court buildings and police stations did not follow any model plan, but they nevertheless form a recognizable group, being designed to fulfil the particular accommodational requirements of these nascent types economically, yet with dignity. He died, apparently unmarried, at Halterworth, Romsey, on 6 December 1866.

CLARE GRAHAM

Sources *DNB* · [W. Papworth], ed., *The dictionary of architecture*, 11 vols. (1853–92) · Boase, *Mod. Eng. biog.* · C. Graham, 'The development of the law court as a building type in England before 1914', PhD diss., University of Sheffield, 1997, 192–3, 220–28 · S. Barson, 'The evolution of metropolitan police stations in the 19th century', MSc diss., U. Lond., 1986, 7–11 · *ILN* (10 Jan 1846), 28 · *ILN* (24 Jan 1852), 67–8 · Colvin, *Archs.* · *Dir. Brit. archs.* · *GM*, 4th ser., 3 (1867) · county court drawings, PRO, work/30 · *VCH Middlesex* · *Shropshire*, Pevsner (1958) · *IGI* · d. cert.
Archives PRO, county court drawings, work/30

Reeves, Helen Buckingham [*née* Ellen Buckingham Mathews; *pseud.* Helen Mathers] **(1851–1920)**, novelist, was born Ellen Buckingham Mathews in the village of Misterton, near Crewkerne, Somerset, probably in August 1851, the fourth of twelve children and third daughter of Thomas Mathews, farmer and manufacturer, and his wife, Maria Buckingham. Little is known about Mathews's parents or siblings, save that her father was both an impecunious businessman and a strict disciplinarian who presided over a harsh regime of outdoor sports and farm labour. At the age of thirteen, Mathews, who was partially deaf, was sent to the Chantry School, Frome, to train as a governess. By this time she had begun to write stories and poetry. When she was about sixteen she sent a version of her poem 'The Token of the Silver Lily' to Dante Gabriel Rossetti, who was encouraging. She also approached G. A. Sala, who was sufficiently impressed to send one of her stories, 'A sketch of Jersey', to Mary Braddon, then editor of the magazine *Belgravia*. Eager for a literary career, Mathews moved to London in the early 1870s, a statuesque figure with red hair, 'a very independent sort of young lady', as she announced herself to the publisher George Bentley (Bentley archives, ILL Reel 48, L9, 30 June 1875). Her first novel and greatest success, the semi-autobiographical *Comin' thro the Rye* (3 vols.), was published under the initials H.B.M. in July 1875. This story of a young girl's education, tyrannical father, and quest for romantic fulfilment was condemned as vulgar, melodramatic, derivative, and full of slang, but proved a hit, selling 35,000 copies for the Bentleys by 1898.

On 6 February 1877 Mathews married Henry Albert Reeves (1841–1914), an orthopaedic surgeon and author of medical textbooks. In domestic life she was known as Helen Buckingham Reeves, but she used the name Helen

Mathers for her literary work. Her only son, Philip Lindley Reeves, was born in March 1878. When interviewed at their home in Grosvenor Street, London, by Helen Black, in 1890, Reeves, like many women writers of the time, gave the impression that her career was little more than a hobby. She explained that she wrote her novels on slips of paper and that she was 'essentially a domestic woman' (Black, 79). In reality, her husband's poor health meant that she had to write constantly in order to support their middle-class standard of living. It is difficult to be precise about the number of novels but between *Comin' thro the Rye* and the unfinished *Eventide* there are at least thirty, as well as numerous short stories and poems. Although dogged by suggestions that she plagiarized her rival, Rhoda Broughton, in her emphasis on 'fast' young ladies, Reeves possessed a greater range than her contemporaries gave her credit for. Besides romantic novels named after song titles, notably *Cherry Ripe!* (3 vols., 1878) and *Land o' the Leal* (3 vols., 1878), she published sensational murder stories (*The Sin of Hagar*, 1896) and collaborated with Bram Stoker and others on the multi-authored *The Fate of Fenella* (1892). Always resourceful, as well as financially needy, Reeves also tried her hand at adapting her novel *The Story of a Sin* (3 vols., 1882) and its sequel, *Eyre's Acquittal* (1884), for the stage. Much in demand as a columnist, she contributed articles on a variety of subjects to magazines (notably *Temple Bar*) and in 1880 established the *Burlington Magazine* with herself as editor. Despite an impressive list of contributors that included Oscar Wilde and Algernon Swinburne, this venture was not a success. The *Burlington* failed to find a niche and was disbanded in 1882, leaving Reeves with large debts.

By the beginning of the twentieth century Reeves's star began to wane. Novels which had once seemed risqué in their sexual frankness came to seem outmoded. These years were also characterized by personal tragedy. In December 1907 Reeves's son, Philip, who had collaborated with her on some of her later works including *Tally-Ho!* (1906), died. Reeves announced her retirement in the same year. In 1909 severe financial hardship caused her to apply to the Royal Literary Fund and the Royal Bounty Fund. Most of her later works were the collections of short stories written much earlier. By the time of her husband's death in 1914, Reeves was severely deaf and very rheumatic, and increasingly irked by her sense that she had lost £20,000 on the still popular *Comin' thro the Rye* since selling the copyright to Bentley & Son for 30 guineas. In July 1915 she resurfaced briefly to bring a lawsuit against the publishers Stanley Paul over a dispute about the copyright of her novel *Love the Thief* (1909). She lost the case when her memory was judged to be at fault. To this period also belongs her interest in spiritualism and her obsessive use of mediums as a way of contacting her dead son. Virtually penniless, Reeves died on 10 March 1920 at the home of her close friend Clara Bone, 26 Callcott Road, in Kilburn, London. She was buried on 13 March in Paddington cemetery.

ANDREW MAUNDER

Sources *The archives of Richard Bentley & Son, 1829–1898* (1976) [microfilm] · H. C. Black, *Notable women authors of the day* (1893) ·

WWW, 1916–28 • J. Shattock, *The Oxford guide to British women writers* (1993) • *The Times* (13 March 1920) • 'Memory at fault', *News of the World* (25 July 1915) • R. Geltman, *A Victorian publisher: a study of the Bentley papers* (1960) • m. cert. • d. cert.
Archives BL, archives of Richard Bentley & Son • U. Cal., Berkeley, archives of Richard Bentley & Son • University of Illinois, archives of Richard Bentley & Son
Likenesses A. Ward, portrait, repro. in Black, *Notable women authors*, 69

Reeves, John (1752–1829), barrister and writer, was born in London on 20 November 1752, the only son of John Reeves, baker, and his wife, Elizabeth. He was educated at Eton College, 1764–71, matriculated at Merton College, Oxford, on 31 October 1771, and graduated BA in 1775. On 11 November 1775 he was elected Michel scholar of Queen's College, Oxford, and on 8 October 1777 a fellow, taking his MA in 1778. He was admitted to the Middle Temple on 11 May 1776, and called to the bar on 18 June 1779.

In 1780 Reeves was appointed commissioner in bankruptcy, soon afterwards withdrawing from practice in the courts in order to concentrate on legal scholarship. He had already published two minor essays before the appearance of the substantial *History of English Law* (1783–4). Reeves rejected an institutional categorization of English law in favour of a historical approach whereby '[t]he law of the time would … be learned in the language of the time, untinctured with new opinions' (2nd edn, 1787, v–vi). In 1789 Reeves was elected fellow of the Society of Antiquaries, and in 1790 fellow of the Royal Society.

Under the encouragement of the home secretary, Lord Sydney, Reeves drafted the London and Westminster Police Bill initially rejected by the Commons in 1785, but enacted in modified form as the Dublin Police Act of 1786 (26 Geo. III, c. 24), and eventually as the Middlesex Justices Act of 1792 (32 Geo. III, c. 53), thereby establishing seven police offices in London. In July 1792 Reeves was appointed receiver of the public offices under the act. As law clerk to the Board of Trade, 1787–1823, he helped to draft proposals establishing a civil court in Newfoundland, sanctioned by 31 Geo. III, c. 29 (1791), and modified, on Reeves's recommendation, by 32 Geo. III, c. 46 (1792). Reeves was appointed successively chief judge and chief justice of Newfoundland in 1791 and 1792, visiting the island from 10 September to 1 November 1791 and from 3 September to 30 October 1792.

On his return to London about 10 November 1792 Reeves was alarmed by the seditious activity which, in his view, threatened to undermine the constitution and government. On 20 November 1792 he established the Association for Preserving Liberty and Property against Republicans and Levellers at the Crown and Anchor tavern in the Strand, installing himself as chairman. Similar associations instituted throughout the country had an immediate impact in suppressing radical agitation. The final meeting of the Crown and Anchor association took place on 21 June 1793. Reeves was hailed as having saved the country from revolution, and rewarded with the Savoy Manor Stewardship (1794–1802).

Reeves published a number of pamphlets on topical political issues, usually from a legal perspective, but his most

John Reeves (1752–1829), by Thomas Hardy, pubd 1793

notorious was the anonymous *Thoughts on the English Government: Letter the First*, dated 29 October 1795. He claimed that the British government was essentially monarchical, and that '[t]he Kingly Government may go on, in all its functions, without Lords or Commons' (p. 13). In the Commons on 26 November 1795 Sheridan denounced the pamphlet as a seditious libel on the constitution, and ascribed its authorship to Reeves. Pitt's intervention ensured its condemnation. A Commons committee found that Reeves was the author, whereupon the attorney-general, Scott, was ordered to prosecute him for libel. On 20 May 1796 Reeves was acquitted by a jury which found his pamphlet to be 'very improper', but his motives not libellous. Reeves reiterated and defended his argument in three subsequent *Letters* (1799–1800).

In 1800, on Pitt's recommendation and possibly in compensation for the prosecution of 1796, Reeves was appointed king's printer. Displaying his classical scholarship and knowledge of Hebrew, Reeves edited and published versions of the Bible (1802) and Book of Common Prayer (1801), as well as a Greek New Testament (1803) and Hebrew Psalms (1804), mainly funded from the emoluments of the office. From 1800 he was one of the treasurers for the literary fund and superintendent of aliens (1803–14). On 7 May 1824 he was elected a bencher and became reader in 1827.

John Reeves died unmarried at his home in Parliament Place, Westminster, on 7 August 1829, and was buried in the Middle Temple vault on 17 August 1829.

PHILIP SCHOFIELD

Sources 'A sketch of the life and character of John Reeves, esq.', *European Magazine and London Review*, 73 (1818), 467–72; 74 (1818), 41–

8, 133–5, 220–25, 322–8, 409–14, 492–4 · *Annual Biography and Obituary*, 14 (1830), 277–99 · *GM*, 1st ser., 99/2 (1829), 468–71, 482 · L. Radzinowicz, *A history of English criminal law and its administration from 1750*, 3: *Cross-currents in the movement for reform of the police* (1956), 108–37 · D. W. Prowse, *A history of Newfoundland from the English, colonial, and foreign records* (1895), 358–60 · *Annual Register* (1796), 20–21 · J. Debrett, ed., *The parliamentary register, or, History of the proceedings and debates of the House of Commons*, 45 vols. (1781–96), vol. 43, pp. 401–27, 480–88, 592–3, 732–4, 749–62 · S. Brooke, *An appeal to the legislature, on the subject of the office of king's printer, in England* (1830) · *Mr Reeves's evidence before a committee of the House of Commons on the trade of Newfoundland* (1793), 102 · *Association Papers* (1793) · 'John Reeves, esq. (with a portrait)', *European Magazine and London Review*, 33 (1798), 363–5 · S. Lambert, ed., *House of Commons sessional papers of the eighteenth century* (1975), 112.94–7 · R. A. Austen-Leigh, ed., *The Eton College register, 1753–1790* (1921) · register of baptisms, St Martin-in-the-Fields, London · Middle Temple bench book

Archives BL, papers of Association for Preserving Liberty and Property against Republicans and Levellers, Add. MSS 16919–16928 · BL, Add. MSS 16929–16931 · Bodl. Oxf., corresp. · Memorial University, Newfoundland, history of government and constitution of Newfoundland | BL, letters to Lord Grenville, Add. MS 58986 · BL, corresp. with earls of Liverpool, Add. MSS 38222–38473 · BL, letters to C. P. Yorke, Add. MS 45038 · Harrowby Manuscript Trust, Sandon Hall, Staffordshire, letters to Dudley Ryder and Richard Ryder · NA Scot., letters to Henry Dundas · PRO, letters to William Pitt, PRO 30/8

Likenesses T. Hardy, engraving, pubd 1793, NPG [*see illus.*] · J. Chapman, stipple (after S. Drummond, *c*.1798), BM, NPG; repro. in 'John Reeves, Esq.', *European Magazine*, 33 (1798) · S. Drummond, oils, Eton College, Berkshire · J. Thomson, stipple (after S. Drummond, 1814), NPG; repro. in 'A sketch of the life', *European Magazine and London Review*, 73 (1818) · oils (after T. Hardy, 1792), NPG

Wealth at death very rich: *Annual Biography* · property was divided amongst four cousins: *GM*

Reeves, John (1774–1856), natural history collector and artist, was born on 1 May 1774, the youngest son of the Revd Jonathan Reeves of West Ham, Essex. Left an orphan at an early age, he was educated at Christ's Hospital and afterwards entered the counting house of a tea broker. He joined the East India Company's office of inspector of tea in England in 1808 and proceeded to China in 1812 as assistant, and subsequently chief inspector of tea, in the company's establishment in Canton.

Before his departure for China Reeves had been introduced to Sir Joseph Banks and had received from him instructions to collect botanical information and natural history specimens. Reeves would never obtain more than basic knowledge of natural history, and he published nothing but a few brief notes in obscure journals. His scientific endeavours in China, however, earned him much respect among naturalists. He was a member of the Horticultural Society and the Zoological Society and was elected to both the Royal Society and the Linnean Society in 1817.

Reeves went to China when the British fascination for Chinese gardening was high. He shipped numerous ornamental plants to the Horticultural Society and became a major channel through which new discoveries in China were introduced; he also acted as the local patron to the botanical collectors sent out by the society. At a time when little was known about China's natural history, Reeves

John Reeves (1774–1856), by George Chinnery, 1826–31

played an important role in gathering information and on his two visits to England in 1816 and 1824, and his final return in 1831, took with him large numbers of natural history specimens (including the famous Reeves pheasant) and other curiosities.

Reeves is best-known by specialists for his collection of natural history drawings, later deposited in the Royal Horticultural Society and the Natural History Museum of London. While in Canton and Macao, Reeves commissioned native artists under his supervision to draw plants and other objects of natural history as scientific data. His fish drawings, which covered more than 300 species, provided British ichthyologists with much new information about Chinese fishes.

Reeves had a gentle personality and was well liked by his colleagues in Canton and naturalist friends at home. After returning to England he lived at Clapham and participated regularly in the affairs of the Horticultural Society. He was frequently consulted by fellow naturalists on Chinese subjects. He died on 22 March 1856 in Old Town, Clapham. His son John Russell Reeves (1804–1877) had joined him in China in 1827 and spent thirty years there. He continued his father's efforts in collecting objects of natural history and was elected to the Linnean Society in 1832 and the Royal Society in 1834.   FA-TI FAN

Sources P. J. P. Whitehead and P. I. Edwards, *Chinese natural history drawings selected from the Reeves Collection in the British Museum (Natural History)* (1974) · E. Bretschneider, *History of European botanical discoveries in China*, 2 vols. (1898) · J. Richardson, 'Report on the ichthyology of the seas of China and Japan', *Report of the British Association for the Advancement of Science*, 15 (1845), 187–320 · J. Reeves, 'An account of some of the articles of the materia medica employed by the Chinese', *Transactions of the Medical Botanic Society* (1828), 24–7 · *DNB* · Desmond, *Botanists*, rev. edn · E. H. M. Cox, *Plant hunting in*

China (1945) • A. M. Coats, *The quest for plants* (1969) • P. Synge, 'Chinese flower paintings: an important purchase by the Royal Horticultural Society', *Journal of the Royal Horticultural Society*, 78 (1953), 209–13 • *Proceedings of the Linnean Society of London* (1855–6), xliii–xlv • *Gardeners' Chronicle* (29 March 1856), 212

Archives BL, corresp. and papers relating to Chinese gazetteer of imperial officials, Add. MS 39255F • NHM, notebooks and drawings; zoological specimens • Royal Horticultural Society, London, Chinese drawings | BL, letters to Sir Joseph Banks, Add. MS 33932 • NHM, Dawson-Turner collection, corresp. of Joseph Banks [copies]

Likenesses G. Chinnery, portrait, 1826–31, FM Cam. [*see illus.*]

Reeves, John Morris [*pseud.* James Reeves] (1909–1978), poet and educationist, was born on 1 July 1909 at 7 Hamilton Road, Wealdstone, Harrow on the Hill, Middlesex, the elder son of Albert John Reeves, company secretary, and his wife, Ethel Mary, *née* Blench. He was educated at Nevill House, Eastbourne, and then from 1923 to 1928 at the recently founded Stowe School. His open scholarship at Jesus College, Cambridge, in 1928 was the first Oxbridge scholarship won by a pupil at Stowe. At Cambridge he read English, taking a second class (division one) in both parts of the tripos, and as an undergraduate he collaborated with Jacob Bronowski to found and edit the influential literary magazine *Experiment*, to which the poet William Empson contributed. Graduating in 1931, in 1933 he embarked on a teaching career. His first post, at Holloway School, was terminated in 1935 on grounds of poor eyesight, a progressive disability that finally compelled him to retire from teaching. On 4 April 1936 he married Mary (1909/10–1966), the daughter of Edward Douglas Phillips, at the parish church of St Peter, Bayswater, in London. At that time Reeves was resident at 54 Lyndhurst Road, Chichester. The couple had one son and two daughters.

James Reeves was a prolific writer: in the course of his career he wrote or edited over a hundred books. After his retirement from teaching in schools and colleges of education in 1952, he turned to full-time freelance writing. His poetry for both adults and children, the first collected in *Collected Poems, 1929–74*, and the second in *Complete Poems for Children* (1973), is generally regarded as his most important work. However, he also contributed significantly to new methods of teaching and presenting poetry to children, first during his own teaching career, and later, after his retirement, through such books as *Teaching Poetry* (1958), *Understanding Poetry* (1965), and (with Martin Seymour-Smith) *Inside Poetry* (1970). His work as teacher and creative writer was integrated in his study *How to Write Poems for Children* (1971). Reeves was a versatile and imaginative anthologist, and also produced many volumes of retold traditional stories for children. In 1951 he was appointed general editor of William Heinemann's Poetry Bookshelf series, and in 1960 general editor of Unicorn Books. His career as a children's poet, now regarded as perhaps the most important part of his achievement, began in 1950, relatively late in life and only a short time before his retirement from teaching, with the publication of *The Wandering Moon*. Much of his work for children was illustrated by Edward Ardizzone, with whom he developed a highly successful collaborative partnership. In

1958 he returned to Cambridge for a short time, in order to research his important book on English folk-songs, *The Idiom of the People*. He became a fellow of the Royal Society of Literature.

Reeves was a friendly and generous man, but intolerant of pretentiousness and falsity, at which he could direct a mordantly satiric intelligence. In some respects he felt out of tune with the modern world, distrusting what he believed to be the distancing effect on individual experience brought about by the media. He complained of the 'nightmare of sensationalism, violence, hysteria and threatened destruction' ('Introduction' to *Collected Poems, 1929–1959*, 19) to which constant second-hand news subjected the individual sensibility, and felt that privacy was threatened in the modern world. Himself a private man, he was nevertheless a natural teacher, held in much admiration and affection by his students.

Having been resident for some time at Danesbury House, Chalfont St Giles, Buckinghamshire, Reeves moved in 1962 to Flints, Rotten Row, Lewes, Sussex, where he spent the rest of his life. Mary Reeves died in 1966. Reeves himself died suddenly of heart failure on 1 May 1978 at his home, and his funeral took place at St Anne's Church, Lewes, on 8 May.   PETER HOLLINDALE

Sources records and obituary, Jesus College, Cambridge • records and correspondence, Stowe School • L. S. Berger, *Twentieth-century children's writers*, 4th edn (1995) • T. Riggs, *Contemporary poets*, 6th edn (1996) • *WW* • b. cert. • m. cert. • d. cert.

Wealth at death £70,624: probate, 3 Nov 1978, *CGPLA Eng. & Wales*

Reeves [*née* Robison], **Magdalen Stuart** [*known as* Maud Pember Reeves] (1865–1953), suffragist and socialist, was born on 24 December 1865 at Mudgee, New South Wales, the third of ten children of William Smoult Robison, a bank manager, and his wife, Mary, a literary and well-travelled relative of the Carr-Saunders family of Surrey. When Maud, as she was always known, was two years old, her parents migrated to Christchurch, New Zealand, an Anglican settlement founded on the colonizing principles of Edward Gibbon Wakefield. She was one of the first pupils at the new Christchurch High School for Girls. A 'keen and spirited' pupil, she developed a passion for the theatre. Tall and striking, with a handsome face, full red lips, dark eyes, and brown hair, Maud met her husband, William Pember *Reeves (1857–1932), a journalist and politician eight years her senior, at a coming-out ball when she was nineteen. The son of a newspaper proprietor, who 'grew up an Englishman', Reeves was an ambitious—if absent-minded—politician whose vision for New Zealand was 'no slums and no poverty'. They married at Christchurch on 10 February 1885.

Newly married, Maud acted, helped her mother-in-law in charitable works, and for three years was the lady editor of the weekly *Canterbury Times*, edited by her husband and owned by his father. The Reeves's first child, William, lived only a few hours. Their daughter Amber [*see* White, Amber Blanco] was born in 1887. After the birth of her second daughter, Beryl, in 1889, Maud took the first part of a BA in French, mathematics, and English at Canterbury

College (founded in 1873). In 1890 the family moved to Wellington, where William Reeves had been a radical member of the house of representatives since 1887. Maud's studies were abandoned for her duties as the wife of a minister and suffragism. She had been converted to women's suffrage by Julius Vogel, a former prime minister and friend of her husband. She had been president and founder of the women's section of the Christchurch Liberal Association. Education, she believed, would both convince women of the need to vote and civilize national debate. Although never a temperance advocate, she worked closely with Kate Sheppard, the Women's Christian Temperance Union's suffrage superintendent, and Ellen Ballance, the prime minister's wife, and she used her considerable charm to influence her husband's colleagues. In September 1893 New Zealand was the first country in the world to grant women the vote, and Maud chaired the first public meeting of enfranchised women in Christchurch on 11 October.

In March 1896 William Reeves was appointed New Zealand agent-general in London. Maud followed him eagerly thither with the three children, Fabian having been born in December 1895. The Reeves immediately made friends with the Fabians, whose essays they had read and who admired Reeves's experience in government. They spent country weekends with the Webbs, Shaws, and Blands, working, bicycling, and talking. Maud joined the Women's Liberal Association, the Fabian Society in 1904, and the executive of the National Union of Women's Suffrage Societies in 1906. At Maud's instigation the Fabian Society's statement of its basic aims included a clause on equal citizenship in 1907, when she was elected, with Ethel Bentham and Marian Phillips, to the society's executive committee. The first meeting of the Fabian Women's Group, which she founded with Charlotte Wilson, the anarchist, was held in her Brunswick Gardens drawing-room early in 1908, after a winter of suffrage agitation.

The Lambeth mothers' project, initiated by Maud, was prompted by the recognition that more infants died in the London slums than in Kensington or Hampstead. It asked 'How does a working man's wife bring up a family on 20s a week?', and from it sprang Maud's *Round about a Pound a Week* (1913), one of the sharpest of the many works of Edwardian social observation. Forty-two families were selected from a lying-in hospital in Lambeth, London, to have weekly visits, medical examinations from Dr Ethel Bentham every two weeks, and 5s. to be paid to the mother for extra nourishment for three months before the birth of the baby and for one year afterwards. The money came from private donations, and the mothers wrote down their weekly expenditure. Eight families withdrew because the husbands objected to this weekly scrutiny. Eight other mothers who could not read or write dictated their sums to their husbands or children. The verbatim accounts of the 'maternal manner of recollecting'—'Mr. G's wages was 19 bob out of that e took thruppons for es diner witch is not mutch e bein sutch a arty man'—is one of the features of the book which is in part an ironic comment on class relations: Lambeth women, familiar with the habits of educated visitors, politely anticipated sitting in draughts, listening to the gospel of porridge, and being advised against marriage.

Poverty, the book argued, and neither maternal ignorance nor degeneration, caused ill health and high mortality. Had the children of Lambeth been 'well housed, well fed, well clothed and well tended from birth' who knows what they would have become. Fabian women were would-be law makers. The state must cast off its 'masculine' guise and 'co-parent'. The individual not the family should be the economic unit, and the state should pay family endowment, train midwives, make burial 'a free and honourable public service', introduce a legal minimum wage, and build clean, light, roomy buildings at economic rents for the working classes. If socialism should address the needs of working mothers then women themselves must want more: 'If people living on £1 a week had lively imaginations, their lives, and perhaps the face of England, would be different.'

Maud's own household was unorthodox. In 1900 Maud's favourite sister, Effie Lascelles, recently widowed, moved in with her two daughters. Amber remembered a house filled with children, relatives, servants, nursemaids, 'frightful rows' in the nursery, and her mother too busy to pay much attention to children. The Reeves marriage after the birth of Fabian was not intimate. William did not approve of birth control. The tensions in their marriage, H. G. Wells—who until his affair with Amber was a close friend—wrote, were about money and birth control. When Amber, then a student at Cambridge, became pregnant by H. G. Wells—a public and political scandal—Maud offended her daughter by suggesting an abortion.

In March 1917 Maud was appointed director of women's services in the Ministry of Food, and in June 1917 Fabian died of wounds sustained during service in the First World War. Maud turned privately to spiritualism, and later to Higher Thought. From the early 1920s her participation in public life declined. She travelled to New Zealand with William in 1925, but while she had conversed with the London poor she had never met a Maori. She was a conscientious grandmother, and she nursed both William and her sister through their final illnesses. Amber described her mother as 'serious-minded' and 'obviously chaste to the last degree'. Her focus on the needs of others was as austere as her prose, but the unflinching eye for detail and clamour of voices in *Round about a Pound a Week* dramatized both the 'almost intolerable conditions' of women's daily lives and Fabian feminism's response. After twenty-one years as a widow, having lived with her sister Effie in Cambridge, Maud died in a nursing home at 27 Powis Gardens, Golders Green, Middlesex, on 13 September 1953.   SALLY ALEXANDER

Sources Nuffield Oxf., Fabian Society MSS · Fabian Society, BLPES, Passfield MSS · M. S. P. Reeves, *Round about a pound a week* (1913) · R. Fry, *Maud and Amber: a New Zealand mother and daughter, and the women's cause, 1865–1981* (Christchurch, New Zealand, 1992) · S. Alexander, interview with Amber Blanco White, Aug 1978, priv. coll. · S. Alexander, ed., *Women's Fabian tracts* (1988) · *The diary of Beatrice Webb*, ed. N. MacKenzie and J. MacKenzie, 4 vols.

(1982–5), vols. 1–3 • G. P. Wells, ed., *H. G. Wells in love* (1984) • K. Sinclair, *William Pember Reeves, New Zealand Fabian* (1965) • M. Holroyd, *Bernard Shaw*, 1 (1988) • J. B. Condliffe, 'Reeves, William Pember', *DNZB*, vol. 2
Archives priv. coll., Blanco White MSS
Wealth at death £22,577 16*s*. 11*d*.: probate, 19 Oct 1953, *CGPLA Eng. & Wales*

Reeves, Marian (1879–1961), feminist activist, was born on 19 February 1879 at 17 Victoria Terrace, Lewisham, London, the daughter of Albert Reeves, a carpenter, and his wife, Emily Hooper Pratt. No records of her early life appear to have survived, but by the time of the First World War she had become active in the feminist movement. Of particular note was her involvement with the Women's Freedom League, the militant suffragist society which under the leadership of Charlotte Despard had in 1907 broken away from the Pankhurst-dominated Women's Social and Political Union; by 1914 it had developed into a body campaigning on a wide range of feminist issues apart from the vote, which it continued to do until its demise in 1961. Marian Reeves was not involved in the initial years of the league (which she later regretted); she joined the league in 1909, and was a member of the Clapham branch, but by 1918 she was already secretary of its Kensington branch. Later she was elected to its national executive and eventually became the league's last president.

In the 1920s Marian Reeves was involved with the Minerva Publishing Company, the Women's Freedom League's publishing branch, and about 1924 she took over the running of the Minerva Club in Brunswick Square, in the Bloomsbury area of London. This residential club had been established by Dr Elizabeth Knight and Mrs Fisher in 1920 as a social centre for members of the Women's Freedom League, and it became the league's headquarters when the lease on the league's own premises at 144 High Holborn ran out in the 1950s. Here she organized many social and fund-raising activities for the league, and for visitors, particularly women from overseas.

Especially notable were her 'tea and politics meetings' (which later became 'supper meetings') when parliament was in session in order to give women (and men) an opportunity to discuss current legislation, and the birthday parties held for Mrs Despard until her death in 1939, for which Mrs Despard came over from her home in Ireland. Marian Reeves's hospitality to feminists of all persuasions at the Minerva Club earned her the sobriquet 'the hostess of the women's movement'.

Marian Reeves also became something of a Bloomsbury figure, including among her friends George Bernard Shaw, Jawaharlal Nehru, E. M. Forster, Harriet Cohen, and Emmeline and Frederick Pethick-Lawrence. She also championed the cause of the small hotels and boarding-houses, then so abundant in Bloomsbury, especially during the Second World War. These businesses had been damaged not only by bombing but by the evacuation of many of their tenants, and Marian Reeves founded the London Emergency Apartment Keepers' Society (known by its initials), which campaigned successfully for the suspension of their rent and rates for the duration of the war.

Marian Reeves was active in a number of other feminist organizations besides the Women's Freedom League, including the Nationality of Married Women Committee, the Equal Pay Campaign Committee, and the Women Peers Committee. She was also a soroptimist. She served on the executive of the Association for Moral and Social Hygiene (campaigning against state regulation of prostitution), on the committee of the Open Door Council (campaigning against legislation that restricted women's right to work in certain occupations), and on the women's advisory council of the United Nations Association. She was an early vice-chairman of the British Commonwealth League, and later of the Status of Women Committee. She felt a special commitment to the International Alliance of Women, whose congresses she regularly attended. In 1961, although in poor health, she visited Dublin for the alliance's congress, and while there placed flowers from the Women's Freedom League on the grave of Charlotte Despard in Glasnevin cemetery. A few days later, on an excursion by motor coach to Killarney on 30 August 1961, she collapsed and died at the railway station, Killarney. Her body was brought back from Ireland for cremation at the Golders Green crematorium on 5 September.

Marian Reeves had never married, devoting herself entirely to the women's cause. Her friend Kate O'Brien saw Marian Reeves as 'a *citizen*, with a highly developed civic sense' and 'a walking manifestation of Voltaire's maxim: "I hate what you are saying, but I will die for your right to say it"' (*The Times*, 1 Sept 1961). However, despite her sustained efforts on its behalf, the Women's Freedom League's numbers had been declining noticeably, especially after the Second World War, and in October 1961, deprived at last of her guiding hand, it finally voted itself out of existence.   DAVID DOUGHAN

Sources *Women's Freedom League Bulletin*, 12 (1961) • *The Times* (1 Sept 1961) • *The Shield* (Oct 1961) • *Catholic Citizen* (15 Oct 1961) • E. Crawford, *The women's suffrage movement: a reference guide, 1866–1928* (1999) • b. cert. • d. cert.
Archives Women's Library, London, Women's Freedom League archives
Wealth at death £871 12*s*. 7*d*.: probate, 10 Nov 1961, *CGPLA Eng. & Wales*

Reeves, Maud Pember. *See* Reeves, Magdalen Stuart (1865–1953).

Reeves, (John) Sims (1818–1900), singer, was born on 26 September 1818 at Woolwich, London, the son of John Reeves, a Royal Artillery bandsman, and his wife, Rosina. He was christened John; 'Sims' was added later. His first professional appearance was as a baritone in H. R. Bishop's *Guy Mannering* at Newcastle in December 1838. Later he performed at the Grecian Saloon, London, under the name of Johnson. His voice settled in the tenor range, and in 1842 and 1843 he was engaged by W. C. Macready at Drury Lane, where the repertory included works by Handel and Purcell. During the summer of 1843 he took some

(John) **Sims Reeves** (1818–1900), by Alessandro Ossani, 1863 [in the title role of *Fra Diavolo* by D.-F.-E. Auber]

lessons with Giulio Bordogni in Paris, and until late 1845 he sang in provincial theatres.

Reeves now took further tuition from Bordogni and from Alberto Mazzucato in Milan. This led to appearances at La Scala, Milan, in Donizetti's *Lucia di Lammermoor* and Verdi's *Alzira* in October 1846 and January 1847, followed by performances elsewhere in Italy and in Vienna. No other British tenor of his generation had such experience. On returning to Britain he swiftly rose to the first rank. In September 1847 he sang in Edinburgh with Jenny Lind, and in December 1847 he joined Louis Jullien's opera company at Drury Lane, where he appeared with great success in works by Donizetti, Balfe, and Berlioz. The last, who conducted, praised his voice and his acting, saying, 'il chante aussi bien que cette effroyable langue anglaise puisse permettre de chanter'—'he sings as well as this frightful English language can be sung' (*Correspondance*, 476). He was now increasingly known as Sims Reeves (a name apparently taken on the advice of a colleague, Madame Puzzi). In 1848 he sang in oratorio performances at Exeter Hall, and was engaged at Her Majesty's Theatre.

On 2 November 1850 Reeves married (Charlotte) Emma Lucombe (1823/4–1895), a soprano, with whom he sang in opera performances and in concerts. They had five children, of whom Herbert Sims Reeves and Constance Sims Reeves became professional singers. In March 1851 Reeves appeared at the Théâtre Italien, Paris. Henceforth, for more than twenty years he was at the forefront of his profession. He sang privately for Queen Victoria and Prince Albert, and Macfarren, Costa, and Sullivan were among the composers who wrote tenor parts specifically for him. His rising reputation is reflected in the fees he could command. From 1848 to 1854 he received 100 guineas for singing at the Norwich festivals; in 1857 he was reported as obtaining £200 per week for appearing in *Guy Mannering* at a theatre in Shoreditch; and in 1858 he was paid 200 guineas for taking part in four concerts of the Leeds festival. His performances in oratorio at the Crystal Palace in 1857 and in the Handel commemoration festival of 1859 received great acclaim, his rendition of 'The Enemy Said' in *Israel in Egypt* being particularly admired. Although Reeves returned to the major London opera stage at various times in the 1860s (for example, in Gounod's *Faust* in 1864), with the growing popularity of mass concerts he now turned increasingly to oratorio and concert work. His interpretations were noted for their declamatory power, founded on his highly admired phrasing. He was also renowned for his moving performances of popular ballads, some of which, such as 'Tom Bowling', and 'In this Old Chair' from Balfe's opera *The Maid of Honour* (in whose première Reeves sang in 1847), he retained in his repertory for years.

In 1868 Reeves campaigned against the high musical pitch common in Britain, and for some years he refused to sing with the Sacred Harmonic Society, the major London organization of its kind, which retained the high pitch. By now he was well known for absences from performances, which were publicly attributed to illness but were often considered due to nerves. Legal judgments for non-performance were given against him at Cheltenham in 1869 and Edinburgh in 1871.

In 1874 Reeves made his final appearance at a Handel festival, and from 1878 he confined himself largely to concerts, though his farewell appearance at the Albert Hall did not take place until 1891. Meanwhile he published *Sims Reeves, his Life and Recollections, Written by himself* and *My Jubilee, or, Fifty Years of Artistic Life* in 1888 and 1889 respectively. Both are unreliable concerning details—for instance, he claimed he was born in 1821. In his later years Reeves was beset by financial worries and he continued to sing intermittently, although his voice was much enfeebled. He joined the staff of the Guildhall School of Music and Drama; his *On the Art of Singing* (1900) gives an impression of his teaching. A month after his wife's death he married, on 17 July 1895, one of his pupils, (Lucy) Maud Madeleine Richard (b. 1873/4), and the following year they toured South Africa. In 1900 he was granted a civil-list pension of £100. He died at Oxford Road, Worthing, on 25 October 1900, and was cremated at Woking.

GEORGE BIDDLECOMBE

Sources C. E. Pearce, *Sims Reeves: fifty years of music in England* (1924) · *DNB* · H. S. Edwards, *The life and artistic career of Sims Reeves*

(1881) · *Correspondance générale: Hector Berlioz*, ed. P. Citron, 3 (Paris, 1978), 482–3 · *The Athenaeum* (7 Nov 1868), 610 · R. H. Legge and W. E. Hansell, *Annals of the Norfolk and Norwich triennial musical festivals* (1896), 116, 144 · M. Musgrave, *The musical life of the Crystal Palace* (1995), 22, 36, 39, 137 · *Edinburgh Evening Courant* (1 Nov 1871), 6 · *The Times* (22 Feb 1869), 5 · C. Gatti, *Il Teatro alla Scala vella storia e nell' arte*, 2 (1964), 46 · *Sims Reeves, his life and recollections, written by himself* (1888) · S. Reeves, *My jubilee, or, Fifty years of artistic life* (1889) · S. Reeves, *On the art of singing* (1900) · *The Athenaeum* (3 Nov 1900), 586 [see also 587n.] · *MT*, 41 (1900), 806–7 · S. Reeves, two letters, BL, BL Add. MS 41637, fols. 159, 307; Add. MSS 41964, fols. 111b, 112, 316 · A. Jacobs, *Arthur Sullivan: a Victorian musician*, 2nd edn (1992) · Grove, *Dict. mus.* · m. cert. · d. cert.

Likenesses C. Baugniet, lithograph, 1850, BM · A. Ossani, oils, 1863, NPG [*see illus.*] · Barraud, photograph, NPG; repro. in *Men and Women of the Day*, 1 (1888) · A. E. Chalon, pencil and watercolour drawing, NPG · Kingsbury & Notcutt, cabinet photograph, NPG · Spy [L. Ward], chromolithograph caricature, NPG; repro. in *VF* (10 May 1890) · cartes-de-visite, NPG · portrait, repro. in Reeves, *My jubilee*, cover

Reeves, William (1667–1726), Church of England clergyman, was born at Flitwick, Bedfordshire, at about Christmas time in 1667, the son of William Reeves. After attending Eton College he matriculated at King's College, Cambridge, at Easter 1685. He received his BA in 1689 and an MA in 1692. He was elected a fellow of King's College in 1688, but resigned on his marriage to Elizabeth (*d.* 1728) in May 1689. They had two daughters. Reeves was ordained deacon in London on 20 December 1689; he was presented on 9 August 1694, by George Berkeley, first earl of Berkeley, to the living of Cranford in Middlesex. On 1 August 1711, on the death of Abraham Brooksbank, he became vicar of St Mary's, Reading, Berkshire, a position he held until his death. He was also a chaplain to Queen Anne (1711–1714).

Among Reeves's published works was his valuable translation, in 1716, of the *Apologies* of Justin Martyr, Tertullian, and Minucius Felix in defence of the Christian religion. This included a discussion of the use of patristic writings, and provided a new translation and critical annotation to each work. The project took seven years to complete. In the 'Preliminary discourse' he sought to defend the authority of the fathers against the challenge posed by the Huguenot divine Jean Daillé and his Anglican followers. For Reeves the church fathers of the first four centuries ranked second only to scripture in authority for the church. William Orme described his translations as 'perspicuous and faithful'. He also stated that the notes 'contain a good deal of learning and frequently illustrate the meaning where it is obscure', making it a useful introduction to patristic study (Orme, 368–9). George Hickes, the nonjuring bishop, suggested that he deserved the 'thanks and praise of all lovers of primitive Christianity' for it spoke 'in our language the same things, with the same united force of wit and reason, and with the same charms of eloquence that they did in their own' (Hickes). His translation of Tertullian's *Apology* was reprinted in the nineteenth century with Jeremy Collier's translation of Marcus Aurelius's *Meditations*.

Reeves was considered an able preacher; a collection of fourteen of his sermons was published posthumously in 1729 from a manuscript that he had already prepared for publication. James Darling described them as having a 'peculiar cast of originality' (Darling, 2521). The collection included an election sermon based on the text of Matthew 27: 3–4 entitled 'The fatal consequences of bribery exemplified in Judas'. He apparently originally published the sermon at low cost to be given away. Many of those who read it were said to have returned the bribes and voted differently (Chalmers, 26.109). The sermon was later reprinted separately in 1733 and 1753. He died at Reading on 26 March 1726, and was buried near the altar in St Mary's Church there.   ROBERT D. CORNWALL

Sources Venn, *Alum. Cant.* · W. Orme, *Bibliotheca biblica* (1824), 368–9 · A. Chalmers, ed., *The general biographical dictionary*, new edn, 26 (1816) · R. Newcourt, *Repertorium ecclesiasticum parochiale Londinense*, 1 (1708), 596 · J. Darling, *Cyclopaedia bibliographica: a library manual of theological and general literature*, 2 vols. (1854–9) · G. Hickes, 'Letter to the author', in R. Laurence, *Lay baptism invalid*, 2nd edn (1709) · Allibone, *Dict.* · J. McClintock and J. Strong, *Cyclopaedia of biblical, theological, and ecclesiastical literature*, 12 vols. (1894–5), vol. 8, p. 980 · W. Sterry, ed., *The Eton College register, 1441–1698* (1943)

Reeves, William (1815–1892), antiquary and bishop of Down, Connor, and Dromore, was the eldest child of Boles D'Arcy Reeves (*d.* 1852), an attorney, and his wife, Mary (*d.* 1832), fourth daughter of Captain Jonathan Bruce Roberts, who fought at the battle of Bunker Hill in the American War of Independence (June 1775), and was afterwards land agent to the earls of Cork. He was born at Charleville, co. Cork, on 16 March 1815 in Captain Roberts's house and was reared in Dublin, where he received his early education. He entered Trinity College, Dublin, in October 1830, became a scholar in his third year, shortly after his mother's death, and graduated BA in 1835. Since he was too young to take holy orders and had the aim of practising among the poor of his parish when ordained, he went on to study medicine and graduated MB in 1837. After being ordained deacon at Hillsborough, co. Down, on 18 March 1838, he became curate of Lisburn, co. Antrim. He was ordained priest at Londonderry on 2 June 1839, and in 1841 became perpetual curate of Kilconriola, or Ballymena, co. Antrim.

Reeves's first publication, printed at Belfast in 1845, was a description of the ancient monastic site of Nendrum, co. Down. On 14 December 1846 he was elected a member of the Royal Irish Academy. In 1847 he published his *Ecclesiastical Antiquities of Down, Connor and Dromore*, which remains the chief work of reference on the ecclesiastical history and topography of that part of Ireland. In 1849 he was made headmaster of the diocesan school at Ballymena, a post which he combined with his existing curacy for the next eight years. When his father died in 1852, he inherited his landed estate in Cork, but generously divided it with his brothers and sisters. In 1850 the Irish Archaeological Society published his *Acts of Archbishop Colton*, a volume which does for the diocese of Derry what his earlier book had accomplished for his own diocese. In both works medieval records are illuminated by a minute knowledge of the modern local topography and of the written records and oral traditions of the districts in question. Sixteen papers of varying importance, but all showing original work, followed, chiefly in the *Proceedings of the Royal Irish Academy* and in the *Ulster Journal of Archaeology*.

In 1857 Reeves published in Dublin his most famous work, *The Life of St Columba, Founder of Hy, Written by Adamnan*. This large volume was the fullest and most learned work on ancient Irish ecclesiastical affairs published since the time of John Colgan. Though no longer the leading edition, it is referred to by scholars nearly 150 years later. The text of the life (which is copiously and carefully annotated) is taken from an early eighth-century manuscript. The preparation of this book helped assuage his grief at the loss of his first wife, his cousin Emma, daughter of Thomas Reeves of Carlisle, whom he had married on 3 January 1838 and who died on 12 October 1855, leaving nine children.

The Life of St Columba earned international scholarly approval and Reeves was elected an honorary member of the societies of antiquaries of Scotland and of Zürich, but he failed to obtain the chair of ecclesiastical history in his own university, Trinity College, Dublin. Dr James Henthorn Todd, a fellow student of Irish ecclesiastical history, was responsible for his appointment to the vicarage of Lusk, co. Dublin, where he took up residence on 30 December 1857. He used the proceeds of his pamphlet *The Ancient Churches of Armagh* (1860) to repair the round tower in Lusk, which was in danger of collapse. (It was by his intervention, too, that Navan Fort—the ancient Emain Macha—near Armagh, was later saved from destruction.) On 19 December 1861 Archbishop Beresford nominated Reeves Armagh diocesan librarian, a post with a greater income than he received from his vicarage, which he continued to hold. He went to live in the librarian's house in Armagh, but maintained a curate at Lusk, where he continued to preach on Sundays. In November 1865 he was appointed rector of Tynan, near Armagh, and resigned Lusk, but remained librarian of Armagh. In 1869 he was unsuccessful a second time in his quest for a post in his alma mater when he was refused the Trinity College librarianship, but in 1871 the university made some amends by conferring on him the honorary degree of LLD; he was already DD, and the University of Edinburgh had conferred an honorary LLD on him in 1860. The College of Physicians in Dublin elected him a fellow in 1864.

In 1875 Reeves was made dean of Armagh, and on 18 March 1886 he was elected bishop of Armagh and Clogher, but soon afterwards Dr Knox, bishop of Down, Connor, and Dromore, was elected archbishop of Armagh, and Reeves succeeded to the consequently vacant see. He was consecrated bishop of Down, Connor, and Dromore on 29 June 1886. He left with regret the library at Armagh, where many volumes of records copied by his hand remain. He went to live at Conway House, Dunmurry, co. Antrim, between Belfast and Lisburn, and administered his diocese with energy. In 1891 he was elected president of the Royal Irish Academy, to whose publications he contributed more than fifty original papers after the publication of his *Life of Columba*, besides editing part of the works of

Archbishop James Ussher and writing many indexes and notes to the work of others. He showed his great knowledge of Irish topography in his paper 'On the townland distribution of Ireland' (1862). His scholarly output came to more than eighty items, including five substantial books and almost a score of lengthy papers.

Reeves did important work on the ninth-century manuscript known as the Book of Armagh, which he purchased for £300 in 1853, at a time when his means were small, and which Primate Beresford bought from him the following year and presented to the library of Trinity College, Dublin. The manuscript, however, did not reach the college for almost forty years; instead it remained with Reeves while he worked on an edition. Beresford paid him £500 in 1860 to defray the cost, but it was not until 1913 that the work appeared in a great edition by John Gwynn, which incorporated many of Reeves's unpublished notes. Reeves used to carry the manuscript about in its original leather sack suspended by straps from his neck. On 26 December 1891 he married, in Dublin, his cousin Charlotte Townley. While still in Dublin, he fell ill with pneumonia on 6 January 1892; he died on the 12th and was buried on the 15th at Armagh. His extensive library was auctioned in Dublin in November 1892 and more than thirty of his valuable Irish manuscripts were acquired by the Royal Irish Academy.

Reeves was a tall man with an aquiline nose and bright expressive eyes. He enjoyed contemporary repute as a lively and erudite conversationalist, and an able raconteur. He was a friend of his fellow antiquary John O'Donovan, and there is evidence that he spoke sufficient Irish to converse in it with the older scholar, whom he promised that he would learn the language 'in right earnest'. He encouraged the pioneering Irish scholar from co. Antrim Róis Ní Ógáin to take an interest in the language. He was also a friend of Todd and of all in Ireland who cared for historical learning. In the districts in which his life was spent he was liked and admired by people in every rank of society and of every shade of opinion. It has been said of him that 'No more notable figure in the field of Irish antiquities and Irish bibliography ever lived ... and no one was more willing to place his great knowledge at the disposal of every inquirer' (*Irish Book Lover*, 99).

NORMAN MOORE, rev. NOLLAIG Ó MURAÍLE

Sources 'William Reeves: bishop and bibliographer', *Irish Book Lover*, 2 (1910–11), 97–100 · D. Breathnach and M. Ní Mhurchú, *Beathaisnéis a Ceathair, 1882–1982*, 4 ([Dublin], 1994), 167–8 · M. C. Ferguson, *Life of the Right Rev. William Reeves, D. D.* (1893) [incl. bibliographical appx by John Ribton Garstin] · B. Ó Cuív, 'A seventeenth-century Irish manuscript', *Éigse*, 13 (1969–70), 143–52 · J. Thompson, 'William Reeves and the medieval texts and manuscripts at Armagh', *Peritia*, 10 (1996), 363–80 · personal knowledge (1896)
Archives Armagh Public Library, papers relating to Irish history · Down, Connor, and Dromore Diocesan Library, Belfast, MSS relating to ecclesiastical history · NL Ire., corresp. and papers · PRO NIre., papers relating to Scottish saints, D2850 · Royal Irish Acad. · TCD, corresp. and papers · TCD, Irish historical collections | Archbishop Marsh's Library, Dublin, corresp. relating to Royal Irish Academy · Limerick University Library, letters to Lord Dunraven · PRO NIre., letters to Lord Dunmore, D3007 · PRO NIre., letters to Lord Dunraven, D3196 · U. Edin., letters to David Laing · University College, Dublin, corresp. with John O'Donovan

Likenesses portrait, repro. in Ferguson, *Life of the Right Rev. William Reeves*, frontispiece
Wealth at death £5877 3s. 3d.: probate, 9 Feb 1892, *CGPLA Ire.*

Reeves, Sir William Conrad (1821–1902), politician and judge in Barbados, was born in Bridgetown, Barbados. His father, Thomas Phillipps Reeves, who was white, was a skilled apothecary and his mother was a free black woman, Phyllis Clarke. As a 'free person of colour', Reeves was born into a slave society whose main divisions were those of colour and legal status. Free people of colour faced a variety of restrictions, including limits on occupations and on participation in political life. During Reeves's childhood, free coloureds in Barbados became the legal equals of white people and slavery itself was abolished in 1834; but the pattern of discrimination against the free people of colour continued after the abolition of slavery.

For Reeves, this meant an education in schools specifically established for free children of colour. As a young man he worked under the leading free coloured journalist of the period, Samuel Jackman Prescod. Prescod edited a radical paper, *The Liberal*, and had a distinguished career in the press and as a member of the Barbadian house of assembly. He was a strong believer in representative institutions as well as in the reform of the house of assembly and, in both areas, had a significant influence on Reeves's subsequent development.

In addition to working on *The Liberal*, Reeves was also a member of the debating club in Bridgetown. His success in debating and in public oratory encouraged some of the leading men of colour as well as the wider coloured community to support his legal education in England. He became a student at the Middle Temple in May 1860 and was called to the bar in January 1863. While in London he also wrote for the Barbados press. He returned to Barbados in 1864, where he practised law. From May 1867 he acted for a short period as attorney-general of St Vincent. In 1868 he married Margaret, eldest daughter of T. P. R. Budder of Bushey Park, St Thomas, Barbados. They had a daughter, who subsequently married and lived in Europe.

In 1874, when he was well over fifty years old, Reeves was elected to the house of assembly for the parish of St Joseph. He was appointed solicitor-general in 1875, but less than a year later resigned from his post in the middle of the federation crisis. This arose because of a Colonial Office plan to federate Barbados with the Windward Islands. Federation would result in Barbados losing its representative system of government and becoming a crown colony, a development which had occurred throughout the West Indies in the wake of the Morant Bay rebellion in Jamaica a decade previously. For the Colonial Office, and for the governor appointed to carry out this task, John Pope-Hennessy, this was desirable not only on administrative grounds but also because of their view (largely justifiable) that the assembly had failed to represent the interests of black people in the post-emancipation period. Advocates of crown colony government maintained that the Colonial Office would act impartially on behalf of the people, something it believed was impossible for a largely white oligarchy in control of the house of assembly.

For Reeves the survival of the house of assembly and of representative institutions in Barbados was a matter of grave importance. He therefore resigned his official post in the government and successfully led the opposition against Pope-Hennessy's proposal of confederating Barbados and the Windward Islands. Similarly, two years later, he opposed a Colonial Office proposal to appoint two crown nominees to represent the government in the house of assembly. Again, he believed that this plan was contrary to the principle of representative government, a system which had been in place in Barbados for well over two centuries.

However, in 1881 Reeves was prepared to modify his views on the relationship between the executive and the assembly. He suggested that a small committee of the legislature prepare bills for the house. After considerable debate the assembly passed an act along these lines: four members of the house and one member of the legislative council would work with the executive to prepare governmental measures. This development was in keeping with Reeves's views about representative government, as the members of the executive committee were representatives of the people rather than responsible to the crown.

For his support of the government, Reeves was appointed attorney-general in 1882 and was created KC in 1883. In 1884 he was instrumental in the widening of the franchise. As part of this process, the freehold qualification was reduced from a £12 freehold to one worth £5. Yet in spite of the reduced franchise requirements, the electorate was not significantly increased. In 1886 Reeves became chief justice of Barbados and was knighted in 1889. His legal judgments were regarded as clear and well worded and were subsequently collected in a volume co-edited by Sir William Herbert Greaves, a future chief justice of Barbados.

Reeves died on 9 January 1902 at his home, the Eyrie, in St Michael, Barbados. He was accorded a public funeral, the first part of which was held in a packed cathedral. The route to the cemetery was lined by thousands of people paying their respects to one of the most illustrious figures of nineteenth-century Barbados.

His role in the confederation crisis and in the subsequent constitutional developments marked him out but, unlike Samuel Jackman Prescod, he was not a radical; instead he espoused a conservative ideology. He believed that property was the only possible basis for the exercise of political power, and he could be complacent about the plight of black people who faced problems of unemployment and emigration. None the less, he was a clever and far-sighted politician. His resignation from the government during the confederation crisis might well have led to political obscurity; instead it brought him financial reward and subsequent political preferment.

GAD HEUMAN

Sources B. Hamilton, *Barbados and the confederation question, 1871–1885* (1956) · H. A. Vaughan, 'Sir Conrad Reeves: the hidden years, 1821–1874' · F. A. Hoyos, *Barbados: a history from the Amerindians to*

independence (1978) · *DNB* · G. Belle, 'The abortive revolution of 1876 in Barbados', *Journal of Caribbean History*, 18 (1984), 1–32 · H. Beckles, *A history of Barbados: from Amerindian settlement to nation-state* (1990)
Likenesses bust, Assembly Chamber, Barbados · photograph, repro. in Beckles, *History of Barbados*, 127

Reeves, William Pember (1857–1932), diplomatist and political activist, was born on 10 February 1857 in Lyttelton, Canterbury, New Zealand. He was the second of eight surviving children of William Reeves (1825–1891), businessman, originally of Clapham, and his wife, Ellen (1833–1919), daughter of John Pember, also of Clapham. Reeves's parents emigrated to New Zealand after incurring losses on the stock exchange. His father dabbled in farming and politics before becoming part owner of the *Lyttelton Times* newspaper. Born within a month of their landfall in the fledgeling colony of Canterbury, Reeves seems to have been influenced by his mother's sense of social and intellectual superiority which, throughout his life in New Zealand, made him distant from his coevals. He was educated in Christchurch: at Lincoln College preparatory school (1862–3), the high school (1866–7), and at Christ's College Grammar School (1867–74). He won scholarships for distinction in the classics, English, languages, and history. In 1874 he intended to enter the University of Oxford to read law, but in 1876 was forced by illness (possibly a nervous breakdown) to return to Canterbury without a degree.

His health restored for a time, Reeves was a determined sportsman who represented Canterbury at cricket and rugby. But he was not physically robust, and was dogged throughout his life by migraines and nervous debility. He became a law clerk, and in 1880 was admitted to the bar in a profession which he loathed. Realizing a talent for journalism, he reported for the *Lyttelton Times*, becoming its editor (1889–91), and wrote outstanding leaders on political and social issues at a time of emergent class politics. In 1887 he entered parliament as an opposition MP on a radical platform of wealth redistribution. In 1890, under the pseudonym Pharos, he published articles on theories of socialism, reflecting his attraction to the ideas of Henry George, Ferdinand Lassalle, and the Fabians, rather than Marx.

On 10 February 1885 he married Magdalen (Maud) Stuart Robison [see Reeves, Magdalen Stuart (1865–1953)], daughter of a bank manager in Christchurch. She was a match for his intellect, a suffragist, and also a Fabian. However, calamity marked Reeves's personal life and caused him great distress. His elder daughter, Amber (1887–1981) [see White, Amber Blanco], was an exceptional Cambridge scholar, but outraged Reeves by having an affair with H. G. Wells (already on his second marriage), and by becoming pregnant before marrying someone else. Wells later depicted the scandal, and caricatured Reeves, in *Ann Veronica* (1909). Beryl, a second daughter, was born in 1889, but to Reeves's lasting grief his son, Fabian (*b*. 1895), died in action as an airman in 1917.

Although he was limited in political experience,

William Pember Reeves (1857–1932), by Howard Coster, 1930s

Reeves's skill as a witty and acerbic debater and his championship of the working class led to a cabinet post as minister of education and justice in the 1891 Liberal ministry. After the 1892 general election he became minister of labour. In a period of industrial strife and class antagonism, he pioneered improvements in the employment conditions of shop workers, seamen, and factory workers. His most renowned achievement was the Industrial Conciliation and Arbitration Act (1894). Although defective in practice, it introduced the principle of compulsory arbitration to resolve industrial disputes. Reeves increasingly cavilled at the cabinet's waning radicalism, but was himself denounced for attempting to prevent the immigration of Asians and paupers.

In 1896 Reeves escaped the hostility of his colleagues to become New Zealand's agent-general in London (a post renamed high commissioner in 1905). He excelled at representing the colony's economic interests, and was much in demand as a speaker and commentator on New Zealand's development. An accomplished poet and historian, he also published one of New Zealand's most admired general histories, *The Long White Cloud: Ao tea roa* (1898). This was followed in 1902 by a scholarly account of social legislation, *State Experiments in Australia & New Zealand* (2 vols.). He also contributed New Zealand entries to the *Dictionary of National Biography*.

In London Reeves revelled in his reputation as a radical legislator, and delighted in the friendship of Herbert Samuel and Fabians such as the Webbs, G. B. Shaw, and H. G.

Wells. A member of the Fabian Society, he wrote a tract entitled *The State and its Functions in New Zealand* (1896). Unable to afford the expense of standing for Westminster, though it was mooted in 1898–1900, he became active in London politics, and helped Sidney Webb to get re-elected to the London county council as a Progressive in 1907. His interest in social and imperial reform coincided with the views of Liberal Imperialists. He influenced Alfred Lyttelton, secretary of state, with a scheme for constitutional reform of the former empire, not as a federation, but with a council and secretariat. By 1907 the scheme was watered down, but the essence of Reeves's approach was ultimately adopted in the form of the British Commonwealth. He also embraced the concept of national efficiency, becoming one of the twelve members of the cross-party Co-Efficient Club founded by the Webbs in 1902. Reeves worked for the adoption of old-age pensions, but by 'socialism' he meant state paternalism to avert social unrest; he disapproved of New Zealand strikers who exploited flaws in the arbitration system. He held orthodox financial views, and abandoned imperial preference as a way of protecting nascent colonial industries, in favour of free trade. Reeves's expertise was recognized in his membership of the commercial intelligence committee of the Board of Trade and of the 1905–9 royal commission on shipping rings.

Obliged by a new prime minister to resign as high commissioner, Reeves was made director of the London School of Economics and Political Science by the Webbs in 1908. He had already been occasionally involved in the school as a lecturer and a crown nominee on the University of London senate. He also fitted the Webbs' requirement for a free-trader in the post. Reeves dramatically improved the school's finances, but he failed to provide leadership and was unpopular with many of the academic staff. He fell out with the chief administrator, and Sidney Webb pressured him to resign in 1919.

Reeves enthusiastically supported the cause of Greek expansion, about which he wrote several articles and pamphlets. He presided over the Anglo-Hellenic League (1913–25), became a supporter and friend of Prime Minister Eleutherios Venizelos, and, although he had rejected the trappings of privilege associated with British honours, accepted the Greek order of the Saviour (1914) and the order of George I (1920), as well as an honorary doctorate from Athens University (1914). He travelled widely but returned only once to New Zealand, in 1925–6, on behalf of the National Bank of New Zealand, of which he was chairman (1917–31). He was fêted as a prodigal son on his tour, but no longer had firm roots there.

In appearance Reeves was tall and lean, and in character reserved and morose. Anxiety-ridden and thin-skinned, he could be kindly and amusing, but was often caustic. Reeves suffered from cancer of the prostate. He died at his London home, 31 Pembroke Square, on 15 May 1932 and was cremated at Golders Green cemetery, survived by his wife and daughters. MICHAEL C. PUGH

Sources K. Sinclair, *William Pember Reeves, New Zealand Fabian* (1965) · *Press Association* (16 May 1932) · 'Past history recalled', *Evening Post (Wellington, New Zealand)* (28 Dec 1938) [letter] · J. Child, introduction, in W. P. Reeves, *State experiments in Australia and New Zealand*, 2 vols. (1902); repr. (1969) · G. R. Hawke, 'W. Pember Reeves: some new evidence', *New Zealand Journal of History*, 7 (1973), 60–69

Archives BLPES, corresp. and papers · London School of Economics · NL NZ, Turnbull L., corresp. and papers | Auckland Public Library, Grey MSS · BLPES, Passfield MSS · Canterbury Museum, Christchurch, Torlesse MSS · General Assembly Library, Wellington, Richmond-Atkinson and Hall MSS · HLRO, letters to Herbert Samuel · Little River, Canterbury, W. H. Montgomery MSS · National Archives, Wellington, Seddon MSS · NL NZ, Turnbull L., Alpers MSS · NL NZ, Turnbull L., Ballance MSS · NL NZ, Turnbull L., Rolleston MSS · NL NZ, Turnbull L., Stout MSS · priv. coll. · Wisconsin State Historical Society, Madison, Wisconsin, letters to Henry Demarest Lloyd

Likenesses double portrait, photograph, *c.*1862 (with his mother), priv. coll.; repro. in Sinclair, *William Pember Reeves* · five photographs, *c.*1875–1932, priv. coll.; repro. in Sinclair, *William Pember Reeves* · W. H. Montgomery, cartoons, *c.*1890, presumed priv. coll.; repro. in Sinclair, *William Pember Reeves* · group portrait, photograph, 1892 (with New Zealand cabinet), NL NZ, Turnbull L.; repro. in Sinclair, *William Pember Reeves* · H. Coster, photograph, 1930–32, NPG [*see illus.*] · M. Beerbohm, cartoon, priv. coll.; repro. in Sinclair, *William Pember Reeves*

Wealth at death £12,547: probate, 14 June 1932, *CGPLA Eng. & Wales*

Refham [le Botoner], **Sir Richer** (*c.*1260–1328), merchant and mayor of London, was the son of Ralph of Refham, vintner, and probably came from Reepham, a centre of the cloth-producing area of Norfolk, although the name was common in the county; he was a relative of a namesake who was a taverner of London. His alternative name Le Botoner suggests he was apprenticed to one of the prosperous Botoners, mercers of London. By 1294 Refham is known to have been buying large amounts of mercery from the Bellardi of Lucca and from Parisian merchants; the frequency of bonds to him may suggest he was a moneylender as well as a supplier to many lesser retailers. He was probably shipping wool from an early date, as he acted as collector of the wool custom from 14 May 1303 to 30 November 1306 (as well as collector of the new custom from 10 February 1303 to 30 November 1306). He was married by 1294 to Joan, the sister of Walter Furner; they had two sons: John, his heir and the only son mentioned in his will, for whom he arranged a prestigious marriage in 1307 to Margaret, daughter of Sir John Blund (mayor 1301–7), and Roger. His own sister, Joan, married another successful mercer, Robert Callere.

Elected alderman and sheriff in 1298, Refham lost his aldermanry in 1300 after a quarrel with Henry le Waleys (*d.* 1302); but he was re-elected in 1302 and was mayor 1310–11. He immediately had a collection of the city's customs read to an assembly of citizens, and gained support for his seeking the king's confirmation of the city's liberties; he endorsed the regulations of at least five guilds during his term; he put down nuisances and proceeded energetically against disturbers of the peace. His term coincided with the crisis between the ordainers and Edward

II. The sparse evidence for the political activities of Londoners is hard to interpret, but as mayor Refham arrested the Frescobaldi on behalf of the ordainers, and subsequently released them at the order of the king. More critical for his civic survival, according to Andrew Horn's brief account, was his enforcement of the law in the matter of the estate of the heir of a mercer, Peter of Sparham, whose widow married William Hackford, one of the dilatory sureties arrested by Refham. Hackford, a politically active mercer who supported the ordainers, was able to sway his fellow mercers against Refham, ensuring that he did not achieve a second mayoralty and lost his aldermanry soon after (1312).

Given Refham's exit from civic office at this time, it seems sensible to identify him with the Richer Refham who was active from 1315 to 1323 on royal commissions concerning such matters as shipwrecked merchandise, illegal trade in victuals to Scotland, and currency, in London, Southwark, and Norfolk (where he had lands), and who was sheriff of Norfolk, 1314–15. The full extent of his usefulness to Edward I and Edward II is not known: but it is on record that he was collector of the customs; that he contributed £100 of the city's 1000 marks for the war with Scotland in March 1311; that he administered the templars' property in London from December 1311 and the temporalities of the bishopric of London, 1316–17; and that he stood surety for the king's horse-dealer when the latter was admitted to the city's freedom during his mayoralty; between 1309 and 1314 he regularly described himself in essoins as in the king's service. He was knighted before October 1317, an honour given to few London merchants. He remained a powerful figure in the city despite his lack of office, not least because of his property there, and he was one of several wealthy citizens unsuccessfully attacked during the eyre of 1321.

Refham was conspicuously successful, but his uncompromising personality made him many enemies. Andrew Horn described him as 'austere and swift to administer justice, sparing no one' (Stubbs, 175–6). This is borne out by the many complaints against him as collector of the new custom that were tried before the exchequer, though he was acquitted of any fraud. Other stories give a similar impression of a harshly just man: he complained of his fellow sheriff's allegation that Refham had defrauded him of 200 marks of their joint profits from office—consequently the accusation was withdrawn and he was offered a cask of wine in propitiation. It is likely that it was Richer rather than his fellow sheriff who insisted on prosecuting no less a person than Henry le Waleys for 50 marks due to their office.

Refham accumulated lands and rents in at least twenty-seven London parishes (including substantial holdings in and near the Mercery, and a great wharf in the Vintry which he sold in 1309) and Southwark, the manor of Stanford Rivers and land at Danbury and Little Baddow, Essex (for his heir, John), and the manors of Aylmerton and Cockthorpe in Norfolk. He died between 17 August and 17 October 1328. Refham's widow, Joan, died in 1343, and his eldest son, John, and grandson, also John, by 1352; much

of his estate then passed via his second son, Roger, and great-granddaughter to Sir Adam Fr{}unceys (d. 1375) and the Charltons of Middlesex.   ANNE F. SUTTON

Sources E. Ekwall, ed., *Two early London subsidy rolls* (1951), 298n. • F. Blomefield and C. Parkin, *An essay towards a topographical history of the county of Norfolk*, [2nd edn], 11 vols. (1805–10), vol. 8, pp. 81–2, 248; vol. 9, pp. 216, 248 • A. Watkin, *Inventory of church goods temp. Edward III*, Norfolk RS, 19 (1947), pt 2, 196 • W. Stubbs, ed., 'Annales Londonienses', *Chronicles of the reigns of Edward I and Edward II*, 1, Rolls Series, 76 (1882), 1–251, esp. 175–6 • R. R. Sharpe, ed., *Calendar of letter-books preserved in the archives of the corporation of the City of London*, [12 vols.] (1899–1912), vol. B, p. 212; vol. C; vol. D, pp. 208–9; vol. E • CLRO, HR 56 (125); HR 35 (24) • PRO, exchequer, queen's remembrancer, accounts various, etc., E101/126/6, mm. 3d, 4 • D. Keene and V. Harding, eds., *Historical gazetteer of London before the great fire* (1987) [microfiche nos. 95/2; 104/24; 105/12, 14, 24–8, 32; 145/9–10, 25–6, 34–5] • *CPR, 1307–24* • T. H. Lloyd, *Alien merchants in England in the high middle ages* (1982), 37–8 • G. A. Williams, *Medieval London: from commune to capital* (1963), 135, 267, 270, 273, 328–9 • V. Harding, 'The port of London in the fourteenth century: its topography, administration and trade', PhD diss., U. St Andr., 1983, 1.141; 2.135–46 • P. Nightingale, *A medieval mercantile community: the Grocers' Company and the politics and trade of London, 1000–1485* (1995)

Archives GL, seal, 25121/1645 • GL, St Paul's Cathedral MSS, GL MS

Regan, Charles Tate (1878–1943), zoologist and museum director, was born at Long Street, Sherborne, Dorset, on 1 February 1878, the only son of Charles James Regan, music master at Sherborne School, and his wife, Maria Jane, daughter of William Tate, author of *The Modern Cambist* (1829). He was educated at Derby School and at Queens' College, Cambridge, where he studied zoology under Adam Sedgwick and was awarded a first class in part 1 (1900) and a second in part 2 (1901) of the natural sciences tripos.

In 1901 Regan was appointed assistant (later known as assistant keeper) in the British Museum (Natural History) and was posted to assist George Albert Boulenger in curating the collection of fishes. At the museum he made his mark, soon taking sole charge of the fishes, becoming keeper of the department of zoology in 1921 and director of the museum in 1927. Regan married on 12 July 1905 Elsie Alice (b. 1882), daughter of George Marlow, land surveyor. They had two sons and two daughters.

Regan's publications numbered some 260. Among these *The Freshwater Fishes of the British Isles* (1911) embodies the results of his observations as an angler and of his museum researches in a way which makes it an authentic and readable reference book for both anglers and naturalists. He edited *Natural History* (1936), in which he wrote the section on fishes. Most of his works, however, were specialist contributions to the zoology of fishes. His anatomical studies were mainly on the skeleton, and aimed to elucidate relationships and evolutionary trends. Modifying and amplifying earlier classifications, he defined and surveyed some forty orders of fishes, producing a comprehensive classification which became accepted as a basis by ichthyologists. This was summarized in his articles on fishes and selachians in the fourteenth edition of the *Encyclopaedia Britannica*. His work on the fish collections of the *Scotia* and *Terra Nova* Antarctic expeditions and on Central American fishes, among others, produced illuminating zoogeographical generalizations.

Regan described the complicated copulatory organs of the tiny East Indian Phallostethid fishes; and in the viviparous fishes of the Cyprinodont family Poeciliidae it was he who first showed that the clue to their classification lay in the detailed structure of the anal fin of the male. It was Regan who, in 1925, first recognized the parasitic dwarf males in certain deep-sea angler-fishes, and he later published two monographs, the second in collaboration, on the *Dana* collections of this remarkable group. To him the Danes also entrusted the description of the Stomiatoid fishes of their Atlantic and Mediterranean expeditions.

In 1925 Regan was president of the zoology section of the British Association meeting at Southampton, and entitled his address 'Organic evolution'. It was his interest in evolution which led him to study and to inspire others to study the species flocks of cichlid fishes in the African lakes, but the completion of this work was left to his successors. He was also interested in the primates and their relationship to the insectivorous mammals. Of this work only a preliminary summary was published in 1930.

Regan was elected FRS in 1917, appointed an honorary fellow of Queens' College, Cambridge, in 1928, and awarded the honorary degree of DSc from Durham University in 1929. The greater part of Regan's administrative duties, when keeper of zoology, was devoted to improving accommodation for the collection. The New Spirit Building, based on his plan, was completed in 1930. One of his first duties as director was to report to the royal commission on national museums and galleries. The commission recommended independence from the British Museum, staff increases and immediate expenditure on new buildings. He was thus enabled to enter on his directorial period in an optimistic atmosphere with a practical plan for the reorganization of the museum according to modern ideas. The financial slump of 1929–31, however, so delayed the building programme that the greater part of the plan remained unrealized when the outbreak of war in 1939 suspended work. The British Museum Act (1930) made the British Museum (Natural History) at South Kensington, and its director, an autonomous institution independent of the British Museum at Bloomsbury. Regan tried then, and again in 1936, to alter the official title to British Museum of Natural History in keeping with English grammar and usage, but at neither time would the trustees permit the change. During Regan's directorship women were admitted to the scientific staff for the first time.

When Regan retired in 1938 it was without the knighthood with which his predecessors had been honoured. He had been in poor health, and his highly strung temperament had made him unpopular with some trustees. Regan died at his home, 8 Carlton Avenue, Feltham, Middlesex, on 12 January 1943. He was survived by his wife.

E. TREWAVAS, *rev.* ANN DATTA

Sources R. H. Burne and J. R. Norman, *Obits. FRS*, 4 (1942–4), 411–26 [incl. bibliography] · E. Trewavas, 'Dr C. Tate Regan, FRS', *Nature*, 151 (1943) · E. Trewavas, 'Charles Tate Regan', *Copeia* (1943), 202–4 · W. T. Stearn, *The Natural History Museum at South Kensington: a history of the British Museum (Natural History), 1753–1980* (1981) · private information (1959) · personal knowledge (1959) · b. cert. · d. cert. · m. cert.
Archives NHM, archives | NHM, letters to Albert Gunther
Likenesses Lafayette, photograph, *c.*1935–1936, NHM · H. Coster, photograph, *c.*1936, NPG · photograph, 1943, repro. in *Obits. FRS*
Wealth at death £1638 15*s.* 2*d.*: probate, 15 March 1943, *CGPLA Eng. & Wales*

Regan, Morice [Muirchertach Ua Riacáin] (*fl.* 1170), administrator, was the trusted personal secretary and interpreter of Diarmait Mac Murchada, king of Leinster. All that is known of him is what can be gleaned from a medieval verse chronicle written in Norman French, and published in 1892 under the title of *The Song of Dermot and the Earl*. From this it is known that Diarmait sent Regan as his ambassador to Wales in 1169, to rally Norman support with offers of land and rich rewards, and that, in September 1170, when Dublin was under siege by Strongbow, Miles de Cogan, and Diarmait himself, the latter sent Regan again as negotiator to demand the surrender of the city and thirty hostages. What is most noteworthy, however, about Morice Regan is that the text cites him as the direct source of the material recorded in the French verse chronicle, which traces the coming of the Normans to Ireland from the abduction of Dervorgilla to the arrival of Raymond le Gros Fitzgerald at Limerick in 1175. The narrator systematically extols the virtues and exploits of Diarmait and his Norman allies and damns his opponents as traitors and felons.

The nature of the material passed on by Morice Regan cannot be stated with any confidence: whether it was a full account or a sketch of events; to what extent in oral or in written form; whether in Latin, Norman French, or, possibly, in Irish. He did, however, supply the anonymous author of the chronicle with a direct link to the events related. The text stresses this link, emphasizing the close relationship between Morice Regan and Diarmait Mac Murchada. Modern historians acknowledge the value of the French narrative as a historical source for the period, in spite of the partisan spirit which pervades it and the naïve craftsmanship of the verses. Morice Regan's role in its composition has been misrepresented in various ways, and he was for a long time held to have been the author. This misinterpretation arises in part from the fragmentary nature of the only surviving manuscript copy, written in a late thirteenth-century hand. Several lines are missing at the start, and the text breaks off abruptly after 3459 verses, at the siege of Limerick in 1175. The date of composition remains a matter of surmise, whether years or decades after the last event recorded. There is a brief allusion to the future canonization of Lorcán Ua Tuathail, archbishop of Dublin (1162–80), which event did not take place until 1225; but that allusion is arguably a later addition and is not adequate ground for placing the composition of the main body of the text at so late a date. Neither can it be known at what period the encounter between Morice Regan and the author of the French verses took place.

JOSEPH LONG

Sources LPL, Carew MS 596 • G. H. Orpen, ed. and trans., *The song of Dermot and the earl* (1892) • J. Long, 'Dermot and the earl: who wrote "the song"?', *Proceedings of the Royal Irish Academy*, 75C (1975), 263–72 • A. Bliss and J. Long, 'Literature in Norman French and English to 1534', *A new history of Ireland*, ed. T. W. Moody and others, 2: *Medieval Ireland, 1169–1534* (1987), 708–36 • E. Mullally, 'Hiberno-Norman literature and its public', *Settlement and society in medieval Ireland*, ed. J. Bradley (1988), 327–43

Regemorter, Assuerus (1615–1650), physician, the son of the Revd Ambrosius Regemorter (*c*.1583–1639), a minister of the Dutch church at Austin Friars, London, and his wife, Johanna, *née* de Fray, was born in London and baptized at the Dutch church on 17 January 1615. He was named after his paternal grandfather, the Revd Assuerus Regemorter, a native of Antwerp, who was minister of the London Dutch church from 1585 until his death in 1603. Regemorter's father became a minister in the church in 1608 and served until his own death in 1639. The Calvinist clergyman Cesar Calandrini (1595–1665) was Regemorter's step-uncle. Regemorter received his earliest instruction from the noted London schoolmaster Thomas Farnaby. In 1630 he entered on the theology line at the University of Leiden, where he remained for five years, transferring to the study of medicine. The change may have been necessitated by current events in England, where the Anglican drive for religious uniformity was threatening the traditional independence of foreign reformed churches. Regemorter's father was prominent in resisting the new episcopal policy. Regemorter received his MD from Leiden on 22 January 1635, dedicating his thesis on agues to his father and to Farnaby. With ambitions of becoming a fellow of the College of Physicians, London, he incorporated on his foreign MD at the University of Oxford on 29 March 1636. A copy of his Leiden thesis, 'De febribus intermittentibus', is held at the Bodleian Library, Oxford.

Regemorter made his first appearance before the College of Physicians on 25 June 1636, only to be told by its president, Simeon Foxe, that he could not be considered for membership until he had at least four years of actual medical practice. On 20 September 1639, more than four years after he had taken his Leiden MD, Regemorter passed the third and final examination of the college censors, and was admitted a licentiate in medicine. But it was not until 30 September 1642 that he appeared at the college again. Forewarned that he would need to prove his English birth before being considered for a fellowship, Regemorter brought the necessary documentation from the Dutch church. He was elected a candidate on 22 December 1642 and elevated, without a single dissenting vote, into a fellow's place on 11 November 1643.

On 13 December 1643 Regemorter was elected a deacon in the London Dutch church, out of a large field of nominees. He was still in this office in 1648 when he contributed money towards the relief of the Dutch church at Colchester. By 1644 he had joined with other college fellows, George Bate and Francis Glisson, as principal investigators in a pioneering study of rickets, *De rachitide*, published in Amsterdam in 1650, with an English translation

appearing in London in the following year. In 1645 Regemorter delivered the college's Goulstonian lecture in morbid anatomy. He was chosen a college censor in 1649, a year which also saw the birth of his son, Assuerus. During and after the civil war Regemorter enjoyed a flourishing practice, based at his London home on Lime Street. He died suddenly, at the height of his fame, still only thirty-five years old, on 25 November 1650. The college was devastated by his death, none more so than the college registrar, Baldwin Hamey, who, as a member of the London Dutch community and the London Dutch church, knew and admired both Regemorter and his father. He made the following entry in the college annals:

> On 29 November of the same year, we extolled Dr Regemorter to whom, most zealous in every way for the continuance of the society, yet it first befell to break through (oh! sad) his swift death, the middle link in the new band of fellows, he is, however, not forgotten among us, to whom he has bequeathed twenty pounds.

In addition to his Leiden thesis and his work on *De rachitide*, Regemorter was the author of the manuscript, 'Of brewing, meliorating, and ordering wines' (BL, Sloane MS 852, fols. 8–27), as well as another manuscript, 'Principia medicinae' (Sloane MS 3326), previously considered to be of anonymous authorship. WILLIAM BIRKEN

Sources W. Birken, 'Dr John King (1614–1681) and Dr Assuerus Regemorter (1615–1650)', *Medical History*, 20 (1976), 276–95 • annals, RCP Lond., 4.30 • B. Hamey, 'Bustorum aliquot reliquiae …', RCP Lond. • Wood, *Ath. Oxon.* • private information (2004) • Munk, *Roll*
Archives BL, Sloane MS 852, fols. 8–27 • BL, Sloane MS 3326
Wealth at death £20 to Royal College of Physicians

Regenbald [Regenbald of Cirencester] (*fl.* 1050–1086), administrator, is presumed from his name to have been of German origin, perhaps one of the several priests who came to England from Lotharingia during the reigns of Cnut and Edward the Confessor, and found service in the royal household. He was Edward's chancellor and perhaps also William the Conqueror's first chancellor. Regenbald began his career as a royal priest in Edward the Confessor's chapel *c*.1050. He appears as a witness to royal diplomas beginning in that year, and continued to attest royal charters throughout Edward's reign. In the early charters, he attests as *presbyter*, but in a charter dated to 1061 he attests as *sigillarius*, and on five subsequent diplomas as *cancellarius*. The title *sigillarius* suggests that he was not only the king's chancellor, but also the keeper of the royal seal and relics. Given his obvious pre-eminence in Edward's chapel, it is surprising that Regenbald never became a bishop. King Edward did, however, confer upon him the legal status of a diocesan bishop in the shires where he held lands, which may suggest that Regenbald was more valuable to the king in his role as chancellor than as a member of the episcopacy.

Regenbald's high status is corroborated by the extent, nature, and value of his pre-conquest landholdings. He held churches and lands, most of which were attached to royal estates, in the five counties of Gloucestershire, Berkshire, Somerset, Wiltshire, and Buckinghamshire. It is likely that he held additional royal minsters in Berkshire and in Northamptonshire in the pre-conquest period, although the evidence dates to Henry I's reign. When the value of five estates he held in his own right in Worcestershire, Berkshire, Dorset, and Somerset is added to the value of the estates he received as a royal priest, Regenbald's pre-conquest income was in the vicinity of £40.

Unlike most important English landholders, Regenbald retained his lands in the post-conquest period, and perhaps even his position as chancellor until late in the year 1067. William the Conqueror issued two writs in his favour, one confirming his rights and privileges and another granting him two estates in Wiltshire that once belonged to Harold Godwineson. At some point after the conquest, Regenbald acquired another 28 hides in Gloucestershire, Berkshire, and Oxfordshire, bringing the total value of his post-conquest acquisitions to about £46. The majority of these estates lay in the vicinity of Cirencester in Gloucestershire, where he probably retired; and from which he was sometimes called Regenbald of Cirencester; both his brother and his son held small estates nearby. Regenbald died some time after 1086 and was probably buried in the church of Cirencester. In the sixteenth century, Leland saw a cross in that church engraved with the inscription: 'Hic jacet Rembaldus presbyter quondam hujus ecclesiæ decanus, et tempore Edwardi regis Angliae cancellarius' ('Here lies the priest Regenbald, late dean of this church, and chancellor in the time of Edward, king of England'; Keynes, 'Regenbald', 212, n. 160).

Historians have challenged the existence of an Anglo-Saxon chancery, and therefore Regenbald's chancellorship, primarily because of the questionable authenticity of the diplomas bearing his title (Brown, 58–63). Given the evidence of Regenbald's wealth and preferment, however, the more persuasive argument is that the authenticity of the charters themselves need not preclude the likelihood that the titles featured on these charters represent genuine and contemporary usage (Keynes, 'Regenbald', 209).   MARY FRANCES SMITH

Sources S. Keynes, 'Regenbald the Chancellor [*sic*]', *Anglo-Norman Studies*, 10 (1987), 185–222 · M. F. Smith, 'Royal clerks in the reign of Edward the Confessor', *Haskins Society Journal*, 9 (1997) · R. Allen Brown, *The Normans and the Norman conquest*, 2nd edn (1985) · A. Farley, ed., *Domesday Book*, 2 vols. (1783), 1.56*v*, 57*r*–*v*, 63*r*, 65*v*, 68*v*, 79*r*, 86*v*, 91*r*, 99*r*, 146*r*, 160*r*, 162*v*, 163*r*, 165*v*, 166*r*–*v*, 170*v*, 174*v*, 180*v*, 219*v*, 220*r* · *AS chart.*, S 1021–3, 1025, 1030, 1033, 1036, 1041, 1043, 1062, 1097, 1154 · *Codex diplomaticus aevi Saxonici*, ed. J. M. Kemble, 6 vols. (1839–48), no. 815 · *Reg. RAN*, 1.9, 19, 213, 379a · S. Keynes, 'Giso, bishop of Wells (1061–88)', *Anglo-Norman Studies*, 19 (1996), 203–71
Wealth at death approx. £86: Farley, ed., *Domesday book*

Regicides (*act.* 1649), were opponents of Charles I and, generally speaking, involved in his death. On 27 January 1649, the last day of his trial for having 'traitorously and maliciously levyed war against the present parliament and the people therein represented' (Wedgwood, 130), Charles I was sentenced to death by the high court of justice, an *ad hoc* tribunal created specifically for the purpose of trying the king. That court, established on 6 January 1649 by 'An Act of the Commons Assembled in Parliament' (ibid., 122),

comprised 135 named commissioners, any twenty of whom were to be a sufficient number for the court to sit. The numbers were a telling indication of the Commons' anxious hope for broad participation in the proceedings and its more realistic anticipation of the difficulties involved. The trial of a sovereign by his subjects was without precedent, and it was soon to be clear that recruiting men to that purpose would be no easy task.

Participation in the trial and execution of Charles I Some commissioners, notably John Lilburne and Bulstrode Whitelock, were on record as having been solicited to serve before the list was drawn, but refused to participate. Most, however, were not given the opportunity to decline in advance, having been named without their prior consent. More than a third of these, forty-seven of the 135 nominated, simply never appeared. Several who did attend one or more preliminary meetings of the court withdrew before the trial began. Sir Thomas *Fairfax, lord general of the army, conspicuous by his absence during the four days of the public trial and later criticized for not having intervened to save the king, was present only at the first private meeting of the court. Algernon *Sidney, who attended three such private meetings, stepped down a day before the trial began and later echoed on jurisdictional grounds the king's own protest at the trial that 'first, the king could be tried by noe court; secondly, that noe man could be tried by that court' (R. Blencowe, ed., *Sydney Papers*, 1825, 237). Others, namely Robert *Wallop, Sir Henry *Mildmay, and William *Monson, first Viscount Monson, attended several meetings, both before and during the trial, but all claimed to have participated only to have a voice for preserving the king's life, and when that proved not to be possible withdrew before sentence was pronounced.

Still, whatever their initial hesitations or subsequent excuses, more than eighty named commissioners were deeply complicit in the proceedings of the high court and were later at risk of being branded as regicides. That, however, did not prove to be the result. Politics, the law, and the weight of tradition have treated most of these commissioners more leniently, limiting the designation of 'regicide' to a maximum of sixty-nine. Of those, sixty-seven were present at the end of the four-day trial and were recorded as having stood to signify their assent to the sentence. On 29 January all but ten of the sixty-seven signed the death warrant. Thomas *Chaloner and Richard *Ingoldsby, two commissioners who were not present at the sentencing, added their names to the warrant, bringing the number of signatories to fifty-nine. The following day, 30 January, Charles I was brought to the scaffold outside the Banqueting House in Whitehall and beheaded. It would therefore appear that there were sixty-nine commissioners directly and most immediately involved in the destruction of the king, either in sentencing him to death on 27 January or in subscribing the warrant for his execution two days later. If these sixty-nine had been the only men proceeded against at the Restoration or the only men singled out by later commentators for condemnation, the designation 'regicide' would be a simple matter, but neither was the case.

Statutory retribution and royal mercy in 1660 In May 1660 the monarchy was restored, and consistent with his declaration of Breda, Charles II sought a general pardon for all except those to be agreed upon in parliament. The king would probably have been content with only a handful of exceptions. In the early years of his exile Charles had even suggested limiting his vengeance to only one member of the high court, its president, John *Bradshaw, and later he spoke of a mere five, or possibly seven, exceptions. When, in summer 1660, the House of Commons seemed vindictively inclined to extend its retribution further Charles implored the members to except none other than the 'immediate murderers' of his father. '[A]s the king saw them quick in their justice, so he thought them too slow in their mercy' (*Englands Triumph*, 115). The result, after months of squabbling and hard bargaining, was that in August a total of 104 men were named and excepted from 'An act of free and generall pardon indemnity and oblivion' and were to be subjected to varying degrees of punishment. Of those, forty-nine named men then living, plus two unknown executioners, were selected to be tried for capital crime, being designated as persons 'to be proceeded against as traitors' for their 'execrable treason in sentencing to death, or signing the instrument for the horrid murder, or being instrumental in taking away the pretious life of our late soveraigne Lord Charles the first of glorious memory' (12 Car. II c. 11).

Nowhere in the act did the word 'regicide' appear, either to define the crime of killing the king or as a label for those responsible for it. The word itself was unrecognizable in law. Regicide was a sin, but it was not a crime. In English law it never had been. The government therefore eschewed the word, abandoning the debate over its use to the arena of popular discourse, where the allegations of regicide were trumpeted from the pulpit and elaborated in the press. Accordingly, every man arraigned, tried, and convicted in 1660 was brought to justice for the crime of high treason, for compassing and imagining the death of the king, as set forth and defined by 25 Edward III (1352). Nor was any reference made in any of the legislative or judicial proceedings to the execution of Charles I. In 1660 such references to the event as there were spoke only to his murder and to the treason of the men who committed it. Men might be damned loosely for regicide, but they would be condemned legally for treason.

The term 'traitor' was wide enough to encompass as many men as parliament chose ultimately to identify and as Charles II in the end would allow. As well as the forty-nine living and the two executioners, a further twenty-four men, since deceased, all of whom save one, John *Fry, had either signified their assent to the sentence on the last day of the king's trial or had signed the death warrant, were to have their property subject to forfeiture. By that count then there were at least seventy-four commissioners on record as having been proximately responsible for taking the life of the king (seventy-five if Fry is to be included) and who might reasonably have been styled 'regicides' if that term had ever been accorded any status in law. And this figure excludes an additional seven men who were excepted from the pardon but not put at risk of punishment extending to their lives, and a further twenty whose lesser punishment was their having been barred by the act from accepting or exercising any ecclesiastical, civil, or military office.

Identifying 'regicides' It was left therefore to contemporaries, and later to polemicists and historians, to apply the regicide label as they might choose, and for that reason there has been considerable disagreement about whom to include. At first relatively few commentators used the word 'regicide' at all, preferring instead the designation 'murderer' to identify anyone associated with the king's trial and execution. Neither word, however, was employed with much precision. John Evelyn, one of the first to use the term in reference to the execution of Charles I, recorded in his diary on 11 October 1660, that 'this day were those barbarous *Regicides*, who sat on the life of our late King, brought to their Tryal in the old baily', implying that he was restricting the word to the king's judges (Evelyn, 3.258). Yet six days later, commenting on the result of the trials, Evelyn noted the execution of ten of these 'murderous Traytors' and included among them Daniel *Axtell, Francis *Hacker, John *Cook, and Hugh *Peter, none of whom were members of the high court and had not therefore passed sentence on the king nor signed the warrant of execution (ibid., 259). Gilbert Burnet ran to even greater imprecision. After the initial executions Burnet indiscriminately labelled all the remaining miscreants as regicides, making no attempt whatever at either enumeration or definition. He merely observed of those still living that 'though the regicides were at that time odious beyond all expression … the king was advised not to proceed further' (Burnet, 1.281). It may therefore have been William Winstanley in 1665 who first offered an exact number, although he too avoided attempting a definition. In his *Loyall Martyrology* he named a total of eighty-four men, counting sixty-nine as the king's judges and then listing an additional fifteen as 'accessory regicides' (Winstanley, 144). Included in the latter group was Sir Henry *Vane the younger, who had refused to serve as one of the high court commissioners and who had no role whatever in the trial of the king, but who was none the less excepted from the pardon and who in 1662 was tried and executed, an unfortunate victim of his republicanism, religious radicalism, and, perhaps most important, his lack of contrition.

Later writers have shown less reluctance to number the regicides, but no greater certainty about whom to include. Those taking the most restricted view have been willing to count only those commissioners who signed the warrant for Charles's execution; others have widened the category to add all who sentenced him to death. But because the 1660 act excepted from pardon any who had been 'instrumental in taking away the [king's] life' the category of regicide has proved seductively elastic. In the early eighteenth century the anonymous author of *A History of King-*

Killers ran the number of 1649 regicides into the hundreds; in 1798 Mark Noble, somewhat less expansively, chose to include all 135 named commissioners in his *Lives of the Regicides*; and at the end of the twentieth century historians were still not agreed on how to either contract or amend that number. Most however have conceded that four men standing outside the category of the king's judges are none the less properly on the list, largely because all were excepted from the Act of Pardon, but more importantly because all were tried, convicted, and executed: John Cook, the principal prosecutor at Charles I's trial; Daniel Axtell, the commander of the guard at the trial; Francis Hacker, commander of the halberdiers charged with custody of the king during the trial; and Hugh Peter, the fiery preacher who had no official function at the trial but who had conspicuously demanded from the pulpit that Charles be called to capital account. Some historians have also accepted several other functionaries at the trial as regicides: Andrew Broughton and John Phelps, the two clerks of the court, and Edward Dendy, the serjeant-at-arms. All three were excepted from the general pardon. Even more elusive are the two masked executioners, who might well be styled regicides. Their identities remain unknown, although it seems very probable that Richard *Brandon, hangman of London, was the one who delivered the fatal blow. In sum, there is no agreement about the length of the list of regicides or about whom to include in that list—nor in the absence of an accepted definition, legal or otherwise, is it reasonable to expect that there could be.

Forfeiture, exhumation, assassination, and exile All that is certain is the number and identity of those named and excepted from the Act of Pardon. Not all, however, proved to be within the reach of the king's justice. Twenty-four men excepted from the pardon had already died. For twenty of these the act limited their post-mortem punishment to the forfeiture of their property, but a more exacting vengeance was reserved for those most despised: John Bradshaw, Oliver *Cromwell, Henry *Ireton, and Thomas *Pride. Their remains were directed by order of parliament to be exhumed and then, on 30 January 1661, the anniversary of Charles I's execution, to be hanged, beheaded, and cast into a pit below the gallows. One other deceased traitor, curiously omitted from those excepted from the Act of Pardon but no less complicit in 'taking away the … life of the king' was Isaac *Dorislaus, counsel to the high court of justice, who was instrumental in drawing up and managing the charges against the king. On an official diplomatic mission to the Netherlands for the republican government in May 1649 Dorislaus was murdered by English royalists, becoming thereby the first of two assassinated abroad for his role in Charles's trial and execution. The other was John *Lisle who, having fled to the continent at the Restoration, was tracked down and murdered in Lausanne in 1664.

In all there were twenty others who chose to become fugitives on the continent rather than face the uncertainties of retribution at home. One, Thomas *Scott, surrendered in Brussels and was returned to England to become

among the first to stand trial; he was convicted and executed in October 1660. A similar end awaited John *Barkstead, Miles *Corbett, and John *Okey, who were apprehended in Delft in 1662 and were also remanded to England for trial and execution. The sixteen remaining exiles fared better in that they all eluded capture and settled, most in the Low Countries or Switzerland, in relative if sometimes anxious peace. Three, John *Dixwell, William *Goffe, and Edward *Whalley, found their way to New England. Dixwell survived under an assumed name in New Haven, while Whalley and Goffe eventually sought a more secure refuge further north in the Connecticut River valley. It was there that, according to local legend, Goffe emerged mysteriously from hiding in 1675 to lead the colonists of Hadley, Massachusetts, in repelling an Indian raid. The best known of the exiles, however, was Edmund *Ludlow, probably the one man at large during the 1660s to be regarded by the government as the most capable of reigniting the threat of republicanism and regicide. Yet over time that perceived threat receded, as did the need to keep the fear of regicide actively alive by retaining the anniversary of Charles I's execution as a national day of fasting and humiliation. The 30 January commemorations were many years from disappearing entirely, but by 1689 they were being observed from significantly fewer pulpits. The result was a post-revolution political atmosphere that prompted Ludlow to return to England but the government's memory of regicide, although dimmed, had been by no means extinguished. After he had been in London for several months a royal proclamation was issued for his arrest, and once again he was obliged to seek refuge on the continent, where, in 1692, he was the last of the regicides to die.

Judicial proceedings and their consequences Those who out of choice or necessity remained in England to negotiate their fate met with differing results. In the regicide trials in October 1660 George *Fleetwood and Sir Hardress *Waller, having pleaded guilty at their arraignment, were sentenced to death without trial, but both avoided execution owing to their useful political connections and their having voluntarily given themselves up pursuant to the proclamation of 6 June 1660 requiring the judges at Charles I's trial to surrender within fourteen days. A further seventeen of the accused who pleaded not guilty and proceeded therefore to trial and conviction on the charge of high treason were similarly spared execution, they too having surrendered themselves in response to the king's proclamation. All nineteen had their sentences temporarily commuted to imprisonment, their executions being suspended pending another act of parliament for that purpose. In the end, whether owing to personal contrition, royal clemency, or family and political connections, none was ever executed, most living out their lives in prison. For others it was a different story. Men like Thomas *Harrison, John *Carew, and Thomas Scott, who were entirely unrepentant, could expect no mercy and were dispatched by the court in 1660 without difficulty. Three others who sat in judgment on Charles I, John *Jones, Adrian *Scrope, and Gregory *Clements, were only slightly less defiant, but they too claimed their secular authority as high court commissioners from parliament and their greater authority from God. They too were convicted and executed. Their punishment, like that of the others condemned, was not only for having blown 'the trumpet of sedition', but for having succumbed to the thrall of 'spiritual pride' (State trials, 5.1055, 1076). It was also convenient to denigrate the origins and status of the regicides. It is true that only one commissioner, Thomas *Grey, Baron Grey of Groby, was a peer, but there were no defining social or economic characteristics to describe the high court of justice as a whole. Despite the impression left by a succession of vengeful royalist writers, the commissioners for the trial of the king were just as often men of education and means as they were base-born adventurers motivated in their treason by the desire for economic and political preferment.

In all only ten men were executed as a result of the trials in 1660, being six of the sixty-nine commissioners who sentenced Charles I to death or signed his warrant of execution, plus four others, Axtell, Cook, Hacker, and Peter, all of whom under the comprehensive yet vague heading of 'being instrumental in taking away the pretious life of our late soveraigne Lord Charles the first of glorious memory' were adjudged equally guilty. Added to the three (Barkstead, Corbet, and Okey) who were captured on the continent and brought back for execution in 1662, there were still only thirteen men hanged, drawn, and quartered for their treason in 1649 (fourteen if Vane is included), far fewer than the original 135 commissioners and others who in some way were regarded by contemporaries, and could just as easily have been regarded by the law, as responsible for the death of the king. Sir Orlando Bridgman, presiding at the trial of the regicides in 1660, was quick to remind all the defendants, whatever their degree of complicity, that '[I]f any of you should say, that we had no hand in the actual murder of the king, remember that they that brought him to the bar, were all as one as if they had brought him to the block' (State trials, 5.1075–6).

Exemption, official restraint, and the national memory Many, of course, were inaccessible to being called to capital account for their crimes because they had died before the Restoration, fled into exile, bargained like John *Hutchinson for nothing worse than being barred from public office, or, like the well-connected John *Milton, escaped without any punishment beyond the burning of his books, despite his having been the most prominent voice during the republic in defence of the killing of the king.

With treason as the normative pattern of official retribution from 1660 the government was free to proceed as widely as it wished. Specifically there was no need to limit its prosecution to the commissioners who sentenced Charles and signed his warrant of execution. The law could, as it did, extend its reach to include Axtell, Cook, Hacker, Peter, and Vane, all of whom were executed, and William Hulet, a trooper in John *Hewson's regiment, convicted as one of the masked hangmen on the scaffold,

but in the absence of further proof never put to death. Yet the government and even parliament proceeded with strategic restraint. In place of widespread retribution it was left to the press, and especially to the church through the vehicle of the 30 January anniversary sermons, to keep the memory of the day alive, to nurture the image of national sin, and above all, by preaching passive obedience and non-resistance, to demonstrate that regicide was the predictable, if not the inevitable, outcome of rebellion.

HOWARD NENNER

Sources 12 Car. II c. 11, 'An act of free and generall pardon indemnity and oblivion' (1660) · 'An act of the Commons of England assembled in parliament for erecting of a high court of justice for the trying and judging of Charles Stuart, king of England' (6 Jan 1649) · State trials, vol. 5 · J. Nalson, A true copy of the journal of the high-court of justice for the tryal of King Charles I (1684) · H. Nenner, 'The trial of the regicides: retribution and treason in 1660', Politics and the political imagination in later Stuart Britain, ed. H. Nenner (1997) · C. V. Wedgwood, The trial of Charles I (1964) · A. W. McIntosh, 'The numbers of the English "Regicides"', History (1982), 195–216 · M. Noble, The lives of the English regicides, 2 vols. (1798) · W. Winstanley, The loyall martyrology (1665) · The history of king-killers, 2 vols. (1719–20) · Englands triumph (1660) · Evelyn, Diary · G. Burnet, History of my own time, 1 (1894) · A. L. Rowse, The regicides (1994)

Likenesses group portrait, line engraving, pubd 1660 (The regicides executed in 1660), BM · line engraving, NPG

Reginald (d. 1097), abbot of Abingdon, was a secular clerk and one of the chaplains of William, duke of Normandy. He became a monk of Jumièges, and William, by then king of England, gave him at Rouen the abbacy of Abingdon on 19 June 1084, his predecessor Æthelhelm, also formerly a monk of Jumièges, having died on 10 September 1083. The king sent him to Walkelin, bishop of Winchester, to be installed in his office. He was received at Abingdon on 18 July 1084, and on 15 August was blessed by Osmund, bishop of Salisbury.

The tenants of the abbey had vigorously resisted the Conqueror's rule, and the house had accordingly suffered; but some return to prosperity seems to have begun under Abbot Æthelhelm, and it increased during the early years of Reginald's abbacy. In 1087 Gilbert of Ghent represented to the monastery a house in the Strand, London, with a chapel dedicated to the Holy Innocents; he had given the property to Abingdon in Æthelhelm's time, but had resumed possession of it on the latter's death. It became the abbot's London lodging. On the accession of William II, Reginald helped him in the distribution of his father's treasure among the minsters and other churches of England and to the poor. Although Reginald disposed of some of the abbey's property to his son and personal friends, he set about rebuilding the church of the monastery, prompted, perhaps, by the collapse of the church tower in 1091. In order to ensure the co-operation of the inhabitants of the abbey's estates, he gathered them together and announced that he would abolish several customs that burdened them, provided that they would give the full tithes of their harvest for the restoration of the church. Robert (I) d'Oilly was led by a dream to restore certain lands that he had unjustly taken from the house in Abbot Æthelhelm's time, and also gave a large sum towards the building.

The abbey's mid-twelfth century chronicle complains, however, that, after a time, enemies of the abbot set William II against him, and that the king deprived the abbey of much of its property. The king having crossed to Normandy in November 1096, Reginald followed him, probably on the abbey's business, and died there on 4 February 1097.

Reginald's son William had been well educated and had taken holy orders. His father presented him to the abbey's living of Marcham, near Abingdon, with some of the abbey's property. When fatally ill, William assumed the monastic habit at Abingdon, and restored to the abbey the church and land that he had received from his father.

WILLIAM HUNT, *rev.* MARIOS COSTAMBEYS

Sources J. Stevenson, ed., *Chronicon monasterii de Abingdon*, 2 vols., Rolls Series, 2 (1858) · *Reg. RAN*, 1.315

Reginald (*supp. fl. c.*1120), supposed chancellor, owes his recorded existence to an error by John Leland, whose account of Montacute Priory, Somerset, names one Reginald Cancellarius as having become prior under Henry I. However, no chancellor named Reginald is recorded from that king's reign, nor is there a Reginald among the early priors of Montacute. The likeliest explanation for the error is that Leland first confused Ranulf, chancellor from 1107 to 1123, who gave Tintinhull Manor in Somerset to Montacute, with Ranulf the king's physician, who perhaps about 1121 (in a grant witnessed by Ranulf the chancellor) gave land in Monmouthshire to that house, and himself became a monk there; Leland then identified this conflation of personalities with the Prior Ranulf who probably died in 1112; and finally gave his creation the wrong name.   HENRY SUMMERSON

Sources *The itinerary of John Leland in or about the years 1535–1543*, ed. L. Toulmin Smith, 11 pts in 5 vols. (1906–10), vol. 1, p. 158 · D. Knowles, C. N. L. Brooke, and V. C. M. London, eds., *The heads of religious houses, England and Wales*, 1: 940–1216 (1972), 121 · *Reg. RAN*, 2.1307, 1399 · *Two cartularies of the Augustinian priory of Bruton and the Cluniac priory of Montacute*, Somerset RS, 8 (1894)

Reginald, earl of Cornwall (*d.* 1175), magnate, was the illegitimate son of *Henry I and Sibyl, daughter of Robert Corbet. It has been generally assumed that he was the Reginald de Dunstanville who held considerable lands in Wiltshire for which he had exemption from geld in 1130, but the Reginald of 1130 is more likely to have been the father of Alan and Robert de Dunstanville. Reginald, the king's son, was, however, known as Rainaldus de Dunstanivilla to Orderic Vitalis in 1137, and certainly Reginald later numbered members of the Dunstanville family among his intimates, but the nature of the link between him and them is never stated.

Reginald appears among those who submitted to King Stephen at Easter 1136, but not long afterwards he was at Argentan in the household of the empress, his half-sister, and he may have left for Normandy in 1136 after the exiling by Stephen of Baldwin de Revières, who appears to have been his friend and ally. Orderic mentions Reginald and Baldwin's activities as militant supporters of the empress in the Cotentin during the winter of 1137–8, until Baldwin's capture by Enguerrand de Say. Reginald may have accompanied his half-brother, Robert, earl of Gloucester, or Baldwin to England in 1139. In 1140 a marriage was arranged between Reginald and a daughter of the Cornish baron William fitz Richard, lord of Cardinan, who had defected from Stephen. The two men combined to attempt to secure Cornwall for the Angevins; William of Malmesbury states that at this time Reginald was made earl of the shire by Robert of Gloucester. There was an energetic and apparently ferocious campaign, in which Reginald made the mistake of alienating the local church by imposing a tax. He was excommunicated and a counter-campaign by the king and Alan, earl of Richmond, seems to have found local support. Reginald was confined to one castle (probably Launceston). Until 1141 Earl Alan maintained himself as earl of Cornwall, and there is a record of his holding a county court at Bodmin, which shows some success on his part. But the king's capture at Lincoln, and Earl Alan's subsequent capture by the earl of Chester, delivered Cornwall back into Reginald's hands, and he remained in unchallenged control of it for the rest of his life. He controlled all the former royal castles and the sheriff was his appointee.

Earl Reginald was at the rout of Winchester in September 1141, leading the party that escorted the empress to safety, according to Florence of Worcester. Reginald was much in evidence as a supporter first of the empress and later of her son, Duke Henry, throughout the civil war. Reginald was acting as intermediary between the empress and King Stephen in 1146, when his royalist nephew, Philip, son of Earl Robert, castellan of Cricklade, captured him and his household. Philip released him not long afterwards when the king expressed his annoyance that Reginald's safe conduct had been broken. In 1149–50 Earl Reginald supported Duke Henry's campaign in England. In Lent 1152 the earl was sent to Normandy by his party to urge the duke (then at Lisieux) to come to England, but without result. On the duke's eventual arrival in 1153 Earl Reginald joined his army and stayed by his side for most if not all of the subsequent campaigns and negotiations. On the duke's departure in April 1154 Earl Reginald was designated as his agent in England in his absence. It is therefore a little curious to find Reginald at the duke's side at both Eu and Rouen in the months leading up to Stephen's death, although no doubt he needed to be in Normandy periodically to give information and to receive instructions from his nephew the duke.

Earl Reginald was a frequent witness to royal acts after his nephew became king, and with Robert, earl of Leicester, and Richard de Lucy was of the group of Henry II's most intimate lay counsellors; Gervase of Canterbury says that Reginald and Richard were the king's only confidants during the election of Archbishop Richard in 1173. It does not seem that the earl often accompanied the king abroad (he appeared with the king at Rouen in 1156–7), although, despite that, two of his daughters were married to French magnates. But the latter marriage (and the former also, perhaps) was at the instigation of King Henry.

Earl Reginald played a significant part in the major crises of his nephew's reign in England. With Robert, earl of

Leicester, the justiciar, Reginald acted as intermediary between the king and Thomas Becket, notably at Northampton in 1164. He played a major part in opposing the rebels of 1173–4 in England, and in late July 1173, with Richard de Lucy, besieged the town of Leicester (the earl of Leicester having joined Henry the Young King, in France) and sacked it, after first evacuating its citizens. They failed to take the castle, however. In October of that year Earl Reginald marched with several other loyalist earls and barons to join the forces opposing the earl of Leicester and his mercenary army in East Anglia, but it does not seem that he was present at Leicester's defeat near Bury St Edmunds.

Sources are confused about Reginald's death. Diceto says that he died on 1 July 1175 at Reading. Roger of Howden and Gervase of Canterbury put his death in December (the former putting the death just before Christmas). According to Howden the earl died at Chertsey and was buried at Reading Abbey; Gervase also records that he died elsewhere and that his body was borne to Reading. Diceto is more likely to be correct as to the date, as the pipe roll for Michaelmas 1175 already has Cornwall under a royal sheriff and the earl's lands in Shropshire in the king's hands. But other sources are unanimous that Reginald died elsewhere than Reading. Reginald and Robert, earl of Leicester, were recognized by contemporaries as 'the most powerful men in the kingdom'. This was no idle assessment. Reginald ruled Cornwall after 1141 as an appanage, having control over the sheriffs, who did not answer at the exchequer. His influence also extended into Devon, where the earl, Baldwin, was a long-time ally and became his son-in-law. Also in Devon his half-brother, Robert, had control of the honour of Okehampton and his sister, Rohese, was married to the local baron, Henry de Pomeray, before 1146. This made him one of the great regional earls of Stephen's reign—to compare with Chester, Leicester, and Hereford—and unusual in that this special position of power remained unchallenged by Henry II. This makes the drastic royal intervention in Cornwall on Reginald's death the more understandable. His legitimate son, Nicholas, predeceased him, but the earl left three legitimate daughters, Mathilda, who married Robert (II), count of Meulan (d. c.1210), Lucy, the second wife of Baldwin, earl of Devon, and Sara, who married the viscount of Limoges. Neither these nor their heirs were allowed to divide the earldom, which was taken into the king's hands, apart from some manors devoted to them. Robert de Torigny reports that the lands of the earldom were intended by the king to be devoted to the upkeep of his son, John. Earl Reginald also left a young illegitimate son, Henry, who in due course was to secure the county of Cornwall from King John, and who assumed the title of earl. Earl Reginald's wife appears as 'M' in a charter to Launceston of her daughter Mathilda. It may be that the *Gesta Stephani* is correct in reporting her fall into insanity in the 1140s; this would account for her near invisibility in Reginald's later career.

DAVID CROUCH

Sources Ordericus Vitalis, *Eccl. hist.* · K. R. Potter and R. H. C. Davis, eds., *Gesta Stephani*, OMT (1976) · William of Malmesbury, *The Historia novella*, ed. and trans. K. R. Potter (1955) · Pipe rolls · GEC, *Peerage* · L. Landon, ed., *The cartae antiquae: rolls 1–10, printed from the original in the custody of the master of the rolls*, PRSoc., 55, new ser., 17 (1939) · cartulary of St Guthlac, Balliol Oxf., MS 271 · LPL, Cartulary of Launceston, MS 719 · W. Stubbs, ed., *Gesta regis Henrici secundi Benedicti abbatis: the chronicle of the reigns of Henry II and Richard I, AD 1169–1192*, 2 vols., Rolls Series, 49 (1867) · J. C. Robertson and J. B. Sheppard, eds., *Materials for the history of Thomas Becket, archbishop of Canterbury*, 7 vols., Rolls Series, 67 (1875–85) · *The historical works of Gervase of Canterbury*, ed. W. Stubbs, 2 vols., Rolls Series, 73 (1879–80) · *Radulfi de Diceto ... opera historica*, ed. W. Stubbs, 1: 1148–79, Rolls Series, 68 (1876)

Reginald (*d.* 1203), abbot of Walden, seems to have originated from Manneville-la-Raoult, Normandy, and may have been connected with the nearby abbey of Grestain. Very little is known of his family and career other than what is found in the foundation chronicle of the Benedictine abbey of Walden. He was apparently a member of King Stephen's household, 'keeping the royal seal in the place of the chancellor' (*Essex Review*, 45.150), though there is no evidence of any Reginald in the king's chancery. He then, possibly as a consequence of the new Angevin regime, became a monk at Reading, where he was appointed prior, and, very shortly afterwards, abbot in 1154. After four years Reginald was obliged to resign 'on account of the king's hostility' (*Flores historiarum*, 75). However, Henry II later supported his appointment as prior of Walden on about 14 January 1166, perhaps through the patronage of Gilbert Foliot, bishop of London (*d.* 1187). Like his predecessor, William, he was also made prior of Luffield by royal appointment, though he only remained there a very short while, if indeed he ever took up office.

As prior of Walden, Reginald was responsible for the expansion and consolidation of the community, providing new conventual buildings, and increasing the endowment. Yet the chronicle of his house is not uncritical: when Reginald was persuaded (probably in 1175) by Hervey de Montmorency, to accompany his nephew, Earl Richard fitzGilbert (Strongbow), to Ireland, in order to take charge of an abbey Richard proposed to found at Bannow, he was rebuked for his departure without taking council. He was also criticized by the chronicler for useless expenditure—he ultimately found no monks willing to move with him from Walden—and for the hostility he thereby provoked on the part of Walden's Mandeville patrons, as well as for the debts incurred in order to restore that patronal friendship. He subsequently came under attack for his insistence on accompanying Earl William de Mandeville (*d.* 1189) on pilgrimage to the Holy Land in 1177.

In 1190 Reginald gained royal support for the elevation of Walden to the status of an abbey and became its first abbot, a post he held until his death on 5 February 1203. During much of this time he had to defend the community against the hostility of Geoffrey fitz Peter (*d.* 1213), who had succeeded the Mandevilles as earl of Essex. Reginald was said by the Walden chronicler to have been well lettered, and to have given the abbey many works, some in verse, which he had composed particularly in old age 'to an excessive degree' (*Essex Review*, 46.220): none of these is known to have survived. His brother, Roger de Manneville, was a benefactor of Walden, and a nephew, Thomas, accompanied him on his pilgrimage.

BRIAN GOLDING

Sources H. Collar, ed., 'The book of the foundation of Walden Abbey', trans. C. H. Emson, *Essex Review*, 45 (1936), 73–85, 147–56, 224–36; 46 (1937), 12–16, 88–98, 164–70, 227–34; 47 (1938), 36–41, 94–9, 150–55, 216–20 [BL, Arundel MS 29] · L. Watkiss and D. E. Greenway, eds., *The book of the foundation of Walden monastery*, OMT (1999) · H. G. Richardson, 'Some Norman monastic foundations in Ireland', *Medieval studies presented to Aubrey Gwynn*, ed. J. A. Watt, J. B. Morrall, and F. X. Martin (1961), 29–43 · *Letters and charters of Gilbert Foliot*, ed. A. Morey and others (1967) · B. R. Kemp, ed., *Reading Abbey cartularies*, 1, CS, 4th ser., 31 (1986) · H. R. Luard, ed., *Flores historiarum*, 3 vols., Rolls Series, 95 (1890), vol. 2

Reginald fitz Jocelin [*called* Reginald Italus, Reginald Lombardus] (*c*.1140–1191), bishop of Bath and archbishop-elect of Canterbury, was the son of Jocelin de *Bohun, bishop of Salisbury, and was related to Earl *Robert of Gloucester (*d*. 1147) and to *Savaric fitz Geldwin (*d*. 1205), whom Emperor Heinrich VI (*r*. 1191–7) in 1191 referred to as his own kinsman. It has been plausibly suggested that Reginald's mother belonged to the family of the Savoyard counts of Maurienne. Reginald was born *c*.1140 and brought up in Italy, whence his epithets Lombardus and Italus. Appointed archdeacon of Wiltshire by his father by 1161, he entered the service of Archbishop Thomas Becket, perhaps in 1162, and went to Paris to study letters (1163–4), carrying a recommendation to Bishop Hugues of Soissons (the French king's chancellor) from Pope Alexander III (*r*. 1159–81) himself. Louis VII (*r*. 1137–80) assigned the abbey of St Exuperius, Corbeil, to him. Philip Augustus of France attested Reginald's long-standing friendship with Louis VII when he wrote in support of his election to Canterbury in 1191.

However, Reginald did not stay at Paris long enough to acquire the title of master, for he is recorded in Henry II's service from *c*.1167. From that moment he was a loyal supporter both of the king and of his father, and so lost the friendship of the exiled Becket circle, although he had provided horses for an anonymous Becket messenger in mid-1164. He became one of Henry II's principal emissaries to the papal curia, representing the king's interests against Becket in 1167–8, 1169, 1169–70, and to the papal nuncios Vivian and Gratian in August 1169. After Becket's murder (29 December 1170) he was sent once more to present the king's case at the papal curia (January–April 1171); and his good service was rewarded in 1173, when Henry II secured his election to the see of Bath, one of four 'enemies of the Martyr' (Bouquet and others, 14.645) to be so promoted. His election and theirs (and also that of Richard of Dover to Canterbury) were challenged by Henry, the Young King, who alleged illegitimacy and uncanonical process against him, and he went to the papal curia in the company of Archbishop-elect Richard to defend his position. Walter Map claimed that Reginald succeeded only through bribery; but the well-informed Ralph de Diceto records that he had to clear himself by oath of complicity

in Becket's death, and provide sworn evidence that his conception had taken place before his father became a priest, before being consecrated at St Jean-de-Maurienne by the archbishops of Canterbury and Tarentaise on 23 June 1174. In the company of Archbishop Richard he met the king at Barfleur (8–9 August) and was enthroned at Bath on 24 November.

Reginald at once began to take his place in the public affairs of the kingdom. In 1175 he attended the provincial council of Westminster in May, and the royal council of Woodstock in July, and in 1176 was present at the king's Easter court at Winchester. Recorded at the Westminster council of March 1177, he attested a royal charter at Rouen in the following September, and may have taken part immediately afterwards in the negotiations with Louis VII which led to the peace of Ivry, although he is not recorded as a witness. These secular duties were interrupted in 1178 by his participation in the joint Anglo-French mission against Cathar heretics in Toulouse, led by Cardinal Pierre of San Crisogono, but Reginald attended that year's Christmas court at Winchester, before going to the Third Lateran Council in March 1179. On his return journey he persuaded Hugh of Avalon to take charge of the Carthusian house of Witham in Somerset, founded by Henry II in partial expiation for Becket's murder. During the 1180s he is only occasionally recorded as attending courts and councils, probably because during that decade his energies were largely devoted to the administration of his diocese, though in 1186 he attended councils at Oxford and Woodstock. But at the coronation of Richard I, on 3 September 1189, he appears in a distinguished position, processing on the king's left hand.

Reginald was by then one of the longest-serving bishops in England, though not yet fifty, enjoying the precedence of noble descent and experience, and in a position to play a more forceful role in the new reign. He attended the Council of Pipewell on 15 September, and was probably the Reginaldus Italus who unsuccessfully offered Richard I £4000 for the chancellorship. On the king's instructions he secured the legatine title for his rival, Bishop William de Longchamp (*d*. 1197), but he then supported Archbishop Geoffrey of York against Longchamp, and in October 1191 colluded in the latter's overthrow. His own long-standing support of the Canterbury monks against Archbishop Baldwin's foundation of a church at Hackington, dedicated to St Stephen and St Thomas the Martyr, made him a strong contender for the archbishopric when Baldwin died at Acre in 1191, and the monks immediately elected him (27 November 1191), rejecting Richard I's candidate, Guglielmo, archbishop of Monreale. The new justiciar, Walter de Coutances (*d*. 1207), challenged the election; but before the matter could be resolved, on 24 December, Reginald was struck down by paralysis at Dogmersfield in Hampshire, having arranged the election of his kinsman Savaric to Bath. In his only surviving letter as archbishop-elect, dictated on his deathbed on Christmas day, he requested the monastic habit from the prior of Christ Church. He died the following day and was buried near the high altar of Bath Abbey on 29 December 1191—

the feast of St Thomas of Canterbury. According to Richard of Devizes, he received the monastic habit from Prior Walter of Bath, with the words, 'God did not wish me to be an archbishop, nor do I. He wished me to be your monk, and so do I' (*Chronicon Richardi Divisensis*, 56). After his death miraculous cures were attributed to his intercession.

Although Becket considered him a turncoat, Peter of Blois (*d.* 1212) wrote first (1169–70) that Reginald desired reconciliation with his old master, but was prevented by his associates and by devotion to his father, whom Becket had suspended and interdicted; and later (1173–4) that his defence of his father was understandable, and that he was not alone in misjudging the martyr. Since Peter and Jocelin were friends, these testimonials may be suspect; but Herbert of Bosham (*d.* 1194) spoke highly of him in his account of the *eruditi sancti Thome* ('St Thomas's learned men'), declaring that he had returned to St Thomas after the murder. This judgement is confirmed both by his dedication of a church of St Thomas the Martyr at St Lô, in Normandy, on his return from Italy in 1174, and by his commission in 1176 of a reliquary pendant containing relics of St Thomas for Queen Margaret of Sicily, mother of William II of Sicily (*r.* 1166–89), whom Henry II's daughter Joanna married in 1177.

Although Peter of Blois recorded Reginald's delight in hawking (and he secured from Richard I the right to have hunting dogs throughout Somerset), he was a hardworking diocesan bishop. More *acta* survive from his episcopate than from that of any other twelfth-century bishop of Bath—122 in all, at least 73 of them datable to the period 1180–91. Moreover, they reveal a conscientious pastoral bishop. He regulated the relationship between monasteries and the vicars of appropriated churches, to the benefit of the latter, by insisting on rights of tenure and adequate endowment, and as a judge-delegate he applied the latest canonical rules in the execution of papal commissions. At Bath he founded the hospital of St John in 1180, so that the poor and sick could have the benefit of the waters. At Wells he built part of the nave of the future cathedral, and provided funds for the completion of work on the fabric by ordering that the incomes of vacant churches should be devoted to it. He confirmed the canons in nine prebendal churches, and increased their common fund. He erected the liberty of Glastonbury Abbey into an archdeaconry, and made the abbot a member of the Wells chapter. He confirmed the burghal status of the town of Wells, defined its boundaries, and added to its privileges. Reginald's early death may well have deprived Canterbury of a distinguished archbishop—as it was, he was commemorated there with archiepiscopal honours.

CHARLES DUGGAN

Sources F. M. R. Ramsey, ed., *Bath and Wells, 1061–1205*, English Episcopal Acta, 10 (1995), xxii, xxix, xlvii–lxxxvi, 48–137, nos. 58–179 · C. R. Cheney and B. E. A. Jones, eds., *Canterbury, 1162–1190*, English Episcopal Acta, 2 (1986), 276 · *Radulfi de Diceto ... opera historica*, ed. W. Stubbs, 1: 1148–79, Rolls Series, 68 (1876), 391, 398; 2: 1180–1202, Rolls Series, 68 (1876) [159] · *Chronicon Richardi Divisensis / The Chronicle of Richard of Devizes*, ed. J. T. Appleby (1963), 7n., 13, 29, 33, 55–6, 96 · W. Stubbs, ed., *Chronicles and memorials of the reign of Richard I*, 2: *Epistolae Cantuarienses*, Rolls Series, 38 (1865), 57, 62–4, 102–3, 105, 150–1, 172, 193, 248–9, 318, 324, 337–40, 342–3, 351–5, 361 · W. Stubbs, ed., *Gesta regis Henrici secundi Benedicti abbatis: the chronicle of the reigns of Henry II and Richard I, AD 1169–1192*, 2 vols., Rolls Series, 49 (1867), 1.69, 74, 84, 144, 154, 155, 160, 165, 199–206, 215–20, 271, 351; 2.79, 81, 83, 105, 218, 226, 227 · J. C. Robertson and J. B. Sheppard, eds., *Materials for the history of Thomas Becket, archbishop of Canterbury*, 7 vols., Rolls Series, 67 (1875–85), vol. 6, p. 643; vol. 7, pp. 181, 195, 471–5, 554 · *Chronica magistri Rogeri de Hovedene*, ed. W. Stubbs, 4 vols., Rolls Series, 51 (1868–71), vol. 2, pp. 25, 171; vol 3, p. 15 · *Materials for the history of Thomas Becket, archbishop of Canterbury*, 3, ed. J. C. Robertson, Rolls Series, 67 (1877), 524 · *The historical works of Gervase of Canterbury*, ed. W. Stubbs, 1: *The chronicle of the reigns of Stephen, Henry II, and Richard I*, Rolls Series, 73 (1879), 511 · R. W. Eyton, *Court, household, and itinerary of King Henry II* (1878) · H. Thurston, ed., 'Visio monachi de Eynesham', *Analecta Bollandiana*, 22 (1903), 225–319 · 'The vision of the monk of Eynsham', *Eynsham cartulary*, ed. H. E. Salter, 2, OHS, 51 (1908), 285–371, esp. 350–51 · R. Foreville, *L'église et la royauté en Angleterre sous Henri II Plantagenet, 1154–1189* (Paris, 1943) · Adam of Eynsham, *Magna vita sancti Hugonis / The life of Saint Hugh of Lincoln*, ed. D. L. Douie and D. H. Farmer, OMT, 1 (1961), 46, 48; repr. (1985) · 'Petri Blesensis epistolae', *Patrologia Latina*, 207 (1855), LXI · W. Map, *De nugis curialium / Courtiers' trifles*, ed. and trans. M. R. James, rev. C. N. L. Brooke and R. A. B. Mynors, OMT (1983) · M. Bouquet and others, eds., *Recueil des historiens des Gaules et de la France / Rerum Gallicarum et Francicarum scriptores*, new edn, 19 vols. (Paris, 1869–80), vol. 14, p. 645 · [H. Wharton], ed., *Anglia sacra*, 1 (1691), 561 · C. M. Church, 'Reginald, bishop of Bath (1174–1191): his episcopate and his share in the building of Wells', *Archaeologia*, 50 (1887), 259–360, 348

Likenesses seal, repro. in Ramsey, ed., *English episcopal acta*, vol. 10 pl. 1

Reginald of Canterbury. See Canterbury, Reginald of (*fl.* c.1100–c.1109).

Reginald of Coldingham. See Coldingham, Reginald of (*d.* c.1190).

Regondi, Giulio (1822?–1872), guitarist and concertina player, was, according to his own account, born in Genoa in 1822. The details of his parentage are unclear, but it appears that he had a German mother and an Italian father and was brought up in Lyons by a foster father, possibly a language teacher who had been a professor in Milan in 1822.

During this period at Lyons, Regondi's musical talent was recognized and cultivated by his foster father, who is said to have locked the child in his room and made him practise five hours a day on the guitar. He also presented the boy in Milan and the major capitals of Europe before he was ten years old, notably in Paris in 1830 and in London in June 1831. When Regondi appeared at the King's Theatre he was described as 'an infant Paganini on the guitar' (*Harmonicon*, 174). His accuracy, expression, and feeling were widely praised and his fame spread.

Regondi spent some time in Dublin, where he became friendly with Felicia Dorothea Hemans, who in 1833 wrote a poem about him entitled 'To Giúlio Regondi, the Boy Guitarist' (*Musical World*, 25 May 1872, 334). In 1840–41, playing the melophone, he made a concert tour with the cellist Joseph Lidel, which included performances in Prague and Leipzig and six very successful concerts in Vienna. Five years later he again toured abroad, visiting Prague and Dresden (26 October 1846), this time with the pianist Madame Dulcken. After his return he appears to have remained in England as a teacher and performer.

Regondi was one of the first to devote serious attention to the concertina, and is said to have shown Charles Wheatstone, its inventor and patentee, the true capabilities of the instrument (Atlas). He certainly helped to popularize it, writing two concertos (Bernhard Molique also composed one for him in 1853), around a dozen chamber works, and several concert pieces, and arranging a great deal of music for it (in particular favourite operatic melodies). Other publications include a concertina tutor, a *New Method* (Dublin, 1857), and numerous solo guitar works.

Regondi died after a long period of ill health on 6 May 1872 at his home, 17 Portsea Place, Connaught Square, London, and was buried at Kensal Green cemetery on 11 May.   DAVID J. GOLBY

Sources *Musical World* (18 May 1872), 315 · *The Harmonicon*, 9 (1831), 174, 200–02, 230 · A. W. Atlas, *The Wheatstone English concertina in Victorian England* (1996) · W. Guernsey, letter to editor, *Musical World* (25 May 1872), 334 · letter to editor, *Musical World* (1 June 1872), 345 · T. F. Heck, 'Regondi, Giulio', *New Grove* · P. J. Bone, *The guitar and mandolin* (1954), 291–6
Likenesses lithographs, BM · portrait, repro. in J. Zuth, 'Eine handschrift von Giulio Regondi', *Musik im Haus*, 6 (1927), 78
Wealth at death under £4000: 1872, stamp office

Regulus [St Regulus, Rule] (*supp. fl.* **8th–9th cent.**), supposed founder of the see of St Andrews, is associated in legend with the establishment of the cult of St Andrew in Scotland. According to manuscript tradition and the account in the Aberdeen breviary of 1510, Regulus was a holy man of Greek origin who, at the instigation of an angel, brought some of the bones of St Andrew from Patras in Greece (or from Constantinople), and landed at Kinrymont in Fife. A Pictish king, Oengus, who had won a victory with the help of St Andrew, gave Regulus land for a church. It was from this that the bishopric, and the town of St Andrews, developed.

It is probable that the cult of St Andrew was indeed initiated among the Picts by a King Oengus (Angus); either the Oengus who died in 761 (who could have been following the earlier King Nechtan's introduction of St Peter, both of them operating under influence from Northumbria) or the Oengus who lived almost a century later, at a time when corporeal relics supposed to be of apostles (as of St James at Compostela in Spain) were being revealed and reverenced. Regulus would have been simply the priestly individual who co-operated with the king in the foundation of church and cult.

The story that Regulus brought bones of the saint from the East introduces chronological confusion, since his removal of the bones is placed when St Andrew's relics were taken from Patras to Constantinople, in 357, or later, about 410. The whole story was presumably constructed to account for the presence of relics at St Andrews, and Regulus antedated, or invented, as the agent of this translation.

W. F. Skene suggested that the legend might owe something to a confusion with St Rieul (or Regulus) of Senlis in France. This saint was said to be a Greek, and Senlis had a later connection with Scotland in that King David I married the widow of Simon (I) de Senlis. However, the life of St Rieul places him in the first or third century, not the fourth or fifth, and there is nothing in his actual legend to connect him with St Andrew or with Scotland. That there was some confusion between the saints at a later date is perhaps indicated by the fact that in the Aberdeen breviary they are given the same feast day, 30 March.

The Aberdeen breviary provided for the feast to be celebrated on a date in October if 30 March fell in Lent. The October date, it appears, should properly be 16 October (though the breviary prescribes the 17th to avoid coincidence with another festival), and this date is that given in some Irish calendars for a St Riagul, called 'of Muccinis in Lough Derg'. It is a possibility that it is this Irish saint who has given his name to the Regulus of the St Andrews legend. It is probable that before the cult of St Andrew was established by King Oengus there was a monastery of the Irish type on the site of Kinrymont. Such a religious establishment, as were others in Scotland, could have been founded in the late sixth or in the seventh century. One tradition took St Cainnech to St Andrews; perhaps a St Riagul was also, or alternatively, involved, and his name preserved as a founder of the monastery there. When in the eighth or ninth century a Pictish King Oengus instituted the cult of St Andrew, Riagul, or Regulus, took a place in a new legend, to account for the presence in St Andrews of relics of the saint.

St Regulus, or Rule, though appearing in Scottish calendars, has had few churches dedicated in his name. There was a 'capella S. Reguli' at Ecclesgreig, St Cyrus, and the oldest church foundation in Monifieth, across the Tay from St Andrews, is known as St Rule's. A church existed there in Pictish times, and it is known from a charter of 1242 that it was served by canons in the old tradition, known as 'culdees'. It is possible, no more, that it was founded by an Irish St Riagul.

As for St Andrews, the ruined church and the surviving tower popularly known as St Rule's should not be regarded as evidence for an ancient dedication to St Regulus, as this church was certainly built in the name of St Andrew, and was the bishop's church until the building of the great cathedral. At a later date the church may well have been rededicated in the name of St Regulus.

URSULA HALL

Sources W. F. Skene, ed., *Chronicles of the Picts, chronicles of the Scots, and other early memorials of Scottish history* (1867), 138–40, 183–8, 375–7 · W. F. Skene, 'Notice of the early ecclesiastical settlements of St Andrews', *Proceedings of the Society of Antiquaries of Scotland*, 4 (1860–62), 300–21 · J. Dowden, 'Notes on the true date of the October festival of St Regulus of St Andrews, as bearing on the suggested identification of St Regulus and the Irish St Riaghail', *Proceedings of the Society of Antiquaries of Scotland*, 27 (1892–3), 247–54 · U. Hall, *St Andrew and Scotland* (1994), 60–77 · R. K. Hannay, *St Andrew of Scotland* (1934), 57–65 · J. M. MacKinlay, *Ancient church dedications in Scotland*, 2 (1914), 473–5 · M. O. Anderson, 'St Andrews before Alexander I', *The Scottish tradition*, ed. G. W. S. Barrow (1974), 1–13 · G. Martine, *Reliquiae divi Andreae, or, The state of the venerable and primitial see of St Andrews* (1797), 16–17, 24, 182 · J. O'Hanlon, *Lives of the Irish saints*, 3 [1875], 1021–3 · *Acta sanctorum: October*, 8 (Brussels, 1853),

163–80 · W. Blew, ed., *Breviarium Aberdonense*, 2 vols., Bannatyne Club, 96 (1854), vol. 1, fol. 82; vol. 2, fol. 128 · A. P. Forbes, *Kalendars of Scottish saints* (1872), 436

Reibey, Mary [*née* Molly Haydock; *alias* James Burrow] (1777–1855), businesswoman in Australia, was born on 12 May 1777 at Bury, Lancashire, the daughter of James Haydock (*d.* 1779), a yeoman, and his wife, Jane Law. Orphaned, and brought up by a grandmother, she was intelligent and literate, and was educated possibly at the free grammar school, Blackburn. On 18 August 1791, dressed as a boy and known by the name of James Burrow, she was arrested for attempting to sell a stolen horse. Her reckless role-play was perhaps rendered plausible by a snub nose and lively brown eyes, and Burrow was duly sentenced at Stafford summer assizes before Haydock's identity was discovered. She was committed to seven years' transportation.

Molly Haydock arrived at Sydney, New South Wales, aboard the *Royal Admiral* on 7 October 1792, optimistic, and pledged 'to make myself as happy as I Can in my Present and unhappy situation' (Haydock to Mrs Hope, 8 Oct 1792, Reibey MSS). Her immediate fate was to sew garments for the government. On 1 September 1794 she married Thomas Reibey (1769?–1811), a merchant seaman turned settler. Thomas qualified for a 30 acre grant at Mulgrave Place, an agricultural settlement on the Hawkesbury River, where their first child was born in May 1796. Besides farming profitably, Reibey carried grain to Sydney and shipped timber and coal along the New South Wales coastline. With a partner, Edward Wills, he later engaged in sealing and trading with the Pacific islands. The growing family moved to Sydney, where at Entally House, their fine home-cum-warehouse, Mary Reibey supervised the sale of merchandise and acquired a hotel licence.

In 1811, shortly after returning with a cargo from India, Thomas died; Wills died a month later. Thomas had named Mary his sole administrator, 'well-knowing and confiding in the natural Love and Affection which she beareth unto her Children, and the steadfast assurance which he hath that she will always do the best in her power to provide for their future Welfare' (Thomas Reibey's will 1811, probates, Supreme Court of NSW, Sydney). Now the mother of seven children (the youngest barely twelve months old), Mary Reibey inherited control of an enterprise that included shipping, farms, and houses. Untypically she did not remarry, but advanced into the capricious frontier economy with assurance. In 1812 she opened a new warehouse in a premier position, and within five years had two ships plying to Van Diemen's Land (where she settled three sons and which later became the family base). She also proved equal to the problem of debt collection endemic in the colony: in May 1817 she was found guilty of assault, having taken her umbrella to a recalcitrant debtor. Her established reputation for 'strictest propriety' and increasingly respectable social status remained unaffected, and were reinforced by the favour of the governor, Lachlan Macquarie.

After failing to find buyers for her assets, generally estimated at over £20,000, Mary Reibey decided in 1820 that her annual rent roll of £1205 would support a voyage to Britain with two of her daughters. In London, Glasgow, and Edinburgh they enjoyed the fashionable sights and entertainments, though, especially at Manchester and Liverpool, Mary Reibey visited factories and warehouses. At her childhood home in Lancashire she was relieved and gratified to meet with consideration and warm hospitality. Back in London, she discussed the future of 'our Colony' with others anxiously waiting for signs of political reaction to the reports of Commissioner Bigge.

During the colonial boom of the 1820s Mary Reibey invested afresh, building and renting high-class property in Sydney and continuing to add to her landholdings, but by 1845 she found herself burdened by 'bereavements and embarrassments', and having to exercise 'the greatest prudence and economy' (Reibey to D. Hope, 20 June 1845, Reibey MSS). A governor of the free grammar school, she had a genuine interest in education, charity, and her Anglican faith. Survived by three of her daughters, whose provision in her will she specified 'shall be free from the … control of … Husbands', Mary Reibey died on 30 May 1855 at Newtown, Sydney, and was buried at Old George Street burying-ground. Disarming in lace cap and pince-nez, an unlikely confidante of sea captains and men of affairs, this small nonconformist remains one of Australia's most original capitalists: fittingly, her portrait appeared on the commonwealth of Australia $20 note from 1994.   MARGARET STEVEN

Sources Mitchell L., NSW, Reibey MSS · New South Wales Archives Office, Supreme Court records · *Sydney Gazette* · F. M. Bladen, ed., *Historical records of New South Wales*, 7 vols. (1892–1901), vols. 5 – 8 · N. Irvine, *Mary Reibey – Molly incognita: a biography of Mary Reibey, 1777 to 1855, and her world* (1982) · N. Irvine, ed., *Dear cousin* (1992) · F. S. Eldershaw, ed., *The peaceful army* (1938) · [F. Watson], ed., *Historical records of Australia*, 1st ser., 8, 10, 14 (1916–22); 3rd ser., 2–4 (1921) · C. J. Baxter, ed., *Musters and lists: New South Wales and Norfolk island, 1800–1802* (1988) · parish register (births and baptisms), 12/5/1777, 29/5/1777, Bury 'old church', Lancashire · church records, St Phillip, Mitchell L., NSW, Mutch MSS · *AusDB*

Archives Mitchell L., NSW | Mitchell L., NSW, Norton Smith & Co. (solicitors) MSS · State Archives of New South Wales, Sydney, supreme court records

Likenesses watercolour on ivory miniature, Mitchell L., NSW

Wealth at death converted and devolved assets to children on their marriage

Reich, Emil (1854–1910), historian, son of Louis Reich, was born on 24 March 1854 at Eperjes in Hungary. After early education in schools at Eperjes and Kassa he went to the universities of Prague, Budapest, and Vienna; at the last he became a doctor of laws. Until his thirtieth year he studied almost exclusively in libraries. He then decided—finding books inadequate for 'a real comprehension of history'—to learn by travelling.

In July 1884 Reich, with his parents, his brother, and two sisters, emigrated to America, where after much hardship he was engaged in 1887 by the Appleton firm of New York in preparing their encyclopaedia. On his father's death, his mother and one sister settled in Budapest; the brother and other sister settled in Cincinnati, the one as a photo-engraver, the other as a public school teacher. In July 1889

Reich went to France. At the end of the year he visited Britain. In February and March 1890 he delivered at Oxford four lectures, subsequently published as *Graeco-Roman Institutions* (1890; French translation, 1891), in which he attempted to 'disprove the applicableness of Darwinian concepts to the solution of sociological problems'. His theory of the hitherto unsuspected influence of *infamia* on Roman law at first aroused opposition, but later was developed in Britain and France. Reich spent his time mainly in France until 1893, when he married Céline Labulle of Paris and settled in Britain for good. There, as a writer, as a lecturer to popular and learned audiences in Oxford, Cambridge, and London, and as a coach at Wren's establishment for preparing candidates for the civil service, he displayed remarkable vigour, versatility, and self-confidence. His breadth of interests appealed to Lord Acton, who described him as 'a universal specialist' and for Acton he wrote on Hungary and the Slavonic kingdoms for volume 1 of the *Cambridge Modern History*.

Reich's work, though full of stimulating suggestions, was often inaccurate in detail, and omission of essential facts discredited his conclusions. A lover of paradox, and a severe censor of established historical and literary reputations, he nevertheless made useful contributions to historical criticism in his lectures on 'Fundamental principles of evidence' and in his *The Failure of the Higher Criticism of the Bible* (1905), in which he combated modern methods of biblical criticism. Of *A general history of western nations from 5000 BC to 1900 AD*, the first part, on *Antiquity*, was published in two volumes in 1908–9. In it Reich laid heavy stress on environmental, geopolitical, and economic conditions. He also unjustifiably charged A. H. J. Greenidge with adopting without acknowledgement some researches of his own (*Antiquity*, 2.339–40n.); the accusation provoked a stout defence from Greenidge's friends in the *Times Literary Supplement* (23 and 30 July, 13 and 20 August 1908). Reich's most successful published work was his *Hungarian Literature* (1897; 2nd edn, 1906). In the dispute between British Guiana and Venezuela (1895–9) in regard to the Venezuelan boundary, Reich was engaged by the British government to help in the preparation of its case. A course of lectures on Plato at Claridge's Hotel, London, in 1906, which were attended by prominent female members of London society, brought him much public notoriety.

Reich published many other works on a wide variety of subjects. Especially notable are his *Handbook of Geography, Descriptive and Mathematical* (2 vols., 1908) and *Woman through the Ages* (2 vols., 1908). His attack on German militarism, *Germany's Swelled Head* (1907), was a best-seller in a revised edition by 'J. B. R.' in 1914. Reich died after three months' illness at his home, 33 St Luke's Road, Notting Hill, London, on 11 December 1910, and was buried at Kensal Green cemetery. His wife, with a daughter, survived him. Reich was fond of music and was an accomplished pianist.   W. B. OWEN, *rev.* H. C. G. MATTHEW

Sources *The Times* (13 Dec 1910) · *Daily Mail* (15 Dec 1910) · *Bevándorló* (16 Dec 1910) · private information (1912) · *WWW*
Archives BL, corresp. with Macmillans, Add. MS 55126

Reichel, Sir Henry Rudolf [Harry] (1856–1931), college head and educationist, was born on 11 October 1856 at Belfast, the second of the nine children of Charles Parsons Reichel (1816–1894), professor of Latin at Queen's College and later bishop of Meath, and his wife, Mary Brown M'Cracken (1827–1885). He was educated at Christ's Hospital (1866–75) and at Balliol College, Oxford (1875–80), where he held a scholarship, taking firsts in classical moderations (1876), in mathematical moderations (1877), in *literae humaniores* (1879), and in modern history (1880). He was a fellow of All Souls from 1880 to 1894. Tall and dignified, he was, in Benjamin Jowett's words, 'quite a gentleman' (Williams, 3.64). In 1884 he was appointed first principal of the University College of North Wales, Bangor, whose fortunes he guided until 1927. He was knighted on 11 July 1907 when the foundation-stone was laid of the fine new college building, completed in 1911.

Reichel's appointment had aroused initial misgivings. He knew practically nothing of Wales; he was an Anglican in a predominantly nonconformist country and he remained a staunch conservative. In public often a halting speaker, he was also disconcertingly direct. Yet, when he died 'Irish' Reichel was hailed as a great Welshman. From the first he was convinced that it was the duty of the privileged few to create an educated democracy. The confident Scots he had known at Balliol were the beneficiaries of a remarkable educational tradition; not so the hesitant Welshmen at Jesus. He was thus much moved when he learnt of the self-sacrifice of ordinary people which had led to the foundation of Wales's first university college at Aberystwyth (1872). He soon recognized the strength of the national movement which found institutional expression in the federal University of Wales (1893), of which he was six times vice-chancellor. After the passing of the Welsh Intermediate Education Act (1889) he energetically supported its effective implementation. He also stressed the importance of technical education, especially educational handwork. He was one of the founders of the Welsh Folk-Song Society (1906) and he learnt Welsh moderately well. He deplored religious animosities and promoted a spirit of reconciliation best exemplified by the establishing of the Bangor School of Theology in which scholars of various persuasions participated. He insisted on the highest standards in academic and public life; his integrity was never questioned and he firmly believed that university training should raise the tone of society. It is a misfortune that he did not write memoirs of his years in Wales and that natural reticence led him to destroy his correspondence.

As is the case with some reserved persons, Reichel came into his own in the lecture room; many regretted that the devouring demands of administration obliged him to discontinue teaching. He cannot be accounted a scholar. He published but one book, a collection of his revered father's sermons. However, his various papers on live educational issues remain crisp and fresh.

Reichel married Charity Mary (1859–1911), daughter of Henry Mulock Pilkington QC, on 1 February 1894; after her death without issue he did not remarry. In 1895 he was appointed chairman of the board of examinations for educational handwork and in 1903 a member of the Mosely commission appointed to study methods of education in the United States. From 1907 to 1915 he served on the consultative committee of the Board of Education. In 1925 his knowledge of the federal system admirably equipped him to chair the royal commission on university education in New Zealand. In 1928 he became chairman of the British Universities Bureau. He held honorary degrees from the universities of Toronto, Perth, Glasgow, Belfast, and Wales. Reichel died suddenly at Biarritz on 22 June 1931 and was buried in the family grave at Whitechurch, Rathfarnham, near Dublin, on 1 July 1931.

J. Gwynn Williams

Sources J. E. Lloyd, ed., *Sir Harry Reichel, 1856–1931: a memorial volume with two photographs* (1934) · *Sermons by Charles Parsons Reichel … with a memoir by his son Henry Rudolf Reichel* (1899) · J. G. Williams, *The University College of North Wales: foundations 1884–1927* (1985) · *The Times* (25–6 June 1931) · pedigree of the family of Reichel, U. Wales, Bangor, Welsh Library, Bangor MS 5538 · U. Wales, Bangor, Belmont MSS · *Liverpool Courier* (16 Nov 1911) · *North Wales Chronicle* (17 Nov 1911) · private information (2004)

Archives U. Wales, Bangor, Welsh Library, obituaries, offprints of speeches, pamphlets, printed papers | All Souls Oxf., Anson MSS · NL Wales, James Hills-Johnes MSS · NL Wales, Thomas Jones MSS · NL Wales, Herbert Lewis MSS · U. Wales, Aberystwyth, T. F. Roberts MSS

Likenesses W. Nicholson, oils, 1913, U. Wales, Bangor · C. Williams, oils, 1924, U. Wales, Bangor, Neuadd Reichel hall of residence

Wealth at death £4538 18s. 5d.: probate, 20 Aug 1931, CGPLA Eng. & Wales

Reid. *See also* Read, Reade, Rede, Reed.

Reid, Alexander (*c.*1570–1641), anatomist and surgeon, was one of the six sons and three daughters of James Reid (d. 1602), first reformed minister of the parish of Banchory-Ternan, Aberdeenshire, in north-east Scotland. Of Alexander's brothers, John was a servant of George Buchanan, Robert succeeded their father in the charge of Banchory-Ternan, Thomas *Reid was Latin secretary to James VI and I, Adam was minister of Methlick, and James, who was left most of Alexander's medical instruments, may also have been a surgeon.

Reid was initially taught by his father in the parish school of Banchory-Ternan, and then in Aberdeen, probably at the grammar school in the 'new' town, before proceeding to study in Old Aberdeen at King's College, from which he graduated before 1600. Next he travelled on the continent, visiting Bohemia and studying in France as well as possibly at Wittemberg. By 1609 he had returned to Britain and was practising surgery in the English midlands and Welsh borders. He was settled for a time at Holt, near Chester, and travelled widely in the course of his practice. The dedications of Reid's published works show him to have been patronized by several prominent members of the gentry and aristocracy of the region, including the earl of Bridgewater, president of the marches of Wales, and Philip Herbert, earl of Pembroke and Montgomery.

In 1616 Reid published his first work, *A Description of the Body of Man*, which was printed in London. Four years later, on 28 May 1620, along with his brother Thomas he was incorporated MA of the University of Oxford. On the following day, by virtue of letters from the king to that effect, he was created doctor of medicine; later he proclaimed his affiliation to Merton College. On 22 December 1621 Reid was admitted a candidate for the College of Physicians; he was made a fellow on 3 March 1624, and on 7 July of the same year he was incorporated at Cambridge University. Having been a 'foreign brother' of the Company of Barber–Surgeons of London since about 1620, and a 'free brother' since at least 25 June 1631, he was appointed on 28 December 1632 to give an anatomy lecture every Tuesday in the Barber–Surgeons' Hall. The king's nominee Richard Andrews had just declined the post, for which Reid was paid £20 *per annum*. Reid continued in this post for three years and subsequently published his lectures under the titles *The Chirurgicall Lectures of Tumors and Ulcers* (1635) and *A Treatise of the First Part of Chirurgerie* (1638). His health was in a state of decline from at least February 1639, when he made his last will and testament, until his death in mid-October 1641.

In the course of his active surgical practice and in his writings, Reid showed himself to be primarily concerned with practicality and utility. In 1618 he was called by Lord Gerard to examine his tailor, whose leg had suffered a serious fracture ten weeks previously. On examination of the tumour which had formed, Reid pronounced that only amputation would save the tailor's life. Having no medicines or medical instruments with him but noting that the house was undergoing repair work, Reid successfully improvised by using a joiner's whipsaw to perform the amputation, and a solution of umber, unslaked lime, egg whites, and hare's fur to stop haemorrhage. He demonstrated a different sort of pragmatism in 1634, when heading a team of surgeons and midwives who, overseen by William Harvey, examined four women who had been convicted of witchcraft some months earlier in Lancashire. The report of the examination, signed by Reid, stated that no sign of witchcraft had been found on three of the four women, and that the 'teats' found on the fourth woman were more consistent with piles or leech marks than anything which might have been used to suckle a familiar spirit. Keevil has also suggested that he was the first surgeon to excise the spleen. Having seen the body of the duke of Buckingham after his assassination by John Felton, Reid showed particular interest in the precise direction of the wound which severed the 'arteria venosa'. Although he did not approve Paracelsus's doctrines, he taught them, so that his students would be better able to disprove them.

An acquaintance of Harvey, Reid has been criticized by some historians (for example Sir Geoffrey Keynes, Walter Pagel, and Wiel) for ignoring, in his published works, Harvey's theories on the circulation of the blood. However, Reid's reputation has largely been rehabilitated by the more balanced work of Roger French, who has highlighted the differences between the target audiences of the two: Reid's was a practical discipline, Harvey's primarily philosophical. French's examination of Reid's annotations to the books in his personal library shows Reid to have been aware of Harvey's doctrine of the circulation of the blood, but to have been more interested in his ideas on pulmonary transit, with which he eventually came to agree. Reid's main concern in his written works, as he made clear in the 1634 edition of his *Description of the Body of Man with the Practice of Chirurgery*, was to provide clear introductory explanations for newly qualified and student anatomists; the aim of *Description* and earlier works was to make available to them, in English, the standard works of such writers as Bauhin and Paré. Reid openly acknowledged that his first work in this genre, the 1616 *Description of the Body of Man*, was actually an abbreviated version of Helkiah Crooke's 1615 work of the same title, which it appears the publisher had asked Reid to abridge into a more manageable form. Reid's works were reprinted several times in the seventeenth century, and show him to have been capable of being moved by an argument to change his own position.

Reid accumulated a considerable fortune in the course of his life and began to disperse it before his death. In 1631 he gifted £100 sterling to augment the provision of the twelve foundation arts bursars (poor students) at King's College, Aberdeen, as well as a wide range of books for the replenishment of its library. His generosity to the university was gratefully acknowledged by several students in John Lundie's *Oratio eucharistica* (1631). This may have prompted the neighbouring university of Marischal College to approach him with a request of its own, and in October 1633 Reid promised that college £100 for the help of poor scholars, as well as books and manuscripts from his own collection. He was later to increase the monetary gift by £10. In his will he assigned equal shares in a debt of £400 sterling due to him by the earl of Annandale to both colleges, and to the grammar schools of the burghs of Old and New Aberdeen, but the debt was not recovered. He also left £100 each to the minister and poor of Banchory-Ternan, as well as £100 and various books to the school of that parish. To the College of Physicians he left £100 towards the erection of an anatomy theatre. The rest of his legacy was to relatives, colleagues, patrons, and friends. In all he left more than £946 and many articles of clothing, jewels, and medical instruments. His will was expressed in strictly orthodox protestant terms, yet his gift of pictures of Christ and the Virgin Mary and of two crucifixes to the firmly covenanted Sir Thomas Burnett of Leys suggests a lack of understanding of the contemporary state of the Church of Scotland into which he had been born. Reid was buried in London in St Mary Woolnoth parish on 27 October 1641.

SHONA MACLEAN VANCE

Sources 'The first double of Doctor Reads latter will and testament', 1641, U. Aberdeen L., special libraries and archives, MS OCC 49, no. 21 • P. J. Anderson and J. F. K. Johnstone, eds., *Fasti academiae Mariscallanae Aberdonensis: selections from the records of the Marischal College and University, MDXCIII–MDCCCLX*, 3 vols., New Spalding Club, 4, 18–19 (1889–98) • L. B. Taylor, ed., *Aberdeen council letters*, 6 vols. (1942–61), vol. 1 • C. Innes, ed., *Fasti Aberdonenses … 1494–1854*, Spalding Club, 26 (1854) • *Fasti Scot.*, vol. 3 • W. B. Menzies, 'Alexander Read, physician and surgeon, 1580–1641—his life, works and library', *The Library*, 4th ser., 12 (1931–2), 46–74 • R. French, *William Harvey's natural philosophy* (1994) • *DNB* • G. Keynes, *The life of William Harvey* (1966) • J. Dobson and R. Milnes Walker, *Barbers and barber-surgeons of London* (1979) • J. F. Kellas Johnstone and A. W. Robertson, *Bibliographia Aberdonensis*, ed. W. D. Simpson, Third Spalding Club, 1 (1929) [incl. complete list of works] • A. Read [Reid], *Workes*, 2nd edn (1650) • W. K. Leask, ed., *Musa Latina Aberdonensis*, 3: *Poetae minores*, New Spalding Club, 37 (1910) • Wood, *Ath. Oxon.*: *Fasti* (1815) • 'Council register of the burgh of Aberdeen', MS, Aberdeen City Archive, Town House, Aberdeen • private information (2004) [M. Pelling]

Archives U. Aberdeen L., annotated works

Wealth at death over £946: 'The first double of Dr Reads latter will and testament', U. Aberdeen L., MS OCC 49, no. 21

Reid, Alexander (1747–1823), painter, was born at Kirkennan, near Dalbeattie, Kirkcudbrightshire, the second son of John Reid of Kirkennan. He may have been the Alexander Read who was an honorary exhibitor of a portrait of Mr Ouchterlony at the Society of Artists in 1770. After spending some time in Paris before the revolution he appears to have had a studio in Dumfries at the end of the eighteenth century. He painted miniatures, oil portraits, and landscapes, some of which have been engraved.

According to a *Glasgow Herald* article of 1917 Reid accompanied Captain Robert Riddell, of Glenriddell, the antiquary and friend of Robert Burns; the antiquary Captain Francis Grose; and 'the Captain's accomplished servant, Thomas Cocking' on tours 'of inspection of the interesting historical remains in Dumfres [sic] and Galloway, Reid or Grose making drawings from them, and Glenriddell writing the descriptions'. A number of the original watercolour sketches made on these tours in 1789 and 1790, along with a few of Reid's watercolours dated 1791 (the year in which Grose died) and 1792, are among the bound volumes of the Robert Riddell manuscript collections in the library of the Society of Antiquaries of Scotland, now part of the National Museums of Scotland Library, Edinburgh. Reid watercolours also illustrate the manuscript of 'A Tour of Nithsdale, 1787' in this collection; the Society of Antiquaries, London, has Riddell's illustrated manuscript of the antiquities of Nithsdale. A series of engravings after drawings by Reid, which included views of Dumfries and Kirkcudbright, was published in *The Copper-Plate Magazine* in the 1790s; a drawing of Glenriddell's seat—Friar's Carse, Dumfriesshire—was sold at Sothebys on 13 May 1925 (lot 123).

Reid is best-known in connection with a miniature of Robert Burns that he painted in Dumfries in 1795. Allan Cunningham, in his life of Raeburn, speaks of 'Read, a wandering limner, who found his way on a time to Dumfries, where he painted the heads of Burn and his Jean on ivory' (p. 215); no miniature of the latter has ever been traced. Burns wrote to Maria Riddell, Glenriddell's sister-in-law, from Dumfries in 1795:

Apropos to pictures, I am just sitting to Reid in this town for a miniature; & I think he has hit by far the best likeness of me ever was taken.—When you are at any time so idle, in town, as to call at Reid's painting-room, & mention to him that I spoke of such a thing to you, he will shew it you; else, he will not; for both the Miniature's existence & its destiny, are an inviolable secret. (DeLancey Ferguson, 343)

In spring 1795 Burns sent the miniature to Mrs Riddell with a note that said 'The painter, in my opinion, has spoilt the likeness', but this change of view may have been because Burns was 'so ill as to be scarce able to hold this miserable pen to this miserable paper' (ibid., 354). In May of that year he wrote to George Thomson:

there is an artist of very considerable merit, just now in this town, who has hit the most remarkable likeness of what I am at this moment, that I think ever was taken of any body.—It is a small miniature. (ibid., 356)

The miniature bequeathed by W. F. Watson to the Scottish National Portrait Gallery, Edinburgh, in 1886 is generally accepted to be that painted by Reid. The bookplate attached to the back refers to Burns's friend John Mitchell, collector at Dumfries, which suggests a possible provenance.

The *Glasgow Herald* article lists a portrait of Captain Grose in sepia ('characteristic but otherwise unpleasing') and miniatures of Edward Cairns of Torr; Cairns's brother George, of Kipp, which was also engraved; his sister Janet and her husband, William Nicol; the Revd Dr James Muirhead, minister of Urr; and Glenriddell. The present locations of these portraits are unknown.

On the death of his elder brother, in 1804, Reid succeeded to the family estate, and settled there. He died, unmarried, in 1823. A portrait of him, by an unknown artist, at one time belonged to his great-nephew Mr G. Corson, architect, of Leeds.

CAMPBELL DODGSON, *rev.* ARIANNE BURNETTE

Sources *The letters of Robert Burns*, ed. J. de Lancey Ferguson, 2nd edn, ed. G. Ross Roy, 2 vols. (1985) · J. M., 'A Burns coterie', *Glasgow Herald* (17 Nov 1917) · A. Cunningham, *The lives of the most eminent British painters, sculptors, and architects*, 2nd edn, 5 (1837) · Graves, *Soc. Artists* · B. Skinner, notes on the Robert Riddell manuscript collections, 1959, National Museums of Scotland Library, Edinburgh, SAS MSS 581–591 [1786–92] [courtesy of the deputy librarian (collections), Andrew Martin] · engraved plates from *The Copper-Plate Magazine*, Courtauld Inst., Witt Library · B. C. Skinner, *Burns: authentic likenesses* (1963) · J. A. Mackay, *Burnsiana* (1988) · P. J. M. McEwan, *Dictionary of Scottish art and architecture* (1994) · private information (2004) [D. Thomson]
Archives S. Antiquaries, Lond., Robert Riddell's MS on antiquities of Nithsdale, MS 117 | National Museums of Scotland, Edinburgh, Library of the Society of Antiquaries of Scotland (National Museum of Antiquities of Scotland Library), Robert Riddell manuscript collections, SAS MSS 581–591
Likenesses portrait

Reid, Alexander (1802–1860), schoolmaster, was born in Thornhill, Dumfriesshire. His father, a merchant, came from Aberdeenshire. Reid was educated at the parish school at Thornhill, and afterwards at Edinburgh University, where, after distinguishing himself in the rhetoric classes, he graduated MA in 1827. From September 1822 onwards he was parish schoolmaster at Dornock, Dumfriesshire, when he prepared himself to enter the Church of Scotland. He was licensed by the presbytery of Annan in 1827. Through his connection with the Presbyterian minister Dr Andrew Thomson (1779–1831), he was appointed

on 27 July 1827 chief master of St George's School, Edinburgh. In 1829 he was appointed to the Circus Place School in Edinburgh, formed about the same time as the Edinburgh Academy, after the model of an English preparatory school with advanced classes. Reid remained connected with it until 1846, except for a short interval in 1832–3, when he took charge of a school in Dublin. In 1833 he married the third daughter of J. Greig, parish minister of Dalmeny, Linlithgowshire.

Between 1833 and 1846 he wrote most of his shorter school books. His most important work was his *Dictionary of the English Language*, which he published in 1844. It cost him much labour, and overwork brought on serious illness. In 1849, partially recovered, he was appointed by the Free Church of Scotland inspector of primary schools. The following year, after receiving from the University of Aberdeen the honorary degree of LLD, he purchased the proprietary school known as the Edinburgh Institution, which aimed to provide a 'modern' education of a high-class character and was energetically run. He moved the school from Hill Street to Queen Street. In 1858 Reid's health gave way entirely. He retired from the school, and died at 20 Scotland Street, Edinburgh, on 29 June 1860.

As well as his *English Dictionary*, Reid published *Rudiments of English Grammar* (1837), *Rudiments of Modern Geography* (1837), *Rudiments of English Composition* (1839), and *An Outline of Sacred Geography* (5th edn, 1840), all of which ran into many editions. A selection from *Rudiments of Geography* was transliterated into the Nagari character for the use of the lower English classes in Indian schools. Reid also adapted Kitto's *History of Palestine* (1843) and P. F. Tytler's *History of Scotland* (1845).

FOSTER WATSON, *rev.* C. A. CREFFIELD

Sources Boase, *Mod. Eng. biog.* · private information (1885)
Likenesses Brodie, replica medallion in stucco (replica in stucco), possibly Edinburgh Institution
Wealth at death £1672 14s. 0d.: inventory, 27 Oct 1860, NA Scot., SC 70/1/106/944

Reid, (Hugh) Alistair (1913–1983), epidemiologist and toxicologist, was born on 2 December 1913 at Annandale, Victoria Road, Great Crosby, Liverpool, the third of the four children of James Martin Reid (1876–1967), physician and surgeon, and his wife, Janet Howie Sturrock (1884–1967). Both parents were Scottish. Reid was educated at Edinburgh Academy (1927–1931), and in 1932 entered the School of Medicine, Edinburgh University, and qualified MB ChB in 1936. He joined the Royal Army Medical Corps in January 1940 and was evacuated from Dunkirk with the British army. He gained his wings and served with the parachute field ambulance division in the north African, Sicilian, and Italian campaigns. He qualified MRCP (Edin.) in 1947 and became fellow in 1958. In 1948 he joined the Anglo-Iranian Oil Company in Abadan as specialist physician but following the nationalization of the Iranian oil industry in 1951 he returned to London. In 1952, having gained the diploma in tropical medicine and hygiene (London), he joined the British colonial medical service and was posted to Penang General Hospital as consultant physician and specialist in tropical medicine to the government of Malaya.

Reid soon observed a fatal case of sea snake bite poisoning. Realizing how little was known of the clinical picture or incidence of sea snake bites he undertook a systematic survey of the fishing villages in Penang, Kedah, and Perlis. Initially, fishing folk were extremely reluctant to discuss snakebite and its outcome, mainly for fear of offending sea snakes and making them aggressive. He overcame this attitude and also the fishing folk's reluctance to seek hospital treatment. The survey revealed that snakes on the defensive often bite man without injecting any significant amount of venom, a finding confirmed in all later surveys of snakebite. However, the survey showed that a medical problem existed as no specific antivenom had been developed at this time for treating serious cases. Reid's careful clinical observation of the victims revealed that in man the venom was myotoxic, resulting in breakdown of skeletal muscle, which was often extensive; the venom was not neurotoxic as reported in animal studies. These findings guided his clinical treatment. The work resulted in his thesis for the degree of MD (Edinburgh) in 1960; for other workers it stimulated an important new field of research into myotoxic phospholipases. Reid founded and was honorary director of the Penang Snake and Venom Research Institute from 1960 to 1964. Common sea snake (Enhydrina schistosa) venom was sent from the institute to the Australian Commonwealth Serum Laboratories which prepared the first specific sea snake antivenom. When clinical use of the antivenom started in Penang in 1961 patient recovery was dramatic.

Reid carried out an epidemiological study of victims of snakebite admitted to hospital in Penang and Kedah. Land snake bites were chiefly from the Malayan pit viper present in the rubber plantations, but also from cobras; he provided clinical guidelines to assess the degree of poisoning and the correct dose of specific antivenom to be used in treatment. Reid observed that patients mildly poisoned by the Malayan pit viper usually had incoagulable blood but that otherwise they were in reasonably good general health. He showed that the venom produced defibrination of blood and suggested that a venom derivative might have an important therapeutic role in the treatment of deep vein thrombosis. This led to the protease ancrod, registered as Arvin, being used clinically in anticoagulant therapy from 1968.

After leaving Malaya, Reid became senior lecturer at the Liverpool School of Tropical Medicine (1964–81) and honorary consultant physician in tropical medicine to the Liverpool Regional Hospital Board (1965–79). As a visiting consultant on clinical research in tropical diseases he investigated and advised on clinical research programmes in relation to drug resistant malaria (Thailand), snakebite (Thailand, Ghana, Nigeria), and scorpion sting (Libya). He was also involved in numerous other consultations and lectures in Asia, Africa, Central America, and Europe. He carried out studies on cerebral malaria in Thailand and Ghana. Reid founded and was head of the Venom

Research Unit (later named the Alistair Reid Venom Research Unit) from 1973 to 1983. At the Liverpool School of Tropical Medicine, which was designated a main National Health Service antivenom centre in 1978, the unit investigated adder bites in Britain and showed that Zagreb viper antivenom was effective against the venom of the British adder. The problem of treatment when the offending snake was unknown was addressed by the unit developing a very sensitive enzyme immunoassay technique to identify and quantify venom in a drop of the victim's blood. Venom antibody in victims previously bitten could also be identified. The technique was used successfully in the field in northern Nigeria and eastern Ecuador and provided further evidence of the serious hazard to health of snakebite in rural populations. Reid collaborated in field studies and clinical research in north-east Nigeria where there was a high incidence of poisoning due to the carpet viper (Echis ocellatus). The efficacy of commercial preparations of specific antivenom produced in different geographical regions was shown to vary markedly. These concerns led to the setting up of the WHO Collaborating Centre for the Control of Antivenoms at the Liverpool School of Tropical Medicine. With Reid as head (1977–83) this unique centre was instrumental in the collection of WHO designated reference snake venoms of medical importance, in the collaborative work of characterizing their biological activities, and in the second stage completed after Reid's death, in organizing the production of monospecific WHO standard antivenoms against these reference venoms.

Reid's achievements were recognized by a succession of honours: he became an OBE in 1963, was elected the first honorary member of the Association of Physicians of Malaysia in 1965 and fellow of the Royal Australasian College of Physicians in 1966. He was a founding member of the International Society on Toxinology and served as president from 1970 to 1972. In 1979 he received the society's Redi award for outstanding merit in the field of toxinology. Reid was the author of more than 130 scientific and clinical papers (many appearing in The Lancet and British Medical Journal), chapters in books, and articles of general interest on the treatment of bites and stings, and on other subjects relating to tropical medicine such as malaria.

Alistair Reid was a tall, well-built man of fair colouring. He possessed a deeply warm personality but nevertheless was capable of being tough when he deemed it necessary. He was a great enthusiast, always positive in his approach to problems, and an outstanding raconteur of rich good humour. Reid was a gifted teacher whose interesting and lively lectures on the problems of bites and stings were appreciated not only by diploma students of tropical medicine in Liverpool, but elsewhere at home and abroad. He encouraged and inspired many to work in the field. On 22 June 1951 Reid married Patricia Anne Harington (b. 1926), a registered nurse who was working in Abadan. They had three daughters. Reid died in the Royal Liverpool Hospital on 10 April 1983 of the aftermath of a repair of a ruptured aortic aneurysm. He was cremated four days later at Thornton Garden of Rest, Liverpool; he was survived by his wife.   BARBARA J. HAWGOOD

Sources *The Times* (14 April 1983) · *BMJ* (7 May 1983), 1522 · B. J. Hawgood, 'Hugh Alistair Reid OBE MD: investigation and treatment of snakebite', *Toxicon*, 36 (1998), 431–46 · private information (2004) · personal knowledge (2004) · b. cert. · m. cert. · d. cert.

Wealth at death £78,536: probate, 5 Aug 1983, *CGPLA Eng. & Wales*

Reid, Andrew (*d.* 1767?), editor and author, was probably a member of the Reid family of Fife, although details of his birth and upbringing are unknown. He is thought to have moved to London about 1720, and from 1728 he edited the *Present State of the Republick of Letters*, a periodical which appeared annually in two volumes under Reid's control until it ceased publication in 1736. In 1732 he published an *Abstract of Sir Isaac Newton's Chronology of Ancient Kingdoms* and in the following year edited, with John Gray, an abridgement of the *Philosophical Transactions and Collections*, covering the twelve years from 1720. His later studies on scientific subjects included *An Account of some Experiments on Tar-Water* (1747); *An Essay on Logarithms* (1767), dedicated to his long-standing friend John Gray; and *Elements of the Theory and Practice of Chymistry* (3rd edn, 1775), a translation of a work by Pierre Joseph Macquer. In 1767 he was employed to edit for press the first two editions of *History of the Life of Henry II* by George, first Baron Lyttelton. It was in connection with this, Reid's last literary project, that he was described by Samuel Johnson as 'a man not without considerable abilities, and not unacquainted with letters and with life', who convinced Lyttelton, 'as he had persuaded himself, that he was master of the secret of punctuation' (Johnson, 1.453). The dates of Reid's death and burial are not known, although the *Dictionary of National Biography* suggests that he probably died in 1767, the third edition of Lyttelton's *History* (1768) being corrected by another editor.   PHILIP CARTER

Sources DNB · Nichols, *Lit. anecdotes* · S. Johnson, *Lives of the English poets*, ed. G. B. Hill, [new edn], 3 vols. (1905)

Reid, Archibald David (1844–1908), painter, was born on 8 June 1844 in Aberdeen, the fourth of the five sons (in a family of thirteen children) of George Reid, blacksmith and later manager of the Aberdeen Copper Company, and his wife, Esther Tait. Archy, as he was known, was the younger brother of the painter Sir George Reid (1841–1913); his younger brother Samuel Reid (1854–1912) was also an artist. In the summer of 1854 Reid's father was declared bankrupt; his brother George was removed from Aberdeen grammar school and Archibald himself was sent to Robert Gordon's Hospital, a charity school. He left school at fourteen and was employed in the counting-house of the flour miller, art collector, and connoisseur John Forbes White. One of the earliest collectors of contemporary Dutch and French painting in Britain, White developed close links with the artists whose paintings he had bought, particularly Gerrit Mollinger and Jozef Israëls. He sent both George and later Archy to study in the Netherlands.

In Aberdeen, Reid gained his first practical training in art at the mechanics' institute. At the age of twenty-three he went to Edinburgh for three years, where he attended the classes of the Trustees' Academy and, later, the life class of the Royal Scottish Academy. This training, however, seems to have had far less effect on his art than did the influence of the realist art of his Dutch and French contemporaries and of his artist friends in north-east Scotland, particularly his brother George, their mutual friend George Paul Chalmers, and the mentor to all three, John Forbes White. White became Archy Reid's guardian, teacher, and promoter. As he had with George, White set out to define Archy's art, to alter his subject matter, and to improve his technique (even to the point of painting on his pictures when he felt it necessary). For Archy the effect of the contact with White was, if anything, still more profound than it had been for George. Reid could, when required, turn out works in an earlier style: minutely realistic, colourful scenes of the local fishing villages such as *Buys and Buoys* (Aberdeen Art Gallery) fall into this category. However, the influence of realism and its accompanying emphasis on tonality soon came to dominate his art, as is revealed in paintings such as *On the Aberdeen Bents* (Aberdeen Art Gallery), which is a direct translation of Israëls's much employed theme of a girl waiting on the shore for the return of the men from fishing. Reid's painting has less sombre realism than many Dutch works on this theme: he relieves the tension somewhat by depicting the girl busy mending nets rather than gazing out to sea. The atmosphere is altogether bleaker, however, in *A Lone Shore* of 1874 (Aberdeen Art Gallery): in this large painting the outcome of the fishing trip—a wrecked boat—is clearly visible. *A Lone Shore* was accepted to hang at the Royal Academy in 1875, but the bleakness of the subject matter and treatment did not appeal to the public and it remained unsold in the artist's studio until his death.

As a young man Reid was dark-haired and blue-eyed, and sported a neat beard and moustache, and a jaunty tam-o'-shanter. Without the same familial responsibilities as his older brother, he was free to travel extensively; a persistent illness (he had an operation in 1887) further reduced the family's expectations of him. He painted in France and in 1874 was in the Netherlands; White funded a journey to Spain. Reid also visited Italy and in 1878 he studied at the Académie Julian in Paris. The careers of the two brothers, George and Archibald, were closely interlinked: George influenced Archibald in his choice of subject matter. (He painted, for example, some of the first still lifes of flowers in Scottish art, a subject which had been introduced to Scotland by his brother.) He also had a career as a portrait painter but this was never as successful as that of George, though he would occasionally take over commissions which George had declined. George was, however, scrupulous in avoiding any hint of nepotism, voting for election to the Royal Scottish Academy other artists in preference to his brother. Indeed, it was not until 1892 that Archy Reid was elected to the Royal Scottish Academy and then only as an associate member. Five years later he became a member of the Royal Institute of Painters in Oils. He was also a member of the Royal Scottish Society of Painters in Watercolour.

From 1883 Reid lived at St Lukes, Kepplestone, George Reid's home in Aberdeen. Ten years later, on 26 July 1893, he married Margaret Sim (*b.* 1839/40), daughter of George Sim, a farmer from Kintore, Aberdeenshire; they had no children. In Aberdeen, Reid moved in a lively intellectual circle. He was a member of the New Deer Academy, which included the theologian and semantic scholar William Robertson Smith and the astronomer David Gill. He was also actively involved in the organization and hanging of the Aberdeen Artists' Society exhibitions which began in 1885. Towards the end of his life he produced many landscapes in charcoal. He made some etchings and also some illustrations, including some for the menus for the meetings of the Aberdeen Pen and Pencil Club, of which he was a member. He died of heart failure at Wareham, Dorset, on 30 August 1908 and was buried in St Peter's cemetery, Aberdeen. His wife survived him.

JENNIFER MELVILLE

Sources J. Melville, 'John Forbes White and George Reid—artists and patrons in north-east Scotland, 1860–1920', PhD diss., U. Edin., [forthcoming] · M. Reid, 'Life of Sir George Reid PRSA', Aberdeen Art Gallery Archives · letters of Sir George Reid, John Forbes White, and others, Aberdeen Art Gallery Archives · *Aberdeen Free Press* (1 Sept 1908) · J. Morrison, 'The academy of Old Deer', *William Robertson Smith—essays in reassessment*, ed. W. Johnstone (1995), 50–59 · P. J. M. McEwan, *Dictionary of Scottish art and architecture* (1994) · J. L. Caw, *Scottish painting past and present, 1620–1908* (1908), 301–2 · R. Billcliffe, ed., *The Royal Glasgow Institute of the Fine Arts, 1861–1989: a dictionary of exhibitors at the annual exhibitions*, 4 vols. (1990–92) · C. B. de Laperriere, ed., *The Royal Scottish Academy exhibitors, 1826–1990*, 4 vols. (1991) · m. cert.

Archives Aberdeen Art Gallery

Likenesses A. Reid, self-portrait, oils, 1882, Aberdeen Art Gallery

Wealth at death £2162 19s. 5d.: confirmation, 21 Dec 1908, CCI

Reid, Beryl Elizabeth (1919–1996), actress and comedian, was born on 17 June 1919 at 8 St Olave's, St Owen Street, Hereford, the only daughter, and one of two children, of Leonard Reid, estate agent and valuer, and his wife, Anne Burton Reid, *née* McDonald. Both parents were Scottish. She was educated in Manchester at the progressive kindergarten Lady Barne House, then at Withington and Levenshulme high schools. At three she began dancing lessons—perhaps a key to her long-term recipe for character acting, 'Get your feet right'. A popular school performer, she was determined to go on stage despite her father's doubts, and after a short period at Kendal Milne's department store she made her professional début in a concert party at the Floral Hall, Bridlington, Yorkshire, in 1936, as an impressionist and soubrette. Subsequently she polished her comic skills in summer seasons, all-day cinevariety, and pantomime, usually as Mother Goose's maid or an Ugly Sister. She toured in variety with such high-flyers as Max Miller and Will Fyffe and also with the Entertainments National Service Association (1940–43).

In 1946–7 Reid played second lead in the famous *Half Past Eight* shows in Edinburgh, Ayr, and Glasgow, for which

Beryl Elizabeth Reid (1919–1996), by unknown photographer, 1984

she had to learn 427 sketches. This led to a wireless breakthrough when on *Henry Hall's Guest Night* she introduced her wicked, posh-voiced schoolgirl character Monica, with beautifully observed catch-phrases including 'She's my best friend and I hate her', and 'Aren't I the absolute terminus!' From 1952 to 1956 Monica featured in *Educating Archie*, and later alongside an even more endearing creation—Marlene, the tough dance-hall raver who put the Brummie accent on the map with her quaint locutions—'But oi doigress …'—and the early rocker's swooning phrase, "E *sends* me!' Reid then became a national institution, a radio monologuist in the Joyce Grenfell league. When she reappeared in pantomime, invariably now as Marlene, or in summer shows such as *Rocking the Town*, at the London Palladium in 1956, it was as a major star, much in demand for television. Meanwhile Reid had also made a career in the more sophisticated world of intimate revue, first at London's St Martin's and New Watergate theatres, then in a great personal success in *One to another* at the Lyric Theatre, Hammersmith, in 1959. Here her gifts as a comic actress as well as a 'turn' became apparent, especially in a doleful sketch by Harold Pinter.

Guest appearances in repertory theatres and in Shakespearian comedy on the radio in 1962 fuelled Reid's ambition to try 'legitimate' acting. The same year she appeared in the West End revue *On the Avenue*, memorably playing a hyperactive Spanish maid. The next turning point came in 1965 when she made her 'straight' West End début in Frank Marcus's *The Killing of Sister George*, playing a hard-drinking, lesbian soap actress. It was a daring play for its time, and a daring career move for Reid, but her performance—truthful, comic, sad, and near-credibly masculine—was acclaimed; after a year and a half's run in London the play transferred to New York, where Reid won a Tony award (1967). She had a further success in Robert Aldrich's turgid film version, but was seen to much greater advantage on screen in Joe Orton's *Entertaining Mr Sloane* (1969). To the part of the ageing nymphomaniac Kath she brought a weirdly graceful near-innocence: Orton's macabre shabby-genteelisms suited her perfectly.

Reid made an impressively serious National Theatre début in *Spring Awakening* (1973); other parts included the

Nurse in *Romeo and Juliet*. In 1977 she played Lady Wishfort in *The Way of the World* at the Royal Shakespeare Company. She won a 1980 Society of West End Theatres award for her performance as a dotty Bristolian mother in Peter Nichols's *Born in the Garden*. On television she made an extraordinary impact in the cameo role of Connie Sachs in John le Carré's *Tinker, Tailor, Soldier, Spy* (1979) and *Smiley's People* (1982, for which she received a BAFTA award). Her decrepit former MI6 researcher was a small masterpiece of wry pathos. Her latter-day career was awesomely crowded: West End theatre, guest roles in films, and appearances in innumerable television plays and series. She remained a beloved popular entertainer on countless game and chat shows. She wrote an autobiography, *So much Love* (1984). In 1986 she was appointed OBE. Despite deteriorating health she worked spiritedly almost to the end.

On and off stage Reid was an exceptionally funny woman. Her very appearance—small, neat, bright-eyed, with a wide mouth, dimples, and tilted nose—betokened mischief. She was also highly intelligent. Throughout her phenomenally varied career she was always learning and enquiring. She revered talent, but had an acute unforgiving eye for pretension and ineptitude. She loved friends and convivial meals, and delighted in human incongruity, yet she had a marked reclusive side, and was happy alone at Honeypot Cottage, her eccentric riverside home at Wraysbury, Buckinghamshire, with her many cats. Perhaps this accounted for the brevity of her two marriages; she was certainly no man-hater. Her first marriage was to William Lister (Bill) Worsley (*b.* 1905/6), a BBC producer, son of Frederick William Worsley, on 1 October 1949; the second to Derek Harold Franklin (*b.* 1920/21), a musician, son of Ernest John Franklin, a salesman, on 23 August 1954. There were no children from either marriage. Reid died from severe osteoarthritis and kidney failure at the Thames Valley Nuffield Hospital, Wexham, Buckinghamshire, on 13 October 1996. JONATHAN CECIL

Sources B. Reid, *So much love* (1984) · private information (2004) [E. Atkins, R. Jessop, J. Tripp] · personal knowledge (2004) · *WWW* [forthcoming] · *The Times* (14 Oct 1996) · *The Independent* (14 Oct 1996) · *Daily Telegraph* (14 Oct 1996) · d. cert. · b. cert. · m. certs. **Likenesses** photograph, 1984, Hult. Arch. [*see illus.*] · photograph, repro. in *The Times* · photograph, repro. in *The Independent* · photograph, repro. in *Daily Telegraph* **Wealth at death** £420,219: probate, 15 Jan 1997, *CGPLA Eng. & Wales*

Reid, David Boswell (1805–1863), physician and inventor of ventilation systems, was born at Edinburgh, the second son of Dr Peter Reid and Christian, eldest daughter of Hugo *Arnot of Balcormo. His younger brother was Hugo *Reid.

His father, **Peter Reid** (1777–1838), educationist, the only son of David Reid, West India merchant, and Elizabeth Boswell, a member of the old family of Boswell of Balmuto, was born at Dubbyside, Fife. He studied medicine at Edinburgh University, and first gained a reputation as editor of Dr William Cullen's great work, *First Lines of the Practice of Physic*. Three editions, published respectively in

1802, 1810, and 1816, with notes by Reid, embodied the results of the most recent experience. Reid's earliest original work was entitled *Letters on the Study of Medicine and on the Medical Character, Addressed to a Student*, published at Edinburgh in 1809. But it was as an educational reformer that Peter Reid chiefly made his mark. In 1824 he published a letter to the town council of Edinburgh urging a thorough reform in the curriculum of the high school, advocating a reduction of the time spent upon the classics and the introduction of such subjects as geography, history, mathematics, and modern languages. Four years later he wrote to the *Caledonian Mercury* a letter proposing that oral examinations should be held in each of the classes in the university, instead of restricting the teaching to the delivery of lectures by the professors and the writing of papers by the students. These innovations, though at first strenuously opposed, were in course of time adopted in both institutions with beneficial results. He died in 1838.

David Boswell Reid, too, was educated at Edinburgh University, obtained his medical diploma on 12 July 1830, and was admitted a fellow of the Royal College of Physicians, Edinburgh, on 2 August 1831. Chemistry was his favourite study, and in 1833 he set up a laboratory in Edinburgh and instituted classes for instruction in practical and theoretical chemistry. These were so successful that he was soon afterwards appointed assistant to Dr Thomas Charles Hope, professor of chemistry at the university. He wrote textbooks and continued to conduct his private chemistry classes until he moved to London in 1847. The ventilation of public buildings was a subject in which he was greatly interested and in 1844 he published *Illustrations of the Theory and Practice of Ventilation*. The book attracted considerable interest among architects and engineers and his system was adopted by Sir Charles Barry in the new houses of parliament, then under construction. Reid was engaged for five years at Westminster upon this work. His method was also applied more fully to St George's Hall, Liverpool—the only building, according to his own statement, in which his system of ventilation was completely carried out.

Reid went in 1855 to the USA where he was professor of physiology and hygiene at the Museum of Practical Science of the University of Wisconsin. In 1856 he became government medical inspector to the national sanitary commission. On the outbreak of the civil war he was appointed inspector of the new military hospitals erected throughout the United States. Reid was about to leave Washington on a tour of inspection when he was seized with a fatal illness, and he died at Washington on 5 April 1863. A. H. MILLAR, *rev.* RALPH HARRINGTON

Sources M. F. Conolly, *Biographical dictionary of eminent men of Fife* (1866) · *Proceedings of the Royal Society of Edinburgh*, 5 (1862–6), 133–6 · *Who was who in America: historical volume, 1607–1896* (1963), 437 · *ILN* (20 March 1852), 237–8 · 'Dr Reid's plan for lighting the new House of Commons', *ILN* (20 March 1852), 229 · Allibone, *Dict.* **Archives** U. Edin., New Coll. L., letters to Thomas Chalmers **Likenesses** wood-engraving (after daguerreotype by Beard), NPG; repro. in *ILN* (20 March 1852)

Reid, **Sir Edward James** [Ned], **second baronet** (1901–1972), merchant banker, was born on 20 April 1901, of Scottish descent, at 28 St James's Place, London, the eldest son of Sir James Reid, first baronet (*d*. 1923), physician to Queen Victoria and later monarchs, and his wife, Susan, formerly maid of honour to Queen Victoria and daughter of the merchant banker Edward Baring, first Baron Revelstoke. Baptized in the Chapel Royal, St James's Palace, on 7 May 1901, Reid's early life was spent in court circles; Edward VII suggested himself as Reid's godfather, and he was a page to George V. He won a scholarship to Eton College and was awarded a first-class degree in classics at King's College, Cambridge, where, three years running (1920–22), he was a Browne medallist for his renderings of epigrams in Greek. He succeeded his father as second baronet in 1923.

A year earlier, Reid had joined Baring Brothers, the London merchant bank then led by his uncle, the second Baron Revelstoke, who in 1924 sent him to learn about cotton trade finance in Barings's Liverpool office. Shortly afterwards he worked with the firm of Kidder Peabody in New York and Boston.

Reid's mastery of languages caused his uncle in 1925 to dispatch him to Barings's Hamburg correspondents, Berenberg Gossler, to watch over the rapidly expanding business they did on joint account with Barings. As a director in London from 1926, he expertly led Barings's banking activities. With rapidly increasing competition, he proved to be an adroit merchant banker, especially in the mid-1920s, when he organized what he reckoned to be 'the greatest coup in cotton financing that Barings Liverpool ever brought off' (Barings archives, DEP 22.xxiii, fol. 29). In December 1928 he was admitted to the partnership, which effectively controlled Baring Brothers. He married on 18 January 1930 Tatiana (*d*. 1992), daughter of Colonel Alexander Fenoult, formerly of the imperial Russian guard, and they had a son and daughter. When Reid retired from Baring Brothers in 1966, in terms of the number of years' service, he was senior partner. He emerged as a distinguished banking technician and for twenty years served as chairman of the Accepting Houses Committee (1946–66), and was president of the Institute of Bankers (1962–4).

The soundness of Reid's German contacts was proved when Baron von Berenberg Gossler gave him early warning of impending difficulties leading Barings to scale down its German business before Germany's economic collapse in 1931. Barings, therefore, escaped the damage inflicted upon its competitors and, with limited conflict of interest, Reid was well positioned to take a major role in the ensuing negotiations concerning German foreign indebtedness. They dominated much of his life for the next thirty years.

While he was much concerned with the negotiation of the German 'standstill agreements', following the suspension of payments on short-term credits by German and other central European countries, Reid's role was subsidiary to that of others, especially Frank Tiarks of Schroders. It was more prominent when Germany defaulted on part of its long-term foreign debt in 1933, when Reid dealt with the Konversionskasse für Deutsche Auslandsschulden on behalf of the London issuing houses of German securities (1933–9). In 1934 it fell to him to put into effect the mechanics of the Anglo-German payments agreement whereby British creditors received Konversionskasse funding bonds.

From 1948 until 1962 Reid was chairman of the British bankers' committee for German affairs, in which role he petitioned the British government for full recognition of the banks' claims. He also served on the distribution committee formed under the Distribution of German Enemy Property Act, and played a key role representing the banks' claims against those of a wide range of creditors, especially holders of United States government bonds, at the 1952 international conference on Germany's pre-war debts. For his City work he was made a KBE in 1967. His close German connections made him especially useful to British intelligence pre-war, and from 1940 to 1945 he was a civil assistant attached to the general staff.

Reid's interests outside banking were closely connected with Scotland. He was especially associated with the Royal Caledonian Schools, which 'took up most of my spare time' (*Scotland*, August 1962). These schools cared for children whose parents could no longer look after them. He was a Church of Scotland elder, a governor of Guy's Hospital (1938–48), and treasurer of London's Infants' Hospital (1938–46). Honorary president of the Clan Donnachaidh Society, Reid was also a member of the council of the Scottish Craft Centre (1966–71).

On retirement Reid returned to his much-loved Scotland about 1969, living in Edinburgh and at Ellon Castle, Aberdeenshire. He died of a 'Stokes Adam attack' at his home, 16 Buckingham Terrace, Edinburgh, on 24 February 1972. His funeral was held at Dean parish church, Edinburgh, followed by cremation. He was survived by his wife.   JOHN ORBELL

Sources M. Reid, *Ask Sir James* (1987) · J. Orbell, *Baring Brothers & Co. Limited: a history to 1939* (privately printed, London, 1985) · R. S. Sayers, *The Bank of England, 1891–1944*, 3 vols. (1976) · ING Barings, London, Barings archives · 'Man of the month', *Scotland* (Aug 1962) · *WWW* · b. cert. · d. cert. · *The Times* (20 Jan 1930) · *The Times* (25 Feb 1972) · *Daily Mail* (20 Jan 1930)
Archives ING Barings, London, Barings archives | GL, accepting houses committee

Reid [*née* Wynne Edwards], **Eleanor Mary** (1860–1953), palaeobotanist, was born on 13 November 1860 in Denbigh, the daughter of John Copner Wynne Edwards, solicitor, and Maria Gitern. After attending Howells School, Denbigh, she enrolled at Westfield College, London University, in 1886. She took a BSc (third-class honours, experimental physics) in 1891 and then taught science and mathematics for four years at Cheltenham Ladies' College.

On 21 April 1897 Wynne Edwards married Clement Reid (1852/3–1916), botanist and geologist with the Geological Survey and a pioneer in the study of fossil seeds and fruits. Almost immediately she began to collaborate in his research. Working backwards from Pleistocene assemblages, the Reids proved conclusively, in the face of some scepticism from the botanical world, that ancient floras could be reliably reconstructed from sources rich in fossil fruiting organs alone. Their thoroughness and persistence set new standards, Clement Reid's *Origin of the British Flora* (1899) reporting record numbers of specimens in some deposits. Between 1907, when their first joint paper appeared, and 1915, they published about a dozen articles; several were of major importance, including their extensive monograph on Pliocene floras of the Dutch–Prussian border (1915).

In 1913 Eleanor and Clement Reid moved to Milford-on-Sea, Hampshire, from where, after her husband died in 1916, Eleanor Reid continued palaeobotanical research. Publication of her analytical review of Pliocene floras (1920) brought her wide recognition. Her home became a centre for palaeobotanical work, housing an ever growing specimen collection, and she was frequently visited by leading botanists and geologists, British and European. Recipient of the Geological Society's Murchison fund in 1919, she was elected a fellow of the society in 1920. That year she was joined by Marjorie Chandler [*see below*], a young palaeobotanist from Newnham College, Cambridge, and the partnership they formed, one of the most remarkable in the annals of palaeobotany, resulted in the production of two monumental treatises on Cenozoic plants.

Bembridge Flora, volume 1 of their *Catalogue of Cainozoic Plants*, appeared in 1926. Based on collections in the British Museum (Natural History), it greatly increased knowledge of the Oligocene flora of the Isle of Wight. Reid and Chandler then studied the museum's extensive collection of fossil seeds and fruits from the Eocene London clay, an undertaking which, expanded to include analysis of their own collections, required seven years of intensive work. The resulting *London Clay Flora* (1933) became a classic of palaeobotany, one of the most important accounts of any Tertiary flora ever published. Both monographs included lengthy introductions in which Reid presented a lucid account of the floral and climatic succession throughout the Tertiary period. The sequence demonstrated was one of gradual change from northern European flora back in time through temperate subtropical to the tropical rainforest of the Eocene London clay. Further, the detailed morphological and anatomical examinations of fossil seeds and fruits that the work involved threw considerable light on evolutionary changes within genera and families. An outstanding contribution towards making knowledge of the Tertiary floras of southern Britain the most complete for any region at the time, the study was recognized with the 1936 award to Eleanor Reid of the Geological Society's Lyell medal.

Reid lived frugally, almost austerely. She worked with primitive, home-made equipment (which probably stimulated her notable development of new techniques); her attic library was said to be 'icy in winter and scorching in summer'. After publication of her second monograph she undertook no more major commitments. She continued

to bring out short papers, however, and followed closely the continuing work on Tertiary floras of Marjorie Chandler, who remained with her as companion and ultimately nurse.

Able, original, persevering and also critical, Reid had uncompromisingly high standards but was unfailingly dependable in helping colleagues. She served on local school, church, and women's committees, getting about until the age of eighty-eight by bicycle. Reading, especially travel books, was her relaxation. She died of cerebral thrombosis on 28 September 1953 at Wedgewood Nursing Home, Milford-on-Sea, and was buried on 2 October.

Marjorie Elizabeth Jane Chandler (1897–1983), palaeobotanist, was born on 18 May 1897 in Leamington Spa, Warwickshire, the oldest of six children of Frederick Augustus Chandler, jeweller, and his wife, Alice Sarah Roberts. She attended a dame-school in Leamington Spa and then, from Leamington high school, she went by scholarship to Newnham College, Cambridge, in 1915, qualifying first class in part one of the natural sciences tripos in 1919. (She received her MA in 1948.)

From 1933, supported mainly by small annual grants from the British Museum (Natural History), she extended the classic Reid–Chandler investigations to other horizons of the Eocene and Oligocene. Her results, which brought her international recognition, are recorded in some twenty papers and in an impressive series of monographs, *The Lower Tertiary Floras of Southern England* (1961–4). These include a 354-page supplement to the *London Clay Flora*, studies of the pipe-clay series of Dorset and the Bournemouth beds, and a general survey. After retiring she occupied herself with gardening and church work, although her contacts with palaeobotanists continued. She died in Swindon, Wiltshire, on 1 October 1983, and was buried on 6 October at Kempsford, Gloucester.

MARY R. S. CREESE

Sources *Proceedings of the Geological Society* (1954), cxl–cxlii · *Nature*, 173 (1954), 190 · *The Times* (1 Oct 1953) · *The Times* (9 Oct 1953) · H. N. Andrews, *The fossil hunters: in search of ancient plants* (1980), 373–81 · Westfield College register of students, Queen Mary College, London, vol. 1 (1882–98), 36 · *University of London, general register*, pt 3 · *Quarterly Journal of the Geological Society*, 75 (1919), xlix [award of Murchison fund] · *Quarterly Journal of the Geological Society of London*, 92 (1936), liv–lv [award of Lyell medal] · The Cheltenham Ladies' College archives, Cheltenham, Gloucestershire · Desmond, *Botanists* [Clement Reid] · [A. B. White and others], eds., *Newnham College register, 1871–1971*, 2nd edn, 1 (1979), 262 [Marjorie Elizabeth Jane Chandler] · K. I. M. Chesters, 'Marjorie E. J. Chandler', *Tertiary Research*, 9 (1988), 1–6 [Marjorie Elizabeth Jane Chandler] · K. I. M. Chesters, *International Organisation of Palaeobotany Newsletter*, 22 (1983), 5–6 [Marjorie Elizabeth Jane Chandler] · *The Times* (5 Oct 1983), 30 [Marjorie Elizabeth Jane Chandler] · b. cert. · d. cert.

Archives BM, collection of modern seeds and fruits

Likenesses M. Chandler?, photograph, 1921 (Marjorie Elizabeth Jane Chandler), repro. in Andrews, *Fossil hunters*, 375 · H. N. Andrews, photograph, 1973 (Marjorie Elizabeth Jane Chandler), repro. in Andrews, *The fossil hunters*, 378

Reid [*née* Sturch], **Elisabeth Jesser** (1789–1866), slavery abolitionist and founder of Bedford College, London, was

women had been Mrs Reid's dream from childhood, and
in 1849 she put up the money to found Bedford College,
London, hoping for hundreds of applications but in fact
receiving at first only a few dozen, including those of her
own friends. The college was founded as a radical, even
visionary institution, being intended to widen women's
culture and thus their whole lives, rather than merely provide vocational training for future governesses. Unlike its
contemporary, Queen's College, Bedford later became
part of the University of London, and among its first outstanding students were Barbara Bodichon and George
Eliot.

One of the college's most innovatory features was the
composition of its governing body, which, at Mrs Reid's
insistence, included three Lady Visitors—the first time
that any British institution had women sharing officially
in its direction. Mrs Reid's religion was the love of humanity and she found it hard that the first women's college
should win so very little understanding or support at its
outset, especially from men. Even her lifelong friend,
Henry Crabb Robinson, thought she carried 'radicalism to
a romantic excess' and had 'bigoted opinions about
female education', but Julia Smith said of her: 'Her failures are better than other people's successes' (Smith to
Robinson, 20 June 1844; Tuke, 17). She played a vital, pioneering role in opening higher education to British women.
She died on 30 March 1866 at her home, 21 York Terrace,
Regent's Park, London. She had no children.

SYBIL OLDFIELD, rev.

Elisabeth Jesser Reid (1789–1866), by unknown photographer

born on 25 December 1789 in London, the second of two
daughters of William *Sturch (1753–1838), a wealthy Unitarian ironmonger, and his wife, Elisabeth (1759/60–1841).
In 1821 Elisabeth the daughter married John *Reid (1776–
1822), physician, from a nonconformist family in Leicester; he died thirteen months later, on 2 July 1822. Mrs Reid
used her independent income to practise warm-hearted
benevolence and was soon well known for her ardent
altruism, supporting, for example, a scheme of Harriet
Martineau to enable poor people in the Lake District to
buy their own houses. She befriended many American
abolitionists, including, during the General Anti-Slavery
Convention in London in 1840, American women delegates, such as Lucretia Mott, who were denied the floor of
the convention. In 1853 Mrs Reid gave hospitality to Harriet Beecher Stowe, who had come to England to speak
about slavery at private gatherings of women, and in 1860
she shared her home with Sarah Redmond, the first black
woman to undertake a public lecture tour in Britain on
the slavery question, who later studied at Bedford College.

Elisabeth Reid, together with her friends Anna Jameson,
Julia Smith (aunt of Florence Nightingale and Barbara
Leigh Smith Bodichon), and Harriet Martineau, form 'the
missing link' in the history of the self-emancipation of
Englishwomen between Mary Wollstonecraft and the
Langham Place circle of the late 1850s. A college for

Sources Diary, reminiscences, and correspondence of Henry Crabb
Robinson, ed. T. Sadler, 3 vols. (1869) • E. J. Morley, The life and times of
Henry Crabb Robinson (1935) • M. J. Tuke, A history of Bedford College for
Women, 1849–1937 (1939) • L. Billington and R. Billington, 'A burning
zeal for righteousness: women in the British anti-slavery move-
ment, 1820–1860', Equal or different: women's politics, 1800–1914, ed.
J. Rendall (1987), 82–111
Archives Royal Holloway College, Egham, Surrey, personal and
family corresp.
Likenesses photograph, repro. in Tuke, History of Bedford College,
frontispiece [see illus.] • photographs, Royal Holloway College,
Egham, Surrey, Bedford New College archives; repro. in L. Bentley,
Educating women: a pictorial history of Bedford College, University of Lon-
don, 1849–1985 (1991), facing pp. 4 and 9
Wealth at death under £25,000: probate, 14 May 1866, CGPLA
Eng. & Wales

Reid, Forrest (1875–1947), novelist and literary scholar,
born at 20 Mount Charles, Belfast, on 24 June 1875, was the
sixth and youngest son of Robert Reid (1825–1881), manager of a felt works, who came from a well-established
upper-middle-class Ulster family, and his second wife,
Frances Matilda Parr (d. 1901), a collateral descendant of
the sixth wife of Henry VIII. He was educated at the Royal
Belfast Academical Institution. After some years as
apprentice in the tea trade, he went to Christ's College,
Cambridge, at the age of thirty and took his degree in 1908
with a second class in the medieval and modern languages
tripos. He then settled down to write in Belfast, which,
apart from periods of travel, remained his home for the
rest of his life.

Reid wrote sixteen novels, two volumes of autobiography, two collections of short stories, critical studies of W. B. Yeats and Walter de la Mare, and a definitive work on the book illustrators of the 1860s and numerous essays and book reviews. The novels fall into two fairly distinct groups. The first includes the books written before the publication of his first volume of autobiography, *Apostate*, in 1926. These include his first published book, *The Kingdom of Twilight* (1904), *The Garden God* (1905), *The Bracknels* (1911), *Following Darkness* (1912), *The Gentle Lover* (1913), *At the Door of the Gate* (1915), *The Spring Song* (1916), *Pirates of the Spring* (1919), and *Pender among the Residents* (1922). Of most of these Reid himself had a low opinion, considering them 'false starts'. *Following Darkness* and *Pirates of the Spring*, however, stand easily with his later and most accomplished writing. The second group of novels, in which he found his subject, that of youth and its adult recall, includes *Demophon* (1927), *Uncle Stephen* (1931), *Brian Westby* (1934), *The Retreat* (1936), *Peter Waring* (1937), and *Young Tom* (1944).

Boyhood and adolescence seen through the understanding eyes of an older man supply the subject of most of Reid's work. It is, however, an exaggeration to claim, as some critics have done, that he could not create a believable character over the age of twelve, but there is a definite sense of a 'King Charles's head' in much of his fiction—his adult characters are invariably less rounded than his juvenile ones. In book after book humorous, gentle, intelligent boys wander on seashores, in woods, along rivers, in the gardens of houses. There is a whole gallery of them—Peter Waring, Denis Bracknel, Brian Westby, Grif Weston, Beach Traill, and his most successful creation, Tom Barber—who would not take happily to life in an industrial city; who all have a sensitive leaning towards the dumb natural life of a landscape, to the extent at times of an adoration of certain phenomena, such as the moon. Graham Greene's observation that obsession lies at the heart of many modern writers applies particularly well to Reid's output, and a fruitful lead was provided by an anonymous reviewer who suggested that 'E. M. Forster's heroes are the sort of men Forrest Reid's boys might have grown into, if Forrest Reid had allowed them to grow up.'

Reid's reputation has perhaps understandably suffered from these apparent obsessions. It is possible to regard him as an 'escapist' novelist. This is the view that his abiding concern with childhood, with youth, and with the loss of innocence, often observed in an unreal quasi-paradisal setting, are the trivial concerns of a hence justifiably minor writer. However, the Elysian landscapes which he evokes again and again in his books are essentially the landscape with which he was most familiar—the Ulster landscape. His landscapes are not alternative imaginative topographies but are based upon firm Ulster realities, and he wrote about the links between personality and landscape in a lucid rhythmic prose.

Reid was unmarried. He led a retired and outwardly lonely life but had many varied interests. He was an expert croquet player, a lover of animals and the country, an opera enthusiast, a discriminating collector, a wide reader, and a stimulating and clear-minded conversationalist. He was close with many writers of his own generation, and was generous with help and advice to young authors.

Reid was one of the founder members of the Irish Academy of Letters and received the honorary degree of DLitt at the Queen's University of Belfast in 1933. He was awarded the James Tait Black memorial prize for his last novel, *Young Tom*. Reid died at 15 Seaview, Warrenpoint, co. Down, on 4 January 1947 and was buried on 7 January in Dundonald cemetery, Knock, Belfast.

JOHN BRYSON, rev. BRIAN TAYLOR

Sources *The Times* (7 Jan 1947) · *Northern Whig and Belfast Post* (7 Jan 1947) · *Belfast News-Letter* (7 Jan 1947) · Burke, *Gen. Ire.* (1912) · R. Burlingham, *Forrest Reid: a portrait and a study* (1953) · B. Taylor, *The green avenue: the life and writings of Forrest Reid, 1875–1947* (1980) · private information (1959, 2004) · F. Reid, *Apostate* (1926)
Archives Belfast Central Library, corresp. and literary MSS · NA Ire., corresp. · New University of Ulster, Coleraine, Northern Ireland · NL Scot., letters · Ransom HRC, corresp. and literary MSS
Likenesses J. A. Greeves, oils, Royal Academical Institution, Belfast · J. S. Sleator, oils, Ulster Museum, Belfast
Wealth at death £3537 7s.: probate, 25 April 1947, *CGPLA NIre.*

Reid, Sir George Houstoun

Reid, Sir George Houstoun (1845–1918), prime minister of Australia, was born at the manse, Johnstone, near Paisley, Renfrew, on 25 February 1845, the fifth of the seven children of John Reid (1800–1867), a Presbyterian minister, and his wife, Marion, *née* Crybbace (1809?–1885). In 1852 the family emigrated to Victoria. Reid attended the Melbourne Academy until 1858, when he moved with his parents to Sydney. After some time in a merchant's office he became a clerk in the public service, and by the age of twenty held a responsible position in the treasury. By 1879, when he was admitted to the bar, he was permanent head of the attorney-general's department. He had also published several works on intercolonial problems, on the colony's resources, and fiscal policy, of which the most significant was *An Essay on New South Wales, the Mother Colony of the Australias* (1876). In 1880 he was elected to the New South Wales legislative assembly, and in 1883 he became minister of public instruction. Unseated on a technicality in 1884, he was again returned the following year, to represent the same area in colonial and federal politics for a generation.

Between 1885 and 1891 Reid was often irregular in his attendance, devoting his time to building up a lucrative legal practice and enjoying an active social life: he thrice declined office under Sir Henry Parkes. When Parkes made a dramatic gesture towards federating the Australian colonies, Reid, suspecting that it would involve a threat to the free-trade policy of New South Wales, was the principal advocate of caution. After a draft constitution was drawn up in 1891 he strongly criticized its illiberal elements, and the movement temporarily petered out. This marked a turning point in his life. He became more active politically, and on 5 November 1891, to the surprise of his bachelor friends, he married Flora Ann, the daughter of John and Suzannah Brumby of Longford, Tasmania, who was twenty-four years his junior. They had two sons and a daughter.

The government fell shortly afterwards, and when Parkes resigned his leadership of the Free Trade Party, Reid, rather unexpectedly, succeeded him. His effective criticism of the new government's protectionism, and his success in putting forward an alternative policy based on direct taxation, won him a resounding electoral victory in 1894, confirmed the following year after a crisis brought about by the upper house. As premier he reshaped the colony's finances, made significant reforms in other areas, and managed the nascent Labor Party very well. He also took up the federal question, which was, after the débâcle of 1891, being pushed by Edmund Barton. Reid convened the premiers' conference which led to the convention in 1897–8 and worked very hard as a delegate. During an adjournment he visited London for the diamond jubilee and the colonial conference. He was sworn of the privy council and entrusted with the Colonial Office's views on the draft constitution. But he was very disappointed at the outcome of the intercolonial bargaining, seeing some of the provisions of the final draft as disadvantageous to his colony, others as potentially undemocratic. He announced his personal intention of voting 'yes' in the referendum on its acceptance in 1898, but his frank criticisms led to its narrow defeat in New South Wales (the critical colony) on 3 June 1898. There followed further negotiations which resulted in substantial improvements, and its endorsement the following June; but the more enthusiastic federalists had already branded him as a fence-sitter, 'Yes–No Reid', and took part in an intrigue which cost him both the premiership of his colony and the first federal prime ministership.

Reid entered federal politics as acknowledged leader of the opposition, but under serious disadvantages. With parliament meeting in Melbourne and his practice, at which he could earn at least ten times his parliamentary stipend, centred in Sydney, he was forced to leave much work to his deputy. Remaining a convinced free-trader, he nevertheless became convinced that the fiscal issue should be compromised in the face of the rise of the Labor Party, which he condemned, rather misleadingly, as 'socialist': his real objections were those of a liberal to the Labor Party's rigid caucus system. The confused political situation produced by the existence of three almost equal parties in the second parliament made Reid prime minister in a coalition from August 1904 to July 1905, but the 'fusion' of the old Free-Trade and Protectionist parties which he advocated did not come until 1909, when he stepped aside to make co-operation between his followers and those of Alfred Deakin (a late convert to the idea) possible. His appointment as first high commissioner in London later in 1909 was in part a reward. He formally held the post from 1910.

Aided by his strong sympathy with English Liberalism, Reid made a great success of what he saw as the primary task: an indefatigable trencherman, with a wit to match his vast waistcoat, he was in constant demand as an after-dinner speaker. On these as well as more formal occasions he let no opportunity pass to emphasize the advantages his country offered to investors and potential emigrants.

He travelled widely and built up an efficient office organization to support his efforts. The outbreak of war widened his responsibilities greatly.

Disappointed when he failed to get his term extended beyond January 1916, Reid was delighted to be returned, without opposition, to the House of Commons. In the winter of 1917–18 he undertook a strenuous semi-official speaking tour of the United States in support of the war effort. He had little time to make a mark in the house, though he did help to defuse an embarrassing resolution on the government's Irish policy. He died suddenly of cerebral thrombosis at his home, 1 Melbury Road, Prince's Gardens, London, on 13 September 1918 and was buried at Putney Vale cemetery on 18 September after a service at St Columba's Church of Scotland, Pont Street. He had been appointed KCMG (1909), GCMG (1911), and GCB (1916). In 1917 his wife had been appointed DBE for her efforts on behalf of wounded servicemen.

Ludicrous obesity, a walrus moustache, thin, sandy hair, and an unruly monocle made Reid a cartoonists' delight. The caricature has often, wrongly, been confused with the man. He was in fact a clever politician, an efficient premier, and a very successful high commissioner; and no one did more to ensure that Australia's federal constitution should be both liberal and workable.   W. G. McMINN

Sources W. G. McMinn, *George Reid* (1989) · L. F. Crisp, *George Houstoun Reid: federation father, federal failure* (1979) · B. Nairn, *Civilising capitalism* (1973) · A. Fairbairn, 'The high commissioner', *Quadrant*, 21/10 (Oct 1977), 60–68 · J. A. La Nauze, *Alfred Deakin: a biography*, 2 vols. (1965) · A. W. Martin, *Henry Parkes: a biography* (1980) · G. H. Reid, *My reminiscences* (1917) · m. cert. · d. cert.
Archives Mitchell L., NSW · NL Aus. | NL Aus., Barton MSS · NL Aus., Deakin MSS · NL Aus., Symon MSS | FILM BFI NFTVA, news footage
Likenesses G. Lambert, oils, Parliament House, Canberra · London Stereoscopic Co., photograph, NPG · J. Longstaff, oils, Parliament House, Canberra · P. N., wood-engraving (after photograph by Kevry), NPG; repro. in *ILN* (15 Sept 1894) · photographs, NL Aus.
Wealth at death £8340: *Morning Post* (11 June 1919)

Reid, George William (1819–1887), museum curator, born in London on 6 July 1819, was the son of George Reid, a draughtsman and teacher of drawing who afterwards became an attendant in the print room of the British Museum. Educated as an artist, in 1842 Reid was appointed an attendant in the department of prints and drawings in the British Museum, from which he was promoted assistant in 1865. On 1 August 1866, following the death of William Hookham Carpenter, he proceeded to the keepership, which he held until he retired, on 20 December 1883.

Reid, who possessed a most exact and comprehensive knowledge of prints, made numerous lists of the holdings, particularly of those after artists of the British school. Great additions were made to the national collection during his tenure as keeper, the most important of which were the John Henderson bequest of watercolour drawings, in 1878, comprising 164 fine examples of the work of J. M. W. Turner, Thomas Girtin, David Cox, William James Müller, Canaletto, and John Robert Cozens; the Frederick Crace collection of maps, plans, and views of London (1880); the Edward Hawkins collection of British satirical prints (Hawkins was a former keeper of the department of antiquities); the Felix Slade bequest of prints; the William Anderson collection of Japanese and Chinese drawings (1882); the collection of proofs and prints of Turner's *Liber Studiorum* formed by John Pye; W. Hollar's great view of Cologne and Deutz, of 1635; and the series of six plates of the triumphs of Petrarch (Florentine, *c*.1460), all in the earliest state, which were formerly in the Sunderland Library at Blenheim Palace, Oxfordshire.

Some departmental catalogues were published under Reid's supervision, including *Catalogue of Political and Personal Satires*, by F. G. Stephens (4 vols., 1870–83); *Descriptive Catalogue of Playing and other Cards*, by W. H. Willshire (1876); and *Descriptive Catalogue of Early Prints in the British Museum: German and Flemish Schools*, also by Willshire (2 vols., 1879–83). Reid likewise selected the examples for the two parts of reproductions of *Italian Prints*, issued in 1882–3. A projected catalogue of early Italian prints by Richard Fisher, Slade's executor, was not completed. Reid was not a scholar, and as the trustees, inspired by the example of Berlin, aimed to publish catalogues of the entire collection so his position became increasingly untenable. His successor as keeper was Sidney Colvin.

Reid's chief non-official work was the *Descriptive Catalogue of the Works of George Cruikshank*, in three quarto volumes (1871). He also wrote introductions and descriptive text to *Designs for Goldsmiths, Jewellers … by Hans Holbein*, containing twenty photographs from the original drawings in the British Museum, published by the Arundel Society in 1869; *A Reproduction of the Salamanca Collection of Prints from Nielli* (1869); *Albert Dürer and Lucas Van Leyden*, a catalogue of works exhibited at the Burlington Fine Arts Club (1869); *Titian portraits: seventeen rare engravings after Titian reproduced in photography by S. Thompson* (1871); *Gems of Dutch Art* (1872); *The Works of Velásquez: a Reproduction of Seventeen Prints in the British Museum* (1872); and *Works of the Italian engravers of the fifteenth century, reproduced in facsimile by photo-intaglio* (1884), of which only the first series was ever published. He also compiled the catalogue of prints and etchings in the Revd Alexander Dyce collection at the Victoria and Albert Museum (1874) and a catalogue in manuscript of the duke of Devonshire's collection of prints and drawings at Chatsworth.

Reid died at his home, Dunkeld, Heathfield Park, Willesden, London, on 20 October 1887, following a long period of depression and ill health, leaving a son, George Robert Reid, an art dealer.

R. E. GRAVES, rev. CHRISTOPHER LLOYD

Sources A. Griffiths, ed., *Landmarks in print collecting: connoisseurs and donors at the British Museum since 1753* (British Museum Press, 1996) [exhibition catalogue, Museum of Fine Arts, Houston, TX, 1996, and elsewhere] · *CGPLA Eng. & Wales* (1887) · trustees' minutes, BM, C 6005; C 10813; C 11037–8 · *IGI*
Archives BM, department of prints and drawings, letter-books, inv. 1969.6.14.47 | BM, trustees' minutes · RGS, letters to Sir David Gill
Wealth at death £1089 5s. 4d.: will, 11 Nov 1887, CGPLA Eng. & Wales

Reid, Sir Hugh Gilzean- (1836–1911), journalist and politician, was born on 11 August 1836 at Thatchill Croft, Cruden, Aberdeenshire, the second of six children of Hugh Reid, crofter and shoemaker, and Christian Gilzean; both his parents had moved early in life to Aberdeenshire from other parts of the north of Scotland. Gilzean-Reid was partly self-educated. His hard formal schooling, firstly at a nearby Episcopalian school and then, when he could walk further, at a Free Church school, was cut short by the need to work. At the age of eight he was employed at a local farm, reportedly taking home 1½d. each week. He seems also in these years to have taught at a local school. The greatest influence on his life at this time was his mother, who, with the rest of the family, 'came out' of the Church of Scotland at the Disruption of 1843 and joined the Free Church. Gilzean-Reid's natural eloquence and constant enthusiasm is attributed to his mother, who herself addressed early Free Church meetings.

After leaving home aged sixteen Gilzean-Reid found work in an art-printing and publishing house in Aberdeen. Art was to remain his lifelong hobby and he was to build up a collection that included signed portraits of those he came to know in later life. In Aberdeen he attended classes at the university—as he was also to do later in Edinburgh—and he first expressed his intention of joining the Baptist ministry. At this time Gilzean-Reid met James Macdonell and William McCombie, the latter editor of the *Aberdeen Free Press*, both of whom played a part in getting him started on a journalistic career. In 1855 he accepted work with the *Banffshire Journal*. This involved him, to his regret, in giving up studies at Aberdeen University. Alexander Ramsay, the editor, was responsible for giving Gilzean-Reid a 'practical and systematic drilling' (Mackay, 143) which, by Gilzean-Reid's own account, was the foundation of his early success. In 1857 he became editor of the *Peterhead Sentinel*, moving in 1859 to a similar, but in this case more secure, position with the *Edinburgh Weekly News*, alongside which he unofficially edited the *Scottish Press*. During the next four years in Edinburgh, Gilzean-Reid was also involved in setting up the Edinburgh Co-operative Building Society in 1861. This grew out of his support for the stonemasons in their long dispute to win a nine-hour working day and out of his related desire to make workmen more independent by enabling them to become home owners. In 1863 Gilzean-Reid returned to Peterhead to start the first newspaper of which he was joint proprietor, the *Buchan Observer*. On 12 June 1863 he married Anne, daughter of John Craig, a saddler in Peterhead; together they had two sons and seven daughters. Anne Gilzean-Reid played a full part in her husband's career and is credited with toning down the more vigorous tendencies in his spirit and with supervising his public appearances. She helped found and became president of the Women's Liberal Association and published a pamphlet on 'Women workers in the Liberal cause'. She died in 1895 following a carriage accident.

Despite the urgings of Gilzean-Reid's friend Macdonell, by then assistant editor of the *Daily Telegraph*, that he should go to London, Gilzean-Reid appears to have made the conscious decision, when he sold his share in the *Buchan Observer*, to move into the English provincial press. His purchase in the mid-1860s of the struggling weekly *Stockton and Middlesbrough Gazette* and his conversion of it in 1869 into the country's first ½d. evening paper, the *North Eastern Daily Gazette*, was a statement of faith in the journalistic possibilities offered by a booming industrial region such as Teesside. For Gilzean-Reid this decision clearly paid dividends, not least in financial terms, as circulation rose to a reported 350,000. His involvement in local movements, especially for the promotion of education, and his identification with the town of Middlesbrough no doubt contributed to this success. Gilzean-Reid saw newspapers as a means of educating and enlightening people politically and otherwise. By 1882 his success and this philosophy led him to be briefly involved with a small syndicate around Andrew Carnegie and Samuel Storey, Liberal MP for Sunderland, which owned and ran nearly twenty daily and weekly papers. In 1883 Gilzean-Reid moved to Worley Abbey near Birmingham, where, freed from operational concerns, he became more active politically. The estate became a meeting place for leading midlanders, including Joseph Chamberlain and Richard Tangye, founder of the Birmingham engineering firm, as well as for leading National Liberals and friends from Gilzean-Reid's past, such as Professor John Stuart Blackie from Edinburgh. Described as a non-doctrinaire radical in favour of reasoned progress, Gilzean-Reid appears to have taken his cue from Chamberlain. He was proud of his achievements in turning Conservative newspapers Liberal, and he expressed the hope to Chamberlain that his activities had given service to the advanced cause.

At the 1885 general election Gilzean-Reid was elected for the Aston Manor division of Warwickshire. Having split politically with Chamberlain over Irish home rule, he lost the seat standing as a Gladstonian Liberal the following year. In 1890 Gilzean-Reid was adopted for Handsworth in Staffordshire, but he failed to win the seat at the 1892 general election. In the meantime he had been active in trying to bolster the Gladstonian presence in a Conservative and Unionist dominated press. Together with T. P. Ritzema, Gilzean-Reid set up a chain of provincial newspapers that included the *Northern Daily Telegraph*, started at Blackburn in 1886, and the *Birmingham Daily Argus*, launched in 1891. The former especially helped to revive the spirit of Gladstonianism in the north-west of England, concentrating its fire on the Conservatives in the hope that Liberal Unionists would return to the fold. In 1893 Gilzean-Reid was knighted, a mark of the prominence he had achieved not only politically, but probably more so as a newspaper proprietor. In addition to the political side of his press activities, Gilzean-Reid played a leading role in attempts to improve the status of journalism, most significantly as the driving force behind the foundation of the National Association of Journalists (from 1889 the Institute of Journalists). This body tried to establish journalism as a recognized profession through education and training, by fixing standards of entry, and by providing measures of social insurance. Gilzean-Reid was its first

president from 1888 to 1890, and in that position he saw the institute's incorporation by royal charter. In 1898–9 he was elected president of the Society of Newspaper Proprietors and Managers. Gilzean-Reid carried his ideals abroad. He took part in pioneering the International Press Congress that met in Belgium in 1894. In 1904 he presided over the first World's Press Parliament which met in St Louis in the United States and had among its aims the improvement of the position of journalists and the encouragement of practical international co-operation.

In contrast to his success as a newspaper proprietor and promoter of journalism, Gilzean-Reid was reputed to be a cautious and laborious writer. Despite this, and in addition to the contributions he undoubtedly made to the journals he at one time owned or managed, he published a fair amount; his books included several that drew upon his experiences from early life, such as *Tween the Gloamin' and the Mirk*, and a biography of his long-standing correspondent James A. Garfield, twentieth president of the United States.

Two other strands in Gilzean-Reid's life stand out; one is his commitment to the international penny post. In the early 1850s he had accompanied Elihu Burritt on his visit to Scotland to promote this in conjunction with Burritt's movement for international peace and arbitration. Gilzean-Reid was at the fore in supporting a motion early in 1886, during his short parliamentary career, for the establishment of such a scheme. The other strand is his attachment to Belgium, and in particular his involvement with colonial and missionary agencies active in the Congo. After his wife's death in 1895 Gilzean-Reid gave up Worley Abbey and spent long periods in Belgium, though he kept a London residence at Dollis Hill and then, from 1906, at Tenterden Hall, Hendon, in Middlesex; the death of his third son, Hugh, in the Second South African War appears to have increased the solace he sought in foreign travel in his later years. For his services to Belgium Gilzean-Reid was made an officer of the order of Leopold in 1897 and a knight-commander of the order of the Crown in 1899.

With honours in general he appears to have been selective. He was made an LLD by the University of Aberdeen in 1897, some compensation for the broken studies of his earlier years, and he accepted the same honour from Columbia State University during his 1904 visit to the United States. His enthusiastic support for R. B. Haldane's reorganization of the volunteers into the Territorial Army, compatible with his Liberal belief in the voluntary principle, led him to accept the vice-chairmanship of the Middlesex County Association. He was also a JP for Warwickshire and Middlesex and deputy lieutenant for Yorkshire. But he apparently refused to become a privy councillor in 1890 or to accept a baronetcy two years later.

As a result of a car accident in 1909 Gilzean-Reid suffered severe shock, and subsequently heart weakness and long periods of illness. He died on 5 November 1911 at Tenterden Hall and was buried at the old cemetery, Middlesbrough, co. Durham, on 8 November. At the time Gilzean-Reid was seen as an example of how it was possible to rise to distinction without the benefits of social rank and fortune, a 'lad o' pairts'. Historically his significance lies in the work he did on the borderline between the press and politics, in particular in the period immediately before the Liberal split of 1886 and in his helping to rebuild the influence of the Gladstonian Liberal Party in its aftermath. In addition his role in trying to improve conditions for groups such as the Edinburgh stonemasons and later, on a wider stage, journalists, were notable achievements.

GORDON F. MILLAR

Sources A. Mackay, *Distinguished sons of Cruden* (1922), 134–86 · *North-Eastern Daily Gazette* (6 Nov 1911) · *The Times* (6 Nov 1911) · *The Times* (9 Nov 1911) · *The Scotsman* (6 Nov 1911) · *WWW, 1897–1915* · *WWBMP*, 2.299–300 · S. E. Koss, *The rise and fall of the political press in Britain*, 1, 1 (1981), 270–71, 290–92, 328
Archives U. Birm., corresp. with Joseph Chamberlain
Likenesses H. Hurst, oils, in or before 1909, U. Aberdeen
Wealth at death £31,551 10s. 7d.: resworn probate, 25 March 1912, *CGPLA Eng. & Wales*

Reid, Hugo (1809–1872), headmaster and educational writer, was born at Edinburgh on 21 June 1809, the third son of Peter Reid (1777–1838), medical writer and educational reformer, and his wife, Christian, eldest daughter of Hugo Arnot, historian of Edinburgh. David Boswell *Reid (1805–1863), chemist and inventor of a system of ventilation, was his elder brother. Reid was a good classical scholar, an able chemist and mechanic, and a writer of popular textbooks on a wide variety of subjects. He was for some years president of the Hunterian Society of Edinburgh, and afterwards lecturer on chemistry and natural philosophy at Liverpool high school, and principal of People's College, Nottingham. He married, on 7 January 1839, Marion, eldest daughter of James Kirkland, a Glasgow merchant. She was the author of *A Plea for Women* (1843), in which she sought to counter the principal disadvantages under which women in Britain then laboured: want of equal rights, enforcement of unjust laws, and lack of access to 'a good substantial education' (p. 48). While presenting a forceful argument against several recent antifeminist tracts, she none the less felt obliged to write under the name of Mrs Hugo Reid.

In 1855 Reid was one of several non-clergyman teachers recruited for Dalhousie College, Nova Scotia. He was appointed headmaster at an annual salary of £300, and commenced teaching in January 1856. Later that year, when Dalhousie briefly resumed university courses, Reid was also professor of logic, grammar, and English, but this higher level teaching ceased after a few months, and Reid reverted to his status as principal of the college until the number of scholars declined. He was a founding member and secretary of the Nova Scotia Literary and Scientific Society and a frequent contributor to its *Transactions*. In 1858 he lectured to the Halifax Mechanics' Institute, and he also prepared a map of Nova Scotia. He left Halifax at the end of 1859, visiting relatives in the United States before returning to Britain.

A prolific textbook author, Reid's 'Catechism' series: *Catechism of Chemistry* (1837), *Catechism of Heat* (1839), *Catechism of Astronomy* (1841); his 'Chemistry' series: *Chemistry of Nature* (1837), *Chemistry of Science and Art*, and *Chemistry of Botany* (1840), and others on aspects of physical geography, chemistry, botany, mathematics, and the steam engine, were published before he left Scotland. Many of these went through later editions while he was in Nova Scotia, during which time he wrote *Elements of Geography Adapted for Use in British America* (1856) and *Remarks on University Education in Nova Scotia*. Among his subsequent publications was *The Art of Conversation* (1862), under the *nom de plume* of Roger Boswell, and several works on social and political aspects of North America. The opening words of one of Reid's essays, 'After a long sojourn in that dullest of all dull places, Halifax, Nova Scotia' (Reid, 9) belie his subsequent comments on Canadian society, which he found admirable in many respects. He died at 7A Wyndham Place, Marylebone, London, on 13 June 1872.

ANITA MCCONNELL

Sources D. C. Harvey, *An introduction to Dalhousie University* (1938) · Mrs Hugo Reid [Marion Reid], *A plea for women* (1843) · H. Reid, *Sketches in north America* (1861) · *DCB*, vol. 10 · *Edinburgh Courant* (20 June 1872) · m. cert. · d. cert.

Reid, James Scott Cumberland, Baron Reid (1890–1975), judge, was born on 30 July 1890 at Drem, East Lothian, the eldest of the three children (all boys) of James Reid (1855–1912), writer to the signet, of Drem House, who also farmed in East Lothian, and his wife, Kate, daughter of William Scott, merchant, of Calcutta. From the Edinburgh Academy, Reid went as a scholar to Jesus College, Cambridge, where he graduated BA, LLB, with first-class honours in part one of both the natural sciences (1910) and law (1911) triposes. His legal studies, which he found arid and remote from the living law practised in London, were his only direct contact with English law until he was appointed lord of appeal. After Cambridge he attended Scots law classes at Edinburgh University, to qualify himself for admission to the Faculty of Advocates. Having by then joined the 8th battalion of the Royal Scots, in November 1914 he was the first advocate to be admitted to the faculty wearing uniform. He transferred to the machine-gun corps, and had an active war in several theatres. Demobilized with the rank of major, he began practice in Parliament House in 1919.

At the outset progress was slow, and Reid found time for legal writing, including a book on the Agricultural Holdings (Scotland) Act of 1923 which established his reputation as an authority on agricultural law. In time he came to be recognized as an exceptionally competent counsel in handling complex cases which gave scope for his quick analytical mind—his arguments in court being presented in a somewhat didactic manner. His practice was distinguished rather than extensive. Partly because of commitment to politics and partly because of prolonged service as law officer, Reid never became a great forensic figure in Scotland. Nevertheless in 1932, the year after his election to parliament, he took silk. In 1933 he married Esther May (d. 1980), widow of Gerald Frank Brierley and daughter of Charles Banks Nelson, advocate, solicitor, and attorney at the Manx bar. They had no children.

A shy man, tall and lean, Reid seemed a somewhat aloof

and Olympian figure in Parliament House. However, as dean of the Faculty of Advocates from 1945 to 1948 he did all he could to be helpful, friendly, and hospitable at the difficult time he held office, but his commitments in London prevented him from giving the guidance and support normally expected of the elected leader of the Scottish bar. Reid's professional career illustrates in striking fashion that eminence at the Scottish bar and a political career cannot be satisfactorily combined.

Long active in Conservative politics, in 1931 Reid was elected member for Stirling and Falkirk burghs, and soon became recognized as a formidable debater and able politician. He lost his seat narrowly in 1935, but in 1937 he was elected for the Hillhead division of Glasgow, which he represented until appointed lord of appeal. In 1936 he became solicitor-general for Scotland and in 1941 lord advocate, holding office until the Labour Party formed a government in 1945. Thereafter he assumed a prominent role in opposition, subjecting to penetrating and devastating criticism much proposed government legislation. He was viewed by certain Labour politicians with hostility, but C. R. Attlee's offer to Reid of a vacancy as lord of appeal was probably prompted more by appreciation of his potential contribution than to remove a powerful critic from the Commons. In fact Reid did not accept until he had consulted the Conservative hierarchy regarding his political prospects and received no adequate encouragement. Appointed lord of appeal and a life peer in 1948, he held office for twenty-six years—a longer period than any before him—and retired in January 1975 at the age of eighty-four with his judicial faculties unimpaired. From 1962 he had been the senior member of the judicial committee, presiding in the absence of the lord chancellor, and responsible for the management of its business. This was an astonishing achievement, since in 1958 he had been operated on for cancer of the stomach and a colostomy had been performed.

Scots lawyers acquiesce unenthusiastically in the curious constitutional fiction which imputes to English lords of appeal on appointment judicial knowledge of Scots law. What was unique about Reid's contribution in the Lords was that, though a Scots lawyer exclusively by professional training, he was accepted by his English colleagues and by the whole legal profession in England as the 'helmsman of the [English] common law'. Since his conception of the judicial function accorded with the older Scottish tradition, his exercise of it in Scottish appeals, though widely respected, was not considered remarkable. Not having been formed in both Scots and English law, he assumed somewhat readily their identity on certain matters where there were latent distinctions. When Reid spoke in House of Lords debates, on matters of Scots law he was accepted as an infallible oracle.

However, the great majority of appeals on which Reid sat—well over 500—concerned English law. In most he wrote a full speech, seldom dissenting since his views usually persuaded his brethren. Presiding in the Lords after Reid's death, Lord Wilberforce observed that the qualities which made him so outstanding a judge were accuracy of thought and precision of reasoning, broad common sense, generous humanity, simple and elegant use of language: '[He] has guided us with the influence of an equal in status, of a superior in wisdom, common sense, and where appropriate imagination.' Reid's 'inside feeling' for English law he attributed to his long and close association with Gray's Inn, of which he was made an honorary bencher (1948). He prescribed criteria for applying creatively but cautiously the practice statement of July 1966 regarding House of Lords precedents, and considered that judges as lawmakers should apply common sense, principle rather than narrow precedent, and regard for an evolving public policy. Some reforms were for parliament alone. His conduct of appeals, probing arguments closely to test principle, was a major contribution. If he kept the law moving in the right direction at the right speed, he was content to influence the present rather than pre-empt the future. His friends were few but close, his refreshment gardening, and, especially in his later years, he was very agreeable and encouraging company to his juniors. Among other contributions, Reid was chairman of the Malaya constitutional commission (1956–7) and of the committee on registration of title to land in Scotland.

Reid was sworn of the privy council in 1941 and appointed CH in 1967. He held honorary degrees from the universities of Edinburgh (LLD, 1945) and Oxford (DCL, 1971). He was elected FRSE, and an honorary fellow of Jesus College, Cambridge (1948). He died on 29 March 1975 in London.

T. B. SMITH, *rev.*

Sources L. Blom-Cooper and G. Drewry, *Final appeal* (1972) · A. Paterson, *The law lords* (1982) · R. Stevens, *Law and politics: the House of Lords as a judicial body, 1800–1976* (1979) · *The Times* (31 March 1975) · *The Times* (3 April 1975) · *The Times* (5 April 1975) · *The Times* (6 April 1975) · *The Times* (17 June 1975) · *WWW* · *The Society of Writers to His Majesty's Signet with a list of the members* (1936) · CGPLA Eng. & Wales (1975)
Archives HLRO, notebooks as a lord of appeal
Likenesses W. Bird, photograph, 1959, NPG · J. Pannett, coloured chalk drawing, 1968, Scot. NPG
Wealth at death £75,813: probate, 30 May 1975, CGPLA Eng. & Wales

Reid, James Seaton (1798–1851), ecclesiastical historian, was born in Lurgan, co. Armagh, on 19 December 1798. He was the eleventh son and the last but one of seventeen children of Forest Reid (1751–1801), master of a grammar school there, and Mary Weir, his wife. Left fatherless at an early age, James spent much of his youth at Ramelton, co. Donegal, under the care of his brother Edward, Presbyterian minister there. After attending a grammar school at Ramelton, at the age of fifteen he entered the University of Glasgow, where he graduated MA in 1816, and afterwards attended the Divinity Hall. He was licensed to preach by the presbytery of Letterkenny in 1818, and in the following year was ordained, and inducted to the Presbyterian church of Donegore, co. Antrim. Four years later he was translated to the Presbyterian church at Carrickfergus. From this time, while active in pastoral duties, he began preparation for a history of the Irish Presbyterian church. This was a task of much difficulty, as there was no existing history of Presbyterianism in Ireland, and many secondary sources proved unreliable. He had to collect his materials from the records of church courts and other manuscripts within his reach, and he made frequent visits to public libraries in Dublin, London, and Edinburgh to pursue his researches. In February 1826 Reid married Elizabeth, daughter of Samuel Arrott, a Belfast surgeon; they had eleven children, of whom nine survived him.

In 1827, aged twenty-nine, Reid was unanimously elected moderator of the synod of Ulster. It was a time of bitter controversy, and, though himself a staunch upholder of the catholic doctrine of the Trinity, Reid had won by his learning and moderation the respect of the Arian party, which was then on the eve of secession. During his term of office he preached before the synod a sermon on the controversy, which he published as *The History of the Presbyterian Church, Briefly Reviewed and Practically Improved* (1828). In 1829 the *Orthodox Presbyterian* was started by Reid and others, and he was a frequent contributor. In 1833 the University of Glasgow conferred on him the honorary degree of DD. In the following year he published the first volume of his *History of the Presbyterian Church in Ireland*. It was at once recognized as valuable, and the Royal Irish Academy unanimously elected him a member. The second volume, containing many original documents relating to the civil war and Cromwell's rule in Ireland, appeared in 1837, and in that year he was appointed professor of ecclesiastical history, church government, and pastoral theology, in the Royal Belfast Academical Institution. In 1841 he was presented by the crown to the professorship of ecclesiastical and civil history in the University of Glasgow. There he had an adequate salary, a great library at his command, and a long vacation of over six months in the year; and under these advantageous circumstances his studies advanced swiftly. He spent part of 1845 and of 1846 on the continent, visiting the sites of historic interest in Germany, France, and Italy. In 1848 he edited James Murdock's translation of J. L. von Mosheim's *Institutes of Ecclesiastical History*, to which he added many valuable notes.

Reid died on 26 March 1851 in Glasgow, from a cerebral tumour, and was buried in Sighthill cemetery, Glasgow. In acknowledgement of his literary work, his widow and family received a government pension. The third volume of his *History* was then ready for the press, and it was completed by Professor Killen of Belfast, who also produced a new edition of the entire work in 1867. Besides the works mentioned above, Reid published *A Brief History of the Irish Presbyterians* (1824); *Seven letters to the Rev. C. R. Eglinton, D.D. regius professor of divinity in the University of Dublin, occasioned by his animadversions in his life of Ussher, on certain passages in the history of the Presbyterian church in Ireland* (1849); 'Indirect influence of the Sabbath on the general prosperity of nations, and especially on their intelligence, trade and commerce, social order, and liberties', in *The Christian sabbath, considered in its various aspects, by ministers of different denominations*, preface by Baptist W. Noel (1850); as well as articles in *Orthodox Presbyterian*, *Banner of Ulster*, *Northern Whig*, and *McComb's Presbyterian Almanac and Christian Remembrancer*. There is a speech by Reid printed in *Sympathy of the Irish Presbyterians with the Church of Scotland: speeches delivered at the great non-intrusion meeting, held in the Presbyterian church, May-Street, Belfast, on Wednesday evening, 26th February, 1840 … on the invaded rights of the church and people of Scotland* (1840). In 1886 W. D. Killen edited *A History of the Congregations of the Presbyterian Church in Ireland* (1886), based on manuscript notes by Reid. There are other unpublished historical and theological writings in the Presbyterian Historical Society, Belfast. Reid's magisterial *History of the Presbyterian Church in Ireland* remains the standard work on its subject, and is a tribute to his painstaking research. G. W. SPROTT, *rev.* I. R. McBRIDE

Sources R. Allen, *James Seaton Reid: a centenary biography* (1951) • T. Croskery, 'The Rev. James Seaton Reid, D. D.', *Evangelical Witness and Presbyterian Review*, 7 (1868) • *Banner of Ulster* (1 April 1851) • *Records of the General Synod of Ulster, from 1691 to 1820*, 3 vols. (1890–98) • W. I. Addison, ed., *The matriculation albums of the University of Glasgow from 1728 to 1858* (1913)

Archives Presbyterian Historical Society of Ireland, Belfast, literary MSS, lecture and sermon notes | U. Edin., letters to David Laing

Likenesses S. Hawskett, portrait, 1841, U. Glas.

Wealth at death £1111 16s. 8d.: probate, Glasgow, SC 36/48/38 120

Reid, James Smith (1846–1926), classical scholar and historian, was born at Sorn, Ayrshire, on 3 May 1846, the eldest son of John Reid, schoolmaster, and his wife, Mary Smith. Among collateral relatives on his mother's side he reckoned Adam Smith, author of *The Wealth of Nations*. He was educated first in Arbroath and then at the City of London School, and entered Christ's College, Cambridge, as a scholar in 1865. Three years later (1868) he was bracketed senior classic, and was awarded the Browne medal for a Latin epigram. He was senior chancellor's medallist in 1869, and the same year was elected a fellow of his college. While studying classics Reid also studied law, and was Whewell scholar in 1870 and graduated LLM in 1872. In the same year he married Ruth, daughter of Thomas Gardner, and sister of Professor Percy Gardner, Professor Ernest Gardner, and Miss Alice Gardner. They had three sons and one daughter.

From 1873 to 1878 and again from 1880 to 1885 Reid was classical lecturer at Pembroke College, and in 1878, having ceased to be a fellow of Christ's on his marriage in 1872, he was elected to a fellowship at Gonville and Caius College, where he remained a fellow for forty-four years. Here, together with the Revd E. S. Roberts (master of the college, 1903–12), he built up a brilliant classical school. In 1899 he was elected first professor of ancient history in the university, and held this chair until 1925. He received the honorary degrees of LittD of Dublin University and LLD of St Andrews University, and in 1917 he was elected a fellow of the British Academy. He was also an honorary fellow of Christ's College, where he had continued to lecture until 1880.

Reid's main interests were in Roman literature and history, and he quickly established himself as a leading Ciceronian scholar, bringing to the elucidation of the texts a particular mastery of idiom. He was greatly influenced by the work of the Danish philologist Johan Nicolai Madvig. In the early stages of his career he produced several compact editions of philosophical and oratorical works of Cicero. These were chiefly designed for undergraduates preparing for the classical tripos, which underwent several revisions in this period. The most important of these editions was of the *Academica* (1874) which appeared in an enlarged edition in 1885, and for which he gained the degree of LittD at Cambridge.

Reid's considerable teaching commitments together with his tutorship at Caius (1885–99) and his tenure of the chair of ancient history (1899–1925) greatly delayed the publication of his major work—an edition of *De finibus*. Although he had produced a translation in 1883, the edition which he had begun to prepare at the same time was not published until 1925 and only covered books one and two. It was unfortunate that Reid's advanced age and failing health made it impossible for him to revise his text in the light of new approaches to the manuscript tradition. Nevertheless the edition shows a deep understanding of the Greek philosophical sources as well as the linguistic idioms of Cicero's work, and its value is increased by the copious illustrations of usage provided.

As first professor of ancient history Reid took on a heavy burden of lecturing which limited his published work. He produced several articles on Roman law and constitutional history, and made contributions to the *Cambridge Companion to Latin Studies*. His only historical book—*The Municipalities of the Roman Empire* (1913)—was the published version of his Lowell lectures. Although the chapters on the theory and history of the Roman municipality in the abstract are valuable, the absence of documentation limits its use.

Reid played a large part in the foundation in 1910 of the Society for the Promotion of Roman Studies, of which he succeeded F. J. Haverfield as president in 1916. He was an active member of the editorial committee of the *Journal of Roman Studies* and of the council of the British School at Rome. For fifteen years he was a tutor of Caius, but his forte was in scholarship and teaching rather than in administration. For university affairs he had little taste. In politics he was a Liberal of the old school, and was for some years chairman of the party in the town of Cambridge. His personality, in which the desire to shine found no place, was gentle and kindly. He retired from his chair on the ground of failing health in 1925, and died at Cambridge on 1 April 1926.

F. E. ADCOCK, *rev.* RICHARD SMAIL

Sources A. Souter, A. C. Clark, and F. E. Adcock, 'James Smith Reid, 1846–1926', *PBA*, 13 (1927), 335–9 · P. Giles, *The Caian*, 34 (1925–7), 134–42 · Venn, *Alum. Cant.* · *CGPLA Eng. & Wales* (1926)
Archives King's AC Cam., letters to Oscar Browning
Wealth at death £6100 1*s.* 1*d.*: probate, 12 June 1926, *CGPLA Eng. & Wales*

Reid [*formerly* Robertson], **John** (1722?–1807), army officer and composer, was probably born on 2 February 1722 at Inverchroskie, near Kirkmichael, Perthshire, the eldest of the three sons of Alexander Robertson of Straloch (*c.*1695–

John Reid (1722?–1807), attrib. George Watson, 1805

1781?) and his wife, Susan or Susanna (*b. c.*1701), the daughter of Patrick Scott, a writer to the signet in Edinburgh, and his wife, Elizabeth Cunningham of Blairquhosh. In a codicil to his will (1806) Reid gave his birthday as 13 February, without naming the year, and expressed a wish that it might be marked with an annual concert; he may, however, have chosen to hold the anniversary back from 2 February (OS) to 13 February (NS) at the calendar reform of 1752, for he was baptized at Kirkmichael on 6 February 1722, and a birth date shortly before that would accord with his declaration on 6 December 1803 that he was then 'in the 82nd year' of his age. As a boy he lived at Reid Hall on the Inverchroskie estate at the head of Strathardle. The Robertsons of Straloch had held land in that area of Perthshire as a barony since the fifteenth century, and successive heads of the family (including John's greatgrandfather John Robertson from 1704, his grandfather Alexander from 1727, and his father from 1742) were known as Baron Reid.

Early military career From the grammar school in Perth, Reid went on to the University of Edinburgh. He studied law there, and a John Reid enrolled in the logic class in 1743–4. Years later he was to remember the university as the place where 'I had my education, and passed the pleasantest part of my youth' (*Will*, 12). In Edinburgh he would also have found opportunities to develop his musical talents and take flute lessons. But the army beckoned. In the hope of getting him a commission his father wrote several letters between December 1744 and May 1745 to Lord Milton, the lord justice clerk and adviser to the third duke of Argyll (NL Scot., MSS 16602, fol. 48; 16611, fols. 111–15).

On 8 June 1745, two months before the raising of the Jacobite standard in Glenfinnan, Reid was commissioned as a lieutenant in the earl of Loudoun's regiment. Although his name was shown as 'John Robertson, or Reid, of Straloch' (Stewart, 2.50), he later used only the surname Reid. He was among more than seventy officers taken prisoner at the battle of Prestonpans on 21 September 1745, but was set free by the Angus militia on 19 January 1746. On 25 March 1746 he helped to capture some 160 Jacobite troops who had been driven ashore in the Kyle of Tongue, Sutherland, along with a large sum of money, the loss of which did much to undermine Prince Charles's campaign. In a letter written to his father from Aberdeen on 8 April 1746 (NL Scot., MS 16635, fol. 116), and in a memorial to Lord Amherst dated 23 July 1794, Reid affirmed the crucial part he had played in this enterprise by ignoring a call to withdraw and deploying the small group of men with him in such a way as to make the rebels think they were surrounded. Loudoun's regiment was in Flanders in 1747–8, where it fought in the unsuccessful defence of Bergen-op-Zoom; but in June 1748, during the armistice that preceded the peace of Aix-la-Chapelle, it was disbanded, and Reid was placed on half pay.

Musical composer On 26 June 1751 Reid bought a commission as captain-lieutenant in the 42nd regiment of foot (the Black Watch), which was stationed at that time in Ireland. Promotion to captain followed on 3 June 1752. Meanwhile he was exercising his musical skills. For his new regiment he composed the piece by which he was to become best known, the march of the 42nd or Old Highland regiment. First published as 'The highland march by Cap[r]. Reid' in the second instalment of Robert Bremner's *Collection of Airs and Marches* (c.1756), it has remained a slow march used by all Scottish regiments, and, with words by Sir Harry Erskine of Alva ('In the garb of old Gaul') fitted to its tune, it became a favourite song of loyal highlanders and was included in the third volume of James Johnson's *Scots Musical Museum* (1790). Reid's first set of *Six Solos for a German Flute or Violin with a Thorough Bass for the Harpsicord* was published in London by James Oswald about 1755–6, and was followed by a second set. The books were dedicated to Horace Walpole's friend Caroline, countess of Ailesbury, whose father (General John Campbell, later fourth duke of Argyll) and second husband (Henry Seymour Conway, later a field marshal) were both distinguished soldiers. When these sets of sonatas originally appeared the composer was cryptically identified as 'I. R. Esq[r], A Member of the Temple of Apollo'—a reference to a 'pretended Society' of amateurs whose music Oswald held a patent to publish—but in an edition of c.1796 he was openly named as 'General Reid'.

Soldiering in North America and the West Indies In 1756 Reid sailed with the 42nd to New York. He was severely ill during the winter of 1757–8: his father was told 'he had the disease of the Country so bade that … he threaten'd a

hectick' (NL Scot., MS 16707, fol. 89). Convalescence prevented him from leading his company in the heroic assault on the French fort at Ticonderoga in July 1758, and he was left in charge of the garrison at Fort Edward instead; but he took part in the advance to Lake Champlain under Major-General Amherst in 1759, when Ticonderoga fell, and during it was raised to the rank of major (1 August). In 1760 the 1st battalion of the 42nd, led by him, was part of the force that advanced on Montreal down the dangerous rapids of the St Lawrence River. Writing to his father on 10 September 1760, two days after Montreal's surrender, Reid reflected on the successful but 'excessively fatigueing' campaign and on his prospects for further promotion (Murray, *Chronicles*, 3.479). Shortly afterwards he submitted to the dukes of Atholl and Argyll a proposal to raise an additional regiment which would draw on highland families that had supported the Jacobite rising (ibid., 477–8; NL Scot., MS 17506, fol. 28), but this was rejected.

In December 1761 Reid's battalion was sent to the West Indies, where it took part in the capture of Martinique under Major-General Monckton. Reid was wounded during the storming of Morne Tartenson, a hill overlooking Fort de France, on 24 January 1762, and suffered 'a violent contusion on one Thigh' (Tullibardine, 389). On 3 February he was made a brevet lieutenant-colonel. From June to August of the same year he was in Cuba at the siege and capture of Havana. His brother Alexander Reid, who after serving in the Scots brigade of the Dutch army had become in 1758 a captain in the 2nd battalion of the 42nd, was also at Havana and died there, either killed in action or from sickness.

After the surrender of Cuba the regiment, now amalgamated into a single battalion under Reid's command, returned to North America. Shortly afterwards he was elected a member of the St Andrew's Society of New York, of which William Alexander, shortly to become his brother-in-law, was president at the time. On 28 December 1762 in New York he married Susannah (1736–1777), the youngest daughter of James Alexander (1691–1756) and his wife, Mary (c.1690–1760). Susannah's parents were both Scottish and her brother William claimed the earldom of Stirling. Her father had settled in America in 1715 and held prominent positions in the government of New Jersey and New York colonies. Her mother was a daughter of John Sprott of Wigtown, and had previously been married to David Provoost, a New York merchant. From them Susannah had inherited considerable wealth, making her one of 'the two greatest fortunes in this Place', according to Richard Shuckburgh (Johnson, 3.323–4). A daughter, Susanna, was born probably in 1763.

Although the treaty of Paris ended the war with France, the 42nd was in action in 1763 against Native Americans at Bushy Run, near Fort Pitt. In 1764 Reid was second in command of an expedition led by Brigadier-General Bouquet to subdue the Native Americans in western Virginia and Ohio. With Bouquet he took part in a series of conferences with native chiefs, and he presided at a meeting at Fort Pitt with representatives of the Seneca tribe in June 1765.

A contemporary chronicler noted that Bouquet 'has taken every occasion of doing justice to the particular merit of Colonel Reid' (Smith, 33), and correspondence between him and Bouquet survives from this time (BL, Add. MSS 21650–51). During 1765–6 Reid obtained from the council of New York colony a grant of a large tract of land beside Lake Champlain, in what is now Vermont. In July 1767, shortly before leaving with his regiment for Ireland, he issued an order expressing satisfaction at the great reputation with which its officers and men had served in America.

Landowner and lieutenant-governor of Jersey The 42nd reached Cork in October. Now that they were stationed in Ireland again, Reid was able to revisit Scotland after an absence of eleven years. In Edinburgh, Alison Cockburn heard him play some of his compositions on the flute at the home of a daughter of Sir John Clerk of Penicuik. On 10 February 1770, after nearly twenty years in the 42nd, Reid was placed on half pay, and shortly afterwards returned to America to supervise his estates. He owned 'about thirty-five thousand acres of very valuable land' near Lake Champlain, with a survey warrant for 15,000 more; he built mills and houses, and his intention was to erect a mansion and settle there with his family (Tullibardine, 390). But his title to some of this land was disputed by claimants from New Hampshire, who in August 1773 evicted his tenants and burned their homes. His claims for compensation achieved little redress. He returned to Britain with his wife and daughter and by March 1775 was in London, where Edmund Burke recommended a compromise over his claims (*Correspondence*, 3.136). On 29 July he wrote from Villiers Street, London, again offering to raise a battalion of Scottish highlanders, but again the proposal was rejected.

In Scotland, Reid found the family fortunes in a sorry state. His father, Baron Reid, who had always been prone to over-optimistic schemes, had not been successful in his management of the Perthshire estate and by 1774 was £12,000 in debt and clearly in his dotage. Trustees were appointed. Reid, who in his will wrote, 'I have made it a constant rule not to be in debt to any man', seems to have done his best to enable his father to go on living at Inverchroskie, but showed no inclination to farm the lands himself. The death of his wife, Susannah, on 27 September 1777 at the age of forty was a further blow. In May 1778 the estate was sold for £13,000 and shortly afterwards was split up. His father seems to have moved to Edinburgh, and when he died, probably in or soon after July 1781, John made no attempt to take the title of Baron Reid.

Meanwhile, in July 1779, as the navies of France and Spain gathered threateningly in the English Channel, Reid had been given permission to raise a regiment, the 95th foot. This was recruited mainly in Yorkshire at his own expense. On 10 October 1779 he was raised to the rank of brevet colonel, and on 7 April 1780 he was appointed the regiment's colonel. The 95th was posted to Jersey, where it played a major role in repelling the French invasion of January 1781. Reid was not on the island when the surprise attack occurred, but on 17 February 1781 he was

sworn in as lieutenant-governor of Jersey in place of the disgraced Moses Corbet and as commander-in-chief during the absence of General Conway, and on 19 October 1781 he was promoted major-general. On 31 May 1782, shortly before he left Jersey for England, the Assembly of States expressed gratitude 'pour l'affection et l'attention qu'il a témoignées envers les habitants de cette Isle durant son Commandement' ('for the affection and consideration that he has shown towards the residents of this island during his command'; Messervy, 14). He relinquished his posts as the island's lieutenant-governor and commander-in-chief on 6 July 1782. On 31 May 1783, in anticipation of the peace of Versailles, the 95th was disbanded.

Further compositions and family affairs During the war years Reid had continued to compose. His *Set of Marches for Two Clarinets, Hautboys, or German Flutes, Two Horns, and a Bassoon* (by 'I. R. Esq'), published by Bremner in 1778–9, contains sixteen marches named for different regiments and their colonels, including the 3rd foot (General Lord Amherst's, to whose wife the volume was dedicated), 17th (Lieutenant-General Monckton's), and 77th (the Atholl highlanders, raised in 1777–8 by Lieutenant-Colonel James Murray, who had commanded Reid's company at Ticonderoga in 1758). These were among the earliest such pieces to be printed in full score and represent a notable contribution to the military music of the period. A companion volume, *A Sett of Minuets and Marches* (c.1780–81), contains his marches for the 42nd and the 3rd foot guards and a slow march for his new regiment, the 95th, together with eighteen minuets for dancing and an affectionate tribute to Blair Castle, *Atholl House*. Reid, who considered that 'the Scots stand unrivalled by all the neighbouring nations in pastoral melody' (*Will*, 13), was a subscriber to William Napier's volumes of *Scots Songs* (1790, 1792), which included nearly 200 of those 'wild but expressive' melodies newly harmonized by Haydn and other masters.

After leaving Jersey, Reid seems to have lived mainly in London. In 1790 his daughter Susanna married, without his consent, the Revd Dr John Stark Robertson (1747–1809), laird of Ballindean in Fife, whose family claimed descent from the Robertsons of Struan. As plain John Stark he had graduated MA at the University of St Andrews in 1766 and in 1773 succeeded his father, the Revd Thomas Stark, as minister of Balmerino, but he had demitted his charge in 1781 in order to study medicine at the University of Edinburgh, where he graduated MD in 1783; he then moved to Bath. By 1788, when he was admitted as a licentiate of the College of Physicians, he had taken the name of Robertson. Reid was greatly vexed by his daughter's marriage and determined to disinherit his son-in-law, whom he referred to as a 'vile apothecary' (Grant, 383). In 1792 he nevertheless offered Susanna use of her mother's property in America if she would go and live there. She and her husband reached New York in the spring of 1793 and took up residence in Cortlandt Street.

Following France's declaration of war on Britain, Reid was made a lieutenant-general on 12 October 1793. On 23 July 1794 he wrote to Lord Amherst, the commander-in-chief, asking for the colonelcy of a regiment not liable to be reduced after the war and setting forth in detail his past services and the ill fortune he and his family had suffered. His request was successful, and on 27 November 1794 he was appointed colonel of the 88th foot.

In March 1796 the death occurred of Major-General John Small, Reid's first cousin, whom he had known since childhood. Small bequeathed to him, 'as a mark of my respect', an estate of nearly 5000 acres beside the River Shubenacadie in Nova Scotia. The executors (who included Reid, his daughter, and her husband) were instructed that these lands should 'be erected into a free barony by the name and description of the Barony of Straloch', which would be passed down to Susanna and her heirs on the condition that 'she and her issue enjoying the same shall bear the name of Reid of Straloch'.

On 1 January 1798 Reid was promoted general. In 1800 Susanna returned to England in the hope of making peace with her father. He sent her presents, but refused to see her. Soon afterwards she settled in Paris with her husband, who was interned when war broke out in 1803 but released after intervention by the American consul.

Last years and assessment Reid continued meanwhile to live modestly in London, at 7 Woodstock Street, off Oxford Street. In 1803, when invasion by Napoleon seemed imminent, an order was published to general officers to communicate their addresses to the adjutant-general. Reid responded on 6 December:

> I am an old man in the 82nd year of my age, and have become very deaf and infirm, but I am still ready, if my services should be accepted, to use my feeble arm in the defence of my King and Country, having had the good fortune on former occasions to have been repeatedly successful in action against our perfidious enemies, on whom, thank God, I never turned my back.   (Jourdain and Fraser, 1.31)

One distinctive contribution that he was able to make to the war effort was to persuade Peter von Winter, who was in London in 1803–5 as composer to the Italian opera company at the King's Theatre, Haymarket, to arrange twelve of his marches for an enlarged military band, and in this form they were published by Thomas Preston. Reid seems to have moved at about this time from Woodstock Street to a house in the Haymarket, where he died on 6 February 1807. He was buried on 13 February at St Margaret's, Westminster, as requested in his will.

Contemporary comments on Reid include one from an officer who had served under him in the 42nd: the men, he recalled, 'were much attached to Colonel Reid for his poetry, his music, and his bravery as a soldier' (Stewart, 1.347). It was said that 'in the meridian of his life he was esteemed the best gentleman German flute performer in England' (GM, 1st ser., 77, 1807, 275). Mrs Cockburn was enraptured by his artistry at a soirée about 1768–9:

> Of all the sounds I ever heard, Colonel Reed's flute—well, it is amazing the powers of it. It thrills to your very heart. He plays it in any taste you please and composes what he plays. You know my taste is the penseroso, and so it is his … He is a gentle, melancholy, tall, well-bred, lean man; and, as for his flute, it speaks all languages. But those sounds that come

from the heart to the heart—I never could have conceived it. It had a dying fall—I was afraid I could not bear it when I heard it perfectly. I can think of nothing but that flute.
(Letters and Memoir, 81–2)

Reid's disposition to melancholy seems to have intensified in later life, partly perhaps as a result of his deafness. A posthumous memoir, accompanied by an engraved portrait, in Kirby's Wonderful and Eccentric Museum caricatured his habit of walking every day at a 'solemn melancholy pace' round Hyde Park, and then to St Paul's and the Bank:

> He never appeared otherwise than in a dirty drab-coloured coat, black breeches, a very small cocked hat, and black stock, with his hair tied in a queue; a cane in one hand, and the other invariably placed within the bosom of his coat. This dress, from which he never deviated, so far from according with the rank of the wearer, seemed to bespeak the pressure of poverty, and this inference was confirmed in the mind of every observer by the appearance of his person, which was tall and very slender … so that he was generally known by no other appellation than the Walking Rushlight.
(Kirby's … Museum, 34–5)

In a painting of 1805, on the other hand, he appears proudly wearing the uniform of colonel of the 88th regiment, holding his flute and with a score of his marches open beside him. This is one of three portraits of himself which he left to the University of Edinburgh: the others depict him as a lieutenant in Lord Loudoun's regiment about 1745 and as a major-general about 1782.

Reid's will: the chair of music at the University of Edinburgh Reid made his will on 19 April 1803 and added a codicil on 4 March 1806. In the latter year he took steps to sell the estate in Nova Scotia that Small had left to him, although there remained property and land in the United States in which he held an interest through his marriage into the Alexander family, and for which his nephew John Rutherfurd (a United States senator from 1791 to 1798) acted as his agent. His residuary estate in Great Britain (which at his death amounted to £52,114) was to be invested by trustees in order to yield a life-rent for his daughter. Although it seemed increasingly likely that she would die without issue, Reid made provision for her children to inherit, on condition that any son or sons should 'use the surname, and bear the arms of Reid' (Will, 8). Failing this, the bulk of his fortune (apart from the American estates and some consols which were to be shared between his nephews and nieces) was to go after her death to the University of Edinburgh, with the primary aim of establishing and endowing Scotland's first chair of music. In the event Susanna died childless in Paris on 31 May 1838. By then Reid's estate had grown to £73,590, from which the university received a benefaction of £68,876 18s. 3d. It came in the form of a stock receipt for 3% consols, transferred into the names of five professors furnished to the court of chancery.

In October 1839 John Thomson was elected as the first Reid professor. Later holders of the chair have included Sir Henry Bishop, John Donaldson, Sir Herbert Oakeley, Frederick Niecks, Sir Donald Tovey, Sidney Newman, Kenneth Leighton, and Nigel Osborne. Donaldson, who was appointed in 1845, protested that his fellow professors, as trustees of the Reid bequest, were obstructing the release of adequate funds for the teaching of the theory of music—the principal purpose specified in Reid's will. When the city council (as patrons of the university) brought a lawsuit against the trustees, the court of session essentially agreed with Donaldson. One consequence was the building in 1858–9 of the Reid School of the Theory of Music (later known as the Reid Concert Hall), designed by David Cousin. The Reid Music Library, which for many years was housed there, possesses some of Reid's own music books. Reid memorial concerts have been given annually by the university since February 1841. During Oakeley's professorship (1865–91) this concert became the centrepiece of a Reid festival. Tovey drew on the resources of the chair to form the Reid Orchestra, which gave concerts in Edinburgh from 1917 to 1982. Commemorative homages to Reid have included two suites arranged and orchestrated by Bishop from music by him (*Introduction, Pastorale, Minuet and March*, 1842; *Introduction, March, Minuetto and Chorus*, 1843) and a set of orchestral variations on his march 'In the garb of old Gaul' by nine composers, among them Lyell Creswell, Edward Harper, James MacMillan, and Nigel Osborne (1994).

CHRISTOPHER D. S. FIELD

Sources Marchioness of Tullibardine [K. M. Stewart-Murray, duchess of Atholl], ed., *A military history of Perthshire, 1660–1902*, 2 vols. (1908) • T. R. Lower, 'General John Reid', *Nova Scotia Historical Quarterly*, 9 (1979), 113–36, 335–61 • Will and codicil of General Reid (1807) • *Letters and memoir of her own life by Mrs. Alison Rutherford or Cockburn*, ed. T. Craig-Brown (1899) • *GM*, 1st ser., 77 (1807), 189, 275 • *Kirby's wonderful … museum*, 6 vols. (1803–20), vol. 4, pp. 34–7 • J. J. H. H. Stewart-Murray, seventh duke of Atholl, *Chronicles of the Atholl and Tullibardine families*, 5 vols. (privately printed, Edinburgh, 1908) • W. M. MacBean, *Biographical register of Saint Andrew's Society of the State of New York*, 1 (1922) [s.v. Gen. John Reid, Dr John Stark Robertson] • H. F. N. Jourdain and E. Fraser, *The Connaught rangers*, 3 vols. (1924) • M. McGregor, ed., photocopies of research notes, PRO documents and army lists relating to officers, 42nd and 73rd foot, Black Watch Archive, Perth, BW Arch 0863/1/2 • *The papers of Sir William Johnson*, ed. J. Sullivan and others, 14 vols. (1921–65) • D. McNaughton, 'The last Baron Reid-Robertson of Straloch', *Scottish Genealogist*, 9/1 (1962), 11–20; 9/2 (1962), 2–4 • J. A. Messervy, 'Liste des gouverneurs, lieut.-gouverneurs et députés-gouverneurs de l'île de Jersey', *Société jersiaise: Bulletins*, 5 (1902–5), 8–26 • J. Ray, *A compleat history of the rebellion* (1749) • D. Stewart, *Sketches of the character, manners, and present state of the highlanders of Scotland: with details of the military service of the highland regiments*, 2 vols. (1822) • F. B. Richards, 'The Black Watch at Ticonderoga', *Proceedings of the New York State Historical Association*, 10 (1910), 1–98 • A. Grant, *The story of the University of Edinburgh during its first three hundred years*, 2 vols. (1884) • [W. Smith], *An historical account of the expedition against the Ohio Indians, in the year MDCCLXIV, under the command of Henry Bouquet, Esq, colonel of foot, and now brigadier general in America* (1766) • J. Redington and R. A. Roberts, eds., *Calendar of home office papers of the reign of George III*, 4: 1773–1775, PRO (1899) • D. T. Rice, *The university portraits* (1957) • J. Robertson, *The barons Reid-Robertson of Straloch* (1887) • C. Rogers, *Memorials of the earl of Stirling and of the house of Alexander*, 2 vols. (1877) • A. McK. Annand, 'General John Reid, 1721–1807', *Journal of the Society for Army Historical Research*, 42 (1964), 44–7 • H. G. Farmer, *A history of music in Scotland* (1947) • D. Johnson, 'Reid, John', *New Grove* • J. M. Allan, 'Reid, John', *Die Musik in Geschichte und Gegenwart*, ed. F. Blume (Kassel and Basel, 1949–86) • *Fasti Scot.*, new edn, 5.129, 163 • ' Matriculation roll of the University of Edinburgh: Arts, Law, Divinity', transcr. A. Morgan, 1933–4, U. Edin. L. • J. V. Duncanson, 'The last Baron Reid-Robertson of Straloch', *Clan Donnachaidh Annual* (1988), 18–19 • 'Record of the service of the 42nd royal highlanders', *Black Watch Chronicle*, 2 (1914), 17–46 • Munk, *Roll*, vol. 2 [John Stark Robertson] • N. B. Leslie, *The succession of colonels of the British army from 1660 to the present day* (1974) • NL Scot., Saltoun MSS 16635, 16652, 16689, 17506 • *The correspondence of Edmund Burke*, ed. T. W. Copeland and others, 10 vols. (1958–78) • J. Richardson, letter to Revd Alexander Brunton, 11 July 1840, U. Edin. L., Box Da 46.10

Archives BL, corresp. with Henry Bouquet, Add. MSS 21650–21651 • BL, corresp. with Frederick Haldimand, Add. MSS 21673, 21729 • BL, petitions to dukes of Newcastle and Cumberland, Add. MS 33057 • NL Scot., Saltoun MSS, corresp., MSS 16635, 16652, 16689, 17506

Likenesses oils, *c.*1745, U. Edin. • oils, *c.*1782, U. Edin. • J. Tassie, medallion, 1797, 28 Charlotte Square, Edinburgh • attrib. G. Watson, oils, 1805, U. Edin. [*see illus.*] • engraving, repro. in Kirby, 'General John Reid' • oils, priv. coll.

Wealth at death £52,114: Grant, *The story*, 231, 351; Lower, 'General John Reid', 358 • £58,226: indenture of trustees, 4 June 1834

Reid, John (1725–1774), thief, was born on 22 November 1725 in the parish of Muiravonside, Stirlingshire, the son of John Reid, flesher, and Joan Dick. His parents being of 'low circumstances' (*Boswell for the Defence*, 357) Reid was sent, aged eight, to work for a series of local smallholders, from whom he gleaned a rudimentary education. In time he became a flesher (butcher), like his father, and with his wife, Janet (*d.* in or after 1774), lived at Hillend, near Avonbridge. Squandering the little money he received on his parents' death, Reid turned in the early 1750s to drink and crime, from which he escaped punishment by enlisting in the army. After another indictment for theft he travelled to London, before he returned to Scotland and began work as a drover. In 1766 Reid was again indicted, this time for stealing 120 sheep, and was tried in Edinburgh, where he was defended by the barrister and later biographer James Boswell. Acquitted, Reid returned to Hillend and resumed his life as a drover, flesher, and, presumably, petty criminal.

Reid committed his final misdemeanour in October 1773, when he was accused either of stealing or of the lesser crime of receiving and selling on nineteen sheep taken from a farm in nearby Peeblesshire. Apprehended after fleeing to England, Reid was brought to trial at Edinburgh's high court of justiciary on 1 August 1774. Here he faced a powerful prosecution counsel which included the lord advocate, James Montgomery, and the solicitor-general, Henry Dundas; on the bench sat Thomas Miller, the lord justice clerk, and lords Kames, Coalston, and Auchinleck (James Boswell's father). Reid was once more represented by Boswell, whose defence depended on revealing the prejudices of a bench which, with the return of a guilty verdict, sentenced Reid to death.

During the remaining six weeks of Reid's life Boswell campaigned vigorously to have the sentence reduced to transportation. At the same time he came to look on Reid as a perfect case study for one of his own enduring interests: man's disposition in the face of death. While still campaigning for the sentence to be revised Boswell had Reid's portrait painted, in a bid to capture the countenance of an individual awaiting execution. In this period

Reid also became a foil in Boswell's attempts to fashion himself as a refined man of sensibility. Writing after a visit to the prisoner's cell on 30 August Boswell claimed 'by sympathy' to have 'sucked the dismal ideas of John Reid's situation', which he took as proof of his own capacity for Humean sympathy. Such correspondence would surely have been sufficient for most men. But the socially competitive Boswell also believed that his sympathy was enhanced by the superior status that he enjoyed as a refined man of feeling: 'the spirits ... when transferred to another body of a more delicate nature' have, he wrote, 'much more influence than on the body from which it is transferred', with the effect that Boswell 'suffered much more than John did' (*Boswell for the Defence*, 300).

Once it became clear that his efforts to save Reid had failed Boswell turned his attention to the possibility of rehabilitation after hanging, a scheme that he hoped to implement at Reid's execution at the Grassmarket, on 21 September 1774. In the end attempts to resuscitate Reid came to nothing, as the body was left to hang for nearly an hour before being taken to Muiravonside for burial. Though only a relatively brief episode in the journal, Reid's trial offers insight into Boswell at his most self-centred and sympathetic, with both themes combining in the melancholic state into which he descended after the sentence had been carried out. In the long term, however, Reid's fate may have prompted a more positive outcome. Shocked by the court's heartlessness, Boswell grew increasingly critical of the legal profession and turned to what he considered the more humane, creative lifestyle of man of letters and, ultimately, biographer of Johnson.

PHILIP CARTER

Sources *Boswell for the defence, 1769–1774*, ed. W. K. Wimsatt and F. A. Pottle (1960), vol. 7 of *The Yale editions of the private papers of James Boswell*, trade edn (1950–89) · G. Turnbull, 'Boswell and sympathy: the trial and execution of John Reid', *New light on Boswell: critical and historical essays on the occasion of the bicentenary of the 'Life of Johnson'*, ed. G. Clingham (1991), 104–115 · V. A. C. Gatrell, *The hanging tree: execution and the English people, 1770–1868* (1994) · F. Brady, *James Boswell: the later years, 1769–1795* (1984) · IGI

Reid, John (1776–1822), physician, was born at Leicester and, after education in Bolton at the school of Philip Holland, a dissenting minister, he attended the Hackney Nonconformist Academy for five years. He then studied medicine at Edinburgh, and there graduated MD on 12 September 1798 reading a thesis, 'De insania'. He became a licentiate of the Royal College of Physicians of London on 25 June 1804. He published in 1801 a translation from the French, *An Account of the Savage Youth of Avignon*; in 1806 *A Treatise of Consumption*, in which he stated his belief that tubercles were inflammatory products, and had no real resemblance to caseous disease of lymphatic glands; and in 1816 *Essays on Insanity*, of which an enlarged edition appeared in 1821 as *Essays on hypochondriasis and other Nervous Affections*. In the same year he married Elisabeth Jesser Sturch (1789–1866) [*see* Reid, Elisabeth Jesser], daughter of William *Sturch (1753–1838), a wealthy Unitarian. Reid was a contributor of medical reports to the *Monthly Magazine*, gave lectures on the theory and practice of medicine,

and was physician to the Finsbury Dispensary. His house was in Grenville Street, Brunswick Square, London, where he died on 2 July 1822, leaving property in London and Glasgow. NORMAN MOORE, *rev.* NICK HERVEY

Sources Munk, *Roll* · General Register Office for England, will/probate 11, 1664, 653

Wealth at death £100 bequeathed to executors; house bequeathed to wife: will/probate, 1822, General Register Office for England, 11,1664,653

Reid, John (1808–1841/2), writer, was born at Paisley, Renfrewshire, on 2 April 1808, the second son in the large family of John Reid (*c*.1765–1830) and his wife, Jean M'Gavin, sister of the controversialist William M'Gavin. His father had been licensed to preach by the Burgher Presbytery of Glasgow in 1799 but later pursued a career as a surgeon and a teacher of oriental languages in Glasgow. The family all adhered to the Secession church and his brother William (1814–1896), later minister of Lothian Road United Presbyterian Church, Edinburgh, and other members of the family played a prominent part in the temperance movement.

Reid received his education mostly from his father and was apprenticed to a firm of booksellers in Glasgow. At the end of his apprenticeship he went to London, where he worked for Black, Young, and Young, booksellers, before returning to Glasgow, where he set up in business on his own account as a bookseller and publisher. When Reid was asked by a friend to catalogue the books in his library which were printed in Gaelic the project grew beyond its original scope until it became a catalogue of all books in the Gaelic language. In 1827 the manuscript came to the notice of Sir John Sinclair, who recommended it to be laid before the Highland Society of London, from which it received a premium in 1831. This was published at a time when dictionaries were systematically recording the Gaelic language, and it includes information about the lives as well as the writings of Gaelic authors, also putting forward some critical assessment. It was published by Reid himself as *Bibliotheca Scoto-Celtica* (1832). Although reluctant to undertake the task by virtue of his youth, Reid prepared William M'Gavin's *Posthumous Works* (1834), to which he prefixed a memoir.

Reid's interests were reflected in his publications. Under the title Illustrations of Social Depravity (1834) he published a series of polemical booklets, many by himself, on topics such as the voluntary controversy. In his *Sketch of the Political Career of the Earl of Durham* (1835) Reid collected his subject's most important speeches, publishing them at a time when Durham's supporters hoped that he might lead a radical party in parliament. He shared the concern of his friend Lord Dudley Stuart for the welfare of Polish exiles in Britain and his circle of friends also included Sir Daniel Macnee, William Weir, and William Motherwell. Reid married, in 1836, Anne, daughter of Captain John McLaren, of Highlaws, Berwickshire; they had a daughter.

In 1838–9 Reid spent nearly a year in Constantinople. The result was *Turkey and the Turks* (1840), an unflattering portrait of the Ottoman empire and its inhabitants. The urge to travel prompted him to give up his business in Glasgow in order to edit an English journal and prepare a Chinese dictionary in Hong Kong, where he died in either 1841 or 1842.   LIONEL ALEXANDER RITCHIE

Sources J. Reid, *Bibliotheca Scoto-Celtica, or, An account of all the books which have been printed in the Gaelic language* (1832), preface · R. Small, *History of the congregations of the United Presbyterian church from 1733 to 1900*, 1 (1904), 466 · *The temperance autobiography of the Rev William Reid DD* (1895) · *United Presbyterian Magazine*, 13 (1896), 470–71 · *DNB* · D. S. Thomson, ed., *The companion to Gaelic Scotland* (1983)
Archives Sandon Hall, Staffordshire, Harrowby MSS, letters

Reid, John (1809–1849), anatomist and pathologist, sixth child of Henry Reid, farmer and cattle dealer, and his wife, Jean Orr, was born at Bathgate, Linlithgowshire, Scotland, on 9 April 1809. He entered Edinburgh University aged fourteen to study Greek, Latin, and mathematics, and later transferred to medicine. He studied physiology in the class of William Pulteney Alison and dissected in the extramural anatomy classes of Robert Knox. As a student he shared lodgings with a friend from Bathgate, James Y. Simpson. Reid graduated MD in 1830 with a thesis 'De aneurismate' and was admitted a fellow of the Royal College of Physicians of Edinburgh on 4 October 1836. He was appointed assistant physician in the clinical wards of Edinburgh Infirmary in 1830, and in the succeeding year went to Paris to pursue his medical studies, returning in 1832.

In 1833 Reid became Knox's assistant in the school of anatomy at Surgeons' Hall which flourished during the time that Alexander Monro tertius held the chair of anatomy at the university. This provided Reid with a foundation for his later work in physiology. In 1836 he was appointed lecturer on physiology at the Edinburgh extraacademical medical school and in the next two years he carried out his most significant experimental work (using animal subjects) on the functions of the ninth, tenth, and eleventh cranial nerves. William Sharpey, professor of anatomy and physiology at the new University of London, noted in a letter to his friend Allen Thomson at this time, 'Reid has given a first rate experimental paper on the nerves of doubtful function' (Jacyna, 16). In 1838 he became pathologist to the Royal Infirmary, Edinburgh, and on the death of Robert Briggs in 1841, Reid was appointed to the Chandos chair of anatomy in the University of St Andrews, where he began a course of lectures on comparative anatomy and physiology, in addition to the regular work of the professorship. He also conducted systematic researches into the natural history of the marine fauna of the Fife coast, and in 1848 published a collection of papers on the subject, entitled *Physiological, Anatomical, and Pathological Researches*, a volume remarkable for originality and accuracy of observation.

Reid died at St Andrews, Fife, from cancer of the tongue on 30 July 1849 after a long, well documented illness in which he endured several painful surgical operations. He was buried at St Andrews on 2 August. Reid left a widow, Ann Blyth, and two daughters.

CAROLYN PENNINGTON

Sources G. Wilson, *Life of Dr John Reid* (1852) · D. F. Harris, 'John Reid, 1809–1849', *Nature*, 81 (1909), 163–5 · I. S. Jacyna, *A tale of three cities: the correspondence of William Sharpey and Allen Thomson* (1989) · J. H. Bennett, 'Observation LVI: cancroid ulcer of the tongue excision', *On cancerous and cancroid growths* (1849) · A. Keith, 'Anatomy in Scotland during the lifetime of Sir John Struthers', *Edinburgh Medical Journal*, 3rd ser., 8 (1912), 7–33 · [W. B. Carpenter], *British and Foreign Medico-Chirurgical Review* (4 Oct 1849), 577–81 · *DNB*
Archives NL Scot., corresp. with George Combe
Likenesses oils, U. St Andr. · photograph, U. St Andr.

Reid, John [*pseud.* David Toulmin] (1913–1998), author, was born on 1 July 1913 at Strathellie Cottages, Rathen, near Fraserburgh, Aberdeenshire, the first of the two children of James Gray Reid (*d.* 1949), farm servant, and his wife, Margaret, *née* Todd (*d.* 1969). After a fitful education at a series of schools he reluctantly followed in his father's footsteps and worked for a succession of masters on the land. The tedium of the farming round was relieved from the start by reading and by visits to the cinema, and then by his marriage, on 5 December 1934, to Margaret Jane Willox (*b.* 1916), followed by the arrival of three sons, Eric, Jack, and Graham. It was not until Reid suffered a serious illness in 1943 that he finally decided that he wanted to become a writer and, while he did not publish until years later he wrote continuously, finding inspiration not only from memory but also from research and excursions. He discovered some old business ledgers in a long-deserted shop, for example, and made good use of them in a masterly re-creation of a First World War airship station and the local inhabitants of Lenabo, now Forest of Deer. He kept diaries, compiled scrapbooks, and wrote obituaries of film stars and other famous people, which he compiled under the title 'Close the door softly'. A man of indefatigable curiosity and dogged persistence, he took the long road leading—after many set-backs, including bouts of depression—to ultimate success.

Under his pen name, David Toulmin, John Reid published a novel, stories, and essays centring on rural life in north-east Scotland, especially the Buchan district. After several years of contributions to such journals as the *Farmer and Stockbreeder* and the *Buchan Observer* his first book, consisting mostly of short stories, *Hard Shining Corn*, was published in 1972; it was soon followed by another such collection, *Straw into Gold* (1973). After several rejections and rewrites came his only novel, *Blown Seed* (1976), which sold about 25,000 copies. *Harvest Home*, resuming the pattern of the first two books, followed in 1978; *Travels without a Donkey* (1980) was an account of the car journeys taken around Scotland and the north of England by the author and his wife. *A Chiel Among Them* (1982) was a mixture of stories and essays, while *The Tillycorthie Story* (1986) was a concise account of a local estate; published in the same year, *The Clyack Sheaf* was a final collection of stories and essays. Reid looked upon the award of an honorary MLitt from the University of Aberdeen in 1986 as an academic culmination to the high acclaim that he had already received, not only from literary critics such as John R. Allan, Isobel Murray, and Maurice Wiggin but also from other readers in Buchan and further afield. There was one more major publication to come, in 1989: a glossary of the language of north-east Scotland, *Buchan Claik*, in collaboration with a Peterhead fisherman, Peter Buchan. *Collected Short Stories*, with an introduction by Robert Smith, was published in 1992.

John Reid died suddenly at his home, 49 West Dyke Avenue, Westhill, Skene, Aberdeenshire, on 13 May 1998, about six years after a debilitating stroke; his body was cremated and his ashes interred at Foveran kirkyard, Aberdeenshire. He was survived by his wife. Many of his unpublished diaries are now in the National Library of Scotland.   PAUL DUKES

Sources private information (2004) [J. Reid; M. Reid; family] · I. Murray, ed., *Scottish writers talking* (1996) · J. R. Allan, introduction, in J. Reid, *Hard shining corn* (1972) · P. Dukes, introduction, in J. Reid, *Hard shining corn* (1982)
Archives NL Scot., David Toulmin diaries
Likenesses photographs, priv. coll.

Reid, Sir John Watt (1823–1909), surgeon and naval officer, born in Edinburgh on 25 February 1823, was the younger son of John Watt Reid, surgeon in the navy, and his wife, Jane, daughter of James Henderson, an Edinburgh merchant. Educated at Edinburgh Academy, at the university there, and at the extra-mural medical school, he qualified LRCS (Edinburgh) in 1844. He entered the navy as an assistant surgeon on 6 February 1845, and spent two years in the Haslar Royal Naval Hospital, Hampshire, before serving a commission on board the *Rodney* in the channel, where he was commended by his commanders-in-chief. He was appointed in March 1849 to the naval hospital at Plymouth, and received Admiralty approval for his services there during the 1849 cholera epidemic. In January 1852 he was appointed acting surgeon to the sloop *Inflexible*, in the Mediterranean; on 12 September 1854 he was promoted to surgeon, and in June 1855 appointed to the line-of-battle ship *London*, on the same station. In these two ships he served in the Black Sea until the fall of Sevastopol; he was thanked by the commander-in-chief, Sir James Dundas, for his services when the crew of the flagship *Britannia* was stricken with cholera in 1854. On 22 October 1856 he was awarded the MD at Aberdeen, and in April 1857 was appointed to the hospital ship *Belleisle*, in which he continued during the Second Opium War, in 1857–9.

In January 1860 Reid was appointed to the *Nile* (90 guns), and served in her for four years on the North American station. On 6 July 1863 Reid married Georgina, daughter of C. J. Hill, of Halifax, Nova Scotia. He earned his captain's commendation for his zeal and professional ability, especially during an epidemic of yellow fever, while he was medical officer in charge of the temporary hospital in Halifax, Nova Scotia. Vice-Admiral Sir Alexander Milne considered him an officer in whom he could invariably place implicit confidence. He served in the Haslar Hospital from 1864 until 1867, being promoted to staff surgeon on 5 September 1866. After further service in the Mediterranean, in the *Duncan* and the *Lord Warden*, he was placed in June 1870 in charge of the naval hospital at Haulbowline, co. Cork, where he remained until 1873. During

the concluding months of the Second Anglo-Asante War he served in the *Active* and in the *Nebraska*, a troopship converted to receive casualties from the naval brigades, at Cape Coast Castle; he was mentioned in dispatches, and on 31 March 1874 was promoted to deputy inspector-general. In that rank he had charge of the medical establishments at Bermuda from 1875 to 1878, when he was appointed to the Haslar Hospital. On 25 February 1880 he was promoted to be inspector-general and was appointed medical director-general of the navy. In this capacity he carried through important and lasting reforms proposed in 1883 by the Hoskins committee, of which he was a member. They included a naval medical school at the Haslar Hospital, the organization of the naval sick-berth branch, and the naval nursing service.

On Reid's retirement in 1888 the Board of Admiralty recorded its high opinion of his zeal and efficiency. He became an honorary physician to Queen Victoria in February 1881 and to Edward VII in 1901. He was created KCB (military) on 24 November 1882, and awarded the LLD of Edinburgh University on 17 April 1884, the jubilee medal in 1897, and a medical good-service pension in July 1888.

Reid died at his London home, 106 Queen's Gate, South Kensington, on 24 February 1909, and was buried on 26 February at Bramshaw, Hampshire.

L. G. C. LAUGHTON, *rev.* J. WATT

Sources Medical officers' services, 1827–61, PRO, ADM 104/38, fol. 197 · *Men and women of the time* (1899), 898–9 · *The Times* (26 Feb 1909) · *The Times* (20 April 1909) · Surgeons' register, PRO, ADM 104/17(3), fol. 380 · Staff surgeons' register, PRO, ADM 104/29, fol. 71 · W. N. Hewitt, letter to secretary of the admiralty, 14 March 1874, PRO, ADM 1/6305, R46 · 'Admiralty committee to inquire into … the training of sick-berth staff', *Parl. papers* (1884), 17.131–149, C. 3959 · Assistant surgeons' register, PRO, ADM 104/24, fol. 212 · Medical officers' promotion submissions, PRO, ADM 104/45 [unnumbered] · Surgeon's journal of HMS *London*, 1 July 1855–26 Jan 1856, PRO, ADM 101/107(3) · CGPLA Eng. & Wales (1909)
Wealth at death £1191 12s. 4d.: probate, 16 April 1909, CGPLA Eng. & Wales

Reid, (Thomas) Mayne [*pseud.* Charles Beach] (1818–1883), novelist and children's writer, was born in Ballyroney, co. Down, Ireland, on 4 April 1818, the son of Thomas Mayne Reid, a Presbyterian minister, and his wife, whose maiden name was Rutherford. Reid entered the Royal Belfast Academical Institution to study for the ministry, but his desire for adventure induced his parents to allow him to abandon his studies, and Reid sailed for New Orleans in December 1839. In America during the next few years he had a variety of jobs, sometimes as a tutor or store clerk, and, according to his widow—though her accounts of her husband's life are not always reliable—he also organized expeditions, on one of which Audubon, the great naturalist, was a companion. In 1843 Reid moved to Philadelphia, where he became friendly with Edgar Allan Poe and published a number of stories and poems in magazines.

In December 1846 Reid joined the American army in the war against Mexico, and sailed for Vera Cruz in January 1847, writing accounts of his experiences for the newspaper *Spirit of the Times*. Although suffering a wound in the thigh which affected his health for the rest of his life, Reid fought with great bravery at the battle of Chapultepec and was promoted to first lieutenant. In 1848 he resigned from the army with the rank of captain, and began his first novel, *The Rifle Rangers*, partly based on his Mexican adventures. Reid returned to Europe in 1849, intending to assist in the Bavarian revolution, but when that collapsed he settled in England as a full-time writer. *The Rifle Rangers* (1850) was a great success and soon followed by *The Scalp Hunters* (1851). Reid also began a series of boys' adventure stories, the first (*The Desert Home*) appearing at Christmas 1851. In 1853 his radical sympathies became evident again when he became involved in Hungarian politics with his friend Lajos Kossuth, but books continued to flow, *The Young Voyageurs* and *The Forest Exiles* both appearing in 1854. On 15 August of that same year Reid married fifteen-year-old Elizabeth Hyde, daughter of George William Hyde, a Nottingham hosier; some account of their courtship may be given in Reid's novel *The Child Wife* of 1868.

In 1856 the couple moved to Gerrards Cross in Buckinghamshire, where Reid subsequently had a striking residence built in the style of a Mexican *hacienda* called The Ranche. Reid's literary career flourished. As well as producing novels and tales, he adapted his novel *The Maroon* (1862) for the stage, and he may have contributed to other books under the pseudonym Charles Beach.

Despite his literary success, Reid's extravagances led to financial difficulties, though the popularity of a new novel, *The Headless Horseman* (1866), saved him from being completely penniless. But his attempt to start a journal, *The Little Times*, foundered, and Reid and his wife returned to America in October 1867. He began to publish a series of 'dime novels', but when a new magazine, *Onward*, also failed, and Reid's health declined, they returned to England in 1870. The recurrence of his war wound weakened him and he found the production of new work increasingly difficult. The flamboyant figure who, wearing a Mexican sombrero, had once galloped his black horse on Gerrards Cross Common was gradually reduced to walking with crutches. He took a house in Herefordshire near Ross and tried farming, and friends helped him obtain backpay and a pension from the American army. Reid moved in 1883 to London, where he wrote his last book for boys, *The Land of Fire*. He died on 22 October 1883 at his home, 12 Blomfield Road, Maida Hill, his wife surviving him, and was buried in Kensal Green cemetery, London, on 25 October.

Reid is best remembered for his boys' adventure stories and his novels, which were often adapted for juveniles. Such children's books as *The Boy Hunters* (1853), with their mixture of adventure, topography, and natural history, have a historical interest, partly because of their lack of imperialistic sentiments, unusual for the time, but they seem unlikely to regain their popularity. The adult novels also seem dated, despite their remarkable combination of romantic plots, their exotic settings described with some attempt at scientific accuracy, and their sympathy for oppressed peoples. His American novels, however, such as *The Scalp Hunters* and *The Lone Ranche* (1871) may continue to attract those readers interested in the powerful physical and metaphysical impressions made by America on nineteenth-century visitors. DENNIS BUTTS

Sources J. Steele, *Captain Mayne Reid* (1978) · E. Reid and C. H. Coe, *Captain Mayne Reid: his life and adventures* (1900) · E. Reid, *Mayne Reid: a memoir of his life* (1890) · M. Q. Holyoake, 'Captain Mayne Reid: soldier and novelist', *Strand Magazine*, 2 (1891), 93–102 · m. cert. · *CGPLA Eng. & Wales* (1883)
Archives BL, agreements with Richard Bentley, Add. MSS 46617–46618, 46643 · PRO NIre., letters, mostly to Charles Ollivant, D2802; Mic258 · Queen's University, Belfast, letters to Reid-Ollivant
Likenesses chromolithograph caricature, NPG; repro. in *VF* (8 March 1873) · photograph, repro. in Reid and Coe, *Captain Mayne Reid*, 155 · wood-engraving, NPG; repro. in *ILN* (3 Nov 1883)
Wealth at death £1258 10s. 7d.: probate, 5 Nov 1883, *CGPLA Eng. & Wales*

Reid, (Anne Margaret) Nano (1900–1981), landscape and figure painter, was born on 1 March 1900 at 17 Magdalene Street, Drogheda, co. Louth, Ireland, the second of four children of Thomas Reid (1862–1933), publican and grocer, and his wife, Anne Downey (*d.* 1924). She was educated by the Dominican nuns at the Siena convent in Drogheda, and while still at school took art lessons from a Miss Sutton at the local technical school. She became a student nurse at the Mater Hospital in Dublin in November 1920 but left in January 1921 to undertake a more formal study of art. She enrolled as a student at the Dublin Metropolitan School of Art in Kildare Street, travelling from Drogheda each day. A fellow student described her as a 'fierce red-head, [staring] with keen green eyes behind spectacles. She was uncompromising, blunt and desperately looking for the truth' (Snoddy, 420). About 1927 Reid went to Paris to study at the Académie de la Grande Chaumière, and she returned to Drogheda about July 1928. In the autumn of 1929 she attended the Central School of Arts and Crafts and the Chelsea Polytechnic, remaining in London, which she loathed, for a year. She admired the work of the Argentinian artist Antonio Berni, whom she had met in Paris, and that of the Belgian painter Marie Howet, though later insisting that external influences on her work were personal, and that she had not been much influenced by her tutors.

Reid first exhibited at the Royal Hibernian Academy in Dublin in 1925 and continued to exhibit there regularly until 1968. Her first solo exhibition was held at The Gallery, St Stephen's Green, Dublin, in 1934. Between 1941 and 1947 she held five solo shows. In 1942 a critic from the *Irish Times* ended a review of an exhibition of her work: 'There seems to be no help for it. This young artist from Drogheda has to be saluted as a genius' (27 Nov 1942). She also exhibited at the first Living Art exhibition in 1943 when the *Dublin Magazine* described her as a 'bold and original painter but inclined to be rather too energetic in her approach and too afraid of colour' (Snoddy, 421).

Reid's early style was reminiscent of the work of Paul Henry. In the 1940s her work became more expressionistic and, as one critic noted, 'much more lyrical [with] the adoption of a bird's eye view of things [which] characterised her work from the 1940s' (Kennedy, 43). In many of her paintings her brushwork is uninhibited and vigorous. There is apparently little attention to composition or perspective. She was fascinated by water and it appears in her work in a variety of forms. Pubs are also a common theme, as are animals, especially cats. She painted landscapes of the Boyne valley which were imbued 'with a strong sense of mysticism' (ibid.). She was not a prolific painter and she supported herself by painting portraits and giving private lessons. In 1962 Reid returned from Dublin to Drogheda to live with her two sisters at the family pub. With the artist Norah McGuinness she represented Ireland at the 1950 Venice Biennale. She also exhibited at the Mostra Internazionale de Bianco e Nero at Lugano, Switzerland, in 1956; at the Guggenheim International Award Exhibition at New York in 1960; and at 'Twelve Irish painters', an exhibition organized by An Comhairle Ealaion (Arts Council of Ireland) and held at New York in 1963. In 1972 she won the Douglas Hyde gold medal at the Oireachtas. In 1974–5 the arts councils in Belfast and Dublin organized a major retrospective exhibition of 108 works dating from 1931, held first at the Municipal Gallery of Modern Art, Dublin, and afterwards at the Ulster Museum, Belfast. Nano Reid died, unmarried, on 17 November 1981 at Drogheda Cottage Hospital. Examples of her work are in the Ulster Museum, Belfast; the City Library and Crawford Municipal Art Gallery, Cork; and the National Gallery of Ireland and Trinity College, Dublin.   MARIA LUDDY

Sources D. Mallon, *Nano Reid* (1994) · T. Snoddy, *Dictionary of Irish artists: 20th century* (1996) [incl. bibliography and list of works] · B. Kennedy, 'Women artists and the modern movement, 1943–49', *Irish women artists: from the eighteenth century to the present day* (1987), 34–45 [exhibition catalogue, NG Ire., the Douglas Hyde Gallery, TCD, and the Hugh Lane Municipal Gallery of Modern Art, Dublin, July–Aug 1987] · *Nano Reid: a retrospective exhibition*, Arts Council of Ireland and Arts Council of Northern Ireland (1974) [exhibition catalogue, Municipal Gallery of Modern Art, Dublin, and Ulster Museum, Belfast] · 'The artist talks: Nano Reid to Marion Fitzgerald', *Irish Times* (2 Oct 1965)
Archives Ulster Museum, Belfast, biographical notes | SOUND BBC Radio Ulster, interviewed by Martin Dillon, 1974
Likenesses E. Solomons, portrait, 1940–49 · photograph, repro. in *Irish Times* (11 Sept 1979) · photograph, repro. in *Irish Times* (14 April 1969) · photograph, repro. in *Irish Times* (2 Oct 1965) · photograph, repro. in Arts Council of Ireland and Arts Council of Northern Ireland, *Nano Reid*
Wealth at death £75,012: probate, 18 Feb 1982, *CGPLA Éire*

Reid, Patrick Robert [Pat] (1910–1990), escape officer and author, was born on 13 November 1910 in India, the son of John Reid, of the Indian Civil Service, and his wife, Alice Mabel Daniell. He was educated at Clongowes Wood College, co. Kildare, and at Wimbledon College, and went on to King's College, London, where he was awarded a BSc in 1932. He qualified as a civil engineer in 1936, while serving his pupillage with Sir Alexander Gibbs & Partners, a leading firm of consulting engineers, from 1934 to 1937. With the outbreak of war in 1939 he was commissioned into the Royal Army Service Corps and was posted to France as an ammunition officer with the British expeditionary force, but he was taken prisoner on 27 May 1940 and sent to the prison camp at Laufen, near Salzburg, in Austria. In that year he was awarded the MBE.

Dressed as a German peasant woman, Reid escaped from Laufen through a tunnel in September 1940, but was recaptured within a week, and on 7 November he was transferred to Colditz Castle, Oflag IVC, in Saxony. Built on top of a cliff overlooking the River Mulde, it was supposedly impregnable and it was the prison to which allied officers were sent if they had already tried to escape from other German prisons. Because every officer regarded it as his duty to escape, each nationality had its own committee, headed by an escape officer, and though they worked in secret the committees to some extent kept each other informed of their plans and benefited from each others' experiences. Reid was made British escape officer in January 1941. The first escape that he masterminded, in June 1941, involved tunnelling from underneath the floorboards of the canteen to a point beyond the outer wall, but it failed when the twelve officers emerging from the tunnel were betrayed by the German sentry who had been bribed to look the other way. He was responsible, however, for the success of the next attempt, by Lieutenant Airey Neave and a companion in January 1942. On 14 October, having resigned as escape officer in order to organize his own escape, he and three others succeeded in escaping from Colditz, having loosened the bars of a window with a saw smuggled in in a food parcel and with the help of a detailed plan of the castle discovered in the British Museum. They made their escape during 'music practice', conducted by Douglas Bader, who was able to signal the movements of sentries by stopping and starting the music. All four reached Switzerland safely. Reid was awarded the MC in 1943 and reached the rank of major.

Reid spent the rest of the war in Switzerland, as assistant military attaché at the British legation in Bern, working under the British air attaché, Air Commodore 'Freddie' West, who was providing an intelligence service behind enemy lines and supervising escape routes from occupied territories. He later helped West to write his autobiography, *Winged Diplomat* (1962). After D-day, Reid was part of the team, in close contact with members of the French resistance, sending and receiving information across the border, and during the winter he was one of those involved in the exchange of sick and wounded prisoners organized by the International Red Cross. In August 1943, while in Switzerland, he married Jane Cabot, one of the Boston Cabots; they had three sons and two daughters, but were divorced in 1966.

After the war Reid remained in the diplomatic service, and was posted to Ankara in 1946, as first secretary for commercial affairs. In 1949 he joined the diplomatic staff of the Organization for European Economic Co-operation (OEEC), in Paris, where he spent three years as chief administrator of the Marshall aid plan. He became famous after the publication of *The Colditz Story* in 1952—his account of life in Colditz and details of the escapes were regarded by some as the best escape story to come out of the Second World War—and its sequel, *The Latter Days at Colditz* (1953). These were followed by a film, *The Colditz Story* (1955), starring John Mills as Pat Reid; the television series, *Colditz* (1972–4), one of the most popular series ever shown on television; and a successful board game, 'Escape from Colditz'. Reid returned to his Colditz experiences in *Colditz: the Full Story* (1984); by this time over sixty books had been written about Colditz, in several languages, including German, Dutch, and Polish. He also wrote *Prisoner of War* (1953), the story of prisoners-of-war throughout history, and *My Favourite Escape Stories* (1975). When criticized for cashing in on his wartime experiences and overshadowing the achievements and sufferings of other escapers he pointed out that he had waited ten years before writing about them, and that any of his fellow prisoners could have done likewise. He was also accused of glamourizing the life of a prisoner-of-war, as in his description of brewing beer from dried fruit received in Red Cross parcels and distilling it by using a large jam tin and lead piping from one of the lavatories.

Prospective Conservative candidate for Dartford and Erith from 1953 to 1955, Reid failed to get elected in the general election of 1955. He returned to engineering and was a director of Richard Costain Ltd from 1959 to 1962 and of W. S. Atkins & Partners, a firm of consulting engineers, from 1962 to 1963; he then established his own business, Kem Estates Ltd, which built houses mainly in Sussex. In 1977 he married Mrs Mary Stewart Cunliffe-Lister, who died in the following year, and in 1982 he married, as his third wife, Mrs Nicandra Hood. He died in Frenchay Hospital, Bristol, on 22 May 1990.

ANNE PIMLOTT BAKER

Sources P. R. Reid, *The Colditz story* (1952) · P. R. Reid, *Colditz: the full story* (1984) · H. Chancellor, *Colditz* (2001) · *The Times* (24 May 1990) · *Daily Telegraph* (24 May 1990) · WW · d. cert.
Archives GL, corresp. with publishers
Likenesses photograph, 1942, repro. in P. R. Reid, *Winged diplomat* (1962), facing p. 203 · photographs, 1955–85, Hult. Arch.
Wealth at death £40,572: probate, 1990, CGPLA Eng. & Wales

Reid, Peter (1777–1838). *See under* Reid, David Boswell (1805–1863).

Reid, Richard Tuohill (1822/3–1883), lawyer and jurist in India, was born at Killarney, co. Kerry, the only surviving son of Herbert Reid (*d.* before 1842), a merchant of Killarney, and his wife, Catherine, *née* Tuohill. He entered Trinity College, Dublin, as a sizar in 1841, and took a degree in 1844–5. On 3 May 1845 he was admitted to the Middle Temple. In 1848 he sailed to India to become a schoolmaster— and soon afterwards professor of English literature and history—at Elphinstone College, Bombay. One of his colleagues was Joseph Patton, professor of mathematics and a fellow Trinity graduate. Both were enthusiasts in the cause of education for Indians and together they founded the Students' Literary and Scientific Society and started a periodical, the *Students' Miscellany*, which published essays by Elphinstone pupils. With the financial and moral backing of Parsi and Hindu benefactors, the society established the first Indian girls' schools in Bombay. It also spawned a network of regional sub-branches run by Indian students.

In 1852 Reid took furlough to Europe. In Trinity term 1853, having by then completed his obligatory residence at a London inn, he was called to the Irish bar at King's

Inns, Dublin. He returned to Bombay in 1854, bearing the degree of LLD, and established a lucrative law practice in the *sadr adalat* (chief court) and the supreme court. In 1855 he was appointed the first Perry professor of jurisprudence at Elphinstone College, and subsequently he was also placed in charge of the government law school. Both institutions were accredited by Bombay University in 1860, and for almost a quarter of a century Reid remained the single most influential figure in the education of lawyers in western India. In 1856 he published a set of his law lectures, *Family Rights, Considered as a Branch of General and Comparative Jurisprudence*. In 1864 he took over the editorship of the reports of the Bombay high court (12 vols., 1862–75), and he also periodically acted as the first judge of the small claims court and as the coroner of Bombay.

Reid was remembered by an Indian law student as 'a fine witty Irishman' (Wacha, 715). From the time of his return to India in 1854, his sister Anna had been his constant companion. She went back with him to Ireland when he retired about 1880, but on a tour of Italy in 1883 both caught pneumonia. Reid died at the Hotel Victoria, via due Marcelli, Rome, on 11 February 1883, Anna having predeceased him by two days. He had earned a small fortune from his law practice in Bombay and he bequeathed his entire estate of some £25,000 in trust for the promotion of education in Ireland. Sir George Birdwood (1832–1917), a former sheriff of Bombay and first keeper of the Indian museum in South Kensington, was named an executor of the trust.

KATHERINE PRIOR

Sources *Bombay Gazette* (10 March 1883), 4 · *The Athenaeum* (5 May 1883), 571 · Burtchaell & Sadleir, *Alum. Dubl.*, 2nd edn · E. Keane, P. Beryl Phair, and T. U. Sadleir, eds., *King's Inns admission papers, 1607–1867*, IMC (1982) · *Bombay Almanac* (1854–68) · D. E. Wacha, *Shells from the sands of Bombay* (1920) · H. A. C. Sturgess, ed., *Register of admissions to the Honourable Society of the Middle Temple, from the fifteenth century to the year 1944*, 2 (1949), 502
Wealth at death £25,107 14s. 5d.: probate, 25 April 1883, CGPLA Eng. & Wales

Reid, Robert (*d.* 1558), Scottish Renaissance humanist, abbot of Kinloss, and Roman Catholic bishop of Orkney, was born at Aitkenhead in Clackmannan parish, son of John Reid of Aitkenhead, who was killed at Flodden in 1513, and Elizabeth Shanwell, sister of John, abbot of Coupar Angus. He was educated in St Andrews under his uncle, Robert Shanwell, vicar of Kirkcaldy, who held office in the university variously as examiner and *quodlibetarius*, dean of the faculty of arts, and rector. Reid entered the university as a student at St Salvator's College in 1511, graduated MA in fifth place in 1515, and served as an examiner in arts in 1517. By 1518 he had become a notary public in the diocese of Moray. Returned to Fife by 1519 he acted as procurator in the courts and in 1521 was styled cleric of St Andrews diocese. Promotion was fast: by 1524 he gained the subdeanery of Moray and by 1527 he was serving as official of the diocese, and he was also provided in 1525 to his uncle's vicarage of Kirkcaldy in Fife. He was entrusted with the rule of Kinloss Abbey, a Cistercian house, in 1526. After visiting Rome in 1527, in the following year he was introduced at Paris to the Piedmontese humanist scholar Giovanni Ferrerio, whom he invited to Kinloss to instruct the monks. There Ferrerio lectured for several years to the monks on philosophy, classical literature, and a little theology—on Aristotle and Cicero, on Sacrobosco's sphere, and the *Sententiarum* of Peter Lombard. He incorporated, too, the humanist scholarship of Jacques Lefèvre, Rudolph Agricola, Erasmus, and Melanchthon, though there was no word of Hebrew, and understandably the Greek authors were taught from Latin translations and not from the original Greek.

In 1528 the pope provided Reid as abbot of Kinloss in succession to Thomas Crystal, with the dispensation that as a secular cleric he took the monastic habit and profession within six months. Reid duly received the Cistercian habit at the hands of Gavin Dunbar, bishop of Aberdeen, in the Franciscan church in Edinburgh, on 11 July 1529. In 1531 he gained the commendatorship of Beauly Priory in the diocese of Ross. At Kinloss he refurbished the buildings, improved the abbot's chamber, added arches to the cloister, built a fire-proof library well stocked with books, covered the roof of the church with lead, decorated three chapels within the church with pictures and altarpieces, and erected a new dovecote, kiln, malthouse, and barns. For ferrying the stone and timber, he provided a longboat of 24 oars; and in addition he brought from Dieppe a gardener who was expert in planting and grafting fruit trees and was also skilled in surgery. At Beauly, Reid built the nave of the church about 1541, covering it with oak pantiles, and restored the bell tower destroyed by lightning. He then turned his attention to the prior's house which he rebuilt in 1544. Five junior monks were transferred from Beauly to Kinloss and their education entrusted to Ferrerio, whom he recalled from France in 1541. In 1550 he resigned the abbacy of Kinloss in favour of his nephew, Walter Reid, but not so Beauly.

An outstanding prelate, Reid's services were sought by the crown: as a lord of council from 1530 and auditor of the accounts of the master of the king's works; as a member of parliament and senator of the college of justice from 1532, and as a diplomat from 1534, first to England to treat for peace with Henry VIII and then to France to seek a bride for James V; as a commissioner for holding the exchequer; and as auditor of the treasurer's accounts—those of the keeper of the privy seal and those of the comptroller. Nominated by James V to the bishopric of Orkney in 1541, Reid secured papal provision, with the right to retain Kinloss and Beauly. He journeyed to his diocese in the same year, though his consecration as bishop took place in Edinburgh in November. Commissioned with others to treat for peace with England, he entered into unsuccessful negotiations at York in 1542; and when an invading English army arrived in Scotland he again was sent by the king to seek peace, though without success.

Following James V's death at the end of 1542 Reid identified himself with Cardinal Beaton's opposition to the pro-English, anti-Roman policy of Governor Arran. A convention of nobles and clergy at Perth in 1543 sent the bishop to Arran to demand that the cardinal, whom Arran had imprisoned, be released, that the circulation of English versions of the New Testament be curbed and that the governor heed their counsel; but Arran refused their requests and summoned the convention to parliament in Edinburgh, where Reid was elected to the influential committee of the articles. Reid encouraged Sir Ralph Sadler, the English ambassador, to visit Beaton in St Andrews, and became the cardinal's spokesman in further negotiations with the English. Although governor and parliament ratified the treaties of Greenwich of 1543 whereby Queen Mary would become betrothed to Prince Edward of England, Arran immediately began to waver: he reached an understanding with the cardinal and renounced his Anglophile and reforming policies. Reid himself was thought to favour Mary's marriage to the governor's son should the English match be abandoned. By September 1543 he was chosen to the council to direct the governor and sought to curb the ambitions of the earls of Lennox and Angus.

As bishop, Reid attended the trial of heretics detected in Perth in January 1544 and in August he set sail for his diocese of Orkney. In Kirkwall he reorganized the cathedral chapter and drew up a new constitution which provided for the endowment of one provost, six other dignitaries, seven canons, thirteen chaplains, and six choristers. To ensure the efficient administration of the cathedral's affairs and the enhancement of the divine service, the qualifications and duties of the dignitaries and canons were carefully defined, with particular attention being given to the musical performance of the liturgical offices. However, Reid's reforms, though praiseworthy, were financed by diverting revenues from hard-pressed parishes to sustain an enlarged cathedral establishment. They testify to his skills as an organizer and lawyer rather than to his capacity as a spiritual leader.

Reid also played a part in public affairs. He had a seat on the privy council, and in 1545 agreed that with the promise of French support Scotland should defend her frontiers against England. In June 1546, after Beaton's murder, he was one of the lords appointed to Governor Arran's privy council. Membership was to rotate in groups, and Reid was one of four men who were to attend between 10 June and 10 July. The scheme was repeated in March 1547, and again Reid was co-opted to the first group. By 1549 he had risen to become president of the college of justice. He attended the provincial council of the Scottish church summoned in 1549 to effect internal reform, and in 1550 he was present in the Blackfriars Church in Edinburgh at the trial for heresy of Adam Wallace, whom he questioned on the doctrine of transubstantiation. Within his own diocese Reid had decided by 1554 to place the choristers and perpetual vicars in St Magnus Cathedral in a separate house where they could prepare for divine service. He also approved a suitable chamber for the subdean's residence so that the subdean might better exercise discipline in the provost's absence and sit at table with the choristers in the hall. The chaplains and choristers were to reside in their chambers, observe the rules laid down by bishop and chapter, and celebrate the stipulated masses annually.

Affairs of state, however, drew Bishop Reid away from

his diocese. When the governor was deposed in 1554 and Mary of Guise, the queen mother, was substituted as regent, Reid acted as curator for the young Queen Mary in these proceedings and presented the documents to parliament for ratification. In 1556 he accompanied the queen regent to Inverness, where she held justice courts before moving to Elgin, Banff, and Aberdeen; and he was appointed a commissioner for resolving disputes with the English on the borders. In that capacity he met with the bishop of Durham at Carlisle. Meanwhile, the English navy made an unsuccessful attempt during the summer to burn Kirkwall in the bishop's absence. In 1558 he was sent to the court of France as one of the commissioners appointed by the three estates to arrange for the marriage of Mary to the dauphin. Before leaving for the royal wedding Reid made his last will and testament, bequeathing an endowment of 8000 merks for founding a college in Edinburgh, the precursor of Edinburgh University. His plan was to erect three schools within one college: a grammar school, an arts school, and a law school, with chambers for the regents, a hall, and other necessary accommodation. Reid's proposed college looked rather as if it would be freed from the conventional university structure with all its clerical emphasis, and while canon law was not neglected, civil law was accorded a greater prominence. Similarly, his intended arts course, with an emphasis on rhetoric, poetry, and the value of the literary text, eschewed the philosophy-based curriculum of existing university courses. Reid completed his testament on the day appointed for sailing from Kirkcaldy to Leith and onward to France. After a stormy voyage to Dieppe which saw the loss of two ships, men, and horses, the bishop survived to witness the contract of marriage between Mary and the dauphin, and he attended the ceremony in Notre Dame on 24 April. As he prepared to return home, Reid fell ill in Dieppe, where he was visited by Lord James Stewart, who used to debate matters of religion with him. He died there on 6 September 1558. Following petitions from Edinburgh town council, an order was given in 1582 that his bequest should be made available for the foundation of his projected college. Only 2500 merks were made available by Reid's executor, but they helped the college to open in 1583, to become the nucleus of the University of Edinburgh.   JAMES KIRK

Sources W. D. Wilson, ed., *Ferrerii historia abbatum de Kynlos*, Bannatyne Club, 63 (1839) • J. Stuart, ed., *Records of the monastery of Kinloss*, Society of Antiquaries of Scotland, 9 (1872) • J. M. Anderson, ed., *Early records of the University of St Andrews*, Scottish History Society, 3rd ser., 8 (1926) • D. E. R. Watt, ed., *Fasti ecclesiae Scoticanae medii aevi ad annum 1638*, [2nd edn], Scottish RS, new ser., 1 (1969) • *APS*, 1424–1592 • *Reg. PCS*, 1st ser., vol. 1 • M. Livingstone, D. Hay Fleming, and others, eds., *Registrum secreti sigilli regum Scotorum / The register of the privy seal of Scotland*, 2–5 (1921–57) • J. M. Thomson and others, eds., *Registrum magni sigilli regum Scotorum / The register of the great seal of Scotland*, 11 vols. (1882–1914), vols. 3–4 • *Letters of James V*, ed. D. Hay (1954) • J. D. Marwick, ed., *Extracts from the records of the burgh of Edinburgh, AD 1528–1589*, [2–4], Scottish Burgh RS, 3–5 (1871–82) • *LP Henry VIII*, vols. 7–21 • J. Kirk, 'Clement Little's Edinburgh', *Edinburgh University Library: a collection of historical essays*, ed. J. R. Guild and A. Law (1982), 1–42 • G. Brunton and D. Haig, *An historical account of the senators of the college of justice, from its institution in MDXXXII (1832)* • *DNB*

Wealth at death bequeathed 8000 merks for endowing a college in Edinburgh: Burton and Masson, *Register*

Reid, Robert [*pseud.* Senex] (1773–1865), topographer and antiquary, youngest son of John Reid (1733–1788), mahogany dealer and cabinet-maker in Glasgow, was born there in the Candleriggs on 27 January 1773. He was educated at Glasgow grammar school (1782–6) and at the University of Glasgow. In 1793 he began business as a muslin manufacturer and in 1800 became a partner with his brother John as a wholesale mahogany dealer. On his brother's death he took over the business, adding to it that of cabinet-making and upholstery. He married, in 1809, a daughter of Robert Ewing, a merchant of London. She died in 1826. With her he had three sons.

In 1832 Reid sold off his stock-in-trade and retired from business. Devoting himself to literature, under the pseudonym of Senex, he contributed for many years attractive and well-informed articles on local memorabilia to the *Glasgow Herald*. These papers were afterwards collected and published, as *Glasgow Past and Present* (3 vols., 1851–6). He also published *Glasgow and its Environs* (1864), and the two works, with additions by other writers, were reprinted in three volumes in 1884. The third volume, entirely by Reid, contains his portrait and a short autobiography. He also wrote on Hebridean history (1850).

During the last years of his life Reid lived at Strahoun Lodge on the Isle of Cumbrae, where he died on 7 June 1865.   GEORGE STRONACH, *rev.* H. C. G. MATTHEW

Sources *Autobiography of the late Robert Reid: with a selection of his papers* (1865) • Boase, *Mod. Eng. biog.*

Archives Mitchell L., Glas., MSS on Glasgow contributed to *Glasgow Herald* | NL Scot., letters to John Buchanan

Likenesses portrait, repro. in R. Reid, *Glasgow past and present*, 3 (1856)

Wealth at death £1170 0s. 11d.: probate, 24 Oct 1865, NA Scot., SC8/35/11, 613

Reid, Robert (1774–1856), architect, was born on 8 November 1774 in Edinburgh, the son of Alexander Reid, a substantial builder and developer in Edinburgh's New Town, and his wife, Mae or May Cochrane. He began by assisting his father in Edinburgh. By 1799 both were styling themselves architect, Robert probably from one of his father's properties in South Castle Street, Edinburgh, although he continued as a builder for at least another five years. He is likely to have been 'the architect agreeable to the Town' suggested by Thomas Anderson to Perth for the designs of his New Town that year, since within two years he was appointed architect of Marshall Place and then Rose Terrace, in Perth (D. Graham-Campbell, *Thomas Moy Marshall*, n.d., 2).

Reid's first two public commissions in Edinburgh were, curiously, in partnership with other architects: the Bank of Scotland, in 1802, with Richard Crichton—an elegant, high-set pavilion—and the Heriot estate (1802–3), jointly with William Sibbald. Heriot Row, for which Reid's elevations exist, was plain if insufficiently majestic for the scale, but of the grandeur of the centrepiece, Great King

Street (if Reid was responsible), there is no doubt. Possibly as a consequence of his father's connections (he feued several of his New Town properties to prominent lawyers) Reid was commissioned for designs to extend the courts in 1802 and for the refacing and extension of Parliament House (1807–10). Reid's refacing of the parliament house of Scotland attracted widespread opprobrium, however, which increased once he extruded the design eastward to complete the south side of Parliament Square after the 1824 fire. Had he had the courage to leave the old building and use it as a foil to his new work, the merit in the latter might have been perceived, for there is a certain dour and massive majesty in Reid's classical buildings which, in the right light, can be powerful. Possibly at the same time, he may have been responsible, judging by its style, for Calder Hall (dem.), Linlithgowshire. His 1806 plan for a new town at Dunkeld remained unbuilt, as did his 1807 design for Inveraray court-house (deemed too expensive); the commission for the latter was awarded to James Gillespie Graham six years later. In 1807 Reid was elected burgess of Edinburgh and began work on 33–34 Charlotte Square. In 1808 he obtained the unremunerated title of king's architect and surveyor in Scotland. In 1809 he submitted an old-fashioned competition design for Glasgow's justiciary courts. His St George's West Church in Charlotte Square (1811) attracted further obloquy: 'a pile of discordancy very rarely to be met with … an object of general disapprobation' (Storer). His architectural popularity never rose. The *New Edinburgh Review* weighed in in 1823: 'Have we not a right to grieve at … the New Church in Charlotte Square … We have no less reason to lament the tastes which produced the Bank of Scotland' ('Architecture', 565).

There may have been a question as to the efficiency of Reid's planning: his authoritarian customs house in Leith (1812) required internal remodelling and a new stair by William Burn only twelve years later. His lunatic asylum, Morningside (1809–10; dem. 1896) formed the subject of his publication in 1809 of *Observations on the Structure of Hospitals for the Treatment of Lunatics*. In 1812 he carried out alterations to the Orphan Hospital, Edinburgh. In 1813 he designed his finest interior, the notable gallery and library in Paxton House, Berwickshire. Edinburgh council had paid him handsomely for abortive plans for completing Edinburgh University in 1810, so he refused to compete for the university in 1816. His plans for the Merchant Maiden's Hospital were equally unsuccessful, and he again refused the 1816 invitation to compete for that, leaving the field to William Burn.

Reid had been asked to report on the contract dispute at Taymouth, of 1811, and the Calton Hill plans in 1813, and was the arbiter between John Paterson and the Eglinton trustees in 1821 in a dispute concerning the construction costs of Eglinton Castle. In 1823 he proposed a new street through Edinburgh's Grassmarket and Cowgate, terminating at the Pleasance. Yet, apart from the county buildings, Perth (1812–14), there appear to have followed some lean years until 'His Majesty's Architect in Scotland' was appointed to design Wick town hall in 1821. In 1824 Reid became 'Sole Master of our Works and General Inspector and Overseer and Architect and Surveyor of all our Palaces and Public Buildings of whatever kind in Scotland' at a salary of £200, with the task to 'superintend and control all repairs to Crown property'. In 1822 he had designed the north wing of Register House, Edinburgh; he also designed Downpatrick gaol in 1824 and carried out works at Holyrood, Fortrose Cathedral, Glasgow Cathedral, Dunfermline, Elgin, Linlithgow Palace, and St Andrews Cathedral. Without his actions, many Scottish monuments might not have survived. He was a pioneering conservationist: 'I conceive that in all cases of this kind, restoration or embellishment should not be the object … but that Repairs … should be executed … with a view solely to their preservation' (NA Scot., SC 21971/2 C ft.1 MW/1/342).

In 1829 Reid was appointed to work at St Salvator's, St Andrews (completed by his successor William Nixon), where he designed the north part of the east range in Scottish seventeenth-century style, added an entrance gate to St Mary's, and extended the library to include a senate house. In 1839, just before he was sixty-five, Reid's post was abolished and he was retired on full pay until his death sixteen years later, dividing his time between his little extended villa, Lowwood, near Kelso, and his house at 44 Charlotte Square, Edinburgh, where he died on 20 March 1856. He was survived by his wife, Sarah, *née* Wisdom. The monument in Edinburgh's Dean cemetery to this prickly, somewhat self-important, old-fashioned, but dedicated architect states that his professional abilities and private virtues 'secured the warm esteem and lasting friendship of a large circle of the most distinguished of his contemporaries'. It would be good to know who these were. CHARLES MCKEAN

Sources Colvin, *Archs.* • J. M. Crook and M. H. Port, eds., *The history of the king's works*, 6 (1973) • P. Ogle-Skan, 'The office of works in Scotland: the early years', *Studies in Scottish antiquity: echoes in stone*, ed. D. Breeze (1984) • N. Allen, ed., *Scottish pioneers of the Greek revival* (1984) • commissariat of Edinburgh, Sheriff court records, SC 70/91 • register of Sasines • private information (2004) [R. Fawcett and D. Walker] • T. A. Markus, ed., *Order and space in society* (1982) • *Tolbooths and town houses: civic architecture in Scotland to 1833*, Royal Commission on the Ancient and Historical Monuments of Scotland (1996) • M. Glendinning, R. MacInnes, and A. MacKechnie, *A history of Scottish architecture* (1996) • *Book of the Old Edinburgh Club*, 18 (1932), 79–99 • 'Architecture', *New Edinburgh Review*, 8 (April 1823), 554–605 • J. Storer and H. S. Storer, *Views in Edinburgh* (1820) • [W. Papworth], ed., *The dictionary of architecture*, 11 vols. (1853–92) • *IGI* • Pevsner (1978–) [The buildings of Scotland series] • C. McKean, ed., *Illustrated architectural guides to Scotland* (1982–)
Archives Mitchell L., Glas., MSS • Paxton House, Berwickshire, MSS • Royal Commission on the Ancient and Historical Monuments of Scotland, Edinburgh, National Monuments Record of Scotland, MSS
Wealth at death £1293 9s. 11d.; plus 191 acres of Borders land; seven flats and one house in Edinburgh; two houses in Melrose: inventory, NA Scot., SC 70/91; will, NA Scot., SC 70/4/45, p. 678

Reid, Sir Robert Basil (1921–1993), railway manager, was born on 7 February 1921 at Park Hill, Britians Lane, Sevenoaks, Kent, the second of the three sons of Sir Robert Niel Reid (1883–1964), sometime governor of Assam and Bengal, and his wife, Amy Helen Disney. Educated at Malvern

College, and from 1939 at Brasenose College, Oxford, where he read history, he was forced to interrupt his studies as a result of the Second World War. In 1941 he joined the Royal Tank regiment and served as a tank commander in the western desert, but was captured and spent four years as a prisoner of war. Having completed his degree at Oxford he joined the railway industry in September 1947 as a management trainee, becoming one of the London and North Eastern Railway's last traffic apprentices in the few months before nationalization. Training in the customary way of the industry in operating and commercial departments at various locations, he was appointed goods agent at York in 1958. His was a comparatively leisurely progression through the ranks. Posts followed as assistant district goods manager, district passenger manager, planning manager (all in the Scottish region at Glasgow), then divisional manager (eastern region, Doncaster). In 1972 he was appointed deputy general manager of the eastern region. Two years later, at the age of fifty-three, he became general manager of the southern region in succession to David Binnie; there he quickly established his authority. In April 1976 he attracted the attention of headquarters with a cost-reduction scheme: secured with the co-operation of the trade unions, it made estimated savings of £1.7 million a year.

On 15 September 1951 Reid had married Isobel Jean McLachlan, a hospital almoner; they had a son and a daughter. His wife's premature death in 1976 turned the ambitious railway manager into a workaholic with considerable drive and purpose. He quickly caught the eye of the recently appointed British Rail chairman, Sir Peter Parker, and played a leading part in the latter's reorganization of the British Railways board in January 1977. Three new full-time posts were established, with direct functional responsibility for engineering and research, marketing, and operations; Reid took on the marketing portfolio, the first of its kind in British Rail. With the chief executive, David Bowick, and his fellow appointees, Jim Urquhart and Ian Campbell, he provided a substantial Scottish or 'MacMafia' presence on the board. Reid flourished at the top level, unlike some of his colleagues. He made a substantial contribution to railway pricing, and in February 1977 joined the board of the neglected subsidiary, British Transport Hotels, where, with Prue Leith and Sir Alexander Glen, he breathed new life into the hotels business before its privatization in 1983. As chief executive in succession to Campbell from March 1980 he inspired a sharpening up of the railway command structure, but this was merely the prelude to a more radical organizational change—sector management—in which he was a main protagonist. Reid had come up through the ranks of the multi-functional region, each with a general manager at the top, but he showed no sentiment in ending the 140-year dominance of the railway barony. Between 1982 and 1989 the regions were effectively replaced with an organization which brought together responsibility for operating and financial performance in each of the five rail businesses or sectors. Reid may not

have been the intellectual architect of sector management, but he immediately saw the benefits of focusing managers more clearly on the bottom line.

Parker stepped down as chairman in September 1983, and when the Department of Transport failed to find a leading businessman to replace him, Reid, who had already taken Campbell's place as a vice-chairman in January, was the natural choice among the professional insiders for the job. His appointment was not universally applauded in Whitehall, however, and the department insisted that he be accompanied by an outsider as deputy chairman, Sir Richard Cave from Thorn/EMI. Characteristically, Reid combined the post of chairman with that of chief executive, though he was soon assisted by two deputy chief executives. Under his direction the board reverted to a planning-style form—Reid called it policy and audit—and the new arrangements gave more authority in a functional sense to the new triumvirate of chief executive and deputies (subsequently known as joint managing directors). Sector directors were progressively given responsibility for the core railway businesses; a firmer grip was imposed on engineering, notably on mechanical and electrical engineering, where the subsidiary British Rail Engineering Ltd was privatized in 1989; and the organizational changes under Reid may be seen as the precursor to the reorganization in 1992 known as organizing for quality, or OfQ, in which the sectors were given full bottom-line responsibility for operating, finance, and engineering. Reid's period also saw the disposal of the subsidiary businesses such as hotels, Sealink (British Rail's shipping arm), and the extensive sale of surplus property. His view on privatization of the rail businesses is more difficult to discern, but the evidence suggests that he was opposed to breaking up the integrated core business.

While Parker was a great motivator of people and appealed to intellectual consensus, Reid was a doer, intent on getting the job finished within the guidelines established by a government whose politics he respected. Happy to see himself as a crusader battling against entrenched opposition, and often uncomfortably abrasive, he had a classic task-oriented approach to management. Indeed, he was described in one journal as '"Neutron Bob" Reid—the one that takes out the people while leaving the buildings standing' (*Modern Railways*, Nov 1983, 601). Determined to manage, he certainly installed some remarkable sector directors—first Cyril Bleasdale, David Kirby, and John Welsby, and later Chris Green, John Prideaux, and John Edmonds. He had inherited a difficult brief from a government which was, at best, indifferent to railways. The last two years of Parker's period had been blighted by the Serpell report, which had been critical of the railways' financial control, by stormy industrial relations, by a patent shortage of investment, and by the government's rejection of British Rail's ambitious electrification programme. Reid rescued the situation. He was clearly in tune with the Conservative administrations he served, enjoying a personal relationship with both Nicholas Ridley and Denis Thatcher, who shared some of his leisure pursuits. He even persuaded the sceptical Margaret Thatcher to make a journey by train in 1987. However, it was his performance in meeting tough government-set financial targets for the industry in the 1980s which caused Thatcher to make him an exception in her customary condemnation of public-sector managers. Reid was able to persuade Ridley, secretary of state for transport, and his successors to support a higher level of railway investment in return for meeting the tougher three-year financial targets of 1983 and 1986 (the central-government subsidy fell below £500 million in 1988/9). Administrative costs were reduced; InterCity became a profitable business, albeit briefly, its newly electrified east coast main line the jewel in its crown; faster and more comfortable new trains were bought for the provincial and network south-east sectors; preparations began for new services through the channel tunnel; passenger traffic increased by 26 per cent from 1982 to 1988/9; and British Rail became one of the world's most cost-effective rail networks. Many people now regard this period as a golden age in the history of Britain's nationalized railways, and it was no surprise when Reid's appointment was extended for a further three years in 1987. Unfortunately, like Parker before him, he came to regret the decision to go beyond his initial term. The years 1988–9 took some of the gilt off the golden age. Battered by the adverse publicity which major rail accidents at Clapham, Purley, and Bellgrove had created, allegations of corruption in the procurement of civil engineering equipment, and a particularly confrontational rail strike in the summer of 1989, he, like Parker before him, retired in a rather bruised condition, in April 1990. In addition, his Conservative sympathies had a less attractive side in a rather hawkish attitude to loss-making rail services, notably the Settle and Carlisle, and an uncompromising approach to industrial relations, evident in the key disputes of his period—flexible rostering, driver-only operation, and the railway unions' support for the miners in 1984–5. Furthermore, critics have pointed out that cost-effectiveness was achieved partly by raising fares, the attention to quality left something to be desired, railway freight business declined sharply, and higher investment levels were financed in large measure by the sale of assets.

Reid, often referred to as Bob Reid I to distinguish him from his successor at British Rail, Sir Robert Paul Reid (Bob Reid II), was arguably the most successful chairman of British Rail in the period of nationalization (1948–97). Shrewd, resilient, and determined, he often appeared shy and remote, but to those who knew him well he was warm, with a wry sense of humour. He never shirked responsibility, no less so at the time of the Clapham accident in December 1988. He certainly had a fundamental impact on both British Rail's organization and its culture. He did much to restore confidence in the railways' financial performance, but was unable to shake off the bewilderment and loss of direction created by the government's early enthusiasm for rail privatization. A freeman of the City of London, he was a president of the Chartered Institute of Transport, chairman of the Council of European Railways and of the Nationalized Industries Chairman's Group (in 1987), and a member of the president's committee of the Confederation of British Industry, of Business in the Community, and of the council of the Prince's Youth Business Trust. He was knighted in 1985. He was also an honorary fellow of Brasenose College and held honorary doctorates from the universities of Bristol and Buckingham. A lover of sailing, fishing, golf, and mountain walking, he was unable to enjoy a well-earned retirement. Already far from well in 1990, he died from cancer on 17 December 1993, at his home, Friday House, White Horse Road, East Bergholt, Colchester.

TERRY GOURVISH

Sources T. Gourvish, *British Rail, 1974–97: from integration to privatisation* (2002) · T. R. Gourvish, 'British Rail's business-led organisation, 1979–90', *Business History Review* (1990) · P. Parker, *For starters: the business of life* (1989) · T. R. Gourvish, *British Railways, 1948–73: a business history* (1986) · *A participative approach to cost reduction in British Railways*, British Railways Board, Southern Region (1976) · *Modern Railways* (Nov 1983), 601; (Dec 1999), 921 · *British Railways Board Annual Report and Accounts* (1977–90) · *The Economist* (21 May 1988) · *New Statesman* (5 Aug 1983) · *Sunday Times* (12 March 1989); (29 May 1983); (17 July 1983) · *Financial Times* (18 May 1983); (3 Sept 1983); (19 July 1989); (27 July 1989) · *The Times* (7 March 1989); (18 Dec 1993) · *The Independent* (18 Dec 1993) · b. cert. · m. cert. · d. cert. · WWW

Archives PRO, board member's papers, British Railways board, AN 192/392

Likenesses portrait, British Railways Board · portrait, repro. in *Annual Report and Accounts*, British Railways Boards (1986–7), 7 · portrait, repro. in *Annual Report and Accounts*, British Railways Board (1989–90), 3

Wealth at death £716,002: probate, 14 June 1994, *CGPLA Eng. & Wales*

Reid, Sir Robert Gillespie (1842–1908), railway contractor and entrepreneur in Canada, was born on 12 October 1842 in Coupar Angus, Perthshire, Scotland, the son of William Robertson Reid, a linen miller, and his wife, Catherine Gillespie. He was educated locally, and trained as a stonemason. In 1865, drawn by the gold rush, he emigrated to Australia, but was disappointed as a prospector and worked on railway viaducts in the Blue Mountains. He was back in Scotland between 1869 and 1871, then moved to Canada, where by 1872 he was working on the Grand Trunk Railway's bridge between Fort Erie (Ontario) and Buffalo (New York). His family—he had married Harriet Duff in Auckland, New Zealand, in 1865—joined him the following year.

During this period Reid established himself as a builder of railway bridges. In the late 1870s and early 1880s he worked in the United States, but returned to Canada in 1883 to take a series of bridge contracts with the Canadian Pacific Railway (CPR). He was closely involved with the line being built by the CPR along the north shore of Lake Superior, including the very difficult Jackfish Bay section. In 1886 he completed the Lachine Bridge near Montreal, where he was then living. The following year he contracted to build his first railway line—the CPR's Sudbury branch—as well as, on Cape Breton, the foundations of the Grand Narrows Bridge and a section of line for the Intercolonial Railway.

By this time Reid was wealthy, well established, respected for his professional skill and reliability, and closely connected to the prominent and influential Montreal businessmen who controlled the CPR, of which he became a director. It is not surprising, therefore, that in 1890 the government of Newfoundland, led by Sir William Whiteway, awarded him, in partnership with G. H. Middleton, the contract to complete a partially built railway from St John's, the capital, to Hall's Bay on the island's north-east coast. In a second contract, settled in 1893, Reid and the government agreed to abandon the idea of a terminus at Hall's Bay and to continue the line across the island to Port aux Basques, where a ferry could connect with the Intercolonial on Cape Breton. In addition, Reid agreed to operate the railway for ten years in return for substantial land grants—10,000 acres per mile, for a total entitlement of nearly 4000 square miles.

Reid's financial stability was threatened in 1894–5, when, in the wake of the collapse of the colony's two banks, the Newfoundland government hung on the edge of bankruptcy. Reid was being paid in government bonds, which suddenly became virtually worthless. His precise role in the events which followed is unclear, but it is probable that he encouraged the Bank of Montreal, with which he was closely connected (he later became a director), to go to Newfoundland, take over the government's accounts, and advance temporary loans. Reid also did his best to facilitate the negotiation of terms of union between Newfoundland and Canada in March 1895. When it proved impossible to arrive at suitable terms he used his influence to help Robert Bond obtain an emergency loan in Montreal, which enabled the colony to avoid default and to stabilize its finances.

The main line of the Newfoundland Railway was completed in 1897. The following year Reid signed a third contract with a new government led by Sir James Winter. It was a complex and wide-ranging document, which represented the aspirations of his family as much as himself. At that point, suffering from 'inflammatory rheumatism', Reid lived in Montreal, spent much time abroad unsuccessfully seeking a cure, and visited Newfoundland infrequently; the business there was looked after by his sons (the eldest, William D. Reid, was general manager). The deal provided that Reid would operate the entire Newfoundland railway system for fifty years, at which time it would become the property of his successors. Reid would pay $1 million and receive an additional 2400 square miles in land grants. He agreed in addition, among other concessions, to take over the government's telegraph system and dry dock, and to operate the Gulf ferry and a coastal steamer service. Clearly, the Reids intended to become much more than railway contractors.

The new contract sparked heated controversy within the colony, and was severely criticized by the colonial secretary, Joseph Chamberlain. The Winter government was eventually defeated in the legislature and replaced by an anti-contract government led by Bond, who was confirmed in office by a landslide election victory in 1900. The result of prolonged negotiations was a revised contract in 1901 whereby 'Czar Reid', as the local press called him, surrendered the reversionary interest in the railway, the telegraph system, and a large amount of land in return for financial compensation (to be decided in part by arbitration) and permission to assign his assets to the Reid Newfoundland Company, of which he became the first president.

It was not long before relations between Bond and the Reid interests deteriorated, so much so that in 1905 Reid offered to sell out to the Newfoundland government. When the offer was rejected, Reid and his sons made a determined and successful attempt to destroy Bond and install a more friendly administration. This was by no means the first time they had intervened in local politics, but perhaps the most blatant example. Their candidate to replace Bond was Sir Edward Morris, who had supported the 1898 contract. In 1907 he left the Bond government, and the following year, funded largely by Reid money, started a new party and a new newspaper. By the spring of 1909 he was prime minister.

Sir Robert Reid—he was knighted in 1907—died at 275 Drummond Street, Montreal, on 3 June 1908, before these plans had come to fruition; he was cremated on 6 June at the city's Mount Royal crematorium. The company he had founded, with its virtual monopoly on public transportation and its extensive land holdings, remained a major factor in the colony's political and economic life into the 1920s. In addition to the operation of the railway and their steamers, the Reids were closely involved with the development of Newfoundland's newsprint and electricity industries. Reid himself, quiet and unostentatious, was remembered more with respect than with affection as a competent, dependable contractor of considerable integrity—the blame for the family's questionable political behaviour being placed, with some justice, on his sons.

JAMES K. HILLER

Sources J. K. Hiller, 'A history of Newfoundland, 1874–1901', PhD diss., U. Cam., 1971 · J. K. Hiller, 'The political career of Robert Bond', *Twentieth-century Newfoundland: explorations*, ed. J. K. Hiller and P. Neary (1994), 11–45 · R. Cuff, 'Reid, Sir Robert Gillespie', *DCB*, vol. 13 · *Daily News* [St John's, Newfoundland] (4 June 1908) · *Daily News* [St John's, Newfoundland] (15 June 1908)

Archives Provincial Archives of Newfoundland and Labrador, St John's, Newfoundland, Reid Newfoundland Company MSS

Reid, Robert Threshie, Earl Loreburn (1846–1923), lord chancellor, was born on 3 April 1846 on the island of Corfu, the second son of Sir James John Reid (1805–1876), of Mouswald Place, Dumfries, and his wife, Mary, daughter of Robert Threshie, of Barnbarroch, Kirkcudbrightshire. His maternal forebears came from Norfolk. Both his father and grandfather were lawyers. Sir James had been appointed chief justice of the Ionian Islands, then a British protectorate, by Lord Grey of the Reform Bill; and Reid spent an exotic boyhood on Corfu, returning with his family to Dumfries when his father's term of office expired. He was educated at Cheltenham College, where

Robert Threshie Reid, Earl Loreburn (1846–1923), by H. Harris Brown, 1911

he proved an outstanding scholar and athlete, becoming head of the school and excelling at cricket, football, and racquets. After winning a demyship at Magdalen College, Oxford, he decided to try for a scholarship at Balliol; and although the president of Magdalen refused his characteristically bold request for permission to make the attempt without forfeiting his demyship, he won the Balliol scholarship anyway. Intellectual and athletic prowess made him the classic Balliol all-rounder. He won his blue for racquets, played cricket for the university, and was reckoned a wicket-keeper of national calibre. 'You will get a Third, Mr Reid', the redoubtable Benjamin Jowett, master of Balliol, warned of these sporting predilections (*Contemporary Review*, 33); but by dint of all-out effort Reid confounded the prediction, gaining first-class honours in both classical moderations and *literae humaniores* (1868) and carrying off the leading classical scholarship, the Ireland.

The bar and politics Failing, however, much to his disappointment, to win a fellowship, Reid decided on a legal career. He was called to the bar of the Inner Temple in 1871 and joined the Oxford circuit. The same year he married Emily Douglas, daughter of Captain Arthur Fleming, of the 1st dragoon guards. His rise at the bar was rapid. He reputedly earned several hundred pounds in his first year. For a time he 'devilled' for Henry James (later Lord James of Hereford), a former pupil at Cheltenham, but soon established his independence. His strong points were common sense, mastery of facts, and ready grasp of issues. Especially able in commercial suits, 'he could

unravel complicated details in a partnership and track a fraud through all its windings' (*The Times*, 1 Dec 1923). A stout, bluff, good-natured man, addicted to his cup of tea and his clay pipe, with a strong physique and a large head (which critics called 'swelled'), determined in his opinions, yet kindly and soft-spoken, he was well liked for his frank, open demeanour, his informality, and his sportsmanship. In an age when first names were less frequently used than later, he was widely known as 'Bob' Reid.

Reid was an admirer of W. E. Gladstone and entertained political ambitions. Through the further influence of Sir Henry James, he stood as Liberal candidate for Hereford in the general election of 1880, and was elected to parliament as the borough's second Liberal member. In 1882 he took silk, only eleven years after call and at the then exceptionally early age of thirty-six. He appeared frequently before the House of Lords and the judicial committee of the privy council; but his performance as a 'leader', though competent, was felt to fall below his early promise, his political pursuits having outstripped his interest in law. When Hereford became a single-member constituency in 1885, Reid sought another seat. He was narrowly defeated at Dunbartonshire, but secured election as a Gladstonian Liberal in June 1886 as member for Dumfries burghs, which he represented for nineteen years until he became lord chancellor in 1905.

Reid made no special mark in the House of Commons, but was much in demand across the country as a popular and attractive speech maker. A lucky chain of events propelled him suddenly from the back benches to high office. In the summer of 1894 the solicitor-general, Sir John Rigby, was made attorney-general, and Reid became a candidate for the vacancy. His main rival was Haldane, strongly supported by Asquith; but Haldane, like Rigby, was a Chancery lawyer, and it was felt that 'it would not do to have him as well as Rigby for Law Officers' (Brooks, 132). With some reluctance, the prime minister, Lord Rosebery, appointed Reid as solicitor-general; he was knighted in the same year. In October 1894, when Rigby was raised to the Court of Appeal, Sir Robert Reid, as he then was, became attorney-general. His tenure lasted only a few months, however, for when the Unionists returned to power the following July, he was out of office for a decade.

During these years in opposition, Reid's practice declined; but the Unionist government thought sufficiently highly of his judgement and character to invite him to act as arbitrator in the boundary dispute between Venezuela and British Guiana in 1899, for which he received the GCMG, and in the Alaska boundary dispute in 1903. A 'Little Englander' (though he repudiated the expression), like the Liberal leader, Sir Henry Campbell-Bannerman, he denounced both the government's policy towards the Boers and its imperialist supporters prominent in his own party. During the Second South African War he continued to speak out for the Boers 'with characteristic disregard of his professional and political interests' (*The Times*, 1 Dec 1923). After the war he helped Campbell-

Bannerman to draw up the settlement which restored self-government to Transvaal and Orange River Colony.

Lord chancellor Even before the Liberals returned to power, there was much intriguing for the office of lord chancellor. As in 1894, Haldane, once more a contender, canvassed the prime minister, again with Asquith's support; but Campbell-Bannerman preferred Reid on both personal and political grounds, and appointed him to the woolsack in December 1905. He took the title of Baron Loreburn of Dumfries (from 'lower-burn', a district of Dumfries, and the city's ancient motto and rallying cry). When Campbell-Bannerman died in 1908, Loreburn's was one of several names proposed to succeed him instead of Asquith. Widowed in January 1904 after a long and happy marriage, in 1907 Loreburn married a close friend of his late wife, Violet Elizabeth, elder daughter of William Frederick Hicks-Beach, of Witcombe Park, Gloucestershire, and niece of the well-known Conservative statesman, Michael Hicks Beach, first earl of St Aldwyn. There were no children of either marriage.

Loreburn was a vigorous, reforming lord chancellor. He established the office of public trustee, a long-awaited measure designed to obviate the defalcations of unscrupulous solicitors. His most important achievement was the establishment in 1907 of the court of criminal appeal, another reform long overdue, which he carried through despite much opposition from his fellow lawyers. He was constantly importuned by Liberal MPs to nominate large numbers of their supporters as justices of the peace after a glut of Unionist appointments by Lord Halsbury. Resolved to appoint on grounds of fitness alone, he indignantly resisted these efforts by what he called 'the caucus' of his party, including the chief whip, as he wrote to George Whiteley on 10 December 1906, 'to force upon me what I regard as a prostitution of my office, and … I will resign the Great Seal sooner than do it' (Heuston, 156). He would gladly redress the political balance, he declared, but on conscientiously investigating the names submitted to him rather than approving them on the nod, as had been customary, he found many which he felt bound to reject. 'I should be a coward', he wrote to Arthur Ponsonby on 22 November 1906, 'if I made what I think unsuitable appointments to appease the clamour of MPs' (Heuston, 154). Chastened by his own experience, in 1910 he introduced the present system of local advisory committees responsible to the lord chancellor for recommending candidates for the magistracy. His impartiality and discernment were likewise apparent in his nominations to the county court and High Court. He showed the same staunch independence of mind in his refusal 'to hawk justice', as he put it (Fitzroy, 335), by bowing to political pressures, which, again, had certainly influenced the process hitherto. As he observed with pride on raising J. C. Bigham to the presidency of the Admiralty, Probate, and Divorce Division in 1909, 'there were no damned politics about the appointment' (Mersey, 227). To a candidate disappointed of judicial office who pleaded his political services, Loreburn explained loftily that politics did not come into it; to which the infuriated aspirant retorted that but for politics Loreburn himself would have risen no higher than a county court bench (Ashley, 224–5). His High Court nominees included such luminaries as Parker, Eve, Bankes, Avory, Horridge, Lush, Scrutton, and Hamilton (later Lord Sumner).

As speaker of the House of Lords, it fell to Loreburn to introduce a succession of radical and controversial measures against strenuous opposition from the hereditary Unionist peers with their huge entrenched majority. Legislation ranged from an act for the taxation of Scottish land values in 1908 to the Trade Union Act of 1913, which, reversing the decisions in the Taff Vale and Osborne cases, empowered trade unions to levy a political fund and to sponsor members of parliament. Loreburn led the house at a period of inter-party strife and constitutional crisis unprecedented in modern times and which intensified when the peers rejected the 'People's Budget' in 1909. Emotions ran particularly high during the debates on the Parliament Act of 1911, which drastically reduced the power of the Lords to delay legislation. Yet unexpectedly, Loreburn established and maintained a marked ascendancy in the upper house, winning respect and even affection for the honesty, straightforwardness, and patience which accompanied and set off his absolute determination. His dignity and pluck and the patent sincerity of his belief in the reforms which he advocated appealed to his opponents' sporting instincts; so did his good humour, as when he offered to go tiger shooting with one of the leading 'die-hards', Lord Willoughby de Broke. 'If he was a strong partisan' the latter recalled, 'no one thought the worse of him for that' (Broke, 259). He also impressed George V, at whose insistence he was raised to an earldom in the coronation honours of 1911 after only five years in office; and he was one of four named councillors of state during the king's absence in India.

As a law lord, Loreburn set high standards of courtesy. He listened to counsel instead of arguing with them: 'an appeal became again a hearing and not a debate' (*The Times*, 1 Dec 1923); and when he did interrupt, it was only for clarification and invariably sweetened by an apology. He was an expeditious and practical judge rather than a great jurist, his first concern being, unusually, for the litigant rather than the law. A leading case on punitive damages, for example, *Addis v. Gramophone Company Ltd* (1909), he saw primarily in human terms as 'a most unfortunate litigation, in which the costs must far exceed any sum there may be at stake'. 'A little common sense', he observed, 'would have settled all these differences in a few minutes.' He deprecated 'long rambling judgments loaded with irrelevant learning' (*The Times*, 1 Dec 1923), and his own rulings, while clear and concise, were often brief to a point. His primary aim in disposing of a case was to do justice between the parties, without enlarging on the legal principles involved. As lord chancellor, this exposed him to justified criticism. In R. V. Heuston's view 'he was not interested in law and his perfunctory judgments are of no interest to the jurist' (Simpson, 445); and it is true that he seldom broke new ground unless his particular interest was aroused, when he could produce a judgment that was workmanlike if not particularly inspiring. In *Hulton & Co.* v. *Jones* (1910), where the defendant newspaper had never heard of the plaintiff, one Artemus Jones, believing that it had merely satirized a fictitious character, Loreburn ruled that once the libel was proved, it was no defence that it was unintentional. In the *Tamplin Steamship Company* case (1916) he explained the principle of frustration of contract as founded on an implied term, absolving the parties under certain untoward circumstances from their future obligations. He took a measured view of the force of precedent. While agreeing that 'great importance is to be attached to old authorities, on the strength of which many transactions may have been adjusted and rights determined', he also insisted that 'when they are plainly wrong', it was 'the duty of this House to overrule them' (*West Ham Union* v. *Edmonton Union*, 1908).

The ardours of office, the long hours and manifold duties, the diverse political pressures on Loreburn at a time of acute political tensions, were compounded by his growing unease at the government's conduct of foreign affairs since the death of Campbell-Bannerman—an issue on which he contemplated resigning. He was never an easy colleague in cabinet. Under Rosebery he 'had shown a good deal of discontent' (Brooks, 133), and even under his friend Campbell-Bannerman, Lloyd George noted, 'he grumbles the first half of the time and sulks the second half' (J. Wilson, 501). He was also much exercised by his public opposition to the Women's Suffrage Bill (1912), which, liberal though he was, he felt to be a 'constitutional outrage' (Vincent, 270). The accumulated strains told on his health: in 1911 he complained in the House of Lords that they 'may prove too much for the strength of anybody'. It was noticed that he was tired, depressed, and eager to leave office. In June 1912 he fell seriously ill with heart trouble and was obliged to resign very suddenly.

Elder statesman and radical Loreburn retired to Kingsdown House, near Deal in Kent, making various subsequent interventions in public life, notably on the Irish Home Rule Bill of 1912. Though hitherto considered 'the best friend of Irish nationalism in the Cabinet' (Vincent, 270), a supporter since Gladstone's day of 'Home rule all round', and vehemently opposed to excluding Ulster from home rule, he feared, not without reason, that the current political crisis might erupt in civil war. In September 1913 he published a letter in *The Times* proposing all-party constitutional talks, to include discussion of special provisions for Ulster. This volte-face, presented 'with a typical elder statesman's show of non-partisan wisdom' (Jenkins, 287) from 'an always disgruntled ex-colleague' (David, 147), annoyed and embarrassed the government; but the king welcomed it, and it prompted his attempt to ease the crisis at the Buckingham Palace conference in 1914.

Loreburn was a self-proclaimed radical, a follower of Bright, Cobden, and Gladstone, who strove to revive traditional Liberal and pacifist values. In advance of the Hague Peace Conference of 1907 he urged the cabinet to champion immunity from prize law of goods at sea, publishing his ideas in a book entitled *Capture at Sea* (1905, reprinted

1913). These efforts were scorned by the Admiralty and the Foreign Office. Lord Hardinge complained of 'the peace at any price section of the Cabinet headed by the Lord Chancellor' (Monger, 255), who, with all the radical's distrust of France, urged rapprochement with Germany and deplored the government's policy of aligning Great Britain with France and Russia. During the Agadir crisis (1911), fearing imminent war with Germany and conscious of his isolation and impotence in the cabinet, Loreburn enlisted C. P. Scott of the *Manchester Guardian* to campaign for British non-intervention. Out of office in the crisis of 1914, he again urged a policy of non-intervention; and while he came to accept that Germany's violation of Belgian neutrality made British involvement inevitable, he never ceased to deplore the secret military conversations between Britain and France which had taken place since 1906, originally without his knowledge, and which he always held to be the underlying cause of the war. He bitterly and somewhat unfairly condemned his former colleagues, 'the Old Gang, who have sold and deceived us' (Heuston, 180)—Sir Edward Grey, Asquith, and Haldane—for what he saw as 'a course of systematic suppression of the truth' (Heuston, 174). He reputedly attended a meeting in 1915 to bring down the Asquith government. But for his pacifism, Lloyd George would have restored him to the woolsack. He never gave up hope of compromise peace with Germany, however. In 1916 he warmly welcomed Lord Lansdowne's 'peace letter' in the *Daily Telegraph* and endorsed it with one of his own in the *Pall Mall Gazette*. In 1919 he published *How the War Came*, a careful but polemical analysis of British foreign policy before 1914. He abominated the treaty of Versailles and the post-war military repression in Ireland. He approved the peace policy of the Labour Party and even voted for a Labour candidate at an election.

Loreburn was justly admired for his independence of character and expression, his moral courage, and fidelity to his Liberal principles. Indifferent to the grandeur of office, he did not stand on ceremony or talk down. On his appointment to the woolsack, a friend, Adolphus Liddell, noted 'the irony of fate that he of all men should be driven into a peerage with all its pomps and vanities! … but Reid accepts it all with dignity, which silences one's tongue inclined to mock' (Heuston, 144). His convictions, in politics and in life, went deep, and he stuck to them. In 1915 he rallied the law lords against an amendment of the Defence of the Realm Act of 1914 which would have made civilians liable to trial by court martial. In 1918, when he gave up sitting as a judge in order to finish his book on the war, he remitted one half of the pension to which he was entitled. Politicians, his fellow Liberals more than his Conservative opponents, were irritated by what they saw as his 'aggressive honesty' (*The Times*, 1 Dec 1923). He once referred to the hereditary whig peers as 'liars, sir and thieves' (Dangerfield, 69), and he fell out with Lord Rosebery by ascribing his resignation as Liberal leader to drink (Vincent, 499). His irascibility, exacerbated by strain and growing alienation from his colleagues, turned in later years to melancholy, embittered by disillusionment at the war and a sense of personal and political betrayal. A visitor in 1915 found that he was 'very depressed, and does not passionately love his old colleagues' (Sandhurst, 305). 'My whole life', he complained in 1919, 'has been a long struggle with men and measures alien to all I value.' (Heuston, 180) He found consolation in translating verse, classical and modern.

In general Loreburn was fair-minded, magnanimous, and kindly. To Haldane, his old rival and successor on the woolsack, he wrote: 'the only thing that makes life worth having is, to my mind, a friendly feeling among men. I think with Sophocles that this alone imparts value to any man's life' (Heuston, 167). His love of games gave him pleasure long after he ceased to be an active sportsman. In 1907 he served as president of the Marylebone Cricket Club. In the same year he received an honorary DCL from the University of Oxford, and in 1912 he was appointed visitor of Balliol College, of which he had been an honorary fellow since 1908. In 1913 he was appointed as chairman of the royal commission on railways. He was a bencher of the Inner Temple, standing counsel to Oxford University from 1899 to 1907, and a freeman of Dumfries and Annan. He was a member of Brooks's and the National Liberal Club. His health declined and he died at Kingsdown House on 30 November 1923. He was cremated at Golders Green and his ashes were interred at the churchyard at Mouswald, in the grave of his first wife. He was survived by his second wife.   A. LENTIN

Sources R. F. V. Heuston, *Lives of the lord chancellors, 1940–1970* (1987) · *The Times* (1 Dec 1923) · 'Ministerial changes. New lord chancellor. Lord Haldane to suceed Lord Loreburn', *The Times* (11 June 1912), 8a–b · 'The cabinet changes', *The Times* (11 June 1912), 9c · *DNB* · F. W. Hirst, 'Lord Loreburn', *Contemporary Review*, 125 (1924), 33–40 · 'Guardians of the Poor of West Ham Union v. Guardians of the Poor of Edmonton Union', *Law reports: appeal cases* (1908), AC 1 HL · 'Addis v. Gramophone Company', *Law reports: appeal cases* (1909), AC 488 HL · 'E. Hulton & Co. v. Jones', *Law reports: appeal cases* (1910), AC 20 HL · 'F. A. Tamplin Steamship Company Limited Appellants' v. Anglo-Mexican Petroleum Products Company, Limited Respondents', *Law reports: appeal cases* (1916), 2 AC 397 HL · *The political diaries of C. P. Scott, 1911–1928*, ed. T. Wilson (1970) · G. Murray and et al., *F. W. Hirst, by his friends* (1958) · A. W. B. Simpson, ed., *Biographical dictionary of the common law* (1984) · J. L. Hammond, *C. P. Scott of the Manchester Guardian* (1934) · R. G. V. de Broke, *The passing years* (1924) · W. M. Sandhurst, *From day to day, 1916–1921* (1929) · A. Fitzroy, *Memoirs*, 1 [1925] · *The destruction of Lord Rosebery: from the diary of Sir Edward Hamilton, 1894–1895*, ed. D. Brooks (1987) · F. W. Ashley, *My sixty years in the law* (1936) · Viscount Mersey [C. C. Bigham], *A picture of life* (1941) · J. Wilson, *C. B.: a life of Sir Henry Campbell-Bannerman* (1973) · *The Crawford papers: the journals of David Lindsay, twenty-seventh earl of Crawford … 1892–1940*, ed. J. Vincent (1984) · *Inside Asquith's cabinet: from the diaries of Charles Hobhouse*, ed. E. David (1977) · G. W. Monger, *The end of isolation: British foreign policy, 1900–1907* [1963] · G. Dangerfield, *The strange death of liberal England* (1936) · R. Jenkins, *Asquith* (1964) · E. Bowen-Rowlands, *In the light of the law* (1931) · *CGPLA Eng. & Wales* (1924)

Archives Cheltenham College, Loreburn MSS · NL Scot. | BL, letters to Sir Henry Campbell-Bannerman, Add. MS 41222 · BL, corresp. with Herbert, Viscount Gladstone · BL, corresp. with Lord Ripon · Bodl. Oxf., corresp. with H. H. Asquith · Bodl. Oxf., Bryce papers · Bodl. Oxf., corresp. with Sir William Harcourt and Lewis Harcourt · Bodl. Oxf., letters to Sir G. J. C. Lewis · Bodl. Oxf., letters to Arthur Ponsonby · CAC Cam., corresp. with Alfred Lyttelton · Surrey HC, corresp. with Lord Onslow

Likenesses H. H. Brown, oils, 1911, Inner Temple, London [*see illus.*] · G. F. Watt, oils, exh. RA 1912, Balliol Oxf. · R. Garnett, portrait, Cheltenham College, Gloucestershire · F. Lockwood, caricature, repro. in H. H. Asquith, *Memories and reflections* · Owl, mechanically reproduced caricature, NPG; repro. in *VF* (24 Sept 1913) · G. Reid, oils, Privy Council Office, London · Spy [L. Ward], chromolithograph caricature, NPG; repro. in *VF* (10 Jan 1895) · B. Stone, photograph, NPG · photograph (as lord chancellor), Hult. Arch. · photograph, Hult. Arch. · portrait, repro. in *ILN*, 104 (1894), 611

Wealth at death £15,979 14s. 5d.: probate, 22 Jan 1924, *CGPLA Eng. & Wales*

Reid, Thomas (*d.* 1624), philosopher, translator, and founder of the first public reference library in Scotland, was one of the family of six sons and three daughters of James Reid (*d.* 1602?), minister of Banchory-Ternan, Kincardineshire, and burgess of Aberdeen. He was educated at Aberdeen grammar school and Marischal College, from where he graduated MA about 1600. On 6 February 1602 he became master of the grammar school, a post he resigned the following year on being appointed one of the three regents of Marischal College on 12 October. He remained in that office until 1607, conducting a university class through the four years of its curriculum, and then travelled to the continent, where he pursued his studies, first in France and then at the universities of Rostock and Leipzig. He was admitted *docent* at Rostock in December 1608, and taught philosophy and humanity there, gaining a considerable reputation. As was the custom of the age, he maintained public disputations, including one on metaphysics with Henningus Arnisaeus, professor of medicine at the University of Frankfurt. Reid's contributions are characterized by elegant scholarship and considerable philosophical talent. At Rostock between 1609 and 1616 he published eight works on metaphysics, while he matriculated at Leipzig in the summer of 1613.

After returning from the continent, Reid settled in London and became in 1618 Latin secretary to James I, a position he held until his death. In collaboration with Patrick Young he produced the Latin translation of the king's collected works (published in London in 1619, reprinted in 1689 at Frankfurt and Leipzig), one of the most important of the several plain and unadorned translations into Latin of original English works produced at the time, and typical of the genre, aiming simply to communicate the text of the original in the universal language. Reid's paraphrase of Psalm 104 was printed in William Barclay's *Judicium de certamine* (1620), and he was, with his brother Alexander *Reid (c.1570–1641), the surgeon, incorporated MA at Oxford on 28 May 1620; Wood asserts that 'he had before been a student in this university' (Wood, *Ath. Oxon.: Fasti*, 1.394) but offers no further specifics. Reid also published Latin poems, several of which appear in the collection *Delitiae poetarum Scotorum* (1637).

It is neither Reid's writings nor his achievements in royal service which form his enduring memorial, however, but the library which he bequeathed to Marischal College and the town of Aberdeen. Reid died, unmarried, in London in 1624, and in his will, made on 19 May that year, he left his entire collection of books and manuscripts 'for the Love I bear to the Town of new Abd. and wishing the new College schools thereof should flourish ... to be put in the Bibliotheck of the sd. new College', along with a bequest of 6000 merks capital to provide an annual salary of 600 merks for a 'Bibliothecar to hold his Door open 4 days a week for the Scholars and Clergy to have the use of the Books of the sd. Bibliotheck, and *no ways* to be astricted in *no* further Duty' (Simpson, 124–5). Reid's manuscript catalogue to his collections (in Aberdeen University Library, AU MS M 70) contains some 1350 titles; the books were duly shipped from London to Aberdeen, where the earliest catalogue of Marischal College Library, that of 1670, contains a list of Reid's printed books and manuscripts. The bequest was described by the contemporary annalist James Gordon as 'the best Library that ever the north pairtes of Scottland saw' (J. Gordon, *History of Scots Affairs*, ed. J. Robertson, 3 vols., 1841, 3.89).

Reid's collection still forms an integral part of what is today the library of the University of Aberdeen, formed by the fusion of the King's College of 'Old' Aberdeen with Marischal, the 'new College', in 1860; his brother Alexander also left books, on divinity and philosophy, to Marischal College, although his medical books he left to King's. The endowment, which had at first made the librarianship the best paid office in the college, was largely frittered away through mismanagement; from 1733 to 1737 the post of librarian was held by Reid's eminent kinsman and namesake, the philosopher Thomas Reid (1710–1796). The Marischal College section of the Aberdeen University Library, of which Reid's bequest forms the core, contains, as Montague Rhodes James put it, 'well-nigh all that is important in the learned and artistic world in general' (James, ix).   T. P. J. EDLIN

Thomas Reid (1710–1796), by Sir Henry Raeburn, *c.*1796

Sources P. J. Anderson and J. F. K. Johnstone, eds., *Fasti academiae Mariscallanae Aberdonensis: selections from the records of the Marischal College and University, MDXCIII–MDCCCLX*, 3 vols., New Spalding Club, 4, 18–19 (1889–98) · M. R. James, *Catalogue of medieval manuscripts in the University Library of Aberdeen* (1932) · W. D. Simpson, 'Historical note on Aberdeen University Library', in M. R. James, *Catalogue of medieval manuscripts in the University Library of Aberdeen* (1932), 121–5 · Wood, *Ath. Oxon.: Fasti* (1815), 394 · J. W. Binns, *Intellectual culture in Elizabethan and Jacobean England: the Latin writings of the age* (1990) · T. Dempster, *Historia ecclesiastica gentis Scotorum* (1829), xvi · H. J. H. Drummond, *A short-title catalogue of books printed on the continent of Europe, 1501–1600, in Aberdeen University Library* (1979) · *DNB* · I. Beavan, 'Secretary Thomas Reid and the early listings of his manuscripts', *Northern Scotland*, 16 (1996), 50–55 · I. Beavan, 'Marischal College, Aberdeen, and its earliest library catalogue: a reassessment', *The Bibliothek*, 22 (1997), 4–19

Archives U. Aberdeen L.

Likenesses portrait, U. Aberdeen, Marischal College; repro. in Anderson and Johnstone, eds., *Fasti*, vol. 1, facing p. 194

Wealth at death exact value unknown; library and 6000 merks left to Marischal College, Aberdeen (Thomas Reid's brother Robert, minister of Banchory, executed/arranged the financial provision): extract from will, repr. in Anderson and Johnstone, eds., *Fasti*, vol. 1, pp. 194–200

Reid, Thomas (1710–1796), natural and moral philosopher, was born on 26 April 1710 in Strachan, Kincardineshire, the son of the Revd Lewis Reid (1676–1762) and his first wife, Margaret, *née* Gregory (1673–1732). After attending the parish school in Kincardine O'Neil for two years, Reid transferred to the Aberdeen grammar school in April 1722

before entering the class of the professor of Greek, Thomas Blackwell the younger, at Marischal College the following October. He was then taken through the philosophy curriculum by the regent George Turnbull, who introduced him to the ideas of Locke, Shaftesbury, the English deists, and natural-law theorists such as Samuel Pufendorf. Turnbull seems to have inspired Reid's empirical approach to the science of the mind, for Turnbull was an early champion of the application of the method perfected by Bacon and Newton to the study of metaphysics and morals. As an undergraduate, Reid may also have attended the lectures of the leading Scottish Newtonian Colin MacLaurin, who was the Liddell professor of mathematics at Marischal from 1717 to 1726.

Early career In 1726 Reid took his MA and immediately began studying divinity under Thomas Blackwell the elder and, after Blackwell's death, James Chalmers. He was licensed to preach by the presbytery of Kincardine O'Neil on 22 September 1731, and served as a clerk to the presbytery and as an occasional preacher from 2 August 1732 until April 1733. Reid returned to Aberdeen as librarian of Marischal College in July 1733, but resigned in 1736 because of a dispute over his salary (which was funded by a bequest from his ancestor Thomas Reid, a secretary to James I). Towards the end of his tenure as librarian, Reid participated in a Philosophical Club based in the college, and his notes from its meetings record that the members discussed morals, metaphysics, and the anatomy of the mind, and addressed a broad array of authors including Joseph Butler, Samuel Clarke, Francis Hutcheson, William King, and G. W. Leibniz.

Accompanied by his close friend from his undergraduate days, the Marischal professor of mathematics John Stewart, Reid visited England in the spring of 1736. In London they attended a meeting of the Royal Society, and made contact with Reid's uncle, George Reid, his fellow physician Alexander Stuart, and Martin Folkes. They also went to Oxford, where Reid had a family connection with David Gregory at Christ Church, and to Cambridge, where they met the legendary Lucasian professor of mathematics, Nicholas Saunderson, along with the principal architect of the Newtonian ascendancy within the university, the classicist Richard Bentley. Back in Aberdeen Reid again took up with the Philosophical Club, and marked time until he was presented with the living of Newmachar, Aberdeenshire, by King's College in February 1737, thanks to the influence of his kinsman James Gregory, the professor of medicine at King's. But his appointment was not welcomed in the parish, and he was given a hostile reception by the people of Newmachar, whose challenge to the college's right to choose their minister was supported by a local evangelical, the Revd John Bissett. By the time he left Newmachar, Reid had apparently made peace with his parishioners, although it is difficult to gauge his success as a minister. He was conscientious in carrying out his pastoral duties, and he seems to have treated his flock with kindness and charity. He was known, too, for his philanthropy, and was a promoter of the Aberdeen Infirmary, which opened in 1742. Yet they must have found his preaching difficult to digest because he was a dry pulpit orator and, following an accepted practice of the day, he insisted on reading them sermons published by other theologians, including Clarke, the latitudinarian John Tillotson, and the English Presbyterian John Evans.

Reid's sojourn at Newmachar saw significant changes in both his personal and intellectual life. He again travelled to London and, on 12 August 1740, married his cousin Elizabeth (1724–1792), the daughter of George Reid. Once settled in the manse, they began a family and eventually had nine children, of whom only their daughter Martha (1744–1805) survived them. The move to Newmachar also brought him into contact with the noted improver Sir Archibald Grant of Monymusk, as well as the clergymen George Campbell and Alexander Gerard, who both shared his philosophical interests and moderate religious outlook. Intellectually, Reid was now in touch with medical and scientific circles in London and, while he was in the metropolis in 1740, he seized the opportunity to attend a meeting of the Royal Society. Having carefully studied Newton's *Principia mathematica* with John Stewart in the late 1720s, Reid kept abreast of the latest developments in mathematical and physical astronomy and, along with Stewart, became part of a network of Scottish observational astronomers affiliated with the Royal Society. Reid explored a variety of mathematical subjects as well, and

was probably at least tangentially involved in the preparation of Stewart's edition of Newton's *Two Treatises of the Quadrature of Curves* published in 1745. Reid's own reflections on the conceptual foundations of mathematics dovetailed with his interest in the *vis viva* controversy in his first publication, 'An essay on quantity', which appeared in the *Philosophical Transactions* for 1748. The 'Essay' shows too that Reid had continued to think about the works of the Glasgow moralist Francis Hutcheson, but the critical tenor of his remarks indicates that he had serious reservations about aspects of Hutcheson's philosophy. Reid's manuscripts from the period reveal that he was much taken with Butler's *The Analogy of Religion*, and there is evidence among his surviving papers which suggests that he was beginning to respond to the sceptical implications of David Hume's *Treatise of Human Nature*.

Regent of King's College Reid's political and family ties led to his unanimous election on 25 October 1751 as a regent at King's College to replace the recently deceased Alexander Rait, who had additionally served as the nominal professor of mathematics. Reid's manifest abilities in mathematics and his competence in the natural and moral sciences made him a worthy successor to Rait, but he hesitated before formally accepting the position on 22 November 1751. Whereas Edinburgh, Glasgow, and St Andrews had all opted for fixed professorships, King's still employed the traditional system of regenting, which meant that Reid was required to teach the whole of the three-year philosophy course. He was evidently soon dissatisfied with the curriculum and other aspects of college life, for he became one of the principal architects of the major reforms undertaken at King's in 1753. Following the example set by their rivals at Marischal College (and partly inspired by the educational ideals of George Turnbull), the masters at King's eliminated the last vestiges of the scholastic curriculum and put in place a course of philosophy which covered mathematics and natural history in the first year, natural philosophy and higher mathematics in the second, and the various branches of moral philosophy in the final year. Yet, unlike Marischal, King's retained the regenting system because Reid and his allies were convinced that regents could regulate the moral development of their charges more effectively than professors. Notwithstanding some of the problematic consequences of the reforms, Reid's pedagogical vision did help briefly to revive the flagging academic fortunes of the college by fostering a polite and more strongly utilitarian attitude towards learning.

Reid was also instrumental in encouraging more contact between King's and Marischal and, although plans for their union were abandoned in 1755, he was one of the founders of the Aberdeen Philosophical Society (1758–73), which brought together men from the two colleges for the purposes of conviviality and intellectual exchange. At the society's meetings, Reid discoursed on and debated a wide range of topics, including the science of the mind, the philosophical foundations of Euclidean geometry, observational astronomy, plant physiology, moral theory, political economy, and the education of the young. Other members, like his friends the former professor of philosophy at Aberdeen, John Gregory, and the physician and naturalist David Skene, shared his fascination with these subjects. Another group Reid was involved in was the Gordon's Mill Farming Club (1758–64?), which served as a forum for the discussion of issues related to agricultural improvement by local academics, merchants, and landowners. The award of an honorary DD by his *alma mater* on 18 January 1762 registered his close personal relations with prominent faculty members at Marischal, and was no doubt intended as a recognition of Reid's efforts to improve relations between the two colleges, as well as his contributions to community life.

The crowning achievement of Reid's King's College years was his *Inquiry into the Human Mind, on the Principles of Common Sense*, published in February 1764. Based on his lectures, graduation orations, and a series of discourses he gave before the Philosophical Society from 1758 to 1763, the *Inquiry* was a sustained attack on the theory of ideas propagated by Descartes, Locke, and Malebranche. According to Reid, the historical evolution of this theory had revealed that it was inconsistent with the dictates of common sense because it had given rise to the paradoxes of George Berkeley and to the more subversive doctrines of David Hume, whose corrosive scepticism threatened to destroy any grounds for belief in the existence of the external world, the self, and God. Believing that philosophy and common sense ought to be reconciled in order to rescue religion and morality, Reid subjected the theory of ideas to extended scrutiny and showed to his satisfaction that it was little better than an unsubstantiated hypothesis which was inconsistent with known anatomical, physiological, and experiential facts. Drawing heavily on concepts found in Berkeley's *Essay towards a New Theory of Vision*, Reid argued that the operations of our five external senses demonstrate that the mind is so constituted that our sensations suggest to us a belief in the existence of the objects which cause them and that our sensations and ideas function as signs in a language which inform us about the things they signify. Consequently, he insisted that the sceptical doubts about our knowledge of the external world and of ourselves raised by Berkeley and especially Hume were groundless, and he presented his alternative account of perception as being entirely consistent with common sense. Reid's refutation of the theory of ideas in the *Inquiry* ranks as one of the most rigorous applications of the Newtonian method to the science of the mind to appear in the eighteenth century, and his discussion of the 'geometry of visibles' vividly illustrates his creativity as a thinker as well as his bluff wit. When David Hume was given part of the manuscript of the *Inquiry* to read by their mutual friend Hugh Blair in 1762, he was not amused by some of Reid's jibes and had perhaps become tired of criticisms written by members of the Aberdeen Philosophical Society, since he had already been the target of works by Robert Traill, Gerard, and Campbell. But Hume subsequently acknowledged Reid's acuity as a critic, and the *Inquiry* firmly established Reid's reputation as Hume's most gifted antagonist within the European republic of letters.

Professor at Glasgow Thanks to the patronage of Lord Deskford and Henry Home, Lord Kames, Reid was elected to succeed Adam Smith by the faculty of the University of Glasgow on 22 May 1764. He was formally admitted as professor of moral philosophy on 11 June and, after he and his family settled at their fashionable address in the Drygate, he was made a burgess and guild brother of the city on 26 September. At first, Reid had difficulty in adjusting to his new surroundings. He found the personal behaviour of some of his new colleagues questionable, and he was disturbed by the religious climate in Glasgow, which was more deeply tinged by evangelicalism than that of his native north-east. His own election had been a highly contentious one and, even though he was no stranger to academic wrangling, he was unprepared for the fractious professorial politics at Glasgow. He was soon caught up in the protracted dispute between Principal William Leechman's party and its opponents which divided the college from 1761 until Leechman's death in 1785, and he became embroiled in a number of other skirmishes because of his friendship with the prickly professor of natural philosophy, John Anderson. Reid's involvement in these disputes did, however, give him a detailed knowledge of college affairs, which meant that he was burdened with a number of senior administrative positions, including serving as the university's representative at the general assembly of the Church of Scotland in 1767 and 1772, and as vice-rector while Edmund Burke was rector in 1784 and 1785. Reid eventually put his knowledge to more profitable use in 1794, when he composed the article on the university which appeared in Sir John Sinclair's *Statistical Account of Scotland* in 1799.

As a Glasgow professor Reid was also obliged to follow a classroom schedule which differed markedly from the one he was accustomed to at King's. He lectured for one hour to his 'public' class each morning of the week during the session, beginning at 7.30 a.m., and then examined his pupils for a further hour at 11 a.m. except on Saturdays. Whereas Hutcheson and Smith had divided their public lectures between natural religion, morals, jurisprudence, and government, Reid split his into pneumatology, ethics, and politics. Reflecting his desire to refute the sceptical doctrines of Hume, Reid devoted the bulk of his course to pneumatology, and began with an anatomy of the intellectual and active powers of the mind, before moving on to consider the immateriality and immortality of the soul, and the being and attributes of God. In his ethics classes, he dealt with the question of human free will, surveyed the history of moral thought from antiquity to his own day, and enumerated the rights and duties of individuals and states as specified in the natural jurisprudence tradition. Lastly, in his politics lectures he classified the basic forms of government, praised the merits of the British constitution, and, under the rubric of 'police', discussed the policies which a nation should adopt to promote the advancement of religion, virtue, learning, and the economy.

Reid also taught an hour-long 'private' class beginning at noon three days per week for part of the session, and here he focused on what (following Bacon) he called the 'culture of the mind', which involved the practical application of his epistemological principles to the study of logic, rhetoric, and the fine arts. Because Reid's Glasgow lectures covered many of the same topics he canvassed in Aberdeen (albeit in revised and expanded form), they should be seen as marking a crucial step in the wider institutionalization which occurred in Scotland during the latter part of the eighteenth century of the common-sense philosophy initially developed by Reid and his Aberdonian circle in the 1740s and 1750s. Moreover, Reid's emphasis on the importance of the anatomy of human nature in his lectures marked a break with the interests of his Glasgow predecessors, and he cultivated a pedagogical style that was opposed to that associated with Francis Hutcheson. For whereas Hutcheson was renowned as a moral preacher who taught in an animated and extemporaneous fashion, Reid was known for the precision and perspicuity of his delivery. But prospective students were not put off by his dry classroom manner; instead, he prospered as a pedagogue and boasted to an Aberdeen friend in 1766 that his classes (and by implication his class fees) were much larger than those of Adam Smith.

Throughout his years at the university, Reid was active in the Glasgow Literary Society, which met at the college and consisted largely of faculty members. This meant that the political divisions among the professors occasionally disrupted the proceedings, and the meetings were sometimes punctuated by sharp intellectual disagreements, such as those which occurred between Reid and the professor of law, John Millar, over the merits of Hume's system. While he was still lecturing, Reid discoursed on various topics related to his analysis of the active and intellectual powers of the mind and discussed questions on morals and political economy. But once he retired from the classroom in 1780 and left his teaching to his assistant Archibald Arthur, his attention shifted to the metaphysical writings of Joseph Priestley, who gradually replaced Hume as Reid's primary philosophical target in the 1770s. Earlier Reid had responded anonymously to Priestley's condemnation of common-sense philosophy in the *Monthly Review* for 1775 and 1776, and he now subjected Priestley's necessitarianism and materialism to searching criticism in a series of discourses read before the society in the 1780s.

Some of this material found its way into the two major works published in his retirement, the *Essays on the Intellectual Powers of Man* (1785) and the *Essays on the Active Powers of Man* (1788). Working steadily from 1783 until 1787, Reid assembled the texts of both volumes out of his lecture notes and various papers given in the Aberdeen Philosophical Society and the Glasgow Literary Society. In the first of the *Essays*, he elaborated on his challenge to the theory of ideas in the context of a broad survey of our powers of perception, memory, conception, abstraction, judgement, reasoning, and taste, while in the second he combined a defence of the concept of human free will with an attack on aspects of Hume's theory of morals. Together, the two *Essays* shaped the teaching of moral philosophy in Britain and America well into the nineteenth century, partly thanks to the influence of his disciple Dugald Stewart, but also because they provided the basis for a systematic account of the faculties of the mind which was both well suited to the practicalities of pedagogy and consistent with most variants of protestant theology.

Later years Based on some of his Glasgow Literary Society discourses, Reid also wrote a detailed critique of Joseph Priestley during the 1780s entitled 'Some observations on the modern system of materialism', which remained in manuscript even though it was apparently intended for publication. At the meetings of the society in the 1790s, Reid discussed Euclid's problematic parallels postulate, muscular motion, and politics. Along with his colleagues Anderson, Millar, and Arthur, he at first welcomed the French Revolution. He joined the Glasgow Friends of Liberty and in 1792 contributed money to support the French national assembly, much to the horror of his former colleague James Beattie. But, being a moderate whig, Reid was disillusioned with the terror and in his discourse 'Some thoughts on the utopian system of government' delivered in November 1794 he condemned revolutionary politics. In the fraught political atmosphere of Glasgow his endorsement of gradual constitutional reform was clearly welcomed by some, for his remarks on the divergent consequences of revolution and reform were printed (with his permission) in the *Glasgow Courier* for 18 December 1794.

Reid was deeply engaged with the affairs of his day in other ways. Within the republic of learning, he was approached by the Parisian projector Pahin-Champlain de la Blancherie to correspond with the Académie des Sciences in 1778, and in 1783 he was elected a fellow of the Royal Society of Edinburgh. He participated in the administration of various philanthropic enterprises, including the Royal Glasgow Infirmary, to which he donated well over £100. In 1790 he was a founder member and first president of the Glasgow Society of the Sons of Ministers of the Church of Scotland, and he was sympathetic to the anti-slavery movement.

After the death of his wife in 1792, Reid increasingly relied on the support of his daughter Martha and his circle in Edinburgh and Glasgow, which included Dugald Stewart, James Gregory, John Robison, George Jardine, and Robert Cleghorn. Beginning in the 1770s Reid suffered from growing deafness, but was otherwise in comparatively good health until he died in Glasgow on 7 October 1796 after a brief but violent illness. He was buried in the city's Blackfriars Church.   PAUL WOOD

Sources U. Aberdeen, Birkwood collection, MSS 2131/1–8 · U. Aberdeen, Reid MSS 3061/1–26 and 2814 · *The works of Thomas Reid*, ed. W. Hamilton, 3rd edn (1852) · T. Reid, *Philosophical orations*, ed. W. R. Humphries (1937) · T. Reid, *Practical ethics*, ed. K. Haakonssen (1990) · P. Wood, ed., *Thomas Reid on the animate creation* (1995) · T. Reid, *An inquiry into the human mind, on the principles of common sense*, ed. D. Brookes (1997) · D. Stewart, *Account of the life and writings of Thomas Reid* (1802) · A. C. Fraser, *Thomas Reid* (1898) ·

P. B. Wood, 'Thomas Reid, natural philosopher: a study of science and philosophy in the Scottish Enlightenment', PhD diss., U. Leeds, 1984 • P. B. Wood, *The Aberdeen Enlightenment: the arts curriculum in the eighteenth century* (1993) • J. Coutts, *A history of the University of Glasgow* (1909)
Archives BL, corresp. • Bodl. Oxf., corresp. • Boston PL, corresp. • NA Scot., corresp. • NA Scot., corresp. • RCP Lond., corresp. • U. Aberdeen, corresp. and family papers • U. Edin., corresp. • U. Edin., New Coll. L., corresp. • U. Glas., corresp. | U. Aberdeen, Birkwood collection, MSS 2131/1–8 • U. Aberdeen, MSS 3061/1–26 and MS 2814
Likenesses J. Tassie, wash drawing, 1789, Scot. NPG • J. Tassie, paste medallion, 1791, Scot. NPG; copy, Royal Ontario Museum, Toronto • plaster medallion, 1791 (after J. Tassie), Scot. NPG • H. Raeburn, oils, *c*.1796, Fyvie Castle, Aberdeenshire [*see illus.*] • R. Scott, engraving, 1800 (after J. Tassie, 1791) • C. Picart, stipple, pubd 1811 (after J. Tassie), BM, NPG • J. Tassie, stipple, pubd 1811 (after C. Picart), NPG • H. Raeburn, oils, copy, Art Gallery of Ontario, Toronto • H. Raeburn, oils, copy, U. Glas.
Wealth at death annuity to stepmother of £10; investment of £5 books; property in Greenhead, Glasgow; legacies of £600: Glasgow testaments, 16 July 1795 – 30 December 1797, NA Scot., CC 9/7/76

Reid, Thomas (1746–1831), horologist, was born in Dysart, Fife, in January 1746. He was apprenticed in 1762 to a cousin, James Cowan, an able watchmaker in Lawnmarket, Edinburgh. After discharge from his indentures, Reid spent eleven years in London, where, in his own words, 'after having received the instruction of the first masters in that profession [he] did carry on business and was employed in the execution of the first-rate work there' (Smith, 311). When Cowan died in 1781 Reid returned to Edinburgh and succeeded to the business. He married Alexandria, *née* Ogilvie, the widow of William Auld, printer, who had died in 1777.

Reid's rise to fame was rapid. Before very long he moved to 8 Parliament Close in Edinburgh. In 1788 a tower clock of his making was put up in St Andrew's parish church. In 1797 he rebuilt that of St Giles's Kirk. His business, however, embraced all aspects of horology. His insistence upon excellence was reflected in his clientele. His enthusiasm, practical ability, and contacts in London and Lancashire ensured success. He corresponded with B. L. Vulliamy (1780–1854) between 1805 and 1826. Reid's best apprentice was his stepson, William Auld (*d.* 1846), who became his partner in 1806 and who remained his lifelong friend. They moved shop to 33 Princes Street in 1809, and later to no. 66. Reid managed to indulge an all-consuming, if unprofitable, interest in improving regulator clocks, experimenting endlessly with different escapements and compensation pendulums. He was particularly proud of his delicate, 'detatched' spring-pallet escapement. This he at first placed outside his movements, where it was vulnerable to damage; however this proved to be an excellent arrangement in a regulator dated 1811 made for Lord Gray's observatory at Kinfauns, Perthshire, and in another dated 1813 for the Royal Observatory, Edinburgh. Both survived, but without Reid's escapements. His later regulators, dated 1816 and 1818, have their spring-pallets within their movements and remain unaltered.

Reid and Auld both retired in 1823. The former had assembled a remarkable horological library and always studied unremittingly. As early as 1793 he was invited by

the scientist John Robison (1739–1804) to co-operate in the writing of 'a magnificent work on the History, Theory and Practice of Horology'. Reid was too busy to comply, but he later addressed long technical letters to the scientific journals and contributed fifteen important horological chapters to Brewster's *Edinburgh Encyclopaedia*. His letter to Vulliamy dated 20 November 1819 reveals, however, that much had been kept back. In 1825 he was elected an honorary member of the Clockmakers' Company. In March 1826 Reid's monumental work *A Treatise on Clock and Watch Making, Theoretical and Practical* appeared. It was dedicated to Auld and was to run to seven editions over more than thirty years; it remained authoritative for much longer. A pirated version appeared in Philadelphia in 1832, the year after the author's death. Reid died in Edinburgh on 20 September 1831 and his former partner caused him to be buried in the Auld family tomb in the Calton cemetery, Edinburgh. He is regarded as Scotland's most celebrated maker of clocks, watches, and chronometers.

CHARLES K. P. ALLIX

Sources *The Star* (23 Sept 1831) • J. Smith, *Old Scottish clockmakers from 1453 to 1850*, 2nd edn (1921) • T. Reid, letters to B. L. Vulliamy, 1805–26, Inst. CE • T. Reid, 'Horology', *The Edinburgh encyclopaedia*, ed. D. Brewster and others, 3rd edn, 18 vols. (1830) • T. Reid, *Treatise on clock and watch making, theoretical and practical* (1826) • T. Reid, 'On the escapements of time pieces', *Journal of Natural Philosophy, Chemistry, and the Arts*, 5 (1802), 55–8 • C. R. P. Allix, 'William Hardy and his spring-pallet regulators ... how Hardy's regulators inhibited sales of similar clocks by Thomas Reid', *Antiquarian Horology and the Proceedings of the Antiquarian Horological Society*, 18 (1989–90), 607–29 [see also 19 (1990–91), 92, for author's letter correcting certain factual misprints] • C. R. P. Allix, Some notes on Thomas Reid and on the astronomical regulator clocks made by Reid & Auld, Edinburgh, 1949 [unpublished, author's copy only]
Archives Inst. CE, letters to B. L. Vulliamy
Likenesses mezzotint, repro. in Reid, *Treatise on clock and watch making* • mezzotint, GL

Reid, Thomas (1791–1825), naval surgeon and prison reformer, was born of protestant parents and educated near Dungannon, co. Tyrone. He passed his examination at the Royal College of Surgeons on 7 May 1813, when he was found qualified to act as 'surgeon to any rate'. He was admitted on 3 November 1815 a member of the College of Surgeons. Reid was appointed as a naval surgeon in January 1814 and, encouraged by Elizabeth Fry, at the end of 1817 he made a voyage in the *Neptune* to New South Wales as superintendent of male convicts. In 1820 he went in the same capacity in the female convict ship *Morley*. Reid, who hated the way the convicts were treated on the voyages, returned to Ireland in 1822, and made an extended tour which resulted in the publication of his *Travels in Ireland* (1823). A year earlier his *Two Voyages to New South Wales and Van Diemen's Land* had been published. In both books Reid considers the treatment of prisoners.

Reid was a sincerely religious man who worked hard to improve the lot of the prison population of the country. He drew attention to the conditions under which convicts, male as well as female, were transported to the penal settlements in Australia. In doing so he showed how bad was the discipline to which they were subjected on board ship during their journey, and how atrocious were the arrangements made for their reception when they arrived in New South Wales. He strongly advocated that convicts should not remain idle, but should be employed in a rational manner.

Reid died at Pentonville, London, on 21 August 1825.

D'A. POWER, *rev.* MICHAEL BEVAN

Sources *GM*, 1st ser., 95/2 (1825), 377 · private information (1896) · *AusDB*

Reid, Sir Thomas Wemyss (1842–1905), journalist and biographer, born in Elswick Row, Newcastle upon Tyne, on 29 March 1842, was the second son of Alexander Reid, Congregational minister of that town from 1830 to 1880, and his second wife, Jessy Elizabeth, daughter of Thomas Wemyss (*d.* 1845) of Darlington, a Hebrew scholar and biblical critic of distinction. After a short stay at Madras College, St Andrews, where he had brain fever, Reid was educated at Percy Street Academy, Newcastle, by John Collingwood Bruce. In 1856 he became a clerk in the Wentworth Beaumont Lead office at Newcastle. He early determined on journalism, at fifteen sending reports on local topics to the *Northern Daily Express*. These attracted the notice of the proprietor, who had him taught shorthand. Reid did occasional reporting work at seventeen; and a local cartoon entitled 'The Press of Newcastle' showed him at the time as a boy in a short jacket perched on a stool taking down a speech. Another youthful exploit was the foundation near his father's chapel of the West End Literary Institute, which included a penny bank.

In July 1861 Reid gave up his clerkship for a journalistic career, becoming chief reporter on the *Newcastle Journal*. His brilliant descriptive report of the Hartley colliery accident in January 1862 was issued as a pamphlet, and raised £40 for the relief of the victims' families. In 1863 Reid varied reporting with leader writing and dramatic criticism; in June 1864 he was appointed editor of the bi-weekly *Preston Guardian*, the leading journal in north Lancashire; and in January 1866 he moved to Leeds to become head of the reporting staff of the *Leeds Mercury*, a daily paper founded and for more than a century owned by the Baines family. He maintained a connection with it for the rest of his life. On 5 September 1867 Reid married his cousin Kate, daughter of the Revd John Thornton of Stockport, a dissenting minister; she died on 4 February 1870, having borne one son. He then married, on 26 March 1873, Louisa, daughter of Benjamin Berry, merchant, of Headingley, Leeds, who bore him a son and a daughter.

From the autumn of 1867 until the spring of 1870 Reid was London representative of the *Leeds Mercury*. In order to gain admission to the press gallery of the House of Commons he had to become an occasional reporter for the London *Morning Star*, then edited by Justin McCarthy. He subsequently took a leading part in the movement that resulted in 1881 in the opening of the gallery to the provincial press. An acquaintance with William Edward Baxter, secretary to the Admiralty, placed at his disposal important political information which gave high interest to his articles. Reid at this time was on intimate terms with Sala,

Sir Thomas Wemyss Reid (1842–1905), by James Russell & Sons

James Macdonell, W. H. Mudford, and other leading journalists. He sent descriptive articles to *Chambers's Journal* and formed a lifelong friendship with the editor, James Payn. To the *St James's Magazine*, edited by Mrs Riddell, he sent sketches of statesmen, which were republished as *Cabinet Portraits*, his first book, in 1872.

On 15 May 1870 Reid returned to Leeds, to act as editor of the *Leeds Mercury*. The paper rapidly developed under his alert control; in 1873 he opened a London office, sharing it with the *Glasgow Herald*, and arranged with the *Standard* for the supply of foreign intelligence.

Reid was a moderate Liberal. A 'writing editor' with an extremely able pen, he was the first to establish a provincial paper as a real rival to the London press, in the quality of its news and comment, and in its access to behind-the-scenes information. His early knowledge of Gladstone's unexpected decision to dissolve parliament in 1874 was the first of many scoops. Reid upheld W. E. Forster's Education Bill against the radicals, and supported, against the teetotallers, Bruce's moderate Licensing Bill. In the 1880 election it was at his suggestion that Gladstone was invited to contest Leeds as well as Midlothian. Reid's relations with Forster were always close, and he vigorously championed his political action in Ireland during 1880–82. The *Mercury* under his editorship continued to support Gladstone when he took up the cause of home rule. While at Leeds, Reid was also on friendly terms with Richard Monckton Milnes, Lord Houghton, at whose house at Fryston he was a frequent guest.

Reid made many journeys abroad, chiefly in his journalistic capacity. In 1877 he visited Paris with letters of introduction from Lord Houghton to the comte de Paris and M. De Blowitz, and was introduced to Gambetta. A holiday trip in Germany, Hungary, and Romania in 1878 he described in the *Fortnightly Review*. He went to Tunis as special correspondent of the *Standard* in 1881, and narrated his experiences in *The Land of the Bey* (1882).

Reid's close association with the Gladstone family led to his most dramatic *coup*, for it was his letter and subsequent encouragement that led in December 1885 to H. J. Gladstone's flying of the 'Hawarden kite', the announcement of his father's 'conversion' to Irish home rule (see Gladstone, *Diaries*, 11, appx I). In 1887 Reid withdrew from the editorship of the *Leeds Mercury*, to which he continued a weekly contribution until his death, in order to become manager of the publishing firm of Cassell & Co. London was thenceforth his permanent home, and his work there was incessant. In January 1890 he added to his publishing labours the editorship of the *Speaker*, a new weekly paper which he founded and which combined literature with Liberal politics, and was a central forum for the discussion of the future of post-Gladstonian Liberalism. Reid became a strong supporter and a personal friend of Lord Rosebery, whose views he mainly sought to expound in the *Speaker*. He was knighted—one of the first journalistic knighthoods—on Rosebery's recommendation in 1894 in consideration of 'services to letters and politics'.

In September 1899 Reid ceased to be editor of the *Speaker*, which in spite of its literary merits was financially only a qualified success. Subsequently he wrote a shrewd and well-informed survey of political affairs month by month for the *Nineteenth Century*, as well as weekly contributions to the *Leeds Mercury*. He was elected president of the Institute of Journalists for 1898–9. He had become in 1878 a member of the Reform Club on the proposition of Forster and Hugh Childers, and he soon took a prominent part in its management, long acting as chairman of committee. He was elected an honorary member of the Eighty Club in 1892, at the instance of his friend Lord Russell of Killowen.

Reid also made a reputation in literature (he received the degree of LLD from St Andrews University in 1893). During his first residence at Leeds he had visited Haworth and interested himself in the lives of the Brontës. Ellen Nussey, Charlotte Brontë's intimate friend and schoolfellow, entrusted to him the novelist's correspondence with herself, and other material which had not been accessible to Mrs Gaskell. With such aid Reid wrote some articles in *Macmillan's Magazine*, which he expanded into his *Charlotte Brontë: a Monograph* (1877). Reid was also, with John Morley, an important biographical historian of Victorian Liberalism. In his lives of W. E. Forster (2 vols., 1888), and Richard Monckton Milnes, first Lord Houghton (2 vols., 1890), he printed much valuable correspondence, and Gladstone helped him by reading the proofs. As Forster's papers subsequently disappeared, Reid's biography has proved of especial importance. He also published memoirs of Lyon Playfair, first Lord Playfair of St Andrews (1899); John

Deakin Heaton MD of Leeds (1883); and a vivid monograph on his close friend William Black the novelist (1902). A *Life of W. E. Gladstone*, which he edited in 1899, includes much still-valuable material, and is excellently illustrated. He further enjoyed success as a novelist, *Gladys Fane: a Story of Two Lives* (1884; 8th edn, 1902), and *Mauleverer's Millions: a Yorkshire Romance* (1886), each selling well. He also left *Memoirs*, which included much confidential matter of a political kind; portions were edited by his brother, Dr Stuart Reid, in 1905.

A diabetic for his last eighteen months, Reid died of pleurisy, active to the last and almost pen in hand, at his house, 26 Bramham Gardens, South Kensington, London, on 26 February 1905, and was buried in Brompton cemetery; his second wife, Louisa, survived him.

G. LE G. NORGATE, *rev.* H. C. G. MATTHEW

Sources S. J. Reid, ed., *Memoirs of Sir Wemyss Reid, 1842–1885* (1905) • *The Times* (27 Feb 1905) • *The Times* (3 March 1905) • *The Times* (4 March 1905) • *Speaker* (4 March 1905) • *Leeds Mercury* (27 Feb 1905) • Gladstone, *Diaries* • S. E. Koss, *The rise and fall of the political press in Britain*, 2 vols. (1981–4); repr. (1990)

Archives BL, corresp. with Lord Gladstone, Add. MS 46041 • BL, corresp. with W. E. Gladstone, Add. MSS 44454–44514 • BL, corresp. with Macmillans, Add. MS 55046 • NL Scot., corresp. with Lord Rosebery

Likenesses S. P. Hall, pencil sketch, 1888–9, NPG • James Russell & Sons, photograph, repro. in Reid, *Memoirs of Sir Wemyss Reid*, frontispiece [*see illus.*] • G. Manton, portrait; in family possession, 1912 • portrait, repro. in *ILN*, 104 (1894), 679 • portrait, repro. in Stead (1891), 129

Wealth at death £9249 17s.: probate, 13 April 1905, *CGPLA Eng. & Wales*

Reid, William (1764–1831), poet and songwriter, was born in Glasgow on 10 April 1764, the son of Robert Reid, baker, and his wife, Christian, *née* Wood, daughter of a farmer at Gartmore, Perthshire. Upon leaving school, he was employed in the type-foundry of Andrew Wilson, leaving that employment to serve an apprenticeship with the Glasgow booksellers Dunlop and Wilson. He then went into business as a bookseller himself in 1790 in partnership with James Brash. The well-known and successful firm of Brash and Reid, in the Trongate, Glasgow, was carried on for twenty-seven years, ending a few years before Reid's death in 1831 and Brash's in 1835. The firm was widely known for a now rare collection, issued in penny numbers, of *Poetry, Original and Selected*, containing some poems by and about Robert Burns, extending to four volumes and published between 1795 and 1798. Reid himself contributed a number of pieces to the collection, as did Brash, but Reid's poems were never separately collected. One historian of music in Scotland stated that Reid wrote the words to the song 'Cauld Kail in Aberdeen', and that his was the most popular version of 'The Lass o' Cowrie'. 'His *forte*', he concluded, 'lay in "eking" out the songs of other poets, rather than in original composition' (Baptie, 156). The firm of Reid and Brash was not only successful but a popular gathering place for Burns, John Galt, Alexander Rodger, and others.

Reid was of a pleasant and sociable nature. According to a contemporary:

In early and mature life Mr. Reid was remarkable both for vivacity, and no mean share of that peculiar talent which, in Scotland, the genius of Burns and its splendid and dazzling course seemed to call forth in the minds of many of his admiring countrymen. He not only shared in the general enthusiasm the appearance of that day-star of National Poetry [Burns] elicited, but participated in his friendship and received excitement from his converse.   (Ewing, 3–4)

Burns left a commonplace book dated 1783–5 which contained a number of poems in manuscript. There are fourteen appended critical remarks by W. R., conjecturally identified by William Scott Douglas, editor of the *Works of Burns* (1877–9, 4.52), as William Ronald, the owner of a 200 acre farm and an acquaintance of Burns. But it was actually William Reid, himself a poet as well as a friend of Burns, who was the W. R. of the commonplace book.

Modern biographers of Burns have very little to say about Reid. However, when Burns died in 1796, Robert Heron, a writer who had once visited Burns in 1789 and had left a less than favourable impression, wrote a memoir of the poet which appeared serially in the *Monthly Magazine* of London in March and June 1797 and was reprinted in various publications thereafter. The memoir was both libellous and inaccurate in detail, and Reid may have been prompted by this to write his 'Monody on the Death of Robert Burns'. This was published at Glasgow in 1797 in one of the Brash and Reid penny chapbooks. The eighteenth stanza of the poem reads:

> But let us not, as chatt'ring fools,
> Proclaim his fau'ts, like envy's tools,
> Wha seek out darkness just like owls
> Dark, dark indeed,
> But a' his failings co'er wi' mools,
> Now since he is dead.

Reid was putting matters to right in his own fashion. He also wrote supplementary verses to Burns's 'Of a' the airts the winds can blaw' and 'John Anderson, my Jo', adding five stanzas to the second of these.

There was a Duck Club in the rural village of Partick near Glasgow whose members have been described as a 'gustative and gormandising fraternity' and of which Reid was the club poet (Strang, 399, 400). This authority states that:

> In the extensive field of Glasgow's social companions, it would have been difficult to find one more courted as a club associate than Mr. Reid. To a peculiarly placid temper, he united a strong smack of broad humour, and an endless string of personal anecdotes, which he detailed with a gusto altogether his own.   (ibid., 402)

Reid died at Glasgow on 29 November 1831, leaving his wife, Elizabeth, daughter of James Henderson, linen printer of Newhall, and two sons and five daughters.

ARTHUR SHERBO

Sources J. C. Ewing, *Brash and Reid, booksellers in Glasgow, and their collection of 'Poetry original and selected'* (1934) • J. A. Mackay, *R. B.: a biography of Robert Burns* (1992) • D. Baptie, ed., *Musical Scotland, past and present: being a dictionary of Scottish musicians from about 1400 till the present time* (1894); repr. (Hildesheim, Olms, 1972) • J. Strang, *Glasgow and its clubs*, 3rd edn (1864) • P. R. Drummond, *Perthshire in bygone days* (1879) • Anderson, *Scot. nat.* • A. Sherbo, 'William Reid in Burn's commonplace book, 1783–1785', *N&Q*, 246 (2001), 117–18 • *DNB*

Reid, Sir William (1791–1858), army officer and meteorologist, fifth child and eldest son of James Reid, minister of the Church of Scotland at Kinglassie, Fife, and his wife, Alexandrina, daughter of Thomas Fyers, chief engineer in Scotland, was born at Kinglassie on 25 April 1791. He was educated at a private school in Musselburgh and at the Edinburgh Academy. He entered the Royal Military Academy, Woolwich, in 1806 and, after learning surveying under William Mudge, was gazetted second lieutenant on 10 February 1809 and promoted first lieutenant on 23 April 1810. From 1810 to 1814 he served with the British army in the Peninsula War, proving a skilled engineer, a brave soldier, and a fortunate man since he survived three wounds, including a severe one to the neck. He returned to England in 1814 and was promoted second captain on 20 December. From 1814 to 1815 he served in the latter stages of the Anglo-American War. In 1816 he returned to Woolwich to become adjutant of the Royal Sappers and Miners and in the same year he accompanied the expedition against Algiers under Lord Exmouth, who, after Reid returned home, joined with Wellington to ensure a promotion to brevet major. On 5 November 1818 Reid married, at Clapham, Sarah, youngest daughter of John Bolland, hop merchant and MP, of Clapham, Surrey. From 1819 to 1824 he was on half pay. Between 1824 and 1827 he served with the Ordnance Survey in Ireland, but found the work under Thomas Colby outdated and frustratingly slow. He was then left without employment until in 1829 he was promoted regimental first captain and sent to Exeter to quell the reform riots.

In 1832–4 Reid was in the West Indies, and in Barbados saw at firsthand the destructive power of storms. He became interested in hurricanes, which were at the time a matter of intense scientific controversy, especially in the United States of America which suffered greatly from storms. One of the three main protagonists in the controversy was William Redfield who, by correspondence with other scientists, established a large body of data to support his contention that the chief underlying determinants of the occurrence and course of storms were gravity and the tendency of fluids to run in whirls. Reid was his most important correspondent, gathering data from ships' logs and coastal stations, and sending them to Redfield, at the same time using them to argue in support of Redfield's ideas and against his rivals, James Espy and Robert Hare. Since Redfield's inductive position depended crucially on access to abundant data, Reid was of great help particularly since he sent data from areas such as Europe to which Redfield had no firsthand access. Reid presented Redfield's ideas before the British Association for the Advancement of Science in 1838 to great acclaim, and the president of the section, Sir John Herschel, publicly thanked Redfield and criticized Espy. In the same year Reid published his *Attempt to Develop the Law of Storms by Means of Facts*, the title of which roundly declared rejection of theoretical positions. For this he was made CB in 1838 and fellow of the Royal Society (with Herschel as one of his proposers) in 1839. Redfield distributed the book in the United States, while his rival Espy reworked some of the data in it to prove that it corroborated his own hypotheses. There was also a practical aim since the book offered advice to shipping caught in storms; British warships were later required to carry a copy and merchant mariners were examined in the contents. Reid published a second book in 1849, called *Progress of the Development of the Law of Storms*, and in that year became vice-president of the Royal Society.

Reid's military career continued meanwhile: in 1835–6 he saw much fighting in the Carlist War and was again wounded in the neck; in 1837 he was promoted lieutenant-colonel and was stationed from then until 1839 in Portsmouth; from 1839 to 1846 he was governor of Bermuda. His first actions there were to secure the island's defences because of the Maine–New Brunswick controversy, and then, by introducing new crops and tillage methods, and even turning the grounds of Government House into an experimental garden, he made the island a profitable supplier of early potatoes and other market crops for the United States—helped by Redfield who sent him equipment and seeds. In 1841 he was promoted regimental lieutenant-colonel, and in 1846 he went to Barbados as governor-in-chief of the Windward Isles; but his efforts to develop the islands were cut short when he resigned in 1848 in protest at the reinstatement of a judge whom he had suspended. He returned to England to become commanding royal engineer at Woolwich, and in 1850–51 chaired the executive committee of the Great Exhibition, being rewarded with a civil KCB in 1851.

In that year Reid was appointed governor and commander-in-chief at Malta. He was promoted colonel in 1854 and major-general in 1856. He met the demands of the Crimean War (during which Malta was a major military entrepôt) with considerable success, and also instituted improvements in agriculture, education, and transport. He returned to England in 1858 and, after a short illness, died on 31 October that year at his home, 117 Gloucester Terrace, Hyde Park, London. His wife had died at St Leonards on 19 February 1858, but their five daughters survived them.

Reid was a member of the Institution of Civil Engineers and of learned societies of many countries. He left many publications, most on military and civil engineering. He is now chiefly remembered for his part in the heated debate on storms which dominated meteorology in the first half of the nineteenth century, a debate in which his importance rested largely on his connection with Redfield. He is also remembered as a successful governor, genuinely concerned with the well-being of those he was sent to govern.

ELIZABETH BAIGENT

Sources O. M. Blouet, 'Sir William Reid, FRS, 1791–1858', *Notes and Records of the Royal Society*, 40 (1985–6), 169–91 · J. R. Fleming, *Meteorology in America, 1800–1870* (1990) · H. Lefroy, *PRS*, 9 (1857–9), 543–6 · *The Times* (6 Nov 1858) · *The Times* (7 March 1860) · War Office Records · Colonial Office Records · Royal Engineers records · 'Bolland', HoP, *Commons* · DNB

Archives Bodl. RH, letters to Labouchere from Malta · National Archives of Malta, corresp. with R. B. P. Lyons; minutes as governor of Malta · NRA, priv. coll., letters to Sir Charles Adam · U. Durham L., letters to Henry George, third Earl Grey · Yale U., letters to Redfield

Likenesses R. J. Lane, lithograph, 1859, NPG · oils, 1896 (after J. Lane), Royal Engineers, Chatham · Graves, engraving (after J. Lane) · granite medallion on obelisk, Hamilton, Bermuda · wood-engraving, NPG; repro. in *ILN* (1851)

Wealth at death under £40,000: probate, 4 Dec 1858, *CGPLA Eng. & Wales*

Reid, William Hamilton (*fl.* 1784–1827), poet and controversialist, was one of a number of anti-government writers who collaborated on the satirical *Criticisms on the Rolliad*, published in 1784. Reid, despite some later (1787) doubt as to his literary abilities, was in the company of Joseph Richardson, R. Tickell, F. Lawrence, Sir J. Anstruther, Sir R. Fitzpatrick, G. Ellis, Lord J. Townshend, and others. The 'Advertisement' to the pamphlet stated that the 'following pieces are without a doubt to be attributed to the first Wits of the age'. There are seven unsigned 'pieces', some necessarily collaborative efforts. A correspondent to the *Gentleman's Magazine* for July 1788 likened Reid to Robert Burns as 'modern untutored bards', prompting a long editorial note in which Reid is described as a 'laborious mechanic', ignorant of prosody and deficient in reading, whose first published efforts were some letters in 'the Gazetteer, signed Philo-Veritas' (*GM*, 58) in 1781.

Reid, however, contributed a considerable number of poems and prose pieces to the *Gentleman's Magazine* in the years 1789 to 1825. In these he displayed a wide-ranging knowledge of languages, both classical and modern, belying the description in the editorial note. It is not known where he was born nor when. His intimate knowledge of London would suggest that he may have been born there. According to the editorial note in the *Gentleman's Magazine*, Reid was married and had a small family and was in straitened circumstances, an object of public charity. Further, he had worked for nine years for a 'silversmith, in Hosier-lane, Smithfield'. Reid himself, in a letter to the *Gentleman's Magazine* in February 1789, commented on the truancy of schoolboys who preferred Smithfield market over their schools, offering 'the line I have moved in', that is, his work in Smithfield, as evidence of the truth of his statement.

What is definitely known is that Reid was a prolific writer, albeit another Grub Street hack, with several books to his credit and the many contributions to the *Gentleman's Magazine*. The former included, among others, books on Hugh Blair (1809) and an edition of Napoleon's *Memoirs* (1827), as well as *The Rise and Dissolution of the Infidel Societies in this Metropolis* (1800). The last included poems of a minor order in many of the conventional genres, as well as translations of poetry in Latin, French, German, Italian, Dutch, Portuguese, and Spanish, despite the lack of any record of formal education. In a letter to the *Gentleman's Magazine* in December 1792 he wrote that 'it has been part of my business to translate some of the papers in the Low Dutch language for a modern print', evidence of employment in some periodical. Probably of most importance is Reid's role in the controversy about the efforts of the London Society for Promoting Christianity among the Jews, opponents of the society accusing him of being in the employment of the Jews. The controversy occasioned several letters in the *Gentleman's Magazine*. Reid's last letter to the magazine was in 1825 (Kuist, 138); in 1784 he contributed a sonnet to the periodical, signing it as from 'Hoxton' that is, Hauxton in Cambridgeshire. Presumably he died and was buried there.   ARTHUR SHERBO

Sources *GM*, 1st ser., 57–95 (1787–1825) · A. Sherbo, 'William Hamilton Reid (*fl.* 1786–1824): a forgotten poet', *Studies in Scottish Literature*, 29 (1996), 245–57 · *BL cat.* · J. M. Kuist, *The Nichols file of the Gentleman's Magazine: attributions of authorship and other documentation in editorial papers at the Folger Library* (1982)

Reidfurd. For this title name *see* Foulis, Sir James, of Colinton, third baronet, Lord Reidfurd (*c.*1645–1711).

Reilly, Sir Bernard Rawdon (1882–1966), colonial governor, was born on 25 March 1882 at Durrington, Wiltshire, the son of Colonel Bradshaw Lewis Phillips Reilly, an officer in the Bombay staff corps, and his wife, Eleanor White. He was educated at Bedford School and entered the Indian army in 1902, transferring to the political department in 1908. He went to Aden, then under the control of the Bombay presidency, as political officer in the Arab town of Shaykh 'Uthman, in the Aden settlement, and remained in Aden throughout the war. He was a member of the delegation to the Yemen led in 1919 by Lieutenant-Colonel Harold Fenton Jacob, assistant resident in Aden, which was intercepted by hostile tribesmen and detained for four months.

Reilly was appointed resident of Aden in 1931. His title changed to chief commissioner in 1932, when the administration of Aden was transferred to the government of India in Delhi, and governor in 1937, when Aden became a British colony, under the control of the Colonial Office in London. The Aden settlement itself covered 75 square miles, but Reilly also had to deal with the Aden protectorate, twenty-five independent states to the north and east of Aden which had signed protection treaties with Britain. As Yemeni raids into the protectorate increased, Reilly persuaded the government that it must honour its treaty obligations and reach an agreement with the imam on the boundary between the Yemen and the protectorate states. In 1933, with Britain and the Yemen close to a state of war, while Yemeni troops occupied the Audhali plateau in the amirate of Dhala and had taken hostages, Reilly was authorized to go to San'a' to open negotiations with the imam, who had accepted a draft treaty. The treaty of San'a', signed in 1934, secured peace on the frontier for a number of years. Britain recognized the imam as king of the Yemen and while the imam never abandoned his claim to the whole of south-west Arabia, on the grounds that the Zeidi imams had ruled there between 1630 and 1730, whereas Britain defined Yemen as the area that had been part of the Ottoman empire, he was prepared to make a temporary settlement, intended to last for forty years. The 1934 treaty marked the beginning of a new phase in the history of the Aden protectorate. Reilly was knighted in 1934.

With the danger of Yemeni raids removed, Reilly turned his attention to internal security in the protectorate. British policy had always been to avoid involvement in internal affairs, but the government could not ignore the interruption of the main trade routes. In 1934 Reilly found money to form groups of tribal guards in each state to police the roads, and trained a force of government guards to escort British officials in the protectorate, and garrison forts on the Aden–Yemen frontier. In addition, there were the Aden protectorate levies, regular soldiers under the command of the RAF regiment. But the bombing of villages by the RAF squadron based in Aden continued to be the favoured method of punishing tribesmen: this was defended by Reilly as plenty of warning was given, there was no loss of life, and the houses were easily rebuilt.

As part of his policy of expanding British involvement in Aden and the protectorate, Reilly appointed a political officer for the protectorate in 1935. He also managed to find government funding for social welfare programmes, including the appointment of an agricultural adviser in 1937. In 1937 he initiated the conclusion of advisory treaties with the main protectorate states, binding the ruler to co-operate with the government of Aden over welfare and development. In 1935 he opened a college for the sons of chiefs and boys from the leading families in the protectorate. It was Reilly who persuaded the British government to take over direct control of Aden in 1937, in response to the desire of the Arab population of Aden to sever the link between Aden and India, worried that Aden might turn into an Indian colony. Although his low-key style meant that he was not widely known outside official circles, Reilly knew how to make the administration work, and was respected by those who served under him, and revered by the Arabs.

In 1940 Reilly left Aden to join the Colonial Office, and spent the war in London. He continued to be involved in Aden affairs and his advice was often sought. He was present at the Anglo-Yemeni conference in London in 1950 to try to settle recent frontier disputes following the assassination of Imam Yahya in 1948, but there was no hope of a final settlement, and no boundary commission was set up. He also attended the meetings held in London in 1957 on the future of the Aden protectorate. He published *Britain and the Yemen* in 1960. He had few interests outside his work, but he was chairman of the Royal Empire Society for the Blind from 1950 to 1959. Sir Bernard Reilly died unmarried on 28 October 1966 at Westminster Hospital in London, and was buried on 3 November at Magdalen Hill cemetery, Winchester.   ANNE PIMLOTT BAKER

Sources R. J. Gavin, 'Air power and expansion', *Aden under British rule, 1839–1967* (1975), 276–317 · T. Hickinbotham, *Aden* (1958) · B. Reilly, *Aden and the Yemen* (1960) · R. Bidwell, *The two Yemens* (1983) · Lord Belhaven, *The uneven road* (1955), 93–107 · H. F. Jacob, *Kings of Arabia* (1923), 202–25 · *The Times* (31 Oct 1966) · *WWW* · *CGPLA Eng. & Wales* (1966) · b. cert. · d. cert.

Likenesses photograph, repro. in Gavin, *Aden under British rule*, 277

Wealth at death £13,741: probate, 9 Dec 1966, *CGPLA Eng. & Wales*

Reilly, Sir **Charles Herbert** (1874–1948), architect and town planner, was born at 3 Manor Villas, Stoke Newington, London, on 4 March 1874, the son of Charles T. Reilly (1844–1928), architect and surveyor to the Worshipful Company of Drapers, and his wife, Annie, formerly Mee. He was educated at Merchant Taylors' School, London, and Queens' College, Cambridge. After graduating in 1895 with a first in mechanical science, Reilly worked for two years as an unpaid draughtsman in his father's office, then moved to John Belcher's office as an 'improver'. Here he came to know a number of leading young architects, including J. J. Joass, Stanley Adshead, E. A. Rickards, and H. V. Lanchester. In 1900 Reilly was appointed part-time lecturer in architectural design at King's College, London, and joined in partnership with Stanley Peach to work on the design of electricity power stations. In 1902 he entered a classical design for the Liverpool Cathedral competition, earning a commendation from the assessors, and made an unsuccessful application for the chair of architecture at University College, London.

On 8 September 1904 Reilly married Dorothy Gladys (1884/5–1939), daughter of J. Jerram Pratt. That same year he was appointed Roscoe professor of architecture at Liverpool University. This conferred on him effective leadership of the university's young school of architecture, which he proceeded to build up with great verve. In 1906 was published the first of a series of volumes promulgating the work of the school, *Portfolio of Measured Drawings*. A second such volume of 1908 was succeeded by *The Liverpool Architectural Sketch Book* (1910, 1911, 1913, and 1920). Reilly's growing authority as an educator led to his becoming in 1906 the first chairman of the Royal Institute of British Architecture's board of architectural education, a position he used to elevate formal and classical standards of architectural training against those who favoured a looser, less academic approach.

Reilly first visited America in 1909, which helped stimulate his interest in Beaux-Arts architecture and educational methods. As a result, with the backing of W. H. Lever (Lord Leverhulme), with whom he had developed a close working relationship, he helped establish at Liverpool University the department of civic design, effectively the first place in Britain where town planning and architecture were taught as integrally related subjects. With the expansion of the school Reilly persuaded Lever to fund a new building. In 1914 he produced designs, but the outbreak of war meant they were not executed and it was not until 1933 that the Leverhulme Building, designed by Reilly in collaboration with his former students Lionel Budden and J. E. Marshall, was finally opened. Earlier Reilly had built the university's students' union (1909–14). Though not primarily remembered as a designer, he could on occasion be impressive, as in the austere church of St Barnabas Shacklewell, London (1909). He also designed one of the many groups of cottages for Leverhulme's model village of Port Sunlight (1906).

Reilly's breadth of interests involved him in 1911 in a campaign to establish the Liverpool Repertory Theatre, of which he was board member (and at one time chairman) until his retirement in 1933. Also in 1911, he was appointed a member of the faculty of architecture at the British School at Rome.

In 1913 Reilly was appointed consulting editor to the *Builders' Journal*. After the war his journalistic output increased and he contributed to the *Manchester Guardian* and *Liverpool Post*, and reviewed for the *Architects' Journal* and *Architectural Review*. Reilly was appointed architectural editor at *Country Life* in 1921, the year in which he published *Some Liverpool Streets and Buildings in 1921*—a collection of articles on the city's architectural stock. In the following year he produced a similar volume on Manchester's architecture, together with two other books, *McKim, Mead and White* and *Some Architectural Problems of Today*. Other books included *Representative British Architects of the Present Day* (1931), *The Theory and Practice of Architecture* (1932), his autobiography, *Scaffolding in the Sky* (1938), and *Architecture as a Communal Art* (1946).

Reilly spent the First World War as an inspector of munitions. In 1919 he again visited America and Canada and subsequently sat as a jury member for the Canadian war memorials competition. He designed the Accrington war memorial, Lancashire (1920), and the Durham war memorial (1928), and acted as assessor for the Liverpool cenotaph competition (1926). He travelled in India with Lutyens in 1927–8. In 1923–4 Reilly was appointed co-architect with Thomas Hastings to design a large Beaux-Arts apartment block: Devonshire House, Piccadilly, London. In 1931 he was successful, with others, in his campaign for the passing of the Architects' Registration Act.

In 1933, with his health failing, Reilly retired to Brighton, but he continued to work on his journalism and acted as consultant architect with William Crabtree (a former student) on the Peter Jones store, Sloane Square, London (1935–9). The design was strikingly modern and much praised. By the late 1930s Reilly had become an enthusiastic advocate for modernism and in 1944 he was proposed as an honorary member of the Modern Architectural Research (MARS) Group, by his former student Maxwell Fry.

In his later career Reilly was involved with town planning issues, writing numerous articles about rebuilding towns and cities. His criticism of the 'Academy Plan' for London brought him into conflict with Lutyens and other former friends. Reilly's planning theories were brought together by Lawrence Wolfe in *The Reilly Plan: a New Way of Life*. Here a series of 'Reilly greens' is described, around which communal housing schemes were to be arranged. The idea was unsuccessful when first proposed for Woodchurch, Birkenhead; the town was eventually designed by Reilly's former student Herbert Rowse. Modified versions of the plan were implemented in Bilston, Staffordshire, and Dudley, Worcestershire. Reilly in collaboration with Naim Aslan published *The Outline Plan for the County Borough of Birkenhead* (1947).

In an obituary written for his former professor William

(Lord) Holford described Reilly as 'an international figure, not only by reputation but by the building up of personal contacts'. His circle of friends encompassed many fields from the arts to politics. Augustus John painted his portrait in 1932, and the fashionable Liverpool photographer E. Chambre Hardman photographed Reilly with hat and ivory-topped cane—which, Holford recalls, he used to knock on the doors of 'peers and poets and the poor'. Maxwell Fry described him as looking like 'a cherub … a laughing, naughty cherub about to direct an arrow where least expected … His fleshy childlike features … in thoughtful repose, his cupid's mouth slightly pursed … wearing a broadbrimmed black hat … from which stray a few white hairs'. Reilly was an enthusiastic joiner and member of clubs, including the Athenaeum, London, and the University and Sandon clubs, Liverpool, as well as being a sponsor of the '1917 Club', London, founded by Ramsay MacDonald to promote world peace. Indeed, Reilly's lifelong socialism informed much of his personal and professional life. Reilly was a charismatic figure and an inspirational teacher, who turned the Liverpool school of architecture into one of the most famous schools in the world during the inter-war years.

Among Reilly's many honours were an honorary LLD from Liverpool University (1934), the royal gold medal for architecture (1943), and a knighthood (1944). He died on 2 February 1948 at the Gordon Hospital, Westminster, London, his wife having predeceased him in 1939, and he was cremated four days later at Golders Green. He had four children, of whom two—a son and a daughter—survived him. The son, Paul *Reilly, Baron Reilly (1912–1990), was closely associated with the Design Council.

SIMON PEPPER and PETER RICHMOND

Sources C. H. Reilly, *Scaffolding in the sky: a semi-architectural autobiography* (1938) • W. Holford, 'Sir Charles Reilly', *ArchR*, 103 (1948), 180–83 • E. Fry, *Autobiographical sketches* (1975) • P. Richmond, *Marketing modernisms: the architecture and influence of Charles Reilly* (2001) • U. Lpool L., special collections and archives, Reilly papers • b. cert. • m. cert. • d. cert. • *CGPLA Eng. & Wales* (1948)
Archives priv. coll., papers • U. Lpool L., corresp. and papers; letter-books | JRL, letters to the *Manchester Guardian* • U. Lpool L., letters to Herbert Thearle
Likenesses A. Lipczinski, group portrait, oils, c.1910 ('New Testament' group, Liverpool University), U. Lpool • R. C. Orpen, pencil drawing, 1910, U. Lpool • Swaine Photography, photograph, c.1914, U. Lpool • E. Chambré Hardman, photograph, 1924, National Museums and Galleries on Merseyside • A. John, oils, 1931, U. Lpool • Lafayette Ltd, photograph, Sept 1933, U. Lpool • T. A. West, oils, c.1933, U. Lpool • M. Brooks, oils, c.1934, University Club, Liverpool • W. Stoneman, photograph, 1944, NPG • K. Pollack, photograph, c.1948, NPG
Wealth at death £40,355: probate, 14 May 1948, *CGPLA Eng. & Wales*

Reilly, (Thomas) Devin (1824–1854), Irish nationalist and revolutionary journalist, was born in Monaghan town, co. Monaghan, Ireland, on 30 March 1824, the son of Thomas Reilly, a solicitor. He was a Roman Catholic all his life. Thomas Devin Reilly was educated at the Revd Bleckley's classical academy in Monaghan town. When his father obtained the office of taxing-master for his services to the Liberal Party in 1836 the family moved to Dublin, where Thomas Devin attended first a school at Usher's Quay and then the seminary at Huddart's. He entered Trinity College, Dublin, in 1842, but never finished his degree because he became involved in O'Connell's Repeal Association, and joined the staff of *The Nation* in 1846. Reilly wrote fiery and eloquent articles, and was one of the most impetuous Young Irelanders. Duffy described him as: 'middle sized, but strongly built, with a head that seemed unduly large even for his sturdy frame, a great crop of light hair, and large, full, protruding blue eyes' (Duffy, *Four Years*, 16).

Reilly became devotedly attached to John Mitchel and his family, but did not work well with Thomas D'Arcy McGee. Duffy was highly critical of him, whereas Mitchel was full of praise for his personality and his work. When Mitchel broke off his connection with *The Nation* in December 1847, and with the Irish Confederation in January 1848, Reilly followed his example, and became the main contributor to Mitchel's newly established paper, the *United Irishman*, preaching republicanism. His articles were as violent as Mitchel's, and one of them, entitled 'The French fashion' (4 March 1848), was used in the indictment on which Mitchel was subsequently tried. Mitchel, who took full responsibility for this article, declared that it was 'one of the most telling revolutionary documents ever penned' (Sillard, 84). Like Mitchel, Reilly hoped that spontaneous uprisings in parts of Ireland would lead to a national rebellion. Reilly was arrested on 22 May 1848 on a charge of drilling and training at a Confederate meeting the previous day. He was freed on bail and consequently helped John Martin to run the *Irish Felon*. In June he took part in a secret meeting of Confederate leaders to organize funds, arms, and support for an uprising. In July he joined other Confederate leaders in co. Tipperary to start the insurrection, but when support of the peasantry was not forthcoming he escaped to America with the help of Jenny Mitchel.

Having arrived starved and impoverished, Reilly made a career in journalism. In 1849 he started *The People*, a paper advocating republicanism in Europe and challenging the American policy of non-intervention in Europe, which was discontinued after six months. Early in 1850 he worked for the *Protective Union*, a paper started by Boston printers to advocate labour rights. In 1851 he contributed to the *American Review* of New York (both Mitchel, *Jail Journal*, 295, and Sillard, 89, called the paper *Whig Review*), but his 'red' republican views did not suit the paper. In 1853 he edited the *Democratic Review*, to which another Young Irelander, John Savage, contributed. In his articles Reilly promoted the election as president of Franklin Pierce, and through his work became known to leading members of the Democratic Party. At the end of 1853 he went to Washington City and edited the *Washington Union*.

On 30 March 1850, in Providence, Rhode Island, Reilly married Jennie Miller (1830/31–1892), originally from Enniskillen, co. Fermanagh, Ireland. The couple endured poverty, hardship, and the death of two infants. Shortly before he was supposed to start a position in the land office, Devin Reilly died suddenly in Washington on 5 March 1854. There were rumours of suicide, but it is more likely that death was caused by an attack of apoplexy. He was buried in St Mathew's cemetery, Washington, on 8 March 1854. (The body was later moved to Mount Olivet, Washington.) Mitchel wrote in his *Jail Journal*: 'Thomas Devin Reilly is dead. The largest heart, the most daring spirit, the loftiest genius of all Irish rebels in these latter days sleeps now in his American grave' (287).

BRIGITTE ANTON

Sources C. G. Duffy, *Young Ireland: a fragment of Irish history, 1840–1845*, rev. edn, 2 vols. (1896) · C. G. Duffy, *Four years of Irish history, 1845–1849: a sequel to 'Young Ireland'* (1883) · C. G. Duffy, *My life in two hemispheres*, 2 vols. (1898) · P. A. Sillard, *The life and letters of John Martin* (1901) · J. Mitchel, *Jail journal … with a continuation of the journal in New York and Paris* (1913); facs. repr. (1982) · T. F. O'Sullivan, *The Young Irelanders*, 2nd edn (1945) · R. Davis, *The Young Ireland movement* (1987) · R. O'Connor, *Jenny Mitchel, Young Irelander* (1988) · J. Phelan, *The ardent exile: life and times of Thomas D'Arcy McGee* (1951) · C. A. Reilly, letters, 8–9 March 1854, PRO NIre., Mic 426, reel 1 · J. Mitchel, letters to C. A. Reilly, PRO NIre., Mic 426, reel 1 [18 Aug 1849, one undated] · T. D. Reilly, letter to J. Martin, 7 July 1848, PRO NIre., D 2137/1/12

Likenesses portrait, repro. in J. Mitchel, *Jail journal* (1982), 272

Wealth at death left 'a few debts': Reilly, letter, 9 March 1854, PRO NIre., Mic 426, reel 1

Reilly, Hugh. *See* Reilly, Hugh (*fl.* 1686–1695).

Reilly, Sir (D'Arcy) Patrick (1909–1999), diplomatist, was born in India on 17 March 1909, the only child of Sir (Henry) D'Arcy Cornelius Reilly (1876–1948), a member of the Indian Civil Service who became chief justice of Mysore from 1934 to 1943, and his wife, Florence Mary, *née* Wilkinson. His family were long-standing servants of the raj and his was the fourth generation to be born in India. He was sent home from India to a preparatory school in the UK where he was a somewhat lonely child, not seeing his parents for five years, before going on to Winchester and later winning a classical scholarship to New College, Oxford. There he was awarded firsts in classical moderations in 1930 and in *literae humaniores* in 1932. He was elected to a fellowship of All Souls in 1932 (in the same election as Isaiah Berlin). After a brief period travelling with a Laming fellowship from Queen's College, Oxford, and studying languages, he passed top into the diplomatic service in October 1933.

Reilly's first overseas posting was to Tehran, from May 1935 to June 1938, where he met and, on 27 July 1938, married Rachel Mary Sykes (*d.* 1984), eldest daughter of Brigadier-General Sir Percy *Sykes, Indian army officer. She came from a family with a tradition of public service similar to Reilly's own, and accompanied him throughout his diplomatic career, developing an enthusiasm for contemporary painting which sometimes clashed with the more traditional tastes of those responsible for embassy décor, but in other respects adhering to a conventional view of the status and role of a senior diplomatic wife.

Sir (D'Arcy) Patrick Reilly (1909–1999), by Walter Bird, 1957

They had two daughters, Jane (*b.* 1939) and Sarah Sophia (*b.* 1941).

Following his return to the Foreign Office Reilly was promoted second secretary, in October 1938. Shortly after the outbreak of the Second World War in September 1939 he was attached to the Ministry of Economic Warfare, which was involved with special operations. He was promoted acting principal in September 1940 and appointed OBE in June 1942, but he became deeply disillusioned by the infighting between the various secret departments in wartime London. He was happier when (having been promoted first secretary in June 1943) he was sent to Algiers in October 1943 on the staff of the minister resident in north Africa. It was there that he first worked for Harold Macmillan and established a rapport that was to further his career in later life. With the liberation of Paris, Reilly moved there, in September 1944, as acting head of Chancery to Duff Cooper and this first introduction to French life was also to prove formative. From Paris he went to Athens, in August 1945, being promoted counsellor in April 1947, and playing an active role during the crucial years of the civil war when Greece was hovering on the verge of communism. He was appointed CMG in the new year's honours list in 1949. A quiet year at the Imperial Defence College from January to December 1949 was a well-earned respite.

Reilly next spent three years (from December 1949 to June 1953) at the Foreign Office as an assistant undersecretary dealing with defence and security subjects. It was during this period that his assessment that Kim

Philby (not yet under suspicion) was untrustworthy probably played a decisive part in preventing the latter's advancement to the head of MI6. From June 1953 to October 1956 he was minister at the embassy in Paris, his modesty providing a useful foil to the more ebullient ambassador, Sir Gladwyn Jebb. He was promoted KCMG in January 1957. A short spell as a deputy under-secretary in the Foreign Office (from October 1956 to February 1957) preceded his next and most challenging appointment.

In February 1957 Harold Macmillan—by now prime minister—chose Reilly to go as ambassador, aged only forty-eight, to Moscow. In East–West relations it was a period both of great danger and of great change: the cold war was at its height, and Khrushchov was in the process of consolidating his personal predominance and—encouraged by the launching of the first (Soviet) spacecraft—of issuing threats to NATO, including an ultimatum to evacuate West Berlin. Macmillan wanted an envoy of high intellect and absolute integrity whom he could trust to report the scene in all its complexity and who would be neither browbeaten nor provocative. Reilly provided this service. He encouraged Macmillan to embark on his celebrated visit to Moscow in February 1959, although warning him that Khrushchov would attempt to use the visit to drive wedges between the NATO allies; and during the visit he helped to stiffen Macmillan's resolve in the face of Khrushchov's bluster and attempted bullying. He painstakingly prepared for the summit conference which was eventually aborted by Khrushchov following the American U2 spy plane incident in May 1960. On occasions when summoned by Khrushchov or Gromeko in the night and subjected to alarming harangues he would return to the embassy residence across the river from the Kremlin and, rather than be rushed into hasty comment, listen to Gregorian chants on the gramophone over a malt whisky until he had thought through the implications of the interview and was ready to interpret it calmly to London. His measured responses did much to steady opinion at home.

On leaving Moscow in April 1960, Reilly returned for a second spell as a deputy under-secretary in the Foreign Office, this time mostly involved with economic work and preparations for the possible entry of the UK to the Common Market. In 1964 he headed (at official level) the British delegation to the UN conference on trade and development. There was some speculation that he might be in line to be the next permanent under-secretary at the Foreign Office, but Reilly himself made clear his desire to finish his career in France—where he had twice served before. His appointment as ambassador in Paris in February 1965 came at a time when relations with France were at a low ebb following President de Gaulle's veto of British entry to the Common Market. From the beginning Reilly's mission was dogged by misfortune. The 150th anniversary of the battle of Waterloo, in June 1965, led to misunderstandings and boycotts of embassy functions; Mary Stewart, wife of the foreign secretary, (Robert) Michael Stewart, took exception to what she considered patronizing behaviour by the embassy; despite painstaking efforts by

Reilly, de Gaulle declined to reconsider his veto; and Reilly's low profile style disappointed many of the more vociferous members of the British community. Misfortune turned to disaster when George Brown (who had succeeded Stewart as foreign secretary) publicly insulted Lady Reilly at an embassy dinner, declaring in front of the French and British guests that she was not fit to be an ambassador's wife. Reilly was deeply incensed by the incident, which he attributed to George Brown's drunkenness. Nevertheless he continued to serve him loyally. His loyalty was not reciprocated: Brown maintained a vendetta against Reilly, whose qualities he altogether failed to appreciate, and whom he mistook for a conventional and disapproving mandarin. It was Brown who arranged to have him replaced (in September 1968) by the more flamboyant figure of Christopher Soames (former Conservative minister, son-in-law of Winston Churchill, and future peer). Reilly took his premature retirement with good grace, but remained permanently scarred by the whole Brown affair. He had been advanced to GCMG earlier in 1968, but only after a number of private representations had been made to the Labour government.

In 1969 Reilly was re-elected a fellow of All Souls College, Oxford, to which he was devoted. He also turned his energies to a number of Anglo-French and European projects: among other activities he was chairman of the Banque Nationale de Paris, formerly the British and French Bank (1969–80), vice-president of the London chamber of commerce and industry (1975–99), and chairman of the board of the British Institute in Paris (1970–79). In 1984 his wife, Rachel, died, and on 23 October 1987 he married Ruth Margaret Norrington (b. 1921/2), author, daughter of Edmund Cude, estate agent, and widow first of Frank Davis, permanent secretary in Enugu, Nigeria, second of Rupert Waterlow (1925–1969), businessman, and third of Sir Arthur Norrington (1899–1982), president of Trinity College, Oxford, from 1954 to 1970. Reilly's elder daughter, Jane, hosted his ninetieth birthday party at the Athenaeum a few months before his death. In his last years he divided his time between his flat in Maida Vale, London, and his rooms at All Souls College, where he spent much time editing and sorting his diaries and letters for preservation in the Bodleian Library. He died of cancer on 6 October 1999, and was survived by his two daughters and his second wife. He lived and died a member of the Church of England.

Reilly's active life spanned three crucial periods of British diplomacy: the intelligence and allied liaison aspects of the Second World War, the height of the cold war confrontation with the USSR, and the British efforts to secure entry to the European Community in the face of French obstructionism. In all he played a quiet but deeply significant role. His great strength lay in the meticulous accuracy and integrity—not only regarding facts but also mood and character—with which he interpreted these far-reaching events to his political masters. He scrupulously resisted the diplomatic temptation to present his reports and comments in a light favourable to himself, not infrequently confessing that he thought he might have failed to get some point properly across. These qualities, together with his outstanding intellect, made him a wise and trusted counsellor to Harold Macmillan and many others. But he lacked the panache to cut a public figure, and the decisiveness to venture into print in any significant way after his retirement. Although always a sympathetic listener and a cheerful companion when with his friends, he had a streak of melancholy and a self-deprecating quality which limited his impact on a wider audience. Nevertheless he was a formidable public servant in the high tradition for which he had been prepared by birth, education, and experience.   JOHN URE

Sources personal knowledge (2004) · private information (2004) · *The Times* (8 Oct 1999) · *Daily Telegraph* (8 Oct 1999) · *The Guardian* (9 Oct 1999) · *The Scotsman* (23 Oct 1999) · WWW · Burke, *Peerage* · m. cert. [Ruth Margaret Norrington]
Archives Bodl. Oxf., corresp. and papers | NL Wales, letters to Desmond Donnelly
Likenesses W. Bird, photograph, 1957, NPG [*see illus.*] · double portrait, photograph, 1957 (with Lady Reilly), Hult. Arch. · group portrait, photograph, 1973, Hult. Arch. · photograph, repro. in *The Times* · photograph, repro. in *Daily Telegraph* · photograph, repro. in *The Guardian* · photographs, priv. coll.

Reilly, Paul, Baron Reilly (1912–1990), designer and design entrepreneur, was born on 29 May 1912 at Dingle Bank, Toxteth, Liverpool, the third child and elder son of the family of four children, of whom only one son and one daughter survived childhood, of Sir Charles Herbert *Reilly (1874–1948), professor of architecture at Liverpool University, and his wife, Dorothy Gladys (d. 1939), daughter of James Jerram Pratt, city merchant, of Highgate, London. His mother was a pupil of Henry Tonks at the Slade School of Fine Art, but her career as a painter was cut short when she developed tuberculosis soon after her marriage in 1904. Reilly was educated at Winchester College. He won an exhibition to Hertford College, Oxford, where he made lasting friendships, dabbled in left-wing politics, and left with a second class in philosophy, politics, and economics (1933). Although not really athletic, he was nimble and at Oxford gained a fencing half-blue. He then spent the year 1933–4 at the London School of Economics on a business administration course. He was always adept at making the best of unpropitious circumstances and his appointment, at a time of poor employment prospects, as a door-to-door salesman for the plywood firm Venesta (1934–6), brought him into contact with leading modernist architects and their clients.

With his innate verbal fluency and buoyant curiosity Reilly was a born journalist. In 1936 he became assistant to the leader page editor of the *News Chronicle*. Gerald Barry, then editor, encouraged him to travel around Britain, with the photographer Barnett Saidman, reporting on buildings and design. He was promoted to features editor in 1940. After a *mouvementé* war, spent mainly in naval intelligence (he joined the Royal Armoured Corps in 1940 and was in the Royal Naval Volunteer Reserve from 1941 to 1946), he worked in New York on *Modern Plastics* magazine in 1946. A chance meeting on board ship returning home to England in 1948 with Gordon Russell, newly appointed director of the Council of Industrial Design (COID), led in

1948 to the offer of a job as public relations officer with the council. The COID had been set up in wartime to 'promote by all practicable means the improvement of design in the products of British industry'. Reilly's aim was to raise consciousness of design standards in a public starved of visual stimulus in the years of austerity and rationing. He organized a series of design weeks in the provinces and drew on his journalistic experience to launch the COID's *Design* magazine. In the early 1950s his energies were focused on the Festival of Britain, an event to which his modernist proselytizing fervour and his liberal left attitudes were perfectly attuned.

The twelve years of double act between Russell, the craftsman–designer of integrity and vision, and the highly political, sophisticated Reilly were enormously successful for the COID. In 1956 the Design Centre in Haymarket, London, a selective exhibition through which the public could locate well-designed products, was opened by the duke of Edinburgh. Reilly was much involved in the setting up of annual Design Centre awards in the next year, and was responsible for the introduction of what became the familiar triangular black and white label affixed to chosen products, the symbol of government-approved design. His wily charm was useful in the COID's struggle to persuade corporate buyers, government and private, to make visually enterprising choices. He was the natural successor as director in 1960, Russell having retired in 1959.

Reilly faced serious underlying problems in the 1960s. In a sense the COID had done its job too thoroughly and commercial outlets began selecting products with more flair and catholicity than the design committees at the COID. Moreover Reilly's own visual aesthetic, based on principles of functional fitness and truth to materials, was, in the more morally mobile 1960s, coming under threat. He identified the problem in an important article in the *Architectural Review* in 1967, 'The challenge of pop'. He subsequently shifted the COID sideways, concentrating on developing design in engineering at the expense of consumer education.

As an ambassador for British visual culture Reilly travelled widely on behalf of the Design Council (as the COID became in 1973) and international crafts organizations: unlike many of his modernist contemporaries, he had great sympathy with the handmade product, and it was under his aegis that the craft advisory committee was set up in 1971. This committee burgeoned to become the Crafts Council. Although he played the power game with great skill and much enjoyment, he also delighted in the personal encounter, and many young craftsmen and designers were spurred on by the warmth of his encouragement.

When he retired in 1977 Reilly became a director of Conran Associates and chairman of the Conran Foundation Boilerhouse, precursor of the Design Museum. He received many awards, and honorary degrees from Loughborough (1977), Aston (1981), and Cranfield (1983). He became an honorary FRIBA in 1965, was knighted in 1967, and became an honorary doctor of the Royal College of

Art in 1978. He was made a commander of the royal order of Vasa (Sweden) in 1961. He was delighted by his life peerage in 1978, regarding the House of Lords, where he sat on the cross-benches (until prevented by encroaching heart disease) as a glorified version of his old newspaper office: a place in which he would never feel unwanted or bored.

Reilly was small, twinkling, and benign enough to be mistaken for the archbishop of Canterbury, Michael Ramsey, whom he much resembled. He was a great gossip and as eclectic a connoisseur of people as of things. His first marriage, in 1939, to the classical ballet dancer Pamela Wentworth Foster (daughter of Major Edward Bayntun Grove Foster, landowner, of Warmwell in Dorset and Clewer Manor in Berkshire), ended in divorce in 1952; their only child, Victoria, a journalist, married the Czech artist–designer Daniel Spicka. In 1952 Reilly married his second wife, Annette Rose, daughter of Brigadier-General Clifton Inglis Stockwell; she had trained as a sculptor and became a fashion and design journalist and cookery correspondent on *The Times*. They had no children and lived and ate convivially in a South Kensington stuccoed terrace house, 3 Alexander Place, designed by George Basevi, surrounded by the paintings, books, and objects of a lifetime's collecting. Reilly died on 11 October 1990 at the Cromwell Hospital in Kensington, London. He was cremated at Putney Vale. FIONA MACCARTHY, *rev.*

Sources P. Reilly, *An eye on design* (1987) · *The Times* (12 Oct 1990) · *The Independent* (17 Oct 1990) · *The Independent* (22 Oct 1990) · personal knowledge (1996) · private information (1996) [family]
Archives V&A, corresp. and papers | University of Brighton, Design Council archive
Likenesses R. Darwin, oils, 1971, Lady Reilly collection
Wealth at death £287,103: probate, 14 Dec 1990, CGPLA Eng. & Wales

Reilly, Sidney George [*formerly* Shlomo ben Hersh Rozenblium] (**1874–1925**), spy, dubbed the Ace of Spies, was born Shlomo (Solomon) ben Hersh Rozenblium on 24 March 1874 in Bedzin, Piotrków Guberniia, Russian Poland, the only son of Hersh (Grigorii) ben Yakov Rozenblium and his wife, Paulina Bramson. He had two sisters, Elena and Mariam. His father was a contractor and minor landowner active in the Jewish emancipation movement. Among his ancestors was the Jewish theologian Elijah ben Solomon, gaon of Vilna (1720–1797).

Details of Reilly's education are uncertain. Despite later claims, he did not attend Heidelberg or Cambridge universities or the Royal School of Mines. Nevertheless he demonstrated sufficient knowledge of chemistry to gain membership in the Chemical Society in 1896 and the Institute of Chemistry in 1897. He had an exceptional command of languages, including English, Russian, Polish, German, and French.

As Sigmund Salomon Georgjevitch Rosenblum he arrived in London in 1895. In 1899 he became Sidney George Reilly by receiving a passport in that name, though he never legally adopted it or became a British subject. A patron, possibly his entrée into British intelligence, was Sir Henry Hozier (1838–1907), powerful secretary of Lloyds connected to the War Office intelligence branch.

With his strong Jewish features and accented English, Reilly was an unconvincing Englishman, but this became his favourite of many alternative identities.

Reilly was married at least four times but never divorced. His first marriage in 1898 was to Margaret Callahan Thomas (1874–1933), a governess and the widow of the Revd Hugh Thomas, from whom he separated by 1904. Between 1904 and 1908 he was married to a Russian woman with whom he maintained a relationship through the mid-1920s. Two children were produced by this union, a son and a daughter, but their names and fates are unknown. In 1910 Reilly took another Russian bride, Nadya Petrovna Zalessky (1888–*c*.1949), the former wife of a tsarist naval official; they separated in 1919. He married a British actress, Pepita Bobadilla (*née* Nelly Louise Burton; 1894–*c*.1970), widow of playwright Charles Haddon Chambers, in 1923.

Reilly was a collector of books and artwork, particularly Napoleona. He was an aviation enthusiast and helped found one of the first aviation firms in Russia, Krylya, in 1910. He also was a member of the Imperial All-Russian Aero Club. He was a freemason.

Reilly's espionage career, as much commercial as political, was long and complex. From 1899 to 1905 he was mostly in the Far East. In 1904 he directed the trading firm M. A. Ginsburg & Co. in Port Arthur, China, and supplied information to both Japan and Russia. The years 1906–14 found him based in St Petersburg, where he developed a wide array of personal and professional contacts extending from the revolutionary underground to the imperial court. In 1914 he went to New York as a war contractor and became a powerful influence in Russian purchasing. His ruthless business tactics earned him a fortune and many enemies. Reilly entered the Royal Flying Corps as second lieutenant in October 1917 and served at that rank until demobilization in April 1920. He received the Military Cross in 1919. An effort to secure his honorary commission as a major in the army failed, in part due to political objections.

The First World War saw Reilly become a formal agent of the British Secret Intelligence Service in whose employ he remained until 1922. In 1918 he spearheaded a bold if unsuccessful plot to topple Lenin's regime, the misnamed Lockhart plot. Thereafter he ostensibly devoted himself to the anti-Bolshevik cause and became the key adviser to one of the Soviets' militant opponents, Boris Savinkov (1879–1924). In 1924 Reilly was a charter member of the International League to Combat the III International and in the same year helped found the American affiliate, the Anti-Bolshevik League. However, Reilly's memoranda to the SIS and various British officials reveal a measured approach to the Soviet regime. He judged the abrupt and total overthrow of the Bolsheviks as unwise and unnecessary and advocated policies aimed at shifting leadership from ideologues to more pragmatic hands. Economic incentives played a vital role in these plans. In pursuit of this goal he returned to Soviet Russia in late 1925 and was captured by Soviet police. Russian records suggest that Reilly was executed in Moscow on 5 November 1925 but this, as with previous contradictory statements on his demise, is by no means definitive. He is said to have been buried in Moscow on 9 November.

Estimates of Reilly's character vary widely. Some saw in him Baron Munchausen, others Mephistopheles. The official verdict, as rendered by the Foreign Office's Sir Nevile Bland, was that Reilly was 'a man of great courage … coupled with a somewhat unscrupulous temperament, [making] him a rather double edged tool' (FO 371/12605). An American business rival, Samuel Vauclain, observed that he was 'not only a keen-witted and resourceful businessman, but, when in a tight place, proved … an ingenious diplomat' (Office of Naval Intelligence, file 21010, 34). Reilly, however, had his champions, among them his wartime SIS chief and later business partner Sir William Wiseman, Sir Robert Nathan, and perhaps most notably Sir Winston Churchill. There remains a division among those who regard Reilly as a martyr to the anti-communist cause (Brook-Shepherd) and those who see him as a devious Soviet double agent (Lockhart, *First Man*). He was all that and more. Reilly was indifferent to matters of ideology; his only true loyalty was to himself.

RICHARD B. SPENCE

Sources Revolt Pimenov, 'Kak ia iskal shpiona Reili', 1968, Radio Liberty SamizdatArchive, Munich, 1089 • SIS Archives, London, File CX2616 • Office of Naval Intelligence, Record Group 45, USA National Archives, Washington, DC, File 21010–3241 • Military Intelligence Division, RG165, USA National Archives, Washington, DC, Files 9140–5091, 9140–6073 • PRO, FO 371/3319, 3350, 3962, 4019, 4022, 11793, 12593, 12602, and 12605 • Russian Federal Security Service, Moscow, Central Archive, 'Operatsiia Trest' records, vols. 37–8 • Hoover Archives, Stanford, California, Paul Dukes, R. H. B. Lockhart, B. I. Nicolaevsky, P. N. Vrangelcollections • V. Krymov, *Portrety Neobychnykh liudei* (Paris, 1971) • R. B. Lockhart, *Ace of spies: the incredible story of Sidney Reilly* (1967) • R. Lockhart, *Reilly: the first man* (1987) • G. Brook-Shepherd, *Iron maze: the western intelligence services and the Bolsheviks* (1998) • P. Reilly and S. Reilly, *The adventures of Sidney Reilly: Britain's master spy* (1931) • M. Kettle, *Sidney Reilly* (1983) • m. certs.
Archives National Archives and Records Administration, Washington, DC, Office of Naval Intelligence, record group 45, files 21010–3241 • National Archives and Records Administration, Washington, DC, Military Intelligence Division, RG165, files 9140–5091, 9140–6073 • PRO, FO 371/3319, 3350, 3962, 4019, 4022, 11793, 12593, 12602, 12605, etc. • SIS Archives, London, file CX2616
Likenesses photograph, 1890, repro. in Kettle, *Sidney Reilly*, following p. 71 • photograph, 1918, repro. in Kettle, *Sidney Reilly*, following p. 71 • H. F. Crowther-Smith, caricature, 1919, repro. in Brook-Shepherd, *Iron maze*, following p. 114 • photograph, c.1923–1924, repro. in Brook-Shepherd, *Iron maze*, following p. 114
Wealth at death approx. $100,000 US—bank deposits, plus undetermined artwork assets: US State Department Report, Aug 1925, in CSA215 file

Reilly, Thomas Rundle [Tommy] (1919–2000), harmonica player, was born in Guelph, Ontario, Canada, on 21 August 1919, the son of Captain James Reilly, a military bandmaster. His father was a versatile musician who not only conducted symphony orchestras but was also the founder of one of Canada's first jazz bands. Himself a keen harmonica player, Captain Reilly also founded and led the Elmdale Harmonica Band, which won many prizes throughout Canada. His son Tommy participated in this band, although, according to one account, he was sacked for

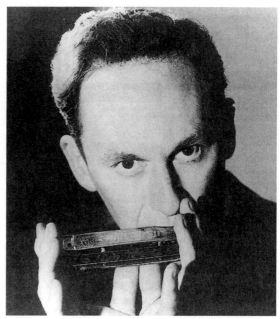

Thomas Rundle Reilly (1919–2000), by unknown photographer

refusing to practise. Reilly also learned several other instruments, including the violin, which he began to study at the age of eight. When the family moved to England in 1935, Tommy was already a virtuoso performer on the harmonica, and toured variety theatres in Britain and Europe. He played in cabaret as a juggler and a tightrope-walker. In 1939 he entered the Leipzig conservatory as a violinist, but in September, as soon as war broke out, he was arrested by the Gestapo and interned. He spent the whole of the war in prison camps in Germany, Poland, and France. Fortunately, however, he was able to keep up his harmonica playing, improving his technique, although he was obliged to surrender his Red Cross parcels in order to bribe the guards so that he could receive the harmonicas sent to him by the famous harmonica manufacturer Ernst Hohner. In his attempt to achieve a smooth legato style of playing, he was much influenced by violinists such as Jascha Heifetz. He ended his days as a prisoner of war at Lüneburg Heath. It is ironic that although he had managed to retain his violin in the prison camps, it was stolen on his return trip to Britain in 1945.

The war over, Reilly embarked on an exciting career as a broadcaster and, subsequently, a film star and television personality, which was to continue for more than fifty years. On 20 October 1946 he married the variety artiste Ena Nabb (b. 1928/9), with whom he had one son. In 1951 Michael Spivakovsky wrote a harmonica concerto for him as part of the Festival of Britain celebrations, a year before Vaughan Williams wrote his *Romance for Harmonica*. Reilly was also the performer of many works written especially for him, including *Five Pieces* for harmonica and piano by Gordon Jacob, a *Concertino* by Vilem Tausky, and concertos by Karl-Heinz Koper and Milton Barnes. Pop works and jazz-based works were written for him by composers such as George Martin and Bob Farnon, while the many film composers writing for him included John Barry, Elmer Bernstein, Bob Farnon, Jerry Goldsmith, Bernard Herrmann, Maurice Jarre, and Dimitri Tiomkin. Reilly was himself also a composer, his notable compositions including the music for the very successful comedy film *The Navy Lark* of 1959. Among his great successes as a performer for television were the theme tunes to *Dixon of Dock Green*, *The Last of the Summer Wine*, and *The Singing Detective*. In the world of film, he achieved great success in 1965 as the performer in Ron Goodwin's music for *Those Magnificent Men in their Flying Machines*, and, in 1969, of the theme tune in John Barry's *Midnight Cowboy*.

Reilly made numerous recordings of many kinds of music, including folk-song arrangements, light music, popular classics, film music, and works by classical composers such as Malcolm Arnold, Heitor Villa-Lobos, and Vaughan Williams. He made several recordings with the Academy of St Martin-in-the-Fields under Sir Neville Marriner, who said of him: 'He achieves remarkable virtuosity with a minimum of fuss. Musically he exploits his instrument with refinement and bravura, and ultimately it does not seem to matter what he plays, but how he plays it' (*The Independent*). Reilly also came into contact with Stravinsky. On one occasion, when Stravinsky's publishers tried to prevent Reilly from playing one of the composer's works, Stravinsky interceded on his behalf, stating: 'After hearing your interpretation of my *Chanson Russe*, I would be happy to let you play anything of mine' (*The Guardian*). He also worked with many leading stars of the day, including Bing Crosby and Marlene Dietrich. In 1967 he commissioned a specially constructed concert harmonica made of silver, which became his trademark. Tommy Reilly did much to prove that the harmonica was a viable concert instrument. The recipient of many awards and prizes, he was a world authority on his instrument, writing a number of manuals and studies, and was an excellent and much sought-after teacher. Perhaps the greatest tribute to his standing as a performer of world significance was made by Larry Adler: 'He was unique, in a class by himself' (ibid.). Reilly died at his home, Hammonds Wood, Frensham, Surrey, on 25 September 2000, at eighty-one years of age; his wife, Ena, survived him.   G. R. SEAMAN

Sources *The Guardian* (28 Sept 2000) · *Daily Telegraph* (29 Sept 2000) · *The Independent* (16 Oct 2000) · *The Times* (5 Oct 2000) · *The Scotsman* (23 Oct 2000) · m. cert. · d. cert. · *New Grove*
Likenesses photograph, News International Syndication, London [*see illus.*] · photograph, repro. in *The Independent* · photograph, repro. in *The Guardian* · photograph, repro. in *Daily Telegraph*

Reilly, William Edward Moyses (1827–1886), army officer, born at Scarvagh, co. Down, on 13 January 1827, was fourth son of James Miles Reilly of Cloon Eavin, co. Down, and Emilia, second daughter of the Revd Hugh Montgomery of Grey Abbey and niece of Bernard Ward, first Viscount Bangor. An elder brother, Sir Francis Savage Reilly QC (1825–1883), was a well-known parliamentary draftsman. Educated at Christ's Hospital, at fifteen William became a cadet at the Royal Military Academy, Woolwich. He was commissioned second-lieutenant, Royal Artillery, on 18 December 1845, being promoted first-lieutenant on 3 April 1846 and second-captain on 17 February 1854. In 1854 he was appointed aide-de-camp to General Fox-Strangways, who commanded the artillery in the Crimea, but on his journey out learned that Strangways had been killed at Inkerman. He went to the Crimea, and volunteered to serve as a battery officer. He was in the trenches through the winter, and in February 1855 he was made adjutant (and subsequently brigade major) of the siege-train. He was at the bombardments and was mentioned in dispatches. He received a brevet majority on 2 November 1855, was made a member of the Légion d'honneur, was awarded the Mejidiye (fifth class), and was created CB (January 1857). After the fall of Sevastopol he was deputy adjutant quartermaster-general at the headquarters of the army until it left the Crimea in June 1856. From December 1856 to April 1859 Reilly was aide-de-camp to Sir Richard Dacres, commanding the Royal Artillery in Ireland, and under Dacres's direction compiled the official account of the artillery operations of the siege of Sevastopol.

During the Austro-Prussian War of 1866 Reilly was sent out as British commissioner with the Prussian army, but could not join it until 19 July, when the fighting was over. He wrote a memorandum on the Prussian army system of supply and transport, as tested in the field, and on its artillery material. While generally favourable, he criticized the hospital arrangements, and he claimed the breech-loading guns inferior to muzzle-loaders and, for some purposes, even to smooth-bores.

Reilly became regimental lieutenant-colonel in 1868, and the next year was the guest of Lord Mayo in India, from where he wrote some descriptive letters to *The Times*. He spoke French fluently, and at the end of October 1870, when Paris was besieged, he was sent as extra military attaché to the British embassy at Tours. He at once joined the headquarters of the French army of the Loire, and became the channel for distributing British contributions to aid the wounded. He was present at Beaune-la-Rolande and at the subsequent battles before Orléans. The hurried French evacuation of Orléans in the night of 4 December took place without his knowledge. He was arrested there next morning by the Prussians and sent to England by way of Saarbrücken and Belgium. He wished to rejoin the British embassy, then at Bordeaux, but the British government refused. The French government raised him to the grade of officer of the Légion d'honneur on 20 March 1872 and to commander on 4 November 1878.

From April 1871 to January 1876 Reilly was assistant director of artillery at the War Office, and made several visits abroad to report on artillery questions: to Berlin in 1872, and to France and to the Vienna Exhibition in 1873. He also accompanied the duke of Edinburgh to Russia in 1874. In his reports he still preferred muzzle-loading guns, and did not think Britain had much to learn from foreign artillery.

Reilly became brevet colonel on 22 August 1873 and regimental colonel on 25 September 1877. In January 1879 he was appointed to command the Royal Artillery at Aldershot, but in the following month he was sent out to South Africa, in a similar capacity, to the Anglo-Zulu War. While he was inspecting one of his batteries his horse fell with him and broke his wrist, and this prevented his being at Ulundi. In 1883 he became director of artillery at the War Office, with the temporary rank of brigadier-general. He resigned this post at the end of 1884 from ill health. On 1 May 1885 he was appointed inspector-general of artillery, with the rank of major-general.

Reilly was a practical and very knowledgeable, but uninnovative, artilleryman. His conservative preference for retaining obsolescent muzzle-loading guns contributed to retarding the modernization of British artillery, and to its temporary *matériel* inferiority to its continental rivals. In his last months Reilly replied trenchantly to Colonel Hope's allegations in *The Times* against the Ordnance department. The royal commission on warlike stores (1887), chaired by Sir James Fitzjames Stephen, investigated the allegations. Its report supported the charge of weak administration, but refuted that of corruption.

Reilly published pamphlets on artillery and other military subjects, and *An Account of the Artillery Operations before Sebastopol* (1859), written for the secretary of state for war. On 28 July 1886 Reilly died on board the steamer *Mistletoe* while engaged in the inspection of the artillery at Guernsey. He was buried with military honours at Cheriton, near Sandgate. A tablet and memorial window were placed in St George's garrison church at Woolwich by his fellow officers.   E. M. LLOYD, rev. ROGER T. STEARN

Sources *The Times* (19 April 1867) · *Pall Mall Gazette* (3 April 1873) · *Morning Post* (29 July 1886) · private information (1896) · W. S. Hamer, *The British army: civil–military relations, 1885–1905* (1970) · E. M. Spiers, *The late Victorian army, 1868–1902* (1992) · J. D. Scott, *Vickers: a history* (1962) · Boase, *Mod. Eng. biog.* · Kelly, *Handbk*
Wealth at death £20,905 14s. 11d.: resworn probate, Feb 1887, *CGPLA Eng. & Wales* (1886)

Reily [Reilly], **Hugh** (*fl.* 1686–1695), royal official and writer, was born in co. Cavan. His parentage and date of birth are unknown. He entered a legal career, qualifying as a barrister. Reily clearly gained royal favour for in May 1686 a warrant appointed him one of the masters of the court of chancery in Ireland, citing his loyalty and ability. The lord lieutenant of Ireland, the earl of Clarendon, sought to block this appointment in favour of Sir John Coghill, who was to be removed, on the grounds of unfitness, to make way for Reily. Despite Clarendon's prevarications it was made clear to him that James II was adamant concerning Reily's appointment. In the correspondence surrounding this affair there is some evidence that Reily came from a relatively modest background, for Clarendon pointedly suggests that the king will be best served in chancery by people such as Coghill who have fortunes of their own. During the Williamite wars Reily's star rose further, for on 5 March 1689 he was made clerk to the privy council, and on 27 August he became a lord commissioner of the Treasury. He followed James II into exile in France, where, it was said, he was appointed lord chancellor of Ireland.

In 1695 Reily published his only known work, *Ireland's case briefly stated, or, A summary account of the most remarkable transactions in that kingdom since the Reformation*, using the pseudonym a True Lover of his King and Country. Paris or Louvain have been suggested as possible places of publication. The book consists of two parts. Part one consciously seeks to provide an alternative reading of recent Irish history to that produced by English and Irish protestant writers. Reily believes that such accounts are partisan attempts to blacken the reputation of Catholic Ireland. His own narrative stresses the long-suffering loyalty of Irish Catholics to the Stuart dynasty, a fidelity which, instead of bringing a much-merited reward, has rather brought further woes. These were fairly standard sentiments among Irish Catholic Jacobites. The second part, however, is unusual in its explicit claim that Charles II was ultimately culpable for this injustice. Though Reily repeats the standard Jacobite claims about wicked advisers and ministers turning the king against his loyal Irish Catholic subjects, he insists that Charles II must be held accountable for the choice of such ministers and the acts of his officials. He also adds a providentialist argument, backed by relevant scriptural texts, that God sometimes punishes the successors of errant rulers, and he even suggests at one point that the Williamite wars themselves might not be unconnected to such divine displeasure. Not surprisingly the publication of this work had fairly serious consequences for Reily. He had taken the precaution of showing the final draft to the exiled king, who, after keeping the material for three weeks, said that there was 'too much Truth in it' (*Whole Works*, 253), but he did not forbid Reily to publish the text. On its publication, however, James showed his displeasure by dismissing Reily from the chancellorship and depriving him of his salary. It is said that Reily took all of this so badly that he died shortly afterwards, though James is also said to have restored his pension just before his death.

Reily's book found favour with later Irish patriotic and nationalist traditions. In the eighteenth century it began to be published, in both England and Ireland, with additional material such as the last speech and dying words of the Catholic primate Oliver Plunket and the Roman Catholic remonstrance to Charles II. The work's title was changed, first to *The Impartial History of Ireland*, and subsequently to *The Genuine History of Ireland*. James MacGeoghegan's *History of Ireland* (1758–62), itself to become part of the classic canon of Irish nationalism, contained extensive citations of *Ireland's Case Briefly Stated*. The work was also translated into Irish. In the nineteenth century it went through many editions in Ireland, including cheap popular editions.   VINCENT GEOGHEGAN

Sources *The whole works of Sir James Ware concerning Ireland*, ed. and trans. W. Harris, rev. edn, 2 vols. in 3 (1764) · *The correspondence of Henry Hyde, earl of Clarendon, and of his brother, Laurence Hyde, earl of Rochester*, ed. S. W. Singer, 2 vols. (1828); repr. (1991) · R. Lascelles, ed., *Liber munerum publicorum Hiberniae … or, The establishments of Ireland*, 2 vols. [1824–30] · W. King, *The state of the protestants of Ireland under the late King James's government*, another edn (1692)

Reinagle family (*per. c.*1760–1877), artists and musicians, came to prominence with Joseph Reinagle (*fl.* 1745–1775), a Hungarian former bandsman with the Empress Maria Theresa's army, who landed in Scotland in 1745 with the Young Pretender, Prince Charles Edward Stuart. After the prince's defeat Reinagle lodged with the Laurie family there, and married the daughter Annie, unconnected with the seventeenth-century Maxwelltown lass. Having taken up composition, he was appointed trumpeter to George III in 1762. Joseph and Annie had a daughter and five sons. Maria Anna Theresa (*d.* 1795), a miniaturist and art teacher, married the Hungarian cellist Johann Georg Christoph Schetky. Of their children, John George (1776–1831) became a cellist and music publisher, while John Christian *Schetky (1778–1874) and John Alexander *Schetky (1785–1824), and Caroline Schetky (1790–1852) were all well-known artists.

The hereditary division of talent between music and art was seen also in Joseph Reinagle's sons. Joseph *Reinagle the younger (1762–1825) was a cellist and composer, his son, Alexander Robert *Reinagle (1799–1877) [*see under* Reinagle, Joseph], being an organist. The elder Joseph's son Alexander (1756–1809) emigrated to the United States and became a composer of distinction, while Philip *Reinagle (1748–1833) entered the newly founded school of the Royal Academy in 1769 and two years later married Jane Austin in London. Of their eleven children, two sons—Ramsay Richard *Reinagle (1775–1862) and Philip Reinagle the younger (*b.* 1784)—and four daughters followed him as artists.

Three daughters of Philip Reinagle the elder were educated at Reading Ladies' Boarding-School, a few years after Jane Austen and with Mary Martha Butt, later Mrs Sherwood, and Frances Arabella Rowden. The eldest, **Amelia Ann Reinagle** (*b.* 1777), was depicted in Mrs Sherwood's reminiscences as dark and handsome. She married, on 3 October 1797, William Henry Souper. The next in line, **Mary Ann Reinagle** (*b.* 1778), who called herself Maria Anna, was small with a plain and pock-marked face, but had a cheerful and vibrant personality and an effortless range of accomplishments which included both drawing and music; as a dare, she smoked until she made herself sick. Although she is said to have died in early youth, she married, on 9 April 1803, Thomas Hayward Budd. **Charlotte Jenetta Reinagle** (*b.* 1782) was baptized on 28 August 1782 at St Marylebone Church, London. She was a junior pupil at Reading, and later married John White, on 14 December 1808.

As Philip Reinagle was chronically short of money, this schooling, at £35 a year for each pupil, was an extravagance, and after the Reading academy went bankrupt in 1794, their provident mother educated the six remaining daughters at home. Jane Reinagle (*b.* 1780) about 1803 married her father's former pupil Henry *Howard (1769–1847), a portrait and history painter.

From 1798–9 onwards Charlotte Reinagle and Frances Arabella Reinagle, known as Fanny (*b.* 1786) exhibited at the Royal Academy and at the British Institution, mostly landscapes. By 1807, to augment the family income, they were copying at great speed parts of old masters (not being allowed to copy the whole) loaned each season to the British Institution. They began by painting with watercolours on the canvas, later working over with oils; in their words, 'Picture painted one day, sold the next, money spent the third' (Farington, *Diary*, 8.3106). They continued to exhibit at London galleries after their respective marriages. Another daughter, Harriet (*b.* 1789), showed landscapes at the Suffolk Street Gallery and the Society of Painters in Water Colours between 1824 and 1862, while the youngest daughter, Oriana Georgina Reinagle (*b.* 1794), exhibited at the Royal Academy and British Institution between 1824 and 1832. Philip Reinagle the younger was an exhibitor at the Royal Academy from 1804 to 1811.

The Reinagle family tradition, of fostering artistic skills, was passed down the generations. Philip Reinagle the elder enrolled his son, Ramsay Richard, and future son-in-law, Henry Howard, as official pupils, and found time to instruct his four artist daughters. Ramsay Richard Reinagle in turn had his son George Philip *Reinagle (*bap.* 1805, *d.* 1835) as pupil, although the latter never became a copyist. He exhibited at the Royal Academy from 1822 onwards. His cousin Frank *Howard (1805–1866), son of Henry Howard, was also an exhibitor there. His death in poverty in 1866, followed by those of John Christian Schetky in 1874 and Alexander Robert Reinagle in 1877, brought to an end the period of celebrity for this talented and sometimes artful clan.
                                                                      T. A. B. CORLEY

Sources DNB · D. Sutton, 'The Reinagles re-considered', *Country Life*, 118 (1955), 1264–6 · *John Constable's correspondence*, ed. R. B. Beckett, 2 (1964), 19–35; 4 (1966), 214–22 · *John Constable: further documents and correspondence*, ed. R. B. Beckett (1975), 266–71 · Graves, *RA exhibitors*, 6 (1906), 256–65 · Graves, *Artists*, 3rd edn, 230–31 · J. Turner, ed., *The dictionary of art*, 34 vols. (1996), vol. 26, pp. 104–5; vol. 28, p. 78 · P. J. M. McEwan, *Dictionary of Scottish art and architecture* (1994), 482–3 · C. Pettys, ed., *Dictionary of women artists before 1900* (1985), 590, 628 · E. Vollmer, *Lexikon für Wasserwesen* (1974), 28 · Waterhouse, *18c painters* · IGI · *New Grove*, 15.714–16; 16.635–7 · M. J. Corry, 'Reinagle, Alexander', *ANB*, 18.320–21 [Alexander Reinagle, 1756–1809] · *Who was who in America: historical volume, 1607–1896* (1963), 437 · W. Gurlitt, ed., *Musik Lexicon, Personenteil L–Z* (1961), 483, 599–600

Reinagle, Alexander Robert (1799–1877). *See under* Reinagle, Joseph (1762–1825).

Reinagle, Amelia Ann (*b.* 1777). *See under* Reinagle family (*per. c.*1760–1877).

Reinagle [*née* Orger], **Caroline** (1817–1892), pianist and composer, was born on 1 May 1817 in London, daughter of Dr Thomas Orger (1767–1853) and his wife, the comic actress Mary Ann *Orger, *née* Ivers (1788–1849). Thomas, a translator of Ovid and Anacreon, and author of a book on Napoleon, was a founder member of the Swedenborg Society and editor of the *Intellectual Repository*. Ever genial, he cheerfully tolerated the career of Mary Ann, who became a Swedenborgian while remaining vivacious and fashionable. Caroline was educated amid theatrical bustle and constant changes of address, but developed a lucid and retentive mind, well read in classical and modern literature.

Caroline Orger studied the piano in London and at Leipzig, where she had lessons with Friedrich Wieck, became friendly with the future Clara Schumann, and acquired an extensive knowledge of contemporary music, especially of Beethoven. Although in 1840 she applied unsuccessfully for the post of organist at St Magnus the Martyr, London Bridge, she was already a much applauded pianist and a founder member of the Society of Female Musicians. On 18 May 1843, at a joint recital in the Hanover Square Rooms with the contralto Charlotte Dolby, she performed her piano trio to some critical acclaim. In 1844 she introduced her piano concerto, and the Society of British Musicians gave her first piano quartet and a cello sonata in G. In 1846 she published a *Tarantella* for piano.

On 10 September 1846 Caroline married Alexander Robert *Reinagle (1799–1877) [*see under* Reinagle, Joseph], son of the cellist and composer Joseph Reinagle (1762–1825) and himself a versatile composer, known for his *Collection of Psalm and Hymn Tunes* (1840) and especially for 'St Peter'. They settled in Oxford, where Alexander was organist at St Peter's-in-the-East. Caroline Reinagle ceased performing in London and withdrew from the Society of Female Musicians, but regularly gave concerts with her husband in Oxford, taught piano (including to the future Lady Stainer), and continued composing. In 1847 the Society of British Musicians presented her piano quartet in E♭, and about this time she wrote her piano sonata (op. 6), the length and technical complexity of which led to its unmerited neglect. A testament to her own virtuosity was the modestly named treatise *A Few Words on Pianoforte Playing* (1854).

Although Caroline contributed a *Rifle March* for the Volunteer craze of 1860, her penchant for programme music found better direction in the art-song. After setting pieces by Adelaide Anne Procter, she attempted Robert Browning, who, in acknowledging 'Would it were I had been false' (1864), encouraged her to set anything she wished by himself or his late wife. In 1868 Reinagle produced what is perhaps her best work, the expressive *Three Songs* to poems by Browning. She later published *Two Songs, Composed to Poetry by Alfred Tennyson and Christina Rossetti* (1880).

Not long after Alexander Reinagle's death on 6 April 1877 at Kidlington, where the Reinagles had been living for some time, Caroline moved back into Oxford. Always interested in women's education, she supported the new Somerville Hall with books, money, and scholarships. But inveterate asthma forced her to retire to Tiverton, Devon, to be close to relatives. Caroline Reinagle died of bronchopneumonia at her house there—which she called 'Somerville'—on 11 March 1892; she was cremated at Woking and her ashes buried at St Mary's, Kidlington, on 18 March.

PATRICK WADDINGTON

Sources Brown & Stratton, *Brit. mus.* · *Tiverton Gazette* (15 March 1892), 5, col. 6 · J. A. Sadie and R. Samuel, eds., *The new Grove dictionary of women composers* (1994) · L. Baillie and R. Balchin, eds., *The catalogue of printed music in the British Library to 1980*, 62 vols. (1981–

7) · 'Orger, Mary Ann', *DNB* · 'Reinagle, Joseph', *DNB* · 'Church and organ music: the tune "St Peter"', *MT*, 47 (1906), 542–3 · *Intellectual Repository*, 14 (1853), 403 [obituary of Thomas Orger] · J. A. A. [J. A. Amor], 'A. R. Reinagle', *Occasional Series* [Kidlington and District Historical Society] [n.d.] · O. Ebel, *Women composers: a biographical handbook of woman's work in music*, 3rd edn (1913) · D. Dawe, *Organists of the City of London, 1666–1850* (1983)
Archives BL, letter to Leigh Hunt, Add. MS 38110
Wealth at death £9036 16s. 5d.: probate, 28 April 1892, *CGPLA Eng. & Wales*

Reinagle, Charlotte Jenetta (*b.* 1782). *See under* Reinagle family (*per. c.*1760–1877).

Reinagle, George Philip (*bap.* 1805, *d.* 1835), marine painter, was baptized at St Marylebone, Middlesex, on 20 March 1805, together with his twin sister Oriana Jane, the youngest of four children (the eldest being sons) of Ramsay Richard *Reinagle (1775–1862), painter, and his first wife, Oriana Bullfinch, a governess. He became a pupil of his father, and decided to concentrate on marine subjects; he began by copying the works of seventeenth-century Dutch sea painters. Apart from some early portraits, all his exhibits at the Royal Academy concerned the sea or coastal scenes. He also composed a pen and wash drawing, *The Landing of George IV at Leith*, in 1822. His most fertile period followed some months at sea. He was present, on board HMS *Mosquito*, at the battle of Navarino in October 1827, publishing a year later a volume of lithographs illustrating the engagement, which he followed up with scenes of preliminary skirmishes between the British and Turkish fleets. His lithographs remain important for their eyewitness reportage of a battle that was instrumental to Greek independence. Five works connected with the battle appeared at Royal Academy exhibitions, the last in 1831. A large number of related pencil sketches are in the National Maritime Museum, Greenwich, which also possesses one of his paintings of the battle.

About 1830 Reinagle married Juliana Eliza Duff, who was to survive him with three infant children, including Agnes Oriana Duff, baptized in January 1832. A typical peacetime composition of his was *French Fishing Boats in a Gale of Wind off Dover*, exhibited in 1833 (National Gallery of Victoria, Melbourne). In 1833 he accompanied Charles Napier, commanding Dom Pedro's fleet in the Portuguese civil war, when Napier defeated Dom Miguel off Cape St Vincent. A picture of this 'glorious triumph' was exhibited at the Royal Academy in the following year. Reinagle also produced some lithographs of the event. His remaining academy exhibits were of the East India Company's vessels, being battered by gales or lightning, or homeward bound or peaceably lying at anchor.

A hypochondriac, Reinagle frequently overdosed himself with medicine. After suffering from '2 or 3 severe gripes [probably attacks of appendicitis]' (*Letters to Leslie*, 193, 146), he died at his home, 11 Great Randolph Street, Camden Town, London, on 6 December 1835. His death at thirty, with much artistic promise unfulfilled, was widely mourned.

T. A. B. CORLEY

Sources *DNB* · D. Sutton, 'The Reinagles re-considered', *Country Life*, 118 (1955), 1264–6 · *John Constable's correspondence*, ed. R. B. Beckett, 2, Suffolk RS, 6 (1964), 19–35; 4, Suffolk RS, 10 (1966), 214–22 · *John Constable: further documents and correspondence*, ed. L. Parris, C. Shields, and I. Fleming-Williams, Suffolk RS, 18 (1975), 266–71 · Graves, *RA exhibitors* · Graves, *Artists*, 3rd edn · Farington, *Diary* · E. H. H. Archibald, *Dictionary of sea painters*, 2nd edn (1989) · 'Reinagle', *The dictionary of art*, ed. J. Turner (1996) · I. Mackenzie, *British prints: dictionary and price guide* (1987), 262 · *Letters of John Constable to C. R. Leslie*, ed. P. Leslie (1931), 146 · *IGI*

Archives RA, papers

Reinagle, Joseph (1762–1825), instrumentalist and composer, was born in Portsmouth, the son of Joseph Reinagle, an Austrian trumpeter who had settled in England and was appointed trumpeter to the king in 1762. He was at first intended for the navy, but became apprenticed to a jeweller in Edinburgh, where his family moved about 1763. Then, having decided on music as a profession, he studied the horn and trumpet with his father, and soon began performing in public. Apparently acting on medical advice, he abandoned wind instruments and studied the cello under Johann Schetky (who married his sister) and the violin under Aragoni and Pinto. He progressed so well that he was appointed leader of the orchestra at St Cecilia's Hall, Edinburgh.

Following appearances as a cellist in London and at the Handel Commemoration in 1784, Reinagle went in the same year to Dublin, where he remained for two years and played under the patronage of the earl of Westmorland. It is reported by Kidson that he gave up the cello around this time, thinking his brother Hugh to be a better player, though he resumed after Hugh's death in 1785. On his return to London he took a prominent position in the chief orchestras, and was principal cello at Salomon's Haydn concerts. It appears from one of his letters that Haydn showed him much kindness and gave him advice on composition. In the 1790s Reinagle was engaged to play at the Oxford concerts and was so well received that he settled in the city. He was evidently a very able cellist, and enjoyed wide popularity. Nathaniel Gow (1766–1831) was one of his Edinburgh pupils. Reinagle composed a good deal of music for violin and cello, particularly duets, as well as piano pieces, and wrote *A Concise Introduction to the Art of Playing the Violoncello* (c.1800), which appeared in several editions and was published as late as 1887. Other published but lost works include six string quartets, a violin concerto, and seven cello concertos. Reinagle died in Oxford, probably on 12 November 1825.

A son, **Alexander Robert Reinagle** (1799–1877), organist, was born in Brighton on 21 August 1799. He studied with his father in Oxford and was organist of St Peter-in-the-East in the city (1823–53). He published *Psalm Tunes for the Voice and Pianoforte* (c.1830), which includes the popular tune 'St Peter', in addition to piano pieces, songs, and teaching manuals and studies for the violin, cello, and piano. In 1846 he married Caroline Orger [see Reinagle, Caroline (1817–1892)], a pianist, teacher, and composer. He died at Kidlington, near Oxford, where he was buried, on 6 April 1877.   J. C. HADDEN, *rev.* DAVID J. GOLBY

Sources F. Kidson and R. Hopkins, 'Reinagle', *New Grove*

Reinagle, Mary Ann (b. 1778). *See under* Reinagle family (per. c.1760–1877).

Reinagle, Philip (1748–1833), painter, was born on 10 February 1748, probably in Edinburgh, and baptized on 22 March at Dover, Kent, the eldest of five sons and a daughter of Joseph Reinagle (*fl.* 1745–1775), a one-time trumpeter in the Hungarian army, and his wife, Annie Laurie. His younger brother, also Joseph *Reinagle (1762–1825), was an instrumentalist and composer. Philip Reinagle was sent by sea from Edinburgh to London in 1762, to begin an apprenticeship with the painter Allan Ramsay: in 1769 he entered the Royal Academy Schools. Ramsay thereafter employed him to produce the plentiful copies of royal portraits (especially of George III and Queen Charlotte) demanded by official bodies. Soon heading a large group of assistants, Reinagle had difficulty in increasing his share from £10 per picture to £42, half Ramsay's fee. On 24 July 1771 he married Jane Austin at St Marylebone, Middlesex; to provide for their nine daughters (Amelia Ann *Reinagle, Mary Ann *Reinagle, Jane, Charlotte Jenetta *Reinagle [see under Reinagle family], Rachel Christiana, Frances Arabella, Caroline, Harriet, and Oriana Georgina) and two sons, Ramsay Richard *Reinagle (1775–1862), and Philip, he had to endure this monotonous toil until Ramsay died in 1784. He also exhibited at the Royal Academy eleven (non-royal) portraits between 1773 and 1787, when he was elected an associate of that body.

Reinagle's later works were mainly of sporting subjects, birds and animals being a speciality. Skilled in blackline etching, he produced hawking scenes, valuable evidence for later historians of falconry. In 1801 he exhibited at the academy what was to be his diploma picture, *A Vulture Disputing with a Hyaena*, becoming royal academician in 1812. His highly praised paintings appeared in William Taplin's *Sportsman's Cabinet* (1803). He was a friend of Thomas Thornton (1757–1823), for whom he painted a number of sporting scenes. The (unrelated) botanical author Dr Robert John Thornton included some of Reinagle's drawings in his *New Illustration of the Sexual System of Linnaeus* (1799–1807) and *Philosophy of Botany* (1809).

All these labours brought Reinagle some fame, but nowhere near enough income for his growing family. In 1798 he had to appeal to the council of the Royal Academy for funds to save them from ruin; he was granted £150. Like other esurient artists, he acquired ready money from the restoration of paintings, and from making copies of old masters, especially of the Dutch school. After many years with Ramsay his versions were plausible enough to be palmed off as originals.

Reinagle lived into an ear-trumpet-and-snuff old age, in the company of his three youngest, and unmarried, daughters; his wife, remembered as prudent and a good manager, predeceased him. Benjamin Robert Haydon found him to be a 'nice old fellow', but deplored the family copyists' work as 'a sort of Reinagle activity without thought' (*Diary*, ed. Pope, 3.57). He died at his home, 5 York Place, Chelsea, London, on 27 November 1833. Both of his sons and four of his daughters followed him as artists.

T. A. B. Corley

Sources *DNB* · D. Sutton, 'The Reinagles re-considered', *Country Life*, 118 (1955), 1264–6 · *John Constable's correspondence*, ed. R. B. Beckett, 2, Suffolk RS, 6 (1964), 19–35; 4, Suffolk RS, 10 (1966), 214–22 · *John Constable: further documents and correspondence*, ed. L. Parris, C. Shields, and I. Fleming-Williams, Suffolk RS, 18 (1975), 266–71 · Graves, *RA exhibitors* · Graves, *Artists* · P. J. M. McEwan, *Dictionary of Scottish art and architecture* (1994) · Waterhouse, *18c painters* · M. A. Wingfield, *A dictionary of sporting artists, 1650–1990* (1992), 235–6 · Farington, *Diary* · *The diary of Benjamin Robert Haydon*, ed. W. B. Pope, 5 vols. (1960–63), 3.57, 140 · *New Grove* · *IGI*
Archives RA, papers
Wealth at death see will, PRO, PROB 11/1829/168

Reinagle, Ramsay Richard (1775–1862), painter, was born on 19 March 1775, and baptized at St James's, Piccadilly, London, on 16 April, the eldest son of Philip *Reinagle (1748–1833), painter, and his wife, Jane Austin. He completed his first picture when only six; in 1788, his *Dead Game* was shown at the Royal Academy. Educated at Wanstead Academy, Essex, he became a pupil of his father. He spent 1793 to 1798 in Europe, first visiting Holland to study the Dutch masters and drawings of rare birds. For his final eighteen months he was in Italy, returning home with £95 and plentiful sketches, mostly views of Rome, Naples, and Florence. He had learned there the techniques of landscape painting, and his own landscapes were to play an influential role in the development of British Romantic art.

In 1799 Reinagle became a friend of John Constable, who was dazzled by his exhaustive knowledge of the London art scene, facility with brush and pencil, and globetrotter's sophistication. The two men soon shared lodgings, Reinagle meanwhile painting a portrait of Constable (NPG) and probably tutoring him in landscape work, as he did in drawing. However, that arrangement lasted only for about a year, when Constable became disillusioned with Reinagle's use of art merely as a source of income and of self-glorification.

On 10 June 1801 Reinagle married Oriana Bullfinch (d. in or before 1836), the well-educated and amiable governess of his sisters, reduced to that servitude by the improvidence of her Welsh landowner father. They had one daughter and three sons, including George Philip *Reinagle. A few years later he was painting scenes for Robert Barker's panorama in Leicester Square, London; he then became partner of Barker's eldest son, Thomas Edward, in order to set up a panorama in the Strand. The latter venture failed, and Reinagle strove to recoup his substantial losses by speculating in sales of old masters and by giving drawing lessons. In 1805 he joined the Society of Painters in Water Colours, and served as its president from 1808 to 1812. He was elected associate of the Royal Academy in 1814.

Two issues of a *catalogue raisonné* of exhibitions of old masters at the British Institution appeared in 1815 and 1816. There being no love lost between that body and the Royal Academy, these anonymous pamphlets were clearly

Ramsay Richard Reinagle (1775–1862), by John Constable, *c*.1800 [retouched by John Hoppner]

counterblasts from the academy side, indicating a fear that the old masters were putting contemporary artists in the shade. Their authorship was variously attributed to the academicians Robert Smirke and Thomas Phillips. However, Reinagle was a far more likely candidate, as suggested by Samuel and Richard Redgrave in *A Century of Painters of the English School* (1866). Reinagle was a fluent writer, composing notices for J. M. W. Turner's *Views in Sussex* (1819) and much of the chapter on Ramsay in Allan Cunningham's *Lives of the most Eminent British Painters* (1832). Unlike Smirke or Phillips, he felt seriously undervalued by his peers, thus having more reason for being spiteful in these works than they had. With an intimate knowledge of the art moguls of the day, he attached insulting epithets to some, such as 'Sillee Foolah' to Sir Abraham Hare, the institution's director. William Hazlitt responded in kind, branding the author as 'a low buffoon' and 'a dirty Grub-Street critic' (*The Examiner*, 3–17 Nov 1816).

In 1823 Reinagle was elected royal academician, and helped to restore Leonardo da Vinci's cartoon *The Virgin and Child* (National Gallery, London), then in the possession of the Royal Academy. His speculations in old paintings soon over-reached themselves; he advertised a sale at his London house with a huge signboard. The sale in 1833 was a flop, and in May 1835 he was gazetted as a bankrupt, his assets being sold off over the next year. On 22 October 1836 he married, at St Pancras Church, Caroline Augusta Flarrent.

Reinagle's reputation plummeted in 1848 when he exhibited at the Royal Academy as his own work (after retouching) a sea picture by J. W. Yarnold. After a full investigation by fellow academicians, he was forced to resign. In 1850 he published two letters of excuse in the *Literary Gazette*, untruthfully boasting that Constable (by then safely dead) had been his pupil and that he had inserted some cattle into one of Constable's paintings. Reinagle continued to submit works to the Royal Academy until 1857; by then he was so hard up that he had to seek (and received) a pension from the academy's funds. He died at his home, 3 Leader Street, Chelsea, on 17 November 1862.

T. A. B. CORLEY

Sources *DNB* · D. Sutton, 'The Reinagles re-considered', *Country Life*, 118 (1955), 1264–6 · *John Constable's correspondence*, ed. R. B. Beckett, 2, Suffolk RS, 6 (1964), 19–35; 4, Suffolk RS, 10 (1966), 214–22 · *John Constable: further documents and correspondence*, ed. L. Parris, C. Shields, and I. Fleming-Williams, Suffolk RS, 18 (1975), 266–71 · Graves, *RA exhibitors* · Graves, *Artists* · Farington, *Diary* · R. Redgrave and S. Redgrave, *A century of painters of the English school*, 2 vols. (1866) · *The complete works of William Hazlitt*, ed. P. P. Howe, 21 vols. (1930–34), vols. 4, 18 · A. Cunningham, *The lives of the most eminent British painters, sculptors and architects*, 6 vols. (1829–33) · *Letters of John Constable to C. R. Leslie*, ed. P. Leslie (1931), 146 · *LondG* (22 May 1835) · *LondG* (2 June 1835) · d. cert. · I. Fleming-Williams and L. Parris, *The discovery of Constable* (1984), 154–8 · parish register, Westminster, St James's, Piccadilly, 16 April 1775 [baptism]

Archives RA, papers · U. Nott. L., commonplace books and papers

Likenesses P. Reinagle, group portrait, oils, exh. RA 1788, Upton House, Warwickshire · J. Constable, retouched by J. Hoppner, *c*.1800, priv. coll.; Sothebys, 9 Nov 1994, lot 58 [*see illus.*] · A. E. Chalon, group portrait, watercolour drawing (*Students at the British Institution, 1807*), BM · R. R. Reinagle, self-portrait?, chalk drawing, NPG · R. R. Reinagle, self-portrait, drawing, BM · plaster death mask, Bodl. Oxf.

Reinhardt, Max [*real name* Max Goldmann] (1873–1943), theatre director and manager, was born Max Goldmann on 9 September 1873 in Baden, near Vienna, of Jewish parents, the eldest of six children of Wilhelm Goldmann (1846–1906), shopkeeper, and his wife, Rosa Weingraf (1851–1924). After attending Realschule and Bürgerschule in Vienna he began acting under the name of Max Reinhardt in 1890, and from 1894 to 1903 performed at the Deutsches Theater, Berlin. In 1901 he founded a cabaret, later to become the Kleines Theater, Berlin, where he devoted himself more and more to directing plays. His first major breakthrough occurred in 1905 at the Neues Theater in Berlin with a spectacular staging of *A Midsummer Night's Dream*, in which a revolving stage was used for the first time in modern theatre as an integral part of the production.

Reinhardt went on to become arguably the most prolific and versatile director of twentieth-century theatre. He brought freshness and excitement to classics that had previously been routinely offered in wooden productions, notably Shakespeare, Goethe, medieval drama, and Greek tragedy; for example, he staged Sophocles' *Oedipus Rex* in a circus arena. He also daringly presented controversial modern works, such as Wilde's *Salome*, Ibsen's *Ghosts*, the banned *Spring's Awakening* by Wedekind, plays by Gorky and Strindberg, and he later provided opportunities for staging expressionist works in his 'Young Germany' seasons at the Deutsches Theater, Berlin.

Max Reinhardt (1873–1943), by unknown photographer, 1923? [with Lady Diana Cooper, rehearsing *The Miracle* by Karl Vollmoeller]

After achieving international fame Reinhardt accepted an invitation in 1911 to première Karl Vollmoeller's *The Miracle*, a mimed religious drama, at Olympia, London. This vast spectacle was a huge success and was subsequently frequently revived; eventually in 1924–5 it was taken on tour across the United States, with Lady Diana Cooper in the lead role. From 1915 to 1918 Reinhardt became the controversial director of the Berlin Volksbühne, saving it from closure. In 1919 he opened his so-called 'Theatre of Five Thousand', a huge arena seating 3200, which, however, soon proved uneconomic. A more successful venture was the founding in 1920 of the Salzburg Festival, at which Reinhardt's production of Hugo von Hofmannsthal's adaptation of the English morality play *Everyman* continues to be performed to this day. In the same year Reinhardt moved back to Vienna, where he refurbished the Theater in der Josefstadt and established himself in a luxury residence at Schloss Leopoldskron, Salzburg. In 1927–8 his ensemble performed in New York, and he lectured at Columbia University: 'On the actor'. In 1932 his production of Offenbach's *La belle Hélène* was performed in London and Manchester.

With Hitler's accession to power in 1933, Reinhardt was forced to hand over his theatres 'to the German people'. Goebbels offered to confer on Reinhardt the status of 'honorary Aryan'. Reinhardt declined, courageously writing a critical open letter to Goering and Goebbels. He now had to spend more of his time abroad, in June 1933 staging his favourite play, *A Midsummer Night's Dream*, with a largely amateur cast on a broad hillside in South Park, Headington, Oxford ('lovely to the eye, ... partaken ... fully of the nature of a dream', reported *The Times* (Styan, 60)). In 1935 he directed for Warner Brothers his sugary film version of *A Midsummer Night's Dream*, with Olivia de Havilland playing Hermia, Mickey Rooney Puck, and James Cagney Bottom. In 1934 he ended his failed marriage (begun in 1910) to the actress Else Heims, with whom he had had two sons, and was at last free to marry his partner and frequent leading lady, Helene Thimig.

In 1937 Reinhardt moved to the United States, and his Austrian property was confiscated by the Nazis the following year. In Hollywood in 1938 he founded the Max Reinhardt Workshop for Stage, Screen and Radio, the last of several institutions created by Reinhardt for the training of the actor. In 1940 he became a United States citizen and continued to direct plays until the last year of his life. He died of a stroke on 31 October 1943 in the Gladstone Hotel in New York, and was buried at Hastings-on-Hudson, New York, on 3 November.

In terms of theatrical style Reinhardt was not particularly innovative, and this, coupled with the fact that he wrote little about his own work, has meant that his importance has been underestimated. Reinhardt's achievement lay not only in the colossal range of his work but above all in the beauty of his stagings and the care that went into them. He nurtured the talents of virtually all the leading German-speaking actors of the day. He gave opportunities to scenic designers to transform the stage into a work of art. He paid attention to detail, working with extras on crowd scenes with hitherto unheard-of solicitude. He was equally skilled at creating pieces for a tiny intimate theatre as mounting a colossal spectacle with hundreds of extras. By offering a fresh reading of great poetic dramas such as those of Greek tragedy or Goethe's *Faust*, he not only established these once more as viable pieces of modern repertory; he also demonstrated to young playwrights the possibility of creating significant drama that went beyond the limits of naturalism and encouraged them in their efforts by enabling the staging of experimental works. The style that emerged from all this has been described as 'impressionistic realism', a style that was unashamedly theatrical in a way that was not possible in naturalism but which, in the search for beauty, eschewed the distorted excesses of expressionism. At a time when most European theatre was being constrained by a misguided pursuit of total realism or being emasculated by commercial pressures to offer mindless entertainment, Reinhardt restored to the stage a respect for quality in acting, design, and writing that has laid the foundations for all that is best in theatre today. As the critic Herbert Ihering summed it up: 'The revolution in theatre was no other than this: that for the first time theatre sought to be an art. Art, measured not against life, but according to its own laws, like painting, music, or poetry' (Ihering, 'Das neue Theater', *Die neue Rundschau*, 1921, 423–4).   MICHAEL PATTERSON

Sources H. Fetting, *Max Reinhardt: Schriften, Briefe, Reden, Aufsätze, Interviews, Gespräche, Auszüge aus Regiebüchern* (1974) · H. Huesmann,

Welttheater Reinhardt: Bauten, Spielstätten, Inszenierungen (1983) · E. Fuhrich and G. Prossnitz, eds., *Max Reinhardt: 'Ein Theater, das den Menschen wieder Freude gibt …', Eine Dokumentation* (1987) · L. M. Fiedler, *Max Reinhardt in Selbstzeugnissen und Bilddokumenten* (1975) · J. L. Styan, *Max Reinhardt* (1982) · M. Jacobs and J. Warren, eds., *Max Reinhardt: the Oxford Symposium* (1986) · O. M. Sayler, ed., *Max Reinhardt and his theatre* (1924) · M. Patterson, *The revolution in German theatre, 1900–1933* (1981)

Archives Max-Reinhardt-Forschungs- und Gedenkstätte, Salzburg, Austria · University of New York, Binghamton, archive | FILM BFI NFTVA, news footage | SOUND BL NSA, documentary recording · BL NSA, performance recording

Likenesses portrait, 1905, repro. in Sayler, ed., *Max Reinhardt*, facing p. 5 · portrait, 1911–12, repro. in Sayler, ed., *Max Reinhardt*, facing p. 5 · photograph, 1923?, Hult. Arch. [*see illus.*] · portrait, 1938, University of New York, Binghamton Archive; repro. in Styan, *Max Reinhardt* · portraits, repro. in Sayler, ed., *Max Reinhardt*, 70, 175

Wealth at death German and Austrian assets seized by Nazis

Reinhold, Frederick Charles (1741–1815), singer and organist, was born in London on 11 February 1741 and baptized that day at St Anne's, Soho, Westminster, one of four children of the singer Henry Theodore *Reinhold (*c.*1690–1751) and his wife, Sarah. He was a chorister at St Paul's Cathedral under William Savage. After Henry Reinhold's death in 1751, his son was quick to appear on the stage, making his début on 5 February 1752 in *Queen Mab*. Between 1755 and 1758 Reinhold seems to disappear from stage notices—presumably his voice was breaking. He reappeared in the chorus for the Foundling Hospital's performance of *Messiah* in April 1758, and two months later greatly distinguished himself in the role of Uberto in an English version of Pergolesi's *La serva padrona* at Marylebone Gardens. In his benefit performance on 9 August Reinhold demonstrated his talent as an organist. He appeared for many years in the gardens' succession of burlettas, of which *La serva padrona* is the most famous. In 1759 at Drury Lane, following his Marylebone success, Reinhold performed in a full range of theatrical entertainments, including singing (and acting) parts in plays, musical 'interludes' or 'entertainments', and comic afterpieces, but he then left London.

In September and October 1760 Reinhold and other London musicians performed in Norwich. In November 1760 Reinhold settled in Colchester as organist of St Peter's Church, and advertised his services in the *Ipswich Journal* of 22 November 1760 as a teacher of harpsichord, guitar, violin, and singing. He made occasional appearances in London during the 1760s, singing in Drury Lane's 'serious English opera', *Pharnaces*, by Lucchini, in 1765, and in the Little Theatre in the Haymarket's *Cure of Saul* (adapted by Samuel James Arnold from the works of Handel and others) in 1768. From 1769 until 1784, however, Reinhold was employed by Covent Garden, earning the relatively high salary of £8 per week from the 1777–8 season onwards. His benefit notices in this period advertise his address as 46 (in 1777) and then 90 Charlotte Street, Rathbone Place. His first role in that theatre was as Giles in *The Maid of the Mill*, by Samuel Arnold and Isaac Bickerstaff, and he continued to feature in many English operas, burlettas, and afterpieces. His most often repeated pieces, along with *The*

Frederick Charles Reinhold (1741–1815), by Johan Zoffany [as Hawthorn in *Love in a Village* by Isaac Bickerstaff]

Maid of the Mill, were Bickerstaffe's *Love in a Village*, *The Padlock* by Bickerstaffe and Charles Dibdin, *True Blue* by Henry Carey, *The Country Madcap*, *The Jovial Crew* by Richard Brome, and R. B. Sheridan's *The Duenna*. A talented singer, he obviously excelled in comic pieces and parody: on 13 October 1783 the *Public Advertiser* commended 'Reinhold's imitation of Italian singing … [which] got … three Peals of Applause.—Why … will not Reinhold *always sing* in this Stile? … his affected Soprano is … *really better* than any contemporary Singer's'.

Reinhold clearly had grander pretensions: for his first benefit performance at Covent Garden, in May 1770, he chose the serious (and extremely popular) opera *Artaxerxes* adapted for London by Thomas Arne, performing as Artabanes for the first time. From 1774 he was a stalwart in the Foundling Hospital charity *Messiah* performances, and from March 1781 he sang in Drury Lane's Lenten oratorios. He was a soloist in the 1784 Handel commemoration in Westminster Abbey, and between 1772 and 1788 he regularly performed in Cambridge's annual Handel benefits for Addenbrooke's Hospital. By 1783 he was organist of St George the Martyr, Queen Square. He continued singing in Handel performances until 1792, appearing finally in 1798, long after he had left the comic stage. Perhaps partly for this reason Reinhold's will asked that his memorial stone should read 'Professor of Music and principal vocal performer under the immortal Handel'. Reinhold had lived in Great Baddow, Essex, but he died on 28 September 1815 at his home, Somers Town Terrace, St Pancras, London, and was evidently separated from his wife, Hannah,

née Reeve, who, according to his will (dated 20 March 1811), lived in Ipswich, Suffolk. Reinhold was buried on 6 October at St Paul's, Covent Garden. From an estate worth more than £7800 in bank annuities alone (in 1811), Reinhold left annuities of £70 to his widow, and £130, the Somers Town property, and all remaining effects after other bequests to Ann Woodbridge (*bap.* 1783), presumably his mistress. A final codicil (3 March 1814) revises these annuities to £50 for his wife and £150 for Woodbridge.

SUZANNE ASPDEN

Sources G. W. Stone, ed., *The London stage, 1660–1800*, pt 4: *1747–1776* (1962) · C. B. Hogan, ed., *The London stage, 1660–1800*, pt 5: *1776–1800* (1968) · Highfill, Burnim & Langhans, *BDA*, 12.306–9 · *Public Advertiser* (13 Oct 1783) · W. Dean, 'Reinhold, Frederick Charles', *New Grove* · Burney, *Hist. mus.*, new edn · J. Doane, ed., *A musical directory for the year 1794* [1794]; facs. edn (1993) · *Cambridge Chronicle and Journal* (June 1772–1788) · *Ipswich Journal* (22 Nov 1760) · *The Euterpeiad* (13 Oct 1821) · M. Hackett and K. I. Garrett, eds., 'A list of some of St Paul's Cathedral choristers before 1873', *Guildhall Studies in London History*, 1 (1973–5), 82–93 · W. Wroth and A. E. Wroth, *The London pleasure gardens of the eighteenth century* (1896); repr. (1979) · *Recollections of R. J. S. Stevens: an organist in Georgian London*, ed. M. Argent (1992), 288 · J. Hawkins, *A general history of the science and practice of music*, 5 vols. (1776); new edn, 3 vols. (1875) · D. Burrows, *Handel* (1994) · private information (2004) [O. Baldwin, T. Wilson] · PRO, PROB 11/1574, sig. 543

Likenesses J. Zoffany, oils (as Hawthorn in *Love in a village*), Garr. Club [*see illus.*] · double portrait, line engraving (with Mrs Farrell in the 25 Jan 1777 performance of *Artaxerxes*), BM

Wealth at death over £4800: will, PRO, PROB 11/1574, sig. 543

Reinhold, Henry Theodore (*c.*1690–1751), singer, is of uncertain origin: one source claimed he was the illegitimate son of the archbishop of Dresden (*New Grove*), although there was no such diocese in Germany at this time. He was perhaps born in Dresden about 1690. It seems likely he was related to the Dresden organist and composer Theodor Christlieb Reinhold (1682–1755), as one of his children was given this name. According to one report Reinhold met Handel at the archbishop's palace and followed the composer to London (Highfill, Burnim & Langhans, *BDA*). If true, Reinhold was slow to act: Handel had last been in Dresden in 1719, though he did visit Germany in 1729.

Reinhold's first London appearance was in 1736, when he sang in the chorus for Handel's *Alexander's Feast* and took the minor role of Mercury in *Atalanta*. Reinhold's arrival in London was fortuitously timed: as Handel shifted from Italian opera (dominated by the soprano voice—female and male) to oratorio in the late 1730s and early 1740s, and concomitantly from aristocratic sponsorship to relative independence, he needed cheap, bilingual singers. Reinhold advanced from the small roles assigned him in operas and early oratorios to become Handel's principal bass by 1743. Handel created major roles for him in every oratorio from *Samson* (1743) to *Theodora* (1750).

Reinhold's talents were widely recognized: after playing the Dragon in J. F. Lampe's and Henry Carey's hugely successful *Dragon of Wantley* (1737), he was regularly employed in the mainstream theatre, appearing in a succession of pantomimes and afterpieces starting with the *Dragon*'s sequel, *Margery* (1738), and *Harlequin Shipwreck'd* and *The*

Fall of Phaeton (1739). Reinhold sang at both major theatres and in a variety of concert venues, but after 1742 was apparently contracted almost exclusively to Covent Garden: in 1744 Handel wrote to a friend that he had had to ask John Rich to release Reinhold and another singer, John Beard, to perform in the oratorios. So firmly was Reinhold a man of the British theatre by 1744–5 that in those years he often appeared at Covent Garden with Beard and Richard Leveridge, singing patriotic songs such as 'Britons, strike home'; in 1745 he was engaged to sing at another national institution, Vauxhall Gardens. He was one of the founders of the Royal Society of Musicians.

Reinhold married his wife, Sarah, in 1740 or before; he died on 14 May 1751 at his home in Chapel Street, Soho, and was buried in St Anne's churchyard. The *General Advertiser* for 16 May declared him 'a man not less admir'd for his private Character than his publick Performance.—He has left behind him a Wife and four small Children in great Distress.' Of Henry and Sarah Reinhold's children, Frederick Charles *Reinhold was born on 11 February 1741, Theodore Christlieb in March 1747, Eleanora on 2 September 1748, and Sarah on 19 May 1750. All the children were baptized at St Anne's, Soho, suggesting that Reinhold conformed to the Church of England. One of the daughters was the Miss Reinhold who appeared as a singer and actor. Drury Lane gave a benefit performance for Reinhold's family, which Cross, the prompter, said raised £101.

SUZANNE ASPDEN

Sources A. H. Scouten, ed., *The London stage, 1660–1800*, pt 3: *1729–1747* (1961) · G. W. Stone, ed., *The London stage, 1660–1800*, pt 4: *1747–1776* (1962) · Highfill, Burnim & Langhans, *BDA*, 12.309–10 · *General Advertiser* (16 May 1751) · W. Dean, 'Reinhold, Henry Theodore', *New Grove* · O. E. Deutsch, *Handel: a documentary biography* (1955) · Burney, *Hist. mus.*, new edn · D. Burrows, *Handel* (1994) · W. Dean, *Handel's dramatic oratorios and masques* (1959) · B. Matthews, ed., *The Royal Society of Musicians of Great Britain: list of members, 1738–1984* (1985) · J. Hawkins, *A general history of the science and practice of music*, 5 vols. (1776); new edn, 3 vols. (1875)

Reinolds [Reynolds], **John** (1584?–1614), Latin poet, probably born at Tuddington, Berkshire, was a scholar at Winchester College in 1597, matriculated at New College, Oxford, and was elected fellow, in 1602. He took the degree of BCL in 1607. Reinolds was thought 'a good Grecian orator and poet', and in Wood's opinion became 'the most noted epigrammatist, next to John Owen and Sir John Harrington, of his time' (Wood, *Ath. Oxon.*, 2.148). He undoubtedly learned this facility at Winchester, and may have edited a collection of Wykehamist poems for a proposed visit by Queen Elizabeth (*c*.1600, Bodl. Oxf, MS Lat. misc. e.23).

Soon after arriving at New College, Reinolds made substantial contributions to the verse collections on the queen's death and on the accession of James, showing his fondness for large numbers of small epigrams; in *Funebre officium* (1603) he had nine poems (seven in Latin elegiacs, one epode, one in Greek) totalling thirty-four lines. Many others adopted a similar strategy of literary multiplication (for instance in that volume Edward James, Richard Carpenter, Thomas Gwynne, Robert Pincke, Edward Evans, Thomas Wint, Thomas Morton, and others); but

Reinolds was beginning to make a mark among older practitioners of the genre. In the volume commemorating Ralph Warcop (1605) Reinolds provided ten poems (some in Greek, and a Latin alcaic ode); his second poem declares that Warcop had a thousand virtues, a hundred arts, and ten languages. He almost certainly contributed to New College's *Musae Hospitales* (1610), where, however, the poems were anonymous. He provided four poems (twenty-six elegiacs in all) on the death of Prince Henry (1612). He had ambitious plans for publishing several thousand of his epigrams; the first 'century' (111 in fact) appeared in 1611 entitled *Epigrammata*, the unfinished first *Chilias* (thousand: in fact two 'centuries') in 1612. They have been found 'too mechanical and uninspired', but 'of considerable interest as an attempt to write epigrams according to a preconceived scheme' (Bradner, 90). The *Epigrammata*, on British kings and queens, have many entertaining, if few brilliant, verses, and help to illustrate contemporary attitudes to earlier history and legend. On King Lear (Leirus, no. 10), for example, Reinolds has a nice, or infuriating, pun: 'Delirus, quando Regna reliquit, erat' ('when he gave up his kingdom, Lear was de*Lear*ious'). No king was worse than the usurper Richard III (no. 88). Henry VII is compared to James as a unifier (no. 89). There is obvious concern to integrate the Stuart dynasty: after Edward VI, Reinolds turns back to James I of Scotland. Henry, prince of Wales (a year before his death), 'will be a British king' (no. 98). After a hundredth epigram on Britain's conversion, Reinolds turns to queens: 'Bowdicea' (no. 103); he is surprisingly, perhaps ambiguously, polite on Mary (no. 106) who was under Philip's thumb, 'sed certe populo praefuit illa suo' ('but was certainly in charge of her people'), and on Elizabeth (no. 107), a proof that female power is not to be scorned. But perhaps, by implication and position in the collection, Elizabeth's grandeur is subordinated to her successor. Reinolds may also be the author of the English poem *Dolarnys Primerose* (1606). He died in 1614, and was buried in New College. Had he lived longer, he might have achieved greater significance as an epigrammatist, though he is unlikely ever to have rivalled the wit and huge international fame of John Owen.

D. K. MONEY

Sources J. Reynolds, *Epigrammata* (1611) · L. Bradner, *Musae Anglicanae: a history of Anglo-Latin poetry, 1500–1925* (1940) · Foster, *Alum. Oxon.* · Wood, *Ath. Oxon.*, new edn, 2.148 · *DNB* · J. W. Binns, *Intellectual culture in Elizabethan and Jacobean England: the Latin writings of the age* (1990) · *Funebre officium*, Oxford University (1603) · *Pietas … erga Iacobum*, Oxford University (1603) · *Encomion Rodolphi Warcoppi*, New College (1605) · *Musae Hospitales Wicchamicae*, New College (1610) · *Justa Oxoniensium*, Oxford University (1612)

Reisen, Charles Christian (*bap.* 1679, *d.* 1725), gem-engraver, the son of Christian (1664–1711) and Isabella Reisen, was born in London, where he was baptized on 3 June 1679 at St Gregory by Paul. His father, Christian Reisen, was a silversmith from Trondheim in Norway. After leaving Norway his father spent two years in Aberdeen, working for a goldsmith named Melvin. He arrived in London in September 1666 shortly after the great fire. George Vertue stated that Christian Reisen then worked as a stone and steel-engraver, employed for a period at the Royal Mint. He was at one stage incarcerated in the Tower for four years, suspected of having engraved dies for coining. According to Vertue, Reisen was a wild and headstrong boy who did not plan for his future. He had a pleasantly humorous character which gained him many friends who promoted his work. He was taught the art of engraving by his father, after whose death at an early age he became the main breadwinner for his widowed mother and several younger siblings. Reisen is said to have learned the technique of engraving very quickly and became a proficient gem cutter. Although he cut arms and crests Reisen was most highly praised for his imitations of antique gems; Horace Walpole described him as that 'celebrated engraver of seals' (Walpole, 698). Under the patronage of Robert Harley, earl of Oxford, Reisen gained access to a library and examined the earl's collection of antique Greek and Roman gems. Reisen himself collected prints, drawings, and medals as well as books and curiosities. He expanded his collection as his wealth and fortune rose with increased commissions and generous payments from his patron. According to Vertue, Reisen was well acquainted with his colleagues in the art world. He was a member of the Rose and Crown Art Club where Sir Godfrey Kneller was also a member. It may have been on the basis of Reisen's virtuosity as an engraver and his knowledge as a connoisseur that Sir Godfrey invited him to become a director of the academy of painting in Great Queen Street, London.

Although of Norwegian descent, Reisen's education had lacked a systematic approach to languages and consequently his knowledge of the Danish language (Norway was then under the Danish crown) was poor. An introduction at the court of Prince George of Denmark was initially indecorous as Reisen was at first unable to understand or reply to the prince. However, Reisen still achieved fame in Denmark, France, and Germany and received royal commissions for engraved gems and seals. James Tassie (1791) listed some of Reisen's gems: Aelius Caesar (chalcedony), Charles I (cornelian), the head of Faustina, and Lucilla, wife of Verus (cornelian); the latter two gems had been part of Horace Walpole's collection. Reisen is described by both Vertue and Walpole as having a 'jovial and free' disposition. He compensated for his lack of linguistic ability by using an invented language when in company with friends. He had a sarcastic sense of humour and enjoyed the good life. He died on 15 December 1725 of gout. He was buried in the churchyard of Covent Garden, London, the area where he had lived for many years.

LORNA COLBERG GOLDSMITH

Sources H. Aars, A. W. Brøgger, and others, *Norsk kunsthistorie*, 2 (1927) · L. Forrer, ed., *Biographical dictionary of medallists*, 8 vols. (1902–30) · R. E. Raspe, *A descriptive catalogue of a general collection of ancient and modern engraved gems, cameos as well as intaglios* (1791), nos. 11.793, 11.874, 11.907, 11.996 · Vertue, *Note books*, 1.147; 3.13, 25–7, 102 · H. Walpole, *Anecdotes of painting in England: with some account of the principal artists*, ed. R. N. Wornum, new edn, 2 (1849); repr. (1862), 697–9 · C. W. King, *Antique gems and rings*, 2 vols. (1872), vol. 1, p. 445 · Thieme & Becker, *Allgemeines Lexikon*, vol. 26 · *Weilbachs Kunstnerleksikon* (1952), 3.38 · I. Bignamini, 'George Vertue, art historian, and art institutions in London, 1689–1768', *Walpole Society*, 54 (1988), 1–148 · N. H. Weinwich, *Dansk, Norsk og Svensk kunstnerlexicon* (1829), 2.100, 137 · *IGI*

Likenesses G. White, mezzotint (after J. Vanderbank), BM, NPG

Reiss [*née* Lucas]**, Phyllis Emily** (1886–1961), garden designer, was born at Ashlyers, Berkhamsted, Hertfordshire, on 3 October 1886, the daughter of Colonel Alfred George Lucas, an army officer and later mayor of Lowestoft and high sheriff of Suffolk, and his wife, Edith Hamilton Crake (*d*. 1925). She was educated at the Allenwood girls' boarding-school in Wimbledon under the principal Madame Souvestre. At the time of her marriage to Lieutenant Ferdinand Edward Reiss (1875/6–1947) on 12 January 1918 she was living with her parents at Hobland Hall, Lowestoft, in Suffolk. The couple lived and gardened at Dowdeswell Manor, near Cheltenham, from 1925 until 1933, when they moved to Tintinhull House, near Yeovil. During the Dowdeswell years Phyllis Reiss, finding herself a neighbour of Lawrence Johnson, had visited his already well-known gardens at Hidcote Manor and appreciated the compartmental garden with its subtle colour schemes. In 1933 she quickly grasped the possibilities of her new garden at Tintinhull, which, although barely more than an acre, lent itself to development in the Hidcote style.

Originally a seventeenth-century Hamstone farmhouse, Tintinhull House was enhanced in the early eighteenth century by a fine façade on the garden front, which looked out on a walled entrance forecourt—the Eagle Court—which was later to become the first of Phyllis Reiss's garden 'rooms'. Using the old walls and an axial pathway already flanked with topiary box, Mrs Reiss added a pattern of yew hedges to complement the existing trees: yews, a cedar of Lebanon, and a holm-oak. She developed six distinct compartments, unifying the whole scheme by repeated planting of silver- and grey-leaved plants, often combined with deep-hued foliage of purple and bronze. She had an architect's eye for shape, form, mass, and repetition, a legacy which still provides the essential bones of the Tintinhull Garden. But she was also a plantswoman, although not an avid plant collector, always choosing good plants carefully to give the effects she sought and to cover all the seasons. Blue and yellow-flowered plants curtained the walls in the Eagle Court, while complements and contrasts were provided by a white garden, an informal semi-woodland area and a border bed of gold and crimson. Finally, after 1945, she designed a garden as a memorial to a nephew killed in the war, in which a wide canal was framed by panels of grass and fine colour borders (one for pale colours, the other for vibrant reds, yellows, and orange) linked together by clumps of gentle silvery foliage.

In July 1939 Mrs Reiss made two broadcasts for the BBC entitled *In my Garden*: she outlined her design plans and planting policies, capturing in her talk the spirit of her convivial yet sophisticated garden. Lanning Roper, the American-born garden designer, described Tintinhull as 'no ordinary garden' in *Gardening Illustrated* in January

1951, and this endorsement was followed by an article on the garden in *Country Life* in April 1956 by Arthur Oswald. More praise and acknowledgement of Phyllis Reiss's remarkable genius came in Sylvia Crowe's *Garden Design* (1958): devoting several pages to Tintinhull, Dame Sylvia praised Mrs Reiss's skill in space division, which made the garden look far larger than it was. After 1945 Mrs Reiss redesigned the forecourt borders at neighbouring Montacute House, designs which have recently been restored by the National Trust. In 1959 Phyllis Reiss gave Tintinhull to the National Trust, although she continued to live there until her death from cancer on 18 September 1961. She was cremated at Weymouth crematorium.

PENELOPE HOBHOUSE

Sources priv. coll., family MSS · b. cert. · m. cert. · d. cert. · A. Oswald, 'Tintinhull House, Somerset', *Country Life*, 119 (1956), 798–801 · L. Roper, 'The smaller garden, IV: Tintinhull House', *Journal of RHS*, 80/1 (1955), 24–32 · S. Crowe, *Garden design* (1958) · G. S. Thomas, 'Phyllis Reiss and her garden', *Gardeners' Chronicle*, 3rd ser., **151** (1962), 118–19, 125 · [J. Malins], *Tintinhull House, Somerset* (1986)

Archives priv. coll., family MSS

Wealth at death £18,372 1s. 6d.: probate, 28 Dec 1961, *CGPLA Eng. & Wales*

Reith, John Charles Walsham, first Baron Reith (1889–1971), first director-general of the BBC, was born on 20 July 1889 at Stonehaven, Kincardineshire. He was the youngest of the seven children of the Revd Dr George Reith (1842–1919), a minister of the Free Church of Scotland long established at the college church, Glasgow, and his wife, Adah Mary Weston (1848–1935), daughter of a prosperous London stockbroker.

Wearing spurs Reith was very much the Benjamin of the family, and the near-decade that separated him from his brothers and sisters meant that his early years were in some ways those of an only child. His father, whom he admired but held in some awe, was a remote figure, busy with sermons and parish visiting. His mother, to whom he was passionately devoted, was taken up with the exacting duties of a minister's wife and was also much given to good works. Reith was accordingly left for much of the time in the charge of nurses; one of them dealt with his fits of temper by holding him upside down by the ankles.

In 1896, like his four elder brothers before him, Reith was entered at Glasgow Academy. 'I had enough brains to get through all the classes without effort, and so scraped through', he wrote later. 'I had no inspiration to excel, although strangely enough I felt a kind of intellectual superiority over others' (Reith, pre-diary narrative). Friendship eluded him. He acquired the nickname Lord Walsham, and it was not affectionately meant.

When he was fifteen Reith was withdrawn from the academy and sent to Gresham's School at Holt, in Norfolk—his eldest brother, Archie, had a church near by. There he did well at German and Latin, played at full-back for the school fifteen, and became a good shot. He discovered that he could run extremely fast and jump very respectably—unsurprisingly, as he was already well on the way to his eventual 6 feet 6 inches—but he always regarded his great height as an affliction.

Reith was bitterly disappointed when his father decreed he was no scholar and that instead of going to university he should be apprenticed to the North British Locomotive Company. The tedium and frustration of the next eight years were relieved only by his military interests. He joined the 1st Lanarkshire rifle volunteers, and in 1911 he was commissioned in the 5th Scottish rifles.

John Charles Walsham Reith, first Baron Reith (1889–1971), by Olive Edis

Three years into his apprenticeship Reith had started his famous diary, which was to absorb so disproportionate an amount of his time and energy over the next sixty years and on which he would draw extensively for his two volumes of memoirs. 'One will try to tell the truth,' he wrote; 'nothing but the truth', but he did so only patchily (Reith, *Into the Wind*, 1).

Reith averred, for instance, that when he took the road to London in search of work in 1914 he was driven by the 'same urge as countless others have felt' (Reith, *Into the Wind*, 13). The overriding reason for going south, however, was that at the age of twenty-four he was infatuated with a seventeen-year-old schoolboy called Charlie Bowser—'a sort of paragon of all infallibilities', as he described him (Reith, summarized diary, Jan 1914). The passionate relationship between them did not end until the early 1920s, and the evidence of Reith's diaries is that bitter memories of their broken friendship returned periodically to trouble him over very many years.

Reith found work at the Royal Albert Dock at north Woolwich, but before the year was out he found himself on the western front as transport officer of the 5th Scottish rifles. He enjoyed his war, although differences with the adjutant led to his transfer to the Royal Engineers. In October 1915, during the battle of Loos, he was struck on the left cheek by a sniper's bullet, a brush with death of which he religiously noted the anniversary for the rest of his life.

It was the end of Reith's active service. The following year he was dispatched by the Ministry of Munitions to the United States as an inspector of small-arms contracts. He would look back on the eighteen months he spent in Philadelphia as among the happiest he had known. He became something of a celebrity, and was sought after as a speaker. Whenever the occasion offered, he harangued his American hosts on their duty to enter the war—'If you have stood by a hundred open graves and seen your comrades laid in that shallow bed' (Reith, enclosure volumes, Jan 1917). He was awarded an honorary master of science degree at Lafayette University. It was quite often in his mind that after the war he would build a future for himself and Charlie Bowser in the United States; he wrote to his mother about buying a house in the country and sending her off on trips to India and Egypt and the Holy Land (ibid., 22 March 1917).

Reith returned to England in the summer of 1917 and spent the remainder of the war there. During a posting to Sussex, where he worked on an improbable project to construct a submarine barrage across the channel, he fell in love with his colonel's driver, Muriel Odhams (*d.* 1977). Charlie Bowser also became attached to her, but after a bizarre triangular courtship, it was Reith who eventually married her (1921), although not before he had impressed on her that she 'must share me with C' (Reith, summarized diary, 7 June 1919). They were to have a son and a daughter (whose lives he attempted to live vicariously). Reith subsequently turned match-maker on Charlie's behalf. He quickly became corrosively jealous of his

friend's fiancée, however, and when Bowser severed relations with him he came close to mental breakdown.

Governing the BBC Reith had been working since the end of the war at Beardmore's, an engineering firm near Glasgow, and had drawn Bowser there in his train as his assistant. He now threw up his general managership and went off to London to explore the job market. He toyed briefly with the idea of politics, and though the family tradition was Liberal, worked as secretary to the London Unionist group of MPs during the 1922 general election.

One day Reith's eye was caught by an advertisement for something called 'The British Broadcasting Company (in formation)'. He had little idea of what broadcasting was, but no more had anyone else. His application for the general managership was successful. Over the next fifteen and a half years he would become a major public figure and preside over the shaping of what quickly became a national institution.

Reith had a great love of the sea and a weakness for nautical metaphor. His memoirs, *Into the Wind*, race through the early part of his life in a short section called 'Fitting out'. For the later years of disappointment and frustration he hit on 'Shipping it green'. The heart of the book, which deals with his BBC career, is headed 'Full and by', which well expresses the exhilaration and fulfilment he felt in those early pioneering days, full of bustle and improvisation. 'Confronted with problems of which I had no experience', he wrote: 'Copyright and performing rights; Marconi patents; associations of concert artists, authors, playwrights, composers, music publishers, theatre managers, wireless manufacturers' (Reith, *Into the Wind*, 89).

The directors of the fledgeling company left Reith to get on with it, and nothing suited him better than sole command and a blank sheet of paper. There were battles with the press over the transmission of news and the publicizing of programmes. Reith's first confrontation with the Newspaper Proprietors Association planted an important idea in his mind, and seven months later the BBC launched *Radio Times*.

Then Reith had to square up to the Post Office over the licence fee. The BBC considered that it was soft on evasion and issuing too many experimental licences, allowing anyone who was handy with a screwdriver to assemble their own receiver from cheap foreign components. The postmaster-general responded by setting up the Sykes committee (April–August 1923), the first of many charged with looking into 'the whole question of broadcasting'. He also—what would be unthinkable today—appointed Reith to sit on it, and it was at the committee's first meeting that the general manager of the British Broadcasting Company gave it as his personal opinion that broadcasting should be conducted as a public service—a bold initiative for the young chief executive of a commercial enterprise. It did not happen immediately, but when the BBC was given its first royal charter in 1926 and turned into a public corporation, Reith, still only thirty-seven, became its first director-general and was honoured with a knighthood (1927). He thought this rather less than his due. 'A KG would not have been too much for what I have done', he confided in his diary; 'An ordinary knighthood is almost an insult' (Reith, summarized diary, 20 Dec 1926).

One of the things Reith had done was to steer the BBC through the minefield of the 1926 general strike. Most national newspapers had ceased publication, and this offered Reith the opportunity he had been waiting for to increase the BBC's news coverage. It also brought him for the first time into dangerous proximity to Winston Churchill, then chancellor of the exchequer and the minister responsible for the government's *British Gazette*. Reith successfully countered Churchill's arguments for commandeering the BBC, but it was a victory he would pay for dearly in later years.

The organization was still small enough in the late 1920s (the BBC's staff numbered just over a thousand at the end of 1928) for the director-general to take a close interest in the appointment of even quite junior employees. Many of them found the experience disconcerting. When Richard Lambert, later the first editor of *The Listener*, was shown into his presence, Reith's first question was 'Do you accept the fundamental teachings of Jesus Christ?' The director-general, Lambert later wrote, reminded him of a giant bird, 'moving restlessly and jerkily on its perch' (Lambert, 25).

Reith was criticized externally for his autocratic ways. Once he took his mother to tea on the terrace of the House of Commons. They fell in with Lady Astor, who asked Mrs Reith if it was from her that the director-general had his 'Mussolini traits' (Reith, summarized diary, 23 July 1929). Another critic was Harold Laski. 'At a conference', he wrote, 'he seems to talk as though he was in charge of the national well-being. He speaks with the urgency of a Pontiff'. Laski also believed that Reith cramped the creativity of some of the talented people he had gathered about him by being 'too dominating in his governance' (*Daily Herald*, 31 March 1931). Inside the BBC, however, Reith's obduracy over such matters as the setting up of a staff association notwithstanding, he was held in considerable affection. When he was ill in bed in the early Savoy Hill days, the female staff sent him a large bunch of roses. On a later occasion, as he was setting off for the House of Commons for what was expected to be a hostile grilling by the 1922 committee of Conservative backbench MPs, a junior member of the accounts staff presented him with a round robin signed by eight hundred members of staff affirming their 'loyalty and gratitude to the Director-General' (Reith, diary, 19 March 1934).

Reith got on less well with one particular chairman of the governors, the earl of Clarendon, whom he was soon referring to as Silly Bertie. He was also at daggers drawn with another member of the board, Mrs Ethel Snowden (wife of the Labour politician Philip Snowden), whom he took to calling the Scarlet Woman. (Years earlier Charlie Bowser's wife had earned her place in his private demonology as Jezebel.) Eventually Clarendon went off to South Africa as governor-general. He was succeeded by J. H. Whitley, a Liberal politician who had been speaker of the House of Commons. Reith came to look on him almost as a second father. When Whitley died in 1935 Reith ordered all flags at corporation premises to be half-masted, and the BBC for the first time in its history went into black-edged letter-paper.

Throughout the twenties and early thirties there had been a steady broadening of the range of BBC activities. By the end of Reith's first year the company had already been broadcasting from ten regional British stations. The first outside broadcast had taken place within days of his arrival—part of *The Magic Flute* from Covent Garden. The first experimental broadcast to America was made within the year, as was the first programme relayed by landline from the continent. National broadcasting to schools had begun in the spring of 1924, and Reith had imposed his views about religious broadcasting on the organization from the start—the BBC's Sunday schedules reflected for many years the unchanging pattern of the sabbath which he had known in the college church manse thirty and forty years previously. If he was aware that numbers of people rolled back the carpet and danced to the music provided by Radio Luxemburg or Radio Normandie, it was a matter of indifference to him.

In programme terms, the twelve months following the granting of the royal charter were especially innovative. There were BBC microphones at Twickenham for a rugby international, at Aintree for the grand national, and on the Thames for the boat race. There was commentary on trooping the colour, coverage of Wimbledon and of the BBC Promenade Concerts from the Queen's Hall—'Today I fixed up a contract with Sir Henry Wood', Reith noted matter-of-factly (Reith, diary, 13 April 1927). The first experimental television transmission began in 1929. A year later the BBC acquired news agency tape machines and began editing the news bulletins itself; 1930 also saw the formation of the BBC Symphony Orchestra.

The newly inaugurated Empire Service, funded from the BBC's own resources, was given a powerful boost when George V made the first of his Christmas broadcasts in 1932 (Reith had originally suggested such a broadcast in 1923). Reith was eager to accelerate the development of the service to meet competition from other countries, particularly Germany, but he failed to persuade the government of the day to loosen the purse strings. In 1934 he was invited by the prime minister of South Africa to advise on how broadcasting should develop there. Unsurprisingly, he recommended the setting up of what was in effect a South African BBC. His powerfully written report (he polished it off in an all-night session in his hotel suite, fortified by a tin of biscuits and a carafe of iced water) emphasized the potential of the medium as an agent of national union and education, drawing together English and Afrikaner, town and country, black and white.

Reith was boundlessly ambitious, and his energy was matched only by his restlessness. As early as 1928 he told the prime minister's secretary that he thought it was time he moved on, and this resulted in a forty-minute conversation with Baldwin. Reith was not short of ideas about what he might do; asked if he had anything specific in mind, he offered a list that included running the electricity board and going to Washington as ambassador or to India as viceroy. He also had talks at that time with the managing director of HMV about the possibility of succeeding him. From 1935 onwards it was no longer a question of whether Reith would leave the BBC but when. No man with a normal appetite for work would have considered himself under-employed—television was developing (although Reith evinced no great enthusiasm for the new medium), the challenge of a renewal of the charter loomed, as did the question of how the BBC should prepare for war. A magazine article of the day said that to find a parallel to the corporation's charter and the powers granted to its director-general it was necessary to go back to the days of the East India Company—'Sir John Reith is as firmly seated in the saddle as Clive or Warren Hastings' (*Nash's Magazine*, September 1937). Reith, however, was increasingly restive and discontented, grumbling endlessly about real or imagined slights—'It is monstrous that the King hasn't given me a GCVO', reads a diary entry early in 1936 (Reith, diary, 1 Jan 1936). At the end of that year it was Reith who announced Edward VIII's abdication broadcast from Windsor.

Two years later Reith was summoned to Downing Street. The prime minister wanted him to leave the BBC and assume the chairmanship of Imperial Airways. Now that the moment had come Reith was filled with misgivings. He eventually agreed to do Neville Chamberlain's bidding, but he later wrote about his own 'monstrous pusillanimity' (Reith, *Into the Wind*, 312). Reith's departure from the BBC was traumatic. He resented not being closely involved in the choice of his successor, and during one altercation with the chairman he broke down in tears. He was still not fifty, and he lived on to his eighties, but there would be nights even in extreme old age when he dreamed that he was back at the helm in Broadcasting House.

Searching for fulfilment Imperial Airways proved profoundly uncongenial. On his first day Reith was asked to approve a £50 bonus and to authorize the expenditure of £238 on the passenger lavatories at Croydon, an executive decision which he declined to take. 'It seemed I was to work in very low gear', he wrote grimly; 'I doubted my capacity' (Reith, *Into the Wind*, 327). He embarked immediately on the creation of an executive management committee, modelled on the control board he had set up at the BBC. Before the end of his first week, he also announced that he intended to bring about an amalgamation of Imperial and British Airways and establish the new entity as a public corporation.

In the late summer of 1939 Reith had taken his wife and their two children on holiday to North America on the *Queen Mary*. He returned alone on the *Aquitania*, and in mid-Atlantic heard the news that war had been declared. He was effectively without an occupation—civil aircraft production had stopped and civil aviation was completely subordinated to the military. He spent the early months of the war waiting for offers of work that never materialized. His name, he was told, had been suggested for both the ministries of information and supply, 'but "they" wouldn't have it' (Reith, *Into the Wind*, 346).

What Reith really wanted was to be minister of war, but Chamberlain's offer, when it came, was of the Ministry of Information. Reith accepted, not particularly graciously. A seat in the House of Commons was found for him—it was arranged that the National Liberal candidate for Southampton should retire with a peerage, and that Reith should be returned unopposed as a national candidate. As he passed through a Southampton hotel lobby on the day of his adoption, he passed a group of officers in battle dress awaiting embarkation. One of them said, 'Good luck, John'. It was Charlie Bowser. Reith took off his hat, and after a slight hesitation they shook hands (Reith, diary, 20 Jan 1940).

Reith's appointment was generally welcomed, although *The Times* noted perceptively that 'his long enjoyment of an independent command may have rendered it difficult for him to collaborate in a team' (*The Times*, 6 Jan 1940). A prominent member of that team was Winston Churchill, now first lord of the Admiralty. At their first encounter he observed that he remembered Reith chiefly as the individual who had kept him from broadcasting his views about India. When Reith told him that he was feeling rather frightened of the Commons, Churchill replied, 'Not nearly so frightened as they are of you' (Reith, *Into the Wind*, 357).

Reith's tenure at information was brief and undistinguished. Within months Churchill had replaced Chamberlain and Reith was made minister of transport—another disappointment, as he had hoped it might be shipping or the new Ministry of Aircraft Production. He felt he was in a backwater. The news that the British expeditionary force was to be evacuated from France he learned from his officials: 'Very odd', he wrote, 'that this information should reach me from below' (Reith, *Into the Wind*, 340).

Reith's attitude to the new prime minister was ambivalent. He frequently expressed his dislike and mistrust of him, but there was also an element of fellow-feeling: 'I wanted a job that would bring me into direct and constant touch with Churchill', he wrote (Reith, *Into the Wind*, 383). It was not forthcoming. In September 1940 the Commons went into secret session for a debate on transport and Reith, although he had been in the house for nine months, made his maiden speech. It was a good one, but it was also his last in that chamber. Two weeks later Churchill summoned him to the cabinet room and said that he wanted him to move to the Ministry of Works and go to the House of Lords.

Clough Williams-Ellis, writing in *The Spectator* (18 October 1940), observed that Hitler had inured the British to large-scale destruction; it was now for Reith to show what dynamite could do when selectively applied in the service of town planning and civic regeneration. More immediate matters, however, clamoured for his attention—he was, for instance, being chivvied to find bomb-proof strongholds for Churchill and other ministers. He also discovered that his routine responsibilities ranged from ancient monuments to Duck Island in St James's Park. The prospects for his being able to establish the ministry as the central authority for post-war planning were never good. The Conservatives in the wartime coalition feared that he would undermine the rights of property in land; Labour wanted nothing done save by themselves.

Reith's move into government had not been good for his bank balance. With a large property in Buckinghamshire to maintain and school fees to be paid (his son Christopher was now at Eton College), his financial circumstances were straitened. His ministerial salary was £3500; his agreement with Imperial Airways had provided for his appointment for eleven years at £10,000 per annum plus fees as a director, and he was slow to agree some not particularly satisfactory severance arrangements. Matters were made worse when he lost his place in a government reshuffle. He later compared the shock of reading Churchill's letter of dismissal with the impact of the bullet that had shattered his cheek in 1915.

Reith was profoundly affected by this reverse. 'On razor-edge of frenzy', he wrote (Reith, diary, 10 March 1942), and he spent more than a week in bed with a high temperature. After three months he could bear the inactivity no longer. He wrote to an old naval acquaintance to ask if he might enlist in coastal forces—'chief clerk or storekeeper or something like that, at a post where there was excitement and danger' (ibid., 16 May 1942).

In the event Reith donned the uniform of a lieutenant-commander in the royal naval volunteer service. At 27s. 2d. a day, plus allowances, his income was one thirtieth of what it had been two years previously. His first job was to organize a special liaison service to reduce delays in the repair of the new craft that were coming into service with coastal forces. His second achievement was to organize his admiral and the chief staff officer who had recruited him out of their jobs and get the supply side of this important functional service established as a department within the Admiralty. Later Reith was transferred to the staff of the third sea lord. He was asked to draw up terms of reference for a new combined operations material department. His proposals, bold and unorthodox, were accepted as they stood. He was promoted captain RNVR and given the job of implementing them. For the next seventeen months, until the invasion of Europe, he had enough on his plate to satisfy even his gargantuan appetite for work.

Not fully stretched Reith left the navy at the end of 1944. His contribution to the war effort received formal recognition in the new year's honours list when he was made a companion of the Bath. He was proud of the fact that it was a military CB, a distinction not previously accorded to any civilian, privy counsellor, or former minister. He was less pleased to note that Lord Portal, his successor at the Ministry of Works, had been made a viscount. 'This is really absolutely shameful', he wrote; 'But of course he is a friend of Churchill's' (Reith, diary, 1 Jan 1945).

The civilian assignment for which Reith left the Admiralty arose from concern in Whitehall about the relationship between Cable and Wireless (of which he had been

made a director in 1943) and the Commonwealth Communications Council. The dominance of Cable and Wireless—commercially owned and London-based—was the cause of some resentment in the dominions. Reith was to be an emissary charged with explaining the British government's view of how relations should develop and be institutionalized. Reith himself had earlier put forward the idea of some sort of imperial corporation—a telecommunications equivalent of what he had envisaged for civil aviation—but this had been countered from Australia and New Zealand by an alternative proposal for a looser arrangement.

Reith and his party left Northolt airport at the end of January in a Consolidated Liberator of RAF transport command. They flew to Australia by way of Washington and Hawaii. 'Bought a pair of fancy Honolulu bathing pants', he wrote; 'Never been in such a warm sea' (Reith, diary, 26 Jan 1945). On to New Zealand, and then to India. In Delhi he was gratified to be put up in the Irwin suite, which had been the viceroy's: 'My bedroom is about 70 feet by 35 and the bed about 8 feet broad' (ibid., 18 Feb 1945).

Reith's first real set-back came in Cape Town. 'My *dear* Lord Reith, you are most welcome to South Africa', said Field Marshal Smuts (Reith, diary, 1 March 1945), but dear Lord Reith failed to budge him. Ascension Island—Brazil—Trinidad—Canada. When there was nothing to see, Reith slept on the 7 foot sofa which had been installed for him on the aircraft. He also played backgammon with his secretary, Joyce Wilson, whom he had winkled out of the Admiralty to accompany him. The British high commissioner in Ottawa, Malcolm Macdonald, was taken aback by the extent to which Reith allowed Miss Wilson to monopolize 'all his available time, attention and affectionate interest' (Boyle, 332).

On his return Reith, characteristically, completed his report overnight and had it printed within seven days. He chaired the subsequent conference of interested parties in London and when it was over devised what he considered an appropriate send-off for the Commonwealth delegates. The Admiralty agreed to lay on a frigate and destroyer to take them over to France to view something of the wartime devastation. Reith rounded off their day by taking them to Canterbury where they were received by the archbishop.

The war was now over, and a Labour government was in power, quickening Reith's hopes of a job from the country's new political masters. Early in 1946 he wrote an extraordinary and poignant letter to Churchill, reproaching him for his failure to make proper use of him during the war: 'Instead of that there has been the sterility, humiliation and distress of all these years—"eyeless in Gaza".' He received a reply which even he was obliged to concede was 'quite decent' (Reith, *Into the Wind*, 526–7).

Reith fantasized endlessly about the tasks he might be called upon to undertake—the secretary-generalship of the United Nations, the bursarship of Wellington College, the chairmanship of the National Coal Board. Meeting the bishop of Gloucester in the Athenaeum one day he told him he would like some honorary job in a cathedral close in return for a house. All that came up was the chairmanship of a committee on new towns, which took up two days a week. The report it produced bears Reith's indelible stamp, especially in the section dealing with social life and recreation: 'Care must be taken to ensure that camouflaged drinking saloons are not allowed … greyhound racing … would bring in its train consequences likely to be specially objectionable' (*Parl. papers*, 1945–6, 14, Cmd 6876). Reith dithered about whether to accept a new town chairmanship, partly because he still hoped for a 'proper job'. While on holiday in Scotland he read some press speculation that he might be considered for the new Iron and Steel Board, but nothing came of it and he eventually took on the chairmanship of Hemel Hempstead.

Reith was now fifty-eight. Christopher had left school and was doing his national service in the navy. His daughter, Marista, had gone away to school for the first time. Reith's mind turned more and more to writing his memoirs. He also, after many years of holding stiffly aloof, began to get back onto terms with the BBC. He lunched with Sir William Haley, the new director-general, and a friendship developed between them. They both lobbied vigorously for Reith to be appointed to the vacant BBC chairmanship, but it went to the Labour peer Lord Simon of Wythenshawe. 'The last straw, it seemed', Reith wrote; 'I felt I absolutely *must* get away from this country' (Reith, diary, 24 May 1947). He explored possibilities in Canada, and was offered the position of dean of the faculty of engineering and applied science at the University of Toronto, but the offer was subsequently withdrawn.

In 1949 the president of the Board of Trade, the 33-year-old Harold Wilson, offered Reith the chairmanship of the National Film Finance Corporation. The salary was only £1500, but Wilson told him that the scope of the job was potentially greater than the terms of the legislation indicated. There was another ray of financial sunshine when his agent secured £1000 from the *Sunday Express* for the serialization of his memoirs.

Reith had once or twice over the years shown an interest in the Moral Re-Armament movement, and there was an attempt at this time to court him; one of their officials told him that his biggest life's work still lay ahead, and that he might be instrumental in bringing about a Christian revolution in Britain. 'I wish I might have some guidance direct', Reith wrote drily (Reith, diary, 7 April 1949). His son was now at Oxford University, and distinguishing himself on the river. His sixteen-year-old daughter was doing well at school, and Reith entertained high ambitions for her: 'Wrote Marista about being first woman PM' (Reith, diary, 20 Feb 1948).

There was an annual holiday pilgrimage to Scotland, and it was on the Isle of Mull in 1949 that Reith was quite seriously smitten by a girl of nineteen called Dawn Mackay. Reith was frequently in her company, and was so carried away with the desire to excel at highland dancing that he set aside his sabbatarian scruples and joined in the rehearsals that were held in the library after dinner.

Reith's memoirs, *Into the Wind*, were published in November that year, and their vigorous and idiosyncratic prose style attracted a good deal of attention. One critic identified a model in Dickens, describing the narrative as being written 'in a series of short snorts, rather as though Mr Jingle had got hold of a dictaphone' (Reith, enclosure volumes, Nov 1949). A former BBC protégée, Mary Somerville, now very much the *grande dame* of educational broadcasting, reproached him for ending on what she termed 'that obituary note'. She could shake him until his teeth rattled, she told him: 'You'll not get again the old sense that God is using you if you just sit girning that the state doesn't!' (ibid.).

Reith, in his seventh decade, still saw himself as a chosen vessel, eager to be used for some high purpose. In October 1950 he was made chairman of the Colonial Development Corporation (CDC). This meant giving up his other appointments. He grumbled about the drop in income which this entailed (from £7500 to £5000) and asked for the official announcement to say that the appointment involved him 'in considerable financial sacrifice'. Reith inherited heavy losses and an organization that he considered over-centralized and top-heavy. As he had done at Imperial Airways, he immediately set about replicating the management structure he had devised at the BBC. He installed an administrative controller of his own choosing: 'It was a comfort to know that another brain of some calibre was at work on the mess' (Reith, diary, 24 April 1951).

Reith was a difficult husband and a demanding father. The family benefited from the new interest offered by his work at the CDC, but only for a short time. Lady Reith's health was not good, and he was miserable at the prospect of Marista's departure for university, particularly as she had gone against his wishes and opted for St Andrews instead of Oxford. He re-read his old diaries obsessively, fretted about his finances, and within a year pronounced himself 'entirely ready to leave the CDC' (Reith, diary, 4 Jan 1952). In the event he retained the chairmanship for nine years, and would willingly have stayed as long again. He was later allowed to accept outside directorships, but to his indignation his CDC salary was reduced. Reith's position did not preclude him from speaking in the House of Lords, and when the government published their plans for introducing commercial television, he launched a ferocious attack, comparing it, in his extravagant way, to the introduction of the black death. A letter he wrote to Churchill inviting him to reconsider the government's proposals was not well received.

Reith travelled abroad a good deal on CDC business. When he sailed to South Africa on the *Winchester Castle*, the shipping line installed a special 7 foot-long bed in his cabin, and transferred it to the *Capetown Castle* for the return voyage. These foreign trips had an unsettling effect on him, largely because of the contrast between the way he was lionized abroad and the neglect he felt he endured in England. The accounts he wrote of his travels are highly entertaining—marvellously vivid, and frequently laced with his distinctive sardonic humour.

In 1955 Reith moved from Buckinghamshire to a flat in Lollards Tower at Lambeth Palace, the London residence of the archbishop of Canterbury. 'Primate takes in £7 a week lodgers', said a headline in the *Sunday Express*. One of the more unusual letters Sir Winston Churchill received on the occasion of his retirement was from Reith, who described himself as 'someone whom you broke and whose life you ruined' (Reith, diary, 8 April 1955). He was never able to see the extent to which he was the architect of his own misfortunes. He took little apparent satisfaction from being able to announce, in the CDC's annual report, that for the first time since it had been set up, the corporation had made a small net income. From the middle 1950s he would become increasingly embroiled in disputes with the Colonial Office, principally over the extent of the CDC's mandate.

The discovery that Reith's daughter had formed a strong attachment to a fellow student at St Andrews both depressed and agitated him. 'God Almighty', he wrote, 'what a crime committed that I should ever have married, or had any children' (Reith, diary, 23 Sept 1955). When he and Lady Reith went to Scotland to inspect a farm for Christopher, they drove through Dunblane, and painful memories stirred, as he and Charlie had shared lodgings there for a time before he was married: 'I launched a curse on the wretched Bowsers' (ibid., 6 Aug 1957).

The government was deaf to pleas that Reith's tenure at the CDC should be extended. 'Saw the squalid Lennox-Boyd at 5', he wrote; 'I knew from his manner that I was to be given *congé*' (Reith, diary, 23 Sept 1958). He went on a final tour of the Far East and on another to east and central Africa. He shook the dust of the corporation from his feet when he was four months short of his seventieth birthday; he departed, as he had done from the BBC, with bitterness and a singular lack of grace.

The last years Reith marked his seventieth birthday by an ascent of Cairngorm, Scotland's fifth highest mountain. He had gone into training by marching up and down the forty-odd steps that led to the flat in Lollards Tower. 'I've a feeling I may meet my father again at the summit', he wrote; 'I'd like to die up there and go away with him' (McIntyre, 338). For a time he once again drew closer to the BBC, although he was soon writing to Sir Arthur fforde, newly appointed as chairman, to complain that Hugh Carleton Greene, 'a divorced man, remarried and an unbeliever', had been made director-general (Reith, diary, 20 July 1959). (He had suggested, a short time previously, that he himself might be the man for the job.) Although he was concerned for the morals of his successor several times removed, he saw nothing remiss in preferring the company of a succession of young women to that of Lady Reith. He took them to dinner and to the theatre and to Ascot. He lavished presents on them from Cartier and Georg Jensen. When one of them accompanied him to some BBC occasion he introduced her as his god-daughter. He later successfully lobbied for her to be appointed headmistress of her old school, although her formal qualifications were slender. When he addressed the pupils of his own old school in Glasgow at a prize-giving, he announced

that he had discovered that 'Life was for Living'. A teetotaller for much of his life, he discovered a taste for champagne and whisky.

Reith retained a number of business interests. He had directorships at the Phoenix Assurance Company and Tube Investments. He was also on the board of the British Oxygen Company, which gave him the use of a Rolls-Royce and a chauffeur. To these now was added the vice-chairmanship of the North British Locomotive Company—'Gosh', he wrote, 'I wish I were chairman' (Reith, diary, 10 Aug 1959)—and the chairmanship of the State Building Society.

In 1960 Reith made his television début, and was interviewed by John Freeman in the *Face to Face* programme. His technique of answering questions caused some amusement, and might well have thrown a less experienced interviewer: 'Have you got that, Mr Freeman? That answer your question?' Was he ambitious? Freeman asked. Only to be fully stretched. His greatest defect of character? An inability to tolerate slow-wittedness. A happy man? Oh no. He received two hundred fan letters, and made a seven-page summary of them in his scrapbook.

Reith made heavy and ungracious weather of his daughter's wedding. He was involved to the point of obsession at the time with Dawn Mackay, and his emotions see-sawed wildly. He was frequently distressed and sometimes violently angry, throwing flower pots across the British Oxygen office and breaking telephones. One one occasion Miss Mackay's training as a Samaritan was put to the test; Reith, alone in his flat in the small hours, harangued her for almost two hours on the telephone with a revolver in his hand.

In 1961 Reith inserted an advertisement in *The Times*, ostensibly seeking advice about what to do with his diaries, which he said he was minded to destroy. In fact he was hoping to sell them, and told Asa Briggs that he would expect £100,000. He received more than 300 replies—from libraries, university colleges, and would-be biographers—but nothing came of it. He had spent hundreds of hours during his director-generalship rewriting passages relating to Charlie Bowser, and he would later persuade a former BBC secretary to edit out the sequences about Dawn Mackay. Eventually, after his death, his children sold the diaries to the BBC for a much smaller sum.

There were further disappointments in store. Reith suggested himself to Sir Roy Welensky as governor-general of the Central African Federation, and the British Transport job he coveted went to Dr Richard Beeching. He was persuaded to attend several celebrations of the BBC's fortieth anniversary in 1962; the corporation presented him with a television receiver and a set of the *Oxford English Dictionary*, which he ranged in order at Lollards Tower before he went to bed that night. In 1966 he published *Wearing Spurs*, an arresting account of his experiences in the First World War. It was widely and favourably reviewed. 'John Reith was born with a claymore strapped to his side', wrote Sir John Elliot: 'The only thing his good fairy forgot was to give him a scabbard for it' (*Daily Telegraph*, 9 Sept 1966).

Reith thought increasingly of retiring to Scotland, but his requirements in the matter of housing were exacting—it had to have a burn, it had to be away from the road (but not *too* far away), it had to have a view. The search for something suitable sent Christopher on many a wild-goose chase. In 1965 Reith was elected lord rector of Glasgow University, defeating Lord Caradon, the British representative at the United Nations, and Iain Macleod, the former health minister and Conservative Party chairman. He gave a highly idiosyncratic rectorial address, and took a closer interest in university affairs than was expected of him, leading to friction with the principal and the university court.

In 1967 Reith was invited to be lord high commissioner to the general assembly of the Church of Scotland—an appointment he had sourly declined when it was offered after his dismissal by Churchill during the war. Installed at the palace of Holyroodhouse, he gloried in his brief season as the queen's representative—'extraordinary how completely naturally I slipped into vice-regality', he wrote (Reith, diary, 5 July 1967). He filled the role a second time the following year, and the queen subsequently appointed him a knight of the Order of the Thistle.

In 1970 Reith accepted the offer of a grace and favour residence in Moray Place in Edinburgh. He and his wife were both now in declining health, and after a fall the following summer he died on 16 June 1971 in the officers' nursing home in Belgrave Crescent, Edinburgh. There was a simple funeral service in the Thistle chapel of St Giles's Cathedral attended only by family and a few friends. His wish that there should be no memorial service was disregarded, and the dean and chapter of Westminster and the BBC collaborated in the organization of a splendidly appropriate occasion. Reith's ashes were buried at the ruined church at Rothiemurchus in Inverness-shire.

The Times, in a leading article, recalled that Reith had felt himself to be elected by providence to do something great in the world, and judged that he had done so. His name passed not only into history, but into the *Oxford English Dictionary*, although 'Reithian', over the years, acquired shades of meaning which were not all complimentary—the BBC, for reasons good and bad, had become a broader church than its outsize founder intended. The Oxford historian Charles Stuart, who edited Reith's diaries in 1975, noted his ability to give excellent advice to all but himself, and applied to him words used by his great enemy Churchill of the French General Michel—'his personality and temperament were not equal to the profound and penetrating justice of his ideas' (Stuart, 70).

IAN MCINTYRE

Sources J. C. W. Reith, diaries (pre-diary narrative, summarized diary, and diary), BBC WAC · Reith's enclosure vols. (scrapbooks), BBC WAC · A. Briggs, *The history of broadcasting in the United Kingdom*, rev. edn, 5 vols. (1995) · *The Reith diaries*, ed. C. Stuart (1975) · J. C. W. Reith, *Broadcast over Britain* (1924) · J. C. W. Reith, *Into the wind* (1949) · J. Reith, *Wearing spurs* (1966) · A. Briggs, *Governing the BBC* (1979) · A. Briggs, *The BBC: the first fifty years* (1985) · P. Scannell and D. Cardiff, *A social history of British broadcasting*, [1] (1991) · A. Boyle, *Only the wind will listen: Reith of the BBC* (1972) · I. McIntyre, *The expense of glory: a life of John Reith* (1993) · personal knowledge (2004) · private information (2004) · R. G. Lambert, *Ariel and all his quality* (1940)

Archives BBC WAC, corresp., diaries, and papers | BBC WAC, corresp. with R. S. Wright · Bodl. Oxf., letters to Robert Bridges · Bodl. Oxf., corresp. with H. A. Gwynne · Bodl. RH, corresp. with Sir Roy Welensky, with a few papers relating to Rhodesia · CAC Cam., corresp. with Sir W. J. Haley · HLRO, corresp. with Lord Beaverbrook · HLRO, letters to Lord Samuel · King's Lond., Liddell Hart C., corresp. with Sir B. H. Liddell Hart · LPL, letters to H. R. L. Sheppard · NA Scot., corresp. with Lord Lothian · NL Scot., letters to Lord Waverley · University of Strathclyde, Glasgow, corresp. with G. L. Pepler · Welwyn Garden City Central Library, Hertfordshire, corresp. with Sir Frederic Osborn |FILM BBC WAC · BFI NFTVA, *Face to face*, BBC, 30 Oct 1960 · BFI NFTVA, *Without walls*, Channel 4, 26 Oct 1993 · BFI NFTVA, 'Auntie — the inside story of the BBC', BBC1, 28 Oct 1997 · BFI NFTVA, performance footage |SOUND BBC WAC · BL NSA, 'Lord Reith looks back', 1967, T8840WTR1 · BL NSA, documentary footage · BL NSA, recorded feature · IWM SA, oral history interview

Likenesses H. Coster, photographs, 1930–39, NPG · E. Kapp, chalk drawing, 1931, Barber Institute of Fine Arts, Birmingham · O. Birley, oils, 1933, Scot. NPG · O. Birley, oils, 1933–4, BBC · W. Stoneman, two photographs, 1934–46, NPG · M. Beerbohm, caricature, 1938, BBC · photographs, 1939–45, Hult. Arch. · W. Bird, photograph, 1962, NPG · G. Kelly, oils, 1967, BBC · O. Edis, photographs, NPG [*see illus.*] · D. Low, caricature, chalk drawing, NPG; repro. in *New Statesman and Nation* (11 Nov 1933) · S. Peet, photograph, repro. in McIntyre, *The expense of glory*, jacket · W. Rothenstein, chalk drawing, NPG · W. Rothenstein, chalk drawing, Laing Art Gallery, Newcastle upon Tyne · F. Topolski, portrait, NPG · D. Wilson, pen-and-ink drawing, NPG · pencil sketches, NPG

Wealth at death £6155: probate, 13 Aug 1971, CGPLA Eng. & Wales

Reitlinger, Gerald Roberts (1900–1978), writer and art collector, was born at 33 Fitzjohn's Avenue, Hampstead, London, on 2 March 1900, the third son of Albert Reitlinger, merchant and banker, and his wife, Emma Brunner. One of his brothers, Henry Scipio, was educated at King's College, Cambridge, where he studied to be an engineer. A sister, Nellie Maude, married Philip Guedalla, the historian, in 1919. Reitlinger was first educated at Westminster School, where his house captain was Roy Harrod, the economist. He then served for a few months with the Middlesex regiment before going up to Christ Church, Oxford, in 1920. There, he read history under Keith Feiling before pursuing his own course of studies at the suggestion of Edward Thurlow Leeds of the Ashmolean Museum, graduating BLitt in 1923. In winter 1921–2 he travelled to Paris to study painting and continued his formal art training after graduating, first at the Slade School of Fine Art in London, under the supervision of Henry Tonks, and later at the Westminster School of Art. During the 1920s and 1930s he exhibited paintings at the New English Art Club and elsewhere. When asked later why he chose not to paint professionally, he replied simply: 'because I wasn't good enough' (Bullock, 10).

Between 1930 and 1932, Reitlinger took part in two archaeological expeditions to Iraq, sponsored by the University of Oxford. The first expedition, organized jointly with the Field Museum in Chicago, was to Kish, where he collected many fragments of local pottery. The second was to Hira, and was co-directed by Reitlinger himself and Professor David Talbot Rice. These experiences helped to influence the former's interest in Islamic and Oriental ceramics, which would later form the basis of his greatest legacy. Later in the decade Reitlinger travelled extensively throughout Persia and Turkish Armenia, as well as the remote Chinese province of Yunnan. Accounts of his travels were included in two books, *A Tower of Skulls* (1932) and *South of the Clouds* (1939). In 1939 Reitlinger entered the Royal Artillery, where he served until 1941. Owing to ill health he was forced to retire from active duty, but remained in the forces as a lecturer until the end of the Second World War.

Following his first marriage, to Dorothy Jardas (1900/01–1951), which ended in divorce, Reitlinger married for a second time on 10 February 1945. His wife was a widow of independent means, Eileen Anne Graham Bell (*b.* 1909/10), the daughter of Charles Stodgson Bilbrough. They had one daughter, Venetia. In addition to his role as husband and father, Reitlinger had an active social life. During the 1920s and 1930s he held regular house parties at Thornsdale, a large cottage near Iden in Kent. In later years legendary gatherings at Woodgate House, in Beckley, Sussex, earned him the title The Squire among his friends. There are vivid glimpses of Reitlinger in *To Keep the Ball Rolling; the Memoirs of Anthony Powell* (1976–8), where the novelist referred to his host as 'tall, bespectacled, jerky in his movements, slightly put-upon in manner, and unpredictable' and added that he 'possessed an extraordinary fund of unlikely information' (*The Times*, 17 March 1978).

In 1953 Reitlinger published a book entitled *The Final Solution*, which included an influential account of the Nazi persecution of the Jews. This work, which continues to hold a place in the literature on the Nazi period, was followed by two more books on related subjects. The first of these, entitled *The SS: Alibi of a Nation*, was published in 1956. The second, entitled *The House Built on Sand*, was published in 1960.

In the succeeding decade, between 1961 and 1970, Reitlinger published a seminal work, consisting of three volumes known collectively as *The Economics of Taste* (*The Rise and Fall of Picture Prices, 1760–1960*, 1961; *The Rise and Fall of Objets d'Art Prices since 1750*, 1963; and *The Art Market in the 1960s*, 1970). Reitlinger's interest in this subject was prompted by what he considered to be the decline of taste in art, which he attributed to a redistribution of wealth and to the inflated price of individual reputation. Reitlinger was also the editor (1927–9) of the art magazine *Drawing and Design*, and a frequent contributor of book reviews and articles on art and antiques to newspapers, periodicals, and journals including the *Daily Telegraph*, *The Observer*, *The Connoisseur*, and *Ars Islamica*.

In summer 1972 Reitlinger began negotiations with the University of Oxford regarding the possible donation of his collection of ceramics to the Ashmolean Museum. This remarkable collection was one of the most important to have been gathered by a single collector, and was the product of over fifty years of collecting, both learned and insatiable. It included over 2000 pieces of Chinese, Japanese, Islamic, and European pottery, as well as a number of Persian and Mughal paintings. For many years the Islamic collection was housed in a room in Reitlinger's home known as the 'Museum'. It was fitted out, from floor to ceiling, with wall cases, each of which was packed full of objects such as tiles, cups, plates, bowls, and jars. Included in Reitlinger's bequest to the Ashmolean were the deeds to Woodgate House, the sale of which was intended to provide the necessary funds to pay for the construction of a proper gallery to display the collection. Before the sale took place, however, a fire ravaged the house in February 1978, while the collection was still *in situ*. Fortunately the majority of the objects were salvaged.

Reitlinger never fully recovered from the shock of the fire that destroyed his home, and died of a cerebral haemorrhage on 8 March 1978 at Clyde House Nursing Home, St Leonards, Sussex. He died knowing that his collection was safe, and that it would be made available for the benefit of future generations. He is remembered as a generous yet enigmatic character, who frowned upon the open expression of feelings and was unpredictable in the alternation of charm and irritability. In 1981 an exhibition of his collection was held at the Ashmolean Museum and at Sothebys in London. Two years later, in summer 1983, the Gerald Reitlinger gallery was opened to house the Ashmolean's collection of Islamic art.   DAVID A. BERRY

Sources A. Bullock, 'Gerald Reitlinger: a portrait', *Eastern ceramics and other works of art from the collection of Gerald Reitlinger* (1981), 9–12 [exhibition catalogue, AM Oxf.] · *WWW, 1971–80* · J. W. Allan, 'The Gerald Reitlinger gift', *Apollo*, 117 (1983), 318–19 · *The Times* (11 March 1978) · *The Times* (17 March 1978) · *The Times* (21 March 1978) · b. cert. · m. certs. · d. cert. · private information (2004) [O. Impey]
Archives AM Oxf.
Likenesses C. Wood, blue chalk on paper, 1926, AM Oxf.
Wealth at death £281,704: probate, 31 May 1978, *CGPLA Eng. & Wales*

Reitz, Deneys (1882–1944), soldier and politician in South Africa, was born at Bloemfontein, Orange Free State, on 2 April 1882, the third of the five sons of Francis William Reitz (1844–1934), and his first wife, Blanca Thesen (1854–1887), a member of a Norwegian family that had settled in Knysna, Cape Colony. Reitz's was an old and cultured family: his grandfather was sent from Cape Town to school in Edinburgh, and according to family tradition once dined with Sir Walter Scott. His father, who was educated in Edinburgh and made lively Afrikaans renderings of Burns, served as chief justice and later president of the Orange Free State; in 1898 he became secretary of state to President Kruger and in that capacity presented the ultimatum which precipitated the Second South African War. After the union he became first president of the senate, retiring in 1918; his sister Frances Hester Reitz married W. P. Schreiner. At home Deneys Reitz grew to be familiar with the English classics; he saw many leading figures in South African public life, and at twelve years of age joined his father on a tour in Europe. He early learned to ride and shoot, and attended Grey College, Bloemfontein, but his formal education ended when at the age of seventeen he joined the Boer forces in the Second South African War.

After serving in the fighting round Ladysmith, Reitz ranged widely for two years, especially with J. C. Smuts through Cape Colony. He later gave a full account, with characteristic charm and generosity, of 'the hairbreadth escapes, the dare-devilry' (to use the words of Smuts) in his book *Commando* (1929), which is an invaluable document on the history of the war from the Boer side. After *Commando* he wrote two further autobiographical volumes, *Trekking on* (1933) and *No Outspan* (1943), which were also marked successes.

After the peace of Vereeniging (1902) Reitz stood by his father in refusing the oath of allegiance and went into exile. Three years in Madagascar brought him hard work, little pay, and much fever, but during this time he produced the first draft of *Commando*. In 1905 Mrs Smuts persuaded him to return and he arrived ill and penniless, but life in the Smuts family restored him to health, and he was able to begin law practice at Heilbron, Orange River Colony, in 1908. Reitz became politically active when he joined the South African Party of Louis Botha and Smuts with its policy of reconciliation between Afrikaans- and English-speaking South Africans, and of full autonomy for South Africa within the British empire. In 1914, in support of Botha and Smuts, he helped suppress the rising which broke out. He then served with Botha in South-West Africa against the Germans. In 1915 Reitz was the South African Party's candidate in Heilbron in the general election. After an emotional and violent campaign, he was soundly defeated by the candidate of the National Party, the political platform of Afrikaner nationalism. He promptly joined the South African forces in east Africa under Smuts. In 1917 this seasoned former enemy of Britain enlisted in the British army and went as a major to the western front where he was twice wounded and in the closing stages of the war was colonel commanding the 1st (Royal Scots) Fusiliers.

On his return to South Africa Reitz entered politics as Smuts's protégé. He was elected to parliament for the constituency of Bloemfontein South in 1920, but lost his seat in the general election of 1921. Within a few months he returned to parliament as the representative of Port Elizabeth (Central). Reitz had one guiding political faith, unswerving loyalty to Smuts. Like Smuts, he firmly believed in the sincerity of British friendship towards South Africa and in the possibilities of building a nation of Afrikaners and English speakers within the empire. He rejected the Afrikaner nationalism of the National Party as race-worshipping 'voodooism'. As a politician he was a doughty campaigner on election platforms where he was a hard hitter who neither asked nor expected any quarter. In the general election of 1929 he left his safe seat to contest Barberton, a seat held by the National Party. Despite the South African Party's crushing defeat in the election, he captured the constituency. He was, however, a poor parliamentary speaker who rarely bothered to prepare his speeches. Although he occasionally excelled in the cut and thrust of debate he was bored by parliamentary life.

In April 1921 Reitz became the minister of lands. He was an ardent conservationist who as minister prepared the way for the inauguration of the Kruger National Park, of which he became a devoted trustee. Out of office between 1924 and 1933, he joined a legal firm in Johannesburg

which provided him with the opportunity to practise some journalism and to travel widely in Africa. In the coalition ('fusion') government of 1933 he was re-appointed minister of lands in General J. B. M. Hertzog's cabinet. He subsequently became minister of agriculture in 1935, of mines in 1938, and of native affairs in 1939. Although paternalistic, he was a pragmatic and enlightened minister of native affairs. He recognized that Africans had major and legitimate grievances and during the Second World War saw the Atlantic charter as a basis for reform. This led to accusations that he was too liberal. After the collapse of 'fusion' in 1939 Reitz became in addition deputy prime minister. Although enterprising, especially with regard to advancing irrigation schemes during his tenure as minister of lands, he was not an outstanding minister. He had a cavalier attitude towards ministerial tasks and despised the drudgery of desk work. But the post did provide him with the opportunity to travel widely. In 1920 Reitz had married Leila Agnes Buissinné (1887–1959), daughter of Dr Claude Wright, of Wynberg, near Cape Town. His wife was a history lecturer at the University of Cape Town, and was the first woman in South Africa to be elected an MP. They had two sons, who both served in the South African forces during the Second World War.

In 1943, troubled by ill health and exhaustion, Reitz was appointed high commissioner in London, South Africa's most important diplomatic posting. Although socially successful and popular, his bad health, wanderlust, and lack of interest in his duties meant that he was not an effective high commissioner. After suffering a stroke he died in the Charing Cross Hospital, London, on 19 October 1944. He was cremated on 25 October.

Although he was incurably indolent, Reitz's physical and moral courage, his forthrightness, tolerance, humour, and talent as a raconteur made him a notable personality and an endearing and popular one. It was sheer force of personality that carried him through a turbulent political career. Reitz's life was a triumph of character. F. A. MOUTON

Sources *DNB* · B. Fourie, *Brandpunte* (1991) · D. B. Sole, 'This above all: reminiscences of a South African diplomat', Library of Africa Institute, Pretoria · L. Blackwell, *Farewell to parliament* (1946) · L. E. Neame, *South African politicians* (1929) · P. Walshe, *The rise of African nationalism in South Africa* (1987) · J. Carruthers, *The Kruger national park: a social and political history* (1995) · L. Egeland, *Bridges of understanding* (1977) · H. Reitz, *The conversion of a South African nationalist* (1946) · J. C. Moll, 'Francis William Reitz en die Republiek van die Oranje-Vrystaat', DPhil diss., University of the Orange Free State, 1968 · *CGPLA Eng. & Wales* (1945) · National Archive, Pretoria, Estate 5697/44 · Dutch Reformed Church Archive, Bloemfontein, South Africa · Grey College, Bloemfontein, South Africa · *DSAB* · unpublished history, Department of Foreign Affairs, South Africa

Wealth at death £6565—in South Africa: Estate 5697/44, National Archive, Pretoria · £1160 13s. 1d.—in England: administration with will, 14 June 1945, *CGPLA Eng. & Wales*

Rejlander, Oscar Gustaf (1813–1875), photographer, was born probably in Sweden; little is known about his parents or his early life. When on 30 September 1862 Rejlander married Mary Bull (*b.* 1837/8), daughter of George Bull, stonemason, the marriage certificate registered his father as Carl Gustaf Rejlander, an officer in the Swedish army.

Oscar Gustaf Rejlander (1813–1875), self-portrait [*The Artist Rejlander Introduces the Volunteer Rejlander*]

According to O. G. Rejlander's obituaries he studied art informally in Rome in the 1830s and supported himself there by working as a portrait painter and copyist of old masters. The reasons for his move to England remain a subject of speculation: one obituary states that it was 'a romantic love adventure' with an Englishwoman which brought him to Britain (*British Journal of Photography*, 22.55) but there is no evidence to substantiate this claim. Rejlander can be placed in Lincoln in 1841; by 1845 he had settled in Wolverhampton, at 42 Darlington Street, where he opened a painter's studio.

It was in Rome in 1852 that Rejlander had first seen photographic reproductions of art and marvelled at their precision. He took up photography in 1853 after an afternoon's tutelage by Nicholaas Henneman, formerly the assistant of William Henry Fox Talbot. His decision to learn photography for himself was based upon his desire to make studies from life which would assist him in his painting; however, he quickly became absorbed in the expressive potential of photography and, in 1855, began to exhibit his photographic compositions. In the same year, he won a bronze medal at the Paris Universal Exhibition; from then until his death in 1875 his photographs were regularly accepted for exhibition and reviewed in the photographic and periodical press. These images consisted of portraits, landscapes, studies from the nude, anatomical studies, *têtes d'expression*, art studies, and subject pictures. Of the latter, it was his genre photographs which earned him his reputation as one of Britain's leading photographers. In photographs such as *Oh Lift me the Veil of the Future* (1855) and *Please Give Us a Copper!* (1860s, both National Museum of Photography, Film and Television, Bradford, Royal Photographic Society collection) he demonstrated his skill for eliciting from his models naturalistic expressions and poses which sustained a narrative and aroused in the viewer the sentiment appropriate to the scene before them. His *Night in Town* (also known as *Homeless* and *Poor Jo*; *c*.1860, National Museum of Photography, Film and Television, Royal Photographic Society collection), depicting a child in rags huddled on a doorstep, was used by the Shaftesbury Society for over a hundred years to highlight the plight of homeless children.

The first photograph which Rejlander exhibited was *Group Printed from Three Negatives*. Unlike most of his contemporaries, he did not view 'combination-printing' as a necessary evil and, in 1857, decided to demonstrate its creative potential by submitting a large-scale composition to the Manchester Art Treasures Exhibition. It took him six weeks, and thirty negatives, to produce *The Two Ways of Life* (1857, two versions, National Museum of Photography, Film and Television, Royal Photographic Society collection), a large-scale (31 in. x 16 in.), elaborate allegory of the choice between the life of virtue and that of vice. The suggestion that photography could fulfil the didactic, morally elevated role ascribed to high art was one which divided the critics: the photograph quickly became a *cause célèbre*. Rejlander's use of semi-clad models to personify a number of the vices proved particularly controversial. Prince Albert, already a patron of Rejlander's, purchased three versions, but this royal endorsement did not prevent the council of the Photographic Society of Scotland from initially refusing to exhibit the photograph on moral grounds. When they did exhibit it in 1858, a curtain was drawn over the offending portion.

In the spring of 1862 Rejlander moved to London and settled in Malden Road. This move brought him into close contact with those who were promoting his exhibition photographs as proof that photography was a fine art. Their insistent claims drowned out Rejlander's own opinion that photography was neither a fine art nor a science but a medium *sui generis*; to his mind, photography and painting were but two of the many media in which the artist could express his inventive faculty. His *Infant Photography Receiving a Fee from the Painter* (*c*.1860) challenged the hypocrisy of artists who publicly claimed that art owed nothing to photography while privately using photographs as studies. For Rejlander, artists had as much to learn from photography about observation and draughtsmanship as photographers had to learn from painting about composition and expression.

Contemporary descriptions of Rejlander, 'the father of art photography', seek to stress his geniality, humour, and childlike enthusiasm for his art (*Photographic News*, 19.42). He had blue-green eyes, a balding pate fringed by long sandy hair, a red moustache, and full beard. He believed that he resembled the Italian patriot Garibaldi and he appears as his hero in two of his own photographs. In his composite self-portrait *The Artist Rejlander Introduces the Volunteer Rejlander* (*c*.1871, National Museum of Photography, Film and Television, Royal Photographic Society collection) he appears as both a bohemian painter and a corporal of the 38th (Middlesex) volunteer regiment, Artists' company. He also appears together with his wife as the personification of married love in his photograph *Happy Days* (*c*.1872–3, National Museum of Photography, Film and Television, Royal Photographic Society collection). Mary Rejlander was a frequent model for her husband and probably worked as his assistant.

As a portrait photographer Rejlander photographed several illustrious sitters, including Alfred Tennyson (c.1863, National Portrait Gallery, London), Charles Dodgson (Lewis Carroll) (1863), Henry Taylor (c.1863, National Portrait Gallery, London), Charles Darwin (c.1871), Gustave Doré (c.1868, National Portrait Gallery, London, and National Museum of Photography, Film and Television, Royal Photographic Society collection), and Prince Albert (c.1861, National Portrait Gallery, London, and Victoria and Albert Museum, London). When, in the mid-1860s, the majority of photographers repudiated their claims to be recognized as artists in favour of staking their claim to professional status on their technical expertise, Rejlander continued to eschew the latter in favour of invention and effect. Despite inspiring a generation of photographers to produce pictorial photographs, his own endeavours became subject to the charge of careless manipulation and his reputation suffered accordingly.

In 1868 Rejlander's fortunes began to revive: he was favourably reviewed in the *Art Journal* and, a year later, opened a new and richly furnished studio opposite Victoria Station in central London. It was soon after this move that Charles Darwin, frustrated in his quest for adequate illustrations of the primary human emotions, sought him out after having seen his photographs in a shop window. Rejlander supplied Darwin with nine illustrations for his *The Expression of the Emotions in Man and Animals* (1872), six of which he posed for himself. The photograph illustrating 'mental distress', that of an infant boy wailing, became known as 'Ginx's Baby' after the popular novel by James E. Jenkins; a contemporary, H. B. Pritchard, claimed that it earned Rejlander £5000 in a year. This period of prosperity was, however, short-lived.

In endeavouring to be both a painter and a photographer, Rejlander found himself increasingly isolated from the fraternities which he hoped to unite. In 1870 a raid upon a print dealer's shop resulted in his art studies being seized with other 'obscene' material. About this time he contracted the 'wasting and painful disease' which led to his death on 18 January 1875 at his home, 23 East Cottages, Clapham (*British Journal of Photography*, 22.54); he was buried in Kensal Green cemetery on 23 January. He left his widow, in the words of one commentator, 'little more than the memory of a reputation, a few debts, and a little knot of friends' (*Photogram*, 59).

JULIET HACKING

Sources S. Spencer, *O. G. Rejlander: photography as art* (1985) • E. Y. Jones, *Father of art photography: O. G. Rejlander, 1813–1875* (1973) • S. Spencer, 'O. G. Rejlander: art studies', *British photography in the 19th century*, ed. M. Weaver (1989) • A. Fielding, 'An elusive quarry: Rejlander in Wolverhampton', *Photographic Journal*, 125 (1985), 226–30 • 'The late O. G. Rejlander', *British Journal of Photography* (29 Jan 1875), 54–6 • A. H. Wall, 'Rejlander's photographic art studies/their teaching and suggestions', *Photographic News*, 30 (1886), 483ff.; 31 (1887), 103ff • A. H. Wall, 'Rejlander's photographic art studies/ their teaching and suggestions', *Photographic News*, 30 (1886), 483ff.; 31 (1887) • O. G. Rejlander, 'An apology for art photography', *British Journal of Photography* (16 Feb 1863), 76–8 • 'Rejlander's legacy', *Photogram*, 1 (April 1894), 59–61 • *Photographic News*, 19 (1875), 42–3 • H. B. Pritchard, *About photography and photographers* (1883); repr. (1973) • 'The photographs of Rejlander', *Art Journal*, 30 (1868), 15 • P. Prodger, 'Photography and *The expression of the emotions*', in C. Darwin, *The expression of the emotions in man and animals*, 3rd edn (1998), 399–410 [incl. introduction, afterword, and commentaries by P. Ekman] • m. cert.

Archives National Museum of Photography, Film and Television, Bradford, Royal Photographic Society collection • NPG • Royal Collection | CUL, Darwin archives • International Museum of Photography, George Eastman House, Rochester, New York • Ransom HRC, Gernsheim collection

Likenesses O. G. Rejlander, self-portrait, photograph, c.1862, National Museum of Photography, Film and Television, Bradford, Royal Photographic Society collection • O. G. Rejlander, self-portrait, photograph, c.1871, National Museum of Photography, Film and Television, Bradford, Royal Photographic Society collection • O. G. Rejlander, double portrait, photograph, c.1872–1873 (with Mary Rejlander), National Museum of Photography, Film and Television, Bradford, Royal Photographic Society collection • O. G. Rejlander, self-portrait, photograph, repro. in sales catalogue, Christies, 10 June 1976 • O. G. Rejlander, self-portrait, photograph, National Museum of Photography, Film and Television, Bradford, Royal Photographic Society collection [*see illus.*]

Relf, Ernest Frederick (1888–1970), aerodynamicist, was born in Beckenham, Kent, on 2 October 1888, the younger child and only son of Thomas Joseph Relf, businessman, and his wife, Marion Weeks. Relf's early education was frequently interrupted by family removals. However, his father, a linguist and very versatile musician, himself took a hand in his son's education. Relf could read music before he could read print, and schooling in the three Rs was matched by musical instruction, both amateur and professional. In 1903 his family home was in Portsmouth; Relf sat the dockyard entrance examination, won first place, and in January 1904 entered the dockyard as an apprentice shipwright: this involved part-time attendance at the Royal Dockyard School. Soon afterwards, at sixteen, he was appointed organist at one of Portsmouth's largest churches, and two years later was nearly persuaded to make music his career. But his record at the Royal Dockyard School was outstanding and in 1909 he won a royal scholarship to the Royal College of Science. Here he read mathematics and physics as principal subjects, won the Tyndall prize, and in 1912 duly obtained his associateship of the Royal College of Science (ARCS) with first-class honours. In August 1912 he was appointed a junior assistant in the aeronautics section of the engineering department of the National Physical Laboratory (NPL) at Teddington; he thus came under the influence of Leonard Bairstow, then head of the section. When Bairstow left in 1917 the section became an independent aerodynamics department; from 1917 to 1920 it was under the direction of T. E. Stanton and from 1920 to 1925 of R. V. Southwell. Relf succeeded Southwell as superintendent in 1925.

Relf's first thirteen years at the NPL showed his brilliance and versatility as a scientist and engineer. Among his hobbies were electrical engineering and photography; he put both to good use in his aerodynamical and related research. In this period he published some forty scientific papers on a wide variety of topics: from the visualization of flow in liquids to the use of an electrical analogue to determine streamlines; from aeroplane stability to the design and manufacture of a special electrical motor, the problems of which had defeated the electrical industry and which now became standard equipment; from the determination of the virtual inertia in yaw of an airship to the 'singing' of bracing wires; these and many more. His work was regarded as of such importance that he was not called up in 1914, although he was attested and served one day in the services. In 1919 the Massachusetts Institute of Technology offered Relf its newly founded chair of aerodynamics; he declined the appointment. Later, he took part in two Oxford expeditions: in 1923 to Spitsbergen and in 1924 to Nordaustlandet, under the leadership of George Binney. Relf was physicist, surveyor, radio officer, and handyman.

From 1925 to 1945 Relf, as head of his department, had to become an administrator. But he never lost his zest for scientific research, even though now it had to be done by others under his direction. A most human man, he ran his team on the lightest of reins, encouraging original thought by his keen and evident interest and his helpful advice, but still keeping everyone on the appropriate road; in this way he brought out the best in his staff, seven of whom were in due course to be elected FRS. Relf himself was elected FRS in 1936 and appointed CBE in 1944: he also became a fellow of the Royal Aeronautical Society (1926) and of the Institute of Aeronautical Sciences (United States) in 1933. He won the George Taylor gold medal of the Royal Aeronautical Society in 1935, and its highest honour, the society's gold medal, in 1953.

At the end of 1945 Relf left the NPL to take up for five years the post of principal of the newly founded College of Aeronautics at Cranfield. He recruited a first-class staff, and set the college on the right lines, so that in his lifetime it became the Cranfield Institute of Technology, Britain's first postgraduate university.

In 1951 Relf left Cranfield to devote the remaining years of his life to consultancy and music. He had already become an independent member of the Aeronautical Research Council, a body to which he gave unbroken service in various capacities for fifty years (1918–68). For four years he acted as a consultant to his former department at the NPL; he also worked with Barnes Wallis and with various research associations. As to music: from his student days, when the proximity of the royal colleges of science and of music enabled him to expand his talents and to make many friends in the musical world, music permeated and supplemented his scientific life. In addition to playing the piano and organ, he composed much chamber music and some 200 songs. Some of his music, with professional performers, has been broadcast by the BBC.

Relf was of medium height, plump and jolly, a man who engendered a real affection in his wide circle of friends. In 1917, at Plymouth, he married Elfreda Grace, daughter of Frank Day, of the Royal Naval Ordnance Service, and his wife, Emily; they had no children. He died at his home, 28 Spinney Hill, Addlestone, on 25 February 1970.

RODERICK COLLAR, rev.

Sources A. R. Collar, *Memoirs FRS*, 17 (1971), 593–616 · personal knowledge (1981) · *CGPLA Eng. & Wales* (1970)
Archives IWM, corresp. with Tizard
Wealth at death £17,692: probate, 28 April 1970, *CGPLA Eng. & Wales*

Relhan, Anthony (1715–1776), physician, was born in Ireland, and educated at Trinity College, Dublin, where he became a scholar in 1734, and BA in 1735. On 15 October 1740 he began to study medicine at Leiden, later returning to Dublin, where he obtained his MD on 12 July 1743. He became a fellow of the King and Queen's College of Physicians in Ireland in October 1747, and was elected president of the college in 1755. Three years later he left Dublin, following disputes with other fellows of the college over the propriety of his prescribing James's Fever Powder, named after Robert James, which was considered by some to be a quack remedy.

Relhan settled as a physician in Brighton in 1759, and in 1761 published *A Short History of Brighthelmstone*, in which he gave an account of the climate, mineral spring, and other advantages of the place as a resort for invalids. In 1763, having been incorporated MD at Cambridge, he became a member of the Royal College of Physicians and he was elected a fellow on 25 June 1764. In the same year he published *Refutation of the reflections* [by D. Rust and others] *against inoculation*. He served as censor at the Royal College of Physicians in 1765 and 1771, and delivered the Goulstonian lectures in 1765, and the Harveian oration on 18 October 1770. In this oration he praised Thomas Linacre and the other benefactors of the college, and dwelt at some length on the friendship of Erasmus and Linacre.

Relhan married twice. He had a son, Richard *Relhan, and a daughter with his first wife, Sarah Breholt. His second wife was the widow of Sir William Hart. He died in October 1776, and was buried in the Marylebone graveyard in Paddington Street, London.

NORMAN MOORE, rev. KAYE BAGSHAW

Sources Munk, *Roll*

Relhan, Richard (1754–1823), botanist and classical scholar, was born in Dublin, the son of Anthony *Relhan (1715–1776), medical practitioner, and his first wife, Sarah Breholt. He was elected a king's scholar at Westminster School in 1767, and was admitted a scholar of Trinity College, Cambridge, on 7 May 1773. He graduated BA in 1776 and MA in 1779, and, having taken holy orders, was chosen in 1781 fellow and conduct (or chaplain) of King's College, Cambridge. In 1783 Professor Thomas Martyn (1735–1825) gave Relhan all the manuscript notes he had made on Cambridge plants since the publication of his *Plantae Cantabrigienses* in 1763. With this assistance Relhan published his chief work, *Flora Cantabrigiensis*, in 1785, describing several new plants and including seven plates engraved by James Sowerby. It appears from his letters that he proposed to issue a 'Flora Anglica', but did not meet with sufficient encouragement. He published supplements to *Flora Cantabrigiensis* in 1787, 1788, and 1793, and second and third, amplified, editions of the whole in 1802 and 1820. In 1787 he gave a course of lectures on botany in the University of Cambridge. Relhan was elected fellow of the Royal

Society in 1787, and in 1788 became one of the original fellows of the Linnean Society. As a botanist he showed most originality in dealing with the non-flowering plants. His name was commemorated by L'Héritier in a genus, *Relhania*, comprising a few species of South African Compositae.

In 1791 Relhan accepted the college rectory of Hemingby, Lincolnshire. Living in retirement there, he devoted himself to the study of Tacitus, publishing editions of *De moribus Germanorum et de vita Agricolae* (1809) and the *Historia*. The identity of his wife is unknown. His children Richard, John Henry, and Charlotte all achieved some eminence in Cambridge life. Relhan died, probably at Hemingby, on 28 March 1823.

G. S. BOULGER, rev. ANITA MCCONNELL

Sources *Old Westminsters*, 2.779 · *GM*, 1st ser., 93/1 (1823), 380 · *N&Q*, 12th ser., 2 (1916), 138 · Venn, *Alum. Cant.* · private information (1896) · D. Lysons, *The environs of London*, 3 (1795), 265–6 · G. C. Gorham and T. Martyn, *Memoirs of John Martyn … and of Thomas Martyn* (1830)
Archives CUL | NHM, letters to members of the Sowerby family

Relly, James (1721/2–1778), Universalist preacher, was born at Jeffreyston, near Saundersfoot, Pembrokeshire, of unknown parentage. He was educated at Pembroke grammar school and apprenticed as a cow farrier.

The preponderance of English speakers in Pembrokeshire drew George Whitefield, John Wesley, and Moravian preachers to the area. According to surviving accounts Relly and his brother John (d. 1777) were converted either by Whitefield in 1741 or by his local adjutant John Harris of South Kennox in 1743. Despite his later modifications to Whitefield's system, Relly retained for him 'the love, the Rev'rence, to a father due' (Clymer, 197).

As a result of his conversion Relly became a Calvinistic Methodist preacher near Narberth, Pembrokeshire. From 1746 he was itinerating through the west and midlands of England, preaching at Bristol, Portsmouth, Exeter, Bath, Tewkesbury, Bromsgrove, and Birmingham.

While Whitefield was in America in 1746, leaving Howel Harris in charge, Relly became an occasional preacher at the London Tabernacle in Tottenham Court Road. Both Whitefield and Harris became concerned about Relly's excessive enthusiasm.

In 1751 there was a Methodist Disruption in Wales arising from a misunderstanding between Howel Harris and Daniel Rowland. John Harris, Relly, and his brother John were among those who separated 'respecting Freeness, and Extent of Grace' (Clymer, 197). Out of this separation emerged a sect known as Rellyites or Rellites, with meeting-houses at Pembroke and Templeton and a hymnbook, *Christian Hymns, Poems and Spiritual Songs* (1754), to which both brothers contributed. The Rellyites were on friendly terms with the Moravians at Haverfordwest.

Meanwhile James Relly was apparently preaching freelance. In 1756 he was in Carrickfergus, co. Antrim, causing problems for John Wesley, who regarded him as an agitator and a representative of antinomianism. In 1761 Wesley wrote to John Green of 'William Cudworth, James Relly, and their associates who abhor us as much as they do the Pope, and ten times more than they do the devil' (Wesley to Green, 2 April 1761, *Letters*, 4.144).

Between 1757 and 1764 Relly preached at Coachmaker's Hall, Addle Street, London, where he incurred the anger of Whitefieldians 'as a man black with crimes; an atrocious offender, both in principle and practice' (Clymer, 199). In 1764 a Yorkshire lady successfully sued him for fraudulently securing her signature on a deed of annuity while in a state of religious frenzy. The deed was cancelled and the money returned. In that year he moved to Bartholomew Close, London, where he remained until 1769, then lived at Crosby Square from 1769 to 1778.

Relly published sermons and polemical material, but is mostly remembered for his *Union, or, A Treatise of Consanguinity and Affinity between Christ and his Church* (1759), which affirmed, on grounds of justice, the co-extension of Adam's sin with Christ's salvation. Relly himself denied that this was implied Universalism, since unbelievers faced a period of post-mortem purgatory before their final salvation; but his critics and disciples clearly inferred the opposite. Relly died on 25 April 1778 and was buried in the Maze Pond Baptist burial-ground, Southwark, London. He was survived by his wife, of whom details are unknown, and a daughter, a Mrs Tongue.

Among Relly's disciples was John Murray (1741–1815). Sent to convince a Rellyian disciple of her error, Murray during the early 1760s became Relly's follower and friend, a Rellyian Universalist, and a founder of the Universalist Church of America (from 1961 the Unitarian Universalist Association). At Relly's death his London congregation split. The remaining members continued to meet in Windmill Street until 1830.

ANDREW M. HILL

Sources W. Wilson, *The history and antiquities of the dissenting churches and meeting houses in London, Westminster and Southwark*, 4 vols. (1808–14) · W. K. Clymer, 'The life and thought of James Relly', *Church History*, 11 (1942), 193–216 · G. M. R. [G. M. Roberts], 'The Moravians and John Relly and his people', *Cylchgrawn Cymdeithas Hanes Eglwys Methodistiaid Calfinaidd Cymru*, 38 (1953), 2–7 · J. Murray, *The life of Rev. John Murray, preacher of universal salvation written by himself* (1870) · T. Prince, ed., *The Christian history containing accounts of the revival and propagation of religion in Great Britain and America for the year 1744* (1747) · G. M. Roberts, ed., *Selected Trevecka letters (1742–1747)* (1956) [of Howel Harris] · *The letters of the Rev. John Wesley*, ed. J. Telford, 8 vols. (1931) · *The journal of the Rev. John Wesley*, ed. N. Curnock and others, 8 vols. (1909–16) · *DNB*
Archives NL Wales, letters
Likenesses S. Harding, etching, BM, NPG · June, engraving

Relph, Harry [*performing name* Little Tich] (1867–1928), music-hall entertainer, was born on 21 July 1867 at Cudham, Kent, the sixteenth child of Richard Relph (1790–1881), a farmer and publican, and his Irish-born second wife, Mary, *née* Moorefield or Murphew (1835–1893). He was born with an extra finger on each hand and both hands were slightly webbed. He also effectively stopped growing at the age of ten and reached a height of only 4 feet 6 inches. This combination of physical characteristics made him extremely self-conscious and resulted in his seeking privacy when off stage. His stature, however,

Harry Relph [Little Tich] (1867–1928), by Steiner

became essential to his act and to the publicity surrounding it.

When he was ten, Harry Relph began work as a lather-boy in a barber's shop in Gravesend, while at the same time performing as a dancer and tin-whistle player in public-house concerts and free and easies. By 1880 he had developed a 'blackface' act and was good enough to secure engagements at the nearby Rosherville Pleasure Gardens and at Barnard's Music Hall, Chatham. He eventually made his London début at the Foresters in 1884. Initially he used the stage name 'the Infant Mackney', an allusion to E. W. Mackney, a leading blackface performer of the period, but by the early 1880s he was billed as 'Young Tichborne'. Finally, in late 1884, he adopted the title 'Little Titch', though the 't' soon disappeared. 'Tichborne', or 'Tich', was a childhood nickname, which he, along with many other children of stout build, had to tolerate at this time. It was originally a reference to the corpulence of a celebrated claimant to the Tichborne family inheritance. It was Little Tich's eventual fame that resulted in the name's gaining its current usage, indicating small stature rather than wide girth.

Little Tich's act matured and gained considerable critical acclaim during a tour of the United States between 1887 and 1889. In particular, Tich dropped the blackface act to concentrate on dancing and character sketches. A major success in *Babes in the Wood* at Manchester in 1889–90 led to a series of engagements at London halls, notably the Pavilion, and in Drury Lane pantomime. By the early 1890s Tich was a leading figure within British music-hall and comic theatre. Between 1896 and 1902 he ran and performed in his own musical theatre company and also spent much of his time in Paris, where he was an enormously popular variety artist; by 1900 he was a good enough linguist to perform in French, and in 1910 he was made an officer of the Académie Française for his services to French theatre. Although he was no longer at the absolute pinnacle of the variety profession by the early 1920s, he remained a popular performer until his death.

Little Tich was famed above all for his talent as what contemporaries referred to as an 'eccentric dancer' and as a character comedian. His most famous routine was the so-called big boot dance, which he developed during his American tour in the 1880s. Each boot was 28 inches in length, and Tich used them as both comic props and the basis for quite remarkable tricks of comic agility. Aided by his being double-jointed, he was able to stand on the points of his shoes and lean out at extraordinary angles. The cry of 'Oo'er' when he appeared to stand on his fingers during the dance was a particular trademark. The act was extremely demanding and he tired of it both physically and mentally in his later years, abandoning it from about 1915. In the 1890s he developed a burlesque of the 'Serpentine dance' used by the American dancer Loie Fuller, which lead to the invention of Little Miss Turpentine, one of his most successful stock characters. Other richly imagined characters included the Tram Conductor, the Gas Inspector, and the Spanish Senora, all of whose tribulations were acted out in meticulously prepared costumes. It is significant that few of Tich's songs ever gained widespread popular currency. J. B. Priestley, a devotee, noted that they were 'sung at a frantic speed, delivered to you as if they were so much routine rubbish, perhaps a minor item in a contract' (Priestley, 189–90). Tich's forte was his agile and acrobatic dancing and mime, his range of facial expression, and his droll, sometimes minimalist, patter: Priestley recalled the simple phrase 'comic business with chapeau' closing a piece which had involved endless failed attempts to pick up a hat.

Little Tich was a member of the charitable Grand Order of Water Rats and was King Rat in 1906. He was also a strong supporter of the 1907 variety strike. He painted in oils and watercolours, played the cello, and was a talented linguist. His personal life was complex. He married an English dancer, Laurie Brooks (d. 1901), in Illinois on 20 January 1889. Their son, Paul (1889–1948), later had a generally unsuccessful theatrical career which borrowed extensively from his father's act. The marriage ended in 1897 when Laurie departed, along with a considerable amount of her husband's savings and furniture. He lived with a Spanish dancer, Julia Récio, from about 1898, and eventually married her on 31 March 1904. Their relationship was far from happy, and Tich had a number of liaisons before meeting the actress Ivy Latimer (1892–1973) (born Winifred Emma Ivey), in 1916. They had a daughter, Mary, in 1918, who was the co-author of an informative biography of her father. The couple married three months after Julia's death in 1926.

Shortly after receiving a heavy blow to the head in an on-stage accident in November 1927, Little Tich suffered a stroke from which he never recovered. He died at his house, 93 Shirehall Park, Hendon, London, on 10 February 1928, and was buried in Marylebone cemetery. He was undoubtedly one of the most popular music-hall and variety acts of all time and influenced a number of British and European performers. Many commentators claimed that the visual trickery employed by many early film comedians owed much to his example and imagination.

DAVE RUSSELL

Sources M. Tich and R. Findlater, *Little Tich: giant of the music hall* (1979) · *The Era* (15 Feb 1928) · J. B. Priestley, *Particular pleasures* (1975), 189–90 · Little Tich [H. Relph] and S. Rohmer, *Little Tich* (1911) · m. cert. · d. cert.
Archives priv. coll., memorabilia, scrapbooks, etc. | FILM BFI NFTVA, performance footage 1909
Likenesses B. Crage, watercolour drawing, 1892, NPG · Steiner, photograph, Jerwood Library of the Performing Arts, London, Mander and Mitchenson Theatre Collection [see illus.] · photographs, repro. in Tich and Findlater, *Little Tich*

Relph, Josiah (1712–1743), poet, was born on 3 December 1712 at Churchtown, a small estate belonging to his father in Sebergham, Cumberland, where his father was the parish priest. He was educated by the Revd Mr Yates at his school in Appleby. In 1727, aged fifteen, he was registered as a student at Glasgow University, but he soon returned to be a teacher in the small grammar school of his native village. Taking holy orders, he also succeeded to the incumbency of the parish of Sebergham, a perpetual curacy with a small salary. He died at the early age of thirty, on 26 June 1743, at his father's house, Churchtown, and was buried at Sebergham.

Relph's poetical works were published posthumously in 1747 and 1798. A wider, national circulation of a few of his poems was achieved by their inclusion in Thomas West's *A Guide to the Lakes* (1784), which was read by Wordsworth, Southey, and early nineteenth-century poets. Similarly, in the twentieth century, his dialect poetry is included in anthologies of Lakeland verse, such as those of the poet Norman Nicholson (*The Lake District: an Anthology*, 1977). Relph's best verses are in the dialect of his native county; they are on pastoral subjects, with classical allusions.

ALBERT NICHOLSON, rev. JOHN WYATT

Sources J. Relph, *A miscellany of poems* (1747) · W. Hutchinson, *The history of the county of Cumberland*, 2 (1794), 415–19 · C. Innes, ed., *Munimenta alme Universitatis Glasguensis / Records of the University of Glasgow from its foundation till 1727*, 4 vols., Maitland Club, 72 (1854) · *GM*, 1st ser., 60 (1790), 1166 · *GM*, 1st ser., 61 (1791), 520
Likenesses monument, Sebergham church, Cumbria
Wealth at death collected antiquities: Relph, *Miscellany of poems*

Rémi [Rémy], **Philippe de** (1205x10–1265), poet, born in France, was the son of Pierre de Rémy, of the Terre Bernard in Remy (Compiègne). In 1237 Philippe was named *bailli* of Gâtinais for Robert d'Artois, a post he held until Robert's death at Mansourah in 1250. In 1239 he succeeded his father in the Terre Bernard, becoming liegeman, therefore, of the abbey of St Denis. After the death of Robert d'Artois, he continued to serve Robert's widow, Mahaut, acting as counsellor and arbitrator, and, no doubt, participating in the literary activities of her court at Arras. In an act of 1255 he is for the first time referred to as 'Phelippes de Remin, chevaliers, *sires de Biaumanoir*', the original *beau manoir* ('fair manor') having been expanded into a small fief by the acquisition of a chapel. Philippe de Rémi married twice. His first wife, Marie, is believed to have been the mother of Girard and Péronelle. His second wife, Alix de Bailleul, mentioned in documents dated 1262 and 1267, survived him. She was probably the mother of Philippe.

There has been much controversy concerning Philippe de Rémi's literary achievements, but most modern scholars reject Bordier's hypothesis (Bordier, 25–39) that all works written by Philippe de Rémi, sire de Beaumanoir, are attributable to his son, the jurist. After Gicquel's discovery that Rudolf von Ems's *Willehalm von Orlens* of 1242 derived from *La manekine*, it is now generally accepted that Philippe de Rémi the younger wrote the *Coutumes de Beauvaisis* (see below) and that between 1230 and 1240 Philippe de Rémi the elder, wrote the works contained in Paris, Bibliothèque Nationale, MS Fr. 1588: *La manekine* (fols. 2–56v), *Jehan et Blonde* (fols. 57–96), *Li salu d'amours* (fols. 97–103v), *La complainte d'amour* (fols. 103v–106v), *Le conte de fole larguece* (fols. 107–109v), *Fatrasie* (fols. 109v–110v), *Lai* (fols. 110v–112v), *Ave Maria* (fols. 112v–113v), *Fatrasie* (fols. 113v–114v), *Chanson d'amour* (fol. 114v) (incomplete).

La manekine ('The Handless Maiden') blends incest folklore, hagiographic *exempla*, and courtly topoi into an 8590-line octosyllabic romance. The widowed king of Hungary, wishing to avoid marriage to anyone who did not resemble his dead wife, planned to marry his daughter, Joïe. To avoid the incestuous nuptials Joïe cut off her left hand which was swallowed by a sturgeon in the river below her window. The heroine, imprisoned, sentenced to burn, set adrift at sea, and subjected to multiple vicissitudes, was eventually rewarded for her virtue and her fortitude. Her identity as Joïe rather than 'la manekine' was reaffirmed when the sturgeon miraculously reappeared in the church's baptismal water, and the pope was instructed to reattach the severed limb. Joïe's husband, the king of Scotland, inherited the territories of Joïe's father, who had now repented and abdicated. Joïe's sons and daughters became kings and queens of sundry lands, and all lived happily ever after. The underlying moral of these peripaties was enunciated at the end of the romance when Rémi urged his public never to succumb to despair, whatever their adversities, but to remember *La manekine*. If the story was perhaps memorable, its manner of composition was less so and, in the prologue of this first youthful work, Philippe de Rémi in fact apologizes for his lack of *clergie* and for never having rhymed before:

molt petit sai de clergie,
Ne onques mais rime ne fis.
(I have very little learning.
I have never rhymed before.)

(Rémi, *La manekine*, ll. 32–3)

Realism rather than the miraculous characterized Philippe de Rémi's second long romance, *Jehan et Blonde*, which narrated the heroic progression of the impoverished hero from *ecuyer* ('squire') of the earl of Oxford to penniless knight who married a rich heiress and who then became, after these inspiring triumphs over adversity, count of Dammartin and Oxford. The moral of this second romance also was made explicit: poor young men should leave home and seek their fortune, and, if not, 'should have their eyes put out' as punishment for their indolence. H.-L. Bordier and H. Suchier interpreted the author's detailed treatment of the geography and customs of England and Scotland in *La manekine* and *Jehan et Blonde*, and *Jehan et Blonde*'s mischievous imitation of aristocratic *franglais*, as proof of his having travelled extensively in those lands. They believed that the author was in England between 1261 and 1265. Subsequent research has separated *père* from *fils*, and has questioned this chronology. Several modern commentators believe that it is not necessary to posit a cross-channel visit to explain the author's textual references to England and Scotland.

Philippe de Rémi [de Rémy, de Beaumanoir] (1250–1296), administrator and jurist, who should not be confused with his father the poet, succeeded to the title of sire de Beaumanoir after the death of his brother Girard. He was *bailli* of Clermont (1279–82), seneschal of Poitou (1284–8) and of Saintonge (1287–8), went on a mission to Rome (1289), then was successively *bailli* of the Vermandois (1289–91), Touraine (1292), and Senlis (1292–6). He died on 7 January 1296, and was buried at Compiègne. This second Philippe de Rémi was responsible for the massive *Coutumes de Beauvaisis* (drafted *c*.1280–*c*.1283, and continually enlarged and emended), an invaluable early codification of French customary law. The ordered expositions and the pragmatic style of his prose, however lengthy its enumerations, specifications, and provisions, reflect his experience as an administrator and jurist in France's civil courts. As he observed, 'clerks have a fine way of talking in Latin, but laymen who must plead against them in civil court do not understand their words even when they say them in French' (Rémi, *Coutumes*, section 196). The *Coutumes de Beauvaisis* employed simple French vocabulary wherever possible, and provided meticulous definitions to clarify technicalities and ambiguities of the law. Philippe de Rémi's codification of legal practices involving treachery, feudal responsibility, property, and, indeed, guilt, crime, and punishment generally, remains a unique source of information about thirteenth-century French law.   JEANETTE BEER

Sources *Actes du Colloque Scientifique International pour la commémoration du VIIe centenaire des 'Coutumes et usages de Beauvaisis' de Philippe de Beaumanoir* (1983) · J. Dufournet, *Un roman à découvrir 'Jehan et Blonde' de Philippe de Rémy* (1991) · Philippe de Rémi, *Jehan et Blonde*, ed. S. Lécuyer (1984) · H. L. Bordier, *Philippe de Rémi, sire de Beaumanoir*, 2 vols. (Paris, 1869–73); repr. (Geneva, 1980) · M. Shepherd, *Tradition and re-creation in thirteenth-century romance: 'La manekine' and 'Jehan et Blonde' by Philippe de Rémi* (1990) · B. Gicquel, 'Le *Jehan et Blonde* de Philippe de Rémi peut-il être une source de *Willehalm von Orlens*?', *Romania*, 102 (1981), 63–72 · Philippe de Rémi, *Le roman de la manekine*, ed. and trans. B. N. Sargent-Baur (1999) · M.-M. Castellani, *Du conte populaire à l'exemplum: 'La manekine' de Philippe de Beaumanoir* (1988) · *Oeuvres poétiques de Philippe de Rémi, sire de Beaumanoir*, ed. H. Suchier, 2 vols. (1884–5) · *Coutumes de Beauvaisis*, ed. A. Salmon, 2 vols. (1899–1900) · A. Jeanroy, 'Les chansons de Philippe de Beaumanoir', *Romania*, 26 (1897), 517–36 · J.-L. Auduc and P. Bonnet-Labordière, 'Philippe de Beaumanoir: sa vie, son oeuvre et son temps', *Bulletin du GEMOB*, 18 (1983), 2–14 · Bibliothèque Nationale, Paris, MS Fr. 1588 · S. N. Rosenberg, 'The lyric poetry of Philippe de Remy', *Romance Philology*, 49/1 (1995), 13–24 · B. N. Sargent-Baur, 'Dating the romances of Philippe de Remi: between an improbable source and a dubious adaptation', *Romance Philology*, 50/3 (1997), 257–75 · F. R. P. Akehurst, *The coutumes of Beauvaisis* (1992)

Archives Bibliothèque Nationale, Paris, MS Fr. 1588

Rémi, Philippe de (1250–1296). *See under* Rémi, Philippe de (1205x10–1265).

Remigius (*d.* 1092), bishop of Lincoln, transferred his see from Dorchester-on-Thames to Lincoln, where he built a cathedral and did much to organize the diocese. Apparently related to the Aincurt family which claimed kinship with the Norman kings, he first appears in 1066 as a monk of Fécamp in Normandy; he was probably its almoner who contributed a ship and twenty knights to Duke William's host and was at the battle of Hastings. In 1067 his reward was nomination by King William to the first English diocese to fall vacant: Dorchester, which straddled England from the Humber to the Thames. The chroniclers Eadmer and William of Malmesbury implied that his succession was simoniacal because part of a bargain of service. More seriously still, Remigius was consecrated by Archbishop Stigand of Canterbury, a schismatic, to whom he made a profession of obedience. On 29 August 1070 he took part in Lanfranc's consecration as archbishop of Canterbury but, under suspension by legates of Pope Alexander II, in autumn 1071 he travelled to Rome with Lanfranc and Archbishop Thomas of York; at Lanfranc's petition he received a papal pardon for the irregularity of his accession. Thereafter, he made a profession of obedience to Lanfranc, saying that, when consecrated, he had been 'neither wholly familiar nor altogether unfamiliar with' Stigand's canonical position.

Remigius's energetic plans for Dorchester were cut short when, in 1072, a royal writ claiming the authority of Pope Alexander and his legates, as well as of Lanfranc and of the English bishops, ordered the transfer of the see to Lincoln and augmented its possessions there and elsewhere. Lincoln was chosen for its population and mercantile wealth, for its commanding situation above the River Witham, and for its good communications at the junction of the Fosse Way and Ermine Street. For the king it became a bulwark against Danish threats; for Remigius the transfer warded off persistent claims, revived in 1070 by Thomas of York, that Lindsey belonged to the diocese of York. Near William I's castle Remigius built his cathedral of St Mary, which was consecrated after his death. Part of the west end survives; it was built in a style reminiscent of St Étienne at Caen but was possibly fortified. In constitution the cathedral was secular, not monastic: by 1092 there were twelve dignitaries who included a dean, a precentor, probably a master of the schools, and seven archdeacons, whose archdeaconries roughly conformed to shire boundaries within the vast diocese. According to Gerald of Wales, Remigius established twenty-one prebends. Before 1086 Remigius restored and re-endowed the abbey of Eynsham in Oxfordshire; but in 1091 he transferred the monks to Stow in Lincolnshire, whence his successor, Robert Bloet, soon returned them to Eynsham. There are insufficient grounds for supposing that Remigius contemplated transferring the monks to his cathedral as a monastic chapter. He was in prolonged dispute with the monks of Ely about episcopal rights.

Remigius was the only English bishop in office, other than Lanfranc, with whom Pope Gregory VII (r. 1073–85) is known to have corresponded (Caspar, 1.34, 2 Dec 1073). Remigius consulted him about a clerk guilty of homicide, whom he sent to the pope with a letter in which he also sought papal absolution for himself and asked Gregory to command how best he might please him; Gregory replied that Remigius should temper justice to the clerk with mercy, while for himself he besought only Remigius's prayers, so that they might together share eternal joys. Little is known of Remigius's dealings with the Norman kings, although the chronicler Henry of Huntingdon mentioned that Remigius had been accused of treason against the king but that, after a servant had undergone an ordeal by hot iron, he was exculpated and restored to royal favour; he may have been suspected of complicity either in the revolt of the earls in 1075 with which Waltheof, earl of Huntingdon, was associated, or in the rebellion of 1088 against William Rufus. In 1086 Remigius was a Domesday commissioner for the Worcester circuit.

Remigius was described as being diminutive in stature but lively in mind. He died at Lincoln on 6 or (more probably) 8 May 1092 and was buried in his cathedral at an undetermined location. In the late 1190s, because Lincoln felt the need for a local saint, Gerald of Wales composed a hagiographical life of St Remigius. Veneration persisted into the thirteenth century, but Remigius was never canonized.　　　H. E. J. COWDREY

Sources D. M. Smith, ed., *Lincoln, 1067–1185*, English Episcopal Acta, 1 (1980) · *Fasti Angl., 1066–1300*, [Lincoln] · E. M. C. van Houts, 'The ship list of William the Conqueror', *Anglo-Norman Studies*, 10 (1987), 159–83 · T. A. M. Bishop and P. Chaplais, eds., *Facsimiles of English royal writs to AD 1100, presented to Vivian Hunter Galbraith* (1957), no. 14 · *Eadmeri Historia novorum in Anglia*, ed. M. Rule, Rolls Series, 81 (1884) · *Willelmi Malmesbiriensis monachi de gestis pontificum Anglorum libri quinque*, ed. N. E. S. A. Hamilton, Rolls Series, 52 (1870) · Henry, archdeacon of Huntingdon, *Historia Anglorum*, ed. D. E. Greenway, OMT (1996) · *Hugh the Chanter: the history of the church of York, 1066–1127*, ed. and trans. C. Johnson (1961); rev. edn, rev. M. Brett, C. N. L. Brooke, and M. Winterbottom, OMT (1990) · *Gir. Camb. opera*, 7.3–80 · D. Whitelock, M. Brett, and C. N. L. Brooke, eds., *Councils and synods with other documents relating to the English church, 871–1204*, 2 (1981), nos. 86, 90–94 · R. Gem, 'Lincoln Minster: ecclesia pulchra, ecclesia fortis', *Medieval art and architecture at Lincoln Cathedral*, ed. [T. A. Heslop and V. A. Sekules], British Archaeological Association Conference Transactions [1976], 8 (1986), 9–28 · D. Bates, *Bishop Remigius of Lincoln, 1067–1092* (1992) · *Das Register Gregors VII*, ed. E. Caspar, MGH Epistolae Selectae, 2/1 (Berlin, 1920)

Rempston, Sir Thomas (d. 1406), soldier and landowner, was the first of the family long established at Rempstone in Nottinghamshire to enjoy a career of any significance. Knighted in the early 1380s, he accompanied John of Gaunt on the Spanish expedition of 1386 and served as Henry Bolingbroke's standard-bearer on crusade against the Lithuanians in 1390–91. So committed was he to the Lancastrian cause that he followed Bolingbroke into exile and was one of the select band that landed with him at Ravenspur in July 1399. He was present at Richard II's abdication and witnessed the formal resignation of the crown. This loyal service brought a handsome reward. Before the end of the year he had been appointed to the constableship of the Tower of London, being responsible for the keeping of the deposed king, and to the stewardship of the royal household. (He lost this office to Thomas Percy, earl of Worcester, in February 1401, as part of the baronial and Commons' reaction to the new king's reliance on lesser men.) The high honour of elevation to the Order of the Garter followed in May 1400, and his military prowess received further recognition in April 1401 with his appointment as admiral of the fleet from the Thames westwards. One of the new king's most intimate associates, he frequently served on diplomatic missions, and accompanied his master's chosen queen, Joan of Navarre, from Brittany early in 1403. With such important national office went the augmentation of his local influence, through appointment to the stewardship of extensive duchy of Lancaster estates in the midlands and the constableship of Nottingham Castle. He was also granted, in November 1399, the custody of the midland estates of the dukedom of Norfolk, during the minority of the heir. In the first half of Henry IV's reign the major administrative offices of Rempston's native county were dominated by his associates, particularly the Leek kinsmen of his wife, Margaret. She, whom he married soon after the death of her first husband in September 1388, was the daughter of Sir Simon Leek of Cotham, with whom Rempston had served in the parliament of May 1382, and the widow of his fellow Lancastrian retainer, Sir Godfrey Foljambe of Hassop in Derbyshire.

Rempston's new-found position, and the wealth that went with it, enabled him to invest heavily in land. His major acquisition was the reversion of the valuable south Nottinghamshire manor of Bingham, which he acquired in singular circumstances. The Binghams, who had anciently held the manor, failed in the male line in the late 1380s, and their feoffees settled the reversion on Richard II. After his deposition, by a fine levied in November 1399, Richard, styled as late king of England, passed the reversion to Rempston and his heirs, saving the life interest of a widow of the Bingham family. This settlement was clearly the result of the new king's favour, but other valuable acquisitions were purchases, including manors in Northamptonshire, Lincolnshire, and Derbyshire. At the end of his life he enjoyed an annual landed income that was probably in excess of £200, together with royal annuities that amounted to about the same sum.

Rempston is said to have been captured by the French

late in 1405 or early in 1406 when accompanying the king across the Thames estuary, but it may be that this tradition is the product of a conflation, on the part of later chronicles, of his career with that of his son. There is, however, no doubt about the manner of his death. The story is told by a London coroner's jury: on 31 October 1406, while being rowed down the Thames towards the Tower, he commanded the boatmen on pain of death to pass under London Bridge, despite their insistence that the strength of the tide against them made the passage extremely hazardous. As they anticipated, the boat collided with one of the pillars of the bridge and capsized: their important passenger was drowned. This fatal episode is not the only indication that Rempston was a ruthless character. His will is that of a man who felt he had done much to threaten the salvation of his immortal soul. It is notable for the generosity of its charitable bequests, and the very considerable sum of 500 marks was set aside for restitution to those he had wronged. He was succeeded by his son, another Sir Thomas *Rempston, and was long survived by his widow, who, on her death in 1454, was buried beside him in Bingham church.   S. J. PAYLING

Sources S. J. Payling, *Political society in Lancastrian England* (1991) · HoP, *Commons, 1386–1421*, 4.189–92
Wealth at death wealthy; annual income of c.£400; disposed of goods worth at least 500 marks; total value of bequests in excess of 1000 marks, part of which was to be satisfied from his goods and part from the revenues of land in the hands of his feoffees: will, Borth. Inst., Arch. Reg. SA, fols. 334–5

Rempston, Sir Thomas (d. 1458), soldier and landowner, was one of the foremost commanders of the English armies in France during the last phase of the Hundred Years' War. The very generous dower and jointure settlement enjoyed by his long-lived mother, Margaret (d. 1454), may have been a factor in determining his choice of career, for although the well-rewarded service of his father, Sir Thomas *Rempston (d. 1406), to the house of Lancaster had very considerably extended the family's estates, centred on Nottinghamshire, the bulk of these gains remained in the hands of his mother. Partial compensation for this loss came through his marriage to Alice, daughter and heir apparent of Thomas Bekering and Isabel, sister and coheir of Sir John Loudham. But though on her father's death in 1425 Alice brought Rempston manors in four counties, it was not until the death of her uncle's widow in 1451 that she inherited her share of the Loudham lands in Nottinghamshire. With so great a part of his own and his wife's expectations frustrated by the survival of two long-lived widows, France was a more natural focus for his ambition than England.

Rempston was knighted on the eve of Henry V's coronation, and he later became a knight of the Garter. His first military experience came during the Agincourt campaign, and from then until the expulsion of the English from Normandy in 1450 he spent little time in England. Appointed captain of the castles of Bellencombre and Meulan in 1419, he took part in the triumphant entry into Paris in December 1420. His experience and ability

brought him further advancement when John of Lancaster, the duke of Bedford, assumed direction of affairs on Henry V's death in 1422. As one of the duke's chamberlains, he was present at the battle of Cravant on 31 July 1423 and commanded the English contingent in the Burgundian campaign that culminated in the capture of Guise in September 1424. During the expedition into Brittany led by William de la Pole, earl of Suffolk, early in 1426, he established himself at St James-de-Beuvron on the border between the duchy and Normandy. There he won a famous victory over a much larger force led by the duke of Brittany's brother, the constable of France. In May 1428 he served under John Talbot (later earl of Shrewsbury), in the retaking of Le Mans.

However, Rempston's fortunes, with those of the English, changed dramatically with the failure of the siege of Orléans, in which he participated at the head of a sizeable retinue, in May 1429. On 18 June of that year he was captured at the battle of Patay when, with other leading English commanders, he foolishly stood to fight a superior French force instead of making a less honourable but more sensible retreat to Paris. A heavy ransom of 18,000 écus was demanded by his captors and, not surprisingly, it proved very difficult to raise. According to his own testimony, he languished 'in harde and streyte prison welnere be the space of vij yere' (Payling, 61), eventually being released late in 1435. Only half the original ransom was paid, the rest being commuted in return for the release of one of the French hostages for payments due under the 1412 treaty of Buzançais; nevertheless, what was paid was more than sufficient to have a dire effect on Rempston's finances. Even though the crown granted him 1000 marks in partial compensation for his misfortune, the refusal of the exchequer officials to deliver the cash led him to petition the parliament of January 1437 complaining of 'the grete losse that he has borne in making chevishans of money' (Payling, 61) for the payment of the ransom.

Rempston's lengthy and expensive captivity did nothing to deter him from further military adventures in France. In November 1437, when the Burgundians were threatening an attack on Calais, he was created the town's lieutenant, but, unfortunately for him, this appointment seems to only have added to his financial difficulties. The wages of his retinue soon fell into serious arrears, and the circumstances of his removal from office suggest he may have been guilty of some serious financial irregularity to make good this deficiency, for, in February 1439, he was committed to prison in Windsor Castle. He was, however, free by the following June, when he enlisted to serve in Gascony under the command of John Holland, earl of Huntingdon, who soon afterwards appointed him to serve as seneschal there. When St Sever fell to the French in July 1442 Rempston was again captured. This period of detention is less well documented than the first but he was still in captivity in March 1445, when a wealthy London merchant, William Estfield, bequeathed £10 'ad financium suam si vixerit' (Payling, 61), and he was not definitely back in England until January 1449, when he attested a Nottinghamshire election. In the following year the final collapse of the English position in Normandy entailed the loss of his lordships of Gacé and Bellencombre.

The death of his very elderly mother—she had been a widow and mother as long before as 1388—in April 1454 finally enabled Rempston to enter the valuable estates from which she had kept him for so long. He had only a few years to enjoy this new-found wealth: he died on 15 October 1458, leaving three daughters as his coheirs. He was buried in the chancel of Bingham church in a fine alabaster tomb now unfortunately lost. His career is a stark illustration of the potential cost of military service in the English cause after the failure of the siege of Orléans.

S. J. PAYLING

Sources S. J. Payling, *Political society in Lancastrian England* (1991) · HoP, *Commons, 1386–1421*, 4.192–4 · A. H. Burne, *The Agincourt war* (1956)
Wealth at death very wealthy: Payling, *Political society*, 62

Rena, Andrea della. *See* Ammonius, Andreas (*bap.* 1476, *d.* 1517).

Renard, Simon (*c.*1513–1573), diplomat, was born at Vesoul in the Franche Comté. Nothing is known about his parentage, but the fact that he attended the University of Louvain, and became *docteur ès droits* there suggests either adequate means or access to patronage. At Louvain he became friendly with Antoine de Perrenot, who was the son of the imperial chancellor Nicolas de Perrenot and who later became bishop of Arras. After leaving the university Renard practised as a notary in Vesoul for several years, but the chancellor had been impressed by his son's friend, and had him appointed lieutenant of the *baillage* of Amont, a district of Franche Comté, in 1540. He continued to impress in these new duties, and in 1547 became *maître des requêtes ordinaires de l'hôtel* for the whole of Burgundy. In 1548 he was made a councillor of state, put in provisional charge of the government of Milan, and sent as a delegate to the Diet of Augsburg. In January 1549 he was created seigneur de Barmont and sent as imperial ambassador to France, a key posting that reflected the degree of trust in which he was held. He remained in Paris until the renewal of war in 1551, when he rejoined the imperial court.

Renard was already interested in English affairs, and well informed about them. He had been proposed for the London posting on his return from Paris, but managed to avoid the responsibility until June 1553 when he was sent as one of a three-man *mission d'honneur*, ostensibly to commiserate with Edward VI on his poor health, but really to watch the situation should the young king die. In spite of the emperor Charles V's strong attachment to Princess Mary, the ambassadors were strictly instructed not to intervene in the crisis that followed Edward's death on 6 July. However Renard, who quickly seized the initiative both from his colleagues and from the existing resident, Jehan Scheyfve, made his master's position clear without formally breaching his instructions. He later claimed that his skill was instrumental in dividing the English council and facilitating Mary's victory. Whether this was true or

Simon Renard (*c.*1513–1573), by unknown artist, 1553

not, Renard quickly established a confidential relationship with the new queen and became her most trusted adviser. This was an anomalous situation, which caused resentment in England and disquiet in Brussels, but the responsibility was Mary's rather than Renard's.

The other ambassadors were withdrawn in September 1553 and Renard embarked upon his most spectacular and successful negotiation, the promotion of a marriage between Mary and Philip of Spain, the emperor's son. Both Charles and Philip gave him a virtually free hand, and the special relationship that he had established with the queen guaranteed success. Mary committed herself in November, and then informed her council and the parliament of her decision. There was widespread resentment, not least among the members of the council, but Renard had some allies, notably Lord Paget, and the decision was undoubtedly the queen's. Renard was only one of the imperial envoys who negotiated the marriage treaty in January 1554, and its generous terms were decided by the emperor and the bishop of Arras, by now his leading minister. However Renard, who remained in London, claimed the credit for stiffening Mary's resolve when the proposed marriage provoked Sir Thomas Wyatt and others to rebel in February, and it was his spies who helped to uncover the plot.

This was the high watermark of Renard's influence. He failed to persuade Mary to execute either Edward Courtenay, earl of Devon, or Princess Elizabeth for their complicity in the rebellion, and was deliberately kept in the dark by Philip about his plans. He was also accused by

Jehan Dubois, the secretary of his predecessor Jehan Scheyfve, of accepting bribes from some of the lesser accused to secure their pardons. The charges were never proved and Perrenot, with whom Renard was still very much in favour, shrugged them off. The ambassador's involvement in internal quarrels between the councillors, however, offended everyone except the queen. With her he maintained his confidential relationship until the arrival of Philip and his marriage to Mary in July 1554. Thereafter Renard's task was really complete, and Philip, who neither liked nor trusted him (largely because he was not a Spaniard), managed to exclude him from confidential business. The emperor kept him at his post, refusing at least two requests for recall, until his own abdication, which commenced in August 1555. Renard left England, generously rewarded by the queen, in September 1555.

Throughout Renard's period in England his dispatches form one of the fullest and most immediate sources for political history, but they are marred as evidence, first by his own agenda of self-aggrandizement, and later by a powerful sense of grievance. Just as he claimed a key role in dividing the council at the time of Lady Jane Grey's attempted usurpation, so he claimed that Mary's resolution in speaking to the Londoners and standing firm against Wyatt were the result of her following his advice rather than the confused and cowardly promptings of her own councillors. There is no independent corroboration for either of these claims. During 1555 he consistently urged Charles to persuade Philip to restrain the persecuting zeal of the English clergy, but the emperor made no recorded attempt to intervene. This failure, and his estrangement from Philip, added a paranoid touch to some of his later dispatches from England.

Renard's career did not immediately suffer from Charles's retirement. In November 1555 he became a member of the council of Flanders, and in the following year he was sent again as ambassador to France. After the Franco-imperial truce broke down, he accompanied Philip on his second visit to England in March 1557. However, after Philip's return to Spain in 1559 he became involved in a bitter quarrel with his former friend and patron Perrenot, now Cardinal Granvelle. The latter used against Renard another accusation levelled by one of his own former servants, Étienne Quiclet, that he had betrayed the emperor's secrets during his mission in England. These charges also were never proved, but they could not be disproved. This time Renard lost favour and his career came to an end. He died in Madrid on 8 August 1573. Renard had married about 1551, and his wife, Jeanne Lullier (b. 1533), survived him by several years. She was with him in London from October 1553 to October 1554; they had six children, three sons and three daughters. All his sons died childless.   DAVID LOADES

Sources E. H. Harbison, *Rival ambassadors at the court of Queen Mary* (1940) • *CSP Spain, 1554; 1554–8*, 12–13 • L'Abbé de Vertot, *Ambassades de messieurs de Noailles en Angleterre*, ed. C. Villaret, 5 vols. (Paris, 1763) • L. Febvre, *Philippe II et la Franche-Comté* (Paris, 1912) • J. Loach, *Parliament and the crown in the reign of Mary Tudor* (1986) • D. Loades, *The reign of Mary Tudor: politics, government and religion in England, 1553–58*, 2nd edn (1991) • M. J. Rodríguez-Salgado, *The changing face of empire: Charles V, Philip II, and Habsburg authority, 1551–1559* (1988) • 'Vunière', *Étude historique sur Simon Renard, chevalier et sieur de Barmont* (Lithograph: Limoges, 1878) • M. Triplen, 'Simon Renard, ses ambassades, ses negociations, sa lutte avec le Cardinal de Granvelle', *Mémoires de la Société d'Émulation du Doubs*, 5th ser., 6 (1881), 109–375
Archives Granvelle Archive, Besançon, dispatches • Imperial collection, Brussels, dispatches • Imperial collection, Vienna, dispatches • Royal Archive, Simancas, dispatches
Likenesses portrait, 1553, Musée du Temps, Besançon [see illus.]

Renault, Mary. *See* Challans, (Eileen) Mary (1905–1983).

Rendall, Montague John (1862–1950), headmaster, the fourth son of the Revd Henry Rendall (1817–1897), and his wife, Ellen Harriette (1830–1905), daughter of Peter Davey and sister of Horace *Davey, Baron Davey, was born on 6 May 1862 at the rectory in Great Rollright, Oxfordshire, where his father was rector. There were in all nine sons of the marriage, united in devotion to their parents and exceptionally influenced by the Christian faith and moral values of their early upbringing. From his preparatory school, Elstree, he won the first entrance scholarship to Harrow in 1876. During his last year at Harrow he was head of the school and first in classics and mathematics. Proceeding to Trinity College, Cambridge, in 1881, he was a Bell scholar (1882) and foundation scholar (1883) and was placed in the first division of the first class in part one of the classical tripos in 1884 and in the first class of part two in 1885. During his last two years at Cambridge he represented the university at association football as goalkeeper. In 1887 he made the first of many journeys abroad to study the masterpieces of continental art, and laid the foundations of his lifelong enthusiasm for medieval and Renaissance Italian painting. In the same year he was appointed to the staff of Winchester College.

Rendall's immediate and striking success as a teacher, especially of classical composition, to 'senior div.', and his enthusiastic and inspiring participation in the life of the school, especially of college, strongly suggested him for appointment as second master in 1899. For the next twelve years his regime in college was both original and highly successful. To his innovative lectures on Italian art he now added holiday trips to central Italy with many of his pupils. 'Scholarship and art … he made a kind of glorious adventure', as one Winchester scholar later recalled (*The Wykehamist*, 18 Dec 1950, 210). In college Rendall upheld high moral standards but softened any severity by his natural sympathy for boys. He was the obvious choice to succeed H. M. Burge as headmaster of Winchester in 1911.

Rendall was not primarily an administrator; indeed, he could be engagingly disorganized in his official habits. Nor was he a reforming headmaster, unlike his predecessor or his successor (A. T. P. Williams). He made no formal changes at Winchester to reflect his own love of art and literature; for any boy particularly interested in such subjects the school remained a somewhat alien environment. He yet impressed all those who served under him as a great headmaster. His educational ideal was a nebulous mixture of traditional Christian values (uncomplicated by

Montague John Rendall (1862–1950), by Glyn Philpot, 1925

twenty-four years of residence in this Suffolk home he was an active and influential figure in the public life of the county.

From 1927 until the end of 1932 Rendall was a governor of the British Broadcasting Corporation. As such he devised in 1927 the BBC's motto 'Nation shall speak peace unto nation' (a felicitous adaptation of Micah 4: 3), which was set aside in the 1930s but rightfully restored after 1946. In 1931 he also composed the Latin inscription for the entrance hall of Broadcasting House. This time he used a direct biblical quotation, 'Whatsoever things are beautiful …' (Philippians, 4: 8), but around it he wove words which are a small reminder of his mastery of the classical languages.

Almost resolutely unmarried himself, Rendall delighted in the marriages and the children of his old pupils, and was a frequent and welcome visitor to their homes, as also to his friends in Winchester. It was only during his last year of life that his splendid vitality was first seen to be failing; he died suddenly in his sleep on 5 October 1950 at Oxenwood, California Lane, Bushey Heath, Hertfordshire, and was buried in the churchyard of Great Rollright, where were the graves also of his parents.

J. D'E. FIRTH, rev. R. D. H. CUSTANCE

Sources J. D'E. Firth, *Rendall of Winchester: the life and witness of a teacher* (1954) · private information (1959) · personal knowledge (1959) · *The Wykehamist* (7 Nov 1950) · *The Wykehamist* (18 Dec 1950) · Headmaster's reports, Winchester College, 1911–24, Winchester College archives · J. P. Sabben-Clare, *Winchester College* (1981); 2nd edn (1989) · BBC WAC [1988] · K. Clark, *Another part of the wood* (1974)
Archives BL, letters to E. H. Blakeney, Add. MS 63088 · Winchester College archives
Likenesses G. Philpot, oils, 1925, Winchester College [*see illus.*]
Wealth at death £5391 10s. 11d.: probate, 9 Dec 1950, *CGPLA Eng. & Wales*

any theology) and neo-medieval chivalry. This ideal he attempted to express in a triptych, still preserved at Winchester, which he commissioned in 1926 from E. Fortescue-Brickdale, showing a knight in armour with his page, their faces those of two of Rendall's last pupils. Whatever the idiosyncrasies of the painting, his vivid and dominating personality enabled him to communicate to the school his intense vision of the noblest aims in life. He also inspired considerable affection, not least on account of his distinctive mannerisms, especially of speech.

The First World War, through which Rendall carried the school with buoyant courage, made the profoundest impression upon him. To his conception and determination the war memorial cloister at Winchester is primarily due; its details also owe much to his sensitive taste. Furthermore, he became convinced that the public schools had a duty and a mission to make their best gifts available to a wider public in the post-war world. These views were reinforced by his visit in 1919 to some leading independent schools in the United States. He gladly accepted, therefore, after his resignation of the headmastership in 1924, an invitation from the Rhodes trustees to visit many of the principal schools in the self-governing dominions; and for the same reason he played a prominent part in the Overseas League, the League of the Empire, and the Royal Empire Society, and became chairman of the public schools empire tours committee. He received the honorary degree of LLD from the University of Toronto in 1921 and was appointed CMG in 1931.

In 1926 Rendall began what was a new life rather than a retirement. He acquired the freehold of Butley Priory, near Woodbridge, a medieval religious foundation of which only the gatehouse remained standing; this he restored with imagination and scholarly care—but with characteristic indifference to its icy draughts. During his

Rendel, Sir Alexander Meadows (1829–1918), civil engineer, was born at Plymouth, on 3 April 1829, the eldest son of James Meadows *Rendel (1799–1856) and Catherine Jane Harris (1797–1884). He was educated at Kings School, Canterbury, and Trinity College, Cambridge, where he read divinity and mathematics. It was originally intended he should enter the church but, following his younger brother Lewis's death in 1851 while engaged upon work at Holyhead, Rendel joined his father's civil engineering firm, based in London. The following year his father was elected president of the Institution of Civil Engineers. The younger Rendel subsequently spent some time on major works at Leith docks and the Portland harbour of refuge, gaining valuable experience. In 1853 he married Eliza Hobson (1835–1915), daughter of Captain William Hobson RN, the first governor-general of New Zealand; they had nine children. They lived initially at 44 Lancaster Gate, London, and later acquired a splendid country residence, Rickettswood, near Charlwood, Surrey.

On their father's death in 1856 it was decided that Rendel and his brother George Wightwick *Rendel should carry on the business, but due to their limited experience the Admiralty appointed new consulting engineers for the great works outstanding at Holyhead,

Portland, and in South Africa. In 1857, due to the intervention of their father's friend, W. G. Armstrong (1810–1900), and Robert Stephenson (1803–1859), Alexander was appointed to succeed his father as consulting engineer to the East Indian Railway. His position was further strengthened by his friendship with Sir Richard Strachey (1817–1908), formerly secretary to Lord Dalhousie, the Indian governor-general and later chairman of the East Indian Railway Company.

In spite of the upheaval caused by the Indian mutiny in 1857, Rendel visited India in order to become acquainted with local conditions, in particular to examine the problems of crossing the Hooghly River between Calcutta and the railway terminus at Howrah. During the next twenty years he was responsible for the construction of many thousands of miles of railway and for bridging many of the great Indian rivers, notably the Upper Son Bridge of Patna, the Alexandra Bridge over the Chenab, the Lansdowne Bridge over the Indus at Sukkur, the Hardinge Bridge over the Ganges, and the Empress Bridge over the Sutlej. He was knighted in 1887. Rendel was also consulting engineer to the strategically important Uganda Railway, reaching Lake Victoria ahead of the German competition. Other notable railway projects were the Egyptian Light Delta Railway and the Mexican Railway. Docks designed by him included those at Kirkcaldy, Llanelli, Milford, and Workington.

In 1894 Rendel's second son became a partner, but he died in 1898. He was succeeded by his youngest brother, who after two years joined his uncle George Wightwick Rendel at Armstrong's Pozzuoli works in Italy. During the same year Frederick Ewart Robertson, formerly chief engineer with the East Indian Railway, entered the partnership and the name of the firm changed to Sir Alexander M. Rendel & Co. Robertson died in 1912 and was replaced by Seymour Briscoe Tritton (1860–1937), a mechanical engineer who had been a key figure in the firm for many years. However, doubts existed in Rendel's mind as to whether a mechanical engineer would be acceptable to the East Indian Railway as his successor, and in 1913 Frederick Palmer (1862–1934), chief engineer to the Port of London Authority, joined the partnership. He had succeeded Robertson as the East Indian's chief engineer and was closely associated with the development of the Calcutta docks. The name of the firm was changed to Rendel, Palmer, and Tritton, and it was closely involved in development of the Port of London and especially construction of the King George V Dock, opened in 1921. Rendel died on 23 January 1918, at 51 Gordon Square, London. At the time of his death he was working on the design of the new Lower Sone Bridge.   MICHAEL R. LANE

Sources priv. coll., family archives · Rendel, Palmer, and Tritton archives, London · *PICE*, 211 (1920–21), 396–7 · M. Stocks, *My commonplace book* (1970) · H. Ricardo, *Memories and machines, the pattern of my life* (1968) · G. Huddleston, *History of the East Indian railway* (1906) · I. S. Greeves, *London docks, 1800–1980: a civil engineering history* (1980) · *The personal papers of Lord Rendel containing his unpublished conversations with Mr Gladstone … and other famous statesmen*, ed. F. E. Hamer (1931) · *The Times* (25 Jan 1918) · d. cert.
Archives NL Wales, Indian travel journals and notebooks

Wealth at death £96,015 18s. 8d.: probate, 25 April 1918, *CGPLA Eng. & Wales*

Rendel, George Wightwick (1833–1902), civil engineer, was born on 6 February 1833 at Plymouth, the third son of James Meadows *Rendel (1799–1856), civil engineer, and his wife, Catherine Jane, daughter of James Harris of Dartmouth. Named after the distinguished architect George Wightwick, his father's lifelong friend, he was educated at Harrow School, but ran away due to a perceived injustice in 1849. Initially he was sent to Grimsby, where his father was engaged in building the Great Grimsby Royal docks (1844–53). Later he joined his father and his elder brother Lewis Rendel (1830–1851) at Holyhead, where they were building the eastern breakwater and new Admiralty pier. He was then apprenticed to his father's great friend, Sir William Armstrong, at his Elswick works, Newcastle upon Tyne, living with Armstrong for a period of three years. He completed his training as an engineer in his father's London office, engaged upon the design of the superstructure of great bridges across the Ganges and Jumna at Allahabad being built for the East Indian Railway.

Following his father's death in 1856 it was decided the business could support only one son. The eldest, Alexander *Rendel (1829–1918), took over the business and, sponsored by Robert Stephenson, continued as consulting engineer to the East Indian Railway. George Rendel, Stuart *Rendel (1834–1913), and Hamilton Rendel (1843–1902) all joined Armstrong, who henceforth treated them like adopted sons.

In 1859 George Rendel became a partner and manager of Armstrong's Elswick Ordnance Company. Later, in 1860, Captain Andrew Noble was appointed joint manager with Rendel. In 1864 Rendel was a signatory to the deed merging the ordnance works and the engine works to form Sir W. G. Armstrong & Co. Stuart Rendel, a barrister and later a notable Liberal politician, whose daughter married Gladstone's son Henry Neville Gladstone, managed Armstrongs' London office until 1883. Hamilton Rendel disliked public life and remained quietly with the firm, dedicated to engineering. Probably his most notable achievement was the machinery for London's Tower Bridge.

During his twenty-four years at Elswick, George Rendel was engaged upon the development, construction, and armament of many warships, especially the design of their gun mountings. He was responsible for the hydraulic systems of mounting and working heavy guns first tried in 1877 in HMS *Thunderer*. Later his designs were used in the admiral class battleships, and soon his hydraulic systems were employed in all British, and some foreign, navy warships.

He was responsible for the introduction to the world of the cruiser type of warship, designed to act as scouts and to fight in fleet actions as secondary line-of-battle ships. In 1881 he designed, for the Chilean and Chinese governments, a series of 1350 ton unarmoured cruisers, protection being offered by light steel decks and coal bunkers. These were followed by the 3000 tons displacement, 18 knots cruiser *Esmeralda* for the Chilean navy. This was the first vessel to be fitted with a steel protective deck.

Rendel and Alfred Yarrow were pioneers in the use of boiler-room forced-draught fans and totally enclosed stokeholds in warships, which dramatically improved their speed and performance. Rendel was responsible also for the design of the twin-screw Staunch class gunboats, and up until 1885 about twenty similar vessels were built. In 1871 Rendel was appointed a member of the British government committee on warship design. He played a major role in the 1877 design of the 11,880 tons displacement HMS *Inflexible*, which carried four 80 ton, muzzle-loading, rifled guns and armour plates 24 inches thick.

Rendel was elected a member of the Institution of Civil Engineers in 1863, and in 1874 contributed a paper entitled 'Gun carriages and mechanical appliances for working of heavy ordnance' (*Minutes of Proceedings of the Institution of Civil Engineers*, vol. 38, 85), for which he was awarded a Watt medal and premium. In 1871 he was awarded the Spanish order of Carlos III, and in 1876 the order of the Cross of Italy. He was elected a member of the Institution of Naval Architects in 1879, and became a vice-president in 1882.

In 1882 Rendel was invited to become an extra-professional civil lord of the Admiralty, a new post allowing the admission of a 'practical man-of-science' to the board. Leaving Armstrongs, Rendel became greatly respected by his colleagues on the board, and it was with great regret that ill health forced his retirement in 1885. His doctors advised that he should live in a warmer climate.

His first wife, Harriet, daughter of Joseph Simpson, British vice-consul at Kronstadt, whom he had married on 13 December 1860 and with whom he had five sons, died in 1878. In 1880 he met and married Licinia Pinelli (1846/7–1934) in Rome, while serving on an Italian ministry of marine warship design committee. They had three sons and a daughter.

In 1885 Rendel rejoined Armstrong and, upon the latter's suggestion, agreed to establish a new ordnance factory at Pozzuoli, near Naples, in 1887, with Admiral Count Albini as joint managing director. Rendel's residence at Posilippo soon became a centre of social activity and it was here he offered hospitality to the ailing and recently widowed Empress Frederick of Germany. She was the eldest daughter of Queen Victoria, and the mother of Kaiser Wilhelm II of Germany. He established also very cordial relations with Lord Rosebery.

Rendel retired to Sandown, Isle of Wight, in 1900 and spent the last two years of his life confined to a wheelchair. He died at his home, Broadlands, in Sandown on 9 October 1902 and, although not a Roman Catholic, was buried in accordance with his wishes at the Kensal Green Roman Catholic cemetery in London. It is said that George Rendel sometimes lacked the commercial instinct of his brother Stuart, but he undoubtedly combined lucidity of intellect and general sagacity with the engineer's exceptional fertile faculty of invention.   MICHAEL R. LANE

Sources private information (1995) · Rendel, Palmer, and Tritton archives, London · M. R. Lane, *The Rendel connection: a dynasty of engineers* (1989) · NL Wales, Lord Stuart Rendel papers · H. Ricardo, *Memories of machines* (1968) · J. D. Scott, *Vickers: a history* (1962) · P. McKenzie, *W. G. Armstrong: a biography* (privately printed, c.1965) · M. Stocks, *My commonplace book* (1970) · *PICE*, 151 (1902–3), 421–2 · *Transactions of the Institution of Naval Architects*, 45 (1903), 332 · *Engineering* (17 Oct 1902) · 'The Armstrong Pozzuoli works', *The Engineer*, 103 (1907), 256–7, 266 · *Men and women of the time* (1899) · *CGPLA Eng. & Wales* (1902) · m. cert. (1860) · d. cert.

Archives NL Wales, papers | NL Wales, Lord Stuart Rendel MSS · Reference Library, Newcastle upon Tyne · Tyne and Wear Archive Service, Newcastle upon Tyne, letters to Andrew Noble · Tyne and Wear Archive Service, Newcastle upon Tyne, letters to Stuart Rendel

Likenesses J. S. Westmacott, plaster cast of medallion, 1853, NPG · A. Gilbert, bust; formerly priv. coll. · H. Hudson, oils, Royal Institution of Naval Architects, London

Wealth at death £370,328 12s. 2d.: probate, 28 Nov 1902, *CGPLA Eng. & Wales*

Rendel, Harry Stuart Goodhart- (1887–1959), architect, was born at Plas Dinam, Newnham, Cambridge, on 29 May 1887, the only child of Harry Chester Goodhart, a lecturer in classics in the university, and his wife, Rose Ellen, daughter of Stuart *Rendel, Baron Rendel (1834–1913). In 1890 his father became professor of humanity at Edinburgh but in 1895 he died, whereupon his widow moved south with her son and, as Goodhart-Rendel expressed it later, 'shut herself up with her grief and me'. The boy had by then shown marked signs of musical talent, inherited from the Goodharts, and a strong aptitude for construction, inherited no less evidently from the Rendels. In 1899 his mother took Chinthurst Hill, near Guildford, a house recently completed by Edwin Lutyens which, with its artful whimsicality, appealed to young Goodhart as 'a symbol of life and adventure'. After less than a year at Eton College he was brought home with a badly poisoned foot and did not return. At home he cultivated music and architecture in his own way, discovering James Gibbs and Nicholas Hawksmoor (a lasting loyalty) and reading, among modern authors, Reginald Blomfield and Henry Heathcote Statham. Lessons from Claude Hayes at this time were the only instruction in drawing he ever received. He next attended Mulgrave Castle, Yorkshire, a school conducted by the Revd Lord Normanby, in whose library he discovered the works of William Chambers and John Soane. In 1902 his mother married Wilbraham Cooper, who had been Goodhart's tutor at Chinthurst. She remained, however, an important factor in her son's development and his subsequent life. Between 1902 and 1905 he spent much time with her not only at Chinthurst but also at Cannes (where Lord Rendel had a villa) and at Valescure, where he became the Francophile Englishman which he always remained. In 1902, at Lord Rendel's instance, he added the name of Rendel to his own.

With unlimited leisure to develop his abilities in the spheres which fascinated him—music and architecture—Goodhart-Rendel composed music imitative of Delibes and Messager, and at the same time devoured the pages of *The Builder* and *Building News*. Of his two pursuits, music

Harry Stuart Goodhart-Rendel (1887–1959), by Augustus John, exh. RA 1940

designed for himself (1912–13) at 60 Tufton Street, London, and in the course of the next twenty years became one of the most prominent and interesting figures in the profession. This was due less to his buildings, which did not generally meet with a warm reception from either critics or the architectural profession at large, than to his vivid personality, keen wit, and willingness to devote himself assiduously to professional affairs. He was president of the Architectural Association in 1924–5, and of the Royal Institute of British Architects in 1937–9, when he aroused some controversy by his strictures on the quality of 'official' architecture. In 1933–6 he was Slade professor of fine art in Oxford. In 1936 he accepted the directorship of the Architectural Association School of Architecture, but failed to attract the loyalty of the young modernists of the 1930s and resigned in 1938.

In the Second World War Goodhart-Rendel rejoined his regiment, then returned to active practice with H. Lewis Curtis, his partner since 1930, and F. G. Broadbent, who joined the partnership in 1945. He was president of the Design and Industries' Association in 1948–50. In 1955 he was appointed CBE for services to architectural criticism. Goodhart-Rendel's architecture was deeply indebted to that of his nineteenth-century predecessors. Many of his contemporaries, influenced by the modern movement, viewed him as something of an anachronism: as David Watkin remarks, he 'seems to have been invented to serve as a warning to historians dedicated to the concept of the *Zeitgeist*' (Watkin, 167). But the architects whose work influenced him in early years—Charles Nicholson, A. Beresford Pite, and Halsey Ricardo—were all remarkable for their eclectic and original perspectives on architectural tradition, and Goodhart-Rendel's own work employed an imaginative stylistic variety which reflects his ability to respond inventively to the demands of each individual commission: it made him a singularly successful designer for restorations and extensions. Although opposed to modern functionalism—he did not disdain the use of ornament—he was equally repelled by the English taste for the picturesque and 'was alive to the dangers of sentimental revivals' (*The Times*, 22 June 1959). Committed to the expression of order and reason in his buildings, he owed much to French architectural theory, and his architecture can be said to be characterized by 'toughness combined with a certain poetry' (Watkin, 169). The sensitivity and resolute originality of his work have invited recent re-evaluations by intrigued architectural historians.

Goodhart-Rendel's most important buildings between the wars were Broad Oak End, Bramfield, Hertfordshire (for R. Abel Smith, 1921–3), influenced by Lutyens; additions to Tetton House, Taunton (for the Hon. Mervyn Herbert, 1924–6), somewhat in the style of Soane; Hay's Wharf, London (1929–31), a challenging attempt to interpret the modern movement through the idiom of the French architect Viollet-le-Duc; St Wilfrid's, Elm Grove, Brighton (1932–4), a modern church with a hard vigour recalling the style of William Butterfield; and Prince's House, North Street, Brighton (1934–5), which introduced

seemed the more promising and it was arranged for him to study with Donald Tovey. There was, however, a hopeless antagonism of tastes: Goodhart-Rendel's love of French light opera seemed to Tovey as incomprehensible as Tovey's obsession with Brahms did to Goodhart-Rendel.

In 1905 Goodhart-Rendel went up to Trinity College, Cambridge, where he graduated MusB in 1909. While at Cambridge he provided designs for a commercial building in Calcutta and from 1909 onwards began to engage in architectural practice, generally working in a Regency revival idiom. His most important work from this period was The Pantiles, Englefield Green, Surrey (1911), for Sophie Weisse and Donald Tovey, a house reflecting—partly through the clients' influence—the progressive German ideas of the period.

In 1913 Lord Rendel died, leaving his grandson a life interest in the bulk of his fortune, including the estate of Hatchlands in Surrey. In 1915 Goodhart-Rendel was commissioned in the special reserve, Grenadier Guards. This precipitated an emotional crisis with his mother and at the same time brought him into a world of rigorous discipline and action where he soon came to believe what he had already suspected, that soldiering was his true vocation. Although ill health prevented his reaching the front (though he spent four months in France in 1917), this was probably the happiest time of his life. A company drill primer of which he was the author was published about 1917.

Demobilized, much against his inclination, in 1919, he resumed architectural practice at the office he had a novel decorative treatment for a frame building. He also built several villas in the south of France.

After 1945 Goodhart-Rendel was concerned mainly with churches, in some of which he was able to develop the ideas originated at St Wilfrid's, Brighton. He built St John the Evangelist in St Leonards (1946–58), Our Lady of the Seven Sorrows, Liverpool (1951–4), and the Sacred Heart, Cobham, Surrey (1955–8); Holy Trinity, Dockhead, and Our Lady of the Rosary, Marylebone, were in progress at the time of his death. The household brigade war memorial cloister, Wellington barracks (1954–5), is a study in Roman Doric. A large and detailed project for the Benedictine abbey of Prinknash, in a modernized Romanesque which has been described as 'stripped Gothic', occupied his last years. Some foundations were laid and Goodhart-Rendel was eventually buried there. His designs, however, were not executed. Although he considered himself primarily an architect, Goodhart-Rendel made an outstanding contribution to the development of architectural history as one of the earliest commentators to examine and appreciate the architecture of the Victorian Gothic revival: in his introduction to the 1950 edition of *The Gothic Revival*, Kenneth Clark aptly described him as 'the father of us all' (p. 6). Goodhart-Rendel possessed the most complete and detailed knowledge of English nineteenth-century architecture of any of his contemporaries and his annotated card index of English churches (which can be consulted at the National Buildings Record and in the library of the Royal Institute of British Architects) remains a work of great value. On broader architectural issues he spoke with insight and charm but without making any significant contribution. Nearly all his writing was in the form of essays, intended to be read as lectures. Studies of a wide range of Victorian and Edwardian architects and their works appeared in the *RIBA Journal* and the *Architectural Review*; his essays also appeared in collections, under the titles *Vitruvian Nights* (1932) and *English Architecture since the Regency* (1953). Of essays or lectures published singly, the sensitive appreciation of *Nicholas Hawksmoor* (1924) is the most memorable.

In early life a devout Anglican, Goodhart-Rendel entered the Roman church in 1924 and his faith thereafter became the core and mainstay of his life. Music remained important to him in later life; he was a pianist with a somewhat brittle touch and a phenomenal capacity for accurate sight-reading. As a composer he was not lacking in invention, and two of his piano pieces were published. He was vice-president of the Royal Academy of Music from 1953 (honorary fellow, 1958) and a governor of Sadler's Wells from 1934.

In appearance Goodhart-Rendel was tall, dark, and spare, with a narrow head, prominent nose, and olive complexion. His *Times* obituarist recalled that 'some chronic disorder gave him a startlingly grey complexion, so that he looked at the point of collapse, which left the unwary unprepared for his vivacity and agility.' In society and in the committee room he was distinguished by a patrician elegance, by an ironic and slightly plaintive manner of speech, and by the sparkle of a wit issuing from a combination of logical thought and a profound love of paradox.

Goodhart-Rendel died, unmarried, at home at 114 Eaton Square, Westminster, on 21 June 1959.

JOHN SUMMERSON, rev. ROSEMARY MITCHELL

Sources *The Times* (22 June 1959) · A. Powers, *H. S. Goodhart-Rendel, 1887–1959* (1987) [exhibition catalogue, Architectural Association] · A. Powers, 'Goodhart-Rendel: the appropriateness of style', *Architectural Design*, 49 (1979), 44–51 · G. Stamp, 'Victorian survival or revival? The case of H. S. Goodhart-Rendel', *A. A. Files: Annals of the Architectural Association School of Architecture*, 15 (summer 1987), 60–66 · D. Watkin, *The rise of architectural history* (1980), 165–9 · b. cert. · d. cert. · private information (1971) · personal knowledge (1971)
Archives NL Wales, corresp. and papers · RIBA BAL, corresp. and papers · Surrey HC, personal and estate papers | RIBA BAL, corresp. with W. W. Begley · St Deiniol's Library, Hawarden, letters to Henry Gladstone
Likenesses D. Gordine, bronze bust, *c.*1938, RIBA · A. John, oils, exh. RA 1940, RIBA [*see illus.*]
Wealth at death £108,549 13*s.* 9*d.*: probate limited to settled land, 2 Nov 1959, *CGPLA Eng. & Wales* · £93,348 15*s.* 10*d.*: probate save and except settled land, 11 Nov 1959, *CGPLA Eng. & Wales*

Rendel, James Meadows (1799–1856), civil engineer, was born at Drewsteignton near Okehampton in Devon, the son of James Rendle, a county surveyor and farmer, and Jane Downy. He was the grandson of John Meadows FRS, a well-known architect. In 1811 he was sent to live with an uncle in Teignmouth to be instructed as a millwright while continuing his education at a local county school. Four years later he went to work for Thomas Telford, surveying roads in north Devon, and subsequently transferred to Telford's London office to learn the art of draughtsmanship. Working with William Provis he was given responsibility for the preparation of drawings for a proposed suspension bridge across the Mersey at Runcorn. His next assignment took him to Scotland where Telford was preparing plans for a ferry across the Tay.

In 1822 Rendel returned to Plymouth, practising upon his own account at 7 Boon's Place. Initially he carried out surveys on behalf of turnpike trusts in north Devon. He became interested in a scheme to build a suspension bridge across the Tamar at Saltash, gaining the support of the earl of Morley. The scheme was abandoned due to difficulties with the Treasury, but Lord Morley advocated Rendel's proposals be employed to provide a bridge across an estuary of the Plym within the harbour of Plymouth. An act of parliament was obtained, but considerable opposition persisted. With the continued support of his mentors, Lord Morley and Telford, Rendel revised his scheme, proposing a 500 feet long, five-span bridge with limestone piers and cast-iron arches. Work on the new bridge was commenced in August 1824 and completed in July 1827. With the exception of John Rennie's Southwark Bridge it was the largest cast iron structure then in use. The Institution of Civil Engineers awarded him its coveted Telford medal, establishing his reputation as being among the leaders of contemporary British bridge design. In 1826 Rendel designed and erected a drawbridge across a navigable branch of the Kingsbridge estuary at Bowcombe, the leaf being uniquely operated by hydraulic machinery. In

James Meadows Rendel (1799–1856), by Richard Cockle Lucas, 1852

1828 he married Catherine Jane Harris (1797–1884), daughter of James Harris, a decorator and picture framer of Dartmouth. His wife was a woman of great strength of character and charm and they had ten children.

Rendel's 1830 design for a suspension bridge over the Avon at Clifton was one of four short-listed, following the rejection of Telford's earlier design. The contest was eventually awarded to I. K. Brunel. Rendel completed other designs for suspension bridges across the Dart and Fowey, but these were not proceeded with. In 1831 he introduced a new system of crossing rapid tideways by means of steam-powered chain ferries. In 1832 he constructed a ferry crossing the Dart, and also others at Torpoint and Saltash across the Tamar in 1832–4, greatly facilitating the movement of traffic between Devon and Cornwall. This work gained him another Telford medal. Similar ferries were later established across the Itchen at Southampton and between Gosport and Portsmouth; he was consulted about proposed schemes for crossing the Severn at Newnham, and also the Hooghly at Calcutta, but these were never implemented due to the rapid development of railways.

During this period Rendel was engaged in the improvement and development of practically every river and harbour in south-west England. He became an acknowledged expert in hydraulic engineering. He designed a new harbour at Par, constructed upon the open beach and used extensively by the china clay industry. He carried out works in connection with Bude harbour and canal, and designed Brixham harbour and Torbay breakwater. Millbay docks at Plymouth were also planned by Rendel, although the work was executed by I. K. Brunel, chief engineer of the Great Western Railway. He supervised extensive work at Looe Pool enabling 300 ton vessels to reach Helston, and also directed improvements at Southampton, Poole, Portsmouth, and Gosport. In 1834, following Telford's death, Rendel was retained by the exchequer loan commission to supervise repairs to Samuel Brown's failed bridge at Montrose. He undertook important work

establishing new guidelines for deep trussing the framing of bridge roadways.

In 1838 Rendel moved to London, leaving his first pupil, Nathaniel Beardmore (1816–1872), in charge of the Plymouth office. A London base was essential when steering bills through parliament and he initially resided at 34 Great George Street, Westminster; later he acquired a mansion in Palace Gardens, Kensington. In 1840 he designed new docks at Hull and reported on Sir John Rennie's plans for embanking the Wash. Engaged by the Admiralty and other government departments in connection with rivers, harbours, docks, and other marine projects, he supervised the construction of new embankment walls on the Avon near Bristol, as well as improvements to a number of ports.

In 1843 Rendel became connected with Birkenhead docks, but difficulties with Liverpool corporation and other vested interests led to parliamentary investigation. In the same period he also undertook important major work at Grimsby, Leith, and Inverness in Scotland, Garston on the Mersey, and for the East and West India docks in London. At Grimsby not only were the dock walls of novel construction, necessitating a 1½ mile long cofferdam, but he introduced a comprehensive system of hydraulically operated machinery, upon which he worked closely with his friend W. G. Armstrong. All the lock gates, sluices, and cranes were hydraulically powered and the 300 feet high hydraulic tower became a feature of the local landscape.

In 1845 Rendel was entrusted with major harbour works at Holyhead and Portland. Both involved depositing hugh quantities of stone for the breakwaters from railway wagons running on overhead timber staging. In the 1850s he undertook a growing volume of overseas work. He designed a harbour of refuge at Table Bay in South Africa and improvements to the Kowie River, Cape of Good Hope. In 1854 he reported upon a scheme for a suspension bridge across the Hooghly at Calcutta, and in due course was appointed engineer-in-chief of the East Indian Railway. In addition to projects in Sardinia, Brazil, and Prussia, Rendel designed the docks for the port of Genoa and the new naval arsenal at La Spezia in Italy. In Spain he designed a railway between Madrid and Oviedo and undertook improvements to the River Ebro.

Rendel was elected president of the Institution of Civil Engineers for 1852–3 and was a council member of the Royal Society. He died at 10 Palace Gardens, Kensington, on 21 November 1856, after twenty-five days of intermittent fever; and was buried at Kensal Green cemetery on 27 November. One of his last acts was to design an ornamental suspension bridge crossing the lake in St James's Park, London, although he died before the work was completed.

Four of Rendel's five sons became prominent in engineering. Sir Alexander *Rendel (1829–1918) became senior partner in his father's business. George Wightwick *Rendel (1833–1902) was a leading naval architect. Stuart *Rendel (later Baron Rendel) became W. G. Armstrong's

London manager, Liberal MP for Montgomeryshire from 1880 to 1894, and the confidant of W. E. Gladstone. Rendel's youngest son, Hamilton, was also employed by Armstrong, and was notably involved in the design and installation of the hydraulic machinery operating the bascules of London's Tower Bridge.   MICHAEL R. LANE

Sources family archives, priv. coll. · Rendel, Palmer, and Tritton archives, London · *PICE*, 16 (1856–7), 133–42 · *PRS*, 8 (1856–7), 279–83 · *The Times* (22 Nov 1856) · *GM*, 3rd ser., 2 (1857), 114–15 · M. Stocks, *My commonplace book* (1970) · H. Ricardo, *Memories and machines, the pattern of my life* (1968) · G. Huddleston, *History of the East Indian railway* (1906) · P. McKenzie, *Sir W. G. Armstrong, a biography* (1983) · I. S. Greeves, *London docks, 1800–1980: a civil engineering history* (1980) · *The personal papers of Lord Rendel containing his unpublished conversations with Mr Gladstone … and other famous statesmen*, ed. F. E. Hamer (1931) · d. cert.

Archives Inst. CE · NL Wales, papers

Likenesses R. C. Lucas, wax medallion, 1852, NPG [*see illus.*] · C. H. Mabey, sculpture, 1855 (after E. W. Wyon), priv. coll. · E. W. Wyon, marble bust; destroyed during WWI

Rendel, Stuart, Baron Rendel (1834–1913), industrialist, politician, and philanthropist, was born in Plymouth on 2 July 1834, the fourth son in the family of four sons and three daughters of James Meadows *Rendel (1799–1856), civil engineer, and his wife, Catherine Jane, daughter of James Harris of Plymouth. Two of his brothers were George W. *Rendel and Alexander *Rendel. He was educated at Eton College and at Oriel College, Oxford, where he graduated in 1856 with a fourth-class degree in classical studies.

He married in 1857 Ellen Sophy, daughter of William Egerton Hubbard of Horsham, Sussex, brother of J. G. Hubbard (later first Baron Addington). In 1861 he was called to the bar (Inner Temple), but before long, through his father's association with the inventor and arms manufacturer W. G. Armstrong, became the London manager of Armstrong's engineering firm, a post which involved business relations with foreign governments. At the time of his death he was vice-chairman of the company.

In 1880 Rendel was elected Liberal MP for Montgomeryshire, and he held the seat for the next fourteen years. His victory there was remarkable, because he had no Welsh connections, and the seat had long been monopolized by the powerful local family of Wynn, a member of which he defeated. He spent £12,000 on the election (to his opponent's £20,000), and thereafter devoted, on his own admission, 20 per cent of his annual expenditure to politics. He soon became known as 'the member for Wales', and was accepted as leader of the Welsh Liberal group in parliament. Under his guidance it began to act coherently, with the result that the Liberal leadership was compelled to pay more attention to Welsh causes.

This process was assisted by Rendel's close friendship with W. E. Gladstone, which became closer still when one of his four daughters, Maude Ernestine, married one of Gladstone's sons, Henry Neville *Gladstone. Sharing Gladstone's Anglican high-churchmanship, he was well qualified for the difficult task of reconciling him to the policy

Stuart Rendel, Baron Rendel (1834–1913), by unknown photographer, 1910

of Welsh disestablishment. A leading opponent of disestablishment, Bishop A. G. Edwards of St Asaph, later wrote of Rendel that he 'read the Welsh character in its strength and weakness', and so achieved unity and discipline within the Welsh party.

Rendel gave much encouragement to the rising generation of authentically Welsh politicians, among whom T. E. Ellis and, above all, David Lloyd George were outstanding. Lloyd George thought very highly of him and used to quote with approval his dictum that in politics 'there are no friendships at the top' (too often attributed to Lloyd George himself). In addition, Rendel took a special interest in Welsh education and culture. He deserves most of the credit for the Welsh Intermediate Education Act of 1889; and from 1895 to the end of his life he was president of the University College at Aberystwyth, to which he regularly contributed £1000 a year. In 1898 he presented the fine site overlooking Aberystwyth on which the National Library of Wales was built.

In Gladstone's later years, Rendel frequently, together with George Armitstead, acted as host, confidant, and companion, regularly playing backgammon with Gladstone in the evening. On Gladstone's resignation in 1894 Rendel was created Baron Rendel of Hatchlands in Byfleet, Surrey. Hatchlands was his English estate, but he also had villas in Italy and the south of France, and in London a succession of grand houses, at the last of which, 10 Palace Green, Kensington Palace Gardens, he died on 4 June 1913, his wife having died in 1912. The peerage became extinct.

Rendel was a shy man, but confident in his views and, to

those who knew him well, a shrewd, witty, and charming companion. Had he been more self-assertive he might have risen higher in politics, but in his chosen field he made good use of his wealth and talents.

JOHN GRIGG, rev.

Sources The personal papers of Lord Rendel containing his unpublished conversations with Mr Gladstone … and other famous statesmen, ed. F. E. Hamer (1931) · K. O. Morgan, Wales in British politics, 1868–1922 (1963) · A. E. Edwards, Memories (1927) · Gladstone, Diaries · H. C. G. Matthew, Gladstone, 1875–1898 (1995) · CGPLA Eng. & Wales (1913) **Archives** Herefs. RO, family corresp.; appointment diaries · NL Wales, corresp.; diary of conversations with W. E. Gladstone · NL Wales, corresp. and papers · NL Wales, diaries · St Deiniol's Library, Hawarden, estate corresp. and papers · Tyne and Wear Archives Service, Newcastle upon Tyne, corresp. and papers | BL, letters to Lord Gladstone, Add. MSS 56053–56067 · Bodl. Oxf., letters to John Morley · NL Wales, letters to T. C. Edwards · NL Wales, letters to A. C. Humphreys-Owen · NL Wales, letters to Josiah Jones · NL Wales, letters to his wife · NL Wales, letters to A. J. Williams · St Deiniol's Library, Hawarden, corresp. with H. N. Gladstone · Tyne and Wear Archive Service, Newcastle upon Tyne, letters to Sir Andrew Noble **Likenesses** photograph, 1910, Hult. Arch. [see illus.] · C. Thompson, oils, NL Wales **Wealth at death** £652,328 11s. 8d.: probate, 31 July 1913, CGPLA Eng. & Wales

Render, Wilhelm (*fl.* 1790–1809), grammarian and translator, was a native of Germany, probably brought up in or near Heppenheim, south of Darmstadt. Nothing is known of his parents. He attended Giessen University, and was ordained to the Lutheran ministry. He was also a member of the freemasons. For a time he acted as 'travelling guardian to the son of a distinguished personage'. He then travelled in western Germany with 'several English gentlemen' (Render, *Tour*, 1.viii), one of whom may have been Francis Rawdon Hastings, afterwards marquess of Hastings, to whom, as earl of Moira, he dedicated his *Tour through Germany*.

Render went to England about 1790 and settled in London. He taught German and other languages in several distinguished families. Later in the 1790s he also became teacher of German at Cambridge, Oxford, and Edinburgh. In 1798 he published an English version of Kotzebue's play *Count Benyowsky* (2nd edn also 1798). In 1800 he published translations of Friedrich von Schiller—*The Robbers, Don Carlos, Maria Stuart*, and *The Armenian*. In 1801 appeared *The Sorrows of Werter*: Render's was the first English translation made direct from the original German. In the preface he speaks of 'his friend the baron Goethe', whom he may have met at Frankfurt. He also claims that at Giessen University a fellow student of his was a brother of the original of Charlotte, and that he was a friend of Werther himself. In the appendix to his translation he recounts at length a conversation he had at Frankfurt am Main with Werther, a few days before the latter's suicide.

Render's *Tour through Germany, Particularly Along the Banks of the Rhine, Mayne …* (2 vols., 1801) provides a detailed account of the geography, history, and people of many principalities and towns. A vocabulary of familiar phrases in German and English is appended. Among Render's educational manuals was the successful *A Concise Practical*

Grammar of the German Tongue (1799); a fifth edition, corrected and enlarged, appeared in 1817. As a token of his appreciation of this work, Alexander I of Russia ordered Vorontsov, his ambassador in England, to present Render with a ring and an autograph letter. Render also published a *Pocket Dictionary* (2nd edn, 1809) in English and German, and other manuals of instruction in German.

G. LE G. NORGATE, rev. JOHN D. HAIGH

Sources W. Render, advertisement, in J. W. von Goethe, The sorrows of Werter, trans. W. Render (1801) · W. Render, appendix, in J. W. von Goethe, The sorrows of Werter, trans. W. Render (1801), 61–75 · W. Render, A tour through Germany, 2 vols. (1801) · [J. Watkins and F. Shoberl], A biographical dictionary of the living authors of Great Britain and Ireland (1816) · Watt, Bibl. Brit. · Allibone, Dict. · D. E. Baker, Biographia dramatica, or, A companion to the playhouse, rev. I. Reed, new edn, rev. S. Jones, 3 vols. in 4 (1812) **Likenesses** Mackenzie, engraving (after Dighton), repro. in W. Render, Recreations (1806)

Rendle, Alfred Barton (1865–1938), botanist, was born in Lewisham, London, on 19 January 1865, the eldest child and only son of John Samuel Rendle, secretary to a London building society, and his wife, Jane Wilson, daughter of John Barton, of Rotherfield, Sussex. Both parents were of Cornish stock.

After local schooling, a series of scholarships which Rendle then won paid almost entirely for his subsequent education. One to St Olave's Grammar School, Southwark, London, was followed by another to St John's College, Cambridge, where he took the natural sciences tripos and graduated in 1887 with first-class honours in botany. Though C. C. Babington was then still professor of botany, he was in his eighties and occupied solely in taxonomic research. This left teaching in the inspiring hands of the then reader, S. H. Vines, an arch-protagonist of the so-called 'new botany', in which taxonomy was abhorred and aspects such as physiology and morphology were emphasized instead. Rendle was captivated by these and planned to pursue postgraduate research on them. Almost at once, however, Vines moved to Oxford on appointment to the chair there, leaving Rendle to choose between a very uncertain future at Cambridge and the security of a post elsewhere. He opted for the latter, but the post he took must have seemed tantamount to deserting to the enemy: an assistantship in the department of botany of the British Museum (Natural History), which promised a lifetime career identifying and describing dried specimens in the museum's collections. However, with the conscientiousness that was always his outstanding characteristic he set about proving he was better fitted for his chosen life's work than his doubters probably suspected.

His future secure, Rendle married Alice Maud, daughter of James Armstrong, in 1892. Two sons (one of whom died in infancy) and a daughter followed, and it was doubtless the extra financial burden that led him to take up evening teaching. Experience as a junior demonstrator at Cambridge had given him a taste for this, and on being appointed head of the botany department at the Birkbeck Institute in 1894 he was to lecture there, with long-remembered lucidity, two or three times a week for the next twelve years. This led to his producing his best-known work, *The Classification of Flowering Plants*, for many years the standard textbook on that subject; the first volume appeared in 1904 but the second, due to heavy competing calls on his time, was not published until 1925.

After only four years of marriage Rendle's wife died, leaving him with a very young family. A second marriage in 1898, however, to Florence (*d.* 1929), daughter of George Brown, was to bring him five further sons (one of whom, again, died in infancy) and another daughter. By a happy chance his marriage occurred just as his first major and important works were about to be published. Ever careful and thorough, he did not hurry into print and it was only after eleven years at the museum that his section on the monocotyledons and gymnosperms (his areas of general responsibility as a staff member) appeared in the department's long-outstanding *Catalogue of the African Plants Collected by Dr. Friedrich Welwitsch in 1853–61* (1899). The previous year his monograph of the genus *Najas* had gained him the degree of DSc from London University, and its subsequent publication in the *Transactions of the Linnean Society* led to his being invited to write the account of the Najadaceae for Adolf Engler's titanic enterprise, *Das Pflanzenreich* (1901). Rendle did particular service to plant taxonomy through his concern with the thorny topic of nomenclature. At the International Botanical Congress held at Vienna in 1905 he was appointed one of the four editors to revise the international code of botanical nomenclature, the publication of which proved of historic importance. He continued to act as an expert in this connection until 1935.

In 1906, Rendle was appointed to the keepership of botany at the museum, a post with significant administrative duties that compelled deferment of much of his scientific work. However, by this time he had won recognition as one of the country's foremost taxonomists, a standing crowned by election as a fellow of the Royal Society in 1909. Further honours began piling up a few years later: botanical secretary of the Linnean Society and president of section K (botany) of the British Association for the Advancement of Science in 1916, the Victoria medal of honour of the Royal Horticultural Society in 1917, and president of the Linnean Society in 1923, in which last capacity he saw that body through a difficult period in its history. Meanwhile his meticulousness and quiet dependability made him an obvious choice as an editor. At first he succumbed in that direction only to the extent of overseeing the botanical contributions to the justly famed eleventh edition of the *Encyclopaedia Britannica* (1911), but, on the death of his colleague, James Britten, in 1924, he finally yielded to a renewed plea to take on the task of editing the *Journal of Botany*, the monthly which was the outlet for much of the museum's botanical work. He remained editor until just before his death.

Rendle was also increasingly in demand in the world of amateur science as a president in that quarter too. In 1919 he was president of the Quekett Microscopical Club, and in 1927 and 1931 respectively of the south of England's two federations of local societies. From 1911 until his death he also acted as president of the South London Botanical

Institute. In this sphere he particularly lent his voice, and the weight of his official position, to furthering the protection of the country's native wild plants, a cause which began to gather considerable momentum in the inter-war years.

Rendle received the Royal Horticultural Society's Veitch memorial medal in 1929, the year that he was widowed for the second time. He retired from the museum in 1930, a year which coincided with a term on the council of the Royal Society. Rendle spent his retirement in a return to his long-deferred scientific work, regularly returning to the department of botany in a long-distance race to complete the comprehensive and deeply scholarly *Flora of Jamaica*, upon which, with his friend and collaborator William Fawcett (*d.* 1926), he had embarked many years earlier. Planned in seven volumes, five had appeared by the time of Rendle's death.

Although Rendle's health had given rise to anxiety, he accompanied a delegation from the British Association to the silver jubilee of the Indian Science Association. But a chill which he contracted on the outward voyage awakened an earlier internal complaint and compelled his premature return from Bombay. Three days after getting back, he died, on 11 January 1938, at Tallard, The Mount, Leatherhead, Surrey, which he had had built as his retirement home. *Rendlia*, a genus of African grasses, serves as his living memorial.   D. E. ALLEN

Sources D. Prain, *Obits. FRS*, 2 (1936–8), 511–17 · J. Ramsbottom, *Proceedings of the Linnean Society of London*, 150th session (1937–8), 327–33 · T. A. Sprague, *Nature*, 141 (1938), 400–01 · W. T. Stearn, *The Natural History Museum at South Kensington: a history of the British Museum (Natural History), 1753–1980* (1981), 299–303 · I. H. Burkill, *Journal of Botany, British and Foreign*, 76 (1938), 65–8 · CGPLA Eng. & Wales (1938)

Archives NHM, corresp. and papers | U. Glas., Archives and Business Record Centre, letters to F. O. Bower

Likenesses W. Stoneman, photograph, 1931, NPG · Sport & General Press Agency, photograph, 1937, repro. in Ramsbottom, *Proceedings of the Linnean Society of London* · photograph, repro. in D. Prain, *Obits. FRS*, 2 (1939) · photograph, Linn. Soc.; repro. in A. T. Gage and W. T. Stearn, *A bicentenary history of the Linnean Society of London* (1988), 100 · photograph, repro. in *Journal of Botany*, 63 (1925), frontispiece · photograph, repro. in Burkill, *Journal of Botany*, facing p. 65

Wealth at death £9971 17s. 8d.: probate, 21 March 1938, *CGPLA Eng. & Wales*

Rendle, John (1758–1815), classical scholar, was born on 20 November 1758 at Tiverton, Devon, the son of Humfrey Rendle, a hop merchant. He was educated at Blundell's School, Tiverton, where he showed a marked proficiency in classics. After winning a scholarship Rendle entered Sidney Sussex College, Cambridge, on 9 April 1777. He graduated BA in 1781, MA in 1784, was appointed lecturer in mathematics, and shortly afterwards made a fellow of the college. After several years' residence he accepted a curacy at Ashbrittle, Somerset, and was afterwards presented with the living of Widdecombe in the Moor, Devon. While there he married; further details of his wife are unknown.

After leaving Cambridge, Rendle devoted his time to the study of classical and early Christian history, and was highly regarded by other scholars. In 1814 he published *The History of Tiberius, that Incomparable Monarch*, a learned work vindicating the character of the emperor Tiberius.

> The main object of the work is to prove that Tiberius was a convert to Christianity, and a great patron of it; and, moreover, that the unfavourable character given of Tiberius by Suetonius, Tacitus, and Dion was occasioned entirely by the partiality which the emperor displayed towards the Christians. (*GM*, 85/2, 87)

He further attempted to prove that Strabo was the father of Sejanus. Rendle was the author of several papers on biblical criticism in the *Orthodox Churchman's Magazine*. He died while visiting friends near Tiverton on 22 May 1815.

J. R. MacDONALD, *rev.* PHILIP CARTER

Sources Venn, *Alum. Cant.* • *GM*, 1st ser., 85/2 (1815), 86–7 • [J. Watkins and F. Shoberl], *A biographical dictionary of the living authors of Great Britain and Ireland* (1816)

Rendle, William (1811–1893), antiquary, son of William Rendle of Polperro, near Fowey, Cornwall, and his wife, Mary, daughter of William and Dorothy Johns of Polperro, was born in the village of Millbrook, Cornwall, on 18 February 1811. He was brought up as a Wesleyan Methodist. At the age of about four he was taken by his father to Southwark in a trader from Fowey, taking six weeks on the passage. He was educated at the British and Foreign Training School in Borough Road, Southwark, and afterwards became the school's honorary surgeon. When he decided upon a medical career, he was sent to Guy's Hospital, and to the medical school of Edward Grainger in Webb Street, Maze Pond, Southwark.

Rendle passed as licentiate of the Society of Apothecaries in 1832 and became MRCS in 1838; in 1873 he was elected FRCS. For nearly fifty years he practised in Southwark, and from 1856 to 1859 he was medical officer of health for the parish of St George the Martyr, Southwark. With a concern for sanitary reform, he was vice-president of the Association of Medical Officers of Health in 1859. A speech he gave on *London Vestries and their Sanitary Work* was published in 1865.

Rendle was also deeply interested in the borough of Southwark, and described his research into its history as 'in the midst of a busy practice … a labour of love' (*Old Southwark and its People*, 1878, vi). Late in life he began to publish his work in two major books and several articles. His two books, *Old Southwark and its People* (1878) and *The Inns of Old Southwark and their Associations* (1888), contain much original information. The latter volume was a joint labour with Philip Norman FSA, who revised and rearranged the manuscript materials, drew the more important illustrations, and superintended the publication. In the same period Rendle wrote articles on Southwark theatres, hospitals, and celebrated residents in the *Antiquarian Magazine* (1882–5), *The Genealogist* (1884–7), *Notes and Queries* (1886), and *The Antiquary* (1888–91).

Rendle lived at Treverbyn, Forest Hill, Lewisham, and died there on 18 September 1893. He had four sons and one daughter, but his wife's name is unknown.

W. P. COURTNEY, *rev.* BERNARD NURSE

Sources G. C. Boase, *Collectanea Cornubiensia: a collection of biographical and topographical notes relating to the county of Cornwall* (1890) • Boase & Courtney, *Bibl. Corn.*, vol. 3 • *N&Q*, 7th ser., 2 (1886), 201–2 • *CGPLA Eng. & Wales* (1893)

Archives U. Edin., corresp. with James Halliwell-Phillipps

Wealth at death £8274 10s. 3d.: probate, 4 Dec 1893, *CGPLA Eng. & Wales*

Reneger, Robert (*d.* 1558?), sea captain, is of unknown parentage. When he is first mentioned, in 1540, he is described as a merchant of Southampton, so it is probable that he was born in that town some time before 1520. According to Hakluyt he was an established trader to Brazil by 1540, and his younger brother John became a burgess in 1542. His active career probably began in the mid-1530s. By 1543 he was a man of some substance, owning at least one ship, and he was one of that tough but dwindling band of English traders who made their main living trading into Spain. At that time Englishmen were favourite targets for the Spanish Inquisition, and although the government of Charles V never sanctioned any campaign of harassment, local officials frequently conducted such campaigns on their own initiative. In April 1543 Reneger was granted letters of marque to 'go upon' the French, and bound in a recognizance of 500 marks not to attack the subjects of the emperor, Henry VIII's ally. Shortly after he was licensed to export 100 quarters of wheat and 100 quarters of barley, and was subsequently informed against in Star Chamber for having exceeded his quotas.

In March 1545, when Charles had ceased to be Henry's ally, Reneger carried out the operation upon which his subsequent fame was to rest. Alleging that a quantity of his goods and at least one ship had been unlawfully seized in Spain, and accompanied by his brother John, he led a small fleet of four ships and one pinnace which intercepted the inward bound *San Salvador* off Cape St Vincent, and relieved her of a cargo valued at over 29,000 ducats (about £10,000). This was no casual depredation. Reneger knew exactly what he was doing. He immediately returned to England, reported his action to the council, and deposited at least some of his loot in the Tower of London. The incident provoked a protracted international wrangle, complicated by the fact that some of the *San Salvador*'s valuables had not been declared to the Spanish authorities. The case was eventually settled in January 1548, when an undisclosed proportion of the plunder was returned.

Meanwhile Reneger's fortune was made. In July and August 1545 he commanded three of his own ships in the fleet that was sent out against the French, and numerous other English freebooters followed his example on the coast of Spain. Anglo-Spanish relations, which had been poor for some time, deteriorated still further, but Henry VIII seems to have approved of his bold seaman's initiative. In May 1548 Robert Reneger, gentleman, was appointed controller of the port of Southampton. He had already been senior steward in 1543, and sheriff in 1546. In December 1548 he purchased the manor of Boughton from the earl of Southampton. In 1549 he is listed as living beside

Godshouse in the town, and in 1550 Robert Reneger, esquire, was named on the commission for the collection of the subsidy. At the same time the lay subsidy roll shows him to have been one of the richest men in the town. In 1553 he was a commissioner for church goods. He appears to have died in 1558 when an inquisition post mortem was taken, and the manor of Boughton was settled on his son John.

The date of Reneger's marriage is not known. His wife appears to have been called Agnes, but nothing else is known about her. John died in December 1569, and Robert's brother (also named John) in 1571. The elder John Reneger seems to have maintained a career as a part-time pirate, and was frequently in trouble with the law, but Robert contented himself with the one major coup which made his fortune and was still being talked about in the days of Drake. DAVID LOADES

Sources LP Henry VIII, vols. 18, 20–21 · APC, 1542–50 · CPR, 1547–53, 1, 5 · G. Connell-Smith, *Forerunners of Drake* (1954) · R. C. Anderson, ed., *Letters of the fifteenth and sixteenth centuries from the archives of Southampton* (1921) · A. B. Wallis Chapman, ed., *The Black Book of Southampton*, 3 vols., Southampton RS, 13–14, 17 (1912–15) · A. L. Merson, ed., *The third book of remembrance of Southampton, 1514–1602* (1955) · R. Hakluyt, *The principall navigations, voiages and discoveries of the English nation*, 3 vols. in 2 (1589); facs. edn, Hakluyt Society, extra ser., 39 (1965), xi
Wealth at death one of the richest men in Southampton

Renehan, Laurence (1797–1857), college head, second son of Laurence Renehan and his wife, Catherine *née* Borden, was born at Longford Pass in the parish of Gurtnahoe, co. Tipperary. After education at Freshford and Kilkenny he entered St Patrick's College, Maynooth, in September 1819 and was ordained priest there in October 1825. The following year he was appointed to the chair of sacred scripture at Maynooth, a post which he held until June 1834, when he reluctantly accepted appointment as vice-president. On 25 June 1845, following the resignation of Michael Montague, Renehan became president of Maynooth, retaining the position until his death there on 27 July 1857; he was buried at Maynooth.

Renehan's presidency coincided with a transformation of the college. Shortly before his appointment the government increased its grant from £9000 to £23,360 per annum, and Renehan commissioned A. W. Pugin to design a new quadrangle, completed in 1850. During his term of office the college underwent a royal commission of inquiry (1853) and came into conflict with Paul Cullen, archbishop of Dublin. Cullen had been appointed to that see in preference to Renehan in 1852 and successfully opposed the latter's candidature for the see of Cashel in 1857.

Renehan was a dedicated antiquary and collector of Irish manuscripts relating to church history. He spent many of his vacations copying such material in continental libraries, was a friend of John O'Donovan, and a vice-president of the Celtic Society, founded in 1845. His manuscripts, bequeathed to Maynooth, were partly edited after his death by the Revd Daniel MacCarthy under the title *Collections of Irish Church History* (2 vols., 1861, 1874). The rest of his library was sold by auction, some of it being acquired by the British Museum. Renehan was the author also of some works on sacred music. G. MARTIN MURPHY

Sources P. J. Corish, *Maynooth College, 1795–1995* (1995) · J. Newman, *Maynooth and Victorian Ireland* (1983) · E. Larkin, *The making of the Roman Catholic church in Ireland, 1850–1860* (1980) · *Freeman's Journal* [Dublin] (28 July 1857) · L. F. Renehan, *Collections on Irish church history*, ed. D. McCarthy, 1 (1861) · *GM*, 3rd ser., 2 (1857), 383
Archives St Patrick's College, Maynooth, historical papers and transcripts, collection of MSS
Likenesses oils, St Patrick's College, Maynooth

Renham, Henry de (*fl. c.*1290), schoolman, is known only for having transcribed and glossed the *corpus vetustius* of Aristotle's works on natural philosophy, in a volume presented to Rochester Cathedral priory by Prior John de Renham, who died in 1294. It is possible that both Henry and John derived their name from Rainham in Kent, a few miles east of Rochester, but this must remain uncertain. The book in question is now BL, Royal MS 12 G.ii; in a note on folio 1v, written in another hand, it is described as one 'which Henry de Renham wrote and heard in the schools of Oxford, and corrected and glossed as he listened'. Each page was carefully prepared for glossing, with blank columns laid out on either side of a central block of text, and plenty of space left both above and below the text, and also between the lines of script. Such meticulous preparation, along with the elaborate flourishes, in red and blue ink, which decorate some of the initial letters, suggest that Renham was also a talented draughtsman. His notes contain frequent citations of the commentaries of Averroes and a few references to the early thirteenth-century writings of Alfred of Shareshill, as well as showing a wide knowledge of the writings of Aristotle. He was probably not the Henry de Reynham who was a fellow of Merton College, Oxford, by 1321, but he may have been identical with the Rainham to whom a commentary, *In Physica Aristotelis*, with the incipit 'Quid sit abstrahere, dicendum', is ascribed by John Bale. CHARLES H. LOHR

Sources BL, Royal MS, 12 G.ii · Bale, *Index* · G. F. Warner and J. P. Gilson, *Catalogue of Western manuscripts in the old Royal and King's collections*, 2 (1921), 68–9 · G. Lacombe and others, eds., *Aristoteles latinus: codices*, 3 vols. (Rome, 1939–61), vol. 1, p. 387, no. 317 · J. C. Russell, 'Dictionary of writers of thirteenth century England', *BIHR*, special suppl., 3 (1936) [whole issue], esp. 47 · Emden, *Oxf.*, 3.1565 · C. H. Lohr, 'Medieval Latin Aristotle commentaries', *Traditio*, 24 (1968), 149–295, esp. 227–8
Archives BL, Royal MS 12 G.ii

Renialme, Ascanius de [known as Ascanius] (*c.*1550–1600), bookseller, was born a Venetian subject. The date of his birth and his parents' names are uncertain. However, since the London bookseller George Bishop described him in 1578 as 'an honest young man who knows his business well' (Plantin-Moretus MS 77, fol. 715) he may be assumed to have been about in his mid-twenties the time of his arrival in London in that year. In 1559 the Antwerp printer and bookseller Christophe Plantin sold books to a Charles de Regnialme, described as 'frere de Bomberghen', brother-in-law to Cornelis van Bomberghen, Plantin's partner (Plantin-Moretus MS 35, fol. 81). This man may have been the father of Ascanius, who was described in his letters of denization of 12 December 1578 as being a Venetian subject.

The first mention of Ascanius's involvement in the book trade is of a payment made to him at the Frankfurt fair in 1576 by Jan Moerentorf (Plantin's son-in-law). Ascanius (as he was generally known) came to England in 1578 'to see the country' with his wife, Elizabeth (Page, 75). He was granted the status of denizen in that year, and the probability is that he came with Plantin's encouragement and assistance. Elizabeth de Renialme was a native of Middelburg, had been married previously, and brought with her a son, James Rimé or Rimius. Her sister Lucy was the wife of another alien bookseller, François Bouvier, who, as a Huguenot refugee, worked in London from about 1577.

Ascanius was admitted as a brother of the Stationers' Company of London on 27 June 1580, and lived in the parish of St Ann Blackfriars until his death in 1600. He rapidly became one of the most substantial importers of books from continental Europe. He regularly visited the Frankfurt fair, and appears prominently as a customer in Plantin's ledgers, though the closure of the port of Antwerp by the Dutch meant that he had to route his cargoes through Middelburg, Flushing, and other ports to London. The Renialmes were protestants, and Ascanius belonged to the French church in London (though his wife seems to have been a member of the Dutch church). He was 'tolerated' by Archbishop Whitgift in 1586 to bring in a few copies of Roman Catholic books for the use of the learned (Strype, The Life and Acts of ... John Whitgift, 1718, 289). Contemporary correspondence—such as that of Abraham Ortelius—shows that Ascanius was regarded as the best source in London for foreign books. It has been said that he printed a catalogue, but extant correspondence with the Cambridge bookseller Hugh Burwell makes it clear that he sent out manuscript catalogues of his wares.

The English version of Christoph Wirsung's Praxis medicinae universalis was entered to Ascanius and George Bishop in the Stationers' register in 1597. Ascanius may have hoped to go on to printing, for the Stationers' Company petitioned the lord mayor and aldermen of the city of London that he might be admitted to the freedom of the city, and thus be made free of the company (and therefore entitled to print). This petition was supported by the privy council on 1 February 1598. Elizabeth, dowager Lady Russell, wrote to Sir Robert Cecil on behalf of 'My neighbour Ascanius the bookseller whom your father [Lord Burleigh] loves exceedingly well' (Salisbury MSS, 8.257). The petition was evidently without effect. Burleigh's affection for Ascanius may well have stemmed not only from his usefulness as a bookseller and binder, but from his role as an international courier and gatherer of intelligence.

Ascanius died in the parish of St Ann Blackfriars shortly after drawing up his will on 29 February 1600. He was buried at St Ann Blackfriars on 5 March. He was survived by his wife. His will shows clearly the eminence Ascanius had attained in the immigrant community and in the London book trade. There were bequests to his brother Jonas and

his sister Groll, and to the French and Dutch churches in London, and to the Bouvier family. He left plate worth £5 to the Stationers' Company, and gold rings to several friends, including George Bishop, and Bonham and John Norton—both already active in the import trade. Ascanius's bequest of £100 to his stepson, James Rimé, was conditional upon his following the trade of bookseller. He also left a conditional gift to his servant Adrian Maroie. Both James Rimé and Adrian Marius (Maroie or Marie) followed Ascanius into the trade of importing books, and were among its most prominent practitioners in the first decade of the seventeenth century.

R. JULIAN ROBERTS

Sources H. G. Aldis and others, A dictionary of printers and booksellers in England, Scotland and Ireland, and of foreign printers of English books, 1557–1640, ed. R. B. McKerrow (1910) · Plantin-Moretus Archive, Antwerp · exchequer records, PRO, E 190 [port-books] · C. Clair, 'Christopher Plantin's trade-connexions with England and Scotland', The Library, 5th ser., 14 (1959), 28–45 · will, PRO, PROB 11/95, sig. 16 · letters from Bouvier and Ascanius to Burwell, Gon. & Caius Cam., K.10.16 · Arber, Regs. Stationers, 2.682 · CPR, 1578–80 no. 908 [letters of denization] · E. J. Worman, Alien members of the book-trade during the Tudor period (1906), 53–4 · R. E. G. Kirk and E. F. Kirk, eds., Returns of aliens dwelling in the city and suburbs of London, from the reign of Henry VIII to that of James I, Huguenot Society of London, 10/2–3 (1902–7) · APC, 1597–8, 290 · W. Page, ed., Letters of denization and acts of naturalization for aliens in England, 1509–1603, Huguenot Society of London, 8 (1893) · I. Scouloudi, ed., Return of strangers ... 1593, Huguenot Society, 57 (1985), 168 · Calendar of the manuscripts of the most hon. the marquis of Salisbury, 8, HMC, 9 (1899), 257 · parish register, St Ann Blackfriars, London [burial], 5 March 1600

Wealth at death   see will, PRO, PROB 11/95, sig. 16

Renison, Sir Patrick Muir (1911–1965), colonial governor, was born on 24 March 1911 at 14 Cavendish Drive, Tranmere, Birkenhead, Cheshire, the son of William John Henry Renison, a marine insurance company assistant secretary, and his wife, Violet Douglas, née Willoughby. He was educated at Uppingham School and Corpus Christi College, Cambridge. A large, rather rubicund individual, he excelled on the rugby field but was a mediocre student.

On graduation in 1932 Renison entered the colonial service, and was seconded for his first three years to the Colonial Office in Downing Street as an assistant principal. In 1935 he went to Ceylon, and in the following year he married Eleanor Hope Gibb. They had one daughter. Renison served in Ceylon until 1944, before returning for another four years to the Colonial Office. This was an unusual career, as few overseas administrators ever served in the Colonial Office in London, which was staffed by members of the home civil service, selected by competitive examination. Ceylon, moreover, with the possible exception of Palestine and Malta, was the most 'advanced' of Britain's colonial territories, already well on the way to dominion status with the full panoply of responsible government and semi-ministerial powers.

In 1948 Renison became colonial secretary in Trinidad and Tobago. Four years later he was appointed governor of

British Honduras, a quiet backwater, and then in 1955 governor of British Guiana, a much more demanding position. In the previous year his predecessor had suspended the left-wing government of Cheggi Jegan, reinstituting direct rule. Renison proved adept at sidestepping political land-mines and made some progress in improving relations between the East Asian and African communities, while reducing suspected communist influence and gradually restoring some power to the elected members of the legislative council. He was made CMG in 1950 and KCMG in 1955.

Renison's success in British Guiana led to his appointment as governor of Kenya in 1959, during the closing days of the Mau Mau emergency, despite the fact that he had never served in Africa. Iain Macleod, the new secretary of state, was determined to transfer power to African moderates as quickly as possible, and decided that there were political advantages in appointing a non-Africanist to this demanding post. He was soon disappointed, as Renison was quickly 'captured' by the Kenya administration and, unlike Macleod, persuaded of the need to proceed slowly. Although Renison remained governor until the end of 1962, policy was increasingly determined in London, driven by Whitehall's response to the demands of African nationalists, and the governor and his advisers in the Kenya administration found themselves increasingly bypassed. The first Lancaster House conference in January 1960 saw the acceptance of African primacy and rapid progress to independence under an African government. This was confirmed by the 1961 election, which centred on Jomo Kenyatta's release from detention, and by the second and third Lancaster House conferences in 1962 and 1963 which devised the new independence constitution.

Renison is best remembered in Kenya for dismissing Kenyatta, still in detention, in a radio broadcast after the election of 1961 as 'the leader to darkness and death' (Kyle, 114). The governor appears to have accepted uncritically the results of an investigation into the origins of Mau Mau, which defended Kenyatta's detention as the organizer of Mau Mau. This report, by F. C. Corfield, was belatedly published in 1960 as part of an attempt by elements in the Kenyan administration to prevent Kenyatta's political rehabilitation. In the end, however, Renison had to back down, first accepting Kenyatta's release, then his election to the legislative council, and finally his appointment as joint leader of government business with Ronald Ngala, leader of the Kenya African Democratic Union (KADU). Renison managed to survive both these changes and the appointment of Reginald Maudling as secretary of state in 1961, but he soon fell out with Maudling's acerbic successor, Duncan Sandys. Many observers had not expected the governor to return from the second Lancaster House conference in spring 1962, which led to the formation of a coalition government between Kenyatta's Kenya African National Union (KANU) and Ngala's KADU, but he had soldiered on, attempting to establish a relationship of trust with the Kikuyu leader.

The marriage of Renison's daughter to the son of the Kenya National Farmers' Union leader, Lord Delamere, did little to reassure Africans, all too vividly highlighting the ties between Government House and the colony's settler aristocracy. Sandys, moreover, quickly became dissatisfied with the pace of progress and disliked Renison's low-profile manner. The new secretary of state wanted a more political, pro-nationalist, and publicity-seeking proconsul to preside over the final stages of the transfer of power. In November 1962 he recalled Renison to London for consultations and then abruptly sacked him to make way for the politically adept Malcolm MacDonald.

Renison was made a GCMG but, at the age of fifty-one, his career was effectively over. A former rugby player, he served briefly in 1963 as adviser to Lord Hailsham on sport and physical recreation before becoming the following year joint vice-chairman of the British Red Cross Society. He was also a governor of Queen Elizabeth House at Oxford. Shattered by his dismissal, Renison's health rapidly deteriorated, and he died in a London hospital, Beaumont House, Beaumont Street, Marylebone, on 11 November 1965.   D. W. Throup

Sources WWW · *The Times* (12 Nov 1965) · D. W. Throup, *Economic and social origins of Mau Mau* (1987) · b. cert. · d. cert. · *CGPLA Eng. & Wales* (1966) · M. Blundell, *So rough a wind* (1964) · K. Kyle, *The politics of the independence of Kenya* (1999)
Archives Bodl. RH, corresp. and papers
Wealth at death £28,945: probate, 28 Jan 1966, *CGPLA Eng. & Wales*

Rennell. For this title name *see* Rodd, James Rennell, first Baron Rennell (1858–1941); Rodd, Francis James Rennell, second Baron Rennell (1895–1978).

Rennell, James (1742–1830), cartographer, was born on 3 December 1742 at Upcot, near Chudleigh, Devon, the younger child and only son of Captain John Rennell (*d.* 1747), of the Royal Artillery, and his wife, Anne, *née* Clarke (*d.* 1776). His father's death in action in the Netherlands forced the sale of the family property, and, when his mother married again, his stepfather found himself unable to provide for both James and his elder sister, Sarah. At the age of ten Rennell was taken in by Gilbert Burrington, vicar of Chudleigh, who brought him up with his own family. Burrington's family connections provided Rennell with an introduction to Captain Hyde Parker, and his naval career began in 1756 as captain's servant under Parker in the frigate *Brilliant*. After experiencing action against the French at St Cast in 1758, Rennell followed Parker to the East India station, rejoining him as midshipman in the *Grafton* at Madras in 1760. After action off Pondicherry, and visits to Trincomalee, Bombay, and Rodriguez Island, Parker recommended Rennell to pursue a career in East India Company service, and in April 1762 allowed him to join Alexander Dalrymple (1737–1808) as 'assistant Draughtsman or Surveyor' in the company's ship *London* on an exploratory voyage to the Sulu islands and China. In Madras again in 1763 Rennell left the navy after the peace with France, to take command of the *Union*, a 'country' vessel in the coastal trade. After the

James Rennell (1742–1830), by George Dance, 1794

start a general survey of Bengal, which he began by cross-country traverses westward through Bengal by quadrant and chain. Rennell was severely injured in northern Bengal in an ambush by tribesmen in February 1766, with a sabre cut through his right shoulder bone, a wound almost a foot long in his back cutting through several ribs, and a hand's breadth of muscle lost from his left arm. Only after several months' convalescence in Dacca could he continue surveys, before returning to Calcutta late in 1766 to prepare maps for Clive's departure. In Clive's last month in Bengal (January 1767) Rennell was appointed surveyor-general, and directed 'to form one general chart from those already made'. Four subordinate surveyors were appointed, and Rennell was thereafter more occupied with map compilation at his chosen headquarters at Dacca than with surveys in the field, though he was liable to be ordered to Calcutta, often at short notice, 'to form a Map of the Provinces, which is to go home by the first ship'.

Though from 1770 Rennell was turning his mind towards financing retirement to England on health grounds, he married, in Calcutta on 15 October 1772, Jane Thackeray (1739–1810), daughter of Dr Thomas Thackeray, headmaster of Harrow School. Jane and her sister Henrietta had accompanied their brother William Makepeace Thackeray, grandfather of the novelist, on his posting from Calcutta to Dacca in 1771. Now settled in Dacca, Rennell continued compiling and improving his maps of Bengal for a manuscript atlas sent to London in 1774. Increasing concern for his health made him apply for retirement on a pension payable in England, proposing, as a *douceur* to the court of directors of the East India Company, a scheme of geographical research and publication of sea charts and maps from documents deposited in East India House. With a pension promised of £600 a year, Rennell and his wife left Calcutta in *Earl of Ashburnham* in April 1777, delaying at St Helena for the birth of their second daughter, Jane, in October. Their first daughter, also Jane, died days after her first birthday in 1774. Two sons were born subsequently, Thomas in 1779, who died unmarried in 1846, and William in 1781, who died without issue at Fatehgarh in 1819. Jane married, in 1809, Admiral Sir Tremayne Rodd, and died in 1863.

In England in 1778 Rennell proposed a new set of maps of Bengal to replace the inadequate small-scale maps published by the East India Company from his earlier surveys, and, with the guarantee of a bulk order from the company, had plates engraved to publish *A Bengal Atlas* first in 1780. The bulk consignment, *en route* for India for the use of company officials, was captured at sea by French and Spanish ships, and Rennell produced a new enlarged *Atlas*, with river maps and tables of distances, in 1781. *A Bengal Atlas* remained the standard administrative map of Bengal for almost fifty years, the river maps being pirated in Calcutta in 1825, and the last recorded London reprint appearing in 1829 or 1830. Rennell's general map of India, first published as 'Hindoostan' in 1782 and dedicated to Sir Joseph Banks, was, on the other hand, a compilation of the surveys, reports, and sketches of others, and subject to

Union sank at Madras in October, Rennell moved to command the *Neptune*, first superintending troop disembarkation for the siege of Madura, and then sailing in February 1764 under owner's orders to Calcutta.

Through introductions to Colonel John Carnac, commander-in-chief, Rennell obtained from the governor, Henry Vansittart, in April 1764 a Bengal army commission as practitioner engineer in the construction of the new citadel at Fort William, and the particular commission, in place of the recently deceased Hugh Cameron, as 'a Surveyor of the New Lands [in Bengal]'. Rennell's credentials as a surveyor and cartographer up to that time were varied. From Burrington's papers have come maps and plans, including some claimed to be, or to be copied from, maps made by Rennell as a boy in Chudleigh, and at St Cast in *Brilliant*. Rennell wrote that he had had instruction from a draughtsman in the ship *America* on his voyage to India, taking a quadrant and *East India pilot* atlas with him. He produced a plan of Rodriguez' anchorage after the visit of *Grafton* in 1761, and though his maps and plans from the *London* voyage were destroyed in the loss of *Union* in 1763, engravings from copies were included by Dalrymple in his chart publication in the 1780s, along with engravings from his coastal surveys in *Neptune* off southern India. For strategic reasons Vansittart first ordered Rennell to survey the Ganges for the shortest perennially navigable creek leading south to the Hooghly River and Calcutta and avoiding the Murshidabad shallows. These river surveys, and the survey of the Brahmaputra to Goalpara, occupied him to October 1765. Clive, on his return to India in that month, gave Rennell new instructions, to constant revision by him. Two versions of the map were published, in 1782 and 1788, the first with two editions of *Memoir of a Map of Hindoostan*, the second with three editions to 1793 of a new *Memoir* and various appendices. Rennell was elected a fellow of the Royal Society in 1781, and awarded the society's Copley medal in 1791.

Rennell's geographical interests widened as his service in India became more remote in time. From his home at 29 Suffolk Street, Portland Place, he entered into the geographical and geo-political discussions of Sir Joseph Banks's circle, and in the dinners of the select Royal Society Club. His research and publication turned increasingly towards the mechanics and interpretation of the geography of classical and biblical times, with papers such as 'On the rate of travelling as performed by camels and its application, as a scale, for the purpose of geography' (1791), 'Concerning the place where Julius Caesar landed in Britain' (1826), and 'On the voyage, and place of shipwreck, of St Paul' (1825), in *Archaeologia* and *Philosophical Transactions*. These supplemented *The Geographical System of Herodotus* (1800), *Observations on the Topography of the Plain of Troy* (1814), and *Illustrations* (*Chiefly Geographical*) *of the History of the Expedition of Cyrus* (1816), and, with them, underpinned his two-volume *A Treatise on the Comparative Geography of Western Asia*, which his daughter, Jane, Lady Rodd, published posthumously in 1831.

Rennell applied this same capacity, to analyse exhaustively the geographical component of apparently unpromising texts and documents, to the developing study of the interior of Africa. Though not a founder member of the African Association in 1788, he was elected an honorary member in 1792, after he had compiled a map of the northern part of Africa, with a memoir on its construction, in 1790. As well as editorial work for the association, producing maps of Mungo Park's routes from his journals, he published papers arguing (incorrectly) that the Niger ended in a lake without reaching the sea, and that a mountain chain stretched along the whole length of Guinea. The wrongness of these conclusions, and the confidence with which they could later be contradicted, validated rather than negated the analytical processes Rennell had used to reach them.

The voyage in *Earl of Ashburnham* from Calcutta to St Helena in 1777 had introduced Rennell to the peculiar patterns of ocean current circulation off the coast of southern Africa. He published his *Chart of the Bank of Lagullus*, with a memoir, first in 1778, and it proved the start of an intensifying interest in ocean circulation patterns. He identified, and explained, in two papers read before the Royal Society in 1793 and 1815, 'Observations on a current that often prevails to the westward of the Scilly islands' and 'Some farther observations on the current', the phenomenon whereby ships approaching the English Channel found themselves set northward unawares towards the Cornish coast and Bristol Channel. Rennell developed, in detail though imperfectly, methods of extracting current information from ships' journals. His theory was published posthumously in 1832, in *An investigation of the currents of the Atlantic Ocean and of those which prevail between the Indian Ocean and the Atlantic*, and forms the historical basis of ocean circulation studies.

Though he continued active for over fifty years in London after his retirement at thirty-six, Rennell did not seek formal employment to complement his geographical research and publication. The story that he turned down the offer of the position of hydrographer to the Admiralty in 1795, before the post was offered to Alexander Dalrymple, is not supported by the documented sequence of events in the summer of that year, and should be treated as apocryphal. All instances of its repetition appear to originate in an unsupported statement of the 1920s in a draft chapter for an unpublished history of the hydrographic office, now in the hydrographic office archives. Though often invoked by the East India Company as an expert referee on surveying and mapping proposals from India, Rennell was inevitably out of touch in later years with the extent of new survey in India. The same straightforwardness with which he advised the East India Company in 1796 against Colebrooke's plan for a canal to link the Ganges with the Hooghly reportedly placed at risk, through Rennell's misunderstanding, Lambton's proposal for the trigonometrical survey of India in 1800, until Nevil Maskelyne explained to Rennell the true mathematical basis of the survey. It was a sign of Rennell's continuing mental acuity that reference, rather than reverence, was made to him even in his eighties: the East India Company, discussing the new *Atlas of India* in 1823, asked his opinion of the scheme and transmitted it to India before accepting the surveyor-general's diplomatic dismissal of his criticisms.

Foreign associate of the Institut de France in 1801, and subsequently also of the Imperial Academy of St Petersburg and of the Royal Society of Göttingen, Rennell was awarded the gold medal of the Royal Society of Literature in 1825. A widower from 1810, he remained active until the age of eighty-seven, when, in 1829, he broke his thigh in a fall from his chair. He died at his home at 29 Suffolk Street on 29 March 1830, and was buried on 6 April in the nave of Westminster Abbey, where a tablet and a bronze bust by Hagbolt in the chapel under the north-west tower mark the event. *The Times* remarked,

> In all his discussions his sole object was the establishment of truth, and not the triumph of victory. … Adapting himself to the level of all who consulted him, he had the happy art of correcting their errors without hurting their feelings, and of leading them to truth without convicting them of ignorance. (30 March 1830)

ANDREW S. COOK

Sources C. R. Markham, *Major James Rennell and the rise of modern English geography* (1895) • R. H. Phillimore, ed., *Historical records of the survey of India*, 1 (1945), 369–78 • J. N. L. Baker, 'Major James Rennell and his place in the history of geography', *History of Geography* (1963), 130–57 • A. S. Cook, 'Major James Rennell and *A Bengal atlas* (1780 and 1781)', *Records Report 1976*, 1978, BL OIOC, 5–42 • R. Hallett, ed., *Records of the African Association, 1788–1831* (1964) • J. Gould, 'James Rennell's view of the Atlantic circulation: a comparison with our present knowledge', *Ocean Challenge*, 4 (1993), 26–33 • M. Bravo, 'James Rennell: antiquarian of ocean currents', *Ocean Challenge*, 4 (1993), 41–50 • A. Downes, 'James Rennell, 1742–1830', *Geographers: biobibliographical studies*, 1, ed. T. W. Freeman, M. Oughton, and P. Pinchemel (1977), 83–8 • A. S. Cook, 'James

Rennell's manuscript maps in the RGS collection', *GJ*, 144 (1978), 157–9 • *The Times* (30 March 1830)

Archives BL OIOC, transcripts and other papers | All Souls Oxf., corresp. with Charles Richard Vaughan • BL, corresp. with R. W. Cox, Add. MS 26653 • BL, corresp. with Lord Grenville, Add. MS 58996 • BL, letters to Warren Hastings, Add. MSS 29140–29193, *passim* • Bodl. Oxf., Rennell of Rodd MSS • Hunt. L., letters to Sir Francis Beaufort • NRA, priv. coll., corresp. with Sir Joseph Banks

Likenesses portrait, *c*.1777, priv. coll. • G. Dance, crayon drawing, 1794, NPG [*see illus.*] • A. Cardon, stipple, pubd 1799 (after Scott), BM, NPG • T. Hagbolt, bronze bust, *c*.1830, Westminster Abbey • marble bust, 1830, NPG • wax medallion, V&A

Rennell, Thomas (1754–1840), dean of Winchester, was born on 8 February 1754 at the rectory, Barnack, Northamptonshire, where his father, Thomas Rennell (1720–1798), prebendary of Winchester, was rector. His mother, Elizabeth, was the daughter of Richard Stone of Larkbear, Devon. He was educated at Eton College (1767–72) and entered King's College, Cambridge, on 20 March 1773. In 1778 he won a bachelor's prize for a Latin essay on 'Government'. He graduated BA in 1777, proceeded MA in 1779, and DD in 1794. At Cambridge he met Thomas James Mathias, who mentions him, along with bishops Horsley and Douglas, in his poem *The Pursuits of Literature* (5th edn, 1798, 159, 350–51). More significantly, he met George Pretyman and his pupil William Pitt, who was to prove an important patron. Rennell was a fellow of King's College from 1776 to 1779, when he was ordained and left Cambridge to become curate to his father at Barnack. In the same year his father resigned his prebend at Winchester in his favour and in 1787 he took charge of the expanding parish of Alton in Hampshire, which he held until 1814, when he exchanged it for Barton Stacy, Hampshire. From 1792 to 1808 he was also rector of St Magnus the Martyr, London Bridge.

In 1786 Rennell married Sarah (*d*. 1830), eldest daughter of Sir William *Blackstone, the judge; they had three sons and two daughters. His two oldest sons, both Anglican priests, predeceased him—Thomas [*see* Rennell, Thomas (1786–1824)] in 1824 and William in 1835. His eldest daughter, Sarah, married William Hart Coleridge, bishop of Barbados. In the 1790s he showed a keen interest in the French Roman Catholic émigré priests who lived at the King's House, Winchester. He was elected as an inspector of the house and spoke highly of 'these persecuted martyrs' (*Principles of French Republicanism*, appx, 24n.). This contrasted with the consistently hostile stance he adopted to the claims of Roman Catholics in England. He inherited a fine library from his father and added to it extensively; it ranged widely but most notably contained 'every book, tract or paper procurable on the Catholic question' (*Catalogue of the … Library*, ix), and many on the Jesuits. The library was sold after his death: the catalogue numbered 3638 items.

Having published a number of sermons separately, Rennell collected fourteen of them in *Discourses on Various Subjects* (1802). These were unfavourably reviewed by Sydney Smith in the first issue of the *Edinburgh Review*, where Rennell was described as 'a holy bully, an evangelical swaggerer' (25 Oct 1802, 88) for his attack on figures of the

French Enlightenment. Pitt, however, had been impressed by the sermons, and called Rennell the 'Demosthenes of the pulpit' following his Cambridge commencement sermon in 1794; a 1796 sermon, preached before Pitt as master of Trinity House, led to Rennell's appointment in 1797 as master of the Temple. He took up this post in 1798 and held it until 1826, making friends with the great lawyers of the day. In 1805 Pitt's patronage led to his appointment as dean of Winchester. A close friend of Henry Handley Norris and the high-churchmen of the 'Hackney phalanx', Rennell was a tory in politics; in 1817 in a letter to Dr James Hook, dean of Worcester, he denounced the 'Democrats' of his day, commenting 'to perish from Anarchy and confusion is bad enough *per se*, but to perish by the hands of Cobbett, Cochrane and Hunt is *intolerable*' (Rennell to James Hook, Ches. & Chester ALSS, Hook MSS, J 5/2). He undertook the restoration of Winchester Cathedral (1815–20), shifting monuments, and repairing and strengthening the nave piers and the presbytery roof. He died at the deanery on 31 March 1840 in his eighty-seventh year and was buried in the epiphany chapel in Winchester Cathedral.   ROBERT HOLE

Sources GM, 2nd ser., 13 (1840) • *Catalogue of the … library of the late Thomas Rennell* (1840) [sale catalogue] • Venn, *Alum. Cant.* • R. A. Austen-Leigh, ed., *The Eton College register, 1753–1790* (1921) • T. Rennell, *The principles of French republicanism essentially founded on violence and blood-guiltiness* (1793) • letters to Dr James Hook, Ches. & Chester ALSS, Hook MS J 5/2 • F. A. Inderwick and R. A. Roberts, eds., *A calendar of the Inner Temple records*, 5 (1936) • B. Given, ed., calendar of Inner Temple records, Inner Temple, London, vol. 7 • chronicle, *Annual Register* (1840), 158–9 • G. H. Blore, *Thomas Rennell, dean of Winchester, 1805–1840* (1952) • *EdinR*, 1 (1802–3), 88 • T. J. Mathias, *The pursuits of literature: a satirical poem in four dialogues*, 5th edn (1798)

Archives Oxon. RO, sermons | Ches. & Chester ALSS, Hook MSS • priv. coll., letters to James Hook

Likenesses S. W. Reynolds and W. Brett, mezzotint, 1824 (after T. Foster), BM, NPG • silhouette, dean and chapter of Winchester; repro. in Blore, *Thomas Rennell*, 14

Rennell, Thomas (1786–1824), Church of England clergyman, only son of Thomas *Rennell (1754–1840), dean of Winchester, and his wife, Sarah Blackstone, was born at Winchester on 22 October 1786. Like his father he was educated at Eton College, where he had a brilliant reputation as a scholar. He won one of Dr Claudius Buchanan's prizes for a Greek Sapphic ode on the propagation of the gospel in India, and a prize for Latin verses on 'Pallentes morbi'. With three of his contemporaries he ran a periodical called *The Miniature*, a successor of *The Microcosm*. In 1806 he was elected from Eton to King's College, Cambridge, where in the same year he won Sir William Browne's medal for the best Greek ode on the subject 'Veris comites'. In 1810 he published, in collaboration with C. J. Blomfield, afterwards bishop of London, *Musae Cantabrigienses*, and he contributed to the *Museum Criticum*, a journal established in 1813 by Blomfield and J. H. Monk. He graduated BA in 1810, MA in 1813, and BD in 1822, holding a fellowship at King's from 1809 to 1816.

Having received holy orders in 1811, Rennell was at once appointed assistant preacher at the Temple by his father, who was the master. Father and son were regarded as equally effective and popular preachers there. He also delivered the Warburtonian lectures at Lincoln's Inn. His interests were wide, and he attended a regular course of anatomical lectures in London. He was a friend of the members of that little group of high-churchmen of whom Joshua Watson was the lay leader and Henry Handley Norris the clerical leader. In 1811 he became editor of, and a frequent contributor to, the *British Critic*, which was the organ of the Hackney Phalanx, as this London coterie was known. His position as a champion of orthodox Anglican divinity was already evident in his critique of Unitarianism, which he published anonymously in 1811 as *Animadversions on the Unitarian Translation or Improved Version of the New Testament*.

In 1816 Rennell was appointed by the bishop of London (Dr Howley) vicar of Kensington, and proved himself an active and conscientious parish priest. In the same year he was elected Christian advocate at Cambridge. In that capacity he published in 1819 *Remarks on Scepticism, Especially as Connected with the Subject of Organisation and Life*, an attack on the materialist philosophical writings of the French physiologist Marie Bichat, of his English popularizer, Thomas Charles Morgan, and the surgeon William Lawrence, whose lectures were considered to be contrary to orthodox religious teaching. Like other high-churchmen Rennell feared that the London medical schools were becoming hotbeds of atheism, and he used his knowledge of anatomy and medicine to attack with effect those medical writers whom he believed to be promoting irreligion. Despite opposition, the book passed through a sixth edition in 1824. He was for several years examining chaplain to the bishop of Salisbury (John Fisher), who in 1823 gave him the mastership of St Nicholas's Hospital and the prebend of South Grantham in Salisbury Cathedral. He was elected fellow of the Royal Society (25 April 1822) in spite of opposition from those who resented his *Remarks on Scepticism*.

In 1822 Rennell produced a reply to the *Apocryphal New Testament* by the radical bookseller William Hone, and in the following year was one of the most distinguished of the churchmen who rushed into print to defend both the established church and its clergy from Henry Brougham's attacks on their wealth and political partisanship. On 14 October 1823 he married Frances Henrietta, the eldest daughter of John Delafield of Kensington, but within a few weeks he was stricken down with a fever. In his final illness he worked on producing a new edition of the English translation (first published in 1773) of a work by Balthasar Münther, *A Narrative of the Conversion and Death of Count Struensee*, wishing to bring its moral lessons to the attention of a new generation of readers. Rennell died at Winchester on 30 June 1824 and was buried in Winchester Cathedral. A touching funeral sermon was preached on him at Kensington (where the shops were shut on the day of his funeral as a mark of respect) by his successor, Archdeacon Pott.

Rennell's promise of intellectual eminence was widely attested and contemporaries regarded his as a talent cut short at its prime. Dr Parr, in his 1819 *Letter to Dr John Milner*, the Roman Catholic writer who had criticized Rennell's views on Catholic emancipation, described him as standing:

> by profound erudition, and by various and extensive knowledge, by a well-formed taste, by keen discernment, by glowing and majestic eloquence, by morals correct without austerity, and by piety fervent without superstition … among the brightest luminaries of our national literature and national church. (*Works of Samuel Parr*, 3.461)

A collection of his sermons (1825) was published posthumously.   J. H. OVERTON, *rev.* M. C. CURTHOYS

Sources [J. Lonsdale], 'Some account of the life and writings of the late Rev. Thomas Rennell', *Christian Remembrancer*, 6 (1824), 490–97; repr. in *GM*, 1st ser., 94 (1824), 178–83 • *GM*, 1st ser., 93/2 (1823), 464 • E. Churton, ed., *Memoir of Joshua Watson*, 2 vols. (1861) • J. H. Overton, *The English church in the nineteenth century, 1800–1833* (1894) • *The works of Samuel Parr … with memoirs of his life and writings*, ed. J. Johnstone, 8 vols. (1828) • Venn, *Alum. Cant.* • G. F. A. Best, *Temporal pillars: Queen Anne's bounty, the ecclesiastical commissioners, and the Church of England* (1964)
Likenesses S. W. Reynolds and W. Brett, mezzotint, pubd 1824 (after T. Foster), BM, NPG • portrait, Trinity Cam.

Rennie, George (1749–1828), agriculturist, was born at Phantassie, Haddingtonshire, Scotland, son of James Rennie (*d.* 1766), farmer, of Phantassie, and his wife, Jean. He was the elder brother of John *Rennie (1761–1821), the engineer. On leaving school he was sent by his father, at the age of sixteen, to Tweedside, to make a survey of a new system of farming which had been adopted by Lord Kames, Hume of Ninewells, and other landed gentry of the district. In 1765 he became superintendent of a brewery which his father had built. His father died in 1766, and, after leasing the brewery for some years, Rennie ran it from 1783 to 1797, when he handed it over to a tenant.

Rennie then turned to farming, on the Phantassie farm, and in 1787 he employed Andrew Meikle (1719–1811), the millwright (to whom his brother John had been apprenticed) to put up one of his threshing machines, which had a revolving drum and was driven by water. When Meikle's claims as the inventor were disputed, Rennie wrote a letter in his support, which was printed in John Shirreff's *Reply to an address to the public, but more particularly to the landed interest of Great Britain and Ireland, on the subject of the thrashing machine*. Rennie was one of the authors of *A General View of the Agriculture of the West Riding of Yorkshire … by Messrs Rennie, Brown, and Shirreff* (1794), written at the request of the board of agriculture.

Rennie died on 6 October 1828. He had a son, George *Rennie (1802–1860), who was a sculptor and who also served as a Liberal MP.

    GEORGE STRONACH, *rev.* ANNE PIMLOTT BAKER

Sources C. T. G. Boucher, *John Rennie* (1963) • Irving, *Scots.* • J. Donaldson, *Agricultural biography* (1854) • W. Anderson, *The Scottish nation*, 3 vols. (1866–77)
Archives NL Scot., corresp. with George Combe

Rennie, George (1791–1866), mechanical and civil engineer, was born in the parish of Christ Church, Southwark, London, on 3 December 1791, the eldest son of John *Rennie (1761–1821) and his wife, Martha Ann, daughter of E. Mackintosh. He was the brother of Sir John *Rennie. Educated first by Dr Greenlaw at a school in Isleworth, he

George Rennie (1791–1866), by John Linnell, 1824

then went to St Paul's School. In 1807 his father sent him to Edinburgh University, where he lodged with John Playfair, the professor of natural philosophy, and studied mathematics, natural sciences, and classics.

In 1811 Rennie entered his father's office, where many great works were in progress. He travelled extensively in Europe, particularly Italy, familiarizing himself with continental engineering and architecture. In 1818, on the recommendation of Joseph Banks and James Watt, he was appointed inspector of machinery and clerk of the irons (that is, dies) at the Royal Mint, which post he held for nearly eight years. Well before his father's death in 1821, he was assisting him in bridge design. Rennie wrote a diary of progress on Waterloo Bridge, appears to have made the theoretical calculations for the iron arches of Southwark Bridge, and claimed to have made the original design for London Bridge in 1820. His government appointment precluded him from acting as engineer to London Bridge (built in 1823–31), however, so that honour and a knighthood went to his brother John, although George wrote the description of the bridge for Cooke's *Views of the Old and New London Bridges* (1833). During the 1820s he designed the bridge over the Serpentine in Hyde Park and materially improved Thomas Harrison's design for Grosvenor Bridge over the Dee in Chester. He designed the stone replacement for Thomas Wilson's iron bridge at Staines (1829–32). Other civil engineering schemes reported on included a proposal for Collier's Dock in the

Isle of Dogs (1824), Denver sluice (1829), and Sunderland docks (1832). Rennie married, in 1828, Margaret Anne, daughter of Sir John Jackson, bt, MP; they had two sons and one daughter.

Rennie later had considerable practice as a railway engineer, and made plans for lines to connect Birmingham and Liverpool, the Vale of Clwyd line, the railway from Mons to Manège, and the Namur and Liège Railway, of which he was appointed chief engineer in 1846. He was consulted about the Liverpool and Manchester Railway following the parliamentary failure of the first bill, and organized a new survey, giving evidence in favour of the successful scheme in 1826. Although generally associated with his younger brother Sir John, he was personally responsible for early proposals for the Midland Counties Railway (1833–6) and Central Kent Railway (1837).

Rennie's genius was chiefly mechanical. He superintended the manufacturing business of the family firm in Holland Street, Southwark, known at first as Rennie Brothers. After his brother Sir John retired from this side of the business about 1850 and George's sons, John Keith and George Banks Rennie, joined him, the firm became George Rennie & Sons and the factory was called the Albion ironworks. During its heyday a great variety of machinery was turned out, including the first biscuit-making machinery, corn and chocolate mills for Deptford victualling yard, and similar machines for the Royal William victualling yard, Plymouth. The firm also made the second tunnelling shield for Marc Isambard Brunel's Thames Tunnel (1835). Many orders for foreign governments were executed, including enormous iron dock gates for Sevastopol.

Rennie Brothers were also employed by the Admiralty in making engines for the Royal Navy, work which dovetailed with the establishment of the shipbuilding yard of J. & G. Rennie at Norman Road, Greenwich, in the 1830s. In all they supplied engines for between forty and fifty steamships for the British navy, and supplied an immense order for the Spanish government. Rennie was much interested in the screw-propeller. In 1840 the Rennies built the *Dwarf*, the first vessel in the British navy propelled by a screw; and they made the engines for the *Archimedes*, the first screw-driven vessel supplied to the Russian navy, in which Francis Petit Smith's screw was installed. Rennie was also interested in floating dry docks, for which he took out a number of patents. Locomotives were also made between 1837 and 1842, for railways in Britain, such as the London to Brighton and the London to Southampton lines, as well as overseas lines in Cuba, Austria, and Italy. But the works were found to be ill suited for manufacturing locomotives and this work was abandoned.

In 1822 Rennie was elected fellow of the Royal Society, his first paper, an account of experiments made on the strength of materials (*PTRS* 2, 1815–30, 118), having been written in 1817. This detailed tests on iron, timber, and stone which were among the earliest test results to be published on the strength of materials in Britain. Further papers followed, on the friction and abrasion of the surfaces of solids (*PTRS* 2, 1815–30, 143–70), and on the friction and resistance of fluids (ibid., 3, 1830–37, 423–42). He presented papers to the British Association of which perhaps the most important were his review papers of 1833 and 1834, *Report on the progress and present state of our knowledge of hydraulics as a branch of engineering*, which were reprinted as a book in 1835. He was elected a member of the Institution of Civil Engineers in 1841. In the same year his revision of Buchanan's *Mills and Millwork* was published.

Rennie was handicapped by physical disability, and in his latter life he appears to have been epileptic. In religion, he was a strict Presbyterian. He died of paralysis on 30 March 1866, at his London home, 39 Wilton Crescent, Pimlico, from the effects of an accident in the street the previous year, and was buried on 6 April at Holmwood, near Dorking. He was survived by his wife.

ANDREW SAINT and MIKE CHRIMES

Sources *PICE*, 28 (1868–9), 610–15 · *GM*, 4th ser., 1 (1866), 749–50 · C. T. G. Boucher, *John Rennie* (1963), 29 · T. Ruddock, *Arch bridges and their builders* (1979) · *DNB* · d. cert. · A. W. Skempton and others, eds., *A biographical dictionary of civil engineers in Great Britain and Ireland*, 1 (2002)
Archives Bodl. Oxf., European travel diary · Inst. CE · LUL, household account books · NL Scot., corresp., journals and papers · U. Edin. L., letters | Birm. CA, letters to Boulton & Watt · BL, corresp. with Charles Babbage, Add. MSS 37183–37194 · NL Scot., letters to John Rennie
Likenesses J. Linnell, miniature, oils, 1824, NPG [*see illus.*]
Wealth at death under £60,000: probate, 10 May 1866, *CGPLA Eng. & Wales*

Rennie, George (1802–1860), sculptor and politician, was born at Phantassie, East Lothian (Haddingtonshire), the son of George *Rennie (1749–1828), agriculturist, and nephew of John Rennie (1761–1821) the engineer. After studying sculpture in Rome, Rennie returned to England in 1828 and in the same year carved his most well-known work, *The Archer* (marble), which he presented to the Athenaeum. Rennie was a regular exhibitor at the Royal Academy from 1828 to 1837 and he exhibited also at the Suffolk Street Gallery of the Society of British Artists. His work, which received varying reviews, included narrative subjects such as *The Gleaner* (marble, 1828) and *The Minstrel* (marble, 1834) as well as classical figures such as *Mars* (marble; Chatsworth, Derbyshire) and *Cupid and Hymen* (marble, exh. RA, 1831). He also exhibited classicizing marble portrait busts including those of the painter David Wilkie (1833), the sculptor Bertel Thorvaldsen (1831), his uncle John Rennie (1831), and William Jolliffe (1832; Amerdown, Somerset). His statue of Lord Harris (1835) is at Throwley church, Kent. In 1834 he carved a series of bas-reliefs for the dividend office of the Bank of England which included such varied representations as *Mercury*, *Britannia*, *Ceres*, *The Thames*, *Industry*, and *Calculation*.

During the 1830s Rennie turned his attention to improving the state of the arts in England. In 1836 he suggested to the Liberal politician William Ewart the formation of the parliamentary committee that led to the establishment of the School of Design at Somerset House. He also worked with the radical politician Joseph Hume to obtain for the public freedom of access to all monuments and works of art in public buildings and museums. He was one of the

first artists to conceive of the idea of bringing Cleopatra's Needle to London. It was to be erected in Trafalgar Square as the main feature of the design and plan he submitted in 1839 for the national monument to Lord Nelson. After failing to win that competition Rennie concentrated his efforts on politics and, as a Liberal, won the Ipswich seat in the 1841 election. He retired after six years in parliament and on 15 December 1847 he was appointed governor of the Falkland Islands. Throughout the eight years he held that position Rennie was acclaimed for his diplomatic skills and the success he brought to the economic development of the islands. Rennie returned to England in 1855 and died at his home, 32 York Terrace, Regent's Park, London, on 22 March 1860, leaving a widow, Jane, and two sons, William Hepburn Rennie, and Richard Temple Rennie, a barrister, of Shanghai, China, and 113 Piccadilly.

CAMPBELL DODGSON, rev. ROBIN L. WOODWARD

Sources R. Gunnis, *Dictionary of British sculptors, 1660–1851* (1953); new edn (1968) · *CGPLA Eng. & Wales* (1860) · *CGPLA Eng. & Wales* (1867) · *CGPLA Eng. & Wales* (1875)
Wealth at death £3000: administration, 7 April 1860, *CGPLA Eng. & Wales* · under £300: further action, 8 Aug 1867, *CGPLA Eng. & Wales* · £200: further action, 9 Jan 1875, *CGPLA Eng. & Wales*

Rennie [*née* Moorhouse], **Isabella Southern** [Belle] (1875–1966), educationist, was born on 17 February 1875 at Lake House, Westoe, near South Shields, co. Durham, daughter of Thomas Firth Moorhouse, analytical chemist, and Isabella, *née* Southern, from a Northumberland coal-owning family. Belle's only brother was born in 1876. Thomas Moorhouse, also described as manager of a chemical works, was killed when conducting an experiment, and his widow returned with her family to live with her mother at Gateshead. When Belle was about twelve Mrs Moorhouse married the family doctor and went to live at Harrogate, at which fashionable resort Dr Rennie built up a large and lucrative practice. The children adopted their stepfather's surname. His overwork brought on a serious illness and the family moved south to Torquay, where the only child of this second marriage, a daughter, died. Dr Rennie never returned to his practice, and the family settled at Lymington in Hampshire and eventually built Quarr House in Sway in the New Forest.

Belle was educated at home and developed an active interest in progressive methods of teaching young children. She herself supposed that a dislocated hip precluded her having children, and the news of the Messina earthquake (28 December 1908) suggested that she might adopt one of its child victims. She travelled to Italy with her friend and former governess, Dr Laura Veale, and found a suitable seven-month-old baby at the Convent of the Annunziata at Naples. Persistence overcame all official difficulties, and the two spinsters brought the child safely back to the New Forest, where the Rennie parents took charge of little Feodora who—to avoid scandal—was brought up as Belle's sister. She was legally adopted by Belle's parents in 1927, after the passing of new adoption legislation, and in 1930 married Walter Chiesman.

Belle Rennie's keen but amateur interest in the education of nursery-infant children developed into well-informed and authoritative knowledge, coinciding with a period of intense interest in new progressive methods and the so-called Child Study Movement—the McMillan sisters opened their nursery school in Deptford in 1914. Miss Rennie played a key part in the foundation of the Conference of the New Ideals in Education in 1912. She had visited the Montessori Institute in Italy and was instrumental in introducing these ideas to Britain; *The Montessori Method* first appeared in English in 1913. In 1914 Miss Rennie helped to organize the first New Ideals conference at Runton, near Cromer, and the second at Stratford upon Avon in 1915, and it was here that Percy Nunn, William Mather, and other like-minded friends suggested that a college for the training of teachers should be founded to reflect their views on nursery-infant education. Miss Rennie became the driving force behind this movement and was responsible for obtaining recognition for Gipsy Hill College from the Board of Education. In 1916 she persuaded Lillian De Lissa, a disciple of Montessori who, at her invitation, had been one of the chief lecturers at the Runton conference, to prepare a scheme for the college, and to accept its principalship, but De Lissa had to terminate her contract in Australia and elude the German U-boats before taking up the post. She arrived in time to welcome the first students. From then on the partnership between these two remarkable women created a unique college.

Miss Rennie had found suitable properties at Gipsy Hill in south London, purchasing two properties at least with her own money. Until 1920, when a bursar was appointed, she was administrative officer for the college, then remained chair of the governors until it passed into the control of the Surrey county council in 1945/6. For this long period Miss Rennie was largely responsible for the government of the college, training teachers for nursery-infant school age, and adopting unusual and enterprising features. This entailed constant and persistent negotiations with the Board of Education, Miss Rennie badgering its officials to allow a unique curriculum and system of examination. For a time the board insisted that the college students underwent two years' probation before being qualified for the teachers' certificate, but each year Miss Rennie and the governors made representations until, in 1923, this slur was removed. In 1927 permanent recognition was granted by the board and in 1928 the college came under a scheme for examination by members of the University of London (Birkbeck College). In 1930 Mather's Manchester College was closed, and its students were taken in as third-year students by Gipsy Hill, making an important contribution to its course and ethos.

It is remarkable that, at this period, a single woman had established herself in a position of such influence and authority. Miss Rennie's wealth, undoubtedly, gave her more independence of operation, and she used it with great generosity to help the impecunious college over several crises. In 1920/21 a bequest of £2000 from Mather came to the rescue and Miss Rennie herself covered the rest of the college's deficit. Another crisis in 1930/31, following a critical report of the college facilities by HM inspectors, was surmounted by a further injection of Rennie money, and the Rommany Nursery School, since 1918 the practising school of the college, had to be rescued financially. The 1938 crisis was the most severe. Queen Mary was induced to pay a much publicized visit to the college; the entire Rommany Nursery School, children, equipment, and staff, was transported to a London meeting before a distinguished audience, and although very little money was raised, enough was secured to tide affairs over until war and evacuation transformed the scene.

Miss Rennie's main interest lay in promoting the Montessori vision of education as the child's own achievement. She was concerned with the application of these theories not only to nursery-infant schoolchildren but throughout schooling. In 1920 she visited the USA and met Miss Helen Parkhurst, who had been asked by Madame Montessori to look after her interests in the States. Miss Parkhurst had begun the application of these methods to the instruction of older children, at first in a small rural school in Wisconsin and later at a mixed state high school at Dalton, Massachusetts. This 'laboratory plan' of giving pupils carefully structured assignments of work covering a broad curriculum came to be known as the Dalton plan. Miss Rennie became its enthusiastic exponent and secretary of the Dalton Association in Britain. Here its ideas spread rapidly, teachers on the whole being free to choose their own methods. While few schools followed the scheme thoroughly and consistently, the Dalton plan had a much wider effect in emphasizing the individual study of the pupil. Miss Rennie, however, remained critical of so-called project methods which were not carefully structured. In 1932, in collaboration with Dr C. W. Kimmins, formerly chief inspector of technical education for the London county council, she published *The Triumph of the Dalton Plan*, claiming that where it had been employed 'there was a new outlook together with a new spirit and a new industry'.

There were not many aspects of educational liberation and progress in the inter-war period with which Miss Rennie was not concerned. She was involved with the rescue of Kurt Hahn from Nazi Germany, and assisted with the foundation of Gordonstoun and with the other reforming public schools of that period—Bryanston and Stowe. She decided to open her own preparatory school, where boys could be taught on the Dalton plan. She formed a company, the Abinger Hill School Limited, appointed Dr Kimmins its chairman, and a school at Abinger Hill was opened in June 1928 by the duchess of Atholl, parliamentary secretary to the Board of Education. G. J. K. Harrison was appointed headmaster, having been sent by Miss Rennie to the USA to study the system at Dalton. Many influential parents sent their sons to this highly successful school. Sir Edward Boyle, for example, remembered his grounding there 'in doing work in one's own time'. Another pupil recalled the careful supervision given to each child's charts of progress and coverage of the curriculum. When in 1946 Gipsy Hill College ceased to be independent and passed into the hands of Surrey county council with premises on Kingston Hill, Miss Rennie remained a member of the governing body until she was too frail for travelling, and became governor emeritus, still taking an interest in its students and hoping and praying that the increase in the size of the college would not swamp the students' individuality.

After the war Miss Rennie lived in Sussex and then in Kent. For the last few years of her life she stayed in bed, not because she was ill, but because she had always hated getting up and saw no reason to continue to do so. A small woman, somewhat lame, meticulously elegant, the secret of her achievements and her influence is difficult to penetrate but their basis was undoubtedly her commitment to her beliefs. To her 'education was a profoundly religious process in which the child's creative powers required to be liberated and strengthened' (*The Times*, 15 April 1966). Her Anglican religion was not perhaps always orthodox—she dabbled in mysticism, thought herself to possess healing powers, and believed in reincarnation, declaring that 'the young souls go to America and the old ones stay in Europe'. She possessed a strange mixture of gullibility and astuteness, and a self-acknowledged eccentricity. Nevertheless, practicality, sound common sense, immense generosity and vitality, a readiness to accept new ideas, and an indomitable spirit enabled her to hold a commanding position in the progressive educational world during a period when forces of change were slowly fermenting. Her shrewdness and enthusiasm had discerned and exploited possibilities for progress within apparently conservative structures. Belle Rennie died at her home, 15 Calverley Park, Tunbridge Wells, Kent, on 11 April 1966.

MARGARET BRYANT

Sources Kingston University, Gipsy Hill College records · private information (2004) · *The Times* (15 April 1966) · *Handbook, 1949–50*, U. Lond., Institute of Education · *Jubilee brochure of Gipsy Hill College* (1967) [Kingston University] · b. cert. · d. cert.
Archives priv. coll. | Kingston University, Surrey, Gipsy Hill College records
Likenesses W. Davey, photographs, priv. coll. · Debenham & Gould of Bournemouth, photograph, priv. coll. · A. Hughes, photograph, priv. coll.
Wealth at death £48,686: probate, 11 July 1966, *CGPLA Eng. & Wales*

Rennie, James (1787–1867), naturalist, was born on 26 February 1787. He was most likely the natural son of Thomas Rennie (or Rainey) of Aldenholme, Sorn, Ayrshire, and Margaret Edwards. He matriculated at Glasgow University in 1810, and won prizes there in logic, ethics, mathematics, and natural philosophy. There were also prizes for his essays on bleaching, on steam and navigation, and on the Huttonian and Wernerian systems of geology—a copy of this last later went to the National Library of Scotland. He graduated MA on 20 July 1815 and proceeded to take holy orders. In 1821 he moved to London. His earliest articles on natural history, some republished in translation in Germany, date from the end of that decade. On 26 November 1830 he was appointed as the first professor of natural history and zoology at King's College, London. (The college's historian describes him as fond of birds, a defender of inductive methods of enquiry, and, in his inaugural lecture, a denouncer of evolutionary speculations.) However,

Rennie's department never flourished; student numbers and expenditure on materials were probably both insufficient, and the council ended the professorship on 1 August 1834. From then on Rennie seems to have made a modest living mostly from his writing.

The majority of Rennie's publications appeared in the 1830s. Ranging over much of natural history, from plants and insects to birds and monkeys, he also took on angling, gardening, and even physics and natural theology (although his titles promised only an 'alphabet' for many of these) A conspectus of British butterflies and moths occasioned a lawsuit over alleged piracy by Rennie. One of his earliest books, *Insect Architecture*, was evidently his best regarded, being reissued in 1857 by the prominent publisher John Murray. Making only a few, small claims to originality, it is a diligent, worthy, orthodox, and conventional work, prefaced with seemingly sincere homilies about the religious and educational virtues attached to close study of such common, accessible objects as wasps' nests and weevil galls. The homilies were well adapted to the book's début in 1830 in the Library of Entertaining Knowledge. Leather bound and gold lettered, the work, like others by Rennie, could make an edifying award to any young, aspiring historian of nature. The brief peaking, at King's, of Rennie's own career acts as a reminder that institutional initiatives in that age of improvement often entailed insecure jobs even for those who had themselves excelled as students. Despite the prizes, the professorship, and the publications, Rennie's life, however respectable and reputable, ended as it began, on the margins of Britain's national society. In 1840 he emigrated to Australia, but nothing is known of his life there except that he died in Adelaide on 25 August 1867.

JONATHAN HODGE

Sources DNB · F. J. C. Hearnshaw, *The centenary history of King's College, London, 1828–1928* (1929) · *Entomologist's Monthly Magazine*, 4 (1868), 191
Archives NL Scot., essay
Likenesses G. T. Allen, photograph, RS

Rennie, John (1761–1821), engineer, was born on 7 June 1761 at Phantassie, Haddingtonshire, the youngest of the nine children of James Rennie, a farmer and owner of a brewery, and his wife, Jean. George *Rennie (1749–1828), the agriculturist, was his oldest brother and took over the family interests when their father died in 1766. John went to the parish school at Prestonkirk. A precocious interest in machinery was nurtured by the well-known millwright Andrew Meikle (1719–1811), inventor of the threshing machine and improver of the windmill, who lived on the estate. Rennie started to work for Meikle when he was twelve, getting a grounding in practical mechanics. For two years (1775–7) he was then at Dunbar high school, where a visitor, David Loch, singled him out for his 'amazing powers of genius' in mathematics and experimental and natural philosophy. Later, when his teacher at Dunbar retired, Rennie was asked to succeed him but agreed to do so only temporarily, as his ambitions lay elsewhere.

After working again for Meikle, with his help and consent Rennie set up on his own as a millwright in 1779.

John Rennie (1761–1821), by Sir Henry Raeburn, c.1800

Among his first jobs was building a mill for his brother to house one of Meikle's earliest threshing machines. Though soon in a good way of business, he opted to combine practical work with studies at Edinburgh University, where he matriculated in November 1780, continuing until 1783. Here he made friends with two eminent teachers, the chemist Joseph Black and the professor of natural philosophy, John Robison, and gained a breadth of scientific interest as well as some grasp of theoretical engineering concepts.

In 1783 Rennie took a study tour into England, making notes on canals, bridges, and machinery along his route. His destination was Birmingham, where a letter from Robison procured him an introduction to James Watt. Watt, in need of a millwright to extend the mechanical scope of his steam engine, was greatly taken with Rennie. The next year Boulton and Watt offered him the job of looking after their London business and erecting the engines they supplied for the Albion Mills, the revolutionary flour mill at the south end of Blackfriars Bridge conceived and designed by Samuel Wyatt. To this end Rennie moved to London, setting up a workshop at a Thames wharf near the mill. The millwork for the twenty sets of grinding stones was supplied by Wyatt, but the substitution of much iron gearing for the customary timber was probably Rennie's idea; there was much friction between the two men.

Rennie opened the Albion Mills to visitors when production began in 1786, despite the secretive Watt's disapproval. The building burned down in 1791, but by then Rennie's reputation was made and he was supplying millwork for customers as far away as France, Spain, and Portugal. He made moving machinery for mills, breweries, and factories of all kinds, including a variety of machines for the new Boulton and Watt factory at Birmingham (erected by his foreman, Peter Ewart). Rolling mills for mints were a speciality, most of the equipment for the new Royal Mint at Tower Hill being Rennie's. He was ingenious in improving mechanical devices. A pioneer in applying steam power to pile-driving and dredging, he was among the first to make regular use of ball-bearings, improved the water-wheel and diving bell, experimented with stone pipes for water supply, and contributed to the evolution of the gantry crane. To meet the demand for his machines, he in 1810 built a larger factory at Holland Street, Southwark, on part of the old Albion Mills site.

The year 1790 proved to be significant for Rennie, both personally and professionally. He married Martha Ann Mackintosh (d. 1806). They had nine children, of whom George *Rennie (1791–1866) and Sir John *Rennie (1794–1874) carried on his work. A daughter, Anna, married the architect C. R. Cockerell. In 1790 a second phase of Rennie's career also began when he was appointed surveyor to the Kennet and Avon Canal. Design and consultancy for civil engineering henceforward took up the bulk of his time. Along the Kennet and Avon (1794–1813), 57 miles long and with twenty-nine locks, many bridges, and several aqueducts and tunnels, Rennie's penchant for solidity first made its mark. But he was hampered by a tight budget and problems of water supply, only in part alleviated by steam-powered pumping stations at Crofton and Claverton. In the same years he laid out the Rochdale Canal and the Lancaster Canal with the noble Lune aqueduct, as well as the Aberdeen Canal, the Crinan Canal, the Royal Canal of Ireland, and the Royal Military Canal (a product of the Napoleonic invasion scare of 1803–4).

Rennie also took on a multitude of river navigation and harbour improvements, fen drainage schemes, and waterworks. In London, he was a key figure in the expansion of the commercial docks during the French wars. He acted as engineer to the London docks (1800–05) and with Ralph Walker to the East India docks (1803–6), and he built extensions and some remarkable sheds at the West India docks (1809–17). For the Admiralty, Rennie made wartime improvements to the Thames naval dockyards, including a superb steam-powered smithy at Woolwich, but his detailed scheme of 1807 for a wholly new dockyard at Northfleet was not carried out. His grandest executed work for government was the mile-long protective breakwater at Plymouth Sound, started in 1811 and completed in 1848. Its scale was admired by Napoleon when he arrived as a prisoner at Plymouth in 1815, to Rennie's gratification.

The thoroughness of his reports was a key to Rennie's reputation. He was often asked to adjudicate on others' projects, and his name was of great value to promoters. He worked well with others and could delegate, but was conscious of his own worth. His foremost collaborative endeavour was with Robert Stevenson, on the famous Bell

Rock lighthouse off Arbroath (1807–10). The apportionment of responsibility for this work led to prolonged disputes between their respective descendants, but it is now certain that while Stevenson designed the lighthouse in the main, Rennie's role too was significant.

Rennie is now chiefly admired and remembered as a bridge-builder. He was designing bridges as early as 1784 and extended their range throughout his career. His masonry bridges were marked by solidity, precision, and a definite structural philosophy. He was alive and receptive to the ideas of French engineers of Perronet's school, but critical of their practical record. The multi-arched road bridges of his maturity all had swept walls to the abutments, elliptical or segmental arches, pointed breakwaters, hidden inverted arches over the piers, and a level surface from end to end.

Rennie's crowning achievement was the trio of metropolitan bridges spanning the Thames: Waterloo Bridge, Southwark Bridge, and London Bridge, all constructed by Edward Banks (1770–1835) of the early contracting firm, Jolliffe and Banks, which had built many of his canals. Waterloo Bridge (1811–17) was his masterpiece. Though privately promoted, it was the most prestigious bridge project Britain had yet seen. The design was based on his earlier bridge at Kelso. It had nine equal arches, facings in granite (then a new building material in London), and twin Doric columns against the piers. Canova is said to have remarked it was worth coming to England merely to see Waterloo Bridge, while a modern authority has described it as 'perhaps the finest large masonry bridge ever built in this or any other country' (A. W. Skempton, *Transactions of the Newcomen Society*, 44, 1971–2, 36). The subsidence of one of the piers led to its destruction by the London county council in the 1930s, despite strenuous and prolonged public protest. Southwark Bridge (1814–19), another private undertaking, had a superstructure of three unequal iron arches on granite piers, the central arch being the widest cast-iron span ever built in Britain. These arches followed on from a previous iron bridge by Rennie (with Thomas Wilson) at Boston, Lincolnshire (1805–8). Though he was keen to vie with Telford in the design of iron bridges, and made an early sketch for crossing the Menai Strait with a single arch and flat deck (1801–2), he was less completely a master of this developing genre. The complexity and expense of the Southwark arches led to the bankruptcy of the iron subcontractors, Walkers of Rotherham, and Rennie was never fully paid for his work; a second large iron bridge, designed on similar principles, was sent out in sections to Lucknow, but not erected there for many years. London Bridge, designed in conjunction with his sons and built posthumously (1823–31), was the last of his masonry bridges. It was removed in 1968 and re-erected in abbreviated form at Lake Havasu City, Arizona, leaving London with no extant memorial to Rennie's genius.

Rennie was elected fellow of the Royal Society in 1798, but declined the knighthood offered to him by the prince regent when Waterloo Bridge was opened. Though strong, Rennie consistently overworked. His one recorded 'holiday', to France and the Low Countries in 1816 with James Watt junior, was largely taken up with visits to docks and harbours. He did however have a country retreat for family life at Frensham Vale, Farnham. Eventually he fell victim to his own energies, and died of liver disease on 4 October 1821 after a short illness at his home in Stamford Street, Southwark. He was buried in St Paul's Cathedral, where a plain granite slab in the crypt marks his grave. Among his many engineering pupils or assistants were, besides his sons, John Aird, Henry Bell, Anthony Bower, William Tierney Clark (also a fine bridge-builder), Peter Ewart, Francis Giles, James Hollinsworth, John Thomas, and Joseph Whidbey.

Rennie was a handsome, big man nearly 6 feet 4 inches tall, with equal determination and charm. In private he had a short temper, but he made and kept friends. Charles Dupin pronounced him 'friendly and welcoming to all foreign engineers who came to England to study his works and profit from his genius' (Dupin, 6). By religion he was brought up and remained Presbyterian. Like every engineer of his day, he took risks and made mistakes. His stone pipes for the Grand Junction Water Company were an abject failure, and the bridge he built at Highgate Archway was to collapse. A common criticism levelled at Rennie was the massiveness and expense of his structures, but Rennie built to last, and for safety and dignity's sake was free with his clients' money. His capacity for combining manufacturing with design derived from his origins as a millwright or mechanical engineer, but it is as a constructor that he is chiefly now remembered. He and Telford were the greatest civil engineers of their day. Although many modern historians of engineering have preferred Telford on the grounds of his originality in structural design, other authorities have been equally impressed by Rennie. He enjoyed a wider range of skills, greater theoretical ability, and more social approbation than Telford, but has been less fortunate in the survival of his major structures. A memorial of 1928 stands on the hill above East Linton, near Phantassie; in London there is only a poor modern plaque under the north end of the present Waterloo Bridge, where foundations of Rennie's bridge still remain.

ANDREW SAINT

Sources C. T. G. Boucher, *John Rennie* (1963) · W. Reyburn, *Bridge across the Atlantic* (1972) · Colvin, *Archs.* · C. Dupin, *Notice nécrologique sur John Rennie* (1821) · D. Brewster and others, eds., *The Edinburgh encyclopaedia*, 3rd edn, 18 vols. (1830) · S. Smiles, *Lives of the engineers*, 2 (1861) · J. Rennie, *Autobiography of Sir John Rennie, FRS* (1875) · T. Ruddock, *Arched bridges and their builders* (1979) · C. Fox, ed., *London, world city, 1800–1840* (1992), 54–6, 311–14 · *DNB*

Archives Inst. CE, drawings, papers, and reports · NL Scot., accounts, corresp., and notebooks · NL Scot., letters · PRO, letters, RAIL 1008/87 · U. Edin. L., corresp. | Bath and North East Somerset RO, Bath, report on Kennet and Avon canal · Beds. & Luton ARS, letters to Samuel Whitbread · Birm. CA, letters to Boulton and Watt · Birm. CA, corresp. with Boulton family · Birm. CA, letters to James Watt · BL, letter and reports to Viscounts Melville, Add. MS 41345 · BL, report on Northfleet New Arsenal, Add. MS 27884 · British Waterways Archive, MS plans · Cambs. AS, reports on fen drainage · Dorset RO, report and corresp. relating to Tamar navigation canal · Lincs. Arch., corresp. and papers relating to Boston

Bridge · Lincs. Arch., reports and papers relating to Lincolnshire River Authority · LUL, specification for rebuilding London Bridge · Mitchell L., Glas., Glasgow City Archives, corresp. and papers relating to Clyde Harbour · NL Scot., papers relating to Whiteadder Bridge · Rochester Bridge Trust, corresp. and reports on Rochester Bridge · Southampton Archives Office, reports on Southampton docks · Staffs. RO, report on Leek canal · U. Birm. L., MS opinion on Shardlow and Nottingham canal · U. Edin. L., letters to Thomas Townshend · Warks. CRO, letters to Sir Roger Newdigate

Likenesses M. A. Shee, oils, c.1794, Scot. NPG · H. Raeburn, oils, c.1800, Scot. NPG [see illus.] · G. Dance, drawing, 1803, NPG · F. Chantrey, marble bust, 1818, NPG; plater cast, AM Oxf. · W. Holl, stipple, pubd 1861 (after A. Skirving), NPG · W. Bain, bronze medallion, NPG · T. O. Barlow, mixed engraving, NPG · F. Chantrey, pencil drawing, NPG · G. P. Harding, pencil drawing (after F. L. Chantrey), NPG · H. Raeburn, portrait · E. Scriven, stipple and line engraving (after S. Kirven), NPG · E. Scriven, stipple and line engraving (after A. Skirving), NPG · J. F. Skill, J. Gilbert, and E. Walker, group portrait, pencil and wash drawing (*Men of science living in 1807–8*), NPG · J. Thomson, stipple (after W. Behnes), BM, NPG; repro. in *European Magazine* (1821)

Rennie, Sir John (1794–1874), civil engineer, was born at 27 Stamford Street, Blackfriars Road, London, on 30 August 1794, the second son of John *Rennie (1761–1821), civil engineer, and his wife, Martha, *née* Mackintosh. His elder brother was George *Rennie, civil engineer. He was educated at Dr Greenlaw's school in Isleworth, where the poet Shelley was a contemporary, and afterwards at Dr Charles Burney's school in Greenwich. In 1809 he entered his father's office and manufactory, where he acquired a practical knowledge of his profession. During the early stages of the building of Waterloo Bridge (1811–13) he was placed under the resident engineer, James Hollingsworth. He produced the working drawings for Southwark Bridge (1814–19) and personally selected the massive blocks of Peterhead granite for the bridge's abutments. During his pupillage he also worked on the Kennet and Avon Canal and helped Francis Giles to survey ports on the Tyne and the Scottish coast.

In 1819–21 Rennie undertook an extensive grand tour which took in France, Switzerland, Italy, Greece, the Turkish coast, and Egypt, visiting antiquities, quarries, and engineering works. In Rome he befriended Sir Humphry Davy, Sir William Gell, Canova, and Thorvaldsen. He returned to find his father dying, and thereafter with his brother George took over the firm, specializing in the civil engineering side of the business. The most important of his undertakings was the construction of London Bridge, the designs of which had been prepared by his father. After many controversies and difficulties the bridge was opened in 1831, when Rennie was knighted—one of the first professional engineers to be thus distinguished.

As engineer to the Admiralty, a post in which he succeeded his father up to 1831, Rennie carried on various works at Sheerness, Woolwich, Plymouth, Portsmouth, and Ramsgate. At Plymouth he completed his father's great breakwater and, using convict labour, constructed the grandiose Royal William victualling yard (1827–35), a 16 acre complex of which 6 acres were reclaimed from the sea; the buildings and machinery alike were almost entirely supplied by Rennie Brothers. Rennie was primarily a hydraulics engineer, and much of his career was

Sir John Rennie (1794–1874), by Simon Jacques Rochard, 1831

spent in adding to or altering commercial harbours and docks. In Britain these included important docks at Whitehaven and Cardiff; abroad, he built the Ponte Delgada breakwater for orange-trade boats in the Azores. He completed the drainage works in the Lincolnshire fens commenced by his father and, in conjunction with Telford, constructed the Nene outfall near Wisbech (1826–31). He also restored the harbour of Boston (Lincolnshire) in 1827–8 and made various improvements on the Welland.

A shipbuilding yard known as J. and G. Rennie was established in the 1830s at Norman Road, Greenwich, and here vessels of widely varying type were built, notably a series of early screw ships incorporating engines made at the brothers' ironworks near Blackfriars Bridge. Among Sir John's personal contributions to this side of the business was the design of fixed floats for paddle wheels. The Rennies were also early in the field as railway engineers, designing a line from Liverpool to Manchester in 1825–6 on a medium gauge of 5 ft 6 in., but their plan was superseded by that of the more aggressive Stephensons. Generally, Rennie's practice in railways was not large. In 1852 he sketched out a system of railways for Sweden, and in 1855 a series of unexecuted railways and harbours for Portugal.

Rennie was elected a fellow of the Royal Society in 1823 and of the Zoological Society in 1825. He joined the Institution of Civil Engineers only in 1844 but was its president in

1845–8 and surveyed the recent history of civil engineering in his inaugural address (1846). His contributions to the institution's *Proceedings* include a learned analysis of the harbour at Ostia, which he had studied in detail in 1819–20. He also published an *Account of Plymouth Breakwater* (1848), a magnum opus entitled *Theory, Formation and Construction of British and Foreign Harbours* (1851–4), and a genial and informative *Autobiography*, written in 1867 and published posthumously in 1875. His memoirs are full on his early life and his travels (including trips to Russia and Poland, about 1830, and to Spain, 1833). Rennie was a connecting link between older engineers such as Brindley, Smeaton, Telford, and his father, John Rennie, and younger men such as the Stephensons and the Brunels. He was more amiable and sociable than his father or brother and enjoyed the comfort and dignity which his family's professional success afforded him. He had one son, C. G. Colleton Rennie, but nothing is known of a wife, or whether the son was adopted within the family. He retired about 1863 and died at Bengeo, near Hertford, on 3 September 1874, just after his eightieth birthday.

ANDREW SAINT

Sir John Ogilvy (Jack) Rennie (1914–1981), by Walter Bird, *c.*1968

Sources J. Rennie, *Autobiography of Sir John Rennie, FRS* (1875) · *PICE*, 39 (1874–5), 273–8 · *Engineering* (11 Sept 1874), 206–7 · L. W. M. Stephens, *A history of the Royal William yard* [typescript] · d. cert.
Archives Inst. CE, life of John Rennie and reports · National Railway Museum, York, accounts · NL Scot., corresp. and papers · NL Scot., account book | BL, reports to Lord Melville, Add. MS 41345 · Cambs. AS, report and papers relating to River Nene · Durham RO, corresp. relating to Seaham harbour · East Kent Archives Centre, reports and surveys of Romney and Walland marshes · Inst. CE, papers relating to London Bridge · NL Scot., letters to his father, John Rennie
Likenesses S. J. Rochard, miniature, 1831, V&A [*see illus.*] · J. Andrews, oils, exh. RA 1853, Inst. CE · engraving, repro. in *Autobiography of Sir John Rennie, FRS*

Rennie, Sir John Ogilvy [Jack] (1914–1981), diplomatist and intelligence officer, was born on 13 January 1914 at 12 Hyde Park Mansions, Marylebone, London, one among the two children of Charles Ogilvy Rennie, match manufacturer, and his wife, Agnes Annette, *née* Paton. He was educated at Wellington College and Balliol College, Oxford, where he showed precocious talent as a painter, exhibiting at the Royal Academy in 1930 and 1931 and at the Paris Salon in 1932. On leaving Oxford in 1935, with third-class honours in modern history, he joined the advertising agency Kenyon & Eckhardt Inc. in New York. In 1938 he married a Swiss subject, Anne-Marie Céline Monica (*d.* 1964), daughter of Charles Godat, of La Chaux-de-Fonds, Switzerland. They had a son.

After the outbreak of the Second World War, Rennie joined the staff of the British consulate in Baltimore, becoming vice-consul there in September 1940. He was then drawn into the British Press Service and its successor, the British Information Services, which were being organized to combat German propaganda in the United States. From 1942 to 1946 he worked in New York as head of the section producing radio programmes designed to put across the British viewpoint. It was during this period that another aspect of his intellectual versatility was shown

when he took up the study of electronics, which later became a hobby. In January 1946 he was formally accepted into the foreign service and on his return to London in December that year was appropriately posted to the Foreign Office's information policy department.

In March 1949 Rennie was appointed first secretary (commercial) in Washington, where he began to establish his reputation in the foreign service, and he was transferred to Warsaw with similar duties in June 1951. It was during the following two years in Poland that he gained firsthand experience of what life behind the Iron Curtain was really like. This enhanced his qualifications for his first senior appointment as counsellor and head of the information research department (IRD) in December 1953. IRD had been set up in 1949 at the instigation of Ernest Bevin and Christopher Mayhew, then his parliamentary under-secretary of state. Its main directive was to disseminate anonymously both at home and abroad evidence about the dangers of Soviet-style communism. Rennie soon found his feet in IRD and was widely admired for his skill and ingenuity, deployed over an unusually long five-year tenure of office, in advancing its reputation. During the 1956 Suez crisis he was appointed to head a committee in charge of British propaganda and disinformation operations in the Middle East. This included a news agency, the Arab News Agency, to feed pro-British material into the Arab media, and a number of radio stations broadcasting anti-Egyptian propaganda. He was appointed CMG in the same year. In April 1958 he was promoted commercial minister in Buenos Aires, a post which led to a similarly successful appointment in Washington in 1960. Soon thereafter his luck turned the other way. His wife fell seriously ill and in 1963 he took a year off in order to be at her side until her death in 1964.

On his return to the Foreign Office in 1964 Rennie was appointed assistant under-secretary for the Americas and headed a special mission to Central America in an effort to resolve the problems between Guatemala and British Honduras. A short period of secondment to the civil service commission as chairman of an interviewing board followed in 1966. On 19 July that year he married Jennifer Margaret, widow of Lieutenant Julian Miles Wemyss Rycroft, Royal Navy officer, and daughter of Lieutenant-Colonel John Gordon Wainwright, army officer, of Penn, Buckinghamshire. They had two sons. In October 1966 he was promoted deputy under-secretary for defence matters, which involved him in chairing a number of cabinet committees and liaising between the Foreign Office and the Ministry of Defence. Recognition of his performance was shown by his appointment as KCMG in 1967.

Amid continuing suspicion within the Labour government over some of the activities of the Secret Intelligence Service (SIS), or MI6, Rennie was appointed in spring 1968 to replace Sir Dick White as 'C', the head of the service. The deliberate choice of an outsider angered many within the service and made life very difficult for Rennie. For three months Maurice Oldfield, who had been White's deputy and as such, under SIS tradition, his anointed successor, ran the service on his own, ensuring that all important operational information came direct to him and not to Rennie. Oldfield's biographer summed up Oldfield's assessment of Rennie, as 'disastrously slow to act, always looking over his shoulder and far too apt to seek unworkable compromises' (Deacon, 152). Although the two men eventually achieved a *modus vivendi*, their relationship was never easy. Oldfield continued to oppose many of Rennie's decisions, including—on the grounds that the SIS traditionally operated only in foreign territory—his agreement to the request in 1971 of the Conservative prime minister Edward Heath that SIS send an officer to Northern Ireland with a brief to make contact with the 'street communities'. It was the initial contacts between this SIS officer, Frank Steele, and two young republicans, Gerry Adams and Martin McGuinness, that led to the so-called 'back-channel' and eventually to the Northern Ireland peace process.

Rennie suffered further family tragedy when his son Charles and his daughter-in-law were sent to gaol on drugs charges in 1973. This incident was widely publicized after the story, involving Rennie's identity, had appeared in the Hamburg magazine *Der Stern*. His offer to resign was turned down and he continued in charge of SIS until his official retirement date in January 1974, when he was succeeded by Oldfield. He then devoted his time to painting and his lifelong love of sailing, with occasional duties as chairman of the English Speaking Union's current affairs committee. He died on 30 September 1981 at St Thomas's Hospital, Lambeth, and was survived by his wife, Jennifer, and his three sons. NIGEL CLIVE, rev. MICHAEL SMITH

Sources R. Deacon, *'C': a biography of Sir Maurice Oldfield* (1985) · D. Leigh, *The Wilson plot: the intelligence services and the discrediting of a prime minister, 1943–1976* (1988) · *WWW* · *FO List* (–1974) · private information (1990) · personal knowledge (1990) · *Balliol College Register* · *CGPLA Eng. & Wales* (1981) · b. cert. · m. cert. [Jennifer Margaret Rycroft] · d. cert.

Likenesses W. Bird, photograph, *c.*1968, priv. coll. [*see illus.*]

Wealth at death £131,469: probate, 5 Nov 1981, *CGPLA Eng. & Wales*

Renniger, Michael (1528/9–1609), Church of England clergyman, was born in Hampshire, of a family connected with Basingstoke (the only place to whose poor he bequeathed money where he had not held ecclesiastical preferment) and apparently of some status. His brother Robert became sheriff of Southampton in 1546 and comptroller of the customs there in 1548. Although entered (probably briefly) in the university registers at Cambridge, Michael Renniger became a demy of Magdalen College, Oxford, in 1544; he graduated in 1546 and became a fellow. He was lecturer in Greek (1548–50), then in natural philosophy (1551) and moral philosophy (1552), proceeding MA in 1549. In 1550 he signed the protestant fellows' petition complaining of President Owen Oglethorpe's preference for the 'unlearned and papists' (Bloxam, 2.309–11), and indeed approached Sir William Cecil privately to complain of Oglethorpe. Yet he joined the other fellows in petitioning against plans to dissolve Magdalen choir as a chantry. At the end of 1550 he visited Zürich 'for the sake of printing the English bible' (Coverdale's translation) and to take letters to Heinrich Bullinger (Robinson, *Original Letters*, 425). According to John Bale, Renniger published in 1550 a Latin translation of the defence of clerical marriage against Richard Smith attributed to John Ponet. He certainly contributed at length to the universities' *Epigrammata varia … in morte[m] duorum fratrum Henrici et Caroli Brandoni* in 1552.

In 1552 Renniger was presented to Broughton rectory, Hampshire, by his brother Robert, who wrote to Cecil to recommend him. He may have vacated his Magdalen fellowship then—Broughton was worth £37 10*s.* p.a. and, according to his epitaph, he left a wife behind on Mary's accession. He had disappeared before the Catholic visitorial purge of the college, but, according to the recollections of Rose Hickman sixty years later, he did not leave England until about March 1554, borrowing £5 from Anthony Hickman to go to study divinity at Louvain. But Bullinger, to whom he was 'much attached', recorded his arrival in Zürich in April 1554 with his Magdalen contemporary John Mullins. He was briefly in Strasbourg, where in November 1554 he signed the letter to the congregation of Frankfurt deploring attempts to be purer liturgically than the Marian martyrs.

After 1558 Renniger returned to England, and Elizabeth made him a royal chaplain, while in 1560 she gave him the rectory of Crawley, Hampshire, and the seventh prebend in Winchester Cathedral (later exchanged for the twelfth). In the 1561 election for the Magdalen presidency, when Laurence Humphrey and John Mullins were the main candidates, he gained only a single vote; the same year, he was one of the eight married men mentioned by Edmund Grindal as possibilities for the Eton provostship, but was passed over in favour of the (then unmarried) William Day. He still resided at court and was noted by Henry Machyn as preaching at Paul's Cross (23 November 1561) and in rapid succession at the funerals of Sir Humphrey Browne and William, Lord Grey of Wilton (15 and 20 December 1562). As proctor for Winchester chapter in the convocation of 1563 he voted for further liturgical reform. At the beginning of 1566 he was instituted to the chancellorship of Lincoln Cathedral at Sir Francis Knollys's presentation, and by 31 March 1567 had also become precentor, an office which under his predecessor had had the prebend of Empingham annexed to it. He resigned as chancellor some time before 23 September 1568, no doubt because he had now been appointed subdean—he was installed on 16 October. Nominated by Bishop Nicholas Bullingham, he acted as cathedral lecturer from 1566 to 1569. By 3 August 1572 he had resigned as precentor, but retained his prebend of Empingham (which had been Bullingham's own before Mary's accession). Perhaps his doing so was regarded as anomalous, for in 1592 the crown re-presented him to the prebend, and he seems to have paid first fruits again. He was in 'major residence' at Lincoln until 1576, and again from 1593.

After proceeding DTh at Oxford in 1573, Renniger gained the archdeaconry of Winchester and the rectory of Chilbolton, Hampshire, in 1575, and yet another prebend, of Reculverland in St Paul's, in 1583. He was also an ecclesiastical commissioner for the dioceses of Lincoln and Peterborough, and for Winchester. His pluralism, if mainly in sinecures, was notable—in 1590, rather late in the day, he obtained a dispensation from the faculty office at Lambeth, and he was the subject of more than one complaint for failing to ensure adequate service at Crawley.

Renniger sought to justify royal favour by his publications. The papally backed expedition to Ireland provoked him to a denunciation, *De Pii V et Gregori XIII Romanorum pontificum furoribus contra … Elizabetham* (1582). Intensified crisis provoked a further anti-Catholic work in 1587—*A treatise containing two parts: An exhortation to true love, loyaltie, and fidelitie to her majestie, and, A treatise against treasons, rebellions, and suchlike disloyalties*—which, stressing his role as 'one of your majestie's old sworne servantes of housholde' (sig. A2r), he dedicated to the queen. In both works he used the Old Testament to show divine approval of political loyalty to monarchy, while also drawing largely on secular history, especially that of the medieval empire (to a degree that might owe something to his exile in German-speaking lands), for papal antagonism to this principle. His last work, *Syntagma hortationum … ad … Regem Jacobum, etc.* (1604), returned to these themes in somewhat calmer mood, hailing James I in specifically imperial terms.

Renniger's putative first wife may have been the mother of his daughter Elizabeth, who married Christopher Peryn of the Winchester chapter in 1583. It appears that on 23 December 1570 Renniger married Margery Ely (d. 1615?), sister of Leonard Ely of Wonsington, Hampshire. Apart from Elizabeth, the three sons and three other daughters mentioned in his will seem mostly to have been

born between c.1574 and 1588. He made this will on 21 August 1609, commending his soul to Christ 'with an assured fayth of my salvation only and wholly by Him' (PRO, PROB 11/144/88). He died at Crawley five days later and was buried in the church with a memorial inscription. Recorded as aged forty-seven in 1576, he would have been about eighty when he died.

Renniger's will, over fourteen sides in a registrar's transcript, perhaps testifies to the potential advantages of multiple middle-tier ecclesiastical posts over a bishopric or major deanery. Directing the payment of debts of over £600, he entailed considerable land in Lincolnshire, Yorkshire, and Hampshire on his three sons, Michael, Samuel, and Raphael (although the latter had gone into the church), with a life interest to Margery. He may very well have inherited family property in Hampshire, but the Lincolnshire lands (largely formerly monastic) were probably his own acquisitions, and raised his descendants to established gentry status in a new county. Renniger also left to Winchester Cathedral a farm valuable enough to fund nearly £170 per annum in charitable donations: to Oxford poor scholars, Winchester and Lincoln cathedral libraries, and paupers in both counties. He remembered his days in exile with 20 French crowns for the Swiss theologian Lewis Lavater, son-in-law of his old mentor Bullinger, and another 20 for the poor of Zürich. Henry Cotton, bishop of Salisbury, formerly a fellow prebendary of Winchester, received a memorial ring, but Renniger had outlived most of his more intimate colleagues.

JULIAN LOCK

Sources J. R. Bloxam, *A register of the presidents, fellows … of Saint Mary Magdalen College*, 8 vols. (1853–85), vol. 2 • will, PRO, PROB 11/114, sig. 88 • C. H. Garrett, *The Marian exiles: a study in the origins of Elizabethan puritanism* (1938) • W. D. Macray, *A register of the members of St Mary Magdalen College, Oxford*, 8 vols. (1894–1915), vol. 2 • Wood, *Ath. Oxon.*, new edn, 2.51–3 • Venn, *Alum. Cant.*, 1/3.441 • H. Robinson, ed. and trans., *Original letters relative to the English Reformation*, 1 vol. in 2, Parker Society, [26] (1846–7), 374–5, 750–51 • A. R. Maddison, ed., *Lincolnshire pedigrees*, 3, Harleian Society, 52 (1904), 817-18 • IGI • C. W. Foster, ed., *Lincoln episcopal records*, Lincoln RS, 2 (1912) • C. W. Foster, ed., *The state of the church in the reigns of Elizabeth and James I*, Lincoln RS, 23 (1926) • R. B. Walker, 'Lincoln Cathedral in the reign of Queen Elizabeth I', *Journal of Ecclesiastical History*, 11 (1960), 186–201 • court of wards and liveries, inquisitions post mortem, PRO, WARD 7/44/106 • exchequer, office of first fruits and tenths, composition books, PRO, E334 • Faculty Office register, LPL, F1/B, fol. 140v • episcopal visitation returns, Hants. RO, Winchester diocesan records, 21M65.B1 • consistory court depositions, Winchester, 1566–71, Hants. RO, Winchester diocesan records, 21M65.C3/4 • A. W. Goodman, 'The cathedral church and archdeaconry of Winchester in 1562', *Proceedings of the Hampshire Field Club and Archaeological Society*, 14 (1940), 63–85, esp. 66–7 • VCH Hampshire and the Isle of Wight, 3.412; 4.215–16, 493–4 • J. R. Lock, '"Strange usurped potentates": Elizabeth I, the papacy, and the Indian summer of the medieval deposing power', DPhil diss., U. Oxf., 1992, 88n., 95, 97–8, 103, 106–8 • J. Shakespeare and M. Dowling, 'Religion and politics in mid-Tudor England through the eyes of an English protestant woman: the recollections of Rose Hickman', *BIHR*, 55 (1982), 94–102, esp. 99 • *Calendar of the manuscripts of the most hon. the marquis of Salisbury*, 1, HMC, 9 (1883), p. 91, no. 366 • B. Usher, 'Backing protestantism: the London godly, the exchequer, and the Foxe circle', *John Foxe: an historical perspective* [Oxford 1997], ed. D. Loades (1999), 105–34 • *The diary of Henry Machyn, citizen and merchant-taylor of London, from AD 1550 to AD 1563,* ed. J. G. Nichols, CS, 42 (1848) • Bale, *Cat.*, vol. 1 • A. B. Wallis Chapman, ed., *The Black Book of Southampton*, 3, Southampton RS, 17 (1915), 90 • F. W. Pledge, *Crawley* (1907), 159 • *Fasti Angl., 1541–1857*, [Lincoln]

Archives BL, letters to Sir William Cecil

Wealth at death £30 cash legacies; £600 of debts; estate valued at over £166 p.a.; ecclesiastical income more than £200 p.a., incl. archdeaconry of Winchester £67 15s. p.a., sub-deanery of Lincoln £35 8s Empingham at £25 6s., Reculverland at £8 7s., Crawley at £35 13s., and Chilbolton at £26 19s.: will, PRO, PROB 11/144/88

Renny, George Alexander (1825–1887), army officer, son of Alexander Renny, a British merchant settled at Riga in Livonia, was born at Riga. A branch of the family had been settled in Russia for more than a century. His mother was widowed shortly after his birth. She went to Scotland with her son and daughter in 1827, and settled at Montrose, Forfarshire, near her husband's relatives. Renny was educated at Montrose Academy and at Addiscombe College (1842–4). He was commissioned second lieutenant, Bengal horse artillery, on 7 June 1844, and went to India in December.

Renny took part in the Sutlej campaign from 24 January 1846, and was present at the battle of Sobraon (10 February 1846). He was promoted first lieutenant on 6 October 1846. He commanded the loyal 5th native troop of the 1st brigade of the Bengal horse artillery during the Indian mutiny, from 1857 to 1858. He was engaged with the mutineers in Jullundur on 7 June 1857, and was at the siege of Delhi from 23 June. When the assault of 14 September was made, he commanded no. 4 siege battery, covering the assault; and when the storming was over he took some gunners of his troop with 12-pounder mortars to shell the houses and streets in front of the attack. During the 14th and 15th a captured gun in the Kashmir bastion was turned on the enemy by his troop. On the 16th he was engaged in the attack on the magazine. After its capture, the enemy advanced to the high walls of the magazine under cover of a heavy crossfire from the high houses on the right and also from the Salimgarh and the palace. Renny bravely climbed to the top of the magazine wall and pelted the enemy with live shells, handed up to him with their fuses lighted. He continued this until the enemy were forced to retire and the safety of the magazine was assured. His troop turned the mortars captured at the magazine on the Salimgarh and the palace. For his conduct he received the Victoria Cross. He was further engaged at the capture of the Salimgarh and of the palace on 20 September. After taking part in the operations in the Muzaffarnagar district, in 1858 he commanded the native horse artillery in Rohilkhand, under Brigadier-General Walpole, and took part in all the operations of the campaigns, including the action of Sisseah, near Pilibhit, on 15 January 1859. Both Walpole and Lord Clyde officially expressed their appreciation of his conduct and that of his troop, which was 'beyond all praise'. Renny was mentioned in dispatches and commended by the government of India.

Renny had been promoted captain on 17 April 1858, and on 20 July he had received a brevet majority for his services at Delhi. He was promoted brevet lieutenant-colonel

on 1 June 1867. He commanded D battery F brigade of the horse artillery throughout the Hazara and Black Mountain campaign of 1868, when his mountain battery was carried on elephants. He was promoted regimental lieutenant-colonel on 28 August 1871, and colonel in the army on 28 August 1876. As colonel he commanded the Royal Artillery in Sind, in the Mau division, and also the station of Ahmednagar. He retired from active employment on 31 December 1878 with the rank of major-general. He married in India Miss Flora McWhirter, who died in 1893; they had three sons and three daughters, who survived him. He died at his home, 24 Rivers Street, Bath, on 5 January 1887, and was buried in the Locksbrook cemetery, Bath.   R. H. VETCH, *rev.* ROGER T. STEARN

Sources Royal Artillery Institution, Woolwich, Royal Artillery records • H. M. Vibart, *Addiscombe: its heroes and men of note* (1894) • G. B. Malleson, *History of the Indian mutiny, 1857–1858: commencing from the close of the second volume of Sir John Kaye's History of the Sepoy War*, 3 vols. (1878–80) • C. Hibbert, *The great mutiny, India, 1857* (1978) • T. A. Heathcote, *The military in British India: the development of British land forces in south Asia, 1600–1947* (1995) • private information (1896) • Boase, *Mod. Eng. biog.* • CGPLA *Eng. & Wales* (1887)

Wealth at death £1192 19s. 7d.: probate, 10 Feb 1887, CGPLA *Eng. & Wales*

Renouard, George Cecil (1780–1867), classical and oriental scholar, born at Stamford, Lincolnshire, on 7 September 1780, was the youngest son of Peter Renouard (*d.* 1801) of Stamford, adjutant in the Rutland militia, and his wife, Mary, daughter of John Henry Ott, rector of Gamston, Nottinghamshire, and prebendary of Richmond and Peterborough. George entered St Paul's School, London, in 1793, and in the same year, on the nomination of George III, was admitted on the foundation of Charterhouse School. In 1798 he proceeded to Trinity College, Cambridge; in 1800 he migrated to Sidney Sussex College; he graduated BA in 1802, MA in 1805, and BD in 1811.

After obtaining a fellowship at Sidney Sussex in 1804, Renouard became that year chaplain to the British embassy at Constantinople. In 1806 he returned to England, and served as curate of Great St Mary's, Cambridge. From 1810 to 1814 he was chaplain to the factory at Smyrna. During his time there he discovered on a rock near Nymphio a figure which he identified with the Sesostris of Herodotus. His priority of discovery was afterwards disputed, but it was finally vindicated by Dr L. Schmitz in the *Classical Museum* (no. 2, 232–3). In 1815 Renouard returned to Cambridge to fill the post of lord almoner's professor of Arabic, which he held until 1821. For a time he also acted as curate of Grantchester, near Cambridge. In 1818 he was presented to the valuable college living of Swanscombe, Kent. While at Smyrna in 1813 he baptized John William *Burgon, whose close friend and correspondent he became. Burgon dedicated to him his *Fifty Smaller Scriptural Cottage Prints* in 1851. Renouard died unmarried at Swanscombe rectory on 15 February 1867, and was buried in Swanscombe churchyard on 21 February.

Renouard was an admirable classical scholar, was acquainted with French, German, and Italian, and gained during his time in the East a thorough knowledge of the

Arabic, Turkish, and Hebrew languages. Although his publications were few, he obtained a wide reputation as a linguist, geographer, and botanist. During the forty-nine years that he lived at Swanscombe he maintained a voluminous correspondence with the most distinguished orientalists and geographers of Europe, and he was an industrious contributor to the journals of learned societies. For the British and Foreign Bible Society he corrected the proofs of the translations of the scriptures into Turkish and other eastern languages. He was a leading member of the translation committee of the Royal Asiatic Society, to which he was elected in 1824, revising many of its publications. His paper on the language of the Berbers was communicated to the society in 1836 (*Journal of the Royal Asiatic Society*, 1st ser., 3, 1836, 131–60). From 1836 to 1846 he was honorary foreign secretary of the Royal Geographical Society, and he actively interested himself in the Syro-Egyptian and Numismatic societies. He wrote on Rome and Greece for the *Encyclopaedia Metropolitana* (1852).   G. C. BOASE, rev. H. C. G. MATTHEW

Sources GM, 4th ser., 3 (1867), 535–7 · *Proceedings* [Royal Geographical Society], 12 (1867–8), 188–9 · E. M. Goulburn, *John William Burgon, late dean of Chichester: a biography*, 2 vols. (1892) · Venn, *Alum. Cant.*

Archives RGS, letters to Royal Geographical Society

Wealth at death under £4000: probate, 15 March 1867, *CGPLA Eng. & Wales*

Renouf, Sir Peter Le Page (1822–1897), Egyptologist and religious writer, was born on 23 August 1822 at St Peter Port, Guernsey, the son of Joseph Renouf, schoolmaster, and his wife, Mary, daughter of John Le Page. He was educated from 1831 at Elizabeth College, Guernsey, and matriculated with a scholarship at Pembroke College, Oxford, in 1840. He soon was drawn by Newman into the Tractarian movement, and was so advanced in his views that he published anonymously in 1841 a pamphlet on the real presence. He converted to the Roman Catholic faith, being received in the church in March 1842 at St Mary's College, Oscott, where he remained as classical tutor. From 1846 to 1854 he was a tutor in a French noble family, travelling with them about the continent and developing his varied scholarly interests. On 25 July 1857 he married in Germany Ludovica Brentano (1836–1921), daughter of Christian Brentano, niece of the poets Achim von Arnim and Clemens Brentano and sister of the philosopher Franz Brentano and the economist Lujo Brentano. She assisted him in his researches and arranged the posthumous publication of his *Life-Work*. They had a son and a daughter.

In 1854 Renouf was appointed by Newman to the faculty of his Catholic university in Dublin, becoming in 1855 professor of ancient history and later also of oriental languages. Here he began his studies in Egyptology, through examining the illustrated funerary held at the college, and began a correspondence with Edward Hincks, the pioneer of Egyptology in Ireland. Renouf published several articles in the university magazine *Atlantis*, including an important refutation of Sir George Cornewall Lewis's criticism of the decipherment of Champollion. He also

published a pamphlet in 1864 advocating a Catholic university in England. In the same year Renouf accepted an appointment as an English inspector of schools, initially visiting Roman Catholic schools but from the 1870s all schools in the Tower Hamlets district. He remained in this service until 1885.

Renouf's Catholicism was increasingly of the liberal variety, opposed to the dominant ultramontanism. He contributed in 1863–4 to the liberal Catholic *Home and Foreign Review*, edited by Acton, and briefly served as a subeditor; he was later to contribute to the *North British Review* in its liberal Catholic phase (1869–71). Anticipating the struggle over the definition of papal infallibility, which he opposed, he published in 1868 a pamphlet entitled *The Condemnation of Pope Honorius*, in which he argued that a pope had been condemned for monothelite heresy. This work, which was translated into Dutch, was placed on the Index and precipitated a controversy which included a rejoinder by Renouf. When papal infallibility was defined, Renouf remained in the Roman Catholic church; but he stayed in contact with those who left the church, including Dr Döllinger and his brother-in-law Franz Brentano. As late as 1890 Renouf and his wife were engaged in seeking the reconciliation of Döllinger to the church at the time of Döllinger's death.

Renouf's Egyptological studies continued; in 1875 he and his wife travelled to Egypt. He had become a member of the Society of Biblical Archaeology in 1872 and contributed to its *Publications*; he was president of the society from 1887 to his death. In 1875 he published *An Elementary Grammar of the Egyptian Language*. In 1879 he was invited to give the Hibbert lectures, published in 1880 as *Lectures on the Origin and Growth of Religion, as Illustrated by the Religion of Ancient Egypt*. His theory of a latent monotheism in Egyptian religion has not been generally accepted. He was more fortunate in his philological researches. In March 1886 Renouf was appointed keeper of Egyptian and Assyrian antiquities at the British Museum, where he carried on the work of arranging, modernizing, and enlarging the Egyptian collection, also working on the Assyrian antiquities, to which he published a guide in 1886. His most important work was on *The Book of the Dead*, in which he published the papyrus of Ani (1890); his translation of the entire work was unfinished at his death and was completed by Edouard Naville. At the end of 1891 Renouf was compulsorily retired from the British Museum, but he continued his work with the Society of Biblical Archaeology until his death. He was belatedly knighted in 1896. He died at 46 Rowland Gardens, South Kensington, London, on 14 October 1897, and was buried on 22 October in the crypt of St Joseph's Church, St Peter Port, Guernsey. His shorter works were republished under the supervision of his widow as *The Life-Work of Sir Peter Le Page Renouf* (4 vols., 1902–7), with a biography by his daughter. His lasting achievement was in furthering knowledge of the language of ancient Egypt, but a century after his death his works were not often consulted by scholars.

JOSEF L. ALTHOLZ

Sources [E. Renouf], 'Biography', *The life-work of Sir Peter Le Page Renouf*, ed. G. Maspero, W. H. Ryland, and E. Naville, 4 vols. (1902–7), 4.v–cxxxiii · W. R. Dawson and E. P. Uphill, *Who was who in Egyptology*, 2nd edn (1972), 246–7 · *Publications of the Society of Biblical Archaeology*, 19 (1897) · *Zeitschrift für Ägyptische Sprache*, 35 (1897), 165–6 · Boase, *Mod. Eng. biog.*, 6.462 · *DNB* · private information (2004) [J. D. Ray]
Archives CUL, corresp. · Pembroke College, Oxford, corresp. and papers · U. Oxf., Griffith Institute, corresp. and papers | BM, Dawson MS 18, fols. 1–94
Likenesses portrait, repro. in *Publications of the Society of Biblical Archaeology*, facing p. 271

Renshaw, (James) Ernest (1861–1899). *See under* Renshaw, William Charles (1861–1904).

Renshaw, William Charles (1861–1904), tennis player, and his twin brother, **(James) Ernest Renshaw** (1861–1899), also a tennis player and sometime doubles partner, were born at Brandon Parade, Leamington, Warwickshire, on 3 January 1861, the sons of James Renshaw, of High Broughton, Manchester, a flax spinner, and his wife, Ellen Knight. James Renshaw died in September 1860, before his sons' birth, leaving an estate valued between £60,000 and £70,000. For two years the brothers attended Cheltenham College as day boys, before leaving in July 1874. Tradition has it that they learned to play tennis on asphalt courts in their home town, where Thomas Gem and J. B. A. Perera had established a club. Five years later they first entered the All England tennis championships at Wimbledon, but, overawed by the crowd, they chose not to play but to watch and learn. Their début on court at the championships came in 1880, when Willie was beaten in the second round and Ernest, for once progressing further than his older brother, reached round three. Then began a period of unparalleled domination. Willie won the men's singles title from 1881 to 1886, Ernest won it the following year, and Willie won his seventh championship in 1889. Playing together they also won five men's doubles titles.

The Renshaw twins revolutionized tennis technique and tactics. Rich enough to be full-time amateurs, they practised hard, including during winter at the Hôtel Beau Site in Cannes on the French riviera. Until they came on the scene most players had attempted to bring to lawn tennis either the heavy cuts of real tennis or the wristy flicks of rackets. The Renshaws, in contrast, developed a distinctive lawn tennis style, often taking the ball early with volleys and smashes rather than waiting for it to bounce. They also radically changed the manner of playing doubles by having one player stand at the net to intercept and volley back returns of service. Willie was the better player, forceful, determined, and full of fire and dash, in contrast to the patient, graceful, and more restrained Ernest. The last appearance of a Renshaw at Wimbledon was in 1893, when the twins were drawn to play each other in the first round—there being no seeding in those days—but Willie withdrew in favour of his younger brother, who lost in the subsequent round.

Ernest Renshaw died on 2 September 1899 at The Grange, Waltham St Lawrence, near Twyford, Berkshire. He had ingested spirits of carbolic acid but the subsequent inquest could find no evidence whether this had been taken intentionally or not. Willie Renshaw, described as a gentleman of independent means, died at Swanage, Dorset, on 12 August 1904 following epileptic convulsions. Neither twin was married. Their relatives donated a trophy, the Renshaw cup, to the All England club, which for many years was presented to the winner of the men's singles at the Wimbledon championships.

WRAY VAMPLEW

Sources *The Sporting Life: British sports and sportsmen* (1908) · E. S. Skirving, ed., *Cheltenham College register, 1841–1927* (1928) · E. Potter, *Kings of the court* (1963) · A. W. Myers, *Lawn tennis: its principles and practice* (1930) · J. Arlott, ed., *The Oxford companion to sports and games* (1975) · Boase, *Mod. Eng. biog.* · *CGPLA Eng. & Wales* (1899) [James Ernest Renshaw] · *CGPLA Eng. & Wales* (1904) · b. cert. · d. cert. · b. cert. [James Ernest Renshaw] · d. cert. [James Ernest Renshaw]
Likenesses engraving, repro. in Myers, *Lawn tennis* (1930), 26 · photograph, repro. in *The Sporting Life*, 2, 203, 313 · portrait, repro. in *Sporting Mirror* (June 1883), 263 · portraits, repro. in *ILN* (9 Sept 1899), 347
Wealth at death £61,604 6s.: probate, 3 Oct 1904, *CGPLA Eng. & Wales* · £49,938 14s. 9d.—James Ernest Renshaw: administration, 18 Dec 1899, *CGPLA Eng. & Wales*

Rentoul, Sir Gervais Squire Chittick (1884–1946), founding chairman of the Conservative 1922 committee, was born on 1 August 1884 at Plumstead, Woolwich, London. He was the elder of the two sons of James Alexander Rentoul (1854–1919), a barrister, Unionist MP for East Down (1890–1902), and then an Old Bailey judge, and his wife, Florence Young (d. 1914). He attended the City of London School from the age of nine, after which he spent over a year in France and Germany before going to Christ Church, Oxford, in 1903, where he read jurisprudence. He had a lifelong passion for the stage; at Oxford he was involved in theatrical productions. In 1906 he was elected president of the Oxford Union. In 1907 Rentoul was called to the bar at Gray's Inn, practising on the south-eastern circuit. He came to public attention in 1912 as a defence counsel in the Seddon murder trial. By this time he was earning about £500 a year, and on 30 March 1912 he married (Christian) Muriel, the only daughter of Harold Alfred Smart, a City banker; they had one daughter. An accident in 1897 left him with limited movement in his right elbow and he was rejected for active duty during the First World War; from 1915 to 1918 he served as legal adviser to eastern command, with the rank of captain.

Rentoul cut his political teeth speaking for the Primrose League and he was always more effective on the platform than in the House of Commons; between 1927 and 1931 he spoke in 300 constituencies. He was adopted as Conservative anti-coalition candidate for Lowestoft in early 1922 after responding to a letter in the *Daily Mail* appealing for someone 'who would scorn to be a mere monkey-on-a-stick' for the party leaders (Rentoul, *This is my Case*, 87). After the Lloyd George coalition fell he won the seat with a majority of just under eight thousand, holding it until he stood down in 1934.

One of 111 Conservatives elected for the first time in 1922, Rentoul, like many of his colleagues, was frustrated by 'the maze of parliamentary procedure' and suggested forming 'a small committee for the guidance and assistance' of new MPs (Rentoul, *Sometimes I Think*, 232). A gathering held on 18 April 1923 approved Rentoul's idea and elected him as chairman. The Conservative Private Members (1922) Committee began as a self-help club for the new intake and was not intended to have any special political role. Under Rentoul's chairmanship the practice developed of inviting a whip to the weekly meeting to brief members on forthcoming business, and in this way the committee found a role which was of practical use to both back-benchers and whips. By 1926 it had expanded to include all Conservative back-benchers, resulting in the permanent renewal of its membership. For most of the inter-war period it functioned as a lecture club rather than a pressure group, and the one occasion when it sought to play a more ambitious role was a fiasco, which resulted in Rentoul's downfall.

In 1932 the committee launched an unofficial inquiry seeking economies in government spending, but the severity of the suggested cuts went far beyond what many Conservative MPs were willing to endorse. Rentoul mishandled the publication of the report in November 1932, appearing both autocratic and incompetent. For the first time his annual re-election to the chairmanship was challenged, and on 5 December 1932 W. S. Morrison defeated him by 117 votes to 76. Rentoul meanwhile had been parliamentary private secretary to the attorney-general from 1925 to 1928; he was knighted in 1929, took silk in 1930, and from 1929 to 1934 was recorder of Sandwich.

Rentoul had grey-blue eyes, a high forehead, a healthy complexion, and a firm mellow voice; beneath his dignified manner lay compassion and a sense of humour. Breezy, genial, and energetic, he was more reflective and ambitious than appeared on the surface. Bruised by the attacks of fellow MPs and the press over the economy inquiry and facing financial difficulties owing to the depression, he could see that office in the National Government was unlikely; as a result he took the 'most grievous and difficult decision' of his life, leaving the Commons on 4 January 1934 to take up the stipendiary position of metropolitan magistrate for West London, a post he found congenial and rewarding (Rentoul, *This is my Case*, 113). From 1941 he was a member of Kensington borough council. He published a volume of essays, *Sometimes I Think*, in 1940 and his memoirs, *This is my Case*, in 1944. His death came suddenly on 7 March 1946 at his Kensington flat at 101 Oakwood Court. He was survived by his wife.

STUART BALL

Sources G. Rentoul, *This is my case* [1944] · G. Rentoul, *Sometimes I think* (1940) · 1922 committee minute books, Bodl. Oxf. · S. Ball, 'The 1922 committee: the formative years, 1922–1945', *Parliamentary History*, 9 (1990), 129–57 · *The Times* (8 March 1946) · *CGPLA Eng. & Wales* (1946)

Likenesses photograph, repro. in Rentoul, *This is my case* [frontispiece]

Wealth at death £1077 9s. 10d.: administration with will, 12 July 1946, *CGPLA Eng. & Wales*

Renwick, James [alias James Bruce] (1662–1688), covenanter, was born on 15 February 1662, the only surviving son of Andrew Renwick (d. 1676), weaver, and his wife, Elizabeth (née Corson), near Moniaive, in Glencairn parish, Dumfriesshire. Reared in a godly home, he gave early promise of a keen mind and was enabled to study at Edinburgh University, from where he graduated MA in 1681. On 27 July that year he witnessed the execution in Edinburgh of the covenanting field preacher Donald Cargill. The spectacle sealed his resolve to side with the 'societies' of more resolute covenanters, soon known also as Cameronians after Richard Cameron (d. 1680). Cameron's issue in June 1680 of the first Sanquhar declaration, renouncing allegiance to Charles II, stimulated their assembly together as the 'united societies' which subsequently developed into the Reformed Presbyterian church. Renwick was among the band of forty armed men who, on 12 January 1682, posted the Lanark declaration again renouncing allegiance to the king. Although not its author Renwick was a rising star among the societies. Through the good offices of Sir Robert Hamilton he was sent to Groningen in the Netherlands for theological training in December 1682. His ordination there on 10 May 1683 would provide the ministerial leadership lost with Cargill and Cameron.

Renwick returned to Scotland via the English Channel, narrowly escaping arrest at Rye, and Dublin, travelling as James Bruce. Reaching Edinburgh by September 1683 he was given and accepted a call to ministry from the united societies meeting on 3 October at Darmead, Cambusnethan, Lanarkshire, after delivering his testimony (which he later admitted was 'too tart' in some expressions). On 23 November he preached his first sermon to the assembled societies at Darmead, on the text of Cargill's last sermon (Isaiah 26: 10).

Renwick now embarked on a wide-ranging ministry, field preaching, baptizing (600 children in a year), counselling, corresponding (especially with the society at Leeuwarden in Friesland), and eluding capture by a hairsbreadth. His letters and sermons are suffused with a sharp-edged but warm devotion to Christ as sole king of his church. Covenanting piety gloried in contrasts—between human wretchedness and Christ's beauty, between earthly distresses and heavenly felicity. It exalted suffering in Christ's cause, and tapped a rich vein of imagery, sometimes to excess. On 30 August 1684 Renwick refused a summons to appear before the privy council and on 24 September an interdiction banned all association with him and ordered all to assist in apprehending him. The societies were provoked into instructing him to draw up 'the Apologetical Declaration and Admonitory Vindication of the true Presbyterians of the Church of Scotland', which was widely posted up on 8 November 1684. It amounted almost to a declaration of war on opponents, and was met with a steep intensification of persecution of covenanters. Renwick regretted its publication, but did not apologize for its terms. The parliament in April 1685 made acknowledgement of the covenant a treasonable offence.

The accession of the Roman Catholic James VII and II

heightened the crisis. Renwick resumed use of his pseudonym James Bruce. On 28 May 1685 his band nailed up the second Sanquhar declaration, recalling Cameron's of five years earlier, but Renwick refused to join the revolt raised that year by Archibald Campbell, earl of Argyll, on the grounds of its insecure grounding in the covenant. For this and other reasons Renwick faced growing criticism, and some isolation. The societies' response, written largely by Renwick with Alexander Shields, his future biographer, was the 'Informatory Vindication', approved at Friarminion near Kirkconnel on 24 March 1687. It was a significant statement of Cameronian principles, explaining why they could not act on the king's indulgences to presbyterians on 12 February and 28 June 1687. Defiance evoked severer proclamations against conventicles, and on 18 October 1687 a high price was offered for Renwick's head.

Renwick still managed to move around, preaching on the Braid hills near Edinburgh and in Fife, and finally, on 29 January 1688, at Bo'ness on the Forth. He was arrested in the Cowgate, Edinburgh, on 1 February and hanged for treason in the Grassmarket on 17 February, almost the last of the covenanting martyrs. He was buried close to the covenanters' monument in Greyfriars churchyard, Edinburgh. In its own terms his trial was fair enough, but he resisted every manner of suasion to escape by compromise. Within a year revolution vindicated the cause for which he died. Renwick was survived by the 'sisters' who had attended him in his last days. Over sixty of his letters are extant, together with *A choice collection of very valuable prefaces* (that is, exhortations), *lectures and sermons*, edited by William Wilson from hearers' notes and first published in 1748.

D. F. WRIGHT

Sources A. Shields, *The life and death of … Mr. James Renwick* (1724) • W. H. Carslaw, *The life and letters of James Renwick* (1893) • W. H. Carslaw, *The life and times of James Renwick* (1901) • J. C. Johnston, *Treasury of the Scottish covenant* (1887) • DNB

Archives JRL, copies of letters and materials connected with drafts of Shields's *Life* • U. Edin. L., copies of letters and materials connected with drafts of Shields's *Life*, La iii 344 • U. Edin., New Coll. L., copies of letters and materials connected with drafts of Shields's *Life* • U. Glas. L., copies of letters and materials connected with drafts of Shields's *Life*, MS Gen 1009/31–1009/47

Renwick, William (*bap.* 1740, *d.* 1814), naval surgeon and author, the son of Andrew Renwick, was baptized in Berwick upon Tweed on 2 March 1740. In August 1760 he was appointed surgeon's mate of a regiment at Plymouth through the influence of General John Crawfurd. Renwick was apparently at the action at Belleisle (7 June 1761) and, after a two years' absence, was invalided, having temporarily lost his eyesight. In June 1763, following the peace, he was reduced, and seems to have unsuccessfully endeavoured to establish a medical practice in Berwick. In the Berwick by-election of January 1765 he was of some use to Sir John Hussey Delaval, who promised him his patronage, on the strength of which, and with no more tangible means of subsistence, he married, in June 1765, Abigail, daughter of Arthur Hindmarsh of Berwick. Poverty pursued him, and for seven years (1766–73) he left his wife,

endeavouring to gain a livelihood as 'journeyman apothecary' in London, Wokingham, and elsewhere. When he rejoined his wife about 1774 his attempt to establish a practice in Berwick met with little success, and in despair he published *Misplaced Confidence, or, Friendship Betrayed* (3 vols., 1777), in which he openly related the story of his sufferings, and attacked his former patron, Delaval.

In October 1778, through the influence of the earl of Lisburne, a lord of the Admiralty, to whom he had been recommended, Renwick was appointed surgeon of the *Countess of Scarborough*, which, on 23 September 1779, was captured off Flamborough Head by the squadron under John Paul Jones and taken to the Texel. He wrote a magniloquent description of the engagement in heroic verse. On being exchanged Renwick was appointed to the *Marlborough*, and, when she was ordered to the West Indies, to the *Egmont*, in which he was present at the relief of Gibraltar, and in the rencounter off Cape Spartel in October 1782. In February 1784 he was surgeon of the sloop *Thorn*, and afterwards of the *Merlin* on the Newfoundland station, and of the *Druid* in the channel and at Lisbon. In 1787 he was put on half pay, and in 1788 published *The Solicitudes of Absence*, mainly composed of correspondence from and to friends at home. From 1795 to December 1800 he was surgeon of the *Vulture*, and of the *Portland* until February 1802, when he was put on half pay. On 20 June 1804 he was, to his disgust, superannuated 'for various infirmities' on 3s. a day.

Renwick retired to Berwick, where he led a solitary and eccentric existence until his death there in October 1814; he was buried on 25 October.

Besides several pamphlets on the state of the medical service of the navy, and the two works already mentioned, Renwick wrote *The Sorrows of Love, with other Poems* (1810), *The Unfortunate Lovers, or, The Genuine Distress of Damon and Celia* (2 vols., 1771), and probably *Damon and Delia, a Tale* (1784). They are all largely autobiographical.

J. K. LAUGHTON, *rev.* MICHAEL BEVAN

Sources D. B. Smith and Royal Navy College, eds., *The commissioned sea officers of the Royal Navy, 1660–1815*, 3 [n.d., c.1954] • IGI • W. Renwick, *Misplaced confidence, or, Friendship betrayed*, 3 vols. (1777) • W. Renwick, *The solicitudes of absence* (1788) • W. Renwick, *Sorrows of love, with other poems* (1810) • W. Renwick, *The unfortunate lovers, or, The genuine distress of Damon and Celia*, 2 vols. (1771)

Renzy, Sir Matthew de (1577–1634), customs official and Gaelic scholar, was born in 1577 in 'Cullen' (probably Cologne), Germany. Having spent some time as a cloth dealer in Antwerp, he moved to London and lived there as a merchant stranger in Bishopsgate, where his brother Lazaro (Lionel) also lived. A courier between Lord Cobham and Count Arenbergh, in November 1603 he testified at the trial of Sir Walter Ralegh and Cobham. As a result of a commercial collapse in London in the winter of 1606, de Renzy fled via Scotland to Ireland bringing, he later claimed, less than £5 with him. He then travelled widely in Ireland, and made himself known to the earl of Thomond and Lord Deputy Chichester. While in co. Clare in 1607 he made contact with the Gaelic learned family of the Mac Bruaideadha, and started learning spoken and written Irish with them. A Mac Bruaideadha praise poem and biography, in his honour, survive. One of a group of land searchers associated with Richard Boyle, by 1613 he had acquired his own property, along the Shannon, in the lordship of Delvin Mac Coghlan in King's county. From 1613 until 1618 or 1619 he lived in the midlands, and his letters and notes reflect his concerns as an isolated planter living in a still functioning Gaelic lordship.

De Renzy married twice after coming to Ireland: his first wife, whom he married about 1608, was Mary Adams (d. c.1610) of Dublin; his second was Ann, daughter of Richard Maypowder, a landed gentleman of co. Roscommon. In the reform of the Irish customs in 1619, the trio of William Massam (De Renzy's brother-in-law), John Pitt, and de Renzy became the agents of the farmers of the Irish customs, under the patronage of Lionel Cranfield (later earl of Middlesex), lord treasurer of England. De Renzy moved to Dublin, and supervised the customs there. The deaths of Massam and Pitt in 1622 increased his official duties: he took on the supervision of the lucrative tobacco farm, and became chief collector of the impost of wines, under James Hay, earl of Carlisle. De Renzy became the chief accountant of the farm of the Irish customs, and succeeded Massam as Middlesex's Irish agent in 1623. He later became Irish agent of the earl of Carlisle, and of Oliver St John, Viscount Grandison, lord high treasurer of Ireland. The lord deputy, Falkland, conferred a knighthood on him in 1627.

The 1619–20 midland plantations, for which de Renzy had campaigned, offered the prospect of further acquisitions. He increased his landholding in King's county through purchase and mortgage, as well as by plantation grant. In 1628 he became one of the first burgesses of the newly established plantation town of Banagher in King's county. De Renzy claimed to have composed a grammar, dictionary, and chronicle in the Irish tongue within the space of three years, a claim noted by John Lynch, in *Cambrensis eversus* (1662). None of these three works is known to have survived. According to the antiquary Roderick O'Flaherty, however, the grammar was the work of De Renzy's tutor, Tadhg Óg O hUiginn. The planter's surviving letters and notes contain topographical and genealogical material in Gaelic script, showing a knowledge of Irish perhaps unparalleled among those who settled in Ireland in the early modern period.

De Renzy died in Dublin on 29 August 1634, and was survived by his second wife, who was still living in 1663. His heir (his son by his first marriage), Matthew (d. 1650x52), a lawyer, married Mary, daughter of Sir John Moore of King's county. He was involved in the commission for defective titles and was an MP in the 1640 parliament. He had landed interests in co. Wexford by the late 1630s and Clobemon Hall, co. Wexford, was the family seat until the 1860s.   BRIAN MAC CUARTA

Sources B. Mac Cuarta, ed., 'Mathew De Renzy's letters on Irish affairs, 1613–1620', *Analecta Hibernica*, 34 (1987), 107–82 • B. Mac Cuarta, 'A planter's interaction with Gaelic culture: Sir Matthew De Renzy (1577–1634)', *Irish Economic and Social History*, 20 (1993), 1–17 • 'Notes on [the De Renzi memorial tablet in] St Mary's Church, Athlone', *Proceedings and Papers of the Royal Society of Antiquaries of Ireland*, 5th scr., 1 (1890–91), 184–5 • B. Mac Cuarta, 'Newcomers in the Irish midlands, 1540–1641', MA diss., University College, Galway, 1980 • V. W. Treadwell, 'Irish financial and administrative reform under James I: the customs and state regulation of Irish trade', PhD diss., Queen's University, Belfast, 1960 • V. Treadwell, *Buckingham and Ireland, 1616–28: a study in Anglo-Irish politics* (1998) • E. Edwards, *The life of Sir Walter Ralegh … together with his letters*, 2 vols. (1868) • B. Mac Cuarta, ed., 'Conchubhar Mac Bruaideadha and Sir Matthew De Renzy (1577–1634)', *Eigse: A Journal of Irish Studies*, 27 (1993), 122–6 • R. Loeber, 'Civilisation through plantation: the projects of Mathew de Renzi', *Irish Midland Studies*, ed. H. Murtagh (1980), 121–35 • B. Mac Cuarta, ed., 'A planter in a Gaelic lordship: Matthew De Renzy's landholding in Delvin Mac Coghlan, 1613–1620', *Studia Hibernica*, 30 (1998–9) • R. E. G. Kirk and E. F. Kirk, eds., *Returns of aliens dwelling in the city and suburbs of London, from the reign of Henry VIII to that of James I*, Huguenot Society of London, 10/3 (1907) • NL Ire., department of manuscripts, L. P. De Renzi • B. Mac Cuarta, ed., 'A planter's funeral, legacies, and inventory: Sir Matthew De Renzy (1577–1634)', *Journal of the Royal Society of Antiquaries of Ireland*, 127 (1997), 18–33 • will of Matthew De Renzy, PRO, PROB 11/224, sig. 225

Archives PRO, MSS, SP46.90–3 | CKS, corresp. with Cranfield, U269/1/Hi95

Wealth at death silver and gold to the value of £1007, and plate to the value of £504; also lands and properties: Mac Cuarta, ed., 'A planter's funeral'

Repington, Charles À Court (1858–1925), army officer and military writer, was born on 29 January 1858, at 15 Chesham Street, London. He was the son of Charles Henry Wyndham À Court Repington (1819–1903), a staunch Anglican and Peelite, MP for Wilton, 1852–5, and of Emily, the eldest daughter of Henry Currie, banker, of West Horley Place, Surrey. The À Courts and Repingtons were wealthy country gentry, well connected with the aristocracy, with a long, distinguished history of service to the church, armed services, and parliament. Following family custom, the extra surname Repington was assumed when, in 1903, Charles succeeded to Amington Hall, Warwickshire. He was educated at Eton College, where he showed no particular distinction (1871–6), and the Royal Military College, Sandhurst (1876–8), before being commissioned in the rifle brigade (1878). His active service was disrupted frequently by ill health. He campaigned in Afghanistan, Burma, Egypt, the Sudan, and South Africa, served five years in army intelligence, was twice military attaché to the Low Countries, and was also a technical delegate to the first Hague peace conference of 1898. By diligent study he became an expert on military affairs, and was generally recognized as 'the most brilliant student' (*DNB*) during his time at the staff college in Camberley (1887–9). When invalided home from the South African campaign he had reached the rank of lieutenant-colonel, had been mentioned in dispatches four times, and created CMG. Bold, tenacious, able, ambitious, and hard-working, he had proved himself a fine regimental, and an outstanding staff, officer. But his considerable virtues were complemented by not inconsiderable faults. He was extravagant, impetuous, and sometimes cavalier in his attitude to authority and routine. He never suffered fools gladly, whatever their rank.

Charles À Court Repington (1858–1925), by unknown photographer

On 11 February 1882 Repington married Melloney Catherine (1860–1938), daughter of Colonel Henry Sales Scobell. They had one son who died in infancy and two daughters. The marriage eventually foundered on Repington's frequent infidelities, and they separated in 1901. While serving in Egypt Repington began a passionate affair with Mary Isabella (née North; 1868–1953), the wife of Sir William Edmund Garstin, a senior official in the Egyptian ministry of public works. Repington was never a discreet lover, and the liaison was soon common knowledge. In order to accept an appointment to General Buller's staff in South Africa, Repington was required by a high-ranking officer, almost certainly the commander-in-chief, Lord Roberts, to give his written promise, 'upon his honour as a soldier and a gentleman' (The Times, 13 Dec 1901), never again to write to or meet with Mary, Lady Garstin. His parole was given to a brother officer in the rifle brigade, Henry Wilson, for safe-keeping. Subsequently, for reasons he considered adequate and of which he advised Wilson, Repington broke his parole. Garstin sued successfully for divorce. Repington was tried for breach of his parole and told to resign immediately. His treatment was undoubtedly harsh. Repington thereafter blamed Wilson for his dismissal, but he contributed to his own downfall by his careless attitude to a superior officer's command. Repington was condemned by most of society, not for the sin of adultery so much as the solecism of being 'found out'. His reputation was permanently tarnished.

Repington turned to journalism. His first regular contributions were to J. A. Spender's Westminster Gazette. But it was his account in The Times of the Russo-Japanese War of 1904–5 that earned him almost instant international recognition as an outstanding military commentator. He frequently disagreed with his editors about defence policy but insisted on his independence. As he told his friend Raymond Marker: 'I take orders from no man ... I say precisely what I think; when I'm asked to support some scheme in which I do not believe I shall stop writing in The Times' (C. Repington to R. Marker, 17 April 1905, BL, Add. MS 52277B, fols. 17–21). Before 1914 international tensions forced changes in British foreign policy that in turn posed complex defence problems. Repington offered solutions that his civilian readers could comprehend. He advocated a general staff, and, believing in the co-ordination of military and naval planning and closer imperial ties, was an enthusiastic supporter of the infant committee of imperial defence. He opposed the dominant 'blue water' strategists, who claimed the navy alone was sufficient to secure Britain against invasion. With Lord Roberts and others he warned of a possible German invasion, a 'bolt from the blue'. He fought a long, peacetime battle for conscription, without success. He was contemptuous of almost all politicians, whatever their party loyalty, dismissing them as 'Tadpoles and Tapers shivering for their shekels ... rabble seeking office and rewards' (C. Repington to L. Maxse, 11 March 1908, West Sussex PRO, MS 458, fol. 671). But he hated the radical Liberals most of all for their sentimentalism; they dubbed him 'the gorgeous Wreckington' (Repington, Vestigia, 256). For the most part he dismissed ministers as 'ignorant ... uncaring ... they know nothing of the Army', but Richard Burdon Haldane he admired as 'the best Secretary of State we have had at the War Office so far as brain and ability are concerned' (C. Repington to R. Marker, 26 Jan 1906 and 15 Aug 1906, BL, Add. MS 52277B, fols. 35–39 and 78–85), and generally supported his military reforms. Repington was long convinced that Germany was Britain's most dangerous rival, and supported alliance with France. In 1905, when the French sought to initiate military conversations with England, they chose Repington to act as intermediary, for which service he was awarded the Légion d'honneur. More clearly than most other commentators in the press, on the brink of war in 1914, he foresaw the likely unfortunate consequences of inconsistent pre-war diplomacy and strategic planning.

In 1911, when Repington was appointed editor of the general staff quarterly, Army Review, many wrongly supposed he had hopelessly compromised his independence. The war confirmed Repington's ideas and some of his predictions, yet his influence waned. He supposed himself martyred for exposing the incapacities of politicians. To those he criticized he appeared too partisan to convince as objective, the willing mouthpiece of the army's high command. He was an unrepentant advocate of war by attrition; a die-hard 'westerner', scathing of 'side-shows' dreamed up by politicians whom he derided as amateur strategists who starved the army of the men and munitions it required. In 1915 his notorious disclosure of a shell shortage contributed to the government's fall. Differences with his editor became increasingly difficult to sustain as Dawson spiked or altered Repington's copy. In January 1918 Repington resigned and joined 'Taffy' Gwynne's *Morning Post*. Given his new editor's blessing he pursued the prime minister with even greater vigour. Within two months he and Gwynne were convicted of a minor breach of the Defence of the Realm Act. Unabashed he continued to censure the government for interfering in matters he judged better left to the military. Lloyd George never forgave Repington and, ten years after the military correspondent's death, unfairly accused him of 'treachery' and 'treason'.

After the war Repington worked for the *Daily Telegraph*. He never again achieved the eminence he had enjoyed at *The Times*. Chronically short of money he decided to publish his war diaries (1920). Though they remain an important historical source, at the time his public recollection of private gossip further damaged his already precarious social position. Repington's wife had refused to divorce him. Nevertheless Mary Garstin, through all their vicissitudes, supported Repington: she took his name, lived with him as his wife, bore him a daughter, and forgave him his not infrequent indiscretions. The last years together in Hove were amicable and peaceful. He died on 25 May 1925 at their home, Pembroke Lodge, Hove, Sussex, penning an article at his desk. He was buried at St Barnabas's Church, Hove, on 29 May.

As a military writer and critic Repington was not without fault. His views on tactics were conventional. He was over-fond of political intrigue although, except in the case of Henry Wilson, he never allowed personal prejudice to cloud his public judgements. But his greatest failing was his inability sufficiently to appreciate the problems that politicians faced during the war. His most important and significant work was completed before the First World War. It is unfortunate that he has been judged largely on the basis of observations by opponents he had wounded in public debate, who sought to salve their self-esteem with lies and cheap jibes, or by deliberately misleading press campaigns, such as that conducted by J. L. Garvin at the behest of Alfred Milner, falsely accusing Repington of giving pusillanimous and contradictory advice. Repington, the *beau sabreur* and 'prince of military correspondents' (Luvaas, 303), deserves a better memorial.

A. J. A. MORRIS

Sources C. À Court Repington, *Vestigia* (1919) · M. Repington, *Thanks for the memory* (1938) · J. Luvaas, *The education of an army: British military thought, 1815–1940*, new edn (1965), 291–330 · W. M. Ryan, 'Lt-Col. Charles À Court Repington: a study in the interaction of personality, press and power', PhD diss., University of Cincinnati, 1976 · A. M. Golin, *Proconsul in politics* (1964) · [S. Morison and others], *The history of The Times*, 3 (1947) · A. J. A. Morris, *The scaremongers: the advocacy of war and rearmament, 1896–1914* (1984) · C. À Court Repington, *The First World War*, 2 vols. (1920) · *The letters of Lieutenant-Colonel Charles À Court Repington CMG: military correspondent of The Times, 1903–1918*, ed. A. J. A. Morris (1999) · *The Times* (13 Dec 1901) · b. cert. · m. cert.

Archives News Int. RO, papers · priv. coll. | BL, H. O. Arnold-Forster MSS · BL, letters to Lord Kitchener and Lieutenant-Colonel R. J. Marker, Add. MS 52277 · BL, corresp. with Lord Northcliffe, Add. MS 62253 · CAC Cam., Esher MSS · HLRO, letters to David Lloyd George · King's Lond., Liddell Hart C., Ian Hamilton MSS · NAM, letters to Lord Roberts · NL Scot., letters to Lord Haldane · U. Durham L., corresp. with Sir Reginald Wingate · W. Sussex RO, Leo Maxse MSS

Likenesses P. A. de Laszlo, oils, *c.*1916, repro. in Repington, *Letters*, frontispiece · W. Rothenstein, pencil drawing, 1916, Man. City Gall. · M. Beerbohm, caricature, 1920, Man. City Gall.; repro. in S. Hynes, *A war imagined* (1990), pl. 20 · photograph, repro. in Repington, *Vestigia*, facing p. 129 · photograph, NPG [*see illus.*]

Repington, Philip. *See* Repyndon, Philip (*c.*1345–1424).

Repton, George Stanley (1786–1858), architect, was born on 30 January 1786, the fifth and youngest son of the seven children of Humphry *Repton (1752–1818), architect and landscape gardener of Hare Street, Essex, and his wife, Mary, *née* Clarke (*c.*1753–1818). His father came from Bury St Edmunds, Suffolk, and his mother from Norwich, Norfolk. In 1801, aged fifteen, he first exhibited a drawing, *View in the Village of Wield, Kent*, at the Royal Academy and in 1802 succeeded his eldest brother, John Adey *Repton [*see under* Repton, Humphry], as a pupil of the rapidly rising London architect John Nash; after many years in Nash's office at 29 Dover Street he eventually became Nash's chief assistant. Repton's earliest work was assisting his father and elder brother in their unexecuted designs in the Hindu style for the Brighton Pavilion. The remodelling of the Italian or Royal Opera House, Haymarket, in London in 1816–20 was described in 1829 as 'a joint design of Mr. Nash and his tasteful pupil Mr. Repton', 'as fine a specimen of the Palladian style of architecture as any in London', and 'eminently theatrical' (Shepherd and Elmes, 148).

Repton often stayed with Nash at his country house, East Cowes Castle, in the Isle of Wight, and it was there that he met and fell in love with another frequent visitor, Lady Elizabeth Scott (1783–1862), eldest daughter of the first earl of Eldon, the lord chancellor. Three years older than Repton, a contemporary described her as 'withered'. The diarist Joseph Farington further commented that 'she is towards 40 years old, & owns to 36 years; Repton is 32 or 33 years old. He is a well looking man & of a placid disposition' (Farington, *Diary*, 15.5134). Her father, who himself had eloped to marry, opposed the match, but she 'had avowed to Him Her determination to marry Mr. Repton' (ibid.). Without his blessing or even his knowledge Repton and she were married, by special licence, on 27 November 1817 at St George's, Hanover Square, London, a popular venue at the time for such marriages. So incensed were her parents that they 'sent Her *Court dress* to Her in a parcel, witht. note or message' (ibid.). Only after the difficult birth of the couple's first child in 1820 were Lord Eldon and the Reptons reconciled, despite his having 'shewn great obstinacy on another occasion when it was supposed He would have relented' (ibid.). Long before his death in 1838 the earl, described in 1818 by James Boswell, son of Dr Johnson's biographer, as 'the first of all our Lawyers', revoked his will, made in anger immediately after his daughter's marriage when he refused to acknowledge her, and instead gave parity both to the Reptons' children, including their only son, George William, and those of his younger daughter.

In Nash's office Repton's

> situation produced him abt. £1500 pr. annum. But Mr. Nash is or affects to be much offended with Him for having married Lord Eldon's daugr ... Mr. & Mrs. Nash are gone to Paris, it is supposed to be out of the way at this time.   (Farington, *Diary*, 15.5134)

Repton began to practise independently as an architect after 1820 and over the next quarter-century of his active career worked on some twenty-five commissions, almost all of which were executed, broadly distributed across the south of England from Norfolk to the west country, the sole exception being one of his few public buildings, the assembly rooms at Aberystwyth (1820). By far the greater part of his curiously desultory output comprised country houses, with a preponderance in the west of England, while churches and chapels represented about a quarter. Some of his buildings have been demolished, but over three-quarters remain extant.

Like many of his fellow architects, Repton was versatile, equally competent in the Greek, Palladian, and Gothic revival styles and the majority of the country houses on which he worked involved remodelling, either thoroughgoing or in the form of minor restyling alterations or additions, clearly influenced by Nash, in the picturesque Elizabethan or Tudor Gothic styles. Alterations to existing buildings accounted for two-thirds of his work, only about ten having been built wholly to his designs. Of the former, *The Dictionary of Architecture* in 1892 noticed particularly three Devon houses: Kitley House (*c*.1820–25), remodelled in the Elizabethan style; Peamore House, Exminster (*c*.1825–30), in the Tudor Gothic; and Follaton House, Totnes (*c*.1826–7). The drawings for these in the RIBA drawings collection are good examples of Repton's fine draughtsmanship. An early work of 1817, the library at Cobham Hall, Kent, was also singled out by the dictionary. These designs contrast with Repton's later classical design in a robust Tuscan Doric style for the porticoed town hall at Chipping Norton, Oxfordshire (1842). Besides the remodelled Royal Opera House, Repton's only other London building was the Waterloo (later St Philip's) Chapel, Regent Street (1819–20; dem.), which he designed for his elder brother the Revd Edward Repton, and erected at a cost of £15,000. Other churches on which Repton worked include St James's, Sarsden, Oxfordshire, where he added an eastern cruciform extension in 1823. At about the same time he added to the adjoining Sarsden House an Ionic portico, colonnade, and conservatory for the distinguished architectural patron James Langston.

The restoration of the chancel at St Peter's Church, Medmenham, Buckinghamshire, in 1845 appears to have been Repton's last executed work and he spent the remaining thirteen years of his life in retirement. He died, on 29 June 1858 at his home at 27 New Norfolk Street, Park Lane, London, aged seventy-two, and was buried in Kensal Green cemetery. He left an estate valued at almost £9000. His

widow, Elizabeth, survived him by almost four years before dying, aged seventy-eight, on 16 April 1862. George William Repton did not follow his father into architecture but was for several years MP for St Albans, Hertfordshire, and later also for Warwick.   RICHARD RIDDELL

Sources Colvin, *Archs.* · Boase, *Mod. Eng. biog.* · [W. Papworth], ed., *The dictionary of architecture*, 11 vols. (1853–92) · *Designs for the Pavilion at Brighton ... by H. Repton, with the assistance of ... G. S. Repton* (1808) · *Recollections of A. N. Welby Pugin, and his father, Augustus Pugin* (1861), 4–5 · J. Summerson, *John Nash: architect to King George IV*, 2nd edn (1949) · D. Stroud, *Humphry Repton* (1962) · E. Hyams, *Capability Brown and Humphry Repton* (1971), 214 · T. H. Shepherd and J. Elmes, *Metropolitan improvements, or, London in the nineteenth century* (1829), 148 · Farington, *Diary*, 15.5134, 5138 · *CGPLA Eng. & Wales* (1858)
Archives Bristol RO, corresp. with J. S. Harford · Hunt. L., letters to his father
Wealth at death under £9000: probate, 24 July 1858, *CGPLA Eng. & Wales*

Repton, Humphry (1752–1818), landscape gardener, was born on 21 April 1752 at Bury St Edmunds, Suffolk, the second of the three surviving children of John Repton (*bap.* 1714, *d.* 1775), a collector of excise, and his wife, Martha (*d.* 1773), the daughter of John Fitch, of Moor Hall, Suffolk. The Reptons moved about 1762 to Norwich, where John Repton, in addition to continuing his professional duties, became a 'proprietor of stage-coaches and waggons' (Farington, *Diary*, 1.198). Humphry Repton received his formal education at grammar schools in Bury St Edmunds and Norwich. In preparation for his intended mercantile career he was sent abroad to learn a commercially useful language—to the village of Workum in the Netherlands, where he was placed for a year in the school of Algidius Zimmerman. After a visit to the Rotterdam home of the banker Zachary Hope, with whom John Repton had lodged money for his son's schooling, Repton was pleased to be invited to move in with the family and continue his education there. Fabulously rich, the Hopes maintained an opulent lifestyle, and Repton learned to mix with high society.

Early career: gentleman, antiquary, writer On his return to Norwich in 1768, aged sixteen, Repton was expensively apprenticed in the textile business. This again took him overseas, to Germany and to the Netherlands, where his interest in gardens was first stimulated by the small, but brilliant, examples along the canals. On 5 May 1773 he married Mary Clarke (1749–1827); subsequently his father made over enough money to set him up in business. Lost ships, failed speculations, a talent for music, drawing, and poetry rather than trade, and a taste for spending money rather than making it contributed to a steep decline in his fortunes. About 1776 after both his parents had died, Repton retired from business, replenishing his capital with his inheritance to fund the life of a gentleman amateur. He took a tenancy on Old Hall, Sustead, on the Felbrigg estate of William Windham, a prominent figure in whig county politics. Sustead was a hamlet 20 miles north of Norwich, but within the cultural and commercial hinterland of the city. Repton's sister Dorothy, married to a lawyer, lived 5 miles away at Aylsham, a centre of the textile trade, where their parents were buried. His elder brother

and comical essays entitled *Variety* (1787), compiling a catalogue, under the pseudonym the Bee, for Boydell's Shakspeare Gallery, and writing a play in the style of Sheridan,
Odd Whims, or, Two at a Time, eventually published in 1804.
It was performed in the eastern counties and read with
approval by Burke and Sir Joshua Reynolds before
another, unnamed cultural celebrity lost the manuscript.
In 1788 Repton decided to exploit his talents as a sketcher
and writer and to pursue his concern for the improvement
of scenery and society by becoming a professional landscape gardener. In little more than a year his 'dread of poverty' receded, and he found himself 'in a state of ease and
comparative affluence' (Repton, 3).

Repton as landscape gardener Repton used his Norfolk contacts, especially William Windham, to launch his career.
His first commission was at Catton, outside Norwich, for
the mayor and textile merchant Jeremiah Ives, and his second was at Holkham (1788), in the north of the county, at
the estate of the powerful magnate Thomas Coke. For the
first two years of his career Repton agreed to undertake
electioneering for Windham and his whig friends, costing
his time at the same rate as his landscape gardening,
although he was never paid. While he complained about
the time spent on whig politics, it helped secure him his
most influential patron, the leader of the party faction,
the third duke of Portland. Commissions at Portland's
seats at Welbeck, Nottinghamshire, and Bulstrode, Buckinghamshire, and visits to the duke's London mansion,
Burlington House, extended Repton's field of work and
helped to establish his name. He was keen to secure
wealthy clients in and around London, especially those
purchasing villa properties. His third client, Lady Salus-
bury, not only paid him handsomely to refashion the
grounds of her villa at Brandsbury, near Willesden, in
1789, but allowed him, in contrast to aristocratic patrons,
great freedom in the design. Repton also relied on more
up-to-date methods of securing new clients, sending
unsolicited circulars (with his trade card) to both old
friends and potential clients.

Repton saw the profession of landscape gardening not
just as a way of making money but as an opportunity to
mix with landed society. His favourite commissions, for
example, at Thoresby (from 1791) and Sheringham (from
1812), were those during which he was invited to stay with
the family, to join in their entertainments, and to return
regularly to monitor improvements and suggest more. In
his Norfolk days he had a reputation as a show-off, for
sporting fine clothes and for giving readings of literature
and recitals on the flute, and this carried over into his career as a landscape gardener. He was dubbed a 'coxcomb'
by aristocratic men for his conceit and exhibitionism, and
also for his flattery of feminine tastes. Repton saw his
socializing more seriously, as a way of helping to fashion
the cultural consensus of polite society.

Repton quickly established the rudiments of his art of
landscape gardening, which he conveyed through the
so-called red book, a handsome morocco-bound report
showing improvements through drawings, maps, and
passages of writing in a copperplate hand. The drawings

Humphry Repton (1752–1818), by William Holl, pubd 1802 (after
Samuel Shelley)

John farmed at nearby Oxnead and was renowned for his
progressive agricultural methods. Repton spent his time
reading (borrowing books from Windham's library), writing, drawing, visiting, improving his small farm, and
roaming the surrounding countryside and sketching its
scenery. He contributed to volume 3 of M. J. Armstrong's
History and Antiquities of the County of Norfolk (1781) both the
text for his district and some drawings of country houses.

After five years Repton was finding life at Sustead difficult to afford. His farming experiments had failed and his
remaining capital was diminishing fast. When Windham
was appointed secretary to the lord lieutenant of Ireland
in 1783, he took Repton with him to Dublin as his private
secretary. Windham resigned after little more than a
month, leaving Repton more impoverished (he failed to
pay him even his travel expenses) but with the consolation of mixing in Dublin society and the opportunity to
develop his sketching skills at picturesque sites around
the city and in north Wales on the journey home. Repton
then headed for Bath, producing some drolls (whimsically
satirical drawings) of the beau monde, and undertaking
an ambitious business venture. He invested most of his
money, and much thought and energy, in a scheme with
the Bath impresario John Palmer to reform the mail-coach
system. The government enthusiastically adopted it, but
Repton received no credit, money, or public recognition.

About 1786 Repton moved his family from Sustead to
Hare Street, Essex, only 13 miles from London, which
brought him closer to the opportunities offered by the
metropolis. Initially he attempted to make a career as a
writer, publishing (anonymously) a collection of moral

illustrated improvements by a hinged cut-out device which, when overlain, would show the present scene and, when removed, the proposed scene. The red books functioned in various ways: as plans, as records of work in progress, as albums of views to be displayed in the patron's library, and were sometimes prepared for clients who never intended to carry out the improvements. There was a standard format to the early red books—a slim oblong quarto. Later there were marked variations: large luxurious volumes for prestigious commissions, such as the books for Longleat (1804), Woburn (1805), and the Royal Pavilion at Brighton (1806), and brief, unbound reports for villas. In 1816, at the end of his career, Repton claimed to have prepared over four hundred red books and reports.

The physical changes to the landscape Repton proposed were often relatively minor, for example, removing some walls or planting some shrubs, but were designed to create striking scenic transformations. His field of operations tended to be small scale, in the pleasure grounds around the house, close to entrance lodges, drives, and approaches, yet the overall scenic improvements, from these vantage points, were often dramatic. The illusionism of his art was greatly influenced by his love of theatre and distrusted as such by some rivals, such as William Marshall and John Claudius Loudon. In contrast to Lancelot 'Capability' Brown, Repton rarely took on the responsibility for organizing the work on the ground—the earthmoving, planting, and building. He was a consultant, not a contractor, charging for visits: for years he charged a famously standard rate of 5 guineas a day plus expenses, and additionally charging for the red book of designs, according to its length and size. It is therefore not surprising that he often found his proposals altered or ignored on the ground. Repton realized that, in contrast to Brown, he would have to establish his reputation through writing, through publishing treatises on the principles, as well as the practice, of landscape gardening.

Publishing and the picturesque Repton's first treatise, *Sketches and Hints on Landscape Gardening*, was planned for publication in 1794 but delayed at the printers until the following year, initially for plates to be re-engraved to a high standard, then to allow Repton to reply to attacks on his work in two publications, *The Landscape: a Didactic Poem* (1794), by Richard Payne Knight, and *Essay on the Picturesque* (1794), by Uvedale Price. The attacks were the more wounding for being unexpected. Repton had become friendly with Knight and Price early in his career, when he was commissioned near their own estates in Herefordshire. He sought their advice, and they thought he would endorse and publicize their ideas. The dispute centred on the relationship between landscape gardening and landscape painting. As connoisseurs of old master paintings, Knight and Price based the improvements of their own grounds on the compositional rules of landscape art and upheld it as a model for all landowners. They saw this not only as raising the cultural register of parks and gardens, but as closely involving landowners in the design and management of their estates, promoting careful stewardship of both scenery and society. They opposed this style

of landscaping to the work of Capability Brown and his followers, which they saw as erasing the picturesque character of many parks and gardens, by clearing away old trees, pathways, and cottages and reducing them to a standardized plan. Radical whigs, Price and Knight also saw the Brown style as representing centralized power, of both courtly and commercial interests. Repton's attempt to assume Brown's mantle, his professional success and cultivation of conservative patrons, and the tempering of his own pictorial inclinations provoked Price and Knight to attack him. Repton defended himself vigorously, challenging his opponents' high opinion of painting as the medium for good design and management—indeed, regarding it, at a time of war, as an unpatriotic distraction from practical issues. The dispute erupted into a full-blown controversy, with thrust and counterthrust, and it drew in others, including William Windham and William Marshall, who took the anti-picturesque line, arguing that landscapes should be lived in, not merely looked at. As a landscape gardener who continued to use watercolours as a key part of his work, Repton had to make careful manoeuvres in the picturesque controversy. The dispute died down as a public issue by the turn of the century but did not dissipate entirely.

Collaboration with Nash From the outset of his career Repton had collaborated with architects on some commissions, notably William Wilkins and James Wyatt. Wilkins was little known outside Norfolk and increasingly gout ridden, and Wyatt was nationally renowned but unreliable. About 1796 Repton formed a partnership with John Nash which he believed would transform his practice and bring him enduring fame and fortune. Nash took Repton's sons John Adey [*see below*] and George Stanley *Repton into his office as assistants and agreed to pay Repton part of the percentage on work he secured. In design terms the partnership worked most successfully at Luscombe in Dorset, for the banker Charles Hoare, where in 1799 Nash's architecture and Repton's landscaping were pleasingly integrated and well executed. Professionally and personally the partnership proved to be a failure: Nash terminated it in 1800, refusing to pay Repton anything and claiming that the money had been absorbed by the cost of accommodating his sons. An embittered Repton took John Adey out of Nash's office and into partnership with himself, whereupon his son's architecture decisively shaped particular designs and his theory of landscape gardening. They developed a domestic style named Queen Elizabeth's Gothic, loosely based on manor houses in Norfolk, which combined an antique-looking exterior with an internal arrangement, including view-framing windows, accommodating the 'comforts of modern life'. George Stanley Repton stayed with Nash and developed a talent for the design of cottages and minor estate buildings, notably Blaise Hamlet, near Bristol.

Repton at the peak of his career Published in a vertical quarto format, Repton's second treatise, *Observations on the Theory and Practice of Landscape Gardening* (1803), reflected the increasing alignment of landscape and architecture: 'I wish to make my appeal less to the eye than to the understanding' (p. 6). Reprinted in 1805, it was a less scenic work than *Sketches and Hints*. So marketable was Repton's work at this time that his publisher also requested a new edition of *Sketches and Hints*, which had become so scarce it was fetching four times its original price. Repton decided not to reissue this expensive book but to extract some passages for a new and much cheaper one, *An Enquiry into the Changes of Taste in Landscape Gardening* (1806). Intended to reach a less affluent audience (perhaps in response to the sales success of works by his rivals in the picturesque controversy), this small, unillustrated octavo volume included extracts from recent red books, a 'History of landscape gardening' (originally commissioned for a new edition in 1807 of *The Gardener's and Botanists Dictionary*), and a response to a recent book by Richard Payne Knight, *An Analytical Inquiry into the Principles of Taste*. In this period Repton also published the two-volume *Odd Whims and Miscellanies* (1804), comprising a revised edition of his play *Odd Whims, or, Two at a Time*, which had been revived in Norwich and Ipswich in 1803, some essays from *Variety* (1787), and some verse and epigrams which had been written for clients or submitted to magazines.

The year 1805, wrote Repton, was the 'pinnacle of my ambition' (Repton, 205). He had begun a prestigious and lucrative long-term commission for the sixth duke of Bedford at Woburn Abbey and secured his most promising commission of all, to refashion the Royal Pavilion at Brighton for the prince of Wales. From the outset of his career Repton had sought royal patronage. When Thomas Sandby died in 1798 he tried unsuccessfully to secure, through his aristocratic contacts, the position of deputy rangership of Windsor Great Park, which Sandby had used to pursue landscaping and architecture. Repton worked on the commission for Brighton Pavilion with three of his sons, John Adey, George Stanley, and Humphry the younger. They chose an Indian style, explicitly modelled on the illustrations in volume 1 of William Daniell's *Oriental Scenery* (1805), and prepared a sumptuous red book. Repton was again disappointed. His design was not implemented, nor was he paid for his work; moreover, John Nash prepared another design loosely based on Repton's which was eventually built. Repton tried to salvage something from the commission by publishing *Designs for the Pavillon at Brighton* (1808).

Decline and death Repton blamed the decline of his fortunes on developments during the Napoleonic wars, especially the imposition of taxes (both on himself and potential clients), and the dramatic inflation and unregulated increase in paper money, which he thought encouraged a spirit of speculation unsympathetic to landscape gardening—or at least to his moral vision of the art predicated on paternalist estate management and domestic propriety. By 1808 he was finding commissions difficult to secure, and those that he did pick up tended to be brief consultations for the *nouveaux riches* whom he despised, men of modest beginnings who had made fortunes during the wars and possessed none of the cultural accomplishments which he valued in more established clients. In January

1811 his career was further blighted by a road accident, when his carriage overturned one icy night on his return home from a ball. He suffered a spinal injury from which he never fully recovered; his heart was also affected, and he endured frequent and painful attacks of angina pectoris.

From 1811 Repton found work scarce, and his fears of personal bankruptcy made him morbid about his own condition and that of the country. When he did secure prestigious commissions he lavished enormous attention on them. That for Sheringham (from 1812) he considered his favourite work, because it was in his home county of Norfolk, and because his young client—Abbot Upcher—shared his social and scenic views, but Upcher's death in 1817 left it unfinished. In 1813 Repton prepared red books to landscape the work of the architect Jeffry Wyatville at Ashridge, Hertfordshire, for the duke of Bridgewater, and the following year at Endsleigh, Devon, for the duke of Bedford. By this time he was in a wheelchair and finding movement of any kind, from travel to a site to getting around the grounds, an often excruciating experience.

From 1814 Repton spent most of his time at home at Hare Street, reading, corresponding with friends and family, and writing his memoirs and his last treatise, *Fragments on the Theory and Practise of Landscape Gardening* (1816). *Fragments* is a valedictory work, charting the break-up of landscape gardening and the society which sustained it. It focuses on small flower gardens and ornate gothic buildings, not the landscape at large. He wondered whether 'the influence of returning Peace may revive its energies, or whether it is hereafter to be classed among the "*Arts Perditae*"' (p. viii). The post-war economic depression and Repton's worsening health brought his practice to an end. He died suddenly, probably of a heart attack, on 24 March 1818 at Hare Street. Three years earlier he had planned his own burial place, a rose garden on the south side of Aylsham church, and penned his own inscription for the tomb: he was interred there on 27 March.

Repton's reputation and influence From the picturesque controversy of 1794 onwards Repton suffered a good deal of ridicule, much provoked by his early success. Professional rivals such as William Marshall and John Claudius Loudon did not hesitate to launch public criticism even while adopting Repton's ideas. In public Repton parried criticism, but in private he was bitter. Towards the end of his life, as he retreated from public view, he was caricatured in Jane Austen's *Mansfield Park* (1814) as a generic name, 'Repton, or any body of that sort', for the fashion-conscious to commission, and in Thomas Love Peacock's *Headlong Hall* (1816) as the obsequious advocate of 'picturesque gardening'.

When a brief and wildly innaccurate obituary appeared in the *Gentleman's Magazine* in 1818, Repton's family announced their intention to publish his memoirs. Brief passages, mainly covering his life before his career as a landscape gardener, were published as a 'Biographical notice' by 'A. B' (probably one of Repton's sons) to preface a collected edition of his works in 1840. Cheap and poorly engraved, it was edited by his former antagonist Loudon, who both tempered his former criticisms and enlisted Repton's work as a precursor of his own patent style, the Gardenesque. Repton had bequeathed his memoirs to John Adey Repton with the intention they should be published: they never were. The surviving manuscript of the second part of Repton's life appears to be a later copy from his original draft and bears some editorial annotations, some dated 1868 and signed M. E. R.—perhaps the wife of his son Edward, Mary Ellis Repton, or their daughter of the same name.

Humphry Repton's reputation spread beyond Britain through influential travellers such as Prince Pückler-Muskau, who observed his works on the ground; his son John Adey was commissioned by Pückler-Muskau during a working trip to Germany and the Netherlands in 1821–2. Repton's principles were expounded for a German audience in E. Petzold's *Landschaftsgärtenerei*, issued in Leipzig in 1862. His writings were a strong influence on the work of the American landscape architect Andrew Jackson Downing, notably on his *Treatise on the Theory and Practice of Landscape Gardening* (1841). The first two of Repton's treatises were edited and published in the United States as *The Art of Landscape Gardening* (1907), without many of the original illustrations and supplemented by modern photographs of English landscape parks, not all Repton sites. In Britain Repton was rediscovered as a theorist in Christopher Hussey's *The Picturesque* (1927) and as a designer in accounts of country houses published in early twentieth-century numbers of *Country Life*. In an article of 1948 Nikolaus Pevsner championed him in the modernist *Architectural Review*. The first modern biography, *Humphry Repton* by Dorothy Stroud, was published in 1961 by Country Life. Stroud journeyed around England and Wales, tracking Repton's red books and other manuscript material in country houses and county record offices, on the basis of which she compiled a chronology of his life and work and documented the condition of Repton landscapes on the ground. The second part of Repton's memoirs came to light in time for the major exhibition 'Humphry Repton: landscape gardener, 1752–1818' held at the Sainsbury Centre at the University of East Anglia, and the Victoria and Albert Museum, London (1982–3). To scholars concerned with Repton's mentality, the memoirs, along with newly available collections of letters, formed a rich seam of evidence. Stephen Daniels's *Humphry Repton: Landscape Gardening and the Geography of Georgian England* (1999) considers not only how Repton fashioned his sense of self through his profession and the journeys which underpinned it but also how the concept of 'character' is central to his portrayal of both places and people. Despite Repton's own pessimism about his career and reputation, his influence on English landscape gardening has proved more powerful than that of any of his predecessors, rivals, or successors. The flexibility of his style, applicable to small gardens and large parks, incorporating a variety of architectural and horticultural features, and accommodating informal, domestic social arrangements, has ensured an enduring appeal. A collection of his poems and sketches is held by the Avery Architectural Library, Columbia University, New York. His red books are in various public and private collections.

John Adey Repton Repton's eldest son, **John Adey Repton** (1775–1860), was born at Norwich on 29 March 1775. He was educated at Aylsham grammar school and then in 1789 in the office of the Norwich architect William Wilkins, who had begun to collaborate with his father that year. Under Wilkins's influence he developed a strong commitment to antiquarian study and the Gothic style; a set of his drawings of Norwich Cathedral was purchased by the Society of Antiquaries. In 1796 he moved to London to be apprenticed to John Nash, who had become his father's partner. He worked with Nash on alterations to Corsham Court (1797–8) but, as his father complained, neither his contribution to this nor any of his other commissions were ever acknowledged. John Adey collaborated with his father on many schemes, and his antiquarian knowledge informed his designs, notably for Bayam Abbey (1800), Magdalen College (1801), and Aspley Wood Lodge (1810) on the Woburn estate. He also worked in a plainer, more modern-looking style, for example, in the design for a villa at Brentry Hill, Bristol, which he exhibited at the Royal Academy in 1802. In 1803 he was elected fellow of the Society of Antiquaries, and he wrote many items for the society's journal, *Archaeologia*. In 1808 he was preparing, in his father's words, 'a great work on Gothic architecture' (Humphry Repton to William Repton, 10 Jan 1808, Hunt. L., HM 40848), which was never published. His drawings of Norwich Cathedral were published in volume 2 of John Britton's *Cathedral Antiquities of Great Britain* (1816).

After his father's death in 1818, John Adey Repton inherited all his manuscripts, sketches, maps, and books. It is likely that he was the author of the 'Biographical notice' that preceded Loudon's 1840 edition of Humphry Repton's works. In 1821–2 he undertook commissions in the Netherlands and Germany. He continued to live at his parents' home in Hare Street until his mother's death in 1827, when he moved with his sister Elizabeth to Springfield in Essex. Profoundly deaf from infancy, he had difficulty dealing with clients during his father's lifetime. His infirmity, together with his scholarly inclinations and disaffection for new tastes in gardens and buildings, contributed to the decline of his practice after his trip to Germany. He entered the competition for the new houses of parliament in 1834, submitting a Gothic design whose austerity was a reaction to the 'Gingerbread-like Gothic Architecture of Germany' (Carter and others, 130). He continued to collect early printed books and to conduct antiquarian researches; his paper on *The Beard and the Mustachio, Chiefly from the Sixteenth to the Eighteenth Century* was privately printed in 1839. He died, unmarried at Springfield on 26 November 1860.   STEPHEN DANIELS

Sources E. Carter, P. Goode, and K. Laurie, *Humphry Repton, landscape gardener, 1752–1818* (1982) [exhibition catalogue, Sainsbury Centre for Visual Arts, Norwich, and V&A, 21 Sept 1982 – 20 Feb 1983] • D. Stroud, *Humphry Repton* (1962) • S. Daniels, *Humphry Repton: landscape gardening and the geography of Georgian England* (1999) •

A. B., 'Biographical notice of the late Humphry Repton', *The land-scape gardening and the landscape architecture of the late Humphry Rep-ton, esq.*, ed. J. C. Loudon (1840) · H. Repton, draft of memoir, pt 2, BL, Add. MS 62112 · Farington, *Diary* · R. W. K. Cremer, *A Norfolk gal-lery* (1948) · K. Laurie, 'Humphry Repton, 1752–1818: new discover-ies', *The Garden*, 108 (1983), 361–5 · *GM*, 1st ser., 88/1 (1818), 648 · *GM*, 1st ser., 88/2 (1818), 102 · C. Hussey, *The picturesque: studies in a point of view* (1927) · E. Malins, *The red books of Humphry Repton* (1976) · H. Prince, *Parks in England* (1927) · K. Sanecki, *Humphry Repton* (1974) · N. Temple, *John Nash and the village picturesque* (1979) · D. Whitehead, 'John Nash and Humphry Repton: an encounter in Herefordshire, 1785–98', *Transactions of the Woolhope Naturalists' Field Club*, 47 (1991–3), 210–36

Archives BL, memoirs, Add. MS 62112 [copy] · FM Cam., note-book of journals made in England · Hunt. L., corresp. and papers · Norfolk RO, Kesten–Gower MS, account book · NRA, corresp. and papers incl. red books | Architectural Association Library, Lon-don, red book · Beds. & Luton ARS, Woburn Abbey landscaping papers · BL, letters to William Windham, Add. MSS 37873–37919, *passim* · BL, red book for Barton Seagrave, Northamptonshire, RP100 [copy] · BL, red book for Montreal, Kent, RP142 [copy] · Bodl. Oxf., red book for Rose Hill, Sussex · Canadian Centre for Architec-ture, Montreal, red book for Burton Park · CUL, red book for Hulme Park, Berkshire · Doncaster Central Library, Doncaster Archives, red book for Ouston, Yorkshire · E. Sussex RO, red book for Heathfield Park, Sussex · Essex RO, Chelmsford, red book for Claybury Hall, Essex · Essex RO, Chelmsford, red book for Hill Hall, Theydon Mount, Essex · Essex RO, Chelmsford, red book for Stansted Hall, Essex · Essex RO, Chelmsford, red book for Stubbers, Essex · Essex RO, Chelmsford, red book for Woodford Hall, Essex [copy] · Glos. RO, corresp. relating to Dyrham Park, Gloucestershire · Herts. ALS, red book for Panshanger, Hertford-shire · Herts. ALS, red book for Tewin Water, Hertfordshire · Holk-ham Hall, Wells-next-the-Sea, political map of Norfolk · Linn. Soc., corresp. with Sir James Edward Smith · NL Wales, red book for Plas Newydd, Anglesey · Norfolk County Library, Colman collection · Norfolk RO, letters relating to Felbrigg, Norfolk, to William Cobb and Robert Marsham · Notts. Arch., red books for Welbeck Abbey · NRA Scotland, priv. coll., red book for Kenwood, Middlesex · NRA, priv. coll., letters relating to Antony House, Cornwall to Reginald Pole Carew, with red book · NRA, priv. coll., corresp. relating to Laxton, Northamptonshire, with George Freke Evans · RA, report on Kippinston House, Kent · RIBA BAL, red book for Sheringham, Norfolk · Royal Horticultural Society, London, red book for Wares-ley Park, Huntingdonshire · Sandwell Community History and Archives Service, Smethwick, red book for Warley, Warwick-shire · Suffolk RO, Ipswich, red book for Henham Hall, Suffolk · University of Bristol Library, red book for Abbots Leigh, Somerset · W. Sussex RO, red book for Little Green, Sussex · W. Sussex RO, red book for Uppark, Sussex · Waltham Forest Archives and Local Studies Library, Walthamstow, red book for Highams House, Essex · Worcs. RO, red book for Hewell Grange, Worcestershire [copy]

Likenesses S. Shelley, portrait, *c.*1800, NPG · W. Holl, stipple, pubd 1802 (after S. Shelley), BM, NPG [*see illus.*] · H. Repton, self-portrait, watercolour, *c.*1814, priv. coll. · H. B. Hall, stipple and line engraving, pubd 1839 (after S. Shelley), NPG

Repton, John Adey (1775–1860). *See under* Repton, Hum-phry (1752–1818).

Repyndon [Repington, Repingdon], **Philip** (*c.*1345–1424), bishop of Lincoln, probably took his name from Repton, Derbyshire, where there was a house of Augustinian canons, small in number but important beyond its size, which was perhaps his point of entry into that order.

Follower of Wyclif By 1369 Repyndon was a canon at Leices-ter Abbey, where he may have gone to study at the almonry school. The dukes of Lancaster were lords of the manor and honour of Leicester, and it was probably thus that Repyndon formed a connection with the Lancastrian dynasty which would prove advantageous to him later. It was certainly at Leicester that he was ordained priest, on 26 May 1369, suggesting that he was born in or before 1345. He continued his studies at Oxford, where he incepted in theology in the spring of 1382, and became DTh later in the year. He also absorbed heterodox reli-gious views, for the Carmelite compilation *Fasciculi zizani-orum* describes Repyndon as having been a supporter of John Wyclif in that year, after he had been previously regarded as 'humble' (perhaps meaning unopinionated, or uncontroversial), 'good-natured' (*benignus*) and well thought of by all. Early in 1382 Repyndon preached a ser-mon upholding Wyclif's eucharistic doctrine at Brackley, on the road between Oxford and Northampton. Later in that year he preached again, in considerably more contro-versial circumstances, when on 5 June he delivered the university's Corpus Christi sermon at the preaching cross in St Frideswide's churchyard, Oxford.

A church council held in May 1382 at the Blackfriars, London, to take action against heresy, had condemned twenty-four of Wyclif's theses as heretical or erroneous, and Archbishop Courtenay wrote to Robert Rygge, chan-cellor of Oxford University, forbidding their circulation there. Nevertheless Rygge and the proctors allotted the prestigious Corpus Christi sermon to Repyndon, even though he was not yet a doctor. As a public act of the uni-versity it was delivered in Latin, in the presence of the chancellor and proctors. According to *Fasciculi zizaniorum*, Repyndon defended Wyclif's theology and suggested that God would illumine the clergy with regard to Wyclif's eucharistic teaching. And he reportedly scaled the heights of defiance in proclaiming that:

> Whosoever offers up the pope or bishops before temporal lords [in prayers of petition] goes against holy scripture, and that his master, Master John Wyclif, is a most catholic teacher, and that Wyclif has never determined or taught with regard to the eucharist other than what the whole church of God holds, and that his opinion on the eucharist is most true. (*Fasciculi zizaniorum*, 307)

Two days later he was said to have declared during univer-sity disputation that his own Augustinian order was better when ten years old than when a thousand. And on 10 June he participated in an open disputation with the Carmelite Peter Stokes, and there defended the proposition from his Corpus Christi sermon that secular lords should take pre-cedence over spiritual ones.

The church authorities were quick to respond. On 12 June a second session of the Blackfriars Council ordered Rygge to suspend Repyndon and other partisans of Wyclif; the order was published on 15 June. Together with Nich-olas Hereford, Repyndon was then summoned to the council, where their refusal to condemn explicitly the twenty-four Wycliffite heresies and errors led on 1 July to their condemnation and excommunication. Hereford continued the struggle, but Repyndon soon backed down and recanted. He was restored to his academic status by

Archbishop Courtenay in a letter of 23 October, and on 18 November 1382 publicly abjured his heresies at St Frideswide's, Oxford. Thereafter he probably became a master teaching theology in Oxford. Indeed, in 1386/7 he rented a room at Queen's College. During this period of his career he is also likely to have been prior or regent master of the Augustinians at Oxford, or, indeed, to have held both these offices, but no records in confirmation of this are known. In May or June 1393 Repyndon was elected abbot of Leicester; his election received royal assent on 12 January 1394. His abbacy saw an important programme of reconstruction and repair both for the abbey church and for the houses and dependencies of the abbey. When Bishop William Alnwick conducted a visitation in 1440, several canons looked back two generations and remarked on how well run and active the abbey had been during their young days in the almonry school.

Bishop of Lincoln His abbacy did not prevent Repyndon from taking on other responsibilities. Not only did he preside at the Augustinian order's general chapter at Northampton in 1401, but he was chancellor of Oxford University from 1400 to 1403. In 1399 Richard II summoned him to a council at Oxford to advise on the papal schism. Just a year later, however, he was referred to as a close friend of Henry IV (formerly duke of Lancaster), and on 4 May 1401 he used his influence to write a letter to the king expressing deep anxiety about lawlessness and injustice in the country. By 1404 he was a chaplain and confessor to Henry. On 19 November in that year Repyndon was papally provided to the see of Lincoln, vacant through the translation to Winchester of the king's half-brother Henry Beaufort. The temporalities were restored on 28 March 1405, he was consecrated at Canterbury on the following day, and was enthroned on 8 April. As bishop, Repyndon usually attended parliaments, but otherwise seems to have eschewed national politics in favour of diocesan business. In his opening months he issued a series of mandates aimed at raising the standard of preaching, preventing unlicensed preachers from spreading heretical opinions, ensuring that the clergy lived properly and performed their proper functions, and encouraging almsgiving and concern for the poor. He encouraged Oxford graduates, especially theologians, to become licensed preachers in his diocese, and sent commissioners to the university to scout for suitable candidates. He also acted against such causes of scandal as the long-running dispute between the dean and chapter at Lincoln, absenteeism from cathedral services, and instances of clerical immorality throughout the diocese. A vivid glimpse of Repyndon in his diocese is provided by Margery Kempe's report of a meeting with him in 1413, at which he treated her with sympathy and discernment, while she commented favourably on his daily alms-giving of a penny and a loaf to each of thirteen poor men.

Margery Kempe was often suspected of religious unorthodoxy. Repyndon's response to heresy in his huge diocese, which included the University of Oxford and

areas in the midlands where Lollardy was rife, is of considerable interest. About 1407 no less a figure than Archbishop Thomas Arundel is reported to have said of Repyndon's treatment of Lollards that 'noo bischop of this londe pursueth now scharplier hem that holden that wei then he doith' (Hudson, 42). But although the Lollards themselves seem to have regarded him with contempt as a renegade, there is little to indicate that Repyndon was in fact an assiduous persecutor. A number of suspected heretics are recorded as having been charged before him, but most were able to clear themselves (some to reoffend later), and none suffered anything worse than imprisonment. It might in fact have been difficult for Repyndon to take a strong line, for he seems to have retained much sympathy for the doctrines he had ostensibly abandoned in 1382, and to have retained links with Lollard circles. In 1402 he was named as an overseer of the will of Dame Anne Latimer, widow of Sir Thomas Latimer, one of the 'Lollard knights', sharing this responsibility with Sir Lewis Clifford, another of the knightly group, and Robert Hoker, parson of Braybrooke, who was a persistent Lollard. When the exhumation of Wyclif's body was ordered in 1415, Repyndon took no action.

Repyndon's sermons The apparent ambiguities of Repyndon's position are less surprising when considered in the light of his *Sermones super evangelia dominicalia*, which were probably composed between 1382 and 1393. Surviving in a number of manuscripts, they draw extensively on works from the late thirteenth and early fourteenth centuries, particularly the gospel commentaries of William of Nottingham and Nicolas de Gorran for the literal or historical analysis of the gospel text, and on the *Sermones dominicales* of Guillaume Peyraut and Jacopo da Voragine for their moral analysis. But these are supplemented by several other authorities, notably Nicholas de Lyre and St Augustine for scriptural problems, and by Robert Grosseteste and Bernard of Clairvaux for contentious issues of canon law. The author addresses individual readers who have access, for instance, to a copy of Lyre's work, in order to verify references, and notes that the gospel for the first Sunday in Advent also serves for Palm Sunday (the former to be read allegorically, the latter literally and historically), so that the reader is provided with one sermon suitable for each occasion. This approach presumes an educated, probably university, readership, an inference supported by the known ownership of the surviving manuscripts.

Repyndon's *Sermones* are composed in an 'ancient' form, expounding the entire gospel reading verse by verse. They differ from patristic models, however, by having a simple initial framing device to organize the discussion of the verses, and as Wyclif proposed, they avoid *exempla* and *curiosa*. Primarily a means of disseminating current biblical scholarship in a liturgical format, they are essentially non-polemical, and contain few contemporary allusions. However, three anomalous sermons do offer insights into Repyndon's personal beliefs: the Ascension day sermon is devoted entirely to the subject of preaching; the sermon on the epistle for the twentieth Sunday after Trinity contains a passage decrying prelates who become too identified with the secular power, and an *excursus* in the Trinity Sunday sermon discusses whether bad ministers may validly confer the sacraments. As well as treating of preaching, these passages deal with the importance of a proper knowledge of scripture, the failings of the friars and (to a lesser extent) the monks, and the proposition that the poor are the true people of God called to preach or evangelize. Elsewhere in his collection Repyndon demonstrates a great concern for the poor and stresses the importance of alms-giving. Opposing himself to the temporal holdings of the church, he regards the primitive and apostolic church as the exemplar for subsequent Christians. He accepts tithing, on condition of its assisting good standards of preaching and helping the poor. On the issue of unworthy priests, he again upholds the orthodox position as propounded by Duns Scotus and Aquinas, that the sacraments do not depend for their validity on the merits of the minister, but in the latter part of his discussion seeks a compromise with Wycliffite criticism of unsuitable or ill-living ministers by exploring the existing powers to punish such priests and exclude them from the sacraments.

Last years, will, and death Such teachings seem to cast Repyndon as a reformer working within the church, albeit one sharing the concerns and priorities of Wyclif, and they offer a bridge between his own teaching in 1382 and his later activities as a bishop; they also suggest that even after his recantation Repyndon occasionally sailed dangerously close to the Lollard wind. Nevertheless his orthodoxy and other qualities were deemed to be such as to justify his creation as cardinal-priest of Sts Nereus and Achilles by Gregory XII on 18 September 1408; however, Gregory's creations were not recognized in England and were revoked after his deposition in 1409, and Repyndon never styled himself cardinal. On 10 October 1419 Repyndon took the unprecedented step of resigning his see; his resignation, which was offered on grounds of frailty, was accepted on 21 November, and he finally relinquished his duties on 1 February 1420. Little is known of the rest of his life, except that he received a papal annuity of 300 marks, later increased to 500, and that he drew up his will, seeing his death as imminent, at the college (and hospital) of St Mary in the Newarke, Leicester. He may have retired there rather than to his former abbey.

Repyndon's will is a remarkable document, and like his sermons suggests that he had retained sympathies with positions he had once held as an avowed follower of Wyclif. Two emphases recur, on the humblest possible treatment of his physical remains, and on a lavish charity to the poor. In a manner not confined to Lollards, but very often associated with them, Repyndon ordered that his most wretched body be buried naked in a sack, out in the open on the north side of the church of St Margaret in Lincoln Cathedral close, there to be food for worms. Only the town crier with his bell was to give notice of Repyndon's death, and ask for prayers for his soul. There was to be an absolute minimum of ceremony, but hundreds of paupers

were to receive carefully graded distributions of food, shoes, and money, with the intention that by the time of his funeral there should be not a halfpenny or farthing of the dead man's money left. After the exequies even the black cloth on the bier was to be given away for clothing. Repyndon was dead by 1 August 1424. He had earlier given Lincoln Cathedral a silver-gilt chrismatory, two silver censers, two silver-gilt basins, six blue copes, and a red cloth of gold for the high altar, while to the cathedral library he gave a copy of Pierre Aureole's *Compendium super totam Bibliam* (now BL, Royal MS 8 G.iii). Such generosity may help to explain why his request for an abjectly lowly burial was ignored, and he was interred in the south-east transept of the cathedral; a plaque now marks the site.

SIMON FORDE

Sources Emden, *Oxf.*, 3.1565–7 · S. N. Forde, 'Writings of a reformer: a look at sermon studies and bible studies through Repyndon's *Sermones super evangelia dominicalia*', PhD diss., U. Birm., 1985 · M. Archer, ed., *The register of Bishop Philip Repingdon, 1405–1419*, 3 vols., Lincoln RS, 57–8, 74 (1963–82) · M. Archer, 'Philip Repingdon, bishop of Lincoln, and his cathedral chapter', *University of Birmingham Historical Journal*, 4/2 (1954), 81–97 · S. N. Forde, 'New sermon evidence for the spread of Wycliffism', *De ore domini*, ed. T. L. Amos, E. A. Green, and B. M. Kienzle (1989), 169–83 · S. N. Forde, 'Social outlook and preaching in a Wycliffite *Sermones dominicales* collection', *Church and chronicle in the middle ages: essays presented to John Taylor*, ed. I. Wood and G. A. Loud (1991), 179–91 · K. B. McFarlane, *Lancastrian kings and Lollard knights* (1972) · A. Hudson, ed., *Two Wycliffite texts*, EETS, 301 (1993) · [T. Netter], *Fasciculi zizaniorum magistri Johannis Wyclif cum tritico*, ed. W. W. Shirley, Rolls Series, 5 (1858) · E. F. Jacob, ed., *The register of Henry Chichele, archbishop of Canterbury, 1414–1443*, 2, CYS, 42 (1937), 285–7 [will] · J. A. F. Thomson, *The later Lollards, 1414–1520* (1965)

Reresby, Sir John, **second baronet** (1634–1689), politician, was born at Thrybergh Hall, in the West Riding of Yorkshire, on 14 April 1634, and was baptized fifteen days later. He was the eldest son of Sir John Reresby (*bap.* 1611, *d.* 1646) and his wife, Frances Yarburgh (*d.* 1668). Like his father, who was created a baronet by Charles I in 1642 and was a staunch royalist during the civil wars, Reresby remained loyal to the Stuarts throughout his political career. He was to rise from relative obscurity to become a prominent local politician and a point of contact between local and national affairs.

Educated initially at home by a tutor until he was almost fifteen, Reresby was then put to school at Whitefriars, London. After six months he moved on to the Blue House school at Enfield Chase, which he attended from 1649 to 1651, making good the inadequacies of his earlier domestic education. In 1652 he was admitted to Trinity College, Cambridge, but because his baronetcy would not be recognized there, as parliament had voided all honours conferred by Charles I after August 1642, Sir John decided to pursue his education at Gray's Inn. In April 1654 he embarked on the grand tour, returning in May 1658 only to leave again the following year. His comment on the 'late disappointment to the king's friends by the discovery of Sir George Booth's plott' (*Memoirs*) to restore the monarchy implies where Reresby's sympathies lay. On his second trip abroad, in 1659, he made his way to the exiled English court in Paris. There he ingratiated himself with the queen mother, Henrietta Maria, and the young Princess Henrietta, duchess of Orléans. He made enough of an impression to carry with him, when he returned to England at the Restoration, a letter of recommendation from the queen, thus putting him on the path of political preferment.

After his return to England, Reresby established himself as a country gentleman at Thrybergh. On 9 March 1665 he married Frances Browne (c.1642–1699), the orphaned elder daughter of William Browne of York, a barrister. He became prominent enough in local affairs to be appointed sheriff in 1665 and justice of the peace a few years later. It was not until a parliamentary seat became vacant that Reresby stepped onto the national stage.

Member of parliament Reresby was elected to parliament in 1673, representing Aldborough in Yorkshire, but it was part of a double return that included another candidate, James Long. The election was significant for two reasons: whereas local selection for office had been the norm, consensus now gave way to contests; secondly, the decisions that were being made by parliamentary committees on double returns became subject to the influence of factions and party interests. Reresby won the contest, and on 24 April 1675 took his seat in parliament.

Mostly an unknown entity in parliament, Reresby knew he had to be careful how he voted in the Commons. Thus he tried to steer a middle path, so as not to offend anyone, while taking opportunities to enhance his position. His initial involvements reflect this cautious approach. In 1675 he was added to the committee for customs appropriation for the navy and to the hearth tax committee. He also backed the chairman of the election committee, Sir Thomas Meres, in a dispute, thus impressing him. Reresby's first speech in the house took place on 13 November on the matter of the Luzancy affair, which implicated the monarchy in an attempt to restore Catholicism to England. Although he was not on the committee to investigate the matter, Reresby was on the committee that complained to the king of the laxness with which the investigation was being carried out. For the rest of Reresby's time in parliament, until its dissolution in 1679, he was involved, for the most part, in committees on routine matters. One issue with which Reresby concerned himself was the hearth tax problem, on which he took a country stance against the court. Yet he was painfully aware of the necessity to curry favour with the Danby ministry. An outstanding illustration of this occurred when Reresby was charged with murdering his black manservant. Although he was cleared of the charge, it was part of a larger design by the duke of Norfolk to confiscate Reresby's properties of Thrybergh and Ickles Mill and an effort to have him removed from parliament. In the end, Reresby declared that 'though a man must not doe mean things to make great men their friends, yet it is follie to omitt such an opportunity of being reconciled to them' (Memoirs, 113–14). His help in defeating an addition to the address which requested the king to put aside 'evil councillors' earned him a commission as governor of Bridlington. He gained a reputation for being 'constantly so faithful both to the King and the Church' (Mexborough MS/R/9-4) and for being a 'very honest and discreet gentleman and of right principles' (Mexborough MS/R/9-11). His vote in favour of the supply bill, in 1679, and his equivocal support of an address by parliament asking the king to back Spain and the Netherlands in their claims in the Nijmegen treaty against the French, earned him Shaftesbury's caustic label of 'doubly vile'.

Reresby thereby gained the backing of the lord treasurer, Thomas Osborne, earl of Danby. Being under the patronage of Danby had its advantages early in Reresby's career, but at the first general election of 1679 it was a distinct disadvantage. Reresby's return was petitioned against, this time by Sir Godfrey Copley. Copley won and Sir John was turned out of the house. Reresby was against excluding the duke of York from inheriting the throne and had, in fact, enlisted the duke's support in his fight against Copley. By the time Reresby stood again for parliament at the second exclusion election, the political crisis was turning in his favour. In the end, Reresby and Copley were returned unanimously and 'without any competition' (Memoirs, 216–17).

Governor of York In 1681 Reresby was elected as MP for York by a clear majority, but parliament was dissolved six days after it was convened in Oxford. In November, following the dissolution, Reresby was appointed justice of the peace for Middlesex and Westminster. As such, he supervised the proceedings over the murder of Sir Thomas Thynne. He also entertained ambitions to be a diplomat. Instead, in April 1682, he was appointed governor of York. In this capacity, he contributed to the king's plan to remodel charters throughout the country. York's charter was among those forfeited.

Reresby's role as JP as well as governor illustrates the fine line between national and local jurisdiction. As governor, he was expected to protect the military's jurisdiction from encroachment by the civilian authority; but as a JP, he appreciated the latter's jealous protection of its powers. The crisis of the Rye House plot accentuated Reresby's role as linchpin between national and provincial politics. When he received orders from Secretary of State Jenkins to search for a couple of conspirators believed to have escaped north, he liaised with the lord mayor of York to obtain a search warrant. Reresby was aware of the need to strengthen his local support without alienating the crown. He succeeded in his aim because he was elected to parliament at the next general election in 1685.

Reresby was seen by James II as a supporter, but the new king was disappointed to learn that Sir John was absent from the vote on supply and the removal of Catholic officers. While he supported the court in a vote to tax London houses in order to pay for the cost of crushing Monmouth's rebellion, Reresby was also acutely aware of his precarious relationship with the corporation of York and the threat by the crown to disgarrison the city. Nevertheless, he continued to support the court by backing a move to vote the king a revenue for life. He also supported a move for a further tax on wines and vinegars in order to grant supply to the king to pay debts from the previous reign, to combat Argyll's invasion, and to enhance the navy, and he spoke in favour of a tax on tobacco and sugars. Still, he voted in favour of having the concurrence of the Lords in the address to the king for dismissing popish officers.

The prorogation and dissolution of James's one and only parliament forced Reresby back to York, but the writing was on the wall when his residence at the manor of York was turned over to the king's chaplain for the purpose of a Catholic school. Although Reresby agreed to stand for parliament in 1688, his heart was not in it, partly because of his infirmities and because he feared having to act against his conscience in the matter of religion. The invasion of William of Orange put a stop to Reresby's dilemma. A conspiracy to seize York was hatched in Yorkshire without Reresby's knowledge. When he agreed with Sir Henry Goodrick's proposal to meet in York in order to send an address of loyalty to the king, coupled with a petition for the replacement of Catholic officers, he was unaware of ulterior motives. Meanwhile, Reresby declined an offer to be made lieutenant-colonel of a regiment of foot on the basis that it would strain his credibility to be associated with Catholic officers and officials. As soon as word was received that William had landed at Torbay, the control of York was taken out of Reresby's hands, effectively snapping the link between the metropolitan and the province. Reresby retired to Thrybergh. He hoped for a place in the new regime, possibly an envoyship, but he died at Thrybergh Hall shortly after, on 12 May 1689. He was buried on 28 May in St Leonard's Church, Thrybergh, where a monument was erected in his memory.

The memoirs Reresby wrote his *Memoirs* for the purpose of recording his accomplishments for his posterity. This was preceded by a draft of the Reresby family history, which included more detail of his offspring. Much of this was eliminated later, probably because of his increasing disappointment in his descendants. The *Memoirs* are a contemporary account of the events of his time. It was first published in 1734 in response to the political events at that time. The publication was followed by more editions in the same year and by the first annotated edition in 1875 by James J. Cartwright. Cartwright's edition was derived from Reresby's genealogy (BL, Add. MSS 29442–29443) and the original *Memoirs* (BL, Add. MSS 29440–29441). In 1936 another edition of the *Memoirs* was produced by Andrew Browning. He relied on the original *Memoirs* and Cartwright's edition. Unfortunately, Browning carried over Cartwright's errors of omission and misread transcriptions. A second edition was made by W. A. Speck and M. K. Geiter (Royal Historical Society, 1991), with corrections and additional materials mainly from the correspondence and estate papers of Sir John Reresby deposited in the Leeds City Archives at Sheepscar, Leeds. Also at Sheepscar are the draft of Reresby's family history and a hitherto unknown French draft of Reresby's diary (1680–81). In addition to the *Memoirs*, two editions of *The Travels and 'Memoirs' of Sir John Reresby, bart.*, the first with pictures, were published in 1813 and 1821. Sir John's letter-book, which contains copies of some of his letters and poems, is in the Bodleian Library, Oxford (MS Rawl. D. 204). Other papers are in the British Library (Add. MSS 6669, 9735, and 28053).

Reresby's marriage to Frances Browne produced five sons and four daughters. The eldest, William, born on 7 January 1668, inherited his father's title and estates. He sold the estate to John Savile of Methley in 1705 because of dissolute living and ended his years in debt working as a tapster in the Fleet prison. The second son, Tamworth, born on 17 September 1670, became a major in Colonel Stanwix's regiment and authored *A Miscellany of Ingenious Thoughts and Reflections in Verse and Prose, with Useful Remarks* (1721). The third and fourth sons, John and George, died in 1683 and 1689 respectively. The last son, Leonard, succeeded to the baronetcy and died unmarried on 16 August 1748, at which time the baronetcy became extinct.

MARY K. GEITER

Sources *Memoirs of Sir John Reresby*, ed. A. Browning, 2nd edn, ed. M. K. Geiter and W. A. Speck (1991) · W. Yorks. AS, Leeds, Mexborough papers · BL, Add. MSS 29440–29443, 28053, 6669, 9735 · Bodl. Oxf., MS Rawl. D. 204 · *CSP dom.*, *1678* · *JHC*, 9 (1667–87) · M. K. Geiter and W. A. Speck, 'The reliability of Sir John Reresby's "memoirs" and his account of the Oxford parliament of 1681', *Historical Research*, 62 (1989), 104–12 · M. K. Geiter, 'Sir John Reresby and the Glorious Revolution', *Northern History*, 25 (1989), 174–87 · J. R. Jones, 'Shaftesbury's "worthy men": a whig view of the parliament of 1679', *BIHR*, 30 (1957), 232–41 · GEC, *Baronetage*, 2.174
Archives BL, memoirs and genealogy of Reresby family, Add. MSS 29440–29443 · W. Yorks. AS, Leeds, Yorkshire Archaeological Society, essays and verses | BL, letters to first marquess of Halifax, C8 · W. Yorks. AS, Leeds, Mexborough MSS
Likenesses portrait; Sothebys, 28 June 1920, lot 314

Resbury, Nathaniel (*bap.* 1643, *d.* 1711), Church of England clergyman, was baptized on 24 September 1643 at Oundle, Northamptonshire, the son of Richard Resbury (1606/7–1674), minister there from 1641, and his wife, Hannah (*d.* 1701). Richard was ordained in 1631 and licensed to practise medicine in 1639; he served at Oundle under the Commonwealth competently enough for Oliver Cromwell to recommend him for the Temple Church, London, in 1658. During this time he also entered into a pamphleteering controversy with the Independent John Goodwin. At the Restoration the crown confirmed him in the Oundle living, but, puritan that he was, he resigned before St Bartholomew's day 1662 and practised medicine in Oundle until his death. In 1672 he took out a licence to preach under the declaration of indulgence as a Congregationalist.

Nathaniel Resbury was educated at Oundle School (1649–52), at the Charterhouse as a poor scholar 'by special recommendation' (1652–7), and at Emmanuel College, Cambridge, where he was admitted pensioner on 8 July 1657. He matriculated the same year, graduated BA in 1661, and proceeded MA in 1672; after incorporation into Oxford in 1673, he was created BD and DD in 1692 from Merton College. Presented to the vicarage of Wandsworth, Surrey, in November 1674, he was also curate of Putney and chaplain to Arthur Annesley, earl of Anglesey, lord privy seal (1673–82), and then to his son. He entered the pamphleteering controversies of the 1680s. Pamphlets he published included *The Texts Examined which Papists Cite for the Visibility of the Church*, to counter current Catholic threat, and *The Case of the Cross in Baptism Considered* (1684), in which he sought to assuage dissenters' fears of Anglicanism. He argued that the sign of the cross at baptism only 'expresseth what hath (already) been done' in the rite—and no more than that. In 1687, with leading churchmen including Thomas Tenison, William Sherlock, and Simon Patrick, he published his contribution, *The Eleventh Note, the Glory of Miracles*, in a series of answers to the fifteen *Notes* of the true church enumerated by Cardinal Bellarmine a century earlier.

Further preferments followed. In August 1687 the crown granted him the living of Broughton Gifford, Wiltshire; this he resigned in 1689 when Edward Stillingfleet, dean of St Paul's, preferred him to the recently created parish of St Paul, Shadwell, Middlesex, which he kept until his death. Two years later, on 15 September 1691, at St Martin Outwich, London, he married Mary Cordell (c.1655–1711), a widow of St Matthew's parish, Friday Street, London, and daughter of Robert Cuthbert, reportedly a wealthy goldsmith of London. In the same year he also became chaplain to William and Mary, and thus preached at Whitehall. Earlier, in the late 1660s, as a young man Resbury had unconsciously caused considerable mirth in the Chapel Royal. While preaching there on the text, 'I am fearfully and wonderfully made' (Psalm 139: 13) he was apparently 'in a sweat, more from apprehension than the warmth of the season' and, wiping his face, 'unluckily blacked himself' with a newly dyed glove (Granger, 2.1.133). Seemingly appropriate to the text, this made the duke of Buckingham, the earl of Arlington, and other courtiers burst into laughter, while Charles II himself was unable 'to keep his countenance' (ibid.). On another occasion an artist in Windsor told Resbury that he 'had the most reproving face he had ever met with' (Granger, *Supplement*, 315).

A sound orthodox churchman, Resbury was also a popular preacher, publishing at least seven sermons, three of which were preached in Queen Mary's presence at Whitehall in the 1690s. His wife died first, on 23 March 1711, and there were no children. He died on 31 July 1711 and was buried in St Giles' Church, Reading, where an epitaph was erected in his honour. WILLIAM MARSHALL

Sources Wood, *Ath. Oxon.: Fasti* (1820) · Wood, *Ath. Oxon.*, new edn, vol. 3 · *Calamy rev.* · Venn, *Alum. Cant.* · Foster, *Alum. Oxon.* · J. Granger, *A biographical history of England, from Egbert the Great to the revolution*, 2 (1769); suppl. (1774) · Ward episcopal register, Wilts. & Swindon RO, D1/2/23 · episcopal register, Morley, Hants. RO, 21M65/A1/33 · Compton episcopal register, 1, 1675–1713, GL · R. Newcourt, *Repertorium ecclesiasticum parochiale Londinense*, 2 vols. (1708–10) · will, PRO, PROB 11/523, fols. 109–110 · *Remarks and collections of Thomas Hearne*, ed. C. E. Doble and others, 11 vols., OHS, 2, 7, 13, 34, 42–3, 48, 50, 65, 67, 72 (1885–1921) · N. Resbury, 'The texts examined which papists cite for the visibility of the church', *A preservative against popery*, ed. J. Cuming (1848) · *IGI* · G. J. Armytage, ed., *Allegations for marriage licences issued by the vicar-general of the archbishop of Canterbury, July 1687 to June 1694*, Harleian Society, 31 (1890), 193 · Oundle School MS register, 1649 · Assembly Order Book B, 1637–58, Charterhouse MS muniments, fol. 139r

Retford [Redford], **Sir Henry** (*c.*1354–1409), soldier and speaker of the House of Commons, may have been son of Ralph Retford (*fl.* 1349–1374) of Castlethorpe, Lincolnshire. Henry Retford seems to have been a man of violent tendencies, twice in 1377 obtaining a pardon for homicide before turning to foreign wars. He served the king in Scotland in 1385, and apparently went with John of Gaunt, duke of Lancaster, to Spain in 1386 (but not as a retainer). About 1384 Retford expanded his interests in Lincolnshire through marriage to Katherine (*fl.* 1383–1397), widow of Sir Ralph Paynel of Caythorpe and Carlton Paynell. He began to serve on royal commissions there and by 25 August 1384 had been knighted. Later he was promoted to sheriff of Lincolnshire, temporarily in 1389, in 1392, and in 1397. Richard II made him a household knight in 1393 and he served in this role on the Irish expedition of 1394. Three years later he pursued a fruitless mission to Rome and Avignon (11 April – 8 November 1397) to seek the resignation of the competing popes.

Though trusted by Richard, Retford was prompt to adapt to the rule of Henry IV, son of his old commander John of Gaunt. His household position was confirmed, and was probably exercised through fighting in Scotland and Wales. In 1402 he was assigned to suppress sedition in Lincolnshire; in 1406 he was sheriff again. Elected to parliament as knight of the shire for Lincolnshire in 1401, he was appointed speaker the next year—presumably for his military and diplomatic rather than parliamentary experience. Under Retford's aegis a sulky House of Commons, while it could not be dissuaded from an unwelcome desire for a joint committee with the Lords, did vote adequate tax grants. He served on great councils and in one more parliament, in October 1404, but thereafter concerned himself principally with Lincolnshire affairs. However, in 1405 he accompanied the king's expedition to Yorkshire against rebels led by Archbishop Richard Scrope, and almost certainly served on the tribunal which passed sentence of execution on Scrope himself. In 1407 he was a commissioner to inquire into the forfeited estates of Henry Percy, earl of Northumberland (*d.* 1408). Henry Retford died shortly before 16 June 1409, when his son's wardship was sold (in error) for £200. His heir and namesake was sheriff of Lincolnshire, in 1427 and 1454, and mayor of Bordeaux in 1452 (just before it fell), but was attainted as a Yorkist in 1459. JULIAN LOCK

Sources C. Rawcliffe, 'Retford, Sir Henry', HoP, *Commons* · J. S. Roskell, 'Two Lincolnshire speakers: 2. Sir Henry de Retford', *Lincolnshire Architectural and Archaeological Society Reports and Papers*, new ser., 7 (1957–8), 117–25; repr. in *Parliament and politics in late medieval England*, 3 (1983), 81–9 · *CPR, 1408–13*, 83 · J. S. Roskell, *The Commons and their speakers in English parliaments, 1376–1523* (1965) · C. Given-Wilson, *The royal household and the king's affinity: service, politics and finance in England, 1360–1413* (1986)
Wealth at death £200—estates' wardship farm: *CPR, 1408–1413*, 83

Reuter, Adam (*fl.* 1608–1626), legal writer, must have emigrated from Cottbus, Silesia, before 3 September 1608, when he was admitted to study at the Bodleian Library, Oxford. The entry in the admission register identifies him as a Silesian 'juris utriusque licentiatus', that is, a licentiate of civil and canon laws (*Reg. Oxf.*, 2/1.266). He is identified in a similar way on the title-pages of his publications (for example, 'Cotbusio L. Siles.'), but not after 1613, when references to his nationality disappear. No evidence has been found to support Anthony Wood's statement that he was 'a learned and ingenious Welshman born in the county of Denbigh'. He may have been a member of Exeter College and later affiliated with New College. Wood describes him as 'a severe Calvinist' who was 'very well read in substantial authors, and had a quick command of his Latin pen' (Wood, *Ath. Oxon.*, 2.420).

Reuter's first book, dedicated to the warden and fellows of New College, was *Ex L. ut vim 3. d. just: et jure. Quaestiones juris controversi 12* (1609); the twelve questions in law take up a little more than fifty pages. In 1610 Reuter apparently presided over two disputations at Oxford: the first, in April, involved the foreigner Andreas Sözinger; the second, in September, involved Georg Wintter of Treptow, Pomerania. Reuter's name appears on the title-pages of both Sözinger's *Disputatio juridica de testamentis* (1610) and Wintter's *Disputatio juridica de injuriis* (1610). Reuter's second book, an oration delivered at Oxford in November 1610, offers an explication of Revelation 17: 8: *Oratio: quam, papam esse bestiam quae non est & tamen est* (1610).

On 5 August and 5 November 1611, respectively, Reuter delivered two orations at Oxford on the Gowrie conspiracy against James VI. These were published as *Contra conspiratorum consilia orationes duae* (1612) and dedicated to George, Baron Carew of Clopton; Henry and Thomas Carey; and William Waller. Reuter's next two works were defences of the monarch and the Church of England: *Libertatis Anglicanae defensio, seu, Demonstratio: regnum Angliae non esse feudum pontificis* (1613), a response to the Jesuit Martin Becanus, and *Eadgarus in Jacobo redivivus, seu, Pietatis Anglicanae defensio* (1614), a reply to Heribert Rosweyde's *Lex talionis XII* of the same year.

Reuter writes on the theme of *consilium* (counsel) in *Delineatio consilii brevissima* (1614), which he dedicates to a community of foreign merchants in London, and responds to *Britannomachia ministrorum* (1614), a polemical work by the Irish Jesuit Henry Fitzsimon, in *Henrici Fitzsimonis, Soc. Jes. contra jus, rationem, Deum, pugna* (1616). Reuter returns to the theme of *consilium* in his final book, *De consilio tractatus*, published at Oxford in 1626. This 220-page treatise is dedicated to Theophilus Howard, second earl of Suffolk, who had succeeded his father, Thomas, a few months earlier. An original letter of about 1615 from Reuter to Sir Robert Cotton survives in the British Library.   EDWARD A. MALONE

Sources Wood, *Ath. Oxon.*, new edn · F. Madan, *Oxford books: a bibliography of printed works*, 3 vols. (1895–1931); repr. (1964) · *Reg. Oxf.*, vol. 2 · *ESTC* [web page] · *A catalogue of the manuscripts in the Cottonian Library deposited in the British Museum* (1802)
Archives BL, letter, Cotton MS Jul. Ciii, fol. 116

Reuter, (Gerd Edzard) Harry (1921–1992), mathematician, was born in Berlin on 21 November 1921, the son of Dr Ernst Rudolf Johannes Reuter (1889–1953), politician, and his wife, (Gertrud) Charlotte, née Scholz (1901–1977). His father, a leading Social Democrat, was twice imprisoned for anti-Nazi activities before escaping, in 1935, to Turkey, where he was professor of municipal theory and practice at the University of Ankara for the duration of the war. After the war he returned to Germany and became burgomaster of what was then left of Berlin. He held office during the Soviet blockade of 1948–9, embodying personally that city's dogged resistance. His memory was enshrined in the Ernst Reuter Platz in Berlin, and in the Free University which he helped to found in 1948.

In 1935 Harry Reuter, like many others, was sent from Germany to England, where he joined the family of (John) Charles and Greta Burkill in Cambridge. They were both for many years notable figures in the university, Charles as a distinguished mathematician and later master of Peterhouse, and Greta later as a principal founder of the Cambridge University Centre. The Burkills also had another adopted mathematical son, Harry Burkill, who said that 'in that household mathematics was in the air' (private information). Reuter was educated at the Leys School in Cambridge from 1935 to 1938, where he was supported by a generous arrangement set up by the school and the Society of Friends' Germany emergency committee. There he distinguished himself on the hockey field. From the Leys he went on to Trinity College, Cambridge, taking part two of the mathematical tripos in 1941. In the latter year he joined the Royal Naval Scientific Service, and spent the war mostly in London. On one occasion he was sent on naval business to the north of Scotland, and was required to show both his Admiralty pass and his British passport. The entry 'Place of birth: Berlin' caused some consternation. On 9 August 1945 Reuter married Eileen Grace Legard (b. 1921), a teacher; they had one son and three daughters.

When the war ended Reuter was sent to Germany to debrief the scientists in various German institutions. There he learned of a mathematical research institute at Oberwolfach in the Black Forest, and reached it just in time to prevent it from being converted into an officers' club. From then on Oberwolfach became the principal European research centre for mathematics. He returned briefly to Cambridge as a research pupil of Frank Smithies, who introduced him to functional analysis. Then, in 1946, he moved to Manchester, where he joined the formidable mathematics department presided over by Maxwell Herman Alexander (Max) Newman. In the late 1940s he worked closely with Dame Mary Lucy Cartwright and John Edensor Littlewood on non-linear differential equations, and with Ernst Sondheimer on the theory of the anomalous skin effect in metals. The latter laid the foundations for subsequent work by Sir Brian Pippard and others on electronic behaviour in metals. In the early 1950s Reuter wrote, with Walter Ledermann, two papers on Markov processes. These were followed by a more extensive collaboration between Reuter and David Kendall on Markov semigroups. This work arose from the recent discovery by the Soviet mathematician A. N. Kolmogorov of two remarkable 'pathological' Markov processes, known as K1 and K2. Reuter and Kendall presented the results of their investigation of these processes in a joint paper at a mathematical congress in Amsterdam at which Kolmogorov was present, and then went on to investigate the associated ergodic theorems and to solve the problem of determining the limits $p_{ij}(\infty)$ directly from a knowledge of the infinitesimal generator.

Reuter spent a brief period at Yale in 1958–9 (where he was able to work with the distinguished American mathematician Will Feller) before moving to Durham to take up the chair in pure mathematics. In 1965 he moved to Imperial College, London, where he remained until his retirement in 1983 as professor of mathematics and head of the mathematics department. He was closely involved, with Kendall and others, in setting up the stochastic analysis group to promote probabilistic activity within both the London Mathematical Society and the Royal Statistical Society. He was a vice-president of the London Mathematical Society and its representative on the Applied Probability Trust, and first chairman of the Rollo Davidson Trust. His work on Markov processes brought him international recognition, especially in China, where 'respect for his achievements stopped little short of reverence' (*The Times*, 9 May 1992). His work in applied fields—including studies of the dynamics of fluid flow, and (with Colin Atkinson and C. J. Ridler-Rowe) studies of the dynamics of epidemics—was also widely appreciated.

Harry Reuter was a great pure mathematician, a great applied mathematician, and an exceptional probabilist. He was also a gifted teacher, leaving behind fifteen distinguished research pupils. His later days were very peaceful, despite a progressive illness which he bore with patience and dignity. After his retirement he and his wife, Eileen, moved to Cambridge, where friends and colleges would always be sure of a warm welcome, and equally sure to find support and wisdom, and a very gentle reproof if they had done something really outrageous. Indeed, for many Reuter was a touchstone of integrity. Many specious compromises were quietly dropped after a chat with him. He died in Cambridge of ischaemic heart disease and bronchopneumonia on 20 April 1992. He was survived by his wife and four children, whose love and support had greatly enriched his life. He was buried at Cambridge.

DAVID G. KENDALL

Sources private information (2004) [Mrs Eileen Reuter] · personal knowledge (2004) · *WWW*, 1991–5 · *Bulletin of the London Mathematical Society*, 27 (1995), 177–88 · *The Times* (9 May 1992) · *The Times* (18 May 1992) · *Daily Telegraph* (25 June 1992)

Likenesses photograph, repro. in *Bulletin of the London Mathematical Society*

Wealth at death under £125,000: probate, 9 June 1992, *CGPLA Eng. & Wales*

Reuter, (Paul) Julius de [*formerly* Israel Beer Josaphat], **Baron de Reuter in the nobility of Saxe-Coburg and Gotha (1816–1899)**, news agency founder, was born on 21 July 1816 in Kassel, Germany, the third son in the family of

(Paul) Julius de Reuter, Baron de Reuter in the nobility of Saxe-Coburg and Gotha (1816–1899), by Thomas Oldham Barlow (after Rupert Lehmann)

four sons and one daughter of Samuel Levi Josaphat, provisional rabbi of Kassel, and his wife, Bette Sanders of Kassel. Soon after the death of his father in 1829, Israel appears to have become a clerk in an uncle's bank in Göttingen.

Reuter moved to England on 29 October 1845, under the name Julius Josaphat. Two weeks later, on 16 November 1845, he was baptized as Paul Julius Reuter at St George's German Lutheran Chapel, Whitechapel, London. And one week after that, on 23 November 1845, he married Ida Marie Elisabeth Clementina, the daughter of Sigismund Matthaeus Magnus, a Berlin civil servant. They had three sons and four daughters, of whom two sons and one daughter reached adulthood. In 1847 Reuter became a partner in a Berlin bookshop and publishing business, Reuter and Stargardt, but the firm's radical pamphlets may have incurred official displeasure and Reuter moved to Paris in 1848. There he first worked as a translator in the news agency run by Charles Havas, and this working relationship later developed into a friendship. He soon switched his attention to bridging the 100 mile gap between the Franco-Belgian telegraph wire which ended at Brussels and the German one at Aachen. By renting pigeons at Aachen, he was able to beat the mail train by several hours, but by Christmas 1850 the gap was finally closed and his service became redundant.

Having now accumulated a small amount of capital and a tiny corps of agents in European cities, Reuter moved to London in June 1851 and set up an office in the Royal

Exchange Buildings. He made use of the new Dover–Calais cable to transmit economic information, which he sold to clients, between the London and Paris stock exchanges. Although he sold a news service to some European papers, he found it hard to sell a news service within the United Kingdom, and *The Times* was particularly recalcitrant. Eventually, in October 1858, he persuaded the *Morning Advertiser* and other newspapers to take his service on a fortnight's free trial. This was a success, and at last even *The Times*, under pressure from rising costs, succumbed.

Reuter, who was naturalized in 1857, energetically expanded and developed his agency, showing a keen appreciation of the value of exclusive news 'beats' and following the cable around the world; 10 January 1859 saw his first major beat, the king of Sardinia's speech which prefaced the war of Italian independence. In 1865 he broke the news of President Abraham Lincoln's assassination several hours ahead of any rivals. In 1865 Reuters opened an office in Alexandria, the first outside Europe, and in 1866 the first Asian office was opened in Bombay. So that his firm could lay its own line to Germany, he floated Reuters as a £250,000 public company on 20 February 1865, taking the post of managing director. The company made a large profit when that line was nationalized. In 1870 Reuter formed a worldwide news agency cartel with Havas in Paris and Wolff in Germany, which survived until the 1930s. He secured his most spectacular coup in 1872 when he won a concession from the shah of Persia covering the exploitation of all industrial and mineral rights. Owing to religious pressure and intervention from Russia, however, this was soon rescinded. Reuter retired in 1878, handing over control of the agency to his son, Herbert de Reuter (1852–1915). The success of Reuter's agency lay in its objectivity, speed, and even-handed treatment of clients. The later profits of the news business were never substantial and much was ploughed back into expansion.

Adorned with lavish side-whiskers, Reuter, succinct of speech but a superb salesman, was short and lively; he gazed sharply at visitors through pince-nez spectacles. A strong supporter of the British empire, he ran his business in patriarchal fashion. In 1871 he was ennobled by Ernst II, duke of Saxe-Coburg and Gotha, as Baron von Reuter, and was from that time known as Baron Julius de Reuter. In 1891 Queen Victoria, to whom Reuter had been careful to send copies of important cables, allowed him to 'enjoy the privileges of the foreign nobility in Britain'.

Reuter died on 25 February 1899 at 97 promenade des Anglais, Nice, France, his wife surviving him. His life became the subject of a film in 1941, released in the United States as *A Dispatch from Reuters* and elsewhere as *This Man Reuter*. It formed a piece of mid-war pro-British propaganda, using Reuter's career as an example of British and American commitment to a free press, showing how, in pursuit of the creation of a news agency that successfully promoted such freedom, Reuter had chosen to leave Germany and set up in London. 'The geographical moral was tacit but obvious' (Read, 276).

Reuter's ultimate impact and influence has been summed up in the following way:

> Julius Reuter had taken the first step in a progression which was to lead in the late twentieth century to instant news and almost instant public reaction—telegraphs, telephone, radio, satellite; still pictures as well as text; newsfilm; and, finally, television. Arguably, the first stage—the making of news quickly available by overland telegraph and undersea cable—was the most important stage of all, in the sense that whereas the first stage brought about a transformation, everything afterwards, however impressive, has been simply a refinement. (Read, 70–71)

Reuters remained under family control until the suicide of Herbert de Reuter in 1915. It then moved into other hands, but continued to develop and operate successfully into the twenty-first century.

CHARLES WINTOUR, *rev.* M. CLARE LOUGHLIN-CHOW

Sources D. Read, *The power of news: the history of Reuters*, 2nd edn (1999) · G. Storey, *Reuter's century* (1951) · Reuters Archives · m. cert.
Archives Reuters Archives
Likenesses T. O. Barlow, mixed engraving (after R. Lehmann), BM, NPG [*see illus.*] · M. Delfico, watercolour caricature, NPG; repro. in *VF* (14 Dec 1872) · London Stereoscopic and Photographic Co., carte-de-visite, NPG · Pet, chromolithograph caricature, NPG
Wealth at death £262,603 12s. 5d.: probate, 17 April 1899, *CGPLA Eng. & Wales*

Revans, Samuel (1807/8–1888), journalist and newspaperman in New Zealand, was born probably in London, the third of the six children of a London surgeon, John Revans, and his wife, Eleanor, *née* Kinsey. After training as a printer he emigrated to Canada, and in 1833, with Henry Samuel Chapman, established Montreal's *Daily Advertiser*. The following year the paper closed and he returned to London. There he joined the radical circle of John Arthur Roebuck, which included many men later prominent in the New Zealand Company. In 1839 he was appointed secretary to the executive committee for inaugurating the settlement of Port Nicholson. In the same year he published in London the first number of the *New Zealand Gazette*, and on 18 April 1840, soon after his arrival in Wellington, New Zealand, the second issue came out, with Revans as editor, printer, and publisher. He helped with his own hands in building an office for the paper, which on 22 August 1840 blossomed into *The New Zealand Gazette and Britannia (Later Wellington) Spectator*. In 1843 he published at this office the first Wellington almanac. Beset by financial difficulties, Revans sold his interests in newspaper publishing in 1845; his subsequent involvement was limited to contributing articles.

In 1845 Revans established a pastoral run near Greytown in the Wairarapa in partnership with Captain William Mein Smith RN. An entrepreneurial expedition to California in 1849 proved a failure, and he returned to sheep farming in New Zealand. From 1853 he represented Wairarapa and Hawkes Bay, both in the general assembly and in the Wellington provincial council, where he espoused radical views. He retired to Greytown after selling his landholdings in 1869, and died there, unmarried, on 14 July 1888, dependent on his friends, but, rather ironically given his continuing radical views, still called a 'gentleman'. C. A. HARRIS, *rev.* JANE TUCKER

Sources K. A. Coleridge, 'Revans, Samuel', *DNZB*, vol. 1 · P. Day, *The making of the New Zealand press: a study of the organisations and political concerns of New Zealand controllers, 1840–1880* (1990) · P. Mennell, *The dictionary of Australasian biography* (1892) · *New Zealand Times* (17 July 1888)
Archives NL NZ, Turnbull L.
Likenesses photograph, NL NZ, Turnbull L.
Wealth at death £163 9s.—interest in estate of W. M. Smith, deceased: probate, 1915, New Zealand

Revel, Richard (*d.* 1213), administrator, was of unknown parentage. He is first recorded in 1166 (unless this is a reference to his father of the same name) holding land in Downhead, Somerset, of the abbey of Muchelney. Pipe roll evidence from the mid-1170s records administrative activity on the king's behalf including, from 1179/80, custody of Carmarthen Castle. In 1190 Richard I granted him the manors of Langport and Curry Rivel, Somerset, for the service of two knights, and land on the royal manor of Somerton, Somerset, which Revel had previously held in socage. From 1191 he was also in receipt of £50 annually from the manor of Horncastle, Lincolnshire. In the exchequer year 1193/4 he was appointed sheriff of Devon and Cornwall, a post he held until 1199. Under King John he fell from favour, losing his sheriffdom and the annuity from Horncastle, and in 1200 was called to account for considerable arrears incurred while sheriff. These were not paid off until 1212. He was dead by July 1213; his body was translated for burial in Muchelney Abbey on 31 March 1215. With his wife (name unknown) he had at least two sons, Richard, his heir, and William, who obtained land in Devon on his marriage to the daughter and heir of William, son of Reginald, but who died without known issue in 1208 or 1209. Richard the younger, who is recorded in 1204 as quarrelling with the sheriff of Somerset, forfeited his lands during the political crisis of 1215, but was reinstated on his making peace with the government of Henry III in July 1217. He married Mabel, sister and heir of Walter of Ashley, lord of Stoke Trister, Somerset, and died in 1222, leaving as heir his daughter, Sabina, married to Henry de l'Orty. ROBERT BEARMAN

Sources H. E. Bates, ed., *Two cartularies of the Benedictine abbeys of Muchelney and Athelney in the county of Somerset*, Somerset RS, 14 (1899) · *Pipe rolls* · L. Landon, ed., *The cartae antiquae: rolls 1–10, printed from the original in the custody of the master of the rolls*, PRSoc., 55, new ser., 17 (1939) · H. C. M. Lyte and others, eds., *Liber feodorum: the book of fees*, 3 vols. (1920–31) · H. Hall, ed., *The Red Book of the Exchequer*, 3 vols., Rolls Series, 99 (1896) · T. D. Hardy, ed., *Rotuli de oblatis et finibus*, RC (1835) · C. Roberts, ed., *Excerpta è rotulis finium in Turri Londinensi asservatis, Henrico Tertio rege, AD 1216–1272*, 2 vols., RC, 32 (1835–6) · T. D. Hardy, ed., *Rotuli litterarum clausarum*, 2 vols., RC (1833–4) · *Curia regis rolls preserved in the Public Record Office* (1922–), vol. 3, pp. 129–30

Reveley, Willey (1760–1799), architect, was the son of William Reveley (*d.* 1806), a younger son of Willey Reveley of Newton Underwood, Northumberland, and Newby Wiske, Yorkshire, whose mother was the daughter and heir of Robert Willey of Newby Wiske. He received his professional education in London as a pupil of Sir William

Chambers from 1777, the same year he was admitted to the Royal Academy Schools. Presumably through Chambers's influence he was assistant clerk of works at Somerset House in 1781–2. He left for Rome in 1784 and accompanied Sir Richard Worsley as 'architect and draftsman' (RIBA BAL, MS Re W/1) for part of his tour through Italy, Greece, and Egypt (1785–6). Reveley was back in Rome in 1788, where he married on 17 April Maria Barnes, daughter of James Barnes, a merchant in Constantinople; their son Henry Willey Reveley (*c.*1789–1875) was also an architect. He returned via Paris to Britain by October, when he made his will.

At this point Reveley's career seemed promising for he had acquired a considerable reputation as an authority on Greek architecture and a number of his designs had been exhibited at the Royal Academy from 1781. However, according to his obituarist in the *Gentleman's Magazine* it was blighted by his 'awkward way of letting loose his real opinions' and his 'sarcastic mode of delivering them' to potential clients. He parted from Worsley on bad terms in 1786 and when in 1794 he edited volume 3 of *Antiquities of Athens*, by J. Stuart and N. Revett, in the preface he replied to some published comments on Greek architecture by Chambers (then still living and the leading architect in England) in terms that were at best unwise. Most of Reveley's designs, often of beauty and elegance, were unrealized, including public baths at Bath, an infirmary at Canterbury, and wet docks on the Thames. The most important works executed by him were All Saints' Church, Southampton (1792–5; dest. 1940), a classical building with a pediment supported by Ionic columns and a cupola; and a country house, Windmill Hill, Sussex, for W. H. Pigou (completed 1798). Minor works include lodges at Parham Park, Sussex (1789), and Stourhead, Wiltshire (1793). Reveley died at his house in Oxford Street, London, on 6 July 1799.

The journal of part of Reveley's tour in the Middle East, together with notes and sketches for a proposed dictionary of architecture and the sale catalogue of his library (Christies, 11–12 May 1801) are in the library of the Royal Institute of British Architects. Some topographical drawings of his tour are in the Victoria and Albert Museum, but the drawings of the pyramids made by him from actual measurement that were in 1814 recorded at New College, Oxford, are now lost. An album containing sixty tracings and sketches of Greek and Roman ornament and other miscellaneous subjects is in Sir John Soane's Museum, London, while a portfolio of early architectural designs (dated 1776–7) was on the London art market in the early 1980s. C. W. HIND

Sources [W. Papworth], ed., *The dictionary of architecture*, 11 vols. (1853–92) · *GM*, 1st ser., 69 (1799), 627 · Colvin, *Archs.*, 805–6 · G. Richardson, *New Vitruvius Britannicus*, 1 (1810), pls. 24–6 [dated 1798] · T. Friedman, 'Willey Reveley's All Saints', Southampton', *Georgian Group Journal*, 12 (2002), 74–95 · C. L. Stieglitz, *Plans et desseins tirés de la belle architecture* (Paris and Leipzig, 1798–1800), pls. 23–4 [orig. designs for All Saints', Southampton, not quite as executed] · notes and sketches for a proposed 'Dictionary of architecture', including a journal of his travels from Rome to Egypt, RIBA BAL, MS Re W/1, fols. 165–88 · will, PRO, PROB 11/1327, sig. 533

Archives RIBA BAL, notes and sketches for a proposed 'Dictionary of architecture', incl. a journal of his travels from Rome to Egypt, MS Re W/1, fols. 165–88
Wealth at death see will, PRO, PROB 11/1327, sig. 533

Revell, Sir Richard. *See* Revel, Richard (*d.* 1213).

Revelstoke. For this title name *see* Baring, Edward Charles, first Baron Revelstoke (1828–1897); Baring, John, second Baron Revelstoke (1863–1929).

Revere, Paul (*bap.* 1734, *d.* 1818), craftsman and revolutionary leader in America, was baptized at the New Brick Church in Boston, Massachusetts, on 22 December 1734, the second of seven surviving children of Apollos Rivoire (1702–1754), a French Huguenot silversmith who emigrated to Boston and Anglicized his name to Paul Revere, and Deborah Hichborn (1703–1777), a Boston native of English descent. Revere learned to read, write, and 'cipher' at the North Writing School in Boston, and was then apprenticed to his father. On 17 August 1757 he married Sarah Orne (1736–1773) of Boston, with whom he had eight children. On 10 October 1773, five months after Sarah's death, he married Rachel Walker (1745–1813) of Boston, with whom he had another eight children. When parliament's colonial taxation policies created a lagging demand for his silver in the mid-1760s, Revere took up copperplate-engraving and dentistry. He engraved trade cards, bookplates, and political cartoons, cleaned teeth, and attached false teeth with gold or silver wire.

Revere regarded Britain's revenue-raising measures to pay off the massive debt of the Seven Years' War and to tighten the reins of empire as unconstitutional attempts to deprive colonists of their liberty and property. His status as a respected silversmith and member of both the artisan-dominated New Brick Church and St Andrew's lodge of freemasons made him a leader among the artisans, mariners, and shopkeepers who joined the Sons of Liberty and Boston's other patriot organizations. As a political cartoonist, albeit one who often copied from English and American sources, he executed masterful works of propaganda. As a trusted express rider from 1773 to 1775, he regularly conveyed vital political information between patriots in Boston and the other colonies.

On 18–19 April 1775 Revere made what became a famous ride to Lexington, Massachusetts, to warn the patriot leaders Samuel Adams and John Hancock that British troops were marching from Boston, either to arrest them or to seize munitions in nearby Concord. Halfway between Lexington and Concord, British officers intercepted Revere and two riders accompanying him: William Dawes, an express rider who had left Boston by an alternative route, and Dr Samuel Prescott, a Concord Son of Liberty. Revere's companions escaped, and the officers released the well-known Revere in Lexington, after he boldly proclaimed that he had alerted the countryside to their secret expedition. Revere then witnessed the opening skirmish of the American War of Independence.

After the war Revere produced some of his finest silver. He also opened a hardware store in 1783, an iron foundry

Paul Revere (*bap.* 1734, *d.* 1818), by John Singleton Copley, 1768

in 1788, which supplied Boston's shipyards, and the first successful copper-rolling mill in the United States in 1801, which produced the dome for the Massachusetts State House. Revere died in Boston on 10 May 1818, at eighty-three, and was buried at Granary burying-ground, Tremont Street, Boston. The *Boston Intelligencer and Evening Gazette* called him one of America's 'most zealous and active of her sons' for his revolutionary service, his hard-earned prosperity, and his post-war philanthropy. Although a relatively obscure figure in his own times, he posthumously reached legendary status through Henry Wadsworth Longfellow's celebrated 1861 poem 'Paul Revere's Ride', which depicts his journey on the night of 18 April 1775. Revere's famous lantern signal for British troop movement of 'one, if by land, and two, if by sea' is a phrase that has been etched into the annals of American folklore. His house at the time, 19 North Square in Boston's North End, is a museum and national historical landmark operated by the Paul Revere Memorial Association.

JAYNE E. TRIBER

Sources J. E. Triber, *A true republican: the life of Paul Revere* (1998) · E. Forbes, *Paul Revere and the world he lived in* (1942) · D. H. Fischer, *Paul Revere's ride* (1994) · N. Zannieri, 'Revere, Paul', *ANB* · E. S. Morgan, *Paul Revere's three accounts of his famous ride* (1976) · P. Leehey and others, *Paul Revere—artisan, businessman and patriot: the man behind the myth* (1988) · D. M. Nielsen, 'The Revere family', *New England Historical and Genealogical Register*, 145 (1991), 291–302 · T. B. Wyman, 'Records of the New Brick Church', *New England Historical and Genealogical Register*, 19 (1865), 235 · R. F. Seybolt, *The public schools of colonial Boston, 1635–1775* (1965) · www.paulreverehouse. org, March 2001 · will and inventory of estate, Massachusetts State archives, Boston, judicial archives, Suffolk probate court record book, case no. 25527, vol. 116, pp. 246, 315, reel 49

Archives Mass. Hist. Soc., family papers | Massachusetts Archives, Boston, Massachusetts archives collection · NYPL, Boston Committee of Correspondence records
Likenesses J. S. Copley, oils, 1768, Museum of Fine Arts, Boston [*see illus.*] · C. B. J. Fevret de Saint-Memin, mezzotint, *c.*1800 (after chalk drawing), Paul Revere Memorial Association, Boston, Massachusetts · G. Stuart, oils, 1813, Museum of Fine Arts, Boston
Wealth at death $37,464.49: will and inventory of estate, Suffolk probate court record book, case no. 25527, vol. 116, pp. 246, 315, reel 49, judicial archives, Massachusetts state archives, Boston

Nicholas Revett (1721–1804), attrib. Thomas Hudson

Revett, Nicholas (1721–1804), architect, was born in May 1721 in Framlingham, Suffolk, the third of four children of John Revett (1691–1756), lord of the manor of Brandeston, and his wife, Elizabeth (d. 1763), only daughter of Edward Fauconberge of London, and great-niece and heir to Dr Henry Fauconberge of Beccles, Suffolk. He was baptized on 11 May 1721 in the church of St Michael, Framlingham.

Little is known of his early education before September 1742, when he left Britain for Italy, travelling through Siena to Rome to study painting under Marco Benefiale. His artistic training eventually served his architectural interests through his measured drawings of antique sites, which were to form the basis of his career and subsequent architectural projects. Revett appears to have studied in Rome for about six years and his interests were shared and encouraged by his compatriots, in particular James Stuart, Matthew Brettingham the younger, and Gavin Hamilton, who in 1748 made up a walking party to Naples. The current excavations at Pompeii and Herculaneum and the temples at Paestum may have inspired their planned expedition to Athens, which Revett described to his father in a letter of 6 January 1749. They intended to record the antiquities in three volumes with a total of 191 plates separating views, sculpture, plans, and elevations. This was expected to take four years and the profit anticipated was at least £10,000. In the event, only Stuart accompanied Revett to Athens and, after many revised proposals, the work amounted to 300 plates and three volumes published between 1762 and 1795, barely covering costs. Funding and support for the project came from dilettanti in Rome, including James Dawkins, the wealthy son of a Jamaican merchant.

Revett and Stuart embarked on their expedition to Athens in March 1750, but an unexpected delay in Venice gave them the opportunity to visit and record the antiquities at Pola in Istria. Many of these drawings were eventually published in the third volume of *The Antiquities* in 1795. The quality of Revett's measured drawings helped to secure further sponsorship and in 1751 Sir James Gray, the British resident in Venice, was responsible for their election to the Society of Dilettanti. This was to prove highly significant for Revett's career. However, the partnership with Stuart ran into difficulties: Stuart prevaricated over producing the text, for which he was responsible, and before publication of the first volume of *The Antiquities of Athens* in 1762, Revett had allowed himself to be bought out of any financial interest by Stuart.

Revett's reputation as a draughtsman was now well established and as an active member of the Society of Dilettanti he was sent on the society's expedition to the coast of Asia Minor in 1764, led by the classicist Richard Chandler. Revett was responsible for the measured drawings of antiquities, while William Pars recorded the views. Lord Le Despenser was chairman of the committee which drew up instructions for the expedition. *The Antiquities of Ionia*, edited by Revett, was published by the society in two volumes in 1769–97. With *The Antiquities of Athens*, these publications represent Revett's greatest contribution to British architecture through the information on Greek architecture which they disseminated to the eighteenth-century cultural élite and the classical sources they provided for the architects of the Greek revival in Britain.

The precise manner in which Revett appears to have completed his work displays the efficient character of this gentleman architect, with the limited private income of a second son which was insufficient to fund his expeditions. That he was a man of letters is evident from his library, which covered architecture, art, history, geography, and literature from Herodotus to Molière. He appears to have been a likeable individual who worked with, and for, friends who were sympathetic to his interests. A portrait attributed to Thomas Hudson depicts a good-looking man with a prominent nose and a high, wide forehead, in the elegant dress of the period with a periwig. A similar portrait was made by Allan Ramsay and it is perhaps no coincidence that Ramsay too had archaeological interests, albeit Roman.

Revett designed a few buildings, incorporating details from his drawings of antique sites; his patrons were friends or fellow members of the Society of Dilettanti. Unfortunately, there is no trace left at Brandeston of what may have been his first building, referred to in a letter of 27 June 1757 now in the Bodleian Library, from his elder brother John at Brandeston. He writes, 'I have almost finished the portico in the garden and beleive [*sic*] Edwards has executed it agreable to your design'. In 1766, before publication of *The Antiquities of Ionia*, he used the unusual Doric order from the temple of Apollo at Delos on the portico which he added to an earlier house for Henry Dawkins at Standlynch in Wiltshire. He was also responsible for decorating some of the interiors, including ceilings and chimney-pieces, in an austere Greek design which anticipated the Greek revival of the next century. Revett used the same feature from the temple of Apollo again on his neo-classical church at Ayot St Lawrence, Hertfordshire (1778–9), for Sir Lionel Lyde. The portico of this remarkable church is connected by columnar screens to lodges. His obituary in the *Gentleman's Magazine* of July 1804 describes it as 'One of the most singular exertions of Mr. R's genius ... fronting the house at the Western extremity of the park, in a style of Architecture not confined to any one Grecian model' (*GM*, 691).

Most of Revett's work was commissioned by Lord Le Despenser, a knowledgeable patron with archaeological interests closely linked through the Society of Dilettanti to Revett. At West Wycombe Park Revett was responsible for the Ionic portico on the west front and several garden buildings; the portico, based on the temple of Bacchus at Teos, was completed in 1771. However, the most intriguing of Revett's buildings is the island temple (1778–80), which had capitals inspired by the Tower of the Winds in Athens. Revett's last recorded payment from Lord Le Despenser was in November 1780, so his work at West Wycombe probably represents his last executed buildings. He died in London on 3 June 1804, presumably from natural causes, given his advanced age, and apparently unmarried. His body was returned to Brandeston for burial at All Saints' Church on 11 June 1804.

ANNE PURCHAS

Sources 'Memoir', *The antiquities of Athens: measured and delineated by James Stuart ... and Nicholas Revett*, ed. J. Woods, 4 (1816), xxi–xxxi, esp. xxviii–xxxi · Colvin, *Archs.* · L. Lawrence, 'Stuart and Revett: their literary and architectural careers', *Journal of the Warburg Institute*, 2 (1938), 128–46 · Brandeston church burial register, Suffolk RO, Ipswich · parish register, Framlingham church, Suffolk RO, Ipswich [baptism] · *GM*, 1st ser., 74 (1804), 690–91 · D. Wiebenson, *Sources of Greek revival architecture* (1969), 62–74 · L. Cust and S. Colvin, eds., *History of the Society of Dilettanti* (1898); repr. with suppl. chaps. (1914), 82–3 · A. Purchas, 'Nicholas Revett's island temple, West Wycombe Park', *Georgian Group Journal*, [5] (1995), 107–10 · *A catalogue of the library, books of prints and drawings of N. Revett* (1804) [sale catalogue, Christies] · BL, Add. MS 22152 · J. Revett to N. Revett, Gough Miscellaneous Antiquities fol. 4, Bodl. Oxf., fol. 174 · E. Harris and N. Savage, *British architectural books and writers, 1556–1785* (1990), 439–48

Archives BL, papers relating to *The antiquities of Athens*, Add. MSS 22152–22153 · BL, proposals for publication of a description of the antiquities of Attica, Lansdowne MS 1056 · RIBA BAL, drawings and proofs for his *Antiquities of Ionia* | BL, works by Richard Chandler with his notes and additions

Likenesses G. Dance, pencil drawing, 1800, BM · W. Edwards, line engraving (after A. Ramsay), probably RIBA, BM · attrib. T. Hudson, oils, RIBA [*see illus.*] · I. Taylor, engraving (after A. Ramsay?), repro. in Woods, ed., *The antiquities of Athens*, frontispiece · engraving (after G. Dance), repro. in W. Daniell, *Collection of portraits* (1808–14)

Wealth at death presumed poor, with possible debts, as library sold three weeks after death; letters to Dilettanti Society show need of funding; not 'in easy circumstances': *GM* (Nov 1821), 423

Revie, Donald [Don] (1927–1989), footballer and football manager, was born on 10 July 1927 at 20 Bell Street, Middlesbrough, the youngest in the family of one son and twin daughters of Donald Revie, journeyman joiner, of Middlesbrough, and his wife, Margaret Emily Haston. His mother died when Revie was twelve. He was educated at Archibald secondary modern school, Middlesbrough, and left school at fourteen to become an apprentice bricklayer, before joining Leicester City Football Club in 1943. Hull City bought him for £20,000 in 1950. On 17 October 1949 he married Elsie May Leonard (*b.* 1927/8), primary school teacher, daughter of Thomas Grosett Duncan, professional footballer, and niece of the Leicester City manager, John Duncan. They had one son and one daughter.

Revie transferred to Manchester City in 1953, and reached his peak as a footballer in the mid-1950s, winning six England caps and being voted footballer of the year in 1955. Manchester City won the Football Association (FA) cup in 1956, using what became known as the 'Revie plan', with Revie, as centre forward, lying deep while feeding the ball to the other forwards and then moving through in the final stage, a tactic copied from the successful Hungarian team by the Manchester City manager.

Revie moved to Leeds United in 1958, after two years with Sunderland. At Leeds he was appointed manager in 1961, at a time when the club was struggling to avoid relegation to the third division. Revie not only avoided this, but brought Leeds to the top of the second division in 1964, and second to Manchester United in the first division in 1965, winning the League championship in 1969 with 67 points, the highest total in the history of the championship, and the FA cup in 1972. His ambitions for the club were not confined to the domestic scene, and in 1968 Leeds won the European Fairs cup (the UEFA cup), beating Ferencváros 1–0, the first British club to win the cup. Despite these successes, Leeds had the reputation of being perpetual runners-up: they lost to Liverpool in the 1965 FA cup final, came second in the League championship in 1965, 1966, and 1970, lost to Chelsea in the FA cup final in 1970, were runners-up to Arsenal in the League championship in 1971, and lost to second-division Sunderland in the 1973 FA cup final. Revie never achieved his ambition for Leeds to win the European cup.

However, encouraged by the British media, which declared Leeds to have the best side in the world at the beginning of the 1969–70 season, Revie was confident of a treble victory: the European cup, the FA cup, and the League championship. In the end all three eluded Leeds, partly as a result of a pile-up of fixtures, compounded by injuries. In 1974, after Leeds United had won the League championship, remaining undefeated for the first twenty-nine games of the season, Revie resigned to take up the position of England team manager, following the sacking

Donald Revie (1927–1989), by unknown photographer, 1969

of Sir Alf Ramsey after England had failed to qualify for the 1974 world cup finals.

After a successful first season as the England manager, with the team undefeated after nine internationals, Revie encountered a set-back when England was eliminated from the European championship early in the 1975–6 season. He was faced with the task of building an international side with players from many different clubs, and it was hard to achieve the family atmosphere that had been so successful at Leeds. Moreover, his difficult relationship with Alan Hardaker, secretary of the Football League, made his task harder. While Revie was manager, England won fourteen out of twenty-nine matches, with seven defeats and eight draws. The poor results were attributed to the uncertainty and lack of continuity caused by frequent team changes rather than to the lack of outstanding players. He used fifty-two players in the twenty-nine games, awarding twenty-nine new caps, and he only once fielded an unchanged side. Morale sagged when England lost 2–0 to Italy in a world cup qualifying match in November 1976, and the press began to forecast England's elimination from the competition and Revie's dismissal.

In July 1977 the *Daily Mail*, to which Revie had sold his story, revealed that he had been in secret negotiations with the United Arab Emirates (UAE) while the England team had been playing in South America, had accepted the post of team manager to the UAE for four years at £60,000 a year, and had resigned from his England job. This led the Football Association to ban him from English football for ten years. Revie successfully appealed against

the ban in the High Court in November 1979, on the grounds that the head of the tribunal, Sir Harold Thompson, chairman of the Football Association, was biased. But the judge made it clear that it was still felt that Revie's conduct in leaving England so abruptly had brought English football into disrepute. He became manager of al-Nasir Football Club in 1980, and moved to the National Football Club, Cairo, in 1984.

At Leeds, Revie had aimed to make the club as famous as Real Madrid. By the time he left in 1974 some argued that Leeds was the greatest club side of all time, and that his achievements lay there, and not in his spell as England manager. He transformed Leeds from a club in danger of relegation into a club aiming at, and achieving, major honours at home and abroad.

Revie was appointed OBE in 1970, and was voted manager of the year in 1969, 1970, and 1972. Always well dressed, he had the pugnacious features of a boxer. He was very superstitious, and had a lucky blue suit, which he always wore on match days.

Revie died on 26 May 1989 in Murrayfield Private Hospital, Edinburgh, of motor neurone disease, survived by his wife and children. He was cremated on 30 May at Warriston crematorium, Edinburgh.

ANNE PIMLOTT BAKER, *rev.*

Sources D. Revie, *Soccer's happy wanderer* (1955) · E. Thornton, *Leeds United and Don Revie* (1970) · A. Mourant, *Don Revie: portrait of a footballing enigma* (1990) · J. Rogan, *The football managers* (1989) · *The Independent* (27 May 1989) · b. cert. · m. cert. · *CGPLA Eng. & Wales* (1989) · A. Mourant, 'The Revie revolution', *Leeds United. The official illustrated history* (1997), 48–102

Likenesses photograph, 1955, repro. in Mourant, *Don Revie*, facing p. 72 · photograph, 1969, Hult. Arch. [*see illus.*]

Wealth at death £67,786: probate, 3 Aug 1989, *CGPLA Eng. & Wales*

Revières [Reviers, Redvers], **Baldwin de, earl of Devon** (*c.*1095–1155), magnate, was the eldest son of Richard de Revières and Adeliz, daughter of William Peverel of Nottingham. The family originated from Reviers (Calvados) but their estates, by the end of the eleventh century, centred on Néhou (Manche) and Vernon (Eure). Richard de Revières was a follower of William I's youngest son, Duke Henry, and when Henry became king in 1100, he rewarded Richard with the grant of extensive estates in Devon, Dorset, Hampshire, and the Isle of Wight, later known as the honours of Plympton, Christchurch, and Carisbrooke. Richard died in 1107 leaving his eldest son, Baldwin, probably little more than twelve years old.

Baldwin acted for Henry I as a minor local administrator in the 1120s and early 1130s, but emerged clearly at the beginning of Stephen's reign when, in the spring of 1136, he seized the royal castle at Exeter. The citizens appealed to the king for help and during the summer the castle was kept under close siege. Baldwin was not among the besieged, but nor was he at Plympton, the *caput* of his Devon estates; for the castle there was handed over to the king by the garrison which Baldwin had left to defend it. It seems he had withdrawn to his castle at Carisbrooke to organize a pirate fleet to prey on shipping running between Normandy and England. Following the fall of

Exeter, Stephen moved quickly to Southampton, intending to invade the island. When the water supply in Carisbrooke Castle failed, Baldwin appeared before the king to plead for mercy and the restoration of his lands. Stephen was unmoved and Baldwin left the country soon afterwards, a landless exile. He took refuge at the court of Geoffrey, count of Anjou, and for the next three years was actively involved in the count's attacks on Normandy. In 1138 he was captured by the Norman baron Ingram de Say outside the castle of Isle Marie (Manche).

Baldwin must soon have regained his freedom as in July 1139 he led the Empress Matilda's invasion of England, landing at Wareham and seizing the nearby castle of Corfe. In the military campaigning of the next three years he remained a firm supporter of Matilda's cause. He fought in her army at the battle of Lincoln early in 1141 and was then among those who escorted her to London, where it was hoped she would be crowned. On her arrival there in midsummer she created him earl of Devon. He stayed with her during her retreat to Oxford and, in July 1141, when she moved her army to Winchester. But when Matilda's forces were routed in September, he may have left her entourage; in any event he is not again recorded in her company. In the late 1140s he may have gone on crusade, but he was at Westminster at the end of 1153 to witness the treaty between Stephen and Duke Henry, Matilda's son.

Baldwin was a prominent benefactor of religious houses. In the 1130s he founded a priory of Augustinian canons at Breamore, Hampshire, and a Cistercian abbey at Quarr, on the Isle of Wight. After becoming earl he established a priory on his manor of St James Church, to the south of Exeter, dependent on the monastery of St Martin-des-Champs, Paris, and gave leave for the abbey of Lyre to found a priory at Carisbrooke. He was a patron of Plympton Priory and of Christchurch Priory, Dorset, where he introduced regular canons.

Baldwin left at least five children from his first marriage, to Adeliz (parentage unknown). Adeliz died around 1146, and between 1151 and 1155 Baldwin married as his second wife, Lucy, the widow of Gilbert de Clare, earl of Hertford. He died on 4 June 1155 and was buried at Quarr Abbey. He was succeeded in his estates and the earldom by his eldest son, Richard. However, neither Richard nor his descendants achieved the prominence of the first earl. Three of the six earls who followed Baldwin either married or were betrothed to important heiresses, showing that they were regarded as potentially men of consequence, but a series of early deaths and often prolonged minorities reduced the family's influence, at court and also in south-west England, which was increasingly neglected in favour of the Isle of Wight. The seventh earl, named Baldwin like his great-great-grandfather, died without a male heir in 1262, when his estates and title passed to his sister Isabella de *Forz, countess of Aumale. She died in 1293, having outlived all her children. In 1335 the earldom of Devon was granted to Hugh Courtenay, lord of Okehampton, a descendant of Isabella's great-aunt Marion.   ROBERT BEARMAN

Sources R. Bearman, ed., *Charters of the Redvers family and the earldom of Devon, 1090–1217*, Devon and Cornwall RS, new ser., 37 (1994) • R. Bearman, 'Baldwin de Redvers: some aspects of a baronial career in the reign of King Stephen', *Anglo-Norman Studies*, 18 (1995), 19–46 • K. R. Potter and R. H. C. Davis, eds., *Gesta Stephani*, OMT (1976) • Ordericus Vitalis, *Eccl. hist.* • R. H. C. Davis, *King Stephen*, 3rd edn (1990) • M. Chibnall, *The Empress Matilda* (1991)

Reymes, Bullen (1613–1672), army officer, courtier, and government official, was born on 28 December 1613 at Petre Hayes, Devon, the eldest son and heir of Bullen Reymes (1586–1652) of Westminster, a courtier and gentleman usher to the duchess of Buckingham, and Mary (1585–1660), daughter of William Petre of Torbryan, Devon. As a young man he attended a small boarding-school run by a Master Herbert and his wife, and received further informal education in the household of the duke of Buckingham at York House. In 1631 he became attached to the household of the English ambassador to Paris, Sir Isaac Wake. Following Wake's death in 1632, Reymes made a tour of southern Europe and the eastern Mediterranean. He was attached to the household of the English ambassador to Venice (1634–5 and 1636–7), interrupted by a brief return to England. In 1635 he acquired from his cousin William Coker the estate of West Chelborough, Dorset, which gave him his first taste of financial security.

Reymes returned to England for good in the autumn of 1637. In 1640 he married Elizabeth (c.1622–1661), daughter and coheir of Thomas Gerrard, of Trent, Somerset, who brought with her the estates at Waddon, Broadway and Nottingham, Dorset. In 1640 Reymes became a captain of foot in the second bishops' war. In 1641 he was named a gentleman of the privy chamber in waiting and attended the king in this capacity at Oxford from the late autumn of 1642 to the spring of 1643. In May of that year he joined the royalist western army, seeing action at Roundway Down, Dorchester, Exeter, Plymouth, Lyme Regis, and Taunton. He was again made a captain of foot by August 1643, became lieutenant-colonel of James Chudleigh's regiment by September, and colonel upon Chudleigh's death in early October. He was present at the surrender of the royalist forces at Exeter in April 1646. In mid-June Reymes served parliament as a go-between with the king. Subsequently he was forced to compound for his estate at £100 (despite its value of £553). During the interregnum he experienced continued difficulties with sequestrators. He was imprisoned in Taunton Castle from August to October 1650. In 1655 he signed a bond of allegiance to Cromwell.

Reymes was elected to the Convention Parliament for Weymouth at a by-election in 1660, and sat for the same borough in the Cavalier Parliament from 1661. He was active on behalf of his constituency, was a frequent committee man, and a parliamentary diarist. Soon after the Restoration he joined the household of the duke of Gloucester, serving until the latter's death in September 1660. He also resumed his position in the privy chamber. Reymes developed a reputation for loyalty and honesty which led to several administrative appointments. He became an assessment commissioner for Dorset in 1660;

vice-admiral of the county in 1661; a commissioner for loyal and indigent officers in 1662; an assistant of the Royal Fishing Company; and a commissioner for Tangier in 1664. In June of that year he was sent as a special emissary to assess the situation at Tangier. The king was highly impressed with the judiciousness of his conduct in attempting to settle disputes and sort out the garrison's pay, as well as by the probity of his final report. In November 1664 he was made a commissioner of sick and wounded for Hampshire and Dorset, and in 1665 deputy treasurer of prizes at Portsmouth. This, plus his position as vice-admiral, made him a significant local figure in the conduct of the Second Anglo-Dutch War: he was a government contractor for sailcloth; responsible for pressing seamen; and an important voice in planning the provisioning and disposition of shipping off the south coast. His persistent attempts to seek adequate funding for the maintenance of sick and wounded sailors—both English and captured Dutch—reveal great humanity, as well as frustration at the inefficiencies and inadequate funding of the crown's ramshackle administrative system.

In 1667 Reymes was nominated FRS by his friend John Evelyn. In September of that year he and Andrew Newport were selected by the new Treasury commission to assist the negotiations with the new farmers of the customs. On 22 November following he was named surveyor of the great wardrobe, one of the least efficient and most prodigal of spending departments. As surveyor, Reymes, in partnership with the Treasury-nominated comptroller, Newport, superseded the existing chain of command of the department, ordering materials for and supervising construction of furniture and clothing, and distributing funds themselves. According to Pepys, Reymes and Newport 'do great things and have already saved a great deal of money in the King's Liverys' by late January 1668 (Pepys, 9.41), though their long-term success in reforming the department was more limited.

In December 1671 Reymes was again named a commissioner for sick and wounded in anticipation of the Third Anglo-Dutch War. But in the autumn of 1672 he retired to Dorset on grounds of ill health, spending most of his days at Weymouth. He died after a mysterious lingering illness on 18 December and was buried at Portisham church. He was survived by his two daughters, Tabitha (b. 1646) and Mary (b. 1651), and by the eldest and only survivor among three sons, also Bullen (b. 1647). His wife, Elizabeth, had died at Waddon in June 1661. Reymes established a business partnership and friendship with Constance Pley (whom, in his will, he referred to both as 'sister' and his 'very intimate dear friend') which has led to some speculation about a more intimate attachment.

In fact, Reymes seems to have been built for friendship: among those in this category he numbered Pepys, Evelyn, Thomas, Lord Clifford, Sir Charles Cotterell, and Sir William Coventry. Despite a passionate temper, he seems to have earned the respect of nearly all who came into contact with him. Contemporaries valued him for his loyalty, honesty, probity, and wry good humour. He was tolerant of the full spectrum of Restoration belief, but died a staunch Anglican. He was also highly cultivated, skilled in music as a youth, an avid theatre-goer and gardener.

R. O. BUCHOLZ

Sources H. A. Kaufman, *Conscientious cavalier: Colonel Bullen Reymes, M. P., F. R. S., 1613–1672, the man and his times* (1962) · M. W. Helms and J. P. Ferris, 'Reymes, Bullen', HoP, *Commons, 1660–90* · Pepys, *Diary*, 5.161, 274–6; 8.68, 294, 512, 519; 9.41 · W. A. Shaw, ed., *Calendar of treasury books*, 2, PRO (1905), 84, 87, 192 [customs farm of 1667]; 3 (1908), 57, 579 [great wardrobe] · CSP dom., 1660–72 [role in local government, second Anglo-Dutch War]
Archives BL, parliamentary diary, Egerton MS 2043 · Wilts. & Swindon RO, manuscript diary, letters, Great Wardrobe entry books (3 vols.) · Wilts. & Swindon RO, papers
Likenesses portrait, repro. in Kaufman, *Conscientious cavalier*, frontispiece
Wealth at death £1000 for daughter Mary; modest wealth: will, PRO, PROB 11/340, fol. 26

Reynard [*formerly* Reinherz], **Helene** (1875–1947), economist and college administrator, was born on 24 August 1875 in Vienna, the daughter (she had a brother and a sister) of Marcus Reinherz and Mina Schapira. Her family emigrated to Bradford, where her father owned a woollen mill. She was educated at Bradford Girls' Grammar School and, from 1893 until 1897, at Girton College, Cambridge, where she gained second-class honours in the moral sciences tripos, subsequently (1905) receiving an MA from Trinity College, Dublin. After leaving Cambridge she lived for a time in London, where she acquired secretarial and bookkeeping skills and worked for several women's clubs. In 1904 she was chosen (out of forty applicants) for the position of junior bursar at Girton College. She held this position, helping to run the residential side of the college and giving occasional instruction in economics, until 1913, when she resigned at her family's urging to help manage her father's factory.

Helene Reinherz was joint director of the Bradford Wool Extracting Company Ltd until 1922, thus gaining a close—and, for a woman, unusual—understanding of managerial and business practices. At the outbreak of the war the entire family changed their name from Reinherz to Reynard. She was an active supporter of the women's suffrage movement and, after 1918, the Society for Equal Citizenship. During the war she was secretary of the Bradford Women Citizens' Association and of the Women's Industrial Interests Society, which was created to protect the interests of women workers employed during the war in occupations previously reserved for men.

In 1922 Reynard returned to the sphere of college administration, becoming the first full-time and salaried treasurer and secretary of Somerville College, Oxford, as well as one of the first fellows of the college. She was also a university lecturer on economics and business administration, and an Oxford MA was conferred on her in 1925. Calm, efficient, and fair-minded, Reynard proved to be a gifted administrator, overseeing the reorganization of the college's structure. With this background, in 1925 Reynard was appointed principal administrative officer of the household and social science department of King's College for Women, which was then in the process of achieving independence as the King's College of Household and Social Science (later Queen Elizabeth College). She held this position until 1945.

The King's College of Household and Social Science lay at the heart of the effort to foster scientific study of all aspects of domestic life. As its head, Reynard helped to shape not only this institution but also the course of development of the 'household science' movement. Her principal goal was to develop new careers for women: thus, while the college did offer a one-year course intended to prepare women 'for the efficient management of their own homes' and a two-year diploma course for teachers of domestic science in secondary schools, Reynard (like the college's early pioneers) concentrated on expanding scientific and professional training. Under her wardenship entrance requirements were made more stringent and new diploma courses were developed to train dietitians and social workers. Yet while the college did develop a monopoly over the new science of nutrition, largely under the guidance of its inspired professor of physiology, V. H. Mottram, its hopes of developing 'an applied science of the household' and of creating a new 'domestic expert' were never fully realized (Blakestad, 394). Difficulties in recruiting the best science students, competition from the domestic science colleges, financial pressures, and a lack of public comprehension of its aims hampered the college's efforts. Reynard was an able administrator and a kind and thoughtful warden, however, and under her leadership the college provided a useful science training to a large number of women students.

Throughout the 1930s Reynard also played an important role within university and professional women's organizations, including the Women's Employment Federation and the Federation of University Women. In 1938 she helped to found the Institutional Management Association. From 1929 to 1939 she was an examiner for the civil service commission. She also published a series of useful and cogent books explaining the basic principles of bookkeeping and of institutional management, including *Institutional Management and Accounts* (1934), *What is a Balance Sheet?* (1935), *Domestic Science as a Career* (1947), and, with D. Hustler, *Book-Keeping by Easy Stages* (1937). She was a regular contributor to the *Economic Journal*.

In 1939, under the threat of air raids, King's College of Household and Social Science was evacuated to Cardiff; when air raids began hitting Cardiff as well it was moved once again to Leicester. Reynard continued to run the college in its Leicester exile, but towards the end of the war her health began to fail. She resigned as warden in 1945, and did not live to see the college rebuilt and re-established. Helene Reynard died at the London Clinic, 20 Devonshire Place, London, on 27 December 1947, and was cremated at Golders Green crematorium on 31 December. SUSAN PEDERSEN

Sources M. Crofts, 'In memoriam: Helene Reynard', *Girton Review*, Lent term (1948), 26–8 • *The Times* (29 Dec 1947), 1 • *The Times* (22 Jan 1948), 6 • N. L. Blakestad, 'King's College of Household and Social Science and the household science movement in English higher education, c.1908–1939', DPhil diss., U. Oxf., 1994 • N. Marsh, *The history of Queen Elizabeth College* (1986) • King's Lond., archives • K. T. Butler and H. I. McMorran, eds., *Girton College register, 1869–1946* (1948) • P. Adams, *Somerville for women: an Oxford college, 1879–1993* (1996) • *CGPLA Eng. & Wales* (1948)

Archives King's Lond.

Likenesses photograph, repro. in Marsh, *History of Queen Elizabeth College*

Wealth at death £3643 18s. 11d.: probate, 24 March 1948, *CGPLA Eng. & Wales*

Reynardson, Sir Abraham (1590–1661), merchant and lord mayor of London, was born at Plymouth, Devon, the eldest son of Thomas Reynardson of Plymouth, a leading west country merchant, and his wife, Julia Brace of the Isle of Wight. He was bound apprentice in 1610 to Edward James of the Merchant Taylors' Company, a merchant trading with Spain and Portugal and a member of the Eastland, Levant, and East India companies. Reynardson gained his freedom on 5 October 1618, was admitted to the livery on 7 May 1627, joined the court of assistants on 20 August 1639, and served as master of the Merchant Taylors in 1640–41. During the same period he rose to become a prominent overseas merchant, trading to the Levant, the East Indies, Spain, and Portugal and sitting on the governing bodies of both the East India Company and the Levant Company (for whom he was treasurer in 1639–41) for much of the 1630s. His wealth and connections had opened up the path to advancement in City governing circles by 1640. Elected alderman for Bishopsgate ward on 12 November 1640, he also served as sheriff in 1640–41 and eventually reached the pinnacle with his election as lord mayor in 1648. His City pre-eminence was further confirmed by his acceptance of the presidency of St Bartholomew's Hospital in February 1649, although he was to resign the office in the following September owing to ill health.

Reynardson was married twice, first, in 1623 at St Peter-le-Poer, to Abigail (d. 1632), third daughter of the wealthy London merchant and customs farmer, Nicholas Crisp of Bread Street, with whom he had two sons born in the parish of St Andrew Undershaft. His second wife, whom he married in 1636, was Eleanor (d. 1674), daughter of Richard Wynne of Shrewsbury; they had three sons and three daughters. A mansion house on the north side of Tottenham Green, purchased in 1639, and a lease of an imposing house in Bishopsgate Street, in 1640, provided appropriate settings for his social advancement.

The developing political crisis and eventual outbreak of civil war found Reynardson initially adopting a deliberately low political profile. He was not a signatory of any of the London petitions of 1641–2 and did not join with fellow members of the London élite in protesting against pro-parliamentary innovations in the City. However, by 1643 his royalist sympathies were becoming well known. His religious views were orthodox in the sense that he was a committed member of his parish church of St Martin Outwich, Threadneedle Street, to which he presented valuable items for the communion table and within which his will directed he should be buried, and he shared in the widespread belief in Calvinist election to salvation. Obadiah Sedgwick, a leading presbyterian divine who was later to plead for the king's life, was chosen to preach Reynardson's election sermon in 1648 when he became lord mayor.

Reynardson's election to the mayoralty placed him directly in the political firing line at a time when events were reaching crisis point as a result of the army's determination to secure the trial and execution of the king. Shortly after his assumption of office he came into conflict with a common council which had been radicalized by a parliamentary ordinance which excluded from membership of that assembly any citizen who had subscribed a recent pro-royalist engagement in favour of a 'personal treaty' with the king (in other words, that the king should go to London to negotiate directly with parliament). When in January 1649 newly elected common councillors came to take their seats, Reynardson insisted on their taking the traditional oath of allegiance to the king. The councillors protested to parliament, which ordered the lord mayor to suspend this requirement. Reynardson proved equally unco-operative when it came to proclaiming in the City the ordinance for erecting the court for the king's trial, making sure that he took no part in the proceedings. A meeting of common council held on 13 January 1649 witnessed a major clash between Reynardson and most councillors. The main business was to be the approval of an official City petition intended for submission to the House of Commons which in effect called for the execution of justice on the king. Reynardson was as obstructive as he could possibly be, arriving late accompanied by only two aldermen, refusing to acknowledge the authority of that meeting of common council, and not allowing the petition to be read. After many hours of debate, Reynardson and his brother aldermen tried one final act of sabotage—they departed the court, thereby technically terminating the meeting. Yet the meeting continued despite their absence and councillors elected their own chairman and proceeded to approve the petition.

After the king's execution Reynardson sought to protect leading fellow citizens from being proceeded against as delinquents by privately burning the subscribed copies in his possession of the London petition for a personal treaty. On 23 March a copy of the 'act' abolishing kingship was sent to him for proclaiming in the City and his resolute refusal to perform that duty, a stance in which he was supported by his wife, resulted in a summons before the bar of the house on 2 April to answer for his recalcitrance. The house voted that he be fined £2000, imprisoned in the Tower for two months, and deposed from the mayoralty. A few days later Reynardson and four other like-minded aldermen were also ordered by the Commons to be discharged from the aldermanic bench. Reynardson was to be replaced as lord mayor by a leading London Independent, Thomas Andrews. Despite these actions, he maintained his defiance of the new regime by refusing to pay his fine, and the seizure and sale of his goods followed. According to his own estimate, the mayoralty had already

cost him £20,000 and he was still being pursued for an unpaid portion of his fine in May 1651 when the seizure of his estate was ordered pending full satisfaction of his fine. During his mayoralty he had two portraits of himself in his robes of office painted but apparently only one of these portraits survives (and currently hangs in the court room at Merchant Taylors' Hall).

After the Restoration Reynardson was knighted by Charles II on his visit to the City on 5 July 1660 and he was formally restored to the aldermanic bench on the following 4 September. However, an offer of the mayoralty for 1660–61 was declined on the grounds of ill health. He died at Tottenham on 4 October 1661 and was buried in the church of St Martin Outwich on 17 October after a period of lying in state at Merchant Taylors' Hall. His will, made on 10 May 1661 at Tottenham and proved on the following 22 October was that of a wealthy City benefactor. Among his bequests was a silver basin and ewer bearing his arms and name to grace the feasts of the Merchant Taylors' Company, as well as provision for the relief of the company's poor. London's five hospitals and the poor of Tottenham also benefited.   KEITH LINDLEY

Sources C. M. Clode, *London during the great rebellion: being a memoir of Sir Abraham Reynardson, knt* (1892) · A. B. Beaven, ed., *The aldermen of the City of London, temp. Henry III–[1912]*, 2 (1913) · J. R. Woodhead, *The rulers of London, 1660–1689* (1965) · will of Sir Abraham Reynardson, PRO, PROB 11/306/163 · *The visitation of London, anno Domini 1633, 1634, and 1635, made by Sir Henry St George*, ed. J. J. Howard and J. L. Chester, 2 vols., Harleian Society, 15, 17 (1880–83) · R. R. Sharpe, *London and the kingdom*, 2 (1894) · *DNB* · Merchant Taylors' Company, apprentice binding books, GL, microfilm 314 · Merchant Taylors' Company, index to freemen, GL, MS MF 324/28 · V. Pearl, *London and the outbreak of the puritan revolution: city government and national politics, 1625–1643* (1961); repr. with corrections (1964), 305–6 · M. A. E. Green, ed., *Calendar of the proceedings of the committee for advance of money, 1642–1656*, 3, PRO (1888), 1188–9 · R. Brenner, *Merchants and revolution: commercial change, political conflict, and London's overseas traders, 1550–1653* (1993)

Likenesses E. de Critz, oils, Merchant Taylors' Company, London · oils (after C. Johnson), Merchant Taylors' Company, London

Wealth at death £18,276 in personalty: will, March 1662, PRO, PROB 11/306/163 · lands in Essex, Sussex and Middlesex, jewellery, etc.: Woodhead, *Rulers of London*; will, PRO, PROB 11/306/163

Reynell family (*per.* 1540–1735), gentry, descended from Hugh of Malston who held the manor of East Ogwell, near Newton Abbott in the east of Devon, in the reign of Edward II. Three generations later Margaret, his great-granddaughter and the Malston heir married Walter [i] Reynell of Bradlingham in Cambridgeshire, a descendant of the Richard Reinell who served as sheriff of Devon in the late 1190s and held the custody of Launceston and Exeter castles. The direct descendant of this marriage was Walter [ii] (1475–1540) who divided his estate between his two older sons. In 1511 he granted the use of the manor of East Ogwell to his heir, John (1488–1547), and his wife, Margery, daughter of William Fortescue of Wood. Then about 1522 the younger son, Thomas [i], and his wife, Cecily, were granted the use of the manor of Malston, further south near Kingsbridge. So arose the two distinct branches of the Reynell family. John Reynell added lands in the parish of North Bovey to the East Ogwell estate. He died on 6 December 1547 and was succeeded briefly by his eldest son, Walter [iii], who was born in 1518 and died childless.

Father and eldest son Richard [i] **Reynell** (1519–1585) of East Ogwell, as the second son of John and Margery Reynell, pursued an adventurous early career of travel and military exploits. He journeyed to Hungary to fight the Turks and was present at the siege of Boulogne. He led a troop of horse in the western rebellion of 1549, was seriously wounded in the action to relieve Plymouth, and was rewarded with lands at Weston Peverell. His brother Walter [iii] was still alive about 1550 when Richard married Agnes, daughter of Thomas Southgate but had presumably died before Richard began to purchase more land in 1555, in particular West Ogwell. In April 1558 Reynell was appointed a captain to defend the county against the French. He sued for a pardon in January 1559 but was trusted enough to begin his long service as a JP later that year, and set a tradition of county service for his descendants. He was sheriff at the time of his death on 29 July 1585. He was survived by five sons, a distinguished generation of whom four were knighted, and two daughters.

The eldest son of Richard and Agnes Reynell, **Sir Thomas** [ii] **Reynell** (1555–1618), entered the Middle Temple with his brother Josias on 13 May 1574. At this time he wrote letters and poems of a devotional nature to his father. He may have pursued a legal career as he refers to himself as 'at law at London' in 1585 (Devon RO, 4652M/F5/1). He kept a slight diary which was continued by his descendants. A typed copy of the original exists and shows that his life centred round his house at West Ogwell which he began building in 1589. Two years later he planted a pear garden and set a row of elms before the house. He consolidated the family estate by buying back land in North Bovey left to his brothers and also purchased Morleigh. He was seldom out of the county: one exception was in July 1603 when he was knighted at Whitehall with his younger brother George [i].

Sir Thomas's public service revolved round his position on the bench from 1588. The quarter session records survive from 1592 and show him attending nearly every meeting. He was also active in taking recognizances and pursuing matters of local concern such as presenting highways in need of repair. The war with Spain made other demands on him. In July 1596 he passed on information gained from merchants to Secretary Robert Cecil. In 1599 he served as a regimental officer and as acting deputy lieutenant in place of his cousin Sir George Carey who was treasurer-at-war in Ireland. Reynell's band and Sir George's guarded Torbay against a possible Spanish invasion.

Sir Thomas married Frances, daughter of John Aylworth, esquire, of London and Polsloe on 3 March 1584. She died on 4 July 1605, survived by three sons and five daughters. On 9 February 1607 he married Elizabeth, daughter of Sir Henry Killigrew and widow of Sir Jonathan Trelawny; they had one son. Sir Thomas died on 8 April 1618 and was buried in the chancel of East Ogwell

next to his first wife. His widow returned to Cornwall and soon married for a third time.

Younger brothers Josias the second son of Richard and Agnes Reynell died unmarried (1556–1614). Their third son and fourth child, **Sir Richard** [ii] **Reynell** (c.1558–1634), became a barrister and was the autumn reader of the Middle Temple in 1617. In 1593 he was a clerk in the office of the lord treasurer's remembrancer and ended his career there as a secondary. It was probably he, rather than Richard [iv] Reynell of Creedy, who was MP for Mitchell in 1593. His wife **Lucy Reynell** (bap. 1577, d. 1652), whom he married in 1600, was the daughter of Robert Brandon, a London merchant. Richard [ii] was able to purchase and enlarge Forde House in the parish of Wolborough, where the life of his wife records that he collected a great library of works of scholarship, befitting a man notable for 'depth of learning and tongues'. He was knighted at Theobalds on 25 July 1622, the year in which his only child, Jane, married Sir William Waller (later the parliamentary general) and 'had a very great marriage of her' (Devon RO, 4652M/F5/1). Sir Richard died in 1634 and was buried on 25 January at Wolborough. His lands were inherited by Margaret, only surviving child of Jane, who married Sir William Courtenay.

Lucy Reynell lived until 18 April 1652. Her character was extolled in the *Life and Death of the Religious and Virtuous Lady* by Edward Reynell. This book reveals her attitude to the religious changes of her times, she 'warily avoided Superstition on one side and Faction on the other' and refused to make new friends by changing her old religion. She strictly observed the sabbath and all fasts and instructed the members of her household. She also managed a 'good spread table' and entertained 'such persons of quality as resorted to her house'—her guests included the king and his household in 1625. When at leisure she worked on tapestry and made clothes for the poor. She built a home for four widows of ministers who were granted £5 p.a. in perpetuity. A charity still exists in her name.

The two youngest sons of Richard and Agnes Reynell, George and Carew, cut their ties with Devon, selling the land inherited from their father to their brother Sir Thomas. George then embarked on three years of travel and Carew made his way at court. In 1597 George Reynell acquired the office of warden of the Fleet prison when he married Elizabeth, daughter of Valentine Browne of Lincolnshire and widow of Edward Tyrell, the previous warden. Later he became marshall of king's bench and was the object of several petitions against his conduct in this office, which he left to Carewe, his only son from his first marriage. Sir George (as he had become in 1603) made a second marriage to Ethelred, daughter of Sir Edward Peacock of Finchley, with whom he had three sons and one daughter. He died in July 1628.

Sir Carew Reynell (c.1563–1624) was a gentleman pensioner of Elizabeth and James. He enjoyed the patronage both of Sir Robert Cecil and of the second earl of Essex, with whom he sailed on the 'islands voyage' of 1597. In 1599 he took a foot company to Ireland, where he was knighted by the earl and entrusted with the keeping of the castle and fort of Duncannon. His association with Essex caused his imprisonment early in 1601, but he was soon cleared of any implication in Essex's rebellion. He had been a member of the parliament of 1593 for Callington, but was returned for Lancaster in 1601 (when he made a speech in the Commons attacking sabbath-breakers) and later for Wallingford in 1614 and Cricklade in 1621. He also gained several profitable offices. He died on 7 September 1624 and was buried at St Martin-in-the-Fields. He had married Susanna, widow of Michael Erneley and daughter of Walter Hungerford of Farley Castle, Wiltshire. He left the earl of Essex a tablet jewel set with more than eighty diamonds, with a picture of the earl's father and £30 in cash to prepare the jewel for the picture in 'Remembrance and full satisfaction of all the favour and benefits which I received from his most noble father' (PRO, PROB 11/144, fols. 201v–202r).

The civil war generation Sir Richard [iii] Reynell (1584–1649), eldest son of Sir Thomas [ii] Reynell, was born at East Ogwell. In 1596 he and his brother Thomas [iii] attended a school at Ashburton; he then went to Exeter College, Oxford, in 1602 and to the Middle Temple two years later. He married Mary, eldest daughter of Richard [iv] Reynell of Creedy, on 12 January 1617. His marriage added Holbeame to his family estates, and he was also rich enough to purchase Ogwell Petyven, part of the parish of East Ogwell. On 5 September 1625 Richard and Thomas were knighted by the king at Ford. The former had followed his father onto the commission of the peace and was almost as assiduous in his attendance. The Reynell presence was strong at quarter sessions; apart from his father-in-law's connection, his sister Francis married Charles Vaughan, clerk of the peace, while another sister, Lucy, married James Welsh, a JP between 1614 and 1647.

Sir Richard [iii] Reynell achieved the higher county position of deputy lieutenant in 1629 but was not a militia officer. He was on the commission of array of 1642 but took no part in the civil war because of illness and from November 1644 'kept to his chamber' suffering from a bladder complaint and thought it 'some mitigation of his affliction that it discharged him from being interested in public affairs'. He was 'very adverse to blood and of a quiet and graceful disposition' (Devon RO, 4652M/F5/1). Sir Richard's first wife died in childbed on 5 July 1626. She had with him nine children, but only two sons and two daughters survived infancy. He married as his second wife in December 1636, Dorothy, the widow of Sir John Chudleigh. She died in March 1642 and was buried at East Ogwell, the first member of the family to be interred in the new vault that Sir Richard had built in the aisle of East Ogwell church in 1633, where he was also buried on 13 February 1649.

The younger sons of Sir Thomas [ii] Reynell and Francis Reynell followed careers at court and in the army. Thomas [iii] Reynell (1589–1665) claimed in 1660 that he had served faithfully in the office of sewer in ordinary for fifty years and suffered much. He lost the grant he had held of the farm of wine licences in Devon, Cornwall, and Exeter and was fined £630 for living in the king's quarters at Oxford.

He had been the member for Morpeth in the parliaments of 1624–9. He married Katherine, daughter of Sir Henry Spiller, and had houses in Weybridge and the Strand. His younger brother, Walter [iv], was born at West Ogwell on 10 March 1591. He served under Count Mansfeld and as a captain under Buckingham on the Île de Ré, where he was killed in 1627. Edward *Reynell, only child of Sir Thomas's second marriage, was educated at Exeter College, Oxford, became rector of West Ogwell and published several religous works. He committed suicide in 1663, soon after the deaths of his son and daughter.

Connections and conclusion The one notable member of the Malston branch of the family was **Richard [iv] Reynell** (c.1565–1631) of Creedy, the fourth son of George [ii] Reynell and Joan, daughter of Lewis Fortescue, a baron of the exchequer. He was the grandson of Thomas [i] and Cecily Reynell. In 1593 he made a profitable marriage to Mary, daughter and coheir of John Periam, twice mayor of Exeter. He was called to the bar on 8 February 1594 and became a bencher and autumn reader in 1614. He was a JP from 1603, attended quarter sessions as regularly as his Ogwell relatives, and was more active in taking examinations and drawing up recognizances. He served as the first recorder of Bradninch until he moved to Creedywiger, just outside Crediton, when his wife inherited the estate in 1618, and spent over £4000 consolidating it. He had a house in Exeter and sometimes acted on behalf of the city. Even though their estates were some distance apart, there were close contacts between the Ogwell and Creedy families which began before they were more intimately linked by the marriage of Richard of Creedy's eldest daughter Mary to Sir Richard [iii] of East Ogwell. Neither of Richard of Creedy's sons married, so a quarter of his estate passed to the Ogwell family by the right of Mary as a coheir. His memorial representing him and his wife kneeling in prayer, survives in Upton Hellions church.

Thomas [iv] Reynell (1624–1698) was the eldest surviving son of Sir Richard [iii] Reynell of East Ogwell and his wife, Mary. On 5 October 1640 he was admitted to Exeter College, Oxford, and stayed in the lodgings of the rector, John Prideaux, who had married his aunt Mary and may well have influenced his religious thinking. He went on to the Middle Temple and was called to the bar in 1649. On 30 June 1648 he married Mary Bennett, niece of Lady Croke, widow of Sir George Croke, judge of the king's bench. They lived with her until they moved to West Ogwell on 6 April 1650.

Thomas Reynell sat on the bench from 1647 through all the changes of government until 1676, when he was removed at the request of the earl of Bath, but even so was appointed sheriff in 1677. On 22 May 1685 he was arrested at his house at night 'to appear before Council to answer for treasonable practices' (Devon RO, 4652M/F5/1) but no grounds could be found for convicting him. He was restored to the bench in October 1687 and resumed the same conscientious attendance characteristic of his family. A later member of his family wrote in the diary that he was 'a hearty well wisher of Revolution' and entertained at West Ogwell part of the company that 'attended our Deliverance' in 1688. He was MP for Devon in 1654 and 1656 and for Ashburton, a borough with a considerable dissenting party, in 1659 and again in 1677, 1679, 1681, and 1689. His younger brother, Sir Richard [v], baronet (1625–1699), who had been deprived of his judgeship of the Irish king's bench, held the seat in 1690.

Thomas Reynell's first wife had died in September 1671, survived by their two daughters. On 28 July 1673 he married Elizabeth, widow of William Vincent and daughter of James Gould of Exeter, merchant. Thomas Reynell died on 15 January 1698. His eldest son, Richard [iv] Reynell (1677–1735), did not marry and was predeceased by his younger brother, so the Reynell estates passed to Rebecca Taylor, the daughter of his half-sister Mary.   MARY WOLFFE

Sources I. Cassidy, 'Reynell, Carew', 'Reynell, Richard I', 'Reynell, Richard II', HoP, *Commons, 1558–1603*, 3.284–5 · *CSP dom., 1553–8*, 328; *1554–80; 1595–1618; Jan 1687 – Feb 1689* · APC, 1591, 1597, 1599–1600 · *Report on the manuscripts of Allan George Finch*, 5 vols., HMC, 71 (1913–2003), vol. 2 · *Calendar of the manuscripts of the most hon. the marquis of Salisbury*, 24 vols., HMC, 9 (1883–1976), vols. 5, 8–11, 14, 16–17 · M. Adams, 'Some notes on the churches and manors of East and West Ogwell', *Transactions of the Devonshire Association*, 32 (1900), 229–48 · R. W. Cotton, 'Ford and its associations', *Transactions of the Devonshire Association*, 33 (1901), 693–713 · H. J. Hanham, 'Ashburton as a parliamentary borough', *Transactions of the Devonshire Association*, 98 (1966), 206–56 · S. Roberts, *Recovery and Restoration in an English county* (1985) · J. L. Vivian, ed., *The visitations of Cornwall, comprising the herald's visitations of 1530, 1573, and 1620* (1887) · M. Wolffe, *Gentry leaders in peace and war* (1997) · W. Pole, *Collections towards a description of the county of Devon* (1791) · quarter sessions minutes, 1592–1618, Devon RO, QS rolls, boxes 1–2, 13–32; 4652M/E5/2; /F5/1, 2; F6/1; T11/22 · H. A. C. Sturgess, ed., *Register of admissions to the Honourable Society of the Middle Temple, from the fifteenth century to the year 1944*, 1 (1949) · inquisition post mortem, PRO, C 142/472/107 [Richard Reynell of Creedy; John Reynell] · will, PRO, PROB 11/144 · will, PRO, PROB 11/154 · will, PRO, PROB 11/450 · will, PRO, PROB 11/165 · E. Reynell, *The life and death of the religious and virtuous lady, the Lady Lucie Reynell of Ford* (1554) · M. O'Hagan, *A history of Forde House* (1990) · J. Prince, *Danmonii orientales illustres, or, The worthies of Devon* (1701) · *Devon*, Pevsner (1989) · Foster, *Alum. Oxon.* · family diary, Devon RO, 4652M/F5/1

Archives Devon RO, 4652M/F5/1, F6/1

Reynell, Sir Carew (c.1563–1624). *See under* Reynell family (*per.* 1540–1735).

Reynell, Carew (1636–1690), writer on economics, was born in Hampshire, the elder son of Carew Reynell (d. 1657), lawyer and marshal of the court of king's bench, and his wife, Mary, daughter of Marcellus Rivers of Southwark and of Rivershill, Hampshire, and grandson of Sir George Reynell, from the family of East Ogwell, Devon; George Reynell (d. 1687), fellow of Corpus Christi College, Oxford, and canon of Lincoln from 1682, was his younger brother. On 16 July 1652 Reynell was admitted a gentleman commoner at Wadham College, Oxford, where John Wilkins was warden, and on 13 November 1654 entered as a student at the Middle Temple. The next year he was implicated in the unsuccessful royalist rising of John Penruddock, and was imprisoned in Exeter. Owing to his

youth he was released by General Desborough on the petition and security of his father. In 1657 he succeeded to the family estate at Rivershill, and at dates unknown married first Anna Metcalfe, a widow, with whom he had a son, Carew, and second Elizabeth, widow of Ralph Took of Took's Court, with whom he had a daughter, Anna.

Reynell greeted the Restoration with *The Fortunate Change … a Panegirick … to his Sacred Majesty King Charles* (1661), a poem with religious as well as political overtones. His wish to obtain public office, perhaps in the embryonic Board of Trade, may be discerned in his *The True English Interest* (1674), a concise and well-argued survey of the British economy from the protectionist and mercantile point of view, which stressed both London and population growth as dynamics for change and prosperity and which gained notice in the Royal Society's *Philosophical Transactions* for 27 April 1674. Chapter 27 of the work may have been intended as the basis for a further study on education and the advancement of learning, possibly foreshadowing the anonymous *Discourse on Humane Reason* (1690).

Reynell remained an out-of-office tory. He died in 1690, leaving properties in London and Hampshire to his son. His writings were influential in the protectionist and protestant cause.

Reynell's grandson **Carew Reynell** (1693/4–1745), Church of Ireland bishop of Derry, was born in Covent Garden, London, one of the sons of Carew Reynell the younger and his wife, whose maiden name was Sheppey. He was educated at Winchester College between 1707 and 1711, and entered New College, Oxford, as a scholar and fellow, matriculating on 29 February 1712, aged eighteen. He graduated BA in 1715, proceeded MA in 1719, and was a proctor of the university in 1728. With his *Prophetia de Messia* (1724), a discourse on the grounds and reasons of Christianity, and *The Resurrection of our Saviour* (1726) he entered theological controversy, exhibiting a firm protestant faith. He was rector of Coleherne, Wiltshire, from 1728 to 1740, and was awarded the degrees of BD and DD in 1730. At an unknown date he became chaplain to William Bradshawe (d. 1732), from 1724 dean of Christ Church and bishop of Bristol. Reynell's two sermons of 1729 preached before the mayor and aldermen of Bristol were published in 1730, and by 1734 he held the living of Sts John and Laurence in the city. He married Elizabeth, daughter of Henry Swymmer, alderman; they had three sons.

In 1737 Reynell went to Ireland, where his family had influential ascendancy connections, as chaplain to the duke of Devonshire, the lord lieutenant. He was installed successively as bishop of Down and Connor in 1739 and as bishop of Derry in 1743; an able ecclesiastical administrator, he was also charitable. He died on 1 January 1745.

His near contemporary and possible kinsman through George Reynell, **Carew Reynell** (1690–1755), Church of England clergyman, was born in Lincolnshire, the son of John Reynell, clergyman, of West Halton, and former rector of West Ogwell, Devon. A scholar at Corpus Christi College, Oxford, in 1708, he graduated BA in 1712, and proceeded MA in 1715 and BD in 1724. He was prebend of

Chichester from 1724 to 1739; his livings included Marston, Oxfordshire (1729–35) and Childrey, Berkshire (1731–55). He died on 29 May 1755.   **V. E. CHANCELLOR**

Sources DNB · Foster, *Alum. Oxon.* · H. A. C. Sturgess, ed., *Register of admissions to the Honourable Society of the Middle Temple, from the fifteenth century to the year 1944*, 1 (1949), 154 · Wood, *Ath. Oxon.*, new edn, 4.730 · Burke, *Gen. GB* (1833–8), vol. 4
Likenesses W. Faithorne, line engraving, BM, NPG

Reynell, Carew (1690–1755). *See under* Reynell, Carew (1636–1690).

Reynell, Carew (1693/4–1745). *See under* Reynell, Carew (1636–1690).

Reynell, Edward (1611/12–1663), Church of England clergyman, was the son of Sir Thomas Reynell (*b.* in or before 1555, *d.* 1621) of East Ogwell, Devon, and his second wife, Elizabeth, daughter of Sir Henry *Killigrew of Cornwall. He was admitted as a fellow-commoner to Exeter College, Oxford, on 30 May 1629, aged seventeen, but left Oxford in 1632 without a degree. He seems not to have entered the law, as suggested by Anthony Wood and John Prince; their reference is perhaps to his cousin Edmund, son of Sir George Reynell of Malston, also in Devon, admitted on 5 May 1627 to the Middle Temple. However that may be, Edward Reynell was ordained a minister and became rector of West Ogwell. He was certainly married, perhaps to Thomasin Shepheard of Braunton, Devon, on 29 January 1642.

During the interregnum Reynell does not appear to have been disturbed in his living, but in *An advice against libertinism, shewing the great danger thereof, and exhorting all to zeal of the truth* (1659) he lamented the 'general viciousness, growth of Schisms, falseness in profession, yea such indifferency therein, without any true warmth, or holy fire of zeal and godliness' (p. 4). But Reynell's spirituality chimed no better with the ethos of the Restoration. His *Celestial Amities, or, A Soul Sighing for the Love of her Saviour*, issued about July 1660, was dedicated to 'the ladies of our times'. Of these, many seem to have aroused his disapproval, in particular those 'that consume your precious time in painting, powdering, perfuming and adorning yourselves … who complain if the least beam pierce through a little hole of your fan, or if a fly chance to light upon it, you (who if a hair be but amis) presently call a council for the reforming thereof'. Urging the contemplation of spiritual delights Reynell was unworldly enough to predict a bleak future for their 'shops of vanity' (sig. A3).

The melancholia for which Reynell became known was deepened by the deaths of two beloved children, a son, 'the joy of his parents, the delight of his friends, the hopes of his country', and soon afterwards a daughter, 'a child in whom did appear so much of perfection', commemorated in *Bracteola aurea, or, Filings of gold drawn from the life and death of that lovely child, Mris Joanna Reynell who died the 26 January 1662 [1663]* (13, 22). Perhaps it was this double tragedy which led to Reynell's suicide at West Ogwell in 1663, apparently by drowning. He was buried at West Ogwell. The antiquary John Prince ascribed his end to 'the furious assaults of predominant melancholy' noting 'how very

weak and feeble the spark of life is, that can be quenched by such unlikely means as a little bason of water' (Prince, 697). Anthony Wood reported the reluctance of his kinsmen to give further information about Reynell, and their desire that 'he might sink into oblivion' (Wood, *Ath. Oxon.*, 3.658).   **STEPHEN WRIGHT**

Sources J. Prince, *Danmonii orientales illustres, or, The worthies of Devon*, 2nd edn (1810) · Wood, *Ath. Oxon.*, new edn, vol. 3 · C. W. Boase, *An alphabetical register of the commoners of Exeter College, Oxford* (1894) · J. L. Vivian, ed., *The visitations of the county of Devon, comprising the herald's visitations of 1531, 1564, and 1620* (privately printed, Exeter, [1895]) · E. Reynell, *Celestial amities, or, A soul sighing for the love of her saviour* (1660) [E1914/3] · E. Reynell, *Bracteola aurea, or, Filings of gold drawn from the life and death of … Mris Joanna Reynell* (1663) · Foster, *Alum. Oxon.* · H. A. C. Sturgess, ed., *Register of admissions to the Honourable Society of the Middle Temple, from the fifteenth century to the year 1944*, 3 vols. (1949)

Reynell, Lucy, Lady Reynell (*bap.* 1577, *d.* 1652). *See under* Reynell family (*per.* 1540–1735).

Reynell, Richard (1519–1585). *See under* Reynell family (*per.* 1540–1735).

Reynell, Sir Richard (*c.*1558–1634). *See under* Reynell family (*per.* 1540–1735).

Reynell, Richard (*c.*1565–1631). *See under* Reynell family (*per.* 1540–1735).

Reynell, Sir Richard (1584–1649). *See under* Reynell family (*per.* 1540–1735).

Reynell, Sir Thomas (1555–1618). *See under* Reynell family (*per.* 1540–1735).

Reynell, Thomas (1624–1698). *See under* Reynell family (*per.* 1540–1735).

Reyner, Edward (1600–1660), Church of England clergyman and writer, was born in Morley, near Leeds, where he attended sermons and the monthly West Riding exercises and early came into contact with moderate protestant nonconformity. He graduated BA in 1621 from St John's College, Cambridge, proceeded MA in 1625, and was ordained deacon and priest at Peterborough in March 1625. After leaving Cambridge he taught first at Aserby in Lincolnshire and then, under the patronage of the countess of Warwick, obtained the mastership of Sir George St Paul's school at Market Rasen. After four years there he became lecturer at Welton. In 1626 he moved to Lincoln, first as lecturer at St Benedict's and in March the following year as rector of St Peter at Arches, the main city church, where, apart from disruptions during the civil war, he performed his pastoral duties for the remainder of his life.

Soon after his arrival in Lincoln, Reyner consulted his friend John Cotton at Boston over cases of conscience, subsequently going on to examine such cases in some of his later writings. Although a nonconformist regarding certain ceremonies in the Book of Common Prayer, he preached freely in Lincoln, attracting the chancellor and other cathedral officials to his sermons. At some point he married, and he and his wife, Elizabeth, had two sons,

John (b. 1634) and Joseph (b. 1640). In 1635 Bishop John Williams offered Reyner the prebend of St Botolph's at Lincoln but Reyner felt unable to accept it for conscientious reasons. In 1639 he also declined an invitation to minister to the English congregation at Arnhem. Probably because of protection in high places only very late in the decade were attempts made to bring Reyner before the high commission court and the calling of the Long Parliament intervened before any further action could be taken.

Having had his goods plundered and fearing for his life during the royalist occupation of Lincoln in the summer of 1643, Reyner fled to East Anglia and secured preaching posts at both Great Yarmouth and Norwich, eventually settling in the latter. At the urgent request of the mayor and aldermen of Lincoln, he returned to St Peter's in October 1645, holding in addition one of the two lectureships at the cathedral with a stipend of £150 per annum. He preached before the parliamentarian army at the siege of Newark on 27 March 1646. In June 1648 Reyner was threatened for a second time by marauding soldiers, who seized him in the cathedral library where he had vainly tried to hide. Only the opportune appearance of the royalist captain, one of Reyner's former pupils at Market Rasen, procured his release. Thereafter, even though he scrupled to take the engagement to the Commonwealth, he was able to fulfil his ministry in Lincoln without hindrance, preaching on Sundays in St Peter's in the morning, in the cathedral in the afternoon.

Reyner published several expositional and devotional works, including *Precepts for Christian Practice* (1644/1645), a short handbook for Christian living which ran to thirteen editions, his sermon preached at the siege of Newark entitled *Orders from the Lord of Hostes* (1646), *Rules for the Government of the Tongue* (1656), and *Considerations Concerning Marriage* (1657). An opponent of antinomianism and Anabaptism, he tended towards the congregationalist way, but he felt that many gathered churches had run into errors. He was not satisfied that every member should preach and insisted on communion and co-operation with other separated churches and a firm stance, publicly and privately, against heresy. While he approved the theology set out in the 1658 Savoy confession of faith he had reservations concerning the form of church government it contained. For his biographical account Calamy may have drawn upon a 'book of remembrance' kept by Reyner, now lost, in which he had 'carefully inserted many particular mercies of God in his education, in the several stages of his life, in his removes, in his wife, son, church, ministry; in preservation from adversaries etc.' (*Nonconformist's Memorial*, 2.154).

Reyner had died in Lincoln by 30 July 1660. His son John Reyner, who had followed closely in his footsteps, having graduated BA from Cambridge in 1654, proceeded MA in 1656, and held a fellowship at Emmanuel College from 1655, inherited his father's papers and from them published *A Treatise of the Necessity of Humane Learning for a Gospel Preacher* (1663)—a passionate justification of the absolute necessity of a classical and academic education for ministers, extending to Semitic languages as well as Greek—and *The being and Well-being of a Christian* (1668). John Reyner was ejected from Emmanuel in 1662 for nonconformity and then practised physic for a time before becoming a schoolmaster in Nottingham; he died of smallpox there in 1675.   CLAIRE CROSS

Sources *The nonconformist's memorial … originally written by …* *Edmund Calamy*, ed. S. Palmer, 2 (1775), 149–54 • *Calamy rev.* • Venn, *Alum. Cant.* • *CSP dom.*, 1660–66, 136 • S. Bush, 'Epistolary counseling in the puritan movement: the example of John Cotton', *Puritanism: transatlantic perspectives on a seventeenth-century Anglo-American faith*, ed. F. J. Bremer (1993) • bishops transcripts for St Peter at Arches; parish register, St Peter at Arches 23/2, Lincs. Arch., Lincoln diocesan archives, MF 4/457 • J. W. F. Hill, *Tudor and Stuart Lincoln* (1956) • R. Marchant, *The puritans and the church courts in the diocese of York, 1560–1642* (1960) • *BL cat.* • Wing, STC • DNB

Reyner, Wilfred [*name in religion* Clement] (**1588/9–1651**), Benedictine abbot, was born near Ripon. It has been conjectured that the name he received at birth was Wilfred. His father, Richard, and his mother both died while in prison for their Catholicism some time after his birth. He was the youngest of three brothers who have often been confused. The two oldest, Christopher and Clement, went to the English College, Douai, in 1598. But their brother became a monk of the community at Dieulouard, Lorraine, some time after 1610, and was then sent to Douai for studies, where he graduated doctor of divinity about 1616 and lectured at the college of St Vedast. For some time he served on the English mission and was imprisoned in Yorkshire until 1618.

In 1626 Reyner published at Douai the *Apostolatus Benedictinorum in Anglia*, a comprehensive survey of all the evidence for the existence of a pre-Reformation English Benedictine congregation in order to refute John Barnes's *Examen trophaeorum congregationis praetensae Anglicanae* (Rheims, 1622), which had contended that the only medieval congregation in England had been that of Cluny and so there could be no historical basis for the claims of contemporary English Benedictines that they were reviving a national body. Reyner was over modest in his claim (*Apostolatus*, 5) 'Non auctor operis sum, sed iussu Congregationis editor et dedicator' ('I am not the author of the work, but by the order of the congregation the editor and reporter'), the researches having been done by Augustine Baker and the rendering into Latin by Leander Jones. But we know from the diaries of John Selden the antiquary that Reyner himself had visited him at Oxford to consult him on historical questions. Although a polemical work the *Apostolatus* was a pioneering study of English monastic history as a whole rather than of individual monasteries.

In 1629 the Catholic forces engaged in the Thirty Years' War had recovered territories in north Germany in which there were many former monasteries. the emperor Ferdinand II restored them to the church, but could not find enough monks to reinvigorate them. At the same time the exiled English Benedictines had too many recruits to be housed in their cluster of small priories on the continent. Reyner was commissioned to negotiate the transfer of some monasteries from the German Benedictine authorities. From 1632 to 1634 he was prior of fifteen English monks settled at Rinteln in Schaumburg, where there was a project to attach to the abbey a university to be sustained by the revenues of three other monasteries that were promised to him. Reyner also acquitted himself well in public disputations, but a three-day debate with the Lutheran Doctor Gesenius, superintendent of Brunswick, as well as the continued existence of Rinteln as an English monastery, was cut short by the invasion of Swedish troops whom Reyner, together with his community, evaded only by swimming across the River Weser.

In 1635 Reyner was not only elected president general of the English Benedictine congregation, a post he held until 1641, but he also became prior of St Peter's, Blandigny—a rich abbey of Ghent, engaged in ambitious building operations but riven by factions because of the abbot's attempt to impose the stricter observance of the congregation of St Vanne in place of that of the Cassinese constitutions. But Reyner refused this abbacy when it was offered him, because negotiations were now in course for English monks to take over Lambspringe, a former nunnery near Hildesheim where the local bishop was agreeable. In 1643 Reyner received the abbacy here and set about the rebuilding of the dilapidated monastery, the reclamation of the local population for the Catholic faith, and the reinvigoration of all monastic rights and dues which had been in abeyance for the best part of a century. Naturally the programme encountered some local hostility, but his community would flourish until its suppression in 1802.

Reyner died on 17 March 1651, aged sixty-two, at St Michael's Abbey, Hildesheim, where he was first buried; on 17 March 1692 his body was reinterred in the grandiose new church at Lambspringe.   DAVID DANIEL REES

Sources B. Weldon, *Chronological notes … of the English congregation of the order of St Benedict* (1881) • D. Lunn, *The English Benedictines, 1540–1688* (1980) • U. Faust, *Germania Benedictina*, vol. 6 (St Ottilien, 1979) • *Monasticon Belge*, vol. 7 (Liège, 1988) • E. H. Burton and T. L. Williams, eds., *The Douay College diaries, third, fourth and fifth, 1598–1654*, 1–2, Catholic RS, 10–11 (1911) • W. K. Browne, J. W. Bone, and M. B., 'Clemens Reynericus', *N&Q*, 7th ser., 10 (1890), 268–9, 349–50 • tombstone, Lambspringe, Germany
Archives Downside Abbey, near Bath
Likenesses portrait (contemporary), Downside Abbey, near Bath

Reynes, John [*formerly* Jan Rijens] (*d.* 1545), bookseller and bookbinder, a native of Wageningen, Gueldres, in the Low Countries, was granted letters of denization on 7 June 1510. Between 1514 and 1535 his name appears regularly in the port rolls as an importer of books. In 1516 Reynes and his first wife, Joan, leased a shop 'at the sign of St George' in St Paul's Churchyard, by the gate leading into Cheapside. In 1523 he was assessed for the subsidy at £40 3s. 4d. In 1542 he and his then wife, Lucy (*d.* 1549), obtained a new lease for the same shop. Reynes's name first appears in the colophon of an edition of Higden's *Polychronycon* (1527), and he continued to publish books at intervals up to 1544. He is, however, better known as a bookbinder, acquiring a number of his own panels. Those most commonly found have on one side a stamp containing the emblems of the passion and the inscription 'Redemptoris mundi arma' and on the other a stamp divided into two compartments containing the arms of England and the Tudor rose. In

1944 Hobson was able to identify 130 surviving books bound by Reynes, and 400 of his bindings.

Reynes's date of death is unknown. His will was proved on 26 February 1545. Long the leading foreign stationer in England, his stock was valued at over £1000. In 1557 John Cawood, who had been apprenticed to Reynes and was then warden of the Stationers' Company, put up a window in Stationers' Hall in his memory.

E. G. DUFF, *rev.* ANITA MCCONNELL

Sources J. Ames, T. F. Dibdin, and W. Herbert, eds., *Typographical antiquities, or, The history of printing in England, Scotland and Ireland*, 4 vols. (1810–19), vol. 3, pp. 266–70 • W. Page, ed., *Letters of denization and acts of naturalization for aliens in England, 1509–1603*, Huguenot Society of London, 8 (1893) • G. D. Hobson, *Blind-stamped panels in the English book trade* (1944) • C. H. Timperley, *A dictionary of printers and printing* (1839), 417, 445 • PRO, E 122/82/3, m. 11 • PRO, E 122/82/8, m. 17v • GL, MS 25.630/1, fol. 132r • PRO, E 179/251/15B, fol. 25r • PRO, PROB 11/30, sig. 23, fol. 180Ar–v • PRO, PROB 11/32, sig. 40, fols. 309v–310v [Lucy Reynes]
Wealth at death £1000—value of stock

Reynold, Joan (*d.* 1483). *See under* Women traders and artisans in London (*act. c.*1200–*c.*1500).

Reynoldes, Edward (*d.* 1623), administrator and politician, was born in Weymouth, Dorset, the second son of Lancelot Reynoldes of Melcombe Regis in that county, who came from a mercantile family which for successive generations had served as collectors of customs. He attended Southampton grammar school, where his schoolfellows included Thomas Lake, who was 'beholding unto me sometymes for his exercises' (PRO, SP 14/18/32). Reynoldes subsequently went to Oxford, where he graduated BA from All Souls on 4 March 1581, became a fellow the same year, and proceeded MA on 13 October 1584.

When Sir Amias Paulet was appointed as keeper of Mary, queen of Scots, early in 1585 Reynoldes entered his service, perhaps at the suggestion of Sir Francis Walsingham, whose secretaries included Lake and Francis Mills, a Southampton man and former fellow of All Souls, and to whom Reynoldes had a connection through his kinship with Lady Walsingham's family, the St Barbs. He remained in Paulet's service until after Mary's execution in February 1587. It is possible that during Mary's imprisonment at Chartley, Reynoldes became known to Robert Devereux, second earl of Essex, whose estate it was. By mid-1588 he had become Essex's man, acting as junior colleague to the earl's secretary, Thomas Smith. He accompanied Essex on the Portugal expedition in 1589 and during the Rouen campaign of 1591. When Smith became clerk of the privy council in mid 1595 Reynoldes became Essex's 'chief confident [personal] secretary' (BL, Harley MS 286, fol. 258v). The appointment of three new secretaries meant that when Essex went on campaign in 1596, 1597, and 1599, Reynoldes remained at Essex House to act as the earl's man of business around the court and the City. However, the prospect of a fourth new appointment to Essex's secretariat (which Reynoldes regarded as a discredit to himself) upset him so greatly that in August 1596 he offered to resign. This additional appointment was abandoned, but he still found himself at odds with one of his new colleagues, Henry Wotton. Reynoldes responded by strengthening his ties with Anthony Bacon, Essex's friend and chief intelligence co-ordinator, himself on poor terms with Wotton.

Compounding Reynoldes's woes in 1596 was the behaviour of his brother Augustine, who misappropriated money which he had collected at Southampton for Essex's impost on sweet wines. Reynoldes was apparently forced to take over his brother's collectorship for the next few years and repay the debt. He had for some time been pursuing office on his own account. By 1597 his chief target was the reversion of a clerkship of the privy seal; with support from Essex, Bacon, and Sir Robert Cecil this was finally granted on 26 June 1598. Essex's attempts to have Reynoldes elected MP for Stafford in 1593 had failed, but in 1597 he was elected MP for Andover, where Essex was high steward. Over this period, possibly already a widower, he had also been conducting a long-distance courtship of Katherine, widow of one John Mills, who owned property in Southampton. After long delays Reynoldes seems to have married her in 1599.

Reynoldes remained in Essex's service after the earl's fall from grace in late 1599. In contrast to other servants like Henry Cuffe and Sir Gelly Meyrick, who increasingly saw force as the only way by which Essex could recover his fortunes, Reynoldes argued that Essex could only 'drawe himself out of this bogg' by 'humble & temperat' conduct (PRO, SP 12/273/38). Several letters from Essex to the queen in 1600 survive in his hand. However, these are copies rather than drafts and provide no evidence that he had a role in their composition. Reynoldes was arrested after Essex's insurrection in London on 8 February 1601, but it is not clear that he took part in the action. He was soon released without being charged or fined.

Although he won election as MP for Weymouth later that year Reynoldes's prospects were hamstrung by the fall of Essex. He spent much of the next few years living at Salisbury or Whiteparish in Wiltshire and was often sick. His wife also suffered chronic ill health and was dead by June 1605. He sustained himself as a moneylender, which caused him great frustrations and forced him to rely heavily upon his brother Owen, a servant of his old colleague Thomas Smith. After years of failed attempts to buy out Thomas Kerry from his clerkship of the privy seal, Reynoldes finally entered the office in mid-1608. Almost immediately he was plunged into an awkward dispute about fees with the lord privy seal, Henry Howard, earl of Northampton, who had been a friend of Essex and whom Reynoldes regarded as a patron. However, his much delayed entry into the privy seal office also made him a close colleague of his old friend Francis Mills. When Mills died in September 1618 Reynoldes succeeded him as registrar of the court of requests. Following the death of his favourite brother, Owen (who had become keeper of the privy council chest), in April 1610, Reynoldes increasingly invested his hopes of family success in his cousin John

Castle, who served as clerk to Levinus Munck, the assistant secretary of state. He ultimately succeeded in establishing Castle as his successor in the privy seal office. Despite his abiding dislike of his brother Augustine, Reynoldes also took a direct interest in Augustine's son Edward *Reynolds (1599–1676, the future bishop of Norwich), whom he sent to Merton College, Oxford, where his old friend and fellow Essexian Henry Savile was provost. In his will of June 1623 Reynoldes named his nephew and namesake as one of his executors. Lacking any children of his own, he specified generous bequests to many members of his extended family. He also left £20 for the schoolmaster of Southampton grammar school and £20 to buy divinity books for All Souls. He died either in late November or early December, or on 18 December, 1623 and was buried at St Margaret's, Westminster.

PAUL E. J. HAMMER

Sources PRO, SP 12, 14 and 15 · will, June 1623, PRO, PROB 11/143, fols. 3v–5r · Cecil MSS, Hatfield House, Hertfordshire · LPL, papers of Anthony Bacon, MSS 647–62 · M. R. Pickering, 'Reynolds, Edward', HoP, *Commons, 1558–1603* · Foster, *Alum. Oxon.* · *Report on the manuscripts of the marquis of Downshire*, 6 vols. in 7, HMC, 75 (1924–95) · *An Elizabethan in 1582: the diary of Richard Madox, fellow of All Souls*, ed. E. S. Donno, Hakluyt Society, 2nd ser., 147 (1976) · Folger, L.a.40, 44, 468 · P. E. J. Hammer, 'The uses of scholarship: the secretariat of Robert Devereux, 2nd earl of Essex, *c.*1585–1601', *EngHR*, 109 (1994), 26–51 · BL, Harley MS 286 · PRO, LR 1/45 · A. L. Merson, ed., *The third book of remembrance of Southampton, 1564–1621*, 3–4, Southampton RS, 8, 22 (1965–79) · H. J. Moule, *Descriptive catalogue of the charters, minute books and other documents of the borough of Weymouth and Melcombe Regis, AD 1252 to 1800* (1883) · *CSP Scot.*, 1585–8 · J. Hutchins, *The history and antiquities of the county of Dorset*, 3rd edn, 4 vols., ed. W. Shipp and J. W. Hodson (1861–74); repr. (1973) · *Notes and Queries for Somerset and Dorset*, 2 (1891); 4 (1894); 11–12 (1909–11) · W. Musgrave, *Obituary prior to 1800*, ed. G. J. Armytage, 6 vols., Harleian Society, 44–9 (1899–1901), 5.131
Archives Hatfield House, Hertfordshire, Cecil MSS · LPL, corresp. with Anthony Bacon, MSS 647–662 · PRO, SP 12, 14, 15
Wealth at death total cash bequests almost £600, plus leases, debts, clothes, and other possessions: will, June 1623, PRO, PROB 11/143, fols. 3v–5r · healthy estate considering oft-repeated claims of poverty (or at least lack of available cash) in early 1600s and his assertion that service to Essex in 1590s cost him more money than it brought in; also claimed late wife left £524 3s. 8d., but her bequest totalled £215 and funeral cost £52, leaving him with net benefit of £257: PRO, SP 14/14/42

Reynolds. *See also* Rainolds.

Reynolds, Alfred (1818–1891), wood-engraver and colour printer, was born on 1 April 1818 at Donnington, near Chichester, Sussex, the youngest of seven children of George Reynolds (1766–1851), naval officer, and his wife, Mary Ann (1783–1833), daughter of Richard Prior, yeoman, of Donnington, and his wife, Ann; he was a grandson of Admiral John *Reynolds. He was baptized on 8 May 1818 at Providence (Independent Calvinistic) Chapel, Chichester, reflecting the religious persuasions of his mother. His father was an evangelical churchman. Alfred probably followed his brother William (*b.* 1815) in attending a school in Southgate, Chichester, before being apprenticed, on 1 August 1832, to George Baxter, colour printer (grandson of the principal founder of Providence Chapel), to learn wood-engraving, at 29 King's Square, Clerkenwell, London, where Baxter lived, and where William Reynolds was already an indentured pupil. About 1836 Baxter moved, with his apprentices, to 3 Charterhouse Square. It appears that Alfred was an inventive pupil but was not alone in finding Baxter's teaching of wood-engraving insufficiently intensive. (He was among former apprentices who in 1849 opposed in court an extension of Baxter's colour printing patent.) Another apprentice was F. W. M. Collins, later joint patentee with Reynolds of the block process.

How Reynolds was employed in 1839–43 is unknown. By 1844 he had joined Collins and another former fellow apprentice, Charles Gregory, in London, as wood-engravers and printers, taking charge of their colour printing. Their skill soon rivalled that of Baxter, and was praised by contemporary critics, including Thackeray. Gregory, Collins, and Reynolds soon specialized in illustrating children's books, including a Home Treasury series (1846) by the versatile Henry Cole, who apparently introduced Reynolds to another entrepreneur, Herbert Minton, pottery manufacturer of Stoke-on-Trent.

On 14 March 1848, Collins, possibly the financier, and Reynolds, usually referred to as the inventor, patented (no. 12079) a process 'for improvements in ornamenting china, earthenware, and glass' by printing several colours exactly on to ceramic or glass surfaces. The result was far superior to the earlier transfer printing. Minton encouraged this project, considering Reynolds as the inventor. Reynolds moved to Stoke-on-Trent in 1848 to manage his process for Minton, who apparently acquired, for fourteen years, a two-thirds share in this patent in May 1849. Reynolds later assumed complete responsibility for Minton's tile department. Some independent evidence shows that at least until the early 1860s Reynolds operated his invention on his own account as well.

Reynolds's technique was immediately used at Mintons for producing large coloured tiles designed by A. W. N. Pugin to decorate the smoking room of the new House of Commons. In 1855 Reynolds's work won a first-class medal at the Universal Exhibition in Paris. In spite of later competition from two breakaway tile firms, particularly after 1868 from Minton Hollins, block printed tile manufacture increased in later years and by 1880 accounted for more than a fifth of Mintons' sales. In 1873 Reynolds was awarded, at a Universal Exhibition in Vienna, another first-class medal. 'He was well placed', Paul Atterbury states, 'to mastermind the great revival in pictorial and decorative tiles that occurred in the 1870s', concluding that 'his technical developments were crucial to Mintons' foremost position as producers of decorative printed tiles' (Atterbury and Batkin, 40, 394). The block process continued in commercial use until the 1920s.

At Stoke, Reynolds, who remained a bachelor, lived in lodgings. Alone among his immediate relations he was a convinced Liberal in politics. His influence secured a clerkship in a local bank for his young nephew Alfred S. H. Reynolds (son of his brother William), who consequently lived with him from 1877 to 1883, and in 1885 married into a Stoke family. In 1886 Reynolds retired on account of

heart trouble, but he continued to enjoy an active interest in books, flowers, astronomy, and local good works until his sudden death at his home, Bank House, Vine St, Stoke-on-Trent, on 9 January 1891. Appreciated by Mintons' workpeople for his kindly character, he was buried on 16 January amid public mourning by an old friend, Bishop Sir Lovelace Stamer, rector of Stoke 1858–92, at Hartshill cemetery. He left a surprising quantity of small house property. Harrison Weir, a contemporary pupil of Baxter, wrote from Kent, 'his memory has ever been fresh and green in my mind' (H. Weir letter to A. S. H. Reynolds, 1891). Anonymous commemorative verses appeared in *Poetical Wild Oats* (n.d.), 100–06, published by Digby, Long & Co., London.

J. S. REYNOLDS

Sources J. S. Reynolds, 'Alfred Reynolds and the block process', *Journal of the Tiles and Architectural Ceramics Society*, 5 (1994), 20–26 · *Staffordshire Advertiser* (20 Feb 1886) · *Staffordshire Sentinel* (10 Jan 1891) · *Staffordshire Courier* (10 Jan 1891) · *Mintons tiles: selected patterns of enamelled tiles* (c.1885); facs. edn (1996) · W. Newton, ed., *London Journal of Arts, Sciences, Manufactures, and Repertory of Patent Inventions*, 33 (1848), 188–9, pl. 7 · incl. typed catalogue compiled by A. Giles Jones, 1971–3, Minton archive, Stoke-on-Trent, vol.1 · L. F. W. Jewitt, *The ceramic art of Great Britain, from pre-historic times*, 2 (1878) · P. Atterbury and M. Batkin, *Dictionary of Minton* (1990) · J. Jones, *Minton: the first two hundred years of design and production* (1993) · J. D. R. McD H. Maclean, *Victorian book design and colour printing*, 2nd edn (1973) · J. D. R. McD H. Maclean, *Joseph Cundall* (1976) · C. T. C. Lewis, *The picture printer of the nineteenth century: George Baxter, 1804–1867* (1911) · C. J. Courtney Lewis, *The story of picture printing in England during the nineteenth century* [1928] · private information (2004)

Likenesses J. Russell & Sons, double portrait, photograph, 1879 (with the Revd J. S. Reynolds), priv. coll.; repro. in Reynolds, 'Alfred Reynolds and the block process'

Wealth at death £1063 7s. 6d.: probate, 23 Feb 1891, CGPLA Eng. & Wales

Reynolds, Sir Barrington (1786–1861), naval officer, second son of Rear-Admiral Robert Carthew *Reynolds (*bap.* 1745, *d.* 1811), was born at his father's seat, Penair, near Truro, Cornwall. He entered the navy in 1795, on the *Druid*, with his father, whom he followed to the *Amazon*. In her he was wrecked in Audierne Bay, Brittany, on 14 January 1797, and taken prisoner. On regaining his liberty he again served with his father in the *Pomone*, then moved to the *Indefatigable*, with Sir Edward Pellew, whom he followed to the *Impétueux* (74 guns). While in her he was present in several boat actions, including that in the Morbihan on 6 June 1800, under the immediate command of Lieutenant John Pilfold. He was afterwards in the *Orion* with his father, and on 18 September 1801 was promoted lieutenant of the *Courageux*. In the following June he was appointed to the *Hussar*, and from August 1803 to September 1808 was in the *Niobe*, during the greater part of the time with Captain John Wentworth Loring, on the coast of France. He was afterwards in the *Russell*, in the East Indies, and in December 1809 was appointed acting commander of the hulk *Arrogant*. His promotion was confirmed by the Admiralty on 3 October 1810, and in the following February he was appointed to the *Hesper* (18 guns), in which he took part in the expedition against Java; in acknowledgement of his conduct he was appointed acting captain of the frigate *Sir*

Francis Drake. On 22 January 1812 he was promoted independently by the Admiralty, probably to mark its appreciation of the services of his father, who had drowned on 24 December 1811. In August 1812 he was moved by Sir Samuel Hood into the *Bucephalus* (32 guns), which he took to England, and paid off in August 1813. Shortly after the peace he was offered the command of a frigate, which he declined on the ground of ill health.

On 28 June 1832 Reynolds married Eliza Anne, third daughter of M. Dick of Pitkerro, Forfarshire, and Richmond Hill, Surrey; she survived her husband. Reynolds did not accept any further employment until 1838, when, in October, he commissioned the *Ganges* (80 guns) for service in the Mediterranean, and commanded her on the Syrian coast during the 1840 operations. He had previously, on 20 July 1838, been made a CB.

On 8 January 1848 Reynolds was promoted rear-admiral, and was shortly afterwards appointed to the command-in-chief at the Cape of Good Hope and on the west coast of Africa; he received the special thanks of the government for his activity and zeal in suppressing the slave trade.

From 1849 to 1852 Reynolds commanded on the south-east coast of South America, eager to implement Palmerston's policy of ending the Brazilian illegal Atlantic slave trade. Despite Brazilian protests, British warships not only captured Brazilian slavers on the high seas and in Brazilian waters, but also, in 1850, entered Brazilian harbours to capture and burn slavers: Reynolds wrote, 'Nothing can be done with the Brazilian government on this matter except by compulsion' (Lloyd, 145). The British naval action contributed much to the virtual ending of the Brazilian slave trade in 1851. On 4 July 1855 Reynolds was promoted vice-admiral; on 4 February 1856 he was made a KCB. From May 1857 to October 1860 he was commander-in-chief at Devonport. On 1 November 1860 he was promoted admiral, and on 28 June 1861 was made a GCB. He died at his seat, Penair, near Truro, on 3 August 1861, and was buried at St Clement's churchyard, near Truro.

J. K. LAUGHTON, rev. ANDREW LAMBERT

Sources D. Syrett and R. L. DiNardo, *The commissioned sea officers of the Royal Navy, 1660–1815*, rev. edn, Occasional Publications of the Navy RS, 1 (1994) • O'Byrne, *Naval biog. dict.* • *GM*, 3rd ser., 11 (1861) • J. Marshall, *Royal naval biography*, suppl. 3 (1829) • W. E. F. Ward, *The Royal Navy and the slavers* (1969) • L. Bethell, *The abolition of the Brazilian slave trade* (1970) • C. Lloyd, *The navy and the slave trade* (1949) • D. Ellis and J. Walvin, eds., *The abolition of the Atlantic slave trade* (1981) • Boase, *Mod. Eng. biog.* • *CGPLA Eng. & Wales* (1861)

Wealth at death £20,000: probate, 20 Sept 1861, *CGPLA Eng. & Wales*

Reynolds, Christopher Augustine (1834–1893), Roman Catholic archbishop of South Australia, was born in Dublin on 11 July 1834, the son of Patrick Reynolds and his wife, Elizabeth *née* Bourke. He was sent to study under the Carmelite brothers at Clondalkin, and showed an early flair for theology. In 1852 he was sent to the Benedictine monastery of Subiaco, near Rome, to be trained for the priesthood. He left Rome for Perth, in Western Australia, for health reasons, and set out with Bishop Serra early in 1855, and he continued his training at New Norcia, where he was especially involved in mission work with the Aborigines. In January 1857, probably for health reasons, he was transferred to South Australia, where he completed his probationary studies at the Jesuit mission at Sevenhills. He was ordained a Jesuit priest in April 1860 by Bishop Geoghan, and he was granted a benefice in the city of Adelaide. He was afterwards transferred to Morphett Vale, where he ran the mission to the workers of the copper mines of Yorke's peninsula and built the parish church at Kadina. He was then transferred to the easier job of parish priest at Gawler.

On the death of Bishop Sheil in March 1872 Reynolds was appointed administrator of the diocese, and on 2 November 1873 he was consecrated bishop of Adelaide by Archbishop Polding. Despite poor means of transport and communication, he visited even the most remote parts of the diocese, travelling over 52,000 miles between 1872 and 1880. Reynolds's major concern during his episcopate was education. He was strongly opposed to the secular education of South Australian government schools. Initially he encouraged the work of Mother Mary McKillop, superior of the sisters of St Joseph, many of whose schools had been closed by Bishop Sheil, though in 1883 Reynolds withdrew this support. He was responsible for the expansion of Catholic education as well as an increase in church building, but this impressive legacy also caused severe financial difficulties within the diocese which amounted to debts of over £56,000 by the time of his death.

Hard work added to Reynolds's health problems, but when he was on the point of resigning the see he was called on by the pope, on 23 April 1887, to fill the archbishopric to which the see was elevated at the time. On 11 September Reynolds was invested by Cardinal Moran in the cathedral at Adelaide. He visited Rome in 1890, but otherwise spent the last six years of his life carrying out his duties as archbishop. He died on 12 June 1893 in Adelaide, where he was buried.

Reynolds had broad sympathies and his tolerance was a marked characteristic, though his genuine kindliness was partly concealed by a certain austerity of manner. He was a good classical scholar, a fine preacher, and filled with missionary zeal. He has been called the 'Father Mathew' of South Australia. C. A. HARRIS, rev. CLARE BROWN

Sources *AusDB* • *The Times* (13 June 1893), 11 • *Adelaide Observer* (17 June 1893) • *The devil is a jackass: being the dying words of the autobiographer William Bernard Ullathorne, 1806–1889*, ed. L. Madigan (1995)

Archives Roman Catholic Archives, Sydney

Reynolds, Edward (1599–1676), bishop of Norwich, was born in November 1599 in Holyrood parish, Southampton, the son of Augustine (Austin) Reynolds, one of the customers of the city, and his wife, Bridget. Educated at Southampton grammar school, he matriculated at Merton College, Oxford, in January 1616 and graduated BA on 15 October 1618. Made a probationer fellow in 1620 owing to his skill in Greek, he proceeded MA on 10 July 1624. Already noted for his preaching, 'tho' of an hoarse voice', remarked Anthony Wood (Wood, *Ath. Oxon.*, 3.1083), Reynolds became preacher of Lincoln's Inn in 1622. In or before 1627 he married Mary Harding (*c.*1610–1683). Instituted vicar of All Saints', Northampton, on 9

January 1628, he resigned the following October. On 1 March 1631 he was instituted rector of Braunston in Northamptonshire, whereupon he resigned from Lincoln's Inn and took up residence at Braunston, a living he held for the next thirty years.

Reynolds was soon recognized as one of the leading moderates among the godly in Northamptonshire, his position epitomized in *A Sermon Touching the Peace & Edification of the Church* (1638). He preached before the House of Commons at the monthly fast on 27 July 1642, was appointed to the Westminster assembly in June 1643, and took the covenant in March 1644. Although not especially active in the assembly, he did preach before it and seems to have had a hand in the preface to the *Directory for the Publique Worship of God*, the confession of faith, and the catechism.

In August 1646 Reynolds was one of the preachers sent to Oxford by parliament to prepare the way for reform of the university, and in May 1647 he was appointed one of the visitors to the university. On 12 April 1648 he was made DD, vice-chancellor, and dean of Christ Church. He refused the engagement when it was tendered to Oxford in November 1649 and ceased to act as a visitor. His promise of obedience to the law but not subscription to the oath in *Humble Proposals of Sundry Learned and Pious Divines* (1649) was insufficient to save him: he lost the vice-chancellorship in September 1650 and the deanery of Christ Church the following March, despite a last minute pledge to subscribe in a limited sense.

Reynolds retired to Braunston, only returning to national prominence from the mid-1650s. He preached before parliament in January 1657 and the same year was appointed minister of St Lawrence Jewry in London. After the death of Oliver Cromwell, he and other presbyterians sought an accommodation with Richard Cromwell, and on 11 October 1658 Reynolds, on behalf of himself and other London presbyterian ministers, delivered an oral address to the new protector. He preached at the opening session of parliament in 1659, and throughout 1659 and 1660 his sermons to parliament and London notables became increasingly pointed about the need for peace, unity, and moderation, codes for the restoration of the monarchy and accommodation with episcopalians.

Reynolds was by now recognized as the leader of the moderate presbyterian divines or 'reconcilers', and he was described as 'the king of their Israel' in September 1660 (*Fifth Report*, HMC, 156). He was the prime mover behind *A Seasonable Exhortation* in January 1660, which condemned sectaries and urged an understanding with Anglicans. In March 1660 he headed the list of commissioners appointed for approbation of ministers; he was also restored to the deanery of Christ Church. In May he led a delegation of presbyterian ministers to wait on Charles at The Hague, where they probably expressed a willingness to work towards a form of reduced episcopacy; at the same time it was reported that Reynolds and Edmund Calamy were willing 'to comply as to episcopacy

and the liturgy with little alteration' (J. Spurr, *The Restoration Church of England, 1646–1689*, 1991, 31). On 26 May, Reynolds was one of the presbyterian divines made royal chaplains, although according to Richard Baxter he preached before the king only once.

Throughout the summer and autumn of 1660 Reynolds continued to push for a moderate episcopacy acceptable to presbyterians and Anglicans, and he helped to draft the king's Worcester House declaration of 25 October 1660. On 7 July 1660 the king nominated him warden of Merton College, Oxford, a post he held only briefly, resigning in February 1661. In the early autumn of 1660 the king nominated him bishop of Norwich as part of a more general overture to the reconcilers: news of the offer was public by 9 September and the official nomination came on 28 September. At about the same time Charles also offered the bishoprics of Hereford to Baxter and Coventry and Lichfield to Calamy; in the event only Reynolds accepted, and he was consecrated on 6 January 1661. Many have pondered Reynolds's acceptance: in Baxter's view Reynolds accepted suddenly (*Reliquiae Baxterianae*, 2.283); according to Wood he was persuaded by his 'covetous and politic' wife Mary (Wood, *Ath. Oxon.*, 3.1085); W. A. J. Archbold suggested that he expected many more to follow (*DNB*). Reynolds's decision, however, was in keeping with his character, his moves towards reconciliation in 1659–60, his advocacy of reduced episcopacy in the Worcester House declaration, and his long-standing call for unity within the church and conformity to its discipline and worship expressed over twenty years earlier in *A Sermon Touching the Peace & Edification of the Church* (1638).

As bishop, Reynolds was noted as 'a frequent preacher and constant Resident' (*The Works of Sir Thomas Browne*, ed. G. Keynes, 6 vols., 1928–31, 5.160); he was also a vigorous promoter of his family, advancing his brother, son Edward, and son-in-law to archdeaconries. He sought to enact a model of reformed episcopacy, ordaining some dissenters, including Samuel Crossman in 1665 and his own son-in-law John Conant in 1670, in the spirit of the Worcester House declaration, and describing the dean and chapter of Norwich in 1661 as his 'ecclesiastical senate' to advise him 'in matters of weight and difficulty' (Reynolds, 5.xiv–xvi). Although Baxter thought Reynolds too mild and timid to be effective, particularly at the Savoy conference (*Reliquiae Baxterianae*, 2.364, 403), Reynolds remained a champion of comprehension.

Reynolds was a prolific writer, the author of more than thirty books, and said by Wood to have been renowned 'by all parties' (Wood, *Ath. Oxon.*, 3.1084–5). His *Treatise of the Passions* was still a common undergraduate text at Oxford at the end of the seventeenth century. His collected works were published in 1658, again in 1679 and, with a memoir of his life by Alexander Chambers, in 1826. Severely afflicted by the stone and strangury in his later years, Reynolds died on 28 July 1676 at his bishop's palace and was buried on 9 August in the bishop's chapel he had newly built at Norwich. He was survived by his wife Mary.

Edward Reynolds (1630–1698), Church of England clergyman, Edward Reynolds's only son, was born on 27 May

1630. He was educated at St Paul's School from 1641 and entered Merton College, Oxford, but on 21 July 1648 was made demy of Magdalen College. On 18 January 1649 he was made a fellow. He graduated BA on 14 March 1650 and proceeded MA on 28 June 1652. In October 1658 he became rector of St Peter's, Northampton.

In August 1660 Reynolds was ejected from his fellowship because he had been put in by parliament's visitors and because he had since then become married—to Frances (d. 1722), daughter of John Alston of Pavenham, Bedfordshire. He was immediately compensated, however, by being presented to a prebend in Worcester Cathedral by the king, and in February 1661 his father collated him as archdeacon of Norfolk. On 6 July 1676 he proceeded DD at Oxford as a grand compounder. The following year he edited his father's *Meditations on the Fall and Rising of St. Peter* (1677).

Reynolds's mother came to live with him after his father's death; she died on 27 September 1683. Edward died on 28 June 1698 and was buried three days later in Kingsthorpe chapel, which was annexed to his living of St Peter's, Northampton.   IAN ATHERTON

Sources E. Reynolds, *The whole works*, ed. J. R. Pitman, 6 vols. (1826) · Wood, *Ath. Oxon.*, new edn, 3.1083–6 · M. Burrows, ed., *The register of the visitors of the University of Oxford, from AD 1647 to AD 1658*, CS, new ser., 29 (1881) · *Reliquiae Baxterianae, or, Mr Richard Baxter's narrative of the most memorable passages of his life and times*, ed. M. Sylvester, 1 vol. in 3 pts (1696) · G. R. Abernathy, *The English presbyterians and the Stuart restoration, 1648–1663* (1965), 5–101 · I. M. Green, *The re-establishment of the Church of England, 1660–1663* (1978) · A. Whiteman, 'The restoration of the Church of England', *From uniformity to unity, 1662–1962*, ed. G. Nuttall and O. Chadwick (1962), 19–88 · C. H. Firth and R. S. Rait, eds., *Acts and ordinances of the interregnum, 1642–1660*, 3 vols. (1911) · W. A. Shaw, *A history of the English church during the civil wars and under the Commonwealth, 1640–1660*, 2 vols. (1900) · *Fasti Angl., 1541–1857*, [Ely] · Foster, *Alum. Oxon.* · *JHC*, 2 (1640–42), 644, 694; 3 (1642–4), 392; 7 (1651–9), 477, 480, 594, 599, 860, 872 · *JHL*, 10 (1647–8), 62–3, 86–7; 11 (1660–66), 11 · biographical notice of Edward Reynolds, junior, BL, Lansdowne MS 987, fol. 125 · BL, Add. MS 22579, fol. 25v [E. Reynolds jun.] · H. I. Longden, *Northamptonshire and Rutland clergy from 1500*, ed. P. I. King and others, 16 vols. in 6, Northamptonshire RS (1938–52), vol. 11, pp. 171, 173 · *Hist. U. Oxf. 4: 17th-cent. Oxf.* · F. J. Varley, ed., 'The Restoration visitation of the University of Oxford and its colleges', *Camden miscellany, XVIII*, CS, 3rd ser., 79 (1948) · G. C. Brodrick, *Memorials of Merton College*, OHS, 4 (1885) · Bodl. Oxf., MS Tanner 130, fol. 144r · Bodl. Oxf., MS Tanner 285, fol. 173r · *CSP dom.*, 1660–61, 262; 1665–6, 40 · CUL, MS Mm 1.51, 96–8 · Kingsthorpe register (transcript), 1539–1789, Northants. RO, p. 134 [burial of Edward Reynolds jun.] · *Fifth report*, HMC, 4 (1876)

Likenesses D. Loggan, line engraving, pubd 1658 (after D. Loggan), BM, NPG; repro. in E. Reynolds, *The works of Edward Reynolds* (1658), frontispiece · D. Loggan, line engraving, pubd 1658, BM, NPG; repro. in Reynolds, *Works* (1658) · R. White, engraving, 1677 (after D. Loggan, 1658), repro. in *The works of ... Edward Reynolds* (1679) · R. Graves, engraving, 1820 (after D. Loggan, 1658), repro. in E. Reynolds, *Whole works* · portrait; in possession of Sir N. Gresley in 1899

Wealth at death monetary bequests of over £1200: will, PRO, PROB 11/351, fols. 386v–90r

Reynolds, Edward (1630–1698). *See under* Reynolds, Edward (1599–1676).

Reynolds, (James) Emerson (1844–1920), chemist, was born on 8 January 1844 at Booterstown, co. Dublin, the only son of James Reynolds, apothecary and playwright, and his wife, a former Miss Campbell. On leaving school Reynolds became assistant to his father, and developed a strong interest in chemistry. He studied medicine, and in 1865 qualified as a licentiate of both the Royal College of Physicians and the Royal College of Surgeons of Edinburgh. He had installed a small laboratory in his home at Booterstown, where he pursued his chemical research. His first paper, 'On the oleaginous matter formed on dissolving different kinds of iron in dilute acids', appeared in *Chemical News* (1861), when he was only seventeen years of age. Reynolds published further articles and, after practising medicine for a short time in Dublin, devoted himself solely to chemistry.

In March 1867 Reynolds was appointed keeper of minerals at the National Museum in Dublin, and in the following year analyst to the Royal Dublin Society. Probably his most significant contribution to chemistry was his discovery of thiourea, the sulphur analogue of urea, in 1868. The existence of this compound was indicated by theory but distinguished scientists of the time such as Liebig and Hofmann had been unable to isolate it. His account of the isolation of thiourea, published in the *Journal of the Royal Dublin Society* and *Journal of the Chemical Society* for 1869, attracted much attention and was promptly republished in several continental scientific periodicals. It at once established Reynolds's position as one of the most promising of the younger British chemists.

While retaining both his other posts, Reynolds was appointed professor of chemistry at the Royal College of Surgeons, Dublin, in 1870. The following year he described the preparation of an interesting compound of propanone (acetone) and mercury (II) oxide. This was the first colloidal derivative of mercury and its formation is the basis of Reynolds's test for propanone. In 1875 he relinquished the museum and Royal Dublin Society positions when he was appointed professor of chemistry at Trinity College, Dublin, as successor to Dr James Apjohn. In the same year, on 12 February, he married Janet Elizabeth, daughter of Prebendary John Finlayson, of Christ Church, Dublin, with whom he had a son, Alfred John, and a daughter, Marion Janet Elizabeth.

At Trinity College Reynolds acted as a public analyst and consultant and helped to produce the *Manual of Public Health for Ireland*. He was also responsible for the analysis of the Dublin water supply. His interest in analytical chemistry included spectroscopy, a subject in its infancy at that time. Though his duties left him little time for research, he published more than a dozen scientific papers during the twenty-eight years that he remained there.

Reynolds also made a significant contribution to silicon chemistry and to the chemistry of minerals containing silicon. He studied organo-silicon compounds including carrying out the syntheses of $Si(NH.C_6H_5)_4$ and $Si(N.C_6H_5)_2$. He synthesized $CaSi_2Al_2$ and the mineral anorthite as described below.

Reynolds was impressed by the concept of periodicity. In 1886 he displayed the elements graphically according to the periodic law and, from a comparison of the specific heat capacities of silver and beryllium, was able to conclude that the relative atomic mass of the latter was nine and that it was therefore a member of the alkaline earth group in the periodic table. Reynolds took a serious interest in his role as a chemistry teacher. T. E. Thorpe, the writer of his obituary, describes how he took particular care with his lecture preparation, his demonstrations and practical work. He was one of the first to introduce quantitative work into a student's early chemical training. His book *Experimental Chemistry for Junior Students* (1882) was favourably received and had considerable success, going through several editions. He worked also as an examiner in chemistry with W. A. Tilden and W. N. Hartley for the Department of Science and Art (1895–7).

Reynolds was elected a fellow of the Royal Society in 1880, and vice-president for 1901–2. He was president of the Society of the Chemical Industry (1891), and of the chemical section of the British Association for the Advancement of Science (1893). In 1903, Reynolds resigned his chair and went to live in London. At the Davy–Faraday Laboratory he continued research, chiefly on silicon compounds, his last work (1913) being the synthesis of a felspar, anorthite, a calcium aluminum silicate, which had the properties of the naturally occurring mineral. His mental capacities were active to the end of his life, but his eyesight, never very good, gradually failed during his later years. He died on 17 February 1920, at his home, 3 Inverness Gardens, Kensington, London.

GRAHAM I. BIRLEY

Sources DNB · T. E. T. [T. E. Thorpe], PRS, 97A (1920), iii–vi · W. R. H., 'Experimental chemistry for senior students', Nature, 37 (1887–8), 388 [review] · W. A. Tilden, A manual of chemistry (1897) · JCS, 22 (1869), 1 · E. A. W., Nature, 105 (1920), 49 · W. J. Davis, 'In praise of Irish chemists', Proceedings of the Royal Irish Academy, 77B (1977), 309–16 · C. Mollan, W. Davis, and B. Finucane, eds., Some people and places in Irish science and technology (1985), 58–9 · 'Great Britain: science and art department', Reports of the examiners, 1878–99, 4 vols. (1879–99) · 'Great Britain: science and art department', Reports and Directories, 1890–1900

Likenesses portrait, repro. in Mollan, Davis, and Finucane, eds., Some people and places in Irish science · wood-engraving, NPG

Wealth at death £1461 0s. 7d.: probate, 20 July 1920, CGPLA Eng. & Wales

Reynolds, Frances [Fanny] (**1729–1807**), painter, poet, and writer on art, was born either on 10 May or on 6 June 1729 in Plympton Erle, Devon, where she was baptized on 6 June, the youngest daughter of seven children of the Revd Samuel Reynolds (1681–1745), master of the local grammar school, and his wife, Theophilia, *née* Potter (1688–1756).

Reynolds moved to London to keep house for her elder brother Joshua *Reynolds (1723–1792), who had returned from Italy in 1752 to establish his career as a painter. Since he discouraged her ambition to become a portrait painter he must have been hesitant to provide her with anything but the most basic instructions. Presumably largely self-taught, according to Northcote, she did draw from the living model, with 'all her figures cloath'd except infants

which she often paints from life' (Wendorf, 79). She executed miniatures after her brother's works—such as her versions of *The Strawberry Girl* and *Cupid as a Link Boy* (reproduced Williamson, 189)—and painted portraits of Samuel Johnson (c.1780; Albright Knox Art Gallery, Buffalo), Charles Burney, John Hoole (c.1783; engraved by Anker Smith), Elizabeth Montagu (1778; engraved by C. Townley), Anna Williams, Hannah More, James Harris, James Beattie and his wife, and others. She also produced *Self-Portrait with her Two Sisters Mary and Elizabeth* (undated; priv. coll.) and in 1774 and 1775 exhibited paintings at the Royal Academy.

Reynolds was, furthermore, known as a writer; she composed poems and published *A Melancholy Tale* in 1790; she completed several drafts of 'Recollections of Samuel Johnson'; and in 1789 she published her aesthetic treatise *Enquiry Concerning the Principles of Taste and the Origin of our Ideas of Beauty &c* (privately printed in 1785), with a dedication to the renowned bluestocking Elizabeth Montagu. Claiming that the moral sense is the governing principle of beauty she sets feminine sensibility at the centre of her aesthetics. 'Virtue, honour, and ornament', she maintains, are:

> three grand co-existing principles of taste … Ornament and honour seem the public character of taste; virtue to be the private and domestic, where, though unperceived by the vulgar, to the eye of taste she appears in her highest ornament, highest honour. (ibid., 41)

Although Samuel Johnson criticized her treatise he also praised it as possessing 'such a depth of penetration, such nicety of observation, as Locke or Pascal might be proud of' (*Letters of Samuel Johnson*, 21 July 1781).

Admired by many of her contemporaries, including Johnson, Frances Burney, and Cornelia Knight—who described her as 'an amiable woman, very simple in her manner, but possessed much information and talent' (*Autobiography*, 1.8)—Reynolds was also regarded by some as overly pious and possessing a 'caprice and queer kind of behaviour' (Radcliffe, 150). In the 1770s relations between her and her brother became increasingly strained. Commenting on their troubled relationship Hester Thrale (later Piozzi) thought that 'perhaps She paints too well, or has learned too much Latin, and is a better Scholar than her Brother: and upon more Reflection I fancy it must be so' (*Thraliana*, 1.80).

In the late 1770s Reynolds left her brother's house. Joseph Moser mentioned that she moved several times and that 'she continued to paint … as long as she could hold the pencil, and her easel used frequently to be set up near her parlour window in order advantageously to display some favourite performance to the admiring passengers' (Whitley, 1.299). It was only on her brother's death in 1792 that she became financially independent, taking a spacious house in Queen Square, Westminster, since, according to Moser, 'her own works were so numerous that a *large* house was absolutely necessary' (Wendorf, 74). She died, unmarried, at her home in Queen Square on 1

November 1807, leaving £200 invested in bank stock to Mrs Mary Shaw, and her furniture to her niece Mary, marchioness of Thomond. ANGELA ROSENTHAL

Sources R. Wendorf and C. Ryskamp, 'A bluestocking friendship: the letters of Elizabeth Montagu and Frances Reynolds in the Princeton collection', *Princeton University Library Chronicle*, 41 (1979–80), 173–20 · R. Wendorf, *Sir Joshua Reynolds: the painter in society* (1996), esp. 68–81, figs. 11–14 · R. W. Jones, *Gender and the formation of taste in eighteenth-century Britain: the analysis of beauty* (1998), 198–210 · F. Reynolds, *Enquiry concerning the principles of taste and the origin of our ideas of beauty &c* (1785) · *Frances Reynolds and Samuel Johnson* (Cambridge, Mass., 1995) · G. C. Williamson, 'Miniatures by Sir Joshua Reynolds' sister', *Magazine of Art* (1902), 188–9 [illustr.] · W. T. Whitley, *Artists and their friends in England, 1700–1799*, 2 vols. (1928); repr. (1968) · C. R. Leslie and T. Taylor, *The life and times of Sir Joshua Reynolds: with notices of some of his contemporaries*, 2 vols. (1865), 1.121–2 · D. Hudson, *Sir Joshua Reynolds: a personal study, with Reynolds' journey from London to Brentford* (1958) · *Thraliana: the diary of Mrs. Hester Lynch Thrale (later Mrs. Piozzi), 1776–1809*, ed. K. C. Balderston, 2nd edn, 1 (1951), 79–80 · E. C. Clayton, *English female artists*, 2 vols. (1876), 1.146–232 · Waterhouse, *18c painters* · *The letters of Samuel Johnson*, ed. B. Redford, 3 (1992), 355–6 · *Autobiography of Miss Cornelia Knight*, 2 vols. (1861), 1.8 · Thieme & Becker, *Allgemeines Lexikon* · Redgrave, *Artists* · G. Meissner, ed., *Allgemeines Künstlerlexikon: die bildenden Künstler aller Zeiten und Völker*, [new edn, 34 vols.] (Leipzig and Munich, 1983–) · N. Penny, ed., *Reynolds* (1986), 21, 24, 33, 167, 170, 174 · S. M. Radcliffe, ed., *Sir Joshua's nephew: being letters written, 1769–1778, by a young man to his sisters* (1930) · *Diary and letters of Madame D'Arblay*, ed. [C. Barrett], 7 vols. (1842–6) · P. de Bolla, *The discourse of the sublime: reading in history, aesthetics, and the subject* (1989), 48–9 · C. Petteys and others, eds., *Dictionary of women artists: an international dictionary of women artists born before 1900* (1985) · Madame D'Arblay [F. Burney], *Memoirs of Doctor Burney* (1833) · J. Northcote, *The life of Sir Joshua Reynolds*, 2nd edn, 2 vols. (1819) · D. Mannings, ed., *Sir Joshua Reynolds: a complete catalogue of his paintings*, 2 vols. (2000) · Graves, *Soc. Artists* · A. Graves, *A century of loan exhibitions, 1813–1912*, 5 vols. (1914) · *Engraved Brit. ports.*, 6.534 · Bénézit, *Dict.*, 4th edn · D. Foskett, *Dictionary of British miniature painters*, 2 vols. (1972) · IGI · PRO, PROB 11/1474, sig. 143
Archives Hunt. L., letters, MSS MO 4650–4651 · priv. coll., commonplace book | BL, corresp. with Samuel Johnson, RP 186 [copies] · BL, corresp. with Elizabeth Montagu, RP 196 [copies]
Likenesses J. Reynolds, oils, *c.*1746, Plymouth City Museum and Art Gallery, Cottonian collection
Wealth at death bequeathed £200 bank stock to Mrs Mary Shaw, and furniture to niece and executor Mary, marchioness of Thormond: will, PRO, PROB 11/1474, sig. 143

Reynolds, Frederick (1764–1841), playwright, was born on 1 November 1764 in Lime Street, London, the youngest of the four sons of John Reynolds (1728–1809?), solicitor, and his wife, Elizabeth (1736–1810?), daughter of Richard West, a retired hosier, and his wife, Susannah. His paternal grandfather came from a rich, long-established Wiltshire family; and John Reynolds's law firm prospered by attracting prestigious aristocratic clients and radicals alike: little surprise that Reynolds was 'reared in the lap of luxury' (Reynolds, 1.7). About 1770 he was sent to a boarding-school of 'good repute' in Walthamstow (ibid., 1.11), before entering Westminster School (22 January 1776), where George Colman junior and the duke of Bedford befriended him. As a schoolboy, he experienced first-hand the mob in the Gordon riots (June 1780) but his father, despite whiggish sympathies, his friendship with John Wilkes, and support for the Bill of Rights, took alarm and temporarily conveyed the family (and 150 guineas) to

the safety of their Kentish estate, at Southbarrow, near Bromley, where they watched the reddened sky as London burned. Being destined for a career in the law, Reynolds commenced work in his father's office and on 12 January 1782 was admitted a student of the Middle Temple, where in the 1790s James Boaden was a contemporary and friend. That summer and again in 1787 he was dispatched abroad to recover money owed to his father, then suffering severe financial difficulties through both bad debts and inefficient estate management in Kent and at his Dominican sugar plantation.

Reynolds's contact with the theatre began at school. He saw Barry as Othello about 1773 and was introduced in the green room to Mrs Barry, playing Desdemona; Garrick was a friend and neighbour at the Adelphi, John Street, in the 1770s. Reynolds witnessed his farewell performance at Drury Lane in 1776, and in 1783 John Kemble's début as Hamlet. His first play, *Werter*, written to impress a girl and originally rejected in London, was staged to a 'dangerously flattering' (Reynolds, 1.312) reception at Bath in November 1785 (when Sir Thomas Lawrence sought an introduction). Reynolds's combined income from this tragedy and a second entitled *Eloisa* (1786) being only £8, he abandoned the genre for the more remunerative realms of comedy.

Reynolds's comedy *The Dramatist* (1789), declined by all three patent theatres but selected by Becky Wells (mistress of his friend Edward Topham) for her Covent Garden benefit, was a success for Lewis as Vapid, the playwright-hero. Probably Reynolds's best play—celebrated for the act IV china closet scene—it was a landmark because the manager, Thomas Harris, purchased two of the traditional author's nights (the sixth and ninth) for fixed sums and also bid for the twenty-first. This was the origin, Reynolds claimed, of an extension to the payment system which actually benefited authors. Following a nervous illness (which recurred at intervals), he collaborated with Miles Peter Andrews and Topham on *Better Late than Never* (1790), but had better success on his own with *Notoriety* (1791), and the aptly named *How to Grow Rich* (1793), the profits of which (including copyright) amounted to £620. *The Rage!* (1794), 'written with the view of lashing the vulgarity of fashion' (Reynolds, 2.181), proved to be the most popular play of the Covent Garden season (thirty-seven performances).

Over several years in the early 1790s Reynolds was involved with a celebrated (but in his autobiography unnamed) actress. She was in fact Becky Wells, Topham's abandoned mistress. They expressed warm regard in their letters (Wells, 1.139–46, 3.161–80) and Reynolds accompanied her 'upon the strictest terms of friendship' (ibid., 1.124), when she fled to France in 1792 to elude creditors. Later, they spent a month in a remote part of Norfolk, where, through Mrs Wells's eccentric behaviour (madness was hinted at), the pair were mistaken by credulous locals for Marie Antoinette and the dauphin.

Reynolds's future wife, Elizabeth Mansel (d. 1848), daughter of Robert Mansel and his wife Alice Landeg, first acted in his comedy *Speculation* (1795) but their courtship began only during rehearsals for *Laugh when you can* (1798). A sister of the actor Richard Mansel (*d.* 1824) who had fled her landed south Wales family for the London stage, she was employed seasonally at Covent Garden on £3 per week. Her final appearance (in *The Heir at Law*) was on 14 March and, with her brother as witness, she married Reynolds at St Clement Danes on 16 March 1799. Since her direct connection with the stage was now severed, Elizabeth's maternal uncle, Colonel Landeg, a Glamorgan landowner and gentleman farmer, dropped his resentment at his niece's conduct and that summer the newly married couple spent 'six Arcadian weeks' (Reynolds, 2.302) (and several subsequent vacations) at Brinwhillach, his estate in Felindre, near Swansea.

Playwriting was a precarious profession but Reynolds's profits on *Delays and Blunders* (1802) were enough to lease a small house in Newman Street, off Oxford Street, where Mrs Siddons was a near neighbour. In 1803 *Three per cents* was damned but the melodrama *The Caravan* became a huge success for author and theatre. Set in bandit-ridden Spain, it famously deployed a dog leaping from a dizzyingly high rock into raging waters to rescue a child. Reynolds enjoyed retailing the story that Sheridan regarded the dog—not himself—as 'guardian angel' and 'preserver of Drury Lane' (Reynolds, 2.352). Trading as far as possible on novelty, Reynolds's comedies up to about 1808 generally netted about £500 apiece; but by the second decade of the new century Reynolds had converted to the new fashion for opera and operatic spectacle. In latter guise are his somewhat ruthless adaptations of Shakespearian comedy (1816–24), beginning with *A Midsummer Night's Dream*, in which, according to Hazlitt, though setting new standards for scenic splendour, '[t]he spirit was evaporated, the genius was fled' (*Complete Works*, 5.275). From 1814 to March 1822 Reynolds was '*maid of all work*' and '*thinker*' (Reynolds, 2.399) to Henry Harris's management at Covent Garden and from 1823, at an annual salary of £200, adviser-reader for Elliston at Drury Lane, where, as 'the great and clever man … who knows everything' he was bitterly resented by Elliston's acting manager, James Winston (*Drury Lane Journal*, 91). Playwriting now became a secondary activity, but the novel *A Playwright's Adventures* (1831) drew on theatrical experiences and in the last phase of his life Reynolds amused himself with pantomime, the last of which was written for the Adelphi in 1840.

An exact contemporary of the playwright Thomas Morton, with whom he was often bracketed because of a certain similarity in their careers, Reynolds wrote about 100 pieces in nearly forty years, generating an unprecedented (though unremarkable) income, for a life of 'incessant labour, struggle, and uncertainty' as a playwright, of just over £19,000 (Reynolds, 2.421). Of sufficiently high profile to have been subjected to two lines of Byron's satire in *English Bards and Scotch Reviewers* (1808), Reynolds as a playwright has now fallen into virtually complete obscurity. Although *The Dramatist* had one performance at the Haymarket in 1927, he is best remembered for his autobiography (2 vols., 1826, repr. 1969), a lively portrayal of mainly late eighteenth-century theatrical, social, and political life.

Reynolds loved cricket with a passion which matched if not surpassed his passion for the drama. Gregarious and well connected, with a host of theatrical, literary, and political friends, he was a member of the MCC as well as other less formalized clubs like 'Keep the Line' (of which he was a founder), the Lion, and the Theatrical Beefsteak. He died at home at 48 Warren Street, Fitzroy Square, London, on 16 April 1841. There were at least two children: Frederick Mansel *Reynolds (1800/01–1850) and Richard (*b. c.*1805).

JOHN RUSSELL STEPHENS

Sources F. Reynolds, *The life and times of Frederick Reynolds, written by himself*, 2nd edn, 2 vols. (1827) · 'Biographical sketch of Frederick Reynolds, esq. (accompanied with an original portrait)', *Monthly Mirror* (Dec 1795), [67]–73 · *The Times* (19 April 1841), 6 · D. E. Baker, *Biographia dramatica, or, A companion to the playhouse*, rev. I. Reed, new edn, rev. S. Jones, 3 vols. in 4 (1812) · G. C. D. Odell, *Shakespeare from Betterton to Irving*, 2 (1920) · *Drury Lane journal: selections from James Winston's diaries, 1819–1827*, ed. A. L. Nelson and G. B. Cross (1974) · C. B. Hogan, ed., *The London stage, 1660–1800*, pt 5: *1776–1800* (1968) · Genest, *Eng. stage* · J. R. Stephens, *The profession of playwright: British theatre, 1800–1900* (1992) · M. D. Wells, *Memoirs of the life of Mrs Sumbel, late Wells*, 3 vols. (1811) · *The complete works of William Hazlitt*, ed. P. P. Howe, 21 vols. (1930–34) · A. Nicoll, *Late eighteenth century drama, 1750–1800*, 2nd edn (1952), vol. 3 of *A history of English drama, 1660–1900* (1952–9), 301 [incl. bibliography] · A. Nicoll, *Early nineteenth century drama, 1800–1850*, 2nd edn (1955), vol. 4 of *A history of English drama, 1660–1900* (1952–9), 391–2 [incl. bibliography] · m. cert. · d. cert. · J. L. Chester, ed., *The reiester booke of Saynte De'nis Backchurch parishe … begynnynge … 1538*, Harleian Society, register section, 3 (1878) [on parents] · Highfill, Burnim & Langhans, *BDA*, vol. 10 [Elizabeth Mansel]
Archives BL, letters, etc., Add. MS 27925
Likenesses G. T. Doo, mezzotint, 1803 (after J. R. Smith), BM, NPG · T. Williamson, stipple, 1804 (after J. R. Smith), BM, NPG; repro. in *European Magazine* (1804) · H. Meyer, stipple (after G. H. Harlow, 1814), BM, NPG; repro. in F. Reynolds, *The life and times of Frederick Reynolds*, 2 vols. (1826) · W. Ridley, stipple (after W. Nash), BM, NPG; repro. in *Monthly Mirror* (1796) · J. R. Smith, portrait

Reynolds, Frederic Mansel (1800/01–1850), writer and journal editor, was the eldest son of the playwright Frederick *Reynolds (1764–1841) and his wife, Elizabeth. He took as his middle name his mother's maiden name, Mansel. Having received a good education, he drifted into a quasi-literary occupation, editing *The Keepsake* for the years 1828 to 1835 and from 1838 to 1839. This annual, in which the engravings were often of a higher quality than the literary contributions, was produced at lavish expense, and was among the best of its class. Literary contributors to *The Keepsake* under Reynolds's editorship included Sir Walter Scott, Lord Byron, Lady Caroline Lamb, Robert Southey, Thomas Moore, Percy Bysshe Shelley, and, under the guise of 'author of *Frankenstein*', Mary Shelley.

The most notable contributor to *The Keepsake*, however, was William Wordsworth, who contributed to the 1829 edition a sonnet on the mysterious gravestone in Worcester Cathedral which bears on it the simple word 'Miserrimus' ('Most Wretched'). Neither Wordsworth nor Reynolds was aware that the person commemorated was Thomas Morris (1659–1748), a non-juring divine. Captivated by Wordsworth's sonnet, and not knowing the true circumstances of Morris's life, Reynolds composed a first-person narrative detailing the crimes of a supposititious Miserrimus. *Miserrimus: a Tale* was originally printed for private circulation in 1832, and then published in 1833 with a dedication to William Godwin; it was reprinted in the same year. By most of the critics it was given the encomium of 'impassioned', but it was denounced in the *Gentleman's Magazine* as a libel on an innocent and helpless person. Jekyll, who called it 'Young Reynolds's extravaganza' (*DNB*), implied that it was the result of a nightmare. In 1836 Reynolds brought out a companion novel entitled *The Parricide, a Domestic Romance*, but it did not meet with equal success. In 1834 he published a three-volume novel, *The Coquette*.

In his later years, Reynolds suffered much from a nervous disorder, and resided at Jersey and abroad. After a long illness he died at Fontainebleau, on his way to Italy, on 7 June 1850. He was survived by a young wife, Jessie, 'whom he had known from her childhood, and whose education he had superintended'. That Reynolds was an educated and cultured man is evidenced in his appreciation for painting and music and in his having tried his hand (albeit amateurishly) at poetry and prose fiction.

DAVID KALOUSTIAN

Sources *GM*, 2nd ser., 34 (1850), 231 · F. Reynolds, *The life and times of Frederick Reynolds, written by himself*, 2nd edn, 2 (1827), 231–7 · R. R. Madden, *The literary life and correspondence of the countess of Blessington*, 3 (1855), 252–4 · *GM*, 2nd ser., 2 (1834), 625–6 [review of *The Keepsake*] · *DNB* · will, PRO, PROB 11/2116, sig. 549 · IGI
Archives NL Scot., letters to *Blackwood's*

Reynolds, George Bernard (1852/3–1925), engineer, was the only son of Commander George Stewart Reynolds (*d.* 1882) RN and his wife, Eliza Susannah; his birth was not registered in England, but his death certificate describes him as a British subject by birth in the UK. His father died a vice-admiral, on the retired list. Details of Reynolds's education are not known, but he graduated from the Royal Indian Engineering College and served in the Indian public works department. He then worked for the Royal Dutch Oil Company in the Sumatra oilfields. Some time before 1895 he married, and although his wife, Lavinia Jane, never seems to have accompanied him on his overseas tours of duty, he wrote regularly to her. They had no children.

In 1901 William Knox *D'Arcy, having obtained an oil concession in Persia, engaged Reynolds as fields engineer there. After prospecting near the border with Mesopotamia (Iraq), Reynolds began drilling operations late in the following year. The wells had to be abandoned in 1904, and he was then instructed to investigate likely sites in south-west Persia. D'Arcy became so short of funds that he persuaded the Burmah Oil Company to finance the Persian venture. Reynolds was too proud and independent-minded to accept the constant interference of his new managers, and he often resorted to uncivil and sarcastic ripostes in his weekly correspondence to them.

Burly and exceptionally robust, Reynolds had the presence and mental strength to face down all his problems in Persia, from troublesome issues concerning drillers and local tribesmen to hardships ranging from polluted water and aggressive insects to extremes of climate. Deriving solace from his pipe, a pet dog, and occasional picnics with cronies, he drove his men hard but was solicitous for their welfare, ordering cider, library books, seeds, and bowling kits for them. Even so, he ironically likened himself to the skipper of a windjammer, forever bombarded with complaints about the rations.

The years 1905 to 1908 were the most arduous and frustrating in the quest for Persian oil. Drilling on an unproductive site wasted two years, and operations did not begin at his favoured location, Masjed-e-Suleiman, until January 1908. Initial setbacks coincided with a severe cash crisis in Burmah Oil, and the directors instructed him to abandon drilling if no oil appeared at 1500 feet. Then, on 26 May 1908, oil was struck in enormous quantities within that limit. This proved to be the first of the massive Middle-Eastern oil fields; and its discovery allowed the Anglo-Persian Oil Company to be floated in London in April 1909.

Relations between Reynolds and his employers thereafter became increasingly fractured. He resented the administrative structure the new company was planning for Persia, refused to co-operate, and deliberately withheld urgently needed information. Early in 1911 he was recalled and dismissed, with a golden handshake of £1000. No word of thanks was offered for his signal achievements.

Sir Henri Deterding shortly afterwards recruited him to work for the Royal Dutch–Shell petroleum group in Venezuela. There he surveyed a potential oil site near Lake Maracaibo on the country's northern coast. Having reported favourably on its prospects, he was appointed fields general manager there. Physical conditions were quite as primitive as they had been in Persia. However, though by then approaching his sixties, his strong constitution and hard-won experience served him equally well there. By 1914 he had begun to produce oil commercially, on a small scale. Venezuela's oil output remained modest until in December 1922 Reynolds secured his second huge find of oil, in La Rosa field, also close to Lake Maracaibo. He must have retired shortly afterwards.

Once back in Britain, Reynolds was asked by the directors of Anglo-Persian to travel to Persia on a courtesy visit. Before he could take up this invitation, however, he died suddenly on 23 February 1925, aged seventy-two, at the Hotel de Inglaterra, Seville. None of the oil journals in that year noticed the man whose initiative, technical skills, and doggedness had opened up the oil riches of the Middle East. Reynolds was survived by his wife who may have seen all too little of him during his eventful career.

T. A. B. CORLEY

Sources R. W. Ferrier, *The history of the British Petroleum Company*, 1: *The developing years, 1901–1932* (1982) · T. A. B. Corley, *A history of the Burmah Oil Company*, 1: *1886–1924* (1983) · R. W. Ferrier, 'G. B. Reynolds of M. I. S. Makers of BP No. 2, *BP Shield*', May 1972, University of Warwick, BP Archives, 14–17 • D. Yergin, *The prize: the epic quest for oil, money and power* (1991) • *CGPLA Eng. & Wales* (1925) • d. cert.

Archives U. Warwick Mod. RC, Burmah-Castrol archive • U. Warwick Mod. RC, BP archive

Likenesses photograph, *c.*1909, U. Warwick Mod. RC, BP Archive

Wealth at death £91,113 15*s.* 7*d.*: administration with will, 8 July 1925, *CGPLA Eng. & Wales*

Reynolds, George Nugent (1770?–1802), poet, was born in Letteryan, co. Leitrim, the son of George Nugent Reynolds, a local landowner, who subsequently entertained O'Carolan the bard. On 16 October 1786, when Reynolds was sixteen, his father was murdered by an attorney named Robert Keon, who was executed for the crime.

Four years later, about 1790, Reynolds took to writing ballads and songs, and managed to publish many quite successfully, generally signed with his initials alone, in various Dublin periodicals including the *Sentimental and Masonic Magazine*, W. P. Carey's *Evening Star*, and Watty Cox's *Irish Magazine*. Reynolds's poems were highly popular both in the papers and when they finally appeared in their own right. The most famous of his short lyrics, 'Kathleen O'More', for example, which was much admired for its pathos, ran through thirteen editions when it was published in 1800.

Reynolds was also a popular dramatist. In 1797, *Bantry Bay*, a loyalist musical collaboration with the composer William Reeve, concerned with the attempted French invasion of Ireland, was successfully performed in Covent Garden, and published later in the same year.

Reynolds combined his literary life with a military career. At the time of his theatrical success in Covent Garden, for example, he was also employed as a yeomanry officer who not only had a flair for wit, but was also in the commission of the peace for Leitrim and Roscommon. In or about 1797, however, Reynolds's loyalty was brought into question, and Lord Clare deprived him of his office. Reynolds managed to turn the affair into literary capital for himself, however, by having his insulting retort to Clare published in the *Irish Magazine*.

In 1801 Reynolds turned over a new leaf and decided to study law. With that purpose he moved to England, but died of exposure early in 1802 at Stowe, while visiting the duke of Buckingham, having generously given up his coach seat to a lady *en route*, thereby enduring a cold journey on the roof. Reynolds was buried in Stowe.

Reynolds's reputation survived well into the twentieth century, thanks in part to the elegy written by fellow poet Patrick O'Kelly, and thanks also to the continuing controversy regarding which of the poems commonly attributed to him O'Kelly actually had a hand in writing. Misattributions included not only a series of three ballads written by a Liverpool composer, Edward Rushton, but also, more comically, a seventeenth-century lyric describing the welcome received by King James in Ireland. By contrast, Reynolds's family claimed that he had originally written, in 1799, Campbell's 'Exiles of Erin'. Reynolds's poems were much anthologized in the nineteenth century and 'Kathleen O'More' still finds a place in the *Field Day Anthology of Irish Writing* (1991). JASON EDWARDS

Sources S. Deane, A. Carpenter, and J. Williams, eds., *The Field Day anthology of Irish writing*, 1 (1991), 472, 492, 497 • O. J. Burke, *Anecdotes of the Connaught circuit* (1885), 152–8 • D. J. O'Donoghue, *The poets of Ireland: a biographical dictionary with bibliographical particulars*, 1 vol. in 3 pts (1892–3), 213 • J. Hardiman, ed., *Irish minstrelsy, or, Bardic remains of Ireland*, 1 (1831), 46–7 • H. Ellis, *Memoranda of Irish matters* (1844) • M. J. Barry, ed., *The songs of Ireland* (1845) • R. F. Cronnelly, *Irish family history* (1865) • *Sentimental and Masonic Magazine* (1792–5) • G. J. Browne, *A report of the whole of the proceedings … on the trial of Robert Keon* (1788) • *DNB*

Reynolds, George William MacArthur (1814–1879), novelist, journalist, and radical, was born on 23 July 1814 in Sandwich, Kent, the elder son of George Reynolds, a captain in the Royal Navy, and Caroline Frances. He was educated at Ashford grammar school, Kent, and in 1828 he entered the Royal Military College, Sandhurst. His temperament, however, unsuited him for a military career. His father had died in 1822, and on his mother's death in 1830 he inherited £12,000 and left Sandhurst for Paris and the continent.

The next six years were to shape Reynolds's literary and political career. France was in a ferment of revolution, and he plunged into radical activities, is reputed to have become a French citizen, and served in the national guard for two years. At this time he published a radical pamphlet, *The Errors of the Christian Religion* (1832), and his first venture in fiction, *The Youthful Impostor* (1835; republished as *The Parricide*, 1847). In 1835 he was running La Librairie des Étrangers in Paris, and was literary editor for the *Paris Literary Gazette* (1835–6), which published the first pieces for which W. M. Thackeray received payment. He invested in the projected *London and Paris Courier*, which was never published. Owing to this and other unwise speculation he declared himself bankrupt in 1836 and returned to London. Although he settled with his French creditors in 1837, this was the first of a series of dubious financial insolvencies, and he was declared bankrupt again in 1840 and 1848.

The following year Reynolds edited the old *Monthly Magazine*, enlivening it with serialized versions of *The Modern Writers of France* (1838) and a racy novel-cum-guidebook to Paris, *Pickwick Abroad, or, The Tour in France* (1837–8), which plagiarized Dickens's characters. This raised the magazine's circulation but offended the proprietors, who terminated his engagement in under a year. Reynolds completed *Pickwick Abroad* in penny monthly parts (1837–8), and the novel was republished in different editions throughout his lifetime. Its success encouraged him to write more fiction, and it was followed by *Grace Darling* (1839), *Robert Macaire in England* (1840), and *Master Timothy's Book-Case* (1841–2), a miscellany in monthly parts loosely modelled on Dickens's *Master Humphrey's Clock* (1839). In an episode characteristic of his impulsive, financially ruinous behaviour a sudden conversion to temperance led him to invest in and edit *The Teetotaller: a Weekly Journal*

Devoted to Temperance, Literature and Science (1840–41). However, the high moral tone of the title was belied by the contents. He included racy fiction and quarrelled with his fellow stockholders. In September 1841 the periodical abruptly ceased, Reynolds advertising from the same address another periodical entitled *The Anti-Teetotaller*, of which no copies have been recorded.

For the next three years Reynolds gave his time to political activities. About 1844 he married the writer Susannah Frances Pearson (1818/19–1858). Brought up in France and Belgium, and herself a minor novelist, Susannah was to share Reynolds's interests and work. Late that year he began the penny-issue serial that made him famous, *The Mysteries of London*, published by George Vickers. This loosely followed Eugene Sue's *Les mystères de Paris* (1842–3), 'mysteries' denoting a new urban Gothic set among the squalor of slums and criminal life, a subject that no doubt appealed to readers living in the rapidly expanding Victorian cities. Reynolds lacked Sue's imaginative flair, but presented a dramatically effective picture of a society split between degenerate wealth on one side and the suffering poor on the other, worlds linked only by crime and a convoluted plot. By the end of the fourth volume Reynolds quarrelled with and left Vickers, who engaged Thomas Miller and then E. L. Blanchard to write a third series. Reynolds continued his own story as *The Mysteries of the Court of London* (8 ser., 1850–55), publishing it himself with John Dicks as printer.

The two serials fill over 100,000 pages of densely printed double-column text. They were phenomenally successful, and have been credited with selling a million copies in ten years, mainly among working-class and lower-middle-class readers. They were dramatized, plagiarized, translated, and imitated. For some fifteen years Reynolds's output was prodigious. He wrote over twenty other novels, besides numerous short stories and articles. They ranged from Gothic and oriental tales, including *Wagner, the Wehr-Wolf* (1846–7) and *The Coral Island* (1848–9), to 'social' novels such as *The Seamstress* (1850) and *Mary Price* (1851–2), and to costume drama and history fiction such as *The Rye House Plot* (1853–4) and *Mary Stewart* (1859).

Reynolds was also active as a journalist. He created a new style of penny-illustrated magazine for the expanding mass readership, influenced by the French newspaper *feuilleton*. Under his editorship the *London Journal* (1845–1912) featured serialized fiction illustrated with a large and often sensational woodcut, a miscellany of general articles, and columns of answers to correspondents which ranged from medical advice to political views. Reynolds raised the circulation to 50,000. However he quarrelled with the owner, the engraver George Stiff, and left to start his own *Reynolds's Miscellany* (1846–69). More sensational and radical than the *London Journal*, the *Miscellany* reached a circulation of 30,000 within a year. It began the business relationship with the printer John Dicks which was to last the rest of Reynolds's life and to make Dicks's fortune.

Reynolds's political career is harder to assess. On 6 March 1848 he came to prominence in a banned Chartist demonstration against the income tax in Trafalgar Square, where he carried through a motion supporting the French Revolution with such effect that he was followed by a crowd to his Wellington Street residence and addressed it from the balcony. He spoke at the Kennington Common meeting on 13 March and represented Derby at the Chartist convention which opened on 4 April. From 1850 to 1851 he was on the Chartist executive. He was proposed as parliamentary candidate for Finsbury in 1850, for Bradford in 1851, and for Lambeth in 1852. An advocate of physical force, he was politically close to Bronterre O'Brien, publishing his treatise 'The rise, progress and phases of human slavery' in *Reynolds's Political Instructor* (1850), and that year presiding over the first meeting of O'Brien's National Reform League. Although he had a popular following and a seat on the national executive Reynolds, however, was not taken seriously by other Chartist leaders, who saw him as a political opportunist and disliked him as the publisher of what Thomas Clark described in his open *Letter* to G. W. M. Reynolds (1850) as 'beastly literature' and 'hellish wares' (*A Letter Addressed to G. W. M. Reynolds, Reviewing his Conduct as a Professed Chartist*). Reynolds quarrelled with other Chartists, and was successfully sued for libel by Ernest Jones in 1859.

Nevertheless Reynolds made a significant contribution to radical journalism in the transition from early working-class papers to the modern mass circulation press. Internal evidence indicates that from about 1842 to 1848 Reynolds was foreign editor for the radical *Weekly Dispatch*, setting up a network of local sources and writing or directing leaders vehemently attacking Louis Philippe, military flogging, and capital punishment. This was also to be a feature of *Reynolds's Weekly Newspaper: a Journal of Democratic Progress and General Intelligence* (1850–1924), which quickly became the leading working-class paper in England, especially in the north, with a weekly circulation in 1872 estimated as over 350,000. It survived under different names until 1967. As in his earlier ventures, Reynolds combined forthright political comment with features of general interest, including cooking recipes (written with the help of his wife), a gardening calendar, and extensive 'Notices to correspondents'.

From 1854 Reynolds lived in Herne Bay, Kent, where he was an active member of the town's improvement commission. On the death of his wife in 1858 he returned to London, where he lived at 41 Woburn Square. He wrote no more fiction, although he edited the new series of *Bow Bells* (the renamed *Reynolds's Miscellany*) in 1864–8, published by Dicks, who had bought the rights to Reynolds's work in the 1860s. Reynolds died at his London home on 19 June 1879. His eldest son, George Edward, had died in 1850, and he was survived by two sons, Ledru and Kossuth Mazzini, and two daughters, Louisa and Emily.

Reynolds offended the respectable Victorian reading public by his sensational portrayal of violence and sexual matters, and his lurid denunciations of royalty and the aristocracy. The middle-class press combined to ignore his presence. Dickens had Reynolds in mind when he denounced 'the Bastards of the Mountain, draggled fringe on the Red Cap, Panders to the lowest passions of the lowest natures', in the first issue of *Household Words* (1850). On the other hand radicals attacked Reynolds's political inconsistency. Marx saw him as 'a rich and able speculator', exploiting working-class sentiments for his own commercial ends. He was accused of attacking wealth while titillating the upper-class aspirations, and the lowest tastes, of his readers.

Yet in his journalism Reynolds remained faithful to radical causes, even when these were generally unpopular, including trade unionism, the Paris commune, Irish independence, and the sepoys in the Indian mutiny. Reynolds simplified and sensationalized the class struggle, but did so with an instinct for popular taste. He helped shape stereotypes of the villainous rich and suffering poor in the popular iconography not only of England but also of Europe and America, where he was widely read. His fiction, while it lacks depth of thought and characterization, has the crude effectiveness of a strip cartoon or a modern soap serial. The cult of 'mysteries' literature that he fostered has been credited with influencing more profoundly imaginative works, including Thackeray's *Vanity Fair* (1847–8) and Dickens's *Bleak House* (1852–3). Reynolds's work makes up a significant part of a large Victorian literature that has been generally ignored by literary histories. *The Bookseller* noted that Reynolds's works outsold those even of Dickens, and in his obituary in 1879 it called Reynolds 'the most popular writer of our time'. Both Reynolds's voluminous output and the huge circulation of his work support this assessment.   LOUIS JAMES

Sources Boase, *Mod. Eng. biog.* · L. James and J. Saville, 'Reynolds, George William MacArthur', *DLB*, vol. 3 · A. Humphreys, 'G. W. M. Reynolds: popular literature and popular politics', *Victorian Periodicals Review*, 16 (1983), 79–89 · E. F. Bleiler, introduction, in G. W. M. Reynolds, *Wagner, the wehr-wolf*, ed. E. F. Bleiler (c.1848); repr. (1975) · E. F. Bleiler, ed., bibliography, in G. W. M. Reynolds, *Wagner, the wehr-wolf* (c.1848); repr. (1975) · J. V. B. Stewart Hunter, 'George Reynolds, sensational novelist and agitator', *Book Handbook*, 4 (1947), 225–36 · R. G. Gammage, *History of the Chartist movement, 1837–1854*, new edn (1894); repr. with introduction by J. Saville (1969) · *The Bookseller* (3 July 1879), 600–01 · F. Jay, 'Peeps into the past', *London Journal* (23 Nov 1918), 1–3 · M. Summers, *A Gothic bibliography* (1940) · C. Pearl, *Victorian patchwork* (1972) · T. Thomas, introduction, in G. W. M. Reynolds, *The mysteries of London* (1996) · R. C. Maxwell, 'G. W. M. Reynolds, Dickens and *The mysteries of London*', *Nineteenth Century Fiction*, 32 (1977), 87–101 · d. cert.
Likenesses F. Mansell, stipple, NPG · portrait, repro. in *Reynolds's Magazine* (7 Nov 1846), 1
Wealth at death under £35,000: resworn probate, Aug 1880, *CGPLA Eng. & Wales* (1879)

Reynolds, Henry (*fl.* 1628–1632), poet, eludes the biographical record, even though he was moving in well-documented London literary circles in the years when he published his few known works. He was the author of *Torquato Tasso's 'Aminta' Englisht* (1628) and, more importantly, *Mythomystes, wherein a short survay is taken of the nature*

and value of true poesy, and depth of the ancients above our modern poets, to which is annexed the tale of Narcissus briefly mythologized. The latter appeared under the initials H. R. and is undated, but it was entered in the Stationers' register on 10 August 1632 with a note identifying the author as 'Henry Reynolds gent'.

Mythomystes is a short but significant book devoted to the belief that the poetry of the ancient world was far superior to modern poetic productions because, at its best, it communicated a secret wisdom relating to the mysteries of nature and the character of the soul to a choice audience of philosophic readers. Reynolds's little treatise is a compendium of Neoplatonic commonplaces which assumes that the ancient (and in some cases mythical) poets of Greece, such as Orpheus, Musaeus, Homer, and Hesiod, were the transmitters of the ancient secrets of creation and of divine mysteries which were concealed in myths and fables. This body of wisdom was similar to and compatible with the secret knowledge that Moses had learned from God and passed down through the traditions of the Jewish cabbala; it was known to the Egyptian sages, who recorded it in hieroglyphic, and also to the magi of the Zoroastrian school. Reynolds interprets many of the Greek myths as parables of natural science or moral philosophy, rather in the manner of Bacon's *De sapientia veterum*. *Mythomystes* is notable for its citation of Florentine Neoplatonic writers, particularly Pico della Mirandola and Poliziano, in support of its arguments. Reynolds shows himself to be familiar with a broad range of modern literature in Italian, Spanish, and French, as well as English, but he assures his reader that modern writing lacks the intellectual loftiness and philosophic acuity of the literature of the ancient world.

Mythomystes was dedicated to Henry, Lord Maltravers, who was the eldest son of Thomas Howard, earl of Arundel. The impression is that Reynolds was part of the Arundel House circle, devoted to the arts, that included Inigo Jones, Henry Peacham, and John Selden. Reynolds's work has some affinity with *De pictura veterum* or 'The pictures of the ancients' (1634), by Francis Junius, Arundel's librarian, which claimed that the paintings of antiquity had a spiritual and inspirational power that was often lacking in modern works; Reynolds's dedication calls attention to the conventional parallels between poetry and painting.

The only literary reference to Reynolds appears to be a verse letter directed to him by Michael Drayton in 1627. Entitled 'Of poets and poesie', it offers a survey of the achievements of modern English poets, and addresses Reynolds as an accomplished critic of sound judgement. Drayton alludes to the long-established friendship between them and the many literary conversations they enjoyed together. Another friend of Reynolds may have been the traveller Thomas Coryate, who is mentioned familiarly in *Mythomystes*. If this was the case then Reynolds would have been associated with the large literary group that showed their colours in the commendatory verses to *Coryates Crudities* of 1611. Reynolds was evidently well read in modern literatures, as his translation of Tasso and his allusions in *Mythomystes* indicate. He also had an unusual range of Greek and Roman reading and a familiarity with Latin Renaissance scholarship. Given these interests and associations, it is surprising that no trace of him is to be found in the documentary record, either of his family or of his education. His provenance and his end remain a mystery. There are verses by Reynolds in Henry Lawes's *Ayres and Dialogues* of 1653 and 1655.

GEORGE THORN-DRURY, *rev.* GRAHAM PARRY

Sources H. Reynolds, 'Mythomystes, wherein a short survey is taken of the nature and value of true poesy … *c.*1632', *Critical essays of the seventeenth century*, ed. J. E. Spingarn, 1 (1908); repr. Bloomington, IN (1968) · M. Drayton, 'Epistle to Henry Reynolds, esquire', *Critical essays of the seventeenth century*, ed. J. E. Spingarn, 1 (1908); repr. Bloomington, IN (1963) · B. H. Newdigate, *Michael Drayton and his circle*, new edn (1961) · *DNB*

Reynolds, Henry Revell (1745–1811), physician, son of John Reynolds, was born at Laxton, Nottinghamshire, on 26 September 1745, one month after the death of his father, and was brought up by his maternal great-uncle, Henry Revell, of Gainsborough, Lincolnshire. He was sent to Beverley grammar school, and from there went in 1763 to Lincoln College, Oxford. Following Revell's death he went to Trinity College, Cambridge, and, after further study at Edinburgh, graduated MB at Cambridge in 1768 and MD in 1773. He first practised at Guildford, Surrey, and married Elizabeth Wilson there in April 1770. Two of their grandchildren were Sir John Russell *Reynolds and Henry Robert *Reynolds.

Reynolds was advised by another doctor, Huck Saunders, to settle in London, and in the summer of 1772 he took a house in Lamb's Conduit Street. On 30 September 1773 he was admitted as a candidate of the Royal College of Physicians, and he was elected a fellow on 30 September 1774. A censor of the college in 1774, 1778, 1782, 1784, 1787, and 1792, Reynolds was also registrar from 1781 to 1783, Goulstonian lecturer in 1775, and Harveian orator in 1776. He did not publish his oration. He was elected physician to the Middlesex Hospital in 1773, and resigned in 1777, when he was elected physician to St Thomas's Hospital, which post he filled until 1783, when his extensive private practice caused him to resign. In November 1787 he was challenged to a duel by a turbulent licentiate, Richard Kentish (1730?–1792), but Reynolds's friends applied to a magistrate, and the court of king's bench intervened to restrain Kentish.

In 1788 Reynolds was asked to attend George III, and in 1797 he was appointed physician-extraordinary, and in 1806 physician-in-ordinary. The fatigue caused by attending the king at Windsor (added to an exhausting examination on the king's illness, during which Reynolds had to stand for two hours before the House of Lords) broke down his strength; but it was with great difficulty that John Latham and Henry Ainslie persuaded him in May to rest. He died at his house in Bedford Square, London, on 22 October 1811 and was buried nearby at St James's cemetery, Hampstead Road.

NORMAN MOORE, *rev.* CLAIRE L. NUTT

Sources Munk, *Roll* · Venn, *Alum. Cant.* · *GM*, 1st ser., 81/2 (1811), 490 · 'Dearest Betsy', *Journal of the Royal College of Physicians of London*, 22 (1988) [editorial], 15
Archives Essex RO, Chelmsford, corresp. · RCP Lond., prescriptions
Likenesses V. Green, mezzotint, 1798 (after L. F. Abbott) · oils, 1798? (after L. F. Abbott), RCP Lond. · T. Blood, stipple, 1812 (after L. F. Abbott) · L. F. Abbott, portrait

Reynolds, Henry Robert (1825–1896), Congregational minister, born at Romsey in Hampshire on 26 February 1825, was the grandson of Henry Revell *Reynolds and the elder son of John Reynolds (1782–1862), Congregational minister, and his second wife, Sarah (*d.* 1868), daughter of Robert Fletcher of Chester and sister of Joseph Fletcher (1784–1843). Sir John Russell *Reynolds was his younger brother. Henry was educated chiefly by his father, and in September 1841 he entered Coward College, London (later incorporated in New College, South Hampstead), to prepare for the ministry. He matriculated at London University in the same year, took a mathematical scholarship in 1844, and graduated BA in 1848, in which year he was made a fellow of University College, London.

In April 1846 Reynolds became pastor of the Congregational church at Halstead in Essex, and was ordained on 16 July 1846. A few months later, on 17 December, he married Louisa Caroline (*d.* 1895), only surviving daughter of Silas Palmer of Newbury. They had no children. In 1849 Reynolds accepted a call to be minister of the East Parade Chapel at Leeds. The ten following years were probably the most strenuous in his life. He took a keen interest in theological controversies of the day, and made a special study of the writings of Auguste Comte, on whom he published a critique in the *British Quarterly Review* in April 1854. In 1855 his health gave way, and over the next five years he visited Egypt, Italy, and the south of France to recuperate from frequent illness. During this period he and his brother, John Russell Reynolds, wrote a novel dealing with the intellectual and religious questions of the time, which was published anonymously in 1860 as *Yes and No, or, Glimpses of the Great Conflict*.

In 1860 Reynolds became president of Cheshunt College. Besides fulfilling the duties of principal of the college and pastor of the college chapel and village churches, he was professor of dogmatic theology, ecclesiastical history, and New Testament exegesis. In addition, from 1866 to 1874 he was co-editor with Henry Allon of the *British Quarterly Review*, and from 1877 to 1882 he edited the *Evangelical Magazine*. In 1870 and 1871 he edited two series of essays on church problems by various writers, entitled *Ecclesia*, and in 1874 he published his lectures on John the Baptist in the new series of *Congregational Union Lectures*. They reached a third edition in 1888, in which year his most important work, the 'Introduction' and 'Exposition' on the gospel of St John, appeared in the Pulpit Commentary.

In 1869 Reynolds received the honorary degree of DD from Edinburgh University, and in the years immediately following he was engaged on the project of enlarging the Cheshunt College buildings, in celebration of the centenary of the institution. This work was completed in 1872.

Reynolds remained at Cheshunt until his retirement in 1894. Despite his devotion to his students, his tenure was marked by declining student numbers, defections to the Church of England, and deepening financial crisis. A theological conservative, he blamed the defections on the influence of the new biblical criticism. Reynolds died at Broxbourne on 10 September 1896, and was buried in Cheshunt cemetery on 15 September.

E. I. CARLYLE, rev. J. M. V. QUINN

Sources Henry Robert Reynolds: his life and letters, ed. [S. F. R. Best and H. R. Vaizey] (1898) · Congregational Year Book (1897), 213–15 · 'Memoir', R. H. Reynolds, Who say ye that I am? (1896) · K. D. Brown, A social history of the nonconformist ministry in England and Wales: 1800–1930 (1988) · C. Binfield, So down to prayers: studies in English nonconformity, 1780–1920 (1977) · ILN (19 Sept 1896), 358 · The Times (12 Sept 1896) · The Times (14 Sept 1896)
Likenesses S. Hodges, portrait, 1882; at Cheshunt College, Hertfordshire in 1901 · J. Cochran, stipple (after W. Gush), NPG · portrait, repro. in Congregational Year Book · portrait, repro. in Henry Robert Reynolds, ed. Vaizey and Best (1898) · print (after photograph by Thomas), NPG · wood-engraving (after photograph by Thomas), NPG; repro. in ILN (19 Sept 1896), 358
Wealth at death £8683 8s. 8d.: probate, 19 Nov 1896, CGPLA Eng. & Wales

Reynolds, Sir James (1685/6–1747), judge, was the son and heir of Robert Reynolds of Steeple Bumpstead, Essex, and his wife, Kesia, daughter of Thomas Tyrell of Gipping, Suffolk. He was a cousin of his near contemporary James *Reynolds (1686–1739), also a judge. From Eton College he went to Peterhouse, Cambridge, in 1702, and three years later—in the same year as his namesake—he was admitted to Lincoln's Inn, where he was called to the bar in 1712. Though he was marginally senior to his namesake, his rise came slightly later. He never practised as a serjeant, but was appointed chief justice of the common pleas in Ireland in 1727 and remained in that post until 1740, when he returned to England as a junior baron of the exchequer. With several other judges he was knighted on the occasion of the loyal address after the rebellion of 1745. After serving on the bench of the court of exchequer for seven years, he died on 20 May 1747 and was buried at Castle Camps, Cambridgeshire, where he lived in a villa called the Greenhouse. J. H. BAKER

Sources Baker, Serjeants · Venn, Alum. Cant. · S. H. A. H. [S. H. A. Hervey], Biographical list of boys educated at King Edward VI Free Grammar School, Bury St Edmunds, from 1550 to 1900 (1908), 326–7 · W. P. Baildon and R. Roxburgh, eds., The records of the Honorable Society of Lincoln's Inn: the black books, 5 vols. (1897–1968) · W. Musgrave, Obituary prior to 1800, ed. G. J. Armytage, 1, Harleian Society, 44 (1899) · GM, 1st ser., 17 (1747), 248 · memorial inscription, Castle Camps, Cambridgeshire · W. P. Baildon, ed., The records of the Honorable Society of Lincoln's Inn: admissions, 1 (1896) · will of Sir J. Reynolds, PRO, PROB 11/755 fols. 110v–111r · F. E. Ball, The judges in Ireland, 1221–1921, 2 vols. (New York, 1927) · R. A. Austen-Leigh, ed., The Eton College register, 1698–1752 (1927) · DNB
Likenesses J. Faber junior, mezzotint, 1748 (after J. Parmentier, 1734), BM, NG Ire.

Reynolds, James (1686–1739), judge, was born on 6 January 1686, the only son of James Reynolds (d. 1690) of Helions Bumpstead, Essex, and later of Bury St Edmunds, Suffolk, and his second wife, Bridget Parker. There were also three sons from his father's first marriage. After attending

Bury St Edmunds grammar school (to which he later left some of his books) he was admitted to Queens' College, Cambridge, in 1702, and to the Middle Temple in 1703, but he migrated to Lincoln's Inn on 19 May 1705, only three months after his cousin and namesake Sir James *Reynolds (1685/6–1747), also a judge. He was called to the bar in 1710, became recorder of Bury in 1712, and three years later, at the remarkably early age of twenty-nine, he was raised to the dignity of a serjeant-at-law. In 1718 he acted as counsel to the prince of Wales in the conference at Serjeants' Inn concerning the guardianship of his children, and in the same year was appointed counsel to the University of Cambridge.

Reynolds's election to parliament in 1717, as member for Bury, was procured through a family connection with the earl of Bristol, and he served until 1725, when he was appointed a justice of the king's bench. This appointment was obtained at the instigation of Bristol, in order to free the seat in parliament for John, Lord Hervey. Reynolds was promoted to be chief baron of the exchequer in 1730. About this time his London residence was in Red Lion Square. His first wife, Mary, daughter of Thomas Smith of Thrandeston Hall, Suffolk, died on 18 July 1736, and the following July he married Alicia Rainbird; there were no children from either marriage. He resigned from the bench on 5 July 1738 after suffering from 'a long nervous and paralytic disorder which took away his speech in large degree' (Abney's Reports), and also affected his sight, and on 24 January he suffered a further stroke at Bury from which he did not recover. He died on 9 February 1739 at Bury St Edmunds, and was buried in St James's Church (now the cathedral), at Bury St Edmunds, where there is an inelegant full-length seated effigy and a magniloquent epitaph.

Sir Thomas Abney wrote at the time of Reynolds's death that he left no great estate or character behind him: 'He had a smattering of almost all sorts of learning and [was] well skilled in title pages, which made him vain and pompous in conversation and on the bench. But his judgments were defective in solidity and substance' (Abney's reports). However, M. Shelton, in dedicating Wotton's short view of George Hickes's grammatico-critical and archaeological treasure of the ancient northern languages (1735) to James Reynolds, added that 'Your Lordship's consummate knowledge in the Law recommended you to the Honour of the Bench sooner than most of the Profession arrive to anything considerable at the Bar' (sig. [a3]). His property in Suffolk passed to the Frere family, with whom he was connected by the marriage of his first wife's sister with Edward Frere of Thwaite. J. H. BAKER

Sources HoP, Commons, 1715–54 · Venn, Alum. Cant. · H. A. C. Sturgess, ed., Register of admissions to the Honourable Society of the Middle Temple, from the fifteenth century to the year 1944, 3 vols. (1949) · W. P. Baildon, ed., The records of the Honorable Society of Lincoln's Inn: admissions, 1 (1896) · W. P. Baildon, ed., The records of the Honorable Society of Lincoln's Inn: admissions, 2 vols. (1896) · Baker, Serjeants · Sainty, Judges · Foss, Judges · Sir Thomas Abney's reports, U. Lond., MS IHR 976, (1), para. 125 · BL, MS Sloane 3984, fol. 145 · Yorke correspondence, BL, Add. MS 32556 · S. H. A. H. [S. H. A. Hervey], Biographical list of boys educated at King Edward VI Free Grammar School, Bury St

Edmunds, from 1550 to 1900 (1908), 326–7 • monumental inscription, Bury St Edmunds cathedral • M. Shelton, 'Dedication', in *Wooton's short view of George Hicke's grammatico-critical and archaeological treasure of the ancient northern languages* (1735)
Likenesses W. Parker, oils, *c.*1730, corporation of Bury St Edmunds • G. Vertue, line engraving, 1730 (after W. Parker), BM, NPG, AM Oxf., FM Cam. • effigy on monument, *c.*1739, Bury St Edmunds Cathedral
Wealth at death not great; property in Suffolk

Reynolds, James (1805–1866), orientalist, was the younger son of Cornwall Reynolds of Clapton. The father, a naval surgeon, had sailed with Lord Nelson, who stood godfather to his elder son. James's mother was daughter of Francis Hayward MD. After education at a private school, he entered St Catharine's College, Cambridge, as a sizar in 1822. He graduated BA in 1826. In the following year he was ordained deacon in London, and on 21 December 1828 took priest's orders. He acted for some time as chaplain to the first earl of Munster, through whose influence he was appointed on 27 October 1837 perpetual curate of St Mary's Chapel, Great Ilford, Essex. In the same year he became secretary to the Oriental Translation Fund of the Royal Asiatic Society, to whose publications he contributed. He retained the post until the fund ceased operating. He died at Great Ilford on 19 April 1866.

Reynolds was a competent Persian and Arabic scholar. He translated several historical books from these two languages, notably the *Kitāb-i-yāmini: Historical Memoirs of Amir Sabaktagin and Sultan Mahmūd of Ghuzni*, from Persian. Reynolds also superintended the publication for the Oriental Translation Fund of Sir Gore Ouseley's *Biographical Notices of Persian Poets (with Critical and Explanatory Notes)* in 1846, and wrote a prefatory memoir of the author.

G. LE G. NORGATE, *rev.* PARVIN LOLOI

Sources *Journal of the Royal Asiatic Society of Great Britain and Ireland*, new ser., 2 (1866), v • J. Foster, ed., *Index ecclesiasticus, or, Alphabetical lists of all ecclesiastical dignitaries in England and Wales since the Reformation* (1890) • Crockford • Allibone, *Dict.* • Venn, *Alum. Cant.* • Boase, *Mod. Eng. biog.* • *CGPLA Eng. & Wales* (1866)
Wealth at death under £2000: probate, 19 May 1866, *CGPLA Eng. & Wales*

Reynolds, John. *See* Reinolds, John (1584?–1614).

Reynolds, John [*alias* Captain Pouch] (*d.* **1607**), enclosure protester, was a leader in the midland revolt of 1607. Since no record appears to have survived of either his examination or trial and the only references to his involvement in the rising omit his place of origin, it is impossible to say anything of his earlier life. A chronicler's later report includes the marginal note that he was either a pedlar or a tinker. If true, then Reynolds was one of those masterless men whose mobility, and the anonymity this brought, alarmed early modern governments.

The background to the midland revolt, and to Reynolds's involvement in it, is to be found in the economic pressures created by the long population growth of the sixteenth century and, as a response to these and the temporary relaxation of restrictive laws, the intensification of enclosure. The latter development was particularly marked in the open-field communities of the heavy clay-lands of the midland counties which formed the heartland of the rising. Protests began in Northamptonshire on May eve 1607, but quickly spread to the adjoining counties of Leicestershire and Warwickshire and crowds numbered in their thousands tore down enclosures. Reynolds's direct leadership and the wider rumours that circulated of his role as Captain Pouch contributed to the scale of operation and to the co-ordination and mobility across county boundaries that distinguished the 1607 episode from other protests against enclosure in the period.

Since there is no direct evidence for Reynolds's role it can only be recovered from the correspondence of the authorities charged with suppressing the protests and from a later well-informed account of the rising added by John Howes to his 1615 edition of John Stow's *Chronicles*. As Howes's account makes clear, Reynolds was a charismatic figure. Adopting the pseudonym of captain, an inversion of military authority, was not uncommon among leaders of protest in this period. According to Howes, Reynolds gained the title of Pouch because of a great leather pouch he wore which, he claimed, contained 'sufficient matter to defend them against all comers' (Stow, 889). His ability to command support was also based, as with other leaders of popular protest in the Europe of his time, on claims to authority from both the king and God. According to Howes, Pouch claimed 'that in this present worke, hee was directed by the Lord of Heaven'. A claim to divine inspiration could challenge the culture of obedience that characterized early modern monarchical states and Reynolds's statement, 'that he was sent of God to satisff[i]e all degrees whatsoever' might indeed be taken to represent such a challenge (Stow, 889). However, Reynolds combined this with a claim to have been given authority from the king to throw down enclosures. Although there was no truth to this, it reflected Reynolds's acute understanding of the need to assert legitimacy for the protest if he was to gain support in a political culture in which popular protest was formally proscribed. His claim to royal authority echoed the protestations of loyalty to the king made in the protesters' petitions in 1607 and commonly in other smaller-scale protests against enclosure in the period. Despite the fact that Reynolds's supporters called themselves Levellers and Diggers, titles which later took on more a more radical meaning in the English revolution, their surviving statements make clear that they saw their activities of levelling and digging up enclosures as being for the good of the commonwealth.

Apart from actively leading the main body of protesters, Reynolds may also have had a hand in the appeal, issued under the name of the Diggers of Warwickshire, which combined professions of loyalty to the king with a biting attack on those enclosers whose greed was thought to have brought poverty and threatened famine. It is also likely that Reynolds was involved in the direct negotiations that took place with the authorities in Warwickshire in which the protesters, again professing their loyalty, promised to disband on news of the king's being informed of their grievances and agreeing to their reformation. Despite the potential for radicalism in Reynolds's leadership, his reported orders to his followers 'not to sweare, nor to offer violence to any person, but to ply their busine[s] and to make fa[i]re works' (Stow, 889) reflected a concern to keep protest within the bounds of order and was intended to contrast the orderly nature of protest with the greater threat to the commonwealth from the disorderly activities of the enclosers. Accounts by Howes and others acknowledged that, while the protesters wreaked violence upon hedges and ditches, they refrained from theft or personal violence. Despite this the central government became alarmed by the persistence of the protests and, angered by what it saw as the failure of the provincial authorities to stop the protests, issued instructions for the suppression of the rising, by force if necessary.

In the first week of June, Reynolds was captured after a clash at Withybrook in Warwickshire, another site of enclosure, and was sent 'as the chiefest leader' (*Hastings MSS*, 4.193) to London. By 9 June he was in custody and had been examined by the privy council. Although no further record survives of him, Howes records that he was found guilty of treason and that his execution was 'made exemplary'. Despite this, rumours of Pouch's activities continued to circulate, with at least one man setting himself up as his lieutenant and claiming from him authority to throw down all enclosures between Northampton and York. Having examined him, James I's privy council described Reynolds as a 'base ringleader and turbulent varlet' (ibid., 4.194) and Howes in a deliberate slight reported that his pouch was found to contain only a piece of mouldy cheese. But the reports of Reynolds's actions suggest that his leadership reflected a level of political knowledge and ability also to be found in other plebeian leaders of protest in this period. Late in the twentieth century the story of 'Captain Pouch and a few ill-armed peasants', written reputedly 'on memory's page', surfaced again briefly as a dramatic motif in one of the novels by the midlands author J. L. Carr (*Battle of Pollocks Crossing*, 1985, 104, 107–8, 129–30). JOHN WALTER

Sources J. Stow and E. Howes, *The annales, or, Generall chronicle of England ... unto the ende of the present yeere, 1614* (1615) · E. F. Gay, 'The midland revolt and the inquisitions of depopulation of 1607', *TRHS*, new ser., 18 (1904), 195–244 · J. E. Martin, *Feudalism to capitalism: peasant and landlord in English agrarian development* (1983) · *Report on the manuscripts of the late Reginald Rawdon Hastings*, 4 vols., HMC, 78 (1928–47), vol. 4 · PRO, STAC 8/221/1 · Warks. CRO, CR 136/C2623 · J. O. Halliwell, *The marriage of wit and wisdom, an ancient interlude* (1846), 140–41 · state papers, James I, PRO

Reynolds, John (*b.* *c.*1588, *d.* after 1655), merchant and writer, was born in Exeter, the first of the three children of Richard Reynolds, a merchant of Exeter (*b.* *c.*1540, *d.* in or before 1593), and his wife, Ann, daughter of John Long of Axminster. Reynolds's mother married, in April 1593, William Waltham, recorder of Treehill, Kenn, Devon. Reynolds was probably educated at the Latin high school at Exeter before possibly matriculating from Exeter College, Oxford. In 1606 he published a poem, *Dolarnys Primrose, or, The First Part of the Passionate Hermit*. Another early work,

The Flower of Fidelitie, a popular romance, dates from his youth but was not published until 1650, with a dedication to his stepfather, William Waltham. Although he continued to write, he did not publish for many years as he developed his career as a merchant. He may have been a member of the Company of Merchant Adventurers; he was fluent in French and had knowledge of other European languages. He was probably based in France from 1619.

In 1621 the first book of Reynolds's collected tales, eventually entitled *The triumphs of God's revenge against the crying and execrable sinne of* (*willful and premeditated*) *murther*, appeared. Although he claimed they were translations from the French, Reynolds wrote the stories himself. *The Triumphs* originally came out as a series of six books of five tales each; they were collected in a lavish folio edition in 1635. The stories were violent cautionary tales and focused on the importance of harmonious family life. Reynolds gave graphic descriptions of murders which were the result of unhappy marriages—half of the tales dealt with the consequences of arranged marriages. Equally lurid details were given for the fates of the execution-bound culprits of the crimes. The murders and the executions are gruesome and realistic. All of the stories illustrate Reynolds's concern with the breakdown of society; greed and drunkenness are two of the problems which lead to cruelty and murder. Reynolds retained sympathy for the victims of crime and was especially concerned with widows and orphans; he undoubtedly contrasted his own family's luck in his mother's happy second marriage to situations in the rest of society. *The Triumphs* was immensely successful; it went into eleven editions by 1660 and was continuously published until 1778 under various titles, and with additional stories on the results of adultery, not written by Reynolds, after the Restoration. Middleton and Rowley's tragedy *The Changeling* (1653) was based on one of Reynolds's violent tales.

Reynolds also translated works from French, such as De Refuge's *A Treatise of the Court* (1622), Leonard Marrauld's *The Judgement of Humane Actions* (1629), and Jean Mestrezat's *The Divine Pourtrait* (1631). His own writings, meanwhile, caused him to find disfavour with King James. In 1624 two political pamphlets, *Vox coeli* and *Votivae Angliae*, caused him to be extradited from France and imprisoned. In the first, Prince Charles's ancestors debate the wisdom of his possible marriage to the Spanish infanta. *Votivae Angliae* was an appeal to restore the Palatinate to protestant control. The date of Reynolds's release from prison is unknown. His *Apologie of the Reformed Churches of France* (1628) was written as if by a French author but is probably his own work; Reynolds may have wished to avoid annoying the new king.

Reynolds married Alice Bucknoll in Exeter on 27 April 1626. Together they had six children, of whom two survived. Alice died in September 1644 and Reynolds's second marriage seems to have resulted in two surviving sons, the last of whom was baptized in 1655. Nothing is known of Reynolds after 1655. K. GRUDZIEN BASTON

Sources J. M. Walmsley, *John Reynolds, merchant of Exeter, and his contribution to the literary scene, 1620–1660* (1991) • P. Salzman, *English prose fiction, 1558–1700: a critical history* (1985) • M. Drabble, ed., *The Oxford companion to English literature*, rev. edn (1995) • R. W. Maslen, 'Walmsley, J. M, *John Reynolds, merchant of Exeter, and his contribution to the literary scene*', *N&Q*, 239 (1994), 98–9 • IGI

Reynolds, Sir John (1625–1657), parliamentarian army officer, a younger son of a substantial Cambridgeshire landowner, Sir James Reynolds (*d.* 1650), and his second wife, Jane Mordaunt, a daughter of Sir Robert Mordaunt, was born on 10 March 1625. He matriculated at St Catharine's College, Cambridge, in 1640, but did not graduate. Like his much older half-brother Robert *Reynolds, the parliamentarian lawyer, John went to the Middle Temple (admitted 1642), but he left without being called to the bar, and joined the parliamentarian army soon after the outbreak of the civil war. He may have been commissioned as early as 1644; by 1645 he was a captain in Oliver Cromwell's cavalry regiment, and he took an active and courageous part in the later campaigns.

The year after the war was won Reynolds emerged as a prominent figure in the army's resistance to the policies being pursued by the presbyterian majority in the House of Commons and in its consequent politicization (April–June 1647). He is said to have acted as chairman of the 'agitators', elected by the regimental officers and other ranks; but this is uncertain, the same source describing him as a great favourite of Cromwell, who is portrayed as having both brought the Agitators into existence and then as having manipulated them to advance his own ambitions—a view which few modern historians would accept. Reynolds is nowhere listed as an elected officer–agitator, and is not recorded as a participant in the debates of the general council of the army at Reading in July or at Putney in October–November 1647; on the other hand he did sign several of the Agitators' petitions and proposals between May and August of that year, his name appearing first at least once. Although he does not seem to have taken any part in the mutinous disturbances of November 1647 he remained sufficiently radical to be involved in a movement, by petitioning and other means, to revive the Agitators and the general council in April 1648. For this activity he was tried before a council of war, and sentenced to three months' imprisonment, followed by cashiering from his commission. Although the sources are either untrustworthy or unclear, it seems that intervention on his behalf, together with his own expressions of regret, led to remission of the sentence, though he did lose his captaincy and the possibility of promotion to major of the regiment.

None the less in the summer of 1648, during the second civil war, Reynolds was allowed to recruit his own regiment as a kind of auxiliary force based in Kent, and this unit seems to have attracted a more than random number of soldiers with Leveller sympathies. Reynolds was one of the officers sent to guard the king (apparently not in a regimental capacity) at Hurst Castle on the south Hampshire coast in late November 1648, prior to Charles's being taken up to Windsor and so to London for his trial. One suggestion is that Reynolds, an educated gentleman, was chosen to balance the more plebeian, less polished future regicide Colonel Thomas Harrison, but this is unlikely. Harrison was only at Hurst briefly on 15 December; on the day the king was moved (18 December) Reynolds was already back in London, taking part in the renewed debates of the army council at Whitehall, where his only recorded vote was in support of the high command's line on church–state relations. This may well indicate that he was veering back in a more conservative direction.

Reynolds was promoted colonel and his regiment established as part of the army early in 1649, when it was earmarked for service in Ireland. The renewed Leveller-inspired unrest in the army (April–May 1649) found Reynolds's regiment deeply and dramatically divided, with whole companies joining the mutineers, while Reynolds and those men who were loyal to the army commanders played a leading, indeed a decisive, part in defeating the mutineers in Oxfordshire and Northamptonshire. Hence the odium which Reynolds incurred among his one-time allies and associates. Presumably the regiment's numbers were made up, to replace those who had defected, before crossing over to Ireland, where they arrived ahead of Cromwell's main expeditionary force in late July 1649. The regiment took part in the important defeat of the Irish confederates by the English under General Michael Jones at Rathmines on 2 August.

During the Cromwellian reconquest and the mopping up operations which followed (1649–52) Reynolds displayed an unusual flair for well-timed, well-executed field movements, and he was promoted commissary-general of horse in 1651. In June 1651, reporting on his several victories against the Irish, he reflected that they were the work of God using 'unworthy instruments … that he may destroy any confidence save in himself, and stir up a spirit of thankfulness in all' (Bodl. Oxf., MS Tanner, fol. 81*v*). He acted as a prop to successive commanders in Ireland, following Cromwell's departure in 1650: Henry Ireton, Charles Fleetwood, and finally Henry Cromwell. He was generously rewarded with confiscated Irish lands, and became a strong supporter of the protectorate. In 1654–5 Reynolds seems to have feared that he might be chosen to command the projected amphibious expedition to attack Spain in the West Indies, but the lot fell to the unfortunate Robert Venables instead. Reynolds sat as an Irish MP in the protectorate parliaments of 1654–5 and 1656–7. He also helped to suppress a planned royalist uprising in Shropshire, and was knighted by the protector shortly after this, in 1655. He married Sarah, daughter of Sir Francis Russell, another Cambridgeshire landowner; her sister Elizabeth was married to Henry Cromwell. So he might seem to have become very much a member of the protectoral inner circle.

In 1657 a rather unenthusiastic Reynolds was chosen to command the English infantry regiments being sent to Flanders, to act in alliance with France against Spain (with English royalist units fighting on the Spanish side). After the allied capture of Mardyke at the end of September Reynolds was appointed its governor; but, in C. H. Firth's words, 'Mardyke was a place easier to take than to keep' (Firth, *Protectorate*, 1.285). Although Spanish attempts to retake it were repulsed the garrison suffered severely from malnutrition and disease. Very sensibly Reynolds wanted regiments to be stationed there in rotation. Meanwhile he had a friendly but noncommittal interview with James, duke of York (the English royalist commander), in no man's land; this was swiftly reported back to Secretary of State Thurloe in London and so, no doubt, to the protector. Reynolds obtained permission to return temporarily to England, probably partly to clear his name over this incident, partly to press his case for reinforcements, and also to see his wife. Together with another former radical from 1647, Major Francis White, he was drowned when their small vessel was shipwrecked on the Goodwin Sands (5 December 1657). So it will never be known whether his conversation with James was a kind of political reinsurance policy, or merely arose from curiosity and amounted to no more than an indiscretion.

Reynolds's will, made in May 1657, before he left Ireland, was disputed between his sister- and brother-in-law (Dorothy and James Calthrop) and his half-brother, Robert. Although administration was granted to Dame Dorothy, the case ended up before the restored Rump Parliament in July 1659, when a compromise settlement was devised. Since Reynolds and his wife had no children she had only a life interest in part of his estate. In any case, most of his Irish property, including Carrick, which passed to Robert, was automatically forfeited in 1660. The times of greatest interest in John Reynolds's career are 1647–9 and 1657. It may be that he should be seen as a conventional East Anglian gentry follower of Cromwell, whose only aberration was his flirtation with democratic ideas in the days of the Agitators and the general council of the army.   G. E. AYLMER

Sources *The Clarke papers*, ed. C. H. Firth, 4 vols., CS, new ser., 49, 54, 61–2 (1891–1901) · C. H. Firth and G. Davies, *The regimental history of Cromwell's army*, 2 vols. (1940) · A. Woolrych, *Soldiers and statesmen: the general council of the army and its debates, 1647–1648* (1987) · I. Gentles, *The New Model Army in England, Ireland, and Scotland, 1645–1653* (1992) · S. R. Gardiner, *History of the great civil war, 1642–1649*, 3 vols. (1886–91) · S. R. Gardiner, *History of the great civil war, 1642–1649*, new edn, 4 (1893) · S. R. Gardiner, *History of the Commonwealth and protectorate, 1649–1656*, 4 vols. (1894–1903), vol. 1 · C. H. Firth, *The last years of the protectorate, 1656–1658*, 2 vols. (1909) · D. P. Massarella, 'The politics of the army, 1647–1660', DPhil diss., University of York, 2 vols., 1977 · K. S. Bottigheimer, *English money and Irish land* (1971), appx · B. Taft, 'Voting lists of the council of officers, December 1648', *BIHR*, 52 (1979), 138–54 · Venn, *Alum. Cant.* · BL, Sloane MS 1707, fol. 11 · 'Chief Baron James Reynolds: Baron James Reynolds', *N&Q*, 3rd ser., 3 (1863), 54 · IGI · *CSP dom.*, 1649–57 · R. Dunlop, ed., *Ireland under the Commonwealth*, 2 vols. (1913) · *The diary of Bulstrode Whitelocke, 1605–1675*, ed. R. Spalding, British Academy, Records of Social and Economic History, new ser., 13 (1990) · PRO, PROB 6/334, fol. 336 (new foliation, fol. 313) · *JHC*, 7 (1651–9), 725–6 · *The memoirs of Edmund Ludlow*, ed. C. H. Firth, 2 vols. (1894) · T. Herbert and others, *Memoirs of the two last years of the reign of … King Charles I* (1702) · Thurloe, *State papers* · J. Rushworth, *Historical collections*, new edn, 8 vols. (1721–2) · *The memoirs of James II: his campaigns as duke of York, 1652–1660*, trans. A. L. Sells (1962) · H. A. C. Sturgess, ed., *Register of admissions to the Honourable Society of the Middle Temple, from the fifteenth century to the year 1944*, 3 vols. (1949)

Wealth at death settled £500 p.a. on wife for life and released her portion of £3000; left £500 to college; £500 to hospital in Dublin; Carrick estate (£500 p.a.) to elder brother; plus £100 p.a. for life to another brother; residue to sister and brother-in-law: administration, PRO, PROB 6/334, fol. 336

Reynolds, John (1668–1727), Presbyterian minister, born at Wolverhampton, Staffordshire, on 19 February 1668, was eldest of five children of John Reynolds (*bap.* 1632, *d.* 1683), who was ejected from his Wolverhampton ministry in 1660, and his wife, Elizabeth Hanbury. His father, a friend of Richard Baxter, was skilled in law and physic as well as divinity, and had taken the degree of MD. Reynolds was educated at the free school of Stourbridge, where the family mainly lived from 1661 to 1683, when they moved to a house in the parish of St Giles-in-the-Fields, London. His father, died intestate in December 1683, but Reynolds equitably shared the property with his four siblings.

Intending to enter the ministry, Reynolds matriculated from Pembroke College, Oxford, on 9 July 1684. In 1687 he left the university, where he had formed an acquaintance with Thomas Gilbert, without taking his degree. He preached his first sermon at Worcester in 1693 on Acts 9:26. Apart from some time in Northamptonshire, he spent much of the next three years in Bristol, where he assisted Isaac Noble in ministerial duties and in the education of candidates for the Presbyterian ministry. At his ordination at Oldbury chapel (30 May 1699) he delivered a Trinitarian confession of faith. His original leaning to the establishment only gradually disappeared after a close study of the points at issue between the church and the dissenters, but he was always well disposed to churchmen, and was on good terms with several of the clergy, including Edward Waddington, bishop of Chichester.

From 1699 to 1706 Reynolds was chaplain to Philip Foley's family at Prestwood. From 1706 to 1708 he was co-pastor with James Forbes (1629?–1712) at Gloucester. In 1708 he and Dr Gyles were jointly appointed to take charge of the High Street congregation and academy at Shrewsbury, previously conducted by Samuel Benion, where Reynolds was especially concerned that the 'students should be able ministers of the New Testament' (Reynolds, 125). The Shrewsbury meeting-house was destroyed in the Jacobite riots of 1715, when Reynolds himself was threatened, the rioters crying out for 'the little presbyterian parson, and they wou'd have him' (ibid., 141). He also served as Whitsun-week lecturer at Dudley. Among several works, he published the funeral sermon he delivered on 24 June 1714 for his friend Matthew Henry. Henry and Isaac Watts wrote commendations of Reynolds's major work, *A Practical Discourse of Reconciliation between God and Man*, which was published in 1729.

Reynolds left Shrewsbury early in 1718, owing to ill health, and, after staying with friends in London, he settled at Walsall, where he gave unpaid assistance to the dissenting minister, John Godley, and preached every Sunday morning. There he remained until his death on 24 August 1727. Although his health was indifferent and his nature retiring, Reynolds was highly esteemed, not least by Sarah Savage, who in 1738 confided to her diary her pleasure at being able to see West Bromwich church from her window, 'where that excellent man, Mr Reynolds, was buried. I have desired that my bones be laid beside his, especially that I may stand with him at Christ's right hand in that day' (Matthews, *Congregational Churches*, 121–2).

W. A. SHAW, rev. ALAN P. F. SELL

Sources J. Reynolds, *Memoirs of the life of the late pious and learned Rev. John Reynolds*, 3rd edn (1735–40) · W. Wilson, *The history and antiquities of the dissenting churches and meeting houses in London, Westminster and Southwark*, 4 vols. (1808–14), vol. 1, p. 83; vol. 4, p.368 · *Calamy rev.* · A. G. Matthews, *The Congregational churches of Staffordshire* (1924?), 121–2 · H. McLachlan, *English education under the Test Acts: being the history of the nonconformist academies, 1662–1820* (1931), 84–5 · F. Willmore, *A history of Walsall and its neighbourhood*, new edn (1972) · A. P. F. Sell, *Dissenting thought and the life of the churches: studies in an English tradition* (1990), 332–3 · Foster, *Alum. Oxon.*

Reynolds, John (*bap.* **1714**, *d.* **1788**), naval officer and colonial governor, the son of John Reynolds (1691–1724), latterly clerk of the cheque, Plymouth Dockyard, and his wife, Frances (*b. c.*1692, *d.* after 1738) was probably born at his parents' house in Gardiner's Lane, Westminster, though baptized at St Paul's, Covent Garden, on 26 November 1714. His relation, Sir Joseph *Jekyll, master of the rolls, arranged for him to enter the navy, as a king's letter boy, on 8 May 1728. For six years he served in a frigate, *Alborough*, under Captain Edward Baker until reaching Port Royal, Jamaica, and thereafter with Captain John Gascoigne, engaged in coastal hydrography southwards from Charles Town, South Carolina. He was midshipman ordinary from 8 May 1730 and midshipman from 30 June 1731. In 1733 Gascoigne surveyed the site of Savannah, Georgia, for James Oglethorpe, who returned to England in the *Alborough* in May 1734; this gave Reynolds early personal links with a trustee colony of which Sir Joseph Jekyll, a friend of Oglethorpe, was one of the leading supporters.

Reynolds passed his examination for lieutenant on 31 July 1734. On 21 January 1735 he joined the first-rate *Britannia*, flagship of Admiral Sir John Norris, with the Mediterranean Fleet. Having received a recommendation from Jekyll, Norris made Reynolds a lieutenant at Lisbon on 14 October 1736. The previous day he had been discharged to the *Griffin*, from which he was paid off on 9 May 1737. After Sir Joseph's death in 1738 Lady Jekyll (a sister of Lord Chancellor Somers) recommended Reynolds to her niece's husband, Lord Chancellor Hardwicke, a former protégé of Jekyll.

From 28 July 1738 Reynolds served as third lieutenant, and from 28 June 1739 as second lieutenant, in the *Argyle* on the home station. He was lieutenant of the fireship *Vulcan*, then in the West Indies, from 28 May 1741, and appointed first lieutenant of the *Jersey* on 14 May 1743; from her, on 11 February 1744, he was discharged as first lieutenant to Sir John Norris's flagship the *Victory*, which he fortunately left before she sank with all hands later that year.

On 23 April 1745 Reynolds was promoted commander of the fireship *Scipio* on the home station. Principally through Hardwicke's influence he was moved, in the rank of post captain, to the *Arundel* on 30 October 1746. During the following year the *Arundel* was employed in the channel, cruising with some success against the enemy's trade,

and afterwards in convoy service in the North Sea. In May 1748 he was sent out to Charles Town, and thence to Jamaica. As commodore of a small flotilla he attended on South Carolina, Georgia, and the Bahama Islands, protecting trade, until the peace of 1749. Reynolds remained off Charles Town during the two following years, though he spent only three months at sea in accordance with Governor James Glen's request 'to be ready to proceed directly on any intelligence the Governor might receive about Pyrates' (PRO, ADM 1/2383). Reynolds returned to England in June 1751. He neglected recent Admiralty orders by putting in for repair and water at Lisbon rather than Gibraltar, and was called to account by Admiral Edward Hawke on arrival at Spithead.

In 1752 the Georgia trustees surrendered their charter, and Reynolds—attracted partly by the prospect of continuous employment—desired to become the first crown governor. In December 1752 the earl of Halifax, president of the Board of Trade and Plantations since 1748, assured Hardwicke in writing that he would nominate Reynolds, though nearly two years passed before his appointment (which Halifax had attempted to discourage) on 6 August 1754. He sailed, with little notice, in the small frigate *Port Mahon*, and reached Savannah on 29 October 1754.

Reynolds's appointment was short-lived. He lacked political talent, and his forceful style of government was unlikely to be acceptable for long in a colony which had been largely accustomed, since Oglethorpe's departure in 1743, to ordering its own affairs. For about a year Reynolds's government in Georgia proved acceptable, after which a series of confrontations gave Halifax the opportunity to recall him in August 1756. William Little, Reynolds's overweening secretary, was also recalled, and Halifax's favoured candidate, Henry Ellis, was appointed lieutenant-governor. Reynolds and Little finally took passage in February 1757 in a regular transit vessel, the *Charming Martha*, which in May was captured by a French privateer, the *Comte de Grammont*. Reynolds was taken a prisoner of war into Bayonne, and though he was quickly exchanged all his working papers were confiscated. He arrived in England in July 1757, but it was not until 14 April 1758 that, by recommendation of the Board of Trade, Reynolds ceased to be governor, and was succeeded by Ellis.

By May 1759, through Lord Hardwicke's continuing favour, Reynolds was appointed to the *Firm* (60 guns), in which he joined the fleet off Brest. In June Hawke made him commodore of a squadron of eleven ships to hinder an intended invasion of Ireland, which Reynolds did by chasing many French frigates and transports into the ports of Morbihan. On 17 November he received news of further French movements, which he transmitted to the Admiralty; but he did not himself succeed in rejoining the British fleet until after the battle of Quiberon Bay three days later. His ship being in bad condition, Hawke sent her home to refit, though not without writing Reynolds a letter appreciative of his recent service. In February 1760 Reynolds was moved to the *Temple*, and in March he was superseded. When in England, Reynolds lived at Newington Butts, Surrey, his home for over twenty years. On 13

November 1761 he married, by licence, as a widower (no certain trace has been found of his previous wife), at St John-at-Hackney, Mare Street, Hackney, Middlesex, Maria Catharina Langin (c.1738–1815), daughter of John and Anna Maria Lange, Swabian protestant refugees who had emigrated to Georgia in 1752. Their daughter, Maria Catharina Reynolds, later married James Sowerby, naturalist and artist. In October 1766 Reynolds had a son George (1766–1851) with Mary Thompson (1737–1829), daughter of George and Mary Thompson.

From 1762 until the end of the Seven Years' War in 1763 Reynolds was in command of the frigate *Milford*. This and his previous commission he owed to Lord Hardwicke, for whom Lord Anson, Hardwicke's son-in-law since 1748, usually mediated while latterly first lord of the Admiralty, until Anson's death in 1762. In April 1763, by influence of James Harris, also a Jekyll connection, and a lord of the Admiralty, Reynolds was appointed captain of the *Guarland*, a commission which for financial reasons he soon resigned. After Hardwicke's death in 1764 the second earl of Hardwicke continued to honour responsibilities assumed by his father, and on 6 May 1766 he obtained a commission for Reynolds to command the *Fame*, guardship at Plymouth. On a stormy night in January 1768 the *Fame* broke the swivel of her chain moorings, and was driven ashore. Although apparently with his senior officer's permission, Reynolds had been sleeping on land. A court martial was not deemed necessary but the *Fame* was taken out of commission on 26 February 1768, and Hawke, then first lord of the Admiralty, though tolerant, was displeased.

Following two short commands, by June 1771 Reynolds was again unemployed, and an interview with the earl of Sandwich, first lord of the Admiralty, proved unsuccessful although Reynolds pointed out that he had been employed at sea for only ten and a half of his twenty-five years as captain. A letter from Lord Hardwicke in 1772, however, brought an admission from Sandwich that 'Captain Reynolds is a deserving officer …' (BL, Add. MS 35610, fol. 207), and a promise of the next guardship. Thus Reynolds commanded the *Dublin* from July 1773, and in November was appointed to the *Ocean* at Plymouth, a ship of which he was relieved at the end of 1774. In 1768 he sent to the Admiralty proposals for moving ships in a calm. In 1771 he submitted a plan for manning the navy without press gangs. Neither proposal, however, appears to have been taken further.

Reynolds was promoted rear-admiral on 31 March 1775 but, contrary to his expectations, remained unemployed. Early in 1777 he sought to bribe Lord Sandwich's mistress, Martha Ray, to speak in his favour, the only immediate result of this being that the well-disposed Hardwicke withdrew his patronage. Nevertheless on 29 January 1778 Reynolds was promoted vice-admiral. A little later he had a serious paralytic seizure, from which he never appreciably recovered. His son George entered the navy in 1781; and in 1782 took part in the battle of the Saints. By 1783

Reynolds had moved to a house on the east side of Edgware Road, St Marylebone, Middlesex. In that year, pleading physical loss equivalent to that of an arm, a leg, and in some degree voice, Reynolds was anxious to petition the king for a pension. The Admiralty lords of 1784 declined to approve such a request. Reynolds was promoted admiral on 24 September 1787, and died in St Marylebone parish on 3 February 1788; he was buried in Paddington churchyard, probably 'in a very private manner' (PRO, will, proved 4 Feb 1788). He desired, it was recalled later, no tombstone; certainly none remains. His death is among the earliest recorded in *The Times*; but it was noticed with more detail in *The Georgia Gazette*.

Reynolds's son George was a survivor of the wreck of HMS *Pandora* (1791) off the Great Barrier Reef, after finding some of the *Bounty* mutineers. He became a retired commander in 1831, and was the father of Alfred Reynolds, wood-engraver and printer.   J. S. Reynolds

Sources N. A. M. Rodger, *The wooden world: an anatomy of the Georgian navy* (1986) • N. A. M. Rodger, *The insatiable earl: a life of John Montagu, fourth earl of Sandwich* (1993) • A. D. Candler, ed., *The colonial records of the state of Georgia*, 27: *Original papers of Governor John Reynolds, 1754–6*, ed. K. Coleman and M. Ready (1977) • *Journal of the commissioners for trade and plantations*, [vol. 10]: *From January 1754 to December 1758* (1933) • W. W. Abbott, *Royal governors of Georgia, 1754–1775* (1959) • T. R. Reese, *Colonial Georgia* (1963) • J. A. Henretta, *Salutary neglect: colonial administration under the duke of Newcastle* (1972) • K. Coleman, *Colonial Georgia: a history* (1989) • J. W. Raimo, *Biographical directory of American colonial and revolutionary governors, 1607–1789* (1980) • S. M. Pargellis, 'Reynolds, John', *DAB* • C. C. Jones, *The history of Georgia*, 2 vols. (1883) • W. B. Stephens, *History of Georgia*, 2 vols. (1847) • captain's letters, 1751–3, PRO, ADM MS 1/2383 • BL, Add. MS 35610, fol. 207 • will, PRO, PROB 11/1162, sig. 92 [proved 4 Feb 1788]

Archives BL, corresp. with earls of Hardwicke, Add. MSS 35607–35622, 35909–35910, *passim* • NMM, naval records, incl. Sandwich MSS • PRO, Admiralty records • PRO, Colonial Office records

Likenesses J. Theus of Charleston, oils, c.1750, Smithsonian Institution, Washington, DC, National Portrait Gallery; repro. in M. S. Middleton, *Jeremiah Theus: colonial artist of Charlestown*, rev. edn (1991); [on loan from NMM] • pencil and wash drawing, 1775–9, priv. coll.

Wealth at death see will, PRO, PROB 11/1162, sig. 92, proved 4 Feb 1788

Reynolds, John Hamilton (1794–1852), writer and lawyer, was born on 9 September 1794 in Shrewsbury, the second of five children of George C. Reynolds (1765–1853), a schoolteacher in Shrewsbury and later at Lambeth School and Christ's Hospital, London, and his wife, Charlotte, née Cox (c.1770–1846). Reynolds grew up in Shrewsbury and in Lambeth, London. He left St Paul's School in 1809 on his fifteenth birthday and in the following year became a clerk, first in a newspaper office, and then, in July 1810, in the Amicable Society for a Perpetual Assurance in Fleet Street, where he stayed for six years until April 1816.

Throughout this period, Reynolds eagerly read and wrote poetry in his spare time, corresponding regularly with John Dovaston, a family friend, on literature and the arts. In 1814 his poem *Safie: an Eastern Tale* was published by James Cawthorn and John Martin, a 'downright imitation of Lord Byron' as Reynolds himself described it (Jones, 47). Reynolds's poem, a watered down version of Byron's *The*

John Hamilton Reynolds (1794–1852), by Joseph Severn, 1818

Giaour (1813) had a brief popularity and generated quali-fied admiration from Byron himself. Later in the same year Reynolds published *The Eden of Imagination: a Poem*, which took as its model the locodescriptive mode of Wordsworth's *An Evening Walk* (1793), and during the same year Reynolds published poems in *The Inquirer* and was soon acting as the journal's poetry editor. He was also beginning to meet a number of other aspiring as well as more established writers, artists, and editors, including Benjamin Bailey, John Scott, Horace Smith, Benjamin Robert Haydon, Leigh Hunt, Charles Lamb, and later William Hazlitt. By December 1815 Reynolds had joined the staff of *The Champion*, a weekly Liberal newspaper edited by Scott, where he worked for two years, contributing the-atre criticism, literary reviews and papers, occasional essays, and twenty-two of his own poems. During this time Reynolds also contributed to other journals includ-ing the *Repository of Arts, Literature, Fashions*, the *Gentleman's Magazine*, the *Ladies' Museum* and *The Inquirer*. By April 1816 he felt well enough established as a writer and poet to resign from his job as a clerk to become a full-time writer. In the summer his volume of poems *The Naiad: a Tale, with other Poems* was published by Taylor and Hessey. Character-ized by a fascination with the supernatural and the nature of evil and by its use of the traditional ballad form, the col-lection owed more to Coleridge than to either Words-worth or Byron. The *Naiad* volume was quite widely and rather favourably reviewed.

In October 1816 Reynolds met Keats at Leigh Hunt's house in the Vale of Health in Hampstead. The two young men had much in common: born within a year of each

other, they were from similar backgrounds and shared a fervent, idealistic commitment to poetry. Established within a small circle of young London writers and artists, both were torn between earning a living on the one hand, and devoting their lives to poetry on the other. Over the next few years—until Keats's departure for Italy in Sep-tember 1820—Reynolds and Keats became firm friends. They often wrote in competition or collaboration with each other, and Leigh Hunt named them (together with Shelley) as important poets of the younger generation in a prominent and controversial article in *The Examiner* in December 1816. At the time of his first meeting with Keats, Reynolds was engaged on one of his most ambitious poems, a long poetic romance entitled *The Romance of Youth*. The poem concerned the growth to maturity of a young poet, and was to influence Keats in such works as *Endymion* and *The Fall of Hyperion*.

From the first, however, Reynolds appears to have rec-ognized the genius of Keats above his own talents, and as 1817 progressed, he became increasingly concerned about his lack of financial security. His predicament was exacer-bated by the fact that his mentor John Scott had resigned as editor of *The Champion*; on a more personal level, his engagement to Eliza Powell Drewe (*b*. 1793), a young woman from Exeter, meant that Reynolds was in need of a more secure financial basis from which to embark on mar-ried life. Through the good offices and with the financial aid of his friend James Rice, Reynolds was articled to Fran-cis Fladgate in November 1817. While his legal work pre-vented him from writing full-time—indeed, he was never to complete the second canto of *The Romance of Youth*—Rey-nolds nevertheless continued to write poems, essays, and reviews for the journals. Influenced by Hazlitt's lecture on Boccaccio of February 1818, Reynolds and Keats decided to collaborate on a collection of modernized versions of a selection of Boccaccio's tales. Keats wrote 'Isabella' in spring 1818, while by September Reynolds had completed two poems for the collection, 'The Garden of Florence' and 'The Lady of Provence'.

In April 1819 Reynolds wrote his most famous poem, *Peter Bell*, after seeing an advertisement for a forthcoming poem of the same name by William Wordsworth. Although he had not read Wordsworth's poem, Reynolds wrote his *Peter Bell* as a parody of some of the more senti-mental of the *Lyrical Ballads*, complete with a mock preface and notes which echoed effects of redundancy, verbosity, and self-importance to which Wordsworth's prose was prone. In particular, Reynolds satirized Wordsworth's ten-dency to base his characters on local Lake District peas-ants, and the older poet's sententious idealization of such figures. Reynolds is said to have written the poem and sent it to the printer within twenty-four hours, and it was pub-lished before its 'original' had appeared. Reynolds's *Peter Bell* was such a success that it went into three editions within two months, and even helped to make a popular success of Wordsworth's poem. Reynolds's relative popu-larity at this time is also evident in the reception of his comic drama *One, Two, Three, Four, Five; by Advertisement* which ran at the English Opera House for fifty nights from 17 July 1819. In June 1820 Reynolds published another light-hearted piece, *The Fancy*, a collection of poems loosely based on sport and especially on prize-fighting, and presented as the poetic remains of a young law student, Peter Corcoran. Once again, the book was something of a success, hailed as among the 'first humourous and satirical productions' by one critic (Jones, 193).

During this period Reynolds was also writing for the periodicals and continuing his legal apprenticeship, and in May 1821 he published *The Garden of Florence and other Poems* under the name John Hamilton (Keats had published his 'Isabella' in his 1820 volume of poetry, the plan for a joint collection having been abandoned). Although there were a number of favourable reviews, the *Gentleman's Magazine* and *Scots Magazine* mocked Reynolds's neologisms and loose versification. From now on, Reynolds's literary ambitions were directed towards more ephemeral productions, including helping John Scott and, after his untimely death, Taylor and Hessey, with the editing of the *London Magazine*, the contents of which, for the next few years, were largely the responsibility of Reynolds and the poet Thomas Hood. This was the start of a long friendship between the two men, which was to be cemented by Hood's marriage to Reynolds's sister Jane in 1825, and by the publication of a collaborative collection of satirical poems, *Odes and Addresses to Great People*, in the same year.

By August 1822 Reynolds had qualified as a solicitor and on 31 August he married Eliza in Exeter. As the 1820s and 1830s progressed, Reynolds published a number of light pieces, including farces and comic operas, occasional poems, and a great deal of increasingly journalistic work in the periodicals, especially in Charles Dilke's *Athenaeum*. In the later 1830s Reynolds contributed to *Bentley's Miscellany*, edited by Charles Dickens, and his increasingly desperate financial affairs led him eventually to edit the *New Sporting Monthly Magazine* between August 1838 and December 1840.

Life became increasingly difficult for Reynolds. After some success as a lawyer (and some fame when he was involved in the trial following the death of John Scott in a duel in 1821) Reynolds seems to have been less and less committed to and effective in his work. He was badly affected by the death of his only child, Lucy, at the age of ten in 1835 and seems to have started drinking heavily during this period; by 1838 things had become so bad that he was declared bankrupt. In 1841, although Reynolds had been Hood's friend and solicitor as well as his brother-in-law for many years, there was a breakdown in relations after which the two saw little of each other. In 1847 Reynolds retired from London and took a relatively modest position as assistant clerk to the county court at Newport on the Isle of Wight, where he died at his home, 36 Nodehill, five years later on 15 November 1852. He was buried in the churchyard of Litten on the island; his wife survived him.   ANDREW BENNETT

Sources L. M. Jones, *The life of John Hamilton Reynolds* (1984) · *The letters of John Hamilton Reynolds*, ed. L. H. Jones (Lincoln, NE, [1973]) · G. L. Marsh, *John Hamilton Reynolds: poetry and prose* (1928) · J. Richardson, *Letters from Lambeth* (1981) · *Selected prose of John Hamilton Reynolds*, ed. L. H. Jones (1966) · H. E. Rollins, ed., *The Keats circle: letters and papers and more letters and poems of the Keats circle*, 1 (1965) · W. J. Bate, *John Keats* (1963) · *The letters of John Keats, 1814–1821*, ed. H. E. Rollins, 2 vols. (1958) · A. Motion, *Keats* (1997) · R. Gittings, *John Keats* (1968) · J. Clubbe, 'The Reynolds–Dovaston correspondence', *Keats–Shelley Journal*, 30 (1981), 152–81 · R. Gittings, 'The poetry of John Hamilton Reynolds', *Ariel*, 1 (1970), 7–17

Archives Bristol Reference Library, commonplace book · Harvard U., Houghton L., papers · Princeton University Library, New Jersey, papers · University of Illinois, Urbana-Champaign, papers · Washington University, St Louis, Missouri, papers | BL, accounts with and letters to Richmond Bentley, Add. MSS 46614, 46632A, 46649–46651 · County RO, Shire Hall, Shrewsbury, Dovaston collection

Likenesses J. Severn, watercolour, *c*.1817, Keats House, London · J. Severn, miniature, 1818, NPG [*see illus.*] · silhouette, Keats House, London

Reynolds, John Henry (1842–1927), promoter of technological education, was born in Salford, Lancashire, on 8 February 1842, the son and eldest of eleven children of John Reynolds, a bootmaker, and his wife, Sarah, *née* Hilton. He attended the Lower Mosley Street day school of the Cross Street Unitarian Chapel and, for one year, Manchester grammar school. At twelve he was apprenticed bootmaker to his father and also became a pupil teacher at the chapel's Sunday school. Here he met William Fairbairn, the Revd William Gaskell, and other leading Unitarians. Apart from a course at Owens College, he was self-educated from this time onward. On 19 August 1868 he married Ellen Ferguson at Cross Street Chapel; they had three children.

In 1879 Reynolds was appointed secretary to the Manchester Mechanics' Institution, which by the 1870s survived mainly by providing elementary school classes. But increasing support for primary education from municipal and other sources had greatly reduced the demand for this service; by 1879 it was clearly in decline. To his new task Reynolds brought vision, administrative skills, integrity (a quality some of his predecessors lacked), and powers of persuasion—gifts made the more effective by his enthusiasm for his work. Within a year he had devised a full programme for the survival and future development of the institution. By this time the need for better technical education was widely recognized. In July 1882 it was decided to transform the institution into a technical school.

In 1887 Reynolds admitted that Manchester was in the third class of English towns in its provision of technical education (*Transactions of the Manchester Statistical Society*, 1887, 118–9). He worked hard to set high standards and to recruit the best-qualified staff for the new school, of which he was the principal. Fortunately, money was becoming available. The new City and Guilds of London Institute was one source of funds, while the acts of 1889 and 1890 empowered local authorities to support technical education. Accordingly, the city took over the Manchester Technical School, now renamed the Municipal

Technical School. At the same time Reynolds became secretary of the Manchester corporation technical instruction committee and director of technical instruction. In that capacity he, with members of the committee, visited the technological schools of Europe in 1891 and 1897 (see his published reports). The fine buildings and lavish equipment they saw, particularly in Germany and Switzerland, impressed everyone. Accommodation in Manchester was quite inadequate: Reynolds had had to arrange courses in widely dispersed buildings. In 1898 he toured the United States and Canada on another fact-finding mission, of which he published a report.

Following a grant of land by the Whitworth Institute, what was claimed to be the finest technical college in Britain was built on Sackville Street, Manchester. It was opened in 1902 by the prime minister and renamed the Municipal School of Technology. Reynolds continued in office as principal and as director for higher education in Manchester. In that year the (federal) Victoria University awarded him an honorary MSc.

In the following year Owens College became the autonomous Victoria University of Manchester. Under Reynolds's supervision several courses had reached university standard, and it was agreed that the new university would establish a faculty of technology in the school (1904). Reynolds became dean of the new faculty, with a seat on the senate. Although ten members of staff had been designated professors by the school, there was room for only three on the university senate. These professors and their staffs, also recognized by the university, were paid by the city. However, most of the school's efforts were devoted to part-time and evening classes. As C. H. Herford remarked, many were involved in this development but it was the idealism, the initiative, and the driving power of J. H. Reynolds that made it possible.

After Reynolds retired in 1912 development of the school was less rapid, and it was only in the era of Dr Bowden that development rivalled that of Reynolds's day. It is now, as the University of Manchester Institute of Science and Technology (UMIST), an autonomous university (1994). It is doubtful if Reynolds would have approved of the ending, in 1956, of part-time and evening courses: these, after all, involved intimate links with local industry and with the wider community, links that he, a Manchester radical, held most important. Reynolds spent his last years at Cheadle Hulme. He died on 17 July 1927 while on holiday in Anglesey and was cremated at the southern cemetery, Manchester.   DONALD CARDWELL

Sources D. S. L. Cardwell, ed., *Artisan to graduate* (1974) · J. D. Marshall, 'John Henry Reynolds, pioneer of technical education in Manchester', *Vocational Aspect*, 16/35 (1964), 176–96 · private information (2004) · *Minerva: Jahrbuch der gelehrten Welt, 1904–6* (1905) · Municipal School of Technology, *Calendar for the session* (1903–4) · Municipal School of Technology, *Calendar for the session* (1904–5) · *Manchester Guardian* (18 July 1927) · *Nature*, 120 (1927), 234 · A. Cobden Smith, *John Henry Reynolds, MSc, 1842–1927: a memorial address* (privately printed, 1927) · *Daily Telegraph* (20 July 1927) · *The Times* (19 July 1927) · m. cert.
Archives Man. CL, pamphlets and short papers · University of Manchester Institute of Science and Technology

Likenesses oils, University of Manchester Institute of Science and Technology · photographs, University of Manchester Institute of Science and Technology · photographs, Man. CL
Wealth at death £3042 15s. 4d.: probate, 15 Oct 1927, CGPLA Eng. & Wales

Reynolds, Sir John Russell, baronet (1828–1896), physician and neurologist, was born on 22 May 1828 at Romsey, Hampshire, the second son of the Revd John Reynolds, a Congregational minister, and his second wife, Sarah, daughter of Robert Fletcher of Chester. He was the grandson of Dr Henry Revell *Reynolds (1745–1811), physician-in-ordinary to George III. Reynolds was educated privately, mainly by his father, and studied medicine at University College, London, where he was awarded three gold medals for medicine, clinical medicine, and obstetrics respectively, becoming the university medical scholar and receiving yet another gold medal in physiology and comparative anatomy when he graduated MB in the University of London in 1851. In 1852 he took the degree of MD and began practice in Leeds, where his brother, the Revd Dr Henry Reynolds, was a minister; he lived in, and practised from, a house owned by his brother-in-law, a member of staff of the *Leeds Mercury*. The neurologist Dr Marshall Hall, one of his teachers, was so impressed by Reynolds's potential that he persuaded him to move to London and to take over the house at 38 Grosvenor Street where Hall had lived. Hall, without Reynolds's knowledge, sent out to his patients a printed circular saying that Reynolds had succeeded him in practice and, in consequence, incurred the censure of the Royal College of Physicians. Reynolds was exonerated from all blame and was duly elected a fellow of the college in 1859. In 1855 he was appointed assistant physician to the Hospital for Sick Children. In 1857 he became assistant physician to the Westminster Hospital, in 1859 assistant physician at University College Hospital, and in 1865 he was elected professor of the principles and practice of medicine at University College. In 1878 he was appointed physician-in-ordinary to the queen's household.

Reynolds's reputation as a physician, and more especially as a neurologist, grew: in 1869 he was elected a fellow of the Royal Society and in 1883 vice-president of the Royal Medical and Chirurgical Society. He delivered the Lumleian lecture at the Royal College of Physicians in 1867, the Harveian oration in 1884, and was elected president of the college in 1893 by a margin of two votes on the second ballot over Samuel Wilks (who subsequently succeeded him after his death). He was re-elected in 1894 and 1895, and on 1 January 1895 was created a baronet. He became president of the British Medical Association in 1894 and presided with grace and distinction over its annual meeting in 1895.

Reynolds was married first at St Pancras Old Church, London, on 28 August 1852 to Margaret Susannah Ainslie (d. 1880), and second, on 8 March 1881, to Frances (b. 1834/5), widow of Charles John Champion Crespigny and daughter of William Plunkett, barrister. Reynolds left no children.

From early in his career Reynolds took a particular interest in disorders of the nervous system, publishing in 1854 *Vertigo*, in 1855 *Diagnosis of Diseases of the Brain, Spinal Cord, Nerves and their Appendages*, and in 1857 *Tables for the Diagnosis of Diseases of the Brain*. In 1861 he published a treatise on epilepsy, embracing the results of experimental studies he had carried out in collaboration with Dr William Squire. 1871 saw the appearance of his *Lectures on the Clinical Uses of Electricity*, and in 1872 he wrote *On the Scientific Value of the Legal Tests of Insanity*. Many other papers in medical periodicals and in the transactions of learned societies flowed from his pen, but perhaps his reputation rested above all upon his editorship of *A System of Medicine*, published in five volumes as a multi-author work between 1866 and 1879. A contemporary commented that while the essays in these volumes were of varying merit, they were generally of high value, having been written by the most eminent physicians who could be induced to write. Reynolds himself wrote several sections on nervous diseases. He was recognized to be proficient in German and an outstanding classical scholar with considerable literary skills; in 1893 he published *Walter Hayle Walshe MD: a Biographical Sketch*.

Studiously grave and quiet in manner, Reynolds nevertheless was a substantial orator with a rigidly strict code of honour and behaviour, but was full of kindness and sympathy towards his patients and his colleagues. He loved precision, order, and systematic classification of diseases, and his lectures were frequently compelling and always well attended. Dr W. R. Gowers was one of his most admiring and devoted pupils. Lady Reynolds, his second wife, supported him devotedly in his final years, during which he became progressively more frail but continued to fulfil his responsibilities to the Royal College and the British Medical Association.

In the winter of 1895–6 Reynolds's health began to fail and he felt unable to offer himself for re-election as president of the college, but early in that year he was able to receive in person honorary LLD degrees from the universities of Aberdeen and Edinburgh. Having lived in Grosvenor Street for forty-four years, he died at his home on 29 May 1896, the result of successive respiratory infections following a fall when leaving his carriage to enter his house. He was survived by his second wife. While he made no fundamental discovery, Reynolds's reputation as a teacher and practising doctor has ensured for him a lasting place in the archives of British neurology.

WALTON OF DETCHANT

Sources *DNB* · Munk, *Roll*, 4.116 · *The Lancet* (6 June 1896) · *Garrison's history of neurology*, rev. L. McHenry, 2nd edn (1969), 305–7 · *BMJ* (6 June 1896), 1422–5 · m. cert. [Frances Crespigny] · *CGPLA Eng. & Wales* (1896)
Archives Essex RO, Chelmsford, corresp. | W. Sussex RO, letters to Richard Cobden
Likenesses S. Hodges, oils, 1882, RCP Lond. · Beynon and Co., coloured lithograph, Wellcome L.
Wealth at death £11,142 4s. 2d.: probate, 13 July 1896, *CGPLA Eng. & Wales*

Reynolds, John Stuckey (1791–1874), civil servant and promoter of teacher training, born in Manchester on 13 September 1791, was the son of John and Ann Reynolds of Manchester. His father later held the office of comptrolling surveyor of the port of London. His mother belonged to the Stuckey family—her brother, Vincent Stuckey, being a banker at Langport in Somerset. Reynolds was educated at the Langport grammar school, but when fourteen years old secured an appointment in the Audit Office in London. In 1806 he was passed on to the Treasury, where he was quickly promoted and received a series of special votes of thanks from the lords of the Treasury, and in 1815 a grant of money. He became private secretary to three successive secretaries of the Treasury. In 1822–3 he was secretary to the Irish revenue commission, and rendered great service in reconstituting the fiscal system. Later on he was one of the heads of the commissariat department. In 1834 his health broke down through overwork, and in March 1835 he retired from the public service. From 1835 to 1837 he had a position in the London Joint Stock Bank, which his uncle Stuckey had raised to a commanding position. He had married in 1819 Mary Anne, second daughter of Robert Bagehot of Langport. Throughout his career Reynolds studied political economy and the currency. On these subjects he wrote much, signed and anonymous, including *Practical Observations on Mr Ricardo's Principles of Political Economy and Taxation* (1822).

During a visit to Dublin in 1823 Reynolds underwent an evangelical conversion experience. Thereafter he combined his official duties and banking interests with work for philanthropic and religious causes. Infant education particularly attracted his interest, and on his return to London he set up an infant school in Fulham. In 1828 he became one of the proprietors of the evangelical *Record* newspaper. He was consulted by David Nasmith, the originator of the London City Mission. After retiring from banking in 1837 he did much charitable work in the parish of St Giles-in-the-Fields, and was an active supporter of the Colonial and Continental Church Society and of African missions. He was involved in an unsuccessful venture to found a Christian college in Malta. Resident at Hampstead from 1836, he secured an evangelical ministry at St John's Chapel in that parish.

Reynolds's work in establishing infant schools in London, and in stimulating their formation elsewhere in England, brought him into contact with Charles Mayo (1792–1846) and his sister Elizabeth Mayo, the earliest English advocates of Pestalozzi's system of education. In May 1836 Reynolds, with John Bridges, founded in Southampton Street, Holborn, an institution to train teachers in Pestalozzian principles. Called the Home and Colonial School Society, it enjoyed the support of a number of peers of evangelical leanings. The training institution opened with three students, but it quickly grew, and in 1837 it was moved to Gray's Inn Road, where one of the practising schools was called after him. Subsequently it was divided into two—a secondary and an elementary branch—the former being located at Highbury and the latter at Wood Green. During his lifetime the college trained some 4000 teachers. Reynolds died at his home, 4 Cannon Place, Squire's Mount, Hampstead, London, on 11 May 1874. He was buried in the graveyard of Langport church.

FOSTER WATSON, rev. M. C. CURTHOYS

Sources *The Record* (15 May 1874) · *Home and Colonial Memorials* (1881) [Christmas] · Boase, *Mod. Eng. biog.* · W. P. McCann and F. A. Young, *Samuel Wilderspin and the infant school movement* (1982) · private information (1896) · D. M. Lewis, ed., *The Blackwell dictionary of evangelical biography, 1730–1860*, 2 vols. (1995)
Likenesses J. Scarlett Potter, high relief medallion; copy, Home and Colonial Training College, Highbury, London in 1896 · engraving (after J. S. Scarlett Potter), repro. in J. Cassell, *Household guide* (1870), 353
Wealth at death under £6000: probate, 6 June 1874, *CGPLA Eng. & Wales*

Reynolds, Sir Joshua (1723–1792), portrait and history painter and art theorist, was born on 16 July 1723 at Plympton, Devon, the seventh of ten (or possibly eleven) children of Samuel Reynolds (1681–1745), schoolmaster, and his wife, Theophila Potter (1688–1756) of Great Torrington, Devon. Reynolds's maternal grandfather was Humphrey Potter, rector of Nymet Rowland and curate-in-charge of Lostwithiel, his great-grandfather being the eminent mathematician the Revd Thomas *Baker. Samuel Reynolds's family also numbered several prominent clergymen. His father, John, had been vicar of St Thomas's, Exeter, and prebendary of Exeter. His uncle, also John, was a fellow of King's College, Cambridge, and Eton College, while another uncle, Joshua, was a fellow and bursar of Corpus Christi College, Oxford, and rector of Stoke Charity, Hampshire. The young Joshua Reynolds was probably named after this uncle. Yet in the baptismal register of Plympton St Maurice, Reynolds's name was entered on 30 July 1723 as 'Joseph son of Samu^l Reynolds Clerk', the entry being amended only after his death. This may have been a simple clerical error, or perhaps Samuel Reynolds had a change of heart and renamed his seventh child.

Education and apprenticeship, 1723–1743 On 9 December 1711 Samuel Reynolds, a former scholar of Corpus Christi College, Oxford, had married at Monksleigh, near Torrington, Devon, having given up his fellowship at Balliol College, Oxford, earlier that year. Four years later, at the age of thirty-four, he was appointed master of the free grammar school, Plympton. It was here that Joshua Reynolds was educated by his father. Classes were small and the curriculum, in line with more advanced Lockean precepts, would have extended beyond the parameters of classical scholarship, to include geography, arithmetic, and drawing. In addition to his teaching Reynolds's father maintained regular correspondence with friends on topics ranging from medicine to metaphysics. He observed the stars through his telescope, cast horoscopes, and wrote treatises on subjects as diverse as theology and gout. Reynolds, too, conversed with his father's friends, notably the Revd Zachariah Mudge, whom Edmund Burke later described as 'very learned & thinking & much inclined to Philosophy in the spirit of the Platonists' (Hilles, *Literary Career*, 7). In addition to formal lessons, the young Reynolds was encouraged to read independently. Into his commonplace

Sir Joshua Reynolds (1723–1792), self-portrait, *c*.1780

book (MS, Yale University) he copied passages from classical authors: Theophrastus, Plutarch, Seneca, Marcus Antonius, and Ovid, as well as Shakespeare, Milton, Pope, Dryden, Addison, Steele, and Aphra Behn. Significantly, the commonplace book also includes extracts from the writings on art theory by Leonardo da Vinci, Charles Alphonse Du Fresnoy, and André Félibien. The most influential text studied by Reynolds, however, was Jonathan Richardson's *An Essay on the Theory of Painting* of 1715. Lost for nearly 200 years, Reynolds's own annotated copy of Richardson's *Essay* turned up in a Cambridge bookshop, bearing the signature 'J. Reynolds Pictor' (G. Watson, 'Joshua Reynolds's copy of Richardson', *Review of English Studies*, 14, 1991, 9–12).

Reynolds's parents encouraged all their children to take a practical interest in art, his elder sister, Elizabeth, recalling how they had been allowed to draw on the whitewashed walls of a long passage with burnt sticks. As James Boswell later noted, Reynolds's 'two eldest sisters did little things … and he copied them. He used to copy all the frontispieces and plates in books' (Hilles, *Portraits*, 20–21). Several of these copies have survived (J. Edgcumbe, 'Reynolds's earliest drawings', *Burlington Magazine*, 129, 1987, 724–6). They include a slight perspective drawing from *The Practice of Perspective* by Jean Dubreuil, a detail of a library from William Parson's English translation of Félibien, *The Tent of Darius Explain'd*, and a figure adapted from Jacob Cats's *Spiegel* of 1656.

Reynolds's first recorded portrait, made at the age of twelve, dates from 1735. The subject was a local clergyman named Thomas Smart, tutor to Reynolds's boyhood friend Richard Edgcumbe. The painting, apparently made at the behest of Lord Edgcumbe, was executed in a boathouse using shipwright's paint and a piece of sailcloth. In 1738, when Reynolds was fourteen, his father entered into correspondence with a neighbouring landowner, James Bulteel, concerning his son's career prospects. Bulteel suggested that Joshua should go to London, offering to introduce him personally to 'those in artistic circles' (Hudson, 14). It was also suggested that Reynolds might train under his father as an apothecary, Reynolds himself declaring that he would rather be an apothecary than 'an ordinary painter' (ibid., 15). However, in the spring of 1740 it was agreed that Reynolds should be bound to the Devonian artist Thomas Hudson for a period of four years, rather than a full seven-year term as stipulated by the artists' guild, the Painter–Stainers' Company.

Hudson lived and worked in Newman's Row, Lincoln's Inn Fields, London, although he still spent a good deal of time catering to his native west country clientele. Reynolds's daily routine at this time involved running errands, preparing canvases, painting accessories in portraits, and perhaps even making replicas of Hudson's pictures. He also made drawings from casts of antique statuary, including one of the Laocoön. Even so, in later life Reynolds regretted that he had not received a proper academic training, lacking 'the facility of drawing the naked figure, which an artist ought to have' (Works, 1.xlix). In 1821 over fifty of his academic studies from both the male and the female figure were sold at auction. In terms of sheer numbers alone these drawings suggest that Reynolds had been in the habit of drawing from the living model, probably at the St Martin's Lane Academy.

In Hudson's studio Reynolds also made copies after pen-and-ink drawings by Guercino. They are uniformly of a very high quality, and Hudson retained several of them among his own old-master drawings collection. Reynolds's knowledge of old-master paintings also developed during this time, principally through attending auctions, Hudson being in the habit of allowing him to bid on his behalf. It was at one such auction, at the sale of the earl of Oxford in March 1742, that Reynolds managed covertly to shake the hand of one of his boyhood heroes, Alexander Pope.

Early career, 1743–1749 Reynolds's apprenticeship with Hudson ended abruptly in the summer of 1743, occasioned apparently by a minor disagreement over Reynolds's refusal to carry out an errand. The quarrel was quickly patched up, and their relationship resumed on a more equal footing. By December 1744 Samuel Reynolds reported that 'Joshua by his master's means is introduced into a club composed of the most famous men in their profession' (Leslie and Taylor, 1.28). This club, composed of artists and connoisseurs with a common interest in old-master prints and drawings, probably met at Old Slaughter's Coffee House in St Martin's Lane, which the contemporary engraver and diarist George Vertue described as 'a rendezvous of persons of all languages and nations, Gentry, artists and others' (Vertue, Note books, 3.91).

By the autumn of 1743 Reynolds was dividing his portrait practice between London and Plymouth Dock. He made the most of the opportunities presented, his father reporting in January 1744 that he 'has drawn twenty already, and has ten more bespoke' (Cotton, Works, 58). In order to expedite the process, he briefly went into partnership with an unnamed artist who painted the bodies while Reynolds concentrated on the heads. On one occasion this resulted in the inadvertent production of a portrait of a man with two hats, one on his head and the other tucked under his arm (Whitley, 1.104). It was during this time, according to Reynolds, that he 'became very careless about his profession, and lived … in a great deal of dissipation with but indifferent company' (J. Prior, Life of Edmond Malone, 1860, 404–5). The few surviving portraits of this period, notably those of the Kendall family (Mannings, Reynolds, 1285–6), indicate that Reynolds was then working very much in the manner of Hudson, turning out competent, if unexceptional, works.

Reynolds's burgeoning talent emerges more clearly in the portraits of his immediate family, painted about 1745–6, notably those of his sister Frances (known as Fanny) *Reynolds, his father (City Museum and Art Gallery, Plymouth), and his own self-portrait (priv. coll.). The principal pictorial influence on all three portraits is Rembrandt, the artist who was to influence Reynolds more profoundly than any other, especially in his earlier career. During this period Reynolds also painted a number of self-portraits in the manner of Rembrandt, of which the most celebrated (c.1749; NPG) shows him peering out towards the viewer, shading his eyes with his hand.

After his father's death on Christmas day 1745 Reynolds's mother, Theophila, vacated the schoolhouse at Plympton and moved to nearby Torrington, where she lived with her eldest daughter, Mary, until her own death in 1756. Reynolds, meanwhile, took a house in Plymouth Dock with his two unmarried sisters, Fanny and Jane. Although he was active in London, his principal patrons were from the west country, notably Richard Eliot, MP for St Germans and Liskeard and auditor and receiver-general to Frederick, prince of Wales, in Cornwall. In addition to his various portraits of members of the Eliot family, Reynolds painted their friend Captain John Hamilton (priv. coll.). When he saw this portrait many years later, Reynolds was 'surprised to find it so well done; and comparing it with his later works, with that modesty which always accompanies genius, lamented that in such a series of years he should not have made a greater progress in his art' (Malone, 1.xi).

By 1747 Reynolds was spending extended periods in London, now maintaining a studio in apartments on the west side of St Martin's Lane. Little is known about his personal life at that time, although he appears to have been romantically attached to a Miss Weston of Great Queen Street, Lincoln's Inn Fields, who may have been related to Bishop Stephen Weston of Exeter. The tone and content of the letters he wrote to her on his way to Italy (including one signed 'From your slave') indicate that they were on intimate terms. Other friends included the painters Robert and

Simon Pine and John Wilkes, the radical. In November 1748 the *Universal Magazine* included Reynolds's name in a list of fifty-seven 'Painters of our own nation now living, many of whom have distinguished themselves by their performances, and who are justly deemed eminent masters'. Of those named only Thomas Gainsborough was younger. In 1748 Reynolds was also commissioned by the corporation of Plympton to paint portraits of Lieutenant Paul Henry Ourry (Saltram, Devon) and Commodore George Edgcumbe (NMM), younger brother of Reynolds's boyhood friend Richard Edgcumbe. Through Edgcumbe, Reynolds became acquainted with Augustus Keppel, a younger son of the second earl of Albemarle, who on 26 April 1749 made an unscheduled stop at Plymouth on board the *Centurion*. Two weeks later, on 11 May, Reynolds set sail with Keppel for the Mediterranean.

Italy and France, 1749–1752 Reynolds travelled with Keppel from Plymouth to Minorca, with brief stops at Lisbon, Cadiz, and Gibraltar, and a detour to Morocco in order to secure the release of the imprisoned British consul. Reynolds had a pleasant journey, taking wine with Keppel in his cabin, reading his books, and observing a bull-fight in Spain. They arrived at Port Mahón on 18 August 1749. Here Reynolds suffered a riding accident in which he sustained injuries to his face, telling Miss Weston that his lips were 'spo[iled now for] kissing' (*Letters*, 7). Reynolds was compelled to remain on Minorca for longer than he had planned, although it gave him the opportunity to paint portraits of the British garrison stationed there, and earned him upwards of £100. Many years later an old soldier recalled to Fanny Burney: 'He drew my picture there, and then he knew how to take a moderate price; but now I vow, ma'am, 'tis scandalous—scandalous indeed! To pay a fellow here seventy guineas for scratching out a head!' (*The Early Journals and Letters of Fanny Burney*, ed. L. Troide, 1994, 3.414).

In January 1750 Reynolds left Port Mahón for Italy, and by Easter was in Rome. There he set about making copies of old-master paintings. They included a small copy of Raphael's *School of Athens* and a full-scale copy of Guido Reni's *St Michael*, which Reynolds recorded having made in Santa Maria della Concezione between 30 May and 10 June, and which his niece later presented to George IV. Reynolds spent many hours in the Vatican scrutinizing the work of Michelangelo and Raphael's frescoes in the Stanze. As he later recalled:

> I found myself in the midst of works executed upon principles with which I was unacquainted: I felt my ignorance and stood abashed. Notwithstanding my disappointment, I proceeded to copy some of those excellent works. I viewed them again and again; I even affected to admire them, more than I really did. (*Works*, 1.xvi)

He also made a thorough inspection of the city's myriad churches and religious foundations, and the spacious private palaces owned by patrician families such as the Colonna, Borghese, and Barberini. His impressions, in the form of both sketches and written description, were recorded in notebooks (MSS, department of prints and drawings, BM; Sir John Soane's Museum, London; Harvard

U., Fogg Art Museum; Metropolitan Museum, New York; Beinecke Library, Yale University; priv. coll.). Collectively the notebooks reveal that while Reynolds respected the high Renaissance he was instinctively drawn to the art of the later sixteenth century and seventeenth century, including a number of lesser-known artists such as Federico Barocci, Andrea Sacchi, and Sacchi's pupil Carlo Maratta.

Reynolds was a diligent student. He also had a keen sense of humour, as the series of caricatures he produced during his time in Rome reveal. Of these, the most ambitious was an inventive parody of Raphael's *School of Athens* (NG Ire.), depicting a rabble of assorted 'milordi', tutors, painters, and picture dealers, many of whom were close personal friends. Unlike many of his contemporaries, Reynolds did not undergo any sort of formal training in Italy. However, he formed friendships with a number of continental artists, including the young French decorative painter Gabriel-François Doyen, with whom he swore a vow of friendship before the statue of Marcus Aurelius, and Claude-Joseph Vernet, then among the most popular painters of Roman landscapes and seascapes. He also met an Italian youth, Giuseppe Marchi, who returned with him to England, becoming his pupil and lifelong factotum.

Reynolds left Rome on 5 April 1752. Following a brief visit to Naples he set out for Florence on 3 May, accompanied by the artists John Astley and Samuel Hone. They travelled via Assisi, Perugia, and Arezzo. In Florence the sculptor Joseph Wilton, whom he had known in Rome and whose portrait he now painted (NPG), acted as Reynolds's guide. Reynolds made a careful study of works in the Pitti Palace, including Raphael's *Madonna della sedia*, Titian's *Mary Magdalen* ('an immense deal of hair, but painted to the utmost perfection'; Reynolds, 'Notebooks', BM, LB 12, fol. 29v), and two large paintings of Henry IV by Rubens (now in the Uffizi gallery, Florence). His predilection for mannerism surfaced once more in his enthusiastic comments on the art of Barocci and Matteo Rosselli and on the sculpture of Giambologna, whom he then rated as highly as Michelangelo.

On 4 July 1752 Reynolds left Florence for Bologna, where he expressed a particular admiration for Lodovico Carracci, an artist whom he was to regard with exaggerated respect throughout the rest of his life. After ten days in Bologna, Reynolds travelled to Venice via Modena, Parma, Mantua, and Ferrara, reaching Venice on 24 July 1752. There he spent time with the Italian painter Francesco Zuccarelli, analysing the technical methods of the great Venetian colourists Titian, Tintoretto, and Veronese. He also found time to make sketches of paintings by Giambattista Tiepolo. Improbably, his greatest praise was reserved for a large crucifixion in the church of San Lio, by the minor baroque artist Pietro Muttoni della Vecchia (1605–1678), a work which he declared to be 'equal to any masters whatsoever' (Reynolds, 'Notebooks', BM, LB 13, fols. 78r and 48v).

Reynolds left Venice on 16 August 1752, and travelled to Padua, Milan, and Turin. Late in August, accompanied by

Marchi, he crossed the Alps, where he had a chance encounter with his old master, Thomas Hudson, and the French sculptor François Roubiliac, who were on their way to Rome. Temporarily short of money, Reynolds journeyed alone to Paris by coach, Marchi following behind on foot. Reynolds arrived in Paris on 15 September, Marchi three days later (sketchbook, Metropolitan Museum, New York, fol. 178). In Paris Reynolds spent time with the architect William Chambers, whose fiancée he then painted (Kenwood House, London). He also looked at works by the old masters, including Van Dyck, Jordaens, Rubens, Rembrandt, and Titian. However, he concluded that the French 'cannot boast above one painter of a truly just and correct taste', Nicholas Poussin (Leslie and Taylor, 1.86–7). After a month Reynolds headed for Calais, where he was reunited with Hudson and Roubiliac. They crossed the channel to England together, Reynolds arriving in London with Marchi on 16 October. Reynolds did not return to Italy. However, he was to make two further visits to Paris in 1768 (9 September – 3 October) and 1771 (15 August to early September).

Appearance and character Reynolds was about 5 feet 6 inches tall, with ruddy, rounded facial features. He was partially deaf, which caused him in later life to affect a large silver ear-trumpet. He blamed the affliction upon a chill caught in the Sistine Chapel, although it was probably hereditary, as was his slight harelip. 'His pronunciation', recalled a female acquaintance, 'was tinctured with the accent of Devonshire; his features coarse, his outward appearance slovenly' (C. Knight, *Autobiography*, ed. J. W. Kate, 1861, 1.9). Although he could, when occasion demanded, dress smartly, he preferred to assume a casual demeanour, taking snuff while he painted, and often spilling it down his waistcoat. Among friends, of whom he had many of both sexes, Reynolds was admired for his generosity, even temper, and capacity for listening. His dinner parties were notorious for their air of anarchic bonhomie, Reynolds invariably inviting far more guests than could be accommodated at his table. He was addicted to card games and was an incorrigible gambler. As a fellow artist observed: 'If He went into a Company where there was a Pharo table, or any game of chance, He generally left behind him whatever money He had abt. him' (Farington, *Diary*, 2.307). Yet in private Reynolds could be cynical and aloof, particularly towards his pupils and his younger sister, Fanny, who acted as his housekeeper during his middle years.

Early maturity, 1752–1760 Following a short reunion with family and friends in Devon, Reynolds resumed his portrait practice in London, initially in apartments at 104 St Martin's Lane and subsequently at a large house at 5 Great Newport Street (afterwards demolished), where his sister Fanny joined him as housekeeper. Among the first portraits he painted on his return one depicted Giuseppe Marchi (RA) in an exotic 'oriental' headdress and crimson coat, which he retained in his studio as an advertisement. He also made portraits of a number of prominent whig grandees, including the fourth duke of Devonshire, Lord

Grafton, and the secretary of state, Lord Holdernesse. However, it was his full-length portrait of Augustus Keppel (NMM) that revealed the extent of his ambition. The figure's pose was modelled on a statue of Apollo by the seventeenth-century French sculptor Pierre Legros the younger, the treatment of light and colour being inspired by Tintoretto.

During the 1750s Reynolds began to experiment increasingly with his painting technique, employing an unusually wide range of pigments, oils, and varnishes. While these experiments often resulted in brilliantly coloured and highly textured works, the instability of certain pigments (notably red lake, carmine, and orpiment) and his incautious combining of incompatible materials resulted in fading and cracking. These shortcomings did not appear to concern Reynolds, who, when challenged, retorted, 'all good pictures crack' (Leslie and Taylor, 1.112–13). At this time Reynolds also began to tender out the painting of costume in his portraits to professional drapery painters, notably Peter Toms and George Roth, who also painted drapery for Hudson. By now Reynolds was extremely busy, producing over 100 portraits a year. And as he became more successful so his prices rose accordingly. In 1753 he charged 48 guineas for a full-length portrait; by 1759 the price had risen to 100 guineas, and by 1764 to 150 guineas (Cormack, 105). Reynolds often worked a seven-day week, save for a hiatus in the months of July and August, when his fashionable clientele deserted the city. From 1755 until he ceased painting in 1790 Reynolds noted appointments with his sitters in small diaries, or 'pocket books', of which most have survived (RA; Cottonian Library, Plymouth), and which provide detailed information on his working life and social engagements.

By the late 1750s Reynolds had established a systematic method of determining the attitudes chosen for portraits, keeping a portfolio of engravings after his own and other artists' works from which sitters could choose and adapt poses. The first mezzotint engraving after one of his paintings was *Lady Charlotte Fitzwilliam*, made by the Irishman James MacArdell, who before his death in 1765 engraved thirty-seven plates after Reynolds. Subsequent engravers included James Watson, John Dean, John Raphael Smith, Valentine Green, and his own pupils, Marchi and William Doughty. These engravings, as much as the paintings themselves, were responsible for promoting Reynolds's work at home and abroad, and were exhibited by engravers in their own right, occasionally even prior to Reynolds's original paintings. Reynolds, who did not charge engravers to copy his works, recognized the importance of prints, allegedly stating after MacArdell's death, 'by this man I shall be immortalized' (Waterhouse, 1973, 20).

By the mid-1760s Reynolds's painting style was emulated by a number of his contemporaries, notably Francis Cotes and Tilly Kettle. Reynolds's own relations with his fellow artists were generally cordial, although he seldom became close. An exception was the Scottish portraitist Allan Ramsay, who exerted a considerable influence over

Reynolds's own work, and whom Reynolds befriended in 1757. As Horace Walpole memorably remarked, 'Mr. Reynolds and Mr. Ramsay can scarce be rivals, their manners are so different. The former is bold, and has a kind of tempestuous colouring; yet with dignity and grace; the latter is all delicacy'. He added somewhat unfairly, 'Mr. Reynolds seldom succeeds in women; Mr. Ramsay is formed to paint them' (Walpole, *Corr.*, 15.47). As his portrait of Georgiana, Countess Spencer, and her daughter reveals (1760–66; priv. coll.), Reynolds was capable of conveying the same air of intimacy and naturalism which pervades Ramsay's portraiture, although he possessed a directness to which Ramsay seldom aspired.

The middle period, 1760–1768 In the summer of 1760 Reynolds purchased a lease on a house at 47 Leicester Square, then among the most fashionable residential areas of the capital. (It was subsequently converted into auction rooms and demolished in 1937.) Reynolds remained there for the rest of his life. He marked his arrival with a grand ball, and set about completely refurbishing the property, adding a series of studios and a picture gallery to the rear of the premises where he displayed his paintings alongside his growing collection of old-master paintings. He also acquired a secondhand coach in which he encouraged his sister to ride, to her considerable embarrassment. Reynolds's studio was a small octagonal room, lit by a single window situated high above the ground. Portrait sitters occupied an upholstered armchair (now in the RA), revolving on castors and raised about 18 inches from the floor on a dais. Reynolds stood, observing his sitters at eye level, looking directly at them or at their reflection in a mirror. According to one sitter he would 'walk away several feet, then take a long look at me and the picture as we stood side by side, then rush up to the portrait and dash at it in a kind of fury. I sometimes thought he would make a mistake and paint on me instead of the picture' (W. P. Frith, *My Autobiography and Reminiscences*, 1888, 3.124).

In April 1760 Reynolds participated in the first annual exhibition of works held by the Society of Artists at the Society of Arts on the Strand. He exhibited five pictures including *Elizabeth Gunning, Duchess of Hamilton and Argyll* (Lady Lever Art Gallery, Port Sunlight), the first in a long line of public female full-length portraits in the 'grand manner'. Reynolds exhibited with the Society of Artists every year (except 1767) until 1768. Among the works he showed there were *Laurence Sterne* (1761; NPG), *Garrick between Tragedy and Comedy* (1762; priv. coll.), *Nelly O'Brien* (1763; Wallace Collection, London), *Lady Sarah Bunbury* (1765; Art Institute, Chicago), and *Mrs Hale as 'Euphrosyne'* (1766; priv. coll.). Of these *Garrick between Tragedy and Comedy* provides the clearest indication of Reynolds's ambition. On a formal level it displays Reynolds's knowledge of the tenets of Western post-Renaissance art theory, the figures of Comedy and Tragedy representing the choice to be made by the artist between the allure of colour and the strictures of line. It also reveals, through a parodic allusion to the classical theme of the Choice of Hercules, how Reynolds perceived that painting could aspire to the level

of poetry and claim its rightful place among the liberal arts.

Like so many of Reynolds's paintings *Garrick* borrowed pictorial devices from a number of other artists (in this case Rubens, Guido Reni, and William Dobson). During his lifetime critics believed that these 'borrowings' indicated a lack of creativity. And it has since been suggested that Reynolds himself hoped that they would not be detected (E. Wind, 'Borrowed attitudes in Reynolds and Hogarth', *Journal of the Warburg and Courtauld Institutes*, 2, 1938–9, 182–5). Yet for Reynolds and his contemporaries, pictorial references to old-master paintings were visual counterparts to the Augustan literary cult of imitation. For Reynolds, as for Johnson, imitation was a 'kind of middle composition between translation and original design, which pleases when the thoughts are unexpectedly applicable, and the parallels lucky' (*The Works of Samuel Johnson*, ed. A. Murphy, 1792, 11.132). To Reynolds these borrowings constituted an intellectual and visual game, as he plundered his own sketchbooks, his portfolios of prints, and paintings in order to enrich the iconography of otherwise formulaic society portraits.

In 1759 Reynolds painted a portrait of George, prince of Wales (Royal Collection), presumably with the hope of securing further royal patronage. In the following year his hopes were dashed when the prime minister, Lord Bute, recommended Allan Ramsay to the post of principal painter to the king. From this moment there was increasing antipathy between Reynolds and the king. Professionally it did Reynolds no harm whatsoever for, as Johnson remarked, 'it is no reflection on Mr. Reynolds not to be employed by them; but it will be a reflection on the Court not to have employed him' (G. B. Hill, ed., *Johnsonian Miscellanies*, 1897, 2.401–2).

Johnson, whom Reynolds had met about 1756, was the single most important influence on Reynolds's life during the 1750s and 1760s. 'For my own part I acknowledge the highest obligations to him. He may be said to have formed my mind and brushed off from it a great deal of rubbish' (Hilles, *Portraits*, 66). Later, in August 1764, when Reynolds was struck with a serious illness, Johnson wrote to him, 'if I should lose you, I should lose almost the only Man whom I call a Friend' (Boswell, *Life*, 1.486). Reynolds painted Johnson on a number of occasions; the earliest (NPG) portrayed him, as Boswell recalled, 'in the attitude of sitting in his easy chair in deep meditation'. Later, in a painting for the wealthy brewer Henry Thrale, Reynolds attempted to capture Johnson's short-sightedness, which resulted in the celebrated retort, 'He may paint himself as deaf if he chuses … but I will not be *blinking Sam*' (H. L. Piozzi, *Anecdotes of the Late Samuel Johnson, LL.D*, 1786, 248). In 1759 Johnson commissioned Reynolds to write three essays for *The Idler*, thus launching his literary career. The essays addressed the concepts of beauty, imitation, and nature, and prefigured arguments that were to underpin his *Discourses on Art*, begun some ten years later.

In the summer of 1762 Reynolds and Johnson made a six-week tour of the west country, which included visits to family and friends. Back in London, in February 1764, Reynolds formed a dining club for Johnson's immediate circle. The Literary Club, or 'The Club', as it became known, was originally restricted to nine members, including Reynolds, Johnson, Edmund Burke, and Oliver Goldsmith, who were then Reynolds's closest companions. Reynolds painted Goldsmith between 1766 and 1767, in a dignified profile (Knole, Kent), Reynolds's sister Fanny referring to it as 'the most flattered picture she ever knew her brother to have painted' (Northcote, *Life*, 1.326). At about the same time Reynolds also painted a half-length portrait of Burke (priv. coll.), and a double portrait of him in the role of private secretary to the earl of Rockingham (FM Cam.). The picture was never completed, possibly owing to the collapse of Rockingham's ministry in July 1766. Even so, it is of great value for the light it sheds on Reynolds's working practices, the slightly sketched outlines of the figures forming a marked contrast to the painstaking details of the Turkey rug and inkstand, produced by his pupils and drapery painters.

Aside from Marchi, Reynolds's first recorded pupil was Thomas Beach, who studied with him from about 1760 to 1762. Other pupils included John Berridge, Hugh Barron, William Parry, and, in the 1770s, James Northcote and William Doughty. These pupils were not formally indentured but exchanged their services in return for board, lodging, and, if they were lucky, a little *ad hoc* tuition. Reynolds's pupils remained surprisingly ignorant of his working methods and, as one remarked, he 'never saw him unless he wanted to paint a hand or piece of drapery from them, and then they were dismissed as soon as he had done with them' (Gwynn, 49). Of Reynolds's pupils, the most successful, if not the most gifted, was James Northcote, who studied under him from 1771 to 1776, and who was to be Reynolds's biographer. Northcote's admiration for Reynolds was tempered by jealousy, and an abiding resentment that he had not enjoyed the same intimacy as Reynolds reserved for his friends and patrons. He later recalled that if 'Sir Joshua had come into the room where I was at work for him and had seen me hanging by the neck, it would not have troubled him' (Leslie and Taylor, 2.601). Reynolds was generally kinder to those who did not work directly under him. He assisted the careers of several young foreign artists, notably the Americans Benjamin West and John Singleton Copley, whose *Boy with a Squirrel* (Museum of Fine Arts, Boston), he exhibited next to his own work at the Society of Artists in 1766. Reynolds's greatest personal encouragement was reserved for the young Irish artist James Barry, who was introduced to him by their mutual friend Edmund Burke in 1764.

The Royal Academy and the *Discourses on Art* In the years immediately following his return from Italy Reynolds took a keen interest in plans by the St Martin's Lane Academy and the Society of Dilettanti to form a Royal Academy. During the early 1760s he was intimately involved in the planning of exhibitions by the Society of Artists. However, in 1765 he quite deliberately distanced himself from the internal politics of the society owing to the growing

rivalry between the committee and its members. Reynolds's name is a notable omission from the twenty-two signatories to the memorial presented to George III on 28 November 1768, requesting his 'gracious assistance, patronage, and protection' in founding a Royal Academy. And it was only after some considerable hesitation, involving private consultation with Burke and Johnson, that on 14 December 1768 Reynolds agreed to accept the presidency of the Royal Academy. In the following year, on 21 April, the king knighted Reynolds at St James's Palace. On that day Johnson broke his vow of abstinence and 'drank one glass of wine to the health of Sir Joshua Reynolds' (Hudson, 93).

Reynolds was intimately involved in the day-to-day running of the Royal Academy, rarely missing council or general assembly meetings. Occasionally he entertained his fellow academicians at home, treating the members of the council on one occasion to a supper of turtle ('callipash and callipee' (*The Letters of Henry Fuseli*, ed. D. Weinglass, 1982, 12). In 1771 Reynolds inaugurated the annual Royal Academy dinner in order to strengthen the link between the academy and connoisseurs. It was held annually on 23 April, the feast of St George, and continues to this day. In 1775, in an attempt to confer increased formality upon the academy, Reynolds proposed the introduction of ceremonial gowns for members. The idea was rejected, principally because of opposition voiced by the academy's treasurer William Chambers, who was from this time increasingly antagonistic towards Reynolds. Chambers features with Reynolds and Joseph Wilton, keeper of the Royal Academy, in an official portrait of 1782 by John Francis Rigaud (NPG).

Reynolds's greatest critic within the Royal Academy was James Barry, who in 1782 was elected as its professor of painting. Barry's differences with Reynolds were primarily ideological. Even so, he used his position and his annual academy lectures to mount increasingly personal attacks on Reynolds, who was apparently reduced 'to so awkward a situation in his chair as an auditor, that he was obliged at last either to appear to be asleep or to absent himself from the place' (Northcote, *Life*, 2.146). Although Reynolds affected indifference, he confessed privately that 'he feared he did hate Barry, and if so, he had much excuse, if excuse be possible' (ibid., 2.196).

The Royal Academy opened on 2 January 1769. To mark the occasion Reynolds read out an address, published the following month as *A Discourse, Delivered at the Opening of the Royal Academy*. Reynolds wrote fifteen discourses between 1769 and 1790, each one (with the exception of the inaugural *Discourse* and the ninth) delivered on the occasion of the distribution of prizes to the academy's students. From 1769 to 1772 they were delivered annually, thereafter biennially. Each discourse was published shortly after its delivery, Reynolds presenting a copy to each member of the academy, and each member of The Club. The first seven discourses were published together in 1778, and were subsequently made available in Italian and German editions. A French edition of thirteen appeared in 1787. The first collected edition of all fifteen, together with Reynolds's other writings, appeared in 1797. A second edition appeared in 1798: William Blake's extensively annotated copy belongs to the British Library. Over thirty other editions of the *Discourses* have since been published, including those by Sir Edmund Gosse (1884), Roger Fry (1905), and more recently by Robert Wark (1975) and Pat Rogers (1992).

One principal difference between the essays in *The Idler* and the *Discourses* was that the latter were addressed to a live audience prior to publication. Even in their published form, the *Discourses* adopt a very personal approach. Even so, Reynolds's measured prose masks the uncertainty of his spoken delivery. He had an undemonstrative speaking voice and the majority of those attending his lectures at the Royal Academy would not have been able to hear what he was saying (Hilles, *Literary Career*, 33–4). Reynolds organized his ideas, as well as the transcriptions taken from various reading materials, in folders with themed headings, including 'Method of study', 'Colouring', and 'Michael Angelo'. In the weeks leading up to the presentation of each discourse Reynolds made copious notes and rough drafts, working late into the night to give form to his thoughts. At the last minute pupils were inducted as scribes, working against the clock to provide a fair copy to be read out at the academy, James Northcote telling his brother, 'I writ out sir Joshua's discourse and he left it till the last day that he was to speak it in the evening so that if Gill had not assisted me it could not have been done soon enough' (Whitley, 2.293). Reynolds also received editorial assistance from friends, notably Samuel Johnson, Edmund Burke, and, latterly, Edmond Malone. Even so, envious contemporaries who underrated Reynolds's abilities as a writer (Hilles, *Literary Career*, 134–40, 217–48) unjustly exaggerated their respective contributions.

In his first discourse Reynolds stressed the vital role played by the living model, a linchpin of academic training since the Renaissance. Subsequent discourses went beyond the scope of art education, synthesizing ideas found in a wide range of aesthetic treatises including classical authors, Horace and Longinus; Renaissance artists, Leonardo da Vinci and Lomazzo; French seventeenth-century theorists, Charles Le Brun, Henri Testelin, André Félibien, and Roger de Piles, as well as more recent texts by Algarotti, Winckelmann, Edmund Burke, and Adam Smith. In the earlier discourses, particularly the third and fourth, Reynolds set out his ideas on the guiding principles of high art, which he believed were embodied in the 'great style'. According to Reynolds, the 'great style' endowed a work with 'intellectual dignity' that 'ennobles the painter's art; that lays the line between himself and the mere mechanick; and produces those great effects in an instant, which eloquence and poetry, by slow and repeated efforts, are scarcely able to attain' (Reynolds, *Discourses*, ed. Wark, 43). Reynolds was in no doubt that the artists who had come closest to this ideal were the Roman, Florentine, and Bolognese masters of the Italian Renaissance, especially Michelangelo, Raphael, and Lodovico Carracci. While he greatly admired the Venetians Titian and Tintoretto, Reynolds considered that their preoccupation with colour and effect militated against the purity and severity of the 'great style'. In his later discourses Reynolds addressed major aesthetic concepts, including the nature of genius, originality, imitation, and taste. Here, again, he explored his themes with reference to the leading masters of the 'great style', although he appears increasingly to acknowledge the contributions of artists lower down the scale, such as Rubens and Rembrandt— both of whom greatly influenced his own art. As it has been argued (Reynolds, *Discourses*, ed. Wark, xxx–xxxii; ed. Rogers, 21–2), Reynolds's *Discourses* do not, with the passage of the years, incline him more towards a more 'Romantic' viewpoint, but retain an essentially empirical outlook that would have satisfied earlier generations. Yet while the *Discourses* collectively represent Reynolds's views on art theory and practice, they do not form a seamless, or even consistent, argument. Over the twenty-year period in which they were written events and experience modified his views. At times he wished to address specific issues: in the tenth discourse sculpture, in the fourteenth the art of Thomas Gainsborough. He also allowed different facets of his own intellectual make-up to surface, tempering his insistence on the primacy of rules with a willingness to countenance arguments based on custom, emotion, or gut instinct.

The 1770s Between 1769 and 1779 Reynolds exhibited over 100 pictures at the Royal Academy, considerably more than he had exhibited during the previous decade at the Society of Artists. These included portraits of close friends, actors and actresses, scientists, clergymen, aristocrats, and children, as well as subject pictures and character studies. Among his friends he showed portraits of Johnson and Goldsmith (1770), Giuseppe Baretti (1774), and David Garrick (1776). John Frederick Sackville, third duke of Dorset, who assembled an entire room of Reynolds's paintings at Knole, purchased all these portraits, excepting that of Baretti (who at the time had been indicted for murder). Lord Sackville also purchased Reynolds's first major history painting, *Ugolino and his Children in the Dungeon*, exhibited at the Royal Academy in 1773. *Ugolino* was based on an episode from Dante's *Divina commedia*. Reynolds regarded this picture as a manifesto for his theories on high art, combining within it motifs from Carracci's *Pietà* (National Gallery, London) and Michelangelo's Sistine ceiling, as well as theories derived from Richardson and Le Brun.

Although history painting formed a relatively small part of Reynolds's artistic output, he devoted increasing time to it from the early 1770s onwards. His acolytes, moreover, promoted Reynolds's history paintings as testimony to his genuine commitment to the cause of high art. In the decades following his death they were even counted among his greatest achievements, fetching great prices at auction and forming the focus of critical attention. Unlike his commissioned portraits, which he dispatched with due efficiency, Reynolds's history pictures are known to have taken months, even years, to complete. During the summer, when his portrait business was slack, Reynolds employed a variety of models, using them to explore his ideas on high art and to test out new painting techniques. In the early 1770s he employed an old beggar named George White who, as well as modelling the figure of Ugolino, sat to Reynolds as a pope, an apostle, and as a captain of *banditti*. He also painted beggar children. Indeed, more successful than Reynolds's history paintings were his character studies of children, known as 'fancy pictures'. They included a *Strawberry Girl* (Wallace Collection, London), the *Infant Samuel* (Tate collection), and the pendant pictures *Cupid as a Link Boy* (Albright-Knox Art Gallery, Buffalo, New York) and *Mercury as a Cut Purse* (Farington Collection Trust, Buscot Manor, Oxfordshire). These last two were not exhibited in public, possibly because of the sexual innuendo they contained. Fancy pictures played an increasingly important role in Reynolds's *oeuvre* in the 1770s and 1780s, allowing him to paint more freely in the manner of old masters such as Murillo, Rembrandt, and Correggio, and to experiment with his technique. According to his pupil James Northcote, when Reynolds:

> was at any time accused of having spoiled many of his portraits, by trying experiments upon them, he answered that it was always his wish to have made these experiments on his fancy pictures, and if so, had they failed of success, the injury would have fallen only on himself, as he should have kept them on his hands.   (Northcote, *Memoirs*, lxxxi)

Reynolds also made imaginative 'character' portraits of women and children. Of these among the most successful are the pendants *Master Crewe as Henry VIII* (exh. RA, 1776; priv. coll.) and *Miss Crewe as 'Winter'* (1775; priv. coll.). At times Reynolds elided the two genres of fancy picture and portraiture, as in the portrait of his niece Theophila Palmer, which he exhibited at the Royal Academy in 1771 as *A Girl Reading* (priv. coll.). She bitterly complained to him that she ought to have been described as 'A Young Lady'. Reynolds retorted, 'don't be vain, my dear, I only use your head as I would that of any beggar—as a good practice' (*Maria Edgeworth: Chosen Letters*, ed. F. V. Barry, 1931, 380).

Aside from history painting and fancy pictures, among Reynolds's most ambitious works were the series of full-length female grand-manner portraits painted during the 1770s. They included *The Duchess of Cumberland* (exh. RA, 1773; priv. coll.), *The Montgomery Sisters* (exh. RA, 1774; Tate collection), *The Countess of Harrington* (exh. RA, 1775; priv. coll.), and *Lady Bamfylde* (exh. RA, 1777; Tate collection). In these portraits the subjects were dressed in voluminous robes which Reynolds hoped would endow them with a timeless quality and elevate the image towards the level of high art. Only occasionally did he resort to quasi-historical costume in male portraits, notably in the double portrait of Colonel John Acland and Lord Sydney (exh. RA, 1770; priv. coll.), portrayed in theatrical tunics as archers, and the Polynesian Omai (exh. RA, 1776; priv. coll.), whom he depicted in white robes and a turban—a form of dress apparently adopted by Omai during his sojourn in England.

Further honours were bestowed on Reynolds during the 1770s. In September 1772 he was elected an alderman of the borough of Plympton, and a year later, on 4 October 1773, he was sworn in as mayor. In 1775 Reynolds was elected a member of the academy at Florence, following the presentation of his self-portrait to the grand duke of Tuscany. The honour Reynolds undoubtedly valued most was the doctorate of civil law awarded him in July 1773 by the University of Oxford: in subsequent self-portraits (notably that painted for the Royal Academy in 1780) he often portrayed himself in his academic robes. In 1774 Reynolds also painted a portrait of his friend James Beattie in doctoral robes, Beattie having received his doctorate at the same ceremony as Reynolds. The portrait (Marischal College, Aberdeen), depicted Beattie holding his *Essay on the Nature and Immutability of Truth in Opposition to Sophistry and Scepticism*, while an avenging angel drives away his enemies, whom Reynolds characterized as David Hume and Voltaire. The painting was attacked by Goldsmith, who told Reynolds that while Beattie's book would soon be forgotten 'your allegorical picture, and the fame of Voltaire will live for ever to your disgrace as a flatterer' (Northcote, *Life*, 1.299).

By the late 1770s Reynolds's most influential patrons were invariably members of the country's leading whig dynasties. Between 1775 and 1778 he exhibited portraits of members of the Crewe, Bedford, and Spencer families, as well as George Townshend (Lord de Ferrars), Viscount Althorp, Lord Palmerston, the duke of Leinster, the duke and duchess of Devonshire, and the family of the duke of Marlborough. He made frequent visits to their country seats and entertained them in London. And although he continued to work hard during the day, evenings were increasingly given over to drinking, gaming, attending masquerades, and even dancing lessons. His pupil James Northcote recalled that 'though the frequent dining-out probably shortened his life, it was of great advantage to him in his profession' (*Conversations of James Northcote R.A. with James Ward on Art and Artists*, ed. E. Fletcher, 1901, 186). He belonged to several prestigious clubs including the Star-in-Garter in Pall Mall, Almacks, and the Society of Dilettanti, where he had been official 'limner' since 1769. Between 1777 and 1779 Reynolds painted two large group portraits of the members of the Dilettanti (Society of Dilettanti, London), enjoying the communal pleasures of wine, conversation, and connoisseurship.

The deterioration of relations between Reynolds and his sister Fanny by the late 1770s resulted in her enforced departure from his house. Their niece Mary Palmer, who remained with Reynolds for the remainder of his life, assumed Fanny's duties as housekeeper. Unlike Fanny, whose artistic efforts Reynolds had belittled, Mary was encouraged to paint. Her own niece Theophila Gwatkin recalled: 'Everybody in the house painted. Lady Thomond [Mary Palmer] & herself, the coachman & the man servant Ralph & his daughter, all painted, copied and talked about pictures' (*The Diary of Benjamin Robert Haydon*, ed. W. B. Pope, 1963, 5.487). At this time Reynolds also volunteered to take on his nephew Samuel Johnson (the eldest son of his sister Elizabeth) as his pupil. His mother refused the offer, on the grounds that she considered Reynolds to be thoroughly degenerate, informing him that his soul was 'a shocking spectacle of poverty' (G. B. Hill, ed., *Johnsonian Miscellanies*, 1897, 2.455–6n.). Reynolds did not attend church. However, he seldom missed a social gathering of the Sons of the Clergy.

In 1779 rumours were circulated in the popular press concerning Reynolds's liaisons with the 'amiable' daughter of a naval officer and 'Lady G—r', who, it was said, sat to Reynolds in the evening as well as the morning so that 'the knight should give a resemblance of her in the most natural way' (*Town and Country Magazine*, Sept 1779, 401–4). His interest in Fanny Burney, whom he met in September 1778, shortly after the publication of her début novel, *Evelina*, is more certain. Over the next few years Reynolds (who was a close friend of her father) met Fanny Burney frequently, fuelling suspicions that he intended to offer her his hand in marriage. However, any prospect of nuptials was diminished in November 1782, when Reynolds suffered a severe paralysis. 'How, my dear Sissy', she told her younger sister:

> can you wish any wishes about Sir Joshua and me? A man who has had two shakes of the palsy! What misery should I suffer if I were only his niece, from terror of a fatal repetition of such a shock! I would not run voluntarily into such a state of perpetual apprehension for all the wealth of the East.   (Leslie and Taylor, 2.385)

Towards the end of his life, in 1788, Reynolds told Boswell he had never married, because 'every woman whom he had liked had grown indifferent to him' (Hudson, 137).

Home and abroad, 1780–1785 In 1780 Reynolds painted several works for the Royal Academy's private rooms at Somerset House, recently completed by Sir William Chambers. They included an allegorical figure, Theory, for the library ceiling, pendant portraits of George III and Queen Charlotte, and portraits of himself and Chambers for the academy's assembly room. At the annual exhibition of 1780 he showed seven works, including a striking full length of Lady Worsley in military riding attire (priv. coll.), a portrait of Edward Gibbon (priv. coll.), and an allegorical figure, *Justice* (priv. coll.). This last painting was one of seven Virtues made as designs for a painted glass window, the west window of New College, Oxford. The central design, a *Nativity*, had been exhibited at the Royal Academy the previous year, although the window itself was not completely installed until 1785. The final result, as Reynolds himself admitted, was disappointing.

In 1781 Reynolds exhibited fifteen works at the Royal Academy. They included a portrait of Charles Burney (NPG), Horace Walpole's nieces, the ladies Waldegrave (NG Scot.), and his young godson, Henry Edward Bunbury (Philadelphia Museum of Art). This picture remained in Reynolds's collection until his death when he bequeathed it to the boy's mother, his close friend Catherine Horneck. The portrait was described in the contemporary press as that of a boy 'supposed to be listening to a wonderful story', a comment which reflected Bunbury's own recollections that Reynolds had entertained him with fairy tales while sitting for the portrait (Whitley, 1.369). That year Reynolds also exhibited two major subject pictures, *Thaïs* (priv. coll.), modelled upon a notorious courtesan,

Emily Pott, and *The Death of Dido* (Royal Collection), a composition inspired by his admiration for seventeenth-century Bolognese art and the antique (the central figure being an adaptation of a classical figure of Cleopatra in the Vatican).

During the 1780s Reynolds turned increasingly for inspiration to the art of Flanders and the Low Countries, an interest which prompted a two-month tour in the late summer of 1781. Accompanied by his Devon friend Phillip Metcalfe, Reynolds embarked from Margate to Ostend on 24 July, travelling to Ghent, Brussels, Malines, Antwerp, Dordrecht, The Hague, Leiden, Amsterdam, Utrecht, Düsseldorf, Cologne, Aachen, Liège, and Louvain, and returning via Brussels and Ostend. Reynolds was already well acquainted with Dutch and Flemish art, owning major works by Van Dyck, Rubens, Jordaens, and Rembrandt, genre paintings by 'old Breughel' and Teniers, and landscapes by Cuyp, Hobbema, Ruisdael, and van Goyen. Reynolds's detailed journal entries, which were intended ultimately for publication, reveal that the tour was organized around major private collections in the Low Countries and the great altarpieces of Flanders. Reynolds admired Dutch art, but its appeal was confined primarily to 'the mechanical parts of the art'. 'Painters', he said, 'should go to the Dutch school to learn the art of painting, as they would go to a grammar school to learn languages. They must go to Italy to learn the higher branches of knowledge' (Reynolds, *Journey*, 110). He was unmoved by Rembrandt's *Nightwatch*, confessing that it was 'with difficulty I could persuade myself that it was painted by Rembrandt' (ibid., 91). He attributed it tentatively to Ferdinand Bol. Reynolds was less ambivalent about Rubens, whose art conformed more closely to his own tenets on the form and function of high art, and to the Italianate ideal, which remained his benchmark. He reserved his highest praise for Rubens's *Conversion of St Bavo* in St Bavo's Cathedral, Ghent, and his *Virgin and Child with Saints* in the Augustinuskerk, Antwerp. Even so, he was disturbed by the poor condition of many of these works which he had only known previously through engravings, observing sadly that the *Descent from the Cross* in Antwerp Cathedral was 'chilled and mildewed' (ibid., 31).

Reynolds went to Flanders once more in late July 1785, this time with the specific intention of purchasing pictures auctioned off by those religious houses and monasteries dissolved by the Holy Roman emperor, Joseph II. As a potential purchaser, Reynolds was deeply disappointed by the standard of work on offer, and bought nothing. However, in order that the visit would not be a complete waste of time he rapidly scoured the country, spending over £1000 in Antwerp on works by Rubens, Van Dyck, Snyders, and Murillo.

During the 1780s Reynolds made some headway in preparing notes from his journeys to Flanders and the Low Countries for publication, although they did not appear in print until after his death, when they were incorporated into the second volume of Malone's *Works of Sir Joshua Reynolds*. In 1783, however, Reynolds published a related piece of work, annotations to William Mason's translation of *De arte graphica*, Charles Alfonse Du Fresnoy's Latin poem of 1667 on colour theory. The timing was significant because, following his visit to Flanders, Reynolds was eager to express his current opinions on the primacy of colour. Less dogmatic than the *Discourses*, Reynolds's annotations on Du Fresnoy allowed him to make extensive comments on the art of Titian, Veronese, Watteau, and Rubens without qualifying his remarks with reference to the Roman school. The lessons learned from an intense study of Flemish art emerged forcibly in Reynolds's paintings of the 1780s. In 1782 Reynolds exhibited the *Infant Academy* at the Royal Academy. According to a contemporary critic the picture was painted immediately after Reynolds had returned from Flanders and thus 'recollected all the beauty and force of colouring so characteristic of the Flemish School' (*St James's Chronicle*, 30 April 1782). In 1786 Reynolds exhibited a portrait of Lady Anne Bingham (priv. coll.), which he himself referred to as 'Sir Joshua's Chapeau de Paille'—a reference to Rubens's celebrated portrait (National Gallery, London), which he had seen in a private collection in Antwerp in 1781.

Reynolds's Victorian biographer, Tom Taylor, was among the first to speculate whether 'Whiggism could have so preponderated his society and sitters had he not been a very decided Whig' (Leslie and Taylor, 2.155). By the 1780s Reynolds's allegiance to the whig party was becoming increasingly evident, both in his choice of friends and in his portrait sitters. When Lord Rockingham finally came to power briefly in spring 1782, many of Reynolds's closest friends assumed key positions in government. They included Augustus Keppel, as first lord of the Admiralty, Lord Ashburton, as privy seal, Charles James Fox, as secretary of state, and Edmund Burke, as paymaster of the forces. In 1783 Burke, in the course of reinstating two Treasury officials accused of embezzlement, was satirically 'observed to have a miniature of Count Ugolino, from Sir Joshua Reynolds, in his hand, in order to give sublimity to the description' (Postle, *Subject Pictures*, 149). Johnson ruefully observed the increasing influence of Fox and Burke on his erstwhile protégé: 'He is under the *Fox star* and the *Irish constellation*. He is always under some planet' (Boswell, *Life*, 3.261). In April 1784 Reynolds exhibited Fox's portrait at the Royal Academy, just as Fox was engaged in a bitter election to retain his parliamentary seat at Westminster. At Fox's suggestion Reynolds included in the portrait his recently defeated East India Bill and his representation of the Commons to the king, the very policies that had precipitated George III into dissolving parliament.

On 1 October 1784 Reynolds was sworn in as principal painter-in-ordinary to the king, following the death of Allan Ramsay. Although the post conferred considerable kudos and a guaranteed income from replicating royal portraits, Reynolds poured scorn on the token annual salary of £50, complaining that the post was 'a place of not so much profit and of near equal dignity with His Majesty's Rat-catcher' (*Letters*, 112). Yet Reynolds coveted the post deeply, to the point of being prepared to resign the presidency of the Royal Academy. Ultimately Reynolds used his influence in the corridors of power to sway the issue in his favour, Thomas Gainsborough remarking that the post was originally to have been his except that Reynolds's friends 'stood in the way' (*The Letters of Thomas Gainsborough*, ed. J. Hayes, 2001, 161). Several weeks later, on 18 October, Reynolds was granted the freedom of the Painter–Stainers' Company at its annual dinner in the City of London.

Among the seventeen works which Reynolds exhibited at the Royal Academy in 1784 were a full-length military portrait of George, prince of Wales, reining in a charger (priv. coll.), a coquettish *Nymph and Cupid* (Tate collection), and a portrait, *Mrs Siddons as 'The Tragic Muse'* (Henry E. Huntington Art Gallery, San Marino, California). This last portrait was greeted by admirers as a form of 'confined' history painting, the general attitude of the figure being modelled upon the figure of Michelangelo's Isaiah from the vault of the Sistine Chapel. The enhanced aesthetic and intellectual appeal of *Mrs Siddons* was mirrored in the 1000 guinea price tag Reynolds placed on the picture. The price proved too high, and in 1786 the picture was still on Reynolds's hands, 'which it would not be was this the period of the Tenth Leo, or the family of the Medici' (*Public Advertiser*, 1 March 1786). In 1790 he sold it to a French collector for 700 guineas, then a record price for a portrait by Reynolds.

The later years, 1785–1790   The death of Samuel Johnson in December 1784 caused Reynolds to forge a closer bond with several mutual friends, and during the summer of 1785 what became known as 'the Gang' was formed by Reynolds, Boswell, Edmond Malone, and John Courtnay. Boswell and Reynolds were seen increasingly in public together, notably on 6 July 1785 when they attended the public execution of a former servant of Edmund Burke at Newgate gaol. In the same year Reynolds painted Boswell's portrait (NPG), which he exhibited at the Royal Academy in 1787. 'This is a strong portrait', observed one critic, 'and shews an artist can do with paint more than nature hath attempted with flesh and blood, viz—put good sense in the countenance' (*Morning Herald*, 2 May 1787). Reynolds also acted as a general adviser on Boswell's *Journal of a Tour to the Hebrides* and, with Malone, encouraged him to complete his biography of Johnson, which was published in May 1791, with a dedication to Reynolds, 'the intimate and beloved friend of that great man; the friend whom he declared to be "the most invulnerable man he knew; whom, if he should quarrel with him, he should find the most difficulty how to abuse"'.

During the mid-1780s Reynolds found new friends and patrons among a younger generation of intellectuals and connoisseurs, including George Beaumont, John Julius Angerstein, Abraham Hume, Henry Englefield, Richard Payne Knight, and Uvedale Price. Of these Beaumont was Reynolds's principal disciple, taking advice and painting lessons from Reynolds, and after his death erecting a cenotaph to his memory in the grounds of his country seat at Coleorton (celebrated in Constable's *Cenotaph* of 1836; National Gallery, London). Reynolds's most prestigious young patron, however, was George, prince of Wales, who in May 1786 sat to Reynolds for a full-length portrait (priv. coll.), commissioned by Louis Philippe, duc d'Orléans, and shown at the Royal Academy the following year. The picture was widely criticized owing to the prominent position in the centre of the composition of a black servant adjusting the prince's ceremonial robes, an idea that apparently came from the duc d'Orléans (*The World*, 27 November 1787). In 1786 Reynolds also painted a full-length portrait of the duc d'Orléans for the prince of Wales. Following its exhibition at the Royal Academy, the portrait was displayed at Carlton House, until early 1792, when it was abruptly moved, following the news that Orléans had voted for the execution of Louis XVI.

By the beginning of 1785 Reynolds's name was a byword for diligence: he was now working harder than ever, exhibiting seventy-nine pictures at the Royal Academy between 1785 and 1790. As *The Times* noted on 10 January 1785; 'Sir Joshua Reynolds is shaved and powdered by nine in the morning, and at his canvass; we mention this as an example to artists, and as a leading trait in the character of this great painter'. Significant portraits from this period include *Mrs Musters as Hebe* (1785; Kenwood House, London), *Georgiana, Duchess of Devonshire and her Daughter* (1786; priv. coll.), *Lord Heathfield* (1788; National Gallery, London), *Lord Rodney* (1789; Royal Collection), and *Mrs Billington as St Cecilia* (1790; Beaverbrook Art Gallery, Fredericton, New Brunswick). *Lord Heathfield*, portraying the subject clasping the key to the rock of Gibraltar, rapidly acquired the status of an icon, Constable referring to it in the 1830s as 'almost a history of the defence of Gibraltar' (Leslie and Taylor, 1.517). It has recently been suggested that the picture may also have had religious overtones, through an intended comparison between Heathfield and St Peter, the great military hero transformed into 'the rock upon which Britannia builds her military interests' (D. Shawe-Taylor, *The Georgians: Eighteenth-Century Portraiture and Society*, 1990, 49).

While portraiture continued to be the mainstay of Reynolds's professional life, he now spent much of his time, particularly during the summer months, working on subject pictures. In 1782 he had exhibited a painting of a young girl leaning on a pedestal, a composition which he repeated on several occasions, and which became popularly known as the *Laughing Girl* (Kenwood House, London). In the mid-1780s he followed this up with a series of fancy pictures depicting little girls with pets: *Robinetta* with a robin, *Lesbia* with a sparrow, *Felina* with a cat, and *Muscipula* with a caged mouse. These paintings, light-hearted allegories on the theme of captive love, proved extremely popular and were extensively engraved and copied into the nineteenth century. In 1784 Reynolds exhibited a more overtly sensual picture on the theme of love, *A Nymph and Cupid* and in 1785 a *Venus* (priv. coll.)—'a picture of temptation from her auburn lock to her painted toe' (*Public Advertiser*, 5 April 1785). The popularity of *Venus* among his aristocratic patrons prompted Reynolds to repeat the composition several times, it being rumoured in 1787 that a version exported to France was destined for Louis XVI (Postle, *Subject Pictures*, 205).

In 1785 Reynolds received a prestigious commission for a historical painting from Catherine the Great. The subject chosen by Reynolds was *The Infant Hercules Strangling the Serpents* (Hermitage Museum, St Petersburg). He devoted more time and attention to this picture than to any picture he had ever painted, working on it intermittently between early 1786 and the spring of 1788, when it was exhibited at the Royal Academy. After completing the painting Reynolds admitted the difficulties he had encountered, observing that there were 'ten pictures under it, some better, some worse' (Northcote, *Life*, 2.219). In addition Reynolds painted two subject pictures for Prince Potemkin, a version of *A Nymph and Cupid* and *The Continence of Scipio*, shown at the Royal Academy in 1789, shortly before its departure for Russia. By this time Reynolds was also working on three subject paintings for Boydell's Shakspeare Gallery: *Puck* (priv. coll.), *The Death of Cardinal Beaufort*, and *Macbeth and the Witches* (both Petworth House, Sussex).

Reynolds's relations with Boydell were invariably strained. Having agreed in December 1786 to paint a scene from *Macbeth*, Reynolds was vexed to see himself described in Boydell's newspaper advertisement for the scheme as 'Portrait-Painter to his Majesty, and President of the Royal Academy'. He sent Boydell a curt note:

> Sir Joshua Reynolds presents his Compts to Mr. Alderman Boydell. He finds in his Advertisement that he is styled Portrait Painter to his Majesty, it is a matter of no great consequence, but he does not know why his title is changed, he is styled in his Patent Principal painter to His Majesty. (*Letters*, 176)

Reynolds was also unhappy at the very idea of being employed by Boydell, believing that he was 'degrading himself to paint for a print-seller' (Northcote, *Life*, 2.226). His reluctance to become involved was eventually overcome through the intervention of the Shakespeare editor George Steevens (Reynolds's friend and fellow member of The Club), and a large cash advance of £500 from Boydell for *Macbeth*, the canvas and stretcher for which he also supplied gratis.

In the late 1780s Reynolds appeared to be in good health, despite a considerable deterioration in his eyesight. His physical appearance at that time can be gauged from his self-portrait with spectacles of about 1788 (Royal Collection). Edmond Malone, to whom Reynolds presented a version of the painting, stated that the self-portrait with spectacles showed the artist 'exactly as he appeared in his latter days, in domestick life', suggesting that it was a private rather than a public image (*Works*, 1.1xxvii, note). That he presented copies of the portrait to Malone, Mason, and Burke suggests that it represented the way in which Reynolds wished to be seen by his close friends. Reynolds had worn spectacles at least since 1783, when he had complained of a 'violent inflammation' in the eyes. He had probably worn them for a lot longer, an examination of two pairs of his spectacles revealing that he was short-sighted, and would have needed spectacles to read and to paint (Penny, 337).

During the spring and early summer of 1789 Reynolds

continued to take portrait clients virtually on a daily basis, including weekends. On Monday 13 July 1789 he had scheduled a 10 a.m. appointment relating to the double portrait of Miss Cocks and her niece (Iveagh Bequest, Kenwood House, London). On the same day he wrote in his sitter book, 'prevented by my Eye beginning to be obscured', the first reference to the failing sight in his left eye. Reynolds attempted to carry on with scheduled portrait sittings over the next few days, although within less than a week he was compelled to stop, the portrait of the misses Cocks being completed by another hand.

Within a fortnight Reynolds's retirement was announced in the press:

Sir Joshua has mentioned to several of his friends that his practice in the future will be very select in respect to portraits, and that the remnant of his life will be applied chiefly to *fancy subjects* which will admit of leisure, and contribute to amuse. Sir Joshua feels his sight so infirm as to allow of his painting about thirty or forty minutes at a time only and he means in a certain degree to retire. (*Morning Herald*, 27 July 1789)

The blank pages of the two remaining sitter books, punctuated only by details of social calls and business matters, reveal that by the end of July 1789 Reynolds had all but retired. His friend urged him to seek medical attention. 'We are all uneasy about him from his plethorick habit', observed Malone to Boswell, 'lest he should have some stroke'. 'If anything should happen to him', he added, 'the chain of our society at least, would be sadly broken:—but let us hope for the best' (*Boswell's Correspondence*, ed. F. Brady, 1986, 4.366).

During the early autumn of 1789 Reynolds's eyesight, and the calibre of medical treatment he was receiving, became a public talking point, as his supporters rallied to counter rumours that the president of the Royal Academy was by now a spent force. 'It is suspected', stated the *Morning Post*, on 9 September 1789,

that some artists who want to bring their own puny talents into estimation have magnified the state of Sir Joshua's disorder in order to injure his reputation, and profit, if possible, by the idea that his faculties begin to suffer too materially to admit of any future works of extraordinary vigour and beauty.

Although he continued to take a keen interest in the affairs of the Royal Academy, Reynolds was also undermined in his presidency. On 22 February 1790, following a disagreement with the academy's general assembly over its opposition to election of the Italian architect Giuseppe Bonomi to the vacant post of professor of perspective, Reynolds tendered his resignation as president, and his membership of the academy. On 13 March he was reinstated, although he never regained the respect he had formerly commanded.

Reynolds's painting activities were by now restricted to retouching and refurbishing works in his collection and those portraits which were already well under way. All the paintings he showed at the 1790 Royal Academy exhibition had been started by the summer of 1789. They included a full-length portrait of Sir John Fleming Leicester in the uniform of the Cheshire provisional cavalry

(University of Manchester, Tabley House, Cheshire), repainted by James Northcote, and Francis Rawdon Hastings, second earl of Moira and first marquess of Hastings (Royal Collection). *Lord Rawdon* may be regarded as Reynolds's final full-length male portrait, since he was working with the sitter right up until the day when he recorded the onset of blindness in his left eye. His final female full-length portrait, completed less than a month earlier, was *Mrs Billington in the Character of St Cecilia*.

Although no longer capable of working full-time as a portraitist, Reynolds in February 1790 discussed sittings for a new portrait of the prince of Wales for Lord Charlemont. 'In short', Thomas Dundas told Lord Charlemont, 'Sir J. is determined that your picture should be an original' (*Charlemont MSS*, 117). However, although Reynolds recorded a single appointment with the prince in his pocket book on 17 February, nothing came of the proposal. By July 1790 Boswell reported that Reynolds was able to do little more than to 'amuse himself by mending a picture now and then' (Reynolds, *Discourses*, ed. Rogers, 405, n.2).

Reynolds remained energetic throughout the spring of 1790, dining out with friends, frequently entertaining, and attending meetings at the Eumelian Club, the Dilettanti Society, and The Club. As usual he spent the summer in London, except for a short stay at Beaconsfield with Edmund Burke, while in October he journeyed to Winchester and to Broadlands, Hampshire, where he was entertained by Lord Palmerston. Reynolds spent the autumn composing his fifteenth, and final, discourse. The discourse, given at the Royal Academy on 10 December 1790, proved a memorable occasion, not least because it appeared that the timbers supporting the floor of the Great Room at Somerset House were about to give way at any moment. Charles Burney recalled:

Sir Jos. had but just entered the room, when there happened a violent and unaccountable crack wch. astonished every one present. But no inquiry was made or suspicion raised of danger till another crack happened, wch. terrified the Comp^y. so much that most of them were retreating towards the door with great precipitation, while others call out—gently! gently! or mischief will be anticipated. (Hilles, *Literary Career*, 182)

Owing to immense sang-froid or possibly deafness, Reynolds was able to complete the reading of his discourse. He did so, succeeding in his desire that 'the last words which I should pronounce in this Academy, and from this place, might be the name of—MICHAEL ANGELO'.

The final years, 1791–1792 Throughout the autumn of 1790 Reynolds was in constant contact with Burke, reading in manuscript form, and heartily approving, his *Reflections on the Revolution in France*. He also began to write down his own 'Reflections' on the causes of the revolution, highlighting the limited and exotic nature of the French court's patronage, which 'cultivated only those arts which could add splendor to the nation, to the neglect of those which supported it', and arguing that the 'people who require Baubles are few and consequently little revenue is acquired to the general purse' (Hilles, *Literary Career*, 188–

9). These notes were written on the back of his fair copy of the fifteenth discourse. It was on the reverse of these sheets also that Reynolds wrote his last extended piece of critical writing, the so-called 'Ironical discourse', an entertaining, if heavy-handed, essay. Drafted in the summer of 1791, the 'Ironical discourse' was the indirect result of the debates among Reynolds and his friends on the seizure of power by the French people, and the ability of the status quo to achieve a rational consensus. Reynolds's view, as expressed in the preface to the 'Ironical discourse', was that the increase in literacy, numeracy, or even the number of practising artists, simply indicated the expansion of mediocrity.

Reynolds remained very active in literary and aesthetic circles, debating the Revd William Gilpin's voguish theories on the 'Picturesque', and vigorously defending the authenticity of his miniature of John Milton by Samuel Cooper in the pages of the *Gentleman's Magazine*. He was even capable of indulging in a little mischief, conning the French picture dealer Noel Desenfans into paying £200 for a copy of a Claude which Giuseppe Marchi had manufactured expressly for the purpose. Reynolds, who eventually gave Desenfans his money back, apparently 'expressed surprise that a man of such discrimination should have thus been taken in by a contemporary work', an allusion to the picture dealer's exclusive interest in old-master paintings (*Letters*, 220–21, n. 1). The trick coincided with a display of Reynolds's own collection of old masters at the Haymarket, and entitled 'Ralph's Exhibition', the 1*s.* entrance fee going to his manservant, Ralph Kirkley. The exhibition contained 183 paintings. All, except three, versions of Correggio's *Marriage of St Catherine*, Michelangelo's *Leda*, and the *Mona Lisa*, were for sale. These pictures were among his most prized possessions, as Reynolds's lengthy catalogue entries revealed. Reynolds, who had acquired his version of the *Mona Lisa* from the duke of Leeds, was convinced that it, rather than the one belonging to Louis XVI (Louvre, Paris), was Leonardo's original. History has proved him wrong.

In May 1791 T. P. Adelcrantz, president of the Swedish Royal Academy, wrote to Reynolds requesting him to sit for his portrait to Carl Fredrik von Breda, who was then working in England. In this painting, von Breda's reception piece for the Swedish Royal Academy, the subject has the appearance of a blind, dispirited old man. Yet to all intents and purposes Reynolds still enjoyed reasonable health. In September 1791 Edmond Malone accompanied him on a 5 mile country walk, recalling that although he was over sixty-eight, Reynolds had 'the appearance of a man not much beyond fifty, and seemed as likely to live for ten or fifteen years, as any of his younger friends' (*Works*, 1.cviii–cix, n.).

Within weeks Reynolds began to experience intense pain and inflammation in his left eye, caused by undiagnosed liver disease. Fanny Burney, who saw him for the last time the following month, noted the rapid decline in his constitution. 'He seemed', she observed,

serious even to sadness, though extremely kind. 'I am very glad', he said in a meek voice and dejected accent, 'to see you

again, and I wish I could see you better! but I have but one eye now,—and scarcely that.'   (Leslie and Taylor, 2.625)

During the remaining few months of his life Reynolds endured tremendous physical pain, and depression. His doctors, Sir George Baker and Dr Warren, ascribed his loss of appetite and low spirits to an attack of hypochondria.

Although he was not aware of the immediate cause of his illness, Reynolds knew he was dying, telling a friend who hoped for a recovery, 'I know that all things on earth must have an end, and now I am come to mine' (Northcote, *Life*, 2.286). On 5 November 1791 he wrote his will, bequeathing the bulk of his estate to his niece Mary Palmer (including a cash sum of £4000), gifts of pictures to his friends, and sums of money to his family and his servant Ralph. In his haste to complete the will Reynolds omitted to mention Giuseppe Marchi, although Mary Palmer ensured that he was granted an annuity after Reynolds's death. On 10 November Reynolds asked Benjamin West to stand in for him at a general meeting of the Royal Academy, requesting him to inform the Academicians that he wished to stand down before the annual presidential election the following month. On 10 December Reynolds was re-elected for the last time. He did not return to the academy. By late January 1792, as the physical pain became unbearable, he found some relief through laudanum, which he took in increasingly large doses. A week or so later Reynolds's friend Dr Blagden realized that there might be a specific reason for Reynolds's rapid decline, aside from self-pity. He sought further medical opinion. Liver disease was diagnosed. Baker and Warren agreed with the diagnosis, but by now it was too late for any effective treatment. Reynolds died, unmarried, at his home at 47 Leicester Square, London, on the evening of Thursday 23 February 1792.

Reynolds's executors, Edmond Malone, Edmund Burke, and Philip Metcalfe, asked permission from the council of the Royal Academy for Reynolds's body to lie in state at Somerset House on the night before his burial. Chambers objected, informing them that, owing to the nature of the lease, it was not possible to use the building for purposes other than had been originally designated. However, George III intervened on behalf of Reynolds's executors, and on the night of 2 March 1792 Reynolds's body was laid out in the Life Room of the Royal Academy, which, for the occasion, was draped in black, and lit by candles mounted in silver sconces. On the following day at half past twelve, the body was conveyed from Somerset House for state burial in the crypt of St Paul's Cathedral. The coffin was accompanied in great ceremony by a cortège of ninety-one carriages. All ten pallbearers were prominent members of the aristocracy, including three dukes, two marquesses, and three earls. 'Everything', Burke told his son, 'was just as our deceased friend would, if living, have wished it to be; for he was, you know not altogether indifferent to this kind of observances' (Leslie and Taylor, 2.634–5).

Reynolds dominated the British art world in the second half of the eighteenth century, and any cultural history of the period would not be complete without some recognition of his central role. Many qualities contributed to his success. First and foremost, Reynolds was the most innovative portrait painter of his generation. Despite technical shortcomings and a tendency to sacrifice quality for quantity, his best portraits retain an unrivalled power and physical presence. His professional skills were underpinned by an unswerving personal ambition, tempered with an awareness of what could be realistically achieved in the current artistic climate, and within the bounds of his own particular gifts. Reynolds appreciated the value of patronage and social networks, and despite his own political preferences (he was a thorough whig), established a wide circle of acquaintance. He was a loyal and generous friend and loved company. And while he was guarded about expressing opinions about those he disliked, he did not suffer fools. Reynolds was a born taxonomist, endowed with an ability to absorb an extraordinary range of ideas and opinions which he could distil, organize, and express with clarity and vigour. The honours conferred upon him, his pre-eminent position at the Royal Academy, his reputation as founder of the British school, together with the seeming ease with which this was achieved, reflect an extraordinary desire to channel his energies into gaining public recognition. In the year before his death Reynolds argued with Chambers as he tirelessly campaigned to erect a monument to Samuel Johnson in St Paul's Cathedral. He wrote then of the importance of conferring and achieving honours. It may serve as his epitaph. 'Distinction', Reynolds affirmed, 'is what we all seek after, and the world does set a value on them [sic], and I go with the great stream of life' (Leslie and Taylor, 2.611).

Reynolds's posthumous reputation Four years after his death, in 1796, Reynolds's executors disposed of the contents of his studio by auction, including all those works not retained by his niece (whose collection was sold after her death in 1821). The most expensive works in these early sales were subject pictures, which were still considered by Reynolds's acolytes to be his most important works. In 1813 the first retrospective exhibition of over 200 of Reynolds's pictures was mounted by the British Institution in Pall Mall. Although the exhibition was lauded by the mainstream press, the essayist Charles Lamb, writing in *The Examiner*, used the occasion to attack Reynolds's history paintings, in particular *Ugolino* and the *Death of Cardinal Beaufort*. 'The one stares and the other grins', he observed, 'but is there common dignity in the countenances?' (Postle, *Subject Pictures*, 293). Over the next two years Reynolds's reputation as a history painter was further undermined in a series of revisionist essays written by William Hazlitt in the radical periodical *The Champion*. While Hazlitt claimed to have no wish to undermine Reynolds's position as founder of the contemporary British school, he stressed that Reynolds's reputation had been inflated by the uncritical attitude of his friends and the vagaries of fashion. In 1797 Edmond Malone had published two volumes of Reynolds's collected writings, prefaced by a short, laudatory, biographical essay. In 1813–15 James Northcote published the first major biography of

Reynolds, which he revised and expanded in a two-volume edition of 1818. In his biography Northcote provided a positive account of his former master's professional career and achievement. However, during the 1820s, in a series of published conversations with Hazlitt, he was far more critical, not least about Reynolds's personal life and character. While Hazlitt confessed that he had exaggerated Northcote's views and even invented some of the opinions attributed to him, his writings none the less contributed to a less reverent attitude towards Reynolds, notably in Allan Cunningham's scurrilous biographical essay of 1829, which appeared in the first volume of his populist *Lives of the most Eminent British Painters*.

Reynolds's reputation, although it was tarnished by the writings of Hazlitt and Cunningham, continued to rise during the second half of the nineteenth century. In 1865 *The Life and Times of Sir Joshua Reynolds* was published, co-authored by the American artist Charles Robert Leslie and the critic Tom Taylor (who completed the volume following Leslie's death in 1859). Leslie's and Taylor's biography, which contained a great deal of contextual matter on Reynolds's friendships and the politics of the period, reasserted the artist's position as a central figure in the Georgian cultural milieu, as well as suggesting for the first time (largely through Taylor's input) Reynolds's close allegiance to the whig party. Major exhibitions of Reynolds's work continued to appear, notably that mounted at the Grosvenor Gallery in the winter of 1883, which was accompanied by a lavish catalogue by F. G. Stephens, who had also published, in 1867, *English Children as Painted by Sir Joshua Reynolds*, a book which, in turn, reflected the immense popularity of the artist's child portraits. Indeed, the appeal of Reynolds's child portraiture to Victorian sentiment is reflected by the fact that *The Age of Innocence* (Tate collection) was copied full-size in oils no fewer than 323 times between 1856 and 1893. During the final decades of the nineteenth century prices for Reynolds's portraits, which had been steadily rising, reached new records, Lord Rothschild paying over £20,000 for *Garrick between Tragedy and Comedy* in 1886.

In 1900 the first catalogue raisonné of Reynolds's paintings, *A History of the Works of Sir Joshua Reynolds*, was published in four volumes by the picture dealer Algernon Graves and William Vine Cronin. This magisterial tome, containing detailed biographies of the artist's sitters and excerpts from contemporary criticism, provided an invaluable basis for Reynolds scholarship over the next hundred years. During the earlier decades of the twentieth century the most significant contribution to Reynolds studies was made by the American scholar Frederick Hilles, who in 1929 edited the first edition of the artist's letters. This was followed up, in 1936, by *The Literary Career of Sir Joshua Reynolds*, a pioneering study of the making of Reynolds's *Discourses* and the artist's other writings, and, in 1952, by *Portraits ... of Sir Joshua Reynolds*, consisting of hitherto unpublished essays and notes by Reynolds discovered among the private papers of James Boswell. The greatest apologist for Reynolds's art in the twentieth century was Sir Ellis Waterhouse, who in 1941 published a book which, as he stated, illustrated 'the bulk of Sir Joshua's major work in portraiture from the beginning of his career to the end' (Waterhouse, *Reynolds*, 1941, ix). Waterhouse's writings on Reynolds were largely confined to short essays, and to the artist's portraits. However, his unrivalled firsthand knowledge of the paintings, combined with his generosity to fellow scholars, ensured that he dominated Reynolds studies until his death in 1986. That year also marked the biggest exhibition of Reynolds's art mounted in the twentieth century, which was held at the Royal Academy, London. This exhibition in turn sparked new initiatives, notably the project for a new catalogue raisonné of Reynolds's oil paintings, which was published by David Mannings (with Martin Postle) in 2000. However, while scholarly interest in Reynolds has been reinvigorated in recent years, this has not been matched either by a rise in public appeal, or by saleroom prices, which have remained below those of contemporaries such as Stubbs, Zoffany, Gainsborough, and Wright of Derby. A marked exception is Reynolds's *Omai* (Tate collection), which sold at Sothebys on 29 November 2001 for £10.3 million.   MARTIN POSTLE

Sources C. R. Leslie and T. Taylor, *Life and times of Sir Joshua Reynolds*, 2 vols. (1865) · J. Northcote, *The life of Sir Joshua Reynolds*, 2nd edn, 2 vols. (1818) · J. Northcote, *Memoirs of Sir Joshua Reynolds, knt.* (1813–15) · *The works of Sir Joshua Reynolds*, ed. E. Malone, 3 vols. (1798) · D. Hudson, *Sir Joshua Reynolds: a personal study* (1958) · D. Mannings, *Sir Joshua Reynolds: a complete catalogue of his oil paintings*, 2 vols. (2000) [the subject pictures catalogued by M. Postle; incl. complete list of works and a comprehensive bibliography] · *The letters of Sir Joshua Reynolds*, ed. J. Ingamells and J. Edgcumbe (2000) · N. Penny, ed., *Reynolds* (1986) [exhibition catalogue, RA, 16 Jan – 31 March 1986] · F. W. Hilles, *The literary career of Sir Joshua Reynolds* (1936) · F. W. Hilles, *Portraits, character sketches of Oliver Goldsmith, Samuel Johnson, and David Garrick, together with other MSS of Reynolds recently discovered among the private papers of James Boswell* (1952) · J. Reynolds, *Discourses on art*, ed. R. R. Wark (1975) · J. Reynolds, *Discourses on art*, ed. P. Rogers (1992) · M. Postle, *Sir Joshua Reynolds: the subject pictures* (1995) · *Sir Joshua Reynolds: a journey to Flanders and Holland*, ed. H. Mount (1996) · R. Prochno, *Joshua Reynolds* (1990) · E. K. Waterhouse, *Reynolds* (1941) · E. K. Waterhouse, *Reynolds* (1973) · A. Graves and W. V. Cronin, *A history of the works of Sir Joshua Reynolds*, 4 vols. (1899–1901) · D. Mannings, *Sir Joshua Reynolds PRA, 1723–92* (1992) · J. Barrell, *The political theory of painting from Reynolds to Hazlitt* (1986) · T. Clifford, A. Griffiths, and M. Royalton Kisch, *Gainsborough and Reynolds in the British Museum* (1978) · W. Cotton, *Sir Joshua Reynolds and his works* (1856) · *Sir Joshua Reynolds's notes and observations on pictures*, ed. W. Cotton (1859) · L. Herrmann, 'The drawings by Sir Joshua Reynolds in the Herschel album', *Burlington Magazine*, 110 (1968), 650–58 · M. Cormack, 'The ledgers of Sir Joshua Reynolds', *Walpole Society*, 62 (1968–70), 105–69 · E. W. Waterhouse, ed., 'Reynolds's "Sitter book" for 1755', *Walpole Society*, 61 (1966–8), 112–64 · E. H. Gombrich, 'Reynolds's theory and practice of imitation', *Burlington Magazine*, 80 (1942), 40–45 · C. Mitchell, 'Three phases of Reynolds's method', *Burlington Magazine*, 80 (1942), 35–40 · D. Mannings, 'The sources and development of Reynolds's pre-Italian style', *Burlington Magazine*, 117 (1975), 212–22 · M. Postle, 'Patriarchs, prophets and paviours: Reynolds's images of old age', *Burlington Magazine*, 130 (1988), 735–44 · G. Perini, 'Sir Joshua Reynolds and Italian art and art literature', *Journal of the Warburg and Courtauld Institutes*, 51 (1988), 141–68 · F. W. Hilles, 'Sir Joshua and the Empress Catherine', *18th-Century studies in honor of Donald F. Hyde*, ed. W. H. Bond (1970) · R. R. Wark, *Sir Joshua Reynolds's 'Portrait of Mrs Siddons as the tragic muse'* (1965) · D. Mannings, 'Reynolds, Garrick and the choice of Hercules', *18th-Century Studies*, 7 (1984), 259–83 · M. Postle, 'Reynolds, Shaftesbury, Van Dyck and Dobson: sources for Garrick between Tragedy and Comedy', *Apollo*, 132 (1990), 306–11 · D. Mannings, 'Reynolds's oil sketches', *Burlington Magazine*, 133 (1991), 491–8 · F. J. P. Broun, 'Sir Joshua Reynolds's collection of paintings', PhD diss., Princeton University, 1987 · S. M. Radcliffe, ed., *Sir Joshua's nephew, being letters written 1769–1778* (1930) · parish register, Devon, Plympton St Maurice, 30 July 1723 [baptism] · W. T. Whitley, *Artists and their friends in England, 1700–1799*, 2 vols. (1928) · S. Gwynn, *Memorials of an eighteenth century painter, James Northcote* (1898) · D. Hudson, *Sir Joshua Reynolds: a personal study* (1958) · Vertue, *Note books* · Farington, *Diary* · Walpole, *Corr.* · Boswell, *Life* · *The manuscripts and correspondence of James, first earl of Charlemont*, 2 vols., HMC, 28 (1891–4)

Archives BL, travel journal, Egerton MS 2165 · BM, sketchbooks with MS notes · FM Cam., letters, ledgers, and MS of *Adaptation of talents* · Metropolitan Museum of Art, New York, sketchbooks with MS notes · Plymouth City Museum and Art Gallery, sitters book and corresp. · RA, pocket books and MSS · Sir John Soane's Museum, London, sketchbooks with MS notes · Wilts. & Swindon RO, receipted account and voucher for paintings for the earl of Pembroke · Yale U., sketchbooks with MS notes · Yale U., Beinecke L., notes on art | Bod., transcript of *A printer's journal* by E. Malone · Sheff. Arch., letters to Edmund Burke · Yale U. CBA, corresp. and papers · Yale U., Beinecke L., corresp. with James Boswell and papers

Likenesses J. Reynolds, three self-portraits, oils, c.1749–1779, NPG, RA · J. Reynolds, four self-portraits, oils, c.1753–1775, Tate collection · J. Reynolds, self-portrait, chalk drawing, 1760, BM · J. Reynolds, self-portrait, oils, c.1766–1773, Society of Dilettanti, Brooks's Club, London · N. Dance, double portrait, pencil drawing, c.1767 (with Angelica Kauffman), Harewood House, Leeds, West Yorkshire · A. Kauffman, oils, 1767, Saltram House, Devon · J. Reynolds, self-portrait, oils, 1769, Woburn Abbey, Bedfordshire · J. Reynolds, self-portrait, oils, 1775, Uffizi Gallery, Florence · G. Ceracchi, marble bust, 1778, RA · J. Reynolds, self-portrait, c.1780, RA [*see illus.*] · J. F. Rigaud, group portrait, oils, 1782, NPG · J. Reynolds, self-portrait, chalk, c.1784, Tate collection · J. Reynolds, self-portrait, oils, c.1788, Royal Collection · J. Flaxman, statue, 1813, St Paul's Cathedral, London · attrib. J. Flaxman, Wedgwood medallion, Nottingham Museum and Art Gallery · O. Humphry, miniature, Corsham Court, Wiltshire · G. Stuart, oils, National Gallery of Art, Washington, DC · J. Zoffany, group portrait, oils (*The academicians of the Royal Academy*, 1772), Royal Collection

Wealth at death approx. £100,000: Leslie and Taylor, *Life and times*, 2.635 and n. 2

Reynolds, Leighton Durham (1930–1999), classical scholar, was born on 11 February 1930 at Greenhill House, Abercannaid, just south of Merthyr Tudful, the son of Edgar James Reynolds, civil servant, and his wife, Hester, *née* Hale. His father was a national health insurance clerk, later an executive officer in the Ministry of Pensions and National Insurance. Reynolds's grandfather William on his mother's side was from a Somerset family who had moved to Wales; he left school at fourteen to become a miner, and eventually occupied a position of some responsibility in the industry. He was a keen gardener and from him Reynolds acquired a love of nature; this led him at thirteen to join a natural history society in Cardiff. This hobby resulted in his first publication: an essay on the flora of the Caerphilly basin. He attended Caerphilly grammar school, and in order to learn Latin had to attend classes at the local girls' school. He would have proceeded to Oxford but for a short-lived regulation that holders of state scholarships had to attend the university nearest their home town; so he went to University College, Cardiff, in 1947, intending to read French. But the professor of Latin, Roland Austin, spotted his linguistic talents and persuaded him to make Latin his principal rather than a subsidiary subject. Having obtained a first-class degree in 1950 he went on to St John's College, Cambridge, as an exhibitioner; a successful career there was crowned by another first-class degree in 1952 and various prizes, including a Craven fellowship. Two years of military service followed, spent mainly in Cambridge as an officer cadet in the Royal Air Force, learning Russian. Later he was staying in Paris with a Russian émigré who drove a taxi, and on finding the taxi driver struggling to repair his engine he was unable to resist the temptation to give his host an exhaustive lecture in Russian on the workings of the internal combustion engine.

Immediately after military service Reynolds was elected, in 1954, to a junior research fellowship at the Queen's College, Oxford, which he held for three years, laying the foundations for his edition of the *Letters* of Seneca, issued in two volumes in 1965 in the Oxford Classical Texts series along with a companion volume on the manuscript tradition of this lengthy and important text. These established his reputation as a leading Latinist. His attainments had already been recognized sufficiently in 1957 for him to be elected to a tutorial fellowship at Brasenose College in succession to Maurice Platnauer, who had become principal. Brasenose was a society he found congenial, and he devoted great energy to his tasks as tutor, while not neglecting other duties; after holding various college offices he became vice-principal in 1984—serving until 1987—and had two spells as acting principal, in 1985 and 1997, in which he acquitted himself with great skill and tact. As a punctilious curator of the senior common room he displayed the aesthetic sense needed for a tasteful refurbishment with antique furniture.

On 3 March 1962 Reynolds married Susan Mary, optometrist, and daughter of Sir Colin Douglas Buchanan, civil servant and later professor of transport studies. A waggish undergraduate, knowing that until recently fellows had required permission from the governing body to marry, sent him an exeat. The marriage was a great success. They had two daughters and a son. At their house, Winterslow Cottage, Lincombe Lane, Boars Hill, Oxford, the atmosphere was always relaxed and cordial. The house was originally a cottage which Reynolds had bought from the college. He enlarged it more than once, doing himself most of what would normally have been done by an architect or clerk of works. The surrounding semi-wilderness became a large and splendid garden; not for nothing did he list among his hobbies in *Who's Who* gardening and plant hunting. Other hobbies were walking and camping, and he practised the latter by driving the family caravan as far as Greece for a summer holiday.

Reynolds's full family and social life did not reduce his scholarly activity. He was co-editor of the *Classical Review* from 1975 to 1987. His edition of Seneca's letters in 1965 was followed by the same author's *Dialogues* (1977), and his edition of Sallust (1991) and of Cicero's *De finibus* (1998). His reputation was further enhanced by two other works. In 1968 he collaborated with his colleague N. G. Wilson to produce *Scribes and Scholars*, which appeared in revised and enlarged editions in 1974 and 1991. An account of how the Greek and Latin classics had been preserved and transmitted had not previously been given in a form accessible to students. The book was at once welcomed, and not merely by students of the classics, and was translated into Italian, Greek, Spanish, French, and Japanese. He also edited and wrote part of *Texts and Transmission: a Survey of the Latin Classics* (1983), a reference book designed as an act of homage to Sir Roger Mynors. He wrote beautifully clear English, and had a knack of finding telling phrases. He was elected a fellow of the British Academy in 1987. He was also visiting professor at Cornell (twice) and at Austin, Texas, and twice visited the Institute for Advanced Study at Princeton. He was elected professor of classical languages and literature at Oxford in 1996, becoming emeritus professor on his retirement in 1997.

When cancer was diagnosed in 1999 Reynolds reacted with a calm that would have earned Seneca's approval. He was persuaded to take a course of palliative treatment. Thanks to this he was able, with amazing intellectual energy, to write his part of a book planned with his Italian colleague Vincenzo Fera about Petrarch's notes on Cicero. He was imposing without any hint of the overbearing, imperturbable without seeming cold, slightly reticent but always ready to display his sense of humour, signalling his appreciation of a good anecdote by a hearty chuckle and the comment, 'That's rich.' He died at his home in Boars Hill, Oxford, on 4 December 1999, and was survived by his wife, Susan, and their three children.   N. G. WILSON

Sources *The Independent* (16 Dec 1999) · *Daily Telegraph* (6 April 2000) · *WWW* · personal knowledge (2004) · private information (2004) · b. cert. · m. cert. · d. cert.
Likenesses photograph, repro. in *The Independent* · photograph, repro. in *The Daily Telegraph*
Wealth at death £420,968—gross; £409,549—net: probate, 29 March 2000, *CGPLA Eng. & Wales*

Reynolds, Osborne (1842–1912), engineer and physicist, was born on 23 August 1842 at Belfast, the son of the Revd Osborne Reynolds and Jane Hickman. The elder Reynolds was a wrangler in 1837, and subsequently a fellow of Queens' College, Cambridge, principal of a school in Belfast, headmaster of Dedham grammar school, Essex, and, like his own father and grandfather, rector of Debachwith-Boulge, Suffolk. The younger Reynolds was schooled at Dedham and because he had a keen interest in mechanics at the age of nineteen entered the workshop of a mechanical engineer, Edward Hayes of Stony Stratford, in order to learn the practical side of the subject. He proceeded to Queens' College, Cambridge, graduated in 1867 as seventh wrangler, and was elected a fellow of the college in the same year. After a short period in the civil engineering office of Lawson and Mansergh of London he was the following year appointed, despite his youth and inexperience, to the newly instituted professorship of engineering in the Owens College, Manchester, a post he held until his retirement, through ill health, in 1905.

After an uncertain start the course of engineering study introduced by Reynolds succeeded in establishing the discipline at Owens, and the more capable among his students later came to occupy posts of distinction. The core of the curriculum was applied mechanics, and his goal was the application of scientific principles to engineering requirements. Reynolds was also instrumental in the foundation of the Whitworth Engineering Laboratory in 1887, in which teaching, research, and testing took place. During the long tenure of his professorship Reynolds investigated and contributed to a wide range of physics and engineering problems. From 1869 to 1873, he focused on questions of electricity and magnetism and their relation to solar and cometary phenomena. Thereafter his investigations dealt almost entirely with mechanical questions, or with physical phenomena so far as they appeared to admit of a mechanical explanation. They were highly original both in conception and in execution.

Reynolds's acute physical insight enabled him to explain phenomena which other minds had regarded as obscure or even paradoxical. Examples of his important work include the study of lubrication, which has led to important practical inventions, especially of bearings capable of carrying high loads at high speeds; the experimental investigation of the laws of the flow of water in pipes, in which he showed that there is a 'critical velocity' (depending on the diameter of the pipe, the kinematic viscosity of the fluid and a quantity now known as the Reynolds number), at which the flow changes its character between streamline and turbulent; the investigation of 'dilatancy', as he called it, a peculiar property of granular media; the development of turbines and pumps; and studies of group-velocity of water waves where he was the first to show that group-velocity also provides the rate of transmission of energy. His most extensive piece of experimental work was a novel determination of the mechanical equivalent of heat; he directly measured the amount of heat required to raise a pound of water from the freezing to the boiling point, the result being thus independent of the thermometric properties of any particular substance, such as mercury or glass. This was an exceptionally deft determination of a physical constant.

Reynolds's scientific papers were published in a collected form, *Papers on Mechanical and Physical Subjects*, in three volumes (1900–03). Of their originality and value there is no question, but it cannot be said that they are always easy to follow. Though Reynolds's approach was always to look for a simple explanation, rather than for one which depended on the concurrence of a number of independent causes, his involved style of exposition had a tendency to perplex all but determined students, with the result that much of his work, especially his theoretical work, was long in gaining general acceptance. The worth of his contributions was, however, early recognized. He was elected a fellow of the Royal Society in 1877, and was awarded its gold medal in 1888. He was an active and dedicated member of the Manchester Literary and Philosophical Society which he served as secretary for many years

and as its president in 1888–9. In 1903 he was its Dalton medallist. In 1884 he received an honorary doctorate from the University of Glasgow.

Reynolds's character was, like his writings, strongly individual. Somewhat reserved in personal matters, and occasionally combative and tenacious in matters of university politics, he was kindly and generous in all ordinary relations of life. He had a keen sense of humour and delighted in starting paradoxes. His first wife was Charlotte Chadwick, whom he married in 1868 and who died the following year; they had one son, who died in childhood. In 1881 he married Annie Charlotte, daughter of the Revd Henry Wilkinson, rector of Otley, Suffolk; they had three sons and a daughter. After his retirement in 1905 Reynolds lived at St Decuman's, Watchet, Somerset, where he died on 21 February 1912. He was survived by his wife.   Horace Lamb, *rev.* Robert H. Kargon

Sources H. Lamb, *PRS*, 88A (1912–13), xv-xxi · private information (1927) · personal knowledge (1927) · D. M. McDowell and J. D. Jackson, eds., *Osborne Reynolds and engineering science today* (1970) · R. H. Kargon, *Science in Victorian Manchester* (1977), 180–92 · *CGPLA Eng. & Wales* (1912)
Archives RS | Air Force Research Laboratories, Cambridge, Massachusetts, Strutt MSS · CUL, letter to Sir George Stokes
Likenesses photograph, 1903, repro. in McDowell and Jackson, eds., *Osborne Reynolds*, facing p. 5 · J. Collier, oils, 1904, University of Manchester
Wealth at death £14,283 13s. 2d.: resworn probate, 10 April 1912, *CGPLA Eng. & Wales*

Reynolds, Richard [St Richard Reynolds] (*d.* **1535**), Bridgettine monk and Roman Catholic martyr, came probably from the yeoman family of Reynolds of Pinhoe, Devon. He was educated at Cambridge University, where William Exmew, later one of the London Carthusian martyrs, was one of his contemporaries. Reynolds graduated BA in 1506, proceeding MA in 1509 and BTh in 1513. In 1509 he became university preacher, and in 1510 a fellow of Corpus Christi College. In 1513 Reynolds entered Syon Abbey, Middlesex, the only English Bridgettine house and one which had promoted religious reform from its foundation in 1415. There he became one of thirteen priest-brethren, responsible for serving the sacramental needs of a larger body of enclosed sisters, and for evangelizing the laity, principally through preaching. He followed this life quietly for twenty years.

Syon's reputation for holiness and its connections with the royal court attracted some leading theologians, who valued the opportunity for study and contemplation within the order, so that in the early sixteenth century the house stood at the forefront of Renaissance learning in England. Reynolds was one of several brethren educated at Cambridge. Unlike other brethren he wrote no books, but was renowned for personal holiness and as a distinguished scholar and preacher. The Catholic scholar and apologist Philippus Montanus reported that Reynolds was a man with the countenance and spirit of an angel, and Cardinal Reginald Pole that he was the only English monk well-versed in Latin, Greek, and Hebrew. Reynolds was known personally to Montanus, More, and Fisher, and certainly by reputation to Pole and Erasmus. Further evidence for his humanist learning is found in the ninety-four volumes he gave to his monastery's library, ranging from works by classical authors to the writings of Italian humanists. The devotional books were a mixture of traditional monastic spirituality and *devotio moderna*, although his theological collection was less innovative than that of John Fewterer, his contemporary at Cambridge who was confessor-general of Syon from 1523 to 1536.

The Bridgettines, Carthusians, and Observant Franciscans, the orders which had encouraged pre-Reformation church reform, all provided martyrs opposed to Henry VIII's divorce and his supremacy over the English church. Syon's association with Elizabeth Barton, 'the Holy Maid of Kent', a political visionary in the mould of St Bridget of Sweden who prophesied against the king's actions, in particular marked that community out as treasonable. Sir Thomas More met Barton twice at Syon through Reynolds, who was allegedly one of two monks to whom Fewterer showed secret correspondence between the king and John Fisher, bishop of Rochester, sent to Fewterer by Fisher with a request for advice. Reynolds was also later reported to have urged Sir George Throckmorton in the confessional, probably in 1532, to stand by Queen Catherine against her husband or risk damnation. After the Act of Supremacy was passed in 1534, Syon's influence made Cromwell anxious to secure the community's endorsement. Opinions in the abbey were divided, and Reynolds may have taken on a position of leadership, as Fewterer became ill under the strain of the crisis. Reynolds was arrested and imprisoned in the Tower shortly before 20 April 1535, when he was interrogated by Cromwell at the Rolls, along with three Carthusian priors, John Houghton, Robert Lawrence, and Augustine Webster. John Hale, vicar of Isleworth, the parish in which Syon stood, was tried separately but executed with them.

The trial of Reynolds and the others took place on 28 April, before a special commission at Westminster. The four monks denied the royal supremacy, but pleaded not guilty to treason. On the following day, before the verdict was pronounced, Reynolds made an impressive speech. Responding to Lord Chancellor Audley's demanding to know why he persisted in standing out against the rest of England, he said that he had intended to keep silence like Our Lord, but in discharge of his own conscience, and those of others, he had all the rest of Christendom in favour of his view, besides the testimony of general councils and the church fathers. The jury had to be persuaded by the judges and Cromwell to return the verdict of guilty. Reynolds asked for two or three days to prepare for death, a request which the king granted, as Cranmer thought the monks might recant. Dr Thomas Starkey, a royal chaplain sent to reason with Reynolds, found him firm in his opinions. On 4 May Reynolds and the others were dragged on hurdles from the Tower to Tyburn, where without having been degraded from holy orders they were executed in their habits, an unprecedented step. Unusually, members of the court witnessed the execution to counteract widespread disapproval as, it was rumoured, did the king in disguise. Reynolds, the last to suffer, comforted the others, promising them a heavenly banquet and supper for their sharp breakfast, taken for their master's sake. When it was his turn, he exhorted the people to pray earnestly for the king, and met his death with fortitude.

Reynolds's remains were exhibited on Syon's gatehouse, on a stone column which the nuns carried into exile. His martyrdom gave Syon a symbolic role in the emerging recusant community in exile and at home, which undoubtedly contributed to the house's tradition, unbroken into the twenty-first century. Reynolds was beatified in 1886 and canonized as one of the forty martyrs of England and Wales in 1970.

Virginia R. Bainbridge

Sources A. Hamilton, *The angel of Syon: the life and martyrdom of Blessed Richard Reynolds* (1905) · *LP Henry VIII*, vol. 8 · Venn, *Alum. Cant.*, 1/3.445 · P. Montanus, *Expositio fidelis de morte Domini Thome Mori et quorundam aliorum insignum virorum in Anglia* (Basel, 1535) · R. Pole, *De unitate* (1538) · M. Bateson, ed., *Catalogue of the library of Syon monastery* (1898) · V. Gillespie, ed., *Syon Abbey, with the libraries of the Carthusians* (2001) · F. R. Johnston, *Blessed Richard Reynolds: the angel of Syon* (1961) · M. B. Tait, 'The Brigittine monastery of Syon (Middlesex) with special reference to its monastic usages', DPhil diss., U. Oxf., 1975 · G. J. Aungier, *The history and antiquities of Syon monastery* (1840) · J. Guy, *The public career of Sir Thomas More* (1980) · M. Chauncy, *Historia aliquot martyrum Anglorum* (1888)

Reynolds [Rainolde], **Richard** (*c.*1530–1606), Church of England clergyman and author, was born of an Essex family, but nothing is known of his early life. He entered St John's College, Cambridge, on 10 November 1546, as sizar for the master, William Bill, and on 11 November 1547 he became a scholar on the Lady Margaret foundation. In 1548 he transferred to the newly established Trinity College, Cambridge, which was dedicated to the new learning and religion. He graduated BA in 1550 and became a fellow in 1551; he proceeded MA in 1553.

There are no records of Reynolds during the Marian years, but his career may have paralleled that of his master, Dr Bill, who in 1551 also had transferred to Trinity, was ejected from his new mastership during Mary's reign, and was restored under Elizabeth. A similar ejection and restoration for Reynolds, with interim employment as a teacher, would help to explain the appearance of his pedagogical treatise, *A booke called the foundacion of rhetorike, because all other partes of rhetorike are grounded thereupon*. It appeared in 1563 from the press of John Kingston, who in that same year reissued Thomas Wilson's *Arte of Rhetorique*, and Reynolds proposes his own treatise as preparation for Wilson's work. The *Foundacion* is an English adaptation of Aphthonius's *Progymnasmata*, a fourth-century series of graduated exercises in written and oral composition. Reynolds expands upon Aphthonius's exercises, domesticates Reinhard Lorich's Latin commentary on the *Progymnasmata*, and offers model orations that stress protestant and English political themes. Some currency for the treatise is indicated by contemporary references in William Fulwood, *The Enimie of Idlenesse* (1563), and John Jones, *The Art and Science of Preserving Body and Soul* (1579), but the *Foundacion* was never reprinted.

Reynolds also produced *A chronicle of all the noble emperours of the Romaines … setting forth the great power, and devine providence of almighty God, in preserving the godly princes and common wealthes* (entered 1566/7, but not published until 1571), and 'De statu nobilium virorum et principum' (*c*.1566, BL, Harley MS 973). Both works used historical material to exemplify Tudor ideas about political order and stability, the first showing divine intervention in political affairs, the second defending monarchy and attacking the papacy. The two works are complementary, in that the second directly addresses the themes which are adduced in the first, and both betray the personal turmoil of the mid-century upheavals. Reynolds sought noble patronage with each of his three works, but did not directly receive any.

Reynolds studied medicine at Cambridge for eight years, starting with the beginning of Elizabeth's reign, and on 14 March 1567 received permission to proceed MD. But instead of keeping his act and being admitted, he was allowed on 17 April 1567 to go to Muscovy with letters of introduction from the university. This unusual proceeding suggests both opportunity and haste. In 1565 Tsar Ivan Vasilyevich (the Terrible) had requested yet again that Elizabeth send him English physicians, surgeons, and craftsmen; and while the tsar paid the English physicians well, few were willing to go, fewer to stay. Reynolds apparently left quickly to sail with the fleet of the Muscovy Company, and on 18 May 1567 Elizabeth replied that she had sent the requested professionals. Reynolds received 50 roubles upon arrival in Moscow that year, but served as a physician only briefly, returning to England either of his own accord, or dismissed by the tsar who had a history of rejecting English doctors he deemed inadequate. The date of his return is uncertain; ambassador Thomas Randolph reported meeting clandestinely with him on 16 October 1568, and Reynolds himself claimed he was serving the tsar as late as 1569.

The queen presented him to the rectory at Stapleford Abbots, Essex, on 7 August 1568, presumably in his absence, and instituted him on 24 May 1569 to the rectory of neighboring Lambourne, on the presentation of Katherine Barefoot, who had inherited her husband Robert's temporary right to grant the benefice. Some time before 1590 he married Elizabeth, the daughter of Hieram Barefoot (or Barfoote) and niece to Thomas Barfoote who inherited Lambourne Manor.

In 1571 Reynolds finally published his earlier *Chronicle*, incorporating material from 'lucubrationes meas Moscoviticas' ('my nocturnal studies in Muscovy') which he had submitted to Elizabeth's councillors, and he signed himself as 'Doctor in Phisicke'. The College of Physicians examined him that same year and rejected him 'as being very ignorant and unlearned' (Goodall, 315); he admitted having practised medicine for the past two years without a licence, and was imprisoned until he paid a fine of £20. He returned to clerical duties, but as late as 1574 his parishioners still referred to him in wills variously as rector and physician. He was instituted to the vicarage of West Thurrock on 2 May 1578, on the presentation of Humphrey Hayes, but he resigned it in 1584, possibly in the wake of a privy council discussion the preceding year about the 'inconveniences' of a Mr Raynolds who was holding multiple benefices. On 25 August 1579 he was summoned to London by Bishop John Aylmer to respond to some allegations, now unknown. However, Reynolds, his wife, and the local constable Francis Bushe jointly assaulted and injured the process-server Morice. All were committed to the Marshalsea, and Reynolds had to petition the privy council before he gained his release on 18 September 1579. The remainder of his life was spent in local clerical duties in Essex, and he died there a few days before 20 December 1606. In his will Reynolds left bequests to his wife, Elizabeth, his brother John Reynolds, his brother's sons John and Thomas, his sister Joan, wife of the 'unthriftie' Ambrose Cragge of Cambridge, and to their daughter Anne.   LAWRENCE D. GREEN

Sources L. D. Green, 'Rainolde, Richard', *The Tudor encyclopedia*, ed. A. Kinney (2000) • M. McClintock, 'Rainolde, Richard', *Sixteenth-century British nondramatic writers: second series*, ed. D. A. Richardson, DLitB, 136 (1994), 273–6 • Cooper, *Ath. Cantab.*, 2.444 • J. Venn, ed., *Grace book Δ* (1910), 65, 87, 204 • Venn, *Alum. Cant.*, 1/3.445 • C. Goodall, *The Royal College of Physicians of London founded and established by law* (1684), 315 • R. Newcourt, *Repertorium ecclesiasticum parochiale Londinense*, 2 (1710), 360, 555, 592 • J. von Hamel, *England and Russia: comprising the voyages of John Tradescant the Elder, Sir Hugh Willoughby, Richard Chancellor, Nelson, and others to the White Sea*, trans. J. S. Leigh (1854), 176–7, 188 • E. D. Morgan and C. H. Coote, eds., *Early voyages and travels to Russia and Persia*, 2, Hakluyt Society, 73 (1886), 277 • F. R. Johnson, 'Two Renaissance textbooks of rhetoric: Aphthonius' *Progymnasmata* and Rainolde's *A booke called the foundacion of rhetorike*', *Huntington Library Quarterly*, 6 (1942–3), 427–44 • T. S. Willan, *The early history of the Russia Company, 1553–1603* (1956), 92 • M. Wretts-Smith, 'The English in Russia during the second half of the sixteenth century', *TRHS*, 4th ser., 3 (1920), 72–102 • *APC, 1578–80*, 268 • *Calendar of the manuscripts of the most hon. the marquis of Salisbury*, 1, HMC, 9 (1883), 347–8, no. 1140 • *CSP dom., 1581–90* • W. C. Waller, ed., 'Old Chigwell wills (continued)', *Transactions of the Essex Archaeological Society*, new ser., 11 (1910), 335–46 • F. G. Emmison, ed., *Essex wills*, 9: *The bishop of London's commissary court, 1569–1578* (1994), no. 369 • E. Stokes, ed., *Index of wills proved in the prerogative court of Canterbury*, 5: *1605–1619*, British RS, 43 (1912), 375 • G. M. Trevelyan, *Trinity College: an historical sketch* (1946)
Archives BL, Harley MS 973

Reynolds, Richard (1674–1744), bishop of Lincoln, was born at Leverington, Cambridgeshire, the son of Richard Reynolds, rector of Leverington, and his wife, Dorothy Conyars. His mother was the granddaughter of Dorothy Bushel, a maid of honour to Henrietta Maria. He was educated at Mr Hayes's school, Moulton, Lincolnshire, and at Mr Warren's school, Peterborough, and was admitted a pensioner at Sidney Sussex College, Cambridge, in 1689, becoming a scholar in 1690. He migrated to Trinity Hall in November 1694, and proceeded LLB in 1695 and LLD in 1701.

Reynolds was ordained deacon in 1697 and priest in 1698 by the bishop of Peterborough. He became rector of Conington, Cambridgeshire, and of Denton, Huntingdonshire, in 1698, and a prebendary of Peterborough and chancellor of the diocese in 1704; these two positions he held until 1718, when he became dean of Peterborough. From 1706 until his death he was rector of St Peter's, Northampton, and in 1715 he became a chaplain to George I. In 1721 he succeeded Benjamin Hoadly as bishop in the poverty-stricken diocese of Bangor.

At Bangor he began a primary visitation before being translated to Lincoln in 1723. He was a conscientious diocesan bishop, spending each summer and autumn in his Lincoln diocese, based at the main episcopal residence at Buckden in Huntingdonshire. He undertook visitations of the vast diocese at least twice—in 1724 and 1727—visiting all the major market towns from Welwyn in Hertfordshire in the south to Gainsborough and Caistor in Lincolnshire in the north. He personally examined ordination candidates, and was able to report to Archbishop Wake, for example, that a candidate for priesthood, after twelve years' diaconate, could:

> just read a verse or two in the Greek Testament, and turn an article out of Latin into English, ... But what is still worse, he is utterly ignorant of everything that relates to the doctrines of the Articles and of every branch of Divinity. (Sykes, 107)

However, because he was 'modest, sober and well-behaved', and his mother was presenting him to a living in succession to his father, he ordained him priest. Reynolds lamented the poverty of the Lincolnshire livings, noting that a great number of parishes comprised only eight or ten houses, and being worth £20 a year or less, required clergy to hold four or five livings to gain 'a scanty subsistence', and that 'neither the public worship, nor any other part of the pastoral charge could ... have due attendance' (ibid.). He supported charity schools, regarding their products as a bastion against a feared resurgence of Roman Catholicism. Reynolds married Sarah, daughter of Richard *Cumberland, bishop of Peterborough; they had at least eight children. She died on 7 April 1740, and was buried at Buckden.

Reynolds was concerned for the city of Lincoln; he rebuked the mayor for not preventing riots in 1726 over a proposal to remove the spires from the cathedral's west towers, and he suggested to the secretary of state, Lord Townshend, that the riots showed disaffection to the state by the inhabitants of the county over the high price of corn, rather than zeal for the church. He contributed to the costs of rebuilding St Botolph's Church, and sanctioned a buttermarket to be built on a strip of the churchyard of St Peter-at-Arches. He was also concerned for the cathedral, and permitted stone from the old palace to be used to repair the cathedral in 1729. In 1735 he requested the dean and chapter to institute a more frequent celebration of holy communion in the cathedral.

In the House of Lords Reynolds was the only bishop to vote against the majority of the bishops, in the South Sea Company divisions during the excise crisis in 1733, when the bishops' votes were crucial to the survival of the ministry. During the later 1730s and early 1740s he became a persistent critic of Robert Walpole's foreign and war policies, and he consistently supported the parliamentary opposition until Walpole's fall. He died at his London home in Charles Street, Westminster, on 15 January 1744, and was buried in Buckden church, Huntingdonshire, adjoining the historic palace of the bishops of Lincoln, with no memorial. In his will Reynolds stated, 'My goods real and personal, by my liberal exhibitions in my lifetime, lye in a small compass.'

Seven of Reynolds's sons were ordained, and six received considerable preferment in the diocese of Lincoln. All became prebendaries of Lincoln Cathedral. George, the eldest, became chancellor of the diocese in 1721, archdeacon of Lincoln in 1725, rector of Farthingstone, Northamptonshire, in 1730–1, rector of Hannington, and of Carlton Scroop, Lincolnshire, and of Walgrave in 1731, and subdean of Lincoln in 1732. W. M. JACOB

Sources Venn, *Alum. Cant.* · N. Sykes, *Church and state in England in the XVIII century* (1934) · F. Hill, *Georgian Lincoln* (1964) · G. G. Perry and J. H. Overton, *Biographical notices of the bishops of Lincoln: from Remigius to Wordsworth* (1900) · D. M. Thompson, 'Historical survey, 1750–1949', *A history of Lincoln Minster*, ed. D. Owen (1994), 210–318 · episcopal act book, 1723–61, Lincs. Arch., Lincoln diocesan archives, Reg 38 · bishops' correspondence, Lincs. Arch., Lincoln diocesan archives, COR B/4/19 & 20 · C. Jones, ed., *A pillar of the constitution: the House of Lords in British politics, 1640–1784* (1989) · DNB

Archives Christ Church Oxf., Wake MSS · Lincs. Arch., corresp. with Sir Gilbert Heathcote · V&A NAL, letters to Lady Sundon

Reynolds, Richard (1735–1816), ironmaster and philanthropist, was born on 1 November 1735 in Corn Street, Bristol, the only son of Richard Reynolds (d. 1769), iron merchant of Bristol, and his wife, Jane Dunne or Doane. He was the great-grandson of Michael Reynolds of Faringdon, Berkshire, one of the first converts to Quakerism. He was educated at Thomas Bennet's Quaker boarding-school at Pickwick, Wiltshire, and on 18 August 1750 was apprenticed to another Quaker, William Fry, grocer, of Castle Street, Bristol. He took up his freedom of the city of Bristol, which he claimed as the son of a freeman, on 14 May 1757. He married, on 20 May 1757, Hannah (1735–1762), daughter of Abraham *Darby (1711–1763), with whom he had a son, William *Reynolds (1758–1803), and a daughter, Hannah Mary (b. 1761), who married William Rathbone in 1786. His second marriage on 1 December 1763 was to Rebecca (d. 1803), daughter of William Gulson of Coventry, with whom he had three children, Richard (b. 1765), Michael (1766–1770), and Joseph (1768–1859).

Reynolds moved to Shropshire in October 1756 as representative of the Bristol merchant Thomas Goldney, who had investments in the ironworks at Coalbrookdale and Horsehay, in which his partner was Abraham Darby II. In 1757 Reynolds took a one-third share of a new ironworks at Ketley, 4 miles from Coalbrookdale, together with Darby and Goldney. After his marriage he initially lived at Ketley, but he moved to Coalbrookdale in 1763 on the death of his father-in-law. He returned to Ketley in 1768, but again removed to Coalbrookdale in 1789. Gradually he bought up the Shropshire interests of the Goldney family, and extended his own property holdings, buying the manor of Sutton Maddock in 1776, and the manor of Madeley in 1780. In consequence he became the principal landlord of the Coalbrookdale Company. The affairs of

Richard Reynolds (1735–1816), by Samuel Percy, *c.*1810

the company in the 1770s and 1780s are not well documented, but it is evident that there were times when only Reynolds's financial resources, derived from his interests in Bristol and elsewhere, kept it from collapse. In 1789 the partnership owed him £20,000 and in December 1793 he advanced a further £4000 to keep the company in business.

Reynolds encouraged the experiments in 1766 of the brothers Thomas and George Cranage, who attempted to forge pig iron into wrought iron in a reverberatory furnace, using coal as the fuel, a process similar to that developed successfully by Henry Cort after 1784. The railway network associated with the Shropshire ironworks was extended in Reynolds's time, and the first use of iron rails in 1767 appears to have been his responsibility. Reynolds was one of the first ironmasters to install Boulton and Watt engines at his works, making an agreement with Boulton and Watt in December 1777 to construct new engines at Ketley.

Reynolds maintained a curiously distant relationship with the project to build the Iron Bridge across the Severn at Coalbrookdale, allowing his brother-in-law Abraham *Darby to put his capital at risk. Reynolds held five shares in the bridge for just a month in 1778, and in 1781–2, after the bridge had been completed, he bought the holding of Abraham Darby III, which in due course he passed to his daughter, Hannah Mary Rathbone.

In 1784–5 Reynolds was prominent among the opponents of a proposed tax on coal, arguing that it would have a detrimental effect on the iron trade, and in 1785 he

became a member of the United Chamber of Manufacturers of Great Britain. He reputedly refused government orders for armaments, although some sources suggest that cannon continued to be manufactured at Coalbrookdale in the period of his management, as they had been during the 1730s and 1740s. He passed his shares in the Ketley and Horsehay works to his sons in 1789, and in 1794 the name of the Coalbrookdale partnership was changed from Richard Reynolds & Co. to William Reynolds & Co. He remained resident at Coalbrookdale, but on 30 March 1803 his wife died, and the following year he settled in James' Square, Bristol.

Reynolds's letters show that he was a seasoned traveller. He was often in London, Liverpool, and Bristol, and visited such sites as the duke of Bridgewater's canal and coal mines at Worsley and Josiah Wedgwood's factory at Etruria. Among his other friends were James Watt, John Howard, John and Mary Fletcher of Madeley, James Montgomery, William Roscoe, MP, and John Wilkinson. Reynolds showed signs of impetuosity in his youth, and even considered a military career, but in his twenties it was remarked that he 'dropped into the sober and steady rut of the Society [of Friends]' (S. Smiles, *Industrial Biography*, 1863, 85). He was nevertheless an enthusiastic horseman, and took a gun on country walks. His character in adult life was marked by caution and discretion. Joseph Banks described him in 1767 as 'a Quaker who seemed Particularly Careful of his Speech' (Trinder, 1988, 28–9). A memorialist commented that 'he held little conversation on trifling subjects as his mind was generally taken up with things of importance' (*Excitements Held out to Mankind*, 8). He was active in the affairs of the Society of Friends, attending the society's yearly meetings, wearing the traditional Quaker dress, and accompanying several American Quakers on tours of England. He was described by one former employee in Shropshire as 'a Quaker—not a thin, withered, crotchety disciple of George Fox, but a full-fed Quaker, fair and ruddy, with eyes of blue that gave back the bright azure of the sky and lightened up a fine and manly face' (Randall, 293).

Reynolds enjoyed rural scenery, and organized picnics on the Wrekin and Benthall Edge for his senior workers and their families. During the 1780s he laid out on Lincoln Hill on the eastern side of Coalbrookdale a network of 'sabbath walks' for the recreational use of his workers. Having a Quakerly concern for good works, he provided generously, but without ostentation, for many deserving causes and individuals and dispensed his philanthropy anonymously. During the grain crisis of 1795 he supposedly spent £20,000 in the relief of poverty. He took a prominent role in the anti-slavery movement, and also encouraged the foundation of Sunday schools in 1786. A Reynolds Commemoration Society was formed in Bristol on 2 October 1816 to continue his philanthropic works. Reynolds died during a visit to Cheltenham on 10 September 1816, following a biliary obstruction, and was interred in the Quaker burial-ground at the Friars, Bristol, on the 18th.

BARRIE TRINDER

Sources H. M. Rathbone, *Letters of Richard Reynolds with a memoir of his life* (1852) · B. Trinder, *The industrial revolution in Shropshire*, 2nd edn (1981) · Mrs E. Greg, ed., *Reynolds-Rathbone diaries and letters, 1753–1839* (privately printed, London, 1905) · J. Randall, *History of Madeley*, ed. B. Trinder, 2nd edn (1975) · A. Raistrick, *Dynasty of iron founders: the Darbys and Coalbrookdale* (1953) · B. Trinder, *The Darbys of Coalbrookdale*, 4th edn (1993) · B. Trinder, ed., *The most extraordinary district in the world*, 2nd edn (1988) · N. Cossons and B. Trinder, *The iron bridge: symbol of the industrial revolution* (1979) · *Excitements to beneficence, held out to mankind in the character and example of Richard Reynolds, esq.* (1817) · M. P. Hack, *Richard Reynolds* (1896) · G. Pryce, *A popular history of Bristol* (1861) · *VCH Shropshire*

Archives Ironbridge Gorge Museum, Shropshire, accounts, incl. as executor of his father · RS Friends, Lond., letters · RS Friends, Lond., corresp. · U. Lpool L., corresp., diary, and papers | Shrops. RRC, financial records of Horsehay ironworks

Likenesses S. Percy, wax bust, *c.*1810, NPG; repro. in *European Magazine* (Feb 1817) [*see illus.*] · W. Sharp, line engraving, pubd 1817 (after W. Hobday), BM, NPG · portrait, 1896; in possession of William Gregory Norris of Coalbrookdale, 1896 · S. Bellin, engraving (after W. Hobday), repro. in H. M. Rathbone, *Letters of Richard Reynolds with a memoir* · Bottomley, engraving, repro. in *Excitements to benevolence* · W. Hobday, portrait; in possession of J. B. Braithwaite, London, 1896 · G. Meyer, engraving (after wax bust by S. Percy)

Reynolds, Sir Robert (1600/01–1678), lawyer and politician, was the son of Sir James Reynolds (*d.* 1650) of Castle Camps in Cambridgeshire, and his first wife, Margaret Melbourne of Dunmow in Essex. John *Reynolds was his much younger half-brother. Robert matriculated from Queens' College, Cambridge, in 1617, entered the Middle Temple on 12 February 1620, and was called to the bar in 1628. He was aged thirty-four when he married, on 29 October 1635, Mary (*b.* 1615, *d.* in or before 1646), daughter of Nathaniel Deards of Dunmow. In 1640 he was elected to represent the Wiltshire borough of Hindon in the Long Parliament.

In October 1642 Reynolds and Robert Goodwin were sent by the House of Commons to Dublin as commissioners representing parliament. They were allowed by the connivance of the lords justices to be present at the meetings of the Irish privy council, and used their opportunities to endeavour to make a party for the parliament among officers and officials. Charles I rebuked the lords justices, and ordered the arrest of the commissioners (1 March 1643), but they left Ireland before the order could be executed. On 3 January 1644 Reynolds was appointed a member of the Westminster assembly, of whose exaggerated claims he subsequently expressed his disapproval. On 26 October 1644 the House of Commons voted him the chambers and library in the Middle Temple belonging to Sir Edward Hyde. His first wife having died, on 23 May 1646 he married Priscilla (1626–1691), daughter of Sir Henry Wyndham of Pillesdon, Dorset.

Politically, Reynolds has been assigned to the middle group, wherein he is said to have occupied the 'peace-party fringe' (Underdown, 231). When the quarrel between the army and parliament came to a head in 1647 he endeavoured to maintain a neutral position, keeping clear of the Commons during successive periods of subservience to presbyterian and Independent interests. Though nominated one of the commissioners for the king's trial he refused to act. Nevertheless he returned to his place in the house after the king's death, thinking, as he said, that he might do some good, and resolving to 'keep as much of the people's rights as I could' (*Diary of Thomas Burton*, 3.209). Contemporary advocates of legal reform saw his procrastination over matters such as reform of the law of debt and land registry as entirely detrimental to popular right. However, Reynolds was pledged to the kingless Commonwealth by his purchases of confiscated lands: 'Besides Abingdon Hall and the lands worth 400*l.* per annum, he hath bought a good pennyworth of bishops' lands', says a contemporary libeller (Hotten, 39). In one of his parliamentary speeches he refers to an investment of £8000 in such property, which he spent in the acquisition of the manor of Bishop's Waltham, Hampshire, from the estate of the bishop of Winchester. In 1650 he also purchased the manor of Elvetham, Hampshire, from the marquess of Hertford. Some time between then and his death twenty-eight years later Reynolds would appear to have built a new house there. On 6 June 1650 he was appointed solicitor-general to the Commonwealth, but failed in the succeeding February to be elected to the council of state.

With the expulsion of the Long Parliament by Cromwell in 1653 Reynolds for a time disappeared from public life. Evidently, though he regarded the Rump's dissolution as long overdue he also saw its bill for fresh elections as the best hope for a firm foundation on which to build lasting political stability. There is no evidence that he ever forgave Oliver Cromwell for jeopardizing that. In 1659 he sat in Richard Cromwell's parliament as member for Whitchurch, Hampshire, and distinguished himself by a long speech against the bill for recognizing Richard's protectorship, while professing the greatest esteem for Richard's person. If proper constitutional securities were given for the rights of the people he was willing to accept the new protector. 'Against the single person there is not one exception; not any other man in this nation would pass so clearly' (*Diary of Thomas Burton*, 3.211). After Richard's fall Reynolds took his seat in the restored Long Parliament and was elected a member of the council of state on 14 May 1659, and again on 31 December 1659. He also became again solicitor-general, and on 18 January 1660 was raised to the dignity of attorney-general. As he had been one of the nine members of the council of state who promised to assist Monck in his action against Lambert (19 November 1659), promoted Monck's policy by his action in parliament, and laboured for the readmission of the 'secluded members', he found no difficulty in making his peace at the Restoration. On 31 May 1660 Reynolds petitioned the king for leave to retire with pardon and protection into the country. Charles II granted his request, and even conferred a knighthood upon him on 4 June 1660. According to Edmund Ludlow, the king was told 'that he had bestowed honour upon one of the veryest knaves of the parliament party', to which Charles replied that Thomas Clarges had presented Reynolds to him 'as one that had done him very good service' (Worden, *Voyce*, 156). The same source also claims that Reynolds was almost excepted from the Act of Indemnity. After this narrow escape Reynolds appears to have passed the remainder of his life quietly; he died in September 1678. He had requested burial at St Mary's, Elvetham. His second wife survived him, and married Henry Alexander, fourth earl of Stirling, in 1683. She died in 1691, her administration being granted on 24 November that year.

C. H. FIRTH, *rev.* SEAN KELSEY

Sources D. Underdown, *Pride's Purge: politics in the puritan revolution* (1971) · B. Worden, *The Rump Parliament, 1648–1653* (1974) · *VCH Hampshire and the Isle of Wight* · R. E. Shimp, 'Reynolds, Robert', Greaves & Zaller, *BDBR*, 86–7 · E. Ludlow, *A voyce from the watch tower*, ed. A. B. Worden, CS, 4th ser., 21 (1978) · J. L. Chester and G. J. Armytage, eds., *Allegations for marriage licences issued by the bishop of London*, 2, Harleian Society, 26 (1887), 224 · Venn, *Alum. Cant.* · H. A. C. Sturgess, ed., *Register of admissions to the Honourable Society of the Middle Temple, from the fifteenth century to the year 1944*, 3 vols. (1949) · IGI · PRO, PROB 11/358, fols. 202–4 · GEC, *Peerage*, new edn, 12/1.284 · *Diary of Thomas Burton*, ed. J. T. Rutt, 4 vols. (1828) · J. C. Hotten, ed., *The mystery of the good old cause briefly unfolded* (1863)
Wealth at death He made gifts worth £2600 in his will and devised annual incomes against sums totalling £2100 when he drew up his will: PRO, PROB 11/358, fols. 202–4

Reynolds, Robert Carthew (*d.* 1804). *See under* Reynolds, Robert Carthew (*bap.* 1745, *d.* 1811).

Reynolds, Robert Carthew (*bap.* **1745**, *d.* **1811**), naval officer, was baptized on 30 July 1745 at Lamorran, Cornwall, the son of John Reynolds and his wife, Elizabeth. He entered the navy in 1759 under the patronage of Captain George Edgcumbe of the *Hero*, and may have been present in the battle of Quiberon Bay and in the operations in the Bay of Biscay during the following years. He was afterwards, for a few months, in the *Brilliant*, with Captain Loggie; for three years in the *Pearl*, with Captain Charles Saxton; and for nearly a year in the *Venus*, with Captain Samuel Barrington. The *Venus* was paid off in June 1769, and on 1 May 1770 Reynolds passed his lieutenant's examination, being described in his certificate as 'more than twenty-one'. He was promoted lieutenant on 26 February 1777, and during the next five years served principally in the Channel Fleet: in the *Royal George*, the flagship of Vice-Admiral Robert Harland; in the *Barfleur*; and in the *Britannia*, with Vice-Admiral Barrington.

In 1783 Reynolds was in the West Indies, where, on 18 April, he was promoted to the command of the armed store ship *Dauphin*, and from 1786 to 1788 he commanded the sloop *Echo* on the Newfoundland station. He was advanced to post rank on 24 September 1790, and in November was appointed temporarily to the command of the *Barfleur*. He was then living at Penair, near Truro.

In 1795 Reynolds commanded the frigate *Druid* and in 1796 the *Amazon*, one of the flying squadron under the command of another Cornish mariner, Sir Edward Pellew (later Viscount Exmouth). In 1797 he was still with Pellew when, on 13 January, they fell in with the French ship *Droits de l'homme* (74 guns), which they engaged in a gale of wind and drove on shore in Audierne Bay on the following morning. The *Droits de l'homme* was utterly wrecked, with many lives lost; the *Amazon* also was wrecked, but, with the exception of six men, her officers and crew got safely to shore, where they surrendered as prisoners of war. In the following September Reynolds was exchanged. Upon his trial by court martial for the loss of his ship he was honourably acquitted.

Soon afterwards Reynolds was appointed to the 24-pounder *Pomone*, a frigate of the largest class, captured from the French in 1794. He continued in her in the channel or the Bay of Biscay until the end of 1800, when he was moved into the *Cumberland* (74 guns), from which in 1801 he again moved, to the *Orion*, in the Channel Fleet. In 1803 he was one of the captains in command of the Cornish sea fencibles; in 1804 he commanded the *Dreadnought* in the channel, and from 1804 to 1807 the *Princess Royal*.

On 28 April 1808 Reynolds was promoted rear-admiral, and early in 1810 he hoisted his flag on the *St George* (98 guns), and followed Sir James Saumarez to the Baltic, as second in command of the fleet on that station. He was employed on the same service in 1811, and on 1 November he sailed from Hanö in charge of a large convoy for England. Three times they were obliged by stress of weather to put back, and it was not until 12 November that they could finally proceed.

On 15 November Reynolds and Saumarez had anchored for the night in the Belt, when a large merchant ship broke adrift and fell on the *St George*, which parted her cable and drove on shore, where she lost her rudder and her masts had to be cut away. By great exertions she was got off and taken to Wingo Sound, where she was refitted as well as circumstances would allow with jury masts and jury rudder, and was, in the opinion of the officers, quite capable of making the voyage. She sailed accordingly on 17 December, the 74-gun ships *Defence* and *Cressy* in company, with orders to attend her on the passage. The weather set in wild and stormy, and on the morning of 24 December in a fierce storm from the north-west, the *St George* was driven, helpless, towards the coast of Jutland, struck on a bank some 300 yards from the shore, near Ringkøb, and broke up. Of the 850 men who formed her crew, twelve only were saved. The *Defence* was lost with the *St George*; the *Cressy* escaped. Reynolds's body was not recovered. Married with two daughters and two sons, he died a widower.

Of Reynolds's two sons Sir Barrington *Reynolds is noticed separately. His first son was **Robert Carthew Reynolds** (*d.* 1804), naval officer. When lieutenant of the *Centaur* off Fort Royal of Martinique, on 4 February 1804, Reynolds commanded the boats which cut out the brig *Curieux* from under the batteries in Fort Royal harbour. For his conspicuous gallantry on this occasion Reynolds was promoted to the command of the prize; but his severe wounds proved mortal, and he died early in September.

J. K. LAUGHTON, *rev.* NICHOLAS TRACY

Sources *Naval Chronicle*, 18 (1808), 454–7 · *Naval Chronicle*, 27 (1811), 44–6, 119–21 · *GM*, 1st ser., 82/1 (1812), 175 · *Steel's Original and Correct List of the Royal Navy* · P. Uhd Jepsen, *St George og defence* (Esbjerb, 1985) · IGI

Reynolds, Samuel Harvey (1831–1897), Church of England clergyman and journalist, was the eldest son of Samuel Reynolds FRCS, a surgeon in practice in High Street, Stoke Newington, Middlesex, and his wife, Elizabeth, younger daughter of Harvey Walklett Mortimer, a gunsmith in the City of London and afterwards a member of the London stock exchange. His paternal grandfather was the Revd John Reynolds, a Wesleyan minister and personal friend of John Wesley. Reynolds was born at Stoke Newington, and was entered at Blundell's School, Tiverton, Devon, on 6 February 1846, but left the following June. On the foundation of St Peter's College, Radley, Berkshire, in 1847, he became in July its first pupil; his reminiscences of the school were published in 1897.

From Radley Reynolds was elected in 1850 to a scholarship at Exeter College, Oxford; he was placed in the first class in classics at moderations at Michaelmas 1852 and in the first class in *literae humaniores* at Easter 1854, and graduated MA in 1857. In 1853 he was awarded the Newdigate prize for English verse for his poem on the theme 'The ruins of Egyptian Thebes'. On 2 February 1855 he was elected probationer fellow of Brasenose, and actual fellow on 2 February 1856. He afterwards became tutor and bursar of the college. In 1856 he obtained the chancellor's prize for an English essay entitled 'The reciprocal action of the physical and moral condition of countries upon each other'.

Intending to be called to the bar, Reynolds became a student of Lincoln's Inn on 23 October 1858, and read in the chambers of equity counsel; but because of an accident that injured his eyesight he abandoned the law and returned to residence in Brasenose. In 1860 he took deacon's orders. He filled in succession the offices of Latin lecturer, tutor, and bursar. In 1865 he was ordained priest, and that year wrote a small treatise, entitled *Rise of the Modern European System*. From 1866 to 1868 he was classical examiner in the university. In 1870 he edited the first twelve books of the *Iliad* of Homer, with a preface and notes, for the series Catena Classicorum.

Reynolds was presented in March 1871 to the college living of East Ham, at that time a comparatively small district of about two thousand people. On 12 April he married Edith Claudia, daughter of the Revd Claudius Sandys, military chaplain at Bombay, and granddaughter of Colonel Sandys of Llanarth, Cornwall; they left no children. He joined the staff of *The Times*, to which he contributed some two thousand leading articles between August 1873 and December 1896 upon literary, political, and financial topics. Some of these were reprinted after his death as *Studies on many Subjects* (1898), which also included a selection of articles written for the *Westminster Review* between 1861 and 1866. He also produced a critical edition of Bacon's *Essays* (1890) and of the *Table-Talk of John Selden* (1892).

Reynolds resigned his living in December 1893, and moved to The Gables, Abingdon, 'to be near enough to the Bodleian for study, and not near enough to Oxford for society'. Here he devoted himself to literary pursuits, but as his health failed he went from time to time to the milder climate of the south of France. He died at the Hotel d'Angleterre, Biarritz, on 7 February 1897, and was buried at Biarritz two days later. He was known as a man of engaging social qualities, a good raconteur with a caustic wit. His literary style was lucid and terse.

I. S. Leadam, *rev.* Joseph Coohill

Sources Boase, *Mod. Eng. biog.* · S. H. Reynolds, 'Some recollections of Radley in 1847', *Sicut columbae: fifty years of St Peter's College, Radley*, ed. T. D. Raikes and others (1897), 35–46 · *Essex Review*, 6 (April 1897) · S. H. Reynolds, *Studies on many subjects* (1898) · private information (1901) · CGPLA Eng. & Wales (1897)
Likenesses P. N., wood-engraving (after photograph by Leigh), NPG; repro. in *ILN* (20 Feb 1897)
Wealth at death £8493 16s. 3d.: probate, 23 April 1897, CGPLA Eng. & Wales

Reynolds, Samuel William (1773–1835), painter and printmaker, was born in London on 4 July 1773. His father, who came from a family of West Indian planters, was educated in England and married Sarah Hunt. Nothing is known of Reynolds's education before his seven-year apprenticeship to the mezzotint engraver Charles Howard Hodges RA, who used him as a servant. After Hodges's sudden departure to the Netherlands in 1793, Reynolds learned quickly, possibly with John Raphael Smith. In 1794 his ebullience and enterprise earned him a reprimand from Joseph Farington RA for presuming to engrave academicians' portraits, Paul Sandby's being a poor first.

Reynolds gravitated to George Morland's bohemian circle and succeeded with mixed mezzotints after that artist from 1795, *A Land Storm* (1798) being outstanding. His versatility enabled the use of etching, aquatint, and stipple, with mezzotint, the finest belonging to the prolific years 1798–1806 and including *Mrs Whitbread*, after John Hoppner (1798). The Napoleonic wars ruined the London print trade, and Reynolds, who had married Jane Cowen in 1793, was unable to support his lifestyle and five children, despite his paintings attracting attention at the Royal Academy between 1797 and 1811. His rescuer, the whig politician and brewer Samuel Whitbread, whose motto was 'industry and sobriety', paid over £1000 between 1801 and 1806 to save Reynolds from creditors, notably John Jeffryes (*fl.* 1785–1804), his print publisher, to whom he owed several plates, and drink merchants. The family moved about 1811 to a cottage at Southill Park, Bedfordshire, where Reynolds developed as a landscape gardener and deputized for Whitbread on estate and artistic business. Reynolds's 1804 landscape scheme at Coleorton Hall had been found impractical, but Sir George Beaumont, aware of his defects, would always value his artistic ability and advice. In 1812 David Wilkie rejected Reynolds's unsatisfactory engraving of *The Cut Finger* (Whitbread collection, Southill, Bedfordshire), paying £140 compensation. Whitbread's Drury Lane Theatre connection led to Reynolds's friendship with Edmund Kean, whom he made up as Othello.

After Whitbread's suicide in 1815 Reynolds, who used young apprentices for the preliminary work, confident of remedying any mistake, resumed engraving at a frenetic pace, and also exhibited paintings once more at the Royal graveur', finding 'quelque chose de l'intelligence et de l'elevation du Poussin avec une main plus Rembrandt-esque et un sentiment plus moderne' ('greater landscape painter perhaps than excellent engraver ... something of the intelligence and elevation of Poussin with a hand more Rembrandtesque and a more modern sentiment'; *Constable's Correspondence*, 10.268). Ary Scheffer, who shared Reynolds's radicalism, and Eugène Delacroix were influenced by his veneration of Rembrandt, whose *Mill* he had engraved in mezzotint in 1822.

In 1825 Reynolds took a four-year lease at 43 rue de Batailles, Chaillot, with local assistants, including Bouchardy and Sixdeniers. He traded between there and London, where his daughter Bessy, later Mrs Elizabeth *Walker [see under Walker, William], supervised the workshop under Lucas. The bankruptcy of Constable's Paris dealer, John Arrowsmith, cost him £200, but Reynolds's prints *à la manière noire*, considered superior to the French, dominated the Paris market up to 1835. Richard Parkes Bonington benefited from Reynolds's small subject mezzotints, and prints after Géricault, Forbin, Horace Vernet, Mme Haudebourt-Lescot, and Charlet were in the 1827 Paris Salon. Reynolds preferred inferior paintings which he could 'paraphrase', and his successes included Mme Dubufe's bosomy ladies; *The Senses-Smelling* (1830) was also published in New York. Reynolds's own small church interiors and Rembrandtesque landscapes sold well, *Le pont de Sèvres* (Musée Condé, Chantilly) being a fine example.

Unlike the figure of Reynolds in A. E. Chalon's *Students Copying at the British Institution* (1806; Print Room, British Museum), Scheffer's 1827 portrait (Dordrecht Museum) shows a dissolute man known to absent himself on long drinking bouts. From 1829 Reynolds remained in England, increasingly assisted by his elder son, Samuel William. He died of 'paralysis' (a stroke) at Ivy Cottage on 13 August 1835. His sale at Christies (19–21 April 1836) yielded £474 6s., and included watercolours by his early friend Thomas Girtin and Bonington. His own bold watercolours and drawings and numerous prints are in the British Museum and the Victoria and Albert Museum. Seven early oils, including a sketch of Whitbread, remain at Southill. Reynolds seldom signed his work, and paintings taken to Germany by the landgravine of Hesse-Homburg (formerly Princess Elizabeth) are untraced.

Samuel William Reynolds (1794–1872), his elder son, was briefly secretary to his benefactor, Whitbread. On the latter's death in 1815 he became the pupil of William Owen. He exhibited portraits at the Royal Academy between 1820 and 1836, one subject painting there in 1845, and five works at the British Institution between 1821 and 1845. He learned mezzotinting from his father, his *Dr Buckler*, after Northcote (1818), being published by Reynolds senior. About 1821 he married Emma Humby; of their five children, the eldest, Frank, practised as a portraitist-cum-photographer at Scarborough up to 1895. From 1821 Reynolds shared a studio with his future brother-in-law, William Walker, at 64 Margaret Street,

Samuel William Reynolds (1773–1835), self-portrait, *c*.1820–25

Academy and the British Institution. In 1818 he moved his Poland Street studio to a family house, Ivy Cottage, Bayswater, and executed in mezzotint two plates for J. M. W. Turner's *Liber Studiorum*, published in 1819. He was appointed portrait engraver to George IV in 1820, having produced a mezzotint after George Dawe of George III, hair and beard shortened to the then prince regent's order.

Reynolds, with the gifted Samuel Cousins apprenticed to him in 1814, next embarked on a prestigious set of 357 small mezzotints after Sir Joshua Reynolds's portraits, to be issued in four volumes between 1821 and 1826, many sold through Moon, Boys, and Graves at 2 guineas. For this in 1821 they toured south Devon, where Reynolds also landscaped Mount Edgcumbe. With steel plates increasing his business, Reynolds recruited another brilliant apprentice, David Lucas. A fine judge of talent, he praised John Constable for *The Lock* (exh. RA, 1824; Thyssen Museum, Madrid) and offered to engrave it at his own expense, but Constable, tired of broken promises, rejected Reynolds's 'soot-bag', which remained unfinished, to await Lucas's engraving at his own risk in 1834. Anonymous reviews by Reynolds eulogizing Constable's *English Landscape*, a series of twenty-two mezzotints engraved under his close supervision by Lucas and issued in parts between June 1830 and July 1832, appeared in *The Athenaeum* of 26 June 1830 and 1 June 1833.

Reynolds's inconsistency increased after he extended his production to Paris in 1824. Despite his poor French, his surname (he was not related to Sir Joshua Reynolds) and his exuberant personality placed him at the centre of the young Anglo-French circle of artists following the re-establishment of the Bourbon monarchy. Paul Huet valued him as a 'plus grand paysagiste peut-être qu'excellent and in the 1840s he moved to 15 Holland Street. Very competent, from 1830 he produced over 120 mixed mezzotints, some jointly with Walker or his father, whom he helped: most of the fifteen after Richard Ansdell, including the very large *Waterloo Coursing Meeting* (1842), were published by Thomas Agnew in Manchester; those after Sir Francis Grant were issued by Paul and Dominic Colnaghi. Reynolds died at Feltham Hill, Middlesex, on 7 July 1872. FELICITY OWEN

Sources A. Whitman, *Samuel W. Reynolds* (1903) · Farington, *Diary*, 1.248, 251; 5.1788; 6.2179; 7.2709–10; 8.2849 · J. Regnante, 'S. W. Reynolds', *L'Artiste*, 10 (1835), 225 · Beds. & Luton ARS, Whitbread papers, W/1 4031–4078 · Graves, *RA exhibitors* · S. Deuchar, *Paintings, politics, and porter: Samuel Whitbread II (1764–1815) and British art* (1984), 21, 71–4, 87–9 [exhibition catalogue, Museum of London, London, 21 Feb – 29 April 1984] · *John Constable's correspondence*, ed. R. B. Beckett, 4, Suffolk RS, 10 (1966), 193–4, 265–9, 351 · F. Owen and D. B. Brown, *Collector of genius: a life of Sir Henry Beaumont* (1988), 121, 155, 211 · P. Noon, *Richard Parkes Bonington: on the pleasure of painting* (1991), 55–6, 158 [exhibition catalogue, Yale U. CBA and the Petit Palais, Paris] · F. Owen, 'Samuel William Reynolds', *Apollo*, 135 (1992), 103–7 · R. P. Huet, ed., *Paul Huet (1803–1869)* (1911), 95–6 · R. Walker, *National Portrait Gallery: Regency portraits*, 1 (1985), 412 · *CGPLA Eng. & Wales* (1872) [Samuel William Reynolds, jun.]

Archives Beds. & Luton ARS, letters to Samuel Whitbread and papers relating to debts · E. Sussex RO, corresp. with Lord Ashburnham

Likenesses J. Opie, oils, *c*.1800, NPG · S. W. Reynolds, self-portrait, oils, *c*.1820–1825, NPG [*see illus.*] · A. Scheffer, oils, *c*.1827, Dordrecht Museum · E. Walker, miniature, *c*.1829, BM, NPG · E. Bell, etching, pubd 1855, BM · A. E. Chalon, pen and wash drawing, BM

Wealth at death under £450—Samuel William Reynolds (1794–1872): probate, 22 July 1872, *CGPLA Eng. & Wales*

Reynolds, Samuel William (1794–1872). *See under* Reynolds, Samuel William (1773–1835).

Reynolds, Stephen Sydney (1881–1919), writer, was born on 16 May 1881 at 63 New Park Street, Devizes, Wiltshire, the first of the two children of Frank Reynolds (1855–1927), a businessman and farmer, and his first wife, Clara (1858–1891), daughter of George Cox, a butcher, and his wife, Ann. His childhood was troubled: his mother died when he was ten and he was constantly at war with his father. He was educated at Devizes College and All Saints' School, Bloxham, where he became a devout Christian, a promising pianist, and, in his final year, head boy. From 1899 to 1902 he read chemistry at Owens College, Manchester, where incipient tuberculosis hampered his studies and he emerged with a third-class degree.

At Owens he came under the influence of the writer and critic Thomas Seccombe and determined to become a writer himself. In the winter of 1902–3 he went to Paris to study at the École des Mines and write for the *Weekly Critical Review*. But poverty and illness drove him back to England where at Sidmouth in the autumn of 1903 he suffered a major breakdown which nearly killed him. He was nursed back to health by his old schoolmistress, Ada Bennett, at Devizes College. He abandoned Christianity for a mystical pantheism.

In Devizes from 1904 to 1906 he wrote his only novel, *The Holy Mountain* (1909), a satirical attack upon the Northcliffe

Stephen Sydney Reynolds (1881–1919), by unknown photographer

press, revivalism, and the petty politicking of his home town. Edward Garnett thought it 'the strongest and most pungent satire' for many years (Scoble, 177), but as a novel it is marred by the weakness of its characterization. Through Garnett and the Tuesday lunches at the Mont Blanc restaurant in Soho, Reynolds became close friends with Edward Thomas and Joseph Conrad.

In August 1906, on a walking holiday with his Great Dane, Margot, he stopped off for a few days in Sidmouth to stay with Bob Woolley, a fisherman friend he had met there in 1903. Robert William Woolley (1865–1947) had lived since 1900 in the tall brick cottage in Bedford Square where he brought up the eight survivors of his fourteen children. Through Reynolds, his catchphrases, like 'you works an' slaves an' worries, an' never gets no for'arder' (*Seems So!*, 186) came to symbolize the frustrations of the Edwardian working class. Reynolds was overwhelmed by the spontaneity and resilience of this large working family as it faced the privations of poverty—what he later called his Sidmouth revelation—and decided to share their lot as both writer and fisherman himself. He lived with them from 1907 until just before his death.

Reynolds wrote a book about this new experience. *A Poor Man's House* (1908) is an Orwellian picture of working-class life from the inside, and its almost anthropological detail provides a mine for sociologists and historians. In it Reynolds first outlined his virulent opposition to Fabian social reform, which destroyed the resilience of working people by forcing middle-class values upon them. But it is the acute observation and living portrayals of the Woolleys, interspersed with the narrator's confessional asides, that turned the book into a minor classic. Joseph Conrad called it 'a book for which one seems to have waited all the time' (*Collected Letters*, 4.134).

Its publication in October 1908 made Reynolds a national figure overnight. He was to be seen regularly in London, a short, sturdy man, with neatly parted hair and small round glasses, dressed in fisherman's jersey, blue serge trousers, and sea boots. Deeply neurotic, he got on well with those who showed sympathy and understanding, most often outsiders like himself, but attacked injustice and self-importance with a fierce temper, inherited from his father. He was homosexual and never married. In 1915 he met Harry Paynter (1894–1958), a young St Ives fisherman, who remained his partner until his death.

Reynolds's second most successful book, *Seems So!* (1911), a collaboration with Bob and Tom Woolley, sought to give a genuine working man's view of the social and political questions of the day. In it he developed in popular form the political themes of *A Poor Man's House*: the superiority of working-class culture, its necessary conservatism, the need to protect it from the depredations of social reformers. He celebrated the instinctive libertarianism of working people, and exposed the hurt of bourgeois class prejudice. His attack upon elementary education caused a political uproar. The book built him a reputation as the voice of working-class opinion and in the pre-1914 industrial unrest he interpreted the strikers to the nation. Much influenced by Henri Bergson and the philosophy of intuition, he saw working-class dissatisfaction as a matter of feeling rather than economics.

His literary success was critical, not financial, and his later books had to be written first as newspaper articles. *Alongshore* (1910) is a lyrical evocation of life where sea and land meet, and *How 'Twas* (1912), a collection of short stories and sketches, though variable in quality, provides a synoptical overview of his writing life. His last work, articles for the *Nation* entitled *Wealth and Life* (1913–14), developed an intriguing new theory of the philosophy of work which he labelled 'psycho-economics'.

The pressures of writing for little financial reward played havoc with Reynolds's nerves, and a further breakdown constantly threatened. Gradually, writing took second place to political support of his fishermen friends. Through his membership of the Harmsworth committee of 1913 and the inshore fisheries committee of 1914 he secured almost single-handed a revolution in longshore fisheries policy: co-operation in marketing, harnessing of motor power, new insurance systems. All of this he personally implemented in the south-west, first as fisheries adviser to the Development Commission and subsequently, after the outbreak of war, as resident fisheries inspector (the idea for which he had developed himself) for the Board of Agriculture and Fisheries.

Worn out by war work and his own relentless drive, he succumbed to the third wave of the influenza pandemic of 1918–19 and, after a six-day illness, died in a nursing home in Seafield Road, Sidmouth, on 14 February 1919. He was buried the following day in Landpart cemetery.

A post-war generation was startled by his *Letters* (1923), edited by Harold Wright, which resurrected his unique voice; and the republication by Edward Garnett in 1928 of *A Poor Man's House* in the popular Travellers' Library ensured its survival through the twentieth century. The emotional power of its narrative, together with the stylistic brilliance of *Alongshore* and many of his short stories, has secured Reynolds's place in literature.

The growth of social history in the 1960s revived Reynolds's reputation as a social observer. For with *A Poor Man's House* and *Seems So!* he also takes his place in the English tradition of middle-class observation of working-class life, stretching from Henry Mayhew in the 1850s to George Orwell and Mass-Observation in the 1930s and 1940s. Like Martha Loane and Lady Bell, whose work he admired, he was a cultural investigator rather than a quantifier, though he rejected their emphasis on cultural 'improvement' as the solution to working-class problems.

As a social explorer Reynolds is unique. He was not driven by motives of class guilt or the desire for quick journalistic copy, academic reputation, or political solutions. He went to live with the poor because he disliked the cold sterility of middle-class culture, and welcomed the honest warmth of the family that was to give him his first real home. For Reynolds it is not working-class, but middle-class, life that is the problem. Unlike other writers in the tradition, he made his whole life with the poor and wrote from the inside looking out.

Reynolds's fishery reforms were overtaken by the industrialization of fishing and have become a part of history, though such a champion would be welcome to fishermen in any age. His sharp journalistic eye and crystalline prose survive in all his works, but it is his human sympathy, in writing and in life, which is arguably his greatest legacy. As Hilaire Belloc wrote, 'He loved the poor: he understood the sea. He was a brother and a support to sailing-men, and he had charity, humility, and justice in equal poise' (Belloc, 130).	CHRISTOPHER SCOBLE

Sources C. Scoble, *Fisherman's friend: a life of Stephen Reynolds* (2000) · *Letters of Stephen Reynolds*, ed. H. Wright (1923) · *The collected letters of Joseph Conrad*, ed. F. Karl and L. Davies, 3–5 (1988–96) · R. McKibbin, *The ideologies of class* (1990) · CGPLA Eng. & Wales (1919) · H. Belloc, *The cruise of the 'Nona'* (1925)
Archives U. Texas | BL, Macmillan papers · HLRO, Strachey papers · Lime Lodge, Egham, Surrey, Cecil Harmsworth papers · Mothecombe, Holbeton, Devon, Mildmay papers · NMM, Pursey papers · Northwestern University, Evanston, Illinois, J. B. Pinker papers · Sheff. Arch., letters to Edward Carpenter · U. Edin. L., corresp. with Charles Sarolea · U. Texas, Edward Garnett papers; John Lane papers; Philippa Powys papers; Jane Reynolds papers
Likenesses photograph, 1897, All Saints School, Bloxham, Oxfordshire · H. Lamb, pencil drawing, 1905, Sidmouth Museum, Devon; repro. in Scoble, *Fisherman's friend* · photograph, 1912, U. Texas · caricature, repro. in Scoble, *Fisherman's friend* · five photographs, repro. in Scoble, *Fisherman's friend* · five photographs, repro. in Wright, ed., *Letters of Stephen Reynolds* [see illus.] · photograph, repro. in *Bookman* (Oct 1909) · photograph, Sidmouth Museum, Devon · three photographs, repro. in *Daily Mirror* (10 July 1912) · two photographs, repro. in S. Reynolds, *A poor man's house*, ed. C. Scoble (2001)

Wealth at death £1499 15s. 1d.: probate, 29 April 1919, *CGPLA Eng. & Wales*

Reynolds, Thomas (*c*.1667–1727), Presbyterian minister, was born in London, perhaps the son of Thomas Reynolds. Being intended for the law, he received his grammar learning from Mr Singleton of Clerkenwell Close before being sent to Oxford, but his tutor there was 'particularly disagreeable to him' and so he returned home (Wood, 31). Prevented by the growth in persecution from attending nonconformist sermons, he heard William Smithies, curate of St Giles Cripplegate, whose preaching awakened in him a sense of conviction and a call to ministry. His father yielded to his wishes despite the difficult times and sent him to the celebrated academy of Charles Morton (1627–1698) at Stoke Newington Green, which he entered on 27 March 1683 in his sixteenth year.

When, as a result of persecution, Morton's academy broke up in 1685, Reynolds, with a number of other ministerial students, went to Geneva. Shortly afterwards he developed serious doubts about his fitness for the ministry, but they were gradually resolved. He studied for a session under François Turretin (1623–1687). In 1686 he moved to Utrecht, where he read philosophy under Gerard de Vries and divinity with Hermann Witsius, despite suffering from ill health. He returned to London in 1689, and in 1690 he was living at the Hand and Pen in Swan Alley, St John's Street, preaching the Sunday evening lecture at Stephen Lobb's meeting in New Street, Fetter Lane. Shortly afterwards he became assistant to John Howe (1630–1705) at Silver Street, where his father had been a member. With Edmund Calamy he lodged in Hoxton Square. After much negotiation he was ordained with Calamy and others on 22 June 1694, the first public ordination of nonconformist ministers in London.

In 1695, after the death of Thomas Kentish, Reynolds accepted an invitation from the Presbyterian congregation in Great Eastcheap, near Cannon Street, despite its small and declining state and the efforts of Howe's congregation to retain him. Though a plain unvarnished preacher, Reynolds soon increased the congregation. In 1697 they built a new meeting-house over the King's Weigh House, at the corner of Love Lane, Little Eastcheap. Reynolds continued as minister until his death. He was elected a manager of the Presbyterian Fund on 25 October 1697. Some years before 1708 a Friday evening lecture was established in Eastcheap for 'the Service of Religion, and particularly the encouraging of Singing' (*Practical Discourses of Singing in the Worship of God*, 1708, iv). Four of the lecture series by Reynolds and the neighbouring ministers were published between 1708 and 1717. Reynolds published a number of sermons, including ones to the Societies for Reformation of Manners (1700) and in celebration of British military victories in 1709 (1710), as well as two with more overtly political themes on 5 November 1712 and following the passing of the Schism Act (1714). He also published funeral sermons for John Ashwood (1706), his sister-in-law Mary Terry (1709), Mrs Clissold (1712), Thomas Clissold (1713), Eleanor Murdin (1713), and William Hocker (1722).

In 1715 Reynolds succeeded John Shower as one of the Tuesday morning merchant lecturers at Salters' Hall. He was named by Dr Daniel Williams as one of the original twenty-three trustees of his charity, but apparently took no part in the management of the trust, never attending any of the meetings. He was also one of the first distributors of the English *regium donum* for poor ministers and their dependants in 1723. Reynolds was liberal with his charity. In 1713 he gave £30 to support the gospel in America, with the promise of more if he had the means. He was engaged in setting up a charity school in Southwark in 1714, though this led to a dispute with Joseph Stedman, the schoolmaster he appointed, when it closed after the passing of the Schism Act. Stedman sued Reynolds, and published *Presbyterian Priest-Craft* (1720) after he had been disciplined by the London ministers.

During the Salters' Hall debate in 1719 Reynolds was one of the leading ministers demanding subscription to a declaration in favour of the Trinity. His orthodoxy had earlier been recognized by Josiah Eveleigh, who wrote to him concerning the Exeter controversy. He joined with three other ministers who subscribed at Salters' Hall to publish the *Doctrine of the Blessed Trinity Stated & Defended* (1719). According to Calamy, 'his zeal for a subscription of doctrinal articles in order to prevent Heterodoxy … rose very high'. As a consequence 'it was the occasion of some coolness between him and me, after an intimate friendship of many years' during which they had shared lodgings (Calamy, 2.510). James Read, Reynolds's assistant, who had voted with the non-subscribers, was dismissed in July 1720 by what Calamy called 'a piece of management' (ibid., 2.511). Reynolds fell ill after the dispute; for three months his life was in danger and his reputation was widely defamed. Read was replaced by James Wood (*d.* 1742), who succeeded Reynolds. In a funeral sermon for Samuel Pomfret (1722) Reynolds reflected upon those who subscribed in the Salters' Hall dispute, thereby provoking further contention. Simon Browne, in *A Letter* (1722), fiercely attacked Reynolds, particularly over the dismissal of Read. Reynolds replied to Browne's second edition in *An Answer* (1723), where he gave a calm rejoinder. James Hawkins, a supporter of Read and a former member of Reynolds's congregation, responded with a further *Answer* (1723) challenging Reynolds's account.

Reynolds married and had at least one son. He died in London on 25 August 1727. His funeral sermon was preached by Wood.   DAVID L. WYKES

Sources J. Wood, *Consciousness of his sincerity, the Christian's rejoicing. A funeral sermon occasioned by the death of the late Reverend Mr Thomas Reynolds; who departed this life Aug 25 1727. Preach'd at the King's Weigh-House in Eastcheap, September 10* (1727) • E. Kaye, *The history of the King's Weigh House Church* (1968) • E. Calamy, *An historical account of my own life, with some reflections on the times I have lived in, 1671–1731*, ed. J. T. Rutt, 2nd edn, 1 (1830), 142, 339–48, 365, 491; 2 (1830), 260, 342, 360, 413, 427, 465, 510–11 • King's Weigh House congregation, minutes of church meetings, 3 July 1699–11 Feb 1794, DWL, MS 38.301 • A. Gordon, ed., *Freedom after ejection: a review (1690–1692) of presbyterian and congregational nonconformity in England and Wales* (1917), 3, 339 • J. Toulmin, *An historical view of the state of the protestant dissenters in England* (1814), 571 • W. D. Jeremy, *The Presbyterian Fund and Dr Daniel Williams's Trust* (1885), 4, 5, 114 • W. Wilson, *The history* *and antiquities of the dissenting churches and meeting houses in London, Westminster and Southwark*, 4 vols. (1808–14), vol. 1, pp. 157–69 · G. S. Klett, ed., *Minutes of the Presbyterian church in America, 1706–1788*, Presbyterian Historical Society Publications, 17 (1977), 18–24, 84–7 · *DNB*

Likenesses T. Gibson, portrait · G. White, mezzotint (after T. Murray), BM

Reynolds, Thomas (1752–1829), antiquary, was the son of Joseph Reynolds, a clergyman, of Marston Trussell, Northamptonshire, and a descendant of Edward Reynolds, bishop of Norwich. He was born at Marston Trussell and matriculated from Lincoln College, Oxford, on 18 October 1769; he graduated BA in 1773 and proceeded MA in 1777. In 1776 he was presented to the rectory of Little Bowden, Northamptonshire, which he held until his death, and to the vicarage of Dunton Bassett, Leicestershire, which he resigned in 1802. He was also vicar of Lubenham, Leicestershire, from 1787 to 1800. He married his wife, Mary, early in life; their eldest son, Joseph Reynolds, died, aged eighteen, in 1805 during his third voyage to China.

In 1794 Reynolds contributed two items to Nichols's *History and Antiquities of the County of Leicester*. These were 'Observations on the Foss and via Devana' (1.154) and 'Remarks on Lubbenham and Frandon camps' (2.700–701). He also wrote several articles on Roman antiquities for the *Gentleman's Magazine*.

Reynolds's principal work, *Iter Britanniarum, or, That part of the itinerary of Antoninus which relates to Britain, with a new comment* (1799), contained much of the new material on the Antonine itinerary which had come to light since the publication of John Horsley's *Britannia Romana* in 1732. It was dedicated to William Bennett, bishop of Cloyne, who had carried out some revision on the original proofs. Bennett felt that Reynolds's work was ingenious and he praised his industry, but he differed greatly from him in his conclusions:

> He was wedded to an hypothesis, and had adopted a very odd idea, that a man was a better judge of Roman Roads and fortifications by consulting books in his closet, than by examining them on the spot. (Nichols, 4.712)

Reynolds died at Little Bowden on 24 December 1829. His wife survived him.

W. W. Wroth, *rev.* J. A. Marchand

Sources *GM*, 1st ser., 100/1 (1830), 373–4 · Nichols, *Illustrations*, 4.712 · Foster, *Alum. Oxon.* · will, PRO, PROB 11/1769, sig. 204 [proved 20 March 1830] · *DNB*

Wealth at death £500 bequeathed to daughter: will, PRO, PROB 11/1769

Reynolds, Thomas (1771–1836), informer, was born on 12 March 1771 at 9 West Park Street, Dublin, in which city his father, Andrew Reynolds (1742–1788), had acquired a considerable fortune as a manufacturer of poplins. His mother was Rose (*d.* 1797), eldest child of Thomas Fitzgerald of Kilmead, co. Kildare, and it was at Kilmead that Reynolds spent the first years of his life under the supervision of a Roman Catholic priest. At the age of eight he was sent to a protestant school at Chiswick, near London, where he remained until the beginning of 1783, when he was removed to a Jesuit seminary at Liège. He returned to Ireland in the spring of 1788, and when his father died

shortly afterwards he inherited considerable property. He subsequently became seriously ill and went for the sake of his health to Rotterdam. In Paris in July 1789, he became alarmed at the progress of the French Revolution, and returned to Dublin. He acquired a fortune on coming of age in March 1792, and proceeded to live a life of leisure. He represented the city of Dublin in the Catholic convention of 1792, and continued to be a member of the committee until its dissolution, after the passing of the Relief Act of 1793. On 25 March 1794 he married Harriet Witherington (1771–1851), whose sister Matilda was the wife of Theobald Wolfe Tone. But, in consequence of the dishonesty of a partner, his business had at that time so far declined that he found himself in serious financial difficulty.

Hitherto Reynolds had avoided politics, but in January or February 1797 he became a United Irishman. Shortly afterwards he obtained an advantageous lease of Kilkea Castle in co. Kildare from the duke of Leinster, through the good offices of Lord Edward Fitzgerald, by whom he was in November persuaded to accept the post of colonel of the so-called Kildare regiment and subsequently, in order to enable him to attend the provincial meeting, that of treasurer of the county. On 19 February 1798 there was a provincial meeting of the Leinster directorate at Oliver Bond's house in Dublin, and it was only then, according to his own account, that Reynolds became for the first time acquainted with the real designs of his fellow conspirators, and of their intention to seize Dublin and to subvert the government by force of arms. In terror—real or feigned—at his discovery, he consulted his friend and creditor Cope, a wealthy Dublin merchant, and was invited to play the part of informer. Cope, who was subsequently rewarded with a pension, was authorized by Cooke, the under-secretary, to stick at no sum—not even £100,000—in order to induce him to turn informer. Reynolds, who was at this time practically bankrupt, was willing to assent on less exorbitant terms. His name was to be kept a secret, and he was to be substantially indemnified for any loss he might sustain. In consequence of information furnished by Reynolds, the government was able to arrest the provincial committee on 12 March, and so practically to destroy the conspiracy. That Reynolds had betrayed them was certainly the opinion of some of the United Irishmen, and more than one attempt seems to have been made to assassinate him. In order to disarm suspicion, he took an oath before a county member that he had not betrayed the meeting at Bond's.

For a time Reynolds's secret was so well kept that on 5 May 1798 he was actually arrested on a charge of harbouring Lord Edward Fitzgerald, and it was not until he had been taken to Dublin, and his identity revealed to undersecretary Cooke, that he was released. It was impossible to return to his house, and so, having promised to give evidence at the forthcoming trials, he was accorded shelter in Dublin Castle until the storm had blown over. The terms of the bargain were arranged by his wife, and, in addition to a pension of £1000 a year, with £5000 in hand, it was agreed that he might settle in any part of England he liked. He was the principal crown witness at the trials of three leading United Irishmen, John McCann, William Michael Byrne, and Oliver Bond, in July 1798. After the suppression of the rebellion, Reynolds emerged from his quarters in the castle and took a house in Leinster Street. By the influence of government he was on 15 October made free of the guild of merchants of Dublin, and on 19 October received the freedom of the city. However, following an attack on his house, he moved to England, going in the first place to Allonby in Cumberland, and subsequently to London. After a short time he was compelled, by his habitual extravagance, to retire to Usk in Monmouthshire; but he returned to London and eventually, in 1810, succeeded in getting himself appointed postmaster or packet agent at Lisbon. He resigned the post when it ceased to be profitable, and in September 1814 returned with his wife to London. In 1817 he accepted the nonresident post of British consul in Iceland.

The government, however, was embarrassed by Reynolds's presence in London, and in July he was quietly shipped off to Copenhagen to take up the duties of his consulship. The salary attached to the post was barely £300, and after a brief trial, including a visit in the summer of 1818 to Iceland, he determined to resign it. He returned for that purpose to London, and was allowed to transfer the consulship to his son, and to travel for his health on the continent. After Lord Castlereagh's death in 1822 he was informed by Canning that the government desired to have as little to do with him and his family as possible, and that the consulship would be abolished but an allowance allotted him. He retired to Paris, where he is said to have undergone a religious conversion in 1831. In the following year he was attacked by cholera, to the effects of which he eventually succumbed in Paris on 18 August 1836. He was interred in the family vault in Welton church, Yorkshire.

ROBERT DUNLOP, *rev.* GERARD McCOY

Sources T. Reynolds, *The life of Thomas Reynolds*, 2 vols. (1839) · W. H. Curran, *The life of the right honourable John Philpot Curran*, 2 vols. (1819) · R. R. Madden, *The United Irishmen: their lives and times*, 1st ser., 2 vols. (1842) · A. J. Webb, *A compendium of Irish biography* (1878) · H. Boylan, *A dictionary of Irish biography* (1978)
Archives TCD | Bodl. Oxf., letters to Sir Francis Freeling · CKS, letters to first Marquess Camden
Likenesses portrait, repro. in T. Reynolds, *Life of Thomas Reynolds, esq.*, vol. 1, preface

Reynolds [Heyne, Heyerne], **Walter** (*d.* 1327), archbishop of Canterbury, is said to have been the son of a Windsor baker named Reginald, and there is considerable evidence for his links with Windsor. The names Heyne and Heyerne, used of him in two chronicles, are unaccounted for and their status unclear.

Early career and promotion He was brought up at the court of Edward I and became one of that king's clerks or chaplains. Chronicle sources describe him as a 'simple clerk' and 'imperfectly educated' but, though not himself a graduate, as archbishop he took an active interest in the universities and became, in a modest way, a patron and promoter of academic learning, even stating in 1324: 'We

Walter Reynolds (*d.* 1327), tomb effigy

take it as the highest responsibility that care be stimulated for those persons reading in the holy writ and that the fervour of their study be augmented' (*Registrum Hamonis Hethe*, 1.341).

Reynolds early became a close confidant of the future Edward II, who in 1309 described Reynolds as one who, 'active in our service from our earliest youth, has came to enjoy our confidence ahead of others' (Rymer, *Foedera*, 2 pt 1, 101). But the tradition that he was the young prince's 'tutor' rests upon no contemporary evidence. He also became a close friend and associate of Piers Gaveston (*d.* 1312). Reynolds was purchaser for Prince Edward's wardrobe by 1297, and was referred to as its clerk two years later, while in 1301 he became keeper of the prince's wardrobe. In 1302–3 he was described as one of the three most important members of the prince's council, and in October 1304 he accompanied Prince Edward overseas to do homage for Aquitaine to Philippe IV at Amiens. Reynolds was with Prince Edward in Scotland when the king died on 7 July 1307, and on 22 August 1307 he succeeded the disgraced Walter Langton (*d.* 1321) in the office of treasurer.

Reynolds owed most of his early ecclesiastical preferments to Edward I or to his son, the prince of Wales. These included the parish churches of Wimbledon, Surrey, Ingram, Northumberland, Horsmonden, Kent, Sawbridgeworth, Hertfordshire, and Snitterley (Blakeney),

Norfolk, the prebend of Weldland in St Paul's Cathedral, and the mastership of St Leonard's Hospital in York, all of which were dispensed to him in plurality by the pope on 7 February 1306 and, or alternatively, on 21 May 1309 for two more years after his consecration, and many of which he remembered in his will. He was also made provost of St John's, Beverley, by royal grant in 1306.

Bishop of Worcester and chancellor of England Edward II soon proceeded to secure Reynolds's provision to the first episcopal vacancy that occurred during his reign, that of Worcester. After long negotiations with the pope Reynolds was finally consecrated bishop at Canterbury on 13 October 1308 by Archbishop Robert Winchelsey (d. 1313), and the king attended the ceremony in person. Clement V (r. 1305–13) must have known of Reynolds's influence with the crown, for in 1309 he wrote telling him to warn the king of his displeasure at various oppressions and grievances of the clergy, and in the same year Clement associated Reynolds with the papal collector Guillaume Testa for the purpose of collecting the arrears of papal tenths in England. In the spring of 1309 Reynolds personally led the first important mission from Edward II to the papal court at Avignon, together with John Salmon, bishop of Norwich (d. 1325), and Adam Orleton (d. 1345). This mission resulted in the recall of Piers Gaveston.

Reynolds became chancellor of England on 6 July 1310, at the same time ceasing to be treasurer. He seldom acted personally in the office of either treasurer or chancellor, however, and his keeping of the great seal was only intermittent. He was regarded by contemporary chroniclers as unequivocally upholding the king's cause against the baronial opposition. Reynolds was one of the English bishops summoned to attend the general council at Vienne, which opened on 16 October 1311, but at the king's instance he was excused by the pope on the ground that he was 'not only useful, but indispensable' at home (Rymer, *Foedera*, 2 pt 1, 101). In November of 1312 he was one of the godfathers of the king's first child, the future Edward III. On 20 December 1312 he attested the peace made at London between the king and the barons, and was the only bishop mentioned there by name.

The king's archbishop On 27 April 1313 Clement V issued a bull reserving to himself the appointment of the next archbishop of Canterbury. Winchelsey died on 11 May, and the monks of Canterbury, anxious not to lose their rights, proceeded immediately after the funeral to the election of Thomas Cobham (d. 1327), with whom they already had close personal and business connections. But Edward had meantime begun negotiations with the pope on Reynolds's behalf, although there is no proof either that Clement's acceptance of Reynolds was made conditional upon payment, as some chroniclers maintained, or that Clement himself preferred Cobham. On 1 October the pope quashed Cobham's election and provided Reynolds to Canterbury, in what was the only translation of an English bishop during Edward II's reign. Reynolds obtained restitution of temporalities on 3 January 1314, and on 17 February 1314 the new archbishop was

enthroned at Canterbury in the presence of the king and many bishops and magnates.

The pope at once allowed Reynolds several special privileges, excusing him from travelling to the curia to receive the pallium and allowing him to delay his personal visit *ad limina* first for five years and then for seven more years. He was also given a papal indult to visit his diocese by deputy for three years but still to receive procurations, and to grant indulgences of 100 days rather than the customary 40. Reynolds retained custody of the great seal for several months after he became archbishop, but ceased to be its official keeper after 3 April 1314. His chancellorship probably ended later the same month, although for some time he had not been styled as chancellor probably because he had not been accepted as such in parliament in accordance with the ordinances of 1311. Nevertheless, Reynolds remained a prominent and active participant in the king's council, and usually supported Edward against his opponents. His influence with the king during this period is shown in the grants of land and custodies made to him, which included weekly markets and fairs, the wardship of lands, the custody of manors, and the fines of all his men and his tenants of the archbishopric.

In contrast to the uncompromising temperament, clericalist claims, and baronial sympathies of his predecessor, Winchelsey, Reynolds often worked to persuade the unwilling clergy to pay liberal taxes, even with papal sanction, to meet the king's necessities, especially for the Scottish wars and against baronial rebellions. In spite of strong protests from the non-episcopal clergy, who saw that Reynolds was not leading them in the same direction as Winchelsey, Reynolds seems to have achieved at least moderate success in persuading the prelates themselves to favour such grants. He was, in this way, opposing entrenched views of clerical privilege and challenging the clergy's customary claim to control ecclesiastical wealth and to determine their own policies in their own separate assemblies. Whereas Winchelsey has been seen as giving a lead to the baronial opposition and drawing up of the ordinances earlier in Edward's reign, Reynolds tried to bring about a reconciliation between the king and Thomas of Lancaster, and in 1318 he attempted a similar pacifying role, with his fellow bishops, in the negotiations that surrounded that year's treaty of Leake.

Ecclesiastical affairs Reynolds's ecclesiastical career achieved some measure of success. An extensive provisory faculty granted by Clement V on 13 January 1314 enabled him to make some thirty provisions by papal authority to canonries of cathedral and collegiate churches of his own province, twelve to the former and eighteen to the latter, even if these resulted in plurality of benefices with cure, and at least twenty-two of his provisions under this faculty were made to members of his own household. This gave a new strength to archiepiscopal patronage, with papal support, and Reynolds's register shows that he did not hesitate to back up these appointments with covering letters, stern rebukes, ecclesiastical censures, assistance from executors, and invocation of the secular arm when necessary. After John XXII ascended the papal throne in August 1316, he sought Reynolds's assistance in obtaining payment of England's long overdue tribute, and in the collection of 'Peter's pence' and of various tenths. Reynolds for his part probably did not understand in any depth either the intricacies of canon law or the high theories of papal centralization implied in the provisions system, but he was ready to take expert advice and then make the best use of opportunities as they occurred. Although he (like Thomas Cobham) had certainly been a pluralist, he soon led the English episcopate in cleverly manipulating the effects of the papal constitution *Execrabilis* against pluralities (1316) to their own advantage. Reynolds also upheld with great zeal the rights of his see against the ancient claim of the archbishops of York to have their cross borne erect before them ('bajulated') within the province of Canterbury. Having won an early battle to have his cross borne before him in the northern province, he obstinately refused to allow reciprocal rights in the south to Archbishop William Melton of York (d. 1340), until in 1325 Edward II gave support to Melton, at least on occasions when he was responding to a royal summons.

Towards the monks of Christ Church, Canterbury, for whom he stood *in loco abbatis*, Reynolds showed both magnanimity and benevolence, selecting them for special favours, encouraging them to pursue university studies as well as to retain their own claustral lecturer, supporting in his household one of their number who had studied at Paris, and bestowing his fullest confidence upon their shrewd and experienced prior, Henry Eastry. During Eastry's time in office, from 1285 to 1331, there were quarrels with Winchelsey, and trouble again under Simon Mepham (d. 1333), but with Reynolds, Eastry and the chapter enjoyed a prosperous and harmonious relationship. In the year before his death Reynolds gave them his archiepiscopal manor of Calcott in the vicinity of Canterbury.

The records of Reynolds's Canterbury administration provide evidence of a number of diocesan and metropolitan visitations, at least some of which were made in person, in spite of the constant pressure of royal business. But it has been established that he did not issue the so-called provincial constitutions of 1322 later attributed to him by William Lyndwood (d. 1446) and David Wilkins (d. 1745). Of some seventy-nine clerks in his archiepiscopal household, no fewer than thirty-eight are styled *magister* in his register and, of these, six were doctors of civil law, one of canon law, one of both laws, and one of medicine. The record of his private library establishes that a number of books were such that only a man of some education and letters could use them, though it must always be a question whether Reynolds himself knew the contents of his books as well as he knew their covers. His personal piety was never impugned; he possessed a relic of the true cross, and his will contains bequests to the shrines of St Thomas of Canterbury and St Mary of Walsingham. Whereas a period of suspension by the pope had been one of the most conspicuous episodes in Winchelsey's primacy, and whereas Mepham too later fell under papal suspension and even died excommunicate, Reynolds

brought an era of comparative peace to the administration of the church in England and also to its relations with the apostolic see.

The deposition of Edward II During Reynolds's early primacy the English bishops collaborated with the crown on many fronts, but following his decision to obey a papal mandate for the transfer of the templars' possessions to the hospitallers, in spite of a royal prohibition and threat of forfeiture both at and after the October parliament of 1320, this policy was less consistently maintained. In 1324 Reynolds even came into open collision with the king, when Edward arrested Adam Orleton, bishop of Hereford, as a traitor for his vigorous support for his patron Roger Mortimer (d. 1330). Reynolds and the whole of the episcopate declared that Orleton was under their protection, and Edward handed Orleton over into Reynolds's custody.

Meanwhile, as the breach between Edward II and his absent queen was widening during the latter's absence in France in 1325 and 1326, Reynolds, on the advice of Prior Eastry, remained largely uncommitted. Remaining at Lambeth, he did publish at St Paul's, on 30 September 1326, an old papal bull of excommunication against Scottish invaders of the north, without reading its date, as if it were directed against the queen and her followers. But finally the rising of the London citizens on 15 October 1326, and the murder on the same day of Bishop Walter Stapledon, caused him to flee to Kent. Consequently Reynolds avoided attending the meeting at Bristol on 26 October of the magnates who proclaimed the young Prince Edward guardian of the realm. However, on 7 December Reynolds left his retreat at Maidstone to make his submission to Queen Isabella, as it became clear that Edward II no longer had any chance of maintaining his position. He played a cautious but crucial role in the parliament that met on 7 January 1327 to consider the king's deposition. About this time Eastry wrote to him, urging him to ensure that the main responsibility for any deposition should not be laid against the archbishop and bishops. The next day, however, when the young Edward was shown to the people in Westminster Hall, Reynolds preached to them on the text 'Vox populi vox Dei', in which he justified the revolution and apparently suggested sending a deputation to renounce homage to Edward II. On Sunday 1 February he crowned his godson Edward III at Westminster. Reynolds's change of allegiance, though delayed, must have given something of a lead in the process whereby a new regime could be installed, with less disorder than might otherwise have been the case.

Death and reputation Although Reynolds was made a member of the new king's council, a reduction in his activities suggests that his powers were failing. He joined with his suffragans in urging on the pope old pleas for the canonization of Winchelsey and Thomas of Lancaster, and on 22 March 1327 he consecrated James Berkeley as bishop of Exeter. But on 16 November 1327 he died at his manor of Mortlake, Surrey, and was buried on 27 November in the south choir aisle of Canterbury Cathedral (rather than next to Winchelsey's tomb in the south-east transept, as his will directed). He was heavily in debt to the crown, and his goods and chattels were therefore taken into the king's hands. He did leave nine chests filled with vestments and precious objects belonging to his chapel and hall, five of which also contained bulls, charters of liberties, muniments, rolls, and memoranda. His will, dated 11 November 1327 and preserved in the archives at Canterbury Cathedral, as well as the subsequent accounts of the king's keepers of temporalities, preserved at the Public Record Office, London, are of considerable interest. Apart from some items left to his successor and eventually delivered to Archbishop Mepham, however, there is no positive evidence that any bequest in his will reached its intended recipient.

The chroniclers of Reynolds's own day vary considerably in their estimates of him, beginning with the totally negative evaluation of that portion of the *Flores historiarum* attributed to the Benedictine monk Robert of Reading:

> A man decidedly unclerkly, and so ill-educated that he was entirely unable to set out the form of his own name …
> Having ceremonially received the insignia of an archbishop, he used them as an ox does its horns, in robbing churches and oppressing the religious, indulging in immoderate filthiness of lust … (*Flores historiarum*, 3.155–6)

There is a group who were suspicious that his appointment to Canterbury might have depended upon a prior financial agreement between Edward II and Clement V (the chronicles of Bridlington and Meaux, and the *Vita Edwardi secundi*), followed by a much larger group who neither denigrate his character nor say they suspect any prior financial promises (notably Adam Murimuth, the London annalists, Higden and Knighton). And finally there is Trokelowe, followed closely by Walsingham, who sounds the most positive note, describing Reynolds as a possible agent for the peace of the English church and king and realm: 'And because the English church was harassed by continual tribulations, the pope took careful thought to provide the bereaved church with a man by whom those tribulations could best be assuaged' (*Johannis de Trokelowe*, 82).

The negative view of Reading was followed by most historians of the nineteenth century, and most notably by Stubbs, but more cautious notes have been sounded in the twentieth century by such scholars as Conway Davies, Maude Clarke, Kathleen Edwards, and May McKisack. Although T. F. Tout, in the *Dictionary of National Biography*, basing his judgements largely upon Robert of Reading, concluded that 'Intellectually and morally Reynolds was, of all the mediaeval archbishops of Canterbury, least deserving of respect', such charges have come to seem less well founded as more about Reynolds has become known. It therefore seems more appropriate, when all the evidence is sifted, to present a less negative picture.

A product of his own turbulent era, Reynolds tried to work with the crown rather than in direct opposition to it, prizing the virtues of moderation, harmony, and stability higher than a reliance on uncompromising standards in which he did not believe. Reynolds desired to see the king and realm at peace, and he used his influence to that end, even when it necessitated a politics based more on expediency than on ultimate principles. What has appeared as indecision to many commentators may in fact have been scrupulous and conscientious deliberation, probably influenced by the king's changing moods as well as by the consistently cautious advice of Prior Eastry. Reynolds lived in a world of complex personal interests rather than in one of clear-cut constitutional conflicts. In spite of his evident personal limitations, his Canterbury appointment was consequently a political triumph for both Edward II and Clement V.   J. ROBERT WRIGHT

Sources J. R. Wright, *The church and the English crown, 1305–1334: a study based on the register of Archbishop Walter Reynolds* (1980) [incl. list of MSS and printed sources] · J. R. Wright, 'The testament or last will of Archbishop Walter Reynolds of Canterbury, 1327', *Mediaeval Studies*, 47 (1985), 445–73 · J. R. Wright, 'The supposed illiteracy of Archbishop Walter Reynolds: 58–68', *The church and academic learning*, ed. G. J. Cuming, SCH, 5 (1969) · *Johannis de Trokelowe et Henrici de Blaneforde … chronica et annales*, ed. H. T. Riley, pt 3 of *Chronica monasterii S. Albani*, Rolls Series, 28 (1866) · H. R. Luard, ed., *Flores historiarum*, 3 vols., Rolls Series, 95 (1890), vol. 3 · J. H. Denton, 'Walter Reynolds and ecclesiastical politics, 1313–1316: a postscript to *Councils and synods II*', *Church and government in the middle ages: essays presented to C. R. Cheney on his seventieth birthday*, ed. C. N. L. Brooke, D. E. Luscombe, G. H. Martin, and D. M. Owen, 2 (1976), 247–74 · J. H. Denton, 'Canterbury archiepiscopal appointments: the case of Walter Reynolds', *Journal of Medieval History*, 1 (1975), 317–27 · F. Woodman, 'Two tombs in the south choir aisle', *Canterbury Cathedral Chronicle*, 69 (1975), 15–22 · *Registrum Hamonis Hethe, diocesis Roffensis, AD 1319–1352*, ed. C. Johnson, 2 vols., CYS, 48–9 (1948) · Rymer, *Foedera*, new edn

Archives CUL, MS Ee.v.31 · LPL, register | Canterbury Cathedral, deanery, cartae antiquae MSS · Canterbury Cathedral, deanery, Christ Church letters · Canterbury Cathedral, deanery, Eastry correspondence · Canterbury Cathedral, deanery, miscellaneous accounts · Canterbury Cathedral, deanery, scrap book A · Canterbury Cathedral, deanery, Sede Vacante scrapbooks I-iii · PRO, ancient correspondence, SC1 · PRO, chancery miscellanea, C 47 · PRO, exchequer diplomatic documents, E 30 · PRO, exchequer accounts various, E 101

Likenesses modern memorial brass, St Mary's Church, Wimbledon, London · portrait (in full pontificals), BL, Add. charter 17353 · tomb effigy, Canterbury Cathedral [*see illus.*]

Wealth at death £115 1s. 5d., value of chapel and hall ornaments; other jewels delivered to successor; £10, value of one other item sold: PRO, E 372/173/44; PRO, SC 6/1128/7, SC 6/1128/8; will, Canterbury Cathedral, MS Cartae Antiquae A14

Reynolds, William (1625–1698), Presbyterian minister, was born on 28 October 1625 at Bures St Mary, Suffolk, the second son of William Reynolds (*d.* 1645) of Abchurch Lane, London, a cloth worker and merchant who traded with Russia. His mother's name is unknown, but she had fled to her family in Suffolk after an outbreak of plague in London. William was educated first by Mr Ashley at Bilson, near Hadley, and then at Charterhouse School in London. On 7 June 1641 he matriculated as a pensioner from Emmanuel College, Cambridge, and in 1643 befriended John *Whitlock, the beginning of a lifelong friendship between the two. After he graduated BA in 1644 difficulties in the family business forced him to abandon his studies when he was sent by his father to Russia to replace his elder brother as a factor. The death of his father the following August revealed more severe financial problems and Reynolds returned to England in 1646 to help resolve them. After arriving in May he found his father's estate gone and a brother imprisoned for debt. When his brother managed to escape Reynolds was imprisoned on suspicion of complicity, but regained his freedom by the end of the summer on the recapture of his brother.

In December 1646, a month after Whitlock was appointed to the living at Leighton Buzzard in Bedfordshire, Reynolds was invited to join him in a shared ministry. For the next fifty-two years they would share the same study desk. In 1647 both men preached at Wokingham in Berkshire and in the following year Reynolds proceeded MA from Cambridge. In 1649 he and Whitlock were incorporated at Oxford and preached at Aylesbury in Buckinghamshire. However, Reynolds's moderate presbyterian views and lack of support for the republic saw him decline to take the engagement in that year and as a consequence lose his post. Appointed an assistant to Whitlock at St Mary's, Nottingham, in 1651 he served as a lecturer and was ordained the same year at St Andrew Undershaft in London. On 10 May 1652 he married Susanna (d. 1671), daughter of alderman Richard Mellor of Derby.

Reynolds was prominent in the establishment of a presbyterian classis in Nottingham and attended all but three of its meetings over the period 1656–60, serving as moderator on several occasions. In 1662 his failure to read common prayer led to his excommunication; however, the sentence was later rescinded on the grounds that it contravened the Act of Indemnity. In July 1662 both he and Whitlock were suspended from their posts and ejected from their livings, a full month before the Act of Uniformity. Sir John Musters at Colwick Hall provided hospitality for Reynolds, Whitlock, and their families from the following October, Reynolds living off the 'considerable portion' he had gained on marrying his wife (Whitlock, 31). Early in 1665 the two men were imprisoned for twelve weeks in Nottingham for preaching. The period of custody severely affected Reynolds's health and many feared for his life. Though still weak, within days of his release in March he had to be carried by coach 10 miles to Derbyshire to fulfil the requirements of the Five Mile Act.

In midsummer 1668 Reynolds and Whitlock moved to the non-corporate borough of Mansfield where they remained for the following nineteen years. Reynolds was licensed as a presbyterian in 1672 and preached at Nottingham once a fortnight. He was described as 'a sound lively, practical preacher' and when circumstances hindered travel he sent his sermon to be read out to the congregation (Calamy, *Abridgement*, 2.524). In 1685 both men were imprisoned for five months for entering the borough town of Newark. They were initially committed to Nottingham gaol, moved to Hull on the duke of Monmouth's landing in July, and gained their freedom in August. Following the 1687 declaration of indulgence Reynolds returned to Nottingham on 14 October to take up pastoral charge with Whitlock of the presbyterian congregation in the town. There they continued their joint ministry until

Reynolds's death in Nottingham, from fever, on 26 February 1698. He was buried on 1 March in St Mary's chancel and was survived by his youngest daughter, Sarah, who married Samuel Coates junior, a dissenting minister. Two sons and another daughter predeceased him. In the year of his death Whitlock published *A Short Account of the Life of the Reverend Mr W. Reynolds* in memory of his friend.

STUART B. JENNINGS

Sources J. Whitlock, *A short account of the life of the Reverend Mr W. Reynolds* (1698) · S. B. Jennings, 'The gathering of the elect: the development, nature and social-economic structures of protestant religious dissent in seventeenth-century Nottinghamshire', PhD diss., Nottingham Trent University, 1999 · B. Carpenter, *Account of the original introduction of presbyterianism in Nottingham and its neighbourhood* (1862) · *Calamy rev.* · E. Calamy, ed., *An abridgement of Mr. Baxter's history of his life and times, with an account of the ministers, &c., who were ejected after the Restauration of King Charles II*, 2nd edn, 2 vols. (1713) · C. G. Bolam and others, *The English presbyterians: from Elizabethan puritanism to modern Unitarianism* (1968) · Venn, *Alum. Cant.* · will, Oct 1698, Notts. Arch. · original church book belonging to the Society of Presbyterians, Nottingham, U. Nott., Hi 2Mi · Nottinghamshire lieutenancy papers of William, marquis of Newcastle, 1660–77, Notts. Arch., DDP 37/3 · J. H. White, *The story of the old meeting house, Mansfield* (1959) · *DNB* · parish register, Nottingham, St Mary's, 1 March 1698, Notts. Arch. [burial]

Wealth at death £139 7s.; plus property at Newark, Nottinghamshire: will and inventory, Oct 1698, Notts. Arch.

Reynolds, William (1758–1803), ironmaster and scientist, was born at Ketley, Shropshire, on 14 April 1758, the elder of the two children of Richard *Reynolds (1735–1816), ironmaster of Coalbrookdale and Bristol, and his first wife, Hannah (1735–1762), daughter of Abraham *Darby (1711–1763). His sister, Hannah (b. 1761), married William Rathbone. He had three half-brothers, the children of his father's second marriage, of whom Joseph Reynolds (1768–1859) lived to adulthood and was his partner in the Ketley ironworks.

Between 1766 and 1769 Reynolds was educated by a resident tutor, George Harrison. Nothing is known of his subsequent education except that he spent some time studying chemistry with Dr Joseph Black (1728–1799), and that by his late teens he was experimenting with Leyden jars and reading the works of Joseph Priestley. Reynolds's interests were concentrated in the Shropshire coalfield, in his lifetime the leading ironmaking area in Britain. By 1777, when he was nineteen, he was employed in his father's ironworks and was negotiating with James Watt (1736–1819) over the installation of new steam engines at Ketley. He was subsequently responsible for similar Boulton and Watt engines at the partners' other works at Coalbrookdale and Horsehay. He was also involved in the establishment of a new blast furnace complex at Donnington Wood in 1783–5.

Reynolds married Hannah Ball of Bridgwater, Somerset, on 3 November 1789. They were first cousins and were consequently disowned by the Society of Friends, from whose tenets they gradually moved away, although Reynolds always wore a Quaker broad-brimmed hat, refused to pay church rates, and was interred in the Quaker burial-ground at Coalbrookdale. They had three sons, William, Joseph, and Michael, all of whom died before reaching

William Reynolds (1758–1803), by Wilson, 1796

adulthood, and two daughters, Susannah, who married the Revd John Bartlett, and Hannah, who lived for less than two months in 1796.

In 1789 Reynolds, with his brother Joseph, received his father's shares in the Coalbrookdale concerns, and took over direction of the works at Ketley. The affairs of the partnerships were becoming increasingly complex, and in 1796 the interests of the Darby and Reynolds families were separated, William and Joseph Reynolds taking charge of the Madeley Wood and Ketley ironworks. The latter was the fifth largest in Britain in 1804 and was valued at £110,000 in 1803 at the time of William Reynolds's death. Reynolds encouraged experiments by Adam Heslop and James Sadler in devising new configurations for steam engines, and in 1782 used one of the first rotative steam engines to work a flour mill at Ketley. His most significant metallurgical achievement was perhaps his process for making manganese steel, which was patented in 1799. His status in the iron trade was shown in 1795–6, when he acted as arbitrator in the bitter dispute between the brothers John and William Wilkinson. After Reynolds died his interests in the Ketley works passed to his brother, Joseph, while those in the Madeley Wood concern and at Coalport passed ultimately to his wife's nephew, William Anstice (1781–1850), who had worked for Reynolds in Shropshire from 1796.

It was due to Reynolds's initiative that tow-paths were constructed along the River Severn between 1796 and 1809, allowing the use of horses for towing vessels. He was responsible for the construction of much of the tub-boat canal system of the east Shropshire coalfield. In 1786–7 he promoted two short private canals at Wombridge and Ketley, the latter incorporating an inclined plane. He personally surveyed the line of the Shropshire Canal, the strategic north–south link across the coalfield, before it received parliamentary sanction in 1788, and supervised the construction of the canal. Reynolds was also an active shareholder in the Shrewsbury Canal, which extended the coalfield network to the county town. He suggested the installation of a cantilevered tow-path through the 970 yard Berwick Tunnel, and the castings for the iron aqueduct at Longdon upon Tern were made at his ironworks at Ketley. Reynolds established the canal port at the eastern end of the Ironbridge Gorge, which from 1794 gained the name of Coalport. He constructed a riverside warehouse for general cargoes, and developed facilities for the downstream dispatch of coal brought to the banks of the Severn by canal. He was a shareholder in the Preens Eddy Bridge, which crossed the Severn near to the interchange. He invested in the potteries established there by John and Thomas Rose, and exploited the natural bitumen found in 1786 when his workmen were digging a canal tunnel into the side of the gorge.

Reynolds was involved with a glassworks at Wrockwardine Wood and an alkali works at Wombridge, both of which used innovative technology. He was probably responsible for the construction at Coalbrookdale by Richard Trevithick in 1802 of the first steam railway locomotive, and his death seems to have ended the project. In 1799 Simon Goodrich was told that Reynolds was experimenting with what appears to have been some kind of oil engine. He had close associations with Archibald Cochrane, ninth Earl Dundonald, and at his ironworks built kilns of Dundonald's design for making coke and extracting by-products, foreseeing that coal gas would be used for lighting and heating. He encouraged Dundonald in his plans, ultimately never realized, to construct an alkali plant at Coalport. At his home at Ketley Bank House, Shropshire, he displayed to visitors his collection of fossils, his library, and his laboratory. He was a pioneer of scientific geology, and influenced the subsequent work of Joseph Prestwich and Roderick Murchison. Part of his collection, after many vicissitudes, passed to the British Museum (Natural History) in 1956. Reynolds's scientific interests were allied with a zany sense of humour. In 1795 he remarked that he hoped when the war was over to construct a flute 150 feet long, blown by a steam engine, and the following year he displayed to visitors a colossal bottle with a capacity of over 70 gallons.

Reynolds's attachment to the Society of Friends did not prevent him from acting sociably within the local community. He presided over a dinner at the Tontine Hotel, next to the Iron Bridge, when a new landlord took over in 1795, and he was accustomed to meet regularly with his contemporaries at a public house known for the quality of its ale. He contributed substantially to the sections on transport and manufactures in Joseph Plymley's *General View of the Agriculture of Shropshire* (1803). His sketchbook, preserved in the library of the Science Museum, London, shows the range of his engineering interests. After some years of ill health, Reynolds died on 3 June 1803 at Coalbrookdale and was interred in the Quaker burial-ground there. He was survived by his wife.   BARRIE TRINDER

Sources B. Trinder, *The industrial revolution in Shropshire*, 2nd edn (1981) · B. Trinder, ed., *The most extraordinary district in the world*, 2nd edn (1988) · Mrs E. Greg, ed., *Reynolds-Rathbone diaries and letters, 1753–1839* (privately printed, London, 1905) · *Thomas Telford, engineer* [Ironbridge 1979], ed. A. Penfold (1980) · A. Raistrick, *Dynasty of iron founders: the Darbys and Coalbrookdale* (1953) · J. Randall, *History of Madeley*, ed. B. Trinder, 2nd edn (1975) · H. W. Dickinson, 'An 18th-century engineer's sketch book', *Transactions* [Newcomen Society], 2 (1921–2), 132–40 · H. S. Torrens, 'The Reynolds–Anstice Shropshire geological collection, 1776–1981', *Archives of Natural History*, 10 (1981–2), 429–41 · N. Cossons and B. Trinder, *The iron bridge: symbol of the industrial revolution* (1979) · B. Trinder, *The Darbys of Coalbrookdale*, 4th edn (1993) · *VCH Shropshire* · R. Reynolds, memorandum, *Pocket companion* (1762) · H. M. Rathbone, *Letters of Richard Reynolds with a memoir of his life* (1852), 69
Archives Sci. Mus. · U. Lpool | Birm. CL, Boulton and Watt MS · Ironbridge Gorge Museum, Shropshire, accounts of Coalbrookdale ironworks · Staffs. RO, executors' accounts
Likenesses Wilson, portrait, 1796, Ironbridge Gorge Museum, Shropshire [*see illus.*] · W. Hobday, portrait, Ironbridge Gorge Museum, Shropshire · Sharp, engraving (after W. Hobday), priv. coll.

Reynolds, William Bainbridge (1855–1935), metalworker and designer, was born on 6 March 1855 in the Royal Military Asylum, in the parish of St Luke's, Chelsea, London, one of the three sons of William James Reynolds, a connoisseur and professor of mathematics to the institution, and his wife, Rosa Russell Bainbridge.

Reynolds's family circumstances were more cultivated than prosperous, but the brothers were encouraged in their various interests. Accounts of Reynolds's early career vary. The most likely sequence of events is as follows. It seems that, at the age of sixteen, in 1871, he was articled to G. E. Street (1824–1881), the leading church architect of the day. Street's office had been the nursery of the arts and crafts movement, and Street himself was particularly interested in metalwork. Perhaps it was then that Reynolds began to be interested in the applied arts, although his principal occupation was the designs for the Law Courts. It was probably in 1874 that he moved to the office of J. P. Seddon, also an important Gothic revival architect, whose friends included Rossetti. However, the most influential meeting for Reynolds was with C. F. A. Voysey, who was apprenticed to Seddon the same year. The two became friends, and Reynolds later made a quantity of metalwork to Voysey's designs.

Reynolds never embarked on an independent career as an architect. He was, perhaps, temperamentally unsuited for it. Although a tall, broad-shouldered man of impressive bearing, he was by character quiet and so self-effacing that he refused to sign or even mark his work. Voysey recalled that 'his personal charm was marked by gentleness … He was intensely musical and more thoughtful than talkative. One often wished he would say more because of his charming voice' (Voysey, *The Builder*, 726).

After a time as a draughtsman for the Royal Engineers, Reynolds, in his late twenties, gave up architecture altogether. He went to work for John Starkie Gardner, a successful metalworker who had recently set up his own premises on the Albert Embankment. About this time Reynolds met the architect Hugh Rumieu Gough, who had worked with Seddon. When Gough was commissioned to build the church of St Cuthbert's, Philbeach Gardens, in 1883, Reynolds became involved in the design of the interior fittings.

Reynolds was a high-church man with 'a profound reverence for ceremonial and symbolism' (Voysey, *The Times*). In St Cuthbert's his devotion to the church and to his craft found a united expression. His work there continued until two years before his death and reveals his development from an unconvincing Gothic revivalist to a harbinger of art nouveau. In 1888 Reynolds was elected a brother of the Art Workers' Guild, founded four years earlier to bring together architects, artists, and designers. The guild, then a vital force in promoting the arts and crafts ideal of integrated art, life, and work, was a catalyst for Reynolds. His mature work at St Cuthbert's, especially the screens and the great repoussé copper lectern, reveals him as an original, indeed bold, designer. In the lectern Pevsner saw something 'much more playful' than most arts and crafts designers (*Buildings of England, London, except the Cities of London and Westminster*, 1952, 244). Made in 1894, it looks back to Pugin in its motif of angels holding Gothic texts, and forward to Mackintosh in the twining towers at its base. The church contains work by many craftsmen and women, both professionals and members of the congregation. The totality, no doubt owing to the influence of Reynolds's own modesty, is harmonious and uplifting.

In the early 1890s Reynolds set up his own business. At first his activities were divided between a drawing office in Victoria Street and workshops in Walworth and Camberwell. In 1904 he established Manor House Metal Works at 7b Old Town, Clapham Common, near his home in Rectory Grove. Here he worked and took on pupils. His standards were high and peculiar to his time. While everything must be 'as flawless as he could make it', this meant ensuring that there were never '2 things quite even or quite equal. Always a twisted rod had to have irregularities so that it would not be mistaken for a casting' (Mills, 83–4).

Reynolds's business throve. After 1904 he designed less on his own account but worked for almost every important architect. The Kitchener chapel gates for Detmar Blow are among half a dozen examples of his work at St Paul's Cathedral. Many cathedrals, several Cambridge colleges and country houses, and innumerable churches have his metalwork. Of his excursions into other media less is known, although St Cuthbert's includes a rare example of his stained glass.

In 1928 Reynolds became semi-retired, and he and his wife moved to Hove. She died in 1932 and Reynolds three years later, on 31 March 1935 at 38 Beaconsfield Villas,

Preston Park, Brighton. They had no children. Their ashes were interred together at St Paul's, Brighton, and their monument, designed by Reynolds, is in the chancel.

ROSEMARY HILL

Sources K. S. Mills, 'William Bainbridge Reynolds (1855–1935), craftsman in metals', *Transactions of the Ecclesiological Society*, new ser., 3/1 (1954), 77–85 · A. Symondson, 'William Bainbridge Reynolds', *Philbeach Quarterly* (autumn 1966), 11–13 · C. F. A. Voysey, *The Builder*, 48 (1935), 726 · C. F. A. Voysey, *The Times* (11 April 1935) · *Victorian church art* (1971), 148–9 [exhibition catalogue, V&A, Nov 1971 – Jan 1972] · I. Anscombe, *Arts and crafts style* (1991), 123 · b. cert. · CGPLA Eng. & Wales (1935) · d. cert.

Wealth at death £16,940 10s. 11d.: administration, 21 May 1935, CGPLA Eng. & Wales

Rham, William Lewis (1778–1843), agriculturalist and Church of England clergyman, was born at Utrecht in the Netherlands. His father, William Rham, originated from Leiden and his mother, of whom very little is known, was Swiss. The family moved to England when he was very young. He initially attended Edinburgh University as a medical student but, determined to seek holy orders, in 1803 he entered Trinity College, Cambridge, where he graduated BA in 1806 (MA 1810). He was vicar of Broad Hinton, Wiltshire, from 1804, a prebend of Bittern in Salisbury from 1806, and from 1808 vicar of Winkfield, Berkshire, where he resided until his death. In addition the Nassau family presented him in 1803 with the living of Fersfield, Norfolk, which he held until 1843. As was common at the time, he was able to retain several livings, paying local curates to maintain his parishes in his absence.

Rham's interest in agriculture probably came from his family background, coupled with a desire to assist his rural parishioners. According to Donaldson, he was one of the greatest agricultural authorities at this time. His lifelong interest in European agriculture led to several tours of the continent, which provided the basis of many of his subsequent accounts. He contributed to the agricultural section of the Library of Useful Knowledge a manual on Flemish industry. He wrote extensively, particularly on practical, utilitarian subjects, for a number of periodicals including the *Gardeners' Chronicle* and the *Penny Cyclopaedia*, sponsored by the Society for the Diffusion of Useful Knowledge, founded by Henry Brougham in 1826. A compilation of these articles was eventually published as *The Dictionary of the Farm* shortly after Rham's death; this popular text was reprinted five times and revised with the addition of supplementary material from other authors including William and Hugh Raynbird. He helped to revise an edition of Martin Doyle's *Cyclopaedia of Practical Husbandry* and contributed several eminent papers on agricultural issues to the Royal Agricultural Society, including an 'Essay on the simplest and easiest mode of analysing soils' (1838), which was awarded a prize by the society. Among his lesser-known agricultural achievements was the introduction of a variety of dessert pear from France, having a characteristic bright green fruit, which eventually turned yellow; it was subsequently sold as the 'Vicar of Winkfield' pear. He was instrumental in establishing the Winkfield School of Industry in 1835, which was widely acclaimed by Mr Tremenheere in his report to the council of education in March 1843. The school, which accommodated fifty boys and fifty girls, had workshops and workrooms where boys were taught to handle tools and girls had lessons in domestic work. The establishment was maintained by private subscription and the sale of produce from the 4 acres of land attached to the school. It was intended to become a model for similar institutions in country parishes.

Rham was a member of the Royal Agricultural Society's journal committee from its foundation in 1838 until his death. During this period, the journal consisted primarily of short articles written by enthusiastic landowners and farmers, many of whom, like Rham, had been founders of the society. His empirical approach to agricultural problems, however, while popular with many contemporary farmers, tended to be rather unscientific. According to Donaldson, Rham suggested that:

> Whatever great chemists may say about the component parts of soils, I am persuaded they never can decide as to the aptitude of any soil to produce a crop till experience has shown it. I believe we have all overlooked some electromagnetic qualities which we have not yet instruments to measure. (Donaldson, 125)

Following a short illness, Rham died, unmarried, on 31 October 1843 at Winkfield vicarage. In recognition of their esteem, the parishioners of Winkfield erected a stone tablet with urn on the west wall of St Mary's Church.

JOHN MARTIN

Sources W. L. Rham, *The dictionary of the farm*, rev. edn (1855) · J. Donaldson, *Agricultural biography* (1854) · Venn, *Alum. Cant.* · N. Goddard, *Harvests of change: the Royal Agricultural Society of England, 1838–1988* (1988) · M. Doyle, *A cyclopaedia of practical husbandry* (1843) · R. Hogg, *The fruit manual*, 5th edn (1884) · Winkfield parish records, Winkfield School of Industry, Berks. RO, D/P151, 25/22/1–26–25/30

Archives LUL, letters · UCL, letters to the Society for the Diffusion of Useful Knowledge | Berks. RO, Winkfield School of Industry MSS · U. Reading, historical records of the Royal Agricultural Society of England

Likenesses R. D. Ansdell, oils, Royal Agricultural Society of England; repro. in Goddard, *Harvests of change*, 9

Rhames, Aaron (d. 1734), printer, is of unknown origins. The first reference to him is as an apprentice to the printer Joseph Ray of Dublin. He was freed of the London Stationers' Company on 7 August 1704 by Ray, and he spent the next few years working both in London and in the printing works at Three Keys, St Nicholas, Dublin. It was in London in 1705 that he married Margaret, daughter of John Millet and stepdaughter of William Onley, both printers. Their first son, Charles, died in 1708 and was buried on 8 February at St Werburgh's Church, Dublin.

Rhames came into his own as a printer in 1709, when he turned out, sometimes using monogram, at least fifteen books and pamphlets, several for his former fellow apprentice, Jeremiah Pepyat. He was given the important task of printing the philosophical writings of George Berkeley, namely his *Essay towards a New Theory of Vision* (1709), and *Treatise Concerning the Principles of Human Knowledge* (1710), at his new printing works situated at the back of Dick's Coffee House, Skinner Row, Dublin.

Rhames established himself as a printer of distinction

when he accepted the order on behalf of William Binauld and Eliphal Dobson of printing the whole of the Bible in folio in 1714, the first extant Irish edition. He then printed for John Hyde and three others an octavo edition in 1722. In 1719 Hyde's company had instructed Rhames to print ten thousand copies of the Bible for charitable distribution and he completed the order in 1722. In 1716 a *Book of Common Prayer* was printed by and for Rhames, Dobson, and Pepyat, with another edition printed in 1724. Rhames took a leading role in the life of the Guild of Printers; admitted in 1714, he served on the council from 1721, as warden in 1723, and then as master in 1728. He was admitted a freeman of the city in 1714.

A tory in politics, Rhames fully appreciated the political value of newspapers and attempted to produce a local newspaper for Dublin on three different occasions, failing each time. In 1705 he produced the *Dublin Courant, or, Diverting Post*, and it folded after two issues; in 1709 he printed five issues, and in 1725 between 25 October and 13 December he printed nine issues. On the last occasion he and the Dublin undertaker William Smith were involved.

Rhames and his wife had three sons who survived infancy: Joseph (*b.* 18 July 1719), John (*bap.* 5 Dec 1727), and Benjamin (*bap.* 6 May 1730). All three followed him in the book trade, Joseph and John as printers and Benjamin as music printer and seller. When Rhames moved in 1725 to a printing works opposite the Pied Horse in Capel Street, it is probable that he began to print sheet music. Rhames was chosen as printer to the newly formed Dublin Society from 1731 to 1736; on 30 October 1731 his proposal for producing *Till's Treatise of Horse Houghing Husbandry* was accepted, and printed by 11 November. By December he was owed £12 10s. 3d. by the society, and in the next five years he printed several pamphlets for the society on a variety of subjects, such as saffron, flax, bees, and hops. Among his other important printing tasks were Joseph Beaumont's *Mathematical Sleaing-Tables, or, Mistery of Weaving Linnen-Cloth Explain'd* (1712), Bishop William Nicolson's *Irish Historical Library* (1724), and the third edition of Gilbert Burnet's *History of the Reformation of the Church of England* (3rd edn, 1730). He produced a number of red and black title pages, rare in the Dublin book trade, and when he died in Dublin on 9 December 1734 he was remembered as a perfectionist in the printing world. He was succeeded by his wife and his sons, and their descendants carried on until 1809.   D. BEN REES

Sources M. Pollard, *A dictionary of members of the Dublin book trade 1550–1800* (2000), 488–9 · R. Hunter, *A dictionary of the print trade in Ireland, 1550–1775* (New York, 1988), 231 · H. Fenning, 'Dublin imprints of Catholic interest, 1701–1739', *Collectanea Hibernica*, 39–40 (1997–8), 106–54

Rhees, Morgan John. *See* Rhys, Morgan John (1760–1804).

Rhees, Rush (1905–1989), philosopher, was born in Rochester, New York, USA, on 19 March 1905, the son of Rush Rhees (1860–1939), Baptist minister and president of Rochester University, and his wife, Harriet Chapin Seelye, daughter of L. Clark Seelye, the president of Smith College. His great-great-grandfather Morgan John Rhys, a

Baptist minister and radical pamphleteer, had emigrated to America in 1794. Rhees read philosophy at his father's university for two years (1922–4), but was expelled from the philosophy class by Professor George M. Forbes, who found his questionings rude and insolent. President Rhees, away at the time, found that his son had left America. He never returned.

Rhees went to Edinburgh in 1924, where A. E. Taylor and Norman Kemp Smith were professors, but the teacher who influenced him most was John Anderson, who later occupied the Challis chair at Sydney. Rhees graduated with first-class honours in 1928. For the next four years he was an assistant to J. L. Stocks at Manchester. In 1932 Rhees went to study for a year with Alfred Kastil at Innsbruck. His interest was in Brentano's theory of relations. He continued to pay visits to Kastil until 1937. In a remarkable reference for Rhees, Kastil comments on how much he looked forward to the visits, for he had become the receiver. In 1933 Rhees had become a research student at Cambridge working on continuity with G. E. Moore. This involved a discussion of various concepts of identity. He never submitted his thesis. Moore regretted this and said, in a letter, how much he had learned from Rhees. In a reference he refers to him as his ablest student.

In 1940 Rhees was appointed to a temporary assistantship at the University College of Swansea, where A. E. Heath was professor. Having taken Wittgenstein's advice to do the job which attracted him least, he was a welder in a factory at the time. The Swansea post was not made permanent until the return, in 1946, of W. B. Gallie and Karl Britton from war service. Rhees's most influential period was during the thirteen years when J. R. Jones, R. F. Holland, and Peter Winch were his colleagues. Although he remained a lecturer, declining all promotion, his influence on staff and students at Swansea was enormous, and he was respected throughout the college, from the principal to the porters.

At Cambridge, Rhees had met and become a close friend of Ludwig Wittgenstein. After the latter's death he became one of his literary executors. He devoted most of his life to editing and publishing Wittgenstein's work, and responding to what he judged to be misunderstandings of it. All Rhees's teachers spoke of his outstanding ability, but his self-assessment was deprecating in the extreme. At various stages people, including Wittgenstein, had to persuade him not to resign his position at Swansea. It was only with reluctance that he consented to the publication of two collections, *Discussions of Wittgenstein* (1970) and *Without Answers* edited by D. Z. Phillips (1969).

After taking early retirement in 1966 Rhees lived in London for a period and was a visiting professor at King's College. He also lived in Cambridgeshire for a period, but, late in life, returned to Swansea, where he became an honorary professor and fellow of the college. He was twice married: first to Jean Henderson, and second, on 5 July 1985, after her death, to Peg, *née* Bovey (*b.* 1924/5), retired lecturer in architectural restoration and the widow of Yorick Smythies. Rhees died at his home, 3 Golwg Hafren,

Derwen Fawr, Swansea, of bronchopneumonia on 22 May 1989. He did not live to see *Wittgenstein: Attention to Particulars*, a Festschrift for him edited by D. Z. Phillips and Peter Winch.

Throughout his career Rhees had denied that he had anything worth publishing and had refused any academic promotion, remaining a lecturer. To the end he denied that there was anything in his papers worth looking at. After his death the department purchased his papers from his widow. The purchase was made possible by the A. E. Heath memorial fund. They amount to sixteen thousand pages of manuscript of various kinds, including copies of work by Wittgenstein. Apart from papers, to date seven books have been edited from the archive by D. Z. Phillips, whom he had first taught as a student in 1952 and who, after early retirement, became Rush Rhees research professor in 1996.

Rhees's most important book, *Wittgenstein and the Possibility of Discourse* (1998) is a far-reaching critique of the analogy between games and language in part one of Wittgenstein's *Investigations*. Games do not make up one big game, but we participate in language games in *the same* language. Rhees emphasizes that language makes sense if living makes sense. Connections between what is said in one context and what is said in others are not contingent. It would not be language without them, and there could be no growth in understanding. But this does not mean that we are engaged in one big conversation. Voices stand in varying relations of proximity and distance from each other. Philosophy's task is to do conceptual justice to them.

This emphasis is to be found in *On Religion and Philosophy* (1997) where Rhees explores what 'reality' means in religion, and various religious concepts. In *Moral Questions* (1999) Rhees opposes the generality of moral theory, and explores substantive moral issues concerning sexuality, issues of life and death, animals, and the meaning of life. He endeavours to show why they are serious questions without providing answers. In *Discussions of Simone Weil* (1999) Rhees engages with her views on political philosophy, philosophy of science, and philosophy of religion, showing how one can learn from one's disagreements with a remarkable writer. Three other books, *What Really Is: in Dialogue with the Presocratics, Plato and Dialectic* and *Wittgenstein's 'On Certainty'* are unpublished hitherto. Other themes such as recursive proofs, the will, and causality remain to be explored.   D. Z. PHILLIPS

Sources D. Z. Phillips, biographical sketch, in R. Rhees, *On religion and philosophy*, ed. D. Z. Phillips and M. von der Ruhr (1997) · D. Z. Phillips, biographical sketch, in R. Rhees, *Wittgenstein and the possibility of discourse*, ed. D. Z. Phillips (1998) · *The Times* (22 June 1989) · J. R. Slater, *Rhees of Rochester* (1946) · d. cert. · B. A. Kimball, 'Rhees, Rush', *ANB* · *CGPLA Eng. & Wales* (1989) · m. cert.
Wealth at death £202,575: probate, 25 Oct 1989, *CGPLA Eng. & Wales*

Rhigyfarch ap Sulien [Ricemarchus] (**1056/7–1099**), scholar and teacher, was the eldest son of *Sulien, sometime bishop of St David's. He was born in 1056 or 1057 (the date is computed from the fact that, according to the *Brut y tywysogyon*, he was in his forty-third year when he died in 1099). According to the obituary notice in that source, 'he was the most learned of all the race of the Britons and there had not been before him his equal nor after him his like nor in his lifetime his peer' (*Brut: Peniarth MS 20*, 21); the same source records that he was trained solely by his father. The result of this training is seen in the small corpus of Rhigyfarch's Latin writings. Of these the earliest is a manuscript (now Dublin, Trinity College, MS A.4.20 (50)), written probably in the year 1079. The principal scribe of the manuscript was one Ithael; the principal illuminator was Rhigyfarch's younger brother Ieuan. The manuscript contains a redaction of the Hieronymian martyrology known as the *Martyrologium Cambrense*, and a copy of Jerome's psalter translation from the Hebrew (*iuxta Hebraeos*). The *Martyrologium Cambrense* is ultimately related to that associated with the name of St Willibrord; it contains various additions not found in other manuscripts of the Hieronymian martyrology, including entries for Irish saints such as Manchín, Laisrén, Colmán, and Brigit, and Welsh saints such as Padarn (the patron saint of Llanbadarn Fawr). These additions indicate that the *Martyrologium Cambrense* was produced at Llanbadarn, conceivably by Rhigyfarch himself. The psalter *iuxta Hebraeos* is accompanied by various patristic materials useful for psalter study (again, these were probably assembled by Rhigyfarch or his father), and by a poem of twenty-five lines' length composed by Rhigyfarch and possibly copied into the manuscript in his own hand (the hand that copied the poem is distinct from that of Ithael, the principal scribe). The poem treats the various versions of the psalter (Hebrew, Greek, Latin); its ascription to Rhigyfarch is confirmed by the inclusion of his signature ('Ergo mihi nostra qui dicor gente Ricemarch'), and shows that he was competently trained in the composition of quantitative verse, though the Latin of the poem exhibits certain syntactic difficulties.

Further examples of Rhigyfarch's skill as a Latin poet are found in an early twelfth-century manuscript (now BL, Cotton MS Faustina C.i), copied from a lost exemplar, which was once in the possession of Rhigyfarch (and was conceivably written by him). The principal content of the manuscript is the *Commentarius in somnium Scipionis* by Macrobius; the text of Macrobius is accompanied by extensive glossing which is the fruit of wide reading in patristic and Carolingian sources (particularly Helperic and Remigius), and there is reason to think that it is the product of Rhigyfarch's learning. The manuscript also includes two poems by Rhigyfarch: the first, a four-line epigram on a harvest destroyed by mice (which has an interesting analogue in the third branch of the *Mabinogi*, namely *Manawydan*); and the second, a passionate lament of ninety lines' length (in a metrical form derived from Boethius) on the devastation of Ceredigion and Dyfed by the Normans in 1093. Rhigyfarch's authorship of the first poem is indicated by its rubric 'Ricemarchus', the second by its inclusion of the line 'Hec ego Ricemarch defleo mestus'. The poetry of Rhigyfarch, taken together with that of his brother Ieuan, indicates that the best classical and Christian poets (especially Virgil, Ovid, Lucan, Juvencus, Prudentius, and Caelius Sedulius) were studied at Llanbadarn Fawr; the glossing to Macrobius shows that the scientific curriculum was studied there as well.

Rhigyfarch's one surviving essay in prose composition is his *Vita sancti Davidis*, which was composed probably in 1095 and is the earliest life of the patron saint of Wales. Rhigyfarch's authorship is announced in the final chapter of the work (*qui Ricemarchus nominor*). He had at his disposal no reliable information concerning either St David or the sixth-century context in which he is supposed to have lived, but his life is a compelling narrative, woven together from legendary materials of Celtic origin, and from hagiographical motifs, many of them apparently drawn from Hiberno–Latin saints' lives, with which Rhigyfarch was thoroughly familiar, perhaps as a result of his father's period of study in Ireland. Rhigyfarch was concerned to show the influence of St David in Ireland; but his life of St David may have had a wider political dimension: the story of the journey of Sts David, Teilo, and Padarn to Jerusalem, and their appeal to the patriarch there, possibly reflects the intention of the Welsh church to show itself independent of (Norman) Canterbury, and perhaps of Rome as well.

When Rhigyfarch died in 1099, he was survived by a son named (after his grandfather) Sulien; this Sulien ap Rhigyfarch lived until 22 September 1146, and was described by the *Brut y tywysogyon* as a teacher at Llanbadarn, and a 'speaker and pleader for his people and a mediator for various kingdoms' (*Brut: Peniarth MS 20*, 54). Nothing further is known of him or of Rhigyfarch's immediate family.   MICHAEL LAPIDGE

Sources J. C. Davies, ed., *Episcopal acts and cognate documents relating to Welsh dioceses, 1066–1272*, 2, Historical Society of the Church in Wales, 3 (1948), 493–506 · T. Jones, ed. and trans., *Brut y tywysogyon, or, The chronicle of the princes: Peniarth MS 20* (1952) · H. J. Lawlor, ed., *The psalter and martyrology of Ricemarch*, 2 vols., HBS, 47–8 (1914) · M. Lapidge, 'The Welsh–Latin poetry of Sulien's family', *Studia Celtica*, 8–9 (1973–4), 68–106 · A. Peden, 'Science and philosophy in Wales at the time of the Norman conquest: a Macrobius manuscript from Llanbadarn', *Cambridge Medieval Celtic Studies*, 2 (1981), 21–45 · *Rhigyfarch's Life of St David*, ed. J. W. James (1967)
Archives BL, Cotton MS Faustina C.i · TCD, MS A.4.20 (50)

Rhind, Alexander Henry (1833–1863), antiquary, was born on 26 July 1833 at Wick, Caithness, where his father, Josiah Rhind (d. 1858) of Sibster, Caithness, was a banker. He was educated at Pulteneytown, Caithness, and at Edinburgh University, where he was a student from 1848 to 1850. He was mainly interested in natural history, physics, and Scottish history and antiquities. He began thus early to study the Picts' houses and cairns of his native district, superintending in 1851 the opening and examination of various tumuli in the neighbourhood of Wick. Later that year he spent several months on the continent, where he visited antiquarian museums in Italy, Austria, Switzerland, Prussia, the Netherlands, and Denmark.

In 1852 Rhind sent rubbings of a slab at Ulbster, Caithness, to Dr John Stuart, of the Society of Antiquaries, Edinburgh, and he was soon elected a fellow of the society. In 1854 he presented to the society the osteological remains from a Pict's house at Kettleburn near Wick and suggested to the Crystal Palace Company, London, the erection in Sydenham grounds of models of early British remains. In 1855 he proposed to Lord Duncan, a lord of the Treasury, that 'all primaeval vestiges should be carefully laid down on the ordnance map of Scotland', in order to furnish an index for archaeological enquiries. Troublesome pulmonary symptoms had now asserted themselves, and Rhind relinquished his intention of studying for the Scottish bar. Thenceforth his health was his foremost consideration. In 1853–4 he wintered at Clifton, near Bristol, in 1854–5 at Ventnor, Isle of Wight, and in 1855–6 and 1856–7 in Egypt, where he made important investigations of the tombs at Thebes, recorded in his chief publication, *Thebes: its Tombs and their Tenants* (1862) and his *Facsimiles of Two Papyri* (1863); he published his observations on contemporary Egypt in *Egypt: its Climate, Character, and Resources as a Winter Resort* (1856). Between 1858 and 1862 he visited Malaga, the north of Africa, the south of France, and Italy (where in 1859 he studied Etruscan antiquities at Rome). Wherever he was he made all possible observations in his own line of work, and sent many papers and specimens to the Scottish Society of Antiquaries. In 1858 he published a pamphlet on the law of treasure trove. In 1862 he went again to Egypt, and some notes which he then made for a projected work on the Nile valley were appended to Stuart's *Memoir* of the author. He had, he said, disentangled two Nubian dialects. After a serious illness in Cairo and Alexandria he managed to struggle homewards as far as the Italian lakes. He died at La Majolica on 3 July 1863, and was buried at Wick.

Rhind's bequests were characteristic and valuable. He left £5000 for two scholarships at Edinburgh University, and £7000 to found an industrial institution at Wick for orphan girls of certain Caithness parishes. To the Society of Antiquaries of Scotland he bequeathed £400 for excavations; a library of about 1600 volumes, of which many were rare and valuable; copyright of his treatise, *Thebes*; and a reversionary sum (which became available in 1874) from the estate of Sibster to found a lecturership on archaeology.   T. W. BAYNE, *rev.* H. C. G. MATTHEW

Sources J. Stuart, *Memoir of the late Alexander Henry Rhind, of Sibster* (1864) · A. S. Bell, ed., *The Scottish antiquarian tradition* (1981) · NA Scot., SC 14/40/7, 101–34
Wealth at death £19,527 16s. 8¼d.: confirmation, 30 June 1864, NA Scot., SC14/40/7, 101–34

Rhind, David (1808–1883), architect, was born in the parish of St Giles, Edinburgh, on 11 January 1808, the son of John Rhind, writer (lawyer), cashier to the Edinburgh Friendly Insurance Company of Scotland, and his wife, Marion Anderson. On his father's death in 1826 his brother succeeded as cashier of the company, and a family trust was established to look after the elder Rhind's property interests in Leith. Rhind was thus embedded into the mercantile milieu of Edinburgh and Leith, and a reasonable inheritance and financial security (as well as a propensity to litigation) may explain the curious lack of urgency in his architectural output. Some eighty projects divided equally between banks, public buildings and churches, and residential projects were evenly spread throughout an almost fifty-year career—an average of under two known projects per year. Other Rhind projects probably remain unidentified, for during his tenure as Commercial Bank architect, that bank constructed some fifty-six branches; and drawings for several unidentified pleasant houses in Rhind's characteristic hand are in the Rowand Anderson Collection, University of Edinburgh.

Although classified as an 'outsider' (Gow), Rhind was at the heart of the establishment between 1835 and 1860. He was architect to the Commercial Bank, to the county prison board of Edinburgh, and to the established Church of Scotland. He was a fellow of the Royal Society of Edinburgh (1836), a founder member of the Institute of the Architects of Scotland in 1840, fellow (1849), convenor of the premises committee and occasional chairman of the Architectural Institute of Scotland (to which he gave a paper on the designer of George Heriot's Hospital, displaying considerable scholarship and research), and mason. His particular interest in sculpture—exemplified in the outsize Miller mausoleum (1848), Craigentinny, Edinburgh, with sculptured panels by Alfred Gatley—was the inspiration for his presidential address to the Royal Scottish Society of Arts in 1855, on the 'practical improvement of all that is requisite for proper construction of our buildings, and such information on art and art-manufacture as is required by the workman for the tasteful execution of his work' (*Building Chronicle*, 1 Jan 1855, 129). Yet by comparison with his near contemporary William Playfair, his few drawings (generally characterized by pale blue roofs, cream walls, orange timberwork, and brown floor plans) display scant interest in construction and detail.

Rhind may have trained with A. C. Pugin in London in the 1820s (when he became firm friends with Charles Barry) and then with George Smith, a former clerk of William Burn, in Edinburgh. That he had visited Italy was emphasized in the strong cosmopolitanism of his principal designs. He was established by 1834 as architect at his mother's address of 6 Forres Street, Edinburgh, but is thought already to have completed two plain late classical Commercial Bank projects: Wick (1829) and Falkirk (1830). In 1834 he designed the plinth for John Greenshields's statue of Sir Walter Scott in George Square, Glasgow. The bulk of his designs were for banks or sheriff courts. Many of the former were routinely Italianate (although some—Banff and Perth—were grand-manner *palazzi*), and his later baronial sheriff courts lacked the vigorous conviction of his contemporaries. His feuing plans (for Merchiston and Pollok, for example) were unremarkable. There was a distinct tailing-off after 1860. Rhind had married Emily Shoubridge on 16 September 1840, and, after her premature death, Mary Jane Sackville Pearson on 24 April 1845. Five of his children predeceased him (two of them in 1856).

Yet between 1843 and 1856 Rhind—or perhaps his award-winning assistants John Alexander Hamilton (who also assisted William Playfair with his later works), Robert

Morham, and Hippolyte Blanc—completed a small number of truly monumental buildings that demonstrate grandeur, flamboyance, and romanticism in a variety of architectural languages. In 1843 he won a competition for the Commercial Bank in George Street, Edinburgh, for which he produced an extraordinarily powerful colour perspective. This Roman classical, Playfair-influenced bank became the outstanding building of George Street, and its success led the trustees of Daniel Stewart's to appoint him for their new hospital/school in 1848. Requesting designs in three styles, they selected what they (and he) called Elizabethan but which was, rather, a flamboyant Scottish Jacobean—a riot of George Heriot's Hospital-style detailing. That this may have been Rhind's own preference is indicated by its choice for his unsuccessful entry for the architectural competition for a design for the Houses of Parliament.

Rhind's design for the Commercial Bank's other principal office, in Gordon Street, Glasgow (1854), took the dignified form of a massively detailed, rusticated Renaissance *palazzo* like a contemporary London club. Through most of the 1850s he was engaged on the troubled refacing of the Life Association headquarters in Princes Street, Edinburgh. It became the most sumptuous three-dimensional façade on the street, a Venetian *palazzo* coruscating with carvings and capped by finials. By contrast, an intriguingly personal romantic reinvention of Scottish historic architecture informed his mid-career houses such as Knockdolian, Ayrshire (c.1840), Carlowrie, Linlithgowshire (1851), and probably the nearby, contemporary Champfleurie (attributed to Rhind).

Rhind's office was reputed to have been a good one to train in, but his architecture left the *Builder* obituarist puzzled, as never being in 'the true spirit' of Gothic. The latter concluded, rather unfairly, that Rhind had been an early Victorian classicist at heart, both unable to adapt and more interested in 'façade effects' than in the intricacies of interior planning. Yet the powerful theatricality of his principal monuments was judged by Lord Cockburn a principal adornment of mid-nineteenth-century Edinburgh. Rhind died at 12 Selwood Terrace, Onslow Gardens, London, on 4 April 1883, and was buried in the combined family tomb, which he had designed in 1834, in St Cuthbert's Church, Edinburgh; he was survived by his second wife.

CHARLES McKEAN

Sources *Building Chronicle*, 10 (11 Jan 1855), 129 · *Building Chronicle*, 21 (1 Dec 1855), 273 · Register of Sasines, NA Scot. · H. Stevenson, 'David Rhind, architect', diss., U. Edin., 1969 [copy in Royal Commission on Ancient and Historic Monuments] · I. Gow, 'David Rhind', *The architectural outsiders*, ed. R. Brown (1985), 153–71 · research notes by Ian Gow, Royal Commission on Ancient and Historic Monuments, MS 643 · D. Rhind, 'Stewart's Hospital Edinburgh', *Civil Engineer and Architect's Journal*, 15 (1852), 121 · D. Rhind, 'On the respective claims of Inigo Jones, Dr Balcanquall, Dean of Rochester, and William Wallace to have been the designer of Heriot's Hospital', *Transactions of the Architectural Institute of Scotland, session 1851–5* (1852) · *The Builder*, 8 (1850), 565; 21 (1863), 354–5, 565; (16 May 1863) · minutes of the Life Association of Scotland, survey of records of Life Association of Scotland, NRA Scotland, 2255 · documents and correspondence relative to Trinity College Church, NL

Scot. • *The Scotsman* (1 May 1883) • *The Builder* (12 May 1883) • *Edinburgh Architectural Association: exhibition catalogue* (1907) [Edinburgh, 19 June – 10 Aug 1907] • *IGI*

Wealth at death £359 13s. 0d.: confirmation, 2 July 1883, *CCI* • £279 10s. 2d.: eik to confirmation, 23 Nov 1886, *CCI*

Rhiwallon ap Cynfyn (*d.* 1069). *See under* Bleddyn ap Cynfyn (*d.* 1075).

Rhodes, Cecil John (1853–1902), imperialist, colonial politician, and mining entrepreneur, was born at Bishop's Stortford in Hertfordshire on 5 July 1853. He was the fifth son of Francis William Rhodes (1806–1878), vicar of that parish from 1849 to 1876, and his second wife, Louisa (*d.* 1873), daughter of Anthony Taylor Peacock of South Kyme, Lincolnshire. The family consisted of nine sons, four of whom joined the army and two of whom died in infancy, and two daughters, both unmarried; one of his brothers was Francis William (Frank) *Rhodes (1851–1905).

Early life As the son of a Church of England clergyman, the young Cecil Rhodes grew up in the reasonably comfortable country vicarage of Bishop's Stortford. For reasons that are unclear he did not follow his older brothers to Eton or Winchester colleges, but was sent in 1861 to the grammar school at Bishop's Stortford (then under the supervision of his somewhat forbidding father), where he completed his education. Wishing for a professional career, and perhaps hoping to acquire the social cachet of his public-school educated older brothers, he was determined to enter Oxford, but this ambition remained unfulfilled until he had begun to amass his African fortune. Instead, in 1871 the seventeen-year-old Rhodes, who had fallen ill in the previous year and who in any case had no vocation to become a clergyman, was dispatched, with £2000 from his aunt, to join his eldest brother, Herbert, then growing cotton in the British colony of Natal. Although it is frequently suggested that he was sent to Natal to cure his consumptive lungs, recent accounts have followed his early biographer Sir Lewis Michell, who remarks that 'his father recognized that he was unfitted for a routine life in England, and resolved to ship him to one of the Colonies' (Michell, 1.21). In later life Rhodes's ill health was occasioned by a weak heart rather than weak lungs.

The decision to send Rhodes to Africa was fateful, if not particularly fortuitous: in 1870 southern Africa was on the eve of its mineral revolution and a period of turbulent economic and political change in which Rhodes was to play a major role. Late in 1870 diamonds, already being exploited along the river banks of the Vaal and Hartz rivers, were discovered on the four farms which were later to make up the Kimberley diamond fields. Five years after the discovery of the first alluvial diamonds in 1867 the region had become the largest producer of these gems the world had known. In 1871, in a series of moves which outraged colonial opinion, the British government first declared the diamond fields the territory of the Griqua under their chief, Nicolas Waterboer, and then annexed them in his name as the British crown colony of Griqualand West,

Cecil John Rhodes (1853–1902), by Bassano

ignoring the rival claims of the Afrikaner republics and the even more substantial claims of the region's indigenous Tswana inhabitants. This marked the beginnings of a new phase of aggressive imperial expansion in southern Africa. The British annexation of Griqualand West was based on dubious title, but the diamond fields were too tempting to allow for any wait upon legal niceties.

For Rhodes the first harbinger of these changes was the absence of his brother Herbert when he arrived at Durban harbour: in January 1871 Herbert had joined thousands of other fortune seekers at the recently discovered Griqualand West diamond fields. Although Cecil Rhodes spent his first year attempting to grow cotton, hoping to use the proceeds to take himself to Oxford, his first crop failed and the second, while more successful, sold for a poor price. By October 1871 he too was on his way to the diamond diggings, riding across the Drakensberg on a pony, the ox-cart behind containing—in addition to his necessary supplies—Plutarch's *Lives* and a Greek lexicon. Rhodes may not have had much success in growing cotton, but he left Natal exuberant at having discovered his ability to direct and control large numbers of African labourers with a shrewdly calculated self-interest. He had also acquired a set of perceptions about African labour and colonial expansion.

Rhodes's managerial skills were to prove important at the diggings for, within two weeks of his arrival, Herbert had departed for Natal and England, leaving Cecil in charge of his claims. That he was able to make his way in the anarchic and at times dangerous social world of Kimberley in the early 1870s is a remarkable tribute to his self-sufficiency and poise, even if Herbert had ensured his entry into the circle of well-connected claim-holders, administrators, and professional men at the diggings. Rhodes set about working his brother's claims and described the diggings in a series of vivid letters to his mother. Within a remarkably short time he had established his reputation in Kimberley. As his brother Frank, who accompanied Herbert back to Kimberley in 1872, wrote to his parents, 'Cecil seems to have done wonderfully well as regards the diamonds'—and he admitted that no one on the fields could believe that he, Frank, was the elder brother (Marlowe, 57). Rhodes was indeed doing 'wonderfully well'. Within two months he was discovering diamonds worth £100 a week and within the year his personal fortune was valued at £5000. By the summer of 1873 he had accumulated £10,000—enough to take him back to England to invest his earnings in land in Hampstead and an education in Oxford.

Despite these financial successes, an illness described as a 'slight heart attack' left Rhodes with a sense of foreboding. On Herbert's return from Britain, the two set off for the Transvaal, partly so that Cecil could recuperate, partly to investigate a recently announced gold strike. Across the Vaal, Cecil purchased a 3000 acre tract of land while the ever-restless Herbert decided to relinquish his diamond claims in order to pursue fortune and adventure in central Africa. He was to die in 1879, when his hut caught fire in what is now Malawi.

The first of Rhodes's eight wills was signed in 1872; in it he left his possessions to the British secretary of state for the colonies, for the extension of the British empire. By the early 1870s the language of imperial expansion was in the air. 'The Anglo-Saxon race', thundered the *Natal Witness* in 1872, 'shall hold undisputed sway from Capetown to the Zambezi' (Newbury, 'Out of the pit', 27)—and there were a number of Natal settlers intent on making this a reality, among them the renowned secretary for native affairs, Theophilus Shepstone, and his agent, Herbert's friend, Frederic Elton, both of whom had subcontinental ambitions. This was heady stuff for the young Rhodes, whose subsequent imperial vision probably owed more to the Natal and diggers' press than to John Ruskin's imperialist lectures which he is believed to have attended at Oxford (ibid.).

On the diamond fields Rhodes soon established a small circle of slightly older male friends. By the end of 1872 he was working claims with Charles Dunnell Rudd, who was nine years his elder. Rudd came from a landowning family with experience in the engineering and machinery industry. An old Harrovian who left Trinity College, Cambridge, without a degree, Rudd was engaged in a variety of entrepreneurial activities in the 1870s and was in charge of Rhodes's claims. His natural caution balanced Rhodes's impetuosity.

Among Rhodes's other close friends at this period was John X. Merriman, described by Basil Williams as the 'best read man and the best talker in South Africa', and already a member of the Cape legislative assembly (he was later to become its last prime minister) (Williams, 32). Merriman represented a long if ambiguous tradition of Cape constitutional liberalism which, with its belief in equality before the law and a colour-blind franchise, ran counter to the dominant social practices of the day; by the mid-1880s the tradition was increasingly under attack, not least from Rhodes himself. Close too was John Blades Currey, secretary to the recently arrived British administration in Griqualand West, whose family nursed Rhodes back to health during his first illness. Merriman and Currey introduced the young man to the world of Cape politics and administration.

Yet Rhodes still hoped to become a barrister and, in the summer of 1873, set off for Oxford. Disappointed to be refused entry to University College (perhaps because of his poor Latin prose), he was accepted by Oriel College, from which he matriculated on 13 October. However, by the end of his first term, during which he passed responsions, his mother's death in November and his own ill health forced him to leave Oxford. Early in 1874 he returned to Kimberley and set about establishing himself on the diamond fields in earnest.

Mining for diamonds The Kimberley to which Rhodes now turned his attention was on the eve of its crucial transformation from the era of small claims and share-workers to the era of joint stock companies and, ultimately, monopoly. With the initial influx of individual diggers, a myriad of claims had been staked out on the four 'dry' diggings that made up Kimberley. At that time each digger was limited to two claims. So long as the interests of small diggers predominated and mining was based on opencast quarrying requiring little capital outlay or technical expertise, black producers were able to compete with white, especially as they had the advantage of family labour. The success of these black diggers now formed a focus for the discontent of the many white small claim-holders, diggers, and share-workers, all of whom operated claims on behalf of owners in return for a percentage of the proceeds. Yet, in Kimberley, infinitely more dreams were shattered than fortunes made. By the time Rhodes returned from Oxford the mines were in a state of crisis. Drought in 1873 followed by floods early in 1874 had sent up food and transport costs in southern Africa, the world price of diamonds had plummeted as a result of a slump on the Austrian stock exchange, and the banks were beginning to foreclose on indebted small diggers. At the same time the mines were threatened with collapsing walls and flooding, the result of haphazard development and primitive technology. As Kimberley's initially opencast operations extended ever deeper underground, the mines demanded increasingly expensive machinery and more sophisticated techniques. When the eroded yellow ground close to the surface gave way to blue, many of the small diggers left the fields.

In the new colony of Griqualand West economic disaster was accompanied by political turmoil as small diggers took the law into their own hands and vented their frustration on what they deemed the unfair competition and illicit diamond selling of black diggers. This culminated in the formation of a white Kimberley Defence League and

Protection Association and the so-called 'black flag' revolt of April 1875. By the end of that year these events had led to the recall of Southey—a supporter of the small claim-holders against the ambitions of larger metropolitan capital—and his replacement as lieutenant-governor of Griqualand West. In 1876 all limitations on claim-holding were lifted, thus allowing for the formation of joint stock companies. There is little evidence that Rhodes took any part in this political and social unrest. From the first he had identified himself with the larger claim-holders and with the colonial administration. Moreover, he was well positioned to take advantage of the new situation. He recognized that, far from spelling the end of the industry, the blue deposits contained larger numbers of more valuable diamonds and that fortunes were to be made by those who could stay the course. On his return from Oxford in 1874 he and Rudd had concentrated their claims in the Vooruitzicht mines (later known as De Beers) and were able to take advantage of the departure of small diggers to consolidate their holdings, once the restrictions on claim-holdings were lifted. By the mid-1870s Rhodes and Rudd were among those advocating rationalization and amalgamation of the mines. By 1879 theirs was the largest concern in the De Beers mine.

Rhodes and Rudd were among the first to see the importance of pumping equipment and, by mid-1874, even before he had acquired a pump, Rhodes had contracted with the De Beers mining board to extract water from the mines. If this was sharp practice, Rhodes's subsequent dealings with the mining board and the pumping contract raised greater question marks over his business probity. In mid-1875 Rhodes's pumps broke down and a temporary contract was awarded to the engineer E. Huteau, pending the arrival of Rhodes's new machines. This arrangement proved satisfactory and the board contemplated transferring the permanent contract to Huteau. When, in December, the temporary pump was sabotaged, Huteau insinuated that Rhodes was responsible. Apparently in order to prevent further public discussion Rhodes forwarded the matter to the attorney-general, a close friend, and Huteau was charged with perjury. The case was never heard in court, however. By March 1876 Rhodes had left for Oxford where he spent most of the next two years. In October 1876 he confessed, 'My character was so battered at the Diamond Fields that I like to preserve the few remnants' (Turrell, *Capital and Labour*, 86).

Return to Oxford If Rhodes had already made his mark in Kimberley, his career at Oxford was undistinguished. When he returned, he read for a pass degree, not for honours; this permitted a pattern of broken residence. He was remembered by his tutor as being part of a set which lived 'a good deal apart from both games and work' (Michell, 1.81). Because of his peripatetic lifestyle, Rhodes completed his pass degree only in 1881, and although he was admitted at the Inner Temple in March 1876 he never seriously pursued a career in the law.

It is easier to see what Rhodes gave to Oxford than what he got from it. Notwithstanding many historical accounts,

he was not in Oxford for John Ruskin's famous inaugural lecture, and there is little evidence that he read his works; nevertheless his Oxford years seem to have reinforced his dreams of expansion with that mix of racial pride and imperial enthusiasm which was beginning to permeate British intellectual and political circles. He seems to have been much impressed by the writings of Winwoode Reade, a social Darwinist who applied notions of the survival of the fittest to the 'races' of mankind and believed that of all the races the 'Anglo-Saxon' was manifestly the finest and fittest. Rhodes was also much taken by such classical authors as Aristotle and Marcus Aurelius as well as by Gibbon, all of whom extolled the virtues of public service.

These many influences came together in Rhodes's 'Confession of faith', a document which, however juvenile and ungrammatical, none the less expressed the philosophy that governed the rest of his life. The 'Confession' was written on 2 June 1877, the day on which Rhodes was inducted as a life member of the Oxford University Apollo chapter of the freemasons (Rotberg, 90). In it he mused on the history of the freemasons and the Jesuits, and advocated the formation of a secret society 'with but one object the furtherance of the British Empire and the bringing of the whole uncivilised world under British rule for the recovery of the United States for the making the Anglo-Saxon race but one Empire'. For Rhodes, 'the absorption of the greater portion of the world under our rule' would mean 'the end of all wars', for he believed that the British were 'the finest race in the world, and … the more of the world we inhabit, the better it is for the human race'. 'What an alteration there would be,' he continued, if 'those parts that are present inhabited by the most despicable of human beings … were brought under Anglo-Saxon influence' (Flint, appx, 248–52).

In September 1877 these notions were embodied in Rhodes's second, vastly ambitious, will. In this he once more appointed as one of his executors the secretary of state for the colonies, who was at that time Lord Carnarvon, whose confederation schemes for southern Africa partly inspired Rhodes's own dream of a unified subcontinent. His endowment of Oxford scholarships, in order to inspire the young élite of empire with ideas of imperial race pride and give effect to his ambitions of world domination, occurred somewhat later. Yet the will proposed the establishment of a secret society for the purposes set out in his 'Confession'. Such proposals recurred in the six wills he wrote thereafter at regular intervals until his death. In 1891, when the journalist and publisher W. T. Stead—appointed at that time one of his executors—wrote asking him for his views on life and politics, Rhodes responded by sending him the 'Confession of faith'. Not only was Rhodes obsessed by this grandiose project, it seems also to have fired the imagination of the coterie of devotees who surrounded him from his early years in Kimberley.

Return to Kimberley There are doubtless many young men who dream of dominating and transforming the world. On his return from Oxford in 1878, the year in which his father died, Rhodes began to collect around him a select band with whom he could share this vision. His ability to recognize other people's talents and to draw them into his enterprises was among his most outstanding characteristics. Prominent among these were the mercurial Leander Starr *Jameson, who established himself in Kimberley as a general practitioner in 1878, Alfred *Beit, financial genius and devoted follower (Galbraith, 59) who helped build Rhodes's mining empire, and Neville Pickering, perhaps his most intimate companion and confidant.

Rhodes's possibly homosexual relationship with Pickering, the first of the young male secretaries with whom he established an intense friendship, has been the subject of much speculation. What is known is that Rhodes moved from his lodgings with the group of friends dubbed the Twelve Apostles, to share a cottage with Pickering, that in 1882 he left Pickering all his 'worldly wealth', and that in 1888, when Pickering lay dying, Rhodes abandoned an exploratory visit to the newly discovered Witwatersrand goldfields to nurse him. Through the 1890s Rhodes continued to befriend and employ unattached young men, whose admiration for him fell little short of adoration. He behaved with great possessiveness when any of them married, and he undoubtedly preferred the company of men to that of women.

There were three exceptions. The first, and probably most important, was the journalist Flora Shaw, who shared Rhodes's imperialist design and lent the support of her columns to his achieving a royal charter in central Africa. She was implicated in the Jameson raid, almost certainly acting as an intermediary between Rhodes and Chamberlain in their collusion, and in 1897 withheld important evidence of this collusion from the House of Commons select committee. There is no doubting Rhodes's admiration for her. He was also intrigued by—and intrigued—Olive Schreiner, who was later to write a damning indictment of his imperialism; and he showed an initial interest in Princess Radziwill, an impoverished Polish fortune-seeker who followed Rhodes to the Cape at the end of his life in the hope of attaching herself to him. When rebuffed, she attempted blackmail but, significantly, did not allege that Rhodes was homosexual.

The rise of De Beers With his already substantial holdings in Kimberley, in the decade after 1878 Rhodes set about accumulating the wealth and political power which were to enable him to shape the destiny of a subcontinent and influence the political culture of the metropole during his lifetime and beyond. In the three years from 1878 to 1880 he and Rudd consolidated their holdings in De Beers mine and in April 1880 were able to float the De Beers Mining Company with a share capital of £200,000. In the following year, during a period of rapid joint stock company formation and 'share mania', they merged their claims with those of the neighbouring Frederic (later Sir Frederic Philipson) Stow and his partners to create the most highly capitalized mine on the fields at £665,550.

During the depression of 1882–5 the De Beers Mining Company became the premier concern on the fields, absorbing the weaker holdings in the old De Beers mine.

By 1886 Stow had established a London office in order to secure metropolitan capital for their endeavours; in 1887 Rhodes, to the same end, brought Alfred Beit onto the De Beers board of directors. The election of Beit caused Stow considerable disquiet, largely because he feared a conflict of interest between the diamond producers in Kimberley and Beit's position as the leading diamond merchant on the fields. But in the battle for the amalgamation of the diamond fields and for the final monopolizing of the diamond mines Rhodes needed the access Beit provided to the markets of Europe. Although the creation De Beers is usually attributed to Rhodes, the contributions of Stow and Beit were at least equally important (Turrell, 'Sir Frederic Philipson Stow', 62–7).

The story of the final contest for control of the diamond fields has frequently been told as a highly personalized encounter between Rhodes, the Oxford-educated Englishman, and Barney *Barnato, the slightly shady upstart from the Mile End Road, the most influential shareholder in Kimberley Central, De Beers's main rival. Recent research suggests that this mythology obscures a highly complex story of financial manoeuvring. Once he realized that Rhodes and Stow held the upper hand, through the assistance of the Rothschilds, Barnato joined forces with De Beers at the expense of his own shareholders, and to his own very considerable advantage. Together with Rhodes, Beit, and Stow—and despite Stow's opposition—Barnato was appointed a life governor of the new De Beers Consolidated Company, entitled to a quarter of all profits apart from the 30 per cent reserved for general shareholders. As a result of amalgamation, De Beers Consolidated became one of the largest British companies of the time (Turrell, *Capital and Labour*, 206–27).

The amalgamation of the mines notwithstanding, Rhodes never gained complete control either over the sale of stones or over the profits of De Beers. There were always tensions between diamond producers and diamond merchants, and between the boards of De Beers in Kimberley and London. There were also tensions between Rhodes and Barnato, which had never been over amalgamation *per se*, but over the immense geopolitical powers Rhodes wanted for the new company. In the end Rhodes's persistence won. The company's trust deed permitted it almost unparalleled power 'to acquire any asset of any kind by any means' (Rotberg, 209). It also permitted the acquisition of African territory by treaty or conquest, and the exercise of political authority over such territory.

So extensive were the company's powers that, when they were challenged in the courts by disgruntled Kimberley Central shareholders, the judge interrupted the litany to say that it would be far quicker to relate what the company could not do than what it could. Counsel for the plaintiffs responded by observing that De Beers 'could do anything and everything, my lord' (Rotberg, 209–10). Despite the misgivings of Barnato and the other life governors, Beit and Stow, Rhodes was able to insist on the retention of these overarching powers. None the less, Rhodes had constraints placed upon his total freedom of action by the board and was not infrequently obliged to employ subterfuge in order to use the profits of De Beers for enterprises which his London board disliked.

Amalgamation had far-reaching consequences beyond the boardroom. It involved the loss of large numbers of jobs for white and black workers. It also saw the streamlining of methods of labour control which had already been pioneered at De Beers. Thus, even before the final stages of amalgamation were reached, Rhodes and his partners in De Beers had begun to reorganize the migrant labour system and establish 'closed compounds' for black workers. These were modelled on the convict station Rhodes had earlier established at De Beers to make use of prison labour. Black workers were rigorously searched before and after being incarcerated in the compounds for the duration of their contracts. Attempts were also made similarly to strip-search and confine white workers, but these attempts failed. The nexus of laws and institutions for the control of African labour established at De Beers provided the model for twentieth-century South Africa.

This control of African labour was made possible both by the imperial conquest and annexation of the remaining independent African kingdoms of southern Africa between 1878 and 1885, and by the increasing role played by Rhodes and his fellow Griqualand West representatives in the politics of Cape Colony. In 1880 Griqualand West was finally incorporated into the colony and Rhodes was elected as member of parliament for Barkly West, amid widespread allegations of vote buying. He rapidly became the most prominent spokesman for the diamond interest, not least because he had secretly bought the colony's leading newspaper, the *Cape Argus*. Rhodes and the Griqualand West representatives had four major concerns in the legislative assembly: to increase their own control over labour migration routes, to improve their disciplinary powers over labour, most essentially through the compound system, to prevent the haemorrhage of diamonds through illicit smuggling, and to secure a railway from the coast to Kimberley.

Politics Rhodes's purpose in being in parliament became immediately evident in his chairmanship of a select committee to inquire into illicit diamond buying, a select committee which framed the Diamond Trade Act of 1882. This draconian piece of legislation, aimed at curbing illicit diamond buying and selling, put the onus on the accused to prove their innocence, allowed for entrapment, and permitted police searches without warrant. Rhodes also demanded flogging for anyone handling stolen diamonds, but this was rejected by the legislative assembly.

Rhodes exercised his influence without being a frequent speaker in parliamentary debates. His maiden speech concerned the affairs of Basutoland, at that time engaged in a costly war with Cape Colony, which had taken over the territory from the British government in 1872. His opposition to the disarmament of the Basuto, as proposed by the legislature, has often been read as showing his early sympathy with African peoples and their rights. However, here too diamond interests were not far

from the surface. The war not only obstructed the construction of the Kimberley railway: Basuto migrants were attracted to Kimberley by the prospect of acquiring firearms. Mine owners feared that disarmament would drastically cut the supply of a particularly reliable source of labour. As one Kimberley man said: 'After all, we sold them the guns; they bought them with their hard-won wages, and it *is* hard lines to make them give them up again' (Williams, 63). In addition, Basutoland served as 'the granary' of the diamond fields and was an important source of firewood. It was crucial to the mine magnates that the war be ended as soon as possible. Rhodes advocated the passage of a Disannexation Bill and the retrocession of Basutoland to the imperial government, a policy that was eventually followed in 1884.

In Basutoland, as a member of a commission to investigate the claims for compensation of 'loyal' Basuto, Rhodes met General Charles George Gordon, then engaged by the Cape government to reorganize the colonial troops who were unsuccessfully contending with the Basuto. Like Rhodes, Gordon came to believe that Cape policy was misconceived, and resigned. The two men are said to have made a profound impression on one another. Gordon invited Rhodes to join him on his ill-fated expedition to the Sudan, and Rhodes was much affected by news of Gordon's death in 1885 at the hands of the Mahdists.

Diamond interests undoubtedly contributed to the regional perspective Rhodes had already set out so grandiosely in his 1877 'Confession'. In his speech on the Disannexation Bill he looked forward to a 'United States of Africa' under the British flag, although, after the débâcle of Lord Carnarvon's confederation schemes for South Africa in the 1870s, he believed Cape Colony should take the lead. By the early 1880s Rhodes was turning his attention to the increasingly anarchic conditions in Bechuanaland on the western flank of Griqualand West. The new market at Kimberley had intensified the struggle between the local Tswana people and Afrikaners for the region's limited arable land and water resources. This conflict was exacerbated when the British withdrew from the Transvaal (which had been annexed in 1877 and then surrendered after the British defeat at Majuba in 1881) and warring Tswana chiefs invited in Transvaal and Cape mercenaries to assist in their internecine battles.

From 1878 Tswana chiefs and their missionary allies appealed for British protection but were ignored. Despite the interest of Cape merchants in the road to the north which ran through Bechuanaland, the colonial legislature was equally reluctant to take any action that would necessitate expenditure. Early in 1882, at the invitation of the contending local chiefs, Afrikaner mercenaries established the little republics of Stellaland and Goshen to the north of Griqualand West, straddling the missionary route to the interior. These freebooters were backed by land speculators in the South African Republic and supported by its recently restored government, which saw the possibilities for using the conflict to test the resolve of the British government and gain additional land.

Rhodes urged action. All his interests were at stake. As in

Basutoland, Bechuanaland represented a source of labour and firewood for Kimberley, and the new republics threatened the supply routes to the west of the Transvaal. Moreover, since he and his fellow diamond merchants were anxious to control any new source of diamonds, it was in Rhodes's interest to argue for the annexation of the territory. This was an objective to which the eastern Cape merchants lent support, since for them the presence in the territory of freebooter Afrikaners threatened to undermine their commercial prospects in the interior. While most of Rhodes's biographers have perceived this episode as indicative of Rhodes's imperial vision, his actions in this case had more to do with immediate and material local imperatives.

By 1883 Rhodes had been dispatched to the region as the Cape's trouble-shooter. The most powerful local chief, Mankurwane, agreed to place his territory under Cape rule, and the Stellalanders were induced to accept Cape incorporation, although the settlers at Goshen proved more intractable. Urged by Rhodes, the British government, after some hesitation, was persuaded by the British high commissioner and Cape governor, Sir Hercules Robinson, to secure the trade route and pacify the region. The resulting London convention of 1884 gave the South African Republic more territory, but left open the vital corridor to the north. John Mackenzie, a missionary, was appointed deputy commissioner, but failed to restore order and was replaced by Rhodes. Initially Rhodes was no more successful in resolving the rival territorial claims, and was forced to withdraw from Goshen in August 1884 when a republican commando invaded the territory and the Transvaal president, S. J. P. Kruger, proclaimed its sovereignty.

By this time, however, the colonial situation had been transformed by the fall of the inert Scanlen ministry and its replacement by one which shared Rhodes's expansionist ideas. Moreover, the geopolitical situation had also been altered by the intervention of Germany in the region: at the end of April 1884 Bismarck had declared a protectorate over the German trading post at Angra Pequeña, and by the end of August had annexed the whole of what became South-West Africa from the Orange River to the as yet unspecified borders of the Portuguese colony of Angola. Despite the efforts of the new Cape ministry, prompted by Rhodes and Merriman, to secure colonial interests in an area long regarded as its commercial hinterland, Germany had acquired its first colony in Africa. Its presence along the Atlantic coast led to fears that the German colony and the South African Republic would act jointly to block the road to the north.

Bechuanaland was now seen as a key imperial interest, and any attempt by the Transvaal to annex the republic of Goshen became unthinkable. At the end of 1884 the imperial government re-entered the region, forced Kruger to withdraw, and sent a military expedition to Bechuanaland under Major-General Sir Charles Warren. He was accompanied by Rhodes and Mackenzie. The triumvirate was doomed to disagreement from the start, divided as they were on matters of principle. Warren and Mackenzie were

determined to defend the land and political rights of local African chiefs; Rhodes was equally determined to reconcile the Stellalanders to British rule and secure the region for white settlement. In February 1885, when Warren repudiated the land titles he had granted the Stellaland settlers, Rhodes resigned.

Despite his resignation, Rhodes nevertheless gained much of what he wanted. Warren re-established order, placed southern Bechuanaland under crown rule, and proclaimed northern Bechuanaland a British protectorate. Transvaal expansion was blocked; the road northwards remained open; and the movement of labour was unimpeded. Moreover Rhodes had been able to prevent Warren's attempt to limit land claims in the new colony to persons of British descent and so had furthered his nascent alliance with the Cape Afrikaners.

Rhodes in 1885 In many ways 1885 was a watershed year for Rhodes, now one of the wealthiest men in South Africa and still only thirty-two years old. The first phase of the amalgamation of the diamond fields and the creation of the De Beers Company had been completed. His Oxford dreams accomplished, he had increasingly identified himself with the subcontinent. In 1883 he had served very briefly as treasurer-general in the Scanlen ministry and had emerged as a leading Cape politician. Majuba and the British withdrawal from the Transvaal, together with imperial indecisiveness over Bechuanaland, had convinced him that for further expansion he needed a local power base, and the increasing hold of the recently formed Afrikaner Bond as the political party of Cape Afrikaners made it clear that this would depend on an alliance with them. The Bechuanaland experience was an object lesson in the importance of local sub-imperialism.

Gold and the Rand The discovery of gold on the Witwatersrand in the South African Republic in 1886 opened a new phase in the history of the subcontinent—and in Rhodes's life. In the next decade the remaining independent African polities south of the Limpopo were conquered and annexed, and both within and without the frontiers of the colonial states, land, labour, and mineral concessionaires were spurred by prospects of further discoveries and the availability of speculative capital. The Limpopo River constituted no barrier to the flood of fortune-seekers, and between 1889 and 1895 all of the African territories as far north as the Congo were annexed in 'a gigantic speculation in mineral futures' (Robinson, Gallagher, and Denny, 250). In central Africa the British competed with the South African Republic, Portugal, Germany, and Belgium. In east-central Africa, to the west and south of Lake Nyasa, the thrust from the south encountered an anti-slavery, missionary, and trading frontier from the east. In this last phase of the scramble for southern African territories, Rhodes played a leading role.

Paradoxically, however, Rhodes was at first somewhat dismissive of the stories of untold wealth on the Rand; he had burnt his fingers on the short-lived Barberton goldfields a couple of years before, and De Beers's American mining engineer in Kimberley was sceptical of the claims being made for the Witwatersrand. During Rhodes's absence prospecting in the Transvaal, Pickering had fallen ill and Rhodes had returned to Kimberley to nurse his dying friend. Always less assured in his appreciation of the goldfields, Rhodes's early investments were haphazard and injudicious. Although he and his partners launched Gold Fields Company Ltd early in 1887 with a share capital of £250,000, initially at least they made more money by manipulating the share market than through the value of their investments. By 1888 it was clear that on the Rand Rhodes had 'cornered the dregs' (Rotberg, 499).

The British South Africa Company Failure on the Rand was an additional spur for Rhodes to move north of the Limpopo, where he believed he would find a 'second Rand', pre-empt rival explorations for diamonds, and outflank an increasingly confident South African Republic. From the 1860s it had been known that there were 'ancient gold workings' between the Limpopo and Zambezi rivers, and by the mid-1880s *Lobengula, king of the most powerful people in that region, the Ndebele (Matabele), was surrounded by concession hunters, including Rhodes's agents. When, at the end of 1887, news came of possible Transvaal expansion across the Limpopo, Rhodes put pressure on Sir Hercules Robinson to act. At Rhodes's insistence, Robinson now authorized J. S. Moffat, son of the famous missionary Robert Moffat, to secure a treaty of amity between Lobengula and the British government, which in effect declared ultimate imperial sovereignty over the Ndebele kingdom (February 1888).

This gave Rhodes his opportunity in Matabeleland, and he set about converting concession into control. In 1888 Rudd, T. Rochefort Maguire (a friend of his Oxford days), and F. R. Thompson, who had established the closed compounds at De Beers, were sent to secure exclusive mining rights in Lobengula's kingdom. Through a mixture of bribery and guile, on 30 October 1888 they secured the king's signature to the Rudd concession permitting the exploitation of minerals in his domains in which were included the lands of his reluctant Shona tributaries. Although the king soon regretted his concession, it strengthened Rhodes immeasurably against his rival concessionaires whom he was now able to buy out.

On 29 October 1889 the British government granted the British South Africa Company (BSAC) a royal charter to exploit and extend its administrative control over a vast, if ill-defined, area of southern and central Africa. Nowhere was Rhodes's conviction that everyone had his price better illustrated than in his dealings to gain and protect the chartered company. An amalgamation of London financial interests and potential competitors, bedecked by an array of aristocratic directors, including the dukes of Abercorn and Fife, the BSAC not only represented a somewhat dubious business enterprise, it also consistently misled the investing public with inspired but false accounts of its new Eldorado. Potential competitors and critics in Britain and the Cape were bought out with substantial shareholdings. Contrary to the impression given at the time, the concession did not include land rights, which the BSAC bought from Edouard Lippert in 1891. Nor, contrary

to what the British government and investing public had been misled into assuming, did the company actually own the Rudd concession. This too had to be acquired by BSAC shareholders for £1 million from the United Concessions Company (formerly the Central Search Company, and in which Gold Fields had a controlling interest), to the great personal profit of Rhodes and his partners.

For the British government the BSAC's great advantage was its promise to people central Africa with white immigrants who would make British occupation effective against contending European powers and bring the necessary capitalist development to the interior at minimum cost. In 1890 a 'pioneer column', consisting of 200 white settlers and 150 black, backed by 500 paramilitary police, occupied Mashonaland, without incident. The 'pioneers' soon scattered over the country in search of gold.

Even before his charter was ratified, Rhodes had sent his agents across the Zambezi, where the British government was anxious to pre-empt its European rivals. Among these agents was the British consul in Mozambique, Harry (later Sir Harry) Johnson, from whom Rhodes probably acquired his slogan of a 'Cape to Cairo' railway and the idea of a telegraph link. In 1888–9, in a flurry of treaty-making, the whole of present-day Malawi and Zambia was staked out for crown and company. The object was to reach the copper deposits of Katanga, but Rhodes's representatives were foiled by the emissaries of the Belgian king, Leopold II, ruler of the Congo Free State. Despite the dubious legality of the treaties, they secured mineral and sometimes land concessions for the BSAC, while the chiefs agreed to accept British jurisdiction over non-Africans in their domains and over external relations. In the European chancelleries, where the frontiers of Africa were then being decided, these treaties provided the British government with useful bargaining counters and helped to establish over the following decade the frontiers of the states which were afterwards to become Angola, Malawi, Mozambique, Namibia, Tanzania, Zambia, and Zimbabwe.

Since events, in South Africa itself and in what was to become Rhodesia, absorbed most of Rhodes's energies and financial capacity, the fact that south-central Africa was now entirely under alien rule meant little north of the Zambezi until the late 1890s. Nor was Rhodes able to gain all the territory he wanted. In 1890–91 the British and Portuguese governments delimited the frontiers of their African territories. Despite the machinations of Rhodes and Jameson, who took command of the new colony of Mashonaland at the end of 1890, and a considerable display of force by company agents, most of Barotseland, Gazaland, and Manicaland remained in Portuguese hands. For the Foreign Office, European diplomacy took precedence over African expansion. Nevertheless, the final Anglo-Portuguese treaty in 1891 left the healthy highlands in the hands of the company and guaranteed freedom of passage between Mashonaland and the sea. Without a railway, however, the pioneers had little future.

In Mashonaland the settlers were also disappointed in their hopes of instant wealth. It was soon clear that any 'second Rand' north of the Limpopo must lie in Matabeleland. Making use of an Ndebele raid on their Shona tributaries around Fort Victoria, Jameson deliberately provoked war against the Ndebele in 1893, and using Maxim machine-guns defeated them. This resulted in the destruction of the Ndebele kingdom, BSAC occupation of Matabeleland, and white settlement there. The war was followed, as Jameson anticipated, by a boom in BSAC shares and huge mining speculation. Nevertheless, by the end of 1894 it was evident to Rhodes's mining engineers that the unviable outcrop mines in Matabeleland could not compete with the deep-level gold of the Witwatersrand. Rhodes's policies towards the South African Republic hardened perceptibly.

Prime minister of Cape Colony Up to this point Rhodes's expansionist schemes were enthusiastically supported within Cape Colony. He had been careful to court the leadership of the Afrikaner Bond through the judicious distribution of BSAC shares, while the rank and file were enticed with promises of cheap land and labour in his new colony. But Bond support for Rhodes had been long in the making and went well beyond mere bribery. On 17 July 1890 he became prime minister of the Cape with the backing of both the Afrikaner Bond and the liberal members of the legislative assembly. On the face of it, both sources of support were surprising and full of contradiction. The Cape liberals differed fundamentally with Rhodes over the place of Africans in Cape society, and had more fastidious standards of public life. Despite their misgivings, however, the three most prominent liberal parliamentarians agreed to join Rhodes's 1890 ministry in order to get rid of the financially irresponsible Sprigg government. In 1892 they were also persuaded to accept the Franchise and Ballot Act. This was passed at the behest of the Bond and raised the property qualifications for voters, but also introduced an elementary literacy test and a secret ballot which they advocated. Nevertheless, they were increasingly disaffected, and when in 1893 Rhodes failed to expel from his cabinet a minister whom they accused of corruption, the liberals, having on 22 June 1893 formally questioned the propriety of his holding the dual position of premier of the Cape and head of the British South Africa Company, resigned. In spite of this, Rhodes easily won the 1894 general election and he re-formed his cabinet with increased Bond representation.

For Rhodes, the alliance with the Bond, which controlled just under half the seats in parliament, was far more important than his association with the liberals, and he had nurtured it since the mid-1880s. His concern to improve colonial agriculture through replacing Cape vines destroyed by phylloxera, encouraging fruit farms, and stamping out scab disease in sheep had endeared him to the more commercially-minded Afrikaner farmers even before he became premier. His interest in controlling African labour was also shared by this wider constituency. In 1886–7 he had given earlier Bond proposals to change the Cape franchise his whole-hearted support,

while in 1890, in the hope of gaining Bond favour, he supported a Masters and Servants Amendment Bill which permitted the flogging of black servants. In the event the bill was defeated, with even some Bondsmen voting against it. In his second ministry Rhodes took on the portfolio of native affairs in addition to the premiership. In 1894 he annexed Pondoland, the remaining independent African territory between the Cape and Natal, where civil strife and the rival claims of Natal provided the pretext for intervention.

More wide-ranging was Rhodes's Glen Grey Act of 1895. This allowed Africans to acquire land under individual tenure on strictly controlled terms, provided for local councils, and imposed a labour tax intended to propel Africans into working for white employers. Widely hailed as 'a bill for Africa', the act was an astute way of satisfying Rhodes's disparate constituencies. Individual tenure and local self-government were long-held liberal demands, while the labour tax and the exclusion of Glen Grey property-holders from the parliamentary franchise were much to the liking of the Bond—even if, in the event, the labour tax soon fell into disuse. The control over the liquor trade, also embodied in the act, appealed to all but western Cape wine farmers.

If Rhodes was mindful of Bond predilections in framing his 'native policy', initially he was also careful to avoid antagonizing their pro-Transvaal sensibilities. This was made easier for him as by the late 1880s the competing interests of Cape and Transvaal farmers, expressed in conflicting tariff policies, had made Bondsmen veer away from uncritical support for the northern republic. Moreover, after the Bechuanaland débâcle, Rhodes came to advocate a Cape sub-imperialism in which Bond Afrikaners were equal partners. His visions for a united South Africa gave the leading role to colonial forces, and had much in common with those of Jan Hofmeyr, the leading Bondsman. Until the mid-1890s he was also prepared to allow the Transvaal to fulfil some of its territorial ambitions in the annexation of Swaziland, and he envisaged the peaceful achievement of South African unification through gradual economic integration.

Rhodes's success in 1892 in constructing a railway between the Cape and the Transvaal was also popular with Bondsmen, who hoped to sell their agricultural products on the burgeoning Rand market. Yet this policy brought him into direct confrontation with Kruger, who was anxious to retain the republic's autonomy and protect its farmers by building a railway to Delagoa Bay and by raising tariffs on Cape produce. In 1894–5 this blew up into a major crisis when, with the imminent completion of its railway to Delagoa Bay, the republic raised tariffs on the Transvaal section of the Cape line. In response, the colonists transported their goods across the Vaal River by ox-wagon. When Kruger closed the fords over the river in an endeavour to exclude Cape produce, war between the two states seemed imminent. It was only averted when Kruger backed down in the face of an imperial ultimatum in November 1895. Through all this Rhodes continued to enjoy the support of Cape Afrikaners.

Nationalism and empire From being in his youth a 'rabid jingo', Rhodes was now a leading exponent of an autonomous South African nationalism, albeit within the British empire. And this form of nationalism was shared by Cape Afrikaners. To this end he began to foster a local South African identity, by extending his patronage to the preservation of Cape Dutch architecture and furniture, cultivating a sense of colonial history and heritage. The statue of Van Riebeeck, the founder of the Dutch settlement at the Cape, which now stands at the foot of Cape Town's main thoroughfare, was paid for by Rhodes. Groote Schuur, his house on the slopes of Table Mountain, which he left in his will as the residence of a future South Africa's prime ministers, was restored in the local idiom at Rhodes's expense by Herbert *Baker, then a young architect, later the architect of Rhodes House in Oxford. Amid the Matabele uprising Rhodes found time to extol the virtues of the colonial historian George McCauley Theal.

So identified was Rhodes with the Cape colonists that in the late 1880s his pro-imperial credentials were in doubt, and he was widely referred to as the 'young Burger'. This was to oversimplify his position: Rhodes's overarching ambition remained imperial expansion and consolidation, as his many wills and his continued support for imperial federation reveal. In 1888, for example, he gave £10,000 to Parnell to support Irish home rule, provided the Irish members of parliament remained at Westminster in the event of home rule. This donation had the added benefit of encouraging, if not ensuring, the support of the Irish parliamentarians for Rhodes's as yet vague schemes of northward expansion. In 1891 he made a secret donation of £5000 to the Liberal Party in the hope of its also supporting his expansionism, and because he had begun to see it as a bulwark against the rise of socialism in Britain (Michell, 2.48). He sat between Gladstone and John Morley at dinner, Gladstone finding him 'A notable man' and Morley observing, 'The African has a fine head; a Gold full eye, and a strong chin' (Gladstone, *Diaries*, 19 Feb 1891). By that time Rhodes was being lionized by liberals in London, while early in 1892 the University of Oxford had decided to grant him an honorary degree.

The Jameson raid Rhodes's respectability in Britain reached its zenith when on 2 February 1895 he was sworn of the privy council on the nomination of Lord Rosebery. By 1899, however, when Rhodes finally came to have the Oxford degree conferred, it had become a matter of some contention. By then his reputation had been tarnished by his identification with the Jameson raid and an increasingly jingoistic pro-war faction in South Africa. It was for these reasons that, although he was elected a member of London's Athenaeum in 1895, he was blackballed by the Travellers' Club. In the 1890s the increasing economic power of the South African Republic had begun to transform the political geography of South Africa. At the same time, by the mid-1890s Rhodes found his hopes of gold in Matabeleland disappointed, and the development of Rhodesia and his deep-level mines on the Witwatersrand were a heavy drain on his capital. The South African Republic's inability to create the conditions necessary for

recruiting a docile and coerced labour force, along with its liquor, railway, and dynamite policies, were all irksome to deep-level mine owners like Rhodes with their huge demand for labour, their tight working costs, and their great need for explosives.

Making use of the largely fomented clamour of unfranchised British immigrants known as Uitlanders ('aliens', that is non-Boers), over their lack of voting rights and other grievances, Rhodes began to plot with leading members of the mining community for the armed overthrow of the republic. He was secretly backed by Joseph Chamberlain, the British colonial secretary, who was anxious to retain control over the political outcome, and by the compromised Sir Hercules Robinson, whose re-selection as British high commissioner at the Cape Rhodes had secured for a second time in 1895.

At the end of 1895 Jameson on his own initiative invaded the Transvaal with some 600 BSAC armed police and volunteers, hoping to be assisted by the planned uprising of Uitlanders in Johannesburg mobilized by Rhodes's brother Frank and members of the Reform Committee. Aware of the lack of support in Johannesburg, Rhodes attempted to postpone the invasion, but was unable to stop Jameson, whose confidence had been greatly enhanced by his success in Matabeleland. Ill-conceived and poorly organized, the Jameson raid, as it became known, was a complete fiasco. There was no Uitlander uprising and the raiders were soon arrested. The leading members of the Reform Committee were sentenced to death, although their sentences were soon commuted to life imprisonment. They were released when Rhodes paid £25,000 per head to the Transvaal treasury.

More significantly Rhodes's unwillingness to repudiate Jameson forced his resignation in January 1896 from the premiership of Cape Colony. The alliance Rhodes had carefully constructed between English-speakers and Afrikaners was finally destroyed when a Cape parliamentary select committee of inquiry showed his collusion in the raid. Previously loyal to the empire, most Cape Afrikaners, now feeling deeply betrayed, began to draw closer to the republic against the British, as did the Afrikaners of the Orange Free State. The Cape electorate was increasingly polarized on ethnic lines.

The raid also threatened Rhodes's charter. Within weeks he was in London negotiating with Chamberlain. Unable to prevent a House of Commons inquiry into the raid or the call for Rhodes's resignation as managing director of the BSAC, the colonial secretary nevertheless agreed to defend the charter in exchange for Rhodes's silence over the 'missing telegrams' which revealed his own complicity in the attempted coup. Rhodes treated the select committee, by which he was questioned, with swaggering contempt. However, its long duration—it reported only in July 1897—and the changed political situation in South Africa also defused the attack on Rhodes, as did his role in settling the Ndebele uprising in Southern Rhodesia in 1896. He was not stripped of his privy councillorship, as many had expected.

The rising in Southern Rhodesia, 1896 In Southern Rhodesia the absence of the British South Africa police, as a result of the Jameson raid, precipitated an uprising by the Ndebele in March 1896. On top of their defeat in 1893, they had been goaded beyond endurance by the rapaciousness of the settlers, who looted their cattle, ravished their women, and stole their land, and who were uncontrolled by the ramshackle government Rhodes had established. The outbreak of the catastrophic cattle disease rinderpest proved the last straw. Rhodes arrived in Salisbury just as the crisis broke, and rapidly took charge, joining in the relief of Bulawayo. For a time the small white colony seemed doomed.

By June, to the amazement of the settlers, who regarded them as abject 'slaves' of the Ndebele, many of the Shona people rose as well. British military assistance became essential to crushing the uprising, although Rhodes was determined to prevent any imperial annexation of a colony he regarded as his own. After the battle of Taba zi ka Mambo on 5 July, he realized that the only hope of saving his charter lay with initiating peace overtures with the Ndebele, which he did secretly, and in the face of virulent settler and military opposition. For many contemporaries, as well as for subsequent historians, Rhodes's physical and moral courage in entering negotiations with the Ndebele in the Matopos made this his finest moment.

By mid-October the Ndebele, exhausted by war, rinderpest, and famine, had accepted his terms, which included a recognition of African communal tenure and his personal purchase of considerable land between Bulawayo and the Matopos on which they could be resettled. Now Rhodes had to 'square' his own side, many of whom were furious at the settlement: by the end of 1897 he had spent more than £10,000 in an attempt to pacify the colonists, and had accepted the idea of settler representation in a proposed legislative council. He also had to end the uprising among the intransigent Shona, which spluttered on for another year. Although this never threatened white settlement in the same way, the continued resistance of the Shona held up white settlement in Rhodesia's eastern province until 1898.

Peace with the Ndebele saved the charter, even if amid the uprisings Rhodes had to resign as managing director of the BSAC. At the same time, the chimurenga, as the uprisings were called by Africans, led for the first time to direct British government intervention in BSAC affairs, with the appointment of a British resident commissioner in Bulawayo responsible to the imperial high commissioner in Cape Town, and the establishment of a legislative council in October 1898. 'Native administration' was put on a more systematic footing and stripped of its more immediately coercive aspects. The age of adventurism was over; the era of settler domination was about to begin.

Cape politics, 1896–1898 By 1898 Rhodes had recovered his position to a remarkable extent. Not only had he rejoined the board of the chartered company but, contrary to those

historians who believe he was a spent force after the Jameson raid, he had also regained a surprising degree of political influence at the Cape, although the political context was changed. In 1896 the Loyal Colonial League had been founded in the Cape, to promote British supremacy in South Africa, and spread as the South African League in the Transvaal and Natal under Rhodes's presidency and patronage. The league engaged in an unscrupulous propaganda campaign against the supposed brutality of the Kruger government directed at the Uitlanders in the Transvaal. In this they were aided by the newspapers, which were largely controlled by Rhodes and his fellow mine magnates. Picked up and reproduced in the British press, these reports contributed powerfully to the creation of pro-war public opinion in the metropole. In South Africa the arrival in 1897 of the ardent imperialist Sir Alfred Milner as the British high commissioner magnified their influence.

In addition, Rhodes became the informal leader of a new grouping of Progressives in the Cape parliament, and spearheaded their efforts in the closely fought general election of 1898, by contributing to party funds and morale. It was in this campaign that he also acquired the reputation for being a liberal supporter of the Cape franchise but this erroneous impression arose out of a typical example of Rhodes's opportunism. In 1897, before the campaign began, he had, with an eye on the Uitlanders in the Transvaal, announced that he favoured 'equal rights for all white men'. This brought an outcry from coloured and African voters but Rhodes took over a year to respond to them and only when it appeared that he might lose their support in the forthcoming election did he reformulate his slogan as 'equal rights for all civilized men south of the Zambezi' (*Diamond Fields Advertiser*, 23 July 1898; *Cape Times*, 10 Aug 1898). Moreover the exigencies of the Cape's non-racial franchise led him to fund the African newspaper *Izwi la Bantu*, which provided an alternative voice to the pro-Bond *Imvo Zabantusundu*.

For all Rhodes's efforts, the Bond-supported W. P. Schreiner became premier in 1898, and this left little scope for Rhodes in Cape politics. Over the next year he travelled restlessly, to Oxford to receive his honorary degree, to Europe, where he met the Kaiser, to inspect Southern Rhodesia, and back to the Cape. He also helped to extend the railway from Vryburg to Bulawayo (4 November 1897), began to arrange for its extension as far as Cairo, and, on 21 April 1898, was re-elected director of the BSAC.

Rhodes's final will It was at this time that Rhodes wrote his eighth and final will; he signed it on 1 July 1899. Increasingly suffering from his heart, he sensed mortality and was concerned to leave a 'monument to posterity'. His sixth and seventh wills, in 1892 and 1893, had begun to focus on the need to inculcate the value of empire in young colonials. This was fully formulated in his last will. Rhodes's estate, when finally settled in 1907, left, after family benefactions, £3,340,000 for the Rhodes Trust (whose assets by 1995–6 were valued at £145,638,000). The will provided for fifty-two scholarships each year to Oxford for young men (women were explicitly excluded) from Canada, Australia, South Africa, Rhodesia, New Zealand, Newfoundland, Bermuda, Jamaica, and the United States (which he still hoped would be restored to the British empire), but not for India. In a codicil to the will in 1901 six scholarships were also set aside for Germans, partly because of Rhodes's liking for the Kaiser, and also because of a vague notion of Teutonic race unity. The young men were to be chosen for their scholarly achievements, athletic abilities, and leadership qualities. Oriel College was to receive £100,000, and land in Rhodesia was left to provide for a university there.

Behind the provisions lurked Rhodes's old ambition of creating a 'band of brothers' who would strengthen the ties of empire. He also left money for more explicitly political purposes: the creation of a pro-imperial political party or interest groups within the existing parties. This fund was to be used in the twentieth century to support a variety of imperial causes, including the closer union movement in South Africa, the pro-imperial Round Table, chairs in imperial history in Oxford and London, and the Royal Institute of International Affairs at Chatham House. The first trustees included his close associates Beit, Jameson, and Earl Grey, as well as the Liberal Lord Rosebery and Milner.

The Second South African War, and Rhodes's death The outbreak of the Second South African War in October 1899 found Rhodes in Kimberley, and he remained there for the four months of the siege (14 October 1899 to 15 February 1900), to ensure its rapid lifting and perhaps hoping by his presence to raise morale. During the siege he quarrelled with, threatened, and once tried to punch the military commander, Lieutenant-Colonel Robert Kekewich. On Rhodes's return to Cape Town he was to find, to his annoyance, that Princess Radziwill, who had followed him to the Cape in 1899, was intriguing to have him restored as premier. He spent considerable time over the next two years fending off her unwelcome attentions. Ultimately, the desperate princess attempted to blackmail him with correspondence she claimed to have in her possession, showing Chamberlain's complicity in the Jameson raid. When she forged Rhodes's signature on promissory notes Rhodes instituted criminal proceedings against her. The final proceedings were heard at Groote Schuur during his last illness, and the verdict—which found her guilty and sentenced her to two years' imprisonment—was rendered after his death.

Rhodes's sojourns in Cape Town in the two years before his death were brief. The war meant that he was no longer at the centre of affairs, and his health was deteriorating. During 1900 he travelled to London to defend himself against the attacks of his former associate W. T. Stead over the raid, and undertook a five-month journey through Rhodesia in an effort both to restore his health and systematically to survey the progress of 'his' colony. The summer of 1901 was spent in Britain and Europe before he returned once more to confront the princess. He died on 26 March 1902 in his cottage in Muizenberg, just outside Cape Town, surrounded by some of his closest associates, and a younger brother. At his own request, he was buried amid the grandeur of the Matopos in Southern Rhodesia on 10 April.

Assessment Cecil John Rhodes has always been the subject of intense controversy. Even in his lifetime he was revered by his intimates, who regarded him as a towering colossus, and reviled by those who saw him as an unprincipled and unscrupulous adventurer. In an age of expanding empire and speculative mining capital, Rhodes was able to give effect to a vast ambition to acquire wealth and power, and to justify this ambition in terms of a vision of Anglo-Saxon world domination. For many of his early biographers, though not all of his countrymen, his life expressed the patriotic aspirations of an imperial age. Later biographers and historians who have not shared his imperialism have been more critical of his methods. They have shown how, for most of the peoples of southern Africa, his ventures hastened the pace of colonialism, capitalist development, and political reconstruction and were accompanied by brutal conquest, ruthless exploitation, sharp business practice, and the insidious corruption of public life. Nevertheless, in his lifetime Rhodes's use of power was often tempered by his ability to engage imaginatively with those who were subject to his control and to bestow largesse upon them, whether fellow mining magnates, Cape Afrikaners, or even, on occasion, African notables and their subjects.

The commemoration and historiography of Cecil Rhodes There are numerous portraits, busts, statues, and photographs of Rhodes and he gave much time to sitting for a variety of portrait painters, sculptors, and photographers. Very few of the portraits have aesthetic merit although Rhodes seems to have been better served by sculptors. He was strongly impelled to bestow his likeness upon posterity and, after his death, a considerable number of portraits and statues were displayed in southern Africa and in Oxford and London. Portraits, busts, and statues were commissioned for, or presented to, government buildings, gardens, and squares, as well as to schools, the new South African universities, and gentlemen's clubs. These are to be found in Cape Town, Grahamstown, Kimberley, Johannesburg, and Bulawayo. In 1911, an elaborate memorial, consisting of a columned Doric portico approached by a long flight of steps flanked by Egyptian lions, was raised to him in the grounds of the Groote Schuur on the slopes of Table Mountain. Among the many portraits in Britain, especially striking are those by Edward Roworth in Rhodes House (brilliantly capturing the power of Rhodes's brooding, slightly sleazy character; this is a copy of the original in the University of Cape Town), A. Tennyson-Cole in Oriel College, Oxford, and G. F. Watts in the National Portrait Gallery.

Rhodes was especially commemorated in Rhodes House, Oxford, built by the Rhodes trustees in 1928 to Sir Herbert Baker's plans with sculptures by Charles Wheeler and carvings by Laurence Turner. In this distinctive building—part memorial, part office, part library—imperial, art and craft, and Cape styles are brilliantly juxtaposed.

Rhodes University at Grahamstown was founded in his memory in 1904.

In the years after Rhodes's death a large number of memoirs and biographies of variable quality were published, but it was not until the 1970s, with the publication of John Flint's biography, that a disinterested scholarly work appeared. This was followed by the works of Robert Rotberg and Apollon Davidson (respectively American and Russian historians), and the Israeli political scientist Mordechai Tamarkin. Economic and business histories by Newbury and Turrell have added much to our understanding of Rhodes's financial affairs. His career was portrayed in the 1936 British film *Rhodes of Africa* and, more critically, in a 1997 British television series.

Shula Marks and Stanley Trapido

Sources R. I. Rotberg and M. F. Shore, *The founder: Cecil Rhodes and the pursuit of power* (1988) · J. Flint, *Cecil Rhodes* (1976) · M. Tamarkin, *Cecil Rhodes and the Cape Afrikaners: the imperial colossus and the colonial parish pump* (1996) · R. V. Turrell, *Capital and labour on the Kimberley diamond fields, 1871–1890* (1987) · C. Newbury, *The diamond ring: business, politics and precious stones in South Africa, 1867–1947* (1989) · R. Turrell, 'Sir Frederic Philipson Stow: the unknown diamond magnate', *Business History*, 28/1 (1986), 62–73 · R. Phimister, 'Rhodes, Rhodesia and the Rand', *Journal of South African Studies*, 5/1 (1974) · R. Turrell, 'Rhodes, De Beers and monopoly', *Journal of Imperial and Commonwealth History*, 10 (1981–2), 309–43 · C. Newbury, 'Cecil Rhodes and the South African connection: "A great imperial university"?', in F. Madden and D. K. Fieldhouse, *Oxford and the idea of commonwealth: essays presented to Sir Edgar Williams* (1982), 75–96 · G. Blainey, 'Lost causes of the Jameson raid', *Economic History Review*, 2nd ser., 18 (1965), 350–66 · R. Mendelsohn, 'Blainey and the Jameson raid: the debate renewed', *Journal of Southern African Studies*, 6 (1980), 157–70 · C. Newbury, 'Out of the pit: the capital accumulation of Cecil Rhodes', *Journal of Imperial and Commonwealth History*, 10 (1981–2), 25–49 · A. Brookner, 'The iconography of Cecil Rhodes', 1953 · L. Michell, *The life of the Rt. Hon. Cecil John Rhodes, 1853–1902*, 2 vols. (1910) · B. Williams, *Cecil Rhodes* (1938) · Vindex, *Cecil Rhodes, his political life and speeches, 1881–1900* (1900) · H. Baker and W. T. Stead, *Cecil Rhodes: the man and his dream* (Bulawayo, 1977) · H. Baker, *Cecil Rhodes, by his architect* (1934) · T. E. Fuller, *The right honourable Cecil John Rhodes: a monograph and a reminiscence* (1910) · P. Jourdan, *Cecil Rhodes: his private life, by his private secretary* (1911) · T. O. Ranger, *Revolt in Southern Rhodesia, 1896–7: a study in African resistance* (1967) · J. S. Galbraith, *Crown and charter: the early years of the British South Africa Company* (1974) · A. Davidson, *Cecil Rhodes and his time*, trans. C. English (Moscow, 1984) · J. G. Lockhart and C. M. Woodhouse, *Rhodes* (1963) · J. van der Poel, *The Jameson raid* (Cape Town, 1951) · W. H. Worger, *South Africa's city of diamonds: mineworkers and monopoly capitalism in Kimberley, 1867–1895* (1987) · B. Roberts, *Kimberley: turbulent city* (Cape Town, 1976) · G. le Sueur, *Cecil Rhodes: the man and his work* (1913) · P. Lewsen, *John X. Merriman: paradoxical South African statesmen* (1982) · P. Lewsen, *Selections from the correspondence of John X. Merriman, 1870–1924*, 4 vols. (Cape Town, 1960–69) · T. R. H. Davenport, *The Afrikaner Bond* (Cape Town, 1966) · J. W. Matthews, *Incwadi Yami, or, Twenty years personal experience in South Africa* (New York, 1887) [repr. 1969] · S. G. Millin, *Rhodes* (1933) · B. Roberts, *Cecil Rhodes and the princess* (1969) · R. Robinson, J. Gallagher, and A. Denny, *Africa and the Victorians: the official mind to imperialism* (1965) · J. E. S. Green, *Rhodes goes north* (1936) · J. Marlowe, *Cecil Rhodes: the anatomy of empire* (New York, 1972) · J. Butler, *The liberal party and the Jameson raid* (1968) · *The Rhodes Trust and Rhodes House* (1996)

Archives Bodl. RH, British South Africa Co. papers · Bodl. RH, corresp. and papers · Bodl. RH, family corresp. · Bodl. RH, notebooks and family corresp. · Cape Archives · National Archives of Zimbabwe, Harare, corresp. and papers | Bodl. Oxf., corresp. with Sir William Harcourt · Bodl. Oxf., corresp. with Lord Milner · Bodl. RH, corresp. with Sir Graham Bower; corresp. with Charles Rudd; corresp. with W. T. Stead, and letters to Edward Ross Townsend [copies] · Brenthurst Library, Johannesburg, letters to Charles Rudd · NA Scot., Primrose papers · NRA, priv. coll., corresp. with Lord Rosebery · Rhodes University, Grahamstown, South Africa, Cory Library for Historical Research, letters to Sir John Sprigg · U. Birm., corresp. with Joseph Chamberlain · University of Cape Town, corresp. with W. P. Schreiner

Likenesses H. von Herkomer, oils, exh. RA 1895, Kimberley Club, South Africa · M. H. Carlisle, miniature, 1896, Oriel College, Oxford · H. von Herkomer, oils, 1896, Bodl. RH · R. Baden-Powell, pencil caricature, 1897, U. Durham · Messrs Downey, photograph, 1898 · V. Rutland, lithograph, 1898, NPG · G. F. Watts, oils, 1898, NPG · lithograph, 1898, NPG · S. March, bronze bust, 1901, Africana Museum, Johannesburg · S. March, bronze bust, 1901, Bodl. RH, NPG · F. D. Wood, bronze bust, 1902, Africana Museum, Johannesburg · H. A. Pegram, marble bust, 1903, Bodl. RH · H. A. Pegram, bust, 1904, Grahamstown, South Africa · W. H. Thornycroft, plaster model of statue, 1904, Tate collection · J. Tweed, statue, 1904, Bulawayo, Zimbabwe · G. F. Watts, equestrian statue, 1904, Burlington House, London · W. H. Thornycroft, equestrian statue, 1907, Kimberley, South Africa · H. A. Pegram, statue, 1910, Botanical Gardens, Cape Town, South Africa · J. Tweed, statue, 1928, Salisbury, Zimbabwe · J. Gunn, oils, 1949, Bodl. RH · Bassano, photograph, NPG [*see illus.*] · O. Birley, oils, Hertford County Hall · M. H. Carlisle, miniature, Bodl. RH · P. T. Cole, oils, Oriel College, Oxford · P. T. Cole, oils, Constitutional Club, London · P. T. Cole, oils, Government House, Lusaka · Felix, oils, Rhodes Trust Office, Oxford · H. Furniss, pen-and-ink caricature, NPG · F. C. Gould, pen sketches, NPG · S. Kendrick, oils, Bodl. RH · S. March, bronze bust, Oriel College, Oxford · M. Menpes, drawings, Bodl. RH, Royal Collection · M. Menpes, drawings, Oriel College, Oxford · M. Menpes, drawings, University of the Witwatersrand, Johannesburg · M. Menpes, drawings, Central African Archives · M. Menpes, etching, BM · L. Orpen, portrait, Kimberley, South Africa · E. Roworth, oils, University of Cape Town; copy, Bodl. RH · Russell & Sons, photograph, NPG · Spy [L. Ward], chromolithograph caricature, NPG; repro. in *VF* (28 March 1891) · Stuff [Wright], chromolithograph caricature (*Empire makers and breakers*), NPG; repro. in *VF* (25 Nov 1897) · J. Tweed, bust, Parliament Buildings, Cape Town · J. Tweed, bust, Bodl. RH · J. Tweed, plaster cast of death mask, NPG · political cartoons, Africana Museum, Johannesburg · political cartoons, Bodl. RH · political cartoons, University of Cape Town

Wealth at death under £5,000,000: R. I. Rotberg and M. F. Shore, *The founder: Cecil Rhodes and the pursuit of power* (1988)

Rhodes, Ebenezer (1762–1839), topographer, was born in Yorkshire, probably at Sheffield. He entered the cutlery trade, and was elected master cutler in 1808. He was in business as a partner in the firm Messrs Rhodes, Brammall, and Jackson, file cutters. Halkett and Laing attribute, in the *Dictionary of Anonymous and Pseudonymous English Literature*, to Rhodes *Alfred* (1789), a tragedy about King Alfred, to which was added some poems, but Rhodes is chiefly remembered as a topographer. He made many excursions with James Montgomery, whom he had first met by chance on an antiquarian tour of Derbyshire. In 1818 Rhodes published the first part of his *Peak Scenery*, illustrated with copper-plate engravings after pencil drawings by Sir Francis Chantrey. Chantrey's illustrations were later republished separately. *Peak Scenery* was completed in four parts by 1824. It was followed by *Yorkshire Scenery* (1826), of which only part 1 was published, and *Derbyshire Tourist's Guide and Travelling Companion* (1837). All his books involved him in financial loss. Apart from these ventures, he turned his attention to journalism, and for a few years was editor of the *Sheffield Independent*. He also published an essay on the manufacture of razors (1824). Meanwhile his cutlery business failed, and before his death he became a bankrupt. A fund was raised for his support, to which Montgomery subscribed £100, while Chantrey privately gave Rhodes £50 a year, acknowledging that Rhodes had been one of his earliest patrons when he himself was struggling for recognition. Rhodes thenceforth made a small income by preparing steel plates for engravers by a novel process. He died of apoplexy in embarrassed circumstances on 16 December 1839 in Victoria Street, Sheffield, leaving his family unprovided for.

CHARLOTTE FELL-SMITH, *rev.* ELIZABETH BAIGENT

Sources J. Hunter, *Hallamshire: the history and topography of the parish of Sheffield in the county of York* (1819) • R. E. Leader, ed., *Reminiscences of old Sheffield*, 2nd edn (1876) • *Memoirs of the life and writings of James Montgomery*, ed. J. Holland and J. Everett, 7 vols. (1854–6) • S. Halkett and J. Laing, *A dictionary of anonymous and pseudonymous publications in the English language*, ed. J. Horden, 3rd edn (1980–) • *Sheffield Iris* (17 Dec 1839) • private information (1896) • J. Holland, *Memorials of Sir Francis Chantrey* [1851] • d. cert.
Likenesses N. Poole, oils, 1830, Cutlers' Hall, Sheffield • F. Chantrey, oils, Graves Art Gallery, Sheffield

Rhodes [*née* Brittan], **Elizabeth** (1759–1836), housekeeper and Methodist leader, was born in Scotland, the daughter of Captain Brittan of the Queen's regiment of dragoons. In 1760 her father resigned his commission and moved to York, his wife's home town, but in 1765 he eloped with her maid. Elizabeth was educated and brought up as a devout Anglican by her mother, who joined the Methodists about 1769. About 1772 Elizabeth went to live with her uncle, who was in the Manchester cotton trade, but hostility from her aunt soon drove her back to York. By 1775 she was in London in search of her father, whom she found in Surrey, living with a married woman. Elizabeth settled and worked as a cook in an indulgent household. She regularly attended church but was also attracted by worldly pleasures and tempted by a career on the stage. She nevertheless rejected the advances of noble would-be seducers, including an offer from an unnamed duke. In the later 1770s she became governess to the daughter of Sir James Pennyman, MP for Beverley, Yorkshire, and witnessed the 1780 Gordon riots from his London residence before returning to York to care for her sick mother. While acting as housekeeper to an unidentified earl of A— in Scotland, she found that he planned to make her his mistress. After a short spell with a family in Wakefield, she became housekeeper to Sir William C— in Bury, Lancashire, apparently the Revd Sir William Clerke, an eccentric rector of Bury from 1778 to 1818, who died as a debtor in the Fleet prison.

Elizabeth appears to have been influenced by Methodists in Beverley and York who helped her towards a conversion experience at some date before 1784. Methodism had probably begun in Bury in the mid-1760s but had encountered persecution for many years. A preaching house was built in an outlying part of the town in 1773 as most land in the area was owned by the lord of the manor or the rector. In 1785, however, Sir William Clerke sold the land for a new central preaching house, dismissing the protests of his fellow gentry with the remark 'It makes no difference to me … if they cover the whole ground with chapels' (*Memoirs*, 61). Sir William was apparently prepared to marry Elizabeth but disliked her Methodist loyalty. She decided in favour of her Methodist allegiance and on 4 January 1787 at Bolton, Lancashire, she married Benjamin Rhodes (1743–1815), a Methodist itinerant preacher and hymn writer. They had three daughters who survived childhood.

Benjamin Rhodes's subsequent ministerial appointments included Bristol, where he was involved in 1787 in the exorcism of the demoniac George Lukyns and the founding of the Stranger's Friend Society for relieving the poor. During their stay in Cornwall in 1788–92 Elizabeth became a class leader and on 7 January 1788 she claimed the experience of 'Christian perfection'. Benjamin finally retired to Margate, Kent, in 1810, where Elizabeth and her three daughters kept a school for young ladies. Here on 1 March 1812 her youngest daughter, Hannah, died painfully as the result of her dress catching fire. Her last days were commemorated in published accounts by her father and brother-in-law. Benjamin died on 12 October 1815. After a serious illness in 1827, Elizabeth moved to Maidstone, Kent. In 1829 she published her *Memoirs*, which included her son-in-law's account of Hannah's sufferings and death. In many respects she gives a typical account of early Methodist experience: a pious upbringing, a period of 'worldliness', the struggle for conversion, and subsequent religious activities. The intention of such narratives was to encourage readers to seek conversion. But in this case the story also illustrates the moral pressures on well-brought-up young women in relatively genteel domestic service. Her story at times reads like that of a *Pamela*, whose virtue is finally rewarded in Methodist rather than worldly terms; and probably this was the underlying message. Elizabeth Rhodes died in Maidstone on 17 April 1836.

HENRY D. RACK

Sources *Memoirs of Mrs Elizabeth Rhodes written by herself* (1829) • B. Rhodes, *Brief account of the sufferings etc. of Miss Hannah Rhodes* (1812) • *Wesleyan Methodist Magazine*, 59 (1836), 399 • B. Rhodes, 'Life of Mr Benjamin Rhodes', *The lives of the early Methodist preachers, chiefly written by themselves*, ed. T. Jackson, 6 (1878), 223–33 • parish register, Bolton, St Peter, 4 Jan 1787 [marriage] • M. Gray, *History of Bury, Lancs. from 1660 to 1876* (1970), 68–107 • J. Williams, *History of Methodism at Pits o' th' Moor, Bury 1774–1924* [n.d.] • J. Brooke, 'Beverley', HoP, *Commons, 1754–90*, 1.432–3 • J. Brooke, 'Pennyman, Sir James', HoP, *Commons, 1754–90*, 3.264–5 • 'Rhodes, Benjamin', *Dictionary of evangelical biography*, vol. 2, pp. 928–9

Rhodes, Francis William (1851–1905), army officer, was the second son of Francis William Rhodes (1806–1878), a Church of England clergyman, and his second wife, Louisa, *née* Peacock (d. 1873); Cecil John *Rhodes was his younger brother. He was born on 9 April 1851 at Thorleybourne, Bishop's Stortford. After attending Goodman's High School in Bishop's Stortford, in 1865 he entered Eton College, where he was in the army class and in the cricket elevens of 1869 and 1870. After passing through Sandhurst he was gazetted lieutenant of the 1st (Royal) Dragoons in April 1873. He saw service in the Sudan as a member of the

Francis William Rhodes (1851–1905), by Elliott & Fry, pubd 1898

staff in 1884, and was present at the battles of al-Teb and Tamai. He was mentioned in dispatches, received the medal with clasp and bronze star, and was promoted captain in October 1884. He accompanied the Nile expedition in 1884–5 for the relief of Khartoum as aide-de-camp to General Herbert Stewart, and distinguished himself at the battles of Abu Klea and al-Gubba, where his horse was shot under him. He was mentioned in dispatches and received two clasps and the brevet of major and lieutenant-colonel (September 1885). Stewart described him as the best aide-de-camp a general could have.

Rhodes next served in the Sudan expedition of 1888, and was present at the action of Gamaiza (Jummaiza) (20 December); he was again mentioned in dispatches, and received the clasp and the order of the Mejidiye (3rd class). He was made colonel in September 1889. From 1890 to 1893 he was military secretary to his old schoolfellow Lord Harris, governor of Bombay; he received the DSO in 1891, and in 1893, as a result of his brother Cecil's importunity, was chief of staff to Sir Gerald Herbert Portal's mission to Uganda. There he nearly succumbed to blackwater fever.

After his recovery Rhodes went out in 1894 to the recently conquered Matabeleland in Southern Rhodesia which had come under the control of Cecil's British South Africa Company over the previous five years. There he joined Dr L. S. Jameson's military council of four which was responsible for expropriating Ndebele (Matabele) land and cattle on a vast scale, a major factor in the Ndebele uprising of 1896. In the following year he went to Johannesburg, ostensibly as representative of the Consolidated Goldfields, of which his brother was a director but in fact to mobilize the Uitlanders against the South African Republic. In September 1895 he was at Ramoutsa negotiating on behalf of his brother for the cession of Tswana territory close to the Transvaal border, which soon came under the jurisdiction of the British South Africa Company and was used as the jumping-off point for Jameson's ill-fated raid against the republic at the end of 1895. As a leading member of the Johannesburg reform movement agitating for Uitlander rights he was one of the five

signatories of the undated letter (November 1895) to Jameson which ostensibly led to the invasion of the Transvaal. On the failure of the raid he was arrested by the republican government, tried for high treason, and sentenced to death (April 1896). The sentence was soon commuted to fifteen years' imprisonment. After being in prison in Pretoria until June, Rhodes and his companions were released, on payment by Cecil of a fine of £25,000 each and on their promising to abstain from politics for fifteen years. Of all the ringleaders, Rhodes was the only one to refuse to accept this condition, and he was banished from the Transvaal. For his encouragement of the raid, Rhodes was placed on the army retired list. Early in July he joined Cecil in putting down the Ndebele uprising in Southern Rhodesia.

In 1898 Rhodes went, as war correspondent for *The Times*, with General Kitchener's Nile expedition; he was wounded at the battle of Omdurman. For his services in that campaign his name was restored to the active list (September 1898).

When war broke out in South Africa in 1899 Rhodes went back and served in the early battles in Natal. He was besieged in Ladysmith. In the fight on Wagon Hill (5–6 January 1900) he showed great courage, and took Lord Ava, who was mortally wounded, out of fire into cover (Amery, 3.194). In the next May he served as an intelligence officer with the flying column under Brigadier-General Bryan Thomas Mahon which hurried to the relief of Mafeking (4–17 May 1900) (ibid., 4.222). For his services in the war he was created a military CB. In January 1903 he was Lord Kitchener's guest at the durbar at Delhi. In the same year he retired from the army, and was, until his death, managing director of the African Transcontinental Telegraph Company.

Rhodes assisted Winston Churchill in preparing his *River War on the Sudan* (1899; new edn by Rhodes, 1902). Churchill found him 'very kind and amiable' (Churchill, 407) and 'a brave and gallant man' (ibid., 415). Rhodes also contributed an introduction and photographs to *From the Cape to the Zambesi* (1905) by G. T. Hutchinson, whom he accompanied in that year to the Zambezi. The strain of this journey is said to have brought on the illness of which he died, unmarried, at his brother's residence, Groote Schuur, Rondebosch, near Cape Town, on 21 September 1905. His body was brought to England to be buried at Dalham, near Newmarket, Suffolk. A memorial tablet was placed by his friends in Eton College chapel in October 1906, and prizes for geography were founded at Eton in his memory. Said to have been a man of charm and a gallant soldier by his contemporaries, he was overshadowed in his lifetime and in the annals of history by his more famous younger brother.   W. B. OWEN, *rev.* SHULA MARKS

Sources G. T. Hutchinson, *Frank Rhodes: a memoir* (1908) · R. I. Rotberg, *The founder: Cecil Rhodes and the pursuit of power* (1988) · L. Michell, *The life of the Rt. Hon. Cecil John Rhodes, 1853–1902*, 2 vols. (1910) · L. S. Amery, ed., *The Times history of the war in South Africa*, 7 vols. (1900–09) · A. Thomas, *Rhodes, the race for Africa* (1996) · R. S. Churchill, *Winston S. Churchill*, 1: *Youth, 1874–1900* (1966) · *CGPLA Eng. & Wales* (1906)

Archives Bodl. RH, corresp. relating to British South Africa Company • NAM, diaries

Likenesses group photograph, 1873 (with family), repro. in Rotberg, *The founder* • Elliott & Fry, photograph, pubd 1898, NPG [*see illus.*] • Spy [L. Ward], chromolithograph, NPG; repro. in *VF* (8 June 1899) • group photograph, repro. in Rotberg, *The founder*, facing p. 266 • photograph, repro. in Amery, ed., *Times history*, vol. 1

Wealth at death £116,993 13s. 4d.: probate, 2 Jan 1906, *CGPLA Eng. & Wales*

Rhodes, Hugh (*fl.* 1545?), writer on education, was the author of *The Boke of Nurture for Men, Servantes and Chyldren, with 'Stans puer ad mensam'*, a courtesy book published in six editions from, probably, 1545 to 1577. Though a member 'of the Kinges Chappell', he remains a shadowy figure. In an apology for his lack of eloquence, Rhodes remarks that he was 'born and bred' in Devon (Rhodes, 71). According to the younger Thomas Warton, Rhodes was also the author of a verse panegyric to Queen Mary:

> the Song of the chyld-byshop, as it was songe before the Queenis Majestie in her privie chamber at her manour of Saynt James in the Feildis on Saynt Nicholas Day and Innocents Day this year nowe present [1555], by the Chyld-byshope of Paules Churche with his Company. (Warton, 4.237)

This has not survived, however.

Rhodes's book is a collection of traditional courtesy material. It begins with the duties of parents and masters in teaching and governing children in learning and good manners: 'for if they learne pure and cleane doctryne in youth, they poure out plentye of good workes in age' (Rhodes, 64–5). Vices and bad language should be reproved: they should read the Bible and other godly books, and not 'fayned fables, vayne fantasyes, and wanton stories, and songs of love' (ibid., 64). There follow prose sections on 'the manner of serving a knight, squire, or gentleman', and on 'how to order your maysters chamber at night to bed-warde'. Then come two pieces in verse—'The Booke of Nurture and Schoole of Good Manners for Man and for Chylde' (384 lines), and 'For the Wayting Servaunt' (796 lines). The final section is 'The rule of honest living', a compilation of proverbial advice in prose and verse. Like other manuals of this kind the aim is to instruct rather than to delight. Modern readers find pleasure in some of the practical instructions—'pronounce thy speeche distinctly'; 'suppe not lowde of thy pottage'; 'blow not your nose on the napkin' (ibid., 75, 76, 78)—rather than in the more high-minded advice.

DOUGLAS GRAY

Sources [H. Rhodes], *The babees book*, ed. F. J. Furnivall, EETS, 32 (1868), 63–114 • *STC, 1475–1640*, nos. 20953–20958 • T. Warton, *The history of English poetry*, new edn, ed. W. C. Hazlitt, 4 vols. (1871)

Rhodes, John Milson (1847–1909), general practitioner and poor-law reformer, was born on 14 September 1847 in Broughton, Salford, Lancashire, the youngest of the three sons of Milson Rhodes (1818–1884), fustian salesman, and his wife, Ann Keith (1818–1885), daughter of Thomas Wemyss, of York, teacher and biblical scholar. Rhodes's parents were both born in Yorkshire. Among his first cousins was Sir Thomas Wemyss Reid, littérateur and editor of the *Leeds Mercury*. Rhodes matriculated at Glasgow University about 1865; his family lived in Glasgow from about 1863 to 1868. After deciding to follow his brothers into the medical profession, Rhodes attended Owens College, Manchester, and the Manchester school of medicine, where he was a major prizewinner. In 1874 he obtained the LRCM and LRCS in Edinburgh; in 1879 he graduated MD in Brussels.

From 1874 until his death Rhodes was a general practitioner in Didsbury, near Manchester. Familiar in the village as a tall, neat, kindly, and scholarly bachelor, he was a member of Didsbury Liberal Club and a sidesman at Emmanuel (Anglican) Church. In addition to running his busy practice, Rhodes was a factory surgeon and a medical referee for an insurance company. A prolific writer, he contributed articles to the medical press on topics as diverse as infant mortality, the alleged increase in insanity, and hospital floors. His article 'The poor law and the medical profession' appeared posthumously in the *British Medical Journal* in 1910.

It was as a poor-law expert and reformer that Rhodes was best-known. In 1880 he was appointed overseer of the poor for Didsbury in Chorlton (south Manchester) union, and in 1882 he was elected to the Chorlton board of guardians. In 1891 he became the first chairman of the Northern Workhouse Nursing Association and in the early 1900s he chaired the central poor-law conference of England and Wales and the Association of Poor Law Unions. He was vice-president of the Société Internationale d'Assistance Publique and held office on international infant-welfare committees.

Rhodes gave evidence before the royal commissions on the care and control of the feeble-minded (1904–8) and on the poor laws (1905–9). He was much in demand as a lecturer to statistical and scientific societies, and a noteworthy lecture to the British Association, entitled 'Pauperism past and present', in 1890, was discussed in a leader in *The Times*; it was also translated into French and widely circulated in pamphlet form. Between 1886 and 1906 Rhodes presented some thirty papers at central and district poor-law conferences, covering such topics as provision for epileptic and weak-minded paupers, the care of infants and children, and the design, nursing, and dietary practices of workhouses. A recurring theme was the iniquities of the 'general mixed workhouse' and the need for separate provision for different groups, the cost of special schemes being mitigated by neighbouring unions working together. Rhodes backed a plan to move 300 workhouse children to the country. In 1898, as chairman of Chorlton union's schools and cottage homes committee, he officially opened Styal Cottage Homes in Cheshire.

Rhodes's chairmanship of the Chorlton board from 1894 to 1898 coincided with a time of great hardship and overcrowding at the union workhouse, and in 1898 he organized a combination with the neighbouring Manchester union to establish joint casual wards in the city centre. He visited rural colonies for epileptics in Germany (1897) and in the USA (1901) and his favourable reports encouraged the authorities in Chorlton and Manchester to build a joint epileptic colony at Langho near Blackburn, which was opened in 1906. Rhodes also helped establish epileptic colonies in Cheshire and Birmingham.

For nearly thirty years a member and chairman of the board of guardians of the huge Chorlton union, south of Manchester, Rhodes spearheaded many reforms which were held up for praise by the Local Government Board and emulated in other unions. In his efforts to control able-bodied paupers while protecting the aged and the feeble 'deserving' poor at as little cost to the ratepayers as possible, Rhodes was no different from the majority of guardians, but his rational investigations into the causes of pauperism and his ability to communicate his findings to others placed him in a class apart. As he observed towards the end of his career:

> If I have done good work for the poor it has been by bringing science to bear upon it, and by trying to show a good many of the causes lying at the root of the evils under the existing system. (*Manchester Evening Chronicle*)

Rhodes's research led him to his major conclusion: that outdoor relief was a perpetuator of pauperism and a waste of the poor rate. He advocated instead the provision by boards of guardians—in combination if necessary—of separate institutions for vagrants, children, the elderly, sane epileptics, and the mentally defective. Such institutions would be kinder to the young, the old, and the sick; would deter wastrels; would ensure that those able to work earned part of their keep; and would help prevent that anathema to eugenicists, 'the multiplication of the unfit'. In response to criticism of such expenditure, Rhodes insisted that *laissez-faire* would no longer do and that this use of public money would, in the long run, result in public benefit.

In 1892 Rhodes became a Liberal councillor (and later alderman) for Lancashire and did sterling work on the Lancashire Asylums Board, particularly in making provision for incurable cases. In 1906 he was appointed a JP and visiting justice to HM prison, Strangeways. Rhodes died at his home, Ivy Lodge, 104 Wilmslow Road, Didsbury, near Manchester, on 25 September 1909, after accidentally taking an overdose of strychnine. A funeral service was held on 29 September at Emmanuel Church and his body was later cremated at Manchester crematorium.

JEAN BARCLAY

Sources R. A. Leach, 'The late John Milson Rhodes, MD, JP', *Poor law conferences held in the year 1909–10*, ix–xxxi · *Poor Law Officers' Journal* (1 Oct 1909) · *BMJ* (9 Oct 1909) · *Manchester Evening News* (27 Sept 1909) · *Manchester Evening News* (30 Sept 1909) · 'Men of mark, no. 50: Dr. J. Milson Rhodes', *Manchester Evening Chronicle* (30 Sept 1907) · J. Stanhope-Brown, *A styal of its own, 1894–1964* (1989) · b. cert. · d. cert.
Likenesses R. Barber, portrait, 1910, Didsbury Liberal Club · W. Brookes, photograph, repro. in *Manchester City News* (2 Oct 1909) · A. Coupe, photograph, repro. in *BMJ* · Matt, caricature, repro. in 'Men of mark, no. 50: Dr J. Milson Rhodes', *Manchester Evening Chronicle* · C. B. Owen, photograph, repro. in *Poor Law Officers' Journal* · effigy on stone clock tower, Didsbury
Wealth at death £657 5s. 9d.: administration, 16 Dec 1909, CGPLA Eng. & Wales

Rhodes, John Nicholas (1809–1842), artist, was probably born in London, the only son of three children of **Joseph Rhodes** (1778–1855), artist and drawing master. His father, baptized in Leeds on 23 September 1778, was largely self-taught; he served an apprenticeship as a house-painter in Leeds, before moving to London to work as a japanner in the furniture trade. He was subsequently employed by M. San Jusse on decorative schemes for houses and as a copyist for a picture dealer. In his spare time he learned the rudiments of anatomy and life drawing at the Royal Academy night schools. He returned to his native city, Leeds, where he exhibited for the first time at the Northern Society for the Encouragement of the Fine Arts in 1811. In Leeds he ran a successful drawing academy from the 1820s; his pupils included his son John Nicholas Rhodes; William Gott, a Leeds merchant; and John Sheepshanks, the merchant and collector of British art. Thomas Hartley Cromek, a watercolour artist specializing in colourful continental views and a contemporary of John Nicholas Rhodes, was also a pupil from 1826, and commented in his autobiographical manuscript that Joseph Rhodes was 'a self-educated man, and had a most elegant mind and a very refined taste for landscape scenery' (Cromek). His reputation as a teacher led to the accolade 'Father of Art in Yorkshire' from the *Huddersfield Chronicle*. He died on 7 April 1855.

John Rhodes was educated at the school of Jonathan Lockwood, whose son Charles bequeathed studies by both father and son to the Leeds City Art Gallery in 1891. Rhodes worked with some success in Leeds and Skipton, exhibiting at the Northern Society in 1822, 1826, and 1830, and assisting his father at their drawing academy. His health started to deteriorate, largely owing to drink, and T. H. Cromek noted in 1833, when he renewed his contact with Rhodes, that he was 'more unsteady than ever' (Cromek). Rhodes moved to London to further his career in the 1830s, and exhibited at the Royal Academy, the British Institution (*Sit up, Sirrah* and *Which is the Tallest?*), and the Suffolk Street Gallery between 1839 and 1842. On his first appearance at the Royal Academy, in 1841, his painting, *The Young Bird*, attracted the attention of a critic who wrote that the northern artist was 'a new name, we believe, and one that we imagine to give good promise' (*Art Union*). His work was purchased and sold by Ackermanns in the Strand and he enjoyed the patronage of a number of Yorkshire collectors. Rhodes specialized in animal and genre subjects and was proficient at rapid sepia sketches, which he produced in abundance. Ill health forced him to return to Leeds, however, where he continued to work despite failing eyesight until his death after an apoplectic fit at his father's home, 1 St Alban's Street, Leeds, on 3 December 1842. Thorp states that Rhodes married in London, but of his wife nothing is known. His work is represented at Leeds City Art Gallery and at Wakefield Art Gallery.

CORINNE MILLER

Sources W. Thorp, *John Nicholas Rhodes: a Yorkshire painter* (1904) · *GM*, 2nd ser., 19 (1843), 541–2 · *Art Union*, 5/50 (1843), 59 · 'The Royal Academy: the exhibition—1841, the seventy-third', *Art Union*, 3/29 (June 1841), 102 · T. H. Cromek, 'Reminiscences at home and abroad, 1812–1855: the story of our lives from year to year', priv. coll. [microfiche in Leeds City Art Gallery] · Graves, *RA exhibitors*, vol. 6 · Graves, *Brit. Inst.* · Graves, *Artists*, new edn · T. Fawcett, *The*

rise of English provincial art: artists, patrons, and institutions outside London, 1800–1830 (1973) • W. Smith, ed., *Old Yorkshire* (1890) • R. V. Taylor, *The biographia Leodensis, or, Biographical sketches of the worthies of Leeds and neighbourhood* (1865) • Redgrave, *Artists*, 2nd edn • Mallalieu, *Watercolour artists* • directories, Leeds, 1816–51 [Joseph Rhodes] • census returns for Leeds, 1841, 1851 [Joseph Rhodes] • d. cert. • d. cert. [Joseph Rhodes]
Likenesses J. Rhodes, portrait (posthumous)

Rhodes, Joseph (1778–1855). *See under* Rhodes, John Nicholas (1809–1842).

Rhodes, Richard (*bap.* 1640, *d.* 1668), playwright, was baptized on 27 December 1640 at St James's, Clerkenwell, Middlesex, the son of Benjamin and Ann Rhodes. He was educated at Westminster School, and from there he was elected to a studentship at Christ Church, Oxford, where he matriculated on 31 July 1658. When he went to the university he was already 'well grounded in grammar and in the practical part of music' (Wood, *Ath. Oxon.*, 3.819). He graduated BA on 22 March 1662. Rhodes is mentioned by Wood as one of the sixteen persons who, like himself, frequented the weekly meetings at the house of Mr Ellis for the cultivation of the 'delightful facultie of musick'; he is also described as 'a junior student of Christ Church, a confident Westmonasterian, a violinist to hold between his knees' (Wood, *Ath. Oxon.*, 1.xxxv).

On 8 January 1664 Rhodes returned to Christ Church for the first performance of his play *Flora's Vagaries*, which was staged by the students. It was entered in the Stationers' register in February 1664 but was not published, presumably because it had been taken up by the King's Company, who performed it at the Theatre Royal, probably as early as March that year. The play, a comedy based on a story from Boccaccio's *Decameron*, must have been relatively successful for the company as it appeared in their repertoire for another two seasons at least. Samuel Pepys went to a performance on 8 August 1664 and wrote that it was 'as pretty a pleasant play as ever I saw in my life' (Pepys). His favourable impression was secured by the character of 'the young jade Flora', who was possibly played by Nell Gwyn in her first major role with the company; she certainly took the part in later performances and appears in the cast list published in the first edition in 1670. Pepys's good opinion of the play did not last, however, and when he saw it again, on 18 February 1668, without his wife and in a bad mood, he thought it 'a very silly play'.

Rhodes, in the company of almost every known writer of the period, appears in *The Session of the Poets*, an anonymous satire of the mid-1660s. He is shown begging for another plot from Apollo, who:

On condition the varlet would never write more,
Gave him threepence to pay for a pipe and a pot.
(Lord, 1.336)

Wood notes that Rhodes took a degree in physic at Montpellier University. Subsequently he travelled in Spain; he died at Madrid in 1668.   ELERI LARKUM

Sources DNB • Wood, *Ath. Oxon.*, new edn, vols. 1, 3 • Foster, *Alum. Oxon.* • *Old Westminsters*, vol. 2 • W. Van Lennep and others, eds., *The London stage, 1660–1800*, pt 1: *1660–1700* (1965) • G. de F. Lord and others, eds., *Poems on affairs of state: Augustan satirical verse, 1660–*

1714, 7 vols. (1963–75), vol. 1 • *IGI* • Pepys, *Diary*, vols. 5, 8 • D. Bond, 'The date of Richard Rhodes' *Flora's vagaries*', *Philological Quarterly*, 65 (1986), 381–6

Rhodes, Richard (1765–1838), engraver, produced mainly small line engravings for book illustrations, closely imitating the popular style of James Heath; this style was continued by Charles Heath, to whom Rhodes was principal assistant for many years. Rhodes engraved plates for John Cooke's *Pocket Edition of Sacred Classics* (1793–6) and *Pocket Edition of English Poets* (1796), for James Woodmason after works commissioned for his Shakespeare Gallery of 1793–4 (after Fuseli, and three others, after Francis Wheatley, Matthew William Peters, and James Northcote, published by John Murray in 1817), and for Cowper's *Poems* (1806). He also produced engravings, after Henry Howard, for *Timon of Athens* in John Boydell's *Shakespeare* (1802) and, after Samuel Woodforde, for *The British Theatre … a Collection of Plays … Acted at the Theatre Royal* (1808), as well as some plates in Taylor Combe's *Ancient Terra-Cottas in the British Museum* (1810). John Thurston's 'most attractive and complete set' (Cannon-Brookes, 40) of illustrations of Shakespeare was engraved by Rhodes and published by Thomas Tegg, in 1812–15.

Rhodes engraved some of Thomas Stothard's designs for Lord Byron's *Poems* (1814); eleven plates for William Somerville's *Poems* (1815); several plates after Richard Westall and others for John Sharpe's editions of English poets (1816–17); and a portrait of Henry Mackenzie, author of *The Man of Feeling*, after Andrew Geddes (1822). Many of the portraits which he engraved were for book illustrations and included those of Thomas Arne (1794) and Colley Cibber (1795), after Robert Dunkarton and Jean-Baptiste Van Loo respectively, both in line, for the *Biographical Magazine*, and of John Southey Somerville, the frontispiece to *Memorie of the Somervilles* (1815), edited by Walter Scott. A number of proofs of Rhodes's engravings are in the print room at the British Museum. He was a governor of the Society of Engravers but resigned his membership in 1806. He was living at 91 Norton Street, London, in 1803 and by 1806 had moved to Titchfield Street. He died at Camden Town on 1 November 1838.

CAMPBELL DODGSON, *rev.* VIVIENNE W. PAINTING

Sources Redgrave, *Artists* • Free Library of Philadelphia, Philadelphia, Pennsylvania, autographs of engravers collection • *Engraved Brit. ports.* • P. Cannon-Brookes, ed., *The painted word: British history painting, 1750–1830* (1991) • J. Pye, *Patronage of British art: an historical sketch* (1845); facs. edn [1970] • *GM*, 2nd ser., 10 (1838), 667 • *GM*, 2nd ser., 11 (1839), 104 • R. Hamlyn, 'An Irish Shakespeare gallery', *Burlington Magazine*, 120 (1978), 515–29 • H. Hammelmann, *Book illustrators in eighteenth-century England*, ed. T. S. R. Boase (1975)
Archives BM, department of prints and drawings | Free Library of Philadelphia, autographs of engravers collection

Rhodes, Thomas (1789–1868), civil engineer, was born on 7 March 1789 at Apperley Bridge, near Bradford, Yorkshire, one of at least four sons and two daughters of the millwright and carpenter James Rhodes. He attended Calverley School and was then apprenticed to his elder brother William, who carried on their father's business. In 1810 Thomas was employed briefly on the Glasgow and

Paisley Canal before obtaining his first important engineering post, on the Caledonian Canal, of which Thomas Telford had overall charge.

Rhodes made three principal contributions to the Caledonian Canal. He designed the lock-gates, originally made from oak, and later from cast iron; he also devised, and built, the equipment for hanging them. It was Rhodes's task to organize the assembly of two of the first steam bucket dredgers in 1816. The parts had been made at Butterley ironworks, and were put together by Rhodes, and his carpenters, on the shores of Loch Oich. During an interval in this work he took charge of the insertion of caissons, and the centering of arches on the Bonar Bridge over the Dornoch Firth.

On leaving Scotland in 1822 Rhodes was immediately engaged by Telford to assist in the building of the Menai and Conwy road bridges in north Wales. His main responsibility was the assembly of the chains for the high-level suspension bridge, at that time the longest ever attempted. The links were manufactured at the Coleham works in Shropshire, and assembled on site. Rhodes observed, from the top of a tower, with Telford and two others, the successful slinging of the first suspension chain across the straits in April 1825. When the bridge was opened in January 1826 he was in the first party to cross by road. Only a week later it was Rhodes's duty to report to Telford the damage caused by a spectacular gale. The introduction of transverse bracings made the bridge safe.

Soon afterwards came a large dock development in London. Telford had been commissioned by the St Katherine's Dock Company, and installed Rhodes as his resident engineer. This scheme was successfully completed (apart from the eastern basin) between May 1826 and October 1828. Telford, always safety conscious, protested against excessive haste. A major novelty of the plan was the provision of two basins within the 10 acre site, and the use of six pumps to draw water through a long culvert from the middle of the river. During his engagement at St Katherine's, Rhodes designed an interlocking-arch swivel bridge, the model for one he later used on the Shannon.

In 1832–3 Rhodes produced major reports on improvements to the River Shannon in the west of Ireland. By 1835 he was one of the Shannon commissioners, who had been given statutory charge over the whole river, with a view to implementing his proposals. The chief purpose was to relieve unemployment, and also to promote passenger transport by steamboat. Much of the work was carried out, especially in the middle sections of the river between Killaloe and Battlebridge. Rhodes was also active in Yorkshire, completing a major survey of the River Ouse in January 1834, which led to many essential repairs. Rhodes was responsible for the twin-bascule bridge, opened in 1840, which carried the Hull–Selby railway over the Ouse. In 1837 he surveyed the River Derwent for Earl Fitzwilliam, and recommended effective improvements.

Rhodes had a wife called Lucy, but little else is known about his private life. More modest, and less celebrated, than several of his contemporaries, Rhodes nevertheless established a sound and well-deserved reputation. He was a member of the Institution of Civil Engineers from 1828. Telford praised his 'dexterity as a mechanic, his superior skill and unremitting attention' (A. Gibb, 185). These skills found outlets in all four countries of the United Kingdom. The period 1849 to 1860 was spent as resident engineer in charge of two harbours in the Channel Islands. After eight years of retirement, Rhodes died at Paignton, Devon, on 6 June 1868.   GERALD CROMPTON

Sources *PICE*, 28 (1868–9), 615–18 · A. Gibb, *The story of Telford* (1935), 185 · V. T. H. Delany and D. R. Delany, *The canals of the south of Ireland* (1966) · A. D. Cameron, *The Caledonian Canal* (1972) · C. Hadfield, *The canals of Yorkshire and north-east England*, 2 (1973) · B. F. Duckham, *The Yorkshire Ouse* (1967) · *The life of Thomas Telford: civil engineer, written by himself*, ed. J. Rickman (1838) · L. T. C. Rolt, *Thomas Telford* (1958) · C. Hadfield, *The canals of the west midlands* (1966) · E. Cresy, *Encyclopaedia of civil engineering* (1847) · *CGPLA Eng. & Wales* (1868) · will, proved, London, 14 July 1868
Archives York Public Library, report on River Ouse navigation
Wealth at death under £12,000: probate, 14 July 1868, *CGPLA Eng. & Wales*

Rhodes, Wilfred (1877–1973), cricketer, was born at Moor Top, Kirkheaton, Yorkshire, on 29 October 1877, the son (another son died in a railway accident) of Alfred Rhodes, coalminer, keen cricketer, and enthusiastic captain of Kirkheaton second eleven, and his wife, Elizabeth Holliday. Rhodes attended Spring Grove School in Huddersfield, left at the age of sixteen, and took a job on the Lancashire and Yorkshire Railway. But this interfered with what was already the inescapable passion of his life, cricket, and Yorkshire cricket in particular. From his own village the great George Hirst, six years older than himself, had already distinguished himself in the Yorkshire eleven; Rhodes was determined to follow, but for the time being he had a season with Kirkheaton first eleven before being appointed professional to the Scottish side of Galashiels, with which he had two successful seasons.

By 1898 there was a vacancy in the Yorkshire side for a slow left-arm bowler, and Rhodes was chosen to fill it. In this season he took 154 wickets and began on the career which over the next thirty-two years made him a record holder of records. No bowler has approached his total of 4187 wickets, and few batsmen have exceeded his aggregate of 39,802 runs. Only his partner George Hirst came near to his record number of sixteen 'doubles' (100 wickets and 1000 runs in a season), and nobody else has taken 100 wickets in a season on twenty-three occasions. In October 1899, at the end of his second season, Rhodes felt secure enough to marry Sarah Elizabeth Stancliffe, of Kirkheaton; they had one daughter.

The first of Rhodes's fifty-eight appearances for England was in the first test against Australia in 1899, the last in which W. G. Grace played. On the next Australian tour in 1902 Rhodes and Hirst had the satisfaction of bowling the opposition out in the first test for 36, with Rhodes taking seven for 17 from eleven overs. The fifth test was the cliffhanger when G. L. Jessop scored 100 in forty-three minutes to make victory possible; 15 runs were still needed, however, when Rhodes, last man in, joined Hirst in a legendary last-wicket partnership. 'Don't worry, Wilf, we'll get 'em in ones', Hirst is alleged to have said, but it seems

Wilfred Rhodes (1877–1973), by Ernest Moore, 1920s

more likely that no words passed between the two Yorkshiremen and that, unlike the spectators, Rhodes remained entirely calm. He never knew 'nerves'. And they got the runs.

Rhodes turned his attention to batting, and worked his way up the order from number eleven to opener. At Sydney on the 1903–4 tour he shared a record last wicket partnership of 130 with R. E. Foster; at Melbourne in 1911–12 he shared a record opening partnership with Sir Jack Hobbs of 323 in four and a half hours. This record stood for thirty-five years. Throughout this prolific period with the bat before the First World War, Rhodes never neglected his bowling. He has frequently been described as the greatest all-rounder after Grace.

As a batsman Rhodes may have been pedestrian compared with some of his dashing contemporaries, but he had unlimited patience and a sufficiency of strokes to keep the score moving. Although some of his youthful slimness had gone by his mid-twenties, and he was becoming the ruddy-faced stocky figure, blue-eyed and phlegmatic, who appeared to be a permanent part of the cricketing scene, his opening partnerships with Hobbs were remarkable for the running between wickets, which was brilliantly opportunist, both men equally nimble and swift. His bowling depended on flight and spin, and deadly nagging accuracy. Off a short economical run, which allowed him to bowl for very long spells, often unchanged throughout an innings, he could tease, tempt, or worry the best batsmen out. His sturdy physique never let him

down; the only vulnerable spot was the spinning finger on his left hand.

In 1914 Rhodes did not join up: he was thirty-eight and chose to work in a weapons factory in Huddersfield. When the game was resumed in 1919, he reverted to bowling as his primary function and headed the national bowling averages in 1919, 1920, 1922, and 1923. At the end of the 1921 season it was generally thought that Rhodes had played in his last test match. But when the Australians returned in 1926, Rhodes was recalled for the final test at the Oval, when the Ashes were at stake. He was forty-eight. Neville Cardus recorded that 'Rhodes at deep third-man did not make a quite decent spectacle.' In the second innings he took four for 44 and won the match and the rubber. In consequence England won the Ashes after fourteen years. In 1929 he toured the West Indies—and became the oldest test cricketer at fifty-two—but already in his last few seasons as a player his eyesight was failing. He won fifty-eight caps for England, forty-one of them against Australia. On retirement he became coach at Harrow School (Hirst had gone to Eton), where he introduced the young gentlemen to the pungent philosophy of the north—'In Yorkshire we don't play cricket for foon.'

When the war came the world was steadily darkening for Rhodes, but he still played golf, gardened, and relaxed at the local Conservative club. In 1945 glaucoma was diagnosed, and in 1952 he was totally blind after an unsuccessful operation. His wife too was old and infirm; after her death in 1952 he lived with his daughter. He still went to the cricket as a matter of course, 'watching' the game by sound, and generally a group of admirers or old colleagues would gather about him. A reserved, reticent man for most of his life, he now became almost garrulous, ready to entertain anybody prepared to listen to him. He died on 8 July 1973 at Southmead, 159 York Road, Broadstone, Dorset.   PETER SUTCLIFFE, rev.

Sources S. Rogerson, *Wilfred Rhodes: professional and gentleman* (1960) · *The Times* (9 July 1973) · *Wisden* (1974) · b. cert. · d. cert. · A. A. Thomson, *Hirst and Rhodes* (1959)

Archives FILM BFI NFTVA, news footage | SOUND BL NSA, documentary recording

Likenesses lithograph, 1905 (after photograph by A. C. Tayler), NPG · E. Moore, oils, 1920–29, Bob Appleyard Collection, Ilkley, West Yorkshire [*see illus.*]

Wealth at death £50,148: probate, 9 Aug 1973, CGPLA Eng. & Wales

Rhodes, William Barnes (1772–1826), writer, was born in Leeds on 25 December 1772, the second son of Richard Rhodes of Leeds, and his wife, Mercy. In early life he was a writer in an attorney's office, but about 1799 he obtained the post of clerk in the Bank of England.

Although he wrote a few books, including *Eccentric Tales* (1808), published under the pseudonym Cornelius Crambo, Rhodes is chiefly known as the author of a long popular burlesque, *Bombastes furioso*, which was produced anonymously at the Haymarket on 7 August 1810, when Charles Mathews took the part of the King of Utopia and John Liston that of Bombastes. It was first printed in Dublin in 1813, but was not published with the author's name until 1822, after which time numerous editions were issued. Rhodes was also a collector of dramatic literature, and made large purchases at the Roxburghe sale in June 1812.

Rhodes continued to work assiduously at the bank, and his able and diligent performance led to his promotion in 1823 to the office of chief teller, which he held until his death. On 24 March 1825 he married Emma Millington at St Clement Danes, London, but he died soon after at his home in Bedford Street, Bedford Square, London, on 1 November 1826. His library had been sold by Sothebys in 1825. He was survived by his wife and a daughter, who was born posthumously.

E. I. CARLYLE, rev. M. CLARE LOUGHLIN-CHOW

Sources GM, 1st ser., 96/2 (1826), 471–2 · Genest, Eng. stage, 8.203 · D. E. Baker, Biographia dramatica, or, A companion to the playhouse, rev. I. Reed, new edn, rev. S. Jones, 3 vols. in 4 (1812) · IGI · admon., PRO, PROB 6/202, fol. 319v

Rhodri ab Owain Gwynedd (d. 1195). See under Hywel ab Owain Gwynedd (d. 1170).

Rhodri Mawr (b. before **844**, d. **878**), king of Gwynedd, was son of *Merfyn Frych, king of Gwynedd, and Nest ferch Cadell of the Powysian ruling line. Rhodri ruled the kingdom of Gwynedd in north-west Wales from 844 until his death in 878. Furthermore, it is possible that he brought Powys in north-east Wales under his control in 855 or at some point after that date, and also annexed Ceredigion in west Wales in 872. He is credited with a number of sons with his various wives, including Angharad ferch Meurig of Ceredigion, and these sons, most notably Anarawd and Cadell, continued his expansionist policy, culminating in the extensive power of his grandson Hywel Dda ap Cadell. Despite the claims of later writers, Rhodri himself never ruled all of Wales, but even so he was relatively well known to contemporaries and is perhaps mentioned in a poem by Sedulius Scottus, an Irishman working on the continent. A majority of Welsh rulers in the tenth and later centuries claimed descent from him and it is probably on account of his contemporary political and later genealogical importance that Rhodri came to be known as 'the Great'. The lists of his sons include *Anarawd, *Cadell, Gwriad, and Merfyn; others, less historically certain, include Aeddan, Gwyddelig, Meurig, Morgan, and Tudwal Gloff.

Rhodri succeeded to the kingdom of Gwynedd and its dependent regions in 844 on the death of his father, Merfyn Frych. In spite of his importance very little is known about his deeds within Wales, and most of that must be surmised from later, brief accounts. More is known of his dealings with the English and Hiberno-Scandinavians. The expansion of Rhodri's authority in Wales seems to have been achieved by a combination of marriage alliance and, no doubt, a certain amount of violence. Rhodri's acquisition of neighbouring Powys is normally dated to 855, when its last known independent ruler, Cyngen ap Cadell, died in Rome. Rhodri is thought to have annexed the kingdom on account of being the son of Cyngen's sister Nest, and the fact that no member of Cyngen's family is mentioned after 855 might support

this view. However, Cyngen is known to have had sons, and the suggestion that Powys was controlled by Rhodri's dynasty this early is not certain. The suggestion of the similar acquisition of Ceredigion on the drowning of its last king, Gwgon ap Meurig, has perhaps more to recommend it, though again there is no explicit statement to substantiate this. Rhodri's wife Angharad was the sister of Gwgon; and the violent nature of Gwgon's death may be suggestive.

Whereas Rhodri Mawr's relations with neighbouring Welsh kingdoms tended to be beneficial to himself, his external relations proved not to be always so. In 853 the combined forces of Burgred of Mercia and Æthelwulf of Wessex entered Wales and acquired Welsh submission; which Welsh ruler or rulers were party to this is not known, but possibly Rhodri was among their number. Two years later he faced trouble from the opposite direction when the vikings known as Dub Gaill ('the Black Host') raided Anglesey. Since Anglesey was the traditional seat of the kings of Gwynedd, such a raid on the island could well have posed a threat. However Rhodri was clearly not intimidated and in 856, a year after this raid, he slew Orm (or Gorm), a viking leader active in Ireland in the early 850s. The site of the encounter is not known. It was possibly this victory over vikings that was celebrated in the poem by Sedulius Scottus. In 865 the English appear to have attacked Rhodri on Anglesey: the Irish annals state that they drove the Welsh from their lands and placed them in bondage on 'Maen Chonáin', possibly Môn (Anglesey). The last years of Rhodri's reign witnessed a number of encounters that were not successful for him. In 877 the so-called 'Sunday battle' was fought on Anglesey. This was possibly against the Dub Gaill for in that year they are said to have driven Rhodri to Ireland. He was back within a year for he was slain, alongside his son Gwriad, by the English in 878. The English in question appear to have been the Mercians if the 'Edryd Long Hair' fought by Rhodri's sons in 881 (in a battle known as the 'avenging of Rhodri') was Æthelred, ealdorman of Mercia.

DAVID E. THORNTON

Sources J. Williams ab Ithel, ed., Annales Cambriae, Rolls Series, 20 (1860) · T. Jones, ed. and trans., Brenhinedd y Saesson, or, The kings of the Saxons (1971) [another version of Brut y tywysogyon] · T. Jones, ed. and trans., Brut y tywysogyon, or, The chronicle of the princes: Peniarth MS 20 (1952) · T. Jones, ed. and trans., Brut y tywysogyon, or, The chronicle of the princes: Red Book of Hergest (1955) · P. C. Bartrum, ed., Early Welsh genealogical tracts (1966) · Ann. Ulster · I. Meyers, ed., Sedulii Scotti carmina (1991) · D. N. Dumville, 'The "six" sons of Rhodri Mawr: a problem in Asser's Life of King Alfred', Cambridge Medieval Celtic Studies, 4 (1982), 5–18 · J. E. Lloyd, A history of Wales from the earliest times to the Edwardian conquest, 3rd edn, 2 vols. (1939); repr. (1988) · N. K. Chadwick, 'Early culture and learning in north Wales', in N. K. Chadwick and others, Studies in the early British church (1958), 29–120

Rhondda. For this title name see Thomas, David Alfred, first Viscount Rhondda (1856–1918); Thomas, Sybil Margaret, Viscountess Rhondda (1857–1941); Thomas, Margaret Haig, suo jure Viscountess Rhondda (1883–1958).

Rhun Hir [Rhun ap Maelgwn Gwynedd] (fl. **547**–c.**600**), king of Gwynedd, was son of *Maelgwn Gwynedd and, according to later genealogies, of Gwallwen, or Gwallt-wen, ferch Afallach. Rhun was probably king of Gwynedd in north-west Wales in the second half of the sixth century. He possibly succeeded to the kingship in 547 if that is the correct date for the death of his father Maelgwn Gwynedd. The date of the end of his reign is not known, though his son and probable successor, Beli, died in 627. Most of the information about Rhun is of a late and unreliable character so that, from a historical perspective, his life and rule remain obscure. For example, the late text *Breiniau gwŷr Arfon* ('rights of the men of Arfon') (*c*.1200) relates that Rhun had to contest claims by north Britons before succeeding his father. He is credited with great height in some later medieval notices, hence his cognomen 'the Tall'. The earliest royal genealogies of Gwynedd would trace the main dynasty of Gwynedd to Maelgwn through Rhun, but later accounts, following Geoffrey of Monmouth, claim rather that the line of descent was through his (alleged) brother Einion and relegate Rhun to the role of fathering a daughter married to a Breton duke. Some late vernacular texts state that his mother Gwallwen was Maelgwn's mistress and that Rhun was therefore illegitimate; this is probably an attempt to explain the discrepancy between the genealogies and Geoffrey's version of events. Rhun's wife is called Perweur ferch Rhun Rhyfeddfawr in late genealogies.   DAVID E. THORNTON

Sources J. Williams ab Ithel, ed., *Annales Cambriae*, Rolls Series, 20 (1860) · R. Bromwich, ed. and trans., *Trioedd ynys Prydein: the Welsh triads*, 2nd edn (1978) · A. W. Wade-Evans, ed. and trans., *Vitae sanctorum Britanniae et genealogiae* (1944) · P. C. Bartrum, ed., *Early Welsh genealogical tracts* (1966) · D. E. Thornton, 'A neglected genealogy of Llywelyn ap Gruffudd', *Cambridge Medieval Celtic Studies*, 23 (1992), 9–23 · T. Jones, 'Gwraig Maelgwn Gwynedd a'r Fodrwy', *BBCS*, 18 (1958–60), 55–8

Rhydderch ab Ieuan Llwyd (*c*.1325–1392×8), literary patron and jurist, was born, possibly *c*.1325 (judging by the course of his later career), into a family and milieu of rich and distinguished cultural associations. The medieval house of Parcrhydderch (of which no trace now remains) stood at the junction of the commotes of Mabwynion and Pennardd, Cardiganshire, jurisdictions in which members of the family served as royal officials in the fourteenth and fifteenth centuries and to which contemporary poets made frequent reference. Barely 10 miles away was situated the Cistercian abbey of Strata Florida, the site of a major monastic scriptorium. Several of Rhydderch's ancestors, in the paternal and maternal lines, were celebrated for their literary patronage. Both his grandfather, Ieuan ap Gruffudd Foel, and his father, Ieuan Llwyd, were addressed by leading poets of the early fourteenth century, while his grandmother, Elliw, daughter of Maredudd ap Cadwgan Fantach, was the subject of a poem addressed to her by Llywelyn Brydydd Hodnant. Dafydd ap Gwilym (*fl*. 1330–1350) composed an elegy on the death of Rhydderch's mother, Angharad, daughter of Rhisiart ab Einion ap Cynfrig of Builth, where she is described as the 'gossamer of Ceredigion' (*gwawn Geredigiawn*) and her associations with the commote of Pennardd are noted.

Distinguished patrons of poets, the family were also directly associated with at least two of the most celebrated manuscript compilations of the fourteenth century. *Llawysgrif Hendregadredd* (the Hendregadredd manuscript), a major source for the poetry of the *gogynfeirdd* or court poets of the twelfth and thirteenth centuries and whose earlier parts were almost certainly written at Strata Florida, may have migrated to the home of Ieuan Llwyd at Parcrhydderch where, it is plausibly suggested, a third stratum, consisting of later poems addressed to members of the Parcrhydderch family, to their neighbours, and to subjects with Ceredigion connections, was written. A second manuscript, *Llyfr gwyn Rhydderch* (the White Book of Rhydderch), one of the most valuable manuscripts in the Welsh language, was almost certainly commissioned and owned by Rhydderch ab Ieuan Llwyd, while the composition of the poetic grammar associated with Einion Offeiriad (*d*. 1353?) may be attributed to the cultural activity focused on Ieuan Llwyd during the second and third decades of the fourteenth century.

The family's outstanding tradition of patronage was continued by Rhydderch, himself the subject of a eulogy by Dafydd y Coed, a mock elegy by Dafydd ap Gwilym, and a celebrated elegy (*marwnad*) composed by Gruffudd Llwyd, while Llywelyn Goch ap Meurig Hen composed a sophisticated *awdl* addressed to Rhydderch and his cousin, Llywelyn Fychan. Rhydderch's sons, from two (possibly three) marriages, the first to Margred, daughter of Gruffudd Gryg (*fl*. 1340–1380), and the second to Maud, daughter of Sir William Clement, lord of neighbouring Tregaron, were likewise addressed by several major poets of the fifteenth century. Noted branches of the lineage were established at Gogerddan and at Morfa Mawr, thus presenting an almost unbroken connection between the family and the region's poetic culture into the sixteenth century. **Ieuan ap Rhydderch ab Ieuan Llwyd** (*fl*. 1430–1470), poet, a writer of considerable distinction and learning, who may well have been university-trained and who wrote mainly on religious themes, was, according to the tradition of manuscripts and pedigrees, one of Rhydderch's sons, almost certainly of his old age. Remembered in later ages as 'the greatest family in that county [of Cardigan]' (Jones, 41), Rhydderch and his kinsmen were also prominent office-holders in the royal counties of Carmarthen and Cardigan. Despite accusations that he was a maintainer of felons and fugitives, Rhydderch himself served as beadle and constable of the commote of Mabwynion and as deputy justiciar of Cardiganshire during the last two decades of the fourteenth century. His sons, Dafydd and Philip, were equally prominent in local administration, the former serving as bailiff itinerant of Cardigan and beadle of Genau'r-glyn, and the latter as beadle of Mabwynion in the early decades of the fifteenth century.

Poetic and record evidence alike testify to Rhydderch ab Ieuan Llwyd's skills as a jurist. Dafydd y Coed, in an *awdl* almost certainly addressed to him, refers to his expertise as an arbitrator ('arail y geirieu cymrodedd'), and describes him as 'strong Solomon' ('cryf Selyf'). Gruffudd

Llwyd, in his elegy, salutes his juristic learning. Nicholas Audley, lord of Cemais, likewise referred to him as 'the wisest and most knowledgeable in the laws and customs of the county [of Cardigan]' ('Baronia de Kemeys', 131–2), a tribute to his legal learning and to his specialist knowledge of the native legal system, which survived and flourished in the counties of Cardigan and Carmarthen in the later middle ages. The royal administration deemed it necessary to engage experts in Welsh legal procedures in the king's courts of the region, and Rhydderch was employed in the capacity of *dosbarthwr* or *legis peritus* in Welsh law between 1380 and 1392. But he was also conversant with English legal procedures, for he held county courts and sessions at Cardigan in 1386 and 1387 and functioned as deputy justiciar of the county. Although there are references to a Rhydderch ab Ieuan Llwyd as beadle of Mabwynion between 1417 and 1442, these are made to another person of the same name. Rhydderch himself was dead by 1398.
LLINOS SMITH

Sources R. A. Griffiths and R. S. Thomas, *The principality of Wales in the later middle ages: the structure and personnel of government*, 1: *South Wales, 1277–1536* (1972) · PRO · *Chancery records* · D. Huws, 'Llyfr gwyn Rhydderch', *Cambridge Medieval Celtic Studies*, 21 (1991), 1–37 · D. Huws, 'Llawysgrif Hendregadredd', *National Library of Wales Journal*, 22 (1981–2), 1–26 · J. B. Smith, 'Einion Offeiriad', *BBCS*, 20 (1962–4), 339–47 · D. H. Roberts, 'Noddwyr y beirdd yn Sir Aberteifi', *Llên Cymru*, 10 (1968–9), 76–109 · D. Johnston, 'Awdl Llywelyn Goch i Rydderch a Llywelyn Fychan', *BBCS*, 35 (1988), 20–28 · *Cywyddau Iolo Goch ac eraill*, ed. H. Lewis, T. Roberts, and I. Williams, new edn (1937) · L. B. Smith, 'Cannwyll disbwyll a dosbarth: gwŷr cyfraith Ceredigion yn yr oesoedd canol diweddar', *Ceredigion* [Cardiganshire Antiquarian Society], 10 (1986), 229–53 · J. Wynn, *The history of the Gwydir family and memoirs*, ed. J. G. Jones (1990) · 'Baronia de Kemeys from the original documents at Bronwydd', *Archaeologia Cambrensis*, 3rd ser., 7 (1861), suppl., 1–36 · 'Baronia de Kemeys from the original documents at Bronwydd', *Archaeologia Cambrensis*, 3rd ser., 8 (1862), suppl., 37–136

Rhydderch Hen (*fl. c.*573–*c.*612), king of Strathclyde, was son of Tudwal Tudclyd ap Clynog. He ruled the north British kingdom of Strathclyde, based at Dumbarton, in the second half of the sixth century. When or whom he succeeded to the kingship is not known; most of the available information about his life and rule is derived from incidental notices in saints' lives. In these texts his pious character is stressed: he was allegedly baptized in Ireland by disciples of St Patrick and had personal contact with the future saints Columba of Iona and Kentigern of Glasgow (whose career he fostered). In the *Historia Brittonum* Rhydderch Hen (the epithet means 'the Old') is represented as one of the four North British kings who fought, ultimately unsuccessfully, against the expanding Northumbrian kingdom of Bernicia. His allies included Urien ap Cynfarch, king of Rheged, Gwallog ap Llinog (whom some would place in Elfed in what is now Yorkshire), and a Morgan (possibly Morgan Mwynfawr). The main Bernician opponents were Theodoric (*supp. r.* 572–9) and Hussa (*supp. r.* 585–92). Later Welsh tradition claims that Rhydderch fought against the Briton Gwenddolau ap Ceidio at the battle of Arthuret in Cumberland in the year 573, but earlier accounts of that encounter do not mention his involvement. Relations with the neighbouring Scottish kingdom

of Dál Riata were not always amicable. A Welsh triad states that the Dál Riatan king Áedán mac Gabráin (*r.* 574–608) ravaged the court of Rhydderch at Dumbarton 'leaving neither food nor drink nor beast alive'. This may reflect some sort of military encounter rather than excessive gluttony on the part of Áedán. Rhydderch is said to have feared that he would be slain by enemies but was reassured by St Columba that he would die a natural death. Later sources date his death to the same year as that of Kentigern, traditionally 612 (though 614 is also possible). Despite his importance for the kingdom of Strathclyde, Rhydderch Hen does not seem to have been succeeded by any of his descendants. He is credited in late Welsh genealogies with a daughter Gwladus.
DAVID E. THORNTON

Sources *Adomnán's Life of Columba*, ed. and trans. A. O. Anderson and M. O. Anderson, rev. edn, rev. M. O. Anderson, OMT (1991) · A. P. Forbes, ed., *Lives of S. Ninian and S. Kentigern* (1874) · T. Mommsen, ed., 'Historia Brittonum', *Chronica minora saec. IV. V. VI. VII.*, 3, MGH Auctores Antiquissimi, 13 (Berlin, 1898), 111–222 · P. C. Bartrum, ed., *Early Welsh genealogical tracts* (1966) · R. Bromwich, ed. and trans., *Trioedd ynys Prydein: the Welsh triads*, 2nd edn (1978) · A. P. Smyth, *Warlords and holy men: Scotland, AD 80–1000* (1984)

Rhydderch, John (*bap.* 1673?, *d.* 1735), printer and poet, is believed to have been the son of David and Elen Roderick who was baptized John on 23 April 1673 in Cemais, Montgomeryshire. By 1713 he was working in Shrewsbury as editor, translator into Welsh, and corrector of the press for Thomas Durston, successor to Thomas Jones as vendor of Welsh books. In 1715 Rhydderch set up his own press in the town, 'Next door to the sign of the Green Man', in Mardol Street; in the past he has been erroneously identified with John Rogers, a contemporary Shrewsbury printer. A steady increase in literacy in Wales provided a ready market for the kind of publication in which Rhydderch, a devout Anglican, specialized: readable religious and moral works, chapbooks, and ballads. He compiled and printed a pocket-sized *English–Welsh Dictionary* (1725) and a Welsh grammar, *Grammadeg Cymraeg* (1728), both of which sold well even though they were justifiably disparaged by scholars.

Rhydderch was a competent if not imaginative poet, best-known for carols and ballads. Editions of his enlarged version of Thomas Jones's anthology of popular verse *Llyfr carolau a dyriau duwiol* were printed by Durston in 1729 and 1745. Poetry featured among the customary components of his almanac *Newyddion oddiwrth y sêr*, which he compiled annually between 1713 and 1735. Also in his almanacs may be found references to his ineffective efforts to promote the Welsh form of literary gathering, the eisteddfod. He rarely acted as publisher, mostly printing on behalf of authors or using the subscription mode. Rhydderch's circle of acquaintances was extensive and commissions came from north Walians and west Walians; in 1716, for example, he printed *A Display of Herauldry ... of North Wales* for John Davies, and *Drych y prif oesoedd*, a seminal if fanciful history of Wales, for Theophilus Evans of Cardiganshire.

An unspecified domestic crisis brought Rhydderch's

printing venture to an end in 1728 and, in a letter written from London in December 1729 to Lewis Morris, he states that he even had to part with his equipment. Rhydderch's interest in old Welsh manuscripts and poetry, together with his efforts to provide his countrymen with books, had endeared him to the renowned Morris brothers. In 1732 Lewis Morris issued a proposal whereby the profits of a press that he would set up by subscription in Llannerch-y-medd, Anglesey, would be used to help Rhydderch, who was by then 'reduced to very low circumstances'. Nothing came of the proposal. The disillusioned Rhydderch suffered a further set-back when Durston failed to honour an agreement to print his almanac for 1734. However, in Carmarthen in 1733 he found some unnamed gentlemen who were prepared to pay Nicholas Thomas to print the issue. By 1735 Rhydderch had returned to Cae Talhaearn, Cemais. He was buried in Cemais churchyard on 27 November 1735. Elegies written on his death testify to the warm regard in which he was held by contemporaries.

EILUNED REES

Sources E. Rees, ed., *Libri Walliae: a catalogue of Welsh books and books printed in Wales, 1546–1820*, 2 vols. (1987) · J. H. Davies, ed., *A bibliography of Welsh ballads printed in the 18th century* (1911) [annotated copy, NL Wales; 1908–11] · *Additional letters of the Morrises of Anglesey, 1735–1786*, ed. H. Owen, 1 (1947), 2–5, 24, 556, 692 · B. Owen, 'Sion Rhydderch yr Almanaciwr, 1673–1735', *Journal of the Welsh Bibliographical Society*, 3 (1925–31), 275–90 · L. Morris, proposals 'for erecting, by subscription, a Printing Press, at Llannerch-y-medd', 1732, BL, Add. MS 14911 · J. E. Lloyd, R. T. Jenkins, and W. L. Davies, eds., *Y bywgraffiadur Cymreig hyd 1940* (1953) · J. Davies, notes on Rhydderch, March 1933, NL Wales, Add. MS 8723B · B. Owen, 'Almanac cyntaf Sion Rhydderch', *Journal of the Welsh Bibliographical Society*, 3 (1925–31), 347–9 · E. W. Rees, 'John Rhydderch', *Transactions of the Carmarthenshire Antiquarian Society*, 7 (1911–12), 88 · W. Waters, 'A short typographical sketch', *Transactions of the Carmarthenshire Antiquarian Society*, 7 (1911–12), 77–81, esp. 77–8
Archives NL Wales, various

Rhygyfarch. *See* Rhigyfarch ap Sulien (1056/7–1099).

Rhyl. For this title name *see* Birch, (Evelyn) Nigel Chetwode, Baron Rhyl (1906–1981).

Rhys ab Owain (*d.* 1078), ruler in Wales, was the son of Owain ab Edwin ab Einion ab Owain ap Hywel Dda. Rhys was one of the leaders defeated by William fitz Osbern (*d.* 1071) in an expedition led by the latter about 1070 against the people of Brycheiniog. On the death of Rhys's brother Maredudd in 1072, Bleddyn ap Cynfyn of north Wales appears to have seized the kingship of Deheubarth, but in 1075 Rhys and the nobles of Ystrad Tywi (east Carmarthenshire) slew the northern ruler, and south Wales was divided between Rhys and Rhydderch ap Caradog, who in the same year defeated Gronw and Llywelyn, sons of Cadwgan ab Elystan, in the battle of Camddwr. One chronicle erroneously states that Rhys was slain in this battle. In 1076 the death of Rhydderch left Rhys in sole possession; he defeated the sons of Cadwgan once again in the following year, in the battle of 'Gweunytwl'. In 1078 Rhys was attacked at Pwllgwdig by Trahaearn ap Caradog, then ruling over north Wales; Rhys's household troops were cut to pieces, and he himself became a fugitive, disasters which were regarded in the north as a judgement for the murder

of Bleddyn. Towards the end of the same year he and his brother Hywel were slain by Caradog ap Gruffudd, lord of Gwynllŵg. J. E. LLOYD, *rev.* DAVID E. THORNTON

Sources J. Williams ab Ithel, ed., *Annales Cambriae*, Rolls Series, 20 (1860) · T. Jones, ed. and trans., *Brenhinedd y Saesson, or, The kings of the Saxons* (1971) [another version of *Brut y tywysogyon*] · T. Jones, ed. and trans., *Brut y tywysogyon, or, The chronicle of the princes: Peniarth MS 20* (1952) · T. Jones, ed. and trans., *Brut y tywysogyon, or, The chronicle of the princes: Red Book of Hergest* (1955) · Ordericus Vitalis, *Eccl. hist.* · J. E. Lloyd, *A history of Wales from the earliest times to the Edwardian conquest*, 3rd edn, 2 vols. (1939) · K. L. Maund, *Ireland, Wales, and England in the eleventh century* (1991) · R. R. Davies, *Conquest, coexistence, and change: Wales, 1063–1415*, History of Wales, 2 (1987)

Rhys ap Gruffudd (1131/2–1197), prince of Deheubarth, was the fourth and youngest son of *Gruffudd ap Rhys (*d.* 1137) and Gwenllian (*d.* 1136), daughter of *Gruffudd ap Cynan.

Early career Before becoming sole ruler of Deheubarth in 1155 Rhys had already joined with his elder brothers Cadell [*see below*] and Maredudd in expeditions against both the Normans in Dyfed and his kinsman, Hywel ab Owain Gwynedd, in Ceredigion. Thus in 1146 Rhys assisted Cadell and Maredudd in capturing Llansteffan Castle, while in 1150 and 1151 he took part in the campaigns that resulted in the conquest of almost the whole of Ceredigion. After Cadell had been seriously injured by a force from Tenby in the latter year, Rhys co-operated with Maredudd in an attack on Gower. In 1153 Rhys and Maredudd completed the conquest of Ceredigion and attacked the castle of Aberafan; Rhys also ravaged Cyfeiliog in Powys. On Maredudd's untimely death at the age of twenty-five in 1155 Rhys succeeded to a kingdom comprising Ceredigion, Ystrad Tywi, and Dyfed; the maintenance and consolidation of this restored kingdom of Deheubarth was the principal objective of his long reign.

Relations with Henry II, 1156–1171 During the first decade of his rule Rhys's fortunes were mixed. In 1156 he built a castle at Aberdyfi in order to defend the northern border of Ceredigion against his uncle, Owain Gwynedd (*d.* 1170). However, Rhys faced a new threat from Henry II, recently established as king of England, who was determined to support the marcher lords who had been dispossessed by the Welsh of their lands in Deheubarth. After an initial show of defiance following Henry's first Welsh campaign of 1157 Rhys submitted to the king the following year, giving homage for Cantref Mawr and some other dispersed lands and surrendering Ceredigion to Roger de Clare, earl of Hertford (*d.* 1173), and Cantref Bychan with its *caput* of Llandovery to Walter de Clifford (*d.* 1190). However, following a raid by Clifford on his territory Rhys captured Llandovery Castle, while the prince's nephew, Einion ab Anarawd, attacked 'Humfrey's castle' (renamed Castellhywel) in Ceredigion. In response to these attacks Henry II led a further expedition to south Wales to secure Rhys's renewed submission before departing for the continent in August 1158. In 1159 Rhys campaigned against the Flemings and Normans in Dyfed and besieged Carmarthen, prompting an expedition against him led by Reginald, earl of Cornwall (*d.* 1175); the forces confronted each other without engaging in battle at Cefn Rhestr Main and Earl Reginald retreated, offering a truce which Rhys accepted.

Rhys captured Llandovery Castle again in 1162, calling forth another campaign against him by Henry II the following year. The prince submitted to the king at Pencader and was taken as a prisoner to England where, together with Owain Gwynedd and Malcolm IV of Scotland, he formally submitted to Henry at Woodstock on 1 July 1163: Rhys gave homage for Cantref Mawr with its castle of Dinefwr, the 'principal seat' of the kingdom of Deheubarth according to sources of the late twelfth century and later. This setback proved only temporary, however, for in 1164 Rhys reconquered nearly all of Ceredigion, in revenge for the killing the previous year (probably during the prince's captivity in England) of his nephew and chief of his retinue, Einion ab Anarawd, at the instigation of Earl Roger de Clare. Then, in the words of the Welsh chronicle *Brut y tywysogyon*, 'all the Welsh made a pact to drive out the garrisons of the French' (*Brut: Hergest*, 145). In August 1165 Rhys joined Owain Gwynedd and other Welsh princes at Corwen to resist Henry II's last campaign against them, which, owing to heavy rain, ended in disaster for the king who was compelled to retreat to England. Later in the year Rhys completed his conquest of Ceredigion, capturing Cardigan and Cilgerran castles together with the constable of the former, his cousin Robert fitz Stephen, the son of Rhys's aunt, Nest (*fl.* 1092–1130). The prince remained in possession of Ceredigion for the rest of his reign. But Rhys's military activities were not confined to Deheubarth: in 1166–7 he joined Owain Gwynedd in campaigns that led to the conquest of Tegeingl in north-east Wales and in 1167 the two princes also attacked Owain Cyfeiliog (*d.* 1197) and captured his castle of Tafolwern, which was given to Rhys.

Cordial relations with Henry II, 1171–1189 Up to 1171 Rhys's relations with Henry II were marked by defiance and hostility punctuated by brief periods of reluctant compliance induced by the exercise or threat of military force. From 1171, by contrast, Henry adopted a fundamental change in his policy towards Rhys, who had become the most powerful native Welsh ruler after the death of Owain Gwynedd in November 1170. This change was closely linked to developments in Ireland which had already served to strengthen Rhys's position in Deheubarth, namely the departure of marcher lords and knights from the region in 1169–70 to assist Diarmait mac Murchada in the recovery of his kingdom of Leinster; Rhys had released Robert fitz Stephen, for example, on the explicit condition that the latter should go to Ireland in Diarmait's service. Aware that military solutions had failed to achieve stability in Wales, and fearful of the increase in marcher power as a result of the conquests in Ireland, Henry II adopted a policy of *détente* with Rhys which lasted for the rest of the king's reign. On his way to assert his authority over the Anglo-Normans in Ireland in October 1171 Henry met Rhys at Pembroke, confirmed him in possession of Ceredigion, Ystrad Tywi, Emlyn, and the commotes of Ystlwyf and Efelffre in Cantref Gwarthaf, and released his son, Hywel Sais, whom he had held hostage. On his return from Ireland after Easter 1172 the king met Rhys again, at Laugharne, and according to *Brut y tywysogyon* appointed him 'justice in all south Wales' (*iustus yn holl deheubarth*; *Brut: Hergest*, 158), thereby probably delegating authority to Rhys, not over his own principality of Deheubarth (of which he styled himself 'proprietary prince' in a charter of 1184), but rather over the native Welsh rulers in Gwynllŵg, Gwent, Glamorgan, Maelienydd, Gwrtheyrnion, and Elfael. As a result of the agreements of 1171–2 it appears that Henry committed himself to uphold Rhys's territorial gains against marcher claims in return for a recognition of his overlordship by the prince, who was furthermore expected to help prevent the Welsh rulers to his east from attacking royal and marcher lands.

1171–2 marked a major turning point in Rhys's reign, opening a period of largely uninterrupted peace with the English crown and also the marcher lords of south Wales which lasted for almost twenty years. The prince's loyalty to Henry is demonstrated by his sending his son, Hywel Sais, to assist the king in France during the revolt of 1173–4, and by Rhys's leading a force of his own on behalf of Henry at Tutbury in 1174. The following year Rhys appeared at the head of the native rulers of south Wales, most of whom were related to him by marriage, to give fealty to Henry at Gloucester (29 June 1175); he appeared likewise at Oxford in May 1177, where he was, in addition, granted Meirionydd by the king. (Rhys may have occupied Meirionydd in support of his son-in-law, Rhodri ab Owain, who rose to dominance in Gwynedd by 1175, a hegemony resisted by, among others, the sons of Cynan ab Owain, who attacked Rhys in 1178.) The agreement with Henry was also subject to strains, however. In 1184 Rhys sought peace for himself at Worcester and later at Gloucester following two years of Welsh attacks on royal lands—including a revolt led by the prince's nephew, Morgan ap Caradog, native ruler of upland Glamorgan, following the death of William, earl of Gloucester, lord of Glamorgan, in 1183—and Ranulf de Glanville was sent to restore peace between Rhys (and other Welsh rulers) and the people of Herefordshire and Cheshire late in 1186. The *détente* with Henry II held despite these tensions, and in Lent 1188 Rhys met Glanville together with Baldwin, archbishop of Canterbury, at Radnor at the start of the latter's journey round Wales to preach the third crusade, and later welcomed the archbishop again at Cardigan.

Gerald of Wales reports that Rhys would himself have taken the cross in 1188 had he not been dissuaded by his wife and first cousin Gwenllian, daughter of *Madog ap Maredudd of Powys (*d.* 1160), who, according to later medieval genealogical tracts, was the mother of three of his sons and two of his daughters. The prince is also recorded by the same sources as having had as many as thirteen other children with other partners, including his own niece, the daughter of his brother Maredudd.

Troubled declining years Henry II's death in July 1189 marked the end of the largely peaceful coexistence inaugurated in 1171–2. The last years of Rhys's reign were dominated by renewed attacks on marcher and royal lands and castles in south Wales, attacks that were in turn quite possibly motivated in large part by the need to satisfy the ambitions of Rhys's sons, whose struggles with each other and with their father are the other main theme of this period. Rhys evidently considered his agreement with Henry II to have been personal and no longer felt obliged to adhere to its terms upon the king's decease. By September 1189 his attacks on royal and marcher strongholds provoked a royal expedition against him under Richard I's brother, John, who concluded a truce with Rhys and escorted him to the king at Oxford. However, since Richard refused to see him, the prince returned to Wales to continue his assaults on marcher lordships in Dyfed, capturing St Clears by Christmas 1189. In the same year Rhys imprisoned his eldest but illegitimate son, *Maelgwn ap Rhys (d. 1231) [see under Gruffudd ap Rhys], afterwards transferring him to the custody of William (II) de Briouze whose prisoner he remained until 1192. Further attacks followed: for example, Rhys took Nevern Castle from his son-in-law William fitz Martin in 1191, and the castles of Llawhaden (belonging to the bishop of St David's), Swansea, and Wiston fell to him the following year. In 1194 the prince rebuilt the castle of Rhaeadr (which he had first erected in 1177), but later in the year was himself captured by his sons Maelgwn and Hywel Sais, and briefly imprisoned in Nevern Castle. In 1195 Rhys suffered further setbacks, as Roger Mortimer of Wigmore conquered Maelienydd, the Flemings recaptured Wiston Castle, and William de Briouze took St Clears. However, the prince succeeded in capturing his sons, Hywel and Maredudd, who had established themselves at Dinefwr and Llandovery respectively, and in 1196 led his last major campaign, in which he burnt Carmarthen, defeated Roger Mortimer, and captured Briouze's castle at Painscastle. Rhys died, aged sixty-five, on 28 April 1197. He was buried in St David's Cathedral after penance had been administered on his corpse to absolve him from a sentence of excommunication incurred for his complicity in an assault on Peter de Leia, bishop of St David's, shortly before his death.

Religious benefactions and historical reputation Despite his conflicts with Bishop Peter during the last years of his life Rhys's relations with the church were amicable on the whole, and the prince patronized a wide variety of religious houses in Deheubarth. He confirmed and augmented the lands of the hospitallers at Slebech and the Benedictine cell of Chertsey Abbey at Cardigan and also protected Malvern Abbey's cell at Llandovery. Most importantly he was almost certainly the first native Welsh ruler to patronize the Cistercians and played a crucial role in encouraging the spread of the order in native Welsh society. As a result of his conquest of Ceredigion in 1165 he acquired the patronage of Strata Florida Abbey, founded by Robert fitz Stephen the previous year, and endowed it generously; he likewise made benefactions to Whitland Abbey, and established a Cistercian nunnery at Llanllŷr. In addition the prince founded the Premonstratensian abbey of Talley, very probably under the influence of Ranulf de Glanville in 1184–9. Rhys was also generous to poets, and *Brut y tywysogyon* describes a festival of music and poetry, often regarded as the first recorded eisteddfod, held by the prince in 1176 at Cardigan Castle, which he had rebuilt in stone in 1171.

Surviving contemporary opinion of Rhys is almost entirely favourable: Gerald of Wales praised him for his generosity, energy, and wit, and his skill and success in warfare were hailed in both the Welsh and the Latin poetry composed in his honour—according to Cynddelw (fl. 1155–1195) the prince was an 'excellent protector' who 'defended the greatness of Deheubarth' (*Gwaith Cynddelw*, no. 9, l. 37), while a Latin elegy on Rhys calls him the 'glory of Wales' (*Brut: Peniarth MS 20*, 77) and a second Alexander. A Latin prose lament preserved in the later thirteenth-century *Cronica de Wallia* likewise lauds his martial exploits as 'the unconquered head of Wales' (T. Jones, 31). From the early modern period onwards historians have stressed Rhys's pivotal role in restoring and defending the kingdom of Deheubarth, over which he was the last native prince to exercise unitary rule. In addition, twentieth-century scholars have suggested, on the basis of later evidence, that the prince organized an administrative reform of his lands and have highlighted his readiness to imitate Anglo-Norman fashions in castle building and religious patronage.

Cadell ap Gruffudd (d. 1175), an elder half-brother of Rhys, is first mentioned in 1138, when he participated with his elder brother Anarawd, ruler of Deheubarth, and Gruffudd ap Cynan's sons Owain Gwynedd and Cadwaladr in an attack on Cardigan, then in Norman hands. After Anarawd's murder by Cadwaladr's men in 1143 Cadell succeeded to the kingship of Deheubarth and led campaigns, often in conjunction with his younger half-brothers Maredudd and Rhys, in Dyfed, Ystrad Tywi, and Ceredigion. In 1146 his forces captured the castles of Dinwileir, Carmarthen, Llansteffan, and Gwyddgrug; the following year they took Wiston Castle. In 1150, in the words of *Brut y tywysogyon*, he 'repaired the castle of Carmarthen, for the splendour and strength of the kingdom' (*Brut: Hergest*, 129) and then ravaged the district of Kidwelly. Later in the same year he occupied the whole of Ceredigion south of the River Aeron, and went on to conquer the rest of the region, apart from the castle of Pengwern in Llanfihangel, from Hywel ab Owain in 1151. However, later in 1151 Cadell was severely injured while hunting by the Normans of Tenby, who left him for dead. The injuries he sustained probably incapacitated him as ruler and may explain why in 1153 (or 1156 according to the *Annales Cambriae*) he went on a pilgrimage to Rome, relinquishing his lands and authority to his brothers, Maredudd and Rhys, until he returned. (Cadell had earlier demonstrated his piety, while king, by granting St Peter's Church at Lampeter to Totnes Priory.) His abdication proved to be permanent, for though he returned to Deheubarth, he never ruled again. Cadell died and was buried at Strata Florida Abbey, where he had taken the monastic habit in his last illness, in 1175.

Referred to in two charters as 'king of south Wales', Cadell played an important role in the restoration of the kingdom of Deheubarth, helping to lay the foundations built upon by Rhys ap Gruffudd. HUW PRYCE

Sources J. E. Lloyd, *A history of Wales from the earliest times to the Edwardian conquest*, 3rd edn, 2 vols. (1939); repr. (1988) • R. R. Davies, *Conquest, coexistence, and change: Wales, 1063–1415*, History of Wales, 2 (1987) • N. A. Jones and H. Pryce, eds., *Yr Arglwydd Rhys* (1996) • D. Crouch, 'The earliest original charter of a Welsh king', *BBCS*, 36 (1989), 125–31 • J. Gillingham, 'Henry II, Richard I, and the Lord Rhys', *Peritia*, 10 (1996), 225–36 • T. Jones, ed. and trans., *Brut y tywysogyon, or, The chronicle of the princes: Red Book of Hergest* (1955) • T. Jones, ed. and trans., *Brut y tywysogyon, or, The chronicle of the princes: Peniarth MS 20* (1952) • J. Williams ab Ithel, ed., *Annales Cambriae*, Rolls Series, 20 (1860) • T. Jones, ed., 'Cronica de Wallia and other documents from Exeter Cathedral Library, MS 3514', *BBCS*, 12 (1946–8), 27–44 • P. C. Bartrum, 'Plant yr Arglwydd Rhys', *National Library of Wales Journal*, 14 (1965–6), 97–104 • W. Stubbs, ed., *Gesta regis Henrici secundi Benedicti abbatis: the chronicle of the reigns of Henry II and Richard I, AD 1169–1192*, 2 vols., Rolls Series, 49 (1867) • *Gir. Camb. opera*, vols. 1, 4, 6 • *Ann. mon.*, vol. 2 • *Gwaith Cynddelw Brydydd Mawr*, ed. N. A. Jones and A. P. Owen, 2 (1995)

Rhys ap Gruffudd (d. 1256). See under Ifor ap Meurig (fl. 1158).

Rhys, Sir, ap Gruffudd (c.1283–1356), soldier and administrator, was the son of Gruffudd ap Hywel (and great-grandson of Ednyfed Fychan) and Nest, daughter of Gwrwared ap Gwilym of Cemais, Pembrokeshire; his lineage and military and administrative service to Edward II, Edward III, and Edward, the Black Prince, helped to stabilize English rule in west Wales. He inherited ancestral lands at Llansadwrn, Carmarthenshire, and Llangybi and Betws Bledrws, Cardiganshire, in August 1308. He was well placed to reconcile the local population to royal rule, and in October 1308 Edward II made him steward of Cardiganshire. His position was strengthened, as a king's yeoman, by the acquisition of further estates in the Tywi valley and south Cardiganshire. A talented soldier, he led local forces against the Glamorgan rebel Llywelyn Bren in 1316, and to Scotland in 1319. Despite complaints about his harsh dominance in west Wales, his value to the crown was demonstrated in the baronial crisis of 1321–2, by which time he had become an esquire of the king's household. He was ordered to resist the marcher opposition to the younger Despenser in south Wales, and his authority was enhanced when he became deputy justiciar in place of Roger Mortimer of Chirk. His loyalty was rewarded with custody of Manorbier Castle and the lordship of Narberth, Pembrokeshire, for life in March 1322, and custody of the castle and lordship of Llandovery in 1323. About this time he married an heiress, Joan Somerville, whose dower included (1325) manors in Staffordshire.

Edward II's dethronement threatened Rhys's position, for the king regarded him as his Welsh protector: he was appointed constable of Carmarthen Castle in June 1326 and sheriff of Carmarthenshire and constable of Aberystwyth Castle in October; he raised men to resist Queen Isabella and Roger Mortimer of Wigmore, and in November was one of Edward's envoys to negotiate with the queen. He even tried to free Edward II from Berkeley Castle in 1327 and afterwards fled to Scotland. Despite a pardon in February 1328, he was accused of supporting the earl of Kent's plot against Mortimer in 1330, and when that failed he fled abroad.

There may have been personal antipathy between Rhys and the Mortimers; after Mortimer of Wigmore was executed in 1330, Rhys was restored to favour and to his estates. His authority in south Wales also increased: as steward of Pembroke and Cantrefmawr, and constable of Dryslwyn Castle, Carmarthenshire. By now he was a knight in Edward III's household and was re-engaged in the 1330s and 1340s as a commander of Welsh armies in Scotland, Ireland, and France, including at Crécy in 1346. Between campaigns he ruled west Wales, as deputy justiciar, steward of Cantrefmawr, and constable of Carmarthen Castle and (until his death) of Dryslwyn Castle.

Rhys was handsomely rewarded by Edward III with grants particularly in the Tywi valley, where his main residence was Abermarlais. Lampeter was confirmed to him for life in 1339 and by August 1343 he was constable of Builth Castle and keeper of the lordship. In 1355 he inherited a kinsman's estate at Llanrhystud, Cardiganshire, and, when his father-in-law died, half the Somerville lands in six English counties passed to Joan and Rhys. He was accused of oppressions, and heavy fines contributed to a debt of £740 by 1349, although all but £50 of this was pardoned by the Black Prince or paid off by 1353. Rhys died on 17 May 1356 and was buried in Carmarthen's Franciscan friary; his widow died in Warwickshire on 8 October 1377. Rhys's passing was lamented by Welsh poets, including Dafydd ap Gwilym and Iolo Goch. He and his sons, Rhys (c.1337–1380) and Henry, united their interests with those of the crown, and were able to dominate west Wales at the same time as they patronized Welsh culture.

R. A. GRIFFITHS

Sources R. A. Griffiths and R. S. Thomas, *The principality of Wales in the later middle ages: the structure and personnel of government*, 1: *South Wales, 1277–1536* (1972) • *Chancery records* • PRO • BL, Stowe 553, Cotton Nero CVIII, Add. MS 35114 • T. F. Tout, 'The captivity and death of Edward of Carnarvon', *Bulletin of the John Rylands University Library*, 6 (1921–2), 69–114 • M. C. B. Dawes, ed., *Register of Edward, the Black Prince*, 4 vols., PRO (1930–33) • *Iolo Goch: poems*, ed. and trans. D. Johnston (1993) • *Gwaith Dafydd ap Gwilym*, ed. T. Parry, 2nd edn (1963)

Rhys ap Gruffudd (c.1508–1531). See under Rice family (per. c.1500–1651).

Rhys ap Gruffudd ab Ednyfed (d. 1284). See under Tudor family, forebears of (per. c.1215–1404).

Rhys ap Maredudd (d. 1292), Welsh rebel, was the son of *Maredudd ap Rhys Gryg (d. 1271), lord of Dryslwyn, Carmarthenshire, and Isabel, daughter of William (II) *Marshal, earl of Pembroke. Although he came to terms with Edward I, Rhys rebelled in 1287–8; his defeat enabled the king's officials to control all Carmarthenshire. Rhys's father had transferred his allegiance from Llywelyn ap Gruffudd, prince of north Wales, to Henry III in 1258; despite attempts at reconciliation with Llywelyn, the treaty of Montgomery (1267) reserved the fealty of Maredudd, alone among Welsh lords, to the king (although Llywelyn purchased it in 1270). Rhys came to an agreement with the new king in 1277 and in return Edward promised (11 April) to consider his claim to Dinefwr Castle and the four commotes of his kinsman, Rhys Wyndod, once they fell into the king's hands; Rhys also agreed to do homage and fealty to the king. By 24 April, however, Rhys Wyndod had submitted and on 1 July swore homage and fealty to Edward; some of his estates were confirmed to him but Dinefwr Castle was seized by the king's lieutenant, Payn Chaworth (5 June). Rhys ap Maredudd's ambition to control the Tywi valley was thus thwarted. Thereafter he was brought under closer royal control: Chaworth asserted the king's right of entry to Dryslwyn Castle and royal justices subjected Rhys to the king's courts in Carmarthenshire. While other Welsh lords re-established contact with Prince Llywelyn (1278), Rhys ap Maredudd nevertheless preferred to remain loyal to the king.

When Edward I and Prince Llywelyn went to war in March 1282, Rhys was loyal to the crown. He was rewarded with two commotes in Ceredigion (28 July) and Rhys Wyndod's forfeited estates; and he acted as the king's agent in receiving Welshmen into Edward's peace. For his part, Llywelyn raided Rhys's estates, yet when Edward discovered that Rhys had already occupied the commotes granted to him their seizure was ordered and Rhys was arrested. The lands were restored to him on 20 October 1283, but only after he had renounced all claim to Dinefwr Castle, the greatest prize. By the end of 1283 he had been made answerable to the king's courts and his surviving kinsmen were powerless; he had little option but to accept his position as a royal vassal.

Rhys rebelled four years later. Although he married Ada, sister of John Hastings, in 1285 'to heal conflicts' (*Littere Wallie*, 92–3), by September 1286 relations with Edward I had deteriorated. In 1279–81 he had lost a dispute at Llandovery with John Giffard, lord of Builth and Iscennen, and the justiciar of west Wales, Robert Tiptoft, was harsh in implementing English procedures. The king, who was in Gascony (1286–9), sought to conciliate, but relations worsened. When in 1287 Rhys refused to attend the Carmarthen county court, he seemed to be denying the king's jurisdiction. As lord of Emlyn, where his father had built a new castle, he maintained that he was not subject to the king's justiciar at Carmarthen but rather to the Pembroke county court. The king and his council in England were prepared to investigate the claims and accusations of Rhys and Robert Tiptoft (1287), but Rhys refused to appear before justices at Carmarthen: the question of the king's jurisdiction had become a matter of principle. He may also have resented his failure to secure Dinefwr Castle and Rhys Wyndod's estates in the Tywi valley. According to Thomas Wykes (*Ann. mon.*, 4.310), he was motivated by selfish ambition, perhaps exacerbated by personal animosity between himself and Tiptoft.

Rhys attacked Llandovery Castle and captured it on 8 June 1287; he then took both Dinefwr and Carreg Cennen castles, carrying destruction as far south as Swansea and westwards; even the new town at Llanbadarn (later called Aberystwyth) and Carmarthen were harassed. In Cardiganshire and north Wales precautions were taken to secure strongholds and patrol the countryside. With the king in Gascony, his brother Edmund, earl of Cornwall, raised forces in the borderland to contain the rebellion, and the justiciar of west Wales was ordered (2 July) to seize Rhys's possessions. A council of war held at Gloucester on 15 July resolved to assemble a great army, mostly from the marcher lordships, to converge on Carmarthen by the first week in August: from Llanbadarn (under John of Havering), Monmouth (under Earl Edmund), Brecon (under Gilbert de Clare, earl of Gloucester and lord of Glamorgan), and west Wales (under Robert Tiptoft). By 12 August 6600 men had reached Llanbadarn; the Monmouth contingent of 2400 men from the midlands and south-east marches reached Carmarthen about 8 August. Tiptoft's force of more than 1000 was composed mainly of Welshmen prepared to serve against a Welsh lord who had not embraced Welsh causes in the past. The earl of Gloucester's army was 5600 strong when it approached Llandovery and grew to 12,500 by 7 August. In addition to subduing the countryside, when Earl Edmund reached Carmarthen on 8 August he planned an assault on Rhys's fortress of Dryslwyn, with siege equipment from Bristol.

This siege lasted three weeks from 13 August, during which mining beneath the castle chapel led to a spectacular roof collapse that killed some leading commanders. Rhys escaped, though most of his adherents surrendered. On 24 September the castle and Rhys's estates were granted to Alan (II) de Plugenet; the stronghold of Newcastle Emlyn was captured too. This was an expensive operation requiring loans from Italian merchants; according to J. E. Morris (219) the total cost exceeded £10,606. Thomas Wykes (*Ann. mon.*, 4.310–11) claims that Gloucester and other marcher lords urged Earl Edmund to grant a truce: they may have sympathized with Rhys's resistance to royal encroachments, and Rhys's mother was related to several of them. When Earl Edmund retired to England, Rhys was still at large.

On 2 November 1287 Rhys suddenly attacked and captured Newcastle Emlyn, and Llandovery was plundered two days later. The earl of Hereford, who was doubtless concerned for his lordship of Brecon, took charge of the defence of the upper Tywi valley; on 14 November other marcher lords and castle constables were told to be vigilant. Yet Rhys still evaded capture, and only at the end of December were steps taken to recover Newcastle Emlyn. The great siege-engine used at Dryslwyn was dragged to the castle by 10 January 1288 and within ten days the castle surrendered. Rhys again escaped, with a price on his head. Detachments of Welshmen scoured the Tywi valley and his Carmarthenshire adherents were pardoned on 6 November 1290, though vigilance was necessary so long as Rhys himself remained at large. Some believed that he planned to sail to Ireland to seek refuge on Gloucester's estates until Edward I returned from Gascony. Eventually, on 2 April 1292, he was betrayed in the Tywi valley by Madog ab Arawdr's four sons; they were rumoured to be Rhys's own men, though Madog had supported Rhys

Wyndod ten years earlier before making his peace with the king. Rhys ap Maredudd was sent in chains to Edward at York, where he was convicted of murder, arson, theft, and the destruction of royal castles; he was drawn and hanged on 2 June. His son Rhys was arrested and still languished in Norwich Castle in 1340; Rhys's widow, Ada, was allowed on 14 June 1293 to retain her own lands.

Rhys's obedience to the Carmarthen courts symbolized his subjection to the king's authority; Edward's seizure of Dinefwr Castle posed a threat to Rhys's personal position. His rebellion seems, with hindsight, to have been inevitable; its failure led to the completion of the English conquest of west Wales. His castle at Dryslwyn and the commotes of the Tywi valley were henceforward ruled by royal officials (from September 1287), and immigrant burgesses of the new town at Dryslwyn reinforced English control.   R. A. GRIFFITHS

Sources J. B. Smith, 'The origins of the revolt of Rhys ap Maredudd', BBCS, 21 (1964–6), 151–63 · R. A. Griffiths, 'The revolt of Rhys ap Maredudd, 1287–88', Welsh History Review / Cylchgrawn Hanes Cymru, 3 (1966–7), 121–45 · J. B. Smith, 'The Cronica de Wallia and the dynasty of Dinefwr', BBCS, 20 (1962–4), 261–82 · J. E. Morris, The Welsh wars of Edward I (1901) · J. G. Edwards, ed., Littere Wallie (1940) · J. G. Edwards, Calendar of ancient correspondence concerning Wales (1935) · Chancery records · PRO · J. C. Davies, ed., The Welsh assize roll, 1277–1284 (1940) · Ann. mon., vol. 4 · J. Williams ab Ithel, ed., Annales Cambriae, Rolls Series, 20 (1860) · A. Gransden, ed. and trans., The chronicle of Bury St Edmunds, 1212–1301 [1964]

Rhys ap Roppert (d. 1377). See under Tudor family, forebears of (per. c.1215–1404).

Rhys ap Tewdwr (d. 1093), ruler in Wales, was the son of Tewdwr ap Cadell ab Einion ab Owain ap Hywel Dda. Some genealogies omit Cadell, and by making Rhys a son of the Tewdwr ab Einion who died in 994, would have it understood that he performed the active deeds of his short reign between the ages of ninety and a hundred. He became king of Deheubarth in 1079, a year after the death of *Rhys ab Owain, his second cousin. According to the unreliable Brut Aberpergwm, he came from Brittany, but Brut Ieuan Brechfa, another late authority, says it was from Ireland, while the medieval chronicles give no hint that he was an exile at all.

For two or three years after his accession Rhys was harassed by the attacks of Caradog ap Gruffudd ap Rhydderch (d. 1081), who had now made himself master of the greater part of Gwent and Morgannwg. According to the twelfth-century Historia Gruffud vab Kenan, when Gruffudd ap Cynan (d. 1137) landed at Porth Glais, near St David's in 1081, he found Rhys a refugee in the cathedral precincts, willing to promise homage and the half of his realm to Gruffudd in return for assistance. While this part of the story may have been coloured by the biographer's provincial zeal, it is certain the two princes marched together against Caradog ap Gruffudd, Trahaearn ap Caradog, and Meilyr ap Rhiwallon, who met them at 'Mynydd Carn', a place not yet identified, but probably in south Cardiganshire. There a decisive battle was fought, in which Caradog, Trahaearn, and Meilyr fell, and the kingships of Gwynedd and Deheubarth were permanently secured to

the descendants of Gruffudd and Rhys respectively. Gruffudd's biographer alleges that he was distrusted by Rhys, who withdrew from him after the battle, and that in revenge he ravaged Rhys's lands.

Rhys was again involved in civil strife in 1088, when Madog, Cadwgan, and Rhirid, sons of Bleddyn ap Cynfyn (d. 1075), drove him into exile in Ireland. Before the end of the year, however, he returned with Irish assistance, and defeated the three in the battle of 'Llech-y-Crau' in which Madog and Rhirid fell. Another movement, due to the conduct of the relatives of Cydifor ap Gollwyn of Dyfed, who set up Gruffudd ap Maredudd against Rhys, was crushed in 1091 at the battle of Llandudoch (St Dogmaels). The Normans were now beginning that vigorous attack on south Wales which marked the reign of William Rufus, and in the Easter week of 1093 (17–23 April) Rhys met the new settlers of Brycheiniog in battle, and was slain. Both John of Worcester and the Welsh Bruts use language which implies that the blow was believed in that age to have put an end to kingship among the Welsh; Dyfed and Ceredigion were at once invaded by the Normans, and many years went by before the descendants of Rhys were able to restore the principality of south Wales. Rhys married Gwladus, daughter of Rhiwallon ap Cynfyn, and left three children: *Gruffudd (d. 1137), who after many years succeeded him; Hywel, who was imprisoned by Arnulf de Montgomery, but escaped with some bodily injury; and *Nest, who married Gerald of Windsor.

The circumstantial account given in the Brut Aberpergwm and in David Powell's Historie of Cambria of the relations between Rhys and Iestyn ap Gwrgan of Glamorgan is without historical authority. So, too, is the statement found in the Iolo manuscripts, that Rhys brought over from Brittany the 'system of the round table', with rules for the bards as they were observed in Arthur's time.

J. E. LLOYD, rev. DAVID E. THORNTON

Sources P. C. Bartrum, ed., Early Welsh genealogical tracts (1966) · J. Williams ab Ithel, ed., Annales Cambriae, Rolls Series, 20 (1860) · T. Jones, ed. and trans., Brenhinedd y Saesson, or, The kings of the Saxons (1971) [another version of Brut y tywysogyon] · T. Jones, ed. and trans., Brut y tywysogyon, or, The chronicle of the princes: Peniarth MS 20 (1952) · T. Jones, ed. and trans., Brut y tywysogyon, or, The chronicle of the princes: Red Book of Hergest (1955) · D. S. Evans, ed. and trans., A mediaeval prince of Wales: the life of Gruffudd ap Cynan (1990) [Eng. trans. of Historia Gruffud vab Kenan, with orig. Welsh text] · Florentii Wigorniensis monachi chronicon ex chronicis, ed. B. Thorpe, 2 vols., EHS, 10 (1848–9) · Ordericus Vitalis, Eccl. hist., 4.260 · A. Farley, ed., Domesday Book, 2 vols. (1783), 1.179b · The historie of Cambria, now called Wales, ed. D. Powell, trans. H. Lhoyd [H. Llwyd] (1584); repr. (1811) · O. Jones, E. Williams, and W. O. Pughe, eds., The Myvyrian archaiology of Wales, collected out of ancient manuscripts, new edn (1870) · T. Williams, ed., Iolo manuscripts (1848) · J. E. Lloyd, A history of Wales from the earliest times to the Edwardian conquest, 3rd edn, 2 vols. (1939) · K. L. Maund, Ireland, Wales, and England in the eleventh century (1991) · R. R. Davies, Conquest, coexistence, and change: Wales, 1063–1415, History of Wales, 2 (1987)

Rhys, Sir, ap Thomas (1448/9–1525), soldier and landowner, was the youngest legitimate son of Thomas ap Gruffudd ap Nicolas (d. c.1474) of Newton, Carmarthenshire, and Elizabeth, daughter of Sir John Gruffudd (d. 1471) of Abermarlais, Carmarthenshire; for forty years

(1485–1525) he was the king's principal lieutenant in south Wales. According to Rhys's biography, written in the 1620s by his descendant Henry Rice, he accompanied his father into exile at the Burgundian court after the Yorkist victory in 1461; he probably returned to Wales early in the 1470s, only to discover that his family was still eclipsed during Edward IV's restored regime. It also suggests that Rhys declined to support Henry Stafford, duke of Buckingham and lord of Brecon, in his rebellion in 1483 because the two families were at odds. Richard III sought to win Rhys's support with an annuity of 40 marks; but this may not have prevented him from communicating with Henry Tudor in Brittany, perhaps even promising to support Henry's invasion in 1485. According to the biography, Richard III demanded the surrender of Rhys's only legitimate son, Gruffudd, as a guarantee of his loyalty. Although the *Life* claims that Rhys welcomed Henry Tudor on arrival in Pembrokeshire on 7 August 1485, he is likely to have been cautious about declaring for the insurgents, and there was uncertainty about his attitude while he shadowed Henry's advance through mid-Wales. Outside Welshpool on about 16 August the forces of Rhys and Henry joined for the march to Bosworth (22 August). Even before they met, Henry seems to have indicated that Rhys would be his chief lieutenant in Wales if Richard III were vanquished. Henry's favour to Rhys immediately after Bosworth, and their intimate relationship throughout Henry VII's reign, suggest that their collaboration in 1485 was well prepared. Rhys's assistance at Bosworth was significant, and one Welsh poet (Guto'r Glyn) seems to imply that he struck the blow that killed the king. Rhys served King Henry primarily as a powerful landowner in south Wales and a skilled soldier.

After 1485 Rhys's position in Wales was second only to that of the king's uncle, Jasper Tudor: 'a man noted for strength of will and military experience' and 'an excellent leader in war' (*Anglica historia*, 52, 97). He offered such steadfast loyalty that seventeenth-century tradition noted that Henry VII called him 'Father Rice'. Knighted three days after Bosworth and a member of the king's household soon after, in November 1485 Rhys was appointed for life the king's lieutenant and steward of Brecon, steward of Builth, and chamberlain of south Wales; he dominated Carmarthen—perhaps Wales's largest town—as its mayor on four occasions between 1488 and 1516. As an outstanding soldier, especially in command of light cavalry, he helped to suppress the Brecon rising of 1486, Simnel's rebellion in 1487, the Cornish rising of 1497, and Warbeck's rebellion of October 1497; he also accompanied the king on his French expedition in October 1492. After Jasper Tudor's death (1495) Rhys acquired further responsibilities, as justiciar of south Wales (January 1496) and constable of Aberystwyth Castle for life (April 1502). His son Gruffudd was close to Prince Arthur (d. 1502) and was buried near Arthur's chantry chapel in Worcester Cathedral in 1521. Henry VII's regard for Rhys led to his election as a knight of the Garter in 1505; the festivities at Carew Castle in April 1506 to celebrate the anniversary of his election are recounted in detail in the later biography.

Henry VIII likewise relied on Rhys's loyalty and military skill: he was confirmed in his Welsh offices, and by August 1509 was steward of Pembroke. In 1513 he commanded 3000 infantry and light cavalry at the sieges of Thérouanne and Tournai, and his energy, daring, and experience contributed to victory over the French at the battle of the Spurs (16 August). He and his son became steward and receiver of Haverford and Rhos in May 1517, and it is likely that Gruffudd ap Rhys, who was frequently at the king's court, was groomed to succeed to his father's position; but Gruffudd died suddenly and intestate in 1521. It was Sir Rhys who was commissioned to guard Milford Sound and defend Ireland in the early 1520s.

Rhys's annual income from land, offices, and annuities was about £1500 by 1509; his estates, acquired by inheritance, marriage, and mortgages, lay mainly in Carmarthenshire, and to a lesser extent in Pembrokeshire and Cardiganshire. He married first Efa, daughter of Henry ap Gwilym of Carmarthenshire, and, second, probably in the early 1480s, Jenet, sister of Sir William Mathew of Radur and widow of Thomas Stradling of St Donats, Glamorgan. He had half a dozen mistresses and at least a dozen children, who were married into gentry houses of south Wales. His greatest coups were the marriages of his heir, Gruffudd, to Catherine St John, daughter of Sir John St John of Bletsoe, Bedfordshire, and the king's kinswoman, and of his grandson, Rhys ap Gruffudd, to Catherine, daughter of Thomas Howard, duke of Norfolk (c.1521). Carew Castle and estate, Pembrokeshire, which he may have acquired in the 1490s, became his main, imposing residence. The family home at Newton was small, though his mother's home at Abermarlais was renovated, and Newcastle Emlyn was used for hunting. Weobley Castle in Gower was also modernized by Rhys. His opulent household attracted poets from Glamorgan and north Wales, most notably Tudur Aled (d. 1525). They lauded his descent and Tudor connections, his military accomplishments in defeating Richard III, the French, and various rebels, and his election to the Garter. He was compared to heroes of romance, and Rhys himself commissioned a copy of the Welsh prose translation of 'La Queste del Saint Graal' (NL Wales, Mostyn MS 184). He spent his last years securing the inheritance of his grandson, Rhys ap Gruffydd (c.1508–1531). He died in the spring of 1525 and was buried at the Greyfriars, Carmarthen; his tomb was transferred to St Peter's Church, Carmarthen, after the dissolution.

R. A. GRIFFITHS

Sources R. A. Griffiths, *Sir Rhys ap Thomas and his family: a study in the Wars of the Roses and early Tudor politics* (1993) · PRO · Carmarthen RO, Dynevor MSS · NL Wales, Dynevor papers · *Chancery records* · 'A short view of the long life of … Rice ap Thomas', *Cambrian Register*, 1 (1796), 49–144 · P. C. Bartrum, ed., *Welsh genealogies, AD 1400–1500*, 18 vols. (1983) · R. A. Griffiths and R. S. Thomas, *The principality of Wales in the later middle ages: the structure and personnel of government*, 1: *South Wales, 1277–1536* (1972) · J. M. Lloyd, 'The rise and fall of the house of Dinefwr (the Rhys family), 1430–1530', MA diss., U. Wales, 1963 · *The Anglica historia of Polydore Vergil, AD 1485–1537*, ed. and trans. D. Hay, CS, 3rd ser., 74 (1950) · *Gwaith Tudur Aled*, ed. J. G. Jones, 2 vols. (1926) · PROB Bodfeld, PRO, 35
Archives Bristol RO, MS 04720 (1)

Likenesses effigy on tomb, c.1525, St Peter's Church, Carmarthen

Rhys ap Tudur (d. 1411). *See under* Tudor family, forebears of (*per. c.*1215–1404).

Rhys Cain (c.1540–1614), poet and herald, was the son of Rheinallt ap Siôn Wyn ap Siôn ab Ieuan Fychan and his wife, Gwen, daughter of Robert ap Siancyn Fychan. He took his bardic name from the River Cain in recognition of his family's association with the parish of Llansanffraid-ym-Mechain, through which that river flows. Rhys himself settled in Oswestry, Shropshire. His paternal grandmother hailed from that town, which was also the home of Wiliam Llŷn, Cain's bardic teacher. In his will of 1580 Llŷn left Cain 'all the books and rolls that I have' (Morrice, xxi), and by 1587 Cain was residing in the house in Willow Street which Llŷn had left to his wife, Elizabeth. Rhys Cain survived his first wife, Gwen (d. 1603), and he himself was buried in Oswestry on 10 May 1614, leaving a second wife, Catrin.

Eulogies and elegies in the *cywydd* metre, addressed primarily to the gentry of north-east Wales, account for approximately 200 of Rhys Cain's 280 or so extant poems. The earliest, to Edward Trefor of Bryncunallt, was composed in 1560. He sang the praises of Wiliam Morgan (in 1583, and again between 1601 and 1604), Dr John Davies, and fellow poets Thomas Price and William Midleton. His best-known poem, however, was his eulogy to Wiliam Llŷn, which features a discourse between the dead and the living, a device skilfully employed by Wiliam Llŷn himself on previous occasions. The rest of his poems are mostly *englynion*, again to members of the gentry or to fellow poets such as Siôn Phylip, but Rhys's religious inclinations are also conveyed. He rues the destruction of holy relics and castigates those responsible. A series of 113 *englynion* exhorts the blessing of the Trinity when a pestilence broke out at Oswestry.

Many of the *cywyddau* that have survived are Rhys's own copies. Several are dated—fifty-six poems in Peniarth MSS 68–69 were composed between 1573 and 1582—but equally interesting are the folds on individual pages which indicate that the poet had carried them on his person during his visits to his patrons' homes. A unique list of payments totalling £23 2s. 6d.—more than 100 items are recorded—which he received during one poetic tour is found in his hand in Peniarth MS 178. Sadly, the year in question is not noted, nor the exact nature of the services rendered. Fragments of genealogical and heraldic material in his hand have survived, together with a bardic grammar. According to nineteenth-century biographies he was also a painter, but none of his work has survived.

Four of Rhys Cain's children were baptized in Oswestry between 1579 and 1592, but **Siôn Cain** (d. c.1649), whose work and career closely mirror those of his father, was probably born earlier (c.1575). Of his 370 surviving poems, all, with the exception of a handful of *englynion*, are eulogies and elegies in the traditional *cywydd* and *awdl* metres, mostly to the gentry of north-east Wales. Significantly, 270 are recorded only in Siôn's own hand. They are found in Peniarth MS 116 (a substantial 900-page compilation of poems composed between 1623 and 1648) and Peniarth MS 117 (composed between 1609 and 1648). Here again, the folds on the individual pages are evident. Although Siôn's earliest known poem is dated 1607, a cursory examination of the surviving material suggests that his most industrious period covered the twenty years between 1625 and 1645. He opens his poems with oft-repeated formulae, and even duplicates parts of his father's compositions.

Heraldic and genealogical material in Siôn Cain's hand survives in several manuscripts. He corresponded with the antiquary Robert Vaughan, as did his father, and many of the manuscripts collected and copied by father and son found their way to Vaughan's library at Hengwrt. Records in his hand in Peniarth MS 327 suggest that Siôn Cain was also involved, at one stage in his life, in husbandry.

A. Cynfael Lake

Sources *Computerized index of Welsh manuscript poetry at the National Library of Wales* (1978) • P. C. Bartrum, ed., *Welsh genealogies, AD 1400–1500*, 18 vols. (1983) • *Report on manuscripts in the Welsh language*, 2 vols. in 7, HMC, 48 (1898–1910) • *DWB* • E. D. Jones, 'Presidential address', *Archaeologia Cambrensis*, 112 (1963), 1–12 • D. Huws, 'Wiliam Llŷn, Rhys Cain a Stryd Wylow', *National Library of Wales Journal*, 18 (1973–4), 147–8 • D. J. Bowen, 'Croesoswallt y Beirdd', *Y Traethodydd*, 135 (1980), 137–43 • D. J. Bowen, 'Cynefin Wiliam Llŷn', *Barn*, 197–215 (1979–80), 206–8, 271–3 • G. Gruffydd, 'Y Beibl a droes i'w bobl draw' (1988) • J. C. Morrice, *Barddoniaeth Wiliam Llŷn* (1908) • J. T. Jones, *Geiriadur bywgraffyddol o enwogion Cymru*, 2 vols. (1867–70) • T. E. Parry, 'Llythyrau Robert Vaughan, Hengwrt', MA diss., U. Wales, Bangor, 1961
Archives NL Wales, corresp. • NL Wales, genealogies • NL Wales, heraldry

Rhys Fychan ap Rhys ap Maelgwn (d. 1302). *See under* Gruffudd ap Rhys (d. 1201).

Rhys Goch ap Rhicert (*fl. c.*1200), supposed poet, was the son of Rhicert ab Einion ap Gollwyn and Ellyw, daughter of *Rhys Gryg [see under* Gruffudd ap Rhys (d. 1201)]. His paternal grandfather, *Einion ap Gollwyn, was a Glamorgan magnate whom tradition held largely responsible for the betrayal of the kingdom of Glamorgan to the Normans; paradoxically many of Einion's descendants became notable professional poets and patrons of professional poetry during the fifteenth and sixteenth centuries. Nothing is known of Rhys Goch apart from his genealogy, which locates him around the turn of the twelfth century, and the origin of his epithet 'Goch' ('the Red') is obscure. In 1799 Edward Williams, Iolo Morganwg (d. 1826), while searching for manuscripts in north Wales, discovered and transcribed five love poems in the 'free' (that is, accentual) metres which were probably composed by the notable later sixteenth-century Anglesey poet Llywelyn ap Hwlcyn. Some time later Williams embellished these five poems and composed a further fifteen in similar style. The twenty poems he then ascribed to Rhys Goch, and they were published as such by Williams's son Taliesin in 1848. Williams's intention was to demonstrate that a species of Welsh courtly love poetry had evolved in twelfth-century Glamorgan under the influence of the troubadours who were supposed to have visited the Norman courts of the region, and that this poetry was later to become important in the literary formation of Dafydd ap Gwilym (*fl.* 1330–1350); Rhys Goch's name was presumably plucked out of the genealogy by Williams because he belonged to an important literary family and because he lived at approximately the right time. Williams's thesis held sway for over seventy years until it was finally demolished by the young Griffith John Williams (1892–1963), later professor of Welsh at Cardiff, in 1920. The success of his deception must largely be attributed to the high quality of the poems which he forged.   R. GERAINT GRUFFYDD

Sources P. C. Bartrum, ed., *Welsh genealogies, AD 300–1400*, 8 vols. (1974), 302 [Einion ap Gollwyn 2] · T. Williams, ed., *Iolo manuscripts* (1848), 228–51, 645–51 · J. H. Davies, ed., *Casgliad o hen ganiadau serch* (1902) · G. J. Williams, 'Rhys Goch ap Rhiccert', *Y Beirniad*, 8 (1918–20), 211–26, 260 · C. W. Lewis, *Iolo Morganwg* (1995), 99–104

Archives BL, Add. MS 14974, fols. 22r–23v, 78v–79r, 84v–85r, 86r–87r · NL Wales, MS 13127A, 579/2–580, 581, 583–584, 585–586, 587–588, 590, 591–595 · NL Wales, MS 13160A, 35–36, 56–57, 59, 61–62, 63–64, 133–136

Rhys Goch Eryri (*fl.* 1385–1448), poet, was the son of Dafydd ab Ieuan Llwyd. According to tradition, his home was Hafod Garegog near Beddgelert; his name means Rhys the Red of Snowdonia. He was a bardic pupil of Gruffudd Llwyd, and is named by him as a promising young poet in his 'Cywydd y cwest', *c.*1385. Rhys composed an elegy on Gruffudd's death (*c.*1420), in which he states that he was almost the same age as his teacher. He in his turn is said to have been bardic teacher to Dafydd Nanmor. The elegy to Gruffudd sparked off a testy exchange with the younger poet Llywelyn ab y Moel, who saw in it an insult to the land of Powys, and that then led to a more fundamental debate on bardic principles with Siôn Cent, who denied Rhys's claim that the bardic inspiration was of divine origin. Rhys lived to sing an elegy on the death of Llywelyn ab y Moel in which he refers to a total eclipse of the sun, probably that of February 1440. None of Rhys's poems refers directly to Owain Glyn Dŵr, but he clearly supported his cause, as can be seen from ironic comments in two poems addressed to members of the Penrhyn family who had opposed Glyn Dŵr. Some fifteen of his poems have survived, mainly praise poetry in a rather opaque style, but also including an account of the death of St Beuno. His last poem, an elegy to Maredudd ap Cynfrig of Anglesey, can be dated to 1448, and Rhys probably died soon after that. He is known to have had one daughter, Margaret, whose son Morus Gethin was an amateur poet in the early sixteenth century.   DAFYDD JOHNSTON

Sources *Cywyddau Iolo Goch ac eraill*, ed. H. Lewis, T. Roberts, and I. Williams, new edn (1937)

Rhys Gryg (*d.* 1233). *See under* Gruffudd ap Rhys (*d.* 1201).

Rhys, Ernest Percival (1859–1946), writer and literary editor, was born in Islington, London, on 17 July 1859, second of the five children of John Rhys (*b.* 1839?), and his wife, Emma, daughter of Robert Percival, a breeder and doctor of horses, of Hockerill, Hertfordshire. John Rhys had been a divinity student who gave up his studies when he married at the age of eighteen, and he was working in a bookshop in London at the time of his son's birth; he later became a wine merchant. Ernest Rhys spent most of his childhood in Carmarthen and in Newcastle upon Tyne. After a home education and two years at Bishop's Stortford, 1866–8, he went to a private school in Newcastle. But he refused to go to Oxford, 'tempted by the open-air life and the chance of horses to ride' offered by mining engineering. He passed his examinations, but in January 1886 he returned to London to earn his living as a writer.

Establishing his base as the British Museum Reading Room, Rhys soon became a familiar figure in literary London. Although he never enjoyed popular success, and was too painstaking and slow a writer to earn a substantial income as a journalist, editors were always glad to have his reviews. He became close friends with W. B. Yeats, who shared his passion for eastern mysticism, Madame Blavatsky, and Celtic gossip. In February 1890 they founded the Rhymers' Club, a group of young poets, including Richard Le Gallienne, Lionel Johnson, Arthur Symons, and Ernest Dowson, who met in an upper room at the Cheshire Cheese, in Fleet Street, 'where long clay pipes lay in slim heaps on the wooden tables between tankards of ale', to recite their verses. The Rhymers published two collections of poetry (1892, 1894); Rhys contributed to both. His first solo volume, *A London Rose and other Poems* (1896), won the admiration of Robert Louis Stevenson, who wrote from Samoa urging him to 'cultivate your native potato'. 'The Leaf Burners', written during the First World War, has been included in several anthologies; but his best poem is generally agreed to be the quatrain 'An Autobiography', with its opening line 'Wales England wed, so I was bred'.

Writers are, however, often remembered by posterity for work by which they themselves set little store, and Rhys is remembered less as a poet than as the editor of Everyman's Library. Sponsored financially by J. M. Dent, this library was planned, in Rhys's words, as 'a collection of the great literatures, beginning with the English, so co-ordinated that if its readers began with one creative book, they would want another and another till the great public had the world literature within its grasp'. Its title was taken from the medieval mystery play, and the quotation:

Everyman, I will go with thee, and be thy guide,
In thy most need to go by thy side

appears on every title-page. Beginning in 1906 with Boswell's life of Johnson, 153 volumes were published in the first twelve months; and when Rhys died, 983 volumes had appeared. In editing this library in face of many difficulties, some of which he has described in his autobiography *Everyman Remembers* (1931), Rhys performed a genuine service to literature. But he regarded this task as the necessary hack work which would buy him leisure in which to write poems and essays.

On 5 January 1891 Rhys married Grace (*d.* 1929), youngest daughter of a country squire, Bennett Little JP, of co. Roscommon, whom he met at a garden party given by Yeats. A lady of great charm and culture, Grace published, among other works, three volumes of *belles-lettres*. The couple worked and lived together as a team, and when

Grace died on Rhys's lecture tour in 1929 in Washington, DC, he was devastated. They had one son and two daughters, and 'Sunday afternoon at the Rhys's' was for many years an opportunity for poets, novelists, and critics to meet and discuss their problems. As his autobiography shows, Rhys was well acquainted with practically every important literary figure in his lifetime—from Robert Browning to Dylan Thomas—but was never too busy to provide kindness, encouragement, and help to the young and struggling. He was a much loved man. He died in a nursing home at 82 Inverness Terrace, Bayswater, London, on 25 May 1946, and was cremated at Golders Green.

ALEC WAUGH, rev. KATHARINE CHUBBUCK

Sources J. K. Roberts, *Ernest Rhys* (1983) · E. Rhys, *Everyman remembers* (1931) · E. Rhys, *Wales England wed* (1940) · N. Alford, *The Rhymers' Club: poets of the tragic generation* (1994) · L. W. Griffith, 'Ernest Rhys', *British Annual of Literature* (1939) · E. Rhys, 'Introduction', in R. F. Sharpe, *The reader's guide to Everyman's Library* (1931) · A. Conran, *The cost of strangeness* (1982)
Archives NRA, corresp. and literary papers | CUL, letters to E. H. Blakeney · JRL, letters to *Manchester Guardian* · NL Wales, corresp. with Thomas Jones · U. Edin. L., corresp. with Charles Sarolea · U. Leeds, Brotherton L., letters to Clement Shorter
Likenesses L. Moholy, photograph, 1938, NPG · D. Bell, pencil drawing, NMG Wales · W. H. Caffyn, pen-and-ink drawing, repro. in Rhys, *Everyman remembers* · photograph, repro. in Roberts, *Ernest Rhys* (1983)
Wealth at death £3615 4s. 4d.: probate, 22 Aug 1946, CGPLA Eng. & Wales

Rhys, Jean. *See* Williams, Ella Gwendoline Rees (1890–1979).

Rhŷs [*formerly* Rees], **Sir John** (1840–1915), Celtic scholar, was born John Rees at Aberceiro-fach, Ponterwyd, Cardiganshire, on 21 June 1840, the eldest son of Hugh Rees (*d.* 1886), a farmer and lead miner, and his wife, Jane Mason (*d.* 1863). Rees received his early education at Brynchwyth, Pantyffynnon, and Ponterwyd, moving in 1855 to the newly opened British School at Penllwyn, near Aberystwyth, where he was a pupil teacher. After a course of study at the Bangor Normal College (1860–61), he was appointed headmaster of the British School at Rhos-y-bol, Anglesey, in January 1861. In 1865 he was introduced by Chancellor James Williams, of Llanfair-yng-Nghornwy, Anglesey, to Dr Charles Williams, principal of Jesus College, Oxford. After a brief oral examination, Rees was offered a place at Jesus College and entered in October 1865. He took a second class in classical moderations in 1867, and a first class in *literae humaniores* in 1869. Towards the end of 1869 he was elected fellow at Merton College. During his time at Oxford he spent his summer vacations studying abroad and visited Paris, Heidelberg, Leipzig, and Göttingen; he matriculated at Leipzig in 1871. While at Leipzig, Rhŷs attended the lectures of, among others, Georg Curtius and August Leskien, and his interest in philology and linguistics was fired.

In 1871 Rhŷs, who adopted the Welsh spelling of his name in early adulthood, returned to Wales as HM inspector of schools for the counties of Flint and Denbigh and made his home at Rhyl. During this time he began publishing articles on Celtic grammar and contributed

Sir John Rhŷs (1840–1915), by James Russell & Sons

important articles on the glosses in the Luxembourg manuscript to the first three volumes of the *Revue Celtique* (1870). A course of lectures delivered at Aberystwyth in 1874, published later under the title *Lectures on Welsh Philology* (1877), established his reputation as a Celtic scholar of the first rank; and when the Jesus professorship of Celtic was founded at Oxford in 1877 he was elected first professor. At the same time he was made an honorary fellow of Jesus College, and in 1881 he became official fellow and bursar. He was bursar until 1895, when he was elected principal of the college, succeeding Dr Hugo Harper.

Rhŷs was first and foremost a scholar, and, although he served as member of the hebdomadal council from 1906 to 1911, the administrative side of academic life had little attraction for him. However, for forty years he worked tirelessly in the cause of educational and social progress. He served on Lord Aberdare's departmental committee on Welsh education (1881), and was secretary to Sir John Bridge's commission on the tithe agitation in Wales (1887) and to the royal commission on Sunday closing in Wales (1889). He was also a member of the royal commission on land tenure in Wales (1893), of the royal commission on university education in Ireland (1901), of Sir Thomas Raleigh's commission on the Welsh university and its constituent colleges (1907), and of Chief Baron Palles's commission for a national university of Ireland (1908). At the time of his death (1915) he was chairman of the Royal Commission on the Ancient and Historical Monuments of

Wales and Monmouthshire. From its formation in May 1886, Rhŷs served as president of the Dafydd ap Gwilym Society at Oxford. He was also chairman of the council of the Honourable Society of Cymmrodorion, and was awarded the society medal in 1912. In recognition of his public services Rhŷs was knighted in 1907, and in 1911 was sworn of the privy council. He received the honorary degree of LLD from the University of Edinburgh in 1893, and that of DLitt from the University of Wales in 1902.

As a scholar, Rhŷs combined with industry and learning a singularly active, reconstructive imagination. Although his principal interest was in Celtic and Welsh philology, his researches took him into many fields. Beginning as a grammarian, he resumed and continued his linguistic and epigraphic investigations in *The Outlines of the Phonology of Manx Gaelic* (1894), and in a series of papers read to the British Academy. He made a substantial contribution to the history of the Celts in Britain and travelled widely across western Europe, studying Celtic inscriptions, particularly the Ogam inscriptions of Wales and Ireland. His historical works included *Celtic Britain* (1879), 'Studies in early Irish history' in the *Proceedings of the British Academy* (1903), *The Welsh People* (with D. Brynmor-Jones, 1900), and 'Celtae and Galli' in *Proceedings of the British Academy* (1905). To the literature of the history of religion, archaeology, ethnology, and folklore he contributed his Hibbert lectures, published as *On the Origin and Growth of Religion, as Illustrated by Celtic Heathendom* (1888), his presidential address to the anthropological section of the British Association (1900), his Rhind lectures at Edinburgh entitled *The Early Ethnology of the British Isles* (1889), *Studies on the Arthurian Legend* (1891), *Celtic Folklore: Welsh and Manx* (1901), and numerous articles in the publications of the Honourable Society of Cymmrodorion. Almost his only excursion into the field of literary research is represented by 'The englyn: the origin of the Welsh englyn and the kindred metres' (vol. 18 of the *Cymmrodor*, 1905). He also collaborated with J. Gwenogvryn Evans in the preparation of three volumes of texts of early Welsh manuscripts, *The Text of the Mabinogion* (Red Book of Hergest) (1887); *The Text of the Bruts* (Red Book of Hergest) (1890); *The Text of the Book of Llan Dav* (Gwysaney MS) (1893).

Rhŷs married Elspeth Hughes-Davies (*d.* 1911) of Llanberis on 6 August 1872; they had two daughters, Myfanwy and Olwen. He died at The Lodgings, Jesus College, Oxford, on 17 December 1915, and was buried on 23 December at Holywell cemetery, Oxford. The British Academy, of which he became fellow in 1903, founded the Sir John Rhŷs Memorial Lecture to be delivered annually in his memory; the first lecture, delivered by his disciple Sir John Morris-Jones, gave a full bibliography of his works. The breadth of knowledge and scholarship exhibited in his numerous publications in the fields of philology, archaeology, folklore, and ethnology serve as testimony of Rhŷs's great contribution to Celtic learning. In these fields he was foremost among the scholars of his time, and his pioneering studies provided a firm foundation for future Celtic scholarship and research for many decades.

JOHN FRASER, *rev.* MARI A. WILLIAMS

Sources J. Morris-Jones, 'Sir John Rhŷs', *PBA*, 11 (1924–5), 187–212 · T. H. Parry-Williams, *John Rhŷs, 1840–1915* (1954) · *Transactions of the Honourable Society of Cymmrodorion* (1914–15), 195–249 · J. Y. Evans, 'Representative Welshmen, VI', *Wales*, 2 (Feb 1912), 91–4 · E. V. Evans and D. Ll. Thomas, 'Sir John Rhŷs, 1840–1915', *Welsh Outlook*, 3 (1916), 12–15 · V. Evans, 'Syr John Rhŷs', *Y Geninen*, 34 (1916), 73–7 · *DWB* · *Archaeologia Cambrensis*, 6th ser., 16 (1916), 98–100

Archives NL Wales, corresp. and papers · U. Wales, Aberystwyth, corresp. and papers | BL, letters to J. Romilly Allen, Add. MSS 37582–37587 · NL Wales, letters and postcards to John Glyn Davies · NL Wales, Dolaucothi corresp. · NL Wales, T. E. Ellis MSS · NL Wales, letters mainly to D. S. Evans · NL Wales, Gregynog Press archives · NL Wales, W. J. Gruffydd MSS · NL Wales, D. R. Hughes MSS · NL Wales, letters to Johnes family · NL Wales, Llwyngwair deeds and documents · NL Wales, D. R. Phillips MSS · NL Wales, Lord Rendel MSS · NL Wales, A. J. Williams MSS · NL Wales, corresp. with A. W. Wade-Evans and J. T. Evans · U. Wales, Bangor, letters from him and his family to William Jones

Likenesses W. G. John, marble bust, exh. RA 1909, NL Wales · C. Williams, oils, 1913, NMG Wales; repro. in Parry-Williams, *John Rhŷs* · S. J. Solomon, oils, exh. RA 1915, Jesus College, Oxford; study, NPG · Elliott & Fry, photograph, NL Wales · Gregynog Press, wood-engraving, NL Wales · Humphreys, carte-de-visite, NL Wales · J. Russell & Sons, photograph, NPG [*see illus.*] · E. Walker, photograph (after photograph by J. Russell & Sons), repro. in *Transactions of the Honourable Society of Cymmrodorion* · oils, British Academy, London

Wealth at death £14,483 9s. 7d.: probate, 22 Feb 1916, *CGPLA Eng. & Wales*

Rhys, Keidrych. *See* Jones, William Ronald Rees (1915–1987).

Rhys, Morgan (1716–1779), hymn writer and schoolmaster, was born on 1 April 1716, in Efail Fach, Cil-y-cwm, Carmarthenshire, one of nine children born to Rhys and Ann Lewis. Little is known of his early life but there is ample evidence in the annual *Welsh Piety* reports of the high praise he received for his successful work as a teacher in the circulating schools of Carmarthenshire and Cardiganshire from 1757 to 1775. He was already known as a 'Methodistical teacher' during this period, although nothing can be said of the personal influences on him. As a teacher in the circulating schools he would have been required to catechize his pupils and prepare them to take their place in the life of the established church. Nevertheless, Morgan Rhys lived in an area where early Methodists like William Richard were active. Howel Harris met what he called the Society of Ministers and Exhorters not far from Cil-y-cwm, in January 1742, and he was present too in the next 'association' in nearby Llwynyberllan in February. Both he and Daniel Rowland preached several times in the district before Rhys began his career as a 'Methodistical teacher'. The young man may well have fallen under the sway of such powerful advocates of the new spirituality. He moved later to a smallholding in the parish of Llanfynydd, where a Methodist chapel was built in 1771, and became known as Morgan Rhys, Llanfynydd.

Morgan Rhys's first collection, *Golwg o ben Nebo ar wlâd yr addewid* (1755), contained only eleven hymns. This was followed two years later by another small collection of seven hymns, *Cascliad o hymau* (1757). In 1760 appeared *Casgliad o hymnau am gwymp dyn*, with twenty-two hymns. By now the demand for his work was growing, and a second and augmented edition of *Golwg o ben Nebo* was published in 1764 (seventy-four hymns) and a third in 1775 (eighty-six). The year 1767 saw the publication of *Golwg ar ddull y byd hwn* (thirty-eight) and 1770 *Golwg ar y ddinas noddfa* (nineteen). Eleven and eight hymns appeared in the two undated parts of *Griddfannau'r credadyn am berffeithrwydd ac anllygredigaeth*. Another undated collection of hymns, *Y frwydr ysprydol*, contained the work of Thomas Dafydd and Morgan Rhys, and a few hymns were included with some of the elegies Rhys wrote. Some hymns were republished in his collections but the greater part of this substantial body of work was original. His popularity was further underlined by the pirated publication in Trefriw (1778) of *Golwg a'r y ddinas noddfa*, under the name of Robert Thomas.

Rhys died at Llanfynydd and was buried there on 9 August 1779. In his will he bequeathed 3 guineas each to such Methodist leaders and hymnists as Daniel Rowland, William Williams Pantycelyn, David Morris Tŵr Gwyn, and David Jones Llan-gan.

Morgan Rhys is generally regarded as second only to William Williams of Pantycelyn as a hymnist. His work was the muscular, comprehensive expression of an intense religious experience and shows a consistent christological emphasis. The precepts of Calvinistic Methodism are the strong guidelines of his experience, keeping him from yielding to human doubt or uncertainty, a virtue in the opinion of later Calvinistic commentators. He sings vividly of the oppressions and dangers to be suffered in this vale of tears, but his theology always enables his hymns to rise to a triumphant thanksgiving for the joys of salvation offered to the predestined elect. This was an irresistibly attractive message in eighteenth-century Wales, and its clarity still recommends it to most denominations.   E. G. MILLWARD

Sources N. Davies, 'Bywyd a gwaith yr emynydd Morgan Rhys', MPhil diss., U. Wales, 1991 · G. M. Roberts, *Morgan Rhys, Llanfynydd* (1951) · J. Thickens, *Emynau a'u hawduriaid*, rev. edn (1961), 133–40 · D. S. Evans, 'Well done, Morgan Rhys!', *Ysgrifau Beirniadol*, 11 (1979), 177–90 · M. Davies, 'Emynyddiaeth', *Y Traethodydd*, 26 (1872), 57–60 · A. Griffiths, M. Rhys, D. Jones o Gaes, and D. William, *Pedwar emynydd*, ed. B. Jones (1970), 52–74 · G. H. Jones, 'Morgan Rhys yr emynydd', *Y Drysorfa*, 100 (1931), 106–10, 241–6, 272–3 · H. Elvet Lewis, ed., *Gwaith Morgan Rhys* (1910) · E. G. Millward, ed., *Blodeugerdd Barddas o gerddi rhydd y ddeunawfed ganrif* (1991), 123–8 · B. F. Roberts, 'The literature of the "great awakening"', *A guide to Welsh literature*, ed. B. Jarvis, 4: *c.1700–1800* (2000), 279–304, esp. 291–2 · G. O. Williams, 'Morgan Rhys', *Gwŷr llên y ddeunawfed ganrif*, ed. D. Morgan (1966), 75–82 · parish records, Cil-y-cwm, Llanfynydd, County Hall, Carmarthen, Carmarthenshire RO · bishop's transcripts, NL Wales

Wealth at death under £100: will as reported by biographers

Rhys, Morgan John (1760–1804), Baptist minister and writer, was born on 8 December 1760 at Graddfa farmhouse, in the parish of Llanfabon, Glamorgan, the fourth of five sons of John and Elizabeth Rhys. John Rhys was a farmer and warden of the parish church; Elizabeth Rhys was a Baptist and a member at Hengoed. Rhys may have received his early education in one of Griffith Jones's circulating schools, and as a youth he helped his father on the farm. It was his father who thwarted Rhys's ambition to become a doctor. After a period as a clerk in London, he booked his passage to Charles Town, but had to return home to Wales because his mother was ill.

Rhys experienced an evangelical conversion and on 6 August 1785 was baptized by full immersion at Hengoed. Encouraged by the church, he undertook ministerial training at the Baptist college in Bristol but left in 1787 without completing his studies, in order to accept a call from the Baptist church at Pen-y-garn, near Pontypool. Ordained in October 1787, he was minister there for four years. He also preached widely in what he called the 'dark places' of south Wales, targeting places where no one had preached before, and made two preaching tours to north Wales in 1788 and 1789.

In the summer of 1791, taking the opportunity of a visit to Kent to take the waters, Rhys impulsively decided to visit revolutionary France to preach protestant civil and religious liberty. He landed at Calais, on the evening of 24 August 1791. Meeting with initial success, he re-opened a former Catholic church at Boulogne. He planned to establish preaching stations at Dunkirk and Calais as well as travelling to Brittany to preach to the Bretons in 'their native language'. He visited Paris and later proudly recalled that he had stood on the ruins of the Bastille.

Before the end of the spring of 1792 Rhys had returned to Wales where he continued his itinerant preaching. His energies turned to the 'poor peasants' of Wales. Using the presses of the Methodists at Trefeca, he published the first volume of his *Cylchgrawn Cynmraeg* ('Welsh magazine') in February 1793. The *Cylchgrawn* has been called the first political journal in the Welsh language, but the subject matter was deliberately diverse and included debate on the reform of the Welsh alphabet, as well as millenarian comments upon the events of the French Revolution. The *Cylchgrawn* was to raise funds to preach the gospel among the 'Welsh' Indians in America (popularly believed to be the descendants of Prince Madoc, who had supposedly discovered America in the twelfth century). Rhys translated the Virginia declaration of religious freedom into Welsh as well as extensive extracts from the millenarian work of James Bicheno, and John Rippon's *Baptist Annual Register*. The *Cylchgrawn* had to be abandoned, for the want of time and sufficient encouragement, in April 1794 after five numbers.

Rhys was a candid critic of oppression in all its forms: in his fast day sermon of February 1794, he stood up for the victims of warfare and attacked the government's policy of waging ungodly war. He defined persecution broadly, and sensing a worsening of conditions for dissenters, he fled to America in August 1794, fearing arrest. None the less, his flight to America was also the fulfilment of a long-held dream. He landed in New York in October 1794 and embarked on a journey which took him to the frontier as well as the eastern states. Applying his millenarian perspective to the contemporary American scene he identified the Antichrist with the institution of slavery. The nadir of his confidence in America as a New Canaan occurred in Savannah, Georgia, in February 1795 where he helped to establish a black church against the opposition of local slaveholders.

In the Northwest Territories, Rhys encountered Major-General Anthony Wayne and his 'legion' who were on the point of signing the treaty of Greenville with the defeated Indian nations. Unpopular with the army officers, in particular the army chaplain, on account of his defence of Indian property rights, he returned to Philadelphia. He married Ann Loxley (1775–1849), the daughter of Colonel Benjamin Loxley, on 22 February 1796 and resided at the home of his in-laws. He paid a brief return visit to the south and it was from Charleston and Savannah early in 1797 that he wrote his *Letters on Liberty and Slavery*.

Back in Philadelphia, Rhys's time was taken up by ministering to a mixed communion of Welsh Independents, Calvinistic Methodists, and Baptists and in paying visits to a site 200 miles west of Philadelphia, where he had purchased lands to site a colony for his fellow Welsh emigrants, which he named Beulah. The land deed was signed in October 1796 and in November the first settlers arrived. The deed provided for a non-sectarian Christian church, but the church at Beulah rapidly became an orthodox Baptist cause, as the paedobaptist element withdrew to form Ebenezer Independent Church, north of Beulah. The rivalry between the two communities contributed to Beulah's decline as a focus for settlement. Rhys busied himself in activities outside the church, opening a day and Sunday school, planning to set up a public library, and running a communal newspaper. In 1802, he abandoned the ministry and became the clerk of the court for Somerset county, where he died on 7 December 1804. He was buried in the cemetery of the First Baptist, Philadelphia. Mostly forgotten in Wales, Rhys came to be remembered in the Baptist historiography of the nineteenth century as a 'man far in advance of his age' (J. Spinther James, *Seren Gomer*, Sept 1898, 257–8). HYWEL MEILYR DAVIES

Sources G. A. Williams, *The search for Beulah land* (1980) · J. J. Evans, *Morgan John Rhys a'i amserau* (1935) · J. T. Griffith, *Revd Morgan John Rhys* (1910) · H. M. Davies, '"Transatlantic brethren": a study of English, Welsh and American Baptists with particular reference to Morgan John Rhys (1760–1804) and his friends', PhD diss., U. Wales, 1984
Archives BL, corresp. with John Rippon, Add. MSS 25386–25389 · NL Wales, Hengoed Baptist Church register
Likenesses silhouette, after 1794, repro. in Griffiths, *Revd Morgan John Rhys*, facing p. 9
Wealth at death $728.11—$532.99 in possessions; $195.12 in cash and fees owed to him: Somerset county will book 1, 1804, testament and estate

Rhys, Siôn Dafydd [John Davies] (*b.* **1533/4**, *d.* in or after **1620**), grammarian, was born at Llanfaethlu, Anglesey, the son of Dafydd Rhys and Sioned or Annes. His immediate forefathers were craftsmen, but a genealogy contained in a manuscript held at the British Library traces his pedigree back to Iarddur ap Cynddelw (BL, Harley MS 5058, p. 90). Richard Davies, bishop of St Asaph (1559–61) and later of St David's (1561–81), may have been his uncle.

Rhys received his early education locally, possibly at a school attached to Bangor Cathedral. Thomas Parry has refuted claims made in Taliesin ab Iolo's *The Doom of Colyn Dolphyn* (1837), based on manuscripts by Iolo Morganwg (Llanover MS C8 and C42), of Rhys's early connection with the Stradlings of Glamorgan.

Wood's *Athenae Oxonienses* states that Rhys was elected a scholar of Christ Church, Oxford, in December 1555, aged twenty-one, when he had already spent three or more years in Oxford. According to college battel records he seems to have ceased payments in August or December of 1556, suggesting he may have left Oxford. Geraint Gruffydd conjectures that he departed for the continent, travelling via the Low Countries to northern Italy in the company of Morys Clynnog, a member of Cardinal Reginald Pole's household and himself a former member of Christ Church.

Four letters at the Biblioteca Palatina at Parma testify to the fact that Rhys was newly arrived in Italy in 1563, coinciding with the Council of Trent's last sitting. They confirm that Rhys was engaged as tutor to the sons of Vincenzo Gheri, brother of the bishop of Ischia, at Pistoia in September 1563. During this period he produced a Greek grammar written in Latin, now lost, as well as a Latin grammar in Italian which was published in Venice in 1567. He subsequently attended the University of Siena, possibly through the sponsorship of a friend, the former privy councillor and now Catholic exile Sir Robert Peckham. Rhys received the degree of doctor of medicine at Siena in July 1567. He then travelled widely within Italy and further afield, visiting—according to his own admission in his 1592 Welsh grammar—Crete and Cyprus.

In Padua in 1569 Rhys published a Latin handbook on the pronunciation of Tuscan Italian which was dedicated to Sir Robert Peckham. *De italica pronunciatione et orthographia libellus* was the first systematic account of Italian phonetics and has been described by Gwynfor Griffith as Rhys's masterpiece. In comparing the pronunciation of Tuscan Italian to that of other European languages, including Welsh, English, Portuguese, and Polish, Rhys reveals a keen ear and an exceptionally wide linguistic knowledge. A work of pioneering linguistic scholarship in its time and still of value to historians of the Italian language today, the handbook may have been inspired by William Salesbury's *A Brief and Playne Introduction*, a guide to the pronunciation of Welsh that was published in 1550.

Rhys returned to Wales early in the 1570s, becoming 'chief schoolmaster' at the newly founded Friars' Grammar School at Bangor in 1574. Late in 1576 or early in 1577 he was summoned by his 'uncle', Bishop Richard Davies, to his palace at Abergwili near Carmarthen, perhaps to assist in translating protestant books into Welsh following the acrimonious departure of William Salesbury. During his stay at Abergwili he claimed to have completed Welsh translations of the official Homilies of the Church of England, parts of the Old Testament, and an elementary catechism by Dean Nowell.

Following the death of Richard Davies in 1581 Rhys proceeded to Cardiff, where he became acquainted with the gentry families of Glamorgan—in particular the Herberts of Wilton and the Stradlings of St Donat's—along with Gervase Babington, later bishop of Llandaff, one of whose catechisms Rhys translated into Welsh. In Cardiff too he met and married Agnes Garbet (*d.* 1617) of Hereford. Early in 1584 they moved to the Brecon area and made their home in the borough, with a retreat at Clun Hir in Cwm Llwch.

Now a burgess of Brecon and a successful physician, Rhys was accused in 1587 of concealing a Roman Catholic printing press in his house and of harbouring recusant beliefs. No corroborating evidence was found but he was forced once again to take the oath of supremacy. Nevertheless, a translation of St Vincent of Lérins's *Tractatus aureus* which may well have been his work, and his presumed part in compiling *Y drych Cristionogawl*, an adaptation of Robert Person's *Book of Christian Exercise Appertaining to Resolution*, suggest that he remained a secret Roman Catholic until the end of his life.

Rhys's Welsh grammar, entitled *Cambrobryttanicae Cymraecaeve linguae institutiones et rudimenta*, was published in 1592 and dedicated to his patron, Sir Edward Stradling. Written in Latin in order to communicate the features of the Welsh language to scholars outside Wales, it comprises a Latin-based grammar of Welsh and a lengthy discussion of the elements of Welsh prosody, which Rhys imperfectly comprehended. The grammar's dedication and preface make reference to Rhys's bitter quarrel with Bishop Marmaduke Middleton of St David's, which dominated his life at this time.

In 1597 Rhys completed two treatises. The first, *Cyngor i feirdd a dysgedigion Cymru* (a letter of advice to the poets and learned men of Wales), contained in the Panton 2 manuscript at the National Library of Wales, is an important example of Welsh humanist literary criticism. The second, contained in the Peniarth 118 manuscript, is a historiographical treatise spanning more than 120 pages, defending the Brutus myth (as expounded in Geoffrey of Monmouth's influential *Historia regum Britanniae* in the early twelfth century) against attacks made by humanist historians such as Polydore Vergil in his *Anglia historia* of 1534. Drawing on arguments employed by other contemporary defenders of Geoffrey—notably Sir John Prise, Humphrey Lhwyd, and David Powel—the work demonstrates Rhys's vast learning and is written in a fine prose style.

Also extant is a manuscript tract by Rhys tracing King James I's Welsh antecedents, which was written in 1604. There is no trace of the dictionary on which he was said to be working by Thomas Wiliems of Trefriw and John Davies of Mallwyd. His Welsh adaptation of Aristotle's *Metaphysics*, a manuscript text belonging to Jesus College, Oxford, and reported to have been in the custody of Henry Vaughan, has also disappeared.

Only one of Rhys's seven sons, Walter Davies, an Anglican clergyman, survived his parents. Agnes died in 1617. There is evidence that Rhys was still alive in 1619; he may

have died about 1620. He was described by his contemporary William Camden as the 'most renowned and most learned' of Welsh humanists.　　ANGHARAD PRICE

Sources Wood, *Ath. Oxon.*, new edn, 2.61–2 • R. Geraint Gruffydd, 'Dr John Davies, "the old man of Brecknock"', *Archaeologia Cambrensis*, 151 (1992), 1–13 • R. G. Gruffydd, 'The life of Dr John Davies of Brecon', *Transactions of the Honourable Society of Cymmrodorion* (1971), 175–90 • T. Parry, 'Siôn Dafydd Rhys', *Y Llenor*, vol. 9, pp. 157–65, 234–41; vol. 10, pp. 35–46 • T. Parry, 'Gramadeg Siôn Dafydd Rhys', *BBCS*, 6 (1931–3), 55–62, 225–31 • T. Gwynfor Griffith, 'De Italica pronunciatione', *Italian Studies*, 8, 71–82 • T. Gwynfor Griffith, 'Italy and Wales', *Transactions of the Honourable Society of Cymmrodorion* (1966), 281–98 • T. Jones, *History of Brecknockshire* (1809), vol. 2 • H. Owen, 'Peniarth MS. 118, fols. 829-37. Introduction, transcript and translation', *Y Cymmrodor*, 28, 115–52 • G. J. Williams, 'Llythyr Siôn Dafydd Rhys at y beirdd', *Efrydiau Catholig*, 4, 5–11 • B. Jarvis, 'Llythyr Siôn Dafydd Rhys at y beirdd', *Llên Cymru*, 12, 45–56 • F. Noble, 'The Radnorshire MSS of Dr. John David Rhys (Siôn Dafydd Rhys)', *Transactions of the Radnorshire Society*, 26, 34–9 • A. B. Melchior, 'Siôn Dafydd Rhys, M. D. (Sienna)', *Sudhoffsarchiv*, 60/3 (1976), 289–94 • N. Maraschio, 'Sulla formazione italiana del grammatico gallese Joannes David Rhaesus (Rhys)', *Studi di Grammatica Italiana*, 9 (1980), 5–18
Archives BL, Cotton MSS Vespasian E.xi, Faustina E.ii • Cardiff Central Library, Cardiff MSS 18 (ii), 50 • NL Wales, Llanstephan MSS 55, 56, 68, 79 • NL Wales, Peniarth MSS 118, 252, 270, 316 • NL Wales, Panton MS 2

Riach, Nancy Anderson Long (1927–1947), swimmer, was born at 9 Allan Street, Motherwell, Lanarkshire, on 6 April 1927, the daughter of Charles Fraser Riach, a police constable who rose through the ranks of the Motherwell police force to become an inspector, and his wife, Agnes Nicol White, a primary school teacher. She attended Dalziel high school and went on to qualify as a teacher employed by Lanarkshire education authority.

Nancy Riach was one of the many young swimmers coached at the Motherwell amateur swimming and water polo club by David Crabb, the remarkable superintendent of the Motherwell corporation baths. He sought for the swimming club, and gave it, international prestige. He aimed to catch future swimming stars early, as young as seven. As a self-proclaimed communist (in a town where the party had some strength, particularly among steelworkers), Crabb led singing of 'The Red Flag' in the club coach and lent members left-wing books. His aim—in the long tradition of working-class 'self-help'—was to assist young people to rise, through sporting excellence, above the social and economic deprivation which they suffered in industrial lowland Scotland. He also created a water polo team which dismissed all opposition in Scotland, and in the years after the Second World War entered and won the English water polo cup competition.

Crabb persuaded the Motherwell and Wishaw council not only to maintain the swimming pool facility in wartime, but to let him train swimmers there until midnight and to open it on Sundays for practice sessions for his club. This dedication enabled him to insert a very young female swimmer into a wartime cultural gap, as the call-up of young males had reduced the status of football as a competitive sport.

The exploits of Nancy Riach brought her immediate and extensive fame. She won her first championship in 1938, competing against girls a year or two her seniors. She broke her first Scottish record at the age of fifteen, and within two years held twenty-eight records: Scottish native, Scottish all-comers, and British. She triumphed in freestyle, breaststroke, and backstroke.

Nancy Riach's background set her apart from other protégés of David Crabb. Her parents were members of the Orange order and voted Conservative, while the family house had two rooms, with kitchen, but also an inside lavatory, at a time when most of her fellow club members lived in tenements with outside lavatories. Nancy, who refused to compete in swimming tournaments on Sundays, echoing the stand taken by the Scottish sprinter Eric Liddell in the 1924 Olympics, attended church regularly, and she sang in the choir.

But Nancy Riach was not strait-laced. She went with the Motherwell 'swimming circus' to perform before capacity crowds in club galas, providing a wide range of aquatic spectacles which included a 'rhythmic swimming display' of a dozen swimmers accompanied by pipe and drum music. Vivacious and independent-minded, Nancy consented to model swimwear, and went along with the promotional efforts of Rex Kingsley, a sports journalist with the Glasgow *Sunday Mail*, who built her up as a 'forces' sweetheart', a clean-living icon of Scottish womanhood. Beating the English was a major part of her appeal. In an obituary piece, Kingsley quoted her saying:

> Oh Rex, remember that time [June 1945] we all went down to the Derby baths, Blackpool, for my attempt on the 880 yards? And all of us paraded along the promenade wearing the kilt. And remember that other night in the Marshall Street Baths in London when I won the 100 yards All Nations Challenge—and the Scots RAF boys in the gallery had the time of their lives? (Walker, 148)

She always swam, Kingsley insisted, not for herself, but 'for Scotland', and she received heavy fan mail from Scottish servicemen as far afield as Burma.

Others began to beat her records, though Riach still held seven at the time of her death. After the war her family moved to Airdrie and she practised in the baths there. Crabb turned his attention to another young swimmer, Cathie Gibson, who set twelve new British records in 1946 when just fifteen, and went on to win a bronze medal in the 1948 London Olympic games.

Nancy Riach had her sights on those Olympics when she went to Monte Carlo in September 1947 with the British team competing in the European championships, having just won the 100 metres freestyle title in the world student games in Paris. A polio epidemic was sweeping Britain, with hundreds of cases reported, many of them fatal. Nancy Riach succumbed to polio, though not before, against doctor's orders, she had insisted on swimming in the 100 metres freestyle heats. The flight of her parents to be at her hospital bedside was front-page news in Scotland. They arrived too late: she died early in the morning of 15 September 1947. Tributes poured in. S. T. Hirst, of the United Nations swimming committee, said that 'She was undoubtedly the finest swimmer that the British Empire

has produced. Nancy Riach has been the finest ambassador of sport that Scotland or any other country within the British Empire has ever turned out' (*The Scotsman*). In her brief life she had become a heroine in Lanarkshire, a sporting idol for all Scots, and a pin-up for Scottish soldiers serving overseas.

Nancy Riach was buried, in Airdrie, on 20 September, dressed in her swimming costume. Thousands lined the route of her last journey to the cemetery. A target of £20,000 was soon set for a permanent memorial to her in Motherwell, but disputes between interested parties prevented this from being created. However, the Scottish amateur swimming association raised a fund which from 1949 provided a Nancy Riach memorial medal for the person judged to have done the most 'to acclaim Scottish swimming during the year'. Nancy Riach's great rival Cathie Gibson won this in 1951. Though other Scottish swimmers later achieved excellence, the sport did not maintain the prominence in national consciousness which it had gained in the 1940s through Nancy Riach's exploits.   ANGUS CALDER

Sources G. Walker, 'Nancy Riach and the Motherwell swimming phenomenon', in G. Jarvie and G. Walker, *Scottish sport in the making of the nation* (1994), 142–53 · *Glasgow Herald* (15–17 Sept 1947) · *Glasgow Herald* (22 Sept 1947) · *Glasgow Herald* (26 Sept 1947) · *The Scotsman* (16 Sept 1947) · *Sunday Mail* (21 Sept 1947) · P. Bilsborough, *One hundred years of Scottish swimming* (1988) · b. cert.

Riall, Sir Phineas (1775–1850), army officer, born in Ireland, probably in Clonmel, on 15 December 1775, was third son of Phineas Riall of Heywood, co. Tipperary, and his wife, Catherine, daughter of Charles Caldwell of Dublin. He was commissioned ensign in the 92nd foot on 31 January 1794, becoming lieutenant on 28 February, and captain on 31 May. On 8 December 1794 he was appointed major in the 128th foot, but the regiment was reduced soon afterwards, and he remained unattached until April 1804, when he became major in the 15th foot. He had been made a brevet lieutenant-colonel on 1 January 1800.

The 15th (1st battalion) went to the West Indies in 1805, and in 1809–10 it took part in the expeditions under General Sir George Beckwith against Martinique and Guadeloupe. In both cases Riall commanded a brigade. He was praised in dispatches. In the capture of the Saintes Islands, which followed that of Martinique, he volunteered to storm Fort Morelli with his regiment, but the risk was thought too great. He was made brevet colonel on 25 July 1810, and on 27 December 1810 he became lieutenant-colonel of the 69th.

On 4 June 1813 Riall was promoted major-general, and in September he was sent to Canada, at that time hard pressed by United States troops. He was employed in Upper Canada, and in the winter, under orders from Lieutenant-General Gordon Drummond, he destroyed Buffalo and other villages on the south side of the Niagara in reprisal for the burning of Newark, and to deprive the enemy of resources. In July 1814 a force of 4000 Americans under General Brown crossed the Niagara and took Fort Erie. Riall had only 1500 regulars and 600 militia and Indians, but he advanced to meet Brown, and attacked him on the 5th at Street's Creek. He was repulsed with a loss of more than 500 men, and fell back on the entrenched camp of Chippewa, near the falls.

Fearing that his communications would be cut off, Riall retreated in the latter part of the month towards Niagara, but was met by General Drummond, who was bringing up reinforcements. These raised the British strength only to 2800 men, but they consisted of veteran regiments from the Peninsula. Drummond at once attacked the Americans (25 July), and, after several hours' fighting, drove them back on Fort Erie. Riall was severely wounded (losing an arm), and was taken prisoner. Drummond wrote of him: 'His bravery, zeal, and activity have always been conspicuous.' He sailed for England on parole in December 1814.

Riall was governor of Grenada from 1816 to 1823, and in December 1819 he married Elizabeth Scarlett. He was promoted lieutenant-general on 27 May 1825, and general on 23 November 1841. He was appointed colonel of the 74th on 20 May 1835, and transferred to his old regiment, the 15th, on 24 April 1846. He was made KCH in 1831 and was knighted in 1833. Riall died in Paris on 10 November 1850.

E. M. LLOYD, rev. ROGER T. STEARN

Sources GM, 2nd ser., 35 (1851) · J. Philippart, ed., *The royal military calendar*, 3rd edn, 5 vols. (1820) · DCB, vol. 7 · *Annual Register* (1814) · R. Cannon, ed., *Historical record of the fifteenth, or the Yorkshire East Riding regiment of foot* (1848) · W. James, *A full and correct account of the military occurrences of the late war*, 2 vols. (1818) · H. J. Morgan, ed., *The Canadian men and women of the time* (1898)
Archives NRA, corresp. and papers

Ribblesdale. For this title name *see* Lister, Thomas, fourth Baron Ribblesdale (1854–1925).

Ribeiro, Samuel [*formerly* Diogo] **Nunes** (*b.* 1667/8, *d.* in or after **1741**), physician, was born and baptized in the parish of Nossa Senhora da Conceição, Idanha a Nova, Portugal, the son of Manuel Henriques Lucena and Maria Nunes, who were of Jewish origin. He qualified as a doctor of medicine after studying at Coimbra, Salamanca, and Piacenza, and commenced practice in Abrantes. In 1698 he settled in Lisbon, where in June 1699 he married Gracia Caetana da Veiga (*b.* 1676).

On 23 August 1703 Nunes and his wife were arrested by the Lisbon inquisition and charged with Judaizing. His initial resistance was broken down, and he confessed and gave information against thirty-six other people. Because he protected his wife he was tortured until he implicated her. On 19 October 1704 he was sentenced at a public *auto da fé*; Gracia held out until she too was tortured and went out in an *auto da fé*, on 6 September 1705. Then further information was extracted from her parents and three sisters. Nunes and his wife were both sentenced again in September 1706 for relapsing, and were imprisoned. Their property was confiscated but they escaped execution, possibly because the inquisitor-general had been one of Nunes's patients. After his release Nunes became one of the leading physicians of Lisbon. His nephew, Antonio Nunes Ribeiro Sanches (1699–1783), who became physician to Empress Anna Ivanovna of Russia, wrote that it was during a visit to his uncle in 1721 that he learnt from

him about the inquisition and was first introduced to Judaism.

In April 1726 the inquisitors learned that Nunes had helped Manoel Rodrigues Sarzedas and his family to escape to England, and Nunes became aware that he was in danger. He then had a house on the banks of the Tagus, from which he planned his family's escape from Portugal. He converted his assets into gold and diamonds; the men put the gold into leather money belts, and the women quilted the diamonds into their dresses. In summer 1726 Nunes held a luncheon party at his house. One of the guests was the captain of an English brigantine, who had promised to carry the family to England for 1000 gold moidores. The captain invited the guests to visit his ship, and while they were taking refreshment in the cabin the vessel weighed anchor and set sail for England with the whole party, including a familiar of the inquisition employed to invigilate the family—leaving their house with its furniture and servants and the lunch set out on tables on the lawn.

In London in August 1726 Nunes and his family converted to open Judaism. Nunes's friend Dr Isaac de Sequeira Samuda acted as godfather at his circumcision. Diogo and Gracia took Jewish names and remarried as Samuel and Ribca Nunes Ribeiro. Nunes found it difficult to establish himself in London, and after seven years decided to emigrate. The trustees for Georgia had appointed three Portuguese Jews, Alvaro Lopes Suasso, Antonio da Costa, and Francis Salvador, as commissioners to promote the new colony. They decided to send some of their poor to Georgia and, to the annoyance of the trustees but to the benefit of the colony, dispatched a ship with forty-two Jewish settlers, including the Nunes family.

On 10 July 1733 Samuel Nunes, his wife, three sons, and two daughters arrived in Savannah, where Governor James Oglethorpe allotted him a 50 acre plot. Nunes's experience of the yellow fever epidemic in Lisbon in 1723 proved valuable. In 1737 Oglethorpe reported that precautionary measures enforced on Nunes's advice had stopped an epidemic, which had killed twenty of the colonists. In August 1740 a Spanish attempt on the colony was expected and, dreading the inquisition, the Nunes Ribeiro family left Savannah for New York, where their daughter Sipora (or Zipra) married David Mendes Machado, the cantor of the Shearith Israel Synagogue. Nunes's name appears in its minute book in 1741, when he was seventy-three, but not thereafter. He probably died in New York, but the burial register for this period has not survived. Nunes and his family suffered severe persecution for their faith. He showed great resilience in establishing himself as a pioneer settler in America.

EDGAR SAMUEL

Sources R. D. Barnett, 'Dr Samuel Nunes Ribeiro and the settlement of Georgia', *Migration and settlement*, ed. A. Newman (1971) · R. D. Barnett, 'Zipra Nunes' story', *A bicentennial festschrift for Jacob Rader Marcus*, ed. B. W. Korn (New York, 1976) · R. D. Barnett, ed., *Bevis Marks records*, 4: *The circumcision register of Isaac and Abraham de Paiba (1715–1775)* (1991) · M. Lemos, *Ribeiro Sanches a sua vida e a sua obra* (Oporto, 1911) · E. M. Coulter and A. B. Saye, eds., *A list of the early settlers of Georgia* (1949) · *The Lyons collection*, 2, Publications of the American Jewish Historical Society, 27 (Baltimore, MD, 1920) ·

L. D. Barnett, ed., *Bevis Marks records*, 2: *Abstracts of the Ketubot or marriage contracts of the congregation from earliest times until 1837* (1949) **Archives** Instituto dos Arquivos Nacionais, Torré do Tombo, Lisbon, Inquisição de Lisboa, processo 2307 de Diogo Nunes Ribeiro · Instituto dos Arquivos Nacionais, Torré do Tombo, Lisbon, Inquisição de Lisboa, processo 3054 de Gracia Caetana da Veiga

Ricardo, David (1772–1823), political economist, was born on 18 April 1772 at 36 Broad Street Buildings in the City of London, the third surviving child of Abraham Israel Ricardo (1733?–1812) and his wife, Abigail Delvalle (1753–1801). Sarah Ricardo *Porter was his sister. The Ricardos belonged to the population of Spanish and Portuguese Jews who had been forced by the Inquisition to emigrate, in their case to Amsterdam, where they were established by the eighteenth century. Abraham Ricardo had followed his father into stockbroking on the Amsterdam exchange. He settled in London around 1760 and in 1769 married Abigail, whose father was a tobacco and snuff merchant, and was granted denizenship in 1771. A wealthy man, Abraham was a devout Jew and a prominent member of the Spanish and Portuguese Jewish community in London. He held strong prejudices, particularly in matters of religion, politics, and education, and insisted on strict, unquestioning compliance from his children. His independently minded son David was to react strongly against his rigid upbringing.

Family and professional life The young Ricardo was groomed to follow in his father's steps and his education was reportedly typical of those who were destined for a mercantile life. Notably, however, his early education included a two-year spell in Amsterdam, though the precise details of the sojourn are unknown. At the age of fourteen he began working for his father as a clerk and messenger on the stock exchange and, although he was apparently allowed to have private tutors, it would seem that his subsequent education contained a strong autodidactic element. Later in life he complained bitterly of his lack of a sustained, formal education, especially in the art of written composition.

In 1792 the Ricardo family moved to Bow, close to the house of Edward Wilkinson, a Quaker and surgeon. Before long David was romantically involved with Wilkinson's reputedly beautiful daughter Priscilla Ann (1768–1849), though it seems that parental obstacles forced the young couple into a courtship by correspondence. In December 1793 David and Priscilla were married, much to the displeasure of both sets of parents. In Ricardo's case the consequences were profound: he was removed from his father's business, disinherited, and disowned by his mother—with whom he never spoke again—and his father, with whom he was reconciled only after his mother's death. The marriage was also the occasion for Ricardo's breach with his Jewish faith, a breach which, according to some accounts, was the culmination of a long period of characteristically independent soul-searching. Subsequently Ricardo attended the meetings of the Unitarians, although there is evidence to suggest that he was, or became, an agnostic. As he wrote:

David Ricardo (1772–1823), by Thomas Phillips, exh. RA 1821

On these difficult points I keep my mind in a state of doubt from which in this world I can never be relieved. To account for evil in a world governed by a being of unbounded benevolence and power is or appears to be impossible. (*Works and Correspondence*, 7.206)

Estranged from his father, Ricardo embarked upon what was to become a hugely successful financial career. As a jobber on the stock exchange, and a loan contractor for government stock, he soon amassed a sizeable fortune, which allowed him in 1815 to begin a gradual retirement from business. From 1814 onwards he invested heavily in land, in loans on mortgages, and in French funds. The total value of his estate at death has been estimated at between £675,000 and £775,000 (1823 prices).

As Ricardo's wealth grew, so too did his family and social standing. Eight children were born between 1795 and 1810. Of the three sons, two—Osman and David—were to become MPs, and the third—Mortimer—became captain in the Life Guards and deputy lieutenant of Oxfordshire. From 1812 the family's prestigious London address was 56 Upper Brook Street, Grosvenor Square. To this was added in 1814 Ricardo's country seat of Gatcombe Park, Gloucestershire. At Gatcombe the Ricardos entertained lavishly, often hosting large, sumptuous dinner parties that would extend well into the small hours. Ricardo, a slim man, below average height with a high-pitched voice, was himself temperate in habits, but he was also sociable, humorous, and addicted to intelligent debate and conversation. Once he had entered the squirearchy (he was high sheriff of Gloucestershire in 1818), acquired his reputation as an intellectual and a political economist, and become a prominent MP (he took his seat in 1819), his company was increasingly sought by luminaries of the aristocracy, the political classes, and the intelligentsia. Ricardo was highly gratified by his success, especially by his success as an authority on his favourite subject (as he described it), political economy.

The bullion controversy Ricardo's interest in political economy was aroused in 1799 by chancing upon a copy of Adam Smith's *The Wealth of Nations* in a travelling library while on a visit to Bath. Before this time it is known (as his brother Moses relates) that his predilection towards subjects of an abstract and general nature had led to a leisurely interest in scientific areas, including mathematics, chemistry, geology, and mineralogy (he was a founder member of the Geological Society in 1807). With political economy, he had stumbled across a subject which (he believed) could be treated abstractly according to the scientific principles of the time, resonated with his own experience, was intensely topical, and appeared to bear on matters no less weighty than the general welfare of society. It was to prove an irresistible mixture. Yet, although his interest was awakened, to the point where he became an avid reader of articles in the whiggish *Edinburgh Review*, he was for several years too preoccupied with furthering his financial career to regard political economy as anything more than 'an agreeable subject for half an hour's chat' (*Works and Correspondence*, 7.246). The turning point came in 1809.

The free convertibility of paper currency into gold had been suspended with the Bank Restriction Act of 1797, after which a disparity had developed between the value of coin and the (depreciated) value of banknotes. The 'bullion controversy' addressed the reasons for the depreciation of the paper currency, and it was this controversy that Ricardo joined in 1809 with an anonymous letter in the popular whig newspaper the *Morning Chronicle*. Ricardo's principal contention, developed subsequently in further letters to the *Morning Chronicle* and in his (signed) pamphlets *The High Price of Bullion* (1810–11) and *Reply to Mr. Bosanquet* (1811), was that the depreciation of the paper currency was owing to the Bank of England's over-issue of notes which, in the absence of convertibility, had resulted in an increase of prices of approximately 20 per cent and a rise in the market over the mint price of gold. The remedy he proposed was a (phased) return to convertibility. His case was prosecuted with syllogistic precision and, also typical of his approach, flourishing references to the 'scientific' principles of the subject.

The contributions to the bullion controversy brought Ricardo to the attention of leading political and intellectual figures, including Thomas Robert Malthus and James Mill. Both Malthus and Mill were to play critical roles in the development of Ricardo's subsequent career. Their influences were, however, profoundly different. At the time of Ricardo's entrance on the public stage, Malthus was a seasoned writer, the author of the controversial *Essay on Population*, and arguably the most prominent political economist of the day. Although he and Ricardo became, and remained, close friends, their intellectual relationship was marked by disagreement over numerous issues bearing on virtually all branches of the new 'science' of political economy. While Ricardo borrowed from Malthus on some points (including population theory and the theory of differential rent), many of the characteristic features of his work evolved dialectically from his long-running intellectual skirmishes with his contemporary. Scholars of Ricardo (and Malthus) are fortunate to find a high proportion of the extensive Ricardo–Malthus correspondence preserved in the superb edition by Piero *Sraffa, *The Works and Correspondence of David Ricardo*.

James Mill also became a close friend of Ricardo but his role was more akin to a manager's. Although he had been an early contributor of articles on political economy to the *Edinburgh Review*, at the time of meeting Ricardo he was engrossed in writing his *History of British India* and it seems unlikely that he directly contributed much to the development of Ricardo's political economy (possibly with the exception of the 'law of markets' and, more uncertainly, the theory of comparative advantage in international trade). But he evidently saw in Ricardo a kindred spirit whose talents were deserving of his nurture. Mill advised, encouraged, cajoled, and even (only semi-humorously) bullied the ever reticent and easily distracted Ricardo, who almost certainly would not have completed his major work without Mill's prodding. It was also Mill, the associate of Jeremy Bentham and popularizer of Bentham's work, who was to push the initially sceptical Ricardo in the direction of political utilitarianism and persuade him to enter parliament. Without Mill, it seems improbable that Ricardo's star would have risen above the general horizon.

On the Principles of Political Economy and Taxation Following his involvement in the bullion controversy, Ricardo's next significant publication was his *Essay on the influence of a low price of corn on the profits of stock; shewing the inexpediency of restrictions on importation* (1815). As its title suggests, the *Essay* was written in opposition to (controversial) proposals for the imposition of new, higher duties on the importation of corn. Ricardo's central argument was as follows. On the assumption that free importation *is* prohibited, the increasing demand for corn from a growing population would have to be met either by the more intensive cultivation of land already under the plough, or from new, less fertile or more disadvantageously situated land. Either way, the expansion of output would tend to encounter diminishing returns which would in turn lead to a higher price of corn, higher money wages (since corn, or bread, was the staple food of the labourers), and therefore a lower general rate of profits. Only the landlords would benefit in virtue of their receiving more *differential* rent; for, as Malthus had argued, rent is a category of income which derives from and is equal to the *difference* in return from the 'best' land and the 'worst' (the assumption being that the 'worst' land yields no income above that required to give farmers the general rate of profit). As for the capitalists (including the capitalist farmers), they would suffer directly from the fall in profitability, while the labourers would shoulder the consequences of a reduction in the demand for labour, itself a result of lower profitability. Hence Ricardo's pithy deduction, which was not to endear him to the country gentlemen (of whom he was now one), that 'the interest of the landlord is always opposed to the interest of every other class in the community' (*Works and Correspondence*, 4.21).

The *Essay* was to prove a watershed in Ricardo's intellectual development; it was a transitional work in which Ricardo repudiated some of the fundamental tenets of the prevailing orthodoxy, as derived from Adam Smith and upheld by Malthus, while failing to supply a fully consistent logical alternative. It was Mill who persuaded Ricardo to develop and publish his ideas in the form of a major treatise. In August 1815 Mill threatened Ricardo with 'no rest, till you are plunged over head and ears in political economy' (*Works and Correspondence*, 6.252). Two years later Mill's exhortations were rewarded with the publication of Ricardo's *On the Principles of Political Economy and Taxation* (1817, hereafter abbreviated to *Principles*), the work for which Ricardo is best remembered. But authorship of his major work had not come easily. Apart from difficulties with the subject matter, Ricardo had also to contend with a hectic social life, recurring bouts of lethargy and defeatism, a 'temptation of being out in the air in fine weather' (*Works and Correspondence*, 6.264), business interests, and the demands of a large family. He was also side-tracked by a commitment he had made to Pascoe Grenfell MP to write a pamphlet subsequently published under the title *Proposals for an Economical and Secure Currency* (1816), in which Ricardo inveighed against the large profits made by the Bank of England as a result of their dealings with the government, canvassed his plan for a return to paper currency convertibility with gold bullion rather than minted coin, and intimated his approval for the establishment of an independent central bank (a proposal developed in the posthumous *Plan for the Establishment of a National Bank*, 1824). All things considered, the *Principles* was the outcome of little more than six or seven months' sustained activity on Ricardo's part.

The 'principal problem in Political Economy' is defined in the *Principles* as the determination of the 'laws' which regulate 'the natural course of rent, profit, and wages' over time. These issues had been addressed in the *Essay* and, indeed, the *Principles* was initially conceived by Ricardo as an *Essay* writ large. In the process of writing the later work, however, its scope was enlarged in previously unforeseen ways as Ricardo developed his ideas. The result was a volume comprising thirty-one chapters, covering not only the 'laws' governing rent, profit, and wages (which were broadly similar to ideas put forward in the *Essay*), but also a newly developed labour theory of value (explaining the relative values of commodities by the relative amounts of labour time expended on their production), a theory of international comparative advantage (according to which a country may benefit from trade even though it has an absolute cost disadvantage in the production of all commodities), monetary theory, several chapters devoted to 'the influence of taxation on different classes of the community', and strictures on the writings of predecessors and contemporaries. Following the publication of an essentially unchanged second edition in 1819, the third edition of 1821 contained a new chapter 'On machinery' in which Ricardo, borrowing from the work of John Barton, famously declared that 'the opinion entertained by the labouring class, that the employment of machinery is frequently detrimental to their interests, is not founded on prejudice and error, but is conformable to the correct principles of political economy' (*Works and Correspondence*, 1.392). It also contained a substantially rewritten chapter 'On value', in which Ricardo attempted to defend himself against penetrating criticisms of his labour theory which had been articulated by Malthus in the latter's own *Principles of Political Economy* (1820).

Political career There was a great deal riding on the success of the *Principles*, not just Ricardo's gathering reputation as a political economist. Mill had suggested in 1815 that Ricardo should enter parliament, a suggestion from which the latter had recoiled with horror. One year later Ricardo was becoming more amenable to Mill's plan, writing to his friend: 'If my book succeeds, perhaps my ambition will be awakened, and I may aspire to rank with senators' (*Works and Correspondence*, 7.113). In fact, though his book did not meet with unanimous acclaim, it did succeed to an extent far surpassing Ricardo's self-deprecatory expectations. With this success Ricardo's circle widened to embrace notables including Lord Grenville (the former prime minister), the marquess of Lansdowne (previously chancellor of the exchequer and now a leader of the whig opposition), and Sir Samuel Romilly (erstwhile solicitor-general and the whig with whom Ricardo had perhaps the greatest affinity); also, around the same time (1817–18), Ricardo was elected to the King of Clubs (associated with the Edinburgh Reviewers) and to Brooks's Club, the centre for the parliamentary whig opposition (he was proposed by Lord Holland and Lord Essex). Ricardo thus succumbed to Mill's plan.

Ricardo took his seat in parliament on 26 February 1819, succeeding his acquaintance Richard 'Conversation' Sharp as the (independent) member for the rotten borough of Portarlington in Ireland—a constituency which Ricardo never visited, where sheep vastly outnumbered the twelve or so electors, and for which Ricardo had advanced the sum of £25,000 to Lord Portarlington as a loan on the mortgage on his estates. At first terrified by the sound of his own voice, Ricardo gradually gained in confidence, availing himself of every opportunity to educate the house in the 'true principles of political economy'. These principles, enunciated both from the floor of the house and in select committees, dictated, *inter alia*: the gradual repeal of trade restrictions generally and of the corn law in particular; the gradual repeal of the poor laws; the repayment of the national debt (which Ricardo believed heroically could be accomplished over two or three years by the imposition of a property tax); minimal taxation and a balanced budget; and a return to a convertible currency. With the signal exception of convertibility (Peel's bill of 1819 for the resumption of cash payments owed much to his proposals), Ricardo found himself on the losing side, but that did nothing to shake his convictions. His parliamentary contributions mark him as a zealous advocate of a free-market capitalist system with minimal government interference—far more zealous and uncompromising than Adam Smith before him—who believed that Great Britain 'would be the happiest country in the world, and its progress in prosperity would be beyond the power of imagination to conceive, if we got rid of two great evils—the national debt and the corn laws' (*Works and Correspondence*, 5.55). Additionally, Ricardo spoke out on a range of liberal issues, including religious tolerance, slavery, freedom of speech, and the right to petition (he opposed the Six Acts). He also aligned himself with the radical cause for the reform of parliament, the subject on which he most clearly distanced himself from mainstream whig opinion.

The contention that good government would not be achieved without a reform of parliament had been put to Ricardo by James Mill in 1815 but was at that time rejected on the grounds that Mill both exaggerated the 'sinister interest' of politicians in pursuing their own ends and undervalued the corrective influence of enlightened public opinion. Three years later Ricardo's position had changed. Partly as a result of Mill's bombardment of Ricardo with radical messages, partly because of Ricardo's growing conviction that the tory government was failing to pursue 'right measures', and finally after reading Jeremy Bentham's *Plan of Parliamentary Reform*, Ricardo was won over to the radical cause. As he came to argue, good government—government 'administered for the happiness of the *many*, and not for the benefit of the *few*' (*Works and Correspondence*, 7.299)—required that politicians should 'legislate for the public benefit only, and not ... attend to the interests of any particular class' (*Works and Correspondence*, 8.275); yet, under present arrangements, politicians fell prey to the interests of particular classes, especially the landed class (*vide* the 1815 corn law); hence the necessity for reform. However, Ricardo's proposals fell some way short of those of his radical contemporaries. The introduction of the secret ballot was, for him, an almost sufficient basis for securing good government under existing circumstances, although he did make a case for triennial parliaments and a modest extension of the franchise to include householders. He might therefore be described as a moderate reformer in the utilitarian tradition of Bentham and Mill: as he once declared, 'I ... am a disciple of the Bentham and Mill School' (*Works and Correspondence*, 8.52).

Ricardo's parliamentary duties made significant encroachments on his time, although they did not prevent him from contributing an article headed 'Funding system' to the *Encyclopaedia Britannica* (1820), making extensive changes to the third edition of his *Principles* (1821), co-founding the Political Economy Club (1821), reiterating his opposition to the corn laws in the pamphlet *On Protection to Agriculture* (1822), drafting his *Plan for the Establishment of a National Bank* (1823), and embarking on a grand tour of continental Europe with his family (1822). In the last year of his life he painted the following picture of

life at Gatcombe to an old friend: 'we shall walk and ride, we will converse on politics, on Political Economy, and on Moral Philosophy, and neither of us will be the worse for the exercise of our colloquial powers' (*Works and Correspondence*, 9.377). But it was not to be. On 11 September 1823 Ricardo died at Gatcombe Park from the effects of an abscess in the middle ear. One week later he was buried in the churchyard of St Nicholas Hardenhuish, near Chippenham, Wiltshire, adjoining the Hardenhuish Park estate of his daughter Henrietta and her husband, Thomas Clutterbuck.

Evaluation Maria Edgeworth, a friend of Ricardo, described him as 'altogether one of the most agreeable persons, as well as the best informed and most clever, that I ever knew' (*Works and Correspondence*, 10.170), a view that seems to have been shared by his many friends and acquaintances. He was also a generous man, who provided almshouses, schools, an infirmary, and a savings bank in his own locality, contributed to a string of charities, and patronized the arts. It is, however, as a political economist that he is best remembered, although the bewildering array of evaluations and interpretations of his work make it impossible to state uncontroversially just what it is that he is best remembered for.

Debate over Ricardo's contribution to political economy began during his own lifetime. The 'new school' of Ricardo, as it came to be known about 1820, was subjected to criticism for a catalogue of perceived errors, including: over-abstraction and the generation of 'noxious' theoretical paradoxes, the use of an absolute concept of value related exclusively to the expenditure of labour, use of a labour theory of value more generally, the neglect of supply and demand considerations in price determination, underestimation of improvements in agriculture, hostility towards landlords, a deficient theory of profits, and the use of the 'law of markets' (the doctrine, in short, that supply creates its own demand, implying that there is no demand constraint on the growth of aggregate output and employment). At the same time, the new school was busily consolidating its position, partly as a result of Ricardo's personal authority, but also owing to the proselytizing efforts of Ricardo's inner circle of disciples, J. R. McCulloch in particular.

McCulloch had published a laudatory review of Ricardo's *Principles* in the *Edinburgh Review*, and thenceforth he was the fount of a stream of literature, including the authoritative entry 'Political economy' for the supplement to the fourth edition of *Encyclopaedia Britannica* (1823), which at least gave the impression of a thriving Ricardian orthodoxy. The youthful J. S. Mill, James Mill, and Thomas De Quincey were also instrumental in championing a Ricardian cause. Yet it is by no means clear that Ricardianism, as it developed in the 1820s, would have commanded Ricardo's personal assent: the virtual abandonment of Ricardo's version of the labour theory of value is a case in point. With Ricardo's death in 1823, his disciples were given licence to apply their own gloss to his doctrines (as they interpreted them, often imperfectly), to incorporate their own innovations, and to trim their sails in the shifting winds of contemporary criticism. By the 1830s aspects of Ricardian economics, now barely distinguishable from the outpourings of McCulloch, were coming under renewed fire from leading intellectuals including Nassau Senior, G. P. Scrope, Richard Jones, and William Whewell. For all the criticism, however, the opponents of the new school were not successful in supplanting Ricardianism with an alternative body of doctrine, partly because they disagreed among themselves, perhaps also because their rejection of orthodoxy was never complete. Where the critics did succeed was in helping to generate an enduring view of political economy as a pseudo-science riven by disagreement among its practitioners. Hence, while it may be true to say that Ricardianism continued to hold sway in the 1830s, and even during the early 1840s, it was more a victory by default than by acclaim.

The publication in 1848 of J. S. Mill's *Principles of Political Economy* did much to revive Ricardo's flagging reputation—Mill hailed Ricardo as 'the greatest political economist'—though debate still continues as to whether Mill's work is truly in the Ricardo (as distinct from the more capacious Ricardian) mould. In 1890 Alfred Marshall argued that, interpreted 'generously', Ricardo's work was wholly consistent with Marshall's version of neo-classical economics. But by that time the question of Ricardo's legacy had been thrown open by the intervention of Karl Marx, who praised Ricardo highly for his attempt to develop a labour theory of value: a project which Marx portrays himself as bringing to a satisfactory completion. By the dawn of the twentieth century the name of Ricardo was still very much alive, although the ideas behind the name were a matter of lively controversy.

Twentieth-century scholarship has done little to resolve the interpretative and evaluative questions thrown up in the previous century. Mention should be made, however, of J. M. Keynes's virtual identification of Ricardo's economics with the law of markets, of which Keynes complained bitterly; of Joseph Schumpeter's indictment of Ricardo for the 'Ricardian vice' (the direct application of simple economic models to the solution of real-world problems); of the view of Ricardo as the brilliant precursor of 'neo-Ricardian' or 'Sraffian' economics, a non-neoclassical species of abstract economic analysis developed by Ricardo's modern editor, Piero Sraffa; and of Samuel Hollander's endeavour, reminiscent of Marshall's, to portray Ricardo as a sophisticated, embryonically neoclassical economist.

Leaving aside the quirks, foibles, and peculiar agendas of his interpreters and critics, and the undoubted confusion between Ricardo's and Ricardian economics, there is an explanation for the differences in interpretation which can be rooted in the nature of Ricardo's own writing. Ricardo was not an academic in the modern sense. He worked only intermittently on his political economy over a relatively short period of his mature life during which he had many other demands on his time. It is therefore unsurprising to find inconsistencies and loose ends in his writings—it would be surprising not to find them—and it

is these which may have facilitated the contradictory readings. Yet—at the risk of pronouncing on a case which may remain forever *sub judice*—there is a core to Ricardo's theoretical system, comprising the labour theory of value (including a conception of absolute value related to labour expenditure), a subsistence treatment of wages (according to which a given, culturally influenced subsistence, or 'natural', wage is an active centre of gravity of market wages), the theory of differential rent, a 'surplus' calculation of profit (that is, profit is equal to net output minus wage costs), the notion of an inverse relationship between wages and profits, and the law of markets. Ricardo was a brilliant, penetrating thinker, capable of working at a level of abstraction far above his contemporaries. It is a tribute to his genius, though not always to that of his interpreters, that his writings remain a continuing source of fascination.   TERRY PEACH

Sources *The works and correspondence of David Ricardo*, ed. P. Sraffa and M. H. Dobb, 11 vols. (1951–73), vols. 1–10 · M. Blaug, *Ricardian economics* (1958) · E. Halévy, *The growth of philosophic radicalism*, trans. M. Morris, new edn (1972) [Fr. orig., *La formation du radicalisme philosophique*, 3 vols. (1901–4)] · S. Hollander, *The economics of David Ricardo* (1979) · T. Peach, *Interpreting Ricardo* (1993)
Archives BLPES, papers relating to estate · CUL, corresp. and papers · Trinity Cam., corresp. · UCL · University of Illinois Library, Chicago, papers | BL, letters to J. R. McCulloch, Add. MS 34545 · UCL, letters to Hutches Trower
Likenesses T. Heaphy, miniature, 1820, priv. coll. · T. Phillips, portrait, exh. RA 1821, priv. coll. [*see illus.*] · V. Bonelli, marble bust, 1822, priv. coll. · T. Hodgetts, mezzotint, pubd *c*.1822 (after T. Phillips), BM, NPG · W. Holl, stipple, pubd 1839 (after T. Phillips), BM, NPG
Wealth at death approx. £675,000–£775,000: Sraffa, ed., *Works*

Ricardo, Sir Harry Ralph (1885–1974), mechanical engineer, was born on 26 January 1885 at 13 Bedford Square, London, the eldest of three children and only son of Halsey Ralph Ricardo (1854–1928), architect, a descendant of the brother of David Ricardo, economist, and his wife, Catherine Jane, daughter of Sir Alexander Meadows *Rendel, civil engineer. He was educated at Rugby School (1898–1903) and Trinity College, Cambridge (1903–7). From the age of ten he was using tools and building engines, and in his first two terms at Cambridge he built a single-cylinder motorcycle engine; riding a machine fitted with this engine he covered 40 miles on a quart of petrol, winning a fuel economy race and bringing himself to the notice of Bertram Hopkinson, professor of mechanism and applied mechanics. Hopkinson persuaded Ricardo to spend his four years at Cambridge helping him with research on the factors limiting the performance of the petrol engine, even though this meant reading for an ordinary rather than an honours degree. While at Cambridge, Ricardo also designed a two-stroke cycle engine to study the flow of air and gas through the cylinder. A 15 hp version of this engine, named the Dolphin, was produced for fishing boats and motor cars by a company started by a cousin.

Ricardo obtained his ordinary degree in 1906 and spent a further year researching at Cambridge. In 1907 he joined his grandfather's firm, Rendel and Robertson (later Rendel, Palmer, and Tritton), first as an inspector of machinery, then as head of a department for designing the specialized mechanical equipment needed for large civil engineering projects. At the outbreak of war he was classified in a reserved occupation but military work was slow in coming, although he designed aero-engines made in 1915 by Brotherhood and Beardmore.

Ricardo's big opportunity came in 1916 with the development of the tank and his appointment as consulting engineer to the mechanical warfare department. He was asked first to explore the willingness of some manufacturers to make a new and more powerful engine and, when they agreed, to undertake its design. The successful design and production of the 150 hp engine and two larger engines giving 225 hp and 300 hp and incorporating features for improving combustion turned Ricardo into a professional and gave him the confidence to start his own company. By April 1917 one hundred of his engines were being produced per week, and the two larger engines were developed. In 1918 he became consulting engineer in aero-engines to the Air Ministry.

In July 1917, after the death of his grandfather, Ricardo launched his own company with the help of a three-year contract from the Asiatic Petroleum Company for research on fuels and detonation. Apart from this research Ricardo & Co. undertook the design of any form of internal combustion or related engine and also offered consulting services. A laboratory designed by his father was built at Shoreham by Sea, Sussex, in 1919 and, except during 1940–5 when it moved to Oxford for security reasons, the company remained at Shoreham. Ricardo communicated his results on the effect of fuel properties to Sir Robert Waley Cohen of the Shell group, whose company sponsored the extensive research on fuels and detonation at Shoreham (1918–21). During this contract Ricardo and his team, which consisted of H. T. Tizard, D. R. Pye, and Oliver Thorneycroft, developed the single-cylinder variable compression engine and the concept of the toluene (later octane) number for rating fuels. In 1922 and 1923 Ricardo's *The Internal Combustion Engine* (2 vols.) was published. In later editions the title was *The High-Speed Internal Combustion Engine*.

Ricardo's lifelong contributions to the development of the internal combustion petrol and diesel engine were based on skilful research and outstanding design. His diffident and polite manner concealed great determination and tenacity in the pursuit of technical achievement. Many notable designs were produced over the years including a side-valve engine (which gave as good performance as the more expensive overhead-valve design), two-stroke and four-stroke cycle diesel engines for automotive and aircraft usage, and sleeve-valve designs for advanced aircraft engines. Most of the world's engine manufacturers used Ricardo's designs at some stage of their history and, after a successful patent case in 1932, paid royalties or consulting fees to the company. In 1939–46 Ricardo was very active in government research and particularly on the sleeve-valve aero-engine. He was a member of the war cabinet engineering advisory committee (1941–5). He also undertook the design of a governor and fuel control for the first Whittle jet engine. Ricardo published extensively in professional journals and long after his retirement in 1964 kept in touch with engineers, young and old, in the company.

In 1929 Ricardo was elected FRS. He was president of the Institution of Mechanical Engineers, 1944–5, and was knighted in 1948. He received honorary degrees from Birmingham (1943), Turin Polytechnic (1960), and Sussex (1970), and an honorary fellowship of Trinity College, Cambridge (1967). He was an honorary member of the British, Dutch, and American mechanical engineering institutions, Manchester College of Technology (1935), and the Deutsche Akademie der Luftfahrtvorschung (1938). He was awarded the Rumford medal of the Royal Society (1944), the Clayton and James Watt (1953) medals of the Institution of Mechanical Engineers, the Lancaster and Crompton medals of the Institution of Automobile Engineers, and medals from the Royal Aeronautical Society, the Institute of Fuel, the Society of Automotive Engineers, USA, and others.

Ricardo married in 1911 Beatrice Bertha (*d*. 1975), daughter of Charles Bowdich Hale, their family doctor; she was an art student at the Slade School. They had three daughters. They lived for most of their happy family life near Shoreham, where his hobby was boating, and after 1945 at Woodside, Graffham, in Sussex, where in his ninetieth year Ricardo broke his leg in a fall. He died six weeks later, on 18 May 1974, at King Edward VII Hospital, Midhurst, Sussex. WILLIAM HAWTHORNE, *rev.*

Sources H. Ricardo, *Memories and machines, the pattern of my life* (1968) · W. Hawthorne, *Memoirs FRS*, 22 (1976), 359–80 · personal knowledge (1986) · *The Times* (20 May 1974), 16 g · *The Times* (22 May 1974), 22g

Archives CAC Cam., papers · IWM, technological papers | IWM, corresp. with Sir Henry Tizard

Likenesses W. Stoneman, two photographs, 1931–43 · photograph, repro. in Hawthorne, *Memoirs FRS*

Wealth at death £168,256: probate, 20 Aug 1974, *CGPLA Eng. & Wales*

Ricardo, John Lewis (1812–1862), politician and entrepreneur, was the son of Jacob Ricardo, financier, and nephew of David *Ricardo. In early life he showed great athletic prowess, on one occasion riding a spirited horse bareback up a staircase and into a dining-room at Aylesbury. He had chosen the army as his profession when he was induced, on the death of his father, to continue the financial business in which the latter had been engaged. In 1841 he became MP for Stoke upon Trent, holding the seat until his death. In conjunction with C. P. Villiers and others, he advocated the repeal of the corn laws and the navigation laws, on which he published *The Anatomy of the Navigation Laws* (1847). It was partly owing to his efforts that the Stade tolls on the Elbe were abolished, and he secured a select committee on the Navigation Acts in 1847, which brought the subject to the fore.

An able administrator, Ricardo took a leading part in the promotion of the electric telegraph. In 1846 he established the Electric Telegraph Company, and was its chairman for ten years (four of the eight shareholders were Ricardos). While acting in that capacity he introduced franked message papers and the employment of female clerks. In 1861, after leaving the Electric Telegraph Company, he proposed to the Treasury the nationalization of the telegraph system, and its administration by the Post Office. He was chairman of the North Staffordshire Railway Company from its inception until his death; chairman of the Norwegian Trunk Railway, for the construction of which he contracted jointly with Sir Samuel Morton Peto and Thomas Brassey; chairman of the Metropolitan Railway Company; and director of the London and Westminster Bank. Ricardo was an accomplished amateur artist.

In 1841 Ricardo married Katherine, daughter of General the Hon. Sir Alexander Duff, and sister of James Duff, fifth Earl Fife; their son, Augustus Lewis Ricardo, was a captain in the Grenadier Guards, and died childless in 1871. Ricardo died at his home, 31 Lowndes Square, London, on 20 August 1862.

W. A. S. HEWINS, *rev.* H. C. G. MATTHEW

Sources GM, 3rd ser., 13 (1862), 495–7 · *The Athenaeum* (30 Aug 1862), 278 · *The Electrician*, 2 (1862) · J. Kieve, *The electric telegraph: a social and economic history* (1973) · S. Palmer, *Politics, shipping and the repeal of navigation laws* (1990)
Archives U. Durham L., letters to Henry George, third Earl Grey
Wealth at death under £50,000: probate, 9 Sept 1862, *CGPLA Eng. & Wales*

Ricardus Anglicus. *See* Morins, Richard de (early 1160s–1242).

Ricart, Robert (*fl.* 1478), town clerk of Bristol, was the compiler of the text known as *The Maire of Bristowe is Kalendar*. The work may be reasonably famous, but very little is known about Ricart apart from scraps in the *Kalendar*. He was elected common clerk of the town of Bristol on 29 September 1478, and compiled the *Kalendar* on the wishes of William Spencer, mayor in 1478–9, who was anxious to have a record of the rights and franchises of Bristol so that they might 'hereafter more duly and freely be executed and exercised, and the more perfectly had in remembrance' (*Maire of Bristowe*, 3). Ricart is referred to once or twice as town clerk and as a witness to proceedings in Bristol's red books, for instance in 1479 and 1483; thereafter, apart from one stray reference in the white book in 1495–6, there is nothing. The date of his death is unknown and attempts to deduce this from the handwriting of the *Kalendar* are unsustainable.

The *Kalendar* is an ambitious work in six books. The first two provide a national, if often apocryphal, history as context for Bristol's fortunes. The third is mainly occupied with a list of Bristol's mayors, sheriffs, and bailiffs from 1217 to 1479 into which descriptions of other events are interpolated. The fourth offers a guide for the town's officers in the discharge of their duties, while the fifth book transcribes a charter of 1374 which conflated three charters issued a year earlier, one of which elevated Bristol to county status; added to this is a précis of King John's charter confirming Bristol's basic liberties. It is odd that no others are included. The final book comprises a series of extracts in French and Latin from London's Liber albus. This material is telling: London was the one city which Bristolians regarded as greater than their own and the one

whose status and franchises they obviously hoped to emulate. Whether the contents and plan of the *Kalendar* reflect Ricart's initiative or Spencer's, or whether they were the results of wider consultation, the extant volume is nevertheless eloquent as to Bristol's determination—and Ricart's brief—to establish its prestige, promote its liberties, and, quite plausibly, protect itself against an increasingly grasping crown. CLIVE BURGESS

Sources 'The maire of Bristowe is kalendar', Bristol RO, MS 04720 (1) · *The maire of Bristowe is kalendar, by Robert Ricart*, ed. L. Toulmin Smith, CS, new ser., 5 (1872) · F. B. Bickley, ed., *The Little Red Book of Bristol*, 2 vols. (1900) · E. W. W. Veale, ed., *The Great Red Book of Bristol*, 5 vols., Bristol RS, 2, 4, 8, 16, 18 (1931–53) · E. Ralph, ed., *The Great White Book of Bristol*, Bristol RS, 32 (1979) · M. Merry, 'Ricart's kalendar: urban ideology and fifteenth-century Bristol', MA diss., University of Kent at Canterbury, 1994
Archives Bristol RO, MS 04720 (1)

Riccaltoun, Robert (1691–1769), Church of Scotland minister, was born at Earlshaugh, near Jedburgh, Roxburghshire, where his father was a farmer. He was educated at Jedburgh grammar school and the University of Edinburgh, but on his father's death he had to take charge of the farm. He maintained his theological studies and was licensed to preach by the presbytery of Kelso in March 1717. On 4 August 1724 he married Anna Scott (*d.* 1764); they had five children including John (*d.* 1800), who later took over the ministry, and Margaret (1731–1786), who married William Armstrong, the parish schoolmaster of Hobkirk, and was mother of two sons, Adam, army officer in the service of Alexander I, and Robert, director of the imperial mint in St Petersburg.

After serving as assistant to the Revd Archibald Deans, minister of Bowden, Riccaltoun was in 1725 ordained to the parish of Hobkirk where he continued the rest of his life. A member of the moderate party within the Church of Scotland, he had a reputation for intelligence, imagination, and extensive learning. In 1722 and 1723 he published anonymously *The Politick Disputant* and *A Sober Enquiry into the Present Differences in the Church of Scotland*, early contributions to the Marrow controversy which pitted the radical evangelicalism of the Marrow men against the more moderate presbyterianism of the general assembly. In both, Riccaltoun criticized James Hadow's earlier attack on supporters of the 'Marrow' for encouraging factionalism. In essays such as 'The original state of mankind' and 'The origin and progress of knowledge', Riccaltoun sought to reconcile scriptural revelation and classical learning, arguing for a parallel between biblical and pagan accounts of natural phenomena. The historian and minister Thomas Somerville considered Riccaltoun's theological opinions 'wild and mystical', but fondly recalled his 'benevolent heart', 'rich imagination', and 'taste for what was beautiful and sublime in the works of nature' (Somerville, 128–9).

Riccaltoun is best remembered for his influence on the poet James Thomson, author of *The Seasons*. As tutor and companion of the young Thomson, Riccaltoun directed his studies and criticized his early poems. Thomson acknowledged that the design of his own 'Winter' was suggested by some 'masterly strokes' in a poem by Riccaltoun (Sambrook, 33) which has never been satisfactorily identified, but which may have been 'A Winter's Day', first published in Richard Savage's *Miscellaneous Poems* (1726) as by David Mallet, reprinted in the *Gentleman's Magazine* (1740) as by a 'Scotch clergyman' and again in the same periodical in 1853 as by Riccaltoun. His wife died on 4 October 1764 and in the following year his son John succeeded his father in the parish. Following Riccaltoun's death at Hobkirk on 17 September 1769 John published a three-volume edition of his father's *Works* (1771–2), with essays on theological and moral philosophical subjects.

WILLIAM GEORGE, rev. MARY CATHERINE MORAN

Sources *Fasti Scot.* · P. Murdoch, 'Account of the life and writings of James Thomson', in J. Thomson, *The seasons* (1836) · H. Nicholas, 'Memoir of Thomson', *The poetical works of James Thomson* (1866) · T. Somerville, *My own life and times, 1741–1814*, ed. W. Lee (1861) · J. Sambrook, *James Thomson, 1700–1748: a life* (1991)

Riccard, Sir Andrew (1603/4–1672), merchant, was the son of Walter Riccard of Dorset. He appears to have come from a poor family, possibly in Dorchester or Swanage, and to have moved to London to learn the trade of a merchant. He duly became involved in the East Indies trade as the apprentice of John Watkins, a middle-ranking official in the East India Company, and he drove himself to become successful and prosperous. He married Catherine, daughter of Robert Bateman, a leading company figure (he was treasurer from 1619 to 1644), and the representative in parliament for Weymouth in 1614 and for the City of London in 1621, 1624, and 1626. Riccard had set up house in the parish of St Olave, Hart Street, in London, where he was one of the highest-rated residents, by 1647; becoming involved in the Levant trade as well, by 1634 he could afford to purchase a coat of arms, whose embellishment of a turbanned head referred to his Eastern trading activities. Riccard's wife died in March 1639, following the birth of their second and only surviving daughter. He later married Susannah (d. 1687).

The Levant Company admitted Riccard as an assistant at their court in 1639, and his industriousness and reputation in the East Indies trade was rewarded when on 27 February 1641 he was admitted to that company by service. Royalist in political sympathies, he joined other leading City figures in signing the petition to parliament of July 1641 in favour of the authority of the lord mayor and aldermen against the claims of the radical-dominated common council. On 16 February 1642 he also signed the royalist merchants' petition against the committee of safety taking control of the city militia, but he took no further part in City politics during the civil war and instead concentrated on augmenting his fortune, in due course becoming a shipowner and also lending vessels in the Mediterranean to Venetian service. On 1 July 1646 he was elected to the East India Company committee and, apart from a year's withdrawal from that body from July 1648, he was thereafter one of their most active members. Accepting the new political order, and indeed benefiting from the withdrawal or exclusion of more established City figures, he became treasurer of the Levant Company

from 1650 to 1652, and he was created an alderman and was admitted to the Drapers' Company in September 1651 in the preliminaries to his year as sheriff of London in 1651–2, his sponsor being his mercantile associate William Williams.

The Drapers' Company was sufficiently impressed with Riccard's abilities to make him master in 1652–3, but his principal concerns lay in Eastern trade, though he also invested in the Caribbean and, in January 1654, led a deputation of the Barbados merchants to Cromwell's council to present a petition concerning the colony's governance. On 7 February 1654 he was elected governor of the Levant Company, and he served in that office for an impressive eighteen years, under both the protectorate and Charles II. In his capacity of governor he had to steer the company through the political dangers of endeavouring to counteract Cromwell's desire to assert his supremacy over the appointment of the ambassador to Constantinople, the post held by the long-standing but royalist envoy Sir Thomas Bendish. He could not prevent Cromwell sending out his own ambassador, Richard Lawrence, in 1654, but Bendish stayed put and the company starved Lawrence of funds and support until he duly returned.

In June 1654 Riccard secured election as MP for London, but he was not prominent in parliament. His reliability and reputation as an administrator was such that, in August 1654, Cromwell called upon him to join the protectorate's leading mercantile supporters—Maurice Thompson, Martin Noell, and William Williams—on the committee planning the 'Western design'. Riccard's knowledge of conditions in the Caribbean and his experience in overseeing the fitting out of ships were both important factors in his appointment. The committee duly advised the government on whom to appoint to govern the various Caribbean islands and the supplies necessary for an expedition of the size and timescale that the regime desired. As such Riccard was one of the signatories to the expedition's instructions to attack the Spaniards on land and sea without a declaration of war and to arrest foreign shipping trading with the colonies in defiance of the Navigation Acts, asserting the theory that there was 'no peace beyond the Line'. Whatever his personal support for the venture, it is clear that his Cromwellian sympathies did not extend to religion—when his daughter Christian married John Geare at St Olave, Hart Street, in March 1656 the civil ceremony, conducted by the powerful Alderman Ireton, was followed by a private episcopal Anglican blessing.

Riccard was appointed in July 1655 to the government's committee for trade, and in November to the trade and navigation committee. He was also chosen on 15 November to help evaluate Manasseh ben Israel's proposal for the readmission of the Jews, and he served as a commissioner for securing peace in the City in March 1656 and for the assessment in June 1657. In his home parish he generously purchased the advowson and in June 1655 gave it in perpetuity to a trust run by five householders, an arrangement that lasted until 1879. In July 1655 he and Thomas

Vyner were entrusted by the government with the custody of the £85,000 that the Dutch had paid in compensation for past East Indies depredations under the 1654 treaty. A loan of £50,000 of this money was duly made to the government, which proved notably tardy in returning it or even finding interest payments; Riccard and Vyner were paid £100 for their services on 24 August. Riccard's other main involvement now became the East India Company, where he was deputy governor from 1653. The company was seeking the renewal of its charter, and Maurice Thompson led a group of merchants in arguing that the next joint stock should be opened to far more investors to enable greater participation instead of control by a small group, a move that was resisted by William Cokayne and the current leadership. Riccard supported Thompson and he signed his second petition to the council of state for a wider joint stock on 21 September 1654, but he did not play a leading role in the negotiations surrounding the reformation of the company under the new charter in 1657. The election court of 10–14 December 1657 elected Thompson governor; Riccard was one of the defeated candidates, but he secured a place on the committee, and in July 1659 he became deputy governor in succession to Thomas Andrews.

Riccard's closeness to the protectorate was cemented when his widowed daughter Christian married on 14 February 1658 Henry, son of Robert Rich, Lord Kensington, who was great-nephew of the earl of Warwick and cousin to Cromwell's son-in-law Robert Rich; the bridegroom, however, died in 1659. Beyond acting as commissioner for assessment in London in January 1660, Riccard took no part in the upheavals of 1659–60, and at the Restoration he was rewarded with a knighthood on 10 July 1660. He served as governor of the East India Company in 1660–62, 1666–8, and 1670–72, combining that role with his similar eminence at the Levant Company. Involved in planning East India Company representation at Macao and the exploitation of the new acquisition at Bombay, he continued his private ventures and was an investor in the new Royal African Company to trade in Guinea. Pepys, a fellow parishioner, called him 'one of our ablest merchants', and on a more domestic level he reported in May 1663 how Riccard's young ward Christian Hawkins, his second wife's heiress niece, was abstracted from Riccard's house and was married by her admirer John Dawes, without Riccard's consent but with that of her aunt.

Riccard's last appearance in national affairs came as an unwilling participant in the confrontation between the Commons and Lords of 1668 in the case of Thomas Skinner, a merchant seeking compensation for goods seized by the East India Company in 1659 who had petitioned the king after refusing derisory damages. Charles passed the matter to the Lords who decided in favour of Skinner's £17,000 claim, but the company persuaded the Commons to deny their jurisdiction. The dispute saw Riccard, as governor of the company, and his officers being summoned on their knees to the bar of the Lords on 8 May 1668 and threatened with the Tower for contempt; he escaped that but spent some days in black rod's custody. He remained active in company affairs until he died in the parish of St Olave, Hart Street, on 6 September 1672 at the age of sixty-eight, having made his will on 23 July. He was buried on 17 September at St Olave, where a statue was later erected of him dressed as a Roman senator; its inscription commended his 'active piety, inflexible integrity and extensive abilities' and praised his 'many instances of love to God and liberal spirit towards Man'. His widow Susannah died in 1687; his daughter Christian became by her third marriage ancestor of the lords Berkeley of Stratton.

TIMOTHY VENNING

Sources A. Povah, *Annals of the parishes of St Olave, Hart Street, and Allhallows Staining, in the City of London* (1894) · Levant Company letter-book, 1647–62, PRO, SP 105/112 · Levant Company court book, 1648–60, PRO, SP 105/151 · *The visitation of London, anno Domini 1633, 1634, and 1635, made by Sir Henry St George*, 2, ed. J. J. Howard, Harleian Society, 17 (1883) · A. B. Beaven, ed., *The aldermen of the City of London, temp. Henry III–[1912]*, 2 vols. (1908–13) · A. H. Johnson, *The history of the Worshipful Company of the Drapers of London*, 5 vols. (1914–22), vol. 3 · *CSP dom.*, 1655; 1657–8; 1660–61; 1667–8 · *CSP Venice*, 1657–9 · *CSP col.*, 1640–43, 1644–9, 1650–54, 1655–9 [East Indies] · Pepys, *Diary*, vols. 4, 6, 7, 9 · C. H. Firth and R. S. Rait, eds., *Acts and ordinances of the interregnum, 1642–1660*, 2 (1911) · W. A. Shaw, *The knights of England*, 2 (1906) · V. Pearl, *London and the outbreak of the puritan revolution: city government and national politics, 1625–1643* (1961) · BL, Add. MS 25116 [records of 1668 Skinner case before House of Lords] · J. Edmondson, *A complete body of heraldry*, 2 vols. (1780), vol. 2 · S. Pincus, *Protestantism and patriotism: ideologies and the making of English foreign policy, 1650–1668* (1996), 408 · J. C. C. Smith and others, eds., *Index of wills proved in the prerogative court of Canterbury*, vol. 9, ed. J. Ainsworth, Index Library, British RS, 67 (1942) · C. H. Ridge, ed., *Index to wills proved in the prerogative court of Canterbury*, 10: *1676–1685*, Index Library, British RS, 71 (1948)

Archives BL OIOC, East India Company archives · PRO, Levant Company archives, letters and documents

Likenesses marble statue, St Olave's Church, Hart Street, London

Wealth at death extensive property in goods, East India Company and Levant Company, with shares in vessels; house in Hart Street, London

Ricci, Marco (1676–1730). *See under* Venetian painters in Britain (*act.* 1708–*c.*1750).

Ricci, Sebastiano (*bap.* 1659, *d.* 1734). *See under* Venetian painters in Britain (*act.* 1708–*c.*1750).

Ricci, Seymour Montefiore Robert Rosso de (1881–1942), art historian and bibliographer, was born on 17 May 1881 at Meadowbank, Twickenham, the eldest son of James Herman de Ricci (1847–1900), barrister and former colonial judge, and his second wife, Helen, *née* Montefiore (*c.*1860–1931). His parents were divorced in 1890, and de Ricci thereafter lived with his mother in Paris, where he attended the Lycée Janson de Sailly (1890–98). He was brought up as an Anglican. His fellow pupils at the lycée nicknamed him Pico della Mirandola because his interests were so eclectic. In a working career of barely forty years, he published over two dozen books. He also wrote several hundred articles, and although many of these are essentially journalistic—for he made a name for himself as an art critic, becoming the Paris art correspondent for the *New York Herald* (1929–32)—they are all distinguished by his attention to detail and, frequently, to the history of who owned whatever he was writing about. While still at the lycée, he was admitted to the École Pratique des Hautes Études, at the Sorbonne, where he proceeded bachelier ès lettres in 1896-7; he attained his licence in 1901. His first publications were in 1896; in the following year they included a substantial repertory of the Roman inscriptions in the Breton department of Côtes-du-Nord. Saturday afternoon visits to the Musée Guimet fired a growing enthusiasm for Egyptology, and he took up the study of hieroglyphs and—again to the level of publishing—of coptic and Greek papyri.

About 1900 de Ricci began to acquire auction sale catalogues: his collection of these ultimately became one of the largest ever formed by an individual, and they underpinned many of his bibliographic and art historical publications. He also gained his first patrons: Émile Guimet, Émile Picot, and, crucially, Salomon Reinach (1858–1932). The last was a member of the Institut de France, director of the Musée National des Antiquités, and founder of the École du Louvre; extremely well connected, he moved with ease in half a dozen scholarly and social worlds, and yet was remarkably prolific as an author. His protégé from about 1896, de Ricci became virtually his adoptive son early in the twentieth century, and owed to him introductions to a glittering array of cosmopolitan friends, such as Bernard Berenson and Princess Bibesco.

On his twentieth birthday, 17 May 1901, de Ricci became a French citizen. He was now eligible for any French state-funded post or for grants for learned missions and the like. With powerful patrons, astonishing talents, and already about twenty scholarly publications to his credit, he might have been expected to scale the heights of the academic world. Instead, he took to the life of an independent scholar, living by his pen and from modest private means; the buying of books (especially bibliographical), coins, and small-scale works of art (such as Renaissance bronze plaquettes) was his only luxury. It was a choice which he occasionally regretted—as when he applied unsuccessfully for a post in the museum of antiquities in Alexandria (1902)—but it was the way of life to which he was temperamentally best suited. He was not a reflective person, but he had an astonishingly retentive and quick memory, and could easily marshal supplementary details from his various and ever growing slip-indexes. He could rapidly turn out a piece of journalistic writing, while he often startled contemporaries by the speed with which he produced more serious works. It took him only a few weeks to compile the catalogue of the Musée Cognacq-Jay (1929) or the *Handlist of Manuscripts in the Library of the Earl of Leicester, at Holkham Hall* (1932). He enjoyed a busy social life, with many friends in the artistic world, but his own lifestyle was hard-working and even austere.

Not until the 1920s was de Ricci to find what was surely his most satisfactory vocation, as a cataloguer of medieval and Renaissance manuscripts, and even then his ever curious mind led him to produce book after book on subjects only tangentially related to this theme. In the century's first decade he perhaps gave primacy to Egyptology and epigraphy; on the other hand, he greatly enjoyed the no less technical problems posed by early typography. Sometimes he would explore such problems in detail, but he eventually decided on the formula of preparing an all-embracing catalogue or census in which he traced the history of each member of some class of materials. In 1906 he proposed to the Bibliographical Society a *Census of Caxtons*; this listing of every recorded copy of each of Caxton's printings duly emerged two years later, to be followed in 1911 by a comparable *Catalogue raisonné des premières impressions de Mayence (1445–1467)*. Perhaps because of an innate modesty that made him a ready annotator of other people's work, his next work in this bibliographic genre was a revision of Henri Cohen's *Guide de l'amateur des livres à gravures du XVIIIe siècle* (1912), detailing all the remarkable copies of French illustrated books of that period.

Enumeration was only one way of acquiring mastery of the subject. Sometimes de Ricci would step back from the task and summarize his knowledge in a different way. His Sandars lectures in bibliography, delivered at Cambridge in 1929, have proved to be among his most enduringly useful works because he offered such a limpidly clear exposition of the subject: *English Collectors of Books and Manuscripts, 1530–1930, and their Marks of Ownership* (1930). However, he was always eager to try out new methodologies or approaches that resulted from new documents or simply from a new way of looking at familiar material. A catalogue of *Twenty Renaissance Tapestries from the J. Pierpont Morgan Collection* (1913) was an exercise in dating through constructing a chronology of female head-dress.

Tall, immaculately dressed, vivacious, and quick, the young de Ricci cut an attractive figure; one friend of his early years, Louis Réau, was later to recall him as a dandy. In these days he moved among fashionable and avant-garde literary and artistic circles in Paris. His bachelor years ended in his mid-twenties, when he married (Jenny Gabrielle) Thérèse Dreyfus (*c*.1886–*c*.1938). Marriage appears to have had little impact on his literary activities, save perhaps to make him veer more towards the remunerative and journalistic side, and he also began to involve himself in the book-trade side of the bibliographic world. From 1911 he had a daughter, Jacqueline, to bring up. In 1914 he launched his own bilingual review, *Art in Europe*. Only three of its monthly issues were published before it was halted by the outbreak of war. From 1914 until 1919 he was mobilized, as a second-class *chasseur à pied* in the French army and then as an interpreter for the British army. His marriage broke down in these years; in 1920 he was married again, to a war widow, Delphine Levy, *née* Feher (*c*.1886–*c*.1977), who had two children from her previous marriage. They rented a flat at 18 rue Boissière; even with the extra capacity offered by cellars that had been specially lined to render them damp-proof, it was never capacious enough for his collections, which filled every little space, not excluding parts of Delphine's bedroom wardrobe.

Just as the war was ending, de Ricci travelled for the first time to the United States, as part of a mission led by Salomon Reinach's brother Théodore; never one to miss an opportunity to inspect rare books or manuscripts, he put the trip to good use. His eyes must have been opened in a more general way to the opportunities that America offered, for henceforth he was at pains to cultivate its rare books world. Almost every year he crossed the Atlantic afresh, and catalogues of private collections were one result, notably of John Clawson's early English printed books (1924) and Mortimer Schiff's Italian maiolica (1927) and French signed bookbindings (1935).

More importantly, a succession of scholarly articles on medieval manuscripts paved the way for de Ricci's most celebrated and colossal piece of work, his *Census of Medieval and Renaissance Manuscripts in the United States and Canada*. Discussions with the American Council of Learned Societies led to this project being adopted by the Library of Congress (1929), thanks to which he was furnished with an assistant, Dr W. J. Wilson, and secretarial back-up. Careful preparation, four extensive journeys around North America (1929–33), and de Ricci's phenomenal speed and his eye for a manuscript's signs of former ownership, combined with his indexes back in Paris, enabled him to complete the work within eight years. Two quarto volumes of 2343 pages contain descriptions of 15,000 books, letters, and groups of charters in 494 libraries (278 of them privately owned), all set out with accuracy and an extraordinary attention to their history and bibliography. These were published in 1935 and 1937; a third volume, with indexes, followed in 1940.

The success of the *Census* owed much to the way in which it had enjoyed institutional support, and de Ricci was at pains to take equal care over the backing that he realized would be required for his next major project, an even more ambitious survey of manuscripts in the British Isles. In 1934 he put such a scheme before the University of London's Institute of Historical Research and gained an undertaking to publish it, and modest financial support. With his characteristic energy de Ricci set to work, aided by just one secretarial assistant. By July 1939 he had completed 40,000 slips of paper for manuscripts and collections in permanent locations and 20,000 slips for existing or dispersed private collections; that summer he had a campaign of work in London, and went far towards completing his work on the British Museum and other institutions. His labours were halted by the outbreak of war, and there remain only the 60,000 slips, now in the Palaeography Room of the University of London Library, and certain other preliminary notes in the Bibliothèque Nationale de France.

Like most Frenchmen, de Ricci failed to anticipate that the war's onset would be followed by so sudden a collapse of the French government; the fall of Paris in the summer of 1940 left him in a state of numbed shock. His health—hitherto generally robust, despite his intensely hardworking lifestyle—now collapsed; he published nothing further. Almost his last recorded action is his deposit in the Bibliothèque Nationale on 10 June 1940 of some thirty of his more precious manuscripts and collections of autograph letters. Prolonged illness was followed by his death, at 10 quai Galliéni, Suresnes, on the edge of Paris, on 25 December 1942. He was buried at the Père Lachaise cemetery in Paris.

De Ricci had long been concerned about what would happen to his extensive collections. In 1935 he gave to the Bibliothèque Nationale his Voltaire papers (including 1500 letters from Voltaire himself). By his will, made in 1938, he gave the pick of his works of art to the Réunion des Musées Nationaux, while to the Bibliothèque Nationale he left all his books, manuscripts, prints, drawings, medals, and working papers. His intention was that these last should be made available to researchers; yet the author of a book on library management (*Le problème des bibliothèques françaises: petit manuel de bibliothéconomie*, 1933) had perhaps not realized what difficulties his will would create for the library. Even after the war, when his old friend Julien Cain returned from deportation and resumed the post of administrator-general, the library was hardly able to cope with cataloguing his manuscripts, sale catalogues, and other printed books (perhaps numbering more than 80,000)—apart from many fifteenth and sixteenth-century books, essentially a scholar's collection that owed much of its value to de Ricci's abundant annotations—never mind his boxes of working notes.

De Ricci was survived for thirty-five years by Delphine. He had reached only the age of sixty-one, and though appointed an officer of the Légion d'honneur (1935) cannot be said to have achieved public recognition commensurate with his talents; his genius was perhaps too wideranging, his spirit too independent. NIGEL RAMSAY

Sources papers of S. de Ricci, Bibliothèque Nationale, Paris · E. P. Goldschmidt, 'Seymour de Ricci, 1881–1942', *The Library*, 4th ser., 24 (1943–4), 187–94 · J. Gibbs, 'Seymour de Ricci's "Bibliotheca Britannica Manuscripta"', *Calligraphy and palaeography: essays presented to Alfred Fairbank*, ed. A. S. Osley (1965), 81–91 · J. Porcher, 'À la Bibliothèque Nationale: le legs Seymour de Ricci', *Bibliothèque de l'École des Chartes*, 105 (1944), 229–33 · L. Réau, 'Seymour de Ricci', *Beaux-Arts* (20 Jan 1943), 16 · J. Adhémar, 'Pour les historiens d'art: avec le legs Seymour de Ricci entre au Cabinet des Estampes une documentation précieuse sur les artistes anciens et moderne', *Arts* (9 March 1945), 1, 3 · private information (2004) · personal knowledge (2004) · d. cert.
Archives Bibliothèque Nationale, Paris · LUL, corresp. and papers relating to Bibliotheca Britannica Manuscripta
Likenesses C. Simatos, drawing (as a young man), priv. coll.

Riccio, David (c.1533–1566), musician and courtier, was born at Pancalieri, near Turin, in the duchy of Savoy, the son of an impoverished musician. Possessed of an excellent singing voice and presumably trained by his father, he seems to have been employed by the archbishop of Turin before moving to the court of the duke of Savoy in Nice. In autumn 1561 he set out for Scotland as secretary to the duke's ambassador, the marquess of Moretto. Aware of Riccio's musical talents, Moretto advised him to seek a position at the Scottish court, for it was well known that Mary, queen of Scots, was fond of music and was herself an accomplished performer. As it happened, Mary was looking for a bass to make up the quartet of French singers who performed partsongs and sacred music for her. Riccio persuaded them to let him sing with them before the queen. She heard him twice, was impressed with his voice, and, when Moretto left for home soon afterwards, she made Riccio one of her *valets de chambre* (gentlemen of the privy chamber). In that capacity he received a payment of £50 Scots on 8 January 1562.

By all accounts Riccio was not old, as some of his detractors claimed, but he was an ugly little man, full of his own importance, with an expensive taste in clothes. 'His appearance disfigured his elegance', George Buchanan commented sourly (Buchanan, 93), but fellow gentleman of the privy chamber Sir James Melville found him 'a merry fallow and a gud mucitien' (*Memoirs of His Own Life*, 131–2) and the queen liked him. When Augustine Raullet, her secretary for French correspondence, fell from favour in December 1564, she gave his place to Riccio. He may have been less than skilful in 'dyting of French lettres' (ibid., 109), but Mary evidently felt that she could trust him. As her secretary he was constantly in her company, and he also seems to have continued some of his previous duties as *valet de chambre*, taking responsibility for bedding in the royal apartments and purchasing cloth for pages' and lackeys' liveries as well as occasionally for the queen herself. At the same time he did everything he could to enhance his own position, and the courtiers soon came to realize that if they wished for favours, they would have to bribe Seigneur Davie, as he was known.

Inevitably, the Scottish lords were jealous. They complained that their access to the queen was restricted and that she should be relying on them for advice, not on this foreign upstart. 'Some of the nobilite wald glowm upon him and some of them wold schulder him and schut [shove] him by when they entrit in the chamber and fand him alwais speaking with hir Majestie', Melville noticed (*Memoirs of His Own Life*, 132). There were also rumours that Riccio was a secret envoy of the pope and after his death it was even said that he had been a necromancer: Robert Murray, a healer and diviner from Glenesle, who was executed for witchcraft in 1588, 'falselie assurit that he was senyeor Davids man' (NL Scot., MS Acc 9769, 4/1/96). Observing the general hostility towards her secretary, Mary urged Melville to befriend 'Seigneur David, who was haited without cause' (*Memoirs of His Own Life*, 138), but Riccio did not help matters by flaunting his new-found wealth in the form of showy garments and expensive furnishings and horses.

By June 1565 Thomas Randolph was telling William Cecil that Riccio now worked all, and was chief secretary to the queen and governor to her goodman. Riccio had ingratiated himself with Henry Stewart, Lord Darnley, on the latter's arrival at the Scottish court in 1565, encouraging Mary to marry him. The dissatisfied lords soon realized that, weak and immature, Darnley was the ideal weapon to use against her. They played on his insecurities, whipped up his resentment at his wife's refusal to grant him the crown matrimonial, and hinted that she was having an affair with Riccio. Darnley was instantly suspicious, complaining that Mary was ignoring him and jealously noting how she and Riccio would sit up playing cards together until the early hours of the morning.

Since Darnley was often absent when he was needed to sign official documents, a stamp with his signature was made for use when he was unavailable, and given into the keeping of Riccio. By now Mary was pregnant, and people began to say that Riccio was the father of the baby. 'Woe is me for you when Davy's son shall be King of England', Randolph told the earl of Leicester, thinking ahead to the death of Elizabeth I and the likelihood of Mary's child inheriting the English throne (*CSP for.*, 8.13). The infant, the future James VI and I, had in fact been conceived in the early months of Mary's marriage, probably during the chaseabout raid when she had shown every sign of being deeply in love with her husband, but Darnley was prepared to believe the lies. Meanwhile, Riccio brushed aside the well-meaning efforts of those who tried to warn him that he was in danger, declaring, 'the Scots are given more to brag than to fight' (*History of the Church*, 2.36–70).

James Stewart, earl of Moray, and the other protestant lords who had fled to England after the chaseabout raid were determined to prevent parliament from meeting as intended in mid-March 1566, for they knew that if it did, they would be forfeited. They therefore set about devising a desperate stratagem and by the middle of February Thomas Randolph was aware that the murder of Riccio was part of the plot. Parliament opened as planned on 7 March 1566 in the presence of the queen, who was now six months pregnant, and it was agreed that a bill of forfeiture against Moray would be passed on 12 March. Three days before that, on 9 March, at about seven o'clock in the evening, the conspirators struck.

The queen was at supper in the little room adjoining her bedchamber at Holyroodhouse. Her half-sister Jean, countess of Argyll, was at one end of the table, David Riccio was at the other, while she herself sat at the side. Light came from a candelabrum on the table. Suddenly Darnley marched in, sat down beside Mary, and put an arm round her waist, chatting to her with unaccustomed geniality. She had scarcely replied when the startling figure of Patrick Ruthven, Lord Ruthven, appeared in the doorway, deathly pale and wearing full armour. 'May it please your Majesty to let yonder man Davie come forth of your presence, for he has been overlong here!' he cried (Keith, 3.266).

The queen rose to her feet in alarm. Terrified, Riccio darted behind her, to cower in the window embrasure, clinging to the pleats of her gown. The royal attendants sprang forward to take Ruthven, but he pulled out a pistol and waved them back. At the same moment the earl of Morton's men rushed into the supper chamber, the table was overturned, and only the countess of Argyll's quick thinking in snatching up the candelabrum prevented the room from being plunged into darkness. While Andrew Ker of Fawdonside held his pistol to the queen's side, George Douglas, Darnley's uncle, snatched Darnley's dagger from his belt and stabbed Riccio. According to Mary's own description of events, this first blow was struck over her shoulder.

'Justice! Justice!' Riccio screamed. 'Save my life, Madame, save me!' (Dalyell, 5n.), but it was too late. The intruders dragged him from the supper room and stabbed him to death at the door of the queen's outer chamber. On Darnley's orders his body, with fifty-six stab wounds, was hurled down the main staircase, dragged into the porter's lodge, and thrown across a coffer where the porter's servant stripped him of his fine clothes. Weeping with anxiety and shock, Mary asked over and over again what had happened to him and sent her servants to retrieve a coffer containing documents and a cipher from his private chamber. Several hours passed before one of her ladies brought her the news that Riccio was dead. At that she dried her eyes. 'No more tears now', she said. 'I will think upon revenge' (Maxwell, 77).

Mary always believed that the events in the supper chamber at Holyroodhouse that night were an attempt on her own life. Lord Ruthven later claimed that the murder was committed in her presence so that the conspirators could taunt her about her friendship with her secretary and her neglect of her husband, but it seems likely that at least some of those involved hoped that their bloody act of violence would send the queen into premature labour and that both she and the child would die. Whatever the truth of it, the killing of Riccio finally ended any lingering affection Mary may still have had for Darnley, although she pretended otherwise so that she could escape from Holyroodhouse. Riccio had been buried hastily in a cemetery outside Holyrood Abbey. When she returned from Dunbar, the queen had his body exhumed and placed in the royal vault in the abbey. She then appointed his young brother Joseph to take his place as her French secretary. Less than a year after that Lord Darnley himself was dead, murdered at Kirk o' Field.   ROSALIND K. MARSHALL

Sources CSP Venice, 1558–80, 375–8 · R. Keith, J. P. Lawson, and C. J. Lyon, History of the affairs of church and state in Scotland from the beginning of the Reformation to the year 1568, 3 vols., Spottiswoode Society (1844–50), vol. 2, pp. 264–8, 411–14 · Memoirs of his own life by Sir James Melville of Halhill, ed. T. Thomson, Bannatyne Club, 18 (1827), 109, 131–6 · Lord Herries [John Maxwell], Historical memoirs of the reign of Mary queen of Scots, ed. R. Pitcairn, Abbotsford Club, 6 (1836), 76–7 · Lettres, instructions et mémoires de Marie Stuart, reine d'Écosse, ed. A. Labanoff, 7 vols. (1844) · J. B. A. T. Teulet, ed., Papiers d'état, pièces et documents inédits ou peu connus relatifs à l'histoire de l'Écosse au XVIème siècle, 3 vols., Bannatyne Club, 107 (Paris, 1852–60), 443, 447–9 · P. Dupuy, Histoires des plus illustres favoris anciens et modernes (1659), 491–9 · D. Calderwood, The history of the Kirk of Scotland, ed. T. Thomson and D. Laing, 8 vols., Wodrow Society, 7 (1842–9), vol. 2, pp. 313–15 · CSP for., 1564–5, 380 · J. B. Paul, ed., Compota thesaurariorum regum Scotorum / Accounts of the lord high treasurer of Scotland, 11 (1916), lvii, lix, lx, lxx, lxxv, 102, 158, 381, 383, 387, 389, 462, 475, 507 · G. Buchanan, The tyrannous reign of Mary Stewart, ed. W. A. Gatherer (1958), 93 · T. Thomson, ed., Diurnal of occurents (1833) · DNB · D. Hay Fleming, Mary, queen of Scots (1897) · J. G. Dalyell, ed., Fragments of Scottish history (1798), 5n. · J. Spottiswood, The history of the Church of Scotland, ed. M. Napier and M. Russell, 2, Bannatyne Club, 93 (1850)

Rice family (per. c.1500–1651), gentry, took their surname from Sir *Rhys ap Thomas (1448/9–1525), whom they regarded as their most illustrious forebear. The family was blighted by the early death of the son and heir of Sir Rhys ap Thomas and his wife Jenet, Sir Gruffudd ap Rhys, and by the execution of the latter's son and heir, Rhys ap Gruffudd, on a charge of treason.

In the sixteenth and early seventeenth centuries the descendants of Sir Rhys ap Thomas were preoccupied with restoring the standing and property of the family, if with modest success. Sir Rhys had anticipated that his son **Sir Gruffudd ap Rhys** (1479–1521) would inherit his position as one of the most prominent Welsh landowners. Gruffudd was well connected with the nobility and served the Tudor crown in war and administration: he joined the household of Arthur, prince of Wales, was knighted at the prince's wedding on 14 November 1501, and was buried near his chantry chapel in Worcester Cathedral. In 1507 he married Henry VII's kinswoman Katherine (d. 1553), daughter of Sir John St John of Bletsoe, Bedfordshire, and Glamorgan, and his wife, Sybil. Sir Rhys assigned them his Gower estate, where the couple may have lived at Weobley Castle. Gruffudd was admitted to Lincoln's Inn in 1509. He joined his father in several offices in south-west Wales but died suddenly in 1521, possibly at a tournament to judge by a contemporary English lament.

Gruffudd's death meant that Sir Rhys ap Thomas, in his last years, sought to secure the future of his grandson, **Rhys ap Gruffudd** (c.1508–1531). As early as 1514 it was arranged with Thomas *Howard, second duke of Norfolk (1443–1524), that Rhys should marry the duke's daughter Katherine (d. 1554). This was a notable match that gave Norfolk an ally in Wales and the west country. The wedding may have taken place soon after Gruffudd's death. However, Rhys proved headstrong and quarrelsome, with high ambitions and expectations with which Henry VIII and his councillors did not sympathize: he was not allowed to assume his grandfather's role in south Wales or on the king's council in the marches of Wales. Rhys was deeply offended, especially when Walter Devereux, Lord Ferrers, was appointed justiciar of south Wales and steward and receiver of Builth for life on 2 August 1525 and, in 1526, chamberlain of south Wales. Rhys and his wife mobilized their noble connections to protest, seeking Cardinal Thomas Wolsey's aid against Ferrers. By 1528–9 their mutual recriminations were at fever pitch, while Rhys alienated the gentry and townsfolk of south Pembrokeshire by exploiting cases of piracy for his own profit. Complaints were lodged in chancery, the council in the marches, and Star Chamber. The most serious incident occurred in June 1529 at the great sessions at Carmarthen, where the retinues of Rhys and Ferrers came to blows as Rhys forced his way into the castle. After Rhys's detention his wife raised more men in south-west Wales to secure his release, causing 'the greate Rebell and Insurreccion of the people' (PRO, SP 1/54, fols. 119r–120r). Eventually the council in the marches decreed that Rhys and Ferrers should provide £1000 bonds to keep the peace, though in Star Chamber Wolsey contented himself with a censure, and their rivalries continued.

Rhys was arrested in October 1530 and put in the Tower of London, though in the following June he was allowed out on bail. His rearrest in September 1531 marked a change in the government's attitude, amid rumours of his intended flight to Scotland and a plot against Henry VIII. The new situation was created by the crisis over the king's wish to divorce Catherine of Aragon and marry

Anne Boleyn. Rhys, a distant kinsman of Henry, was a victim of uneasy times: he was accused of plots in London, amid rumours and prophecies involving a Scottish invasion, and suggestions that he be installed in the principality of Wales. The government's reaction reflected the king's dynastic anxieties, memories of Edward Stafford, third duke of Buckingham, whose name was linked with Rhys's, and the royal divorce. Wolsey's fall from grace and the insecure position of Thomas *Howard, third duke of Norfolk (1473–1554), deprived Rhys of a strong patron. He was indicted of treason in king's bench on 22 November and found guilty five days later. He was attainted, condemned to death, and beheaded on 4 December. Testimony had been contrived and witnesses seemingly coached in what amounted to a show trial in which Thomas Cromwell played a final part. Rhys was buried in Holy Cross Friary, London. His attainder destroyed one of Wales's most important families at a time when others were prospering; it may have been taken as a warning on the eve of the union with England (1536).

The two sons of Rhys ap Gruffudd were placed in the household of Cuthbert Tunstall, bishop of Durham, where they were brought up. Thomas ap Rhys (d. 1544) fled to Scotland and entered the service of Mary, queen of Scots, until he was killed in battle in 1544. **Gruffudd Rice** [Gruffudd ap Rhys] (c.1526–1592) sought to rehabilitate his family's reputation and recover its property. This was not easy in the volatile environment of the mid-sixteenth century, and much of Rhys's property had been disposed of by grants and leases. About half of the estate—worth £360 per annum—remained in the possession of three widows after Rhys's execution: Jenet (d. 1535), widow of Sir Rhys ap Thomas, whose dower property was around Carmarthen; Katherine, widow of Sir Gruffudd ap Rhys, who had married Sir Peter Edgcumbe of Cotehele in Cornwall, and whose dower estate was in Gower; and Katherine, widow of Rhys ap Gruffudd, who had married Henry Daubeney, second Baron Daubeney, whose lands were mostly in Pembrokeshire, including Carew Castle. The rest was disposed of piecemeal, mostly to Rhys's kinsmen. By January 1547, when Henry VIII died, two-thirds of the Carmarthenshire estates and all those in Cardiganshire had been dispersed. Rice began his campaign with a petition to Edward VI's first parliament in November and December 1547, seeking to overturn his father's attainder. He secured a pardon but only by acknowledging Rhys's treason and the disposal of his property. Rice could only recover a small part of the estate, and then by acknowledging crown lordship. He benefited from his mother's death (by May 1554) and Mary I's favour, but much property was still being leased to others, notably Sir John Perrot, who gained the castle and lordship of Carew in 1555. Rice's campaign was also hindered by involvement in the murder of Mathew Walshe in co. Durham in 1557, which led to his own attainder and forfeiture. However, early in Elizabeth I's reign he arranged to marry Elinor, daughter of Sir Thomas Jones of Carmarthenshire, one of his father's kinsmen and a beneficiary of the crown's largesse from the Rice properties. A pardon for the Durham murder followed in 1560, and Rice

resumed his efforts to recover the family inheritance. Although a suspected Catholic, he made modest progress in his campaign of recovery, in the course of which he stressed Rhys's signal service to the Tudor crown and intimated that his father had been duped in 1530–31. He received a further partial restoration of the estate. Newton was returned in 1561, with property in Pembrokeshire and Carmarthenshire worth £105 10s. 4d. per annum. He gradually achieved local standing, as JP of Carmarthenshire from 1564 to his death, sheriff of the county on a number of occasions between 1567 and 1583, and mayor of Carmarthen in 1571. Rice died on 1 September 1592. The crown continued to enjoy the forfeited Rice estates, titles to some properties had been alienated, and kinsmen—especially Perrot and Jones—officers from south Wales, and loyal crown servants benefited most.

Rice's eldest son, **Sir Walter Rice** (c.1562–1636), continued his father's efforts throughout his life. He entered Elizabeth's service, and based his family's case on the reputation of Sir Rhys ap Thomas and the malicious nature of the accusations against Rhys ap Gruffudd, as well as pleading poverty. He submitted a formal petition in 1597 to secure the lordship of Narberth, Pembrokeshire, but it was unsuccessful. Meanwhile he consolidated an official reputation in south-west Wales, as JP of Carmarthenshire from about 1583 to 1615, MP for the county in 1584, and for Carmarthen Boroughs in 1601 and 1604, and sheriff of Carmarthenshire from 1585 to 1586. Rice was knighted by James I on 23 July 1603 and he hoped that the new dynasty would prove more amenable. He showed a deep interest in his family's history and its royal and noble links. Another petition (1607) sought restoration of those estates still in crown hands, estimated by him to be worth about £200 per annum; but James's privy councillors were not helpful until, in 1623, Walter Rice and his son secured the reversion of ancestral lands in and around Newton, Carmarthenshire. By then Rice was in financial difficulties, and he agreed to dispose of the Pembrokeshire estates and to mortgage Newton and others. He married Elizabeth, daughter of Sir Edward Mansel of Margam, Glamorgan, and his wife, Jane. He died in 1636.

It was Henry Rice (1585/6–1651), Walter Rice's eldest son and heir, who most imaginatively exploited antiquarian interests to restore the family's reputation and wealth. He matriculated from Jesus College, Oxford, aged twenty-one, on 7 December 1607, and graduated BA on 17 December. In the late 1620s he wrote the so-called 'Life of Sir Rhys ap Thomas' as well as 'Objections against Rice Griffith in his indictment, with the answers thereunto'. Henry and his brother Thomas Rice (b. 1587/8), who attended Oxford University at the same time as him, became part of the humanistic circle of Welsh gentry in south-west Wales with links to William Camden, Francis Bacon, and Thomas Jones. Henry Rice was also a gentleman of Charles I's privy chamber and felt able to petition the king in 1625 for the return of estates worth £200 per annum. A further petition was approved in 1629. The accompanying life was replete with classical allusions and Rice also had access to royal archives at Westminster, family tradition, eulogies of Welsh poets, and popular sixteenth-century chronicles like those of Polydore Vergil and Raphael Holinshed. The life was published in 1796 in the *Cambrian Register* and became an important source for the fifteenth- and early sixteenth-century history of south Wales and of the Rice family until the twentieth century.   R. A. GRIFFITHS

Sources 'A short view of the longe life of … Rice ap Thomas', *Cambrian Register*, 1 (1796), 49–144 · 'Objections against Rhys ap Gruffydd', *Cambrian Register*, 2 (1797), 270–77 · R. A. Griffiths, *Sir Rhys ap Thomas and his family* (1993) · 'The epitaph of Sir Gryffyth Apryse', *Anglia*, 31 (1908), 347–50 · *LP Henry VIII* · W. Ll. Williams, 'A Welsh insurrection', *Y Cymmrodor*, 16 (1902), 1–94 · *The reports of Sir John Spelman*, ed. J. H. Baker, 2 vols., SeldS, 93–4 (1977–8) · H. A. Lloyd, *The gentry of south-west Wales, 1540–1640* (1968) · E. A. Lewis, 'Materials illustrating the history of Dynevor and Newton', *West Wales Historical Records*, 1 (1910–11); 2 (1911–12) · *CSP Spain, 1529–38* · Carmarthenshire RO, Dynevor MSS · NL Wales, Dynevor papers · HoP, *Commons, 1558–1603*, 3.289–90 · *DWB* · E. Davies and B. Howells, eds., *Pembrokeshire county history, 3: Early modern Pembrokeshire, 1536–1815* (1987)
Archives Carmarthenshire RO, deeds, family and estate papers · NL Wales, deeds, family and estate papers

Rice, Sir Cecil Arthur Spring- (1859–1918), diplomatist, was born in London on 27 February 1859. He was the second son of the Hon. Charles Spring-Rice (1819–1870), second son of Thomas Spring-*Rice, first Baron Monteagle (1790–1866), and his wife, Elizabeth (*d.* 1883), daughter of William Marshall MP of Halsteads and Patterdale Hall, Cumberland. Educated at Eton College and Balliol College, Oxford, he achieved distinction as a scholar both at school and at college, and his first efforts at poetry appeared in an Eton booklet, while his *Oxford Rhymes* had a more than ephemeral vogue. Later on it was in poetry of a more serious order that he often revealed his innermost thoughts, and sometimes with rare felicity of expression and depth of feeling.

Spring-Rice's father had been at one time under-secretary of state for foreign affairs, and he himself was appointed clerk in the Foreign Office on 9 September 1882. He had the advantage almost at the outset of his diplomatic career of serving directly under two secretaries of state, first as assistant private secretary to Lord Granville and then as précis writer to Lord Rosebery. His first post abroad, as well as his last, was Washington, where, with brief intervals, he spent several years between 1886 and 1895; he was then transferred to Berlin. He remained in the German capital until 1898 and he had there the opportunity, which he always regarded as having been of the greatest educational value to him, of watching at close quarters the 'new course' upon which the policy of the German empire was being set by Wilhelm II after he had emancipated himself from Bismarck's tutelage. From Berlin, Spring-Rice went in 1898 first to Constantinople and then to Tehran. He was seconded thence in 1901 as British commissioner on the Caisse de la Dette Publique in Cairo, where, as he put it, he went 'back to school' under Lord Cromer.

From Cairo, Spring-Rice was promoted in 1903 to be secretary of embassy at St Petersburg during the stormy years of the Russo-Japanese War and the first revolutionary upheavals in Russia. While serving in Russia he married,

Sir Cecil Arthur Spring-Rice (1859–1918), by unknown photographer, 1913

in 1904, Florence, the only daughter of his former chief Sir Frank *Lascelles, then still ambassador in Berlin; one son and one daughter were born of the marriage. In 1906 he was created KCMG and he returned to Persia as British minister. There he supported the constitutionalist movement, and in troublous times thousands used to take sanctuary within the grounds of the British legation in Tehran. None the less he faithfully carried out the policy of the Anglo-Russian agreement of 1907, which effectively partitioned Persia. Having been passed over for the Washington embassy in 1907, he enjoyed from 1908 to 1913 five years of relative ease and rest at Stockholm as British minister to Sweden. In April 1913 he was appointed ambassador at Washington, and shortly after his arrival there he signed the agreement renewing the Anglo-American arbitration convention of 1908. He was at home on leave after a somewhat serious illness when the Sarajevo tragedy precipitated the European conflict, which he had long foreseen.

Spring-Rice returned to Washington immediately war began in Europe and signed the Bryan–Spring-Rice treaty, providing for a permanent International Peace Commission. Spring-Rice's view was that 'the President [Wilson] will be with us by birth and upbringing, but he is very much in the hands of some of our worst enemies' (Gwynn, 2.220). He found William Jennings Bryan, the secretary of state, hard to take seriously and he was not successful in striking up a good relationship with Colonel House, Wilson's confidential adviser. Indeed, House argued that Spring-Rice's approach delayed American entry into the war by two years (Gwynn, 2.216). Certainly, Spring-Rice believed that it was important that Britain should not seem to be inveigling the United States into the war, and in his approaches to Wilson he maintained a scrupulous neutrality, waiting for Germany to show herself even more clearly in the wrong than she had done in August 1914. He felt more comfortable in the company of pro-war republicans—especially Roosevelt and Cabot Lodge—than of democrats, and the latter were quick to notice this. But he had good relations with J. P. Morgan (the banker who acted as British purchasing agent in the USA) and once assisted in disarming a German assassin who had attacked him. Spring-Rice proved himself a shrewd commentator on the internal politics of the USA, and on understanding the difficulties of Wilson's position. He was personally much affected by the carnage of the war; this and the heavy demands of his position caused very considerable strain. Some saw him as physically and morally unequal to the requirements of his position (Gwynn, 2.217). At least by Colonel House's account, he on several occasions lost his temper. He was undoubtedly reticent about combating German propaganda; in the whole of his time as ambassador he spoke in public only once (a few words spoken at Harvard in 1917). But he countered Wilson's proposals for a League of Nations in 1916 by warning the Foreign Office that Congress would make isolationist objections, and in that sense House was right to see Spring-Rice as working against himself and Wilson (Gwynn, 2.334). His reticence and caution were regarded as feeble and ineffective by Lloyd George and his group, and he became the focus of what was really a more general attack on traditional Foreign Office methods.

When America entered the war in April 1917, A. J. Balfour led a mission to the USA which effectively superseded Spring-Rice, though it was not until January 1918 that he was replaced as ambassador by Lord Reading. Just as he was leaving Washington, Spring-Rice was sent some verses by W. J. Bryant; in response he penned the famous lines 'I vow to thee, my country' (Gwynn, 2.432). After a day's skiing in Ottawa on his way home, he died suddenly on 14 February 1918 at Government House. Death meant the end of his pension; American friends raised $75,000 for his widow and family, the money to go subsequently to Balliol College, Oxford, for travelling scholarships. His poems were edited in 1920 by Bernard Holland.

H. C. G. MATTHEW

Sources *The letters and friendships of Sir Cecil Spring Rice: a record*, ed. S. Gwynn, 2 vols. (1929) • V. Chirol, *Cecil Spring-Rice* (1919) • E. M. House, *The intimate papers of Colonel House*, 4 vols. (1926–8) • *FO List* (1918) • G. P. Gooch and H. Temperley, eds., *British documents on the origins of the war, 1898–1914*, 11 vols. in 13 (1926–38) • F. H. Hinsley, ed., *British foreign policy under Sir Edward Grey* (1977) • K. Robbins, *Sir Edward Grey* (1971)
Archives CAC Cam., diplomatic and personal corresp. and papers • PRO, corresp., FO 800/241–2 | BL, corresp. with Arthur James Balfour, Add. MS 49740 • BL OIOC, corresp. with Lord Curzon, MSS Eur. F 111–112 • BL OIOC, letters to Lord Reading, MSS

Eur. E 238, F 118 • Bodl. Oxf., corresp. with Herbert Asquith • CAC Cam. • CUL, corresp. with Lord Hardinge • Cumbria AS, Carlisle, letters to Lord Howard of Penrith • HLRO, letter to David Lloyd George • HLRO, corresp. with John St Loe Strachey • JRL, corresp. with S. E. Spring-Rice and Julia Spring-Rice • Mass. Hist. Soc., letters to Mrs James D. Cameron • NA Scot., letters to G. W. Balfour • NL Scot., corresp. with Lord Rosebery • NRA, priv. coll., letters to Sir Norman Moore • Plunkett Foundation, Long Hanborough, Oxfordshire, corresp. with Sir Horace Plunkett
Likenesses photograph, 1913, Hult. Arch. [*see illus.*]
Wealth at death £27,254 19s. 4d.: probate, 22 May 1918, *CGPLA Eng. & Wales*

Rice, Charles (*bap.* 1820, *d.* 1880), actor, theatre manager and playwright, was born in Brompton, London, where he was baptized on 6 February 1820, the son of Thomas Rice, a mason, and his wife, Mary. His father is said to have undertaken building work at Buckingham Palace. An inclination towards art led to Charles Rice's being apprenticed to an engraver and to his preparing drawings for publication by the Royal College of Surgeons. However, finding some of his subjects—especially the head of a murdered woman—too distressing, he ran away from home and joined a company of players on a circuit in the southern counties.

Rice's career reflects the major changes in nineteenth-century provincial theatre, from the days when an actor–manager depended on providing an annual season at each of a circuit of theatres to maintain his stock company, to the era of considerable investment in new theatre buildings, open for most of the year, to host touring productions, usually from the London stage.

As an actor Rice's chief talent was for low comedy, but he was versatile enough to succeed in roles as varied as those of the Artful Dodger, Rip van Winkle, played with 'quaint humour and pathos' (*Bradford Observer*, 13 April 1880), and King Lear. He delighted in stage machinery and applied his artistic skills to set design and painting scenery. In 1844 he formed a partnership with John Mosley, which lasted until 1847, to run a west Yorkshire circuit of theatres in Bradford (for which Rice designed a new façade), Huddersfield, and Wakefield. Rice dramatized episodes of local significance for the Bradford theatre, including *The Gibbet Law of Halifax, or, A Legend of Kirklees Abbey* (c.1846).

In August 1850 Rice's adaptation of *The Three Musketeers* was performed in Manchester. From 1851 to 1868 he was associated primarily with London theatres, including the Grecian Theatre, where his pantomime *The Fairy and the Fawn* was put on in 1852, and the Surrey, Britannia, and Strand theatres, as a playwright and actor, but he starred also at Glasgow and at provincial theatres. On 24 December 1856 he married Hoxton-born Harriet (or Harriot) Hart, who, although not herself an actress, shared his love of design and worked with him in management.

Rice began management on his own account at Oldham, where he took a three-year lease of the Working Men's Hall at £300 a year, opening it with a stock company as the Theatre Royal in August 1865 with his own play *The Stricken Oak*, in which he made use of Professor Pepper's ghost illusion and which had already been put on that same year in

Glasgow and York. His first Christmas pantomime at Oldham that year was his own *Koh-i-noor*, which contained 'extraordinary mechanical effects rather surprising to see attempted on this stage' (*Oldham Evening Chronicle*, 23 Dec 1865). In 1868 Rice moved to Bradford, where he leased the recently built Theatre Royal, Manningham Lane, and where he remained until his death, from cirrhosis, at his home, 1 Drewton Street, Bradford, on 12 April 1880. For much of the year the Bradford theatre served as a receiving theatre for touring productions, but Rice created an annual in-house pantomime, for which he was widely celebrated.

In 1873 Rice took over the running of Covent Garden theatre for the Christmas period, putting on his own *Red Riding Hood and Little Bo-Peep* with a profusion of bad puns, a transformation scene that was a 'triumph of mechanism and art' (*The Times*, 27 Dec 1873), and allusions to the new school boards and to the Tichborne claimant. The following year saw his *Babes in the Wood and the Big Bed of Ware*. *Cinderella and the Little Glass Slipper* followed in 1875, when he 'shone above his competitors in manufacturing the worst imaginable play upon words' and when the transformation scene included 'all sorts of ladies suspended in all sorts of happily impossible positions from all sorts of fabulous trees and branches of extraneous growth' (*The Times*, 28 Dec 1875).

Rice was spoken of as a 'kindly and genial gentleman' (*Bradford Observer*, 13 April 1880), and he had a reputation for generosity in providing benefits for various causes at his theatres. He was a freemason and was a member of the Hope Lodge at Bradford. The Rices had no children, and Mrs Rice continued to manage the theatre until her own death in 1887.　　　　　　　　　　　C. M. P. TAYLOR

Sources W. Scruton, *Pen and pencil pictures of old Bradford* (1890) · A. Nicoll, *A history of English drama, 1660–1900*, 6 vols. (1952–9); repr. (1963) · W. A. Hulme, 'Oldham theatres and plays during the 19th century', July 1960, 84 Union Street, Oldham, Oldham Local Studies and Archives · *The Britannia diaries, 1863–1875: selections from the diaries of Frederick C. Wilton*, ed. J. Davis (1992) · W. Baynham, *The Glasgow stage* (1892) · S. Rosenfeld, *The York theatre* (1948) [MS in York Library] · K. Barker, *The Theatre Royal, Bristol, 1766–1966* (1974) · d. cert. · b. cert. · *CGPLA Eng. & Wales* (1880) · *Bradford Observer* · *The Wakefield and Halifax Journal* · *Oldham Chronicle*

Wealth at death under £2000: probate, 21 Aug 1880, *CGPLA Eng. & Wales*

Rice, David Talbot- (1903–1972), Byzantine scholar and farmer, was born in Rugby on 11 July 1903, the third son of Henry Charles Talbot-Rice (1862–1931), landowner, of Oddington House, near Stow on the Wold, Gloucestershire, and Cecil Mary Lloyd (d. 1940), daughter of Edward Lloyd (1824–1869) and Rosabella Susan Lloyd (1834–1909) of Lingcroft, near York. He was educated at Eton College and Christ Church, Oxford, where he read archaeology and anthropology, an unusual combination at the time. He graduated in 1925.

At Oxford, Talbot-Rice was part of a convivial group known as the Hypocrites Club, the scope of whose members, according to the novelist Anthony Powell, ranged from the aesthete Harold Acton to Talbot-Rice who 'could not have been less aesthete-like' (Powell, 155)—though

among undergraduates in Edinburgh rumour later had it that he wore ties fashioned from the silk of emperors. He combined this social life with the discipline of academic study. Evelyn Waugh, a fellow Hypocrite and lifelong friend, wrote some years later: 'There was David Talbot-Rice, who seemed to live a life of carefree pleasure but was secretly studious, so that he is now full of academic honours' (Waugh, 200). This discipline never left him as his wife, Tamara, recorded in her autobiography:

> Although giving no indication of it, he in fact worked more than most of the Hypocrites, studying daily from breakfast to lunch time and from tea to dinner time, a practice to which he kept for the rest of his life. (*Tamara*, 116)

After his death his friend David Lindsay, twenty-eighth earl of Crawford and eleventh earl of Balcarres, wrote: 'The wonder is that any man could do so much without ever seeming to be in a hurry, yet always able to find time for more' (Robertson and Henderson, foreword), a statement borne out by the extent of Talbot-Rice's written legacy, his impact as a university teacher and administrator, and his active husbandry of his Cotswold farm.

On leaving Oxford in 1925 Talbot-Rice began a career in archaeology, first in Iraq, though it was in this year, as he later wrote, that he 'first fell in love with Constantinople' (Robertson and Henderson, foreword). This infatuation coincided almost exactly with that of the poet W. B. Yeats. They had been in Oxford at the same time, although there is no notice of Talbot-Rice's own meeting with the poet, but his wife, as an undergraduate, did do so. Their separate approaches to Byzantium are, however, complementary. Yeats's sense of its spiritual significance is overlaid with images of its artefacts. Talbot-Rice, beginning with the artefacts themselves, intuited from them the significance of Byzantine art and culture in the continuity and development of both Eastern and Western Christendom. Indeed, his first major contribution to the study of Constantinople itself were his reports for the Royal Academy's expedition of 1927 to excavate the great palace of the emperors—a project finally completed under his direction some thirty years later. The specific archaeological discoveries were published in his *Byzantine Glazed Pottery* of 1930. In this same year his interest in the broader significance of Byzantine painting for the development of western European art, inspired by studying in Paris with the eminent Byzantinist Gabriel Millet, and rooted in an earlier visit to Mount Athos with his mercurial Oxford friend Robert Byron, came to fruition in *The Birth of Western Painting*, which Byron and he wrote together. This initial interest became a lifelong devotion first demonstrated independently in his own seminal *Byzantine Art* of 1935 and culminating in his *Byzantine Art: the Last Phase*, published but five years before his death, where he returned to the theme first mooted in 1930. Although he aimed to inspire an interest in things Byzantine as much among the public as among scholars—the exhibition of Byzantine art he arranged in London and Edinburgh in 1958 being an example of this—his views were always underpinned with a firm armature of archaeological and historical evidence. He maintained throughout a 'hands-on' approach, supervising the excavations of the church of Haghia Sophia at Trebizond from 1957 to 1968, when the findings were eventually published as *The Church of Haghia Sophia at Trebizond.*

This sense of the primacy of the practice of art and the significance of artefacts informed Talbot-Rice's teaching of art history as an academic discipline, which he was one of the first to develop in Britain. In 1932 he was made lecturer in Byzantine and Near Eastern art at the newly founded Courtauld Institute in London, but in 1934, at the age of thirty-one, he succeeded the eminent critic Herbert Read to the Watson Gordon chair of fine art at Edinburgh University. There he drew together his respect for the production of art and his belief in its historical and cultural significance in the curriculum of the fine art degree which he designed with the Edinburgh College of Art in 1946 on returning from war service as head of the Near East section of military intelligence. This degree course, innovative when set up and subsequently influential nationally, remains at the core of art history at the university. Talbot-Rice held the chair until his death and during thirty-eight years his impact on the character of the university was profound. He held the offices appropriate to his chair and, later, to his position as vice-principal, but his influence was felt most through the university's own cultural life and through its standing in the wider community. Two of his initiatives demonstrate this: first, the acquisition of Raymond Russell's internationally renowned collection of keyboard instruments now housed in the university's St Cecilia's Hall and, second, the foundation of an art centre—now called the Talbot-Rice Art Gallery—to house the university's nineteenth-century Torrie bequest of works of art and to mount contemporary exhibitions. Many generations of students, some equally distinguished in their fields, benefited from his inspiration and generosity as a teacher and from his great kindness. He had a natural sympathy with the young, and so he was all the more distressed at the unfair criticism he suffered as chairman of the disciplinary committee set up to adjudicate on the student unrest of 1968.

Alongside his distinguished academic, military, and public career—Talbot-Rice was an influential trustee of the National Galleries of Scotland, served on various national advisory committees, and was made CBE in 1968—he maintained a profound interest in his native Gloucestershire. In 1931 he and his wife acquired a charming Cotswold house with a demesne through which the River Coln quietly flowed. Late in his life, with characteristic practicality, he rebuilt a bridge over the river with his own hands, an act perhaps emblematic of the bridge between east and west that he sought to find in his chosen field of study. Here, at Pigeon House, once more practice and intellect came together. To the outside world the house, with its smallholding of livestock and the polled Hereford cattle he introduced into Britain in 1949 from an American pedigree herd, spoke of the gentleman farmer he most certainly was. To his friends and family, however, the house contained within it the many fascinating and rare things that he and (Elena) Tamara Abelson [*see below*]—the beautiful and spirited Russian émigrée he met at Oxford and married on 31 December 1927—had unearthed on their many journeys. Above all, it contained a magnificent library, a further testimony to the intellectual life which sustained them and to the scholarship which they shared. A distinguished scholar in her own right, Tamara excavated with him, and they wrote together. As the earl of Balcarres writes:

> If he gave her the keys of the Golden Gate in the Walls of Byzantium, she in turn opened for him new vistas among the Seljuks, the Scythians and other civilizations of Central Asia, no less than the art, history and architecture of her native Russia. (Robertson and Henderson, foreword)

They had three children: Elizabeth (*b.* 1931), Nina (*b.* 1941), and Nicholas (*b.* 1944).

Although best-known as a Byzantine scholar, Talbot-Rice also pioneered the post-war study of Islamic art in Britain, and his *English Art, 871–1100* (1952) in the Oxford History of English Art shows that he was equally at home with the art and culture of his native land. This came naturally, for, in spite of some Welsh blood on his mother's side, he came from a stratum of society whose roots lay long-planted in the English soil. He died at home at Pigeon House, Coln Rogers, near Cheltenham, on 12 March 1972, cut down by cancer, at a time which coincided, as his wife Tamara wrote, 'with the death of the elm trees he so greatly loved for their intrinsic beauty, as well as for their role in English painting' (*Tamara*, 239); he was buried at Coln Rogers. As with the elms, his death, along with that of others of his generation, changed the landscape of English life forever and marked the passing of an older, and perhaps more noble, order.

Talbot-Rice's wife, **(Elena) Tamara Talbot-Rice** (1904–1993), art historian, was born in St Petersburg on 19 June 1904 into the non-practising Jewish family of Israel Boris Abelevich Abelson, a wealthy businessman and senior official in the tsar's treasury, and his wife, Louisa Elizabeth (Lifa), *née* Vilenkin (*d.* 1954). A goddaughter of Lev Tolstoy, she was educated by governesses—she later attributed her Anglophilia to a beloved English governess—and at the Tagantzeva Girls' School, St Petersburg. Following the Bolshevik revolution of 1917 she and her mother escaped via Finland, and her father and brother escaped separately; they lived in London, then in Paris. After a brief spell at Cheltenham Ladies' College and further education at home she went as an exhibitioner to St Hugh's College, Oxford, in 1921 to read philosophy, politics, and economics. She disliked the accommodation, paucity of bathrooms, chaperonage, and other restrictions, and after one term transferred to the Society of Oxford Home Students (later St Anne's College), living in lodgings. Busy socializing, she neglected her studies and in 1924 failed schools. She returned to her family, by then relatively impoverished, in the Russian exile community of Paris, and was variously employed, taking jobs as, among others, a film extra, a fashion journalist, and a social researcher under Professor Carlton Hayes of Columbia University, New York. After their marriage in 1927 she accompanied Talbot-Rice on his travels and excavations in

Greece, Yugoslavia, Bulgaria, Georgia, Persia, and Turkey, supervising some of the excavation. During the Second World War she worked in the Turkish section of the Ministry of Information. Among her publications were *The icons of Cyprus* (1937), *The Scythians* (1957), *The Seljuks in Asia Minor* (1961), and an unusually favourable biography, *Elizabeth, empress of Russia* (1976). Small, blue-eyed, vivacious, and hospitable, she was a notable raconteuse. Following Talbot-Rice's death in 1972 she began but never completed her memoirs. (These were edited and published in 1996 by her daughter Elizabeth.) She died on 24 September 1993 at Bourton on the Water, Gloucestershire, survived by her three children.   ROGER TARR

Sources WW (1971) · private information (2004) [family] · G. Robertson and G. Henderson, eds., *Studies in memory of David Talbot-Rice* (1975) · J. H. Burnett, D. Howarth, and S. D. Fletcher, *The university portraits: second series* (1986) · *Tamara: memories of St Petersburg, Paris, Oxford and Byzantium*, ed. E. Talbot-Rice (1996) · E. Waugh, *A little learning: the first volume of an autobiography* (1964) · A. Powell, *Infants of the spring* (1976) · b. cert. · d. cert. · *The Independent* (29 Sept 1993) · *The Guardian* (2 Oct 1993) · *Daily Telegraph* (11 Oct 1993) · *The Times* (14 Oct 1993)
Archives GL, corresp. with publishers
Likenesses E. Coia, pencil and ink drawing, *c.*1971, U. Edin.
Wealth at death £182,726—Elena Tamara Talbot-Rice: probate, 9 Dec 1993, *CGPLA Eng. & Wales*

Rice, Edmund Ignatius (1762–1844), founder of the Irish Christian Brothers and educationist, was born on 1 June 1762 at Westcourt, near Callan, co. Kilkenny. He was the fourth of the seven sons of Robert Rice, a farmer, and his wife, Margaret Murphy, *née* Tierney, of Maxtown. After attending schools at Callan and Kilkenny, at the age of seventeen he was taken into the business of his uncle, Michael Rice, a prosperous provision merchant and meat exporter at Waterford. On the latter's death about 1790 Rice succeeded to the business, which he managed with great success. In 1785 he married Mary, *née* Elliott, of Annestown, Tramore. She died in 1789, after giving birth to a mentally handicapped daughter, Mary, who was cared for by an aunt. Rice was profoundly affected by the loss of his wife. He dedicated himself to charitable work, being a founding member of the Trinitarian Orphan Society (1793) and of the Waterford Society for Visiting and Relieving Distressed Room-Keepers. Among the beneficiaries of his charity was the young Italian immigrant Charles Bianconi, later a pioneer of coach transport in Ireland. In the course of his charitable work Rice saw at first hand the consequences of ignorance and unemployment among the young. Roman Catholics were still officially disqualified from public teaching, and the children of the poor had either to attend the so-called 'hedge schools', which charged fees, or to become pupils at the free schools set up by proselytizing protestant societies. In 1798 Rice helped to establish the Presentation Sisters at Waterford, and their educational work for girls inspired him to make similar provision for boys. In this undertaking he was supported by the bishop of Waterford, Thomas Hussey, who was concerned at the possible effect of the proselytizing schools. Rice sold his business to finance the venture, and in 1802 began teaching with two companions in a disused

stable. In June 1803 permanent buildings were opened at Ballybricken by Bishop Hussey, who at his death later that year left Rice the greater part of his estate. By 1804 there were more than 300 boys on the school roll.

Rice was soon joined by four friends of similar background, who lived as brothers in a religious community under his direction. A further school was opened at Carrick-on-Suir in 1806. In August 1808 the brothers, now nine in number, took formal vows according to the rule and constitutions of the Presentation order, under the authority of the bishop of Waterford. Henceforward they were known as Christian Brothers. Their educational system, in place by 1810, gave priority to religious and moral formation and, unusually, put strict limits on corporal punishment. The first school at Cork was established in 1811, and the following year the first of several schools was established at Dublin at the invitation of Archbishop Daniel Murray. Each school received postulants and trained novices, and expansion was now rapid. The first foundation in England was made at Preston in 1825, followed within a year by establishments in Manchester and London (Soho).

With the support of Archbishop Murray, Rice petitioned Rome to grant his community the status of a pontifical institute independent of episcopal control. A papal brief of 5 September 1820 granted this request, and in 1822 Rice was unanimously elected the first superior-general of the new congregation, known as Religious Brothers of the Christian Schools (Ireland). Its rules and constitutions were modelled on those of the French congregation of De La Salle Brothers. The new institute had to face the determined opposition of Bishop Robert Walsh of Waterford and Bishop John Murphy of Cork. The latter persuaded some of Rice's brethren at Cork to form a diocesan congregation there under his authority and with the name of Presentation Brothers. From 1826 the two congregations were separate.

The foundation stone of a permanent school in North Richmond Street, Dublin, was laid by Daniel O'Connell in 1828. The event, attended by a crowd of 100,000, turned into a mass demonstration in the cause of Catholic emancipation. When the school opened in July 1832 it admitted over 600 students. From 1831 the brothers co-operated with the non-denominational Irish board of education but withdrew in 1836 over the issue of religious education. Rice wished to integrate the teaching of religion into the general curriculum, whereas under the board's scheme it was restricted to specific days; his brethren also objected to what they perceived as an English bias in the board's textbooks. The brothers' withdrawal from the national scheme and consequent loss of state subsidy led to a severe financial crisis. Rice proposed the establishment of fee-paying schools for the better off, as a means of raising funds for the free schools, but was opposed by a group led by Michael Riordan. The latter succeeded him as superior-general on his resignation in 1838. In 1841 he suffered the humiliation of being excluded from the general chapter of the congregation he had founded. The division among his brethren clouded his final years. He died at Mount

Sion, Waterford, on 29 August 1844, aged eighty-two, and was buried in the adjoining cemetery, where a memorial church was later erected in his honour. By the end of the century the institute, numbering some thousand brothers, had spread to Canada, India, and Australia and was responsible for about 300 schools in Ireland.

Rice played a vital role in providing the Catholic poor with the means of self-improvement. He was a close associate of Father Theobald Mathew, the apostle of temperance, and sedulously cultivated in his pupils the virtues of discipline, hard work, and sobriety. Though driven by religious, rather than political, motives, he contributed to the modernization of Irish society and to the creation of an educated Catholic working class, which was to produce the leaders of the nationalist movement. Edmund Rice was beatified at Rome on 6 October 1996.

G. MARTIN MURPHY

Sources D. Keogh, *Edmund Rice, 1762–1844* (1996) · M. C. Normoyle, *A tree is planted: the life and times of Edmund Rice* (1976) · D. Blake, *A man for our times: a short life of Edmund Rice* (1994)
Archives Archives of the Christian Brothers, Rome
Likenesses portrait, repro. in Keogh, *Edmund Rice*, 95

Rice, George (1724?–1779), politician, was the only son of the three children of Edward Rice (d. 1727), politician, of Newton, Carmarthenshire, and his wife, Lucy, the daughter of John Morley Trevor of Glynde, Sussex. The family traced its ancestry to the medieval princely house of Dinevor, and George Rice was a direct descendant, tenth in the male line, of Sir *Rhys ap Thomas, who in 1485 joined Henry Tudor in his Bosworth campaign. He matriculated at Christ Church, Oxford, in 1742 but did not graduate, and devoted himself to politics and management of the family estate, inherited from his paternal grandfather, Griffith Rice, in 1728. The Rice family formed a leading whig house in Carmarthenshire, and George's grandfather and father had both sat for the county before he won the shire seat in a fierce contest of 1754. Thereafter he was unopposed until his death. His mother was a relative of the then prime minister, the duke of Newcastle, and young Rice, whom the duke had known since infancy, was assimilated into the ruling whig oligarchy. He acted as the duke's south Wales manager for the general election of 1761.

Rice's career was not blighted by the political changes caused by the accession of George III in 1760, for on 16 August 1756 he had married Cecil (1735–1793), the only daughter of William Talbot (1710–1782), second Baron Talbot of Hensol, a man so high in favour at the new royal court that he was elevated to an earldom and appointed lord steward of the household. In 1761 Rice, at the personal behest of the king's favourite, Lord Bute, was appointed a lord of trade, with a salary of £1000 a year, an office he held until 1770 throughout all the ministerial changes of that period. Lord North then gave him the more lucrative post of treasurer of the chamber, which involved appointment to the privy council. Rice was neither a tame office-holder nor a sinecurist. His vestigial role as a country gentleman was reflected in his opposition to government on such popular issues as the land tax in 1767,

a Nullum Tempus Bill of 1768, and Grenville's Election Act in 1774. But the significance of his parliamentary career was his role as a ministerial spokesman on America, for he had become a colonial expert when at the Board of Trade. In 1764 he masterminded the passage of the American Currency Act, and as the colonial crisis worsened he emerged as a hardliner. He opposed repeal of the Stamp Act in 1766 even when in office. In 1769 he reminded the Commons that the economic advantages of the empire to Britain, which was the American argument against taxation, depended on enforcement of the trade laws which the colonists were also resisting. They were trying to have it both ways. After the Boston Tea Party of 16 December 1773 it was Rice who, on 7 March 1774, moved the ministerial address. The question, he declared, was whether 'the colonies of America are, or are not, the colonies of Great Britain'. He argued that their retention was essential to Britain's role as a great power. 'The station we hold in Europe, so much beyond our natural power, we hold by means of our commercial advantages' (Simmons and Thomas 4.37). In a debate on 19 April 1774 on the American tea tax, he asserted that the colonists had 'a system to gain step by step, to clear themselves from the control of this country'. After denial of Britain's right of taxation, 'the next step to be taken is you have no right to make laws binding upon them in any case whatever' (ibid., 4.182–3). Rice spoke less often after war followed his prediction of events, and he died during the conflict, on 2 August 1779. He was buried at Llandeilo, Carmarthenshire. The income from his estate, which Capability Brown had laid out in 1775, was then about £2500. In 1780 Lord Talbot obtained the title of Baron Dinevor, with special remainder to his daughter. On his death in 1782, Rice's widow therefore became a peeress in her own right, and their eldest son, George, succeeded as third Baron Dinevor when she died on 14 March 1793, leaving two sons and two daughters.

PETER D. G. THOMAS

Sources P. D. G. Thomas, *Politics in eighteenth-century Wales* (1997) · P. D. G. Thomas, *Tea party to independence: the third phase of the American Revolution, 1773–1776* (1991) · D. W. Howell, *Patriarchs and parasites: the gentry of south-west Wales in the eighteenth century* (1986) · HoP, *Commons* · R. C. Simmons and P. D. G. Thomas, eds., *Proceedings and debates of the British parliaments respecting North America, 1754–1783*, 4 (1985) · GEC, *Peerage*
Archives BL, corresp. with duke of Newcastle and Charles Jenkinson · Carmarthenshire RO, Carmarthen, Dynevor MSS · NL Wales, letters to John Johnes
Wealth at death approx. £2500 p.a.: Howell, *Patriarchs and parasites*, 54

Rice, Gruffudd (c.1526–1592). See under Rice family (*per.* c.1500–1651).

Rice, (Samuel) James (1844–1882), novelist, was born at Bridge Street, All Saints, Northampton, on 26 September 1844, the son of Samuel Rice and his wife, Ann Jane. On 1 November 1865 he was admitted at Queens' College, Cambridge, where he resided for nine terms.

In 1868 Rice became editor and proprietor of *Once a Week*, which he conducted at a financial loss until 1872. At the same time he was studying for the bar, and was called at Lincoln's Inn in 1871, but never obtained much practice. At Dublin in 1871 he married Lillie, daughter of George Latouche Dickinson of St Stephen's Green, Dublin; they had a son, Fabian Arthur Besant Rice. In 1872 Rice became London correspondent of the Toronto *Globe*.

Rice's reputation was assured by the publication in 1872 of *Ready-Money Mortiboy*, the first of the series of novels he issued in conjunction with Walter Besant, in a remarkable literary partnership. Rice numbered Besant among the contributors to *Once a Week*, and, after attempting single-handed a novel in its pages and publishing *The Cambridge Freshman* (1871) under the pseudonym Martin Legrand, Rice proposed that they should jointly write the novel which they entitled *Ready-Money Mortiboy*. The idea on which the story is founded was Rice's own; he had already written two or three chapters before inviting Besant's aid. It was published anonymously at the authors' risk, and proved a great literary, though not a great commercial, success; it was subsequently dramatized, under the title of *Ready-Money*, by the authors. The piece was produced at the Court Theatre on 12 March 1874, and printed.

After the appearance of its successor, *My Little Girl*, the partnership was for a time placed in jeopardy by Rice's resolution to devote himself to the bar; but he found little encouragement there, and soon returned to literature. *With Harp and Crown* appeared in 1874, and *This Son of Vulcan* in 1875. In 1876 the partners obtained a great success with *The Golden Butterfly*, which was very popular owing in part to the advantage it derived from publication in *The World*. *The Monks of Thelema* (1877) also appeared in *The World*, and in 1878 and 1879 *By Celia's Arbour* and *The Chaplain of the Fleet* were published in *The Graphic*. The last novel in which Rice had a share was *The Seamy Side* (1881). He and his colleague had for some time past been writing Christmas stories for *All the Year Round* and *The World*, and had made some unsuccessful experiments in the drama. In 1879 Rice published a *History of the British Turf* in two volumes, which was more of a lively contribution to the subject than a serious history, consisting mainly of gossip and desultory essays.

In January 1881 Rice, whose health had hitherto been excellent, was attacked by a serious illness, and, although he apparently recovered, could never rally from its results. He died at his home, Hill Bank, Reigate Road, Redhill, of heart failure combined with an unspecified throat ailment on 26 April 1882.

Besant, writing to *The Athenaeum* on the day of his death, spoke of Rice as eminently large-minded, thoroughly businesslike, and full of loyalty and goodness of heart.

RICHARD GARNETT, *rev.* MEGAN A. STEPHAN

Sources Venn, *Alum. Cant.* · W. Besant, 'Preface', in W. Besant and J. Rice, *Ready-money Mortiboy*, 1887 edn · W. Besant, *The Athenaeum* (29 April 1882) · Allibone, *Dict.* · Boase, *Mod. Eng. biog.* · *CGPLA Eng. & Wales* (1882) · b. cert.

Likenesses A. S. Wortley, double portrait, oils, 1882 (with W. Besant), NPG · wood-engraving (after photograph by London Stereoscopic Co.), NPG; repro. in *ILN* (13 May 1882)

Wealth at death £3281 15s. 2d.: probate, 6 July 1882, *CGPLA Eng. & Wales*

Rice, Marcia Alice (1868–1958), headmistress and historian, was born at 6 Ainslie Place, Edinburgh, on 5 December 1868, the second child and eldest daughter of Lieutenant-Colonel Cecil Rice of the Seaforth Highlanders and his wife, Frances Anne Napier. She was educated privately and knew Latin and Greek when she went up to St Hugh's Hall in Oxford at the age of twenty-five. She was awarded a brilliant first in English in 1898, though she could not take her degree formally until 1920 (MA). She was awarded an MA by the University of Dublin in 1906.

In 1899 Marcia Rice became a housemistress and teacher of classics and English at Godolphin School, Salisbury. A tall and dignified woman with a sense of humour, she had few disciplinary problems. In 1900 she was appointed headmistress of St Anne's School, Abbots Bromley, begun by the Woodard foundation in 1874. When Marcia Rice arrived, there were fifty-four girls. By 1913 numbers had increased to more than 100 as a result of her efficient and enlightened regime. She introduced grouping into four houses, which entailed the purchase of neighbouring property, a prefect system (1910), and a debating society—the St Anne's Political and Social Problems Club (1905). Successful school certificate and university entrance results did not lead to neglect of technical and practical subjects, and games for the less academic pupils. Miss Rice showed tact during the amalgamation of St Anne's with the sister school of St Mary's, where the girls came from modest backgrounds, in 1921. During the First World War a girls' cadet corps was formed, which became the Girl Guides on the coming of peace. Marcia Rice had strong Scottish episcopalian religious principles, and combined these with the ideals of international brotherhood of man through support for the League of Nations. As part of a progressive education policy, some disciplinary powers were transferred from staff to girls, visits from outside lecturers were encouraged, and there was concern for the poor in urban areas and industry. However, the chapel remained central to the school and contributions continued to be made to the overseas missions of the Church of England.

Marcia Rice retired to Oxford in 1931, when school numbers at St Mary and St Anne had risen to over 300. She had long collected material relating to the history of Abbots Bromley through documentary evidence as well as topographical and archaeological study of the area. She had a wide circle of social contacts among the gentry, the professional and trading classes, and the servants and poor, whom she assisted through charitable work and contributions to local social clubs. Thus she was able to become a pioneer of oral history, meticulously recording conversations as they occurred and examining the validity of family memories over several centuries. Her well-illustrated and comprehensive *Abbots Bromley* (1939) was notable for her dispassionate consideration of theories as to the origin of the horn dance and her use of varied folk material. The work was of anthropological as well as historical significance.

In spite of wartime difficulties and increasing infirmity, Marcia Rice completed *The Story of St Mary's, Abbots Bromley*

(1947), which provided useful information on the history of the school up to the point when she became headmistress, though she was modest and discreet about her own achievements. Otherwise it was a classic of the history of women's education in pioneering times. Marcia Alice Rice died at St Josephs Nursing Home, Boars Hill, Sunningwell, Berkshire, on 22 April 1958 of coronary thrombosis. Her life had been important to acceptance of female academic achievement at Oxford University and to the study of history generally. She stands out among early headmistresses of Anglican public schools for her progressive ideas and scholarship.   V. E. Chancellor

Sources M. E. Hall and V. M. Macpherson, *Marcia Alice Rice: the story of a great headmistress* (1961) · V. M. Macpherson, *The story of St Anne's, Abbots Bromley, 1874–1924* (1924) · M. A. Rice, *Story of St Mary's (School)*, Abbots Bromley (1947) · A. Wells and S. Meads, *St Mary and St Anne: the second fifty years* (1974) · K. E. Kirk, *The story of the Woodard schools* (1937) · L. W. Cowie and E. E. Cowie, *That one idea: Nathaniel Woodard and his schools* (1991) · *St Mary's Magazine* (1903) · *St Anne's Guild Magazine* [with St Mary's after 1921] (1907) · T. Pape, 'Foreword', in M. A. Rice, *Abbots Bromley* (1939) · *St Hugh's Chronicle*, 31 (1959) · B. Heeney, *Mission to the middle classes: the Woodard schools, 1848–1891* (1969) · F. Watson, ed., *The encyclopedia and dictionary of education, 1848–1891*, 4 vols. (1922) · St Hugh's College, Oxford · d. cert.

Archives St Hugh's College, Oxford · Woodard School, Lancing, Sussex, archives

Likenesses T. W. Holgate, oils, 1931, School of St Mary and St Anne, Abbots Bromley, Staffordshire · photographs, repro. in Rice, *The story of St Mary's* · photographs, repro. in Macpherson, *The story of St Anne's* · photographs, repro. in Hall and Macpherson, *Marcia Alice Rice*, facing pp. 28 and 56

Wealth at death £11,318 17s. 9d.: probate, 11 July 1958, *CGPLA Eng. & Wales*

Rice, Margaret Lois [Margery] **Spring** [née Margaret Lois Garrett] (1887–1970), advocate of birth control, was born on 10 June 1887 at 25 Hamilton Terrace, Marylebone, London, the only daughter of Samuel Garrett (1850–1923), a solicitor in the City of London who became president of the Law Society, and his wife, Clara Thornbury. Her father, who was one of the first solicitors to accept women pupils, was the ninth child of Newson Garrett, a progressive-thinking and wealthy Suffolk maltster who built the Maltings at Snape. Garrett's paternal aunts included both Dame Millicent Fawcett and Elizabeth Garrett Anderson, who may well have sown the seeds of her lifelong interest in social welfare and reform. Her brother was Sir Ronald Garrett (1888–1972), a director of a shipping line and chairman of Lloyds.

After education by private governesses (Isabel Fry and Constance Crommelin) at home and in Paris, Garrett went to Bedford College and then read moral sciences at Girton College, Cambridge, from 1907 to 1910, gaining a second in part one of the tripos. Her subsequent training as a factory inspector was cut short by her marriage on 28 April 1911 to Captain Charles Edward Coursolles Jones, who, five years later, was killed on the Somme. They had two sons, Ronald and Charles Garrett-Jones. With her second husband, the financier (Edward) Dominick Spring Rice (1891–1940), whom she married on 26 July 1919, she had two children, Stephen and (Theodosia) Cecil; the latter,

like her mother, was a Girton graduate. Spring Rice and her second husband divorced in 1936.

Spring Rice was active in public life during the war as first secretary of the League of Nations Society (the forerunner of the League of Nations Association). Her public work grew steadily during the 1920s. From about 1922 to 1927 she was honorary treasurer of the Women's National Liberal Federation, and in 1924, in response to concerns expressed by her friends Mrs Lloyd and Margaret Pollock (later Margaret Pyke) about the appalling levels of poverty and overcrowding in North Kensington, she helped to set up the North Kensington birth control clinic and became its first chairman. This was at a time when contraception was still very little discussed; North Kensington had only the third such clinic in the country. For the next thirty-four years Spring Rice oversaw the work of the clinic; she pressed for its expansion in 1932, when the building was doubled in size and the provision of treatment and advice for minor gynaecological ailments was introduced, and she set up satellite clinics in Hounslow, Edgware, and Hayes.

Spring Rice's experience and contacts led her to get involved in the wider birth control movement. She wanted an independent co-ordinating body to advance the movement and to provide support for clinics to promote medical research. In 1930, with others, she persuaded Lady Denman, like Spring Rice a member of the Women's Liberal Federation, to become the founding chairman of the National Birth Control Association (from 1939 the Family Planning Association), which initially co-ordinated the work of and eventually absorbed the five existing national birth control bodies. Spring Rice served on the executive from 1930 to 1958, when she felt compelled to resign over proposed organizational changes. In 1930 she attended a conference on birth control in Los Angeles with the American family planning pioneer Margaret Sanger. 'The principle of democracy is inherent', she wrote in February 1939, 'in the right of the individual to decide for himself the degree to which he exercises the most important and far-reaching of his functions, that of procreation' (Family Planning Association archives A 1/2, p. 1).

In 1933 Spring Rice became a member of the women's health enquiry committee which was made up, on a non-political basis, of representatives from several women's organizations and to which she was appointed honorary secretary. She used the material collected by the committee on the health and living conditions of 1250 married working women from many parts of Britain as the basis for her book *Working-Class Wives: their Health and Conditions* (1939; repr. 1981), which had an introduction by Barbara Wootton. This painted a detailed picture of widespread poverty and poor health, much of it due to repeated pregnancies, miscarriages, and minor gynaecological problems, and gave rise to much public concern. Spring Rice was subsequently invited by the Eugenics Society to give a lecture on the subject and on the importance of women's health to the nation in wartime. An abstract of her text appeared in *The Lancet* (3 February 1940) and, in a slightly different version, in the *Eugenics Review* (32/2, 1940). Her other writings include three articles on wartime child evacuation in the *Times Education Supplement* and an article on population in the *Fortnightly Review*. She herself spent much of the Second World War in Woodbridge, near Aldeburgh, where at her home, Iken Hall, she ran a residential nursery for pre-school children evacuated from London without their parents.

Spring Rice was a passable pianist and had a keen interest in music. During the 1930s she acted as unpaid agent for the Rothschild Quartet, and after the war she founded the Suffolk Rural Music School in memory of her son Stephen, who was lost in a submarine in the Mediterranean in 1943. She also played a major role in founding the Aldeburgh festival, providing considerable financial support in the early years and, as a key member of the organizing committee, making suggestions for programmes and artists, and allowing Iken Hall to be used almost as a hotel for performers and guests. Her other interests included gardening, sailing, and countryside protection.

During the 1950s Spring Rice continued to further the development of family planning services, particularly in Suffolk where she helped to establish several clinics, including one at Ipswich of which she became chairman. She was also a co-opted member of the East Suffolk county council health committee. She spent her last few years at a nursing home in Aldeburgh and died from pneumonia in Aldeburgh Cottage Hospital on 21 April 1970.

Spring Rice made an invaluable contribution to the expansion and social acceptance of family planning. Not only was she prepared to take practical steps to provide information and treatment at a time when contraception was virtually a taboo subject, but she also recognized the importance of broadening the scope of the work and regularly argued for the provision of other family welfare services, such as advice on psychological difficulties in marriage and even on infertility—often with a sense of frustration at the more cautious approach of her colleagues and the continuing lack of financial resources.

In 1955, the silver jubilee year of the Family Planning Association, the health minister, Iain Macleod, paid a visit to the North Kensington clinic and asked the association to make the '"most of the occasion" by full-scale publicity' (Leathard). This was the first official ministerial visit to a family planning clinic and marked a significant turning point in social and governmental attitudes to contraception. For women like Spring Rice, whose vision, driving force, and 'combative spirit' (Margaret Pyke's phrase) had nurtured the movement in its early days, it was a momentous occasion. In a letter to Sir Theodore Fox who spoke at the Family Planning Association dinner in 1966, Spring Rice rejoiced in the fact that 'there is nothing and nobody to be afraid of anymore, and that all in good time we will conquer the world with the most merciful "movement" that has ever been' (Spring Rice papers).

SYLVIA DUNKLEY

Sources K. T. Butler and H. I. McMorran, eds., *Girton College register, 1869–1946* (1948) · A. Leathard, *The fight for family planning: the development of family planning services in Britain, 1921–1974* (1980) · M. Spring Rice, *Working-class wives* (1981) · *The Times* (30 April 1970) · *Family Planning* (July 1970) · Wellcome L., Family Planning Association archives, Spring Rice papers · *Making Music* [Rural Music School Association] (summer 1970) · letter to Rosamund Strode from Ronald Garrett-Jones, Benslow Music Trust, Little Benslow Hills, Hitchin, Hertfordshire · b. cert. · d. cert. · Burke, *Peerage* (2000) [Monteagle of Brandon] · archives of the Family Planning Association, University College, Cardiff, David Owen Centre for Population Growth Studies

Archives Wellcome L., Family Planning Association archives, papers | Britten–Pears Library, The Red House, Aldeburgh, Suffolk, corresp. with B. Britten · Wellcome L., North Kensington Women's Welfare Centre archive | SOUND Francis A. Countway Library of Medicine, Boston, Norman Hime collection, transcripts of interviews with people running birth control clinics, incl. Spring Rice

Likenesses photograph, Little Benslow Hills · photograph, repro. in Leathard, *Fight for family planning*, pl. 4

Wealth at death £8448: probate, 3 July 1970, *CGPLA Eng. & Wales*

Rice, Peter Ronan (1935–1992), structural engineer, was born on 16 June 1935 at 26 Upper Pembroke Street, Dublin, the son of James Patrick Rice of Dundalk, chief education officer for co. Louth, and his wife, Maureen, *née* Quinn. He was educated at the Christian Brothers' school in Dundalk and at fifteen was sent to Newbridge, a boarding school, before entering Queen's University, Belfast, to read civil engineering. He graduated in 1956, and after a year working for Ove Arup & Partners in London he spent the year 1957–8 at Imperial College, London. He then rejoined Arup in 1958 to work on the geometry of the shells forming the roof of the Sydney Opera House, designed by the Finnish architect Jorn Utzon, before moving to Australia as site engineer in 1963. Arup believed in the concept of total design, stressing the importance of the integration of design and construction, and Rice later described him as his 'father in engineering'. Like Arup, Rice wanted to be involved from the conception of a project, and he regarded the distinction between creation and invention as the key to understanding the difference between the architect and the engineer, and how they could contribute in different ways to the same project: the role of the engineer was to realize the architect's vision. After his return from Sydney he spent the year 1966–7 at Cornell University, New York, applying pure mathematics to engineering problems, and worked with Frei Otto on the mathematics of lightweight roof structures. Meanwhile, on 7 December 1960 he had married Sylvia Watson, bookkeeper and daughter of Robert James Watson, porter; they had one son and three daughters.

Rice's career took off in 1971 when the architectural partnership of Renzo Piano and Richard Rogers won the competition to design the Centre Beaubourg in Paris (renamed the Centre Georges Pompidou in 1974), intended as a popular palace of culture, containing a museum of modern art. Their idea was to have a large open steel framework: Ove Arup & Partners were appointed consultants, and Rice was put in charge of the structural engineering team. He was appointed a director of the partnership in 1978. Continuing his collaboration with Richard Rogers he worked on the Lloyds building (1978) in London, and PA Technology (1982) in Princeton,

USA. With Norman Foster he worked on the new terminal at Stansted airport (1981), and in collaboration with Michael Hopkins he designed the Mound stand (1985) at Lord's cricket ground. The stone arcade forming the façade of the Pavilion of the Future for Expo '92 in Seville (1989) was the last project he finished.

After their collaboration on the Centre Georges Pompidou, Piano and Rice Associates was formed in 1977 to take on experimental projects that would benefit from integrating architectural and engineering input. Fiat commissioned them to reconsider the car from first principles, and to develop ideas for a car of the future, the Fiat VSS, setting up a research institute in Turin. Another commission for Fiat was the Flying Carpet, a car designed for use in north Africa. With a reinforced concrete chassis, the 'mechanical mule' could be fitted with Fiat components, but it was never built. For UNESCO they devised a strategy for regenerating rundown historic town centres, which they implemented in 1979 in Otranto, in southern Italy, where they set up a mobile neighbourhood urban reconstruction workshop in the piazza, to demonstrate how to use up-to-date technology to repair the town. Although the partnership was dissolved in 1980 Rice continued to work on many of Renzo Piano's buildings, including the Menil Collection Gallery (1981) in Houston, Texas, with a roof of ferro-cement leaves, and the World Cup football stadium (1986) in Bari, Italy.

While remaining a director and partner of Arup, in 1981 Rice established his own practice, RFR Consulting Engineers, in Paris, with Martin Francis and Ian Ritchie, to take on projects in France. The first was at the Musée des Sciences et de l'Industrie at the Parc de la Villette in Paris, where he designed the structures for the *grandes serres* (1981), the conservatories that linked the museum to the park. Here he developed a new method of using glass as a structural material to create a lighter effect, and with Hugh Dutton he published *Le verre structurel* (1990; translated as *Structural glass*, 1995). He also used his new technique in the construction of the *grande pyramide* of the Louvre (1985) for the American architect I. M. Pei. One of his last projects for RFR was the Full Moon Theatre (1988), near Montpellier in southern France, lit entirely by reflected moonlight.

A supporter of Queen's Park Rangers, Rice loved football and going to the races—he designed the queen's stand at Epsom racecourse (1989)—and he also liked to read poetry and philosophy. He was a devout Roman Catholic. Described by Richard Rogers as one of the greatest engineers of the twentieth century he was awarded the royal gold medal for architecture of the Royal Institute of British Architects in June 1992. On 25 October 1992 he died from a brain tumour at the Hospital of St John and St Elizabeth, Westminster.

Among the projects unfinished at Rice's death were the TGV railway station at Lille (1991), one of several TGV stations he designed, including the Paris–Roissy *aérogare*; a second pyramid for the Louvre (1991) to reflect daylight into the underground shopping areas; the west façade of Lille Cathedral (1991); and the terminal building at Kansai international airport (1988) at Osaka, Japan, with Renzo Piano. During his illness he wrote *An Engineer Imagines* (1994), less an autobiography than an exploration of some of his engineering projects, which conveyed his exuberance and his enthusiasm for his profession. A Peter Rice scholarship was established in 1994 at the Harvard Graduate School of Design. ANNE PIMLOTT BAKER

Sources P. Rice, *An engineer imagines* (1994) · P. Rice and H. Dutton, *Structural glass* (1995) · P. Buchanan, *Renzo Piano building workshop*, 1 (1993), 64–77 · R. Piano, *The Renzo Piano logbook* (1997) · *The Guardian* (2 July 1992) · *The Independent* (29 Oct 1992) · *Daily Telegraph* (30 Oct 1992) · *The Times* (7 Nov 1992) · WWW · b. cert. · m. cert. · d. cert. · *CGPLA Eng. & Wales* (1993)
Archives FILM BBC WAC
Likenesses photograph, 1992, repro. in *Daily Telegraph* · photograph, repro. in *The Times* · photograph, repro. in P. Rice, *An engineer imagines* (1994), 18
Wealth at death £193,400: probate, 29 March 1993, *CGPLA Eng. & Wales*

Rice [Price], **Richard** [Richard ap Robert ap Rhys] (1511–1589), abbot of Aberconwy and translator, came of a noted north Wales family. His grandfather Rhys Fawr had been standard-bearer to Henry VII at Bosworth and placed Richard's father, Robert, into the church, where his career included time as Cardinal Wolsey's personal chaplain. On returning to north Wales as chancellor and vicar-general of St Asaph, Robert became a wealthy and powerful man. It was at his estate at Plas Iolyn, near Pentrefoelas, that Richard Rice was brought up, one of twelve sons and four daughters. Rice's elder brother Ellis *Price (Y Doctor Coch) followed his father as chancellor of St Asaph. It was as member of a visitation of monastic houses in 1536 that he managed to secure Rice's appointment as abbot of the Cistercian house of Conwy or Aberconwy, despite Rice's being only twenty-four and thus under the canonical age. The family already had strong links with the house: as far back as 1506 Robert ap Rhys was said to have had ninety-nine-year leases of many of the abbey farms. In addition, Rice's brother Huw had been abbot from 1526 to 1528, dying in office while still a student at Cambridge. Even more recently, in 1534, the then abbot of Conwy had mortgaged 12,000 acres of Hiraethog to Ellis (the money being left under Robert ap Rhys's will in trust for his six children who were still minors).

At the time of his election to the abbacy Rice was already a monk, although whether he was studying at a university or attached to a house is not known. At the same time John, another brother, was abbot of Strata Marcella. The dominance of the north Wales church by the family was a concern to some, and prompted Richard Bulkeley to protest strongly to Thomas Cromwell about Rice's appointment, describing him as 'a wilful and misruled person, who would utterly destroy the said abbey within a short space' (Hays, 161). The complaint was not heeded and, as it turned out, external events brought a swifter and more conclusive demise for Aberconwy. Henry VIII's ecclesiastical policy saw to it that, after less than a year in office, Rice was petitioning Cromwell in an attempt to ensure that if his house was not spared dissolution its possessions could be farmed by one of his 'poor brethren' (ibid., 177).

His correspondence with Cromwell suggests a certain desperation at having paid heavily for his election and then seen little return for his money. As part of the dissolution settlement, Rice received the rectories of Llanbadrig and Eglwys-bach (previously possessed by the abbey) as well as a pension of £20 a year, which he is known to have received until at least 1553. He later married Janet ferch Elis ap Harri ap Cynwrig ab Ithel Fychan of Ysgeifiog, and became parson of Cerrigydrudion, Denbighshire (the Star Chamber proceedings record that a previous holder of this benefice had been terrorized by Rice's father).

In the post-Reformation period Rice published *The right institution of baptism set forth by the Reverend Father in Christ Herman, archbishop of Cologne, whereunto is also annexed a godly treatys of matrimonie* (1548). These translations of pastoral works by a cautious would-be reformer of Cologne, and the reformer and preacher of Augsburg, Wolfgang Musculus, were thoroughly unexceptionable. Rice may well have held hopes of a Welsh bishopric, but unlike some of those Englishmen who had been abbots before the dissolution no former Welsh abbots ever gained episcopal rank. Over thirty years after his first publication he added to it his second and last, *An invective against vices taken for virtue; also certeine necessary instructions meet to be taught the younger sort before they come to be partakers of the holy communion* (1579). Rice died at his living of Cerrigydrudion in 1589. His son and heir, Thomas Wynn of Plas Newydd, Llanrwst, was high sheriff of Denbighshire in 1595.

MIHAIL DAFYDD EVANS

Sources G. Williams, *Wales and the Reformation* (1997) · G. Williams, *The Welsh church from conquest to Reformation* (1962) · R. W. Hays, *The history of the abbey of Aberconwy* (1963) · D. R. Thomas, *Esgobaeth Llanelwy: the history of the diocese of St Asaph*, rev. edn, 3 vols. (1908–13) · J. Y. W. Lloyd, *The history of Powys Fadog* (1881–7) · *Heraldic visitations of Wales and part of the marches ... by Lewys Dwnn*, ed. S. R. Meyrick, 2 vols. (1846) · A. I. Pryce, *The diocese of Bangor in the sixteenth century* (1923)

Rice, Sir Stephen (1637?–1715), judge, was probably the eldest son of Edward Rice (*d.* in or before 1672), of Dingle, co. Kerry, and Christian, daughter of Peter Nagle, although some doubt as to his parentage remains. Raised a Roman Catholic, the religion he continued to profess, Rice was admitted a student of the Middle Temple in January 1672. Two years later, in 1674, Rice joined King's Inns, the Irish inn of court. William King, later archbishop of Dublin, described Rice at this juncture as 'a rook and a gamester'—a possible partisan slur on the part of a political adversary—but conceded that Rice's subsequent acquisition of a substantial practice was merited since he was 'well enough versed in the law' (King, 80). Rice developed special expertise in handling cases involving crown revenues, but it was his religion which secured his advancement when James II, on his accession in 1685, initiated a policy of appointing Catholics to offices in the gift of the crown. In the spring of 1686 Sir Standish Hartstonge was summarily removed as a baron of the exchequer and replaced by Rice. The Anglican Lord Clarendon, as lord lieutenant of Ireland, protested over the manner of the appointment. Straightaway Rice was elevated to the privy council—again over Clarendon's protests—and the following year he was promoted to chief baron of the exchequer and knighted. Beside the diet of civil suits heard in Dublin and the criminal work of the assize circuits, in all of which Rice participated, the exchequer court, over which Rice now presided, oversaw a rash of *quo warranto* proceedings, the avowed object of which was to secure the replacement of existing borough charters by new ones that would restore Catholics to a prominent role in Irish municipal affairs.

As a privy councillor, Rice was intimately concerned in the execution of the policies of the earl of Tyrconnell, who replaced Clarendon in Ireland in January 1687, to consolidate the Catholic interest in Ireland, being one of 'les chefs de toutes les affaires qui regardent le dedans du royaume' ('the leading men who attend to the internal affairs of the kingdom'; Hogan, 55). In August 1687 Rice accompanied Tyrconnell, Thomas Sheridan, Tyrconnell's secretary, and Richard Nagle, the attorney-general, to Chester for a meeting with the king, at which two pressing matters of Irish business, the shortfall in the crown's revenue and the Restoration land settlement, were both discussed. The Irish delegation had dinner with Bishop Cartwright of Chester, but accounts differ over the political decisions taken at the meeting with James and over how these were reached. That James sympathized with the arguments in favour of some modification of the 1662 and 1665 Acts of Settlement and Explanation—arguments which Rice can be presumed to have forcefully reiterated—seems plain enough, but James for the moment held back, troubled at the prospect of loss of support in England if he moved too precipitately in favour of his Irish Catholic subjects.

It was, however, accepted that emissaries should again travel to England carrying detailed drafts of alternative bills to be introduced in the Irish parliament to reshape the land settlement. In February 1688 Rice, accompanied on this occasion by Thomas Nugent, the chief justice of king's bench, went to London, hoping to take things further, but the mission was not a success. Word had spread as to the aim of Rice and Nugent's visit and a London mob reportedly demonstrated carrying potatoes impaled on sticks and shouting, 'Make way for the Irish ambassadors' (Simms, 41). It was only at James's Irish parliament in the early summer of 1689 that the nettle was finally grasped, and an act of forty-one tortuous sections adopted (5 James II c. 4), repealing outright the Acts of Settlement and Explanation. In the intervening period much occurred in which Rice had a leading role. Most of May 1688 Rice spent, in the company of four other judges, in the conduct of the private investigation into charges of corruption against Thomas Sheridan, Tyrconnell's secretary, and, as it happened, a fellow Middle Templar. Miller has pronounced the charges against Sheridan 'false and malicious' (Miller, 'Thomas Sheridan', 105). None of the judges emerges with credit over the eventual outcome, a decision adverse to Sheridan.

In January 1689, following James's flight from England,

Rice was entrusted by Tyrconnell, to whom he remained extremely close, with yet another mission: this time to travel to France in the company of Viscount Mountjoy to sound out James on his plans. Mountjoy understood that their instructions were to dissuade the king from attempting any incursion in Ireland, since by resorting to such action 'he could ruin it and make it a heap of rubbish' (*Ormonde MSS*, new ser., 8.14), but it seems Rice carried other instructions: a possible champion of Irish protestants, Mountjoy was adjudged traitorous and dangerous and, on arrival on the continent, was to be instantly incarcerated by the French. James himself may have mildly protested, but to no avail, and Mountjoy was lodged in the Bastille. Rice accompanied James when the latter went to Ireland, landing at Kinsale, co. Cork, in March 1689 and returning with him into exile after the defeat at the Boyne in July 1690. In one Frenchman's view, neither Rice nor Nugent, another member of the inner circle, impressed during what proved a critical phase for the Jacobite cause. These two lawyers, wrote Auffroy, the French army contractor, in December 1689:

> ne se picquent pas d'en scavoir davantage, et lorsqu' il y a quelques difficultez (ce que arrive souvent) il faut nommer des personnes pour les terminer, et cela cause des longueurs et des retardemens aux affaires les plus pressées (do not boast any great knowledge of things, and when there are difficulties (which frequently occurs), one has to name others to resolve them, and that causes endless discussion and delays in dealing with the most urgent business). (Molloy, 215)

Rice was back in Ireland in January 1691 in time for the final collapse of the cause itself. Though listed for attainder by the English Commons in August 1689, he was adjudged to come within the terms of the articles of Limerick; he thus remained in possession of his estates. Deprived of office but perhaps resuming legal practice, Rice survived as a voice prepared to speak out on public matters. In 1695 he joined a group that protested unavailingly at double taxes levied on Catholics under a poll tax measure. More memorably, in February 1704 he joined Theobald Butler and Counsellor Malone in vainly presenting an address to both the Irish Commons and the Irish Lords against the bill that was to become the infamous 1704 Act to Prevent the Further Growth of Popery.

Rice married Mary, daughter of Thomas Fitzgerald of Ballylaghan, co. Limerick. They had three sons and a daughter. The eldest son, Edward, converted to protestantism, and thus secured the family's estates against the operation of the gavel authorized by the penal laws (though evidence was presented in litigation in 1738 that Edward may have relapsed before his death in 1720). Rice died on 16 February 1715 and was interred in St James's Church in Dublin, a popular choice by the city's Catholics at the time. In 1726 Robert Dickson of Dame Street, Dublin, published a curious volume on litigation strategy, ascribed to 'Sir S. Rice, kt', but of questionable authenticity, given the length of time since Rice's death, titled *The great law of the crown, or, A sure guide for all persons concerned in the bishop's court, also a concise body of more immediate direction, for any one endited therein, how to evade the exorbitant expences usually attending suits there, collected from the statutes.*

W. N. OSBOROUGH

Sources H. A. C. Sturgess, ed., *Register of admissions to the Honourable Society of the Middle Temple, from the fifteenth century to the year 1944*, 1 (1949) · B. O' Connell, 'The Nagles of Mount Nagle', *Irish Genealogist*, 2 (1943–55), 377–89 · M. A. Hickson, *Selections from old Kerry records* (1872) · *The correspondence of Henry Hyde, earl of Clarendon, and of his brother Laurence Hyde, earl of Rochester*, ed. S. W. Singer, 2 vols. (1828) · W. King, *The state of the protestants of Ireland under the late King James's government* (1768) · J. T. Gilbert, ed., *A Jacobite narrative of the war in Ireland, 1688–1691* (1892) · J. Miller, 'The earl of Tyrconnell and James II's Irish policy, 1685–1688', *HJ*, 20 (1977), 803–23 · J. Hiller, 'Thomas Sheridan (1646–1712) and his "Narrative"', *Irish Historical Studies*, 20 (1976–7), 105–28 · J. G. Simms, *Jacobite Ireland, 1685–91* (1969) · J. Brown, *Reports of cases upon appeals and writs of error determined in the high court of parliament*, 2nd rev. edn (1803) · *CSP dom.*, 1686–7; 1695 · C. McNeill, 'Reports on the Rawlinson collection', *Analecta Hibernica*, 1 (1930), 12–178 · *Calendar of the manuscripts of the marquess of Ormonde*, new ser., 8 vols., HMC, 36 (1902–20), vols. 7–8 · *Report on the manuscripts of Allan George Finch*, 5 vols., HMC, 71 (1913–2003), vols. 2–3 · J. D'Alton, *Illustrations, historical and genealogical, of King James's Irish army list, 1689* (1855) · J. G. Simms, *The Williamite confiscation in Ireland, 1690–1703* (1956) · *An Act for Repealing the Acts of Settlement, and Explanation, Resolution of the Doubts, and all Grants, Patents and Certificates Pursuant to Them or Any of Them* [5 James II c. 4] · R. H. Murray, *Revolutionary Ireland and its settlement* (1911) · E. Keane, P. Beryl Phair, and T. U. Sadleir, eds., *King's Inns admission papers, 1607–1867*, IMC (1982) · T. Power, 'The "black book" of king's inns: an introduction with an abstract of contents', *Irish Jurist*, new ser., 20 (1985), 135–212 · F. E. Ball, *The judges in Ireland, 1221–1921*, 1 (1926) · *The diary of Thomas Cartwright, bishop of Chester*, ed. J. Hunter, CS, 22 (1843) · *Négociations de M. le Comte d'Avaux en Irlande, 1689–90*, ed. J. Hogan, 1, IMC (1934) · S. Molloy, ed., *Franco-Irish correspondence, Dec. 1688–Feb. 1692*, 1 (1983) · J. Strange, *Reports of adjudged cases in the courts of chancery, kings bench, common pleas and exchequer*, 3rd edn, 2 (1795) · S. Rice, *The great law of the crown* (1726) · *DNB* · *Calendar of the Stuart papers belonging to his majesty the king, preserved at Windsor Castle*, 7 vols., HMC, 56 (1902–23), vol. 6

Rice, (Elena) Tamara Talbot- (1904–1993). *See under* Rice, David Talbot- (1903–1972).

Rice, Thomas Spring, first Baron Monteagle of Brandon (**1790–1866**), politician, was born on 8 February 1790 at 21 Mungret Street, Limerick, the elder son of Stephen Edward Rice (*d.* 1831) of Mount Trenchard, co. Limerick, and his wife, Catherine, daughter and sole heir of Thomas Spring of Ballycrispin, co. Kerry.

Spring Rice was born into a well-connected Irish gentry family (his paternal grandmother was a daughter of the knight of Kerry) only recently converted to protestantism. He matriculated at Trinity College, Cambridge, in 1809. His university career was terminated prematurely by his marriage on 11 July 1811 to Theodosia (1787–1839), daughter of Edmond Henry *Pery, the first earl of Limerick. They produced eight children while he studied law and laid the foundations for a political career. Spring Rice was a kind and generous parent, a loving husband, and a responsible landlord.

In 1820 Spring Rice won a seat in parliament for Limerick. He continued to sit for his native town until the Reform Act (1832) made his return there unlikely and he

Thomas Spring Rice, first Baron Monteagle of Brandon (1790–1866), by Francis Holl (after George Richmond, 1850s)

transferred to Cambridge where he remained for the rest of his Commons career. Spring Rice came to the notice of the third marquess of Lansdowne, who remained his patron for many years. The Bowood House circle mixed Benthamite utilitarianism and *laissez-faire* economics with traditional constitutional whiggism. The members had literary tastes: Spring Rice loved poetry and contributed articles to the *Edinburgh Review*. They were frightened by even a hint of boldness in the advocacy of reform. Spring Rice followed his leader into Canning's coalition ministry as under-secretary for the Home Office in July 1827, even though this required accepting deferral of Catholic emancipation. He resigned in January 1828 from the brief administration that followed Canning's death, although he had hoped to keep the centrist amalgamation together almost at any cost.

When the whigs returned to power as a unified party in November 1830, Spring Rice was made secretary of the Treasury. He worked closely with Lord Althorp on budgetary policy. In a government with a weak front bench in terms of speaking talent, his fluent debating style was much valued. In 1833 he expressed interest in gaining election as speaker, and made successive quests for the position in 1834–5, 1837, and 1838–9. His continual canvass for the chair made him increasingly unpopular in the House of Commons. He turned down the Irish secretaryship in May 1833, but was appointed colonial secretary with a seat in the cabinet after Stanley's resignation in 1834. In the latter position he did little to head off trouble in Canada, although his lifelong attachment to the antislavery movement and friendship with Thomas Fowell Buxton helped smooth the process of emancipation.

Spring Rice succeeded Althorp as chancellor of the exchequer after Peel's abortive attempt to form a government collapsed in April 1835. He was widely regarded as not up to the job both by contemporaries and later historians, and admitted his own 'inadequacy' (Murphy, 133–4; *Greville Memoirs*, 3.332, 4.19). His Church Rate Bill of 1837 was ignominiously abandoned, and his attempt to revise the charter of the Bank of Ireland was also a humiliating fiasco. His budgets were pedestrian, adequate when trade remained favourable and expenditures were controlled, but depression and crop failures, combined with rebellion in North America and the compensation charges due to plantation owners in the West Indies, created large deficits. In 1839 he departed from office in the face of withering criticism, consoled by a peerage (5 September 1839). In the Lords he was an active but peripheral figure.

Lady Theodosia died soon after her husband's resignation, and on 13 April 1841 Spring Rice married Mary Anne (1800–1889), daughter of John *Marshall, the Leeds industrialist. His second wife's fortune came in the nick of time. The Limerick estate had never been sufficient to support the family without the supplement of an official salary. Then the terrible famine of the 1840s wiped out much of Spring Rice's Irish income, and he spent the remainder on ameliorative measures. He responded to the catastrophe with compassion and intelligence. He lectured the men responsible for relief, especially Bessborough, Wood, Russell, and Trevelyan, about the condition of the starving masses and the necessity for effective remedies, urging the abandonment of the economic theories he had upheld for a lifetime in face of the immediate need 'to keep society together' (Howell-Thomas, 297, 308).

Spring Rice was a conventionally devout Anglican 'in a lowish sort of way' (Hilton, 237) who led his family in regular prayers and scripture readings, but he was ecumenical in the political and educational controversies surrounding religion, most notably in his support for appropriation of surplus revenues from the Church of Ireland to lay purposes. In 1835 Spring Rice declared that a 'clergy without flocks and parsons without congregations were scandals which endangered the existence of the Protestant establishment' (Murphy, 111). He believed moral and religious education was 'the greatest of all national duties' (Brent, 58, 246). Historians disagree about the extent of his commitment to state-supported education. Some see his role as central to the formation of whig policy in this area during the 1820s and 1830s (Newbould, 281; Paz, 70–71). Others question his commitment and cite his 'niggardly' allocation of funds to support innovation (Mandler, 183, 188, 190–91).

Spring Rice was a strong unionist and even went so far as to suggest in 1834, in a parliamentary speech which he later published, that Ireland be renamed 'West Britain' (Brent, 51). He feared repeal legislation would unleash dangerous conflict between the upper and lower classes in an already fragile social order. By showing what Lord Holland called 'injudicious reluctance' in conceding reductions in the stamp duty on newspapers and when introducing the penny post (1839), he alienated Liberal and radical opinion (Holland, 409). He took pride in his traditional whiggism, which, he told the poet Wordsworth, he 'had not added to … nor taken therefrom' over his whole career (Newbould, 316). His conservative opinions made him more comfortable with the Canningites and the 'Derby Dilly' than the mainstream of his party. It was characteristic of both his politics and his need for cash that he spent his last years enjoying the proceeds of the comptrollership of the exchequer, one of few sinecures that had survived from the era of 'Old Corruption', and was only dislodged from it in 1865 by Gladstone's determined efforts. He was never fully welcomed into the circle of the whig grandees and remained more Lansdowne's protégé than friend. One grandee thought so little of Spring Rice's dignity that he leap-frogged over his back in the lobby of the House of Commons. Though as a young man he had once escaped the Dublin police bent on preventing a duel by disguising himself as a servant and hiding on a roof-top, his life was otherwise curiously devoid of incident and enterprise. He left a blank silhouette on a political landscape teeming with colourful and distinguished characters. The diarist Charles Greville judged him 'indolent but full of vivacity'. He chaired the royal commission on decimal coinage from 1855 to 1859, when he resigned following parliamentary criticisms of the commissioners' slowness in producing a report. He was a commissioner of the state paper office, a trustee of the National Gallery, a member of the senate of the University of London and of the Queen's University in Ireland, and FRS and FGS (*DNB*). Spring Rice enjoyed the ease and privilege of the London cultural and political worlds, but he was ultimately unwilling to pay the cost of his pleasures by bearing the burden of ministerial responsibility. He died in Ireland at Mount Trenchard, co. Limerick, on 7 February 1866, and was buried at Shanagolden, co. Limerick.

ELLIS ARCHER WASSON

Sources C. M. Murphy, 'The life and politics of Thomas Spring Rice, 1st Baron Monteagle, 1790–1866', MA diss., University College, Cork, 1991 · I. Newbould, *Whiggery and reform, 1830–41* (1990) · R. Brent, *Liberal Anglican politics: whiggery, religion, and reform, 1830–1841* (1987) · P. Mandler, *Aristocratic government in the age of reform: whigs and liberals, 1830–1852* (1990) · D. Howell-Thomas, *Duncannon: reformer and reconciler, 1781–1847* (1992) · Lord Holland [H. R. V. Fox] and J. Allen, *The Holland House diaries, 1831–1840*, ed. A. D. Kriegel (1977) · A. Mitchell, *The whigs in opposition, 1815–1830* (1967) · E. A. Wasson, *Whig renaissance: Lord Althorp and the whig party, 1782–1845* (1987) · D. G. Paz, *The politics of working-class education in Britain, 1830–50* (1980) · *The Greville memoirs, 1814–1860*, ed. L. Strachey and R. Fulford, 8 vols. (1938) · B. Hilton, *The age of atonement: the influence of evangelicalism on social and economic thought, 1795–1865* (1988) · C. B. F. Woodham-Smith, *The great hunger: Ireland, 1845–1849* (1962) · GEC, *Peerage* · *Wellesley index* · *DNB*
Archives JRL · NL Ire., MS · priv. coll., MSS | BL, Babbage MSS · BL, Gladstone MSS · BL, Holland MSS · BL, Macvey Napier MSS · Bodl. Oxf., Theodosia Taylor MSS, MS Eng lett. d.27 · Bodl. RH, Buxton MSS · Borth. Inst., Halifax MSS · Derbys. RO, Wilmot-Horton MSS · Lpool RO, fourteenth earl of Derby MSS · NA Scot., Dalrymple MSS · NL Wales, Williams-Wynn MSS · PRO, Lord John Russell MSS · Royal Arch., Melbourne MSS · State Library of New South Wales, Sydney, Bourke MSS · Trinity Cam., Whewell MSS · U. Durham, Grey MSS · U. Edin., Chalmers MSS · U. Southampton L., Palmerston MSS · U. Southampton L., Wellington MSS · UCL, Brougham MSS · UCL, SDUK MSS · W. Sussex RO, Gordon Lennox MSS
Likenesses W. Turner, oils, 1820, Limerick chamber of commerce · R. Cooper, stipple, pubd 1825 (after J. Comerford), NG Ire. · E. U. Eddis, oils, *c.*1830–1839, Templenoe, Fermoy, Cork · J. Doyle, group portrait, lithograph, pubd 1834 (*The road to ruin*; after pencil and ink drawing), NG Ire. · J. Linnell, etching and mezzotint, pubd 1836 (after oil portrait, exh. RA 1835), NG Ire. · J. Linnell, mixed print, pubd 1836, BM, NPG · J. Doyle, group portrait, lithograph, pubd 1839 (*Another heavy blow …*), NG Ire. · L. MacDonald, marble bust, 1843, NG Ire. · C. Silvy, two photographs, 1861, NPG · J. Doyle, drawings, BM · G. Hayter, group portrait, oils (*The House of Commons, 1833*), NPG · F. Holl, stipple (after G. Richmond, 1850–59), NPG [*see illus.*] · J. Linnell, oils, Templenoe, Fermoy, Cork · M. A. Shee, oils, Limerick chamber of commerce
Wealth at death under £16,000: probate, 18 May 1866, *CGPLA Eng. & Wales*

Rice, Sir Walter (*c.*1562–1636). *See under* Rice family (*per. c.*1500–1651).

Rich, Barnaby (1542–1617), soldier and author, led a life which has been only lightly documented.

Life story Rich is thought to have been Essex-born, a suggestion supported by his service with troops from that county in 1562, by a business interest there in 1565, and by the titling of a treatise *A Martiall Conference … Newly Translated out of Essex into English* (1598). Rich also saw action under both earls of Essex. Arriving in Ireland on the ill-fated expedition to colonize Ulster in the company of the first earl of Essex, Walter Devereux, in July 1573, Rich participated in the equally disastrous campaign of Devereux's son in 1599, and was on hand to suppress the subsequent Essex rebellion of 1601. Other noteworthy participants in that early expedition to Ulster were lords Rich and Darcy, both from Essex, the latter married to Frances, Lord Rich's sister. These family connections may have afforded Barnaby Rich his opportunity to sail with Walter Devereux.

Rich lived under five monarchs, fighting or writing under three of them. He first saw action in France at the end of Mary's reign, then again in the Low Countries at the beginning of Elizabeth's. His promotion to military captain about 1574 coincides with his decision to become a writer. He was named a sea captain on 5 January 1586, but it is doubtful whether he saw action at sea. One week later, on 12 January 1586, at the church of St Mary Somerset, near Broken Wharf, Rich married Katheryn Easton. She was possibly a relative of Joyce Aston, to whom he dedicated *The Adventures of Brusanus* (1592), addressing her as 'My very good cosyn' (Cranfill and Bruce, 38). New evidence points to Rich having been married before, and this became a serious issue for him in the wake of the Bigamy Act of 1604. While he was away in Ireland in the summer of 1605 his (second) wife appeared before the commissary court of London on 22 June to answer accusations of bigamy. Rich was probably informed on by Captain Robert Gosnold, whom Rich had branded a traitor in letters to Robert Cecil after an acrimonious dinner party in the Isle of Wight on 3 September 1604. This tale of the arch-informer hoist with his own petard neatly captures the volatile mix of double-dealing, hypocrisy, and outrage characteristic of Rich.

Thus far the life. As one modern critic notes, 'The man who left such a sparse biographical account of himself also left a written record in excess of a half-million words' (Flanagan, 161). Rich is eminently quotable, but as such is merely mentioned in passing rather than mined or mulled over. The tendency to concentrate on *Riche his Farewell to Militarie Profession* (1581) and on the *New Description of Ireland* (1610) makes him appear more eccentric and idiosyncratic than he is. Even when its quality is questionable, Rich's writing retains a remarkable consistency. Taken as a whole his is undoubtedly the most comprehensive corpus covering early modern Ireland of any English author.

Multiple expertise If he is somewhat neglected as a literary figure in his own right and as an authority on Ireland, Rich is an acknowledged expert on military matters. Blooded in battle from boyhood, in *A Short Survey of Ireland* (1609) he remarked: 'I am a Souldier, a professed souldier, better practised in my pike then in my penne' (A3). A self-styled professional soldier, who attained gentle status through the title of captain, Rich professed experience and expertise, but also showed evidence of study. Military historians have noted that his arguments on warfare were based on considerable reading as well as experience in the front line. While privileging battle over books, Rich prescribed study as a crucial means of forming future strategy. In *A Right Exelent and Pleasant Dialogue* (1574) Rich recommends reading the ancients as perfect preparation for prosecuting a successful war, for by this means 'Alfonsus king of Aragon … learned boath armes, and the order of armes: and did not Lucullus by the study of his Bookes, become one of the noblest Captaines of all the Romaines?' (*A Right Exelent and Pleasaunt Dialogue*, 50; Webb, 244).

From the early 1570s until the last year of his life Rich published some twenty-six tracts and treatises: he was a prolific and popular writer. The subtitle of his last published pamphlet, *The Irish Hubbub, or, The English Hue and Crie* (1617) reflects the serio-comic tone of his texts as a whole: 'No lesse smarting then tickling'. His biographers have stressed the extent to which Rich was a self-made, self-taught writer whose twin careers rested on his colonial experiences. In his *Allarme to England* (1578) Rich remarked 'what I have written, was onely done in Ireland' (iii), while in the preface to *Riche his Farewell* he says the tales he is presenting to the public were composed or compiled 'in Ireland at a vacant tyme' (sig. B1). *The Irish Hubbub* opens with the lines: 'For want of a better cloake whereby to shelter these indeavours of my untutored penne, I have borrowed an Irish Mantle' (sig. A2). Although he was largely in England between 1592 and 1608, Rich continued to write on Irish topics and to see himself as an expert on Ireland, which he certainly was. His service to the crown included intelligence gathering and informing.

Problems of assessment Like Edmund Spenser, Rich claimed a connection with a noble family of the same name, in his case that of Lord Rich, the lord chancellor,

with whom he was 'distantly connected' (*DNB*). Like Spenser too, Rich has suffered the consequences of attracting a diverse readership. Irish historians value him as a chronicler of Dublin life at the turn of the century, and for his best-known treatise on Irish affairs, *A New Description of Ireland* (1610). He interests literary critics as a close contemporary of a host of Elizabethan writers and translators who found themselves in Ireland, Spenser and Ralegh being the most famous. Fellow 'minor Elizabethans' include Lodowick Bryskett, Thomas Churchyard, Geoffrey Fenton, and Barnaby Googe. Rich is remarkable for the length of his Irish association. One of his editors observed: 'Of all Elizabethan or Jacobean writers on Ireland Rich's acquaintance with the country was the closest and most continuous' ('Barnaby Rich's "Remembrance"', 126).

Rich was a colonial contemporary of Spenser, although students of literature look to him mainly as a source for Shakespeare. His 'Apolonius and Silla' in *Riche his Farewell to Militarie Profession* (1581) provided the plot for *Twelfth Night*. Shakespeare may have drawn on two other stories for that play and for *The Merry Wives of Windsor*, while *Othello* owes a debt to Sappho, duke of Mantona. It was suggested by Sidney Lee in the *Dictionary of National Biography* that one of the characters in *The Adventures of Brusanus* (1592) has a close kinship with Armado in *Love's Labours Lost*. Rich's own influences are diverse. He was versed in the work of his contemporaries: *The Straunge and Wonderful Adventures of Don Simonides* (1581) suggests an engagement with Lyly's *Euphues*, and one of the speakers in his dialogue 'Anothomy of Ireland' bears the name Philautus, borrowed from *Euphues*. The tale by Bandello forming the second part of *A Right Exelent and Pleasant Dialogue* had already been translated and published by Geoffrey Fenton, himself later a key figure in the Anglo-Irish administration, as part of his *Tragicall Discourses* (1567).

Rich suffers from a lack of credibility. His status as a source for Shakespeare notwithstanding, he is regarded as a minor writer, modest in terms of literary talent if not output. Sidney Lee voiced a common conception when he declared: 'His verse is contemptible, but much literary feeling is often apparent in his prose' (*DNB*). Irish historians have been less enamoured of his prose style, taking his outpourings on Ireland less seriously than those of his more accomplished contemporaries, such as Spenser and Sir John Davies, so that Rich 'for all his persistence and literary workmanship, remains an excluded figure' (Flanagan, 159). Lacking the seniority or high office of his fellow English colonists, or the critical acclaim of literary contemporaries, Rich has languished in that limbo between literature and history, the last resort of historian and literary critic alike. Both sets of critics regard Rich as a rather low character—popular, polemical, and prolific, superficial rather than serious—who wrote for a rude and untutored readership. In this they are merely echoing the prejudice of Rich's contemporaries. In *Have with You to Saffron Walden* (1596) Thomas Nashe depicts Rich as 'the favourite reading of Lichfield, the Cambridge barber' (*DNB*).

Writer on war　At least six of Rich's works were devoted to the art of war: *A Right Exelent and Pleasant Dialogue, betwene Mercury and an English Souldier* (1574); *Allarme to England* (1578); *A Path-Way to Military Practise* (1587); *A Martiall Conference* (1598); *The Fruites of Long Experience* (1604); and *Faultes Faults, and Nothing Else but Faultes* (1606). Similarities have been noted between Rich's first military tract and *The Arte of Warre* (1560), Peter Whitehorne's translation of Machiavelli. Rich has been credited with elaborating ten key ideas about armed conflict, some derivative, but all relevant to contemporary theories of warfare: preparedness; training; selection of soldiers; education; leadership; wages; the consideration due to soldiers; care of veterans; discipline; and the nobility and the military profession. Rich's chief bugbears were peacemongers or 'carpet knights', their peace and pleasure purchased with the lives of the soldiers they neglected (*A Right Exelent and Pleasant Dialogue*, sig. Miii).

The most important essay on Rich's military writings, written during the Second World War, argues that his work as an engaged and committed ideologue has to be understood in the context of contemporary conflict:

> He shows himself to be, not a great man, but certainly a solid man whose contributions to military literature are historically speaking every bit as important as Shakespeare's contributions to drama. Only in war time, unfortunately, does the obviousness of that fact become apparent.　(Webb, 252)

The irony of these words is that Rich of course contributed to Shakespeare's drama as well as augmenting military literature. From an Irish perspective, Rich has suffered from an overwhelming concern with his most mature works, notably *A New Description of Ireland*, arguably his least interesting political treatise. His three earliest works remain his most significant—*A Right Exelent and Pleasant Dialogue*, *Allarme to England*, and *Riche his Farewell*. In many ways the first two are preparations for the third, and all are variations on a lifelong theme of the ingratitude of the citizenry towards soldiers.

Riche his Farewell (1581) is dedicated to warriors and women, linked through the trope of effeminacy—and with it entertainment and indolence—won by waging war. It is read as a resentful response to George Pettie's *Petite Pallace of Pettie his Pleasure* (1566; 1576), and other attempts by male authors to find favour with women readers, 'a story both of self-loathing and of political discontent' (Fleming, 166). Critics regard this collection of fictions, one of many long goodbyes that Rich took from military service, as a genuine if short-lived turning away, when in fact his work flits constantly between fighting and its fruits, both bitter and sweet.

Irish images　Rich benefited from being in Ireland, a highly marketable literary commodity in the period, as well as the site of more or less permanent conflict—indeed, the perfect home for an aspiring soldier–poet. If Ireland was a land of ire, it was also a place of safety and retreat, a secure site from which to critique England, often under allegorical cover of attacking Irish habits. *The Irish Hubbub*'s alternative title was *The English Hue and Crie*, and the full title of *Roome for a Gentleman, or, The Second Part of Faultes* (1609) is also revealing: 'collected and gathered for the true Meridian of Dublin in Ireland, and may serve fitly else whereabout, London &c'. This lends weight to the claim that English writers intent upon reforming Ireland had one eye on England. Professions of loyalty notwithstanding, the most vexed element of such a covert critique is the attitude to female rule. Rich's attacks on the extravagance of English women are a case in point. When Elizabethan Englishmen in Ireland complain of female profligacy amid under-funding for the army, they are attacking royal policy.

Rich began his career berating the wild Irish and ended it rebuking the wild English. He portrays Ireland, through his intimate knowledge of Dublin, as a modern metropolis obsessed with the latest fashions, bourgeois ahead of its time, a perspective at odds with standard English views. Ireland afforded Rich his muse and military acumen. The very licence and liberty he complained of gave him the freedom to forge his own identity and frame his narratives. Ireland was a country without a resident monarch, and as a virtual republic it afforded English writers the time and space to breathe and think at a safe distance from the policing and patronage of the court. As Rich put it in one of his last works, unpublished in his own lifetime: 'thos wordes that in *Englande* would be brought wythin the compasse of treason, they are accounted wyth us in *Ireland* for ordynary table taulke' (Hinton, 91).

Where better to denounce treason and tobacco, two of Rich's subjects of loathing, than in England's first colony? In *The Irish Hubbub* Rich turns to the topic of tobacco when four youths pass his window in Dublin, the fumes from their pipes giving offence: 'I began to wonder how a filthy stinking Antidot could so bewitch men to forget themselves.' Rich observes that some physicians take it, 'But I have heard as wise, as learned, and as honest Phisitians, as any bee in England, that have said Tobacco hath both killed, and shorted many mens lives' (pp. 37–8). Rich warms to his subject, managing to mingle smoking and sedition. Rather perversely, perhaps minded of the burning of incense, Rich sees pipe smoking as a peculiarly 'papist' pastime:

> Tobacco is like a Popes Bull, that Papists doe thinke to be a good discharge of all the sinnes they can commit, from the meanest to the maynest, from the eating of an egge, to the murthering of a King.　(*Irish Hubbub*, 43)

Aware of straining credulity, he blames the nebulous nature of his prose on the subject matter (or lack thereof): 'The text that I have taken in hand is but of smoake, and why should I use any forcible battery against so vaine a vapour' (ibid.).

Rich, incurable opportunist and moralizing gossip, railed against tobacco as a ruinous import, and by extension criticized the out-of-favour Ralegh: 'I have formerly said, that the first transportation of Tobacco into England, was not performed by any man that was eyther of worth, or of any great account' (Rich, *Irish Hubbub*, 44). Rich's descriptions of smoking would deter anyone for life:

First, it is drawne in at the mouth, then it is snuffled out at the nose, whereby the ayre is infected with such a loathsome fume, that those that bee standers by cannot draw their breath, but they must sucke downe some of that filthy vapour, that hath beene blowne out (if not through a pocky nostrill) yet (for the most part) through a snottie Nose. (ibid.)

This whole digression on smoking is vintage Rich, and typically humdrum. Rather than upbraid the Irish for drinking blood, he chastises them for taking tobacco. The pat preaching masks a sharp eye for social observation and an archiving awareness of the everyday.

War and peace in Ireland Juliet Fleming insists on 'the sharp division between Rich's serious writing and the products of his "prodigal" period', those few years in which he wrote romances (Fleming, 170). But Rich's work is characterized from start to finish by a playfulness that undermines claims to seriousness. There is always a tickle with the smart. In the *Dialogue*, Mars asks: 'But how should these womanlike mynded men, or any other of these loving wormes, injoy their delightes in such quiet maner, were not the noble Souldier to backe them who is the very Wal and Bulwark to defend them.' Venus relents, pledging 'henceforth I will yield myself beholding unto Souldiers, promising them my furtheraunce in any thing, wherin I may pleasure them' (Miii). *A Path-Way to Military Practise* (1587) continues the theme of complaint. War is the means by which culture is created. Neglect of soldiers weakens a culture. War, itself an art of great antiquity, enables other arts: 'Is it not the Souldiour by hasarding his life abroade, that upholdeth the Artificer to sit quietly by his worke at home' (B3). Phrasemonger and warmonger, Rich saw peace as a corrosive power. In *Roome for a Gentleman*, he reminds his readers that 'it is the surfets of peace, that hatcheth uppe war' and maintains that:

Warre, stirs up the bloud, it cals courage to the field, and it is the Theatre where on Nobilitie was borne to shew himselfe. Peace breedes Cowards, it effeminates our mindes, it pampers our wanton wils, and it runs headlong into all sorts of sinne. (B)

In *The Irish Hubbub* Rich blames Englishwomen for the fashion for idleness—and the indolence of fashion—in Ireland:

There is not a people under the face of Heaven, that is of a more haughty and proud spirit then are the Irish: proud mindes they have ever had, but for any pride in their apparell, they never knew what it meant, till they learnt it from the English. (G3 47)

It is the new English colonial classes who are bringing in destructive habits:

these proud and new upstart Changelings, that never knew what Gentry meant ... They be these that have filled Ireland so full of new fashions, by their strange alterations in their Ruffes, in their Cuffes, in their huffes, in their puffes, in their Muffes, and in many other vanities, that Ireland was never acquainted withall, till these women brought them up. (H49)

English upstarts are answerable for the crisis of authority in Ireland.

Many of the ills of Ireland are imputed to 'the ill

example of the English'. Ireland acts as a magnet for disaffected and unprincipled social aspirants. Writing without irony, Rich informs his readers that:

Ireland for these many yeares hath been the receptacle for our English runnagates, that for their mis-led lives in England, do come running over into Ireland, some for murther, some for theft, some that have spent themselves in ryot and excesse, are driven over for debt, some come running with other mens goods, some with other mens wives, but a great number now lately, that are more hurtfull then all the rest, and those be Recusants.   (*Irish Hubbub*, sig. H2, 51)

Critique of colonialism Despite the reference to recusants, there is a glibness to Rich's anti-Catholicism that speaks of other priorities. The pamphlet that deals most explicitly with religion is *A Catholicke Conference* (1612). The dialogue form, a familiar feature of Rich's writing, makes it more open than a straightforward prose polemic. Like Spenser, Rich was so preoccupied with the character and customs of the three main Irish communities—the Gaelic Irish, the Old English, and the New English—that he left little time for religion. However heartfelt were his denunciations of Irish Catholicism, Rich's main business was with culture in the broadest sense, reserving his strongest criticisms for an unappreciative English audience, and particularly those recalcitrant and reprobate colonists who had settled in Ireland, rather than the native culture corrupted by their novelties and vanities. *Riche his Farewell* reprises the debate of *A Right Exelent and Pleasaunt Dialogue*, only this time the dedication 'To the right courteous Gentlewomen, bothe of Englande and Irelande' implies that Venus has won the day, securing victory over Mars (sig. B2). The barbed prefatory matter—deadly deadpan dedications are Rich's forte—is aimed at a wasteful effeminacy that profits from war but slights the soldier's art.

Allarme to England (1578) is arguably Rich's most significant work, setting the scene for the next three decades of conflict in Ireland. Its discussions of garrisons and standing armies anticipate the Ulster plantation and the policies advocated by those such as Spenser. *Allarme to England* is a wake-up call for an England that must, in Rich's view, put itself on a war footing if it is to survive in a hostile Europe. Ireland was to be the testing ground for English military might, and its strategic importance is emphasized. In 1609 Rich describes Ireland as a country 'invironed with *England, Scotland, France* and *Spaine*' (*A Short Survey of Ireland*, 1–2). Since two of these countries are newly allied as Britain, and the other two are long-standing enemies, Ireland emerges as an exemplary site of interest and investment.

The blurring of gender roles is one of Rich's constant complaints: 'To be shorte, in Englande, Gentlemen have robbed our women of theyr mindes, & our women have bereaved us of halfe our apparell' (*Allarme*, sig. Gi). The message of the *Allarme* is that England must prosecute the wars in Ireland 'without compassion' (sig. D). Rich's view was to be taken up by Spenser and others:

who so ever will thinke to prevaile in Ireland, it must be by using of justice with extremitie, and not with lenitie. And what pittie is to be used to those, that so without pittie will not spare to oppresse the poore and simple farmer, suche as laboureth only for his living? (*Allarme*, sig. Dii)

This notion of colonial justice anticipates the severe strategies advocated in book 5 of *The Faerie Queene*.

Assessment *Riche his Farewell*, dedicated to Sir Christopher Hatton, later one of the undertakers of the Munster plantation alongside Spenser and Ralegh, 'was apparently intended as a valediction to his career as a soldier; but it proved premature' (*DNB*). But Rich had used the trope of writing as both escape from and incitement to war in his first published work, and the pose of peace at a price through penmanship was standard fare for Elizabethan soldier–poets.

Although he continued to lament the neglect of soldiers, Rich's own years of loyal service did not go unrewarded. In 1587 Elizabeth granted him a pension of 2s. 6d. daily for life, to be paid through the Irish treasury, and in July 1616 James awarded him £100 as 'the eldest Captain of the Kingdom' (Cranfill and Bruce, 39, 126; Eccles, 606). His new-found wealth was short-lived. Rich died on 10 November 1617, outlived by his wife.

Rich, by no means a slight figure, remains a slighted one. His writings have been divided into four categories: military tracts, romances, books of informations, and social satire and Irish chronicle. Yet these generic lines bleed and blur into one another. Throughout his position papers and prose fictions Rich displays a penchant for the dialogue form—even his most explicitly religious pamphlet is staged as a 'conference'. He is also partial to scandalmongering.

Always allusive and alliterative, Rich writes as though he has only just discovered language and wants to play with his new toy. His driest sounding treatise on warfare is flippant as well as forthright. His motto, prominently posted on his publications, was *Malui me divitem esse quam vocari*, rendered by his most recent biographers as 'I have preferred to be rich rather than to be called so' (Cranfill and Bruce, 126). Cranfill and Bruce spoke of 'wistful posy' and 'pathos', while Sidney Lee called it 'prudent', but, with his rich and resourceful rhetoric, Barnaby really was wealthy by name and nature. He lived most of his life in penury, but his corpus embodies an embarrassment of riches. Imprudent and impudent, playful and punning, Rich remains one of the most major of minor Renaissance writers. As margins become increasingly important to studies of literature and history, he may assume the more mainstream position to which he aspired.

WILLY MALEY

Sources B. Capp, 'The marital woes of Barnaby Rich', *N&Q*, 245 (2000), 469–70 · T. M. Cranfill and D. H. Bruce, *Barnaby Rich: a short biography* (1953) · M. Eccles, 'Rich, Barnaby (1542–1617)', *A Spenser encyclopedia*, ed. A. C. Hamilton (1990), 606 · E. Flanagan, 'The anatomy of Jacobean Ireland: Captain Barnaby Rich, Sir John Davies and the failure of reform, 1609–22', *Political ideology in Ireland, 1541–1641*, ed. H. Morgan (1999), 158–80 · 'Barnaby Rich's "Remembrance of the state of Ireland, 1612", with notices of other manuscript reports, by the same writer, on Ireland under James the First', ed. C. L. Falkiner, *Proceedings of the Royal Irish Academy*, 26C (1906–7), 125–42 · J. Fleming, 'The ladies' man and the age of Elizabeth', *Sexuality and gender in early modern Europe: institutions, texts,*

images, ed. J. G. Turner (1993), 158–81 · R. Helgerson, 'Lyly, Greene, Sidney and Barnaby Rich's *Brusanus*', *Huntington Library Quarterly*, 36 (1972–3), 105–18 · E. M. Hinton, ed., 'Rych's *Anothomy of Ireland* [1615], with an account of the author', *Publications of the Modern Language Association of America*, 55 (1940), 73–101 · *DNB* · W. Maley, 'Gender and genre: masculinity and militarism in the writings of Barnaby Rich', *Irish Studies Review*, 13 (1995–6), 2–6 · R. M. Smith, 'Spenser's scholarly script and "right writing"', *Studies in honor of T. W. Baldwin*, ed. D. C. Allen (1958), 66–111 · H. J. Webb, 'Barnabe Riche: sixteenth century military critic', *Journal of English and Germanic Philology*, 42 (1943), 240–52

Rich, Christopher (*bap.* 1647, *d.* 1714), lawyer and theatre manager, was baptized in Over Stowey, Somerset, on 30 December 1647, the second son of John and Susanna Rich, according to genealogical work done by Paul Sawyer. Nothing is known about Rich's early education or when he moved to London. At an unknown date he became law clerk to the serjeant-at-law Thomas Skipwith, later a baronet. On 6 June 1676 Rich was admitted as a student to Gray's Inn, where he maintained chambers as long as he lived. He became man of business for Skipwith's son Thomas, and eventually his partner and manager of his theatrical investments. Identical names in the Skipwith family confuse the record, but prior to 2 June 1694, when the baronet died, the 'esquire' signing legal documents is presumably the son.

Rich married Sarah Bewley (1662–1694), of Eltham, Kent, on 25 December 1684 at St Stephen Walbrook. Sawyer shows that they lost at least five daughters in childhood, but their sons John *Rich and Christopher Mosier (*b.* 1693) flourished. Sarah Rich died, probably in childbirth, and was buried at St Andrew's, Holborn, in late October 1694. Highfill, Burnim, and Langhans mention a Susanna Rich who died in 1726 as a possible second wife, but Rich's will mentions no such person.

Rich joined the younger Thomas Skipwith as an investor in a variety of businesses through the years, two of which are known from lawsuits. The token amounts that Rich could afford to put up were enough to allow him to represent Skipwith and at the same time participate as a shareholder in his own right. Together, the two were a potent team. On account of rank Skipwith's name usually comes first in legal documents, creating the initial impression that he was the active partner, but other evidence suggests that Skipwith was more figurehead than leader.

The partners' investments in theatre produced many lawsuits. Skipwith first bought a part-share in the Duke's Company on 31 March 1682, shortly before it absorbed the remnants of the King's Company (Milhous and Hume, 1795). The monopoly, housed in the Drury Lane Theatre, proved profitable enough; so when the hereditary patentee, Charles Davenant, wanted to sell, his brother Alexander was able secretly to borrow £2400, the price of a controlling interest, from Skipwith and Rich. As Davenant slipped behind in payments on his loan, he transferred shares to them, and in October 1693, following a chancery audit, he fled to the Canary Islands (ibid., 1369, 1467). Rich and Skipwith had apparently done no more than collect profits until then, but at this crisis they revealed themselves as shareholders and 'patentees' equal in power to Charles Killigrew. Chiefly concerned to protect their investments, the uneasy trio soon disagreed over means. Killigrew, having inherited management of the King's Company, accepted traditional patterns of running a theatre, which would normally include large reinvestments in the fabric and stock of Drury Lane. Rich, who spoke for Skipwith, was intent on restructuring the organization.

The patentees' reforms aimed at enhancing profits by stringently cutting costs. The changes limited actors' possession of roles and hence their workloads and salaries. Refurbishment of scenery, costumes, and buildings was curtailed. The patentees intended to penalize actresses for getting pregnant and to stop paying duties to the parish. These policies, while not wholly wrong, were badly timed and were implemented too drastically. The senior generation of actors could have been allowed to give up their roles gradually, as Thomas Betterton had already begun to do. However, when change was forced, Betterton led his colleagues in protest, first within the theatre and then to the lord chamberlain. In the 'petition of the players' they objected to departures from 'the whole Course & Method' of past managements, 'tending to the ruine & destruction of the Company' that amounted to treating them 'not as … the Kings & Queenes servants but the Claimers slaves' (Milhous and Hume, 1483). Confrontation made Rich intransigent. The 'Reply of the Patentees' of 10 December 1694 argued that the changes were all business necessities and were entirely legal. Personal influence rescued the actors: Betterton turned to the lord chamberlain, Charles, earl of Dorset, whom he had known for decades (ibid., 1056). To resolve the impasse Dorset issued a licence to the 'rebels' which entitled them to set up on their own at the old theatre in Lincoln's Inn Fields.

While resenting the loss of their monopoly, Rich and Skipwith wisely focused on building up their weakened company in order to perform, lest the patent die through lack of use. The next generation of actors, Colley Cibber among them, were given contracts based on shares of profits, and when at first there were none Skipwith advanced money to pay them token sums (for example, Milhous and Hume, 1502). As losses mounted Skipwith soon dropped out of sight except in lawsuits, where he testified that he had nothing to do with management (Hotson, 306).

The ironic, negative picture of Rich that Cibber paints in his *Apology* (1740) was the chief source of information about the partnership until lawsuit records were discovered in the twentieth century. He dismisses Skipwith as a mere socializer—other contemporaries implied womanizer—unimportant to the running of the company (Cibber, 1.217). Cibber's main charges against Rich were that he consistently short-paid his actors, even after the company began to make money, that he regarded performers as interchangeable and expendable, and that he had no knowledge of, or taste in, theatre. Legal documents confirm Cibber's generalizations, and contemporary opinion often, though not always, agrees with the more subjective aspects of his evaluation. According to Cibber,

in the long term Rich's 'tastes' reflected profitability: 'He look'd into his Receipts for the Value of a Play, and from common Fame he judg'd of his Actors' (ibid., 1.262). An eager junior, Cibber recognized the opportunity to improve his position in the company and so ingratiated himself with Rich that he became a regular consultant and even drinking companion, though he never had Rich's full confidence. He reports that Rich would 'laugh with [the actors] over a Bottle, and bite them [cheat them] in their Bargains: He kept them poor, that they might not be able to rebel; and sometimes merry, that they might not think of it' (ibid., 1.252).

Rich's actors were not popular, and while they were learning their trade there really was no money to pay employees. Hence from 1698 or earlier the privilege of a benefit performance was extended to many not previously eligible for one, so that they might earn enough money to survive. Rich also permitted attendants of 'People of Quality' to enter the upper gallery of Drury Lane without paying, a decision that proved difficult to reverse (Cibber, 1.233–4). He continued but did not originate the practice of allowing customers to pay a reduced rate after the third act, called 'aftermoney' in the theatre's accounts (Hotson, 289–90). At an unknown date Rich cut back the forestage that projected into the auditorium, so as to fit in more seats (Cibber, 2.81, 85). He preferred verbal to written agreements and made sure to pay himself 2s. from every pound first, 'which in effect made them all, when he pleas'd, but limited Sharers of Loss, and himself sole Proprietor of Profits' (ibid., 1.253). Mere hirelings had no right to inspect the company's books, but the actors could see that over time the operation took in enough money to be profitable, while arrears accumulated. Cibber says that during the first run of Steele's *Funeral* (1702) they were paid for nine days in one week—but that was all they saw of fifteen years' worth of back pay. To find acting managers who could quell the growing dissatisfaction among employees was not easy.

Rich took the pragmatic view that talent was replaceable, either in kind or with such alternatives as singers, dancers, tightrope walkers, weightlifters, bird-imitators, and elephants—until his architect advised against the last (Cibber, 2.6). Rich did judge correctly one popular trend with long-reaching consequences. After hurried preparations, on 16 January 1705 his company mounted the first successful production of an Italian opera in English translation, Thomas Clayton's *Arsinoe*. Rich was so convinced that opera would be profitable that in autumn 1706 he allowed his best actors to move to John Vanbrugh's new theatre in the Haymarket.

Over the years financial pressures gradually eased, yet Rich continued to defraud his employees, not to mention his fellow shareholders in the patent and the building. While the actors could not afford to bring suit against him, shareholders could. For more than ten years Charles Killigrew tried in court to recover profits from the theatre, entirely without success. Rich was adept at all the delaying tactics the law allowed, and when finally found in contempt and threatened with arrest, 'he conjur'd up a Spirit, in the Shape of Six and eight Pence a-day, that constantly struck the Tipstaff blind whenever he came near him' (Cibber, 1.328; PRO, C 33/310, decrees, 1707B, fol. 78v). In May 1704 another disgruntled shareholder, Sir Edward Smith, began a suit against all participants in the London theatre since 1695, attempting to find out why his investment had not prospered. After five years of legal wrangling he gave up. In October 1707 Skipwith despaired of making any money and assigned his share to Henry Brett for 10s., though he reclaimed it seventeen months later. Rich's manifest indifference to his employees' well-being bred disloyalty to him. A constant stream of complaints made their way to a succession of four lord chamberlains after Dorset. The courts spent years trying to sort out lawsuits arising from the theatre. Rich went so far as to sue the chief actors he had let go in 1706, while simultaneously abrogating agreements with his singers. Thus the theatre's internal problems became public knowledge.

When Vanbrugh persuaded the lord chamberlain to grant him a monopoly on Italian opera in the Queen's Theatre, Haymarket, effective from 31 December 1707, all Rich's actors perforce returned to Drury Lane. Brett, taking Skipwith's place, was then sharing authority with Rich, and the rest of that season went quietly. In March 1708 Brett negotiated a change in benefit arrangements. To guarantee that the theatre would not lose money, actors were required to post a security deposit of £40, rather than have losses deducted from future earnings. Furthermore, the benefit income of most actors would be taxed by as much as half, depending on rank. Yet Rich schemed to rid himself of Brett and regain complete authority. Skipwith demanded the return of his 'gift' shares after Rich declared an unexpected dividend. As the benefit season approached in spring 1709 Rich cautiously required the actors to sign a document agreeing to the new tax, unaware that he was about to precipitate a second rebellion on the pattern of 1695. The most senior actors had privately approached the lord chamberlain's office, where they received a sympathetic hearing. As expected, Rich taxed Anne Oldfield's benefit of 3 March 1709, whereupon she protested. The lord chamberlain cautioned him to cease on pain of being silenced—that is, forbidden to perform plays. Rich ignored the warning, and on 6 June 1709 the lord chamberlain silenced him (Milhous and Hume, 2023).

With his theatre closed despite vigorous protests and lobbying, Rich chose to retire and concentrate on other undertakings. In the late 1680s he and Skipwith, along with other investors, had begun a building project in St Andrew's, Holborn, but the Society of Gray's Inn had resisted it as 'a hindrance to [their] prospect' (PRO, C 33/310, decrees, 1707B, fol. 75v). The project, under way by 1687, was hampered by litigation and may not have got very far until February 1709, when the court finally allowed the partners 'to goe on with Buildings on Gravell Pitt feild and Warwick ffeild' (PRO, C 33/312, 1708B, fol. 218v). Rich used his holdings in this enterprise as collateral for loans in 1713 to build the third Lincoln's Inn Fields

Theatre. Since at least mid-May 1708 he had also been paying rates on the unoccupied playhouse in Lincoln's Inn Fields. Baulked of Drury Lane, but confident that his patent rights could be reasserted, Rich built an essentially new theatre on the old site. At least as important, among the investors he cultivated to help finance the project was James Craggs the younger, who in 1714 carried out the delicate negotiations with Prince George of Hanover that resulted in royal approbation of a second theatre, in effect nullifying the order of silence.

Rich died on 4 November 1714, just six weeks before the new company held its première performance. John Philip Kemble, a one-time owner of the manuscript chronicle known as 'Rich's register', added to it a note that Rich suffered 'a Mortification, occasioned by a Hurt in his Leg, received as he was stepping out of a coach' (Washington, DC, Folger Shakespeare Library, MS W.a.32). The will Rich wrote the day before he died provided that the patent be left to his sons, three-quarters to John and one-quarter to Christopher Mosier, with the rest of his estate divided equally between them. Rich was buried on 7 November 1714 in the family tomb at St Andrew's, Holborn. He ran his theatre on a relentless business model, defrauding both employees and shareholders to an extent that amazed Cibber, who learned much from him. Rich's passing was not much mourned, but he did leave London a new theatre and a talented Harlequin, his son John.

JUDITH MILHOUS

Sources J. Milhous and R. D. Hume, eds., *A register of English theatrical documents, 1660–1737*, 2 vols. (1991) · P. Sawyer, *Christopher Rich of Drury Lane: the biography of a theatre manager* (1986) · C. Cibber, *An apology for the life of Mr. Colley Cibber*, new edn, ed. R. W. Lowe, 2 vols. (1889) · J. Milhous, *Thomas Betterton and the management of Lincoln's Inn Fields, 1695–1708* (1979) · L. Hotson, *The Commonwealth and Restoration stage* (1928) · Highfill, Burnim & Langhans, *BDA*, vol. 12 · P. Fitzgerald, *A new history of the English stage*, 2 vols. (1882) · J. Milhous, 'An inventory of the theatrical possessions of Christopher Rich, 1715', *Du verbe au geste: mélanges en l'honneur de Pierre Danchin* (1987)
Archives PRO, estate papers, C107/171

Rich, Claudius James (1786/7–1821), traveller and collector of manuscripts and antiquities, was born on 28 March 1786 or 1787 at Dijon in Burgundy. He was probably the illegitimate son of Colonel Sir James *Cockburn, fifth baronet (1723–1809), whose mother's maiden name was Rich, and who lived in Bristol. His half-brother was General Sir William *Cockburn. His mother is unknown. Claudius Rich spent his childhood between Bristol and Kilkenny, where the Cockburn family had connections. As early as the age of nine his curiosity was roused by some Arabic manuscripts, and under the tutelage of Charles Fox and Dr Marshman of Bristol he began to study various oriental languages. In 1803, by the influence of friends, he was appointed a cadet in the East India Company's service. At the time he was described by Robert Hall (1764–1831), Baptist minister and sometime preacher in Bristol, in a letter to Sir James Mackintosh as

a most extraordinary young man. With little or no assistance he has made himself acquainted with many languages, particularly with the languages of the East. Besides Latin,

Greek, and many of the modern languages, he has made himself master of the Hebrew, Chaldee, Persian, Arabic, and is not without some knowledge of the Chinese, which he began to decipher when he was but fourteen. He is a young man of good family, and of most engaging person and address. ('Notice of Mr Rich' in C. J. Rich, *Narrative of a Residence in Koordistan*, 1836, 1.xviii)

Charles Wilkins, librarian of the East India Company, was so impressed by Rich's linguistic skills that he persuaded the directors in 1804 to present him with a writership on the Bombay establishment, and thus changed his career from the military to the civil side. At the same time he was provisionally attached as secretary to the consul-general in Egypt to improve his Arabic and Turkish. Rich embarked early in 1804 in the *Hindostan*, which was burnt in the Bay of Rosas, when Rich escaped to the Catalonian coast. Thence he made his way to Malta, after a stay of three months in Naples, where he learned Italian and studied the flute and the guitar. The consul-general died before Rich reached Egypt, and Rich, by permission of the directors, continued his oriental studies at Constantinople and Smyrna.

After several journeys into the interior of Asia Minor to explore and gather intelligence, Rich was appointed assistant to the new consul-general in Cairo, and in this post he improved his Arabic and amused himself by acquiring the skill in horsemanship and the use of the lance and scimitar in which the Mamlûks, descendants of Caucasian slaves, excelled. From Egypt he travelled in Mamlûk disguise over much of Syria and Palestine, visited Damascus in the pilgrimage time, and even entered the great mosque, undetected. Thence by Mardîn and Baghdad, he went to Basrah, where he took ship for Bombay, arriving on 1 September 1807. There he lived with the governor, Sir James Mackintosh, who held him in high regard. On 22 January 1808 Rich married Sir James's eldest daughter, Mary (1789–1876), a few days after being appointed the East India Company's resident at Baghdad.

The residency had been established at the end of the eighteenth century to counteract growing French influence in the *pashaliq* of Baghdad. It was placed under the control of the government of Bombay in 1806 and its remit redefined to exclude most political activity. Rich's term in Baghdad was marked by violent struggles as the Wahabi people sought to extend their power, and as Qawasim piracy in the Persian Gulf increased. It also saw action by British forces after 1819 to bring piracy to an end. Rich played a very minor part in these events, although he was able to give asylum to individuals whose lives were threatened by internal political disturbances. However, he conscientiously passed sound information to Bombay and won some commercial concessions for Britain. For six years he lived at Baghdad, collecting coins, rare manuscripts, and other materials in his leisure time for a history and statistical account of the *pashaliq*. Christian communities in the East were a particular concern of his, and he acquired many manuscripts and artefacts from them. An excursion to Babylon in 1811 led to the *Memoir on the Ruins of Babylon* (1815), which was amplified, after a second visit to the site, in the *Second Memoir on Babylon* (1818).

In 1813 ill health compelled Rich to go to Constantinople with his wife, and in 1814 he prolonged his journey through the Balkans to Vienna, and thence to Paris, then in the hands of the allies. On his return through Asia Minor and Mesopotamia to Baghdad, he resumed his studies and collections, made his second visit to Babylon, and in 1820, being again in bad health, travelled in Kurdistan. This tour was described in his most important work, *Narrative of a Residence in Koordistan*, published posthumously in two volumes in 1836. The work long remained valuable, as the first nineteenth-century geographical and archaeological account of the region and also as an interesting narrative of travel. It was reissued in 1984 in recognition of its continuing value. In May 1821 Rich removed the residency from Baghdad after quarrelling with the *vali* Daud Pasha. He then retired to Bushehr. At the same time the residency at Basrah was also withdrawn, and Mountstuart Elphinstone in 1822 undertook a fundamental review of the East India Company's representation in the Gulf. In connection with this it is stated that Rich had been appointed to an important office (said to be as member of council and governor of Surat) at Bombay by Elphinstone when he contracted cholera during a visit to Shiraz. He died on 5 October 1821 and was buried in the Jan Numa at Shiraz, in which he was living at the time of his death. His remains were exhumed and reinterred in the Armenian cathedral of Jolfa in Esfahan in 1826. He was childless. Parts of his collections were purchased by the trustees of the British Museum, and consisted of about 900 volumes of manuscripts in Arabic, Persian, and Turkish, and a great number in Chaldee and Syriac; a large collection of coins, Greek and oriental; and gems and antiquities dug up at Babylon and Nineveh, including the first cuneiform inscriptions ever brought to Europe.

STANLEY LANE-POOLE, *rev.* ELIZABETH BAIGENT

Sources C. M. Alexander, *Baghdad in bygone days from the journals and correspondence of Claudius Rich* (1928) · J. B. Kelly, *Britain and the Persian Gulf, 1795–1880* (1968)
Archives BL OIOC, journals, notes, sketches, etc., MSS Eur. A 12–19, B 44–49, C 38, D 232–235, G 34–35 · NRA, priv. coll., letters and journals · priv. coll., letters of Rich and his wife, travel journals | Herefs. RO, corresp. with Sir Harford Jones Brydges · PRO, letters to Strafford Canning, FO 352
Likenesses T. Phillips, oils, BM · portrait, BM; repro. in Alexander, *Baghdad in bygone days*, frontispiece

Rich, Edmund. *See* Abingdon, Edmund of (c.1174–1240).

Rich, Henry, first earl of Holland (*bap.* **1590**, *d.* **1649**), courtier, was baptized at the church of Stratford-le-Bow, Middlesex, on 19 August 1590, the second son of Robert *Rich, third Baron Rich (1559?–1619), and his wife, Lady Penelope *Rich (1563–1607), daughter of Walter Devereux, first earl of Essex, and sister to the Elizabethan favourite, and the Stella of Sidney's sonnets. The couple divorced in 1605 after many years in which she lived in open adultery with Charles Blount, later Lord Mountjoy and earl of Devonshire, whom she eventually married. This liaison produced a son, Mountjoy Blount, who became earl of Newport. Henry's elder brother, Robert

Henry Rich, first earl of Holland (*bap.* 1590, *d.* 1649), studio of Daniel Mytens [original, *c.*1632–3]

*Rich (1587–1658), inherited the title earl of Warwick, which Lord Rich acquired in 1618; the greatest landowner in Essex, he was a leading puritan famous for investing in privateering ventures, who secured control of the navy for parliament in 1642.

Early years After attending Emmanuel College, Cambridge, Henry Rich was installed knight of the Bath on 4 June 1610 at the creation of Henry as prince of Wales. He sat in parliament that year and again in 1614. According to Clarendon he spent some time in France before embarking on a military career in the Netherlands. In 1612 he married Isabel (*d.* 1655), daughter and heir of Sir Walter Cope, whose death two years later left him possessed of a substantial estate in Kensington and Cope Castle, a new mansion designed by John Thorpe, which Rich later enlarged and renamed Holland House. Rich visited the court in 1613, attracting notice by his good looks, pleasant manner, and skill at jousting. In 1616 he joined the entourage of Lord Hay on an embassy to France and was appointed a bedchamber servant of Prince Charles. The next year he won the post of captain of the yeomen of the guard through the support of Queen Anne, reportedly paying

£5000 to the previous incumbent. This office brought him into frequent contact with the king and other notables.

Client of Buckingham Rich set out to win Buckingham's patronage but was opposed by the favourite's brother, Sir Edward Villiers, whom he challenged to a duel. This incident did not prevent him from becoming a Buckingham client, however, and continuing his ascent at court. He was mentioned as a possible ambassador to Brussels in 1620 and two years later lent his house in Drury Lane to the Huguenot duke of Soubize. On 8 March 1623 he was created Baron Kensington and, three months later, summoned to attend Prince Charles in Madrid. The following February he was sent to Paris to assess French interest in a marriage alliance with England and joint military action against the Habsburgs. The encouraging reports he sent back resulted in his being joined by James Hay, earl of Carlisle, with a commission to conclude the treaty that made Henrietta Maria wife to Charles I. Kensington was usually more optimistic than Carlisle and the previous ambassador, Edward Herbert, about French intentions, overestimating the willingness of Cardinal Richelieu, who rose to power during his embassy, to pursue a policy of open alignment with protestant states, against the opposition of powerful groups within France. This mistake may have influenced Buckingham to place excessive confidence in the French alliance, with results that ultimately proved disastrous. French court politics were extremely fluid during this period, however, making assessments difficult.

In Paris, Kensington already displayed a penchant for political dealings with women that later marked his career at Whitehall. He established cordial relations with Marie de' Medici and began an affair with the duchess of Chevreuse, a famous beauty who was soon to establish herself as an indefatigable political conspirator. Through Chevreuse he arranged for Buckingham to initiate a romantic pursuit of Anne of Austria, queen of Louis XIII, which caused considerable scandal. He also began the relationship with Henrietta Maria that blossomed in the 1630s. Kensington's good looks and charm undoubtedly made him attractive to women but he also genuinely respected their political skills and valued their advice. In addition to the queen and court ladies such as the countess of Carlisle his confidantes during the years of prerogative rule appear to have included the wives of a number of puritan peers, such as his brother Warwick and the earl of Essex.

Kensington's mission left him heavily indebted but also solidified the favour of the duke and the prince of Wales. He was created earl of Holland in September of 1624, sworn of the privy council on 31 July 1625, and inducted into the Order of the Garter in December. He accompanied Buckingham on an important diplomatic mission to the Netherlands before returning to Paris in January 1626, accompanied by Sir Dudley Carleton, with instructions to mediate between Louis XIII and the Huguenots, who appeared about to launch a rebellion that would have ended any prospects for French assistance against the Habsburgs. Thanks to English pressure the Huguenots were induced to reach an accord with Louis, on terms they considered disadvantageous. Charles shared their disappointment and almost repudiated his ambassadors' work but the Dutch, who had a better appreciation of military realities, thought Carleton and Holland had saved French protestantism from disaster. Charles regarded himself as a guarantor of the treaty's terms, an attitude that precipitated him into war with France when a new dispute broke out the following year.

During the parliament of 1626 Holland was one of Buckingham's staunchest supporters in the House of Lords. His loyalty was rewarded in early August when, along with Carlisle, he was sworn a bedchamber servant to the king. In 1627 he was given command of the large force being gathered to reinforce Buckingham's ill-fated expedition to the Île de Ré. Slow preparations and adverse winds kept him from sailing until 6 November, ironically the very day on which the duke left the French coast with his defeated army. Despite rumours that he would be made a scapegoat, Holland soon recovered. He served briefly as master of the horse from September to November 1628 before being appointed constable of Windsor (27 October 1629), high steward to the queen (1 December 1629), and chancellor of the University of Cambridge. He also received numerous gifts and lucrative privileges that by the 1630s provided him an income estimated in the range of £10,000 to £13,000, mostly from court offices and monopolies. His expenditures probably at least matched these profits. In 1629 both Rubens and the Venetian ambassador independently singled out Holland and the earl of Carlisle as prime examples of court nobles whose taste for splendour had resulted in crushing debts.

Court intriguer Following Buckingham's assassination in August 1628 Holland was frequently mentioned as a prime candidate to succeed to his position as chief minister, in rivalry with Carlisle and Lord Treasurer Weston. He co-operated with the French ambassador, the marquis de Châteauneuf, in teaching Henrietta Maria to use her personal influence over Charles as a source of political power. Thereafter he was often mentioned as leader of the queen's party within the court. With the support of Henrietta Maria and Châteauneuf he pressed Charles to renew his alliance with France, summon a new parliament, and continue the war against the Habsburgs, in opposition to the advice of Weston, Carlisle, Sir Francis Cottington, and others, who advocated an accommodation with Spain. He also attempted, unsuccessfully, to gain the post of lord admiral and sought to undermine Weston, who was emerging as Charles's most influential adviser.

Although the queen's faction had supported French interests in 1629, she and Holland were drawn into a conspiracy against Richelieu that Châteauneuf devised after his return to France in 1630, in which Chevreuse was also involved. When Châteauneuf was arrested in February 1633 his papers were found to contain correspondence with Holland and Henrietta Maria. Another packet of letters from Holland and the queen was intercepted by Weston's son, Jerome, while on a mission to Paris, and sent to Charles I. The French ambassador, Fontenay, reported that the king also had evidence implicating 'puritans' in

the intrigues of the queen's party. Holland worsened matters by challenging Jerome Weston to a duel and was placed under house arrest in April. The large number of distinguished guests who visited him during his confinement, reportedly including two leading puritan lords, increased Charles's annoyance, though the queen still managed to win Holland a pardon by the end of the month.

Holland's credit with both Charles and Richelieu was badly strained by this episode, but he eventually re-emerged as a leading advocate of a French alliance against the Habsburgs at Whitehall. He was also reputed a benefactor and leader of the puritans, by several Catholic ambassadors as well as some English observers. His penchant for duels and love affairs appears to contradict this view and he left no evidence of deep spirituality, but he did maintain a puritan chaplain, John Everard, and he had extensive kinship connections to puritan peers and gentry. He was repeatedly elected governor of the Providence Island Company, which colonized several islands off the Mosquito Coast of Central America intended as bases for trade and privateering. Other shareholders included the earls of Warwick and Bedford, Lord Saye, and John Pym. Although inactive in the company's business affairs, Holland used his influence at court to obtain a charter and other legal privileges for it.

When Charles's relations with Spain and Austria deteriorated in 1636, Holland's stock rose at court. In that year he was appointed groom of the stole, succeeding his one-time friend and later rival, the earl of Carlisle. Even at this juncture, however, Holland's real influence remained limited and he never obtained an office of the first rank. His chief administrative contribution to the personal rule derived from his appointment as chief justice in eyre south of the Trent in 1631, which gave him jurisdiction over royal forests and, consequently, the task of levying forest fines, which earned him the lasting resentment of several victims. Although Pym exonerated Holland from personal responsibility for the king's forest policy in the Short Parliament, others, such as the earl of Leicester and Lord Willoughby, proved less forgiving. Holland made other enemies, including Thomas Wentworth, earl of Strafford, by intriguing against them at court. On the other hand he does not seem often to have inspired lasting devotion: by the end of the 1630s former associates such as Henry Jermyn, Henry Percy, and the countess of Carlisle had all become antagonistic. His relations with the queen grew more strained after she obtained the post of lord admiral, which he continued to covet, for the earl of Northumberland in 1638. Holland's inability to hide his disappointment at the news inspired considerable merriment among his court enemies. When the duchess of Chevreuse arrived in England in April 1638, having fled France after the collapse of yet another conspiracy, Holland met her at Brainford at the head of a cortège of twenty-four carriages filled with gentlemen of the court and two containing Henrietta Maria's ladies. He attempted to rekindle their old relationship, writing love poems to the duchess and pretending to take seriously her attempts to convert him to Catholicism and Hispanophile policies, but this did not prevent her from forming a friendship with his enemy, Wentworth. Under the influence of Chevreuse, the papal envoy Rosetti, and Marie de' Medici, who arrived in England in 1639, Henrietta Maria became more aggressive in her advocacy of Catholic interests and less interested in anti-Habsburg alliances. This left Holland in an increasingly isolated position.

Royalist and parliamentarian The queen's support did win him appointment as general of the horse in the first campaign against the Scots in 1639. He led the English cavalry to a fateful encounter at Kelso, just over the border, where he was persuaded by the Scots' clever deployment along the crest of a hill that their force was larger than it actually was. He therefore ordered a retreat and urged Charles to negotiate a truce, when a sharp attack might have defeated the Scots, preserving the king's authority in all three of his kingdoms. Holland's cordial relations with the Scots commissioners in the ensuing negotiations aroused Charles's suspicions, further damaging his position at court. His connections to oppositionist peers and reputation for favouring protestant interests gave him much more credit, however, within the Short and Long parliaments. In June of 1640 Viscount Conway described Warwick and Holland as the temporal and spiritual heads of the puritans:

> or rather the one is their visible and the other their invisible head, not because he means to do either good or hurt, but because he thinks it is a gallantry to be the principal pillar on which a whole cabal must rely. (*CSP dom.*, 1640, 278)

Holland opposed the dissolution of the Short Parliament in a privy council meeting on 5 May 1640 and gave evidence against Strafford in the Long Parliament, although he absented himself from the final vote on attainder. In April 1641 the court tried to win him back by appointing him captain general of military forces north of the Trent, and in this capacity he oversaw the paying off and disbanding of the army levied to fight the Scots the previous year. On 17 November parliament appointed him to take charge of the trained bands north of the Trent. In addition to his military duties he was often used as an intermediary with the king and queen, for example being given the delicate task in October 1641 of explaining to Henrietta Maria why parliament wished to restrict Prince Charles from visiting her, out of concern for his religion.

Holland declined to accompany the royal family when it departed London in January 1642 and refused a summons to attend the king at York in March, although this meant surrendering his court appointments. He was chosen in July to join the delegation that presented parliament's negotiating terms to the king but met with a cold reception. In the same month he was named to parliament's committee of safety. He marshalled parliament's forces at Turnham Green on 13 November where, according to both Ludlow and Whitelocke, he dissuaded the general, Essex, from ordering an attack. By early 1643 he had become an advocate of a negotiated settlement with the king and in

August he deserted parliament for the king's headquarters at Oxford. He fought for the king at the battle of Newbury but failed to regain Charles's favour and returned to Kensington by November. Arrested by order of the Lords, he was soon released but not permitted to resume his seat in the upper House. He published a declaration attributing his return to his parliamentary allegiance to the influence of papists at Oxford and the king's willingness to employ Irish Catholic troops, but many others attributed his behaviour to selfish motives.

Holland continued to seek a compromise settlement. In 1645 he attempted to mediate between Charles and Scottish presbyterian leaders. Two years later he was one of the authors of a scheme advanced by presbyterian peers for a treaty between parliament and the king. At the outset of the second civil war he opened secret negotiations with the court and, in collaboration with the duke of Buckingham, attempted to raise a cavalry force for the king. The two peers raised a disappointing total of about 600 men, who were defeated by a detachment under Sir Michael Livesey on 7 July 1648. Three days later Holland was captured at St Neots. Although the Lords voted on 18 November to punish him by banishment, the army had resolved on sterner measures. In February 1649 he was tried, along with the duke of Hamilton, George Goring, and Lord Capel, by a special court under John Bradshaw, which condemned him to death. Despite the intercession of the earl of Warwick and Sir Thomas Fairfax, parliament declined to reprieve him by a vote of thirty-one to thirty. The news of this vote plunged Holland into an anguished spiritual crisis, resolved by a typically puritan experience of religious conversion. At his execution in New Palace Yard, Westminster, on 9 March 1649, he delivered a long speech protesting his lifelong devotion to parliament, the protestant religion, and the principles of honour in which he had been raised. He was buried in Kensington the next day. His second daughter, Susanna [see Howard, Susanna], who had supported him up until his death, died only months later.   R. MALCOLM SMUTS

Sources B. Donagan, 'A courtier's progress: greed and consistency in the life of the earl of Holland', *HJ*, 19 (1976), 317–53 · R. M. Smuts, 'The puritan followers of Henrietta Maria in the 1630s', *EngHR*, 93 (1978), 26–45 · J. L. Beatty, *Warwick and Holland, being the lives of Robert and Henry Rich* (1965) · K. Sharpe, *The personal rule of Charles I* (1992) · *CSP dom.*, 1625–49 · PRO, SP16 · Baschet transcripts of dispatches by French ambassadors to London, 1625–40, PRO, PRO 31/3/62–72 · *CSP Venice*, 1625–48 · Clarendon, *Hist. rebellion* · *Cabala, sive, Scrinia sacra: mysteries of state and government in letters of illustrious persons*, 3rd edn (1691) · PRO, SP78/72–74, 77–78 · R. E. Schreiber, *The first Carlisle: Sir James Hay, first earl of Carlisle as courtier, diplomat and entrepreneur, 1580–1636* (1984), 55–102 · *The letters of John Chamberlain*, ed. N. E. McClure, 2 vols. (1939) · *Report on the manuscripts of Lord De L'Isle and Dudley*, 6, HMC, 77 (1966) · [B. Whitelocke], *Memorials of the English affairs* (1682) · *State trials* · GEC, *Peerage* · correspondence of Salvetti, ambassador to the English court of the duke of Tuscany, BL, Add. MS 27962, vols. E–I · S. R. Gardiner, *History of England from the accession of James I to the outbreak of the civil war*, new edn, 10 vols. (1893–4) · G. E. Aylmer, *The king's servants: the civil service of Charles I, 1625–1642* (1961) · J. Rushworth, *Historical collections*, 5 pts in 8 vols. (1659–1701) · *DNB* · V. Cousin, *Madame de Chevreuse* (1862) · W. J. Loftie, *Kensington picturesque and historical*

(1885) · C. Andrews, *The colonising activities of the English puritans* (1914) **Archives** NRA, priv. coll., corresp. | CUL, corresp. relating to Cambridge University · PRO, dispatches of Holland and Carlisle from Paris, SP78/72–74, 77–78 **Likenesses** W. Passe, line print, *c.*1625, BM, NPG · A. Van Dyck, oils, *c.*1640, Buccleuch estates, Selkirk, Scotland · circle of J. Hoskins, miniature, *c.*1645, Ham House, London · C. Turner, mezzotint, pubd 1810 (after A. Van Dyck), BM, NPG · P. Clouwet, line print (after A. Van Dyck), BM, NPG · J. Godefroy, line engraving (after S. Cooper), BM, NPG · studio of D. Mytens, oils (after original, *c.*1632–1633), NPG [*see illus.*] · pen-and-ink drawing (after W. Faithorne senior), NPG · portrait (after A. Van Dyck, *c.*1640), NPG **Wealth at death** £20,000 owed to him by king: will

Rich, Jeremiah (*d.* 1666×9), stenographer, has left no trace of his birth or parentage. Although several of his works are dedicated to the members of the Rich family of the earls of Warwick, he claimed no family connection with them, and none is known. Rich appears to have been living in London by 1642, when he published *Semography*, a system of shorthand invented and taught by his deceased uncle, William Cartwright. Rich produced several subsequent re-entitled versions of *Semography*, none of which made mention of Cartwright. The first, *Charactery* (1646), signed from St Olave's parish, Southwark, was dedicated to Robert Rich, Lord Rich, son of the second earl of Warwick. It reappeared as *Semigraphy* (1654; signed from Mill Lane), and finally in 1659 as *The Penns Dexterity*. The posthumous *Pens Dexterity Compleated* (1669) went to many editions, the last being published in Leeds in 1792.

Rich was himself a skilled and celebrated shorthand writer, claiming to have recorded the trial at the Old Bailey of John Lilburne in August 1653 (no copy has survived). A tiny volume only ⅝ inch square in the Bodleian Library (MS Eng. misc. g.2) contains his own shorthand notes of a contemporary sermon. Rich may at one time have been employed as a writing-master at the free school in the Old Jewry, London. However, he was also active in other fields. By 1648, if not earlier, he was a cavalry trooper in Colonel Nathaniel Rich's regiment of the New Model Army. He has been identified as the Mr Rich who in June 1650 was directed to submit to the council of state evidence relating to the suppression of unlicensed printers in Leicestershire. During the First Anglo-Dutch War (1652–4) Rich served on board the frigate *Portland* under Captain William Rowse, and saw active service at the battle of the Texel (July 1653). In July 1654 the admiralty committee recommended him for employment as clerk of the check.

Rich produced several works that were not connected with shorthand. His *Elegie on John Warner* (1648?) marked the death of Warner, Independent lord mayor of London installed by the New Model Army in September 1647, who died in November 1648. This was followed by *Jeremiah's Contemplations* (1648?), written in the immediate aftermath of the army purge of parliament on 6 December 1648 (Pride's Purge), in which Colonel Nathaniel Rich's regiment of horse, and therefore possibly Jeremiah Rich himself, was closely implicated. The poem, which reflects on the chaos and confusion then prevailing in London, is

dedicated to Eleanor Rich, wife of the second earl of Warwick; Warwick disapproved of the purge, remaining loyal to the unpurged Long Parliament. In 1650 Rich published *Mellificium musarum*, a series of soliloquies, dedicated to 'my Noble Colonel', Nathaniel Rich. *The Mirrour of Mercy* (1654) was written, the title-page records, 'in a fit of Sickness'.

Immediately before the restoration of Charles II in May 1660 Rich issued *Logomachia*, an address of loyalty to the king. It was probably in the same year that he produced his shorthand edition of *The Whole Book of Psalms in Meter*, engraved by Thomas Cross (*fl.* 1632–1682) and measuring only 2½ by 1½ inches, with a frontispiece portrait of Rich. In November 1663 he was apparently teaching shorthand at Reading, Berkshire. *Death's Envious Triumph* (1664) marked the death of Andrew Rutherford, Lord Rutherford, governor of Tangier, killed in an ambush there on 3 May 1664, while Rich's shorthand version of *The Book of the New Testament* probably appeared in 1666 or 1667. He died some time shortly before the appearance in 1669 of *The Pens Dexterity Compleated* which refers to 'our deceased Author' (p. 31). Rich's shorthand system was widely used and after his death was taught and republished by Samuel Botley as *Maximum in minimo* (1675?) and by Rich's pupil, Nathaniel Stringer, as *Rich redivivus* (1677?). During the eighteenth century the Revd Philip Doddridge devised his own 'improved' version, *A Brief and Easy System of Short-Hand* (1799). FRANCES HENDERSON

Sources W. J. Carlton, ed., *Shorthand books* (1940), 55–67 · R. C. Alston, ed., *Treatises on shorthand* (1966), 17, 20, 22–4 · A. T. Wright, *Jeremiah Rich* (1911) · S. Botley, *Maximum in minimo* (1675?) · N. Stringer, *Rich redivivus* (1677?) · *CSP dom.*, 1650, 192; 1654, 514, 523 · [J. Rich], *A brief and easy system of shorthand ... improved by Dr Doddridge* (1799) · [Hatton], *A new view of London* (1708), 2.705 · *The manuscripts of the duke of Leeds*, HMC, 22 (1888), 195 **Likenesses** line engraving, 1659, BM, NPG · T. Cross, line engraving, NPG, V&A; repro. in J. Rich, *Semigraphy* (1654) · line engraving (aged twenty-four), BM

Rich, John (1692–1761), pantomimist and theatre manager, the fifth of the seven children (of whom only two sons survived) of Christopher *Rich (*bap.* 1647, *d.* 1714), a London attorney and theatre manager, and his wife, Sarah Bewley (*bap.* 1662, *d.* 1694), was baptized on 19 May 1692 at St Andrew's, Holborn. He apparently grew up without formal education. At the age of twenty-two, upon the death of his father, Rich, as the elder son, received three-quarters possession of the patent to operate a theatre, which had originally been given to Sir William Davenant by Charles II in 1663; his brother, Christopher Mosyer Rich, one year younger, received one-quarter of the patent.

For the next forty-seven years Rich implemented his father's vision, first as manager at Lincoln's Inn Fields and later at Covent Garden, where he opened a lavish new theatre in 1732. He distinguished himself as the originator of English pantomime, introducing elaborate scenery and extravagant costumes into his productions, and he became the most celebrated comic dancer of his age.

At Lincoln's Inn Fields, which opened on 18 December 1714, Rich acted on two occasions; in his third season he began to appear as a comic dancer, using the stage name

John Rich (1692–1761), by unknown artist, 1753 [as Harlequin]

Lun. Because his theatre experienced serious financial problems, in October 1717 he leased the patent and playhouse to two actors, Christopher Bullock and Theophilus Keene, and he did not resume full managerial responsibility until the 1719–20 season. By October 1716 he had begun to feature dance compositions, using well-known characters from the Italian *commedia dell'arte*. On 29 April 1717 he danced the role of Harlequin in *The Jealous Doctor, or, The Intriguing Dame* and on 30 May 1717 *Harlequin Executed*; his customary costume was a short, loose jacket, tight, crossed trousers, and a black vizard.

Whereas Drury Lane's treatment of dance was serious, Rich exploited the comic possibilities of Italian *commedia dell'arte*. In response to Drury Lane's *The Loves of Mars and Venus*, performed on 2 March 1717, on 22 November he brought out *Mars and Venus, or, The Mouse Trap*; answering John Weaver's *Harlequin Turned Judge* on 5 December 1717, Rich performed *Colombine, or, Harlequin Turn'd Judge* within a week. Thomas Davies gave the fullest contemporary description of this new form of entertainment, explaining that Rich first depicted in dance a serious tale from mythology, interweaving between the episodes 'a comic fable consisting chiefly of the courtship of Harlequin and Columbine, with a variety of surprising adventures and tricks which were produced by the magic wand of Harlequin' (Davies, 1.130).

Rich's first great success of the 1720s, *The Necromancer, or, Harlequin Doctor Faustus*, performed on 20 December 1723 in response to John Thurmond's *Harlequin Doctor Faustus* at Drury Lane on 26 November 1723, brought the house £260. Within the decade Lincoln's Inn Fields developed an enviable record of additional pantomimes, including *Jupiter and Europa* (1723), *Harlequin a Sorcerer* (1725), *Apollo and Daphne* (1726), *The Rape of Proserpine* (1727), *The Loves of Damon and Clemene* (1727), *Harlequin Anna Bullen* (1727), *Italian Jealousy* (1729), and *Perseus and Andromeda, or, The Spaniard Outwitted* (1730).

Rich's pantomimic success was matched by his managerial good fortune. In John Gay's *The Beggar's Opera* (1728) he produced the greatest commercial theatrical success of the century, earning between £7200 and £9000 within two years; thus encouraged, he planned a new theatre in Covent Garden. Rich leased the land from the duke of Bedford, whose family had owned it since the dissolution of the monasteries, and on 11 December 1731 he published a prospectus offering shares to London notables. He contracted with Edward Shepherd to build the theatre and employed Jacopo Amiconi, John Harvey, and George Lambert to paint the scenery. The sumptuous new theatre opened on 7 December 1732, and, although he realized only £6700 of the £15,000 originally pledged to him, Rich netted a profit of £200 from the subscriptions.

During the 1730s and 1740s Rich maintained a busy schedule of dancing and producing new works and renovating previous pantomimes. Although it is difficult to assess his precise contribution to each, the following works are usually credited to him: *Harlequin Executed* (1716); *The Jealous Doctor* (1717); *Amadis* (1718); *The South-Sea Director* (1720), which was probably the same as *The Magician, or, Harlequin a Director* (1721); *Jupiter and Europa* (1723); *The Necromancer* (1723); *The Sorcerer* (1724), probably the same as *Harlequin a Sorcerer* (1725); *Apollo and Daphne* (1725); *The Rape of Proserpine* (1727); *Orpheus and Eurydice* (1740); *The Fair* (1740); and the comedy *The Spirit of Contradiction* (1760).

Audiences appreciated Rich's gift of expressing emotion through dance. David Garrick wrote in the prologue to *Harlequin's Invasion* (1759), 'He gave the power of speech to every limb.' Rich transformed the original *commedia* role of Harlequin into a dancing character, and excelled in statue scenes, in catching the butterfly episodes, and in 'graceful and affecting' scenes in which he parted from Columbine (Davies, 1.369). He was widely acclaimed for miming in elaborate detail the hatching of an egg by the rays of the sun in *Harlequin a Sorcerer*. At the age of sixty he performed his last dance on 8 November 1752.

Rich continued throughout his career to develop lavish stage effects, revolutionizing stage production in his day. The *Scots Magazine* describes the famous serpent that appeared in *Orpheus and Eurydice* (1740) as:

> a piece of machinery, that enters, performs its exercise of head, body, and tail in a most surprising manner, and makes behind the curtain with a velocity scarcely credible. It is about a foot and a half in circumference of the thickest part. … It is believed to have cost more than £200. (*Scots Magazine*, March 1740)

In 1740 John Hill insisted that Rich's pantomime *Orpheus and Eurydice: with the Metamorphoses of Harlequin*, performed on 12 February 1740, was plagiarized from Hill's *Orpheus, an English Opera*, published the previous December. Rich rejected Hill's claim, maintaining that he had merely devised a pantomime for Lewis Theobald's *Orpheus* (1740). The dispute was resolved when Hill and Rich agreed to read their works before an assembly. Hill delegated the reading of his text, whereas Rich read his own work, 'with his best Grace of Diction' (Hill, preface to *Orpheus*). The company resolved the dispute in favour of Rich.

This incident argues against the charge that Rich was illiterate, but he was admittedly ill-spoken, often mistaking the meaning of words and sometimes mispronouncing them, resulting in what Davies described as a 'vulgar and ungrammatical' use of language (Davies, 1.370). He irritated many of his associates by claiming he was unable to remember their proper names and devising his own versions of them, such as Griskin for Garrick, Shuttleworth for Shuter, and Footseye for Foote, or by addressing them simply as 'Muster'.

Rich survived unrest in managing his theatre, including theatrical accidents and riots, as well as the complaints of playwrights that he neglected to read their plays. He was accused of failing to engage excellent performers and to develop the talent already in his company, and was said to be ungenerous in bargaining with players over salary. He was also the target of attacks by such reputable persons as Alexander Pope, Henry Fielding, Aaron Hill, and James Ralph for allegedly pandering to popular taste.

Despite the turbulence, Rich held his own against Garrick, who managed the rival theatre at Drury Lane from 1747 through the last fourteen years of Rich's life. Rich was especially effective in staging spectacles, such as the splendid procession which he added to his 1756 revival of Nathaniel Lee's *The Rival Queens*. On several occasions the two theatres entered into direct competition in the staging of spectacles: in September and October 1750 *Romeo and Juliet* was performed by both patent theatres for twelve consecutive nights; both enhanced their performances with an elaborate funeral procession for Juliet. In 1761 both theatres staged spectacular processions to mark the coronation of George III; Rich's genius for orchestrating dress, decoration, and motion made his production clearly superior, according to Count Frederick Kielmansegg, a visitor, who claimed that the procession he witnessed at Drury Lane 'was nothing compared with the representation at Covent Garden' (Kielmansegg, 192). Rich constantly sought new ideas for productions, as attested by unidentified newspaper clippings in the New York Public Library, which tell of his trips to Paris in 1753 and 1758 'to Furnish himself with proper Hints for New Entertainments in the Grotesque way' (New York Public Library, file MGZR). Horace Walpole praised the pantomimes of Rich for their wit and coherence.

Rich seems to have been popular with most of his performers, to whom he was exact in the payment of salary and generous in allowing benefit performances. He was extremely solicitous of his actresses, especially George Anne Bellamy, whom he protected from Lord Byron, and Hannah Norsa, whom he took into his own home when she was left destitute in 1751; she remained there for over thirty years. Davies indicates that Rich supported many theatrical pensioners, both male and female, and was generous to them, as well as to his tenants at Uxbridge, where he was known as 'an obliging neighbour, a hospitable country gentleman, and a very kind landlord' (Davies, 1.372).

Rich married Henrietta Brerewood of the parish of St James, Westminster, on 7 February 1717 in St Clement Danes. Their son, John, was born on 3 May 1720 and was buried on 28 February 1721. Henrietta also died, and was buried on 28 September 1725. Rich's second wife, Amy, sometimes called Anne, was the mother of seven of his children: two sons and five daughters. She died 'of a Hectick fever' on 26 November 1737 (*Read's Weekly Journal*, 3 Dec 1737) and was buried at Hillingdon, near Uxbridge.

Rich lived in Southampton Street, in elegant Bloomsbury, having moved there from the parish of St Martin-in-the-Fields. About 1739 he moved to the parish of St Paul's, Covent Garden, and in 1744 he purchased a country house in Cowley, near Uxbridge, where he lived in fine style, keeping horses, dogs, and a multitude of cats, collected paintings, and lavished entertainment on various ladies. He was a convivial man who became somewhat corpulent in his later years, and his fine appearance was marred only by a disfiguring blemish in one of his eyes.

After Rich's third marriage, on 25 November 1744 to Priscilla Wilford (*c*.1713–1783), a minor actress in the company who used the stage name of Stevens, his lifestyle became austere. The strong-willed Priscilla, said to have been first a barmaid and then housekeeper to Rich for several years before their marriage, was converted to Methodism and insisted that Rich adapt himself to her mode, prompting Tobias Smollett's depiction of her in *Roderick Random* as a tyrant.

As a man who enjoyed sociability, Rich founded the Sublime Society of Beefsteaks in 1735, an eating club which counted among its twenty-four original members William Hogarth and George Lambert; other members were Samuel Johnson, Charles Churchill, Theophilus Cibber, and John Wilkes. He was welcome at court and acted as host to Frederick, prince of Wales, on his 1740 visit to Bartholomew fair. George Frideric Handel, a long-time friend, left his great organ at Covent Garden to Rich upon his death in 1759.

Rich died on 26 November 1761 at his home, next to his theatre in Covent Garden, of 'gravel and stone' according to *Lloyd's Evening Post* (25–7 November 1761). The *Public Advertiser* called him a man 'to whom the Public is indebted for many years agreeable Entertainment, and who adorn'd domestic Life with all the virtues of Humanity' (27 Nov 1761). He was buried on 4 December in the churchyard at Hillingdon, near Uxbridge, close to his second wife, Amy, and their two infant children John and Elizabeth.

Rich's will, dated 21 May 1761 and proved on 7 December 1761, left Covent Garden Theatre and the letters patent awarded to both Killigrew and Davenant to Priscilla and stipulated that the theatre be managed by Priscilla and

their son-in-law, the tenor John Beard, until Covent Garden be sold for an adequate sum. After the sale the proceeds were to be divided equally among Priscilla and Rich's four remaining daughters. Rich also provided for Catherine Benson, his 'reputed natural daughter'; it has been suggested that she may have been the daughter of Mrs Benson, a member of Rich's company at Lincoln's Inn Fields from 1728 to 1731. Covent Garden was managed by Beard until 1767, when it was sold for £60,000 to George Colman, Thomas Harris, William Powell, and John Rutherford.
PHYLLIS T. DIRCKS

Sources T. Davies, *Memoirs of the life of David Garrick*, 2 vols. (1808) · Highfill, Burnim & Langhans, *BDA* · P. Sawyer, 'John Rich's contribution to the eighteenth-century London stage', *Essays on the eighteenth-century English stage* [Manchester 1971], ed. K. Richards and P. Thomson (1972), 85–104 · P. Sawyer, 'Father and Lun', *Restoration and Eighteenth Century Theatre Research*, 12 (1973), 51–8 · P. Sawyer, 'Was John Rich illiterate?', *Theatre Notebook*, 27 (1972–3), 36–9 · P. Sawyer, *The New Theatre in Lincoln's Inn Fields* (1979) · B. Francis, 'John Rich's "proposals"', *Theatre Notebook*, 12 (1957–8), 17–19 · C. F. Burgess, 'Some unpublished items of John Rich and something of a puzzle', *Restoration and Eighteenth Century Theatre Research*, 7 (1968), 34–7 · J. Hill, *Orpheus: an English opera* (1740) · F. von Kielmansegge, *Diary of a journey to England in the years 1761–1762*, trans. Countess Kielmansegge [S. P. Kielmansegg] (1902) · P. T. Dircks, 'The eclectic comic genius of John Rich in *The necromancer*', *Theatre Notebook*, 49 (1995), 165–72 · G. Barlow, 'A first-night prologue for the New Theatre, Lincoln's Inn Fields', *Theatre Notebook*, 38 (1984), 51–3 · parish register, Holborn, St Andrew's, GL, MS 6667/5 · *Lloyd's Evening Post* (25–7 Nov 1761)
Archives Chatsworth House, Derbyshire, MS register, pt 3 · Folger, MS register, pt 1 · Garr. Club, MS register, pt 2 · PRO, legal papers, C107/171
Likenesses engraving, 1723, Harvard TC · W. Hogarth, group portrait, oils, *c*.1729–1731, Yale U. CBA; version, Tate Collection · W. Hogarth, group portrait, 1732, priv. coll. · B. Vandergucht, engraving, 1739, repro. in J. Miller, *Harlequin Horace* (1729), frontispiece · engraving, *c*.1749, Folger · watercolour, 1753, Garr. Club [*see illus.*] · engraving, 1755, repro. in *An epistle from Mr Theophilus Cibber to David Garrick esq.* (1755), frontispiece · R. Wilkinson, engraving, 1818 (after watercolour, 1753) · attrib. J. Highmore, group portrait, oils (with family), Garr. Club
Wealth at death left Covent Garden Theatre to be sold; fetched £60,000, 1767

Rich [*née* Boyle], **Mary**, countess of Warwick (1624–1678), noblewoman, was born, according to her father, on 11 November 1624 at Youghal, co. Cork, Ireland, the thirteenth of fifteen children of Richard *Boyle, first earl of Cork (1566–1643), Irish landowner and politician, and his second wife, Catherine (*c*.1588–1630), only child of Sir Geoffrey Fenton, principal secretary of state for Ireland. At the age of three, Mary Boyle was sent to live in the household of Sir Randall Cleyton, her father's agent, on a farm near Cork. Having no children of her own, Lady Cleyton treated Mary like a daughter, taking 'great care to have me soburly educated' as Mary recalled (BL, Add. MS 27357, fol. 2*v*). With tutorial assistance from two gentlewomen and a Frenchwoman, Mary learned English and French, which facilitated her youthful addiction to plays and romances (she was reading Sidney's *Arcadia* at twelve). She also learned her catechism and Bible, and fancy needlework.

In 1638 Mary Boyle was presented with a marriage treaty

Mary Rich, countess of Warwick (1624–1678), by Robert White, pubd 1678

her father had arranged. The prospective groom was James Hamilton, son and heir of Cork's friend Viscount Claneboye, with an estate of £8000 per annum. Although James professed a 'great passion' for Mary, she failed to return it: 'my aversion for him was exstrordnary' (BL, Add. MS 27357, fol. 3*v*). She defied the entire Boyle clan and refused the match. Presented subsequently with many advantageous offers, she rejected them all, having meanwhile fallen in love with Charles Rich (1616–1673), second son of the second earl of Warwick, whom she had met through the court connections of her sister-in-law Elizabeth Boyle (*née* Killigrew). Again in defiance of her father, Mary informed her family that, while she would not marry Charles without her father's consent, she refused to marry anyone else. Finally obtaining the earl of Cork's consent to the union and his agreement to a marriage portion of £7000 (which, in the event, he never finished paying), the couple stole away to be married privately. Instead of the grand London wedding Cork planned, the ceremony took place at Shepperton near Hampton Court on 21 July 1641, Mary having declared herself 'a great enemy allwayes to publicke maredge' (BL, Add. MS 27357, fol. 15*v*).

The couple began married life in the earl of Warwick's household at Leighs, Essex. Mary bore a daughter (Elizabeth) in 1642, and a son (Charles) in 1643. Worried that they might have too many children for their slender means (Charles remarked he 'feared he should have so many as wold undoe a younger brother'), and that frequent child bearing would spoil Mary's beauty, they stopped having children, though both parents were devoted to their son and daughter (BL, Add. MS 27357, fols. 33v–34). When Elizabeth died at fifteen months, Mary was very distressed, while Charles was 'pationately so … he being most exstrordnarely fond of hur' (BL, Add. MS 27357, fol. 18v). In 1647 the sudden illness of four-year-old Charles accelerated a conversion process that Mary had begun at Leighs, encouraged by the earl's household chaplain Anthony Walker. Before her marriage Mary had been hostile to religion, being 'stedfastly sett against being a Puritan' (BL, Add. MS 27357, fol. 23). Now, vowing she would become a 'new Creature' if her son were restored to health, she transformed herself into a paragon of piety, beginning an all-encompassing devotional routine to which she adhered for the rest of her life (BL, Add. MS 27357, fol. 19v).

After the successive deaths in 1658 and 1659 of Charles's father and elder brother, Charles succeeded as fourth earl of Warwick. The succession was an ironic turn of events: Charles was already disabled by the gout which was to kill him, and in 1664 young Charles, the couple's sole surviving child, died of smallpox. On hearing the news the earl 'cryed out so terably that his cry was herd a great way' (BL, Add. MS 27357, fol. 31v). But, as Anthony Walker recalled, the earl was even more concerned that the news would kill his wife, 'which was he said more to him than an hundred sons' (Walker, Eureka, 91). Mary confessed she loved her son so dearly she would willingly have died either 'for him, or with him' (BL, Add. MS 27357, fol. 31v). Yet aided by religious discipline, the countess survived to nurse her increasingly crippled and irascible husband until he succumbed to his illness on 24 August 1673. She also raised and married off her three nieces, the daughters of the third earl. Both before and after her husband's death, the countess was a revered leader in her local Essex community, settling disputes between neighbours, arranging an equitable distribution of income to ministers of various denominations, and giving away a third or more of her income to the poor, the clergy, and local institutions such as Felsted School. Although she led a quiet life at Leighs, Mary remained close to her siblings and other relations, especially her sister Katherine *Jones, Lady Ranelagh, and her younger brother Robert *Boyle, the natural philosopher, who had dedicated his Some Motives and Incentives to the Love of God (1659) to Mary in gratitude for her pious influence.

During the 1660s the countess embarked on various forms of spiritual and autobiographical writings. From about 1663 she wrote intermittent 'Occasional meditations' (BL, Add. MS 27356), using homely analogies from housewifery and other feminine concerns to draw godly morals. In July 1666 she began a diary (now BL, Add. MSS 27351–27355), in which she recorded her devotional routine and daily events until the end of her life, and in February 1672 she set down her autobiographical reminiscences, 'Some specialties in the life of M. Warwicke' (BL, Add. MS 27357).

The countess died at Leighs on 12 April 1678 and was buried in Felsted church on 30 April. The funeral sermon, with biographical reminiscences and selections from her 'Occasional meditations', was preached by the Revd Anthony Walker, and published in 1678 as Eureka, eureka. The virtuous woman found, her loss bewailed, and character examined in a sermon preached at Felsted in Essex, April 30, 1678, at the funeral of … Mary, countess dowager of Warwick, the most illustrious pattern of a sincere piety, and solid goodness his age hath produced. In addition to this lengthy public eulogy, there was a touching private tribute by her friend Elizabeth Walker in the latter's autobiographical memoirs:

> April 12. 1678. It pleased God to take to himself the Most Excellent Lady, the Countess of Warwick. She was Eminent in Religion; a sound Christian in Knowledge and Practice; exceeding Charitable; did very much good; a very sincere and obliging Friend; very sweet in Disposition, and in Condescention to all; even to those much below her; she did excell both in Religion, and in all other commendable Vertues; she lived very desirable, and dyed much bewailed, as a deep Loss to her Relations, to the Neighbourhood, to the Church, and People of God, to all that knew her … to my Dear Husband … she was a most entire Friend, and to my self.   (Walker, Holy Life, 128)

By the time she died, the countess had attained almost legendary status as a pattern of the saintly life. After her death her writings, including her diaries and occasional meditations, were preserved and annotated by her household chaplain, Thomas Woodroffe, who transcribed exemplary passages under the title 'Collections out of my Lady Warwick's papers' (now BL, Add. MS 27351). Extracts from 1666 to 1672 taken from another transcript of the diaries in the possession of the Revd Nathaniel Woodroffe were published by the Religious Tract Society in 1847. The following year the countess's manuscript autobiographical memoir was edited by Thomas Crofton Croker for the Percy Society. Two biographies of the countess were published in 1901, by Charlotte Fell Smith and Mary E. Palgrave respectively.   SARA H. MENDELSON

Sources DNB · S. H. Mendelson, *The mental world of Stuart women: three studies* (1987), 62–115 · diary, BL, Add. MSS 27351–27355 · 'Occasional meditations', BL, Add. MS 27356 · 'Some specialties in the life of M. Warwicke', BL, Add. MS 27357 · A. B. Grosart, ed., *Lismore papers*, 1st and 2nd ser., 10 vols (1886–9) · A. Walker, *Eureka, eureka. The virtuous woman found, her loss bewailed, and character examined in a sermon preached at Felsted in Essex, April 30, 1678, at the funeral of … Mary, countess dowager of Warwick* (1678) · A. Walker, *Planctus unigeniti …, or, … the bitter sorrows for a first-born* (1664) · A. Walker, *Leez lachrymans, sive, Comitis Warwici justa. A sermon delivered at the funeral of the Right Honourable Charles, earl of Warwick …* (1673) · A. Walker, *The holy life of Mrs. Elizabeth Walker* (1690) · C. Fell Smith, *Mary Rich, countess of Warwick (1625–1678): her family and friends* (1901) · *Autobiography of Mary, countess of Warwick*, ed. T. C. Croker (1848) · T. O. Ranger, 'Richard Boyle and the making of an Irish fortune, 1588–1614', *Irish Historical Studies*, 10 (1956–7), 257–97 · GEC, *Peerage*

Archives BL, diary, meditations, autobiography, etc., Add. MSS 27351–27358

Likenesses attrib. E. Ashfield, oils, Burghley House, Northamptonshire · R. White, line engraving, BM, NPG; repro. in Walker, *Eureka, eureka* (1678) [*see illus.*]

Rich, Sir Nathaniel (*c.*1585–1636), colonial investor and politician, was probably born at Leighs in Essex, a son of Richard Rich (*d.* 1598), landowner, and Jane Machell or Mitchell, daughter of John Machell or Mitchell, clothier and sometime sheriff of London. His father was one of the illegitimate children of the first Baron Rich [*see* Rich, Sir Richard], chancellor of Henry VIII's newly founded court of augmentations and lord chancellor under Edward VI. Unlike his father, but in keeping with other senior members of the Rich family for the next three generations, Richard Rich adopted advanced protestant views, organizing unauthorized fasts and holding prophesyings and sermons in the great hall of the second Baron Rich's house at Rochford in Essex, in company with the domestic chaplain, Robert Wright. The bishop of London considered he had never been so abused in his life as by Richard Rich, who, though he was detained for a year in the Marshalsea prison, was in trouble again in 1586 for attending an illegal baptism.

Education and legal training Nathaniel Rich was to exhibit a moderate puritan attitude throughout his life. If they were not inspired by the father who died when he was about thirteen, his religious views would surely have been strengthened and sustained by his time at Emmanuel College in Cambridge, and by the puritan households of the two successive heads of the Rich family, the earls of Warwick, whom he served loyally from the second to the fourth decades of the seventeenth century.

Walter Mildmay's foundation at Emmanuel College in Cambridge had been the nursery for numerous late Elizabethan and Jacobean puritan-minded gentry, including Nathaniel's relatives the earls of Warwick and of Holland, the latter a chancellor of the university. The noted puritan minister Nathaniel Ward, whom Rich was to appoint as rector of his parish at Stondon Massey in Essex, was an Emmanuel graduate, as was William Bedell, an Essex man by birth and a distinguished scholar and churchman, who was encouraged by Rich into the posts of provost of Trinity College, Dublin, and bishop of Kildare and Ardagh. In later life Rich corresponded with his old college master, Laurence Chaderton, and his successors, John Preston and William Sandcroft. In 1628 Rich was to be a leading participant on Cambridge's side in a vigorous parliamentary debate over the matter of precedence between the ancient universities. When he came to make his will in 1636 he left money to enable his nephew and heir to attend Cambridge, and he also urged him to study the law at Lincoln's Inn.

Colonial administration In 1610, five years after graduating, Rich had himself entered Gray's Inn, where he developed a deep interest in both legal argument and precedent, which was to stand him in good stead not only as a man of business for Warwick and Holland but also as a board member of the Somer Islands, Virginia, and Providence Island companies. In this role Rich could combine

Sir Nathaniel Rich (*c.*1585–1636), by unknown artist

his powerful connections at court and his incisive legal and administrative skills with his puritan zeal for exploring new worlds and combating the Spanish threat. From the time that he was called in to examine the Somer Islands company's charter in 1616 until his death twenty years later, Rich was a key member of the Warwick interest. By 1619 he owned twelve shares in the Somer Islands, concentrated near Port Royal into a substantial estate of nearly 500 acres and surpassed in extent only by the holdings of the earl of Warwick himself. Through his agent in the islands, his younger brother Robert, Nathaniel Rich established and supplied tenants, developed a scheme for using young indentured servants, experimented with wine, sugar cane, figs, and exotic plants, provided many cattle, and, by 1628, was to see his estate produce almost one sixth of the tobacco crop from the islands. By the 1630s, after some years of limited success in tobacco sales, Rich was strongly advocating juniper cultivation and cedar wood exports. Moreover he was interested in more than the economic life of the islands and supported the minister Lewis Hughes, whose remarkable liturgy, *The Manner of Public Worship*, was sent to him in 1618 in hopes that it would be promoted in English puritan circles. That Rich had confidence in the islands' future may be gauged by his bequests in 1636 of four shares to establish a free school and of his library to stock it. Rich's executor, Lord Mandeville, was unable to persuade the community to establish the school, and the matter remained unresolved into the 1660s.

Except for two brief periods in the early 1620s, Rich was a very active member of the Virginia Company. At all times he acted in the earl of Warwick's interest, and it is striking how often both men were present at meetings together. Rich's astute legal mind made two particular contributions to the company's affairs: vigorous attempts to obtain more favourable terms for the tobacco contract; and the meticulously detailed analysis of the failures of the Sandys party during the bitter factional disputes from 1620 to 1623, which culminated in the company's dissolution. In the matter of the contract Rich finally advocated that the trade should be vested in the king's hands—much as the gabelle was in France—not only to increase royal revenues but also to illustrate the king's direct interest in the plantation's welfare. For the king's commissioners investigating the company, Rich provided evidence of the excessive number of emigrants dispatched into the poorly provisioned colony, of the over-optimistic reports of conditions there, and of the promotion of unworkable economic projects, all of which had characterized the self-aggrandizing policies of the Sandys administration. For their part this group took into the parliament of 1624 the charge that the company's misfortunes had derived from the prejudiced judgments of Lord Treasurer Cranfield and Nathaniel Rich. The Sandys group was severely rebuffed when the new royal commission to oversee Virginia's affairs included Rich and the earl of Warwick.

Three years earlier, in 1621, Sandys and Rich had both promoted the idea of a West India Company to enhance trade and reduce the export of bullion. By 1626 Rich took the lead in parliament for this project, which had now become part of the desire for a colonial war with Spain. Arguing that Bermuda could be used as a base for the company's naval vessels, Rich and his friends were seeking to place the war at sea into the hands of private individuals. Rich himself offered to put up £100 in May 1636 to assist in sending a warship to the West Indies. Warwick had been active in privateering ventures in the Caribbean region and it was these which led to the discovery and settlement of islands off the Nicaragua coast which were to be administered through the Providence Island Company from 1630. Rich encouraged relatives to settle there, and he himself became the company's deputy governor in 1635. While John Winthrop urged him to continue expansion in the south, Rich helped Winthrop's son to acquire knowledge of fortifications to take back to Massachusetts by gaining him access to the recently constructed forts at Harwich in Essex. He himself kept his interests in the northern colonies by joining the scheme in the 1630s to establish communities along the Connecticut River. Rich also had an investment in the East India Company, which he bequeathed to his secretary, William Jessop, in 1636, but he was not involved in the governing body.

Parliamentary interests In domestic affairs, and especially in parliament, Rich achieved great respect as a political strategist and trusted colleague—'my partner' as Sir Dudley Digges described him in 1622 (NL Ire., MS 18653). Member for Totnes in 1614, for East Retford in 1621, for Harwich in 1624, for Newport in the Isle of Wight in 1625, and for Harwich again in 1626 and 1628, Rich first obtained his seat through the patronage of such relatives as Sir George Carey, the recorder of Totnes, and Sir Gervase Clifton. Both men had married daughters of Penelope Rich and Robert Rich, first earl of Warwick. At Newport, Rich was sponsored by Secretary Conway; in Essex his own connections and influence secured his return. His several diaries were quite brief and most often they dealt with proceedings in the earlier weeks of a parliament. Save for the fragments surviving from 1614 and 1625, each had a specific emphasis: that for 1621 reported the speeches of Sir Edwin Sandys especially fully and demonstrated a keen interest in matters of trade; that for 1624 focused on relations with Spain and foreign affairs; and that for 1626 reflected Rich's outspoken criticism of Buckingham by emphasizing the mismanagement of naval affairs. His short notes from 1628 were concerned with the Lords' adding a clause to the petition of right saving the king's prerogative and with the Commons' preparing a remonstrance to the king.

Rich made a brief appearance as a committee man in the parliament of 1614 and thereafter his influence grew steadily. His record of 57 committees and 75 speeches in 1621 was surpassed only by the 74 committees and 136 speeches of 1628, but he was clearly of great political importance by 1626 and had come to appreciate the vital role to be played by communication between the two houses. By 1628 he was chairman of eight important committees and he and John Pym had become much more than neighbours in St Andrew's Holborn. Throughout the 1620s both men and several of their colleagues, Digges, Rudyard, Knightley, Eliot, and Strode in the Commons and Warwick, Saye and Sele, Brooke, and Pembroke in the Lords to name a few, became increasingly disturbed by the state of religion and the direction of foreign policy. The prosecution of war with Spain and concerns for the recovery of the Palatinate and for the condition of Germany were of central importance. Rich and Pym also had a distaste for monopolists, and Rich saw Giles Mompesson's case in 1621 as one requiring exemplary punishment. The issue of monopolies, like that of impositions, was one branch of their care for the state of the king's revenue and the manner in which it was obtained and spent. Rich was anxious that members of parliament should be present in the Commons, working hard at formulating and passing bills. He was less keen than Eliot or Coke, for example, that the Commons should identify and resolve grievances as a first item of business. He was a stickler for procedure and legal forms and his interventions in debate commonly dealt with matters of precedent. This was a part of his role as a mediator, suggesting lines of action that would produce workable compromises. His essentially cautious parliamentary style was, however, cast aside when he vigorously joined the attack on Buckingham in

1626. By then he had become increasingly alarmed by the threat of militant Arminianism in the context of a spread of Jesuit and papal influence made especially dangerous by the presence of Irish troops in the armies of 1627 and 1628 billeted in southern England. These fears were doubtless heightened by his membership of the committee of religion examining the Arminian Richard Montagu in 1626, and also by his personal experiences in Ireland a few years earlier.

Irish affairs Rich was appointed to the several commissions for Irish affairs between 1622 and 1625, and he also served on the 1625 commission on the wool trade, which closely examined its Anglo-Irish dimension. There is no contemporary evidence to warrant the oft-repeated view that the members of the Irish commission of 1622 were sent there as punishment for their criticism of royal policy in the parliament of 1621: 'an employment not much preferable to prison' (R. Zaller, *The Parliament of 1621*, 1971, 188). While several commissioners undoubtedly had been outspoken members of that parliament—Rich, Digges, and Crew among them—they were also well-connected politicians, experienced in colonial administration. Transatlantic settlement shared features with the problems of Ireland, including plantation, economic uncertainty, unreliable native populations, doubtful religious loyalties, and financial concerns. Those experienced in colonial matters were probably considered ideal figures to study Irish conditions. Furthermore it was such men as Sandys and Rich who first argued in the parliament of 1621 for the need to study Ireland, a fact acknowledged by the privy council when it came to discharge the commission. The council was unlikely to have appointed men under a cloud to a commission so central to Lord Treasurer Cranfield's political and fiscal strategy. Rich took up the challenge with deep seriousness, taking extensive notes of the daily activities of the commission from its beginning in Dublin in April 1622 throughout the summer, with a view to preparing a detailed journal of its proceedings.

While in Ireland, Rich was closely involved in the recommendations for improving the courts of justice and for ruthlessly paring the establishment, and in the strenuous efforts to reduce the heavy government indebtedness to the soldiery. He also joined in the revulsion at 'the hardening of the recusants in their obstinacy' (BL, Add. MS 4756, fol. 70). Together with Digges and the master of the ordnance, Lord Caulfeild, he surveyed Armagh and co. Tyrone and kept meticulous notes of their proceedings. The commission's prodigious amount of work was recognized by the privy council's statement 'that his Majestie's and their Lordshipp's good opinion of theire service should be kept in memory and registered in the booke of councell causes' (*Acts of the Privy Council, 1621–3*, 422). It later appeared that the king was especially impressed with the chairman, Sir William Jones, and with Rich, who was seen throughout 1623 and 1624 as an effective negotiator with the lord treasurer on behalf of his friends in the Irish administration, who felt that fiscal mismanagement and wrongly directed patronage were still rampant. As Sir Francis Blundell put it in July 1623, 'your letters … doe

come to mee like the dove to Noah [and] bringe with them toakens of peace and comforte to mee whoe have suffered much … by malice and misinterpretation' (NL Ire., MS 18661). Matters were no better in religion. William Bedell reported pessimistically to Rich in 1627 of a country 'wholly given over to Romish superstition … abandoned by those who should have care and charge of it. … Yourselfe I beleeve would scarce beleeve it possible that in a few years since your being there it should receive such a headlong downfall' (Shuckburgh, 270).

The alarm which Rich felt at the spread of Irish and English recusancy was to be expected in one so committed to a zealous, evangelical religion. Several divines dedicated works to him. In *The Return of Prayers* (1636) Thomas Goodwin remarked 'you have beene long a frequent and constant dealer in the blessed way of entercourse with God in private'. In *God's Three Arrows* (1631) William Gouge dedicated to his friend of many years the reprint of the sermon he had preached as vicar of Blackfriars on 5 November 1623, rejoicing at the death of those Catholics unfortunate enough to have attended the Jesuit sermon in the French ambassador's chapel when it collapsed under the weight of numbers. Richard Sibbes, the exceptional Gray's Inn lecturer, Cambridge college master, and mentor to Gouge, commended Rich's 'sincereity, wisdom and right judgement' to Ussher, the Irish primate (*The Whole Works of the most Rev. James Ussher*, ed. J. Elrington and J. H. Todd, 1847–63, 16.395). Throughout the 1620s Rich was active in the circles of puritan clergy in Essex and supported young clerics like Stephen Marshall whose divinity degree was obtained under his patronage. Rich counted many fiery London preachers among his correspondents and received controversial protestant literature from abroad. He urged young men to go to Leiden for their spiritual education and he gave financial backing and political support to the eirenicist John Dury (himself educated at Leiden) and the Comenian Samuel Hartlib. He was not prepared to jettison the Book of Common Prayer in favour of an independent liturgy but he was somewhat ahead of John Dury in England when he advocated in the parliament of 1621 the union of the protestant churches in Europe to counter the threat of Rome and Spain. Dury, with whom Rich regularly corresponded, recommended Hartlib to him in 1633. Both Hartlib's vision of Virginia as one potential location for his model state and his desire to overthrow the Antichrist doubtless appealed to Rich, whose keenness to see Indian children educated in the Americas was shared by the Comenian. Certainly some contemporaries felt that Hartlib lost a good friend when Rich died in 1636.

Society life Despite his interest in the continental reformation and in overseas enterprise Rich only once travelled abroad. He was in Paris in 1612 and passed on correspondence from London to John Donne. He was perhaps accompanying Sir Robert Rich and Sir Henry Wotton on an embassy to Savoy, and in Paris he may have witnessed the betrothals of Louis XIII to Anne of Austria and Philip IV of Spain to Princess Elizabeth of France. He was well known in London society. He owed his knighthood in 1617 to Lady Hatton and he lived for much of the time after 1618 at Warwick House in Holborn. He helped to arrange several marriages to young aristocrats and politicians in the Warwick circle. He had excellent Latin and Greek and was familiar with Hebrew literature. He enjoyed scholastic debates through Latin correspondence with friends. He may have suffered from gout and a form of vertigo and was sometimes unable to stand for long in debates.

Rich's death, which occurred between 10 November and 1 December 1636, was rumoured to have been hastened by the immoderate use of an antimonial cup, a remedy much in demand following the publication in 1634 of John Evans's *The Universal Medicine, or, The Vertues of the Antimoniall Cup*. The author claimed that one could not take too much of this powerful concoction of mercury, sulphur, and salt, which was placed in an earthenware pot and heated in wine or ale. Predeceased by his sister Margaret Wroth (*née* Rich) and his brother Robert, Rich left three surviving sisters and many friends and relatives in Essex society, notably in the Warwick and Barrington connections. To his closest friend, John Pym, he left a gold ring and his best gelding. All the property recorded in his will had been acquired early in his career: the manor of Stondon Massey by 1611; the rectory in Pembrokeshire in 1615; his estate in the Somer Islands, and his East India Company stock before 1620. He urged one sister to take up residence in the Somer Islands with her family on property to be bequeathed to her with that condition. The others already there or in Providence he expected would stay. He appointed Lord Mandeville his executor and gave a substantial annuity to the 'dear and most noble religious lady', his executor's wife. He himself was unmarried and left the balance of his estate to his nephew Nathaniel, later to become a colonel in the parliamentary army.

ROBIN J. W. SWALES

Sources V. A. Ives, ed., *The Rich papers: letters from Bermuda, 1615–1646* (1984) • S. M. Kingsbury, ed., *The records of the Virginia Company of London*, 4 vols. (1906–35) • W. Notestein, F. H. Relf, and H. Simpson, eds., *Commons debates, 1621*, 7 vols. (1935) • M. Jansson and W. B. Bidwell, eds., *Proceedings in parliament, 1625* (1987) • W. B. Bidwell and M. Jansson, eds., *Proceedings in parliament, 1626*, 4 vols. (1991–6) • R. C. Johnson and others, eds., *Proceedings in parliament, 1628*, 6 vols. (1977–83) • C. Thompson, *Sir Nathaniel Rich's diary of proceedings in the House of Commons in 1624* (1985) • W. Notestein and F. H. Relf, eds., *Commons debates for 1629* (1921) • C. Thompson, 'The origins of the politics of the parliamentary middle group, 1625–1629', *TRHS*, 5th ser., 22 (1972), 71–86 • C. Russell, *Parliaments and English politics, 1621–1629* (1979) • W. F. Craven, *Dissolution of the Virginia Company: the failure of a colonial experiment* (1932) • T. W. Moody and others, eds., *A new history of Ireland*, 3: *Early modern Ireland, 1534–1691* (1976) • E. S. Shuckburgh, ed., *Two biographies of William Bedell, bishop of Kilmore, with a selection of his letters and an unpublished treatise* (1902) • Venn, *Alum. Cant.* • will, PRO, PROB 11/172, sig. 253 • T. Webster, *Godly clergy in early Stuart England: the Caroline puritan movement, c.1620–1643* (1997) • T. K. Rabb, *Jacobean gentleman: Sir Edwin Sandys, 1561–1629* (1998) • V. Treadwell, *Buckingham and Ireland, 1616–28: a study in Anglo-Irish politics* (1998)

Archives Bermuda National Trust, MSS • HLRO, parliamentary diary • NL Ire., corresp. and papers • NRA, priv. coll., colonial papers | Cambs. AS, Huntingdon, Manchester MSS

Likenesses P. van Somer, portrait, repro. in Ives, ed., *The Rich papers*, 386 • portrait; formerly Kimbolton Castle, Huntingdonshire [*see illus.*]

Wealth at death manor of Stondon Massey, Essex; over 500 acres in Somer Islands; financial interests in Providence Island and East India Company; rectory at Nevern, Pembrokeshire, purchased in 1615: will, PRO, PROB 11/172, sig. 253; Cambs. AS, Huntingdon, M28/1/16

Rich, Nathaniel (*d.* 1700×02), army officer, was the eldest son of Robert Rich of Felsted, Essex, and Elizabeth, daughter of Sir Thomas Dutton. Sir Nathaniel *Rich, who was probably his uncle, left him his manor of Stondon, Essex, in 1636, at which time he was still a minor. He matriculated from St Catharine's College, Cambridge, in 1637, and on 13 August 1639 was admitted to Gray's Inn. Some time during the 1640s Rich married Elizabeth (*d.* 1655), daughter of Sir Edmund Hampden, and sister of John Hampden of ship money fame. Together they had three children, including two sons, Nathaniel and Robert.

When the civil war broke out Rich, along with other young gentlemen from the inns of court, joined the earl of Essex's life guard regiment. In the summer of 1643 he was commissioned captain of horse, and returned to Essex to raise a troop for the earl of Manchester's army. By December 1644 he had risen to the rank of lieutenant-colonel. In the parliamentary inquiry into the quarrel between Manchester and Oliver Cromwell, Rich sided with Cromwell, giving damning testimony about Manchester's reluctance to fight the king, and his dilatoriness in obeying the orders of the committee of both kingdoms.

At the time of the New Model Army's formation in February and March 1645, Rich's nomination as colonel of horse was rejected by the House of Commons; the parliamentary diarist Sir Simonds D'Ewes claimed that this was on account of his youth, but his recent identification with Cromwell is the more likely explanation. However, he was permitted to take up his colonelcy later that spring. He and his regiment saw action at the battle of Naseby (14 June 1645). In March 1646 he led a party of horse and dragoons that routed a royalist outpost at St Columb, Cornwall. He was also one of Fairfax's commissioners who negotiated the surrender of Oxford in May and June of that year. Early in 1647 he stood, along with Sir Thomas Fairfax, for Cirencester in the recruiter election. Their return as MPs was blocked by cavaliers who prevented the poll from being taken.

During the conflict between army and parliament in 1647 Rich played a moderating role, which prompted the Leveller leader John Lilburne to rail against him as 'a juggling, paltry, base fellow' (Lilburne, 8). At first, according to the Leveller John Wildman, Rich tried to suppress the petitioning activity of the soldiers. Later, however, he changed tack, and merely strove to remove those demands made by his regiment that were 'impertinent and extravagant' (*Clarke Papers*, 1.63). He spoke forcefully against the Irish expedition, especially under a strange or new commander, and urged parliament to settle the soldiers' pay arrears before giving them fresh assignments. In July he was one of three officers who acted as intermediaries between the army and lords Wharton and Saye while they drafted 'The heads of proposals'. He was also a member of the delegation of officers that presented the 'Heads' to the king and spent three hours debating with him, removing some of the parts to which he objected most. Rich's participation in these and other negotiations marked him as one of the senior officers of the army, despite his youth. Such was his reputation for moderation that when the counter-revolutionary presbyterians briefly recaptured control of parliament at the end of July they appointed Rich to their reconstituted committee of public safety.

During the army's debates at Putney over the Leveller *Agreement of the People* Rich backed Henry Ireton in opposing a democratic franchise, reminding his listeners of the disaster that had befallen ancient Rome when it had followed the same route. He was appointed to an eighteen-man committee of officers and agitators to review the *Agreement* to see whether it conflicted with any of the army's previous engagements and declarations.

In January 1648, on the eve of the second civil war, Rich's regiment was one of two quartered at the Mews in Westminster to guard parliament and keep a watch on the City. It was instrumental in quelling the crypto-royalist Easter rising of London apprentices on 2 April, in which several apprentices and watermen were killed. On 1 June it was part of the army with which Fairfax defeated the royalists at Maidstone. Rich was then detached to relieve Dover. With efficient professionalism he overran Dover and then retook Walmer, Sandwich, Deal, and Sandown castles before the end of August.

In December 1648 the army resumed its debate on the *Agreement of the People*. While he had shown himself a conservative on the franchise question, Rich parted company with Ireton on religious toleration. A radical libertarian, he spoke out against allowing the magistrate any power over men's consciences. He felt uneasy about the legality of the king's trial, and significantly was not named to the high court of justice, but he did approve of the establishment of the republic. In February 1649 he was at last admitted to parliament, as member for Cirencester. In December 1650 he took charge of the suppression of a royalist rising in Norwich.

Rich remained an active supporter of the republican regime, working diligently to promote the army's reform programme until the downfall of Barebone's Parliament at the end of 1653. Having supported Cromwell's expulsion of the Rump, he was appointed to the commission of the admiralty and navy, and was one of a three-man committee to consider what to do about the Post Office. Concerned chiefly with national security and guarding the regime against subversion, the committee recommended that the Post Office ought to be in the hands of those 'who have given evidence of their good affeccion', and should principally serve the strategic needs of the navy (BL, Add. MS 22546, fol. 109). Between 1651 and 1653 Rich was one of the largest purchasers of confiscated crown land, acquiring the manors of Eltham, Kent, where he took up residence in 1653, and High Easter, Essex. The value of the two properties was well in excess of £36,000. He was also part of a consortium each member of which obtained a sixth of Newfoundland.

In 1654 Rich began to show his millenarian colours by associating with Fifth Monarchist critics of the Cromwellian regime. Before the end of the year he had been removed from the army, possibly in connection with the petition that the three colonels—Okey, Saunders, and Alured—had drawn up against the protector and circulated in the army. As part of a Fifth Monarchist deputation Rich criticized the parliament, 'whereby power is derived from the people, whereas all power belongs to Christ'. Because the present government was 'carnall' and illegitimate, 'armes may bee taken upp againste it' (*Clarke Papers*, 2.244). Furious, Cromwell accused Rich of hindering tax collection, and placed him and three others under house arrest. Rich was allowed to attend to his wife, Elizabeth, who died in 1655, but was later incarcerated at Windsor Castle and then Carisbrooke on the Isle of Wight. He was not freed until March 1656. Despite the displeasure of Cromwell and the major-generals, he was then apparently elected to the parliament of that year, though barred from sitting.

When the Rump was restored in 1659 Rich was given a regiment and offered the post of English resident in the Netherlands, which he declined. When Lambert again expelled the Rump in October, Rich, who managed to hang on to his command, backed Ludlow in the latter's campaign for parliament's restoration. When his regiment was sent to Portsmouth to subdue the garrison that supported the Rump, Rich joined his forces and the whole regiment declared for parliament, and united with the garrison in marching to London. This led to the restoration of the Rump, which thanked Rich and gave him a new commission. His triumph was short lived, for by February General Monck had recalled the excluded members of the Long Parliament, and a Restoration had become all but inevitable. Dismissed from his regiment, Rich tried to make a last stand in East Anglia, but was arrested and imprisoned. He was released a few days later, and since he had not been one of the king's judges he was allowed to benefit from the Act of Indemnity.

Nevertheless the government distrusted Rich, and in the panic over Venner's plot he was once again arrested, on 10 January 1661. In the following August he was imprisoned at Portsmouth. In addition to losing his freedom he had been compelled to surrender his crown lands, which reduced his income by £800 a year. Despite his penurious imprisonment he none the less found favour with a high-born lady, Elizabeth, daughter of Robert Kerr, first earl of Ancram, whom he had been courting for several years. Writing to her brother William, the third earl of Ancram, she boasted of Rich's connection with the family of the earl of Warwick, though more important to her was 'his nearer relation to the Lord, who has soe well accomplished him with the best qualifications, that I have reason to think myselfe unworthy of him' (*Correspondence*, 2.454). The two were married some time before 13 August 1663, but had no children.

Thanks to his wife's persistent lobbying, and the intervention of Lord Falmouth, Rich obtained his release in 1665. From that point onwards he lived quietly at his ancestral manor of Stondon until the beginning of the next century, though he is known to have taught at sectarian conventicles. When James II was trying to create a parliament to repeal the penal laws he made Rich a JP for Essex, to the great disgust of Sir John Bramston, deputy lieutenant of Essex. When he died at Stondon, some time between signing his will in October 1700 and March 1702 when it was proved, he left the manor, burdened with a mortgage, to his wife during her lifetime, and to his elder son, Nathaniel, in reversion. Apart from a small bequest to 'Mr Pagit, minister of Stondon meeting', he appears to have had little other disposable wealth (will, PRO, PROB 11/464, fol. 54v). A scion of the Warwick family of Essex, Rich was an example of those pious puritan gentlemen who were inspired by the ideals of the English revolution.   IAN J. GENTLES

Sources I. Gentles, *The New Model Army in England, Ireland, and Scotland, 1645–1653* (1992) · B. S. Capp, *The Fifth Monarchy Men: a study in seventeenth-century English millenarianism* (1972) · *The Clarke papers*, ed. C. H. Firth, 1–3, CS, new ser., 49, 54, 61 (1891–9) · *CSP dom.*, 1644–5; 1652–4; 1656–62; 1664–5 · *The memoirs of Edmund Ludlow*, ed. C. H. Firth, 2 vols. (1894) · *Correspondence of Sir Robert Kerr, first earl of Ancram, and his son William, third earl of Lothian*, ed. D. Laing, 2 vols., Roxburghe Club, 100 (1875) · H. Cary, ed., *Memorials of the great civil war in England from 1646 to 1652*, 2 vols. (1842) · J. Sprigge, *Anglia rediviva: England's recovery* (1647) · C. H. Firth and G. Davies, *The regimental history of Cromwell's army*, 2 vols. (1940) · J. Lilburne, *Jonah's cry out of the whale's belly* [1647] [Thomason tract E 400(5)] · J. Lawmind [J. Wildman], *Putney projects, or, The old serpent in a new forme* (1647) · naval papers, BL, Add. MS 22546, fols. 109, 118–19, 141 · Z. Grey, *An impartial examination* (1738), appx, 105 · J. Rushworth, *Historical collections*, 2nd edn, 7 (1701) · *Seventh report*, HMC, 6 (1879) [Lowndes MSS] · *The manuscripts of his grace the duke of Portland*, 10 vols., HMC, 29 (1891–1931), vol. 1 · *JHC*, 4 (1644–6); 7 (1651–9) · Thurloe, *State papers*, vol. 6 · P. Morant, *The history and antiquities of the county of Essex*, 2 vols. (1768) · J. Foster, *The register of admissions to Gray's Inn, 1521–1889, together with the register of marriages in Gray's Inn chapel, 1695–1754* (privately printed, London, 1889), vol.1, p. 223 · Venn, *Alum. Cant.*, 1/3.449 · J. R. Brown, 'Sir Nathaniel Riche', *N&Q*, 5th ser., 10 (1878), 155 · W. D. Pink, 'Sir Nathaniel Rich', *N&Q*, 8th ser., 1 (1892), 66–7 · R. Baker, *A chronicle of the kings of England* (1670) · chancery close rolls, PRO, C 54/3610/57 (High Easter); 54/3711/30 (Newfoundland); 54/3745/28 (Eltham) · will, proved, 3 March 1702, PRO, PROB 11/464, fols. 53v–54v

Archives BL, Egerton MS 2647, fol. 363

Wealth at death perhaps a few hundred pounds; manor of Stondon, Essex, was mortgaged; left £10 to a Mr Pagit, 'minister of Stondon meeting': will, proved, 3 March 1702, PRO, PROB 11/464, fols. 53v–54v

Rich [*née* Devereux], **Penelope**, **Lady Rich** (1563–1607), noblewoman, was born in January 1563 at Chartley, Staffordshire, the eldest child of Walter *Devereux, first earl of Essex (1539–1576), and his wife, Lettice (c.1539–1634), daughter of Sir Francis Knollys. She was educated by tutors at home until her father's death in September 1576, then confided to the guardianship of Henry *Hastings, third earl of Huntingdon (1536?–1595), living at his house in Leicestershire. She knew French well and her talents in languages and music were later praised, as was her beauty. Before his death her father had sought a contract for her

marriage to Philip Sidney, but Sidney did not wish to marry then, although later he regretted his decision. In January 1581 Penelope arrived at court to become one of Queen Elizabeth's maids of honour. Huntingdon soon arranged for her marriage to Robert *Rich (1559?–1619) of Leighs, Essex (then Lord Rich, later first earl of Warwick), and the wedding took place about 1 November 1581. The high-spirited young Penelope Rich thereafter frequently visited her mother (now wife of the earl of Leicester) and the court, staying with her brother Robert, earl of Essex [see Devereux, Robert], in London.

About the time of her marriage, Philip Sidney, who was at court during 1581, apparently fell in love with her; his *Astrophil and Stella* supposedly describes Sidney's own passion for the married Lady Rich. Some of the sonnets depict a conflict between virtue and passion. Many clues suggest that Penelope Rich was the object, especially the riddle which plays on the word rich, applied to a woman at 'Aurora's court', and ending 'hath no misfortune, but that Rich she is' (Sonnet 37). Sonnet 35 includes the words:

> long needy Fame
> Doth even grow rich, naming my Stella's name.

Hudson argued that other writers of her time believed Penelope Rich was the model for Stella. They included John Harington, who commented that Sidney's sonnets of Stella called her inestimably rich. In 1595 Thomas Campion wrote an outline in Latin for a poem touching 'stella Britanna, Penelope, Astrophili quae vulta incendit amores' ('the British star, Penelope, who sometime kindles the love of Astrophil'). Unfortunately we do not know what Penelope herself thought of Sidney's poems, or even if she saw them. They were probably written in 1582, but did not appear in print until after Sidney died in 1586. There is no evidence that the two became lovers, although many have assumed that they did. Sidney was away from court for much of 1582, and he married in 1583. On his deathbed in 1586 Sidney reportedly told the preacher George Gifford of a vanity in which he had taken delight, of which he must now rid himself, naming Lady Rich (Robertson, 296–7). Sidney's widow, Frances, married Penelope Rich's beloved brother Essex and the two women were often together. This might suggest that if there had ever been an affair between Sidney and Lady Rich it was over before Frances married Sidney in 1583.

The relationship between Lady Rich and her husband was not simple. They had five children, four of whom, two daughters and two sons, survived; the last was born in August 1590. The elder son, Robert *Rich, became second earl of Warwick, the younger, Henry *Rich, first earl of Holland. But Lady Rich would not stay at home as a country wife, and continued her life at court. At the age of twenty-seven she inspired the love of another prominent Elizabethan: her affair with Sir Charles *Blount (1563–1606) was public by 17 November 1590, when he wore her colours for the accession day tournament. It was a lasting devotion. The first of their six children, Penelope, was baptized on 30 March 1592 at St Clement Danes in London (she was not born in 1589 as has been thought), but given the surname Rich and brought up with the other children.

Their next child, baptized in 1597 with the Christian name Mountjoy (in 1594 Blount had become eighth Baron Mountjoy), was not included on the Rich pedigree [*see* Blount, Mountjoy]. Another son was baptized at Essex House, but soon died; two more sons and a daughter followed. Mountjoy's careful trusts and his will provided appropriately for all five, and for any posthumous birth, giving most to the eldest son, Mountjoy. The eldest daughter, Penelope, was to have a £5000 dowry. Yet until 1603 at least Lady Rich still spent some time with Lord Rich—in 1600 she nursed him in a serious illness. He accepted the strange situation for years, with all the children brought up together, perhaps because of her contacts, especially her brother. When Rich's landholdings were threatened in 1599 he importuned his reluctant wife to come to London to use her influence to stop a lawsuit proceeding (*Salisbury MSS*, 15.175, 179, wrongly dated 1603). Lord Rich had intended to go with Mountjoy and Essex on the islands voyage, but was too seasick to go.

Penelope Rich wielded some power at court. She wrote to Lord Burghley in 1588 for a wardship. People seeking favours, such as a knighthood, asked for her mediation, and she would make their requests to Sir Robert Cecil. In 1595 and 1596 she thanked Cecil for his kindnesses, assuring him of her constancy, and after her brother's execution (discussed below) she continued the correspondence. In 1599 she asked Sir Julius Caesar, a judge of the admiralty court and master of requests, to continue his favour to a Captain Isard, for which she was beholden to Caesar. Rowland Whyte often mentioned her in his reports to Sir Robert Sidney. In order to help Sir Robert, who hoped to become warden of the Cinque Ports, Lady Rich cleverly raised his name when discussing the choice of warden with the queen. Whyte also reported such matters as Lady Rich's agreement to be a godmother to Sir Robert's son (Mountjoy was to be godfather), her efforts to buy hangings for Lord Rich, and her smallpox in April 1597, from which she recovered 'without any blemish to her beautiful face' (*De L'Isle and Dudley MSS*, 2.268). Her independence in the 1590s derived from her own personal qualities, as well as from Essex's position as the queen's favourite. Brother and sister had a very close, affectionate, and sometimes playful relationship, as shown by his undated 'fantastical' letters to her (printed in A. Freedman, 'Essex to Stella: two letters from the earl of Essex to Penelope Rich', *English Literary Renaissance*, 3, 1973, following p. 248; Margetts, '"Wayes of mine owne hart"').

But her brother's disgrace in 1599 prompted Lady Rich to overestimate her influence, when she wrote a strong letter to Queen Elizabeth on 1 January 1600, defending Essex, castigating his enemies, and complaining that the queen would not see him to allow him to answer them. Elizabeth was angry. She thought Lady Rich should not meddle in such matters, and must answer for it if she wished to recover the queen's favour. Elizabeth was equivocal, but never fully forgave her for her 'stomach and presumption' in writing that letter (*Salisbury MSS*, 7.167–8). Worse was to come. Lady Rich was named as one of the chief conspirators in the abortive Essex rising of February 1601 in London; she had dined at Essex House with the leaders the previous night, and went to fetch the earl of Bedford on the morning of the revolt. After the trial, Essex reportedly insisted that she had urged him on by saying that all his friends and followers thought him a coward. She maintained that she had been more like a slave, and that her brother had wrongly accused her. After brief confinement, and examination by the privy council, she was released.

Lady Rich may have owed such leniency to her relationship with Mountjoy, who was then in Ireland at the head of an army sent to defeat the rebels, and vital to English policy; and the queen was fond of Mountjoy. Lady Rich retrieved her influence when James I ascended the throne; she escorted his queen from the border, and performed in court masques by Samuel Daniel and Inigo Jones alongside Queen Anne. In August 1603 James conferred on her the precedence of the earldom of Essex created for Henry Bourchier in 1461. Sir Humphrey Ferrers considered her powerful enough to ask the king or queen to procure him a barony (BL, Stowe MS 150, fol. 192). Later in 1603 Mountjoy returned to England, and to Lady Rich, after three and a half years away in Ireland; James created him earl of Devonshire in gratitude for his victory. After another two years the marriage of Lord and Lady Rich ended, with a decree in the London consistory court on 14 November 1605, on the ground of Lady Rich's acknowledged adultery, although she named no one. The legal separation did not allow remarriage while the former spouse lived. However, the lovers were married on 26 December 1605 by Devonshire's chaplain, William Laud, at Wanstead House, Essex. Devonshire prepared a long, learned defence of Lady Rich's marriage to him, quoting Old Testament texts, and maintaining that the laws of God did not expressly forbid such unions when the magistrate had made a decree. In a letter to King James he claimed that she had protested during the wedding with Rich, that after it Rich had tormented her, and had now not 'enjoyed her' for twelve years; the last is more likely to be correct (BL, Add. MS 4149, fols. 306–319v; BL, Lansdowne MS 885, fols. 86–7). The claim of an earlier secret pre-contract with Devonshire was not made in these defences, and was probably invented later, possibly by Laud or his biographer to justify his part in the marriage. The king was angry, but just over three months later, on 3 April 1606, Devonshire died. Penelope Rich died at Westminster on 7 July 1607.

Lady Rich was a fascinating and forceful woman. She was celebrated by other writers besides Sidney: in dedications, in panegyrics, in sonnets by Henry Constable, in songs and sonnets by Coperario as 'the starre of honor, and the sphere of beautie', and the happiness of her union with Mountjoy by John Ford in the elegy *Fame's Memorial*. Many praised her mind as well as her beauty. Such descriptions owe something to literary hyperbole and hope of patronage, yet they indicate her reputation. Nicholas Hilliard painted her (his portrait is now lost), and named his daughter after her. Other pictures were listed in inventories at the time although no definitive portrait of her survives. A picture at Lambeth has on the back 'a countess of Devon', and is taken to be Penelope, with her blond hair and black eyes.   ALISON WALL

Sources *Report on the manuscripts of Lord De L'Isle and Dudley*, 2, HMC, 77 (1933) · *Calendar of the manuscripts of the most hon. the marquis of Salisbury*, 24 vols., HMC, 9 (1883–1976), vols. 7, 9, 15 · H. H. Hudson, 'Penelope Devereux as Sidney's Stella', *Huntington Library Bulletin*, 7 (1935), 89–129 · Lady Rich's letter to the queen, 1/1/1600, BL, Stowe MS 150, fol. 140 [many other copies available] · *CSP dom.*, *1598–1601*, 396, 414, 439, 546–51, 572 · decree of London consistory court, 1605, BL, Add. MS 38170, fols. 82–4 · Lord Mountjoy's will, PRO, PROB 11/108, fols. 1–3r · 'A discourse … by the earl of Devonshire in defence of his marriage with the Lady Rich', BL, Add. MS 4149, fols. 306–319v · 'Earl of Devonshire … epistle to the king', BL, Lansdowne MS 885, fols. 86–7 · J. Robertson, 'Sir Philip Sidney and Lady Rich', *Review of English Studies*, new ser., 15 (1964), 296–7 · S. Freedman, *Poor Penelope: Lady Penelope Rich, an Elizabethan woman* (1983) · M. Margetts, '"The wayes of mine owne hart": the dating and mind frame of Essex's "fantasticall" letter', *Bodleian Library Record*, 16 (1 April 1997), 101–10 · Devereux letter book, Warks. CRO, MI229 [microfilm] · P. E. J. Hammer, *The polarisation of Elizabethan politics: the political career of Robert Devereux, 2nd earl of Essex, 1585–1597* (1999) · BL, Stowe MS 150, fol. 192 · PRO, PROB 11/109/322 · PRO, PROB 11/109/323 · M. Margetts, 'A christening date for Lady Penelope Rich', *N&Q*, 238 (1993), 153–4
Wealth at death illegal marriage to earl of Devonshire, 1605; his will of 1606 leaving much to her still in dispute at time of her death: PRO, PROB 11/108, fols. 1–3r; PRO, PROB 11/109/322; PRO, PROB 11/109/323

Rich, Richard, **first Baron Rich** (1496/7–1567), lord chancellor, was born at Basingstoke, Hampshire, the son of John Rich (*d.* 1509?), of Penton Mewsey in Hampshire, and his wife, Agnes; he was described as aged fifty-four in January 1551. Rich may have had connections to the Rich family of London, prominent in the Mercers' Company in the fifteenth century, but earlier pedigrees claiming him to be the son of Richard Rich of St Lawrence Jewry in the city are clearly incorrect. There was a London connection, however, for Rich's father owned a house in Islington, Middlesex, which he left to his son in 1509, and Richard Rich may have grown up in the city (at his trial in 1533 the Londoner Sir Thomas More declared that he had known the young Rich).

Common lawyer and administrator, 1516–1547 The young Rich may have studied at Cambridge University before entering the Middle Temple in February 1516. At some point between 1520 and 1525 he was reader at New Inn: a window in the hall there bears the inscription 'Ricardus Riche dominus cancellarius Anglie lector' (BL, Harley MS 1042, fol. 47v). He served as butler of Middle Temple from 1519 to 1520, and (searching for a powerful patron) wrote to Cardinal Thomas Wolsey in 1528 with suggestions for reforming the common law. His earlier effort to secure election as common sergeant of London in 1526 had been unsuccessful, as he lost to Henry VIII's favoured candidate, William Walsingham. It may have been no coincidence that the letter to Wolsey of 1528 was followed shortly afterwards by Rich's appointment to the commission of the peace for Essex and Hertfordshire. Already a

Richard Rich, first Baron Rich (1496/7–1567), by Hans Holbein the younger

member of the council of the Essex magnate John de Vere, fifteenth earl of Oxford, Rich now cultivated the friendship of Thomas Audley, knight of the shire for Essex, who helped to ensure his return for the borough of Colchester in the parliament of 1529; Audley was himself chosen speaker. That same year Rich was named autumn reader at the Middle Temple. In 1530 he was placed on the Colchester gaol delivery commission, and on 30 September 1532 he was chosen as recorder of Colchester, no doubt with the backing of Oxford and Audley.

After he was appointed attorney-general for Wales on 13 May 1532 and deputy chief steward of the south parts of the duchy of Lancaster later that year, Rich's professional career began to prosper. With the promotion of Audley as lord chancellor, Rich finally enjoyed a powerful patron who provided him with his first important legal post: that of solicitor-general, to which he was appointed on 10 October 1533 (he was knighted on the same occasion). As solicitor-general Rich assisted Audley in the House of Lords, working on drafting a number of important bills, including those in restraint of appeals to Rome and establishing the court of augmentation (24 Hen. VIII, c. 12; 27 Hen. VIII, c. 27). He was responsible for the prosecution of opponents of the royal supremacy, including the two principal critics of it, John Fisher, bishop of Rochester, and More. He participated in the examination of Fisher in the Tower of London in May 1535, having been sent to ascertain the bishop's opinion of the royal supremacy but promising him to divulge his views only to the king. Fisher's answers furnished the necessary evidence for his conviction of treason.

Although Rich has usually been attacked for his dealings during More's imprisonment, their relationship was complicated. The two men had known one another since Rich's youth, having lived in the same parish of London, and at the time of his trial More accused him of being

> as yourself can tell (I am sorry you compel me to say) you were esteemed very light of your tongue, a great dicer, and of no commendable fame. And so in your house at the Temple, where hath been your chief bringing-up, were you likewise accompted. (Sylvester and Harding, 245–6)

However, the sources recounting Rich's dealings with More are invariably hostile to him because they were written by members of More's family, their descendants, and Catholic apologists. According to this evidence, on 12 June 1535 Rich had an interview in the Tower with More, who as a skilled lawyer was more circumspect in his responses than he. The two lawyers engaged in a hypothetical discussion of the power of parliament to make the king supreme head of the church. Yet at More's trial on 1 July Rich testified (falsely) that during their conversation the former lord chancellor had explicitly denied the supremacy. The alternative view is that More relaxed somewhat during the interrogation by Rich in what was a bit of professional jousting, but that Rich did not see or report this as something new. However, someone, possibly Cromwell, saw that More's statements could be used to convict him of denying the royal supremacy. Hence Rich's evidence was not dishonest, merely used in a way he never foresaw. As solicitor-general he had a duty to use whatever evidence there was to secure convictions for the crown. Despite the fact that neither of his companions that day in the Tower later corroborated this testimony, Rich's words did suffice to convict More. His alleged perjury received its full reward: on 27 July 1535 Rich was named chirographer of the court of common pleas (a post which he occupied until 3 July 1537), but at the cost of his historical reputation. However, his subsequent acceptability to Mary I suggests that, although he was *persona non grata* with the More and Roper families, this cannot have been the case generally with Catholics and conservatives in public life.

Rich married about 1535, and certainly before May 1536, Elizabeth (d. 1558), daughter and heir of a London grocer, William Jenks. The couple had at least three sons, including Hugh (d. 1554) and Robert Rich, later second Baron Rich (c.1537–1581), and nine or ten daughters. Rich also had one illegitimate son, Richard (d. 1598), the father of Sir Nathaniel *Rich (c.1585–1636). Drawings of Richard and Elizabeth Rich by Hans Holbein the younger survive.

The fiscal and legal consequences of the Henrician reformation soon brought Rich fresh responsibilities. Having resigned as solicitor-general, on 20 April 1536 he was appointed surveyor of liveries, and four days later was named chancellor of the newly erected court of augmentations, charged with overseeing the dissolution of the monasteries, a task for which he showed a particular relish and acquisitiveness that has contributed to the tarnishing of his posthumous reputation. Further recognition of Rich's rising status followed with his selection as a knight of the shire for Essex in the parliament of 1536,

and his subsequent election as speaker of the House of Commons (although the election may have encountered opposition, as it required more time than usual). Displaying a talent for flattery which no doubt helped to advance his career on several occasions, in his opening oration the new Commons speaker likened Henry to Solomon (for wisdom and justice), to Samson (for bravery and strength), and to Absalom (for beauty!). Rich subsequently sat as a knight of the shire for Essex in the parliaments of 1539 (in which he secured a private act, 31 Hen. VIII, c. 23), 1542, and 1545.

Despite having been a protégé of Cromwell during the later 1530s, Rich hastily abandoned his patron in the summer of 1540, and willingly provided damaging testimony against him (as he had done against More). He was a privy councillor by August 1540. By the early 1540s Rich had achieved great success as chancellor of the court of augmentations (the largest of the royal revenue courts), whose coffers were swollen with the profits of the dissolutions. The possibilities of such an office were great, and Rich managed to amass a considerable landed estate in Essex, centred on Leighs Priory (a gift from the king in 1536), which he enlarged. The temptations it presented were equally great, however, and several times Rich was called to clear himself of accusations of corruption, as in April 1541 when John Hillary alleged (unsuccessfully) that Rich had defrauded the crown. On 24 April 1544 he was succeeded as chancellor of augmentations by Sir Edward North (previously treasurer of the court), and in the following month Rich was named treasurer of the French war. He spent five months across the channel handling finances and logistics, before resigning and returning to England in November 1544. It was claimed that ill health prompted him to relinquish his treasurership, but his resignation may have been forced, for the king himself had raised questions about Rich's probity, and had personally challenged his accounts. Despite holding no major office, Rich remained an active privy councillor during the mid-1540s, serving on various commissions and eagerly assisting Edmund Bonner, bishop of London, in pursuing heretics in Essex. In June 1546 he and Thomas Wriothesley, first Baron Wriothesley and lord chancellor, personally tortured Anne Askew, who charged that they 'took pains to rack me with their own hands' (*Acts and Monuments*, 5.547). Despite conservative religious sympathies, Rich consolidated his position by prudently keeping on good terms with the Seymours, and by collaborating in the destruction of the conservative Thomas Howard, fourth duke of Norfolk, and his son Henry Howard, earl of Surrey, in the months before the king's death on 28 January 1547.

Lord chancellor and hunter of heretics, 1547–1558 An assistant executor of Henry's will, soon after the accession of Edward VI, Rich was created Baron Rich, with a grant of lands worth £66 13s. 4d. per annum, on 16 February 1547. A staunch supporter of the creation of the protectorship of Edward Seymour, duke of Somerset, Rich backed the removal of Wriothesley from the chancellorship, and on

23 October he was himself appointed lord chancellor as a reward for his loyalty. As lord chancellor Rich was active in the court of chancery, and promoted the regime's programme of moderate religious reform. He also managed Somerset's legislative agenda during the parliament of 1547, including the repeal of the harsh Henrician treason statutes, and secured for himself a private act guaranteeing certain lands (1 Edward VI, c. 11; 1 Edward VI, c. 13). Despite his close ties to Somerset, Rich demonstrated little loyalty to the lord protector and was instrumental in ensuring the success of the coup of October 1549, when he used the authority of the great seal to countermand the protector's personal orders and drew upon his family's London connections to secure the support of the corporation. Despite this abandonment of Somerset, Rich was soon out of favour with his replacement, John Dudley, earl of Warwick, and late in 1551 there were suspicions that he was involved in a plot by Somerset to recover power. One story (perhaps apocryphal but nevertheless indicative of Rich's growing reputation for treachery) relates how Rich sent a secret message of support to 'the Duke', meaning Somerset, but the messenger misunderstood and delivered the incriminating letter to Norfolk instead, who informed Warwick, now duke of Northumberland, of its contents. Aware of the chancellor's disloyalty, on 31 December 1551 Northumberland personally took possession of the great seal from Rich; rumours circulated that the disgraced chancellor would be sent to the Tower, but he was saved by a timely illness. Even following Somerset's execution on 22 January 1552 it was widely thought that Rich would be imprisoned. Although he remained a privy councillor and was made lord lieutenant of Essex on 16 May 1552, Rich returned to Essex and was rarely at the council board until mid-June 1553, when the succession crisis necessitated his recall. On 23 June he subscribed to Northumberland's device to alter the succession in favour of Lady Jane Grey, and he received the honour of Rayleigh in Essex on 24 June as the price of his support. The king died on 6 July and, despite this bargain, Rich ignored an order of 19 July to raise men in support of Jane, wasted little time in declaring his support for Mary, and worked to raise troops in Essex for her cause.

Rich and his wife entertained Mary on her progress to the capital early in August 1553, and he was named a privy councillor on 28 August. Having profited greatly from the dissolutions, Rich was forced by Mary to restore some properties, and he opposed the restoration of land to the see of Durham on the same grounds. Although not active as a privy councillor, he was busy in Essex, where he was soon infamous for his energetic persecution of heretics. He was consistent in suppressing conventicles during Edward's and Mary's reigns. Rich's earlier support for moderate religious reform under Somerset led Thomas Watts, burnt at Chelmsford in June 1555, to rebuke him: 'My Lord, beware, beware! For you do against your own conscience herein, and without you repent, the Lord will revenge it' (*Acts and Monuments*, 7.123). Yet it seems clear that Rich remained a conservative in religion throughout his life, and his earlier endorsement of reform was motivated more by politics and greed than by personal faith.

Last years, 1558–1567 Following the accession of Elizabeth I, Rich accompanied the new queen to the capital, but she did not name him to her privy council. He did retain some status, however, and was even suggested as a potential lord chancellor late in 1558. As a former chancellor of augmentations Rich supported the restoration of the royal supremacy, but his Catholic faith prompted him to vote against the Act of Uniformity in 1559. Although excluded from the privy council, Rich none the less continued to offer advice to the queen, as in February 1563 when he requested an audience to discuss the succession and the security of the realm; three years later he joined a delegation of Lords and Commons who addressed Elizabeth on the sensitive subject of her marriage. His wife died at St Bartholomew's in London and was buried on 18 December 1558 at Rochford in Essex. Although no longer active at court, as a leading landowner and JP Rich remained an influential figure in Essex during the early 1560s. As well as caring for his estate at Leighs he took an interest in promoting education. Upon the death of his eldest son he had endowed a chantry at Felsted on 26 April 1554, but the endowment was converted in May 1564 to establish the 'Free School of Richard Lord Rich' there, intended to educate the youth of Essex (its celebrated alumni included the sons of Oliver Cromwell). He also founded almshouses at Felsted, and erected the tower of Rochford church.

Having drawn up his will on 12 May 1567, Rich died on 12 June at Rochford and was buried at Felsted on 8 July 1567. His surviving son, Robert Rich, inherited his title and estates, while his nine surviving daughters and his illegitimate son received legacies. About 1620 his great-grandson erected a monument by the sculptor Epiphanius Evesham at Felsted, celebrating the achievements of his illustrious ancestor in carved panels which depict Rich as speaker of the Commons and as lord chancellor (holding the great seal purse and entering in state).

Historical reputation While Evesham glorified Rich's accomplishments in marble, the judgment of posterity has not been so kind. Indeed, since the mid-sixteenth century he has enjoyed a reputation for amorality and treachery with few parallels in English history. In large measure this is due to his role in securing More's conviction, which prompted More's devastating denunciation of Rich's character. More's stinging words were preserved by his son-in-law William Roper in his account of the trial:

> neither I nor no man else to my knowledge ever took you to be a man of such credit as in any matter of importance I or any other would at any time vouchsafe to communicate with you. And I, as you know, of no small while have been acquainted with you and your conversation, who have known you from your youth hitherto. (Sylvester and Harding, 245–6)

As chancellor of augmentations, Rich earned the enmity of Aske and the pilgrims during the risings of 1536 for his role in dissolving monasteries. Nor did he escape protestant censure: John Foxe portrayed him as taking perverted delight in torturing Askew, in particular. Rich's ability to survive and prosper by adapting to changing political and religious regimes (and betraying his former associates) attracted some hostile comment from contemporaries (although he was scarcely alone in this), and has subsequently served to confirm his historical reputation as an unscrupulous time-server. For J. E. Oxley 'principles had no meaning for Rich', while A. G. Dickens describes him as 'odious' and 'unprincipled' (Oxley, 253; Dickens, 144, 211). Such universal opprobrium has been reinforced in the popular imagination by Robert Bolt's play *A Man for All Seasons* (1960), a study of the downfall of More. While seeking to present a more rounded view of Rich's character, Bolt none the less draws heavily upon Roper's account of the trial, presenting Rich as a talented young man prepared to do wrong to promote his career, who possessed 'a studious unhappy face lit by the fire of banked-down appetite … [and] longed to be rescued from himself' (Bolt, xxiii). The popular success of Bolt's play (and Fred Zimmerman's film of 1966, in which John Hurt played Rich) has made Rich's name synonymous with treachery, and confirmed his historical reputation as a man without scruples who betrayed a saint to advance his career. His lengthy service to the crown, his legal and administrative talents, and his educational endowments could not efface the stain upon his character resulting from his possible perjury in 1535 and his later acts of duplicity, and failed to refute More's charge that Rich was a man 'of no commendable fame'.

P. R. N. CARTER

Sources HoP, *Commons, 1509–58*, 3.192–5 • R. Bolt, *A man for all seasons: a play in two acts* (1960) • W. C. Richardson, *History of the court of augmentations, 1536–1554* (1961) • *The acts and monuments of John Foxe*, new edn, ed. G. Townsend, 8 vols. (1843–9); facs. edn (1965) • J. E. Oxley, *The Reformation in Essex to the death of Mary* (1965) • A. Esdaile, 'The monument of the first Lord Rich at Felsted', *Transactions of the Essex Archaeological Society*, new ser., 22 (1936–9), 59–67 • D. E. Hoak, *The king's council in the reign of Edward VI* (1976) • S. E. Lehmberg, *The later parliaments of Henry VIII* (1977) • N. L. Jones, *Faith by statute: parliament and the settlement of religion, 1559* (1979) • R. S. Sylvester and D. P. Harding, eds., *Two early Tudor lives* (1962) • *VCH Essex* • *CSP Spain, 1547–53* • A. G. Dickens, *The English reformation* (1964) • L. M. Higgs, *Godliness and governance in Tudor Colchester* (1998) • J. Guy, *Thomas More* (2000)

Archives Herefs. RO, valuation of his estates • JRL, papers as chancellor of the court of augmentations

Likenesses attrib. E. Evesham, effigy on monument, *c.*1620, Holy Cross Church, Felsted, Essex • H. Holbein the younger, chalk drawing, Royal Collection [*see illus.*]

Rich, Richard (*fl.* 1610), adventurer and author, has been linked to various members of the illustrious Rich family. He was possibly a younger son of Edward Rich of Horndon, or a brother of Robert Rich (*d. c.*1646), master in chancery, or the third son of Sir Edwin Rich, who was half-brother of Robert Rich, earl of Warwick (*d.* 1619), or related to Barnabe Rich. One early biographer's claim that he was the illegitimate son of Richard Rich, first Baron Rich (1496/7–1567), and father of Sir Nathaniel Rich (*c.*1585–1636), now appears mistaken. All that is known for certain is that Rich was the author of a small tract, written in verse, describing his voyage to Bermuda and Virginia in 1610. He travelled in the nine-ship fleet of Sir George Somers together with Sir Thomas Gates and Lord De La Warr

('Delware' in Rich's pamphlet), both, like Somers, commissioners of the Virginia colony, and George Percy, a younger son of the earl of Northumberland, whose own account of the English settlement of Virginia was published in 1625 by Samuel Purchas.

Rich's poem, entitled *Newes from Virginia. The lost flocke triumphant. With the happy arrival of that famous and worthy knight Sr. Thomas Gates: and the well reputed & valiant Captain Mr. Christopher Newporte, and others, into England*, was published in London in 1610 by Edward Allde, who was later fined for printing without a licence. Rich identified himself as one of the gentlemen on the voyage, and promised his readers information about the travels of the *Sea Venture* during its fateful shipwreck on Bermuda ('Bermoothawes'), the survival and resiliency of the crew, and their eventual passage to Virginia. The poem consists of twenty-two eight-line verses, as well as a brief prose preface in which Rich notes that he is 'a Soldier, blunt and plaine, and so is the phrase of my newes'. He planned the poem to be the first instalment of his published views about his journey, but, although the Stationers' register records a book entitled *Good Speed to Virginia* on the same date (1 October 1610) as *Virginia Newes*, there is no known surviving copy of that work.

Rich claims that the shipwrecked crew arrived on Bermuda with few resources. But the island boasted a large supply of fowl, hogs, and tortoises, ample food to keep the men alive once they realized that their one dog could kill the swine for them. Although the crew spent forty-two weeks on the island, only two of them died there and the survivors managed to build two cedar pinnaces to continue their journey to Virginia. When they arrived they found the settlers in desperate circumstances, though De La Warr brought supplies that provided at least temporary sustenance. Like other promoters of the colonization of North America, Rich claimed that the sorrowful state of the Virginia experiment should not be taken as a sign of imminent failure:

> Let England knowe our willingnesse,
> For that our worke is good,
> Wee hope to plant a Nation,
> Where none before hath stood.

His enumeration of the natural bounty of Virginia aimed to assure readers that success seemed inevitable, and he also provided information for any prospective colonists about the organization of the colony.

Rich's brief account of Bermuda possibly had an influence on Shakespeare's *The Tempest*, though other early seventeenth-century works—such as Silvester Jourdan's *A Discovery of the Barmudas, otherwise called the Ile of Divels* (1610) and William Strachey's account of Gates's story (published by Purchas in 1625)—provided more details about that island. No further details of Rich's life or death are known.

CHARLOTTE FELL-SMITH, rev. PETER C. MANCALL

Sources R. Rich, *Newes from Virginia*, ed. W. F. Craven (1937) • Arber, *Regs. Stationers*, 3.444 • STC, 1475–1640, no. 21005

Rich, Robert. *See* Abingdon, Robert of (*d.* 1243).

Rich, Robert, first earl of Warwick (1559?–1619), nobleman and politician, was the second son of Robert Rich, second Baron Rich (c.1537–1581), and his wife, Elizabeth Baldry (d. 1591). He was baptized in early January 1560. His accession to the Rich barony was unexpected and sudden. In 1578 he was enrolled at Gray's Inn, presumably in preparation for the life of a country magistrate, but in 1580 his elder brother, Richard, died without issue. He entered the Commons at a by-election on 7 February 1581 as knight of the shire for Essex, and succeeded his father twenty days later.

With landed estates worth perhaps £5000 per annum, mainly in central Essex, Rich found himself the most eligible bachelor in England. Lord Burghley, guardian of Robert Devereux, earl of Essex, and Henry Hastings, third earl of Huntingdon, guardian of Essex's sister Penelope (1563–1607) [see Rich, Penelope], swiftly arranged a match: Rich and Penelope were married probably on 1 November 1581. That 'being in the power of her friends' Penelope was wedded against her will 'unto one at whom she did protest at the very solemnity', and that Rich thereafter 'did study in all things to torment her' (BL, Lansdowne MS 885, fol. 86), were pieces of special pleading composed over twenty years later by her then lover, Lord Mountjoy. Mountjoy's aspersions, together with Sir Philip Sidney's cuckolding of Rich in print in the sonnet sequence *Astrophil and Stella*, have combined to ensure that Rich has been dismissed as a boorish and talentless puritan zealot. By perverse contrast Sidney's less than honourable wishful thinking did nothing, even among Victorian commentators, to dent his reputation as the pattern of chivalry.

The more sober facts are that the couple had five children, that Essex was attached to Rich, and that he proved an energetic, if often rash and impulsive, leader of county society. He began his thirty-eight years as head of the family under the domination of his bastard uncle Richard, who had encouraged the second baron to espouse radical protestantism. In September 1581 Richard and his nephew visited John Aylmer, bishop of London, to solicit a preaching licence for their chaplain Robert Wright, recently ordained in Antwerp. When Aylmer refused to grant one without knowledge of Wright's orders and assurances of his conformity, Richard Rich physically assaulted him. The affair led to the high commission trial and imprisonment of Richard and Robert Wright but not, as sometimes stated, of Lord Rich himself.

Although sternly advised by Aylmer not to follow his uncle's counsels, Rich took no notice. As patron of eighteen Essex livings he was uniquely placed to become the lay leader of the county's godly clergy. Aylmer's hostility ensured that during the 1580s he met with limited success, the bishop refusing on three occasions to institute his presentees. From 1583, however, Rich successfully claimed ordinary jurisdiction at Good Easter, whilst in 1585 Aylmer accepted three of his candidates, including William Negus. In 1586 Rich imported as his household chaplain Ezekiel Culverwell, who remained with the family until 1592 despite a severe mauling from Aylmer during his triennial visitation in 1589.

Rich also used his position as a member of the upper house to promote the godly party in the Commons. He turned himself into an efficient campaign manager for Essex's county seats and influenced elections in the borough of Maldon. In 1586 he organized petitions to himself on behalf of ecclesiastical reform. In 1588 the privy council ordered him to cease canvassing on behalf of an alternative candidate to the government's nominee as junior knight of the shire. While during the eclipse of 'political puritanism' in the 1590s Rich probably remained quiescent, these early experiences of electioneering stood him in good stead thereafter. He also had contacts with his godfather, the earl of Leicester; Leicester asked for Rich's services in the Low Countries, but there is no evidence that he went, and the command of fifty lances allotted to him was soon assigned elsewhere.

With the birth in 1590 of their second son, Penelope regarded her duty to Rich as fulfilled and thereafter they lived apart. In the same year she began a liaison with Charles Blount, future Lord Mountjoy. Their first child, Penelope, baptized on 30 March 1592, their daughter Isabella, and their second son, Charles, all brought up as if they were Rich's, are found in the Rich pedigrees. Their eldest son, Mountjoy (b. 1597), is not. Meanwhile, Rich remained close to his brother-in-law Essex. In 1591 he was a commissioner for the trial of Ruy Lopez, whose (possibly) treasonable activities Essex had unmasked. In 1596, having advanced Essex £1000 (never recovered in Rich's lifetime) to finance the expedition to Cadiz, Rich sailed with the fleet but left it early, joining the earl of Shrewsbury's embassy to France. He abandoned the Islands voyage in 1597 because of seasickness.

Suffering a serious illness in late 1600, through which Penelope nursed him, Rich remained at a safe distance from her brother's rebellion and was, presumably unwillingly, one of the twenty-five peers summoned as judges to Essex's trial on 17 February 1601. If it was their incompatibility which initially drove Rich and Penelope apart, Essex's fall severed all further connection between them. Henceforth Rich abandoned his wife to her own devices. He was presumably influential in the election of Francis Barrington as junior knight of the shire for Essex in 1601, since in 1604 he exhibited great energy in securing his re-election. In 1605, Penelope being prepared to admit to adultery with a stranger, Rich sued for divorce. Archbishop Bancroft granted it on 14 November, strangely commending Penelope, berating Rich for his behaviour to her, and finally bidding him to 'go amongst his puritans' (BL, Egerton MS 2804, fol. 203r).

Rich had certainly continued to patronize them. After Aylmer's death in 1594 he had no difficulty in getting his candidates instituted, and most proved to be sturdy nonconformists. Of the five clergymen deprived in Essex between 1606 and 1609, three owed their benefices to Rich, and another was Ezekiel Culverwell. A privy counsellor from 1608, Rich married in 1616 Frances (d. 1634), daughter of Sir Christopher *Wray and widow of Sir George St Poll. John Chamberlain crowed that she had 'so conveyed her estate that he has little or nothing the better by her and, if she outlive him, like to carry away a great part of his' (*Letters of John Chamberlain*, 2.101). In fact Rich's will shows that by the terms of the marriage settlement she was entitled to £1000 per annum for life as his widow but to none of his property.

On 6 August 1618 Rich was created earl of Warwick on payment of £10,000 into the exchequer. Since he had no territorial connection with the county, his choice of title was assuredly a statement of his religious predilections: he was assuming the mantle of the last holder, the godly Ambrose Dudley. Rich had made his will on 15 September 1617, requesting burial in Felsted church ('all pomp and unnecessary charge therein to be avoided') and directing his eldest son Robert *Rich (1587–1658), the second earl and his sole executor, to erect 'a comely and decent tomb' for his grandfather, father, brother Richard, and himself. He left probably in excess of £5000 in liquid assets, plus property in London, Essex (over seventy manors), Suffolk, and Norfolk. Children, grandchildren, and friends were generously remembered and £100 was bequeathed to the poor of Essex. All his servants were granted a full year's wages over and above what was due to them. His overseers, Sir Francis Bacon and Lord Darcy of Chiche, each received £40 in plate.

Rich died on 24 March 1619 at his London mansion, Warwick House, Holborn, and was buried on 7 April at Felsted. His second son, Henry *Rich, was created earl of Holland. His eldest daughter, Lettice, married Sir George Carey, and his second, Essex, Sir Thomas Cheke. His third, Mary, died young.   BRETT USHER

Sources HoP, *Commons, 1558–1603* · W. C. Metcalfe, ed., *The visitations of Essex*, 2 vols., Harleian Society, 13–14 (1878–9) · L. Stone, *The crisis of the aristocracy, 1558–1641* (1965) · W. A. Ringler, ed., *The poems of Sir Philip Sidney* (1962) · S. Freedman, *Poor Penelope: Lady Penelope Rich, an Elizabethan woman* (1983) · M. E. Bohannon, 'The Essex election of 1604', *EngHR*, 48 (1933), 395–413 · C. Thompson, 'The third Lord Rich and the Essex election of 1604', *Essex Journal*, 14 (1979), 2–6 · A. Peel, ed., *The seconde parte of a register*, 2 vols. (1915) · *The letters of John Chamberlain*, ed. N. E. McClure, 2 vols. (1939) · C. F. D. Sperling, 'Robert Rich, first earl of Warwick', *Essex Review*, 42 (1933), 119–22 · A. Searle, ed., *Barrington family letters, 1628–1632*, CS, 4th ser., 28 (1983) · PRO, PROB 11/135, sig. 51 [registered will] · S. Adams, ed., *Household accounts and disbursement books of Robert Dudley, earl of Leicester, 1558–1561, 1584–1586*, CS, 6 (1995) · GEC, *Peerage*
Archives JRL, papers | BL, Egerton MSS, Barrington papers · BL, Lansdowne MSS, letters to Robert earl of Essex
Likenesses memorial plaque, Snarford church, Lincolnshire; repro. in *Essex Review*
Wealth at death over £5000 incl. £1000 p.a. to widow; also £900 bequeathed to family and friends; £100 to poor of Essex; year's wages to all servants; £40 each to two overseers; plus property in London, Essex (over seventy manors), Suffolk, and Norfolk; debtors £1500: will, PRO, PROB 11/135, sig. 51

Rich, Robert, second earl of Warwick (1587–1658), colonial promoter and naval officer, was born in May or June 1587, probably at Leighs Priory, Essex, the eldest son of Robert *Rich, third Baron Rich and later first earl of Warwick (1559?–1619), courtier and privateer, and his first wife, Penelope *Rich (1563–1607), daughter of Walter

Robert Rich, second earl of Warwick (1587–1658), by Sir Anthony Van Dyck, c.1634

Devereux, first earl of Essex, best known as Sir Philip Sidney's 'Stella' and notorious for her adultery.

Early life Robert was admitted to Emmanuel College, Cambridge, on 4 June 1603. He was knighted on 25 July 1603 at the coronation of James I. On 24 February 1605 he married Frances (1590–1623), daughter and heir of Sir William Hatton (formerly Newport) and Elizabeth Gawdy; they had at least five children. Sir Robert appears to have been admitted a member of the Inner Temple in the Lent term of 1604 or 1605 by a special arrangement with the reader, John Harris, which was not confirmed until 20 April 1605. He then proceeded to make an impressive entry onto the stage of the Jacobean court. His earliest bent was for drama, performing to acclaim in Ben Jonson's *Masque of Beauty* in 1609. He also excelled at the tilts.

Robert's public life began with his election to the House of Commons for the borough of Maldon in Essex in 1610, though he left no impression on parliamentary business. Two years later he accompanied Sir Henry Wotton's embassy to Turin. In 1614 he was again returned by the voters of Maldon to sit in parliament, and again maintained a low profile, his mind possibly elsewhere. On 29 June 1614 he became a founding member of the Bermudas

Company for the plantation of the Somers Islands. His emerging colonial and commercial interests naturally encouraged him to follow in the wake of his father's highly profitable semi-piracies. In 1616 he obtained commissions from the agent of the duke of Savoy to attack Spanish shipping, fitting out two vessels for a roving voyage in the East Indies. Finding no Spaniards, his captains showed a suitable lack of discretion, attacking and plundering instead a richly laden craft belonging to the mother of the Mughal emperor of India, causing a diplomatic incident which threatened with ruin the legitimate trade of the East India Company. In reprisal the company seized Warwick's own ships. The resulting dispute was not settled for more than a decade, when under pressure from the House of Lords the company consented to pay off a fraction of the privateer's claim to £20,000 compensation. Undaunted, in April 1618, under the same Savoyard commission, Sir Robert sent to Virginia and the West Indies a ship called the *Treasurer*, commanded by Captain Daniel Elfrith, whose mission ended up landing his patron in further trouble, almost costing him his life.

Ennoblement, politics, and opposition In the same year, supposedly under considerable pressure from the marquess of Buckingham, Rich's father agreed to purchase an earldom for £10,000. Rich was instrumental in the negotiations which eventually secured his father the earldom of Warwick, having been denied that of Clare on the grounds, subsequently proved specious, that the more senior title was reserved for the blood royal. The first earl did not have the satisfaction of enjoying his title for long, and Rich succeeded as the second earl on 24 March 1619. He was soon embarked on a substantial career in English political life. In the parliaments of 1621 and 1624 he chaired the important subcommittee of the House of Lords' grand committee on the privileges of the upper house. He also took part in legislation for the more effective prosecution of recusants. Beginning already to establish himself as a patron of orthodox Calvinist interests, Warwick found himself temporarily befriended by Buckingham in the aftermath of the 'blessed revolution', which swung English foreign policy away from an intended marriage alliance with Spain in 1623 in the direction of a more warlike posture. As Charles I prepared to fight with Spain in vindication of the rights of his sister, the queen of Bohemia, Warwick was appointed in September 1625 to oversee the preparation of defences against invasion in his home county of Essex, much to the disgust of the lord lieutenant of the county, the earl of Sussex. With no real resources to commit to it, the exercise was regarded by the privy council as very largely cosmetic. The secretary of state Sir John Coke wanted the defences repaired at least in order that 'the varie noise of arming and training' might dissuade Spinola from mounting an attack from Dunkirk designed to divert from preparing the English fleet off the south coast (Quintrell, 'Towards a "perfect militia"', 97). But Warwick's enthusiasm for the task gravely threatened good order in the county, and had a number of unforeseen consequences which appear ironic in light of his later career in opposition to the court. His efforts to improve the training of the local auxiliaries gave a spur to the king's aspirations for a 'perfect militia', while his recommendations for financing the county's defence from contributions raised in contiguous shires may well have inspired the levying of ship money nationwide. In the meantime, his first wife having died shortly before 21 November 1623, Warwick married Susan Halliday (*bap.* 1582, *d.* 1646), daughter of Sir Henry Rowe, one-time lord mayor of London, and Susan Kighley, and the widow of William Halliday (*d.* 1624), alderman. The marriage took place between 12 March 1625 and 20 January 1626.

From 1626 onwards, although Warwick retained some influence there, he became gradually estranged from a court set on policies with which he evidently felt little sympathy. In 1625 he and the duke of Buckingham had co-operated in a new commercial venture for the discovery of a north-west passage to the Orient. The passing of any threat of Spanish invasion and the receding of any prospect of major conflict with Spain brought to an end Buckingham's uses for Warwick and the other puritan leaders such as Viscount Saye and Sele. The breakdown was precipitated by Warwick himself, who procured the disputation at York House in February 1626 designed to push Buckingham off the fence in the matter of Arminian innovation. After Buckingham came down firmly on the opposite side from Warwick, the earl's dependants in the House of Commons led the attack on the duke in the parliament of 1626. Although Warwick was evidently opposed to the forced loan, he avoided open hostility in order to protect his privateering interests, and instead preferred 'a moderate strategy' of encouraging the opposition of others (Cust, 229). Consequently, he was able to secure a potentially valuable privateering commission with complete independence from Buckingham's admiralty jurisdiction in 1627, but by then he had received his punishment for disloyalty, for he and his clients lost office and influence in their power base of Essex. Warwick himself lost the lieutenancy powers granted the year before, while Sir Francis Barrington, Sir Thomas Barrington, Sir William Masham, and Sir Harbotle Grimston found themselves ejected from the deputy lieutenancy. In the struggle for the petition of right Warwick was one of the band of peers who supported the lower house, and on 21 April 1628 he made a spirited speech against the king's claim to imprison without showing cause. His stand no doubt helps to explain the persistent frustration of his ambitions for sole control over the Essex lieutenancy, and for the further flourishing of his outward-looking personal foreign policy.

Colonial interests The experiences of the 1620s deepened Warwick's contacts with the leading men of the puritan party, adding significantly to his maturing association with colonial ventures in the Americas. On 16 November 1618 he had become an original member of the Guinea Company and Amazon River Company. On 9 June 1619 he had additionally become a councillor of the Virginia Company. But Warwick's aggressive exploitation of his stake in the Bermudas to further his privateering interests in the west, as well as incidents such as Captain Elfrith's plundering expedition to the Caribbean in 1618, exposed the Virginia Company's investments to the risk of Spanish retaliation. The leadership of the company consequently split into two factions in 1620, one headed by the earl of Southampton, Lord Cavendish, and Sir Edwin Sandys, the other by Warwick and his kinsman, Sir Nathaniel Rich. Although a duel to settle the dispute between Cavendish and Warwick was narrowly avoided, the company was fatally stricken and its business wound up four years later. The earl had himself long since moved on by then.

In 1620 Warwick had attempted to persuade the original puritan 'pilgrims' to settle on the coast of Guiana at the mouth of the Orinoco, in accordance with a plan drawn up long before by Sir Walter Ralegh. When they made landfall more than 1000 miles north, Warwick was instrumental in securing the patent to John Peirce, which he himself signed on 1 June 1621 as a member of the Council for New England, under which Plymouth colony existed for the first eight years of settlement. It was as president of the council that he signed the second patent, to William Bradford, on 13 January 1630. The patent for the Massachusetts colony to John Endecott and his associates, dated 19 March 1628, was procured by them through the influence of Warwick also, although it has been said that the enterprising earl looked to relocate the settlement there to the Caribbean as part of his consistent efforts to thrust to the heart of the western Spanish empire. On 19 March 1632 Warwick granted to Lord Saye, Lord Brooke, John Hampden, and others what is known as the old patent of Connecticut, under which the town of Saybrook was established, but the earl's authority for making this grant was disputed. The conflict within Massachusetts which arose in consequence was part of a wider struggle between the 'merchant interest', led by Sir Ferdinando Gorges, and the puritan interest led by John Winthrop. Three months after his grant to Saye and the others, Warwick was ousted from the presidency of the council. However, he remained sympathetically disposed to Winthrop and the eventual victors in the struggle for the soul of the American venture.

Apart from turning his attentions to the management of his extensive interests in Bermuda, Warwick now became heavily involved in the colonial adventure with which his name is associated most intimately. On Christmas eve 1629 the redoubtable Captain Elfrith and his companion Captain Chamock landed on the island of Catalina, known thenceforth as Providence, 60 miles off Nicaragua's Mosquito Coast. On 4 December 1630 the patent founding the company of adventurers for the island was granted to Warwick, Lord Saye, Lord Brooke, Oliver St John, and a number of other noted English puritans. John Pym was treasurer of the company. Warwick's house in St Bartholomew's was frequently the venue for its meetings. Despite high hopes for the opportunities the new settlement might afford for the exploitation of the region's wealth, the venture became an enormous financial burden on its principal backers. Envisaged by Warwick as a base for his privateering activities against Spanish shipping, the island was far too exposed to survive for long the hostile attentions it inevitably attracted. The first attack came in 1635. Smelling an opportunity, the Dutch West India Company made an offer to buy as early as 1636, but Warwick did not respond favourably until 1639, by which time he had incurred debts of £2430. But Warwick had failed to disengage himself from his expensive commitment by the time the colony was finally overrun in 1641. In 1638 he had purchased the fourth earl of Pembroke's patent for the islands of Trinidad and Tobago, and he spent much of the 1640s trying to turn them into a more viable platform from which to attack Spanish interests.

The personal rule If Warwick was effectively trying to conduct an independent foreign policy by charter company, in parallel with and often at cross-purposes to that of his king during the 1630s, then that was an accurate indication of his standing in the politics of the personal rule. Unhappily, his fortunes at home very largely mirrored those of his enterprises in the Caribbean, perhaps helping to explain his periodic consideration of the possibility of taking up the reins of Providence in person. Warwick was the undoubted leader of the body politic of Essex, one of the greatest landowners and clerical patrons of the county. It has been estimated that between 1603 and 1640 candidates sponsored by Warwick and his father before him were returned in forty-one of sixty-four parliamentary elections. Not surprisingly, in the absence of parliaments, leadership of local opinion fell to the earl himself, although thanks to his repeated failure to monopolize the lieutenancy, shared with the lord treasurer Weston from 1630, and Lord Maynard from 1635, he never quite had it all his own way in his home county.

In 1634 Warwick came into sharp conflict with the king over the revival of the forest laws, which effectively subjected the whole of Essex to the threat of an arbitrary mulct. Being the largest landowner in the county, the earl was deeply concerned in this perceived extension of the prerogative, and at the forest court held for Waltham Forest in October 1634 he opposed Sir John Finch, the attorney-general, on behalf of the gentlemen of Essex. Warwick's brother the earl of Holland was warden, chief justice, and justice on eyre for all forests south of the Trent, and he used his authority to adjourn the court for a time, but was ultimately unable to hold off judgment. Almost the whole county was fined, but Holland appears to have secured an otherwise suspiciously low imposition on his brother, who paid no more than £1600 despite owning an estate estimated at 16,000 acres. Warwick's leadership of the opposition to ship money in Essex was hardly any more effective. The county was among the most abject in its refusal until 1637, and those areas under Warwick's control in the van of resistance, prompting *quo warranto* proceedings in investigation of his right to appoint the bailiffs of certain royal bailiwicks under his control. But thereafter, in light of the successful exchequer proceedings against refusers, the failure of a bold personal appeal to the king made by the earl himself, and the subsequent threat of loss of office, the mood in Essex was radically altered. Warwick demonstrated his leadership credentials by shifting from resilience to damage limitation, petitioning for the tax to be levied at the relatively mild rates settled during the shrievalty of Sir Humphrey Mildmay, rather than the more stringent exactions demanded by the new sheriff, Sir John Lucas.

Recognizing a no-win situation when he saw one, the earl, in his opposition to Laudian church policy, also avoided recklessly picking fights. He was, without any doubt, 'the most visible and consistent supporter of the Puritan cause among the English nobility in the first half of the seventeenth century' (Donagan, 388). But equally beyond question are the limits to his powers to protect and to reward, powers sometimes praised beyond reasonable measure, albeit often by men with reason to be grateful for Warwick's real generosity. At one time or another Jeremiah Burroughes, Thomas Hooker, and Hugh Peter all had reason to thank the earl for his protection, yet all of them also ended up undergoing periods of exile which Warwick was powerless to prevent.

The coming of war Tellingly, it was also Warwick who afforded protection to Calybute Downing amid the furore which surrounded the preacher's sermon, given before the Honourable Artillery Company in September 1640, justifying armed resistance to authority in defence of religion. By then Warwick and his party had been frustrated in their attempts to place a check on the actions of the king, with the dissolution of the Short Parliament which assembled that spring, during which Warwick and ten other earls had opposed a motion that supply be considered before grievance, and after which Warwick himself was arrested and his papers searched. In September Warwick was one of the twelve peers who petitioned the king, beseeching that he call another parliament. It is also clear that Warwick was not above using means of persuasion considerably less elevated than the king's great council, and he certainly appears to have turned to his own advantage the increasingly violent protests of the numerous and well-organized 'godly party' in Essex in 1640, even if he did not actively connive in them. In the Long Parliament, which assembled in November, the earl was, reportedly, fairly prominent by his absence from many of the key debates. But his presence was one of the focal points for 'middle group' opposition, organized by John Pym in the Commons, which traced its pedigree back to the parliaments of the late 1620s. It was he who secured Sir John Clotworthy the seat for Maldon in Essex, thus ensuring a place at Westminster for one of the leading opponents of the hated lord deputy of Ireland, Thomas, first earl of Strafford. Then in December it was Warwick who was put in charge of overseeing payment of the Scottish army still occupying Newcastle, a responsibility which involved him in lengthy negotiations with merchants and financiers in the City of London, as well as the channelling of almost £300,000 in 'brotherly assistance' to the invaders. In April 1641 Warwick was admitted to the privy council, and he was also appointed to the council of regency which

was set up in advance of the king's departure for Scotland that summer. But his admission to the inner circle of government in the spring certainly failed to curtail his hostility to the earl of Strafford, and it was Warwick who took charge of the bill of attainder in the Lords; while the king was evidently no more sure of him by the time of his return to England late in 1641, placing Warwick, along with Essex, Holland, Saye, and Wharton, on the list of those he wished to call as witnesses for the prosecution against the six members whom he intended to impeach for treason in January 1642.

After the king departed Whitehall, Warwick was one of the most active champions of the parliamentary cause. On 28 February 1642 he was nominated lord lieutenant of Essex and Norfolk, at long last realizing one of his principal ambitions, personally putting the militia ordinance into execution in his home county. On 22 October 1642 he was appointed captain-general of a second army which the parliament intended to raise in addition to that under Essex in order to safeguard London and the south-east while their lord general was occupied fighting the king in the midlands. Much of this new force was to be raised in Essex, indicating the extent of its dependence on Warwick's personal lordship. Notably, however, he himself was keen that it be officered by experienced Scottish captains, incurring some mislike among the Essex men, who probably thought of the second army as more of a local defence force than the offensive instrument which Warwick seems to have seen it as. In the event, with the passing of any immediate threat to the capital to which existing forces could not respond adequately, the planned 'running army' was allowed to lapse, and Warwick resigned his commission on 23 November, not wishing to give offence to parliament's supreme commander of land forces for any longer than absolutely necessary.

Naval command Throughout the first war Warwick took a leading part in the parliamentarian war effort, joining the committee of both kingdoms at its inception in February 1643, and taking command of the army of the eastern association in August 1645. It was, however, as commander of the English navy that Warwick did most service, and his swift action in the early summer of 1642 in securing the fleet for parliament placed the king at a strategic disadvantage from which he never fully recovered. Charles seems to have fallen prey to a criminal complacency in assuming that the seamen would remain loyal to him, obey the orders of his appointed admiral, Sir John Pennington, and repudiate Warwick's treasonable claim to command, based as it was on the dubious authority of a parliamentary ordinance. However, the mood of the mariners was better indicated by those detachments prominent in the protests at Westminster against bishops and popish lords in 1641. Seamen had also provided the five MPs with an armed escort at their return from the City to the House of Commons in January 1642. Moreover, the king failed to take into account the significance of parliament's appropriation of tonnage and poundage revenues to the upkeep of the navy, which had not only constituted as grave an attack on his personal prerogative as the militia ordinance, but had also given the seamen an important interest in seeing parliamentarian designs succeed. Additionally, and no less influentially, Warwick's appointment marked a dramatic reversal in the navy's strategic responsibilities. Many mariners had deeply resented the role they had been expected to perform during the 1630s, when they had escorted, even transported, Spanish troops and gold to the Netherlands. Warwick, on the other hand, had a well-earned reputation as the scourge of Spain, and his antipathy towards his Catholic majesty had not been lessened when, just months earlier, Providence Island had finally succumbed to Spanish attack. Consequently, the Spanish ambassador in London watched developments with mounting anxiety in the months from Warwick's first appointment in the spring of 1642 as commander of the fleet, by commission from the lord high admiral, the earl of Northumberland, through to Warwick's bold assertion of his parliamentary authority on 2 July, when he went aboard the fleet even while Sir John Pennington hesitated to put his own commission in execution. Warwick was welcomed almost unanimously within the fleet as an admiral who might lead the navy back to glory, self-respect, and regular pay, and the few dissenting voices were rapidly silenced.

Under Warwick's command, the ships of the parliamentarian fleet guarded the seas, intercepted vessels bringing supplies from the continent to the king or the Irish rebels, and acted as auxiliaries to the land operations of the earl of Essex. They helped in the defence of Hull against the king, removing its magazine to safe keeping in the Tower of London, and in August 1642 in the capture of Portsmouth. In August 1643 Warwick attempted unsuccessfully to relieve Exeter, but in the following May he did manage to relieve Lyme. When the earl of Northumberland withdrew his support for the prosecution of the war, Warwick was appointed lord high admiral in his stead on 7 December 1643, but, when he failed in his efforts to intercept the queen's departure from Falmouth for France on 14 July 1644, his own loyalty was called in question. Warwick blamed the lack of shipping relative to the range of tasks he was expected to perform, as well as parliament's failure adequately to support the ships he had, a grievance which the earl repeatedly protested during the war. However, it was the unavoidable inconvenience of contrary winds that prevented Warwick from lending assistance to the earl of Essex on his ill-advised march into Cornwall later that summer, which ended with the catastrophe of Lostwithiel.

Parliamentarian politics Parliament was nevertheless sufficiently confident in its naval commander to insist on Warwick's elevation to a dukedom at one stage in its negotiations with the king. Yet in spite of his relative efficiency and popularity in the performance of his lord high admiralty, Warwick was displaced from his command with the passing of the self-denying ordinance in 1645. He laid down his commission on 9 April, declaring that he resigned it back to parliament with the greatest cheerfulness, and should be ready to serve 'the great cause of religion and liberty' in any capacity (DNB). However, it is doubtful whether this was anything more than diplomatic platitude, adopted to mask political defeat and the frustration of ambition. The clue probably lies in the earl's protestation of devotion to that 'great cause' which was in fact increasingly apt to splinter under the force of a violent struggle for political control. It has been plausibly suggested that the presbyterian faction at Westminster, which was so badly crossed by the passage of the self-denying ordinance and the movement for the remodelling of the army command, would have much preferred to see Warwick stay in control of the navy. Having lost the battle, they renewed the struggle, however. On 19 April the government of the navy was entrusted to a committee of six lords, of whom Warwick was the chief, and twelve commoners. It was clear from the composition of the new body that 'Holles and his followers had won one of their occasional successes', and within a short time Warwick had resumed his grip over the command of the navy (Rowe, *Sir Henry Vane*, 126). In 1646 he was named among the presbyterian and pro-Scottish party in the House of Lords, and in January 1647 he acted with other moderates in the endeavour to formulate a scheme of settlement which would be acceptable to the king. He was also one of the commissioners employed by parliament in April 1647 to persuade the army to engage for service in Ireland.

However, Warwick seems likely to elude any attempt to pen him firmly on any one side of the political and religious arguments internal to the wartime parliamentarian coalitions. He headed the commission of six lords and twelve commoners appointed on 2 November 1643 to govern the colonies of North America and the Caribbean, and his name is inextricably linked with the foundation of the state of Rhode Island, which began with the incorporation of Providence plantation under the governance of Roger Williams in March 1644. So far as his personal commitments may be discerned in this and the other undertakings of his government of the colonies, it is clear that Warwick consistently used his influence in favour of religious freedom. He intervened with the Massachusetts government on behalf of Samuel Gorton, who called his settlement at Shawomet by the name of Warwick. The earl also issued, on 4 November 1645, a declaration establishing freedom of worship in the Bermudas. More importantly for domestic politics, despite his alignment with the presbyterian leaders early in 1647, he abandoned them at the time of the City putsch in July 1647, retiring into Essex, pledging himself to co-operate with Fairfax in vindicating the independence of parliament, and refusing to obey the summons of the Lords to return to his seat in the house. Clarendon remarked that Warwick and Manchester threw in their lot with the New Model Army in such dramatic fashion because 'they were resolved to have their particular shares in the treaty which they believed the chief officers to have near concluded with the king' (Clarendon, *Hist. rebellion*, 4.245). By this point Warwick had married for the third time, on 30 March

1646, two months after Susan's death on 16 January 1646. His new wife was Eleanor Radcliffe (*née* Wortley), dowager countess of Sussex (*d.* 1667), the widow of the sixth earl and also the widow of Sir Henry Lee, first baronet; she was the daughter of Richard Wortley, of Wortley, Yorkshire, and Elizabeth Boughton.

Revolution Hopes of a peaceful settlement were dashed late in 1647. Warwick used his influence to hinder the presentation of a royalist presbyterian petition from the county of Essex in the spring of 1648, grounds for the rejection of Clarendon's assertion that Warwick was privy to his brother Holland's engagement for the king, and had even promised to join him when Holland raised the county against parliament. The earl's steward, the historian Arthur Wilson, was, however, put to it to deny the charge of complicity at the time, claiming later that the allegations were easily enough rebuffed in the absence of evidence, for 'though falsehood gives Report a Birth, yett Truth gives it a Buriall' (CUL, Add. MS 33, fol. 101).

However, as the events of 1648 unfolded, some of the ambiguities of Warwick's position appear rather to have deepened than to have diminished. On 27 May 1648 the greater part of the parliamentary fleet in the Downs mutinied against the command of Colonel Thomas Rainsborough, appointed in place of the politically suspect William Batten. Two days later parliament reappointed Warwick to the post of lord high admiral, in the hope that his popularity would secure the fidelity of the sailors. He went on board at once and, finding, after some futile negotiations, that it was impossible to win back the crews of the nine revolted ships, devoted himself to getting together a new fleet and discharging disaffected sailors and officers. By the end of August Warwick felt strong enough to offer battle to Prince Charles and the revolted fleet off the mouth of the Medway, but a storm prevented the intended action, and want of provisions obliged Prince Charles to retreat to Holland without fighting. Warwick blockaded the prince's ships in Helvoetsluys in September, remaining off the Dutch coast until the end of November, when the winter weather obliged him to return to England. He had succeeded in regaining four of the prince's fleet, and in preventing the rest from preying upon English trade. But he came under fire nevertheless, his loyalty to parliament called in question in consequence of his apparent reluctance to engage the mutineers in battle, and also because his withdrawal in November freed the royalists to resume their lucrative plunder of English shipping. Moreover, all throughout the crisis there had been persistent rumours about the nature of the contacts back and forth between Warwick and representatives of the prince of Wales. Suspicion also fell on the earl's eldest son, Lord Rich, who went to the Isle of Wight in July 1648 on the pretext of being touched for the king's evil. In the autumn of 1648 Warwick's name was invoked in connection with strong support for the negotiations at Newport in the face of growing Independent misgivings, and it was feared that the earl would too readily support the successful conclusion of a personal treaty. Evident royalist expectations of the lord high admiral's loyalty to the king were seemingly dashed by his acquiescence in the new political realities which pertained after Pride's Purge in December. But Warwick remained an object of suspicion to many of the new rulers at Westminster, although some of them may have approved the useful interventions of Edmund Calamy and John Gauden, two of Warwick's closest spiritual counsellors, as moderating influences in the all-important January 1649 debate about what to do with Charles I.

Quiescence, senescence, decease The execution of Charles I and the abolition of the monarchy and the House of Lords need not necessarily have spelled the end of Warwick's authority. However, it clearly could not survive the abolition of the lord high admiralty on 23 February 1649 and the assumption of its powers by the new executive council of state. Neither was there much prospect for the continuation of his personal influence given the political preponderance at Westminster of an Independent faction with more sympathy for Spanish interests than their presbyterian colleagues had ever had. But, with long-time associates such as Sir William Masham firmly ensconced at the helm of the new regime, Warwick is unlikely to have lost touch with political power entirely. Nevertheless, it was clearly not until the fall of the Rump, and then Barebone's parliaments, the ending of the war with the Dutch, and the freezing of hitherto cordial relations with Spain that Warwick resumed any significant interest in affairs of state. Cromwell's western design was justified at least in part by explicit reference to the Spanish despoliation of Providence Island, at which the earl's hopes can reasonably be expected to have been raised. It is probably no coincidence that, at the lord protector's second inauguration on 26 June 1657, Warwick personally bore the sword of state and helped to invest Cromwell in his robe of purple velvet. Although the earl declined to sit in the other house, the marriage on 14 November 1657 of Cromwell's daughter Frances with Warwick's grandson and heir Robert Rich clearly indicated the level of respect the two men had for each other. Robert Rich died on 16 February 1658. In his touching answer to the protector's letter of condolence, Warwick ended by congratulating Cromwell on his 'prudent, heroic and honourable management' of public affairs (*DNB*). Warwick himself died, apparently much lamented by his lord protector, at Warwick House on 19 April 1658, and was buried at Felsted, Essex, on 1 May. He was survived by his wife.

Assessment Clarendon's view that Warwick was a jovial hypocrite is informed largely by the dyspepsia induced in the lord chancellor whenever he contemplated the lives and actions of peers of the realm who had had a hand in the rebellion against their king. There is every indication of sincerity in Warwick's godly carriage, while his convivial good humour was evidently much cherished by those zealous Calvinists with an ear for disputation upon whom he placed especial trust. His patronage of the 'puritan' interest in England during the 1620s and 1630s did not create a uniformly 'puritan' grouping, however, and indeed even among those of his clients who can be identified as rigid Calvinists there were sown the seeds of faction which emerged in the 1640s, condemning Calvinist orthodoxy to ultimate defeat and long-drawn-out decline. The earl's lasting legacy must be sought instead in the American colonies, where his influence had equally complex and unpredictable, yet eminently more fruitful, long-term consequences.　　　　　　　　　SEAN KELSEY

Sources DNB · CUL, Add. MS 33 · *Autobiography of Mary, countess of Warwick*, ed. T. C. Croker (1848) · W. F. Craven, *The Virginia Company of London, 1606–1624*, Jamestown 350th anniversary booklet, no. 5 (1957) · V. A. Rowe, 'Robert, second earl of Warwick and the payment of ship-money in Essex', *Transactions of the Essex Archaeological Society*, 3rd ser., 1 (1961–5), 160–3 · D. E. Kennedy, 'The establishment and settlement of parliament's admiralty, 1642–1648', *Mariner's Mirror*, 48 (1962), 276–91 · W. F. Craven, *Dissolution of the Virginia Company: the failure of a colonial experiment* (1964) · B. W. Quintrell, 'The government of the county of Essex, 1603–1642', PhD diss., U. Lond., 1965 · J. L. Beatty, *Warwick and Holland, being the lives of Robert and Henry Rich* (1965) · V. A. Rowe, *Sir Henry Vane the younger: a study in political and administrative history* (1970) · C. Thompson, 'The origins of the politics of the parliamentary middle group, 1625–1629', *TRHS*, 5th ser., 22 (1972), 71–86 · C. Holmes, *The eastern association in the English civil war* (1974) · C. T. Maples, 'Parliament's admiral: the parliamentary and naval career of Robert Rich, second earl of Warwick', PhD diss., University of Alabama, 1975 · B. Donagan, 'The clerical patronage of Robert Rich, second earl of Warwick, 1619–1642', *Proceedings of the American Philosophical Society*, 120 (1976), 388–419 · W. Hunt, *The puritan moment: the coming of revolution in an English county*, Harvard Historical Studies, 102 (1983) · R. McCaughey, 'The English navy, politics and administration', DPhil diss., University of Ulster, 1983 · W. B. Cogar, 'The politics of naval administration, 1649–1660', DPhil diss., U. Oxf., 1983 · B. W. Quintrell, 'Towards a "perfect militia": Warwick, Buckingham, and the Essex alarum of 1625', *Transactions of the Essex Archaeological Society*, 15 (1984), 96–105 · R. P. Cust, *The forced loan and English politics, 1626–1628* (1987) · C. Thompson, *Two puritan commonwealths: Providence and New England* (1987) · B. Capp, *Cromwell's navy: the fleet and the English revolution, 1648–1660* (1989) · K. O. Kupperman, *Providence Island, 1630–1641: the other puritan colony* (1993) · J. Walter, *Understanding popular violence in the English revolution: the Colchester plunderers* (Past and Present Publications, 1999) · C. Thompson, *The earl of Warwick's 'running army', the county of Essex and the eastern association* (c.1999) · GEC, *Peerage*
Archives Bodl. Oxf., Tanner MSS, corresp. | BL, papers and letters, Add. MSS; Egerton MSS
Likenesses D. Mytens, oils, 1632, NMM · A. Van Dyck, oils, c.1634, Metropolitan Museum of Art, New York [*see illus.*] · W. Hollar, etching, 1642, BM, NPG · R. Earlom, mezzotint, pubd 1810 (after A. Van Dyck), BM, NPG · D. Mytens, oils, Hardwick Hall, Derbyshire · A. Van Dyck, oils, Buccleuch Estates, Selkirk · silver medal, BM
Wealth at death extensive real estate in Essex and London; patrimony valued at £6000 p.a. in 1635: will, PRO, PROB 11/276, fols. 244r–247r; Thompson, *Earl of Warwick's 'running army'*, 9

Rich, Robert (d. 1679), Quaker adherent and sectary, is of unknown parentage. He was described as 'born of a worthy family, and having many great and noble relations' (*DNB*); perhaps he came from a branch of the family of the earls of Warwick. By the early 1650s he was a prosperous London merchant with estates in New England and Barbados, and part-owner of the privateer *Negro*. By 1654 he was an active member of the newly established Society of Friends, or Quakers. In September 1655 he was imprisoned at Banbury, and wrote an address to the magistrates and recorder of that town.

About that time Rich attached himself to James Nayler, whose re-enactment of Christ's Palm Sunday entry into Jerusalem, at Bristol in October of 1656, led to a celebrated trial in parliament for blasphemy. Rich was not one of the small group that accompanied Nayler into Bristol, but was with him the previous night, as Nayler mentioned years afterward. In due course the parliamentary committee of investigation released a report which Rich and a colleague, William Tomlinson, later reprinted with indignant marginal glosses, many of which defiantly stressed Christological parallels, as *A True Narrative of the Examination, Tryall and Sufferings of James Nayler*. When the full parliament took up the case in December Rich began to pour out a series of petitions in Nayler's defence, urging that his prophetic act was entirely in keeping with scriptural precedent—'Did not the prophets do many things that the wisdom of the flesh might count foolishness, and to be ridiculous?' (Rich and Tomlinson, 35)—and pointing out that since Nayler never opened his mouth during the fatal ride in Bristol it was hard to see how he could be said to have blasphemed. After a debate that lasted ten days Nayler narrowly escaped a death sentence and was condemned to receive 300 lashes, have his tongue bored through with a red-hot iron, and have the letter B (for 'blasphemy') branded on his forehead. Thomas Burton, an MP whose diary is the chief source of information for the trial, joined the crowd at the pillory to see Nayler punished and reported, 'Rich, the mad merchant, sat bare [headed] at Nayler's feet all the time. Sometimes he sang and cried, and stroked his hair and face, and kissed his hand, and sucked the fire out of his forehead' (*Diary of Thomas Burton*, 1.266). Another hostile witness commented that Rich licked Nayler's wounds in imitation of the dogs that licked Lazarus, and complained that he was permitted to put up a sign that read 'This is the King of the Jews' (J. Deacon, *An Exact History of the Life of James Nayler*, 1657, 36–7). Rich subsequently accompanied Nayler to Bristol, where he was compelled to retrace his ride backward, and two decades later pointedly described this punishment as 'his crucifixion there' (Rich, 37).

By 1658 Rich had been rejected by the Quakers and emigrated to Barbados, where he remained for twenty years: a list of the leading planters on the island records him as holding 350 acres. He kept up his interest in religious topics, having acquired a remarkably ecumenical collection of spiritual works, and when the great fire of 1666 devastated London he arranged for the considerable sum of £210 to be distributed among 'the Seven Churches', which he identified as the Roman Catholics, Church of England, presbyterians, Independents, Baptists, Quakers, and 'Church of the First-Born'. This last was a universalist experiment that may never have existed as an organization, but that embodied Rich's hopes for religious reconciliation. In so far as he remained in touch with the Quakers he was a consistently hostile critic. He sided with John Perrot, whose refusal to remove his hat when praying was denounced by George Fox in a sort of test case for group loyalty, and he roundly condemned the movement for accepting the disciplinary leadership of Fox, arguing that they had:

betrayed their great principle of the light in every man his unerring guide, and even the principle of Protestantism and all the Reformation, which requires every man to judge for himself, and follow his own judgment against any number whatsoever. (Rich, preface)

George Whitehead, who published a large collection of Nayler's writings early in the next century, remembered that, in Barbados, Rich was reported to have been 'turbulent in our Friends' meetings with noisy singing, &c. to the offence of sober Friends there', and that when he returned to London in the last year of his life:

he came into some of our meetings, and walked up and down therein in a stately manner (having a very long white beard) in his black velvet coat, with a loose hanging cloth one over it. When he heard something declared that pleased him, he would cry 'Amen, amen, amen'. (Whitehead, xvii)

Rich died on 16 November 1679, two months after returning to London. A collection of his writings was published in the next year by his friend John Pennyman as *Abstracts of some letters written by Mr. Robert Rich … for promoting universal love amongst all sorts of people.* LEO DAMROSCH

Sources R. Rich and W. Tomlinson, *A true narrative of the examination, tryall and sufferings of James Nayler* (1656) • R. Rich, *Hidden things brought to light, or, The discord of the grand Quakers among themselves, discovered in some letters, papers, and passages written to and from George Fox, James Nayler, and John Perrott* (1678) • G. Whitehead, ed., *A collection of sundry books, epistles and papers, written by James Nayler … with an impartial relation of the most remarkable transactions relating to his life* (1716) • *Diary of Thomas Burton*, ed. J. T. Rutt, 4 vols. (1828), vol. 1 • G. F. Nuttall, 'The last of James Nayler: Robert Rich and the church of the first-born', *Friends' Quarterly*, 23 (1985), 527–34 • W. C. Braithwaite, *The beginnings of Quakerism*, ed. H. J. Cadbury, 2nd edn (1955) • W. C. Braithwaite, *The second period of Quakerism*, ed. H. J. Cadbury, 2nd edn (1961) • L. Damrosch, *The sorrows of the Quaker Jesus: James Nayler and the puritan crackdown on the free spirit* (1996) • J. Nayler, *A short answer to a book called 'The fanatick history'* (1660) • *CSP dom., 1651–4* • *CSP col.*, vols. 5, 7

Rich, Sir Robert, fourth baronet (1685–1768), army officer, born on 3 July 1685 and baptized at Beccles on the 13th of the same month, was the second son of Sir Robert Rich, second baronet (1648–1699), of Roos Hall, Suffolk, lord of the Admiralty from November 1691 to October 1699 and MP for Dunwich from 1689 until his death in 1699. His father was descended from the elder branch of the powerful family of Rich, earls of Warwick and Holland. Robert's mother was Mary (d. 1714), the second daughter of Sir Charles Rich, first baronet, whose baronetcy was limited in the patent to the husband of Mary Rich.

Rich was senior of the four pages of honour to William III between 1700 and 1702. He was granted a commission as ensign in the Grenadier Guards on 10 June 1700 and saw service in the wars under the duke of Marlborough. Before he attained his twentieth year he was twice wounded, first at Schellenberg on 2 July 1704, and afterwards at Blenheim on 13 August of the same year. He became lieutenant and captain in Brigadier-General Tatton's regiment of foot (the 24th foot) soon afterwards. In October 1706 he succeeded to the family baronetcy and estates on the death of his brother Sir Charles Rich, and in June 1708 he fought a duel in Suffolk with Sir Edmund Bacon, bt, whom he

injured, but not mortally. On 9 March 1708 he returned as captain, with the rank of lieutenant-colonel, to the Grenadier Guards, and in January 1710 he was promoted colonel of the 18th regiment of foot (late Colonel Watkins's regiment). The regiment was stationed at Gibraltar from 1710 until the peace of Utrecht in 1713, when it was disbanded. Together with other officers, Rich was taken prisoner *en route* for Gibraltar in October 1710, by the capture of the frigate HMS *Hunter* by three French privateers, though he was later paroled.

On 28 September 1714 Rich married Elizabeth (1691/2–1773), the daughter and coheir of Colonel Edward Griffith, clerk of the board of green cloth to Queen Anne and secretary to Prince George of Denmark. They had three sons, including Sir Robert *Rich, fifth baronet, and a daughter, who married George, first Baron Lyttelton.

In 1715 Rich entered parliament as MP for Dunwich. At the outbreak of the Jacobite rising he was commissioned to raise a regiment of dragoons; however, he was one of a group of colonels who were deprived of their regiments for voting against the government in the division on Lord Cadogan in 1717. Rich served as groom of the bedchamber to the prince of Wales and later to George II, from March 1718 until his resignation on grounds of advancing years in 1759. (His salary in 1727 was £500 per annum.) After being defeated at Dunwich in the general election of 1722 he was made colonel of the 13th light dragoons (later the 13th hussars) on 19 November of that year. He was returned as MP for Bere Alston at a by-election in February 1724 and sat for St Ives from 1727 until 1741, when he retired from parliament.

As a consistent supporter of Walpole, military promotion came Rich's way. He transferred in succession to the command of the 8th light dragoons (23 September 1725), the 6th dragoon guards (1 January 1731), the 1st troop Horse Grenadier Guards (July 1733), and the 4th dragoons (13 May 1735). The last command he held until his death over thirty years later. He was promoted to the ranks of brigadier-general (March 1727), major-general (November 1735), and lieutenant-general (July 1739). In May 1740 he received the life appointment of governor of the Chelsea Hospital, with a salary of £500 per annum.

Rich was executor to his old friend Field Marshal Sir Charles Wills, who, at his death on 25 December 1741, left him the bulk of a considerable estate. On 24 April 1742 he embarked with his regiment of dragoons for Flanders to join the earl of Stair's army; he fought at Dettingen on 16 June 1743, and on 14 December 1745 his was one of the regiments which marched through London on their way to Kent and Sussex to oppose any landing of the French there. He was one of the three lieutenant-generals placed upon the staff of the army formed under the chief command of the earl of Stair to oppose an apprehended invasion from France (26 February to 8 August 1744), and he was advanced to the rank of general on 29 March 1747. In May 1749 he was one of the officers' board convened to consider possible reform of the cavalry. In an age when the tactical role of cavalry was well established, and when manoeuvres were few and well understood, no innovations were proposed to the 1728 regulations. In August 1756 he was president of the court martial of Lieutenant-General Thomas Fowke, governor of Gibraltar, for disobedience of orders in connection with the loss of Minorca, and on 28 November 1757 he was made field marshal of his majesty's forces. He was reappointed governor of Chelsea Hospital on 27 October 1760. In the summer of 1762 an acrimonious dispute arose between Rich and his regimental agent, Thomas Fisher, of Axe Yard, Westminster. Rich pressed the matter to a full court martial in December before accepting an agreement reached by arbitration. He died on 1 February 1768, aged eighty-two.

W. R. WILLIAMS, *rev.* JONATHAN SPAIN

Sources Burke, *Peerage* · B. Burke, *A genealogical history of the dormant, abeyant, forfeited and extinct peerages of the British empire*, new edn (1866) · C. Dalton, ed., *English army lists and commission registers, 1661–1714*, 6 vols. (1892–1904) · HoP, *Commons, 1715–54* · J. A. Houlding, *Fit for service: the training of the British army, 1715–1795* (1981) · A. J. Guy, 'Regimental agency in the British standing army, 1715–63: a study of Georgian military administration [pts 1–2]', *Bulletin of the John Rylands University Library*, 62 (1979–80), 423–53; 63 (1980–81), 31–57 · *The manuscripts of the earl of Carlisle*, HMC, 42 (1897) · N. Luttrell, *A brief historical relation of state affairs from September 1678 to April 1714*, 6 vols. (1857)
Archives Folger, estate and family MSS and corresp.
Wealth at death £100,000: *The manuscripts of the earl of Carlisle*, HMC, 238

Rich, Sir Robert, fifth baronet (1717–1785), army officer, was the eldest son of Field Marshal Sir Robert *Rich, fourth baronet (1685–1768), and his wife, Elizabeth (1691/2–1773), the daughter of Colonel Edward Griffith. After attending Westminster School between 1727 and 1735 he entered the 1st foot guards as an ensign on 5 July 1735. He served for seventeen months as a cornet in his father's regiment, the 4th dragoons, and then returned to the 1st foot guards as a lieutenant and captain on 9 July 1739. He was subsequently appointed aide-de-camp to his colonel, General Sir Charles Wills, on whose death (25 December 1741) he came into a legacy of £5000. Rich served in Flanders and Germany during 1742–3 and spent some months under arrest: he had struck a fellow officer on parade. In June 1744 he sold out from the guards and purchased the lieutenant-colonelcy of the 4th foot, or Barrell's regiment. He commanded the regiment at the battle of Falkirk (17 January 1746) and was with it at Culloden three months later, when Barrell's bore the brunt of the highlanders' charge, suffering 125 of the British army's 309 casualties. Rich was himself terribly wounded, his left hand being clean cut off and his right arm almost severed above the elbow; he also received six cuts to his head. So serious were his wounds that his death was reported in the *Gentleman's Magazine*. A year later, when Rich was once again fit for duty, there appeared a satirical print, *The Old Scourge Return'd to Barrels*. It depicts Rich, who had a reputation as a disciplinarian, ordering the mass flogging of his men. On 22 August 1749, following the death of Lieutenant-General Sir William Barrell, Rich succeeded to the colonelcy of the 4th foot.

In 1753 the regiment sailed for Minorca, but by the time

Sir Robert Rich, fifth baronet (1717–1785), by Arthur Devis, 1756–8

of the famous siege three years later Rich had already returned home: he resigned the colonelcy on 12 May 1756 upon his appointment as governor of Londonderry and Culmore Fort. He was promoted to the rank of major-general on 17 January 1758 and advanced to lieutenant-general on 10 December 1760. On 8 February 1771 he resigned his post as major-general on the Irish establishment because of ill health. He solicited in vain a post on the English establishment.

In 1768, upon the death of his father, Rich inherited the baronetcy and family estates. General Henry Seymour Conway, meanwhile, was appointed to the colonelcy of the 4th dragoons in the room of Rich's father. On making his inspection of the regiment Conway found fault with the men's accoutrements and called upon Rich, Viscount Orwell, and Lieutenant-Colonel John Bradford, who were the elder Rich's executors, to make good the deficiencies. After vainly seeking relief, the executors agreed to satisfy the claim; but by then Conway had made a further demand for horse furniture, with which the executors declined to comply. In 1774 the board of general officers decided that the claim was justified. Lord Orwell and Colonel Bradford obeyed the order, but Rich continued his resistance. On 1 October 1774 he was therefore dismissed from his post as governor of Londonderry and from the service. In response Rich published a letter to the secretary at war, Lord Barrington, accusing him of partiality and stating his case at length. On the basis of this, one writer, Francis Ayerst, somewhat fancifully claimed Rich as the author of *The Letters of Junius*.

Rich had married, in 1752, Mary, the daughter of Peter Ludlow of co. Meath. She died in 1755, aged thirty, after giving birth to a daughter, Mary Frances (1755–1833). In 1771 Rich married a widow, Elizabeth Williams (*d.* 1788), the daughter of Richard Bell of Brampton, Cumberland. They had a son, Charles, who died on 4 February 1782 aged seven. After the death of his son Rich made the unwelcome discovery that, in default of a male heir, his father's will stipulated that the family estates, notably Roos Hall, Suffolk, and Waverley Abbey, Surrey, should go to Mary Frances, with whom Rich had long been on the worst of terms. Having characteristically decided that the lawyer who drafted the will had misinterpreted his father's wishes, Rich sought the agreement of his daughter to have the will changed; but Mary Frances, realizing that she was now an heiress, contracted instead a marriage to the Revd Charles Bostock. Rich vehemently disapproved.

Rich died at Bath, aged sixty-seven, on 19 May 1785. He was buried on 29 May in Grosvenor Chapel, South Audley Street, a short distance from his chief London home in Grosvenor Square: there are memorial tablets to Rich, his son, and his first wife on the chapel wall. The baronetcy went to Rich's brother George and became extinct on the latter's death in 1799. The Revd Bostock, however, assumed the surname and arms of Rich and was created a baronet on 28 July 1791. **ALASTAIR W. MASSIE**

Sources 'Two letters from Sir Robert Rich, Bart. to E. B. Esq.', 1783, Suffolk RO, Lowestoft, Acc. 541 • *A letter from Sir Robert Rich, baronet … to the Right Honourable Lord Viscount Barrington, his majesty's secretary at war*, 2nd edn (1776) • Burke, *Peerage* (1924) • *Report on the manuscripts of Mrs Frankland-Russell-Astley of Chequers Court, Bucks.*, HMC, 52 (1900) • J. Redington and R. A. Roberts, eds., *Calendar of home office papers of the reign of George III*, 3: 1770–1772, PRO (1881); 4: 1773–1775, PRO (1899) • will, PRO, PROB 11/1131 (331) • *GM*, 1st ser., 16 (1746), 328 • *GM*, 1st ser., 26 (1756), 206 • *GM*, 1st ser., 55 (1785), 406 • *Old Westminsters*, vol. 2 • F. Ayerst, *The ghost of Junius* (1853) • J. L. Chester, ed., *The marriage, baptismal, and burial registers of the collegiate church or abbey of St Peter, Westminster*, Harleian Society, 10 (1876) • L. I. Cowper, ed., *The King's Own: the story of a royal regiment*, 1 (1939) • *Army List* • memorial tablets, Grosvenor Chapel, South Audley Street, London

Archives Suffolk RO, Lowestoft, notebook relating to inheritance dispute | Suffolk RO, Lowestoft, letters to E. B., esq.

Likenesses A. Devis, portrait, 1756–8, King's Own Royal Regiment Museum, Lancaster [*see illus.*] • satirical print, BL

Wealth at death estates in Suffolk and Surrey; property in London and Bath: will, PRO, PROB 11/1131; notebook, 1783, Suffolk RO

Richard [Richard (I) of Fountains] (*d.* **1139**), abbot of Fountains, had previously been prior of the nearby Benedictine house of St Mary's, York; nothing is known about his early life. The part played by Richard in the establishment of the Cistercian house of Fountains is related in the so-called *Narratio fundationis* of Fountains, a chronicle dictated in his last years (probably *c.*1206) by the monk Serlo, who had himself witnessed many of the events he recorded, and in letters preserved in the narrative of this text. Doubts have been cast on the authenticity of the most important letter of the collection, that from Archbishop Thurstan of York to Archbishop William of Canterbury, reporting the happenings at St Mary's and attributing a key speech to Richard. However, even if this speech was embellished by a later hand, there are no grounds for doubting that its substance accurately reflects the mood at St Mary's in the early 1130s.

St Mary's was a Benedictine abbey founded in the late eleventh century. Despite, or perhaps because of, its newness as a house, its morale was easily upset by the arrival in the neighbourhood in 1132 of monks from the Cistercian order. Geoffrey, abbot of St Mary's, saw no reason to be influenced by the newcomers, but a number of his monks, led by Richard the sacrist, thought otherwise. These monks, after secret deliberations among themselves, and despite trepidation about his reactions, decided to open their hearts to Prior Richard—according to the *Narratio* a much respected figure in the community and a man with influential friends. Richard listened to the cabal with sympathy and became their leader. On 28 June 1132 Richard decided the time had come to approach Abbot Geoffrey with the group's plans for reform. Geoffrey responded by asking for these proposals to be put in writing. Richard presented these in mid-July; Geoffrey again procrastinated. These delays had the effect of making the debates in the community at St Mary's between reformers and conservatives so acrimonious that Richard decided to appeal for help and arbitration to Thurstan, with the result that a date in October was fixed for Geoffrey's reply, to be given now in full chapter in Thurstan's presence. When the day arrived Geoffrey refused Thurstan entry into the chapter. Uproar followed; the conservatives attempted to lay hands on Richard and his party, who in turn succeeded in breaking free and joining Thurstan with whom they escaped from the abbey.

The reformers now numbered fourteen. Until Christmas they lived with Thurstan who then gave them land in Skeldale near Ripon on which to build a monastery. On 27 December 1132 Richard was confirmed as its abbot. Under his aegis the new community turned to the Cistercians to ask for instruction in their way of life, with a view to joining the order. But, despite success in attracting recruits to join the venture, the poverty of Fountains was such that in 1134 Richard went to visit Bernard of Clairvaux, to ask for a new site for the community in France. Bernard was ready to provide him with a Cistercian grange, but while Richard was away Fountains had the good fortune to be joined by three wealthy recruits, Hugh, dean of York, and two of his canons; the value of their endowments, in particular Hugh's, made any projected move unnecessary.

Fountains, far from being an endangered settlement, was now set to become a rich and influential mission centre. In 1135 Richard successfully applied for formal admission into the Cistercian order, and Fountains thus became a daughter house of Clairvaux. Before Richard's death Fountains had itself founded daughter houses at Haverholme (1138), Newminster (1139), and Kirkstead (1139). At Fountains a stone church, similar in design to the earliest Cistercian churches of Pontigny and Cîteaux, had been built in place of the original wooden oratory. On the surrounding moors Cistercian sheep were now grazing; it was flocks such as these that would guarantee the future prosperity of the Cistercian order in England.

As abbot of Fountains, Richard became an influential figure in ecclesiastical circles. In 1138 he was chosen by Alberic, cardinal-bishop of Ostia and legate in England, to go with him on his tour of visitation. The following year he accompanied Alberic back to Rome in order to act as the representative of Archbishop Thurstan at the Second Lateran Council. His mission seems to have been to arrange for Thurstan's retirement in favour of the latter's brother, though Serlo in the *Narratio* suggests that Alberic wanted to find a curial post for Richard. But while in Rome Richard caught a fever. He died on 30 April and was buried in Rome.   HENRIETTA LEYSER

Sources J. R. Walbran, ed., *Memorials of the abbey of St Mary of Fountains*, 3 vols., SurtS, 42, 67, 130 (1863–1918) • D. Knowles, *The monastic order in England* (1940) • D. Bethell, 'The foundation of Fountains Abbey and the state of St Mary's York in 1132', *Journal of Ecclesiastical History*, 17 (1966), 11–27 • L. G. D. Baker, 'The foundation of Fountains Abbey', *Northern History*, 4 (1969), 29–43 • G. Coppack, *English Heritage book of Fountains Abbey* (1993) • J. Wardrop, *Fountains Abbey and its benefactors, 1132–1300* (1987) • D. Baker, 'The genesis of English Cistercian chronicles: the foundation history of Fountains Abbey', *Analecta Cisterciensia*, 25 (1969), 14–41; 31 (1976), 179–212 • D. Nicholl, *Thurstan: archbishop of York, 1114–1140* (1964)

Richard [Richard (II) of Fountains] (*d.* 1143), abbot of Fountains, is first mentioned in the *Narratio fundationis* of the Cistercian monastery of Fountains, Yorkshire, as the moving spirit behind the reforming party at St Mary's Abbey, York, which in 1132 broke away to found what was to become Fountains Abbey. As the party gained strength Richard ceded his place of leadership among the rebels to the prior, also called Richard, who subsequently became the first abbot of Fountains. When this Richard died in 1139 the monks of Fountains, on the advice of Bernard of Clairvaux—for Fountains was by now a daughter house of Clairvaux—elected the former sacrist, now their prior, to be abbot, though there is no proof that he took up office before 16 September 1141.

Fountains was now a very different place from the Fountains of 1132, with a new stone church and three daughter houses. Under the second Abbot Richard the keynote was to be consolidation rather than further expansion. The change in tempo may in part be explained by the extent to which Richard as abbot was embroiled in the controversy, unresolved in his lifetime, that followed the death of the abbey's benefactor, Archbishop Thurstan of York, on 6 February 1140. The election as archbishop in 1141 of William Fitzherbert (*d.* 1154), the candidate favoured by King Stephen and his brother, the papal legate Henry of Winchester (*d.* 1171), was strongly opposed by a northern monastic party which, despite his distaste for public life, included Richard. Galvanized by Bernard, this party maintained a resolute stand against William, accusing him of intrusion, simony, and lack of chastity, charges that Richard and others were called to Rome to substantiate in 1143.

As a raid on the monastery in 1146 was to show, such sustained resistance to William put the property of Fountains at risk, though the abbey possibly gained some measure of immunity through the bull that Pope Innocent II (*r.* 1130–43) gave to Richard, placing the abbey under his direct protection.

According to the sixteenth-century antiquarian John Leland, Richard, known to Leland as Fastolf, wrote a treatise on harmony and a book of homilies, but no such works have been identified; there are further problems with Leland's testimony since he seems to confuse Richard with the sixth abbot of Fountains, also *Richard (d.* 1170).

The *Narratio fundationis* contains a warm portrayal of the second Abbot Richard, drawn from the memory of the monk Serlo who had joined Fountains during his abbacy. In contrast to Bernard's next appointee, the combative Henry Murdac (*d.* 1153), Serlo depicts Richard as an abbot more interested in his pastoral than his administrative role, a wise confessor, and a contemplative who regularly tried to resign his office as abbot. Every year after his election he asked Bernard for permission to do so; on the fourth occasion Bernard agreed to grant his request, provided he could gain the consent of the monks of Fountains. This they refused to give but, as Richard himself had prophesied, his days were numbered, and in the same year, on 12 October 1143, he died while attending the Cistercian general chapter. He was buried at Clairvaux by Bernard.   HENRIETTA LEYSER

Sources J. R. Walbran, ed., *Memorials of the abbey of St Mary of Fountains*, 3 vols., SurtS, 42, 67, 130 (1863–1918) • D. Knowles and R. N. Hadcock, *Medieval religious houses, England and Wales*, new edn (1971) • D. Knowles, 'The case of Saint William of York', *Cambridge Historical Journal*, 5 (1935–7), 162–77, 212–14 • D. Knowles, *The monastic order in England* (1940) • G. Coppack, *English Heritage book of Fountains Abbey* (1993) • *DNB* [Richard, called Fastolf]

Richard [Richard (III) of Fountains] (*d.* 1170), abbot of Fountains, was elected to that office in 1151. During the later middle ages he was reckoned as the fourth, not the sixth, abbot, neither Maurice (1147–8) nor Thorold (1148–50) being considered worthy of commemoration.

Born in York, Richard spent some years in France, where he first became abbot of Vauclair in the diocese of Laon, and then precentor at Clairvaux. Bernard of Clairvaux, who had chosen all but the first of the abbots of Fountains, now put forward Richard as his nominee; in this he was backed by the former abbot of Fountains, Henry Murdac, now archbishop of York. The deaths of both men in 1153 deprived Richard of much needed support, and he soon found himself faced with a party of rebellious monks whose ringleaders he had to expel. What the issues were is not clear, but the disputed election to the see of York, finally settled only in 1154, had had serious repercussions for Fountains, and may have contributed to the formation of factions within the community. In May 1154 peace was celebrated between the monastery and William Fitzherbert, the archbishop Fountains had long resisted, but in June William died, allegedly the victim of poisoning; it is reasonable to infer from the account in the

Narratio fundationis of Fountains that the rising against Richard was a sequel to this drama.

With these initial troubles behind him Richard was able to give Fountains the benefit of an unusually long period of office, only three later abbots serving longer than he. Except in the first years of his office this was not, however, an era of great expansion for Fountains, the gifts of the late 1140s and early 1150s not being matched again until the final quarter of the century. Thus 1150 saw the foundation of the abbey's last daughter house, Meaux in Holderness, and only two new granges (Kilnsey and Morker) were established in Richard's time. None the less, Richard's period of office was of considerable importance, for to it belongs on the one hand a policy of careful consolidation of the abbey's original holdings, on the other the inauguration of an ambitious building programme that in many ways marks the new status the abbey was now claiming for itself within the Cistercian order and within the society of northern England.

Richard's church, thought to have been begun in 1154, was designed both to imitate and to surpass the abbey church of nearby Rievaulx. Similar in plan, the church at Fountains was yet longer, taller, and less austere than its counterpart at Rievaulx, and, in the words of the *Narratio fundationis*, was 'far more lavish' than the church it replaced. It is still possible to see Richard's transepts with their eastern chapels, and to reconstruct the design of the west front as built under his aegis. Particularly striking would have been its large rose window, a novelty in a Cistercian setting. By the time of Richard's death the building of the church was all but complete, slowed down only by the need in the early 1160s to rebuild the cloister ranges to house the growing community. To Richard's period of office belongs also a new chapter house, two guest houses, and an abbot's lodging.

Richard died on 31 May 1170. Fittingly he was buried in his chapter house, thus becoming the first abbot of Fountains to be buried within the precincts of his monastery. Richard was confused by the sixteenth-century antiquarian John Leland with Richard (d. 1143), the second abbot of Fountains. Which Richard, if either of them, wrote the book of homilies and the psalmody described by Leland is unclear. HENRIETTA LEYSER

Sources J. R. Walbran, ed., *Memorials of the abbey of St Mary of Fountains*, 3 vols., SurtS, 42, 67, 130 (1863–1918) · D. Knowles, 'The case of Saint William of York', *Cambridge Historical Journal*, 5 (1935–7), 162–77, 212–14 · D. Knowles, *The monastic order in England* (1940); repr. with corrections (1950) · R. Gilyard-Beer and G. Coppack, 'Excavations at Fountains Abbey, North Yorkshire, 1979–80; the early development of the monastery', *Archaeologia*, 108 (1986), 147–88 · G. Coppack, *English Heritage book of Fountains Abbey* (1993) · J. Wardrop, *Fountains Abbey and its benefactors, 1132–1300* (1987) · W. T. Lancaster, *Abstracts of the charters and other documents contained in the chartulary of the Cistercian abbey of Fountains*, 2 vols. (1915) · J. E. Burton, ed., *York, 1070–1154*, English Episcopal Acta, 5 (1988) · DNB

Richard (d. 1178), bishop of St Andrews, was a nephew of Alwin, first abbot of Holyrood, and was probably English. He was chaplain to Malcolm IV before his election to St Andrews in early 1163. The archbishop of York pressed his claims as metropolitan, secretly but unsuccessfully asking the pope 'that he would compel the bishop-elect of St Andrews to come to York for his consecration, and, if he did not come, that the archbishop might suspend him' (Somerville, no. 61). Then, since both Glasgow and St Andrews were without consecrated bishops, the archbishop tried to summon the Scottish clergy to him as legate. Ingram, archdeacon of Glasgow (who had been the king's chancellor, while Richard was only his chaplain), was chosen to intimate refusal and to carry the appeal to the pope, from whom he secured authority for the consecration of Richard by Scottish bishops; this took place before Malcolm IV on 28 March 1165 at St Andrews, possibly in the cathedral whose foundations had been laid out by Richard's predecessor, Arnald.

Between 1173 and 1177 the pope confirmed to Richard and the other Scottish bishops their 'ancient liberty' in consecrating bishops—that is, without an archbishop. Richard's episcopate was the first for some decades in which no attempt was made to secure metropolitan status for his see, a sign of the cautious spirit of the times: the ecclesiastical order was best not disturbed, but should be given the cloak of canonical respectability. Richard left about fifty charters and was clearly active in the affairs of his diocese, in response to rapidly developing canon law.

The greatest threat to this conservatism came from the secular power. When King William was taken prisoner in 1174, Richard was one of those sent to Normandy to secure his release, and he presumably knew the terms of the treaty of Falaise, including 'customary' subjection of the Scottish church to the 'English church'. Richard did fealty to Henry II along with other prelates and barons at York on 10 August 1175, but, when it came to the ecclesiastical order, he rejected the metropolitan claims of York at Northampton in January 1176, in a debate in which Jocelin, bishop of Glasgow, clearly played the leading part. Pope Alexander III bailed out the Scottish bishops on 30 July 1176 by rejecting York's claims in *Super anxietatibus*.

Richard died in the infirmary of the priory of St Andrews on either 5 or 13 May 1178 and was probably buried at St Andrews. His sister lived at St Andrews, and his chaplain brother and two nephews were also possibly in his *familia*. Richard may have represented an unduly weak response to royal influence in the church, for on his death the clergy hastened to elect Master John the Scot, probably nephew of Bishop Robert (d. 1159), without royal leave. A. A. M. DUNCAN

Sources J. Dowden, *The bishops of Scotland ... prior to the Reformation*, ed. J. M. Thomson (1912), 7–8 · O. Engels and others, eds., *Series episcoporum ecclesiae Catholicae occidentalis*, 6th ser., 1, ed. D. E. R. Watt (1991), 86–7 · G. W. S. Barrow, 'The early charters of the family of Kinninmonth of that Ilk', *The study of medieval records: essays in honour of Kathleen Major*, ed. D. A. Bulloch and R. L. Storey (1971), 107–31 · N. P. Brooks and G. Whittington, 'Planning and growth in the medieval Scottish burgh: the example of St Andrews', *Transactions of the Institute of British Geographers*, new ser., 2 (1977), 278–95, esp. 259–71 · A. O. Anderson, ed., *Scottish annals from English chroniclers, AD 500 to 1286* (1908), 259–71 · A. O. Anderson, ed. and trans., *Early sources of Scottish history, AD 500 to 1286*, 2 (1922), 251–99 · The *'Original chronicle' of Andrew of Wyntoun*, ed. F. J. Amours, 4, STS, 1st

ser., 54 (1906), 431 · R. Somerville, ed., *Scotia pontificia: papal letters to Scotland before the pontificate of Innocent III* (1982)
Likenesses seal, U. Durham L., Durham dean and chapter archives, misc. ch. nos. 985–987x, 1302, 1319, 1330

Richard [Richard of Dover] (d. **1184**), archbishop of Canterbury, was born in Normandy, educated in the liberal arts, and entered the Benedictine monastery of Christ Church, Canterbury, as a young man. He became a chaplain to Archbishop Theobald of Canterbury (d. 1161), and prior of St Martin's at Dover (a dependency of Christ Church) from 1157 until his election as archbishop of Canterbury.

Election to Canterbury That an otherwise obscure monk, lacking scholarly distinction or aristocratic connections, was chosen to succeed Thomas Becket as archbishop of Canterbury in 1173 reflects a desire for peaceful relations between church and state in the aftermath of Becket's murder (1170), rather than recognition of his ability. His was a compromise election. After Henry II's initial preference for a Norman successor had failed (Bishop Henri of Bayeux, Abbot Roger of Bec, Abbot Martin of Cérisy), the monks at Canterbury favoured their prior, Odo, later abbot of Battle (d. 1200), but the bishops and the king preferred Richard of Dover, and their opinion, expressed by Bishop Gilbert Foliot of London (d. 1187), secured his election in St Katherine's Chapel, Westminster, on 3 June 1173. The justiciar Richard de Lucy (d. 1179) confirmed the election immediately, and the archbishop-elect took the oath of fealty to Henry II. Ralph de Diceto, as archdeacon of Middlesex, a probable eyewitness of the ceremonies, was careful to record that Richard's oath was taken 'saving his order' and 'without any mention of observance of the "customs of the realm"' (*Diceto … opera historica*, 1.369)—implying that the constitutions of Clarendon had been tacitly abandoned.

Although Richard was formally received at Canterbury on 8 June, his consecration was delayed by the action of Henry II's son, Henry, the Young King, who, with the encouragement of Louis VII of France (r. 1137–80), was in the early stages of his rebellion against his father. The Young King opposed the five episcopal elections that had just been made, including Richard's, on the grounds that he had not been consulted and that the elections had not been conducted in canonical form. All interested parties appealed to the pope, and Richard, accompanied by Reginald fitz Jocelin (d. 1191), bishop-elect of Bath, pursued his appeal in person. The charges laid against him by the Young King and Louis VII of France (of simony, taking an unqualified oath of fealty—without the clause 'saving my order'—and illegitimate birth) were all rebutted, and Pope Alexander III (r. 1159–81) confirmed his election on 2 April 1174, consecrated him at Anagni on the 7th, conferred the pallium, appointed him legate, and confirmed the primacy of Canterbury. Richard of Dover thus began his pontificate with all aspects of his position intact: more securely than any incoming archbishop of Canterbury he combined the primacy with a papal legation, which set his authority in the English church apparently beyond challenge.

Richard's return to England reads like a triumphal progress. He left Ostia by sea on 26 May and landed at Genoa; he proceeded to St Jean-de-Maurienne where, with Archbishop Pierre of Tarentaise, he consecrated Reginald fitz Jocelin as bishop of Bath on 23 June 1174. From there he travelled by easy stages to Normandy, where he met Henry II at Barfleur in early August and was received with every mark of favour, including dinner with the king. On the king's instruction, he returned to England, being received in London on 3 September, where he learned of the great Canterbury fire, which had destroyed the choir of his cathedral on 5 September. Nevertheless, he did not proceed to Canterbury for some weeks, having been instructed by the pope to spend some time in London. He entered his cathedral city on 5 October, amid general rejoicing, and was enthroned; and he crowned his triumphant return by consecrating four new bishops (Richard of Winchester, Robert of Hereford, Geoffrey of Ely, John of Chichester) in a spectacular ceremony at Canterbury on 6 October, and then displayed his authority on a broader canvas, by conducting a visitation of his province, as metropolitan and legate.

Disputes and controversies This energetic beginning to Richard's pontificate, however, awakened old grievances. Religious houses resented his intrusion into their affairs (and the costs associated with his reception), and clerks and officials of Archbishop Roger de Pont l'Évêque of York (d. 1181) resisted his attempt to visit the priory of St Oswald at Gloucester, over which York claimed jurisdiction. His suspension of the defiant clerics renewed the dispute between Canterbury and York. Archbishop Roger appealed to the pope, and an unsatisfactory settlement was reached in November 1175, when, under pressure from Cardinal Hugo Pierleone and the king, Richard abandoned his claim over St Oswald's and absolved Roger's clerks. The dispute between the two archbishops rumbled on inconclusively throughout the pontificate, despite the efforts of Pierleone and the king to resolve it. Roger claimed the right to have his archiepiscopal cross borne before him in the southern province, and lodged a claim to the bishoprics of Chester, Worcester, and Hereford at Richard's Council of Westminster in May 1175 (which he chose not to attend, although he was in London), claimed jurisdiction over the Scottish bishoprics of Glasgow and Whithorne at the royal Council of Northampton in January 1176, and challenged Canterbury's precedence at the legatine Council of Westminster in March 1176, after which Henry II imposed a five-year truce at the Council of Winchester in August that year.

The dispute about archiepiscopal claims to a profession of obedience from the abbot of St Augustine's, Canterbury, was another distracting inheritance from the past. Roger, the new abbot-elect, offered only a qualified profession, which Richard would not accept, appealed in person to the pope, and obtained papal confirmation of his independence on the basis of privileges, later shown to be spurious, and a commission ordering the bishop of Worcester to confer the abbatial blessing. Richard's attempt to circumvent this manoeuvre by going in person to St Augustine's in 1178 was foiled by Roger's deliberate absence, and Richard appealed to Alexander III, with royal backing, since it was alleged that the abbot-elect had submitted the abbey to the papacy and promised an annual tribute. Roger returned a second time to the papal curia, where he charged the archbishop with disobedience to the pope's earlier mandate and secured benediction from the pope's own hands in February 1179, saving the rights of the see of Canterbury. Roger's victory seemed to have been sealed in 1180, when Alexander III sent letters to him and to Henry II declaring that the archbishops of Canterbury were to bless future abbots without profession. Richard strenuously opposed the abbey's claims, and in 1183 successfully challenged the authenticity of its documents, but it was royal pressure that compelled the monastery to make a satisfactory peace with him. It was in fact the St Augustine's case which compelled him to follow the king's court to the continent in 1182–3. He returned to England on 11 August 1183, and is recorded at Canterbury in August and September of that year. He was struck down by colic on 14 February 1184, at Halling, Kent, where he died on 16 February; he was buried in the lady chapel of Canterbury Cathedral, which was then in the nave north aisle, on 18 February 1184.

Relations with Henry II Richard's election, in June 1173, just three months after the canonization of his murdered predecessor, occurred at a moment of transition. Many contemporaries saw him as weak and ambivalent. According to Richard of Ilchester, bishop of Winchester (d. 1188), he threw away the gains made by Thomas Becket; the anonymous annotator of the earliest manuscript of Becket's letters thought him 'unworthy of the name of archbishop, both in word and in deed' (BL, Cotton MS Claudius B.ii, fol. 354rb); and it is certainly possible to construct an image of a time-serving primate committed to collaboration with the crown. On the debit side are his acquiescence in the king's ecclesiastical policies: in 1175 collaborating in the deposition of the abbot of Peterborough and in the king's appointment of some twelve abbots, and also accepting the royal appointment of bishops. On one occasion he was rebuked by Alexander III for confirming episcopal elections in the king's chamber. He was often in the king's company. In 1175 he was with Henry II at Westminster and Canterbury in May, and at the royal Council of Woodstock in July; in 1176 he attended the Council of Northampton, the Easter court at Winchester, and the Council of Winchester (15 August). On 13 March 1177 he is recorded at the splendid Council of Westminster, where Henry II adjudicated between the claims of Sancho VI of Navarre (r. 1150–94) and Alfonso VIII of Castile (r. 1158–1214), and on 22 May at Amesbury, presiding at the introduction of nuns from Fontevrault. In 1178 Richard attended the Christmas court at Winchester, and in the summer of 1181 he was with the king at Nottingham. In 1182 he was at Henry II's Christmas court at Caen; and in 1183 he is recorded at Poitiers, at Caen, where on 26 May he excommunicated those disturbing the peace between the king and his sons, and at Le Mans, for the disinterment of the body of Henry, the Young King, and its transfer to Rouen (24 June).

Attendance at royal courts and councils can be construed as subservience, but it was a part of the archbishop's duty of counsel, as indeed were Richard's two recorded diplomatic missions: from September to November 1176 escorting the king's daughter Joanna to St Gilles in Provence, on her journey to marry William II of Sicily (r. 1166–89), and representing the king in Flanders in January and February 1177. More significantly, perhaps, he did not, it seems, attempt to oppose the compromise over clerical immunity worked out with the papal legate, Cardinal Pierleone, in 1175–6, which Howden criticized because it exposed clergy to the perils of the forest law, nor did he oppose the concession of secular jurisdiction over advowson and lay fee, and he did not attend the Third Lateran Council in 1179 (having turned back at Paris), although he was represented by his chancellor, Master Peter of Blois (d. 1212). Moreover, he strongly defended the secular activities of the bishops of Winchester, Ely, and Norwich.

The Council of Westminster and canon law Nevertheless, a different picture emerges from a consideration of Richard's legislative and judicial actions as primate. Although there is no evidence that he had had legal training, his pontificate was highly important in the development of canon law in England. Having gathered round himself a household of learned clerks, called by Peter of Blois 'an assembly of cultivated and acute minds' (*Patrologia Latina*, ep. 6), including masters Gerard Pucelle (d. 1184), Peter of Blois, and Henry Pium of Northampton—all canonists of repute—he confronted many serious questions in the provincial council that he held at Westminster (11–18 May 1175) early in his pontificate. Of the council's nineteen canons, thirteen deal with various aspects of clerical behaviour—clerical marriage (1), frequentation of taverns (2), involvement in sentences of blood (3), tonsure (4), indiscriminate ordination (5), trial of secular cases in churches or cemeteries (6), simony (7–10), bearing of arms (11), vicars (12), and the payment of expenses in financial lawsuits between clerks (14)—while five concern the eucharist (16–17), tithe payments (13), and clandestine and child marriages (18–19). Although issued in the presence of Henry II and his son, two of the decrees (canons 1, 12) cited the latest papal pronouncements as expressed in decretal letters addressed to English recipients. Moreover, it is clear that a schedule of thirty-seven propositions listed in the collection of decretals found in BL, Cotton MS Claudius A.iv had been prepared for discussion, of which twenty-two appeared in the council's decrees; and, of the fifteen which were not adopted, seven or eight became the subject of consultations submitted by Richard to the pope for guidance, and resulted in a series of decretal letters addressed jointly to Richard and his suffragans on such matters as hereditary benefices, Cistercian possession of churches and advowsons, Jewish holding of churches or church revenues, appeals by men who had deserted their wives, promissory pensions to secure appointments, the repayment of pledges, and the treatment of lepers. This council, and the consultations which followed it, show the new primate seizing the legislative initiative and laying down important rules for the reform of the English church.

Moreover, Richard and the canonists in his circle made a notable contribution to the reception and enforcement of papal jurisdiction in England. Like his suffragan bishops, notably Bartholomew of Exeter (d. 1184) and Roger of Worcester (d. 1179)—described by Alexander III as 'the twin lights of the English church' (Gir. Camb. opera, 7.57)—he received numerous papal commissions as judge-delegate in specific cases, and diocesan and archival sources record his involvement at various stages in the judicial process—endorsement or confirmation of judgment, mandate for execution of sentence, and other comparable ways. At the same time early English decretal collections, notably the Canterbury and Rochester collections, drew heavily on the corpus of papal commissions addressed to him. A remarkable number of decretal letters to Richard, occasionally with a fellow commissioner, or jointly with his suffragans, is contained in canonical collections from the mid-1170s onwards, and many of them can be traced in the professional compilations of decretal law, from the *Compilatio prima*, made after 1188 at Bologna by Bernardo da Pavia, to the papally promulgated Gregorian *Decretals* or *Liber Extra* of 1234, compiled by Ramon de Peñafort, which became the second component in the official corpus of canon law in the Latin church. In this way, together with many other decretals received by him, four of Richard's questions put to Alexander III in the wake of the Westminster council of 1175 evoked answers which became part of the permanent law of the western church.

A paradoxical primate Archbishop Richard's pontificate is therefore something of a paradox. On the one hand, there is the manifest evidence of continuing good relations with Henry II—which some contemporaries found unpalatable, in the wake of the Becket controversy; on the other, there is the less well-known evidence of active participation in the application of the principles of papally defined canon law, operating through appeals, consultations, and the regular processes of ecclesiastical courts. Richard emerges not so much a compromiser as a judicious peacemaker. Lacking social or educational status, Richard did not apparently command the universal respect of his contemporaries (even his chancellor, Peter of Blois, was ambivalent in his judgements), but his pontificate was not the weak capitulation that is sometimes suggested. His recommendation of active collaboration with the royal courts in the punishment of laymen convicted by the church of the murder of clerks did not in his view constitute double punishment, since 'what was begun by one authority was completed by another' (*Patrologia Latina*, ep. 73). William of Newburgh's description of him as 'a man of modest education, yet laudably innocent and prudently content with his limited capacity, so that he did not venture into great matters' (William of Newburgh, *Historia rerum Anglicarum*, ed. R. Howlett, Rolls

Series, 1884, 235–6) seems only partly valid. Like Archbishop Theobald, Richard of Dover could exploit his monastic simplicity when it suited him—Gervase of Canterbury stresses his mildness and affability—but his cultivation of Henry II's goodwill enabled him to pursue canonical policies that consolidated the jurisdictional position of the English church in harmony and co-operation with secular authority.

CHARLES DUGGAN

Sources C. R. Cheney and B. E. A. Jones, eds., *Canterbury, 1162–1190*, English Episcopal Acta, 2 (1986), 28–202 · S. Chodorow and C. Duggan, eds., *Decretales ineditae saeculi XII: from the papers of the late Walter Holtzmann* (Vatican City, 1982), 9, 64–77 [nos. 38–43a] · *Radulfi de Diceto ... opera historica*, ed. W. Stubbs, 2 vols., Rolls Series, 68 (1876) · D. Whitelock, M. Brett, and C. N. L. Brooke, eds., *Councils and synods with other documents relating to the English church, 871–1204*, 2 (1981), 957–93, 993–1010 · *The historical works of Gervase of Canterbury*, ed. W. Stubbs, 2 vols., Rolls Series, 73 (1879–80), 1.3ff., 20, 250, 275–6, 296; 2.397–400 · W. Stubbs, ed., *Gesta regis Henrici secundi Benedicti abbatis: the chronicle of the reigns of Henry II and Richard I*, AD 1169–1192, 2 vols., Rolls Series, 49 (1867), vol. 1 · 'Petri Blesensis epistolae', *Patrologia Latina*, 207 (1855), 5–6, 38, 68, 73 · *Gir. Camb. opera*, 1.53, 144; 7.57, 69–70 · R. Howlett, ed., *Chronicles of the reigns of Stephen, Henry II, and Richard I*, 1, Rolls Series, 82 (1884), 235–7 · R. W. Eyton, *Court, household, and itinerary of King Henry II* (1878) · M. G. Cheney, 'The Council of Westminster, 1175: new light on an old source', *The materials, sources, and methods of ecclesiastical history*, ed. D. Baker, SCH, 11 (1975), 61–8 · C. Duggan, *Twelfth century decretal collections and their importance in English history* (1963) · C. Duggan, *Canon law in medieval England: the Becket dispute and decretal collections* (1982) · R. Foreville, *L'église et la royauté en Angleterre sous Henri II Plantagenet, 1154–1189* (Paris, 1943) · C. R. Cheney, *From Becket to Langton: English church government, 1170–1213* (1956); repr. (1965) · Thomas of Elmham, *Historia monasterii S. Augustini Cantuariensis*, ed. C. Hardwick, Rolls Series, 8 (1858), 420ff. · A. Saltman, *Theobald, archbishop of Canterbury* (1956) · *Chronica magistri Rogeri de Hovedene*, ed. W. Stubbs, 2, Rolls Series, 51 (1869), 171 · R. Howlett, ed., *Chronicles of the reigns of Stephen, Henry II, and Richard I*, 4, Rolls Series, 82 (1889), 37 · Dugdale, *Monasticon*, new edn, 4.530 · BL, Cotton MS Claudius B.ii · BL, Cotton MS Claudius A.iv
Archives BL, Cotton MS Claudius A.iv
Likenesses seal, Canterbury dean and chapter archives, C.A.D. 19 · seal, Bodl. Oxf., Deposited Deeds, Ch. O. 627 · seal, CKS, T. 264/12

Richard [Richard Palmer] (d. 1195), archbishop of Messina, was described in the inscription on his funeral monument as having been born in England and educated in France before making his career in Sicily. There appears to be no medieval evidence for the surname Palmer, first attributed to him by Pirri, who thought he was a member of the Palmeri family; in twelfth-century documents his first name only is given. He probably owed his initial post in royal service to the backing of one of the several well-placed Englishmen in the kingdom, perhaps that of the chancellor Robert of Selby. As early in the reign of William I (r. 1154–66) as 1157 he had already been nominated by the king as bishop-elect of Syracuse, a see directly dependent at that time on the papacy. In the disturbances of 1160 Richard took a leading part in the successful attempt to secure the release of the king from captivity, and himself delivered the king's promises of better government to the people. Together with Matthew of Salerno, the vice-chancellor, he is said to have dissuaded the king from carrying out his plan to destroy the city of Salerno after its rebellion in 1161. In the king's last years he is called royal *consularis et familiaris* and he was one of the three familiars whom the king appointed on his deathbed (1166) to advise Queen Margaret during the regency for the young William II. Adroitly he survived intrigues aimed at securing his removal from court by bringing papal pressure to bear on him to be consecrated and attend properly to his diocese.

Richard was unpopular with those who found him proud, scornful, unbending, and, in the way of northern Europeans, unfriendly to the Lombards (southern Italians). His ambition to become archbishop of Palermo was opposed by rivals such as Gentilis of Agrigento. More seriously still, the queen, who had resented his influence over her husband, preferred the eunuch Peter as chief counsellor, until Peter was chased out of Sicily by her cousin Henry, count of Gravina. When Gravina too lost power, Richard proved to be an indispensable ally to Gravina's enemy Richard, count of Molise. Although he survived, probably on account of his real abilities, he was thwarted in his ambition to become archbishop of Palermo, because the queen offered this post to her young cousin Stephen of Perche, whom she had made chancellor. As such Stephen attempted to recover the rights and revenues belonging to the chancellor's office, some of which Richard had been holding. Although Stephen was prepared to give up claims on two valuable properties in return, Richard was not mollified. He continued his opposition to Stephen by championing the case of a court notary arrested by the chancellor's order, on the grounds that, whatever might be the case in France, notaries of the court in Sicily could not be summarily arrested.

It is not clear what part Richard played in Stephen's downfall in 1168, but from that time on he was one of the three or four longest-serving members of the king's inner council, which ran the government throughout the reign of William II (r. 1166–89). He was at last consecrated bishop of Syracuse in 1169, but Alexander III appeared to be more concerned to secure Richard's recognition of the papacy's direct authority over his see than to require him to leave Palermo—probably because Alexander appreciated the importance of Richard's political influence at court. He was treated with comparable respect by Thomas Becket. Richard had given some of Becket's fellow exiles and kinsmen a charitable reception in Sicily as his compatriots. Becket presumed so far on his benevolence as to think he might be prepared to intercede with the king on behalf of Stephen de Perche. Becket himself was so well aware of Richard's power that he regarded it as natural that Henry II should attempt to win Richard over by offering him the see of Lincoln (vacant since 1166) in return for his good offices in arranging the marriage of William II to Henry's daughter Joanna, and he praised Richard's eloquence and prudence shown in a letter Richard had written on behalf of William, cardinal of Pavia. Some time after Becket's murder, Peter of Blois explained in a letter to Richard why he could not contemplate returning to Sicily as Richard desired, and preferred to breathe the air of Richard's

native country. Complaining bitterly of the treacherous behaviour of the Sicilians, Peter claimed to be sure Richard would sympathize with these criticisms, and urged him to return to England, where Henry II would welcome him. Richard was one of the party that left for France in 1176 to meet Joanna and escort her to Sicily for her marriage to William II. He was certainly one of the bishops Richard, archbishop of Canterbury (d. 1184), had in mind when he wrote to the pope in the same year about Sicilian bishops who did not leave court for seven, even ten, years at a time.

Richard was not tempted back to England. His great eminence in Sicily clearly satisfied his ambition. How much time he ever spent in his diocese is not known. Pirri gave Scobar's book of 1520 (now no longer extant) as authority for his statement that Richard had painting and mosaic work done for his cathedral in Syracuse. He certainly had a silver reliquary made for the arm of St Marcian, patron saint of Syracuse, which, however, he rather meanly and inappropriately took with him to Messina, when he was translated to the archbishopric there early in 1183. An archbishop at last, Richard promptly set about ordering his new province, obtaining papal injunctions to the suffragan sees of Cefalù and Patti confirming his rights. He was a prominent member of the delegation sent by the city of Messina to negotiate with Richard I while he was staying in the city in 1190. Documents survive that show Richard giving judgment in his consistory court in 1192 and receiving in February 1195 a privilege from the new king of Sicily, Henry VI, which restored to him the metropolitan's privilege of judging cases of adultery in his courts. He set about completing the new cathedral for his church at Messina and he also provided for it a large number of decorated cathedral service books and theological works. Since the new cathedral was not ready for consecration when Richard died on 7 August 1195, he was buried in the old cathedral of St Nicholas. On his funeral monument he was portrayed bearded and in his vestments, and a verse inscription endorsed his reputation as a man of learning and eloquence. For forty years he played a prominent part in the affairs of the kingdom, proving himself to be indispensable in the management of public affairs and discharging his ecclesiastical responsibilities with credit. D. J. A. MATTHEW

Sources H. Falcandus, *La Historia, o, Liber de Regno Sicilie*, ed. G. B. Siragusa, 2 vols. (Rome, 1897–1904) • *Romauldi Salernitani chronicon*, ed. C. A. Garufi, 1 (Città di Castello, 1914), 247, 253, 268–9 • R. Pirri, *Sicilia Sacra disquisitionibus et notitiis illustrata*, ed. A. Mongitore, 3rd edn, 1 (Palermo, 1733), 98, 110, 398–400 • P. F. Kehr, *Italia Pontificia*, 10 (1975), 341 • A. Garofalo, *Tabularium regiae et imperialis capellae collegiatae divi Petri in regio Palermitano palatio* (1835), 25, n.11 • A. Amico, ed., *I diplomi della cattedrale di Messina* (Palermo, 1888), 21–2, 24–7 • P. Jaffé, ed., *Regesta pontificum Romanorum*, rev. G. Wattenbach, 2nd edn, 2 (Leipzig, 1888), n.11619 • J. C. Robertson and J. B. Sheppard, eds., *Materials for the history of Thomas Becket, archbishop of Canterbury*, 7 vols., Rolls Series, 67 (1875–85), vol. 6, pp. 396–7; vol. 7, pp. 26, 143–4 • Peter of Blois, *Letters*, cc. 1337, n.46 • Richard of Dover, *Letters*, cc. 1459–61 • *Chronica magistri Rogeri de Hovedene*, ed. W. Stubbs, 4 vols., Rolls Series, 51 (1868–71) • *Chronicon Richardi Divisensis / The Chronicle of Richard of Devizes*, ed. J. T. Appleby (1963), 22 • F. Nitti di Vito, ed., *Le Pergamene di S. Nicola di Bari*, 6 vols.

(Bari, 1900–50), vol. 2, p. 252, n.147 • C. A. Garufi, *I documenti inediti dell'epoca normanna in Sicilia* (1899), 109–11, 188 • I. La Lumia, *Storia della Sicilia sotto Guglielmo II il Buono* (1867), 5–7, 66, 68–9, 78, 124, 174 • K. A. Kehr, *Die Urkunden der Normannische Sizilischen Könige* (1902), 86–8 • F. Chalandon, *Histoire de la Domination Normande en Italie et en Sicile* (1907), vol. 2, pp. 348–9, 633 • G. La Corte-Cailler, 'Un monumento del secolo xii nel duomo di Messina', *Archivio Storico Messinese* (1900), 240–45 [anno 1] • H. Buchtal, 'A school of miniature painting in Norman Sicily', in H. Buchtal, *Late classical and medieval studies in honour of Albert Matthias Friend Jr.* (1955), 312–39, esp. 325–9

Likenesses effigy on sepulchral monument, Messina Cathedral, Sicily

Richard [*called* Richard the Premonstratensian] (*fl.* **1150–1199**), Premonstratensian abbot and religious writer, was abbot of an unknown house of the order and the author of a widely read commentary on the mass (*De canone missae*). The commentary was often attributed to other writers, but in 1876 Barthélemy Hauréau restored it to its true author. The date of foundation of the Premonstratensian order and the dates of the earliest manuscripts of the commentary indicate that Richard flourished in the second half of the twelfth century, but it is impossible to be more specific.

That Richard was English is probable but not certain. John Bale maintains that he was, but Bale is a dubious authority. Another prominent early English antiquary, John Leland, does not mention him, and the evidence of the manuscripts is inconclusive. It is possible that he was French. He certainly visited Clairvaux, for a manuscript now at Troyes (Troyes, Bibliothèque Municipale, MS 302) contains a copy of his commentary which, it is stated, was delivered as a sermon at Clairvaux 'by a certain canon of the Order of Prémontré'. And, since some later manuscripts refer to him as an abbot, it may be presumed that some time after his visit he was so elevated, but as abbot of which abbey is unknown. Again, it is probable, but not certain, that it was in England.

There is a tradition that *c.*1180 Richard left England, made his way via Cologne to the Premonstratensian abbey of Wedinghausen–Arnsberg, and there wrote his commentary. This tradition is the result of an amalgamation of Bale's assertion of his English ancestry with Caesarius of Heisterbach's story of a Richard who was an English scribe at Wedinghausen, and whose hands had laboured so long in holy pursuits that they were preserved incorrupt after his death. The first to associate the two ideas was John Pits in 1619, and Pits's suggestion was adopted by Jean Le Paige in 1633, Casimir Oudin in 1722, and Barthélemy Hauréau in 1876. There are, however, no good grounds for identifying the two Richards, and the legend of the peripatetic Premonstratensian has no firm foundation.

Whether Richard wrote any other treatises besides his commentary is unclear. Bale says that he did, but Bale is unreliable, and the other early bibliographers do little more than echo his account. Apart from the commentary, Bale attributes to Richard a *De computo ecclesiastico*, a poem *De mysteriis sacrorum*, and a life of St Ursula. But the *De computo* remains untraced; *De mysteriis sacrorum* is by Hildebert de Lavardin; and the *Vita S. Ursulae* is a work of the Premonstratensian visionary Hermann of Steinfeld. Thomas Tanner also attributes to Richard a chronicle of the years from 1064 to 1284, but on no good authority.

In short, all that can be stated with certainty of Richard is that he was a twelfth-century Premonstratensian abbot; that he wrote a commentary on the mass; and that he once visited Clairvaux. All else is a matter of conjecture.

DAVID N. BELL

Sources B. Hauréau, 'Notice sur une exposition du canon de la messe', *Notices et Extraits*, 24/2 (1876), 145–56 • G. Macy, 'A bibliographical note on Richardus Praemonstratensis', *Analecta Praemonstratensia*, 52 (1976), 64–9 • Bale, *Cat.*, 1.232 • J. Pits, *Relationum historicarum de rebus Anglicis*, ed. [W. Bishop] (Paris, 1619), 255–6 • J. Le Paige, *Bibliotheca Praemonstratensis ordinis* (1633), 305 • C. Oudin, *Commentarius de scriptoribus ecclesiae antiquis*, 3 vols. (1722), 2.1521–3 • Tanner, *Bibl. Brit.-Hib.* • Caesarius of Heisterbach, *Dialogus miraculorum*, ed. J. Strange, 2 vols. (1851), 2.354 • *Acta sanctorum: October*, 9 (Brussels, 1858), 9.92–3 • W. Levison, 'Das Werden der Ursula-Legende', *Bonner Jahrbücher*, 132 (1927), 1–164, esp. 134–5 • F. Petit, *La spiritualité des Prémontrés aux XIIe et XIIIe siècles* (Paris, 1947), 226–30 • Bibliothèque Municipale, Troyes, MS 302

Archives Bibliothèque Municipale, Troyes, MS 302

Richard (*fl.* **1216–1222**), Augustinian canon and historian, may be identifiable with the Richard de Templo who was chaplain to Archbishop Stephen Langton (d. 1228) and prior of the Augustinian house of Holy Trinity, London, from 1222 until his death in 1250. Canon Richard wrote his *Itinerarium peregrinorum et gesta regis Ricardi* between 1216 and 1222. This was an almost entirely derivative work, divided into six books and covering events in the Holy Land between 1187 and 1192, including the third crusade, and the reign of Richard I. The first book is a transcription of a vivid eyewitness account of the years 1187–90, written by a chaplain attached to the order of the knights templar. The last five books translate into Latin a French account of the crusade, possibly in prose, in all probability composed in 1195–6 by a Norman clerk from the region around Évreux, who had been on the crusade and had links with Robert de Breteuil, earl of Leicester (d. 1204). Apart from Richard's translation of this work there has survived a French verse version of the original, the *Estoire de la Guerre Sainte*. There is little evidence of any originality from Canon Richard, whose authorship is attested by two independent sources, the contemporary anonymous *Libellus de expugnatione Sanctae Terrae* and, a century later, the English Dominican chronicler Nicholas Trevet (d. 1328). It is possible, however, that Richard added documentary evidence for aspects of royal administration to his source. If so, this would strengthen the case for his identification with Prior Richard de Templo (perhaps a family name), since the latter was ordered in 1227 to return to the royal archives documents that had belonged to the former justiciar Geoffrey fitz Peter (d. 1213). According to Trevet, in addition to the prose *Itinerarium*, Richard composed a metrical verse account of the crusade; this survived into the sixteenth century when it was seen by Leland. It is not to be confused with the *Estoire* which was derived separately from the common Norman source. The *Itinerarium* has been published twice, by Thomas Gale in 1687, and by William Stubbs for the Rolls Series in 1864.   C. J. TYERMAN

Sources W. Stubbs, ed., *Chronicles and memorials of the reign of Richard I*, 1: *Itinerarium peregrinorum et gesta regis Ricardi*, Rolls Series, 38 (1864) · [Richard], *Itinerarium peregrinorum*, ed. H. E. Mayer (1962) · Ambroise, *L'estoire de la guerre sainte*, ed. G. Paris (1897) · N. Trevet, *Annales sex regum Angliae, 1135–1307*, ed. T. Hog, EHS, 6 (1845) · *Radulphi de Coggeshall chronicon Anglicanum*, ed. J. Stevenson, Rolls Series, 66 (1875) [incl. *De expugnatione terrae sanctae libellus*] · J. G. Edwards, 'The *Itinerarium regis Ricardi* and the *Estoire de la guerre sainte*', *Historical essays in honour of James Tait*, ed. J. G. Edwards, V. H. Galbraith, and E. F. Jacob (1933), 59–77 · A. Gransden, *Historical writing in England*, 1 (1974), 239–42

Richard, first earl of Cornwall and king of Germany

(1209–1272), was born at Winchester on 5 January 1209, the second son of King *John (1167–1216) and his queen, *Isabella of Angoulême (*c*.1188–1246).

Early life and rebellion Baptized in memory of his uncle, *Richard I, Richard was brought up at first in his mother's household at Marlborough Castle, where, in 1212, it was falsely rumoured that he had been murdered as part of a wider conspiracy against the crown. In 1213 he joined his father on a progress through the north of England, and in the following year accompanied the king's military expedition to Poitou. With the outbreak of baronial rebellion he was transferred, in April 1215, to the keeping of the Poitevin courtier Peter de Maulay at Corfe Castle. There he was placed under the supervision of a tutor, Roger of Acaster, probably a Yorkshireman native to Maulay's lordship of Mulgrave, later rewarded by his pupil with land in Cornwall. Following the death of his father, the accession to the throne of his elder brother, *Henry III, and the departure of his mother, Isabella, for her homeland in France, Richard remained at Corfe in Maulay's charge until May 1220, when he was brought to London for his brother Henry's coronation. Thereafter, with Maulay's disgrace, Richard may well have resided at court. In 1221 he received a nominal grant of the honour of Eye in Suffolk, and in 1223 accompanied Alexander II of Scotland on a pilgrimage to the newly rebuilt shrine of St Thomas at Canterbury. He was knighted by his brother at Westminster on 2 February 1225, shortly after his sixteenth birthday, and a few days later received the county of Cornwall to hold during the king's pleasure, pending Henry III's majority.

A month later, in the company of William (I) Longespée, earl of Salisbury, and Philip d'Aubigny, Richard was appointed leader of an expedition sent to recover Poitou and to rescue Gascony from the threat of a French invasion. Although promoted merely as a figurehead, from August 1225 he assumed the title of count of Poitou. The chronicler Matthew Paris was to claim, much later, that in 1225 Richard was also granted Gascony in a secret charter from the king. This story is implausible, not only because the king was prevented from issuing charters until 1226, but because the surviving records suggest that Richard's activities in Gascony were subject to control by the other leaders of his expedition. He did, however, appoint an official to administer his rights at La Réole in Gascony, and

Richard, first earl of Cornwall and king of Germany (1209–1272), seal [as king of the Romans]

issued at least one charter, styling himself 'count of Poitou and brother of the king of England', confirming the monks of Granselve in a pension at Bordeaux, and right of passage in the waters of the River Garonne, first granted to them by his uncle Richard during his own time as count of Poitou before 1189. Probably there was no clear distinction in Richard's mind between his rights as count of Poitou and the more extensive franchises exercised further south by the dukes of Aquitaine. Financed by an enormous treasure raised from taxation in England, Richard's expedition succeeded in stabilizing Plantagenet power over Gascony, but enjoyed little success against the barons of Poitou. Negotiations for a marriage between Richard and a daughter of the king of the Spanish realm of León were terminated following intervention from Henry III's council in England, and with the retirement of the earl of Salisbury after October 1225 little further was achieved. Following the death of the French king, Louis VIII, in November 1226, various of the great magnates of Poitou considered rejoining the Plantagenet camp, and in February 1227 Richard engaged in negotiations at Thouars in an attempt to establish an alliance with the northern French counts of Champagne and Bar. This projected alliance came to nothing, however, and in April 1227 Richard returned to England after two years abroad.

By now, aged eighteen, Richard could expect considerable favours from his brother Henry, who had only recently cast off the shackles of his prolonged minority council to assume personal rule as king. On 30 May 1227, at Westminster, Richard was belted with the earldom of Cornwall, effectively as the first earl of Cornwall since 1175 and the death of Earl *Reginald, an illegitimate son of *Henry I. However, the Cornish lands and the other honours that Richard had received since 1221 were conferred upon him merely during the king's pleasure, without any award in hereditary fee. In July 1227, when Richard attempted to eject Waleran the German, a royal mercenary and former servant of his mother, from a manor belonging to the earldom of Cornwall, Waleran complained to the king who ordered his immediate restitution, perhaps even threatening Richard with banishment should he fail to comply. Richard left court in fury, and at Reading entered into an alliance with his brother-in-law William (II) *Marshal, earl of Pembroke, subsequently extended to include the earls of Chester, Gloucester, Warenne, Hereford, Ferrers, and Warwick. The earls and their followers gathered in arms at Stamford, issuing demands to the king and his chief minister, Hubert de Burgh, protesting against a recent perambulation of the royal forests, and demanding that curbs be placed upon the personal power of de Burgh. Richard himself was at odds with de Burgh over their respective claims to the honour of Berkhamsted, which Richard had been forced to surrender in July 1227 to Hubert's nephew Raymond. About 11 August 1227 Richard travelled under safe conduct to parley with the king at Northampton, and was there bought off with an award of the dower lands recently confiscated from his mother, Queen Isabella, and with English lands seized from the lords of St Valéry-sur-Somme, including the Oxfordshire honour of Beckley. With Richard's defection, the baronial alliance collapsed in disarray: the first of many occasions in his life when Richard was to affect sympathy for the barons, only to abandon his baronial allies once his own, personal grievances had been settled with the king.

Politics and lordship, 1227–1235 Over the next two years, Richard was able to consolidate his burgeoning lordship. In November 1229 he received the vast honour of Wallingford during pleasure, and at much the same time was restored to control of Berkhamsted. In 1230, on coming of age, he was confirmed in his previous, nominal, award of the honour of Eye, granted 1000 marks, and appointed custodian of the lands and heirs of Theobald Walter in England and Ireland. His whereabouts are uncertain before May 1230, when he joined Henry III's ill-fated expedition to France, landing at St Malo in Brittany and thereafter, in September 1230, serving as one of the English envoys to arrange a truce with France and a prolongation of the king's alliance with Pierre, duke of Brittany. In October, having fallen ill with the king at Redon, he returned to England, the expedition having been abandoned as a costly fiasco. In all likelihood, given his own, personal interest in restoring English lordship over Poitou, Richard was dissatisfied with the conduct of the campaign, and above all with the timidity shown by the king's chief minister, Hubert de Burgh, who had counselled against any major engagement with the French, either in Poitou or in Normandy.

Shortly after his return, on 30 March 1231, Richard was married to Isabella Marshal, sister to the earl of Pembroke and widow of Gilbert de Clare, late earl of Gloucester. The marriage took place at the Marshal manor of Fawley near Henley, and marks a significant breach in the relations between Richard and his brother the king. By allying himself to the Marshal, Richard threatened to bring together two of the greatest baronial power blocs in opposition to the king and de Burgh. Added to this, Richard's marriage opened the prospect that Richard himself might inherit the throne should his brother die, since Henry III was himself unmarried and destined to remain a bachelor for the next five years. In the meantime, the royal succession would pass to any children that Richard might have with Isabella. The first such child was born on 31 January 1232 and baptized John: a controversial choice of name, given the evil reputation that had already begun to cling to the memory of Richard's father, the late king. In the immediate term, the threat of an alliance with the Marshal was ended in April 1231 with William Marshal's death and the dispute that erupted thereafter over the accession of his younger brother, Richard *Marshal, a subject of the kings of France. Richard of Cornwall received custody of the Briouze lands in England and of various Irish estates, previously held by William Marshal. However, suspicions still lingered that he intended throwing in his lot with the Marshal heir. In early May 1231 he was ordered to surrender the honour and castle of Wallingford, and on 20 May Hubert de Burgh took control of the Briouze lands for himself.

Once again, as in 1227, Richard was poised on the edge of rebellion, and once again he preferred to seek a reconciliation with the court. At Painscastle in the Welsh marches on 10 August 1231 he was at last granted royal charters establishing his control over Cornwall, Wallingford, Eye, and Beckley in hereditary fee, rather than as previously during the king's pleasure. This settlement, which was accompanied by the recognition of Richard Marshal as earl of Pembroke and the admission to court of Simon de Montfort, heir to the earldom of Leicester, marked the beginning of the end for the king's chief minister, Hubert de Burgh, thereafter supplanted in the king's favour by the alien bishop of Winchester, Peter des Roches, and by des Roches's nephew, Peter de Rivallis. Richard of Cornwall had good cause to ally himself to this new order at court: he had been raised in the household of Peter de Maulay, a close associate of Bishop des Roches, and in 1227, at the time of his first threatened rebellion, had received entertainment and provisions from des Roches's estate bailiffs. Like Richard Marshal, des Roches, Maulay, and Simon de Montfort (and unlike Hubert de Burgh), Richard possessed a strong personal interest in pursuing a more aggressive policy towards Poitou and the king's French dominions. On the fall of de Burgh, in the summer of 1232, Richard duly fell into line behind the new regime. He was present in mid-September, when discussions were held over the advisability of putting de Burgh on trial, and in November was one of the four earls appointed to ensure de Burgh's close confinement at Devizes. At the same time he was allowed possession of the dower of his wife, Isabella, which seems previously to have been retained by de Burgh in his capacity as custodian of the honour of Gloucester. He seems also to have bestowed land in Cornwall upon Peter de Rivallis, the chief executive of the new regime. However, on 10 November the regime authorized a visitation of the judicial eyre, set to hear pleas in Cornwall in January 1233, the first such visitation of the county in more than thirty years, and an obvious challenge to Richard's autonomy as earl. Two weeks later the eyre was postponed until April, but the breach between Richard and the king's ministers, far from being healed, appears to have grown wider as des Roches and his supporters persuaded the king to dispense with the counsels of Richard Marshal, and to rule in a more arbitrary way, reminiscent of the practices of King John. The crisis came in the spring of 1233, with the arbitrary seizure of the manor of Upavon, previously conferred by royal charter upon one of the Marshal's dependants, now awarded to Peter de Maulay, Richard of Cornwall's former guardian, who had held the manor under King John. Far from supporting Maulay and des Roches in their moves against the Marshal, Richard of Cornwall appears to have withdrawn his support from des Roches's regime, and in March 1233, in alliance with Richard Marshal, conducted a brief but provocative campaign to drive the Welsh from Radnor. Here he was motivated both by a desire to protect the Brouze lands, then in his custody, and also by annoyance that the regime had denied him his claims to act as custodian to the young earl of Gloucester, his stepson, who was instead placed under the wardship of Bishop des Roches. Richard's offensive against Radnor was conducted without the approval of either the king or his ministers, and effectively wrecked the chances of any truce with the Welsh. Richard made no further appearance at court until June 1233, when various conciliatory awards were made to him, including the profits of the Cornish eyre that had duly convened in April amid considerable local disturbance. In August, when Richard Marshal approached the court to attempt a settlement, it was Richard of Cornwall's wife, Isabella, the Marshal's sister, who warned him to flee or face arrest. Thereafter, the chronicler Roger of Wendover implies that Richard was bribed by des Roches to abandon the Marshal. In support of this allegation, in August Richard received custody of the earldom of Devon together with Christchurch and Carisbrooke castles, which des Roches had previously controlled.

Henceforth the Marshal and his supporters appear to have regarded Richard as a traitor to their cause. It was against the Brouze castle of Hay-on-Wye, then in Richard's custody, that the Marshal's men launched the first of their acts of violent rebellion in August 1233, followed that winter by a campaign of daring raids in which Richard's property was singled out for destruction. In December 1233 his favourite seat at Beckley was attacked and burnt in a raid led by Richard Siward, a Marshal supporter. Richard himself continued to stand aloof from des Roches's regime, and made only one appearance at court over the next few months, on 14 March 1234, on which occasion he was granted the manor of Haughley in Essex in perpetual fee, confiscated from the estate previously controlled by Hubert de Burgh. Three weeks later he was at Canterbury on 2 April for the consecration of Archbishop Edmund, an event that marked the end of des Roches's ascendancy at court. Thereafter Richard proved one of the chief beneficiaries of des Roches's fall, over the next twelve months receiving the Yorkshire honour of Knaresborough, confirmation of the manors of Haughley and Kirton previously held by de Burgh, and custody of the entire Brouze estate in Sussex and the Welsh marches, subsequently sold to Gilbert Marshal for 3000 marks. In general, the events of 1232–4 had confirmed Richard's untrustworthiness as an advocate of the barons, first supporting Richard Marshal and then abandoning him after June 1233 in return for rich favours from his brother the king. In the process, Richard acquired enormous personal wealth combined with a reputation for duplicity among his erstwhile allies. The tensions to which this gave rise lingered for at least a further two years, resulting, in 1236, in the banishment from court of Richard Siward, disgraced at the behest of Richard of Cornwall in revenge for Siward's earlier attack upon the manor of Beckley.

Diplomacy and crusade, 1235–1241 By 1236 Richard was undoubtedly the richest earl in England, with a vast personal fortune and an effectively autonomous authority over Cornwall. His marriage to Isabella Marshal, which in 1235 had been subject to strain and the threat that Richard might seek a papal annulment following the death in infancy of their first two children, was stabilized following the birth on 2 November 1235 of a son and heir, *Henry of Almain. His wealth and ambition were sufficient to attract the attention of the Holy Roman emperor, Frederick II, recently married to Richard's sister *Isabella. Early in 1236 Frederick sought Richard's participation in a proposed anti-French alliance. In the event, Richard was prevented from taking up this proposal by the king and by concerted baronial disapproval. None the less, in June 1236 he took the cross at Winchester, immediately felling his woods to pay for his crusade. In January 1237 he obtained a forced levy of 3000 marks from the Jews. His departure was postponed, after February 1237, following the receipt of papal letters addressed to Richard, Simon de Montfort, and the earl of Salisbury, no doubt solicited by the king, urging them to consider the dangers in which England itself was placed, and not to set out without specific papal licence. As a result, Richard witnessed, disapprovingly, the new ascendancy at court being obtained by the king's uncle by marriage, William, bishop-elect of Valence, and the other Savoyard kinsmen of the queen, *Eleanor of Provence, who had married Henry III in January 1236. These tensions exploded in January 1238, following the secret marriage of the king's younger sister *Eleanor to the French-born Simon de Montfort. Richard entered into a hasty alliance with Gilbert Marshal, earl of Pembroke, and the earl of Winchester, which met in armed opposition at Kingston. In all likelihood, Richard was spurred into rebellion by hopes of repeating his earlier successes of 1227 and 1233, and out of a sense of pique that the resources of the crown, to which he was still heir presumptive, were being squandered on the king's foreign favourites. The threatened rebellion led the king to write to the Cinque Ports, urging them to enter into no arrangement with Richard, but as before Richard almost immediately made peace with his brother. Late in February 1238 he abandoned the barons, who received nothing more than a series of empty promises of reform.

On 4 March both Henry and Richard attended the deathbed of their sister *Joan, queen of Scotland, and in May the king made arrangements to dispatch 6000 marks to France for the use of Richard on his forthcoming crusade. Amid attempts by both Pope Gregory IX and the emperor, Frederick II, to divert Richard's crusading ardour towards their own internecine wars in Italy, in April 1238 Richard was granted papal licence to put all legacies to the Holy Land or sums paid for the redemption of crusader vows to his own use. A further attempt by the pope to persuade him to divert his expedition from the Holy Land to the needs of the Latin empire of Constantinople, and fears for the safety of England during his absence, delayed his departure for a further year, during which Richard stood as godfather to the king's eldest son, the Lord *Edward, born in May 1239, sought to mediate between the king, Gilbert Marshal, and Simon de Montfort, and spent Christmas 1239 with the royal court at Winchester, where he persuaded Henry to admit his ward, Baldwin de Revières, to the earldom of Devon. Further delay was caused by the death of Richard's wife, Isabella, at Berkhamsted on 17 January 1240, shortly after her delivery of a stillborn son. In May 1240 Richard served as one of the commissioners to make peace with the Welsh, before travelling to London where on 5 June he appointed Henry III to serve as guardian to his son and heir, Henry of Almain, and the abbots of Wardon and Beaulieu and his clerk Robert of Astill to take care of his ecclesiastical patronage. He embarked at Dover on 10 June in company with the earl of Salisbury and several dozen knights, including his former tutor, Peter de Maulay. At Paris he was entertained by Louis IX, and assisted in the renewal of the Anglo-French truce. His journey down the Rhône was disturbed by a violent encounter with the men of Vienne, who impounded his transport ships, and by attempts by papal agents to dissuade him from sailing or at least to divert his departure from Marseilles to Aiguesmortes. In response, Richard sent a notorious anti-papalist, Robert of Thwing, to serve as his spokesman at Rome. Richard himself sailed from Marseilles in mid-September, landing at Acre on 8 October 1240. In the Holy Land he found a disturbed situation, in which the leaders of the military orders were at odds with one another over whether to seek an alliance with the Muslims of Egypt or of Damascus, and in which the recent crusade of the count of Champagne had only fuelled the long-standing disputes in the East between those who favoured the claims to the throne of Jerusalem advanced by Emperor Frederick II, and those who preferred rule by the local aristocracy of Outremer. Richard, although officially recognized as the emperor's delegate, attempted to stand apart from these disputes, joining the duke of Burgundy in an effort to rebuild the fortifications of Ascalon, and in April 1241 ratifying a truce that had been arranged between Count Thibault of Champagne and the Ayubid sultan of Egypt. As a result of this truce, various Frankish prisoners were released from captivity, including Aimaury de Montfort, the brother of Simon. Without engaging in any further military venture, Richard then set sail for Europe, landing at Trapani on 1 July 1241 to spend several months at the court of his brother-in-law Frederick II. His crusade had proved a qualified success, helped by the divisions within the Muslim world. However its brevity and its lack of military vigour only reinforce the impression that Richard was no great warrior, but a negotiator and schemer of genius.

Continental activity and second marriage, 1241–1246 Lavishly entertained by Frederick II with a series of spectacles, including a performance by dancing girls balanced on rolling spheres, Richard failed in his attempts to make peace between emperor and pope. Late in 1241 he set out for the north, stopping at Cremona where he was shown an elephant, later described to the chronicler Matthew Paris. On 7 January 1242 he landed at Dover where he was greeted by the king and queen. At London a triumph was held in his honour, but almost immediately he was forced to cross overseas once more, to assist his brother's projected expedition to Poitou. Possibly, it had been foreknowledge of the intention of the French king, Louis IX, to invest his younger brother Alphonse with the county of Poitou—an event that took place in June 1241—that had persuaded Richard to cut short his expedition to the Holy Land. As titular count of Poitou since 1225, he could not ignore this new threat from France, or the decision of his mother, Isabella of Angoulême, and her husband, Hugues de Lusignan, count of La Marche, to seek an anti-French alliance with Henry III. Neither Richard nor Henry, however, could persuade the English barons to support a continental expedition with a grant of direct subsidy. The expedition set sail from Portsmouth in May 1242, landing at the mouth of the River Gironde and from there proceeding via Pons to Saintes, where half-hearted negotiations were opened with the French. In July, Henry and Richard marched eastwards into the county of Angoulême, but their failure to secure the bridge at Taillebourg enabled Louis IX to cut off the English from their base. On 20 July 1242 the two armies faced one another, divided only by the waters of the Charente. In the English camp there were bitter recriminations between Richard and Hugues de Lusignan, with Richard blaming the latter for the failure of military supplies, and Lusignan attributing the entire affair to Richard's mother, Isabella. Despairing of victory in battle, Richard set out across the bridge at Taillebourg to negotiate, putting aside his armour and carrying nothing but a pilgrim's staff. The French, some of whom had been freed from captivity in the Holy Land by Richard's endeavours the previous year, agreed to a twenty-four hour truce. Spurred on by Richard's cry to them to flee as quickly as possible, the English made an inglorious retreat to Saintes. Thereafter, abandoned by Lusignan, and forced to fall back across the Gironde, the expedition disintegrated into a futile, year-long progress through Gascony.

Richard had meanwhile quarrelled with his brother in late August 1242, almost certainly over Richard's claims to

Gascony. At Saintes, either shortly before the débâcle at Taillebourg, or in reward for Richard's services as peacemaker in late July, the king had issued a charter granting him Gascony as his personal possession. This met with bitter reproval from Queen Eleanor, who perhaps already hoped that Gascony might pass to her son, the future Edward I. According to Matthew Paris, Henry went so far as to bribe the men of Bordeaux to imprison Richard, who was forced to take refuge in the city's church of Ste Croix. Richard may also have been angered by the king's treatment of William de Ros, a north-country knight who was forced to leave the expedition because of his poverty. Richard was licensed to return to England on 22 August, and again on 2 September, although he did not in fact sail for several weeks, arriving at the Isles of Scilly on 18 October 1242. According to one source, he may have spent the intervening weeks in a fruitless attempt to visit Provence, where he had hoped to view his future bride, Sanchia, sister of Queen Eleanor, to whom he had been betrothed by proxy in July 1242 following negotiations carried out at Tarascon by Peter of *Savoy and the Savoyard bishop of Hereford, Peter d'Aigueblanche. In the event, Richard broke off his projected journey to Provence, fearing ambush, and came close to shipwreck on his return voyage to England, vowing to build an abbey should he escape with his life. This vow was fulfilled in 1246 with his foundation of the Cistercian abbey of Hailes in Gloucestershire. Sanchia herself arrived in England in 1243, and was married to Richard at Westminster on 23 November. Having granted Richard £2000 in cash and a promise of 1000 marks a year at the time of his marriage, in December 1243 the king demanded a written renunciation of any rights that Richard might possess in Ireland or Gascony, together with an explicit disclaimer of the award that had been made at Saintes. In return, Richard was confirmed in possession of Cornwall and of the honours of Wallingford and Eye. By his marriage to Sanchia, Richard acquired an interest in the affairs of both Provence and Savoy. In 1246, together with Henry III, he sought, unsuccessfully, to oppose the efforts of Charles of Anjou, brother of Louis IX, recently married to Sanchia's younger sister Béatrice, to claim the entire dominion of Count Raymond-Berengar (V) of Provence, who at his death in August 1245 had deliberately excluded all of his daughters save for Béatrice from any claim to his lands. With respect to Savoy, Richard's marriage greatly improved the relations that he had already established with the Savoyards in England, and in particular with Peter of Savoy, titular earl of Richmond, whom Richard henceforth served as banker and political ally.

Diplomacy and regency, 1244–1254 In domestic politics, Richard continued to act as a mediator between king and barons. In 1244, besides negotiating a treaty with Alexander II of Scotland, he was named as one of the committee of twelve, appointed to supervise reforms of the realm, encapsulated in a surviving but never implemented 'paper constitution'. By this time, with the collapse in royal finances brought about by the expedition to Poitou, and with the mounting pressure to find money and lands

to reward the various foreign favourites at court, Richard was already serving to prop up royal government by a series of ever more massive loans to his brother, financed in part from the profits of the Cornish tin mines, and in part from Richard's other perquisites, including the collection of redemption fines from those who failed to fulfil their crusading vows, a privilege first granted to Richard in 1238, but which he had continued to exercise long after his return from the East. In 1245 Richard loaned £2000 to the king to support an expedition against the Welsh. None the less, still smarting from his disappointments over Gascony, he is rumoured to have shown too great a sympathy for the king's enemies. In the following year he at first urged resistance to demands for papal taxation, and then persuaded his brother to accede to the pope's requests. It is possible that this change of mind was the result of papal bribery, since in the meantime Richard had received the pope's licence to continue his lucrative collection of crusader fines and legacies. His financial situation was further strengthened in 1247 when he was granted powers to supervise and to profit from the minting of new coin, a lucrative privilege that he was to continue to exercise for the next ten years and which brought him several thousand pounds in profit. In 1247 he crossed overseas with his son Henry, in a vain attempt to persuade Louis IX to relinquish Normandy on the eve of the French king's departure for crusade, and in order to visit the shrine of the newly canonized St Edmund of Canterbury at Pontigny, Richard paying one quarter of the cost of the shrine. At Easter 1249 he refused to attend the king's parliament, claiming the pressure of his own private business in Cornwall, but perhaps still angered by the king's attitude to Gascony, which in September 1249 was formally promised to the future Edward I.

In March 1250, together with Peter of Savoy, Richard travelled to France for a renewal of the Anglo-French truce. From Paris, with a magnificent retinue, he travelled on to the papal court at Lyons, where in early April he secured a mandate from Innocent IV awarding a tax of one-tenth of clerical incomes to Henry III, who had taken the cross on 6 March. Rumour suggests that at this meeting the pope made his first offer to Richard of the crown of Sicily, should Richard be prepared to lead a military expedition to expel the island's Hohenstaufen rulers. Returning home, he made a second pilgrimage to St Edmund at Pontigny, and at St Denis arranged the purchase of the alien priory of Deerhurst in Gloucestershire, apparently intending to convert the site into a castle, a project that was never put into effect. In London, acting together with Simon de Montfort, he served as mediator between the citizens and the monks of Westminster, and in 1251 he made a further visit to Westminster, to arbitrate between the monks and their abbot over the division of monastic property. In January 1252 he served once again as arbiter, in the bitter dispute between Simon de Montfort and the king over Simon's expenses and record as seneschal in Gascony since 1248. When this was followed by a further renewal of the promise that Gascony should pass to the Lord Edward, Richard left court in disgust, being bought off thereafter with a series of significant grants from the crown, including the manors of Oakham in Rutland and Lechlade in Gloucestershire.

The king then determined on personal intervention in Gascony. On 22 June 1253 the great seal was entrusted to Queen Eleanor, and on 7 July the queen was formally appointed to serve as regent in Henry's absence, acting with the counsel of Richard. In fact, the burden of the regency fell on Richard alone. In December 1253 he summoned a parliament to discuss aid for the king, himself promising 300 knights for Gascony, but failing to secure any grant of taxation from the laity. By the end of January 1254 Richard was preparing to sail in person to assist his brother, and in the following month took the unprecedented step of summoning two knights from each shire to represent lay opinion in parliament, the first occasion that elected delegates or representatives of the shires had been summoned in this way. In March 1254 he presided over the publication of a reissue of Magna Carta that had been formally agreed in May 1253. But in the event, neither Magna Carta nor the parliamentary summons excited support, and when the queen eventually sailed to Gascony in May, without Richard, she was accompanied by only forty knights. For his services as sole regent in England after May 1254, and in repayment of the vast loans that he had made to the crown since the mid-1240s, Richard was henceforth awarded ever greater control over the Jews of England. Matthew Paris reports that in 1254 Richard sought to protect Abraham of Berkhamsted, a Jew accused of desecrating an image of the Virgin and child, released from imprisonment at Richard's request and in return for a substantial fine. Two years later, he is said to have intervened on behalf of the Jews of Lincoln, victimized following the supposed martyrdom of Little St Hugh. As early as 1235 he had secured licence to have the Jews reside at his manor of Berkhamsted, and in 1242 this community had been transferred, together with their loan chest, to Wallingford, thereafter playing a significant role in Richard's financial dealings.

King of Germany During his Gascon expedition Henry III had accepted the pope's offer of the throne of Sicily, prudently refused by Richard in 1250 and again, at least twice more, between 1252 and 1254. As a result, the king was committed to vast expenditure in mounting a campaign for the island's conquest, even despite his overextended domestic expenditure. Richard, who seems to have regarded 'the Sicilian business' as mere folly, henceforth withdrew the financial support that had previously propped up his brother's regime. In 1255 he refused to lend 5000 marks to the pope, arguing that no adequate security had been offered, and in parliament, in October 1255, he openly spurned his brother's request for a further loan.

Almost immediately, however, Richard became embroiled in an adventure just as ambitious as that of his brother in Sicily. William of Holland, papal candidate for the title of Holy Roman emperor, died on 28 January 1256. Barely a week later, at Richard's petition, the royal exchequer granted a pension to Jean d'Avesnes, count of Hainault, and before the end of February Henry III had dispatched ambassadors to Rome, empowered to work for the promotion of a suitable successor to William as king of Germany. There seems little doubt that Richard's name was already being canvassed in papal and imperial circles. More intelligent and more forceful than his brother Henry, Richard had none the less been prevented from assuming the crown of England through the accident of primogeniture. He had turned down the pope's offer of the throne of Sicily, judging it to be a hopeless and potentially disastrous enterprise, but when the throne of Germany fell vacant his ambitions at last found an appropriate outlet. To become king, let alone Holy Roman emperor, Richard would need to overcome a number of formidable obstacles: he would first have to obtain the support of a majority of the imperial electors before being recognized in Germany. He would then require papal recognition to be crowned emperor, and to obtain this he would have to ensure that no significant voices were raised against him either in Germany or in France. Even then, the imperial title would be an empty bauble unless he could provide men and money to secure the imperial lands south of the Alps, hotly disputed since the death of Frederick II. Since no allodial lands were attached to the throne of Germany, successive kings and emperors had been forced to depend upon their own personal resources to finance armies and administration—a situation in many ways resembling that already encountered by Richard during his years as count of Poitou. Set against these potential difficulties, Richard could count upon the support of his brother, Henry III, to whom it was important that a sympathetic ally be placed upon the throne of Germany, in order to further Henry's own ambitions in Sicily. Richard possessed great wealth, considerable diplomatic skills, and a standing both in France and at the imperial court sufficient for his enterprise.

Richard's first task was to win over the imperial electors, which he proceeded to do through open bribery. A total of 28,000 marks was paid to Ludwig, count palatine, and the archbishops of Cologne and Mainz to secure three of the seven potential votes. At London on 26 December 1256 the crown of Germany was solemnly offered to Richard by the archbishop of Cologne, and at Frankfurt on 13 January 1257 his three supporters conducted a formal ceremony of election. The remaining four electors—of Saxony, Brandenburg, the archbishop of Trèves, and Ottokar of Bohemia—a clear majority, proceeded shortly afterwards to the election of King Alfonso of Castile, a Hohenstaufen candidate. But Ottokar's support for Alfonso was by no means unwavering, while Alfonso himself was in no position, either financially, or in light of his own problems in Castile, to make a personal appearance in Germany. As a result, on 29 April 1257 Richard set sail from Yarmouth with a large entourage, having earlier that month received the homage of the archbishop of Cologne and Count Florence of Holland. He landed at Dordrecht on 1 May, and from there made his way to Aachen where he and Sanchia were crowned as king and queen of Germany by the archbishop of Cologne on Ascension day (17 May).

Richard provided a splendid feast for his supporters before proceeding down the Rhine, reaching Mainz in September where he held his first royal parliament or diet. He retired northwards to the lower Rhineland for the winter, before making a similar progress in the spring of 1258, travelling as far south as Worms and at Aachen paying for the construction of a new town hall. Throughout this period, using his imperial style as king of the Romans and a new royal seal that had been cast for him, he confirmed existing imperial privileges and issued charters of his own to the towns of the upper Rhine. Without possessing anything in the way of lands or a settled administrative capital, and without subduing the opposition of three of the German electors, he had none the less achieved a remarkable success, gaining recognition for his authority throughout the Rhineland and as far north as Lübeck and Ratzeburg. He lacked only papal approval for his election, to obtain which it was essential that he reduce Alfonso of Castile's standing with the papacy. This in turn required that Alfonso be deprived of the support of Louis IX of France, the pope's chief protector, who was naturally apprehensive of the appearance of an English king in Germany. In June 1258 Richard sent his protonotary Master Arnold of Holland to seal a preliminary draft of the Anglo-French treaty of Paris, resigning any interest that Richard might have in the Plantagenet lands in France save for his claims to the Angoumois which had been ruled by his mother, Isabella of Angoulême, as countess in her own right.

Domestic turmoil, 1258–1260 In the winter of 1258 Richard made his way back towards the channel. His departure from England two years previously had served as a catalyst to rebellion. No longer cowed by fear of Richard, the baronage rose up against Henry III, who himself had been deprived of the financial and political support that Richard had previously brought to royal government. Clearly there was apprehension that Richard might seek to overturn the programme of reform that had been enacted in his absence, and to restore the king's hated Lusignan half-brothers to their English estates. Before crossing to Dover he was several times asked to swear an oath to uphold the reforming provisions of Oxford. Having initially refused this, in the end he complied at Canterbury on 28 January 1259, taking the prescribed oath in the presence of the king and of Boniface of *Savoy, archbishop of Canterbury. London was once again decorated to mark his return, and at Westminster on 10 February he ratified a second version of the treaty of Paris, essential in his strategy against Alfonso of Castile. Thereafter, for the remainder of the year, he seems entirely to have avoided political involvement, retiring to his own estates, no doubt to raise money and to set his own affairs in order. In July 1259, at Westminster, he served as arbiter in a long-standing dispute over jurisdiction between the archbishop of Canterbury and Bishop Lawrence of Rochester. In March 1259 came the first signs that his overtures to the pope were taking effect, with papal letters to the duke of Burgundy urging him to support Richard in his bid for the imperial title, followed by an invitation to Richard himself to come to Rome. Initially, Richard proposed accompanying Henry III to Abbeville in December 1259 for the solemn ratification of the Anglo-French treaty. In the event he remained behind, perhaps to counter baronial infringements upon his liberties, threatened by the terms of the provisions of Westminster and by the activities of a special judicial inquiry. To forestall such infringements, Richard obtained licence in October 1260 to oversee the appointment of nominees from his own tenantry to investigate abuses, a measure that continued to protect him until January 1262 when it was commanded that his own nominees answer to three justices appointed by the council. Meanwhile, in April 1260, at the king's request, he was instrumental in excluding the rival parties of the Lord Edward, Simon de Montfort, and the earl of Gloucester from London which was thus secured for Henry III. Subsequently, he reconciled Edward to his father, and in June 1260 presided over a treaty of peace between Edward and the earl of Gloucester, before leaving London on 17 June *en route* for Dover and his German realm. Throughout this period, although standing outwardly aloof from either the baronial or the royal camp, there can be little doubt that he approved entirely Henry III's attempts to undermine the baronial programme of reform.

Hindered imperial ambition Richard's second visit to Germany had been planned as a triumphant progress, set to culminate in his coronation as emperor at Rome. In the preceding months, he had continued to issue charters from England for his German subjects, including an award to his brother-in-law, Peter of Savoy, of the strategically significant lordship of Gummingen. Following an extended stay at Cambrai where he invested Marguerite, countess of Flanders, and her son Gui with their imperial lands, he travelled on to Worms where he remained from early August until 17 September 1260, declaring his imminent intention to cross the Alps to Bologna. He then turned back, retracing his journey up the Rhine, to arrive in England on 24 October. His loss of confidence is to be explained first and foremost by the defeat of the anti-Hohenstaufen armies of northern Italy at Montaperto on 4 September, after which Richard could no longer hope for a safe passage through to Rome. In addition, following much lobbying by Alfonso of Castile, the pope had reverted to his former neutrality, depriving Richard of any expectation of a speedy recognition as emperor. Richard's best opportunity to obtain the imperial throne had been let slip, and with it he lost much of his previously high reputation within Germany. Despite spending Christmas 1260 with the king at Windsor, he continued to live for most of his time on his own estates. With the approaching crisis in royal government, in January 1261 he was licensed to munition his own castles, and he was present in London in the following month when the citizens were made to swear oaths of fealty to the king. Thereafter he disappears once again from public life until October 1261. Behind the scenes he was almost certainly active in counselling Henry to obtain papal annulment of the baronial provisions and to throw off the limitations that had been placed upon royal power. By October Richard was offering the king his services, if need be, to land foreign mercenaries in Cornwall, and thereafter acted as mediator to reconcile Henry to the earl of Gloucester. In the spring of 1262 he once again served as arbiter, over the king's demand to control the appointment of sheriffs, entirely vindicating the king's prerogative rights. In the meantime he suffered the death of his second wife, Sanchia, on 9 November, buried at Hailes on 15 November 1262 but in the absence of her husband, an indication perhaps that Richard's affections for her had long cooled.

In April 1261 Richard had been elected senator of Rome for life, a purely honorary title which he made no attempt to exercise in person and in which he was subsequently supplanted by Charles of Anjou, brother of Louis IX. The death of Pope Alexander IV and the accession of Urban IV in August 1261 had brought the papacy no closer to a decision over the imperial election. However, in May 1262 news reached England of a threat to elect Conradin, the grandson of Frederick II, as king in Richard's stead, supported by the Count Palatine Ludwig, the newly elected Archbishop Engelbert of Cologne, and the archbishop of Mainz. This threat, exacerbated by disputes between Richard and Conradin over Conradin's claim to Swabia, and by tensions between the archbishop of Mainz and Richard's official Philip von Hohenfels, could not be ignored. On 20 June 1262 Richard set out once more for Germany, making a third progress through the Low Countries and thence down the Rhine. At Aachen, on 13 July, he deposited a duplicate set of imperial regalia, apparently fearing that in future he might be unable to obtain access to the true regalia, stored in the great imperial fortress of the Trifels. On 6 August, to ensure the support of Ottokar of Bohemia and to reward him for his earlier abandonment of King Alfonso, Richard issued a charter granting Ottokar the duchies of Austria and Styria, an indication of the extent to which he was prepared to tolerate the disintegration of his own German realm east of the Rhine, albeit in a region that had long since slipped from imperial control. A day later, Pope Urban announced that both Richard and Alfonso were to be granted equal recognition as king-elect, and that both were to be summoned to Rome. By November Richard was in sight of the Alps, taking Zürich under his protection and perhaps visiting Basel. This was the furthest south he was ever to reach, and in November he turned back, making his way down the Rhine to the coast, landing in England on 10 February 1263.

Civil war in England The political situation to which Richard returned was a troubled one. England stood on the brink of civil war between the king and the supporters of Simon de Montfort, with the Welsh already in open rebellion. On Richard's arrival from Germany it was rumoured that he had come to seize the throne and to rule in place of both Henry and the as yet untested Lord Edward. In fact, once again, he attempted to steer a middle course, retiring to his own estates and offering only muted support to his brother the king. In April 1263 he may have been among the barons who met at Oxford to renew the reforming provisions. In June he was with the royal court in London

when Henry received the barons' petition. Thereafter he attempted, in vain, to act as a mediator with Montfort. In July 1263 he undertook to seal the king's agreement to respect the baronial provisions, but his show of neutrality seems by this stage to have left him isolated from both the baronial and the royalist camps. In September Pope Urban IV was persuaded to write to Richard, accusing him of conniving in the barons' rebellion by lending insufficient support to his brother the king. These letters would not have been written without approval from Henry's proctors at Rome, although they should be set in the context of Urban's attempts to mediate in the imperial election dispute, where in August he had summoned both Richard and Alfonso to appear in Rome on 2 May 1265. In addition, they may reflect the king's anger with Richard's son, Henry of Almain, who throughout the summer of 1263 had openly sided with Montfort.

With the king's resumption of personal power in October, Richard was granted wardship of the major northern estate of the Mowbrays, and he joined Henry in late November 1263 in an unsuccessful attempt to seize Dover Castle from the barons. On the king's crossing to France in January 1264, for the publication of formal arbitration by Louis IX, Richard remained behind in England, effectively as Henry's regent. On 4 February, shortly before making a personal tour of the marches, he ordered the destruction of all bridges across the Severn save for that at Gloucester, in an attempt to prevent incursions by the Welsh. He rejoined the king at Windsor in March, and thereafter was in constant attendance at court. Meanwhile his manor of Isleworth was attacked by the London mob, who also sacked his mansion at Westminster, actions that were to transform Richard into one of the most outspoken of royalists, determined upon armed confrontation with Montfort. The attack on Isleworth had been led by Sir Hugh Despenser, Montfort's keeper of the Tower of London and a tenant of Richard in Rutlandshire, perhaps in an attempt to provoke a royalist attack upon London. At Lewes in early May Richard and the king were offered a huge sum, £30,000, in compensation from the barons, in return for peace, but the offer came to nothing. The chronicler William Rishanger blames Richard for the collapse of negotiations and his action in persuading the Lord Edward to join with him in a letter of defiance, preserved in several sources, which in turn provoked the barons into a formal withdrawal of their homage to the king, on 12 or 13 May.

In the battle fought at Lewes on 14 May 1264 Richard failed to distinguish himself before being taken prisoner by John Giffard, a knight of the earl of Gloucester. At some time during the battle he was confined in a windmill, where, according to the Melrose chronicler, he was taunted by the victorious barons who mocked at his grand titles as king of the Romans, *semper augustus*, calling to him to come out of the mill: 'Come down, come down, you worst of millers: Come out, come out, you evil master of the mill' (Stevenson, 196). From Lewes he was conveyed to the Tower of London, and thereafter placed in the charge of his sister, Simon de Montfort's wife Eleanor, at Wallingford, despite the prior claims to his ransom advanced by the earl of Gloucester. His estates were seized and thereafter administered by Montfort's son Guy. A rescue attempt led by Robert Waleran was foiled in November, whereafter Richard was transferred for safer keeping to Kenilworth, where he was placed in chains following the escape from prison of the Lord Edward in May 1265. The Melrose chronicle alleges that in the winter of 1264 he procured his release in return for a ransom of £17,000 of silver and £5000 of gold, but, although he may have offered such a sum, in the event he was destined to remain a prisoner until after the baronial defeat at Evesham. He was released on 6 September 1265 by Simon de Montfort the younger and the bishops of Worcester and Coventry, in return for an oath sworn by Richard later that day in Kenilworth Priory, promising to do his best to protect his sister Eleanor, Montfort's widow, from any reprisals by the royalists. Rishanger claims that the garrison of Kenilworth would have killed him, but for the intervention of the young Montfort. From Kenilworth he made his way to Wallingford where he was joyfully received by his household on 9 September, and where he received royal letters intended to assist him in the recovery of his ravaged estates. On 31 October 1265 he was at Canterbury to welcome the newly arrived papal legate Ottobuono, with whom he later made arrangements for the surrender of Eleanor de Montfort and her children.

Thereafter Richard seems to have retired once again from court, preoccupied with his own affairs including, on 18 April 1266, his foundation of an Augustinian nunnery at Burnham in Buckinghamshire. Although a beneficiary of the confiscation of rebel estates, he none the less seems to have counselled clemency towards the defeated barons. In March 1267 he joined the king at Cambridge, lodging at Barnwell Priory during the negotiation of a surrender by the earl of Gloucester and other malcontents who had occupied Ely and the city of London. In April he was one of two royalist leaders commissioned to parley with Gloucester, and in the following month loaned money to the king to relieve the hardships of the royalist army encamped outside London. The final award which he negotiated between 4 and 15 June allowed for the surrender of London in return for an amnesty for the earl of Gloucester. Thereafter, having failed in his attempts to negotiate a further peace with the Welsh, he attended the court at Marlborough in November 1267, where the king issued his statute incorporating various of the baronial reforms, now reclothed as a royalist programme. In March 1268 he was present for the final settlement with the Londoners, insisting upon a separate inquiry into the outrages that the Londoners had committed against his own estates in 1264. On 10 July he obtained letters of protection for those of his followers who were to accompany him overseas, and on 4 August 1268 he sailed for Germany.

Final years and death During Richard's absence and imprisonment the dispute over the German throne had come no closer to solution, albeit that, with the execution of Conradin in 1268, one of the three principal claimants had been removed from the scene. Between August 1268 and August 1269 Richard made a fourth and final progress down the Rhine, in April 1269 holding a diet at Worms, where the assembly sought to abolish most tolls on the Rhine, and where a new *Landfriede* or royal peace was proclaimed, to curb the activities of the region's warring barons. At Kaiserslautern on 16 June 1269 he married, for a third time, Beatrix von Falkenburg, a niece of the previously hostile Archbishop Engelbert of Cologne. However, lacking an army, and powerless to influence events elsewhere in his realm, he was in no position to press home his claim to the imperial title or to answer the pope's demand that he visit Rome. In 1265, at the time of his first summons, he had been a prisoner, and in 1267, although free, he had preferred to send his son, Henry of Almain, to serve as his proctor at the papal court. He was cited again in 1268 and 1269, together with Alfonso, but by this time had clearly become reconciled to deadlock in the imperial election dispute.

With his new bride Richard returned to Mainz in July, and landed at Dover on 3 August 1269, where he was greeted by the Lord Edward. By this time Henry III was in failing health, so that for the next two years Richard was to occupy a leading role in royal government. By an elaborate award, in May 1270 he mediated in the disputes between the Lord Edward and the earl of Gloucester, over Gloucester's obligations to the forthcoming crusade. When Edward set out on crusade in August, Richard was one of five counsellors appointed to manage his English affairs, and on 7 March 1271, when the king fell seriously ill, received a formal commission to act as protector of the realm. During these same months he was present in parliament, when the disinherited barons of the late rebellion were at last promised restoration of their estates, and in July 1271 witnessed major new legislation intended to limit the activities of the Jews. By this time news had reached him from Italy of the death of his eldest son, Henry of Almain, murdered at Viterbo on 13 March by Guy de Montfort, son of the late Earl Simon. These events cast a shadow over Richard's final months, compounded in August 1271 by the death of the Lord Edward's five-year-old heir, John, who had been left in his care, and whose funeral cortège Richard joined at Westminster on 8 August. On 12 December, while staying at Berkhamsted, and shortly after having been bled, Richard suffered a seizure, probably a stroke, which left him partially paralysed and unable to speak. He died at Berkhamsted on 2 April 1272; his body was buried beside his son and second wife, Sanchia, at Hailes, his heart being interred in the choir of the Franciscan church at Oxford.

By his will Richard left 8000 marks to the Holy Land, 500 marks to the Dominicans of Germany, and money to found a college of canons at Oxford, later diverted by his son and successor as earl, Edmund, towards the establishment of the Cistercian abbey of Rewley. His widow, Beatrix von Falkenburg, survived until 17 October 1277, being buried before the high altar of the Oxford Franciscans, close to her husband's heart. Richard fathered several children. With Isabella Marshal, his first wife, he had at least three sons and a daughter: John, who was born on 31 January 1232, died at Great Marlow on 22 September 1232, and was buried at Reading Abbey; Isabella, who was born about 9 September 1233, died on 6 October 1234, and was also buried at Reading; Henry of Almain, who was born on 2 November 1235 and who was murdered at Viterbo in 1271; and Nicholas, who was born and died at Berkhamsted in January 1240, shortly before the death of his mother. With his second wife, Sanchia of Provence, he had at least two children: a son born in July 1246, who died on 15 August that same year; and a second son, *Edmund of Almain, Richard's eventual heir, born on 26 December 1249, who died as earl of Cornwall in 1300. Besides these legitimate offspring, Richard fathered at least one and perhaps several bastards, including the Richard of Cornwall, brother to Earl Edmund, who was killed during the storming of Berwick in 1296.

Reputation Contemporary satire made much of Richard's eye for the ladies, branding him 'a great lecher towards all women of whatever profession or condition, a most greedy storer-up of treasure, and a most violent oppressor of the poor' (*Ann. mon.*, 4.xxx). To an anonymous author, commemorating the baronial victory at Lewes, Richard was a trickster and cheat: 'Richard thah thou be ever trichard, trichen shalt thou never more' (Wright, 69). Certainly, he several times proved an untrustworthy ally of the barons, in 1227, 1233, and 1238 joining wider baronial confederacies only to abandon his allies once his own grievances with the crown had been settled. Although a crusader in 1240, and one of the most outspoken advocates of a military solution to the political crisis of 1264, he generally preferred negotiation and arbitration to armed conflict. According to Matthew Paris, his unwarlike nature was to be explained not by any specific physical infirmity but by a general lack of either martial spirit or good health.

As an arbiter and author of settlements to other men's disputes Richard was unrivalled in his day, making peace again and again between king and barons, and frequently serving as mediator in both baronial and ecclesiastical disputes. The richest earl in England, and one of the richest men in Europe, he spent a large part of his fortune in supporting the regime of his feckless elder brother, Henry III. Advanced in the form of loans, without usury, this money was crucial in maintaining royal government before 1255. Its withdrawal thereafter was a key element in the collapse of Henry's personal rule. As a financier, Richard served as principal governor of the mint between 1247 and 1258, an office from which he derived considerable profit. He was also closely involved with the Jews. Of his 100 or more surviving charters, a large number concern the boroughs of Cornwall, where Richard granted markets or other privileges to the men of Bodmin, Bossinney, Camelford, Dunheved, Helston, Launceston, Liskeard, Lostwithiel, Marazion, Tintagel, and West Looe. Elsewhere he issued communal charters to the men of Exeter and of Corsham in Wiltshire, and in 1265 the men

of Helston, Truro, Bodmin, and Exeter are to be found acting as Richard's brokers in the export of tin from the Cornish stannaries.

However, with the exception of his dealings with the Cornish boroughs and the mint, Richard seems to have been neither an innovative nor a particularly grasping man of business. An analysis of his property transactions suggests that in 40 years he spent only £2000 or so on the purchase of land, at a time when his annual income from estates granted to him by the crown exceeded £5000. Most of his money went in supporting the king, financing his own vastly expensive bid for the throne of Germany after 1257, and in conspicuous consumption within his own household, hinted at by the luxuries with which he was supplied by his sister Eleanor while in captivity at Kenilworth in 1264–5, including dates, ginger, almonds, raisins, and 12 measures of scarlet cloth for his robes at Whitsun. His interventions in the Cornish property market may have fuelled opposition to his lordship within the county, ensuring that the men of Cornwall lent him only lukewarm support during the period of baronial rebellion. His chief residences lay in the Thames valley, and he only infrequently ventured into his Cornish estates, despite rebuilding Tintagel Castle, almost certainly because of its supposed association with the semi-mythical King Arthur.

Richard founded several religious houses, most notably the Cistercian abbey of Hailes in Gloucestershire, established as a daughter house of King John's foundation at Beaulieu, the Augustinian nunnery at Burnham in Buckinghamshire, and a Trinitarian friary at Knaresborough, home to the shrine of the hermit St Robert. He also allowed the Franciscans of Chichester to transfer their community to the site of the former castle, and bestowed less significant patronage upon the English monasteries and upon the order of Cîteaux, which in 1240 received a pension from Richard's mills at Boroughbridge and the church of Stanley in Yorkshire, intended to finance the meetings of the Cistercian general chapter. As a patron of the religious, Richard's piety was conventional rather than fanatical, and in the same way, despite his great wealth, he made little impression as a patron of the arts or of learning. In Germany, although never a great king, through skilful negotiation and the renewal of privileges granted by his predecessors to the towns and monasteries of the Low Countries and the Rhineland he obtained widespread recognition for his authority during his own lifetime. Only in retrospect, and as a result of the imperial election dispute that followed his death, between Ottokar of Bohemia and Rudolf von Habsburg, was the memory of Richard's reign transformed into one of bloodshed, royal weakness, and princely anarchy.

The essential features of Richard's career lay in his skills as negotiator and in his loyalty to his elder brother, Henry III. It was this loyalty from which he derived his landed estates and his wealth. Had he turned traitor, he might have supplanted his less able brother on the throne of England. As it was, he preferred a supporting role at home, and exhausted his own, personal ambitions in the pursuit of kingship in Germany. His failed bid for the imperial title established no permanent relations between Germany and the crown of England. None the less, Richard remains the only Englishman ever to have laid claim to the Holy Roman empire. NICHOLAS VINCENT

Sources Chancery rolls • Paris, Chron. • Ann. mon. • J. Stevenson, ed., Chronica de Mailros (1835) • N. Denholm-Young, Richard of Cornwall (1947) • J. F. Böhmer, Regesta imperii, 1198–1273, ed. J. Ficker and E. Winkelmann (Innsbruck, 1881–94) • E. Winkelmann, ed., Acta imperii inedita seculi xiii, 2 vols. (Innsbruck, 1880–85) • B. Weiler, 'Image and reality in Richard of Cornwall's German career', EngHR, 113 (1998), 1111–42 • G. C. Gebauer, Leben und denkwürdige Thaten Herrn Richards, erwählten römischen Kaysers, Grafens v. Cornwall und Poitou (Leipzig, 1744) • N. Vincent, Peter des Roches: an alien in English politics, 1205–38, Cambridge Studies in Medieval Life and Thought, 4th ser., 31 (1996) • J. R. Maddicott, Simon de Montfort (1994) • R. C. Stacey, Politics, policy and finance under Henry III, 1216–1245 (1987) • PRO, MS E36/57 [earldom of Cornwall cartulary] • Bibliothèque Nationale, Paris, MS Doat 80, fols. 307r–308r • BL, Cotton MS Julius D.v, fol. 27r • Archives départementales Côte-d'Or, Dijon, MS 11H22 • I.PI., MS 1212 [Canterbury cartulary], fols. 76r–76v • T. Wright, The political songs of England, ed. P. Cross (1996) • The chronicle of Walter of Guisborough, ed. H. Rothwell, CS, 3rd ser., 89 (1957) • J. Thorpe, ed., Registrum Roffense, or, A collection of antient records, charters and instruments … illustrating the ecclesiastical history and antiquities of the diocese and cathedral church of Rochester (1769), 82–4 • A. Magen and G. Tholin, eds., Archives municipales d'Agen: chartes première série (Villeneuve-sur-Lot, 1876) • M. W. Beresford and H. P. R. Finberg, English medieval boroughs: a handlist (1973) • F. Liebermann, 'Zur Geschichte Friedrichs II und Richards von Cornwall', Neues Archiv, 13 (1888) • H. Marc-Bonnet, 'Richard de Cornouailles et la couronne de Sicile', Mélanges d'histoire du Moyen Âge: dédiés á la mémoire de Louis Halphen, ed. [C.-E. Perrin] (Paris, 1951) • A. Busson, Die Doppelwahl des Jahres 1257 und das römische Königthum Alfons X von Castilien (Münster, 1866) • S. Raban, 'The land market and the aristocracy in the thirteenth century', Tradition and change: essays in honour of Marjorie Chibnall, ed. D. Greenway, C. Holdsworth, and J. Sayers (1985) • K. Hampe, 'Ungedruckte Briefe zur Geschichte König Richards von Cornwall', Neues Archiv, 30 (1905) • J. F. Bappert, Richard von Cornwall seit seiner Wahl zum deutschen König, 1257–1272 (Bonn, 1905) • F. Trautz, 'Richard von Cornwall', Jahrbuch des Vereins für Geschichte von Stadts und Kreis Kaiserlautern, 7 (1967) • H. Koch, Richard von Kornwall. Erster Theil, 1209–1257 (Strassburg, 1888) • G. Lemcke, Beiträge zur Geschichte König Richards von Cornwall (Berlin, 1909) • H.-E. Hilpert, 'Richard of Cornwall's candidature for the German throne and the Christmas 1256 parliament at Westminster', Journal of Medieval History, 6 (1980), 185–98 • F. R. Lewis, 'Beatrice of Falkenburg the third wife of Richard of Cornwall', EngHR, 52 (1937) • F. R. Lewis, 'The election of Richard of Cornwall as senator of Rome in 1261', EngHR, 52 (1937) • F. R. Lewis, 'Ottakar II of Bohemia and the double election of 1257', Speculum, 12 (1937) • H. Schiffers, Die deutsche Königskrönung und die Insignien des Richard von Cornwallis, Veröffentlichungen des Bischöflichen Diözesanarchivs Aachen, 2 (Aachen, 1936) • M. Page, 'Royal and comital government and the local community in thirteenth-century Cornwall', DPhil diss., U. Oxf., 1995 • M. Page, 'Cornwall, Earl Richard and the barons' war', EngHR, 115 (2000), 21–38

Archives Archives départementales Côte-d'Or, Dijon, MS 11H22 • Bibliothèque Nationale, Paris, MS Doat 80, fols. 307r–308r • BL, Cotton MS Julius D.v, fol. 27r • PRO, MS E36/57

Likenesses seal, Landeshauptarchiv, Koblenz, Bestand 133, Nr. 18 [see illus.]

Richard [Richard of Conisbrough], **earl of Cambridge** (1385–1415), magnate, the second son in the family of *Edmund of Langley, duke of York (1341–1402), and Isabel, daughter and coheir of Pedro the Cruel, king of Castile and Leon, was born at Conisbrough Castle, Yorkshire, where he was also baptized about 20 July 1385. Richard was twelve years younger than his brother *Edward, duke of York (c.1373–1415), and may have been the product of his mother's illicit liaison with John *Holland, earl of Huntingdon (d. 1400), for neither his father nor his brother provided him with land or income and neither mentioned him in his will. It was left to his mother to persuade his godfather, Richard II, in her own will of 1392, to grant him an annuity of 500 marks. This Richard did in 1395, but any further royal beneficence was cut short by that king's deposition in 1399 and he received no favours from Henry IV.

From April 1403 to October 1404 Richard commanded a small body of men defending Herefordshire against Owain Glyn Dŵr but his lack of resources and, probably, aptitude kept him on the fringe of the aristocratic commanders around Prince Henry. Knighted in 1406, he was appointed to accompany the king's daughter Philippa to her marriage with Erik, king of Denmark, but otherwise he held no political or military office. His hurried and possibly clandestine marriage to Anne Mortimer, the elder of two sisters of Edmund, earl of March, early in 1408 was validated by papal bull on 23 May, and his annuity was henceforth charged upon the Mortimer estates in the custody of her stepfather, Sir Edward Charleton. She died soon after the birth, on 22 September 1411, of a son, Richard, who was eventually heir to both the York and Mortimer inheritances.

As his second wife Richard married Maud, daughter of Thomas *Clifford, Lord Clifford, and formerly wife of Lord Latimer from whom she held five manors in dower. These apart, he had no lands and was dependent on his crown annuity; he had won no patronage, and had no record of service to the crown. Yet as heir to his childless brother Edward, duke of York, and as a grandson of *Edward III, he could not be left in obscurity. By creating him earl of Cambridge in the parliament of 1414 Henry V ostensibly acknowledged his expectations, but the king's insistence that reward be earned by service made it an invitation to seek his fortunes in France. For the title was empty: it brought neither land nor money from the king or his brother. If anything, it worsened his predicament; for, as the poorest of the earls, he lacked the resources to equip himself for the impending expedition as his rank demanded.

It is in terms of disappointed expectations that Cambridge's instigation in 1415 of a plot to dethrone Henry V is most plausibly (though not wholly) explained. He sought to raise a rebellion either in the name of Richard II, using the impersonator who had been harboured at the Scottish court and appealing to supporters of the exiled Percy earl, a refugee in Scotland, or in the name of his brother-in-law the earl of March, as legitimate claimant to the English crown.

Both schemes proved impractical, the first because the pretender had died and Henry V was already offering to restore Henry Percy, the second because March was a vacillating and contemptible figure who commanded neither baronial nor popular support. March was indeed prepared to listen to Cambridge's scheme, for he was aggrieved and unnerved by the punitive fine imposed on him for his marriage to Anne, sister and heir to the earl of Stafford, and by the urgings of his confessors to assert his claim to the throne. Cambridge also managed to implicate Sir Thomas Grey of Castle Heaton, near Wooler, who was in debt to the duke of York, and Henry, Lord Scrope of Masham, who claimed to avenge the death of his uncle, Archbishop Scrope, at the hand of Henry IV. But at his trial Scrope also maintained that he had joined the conspirators only to try and dissuade them. With their disparate personal motives and in the absence of any widespread opposition to Henry V it is difficult to understand how they could have expected to succeed. Nor is it clear that they had any concrete plans. Discussions about how to raise revolt in Wales in the name of the earl of March were still in progress, with a minimum degree of security, at the end of July when the earl lost his nerve and disclosed the plot to the king, thus saving his life. Cambridge, Grey, and Scrope were at once arrested on a charge of treason and detailed confessions were extracted from them.

Grey was promptly executed on 2 August but Cambridge and Scrope claimed trial by their peers and a special commission was appointed. Cambridge admitted his guilt but wrote piteous letters to Henry appealing for clemency. 'He reckoned without the rigour of Henry V's justice', and both were beheaded on 5 August 1415 (Pugh, 126). Cambridge was buried in the chapel of God's House, Southampton. His honours were forfeited but he had not been attainted and his inheritance passed to his son *Richard, third duke of York, aged four, whose son, Edward IV, in the parliament of 1461 annulled the sentence on his grandfather. Within three months Edward of York had perished at Agincourt and the boy Richard became duke, a title which Cambridge would have held. His conspiracy was thus not merely ill-judged but, if undertaken to improve his own fortunes, unnecessary.

Contemporaries as well as historians found it a puzzling affair, resorting to the improbable theory of bribery by the French. Though indicative of the lingering resentments and divisions engendered by the policy of Richard II, its failure ensured that these no longer posed a threat to the Lancastrian crown. Cambridge appears as not only the moving spirit but also the most deluded of the three, his plight and sense of grievance exciting an already ill-balanced personality to a doomed venture.

G. L. HARRISS

Sources T. B. Pugh, *Henry V and the Southampton plot of 1415*, Southampton RS, 30 (1988) [incl. all documents in trans.] • J. H. Wylie, ed., *The reign of Henry the Fifth*, 1 (1914) • *RotP*, vol. 4 • N. H. Nicolas, ed., *Proceedings and ordinances of the privy council of England*, 7 vols., RC, 26 (1834–7), vol. 2 • F. Taylor and J. S. Roskell, eds. and trans., *Gesta Henrici quinti / The deeds of Henry the Fifth*, OMT (1975) • *Thomae Walsingham, quondam monachi S. Albani, historia Anglicana*, ed. H. T. Riley, 2 vols., pt 1 of *Chronica monasterii S. Albani*, Rolls Series, 28 (1863–4), vol. 2 • *Chancery records* • N. B. Lewis, 'The last medieval summons of the English feudal levy, 13 June 1385', *EngHR*, 73 (1958), 1–26 • PRO

Archives BL, Cottingham MSS, letters • PRO, confessions of conspirators, deputy keeper report 43
Likenesses stained-glass window, Christ Church, Canterbury

Richard, duke of York and duke of Norfolk (1473–1483), prince, the second son of *Edward IV and his queen, *Elizabeth Woodville, was born at Shrewsbury on 17 August 1473. He was created duke of York on 28 May 1474, and knighted on 18 April 1475. He and his elder brother were made knights of the Garter a month later, on 15 May. His landed endowment was under consideration in the same year, and in March 1475 land formerly belonging to the Welles and Willoughby families was settled on him. Edward IV's will, drawn up before the French expedition of 1475, suggests that the king was then planning an apanage for York based on the duchy of York lordships of Fotheringhay, Stamford, and Grantham, with the duchy of Lancaster estates in the same region. But these plans were superseded by the decision to marry Richard to Anne Mowbray (1472–1481), the sole heir of John (VII) Mowbray, duke of Norfolk. Negotiations began almost immediately after the duke's death in January 1476, although the necessity for a papal dispensation (on the grounds of consanguinity in the third and fourth degrees) meant that the marriage itself did not take place until 15 January 1478, in St Stephen's Chapel, Westminster.

Richard received all the former Mowbray titles. He was made earl of Nottingham on 12 June 1476, and duke of Norfolk and Earl Warenne on 7 February 1477. He also became earl marshal, and lord of Seagrave, Mowbray, and Gower. By an agreement embodied in an act of parliament of 1478, he was given a life interest in the Mowbray lands even if his wife died childless (as in the event she did, at Greenwich on 19 November 1481). This deferred the claims of the two heirs general: William, Lord Berkeley, and John, Lord Howard. In addition Berkeley had been persuaded in May 1476 to surrender his claim altogether in return for the cancellation of debts of £34,000—a surrender confirmed in 1482 by a further act of parliament. In May 1479 Richard was appointed lord lieutenant of Ireland, an appointment renewed for a further twelve years in the following year. By 1480 he had his own officers, although they were probably seconded from his father's household, as his chamberlain (the East Anglian knight of the body Thomas Grey) certainly was.

After the death of Edward IV on 9 April 1483 York was probably with his mother. He went with her into sanctuary at Westminster at the very end of the month, when word reached London that the dead king's brother, Richard, duke of Gloucester, had taken control of *Edward V and was accusing the Woodvilles of a conspiracy to seize power. On 16 June the queen was persuaded by Cardinal Bourchier to hand over her son, and York joined his brother in the Tower of London. Gloucester immediately postponed Edward V's coronation, which had been scheduled for 22 June, and on 26 June took the throne for himself on the grounds that the two sons of Edward IV were illegitimate because their father's precontract to Eleanor Butler, *née* Talbot, rendered his marriage to Elizabeth Woodville bigamous.

Opposition to *Richard III's seizure of power surfaced quickly, and in July 1483 there was an unsuccessful conspiracy to rescue the two princes from the Tower. But by September Richard's opponents had adopted Henry Tudor as their claimant for the throne, which strongly implies that they believed Edward V and his brother to be dead. The fate of the princes has been the subject of considerable controversy, but their murder on Richard's orders late in the summer of 1483 remains the most probable explanation for their disappearance. The lack of any public statement about their death meant that uncertainties persisted. No pretender emerged in Richard III's own brief reign, but in the 1490s Perkin *Warbeck's claims to be Richard, duke of York, gained considerable backing, not all of it factitious.   ROSEMARY HORROX

Sources *RotP* · *Chancery records* · GEC, *Peerage* · Rymer, *Foedera* · C. Ross, *Edward IV* (1974) · C. L. Scofield, *The life and reign of Edward the Fourth*, 2 vols. (1923) · A. Crawford, 'The Mowbray inheritance', *Richard III: crown and people*, ed. J. Petre (1985), 79–85 · N. H. Nicolas, ed., *Privy purse expenses of Elizabeth of York: wardrobe accounts of Edward the Fourth* (1830)
Likenesses stained-glass window, c.1482, Canterbury Cathedral

Richard I [*called* Richard Coeur de Lion, Richard the Lionheart] (**1157–1199**), king of England, duke of Normandy and of Aquitaine, and count of Anjou, was born on 8 September 1157 at Oxford, the third son of *Henry II (1133–1189) and *Eleanor of Aquitaine (c.1122–1204). Richard's early upbringing would have been the responsibility of his mother and of his nurse, Hodierna, to whom he granted a substantial pension as soon as he became king. Although nothing is known of his education, it is clear he obtained a conventionally good one, and not only in the arts of war. He was able to enjoy a Latin joke at the expense of a less learned archbishop of Canterbury. His interest in words and music was such that he became not just a patron of troubadours, but also a songwriter with a poetic voice very much his own. Muslim sources noted his interest in Arabic culture.

Duke of Aquitaine Richard's association with the duchy of Aquitaine began early. Henry II's conquest of the Quercy at the expense of Raymond (V), count of Toulouse, in 1159 had been preceded by an alliance with the house of Aragon–Barcelona involving Richard's betrothal to a daughter, whose name is unknown, of Raymond-Berengar (IV), count of Barcelona, on the understanding that in due course he would inherit Aquitaine. Until 1196 much of Richard's life was to be shaped by the diplomatic configuration of 1159. The betrothal itself was to prove more ephemeral. By the late 1160s Henry was planning a division of his dominions between his sons and he needed the consent of Louis VII of France. In January 1169, as part of the peace of Montmirail, Richard's betrothal to Louis's daughter Alix was confirmed and he did homage to Louis for Aquitaine. In June 1172 he was formally installed as duke.

However, the status of his duchy was put in doubt as early as February 1173 when Raymond (V) did homage to Richard's older brother *Henry, the Young King, as well as to both Henry II and Richard. This seemed to presage the

Richard I (1157–1199), tomb effigy

permanent absorption of the great duchy of Aquitaine into the Angevin empire. It may explain why when the Young King, for reasons of his own, rebelled, Eleanor herself joined in the rising against her husband and was followed by most of the barons of Poitou and the Angoumois as well as her third and fourth sons, Richard and *Geoffrey, whom she sent to join their older brother at the court of her former husband Louis VII. In this crisis Louis knighted Richard, now fifteen years old. In July 1173 he took part in an invasion of eastern Normandy—his first known military action. In the autumn Henry offered Richard four castles and half the revenues of Aquitaine (and similar terms to his brothers). On Louis's advice they rejected this offer and the family war continued. After Eleanor's capture in November 1173, Richard took command of the revolt in Aquitaine, establishing his headquarters at Saintes. Here at Whitsun 1174 he was taken by surprise by his father's sudden attack. He and a few followers managed to escape to Geoffroi de Rancon's formidable castle of Taillebourg and despite the loss of the 60 knights and 400 archers, whom Henry captured at Saintes, he fought on stubbornly. However, when he learned that both Louis VII and the Young King had made peace, further resistance became pointless. On 23 September 1174 he submitted. At a Michaelmas peace conference at Montlouis, Richard and his brothers accepted terms slightly less generous than the ones they rejected the year before; their mother remained her husband's prisoner.

Presumably the young duke's conduct had impressed his father. The following year Richard was given full control of the duchy's armed forces, and orders to punish rebels and to 'pacify' Aquitaine, in particular those parts of the duchy that lay south of the more securely governed Poitou. These two tasks were to dominate the next thirteen years of Richard's life; in executing them he acted as his father's agent—as is clear from the written reports that Richard sent his father, which Roger of Howden then included in his history of the *Gesta regis Henrici secundi*. In 1175 one of Henry's deeds was to cause Aimar, vicomte of Limoges, to join the ranks of the disaffected nobles. As son-in-law of Reginald, earl of Cornwall, Aimar felt disinherited when the earl died that year, and Henry II reserved his estates for his youngest son, *John (1167–1216). However, Henry II responded generously to Richard's request for the resources to meet this additional threat. In 1176 the young duke rapidly routed the rebels, defeating Brabançons hired by Guillaume, count of Angoulême, in battle at Barbezieux in May, and then capturing both Limoges and Angoulême as well as a number of castles. Guillaume and Aimar surrendered and were dispatched to seek mercy from Henry II. Immediately after Christmas, Richard took up arms against the count of Bigorre and the vicomtes of Dax and Bayonne, capturing their towns and strongholds as far south as the castle of St Pierre at 'the gate of Spain' at Cize. In a report sent to his father on 2 February 1177 Richard announced that he had made safe the road to Santiago de Compostela, forced Basques and Navarrese to swear not to molest pilgrims, and had brought peace to all parts of Aquitaine.

But the devastating military success with which Richard carried out his father's policy left resentments, reflected in the words with which the Limousin troubadour Bertran de Born described the duke's treatment of his nobles: 'he besieges and pursues them, takes their castles, and smashes and burns in every direction' (*Poems*, 188–9). Thus there were some regions in which the duke's peace did not last very long: Gascony where Richard campaigned again in 1178 and 1181; and above all the Limousin and Angoumois—the soft underbelly of the Angevin empire. In 1179 Count Vulgrin of Angoulême and Geoffroi de Rancon rebelled again but surrendered their castles after the shock of Richard's capture of Taillebourg in May. According to Ralph de Diceto, the reputedly impregnable castle fell to an assault in which Richard himself fought in the thick of the fray. When Vulgrin died on 29 June 1181 Richard took custody of his heiress daughter. Applying the Anglo-Norman custom of wardship to Angoulême was bound to anger Vulgrin's brothers, Guillaume and Audemar. They rebelled and were joined by Aimar de Limoges. In May 1182 Henry II and his eldest son helped Richard to suppress the revolt, but the Young King was evidently jealous of his younger brother's success and, as they surrendered, the rebels took care to inform him of their grievances. By this channel English historians came to learn something of Richard's style as a ruler. According to Gervase of Canterbury, 'the great nobles of Aquitaine hated him because of his great cruelty' (*Works of Gervase of Canterbury*, 1.303); according to Howden, 'he carried off his subjects' wives, daughters and kinswomen by force and when he had sated his own lust, handed them down to his soldiers' (*Gesta … Benedicti*, 1.292).

At Christmas 1182, as in 1173, Henry II lost control of his family. He asked Richard and Geoffrey to do homage to their elder brother. Richard reluctantly consented to do so as long as it was agreed that Aquitaine should belong to him and his heirs. But the Young King refused to accept Richard's homage on these terms; in a series of explosive quarrels it emerged that he wanted to be duke of Aquitaine himself, and that to this end he had already encouraged Viscount Aimar and other rebels to take up arms again. In the hope of imposing peace on both Aquitaine and his own family, Henry sent Geoffrey to the Limousin to prepare the ground for a conference. Instead Geoffrey joined the rebels. When Henry then allowed his eldest son to go to Limoges, also ostensibly in the role of peacemaker, Richard refused to remain at court any longer. After an angry scene with his father he rode off to fight for his duchy. Aristocratic resentments and fraternal tensions had combined to bring Richard's rule to crisis point.

On 12 February 1183 Richard surprised Aimar's *routiers* near Limoges and put them to the sword. Belatedly Henry II remembered that his son's view of ducal authority was his own. He joined Richard and they laid siege to the citadel of St Martial at Limoges, where Viscount Aimar was entrenched with virtually all the rebel leaders. At this stage Philip Augustus of France (r. 1180–1223), Raymond (V), count of Toulouse, and Hugues, duke of Burgundy, moved to help the Young King; Alfonso II of Aragon came to the aid of Henry and Richard. A massive showdown seemed to threaten, but the unexpected death of the Young King on 11 June deprived the rebels of their public cause, the replacement of a tyrannical duke by an easygoing one. On 24 June Aimar surrendered to Henry and Richard; other rebels, including Bertran de Born, followed suit and were forced to see their strongholds confiscated or dismantled. In the following years Richard continued to extend ducal authority. By 1189 there were fifteen ducal provostships in Aquitaine compared with ten in 1174.

Uncertain inheritance Since Richard was now his principal heir, with expectations of inheriting Anjou, England, and Normandy, Henry sought a new family settlement. He reconciled Richard with Geoffrey and then, at Michaelmas 1183, he ordered him to transfer Aquitaine to his youngest brother, John. But it was for Aquitaine that Richard had, in Bertran's words, 'given and spent so much money, handed out and taken many a blow, and endured so much hunger and thirst and fatigues' (*Poems*, 286–7), and he would not do so. From now on Richard's relations with his father were tense. Angrily Henry gave John permission to take the duchy by force. In discussions with Philip Augustus he raised the possibility of the marriage of Alix (who had remained in his custody ever since 1169) with John instead of Richard. During 1184 Richard found himself at war with both John and Geoffrey, while his father negotiated a new marriage for him with a daughter of Frederick Barbarossa—she, however, died before the end of the year. Henry summoned all three brothers to England and in December 1184 they were publicly reconciled. But almost immediately Henry revived the rivalry between Richard and Geoffrey by giving the latter a command in Normandy which seemed to threaten Richard's expectations there. Richard's reaction was to take up arms against Geoffrey. In April 1185 Henry began to muster an army against Richard but then thought better of it, released Eleanor from custody, and commanded Richard to surrender Aquitaine to his mother, the lawful duchess. Richard obeyed. It was likely, after all, to strengthen his own position as well as his mother's. This was followed not only by a confirmation of Richard's betrothal to Alix in March 1186, but also by a renewal of the Aquitanian claim to Toulouse. In April 1186, with a large subsidy from his father and in alliance with Alfonso II, Richard invaded the county and made substantial conquests—in part at least reconquests, since it seems that the rebellions and distractions faced by Richard in and after 1182 had allowed Raymond (V) to recover the territory lost in 1159.

However, now that he was his father's principal heir, Richard found himself increasingly involved with his father's chief opponent: the king of France. Episodes such as Philip's threat to invade if he were not given custody of Geoffrey of Brittany's daughters following their father's death in August 1186 drew Richard north to help with the defence of Normandy. In June 1187 Philip invaded Berry, precipitating a confrontation at Châteauroux which nearly led to a pitched battle. In the event both sides drew back and a two-year truce was agreed. When Philip returned to Paris, Richard rode with him. In Howden's words:

> Philip honoured Richard so highly that every day they ate at the same table and shared the same dishes; at night the bed did not separate them. The king of France loved him as his own soul and their mutual love was so great that the lord king of England was stupefied by its vehemence.   (Gesta … Benedicti, 2.7)

This political—not sexual—demonstration had the desired effect. Henry promised to grant Richard all that was rightfully his, but Richard, still distrusting his father, rode to Chinon, took possession of the Angevin treasure stored there, and spent it on restocking the castles of Aquitaine. When he was eventually reconciled with his father, he admitted that he had been listening to people (presumably Philip Augustus above all) who were out to sow dissension between them.

That autumn Richard took the cross in response to the news of the catastrophe that had overwhelmed Jerusalem. North of the Alps he was the first prince to do so—the first of many indications of his commitment to the crusading cause. That he took the cross without consulting his father added to the tension between them, so much so that it was alleged that early in 1188 Henry encouraged Geoffroi de Lusignan, Count Audemar of Angoulême, and Geoffroi de Rancon to rebel in order to detain Richard in the West. No sooner had he suppressed this revolt, once again capturing Taillebourg in the process, than a quarrel with Raymond (V) of Toulouse escalated into war. In a brief campaign Richard took no fewer than seventeen castles and installed garrisons in Cahors and Moissac to ensure firm control of the Quercy. Raymond appealed for help

to Philip, who invaded Berry in June and captured Châteauroux. Richard then joined his father in Normandy, and cross-border raids and peace conferences followed in swift succession. Philip consistently offered to return his gains in Berry, if Richard would restore his conquests to Raymond. Since the Quercy meant more to Richard than it did to Henry, Philip's offer was shrewdly chosen to drive a wedge between father and son. Diceto believed that Richard had in any case been dismayed by the reports that the recent revolt had been inspired by Henry. Richard began to negotiate directly with Philip. At a conference held at Bonsmoulins on 18 November 1188 Philip offered to return all his gains on condition that Henry gave Alix in marriage to Richard, and had his barons swear an oath of fealty to Richard as heir. Whatever Henry's real intentions, his blunt refusal to do this inevitably appeared to be public confirmation of the rumours that he was planning to disinherit Richard in favour of John. Richard at once did homage to Philip for all the Angevin continental dominions, including his own recent conquests in Toulouse.

War broke out when the truce expired in mid-January 1189. As his barons began to transfer their allegiance to Richard, Henry, now a sick man, favoured John's cause more openly. A papal legate, Giovanni di Anagni, arrived to bring the kings to peace for the sake of Jerusalem but, at a conference held at Whitsun, Richard said he would not go on crusade unless John went too. Henry's reply was to suggest that John should marry Alix. This brought negotiations to an abrupt end. Philip and Richard attacked at once, and by advancing on Le Mans forced Henry to flee. The capture of Tours on 3 July brought him to submission. Next day he acquiesced in the terms they dictated, including a payment of 20,000 marks to Philip and an agreement that the marriage of Alix and Richard would take place after Richard's return from crusade. On 6 July Henry died at Chinon.

Duke of Normandy, king of England A courtly king, in Chrétien de Troyes's view, should not show the grief he felt. Richard's reign began in the abbey church of Fontevrault where, in the presence of his father's body, he immediately tackled the business of patronage which was at the heart of politics. He gave generously to those such as André de Chauveny who had consistently supported him, but equally generously to those such as his half-brother Geoffrey (d. 1212) and William (I) Marshal who had stayed with the dying king to the end. Anticipating that the Lord Rhys would attack English castles in Wales as soon as he heard of Henry's death, he dispatched Rhys's cousin Gerald of Wales to south Wales. On 20 July he was formally installed as duke of Normandy at Rouen. Two days later he met Philip, confirmed their treaties, and agreed to pay him an additional 4000 marks; in return he received all his father's continental dominions except for the lordships of Graçay and Issoudun which Philip had held since 1187. He restored to Robert de Breteuil, earl of Leicester (d. 1190), estates of which Henry had disseised him, and promised to do the same for all whom Henry had disinherited. The prospect of a general restoration of rights ensured that jubilation greeted his landing at Portsmouth on 13 August. On 3 September 1189 he was crowned and anointed at Westminster; Howden's account affords the first detailed description of a coronation in English history. However, the celebrations were marred by anti-Jewish riots in Westminster and London; these riots spread after Richard left England and culminated in the massacre at York in March 1190.

In the autumn of 1189 Richard reorganized the government of England, appointing two new justiciars, replacing or reshuffling the sheriffs, confirming old and making new grants. Those who received the offices and privileges they wanted paid for them. He had, in Howden's words, 'put everything up for sale' (*Gesta … Benedicti*, 2.90). This was standard practice; what was not standard was the speed and scale on which it was done in 1189. If a crusade against the great Saladin was to have any chance of success, it had to be properly resourced, and although Richard had taken over the treasure accumulated by his father—some 100,000 marks according to Howden's estimation—the greater the financial resources the better. He is alleged to have said that he would have sold London if he could have found a buyer. But preparing the crusade was more than just filling a war chest, assembling and equipping a fleet and army, though all this was done on a prodigious scale. In addition his frontiers had to be made secure. To this end he sent John to deal with the Lord Rhys, while he met the other Welsh princes at Worcester in September. Although he refused to meet Rhys himself, the fact that no Welsh prince is known to have supported John's revolt while Richard was in prison suggests that the measures taken in 1189 were effective. His dealings with Scotland were even more successful. He met King William at Canterbury in December 1189; in return for 10,000 marks he restored Roxburgh and Berwick and freed the kingdom of Scotland from 'the heavy yoke of servitude' (*Chronica de Mailros*, 98) to which Henry II had subjected it. Far from invading the north in 1193, William contributed 2000 marks towards Richard's ransom. Internal political arrangements presented a more intractable problem; his brother John had not taken the cross and was evidently not going to be satisfied with his lordship of Ireland. Richard's solution was to endow him with great estates while keeping real power—in the shape of castles—in the hands of ministers whom he trusted, above all William de Longchamp and then Walter de Coutances. It did not prevent John from rebelling but probably nothing could have done. On 11 December 1189 Richard crossed from Dover to Calais, and before the end of the year met Philip to confirm that their joint crusade would start from Vézelay on 1 April 1190.

On 15 March Queen Isabella of France died. On 16 March the two kings met again; their departure was postponed. This may well have suited Richard. His frontier with Toulouse also had to be made secure. Alone of all the major French princes, Raymond (V) had not taken the cross, and he was still smarting from the defeats of 1186–8. Richard's solution was to make a marriage alliance with Navarre—not at all easy when his promise to marry Alix had only recently been confirmed, and when to humiliate Philip by publicly discarding his sister would jeopardize the already long-delayed crusade. It might work if he could postpone the Navarre match until the crusade was well under way, but it cannot have been easy to persuade Sancho VI of Navarre to agree that at some future date he would send his daughter *Berengaria (*c.*1165–1230) to be married somewhere in the Mediterranean to a man who had just broken off another betrothal. Richard had visited Gascony in February, but very probably he needed more time to complete such delicate negotiations; May and early June found him once again close to the border with Navarre. As subsequent events show, somehow or other the terms of the alliance were agreed.

Winter in Sicily, 1190–1191 The two kings left Vézelay on 4 July 1190. It had been agreed that they would share the spoils of war equally between them. At Lyons the two armies separated. Richard had arranged to rendezvous at Marseilles with the huge fleet that he had raised in England, Normandy, Brittany, and Aquitaine, which was to transport his troops to join the Christian army at the siege of Acre. But a drunken spree at Lisbon led to the fleet's being delayed, and, after waiting a week at Marseilles, Richard hired ships to send one contingent on ahead to Outremer (as the crusading settlements in the Levant were known), while he with ten transport ships and twenty galleys took a leisurely trip along the Italian coast, visiting places of interest, including the medical school at Salerno, in order to give his fleet time to meet him at the next rendezvous in Sicily. On 23 September he staged a grand entrance at Messina and conferred with Philip. Since Philip immediately set out for the Holy Land, it seems probable that Richard broached the subject of his revised marriage plans. However, the wind shifted and Philip, to his dismay, was forced to return to Messina.

Richard had family and crusade business in Sicily. King Tancred (r. 1189–94) had held Richard's sister *Joanna in close confinement ever since the death of her husband, William II, in 1189. By 28 September Richard had secured her release, but Tancred continued to withhold her dower as well as the legacy—money, gold plate, and galleys—that William II had left as a crusade subsidy to Henry II, and which Richard now claimed as his. Tension mounted, exacerbated by friction between the newly arrived troops and the mainly Greek population of Messina. On 2 October Richard unloaded his ships as though planning to take over the island by force. When rioting broke out on 4 October, Richard ordered an assault on the city. It was taken in less time, said the minstrel–historian Ambroise, than it would have taken a priest to say matins. Tancred rapidly came to terms—the treaty of Messina concluded on 6 October 1190. He paid 20,000 ounces of gold in lieu of Joanna's dower, plus a further 20,000 which Richard promised would be settled on Tancred's daughter when she married Arthur of Brittany (d. 1203), now declared his heir presumptive. In return Richard agreed that while he was in Sicily he would help Tancred against any invader—a provision directed against Heinrich VI of Germany (r.

1190–97), in whose eyes Tancred was a usurper. The customary winter closure of shipping lanes in the Mediterranean meant that the crusaders would now have to stay in Sicily until the spring. Presumably at about this time a messenger was sent to Navarre.

The winter months were spent refitting the fleet and building siege-machines. Richard visited Abbot Joachim di Fiore, who prophesied that he would drive the infidels out of the Holy Land. In February 1191 Richard's mother, Eleanor, and Berengaria, escorted by Philippe, count of Flanders, reached Naples. The count was allowed to sail on to Messina but they were detained by Tancred's officials. Howden believed that Philip Augustus, desperate to save Alix, had been feeding Tancred with stories about Richard's designs on Sicily. At a meeting with Tancred on 3 March Richard succeeded in dispelling these fears, and Philip now had to acquiesce in his sister's abandonment. If he had not, wrote Howden, Richard would have produced many witnesses to testify that she had been Henry II's mistress. Faced with this terrible threat to his sister's honour Philip released Richard from his vow. In return for 10,000 marks he allowed Richard to retain the strategically vital district of the Norman Vexin (including the great castle of Gisors) which he had hitherto regarded as his sister's marriage portion. He set sail from Messina on 30 March, a few hours before Eleanor and Berengaria arrived. For the moment the marriage of Richard and Berengaria was postponed; no one could enjoy a good wedding in Lent.

The conquest of Cyprus On 10 April Richard's immense force of some 200 ships and as many as 17,000 soldiers and seamen left Messina. On the third day out a storm blew up and at their first rendezvous off Crete it was discovered that twenty-five ships were missing, including the great ship carrying Joanna and Berengaria. While the main fleet sailed on to Rhodes, the galleys scattered in search of the lost ship. It was found at anchor off Limasol, and in danger of being arrested by Isaac Ducas Komnenos, the self-proclaimed emperor of Cyprus, who had already seized the cargoes and survivors from two wrecked crusader ships. On 6 May Richard arrived on the scene. When Isaac refused to return prisoners and plunder, he ordered—and led—an amphibious assault. Limasol was quickly captured. Isaac announced that he would give battle next day but he had underestimated his opponent. During the night Richard had the horses disembarked and exercised. Before the Cypriots were fully awake, their camp fell to a surprise attack. Isaac managed to get away but he lost arms, treasure, and reputation. On 12 May Richard and Berengaria were married in the chapel of St George at Limasol. Soon afterwards peace talks with Isaac broke down, and Richard set about the conquest of Cyprus. Giving command of the land forces to Gui de Lusignan who had arrived on 11 May with news and troops from Acre, Richard himself took charge of one of the two galley fleets that sailed round the island in opposite directions, seizing ports and shipping. Isaac might well have held out in the mountains, but, when Richard captured his daughter at

Kyrenia, he surrendered. He made, it was said, just one condition—that he should not be put in irons; Richard had him fettered in silver. By 1 June Richard was master of the whole island. He imposed a heavy tax on the population in return for confirming their customs. Whether or not the conquest of Cyprus had been planned during the winter months in Messina, it proved to be a strategic masterstroke, vital to the survival of the Latin kingdom.

In the kingdom of Jerusalem: Acre and Arsuf On 8 June 1191 Richard joined the army that had been besieging Acre for nearly two years. Since his arrival on 20 April the French king had been supporting Gui de Lusignan's bitter rival Conrad de Montferrat, so it was inevitable that the quarrel of the two kings would intensify, as did the military pressure on Acre, once Richard's siege equipment was disembarked and his galleys had completed the blockade. After Saladin's final attempt to take the besiegers' heavily fortified camp by storm was beaten back on 4 July, the exhausted defenders capitulated. Terms were agreed on 12 July: the garrison to be ransomed in return for 200,000 dinars, the release of 1500 of Saladin's prisoners, and the restoration of the relic of the True Cross—all to be found by 20 August. As the banners of the two kings were raised over Acre, so too was a third banner, the standard of Leopold, duke of Austria, leader of the small German contingent. Richard's soldiers tore it down. The two kings had no intention of letting Leopold claim a share of the spoils that they had agreed to divide equally between them. But Philip Augustus was already keen to return to France. Count Philippe of Flanders had died on 1 June, and Philip could now claim possession of Artois. At Acre, Philip was daily outbid by a king whose war chest had been replenished in Cyprus. Richard, as Saladin's secretary Baha ad-Din observed, was greater than Philip in wealth, reputation, and valour. Philip stayed long enough to sit with Richard in judgment on the competing claims of Gui and Conrad; on 28 July they awarded the kingdom to Gui for his lifetime and then to Conrad. On 31 July Philip left Acre. He left Hugues of Burgundy to collect his share of the ransom (on which Richard advanced 5000 marks) and to command those of his followers who chose to remain. Philip's departure eased one problem. In relation to Richard he had been, wrote Richard of Devizes, 'like a hammer tied to the tail of a cat' (*Chronicon*, ed. Appleby, 78). On the other hand, in Leopold and Philip, Richard had made two enemies, and they returned to Europe ahead of him.

By 20 August Saladin had not paid even the first instalment of the ransom; it may be that he could not, or he may have been trying to delay things. The crusaders had to move on towards Jerusalem and Richard and his fellow commanders doubtless calculated that they could not afford to leave 3000 prisoners to be guarded and fed in Acre. In the afternoon the captives were slaughtered, only the garrison commanders being spared. According to Ambroise, the Christian soldiers enjoyed the work of butchery. On 22 August the march south to Jaffa began. The army kept close to the sea, its right flank protected by the fleet, which now included the Egyptian galleys captured in Acre. Heat and incessant harassing by mounted archers meant that the pace was painfully slow, but Saladin could not break their disciplined advance. On 7 September at Arsuf he decided to risk battle. He eventually succeeded in provoking the hospitallers into launching a premature charge, but Richard's swift response conjured victory out of imminent confusion. On 10 September the crusaders reached Jaffa. The soldiers needed a rest and Jaffa's walls, which Saladin had dismantled, had to be rebuilt.

A letter Richard wrote in October shows that he was already thinking in terms of the thirteenth-century maxim that the keys of Jerusalem were to be found in Cairo. Nearly all the troops, however, were passionately in favour of the direct route and not even the victor of Acre and Arsuf enjoyed sufficient prestige to persuade them otherwise. November and December were spent rebuilding the castles on the pilgrims' road from Jaffa to Jerusalem. Soon after Christmas the army reached Beit Nuba, 12 miles from Jerusalem. They could avoid military realities no longer. Even though Richard's patient war of attrition had at last forced Saladin to disband the bulk of his troops, he stayed in Jerusalem; while he was there the crusaders' own logistical problems meant that laying siege to the city was impossibly risky. In any case even if they managed to take Jerusalem, they did not have the numbers to occupy and defend it—especially since many of the most devout crusaders, having fulfilled their pilgrim vows, would at once go home. Reluctantly an army council decided to go to Ascalon, a step in the direction of Egypt which the duke of Burgundy refused to take.

The end of the crusade Richard reached Ascalon on 20 January 1192, and its rebuilding began—mostly at his expense. As a base from which caravans travelling between Syria and Egypt could be raided, it should in due course be a source of profit for its new lord, Richard's old enemy, Geoffroi de Lusignan. Hugues of Burgundy then appeared wanting to borrow more money; when Richard refused, he withdrew to Acre and in alliance with Conrad de Montferrat and the Genoese tried to seize control of the city. Gui's allies, the Pisans, kept them at bay until they fled to Tyre on hearing that Richard was on his way. He remained at Acre for six weeks, managing to reconcile the Pisans and Genoese, but failing to shift Conrad from the policy of non co-operation which he had pursued ever since Philip's departure. On 15 April, two weeks after his return to Ascalon, Richard received disquieting news which forced him to think about returning to his dominions and hence about what would happen if he left behind a kingdom torn apart by faction. Recognizing that Gui would be no match for a politician as clever and ambitious as Conrad, he summoned a council to pronounce in favour of Conrad as king; he compensated Gui by selling him Cyprus in return for a down payment of 60,000 bezants. He then sent Count Henri of Champagne to Tyre to inform the new king of his good fortune. No sooner had this been done than, on 28 April, Conrad was murdered by two

Assassins. Local chronicles give the simplest explanation of the murder as the outcome of a quarrel between Conrad and Rashid al-Din Sinan, the head of the Syrian branch of the Assassins. Naturally, however, rumours abounded. Many people said Richard had bribed Sinan, the 'Old Man of the Mountain'; others said Saladin had; yet another candidate for this secret role was Humphrey de Toron, the discarded first husband of Conrad's wife, Isabella. As the most favoured claimant to the title of queen of Jerusalem, Isabella could not remain without a third husband for long. On 5 May she was married to Henri of Champagne. As nephew of both Richard and Philip Augustus he was well placed to reconcile the factions—as was shown when both he and Duke Hugues answered Richard's summons to the siege of Darum, 20 miles south of Ascalon. In the event Richard captured it on 22 May, the day before they arrived.

A week later reliable news came to Richard of his brother's treasonable dealings with Philip. To complicate matters further, a meeting of the army council decided to make another attempt on Jerusalem. Faced by impossible choices Richard retired to his tent for several days before announcing that he was ready to stay until next Easter and would go with them to Jerusalem. (As it happened, Eleanor held John in check, and his own nobles restrained Philip.) By 29 June the entire crusader army was at Beit Nuba again. Confronted by the realities, the army hesitated. Richard urged an attack on Egypt. According to Ambroise, on one patrol he rode to the top of a hill from which he saw Jerusalem. In later legend it was said that he covered his eyes with his shield so that he did not see what he could not take. A committee of twenty (five templars, five hospitallers, five barons of Outremer, and five of France) was set up; it was agreed that all would abide by its decision. But when it opted for Egypt the duke of Burgundy refused. Hopelessly split, the army could only retreat.

Richard reopened negotiations with Saladin, dismantled Darum, and strengthened Ascalon, before returning to Acre on 26 July. Next day Saladin launched a surprise attack on Jaffa. Richard sailed south as soon as he heard, but by the time his galleys reached Jaffa (1 August) the town had been captured and only the citadel was still holding out. Richard himself led the assault up the beach and into the town. That day, said Ambroise (and not for the first time), his prowess exceeded Roland's at Roncesvaux. Three days later when Saladin attacked again, Richard combined spearmen and crossbowmen in a solid defensive formation which the Muslim cavalry could not break. By now both sides were weary, and Richard himself fell seriously ill. A three-year truce was agreed on 2 September; Richard had to hand back Ascalon and Darum; Saladin granted Christian pilgrims free access to Jerusalem. Many crusaders took advantage of this facility, but not Richard. Finally he was well enough to set sail on 9 October, worryingly late in the year. He had failed to take Jerusalem, but the entire coast from Tyre to Jaffa was now in Christian hands; and so was Cyprus. Considered as an administrative, political, and military exercise, his crusade had been an astonishing success.

Prisoner in Germany By mid-November 1192 Richard had reached Corfu. There, if not before, he must have calculated that the enmity of Raymond (V) and Emperor Heinrich VI (and the latter's alliances with Pisa and Genoa) had in effect barred the most promising route back to his own dominions via Barcelona. Weather conditions at sea now meant that the most plausible alternative was to travel through eastern Germany, where a group of princes led by Richard's brother-in-law Henry the Lion, formerly duke of Saxony and Bavaria, was in opposition to Heinrich VI. It was a gamble because it involved passing through the territory of Leopold of Austria, but at least he would be going where he was not expected. At Corfu he hired galleys and went north with a handful of trusted companions. They survived shipwreck on the Istrian coast and then headed for Moravia disguised as pilgrims. Suspicions were soon aroused and, although they evaded the hunt for three days, they were finally captured near Vienna (only 50 miles from safety). By 28 December the emperor had been informed that Leopold held the king of England prisoner in the castle of Dürnstein. Heinrich wrote to Philip, 'We know this news will bring you great joy' (*Chronica magistri Rogeri de Hovedene*, 3.195–6). By mid-January 1193 John also knew, and hastened to do homage to Philip. The church claimed to protect returning crusaders and the pope excommunicated Leopold, but no one took any notice. For more than a year kings and princes haggled over the price of Richard's freedom. Heinrich and Leopold agreed terms on 14 February 1193 and Richard was then transferred to the emperor's custody. At an imperial court held at Speyer (21–25 March) he had to defend himself against charges of betraying the Holy Land and plotting the death of Conrad de Montferrat. Even his enemies were impressed by his self-possessed bearing. In the words of Guillaume le Breton, Richard 'spoke so eloquently and regally, in so lionhearted a manner, it was as though he were seated on an ancestral throne at Lincoln or Caen' (Delaborde, 2.112). The charges were dropped, but fortune had dealt Heinrich—who had been in considerable political difficulties—a trump card and he had no intention of giving it away. At Speyer, Richard agreed to pay a ransom of 100,000 marks and to supply the emperor with 50 galleys and 200 knights for a year.

Had Richard returned safely early in 1193 he would have found the Angevin empire in good shape. In England the justiciar, Longchamp, had failed to survive a political crisis orchestrated by John in the autumn of 1191 but, to John's chagrin, Longchamp had been replaced by the archbishop of Rouen, Walter de Coutances, whom Richard had sent back from Sicily earlier that summer in order to take care of just such an eventuality. In 1192 Philip and Raymond (V) managed to stir up rebellion in Aquitaine, but Richard's marriage alliance proved its worth. With the aid of Berengaria's brother, Sancho of Navarre, the seneschal Elie de la Celle was able to suppress the revolt and launch a punitive raid against Toulouse. Another Aquitanian rebellion early in 1193 was also suppressed,

and its leader, Count Audemar of Angoulême, captured. But on 12 April 1193 Philip at last inflicted a severe blow when the castellan of Gisors, Gilbert de Vascoeuil, surrendered without a fight. Presumably Gilbert calculated that John, Philip's eager ally, would soon be duke of Normandy, and that he had best align himself with the likely victors. In this sense John's rebellion against his brother, though it had small success in England, turned out to be critical. Philip arranged to meet Heinrich VI on 25 June, an indication that Richard's position was continuing to deteriorate. To persuade the emperor to cancel the conference with Philip, Richard had to renegotiate his ransom terms; he would now be released only after 100,000 marks had been paid and hostages for an additional 50,000 handed over. (However, the emperor's promise to remit the 50,000 if Richard could persuade Henry the Lion to make peace on acceptable terms indicates the extent to which, even in captivity, Richard had political weight and the diplomatic skill to make it count—as indeed he had already demonstrated in bringing about a reconciliation between the emperor and some of his other opponents.)

The king returns The cancellation of his conference led Philip to believe that, as he wrote to John, 'the devil is loosed' (*Chronica magistri Rogeri de Hovedene*, 3.216–17). Even so the terms of the treaty of Mantes (9 July 1193), which he negotiated with Richard's agents, show just how strong the French king's position was. He insisted on the release of Count Audemar, kept all his gains, and in addition was given four key castles—Loches, Châtillon-sur-Indre, Drincourt, and Arques—as security for Richard's promise to pay him 20,000 marks. In the event not until Christmas did the emperor receive enough of the ransom to fix a day for Richard's release: 17 January 1194. Philip and John at once put in a counter-offer. Heinrich was tempted and summoned the German princes to an assembly at Mainz on 2 February 1194. Here Richard's good relations with the princes bore fruit. On 4 February he was set free; two of Henry the Lion's sons were among the hostages he provided. On his mother's advice he resigned his kingdom to Heinrich VI and received it back as an imperial fief. In return emperor and princes wrote to Philip and John, threatening war if they did not restore all they had taken. On his way back to England, Richard renewed his alliances with the major princes of the Rhineland. On 13 March he landed at Sandwich and then, after visiting the shrines of Canterbury and Bury St Edmunds, went to Nottingham where the last of John's garrisons still held out. After some fierce fighting the castle surrendered on 28 March. On 17 April at Winchester, Richard wore his crown in state. On 12 May he sailed to Normandy, never to return, leaving the government of England in the remarkably capable hands of Hubert Walter (*d.* 1205), with whom he had become well acquainted on crusade, and whom in 1193—while in prison—he had appointed archbishop of Canterbury and justiciar.

Unlike England, the duchy was in a parlous state. In January 1194 John had granted Philip the castle of Vaudreuil and the lands south and east of the River Itun, as well as the whole of the duchy east of the Seine except for

Rouen itself. By the time Richard landed at Barfleur, Philip had succeeded in taking possession of much of this territory, including channel ports such as Dieppe and Le Tréport in the lordships of Arques and Eu. Yet, although the tide of war in Normandy appeared to be flowing in Philip's favour, no sooner had Richard returned than John rushed to beg—and receive—forgiveness. On 29 May Richard raised Philip's siege of Verneuil, then moved south to enter Tours (which John had also given away) on 11 June, before taking Loches with the help of Navarrese troops on 13 June. Philip followed Richard into the Loire valley in the hope of inhibiting his freedom of movement but, as soon as Richard threatened to engage him in battle, at Fréteval on 4 July, he took flight, losing his entire baggage train, including treasure and archives. Richard now had a free hand to deal with Philip's friends in Aquitaine. On 22 July he sent a boastfully laconic note to Hubert Walter:

> Know that by God's grace which in all things upholds the right, we have captured Taillebourg and Marcillac and the whole land of Geoffroi de Rancon; also the city of Angoulême, Châteauneuf-sur-Charente, Montignac, Lachaise and all the other castles and the whole land of the count of Angoulême; the city and citadel of Angoulême we captured in a single evening; in all we took 300 knights and 40,000 soldiers.   (*Chronica magistri Rogeri de Hovedene*, 3.256–7)

War for Normandy So emphatic a restoration of Angevin authority could not be achieved in Normandy. The Norman castles of the Seine valley and the Vexin were of such importance to the French king at Paris that a campaign to wrest them from his grasp would require massive and expensive preparation. Hence Richard's acceptance until 1 November 1195 of the truce that his representatives in Normandy negotiated on 23 July 1194. In fact the truce was always poorly kept and by the summer of 1195 full-scale war had broken out. Richard's strategy involved pressure both in Normandy and in the Auvergne and Berry where his forces captured Issoudun. To add to Philip's worries, Heinrich VI, enriched by the spoils of Sicily which he had conquered with Richard's money, announced his intention of helping his vassal. By August Philip was ready to restore virtually all his conquests in return for a marriage treaty between his heir, Louis, and Richard's niece Eleanor, which would guarantee him secure possession of the Vexin; indeed, realizing he could not hold castles like Vaudreuil, he had begun to dismantle them. Although completion of peace talks was deferred until the emperor had been consulted, Richard returned Alix to Philip who promptly (20 August) gave her in marriage to the count of Ponthieu with Eu and Arques as her dowry. In consequence the struggle for Dieppe was renewed and the port sacked in November 1195. Later that month Philip laid siege to Issoudun, but was outmanoeuvred by Richard's speed of response and had to agree to the treaty of Louviers in January 1196. Not only did Philip resign all his conquests except the Norman Vexin and six castles elsewhere on the Norman–Capetian border; he was also forced to abandon the new count of Toulouse, Raymond (VI). This paved the way for the diplomatic revolution finalized at Rouen in October 1196 when Richard renounced his claim to Toulouse, restored the Quercy, and gave his sister Joanna, together with the Agenais as her dowry, in marriage to Raymond (VI). This, wrote William of Newburgh, marked the end of an exhausting forty years' war and freed Richard to concentrate his resources on the struggle against Philip.

This was just as well, since elsewhere 1196 went badly for Richard. The threat to his control of the channel posed by Philip's allies, the counts of Ponthieu and Boulogne, was increased when Philip won over the new count of Flanders, Baudouin (IX). Then the commercially vital shipping lanes to Poitou were put at risk, when the Bretons responded to Richard's demand for custody of his nine-year-old nephew *Arthur by appealing for help to Philip. A massive invasion of Brittany by naval and land forces in April 1196 countered that threat, but not before Arthur had been given asylum by the king of France. In the war that followed Richard suffered set-backs. He was wounded in the knee by a crossbow bolt while vainly besieging Gaillon; he was defeated by Philip and Baudouin when he tried to lift their siege of Aumale. When Aumale surrendered late in August it cost him 3000 marks to ransom the garrison. Yet by July 1197 Philip's most valuable ally had been persuaded to change sides. Richard first imposed a crippling embargo on Flemish trade and then rewarded Count Baudouin's new allegiance with generous gifts of cash and wine. From then on the tide of diplomacy and war flowed strongly in Richard's favour. While he campaigned in Berry, capturing Vierzon and other castles, Baudouin invaded Artois, taking the rich town of Douai. A truce based on the status quo of September 1197 meant that Philip had lost territory on two fronts. In February 1198 a group of German princes, at Richard's suggestion, elected his nephew Otto as king in succession to Heinrich VI. Some of Philip's most powerful vassals, the counts of Boulogne, St Pol, Perche, and Blois, decided that the time had come to join the winning side.

Reconquest of the Vexin When the truce expired in September 1198 Richard at last set about the systematic recovery of the Vexin. This Philip had to prevent; in consequence Baudouin, given a free hand in Artois, was able to take Aire and St Omer. And by forcing Philip to march to the relief of his castles Richard had him where he wanted him. Twice Philip had to run for safety. On the second occasion, on 28 September, so hot was Richard's pursuit that the bridge of Gisors collapsed under the weight of knights struggling to reach safety. Philip himself was dragged out of the river, but more than 120 Capetian knights were drowned or captured. 'We ourselves unhorsed three knights with a single lance' wrote Richard (*Chronica magistri Rogeri de Hovedene*, 4.58). After this Philip was left with little but Gisors. The reconquest had been well prepared. For this Richard had embarked on the greatest building project of his life at Les Andelys—not just the castle, Château Gaillard, high on the Rock of Andelys, but also a new river-port, a new town (Petit-Andelys), and the new palace (on the Isle of Andelys), which became his favourite residence. Recorded expenditure here for the two years ending September 1198 was more than recorded expenditure on all royal castles in England during his entire reign. Merely to acquire the site he had to bully the church of Rouen into accepting two manors and Dieppe in exchange. But Andelys was vital, for it constituted one end of the strategic lifeline of the Angevin empire; at the other lay Richard's new port, palace, and town of Portsmouth. Linked to the arsenal at Rouen by cart and barge—the latter sailing under the protection of galleys—it was the great forward base, only 5 miles from Philip's castle of Gaillon, from which the recovery of the Vexin had been organized.

Death Richard had always proclaimed his intention of returning to the East once he had regained his own lands. Now Pope Innocent III (r. 1198–1216) summoned a new crusade and sent a legate to make peace. On 13 January 1199 the kings met and agreed to a five-year truce. Philip was ready to hand back everything else in return for a marriage treaty that left Gisors securely in the hands of his heir. In March, while negotiations continued, Richard took an army to the south. On 26 March he was wounded in the shoulder by a crossbow bolt while reconnoitring Châlus-Chabrol, a small castle belonging to Aimar de Limoges. When the wound turned gangrenous, Richard named John as his heir, bequeathed his jewels to Otto, and forgave the man who shot him. He died on 6 April and was buried at Fontevrault, beside his father (his heart was buried in Rouen Cathedral). The rumour spread—and was reported by a number of French and English historians— that he had gone to Châlus to claim treasure trove. However, Bernard Itier, the local historian from the abbey of St Martial at Limoges, certainly better informed about the circumstances that led to his death than any other reporter, had not a word to say about treasure. Once again Richard had been drawn to the Limousin in order to suppress a rebellion encouraged by King Philip and led by the vicomte of Limoges and the count of Angoulême. He had not been killed in a trivial sideshow, but in confronting what had long been the most serious problem in the politics of Aquitaine.

The sinews of war Opinions were divided as to the justice of the wars that Richard fought as duke, but there was no division of opinion within the Angevin empire about the wars he undertook as king. All agreed that they were just wars fought for the recovery of legitimate rights, whether in Outremer or in the West. For his crusade, for his ransom, and then for his war against Philip, he made heavy financial demands on his subjects everywhere, from Cyprus to England. Although the records do not permit useful global estimates to be given, it is clear that huge sums were raised. On crusade Richard was, in the words of a German chronicler, greater in wealth and resources than all other kings. The bulk of his ransom must have been raised by an extraordinary 25 per cent levy of the value of all rents and moveables (the highest rate in the history of this tax), but after his release more traditional fiscal methods were generally employed: scutages, carucages, reliefs, and the profits of royal patronage.

It was done systematically and with a ruthless efficiency which at times smacked of chicanery. Men who thought they had bought their offices in 1189 were dismayed to be told in 1194 that in reality they had only leased them for a term of years, that the term had expired, and that new bids were now in order. In 1198 charters granted under the king's seal were declared void unless renewed under a new seal. In Coggeshall's opinion, Richard's cupidity endangered his soul; 'no age can remember or history tell of any king who demanded and took so much money from his kingdom as this king extorted and amassed within the five years after his return from his captivity' (*Chronicon Anglicanum*, 93). Yet there was a grudging acceptance that the money was raised for honourable causes and efficiently expended. Hence Newburgh's comment that, although Richard taxed more heavily than his father had done, people complained less. Whereas English historians give the impression that English taxpayers bore the brunt, a comparison of the Norman and English exchequer rolls suggests that the Norman taxpayers were particularly hard-pressed.

The fact that such vast sums were raised suggests an efficient administration, and implies that, when appointing chief ministers, Richard generally chose competent men for his continental dominions—men such as Robert of Thornham (d. 1211) in Anjou, Geoffroi de la Celle in Aquitaine, and William Fitzralph in Normandy—as well as for England. In England no new assizes were issued while he was on crusade and in Germany (though routine judicial and financial government continued), but once he was back in his dominions administrative innovation resumed. Unquestionably much of the credit for this must go to Hubert Walter, one of the ablest ministers in English history, but it was the king who made him justiciar and who, against mounting ecclesiastical pressure, persuaded the archbishop to stay in government office until 1198. It was the king who, when Hubert resigned the justiciarship, found a highly competent replacement in Geoffrey fitz Peter (d. 1213). Political and military obligations and pressures meant that Richard's presence was required not in England but on the continent and in the Mediterranean. However, like other masterful kings of England, he found no difficulty in governing it from abroad. He intervened frequently and decisively in English secular and ecclesiastical business, even during Hubert Walter's justiciarship, and there is certainly no evidence that he neglected his duties. In 1189, according to Howden, after he had imposed a settlement on the long-drawn-out dispute between the archbishop and monks of Canterbury, provided for Scotland and for his brother John, 'everyone went home commending and praising the king's great deeds' (*Gesta ... Benedicti*, 2.99). It is not surprising that hopeful English litigants visited him even when in Sicily or in prison. There is no evidence that anyone thought him addicted, as were many of his contemporaries, to the pleasures of the chase or the tournament, though he appreciated the latter's value as training for real war, and by organizing the holding of tournaments in England—and charging fees for them—he broke with the cautious custom of his predecessors.

The character of a legend It was entirely in character that Richard should have been fatally wounded while engaged in close reconnaissance. From 1173 onwards a series of wars dominated his life. Although good-quality armour could make participation in war a safer pursuit than hunting, the fact that he was prepared to plunge into the thick of the fray meant that at times he took his life in his hands. Even an admirer as fervent as Ambroise could imagine that Saladin would judge Richard to possess 'courage carried to excess' (*Crusade of Richard Lionheart*, l.12,152). It was not, however, mindless courage. In part it was based upon a morality of command. Hence the words attributed to him when, against advice, he went to the rescue of a foraging party in difficulties: 'I sent those men there. If they die without me, may I never again be called a king' (ibid., ll.7345–8). In part it was based upon a commander's perception of morale. Knowing that he would share the risks they ran, his men, in the words of Richard of Devizes, 'would wade in blood to the Pillars of Hercules if he so desired' (*Chronicon*, ed. Appleby, 21). In planning and organizing wars on the scale of the crusade or the recovery of his dominions in France he was a cool and patient strategist, as much a master of sea power as of land forces. Defeated opponents commonly complained that he had cunningly taken them by surprise. But friends and rivals alike testified to his individual prowess and valour. In his lifetime he was already known as Coeur de Lion. These qualities endangered his life, but they impressed enemy troops as well as his own, and while he lived they made him a supremely effective soldier. After his death they ensured that the image of the legendary warrior–hero lived on. Understanding the value of a legendary reputation, he preached what he practised. The letters in which he inflated his own achievements were intended for wide circulation. He consciously associated himself with the world of romance, as when he rode out of Vézelay bearing Excalibur. But he was also a businesslike king; in Sicily he exchanged King Arthur's sword for four transport ships and fifteen galleys.

The evidence is too fragmentary and contradictory to give a reliable impression of Richard's physical appearance. The effigy on his tomb at Fontevrault dates from several decades after his death. The chronicler Ralph Coggeshall, who vividly remembered the ferocious look and tone with which Richard greeted anyone who interrupted him at work, implies that by 1199 he was running to fat; if so he still remained a fighting knight. On several occasions the magnificence of his dress drew admiring comment—another aspect of his awareness of the impact of display. (He is the first king of England whose charters employed the royal 'we' of majesty.) He participated in the music of the royal chapel and took the ritual of the church seriously—it was, after all, a ritual that exalted kings, an ecclesiastical drama in which the king, enthroned, played a central role. On crusade Richard insisted on playing a starring role, but he was also deeply committed to the religious obligation to recover the patrimony of Christ; it happened to coincide with his duty as family man and lord to restore the kingdom of Jerusalem to his cousins, the junior branch of the Angevin family, and to its rightful king, Gui de Lusignan, one of his own vassals. He founded several religious houses: a Premonstratensian abbey (Le-Lieu-Dieu-en-Jard) and a Benedictine priory (Gourfailles) in the Vendée; and an abbey for the Cistercians, with whom he had a close relationship, at Bonport in Normandy.

William of Newburgh assumed that Richard would find pleasure in his marriage to Berengaria. But they seem to have spent little time together after 1192 and they had no children. He had an illegitimate son, Philip, to whom he gave the lordship of Cognac. Contemporaries and near contemporaries clearly assumed he was heterosexual. The late twentieth-century idea that he was homosexual is based upon an anachronistic interpretation of the evidence, though in the final analysis his sexuality must remain unknown. He comes across as an intelligent man—famous for his pointed witticisms—and as a ruler driven by the tasks he had to deal with. Even his songs were composed with politics in mind. His main sin was arrogance, the confident assumption that there was no problem he could not solve: in consequence he sometimes made enemies casually, but he then faced them, even when in prison, in a calm and self-possessed manner.

Historiography Inevitably historians attached to the courts of Philip Augustus and his allies took a hostile view, but not even Philip's panegyrist conceals his underlying admiration for Richard. According to Guillaume le Breton, had Richard been more God-fearing, and had he not fought against his lord, Philip of France, England would never have had a better king. Some English historians such as Coggeshall and William of Newburgh mix praise with criticism. Newburgh disapproves of Longchamp and thinks Richard overgenerous to John. A German contemporary, Walther von der Vogelweide, believes that it was precisely Richard's generosity that made his subjects willing to raise a king's ransom on his behalf. Richard's reputation, above all as a crusader, meant that the tone of contemporaries and near contemporaries, whether writing in the West or the Middle East, was overwhelmingly favourable. According to Baha ad-Din, Richard was a man of wisdom, experience, courage, and energy. Ibn al-Athir judges him the most remarkable ruler of his time for courage, shrewdness, energy, and patience. In France St Louis's biographer Joinville portrays Richard as a model for St Louis to follow. In England he became a standard by which later kings were judged. Even in Scotland, thanks to the quitclaim of Canterbury, he won a high place in historical tradition; according to John Fordun, he was 'that noble king so friendly to the Scots' (*Chronica gentis Scottorum*, 2.271).

For at least four centuries Richard remained what he had always been: a model king. Holinshed in his *Chronicles* calls him 'a notable example to all princes' (R. Holinshed, *Chronicles of England, Scotlande and Irelande*, 1578, 2.266); for John Speed he is 'this triumphal and bright shining star of chivalry' (J. Speed, *The Historie of Great Britain*, 1611, 481). The first serious note of dissent comes from the Stuart courtier–poet and historian Samuel Daniel who criticizes

Richard for wasting English resources on the crusade and other foreign projects—'gleaning out what possible this kingdom could yield, to consume the same in his business of France' (S. Daniel, *The Collection of the History of England*, 1621 edn, 105). In later centuries Daniel's remarkably original and consciously anachronistic interpretation gradually became the common opinion of scholars. David Hume, for example, the most influential eighteenth-century historian of England, breaking with Scottish tradition, describes Richard as 'better calculated to dazzle men by the splendour of his enterprises, than either to promote their happiness or his own grandeur by a sound and well-regulated policy' (D. Hume, *History of England*, 1871 reprint of 1786 edn, 1.279). In consequence, although works of literary fiction, most notably *Ivanhoe* (1819) and *The Talisman* (1825) by Walter Scott, continued to present a glamorous image of Richard I, one given lasting visual form by the equestrian statue of the king by Carlo Marochetti which was financed by public subscription and placed outside the houses of parliament in 1860, virtually all historians came to think of Richard as 'a bad ruler' (Stubbs, *Gesta*, xxvii), an absentee king who neglected his kingdom. This perception came to be so powerful that the early twentieth-century historians who worked in most detail on his reign, Kate Norgate and Maurice Powicke, challenged it only by implication. At a popular level the idea of a king who was 'never there' was reinforced by Richard's legendary association with Robin Hood. The 'Little England' view of Richard is summed up by A. L. Poole in the *Oxford History of England*. 'He used England as a bank on which to draw and overdraw in order to finance his ambitious exploits abroad' (*From Domesday Book to Magna Carta*, 2nd edn, 1955, 350). Since 1978 this insular approach has been increasingly questioned. It is now more widely acknowledged that Richard was head of a dynasty with far wider responsibilities than merely English ones, and that in judging a ruler's political acumen more weight might be attached to contemporary opinion than to views which occurred to no one until many centuries after his death.

JOHN GILLINGHAM

Sources W. Stubbs, ed., *Gesta regis Henrici secundi Benedicti abbatis: the chronicle of the reigns of Henry II and Richard I, AD 1169–1192*, 2 vols., Rolls Series, 49 (1867) · *Chronica magistri Rogeri de Hovedene*, ed. W. Stubbs, 4 vols., Rolls Series, 51 (1868–71) · *Radulfi de Diceto … opera historica*, ed. W. Stubbs, 2 vols., Rolls Series, 68 (1876) · *Radulphi de Coggeshall chronicon Anglicanum*, ed. J. Stevenson, Rolls Series, 66 (1875) · *Cronicon Richardi Divisensis tempore regis Richardi primi*, ed. and trans. J. T. Appleby (1963) · R. Howlett, ed., *Chronicles of the reigns of Stephen, Henry II, and Richard I*, 4 vols., Rolls Series, 82 (1884–9), vols. 1–2 · A. Holden, S. Gregory, and D. Crouch, eds., *The history of William Marshal*, 3 vols., Anglo-Norman Texts [forthcoming] · *Œuvres de Rigord et de Guillaume le Breton, historiens de Philippe-Auguste*, ed. H. F. Delaborde, 2 vols. (Paris, 1882–5) · Geoffrey de Vigeois, 'Chronica', *Novae bibliothecae manuscriptorum*, ed. P. Labbe, 2 vols. (1657) · *The crusade of Richard Lionheart by Ambroise*, ed. and trans. M. Ailes and M. Barber (2003) · H. J. Nicholson, ed. and trans., *Chronicle of the third crusade: a translation of the Itinerarium peregrinorum et gesta Regis Ricardi* (1997) · E. Mabille, 'Chronicae Sancti Albini Andegavensis', ed. P. Marchegay, *Chroniques des églises d'Anjou* (Paris, 1869), 17–61 · J. Stevenson, ed., *Chronica de Mailros*, Bannatyne Club, 50 (1835) · *The historical works of Gervase of Canterbury*, ed. W. Stubbs, 2 vols., Rolls Series, 73 (1879–80) · *The poems of the troubadour Bertran de Born*, ed. W. D. Paden, T. Sankovitch, and P. H. Stäblein (1986) · Baha al-Din Abu al-Mahasin [Ibn Shaddad], *The rare and excellent history of Saladin*, trans. D. S. Richards (2001) · *Pipe rolls* · T. Stapleton, ed., *Magni rotuli scaccarii Normanniae sub regibus Angliae*, 2 vols., Society of Antiquaries of London Occasional Papers (1840–44) · F. M. Powicke, *The loss of Normandy, 1189–1204: studies in the history of the Angevin empire*, 2nd edn (1961) · K. Norgate, *Richard the Lionheart* (1924) · L. Landon, *The itinerary of King Richard I*, PRSoc., new ser., 13 (1935) · J. Gillingham, *Richard I* (1999) · J. O. Prestwich, 'Richard Coeur de Lion: rex bellicosus', *Richard Coeur de Lion in history and myth*, ed. J. L. Nelson (1992), 1–16 · J. C. Holt, 'Ricardus rex Anglorum et dux Normannorum', *Magna Carta and medieval government* (1985) · J. Gillingham, *Richard Coeur de Lion: kingship, chivalry and war in the twelfth century* (1994) · R. V. Turner and R. R. Heiser, *The reign of Richard Lionheart* (2000) · *Johannis de Fordun Chronica gentis Scotorum / John of Fordun's Chronicle of the Scottish nation*, ed. W. F. Skene, trans. F. J. H. Skene, 2 (1872)
Likenesses tomb effigy, 13th cent., Rouen Cathedral · Proud, line engraving, BM, NPG · coins · line engraving, NPG · seals · tomb effigy, Fontevrault Abbey, Maine-et-Loire, France [*see illus.*] · wax seal, BM, PRO

Richard II (1367–1400), king of England and lord of Ireland, and duke of Aquitaine, was born in the abbey of St André at Bordeaux on the feast of the Epiphany, 6 January 1367.

Infancy and early life, 1367–1377 Richard was the second son of *Edward, prince of Wales (the Black Prince) (1330–1376), and *Joan, the 'Fair Maid of Kent' (c.1328–1385), widow of Thomas Holland, earl of Kent (d. 1360). His father had been created prince of Aquitaine in 1362 and established his court at Bordeaux. According to the chronicle of William Thorne, a monk of St Augustine's Abbey, Canterbury, three 'magi' were present at his birth, 'the king of Spain, the king of Navarre and the king of Portugal, and these kings gave precious gifts to the child' (Thorne, 91). The symbolism of the story meant much to Richard and throughout his life the feast of the Epiphany remained of special significance to him. He was baptized three days later, on 9 January 1367, by the archbishop of Bordeaux, with Jaume, the titular king of Majorca, acting as his chief sponsor. Richard remained at his father's court in Bordeaux for the first four years of his life. In January 1371, however, his elder brother, Edward of Angoulême, who had been born in 1364, died, and shortly afterwards Richard left for England with his father and mother.

With his elder brother dead Richard stood in the direct line of succession to the English throne, and the prospect of his succeeding while he was still a child was brought appreciably nearer by the deepening illness of his father, who played only a limited role in politics after his return to England, and who died on 8 April 1376. Richard was now heir to the throne, and with the health and mental capacity of his 63-year-old grandfather, Edward III, beginning to fail, his accession would probably not be long delayed. With this in mind, and perhaps to silence rumours that Edward III's eldest surviving son, *John of Gaunt, duke of Lancaster, had designs on the crown, the Commons in the Good Parliament of April–July 1376 required Richard to be brought before them on 25 June that they 'might see and honour [him] as the true heir

Richard II (1367–1400), by unknown artist, c.1388

apparent' (*RotP*, 2.330). Later that year, on 20 November, his father's titles of prince of Wales, duke of Cornwall, and earl of Chester were conferred on him, and he presided over the next parliament on 27 January 1377 in place of the ailing king.

Little is known about the companions of Richard's childhood. His household first emerges into the light with his creation as prince of Wales in 1376. Sir Simon Burley, a long-standing retainer of the Black Prince, was one of Richard's tutors and was appointed chamberlain of his household in 1376; Sir Richard Abberbury, another servant of the Black Prince, was described as Richard's 'first master' in 1376, and another close associate of the Black Prince, Sir Guichard d'Angle (*d.* 1380), was also named as his tutor. The influence these men had upon the young Richard is largely a matter of conjecture, though some historians have argued that Richard's personality and his

ideas of kingship were shaped by them. Anthony Steel, for instance, suggested that the Black Prince's choice of Burley and d'Angle as Richard's tutors was intended to ensure that 'the son was to be formed in the image of his father' (Steel, 41), though if this is so they clearly failed in their task. R. H. Jones, on the other hand, has suggested that Burley may have introduced Richard to the quasi-absolutist ideas of kingship in the writings of Giles of Rome. Unfortunately little of this can be shown to have any substance. Richard's reluctance to lead military campaigns in France as his father had done probably owes more to financial and diplomatic considerations than to any physical or psychological aversion to warfare. The development of his concept of kingship probably derives from the pressure of events and, in the 1390s, from the influence of the French court, rather than from books which his tutors may or may not have read and understood.

The king's minority, 1377–1381 Richard succeeded to throne on 22 June 1377. The day after his accession was the vigil of the feast of St John the Baptist, and throughout his reign he showed particular devotion to the saint. The most significant evidence for this is the Wilton diptych, in which the Baptist is one of the three saints who present Richard to the Virgin, but there are other representations of Richard in association with the saint, and Richard invoked him in the preamble to his will. His coronation took place nearly a month later, on 16 July. The record of the ceremony in the *Liber regalis* is the earliest detailed account of the English coronation ritual to survive, and several contemporary chroniclers describe the elaborate pageantry of the occasion. More significantly for the future, perhaps, the bishop of Rochester, Thomas Brinton, preached a sermon on the following day exhorting the nobles to show loyalty to their young and innocent king, and to strive to ensure that king and kingdom were not brought into danger.

The accession of a child king was acknowledged as a time of political peril, and there were few precedents to guide the English nobility in establishing an appropriate form of government during the king's minority. In 1216, when Henry III became king at the age of nine, William (I) Marshal had been appointed *rector regis et regni*, and discharged the functions of kingship until his death in 1219. Nine years later in France, at the death of Louis VIII, the queen dowager, Blanche, had acted as regent for the young Louis IX. In England in 1377, however, neither of these precedents was followed, and Richard nominally exercised all the powers of kingship from the time of his accession. The implications of the lack of a formal regency were substantial. A series of continual councils held office between 1377 and 1380 and discharged much routine government business, while the leading nobles, especially Gaunt and his youngest brother Thomas of Woodstock, earl of Buckingham, exercised informal influence and attended great councils from time to time. The royal household, however, increasingly became the centre of real, rather than just formal, power. Burley and Aubrey de Vere, who were both knights of the new king's chamber, dealt with petitions submitted to the king, signing those that were successful and sending them on to the council for action: from very early in the reign these two courtiers were able to exercise some control over the direction of royal patronage.

The influence which Burley and Aubrey de Vere, along with other chamber knights who were also former servants of the Black Prince, exercised over Richard soon attracted the critical attention of the Commons. In October 1378 the Commons asked to be told 'who would be the king's councillors and governors of his person' (*RotP*, 3.35), and in order to establish closer links between the household and the council Aubrey de Vere and another chamber knight, Sir Richard Rous, were appointed to the third continual council which took office in November 1378. The Commons continued, however, to complain about the extravagance of the royal household, and following the parliament of April 1379 Sir John Cobham was appointed 'to remain in the household for the safeguard of the king's person' (PRO, E 403/475 m. 8). There is little sign that his supervision had any effect, and in January 1380 the Commons successfully sought the ending of the continual councils, on the ground that Edward III at his accession had had no councillors except the five principal officers of state. They also asked for another committee of inquiry into the crown's finances and the state of the royal household. Although their petition was accepted, there is no evidence that the committee ever got down to business.

The criticisms of the Commons in the early years of Richard's reign were focused not just on the royal household but also on the heavy taxation that was levied to finance England's standing military commitments such as Calais and the Scottish border, and to fund various military expeditions to France which achieved very little. Resentment over taxation with little or nothing to show for it was not new, however, and no major military or diplomatic initiative could have been expected until the king himself came of age. Yet the perception that the country was suffering under the burden of heavy taxation was widespread, and was enhanced by the imposition of three poll taxes between 1377 and 1381 which substantially extended the range of those liable to pay.

The peasants' revolt, 1381 Although the revolt was sparked off by the activities of the poll-tax collectors in south Essex in late May and early June 1381, the demands which the peasants put forward during the revolt, notably for the emancipation of the serfs, had their roots in the growing tensions between landlords and peasants that followed the widespread mortality from successive outbreaks of plague. In early June there was rioting in Essex and Kent, and bands of rebels from both counties headed for London. Within London there was some sympathy for the rebels among the commons of the city, who had their own grievances with the merchants, and the Kentish rebels were able to enter the city on Thursday 13 June, and to make common cause with the Londoners. They showed particular hostility to John of Gaunt, burning his palace of the Savoy to the ground. Richard, meanwhile, was in the Tower of London with a group of nobles and councillors, who urgently discussed with him how to deal with the rebellion. Richard's own part in the discussions is almost impossible to determine, though some historians have suggested that he took the initiative in seeking to negotiate with the rebels, despite the fact that he was only fourteen when the rebellion occurred. Even before the Kentish rebels entered London, Richard had apparently suggested negotiation with their leaders at Greenwich, but the talks had broken down almost as soon as they began. Faced with an even more serious situation once the rebels had begun creating mayhem within the city itself, Richard undertook on Friday 14 June to ride to Mile End to seek to disperse the Essex rebels by offering them charters of freedom and pardon for their rebellion. Although the Anonimalle chronicle attributes the proposal to the king himself, it is not certain that it emanated from him. Even if it did, it may have been merely a tactical device to persuade the rebels to go home rather than an indication of genuine sympathy with their grievances. The danger inherent in this course of action is well conveyed by the contemporary chroniclers: indeed, Henry Knighton records that the knights who should have accompanied Richard to Mile End lost their nerve and stayed in the Tower. Richard's outwardly courageous bearing did much to ensure that the meeting achieved its immediate purpose. The rebels' attitude to the king was one of respectful loyalty: the hostility they showed to royal officials and to the landowning nobility did not extend to the king, whom they affected to perceive as ill-advised, and his apparent willingness to grant them charters of freedom brought about their dispersal. But while Richard was at Mile End a group of rebels within London broke into the Tower and murdered the chancellor, Simon Sudbury, archbishop of Canterbury, and the treasurer, Robert Hales.

Richard and his party took refuge in the great wardrobe, near Blackfriars, and on the following day (Saturday 15 June) had it proclaimed in the city that all the rebels who were still in London should assemble before him at Smithfield. The intentions of the king and those round him have been the subject of some controversy. Wat *Tyler, the leader of the Kentish rebels in London, approached the king and addressed him as *Frer* ('brother'; *Anonimalle Chronicle*, 147). The king asked why he and his fellows would not go home, to which Tyler replied that they would not disperse until their demands had been met. Tyler's demeanour antagonized some of those round the king; an altercation took place, and William Walworth, lord mayor of London, struck Tyler and killed him. With some presence of mind, Richard then rode towards the rebels saying, according to the monk of Evesham, 'I am your leader: follow me' (*Historia vitae et regni Ricardi secundi*, 66). This drew many of the rebels away from the fracas around the dead Tyler; the London militia now arrived and under the command of Walworth and Sir Robert Knolles dispersed the rebels, with Richard still promising them their charters of freedom.

Whether the sequence of events at Smithfield was as unplanned and unexpected as the chroniclers suggest may be doubted. The rapid arrival of the militia suggests some element of advance planning, and those around the king, even perhaps the king himself, may have intended to create an opportunity to kill or capture Tyler and separate him from the main body of his followers. If this is so, it was a risky strategy, as the Mile End meeting had been, and again Richard's personal courage is not in doubt. His promise both at Mile End and at Smithfield to give the rebels their charters of freedom might suggest that he had some sympathy with them. However, at the end of June he accompanied his chief justice of king's bench, Sir Robert Tresilian, into Essex to witness the execution of some of the rebels, and on 2 July he formally revoked the charters of manumission and pardon. It seems likely that the promises of freedom he had made at Mile End were empty, designed to placate the rebels and make it easier to disperse them. Serfs were the property of their lords and, as was pointed out in the subsequent parliament, manumission was a matter for individual lords rather than the king. In all probability the conclusion Richard drew from the revolt was not that the serfs deserved their freedom, but rather that disobedience was a threat to order and stability in the realm and should not be tolerated. In the parliament of October 1383 Michael de la Pole, who was one of the more influential of Richard's courtiers, observed that 'obedience is the foundation of all peace and quiet in the realm', and that 'disobedience … was the source and chief cause of the treasonable insurrection recently made by the commune of England' (*RotP*, 3.150). As Richard's own ideas of kingship developed, so this interpretation of the revolt perhaps gained ascendancy in his mind.

Marriage, 1381–1382 Richard's own part in bringing the revolt to an end had been significant, and showed that he was no longer a child. Although he had been formally competent to discharge all the functions of kingship from the day of his accession, the revolt marked an important stage in the development of his personal authority and, perhaps, of his idea of kingship. At the same time, as befitted a king of fourteen years of age, the question of his marriage was being resolved. A number of proposals had been discussed since his accession, including marriage to a Navarrese princess and to the daughter of the ruler of Milan. But for the English government, a marriage between Richard and *Anne of Bohemia (1366–1394), daughter of the late Emperor Charles IV (*d*. 1378), and sister of the emperor-elect and king of Bohemia, Wenceslas IV, seemed to offer several advantages. The house of Luxembourg had traditionally been allied to France, but the outbreak of the schism in the church and rivalry over the succession in Hungary drove a wedge between the courts in Prague and Paris. England and the empire both recognized Pope Urban VI, in Rome, whereas the French supported the claim of his Avignon rival, Clement VII. The English perhaps hoped for a revival of an Anglo-imperial alliance directed against the French, whom both parties now regarded as schismatics. Negotiations between Wenceslas and the English, in which Burley and Michael de la Pole played a leading part, went ahead successfully and a marriage treaty was agreed on 2 May 1381. Anne

arrived in England in December, and the marriage took place on 20 January 1382.

The marriage aroused little enthusiasm in England. Some of the queen's Bohemian retinue made themselves unpopular; the desired Anglo-imperial alliance never bore fruit, and the marriage seemed a financial liability, for Richard promised to lend Wenceslas over £16,000. Several chroniclers maintained that the marriage merely served Wenceslas's financial interests. Richard's own relationship with Anne, however, seems to have been based on genuine affection. She did not produce an heir (there are no reports of stillborn children, or children who died in infancy: in all probability she never became pregnant), but no chronicler reports any other liaisons on the king's part. When she died, on 7 June 1394, Richard gave himself over to an outburst of destructive grief and ordered Sheen Palace, where she had died, to be razed to the ground. Richard may also have seen the marriage as enhancing his status in Europe: his wife was the daughter of an emperor and sister of the emperor-elect, and after the death of his mother-in-law, the dowager Empress Elizabeth, the Westminster chronicler records that Richard had 'a very unusual imperial shrine' of a hitherto unheard-of design constructed in St Paul's Cathedral (*Westminster Chronicle*, 516–17).

The king and his courtiers, 1381–1386 In the months that followed the peasants' revolt and Richard's marriage some of those who had served the king in the early years of his reign moved away from the court. Many of these men were former servants of the Black Prince, and it was only to be expected that as Richard grew to manhood he would wish to surround himself with people of his own choosing. Young knights of the chamber such as James Berners, John Beauchamp of Holt, and John Salisbury now came to prominence at court. Some of the courtiers of Richard's youth, such as Simon Burley, remained close to the king and indeed increased their influence, but the king himself was largely responsible for his choice of advisers and friends from 1381 onwards.

The chamber knights were an important and distinctive group around Richard, but perhaps even more influential were two men, Michael de la Pole and Robert de Vere, earl of Oxford, who came to enjoy the king's favour and patronage above all others. De la Pole was the son of the Hull merchant and financier William de la Pole, but he had chosen a military career and had been a follower of the Black Prince. His association with the king probably began in November 1381 when parliament appointed him, together with Richard (III) Fitzalan, earl of Arundel, to 'advise and govern' the person of the king. He seems, however, to have identified himself with the circle around the king, and he soon rose high in Richard's favour: he was appointed chancellor in March 1383. De Vere was a younger man, only five years older than the king; he had probably been introduced to the king by his uncle Aubrey de Vere, and Richard evidently found him a most congenial companion. None of Richard's courtiers in these years was as much disliked as de Vere. Little in his personality or career seemed to justify the lavish favours he received from the king, and the parallels that were drawn in 1386 with the events of Edward II's reign suggest that he was regarded as a second Gaveston.

Richard's patronage of his courtiers and friends in these years was lavish to the point of foolishness, not least in view of the financial demands that the government continued to make on its subjects to finance the war. De la Pole was created earl of Suffolk in 1385, despite the feeling in some circles, recorded by Thomas Walsingham, that he was not worthy of such an honour. At the same time de Vere was promoted to the hitherto unheard-of rank of marquess, taking his title from Dublin and receiving quasi-regal authority over Ireland. The title of marquess gave him precedence over all the earls, but when in October 1386 he was created duke of Ireland he ranked alongside the king's three uncles of Lancaster, York, and Gloucester. In all probability only parliamentary opposition prevented Richard conferring the earldom of Huntingdon on Simon Burley in 1385, and in 1387 Richard succeeded in elevating another of his chamber knights to the peerage, when he created John Beauchamp of Holt Baron Kidderminster. These grants of titles were accompanied by grants of lands and offices to the point where nobles such as Thomas of Woodstock, who depended on exchequer annuities for part of his income, felt increasingly excluded from royal patronage.

Growing unpopularity, 1383–1386 The direction of royal patronage in these years was one reason for the growing unpopularity of Richard's associates. Royal resources, it seemed, were being lavished on favourites, and the king's chamber was increasing its income while at the same time falling into debt. Such apparent extravagance, in years when the Commons were being asked to vote taxes for the defence of the realm and for expeditions to France, was unacceptable to a wide body of opinion. Furthermore, hostility to the king and his advisers on these grounds was compounded by criticism of their lack of success in the war with France. In 1383 an inept attempt by the bishop of Norwich to prevent Flanders falling under the control of the duke of Burgundy, the king of France's uncle, failed ignominiously, and although Ghent held out against Burgundy until 1385 the government made little effort to send help to the town. In the circumstances de la Pole's advocacy of negotiations for a peace with France made sense, and he evidently had Richard's support; but the policy of peace was unpopular with nobles such as Arundel and Woodstock, who still perhaps had hopes of a successful military career in France, and who believed that more might have been done to maintain English influence in Flanders.

At this stage, however, neither the French nor the Scots were seriously prepared to negotiate a lasting settlement with England, and in 1384, as Richard neared his eighteenth birthday, he was encouraged to undertake a military expedition himself. A campaign in France in 1384 or 1385 was scarcely feasible but, following the renewal of the Anglo-Scottish war in 1384 and Scottish incursions into England, the council resolved that in July 1385 Richard should lead an expedition to Scotland. Richard now prepared to lead his nobles in war as his father and grandfather had done; at his army's entry into Scotland he ceremonially created new knights, and bestowed the titles of duke of York and duke of Gloucester on his uncles Edmund Langley (d. 1402) and Thomas of Woodstock (d. 1397). From the symbolic point of view, the expedition was intended to mark Richard's coming of age as a warrior and the opening of his military career. The expedition cut a swathe of destruction from the border to Edinburgh, but ended in acrimony when Richard rejected Gaunt's advice to advance beyond the Forth. Richard is said to have insisted that his men, who had loyally accompanied him thus far, should not be exposed to danger and privation by marching further into Scotland as autumn approached; the expedition had achieved its aim of retaliation for Scottish raids into northern England, and Richard declared that he was now going home.

The tension between Richard and Gaunt, which the Scottish expedition revealed, had been rising since the previous year. Rumours of plots against Gaunt had circulated at court, and it is possible that de Vere was seeking to exclude Gaunt from any influence over the king. Richard, who was too ready to listen to de Vere, did little to prevent the deterioration in his relationship with the most powerful of his nobles, and in July 1386 Gaunt set sail for Spain in pursuit of his claim to the Castilian throne.

Murmurings of hostility against Richard's advisers had surfaced in parliament in 1384, and in the parliament of October 1385 which followed the Scottish expedition the Commons complained about the king's extravagance and his misuse of patronage. They demanded an inquiry into the finances of the royal household, but although a committee of nine was appointed to investigate royal finances it never met, and it was later alleged that de la Pole had sabotaged its proceedings. Gaunt's departure, however, left the way open for more overt hostility to make itself felt. Although Gaunt's influence over the king had been waning over the previous two years, he still represented a powerful force for political stability in the realm, and only with his departure did his younger brother Thomas of Woodstock, duke of Gloucester, together with Woodstock's political ally the earl of Arundel, come to the forefront of politics and assume the leadership of those who sought to break the influence over the king exercised by de la Pole and other favourites.

The Wonderful Parliament of 1386 The policy of *rapprochement* with France made little headway in 1385 and 1386. Indeed, Gaunt's expedition to Castile may have encouraged the French to prepare an invasion of England in the summer of 1386 which was to be led by Charles VI himself and which was intended to force the English to accept peace on French terms. The French assembled the largest force so far raised by either side during the war, and their preparations induced widespread panic and insecurity in England. Although in the event the invasion never took place, these feelings were at their height when parliament opened in October 1386. The Commons were immediately confronted with a request from the chancellor,

Michael de la Pole, for an unprecedented quadruple subsidy to cover the cost of defence against the threatened invasion, and the hostility to him that had been gathering over the past two years now came to a head. The Commons, probably with the support of Gloucester and Arundel, refused to proceed with the business of parliament until the chancellor was removed from office. Richard for his part refused to meet parliament and from his manor of Eltham sent his famous message that he would not dismiss so much as a scullion from his kitchen at parliament's request.

The demand made by the Commons for de la Pole's removal raised the issue of the king's prerogative to appoint and dismiss ministers, and the situation now escalated into a major crisis. Gloucester, with Arundel's brother Thomas, bishop of Ely (d. 1414), confronted Richard at Eltham and told him that if he did not attend parliament it could dissolve itself after forty days. Richard then apparently raised the temperature still further by ill-advisedly threatening to seek help from the French against those who infringed his liberty. It is not clear what Richard meant by this: even in the bad-tempered and emotional atmosphere of the Eltham meeting it is unlikely that he seriously contemplated invoking the aid of those who had been threatening to invade his kingdom. Perhaps, as has sometimes been argued, he was recalling the precedent of Louis IX's arbitration between Henry III and Simon de Montfort in the mise of Amiens of 1264; perhaps, on the other hand, it was no more than a spontaneous but foolish riposte to Gloucester and Arundel.

Richard's threat, however, provoked Gloucester and Arundel into raising the stakes still further by reminding him of the fate of Edward II. In effect, they threatened him with deposition if he did not give way. The threat was sufficient. Richard agreed to meet parliament, and to dismiss not only the chancellor but the treasurer and the keeper of the privy seal as well. The chancellor was then impeached by the Commons on charges arising out of his conduct in office. These charges have sometimes been dismissed as trivial or trumped-up, but detailed analysis has shown that most of them had substance. De la Pole was condemned to imprisonment, but Richard set aside the penalty and de la Pole remained at the king's side. Parliament then established a commission which was to hold office for a year and which was to conduct a thorough review of royal finances. It was to have control of the exchequer and the great and privy seals, and Richard was required to take an oath to abide by any ordinances it made.

The king's 'gyration', 1387 In Richard's eyes the dismissal, impeachment, and imprisonment of his minister and the imposition upon him of the commission constituted an infringement of his prerogative, in that they had been undertaken against his will and without his genuine consent. His reaction, however, need not imply that he had developed any novel or exaggerated concept of his royal rights and powers. Although his resistance to parliament's demands had been expressed in ill-judged and intemperate language, the removal of ministers and the

restriction on royal power implicit in the commission's terms of appointment would have been regarded by his predecessors as unacceptable infringements of the prerogative. Richard's protest at the end of the parliament that nothing that had been done should be to the prejudice of his person or his crown, so that the liberties and prerogatives of his crown were safeguarded, would not have seemed out of place to Edward I or Edward III. The rhetoric of the conflict of 1386 may have been more colourful and violent than in earlier political crises, but the issues were not substantially different.

Had Richard acquiesced, at least outwardly, in the work of the parliament and merely allowed the commission to serve its time out before he resumed personal power, the crisis might have blown over. However, his response to what he saw as the infringement of his prerogative not only prolonged the crisis but did much to provoke its escalation from constitutional measures to violence. While the commission set about its duties in Westminster, Richard embarked on a progress, or 'gyration', round England which took him away from the centre of government for nine months between February and November 1387. If part of the purpose of his progress was to avoid personal contact with the commission, another and more important part was to assess the extent of support for him in the country and plan a counter-attack against his opponents. An attempt to recruit supporters in East Anglia came to nothing when one of his agents was captured and imprisoned in Cambridge, and there was little evidence that the shire gentry were prepared to rally to Richard's cause. However, by appointing de Vere as justice of Chester on 8 September, Richard took the first step towards recruiting a force in a county where men felt a personal loyalty to the king as their earl.

Richard was concerned, however, not just to gauge the extent of support for his cause, but also to obtain assurance about his legal rights. In August 1387 he twice sought the opinion of his judges, first at Shrewsbury and then at Nottingham. According to Knighton, his question to them at Shrewsbury was couched in general terms and asked whether he could oppose and resist the ordinances which he had been compelled to accept in the last parliament. They replied that he could annul and change them because he was 'not subject to those laws' (supra jura). Encouraged by this Richard put a series of more specific questions about the parliament of 1386 to the judges at Nottingham on 25 August. This time, led by Chief Justice Tresilian, they told him that the commission of government was an unlawful infringement of his prerogative because it had been imposed against his will, and that those who had accroached the royal power in this and other ways should be punished 'as traitors' (ut proditores). Such a declaration implicitly widened the scope of the treason law, for the Statute of Treason of 1352 had not included accroaching the royal power as a treasonable offence, and it presented those who had demanded de la Pole's dismissal and the establishment of the commission with a threat to their lives and property.

Radcot Bridge and the Merciless Parliament, 1387–1388 In November Richard returned to London and both sides began to prepare for armed conflict. Richard had little support: the Londoners refused to rally to him, despite the efforts of their mayor, Nicholas Brembre; few nobles were willing to fight (as some saw it) for de Vere; and the sheriffs had earlier stated that they could not raise troops for the king because the commons all supported the lords. Gloucester and the earl of Arundel, together with the earl of Warwick, met at Harringay on 13 November, and four days later, in a formal audience with the king at Westminster, presented an indictment of treason in the form of an appeal (a civil law procedure) against five of the king's favourites, de la Pole, de Vere, Brembre, Chief Justice Tresilian, and Alexander Neville, archbishop of York (d. 1392), who had been closely associated with the court over the previous two years. Richard's response was to play for time, to give de Vere a chance to raise troops in Cheshire.

The three *lords appellant assembled in arms at Huntingdon on 12 December, where they were joined by Gaunt's son Henry, earl of Derby (the future Henry IV), and the earl of Nottingham, Thomas (I) Mowbray (d. 1399); some chroniclers reported that they discussed whether Richard should now be deposed. The immediate threat, however, came from de Vere's Cheshire army which was marching south to support Richard. The appellants intercepted and routed it at Radcot Bridge on 20 December. De Vere escaped and fled overseas, while the appellants marched triumphantly to London and confronted Richard in the Tower on 27 December. Some chroniclers suggested that Richard was deposed for three days at the end of the month and was restored to the throne only because the appellants could not agree on a successor. Gloucester's confession in 1397 lends some support to the story: it is possible that he had designs on the crown but was forestalled by Derby, who as Gaunt's heir represented the senior male line of descent from Edward III.

Richard survived with little but his formal kingship intact. He agreed to summon a parliament in which his favourites would be put on trial for treason. The lack of widespread support for him in the country, and the superior military force of the appellants, had put him at the mercy of his opponents, and the judges' declaration about his prerogative counted for little in the face of his opponents' determination to destroy Richard's inner circle of favourites and courtiers once and for all.

De la Pole, Neville, and de Vere, however, had all fled overseas when the so-called Merciless Parliament opened on 3 February 1388 and the appeal of treason was formally presented. De la Pole and de Vere were condemned to death in their absence and all three sentenced to loss of their lands and property. Of those against whom the appeal was directed, only Brembre and Tresilian (who was dragged out of sanctuary in Westminster Abbey) were in the hands of the appellants, and they were now condemned and executed. With strong support from the Commons the appellants then turned their attention to Richard's chamber knights. Burley, Berners, Salisbury, and John Beauchamp of Holt were impeached on sixteen counts, most of which amounted to accroaching the royal power. They, too, were sentenced to death and executed, though Richard, with support from some of the more moderate nobles, struggled hard to persuade Gloucester, Arundel, and Warwick, and the Commons, to spare Burley. His pleas were in vain, however, and Richard never forgave them for sending his former tutor to his death. The judges who had suggested at Nottingham in the previous year that accroaching the royal power might incur the penalties of treason were now themselves arraigned on charges of treason; they too were sentenced to death, but their lives were spared and they were exiled to Ireland.

The appellants had achieved their goal of destroying the group of favourites around the king, and they had encountered little opposition in doing so. Few nobles, and few of the shire gentry who sat in the Commons, were willing publicly to declare their support for the king and his unpopular courtiers. Indeed, over forty members of the Commons can be shown to have had links with the appellants. Yet the appellants made no attempt to institutionalize their power by establishing a council with responsibility for government, and with the removal of de la Pole, de Vere, and Burley much of the venom went out of the opposition to the king and his court.

The recovery of royal authority, 1388–1389 By the autumn of 1388 there were signs that power was beginning to move back towards the king, and on 3 May 1389 Richard formally assumed responsibility for the conduct of government. According to the monk of Westminster, he declared that now he had reached the age of twenty-one he was entitled to claim his inheritance, and the lords agreed that he should assume sole responsibility for government. He disavowed personal responsibility for past events by saying, somewhat disingenuously, that for twelve years he and his kingdom had been ruled by others: such an assertion enabled him to make a fresh start and claim that he now intended to work tirelessly for the well-being and profit of his people.

Although Richard had now formally regained power, he made no attempt over the next seven years to revive the style of government which had brought about the crisis of 1386–8. De la Pole, de Vere, and Neville were left to die in exile; the judges were not recalled from Ireland until 1397; and for the time being no new inner circle of courtiers emerged to enjoy Richard's favour and patronage. Outwardly at least, political stability had been restored. Richard was apparently reconciled with Gloucester, Arundel, and Warwick, and Arundel's brother the bishop of Ely returned in 1391 to the chancellorship which he had first held from 1386 to 1389. John of Gaunt's return to England in November 1389 was another factor making for stability. He and Richard exchanged the kiss of peace, and Richard placed upon himself Gaunt's livery collar in the form of a double S. Gaunt now attended the council regularly, and his conciliatory role was important in preventing any simmering tensions between Richard and his former opponents from coming to the surface.

Although Gaunt's influence was important in maintaining stability and upholding the authority of the crown,

Richard sought in the early 1390s to broaden the basis of support for the crown by retaining members of the shire gentry. This policy was prompted by his failure to win much support from this section of society between 1386 and 1388. Between 1391 and 1393 he retained thirty-six knights and thirty-three esquires; they were recruited from all parts of the country, and many of them were prominent in local administration. They were expected to provide an important nucleus of support for the crown in any future political conflict.

In the early 1390s, too, Richard developed the ceremonial and cultural aspects of monarchy. Perhaps in imitation of the French court, the language of address at court became more elaborate: the king was frequently addressed as 'royal majesty', or 'high majesty', rather than just 'highness', and the author of the continuation of the *Eulogium* presents a vivid picture of the king sitting enthroned in state in his chamber after dinner and requiring anyone upon whom his glance fell to bow the knee to him. His court also became a centre of artistic and literary patronage: Froissart visited the court in 1395 and presented Richard with a manuscript of his poems; the poetry of one of Richard's courtiers, Sir John Montagu, was admired in France by Christine de Pisan; and Gower's *Confessio amantis* was said to have been written at Richard's request. Perhaps the most important visual expression of Richard's patronage was the rebuilding of Westminster Hall, in the form which survives today.

This work was put in hand in 1393 under the direction of two of the most important architect–masons of the day, Henry Yevele and Hugh Herland. Yevele had already worked on the reconstruction of the nave of Westminster Abbey. The work had been initiated in 1376, and Richard made a contribution of £1685 towards the cost. He perhaps intended that the buildings at Westminster should express the wealth and magnificence of the English monarchy. Richard also identified his kingship with the royal saints of England. About 1395 he had the royal arms of England impaled with those of Edward the Confessor. Many representations of this symbol of his cult of the Confessor survive at Westminster and elsewhere, and he invoked the royal saint in the opening phrases of his will. He also expressed his devotion to the cult of St Edmund, the martyred king of the East Angles who, like Richard, had become king in his youth. The two royal saints, together with John the Baptist, are portrayed presenting Richard to the Virgin and Child in the Wilton diptych, painted perhaps around 1395, which represents more than any other surviving work the image of sacred majesty which Richard sought to create. Richard also took some steps towards the establishment of the cult of another murdered king, Edward II, whose experiences at the hands of his nobility had obvious significance for Richard. He sought to ensure that the abbey of Gloucester, where Edward was buried, observed his anniversaries, and in 1395 he proposed to the pope that Edward should be canonized. Political resonances from Edward's reign punctuated the 1380s and 1390s: Walsingham reported the execution and subsequent veneration of the earl of

Arundel in 1397 in terms that are reminiscent of the cult of Thomas of Lancaster, but Richard's wish to canonize his predecessor was not to be granted.

Relations with France: second marriage, 1389–1396 It is likely that some of Richard's ideas about court ceremonial and the majesty of kingship derived from the court of France, and it is no coincidence that the two courts drew closer in the 1390s as both sides embarked on a series of negotiations designed to bring about a lasting peace between the two kingdoms. In 1387, during discussions about the possibility of a final peace with France, the monk of Westminster reported Richard as saying that 'if he was going to have to maintain a ceaseless state of war against the king of the French, he would inevitably be compelled to be for ever burdening his people with new imposts, with damaging results for himself' (*Westminster Chronicle*, 204–5). The political and financial arguments for a lengthy truce or a final peace were powerful. The lesson of October 1386, when the Commons had resisted de la Pole's demand for a subsidy to meet the costs of the threatened French invasion until he was removed from office, had not been lost on Richard. The series of truces from 1388 onwards were accompanied by a lower level of taxation, and by significantly less friction between Richard and his parliaments than had been the case in the early 1380s.

The French, too, saw advantages in a final peace. Their belligerent attitude in 1386 had not brought a settlement any nearer, and the abortive invasion had proved costly. Furthermore Charles VI's uncle the duke of Burgundy wished to consolidate his authority in Flanders and ensure good relations with England, the source of most of the wool on which the prosperity and social peace of the Flemish towns depended. Both sides therefore were genuinely prepared to seek a final peace. Whether this is evidence of a more general aversion to war, or war weariness, on the English side is open to doubt. Although the rhetoric of both sides dwelt on the need to avoid the shedding of Christian blood, and although some writers opposed the war for its destructive effects, and some Lollards on religious principle, there is little sign of any general will to end the war except on favourable terms. Richard himself was not averse to war on principle, as his expeditions to Scotland in 1385 and to Ireland in 1394–5 and 1399 show. His court embodied the chivalric and military ethos to a significantly less obvious degree than the courts of Edward III and the Black Prince, but this probably reflected the experience and circumstances of his generation. Some twenty years later Henry V was to have little difficulty in marshalling the nation once again for war against the French.

A draft treaty was drawn up in 1393 which sought to settle the status of Aquitaine, the most intractable of the issues in contention between England and France. The territory to be held by the English king would be greatly enlarged, but in a crucial concession Richard agreed that he would hold the duchy of the king of France by liege homage. However, the draft was severely criticized by parliament in England in 1394; the suggestion that the king should perform liege homage to the king of France was particularly unpopular, and in the face both of this hostility at home and of the simmering resentment of the Gascons the peace proposals were abandoned. Neither side had the will to resume the war, however, and in 1396 they concluded a twenty-eight years' truce. The truce was accompanied by an agreement for Richard, a widower since 1394, to marry *Isabella (1389–1409) the seven-year-old daughter of Charles VI.

The close relationship between the two kings which followed the truce and the marriage treaty was unpopular in England. The new queen was not seen as a suitable bride for Richard, not least perhaps because she was unlikely to produce an heir for some years. Furthermore, Richard now acted as though the war was over. Brest, which had been ceded to England 'until the end of the war' was handed back to the duke of Brittany; Cherbourg, leased from the king of Navarre, had been returned in 1393, and rumours began to circulate that Richard intended to surrender Calais as well. The draft treaty may have provided some basis for this, for it left the status of Calais to be determined by the two kings.

However, the ending for the time being of the French war gave Richard the opportunity to turn his attention to Ireland, where the English lordship was on the defensive against the resurgent Irish. The government in Dublin had made several appeals to Richard to come over in person and rescue the lordship from the threat of extinction. In the autumn of 1394, free from other preoccupations, he took an army of about 5000 men to Ireland. In the few encounters that took place the English archers put the Irish forces to flight, and over the first five months of 1395 Richard received the submissions of most of the Irish rulers. He had apparently restored the English lordship and the authority of the crown quickly and easily, and although the settlement soon broke down he returned home in May 1395 with his reputation in many quarters enhanced. On the other hand, if Froissart is to be believed, the duke of Gloucester took a less sanguine view of the Irish campaign. He had accompanied Richard on the outgoing voyage in 1394, but he had returned early. He later asserted that Ireland was 'a land neither of conquest nor of profit' and that what was gained in one year in Ireland would be lost in the next (*Œuvres*, 16.5). The political and personal advantages which Richard gained from his Irish expedition proved short-lived.

The destruction of the king's opponents, 1397 Richard's relationship with the French court contributed to the raising of political tension in 1396 and the early months of 1397. Froissart stresses the duke of Gloucester's opposition to the *rapprochement* with France, but others also had misgivings. Richard's proposal to send an expedition to Milan in support of Charles VI's ambitions there was received coldly by the Commons in the January parliament of 1397, and the Commons presented a petition complaining about the extravagance of the royal household. Richard's reaction revealed once again his sensitivity about his prerogative. He accused the Commons of giving 'great offence', and the Lords declared that whoever engaged in such criticism was guilty of treason. The ostensible author of the petition, a clerk named Thomas Haxey (d. 1425), was convicted of treason but spared because of his cloth.

In July 1397, without any warning, Richard arrested the duke of Gloucester and the earls of Arundel and Warwick. Contemporary interpretations of his actions differed sharply. Walsingham portrayed Richard as wilfully plotting the downfall of his opponents, the arrests coming out of a clear blue sky. The Kirkstall chronicler, however, linked the arrests with the events of 1386–8, saying that Richard now 'called to mind' his former humiliations. French writers, on the other hand, especially the author of the *Chronique de la traison et mort de Richart Deux roy Dengleterre*, sought to portray Richard as a Christlike king betrayed and destroyed by his opponents. They suggested that Gloucester, Arundel, and Warwick had plotted to seize Richard along with Gaunt and other nobles, and depose him: Richard's arrest of the three lords was thus a pre-emptive strike. There is, however, no evidence that a plot was hatched against Richard, and the three lords were never accused of plotting in the way described by the *Traison*.

It is possible that Richard believed the three lords might move against him if he did not strike first, but such an argument rests on an assumption about Richard's state of mind rather than any objective evidence. It is not, however, incompatible with the view that Richard intended to revenge himself on those who had violated his prerogative and humiliated him between 1386 and 1388. He was well prepared: the truce with France meant there was little likelihood of any unexpected military emergency, and his policy of retaining members of the shire gentry should have ensured him a body of supporters in the country. He had the loyal support of John of Gaunt, and also of a group of younger nobles including his half-brothers John *Holland (d. 1400) and Thomas *Holland (d. 1400), earls of Huntingdon and Kent, John Beaufort (d. 1410), Gaunt's eldest son with Katherine Swynford, Edward, earl of Rutland (d. 1415), the heir to the duke of York, John Montagu, now earl of Salisbury (d. 1400), and Thomas Despenser (d. 1400), a name with a resonance from a remoter past. The promotion of these earls to dukedoms, and of Despenser to an earldom, in 1397 aroused public hostility, and according to Walsingham they were derisively known as 'duketti' (*Johannis de Trokelowe … Chronica*, 223).

Parliament opened at Westminster on 17 September 1397. The monk of Evesham describes how the building was surrounded by 200 of the king's Cheshire archers, and both he and Adam Usk convey the sense of terror they were evidently intended to induce. The chancellor, Edmund Stafford, set the tone for the parliament by preaching a sermon in which he declared that the power of the king lay singly and wholly with the king, and that those who usurped or plotted against it were worthy of the penalties of the law. These penalties were now to be visited on Gloucester, Arundel, and Warwick. The three lords were appealed of treason by the king's noble supporters in a trial presided over by Gaunt, as high steward of England. Arundel was condemned and executed after a trial which included a bitter exchange of words with the king, who attacked him for his part in Burley's death in 1388. When Gloucester's trial began, however, Thomas Mowbray, earl of Nottingham, announced that he was dead. After his arrest he had been taken to Calais, of which Mowbray was captain, and imprisoned there. In all probability he was murdered there, on Richard's instructions, for Richard perhaps feared the reaction both of the populace and of Gaunt if Gloucester was brought to stand trial. On the same day Thomas Arundel, now archbishop of Canterbury, was accused of treason for his participation in the events of 1386–8 and sentenced to exile for life. Finally, Warwick was arraigned and condemned, but his life was spared and he was sentenced to exile in the Isle of Man.

The 'tyranny' of Richard II, 1397–1399 Richard now rewarded his friends with the spoils of victory. The estates of the three lords were confiscated; many of them were granted to Richard's supporters, who were also rewarded with enhanced titles. Arundel's lands in north-east Wales, however, were annexed to the earldom of Chester, which was elevated to the status of a principality. Finally, in a ceremony of symbolic significance, the Lords and Commons were required to swear an oath on the shrine of St Edward at Westminster that they would uphold the judgments and ordinances of the parliament or suffer the penalties of treason.

Richard's triumph, it seemed, was complete. His prerogatives had been upheld and those who violated them condemned as traitors. He had lived up to his epitaph, which he had composed for his tomb in Westminster Abbey, commissioned in 1395: 'He threw down all who violated the royal prerogative; he destroyed heretics and scattered their friends' (*Inventory of the Historical Monuments*, 1.31). It had all been accomplished with surprising ease: Richard had had Gaunt's support, and the support of a carefully managed Commons. The speaker, John Bussy, was a life retainer of both Richard and Gaunt, and twenty-nine of the knights were royal retainers or crown office-holders. Yet Richard now acted as though he had little confidence in his own security. He believed that the affinities of Gloucester, Arundel, and Warwick presented a threat to him, and between October 1397 and September 1398 many of those who had ridden with the appellants in the Radcot Bridge campaign were summoned before the council and required to pay a fine in return for a pardon. The men of Essex and Hertfordshire, where Gloucester's influence had been strong, were collectively pardoned in return for a payment of £2000, and in the summer of 1398 the inhabitants of London and sixteen counties in the south and east of England were required to seal charters giving the king *carte blanche* to do what he wished with them and their goods. Chroniclers alleged, though there is no firm evidence, that under colour of these 'blank charters' Richard extorted fines of £1000 or 1000 marks from the sixteen counties.

The treason law was used as a means of political oppression: in March 1398 the dukes of Albemarle and Surrey (formerly earls of Rutland and Kent respectively) were given power to arrest all traitors and punish them according to their deserts. Albemarle, as constable of England, was also empowered to use the court of chivalry, which employed civil law, to hear cases involving alleged slander of the king. It was measures of this kind that gave substance to the accusation at Richard's deposition that he had violated clause 39 of the 1215 text of Magna Carta (clause 29 of the reissue of 1225) guaranteeing that an offender would be be dealt with 'according to the lawful judgement of his equals and the law of the land'. Richard also sought to escape from the financial insecurity which arose from the Commons' grant of customs revenue for only a year or two at a time. When the adjourned parliament of September 1397 reconvened at Shrewsbury in January 1398, the general pardon promised in September was made conditional upon a grant of the customs revenue to the king for life, and if at any time in the future the grant was revoked the pardon would lapse.

These measures in themselves were unlikely to bring Richard down. It is difficult to assess how unpopular they were in the country; oppressive government was nothing new, and most of the surviving accounts were influenced by hindsight and in particular by Henry Bolingbroke's use of the evidence for Richard's 'tyrannical' government to fashion a case for deposing him in 1399. In 1398 and early 1399 there was no obvious figure around whom opposition could rally, and the steps Richard took to impose his authority, however tyrannical they may have seemed, were apparently effective.

At court, however, there were rumours of plots against the house of Lancaster. It is possible that Richard wanted to get the duchy of Lancaster into his own hands, but it is also possible that the murmurings against Gaunt and his son Henry, who had cautiously supported Richard in 1397 and had been rewarded with the title of duke of Hereford, may have arisen because of a wish on the part of some of Richard's courtiers to exclude Gaunt and his son from the succession to the crown. Richard's childlessness inevitably raised some speculation about who might succeed him. Roger Mortimer, earl of March (d. 1398), was Richard's heir-general, being descended from Edward III's second son, Lionel, duke of Clarence (d. 1368), but through the female line. Richard may have nominated Mortimer as his heir in the Michaelmas parliament of 1385, at a time of some tension between him and Gaunt. Gaunt, however, was Richard's heir male, and in 1376 Edward III had entailed the crown on his heirs male. Gaunt must have been aware of this entail, and might well have believed that he (or his son Henry) should be regarded as Richard's heir if he died childless.

At some time in December 1397 Thomas (I) Mowbray, who had been created duke of Norfolk in 1397 but whose position at court was insecure, spoke to Henry about plots at court and the dangerous position he believed both of them were in. Henry reported the conversation to his father, from whom it presumably reached the king. Henry's action precipitated a quarrel with Norfolk, and each accused the other of treason. In the absence of evidence, Richard ordered the matter to be put to trial by battle at Coventry on 16 September 1398. A large crowd assembled to watch the eagerly anticipated spectacle, but Richard ordered that the combat should not begin. Instead, he imposed sentence of exile on both parties: Norfolk for life and Henry for ten years. Henry was, however, given leave to sue for livery of his inheritance if Gaunt died before Henry's term of exile came to an end.

The overthrow of the king, 1399 John of Gaunt died on 3 February 1399, and his death presented Richard with an awkward dilemma. Henry was now entitled in law to claim his inheritance, and though in exile he would control the revenues and patronage of the vast duchy of Lancaster. An exiled but wealthy and influential duke of Lancaster posed an obvious threat to Richard's security, but the alternative was disinheritance. This was the course that Richard chose: by altering the terms of reference of the committee set up to deal with business outstanding at the end of the Shrewsbury session of parliament, Richard gave a cloak of legality to the repeal of the letters allowing Henry to sue for his inheritance, and his term of exile was extended to life. Richard may have believed that Henry could do little about his disinheritance. He had taken up residence in Paris, where he was under the surveillance of the duke of Burgundy, who had no wish to see Richard, who was committed to the *rapprochement* with France, once again brought under the control of a council dominated by his aristocratic opponents and supported by a bellicose Commons. In May 1399 Richard believed that he was safe from any counter-move on Henry's part, and began preparations for an expedition to Ireland to rescue what remained of his settlement of 1395. He landed at Waterford on 1 June 1399.

At this point, however, events in France took a turn which Richard could not have foreseen. Burgundy's enforced absence from Paris in May and June allowed his rival, the duke of Orléans, to establish his ascendancy over the intermittently insane Charles VI, and Orléans now allowed Henry freedom to prepare an invasion of England. He concluded an alliance with Henry, and may secretly have given him some help. His motives were opportunistic: he hoped to destabilize Richard's regime in England, undermine the Anglo-French accord, and thereby weaken Burgundy's standing at court in France. With a small body of supporters, including Archbishop Arundel, Henry landed at Ravenspur in Yorkshire about 1 July 1399. Many duchy of Lancaster retainers rallied to him, and he was soon joined by the earls of Northumberland and Westmorland, who had their own grievances against the king. With the north thus quickly secured, Henry marched south, gaining support as he went.

The duke of York, who was keeper of the realm during Richard's absence, had kept himself well informed about Henry's movements, and even before Henry landed he had begun to muster an army from the shire militias and the few pro-Ricardian nobles left in England. However, many of the knights and esquires whom Richard had retained in earlier years were with him in Ireland, along with most of the nobles who were most deeply committed to his cause. Richard's real supporters never got the chance to fight for him; York threw in his lot with Henry, perhaps believing that the localized pockets of resistance to Henry's advance could not halt or delay it, and by the end of July England was Henry's. Although Henry may initially have allowed his supporters to believe that he had returned to England only to claim his inheritance as duke of Lancaster, by the time he took Bristol on 28 July he had little compunction about usurping royal authority. He had three of Richard's councillors, William Scrope, earl of Wiltshire, John Bussy, and Henry Green, executed there, and a few days later he made a grant of the wardenship of the west march to the earl of Northumberland under the great seal of the duchy of Lancaster.

News of Henry's invasion probably reached Richard by 10 July. He sent the earl of Salisbury across to north Wales to rally troops, but he himself did not leave Waterford until some time between 20 and 25 July. It has sometimes been argued that Richard was persuaded to delay his departure by the earl of Albemarle, who was allegedly in league with Henry; but, whether or not the earl was disloyal, the assembly of Richard's scattered army necessarily took some time. Richard landed in south-west Wales, perhaps at Milford Haven or Pembroke, but his movements thereafter are uncertain: all we can be sure of is that he had reached Conwy by 11 August at the latest. What is more certain is that much of Richard's army now deserted him, and when he arrived at Conwy he found that most of Salisbury's troops had deserted too. News of York's defection and the executions at Bristol probably persuaded most of Richard's followers that his cause was lost.

Henry meanwhile had moved from Bristol to Chester, and from there Northumberland, probably accompanied by Archbishop Arundel, went to Conwy to negotiate with the king. Contemporary sources give widely varying accounts of this meeting, but it seems likely that Northumberland mendaciously promised Richard that Henry sought only his inheritance, and on the strength of this promise persuaded Richard to leave Conwy and meet Henry at Flint. But, in leaving Conwy, Richard in effect walked into a trap and arrived at Flint on 16 August as a virtual prisoner. From Flint, Henry took him to Chester and thence to London, where on 2 September he was lodged in the Tower.

The deposition of Richard, 1399 Henry's intentions were now clear. While still at Chester he had authorized the issue of writs summoning a parliamentary assembly for 30 September 1399. After his arrival in London, according to Adam Usk, he set up a committee to inquire how Richard was to be set aside, and for what reasons. It concluded that his 'perjuries, sacrileges, sodomitical acts, dispossession of his subjects, reduction of his people to servitude, lack of reason, and incapacity to rule' (*Chronicle of Adam of Usk*, 63) were sufficient grounds for his deposition in accordance with canon law as established in the deposition of the emperor Frederick II by Pope Innocent IV at the Council of Lyons in 1245. Usk also reported that, although the committee believed that Richard was ready to abdicate, it was determined 'as a further precaution' that he should be deposed 'by authority of the clergy and people' (*Chronicle of Adam of Usk*, 63). The official record of the deposition proceedings also insisted that Richard declared at Conwy that he was willing to resign his crown. A deputation of lords, including Henry and Archbishop Arundel, visited Richard in the Tower on 29 September and Richard supposedly repeated the promise to abdicate which he had allegedly made at Conwy. He then, it was said, expressed a wish for Henry to succeed him, and as a token of his goodwill gave Henry his signet ring. Other sources, however, give a different impression. Usk himself visited Richard in the Tower on 21 September and heard him denounce a country which had 'exiled, slain, destroyed, and ruined so many kings, so many rulers, so many great men'. 'Seeing therefore the troubles of his soul,' Usk went on, 'I departed much moved at heart' (*Chronicle of Adam of Usk*, 65). The author of the *Traison* portrayed a furious Richard, accusing his captors of treason and becoming almost speechless with rage. In a more elegiac account, the Dieulacres chronicle suggested that Richard placed his crown on the ground and resigned his right to God rather than to Henry. The official version is almost impossible to believe: Richard was probably resigned to his fate, but not at all disposed to co-operate with his supplanter or voluntarily resign his God-given kingship.

Although Henry had not obtained from Richard the voluntary resignation which he sought, the assembly that opened on 30 September was none the less told that Richard was willing to abdicate. His abdication was formally accepted; thirty-nine accusations against him were then read out, and it was agreed that they formed sufficient grounds for his deposition. The charges began with a recital of the king's coronation oath, and their purport was to argue that by his actions between 1397 and 1399 Richard had broken his oath and thus broken the legal bond between himself and his people. The charges amount to the prosecution version of events, mainly in the last two years of his reign, and they singled out his treatment of Henry himself, Gloucester, Arundel, and Warwick, and Archbishop Arundel. But they also criticized the principles underlying Richard's kingship. Article 16 in particular maintained that the king did not wish 'to uphold or dispense the rightful laws and customs of the realm, but [preferred] to act according to his own arbitrary will and do whatever he wished', and that he 'frequently replied and declared expressly ... that his laws were in his mouth ... or in his breast, and that he alone could change or make the laws of his kingdom' (*RotP*, 3.419). The issue of the relationship of the king's will to law had been raised in the crisis of 1386–7, and in returning to it in the articles of deposition the king's opponents were condemning him not just for his practice of government but also for the ideology of his kingship which had first been articulated in 1386 and 1387.

The proceedings in the assembly were conducted with no overt opposition. Several of the knights elected to the assembly were retainers of Henry or former retainers of Gaunt, and the sheriffs whom Henry had appointed in August may have played their part in ensuring that a nucleus of pro-Lancastrian members were elected to the Commons. The author of the *Traison* suggested that Thomas Merks, the bishop of Carlisle, spoke up in Richard's defence and called for him to be brought before the assembly to answer the charges against him in person; but this is not confirmed in any other account and may be a misunderstanding of a speech the bishop subsequently made in his own defence. There are hints in a later source that the earl of Northumberland and his son were unhappy about the proceedings, but this was probably a view heavily influenced by the Percys' later enmity towards Henry IV; it is hard to believe in face of Northumberland's evident willing participation in the plan to lure Richard out of Conwy. The day after the assembly agreed on Richard's deposition, a deputation led by William Thirning, chief justice of the king's bench, brought Richard news of what had happened. According to the official record, which for once has the ring of truth, Richard said that 'he looked not hereafter, but hoped that his cousin would be a good lord to him' (*RotP*, 3.424).

Imprisonment, death, and burial Little is known for certain about the rest of Richard's life. He evidently remained in the Tower for some weeks, but before Christmas 1399 he was taken under escort first to Knaresborough and then to the duchy of Lancaster castle of Pontefract, where he was guarded by two trusted duchy retainers, Sir Robert Waterton and Sir Thomas Swynford. His fate was probably sealed by the Epiphany rising of 1400. The earls of Huntingdon, Kent, and Salisbury, and Sir Thomas Despenser (all now reduced to their former ranks), plotted to seize and murder Henry and his sons, and to restore Richard to his throne. Henry, however, was forewarned of the conspiracy, which received little popular support, and the leaders were seized and executed by townspeople in Bristol, Cirencester, and Pleshey. In February the council ordered that if Richard were still alive he should be 'placed in appropriate safe keeping', but if dead he should be 'shown openly to the people' (*Proceedings ... of the Privy Council*, 1.111). Most chroniclers believed that he died on 14 February, but how he died will never be known for sure. The *Traison*'s story that he was hacked to death by Sir Piers Exton is almost certainly fictitious; three accounts, by John Hardyng, the Whalley Abbey chronicler, and the monk of Evesham, suggest he was deliberately starved to death; while other chroniclers, including Walsingham, describe how he refused food and drink and gradually starved himself to death. On 17 February instructions were given for his body to be transported to London, and on 6 March his obsequies were performed at St Paul's. In his will, drawn up before his departure for Ireland in 1399, he had expressed a wish to be buried in the tomb in Westminster Abbey that he had commissioned in 1395. Henry, however, ignored Richard's wishes and had him buried in the priory of the Dominican friars at the royal manor of Kings Langley. The priory had been founded by Edward II, and Edward III had made substantial contributions towards the cost of building the church and the conventual buildings.

Rumours persisted, however, that Richard was still alive. Some suggested that he had escaped to Scotland, and these rumours were given particular currency by the Franciscans, who had enjoyed Richard's patronage during his reign. The Scots, for their own purposes, gave a pension to an impostor (believed by the English to be Thomas Warde of Trumpington) who survived until 1419. It is impossible to credit these stories: they are not dissimilar to other survival legends that gathered round kings who died in mysterious circumstances and which proved useful to politically disaffected elements within the realm and to external enemies.

Kings Langley did not prove to be Richard's last resting place. The tomb that he had commissioned for himself in 1395 remained in Westminster Abbey, and in early December 1413 Henry V had him ceremonially reburied there, beside the tomb of Queen Anne. The reburial was intended to symbolize a healing of the political wounds opened by Richard's deposition, and to be a gesture of piety towards a king who is said to have knighted the young Henry when he had been taken to Ireland with Richard in 1399, in effect as an honourable hostage.

Richard's tomb was opened in 1871 and when his remains were examined they suggested that he had been a man almost 6 feet in height. Perhaps the effigy of the king on his tomb is the best likeness of him as a mature adult, and with other surviving portraits suggests that he was bearded from c.1386. However, the idealized representations of him in the Wilton diptych, and in the so-called coronation portrait in Westminster Abbey, which are both icons of kingship and which both date from c.1395, perhaps reveal more than a true likeness would of a king whose belief in the majesty of kingship and the sanctity of his own prerogative ultimately brought him to destruction.

The significance of the reign and Richard's historical reputation The deposition of Richard II cast its shadow over much of fifteenth-century English history. Although Henry IV was succeeded on the throne by his son and grandson, none was free from challenge on the grounds that he was not the true heir of Richard II and that the dynasty had gained the throne by an act of usurpation. By 1460 Henry VI's ineptitude had brought the dynastic issue to the forefront of English politics. In that year Richard, duke of York, formally claimed the throne on the ground that he and not Henry was the legitimate heir of Richard II, and York's son repeated the claim the following year when he became king as Edward IV. Edward declared that Henry IV had 'usurped and intruded upon the Roiall power' even though the 'right and title' of the crown after Richard's death belonged to Edmund Mortimer, and therefore all three Lancastrian kings had reigned unlawfully (*RotP*, 5.463). Richard's deposition thus introduced an element of uncertainty, and potential instability, to the fifteenth-century monarchy which was exploited with varying degrees of conviction and success by nobles who wished to undermine royal authority. This was perhaps

the abiding legacy of Richard's reign. Parallels can be drawn, in terms of misuse of royal patronage and lack of enthusiasm for the French war, between Richard and Henry VI, and there are certain similarities between Richard's emphasis on the subject's duty of obedience and that of the Tudors, though this is not to suggest that Richard was a premature exponent of the Tudor approach to government. Richard's manner of rule in the last two years of his reign, however, was not imitated by his successors: it was the deposition, the consequence of that manner of rule, that had the greatest impact on the monarchy in the fifteenth century.

In Elizabethan and Stuart times writers and rulers continued to draw lessons from the fate of Richard II. Shakespeare's *Richard II*, probably written in 1595, has been interpreted as a political allegory, and it was certainly seen in that light by Elizabeth I in 1601, when associates of the earl of Essex financed stagings of the play to whip up support for the earl. 'I am Richard II, know ye not that?' asked the indignant queen (Nichols, *Progresses*, 3.52–3). Holinshed's view of the king was friendly, perhaps because of his knowledge of the French narratives of Richard's last years; but Edward Hall adopted a distinctly hostile tone in his interpretation of the king: both chroniclers may have had some influence on Shakespeare's characterization of Richard. In the early 1640s both Thomas Favent's pro-appellant account of the Merciless Parliament and the *Traison*'s account of the bishop of Carlisle's defence of Richard in 1399 were translated and printed, while in 1681 an anonymous life of Richard referred to Richard's courtiers as a 'cabal', a reference to the group of courtiers whose influence over Charles II attracted hostility in the late 1660s and early 1670s.

Only in the nineteenth century did a full-length biography of Richard appear. This was *Richard II: épisode de la rivalité de la France et de l'Angleterre*, by Henri Wallon, published in 1864. Perhaps influenced by whig historians in England, Wallon argued that Richard's reign was: 'l'époque où commence, avec le premier exemple d'un roi mis en tutelle et à la fin jugé en parlement, la longue histoire de la Révolution en Angleterre' ('the point at which, when for the first time a king was brought under control and eventually judged in parliament, the long history of the English revolution begins'; Wallon, 1.iv). Wallon portrayed a king brought down by his own poor judgement and his alienation not just of ambitious nobles but of the whole political community. At much the same time William Stubbs delivered his verdict on the king. He argued that Richard had tried to act on a theory of the 'supremacy of the prerogative'; in doing so, he had 'resolutely, and without subterfuge or palliation, challenged the constitution', and this had brought about his downfall (Stubbs, 2.533).

In the twentieth century historians began to consider Richard's personality rather than the place of his reign in constitutional history. Perhaps the most original assessment from this point of view was provided by Anthony Steel in his *Richard II*, published in 1941. Steel attempted psychoanalysis of the king, suggesting that he felt unable to live up to the standards of knightly prowess exemplified by his father, was traumatized by the murder of his friends in 1388, and in his later years became 'a pitiful neurotic' (Steel, 8) probably suffering from schizophrenia. V. H. Galbraith, in a celebrated review which showed how good a book on Richard he could have written, criticized this colourful interpretation of Richard as lacking any real basis in the evidence; in particular, he argued, there is no justification for the belief that he went mad at the end of his reign. None the less, Steel's interpretation has had some influence on subsequent accounts. May McKisack, for example, in her volume on the fourteenth century in the *Oxford History of England*, argued that Richard's actions in his last two years suggest 'a sudden loss of control, the onset of a mental malaise' (McKisack, 498). Historians who worked on the reign in the 1970s and 1980s, such as Anthony Goodman and Anthony Tuck, eschewed this approach, but it came once again to the forefront of discussion about the king with the publication in 1997 of Nigel Saul's biography of the king. This is the most substantial treatment of Richard since the nineteenth century, and represents the state of knowledge of the king and his reign at the end of the twentieth century. Saul rejects Steel's assertion that Richard was insane, but suggests that the king had a 'narcissistic' personality, and that by the end of his reign his grasp on reality 'was becoming weaker' (Saul, *Richard II*, pp. 459–60).

The character of the king and his reign However, it remains doubtful whether the impetuousness and touchiness which characterize Richard's adolescent years as king, the concern about his prerogative rights which is apparent in 1386 and 1387, and the image of kingship which he cultivated in the 1390s amount to evidence for a personality disorder, though they made for an uneasy political relationship with his nobility. Indeed, his courage at the time of the peasants' revolt and his effective conduct of the limited military campaigns he undertook in Scotland and Ireland suggest qualities which would have been readily comprehensible to his contemporaries, though they might have preferred him to fight in France. Many of the difficulties of the early years of his reign arose from misjudgements of men and events that suggest parallels with earlier and later rulers who met similar fates, such as Edward II and Henry VI. His emphasis on the majesty and sacred character of kingship may have been received uneasily by some of his nobles—although there is no direct evidence for this—but it was not dissimilar from, indeed may have been derived from, ideas of kingship current at the French court, and his concern for his prerogative rights would not have seemed unusual to some of his English predecessors, notably Edward I.

Richard's patronage of literature and the arts, too, was perhaps similar to that of his royal predecessors, but it has particular significance because several of the poets who enjoyed the patronage of the court wrote in English. Chaucer especially developed English into a language suitable, in the distinction that Dante made in *De vulgari eloquentia*, for 'eloquence' rather than mere 'speech'. This is not to say that Richard specifically encouraged the use of English: like most contemporaries of noble birth he was probably bilingual in English and Anglo-Norman, and he was probably able to read Latin: his cousin and supplanter, Henry IV, was certainly competent in all three languages.

In his tastes and beliefs Richard appears to have been conventional. Although some of the knights of his chamber sympathized with Lollardy, Richard's own piety was orthodox. His cult of royal saints has already been discussed, but he seems to have shared the enthusiasm of some of his nobles for the Carthusian order, which was also fashionable on the continent, and in 1385 he laid the foundation stone of the Coventry Charterhouse. Like many of his contemporaries he had an interest in astrology and divination. The *Libellus geomancie*, a treatise compiled in 1391 'for the solace of our lord king Richard' (Bodl. Oxf., MS Bodley 581 fol. 9) contains material on astrology, geomancy (divination by casting earth or small pebbles and drawing conclusions from the random patterns they form), and physiognomy (how a person's character may be deduced from the shape of his limbs and his facial features).

Thus Richard was a king who shared many of the tastes and interests of his generation, yet aspects of his personality prevented the emergence of the same rapport with his nobility that had contributed so much to Edward III's popularity, especially in the 1340s and 1350s. His failure to lead his nobles in arms against the French is one reason for this, however explicable such failure may be in political and financial terms. In explaining his eventual downfall, however, both contemporaries and modern historians have focused attention on the unwisdom and extremism of his actions in the last two years of his reign, when he sought to impose his own concept of kingship on a reluctant community, and to enforce his authority by means considered by many in the community as barely lawful. It is the immoderation of his behaviour in these years that has persuaded some historians that by then Richard was inhabiting the borderlands of sanity. Yet although at his deposition his rule was condemned as oppressive, unjust, and contrary to law, running through the charges against him is the assumption that his conduct had been rational, if unacceptable. Walsingham maintained that in 1397 Richard had begun to 'tyrannise' his people (*Johannis de Trokelowe … Chronica*, 199). In terms of the Aristotelian definition of a tyrant as one who rules for his own advantage rather than the well-being of his people, such an accusation was an understandable judgement on Richard's kingship during the last two years of his reign. When Henry Bolingbroke claimed the throne on 30 September 1399, he maintained that 'the realm was on the point of being undone for default of governance and undoing of the good laws' (*RotP*, 3.423). Richard's rule from the summer of 1397 onwards was characterized by a combination of ideology and a sense of insecurity which in the eyes of his opponents amounted to a lack of good governance, and for this he was rejected.

ANTHONY TUCK

Sources PRO, Exchequer, king's remembrancer, E 101, Accounts, various · PRO, Treasury of receipt issue rolls, E 403 · Bodl. Oxf., MS Bodley 581 · *Chancery records* · RotP, vols. 2–3, 5 · F. S. Haydon, ed., *Eulogium historiarum sive temporis*, 3 vols., Rolls Series, 9 (1858–63) · *Thomae Walsingham, quondam monachi S. Albani, historia Anglicana*, ed. H. T. Riley, 2 vols., pt 1 of *Chronica monasterii S. Albani*, Rolls Series, 28 (1863–4) · *Johannis de Trokelowe et Henrici de Blaneforde … chronica et annales*, ed. H. T. Riley, pt 3 of *Chronica monasterii S. Albani*, Rolls Series, 28 (1866) · *Knighton's chronicle, 1337–1396*, ed. and trans. G. H. Martin, OMT (1995) [Lat. orig., *Chronica de eventibus Angliae a tempore regis Edgari usque mortem regis Ricardi Secundi*, with parallel Eng. text] · L. C. Hector and B. F. Harvey, eds. and trans., *The Westminster chronicle, 1381–1394*, OMT (1982) · *The chronicle of Adam Usk, 1377–1421*, ed. and trans. C. Given-Wilson, OMT (1997) · *Œuvres de Froissart: chroniques*, ed. K. de Lettenhove, 25 vols. (Brussels, 1867–77) · G. B. Stow, ed., *Historia vitae et regni Ricardi Secundi* (1977) · C. Given-Wilson, ed. and trans., *Chronicles of the revolution, 1397–1400: the reign of Richard II* (1993) · B. Williams, ed., *Chronicque de la traïson et mort de Richart Deux, roy Dengleterre*, EHS, 9 (1846) · W. Thorne, *Chronicle of St Augustine's Abbey, Canterbury*, trans. A. H. Davis (1934) · V. H. Galbraith, ed., *The Anonimalle chronicle, 1333 to 1381* (1927) · H. Wallon, *Richard II: épisode de la rivalité de la France et de l'Angleterre*, 2 vols. (Paris, 1864) · Tout, *Admin. hist.* · A. B. Steel, *Richard II* (1941) · R. H. Jones, *The royal policy of Richard II: absolutism in the later middle ages* (1968) · A. Goodman, *The loyal conspiracy: the lords appellant under Richard II* (1971) · A. Tuck, *Richard II and the English nobility* (1973) · J. J. N. Palmer, *England, France and Christendom, 1377–99* (1972) · C. Given-Wilson, *The royal household and the king's affinity: service, politics and finance in England, 1360–1413* (1986) · N. H. Nicolas, ed., *Proceedings and ordinances of the privy council of England*, 7 vols., RC, 26 (1834–7) · A. Goodman, *John of Gaunt: the exercise of princely power in fourteenth-century Europe* (1992) · M. McKisack, *The fourteenth century* (1959) · W. Stubbs, *The constitutional history of England in its origin and development*, new edn, 2 (1887) · J. S. Roskell, *The impeachment of Michael de la Pole earl of Suffolk in 1386* (1984) · HoP, *Commons* · J. Sherborne, *War, politics and culture in fourteenth century England*, ed. A. Tuck (1994) · C. M. Barron, 'The tyranny of Richard II', *BIHR*, 41 (1968), 1–18 · D. Gordon and others, *Mastery and meaning: the Wilton diptych* (1993) [exhibition catalogue, National Gallery, London] · A. P. Stanley, 'On an examination of the tombs of Richard II and Henry II in Westminster Abbey', *Archaeologia*, 45 (1880), 309–27 · J. E. Powell, 'A king's tomb', *History Today*, 15 (1965), 713–17 · V. H. Galbraith, 'A new life of Richard II', *History*, new ser., 26 (1941–2), 223–39 · *An inventory of the historical monuments in London*, Royal Commission on Historical Monuments (England), 1 (1924) · J. Nichols, *The progresses and public processions of Queen Elizabeth*, new edn, 3 (1823) · R. Brown, H. M. Colvin, and A. J. Taylor, eds., *The history of the king's works*, 1–2 (1963) · J. Taylor, ed., *The Kirkstall Abbey Chronicles*, Thoresby Society, 42 (1952) · M. V. Clarke and V. H. Galbraith, eds., 'The deposition of Richard II', *Bulletin of the John Rylands University Library*, 14 (1930), 125–81, esp. 164–81 [chronicle of Dieulacres Abbey] · J. H. Wylie, ed., *The reign of Henry the Fifth*, 1 (1914) · N. Saul, *Richard II* (1997) · [J. Nichols], ed., *A collection of … wills … of … every branch of the blood royal* (1780), 191–202 · E. B. Fryde and others, eds., *Handbook of British chronology*, 3rd edn, Royal Historical Society Guides and Handbooks, 2 (1986) · M. Bennett, 'Edward III's entail and the succession to the crown, 1376–1471', *EngHR*, 113 (1998), 580–609 · N. Saul, 'Richard II and the vocabulary of kingship', *EngHR*, 110 (1995), 854–77

Archives BL · PRO · PRO, E 101, E 403

Likenesses manuscript, 1380 (*The Ipswich charter*), Suffolk RO, Ipswich · oils on panel, *c*.1388, Westminster Abbey, London [*see illus.*] · manuscript, 1389 (*The Shrewsbury charter*), Guildhall, Shrewsbury · manuscript, *c*.1389 (*Book of Statutes*), St John Cam., MS A.7, fol. 133 · attrib. Herebright of Cologne, stained-glass window, *c*.1393, Winchester College, Hampshire · R. Dymmock, manuscript, *c*.1395 (*Liber Contra Duodecim Errores et Hereses Lollardorum*), Trinity Hall, Cambridge, MS 17, fol. ia · group portrait, oils, *c*.1395 (*The Wilton diptych*), National Gallery, London · P. de Mazières, manuscript,

1395–6, BL, Royal MS 20 B.vi, fol. 2 · N. Broker and G. Prest, gilt copper tomb effigy, *c*.1395–1397, Westminster Abbey; electrotype, NPG · W. Hollar, portrait, NPG · illuminated initial, BL, Cotton MS Nero D.vi, fol. 85; *see illus. in* Mowbray, Thomas (I), first duke of Norfolk (1366–1399) · silver half-groat, BM

Wealth at death see will, Nichols, *Royal wills*

Richard III (1452–1485), king of England and lord of Ireland, was born on 2 October 1452 at Fotheringhay, Northamptonshire, the youngest surviving child of *Richard, third duke of York (1411–1460), and *Cecily, duchess of York (1415–1495), the daughter of Ralph *Neville, first earl of Westmorland, and Joan Beaufort.

Childhood 1452–1468 Little is known of Richard's early life, although he can occasionally be glimpsed on the margins of the developing struggle for power between his father and the circle around Henry VI's queen, Margaret of Anjou. After the Yorkist rout at Ludford in 1459 Cecily Neville submitted to Henry VI and was placed in the keeping of her sister Anne, duchess of Buckingham, with an annual allowance of 1000 marks for the maintenance of herself and her younger children. It may be during the months after Ludford that Richard and his elder brother *George were in the care of the archbishop of Canterbury, Thomas Bourchier, who was later (in December 1471) to be rewarded by Edward IV for supporting the king's brothers 'for a long time at great charges' (Ross, *Richard III*, 7).

In July 1460 the political situation was transformed by the Yorkist victory at Northampton. In September Cecily and her three youngest children, Margaret, George, and Richard, arrived in London to await the return of the duke of York from Ireland. They stayed in the Southwark house formerly owned by Sir John Fastolf, where the children remained (visited daily by their eldest brother, Edward, earl of March) while the duchess travelled to meet her husband. On his return York asserted his claim to the throne, and, in a compromise solution, was recognized as Henry VI's heir. This agreement, which disinherited Edward of Lancaster, was never likely to hold, and on 30 December York's forces clashed with those of the queen near Wakefield, and York and his second son, Edmund, were killed. The royal army then advanced towards London, meeting and defeating an army under the command of the earl of Warwick at St Albans on 17 February.

With the Lancastrian army at the gates of London, George and Richard were sent for safety to Burgundy. Their arrival was something of a diplomatic embarrassment for Duke Philip and they were initially placed in the household of the bishop of Utrecht, one of the duke's illegitimate sons. News of the battle of Towton (29 March) and Edward IV's accession transformed them into visitors of consequence, and the brothers were invited to the ducal court at Bruges before returning to England early in June. On 26 June, as part of the ceremonial preceding Edward's coronation two days later, both brothers were created knights of the Bath, but, whereas George was made duke of Clarence at the coronation, Richard had to wait until 1 November before becoming duke of Gloucester. He was still only nine, and his early grants were clearly regarded as provisional, with much of what he was given

Richard III (1452–1485), by unknown artist, *c*.1516

in August 1462 subsequently regranted, including the forfeited de Vere estates, which were restored to the earl of Oxford at the beginning of 1464.

Richard was left with a geographically scattered collection, designed to provide him with an income rather than any sort of power base. In 1465 he was granted the duchy of Lancaster lordships of Bolingbroke, Lincolnshire, and Pickering and Barnoldswick, Yorkshire, but evidently enjoyed no direct influence within the lordships, where the officers remained unchanged. The three lordships yielded £1000, and the grant was probably designed to meet Richard's costs within the household of his cousin, Richard Neville, earl of Warwick, which he had entered by Michaelmas 1465. He had spent some, at least, of the previous years with Margaret and George at Greenwich, in an establishment under the aegis of the royal household. It is possible that the period when he was in Archbishop Bourchier's care should also be dated to the early 1460s rather than to 1459–60.

First steps in war and politics, 1468–1471 Richard probably remained in his cousin's household until late in 1468, when he was sixteen; it is likely that, as with his brother Clarence, he was then deemed to have come of age. In February 1469 he was with the king, and took an active role in the trial for treason of Henry Courtenay and Thomas Hungerford. Late in 1468 Richard had been granted the forfeited estates of Thomas's father, Robert, Lord Hungerford: a sign that Edward was trying to put together an

endowment for his youngest brother. But royal resources were in short supply. When in May 1469 Richard was granted a significant collection of duchy of Lancaster land, including Clitheroe, Liverpool, and Halton, the grant cut across the existing interests of Thomas, Lord Stanley, and triggered a dispute in which Edward IV had to intervene in 1470.

Richard's emergence on the public scene took place against a background of growing opposition to Edward IV from Clarence and Warwick. In spite of his links with the earl, Richard's loyalties remained with Edward, and he was with the king in Norwich when trouble finally erupted in June 1469. His movements over the next few months are unclear. He was apparently not with the king when Edward was captured by the rebels in July and is next mentioned in October, when Edward, having reasserted his freedom of action, returned to London. The death of several of Edward's leading allies in the rebellion meant that Richard's loyalty could now be rewarded. On 17 October he became constable of England in succession to the king's father-in-law, the executed Earl Rivers. A month later Richard was granted the castle and manor of Sudeley, Gloucestershire, but his major gain from the events of 1469 was the acquisition, for the first time, of a regional sphere of influence. The rebels' execution of William Herbert, earl of Pembroke, had seriously compromised royal authority in Wales, and the grant to Richard of Herbert's key offices, including the justiciarships of north and south Wales and the stewardship of the principality, cast him, in effect, as Herbert's replacement. His influence, unlike that of Herbert, did not have a territorial base, apart from Chirk, which he had held since September 1462 and where he was retaining men in 1470. He was essentially intended to act as a focus for lesser royal servants in the region. But that role was an important one, actively pursued. Richard probably left for Wales in November 1469 and may have spent most of the next few months there. He was certainly in Wales in mid-June 1470 when he presided as justiciar over the Carmarthenshire great sessions.

By that date Edward had weathered another rebellion by Clarence and Warwick, who, after gaining little support, had fled to France. There is no evidence that Richard played any part in the suppression of the rebellion itself, but in July he joined Edward in mopping up one of the after-effects: the rebellion of Warwick's kinsman, Lord Fitzhugh, in Yorkshire. In August he was granted Warwick's forfeited office of warden of the west march, although there is no other suggestion that he was intended to take over the Neville role in the north. The king's plans must, however, remain doubtful, for in September Warwick and Clarence invaded with French backing to restore Henry VI and it was the turn of Edward and Richard to escape into exile, sailing from Bishop's Lynn on 29 September. Their ships were scattered by storms, and Richard landed at Weilingen in Zeeland, while Edward put ashore further north, at Texel, but by the middle of October the exiles had assembled at The Hague as the guests of Louis, Lord Gruthuyse.

Charles, duke of Burgundy, was initially not convinced that he wished to help his brother-in-law regain the throne, but the alliance of the new regime in England with France, and the increasingly bellicose stance taken by Louis XI, changed his mind, and at the beginning of January 1471 he agreed to support Edward's invasion of England. The fleet sailed early in March and, after an abortive landing near Cromer, where they were opposed by the earl of Oxford, landed in Holderness on 14 March. The Yorkist army defeated Warwick at the battle of Barnet on 14 April and then the Lancastrian army at Tewkesbury on 4 May. Richard commanded the vanguard in the second battle, and may also have held a command at Barnet, where none of the Yorkist commanders, other than the king, is named by the chroniclers. After returning with his brother to London, Richard was sent ahead of the king into Kent to deal with Thomas Neville, the Bastard of Fauconberg, who had led an assault on London in the king's absence. Neville submitted to Richard at Sandwich on 27 May.

Heir of Neville: marriage Richard, predictably, was the chief beneficiary of Edward's restoration, emerging as the heir to Neville power in the north. On 29 June he was granted the Neville strongholds of Middleham, Sheriff Hutton, and Penrith. On 14 July this was superseded by a grant of all the lands in Yorkshire and Cumberland entailed to Richard Neville and his heirs male. He also assumed the key offices held by Warwick in the region, notably the chief stewardship of the duchy of Lancaster in the north, which he was formally granted on 4 July but which he had been exercising at least since the beginning of June, and which gave him extensive influence from Lincolnshire and Leicestershire northwards. These grants formed the foundation of what became a great northern power base for Richard. The grant of the Neville lands meant that the earl's retainers, in urgent need of effective lordship following Warwick's death at Barnet, turned naturally to Richard, and he was retaining within the lordship of Middleham by August 1471. The grant of the duchy stewardship put him at the head of the royal servants in the north, for whom duchy patronage provided the major source of reward and influence.

The grants thus benefited Richard. But they also benefited the king. There had been disaffection in the north for much of Edward's first reign: in the beginning from committed Lancastrians, and later from Warwick. The assertion of Richard's authority was *de facto* the assertion of royal authority. The reverse was also true, and much of Richard's authority in the north derived from contemporary awareness that he had royal backing. The steady extension of Richard's hold on the north after 1471 should therefore not be seen as unilateral empire building by an 'over-mighty' subject. It was achieved with royal approval and was dependent on the continuance of that approval.

Warwick's patrimony had come to Richard by an exercise of royal patronage: since it was held in tail male it should have passed to Warwick's nephew George on the earl's death. But *c.*1472 Richard married Warwick's second daughter, *Anne (1456–1485), the widow of Edward of

Lancaster, and thus became eligible for a share of the Beauchamp and Despenser lands that had come to the earl by marriage. Clarence, who had married Anne's sister Isabel in 1469, was strongly opposed to the prospect of Anne's marriage, reputedly even to the extent of trying to hide her from his brother. The ensuing dispute between the two men was not finally resolved until 1474, when the land was divided between them as if the dowager countess were dead. Richard's major gain in the north was Barnard Castle, which allowed him to extend his influence into the county of Durham, but he also acquired land in Derbyshire and Hertfordshire, which he exchanged in 1475 for land in Yorkshire, notably the castle and lordship of Scarborough. In another exchange accomplished under the royal aegis in 1475, Richard received the Clifford barony in the West Riding, consisting of Skipton and Marton in Craven, from William Stanley in exchange for Chirk. In the same year Richard was made sheriff of Cumberland for life, with the demesne lands of the castle of Carlisle.

Northern pre-eminence By 1475 Richard had emerged as the pre-eminent nobleman in the north-east and far north-west. The only area outside his sphere of influence was Lancashire and Cheshire. The grant made to him of land there in 1469 had been replaced in 1471 by a grant of office, but even that trespassed on Stanley interests, and there seems to have been continuing friction between them. By 1475 it was clear that Richard was not going to absorb central Lancashire into his sphere of influence, in spite of his duchy office, although he was the leading figure in Clitheroe and Furness (which complemented his West Riding and Westmorland interests respectively). Elsewhere in the north, however, local noblemen, including the restored earl of Northumberland, apparently accepted a place within the duke of Gloucester's connection.

Richard was never an exclusively northern figure. Although the role envisaged for him in Wales in 1469–70 was abandoned in Edward's second reign, his share of the Warwick inheritance, including Glamorgan and Abergavenny, ensured him a continuing interest in the region, which was strengthened in 1478 when he exchanged the Neville lordship of Elfael for Ogmore. He also held land in East Anglia, where he was granted the lion's share of the forfeited de Vere lands in 1471. These did not include the lands held by the widow of the twelfth earl of Oxford, who was persuaded to make an estate in her lands to Richard in 1473. According to her servants she capitulated under threat of a forced removal to Middleham, which 'considering her great age, the great journey, and the great cold there then was of frost and snow' (Hicks, 'Last days', 91) she thought would be the death of her. Richard's East Anglian grants from the crown were reordered and somewhat reduced in 1475, and he was subsequently prepared to sell off parts of the de Vere dower lands, implying that he now saw them as peripheral to his main concerns. Similarly, in 1478, he was prepared to exchange Sudeley in Gloucestershire, Farleigh Hungerford in Wiltshire, and

Corfe in Dorset for land in Yorkshire forfeited by his executed brother, Clarence, including the castle of Richmond which filled an obvious gap in his Middleham-based domination of Richmondshire.

As brother of the king, Richard's importance was national as well as regional. Throughout Edward's second reign the duke was constable and admiral of England, and was active in both capacities. As constable he presided over the trial of the Lancastrian captives after Tewkesbury, and in 1473 looked into a dispute between two London goldsmiths which was thought to have treasonable overtones: an example of Edward IV's willingness to extend the constable's jurisdiction beyond military and chivalric matters. In 1475 Richard led the largest private retinue on the campaign against France which was ended by the treaty of Picquigny. He did not attend the meeting of Louis and Edward at which the treaty was agreed, and evidently disapproved, although he later paid a courtesy visit to Louis at Amiens. His military skills, unused in France, were not called upon until the end of Edward's reign when the war against Scotland was resumed. Little came of the planned invasion of 1481, which was to have been led by the king in person, but the campaign of 1482 led by Richard penetrated as far as Edinburgh in support of the duke of Albany, who had sought English help against his brother James III. At that point, however, Albany backed down, and the English forces had little option but to retreat, with only the capture of Berwick to show for their efforts. English opinion was divided on the value of the campaign, but in the parliament of 1482–3 Richard was rewarded with the grant of palatine authority in any land that he could capture in the Scottish dales along the west march. He was also given the wardenship of the English west march in hereditary right, along with extensive lands and royal rights in Cumberland, where the shrievalty of the county and control of Carlisle were vested in him and his heirs.

Protector of the realm Edward IV died on 9 April 1483. His death seems to have taken the political community by surprise. Richard was in the north, and the prince of Wales was with his senior maternal uncle, Anthony Woodville, Earl Rivers, at Ludlow. Immediate authority thus rested with the royal council. Edward's own plans for the succession are unclear, but the implication of the Crowland chronicle is that he favoured the immediate coronation of his twelve-year-old son. Some of the council, however, evidently preferred the idea of a protectorate, for which the obvious candidate was Richard, now Edward IV's only surviving brother. There were clearly anxieties within the council about the degree of influence likely to be wielded over the young king by his maternal kinsmen, the Woodvilles. The debate was, however, overtaken by events at the end of the month, when Richard, *en route* for London, took possession of the prince at Stony Stratford, and arrested Rivers and other members of the prince's circle. By the time the prince and his uncle entered London on 4 May it seems to have been generally believed that Richard would indeed be protector, and he assumed the office almost immediately.

For the next few weeks the regime functioned smoothly. Richard's claims that the Woodvilles had been threatening to take power by force may not have been believed in detail (and he was unable to secure their execution on the grounds that their actions against him constituted treason) but there seems to have been little sympathy for them, and the protector was able to call on the support of Edward IV's former servants against Rivers's brother Edward Woodville, who was in command of a fleet in the channel. The regime's main problem was financial rather than political. Edward IV had left little cash in hand at his death and it was unclear where the money was to be found for the coronation, now scheduled for 22 June. Richard himself paid £800 towards the king's household expenses within this period. This period of harmony is ignored by the chroniclers, who tend to telescope the seizure of the prince and Richard's usurpation, as if one led inexorably to the other. That was not the case, and the protectorate was still viable when Richard chose to end it.

The usurpation of the throne The date of that decision can be fixed fairly precisely. On 9 June government was still proceeding as normal, and the council meeting that day was still absorbed in how to meet the costs of the coronation. On 10 June 1483 Richard wrote to York for military help against Queen Elizabeth and her associates 'which have intended and daily doth intend to murder and utterly destroy us' (Attreed, 714). A Woodville conspiracy against Richard is not improbable—the measures he had taken against the family since seizing power gave them grounds for resentment—but given their political isolation it is hard to see them as a serious threat. It is more likely that, as at the beginning of May, Richard was maximizing the danger of disaffection as an argument for increasing his own authority as a bulwark against political instability. In April and May it had justified his assumption of the protectorship; now it was tacitly to justify his taking the throne.

On 13 June Edward IV's chamberlain and friend, William, Lord Hastings, was seized and executed at the Tower of London; again, it was claimed, this action was in response to an attempt by him to attack the protector. A more likely explanation is that Hastings had been sounded on Richard's plans to claim the throne and had refused to be party to them. Other councillors were arrested: Lord Stanley, the archbishop of York, and the bishop of Ely. With hindsight it seems a clear avowal of Richard's designs on the throne, but contemporaries apparently still hesitated to draw that conclusion. On 16 June the queen (who had taken sanctuary at Westminster at the end of April) was persuaded by the archbishop of Canterbury and the bishop of Lincoln to hand over her second son, the duke of York, to attend his brother's coronation. With both the sons of Edward IV in his hands, Richard immediately postponed the coronation, this time until 9 November.

From this point government business began to wind down as men awaited a change of ruler. On 22 June Dr Ralph Shaw publicized Richard's claim to the throne in a sermon at Paul's Cross. According to Dominic Mancini, Richard initially claimed that his brother had been illegitimate, but, if so, this line was afterwards abandoned and it was argued instead that his sons were illegitimate, on the grounds that Edward IV, before his marriage to Elizabeth Woodville, had been precontracted to another woman— later identified as Eleanor Butler (*née* Talbot). Contemporaries, and most subsequent historians, have regarded this as an *ex post facto* justification for a decision taken on other grounds: Richard took the throne because he wanted it. But that still leaves open the question of Gloucester's motivation. Ambition no doubt played a part, but Richard may also have persuaded himself that he was genuinely the best man to preserve the polity created by his brother. In one sense he was probably right, but many contemporaries were not prepared to accept that the end (the accession of an experienced adult) justified the means (the deposition of a child king).

That hostility was not, however, immediately apparent. Richard's seizure of power evidently happened too quickly, and was too shockingly unexpected, for people to concert opposition. He took his seat at Westminster on 26 June, in a ceremony modelled on that of his brother in 1461, and was crowned on 6 July. At that stage Richard clearly still believed that he had carried all his brother's servants with him, save for the Woodvilles and their immediate circle, and the opening weeks of his reign are marked by almost complete continuity of personnel in central and local government.

The rebellion of 1483 After the coronation Richard set off on a progress around his realm, which was to culminate in his triumphant entry into York on 29 August. Shortly after he left London late in July news reached him of an attempt to rescue the princes from the Tower of London. The attempt had failed, but it probably prompted the princes' death. Certainly contemporaries quickly came to believe that the princes were dead, for, when opposition next surfaced, it did so with Margaret Beaufort's son, Henry Tudor, as its figurehead: an inconceivable choice if Edward V and his brother were thought to be still available. News of the rebellion in Tudor's favour reached Richard as he travelled south through Lincolnshire in the second week of October, although it took time for the full extent of the unrest to become apparent. The rebellion affected English counties south of a line from the Wash to the River Severn. It was probably also intended to include Wales, where the elevation during the protectorate of Richard's ally, the duke of Buckingham, had challenged the power of Edward IV's servants in the region; but Buckingham's decision to join the rebels neutralized that element of the rising directed against him, and Tudor writers were agreed that it was the failure of Buckingham to win support that led to the collapse of the rising elsewhere. By the beginning of November the rebellion was effectively over.

Although the rebellion had collapsed without coming to battle, it left Richard III with two uncomfortable legacies. One was the existence, for the first time since 1471, of an acknowledged rival claimant to the throne. The other was the revelation that Richard did not, as he had assumed, enjoy the support of his brother's former servants in the south, many of whom had joined the rebels. The king's response was to use the land and offices forfeited by the rebels to establish trusted servants, many of them from the north-east, in the areas most badly affected by the rebellion, where they could spearhead the reassertion of royal authority: a process which was already under way before the attainder of the rebels in the parliament of January 1484. This 'plantation' of outsiders was deeply unpopular, and was to breed further disaffection in the counties concerned.

Continuing unrest In the short term, however, the rebellion's failure brought Richard a few months of apparently unchallenged authority. Parliament endorsed his title to the throne and granted him the customs revenues for life. Some rebels had sued for pardon before parliament rose, and escaped attainder; others returned to the fold in the course of the spring. But in July 1484 there were further signs of unrest. A commission was appointed to investigate 'great treasons' in the south-west, and, in London, William Collingbourne and others conspired to incite Tudor to invade. On 18 July Collingbourne pinned rhymes and ballads of seditious language on the doors of St Paul's including, presumably, the doggerel credited to him by Tudor writers:

> The Cat, the Rat and Lovell our Dog
> Rule all England under a Hog.
> (Ross, *Richard III*, xxxiii)

Although Richard's inner circle was not limited to William Catesby, Richard Ratcliffe, and Francis, Viscount Lovell (the others, including James Tyrell and Marmaduke Constable, did not lend themselves to animal imagery), the verse highlights Richard's identification with an unacceptably narrow clique.

There was more unrest in the winter of 1484–5, centred on Essex and Hertfordshire but with links to the Calais garrison, where the commander of Hammes, James Blount, freed the Lancastrian earl of Oxford and went with him to Tudor. Again the unrest came to nothing, partly at least because Tudor was not yet ready to act. But it involved members of Richard's own household: former servants of Edward IV who had initially supported Richard but had now reconsidered their position. This continuing seepage of loyalty reflects the growing credibility of Henry Tudor. At Christmas 1483 Tudor had strengthened his appeal to disaffected Yorkists by promising to marry Edward IV's daughter Elizabeth were he to gain the throne. Of more practical consequence, however, was his acquisition of military backing from France. After the collapse of the rising of 1483 Tudor had returned to Brittany, and during 1484 Richard had been negotiating with Pierre Landais, the Breton treasurer, for Tudor's surrender. By autumn the negotiations were close to success, but Tudor was alerted and escaped to France, offering Charles VIII a chance of putting pressure on England. Polydore Vergil, who was well informed about this stage in Tudor's career, noted that once he was based in France men began to make their way from England to join him.

The search for stability Richard's response to Tudor's growing authority was to seek an understanding with the Woodvilles. Edward IV's daughters had left sanctuary and entered Richard's care in March 1484, but the first indication of a real thaw in relations came at Christmas 1484, when the attention paid by Richard to his niece Elizabeth scandalized the Crowland chronicler. The king's motives were, however, likely to have been political rather than sexual. In January Richard Woodville and John Fogge bound themselves to be faithful lieges of the king, and in March Richard Haute of Ightham, like Fogge a close Woodville associate, secured a royal pardon. Richard had also won over Elizabeth Woodville and it was probably about this time that she persuaded her son the marquess of Dorset to abandon Tudor and return to England, although the plan was foiled by Humphrey Cheyne, one of the other exiles in Tudor's company.

In England, too, there were powerful vested interests opposed to the Woodvilles' rehabilitation. On 16 March 1485 Queen Anne died and Richard, whose only legitimate son had died the previous year, began the search for a second wife. Joanna of Portugal was among the candidates under consideration and so, evidently, was Elizabeth of York. Indeed the rumour that reached Tudor claimed Richard had already married her—news which, in Vergil's graphic phrase, 'pinched him by the very stomach' (*Polydore Vergil's 'English History'*, 215). But Henry's anxiety was premature. According to the Crowland chronicler, Catesby and Ratcliffe were intent on blocking the proposed marriage. They found canonists to argue that it would be impossible to secure a dispensation for an uncle's marriage to his niece, and further claimed that such a marriage would lose Richard the support of his northern allies, who would think that Richard had murdered Anne Neville in order to marry Elizabeth. The claim echoes the Crowland chronicler's own suspicions of Richard's relationship to Elizabeth, but he adds that the counsellors' real motive was unwillingness to see the restoration of the Woodvilles.

Faced with such opposition Richard publicly denied that he had considered marriage to Elizabeth. His declaration, made before 'the substance of all our household' (Attreed, 360), was a tacit assurance that the interests of his servants who had benefited from the forfeitures of the Woodvilles and others would be protected. The episode reveals the extent to which Richard's reliance on trusted associates in the aftermath of the rebellion of 1483 had created a power base that was not only limited but self-limiting. Richard therefore had little hope of winning over former opponents, and instead had to deal with opposition as it occurred. Although he issued orders against seditious speech and probably engaged in counter-espionage, the efficacy of such measures is likely to have been limited.

Even so, time was probably on Richard's side. Much of Henry Tudor's credibility derived from French backing and, if French policy towards England changed, that backing would be withdrawn. As king, Richard still commanded obedience. Although there are signs that the associates of the inner circle to whom he turned for particularly sensitive assignments were finding themselves overstretched, the routine manifestations of royal government (such as local commissions) could still be maintained. In spite of the erosion of loyalty, in practical terms Richard's regime had not ceased to be viable.

The king's difficulties in 1485 were not only political. Finance was evidently also a problem. Richard had inherited an empty treasury from his brother, although he may have taken over Edward's jewels and plate, the fate of which is unknown. One measure of financial stringency is likely to be the truce with Scotland in September 1484. Richard had probably regarded the campaigns of 1481–2 against Scotland as 'his' war, and he agreed to the truce grudgingly. Another sign of difficulty is his request for loans from his subjects in February and March 1485. These were not the same as the 'benevolences' to which Edward IV had resorted and which Richard had outlawed in parliament—which were gifts rather than loans—but the Crowland chronicler thought that there was nothing to choose between them, and the insistence of Tudor chroniclers that Richard had squandered the wealth left by Edward IV, although assuming a royal hoard which (in cash terms, at least) did not exist, may also be testimony to contemporary dislike of his financial expedients. Those expedients also included maximizing the yield from the royal lands, and from what would later be called 'prerogative' revenues—tactics previously employed by Edward IV.

The Bosworth campaign The military defeat of Tudor would have resolved many of Richard's problems, as well as giving him the divine sanction that his regime signally lacked, and it is likely that Richard genuinely welcomed his rival's invasion. According to the Crowland chronicler, when the king heard of Tudor's landing he rejoiced; after his victory he would 'comfort his subjects with the blessings of unchallenged peace' (Pronay and Cox, 176). But the king's public confidence was misplaced. When the two armies met near Dadlington, Leicestershire, on 22 August 1485 the victory was Tudor's, although Richard, who had the larger army, seems to have come close to success. Almost nothing is known of the course of the battle, now known as the battle of Bosworth after the nearby town of Market Bosworth, but it is generally assumed that the climax of the engagement was a charge against Tudor's position led by the king in person. The Yorkist forces apparently came very close to Tudor himself, but at the last moment William Stanley threw in his troops, hitherto unengaged, on Tudor's side, and Richard was overwhelmed and killed, 'fighting manfully in the thickest press of his enemies' (*Polydore Vergil's 'English History'*, 224).

Richard had already been aware of the risk from the Stanleys. Indeed he had probably expected Thomas, Lord Stanley, to support his stepson Henry Tudor in 1483. In the event he did not, and Richard's surprise as much as his gratitude is reflected in the rewards that Stanley received and in the lenient treatment accorded to his wife, Margaret Beaufort, who was Tudor's mother. This harmony had eroded by the summer of 1485, when Richard was not prepared to allow Lord Stanley to leave court unless he left his son George, Lord Strange, as hostage for his good behaviour. This subsequently kept Lord Thomas from the battle, and the family forces were led instead by his brother William. In spite of Richard's manifest hostility, William Stanley seems to have hesitated before committing his men on Tudor's side, which may imply that even when battle was engaged Stanley thought Richard likely to win.

Richard III and the north By the time William Stanley acted, Richard's numerical superiority had probably been eroded by the failure of the earl of Northumberland to engage his troops. Recent writers have been divided on whether the earl's inactivity was deliberate, but most have regarded him as the leader of the many who, according to Vergil, 'forbore to fight … and departed without any danger, as men who desired not the safety but destruction of that prince whom they hated' (*Polydore Vergil's 'English History'*, 224). If Northumberland was sufficiently disenchanted to withhold his support, it was presumably as a result of Richard's manifest unwillingness to allow him to take over his own former role in the north. Once the rebellion of 1483 had shown the limits of southern support for the new regime, Richard's northern retinue became a vital prop to royal authority, and something which he could not risk allowing to pass under other control. Initially Richard's former ducal council, now nominally acting for his son *Edward, served as a focus for the king's affinity. After Edward's death in April 1484 the council was reconstituted as the council in the north, and was headed, not by Northumberland, but by the king's nephew John, earl of Lincoln, whose independent standing in the north was negligible. In spite of Lincoln's royal status (he may by this date have been regarded as Richard's heir apparent), Northumberland must have seen the appointment as a snub.

Richard's accession had brought the north into a new, and much more immediate, relationship with the crown. The treatment of Northumberland suggests that the change might not have been without its problems, but, for those of Richard's northern associates who benefited from the forfeitures of his opponents, his brief reign must have seemed a golden age. Francis Bacon, writing of the rising of 1489 in which Northumberland was killed, blamed it on the fact that in the north 'the memory of King Richard was so strong that it lay like lees in the bottom of men's hearts, and if the vessel was but stirred it would come up' (Bacon, 94). Richard's self-identification with the north is reflected in his plans for a chantry of 100 priests in York Minster, where he surely hoped to be buried. In the event his body was taken from the battlefield for burial in the church of the Franciscans at Leicester. In 1495 Henry VII paid for a tomb, but the body was never (as in the case of other deposed kings) translated to a more prestigious burial site, and the tomb was destroyed at the Reformation.

Image and reputation One strand of Henry Tudor's justification for taking the throne was that he was rescuing England from a tyrant, and Richard III's reputation inevitably darkened under his successors in a way that Edward IV's did not—partly because of Henry VII's marriage to Elizabeth of York and partly because the early Tudor regime was very largely staffed by Edward IV's men. This initial image of a king who seized power and ruled unjustly, best exemplified in the work of Polydore Vergil, gradually developed into a more elaborate picture of an ambitious man intent on clearing his way to the throne from at least 1471. This picture, most potently embodied in Shakespeare's tetralogy (of which *Richard III* is the shocking denouement), presented Richard's career as a series of calculating murders: Edward of Lancaster and Henry VI in 1471; Clarence in 1478; Hastings, Rivers, Vaughan, and Grey in June 1483; Edward V and his brother later that year; and finally Richard's own wife in 1485. Shakespeare's Richard III was compellingly depicted on film by Laurence Olivier (1955) and Ian McKellen (1995).

Much subsequent writing about the reign centred on whether what came to be called the 'Tudor myth' was true or not. Sir George Buck, who died in 1622, and Horace Walpole, whose *Historic Doubts* appeared in 1767, were early defenders of the king (although Walpole did have second thoughts), and efforts to reverse the Tudor view culminated in Clements Markham in 1906, who saw all hostile references to Richard as the product of Tudor propaganda. Twentieth-century scholarly treatments of the reign have tended to occupy a middle ground, although some popular treatments have remained polarized, including A. L. Rowse's *Bosworth Field* (1966), which accepts Shakespeare as a legitimate historical source for the reign, and P. M. Kendall's sympathetic *Richard III* (1955).

It is easy to refute the 'Tudor myth', with its cold-blooded schemer who revels in evil. Responsibility for the death of Henry VI and Clarence rests at Edward IV's door, although in the latter case it is probably fair to say that Edward could not have executed one brother without at least the tacit acquiescence of the other. There is no evidence that Richard had ambitions to seize the crown before Edward's death, and no evidence that he was someone who enjoyed violence for its own sake. When he ordered the death of his nephews he may very well have justified it to himself (as he justified his own usurpation) as a way of averting unrest, although that, of course, was synonymous with securing his own position. It is unlikely in the extreme that Richard murdered his own wife. But Richard's bad reputation was not entirely a Tudor creation. His usurpation was profoundly shocking, and it is striking that many of the rebels in 1483 had no material motive to rebel, since Richard had shown himself willing to keep them in office. The continuing seepage of loyalty later in the reign also suggests growing reservations in some circles about the propriety of Richard's regime.

These reservations derived from Richard's inability to deliver the continuity and stability that he had promised—the tacit justification of his usurpation. In 1483 he had identified the Woodvilles with factionalism, but his own regime came to be perceived as dominated by a regional clique. Although he expressed a strong commitment to the maintenance of law and order, his reign was marked by unrest and the large-scale seizure of forfeited land, which would have been unsettling in itself, but also led to actions of dubious legality. Richard was condemned out of his own mouth, and it is significant that one of the early criticisms of him was that he was a hypocrite: the word used by William Burton of York in 1491.

Burton also described Richard as a 'crochebak', a description that was to figure largely in later accounts of the king. If Richard did have some physical deformity it is likely to have been slight, probably no more than the uneven shoulders mentioned by Rous and Vergil. Contemporary chroniclers seem agreed that he was small and slight, and the Crowland chronicler refers to his haggard face, a detail that gains support from the most nearly contemporary portraits. These also show Richard fiddling with his rings and tight-lipped, an image of nerviness that recurs in the chronicles, most graphically in Vergil's description of him biting his lower lip, and 'ever with his right hand pulling out of the sheath to the middle, and putting in again, the dagger which he did always wear' (*Polydore Vergil's 'English History'*, 227).

The king's character   Richard's character is even more contentious than his appearance. Many of his attributes were conventional: he enjoyed splendour, he was devout, committed to law and order, an accomplished soldier. But these were the attributes to which anyone of his social standing would aspire. Some traits, however, were more personal. Richard's piety, which manifested itself in conventional ways, seems to have been coloured in his later years by a deep sense of insecurity, at least judging by the prayer for King Richard copied into his book of hours, in which the king identifies himself with unjustly persecuted heroes and heroines of the Old Testament. Earlier in his career he may more naturally have associated himself with the judges and commanders of Israel. His career as a soldier was evidently important to him, and was accompanied by the physical bravery to which Vergil testifies. But it is his role as arbiter and judge that appears most strongly in the records, and there is no reason to doubt his assertion, uttered twice in the course of an Essex legal dispute, that 'we intend, nor will none otherwise do at any time, but according to the king's laws' (Horrox, *Richard III: a Study of Service*, 66).

Richard's career in the north showed him capable of inspiring great loyalty, although this is much less marked after his accession, perhaps in part because of the strain he found himself under. His sense of insecurity may explain the apparent deviousness that Tudor writers thought they could identify in him. In other respects he does not seem to have been the calculating schemer of later writing. On the contrary, confronted with a problem, Richard seems to have had a preference for immediate action. His usurpation and reign rested on a whole series of short-term solutions, and many of the difficulties of his reign had their roots in his apparent failure to think through the likely consequences of his actions. Impulsiveness of a rather different kind comes across in Nikolaus von Poppelau's account of his meeting with the king in 1484. It was to Poppelau that Richard blurted 'With my own people alone and without the help of other princes I should like to drive away not only the Turks, but all my foes' (*Usurpation of Richard III*, 137). Poppelau may have been responding to this openness in Richard when he praised the king's 'great heart', and Vergil, for all his belief in Richard's dissembling, paid a similar tribute to his 'courage … high and fierce' (*Polydore Vergil's 'English History'*, 227).

Richard and his wife had only one surviving son: Edward, who was probably born in 1476 and died in April 1484. Richard also had two acknowledged bastards: John and Katherine. It is not known when they were born. John, variously described as of Gloucester and of Pontefract, was made captain of Calais in March 1485, and went there in person. He was presumably back in England by the first year of Henry VII's reign, when he was granted an annuity of £20 from Kingston Lacy, Dorset. The manor had previously been Richard's, and the annuity may therefore be a confirmation of provision earlier made by Richard himself. John's later career is not known, but he is presumably the illegitimate son of King Richard who died in captivity in the Tower at about the time of the Warbeck–Warwick conspiracy. Katherine was betrothed in February 1484 to William Herbert, earl of Huntingdon, the marriage to take place before Michaelmas. At the coronation of Queen Elizabeth on 25 November 1487 Herbert is described as a widower, so Katherine may then have been dead, or Herbert may have repudiated the marriage.

ROSEMARY HORROX

Sources   R. Horrox, *Richard III, a study of service*, Cambridge Studies in Medieval Life and Thought, 4th ser., 11 (1989) • C. Ross, *Richard III* (1981) • C. Ross, *Edward IV* (1974) • N. Pronay and J. Cox, eds., *The Crowland chronicle continuations, 1459–1486* (1986) • *The usurpation of Richard the third: Dominicus Mancinus ad Angelum Catonem de occupatione regni Anglie per Ricardum tercium libellus*, ed. and trans. C. A. J. Armstrong, 2nd edn (1969) [Lat. orig., 1483, with parallel Eng. trans.] • F. Bacon, *The history of the reign of King Henry the Seventh*, ed. R. Lockyer (1971) • M. A. Hicks, 'False, fleeting, perjur'd Clarence': George, duke of Clarence, 1449–78 (1980) • P. W. Hammond, 'The illegitimate children of Richard III', *Richard III: crown and people*, ed. J. Petre (1985), 18–23 • C. Weightman, *Margaret of York, duchess of Burgundy, 1446–1503* (1989) • J. Potter, *Good King Richard?* (1983) • R. Horrox, ed., *Richard III and the north* (1986) • *Three books of Polydore Vergil's 'English history'*, ed. H. Ellis, CS, 29 (1844) • C. R. Markham, *Richard III: his life and character, reviewed in the light of recent research* (1906) • P. M. Kendall, *Richard the third* (1955) • H. Walpole, *Historic doubts on the life and reign of King Richard III* (1768); repr. in P. Kendall, ed., *Richard III: the great debate* (1965) • A. L. Rowse, *Bosworth Field and the Wars of the Roses* (1966) • P. Tudor-Craig, *Richard III* (1973) [exhibition catalogue, NPG, 27 June – 7 Oct 1973] • G. Buck, *The history of King Richard the Third*, ed. A. N. Kincaid (1979) • M. A. Hicks, 'The last days of Elizabeth, countess of Oxford', *EngHR*, 103 (1988), 76–95 • L. C. Attreed, ed., *The York House books, 1461–1490*, 2 vols. (1991) • A. J. Pollard, ed., *The north of England in the age of Richard III* (1996)

Likenesses   oils, 15th cent., Royal Collection; version, NPG • manuscript, 1483–5 (Rous roll), BL, Add. MS 48976; Latin version, Coll. Arms • manuscript, 1483–5 (*Salisbury roll*), Buccleuch estates,

Selkirk · oils on panel, c.1516, S. Antiquaries, Lond. [see illus.] · silver halfpenny, BM

Richard ap Robert ap Rhys. See Rice, Richard (1511–1589).

Richard de Abyndon. See Abingdon, Richard (d. in or before 1322).

Richard de Capella (d. 1127), administrator and bishop of Hereford, was a royal chaplain and, from at least 1112, keeper of the seal under Ranulf, the chancellor of Henry I. William of Malmesbury's reference to him as clerk of the seal simply reflects the relative lack of organization of Henry I's chancery. In 1121 Henry appointed him to the bishopric of Hereford; the election took place on 7 January at Westminster, and the consecration on 16 January at Lambeth. His episcopate is not well documented; his part in public life seems to have been small. He is known to have attested only one unquestionably genuine charter of Henry I, probably issued on 15 April 1123. His own surviving charters are too few to give a clear impression of his activities as diocesan; however, when Henry I granted the large ancient estate and church of Leominster to his new foundation, Reading Abbey, in 1123, Richard presided over an inquest to establish the extent of the parish. He appears to have tried to strengthen his political position in the area by seeking the friendship of Walter of Gloucester, a powerful local magnate, and he improved the economic basis of the bishopric by obtaining in 1121 the grant of a three-day fair at Hereford from Henry I. At the legatine council of Westminster, 13–16 May 1127, Urban, bishop of Llandaff (d. 1134), disputed the claim of the diocese of Hereford to include Ergyng and Ystradŵr, but the proceedings were inconclusive. Richard died at Ledbury, an episcopal manor, on 15 August 1127, and was buried in Hereford Cathedral. JULIA BARROW

Sources Eadmeri Historia novorum in Anglia, ed. M. Rule, Rolls Series, 81 (1884), 29 · Reg. RAN, 2.846, 1010, 1015, 1017, 1091, 1183, 1204, 1222, 1243, 1245, 1265, 1267–8, 1294, 1300–01, 1312, 1391–2, 1400–01, 1411, 1428 · The chronicle of John of Worcester, 1118–1140, ed. J. R. H. Weaver (1908), 15–17, 25 · J. Barrow, ed., Hereford, 1079–1234, English Episcopal Acta, 7 (1993), xxxvi, 11–13, 311–12 · D. Whitelock, M. Brett, and C. N. L. Brooke, eds., Councils and synods with other documents relating to the English church, 871–1204, 2 (1981), 744–5 · M. Brett, The English church under Henry I (1975), 108 · Willelmi Malmesbiriensis monachi de gestis pontificum Anglorum libri quinque, ed. N. E. S. A. Hamilton, Rolls Series, 52 (1870), 304 · Fasti Angl., 1066–1300, [Hereford], 3, 135–6

Likenesses effigy, Hereford Cathedral

Richard fitz Nigel [Richard fitz Neal] (c.1130–1198), administrator, writer, and bishop of London, was the son, presumably illegitimate, of *Nigel (c.1100–1169), Henry I's treasurer and bishop of Ely, who in turn was nephew of Roger of Salisbury (d. 1139). Contemporaries referred to him at various stages of his life until he became bishop of London as Richard of Ely or as Richard the Treasurer, and the closeness of family feeling within the group is best illustrated by the devoted tone of Richard's Dialogus de Scaccario ('Dialogue of the exchequer'). His mother was probably English—a document of 1184 follows Richard's name with that of 'William the Englishman, brother of the treasurer' (Madox, 1.215–16). His youth was far from

tranquil; in 1144, and also earlier in the reign, King Stephen took him as a hostage for the good behaviour of his father, Nigel. However, his paternal family, and also the monastery of Ely, ensured that his education was a learned one. His later writings display a fondness for classical phrases, at least a basic knowledge of the categories of logic, and some learning in Roman law.

At the exchequer Henry II's reign saw Nigel securely restored to royal favour; according to Richard, writing two decades later, his father was brought in to revive the ancient learning and practices of the exchequer. Within the first few years of the reign Richard became treasurer, having already perhaps held the post of chief writing clerk in the exchequer. The Liber Eliensis states that Henry II, eager for money for his Toulouse campaign of 1159, accepted £400 from Nigel so that his son might be treasurer. While the link between Nigel's payment and the treasurership may not be quite so close, and while no other source gives an exact date for Richard's assumption of the treasurership, the association with Nigel's influence and the period 1156–60, and quite possibly with some kind of payment, seems sure. His tenure of the office was lengthy, lasting until just before his death in 1198. If initially he may have been overshadowed by his father, he long enjoyed personal control of the office. His financial activities were wide-ranging. In 1173 Richard, Nicholas de Sigillo, and Reginald de Warenne were responsible for taxing the royal demesnes in Bedfordshire, Buckinghamshire, Kent, Oxfordshire, and Sussex. The pipe roll of 1175 records a payment concerning the king's horses which the treasurer took with him to the continent. It is conceivable, although unprovable, that Richard's trip was connected to financial reorganization in Normandy during 1176. In the late 1170s he was at work on the Dialogus de Scaccario, which is both a manual of exchequer business and a celebration of Richard's family as royal servants. Indeed, the family connection with the treasury was continued after Richard's time, for his successor was described as William of Ely 'our kinsman'.

In common with other royal servants of the time, Richard's involvement in administration was not limited to one field, in his case that of finance. In 1179 he was an itinerant justice, going on a circuit through Hampshire, Wiltshire, Gloucestershire, Dorset, Somerset, Devon, Cornwall, Berkshire, and Oxfordshire. Final concords also record him serving as a royal justice at Westminster, sometimes, but far from always, at the exchequer. Other final concords were made before him elsewhere, for example on 27 January 1188 and 20 January 1189 at Oxford. He also dealt with a variety of other tasks for the king; for instance in the late 1180s he kept a falcon for Henry's use, and in 1189 was one of those sent by the king to Canterbury concerning a dispute between the archbishop and Christ Church. The pipe rolls record some of his reward, with Richard from 1177 receiving £20 a year from the manors of Essendon and Bayford in Hertfordshire.

Promotion in the church Meanwhile Richard was also occupying various positions in the church. He first occurs as archdeacon of Ely *c*.1158, and may have controlled diocesan affairs during his father's lengthy terminal illness in the 1160s. He also held the prebend of Chiswick from St Paul's Cathedral. Probably in December 1183 Richard was appointed dean of Lincoln. One of his major acts was to buy certain ruinous houses in the churchyard, rebuild them from their foundations, and give them to the deanery as the dean's first proper residence. In 1186 the canons of Lincoln, wanting to please the king, proposed Richard as their bishop. Henry refused to accept either Richard or two other candidates put forward by the canons, and chose the saintly Carthusian Hugh instead. However, Richard was soon to have a bishopric. Following the death of Gilbert Foliot in 1187 Richard was elected bishop of London on 15 or 16 September 1189 at Pipewell, and on 31 December following he was consecrated at Lambeth in the presence of twelve bishops. As bishop he can be seen looking after his diocese in various ways, for example by constructing buildings, by pursuing a dispute with a certain John Picot concerning lands in the bishop's fee at Barnet, Hertfordshire, and by endowing the master of the cathedral school with tithes. That St Paul's was a centre of learning in his time is confirmed by the presence of Ralph de Diceto as dean.

Before setting off on the third crusade Archbishop Baldwin of Canterbury held a council at Westminster on 19 February 1190 where he made Richard his deputy. Richard took up the pastoral care both in the territory of Kent and in the churches of the archbishop's manors. This position involved Richard in the case of Hugh de Nonant, bishop of Coventry, whom Baldwin had suspended for accepting the shrievalties of Warwickshire, Staffordshire, and Leicestershire. Hugh promised to resign the offices, and not to accept their like in future, whereupon Baldwin wrote to Richard asking him to ensure that Hugh kept his promise, and Hugh duly resigned his offices, and wrote to Richard about his decision.

On 15–16 October 1190 Richard attended a council held by William de Longchamp as papal legate at Westminster. Ralph de Diceto reports simply that Richard, as the third most important bishop according to the custom of the realm, sat at the legate's right hand. However, Gervase of Canterbury records a long dispute involving the bishop of Rochester concerning the relative claims of the latter and the bishop of London as to the consecration of the bishop of Worcester and the seat at the legate's right hand. Following Archbishop Baldwin's death on crusade in 1190 Richard took a leading role in assembling the bishops for the election of a successor in November and December of the following year. However, in part because Richard was detained in London on the king's business, the bishops were pre-empted by the monks of Canterbury who succeeded in electing their own candidate, Reginald de Bohun, bishop of Bath. But Reginald died on 26 December 1191, and Richard was once more responsible for assembling the bishops for an election on 30 May 1193. Again the monks anticipated any action by the bishops, and on 29 May elected Hubert Walter. This time, despite the infringement of what the bishops regarded as their privilege, the monks' choice was acceptable, and was confirmed the next day when the bishops also elected Hubert at Westminster, and Richard made the public announcement of the election. Hubert was enthroned on 7 November, but this too was an occasion for controversy. Richard, as bishop of London and hence as dean among the bishops of the church of Canterbury, and the bishop of Rochester, as the archbishop's chaplain, both claimed precedence in the ceremony. A compromise was finally reached, allowing Richard to take his place at the archbishop's right hand, and to say prayers when the pall was placed on the archbishop's shoulders and when he was enthroned. As at other times in his episcopate, Richard seems highly attached to the privileges and traditions of his see, just as he was to the customs of the exchequer.

Relations with Count John, and death During Richard I's absence from the realm much of Bishop Richard's time was occupied with the dispute between the king's brother Count John and the chancellor William de Longchamp. On 28 July 1191, at a conference at Winchester, Richard, along with other great churchmen, was a mediator in the peace between John and Longchamp. By the agreement, Richard undertook the keeping of the castle of Bristol. However, in mid-September Geoffrey, the king's half-brother and newly consecrated archbishop of York, landed at Dover, only to be seized by supporters of Longchamp, who violently dragged him from St Martin's Priory wherein he had taken refuge. Richard took a prominent part in the condemnation of this act; he travelled to see Longchamp in the region of Norwich and according to Gerald of Wales threatened an interdict unless Geoffrey were released—according to Diceto having to pledge his bishopric as the condition for Geoffrey's release. Following his release Geoffrey went to London, where he was received by Richard with great honour on 2 October.

Meanwhile John had summoned a council at Loddon Bridge, between Reading and Windsor. On 5 October Richard, together with other great men, accompanied William de Longchamp from Windsor towards the meeting, but Longchamp, his position undermined by the scandal of Archbishop Geoffrey's arrest, then turned back to Windsor and proceeded to flee to London. On 8 October a meeting of barons and bishops was held at St Paul's, where all swore an oath of loyalty to the king. According to Diceto only Richard added to his oath 'saving his order and ecclesiastical justice' (*Diceto … opera historica*, 2.99). On 9 October the monks of Westminster elected their prior William Postard as abbot, in preference to William de Longchamp's brother, and the new abbot received his staff and a blessing from Richard before the altar of St Paul. On 10 October Richard was present when Longchamp was deprived of his temporal authority. In 1192, however, it was the turn of Archbishop Geoffrey to be cast as Richard's opponent. In March he stayed in London at the New Temple while he attended a council. When he went from his residence to the council, he had his processional cross carried before him, an act that Richard and the other bishops of the southern province declared to be contrary to right. They would hold Geoffrey as excommunicate, and threatened that, if the act was repeated, they would break the cross, as they would already have done if he had not been a king's son, a king's brother, and a new archbishop. Richard also suspended the New Temple from celebration of divine office and sounding of bells because Geoffrey had stayed there. Richard seems to have won this conflict, as Geoffrey was careful not to have his cross carried before him when he left London on his return to York.

Throughout this period Richard retained his importance to the king and to royal administration. In April 1193 he was made one of the guardians of Richard's ransom. On 10 February 1194 he was one of the bishops who excommunicated John and his supporters in the infirmary chapel at Westminster Abbey as disturbers of the king's peace and of the realm. On the king's return the bishop of London was prominent at the king's formal crown wearing on 17 April 1194. Gervase of Canterbury records that he owed his important position in the procession to the seniority of his see, and that he sat on the left-hand side of the enthroned king. Richard's loyalty to the king was also apparent at the Council of Oxford in 1197, when Hubert Walter put forward the king's request for 300 knights to serve him abroad for an entire year. The incident is famous for the refusal of Hugh of Lincoln to provide such service, but before this occurred Richard had declared his support for Hubert's request. Richard's judicial activities also continued, and he sat regularly as a justice at Westminster until 1196, and then more occasionally until his death. Other final concords show his sitting as a royal justice elsewhere, for example on 22 July 1192 at Hertford. Final concords and the pipe rolls of the fifth and seventh years of the reign show him serving as an itinerant justice in Essex, Hertfordshire, Norfolk, and Suffolk, and perhaps Cambridgeshire and Huntingdonshire. Richard died on 10 September 1198.

Writings Richard retains his prominence in historians' eyes not only because of his active life but also because of his writings. Unfortunately not all of these survive, but Richard himself records that before the late 1170s he had written

> a little book ... about the history of the realm of England under the illustrious king of the English Henry I. ... I called it *Tricolumnis* because I arranged it all in three columns. The first column dealt with very many affairs of the English Church and some papal bulls. The second dealt with the king's noble deeds, which are beyond human belief. In the third are many matters of public or private interest, and also judgments of the King's court. (*Dialogus*, ed. and trans. Johnson, 27)

This description comes from Richard's famous surviving work, the *Dialogus de Scaccario*. This was composed in the late 1170s, although the existing text includes passages which are probably later interpolations, some not necessarily by Richard. The work takes the form of a dialogue between a master and a student. It is divided into two parts, the first dealing primarily with the staff and structure of the exchequer, the second with the operation of one of its sessions. Also included is a variety of incidental,

often historical, material. With the slightly later *Tractatus de legibus*, attributed to Glanvill, Richard's *Dialogus* marks the emergence of a new type of work, the secular administrative manual.   JOHN HUDSON

Sources Richard fitz Nigel [Richard Fitzneale], *De necessariis observantiis scaccarii dialogus: commonly called Dialogus de Scaccario*, ed. A. Hughes and others (1902) · R. Fitz Nigel [R. Fitzneale], *Dialogus de scaccario / The course of the exchequer*, ed. and trans. C. Johnson, rev. edn, rev. F. E. L. Carter and D. E. Greenaway, OMT (1983) · F. Liebermann, *Einleitung in den Dialogus de scaccario* (Göttingen, 1875) · J. G. H. Hudson, 'Richard Fitznigel and the "Dialogue of the exchequer"', *Perceptions of the past in twelfth-century Europe*, ed. P. Magdalino (1992) · Pipe rolls · *Radulfi de Diceto ... opera historica*, ed. W. Stubbs, 2 vols., Rolls Series, 68 (1876) · *Chronicon Richardi Divisensis / The Chronicle of Richard of Devizes*, ed. J. T. Appleby (1963) · D. M. Stenton, ed., *Pleas before the king or his justices*, 4 vols., SeldS, 67–8, 83–4 (1952–67) · *The historical works of Gervase of Canterbury*, ed. W. Stubbs, 2 vols., Rolls Series, 73 (1879–80) · E. O. Blake, ed., *Liber Eliensis*, CS, 3rd ser., 92 (1962) · *Gir. Camb. opera* · M. Gibbs, ed., *Early charters of the cathedral church of St Paul, London*, CS, 3rd ser., 58 (1939) · J. C. Robertson and J. B. Sheppard, eds., *Materials for the history of Thomas Becket, archbishop of Canterbury*, 7 vols., Rolls Series, 67 (1875–85) · C. W. Foster and K. Major, eds., *The registrum antiquissimum of the cathedral church of Lincoln*, 3, Lincoln RS, 29 (1935) · Adam of Eynsham, *Magna vita sancti Hugonis / The life of Saint Hugh of Lincoln*, ed. D. L. Douie and D. H. Farmer, 2 vols., OMT (1961–2) · T. Madox, *The history and antiquities of the exchequer of the kings of England*, 2nd edn, 2 vols. (1769)

Richard fitz Turold (*d.* before 1123). See under Cardinan family (*per.* 1066–*c.*1300).

Richard, St, of Chichester. See Wyche, Richard of (*d.* 1253).

Richard of Devizes. See Devizes, Richard of (*c.*1150–*c.*1200).

Richard of Ely. See Ely, Richard of (*fl.* 1177–1189).

Richard of Hexham. See Hexham, Richard of (*d.* 1155×67).

Richard of Ilchester. See Ilchester, Richard of (*d.* 1188).

Richard of St Victor. See St Victor, Richard of (*d.* 1173?).

Richard of Wallingford. See Wallingford, Richard (*c.*1292–1336).

Richard of Wendover. See Wendover, Richard of (*d.* 1252).

Richard of York, third duke of York (1411–1460), magnate and claimant to the English throne, was the only son of *Richard of Conisbrough, fourth earl of Cambridge (1385–1415), and Anne Mortimer (*b.* after 1388, *d.* before 1414), daughter of Roger (VII) *Mortimer, fourth earl of March. He was descended from Edward III through both parents, his father being the son of that king's fourth son, *Edmund of Langley, first duke of York, and his mother the great-granddaughter of Edward's second son, Lionel of Antwerp, duke of Clarence. It was this distinguished ancestry that provided the basis for his explosive participation in the troubled politics of the 1450s. In October 1460, after a decade of agitation and intervention, he attempted to seize the throne on the grounds that his descent from Clarence made him rightful king in place of Henry VI, who, like the other Lancastrian kings, was descended from Edward III's third son, John of Gaunt, duke of

Lancaster. The attempt failed, and York died a few months later at the battle of Wakefield, but the claim, of course, lived on to provide the basis for Edward IV's succession in March 1461.

Youth and inheritance Richard of York was born on 22 September 1411, to parents who had married in secret and were soon to be dead. His mother was gone within a year or two; his father, who married again in 1414, was executed the following year when details of his plot to depose Henry V came to light. Cambridge's plan to raise the north and (apparently) to put Edmund (V) Mortimer, earl of March, on the throne must have thrown his son's dynastic position into sharp relief: the young Richard's mother had been the elder of March's sisters, which made the boy himself a possible heir to the Mortimer–Clarence claim to the throne. On Cambridge's death he became a royal ward, and it is not altogether surprising that in March 1416 he was placed in the custody of the Lancastrians' leading gaoler, Sir Robert Waterton. Three years into his reign, however, Henry V was busy laying to rest the divisions of his father's time and Richard of York was destined for rehabilitation. He was protected from the effects of his father's attainder and, on the death of his uncle *Edward, duke of York, at Agincourt, the boy was recognized to be his heir. Not long after Henry VI's accession York's wardship and marriage were sold to Ralph Neville, earl of Westmorland. At 3000 marks the price was a high one, but Neville's investment was amply repaid when, in January 1425, Edmund, earl of March, died childless, and York, as his nephew, became heir to the extensive Mortimer inheritance. At some stage in the 1420s, possibly as early as 1424, the young duke was married off to *Cecily Neville (1415–1495), one of Westmorland's daughters with Joan Beaufort. From the point of view of the Nevilles, who had married into most of the leading magnate families of the day, it was a prestigious match that helped to confirm the family's growing pre-eminence; from the point of view of Henry VI's government, it was an ideal way to absorb a potentially dangerous figure by attaching him to some of the dynasty's staunchest supporters.

Over the next few years York was drawn more closely into the circle around the young king. In 1426 he was knighted, and two years later he was appointed to take up residence in the royal household. In 1430 York took part in the king's coronation expedition to France. His retinue was small, but he was handsomely rewarded for his involvement: over 1000 marks by the summer of 1431. Soon after his return, and still a minor (though there appears to have been some uncertainty over this at the time), he was granted livery of his estates on 12 May 1432. At the time both inheritances were encumbered with debts, dowers, and obligations, while the duchy of York was mainly in the hands of feoffees. By the summer of 1434, however, a series of financial settlements and the deaths of the two remaining dowagers had lifted the worst of these burdens, and the duke was free to enjoy his extensive patrimony undisturbed. The acquisition of his inheritance had cost him quite a lot, but he had received fair—even generous—treatment from the government.

York's proximity to the king, both in blood and in person, and his links with the families of Neville and Beaufort had stood him in good stead.

Service in France In 1433 York was admitted to the Order of the Garter—a mark of favour, a certificate of loyalty, and perhaps a token of martial expectations. His first taste of military command was to be as successor to John, duke of Bedford, in the lieutenancy of France, a post for which he was, in many ways, the obvious candidate: the royal commission, dated 8 May 1436, recited the king's desire to see France ruled by 'some great prince of our blood' (Johnson, *York*, 226), and there was no one else who fitted the bill, apart from Humphrey, duke of Gloucester. York had agreed to serve in France as early as February 1436, but his army did not reach Harfleur until 7 June. Had it left England more promptly, it might have been able to prevent the French reconquest of Paris and the Île-de-France, which took place during the spring, though it is difficult to know where the blame for the expedition's dilatoriness should lie: York was also to be late leaving for his second tour of duty in 1441, and the government was sceptical of his excuses on both occasions, but recruiting an army was no easy feat in the later stages of the Hundred Years' War, and delays were probably unavoidable. In the event the French advance was halted by York's forces. The brilliant campaign of autumn 1436, which ensured the safety of Rouen, was actually commanded by John, Lord Talbot, but Duke Richard too seems to have carried out some useful work, regaining most of the Pays de Caux after the rebellion of 1435, attending to the grievances of the Normans, and surveying the English garrisons. During both of York's lieutenancies it seems to have been a policy of his to delegate the basic management of the war to leading captains: his retainer Talbot, as marshal, in 1436; his brother-in-law Richard Neville, earl of Salisbury, as lieutenant-general in 1437; and Talbot again as 'lieutenant-general for the conduct of the war' (Pollard, 39) during York's second tour of duty from 1441. Although the duke and his council retained overall control of military policy throughout, it may be that York saw himself more as a viceroy, responsible for government as a whole, than as a warrior. This is certainly implicit in the attention that he gave to matters of domestic governance in Normandy and the *pays de conquête*: it was for his good rule of the duchy and for his genuine attempts to deal with the problems created by a declining military occupation that York would be remembered in France. His role in the fighting of the war was undistinguished, and a number of English chroniclers noted the fact.

Faced with the imminent expiry of his indentures—though not of his lieutenancy, the term of which was indefinite—York sought permission to return home in the spring of 1437. His successor was to be the earl of Warwick, and York was instructed to remain in Normandy until his arrival, which was delayed until the following November. It is difficult to know whether the decision to replace York reflects disappointment with his performance or not: the duke may even have wished to stand down, possibly because of difficulties in extracting money from the Norman exchequer for the payment of his troops. In any event Warwick's service was soon cut short by his death in April 1439, and Henry VI's government found itself once again faced with the task of providing for the rule of Lancastrian France. It was apparently as a compromise candidate that York emerged as the new lieutenant on 2 July 1440: Gloucester appears to have sought his own appointment, while Cardinal Beaufort, the regime's paymaster, probably pressed the claims of his nephew John Beaufort, earl of Somerset. York, however, was the most suitable choice for a post which now, more than ever, demanded a flexible, diplomatic, and authoritative holder: as the government pursued both peace and war with greater vigour than before, the duke was sufficiently neutral, consultative, and grand to act effectively on its behalf; he was also well connected with all parties, including the military establishment in France.

On this occasion York demanded adequate funding and increased powers before he would accept the job: he went to France as a second Bedford, with all the powers that Duke John had enjoyed after 1432 and a promise of £20,000 a year from the English exchequer to fund his troops. Apart from these improved terms of service, however, the patterns of the first lieutenancy were repeated. York left England late, not arriving in Normandy until the end of June 1441. He then moved speedily down the Seine to Pontoise where Talbot was struggling to lift Charles VII's siege, but this was to be his only military action in the three years before the truce of Tours. It was not a particularly impressive one: if York had helped to secure Pontoise for a further few months, he may also have frustrated a daring scheme of Talbot's that could have resulted in the capture of the French king. Caution, it seems, got the better of York, and not for the last time in his career.

Over the next few years the duke busied himself with matters of governance and diplomacy while the war effort in Normandy ground slowly to a halt. In part this was because Charles VII had turned his attention to the southwest, but it is clear that York's reluctance to engage the French directly caused dissatisfaction in the English government and it may help to explain why Cardinal Beaufort was able to engineer a major military command for his nephew John. The earl of Somerset's expedition, planned from late 1442 and launched in the summer of 1443, involved a major diversion of men, funds, and authority away from York and the Norman theatre. Duke Richard dispatched an embassy to remonstrate with the English government in June 1443, but it had no effect, and the campaign itself added injury to insult: Somerset's attack on Brittany and the duke of Alençon's stronghold of La Guerche disrupted York's attempts, conducted during 1442–3, to involve the English in an alliance of French princes. In the light of all this it is hardly surprising that, following the expedition's failure, the government seems to have felt the need to appease York: tallies for the payments due at Michaelmas 1443 arrived in February 1444 and, later in that year, the duke was given a major apanage in southern Normandy, while earldoms (and, in Edmund's case, lands) were granted to his eldest sons. After this no more of York's wages were paid until 1446, but at least the truce contracted in May 1444 reduced his expenses and removed the need for further military activity. In September 1445 York returned to England: his indentures were about to expire, parliament was in session, and—rather ironically, given the government's own failures in this regard—his management of Norman finances was under investigation.

York and English politics before 1450 It now seems clear that Cardinal Beaufort, William de la Pole, earl of Suffolk, and the other leading councillors and courtiers who, in the first instance, managed Henry VI's authority in the 1430s and 1440s intended Richard of York to be a pillar of the Lancastrian regime. This did not mean that the already wealthy duke was to be showered with gifts, nor did it mean that he was to be given a formal role in the government of England. York was not, for example, appointed to the re-established council in November 1437, but nothing should be inferred from this: at twenty-six the duke would have been considered rather youthful for what was in any case a rather anomalous role; exclusion from the council would scarcely have excluded him from influence; and it is likely that already the expectation was that his service to the crown would be overseas, at least while he was of military age. It is not known what part, if any, York played in the politics of 1437–41, during which time he was in England and Henry VI, somewhat uncertainly, came of age. There is no reason to suppose that he supported the moves of Humphrey, duke of Gloucester, against Cardinal Beaufort in 1439–40, despite Gloucester's suggestion that York and other lords had been wrongfully kept out of power; nor should it be assumed that he was opposed to the release of the duke of Orléans. He seems to have kept a low profile at this time, participating in a scheme to restore order in Wales in 1437–8, sharing in the custody of the Beauchamp wardship in 1439, and touring his estates. When, in early 1441, the 'longe bareynesse' of his marriage was suddenly ended and a son born, York named him Henry (*Bokenham's Legenden*, 273). This demonstration of dynastic loyalty earned a gift of £100 worth of jewels from the grateful king: the restoration of the heir of Cambridge and Mortimer must have seemed to be complete.

As lieutenant of France for the second time York became embroiled in the government's various diplomatic initiatives, including the moves associated with the truce of Tours. It has often been assumed that Duke Richard was hostile to the peace negotiations of the 1440s, but there is absolutely no evidence for this. While the confusions of policy in the early years of the decade must have been exasperating for anyone charged with responsibility for the defence of Lancastrian France, there is nothing to suggest that York preferred war to diplomacy as a means of preserving English interests. As the plan to seek a truce with Charles VII and a marriage alliance with the house of Anjou emerged as the central plank of royal policy in 1444, York seems to have given it his full support. In the new spirit of Anglo-French amity, for example, he sent forces to assist the dauphin's campaign in Alsace in the summer of 1444. The following year, and possibly in response to promptings from the government, he opened negotiations for a marriage between his eldest son (now Edward of Rouen—the future Edward IV—born on 28 April 1442) and one of the French king's daughters. The duke may even have been sympathetic to the government's plans to surrender Maine, which proceeded alongside the truce negotiations and formed an integral part of the alliance policy. Because of the postures that York struck after 1450 historians have tended to assume that he was opposed to this notorious scheme, but that is by no means clear. It is very likely that he knew what was planned by the end of 1445 (if not earlier, since he met Suffolk's embassy as it travelled through Normandy in 1444) and he was certainly involved in the arrangements for compensating Maine's English landholders in 1447. Interestingly York was never explicitly to condemn the handover of the territory, although its loss was certainly a prominent feature of popular and parliamentary criticism of William de la Pole, by then duke of Suffolk, Edmund Beaufort, duke of Somerset, and the other so-called 'traitors' of 1450.

It is from the period following his return to England in 1445 that York's alienation from Henry VI's ministers is often supposed to have dated. The duke found himself accused of mishandling the funds he had been paid for the defence of Normandy, and his chief accuser, it appeared, was a central figure in the government, Adam Moleyns, bishop of Chichester. York had returned to England confident of reappointment to the French lieutenancy, but he was obliged to wait for more than a year and then to see the office go to Edmund Beaufort instead. It used to be thought that because of his alleged hostility to the peace policy, and his putatively close links to the duke of Gloucester (who died mysteriously in 1447), Duke Richard was *persona non grata* with Suffolk's regime: his appointment to the lieutenancy of Ireland on 30 July 1447 has sometimes been seen as a form of exile, the government's hope being that, like the earls of March, his predecessors, he would go there and die.

However, events thus far do not support this interpretation. York was certainly dismayed by the rumours concerning his performance in Normandy, but he was explicitly vindicated by king and lords both in and outside the parliament of 1445–6; it is not even known that Moleyns had made the accusations York claimed, only that the duke saw in a public attack on the bishop the opportunity to clear his own name. Similarly, while York was probably disappointed not to regain the lieutenancy of France, too much should not be made of this: the lieutenancy of Ireland, which he was granted in return, was a post that his most distinguished ancestors (notably Clarence himself) had held; it bestowed upon him almost sovereign powers in the island; and it gave him the opportunity to combine military service with the exploitation of his interests as an Irish landlord. Finally, since the terms of his commission permitted him to appoint a deputy and return to England, it cannot be seen as a form of banishment. In some ways, indeed, 1446 and 1447 saw York more closely involved in

the governing regime than he had ever been: in October 1446 he was granted the abbey and town of Waltham because he 'will come often to London for the king's business and his own' (*CPR, 1446–52*, 43); over the next year he attended a number of council meetings and was named as a witness to more than three-quarters of the charters issued from 1446 to 1448; during 1447–9 he was added to the peace commissions of eleven counties beyond those to which he had been named at his inheritance (and in some cases beyond the scope of his landholdings); and finally, almost for the first time, he began to enjoy the kind of rewards more commonly bestowed on courtiers— most notably, perhaps, the wardship and marriage of the Holland heir (Henry) and a series of lands and offices once held by Gloucester. This last detail is a reminder that there was almost nothing to link York with Duke Humphrey in the latter's lifetime: in no sense can York be considered his supporter, and it is not improbable that, like other members of the nobility, he witnessed Gloucester's destruction at the Bury parliament and, tacitly at least, assented to it.

When he finally left for Ireland, in June 1449, Duke Richard did so as a loyal and well-regarded member of the Lancastrian establishment. If he had been less involved in affairs during the preceding year or so, this may well have been at his own choice. Many of the nobility seem to have withdrawn from the court during 1448 as the government's troubles began to mount. York cannot have wished to be associated with the humiliating surrender of Le Mans in March 1448 and he may well have feared the consequences of the extraordinary coup at Fougères. A tour of duty in Ireland must have appeared an attractive alternative. During his fourteen months in the province York scored a series of easy (if short-lived) victories, receiving the submission of most of the island's leaders and campaigning effectively in Wicklow. At the Drogheda parliament of April 1450 he followed the lead of the Commons at Westminster by introducing an Act of Resumption. Like the lieutenant of France he was short of money, and this limited his achievements, but the contrast between this vigorous performance and the demoralizing stasis of Somerset's rule in France must have impressed itself upon contemporaries.

Estates and connections By the mid-1430s, when he had gained full control over his estates, York was the richest and most extensive landowner among the king's subjects. Estimates of his wealth have varied between £2874 and £5800 net, but the most recent and reliable estimate suggests that his estates in England and Wales were worth about £4000 a year (net) when he came into them, and that his exchequer annuities yielded an average of £600 a year. York's lands were scattered through England and the march of Wales, with notable concentrations in the West Riding of Yorkshire; in Lincolnshire and Northamptonshire; in Dorset and Somerset; in Herefordshire, Shropshire, and the middle march of Wales; and in the centre of East Anglia along the border of Norfolk and Suffolk. Beyond this he held the earldom of Ulster and the lordships of Connacht and Trim, although only the last of these Irish estates is likely to have yielded York any real influence or income.

The possession of such vast holdings shaped York's activities as a lord: like John of Gaunt before him he was a truly national figure, with interests so widespread and diverse that it was difficult for him to exert the kind of local authority typical of later medieval magnates. He had no real 'country'—no county-sized area of concentrated influence where local gentlemen might turn first of all to him for lordship—and this helped to determine both the nature of his affinity and the role that he and it were to play in the politics of the realm. York's following, like Gaunt's or indeed the king's, was a disparate group of often important men, many of whom had their own local allegiances and whose links with York were forged mainly through military service and the tenure of estate or household office. In part, of course, this pattern was a consequence of the duke's long minority and his prolonged service in France: many of the servants of the duchy of York had melted away in the 1420s into Gloucester's service, for example; while Duke Richard's appointment as Bedford's successor in Normandy presented him with a ready-made following looking for a lord. A spry comment from an anti-Yorkist chronicler has promoted the suggestion that York was unduly influenced by the men who gathered round him in Normandy—in particular, by Sir William Oldhall, who was one of York's most reliable agents during the 1450s—but there is little to support this notion, particularly when the duke's involvement in the peace policy of the mid-1440s is taken into account. On the contrary, it seems likely that York's high status, his extensive interests, and his relative disengagement from the affairs of any particular locality beyond his estates meant that he was exposed to a wide array of different voices. If anyone besides the king and his ministers was likely to hear the counsel of the realm, it was surely York, who numbered lords such as Talbot, Ralph Cromwell, and Thomas Scales among his councillors, but also enjoyed links with exchequer clerks, lawyers, the widows of Norman soldiers, and local worthies from all parts of the country. The maintenance of this kind of connection may have cost York dear—as much as £1300 a year, according to one recent estimate—but it seems that this money was well spent. Despite his inability to offer really consistent local support, he was apparently able to co-ordinate the raising of large retinues throughout the 1450s. If some of his servants kept away from the duke's more controversial ventures, a sizeable and prestigious core remained loyal to the end.

The making of York's rebellion The last and best-known period in York's political life began in September 1450, when he suddenly returned from Ireland and took up the common cry for the traitors surrounding the king to be brought to justice. This was a significant change of political direction for the duke, and one that shaped the remainder of his career, but the reasons for it are not immediately obvious. Modern historians have mostly rejected the traditional interpretation, which laid stress on York's dynastic interests and saw his participation in

the popular ferments of the 1450s as a device for seizing the crown. Instead, the search has been for the causes of personal grievance on Duke Richard's part: was he moved to anger, or even desperation, by the government's enormous debts to him? Was he incensed by the new pre-eminence of Edmund Beaufort, duke of Somerset, the man who had so recently lost France? Did he fear for his own position, as an old rival took control of Henry VI's government? Alternatively, was York simply an opportunist, moving (typically late) to exploit the regime's difficulties, but without any fixed idea of where his dissidence might take him?

One difficulty in reaching any conclusions lies in trying to establish which elements of York's programme, as this slowly unfolded, were intentional, and intended from the start. It is certainly unlikely that the duke was seeking to gain the throne in 1450: previous legitimists had soon revealed their desire to improve the realm by changing the king, but York was not to assert his Mortimer–Clarence claim until 1460, after ten years of activism explicitly devoted to other ends. Even in that year, moreover, his move was greeted with hostility, and it seems reasonable to suggest that the duke would have known all along that this was a likely reaction and would have trimmed his policy accordingly. It is possible that, in 1450, York was concerned to secure recognition as heir presumptive to Henry VI: the king was still without a child and there was a (somewhat faint) possibility of dynastic competition from the house of Beaufort. Like most noblemen York took an active interest in the claims and titles he possessed—in 1445 he had sought information on his interest in the throne of Castile and in 1451 an agent of his was to argue in parliament that the duke should be named as heir apparent—but, at best, this can provide only a partial explanation for his actions in 1450.

As far as personal grievances are concerned, meanwhile, it is difficult to see what grounds York had for complaint. That the duke was part of the establishment in the 1440s has already been illustrated. Financially he had fared no worse than any of Henry VI's other major accountants: indeed, somewhat remarkably, given the state of royal finances, he received £1200 from the crown at the end of 1449, and even in May 1450 efforts were being made to find him money. He may have decided to return to England to seek funds—a letter to Salisbury, written in June 1450, suggests that he feared serious losses in Ireland unless he received further payments—but this is rather a different matter from acting on a sense of grievance, and if seeking money was York's initial aim, it was soon overwhelmed by other purposes.

What, finally, of York's famous antagonism towards Somerset: was this the motivation for his assault on the king's ministers? The problem here is one of disentangling the personal feud between the two men from the relative positions in which a wider politics had placed them: did York attack the government because it contained Somerset, or did he attack Somerset because he was the leader of the government? It is certainly possible to find grounds for animosity between the two men: Beaufort's performance in the last years of the war was undistinguished to say the least, and York may have thought that he himself could have achieved more; it has recently been suggested, moreover, that the lieutenant's casual surrender of Rouen would particularly have rankled with Duke Richard, since he had continued to be its captain. At the same time, however, it is clear that once York had made his inflammatory moves of September 1450 (and possibly even before then), he and Somerset were destined to be at odds: Duke Richard's political standing came quickly to depend on the argument that the government was run by traitors, and a large part of his justification for taking up arms in 1450, 1452, and 1455 was that the enmity of leading ministers obliged him to take action to defend himself; Duke Edmund, on the other hand, was not unjustified in regarding much of York's behaviour as threatening, both to himself and to the order of the realm; if he sought, in 1450, in 1452–3, and in 1455, to deal with the problem by repression instead of indulgence, it was an understandable approach. Politics, as much as personality and private interest, determined the conflict between York and Somerset.

Pursuing this further, it may be suggested that it was in the extraordinary politics of 1450 that the most likely reasons for York's sudden attack on the government are to be found. As Normandy fell to the French and the king's bankruptcy was exposed in parliament, the authority of Henry VI's ministers disintegrated. MPs and more lowly members of society appeared to be united in the belief that the king had been betrayed by a self-serving clique who had pillaged his possessions in England and surrendered those in France. If Suffolk's trial and murder had removed the leader of the gang, the rest remained in positions of power, and until the king and the 'true lords' took action against them, there could be no justice or order in the realm. This judgement on the recent past dominated public life in England between 1449 and 1451, and it continued to exert a certain influence over the public imagination thereafter. York, like other members of the nobility, must have known that in certain ways it was wide of the mark, but this did not mean that it could be ignored. In particular, in fact, it could not be ignored by York, who had already been identified by some of the government's critics as the figure most likely to visit retribution upon the 'traitors'. This appears to be the explanation for the rough reception that York and his men received at their landing in north Wales in September: local agents of the royal household, and possibly their commanders at the centre, had become alarmed about the duke's intentions. It was at this point, perhaps, and not in 1447, that 'by treating [the duke] as an enemy the court had made him one' (McFarlane, 405): if both the king's ministers and his subjects were going to cast York as the agent of justice, he might as well fulfil their expectations. Certainly, the moment must have seemed ripe for someone to take drastic action: the king's officers could not govern without public confidence, and it may have appeared that the removal of some of the discredited men—not least, perhaps, the duke of Somerset—was the best way to restore it.

Beyond all this, it might be added that, even if the government had not moved against him in 1450, everything in York's make-up would have given him the sense that he was the man to restore the situation. He was the greatest prince of the royal blood, head and shoulders above other lords, the natural successor to Bedford and Gloucester in the protection of Henry VI's interests. He had already acted as the king's viceroy in France and Ireland; why not in England too? What, if anything, York knew of the deeds of men like Gaunt and Woodstock (or those of Montfort and Lancaster), whose status was much the same as his and whose actions were to prefigure his own, is not known; but one model of proper noble service had been made available to him when, probably in 1445, York was presented with an elegantly decorated translation of Claudian's life of the consul Stilicho. It was an account of how the people of Rome and other nations implored this virtuous prince to accept the office of consul and restore good government to a city torn apart by the evil advisers of a child emperor. Its translator had invited York to 'marke stilicoes life' ('Mittelenglische Claudian–Übersetzung', 256): in 1450 the moment had arrived when he might put this teaching to good use.

York and the politics of the 1450s It was with a volley of bills and open letters addressed to the king that York returned to English political life in September 1450. The first of these sought to establish the duke's loyalty; the second advertised his intention to seek justice against his accusers; but it was the third that was truly controversial—it drew the king's attention to the universal complaint that justice was not being done to those who broke the king's law with impunity (in particular, the so-called 'traitors'), and offered York's services in bringing the guilty to book. This was an open defiance of the government's authority, since the essence of the 'traitors' idea was that it was the men about the king who were most of all responsible for the disasters that had befallen the realm. As far as York was concerned, this meant that a true subject was obliged to act against the inner circle of authority in order to fulfil the terms of his allegiance to king and realm, and this explains the duke's many affirmations of loyalty to King Henry: it was the essential justification for actions that, on the face of it, appeared disloyal. Under normal circumstances, of course, attempts to separate a king's chosen counsellors and servants from the ruler himself were unlikely to succeed: defiance of royal agents easily shaded into defiance of the king, and that was treason. As York and all the rest of the nobility knew, however, these circumstances were not normal: Henry VI had shown no more discernment than a child in the government of his realm; his ministers were virtually self-appointed, and the policies pursued during the 1420s, 1430s, and 1440s were essentially theirs. If this makes nonsense of one aspect of the 'traitors' thesis, it exposes the truth of another aspect: the government was not in any real sense the vehicle of the king's will, and thus defiance of it was not treason; the regime could legitimately be reshaped, and, with large sections of the public arguing that it should be, York's actions had a certain justice in them. In reality he was appealing not to the king with these manifestos, but to the Lords and to the wider public: his plea was that those who were less compromised by the disasters of 1449–50 must abandon those who were more immediately responsible; a new government, in which the duke was to play a more prominent role, must be established.

Not surprisingly York's demands fell on deaf ears. The king's circle saw little reason for a general blood-letting, and the nobility, who had begun to lend support to the beleaguered regime as the crisis mounted, appear to have taken a similar view. In a public reply to York's bills, his offers of assistance were politely rebuffed, and the duke left London to prepare for the parliament summoned to meet in November 1450. When it gathered on the 6th, MPs demonstrated their continuing enthusiasm for reform by electing Oldhall, York's chamberlain, as speaker and loudly calling for the traitors to be brought to justice. When the duke himself arrived, with sword borne upright before him and a large army at his back, the initiative was his: Somerset was promptly imprisoned and the Lords waited to see what would happen next. What followed was in part a demonstration of Duke Richard's hesitancy and conservatism, and in part a reflection of the constraints of his position. Elements of the Commons' programme were put into effect, but the duke made no attempt to alter the institutional framework of Henry's government, and the result was that, during the Christmas recess, authority drifted back to the king and his household, Somerset was released, and the Lords, many of whom had flirted with York while he was in the ascendant, resumed their former obedience. During the sessions of the parliament in 1451 York's power waned, and Thomas Younge's notorious attempt to have him recognized as heir apparent must have seemed to many an act of desperation. Why had York not done more to secure himself during his brief ascendancy? It is not, of course, clear what he wanted: if only the restoration of order, then this was being achieved without his help; if a role for himself in the government, then his actions had made this unthinkable unless the king himself were to be altogether displaced—the men of Henry's household, who effectively disposed of royal power, were hardly going to welcome a man who had posed as their nemesis. What York had done, in effect, was to go too far without going far enough. Perhaps he should have cut his losses and risked a direct assault on the throne; but such a move was almost certain to fail. The duke had cast himself as the true liegeman of Henry VI: any deviation from this role was sure to be seen as the grossest kind of betrayal; York had many potential supporters, but—apart, perhaps, from his own servants—their support was for his public, not his private, interests.

It has been worth looking at the events of 1450 in some detail, because for the next two years Duke Richard's options were very largely shaped by what had happened in that year. He could not be secure while Somerset and the household retained both control of the king and the support of the Lords, yet there was little he could do to improve his lot. Moves against Oldhall were under way by the end of 1451, and when, in January 1452, York reacted publicly against them and against their implications for himself, he was thinly supported. Apart from the duke's own men only the malcontent Thomas Courtenay, earl of Devon, and his crony Lord Cobham were persuaded to join the rising that attempted to repeat the coup of 1450: the rest of the nobility gathered around the king and Somerset, and York was forced to capitulate at Dartford in early March. His failure left him worse off than before. He was obliged to swear a humiliating oath of submission, his supporters and tenants were harried by judicial commissions, and his attempts to discredit Somerset were treated as part and parcel of a private quarrel. As the common people were reduced to order and the government enjoyed the unfamiliar taste of victory in Gascony, it seemed that York's political career was at an end: never again would he be able to take his proper place in the Lancastrian establishment.

At this point, however, fate combined with the contradictions of Henry VI's regime to bestow new opportunities upon Duke Richard. In the summer of 1453 Somerset's governing consensus suddenly collapsed, as the victories in Gascony were reversed, the king lost his mind, and war broke out in the north between the Nevilles and the Percys. In the resulting crisis York was the only person of sufficient stature to restore the situation, and it must be this factor, above all, that explains the decision of a nonpartisan group of councillors to summon him to London in October 1453, and the agreement in parliament to appoint him protector and defender of the realm on 27 March 1454. Here was a means for York to wrest control of government from Somerset and the king's household men without bringing his loyalty to Henry VI into question; and here was a means for the rest of political society to contain the powerful duke and to create an effective government without the kind of sacrifices that had been demanded in 1450. York certainly did his part: he went to London full of emollient promises to attend the council and do all 'that sholde or might be to the welfare of the king and of his subgettes' (*CPR, 1452–61*, 143); he made no attacks on Somerset or other sometime 'traitors' (though his ally, Norfolk, did); and, on taking up the post of protector, he committed himself to rule consultatively and representatively with the Lords. During the succeeding months York made serious and well-founded attempts to pacify the disputes in the north and north midlands, and he enjoyed some success. Making genuine efforts to consult widely, he demonstrated the same statesmanlike qualities that had marked his management of France and Ireland: 'for a whole year', wrote one chronicler, 'he governed the whole realm of England most nobly and in the best way' ('Benet's chronicle', 212). There were certainly limits to his achievement, and his tenure of office was to be brought to an abrupt halt in February 1455, but the duke's performance may have prompted many of his peers to look more sympathetically at his claims in the years to come.

Unfortunately, however, the moulds of politics were changing in these years, and the broad unity that had so long been preserved among the nobility was breaking down. The deterioration of order in the localities, which had become so dramatic and extensive by 1453, was now combined with the emergence of a more aggressive Lancastrian dynasticism to promote significant divisions among the élite. These had begun to emerge even before York's protectorate: one of the reasons why it had taken so long to arrange the duke's appointment was that a substantial group of lords had grouped themselves around the queen, Margaret of Anjou, who—since the birth of her son Edward in October 1453—was attempting to secure a regency for herself. In the winter of 1453–4, indeed, civil war looked a distinct possibility. It was held off by York's readiness to make explicit his submission to the dynastic claims of the new prince, and by the agreement of all but the most extreme figures to join a broadly based regime under the duke's headship. When Henry VI recovered his sanity, however, at Christmas 1454, those in the household and the north who had opposed the protectorate seized the opportunity to assert their interests. York was removed from office on 9 February 1455, and by early March a more hard-faced government was taking steps against the duke. The fact that the Neville earls of Warwick and Salisbury also fell under attack at this time reveals the factional and divisive aims of those in control: although the government proceeded with the language of treason and obedience, its narrowing base and its sponsorship of conflict began to undermine its claims to such public goods; when York and the Nevilles confronted the king, Somerset, and the Percys at St Albans on 22 May 1455, there was a broad equivalence between the two sides, and the first blows of a civil war were struck.

The Yorkist victory, however, brought this war to a rapid halt. Just as he had done in the early 1450s, the duke submitted to the king and attempted to rebuild unity. This was to remain his posture and that of his allies right up to the disasters of 1459. York was certainly prepared to strain his allegiance to its very limits—securing appointment to a second protectorate on 15 November 1455 and depriving the king of personal authority a week later—but he would not cross the bounds to an outright repudiation of Henry VI's sovereignty. As a consequence his pre-eminence remained insecure. His protectorate was soon terminated (on 25 February 1456) when parliamentary pressure for a resumption weakened his support among the Lords, but the aim of preserving unity, or *oonhede*, among the nobility lingered on for some years and ensured that if York was not to be admitted to any special power, he was not to be destroyed either. It seems likely that, provided he behaved himself, most of the peerage had some respect for the duke. Pressure from Queen Margaret and her growing band of partisans meant that he was obliged to repeat his submission of 1452 on a number of occasions between 1456 and 1459, but he was confirmed in possession of the lieutenancy of Ireland, and even seems to have been able

to direct policy for a time in the wake of the 'loveday' settlement of 1458. Only in 1459 did the bulk of the Lords finally accept the case for war against the duke, and then the fault-lines of 1453–4 and 1455 were recreated and York received the support of the Nevilles. Rather as at St Albans, York, Warwick, and Salisbury revived the case that evil counsellors around the king were destroying the common weal of the realm and threatening their own security. On this occasion, however, their propaganda cut no ice: finding most of the nobility in arms against them at Ludford Bridge (near Ludlow, Shropshire) and deserted by a part of the army, York and his allies fled the field during the night of 12–13 October 1459.

Exile, return, and death The duke and his second son, Edmund, earl of Rutland, spent the next eleven months in Ireland, attempting to gain the men and money for an armed return to England, where the duke's estates were in royal hands as a result of his attainder at the Coventry parliament (about the end of November 1459). His younger children, including *George, were all placed in the custody of the duchess of Buckingham. An incidental result of York's efforts was the famous Drogheda parliament of 8 February 1460, in which the Anglo-Irish establishment obtained recognition as a distinct political community, separate from England, ruled by its own laws and financed by its own currency. In return for these concessions York gained resources, protection for his person, and an extensive army of archers, which he must have intended to take to England. Plans for a co-ordinated invasion of the mainland were apparently made during a conference with Warwick at Waterford in the spring of 1460, and the duke's Neville allies, accompanied by his eldest son, Edward of March, duly landed in Kent in June professing loyalty to Henry VI and protesting about the misgovernment of the realm. With startling success, they won support in London and the south-east and proceeded to defeat the royal army at Northampton on 10 July, submitting to the king at the battle's end. Over the next few weeks March and the Nevilles began to secure the realm and to await York's return, which finally occurred near Chester on or about 9 September 1460.

Much about the next few weeks is obscure: it is not known why it took York so long to join his allies on the mainland; it is not known when he began so famously to assert his claim to the throne (13 September is the first date for which a plausible case can be made); it is not known whether or not the initiative had been agreed, or even discussed, with the Nevilles. It seems clear that there was no option for York but to attempt to make himself king: all other avenues, as has been shown, led nowhere; the duke could neither secure himself nor restore political order without taking the drastic step from which he had so far shrunk; and it may have seemed that by 1460 the polity of Henry VI was sufficiently dislocated to permit a direct assault on the king. Unfortunately for the duke, however, his own options were different from those of his allies, even his sons. These men had gained support on the old plea of reforming Henry VI's government. They had recently made their loyalty to the king explicit. As the managers of a large and diverse alliance, they could not easily abandon what they had promised, and it seems clear that the message from the London élite, who played an important role in the frantic politics of 1459–61, was that a deposition could not be tolerated. York marched into London, seized the king, and entered parliament on 10 October, announcing that he intended 'to challenge his right' to the crown (Johnson, *York*, 214). The Lords' response was unpromising: they went into conclave at Blackfriars and sent the young earl of March to persuade his father to accept a negotiated settlement. By 13 October York had been brought to abandon his plans for an immediate coronation, and a few days later he submitted his claim for discussion in parliament. An accord emerged on 31 October, and its central feature was to leave Henry VI on the throne, while settling the succession on York and his sons. It is possible that even after this York attempted to get his way by inducing Henry to abdicate. He must have realized that, like the treaty of Troyes on which it was apparently based, the accord promised immediate war with the disinherited heir. In any event, the king was moved to safety and the duke was obliged to accept the terms agreed in October, at least for the time being. Acting more or less as protector he marched north in early December to deal with the forces of the prince of Wales and Queen Margaret, which had regrouped in Yorkshire after the defeat at Northampton. Venturing forth from his castle at Sandal on 30 December 1460, in what may have been an uncharacteristic attempt to surprise his enemy, York was set upon by an unexpectedly large Lancastrian force. In the ensuing battle of Wakefield, he and his second son, Edmund of Rutland, were killed. As a macabre riposte to Duke Richard's recent pretensions, his head was severed from his body and displayed on the walls of York bearing a paper crown.

So ended the life of this curious figure, who, having played safe in the prime of his years, abruptly changed tack at the age of thirty-nine, pursuing ever more ambitious and dangerous policies until, with victory almost in his grasp, he fell on an ill-chosen battlefield. Duke Richard was the true founder of the royal house of York, but despite a career that a recent biographer has described as 'the most successful failure of the middle ages' (Johnson, 'Political career', abstract), he has inspired little interest and even less sympathy among historians. Notwithstanding his many claims to be acting for the 'common weal' of the realm, York has usually been presented as a somewhat colourless bungler: all along, it seems, he wanted power, but he could not decide how far to go until the last minute, whereupon—fatally—he went too far. In 1964 B. Wilkinson set the tone for most modern accounts of the duke's career with his judgement that 'it would be folly to make a statesman out of this fifteenth-century worldling' (Wilkinson, 88). This view seems unfairly harsh: like many of his peers, his instincts were to make the best of things in Henry VI's England, a world in which there were no easy answers. York's opportunities were closely circumscribed and his intentions in opposing Henry VI's government are far from clear; in fact there may be a case for seeing him

more as the victim of circumstances than as their creator. His cautiousness, if ultimately unproductive, was justified by the sheer impropriety of opposition to the government. On the other hand, the recklessness that he demonstrated in 1450, 1452, 1455, 1459, and 1460 was also justified: sometimes by its results; always by the need to do something to restore the authority that the king, in his feebleness, had frittered away. In medieval England, however, the restoration of authority could only be carried out from the throne. York's final and most destructive venture was thus his best-conceived one, but it is easy to see why it has won him few plaudits. JOHN WATTS

Sources P. A. Johnson, *Duke Richard of York, 1411–1460* (1988) · T. B. Pugh, 'Richard Plantagenet (1411–60), duke of York, as the king's lieutenant in France and Ireland', *Aspects of medieval government and society: essays presented to J. R. Lander*, ed. J. G. Rowe (1986), 107–41 · J. L. Watts, *Henry VI and the politics of kingship* (1996) · R. A. Griffiths, *The reign of King Henry VI: the exercise of royal authority, 1422–1461* (1981) · Chancery records · J. T. Rosenthal, 'The estates and finances of Richard, duke of York, 1411–1460', *Studies in Medieval and Renaissance History*, 2 (1965), 117–204 · G. L. Harriss, *Cardinal Beaufort: a study of Lancastrian ascendancy and decline* (1988) · A. J. Pollard, *John Talbot and the war in France, 1427–1453*, Royal Historical Society Studies in History, 35 (1983) · C. T. Allmand, *Lancastrian Normandy, 1415–1450* (1983) · M. K. Jones, 'Somerset, York and the Wars of the Roses', *EngHR*, 104 (1989), 285–307 · R. A. Griffiths, 'Duke Richard of York's intentions in 1450 and the origins of the Wars of the Roses', *Journal of Medieval History*, 1 (1975), 187–209 · M. L. Kekewich and others, eds., *The politics of fifteenth-century England: John Vale's book* (1995) · J. L. Watts, '*De consulatu Stiliconis*: texts and politics in the reign of Henry VI', *Journal of Medieval History*, 16 (1990), 251–66 · J. M. W. Bean, 'The financial position of Richard, duke of York', *War and government in the middle ages*, ed. J. Gillingham and J. C. Holt (1984), 182–98 · T. B. Pugh, *Henry V and the Southampton plot of 1415*, Southampton RS, 30 (1988) · A. J. Otway-Ruthven, *A history of medieval Ireland* (1968) · 'John Benet's chronicle for the years 1400 to 1462', ed. G. L. Harriss, *Camden miscellany, XXIV*, CS, 4th ser., 9 (1972) · E. Flügel, 'Eine mittelenglische Claudian-Übersetzung (1445)', *Anglia*, 28 (1905), 255–99 · P. A. Johnson, 'The political career of Richard, duke of York, to 1456', DPhil diss., U. Oxf., 1981 · B. Wilkinson, *Constitutional history of England in the fifteenth century (1399–1485)* (1964) · *Osbern Bokenam's Legenden*, ed. C. Horstmann (Heilbronn, 1883) · 'William Gregory's chronicle of London', *The historical collections of a citizen of London in the fifteenth century*, ed. J. Gairdner, CS, new ser., 17 (1876), 55–239 · K. Dockray, 'The battle of Wakefield and the Wars of the Roses', *The Ricardian*, 9 (1991–3), 238–58 · R. Knowles, 'The battle of Wakefield: the topography', *The Ricardian*, 9 (1991–3), 259–65 · C. Ross, *Edward IV* (1974) · *Itineraries [of] William Worcestre*, ed. J. H. Harvey, OMT (1969) · K. B. McFarlane, 'The Lancastrian kings', *Cambridge Medieval History*, 8, ed. C. W. Previté-Orton and Z. N. Brooke (1936), 363–417 · *CPR, 1446–61* · *CEPR letters*, 8.132

Archives BL, letters relating to a truce between England and Burgundy, Add. Ch. 75479

Likenesses stained-glass window, Cirencester; repro. in S. Lysons, *A collection of Gloucestershire antiquities* (1804)

Wealth at death under £4600 p.a. net: Johnson, *Duke Richard*, 7, 21–4

Richard Rufus of Cornwall. *See* Cornwall, Richard of (*fl.* c.1238–c.1259).

Richard Scrob (*fl.* 1052–1066), soldier and landowner, was a Frenchman of unknown origins (not for certain a Norman) who came to England in the early years of the reign of Edward the Confessor (*r.* 1042–66) and was given land on the Welsh border. The twelfth-century chronicler John of Worcester mistook his additional or alternative name Scrob for a patronymic, and Richard has ever since been widely miscalled Richard fitz Scrob.

Richard married the daughter of another French settler, Robert the Deacon (possibly to be identified with Robert fitz Wimarc); his sons Osbern and William were adults by 1066. Richard's main base was the Herefordshire manor of Auretone, where he built the earthwork of Richard's Castle, one of the handful of pre-conquest castles in England. His lands were concentrated within a few miles, in Worcestershire and Shropshire as well as Herefordshire. Richard was one of the king's housecarls, and was exempted from the expulsions of Frenchmen which followed Earl Godwine's return to power in 1052. In the 1050s and early 1060s he was possibly sheriff of Worcestershire and certainly a man to whom the king entrusted important business there. In 1066 he and his family threw in their lot with the Normans as fighting broke out in Herefordshire between the French and Eadric the Wild. The date of his death is unknown.

Osbern fitz Richard (*fl. c.*1066–1088), landowner, Richard's son, owned an estate abutting his father's during the latter's lifetime, including a large tract on the border probably reconquered from the Welsh by Earl Harold in 1063–4. Osbern added greatly to it under Norman rule: by inheritance from his father; by gift from King William, especially in Worcestershire and Warwickshire; by marriage to Nest, daughter of *Gruffudd ap Llywelyn and *Ealdgyth, Earl *Ælfgar of Mercia's daughter, which seems to have brought him five valuable Mercian manors; and by taking manors as a tenant of the bishop of Worcester, the sheriff of Gloucester, and the earl of Shrewsbury. The last connection, with Roger de Montgomery, was perhaps the key to his success: it is striking that an apparently independent and wealthy baron was in 1085 in the earl's household.

By 1086 Osbern's manors straggled from the Welsh border as far as Worcester and Warwick, with outliers in Nottinghamshire and Bedfordshire; they were worth over £100 a year, more than three times his and his father's combined value in 1066. He was especially important in Worcestershire, where in the 1080s he was a judge alongside the sheriff and Geoffrey, bishop of Coutances, in a case between the bishop of Worcester and Evesham Abbey. He was also a benefactor of Worcester.

Osbern joined the Welsh marcher rebellion of 1088, but was not one of those whose calculations were complicated by property in Normandy and he was later loyal to William II, his honour of Richard's Castle passing on his death at an unknown date intact to his descendants.

C. P. LEWIS

Sources A. Farley, ed., *Domesday Book*, 2 vols. (1783) · John of Worcester, *Chron.* · F. E. Harmer, ed., *Anglo-Saxon writs* (1952), nos. 50, 116–17 · *Reg. RAN*, 1.10, 221, 230, 282 · C. P. Lewis, 'The French in England before the Norman conquest', *Anglo-Norman Studies*, 17 (1994), 123–44 · K. L. Maund, 'The Welsh alliances of Earl Ælfgar of Mercia and his family in the mid-eleventh century', *Anglo-Norman Studies*, 11 (1988), 181–90 · V. H. Galbraith, 'An episcopal land-grant of 1085', *EngHR*, 44 (1929), 353–72 · F. Barlow, *William Rufus* (1983) · F. Barlow, *St Wulfstan of Worcester, c.1008–1095* (1990)

Richard, Edward (1714–1777), schoolmaster and poet, was born in March 1714 in Ystradmeurig, Cardiganshire. He was the second son of Thomas Richard, a tailor and innkeeper, and Gwenllian (*d.* 1763), who kept the inn when Thomas was away tailoring. His brother Abraham was a student at Jesus College, Oxford, and it was he who introduced Edward to Greek and Latin. Edward then spent some time at the Queen Elizabeth Grammar School, Carmarthen, and later a cleric in a nearby parish worked with him to improve his Greek. He returned to Ystradmeurig about 1735 to open a school, where he quickly became known as an excellent classical scholar and a successful teacher, numbering among his pupils such poets as David Richards (Dafydd Ionawr) and Evan Evans (Ieuan Brydydd Hir). He closed his school about 1740 in order to perfect his knowledge of Greek and Latin and their literatures, and reopened it in 1746. In subsequent years his brilliant contemporary Lewis Morris of Anglesey, who lived in Cardiganshire from 1742 to 1765, and his erstwhile pupil Ieuan Brydydd Hir tried to further his Welsh studies but, unlike them, he had little interest in early Welsh literature, preferring the 'free' verse of the sixteenth and seventeenth centuries—that is, verse not in the traditional bardic metres.

Richard's poetical output was small. He translated John Gay's ballad ''Twas when the seas were roaring', and wrote two songs about a local bridge in the popular *tri thrawiad* metre, embellished with *cynghanedd*. His *englynion* (epigrammatic stanzas in the strict metres), 'In sepulchrum infantoli', win a place in most anthologies, but he is best remembered for two pastoral poems which look back to the pastorals of Theocritus and Virgil. The first appeared in 1767 in Gwilym Howels's almanac, and Richard believed it to be 'the first Essay of the kind in our Language'. The second was published in Shrewsbury in 1776. Richard's pastorals were not slavish imitations of the classical models he knew well. He had studied Rapin on the pastoral, possibly in the original French, and he was familiar with Joseph Trapp's lectures on poetry. Retaining respect for his admired masters, he adapted their standards to Welsh idiom and practice, again using the *tri thrawiad* metre, setting the poems to be sung to Welsh tunes. Like those of his predecessors his pastorals are dialogues between two shepherds; these exchange thoughts on death and the vicissitudes of life in a local, rural setting, with ample moral exhortations. The first pastoral was written on the death of his mother; the second was described as a complaint 'of the evils of life, and the infelicities of old age, intermixed with censures of the supposedly increasing luxuries and immoralities of the age'. He used colloquialisms in the language of his shepherds and stoutly defended this against his friends' criticism, quoting Horace and Theocritus as his authorities. In all he sought to create a new genre: a truly Welsh pastoral. His work was collected in *Yr eos* (1803), with additions in several later editions in 1811, 1813, 1851, 1856, and 1912. Richard died of 'gravel and stone' on 4 March 1777 and was buried at Ystradmeurig having remained, throughout his life, unmarried, in the Ystradmeurig area.

E. G. MILLWARD

Sources D. G. Osborne-Jones, *Edward Richard of Ystradmeurig* (1934) · S. Lewis, *A school of Welsh Augustans* (1924), chap. 3 · D. E. Evans, 'Edward Richard', *Y Beirniad*, 7 (1917), 252–62 · *Additional letters of the Morrises of Anglesey, 1735–1786*, ed. H. Owen, 2 vols. (1947–9) · T. Ellis, 'Nodyn ar Edward Richard, Ystradmeurig, a'i waith llenyddol', *Y Llenor*, 27 (1948), 173–82 · D. G. Jones, ed., *Blodeugerdd o'r ddeunawfed ganrif* (1947), xxxiii–xxxvii, 28–35, 116–21 · J. G. Jones, 'Edward Richard ac Evan Evans (Ieuan Fardd)', *Gwŷr llên y ddeunawfed ganrif a'u cefndir*, ed. D. Morgan (1966), 121–8 [56–65] · A. Lewis, 'Edward Richard ac Ieuan Fardd', *Ysgrifau Beirniadol*, 10 (1977), 267–89; repr. in *Dysg a dawn: cyfrol goffa Aneirin Lewis*, ed. W. A. Mathias and E. W. James (1992), 170–85 · E. G. Millward, ed., *Blodeugerdd Barddas o gerddi rhydd y ddeunawfed ganrif* (1991), 111–16

Archives NL Wales, Panton MSS

Likenesses portrait, repro. in Osborne-Jones, *Edward Richard of Ystradmeurig*, frontispiece

Wealth at death comfortable; mill; several farms; land

Richard, Henry (1812–1888), politician, was born at Tregaron, Cardiganshire, on 3 April 1812, the second son of the Revd Ebenezer Richard (1781–1837) and his wife, Mary, only daughter of William Williams of Tregaron. Ebenezer Richard was a Calvinistic Methodist minister, an eloquent speaker and an administrator of some repute, who co-ordinated the affairs of his denomination in south Wales. His life was commemorated by his sons Henry and Edward, a London doctor, in a biography written two years after his death (*Bywyd y Parch. Ebenezer Richard, gan ei Feibion*, 1839, with a portrait).

Education and religious career Henry Richard was educated at Llangeitho grammar school, an institution better known for the training of potential Anglican clergymen, and then went to the commercial and mathematical school run by John Evans in Aberystwyth. Following this, he was apprenticed for three years to Mr Lewis, a draper at Carmarthen, a calling he viewed with 'unbounded disgust'. After a further purgatorial period as a draper's assistant in Aberystwyth, he approached his father in April 1830 to confess that he had 'an inclination for the ministry'. Unlike his father, however, Henry Richard became a Congregationalist, and entered Highbury College in Middlesex in September 1830. He was ordained, on 11 November 1835, pastor of Marlborough Chapel, on the Old Kent Road, a position he held until May 1848, when he chose to devote himself himself wholly to his political work. He ceased to use the title Reverend about 1853, but remained attached to the denomination throughout his life and filled the chair of the Congregational Union in 1877. In addition, he was chairman of the dissenting deputies from January 1875 until his death in 1888. The political battles of nonconformism occupied him throughout his public life, and religious conviction underpinned all that he was to achieve as a member of the Peace Society, of the Liberation Society, as an MP, and as the champion of Welsh interests.

Henry Richard (1812–1888), by Elliott & Fry

The Peace Society Richard's interest in the Peace Society, and its commitment to arbitration as the only moral means of settling international disputes, was evident from the early 1840s. He first publicly enunciated his principles on 5 February 1845 at the Hall of Commerce, Threadneedle Street, in a lecture on *Defensive War* (1846; 2nd edn, 1890) and on 22 May 1848 was appointed to succeed John Jefferson as secretary to the Peace Society. In this role he edited the *Herald of Peace*, the society's newspaper, a job that undoubtedly played an important part in developing his polemical skills. More important, in view of his long-term career, was the close contact into which he was now brought with men such as Richard Cobden and other leading radicals in the House of Commons.

Richard's new position as secretary of the Peace Society led him to promote a series of conferences designed to mobilize public opinion behind the principle of international arbitration. In the wake of Cobden's motion in parliament in favour of arbitration (June 1849), Richard organized, in association with Elihu Burritt and Joseph Sturge, peace conferences at Paris in August 1849 (under the presidency of Victor Hugo), at Frankfurt am Main in August 1850, at London in July 1851, and at Manchester and Edinburgh in January and October 1853 respectively. After the first of these he was presented with a cheque for

£1000 by his friends. Although the progress of the peace movement was stayed by the outbreak of the Crimean War (which Richard condemned in his pamphlet *A History of the Origin of the War with Russia*, 1855), the treaties that marked its conclusion were to provide him with one of the high points of his early career. In the company of Joseph Sturge and Charles Hindley, he travelled to Paris in March 1856, and persuaded the plenipotentiaries there assembled to insert a declaration in favour of arbitration into the treaty of Paris.

The Liberation Society and political career Richard was a keen opponent of all state interference in religious matters. A committed supporter of the Liberation Society, he opposed government involvement in education on the grounds that education was properly a religious function, and that it should thus be entirely voluntary. He was a member of the deputation sent to the principality by the Congregational Union of England and Wales in 1844, which did so much to convince his co-religionists in Wales to support the union's anti-government line on education. He also took a leading part in the foundation of a normal school in Brecon, the principalship of which he declined in 1853. In 1847, assisted by Edward Miall and Samuel Morley, he founded the Voluntary School Association, of which he was the secretary.

It was in connection with the Liberation Society that Richard took his first steps towards a seat in parliament. He was a member of the deputation that held a large conference in Swansea in September 1862, and a key figure in the administration of the society. He was appointed in 1865 to its central committee, and henceforth all matters relating to Wales passed under his control. The Liberation Society did not confine its attention to speechifying; it also aimed to return to parliament members sympathetic to its aims, and in pursuit of this it paid considerable attention to the registration of voters in especially targeted constituencies. One of these was Richard's native county of Cardiganshire, which was nursed for two years on his behalf. A preliminary canvass prior to the general election of 1865, however, convinced Richard that he was unlikely to succeed, and, given the number of other candidates who had already declared, he withdrew from the contest. In the following year, on 20 August, he married Matilda Augusta, third daughter of John Farley of Kennington.

The Liberation Society had hoped that Richard would contest Cardiganshire again in 1868. The second Reform Act (1867), however, had given Merthyr Tudful a second seat, and Richard accepted an invitation to stand there, specifically as the representative of the nonconformists. Sporting white favours as a symbol of the purity of his election campaign, he was returned as the senior member ahead of Richard Fothergill, who, in an intensely dramatic twist, ousted Henry Austin Bruce. In this election, as in all his other contests for the borough, Richard's expenses were met by public subscription. He held the Merthyr seat until his death, and although it was rumoured that he might contest one of the new Carmarthenshire seats

against the aristocratic Lord Emlyn in 1885, this came to nothing.

The 'Member for Wales' From the first, Richard was known as the 'Member for Wales'. Running alongside all the activities described above was Richard's commitment to the needs of the principality. He was always self-consciously Welsh: as he said at the end of his life, part of his role on the national stage had been to 'interpret' Wales for the English. It was a responsibility that took many forms. In 1843, for example, he wrote to the *Daily News* on the subject of the Rebecca riots and, in line with his wider views on peace, helped to distribute leaflets urging the rioters to forsake the gun and the torch in pursuit of redress on the toll-gates issue. In 1848, under the auspices of the Congregational Union, he delivered a bitter defence of his countrymen against the accusations of immorality and backwardness contained in the report of the commissioners for education in Wales.

Of wider significance than any of these initiatives, however, was Richard's series of articles on the nature of society in Wales, written during 1866. They appeared in the *Morning Star*, a paper founded in 1855 to propagate the views of the Peace Society in a somewhat less didactic form than the *Herald of Peace*, with which Richard had been connected from the beginning. The articles were collected and published under the title *Letters on the Social and Political Condition of the Principality of Wales* (1866), and represent perhaps the most significant legacy of Richard's long career. Violently anti-landlord and anti-establishment in their tone, the *Letters* offered a coherent definition of an essentially new kind of 'Welshness'. Birth in the principality was no longer the chief qualification; henceforth, to be 'Welsh' implied that one was a nonconformist, Welsh-speaking, and a Liberal. The articles were also translated into Welsh, but their initial appearance in English is significant; the *Letters* were an attempt to raise public consciousness of the reality of nonconformist, Liberal Wales as a nation on a par with Scotland and Ireland.

It was thus as a well-connected and well-known figure that Richard entered the House of Commons. He appears to have handled the transition from platform demagogue to parliamentary orator with less trouble than friends such as C. S. Miall feared. He became an active member of the house immediately, and made his maiden speech, in support of the second reading of the Irish Church Bill, on 22 March 1869. While this made a good impression, what really caught the eye was his motion of 6 July 1869, condemning the actions of some landowners in Wales who had apparently evicted such of their tenants as had voted for the Liberal candidates at the recent election. The motion was withdrawn without being put to the vote, but it offered an early indication that the problems of Wales as a distinct community were now being championed by some of the principality's members. Richard nevertheless continued to agitate the cause of the evicted tenants, and was the chief speaker at a number of conferences held in England and Wales in the winter of 1869–70 which raised a fund of nearly £4000, from which the victims might be compensated. An attempt to translate this unity of action among some Welsh members into a more formal arrangement in parliament, however, failed, despite Richard's being the key speaker at a conference in Aberystwyth during November 1871 which aimed to promote the scheme. His acknowledged leadership of the Welsh members in the house was an informal convention.

In parliament Richard continued to champion the same range of interests as had occupied him before his election. When W. E. Forster's Education Bill was before the house in 1870, Richard, who had reluctantly accepted the principle of state aid in education, opposed the 'conscience clause compromise', and proposed that 'religious instruction should be supplied by voluntary effort and not out of public funds'. His speech against the third reading of the bill (11 July) was, as Daniel Lleufur Thomas remarked, 'bitter and sarcastic' (*DNB*), and he subsequently made repeated attempts to get rid of the clauses that were considered obnoxious to nonconformists. In later years his involvement in issues touching education in Wales grew markedly. In 1880 he was the only nonconformist on the departmental committee established under Lord Aberdare to investigate the state of intermediate and higher education in Wales. The recommendations of this committee led to the Intermediate Education Act (Wales) of 1889, and to the establishment of the University of Wales in 1893. In January 1886 Richard became a member of the royal commission on education, which, at his prompting, recommended a scheme for using the Welsh language in elementary schools.

Richard's parliamentary efforts in pursuit of the goals of the Liberation Society were also notable: he seconded both Edward Miall's motion (9 May 1871) for the disestablishment of the British churches, which was lost by 374 votes to 89, and (on 9 March 1886) the motion brought forward by Lewis Llewelyn Dillwyn to disestablish the church in Wales, which failed by the closer margin of 241 votes to 229. More generally, he took an active part in attempting to redress the long-standing nonconformist grievance over the inability of dissenting preachers to officiate in Anglican burial-grounds. He was not satisfied with the Burials Act of 1880, and introduced, unsuccessfully, an amending cemeteries bill in both 1883 and 1884. In 1885 he wrote, with John Carvell Williams, *Disestablishment*.

Richard and internationalism Richard also remained an active proponent of international arbitration. On 8 July 1873 he carried a motion in the House of Commons in favour of the principle, similar to that moved by Richard Cobden twenty-five years earlier. This success prompted Richard to undertake a tour of the continent, and between October and December 1873 he visited Brussels, the Netherlands, Berlin, Dresden, Vienna, Rome, Venice, Florence, and Milan, holding public meetings and having private interviews with prominent figures in each city. He continued this work throughout the 1870s, and was present at the talks held to conclude the treaty of Berlin in 1878, when he succeeded in getting reaffirmed the declaration inserted in the treaty of Paris in 1856. Two years

later, on 16 June 1880, he introduced in the House of Commons a motion in favour of gradual and mutual disarmament, which was accepted by the government in a modified form. In 1882 he was placed in an awkward position by the involvement of Gladstone's government, of which Richard was a supporter, in the Abyssinian war; his urgent letters to the premier, containing copies of articles taken from the *Herald of Peace*, had, however, no discernible impact on government policy. In 1885, because of increasing ill health, he retired from the secretaryship of the Peace Society and accepted the testimonial of 4000 guineas that was presented to him.

Death and assessment Richard died three years later, on 20 August 1888, while on a visit with his wife to Richard Davies, of Treborth, formerly MP for Anglesey and then the county's lord lieutenant. He was buried on 24 August 1888 at Abney Park cemetery, where a monument provided by public subscription was erected over his grave in November 1889. A statue, provided by public subscriptions, was unveiled in his native town of Tregaron in August 1893. His wife survived him; they had no children.

Henry Richard's public career encapsulated a broad range of interests. Daniel Lleufur Thomas described his activities with the Peace Society as the 'chief work' of his life; modern historians have been anxious to place greater emphasis on his role in the mainstream of Victorian radical politics. Certainly, one may list alongside his commitment to international arbitration a lifelong interest in educational reform and to disestablishment, keen support for parliamentary reform and franchise extension, and support for retrenchment in government spending. His role as the biographer of Joseph Sturge and his involvement in the preparation of Cobden's papers for John Morley underline this aspect of his career. Yet the most striking aspect of Richard's long career was undoubtedly his attachment to the interests of the principality. A remark made in the *South Wales Daily News* during the 1874 general election campaign may stand for his whole career: 'He has been MP for the Liberation Society, MP for the Education League, MP for the Peace Society, but withal and beyond, MP for all Welshmen and all Wales' (3 Feb 1874). A stirring orator, on the platform or in parliament, a forceful polemicist, and an organizer of considerable talent, Henry Richard was not only the consummate Victorian radical, but also the consummate Victorian Welshman. MATTHEW CRAGOE

Sources C. S. Miall, *Henry Richard, MP* (1889) · L. Appleton, *Memoirs of Henry Richard, the apostle of peace* (1889) · J. Vyrnwy Morgan, 'Henry Richard, M.P.', *Welsh political and religious leaders of the Victorian era*, ed. J. Vyrnwy Morgan (1908), 271–90 · I. G. Jones, 'The election of 1868 in Merthyr Tydfil', *Explorations and explanations: essays in the social history of Victorian Wales* (1981), 193–214 · I. G. Jones, '1848 and 1868: brad y llyfrau gleision', *Mid-Victorian Wales: the observers and the observed* (1992), 103–65 · B. L. Davies, *Henry Richard and education* (1993) · G. A. Williams, *Peace and power: Henry Richard* (1989) · I. G. Jones, 'The Tregaron of Henry Richard', *Ceredigion* [Cardiganshire Antiquarian Society], 11 (1988–9), 147–69 · *CGPLA Eng. & Wales* (1888)

Archives NL Wales, corresp., diary, travel journals | BL, corresp. with Richard Cobden, Add. MSS 43657–43659 · BL, corresp. with W. E. Gladstone, Add. MSS 44425–44507, *passim* · Fellowship

House, London, Peace Society MSS · NL Wales, letters to Lewis Edwards · NL Wales, letters to his father, with related items · W. Sussex RO, corresp. with Richard Cobden

Likenesses F. S. Moscheles, oils, 1883, NMG Wales · J. Cochran, stipple (after a photograph), NPG · W. Davis, plaster bust, U. Wales · Elliott & Fry, carte-de-visite, NPG [*see illus.*] · bronze statue; known to be at Tregaron, Cardiganshire, in 1893 · photograph, repro. in Appleton, *Memoirs of Henry Richard*

Wealth at death £12,243 9*s*. 8*d*.: probate, 25 Sept 1888, *CGPLA Eng. & Wales*

Richard, Timothy (1845–1919), missionary, was born on 10 October 1845 in Ffaldybrenin, Carmarthenshire, the ninth and last child of Timothy Richard, blacksmith and farmer, and his wife, Eleanor Lewis, who were devout Baptists. The family moved permanently to Tan-yr-esgair farm soon after his birth. Richard left the local Congregational school at the age of fourteen, and briefly attended a private school at Cross Inn near Llanelli and a grammar school at Llanybydder. He taught in the mining village of Pen-y-groes while completing a short course at the Swansea normal school, and at eighteen he became master of the 120 pupil endowed school at Cynwyl Elfed, where he remained for two years.

Richard had experienced spiritual rejuvenation during the great revival that swept over northern Europe and the British Isles between 1858 and 1860, and as a twelve-year-old was baptized—along with fifty others—by the Revd John Davies in the River Caeo near his home, joining the Caeo Baptist Church. In 1865 he enrolled in Haverfordwest Theological College (Baptist) in Pembrokeshire; he distinguished himself academically and played a prominent role in the student-led reformation of the curriculum. An address in 1868 by Mrs Grattan Guinness on the work of the China Inland Mission moved Richard to pursue a missionary vocation.

After graduating at Haverfordwest in 1869 Richard was accepted by the Baptist Missionary Society (BMS); he departed for China in November of the same year and arrived in Chefoo (Yantai) on 27 February 1870. He then commenced a missionary career of forty-five years which was remarkable enough to make *Li T'i-mo-tai* a household name throughout China in his day; he also earned Chinese honours rarely, if ever, bestowed upon foreigners ('Mandarin with a red button', the highest grade, in 1903; member of the order of the Double Dragon—second order, second grade—in 1907), which ensured him a place in both contemporary Chinese and mission history.

Disenchanted by traditional mission stratagems, Richard's role in combating the effects and discerning the causes of the great famine of 1876–9 convinced him of the need for a radical transformation of China's social and political infrastructures—reform that could be best achieved by providing the Chinese 'thinking classes' with a modern education. Accordingly he began to concentrate on reaching Chinese literati and governing officials, reasoning that in their re-education lay the key to the transformation of China. 'Conversion by the Million' would, according to Richard, be accomplished by 'three radical reforms in mission methods': first by presenting Christianity 'as the kingdom of God to be established, not only in the hearts of men, but also in all institutions on earth'; second by preaching not merely or even primarily to the millions of poor and needy, but 'to the leaders of the millions (who made the law of the land and held the poor in bondage)'; and third by 'preaching to devout souls, the worthy … the born ambassadors of God'—pious Confucianists, Buddhists, Taoists, and secret sect members— 'the natural messengers of peace and salvation in all lands, [whom] the multitudes follow … as certainly as the swarming bees follow the queen bee' (Richard, *Conversion by the Million*, 13–15).

Richard's scheme was regarded by the Baptist Missionary Society as rather larger than either their means or vision could accommodate. His more evangelical peers viewed his association with non-Christian religions with marked suspicion, and his dream of a Christian college for every Chinese province never materialized. Deeply disappointed he parted company with the BMS (though he continued to receive financial support from the society) and became editor of a Chinese daily newspaper, the *Shibao* ('The Times') in 1890, before moving in 1891 to Shanghai to serve as secretary of the Society for the Diffusion of Christian and General Knowledge, later known as the Christian Literature Society, an association that continued until his retirement from active missionary service in 1915.

Writing and translating numerous books and pamphlets, Richard gained a reputation among reform-minded Chinese leaders and intellectuals; this reached its apogee in 1898 when he was invited to become adviser to the emperor. While the empress dowager's bloody ascent to power, precipitating the Boxer uprising of 1900, brought a temporary halt to reform, Richard played a vital role in the establishment in 1901 of Shansi (Shanxi) University. The institution was modelled on Western lines, funded with indemnity moneys, and widely emulated throughout China, and Richard served as the school's chancellor, with jurisdiction over the curriculum.

Internationally Richard exerted considerable influence as a consultant to statesmen, educators, and missionaries, and he is credited with creating and fostering seminal ideals that would eventually take form as the League of Nations. During the Russo-Japanese War of 1904–5 he was made secretary of the International Red Cross Society in Shanghai.

Richard's marriage to Mary Martin (*b*. 1843) in October 1878 produced four daughters, Eleanor, Mary Celia, Florence, and Margaret, and lasted until his wife's death from cancer on 10 July 1903. Born in Edinburgh, Mary Martin was a person of marked musical and intellectual ability; she served the six years prior to her departure for China (where she arrived to work with the United Presbyterian Mission in Chefoo in 1877) as a teaching governess on the staff of the Merchant Company's College School in Edinburgh. After their marriage she made notable use of her gifts in publishing a considerable body of Chinese literature—in some instances translations of existing works— and in the training and supervision of 'Biblewomen'.

Richard's second marriage, in August 1914, was to Dr Ethel Newton Tribe of the London Missionary Society

(LMS). Ethel Tribe was born on 5 July 1860 at Bristol. She studied medicine at the London School of Medicine for Women, and at University College Hospital, London. From 1895 to 1912 she served as a medical missionary of the LMS—in Amoy (Xiamen) until 1909, then in Shanghai, where she was director of the women's hospital and instrumental in founding the children's ward. She retired from active service with the LMS in 1912.

In addition to his Chinese honours Richard received an honorary DD degree from Emory University in 1895, an honorary LittD degree from Brown University in 1901, and the LLD degree of the University of Wales in Aberystwyth in 1916. Having returned to Britain in 1915 because of illness, he died unexpectedly in London at Hendon Cottage Hospital on 17 April 1919, following surgery. He was cremated and his remains interred in Golders Green cemetery; he was survived by his second wife.

JONATHAN J. BONK

Sources P. R. Bohr, *Famine in China and the missionary: Timothy Richard as relief administrator and advocate of national reform, 1876–1884* (1972) · P. A. Cohen, 'Missionary approaches: Hudson Taylor and Timothy Richard', *Papers on China* (1957) · J. S. Dennis, *Christian missions and social progress: a sociological study of foreign missions*, 3 vols. (1897–1906) · R. T. Johnson, 'Timothy Richard's theory of Christian missions to the non-Christian world', PhD diss., St John's University, New York, 1966 · W. E. Soothill, *Timothy Richard of China: seer, statesman, missionary & most disinterested adviser the Chinese ever had* (1926) · T. Richard, *Conversion by the million in China: being biographies and articles by Timothy Richard*, 2 vols. (1907) · T. Richard, *Forty-five years in China: reminiscences* (1916) · K. S. Latourette, *A history of Christian missions in China* (1929) · D. MacGillivray, *Timothy Richard: a prince in Israel* (1920) · *CGPLA Eng. & Wales* (1919)
Archives NL Wales, corresp. and papers | Mitchell L., NSW, letters to G. E. Morrison · Regent's Park College, Oxford, Angus Library, letters to Baptist Missionary Society
Wealth at death £1847 1s. 8d.: probate, 19 June 1919, *CGPLA Eng. & Wales*

Richards, Alfred Bate (1820–1876), writer and promoter of the volunteers, was born on 17 February 1820 at Baskerville House, Worcestershire, the eldest son of John Richards of Wassell Grove, near Stourbridge, Worcestershire, who was MP for Knaresborough in the West Riding of Yorkshire from 1832 to 1837, and his wife, Frances Smith. He was educated at Edinburgh high school and at Westminster School, London, where he was admitted on 18 January 1831. He matriculated at Exeter College, Oxford, on 19 October 1837, and entered his name as a law student at Lincoln's Inn, London, on 16 May 1839. He graduated BA in 1841.

On 18 November 1841 Richards brought out an anonymous pamphlet, 'Oxford unmasked', in which he denounced abuses in the organization of the university, which were afterwards removed by parliament. The brochure rapidly passed through five editions. On its authorship becoming known, Richards deemed it prudent to move to London. He was called to the bar at Lincoln's Inn on 20 November 1845 and for a brief time went on circuit, but he soon devoted himself entirely to literature. His first published work was a five-act tragedy, *Croesus, King of Lydia* (1845). Four other five-act dramas followed between 1846

and 1850. In 1846 he published his first volume of poems, *Death and the Magdalen*, and in 1848 published another, *The Dream of the Soul*.

From 1848 to 1850 Richards gained early experience as a journalist by editing a weekly newspaper, the *British Army Despatch*. Of patriotic temperament and strongly opposed to the Manchester school of politicians, in 1848 he issued a fierce denunciation of the peace-at-any-price party in the form of a letter addressed to Richard Cobden entitled *Cobden and his Pamphlet Considered*, as well as a volume called *Britain Redeemed and Canada Preserved* in which he foreshadowed, some thirty years before its actual construction, the transcontinental railway between the Atlantic and the Pacific. On 15 February 1849 he married Emma Camilla Angela Maria, daughter of Camillo Gaggiotti, then minister of war in Rome.

On 3 August 1850 Richards started a new weekly journal, the *Mirror of the Time*, which lasted only a year. His chief contributions to it he reissued under the titles of *Poems, Essays, and Opinions* (2 vols., 1851) and *Essays and Opinions* (2 vols., 1852). During the Crimean War he brought out, in 1854, a collection of lyrics, *The Minstrelsy of War*. From 29 June to 31 December 1855 he held the office of first editor of the *Daily Telegraph*.

Richards had previously advocated the enrolling of rifle corps throughout the three kingdoms as a precaution against invasion; and when editor of the *Daily Telegraph*, he brought the subject prominently to public notice. In 1858 he was appointed secretary of the National and Constitutional Defence Association, which was formed to give effect to the scheme. Through his efforts a public meeting was held in St Martin's Hall, Long Acre, London, on 17 April 1859; Admiral Sir Charles Napier presided, and, as a result of this, and of pressure from the *Daily Telegraph* and *The Times*, the War Office issued, on 12 May 1859, a circular which authorized the enrolling all over the United Kingdom of rifle volunteers. On the publication of that circular, Richards, who had been honorary secretary to the workmen's volunteer brigade, strove hard to have working men admitted. This had been a sticking point with those in authority for some time, but his persistence meant that his 'brigade' had been accepted as the 3rd City of London rifle volunteer corps before the end of 1860. This gave him something of a right to the title Father of the Force (Cunningham, 24), and he was appointed major of the corps, and soon afterwards colonel. He held his commission until 1869, when a testimonial was presented to him in recognition of his efforts. The rifle volunteer movement grew rapidly; 337,072 volunteers were enrolled in 1907, when the force was absorbed in the Territorial Army.

In 1869 Richards published *Medea*, a poem on the well-known painting by Frederick Sandys; a photograph of the work formed the frontispiece to the volume. In 1870 he was appointed editor of the *Morning Advertiser* in succession to James Grant, and he held that position until his death. In 1871 his only novel, *So Very Human*, was published; its title was suggested by a chance phrase spoken by Dickens. Richards died on 12 June 1876 at his home, 22 Brunswick Square, London, and was buried in St Peter's churchyard, Croydon, Surrey.

CHARLES KENT, *rev.* MEGAN A. STEPHAN

Sources *Old Westminsters*, vols. 1–2 · Foster, *Alum. Oxon.* · *The Athenaeum* (17 June 1876), 832 · H. Cunningham, *The volunteer force: a social and political history, 1859–1908* (1975)
Archives NL Scot., letters to Blackwoods
Wealth at death £8000: administration with will, 30 Sept 1876, *CGPLA Eng. & Wales*

Richards, Arthur Frederick, first Baron Milverton (1885–1978), colonial governor, was born at 7 Nelson Parade, Bristol, on 21 February 1885, the second of the four children (all boys) of William Richards, timber merchant, of Bristol, and his wife, Amelia Sophie Elizabeth Orchard. He was educated at Clifton College, winning an open classical scholarship to Christ Church, Oxford, in 1904; but a serious illness restricted him to taking a pass degree. He nevertheless sat the eastern cadetship examination and entered the Malayan civil service in 1908.

Quickly making his mark as an administrator of conspicuous efficiency, in both field and secretariat posts, Richards rose steadily and in 1926 became under-secretary to the government of the Federated Malay States. In 1927 he married Noelle Benda, daughter of Charles Basil Whitehead, of Torquay, and chief police officer of Province Wellesley, Straits Settlements; they had two sons and one daughter. After acting as adviser to the government of Johore in 1929, he was seconded in 1930 as governor of North Borneo, then administered by the Chartered Company.

By now Richards had been singled out by the Colonial Office, and his appointment to his first governorship came in 1933, to the Gambia. Further recognition followed in quick succession, with a spell as governor of Fiji and high commissioner for the Western Pacific from 1936 being interrupted, in 1938, by a crisis transfer to the first-class governorship of Jamaica, where the incumbent, Sir Edward Denham, had died suddenly. The West Indies were then in a state of violent unrest (grave enough subsequently to warrant the appointment of a royal commission, headed by Lord Moyne), and Richards saw his task as that of restoring order to the island.

It had been expected that after Fiji Richards would succeed Sir T. Shenton Thomas in Singapore, a posting dear to his hopes, but the war meant fewer inter-territorial transfers. By the time he concluded his term in Jamaica, not only was Malaya under enemy occupation but Richards was nearing the conventional retiring age. However, his innate talents, added to the political experience gained from the characteristic rough-and-tumble of a grooming Caribbean governorship, persuaded the Colonial Office that it could not afford to let Richards go. He was offered one of the plums of the service, and in 1943 returned to west Africa as governor of Nigeria.

Exactly why Richards, with his reputation for firm leadership linked to a trenchant tongue and a name for no-nonsense administration, as his decisive government of Jamaica had shown, was selected for the sensitive

Arthur Frederick Richards, first Baron Milverton (1885–1978), by Elliott & Fry, 1950

Nigerian post is still not totally clear. He was known in the Colonial Office as 'the toughest governor of them all', and in Nigeria he earned the nickname Old Sinister. Many (Richards among them) thought he was the right man to rebuild Malaya, shattered by the Japanese occupation, but the Colonial Office felt the task might impose too much strain on an older man. With neither Ceylon nor Kenya vacant, it had, for a governor of Richards's seniority and stature, to be Nigeria or nothing.

Nigeria, whose size and complexity led Richards to describe it as more of an empire than a colony, was already beginning to prepare for the post-war world. With his usual thoroughness, Richards at once set his own stamp on the level of constitutional advance that he thought best. His dispatches home, on what became known as the Richards constitution, mastered the problems as he saw them and devised incisive solutions to what he believed the shape of politics in Nigeria should be. As Sir Hugh Foot, his chief secretary in Lagos, said of Richards's role in the constitutional plans, he 'often allowed his intelligence to overcome his delight in pretending to be a cynical reactionary' (Foot, 103).

Whether Richards gave enough credit to the spadework undertaken by his predecessor, Sir Bernard Bourdillon, is a moot point; Richards himself found those ideas too imprecise to accept them as plans and, in the opinion of the former's biography, consigned them to oblivion with the characteristic minute 'R.I.P.'. Once again, he saw his role as one of action, and he was never loath to make up his own mind. This brought him into conflict with the emergent political class in Nigeria, who protested against what they called his 'obnoxious ordinances' as well as his refusal to consult Nigerians on his constitutional reforms (Richards later argued that in a country as divided as Nigeria, consultation would only have led to confusion). On the initiative of its leader, Nnamdi Azikiwe, the nascent National Council of Nigeria and the Cameroons sent a protest delegation to London, but the secretary of state paid them scant attention. In his classic study, James Coleman has pointed to Richards's 'special knack for antagonising the educated elements' and concluded that his appointment was an unfortunate one (Coleman, 275).

In the event, the new constitution, envisaged to last nine years, was quickly replaced by Richards's successor, Sir John Macpherson. In retrospect, it is arguable how far Richards's plan to emphasize the essential unity of the country by fully involving the reluctant northern emirs in the constitutional process for the first time, while providing for its underlying diversity through the device of elected regional assemblies in addition to a strong central legislature (originally envisaged on a peripatetic basis, sitting in each regional capital), represented the limit of Nigeria's fragile unitary potential or the irrevocable first step in its subsequent history of creeping federalism.

Richards left Nigeria in 1947. In the same year his outstanding pro-consular career was recognized by his elevation to a peerage. Unlike lords Lugard and Hailey but like Lord Twining, Richards incorporated the name of Nigeria's capital into the title of his barony, becoming Baron Milverton of Lagos and of Clifton in the city of Bristol. Although retired, he at once threw himself into political affairs. In the House of Lords his attachment to the Labour Party did not survive its views on nationalization or its handling of the Indonesian question, and in June 1949 he resigned. His association with the Liberals lasted no longer, and within eighteen months he declared for the Conservative Party.

Outside parliament, Milverton showed himself the indefatigable administrator he had ever been. At various times he became a part-time director of the Colonial Development Corporation; director of the Bank of West Africa, the Perak Rubber and Tin Company, and the West Indian Sugar Company; member of the board of governors of Clifton College; chairman of the council of the London School of Hygiene and Tropical Medicine, the Empire Day Movement, the British Leprosy Relief Association, and the Royal African Society; vice-president of the Royal Empire Society; and president of the Association of British Malaya. During the tragic years of the Nigerian civil war, he restored some of the shine to his reputation in Nigeria by speaking out forcefully against secession.

Milverton published only a few, short articles. He excelled as a raconteur and had an enviable memory for quotations. He did not find accessibility easy to practise, preferring to live up to his image of one who spoke his mind, often in sharp epigrams or with a wit tinged with irony. Unwilling to suffer fools gladly, he never disguised

his contempt for the glib or hasty and was prouder of being right than popular or fashionable in his views. Sarcasm he knew, but never cynicism. Golf, sailing, snooker, tennis, and his library were among his hobbies; and, to the consternation of his Government House aides, late nights and dawn rising.

Appointed CMG in 1933, he was advanced to KCMG in 1935 and GCMG in 1942. He was made knight of the order of St John of Jerusalem in 1945. Milverton died on 27 October 1978, at his home, The Lodge, Woodlands Park Road, Cox Green, Bray, near Maidenhead. The barony passed to his eldest son, the Revd Francis Arthur Richard Richards. He was survived by Lady Richards.

A. H. M. KIRK-GREENE

Sources R. Peel, *Old Sinister* (1986) · *The Times* (28 Oct 1978) · interview (recording and transcript), 22 Feb 1969, Bodl. RH · 'Leadership or platitudes? Lord Milverton voices the challenge', *West Africa* (2 Oct 1948), 997–9 · *West Africa* (6 Nov 1978), 2182–3 · J. S. Coleman, *Nigeria: background to nationalism* (1958) · R. D. Pearce, *Sir Bernard Bourdillon* (1987) · H. Foot, *A start in freedom* (1964) · R. D. Pearce, 'Governors, nationalists, and constitutions in Nigeria, 1935–51', *Journal of Imperial and Commonwealth History*, 9 (1980–81), 289–307 · J. E. Flint, 'Governor *versus* colonial office: an anatomy of the Richards constitution for Nigeria, 1939–1945', *Historical Papers* [Canadian Historical Society] (1981), 129–43 · A. H. M. Kirk-Greene, *A biographical dictionary of the British colonial governor* (1980) · CGPLA Eng. & Wales (1979) · b. cert. · d. cert. · private information (1986)
Archives Bodl. RH, uncatalogued MSS [microfilm] · Bodl. RH, tape-recorded reminiscences with transcripts | Bodl. RH, corresp. with Lord Lugard · Bodl. RH, corresp. with Sir R. R. Welensky · CAC Cam., corresp. with Sir L. E. Spears · Derbys. RO, papers relating to British South Africa Society | SOUND Bodl. RH, tape-recorded interview
Likenesses Elliott & Fry, photograph, 1950, NPG [*see illus.*] · portrait, repro. in Peel, *Old Sinister*, frontispiece
Wealth at death £80,887: probate, 9 Feb 1979, CGPLA Eng. & Wales

Richards, Audrey Isabel (1899–1984), social anthropologist, was born on 8 July 1899 in London, the second of the four daughters of Sir Henry Erle Richards (1861–1922), professor of law, and his wife, Isabel (1867–1945), daughter of Spencer Perceval Butler of Lincoln's Inn. Her girlhood was spent in India; the family returned to England in 1911, when her father, then a member of the viceroy's council, was appointed Chichele professor of international law at Oxford. She was educated at Downe House School near Newbury, where she boarded, at Newnham College, Cambridge (1918–21), where she read natural science (part one 1921, second class), and at the London School of Economics (LSE; PhD 1931). After graduation she taught at her old school for a year, then worked for Gilbert Murray for a year in Oxford. From 1924 to 1928 she was secretary to the League of Nations labour department before becoming a student at the LSE under the supervision of Charles Seligman. At the same time she was teaching at Bedford College, London. Her PhD thesis, published as *Hunger and Work in a Savage Tribe* (1932), was a library-based assemblage of information on nutrition that took a functional approach, though it was finally finished in the field. This interdigitation of habitats typified her work for the next twenty-five years.

Richards first went to Northern Rhodesia (later Zambia)

Audrey Isabel Richards (1899–1984), by Ramsey & Muspratt, 1968

rather 'intermittent'. Something of the scale of Richards's institute-related work (she was co-ordinating over thirty ethnographic and linguistic surveys) is reflected in collected volumes such as *Economic Development and Tribal Change* (1954) and *East African Chiefs* (1960).

After her final return to England in 1956 Audrey Richards took up a fellowship at Newnham College, Cambridge, was college vice-principal (1958–9), and from 1966 an honorary fellow. She founded the African studies centre at Cambridge University, and held a Smuts readership from 1961 to her retirement in 1966. During this period she gave a Royal Institution discourse (1963) and the Frazer lecture (1965), and held the presidency of the African Studies Association (1963–6). Her move to the Essex village of Elmdon in 1962 whetted her ethnographic appetite, and both before and after retirement she encouraged students to take their first steps in interviewing her fellow villagers, a project initially instigated with Sir Edmund Leach. The eventual result was a short study produced for the people of Elmdon, and two volumes by colleagues which drew on much of this material. She died at the King Edward VII Hospital, Midhurst, Sussex, on 29 June 1984, having been staying with one of her two younger sisters, and was cremated at Chichester. A memorial service was held in King's College chapel on 10 November 1984.

Audrey Richards held her own among the best-known British social anthropologists of her day. She was honoured with the Wellcome medal (1941) and the Rivers memorial medal (1945), and was appointed CBE in 1955. She held the presidency of the Royal Anthropological Institute (1959–61), the first woman to hold the post, and was elected to the British Academy in 1967, the first woman anthropologist to be so honoured. She knew before she died about the lecture established in her name at the centre for cross-cultural research on women at Oxford University; the inaugural address was given by her distinguished pupil Professor Jean La Fontaine. She made a lasting contribution to the study of African nutrition and agricultural economics, but is more widely known for what she contributed to the anthropological understanding of matrilineal kinship structures and to the twinned issues of politics and ritual. These were the subject of two separate and substantial sets of essays in her honour, both published in her lifetime. She had an abiding interest in anthropological methods, and in the virtues of systematic data collection, one of the inspirations she always attributed to Bronislaw Malinowski at the LSE, who had the most profound influence on her early anthropology. The functional theory she learned from Malinowski was suited to the kinds of understandings of 'total systems' which tackled prejudice and ignorance about 'savages'. Some of her colleagues in later years became impatient at her loyalty to these tenets, but she never sought to impose her ideas. Indeed one anecdote must stand for the many which give a flavour of her robustness and sense of the ridiculous. Audrey told Jean La Fontaine that she had been sent to study the Bemba because both nutrition and matrilineal organization were felt to be suitable topics for a

in 1930, where she worked among the Bemba people for fifteen months. She returned in 1933 for a further eighteen months, having taught in the intervening period at the LSE. The result of her fieldwork was the monumental *Land, Labour and Diet in Northern Rhodesia* (1939), written during her continuing appointment as a lecturer at the LSE. By the time it was published she was in Africa again, having left her London lectureship for a post as senior lecturer and head of department at the University of the Witwatersrand, Johannesburg. This led to a brief spell of fieldwork in the Transvaal. However, the war brought her back to England in 1940 to work on the nutrition committee in the Colonial Office, where she became a temporary principal. She subsequently collaborated with Lord Hailey in planning, among other things, the Colonial Social Science Research Council and one of its institutes, the East African Institute of Social Research. She served on the council's committee from its founding in 1944 until 1950. As special lecturer in colonial studies at the LSE (1943–5) she promoted the training of local administrators, becoming reader in 1946. Then in 1950 she moved again, and from 1950 to 1956 she was director of the East African Institute of Social Research at Makerere College, Uganda, an affiliate of London University. During this period she went back to her notes from the 1930s and wrote what has become her most widely read book, *Chisungu* (1956), a study of female initiation rites in Bemba. Apart from a brief return trip to the Bemba, her focus moved to Uganda, though she records her own activities as being woman. She did not, La Fontaine remarks, take it as a compliment. It was also thought appropriate for her as a woman to study women. However, as she was forced to report, she found as many men as women in Bemba.

Audrey Richards's interest in method was allied to her promotion of 'applied anthropology' and the practical questions it might answer, pressing anthropological findings into the service of administration, education, and social welfare. Thus at the East African Institute she probed problems arising from the effects of wage labour on rural families, the conditions of migration, changing land use, and so forth, stimulating a set of studies which contributed to what indeed must count as, in her words, a pioneering 'experiment in applied research'. She also stimulated primary ethnographic surveys, since she regarded these as basic for any future work. Her own work was exemplary in this.   MARILYN STRATHERN

Sources R. Firth, *Man*, new ser., 20 (1985), 341–4 · *International encyclopedia of social sciences*, 18 (1979), 658–60 [biographical suppl.] · M. Strathern, *PBA*, 82 (1993), 439–53 · *Cambridge Anthropology* [memorial issue, ed. J. La Fontaine], 10 (1985) · J. Gladstone, 'Significant sisters', *American Ethnologist*, 13 (1986), 338–62 · A. Robertson, 'An appreciation', *African Affairs*, 84 (1985), 136–8 · A. Richards, 'The colonial office', *Anthropological Forum*, 33 (1978), 168–89 · *WW* (1983) · *ASA annals* (1974) [Association of Societal Anthropologists, register of members] · *DNB* · *Newnham College register* (1959) · J. La Fontaine, *Newnham College Roll Letter* (1985) · private information (2004) [T. Faber, nephew and executor]

Archives BLPES, field notes and work papers · BLPES, papers · priv. coll., personal papers · Royal Anthropological Institute, London, notes relating to the Buganda | Bodl. RH, corresp. with Margery Perham · CUL, corresp. with Meyer Fortes · priv. coll. · priv. coll., corresp. with executor Tom Faber · priv. coll., corresp. with Sir Raymond Firth | FILM U. Cam., department of social anthropology archives, film on video (1982), 'On fieldwork', Audrey Richards talking with students, 1.5 hrs | SOUND U. Cam., department of social anthropology archives, two audio tapes of reminiscences

Likenesses B. Malinowski?, photograph, c.1930, Royal Anthropological Institute archives; repro. in La Fontaine, ed., *Cambridge anthropology* · Ramsey & Muspratt, photograph, 1968, Cambridge Central Library [*see illus.*] · photograph, c.1970, repro. in La Fontaine, ed., *Cambridge anthropology* · B. Gaye, photograph, British Academy archives; repro. in Strathern, *PBA* · photograph, U. Cam., department of social anthropology

Wealth at death £120,644: probate, 19 Dec 1984, *CGPLA Eng. & Wales*

Richards, Ceri Giraldus (1903–1971), artist, was born on 6 June 1903 at Dunvant near Swansea, the eldest of three children and elder son of Thomas Coslette Richards, tinplate worker, of Preswylfa, Dunvant, and his wife, Sarah Jones. He was educated at Dunvant council school and Gowerton intermediate school, and followed an interest in mechanical drawing by a brief apprenticeship to an electrical firm in Morriston. From 1920 to 1924 he studied at Swansea School of Art, and from there won a scholarship to the Royal College of Art (1924–7). Ceri Richards married Frances (d. 1985), daughter of John Clayton, kiln fireman at Stoke-on-Trent, in 1929. They were contemporaries at the Royal College of Art, and she also became a distinguished painter and graphic artist; they had two daughters.

Richards continued to live in London until 1939, where he became a leading contributor among the small group of artists interested in the international modern movement. At the Royal College his skill in drawing had been remarked, and his best works of the early 1930s are rhythmical and confident life and figure drawings. In March 1934 he showed two paintings at the one and only 'Objective abstractions' exhibition (neither of them abstract), which indicated his distance from the more purely abstract artists gathered around Ben Nicholson. Also in 1934 he began to make pictorial relief constructions assembled from pieces of wood, which were associated at first with a number of drawings of an artist contemplating a piece of abstract sculpture. The abstraction of the figures in the reliefs is comparable to contemporary work by Picasso and Hans Arp which he had seen in reproduction, and which were then also influencing others in London. His early relief constructions were never totally abstract, and the extraordinary variety of material he used implied uniquely ironic references to their figure subjects. He first exhibited these at the 'Surrealist objects' exhibition at the London Gallery in 1937. He joined the staff of Chelsea College of Art the same year.

In 1939 Richards moved to Cardiff where he remained during the war, teaching graphic art at Cardiff School of Art. He was commissioned by the Ministry of Information to record tin-plate workers in south Wales, and the series of black and white ink drawings that he made both referred to his father's occupation and became a means of developing the rhythms of the relief constructions into a popular and realistic subject.

Richards's response to the poetry of Dylan Thomas—whom he met only once, in 1953—which was in the first place a print commission for *Poetry London* (1947), became the major theme of his post-war work. *The Cycle of Nature* (of which there are several oil paintings, from 1944) was inspired by Thomas's poem 'The force that through the green fuse' and extends the allusive subjects of the later constructions into an active display of human and botanical sexuality. It led on to associated subjects, notably *The Rape of the Sabines* and a number of interiors with a woman at a piano, which exploit bright colours and rapid application reminiscent of Matisse, although the decorative surface rhythms are typical of Richards. Following his own illness, and after the death of Dylan Thomas in 1953, another group of works deals with these subjects, including two church commissions, *The Deposition* (1958; St Mary's, Swansea) and *The Supper at Emmaus* (1958–9; St Edmund Hall, Oxford).

Retrospective exhibitions were held at the Whitechapel Art Gallery in 1960, the Venice Biennale in 1962–3, Fischer Fine Art Ltd in 1972, and, after Richard's death, at the Tate Gallery in 1981. In 1985 there was an exhibition of his work entitled 'The lyrical vision' at the Gillian Jason Gallery in Camden Town, London. During the 1960s he returned to more abstract paintings, and also constructions, often based on Debussy's 'La cathédrale engloutie', which he himself played on the piano. Some of these paintings were large, with a technique variously geometrical or painterly, but also with, most importantly, intense and unusual colour harmonies. From the 1950s he continued to work on many of his subjects as lithographs and screen prints, often working with the Curwen Press. In 1964–5 he designed stained glass for Derby Cathedral and in 1965 was commissioned to design the Blessed Sacrament Chapel at Liverpool Roman Catholic Cathedral, for which he made stained glass, the painted reredos, the tabernacle, and the altar frontal.

Richards was a trustee of the Tate Gallery from 1958 to 1965. He was appointed CBE in 1960 and was made an honorary DLitt by the University of Wales in 1961. He won the gold medal at the national eisteddfod in 1961 and the Einaudi prize for painting at the Venice Biennale of 1962–3. He died in London on 9 November 1971. In 1984 an inaugural exhibition was held at the Ceri Richards Gallery, University College, Swansea.

A. D. F. JENKINS, rev.

Sources D. Thompson, *Ceri Richards* (1963) · R. Sanesi, *The graphic work of Ceri Richards* (1973) · R. Sanesi, *Ceri Richards: rilievi, desegni e dipinti, 1931/1940* (1976) · J. Ormond, *Arddangosfa goffa Ceri Richards* (1973) [exhibition catalogue, Welsh Arts Council, NMG Wales, 1973] · M. Gooding, *Ceri Richards graphics* (1979) [exhibition catalogue, NM Wal.] · *Ceri Richards* (1981) [incl. introduction by B. Robertson; exhibition catalogue, Tate Gallery, London, 22 July – 6 Sept 1981] · private information (1986) · *The Times* (11 Nov 1971) · *CGPLA Eng. & Wales* (1972) · *Ceri Richards: an exhibition to inaugurate the Ceri Richards Gallery* (1984) [exhibition catalogue, Ceri Richards Gallery, University College, Swansea]
Archives NL Wales, corresp. and papers | NL Wales, letters to Dr Hughes Jones and Mrs Hughes Jones · NL Wales, corresp. with Vernon Watkins · W. Sussex RO, letters to Walter Hussey relating to commission for Chichester Cathedral
Likenesses O'Meara, photograph, c.1963, Hult. Arch.
Wealth at death £30,728: probate, 17 Feb 1972, *CGPLA Eng. & Wales*

Richards, David [*pseud.* Dafydd Ionawr] (1751–1827), schoolmaster and poet, son of John and Anne Richards, was born at Glanymorfa, near Tywyn, Merioneth, on 22 January 1751. His father, who owned a small estate, neglected his education, and it was not until he was about twenty-one that he entered Edward Richard's school at Ystradmeurig with a view to preparation for orders. There he made rapid progress, not only in his school studies but also in the writing of 'strict' Welsh verse, an art he had learned from Evan Evans (Ieuan Brydydd Hir), for a time curate of Tywyn. After a year his father refused him further help, and he took a situation as usher to C. A. Tisdaile of Wrexham grammar school. He then made his first appearance in Welsh literature, contributing to *Yr Eurgrawn*, the first Welsh magazine.

On 16 May 1774 Richards matriculated at Jesus College, Oxford, but found university life so uncongenial that in a few months he again became usher to Tisdaile, now headmaster of Oswestry grammar school; some years afterwards he became assistant to W. H. Barker, headmaster of Carmarthen. At Carmarthen he experienced a double disappointment: he competed unsuccessfully in 1779 for the prize offered by the Cymrodorion Society for the best elegy upon Richard Morris (d. 1779), and not long afterwards Bishop Watson declined to ordain him to the curacy

of Llandough. He resolved never again to enter a competition or seek orders.

In 1790 Richards returned to Tywyn to take charge of the free school, but after two years' labour abandoned teaching that he might carry out more effectually what he conceived to be the true mission of his life, that of the religious poet. His *Cywydd y Drindod* ('Ode to the Trinity') had been in preparation for twenty years; in 1793 it appeared, a poem of over 13,000 lines, published at Wrexham under the name of Dafydd Ionawr, Richards having mortgaged his interest in the family estate in order to defray the cost of printing and having also received assistance from Thomas Jones of Dolgellau. The work was not popular, and two-thirds of the issue remained unsold, although it was reprinted in Carmarthen in 1834. In 1794 he moved to Dolgellau, and four years later, on the death of his father, gave still further proof of his devotion to the life of the poet and the recluse by making over his inheritance to his friend Thomas Jones on condition of receiving maintenance for the rest of his life. From 1800 to 1807 he took charge of the free school at Dolgellau, but devoted his closing years entirely to the writing (as Dafydd Ionawr) of Welsh religious verse, including *Joseph, llywodraethwr yr Aipht* (1809), *Barddoniaeth Gristianogawl* (1815), and *Cywydd y Diluw* (1821). 'My motive to write', says Richards in his preface to *Cywydd y Drindod*, 'was a very strong impression made upon my mind very early in life, which would not suffer my thoughts to rest, and which I regarded as a call from heaven.' His power as a poet, however, was not on a level with his loftiness of purpose, and his works have exercised little influence.

Richards lived with Thomas Jones (d. 1819), and then with Jones's son Griffith, at Bryntirion, Dolgellau, until his death on 11 or 12 May 1827. He was buried in Dolgellau cemetery. In 1851 a collected edition of his poems, with portrait, memoir by R. O. Rees, and critical essay by Evan Jones (Ieuan Gwynedd), was published under the supervision of Morris Williams (Nicander).

J. E. LLOYD, rev. D. BEN REES

Sources *DWB* · M. Stephens, ed., *Cydymaith i lenyddiaeth Cymru* (1986), 503 · D. G. Jones, 'Dafydd Ionawr', *Y Genhinen*, 1 (1950–51), 135–142 · R. O. Rees, 'Memoir', in *Gwaith Dafydd Ionawr, dan olygiad y parch Morris Williams* (1851), 5–26 · C. Ashton, *Llyfryddiaeth Gymreig o 1801 i 1810* (1908), 481–8 · Foster, *Alum. Oxon.* · R. Williams, *Enwogion Cymru: a biographical dictionary of eminent Welshmen* (1852)
Likenesses portrait, repro. in M. Williams, ed., *Gwaith Dafydd Ionawr* (1851)

Richards [née Pilley], **Dorothy Eleanor** (1894–1986), mountaineer, was born at 167 The Grove, Camberwell, London, on 16 September 1894, one of four children of John James Pilley, science lecturer, and his wife, Annie Maria Young. She referred to herself as belonging to the era of finishing schools, and believed that her early climbing days were akin to a university education. Her first exposure to the mountains was on a family holiday in Beddgelert, north Wales, but her parents were not dedicated climbers, so Dorothy made independent trips back to the locality to pursue her interest. Introduced to rock climbing by Herbert Carr in 1915, through willingness and

Dorothy Eleanor Richards (1894–1986), by unknown photographer

aptitude she secured a place in the predominantly male climbing circles of the time. She ignored protests from her conventional middle-class family, who felt the activity too dangerous, and continued to pursue her climbing ambition.

Dorothy Pilley climbed existing and new routes with mostly male companions on Tryfan, Lliwedd, Cwm Idwal, and the Devil's Kitchen. A highlight was a first ascent of Holly Tree Wall on Idwal Slabs (1920). A similar pattern of activity followed in the English Lake District, the stamping ground of the Fell and Rock Climbing Club. She consolidated her contacts by joining its ranks in 1918, was quickly elected a committee member, and in 1920 was a founder of its London section. The club was unusual in its day for being mixed, and her membership brought her closer to other innovative female climbers.

During her first and guided season in the French Alps, Pilley led ascents of the Aiguille de l'M and the Petit Charmoz. This early promise and a list of classic alpine climbs qualified her for membership of the Ladies' Alpine Club. During her second season in 1921 she made guideless ascents of the Egginergrat and the Portjengrat with two other female climbers. This was pioneering work, in days when it was highly unusual for women to lead an alpine climb, let alone do so as part of an all-female party. The conviction that women should take responsibility for their own climbing ropes was reflected by Dorothy's involvement with the founding movement of the Pinnacle Club. Predominantly a rock climbing club and exclusively for women, it was dedicated to nurturing the skills of female climbers. Its founding in 1921 was a radical move, and constitutes the lasting legacy of pioneers such as Dorothy Pilley, who, while being an exceptional climber in her own right, was committed to furthering the standard of women's climbing in general.

Throughout the 1920s Dorothy Pilley climbed extensively in Britain and Europe. In the Mont Blanc chain, the Spanish and French Pyrenees, the Italian Alps, the Oberland, and Valais she tackled some of the most formidable climbs of the day. During a two-year world tour, 1925–7, she climbed in the Canadian Rockies, the Selkirks, the Bugaboo, and the American Rockies. In 1926 first ascents of Mount Baker and Mount Shuksau, Washington, were made with the Cambridge scholar and fellow climber Ivor Armstrong *Richards (1893–1979). They sealed their climbing partnership on 31 December that year by marrying in Honolulu. The tour ended with a trek in the Himalayas and an immediate return to the Alps. Incessant climbing and social activities—the latter usually at the behest of Dorothy—were to remain a hallmark of their lifestyle.

The high point of Dorothy's climbing career came in 1928, when she made the celebrated first ascent of the north ridge of the Dent Blanche, with her husband, the guide Joseph Georges, and Antoine Georges. This was acknowledged as one of the last great alpine climbing problems. The achievement is central to the final chapter of her reflective autobiographical work, *Climbing Days* (1935; 2nd edn, 1965). This early publication remains the only comprehensive account of her climbing exploits. Thereafter she intermittently contributed articles to climbing club journals and, having already made a career in journalism, wrote anecdotally about her sport on a freelance basis.

During the next thirty years, through the circumstances of Ivor Richards's academic appointments, new climbing horizons opened and many unclimbed peaks were attained, mostly guideless. While in Peking (Beijing) in 1929–30 and 1936–8, Dorothy climbed in the nearby Western Hills, the upper Yunnan, the Japanese Alps, and the Diamond Mountains of Korea. In 1938, still an independent spirit, she alone followed the 200 mile Old Jade Trail from Tali (Dali) in Yunnan to Bhamo on the Irrawaddy in Burma. When they were living in Cambridge, Massachusetts, from 1939 to 1974, the couple went weekend climbing in the White Mountains, and among innumerable expeditions ascended all but three of the winter 4000 foot mountains of New Hampshire.

The scale of Dorothy's climbing was prematurely reduced after a car accident in 1958, but her enthusiasm remained undiminished. She continued to endorse mountain activity through support of the clubs she had joined in her youth and in 1975 was appointed the first vice-president of the Alpine Club (the amalgamated Ladies' Alpine Club and all-male Alpine Club). This best demonstrates the respect she had attained within climbing establishment circles. Certainly, her prolific activity and her achievements all over the world marked her as one of the most outstanding mountaineers of the inter-war and post-war periods. One of the mountaineering world's most irrepressible personalities, she characteristically spent her last new year, aged ninety-one, at the climbers' hut at Glen Brittle, Skye, drinking whisky and talking mountains with a party of Scottish climbers. She died at Addenbrooke's Hospital, Cambridge, on 24 September 1986.

CAROL A. OSBORNE

Sources D. Pilley [Mrs I. A. Richards], *Climbing days*, 2nd edn (1965) · M. Files, 'In memoriam', *Fell and Rock Climbing Club Journal*, 24 (1985–8), 591–3 · J. Adam Smith, *Alpine Journal*, 92 (1987), 308–10 · K. Chorley, *Alpine Journal*, 85 (1980), 263–5 [obit. of Ivor Armstrong Richards] · D. Pilley-Richards, climbing list, 1916–69, Alpine Club Library, London, Ladies' Alpine Club, G25 · *The Times* (30 Sept 1986) · D. Pilley, application form to Ladies' Alpine Club, 1920, Alpine Club Library, London, G25 · private information (2004) · b. cert. · d. cert.
Archives Magd. Cam., diaries
Likenesses two photographs, Alpine Club [*see illus.*]
Wealth at death £1,129,140: probate, 6 April 1987, *CGPLA Eng. & Wales*

Richards, Francis John (1901–1965), agriculturist, was born on 1 October 1901 at Newton Road, Burton upon Trent, the third child of Robert Richards, a retail butcher, and his wife, Mary Ann Mayger. Frank Richards was educated at Burton grammar school where he was an outstanding pupil and where an early interest in biology, fostered at home, was developed by an enthusiastic schoolmaster. He also showed an early talent for mathematics. He was awarded a major borough scholarship and in 1921 he went to the University of Birmingham, whence he graduated BSc in 1924 with first-class honours in botany. After eighteen months as a demonstrator he obtained his MSc; he was later awarded the DSc for published work.

In 1926 Richards joined the Research Institute of Plant Physiology at Imperial College, London, under the general direction of Professor V. H. Blackman, to assist F. G. Gregory, later director of the institute, in investigations of the mineral nutrition of barley. After six months in London he moved to Harpenden, where field facilities were provided at Rothamsted Experimental Station. He remained in Harpenden for thirty-five years. When responsibility for the institute passed from the Ministry of Agriculture to the Agricultural Research Council he became a principal scientific officer, subsequently, by two special merit promotions, becoming senior principal scientific officer and deputy chief scientific officer (1963). In 1928 Richards married Lilian Kingsley Mason, daughter of a Burton timber merchant. They had two daughters and led a quiet domestic life in Harpenden.

At Harpenden, Richards gradually took over from Gregory responsibility for the nutritional aspects of the institute's research and for training research students in plant physiology, in which he himself continued to work throughout his career. On Gregory's retirement in December 1958 the institute was disbanded. To provide for the continuation of Richards's work a research unit was set up, with Richards himself as director. The unit was based at Wye College, Kent (University of London), and Richards moved there in 1961, accompanied by his senior colleague, W. W. Schwabe.

In 1929 Richards published (with Gregory) in the *Annals of Botany* the first of a series of papers on the mineral nutrition of barley which indirectly contributed much to modern fertilizer practice. Making meticulous measurements and exploiting R. A. Fisher's new techniques for statistical interpretation, he established the effects of nitrogen, phosphorus, and potassium deficiencies on assimilation and respiration rates of barley leaves. Subsequent studies examined the roles of phosphorus and potassium in protein synthesis and in the general nitrogen metabolism of plants. He demonstrated that the amine putrescine, itself toxic, was produced as the ionic substitute for a lack of potassium.

Richards took an interest, which possibly arose from his mathematical inclination, in the problem of the patterns of leaf arrangements in plants—phyllotaxis. His studies led to a new understanding of the relations between the growth of the shoot tip and organ formation. He devised a means of defining the patterns—the Phyllotaxis Index for plane projection and the Equivalent Phyllotaxis Index for a conical surface. As a result it became possible to describe phyllotactic systems in terms of radial distances from the centre of the growing point and the angular divergence between primordia which was free from implied hypotheses about the origin of the system. While Richards did not proceed to prove formally the necessity of the Fibonacci angle being the limiting divergence, his contributions, published in several papers, stimulated renewed interest in this, perhaps the oldest, problem of plant morphogenesis. Richards was elected a fellow of the Royal Society in 1954.

While still a student Richards had joined a volunteer party to assist Professor R. H. Yapp in a study of the salt marshes of the Dovey estuary of which an important aspect was the vertical accretion of the sward association. After Yapp's death Richards completed the project and published the results in 1934. His use of statistical methods in the analysis of the data was pioneering in ecological studies.

Richards was a modest man with a diffident manner which concealed remarkable talents and a wide range of general as well as biological knowledge. His reluctance to express his views restricted his influence, but his colleagues had deep respect for his shrewd analytical mind and clarity of thought. Richards had a number of hobbies. As examples, he assembled and mounted a superb collection of Lepidoptera and made a collection of palaeolithic artefacts from the classical fields of Rothamsted; he also made a reflecting telescope, grinding the parabolic mirror himself. Soon after the move to Wye Richards's health began to deteriorate and he died there, at his home, Orchard Bank, Oxenturn Road, on 2 January 1965.

H. K. PORTER, *rev.* V. M. QUIRKE

Sources H. K. Porter, *Memoirs FRS*, 12 (1966), 423–36 · personal knowledge (1981) · *The Times* (4 Jan 1965) · *CGPLA Eng. & Wales* (1965)
Wealth at death £11,200: probate, 9 March 1965, *CGPLA Eng. & Wales*

Richards, Frank. *See* Hamilton, Charles Harold St John (1876–1961).

Richards, Frank (1884–1961), soldier and author, was born in Newport, Monmouthshire. According to Robert Graves (who was sometimes inaccurate) Richards grew up believing himself illegitimate but later learned that his mother, a servant at the house of a rich colliery owner, had been secretly married to his father, the colliery owner's ne'er-do-well son. According to Richards he was orphaned in 1893 at the age of nine. He was adopted by his mother's twin brother, a tinplate worker, and his wife, and brought up with their children at Blaenau, Monmouthshire, then a thriving industrial town. He later wrote, 'no boy could have had better parents than what they were to me' (Richards, *Old Soldier Sahib*, 9). His aunt taught him some Welsh but he later forgot it. He was educated at the local board school in Blaenau, which he disliked and from which he latterly often played truant. On his twelfth birthday he left school and began work as a door boy, working ventilation doors in a colliery. After two months he worked briefly greasing cold rolls in a tinworks, then went back to the colliery as an assistant employed by a coal-face worker ('buttie'), 'an excellent man' (ibid., 12) who treated him well.

Richards's cousin had enlisted and enjoyed the army. In April 1901, having added eighteen months to his age, Richards enlisted in the regiment of his choice, the Royal Welch Fusiliers. His service coincided with a peaceful, relatively uneventful period for them, and he had no active service. He served in the 2nd battalion in England—gaining his marksman badge and in 1902 training as a signaller—and in Jersey, 'the happiest six months of my life' (Richards, *Old Soldier Sahib*, 61). Known to his fellow soldiers as Dick or Big Dick, he was tough, sociable, humorous, and cynical, and took easily to army life. He enjoyed women, beer, gambling, music, reading—especially historical fiction, with Dumas his favourite, and history—and army signalling. Robert Graves later described him as 'tall, resourceful, very Welsh, the company humorist' (Richards, *Old Soldiers Never Die*, 3). From 1902 to 1907 he served in India, 'a land of milk and honey' (Richards, *Old Soldier Sahib*, 82), mostly at Agra—gaining the army third-class certificate of education to qualify for more pay—and from 1907 to 1909 in Burma, at Shwebo. He decided not to complete twelve years with the colours, and in 1909 returned home. When a soldier he was tattooed 'with designs of animals, snakes and celebrities' (ibid., 335) which he later regretted. His uncle and aunt had moved to Liswerry, near Newport, Monmouthshire. He did various jobs there and around Newport, then was employed in the Caerleon tinworks near Newport. He missed the army and the tropics and wished he had not left, but as a reservist was not permitted to re-enlist. He returned to Blaenau and worked as a timberman's assistant in a mine, suffering from recurrent malaria. In 1912 he extended his reserve service for another four years.

In August 1914 reservists were recalled and Richards rejoined the 2nd battalion. On 10 August they arrived in France, Richards's first time there. They were at Mons, though not in action, and on the long, tiring retreat—when he and others became separated from the unit—to the Marne. He fought at first Ypres (October–November 1914), and from November 1914 he served in the trenches of the western front, from 1915 again as a signaller. A 'sterling fellow' (Dunn, 347), brave and resilient, he endured trench warfare—including the battles of Loos, the Somme, and third Ypres, and the German spring 1918 offensive—with the intermittent consolations of women, drink, gambling, and occasional home leave. Among the officers of the battalion were Siegfried Sassoon, Robert Graves, and Dr James Churchill Dunn, the regimental medical officer. Richards was exceptionally fortunate not to be killed or severely wounded. In 1916 he was awarded the distinguished conduct medal for maintaining communications under heavy fire during a trench raid, and in 1917 the military medal for bravery in the unsuccessful attack on Polygon Wood. As earlier, he refused promotion, according to his memoirs because he did not want to be separated from his friends (NCOs were forbidden to socialize with privates), but according to Graves because, believing himself illegitimate, he feared having to show his birth certificate. After the war ended miners were given priority for release, and Richards was demobilized on 5 December 1918 at Liverpool.

Richards's post-war years were difficult. His health was impaired by his war service, preventing his working in the pit, and unemployment was high in south Wales. He worked, initially temporarily, for about thirteen years as a labour exchange clerk, though he disliked 'pen-pushing', and retired on a pension. After reading officers' war memoirs—'a different war to what I knew, being in the ranks' (Richards, *Old Soldiers Never Die*, 4)—in 1930 he started writing his memoirs of the war. He sent the manuscript to Graves, asking his opinion. Graves edited it—'he didn't half lick it into shape' (ibid., 5)—and arranged its publication by Faber and Faber in 1933. *Old Soldiers Never Die* was lucidly written—Graves attributed Richards's style to his signals training—vivid, cynical, and sometimes bawdy. It recounted his experiences, with vignettes of military stupidity, and expressed his attitudes, including his contempt for hypocrites, war correspondents—who wrote 'the biggest B.S. imaginable' (ibid., 134)—staff officers, chaplains, and Portuguese. It was favourably reviewed, was praised by Liddell Hart, sold well, and brought Richards welcome royalties which he largely spent on betting and trips to London. However, it was privately criticized by Dr J. C. Dunn, who considered Graves inaccurate and hyperbolic, as having 'far too much of the Graves flavour' (Dunn, xlviii). Its success led Richards to write, again with Graves's encouragement and assistance, his memoirs of his early life and Edwardian soldiering, *Old Soldier Sahib* (1936). Vivid and proudly imperialist, it expressed his and his fellow soldiers' attitudes, including their dislike of Curzon, the viceroy of India, and Lady Curzon. Richards's books are unique as accounts by a socio-economically and educationally typical regular army private infantryman of Edwardian imperial soldiering and the western front.

They are considered classics and have been repeatedly cited by military historians. The two books and Graves's prefaces to their paperback editions of the 1960s are the main sources for Richards's life: his army file did not survive the blitz or official 'weeding', and there remain gaps in his life story. He was also the only royal Welch fusilier private to contribute to Dunn's *The War the Infantry Knew, 1914–1919* (1938). Dissatisfied with the official war history of the 2nd Royal Welch Fusiliers, Dunn contacted survivors and compiled his 'Chronicle of service in France and Belgium', a work highly regarded by military historians.

After he wrote *Old Soldier Sahib* Richards married a shop assistant, and they had a daughter. He died on 26 August 1961 at Waen Ebbw Nant-y-glo, Abertillery, Monmouthshire. He is to be distinguished from his pseudonymous namesake, the author of children's books, who died in the same year.

ROGER T. STEARN

Sources F. Richards, *Old soldiers never die* (1964) · F. Richards, *Old soldier sahib* (1965) · J. C. Dunn, *The war the infantry knew, 1914–1919: a chronicle of service in France and Belgium* (1989) · private information (2004) [Royal Welch Fusiliers regimental museum, Caernarfon Castle] · M. Glover, *That astonishing infantry: three hundred years of the history of the Royal Welch Fusiliers* (1989) · M. Barthorp, 'Frank Richards', *Military Illustrated*, 33 (Feb 1991), 45–50 · H. Cecil and P. Liddle, eds., *Facing Armageddon: the First World War experienced* (1996) · I. W. F. Beckett and K. Simpson, eds., *A nation in arms: a social study of the British army in the First World War* (1985) · D. Winter, *Death's men: soldiers of the Great War* (1978)
Likenesses photograph, *c.*1902, repro. in Glover, *That astonishing infantry*, facing p. 198 · photograph, *c.*1930, repro. in Dunn, *The war the infantry knew*, following p. 296

Richards, Sir Frederick William (1833–1912), naval officer, was born at Ballyhally, co. Wexford, on 30 November 1833, the second son of Captain Edwin Richards RN, of Solsborough, co. Wexford, and his wife, Mary Anne, daughter of the Revd Walter Blake Kirwan, dean of Killala. After the Royal Naval School, New Cross, he became a naval cadet in 1848. He served several years on the Australian station and was promoted acting mate, HM sloop *Fantome*, on the same station in January 1854. He was promoted lieutenant in October 1855, and on returning home in 1856 went on half pay for a year, after which he was appointed to the *Ganges*, flagship on the Pacific station. The commander-in-chief, Rear-Admiral R. L. Baynes, appointed him flag-lieutenant in April 1859, and in February 1860 he was promoted commander in command of the paddle-sloop *Vixen* on the China station. He brought home and paid off this vessel in 1861. From March 1862 to January 1866 he commanded the *Dart*, a gunboat, on the west coast of Africa, and on his return was promoted captain in February 1866. Later that year he married Lucy, daughter of Fitzherbert Brooke, of Horton Court, Gloucestershire. They had no children, and she died in 1880.

After four and a half years on half pay Richards commanded the Indian troopship *Jumna* until June 1873, and was then selected to command the *Devastation*, the first steam turret battleship designed without any sail power. This command was of great importance, as the loss in 1870 of the turret ship *Captain* had caused great anxiety as to the stability of such vessels. Richards's conduct of the exhaustive steam trials and his able reports on them completely satisfied the authorities and allayed public anxiety. This was the key to his later career. It established him as a man of energy and resolve.

In 1874 Richards took the *Devastation* to the Mediterranean and remained her captain until June 1877. The following January he became captain of the steam reserve, and in October 1878 he was appointed commodore and senior officer on the west coast of Africa, HMS *Boadicea*. When he arrived at the Cape the disaster at Isandlwana in the Anglo-Zulu War had just occurred (22 January 1879), and he promptly went up the east coast outside the limits of his station, and landed in March 1879 with a small naval brigade and commanded it at the battle of Gingindlovu (2 April) and in the relief of Echowe (3 April). For these services he was gazetted and made a CB (1879). He remained as commodore in South Africa until June 1882, having taken part in the defeat at Laing's Nek (28 January 1881) in the First South African War, and having been promoted KCB that year.

After promotion to flag rank in June 1882 Richards was appointed junior naval lord at the Admiralty under the second earl of Northbrook. In May 1885 he received the command of the East India station with his flag in HMS *Bacchante*. In the course of this three years' command he organized and equipped the naval brigade in the Third Anglo-Burmese War and was thanked by the government of India. After his return to Britain in 1888 he was appointed, with admirals Sir William Montagu Dowell and Sir Richard Vesey Hamilton, to report on the lessons of the naval manoeuvres of that year. Their report, most of which was acknowledged to be by Richards, presented a most convincing discussion of the conditions of modern warfare and a clear statement of the vital importance of sea power to the existence of the British empire, and set forth what became known as the two-power standard as the principle on which the British naval construction programme should be based. It re-established the strategic principles of previous generations as the basis for naval planning. This able report, though challenged at first by official naval opinion, made a great impression, and was one of the causes of Lord George Hamilton's 1889 Naval Defence Act, which overhauled the Royal Navy. Richards was also the naval representative on the royal commission on naval and military administration (1890), in the proceedings of which and in the drafting of its conclusions he bore a leading part.

Richards was promoted vice-admiral in 1888, and in 1890 went as commander-in-chief to the China station until June 1892, when he rejoined the Board of Admiralty under Lord George Hamilton as second naval lord. He was promoted admiral in September 1893, and in November of that year was selected by the fifth Earl Spencer to succeed Sir Anthony Hiley Hoskins as first naval lord, a position which he retained for nearly six years. His career as first naval lord was of great importance in the history of naval administration. Richards had a clear understanding of the needs of the navy, and he had the confidence of his political chiefs, Lord Spencer and Mr Goschen. This period was marked by a great development of the shipbuilding programme begun under the Naval Defence Act of 1889, and, at Richards's particular instigation, by a series of large naval works carried out under the Naval Works Acts of 1895 and subsequent years. The result was that the naval ports and dockyards at home and abroad were renovated and brought up to date to meet the requirements of the modern navy. Under this scheme naval harbours were constructed at Portland, Dover, Gibraltar, and Simon's Bay, and great extensions of the dockyards at Portsmouth, Devonport, Malta, Gibraltar, Hong Kong, and Simon's Bay. In carrying his naval programme against the opposition from Sir William Harcourt and Gladstone, Lord Spencer was supported by the foreign secretary, Lord Rosebery, and could rely on the unwavering determination of Richards and his colleagues on the board. The cabinet's acceptance of the naval 'Spencer' programme was in large measure responsible for Gladstone's final decision to resign from office in 1894.

In June 1895 Richards was promoted GCB on the resignation of the Rosebery ministry. Mr Goschen, who then again became first lord after an interval of over twenty-one years, wisely decided to follow the precedent set by Lord Spencer and to retain the naval advisers of the outgoing government. He and Richards worked together with remarkable unity of purpose during the next four years. This was particularly obvious in the field of coercive diplomacy, where the 1893 programme provided a powerful political instrument. Sending the fleet to the Dardanelles in 1895 put pressure on the Turkish government over the Armenian massacres; the 1896 flying squadron warned the Kaiser of the possible consequence of his telegram to President Kruger; in 1897 and 1898 the British fleet at length restored order in Crete; while the vigorous handling of the naval situation in the Fashoda crisis in 1898 was the chief preventive of war with France over that incident; and, finally, the firm attitude of the government based on the readiness of the fleet stopped any interference by European powers in the Spanish-American War. There was thus a widespread and well-founded feeling in the naval service that its interests were safe in the hands of Richards.

In November 1898 Richards would have been retired for age, but Goschen obtained a special order in council promoting him to be admiral of the fleet in order that he might remain on the active list until the age of seventy. The following August Goschen decided that it was time that Richards should give place to a younger officer as first naval lord, though Richards was much disappointed at being superseded after the special promotion to keep him on the active list. He was succeeded by Lord Walter Kerr, who agreed with Admiralty policy during Richards's term of office.

Richards was one of the leading administrators in the history of the navy. He quickly won the confidence of his superiors, and was selected for successive important duties, performing them successfully until he became chief naval adviser to the government at a time when a firm and clear restatement of the essentials of maritime policy was invaluable. Richards was a man of prudent foresight, clear, if limited, vision, and firm determination. His powerful intellect was somewhat slow in operation; but, though taciturn and not ready in council, he could and did express his views in admirable, if sometimes monosyllabic, English which left no doubt of his intention or of the strength of will that lay behind it. His official minutes were models of vigorous style and well-chosen language. As a sea officer it was not his fortune to command a battle fleet or to win the renown of such peacetime fleet commanders as Sir Geoffrey Thomas Phipps Hornby and Sir Arthur Knyvet Wilson. His natural qualities of a clear brain and indomitable will, combined with a gift for organization, found their best opportunity in his work at Whitehall. Though he was of a retiring disposition, avoiding publicity and loathing controversy, his character was so transparently honest and just and his devotion to his service and country so marked that he was regarded throughout the naval service with confidence and trust. In private life he was a constant friend and, though a ruler among men and of a stern exterior, he also had sympathy, humour, and kindness.

After his retirement Richards maintained his interest in naval affairs, and although he was not in sympathy with many of the changes carried out by Sir John Fisher's administration, he seldom expressed his mind in public and took no share in controversy. In 1904, shortly after the election of Lord Goschen as chancellor of Oxford University, Richards was given the honorary degree of DCL. He died at his residence, Horton Court, Chipping Sodbury, Gloucestershire, on 28 September 1912.

After the successful struggle over the naval programme in the cabinet of 1893–4, the officers of the fleet had Richards's portrait painted by Arthur Cope RA, and presented it 'from the navy to the nation'. It was hung in the Painted Hall at Greenwich. In November 1912 a Sir Frederick Richards memorial fund was established by a large representative meeting of admirals, friends, and admirers, the trustees of which make charitable grants to naval and marine officers and their dependants. A memorial tablet is in the crypt of St Paul's Cathedral. A formidable champion of naval preparedness, and legendarily taciturn, Richards's reputation rests largely on his defeat of Gladstone's last campaign.

V. W. BADDELEY, *rev.* ANDREW LAMBERT

Sources A. J. Marder, *The anatomy of British sea power*, American edn (1940) · *The Red Earl: the papers of the fifth Earl Spencer, 1835–1910*, ed. P. Gordon, 2 vols., Northamptonshire RS, 31, 34 (1981–6) · R. F. MacKay, *Fisher of Kilverstone* (1973) · J. B. Hattendorf and others, eds., *British naval documents, 1204–1960*, Navy RS, 131 (1993) · H. C. G. Matthew, *Gladstone*, 2 vols. (1986–95); repr. in 1 vol. as *Gladstone, 1809–1898* (1997) · *WWW* · CGPLA Eng. & Wales (1912)

Archives BL, Spencer (Althorp) MS

Likenesses A. S. Cope, oils, 1894, NMM

Wealth at death £18,108 11s. 3d.: probate, 6 Nov 1912, CGPLA Eng. & Wales

Richards, George (*d.* **1694**), merchant, was a younger son of Captain Edward Richards (*c.*1617–1664) of Southampton. Of a very respectable gentle pedigree, in March 1653 his father chose to put him out as an apprentice, at the cost of £80, to Matthew Atkins, a member of the Weavers' Company. Thereafter he passed under the guidance of Philip Forter of the Barber–Surgeons' Company, and did not take his freedom in the Weavers' Company until May 1669. He married Anne (*d.* 1683), with whom he had at least two sons and a daughter, and the family settled in Gravel Lane, in the East End of the City.

Richards made his fortune by importing Virginia tobacco. In 1672, and again in 1676, he was the second largest dealer, and still ranked fifth in the much greater trade of 1686. His prominence in colonial commerce was attested by his appearance among the signatories of a petition to the privy council in June 1677 for the payment of bills of exchange by the governors of Virginia. Moreover, he also signed a petition of tobacco importers in September 1685 which implored the government to encourage a trade undergoing 'difficulties' (*CSP col.*, 12.98). Under James II he gained new prominence in civic circles, being appointed in July 1685 to the court of assistants of the Weavers' Company. Two years later he was removed from both the court and the livery, only to be restored in February 1688 as the government desperately sought support in the capital. Despite these political and mercantile upheavals, his finances remained sound, and he valued himself in June 1690 at 'above £8,000 in goods and good debts and money' (PRO, PROB 11/421/138).

Richards was buried on 13 June 1694 at St Botolph's, Aldgate, London. Judging by his will, he was a most scrupulous businessman, having set aside sums to pay duties for tobacco 'which the waiters of several Virginia ships did order me to post short of what I ought and should have done' some eighteen years previously (PRO, PROB 11/421/138). He also proved a generous benefactor to several good causes, most notably Christ's Hospital, which received a legacy of £200. His wife having predeceased him, the bulk of his estate passed to his only surviving son, Philip, who died in April 1695. The Richards fortune thus passed to George's daughter, Sarah, who, through her marriage to the influential tobacco merchant Richard Perry, united the business and wealth of two of the most prominent families in that trade.　　PERRY GAUCI

Sources wills, PRO, PROB 11/314, sig. 71 [Edward Richards]; PROB 11/421, sig. 138 · GL, MSS 4657/2, p. 80 · GL, MSS 9232/1 · *CSP dom.*, 1685, 277 · *CSP col.*, 10.259–60; 12.98 · W. Berry, *County genealogies: pedigrees of the families of the county of Hants* (1833), 18–19 · G. D. Squibb, ed., *The visitation of Hampshire and the Isle of Wight, 1686*, Harleian Society, new ser., 10 (1991), 78 · Foster, *Alum. Oxon.* · private information (2004) · *The manuscripts of the House of Lords*, 4 vols., HMC, 17 (1887–94), vol. 2, pp. 24*v*, 34, 55 [2–7 Nov 1689] · W. L. Grant and J. F. Munro, eds., *Acts of the privy council of England: colonial series*, 1: *1613–80* (1908), 782 · J. M. Price and P. G. E. Clemens, 'A revolution in overseas trade: British firms in the Chesapeake trade, 1675–1775', *Journal of Economic History*, 47 (1987), 1–43 · J. M. Price, *Perry of London: a family and a firm on the seaborne frontier, 1615–1753* (1992), 21–2, 66

Wealth at death probably over £8000 in 1690: will, PRO, PROB 11/421, sig. 138

Richards, George (*bap.* **1767**, *d.* **1837**), poet and Church of England clergyman, was baptized on 15 September 1767 in Halesworth, Suffolk, the son of James Richards, later vicar of Rainham, Kent. He studied at Blundell's School in Tiverton and was admitted at Christ's Hospital, London, in June 1776, when he was described as from Hadleigh in Suffolk. Charles Lamb knew him at school, and called him 'a pale, studious Grecian'. On 10 March 1785 he matriculated from Trinity College, Oxford, becoming a scholar of his college in 1786. He gained two chancellor's prizes: in 1787 for Latin verse, on the subject *Rex, a violenta regicidae manu ereptus, cum regina Oxoniam invisens*, and in 1789 for an English essay entitled *On the Characteristic Differences between Ancient and Modern Poetry*. In 1791 George Simon, Earl Harcourt, gave anonymously a prize for an English poem *The Aboriginal Britons*, which Richards won, and the donor of the prize became his lifelong friend. The poem was printed separately and in sets of *Oxford Prize Poems*. It was called by Charles Lamb 'the most spirited' of these poems, and lauded by Byron in *English Bards and Scotch Reviewers*; De Morgan described it as 'a remarkable youthful production' (431–2).

Richards graduated BA on 4 November 1788, MA on 11 July 1791, and BD and DD in 1820. In 1790, when he took holy orders, he was elected to a fellowship at Oriel College, and remained there until 1796. In 1791 he published *An Essay on the Characteristic Differences between Ancient and Modern Poetry*. He was appointed Bampton lecturer in 1800, and select preacher in 1804 and 1811. From 1796, when on 6 October he married Anna Maria Parker of Oxford, to 1824, he was one of the vicars of Bampton, and from 1795 he was rector of Lillingstone Lovel in Oxfordshire. In July 1824 he was appointed to the more valuable vicarage of St Martin-in-the-Fields, Westminster. There he erected at his sole cost a new vicarage, largely contributed towards the erection of the church of St Michael in Burleigh Street, Strand, and served for some years as treasurer of Charing Cross Hospital. He became in 1822 a governor of Christ's Hospital, and founded there the Richards gold medal for the best copy of Latin hexameters. In 1799 he was elected FSA.

Besides the works already noted Richards published: *Songs of the Aboriginal Bards of Britain* (1792); *Modern France: a Poem* (1793); *Matilda, or, The Dying Penitent* (1795); *The Divine Origin of Prophecy Illustrated and Defended* (Bampton lectures, 1800); *Odin*, a drama (1804); *Miscellaneous Poems* (2 vols., 1804), the first volume of which was dedicated to Lord Harcourt and the second to the Revd William Benwell; most of the poems which he had previously published were reprinted in this collection. Richards died at Russell Square, London, on 30 March 1837, and was buried on 6 April in a special vault in the churchyard of St Martin-in-the-Fields. His wife survived him.

W. P. COURTNEY, *rev.* REBECCA MILLS

Sources will, PRO, PROB 11/1879, sig. 405 · Foster, *Alum. Oxon.* · [J. Watkins and F. Shoberl], *A biographical dictionary of the living authors of Great Britain and Ireland* (1816), 293–4 · *The clerical guide, or, Ecclesiastical directory* (1817), 260 · W. Trollope, *A history of the royal* foundation of Christ's Hospital (1834), 304 • J. A. Giles, History of the parish and town of Bampton (1847) • A. W. Lockhart, Christ's Hospital, list of university exhibitioners, 1566–1875 (1876), 17 • A. De Morgan, A budget of paradoxes (1872), 431–2 • GM, 1st ser., 66 (1796), 878 • GM, 2nd ser., 7 (1837), 662–3 • Watt, Bibl. Brit., 2.802 • [D. Rivers], Literary memoirs of living authors of Great Britain, 2 (1798), 197–8

Likenesses C. Turner, mezzotint, pubd 1832 (after C. Ross), BM, NPG

Wealth at death extremely wealthy; gave more than £20,000 to charity schools, Christ's Hospital, Oxford colleges, and servants; wife receiving bulk of estate, incl. much land and investments held in trust for her: will, PRO, PROB 11/1879, sig. 405, fols. 37–41

Richards, Sir George Henry (1820–1896), naval officer and hydrographer, was born in Antony, Cornwall, on 13 January 1820, the eldest of three sons and second of four children of Captain George Spencer Richards RN, and his wife, Emma Jane, daughter of Samuel Harvey. Richards entered the Royal Navy in 1832 and in 1835 was appointed midshipman in the survey ship *Sulphur*, serving in the Pacific under Captain Edward Belcher. Belcher was notoriously difficult to please, and, of the surveyors who piloted the fleet to Canton (Guangzhou) during the First Opium War (1839–42), Richards was one of the few to receive his praise. In 1842, as lieutenant, Richards served in the surveying brig *Philomel* off the Falkland Islands and the coast of South America. He commanded the *Philomel*'s small-arms men at the storming of the forts in the Parana River, Argentina, in 1845, and was promoted commander. On 24 July 1847, in Hampshire, he married Mary (d. 1881), daughter of Captain Richard Spackman Young RE. They had four daughters and four sons, the eldest, George, becoming a rear-admiral. From 1847 to 1851 Richards served under Captain John Lort Stokes surveying the coasts of New Zealand in arduous conditions, sometimes from open boats. In 1852 he served again under Belcher, this time on a voyage to the Arctic in search of the Franklin expedition. No sign of Franklin was found, despite a number of prodigious sledge journeys, including one by Richards which lasted for ninety-three days. Belcher proved more overbearing and unreasonable than ever on this mission and Richards's tact and judgement were critical in holding the operation together. He was promoted captain in 1854. Between 1856 and 1863 he carried out surveys of Vancouver Island and parts of British Columbia.

In 1863 Richards was appointed hydrographer to the Royal Navy, and began work in January 1864. Among his innovations was to make charts readily available for general use on Royal Navy ships, so that all officers, not only those responsible for navigation, would become familiar with them. He also organized the compilation and publication of charts showing prevailing winds and currents for each quarter of the year and improved the training of pilots. Under Richards hydrographic activity concentrated on areas of strategic importance, such as Canada when the USA was expanding into Alaska, or the newly opened Suez Canal in 1870, and areas of economic expansion such as Japan and Chile in the 1860s. Following the successful laying of an Atlantic submarine cable from the *Great Eastern* in 1866, British ships began laying cables

Sir George Henry Richards (1820–1896), by Stephen Pearce, 1865

in other parts of the world. Naval surveying ships undertook preliminary work, taking soundings along the proposed routes and sampling the seabed: these activities coincided with a surge of interest in the scientific exploration of the sea. Richards worked with the Royal Society, of which he was elected a fellow in 1866, to arrange for scientists to accompany hydrographic cruises from the Faro Channel to the Strait of Gibraltar, and for the *Challenger*, with scientists chosen by the Royal Society on board, to set out in 1872 on a scientific voyage of three years. In 1868 Richards privately circulated his *Memoir* of the hydrographic office, which is an important source for the history of the department. During his period of command the workload of the service increased substantially, in part because of increasing scientific demands and in part because of the transfer to it of Indian hydrographic work.

Richards was promoted rear-admiral in 1870, and became CB in 1871. He retired as hydrographer in 1874, and became managing director of the Telegraph Construction and Maintenance Company, which laid 76,000 miles of submarine cables during his period there. He was knighted in 1877, and in the same year became a vice-admiral on the retired list. In 1882 he married, as his second wife, Alice Mary, daughter of the Revd Robert Tabor of Cheam School; she survived him, but they had no children. Richards died in Bath on 14 November 1896.

G. S. Ritchie, *rev.* Elizabeth Baigent

Sources L. S. Dawson, Memoirs of hydrography (1885) • A. Day, The admiralty hydrographic service, 1795–1919 (1967) • Proceedings [Royal Geographical Society], 14 (1869–70), 259 • ILN (28 Nov 1896) • CGPLA Eng. & Wales (1897) • m. cert. [GRO] • private information (1990) • W. J. L. W., PRS, 60 (1896–7), xxxii-xxxv

Likenesses S. Pearce, oils, 1865, NPG [*see illus.*] · group portrait, wood-engraving (after photograph by Beard), NPG; repro. in *ILN* (1 May 1852) · portrait, repro. in *ILN*

Wealth at death £35,571 6s. 4d.: resworn probate, Sept 1897, *CGPLA Eng. & Wales*

Richards, Sir Gordon (1904–1986), jockey and racehorse trainer, was born on 5 May 1904 in Ivy Row at Donnington Wood, a district of Oakengates, Shropshire, the fourth child and third son of the eight surviving children (four died) of Nathan Richards, coalminer, and his wife, Elizabeth, a former dressmaker, daughter of William Dean, miner and lay preacher. He was given a strict Methodist upbringing, and educated at the infant school at Donnington Wood. In 1917 he became a junior clerk in the warehouse of the Lilleshall engineering works, Oakengates. Finding the work monotonous, he answered a newspaper advertisement for an apprentice to Martin Hartigan, who had the Foxhill stable near Swindon, Wiltshire, and on new year's day 1920 left home for the first time to go to Foxhill.

Short, stocky, and very strong for his weight, Richards had the ideal physique for a jockey. He had dark brown eyes and a thick shock of black hair, which gave him the nickname Moppy. He weighed out at 6 stone 9 pounds for his first mount in public on Clock-Work at Lingfield on 16 October 1920, and rode his first winner on Gay Lord at Leicester on 13 March 1921, but it was not until he had ridden forty-nine winners, and lost his apprentice allowance, in 1923, that his career got under way.

After coming out of his apprenticeship in 1924, Richards was first jockey to Captain Thomas Hogg's stable at Russley Park, Wiltshire, in 1925, and became champion jockey by winning 118 races. By the outset of 1926 his career was put in jeopardy by the diagnosis of a tubercular lung after he had ridden just five more winners, and he spent the rest of the year in a sanatorium. In the 1927 season he regained the championship with 164 winners. The first claim on his services in 1928 was held by the shipping magnate the first Baron Glanely, to whom Captain Hogg had become private trainer at Newmarket. Richards obtained his first classic successes in 1930 by winning the Oaks on Rose of England and the St Leger on Singapore for Lord Glanely, but he narrowly lost the championship. After landing the Manchester November handicap on Lord Glanely's Glorious Devon, on the final day he had ridden one more winner than Freddie Fox, but Fox won the fourth and fifth races to be champion with 129 successes.

Richards was champion again with 141 winners in 1931, during which the Beckhampton trainer Fred Darling offered a substantial sum for first claim on him. With typical loyalty, he first asked Lord Glanely to match the offer, but on Glanely pleading poverty, he became first jockey to the Beckhampton stable. Always immensely popular with the public, Richards was a national hero in 1933, as he bid to break the seasonal record of 246 winners established by Frederick Archer in 1885. After eleven consecutive successes at Chepstow in October, he rode his 247th winner on Golden King at Liverpool on 8 November, and finished the season with 259 winners. In 1934 he rode Easton to be

Sir Gordon Richards (1904–1986), by James Jarché, 1931

second in the Derby, a race he was yet to win, and in 1936 may have been unlucky not to win it on the Aga Khan's Taj Akbar, who was badly hampered before being runner-up to the Aga Khan's second string Mahmoud. By 1938 his bad luck in the Derby was proverbial. In that year Darling ran both Pasch, on whom Richards had won the Two Thousand Guineas, and the recent French importation Bois Roussel. Richards chose to ride Pasch, and was third to Bois Roussel.

As his tubercular record made him ineligible to serve in the armed forces, Richards continued to ride during the Second World War but, after breaking a leg at Salisbury in May 1941, he missed the remainder of that season and lost the championship for the third time. In 1942 he wore the colours of George VI when winning substitute races for the One Thousand Guineas, Oaks, and St Leger on Sun Chariot. He also won a substitute Two Thousand Guineas for the king on Big Game, and was champion again. In 1943 he surpassed Archer's career total of 2748 winners on Scotch Mist at Windsor, and was champion for the sixteenth time. After winning the Two Thousand Guineas by an extraordinarily easy eight lengths on that great miler Tudor Minstrel in 1947, Richards seemed certain to win the Derby at last. Heavily backed by the public, Tudor Minstrel started hot favourite, but failed to stay the course and finished only fourth. Champion for the twentieth time in 1947, Richards broke his own record of 1933 by riding 269 winners. After the retirement of Fred Darling at the end of that season, the Beckhampton stable continued to hold first claim on him when it was taken over by Noel Murless. The best horse he rode for Murless was the brilliant grey sprinter Abernant, on whom he won the Nunthorpe Stakes at York in 1949 and 1950.

The knighthood that Richards received in the coronation honours in 1953 was as much in recognition of his exemplary integrity as of his professional achievement; he was the first jockey thus honoured. A few days after the queen had conferred it upon him, he won the Derby at his twenty-eighth and final attempt by riding Sir Victor Sassoon's Pinza to beat the queen's colt Aureole. A little over a year later, Richards had to retire from riding after breaking his pelvis and four ribs when he was thrown by Abergeldie in the paddock at Sandown Park on 10 July 1954.

With his body slewed round to the left, so that his weight was unevenly distributed as he rode his powerful finish, Richards had a most unorthodox style. All the same, horses ran as straight as a die for him. From 21,843 mounts, he rode 4870 winners and was champion jockey twenty-six times.

Subsequently Richards trained at Beckhampton, Ogbourne Maisey, and finally Whitsbury, Hampshire. Although his success was not comparable to that which he had enjoyed as a jockey, he won a number of valuable races, notably the Middle Park Stakes with Pipe of Peace, who was to be third in the Derby in 1956, and the Champion stakes with Reform in 1967. Richards also managed the horses of Lady Beaverbrook and Michael Sobell. He closed his stable in 1970. He was elected an honorary member of the Jockey Club in the same year.

On 1 March 1928 Richards married Margery Gladys (d. 1982), daughter of Thomas David Winckle, railway carriage fitter. They had two sons and a daughter. A third son, the daughter's twin, lived only a few hours. Richards died of a heart attack at his home, Duff House, Kintbury, Berkshire, on 10 November 1986. RICHARD ONSLOW, rev.

Sources G. Richards, *My story* (1955) · M. Seth-Smith, *Knight of the turf: the life and times of Sir Gordon Richards* (1980) · *Sporting Life* (11 Nov 1986) · *The Times* (11 Nov 1986) · personal knowledge (1996) · CGPLA *Eng. & Wales* (1987)
Likenesses photographs, 1923–58, Hult. Arch. · J. Jarché, photograph, 1931, NPG [*see illus.*] · cigarette card, NPG
Wealth at death £835,624: probate, 18 June 1987, CGPLA *Eng. & Wales*

Richards, Gordon [*known as* Gordon W. Richards] (1930–1998), racehorse trainer, was born at 5 Petersburgh Place, Bath, on 7 September 1930, the eldest of the ten children of Thomas Herbert Richards, master haulier and later timber merchant, and his wife, Florence Gladys, *née* Thompson. He was educated locally. His parents were racing enthusiasts—his father once held a trainer's licence—and named him after the famous champion jockey. Almost inevitably young Gordon determined to become a flat race jockey. Aged eleven, he was apprenticed to Louie Dingwall, who combined training with selling petrol and second-hand cars at Poole, though her licence had to be held by her head lad as the Jockey Club refused to sanction women trainers until 1966. He switched his indentures to

J. C. Waugh at Didcot and at thirteen had his first ride in public at Salisbury, where he finished fourth. It was when riding for Waugh that a fastidious clerk of the scales insisted that Gordon should have a middle initial to distinguish him from his champion namesake and W. (later elongated to Waugh) came readily to mind. However, he became too heavy for the flat, and finished his time in the Wroughton jumping stables of Ivor Anthony. He then rode for Johnny Marshall's yard at Chatton in Northumberland and later became first jockey for Major Renwick, another Northumberland trainer. On 9 September 1955 he married Jean Charlton (b. 1931/2, d. before 1980), of Chathill, Northumberland, daughter of Gordon Southern Charlton, wine merchant. They had a daughter, Joey, and son, Nicky.

A bad fall at Perth on Sea View, in which he broke his back, finished Richards's undistinguished riding career and, aged twenty-nine, he moved to Town Farm, Beadnell, on the Northumberland coast, where he established himself as a horse dealer and livery stable proprietor. In 1964 Adam Pringle, a local farmer, persuaded him to take an unbroken two-year-old horse, Playlord, for training and Richards set up with eight horses from seven owners, including both himself and his wife. Pringle died before Playlord ran and Richards borrowed £1400 to purchase the animal, before selling a half-share for £1500 to Joe Lisle, a prominent northern owner, with the proviso that he could buy it back at the same price if the two men ever fell out, which they duly did. He then sold the share to millionaire Newcastle builder Philip Cussins. It was with Playlord that Richards won his first race as a trainer, a novice hurdle at Bogside. Both horse and trainer went on to greater things. Playlord, in Cussins's colours, won both the Great Yorkshire chase and the Scottish national.

In 1968 Richards took a tenancy at Castle Stables, Greystoke, Cumberland, where he trained until he died, though never losing his distinctive west country burr. Soon after that move he persuaded Cussins to pay £14,750 for Titus Oates, a then record price for a National Hunt horse. Under the guidance of Richards victories were secured in seventeen races, including the Massey Ferguson gold cup at Cheltenham, the King George VI chase at Kempton, and the Whitbread gold cup at Sandown. His other famous horse came late in his career. One Man was bought at the dispersal sale following the death of trainer Arthur Stephenson and the grey gelding twice won the King George VI chase, in record time on the second occasion. Although never champion trainer, he was one of the more successful trainers of his time and saddled over 2000 winners, mainly in the north of England and Scotland, and including the grand nationals of 1978 (with Lucius) and 1984 (with Hello Dandy). On three occasions he saddled over 100 winners in a season, a figure beaten only by Martin Pipe.

Not for nothing was Richards known as 'the Boss'. A successful amateur boxer during his apprenticeship, he was a hard man, not averse to giving his jockeys a public dressing down for not riding to his orders, even if they had won.

His attitude was simple: he would listen to his stable staff and riders but ultimately they did what they were told or they were sacked. Nevertheless he had a softer side, and when one of his stable jockeys, Brian Harding, was seriously injured, Richards promised to look after him for life. Possibly he had a better rapport with horses than with people. Certainly he left Aintree in tears when One Man was killed in a fall.

Richards's first wife, Jean, assisted him in the stables but predeceased him; their daughter, Joey, and son, Nicky, continued to work with him. His second marriage, on 17 June 1980, was to Joan Dacre Lacey (b. 1946), former wife of William J. Lacey and third of the five daughters of the Hon. Henry Anthony Camillo Howard, colonial governor, and granddaughter of Esme William Howard, first Baron Howard of Penrith, diplomatist. Richards and his second wife separated after fifteen years of marriage. Richards fought cancer and continued to ride out up to only a few weeks before his death at the Cumberland Infirmary, Carlisle, on 29 September 1998. The funeral took place at St Andrew's Church in Greystoke on 5 October 1998. As a sign of the respect in which he had been held in the racing industry, a minute's silence was observed at Newcastle races. He was survived by his second wife and the son and daughter of his first marriage.   WRAY VAMPLEW

Sources *The Times* (1 Oct 1998) · *The Independent* (1 Oct 1998) · *The Scotsman* (1 Oct 1998) · *The Guardian* (1 Oct 1998) · *Daily Telegraph* (1 Oct 1998) · *WWW* · b. cert. · m. certs. · d. cert.
Likenesses photograph, 1992, repro. in *The Times* · photograph, 1996, repro. in *The Independent* · photograph, 1996, repro. in *Daily Telegraph* · photograph, repro. in *The Scotsman* · photograph, repro. in *The Guardian*
Wealth at death under £200,000: probate, 19 April 1999, *CGPLA Eng. & Wales*

Richards, (Franklin Thomas) Grant

Richards, (**Franklin Thomas**) **Grant** (1872–1948), publisher and writer, was born on 21 October 1872 at University Hall, Hillhead, Partick, Lanarkshire, the first of two children of Franklin Thomas Richards (d. 1905), at the time assistant to the chairman of Latin at the University of Glasgow, and his wife, Emily, née Jerrard. He spent his early years in Oxford, where his father by 1894 had assumed the post of fellow and tutor in Latin at Trinity College. He attended school at Langdale House, Oxford, from 1880, and later the City of London School. Known from his early years as Grant, as a child he remained emotionally distant from his family but was influenced strongly by an uncle, (Charles) Grant Blairfindie *Allen (1848–1899), a prolific author of works of fiction and natural science. Grant Allen recognized Richards's interest in publishing and in 1888 arranged a job for him as junior clerk with the wholesale booksellers Hamilton, Adams & Co., and in 1890 obtained him a position with W. T. Stead on the *Review of Reviews*, where for the next six years he was involved with editorial work and reviewing.

With financial backing from Allen, another uncle, and his father, Richards opened his own publishing house in January 1897 at 9 Henrietta Street, Covent Garden, London. Under the imprint of Grant Richards, his substantial

list that year included the first volumes in Grant Allen's Historical Guides series, *Paris* and *Florence*, Allen's *The Evolution of the Idea of God*, E. V. Lucas's *A Book of Verse for Children*, and Stead's *Real Ghost Stories*. In 1898 Richards published works by two of the major authors on which his reputation rests: G. B. Shaw's *Plays Pleasant and Unpleasant*, and A. E. Housman's *A Shropshire Lad*. He was also married in 1898; he and his first wife, Elisina Richards, had three sons, Gerard, Geoffrey, and Charles, and a daughter, Gioia. Richards remained Housman's publisher throughout the rest of his career, but more commonly authors published a few books with his firm and then moved on to more prominent houses; G. B. Shaw, G. K. Chesterton, Alfred Noyes, John Masefield, Hector H. Munro (Saki), Arnold Bennett, and Maurice Baring were of this number. Nevertheless, Richards's inspiration, energy, and taste served in identifying rising or under-appreciated writers of fiction and poetry (such as Samuel Butler, whose *The Way of All Flesh* he published in 1903), in producing expensive multivolume collected works of Shakespeare and Jane Austen, and in initiating series including the World's Classics and the Dumpy Books for Children (which included Helen Bannerman's now infamous *Story of Little Black Sambo* in 1899). He was particularly attentive to the design of his books, many of which featured a distinctive fleuron on the title-page.

Richards's move in 1902 into larger London offices at 48 Leicester Square was a sign of his financial overreach, which led, in April 1905, to bankruptcy. Undaunted, he reorganized the firm, adding to his imprint the initial of his wife's name (trading as E. Grant Richards), and moving later that year to smaller offices at 7 Carlton Street. In 1908 the firm reverted to Richards's name and moved to 8 St Martin's Street. In the ensuing two decades Richards honed his already sharp eye for authors. In 1914, after nine years of sporadic negotiation with James Joyce over the blunt language of some of his short stories, Richards published *Dubliners*, and while declining Joyce's *A Portrait of the Artist as a Young Man*, followed it with Joyce's play *Exiles* in 1918. A critical and financial success despite similarly risqué allusions was Thomas Burke's collection of stories about London's Chinatown, *Limehouse Nights* (1916). Alec Waugh's revelatory novel of public-school life, *The Loom of Youth* (1917), was a further success which led to his publication of six further books with Richards. Other authors of critical note that Richards published during these years included Osbert and Sacheverell Sitwell, Eden Phillpotts, and T. Sturge Moore. He published his own novel *Caviare* in 1912, following it with seven other novels. In 1917 he began a series of distinctive advertisements in the form of chatty columns in the *Times Literary Supplement*.

Richards moved from London to Cookham Dean, Berkshire, after his bankruptcy, commuting via train to London. His first marriage ended in divorce in 1914, and on 2 July 1915 he married Maria Magdalena de Csanády (b. 1889/90), a widow, and the daughter of Emil Csanády, an officer in the Hungarian army. He entertained friends and authors at Sunday night dinner parties, spent a good deal of time travelling in France, and recorded his appreciation for the Riviera in *The Coast of Pleasure* (1928). The monocle that he wore in his right eye for most of his adult life—along with his taste in clothing, food, and wine—manifested the social grace for which he was known, and which for him was inextricable from the conduct of business.

Financial mismanagement led Richards for the second time into bankruptcy in 1926. The firm was renamed the Richards Press; Richards himself continued partial involvement for the next few years, but gradually left publishing to write his desultory but engaging memoirs *Memories of a Misspent Youth, 1872–1896* (1932), *Author Hunting by an Old Literary Sportsman: Memories of Years Spent Mainly in Publishing, 1897–1925* (1934), and *Housman, 1897–1936* (1942). He sold his home in Cookham Dean in 1927, and lived at several addresses in London until moving to Moor Park, Surrey, in 1946. He died in Monte Carlo following a long illness on 24 February 1948; his wife survived him.

WILLIAM S. BROCKMAN

Sources G. Richards, *Memories of a misspent youth, 1872–1896* (1932) · G. Richards, *Author hunting by an old literary sportsman: memories of years spent mainly in publishing, 1897–1925* (1934) · G. Richards, *Housman, 1897–1936* (1942) · W. S. Brockman, 'Grant Richards', *British literary publishing houses, 1881–1965*, ed. J. Rose and P. J. Anderson, DLitB, 112 (1991), 272–9 · G. Sims, 'Grant Richards: publisher', *Antiquarian Book Monthly Review*, 16 (1989), 14–27 · 'Mr Grant Richards: an adventurous publisher', *The Times* (25 Feb 1948) · 'Mr Grant Richards's affairs', *Publishers' Circular* (22 April 1905), 434 · M. Horder, 'Grant Richards: portent and legend', *London Magazine, a Monthly Review of Literature*, new ser., 31/1–2 (1991), 36–46 · b. cert. · m. cert., 1915

Archives Georgetown University Library, Washington, DC, papers · L. Cong., corresp. and papers · NL Ire., corresp. and papers · Princeton University, New Jersey, corresp. · University of Illinois, Urbana-Champaign, corresp., literary MSS, and papers | BL, corresp. with Samuel Butler, Add. MS 44041 · Col. U., Ronald Firbank manuscripts and letters · Col. U., E. V. Lucas papers · Ransom HRC, corresp. with John Lane

Likenesses W. Rothenstein, pastel drawing, 1893, repro. in Richards, *Memories of a misspent youth*, frontispiece · photograph, 1932, repro. in Richards, *Author hunting: memories of years spent mainly in publishing*, [new edn] [1960], frontispiece · H. Lamb, drawing, repro. in Richards, *Author hunting*, frontispiece

Richards, Henry Brinley [*pseud.* Carl Luini] (1819–1885), pianist and composer, was born on 13 November 1819 at Carmarthen, the son of Henry Brinley Richards, organist of St Peter's Church, Carmarthen, and keeper of a music shop, and his wife, Elizabeth. He intended to become a doctor, but abandoned medicine after winning a prize for composition at the Gwent and Morgannwg eisteddfod in 1834. That year he entered the Royal Academy of Music, and in 1835 he was the first to be awarded the king's scholarship, which he won again in 1837. In 1839 he went to study in Paris, and met Chopin. On his return to London he gained the reputation of being the finest pianist in England. He became a professor of piano at the Royal Academy of Music, and was later a director. At the Royal Academy he was responsible for starting the regional examinations system, and in 1881 he became superintendent of examinations.

Although he lived in London, Richards remained interested in Wales and the history of Welsh music, a subject on which he lectured widely. He adjudicated at eisteddfods, and encouraged the South Wales Choral Union during its visits to the Crystal Palace in 1872 and 1873. He was a leading member of the Society of Cymmrodorion, which sought to foster Welsh culture through eisteddfods, from 1873 until his death. Most of his 550 compositions were inspired by his love of Wales. He is remembered mainly for his setting of J. C. Hughes's 'God Bless the Prince of Wales' (1862), which became in effect a second Welsh national anthem. He was presented to the prince on St David's day 1867. Several of Richards's orchestral works were performed in Paris, including his overture in F minor (1840). He wrote some additional songs for the English version of Auber's *Crown Diamonds* for its performance at Drury Lane in 1846. His most popular songs included 'Up, quit thy bower', 'Cambrian War Song', 'The Harp of Wales', and 'Let the hills resound', and his *Songs of Wales* (1873) sold well. He was also a popular composer of drawing-room piano music. He published several pieces in the late 1860s under the pseudonym Carl Luini, including 'Just after the Battle, Mother' (1866).

Richards died on 1 May 1885 at his home, 25 St Mary Abbott's Terrace, Kensington, leaving a widow, Harriet, and a son, also called Henry Brinley Richards. He was buried in Brompton cemetery.

ANNE PIMLOTT BAKER

Sources DWB · *The Times* (5 May 1885) · Boase, *Mod. Eng. biog.* · J. D. Champlin, ed., *Cyclopedia of music and musicians*, 3 vols. (1888–90) · *New Grove* · *CGPLA Eng. & Wales* (1885)

Archives Carmarthenshire RO, letters and papers | NL Wales, letters to D. S. Evans

Likenesses portrait, repro. in *Red Dragon*, 2 (1882), following p. 385 · portrait, repro. in Champlin, *Cyclopedia of music and musicians*

Wealth at death £4411 17s. 3d.: probate, 10 June 1885, *CGPLA Eng. & Wales*

Richards, Ivor Armstrong (1893–1979), literary scholar and educationist, was born at Hillside, Sandbach, Cheshire, on 26 February 1893, the third son and third and youngest child of William Armstrong Richards (1849–1902), a chemical engineer originally from Swansea, and his wife, Mary Anne (b. 1859), daughter of William Haigh, a Yorkshire wool manufacturer. On his father's death in 1902 Richards moved with his mother and brothers to Bristol, where he attended Clifton College from 1905 to 1911.

Cambridge, 1911–1939 Richards's formal education was interrupted by an attack of tuberculosis in 1907 which kept him away from school for over a year, but in 1911 he proceeded to Magdalene College, Cambridge, with an exhibition to study history. Within a few months he had switched to moral sciences, studied under the three headings of ethics, logic, and psychology, and this brought him into contact with the Cambridge philosopher G. E. Moore, who remained a profound influence on his thinking throughout his career (his working title for *Principles of Literary Criticism* was 'Principia critica' after Moore's *Principia ethica*). At Cambridge Richards also began a long intellectual collaboration with C. K. Ogden, a Magdalene graduate several years his senior. Another attack of tuberculosis in 1912 interrupted his studies, but he was awarded a first class in part one of the moral sciences tripos in 1915 and graduated BA in the same year. He spent some time in Wales, convalescing after a third and final attack of tuberculosis, but returned to Cambridge in 1918 to pursue various studies informally.

Richards was hoping to find academic employment of some kind, but by 1919 was growing restless in Cambridge and considering an alternative career as a Scottish mountain guide. At this point he was unexpectedly invited by Mansfield Forbes and H. M. Chadwick to contribute to the programme of lectures they were organizing for the new Cambridge English tripos. The story of how Richards went to the eccentric Forbes to ask for some letters of introduction to his many Scottish contacts, fell into a long conversation with him about Wordsworth, at the end of which Forbes threw the letters in the fire and told Richards he must lecture for the English tripos instead, has become part of the mythology of the origins of 'Cambridge English'. The English tripos had only just been established (the first students were examined in 1919) and at that time the 'Cambridge English school' consisted mainly of a group of freelance lecturers recruited by Forbes from a range of different disciplines. Richards offered two courses of lectures in 1919–20, 'Modern Novels' (for which students paid 1 guinea) and 'Theories of criticism' (for which they paid half a guinea), and gave similar courses every year thereafter. His lectures proved popular and his position in Cambridge was further strengthened in 1922 when Magdalene College appointed him college lecturer in English and moral sciences. Richards's lectures on modern novels, and later on modern poetry, helped to give the Cambridge English course a contemporary edge which most other English courses at that time lacked. But it was the opportunity to explore the theory of literary criticism that stimulated him to produce his most important work. He had started publishing articles on aesthetics and semantics in 1919, and was co-author, with C. K. Ogden and James Wood, of *The Foundations of Aesthetics* (1922) and, with C. K. Ogden again, of *The Meaning of Meaning* (1923), which showed a lively interest in demystifying the discussion of language and aesthetics. When Richards applied the same interest to literary studies, the result was *Principles of Literary Criticism*, published at the end of 1924, his first independent book and a foundational text for Anglo-American literary studies in the twentieth century. The book was originally published as part of Ogden's International Library of Psychology, Philosophy and Scientific Method series, and Richards particularly emphasized the role of modern psychology in bringing order to what he called 'the chaos of critical theories' (p. 5). But the real achievement of the book was to convince readers that evaluative literary criticism could be an intellectually respectable and rigorous discipline in its own right, with a vital role to play in the modern world. Richards summarized and developed this argument further in a shorter book, *Science and Poetry* (1926), in which he famously claimed that poetry was 'capable of saving us' and 'a perfectly possible means of overcoming chaos' (p. 82), and emphasized the distinction between poetry and belief: 'it is never what a poem *says* which matters, but what it *is*' (p. 25). Richards was on friendly terms with T. S. Eliot, and the combination of formalism and modernism in his work dovetailed very effectively with similar emphases in Eliot's poetry and criticism in the 1920s, helping to establish an academic base for Eliot's growing influence.

When a separate English faculty was created at Cambridge in 1926, as part of a general restructuring of the university's teaching arrangements, Richards was confirmed in a permanent post as a university lecturer. In the same year he was elected to the Millington fellowship at Magdalene College. Financially secure at last, he took a year's leave and travelled to America, Japan, and China. In Honolulu, on 31 December 1926, he married Dorothy Eleanor (1894–1986) [see Richards, Dorothy Eleanor], daughter of John James Pilley. The couple had first met on a climbing holiday in Wales in 1917, and they shared a lifelong passion for mountaineering. Dorothy later described some of their many climbing adventures and achievements, which included the first ascent of the north ridge of the Dent Blanche in the Alps in 1928, in her book *Climbing Days* (1935).

Back in Cambridge, Richards started writing his next book, the idea for which had first come to him in 1923 while devising a test for Magdalene undergraduates competing for a literary prize. From 1925 onwards he had given several university lecture courses entitled 'Practical criticism' at which he had distributed copies of poems, without any note of date or author, asking his audience (including some academic colleagues) to 'comment freely in writing upon them'. The responses that were returned, which Richards called 'protocols', became the material for *Practical Criticism: a Study of Literary Judgment* (1929). In the fascinating middle section of this book, Richards sampled and analysed the protocols for thirteen short poems, highlighting what he saw as numerous misreadings and classifying these as the 'chief difficulties of criticism'. The book succeeded at several different levels. It engaged the reader in an interesting discussion and close reading of the thirteen poems; it demonstrated a useful 'unseen' method for teaching and examining in English, which was widely adopted in schools and universities; and it also provided what Richards called 'a new kind of documentation to those who are interested in the contemporary state of culture' (p. 3). The book was brilliantly successful, but for Richards it also suggested failure, since it seemed to confirm that, as he later noted in *Basic in Teaching: East and West* (1935), 'our most careful and expensive methods of teaching people to read are, judged by their results, at present almost ludicrously inefficient' (p. 49).

Richards received the degree of LittD from Cambridge in 1932, and officially remained a lecturer in the Cambridge English faculty until 1939, but he was increasingly looking beyond Cambridge for other fields of action in education. He was visiting professor at Tsing Hua National

University in Peking (Beijing) in 1929–30 and visiting lecturer at Harvard in 1931. On his return from China he wrote *Mencius on the Mind* (1932), an attempt to relate his ideas about language to the problems of translating Chinese philosophy. This was followed by *Coleridge on Imagination* (1934), which registered another new development in his thinking. He returned to analysis of the mechanics of meaning in *The Philosophy of Rhetoric* (1936), which is notable for the introduction of the terms 'tenor' and 'vehicle' to describe the workings of metaphor. For *Interpretation in Teaching* (1938), Richards again collected sets of 'protocols' from his Cambridge students, but based this time on their readings of prose passages rather than short poems. The book was designed to do for the reading of prose what *Practical Criticism* had done for poetry, and Richards later envisaged it as the potential 'beginning of a vast collective *clinical* study of the aberrations of average intelligence' (Russo, 148). It was not as well received as *Practical Criticism*, but Richards regarded it as one of his most important works.

The need to correct 'aberrations' in communication was becoming central for Richards and by this time he had become heavily involved in another of C. K. Ogden's enterprises, the promotion of 'Basic English' as an international language. Richards had assisted Ogden in the invention of 'Basic' (acronym for British American Scientific International Commercial), and as the project gathered momentum in the 1930s he became one of its leading ambassadors, travelling around the world to promote it and publishing numerous articles and short books such as *Basic Rules of Reason* (1933), *Basic in Teaching: East and West* (1935), and *Basic English and its Uses* (1943). Richards spent most of 1936 and 1937 back in China, working with the Orthological (Basic English) Institute of China to promote Basic English as the most effective foundation for Chinese students studying western subjects. He met with some initial successes, but his efforts were frustrated by the outbreak of war between China and Japan in 1937, although he was still able to publish *A First Handbook of English for Chinese Learners* in Peking in 1938.

Harvard, 1939–1974 In early 1939 Richards was offered a position as lecturer in the school of education at Harvard, with a large grant and the chairmanship of a special committee on communication through which he could co-ordinate Basic English and other literacy projects in America. He was persuaded to take up the post, despite the outbreak of war, and moved to America with Dorothy in September 1939. Harvard remained his base for the next thirty-five years. He was made university professor in 1944 and was a member of the committee that produced the influential Harvard 'Redbook' report *General Education in a Free Society* (1945). Although the move to America precipitated a break with Ogden, and Basic English began to fall out of favour after the war, Richards remained actively committed to improving world communication through better language training and clearer thinking about language. Working with a team of collaborators, and later through the non-profit-making Language Research Inc., he was involved in numerous experimental projects using a range of different media for language teaching, including records, film, and (though he never owned a set himself) television. He spent some time at the Walt Disney studios, learning to draw cartoons, and with Christine Gibson, his chief collaborator at Harvard, he edited *French through Pictures* (1950) and a subsequent series of Language Through Pictures books, which sold over a million copies.

In his own writing Richards continued to experiment with different applications of Basic English, ranging from 'translations' of Plato's *Republic* (1942) and Homer's *Iliad* (1950) to *Nations and Peace* (1947) which combined a Basic English text with cartoons to argue for disarmament and world government through the United Nations. He also began to experiment with different genres. His first play, *A Leak in the Universe*, was performed and published in 1956 and this was followed by *Tomorrow Morning, Faustus!* (1962) and *Why so, Socrates?* (1964). In the 1950s he started writing poetry, published in four volumes: *Goodbye Earth* (1958), *The Screens* (1960), *Internal Colloquies* (1971), and *New and Selected Poems* (1978). He continued to write and lecture on language, education, and (occasionally) literature, and collected these writings in *Speculative Instruments* (1955), *So much Nearer: Essays towards a World English* (1968), and *Design for Escape: World Education through Modern Media* (1968). His later books added little to his reputation, but his 1920s books remained influential to the end of his life and he received numerous honours towards the end of his career, including the CH in 1963 and the Emerson-Thoreau medal of the American Academy of Arts and Sciences in 1970. On his eightieth birthday in 1973 he was presented with the volume *I. A. Richards: Essays in his Honour*.

Last years and reputation In 1974 the Richardses finally left Harvard and moved back to the English Cambridge, taking up residence in Wentworth House in the grounds of Magdalene College. Richards's last book, *Beyond* (1974), was as innovative as ever: a theological meditation which included one chapter in verse. Further collections of his essays were made by admirers in *Poetries: their Means and Ends* (1974) and *Complementarities* (1976). In 1979 Richards returned to China once more, for a lecture tour, but was taken seriously ill while there and had to be flown back to England. He died in Cambridge on 7 September 1979. He was survived by Dorothy, who died in 1986. They had no children.

Although I. A. Richards was active in many different intellectual and educational fields, it is primarily for his Cambridge-based work in the 1920s that he is considered a significant figure. He inspired a generation of critics and teachers, and developed a basic theoretical framework and teaching method for academic literary studies that became dominant in Britain and America for much of the twentieth century. His emphasis on the poem, rather than the poet or context, was successfully taken up by the 'New Criticism' tradition in America. In Britain he was a key figure, both as teacher and writer, for the critics who carried on the 'Cambridge English' tradition in the 1930s. William Empson's *Seven Types of Ambiguity* (1931) had its origins in supervisions with Richards, and they remained closely associated throughout their careers. Q. D. Leavis's *Fiction and the Reading Public* (1932) was based on a PhD thesis supervised by Richards. His significance for the work of F. R. Leavis has also been recognized, and was acknowledged by Leavis himself, although the Leavises broke with Richards in the mid-1930s and several of Richards's later books were savagely reviewed in *Scrutiny*, the journal they edited. Richards himself remained detached from the boom in academic literary criticism which he had helped to make possible. His writings contain little in the way of conventional literary scholarship, and he tended to reserve close reading of texts for his memorable lectures. He was well described by T. E. B. Howarth, in *Cambridge between Two Wars* (p. 121), as combining 'a curiously benign personality with an exceptionally astringent mind'.

RICHARD STORER

Sources J. P. Russo, *I. A. Richards: his life and work* (1989) · *Selected letters of I. A. Richards*, ed. J. Constable (1990) · R. Brower, H. Vendler, and J. Hollander, eds., *I. A. Richards: essays in his honour* (1973) · *Cambridge University Reporter* (1910–39) · H. Carey, *Mansfield Forbes and his Cambridge* (1984) · I. A. Richards, 'The lure of high mountaineering', in I. A. Richards, *Complementarities: uncollected essays*, ed. J. P. Russo (Cambridge, MA, 1976) · I. A. Richards, 'An interview', in I. A. Richards, *Complementarities: uncollected essays*, ed. J. P. Russo (Cambridge, MA, 1976) · T. E. B. Howarth, *Cambridge between two wars* (1978) · D. Pilley [Mrs I. A. Richards], *Climbing days* (1935) · E. M. W. Tillyard, *The muse unchained: an intimate account of the revolution in English studies at Cambridge* (1958) · *Magdalene College Magazine and Record*, 8 (1926) · *Magdalene College Magazine and Record* (1979) · C. Baldick, *The social mission of English criticism, 1848–1932* (1983) · P. McCallum, *Literature and method: towards a critique of I. A. Richards, T. S. Eliot and F. R. Leavis* (1983)

Archives Harvard U., Widener Library · Harvard U., Houghton L., corresp. and literary papers · JRL, corresp. and literary papers · King's Cam., corresp. and literary papers · Magd. Cam. | CUL, letters to Charles Ogden · King's Cam., letters and postcards to G. H. W. Rylands

Likenesses J. Wood, drawing, 1933, repro. in Brower, Vendler, and Hollander, eds., *I. A. Richards* · R. Stone, oils, 1979, Magd. Cam. · photographs, repro. in Brower, Vendler, and Hollander, eds., *I. A. Richards* · photographs, repro. in Russo, *I. A. Richards*

Wealth at death £113,814: probate, 17 Dec 1979, *CGPLA Eng. & Wales*

Richards, Jacob (*bap.* 1664, *d.* 1701), military engineer, was baptized on 19 February 1664 at St Martin-in-the-Fields, London, the son of Jacob Richards and his wife, Anne. John *Richards (*bap.* 1668, *d.* 1710) and Michael *Richards (1673–1722) were his brothers; his sister Elizabeth married James *Craggs (*bap.* 1657, *d.* 1721). There is a longstanding belief that the Richards brothers were the sons of Solomon Richards (*d.* 1691), of Solsborough, co. Wexford, a commissioner in Ireland and lieutenant-colonel of Henry Cromwell's regiment and governor of Wexford, but the tradition seems to be based on unreliable pedigrees.

Jacob Richards was commissioned as an engineer on 30 January 1684, with an allowance of £100, to 'go to Flanders in order to go to the Imperial Corps in Hungary' (Porter, 1.51), at war with the Turks, with some other officers and instructions to note 'Fortifications and Artillery not only that of Hungary but of places on your way thither' (ibid.). His methodical journal (in the Stowe MSS, BL) therefore included accounts of defences, work in progress, and the

state of troops on the way from the Netherlands to Austria. He joined the staff of Viscount Taaffe, under the duke of Lorraine, at the siege of Buda in 1686. There were possibly twenty British officers present. Richards wrote a full account of the siege, later published as *A Journal of the Siege of Buda Taken by the Imperial Army* (1687).

To gain professional experience Richards joined the Venetian service, keeping the usual journals on the way. Having arrived at Venice he visited Lombardy, apparently using the travels of Dr Edward Browne, published in 1685, as a guidebook. In March 1687 he sailed to Zante (Zakynthos) and joined the Venetian forces in the Morea: his diary includes neat sketches of the Italian coastline. In August he was at Patras. In April 1688 he was back in England inspecting the defences of Hull, and in June he was appointed third engineer of Great Britain, with effect from 25 March 1688. He was appointed to the ordnance train assembled to oppose an invasion by William of Orange in October, but after some deliberation both Jacob and Michael Richards decided that they could conscientiously transfer their loyalty to William. After some further coastal inspections (Sheerness and the Mersey), Richards went to Ireland in June 1689 under Percy Kirke, served at Carrickfergus (where he was wounded) under Marshal Schomberg, and was appointed chief engineer in Ireland in March 1690. He was at the Boyne and served later under Marlborough at Cork and Kinsale. He was with Ginkell at Athlone and Aughrim, and was present at the siege of Limerick that ended the war in Ireland in September 1691.

At some point Richards translated a German treatise of 1685 into French as 'Traité de l'artillerie par le sieur Guillaume Dilich traduit de l'allemand en français', an account of not only artillery but firearms in general, with notes on the composition of powder, the capability of weaponry, and the requirements of arsenals and fortresses. To this he added further unpublished papers dealing with artillery, well illustrated, and, later, part of Euclid.

In February 1692 Richards was appointed second engineer of the ordnance train to serve in Flanders, as lieutenant-colonel. He and his brother Michael saw much action, including the battles of Steenkerke and Landen. During this time there was much pressure on the government to counter the considerable damage to merchant shipping by the numerous French privateers; to this end the channel ports (Dunkirk, Calais, Dieppe, and Le Havre) were bombarded, Richards commanding the artillery on the bomb vessels. He enhanced the ordnance on the ships, devising ways of traversing mortars and improving gun carriages, and also patented devices for the defence of merchant vessels—'several small engines of various kinds whereby any number of French or other enemies shall be inevitably destroyed upon boarding any such merchant ships' (*CSP dom.*, warrant books 37, 270). On 16 March and 16 May 1695 he demonstrated, effectively, newly devised mortar shells to the master-general of the ordnance (Romney) and the Admiralty. In 1695–6, as acting second engineer, he took part in further raids on French ports, notably St Malo.

In 1697, following the treaty of Ryswick, a peacetime train of ordnance was founded, with Richards as colonel. He continued to be third engineer until his death. On 7 March 1697 he and his brother John were issued passes to go to Venice again, and they sailed for Zante on 17 June. As ever, interesting observations were made *en route*, not only technical but historical and classical. There was much to be done on fortification of newly won territory, and one of Richards's suggestions to the senators of Venice concerned the possibility of settling Irish soldiers as military colonists. The peace of Carlowitz ended hostilities, but Richards continued to submit memoranda. Ultimately, following some disagreements with the Venetian government, and also because his pay was irregular, he left for Poland to serve Augustus the Strong, elector of Saxony and king of Poland. Here he was well received, and sent for John, who joined him in February 1701. The brothers accompanied the king to a conference with Peter the Great, his ally against Charles XII of Sweden. The tsar was impressed by Richards and offered him employment, which he declined. The brothers then parted, John to Saxony to cast artillery and Jacob to Koenigsberg, where he died after a brief illness in March or April 1701. His health, apart from some episodes of malaria, had always been good, and John attributed his death in part to unaccustomed heavy drinking with a bibulous monarch: 'in effect it was burning the candle at both ends which soon consumed' (Stowe MS 466). Richards was a highly professional and hard-working officer, and seems to have contributed much to improving the engineer and artillery service, a task continued later by his brother Michael.

F. J. HEBBERT

Sources the military collection of the 3 brothers, Jacob, John and Michael Richards of Solsborough, co. Wexford, 1685–1716, BL, Stowe MSS 447–462, 466, 481 · Burke, *Gen. Ire.* (1912) · E. A. Webb, *A history of the service of the 17th (Leicestershire) regiment* (1912) · W. Porter, *History of the corps of royal engineers*, 2 vols. (1889) · J. C. R. Childs, *Nobles, gentlemen and the profession of arms in Restoration Britain, 1660–1688: a biographical dictionary of British army officers on foreign service* (1987) · CSP dom., 1684–1701 · C. Dalton, ed., *English army lists and commission registers, 1661–1714*, 6 vols. (1892–1904) · J. Childs, *The army, James II, and the Glorious Revolution* (1980) · F. J. Hebbert, 'The Richards brothers', *Irish Sword*, 12 (1976), 200–11 · *IGI* · private information (2004) [T. Woodcock] · will, PRO, PROB 11/461, sig. 117
Archives BL, corresp., diaries, and papers, Stowe MSS 447–480 · Royal Irish Acad., diaries

Richards, James Brinsley (1846–1892), journalist, was born in London on 29 August 1846. He was at Eton College from 1857 to 1864, and the details of his school career are given in an entertaining form in his *Seven Years at Eton, 1857–64* (1883). At a comparatively early age he went abroad, and lived for several years in France. He acted for some time as secretary to Drouyn de Lhuys, and then as secretary to the Duc Decazes, and it was during this period that he acquired an intimate knowledge of French politics and politicians, which was conspicuous in all he wrote. On 7 January 1880 Richards married Blanche, the daughter of J. Caldecott Smith, in Brussels; they had four children.

In 1882 Richards sent voluntary contributions to *The Times*, and on the death of General Eber in February 1885 he was appointed to succeed him as the paper's correspondent in Vienna, in which capacity he contributed a series of letters and articles on a variety of foreign topics, as well as lives of foreign statesmen and politicians, many of which attracted attention on the continent. In addition to his journalistic publications, he wrote three novels. The first, which was published in 1886 and entitled *The Duke's Marriage*, was a tale of high society set in the France of the Second Empire. It was followed by *Prince Roderick* (1889) and *The Alderman's Children* (1891).

On 2 January 1892 Richards was transferred by *The Times* to Berlin. There he died from a stroke at 1 Von der Heydt Strasse on 5 April 1892; his wife survived him. Richards was buried in the Twelve Apostles cemetery, Berlin, on 9 April; the Empress Frederick sent a wreath of laurels fringed with gold.

G. C. BOASE, *rev.* JOANNE POTIER

Sources *The Times* (6 April 1892), 9 · *The Times* (11 April 1892), 9 · [S. Morison and others], *The history of The Times*, 3 (1947), 139–40 · D. Griffiths, ed., *The encyclopedia of the British press, 1422–1992* (1992) · *Wellesley index* · *Daily Graphic* (7 April 1892)
Likenesses portrait, repro. in *Daily Graphic*
Wealth at death £189 15s.: probate, 13 Aug 1892, CGPLA Eng. & Wales

Richards, Sir James Maude [Jim] (1907–1992), architectural writer and critic, was born on 13 August 1907 at Ladypath, Park Lane, Carshalton, Surrey, the second son of Louis Saurin Richards, a London solicitor of Irish protestant ancestry, and his wife, Lucy Denes, *née* Clarence, who was born in Ceylon. As a child he was isolated and obliged to wear a splint to cure a tubercular hip joint. Only in 1921 did he go to Gresham's School, Holt, where his contemporaries included the future architect Christopher Nicholson as well as Benjamin Britten, W. H. Auden, and Donald Maclean. Owing to a family financial crisis he did not then go up to Cambridge University as intended but studied architecture at the Architectural Association Schools from 1924 until 1929.

Richards first worked in the architect's department of J. Lyons & Co., where he assisted Oliver P. Bernard on the drawings for the illuminated entrance of the Strand Palace Hotel. Bernard, sensing that his assistant did not care for that style of decorative design, sent him on to work for the engineer Sir Owen Williams. In 1930 Richards crossed the Atlantic to travel in Canada and the United States, and then worked in Dublin before joining the office of C. Cowles Voysey in 1932. He was by now acquainted with the new architecture of Europe and out of sympathy with Voysey's classical designs for civic buildings; nevertheless another assistant, John Brandon-Jones, recalled that

> he was a first-rate draughtsman and did some excellent work on Voysey's competition drawings … He also shared with me a nearly disastrous adventure in a small boat on the Tideway at Greenwich when we were nearly lost by being swept under the bows of a moored lighter. (private information)

Richards found his true métier as a journalist in 1933, when he was hired as an assistant editor of the *Architects' Journal* by Hubert de Cronin Hastings, the inspired and eccentric chairman of the Architectural Press. Two years later Richards became assistant editor of the *Architectural*

Review, working from the same office in Queen Anne's Gate. In 1937 he became the resourceful and imaginative editor of that monthly journal, a position he held until 1971. Among his colleagues was Nikolaus Pevsner. Both the *Architects' Journal* and the *Architectural Review* were influential in promoting the new architectural ideas coming from Europe, and Richards became an enthusiastic propagandist for the modern movement. He embraced the social ideals of the new architecture and recalled in his autobiography, *Memoirs of an Unjust Fella* (1980), how at that time

> I and my friends and acquaintances joined and subscribed and protested and marched—marched in support of left-wing and anti-Fascist causes that seemed desperately to matter … decades of disillusioning happenings in Hungary and Czechoslovakia were needed before we relinquished our deep-seated belief that in seeking the social ideal we should look always towards Russia.   (Richards, 119)

In consequence, John Betjeman, Richards's sometime colleague at the Architectural Press, often referred to him as Karl Marx. He was a member of the Modern Architectural Research (MARS) Group and in 1940 published the influential Pelican paperback *Introduction to Modern Architecture*. On 31 July 1936 he married Margaret MacGregor (Peggy), (1904–1993), a painter, daughter of David Angus, a civil engineer. They had one son, who died young, and one daughter.

At the beginning of the Second World War Richards served in the night watch at St Paul's Cathedral—which he much enjoyed—and, with John Summerson, published a photographic survey of *The Bombed Buildings of Britain* (1942; 2nd edn, 1947). In 1942 he joined the Ministry of Information, and he was posted to Cairo in the following year. In 1946 he returned to the Architectural Press. In 1947 he helped to organize the first post-war congress of the Congrès Internationaux d'Architecture Moderne (CIAM) at Bridgwater, and in the same year he became the architectural correspondent of *The Times*. His first marriage ended in divorce in 1948, and on 31 July 1954 he married Kathleen Margaret (Kit), a painter, widow of Morland Lewis, a painter, and second daughter of Henry Bryan Godfrey-Faussett-Osborne, a probate officer. They had one son.

In 1951 Richards was invited to become a member of the Royal Fine Arts Commission. Through that committee and the others on which he served, as well as in the publications he edited or contributed to, Richards became, in the 1950s, the most influential architectural commentator in Britain, wielding considerable power which he used to promote architects committed to the modern movement while denying opportunities to even the most talented traditionalists. However, despite this public and bureaucratic orthodoxy, there was another side to him. Reyner Banham, his colleague on the *Architectural Review*, concluded that he

> was much less committed to the Modern Movement than even he himself had supposed … his position in 'the middle' of it may have been to some extent protective colouring, part of the public façade of his guarded person, part of the

programme of holding things and people at arm's length. (Banham, 31)

On his return from Egypt he had published *The Castles on the Ground* (1946), a nostalgic but perceptive social study of suburbs, illustrated by John Piper, one of his many artist friends, but, as he recalled, 'The book was scorned by my contemporaries as either an irrelevant eccentricity or a betrayal of the forward-looking ideals of the Modern Movement' (Richards, 188). His intelligent interest in historical architecture was shown when he encouraged the founding of the Georgian Group in 1937 and when he published his study of *The Functional Tradition in Early Industrial Buildings* in 1958—the year in which he became a founder member of the Victorian Society.

Richards joined the campaign to prevent the demolition of the Euston Arch and was mortified when in 1961 the editor of *The Times*, Sir William Haley, published a leading article arguing that it was not worth saving. He became increasingly frustrated with the newspaper, and was not disappointed when his contract was terminated in 1971, shortly before he left the Architectural Press (and the editorship of the *Architectural Review*) in unhappy circumstances following disagreements with de Cronin Hastings. By this time he was also disillusioned with the consequences of the architectural ideals he had espoused, and when invited to give the annual discourse of the Royal Institute of British Architects for 1972, the year he was knighted, he shocked many in the audience by questioning the policy of comprehensive redevelopment associated with the modern movement, as well as architects' eagerness for self-expression. More and greater unhappiness followed when, also in 1972, Richards's second son, Alexander, was killed by a speeding car at the age of sixteen.

Richards was particularly happy in the company of artists, including Eric Ravilious with whom he published *High Street* in 1938, and he wrote about the work of Edward Bawden. His many other books included *New Buildings in the Commonwealth* (1961), *An Architectural Journey in Japan* (1963), *A Guide to Finnish Architecture* (1966), and *Modern Architecture in Finland* (1964). Finland was a country of which he was particularly fond.

Richards was short in height and exuded an air of puzzled melancholy, particularly in his later lonely and isolated years. Banham recalled that he was 'grey and grave, with a face whose musculature sagged all too easily into an expression of guarded sadness' (Banham, 31). This dogged advocate of modernity was notably punctilious in his old-fashioned courtesy, particularly to women. He died on 27 April 1992 at Charing Cross Hospital, Fulham, London, after suffering a stroke. He was survived by his second wife and the daughter of his first marriage, Victoria, who married Richard Gibson, the leading architect in Shetland.　　　　　　　　　　　　　　GAVIN STAMP

Sources J. M. Richards, *Memoirs of an unjust fella* (1980) · *The Independent* (30 April 1992) · *The Times* (28 April 1992) · *Daily Telegraph* (30 April 1992) · *The Guardian* (28 April 1992) · R. Banham, 'Sir Jim', *London Review of Books* (22 May–4 June 1980) · WWW, 1991–5 · personal knowledge (2004) · private information (2004) · b. cert. · m. cert.

[Margaret MacGregor Angus] · m. cert. [Kathleen Margaret Lewis] · d. cert.

Archives University of Middlesex, Museum of Domestic Design and Architecture

Likenesses photograph, repro. in *The Times* · photograph, repro. in *The Guardian* · photograph, repro. in *Daily Telegraph* · photograph, repro. in *The Independent*

Wealth at death under £125,000: probate, 22 July 1992, *CGPLA Eng. & Wales*

Richards, John (*bap.* 1668, *d.* 1710), army officer, was baptized at St Martin-in-the-Fields, Westminster, on 5 March 1668, the third son of Jacob Richards of Westminster and his wife, Anne, and was the brother of Jacob *Richards and Michael *Richards. He was in Spain before 1690, when he travelled to Ireland to become adjutant to Hugh Balldearg O'Donnell. Towards the end of the Williamite war he was a trusted intermediary between Ginkel and O'Donnell, and for his services he was given a cash grant and, later, a pension of £200 per annum, 'payable out of the Royal Oak Lottery' (*CSP dom.*, *1692*, 126). In 1696 he joined the Venetian army with his brother Jacob, to serve in Greece.

Richards's journals on service are well written and amusing at times, showing evidence of wide general interests as well as professional comments. After the peace of Carlowitz he travelled in the Aegean and reached Turkey. From there he went to Poland to join Jacob, but decided to quit the Polish service after Jacob's death in 1701. His pension had lapsed on the accession of Queen Anne, but his 'friends at Court' hoped to employ him in the Iberian peninsula. Richards pointed out that as a Roman Catholic he could not hold the queen's commission, and that as a man of honour he could not leave the Polish army without permission. Diplomatic pressure was used to solve these problems, and within the provisions of the treaty with Portugal he was appointed lieutenant-general of the ordnance in the Portuguese army at 20s. a day (*Calendar of Treasury Books*, 1704–5, 198).

Despite the many difficulties that a less industrious and patient officer might have found impossible, Richards obtained a more active role as colonel of artillery and succeeded in putting a satisfactory service in the field in actions at Monsanto and the Agueda in 1704, and in successful sieges at Valenza and Albuquerque in 1705. At the siege of Barcelona he was on Peterborough's staff. By this time he had come to be regarded as an expert in the military situation in Spain, and he was twice recalled to London, in 1705 and again in 1706, to report to Marlborough and the privy council. He gave advice on a projected operation against Cadiz, but, this being cancelled, he landed at Alicante, a vital base for allied operations throughout the kingdom of Valencia. Most of the forces went on to reinforce Galway's army, while he remained as governor of Alicante, with the rank of major-general. After the disastrous battle of Almanza on 25 April 1707, Richards exerted himself to make Alicante as defensible as possible, laying in stores of all kinds with the co-operation, sometimes grudging, of the navy and the allied military command at Barcelona. The Bourbon armies lost no time in invading Valencia, and soon the coastal fortresses of Alicante and Denia were under threat. With an adequate garrison in the castle, well furnished with ordnance, food, and water in a new underground cistern, Richards was reasonably confident of sustaining a prolonged siege.

In 1708 an assault on Denia failed, but on 18 November 1709 this town, defended by a small Spanish garrison supported by irregulars, fell to an army of 12,000 men commanded by d'Asfeld (a future director-general of fortifications and marshal of France). Alicante was invested on 28 November, and the town itself, indefensible against a formal siege, had soon to be surrendered, Richards obtaining honourable terms for the Spanish garrison to proceed to Catalonia. The Castillo de Santa Barbara, the citadel of Alicante, stands on a high rock and could not be effectively bombarded; d'Asfeld commenced mining operations. Richards, hopeful of relief for his force of 700 men, reported to Stanhope on the progress of the mine. Five British ships arrived on 15 January 1710 but departed after a brief exchange of fire. On 20 February d'Asfeld offered terms of surrender, inviting Richards to send two officers to inspect the mine, which now contained 1200 barrels of powder. They reported that the mine was now ready but that the nature of the rock might limit its effect. Richards refused to surrender. His reasons for doing so are listed at length in his papers. A further offer was made a few days later, and again declined. On 3 March 1710, when the mine was to be sprung, he placed most of the garrison in positions of safety, retaining the minimal guards necessary to meet an immediate assault. To reassure his men he took post on the parade ground with some of his staff. Against all expectation the tremendous explosion split the ground into numerous fissures. Richards, eleven other officers, and forty-two men were buried and killed. The actual defences, as had been predicted, were little affected, and the garrison, under Lieutenant-Colonel d'Albon, continued to defend the castle until 15 April, when Stanhope and Byng arrived with the relieving fleet—only to negotiate the usual honourable terms of surrender.

Richards was an officer of real distinction. It is tragic that his heroism should have ended thus, but his conduct at Alicante had tied up a large enemy army for three months. A little more effort on the part of his colleagues by land and sea might have saved all.   F. J. HEBBERT

Sources Stowe MSS, BL, Richards Collection · *CSP dom.*, 1690–1704 · A. Parnell, *The war of the succession in Spain during the reign of Queen Anne, 1702–1711* (1888); repr. (1905) · A. D. Francis, *The First Peninsular War, 1702–1713* (1975) · C. Dalton, ed., *English army lists and commission registers, 1661–1714*, 6 vols. (1892–1904) · D. Chandler, 'The siege of Alicante', *History Today*, 19 (1969), 475–85 · F. J. Hebbert, 'The Richards brothers', *Irish Sword*, 12 (1976), 200–11 · C. Sevin, *Histoire militaire du regne de Louis le Grand*, 6 (1726), 256–9 · N. Tindal, *The continuation of Mr Rapin de Thoyras's 'History of England'*, 2 vols. (1744–7) · W. A. Shaw, ed., *Calendar of treasury books*, [33 vols. in 64], PRO (1904–69) · Burke, *Gen. Ire.* (1912) · private information (2004) [T. Woodcock] · will, PRO, PROB 11/529, sig. 218

Archives BL, corresp., diaries, and papers, Stowe MSS 447–480

Likenesses oils, 1706, priv. coll. · photograph, Courtauld Inst.

Richards, John Inigo (1730/31?–1810), landscape and scene-painter, was born in London. The precise year of his birth cannot be confirmed: in June 1810 his daughter reported to Joseph Farington that Richards would be '80 yrs old the 2d. of August next, born London' (Farington, *Diary*, 3668); however, this information conflicts with that given in the burial registers of St Paul's, Covent Garden. Richards himself claimed to Farington that William Hogarth was his godfather, and that his father, also John Richards, was a scene-painter (ibid., 2355). His father is thought to have assisted Hogarth with the mural decorations for St Bartholomew's Hospital in 1737. A drawing Richards made on the occasion of the execution of the Swiss enamellist Theodore Gardelle in 1761, and reputedly corrected by Hogarth, was etched by Samuel Ireland in 1786 and included in his *Graphic Illustrations of Hogarth* (1794–9). Ireland, who owned the sketch, relates how, on having amended it, Hogarth added, 'There, Richards, I think the drawing is now as like as it can be' (Ireland, 172). Richards conducted an extramarital relationship with the actress Mrs Ann *Pitt (c.1720–1799); their daughter, Mary Ann, was baptized on 22 October 1759 at St Martin-in-the-Fields, London. On 28 September 1769 Richards married Elizabeth Wignell in Orpington, Kent. His brother-in-law was Thomas Wignell (1753–1803), proprietor of the Cherry Theatre in Philadelphia, USA.

Richards studied with the landscape and scene-painter George Lambert, and from 1759 collaborated with Nicholas Thomas Dall and Giovanni Battista Cipriani on scenery for productions at Covent Garden. His designs received acclaim and, succeeding Dall, he was principal scene-painter from 1777 to 1803. In 1792 he assisted the architect Henry Holland on rebuilding the interior of Covent Garden Theatre. From 1768 to 1783 he contributed eighteen paintings to the Free Society of Artists, and from 1762 to 1768 he exhibited twenty-nine, mainly landscapes, at the Society of Artists, where he was elected a fellow in 1766.

Richards was a founder member of the Royal Academy in 1768, and became secretary in 1788, living in apartments at Somerset House. Between 1768 and 1808 he exhibited thirty-nine paintings there, and was said by William Sandby to have catalogued the academy's collection, though no manuscript now exists. In 1791 he was paid 12 guineas to restore Leonardo's *Holy Family* cartoon, then belonging to the academy. He executed his secretarial duties ably, if unimaginatively, his chief strength being that of administrator rather than innovator. His relations with other royal academicians could be tense. He became embroiled in factionalism during Benjamin West's presidency, Farington noting 'that Richards was no longer a neutral person, but had violated the trust reposed in him, which required that the secretary shall be neutral' (Farington, *Diary*, 1379).

Richards's landscape practice competed with the success and demands of his theatre work, and in later life he largely abandoned it owing to other commitments and ill health. However, his early landscapes are accomplished and follow the principles of picturesque composition then finding favour. *Orpington* (1768; Lady Lever Art Gallery, Port Sunlight), *Cascade at Hestercombe* (1770; Stourhead, Wiltshire), *Halswell House, Somerset* (NMG Wales), *Ivy Bridge, Devon* (Tate collection), and *Penllyn Castle* (Laing Art Gallery, Newcastle upon Tyne) illustrate his broad topographical range. His watercolours are represented in the Oppé collection (Tate collection) and by a group at the British Museum which includes his earliest known, *St Regadon's Abbey, Kent*, of 1753. It is uncertain to what extent Richards copied after others rather than making original sketches. He also painted imaginary Italianate views and capricci such as *View of the Colosseum* (1776; Yale U. CBA), or scenes based on his own designs for theatrical productions. *The Maid of the Mill* (1765; Yale U. CBA) is based on his set for Samuel Bickerstaffe's comic opera of the same name, and his drawing *Gothic Hall* (1794; Royal Collection) derives from the production of *Netley Abbey* (1793–4).

Richards died at his home in Somerset House after a lengthy decline on 18 December 1810, and was buried at St Paul's, Covent Garden, on 24 December; his wife survived him. His impoverished state was noted by Farington, who reported, on the occasion of the sale of Richards's personal collection (12–14 March 1811), that 'Barlow, an agent of Mr. Harris, principal proprietor of Covent Garden Theatre has gone to Squibbs and selected about 80 drawings … as compensation for £100 advanced to Richards to be repaid for his professional work' (Farington, *Diary*, 3885).

TINA FISKE

Sources *GM*, 1st ser., 80 (1810), 665 • S. Ireland, *Graphic illustrations of Hogarth*, 2 vols. (1794–9) • Farington, *Diary* • J. Turner, ed., *The dictionary of art*, 34 vols. (1996) • A. Lyles and R. Hamlyn, *British watercolours from the Oppé collection* (1997) [exhibition catalogue, Tate Gallery, London, 10 Sept – 30 Nov 1997, and elsewhere] • E. Croft-Murray, *Decorative painting in England, 1537–1837*, 2 vols. (1962–70) • W. T. Whitley, *Artists and their friends in England, 1700–1799*, 2 vols. (1928) • Graves, *RA exhibitors* • S. C. Hutchison, *The history of the Royal Academy, 1768–1986*, 2nd edn (1986) • Waterhouse, *18c painters* • C. B. Hogan, ed., *The London stage, 1660–1800*, pt 5: *1776–1800* (1968) • M. H. Grant, *A dictionary of British landscape painters, from the 16th century to the early 20th century* (1952) • E. Einberg, *George Lambert* (1970) [exhibition catalogue, Iveagh Bequest, Kenwood, London] • W. H. Hunt, ed., *The registers of St Paul's Church, Covent Garden, London*, 5, Harleian Society, register section, 37 (1909) • *IGI* • will, PRO, PROB 11/1519, sig. 86 (1811)

Likenesses J. Zoffany, group portrait, pencil drawing, 1772 (*Royal Academicians*), NPG • J. Zoffany, group portrait, watercolour drawing, 1773 (*Royal Academicians*), NPG • G. Dance, drawing, RA • W. Daniell, pencil and red chalk drawing (after G. Dance), Yale U. CBA • H. Singleton, group portrait, oils (*Royal Academicians*, 1793), RA • J. Zoffany, group portrait, oils (*Royal Academicians*, 1772), Royal Collection

Wealth at death household items, personal effects, paintings, drawings, etc., incl. those by other artists such as Tilly Kettle; money owed to sister-in-law; also other debts: Farington, *Diary*; will, PRO, PROB 11/1519, sig. 86

Richards, Michael (1673–1722), army officer, was the fifth son of Jacob Richards of Westminster and his wife, Anne. Jacob *Richards and John *Richards were his brothers. His name appears on the list of officers in Colonel Solomon Richards's regiment in Ireland in December 1688; contrary to a widely accepted tradition he was not Solomon

Richards's son. He served with Jacob as an engineer in Ireland in 1691 in the artillery train under Ginkel. The following year he was commissioned as lieutenant in the Queen Dowager's regiment. Having been appointed as an engineer in the train of artillery in Flanders he was present at the battles of Steenkerke and Neerwinden and was wounded in the assault on the castle at the siege of Namur (20 August 1695). By 1696 he was sufficiently experienced to be appointed chief engineer in Newfoundland by royal warrant. He constructed defences and barracks at St John's and was promoted captain on 1 September 1701. In the autumn of 1703 he returned home on sick leave.

In March 1704 Richards's report on the Newfoundland defences was considered by the privy council in the presence of the queen. That spring he joined Marlborough's force in the Netherlands and took part in the battles of the Schellenberg and Blenheim. On 25 March 1705 he was awarded a captain's commission in the 1st foot guards and later in the same year he was present at the recapture of Huy. He was in charge of bridging operations at the forcing of the lines of Brabant, and as a mark of approval he was sent with dispatches to report to the emperor Joseph at Vienna.

In 1706 Richards was at the battle of Ramillies, where he acted as aide-de-camp to Marlborough, and he carried home dispatches to Queen Anne, Prince George of Denmark, and Harley. Marlborough was so fatigued after the battle that he could only scribble a few lines stating that Richards would supply details. Richards wrote an account of the battle, which was published in the *Historical and Political Mercury* of May 1706.

Richards, who had been promoted lieutenant-colonel, was on Marlborough's recommendation appointed on 31 January 1707 chief engineer and commander of the field train of artillery in the army which landed at Alicante in February 1707 to reinforce Lord Galway. In April Galway, with Richards as his chief engineer, concentrating his forces between Elda and Xativa and advancing on Yecla and Montalegre, captured Berwick's principal magazines. He then laid siege to Villena, but, on hearing that the French were near Almanza, with the marqués das Minas he raised the siege on 24 April and marched on that town. Richards commanded the British train of six field pieces. The battle of Almanza began at three o'clock in the afternoon of 25 April, and by five o'clock Galway and his allies were defeated, but before the end the train of six guns, camp equipment, baggage, commissariat stores, and ambulances with the sick and wounded had already been sent off the field under the command of Richards, who got safely to the Grao of Valencia. On 11 May he arrived with the field train at Tortosa and sent engineers to superintend the defences of the various towns along the Aragon frontier.

Early in September 1707 Galway concentrated his forces at Tarragona to relieve Lerida, Richards commanding the train. But on 14 November Lerida capitulated. Richards was promoted colonel in the army on 15 May 1708, when he occupied the post of chief engineer at Barcelona, and also commanded the train with Stanhope's force under Field Marshal Count Guido von Starhemberg. In December he took part in an unsuccessful attempt to recover Tortosa by surprise. In 1709 he spent some time at Gibraltar examining the defences and advising on improvements. He sent home plans involving an expenditure of £9000. In July 1710 he was appointed colonel of his own regiment, formerly Lepell's, and commanded the train of Stanhope's force of 4200 British under von Starhemberg at Agramont. Taking the offensive, von Starhemberg reached the River Noguera unopposed on 27 July. Richards bridged the river, and Stanhope was able to place his horse advantageously on the Almenara heights. After a short fight in the evening of the same day, King Philip and Villadarias were defeated and fell back on Lerida. The following month they retreated to Saragossa, where they were heavily defeated on 20 August. Following this victory the allied forces occupied Madrid at the end of September, but they withdrew on 3 December on account of the hostility of the Spaniards and the approach of the Bourbon army under Vendôme. Richards, in a letter to James Craggs, expressed strong views on the part that lack of supplies and pay, and consequent indiscipline, had played in this situation, and in the surrender of the British contingent at Brihuega. Richards's artillery and his own regiment contributed to the nominal allied success at Villaviciosa. Unfortunately, a cavalry raid on the baggage lines deprived them of transport and draught animals, and in their further retreat to the safety of Catalonia they had to abandon supplies and most of the artillery. This concluded Richards's field service, and he arrived at Barcelona on 6 January 1711. He was promoted brigadier-general on 17 February and remained in Barcelona to work on the town defences, which had been neglected.

On 11 September 1711 Richards, having been highly praised by Marlborough, was appointed chief engineer of Great Britain and returned to England. In August 1712 he submitted to the Board of Ordnance a long report on the defences of Port Mahon. On 19 November 1714 he was appointed master surveyor or surveyor-general of the ordnance and assistant and deputy to the lieutenant-general of the ordnance. While holding this position he was most active in visiting the works in progress at Sheerness, Portsmouth, Plymouth, and elsewhere. In 1716, at his instance and under his direction and that of Colonel Armstrong, a colleague on the Board of Ordnance and his successor as chief engineer of Great Britain, the ordnance train was converted into a regiment (the present Royal Artillery) independent of the king's engineers, while at the same time the mother corps was increased and reorganized. In 1720 the same officers founded the Royal Military Academy at Woolwich.

Richards died, unmarried, on 5 February 1722, probably at the Tower of London, and was buried at Old Charlton, Kent, where there is an imposing effigy. In his will he left legacies of over £8000, including £3000 each to two of the illegitimate children of his nephew James *Craggs, James and Henrietta Smith, and £2000 to a third, James Walters; the remainder of his estate was inherited by his nieces, the daughters of James *Craggs the elder, who had married Richards's sister Elizabeth: Ann, the wife of John Newsham MP; Elizabeth, the widow of Edward Eliot of Cornwall; and Margaret, the widow of Samuel Trefusis MP, who later married Sir John Hynde *Cotton.

R. H. VETCH, rev. F. J. HEBBERT

Sources BL, Richards Collection, Stowe MSS 463, 464, 465, 469, 472, 473, 476, 477 · CSP col., vol. 21 · CSP dom., 1703–4 · W. A. Shaw, ed., Calendar of treasury books, [33 vols. in 64], PRO (1904–69) · C. Dalton, ed., English army lists and commission registers, 1661–1714, 6 vols. (1892–1904) · W. Coxe, Memoirs of the duke of Marlborough, with his original correspondence, rev. J. Wade, 3rd edn, 3 vols. (1847–8) · The letters and dispatches of John Churchill, first duke of Marlborough, from 1702 to 1712, ed. G. Murray, 5 vols. (1845) · A. D. Francis, The First Peninsular War, 1702–1713 (1975) · A. Parnell, The war of the succession in Spain during the reign of Queen Anne, 1702–1711 (1888); repr. (1905) · F. J. Hebbert, 'The Richards brothers', Irish Sword, 12 (1976), 200–11 · PRO, PROB 11/583, sig. 34 · private information (2004) [T. Woodcock] Archives BL, corresp., diaries, and papers, Stowe MSS 447–480 Likenesses statue on monument, 1721, St Luke's Church, Charlton Village, Greenwich · J. Faber, mezzotint, pubd 1735 (after G. Kneller, 1719), BM, NPG Wealth at death over £8000: will, PRO, PROB 11/583, sig. 34

Richards, Nathanael (fl. **1630–1660**), playwright and poet, whose origins are obscure, may have been born in Kent. He should, however, be distinguished from the clergyman Nathaniel Richards (1611–1660), with whom he has often been confused (see Moore Smith). What is certain is that during the 1630s Richards the writer was closely associated with London circles, in particular, groups surrounding the Salisbury Court and Red Bull theatres.

Richards published three closely related collections of poetry. The first, in 1630, was entitled The Celestiall Publican. A Sacred Poem. The title poem, which contains a number of pictograms (a fashionable 1630s form), considers themes of worldly sin. The collection includes several poems on religious topics, a series of epitaphs, including one for King James VI and I, epigrams, and acrostics. Some of these poems are reprinted in Seven Poems: Divine, Morall and Satyricall (1631) which was reprinted as Poems Sacred and Satyricall (1641). The latter includes several new poems on familiar themes of worldly corruption and, most significantly, a topical poem 'Prayers Paradise' which makes direct reference to the 1641 parliament and fears about the collapse of King Charles I's supposed peace of the 1630s (the period of non-parliamentary personal rule, 1629–40). Also of interest is the poem 'Death's Masquing Night' which in its employment of the masque trope echoes themes in his one published play.

Richards's The Tragedy of Messalina was published in London in 1640 and dedicated to John Cary, Viscount Rochford, with verses by Robert Davenport, Thomas Jordan, Thomas Rawlins, and others. An edition by A. R. Skemp appeared in 1910. A Roman tragedy based on the writings of Pliny, Tacitus, Suetonius, Plutarch, and Juvenal, the play depicts a Rome where actions are influenced by the sexual depravity of the empress. The play has much to say on decadent courts and the perils of performance that is relevant to the contemporary situation in Caroline England. The prologue to the play claims the author has written much 'comic fare' but none of this survives, although a play in the British Library, 'Pyramus and Thisbe' (BL, Add. MS 15227), may be by Richards.

Richards's later poetry includes Upon the Declaration of his Majesty King Charles the Second (1660) and Truth's Acrostick (1650), an elegy for the diplomat and financier Sir Paul Pindar. Richards wrote a dedicatory verse for the printing by Humphrey Moseley of Thomas Middleton's Women Beware Women (1657). Since Richards's poem is so specific about the play, it has been suggested he may have been responsible for the rediscovery of the play text some thirty years after its composition.

JULIE SANDERS

Sources A. Harbage, Cavalier drama: an historical and critical supplement to the study of the Elizabethan and Restoration stage (1936) · M. Butler, Theatre and crisis, 1632–1642 (1984) · S. Wiseman, Drama and politics in the English civil war (1998) · G. Langbaine, An account of the English dramatick poets (1691); facs. edn with preface by A. Freeman (New York, 1973) · J. O. Halliwell, A dictionary of old English plays (1860) · Genest, Eng. stage · DNB · G. C. Moore Smith, 'Nathanael Richards, dramatist', N&Q, 10th ser., 11 (1909), 461–2 Likenesses engraving, BL; repro. in N. Richards, The tragedy of Messallina (1640) · line engraving, BM, NPG; repro. in N. Richards, The tragedy of Messallina (1640)

Richards, Owain Westmacott (1901–1984), entomologist, was born on 31 December 1901 at Croydon, the second of the four sons (there were no daughters) of Harold Meredith Richards MD, medical officer of health for the district, and his wife, Mary Cecilia, daughter of W. J. Todd, a civil servant from Cumbria. He entered Brasenose College, Oxford, in 1920 from Hereford Cathedral school as an exhibitioner in mathematics, but his boyhood devotion to natural history, shared with his brother Paul Westmacott Richards (1908–1995), and encouraged by their mother, led him to abandon mathematics for zoology. He took a first in 1924 and after election as senior Hulme scholar and Christopher Welch scholar he spent three postgraduate years in the Hope department of entomology under Professor Edward Poulton (1856–1943).

In 1927 Richards left Oxford for London, where he was research assistant to J. W. Munro at Imperial College, becoming lecturer and then reader in entomology, and succeeding Munro in 1953 as professor of zoology and applied entomology and director of the college field station. Even after retirement in 1967 he remained actively associated with his department and continued research at the Natural History Museum, working there almost every day until he was over eighty.

In 1931 Richards married Maud Jessie, daughter of Captain Colin M. Norris RN, and herself an entomologist of some note; they had two daughters. She died in 1970 and in 1972 he married Joyce Elinor, daughter of John Morrison McLuckie, minister of the Church of Scotland, and widow of his friend and fellow entomologist Robert Bernard Benson.

Before leaving Oxford, Richards had already started publishing in the three fields in which he was to specialize: systematics, ecology, and evolution theory. He was an authority on the Sphaerocerid flies and celebrated internationally for his work on the aculeate Hymenoptera, combining detailed revisionary studies with broader biological, behavioural, and evolutionary considerations, all based on extensive field experience. Notable among his many taxonomic publications were those on the Bethylidae, the Dryinidae, and the genera *Bombus*, *Belonogaster*, and *Mischocyttarus*, together with his books *A Revisional Study of the Masarid Wasps* (1962) and *The Social Wasps of the Americas* (1978).

In addition to work in his three specialist fields, Richards made major contributions to insect ecology, becoming a leading figure in the quantitative investigation of insect population dynamics. His pioneering study of the butterfly *Pieris rapae* in the 1930s was followed by others on *Ephestia*, *Phytodecta*, and the British Acrididae, in collaboration with his colleague Dr Nadia Waloff. An early interest in evolutionary mechanisms led him also to collaborate with the malacologist G. C. Robson. Their joint book, *The Variation of Animals in Nature* (1936), displayed to the full Richards's powers of critical analysis and his ability to co-ordinate large bodies of fact, though its sceptical attitude to selectionist theories (a reaction to the views of Sir Edward Poulton) has not stood the test of time, as Richards himself later recognized.

Richards was deeply involved in the affairs of the Royal Entomological Society of London, serving as honorary secretary (1937–40) and as president (1957–8). He was president of the British Ecological Society (1944–5), and editor of the *Journal of Animal Ecology* from 1963 to 1967. Both societies elected him to honorary fellowship, as did the Société Entomologique d'Égypte, the Nederlandsche Entomologische Vereeniging, and the Accademia Nazionale Italiana di Entomologia. He was elected a fellow of the Royal Society in 1959 and was president of the thirteenth international congress of entomology at London in 1964.

Almost excessively conscientious, Richards never allowed his personal research to overshadow other academic obligations. He was not an exciting teacher, but his many postgraduate research students found him patient, helpful, and surprisingly approachable. Visiting professorships at the University of California, Berkeley, and in Ghana and his joint authorship of the two revised editions of A. D. Imms's *General Textbook of Entomology* (1957 and 1977) helped to extend his influence as a university teacher.

Despite his reputation and the great respect in which he was held, Richards was regarded by contemporaries as a modest man, shunning anything that suggested ostentation or flamboyance. Tall, sparely built, and distinguished in appearance, he could seem austere, remote, or even formidable to those who hardly knew him, an impression enhanced by his capacity for penetrating comment and a reluctance to waste words. But with friends, colleagues, and especially younger people, he was always interesting, and gifted with a boyish sense of humour. He was well read and well informed and he enjoyed travel, the theatre, and the open air. Richards died at the Whitehanger Nursing Home, Haslemere, on 10 November 1984.

R. G. DAVIES, rev.

Sources R. Southwood, *Memoirs FRS*, 33 (1987), 539–71 · W. T. Stearn, *The Natural History Museum at South Kensington: a history of the* British Museum (Natural History), 1753–1980 (1981) · personal knowledge (1990) · CGPLA Eng. & Wales (1985)

Archives Bodl. Oxf., corresp. with T. R. E. Southwood · Royal Entomological Society of London, letters to C. J. Wainwright

Likenesses black and white photograph, repro. in Southwood, *Memoirs FRS*, 539

Wealth at death £121,922: probate, 17 Jan 1985, CGPLA Eng. & Wales

Richards, Sir Richard (1752–1823), judge, was born at Coed, Brithdir, near Dolgellau, Merioneth, on 5 November 1752, eldest son of Thomas Richards of Coed and his wife, Catherine, sister of the Revd William Parry, warden of Ruthin, Denbighshire. He was educated at Ruthin grammar school, where his grandfather was headmaster, and at Jesus College, Oxford, where he matriculated on 19 March 1771. He migrated to Wadham College on 7 May 1773, and proceeded BA on 10 October 1774. Elected to a Michel scholarship at Queen's College on 17 December 1774, he became a Michel fellow on the same foundation on 20 June 1776, graduating MA on 15 July 1777.

Richards was admitted to the Inner Temple on 10 May 1775, and was called to the bar on 12 February 1780. At the general election in May 1796 he became one of the members for Helston, representing that borough until March 1799, when, as always intended, he made way for the eldest son of its 'owner', the duke of Leeds, his compliance being rewarded with a patent of precedence dated 21 February 1799. He again became a caretaker member for Helston at the general election of May 1807, resigning on 29 July. Like his patron, he supported Pitt's ministry and made only one reported speech, on 24 February 1797, opposing the Quakers' Relief Bill as unnecessary and inconvenient, because it would alter the law of the land.

Richards practised chiefly in the court of chancery. He became counsel to Queen Anne's Bounty in 1789 and was one of the three principal registrars to the prerogative court of Canterbury from 1788 to 1800. In 1794 he became solicitor to the queen and in 1801 succeeded Sir William Grant as the queen's attorney. He was made a bencher of his inn on 19 April 1799, was reader in 1804, and treasurer in 1806. On 7 October 1785 Richards married Catherine (1758–1825), daughter and heir of Robert Vaughan Humphreys, through whom he acquired the estate of Caerynwch in Merioneth, of which county he became a deputy lieutenant. The couple had eight sons and two daughters. He was in the running for the vice-chancellorship of the court of chancery when that post was created in 1812. As senior chancery counsel outside parliament, earning £7000 a year, Richards had a strong claim to the post, and Lord Chancellor Eldon, a personal friend, led him to expect it. But though Richards was certainly the best qualified for it, Eldon yielded to party pressure and bestowed it on Sir Thomas Plumer, the attorney-general. Richards did not conceal his indignation and was mollified only when appointed chief justice of the county palatine of Chester on 17 May 1813. He resigned that office on accepting the offer to be a baron of the exchequer in February 1814, allegedly made by a note to 'Taffy' tossed by Eldon into the well of the court. He was made a serjeant on

26 February, and was knighted at Carlton House by the prince regent on 11 May 1814. Richards had refused a similar offer in 1807, but this time it was understood that he would succeed as chief baron, and on the death of Sir Alexander Thomson he was promoted to the head of the court. He took his seat as lord chief baron of the exchequer on 21 April 1817, and was sworn of the privy council on 26 April in the same year in order to hear equity appeals.

During Lord Eldon's indisposition in January 1819, Richards took his place as speaker of the House of Lords, by commission dated 8 January 1819, and was thought likely to become lord chancellor if Eldon did not recover. Richards died at his house, 41 Great Ormond Street, London, on 11 November 1823, aged seventy-one, and was buried in the Inner Temple vault on 17 November. His wife was buried in the same vault on 12 October 1825. His eldest son, Richard (known as 'Double Dick'), MP for Merioneth from 1832 to 1852, was a master in the exchequer court, then a master in chancery in 1841 when the exchequer's equity jurisdiction was abolished. Robert Vaughan, the third son, and Griffith, the sixth son, were both appointed queen's counsel in Hilary vacation 1839, and were elected benchers of the Inner Temple in the same year; a grandson and a great-grandson also became benchers of the same inn.

Though not a brilliant lawyer, Richard Richards senior, who was known as Stumpy Dick, was a sound and capable judge, who assumed an asperity in court out of fear of seeming partial. Aided by a statute that enabled him to dispose of cases sitting alone, he rapidly cleared the backlog of equity arrears. He also presided over the treason trials of Brandreth and two of the Cato Street conspirators. In private life he was greatly respected for his amiability and benevolence. He was an intimate friend of Lord Eldon, and is said to have twice declined the offer of a baronetcy. He was president of 'Nobody's Club', founded in 1800 by his friend William Stevens, treasurer of Queen Anne's Bounty office.

G. F. R. BARKER, rev. PATRICK POLDEN

Sources R. L. Lloyd, 'Welsh masters of the bench of the Inner Temple … to the end of the eighteenth century', *Transactions of the Honourable Society of Cymmrodorion* (1938), 155–245 · H. J. Owen, 'Chief Baron Richards of the exchequer', *Journal of the Merioneth Historical and Record Society*, 4 (1961–4), 37–45 · HoP, *Commons, 1790–1820* · Foss, *Judges*, 7.24, 9.36–7 · B. Parry-Jones, 'A calendar of the Eldon–Richards correspondence, c.1809–22', *Journal of the Merioneth Historical and Record Society*, 5 (1965–8), 39–50 · H. Twiss, *The public and private life of Lord Chancellor Eldon, with selections from his correspondence*, 2 (1844), 242–3 · S. Romilly, *Memoirs of the life of Sir Samuel Romilly*, 3 (1840), 31, 102 · GM, 1st ser., 94/1 (1824), 82 · T. P. Ellis, 'Merioneth notes', *Y Cymmrodor*, 38 (1927), 37 · B. Parry-Jones, 'Aunt Emily's Caerynwch journals', *Journal of the Merioneth Historical and Record Society*, 4 (1961–4), 47–59 · *The correspondence of Charlotte Grenville, Lady Williams Wynn, and her three sons … 1795–1832*, ed. R. Leighton (1920), 50 · JHL, 72 (1840), appx 3, pp. 434ff. · J. A. Park, *Memoirs of William Stevens*, 4th edn (1859), 163 · Foster, *Alum. Oxon.* · I. R. Christie, *Non-elite British M.P.s, 1715–1820* (1995), 14 · W. Ballantine, *Some experiences of a barrister's life*, 2 (1882), 112–13 · *The letters of Sydney Smith*, ed. N. C. Smith, 1 (1953), 313 · N. Carlisle, *A concise description of the endowed grammar schools in England and Wales*, 2 (1818), 944 · probate of will of Sir R. Richards, PRO, IR 26/973

Likenesses J. S. Copley, oils; in possession of the family, 1960s · J. Jackson, oils, repro. in Owen, 'Chief baron Richards', p. 40; priv. coll. in possession of the family, 1960s

Wealth at death under £35,000 personal estate: PRO, death duty registers, IR 26/973

Richards, Thomas. *See* Rychard, Thomas (*d.* 1563/4).

Richards, Thomas (1709/10–1790), lexicographer and Church of England clergyman, was born in Carmarthenshire. Nothing is known of his family except that he had a brother called Lewis. He did not receive a university education. Before taking holy orders he was the master of a charity school supported by the principal of Jesus College, Oxford, in Llandysul, Cardiganshire. He was ordained deacon in September 1733 and at the same time was licensed to the curacy of St Ishmaels and Llan-saint, Carmarthenshire. He was ordained priest in 1734, and remained at St Ishmaels until August 1737. By November 1737 he was the curate of Llanilid, Glamorgan, and remained there until the following April. In May 1738 he moved to Coychurch, where he had occasionally taken services during his curacy of Llanilid, and remained there until he died.

Richards married Beatrice Evans (*d.* 1746) in October 1740, and they had two sons and two daughters. Beatrice, his wife, died a few days after the birth of their fourth child, also Beatrice, who died in March 1747. The eldest child, Thomas, became a clergyman, but nothing is known of the lives of the other children, David and Mary. On 24 May 1759 Richards married his second wife, Rachel Lewis (*d.* 1781). In December 1765 she gave birth to their only child, Einion. Richards was appointed vicar of Eglwysilan in 1777, although he remained curate of Coychurch and paid a curate to serve the churches of Eglwysilan, Caerphilly, and Llanfabon on his behalf. When Rachel died in April 1781 Richards gave up his clerical duties and lived off his income from Eglwysilan and his small farm.

Richards published a translation of the anti-Catholic tract by Philip Morant, *The Cruelties and Persecutions of the Romish Church Displayed*, under the title *Creulonderau Eglwys Rufain gwedi eu tannu ar led* in 1746. He may have also translated an abridged version of Foxe's book of martyrs, but it was never published. His chief work, however, was his Welsh–English dictionary, *Antiquae linguae Britannicae thesaurus*, published in 1753. It was basically an adaptation of the Welsh–Latin section from John Davies's *Dictionarium duplex* (1632), with additions from Edward Lhuyd's *Archaeologia Britannica* (1707), the glossary of William Wotton's *Cyfreithjeu Hywel Dda ac eraill* (1730), and vocabulary supplied by Richard Morris (1703–1779) and various other sources, including some dialect words from Carmarthenshire and Glamorgan. A Welsh grammar, based on John Davies's *Antiquae linguae Britannicae … rudimenta* (1621), was also appended to it. Although not a work of great originality, Richards's *Thesaurus* was a useful dictionary, given the rarity of Davies's *Dictionarium duplex*, and since it was a Welsh–English dictionary it was more accessible than Davies's Welsh–Latin section. A second edition was published in Trefriw in 1815, a third in the same year in Dolgellau, and a fourth in Merthyr Tudful in 1838.

Supported and encouraged by Dr John Richards of the neighbouring parish of Coety, Richards started to compile an English–Welsh dictionary, but it was not published and nothing is known of the manuscript. However, when a new version of William Evans's English–Welsh dictionary was published in 1812 (first published in 1771) the title-page said that it was 'improved by the late Rev. Mr. Richards, of Coychurch'. Richards died on 20 March 1790 and was buried in Coychurch. RICHARD CROWE

Sources B. L. James, *Thomas Richards, 1710–1790, curate of Coychurch, scholar and lexicographer* (1990)
Wealth at death under £600; incl. £5 each to nephew and two nieces; books and MSS to Edward Thomas of Tregroes: James, *Thomas Richards*, 12–13

Richards, William (1643–1705), Church of England clergyman and author, was born at Helmdon, Northamptonshire, the son of Ralph Richards (1611/12–1668), who had been rector there since 1641. Nothing is known of his mother. Richards entered Trinity College, Oxford, as a commoner in 1658, matriculated on 3 May 1659, and became a scholar on 13 June 1661. He graduated BA on 24 February 1663, MA in 1666, was elected to a fellowship on 15 June 1666, and was chosen preacher at Marston, Oxfordshire. On his father's death in 1668, Richards appointed Thomas Richards, probably a relative, to the living at Helmdon. In 1675 Richards instituted himself to Helmdon.

The first part of Richards's *The English Orator* (1680) consists of a series of declamations, for and against certain positions, for example, the view that a 'certain Damsel reduc'd to want' should have sold her hair to relieve her poverty. The style is jaunty, with some pretence to serious moral observation. The second part discusses such questions as whether 'Vertues are implanted in man by Nature'.

Wallography, or, The Briton Described (1682) was published under Richards's initials only. The early perception, that this humorous account of a journey to Wales was a poor imitation of Swift's style, is defective chronologically and as stylistic criticism. Of a 'Fellow driving a tyr'd cow … by wringing the *Pendulum* of her tail', Richards writes:

> We began to subscribe to Cartesius's opinion, that Animals were Engins; For tis like, the *Clock-work* of the Cow was somewhat disorder'd, and the Machine (like a Jack) was run down and stood still, till this Artist wound it up, and set the motions going.

This production of humour by bringing 'learned' observation to a bucolic subject is on a higher level than some other passages, which resemble the playground conversation of schoolboys. Nevertheless *Wallography* is entertaining, if undemanding.

The History of many Memorable Things Lost … and an Account of many Excellent Things Found (1715), a translation of the *Nova reperta, sive, Rerum memorabilium libri duo* of Guido Pancirelli, is anonymous. Its ascription rests on Wood's statement that Richards had translated and annotated Pancirelli's work and that it was ready for the press by 1690. It is reasonable to surmise that its subject matter

William Richards (1643–1705), by John Smith, 1688 (after Sir Godfrey Kneller)

would have been congenial to the author of *The English Orator*; its style also supports the ascription.

Richards, who was a nonjuror, was appointed on 25 July 1689 by the corporation of Newcastle upon Tyne lecturer of St Andrew's in that city. He was buried in the chancel of St Andrew's on 22 August 1705. His portrait, painted by Kneller, was engraved by T. Smith about 1688.

CHARLOTTE FELL-SMITH, *rev.* ALAN RUDRUM

Sources Wood, *Ath. Oxon.*, 2nd edn, 2.1072 • Wood, *Ath. Oxon.*, new edn, 4.269, 678 • J. Brand, *The history and antiquities of the town and county of the town of Newcastle upon Tyne*, 1 (1789), 194 • J. Bridges, *The history and antiquities of Northamptonshire*, ed. P. Whalley, 1 (1791), 191 • J. D. Stewart, *Sir Godfrey Kneller and the English baroque portrait* (1983) • Foster, *Alum. Oxon.*
Likenesses J. Smith, mezzotint, 1688 (after G. Kneller), BM, NPG [*see illus.*]
Wealth at death £100 p.a. salary at Helmdon: Brand, *History*, vol. 1, p. 194

Richards, William (1749–1818), General Baptist minister and historian, was born in early 1749 in Boncath, Penrhydd parish, Pembrokeshire, the son of Henry Richards (1708/9–1768), a farmer, who moved in 1758 to Pen-coed, Meidrim, Carmarthenshire, and his wife, Mary (c.1717–1801); both parents were committed Particular Baptists. He received only a year's schooling, in his twelfth year; nevertheless, with paternal backing, he successfully educated himself. On 3 March 1769 he received believer's baptism at Rhydwilym; later he became a member of and preacher at Salem, Meidrim, a chapel his late father had projected. In a letter (21 August 1793), he told Joseph Hughes (1769–1833) he had spent only a year—unprofitably—at Bristol Baptist college (apparently from September 1774). He was gaining more, it seems, from assisting John Ash, the minister at Pershore, Worcestershire, when in May 1776, on the recommendation of Hugh Evans, the college's president, he was invited to an unsettled congregation in Broad Street, King's Lynn, Norfolk. He arrived on 5 July. Through his guidance and hard, systematic work, this people formally became a Particular Baptist church by 1778; he was probably ordained about 1777.

Ever a defender of distinctively Baptist tenets, Richards championed believer's baptism against John Carter, Independent minister at Mattishall, Norfolk, in three pamphlets, the last, *The History of Antichrist* (1784), adumbrating his conviction that most contemporary churches were apostate, thus fulfilling prophecy. In his pamphlets *Reflections on French Atheism and on English Christianity* (1794) and *Food for a Fast-Day* (1795), Richards denounced the war against revolutionary France, contending that war was incompatible with New Testament Christianity; that the allies were provoking a libertarian France to ferocity; and that the allies' anti-Christianity, which lent their evil courses a religious colouring, was akin to the established French pseudo-Christianity which, by crediting the abominable *ancien régime* with divine approval, had engendered atheism as a scandalized reaction.

During sojourns in Wales (September 1795 to 1798 and 1799 to 1801), meant to alleviate his depression and physical illnesses, Richards took up causes there, meanwhile striving to resign his pastorate, left to his lay assistant Timothy Durrant of Leziate. For poorer folk he published his *Geiriadur Saesneg a Chymraeg: an English–Welsh Dictionary* (1798). To emigrants seeking escape from crisis or pursuing ideals, he gave letters addressed to Samuel Jones, the influential Baptist minister of Pennepek, Philadelphia, who might advise them. When Richards's relative Thomas John was accused of complicity with the French invaders of Pembrokeshire—the fabrication described in Richards's anonymous *Cwyn y cystuddiedig* ('The complaint of the afflicted') (1798)—he aided the successful defence, probably by subsidizing it, drawing upon the modest fortune inherited about 1792 from a King's Lynn congregant. He opposed the incursion of hysterical, 'Methodistical' behaviour into Welsh Baptist worship; and sided in fierce Welsh pamphlets with the Arminians and others who broke away from the South-West Wales Baptist Association rather than subscribe to a confession of Calvinistic orthodoxy when seeking grants. He himself was by now anti-Calvinist and recognized no standard of doctrine or, indeed, of church organization but that of scripture, from which he had deduced that Christ is divine because the Father indwells him. Rumours, however, reaching King's Lynn and America, accused him of Socinianism and deism. Understandably, given these slanders, his impaired health, and his alienation from strictly orthodox Calvinism, his King's Lynn pastorate petered out. He did not pursue it after 1802, though the connection was never formally dissolved. During a part of 1802 he conducted a morning service in the vacant presbyterian chapel at King's Lynn.

Richards married, in 1803, Emiah Owens (1775/6–1805), daughter of the stoutly nonconformist farmer Evan Owens of Maneian-fawr Farm near Parc Nest. She strongly supported Richards's literary enterprises, but died on 3 January 1805, aged twenty-nine. Profoundly distressed, Richards could not for several years go out into society. He must have received callers, however; and in these years he produced historical essays—collected in *The Welsh Nonconformists' Memorial* (1820)—and his masterly, illustrated, two-volume *History of Lynn* (1812). He was denied proper access to the municipal records, but friends brought him materials; and in lucid prose, with sardonic humour and occasional startling violence—like the sneer about the Walcheren expedition's losses through fever in 1809—he took the story of King's Lynn to 1812, and included biographical sketches, statistics, and accounts of King's Lynn's former religious houses and of the progress of local dissent. Moreover, he dinned into his readers' minds the wrongness of slavery, of religious intolerance, and of war, and the need for enlightenment, municipal and national reform, and New Testament Christianity. Exceptionally meritorious as he said the contemporary local clergy were, he had to observe, 'We know of no period in the history of this town, from the reformation to the present time, when a great majority of its population was not involved in deplorable and heathenish darkness' (W. Richards, *The History of Lynn*, 2 vols., 1812, 2.679).

The *History*, published by subscription, was written at the request of 'the principal inhabitants' (W. Richards to S. Jones, 5 Feb 1806, Philadelphia, Historical Society of Pennsylvania, Jones MSS); and Richards achieved at King's Lynn almost guru status. Among his medley of associates, admirers, and disciples were his friends the attorney Harvey Goodwin, grandfather of the Egyptologist Charles Wycliffe Goodwin and Bishop Harvey Goodwin; Dr James Adams, formerly master of the Eye and Boxford grammar schools; James Keed, a dissenting tradesman; and Thomas Finch, whom Richards equipped with a new, free Christian chapel, Salem (1811), when Finch was forced out of Broad Street's pastorate for scripture-sufficiency anti-Calvinism. Richards lent Goodwin and Keed substantial sums at interest, cancelling these debts in his will (6 September 1818). In 1793 he had become MA of Brown University, Rhode Island, a Baptist foundation, and in 1818 he was made an LLD, but this latter diploma reached King's Lynn after his death. He admired the American constitution, and, like other Welsh intellectuals, followed the quest for the 'Welsh Indians', supposed descendants of the medieval prince Madoc and his companions, fancied discoverers of America.

Tall, strongly built, with a solid Welsh accent, and genuinely affectionate, Richards was, however, a depressive and liable to flare up furiously. Latterly he suffered from angina pectoris; he died, probably of heart disease, in his house, 122 Norfolk Street, King's Lynn, on 13 September 1818. He had no children. He was buried on 17 September in his wife's plot in the Unitarian General Baptists' graveyard at Wisbech, the site of which, between The Crescent and Love Lane, is now partly occupied by the Masonic (formerly Wesley) Hall. In his will he provided for his widowed sister, Martha Evans of Llanfihangel Abercywyn, St Clears, with a life income from his £800 or so of United

States stock. He bequeathed his notable library to Brown University. His executor and biographer, John Evans (1767–1827), had access to a considerable archive, including an estimated total of 600 letters Richards had received. This subsequently disappeared; even so, modern scholarship has been able to elucidate Richards's ideas and map his milieux.   J. A. ODDY

Sources J. Evans, *Memoirs of the life and writings of the Rev. William Richards* (1819) · R. T. Jenkins, 'William Richards o Lynn', *Trafodion Cymdeithas Hanes Bedyddwyr Cymru* (1930), 17–61 · R. T. Jenkins, 'Briwsion o hanes y Bedyddwyr Cyffredinol Cymreig: William Richards', *Trafodion Cymdeithas Hanes Bedyddwyr Cymru* (1931), 31–3 · Hist. Soc. Penn., Jones papers, Mrs Irving H. McKesson collection · J. A. Oddy, 'The dissidence of William Richards', *Baptist Quarterly*, 27 (1977–8), 118–27 · W. Richards, letter to J. Hughes, 21 Aug 1793, NL Wales, Isaac Mann papers, MS 1207 · PRO, PROB 11/1610, sig. 528, fols. 342v–343v · *DWB* · *DNB* · private information (2004) [Haverfordwest Public Library; Norfolk RO] · R. Wright, *A review of the missionary life and labors of Richard Wright* (1824)
Archives Hist. Soc. Penn., Mrs Irving H. McKesson collection, letters to Samuel Jones of Pennepek · NL Wales, Mysevin collection, letters to William Owen (Pughe), MSS 13221 E, pp. 403–5, 349–51, 353–6, 461–3; 13222 C, pp. 491–4; 13224 B, pp. 375–7, 378–81; 13223 C, pp. 751–3, 785
Likenesses J. Hopwood?, stipple, NPG; repro. in Evans, *Memoirs*
Wealth at death approx. £1601; incl. £601 in pecuniary legacies; plus £800 [$5527.23] in US stock; plus library valued at £200: will, PRO, PROB 11/1610, sig. 528; letter of Charles Hursthouse, executor, to William H. Nevett, 24 June 1819, Brown University, 1-X-R39 Archives

Richards, William Upton (1811–1873), Church of England clergyman, only son of William Richards of Penryn, Cornwall, and his wife, Elizabeth Rose Thomas, was born at Penryn on 2 March 1811. He was tutored at Greenwich, Kent, by Archdeacon Charles Parr Burney before entering Exeter College, Oxford, in April 1829. He graduated BA in 1833 and MA in 1839. In 1833 he joined the manuscript department of the British Museum, where he compiled a printed index to the Egerton manuscripts and the Additional manuscripts acquired between 1783 and 1835. Ordained in 1837, he served a brief curacy at Bushey, Hertfordshire, before being appointed, later that year, assistant minister at Margaret Street Chapel, west London. He became minister there in 1845, and four years later gave up his post at the British Museum.

Richards was a committed Tractarian and a close friend of E. B. Pusey; it was to him that Pusey addressed the letter he published in 1850 on the place of private confession within the Church of England. Richards had been appointed minister at Margaret Street on the secession to Rome of Frederick Oakeley (1802–1880), and he steadfastly held the fort at a time of crisis. In 1848 he helped to found within his parish the Society of All Saints, one of the first Anglican sisterhoods. He commissioned William Butterfield (1814–1900) to design the new chapel which was opened in 1859, when Margaret Street was erected into the separate parish of All Saints, Richards becoming its vicar. He was conservative in matters of ritual, and though he published devotional works and a substantial volume on *The Great Truths of the Christian Religion* (1862), he made his mark chiefly as a pastor of unaffected simplicity and practical wisdom. He died at his home, 10 St Andrew's

Place, Regent's Park, on 16 June 1873, and was buried at Brompton cemetery, London, on 21 June. Richards was survived by his wife, Caroline, and their daughter.
                                                              G. MARTIN MURPHY

Sources P. Galloway and C. Rawle, *Good and faithful servants: the vicars of All Saints', Margaret Street* (1988) · P. Mayhew, *All Saints: birth and growth of a community* (1987) · H. P. Liddon, *The life of Edward Bouverie Pusey*, ed. J. O. Johnston and others, 4 vols. (1893–7), vol. 3, pp. 18, 266, 269 · Foster, *Alum. Oxon.* · *Church Times* (30 June 1873) · *The Guardian* (25 June 1873), 2–3 · E. G. K. Browne, *Annals of the Tractarian movement*, 3rd edn (1861), 230–32 · P. F. Anson, *The call of the cloister: religious communities and kindred bodies in the Anglican communion* (1955), 318–19 · *CGPLA Eng. & Wales* (1873) · *DNB*
Archives BL, corresp. with W. E. Gladstone, Add. MSS 44361–44422 · LPL, corresp. with A. C. Tait · NRA, priv. coll., letters to W. F. Hook · Pusey Oxf., letters to E. B. Pusey
Wealth at death under £14,000: probate, 5 July 1873, *CGPLA Eng. & Wales*

Richards, W. J. [alias William Oliver; called Oliver the Spy] (1774?–1827), spy and agent provocateur, claimed to have been born at Pontesbury, Shropshire. He may have been the Richard Richards baptized there on 21 October 1774, son of a father of the same name and his wife, Margaret. He was 'a person of genteel appearance and good address, nearly six feet high' (*Hansard 1*, 16 June 1817), with light hair and marked by smallpox. Little is known of his early life: he moved to London in the 1780s, marrying Harriet Dear (d. 23 Feb 1851) of Fulbourn, Cambridgeshire, at an unknown date. A son, William, was born in 1810, by which time the father was employed as a foreman carpenter. In 1816 Oliver spent five months in the Fleet debtors' prison.

Oliver was working as a surveyor when he sought an interview at the Home Office on 28 March 1817, offering 'material information': he was immediately offered employment on the direct authority of the home secretary, Sidmouth. The latter's interest in Oliver, at a time of widespread industrial discontent and rumoured revolution, stemmed from his close association with the Spenceans, the ultra-radical group responsible for the Spa Fields riots the previous December. Spencean strategy centred upon engineering a violent incident in the capital that would serve as a signal for a provincial rising. Spa Fields had failed in this respect, but the arrest of its protagonists Arthur Thistlewood and James Watson had not stilled the possibility of insurrection. The Spencean group was now mainly directed by Charles Pendrill, a veteran of the 'Despard conspiracy' of 1802 and one of the friends who had secured Oliver's release from prison the previous year. Meanwhile, provincial delegates present at Spa Fields, notably Joseph Mitchell from Lancashire, still maintained a covert network of potential conspirators which Oliver infiltrated.

Oliver met Mitchell at Pendrill's home in mid-April 1817. As the sole 'London delegate' he accompanied Mitchell on an intensive tour of the midlands and north (23 April to 16 May); but Mitchell was arrested on 4 May, permitting Oliver to improvise a more ambitious role for himself. He became, in effect, the only metropolitan contact for conspiratorial groups in the textile districts. He cut a persuasive figure in London upon his return, both at the Home

Office and in the Spencean circle. He convinced both that a general rising was not only possible but imminent, and on 23 May returned north.

Sidmouth informed authorities in Birmingham, Manchester, Leicester, and Derby of Oliver's activities, but Oliver concentrated on putative revolutionary cells in Nottinghamshire and west Yorkshire. These districts had seen the suppression of the last Luddite risings the previous year and were plausible focal points for revolution. Just how plausible has long been a matter of debate, with Oliver widely seen as having overstepped the role of informer to become an agent provocateur. His apparent deviation from Sidmouth's instructions placed his mission in jeopardy when he came close to arrest in both Sheffield and Leeds. Touring the south Pennine villages he visited Jeremiah Brandreth, whom he had previously met at a delegate meeting in Wakefield on 5 May. Finally, he was arrested with ten other Yorkshire 'delegates' at Thornhill (between Huddersfield and Wakefield) on 6 June, but escaped with the connivance of the commander of the army's northern district who was aware, through Sidmouth, of his identity. Oliver proceeded at once to meet delegates (but not Brandreth) in Nottingham, immediately after which he returned to London.

Three days later Brandreth led some two or three hundred artisans and labourers in a disastrous rising centred on the Derbyshire village of Pentrich. Its timing—if not actual occurrence—was largely Oliver's responsibility. During his intensive tours, his visits to individual conspiratorial cells can only have been brief. It is highly unlikely that he could single-handedly have fomented a rising had the mood not already been heavily disposed to insurgency. Oliver fuelled this mood with exaggerated reports of readiness to revolt elsewhere, and the insurgents acted under the impression that they were participants in a wider movement. There were indeed smaller disturbances in Huddersfield the same night, while similar actions in Leeds, Sheffield, and Wakefield were abandoned at the last moment. Nottingham, on which the rebels were marching, saw disturbances the following day.

Oliver was exposed by Edward Baines (1774–1848) through a series of articles in his newspaper the *Leeds Mercury*. With the light of hindsight, and drawing particularly on the testimony of two constitutional reformers whom Oliver had recklessly sought to involve in insurgency, Baines was able to construct a plausible case that Oliver had instigated the Pentrich rising. In parliament the affair was taken up by Sir Francis Burdett, Sir Henry Holland, and especially Henry Grey Bennett. The episode significantly damaged the reputation of Sidmouth and the government, but at Brandreth's trial his defence declined to call Oliver for fear that his evidence would be widely incriminating. Brandreth was executed with two accomplices in November. Oliver immediately emigrated to the Cape Colony where, as William Oliver Jones, he was employed by the governor as an inspector of works. He was implicated in fraud and other misdemeanours, but never tried. He is presumed to have died and been buried in Cape Town in August 1827, survived by his wife and his son. Ultimately, Oliver is significant not so much for his actual role in the events of June 1817 than for what his career betokened, in the eyes of contemporary critics and historians alike, of the government's handling of reform and unrest in the post-Waterloo years.

MALCOLM CHASE

Sources J. L. Hammond and B. Hammond, *The skilled labourer, 1760–1832* (1919) · J. Stevens, *England's last revolution: Pentrich, 1817* (1977) · A. F. Fremantle, 'The truth about Oliver the spy', *EngHR*, 47 (1932), 601–16 · E. P. Thompson, *The making of the English working class*, new edn (1968) · narrative of Oliver, PRO, HO 40/9 · examination of person known as W. J. Richards, PRO, HO 42/166 · 'Oliver's Tour' and 'Rex v. Thomas Bacon', PRO, TS 11/351 · *Leeds Mercury* (14 June 1817) · *Leeds Mercury* (21 June 1817) · *Leeds Mercury* (28 June 1817) · *Leeds Mercury* (5 July 1817) · *Leeds Mercury* (12 July 1817) · *Leeds Mercury* (26 July 1817) · *Hansard 1* (1817), 36.949–56 · M. I. Thomis, *Politics and society in Nottingham, 1785–1835* (1969) · *Cobbett's Weekly Political Register* (16 May 1818) · parish register, Shropshire, Pontesbury, 21 Oct 1774, Shrops. RRC [baptism] · will, Cape Town Archives, South Africa, MOOC 7/1/103, no. 104 · Cape Town Archives, South Africa, MOOC 6/9/53, no. 636
Archives Devon RO, Sidmouth MSS · PRO, home office and treasury solicitors' papers
Wealth at death less than 6000 guilders (Cape Colony); plus gold watch and chain: will, Cape Town Archives, South Africa, MOOC 7/1/103, no. 104; Stevens, *England's last revolution*

Richardson, Alan (1905–1975), dean of York, was born in Highfield, Wigan, on 17 October 1905, the younger son of William Richardson, company director, and his wife, Anne Moss. He was educated at Ashfield high school, Wigan, and Liverpool University, where he took first-class honours in philosophy in 1927. After preparing at Ridley Hall, Cambridge, for ordination (1927–8), he became in 1928 intercollegiate secretary of the Student Christian Movement (SCM) in Liverpool, a post which he held until 1931 when he was appointed chaplain of Ripon Hall, Oxford; he also took a first in theology at Oxford in 1933. In 1933 Richardson married Phyllis Mary, third child of William Alfred Parkhouse, company director of Blundellsands, who identified himself with his work in every way and made notable contributions to it, particularly at York. There were no children.

From 1934 to 1938 Richardson was vicar of Cambo, a sparsely populated rural parish in Northumberland. In 1938 he returned to the staff of the SCM as study secretary and editor, before becoming a canon residentiary of Durham in 1943. Ten years later he succeeded to the chair of Christian theology at Nottingham University. These were to be some of his happiest days. The department grew in range and influence. Richardson was noted for his accessibility and lack of pomp. He played a large part in university life, and was dean of arts from 1962 to 1964. His home was a centre of hospitality for staff, students, and distinguished visitors. He demonstrated that the place of theology in the university went far beyond the training of ordinands; it was a central, humanistic intellectual discipline in its own right, and the basis of a sound general education.

In 1964 Richardson became dean of York, but almost

immediately suffered the first of a number of heart attacks which were to slow him but the effects of which he bore with courage, taking care but making no fuss. It was soon discovered that York Minster was in imminent danger of collapse owing to the fall in the level of the water table because of the growth of York. The minster had literally to be re-founded. The necessary engineering works required the raising of over £2 million. Richardson had the wisdom to seek the best advice and secure the best people for each job, and with their combined efforts that money was raised and the minster saved and improved. Richardson's establishment of the York Glaziers' Trust made it a leading European centre of stained-glass restoration and conservation. His achievements were recognized when he was appointed KBE in 1973. Amid this work, as at Nottingham, he was noted for the calmness and peaceableness he exemplified and created around him.

Throughout Richardson's life academic work continued. His many books and writings reflect the range of his scholarship, from biblical studies, the history of ideas, and the philosophy of history, to contemporary theology and apologetics. He was an extremely lucid lecturer and writer at both a scholarly and a popular level. Several of his books were reprinted many times, and translated into up to ten languages. Among the best-known were *Christian Apologetics* (1947), *An Introduction to the Theology of the New Testament* (1958), and *History Sacred and Profane* (1964). All but two were published by the SCM Press, of which he was chairman from 1957 to 1973 and to which he gave a great deal of care.

Richardson's connection with the SCM led him to have a large number of friends in different confessional traditions from an early age, and made the ecumenical movement his constant concern. He was a frequent participator in ecumenical meetings before and after the formation of the World Council of Churches in 1948. After the Second Vatican Council, Roman Catholic links developed, particularly with Ampleforth Abbey. Richardson lectured and preached all over the world, and was one of the two or three best-known Anglican theologians of his day. His aim was to expound the Christian faith as a convincing understanding of human life amid the intellectual heterogeneity of the twentieth century. He moved from a position akin to that of Anglican modernism of the 1930s to what was known as 'biblical theology', with which he came too neatly to be associated, for he was never the kind of 'neo-orthodox' to whom the term 'liberal' was merely one of condemnation, and he maintained the traditional Anglican position of seeking to understand and maintain the use of 'right reason' in theology. However, in spite of his philosophical training he distanced himself from the current positivist and analytical preoccupations of British philosophy, and the problems of York did not give him the opportunity to come to terms with the collapse of biblical theology by the 1960s. He gained a DD from Oxford in 1947, and the honorary degrees of DD (Glasgow) in 1952 and DUniv (York) in 1973.

Richardson died after the end of evensong on 23 February 1975 in the minster, from which he had intended to retire later in the year. RONALD H. PRESTON, *rev.*

Sources *The Times* (24 Feb 1975) · *The Times* (3 March 1975) · R. H. Preston, ed., *Theology and change* (1975) · private information (1986) · personal knowledge (1986)
Archives U. Nott. L., personal and academic papers
Likenesses photograph, Castle Museum, York
Wealth at death £71,744: probate, 15 May 1975, *CGPLA Eng. & Wales*

Richardson, Sir Albert Edward (1880–1964), architect, was born on 19 May 1880 at 33D Middleton Road, Hackney, London, the eldest of the three children of Albert Edmund Richardson, printer, and his wife, Mary Ann, daughter of Thomas Richardson (not related), of Highgate. He was educated at the Boys British School, Highgate, where he already showed pleasure in buildings and a talent for drawing. In 1895 he was articled to an architect named Thomas Page, in Gray's Inn Road, and he subsequently served in the offices of Evelyn Hellicar (1898–1902), Leonard Stokes (1902–3), and Frank T. Verity (1903–6). On 31 May 1904 he married Elizabeth (1882/3–1958), daughter of John Byers, a warehouseman from Newry, co. Down; they had one daughter. As Verity's leading assistant he designed 'mansion flats' in Cleveland Row, St James's, and in Bayswater Road (both 1906), the middle section of 169–201 Regent Street (1908–9), and the façade of the Regent Street Polytechnic; the latter was executed after he had severed his connection with Verity and set up in practice with another of Verity's assistants, Charles Lovett Gill. The contemporary French influence seen in the work for Verity is reflected again in the early works of the partnership, notably flats in Berkeley Street (nos. 10 and 19) executed between 1910 and 1916. A developing taste for an earlier and more distinguished type of neo-classicism is shown in the New Theatre (now the Opera House), Manchester, built in association with Horace Farquharson in 1911–13. The most substantial commission, however, obtained by the partnership before the First World War was Moorgate Hall, Finsbury Pavement, London (1913–17), a thoughtful solution to the problem of combining office fenestration with shop windows. This led to a series of similar commissions which formed the backbone of the practice for twenty-five years.

With the exigencies of practice, Richardson combined an enthusiastic devotion to the architecture of the past, especially the then neglected history of English domestic classicism from the seventeenth century to the nineteenth. With the encouragement of Harry Batsford he wrote, in collaboration with C. Lovett Gill, his first book, *London Houses from 1660 to 1820* (1911), a pioneering appreciation of the simple elegance of Georgian streets and squares. This was followed by *Monumental Classic Architecture in Great Britain and Ireland in the Eighteenth and Nineteenth Centuries* (1914), a superbly illustrated folio work demonstrating the progress of the classical tradition from the Palladian movement to the mid-Victorian period. This offered a new perspective of stylistic continuity and

Sir Albert Edward Richardson (1880–1964), by Sir Cecil Beaton

became a landmark in British architectural historiography.

Between 1916 and 1918 Richardson served as a lieutenant in the Royal Flying Corps, working at the school of military aeronautics at Reading. In 1919 his combination of practical experience and historical learning made him eligible for the chair of architecture at the Bartlett school of architecture, University College, London, where he succeeded F. M. Simpson. This chair he held for twenty-seven years, before retiring as professor emeritus in 1946. At University College he effectively exploited his personal qualities as a teacher. Not by temperament an academic, nor indeed a scholar of the more disciplined kind, his history lectures were rhetorical improvisations made wonderfully vivid by a rare talent for impromptu graphic demonstration. In the studios the same ready pencil, accompanied by an enthusiastic flow of talk and the random play of ideas, endeared him to a whole generation of students. Richardson's personal interests and distaste for modern art and architecture ensured that classical and Renaissance architecture was studied at the Bartlett School virtually to the exclusion of anything else. Yet even this was tolerated by his students as an aspect of his ebullient eccentricity, as were his perpetual haste and the general waspishness which increased as he grew older.

Meanwhile the practice of Richardson and Gill developed remuneratively through the 1920s and 1930s with offices in the City, flats in the West End, and a few churches and country houses. In the City, 47–57 Gresham Street (1924) show a departure from classical compromise towards direct statement and this became more manifest in the premises built for Sir Arthur Sanderson & Sons in Wells Street (1930–32), which was awarded the London architecture medal at the Royal Institute of British Architects in 1932. But although Richardson was sympathetic to the modern tendency towards simplification, he rejected

contemptuously the intellectual premises of the continental Modern Movement as expounded in the teaching of Walter Gropius and the publications of Le Corbusier. *The Art of Architecture* (1938), which he wrote in collaboration with his colleague H. O. Corfiato, was an attempt to defend traditional architectural principles, but its influence was negligible and in the late 1930s Richardson found himself increasingly alienated from the younger generation of architects.

During the Second World War the Bartlett School was transferred to Cambridge, where Richardson spent happy years in a privileged environment which appealed to his sense of tradition. In the post-war world he emerged as a stalwart reactionary, a lively castigator of bureaucracy, and a champion of the preservationist movements then gathering strength. Elected ARA in 1936, he became a full academician in 1944 and president of the Royal Academy ten years later. In this high office he was at once recognized as an agreeably controversial public figure who could be relied upon to say something original, paradoxical, and quite possibly irresponsible, on any subject to which his attention was directed. As a member of the Royal Fine Arts Commission from 1939 to 1956 his insights were often valuable and his criticism unsparing. In 1947 he was awarded the gold medal for architecture of the Royal Institute of British Architects and in 1956 he was appointed KCVO. He was also an FSA, an honorary member of the Royal Society of Painters in Water Colours, an honorary MA of Cambridge, an honorary LittD of Dublin, and an honorary fellow of St Catharine's College, Cambridge.

The partnership with Gill having terminated in 1939, Richardson found, in 1945, a new partner in his son-in-law, Eric Alfred Scholefield Houfe, and together they produced an admirable sequence of designs during this final phase of his career. Their works included in and around London the Chancery Lane safe deposit (1945–9), the *Financial Times* building, Cannon Street (1955–8), the AEI building, Grosvenor Place (1958), and the chapel and library, St Mary's College, Twickenham (1961). Restoration and alteration work featured prominently during this period and included the repair of war-damaged buildings such as Merchant Taylors' Hall (1953), Trinity House, Tower Hill (with an important extension, 1956), and the churches of St Alfege, Greenwich (1959), and St James, Piccadilly (1947–54). In 1950 Richardson and Houfe also undertook alterations to Woburn Abbey, Bedfordshire, and in 1954 they restored the assembly rooms in Bath. Written work of this period includes his notice of the architect Sir (Thomas) Edwin Cooper for the *Dictionary of National Biography*.

In appearance Richardson was of medium height, inclining to stoutness in middle age; his face was somewhat fleshy with dark hair brushed back, an aquiline nose, and fine grey eyes, heavy-lidded. In deportment and gesture he had something of the air of an old-fashioned actor. Richardson died on 3 February 1964 at Avenue House, Ampthill, a beautiful late eighteenth-century house which he had acquired in 1919 and where he brought together a remarkable collection of furniture and works of art, including architectural drawings. He was buried in the churchyard at Millbrook, Bedfordshire.

JOHN SUMMERSON, *rev.* CATHERINE GORDON

Sources S. Houfe, *Sir Albert Richardson* (1980) · A. K. Placzek, ed., *Macmillan encyclopedia of architects*, 3 (1982), 556–7 · *Architect and Building News* (12 Feb 1964), 255–6 · N. Taylor, 'A classic case of Edwardianism', *ArchR*, 140 (1966), 199–205 · personal knowledge (1981) · private information (1981) · m. cert.

Archives Beds. & Luton ARS, diaries | RIBA, corresp. with W. W. Begley

Likenesses K. Parbury, bronze bust, 1953, priv. coll. · W. Stoneman, photograph, 1955, NPG · C. Beaton, photograph, NPG [*see illus.*] · M. Codner, portrait · J. Gunn, portrait, Clarendon School, Haynes Park, Bedfordshire · D. McFall, bronze memorial tablet, St Paul's Cathedral, London · E. S. Rose, portrait

Wealth at death £160,827: probate, 19 May 1964, *CGPLA Eng. & Wales*

Richardson, Alexander (*fl.* 1579–1629), logician, came from Surrey and matriculated from Queens' College, Cambridge, in 1579 (BA, 1583–4; MA, 1587). Nothing more is known of his life and antecedents. A course of lectures given on graduating MA was probably the origin of his book *The Logicians School-Master, or, A Comment upon Ramus 'Logicke'* (1629). It was indeed principally concerned with Ramus, whose Latin work *Dialectica* appeared in English translation by Roland MacIlmaine in 1574 as *Logike*. (The second edition of Richardson's work, published in 1657, adds a commentary, also styled 'prelections', on Ramus's grammar, and other material.) Richardson's is probably the tenth logic book published in English (the next was by Zachary Coke). Book 1, on 'invention', discusses argument, the four causes, subject, adjunct, contraries, and definition, after a consideration of what *dialectica* is, which concludes (p. 39) that 'Logicke and it are all one'. Book 2 is mainly about types of propositions ('axiomes') and syllogisms (ch. 9), though he avoids giving all the rules. Clearly the pattern of Ramus's book is being followed throughout.

Many of the terms in Richardson's work are left in Latin, for example, *definitio* (p. 215) and *prosyllogismus* (p. 295), also in English at page 289, or in Greek form, as *enthymema* ('it is nothing but a syllogisme wanting a leg,'; p. 295). In fact much of the discussion is about Latin expressions and propositions as used by previous logicians such as 'Kickerman' (Bartholomew Keckermann). Richardson often uses the formula 'Ramus doth *commorari*,' (p. 276) 'for hee could not well tell what to say'.

Though rather unoriginal as a commentator, Richardson is the first known user of some terms, such as 'contradicent', 'distributively', 'heterozetesis', 'polyzetesis', 'privant', 'privately', and 'relate' (noun). He is the only known user of 'adjunctity', 'axiomation', 'inartificial' (noun), 'quadrichotomy', and 'unmatch' (noun).

ROLAND HALL

Sources R. Hall, 'Antedatings in logic', *N&Q*, 215 (1970), 322–32 · R. Hall, 'Unnoticed terms in logic', *N&Q*, 217 (1972), 131–7, 165–71, 203–9 · Venn, *Alum. Cant.*

Richardson [*née* Atkins], **Anna** (1806–1892), slavery abolitionist and peace campaigner, was born in Chipping Norton, Oxfordshire, on 5 January 1806, the fourth of the eight children of Samuel Atkins (1772?–1821), mealman, of Chipping Norton and his wife, Esther (1776–1833), daughter of John Millard, silversmith, of Tewkesbury and his wife, Anna. Her parents were members of the Society of Friends and her mother was a supporter of the anti-slavery campaign. Anna Atkins spent from 1817 to 1819 as a pupil at Ackworth, a leading Quaker school in Yorkshire. On her father's death in 1821, her widowed mother had to bring up a large family in difficult financial circumstances.

On 5 July 1833 Anna Atkins married another Quaker, **Henry Richardson** (1806–1885), whom she had met at Ackworth (where Henry was a pupil from 1818 to 1820). Born on 18 September 1806, he was the third of the seven children of George Richardson (1773–1862) of Newcastle upon Tyne, a grocer, philanthropist, reformer, and travelling minister in the Society of Friends, and his wife, Eleanor (1778–1846), daughter of John and Rachel Watson, also of Newcastle. Henry and Anna Richardson settled in Newcastle and had a long and happy marriage, although they had no children, and they devoted their energies to philanthropic and reform activities in the town. Henry Richardson took over his father's grocery shop, but retired from the business in 1858. He became an elder in the Society of Friends, and he was the founder of the Boys' ragged school, superintendent of the Friends' Sabbath School, leader of the Newcastle Bible Society, editor of the periodical the *Peace Advocate* (1843–51), and an active member of Newcastle Peace Society.

Anna Richardson was even more prominent as an activist than her husband. During the 1840s and 1850s she was the leader of the British free produce movement, an arm of the anti-slavery campaign which aimed to discourage the use in Britain of American slave-grown cotton. In 1846 she founded the Newcastle Ladies' Free Produce Association, and issued a circular encouraging women nationwide to form similar groups. In 1850 she persuaded the American former slave Revd Henry Highland Garnet to come to Britain to promote the cause; as a result, about twenty-six free labour associations were rapidly formed, progress that was recorded in *The Slave*, a periodical promoting the free produce movement which she edited between 1851 and 1854. She was recognized by the British and Foreign Anti-Slavery Society as the national co-ordinator of the free produce movement. She also promoted the anti-slavery cause by assisting her sister-in-law, Ellen Richardson, in raising funds to purchase the freedom of the African-American abolitionist Frederick Douglass, and by compiling monthly 'Illustrations of American slavery', which she distributed free to newspaper editors throughout Britain from 1847 onwards.

Anna Richardson's promotion of the free produce movement was closely linked to her second major preoccupation: the peace movement. Anna and Henry Richardson both attended the 1849 Paris Peace Congress, and between 1844 and 1857 Anna edited the *Olive Leaf*, a peace magazine for children. She belonged to the network of Ladies' Olive Leaf circles, which were linked to the League of Universal Brotherhood. The league had been founded by an American, Elihu Burritt, who came to live in Britain in 1846, and it combined promotion of international peace with support for the free labour movement.

Anna Richardson was also involved in a wide variety of other philanthropic and reform activities in Newcastle. She was secretary and district visitor for the Ladies' Branch Bible Society and set up a Bible women's mission to spread religious knowledge to working-class homes, and she was an active member of the Society of Friends. In 1834, at the suggestion of Elizabeth Fry, she became a visitor of Newcastle prison. She became a teetotaller, and she and her husband established temperance refreshment rooms in 1853. Anna was also involved in aid to European immigrants into Britain: in 1839 she produced a book to raise funds in support of Lutheran refugees from Prussia.

Henry Richardson suffered from poor health from 1840 onwards, but lived to the age of seventy-eight, dying on 24 April 1885 at their home, 116 Park Road. He was buried on 28 April at Elswick general cemetery, Newcastle. Anna Richardson died on 27 March 1892 at 116 Park Road, and was buried on 30 March, also in Elswick cemetery. Surviving portraits show a large-featured woman, neatly attired and wearing a Quaker bonnet. She was clearly a serious and religious woman, with a lifelong commitment to philanthropy and reform, and considerable organizational abilities and leadership skills. CLARE MIDGLEY

Sources T. Pumphrey and E. R. Pumphrey, *Henry and Anna Richardson: in memoriam* (1892) · C. Midgley, *Women against slavery: the British campaigns, 1780–1870* (1992), 137–9 · J. W. Steel and others, *A historical sketch of the Society of Friends … in Newcastle and Gateshead, 1653–1898* (1899), 189–201 · *Annual Monitor* (1893) · *The Slave*, 1–48 (Jan 1851–Dec 1854) · *Olive Leaf*, 11–14 (1854–7) · A. Richardson, *Antislavery memoranda* (privately printed, Newcastle upon Tyne, [1860]) · *Peace Advocate*, 1st ser., 1–12 (1843) · *Digest registers of births, marriages and burials for England and Wales, c.1650–1837* [1992] [Berkshire and Oxfordshire quarterly meeting; microfilm] · d. cert. · digest registers of births, marriages, and burials, RS Friends, Lond. [microfilm] · digest of deaths, 1837–1961, RS Friends, Lond.
Archives Bodl. RH, anti-slavery MSS
Likenesses double portrait (Henry and Anna Richardson), repro. in Pumphrey and Pumphrey, *Henry and Anna Richardson* · portrait, repro. in Pumphrey and Pumphrey, *Henry and Anna Richardson*
Wealth at death £561 12s. 9d.: probate, 26 April 1892, CGPLA Eng. & Wales · £7358 9s. 5d.—Henry Richardson: probate, 27 May 1885, CGPLA Eng. & Wales

Richardson, Sir Benjamin Ward (1828–1896), physician, was born at Somerby, Leicestershire, on 31 October 1828, the only son of Benjamin Richardson and Mary Ward (c.1800–1838), his wife. He was educated locally at a dame-school, and then at the Burrow Hill School, Leicestershire, under the Revd W. Young Nutt. The direction of his life was set in 1838, when, on the deathbed wish of his mother, he dedicated himself to the study of medicine. He later recorded that she was inspired by a deep admiration for the eighteenth-century surgeon William Chesleden, whose portrait she had inherited (Richardson, 6).

Richardson was therefore apprenticed at an early age to Henry Hudson, a surgeon at Somerby. In 1847 he entered Anderson's University, Glasgow, but he was forced to leave before completing his training after he contracted slum fever, probably while attending the delivery of a poor Irishwoman in a cellar dwelling. After a period of convalescence he became assistant to Thomas Browne, of Saffron Walden in Essex. Later he worked for Edward Dudley Hudson, the elder brother of his first master, who practised as a surgeon at Littlebury, Narborough, near Leicester. While working for Hudson, Richardson met Professor Taylor, lecturer in chemistry at the Middlesex Hospital in London. Taylor, impressed by the young man, arranged in 1849 for him to become the partner of Robert Willis of Barnes, Surrey; Willis was well known as the editor of the works of William Harvey, and the librarian of the Royal College of Surgeons from 1828 to 1845. Richardson then returned briefly to Glasgow in 1850, to be admitted a licentiate of the Faculty of Physicians and Surgeons of Glasgow; later he was made faculty lecturer (1877) and fellow (1878). Also in 1850 Richardson moved to Mortlake in Surrey, near Barnes, where he set up a household of his own and began to practise alongside Willis.

At Mortlake, Richardson's scientific and medical interests developed. In the laboratory he established in his house, he began to research a range of subjects, including the coagulation of blood, antiseptic properties of gasses, and resuscitation. In response to the threat of cholera Richardson established the East Surrey Society for the Investigation of Cholera, in 1853. Through Willis he was introduced to many of the best-known physicians of the time, including Richard Bright, Thomas Hodgkin, and Thomas Addison. At the same time, thanks to an accidental meeting with Douglas Jerrold, he became a member of the circle of literary figures and wits known as 'Our Club', where he met, among others, W. M. Thackeray and George Cruikshank, whose executor he later became.

In 1854 Richardson was admitted MA and MD by St Andrews University. He later became a staunch defender of the university: when a bill sponsored by Edinburgh, Glasgow, and Aberdeen universities threatened to remove its right to award MDs, he established the St Andrews Medical Graduate Association to help in its defence. He was president of the association for thirty-five years, also becoming a member of the university court and assessor of the general council. In 1877 he was awarded an honorary LLD degree for his services.

Richardson had moved to London early in 1854. He took a house at 12 Hinde Street, where he remained until 1880, when he moved to 25 Manchester Square. He rapidly established himself in the capital; he was made physician to the Blenheim Street Dispensary and in 1854 lecturer on forensic medicine at the Grosvenor Place school of medicine. In the same year he was awarded the Fothergillian gold medal of the Medical Society of London for his essay, 'Diseases of the foetus in utero'. In 1856 Richardson's researches at Mortlake again bore fruit, when he won the Astley Cooper prize of 300 guineas for his essay on the coagulation of the blood. That year he was made physician to the Royal Infirmary for Diseases of the Chest, and to the Metropolitan, Marylebone, and Margaret Street dispensaries. One of the earliest English followers of

Laënnec's work on chest diseases, he helped to found the Society for the Study of Chest Diseases, and was among the first to use the stethoscope.

Helped by his prizes and developing reputation as a medical researcher, Richardson quickly built up an extensive practice. By 1857 he was secure enough to marry, on 21 February, Mary J. Smith of Mortlake, where the couple had met through the local musical circle. They had three children: two sons, Bertram and Aubrey, and a daughter, Mary Stella. Even on their honeymoon in Hastings, Richardson did not leave behind his involvement with medicine: while there he befriended another young physician, William Greenhill, with whom he long maintained a fruitful correspondence.

Richardson's upward progress within his profession continued through the 1850s and 1860s. In 1856 he was admitted a member of the Royal College of Physicians, London, of which he was elected fellow in 1865 and chosen lecturer on materia medica in 1866. Meanwhile he held several posts at the Grosvenor Place school, lecturing on public hygiene and physiology before becoming dean of the school. Richardson remained dean until 1863, when the premises were sold and demolished. He also lectured to the College of Dentists in this period. He was elected a fellow of the Royal Society in 1867 and in 1873 delivered the Croonian lecture, entitled 'The muscular irritability after systemic death'; it was based on his research into resuscitation. In 1868 he was elected president of the Medical Society of London.

Richardson was best-known for his research into anaesthetics and for his involvement in public health and the sanitary movement. He was a close friend of John Snow, who shared his laboratory on occasion; Richardson edited Snow's classic work, Chloroform and other Anaesthetics (1858) after the latter's death. Both pursued the pharmaceutical action of simple molecular structures, seeking safe, effective, and economical anaesthetics. Starting with amyl nitrate, Richardson systematically investigated an extensive range of compounds in the methyl and ethyl series. Between 1863 and 1871 his work was subsidized by the British Association for the Advancement of Science, an unusual favour for that time. He was highly productive, discovering fourteen new anaesthetics, several of which were soon widely used (particularly methylene bichloride), and inventing the first double-valved mouthpiece for the administration of chloroform. He also invented the ether spray, the only known method of local anaesthesia until the introduction of the topical use of cocaine in 1884. In addition he investigated the potential of mesmerism, electricity, and other possible alternatives to chemical anaesthetics. These researches were far from confined to this field, however; Richardson explored a variety of questions, including the uses of colloids and methods of embalming. A by-product of this work was the introduction of hydrogen peroxide, both as a medicinal substance and as a bleach for hair dyes. Richardson's interest in the prevention of suffering extended to animals: in 1853 he invented a lethal chamber for the painless slaughter of

animals, and thirty years later he installed a large version of it at the Battersea dogs' home. The issue of humane slaughter combined his concerns with suffering and his public health interests (in preventing the deterioration of meat). He established the Model Abattoir Society in 1882 and remained its president until his death.

Richardson's investigation of anaesthetics came to convince him that alcohol was a potent and dangerous drug. Although for many years a believer in the pleasure and value of drinking, while giving his Cantor lectures on alcohol for the Society of Arts from 1874 to 1875 he became a committed teetotaller. He later lectured influentially on temperance across the country, and in 1892 he joined the staff of the London Temperance Hospital. Although some of his acquaintances were offended by his abstinence, one feeling unable 'to acquit it of some shame in bringing about a death which at least was premature' (Transactions of the Epidemiological Society, 292), others thought he 'proved that alcohol is not essential to postprandial eloquence' (BMJ, 1612).

Through his interest in cholera and his friendship with Snow, Richardson became one of the pioneers of the sanitary movement. He became a friend of William Farr and Edwin Chadwick, whose work he later reviewed and collected as The Health of Nations (1887). He founded and edited the first journal dedicated to public health, the Journal of Public Health and Sanitary Review, in 1855, and was a senior officer of the Sanitary Institute for many years, helping to establish examinations for sanitary inspectors. He gave a celebrated address to the Social Science Association in 1875, in which he described a health utopia, a city of spotless cleanliness and hygiene; this was later published as Hygiea, a City of Health (1876). Richardson's conviction of the importance of environmental factors in disease led him consistently to oppose Pasteur's germ theory, rather emphasizing cleanliness and preventive medicine.

Richardson was a man of wide interests. A prolific writer, he wrote plays, biographies, poems, songs, and even a romantic novel, The Son of a Star (3 vols., 1888). Much of his work was printed in The Asclepiad, a journal of researches in science, art, and medicine, which he edited and published from 1861 until his death. He was also an early cycling enthusiast, advocating bicycle use for the preservation of health. In the parliamentary election of 1892 he (unsuccessfully) contested the Walton division of Liverpool as a Gladstonian Liberal. He practised extensively as a physician throughout his life, serving several bodies, including the Newspaper Press Fund and the Royal Literary Fund.

Recognition of Richardson's scientific and humanitarian work led to his election as a fellow of numerous international bodies, including the Philosophical Society of America, the Pathological Society of Berlin, and the Imperial Academy of Sciences at Dresden. In 1877 he became a fellow of the Society of Antiquaries. He was knighted in June 1893.

Richardson died at his house, 25 Manchester Square, London, on 21 November 1896, and his body was cremated at Brookwood, Surrey. Active to the end, he had dictated the final chapter of his autobiography only two hours before falling ill with his final sickness.

PATRICK WALLIS

Sources A. S. MacNalty, *A biography of Sir Benjamin Ward Richardson* (1950) · B. W. Richardson, *Vita medica: chapters of a medical life and work* (1897) · W. F. Bynum, 'Chemical structure and pharmacological action: a chapter in the history of 19th century molecular pharmacology', *Bulletin of the History of Medicine*, 44 (1970), 518–38 · *PRS*, 75 (1905), 51–2 · *Transactions of the Epidemiological Society of London*, 16 (1896–7), 289–93 · *Journal of the Sanitary Institute*, 17 (1896–7), 618 · *BMJ* (28 Nov 1896), 1612 · *The Lancet* (28 Nov 1896), 1575 · E. H. Ackerknecht, 'Sir Benjamin Ward Richardson and the Jews', *Gesnerus*, 45/3–4 (1988), 317–21 · *DNB*
Archives RCP Lond., corresp. and papers · Wellcome L., lecture notes | UCL, letters to Sir Edwin Chadwick
Likenesses S. Pearce, oils, 1865, NPG · group portrait, wood-engraving, 1875 (*A group of starving and emaciated physicians lamenting their lack of work*; after G. Du Maurier), Wellcome L. · G. Cruikshank, group portrait, wood-engraving (*Lecture at the Charterhouse on Stephen Gray's discoveries in electricity*), NPG; repro. in *ILN* (21 Feb 1874) · Lock & Whitfield, photograph, Wellcome L. · Lock & Whitfield, woodburytype photograph, NPG; repro. in T. Cooper, *Men of mark: a gallery of contemporary portraits* (1883) · group portrait, wood-engraving (*Departure of the Arctic Searching Expedition*; after photograph by Beard), NPG; repro. in *ILN* (1 May 1852) · photograph, repro. in G. B. Rushman, N. J. H. Davies, and R. S. Atkinson, *A short history of anaesthesia* (1996), 138, fig. 15.1
Wealth at death £8726 7s. 0d.: probate, 3 Feb 1897, *CGPLA Eng. & Wales*

Richardson [*née* Scott], **Catherine Eliza** (1777–1853), poet and novelist, was born at Forge House in the parish of Canonbie, Dumfriesshire, on 24 November 1777. She was one of the seven children of James Scott (*d.* 1799), captain and JP, and Phoebe Dixon. In 1799 she travelled to India and on 29 April of that year married her first cousin, Gilbert Geddes Richardson, a mariner, in Madras. The first of their five children, a son, was born in 1802. In the meantime, her anonymous novel, *Adonia, a Desultory Tale*, written before she left England, had been published in London in four volumes in 1801. It is a sentimental narrative of the love of a young French aristocrat for an Englishwoman and of the opposition he encounters from his own family, and it was reviewed indulgently by the *Monthly Review*. The evidence that the novel is hers depends on the tradition that she had written a novel, the fact that the author refers to herself as having been nineteen at the time when it was written, and, most materially, that it is dedicated to the duchess of Buccleuch (Richardson's dedication of her *Poems* of 1834 to the next duchess of Buccleuch mentions that the duchess's mother-in-law had patronized her earlier writing).

After her husband's death Catherine Richardson remained in India for some years, returning to Britain in 1827 with three of her children to live in Dumfries. Between 1827 and 1829 she contributed short poems, over the initials R., C. E., or C. E. R., to the short-lived *London Weekly Review*, a journal edited by another recent returnee from India, David Lester Richardson. According to her own account he encouraged her to bring out a collection,

and in 1828 her *Poems* appeared. She mentions in the preface that 1700 copies had been spoken for before publication; there was a second edition in 1828 and a third in 1829. The collection is a miscellaneous one made up of legendary tales, ballads, elegies, and verse in dialect. The only trace of her Indian experience is the poem 'Kishen Kower' and an explanatory note on 'Hindoo' mythology. In 1834 she brought out her *Poems: Second Series*. In 1836 she dedicated her *Grandmamma's Sampler; with Some Other Rhymes for Children* to two granddaughters of her own.

Catherine Richardson was acquainted with the Carlyles in Dumfries between 1828 and 1831, Thomas Carlyle referring to her in one of his letters as 'really a good worthy woman' (*Collected Letters*, 5.21), and mentioning in his *Reminiscences* that when the critic Lord Jeffreys visited Dumfries he made a point of calling on her as a friend from the days before her marriage. Richardson died in Canonbie on 9 October 1853. J. R. DE J. JACKSON

Sources parish records, Dumfries and Galloway county archives · K. Scott, *James Scott of Forge* (1923) · 1851 census, Canonbie, index · *The collected letters of Thomas and Jane Welsh Carlyle*, ed. C. R. Sanders and K. J. Fielding, 5 (1976), 21 · T. Carlyle, *Reminiscences*, ed. C. E. Norton, 2 (1887), 247 · *The East India kalendar, or, Asiatic register* (1800), 172 · *Asiatic Journal*, 23 (1827), 887–9 · *Monthly Review* · *GM* · *Edinburgh Annual Register* · *Lloyd's Shipping Registers* · *Asiatic Annual Register*, 4 (1802), 113 · *Asiatic Annual Register*, 5 (1803), 149 · *Asiatic Annual Register*, 1 (1799), 177 · F. Miller, *The poets of Dumfriesshire* (1910), 265 · *Eskdale and Liddesdale Advertiser* (2 Nov 1853)

Richardson, Cecil Antonio [Tony] (1928–1991), theatre and film director, was born on 5 June 1928 at 28 Bingley Road, Saltaire, Shipley, Yorkshire, the only son of Clarence Albert Richardson (*d. c.*1967), pharmacist, and his wife, Elsie Evans, *née* Ingle (*d. c.*1975), the daughter of a bankrupted West Hartlepool shipbuilder. After attending Ashville College, Harrogate (1939–45), he went up to Wadham College, Oxford, in 1948, where his audacious production of *Dr Faustus* prompted his election as president of both the Experimental Theatre Club and the Oxford University Dramatic Society. Richardson graduated with a third in English in 1951 and he joined the BBC, where he made his professional directing début with Giraudoux's *The Apollo of Bellac* in 1953. However, he was fired from his West End bow, *Mr Kettle and Mrs Moon* (1954), although, thanks to J. B. Priestley, he retained his credit. It was about this time that he befriended the actor George Devine, with whom he had worked on a BBC adaptation of Chekhov's *The Actor's End* (1955). Later that year they co-formed the English Stage Company, which began its tenure at the Royal Court Theatre with the première of John *Osborne's prototype 'angry young man' drama, *Look Back in Anger* (1956). Although several early reviews were hostile, it was hailed as a watershed in British theatre after *The Observer* critic Kenneth Tynan wrote, 'I doubt if I could love anyone who did not wish to see *Look Back in Anger*' (Richardson, 79). The English stage was seemingly in his thrall. Yet the angular, garrulous Richardson was something of a young man in a hurry and he had already moved into films. In 1955 he co-directed, with Karel Reisz, *Momma Don't Allow*, a short documentary study of a north London jazz club that was screened at the National Film

Cecil Antonio [Tony] **Richardson** (1928–1991), by Roger Mayne, 1960

Theatre in February 1956 as part of the influential Free Cinema programme. Indeed, the movement's motto, 'Perfection is not an aim' (ibid., 69), would long remain Richardson's rallying cry.

Shortly after directing Laurence Olivier in the Royal Court production of Osborne's *The Entertainer* (1957), Richardson and Osborne co-founded Woodfall Films. Having brought *Look Back in Anger* (1959) and *The Entertainer* (1960) to the screen, he continued to embrace the social realist, or 'kitchen sink', tradition with his versions of Shelagh Delaney's *A Taste of Honey* (1961) and Alan Sillitoe's *The Loneliness of the Long Distance Runner* (1962). However, it was his first colour feature, *Tom Jones* (1963), that earned him international recognition and a reputation for literate filmmaking. However, he would never repeat the success of this reworking of Henry Fielding's picaresque novel, which became only the second British feature to win the Oscar for best picture; it also brought Richardson the Oscar for best direction. Following Osborne's *Luther* (1961), Richardson grew increasingly disillusioned with what he described as 'totem theatre' (*The Independent*, 16 Nov 1991). Nevertheless he drew praise for his staging of *The Seagull* (1964), *The Threepenny Opera* (1972), and *Antony and Cleopatra* (1973), all three of which starred Vanessa Redgrave (b. 1937). Richardson had married Redgrave, the elder daughter of Sir Michael *Redgrave and Rachel Kempson, on 28

April 1962; they had two children, Natasha (b. 1963) and Joely (b. 1965), who would both become actors. The couple divorced in 1967, following Richardson's affair with Jeanne Moreau—whom he had directed in Jean Genet's *Mademoiselle* (1966) and in Marguerite Duras's *The Sailor from Gibraltar* (1967)—and Redgrave's liaison with the Italian star Franco Nero.

Now based at Le Nid du Duc in the south of France, Richardson embarked on a sequence of literary adaptations—Evelyn Waugh's *The Loved One* (1965), Vladimir Nabokov's *Laughter in the Dark* (1969), Shakespeare's *Hamlet* (1969), Edward Albee's *A Delicate Balance* (1973), and even a version of Dick Francis's horse-racing whodunit *Dead Cert* (1974). Only his extravagant slice of costume realism, *The Charge of the Light Brigade* (1968), found widespread critical favour, although both his biopic of the Australian outlaw *Ned Kelly* (1970), with Mick Jagger in the title role, and a return to Fielding, with *Joseph Andrews* (1977), had their adherents. Nevertheless, Richardson never broke the cinematic mould in the same way he had done with the stage. He was removed by producer Berry Gordy jun. from *Mahogany* (1975), for failing to 'capture the black point of view' (Lyon, 446), and he had to endure his collaboration with Jack Nicholson, *The Border* (1982), being saddled with an upbeat ending. Largely ostracized from Hollywood after his faithful adaptation of John Irving's *The Hotel New Hampshire* (1984), he had to content himself with a succession of teleplays and miniseries.

From the early 1970s Richardson was resident in Los Angeles, California, with Grizelda Grimond, the only daughter of the former Liberal Party leader Jo Grimond. They had one daughter, Katherine (b. 1973). Having been diagnosed as HIV positive, he completed a memoir, *Long Distance Runner* (1993), and his final feature, *Blue Sky*, which was released three years after his death in Los Angeles from a neurological condition brought on by AIDS on 14 November 1991.   DAVID PARKINSON

Sources T. Richardson, *Long distance runner* (1993) • V. Redgrave, *Vanessa Redgrave: an autobiography* (1991) • *The international dictionary of films and filmmakers: directors*, 2nd edn, ed. C. Lyon (1991) • D. Thomson, *A biographical dictionary of film*, 3rd edn (1994) • *The Times* (16 Nov 1991) • *The Independent* (16 Nov 1991)
Likenesses R. Mayne, photograph, 1960, NPG [*see illus.*] • double portrait, photograph (with John Osborne), repro. in *The Independent* • photographs, repro. in *The Times*

Richardson, Charles (1775–1865), lexicographer, was born at Tulse Hill, Norwood, London, in July 1775 and studied law, but left it early for scholastic and literary pursuits. He kept a well-known school on Clapham Common from about 1800 to 1827, and among his pupils there were Charles James Mathews, who assisted Richardson as a copyist, John Mitchell Kemble, and John Maddison Morton, the dramatist. Mathews says:

> He was fond of horse exercise, and I was allowed a pony, and at five o'clock on summer's mornings we used to sally forth together over the Surrey hills. … Among the many obligations I owe to Dr. Richardson, one of the deepest is that of first having my eyes opened by him to the real enjoyment of the ancient classics. (Dickens, 1.25, 27)

On 23 May 1835 Richardson married Elizabeth Wemyss

*Nasmyth (1793–1862) [see under Nasmyth family], daughter of Alexander *Nasmyth (1758–1840), landscape painter, and widow of Daniel *Terry (1789–1829), the actor, whose son was at his school. Richardson later bequeathed his house at Tulse Hill to her daughter, Jane.

Richardson was an ardent philologist of the school of Horne Tooke, 'whose extraordinary assumption that the etymology of all words could be traced back to a few simple roots … held back the subsequent comparative study of etymology in Britain for several decades' (Hausmann and others). In 1815 he published *Illustrations to English Philology*, consisting of a critical examination of Samuel Johnson's *Dictionary*, and a reply to Dugald Stewart's criticism of Horne Tooke's *Diversions of Purley*. The book was reissued in 1826. In 1818 the opening portions of an English lexicon, by Richardson, appeared in the *Encyclopaedia metropolitana*. In 1834 he issued the prospectus of a *New English Dictionary*, and the work itself was published by Pickering in parts between January 1835 and the spring of 1837. The dictionary is a republication of the lexicon, with improvements and additions. Richardson's avowed aim was to arrive at the original and proper meaning which was inherent in a word from its etymology. He was severely criticized by Daniel Webster in his *Mistakes and Corrections* (1837), especially for his ignorance of oriental languages. The spelling was antiquated; the etymologies frequently wrong; sounds were not distinguished by signs; the wrong word often headed the lemma. Nevertheless, the work was generally approved, especially by *The Quarterly*, *The Spectator*, and the *Gentleman's Magazine*. An abridged edition, without the quotations, appeared in 1839, with a new preface, but uncorrected. In fact Richardson's work had much value, and made notable advances in lexicography. In quotations from authors the dictionary was far more copious than Johnson, or any previous work of its class in English. Its citations go back to the fourteenth century, and point the way to the *Oxford English Dictionary*. In addition to the above works, Richardson published *On the Study of Language: an Exposition of the 'Diversions of Purley'* (1854), and he contributed several papers to the *Gentleman's Magazine*.

Richardson gave up his school after 1827, and moved to Lower Tulse Hill, Norwood. Before 1859 he moved to 23 Torrington Square, Bloomsbury. In 1852 a pension of £75 p.a. was granted to him from the civil list and in 1856 another of £25. He died at Feltham, Middlesex, on Friday 6 October 1865, and was buried in his mother's grave at Clapham. Chantrey's bust of Horne Tooke at University College, London, was bequeathed by him.

E. C. MARCHANT, rev. JOHN D. HAIGH

Sources *N&Q*, 8th ser., 5 (1894), 144 • *GM*, 3rd ser., 19 (1865), 796 • *The life of Charles James Mathews*, ed. C. Dickens, 2 vols. (1879), 1.25, 29 • Richardson's will [*DNB*] • *QR*, 51 (1834), 172 • H. B. Wheatley, *Transactions of the Philological Society* (1865), 276–7 • C. Richardson, 'Preliminary essay', *A new dictionary of the English language*, 1 (1836), 1–36 • F. J. Hausmann and others, eds., *Wörterbücher: ein internationales Handbuch zur Lexikographie / Dictionaries: an international encyclopedia of lexicography*, 2 (Berlin, 1989), 1956–7 • Allibone, *Dict.* • J. Green, *Chasing the sun: dictionary-makers and the dictionaries they made* (1996), 292–3 • S. I. Landau, *Dictionaries: the art and craft of lexicography* (1984), 66 • Boase, *Mod. Eng. biog.*, 3.143–4 • *The Times* (12 Oct 1865) • *CGPLA Eng. & Wales* (1865)
Wealth at death under £1500: probate, 23 Nov 1865, *CGPLA Eng. & Wales*

Richardson, Charles (1814–1896), civil engineer, was born at Capenhurst Hall near Chester on 14 August 1814, the third son of Richard Richardson JP, a deputy lieutenant for Cheshire, who died when Charles was six years old, and his wife, Dorothea. He was educated privately in England and France, and then at Edinburgh University which he left in 1833. From his earliest years he showed exceptional ability in mechanics and a natural talent for engineering, which his mother in particular did much to foster.

At the age of nineteen Richardson was apprenticed to Isambard K. Brunel who employed him on the Box and Sapperton tunnels and on other sections of the Great Western Railway. In 1858 he was appointed resident engineer under Brunel of the Bristol and South Wales Union Railway, which was to involve a ferry crossing of the River Severn. After the death of Brunel in 1859 he was promoted engineer-in-chief, and it was while working on the ferry piers in 1862–3 that the idea of the Severn railway tunnel came into his mind. Although the plan was at first rejected on the grounds of cost, eventually in 1872 the Severn Tunnel Bill was passed by parliament and construction began the following year. In October 1879 the headings from the English and Welsh sides were only 138 yards apart when a great inrush of water occurred, and the work was brought to a standstill. At this stage Richardson was replaced as engineer-in-chief by John Hawkshaw, and the former's role was much diminished. It was the end of 1881 before the most strenuous efforts of the engineers, contractors, and divers enabled the tunnel to be pumped dry and work to continue. At the end of 1886 the tunnel was opened to passenger and goods traffic; it was more than 4 miles long and its construction occupied almost fourteen years, at a cost of more than £2 million. Much credit is due to Richardson for the conception of the scheme. He developed a system for successfully aligning the two headings with unparalleled accuracy, and on occasion his advice was ignored when it might better have been followed.

Richardson was the inventor of the cane-spliced cricket bat and a catapult for bowling which was successfully used for many years. He was elected a member of the Institution of Civil Engineers in 1875. In his later years he wrote three papers on the Severn tunnel, one on arches, and one on the disposal of sewage. He died at his home, 10 Berkeley Square, Bristol, on 10 February 1896, survived by his wife, Mary Frances, and two sons.

RONALD M. BIRSE, rev. MIKE CHRIMES

Sources *PICE*, 124 (1895–6), 417–19 • T. A. Walker, *The Severn tunnel: its construction and difficulties, 1872–1887*, 3rd edn (1891) • *Engineering*, 61 (1896), 219 • A. W. Metcalfe and F. Richardson, unpublished memoir, Oxford University Press, Oxford DNB archives • *CGPLA Eng. & Wales* (1896)
Archives Inst. CE, Thames Tunnel MSS • PRO, railway records
Likenesses W. R. Gibbs, engraving (after photograph by Maull & Fox), repro. in Walker, *Severn tunnel*, 12

Wealth at death £25,832 6s. 7d.: resworn probate, Sept 1896, *CGPLA Eng. & Wales*

Richardson, Charles James (1806–1871), architect and art collector, was born in London. Of his parents, nothing is known. He was a pupil of Sir John Soane from 1824 to 1830 and was then his assistant until Soane's death in 1837. He tried unsuccessfully to establish his own academy of architecture; from 1845 to 1852 he was master of the architectural class at the School of Design at Somerset House. He married a Miss Cuttin, with whom he had one daughter.

In 1851 Richardson became surveyor to the fifth earl of Harrington, whose house at 13 Kensington Palace Gardens he designed. This was a curious semi-Tudor mansion which was praised by Harrington for its comfort and convenience. He helped design the houses on the earl's South Kensington estate, principally in Queen's Gate, and the entrance lodge from the estate into Hyde Park. Subsequently he worked for other landowners in the same area. Elsewhere in London he designed houses in Belsize Park, and he also had clients abroad in Denmark, Sweden, and Austria.

Richardson is chiefly remembered as a pioneer of the Victorian appreciation of Tudor and Elizabethan architecture and as an architectural draughtsman and collector of architectural drawings. He toured England (on at least one occasion in the company of John Britton) sketching historic buildings and from these tours, and his studies of historic architectural drawings, he compiled three of his most famous books: *Observations on the Architecture of England during the Reigns of Queen Elizabeth and James I* (1837), *Architectural Remains of the Reigns of Elizabeth and James I* (1840), and *Studies from Old English Mansions* (4 vols., 1841). His enthusiasm for the picturesque qualities of Tudor architecture characterizes his *Picturesque Designs for Mansions, Villas, Lodges, etc.* (1870), which subsequently went through at least four later editions under the title *The Englishman's House*. He also wrote about the services in domestic buildings, for instance in *A Popular Treatise on the Warming and Ventilating of Buildings* (1837), and worked as an architectural draughtsman for the *Art Journal*.

Richardson's historical interests led him to amass a large collection of architectural drawings and copies of drawings by others. It has been established that many of these were removed by him from the collection of Sir John Soane before the latter's death, including original drawings by Robert Adam, Sir William Chambers, and Soane himself. The best interpretation that can be put on this is that Richardson allowed his antiquarian enthusiasm for English architecture to get the better of him (Rowan, 22–3). He sold two substantial groups of drawings to the Victoria and Albert Museum in 1863–4. He also presented drawings by himself to the Royal Institute of British Architects and to the Soane Museum. Richardson lived for most of his professional life in the area of South Kensington where his work was concentrated. He died in 1871 in reduced circumstances.

CAMPBELL DODGSON, *rev.* ROBERT THORNE

Sources [W. Papworth], ed., *The dictionary of architecture*, 11 vols. (1853–92) • F. H. W. Sheppard, ed., *Northern Kensington*, Survey of London, 37 (1973) • F. H. W. Sheppard, ed., *The Grosvenor estate in Mayfair*, 1: *General history*, Survey of London, 39 (1977) • *The museums area of South Kensington and Westminster*, Survey of London, 38 (1975) • P. de la Ruffinière du Prey, *Sir John Soane* (1985) • A. Rowan, *Robert Adam* (1988) • M. Girouard, 'Attitudes to Elizabethan architecture, 1600–1900', *Concerning architecture*, ed. J. Summerson (1968), 13–27 • Mallalieu, *Watercolour artists* • census returns • *The Post Office directory* [annuals]

Archives RIBA BAL, architectural sketchbook and drawings • Sir John Soane's Museum, London, sketchbook and drawings

Richardson, Sir Charles Leslie (1908–1994), army officer, was born on 11 August 1908 in Guernsey, the only son and elder child of Lieutenant-Colonel Charles William Richardson (d. 1928), of Springfield, Lurgan, co. Down, Royal Artillery officer, and his wife, Eveline Adah, daughter of Richard Paul Wingrove, merchant. 'My mother is English,' he once remarked, 'for which I have always been grateful, for a little of the Irish temperament goes a long way' (Richardson, 15). He was educated at Wellington College, where he was a scholar, and the Royal Military Academy, Woolwich, where he passed out first and was awarded the king's medal. He was commissioned into the Royal Engineers in 1928 and then went to Clare College, Cambridge, as an exhibitioner. He graduated with first-class honours in mechanical engineering. Having lived in French Switzerland for two years as a boy, he was bilingual. After graduating from Cambridge he was posted to India to join the Royal Bombay sappers and miners, first in Mhow and then in Rajputana, where he enjoyed pigsticking, shooting sandgrouse, and riding; though when he first took up pigsticking, he said, he found himself 'too frequently galloping, spear aloft, into a thorn tree' (ibid., 33). Later he served at Quetta, Chitral, and Kohat, latterly as brigade-major on frontier operations. He recalled that soldiering was entirely on horseback, with primitive engineering equipment and no radios. Stores ordered five months in advance had to be carried some 60 miles over a 10,000 foot ridge.

Richardson returned to England in 1938, and in 1939 he was sent to France as adjutant of 1 corps engineer troops, whose task was to build pillboxes along the northern extension of the Maginot line. Later that year he was posted back to England to take the staff college course at Camberley. However, in May 1940 he returned to France to demolish bridges, lay minefields, and strengthen potentially defensible positions. In ten days he had a total of 24 hours sleep and, after being evacuated to England via Dunkirk, he slept for 36 hours. He was then assigned to defend 100 miles of English coastline with fifteen French 75 mm guns, each with only ten rounds, and twelve boxes of small arms ammunition. His next posting was to the Haifa Staff College for a nine months' tour as an instructor. From there he went on to become GSO1 (operations) with Special Operations Executive (SOE). 'I am surrounded by mountebanks,' he wrote, 'but there are no dull moments' (Richardson, 84). His charges had conflicting aims: MI6 wished to gather intelligence without attracting attention, while SOE wished to celebrate its triumphs with as much publicity as possible. The long range desert group conducted deep reconnaissance behind the German lines as unobtrusively as possible, while the SAS wished to destroy any enemy material it could reach. In the Balkans the SOE controllers were jealous of each other and were reluctant to disclose information. The Royal Navy was helpful but the RAF less so, and when Richardson complained to the air vice-marshal, Sir Philip Wigglesworth, the latter tried (in vain) to have him sacked 'for truculence'.

In 1942 Richardson was appointed GSO1 (plans) at the Eighth Army, then under the command of General Auchinleck. He survived Auchinleck's dismissal by Churchill and was employed by Montgomery to help prepare the Alamein deception plans. These involved bogus dumps, vehicles, tanks, and even a pipeline, and led Rommel to believe the next British attack would be in the south. Richardson continued as GSO1 (plans) through the remainder of the north African campaign. From there he went on to Sicily, where he was appointed brigadier, general staff, and then British deputy chief of staff in the United States Fifth Army, commanded by General Mark Clark. He landed at Salerno, had several narrow escapes from death, and stayed with the Americans until Cassino. He was then recalled to Montgomery to be brigadier general staff (plans) for the D-day landings and subsequent operations in Europe. He was present at the German surrender and also spent two days at the Nuremberg trials. In 1945 he was appointed chief of the military division of the Allied Control Commission, from which he went on to command an engineer regiment in the British army on the Rhine. On 10 May 1947 he married Audrey Elizabeth Styles (b. 1915/16), widow of Wing Commander Hugh Mortimer Styles, air force officer, and daughter of Captain Conrad Reginald Eric Jorgensen, army officer. They had a son and a daughter, and Richardson became stepfather to his wife's daughter by her previous marriage.

In 1953 Richardson was appointed to command the infantry brigade of 6th armoured division. He then became commandant of the Royal Military College of Science for three years, from 1955 to 1958. He found that commanding professors was a 'daunting but enlightening experience' (Richardson, 212). From 1958 to 1960 he was general officer commanding, Singapore district, from where he went on to become director of combat development at the War Office. Then followed appointments as director of military training (1961–3), and general officer commanding, northern command (1963–5). In 1965 he became a member of the army board, first as quartermaster-general to the forces (1965–8), then as master-general of the ordnance (1968–71). In the former position he was closely involved with the logistical arrangements for the army's withdrawal from east of Suez, and in the latter he was responsible for the initial stages of development of a wide range of new weapons systems. He was aide de camp (general) to the queen (1967–70), chief royal engineer (1972–7), and colonel commandant of the Royal Army Ordnance Corps (1967–71); he was awarded a DSO in 1943, and appointed CBE in 1945, CB in 1957, KCB in 1962, and GCB in 1967.

After retiring from the army Richardson (who lived in Betchworth, Surrey) became a consultant to International Computers Ltd (1971–6), treasurer of the Kitchener National Memorial Fund (1971–81), and chairman of the Gordon Boys' School (1977–87). He wrote three books: *Flashback* (1985), an autobiography; *Send for Freddie* (1987), a biography of General Sir Francis de Guingand; and *From Churchill's Secret Circle to the B.B.C.* (1991), a biography of Sir Ian Jacob. A brilliant intellect, clarity of mind in confusing situations, and an ability to get things done, were tempered by a lively sense of humour. He died at the East Surrey Hospital, Redhill, on 7 February 1994, following a heart attack. He was survived by his wife, son, daughter, and stepdaughter. A memorial service was held in the chapel of the Royal Hospital, Chelsea, on 27 April 1994.

PHILIP WARNER

Sources C. Richardson, *Flashback: a soldier's story* (1985) · Royal Engineers Library, Brompton Barracks, Chatham, Kent, archives of the Royal Engineers · *The Times* (8 Feb 1994) · *The Times* (28 April 1994) · *Daily Telegraph* (11 Feb 1994) · *WWW*, 1991–5 · Burke, *Peerage* · private information (2004) · m. cert. · d. cert.
Likenesses photograph, repro. in *The Times* (8 Feb 1994) · photograph, repro. in *Daily Telegraph* · photographs, repro. in Richardson, *Flashback*

Richardson [*née* Smith], **Charlotte** (1775–1825), poet, was born in York on 5 March 1775. Her 'uncommon quickness, docility, and great desire of information' were noticed at Sunday school, and when she was twelve years old a place was found for her at the Grey Coat School, a charitable establishment that prepared girls to be domestic servants, training them in practical skills and teaching them to read the Bible and to do simple accounting. She left school for work four years later, and after a succession of jobs that left her insufficient leisure either to attend church or to read, was taken on as a cook-maid for £4 per annum by a widow who was sympathetic to her religious and literary inclinations and who had a small collection of books. Charlotte's mother, the one parent she had known, died in 1790, and her only brother, who was disabled, died in a poorhouse a few years later, leaving her alone in the world. In 1802 she married R. Richardson, a shoemaker, and gave up her employment. When he died of consumption in 1804, she found herself destitute and ill, with a sickly infant to support.

Charlotte Richardson's plight came to the attention of the York educational reformer Catherine Cappe, who had been closely involved with the Grey Coat School and whose brother had attended the Richardson family as a physician. Impressed by Richardson's verse as well as by her worthy character, Cappe arranged to have a volume of it published by subscription, contacting publishers and appealing for subscribers through the leading literary periodicals. The *Gentleman's Magazine* published her account of Richardson's circumstances and two sample poems. *Poems on Different Occasions* appeared in 1806, with a biographical memorial as an introduction and a subscription list of 620, some of the subscribers contributing more than the 5*s*. cost of the book and a number purchasing extra copies. This substantial response led to a second edition in 1806. Richardson briefly kept a school with some success, but ill health prevented her from persisting with it. Mrs Cappe once again arranged for a subscription publication, this time of *Poems Chiefly Composed during the Pressure of Severe Illness*, which appeared in 1809 as a second volume uniform with the first. 617 subscribers responded. A third edition of the first volume was advertised but apparently did not appear (an edition had also appeared in Philadelphia in 1806).

Richardson belongs to the group of Romantic poets to whom Southey applied the term 'uneducated'. They were valued by critics for their ingenuous spontaneity and by reformers for their uncomplaining struggle against social disadvantages. Richardson's verses were competent and sincere. Along with poems about domestic life and about the comforts of religion she offers thoughts on current topics such as the slave trade and the fears of French invasion, and she responds with discernment to the writings of Thomas Clarkson and Walter Scott. A resident of Acomb, Yorkshire, she died there, after a long illness, on 26 September 1825.   J. R. DE J. JACKSON

Sources DNB · C. Cappe, preface, in C. Richardson, *Poems written on different occasions* (1806), v–xxii · C. Richardson, *Poems chiefly composed during the pressure of severe illness* (1809) · GM, 1st ser., 75 (1805), 813, 846 · GM, 1st ser., 78 (1808), 697 · *Yorkshire Gazette* (1 Oct 1825)

Richardson, Charlotte Caroline (1796–1854), poet and novelist, was born on 15 May 1796 in Lambeth, London, the youngest of the three daughters of Robert Richardson (d. 1804), clerk, and Elizabeth Smales (c.1759–1841). When Charlotte's father died in 1804, her mother opened a boarding-school in Vauxhall, in order to combine a source of income with supervision of the education of her older daughters, but she sent the youngest to live with an aunt in Hinderwell, Yorkshire. What had begun as a temporary measure was prolonged for more than ten years, apparently contrary to the wishes of both mother and daughter.

Charlotte Richardson's parents had become acquainted through the pages of the *Ladies' Diary*, an almanac that featured verse enigmas, charades, and rebuses, along with prose mathematical puzzles, and offered prizes for verse answers. The mode of question and reply fostered a degree of courtly flirtation between the various contributors, and Robert Richardson, who had been contributing since the 1780s, was so taken with the contributions of Miss Smales that he tracked her down and after a short correspondence they were married. Charlotte Caroline in turn seems to have regained contact with her mother by publishing a poem in the *Ladies' Diary* in 1815, identifying herself as the youngest daughter of Mrs Richardson, 'formerly Betty Smales'. Mrs Richardson, who was familiar to readers by both names, replied in a poem the following year, greeting her 'long-lost child', and in the meantime arrangements were made for Charlotte to visit her family in London. The two generations of Richardsons were steady contributors to the *Ladies' Diary* (and its successor the *Lady's and Gentleman's Diary*) for over seventy years, Charlotte's sisters Elizabeth Anne (later Mrs Baker) and

Eleanor (later Mrs Long) playing their part, and in 1846 Charlotte and Elizabeth Anne edited a volume of their mother's *Poems*, drawn from her contributions, and provided a memoir of her life.

Charlotte, however, was the most successful writer in the family. Her brief volume *Waterloo, a Poem on the Late Victory* (1817) and her book of verse for children, *Isaac and Rebecca*, of the same year, were followed by the more ambitious *Harvest, a Poem, in Two Parts: with other Poetical Pieces* (1818), which was dedicated to the mathematician Charles Hutton, editor of the *Ladies' Diary*. Charlotte's last substantial work was a complicated 'legendary tale', *Ludolph, or, The Light of Nature, a Poem* (1823). Her sentimental-gothic novel, *The Soldier's Child, or, Virtue Triumphant* (1823) was not well received, but it contains a minor character called Clara Roberts whose childhood closely parallels Charlotte's and may reflect her feelings about having been separated from her family. Charlotte continued to write for the *Ladies' Diary* until the year of her death, and contributed occasional verse to other periodicals such as *Pawsey's Ladies Fashionable Repository*.

On 5 November 1827 Charlotte married John Richardson, a wharfinger; they do not seem to have had any children. Thereafter she styled herself variously Mrs Charlotte Caroline Richardson, Mrs C. C. Richardson, and, after her mother's death in 1841, Mrs Richardson of Vauxhall. As a consequence she has been regularly confused in library catalogues and elsewhere with her mother and with Mrs Charlotte Richardson of York and Mrs C. E. Richardson of Dumfries. She died after an attack of paralysis on 29 March 1854 at her home, 25 Vauxhall Street, Vauxhall, Surrey.   J. R. DE J. JACKSON

Sources *Ladies' Diary* · *Lady's and Gentleman's Diary* (–1855) · d. cert. · E. Richardson, *Poems* (1846) [incl. memoir of Elizabeth Smales and family] · E. Baker, *The fruits of the spirit* (1847) · *Pawsey's Ladies Fashionable Repository* (–1855)

Richardson, Christopher (bap. 1619, d. 1698), clergyman and ejected minister, the son of Thomas Richardson of Sheriff Hutton, Yorkshire, and Frances, his wife, was baptized at St Mary Bishophill Junior, York, on 17 January 1619. He was educated at Trinity College, Cambridge, where he matriculated as a sizar in 1633; he graduated BA in 1637 and MA in 1640. In 1646 he obtained the sequestered rectory of Kirkheaton, near Huddersfield, Yorkshire, which he held until removed under the Act of Uniformity in 1662. In 1661 he bought Lascelles Hall and he continued to preach there after his ejection, using the staircase as a pulpit 'so as to enable him to escape in case constables should come in to apprehend him for holding a conventicle'. He was an intimate friend of Oliver Heywood, in whose diaries are to be found frequent mention of visits to Lascelles Hall for religious exercises. He was chaplain to William Cotton of Denbigh Grange, Penistone, and was licensed as a presbyterian at Cotton's house on 8 May 1672, with Lascelles Hall also being licensed as a meeting-place. He also preached in Sheffield and at Norton, Derbyshire.

Sons Richardson had with his first wife, Elizabeth (d. 1668), were educated with Oliver Heywood's sons, first at Henry Hickman's academy, Bromsgrove, Worcestershire, in 1673, then with Richard Frankland at Natland, Westmorland, commencing in 1674. Heywood was in some doubt as to the suitability of Richardson's sons as companions for his sons and made the mistake of confiding this to Frankland, whom he suspected of passing on his doubts to Richardson. Heywood detected a cooling of their relationship in 1674 but it was not enough to destroy the friendship. On 12 September 1676 Heywood records that he and 'Mr. Richardson' met Christopher Richardson and 'my two sons' at Marton Scar near Horton in Craven, Yorkshire (Turner, 3.174). Heywood and Richardson were there to see their sons off to university in Edinburgh. Christopher Richardson junior and John and Eliezer Heywood all graduated MA together at Edinburgh in 1677. John Heywood and 'Christopher Richardson, my sons companion', were present at the first nonconformist ordination in Yorkshire that was held at Pasture House near Horton in Craven on 8 July 1678, with Oliver Heywood and Richard Frankland presiding (ibid., 2.194–7).

On 23 January 1682 Richardson married again; his second wife was Hephzibah (1655–1735), daughter of Edward Prime, the ejected curate of Sheffield. The following year Christopher Richardson gave his son the Lascelles Hall estate, where Christopher junior lived until his death in August 1721.

Having settled his earthly affairs, Richardson set about the work of God. According to Calamy, in 1687 Richardson, at almost seventy years of age, left Lascelles Hall and began a ministry in Liverpool. He took advantage of James II's declaration of liberty of conscience and conducted worship in a building in Castle Hey. Tradition has it that his services were fortnightly, and that he preached alternately at Toxteth Park Chapel outside the town. Evidence from the 1660s suggests that Toxteth Park Chapel, founded about 1618 by Richard Mather, was shared by two congregations, possibly representing Independents and presbyterians; and it may be that as a presbyterian Richardson alternated with Samuel Angier, who may have had Independent leanings. Richardson may have been responding to a call from the dissenters resident in Liverpool, keen to establish a congregation at the inception of a measure of toleration. Tradition certainly asserts that it was Richardson who was the 'founder' of nonconformity in the parish of Liverpool. However, when the Toleration Act of 1689 allowed the dissenters a presence in the town, it was Samuel Angier who registered 'the new chapel in Castle Hey' at the Preston quarter sessions on 22 July 1689. The first evidence to place Richardson in Liverpool is the Common Fund survey of 1690–92, which states that he had 400 hearers, with £75 split at Toxteth Park between him and Angier, who is also described as 'assistant to Mr Richardson in Liverpoole' (Gordon, *Freedom after Ejection*). Clearly Richardson was the nucleus of the urban congregation in Liverpool parish in the late 1680s. He may have shared his pulpit with Angier but despite Calamy's assertion that 'He had a healthful constitution, which continued till old age' (Calamy, *Abridgement*, 2.795) it was Angier who was left with the bulk of the administrative duties, registering the meeting-house and attending the

provincial meeting of United Brethren between 1693 and 1700.

Richardson died in November or December 1698 and was buried in the graveyard of St Nicholas's, Liverpool, on 5 December 1698. Oliver Heywood began a life of his old friend in October 1699 (from which Edmund Calamy derived his account) but never finished it. In 1884 a tablet to Richardson's memory was erected in Kirkheaton church by his descendants. His widow remarried in July 1722, her second husband being Robert Ferne (d. 1727), the nonconformist minister of Wirksworth, Derbyshire.

JONATHAN H. WESTAWAY

Sources W. R. Richardson, 'Some account of the probable ancestry of the Rev. Christopher Richardson, M.A., Trin. Coll. Camb., of Lascelles Hall, and rector of Kirkheaton, Yorks., 1646–1661', *Northern Genealogist* (1896), 1.9–12 [with pedigree] · A. Holt, *Walking together: a study in Liverpool nonconformity, 1688–1938* (1938), 35–42 · *Calamy rev.*, 410 · E. Calamy, ed., *An abridgement of Mr. Baxter's history of his life and times, with an account of the ministers, &c., who were ejected after the Restauration of King Charles II*, 2nd edn, 2 vols. (1713), vol. 2, p. 795 [the account of Richardson is 'derived from Oliver Heywood, who began a life of Richardson on 2 Oct 1699'] · *The Rev. Oliver Heywood … his autobiography, diaries, anecdote and event books*, ed. J. H. Turner, 1 (1881), 230, 232, 234, 243, 256, 260, 288, 293–5, 296, 298, 334, 350; 2 (1883), 9, 38, 45, 64, 65, 66, 71, 95, 197; 3 (1884), 69, 119–21, 123, 138, 161, 174; 4 (1885), 85, 132, 184 · A. Gordon, ed., *Freedom after ejection: a review (1690–1692) of presbyterian and congregational nonconformity in England and Wales* (1917), 58–9, 245–6 · *DNB* · F. Nicholson and E. Axon, *The older nonconformity in Kendal* (1915), 540 · B. Nightingale, *Lancashire nonconformity*, 6 vols. [1890–93], vol. 6, pp. 83–90, 110–12 · Alexander Gordon to Lawrence Hall, 1919, JRL, Unitarian College collection, B143 [possibly a draft letter from Hall to Gordon] · T. Whitehead, *History of the dales congregational churches* (1930), 114–18 · B. Dale, *Yorkshire puritanism and early nonconformity*, ed. T. G. Crippen [n.d., c.1909], 121–2, 264 · H. Peet, ed., *The earliest registers of the parish of Liverpool (St. Nicholas's Church) christenings, marriages and burials, 1660–1704, with some of the earlier episcopal transcripts commencing in 1604*, Lancashire Parish Register Society (1909), 195 · D. Thom, 'Liverpool churches and chapels; their destruction, removal, or alteration: with notices of clergymen, ministers, and others [pt 2]', *Proceedings and Papers of the Historic Society of Lancashire and Cheshire*, 5 (1852–3), 3–56 · J. H. Turner, T. Dickenson, and O. Heywood, eds., *The nonconformist register of baptisms, marriages, and deaths* (1881), 45, 114, 217, 297 · J. Walker, *An attempt towards recovering an account of the numbers and sufferings of the clergy of the Church of England*, pt 2 (1714), 374 · J. Westaway, 'Scottish influences upon the reformed churches in north west England, c.1689–1829: a study of the ministry within the congregational and presbyterian churches in Lancashire, Cumberland and Westmorland', PhD diss., University of Lancaster, 1997

Likenesses double portraits (with Hephzibah Richardson), repro. in Nightingale, *Lancashire nonconformity*, vol. 6, pp. 86, 88

Richardson, David Lester (*bap.* 1801, *d.* 1865), poet and writer, was baptized on 15 February 1801 at St Marylebone, Middlesex, the son of David Thomas Richardson, a lieutenant-colonel of the East India Company's Bengal army, and his wife, Sarah, *née* Lester. He became a cadet in the Bengal army, and went to India in 1819, where he contributed poetry to the *Calcutta Journal* in 1820, and published *Miscellaneous Poems* (1822). In 1824 he returned to England for health reasons, and founded the *London Weekly Review*, which afterwards became *Colburn's Court Journal*. He also published another volume of poetry, *Sonnets and* *other Poems* (1825), which was reprinted as *Sonnets and Miscellaneous Poems Written in India*, in *Jones's Diamond Poets* (1827), and again in *Jones's Cabinet of the British Poets* (1837). The inflated nature of the notes to these reprints was criticized by John Wilson (Christopher North), who thought little of Richardson's work, referring to him as 'The Diamond Poet, who published three hunder and sixty-five panegyrics on his ain genius, by way of Notes and Illustrations to his Sonnets' (*Noctes Ambrosianae*, 60, December 1828).

In 1829 Richardson went back to military service in Calcutta. He was promoted captain in 1832, and retired on 19 July 1833 as a major, after being invalided out. He was soon given employment in the civil service. Initially he served on the staff of the governor-general, Lord William Bentinck, and in the education department at Calcutta. From 1830 to 1837 he acted as editor of the *Bengal Annual*, afterwards editing the *Calcutta Monthly Journal*, and from 1834 to 1849 the *Calcutta Literary Gazette*. In 1836 he became professor of English literature of the Hindu College at Calcutta, largely on Lord Macaulay's recommendation, and in 1839 he was promoted to the newly created post of principal of the college, while retaining his professorship. He continued to produce volumes of poetry at this time, publishing *Literary Leaves* in Calcutta in 1836, and reissuing it in London in an expanded second edition in 1840. *Selections from the British Poets, from the Time of Chaucer to the Present Day* … (1840) was published in Calcutta, compiled at the request of Macaulay. In 1845, the same year in which Richardson was appointed principal of Krishnagar College, he produced *The Anglo-Indian Passage*. In 1848 he was appointed principal to Hughli and Hindu College and published *Literary Chit-Chat, with Miscellaneous Poems*. His other Indian publications included *Literary Recreations* (1852) and *Flowers and Flower Gardens, with an Appendix … Respecting the Anglo-Indian Flower Garden* (1855).

Richardson finally left India in February 1861, and became proprietor and editor of the *Court Circular* and editor of *Allen's Indian Mail*. He died at Lambourne Road, Clapham, London, on 17 November 1865.

G. S. BOULGER, rev. REBECCA MILLS

Sources IGI · C. E. Buckland, *Dictionary of Indian biography* (1906), 356 · J. Britten and G. S. Boulger, eds., *A biographical index of British and Irish botanists* (1893), 142 · *GM*, 4th ser., 1 (1866), 147 · Allibone, *Dict.* · d. cert.

Wealth at death under £100: probate, 8 Dec 1865, *CGPLA Eng. & Wales*

Richardson, (Frederick) Denys (1913–1983), chemist and metallurgist, was born on 17 September 1913 in Streatham, London, the third son of a family of three sons and one daughter of Charles Willerton Richardson (*d.* 1916/17), managing director of Asquith and Lord, of Bombay, and his wife, Kate Harriet Bunker, a schoolteacher. Both Richardson's parents died while he was young, and from 1919 the family was raised by his maternal aunt, Omie, and her friend, a Mrs Parrot.

Richardson was educated at University School in Hastings, and at University College, London (of which he became a fellow in 1971), where he graduated in chemistry in 1932. Charles Goodeve, lecturer in chemistry, steered him to carrying out a PhD on the oxides of chlorine, which he completed in 1936.

In 1937–9 Richardson was a Commonwealth Fund fellow at Princeton, USA. Soon after the start of the Second World War he joined the Royal Naval Volunteer Reserve to help Goodeve counter the magnetic mine. This partnership found Richardson in the department of miscellaneous weapon development (DMWD) of the Admiralty, where he rose to be deputy director (1943–6) with the rank of commander RNVR. The work he carried out in DMWD was varied and extensive, embracing such topics as minesweeping, radar deception, anti-aircraft weapons, illuminating shells, artificial harbours, rockets, and anti-submarine techniques. He gathered about him a heterogeneous collection of scientists, engineers, and naval personnel, encouraging them to get on with urgent problems, often in the face of official scepticism. The work of DMWD is entertainingly outlined by Gerald Pawle in *The Secret War* (1956). While at the DMWD Richardson married, in 1942, Irene Mary Austin, a graduate engineer, daughter of George Edward Austin, a Lancashire textile manager. The couple had two sons.

After the war Richardson became head of the chemistry department of the British Iron and Steel Research Association under the leadership of Goodeve. He organized research into the physical chemistry of iron and steel making, applying the theories of chemical thermodynamics and kinetics to the high temperature processes hitherto governed by empirical methods. During the next six years his group received wide recognition.

In 1950 Richardson moved as Nuffield fellow to the metallurgy department of Imperial College, London; he remained there until his death, from 1957 until 1976 as professor of extraction metallurgy. He founded the Nuffield and John Percy research groups which made important contributions in the fields of physical chemistry and process engineering respectively, and during this period published about 125 substantial papers and a two-volume book, *The Physical Chemistry of Melts in Metallurgy* (1974).

Richardson travelled widely and delivered many prestigious lectures. Between 1956 and 1983 he received numerous honours and awards, among them the Sir George Beilby memorial award, the Bessemer gold medal, gold medals of the Institution of Mining and Metallurgy (of which he was president in 1975) and of the American Society of Metals, the Peter Tunner medal of the Verein Eisenhütte Österreich, grande medaille de la Société Française de la Métallurgie, Carl Lueg medal of the Verein Deutscher Eisenhüttenleute (1978), and Kelvin medal of the Institution of Civil Engineers (1983). He had honorary doctorates of the Technische Hochschule, Aachen (1971), and the University of Liège. He became FRS in 1968 and FEng in 1976.

Richardson's quickness of mind together with his slight build and spruce appearance marked him out in any discussion, and his ready wit and sense of timing made him a popular speaker at formal and informal occasions. He was a meticulous experimentalist and writer and his colleagues remembered wryly the formidable cross-examinations they underwent before their results were accepted. They also remember his generous support and loyalty. He was an accomplished water-colour landscape painter and an enthusiastic gardener. Richardson died on 8 September 1983 at St George's Hospital, Tooting, survived by his wife.   J. H. E. JEFFES, *rev.*

Sources J. H. E. Jeffes, *Memoirs FRS*, 31 (1985), 493–521 · F. D. Richardson, autobiographical notes · personal knowledge (1990) · private information (1990)
Likenesses G. Argent, black and white photograph, RS
Wealth at death £41,801: probate, 29 Nov 1983, *CGPLA Eng. & Wales*

Richardson [*married name* Odle], **Dorothy Miller** (1873–1957), novelist and journalist, was born on 17 May 1873 at Albert Park, Abingdon, Berkshire, the third of the four daughters of Charles Richardson (1836–1915), grocer and tradesman, of Abingdon, and his wife, Mary Miller (1843–1895), daughter of Edward Taylor, manufacturer, of East Coker, Somerset. She attended schools in Abingdon and in Worthing, Sussex, where the family settled in 1880. In 1883 the Richardsons moved to Putney, London. There Dorothy was educated first by a governess and then in the intellectually stimulating environment of Southborough House, which provided the only formal education she valued in retrospect.

Charles Richardson's aspirations to rise socially and live the life of an intellectual gentleman, combined with his unwise investments, led the family into bankruptcy. Dorothy thus had to start earning her own living when she was seventeen. In 1891 she taught at a finishing school in Hanover, Germany, for six months. After her return to England she taught at a school in Finsbury Park, Middlesex. She considered teaching to be an unduly confining experience and resigned her subsequent post as a governess in 1895 in order to look after her mother, who suffered from severe depression. Her parents, who had been forced to sell their house in London, had moved to Chiswick in 1893, and Mary Richardson's ordeal came to a tragic end when she committed suicide during a stay in Hastings with her daughter Dorothy in November 1895.

In 1896 Richardson moved to Bloomsbury and earned a meagre living as an assistant to a Harley Street dentist. In London she showed an interest in a wide range of political, feminist, philosophical, and religious avant-garde movements of her time. She was a close friend of H. G. *Wells (1866–1946), who, among others, encouraged her to write. She had a brief affair with him, became pregnant, miscarried, and subsequently suffered a breakdown in 1907. As a result of these events, she gave up her job, spent the following winter in Switzerland, and then lived on a farm in Sussex for several years. There she felt attracted to Quakerism, which became the topic of her first two books, *The Quakers Past and Present* (1914) and *Gleanings from the Works of George Fox* (1914). From 1907 she devoted

Dorothy Miller Richardson (1873–1957), by unknown photographer

herself to a journalistic career, publishing periodical articles on topics which ranged from literature and politics to dentistry, as well as reviews, sketches, short stories, and poems. She also engaged in translation work from German and French originals. In 1912 she began to write fiction while staying in Cornwall with friends. Twelve books of her best-known work, *Pilgrimage*, were published between 1915 and 1938; the first collected edition of all thirteen volumes of this novel, comprising *Pointed Roofs* (1915), *Backwater* (1916), *Honeycomb* (1917), *The Tunnel* (1919), *Interim* (1919), *Deadlock* (1921), *Revolving Lights* (1923), *The Trap* (1925), *Oberland* (1927), *Dawn's Left Hand* (1931), *Clear Horizon* (1935), *Dimple Hill* (1938), and *March Moonlight* (1967), appeared posthumously in 1967.

In *Pilgrimage* Richardson provided an impressionistic account of the experiences of the central character, Miriam Henderson, which are modelled on the author's own migratory life between 1891 and 1915. Her writing technique is experimental and has frequently been compared to James Joyce's and Virginia Woolf's style. Richardson believed that reality in the early twentieth century could no longer be captured by imposing a plot through conventional narrative devices. Instead she immersed herself in Miriam's multilayered consciousness and narrated everything through the mind of her heroine. In doing so she frequently sacrificed conventional form and selectivity, which she considered to be characteristics of male writing. She attempted to portray life as continually fluctuating, blurred, and opaque, as well as an open-ended and timeless experience without fixed meanings. What is more, she considered her technique to be a specifically female way of writing. In her foreword to the 1938 edition of *Pilgrimage* she pointed out that feminine prose should be 'unpunctuated, moving from point to point without formal obstructions', and Virginia Woolf claimed that Richardson had invented 'the psychological sentence of the feminine gender' (*TLS*). In a review of *Pointed Roofs*, which was published in *The Egoist* in April 1918, May Sinclair first applied the term 'stream of consciousness' to literature in her discussion of Richardson's stylistic innovations. Even though Richardson despised Sinclair's term, it is today closely associated with her writing.

On 29 August 1917 Richardson married the artist Alan Odle (1888–1948), son of Samuel Odle, a bank clerk. Her husband was fifteen years younger than she and had consumption, and she looked after him until his death in 1948. Between 1917 and 1939, when the Odles had to give up their rooms in Queen's Terrace, St John's Wood, the couple lived alternately in London and Cornwall. After 1939 they settled in Cornwall, and Richardson remained there after her husband's death. There were no children of the marriage.

In 1954 Dorothy Richardson moved to a nursing home at 131 Albemarle Road, Beckenham, Kent, where she died on 17 June 1957. In accordance with her wishes her body was donated to medicine, and over two years after her death was interred at the Streatham Park cemetery, London.

SUSANNE STARK

Sources G. G. Fromm, *Dorothy Richardson: a biography* (1977) · J. Rosenberg, *Dorothy Richardson: the genius they forgot* (1973) · G. E. Hanscombe, *The art of life: Dorothy Richardson and the development of feminist consciousness* (1982) · J. Radford, *Dorothy Richardson* (1991) · J. C. Powys, *Dorothy M. Richardson* (1931) · J. Todd, ed., *Dictionary of British women writers* (1989) · J. Shattock, *The Oxford guide to British women writers* (1993) · *The Times* (18 June 1957) · *Manchester Guardian* (18 June 1957) · M. Sinclair, 'The novels of Dorothy Richardson', *The Egoist* (April 1918), 57–9 · [V. Woolf], review of *The tunnel*, *TLS* (13 Feb 1919); repr. in V. Woolf, *Women and writing*, ed. M. Barrett (1979), 188–91 · [V. Woolf], review of *Revolving lights*, *TLS* (19 May 1923); repr. in V. Woolf, *Women and writing*, ed. M. Barrett (1979), 191–2 · b. cert. · *CGPLA Eng. & Wales* (1957)

Archives NRA, priv. coll., corresp. · NYPL, corresp. and literary papers · Ransom HRC, corresp. | BL, letters to E. B. C. Jones, Add. MS 53788 · BL, letters to S. S. Koteliansky, Add. MS 48972 · New York Historical Society, letters to P. P. Wadsworth · Princeton University, New Jersey, Sylvia Beach MSS · Ransom HRC, Edward Garnett MSS · Ransom HRC, Claude Houghton MSS · Ransom HRC, journals of and letters to Hugh Walpole · Ransom HRC, H. G. Wells MSS

Likenesses photograph, 1917, repro. in Fromm, *Dorothy Richardson*, p. 41 · double portrait, photograph, 1920–29 (with Alan Odle), repro. in Fromm, *Dorothy Richardson*, p. 203 · double portrait, photograph, 1930–34 (with Alan Odle), repro. in Rosenberg, *Dorothy Richardson*, p. 1 · A. Allinson, oils, 1936–7, repro. in Fromm, *Dorothy Richardson*, pp. 304–5 · photograph, Yale U., Beinecke L. [*see illus.*]

Wealth at death £9214 2s. 7d.: probate, 6 Nov 1957, *CGPLA Eng. & Wales*

Richardson, Edward M. (1812–1869), sculptor and archaeologist, was born in London; nothing is known of his parents or his early life. In 1832 he entered the Royal Academy Schools at the special recommendation of Francis Chantrey, though his first work had appeared at the academy in 1829—a restoration of the head of a figure from the Elgin marbles. He continued to send sculpture to the academy until 1866, at first mostly classical subjects and treatments, but then works in a variety of other genres and on many themes, ranging from equestrian statues such as *Study of a Horse* (1832) to mythological and literary works including *Mercury and Pandora* (1836) and *Master Puck* (1848), from Shakespeare.

Alongside his twenty-eight academy pieces, Richardson also exhibited more controversial work at the Society of British Artists in Suffolk Street, the British Institution, and at the Great Exhibition of 1851. In 1842 he was commissioned to restore the effigies of the knights templar in the Temple Church in London, but the effigies unfortunately suffered considerable damage prior to their restoration, having been left in a damp shed the previous winter. Although considerable restoration was consequently needed, his work was considered insensitive: he was refused admission to the Society of Antiquaries and was characterized by Augustus Hare as 'a charlatan' who had simply 'plane[d] down the effigies' (Gunnis, 320–21). Two years later Richardson was again under attack, his statue of the medieval poet John Gower for Westminster Hall at the houses of parliament causing the astonished art critic of the *Literary Gazette* to ask 'how a man could be audacious enough to send such an abortion ... to a competition' (cited in Gunnis, 320–21).

Despite the opprobrium raised by his work, Richardson was, however, increasingly respected as a sculptor and commentator, particularly in the field of ecclesiastical decoration and restoration. In 1844 he was chosen to restore the Arundel monument in Chichester Cathedral, and two years later that of Bishop Richard de Wyche in the same place, to which he added seven new statuettes. His reputation reached its peak in the 1850s, when he was commissioned to make or procure many of the casts of sepulchral effigies for the Crystal Palace, and when he was called in by the keepers of Wells Cathedral to repair the seated statue of the saxon king Edward the Elder on the west front, which had fallen from a height of 60 feet, narrowly missing the carriage of a judge who was luckily listening to the assize sermon inside the cathedral. Richardson also increasingly turned his hand to portrait busts and recumbent effigies, many in alabaster, of various Victorian civic dignitaries and members of the aristocracy, particularly in Madras and Chichester where his work was most popular. In the 1850s he also received many military commissions, including, in 1855, a marble relief of a light cavalry officer, again for Madras, and, in the wake of the Crimean War, many large-scale monuments to the officers and men of the North Lincolnshire regiment (1851), the Royal Welch Fusiliers (1859), the Duke of Cornwallis's light infantry, and the 51st regiment (both 1861).

Throughout his life Richardson combined his passion for sculpture with a love of archaeology, being an active member of the London and Middlesex Archaeological Society, publishing several papers in the *Archaeological Journal*, and lecturing on monumental effigies and tombs and ancient stone and leaden coffins. After some years of ill health he died of erysipelas on 17 May 1869 at 19 Egremont Place, Brighton, Sussex. Despite the controversy surrounding much of his work, Richardson's reputation survived well into the twentieth century, when he was still being characterized, by M. H. Grant, as one of the most 'notable sculptor[s] and archaeologist[s] of his day' (Grant).   CAMPBELL DODGSON, *rev.* JASON EDWARDS

Sources T. Cooper, ed., *The register, and magazine of biography, a record of births, marriages, deaths and other genealogical and personal occurrences*, 1 (1869), 486 · *GM*, 2nd ser., 27 (1847), 258 · *GM*, 2nd ser., 38 (1852), 66 · *GM*, 2nd ser., 40 (1853), 288 · *Archaeological Journal*, 7 (1850), 201 · *Archaeological Journal*, 10 (1853), 116 · *Archaeological Journal*, 12 (1855), 298 · *Graves, RA exhibitors* · M. H. Grant, *A dictionary of British sculptors from the XIIIth century to the XXth century* (1953), 203 · R. Gunnis, *Dictionary of British sculptors, 1660–1851* (1953), 320–21 · *The Builder*, 11 (1853), 560 · *CGPLA Eng. & Wales* (1869)

Wealth at death under £4000: probate, 14 June 1869, *CGPLA Eng. & Wales*

Richardson [*née* Beaumont; *other married name* Ashburnham], **Elizabeth**, *suo jure* baroness of Cramond (**1576/7–1651**), writer, was the eldest of the ten children of Sir Thomas *Beaumont (*d.* 1614) [*see under* Beaumont, Huntingdon] of Stoughton, Leicestershire, and St Botolph, Aldersgate, London, and his wife, Catherine (*d.* 1621), daughter and heir of Sir Thomas Farnham of Stoughton and his wife, Helen. On 27 November 1594 she married, as her first husband, John Ashburnham (*c*.1571–1620) of Ashburnham, Sussex, who was knighted in 1604. They had ten children, six of whom lived to adulthood, including John (1603–1671) and William (*d.* 1679). Elizabeth's husband's death on 29 June 1620 left the family in financial straits, but his widow was able to exercise considerable influence at court since Mary, countess of Buckingham, mother of the favourite, was a cousin. Elizabeth's attempts to gain advancement for her son-in-law Sir Edward Dering ended eventually in a baronetcy on 1 February 1627. A letter to the duke of Buckingham of the same year indicates that she enjoyed the society of his wife, of Lady Carlisle, and of the queen (*CSP dom.*, 1627–8, 326); in 1627 she also waited on the queen of Bohemia in The Hague.

On 14 December 1626 Elizabeth married, as his second wife, Sir Thomas *Richardson (*bap.* 1569, *d.* 1635), later lord chief justice, and through his influence was created baroness of Cramond on 29 February 1628, an occurrence which apparently elicited 'many gibes and pasquinades … for the amusement of Westminster Hall' (Campbell, 2.15). On 9 September 1629 she was granted an annual pension of £300 for the duration of her life. In 1645 her collection of prayers, *A Ladies Legacie to her Daughters*, was printed. The text was in three parts; the first had been written in 1625 and the second in 1635. Richardson gave a manuscript copy of her prayers to her eldest daughter, Elizabeth Cornwallis, in 1635 (E. Sussex RO, ASH 3501), but a Folger Shakespeare Library manuscript (MS V.a.511), headed 'Instructions for my children or any other Christian', is dated 1606, indicating that she began her writing of mother's advice many years earlier. She died, in her seventy-fifth year, at Covent Garden, London, and was buried next to her first husband on 3 April 1651 at St Andrew's, Holborn.   VICTORIA E. BURKE

Sources GEC, *Peerage*, new edn, vol. 3 · *Collins peerage of England: genealogical, biographical and historical*, ed. E. Brydges, 9 vols. (1812) · J. Nichols, *The history and antiquities of the county of Leicester*, 4 vols. (1795–1815); facs. edn (1971) · J. Bruce, preface, *Proceedings, principally in the county of Kent, in connection with the parliaments called in*

1640, *and especially with the committee of religion appointed in that year*, ed. L. B. Larking, CS, old ser., 80 (1862) · patent rolls, 1629, PRO, C 66/2497–66/2532 [5 Charles 1] [Richardson's annual pension of £300] · *CSP dom.*, 1625–8 · *APC*, 1627 –8 · chancery, privy seals, 1627, PRO [baronetcy for son-in-law Sir Edward Dering which Richardson helped secure] · F. W. Steer, *The Ashburnham archives: a catalogue* (1958) · W. Camden, *The visitation of the county of Leicester in the year 1619*, ed. J. Fetherston, Harleian Society, 2 (1870) · W. B. Bannerman, ed., *The visitations of the county of Sussex … 1530 … and 1633–4*, Harleian Society, 53 (1905) · W. A. Shaw, *The knights of England*, 2 vols. (1906) · John, Lord Campbell, *The lives of the chief justices of England*, 3rd edn, 4 vols. (1874) · E. Richardson, *A ladies legacie to her daughters* (1645) · monument, parish church, Ashburnham, Sussex · monument, St Botolph, Aldersgate, London [Thomas and Catherine Beaumont] · will, PRO, PROB 11/216/63, fol. 78*v* · parish register, St Andrew's, Holborn, London [death, burial] · parish register, Stoughton, 27 Nov 1594 [marriage]

Archives E. Sussex RO, papers · Folger, papers

Wealth at death bequests of £730; plus two bequests for children of £20 p.a. from lease of lands 'in or neere' Lambeth for 14 years; £300 funeral expenses; smaller bequests to the poor: will, proved 7 April 1651, PRO, PROB 11/216/63, fol. 78*v*

Richardson [*married name* Robertson], **Ethel Florence Lindesay** [*pseud.* Henry Handel Richardson] (**1870–1946**), novelist, was born on 3 January 1870 at 1 Blanche Terrace, Fitzroy, Melbourne, Australia. She was the elder daughter of Walter Lindesay Richardson (1825–1879) and Mary Bailey (1835–1896). Her father came from a Dublin protestant family, trained as a doctor in Edinburgh, and went out to the Australian goldfields in Victoria in 1852. Gold-digging and being a squatters' storekeeper proved unsatisfactory, and by 1856 he had established a medical practice in Ballarat. Mary Richardson, an energetic and resourceful woman, had emigrated to Australia from Leicester as a teenager; she and Walter Richardson were married in Ballarat in 1855. Although the future novelist was not born until her parents had been married for fourteen years, their married life, and particularly the career and later devastating illness and death of her father when she was nine years old, provided the material for perhaps her greatest novel, and certainly the one by which she is best known, *The Fortunes of Richard Mahony*. This novel was originally published as a trilogy: *Australia felix* (1917), *The Way Home* (1925), and *Ultima Thule* (1929).

As a child Ethel Richardson lived in several small towns, where her mother worked as a postmistress. When she was thirteen she was sent to the Presbyterian Ladies' College in Melbourne. She proved to be a good scholar and an exceptional musician; consequently, in 1888 her mother was persuaded to take her and her younger sister, Lilian, to Europe, so that she could continue her musical studies. Except for a very brief visit in 1912 to check details for *Richard Mahony*, she never saw Australia again.

In 1889 Richardson entered the Leipzig conservatory, where she studied for three years, with the intention of becoming a concert pianist. However, her engagement to John George *Robertson (1867–1933), a brilliant Scottish student of European languages, and her own distaste for public performances brought her studies to an end in 1892. Under Robertson's guidance she read widely in European literature and translated two novels (published under her married name): *Siren Voices: Niels Lyhne*, after *Niels*

Ethel Florence Lindesay Richardson [Henry Handel Richardson] (1870–1946), by Howard Coster, 1934

Lyhne, by the Danish writer J. P. Jacobsen; and *The Fisher Lass*, after *Fiskerjenten*, by the Norwegian Bjornstjerne Bjornsen.

Richardson and J. G. Robertson were married in Dublin on 30 December 1895. The early years of their marriage were spent in Strasbourg. Richardson's husband was appointed to a university lectureship and she began, rather hesitantly, to write a novel. They walked, read, listened to endless concerts, and enjoyed European intellectual life. This satisfying pattern came to an end in 1904 when J. G. Robertson, who had published *A History of German Literature* in 1902, was invited to become the first professor of German at London University. For Richardson, England and London proved much less congenial than Germany and Strasbourg. She turned inwards, concentrated on writing, and for the rest of her life restricted her company to her husband and a few close friends.

Her first novel, *Maurice Guest* (1908), for which she adopted the pseudonym Henry Handel Richardson, is set among music students in Leipzig. Nobody questioned that she was a male writer, and she was thereafter widely known as HHR or even Henry. Her second novel, *The Getting of Wisdom* (1910; filmed by Bruce Beresford in 1977), is based on her schooldays in Melbourne. She began work on *The Fortunes of Richard Mahony* in 1912, but the First World War delayed publication of the first volume; she eventually achieved fame with the publication of the final volume in 1929. In that year she was awarded the Australian Literary Society's gold medal for *Ultima Thule*, and in 1932 was nominated for the Nobel prize for literature.

After her husband's death in 1933 Richardson struggled to continue writing, but her collection of short stories and the late novel *The Young Cosima* (1939) did not match her earlier work. She had moved to a house at Fairlight, near Hastings, in 1934, and here, during the Second World War, she worked on an autobiographical memoir. It was unfinished at the time of her death and published as *Myself when Young* in 1948. She died, childless, of cancer of the colon on 20 March 1946, and was cremated at the Golders Green crematorium on 25 March.

Richardson was Australian by birth and British by residence (for the last forty-two years of her life), but her great achievement is to have written two major novels which are rooted in continental European realism. They owe little to English traditions. She was influenced by German philosophy and by Russian, Scandinavian, and French fiction, most notably in *Maurice Guest*, a novel which is remarkable for its unblinking treatment of sexual obsession and for its depiction of male homosexuality which is neither effete nor coy. The same sympathetic but intransigent realism is applied to her examination of her restless and obsessive hero in *The Fortunes of Richard Mahony*. Even the short novel *The Getting of Wisdom* avoids adolescent whimsy; it is witty and caustic about a difficult child.

As a writer Richardson was not linguistically inventive and she lacked the modernist sensibility of many of her contemporaries. But her respect for her characters, her brilliant evocation of their social environments (including her lengthy study of colonial Australia), and her unwavering depiction of the conflict between the hard facts of circumstance and the human yearning for freedom turned her, despite her limitations, into a major novelist.

Richardson was a pale, dark-haired, slightly built woman, who combined energetic enthusiasm for music, tennis, swimming, and walking with a lifelong tendency to withdraw into ill health. Her own view of herself was of a square peg failing to fit into a round hole, but this was a failure that she explored without self-pity. The effect on other people could be daunting, especially since she combined her objectivity with personal shyness. The transition from Germany to England was particularly difficult, since she had no small talk, and ditherers or chatterers would find themselves facing scrutinizing intelligent eyes and silence. However, given the opportunity to explore the unorthodox, she flourished. She had a lifelong sceptic's interest in spiritualism; she loved fast cars; and, as a researching novelist, she enjoyed investigating boxing booths and opium dens.   KAREN MCLEOD HEWITT

Sources H. H. Richardson [E. F. L. Robertson], *Myself when young* (1948) · E. Purdie and O. M. Roncoroni, eds., *Henry Handel Richardson: some personal impressions* (1957) · D. Green, *Ulysses bound: Henry Handel Richardson and her fiction* (1973) · K. McLeod, *Henry Handel Richardson: a critical study* (1985) · A. Clark, *Henry Handel Richardson: fiction in the making* (1990) · G. Howells, *Henry Handel Richardson, 1870–1946* (1970) · N. Palmer, *Henry Handel Richardson: a study* (1950) · L. Gibson [L. J. Kramer], *Henry Handel Richardson and some of her sources* (1954)

Archives NL Aus. | Mitchell L., NSW, M. A. Kernot MSS |SOUND Australian Broadcasting Corporation, Sydney, 'Life of HHR'—record of short talks by personal acquaintances
Likenesses H. Coster, photograph, 1934, NPG [*see illus.*] · S. Botzaris, photograph, repro. in Howells, *Henry Handel Richardson* · R. Eves, drawing, National Gallery of Victoria, Melbourne, Australia · photograph, repro. in McLeod, *Henry Handel Richardson* · photograph, repro. in Clark, *Henry Handel Richardson* · photographs, NL Aus., Henry Handel Richardson MSS

Richardson, Gabriel (*d.* 1642), author, the son of a Lincolnshire clergyman, was admitted to Brasenose College, Oxford, in 1602 and graduated BA on 20 July 1604. Having become a fellow of the college on 20 November 1607, he proceeded MA on 7 July 1608 and BD on 8 July 1619.

'Admirably well read in histories and geography' according to Anthony Wood (Wood, *Ath. Oxon.*, 3.37–8), Richardson published in 1627 *Of the state of Europe: XIIII bookes conteining the historie and relation of the many provinces hereof, continued out of approved authours*, 'a book much valued by learned men'. Dedicated to John Williams, bishop of Lincoln, the visitor of Brasenose College, it gives a general survey of the topography, languages, civil government, and religion of much of western, central, and northern Europe; the author does not claim to have travelled. Largely descriptive and without polemic, its critique of the imperfections of the great powers—Spain, France, and Germany—is bland: 'a short censure of the present Spanish greatnes' relates only to the 'empty, scattered and ill-affected dominions, rather to be a trouble, and burthen, then to add any great advantage, and strength' to their monarch (5.1, 13), Germany is 'vast, unwieldie and ill-united' and subject to 'disorders' (11.1), and the king of France's comparative, though not to be overrated, strength is at the expense of the Huguenots whose wealth he confiscated (8.11). Wood states that Henry Bridgman was responsible for the neglect or mutilation of several other unpublished volumes of the original manuscript. In 1635 Richardson became rector of Heythrop, Oxfordshire. He died on 31 December 1642, possibly in Oxford, and was buried on 1 January 1643 in St Mary the Virgin, Oxford.

W. A. SHAW, rev. VIVIENNE LARMINIE

Sources [C. B. Heberden], ed., *Brasenose College register, 1509–1909*, 1, OHS, 55 (1909), 97 · Wood, *Ath. Oxon.*, new edn, 3.37–8 · Wood, *Ath. Oxon.: Fasti* (1815), 302, 326 · G. Richardson, *Of the state of Europe: XIIII bookes conteining the historie and relation of the many provinces hereof, continued out of approved authours* (1627)

Richardson, George (1737/8–*c*.1813), architectural draughtsman and decorative designer, was by 1756 or thereabouts in the service of the Adam brothers in Edinburgh as an apprentice, possibly having been recruited by John Adam. It is likely that he was a native of Edinburgh or Edinburghshire, perhaps the village of Inveresk, where he had a patron. However, nothing is known of his family background, parentage, education, or early years. Doubtless his circumstances were humble. Richardson was involved about 1759, albeit in a minor capacity and under James Adam's direction, in the complex and lengthy business of turning Robert Adam's plates of and commentary on Diocletian's Palace at Split into a publishable book

(*Ruins of the Palace of the Emperor Diocletian at Spalatro in Dalmatia*, 1764). In 1760 he was given his great opportunity to encounter antiquity at first hand.

With the intention that he should accompany James Adam on his grand tour, Richardson had been sent from Edinburgh to London to work with Robert Adam after the latter's return from abroad. Robert's advice to James was that he should take a Scots draughtsman with him: 'the Scots are more faithful and in every way preferable to the English if well chosen' (Fleming, 262). James Adam was to find in Richardson an able assistant, although (if Richardson is to be believed) his master took advantage of him and treated him with less consideration than he deserved. Adam was mean and suspicious, and jealous of Richardson's attempts to draw for his own pleasure and instruction: a ludicrous dispute arose between the two centred on the quality of clothing (rough, unlined breeches and the like) which Adam intended to provide for Richardson when they planned to extend their travels from Italy and Istria to Greece and the Levant. But Richardson was certainly enabled to see and study antique sources in a way that otherwise he would never have been able to do. The handful of his surviving letters from Italy are exemplary statements of what Rome meant to an impressionable young man of a class not often given such chances. Though the Aegean expedition came to naught, Richardson remained ever afterwards under the spell of Rome, 'the fittest place in Europe for our profession' (Brown, 37); and in many of his subsequent publications he would refer to the classical buildings he had seen as a young man and to the decorative motifs of antiquity on which he modelled his own elegant version of the 'Adam' style.

Well knowing his own self-confessed 'incapacity, small fortune, want of Books & little hopes of Interest' (Brown, 39), Richardson was resigned to continuing in the Adams' London office after his return from Italy in 1763. Shortly, however, the growing self-worth already evident in his letters asserted itself, and he was practising in his own right. In 1765 he gained a premium from the Society of Arts, and from 1766 he exhibited regularly architectural and decorative works both at the Society of Arts and at the Royal Academy. In the later 1760s he was in active practice as a decorative designer, supplying ceiling designs for Lord Scarsdale at Kedleston Hall, Derbyshire. He also offered his services as a drawing master.

By the 1770s Richardson's career as author, engraver, and publisher of architectural books was launched: the various productions of the man who had once lamented his own lack of books provided many a builder, gentleman amateur, and would-be patron with an extensive repertoire of designs, and inspiration for almost endless variation on classical themes and sources. This was Richardson's real claim to distinction. In publishing collections of his designs he was surely influenced by the production of *The Works in Architecture of Robert and James Adam* (1773–5). Ironically the publication, and therefore the availability of his works for imitation and execution by others, rendered unnecessary his actual employment as an architect.

Richardson's architectural output was small: he entered the competition for the Royal Exchange, Dublin, in 1769, and conceived a Gothic church for Stapleford, Leicestershire; he may have designed two others for the same patron, Robert Sherard, fourth earl of Harborough. His architectural achievements on paper were, by contrast, large: his designs fill the pattern books (mentioned below) which—often with his son William—he engraved in aquatint. The great majority of these were for elegant villas and small country houses (some even provided with estimates of building costs based on London prices of labour and materials between 1788 and 1792), and he specialized in inventing sophisticated decorative schemes for ceilings and wall surfaces.

From two addresses in Great Titchfield Street, London (number 95 and subsequently 105) Richardson issued an important series of publications. These books were very well subscribed: most of the leading architects of the day patronized his *Book of Ceilings* (1776), and most of the principal architects, painters, sculptors, designers, craftsmen, manufacturers, patrons, and connoisseurs bought his *Iconology, or, A Collection of Emblematical Figures* (2 vols., 1779), a useful English version of Cesare Ripa's original, which bore a dedication to George III. The Adam brothers (invariably mentioned with admiration and respect by Richardson in his publications) feature in all these lists, as do a fair number of Edinburgh builders, craftsmen, and superior tradesmen: Richardson's continued contact with Scottish members of the profession is particularly evident in the subscriptions to his *Treatise on the Five Orders of Architecture* (1787) and *New Designs in Architecture* (1792).

Eclecticism and imitation were the keys to Richardson's elegant style. Inspired by the painted and stucco decoration of the villas and baths of imperial Rome, Tivoli, and 'the Baian shore' of the Bay of Naples, Richardson considered that by 'blending particular parts' his patrons might 'form new designs according to their fancy' with 'an almost infinite variation' ('Preface', *Book of Ceilings*). The theory demonstrated in his books found practical expression in his own work at Kedleston. All Richardson's fields of interest were made manifest in his *Series of Original Designs for Country Seats or Villas* (1795); it contained plans, elevations, and sections, details of 'ornaments' and 'Interior Decorations in the Antique Style', the latter being examples of 'the unlimited excursions of Fancy and Taste in Design'. Later Richardson, always motivated by didactic purpose, recorded the achievements of British architecture of the late eighteenth century in the two-volume *New Vitruvius Britannicus* (1802–8 and 1808–10), a conscious attempt to emulate and continue the great works of Colen Campbell, and John Woolfe and James Gandon.

The success of his publications notwithstanding, Richardson's later years were passed in social and financial distress. He was, according to Farington (*Diary*, 12.1452), long a widower: his wife 'drank & had no proper conduct'. His son and daughter were 'equally irregular & witht. conduct'. From 1807 Richardson was in receipt of donations from Royal Academy funds, and Nollekens, finding him 'glumpish' (Smith, 1.119), helped to relieve his hardship with an annuity. Nollekens stated in July 1812 (Farington, *Diary*, 12.1457) that Richardson, whom he had known in Rome as an 'industrious good natured creature', was then seventy-four years old, and that he would not 'live another year'. His collections of prints and drawings were sold on 29 November 1813, so his earlier death is to be presumed.

IAIN GORDON BROWN

Sources Colvin, *Archs.* · E. Harris and N. Savage, *British architectural books and writers, 1556–1785* (1990) · I. G. Brown, '"The fittest place in Europe for our profession": George Richardson in Rome', *Architectural Heritage*, 2 (1991), 29–40 · J. Fleming, *Robert Adam and his circle in Edinburgh and Rome* (1962) · G. Richardson, *A book of ceilings, composed in the style of the antique grotesque* (1776) · G. Richardson, *Iconology, or, A collection of emblematical figures*, 2 vols. (1779) · G. Richardson, *A treatise on the five orders of architecture* (1787) · G. Richardson, *New designs in architecture* (1792) · G. Richardson, *A series of original designs for country seats or villas* (1795) · J. T. Smith, *Nollekens and his times*, 2 vols. (1828) · Farington, *Diary*, vols. 12–13
Archives NL Scot.

Richardson, George (1773–1862), Quaker minister, born on 18 December 1773 at Low Lights, near North Shields, Northumberland, was the fourth son of the seven surviving children of John Richardson (*d.* 1800), a tanner there, and his first wife, Margaret Stead. Richardson's mother died in 1781, and he was sent to live with an aunt who kept a shop at Shields. There he read extensively in Quaker literature. At fourteen he was apprenticed to Joshua Watson, a grocer in Newcastle upon Tyne, where he settled for life, and soon took charge of a branch of his master's business. He began preaching at twenty, and was recorded a minister by his monthly meeting at twenty-four. After travelling 700 miles or more as 'guide' to Friends from America, he began religious tours on his own account, and during the next forty years visited every county in England, as well as Wales, Ireland, Scotland, Jersey, and Guernsey. He was often accompanied by his friend Daniel Oliver of Newcastle. He also interested himself in missions, and was for fifty years connected with the Bible Society. He helped to found the Royal Jubilee Schools at Newcastle by way of celebrating the jubilee of George III in 1809. He spent his leisure among the fishing population of Cullercoats, Northumberland, and provided an efficient water supply and schools for the village. Even in advanced age he would, when at Cullercoats, put out to sea with Bibles for French sailors in ships off the coast.

Richardson married in 1800 Eleanor Watson (1778–1846), niece of his first employer, and they had seven children, of whom five reached maturity. Of a son Isaac, who died young, Richardson wrote a brief *Memoir* (1841). He also wrote tracts and pamphlets on tithes and other subjects, and *Annals of the Cleveland Richardsons and their Descendants* (1850). He died on 9 August 1862 at his home in Albion Street, Newcastle, and was buried in the Quaker burial-ground, Pilgrim Street, Newcastle.

CHARLOTTE FELL-SMITH, *rev.* K. D. REYNOLDS

Sources *Journal of the gospel labours of George Richardson* (1864) · A. O. Boyce, *Records of a Quaker family: the Richardsons of Cleveland* (1889) · G. Richardson, *Annals of the Cleveland Richardsons and their* *descendants* (1850) · *Annual Monitor* (1863), 147–66 · *Northern Daily Express* (11 Aug 1862) · *CGPLA Eng. & Wales* (1863)

Archives RS Friends, Lond., corresp. and papers, incl. papers relating to Quakers in Norway

Wealth at death under £800: probate, 7 Jan 1863, *CGPLA Eng. & Wales*

Richardson, George Bourchier (1822–1877). *See under* Richardson, Moses Aaron (1793–1871).

Richardson, George Fleming (1796–1848), geologist and itinerant lecturer, was born on 8 December 1796 in Lewes, Sussex, son of George Richardson (1763–1843), Brighton linen draper and lodging-house keeper and his wife, Martha, *née* Fleming. Probably educated at local schools, Richardson entered his father's businesses, but being an avid reader with a most retentive memory, he found time to master several European languages while so employed. His first publication was a volume of poems in 1825, the same year that he was involved in the founding of the Brighton Mechanics' Institution.

In 1833 the fossil museum of Dr Gideon Algernon Mantell (1790–1852) moved to Brighton, under the patronage of the third earl of Egremont. However, by the end of 1835 the rush of 6000 visitors had forced its closure, and the following year a Sussex Scientific and Literary Institution was set up to rent the collection from Mantell and to administer access. Richardson, having now given up his profession, was its first librarian and curator. He set about establishing the new institution with enthusiasm, lecturing on an enormous range of topics, guiding visitors, issuing descriptive catalogues of the collections, translating articles for Mantell, and acting as his literary agent. But, late in 1837, the death of the earl of Egremont threw the future of the Mantellian Museum into doubt.

In 1838 the British Museum purchased both the collection and Richardson's services. He was appointed sub-curator in the mineralogical and geology branch of the museum. But the wage paid, initially 7s. for each day worked, was derisory—only about half the £200 per annum which was considered 'scarcely enough to support a gentleman in a life of science' (Rudwick, 461). As a result, although expected to catalogue and curate museum collections, Richardson returned to Brighton as a professional lecturer. Continuing to write, he issued the second of his two volumes of *Sketches in Prose and Verse* (1838) and edited Mantell's highly successful *Wonders of Geology* (1838), from notes he had taken at Mantell's lectures.

Richardson was elected a fellow of the Geological Society in 1839, and then became a peripatetic lecturer, mainly on geology, to many general and learned bodies, including the Royal Institute of British Architects. In 1840 he started attending meetings of the British Association for the Advancement of Science as a paid, scientific, newspaper correspondent and was clearly seen as expert on geological matters. The following year, he issued proposals for his own *Geology for Beginners*. This successful book, published in May 1842, was regarded by Mantell as 'scandalous piracy' (Spokes, 154) and open warfare erupted between the two men.

The mid-1840s brought a steep decline in the audiences for such itinerant lecturers. Richardson's attempts to earn a more gentlemanly living from his life on the edge of professional science had not succeeded. Although also busy as a consultant geologist by 1842, and despite increased income from his museum duties (£215 per annum by 1847 as senior assistant), he was in arrears with his Geological Society subscription in the mid-1840s. He was later rumoured by Edward Forbes to have got into financial difficulty through having had expensive habits and possibly a mistress. His hopes of augmenting the wages earned at the museum with royalties from books and fees from lectures had been dashed. His 'war' with Mantell caused problems with book sales, and the declining audiences for lectures had the same effect with fees. Richardson was passing through the 'insolvent court' when, in the night of 30 June – 1 July 1848, he committed suicide in Somers Town, London. H. S. TORRENS

Sources H. S. Torrens and J. A. Cooper, 'George Fleming Richardson (1796–1848): man of letters, lecturer and geological curator', *Geological Curator*, 4 (1984–5), 249–72 · S. Spokes, *Gideon Algernon Mantell LL.D., F.R.C.S., F.R.S., surgeon and geologist* (1927) · E. C. Curwen, *The journal of Gideon Mantell, surgeon and geologist* (1940) · H. S. Torrens and M. A. Taylor, 'Geological collectors and museums in Cheltenham, 1810–1988', *Geological Curator*, 5 (1988–94), 173–213 · [J. W. Judd], 'Samuel Sharp', *Journal of the Northamptonshire Natural History Society and Field Club*, 2 (1882), 71–3 · E. Forbes, letter to Andrew Ramsey, 4 July 1848, ICL, archives, Ramsey 8/389 · M. J. S. Rudwick, *The great Devonian controversy: the shaping of scientific knowledge among gentlemanly specialists* (1985) · *Brighton Herald* (8 July 1848) · *Lewes registers*, 6 (1791–9), 43

Archives BM, archives · NHM | BGS, Buckman MSS · McGill University, Montreal, Woodward MSS · NL NZ, Mantell MSS

Wealth at death bankrupt: *Brighton Herald*

Richardson, Henry (1806–1885). *See under* Richardson, Anna (1806–1892).

Richardson, Henry Handel. *See* Richardson, Ethel Florence Lindesay (1870–1946).

Richardson, James (1806–1851), traveller in Africa and anti-slavery campaigner, was born in Lincolnshire, and was educated for the evangelical ministry. He joined the British and Foreign Anti-Slavery Society on its foundation in 1839 and helped to direct the attention of the society to the hitherto neglected trans-Saharan and Mediterranean slave trade. He was probably behind the successful attempts of the society in 1840 to interest the British government in the trade in this area. The government opened negotiations to try to halt the trade and Richardson went as the society's agent to report on progress on the area from a base in Malta. There he set up a branch of the anti-slavery society, helped edit the *Malta Times*, and established contact with all British consular agents in north Africa, becoming a warm friend of Colonel Hanmer George Warrington, consular-general in Tripoli and a particular enemy of the slave trade. Having heard that, under British pressure, the bey of Tunis had agreed to stop the export of slaves from Tunis and the public sale of slaves there, Richardson travelled there in 1842 to present him with a petition of lavish praise (cited in the *Anti-Slavery Reporter*, 23 March 1842, 45). In 1843 he set off on a mission to gather statistics on slavery for the anti-slavery society and to persuade the sultan of Morocco to reject slavery. He was refused an audience with the sultan, but gathered some information, which was published in the *Anti-Slavery Reporter* of 1 May 1844. Richardson returned briefly to England in 1844 but returned to his mission later that year, undeterred by his failure with the sultan. He found that the bey's income had been greatly diminished by the effective abolition of the slave trade in Tunis, and in an unpublished book manuscript, 'The regency of Tunis' (PRO, FO 100/29), urged British support for the bey's development of other sources of income. In 1845 Richardson set out across the desert to gather information on the legitimate and slave trades in the interior and in the (unfulfilled) expectation that he would be made vice-consul at Ghadames, a strategically important market town. From Ghadames he travelled to Ghat, a very important slave market, but there was forced by ill health and lack of equipment to turn back, travelling via Fezzan and reaching England in 1846. His report for the society and the government gave details of the slave trade in the area and its geography, and warmed to his old theme of the encouragement of legitimate trade and the abolition of slavery.

In 1846 Richardson had an interview with Palmerston to try to interest him in his plans for a second expedition, with both geographical and anti-slavery objectives, which was to approach the interior of Africa over the Sahara, not via west Africa where expeditions had proved so susceptible to disease. Richardson originally envisaged travelling alone, for about a year, at a cost of about £500, but, aware that his ignorance of surveying would cause difficulties and limit the accuracy of the geographical information he could gather, he asked for help. He tried unsuccessfully to gain French support for the venture on a visit to Paris in September 1849, but, with the aid of Carl Ritter, the German geographer, Charles Bunsen, the Prussian ambassador in London and fellow of the Royal Geographical Society, and August Petermann, the Prussian cartographer, then also living in London, he gained the co-operation of the Germans Heinrich Barth and Adolf Overweg, who accompanied him at the expense and under the direction of the British government. Sir Roderick Murchison, president of the Royal Geographical Society, later regretted the Prussian involvement in the expedition, particularly as the Prussians survived to publish their findings, while Richardson did not. The object of the expedition was to explore Lake Chad, which, in spite of the visits of Oudney, Denham, and Clapperton (1822–4), remained little known to Europeans. Richardson's wife, whom he had married shortly before the start of this his third and final venture, went with him as far as Tripoli, where she stayed to wait for his return. On 23 March 1850 the three explorers set out from Tripoli, arriving at Ghat on 24 July. They reached Aïr on the southern edge of the Sahara on 4 September, and Damergu in December of the same year. At this point they were delayed some time, and at last decided to take different ways to Lake Chad. Richardson went straight by Zinder (now in Niger), Barth by Kanou and Kuka, Overweg by Tessaoua and Maradi. This last part of the journey, however, was too much for Richardson, whose constitution had already been undermined by the African climate. With great exertion he advanced to Ungouratona—about twelve or fifteen days' journey from Lake Chad—where, on 4 March 1851, he died of fever, brought on by the heat and compounded by injudicious use of medicines. The villagers buried him with honour; his notes, journal, and papers were collected and returned to England.

Richardson's *Travels in Morocco* (2 vols., 1860) was the record of his earliest journey, but the last to be published. His widow edited the book and wrote a short preface. It was a largely unoriginal work about fairly well-known areas. More original was *Travels in the Great Desert of Sahara in the Years of 1845 and 1846* (2 vols., 1848). *Mission to Central Africa* was also published posthumously (2 vols., 1853), and is his most important work. As in his Saharan journey, he was going through territory little known to, and certainly seldom described by, Europeans. Besides his longer works Richardson wrote on various African languages and translated part of the New Testament into these languages.

Boahen considers that Richardson's contributions to both the anti-slavery campaign and to African exploration in the nineteenth century have been most unjustifiably neglected. Though his own time in Africa was limited, it was entirely due to his persistence that the 1850 expedition happened at all and that the German survivors had joined it, and in considerable part due to him that the slave trade in the area was fought with such tenacity and some success.

ELIZABETH BAIGENT

Sources A. Adu Boahen, 'James Richardson: the forgotten philanthropist and explorer', *Journal of the Historical Society of Nigeria*, 3 (1964–7), 61–71 · private information (2004) [D. J. Goodsir-Cullen] · J. Richardson, preface, in J. Richardson, *Travels in Morocco* (1860) · R. A. Stafford, *Scientist of empire: Sir Roderick Murchison, scientific exploration and Victorian imperialism* (1989) · *The Times* (20 Sept 1851) · review, *The Athenaeum* (29 Jan 1848), 103–4 · review, *The Athenaeum* (10 Dec 1859), 768–70 · *The Athenaeum* (18 Feb 1860), 245–6 · Boase, *Mod. Eng. biog.* · Allibone, *Dict.* · J. Irving, ed., *Annals of our time* (1871), 321 · A. Adu Boahen, *Britain, the Sahara and the western Sudan, 1788–1861* (1964)

Archives RGS, papers relating to travels in Africa

Likenesses G. Cook, engraving, repro. in J. Richardson, *Travels in the great desert of Sahara in the years of 1845 and 1846*, 1 (1848), frontispiece

Richardson, James Nicholson (1846–1921), industrialist and politician, was born on 7 February 1846 in Belfast, the only child of John Grubb Richardson, an industrialist, and his first wife, Helena Grubb, originally of Cahir Abbey, co. Tipperary. Helena died in childbirth in 1849 and John Grubb remarried in 1853; he had one son and seven daughters by his second wife. James lived with his father and stepmother, between 1853 and 1858 at Brookhill, Lisburn, co. Antrim, and then at Moyallon House near Lisburn. He was educated at home until 1857, and was then sent to a small private school, which closed nine months later. From 1858 to 1862 he attended Grove House School in Tottenham, Middlesex. He married Sophie Malcolmson of Portlaw near Waterford, Ireland, in 1867, after which he made his home at Mount Caulfield, Bessbrook, near Newry, on the border of counties Down and Armagh.

Richardson was a member of a long established linen-manufacturing family in Ireland. Although his father was originally involved in linen bleaching, in 1846 he diversified into flax spinning, erecting a purpose-built mill and creating the model village of Bessbrook for the employees. Six years later he introduced power-loom weaving to Bessbrook. Finally in 1863 John Grubb Richardson bought out the entire business, works, and village of Bessbrook from its parent company, J. N. Richardson Sons and Owden, and formed the Bessbrook Spinning Company. The timing of the formation of the new company proved extremely fortuitous in that it coincided with a sudden and unexpected upturn in the fortunes of the Irish linen industry, caused by the cotton famine in Britain. In the first two years of its existence, annual profits rose from just over £8000 to over £41,000.

James began his apprenticeship in his father's firm in the year of its formation. He was treated exactly the same way as any other apprentice, learning through practical experience about each of the processes involved in flax spinning—hackling, sorting, preparing, and spinning—as well as having to observe 'every rule as to hours and routine' (Smith, 199). He became especially good at judging and buying flax, and he showed an aptitude for 'industrial management and for dealing with men of all shades of opinion' (ibid., 42). As his competence to run the firm became increasingly apparent, his father left it more and more in his hands.

Among the developments at Bessbrook in Richardson's early years of management was the introduction of damask weaving in 1867 and the consequent innovation of the 'Bessbrook machine' two years later. In 1868 the firm purchased the nearby Craigmore factory in order to extend its power-loom weaving operations.

In 1878 the Bessbrook Spinning Company was incorporated as a limited company, with Richardson as its first chairman. This allowed him the freedom to participate in other interests. He had for a number of years been committed to land reform in Ireland. Because of this he was persuaded to stand for parliament in 1880. He was elected as Liberal MP for co. Armagh. In parliament he was very involved in promoting land purchase legislation (later achieved in the Ashbourne Act of 1885. However, he found that public life 'was contrary to his own feelings and desires' (Smith, 62). Furthermore, during his years as an MP his wife's health deteriorated badly. By the beginning of 1884 the strain was beginning to tell and he felt he needed a break. He took a year travelling round the world, after which he decided to retire from politics. He had become disillusioned because of Gladstone's failure to address the temperance question and his support of Irish home rule. During the next five years Richardson suffered from 'temperamental depression', as in 1886 first his wife and in 1890 then his father died. After each bereavement he travelled abroad to find solace. In 1886–7 he toured the Holy Land and in 1890 he went on his second world trip.

On his return to Ireland in 1891 Richardson became very actively involved in unionism, addressing a huge convention in the botanic gardens in Belfast in 1892 and another in Enniskillen in co. Fermanagh in 1893. In that year he remarried. His second wife was Sarah Alexander Bell of Lurgan, co. Armagh. After a honeymoon in Palestine the couple returned to Mount Caulfield. In 1916 Richardson resigned as chairman of Bessbrooks. His physical health began to fail, and he died on 11 October 1921 in a hospital in Edgbaston, Birmingham, after an unsuccessful operation. He had no children by either marriage.

Throughout his life Richardson was a prominent member of the Society of Friends and was renowned for his altruism, especially towards the people of Bessbrook. He provided an orphanage for the children and a convalescent home for the working women. He also laid out a cricket field and built a pavilion, created a bowling green, and bought ground for a golf course. Furthermore, he sold some 5000 acres of his land to his tenants under the terms of the Wyndham Land Act of 1903 and installed electric lighting in the village in 1911.

Richardson had a sensitive and romantic nature and a love of poetry and art. He wrote many poems and published a variety of pamphlets for the people of Bessbrook. He was also a 'born mimic' and an excellent public speaker. His speeches 'were brimful of wit and humour' (*Belfast News-Letter*, 12 Oct 1921). At his death his estate was estimated at £75,000 (£32,665 of it in England).

EMILY BOYLE

Sources C. Smith, *James Nicholson Richardson of Bessbrook* (1925) · *Belfast News-Letter* (12 Oct 1921) · E. Boyle, 'The economic development of the Irish linen industry, 1825–1913', PhD diss., Queen's University, Belfast, 1979

Archives PRO NIre., corresp.

Wealth at death £74,604 6s. 10d.; incl. est. £32,665 in England: probate, 1922, *CGPLA NIre.*

Richardson [*née* Hunting], **Jerusha Davidson** [*known as* Mrs Aubrey Richardson] (1864–1938), philanthropist and author, was born at 12 Burlington Road, Paddington, London, on 10 August 1864, the daughter of Richard Hunting, a manufacturer who apparently introduced the sewing machine to Great Britain, and his wife, Margaret Davidson. She was educated at a boarding-school, and on 20 May 1893 she married a solicitor, Aubrey Richardson (*b.* 1862/3), son of Sir Benjamin Ward *Richardson (1828–1896), physician and sanitary reformer, and his wife, Mary J. Smith. He died some years later, apparently leaving her a childless widow.

As a girl, Jerusha Hunting had contributed articles on social and literary subjects and short stories to various magazines. In 1899 she published *Famous Ladies of the English Court*, in the preface of which she pointed to the few opportunities of exercising political power open to women, both past and present. She celebrated, however, the broadening sphere of moral, humanitarian, and religious activities offered to her sex. That women should rest content with influence in these spheres is the burden of many of Mrs Richardson's later publications: her first novel, *A Drama of Sunshine, Played in Homburg* (1903) condemns an unhappily married socialite who neglects her husband and child to seek behind-the-scenes political influence; the 'raving female suffragist' (*A Drama of Sunshine*, 171), though equally mistaken, is seen to be more honest. This theme is reiterated in her biography of Catherine of Siena, *The Mystic Bride* (1911), where Mrs Richardson deplores the saint's intervention in international politics as a departure from her more womanly exercise of religious and moral influence; she explicitly rebukes suffragettes for their use of violence and their (alleged) neglect of their families. The historical dimensions of women's religious mission were explored in her *Women of the Church of England* (1907), an unusually comprehensive survey which was a real contribution to the establishment of women's history. *They Twain* (1904), another (possibly semi-autobiographical) novel, pursues a different tack: here Mrs Richardson explores the early married life of a tomboyish girl, who learns painfully the responsibilities of her new position and the different social roles allotted to men and women. *Gates of Brass* (1909), a sensationalistic novel about the necessity for the virtuous to learn wisdom, reflects both Mrs Richardson's recognition of the limitation of women's moral influence (the heroine fails to reform her parents) and her open-mindedness: the characters include an unmarried mother and her child. Mrs Richardson also published *The Lover of Queen Elizabeth* (1907), a biography of Robert Dudley, earl of Leicester, and *The Doges of Venice* (1914). The latter was the last of her publications: with the outbreak of the First World War, Mrs Richardson found herself pursuing the apolitical role of social and moral benefactor which she had outlined for her female readers.

From 1914 Jerusha Richardson served as quartermaster in a hospital for the wounded in Willesden until the end of 1915. She was then appointed commandant of voluntary aid detachment 58, and early in 1916 she opened Dollis Hill House auxiliary military hospital; it received its first intake of patients in February, and later accommodated up to sixty patients at a time. Here her 'powers of organisation and forceful personality' (*Willesden Chronicle*) were used to much effect. Succeeding in attracting the loyalty of her staff, she was less successful with the management committee: stormy meetings were sometimes followed by resignations among its members. She realized that many former soldiers still needed care after the hospital had closed in April 1919, and accordingly opened a clinic in Priory Road, Willesden, in 1920. This later became a surgery clinic, to which doctors sent their patients for specialized treatment at reduced fees; by the 1930s it was specializing in the treatment of rheumatism and related diseases. Mrs Richardson secured the patronage of high-ranking ladies and organized fund-raising events, such as sales of work and pageants; she also acted as commandant, before finally retiring in 1935. She was made an OBE for her war work.

Jerusha Richardson was also involved in other local philanthropic ventures. A founder member of the Willesden Housing Society, she acted as honorary secretary and as chair of the propaganda subcommittee; she was also a member of the Mansion House council of health and housing. An attendant at St John's Church in Cambridge Gardens (where her brother-in-law was sometime vicar), she supported many church activities; she was one of the founders, and for many years the leader, of the Kilburn branch of the Phoebe girls' club. She also helped to establish the Willesden Christian social crusade and the Willesden branch of the Women Citizens' Association, of which she was for many years the chair. She was clerk to the Chadwick trust from 1912, and a member of the Model Abattoir Society (founded by her father-in-law), besides serving on a committee working to secure a maternity ward in Willesden General Hospital.

Mrs Richardson was taken ill in the clinic on 20 January 1938, and died of broncho-pneumonia and heart disease at her home, 75 Carlton Hill, Maida Vale, on 8 February. Her funeral, at which the bishop of Willesden officiated, was held on 11 February 1938 at the crematorium at Golders Green (in the year of their marriage, 1893, her husband had published *The Law of Cremation*). It was preceded by a memorial service in St John's, Cambridge Gardens.

ROSEMARY MITCHELL

Sources *Willesden Chronicle* (11 Feb 1938) · *Willesden Chronicle* (18 Feb 1938) · *The lady's who's who: who's who for British women ... 1938–9* (1939) · b. cert. · m. cert. · d. cert.
Likenesses portrait, c.1916–1919, repro. in *Willesden Chronicle* (11 Feb 1938)
Wealth at death £2841 17s. 7d.: resworn probate, 2 April 1938, CGPLA Eng. & Wales

Richardson, John (d. 1625). *See under* Authorized Version of the Bible, translators of the (*act.* 1604–1611).

Richardson, John (1579/80–1654), Church of Ireland bishop of Ardagh, was born in Cheshire. He was one of the earliest students at Trinity College, Dublin, obtaining his MA and a fellowship by 1601, his BD by 1610, and his DD by early 1614. On 10 August 1612 he married Elizabeth, the daughter of Sir Henry Bunbury, described by William Brereton in 1635 as 'a tall handsome fat woman' (Brereton, 140). During the early seventeenth century Richardson combined two roles: fellow of Trinity and godly preacher in Dublin city. He gave weekly public lectures with James Ussher at Christ Church, Dublin, Richardson covering the book of Isaiah on Fridays. By 1604 he was prebendary of St Audoen's (attached to St Patrick's Cathedral, Dublin), a post he held until about 1617, when he left Dublin for the new Ulster plantation, where protestant preachers were urgently needed. Richardson, who had held the rectory of Granard (diocese of Ardagh) since 1610 as a non-resident, was presented by Trinity College to the rectory of Ardtrea (diocese of Armagh) and by the crown to Ardstraw (diocese of Derry), both in 1617, and by 1622 also held the archdeaconry of Derry.

James Ussher thought highly of his former Trinity colleague, recommending him for the see of Raphoe in 1630. Though unsuccessful then, he was soon proposed by Bishop William Bedell of Kilmore as his own successor in Ardagh. Richardson was nominated on 8 April 1633 and consecrated later that year in Armagh. Because of the poverty of the see, he was allowed to retain his archdeaconry *in commendam*, exchanging it in 1639 for the archdeaconry of Connor. Richardson himself, however, was not poor, living 'very plentifully' as bishop and owning the 1000 acre manor of Carrickglass, in co. Longford, while also having extensive landholdings in Donegal, which he rented from Trinity for £422 p.a. during the 1630s. When William Bedell was suspected of deviating from Calvinist orthodoxy on grace and free will in the early 1630s, Richardson was deputed by Ussher and other concerned bishops to investigate his views. Though Bedell and Richardson, during a lengthy correspondence, agreed to differ over the efficacy of grace in baptism, the tone of their exchanges remained friendly.

Though his first work, published in 1625, was a general defence of the protestant doctrine of justification by faith, Richardson specialized in the Old Testament, contributing to the second edition of the Westminster assembly *Annotations* (1657). After his death, his additional Old Testament notes were printed with the help of Ussher and Thomas Gataker. Richardson also had historical interests, contributing to Sir James Ware's researches on the origins of Irish round towers. Whether through foresight or luck, he retired to England just before the 1641 rising broke out, and remained there, dying in Cheapside, London, on 11 August 1654, aged seventy-four. In his will he left Carrickglass to be sold on the death of his wife, the proceeds to go to support Trinity students from the four parishes in which he had served (St Audoen's, Granard, Ardstraw, and Dunboe).   ALAN FORD

Sources *The whole works of Sir James Ware concerning Ireland*, ed. and trans. W. Harris, 1 (1739), 255f • E. S. Shuckburgh, ed., *Two biographies of William Bedell, bishop of Kilmore, with a selection of his letters and an unpublished treatise* (1902), 371–96 • Bodl. Oxf., MS Tanner 458, fols. 188r–218v • J. P. Mahaffy, ed., *The particular book of Trinity College, Dublin* (1904) • muniments, TCD, P/24/122, P/27/2 and 5 • deeds, TCD, 81–2, 85, 122, 131–2 • J. B. Leslie, *Armagh clergy and parishes* (1911) • W. Brereton, *Travels in Holland, the United Provinces, England, Scotland, and Ireland, 1634–5*, ed. E. Hawkins, Chetham Society, 1 (1844) • J. B. Leslie, *Derry clergy and parishes* (1937) • J. B. Leslie, ed., *Clergy of Connor: from Patrician times to the present day* (1993) • Burtchaell & Sadleir, *Alum. Dubl.*, 2nd edn • C. McNeill, ed., *The Tanner letters*, IMC (1943) • T. W. Moody and others, eds., *A new history of Ireland*, 9: *Maps, genealogies, lists* (1984)

Archives Bodl. Oxf., letters

Likenesses T. Cross, line engraving, BM, NPG; repro. in J. Richardson, *Choice observations* (1655); facsimile, pubd 1804, NG Ire.

Richardson, John (1647–*c.*1725). *See under* Richardson, William (1698–1775).

Richardson, John (1667–1753), Quaker minister, was born in North Cave, Yorkshire, the son of William Richardson (1624–1679), an early Quaker convert. William died when John was about thirteen years old, leaving five children, and a grazing farm that kept young Richardson hard at work. Following his father's death he sought spiritual knowledge from religious teachers and in solitary meditations. But he did not initially turn to the scorned Friends, who lived plainly and met far from his home. By age sixteen, however, Richardson's religious openings led him to adopt Quaker beliefs and faithfully to attend Quaker meetings.

Richardson's life took a momentary turn for the worse when his mother married a presbyterian who disapproved of Richardson's Quakerism and discouraged the teenager from attending meetings. On Sunday mornings his stepfather asked Richardson to check up on the most distant herds, and would not allow him a horse to ride on unless a difficult horse needed to be broken in. When these subterfuges failed to deter Richardson's religious commitment, the stepfather forced him to leave home. Left with no means to make a living, he bound himself to a Quaker weaver, and later learned to repair clocks. During his twenties, Richardson became an itinerant minister, travelling through England four times and twice through Wales. Though he hoped eventually to visit America, in 1695 Richardson settled down in Bridlington, opened a repair shop, and married Priscilla Canaby (1672?–1700?); her death left Richardson with three small children.

When Richardson's youngest child also died, the minister felt a stronger call to visit America. Leaving his older children, he headed for London where a premonition caused him to decline passage on a ship that later sank in the English Channel. Instead, he and several friends boarded the *Arundel*, which arrived in Maryland in 1701 after a miserable sixteen-week crossing. Here Richardson purchased a white horse that he had dreamed about; the horse eventually carried him over 4000 miles as far north as New England and as far south as Virginia. He visited friends, attended meetings, and argued with both Quakers and non-Quakers over issues such as baptism, church tithes, and war taxes. His most famous dispute took place in Lynn, Massachusetts, where he charged George Keith with misrepresenting Quaker beliefs when he accused Friends of slighting Jesus. Richardson attended an Indian treaty with William Penn and found the American Indians to be 'commendable', travelled with other notable Quaker ministers such as Elizabeth Webb and Thomas Story, and met many powerful people including several governors and proprietors. He concluded the journey in the Caribbean, where he found 'much love' in Bermuda, but 'little truth' in Barbados. During this voyage he narrowly escaped many near-drownings and capture by two pirate ships.

Upon returning to England in 1703 Richardson married Anne Robinson. Her virtues included a gift for ministering and her acquiescence in Richardson's travels. She died on 18 February 1711. Richardson continued to preach throughout England and Ireland. He made a second journey to America in 1731. He died on 2 June 1753, aged eighty-seven, near Hutton-le-Hole and was buried in the Quaker burial-ground at Kirkby Moorside.   CARLA GERONA

Sources *DNB* • 'An account of the life of that ancient servant of Jesus Christ, John Richardson', *The Friends' library*, 4 (Philadelphia, 1840), 60–127 • *The journals of the lives and travels of Samuel Bownas and John Richardson* (Philadelphia, 1759)

Richardson, John (1668/9–1747), Church of Ireland dean of Kilmacduagh, the son of William Richardson, was born in co. Tyrone. After attending John Morris's school, he entered Trinity College, Dublin, in 1683, where his tutor was St George Ashe. He became a scholar in 1686, and graduated BA in 1688. He was ordained, and in 1694 was appointed to the rectory of Derryloran, co. Tyrone. This he left in 1709 for Annagh, a parish in co. Cavan that includes the town of Belturbet, where he lived for the rest of his life.

Recent laws intended to suppress the Catholic priesthood and ultimately to destroy Catholicism in Ireland stimulated Richardson to propose a more constructive approach among protestants. He revived preaching in the Irish language, a policy adopted intermittently in the previous century but always contentious. In 1711 he secured the backing of the lord lieutenant, Ormond, his diocesan and former tutor, Ashe, and Archbishop King of Dublin. His proposals were approved by the Irish House of Commons, but soon ran into trouble in convocation. There they were drawn into the acrid debates about how best the Church of Ireland should fulfil its mission. Richardson turned instead to England for help, enlisting the SPCK, of which he was a member and the meetings of which he attended in 1711 and 1712. His programme coincided with that of the SPCK, so that the latter assisted the publication and distribution of manuals which he had prepared. These included sermons, a catechism, prayers, and an elementary Irish grammar, each printed in parallel English and Irish texts.

In 1712 Richardson published *A Short History of the Attempts that have been Made to Convert the Popish Natives of Ireland*. This exposed the inconsistencies and hesitancy which had hitherto characterized protestant policy. He boasted of his own successes, but the results of his exertions disappointed his extravagant hopes. Few converted to protestantism and much of the stock of instructional books remained undistributed. Clerical opponents, principally high-churchmen, not only obstructed the project but sought to have him deprived of his living for neglecting it while he lobbied in Dublin and London. Nothing daunted, he reverted to the design in a sermon on 23 October 1715 occasioned by the public recantation at Belturbet of Captain Bryan Reily. Official efforts were increasingly directed into protestant education in English, a policy that Richardson himself furthered through a school at Belturbet. Having spent heavily from his own funds he looked for recompense, but received only the deanery of Kilmacduagh (worth about £120 p.a.) in 1731. His interests had brought him into contact with others proficient in Irish, such as the Revd Philip MacBrady and John O'Mulchroni, and encouraged him to investigate the antiquities and history of Ireland. Nevertheless, the aim remained the eventual eradication of the Irish language and indigenous customs, some of which he attacked in an account of the popular place of pilgrimage, St Patrick's Purgatory, published in 1727 as *The Great Folly, Superstition, and Idolatry, of Pilgrimages in Ireland*.

Richardson died in Archdeacon John Cranston's house at Clogher on 9 September 1747.   TOBY BARNARD

Sources minutes and correspondence, CUL, SPCK MSS · J. Richardson, letter to H. Newman, 19 Nov 1711, BL, Add. MS 4276, fol. 100 · W. King, correspondence, TCD · Burtchaell & Sadleir, *Alum. Dubl.* · J. B. Leslie, *Clogher clergy and parishes* (1929), 72 · J. B. Leslie, *Supplement to 'Armagh clergy and parishes'* (1948), 74 · Letters of

H. Boulter, 2 vols. (1770) · T. C. Barnard, 'Protestants and the Irish language, c.1675–1725', *Journal of Ecclesiastical History*, 44 (1993), 243–72 · *DNB* · *GM*, 17 (1947), 447–8 · H. Cotton, *Fasti ecclesiae Hibernicae*, 4 (1850), 204

Archives BL, letter to Henry Newman, Add. MS 4276, fol. 100 · BL, letter to C. J. Parker, Sloane MS 750, Col. 74

Richardson, John [styled Sir John Richardson, ninth baronet] (**1740/41–1795**), orientalist, was the third son of George Richardson, writer to the signet, of Edinburgh, and of his wife, Jean, daughter of James Watson of Cornton, Stirling. He was apprenticed in 1753 at the age of twelve to the notable Edinburgh printers Thomas and Walter Ruddiman. By 1767 he had moved to London to study law. On 12 November 1767 he was proposed for the Society of Antiquaries of London as of Furnival's Inn. In London he pursued both the law and the study of Arabic and Persian. In his oriental interests Richardson was much influenced by another young man, William Jones, who was already coming to be regarded as a prodigy of learning in Asian languages. With the growth of British territorial power in India the potential market for a Persian dictionary had aroused the interest of London publishers and by 1770 Jones and Richardson were working on a new version of Franciscus Meninski's *Thesaurus linguarum orientalium*, first published in 1680–87. Progress was very slow, and Jones withdrew to concentrate on his legal career, leaving the field to Richardson. Thanks to his 'ingenuity and perseverance' (memorial of A. Hamilton and G. Nicol to East India Company, 6 Feb 1776, BL OIOC, E/1/60, no. 26), an abridged version of the original project eventually appeared in two volumes in 1777 and 1780 as *A Dictionary, Persian, Arabic and English*. Fundamentally revised by others, notably by Charles Wilkins in 1806 and 1810, the dictionary was to have a long life, but although the company took 150 sets, there were few other subscribers and Richardson got little reward for the huge effort he had expended on it.

Richardson made another attempt to tap the British-Indian market in 1776 with *A Grammar of the Arabick Language*, aimed at the East India Company's servants. He modelled his work on Jones's very well received Persian grammar of 1771, stressing, as Jones had done, that what he was offering was a work in which 'instruction' and 'entertainment' would be mixed, and that it would therefore be very different from the turgid linguistic studies of the old orientalists (Richardson, *Grammar*, viii). Richardson, like Jones, wished to be taken for a man of taste as well as of learning. In 1774 he published *A Specimen of Persian Poetry, or, Odes of Hafez*. He matriculated at Wadham College, Oxford, in 1775, at the age of thirty-four. The first volume of his dictionary was prefaced by a long, intellectually ambitious and highly polemical 'Dissertation on the languages, literature and manners of Eastern nations'. Those who tried to write the history of Eastern peoples without using Eastern sources were particular objects of his disdain. One of those thus attacked, Jacob Bryant, retaliated in *An Apology to John Richardson*, to which Richardson replied in a second edition of his 'Dissertation', published separately in 1778. James Boswell, who 'had known Richardson as a printer in Edinburgh' and 'wondered at the great benefit that he had received by studying at Oxford', criticized his style in the 'Dissertation' as 'frequently incorrect and sometimes absurd from his ambition for pomp and metaphor', but was still surprised by its 'abundance and choice of words' (*Boswell in Extremes*, 211).

While pursuing his scholarly and literary ambitions, Richardson had also maintained his study of the law. He was admitted to the Middle Temple in 1775 and called to the bar in 1781. Judging by testimonials given to him by legal luminaries, he developed a successful practice in London. Yet again following the example of Jones, however, Richardson hoped that he might be able to combine the law and oriental scholarship by going to India. In 1783 he asked for leave 'to accompany my friend Sir William Jones' to Bengal, where he hoped to practise as a barrister in the supreme court at Calcutta (Richardson to East India Company, 31 March 1783, BL OIOC, E/1/72, fol. 318). Leave was given, but he did not go to India until after renewing his application in 1790. In Calcutta, where his 'broad Scots dialect' drew comment (*Memoirs of William Hickey*, 4.82–3), he called himself Sir John Richardson, asserting his claim to succeed to a baronetcy revived by his elder brothers, since the second one had died in December 1791, leaving as his heir a child born out of wedlock but legitimized by subsequent marriage. Richardson, who seems neither to have married nor to have had children, died in Calcutta of 'Bengal fever' on 5 May 1795.　　　　P. J. MARSHALL

Sources J. Richardson, 'Preface', *A specimen of Persian poetry, or, Odes of Hafez* (1774) · J. Richardson, 'Preface', *A grammar of the Arabick language* (1776) · letters from or about Richardson, BL OIOC, Home correspondence series E/1 · *Boswell in extremes, 1776–1778*, ed. C. M. Weis and F. A. Pottle (1971), vol. 10 of *The Yale editions of the private papers of James Boswell, trade edn* (1950–89) · F. Johnson, 'Preface', *A dictionary of Persian, Arabic, and English* (1852) · H. A. C. Sturgess, ed., *Register of admissions to the Honourable Society of the Middle Temple, from the fifteenth century to the year 1944*, 1 (1949) · minutes, S. Antiquaries, Lond. · C. B. B. Watson, ed., *Register of Edinburgh apprentices* (1929) · H. Paton, ed., *The register of marriages for the parish of Edinburgh, 1701–1750*, Scottish RS, old ser., 35 (1908) · Foster, *Alum. Oxon.* · minutes of court of directors of the East India Company, BL OIOC, series B · minutes of committee of correspondence, BL OIOC, D/29, fols. 314–15; D/31, fols. 193–4 · GEC, *Baronetage* · *Memoirs of William Hickey*, ed. A. Spencer, 4 vols. (1913–25) · will, PROB 11/1417, fol. 791 · inventory, BL OIOC, L/AG/34/27/17, no. 111
Archives BL OIOC, memorials, petitions, etc.
Wealth at death Rs12,700—value of property in India: inventory, BL OIOC, L/AG/34/27/17, no. 111

Richardson, John (1743–1815), brewer, was born at Folksworth, near Stilton in Cambridgeshire. Sometime resident in London and Liverpool, by his own account he travelled throughout Britain and Europe while practising as a brewer, before settling in Hull and forming a partnership at the North Brewery, Wincolmlee, about 1783. A pioneer in bringing scientific measurement to brewing, he published two major books, *Theoretic Hints on an Improved Practice of Brewing Malt-Liquors* (1777) and *Statical Estimates of the Materials for Brewing* (1784). (These were bound together into one volume with consecutive pagination in 1788 as *The Philosophical Principles of the Science of Brewing*.) His most

influential work was *Statical Estimates*, in which he demonstrated how the hydrometer could be applied in brewing practice. Though he was not the first to use this instrument in brewing, it was he who coined the term saccharometer to describe a hydrometer calibrated in a scale of his own devising, which when used in conjunction with a thermometer allowed accurate measurement of the amount of fermentable matter in wort, in units of direct relevance to the brewer. His work alerted brewers to the economic importance of the hydrometer in providing a means of obtaining uniformity of strength of the subsequent beer, and allowed informed choice of the best yielding malts at a time when increases in the scale of production in the major London breweries were beginning to make accurate measurement imperative. By 1800 many of these breweries had adopted Richardson's instrument and he was destined to become regarded as the father of methodical brewing. The third and final revised edition of his *Philosophical Principles* appeared in 1805. Richardson's brewery was successful and, unusually for the period, the firm had built up a pub estate by the time he sold out in 1810. He took part in the intellectual life of his adopted town and wrote articles on theological matters. He died at Welton, near Hull in 1815.　　　RAYMOND G. ANDERSON

Sources J. Sumner, 'John Richardson, saccharometry and the pounds-per-barrel extract: the construction of a quantity', *British Journal for the History of Science*, 34 (2001), 255–73 · P. Aldabella and R. Barnard, *Hull and East Riding breweries* (1997), 80–81 · *Treatises on brewing*, ed. J. H. Baverstock (1824) · H. S. Corran, *A history of brewing* (1975) · P. Mathias, *The brewing industry in England, 1700–1830* (1959) · T. A. Glendinning, 'A short account of the brewers' saccharometer', *Journal of the Institute of Brewing*, 6 (1900), 357–64 · H. Stopes, *Malt and malting* (1885) · W. Bell, 'One man and his saccharometer', *Brewers' Guardian* (5 Dec 1990), 16–17

Richardson, John (1766–1836), showman, was born in the workhouse at Great Marlow, the town in which he eventually chose to be buried. After working at various menial jobs there and in London, in 1782 he joined an itinerant theatrical troupe led by Mrs Penley, then playing in the club room of the Paviour's Arms tavern, at Shadwell, near Wapping. The company consisted of two men and two women, but staged burlettas requiring a much larger cast, such as *Chrononhotonthologos* and *Midas*, and shared takings of between 4s. 6d. and 5s. a night. Carrying their costumes and scenery on their backs, they took the Gravesend boat to Brompton, near Chatham, where they were engaged by Timothy Moore to perform in a public house. Soon afterwards, Richardson left Mrs Penley and set up as a broker in London. By 1796 he had accumulated enough money to rent The Harlequin tavern, near the stage door of the Theatre Royal, Drury Lane.

In 1798, first at Bartholomew fair and next at Edmonton fair, Richardson began his long career as manager of his own itinerant theatrical show, assembling his company from among the actors who frequented his tavern. He hired two Drury Lane scene-painters, a carpenter, and a dressmaker, and selected three blind Scotsmen, noted as clarinet players, for his band. He constructed his platform above a gingerbread stall, outside the first-floor window of a public house, and attracted so many customers, he later recalled, that he repeated his show twenty-one times a day. During the off-season he acquired caravans in order to travel the circuit of fairs, and for nearly forty years his show was the most prominent attraction of the English fairground, celebrated at the time of his death by William Jerdan as 'the National Theatre' (Jerdan, 184). By the end of his career Richardson had visited some sixty fairs, and after his death the show, still billed as 'Richardson's', carried on until 1852 under the management of John Johnson and Nelson Lee.

Each season generally began at Greenwich fair at Easter and concluded at Bartholomew fair in September. In his second season, 1799, at Stourbridge fair, all but three of Richardson's horses were drowned in a flood, and he lost all his money. After being arrested for failing to pay his ground rent, he was rescued by the generosity of Brunton, the manager of the Norwich theatrical circuit, who presented him with a gift of £5. Even that was insufficient to relieve his financial difficulties, and he was reduced to busking at public houses with Jeffries, the clown, and Brown, a musician, and only finally recouped his losses when the magistrate at Waltham Abbey bespoke a performance by Richardson's company. The next season he was again threatened with arrest when he circulated bills advertising a performance at Twickenham the day after the fair there ended, but he was saved by the great actress Dorothy Jordan, who made up a party to attend the play. Thereafter Richardson met with unparalleled success, and he amassed a fortune, charging 2s. for boxes, 1s. for the pit and 6d. for the gallery at a time when provincial theatres charged 3s., 2s., and 1s. for an entire evening's performance, and when only menageries, among other fairground attractions, charged as much as 6d. His portable theatre booth was capable of holding a thousand spectators at each of a dozen or more performances a day. According to his obituary in the *Gentleman's Magazine*, his estate was worth £20,000 when he died, although Pierce Egan, whose lengthy interview with Richardson is the primary source of information about the showman, states that he possessed less than half that amount (Egan, *Pilgrims*, 116). In 1826, when the fairs were in serious decline, Richardson attempted to sell up, but withdrew his properties when only £2000 was bid at auction. The front of his theatre alone was worth £600, and Jerdan reported that 334 lots of properties were sold, at a fraction of their value, after the showman died in 1836.

Richardson was decidedly a 'character'. He dressed in a blue coat, corduroy breeches, and worsted stockings, and spoke with a broad accent, but styled himself a gentleman, and in his only known portrait sports a top hat. Abstemious in his habits, he never married and lived in a caravan until the final three days of his life. Although shrewd and calculating, he was renowned for his generosity, punctiliously paying good wages to his actors and giving assistance to fellow showfolk in distress, without ever asking for repayment. In an often-repeated anecdote, he paid a subscription of £100 to relieve victims of a fire in St Albans and, when asked his name, proudly replied, 'Richardson, the penny showman'.

A typical performance at Richardson's consisted of a play with numerous scene changes, a comic song, and a pantomime, which sometimes concluded with a panorama. On the large platform outside the theatre, the actors paraded, the clown told jokes, and a barker harangued the crowd—a spectacle which Oxenford judged more exciting than the performance within. The play itself was a brief, vigorous, spectacular melodrama, such as *Virginius*, *The Wandering Outlaw*, *Wallace*, or *The Warlock of the Glen*, in which lurid action, fights and death scenes, and last-minute escape were invariably resolved by the appearance of a ghost. Although a different play was staged daily, the basic formula was pretty much the same. Charles Dickens, who recalled 'the ten thousand million delights' (*Memoirs of Grimaldi*, 1838, 1.xii) he experienced when Richardson's waggons came lumbering into the dull little town where he grew up, described the plot as a confrontation of rightful heir and wrongful heir, then of good assassin and bad assassin, before the heroine is rescued from the villain by the ghost. Once, when the play was going badly, Richardson instructed his leading man to go on and improvise; on being told that he had just been killed on stage, the manager exulted, 'Then the piece is saved—on with his ghost!' (Rosenfeld, 114).

Richardson prided himself on the high quality of his shows. Unusually for the era, his actors were well rehearsed and well paid. He claimed there was not a theatre in London at which some of his performers had not been engaged at one time or another, and he declared that he had seen 'more real talent exhibited at *Feers* than I ever saw at any of the licensed theatres' (Egan, *Pilgrims*, 112). Tom Jeffries, William Oxberry, and John Cartlitch were among those who worked for Richardson, and throughout the 1799 season the ten-year-old Edmund Kean performed along with his mother, Mrs Carey, so successfully that he was invited to give a command performance for George III at Windsor Castle.

Richardson died on 14 November 1836 at Horsemonger Lane, Southwark, and was buried, at his own request, beside George Alexander, the 'spotted boy' whom he had exhibited at the fairs in 1810, in Great Marlow churchyard. Egan states that he left £500 to the actor Johnson and £1000 to Cartlitch. He left annuities for nephews and a niece, and the rest of his estate to Charles and Elizabeth Reed, musicians in his company. In the authoritative judgement of Sybil Rosenfeld, Richardson's achievement was to 'infuse new dramatic life into the fair in the nineteenth century' (*The Theatre of the London Fairs in the 18th Century*, 1960, 70).

PAUL SCHLICKE

Sources S. Rosenfeld, 'Muster Richardson, the great showman', *Western popular theatre*, ed. D. Mayer and K. Richards (1977), 105–21 • P. Egan, *The life of an actor* (1825), 206–18 • P. Egan, *The pilgrims of the Thames* (1838), 81–119 • W. Hone, *The Every-day Book and Table Book*, 1 (1838), 1182 • W. Jerdan, 'Biographical sketch of Richardson the showman', *Bentley's Miscellany*, 1 (1837), 178–86 • *GM*, 2nd ser., 7 (1837), 326–7 • J. Oxenford, 'Richardson's show', *Era Almanack and Annual* (1869), 82–3 • P. Schlicke, 'The showman of *The Pickwick papers*', *Dickens Studies Annual*, 20 (1991), 1–15

Archives GL | Theatre Museum, London, Enthoven collection
Likenesses engraving, repro. in Egan, *The pilgrims of the Thames*, 89 · print, Harvard TC
Wealth at death 'his property altogether did not reach ten thousand pounds, and his theatrical concern, dresses etc, did not fetch, when sold by auction, one thousand pounds': Egan, *Pilgrims*, 116

Richardson, Sir John (1771–1841), judge, was born on 3 March 1771 at Copthall Court, Lothbury, in the City of London, third son of Anthony Richardson, a merchant of London. He was educated at Harrow School before matriculating on 26 January 1789 at University College, Oxford, where he graduated BA in 1792, winning the Latin verse prize for a poem on Mary, queen of Scots, and was awarded his MA in 1795. He was admitted in June 1793 as a student at Lincoln's Inn, where, after practising as a special pleader for several years, he was called to the bar in June 1803. In early life he was closely associated with William Stevens, treasurer of Queen Anne's Bounty, who gave him money while at Oxford. They worked together for the repeal of the penal laws against the Scottish Episcopal church. Richardson was an original member of the Nobody's Club, founded in his honour.

Richardson acted as counsel for William Cobbett at his trial on 24 May 1804 for printing and publishing libels on the lord lieutenant of Ireland and other officials; he also defended him in the civil action brought against him by William Conyngham Plunket. The author of the alleged libel on the Irish officials was an Irish judge, Robert Johnson. On his indictment at Westminster in June 1805 Richardson argued that the court of king's bench had no business to be concerned with offences committed by Irishmen in Irish territory. The plea being disallowed, Richardson appeared for Johnson in the trial which followed, and which ended in a *nolle prosequi*. About the same time Richardson defended Henry Delahay Symonds on a charge of libelling the Roman Catholic archbishop of Dublin, John Thomas Troy. Richardson's defence speech was in effect an attack on the Catholic religion. Not long afterwards he was chosen to fill the post of devil to the attorney-general, and on 30 November 1818 he succeeded Sir Robert Dallas as puisne judge of the court of common pleas, being at the same time made serjeant-at-law. On 3 June 1819 he was knighted by the prince regent at Carlton House.

Richardson's tenure was brief, since illness forced him to retire in May 1824. After retirement he spent much of his time in Malta, where he edited *The Harlequin, or, Anglo-Maltese Miscellany* and drafted a code of laws for the island. He died at his house in Bedford Square, London, on 19 March 1841. His wife Harriet, about whom little is known, died in 1839; they had a son, John Joseph, who was called to the bar at Lincoln's Inn in 1832.

J. M. RIGG, *rev.* HUGH MOONEY

Sources *Annual Register* (1818) · *Annual Register* (1819) · *Annual Register* (1841) · *The Times* (20 March 1841) · Foss, *Judges* · E. Henderson, *Recollections of the late John Adolphus* (1871) · J. A. Park, *Memoirs of William Stevens*, 4th edn (1859), 29, 115, 125, 175 · *GM*, 2nd ser., 16 (1841), 193, 417

Richardson, John (1780–1864), lawyer, was born on 9 May 1780 at Gilmerton, Midlothian, the son of John Richardson (*d.* 1781), farmer at Gilmerton, and his wife, Hope Gifford (*d. c.*1785), niece of Principal William Robertson. His father died when he was eight months, and his mother when he was a few years old. On his mother's side he was related to the Brougham family, and Eleanor Brougham, Henry Brougham's mother, was very kind to him in youth and his friend in later years. He was sent to school at Dalkeith, where he remained until 1794, and then he was entered at the University of Edinburgh, where he was friendly with Henry, James, and Peter Brougham. His other friends in early life included Henry Cockburn and Francis Jeffrey, Francis Horner, James Grahame, John Leyden, Thomas Campbell, and Walter Scott. In his youth he was a strong democrat, and he wrote songs which were sent to the Irish and British refugees at Hamburg; these he characterized in later life as 'sad trash'.

In 1796 Richardson was apprenticed to a writer to the signet. After qualifying as a solicitor, he decided in 1806 to move to London and to conduct Scottish cases in parliament. Lord Cockburn noted that Richardson was the last of a band of young and ambitious Scotsmen 'to be devoured by hungry London', the hunger being not wholly on London's side. With a patrimony of £1000, Richardson took up residence in Fludyer Street, Westminster, where he lived for many years, though his start as a solicitor was slow with 'many a heavy and sorrowful day'. On 5 August 1811 he married Elizabeth (*d.* 1836), daughter of Lawrence Hill, writer to the signet. His ultimate success as a parliamentary solicitor was great, and his firm, Richardson, Loch, and Maclaurin, had a high reputation. For thirty years Richardson was crown agent for Scotland, and solicitor for the city of Edinburgh; he was also the London law agent of the University of Glasgow, which made him an honorary LLD on 2 December 1830. On 13 November 1827 he was admitted a writer to the signet.

Richardson moved in literary society in London and in Scotland. He was the legal adviser of Thomas Campbell, also a friend of his wife. In 1821 he introduced George Crabbe to Campbell in Joanna Baillie's house at Hampstead, which was near his own. Sir Walter Scott, who regularly corresponded with him, said of him in a letter to Joanna Baillie on 10 December 1813 'Johnnie Richardson is a good honourable kind-hearted little fellow as lives in the world with a pretty taste for poetry which he has wisely kept under subjection to the occupation of drawing briefs and revising conveyances' (*The Letters of Sir Walter Scott*, 3.389). Scott confided to Richardson the secret of the Waverley novels. In 1806 Richardson recorded that he met Scott in Campbell's house at Sydenham, where they had 'a very merry night', and Scott, for the only time in his life, attempted to sing. He acted for Scott's children over a legacy. On Scott's recommendation in 1830 he bought the estate of Kirklands, Ancrum, Roxburghshire, where he spent the autumn months every year thereafter until 1860. Richardson saw Scott in London in June 1832 when he stopped there on his return, a dying man, from Italy to Abbotsford; the sound of a familiar voice roused Scott from his lethargy and made him ask, 'How does Kirklands get on?' In his eightieth year, Richardson retired to Kirklands. He died there, after three years of illness, on 4 October 1864, leaving several children. Some of his poems were published in Joanna Baillie's *Collection of Poems* (1823).   W. F. RAE, *rev.* H. C. G. MATTHEW

Sources J. G. Lockhart, *Memoirs of the life of Sir Walter Scott*, 2 vols. (Philadelphia, 1837) · *The letters of Sir Walter Scott*, ed. H. J. C. Grierson and others, centenary edn, 12 vols. (1932–79) · *The journal of Sir Walter Scott*, ed. W. E. K. Anderson (1972) · *GM*, 3rd ser., 18 (1865), 239 · *Memorials of his time, by Henry Cockburn* (1856) · *Life and letters of Thomas Campbell*, ed. W. Beattie, 3 vols. (1849)
Archives NL Scot., corresp. and papers | NL Scot., corresp. with John Lee · NL Scot., corresp. with Robertson-Macdonald family · NL Scot., letters to Andrew Rutherford · NL Scot., corresp. with Sir Walter Scott
Wealth at death £18,473 9s. 3d.: confirmation, 13 Dec 1864, *CCI*

Sir John Richardson (1787–1865), by Bernhard Smith, 1842

Richardson, Sir John (1787–1865), physician, naturalist, and Arctic explorer, was born on 5 November 1787 at 11 Nith Place, Dumfries, Scotland, eldest of the twelve children of Gabriel Richardson and Anne, daughter of Peter Mundell of Dumfries. Gabriel Richardson was a prosperous brewer, provost at one time, and chief magistrate of Dumfries for many years. Both parents taught their son to be thoughtful of others and deeply religious. He was precocious in his studies, encouraged by Robert Burns (a neighbour and frequent visitor), and entered Dumfries grammar school at an early age. In 1800 he was apprenticed to his uncle James Mundell, a retired naval surgeon in practice at the infirmary in Dumfries, on whose death he transferred to Dr Samuel Shortridge. In 1803 he went to Edinburgh University, following medical courses and also studying natural history with geologist Robert Jameson.

In 1804 Richardson interrupted his studies to serve as temporary house surgeon in the Dumfries and Galloway Infirmary. In 1805, he became FRCS (Lond.). In 1807 he became assistant surgeon aboard the frigate *Nymphe*. With successive service on the *Hibernia*, *Hercules*, *Blossom*, and *Cruiser*, he advanced to senior surgeon. He enjoyed life at sea, and saw action at the battle of Copenhagen and the blockade of the Tagus, and was commended for coolness and bravery. After cruising off the Scottish coast against American privateers in the Anglo-American War of 1812–14, he went to North America as surgeon to the 1st battalion, Royal Marines, taking part in raids on St Mary's and Cumberland Island, Georgia. He thought the pillaging and assaults on noncombatants and their property degrading to the British character.

When peace returned in 1815 Richardson resumed study in Edinburgh and became doctor of medicine in 1816 after submitting a thesis on yellow fever, *De febre flava*. He started a private practice in Leith and on 1 June 1818 married Mary (1795–1831), daughter of Alexander Stiven, brewer of Leith. When his practice faltered, he applied to join an Admiralty expedition to the Canadian Arctic. Surgeons who could double as naturalists were preferred in the peacetime navy; they could bring back data on weather and specimens of minerals, plants, and animals for possible commercial use. Recommended by Jameson and others in Edinburgh, he attained the appointment, which

he saw as a chance for advancement and contact with leaders in science. The expedition was to search for the north-west passage, under the command of John Franklin. Richardson became the lifelong friend and loyal supporter of a leader to whom he was perhaps superior in ability. Others in the party were George Back, Robert Hood, and John Hepburn.

The expedition left England in May 1819 and reached the Northwest Fur Company's Fort Providence in July 1820. From there they pushed on to the confluence of the Yellowknife and Coppermine Rivers, where they built Fort Enterprise, their quarters for the winter. In the summer of 1821 they descended the Coppermine River in canoes to the Polar Sea, and charted 500 miles of difficult, unexplored coastline eastward, until bad weather and short rations halted them at Point Turnagain. The journey back over the Barren Lands was calamitous because of early storms, freezing temperatures, and lack of food. At one point Richardson nearly lost his life trying to swim across the icy Coppermine River with a lifeline. While the others struggled on towards Fort Enterprise, he and Hepburn volunteered to stay behind with Hood, who was too weak to travel further without resting.

Two days later, on 9 October 1821, Michel Terohaute, an Iroquois voyageur, rejoined them. Previously a valued companion, he had become unco-operative, dictatorial, and threatening and Richardson and Hepburn became convinced that meat he brought in, saying it was wolf, was human. On 20 October 1821 they heard a shot and found Hood dead. Terohaute, standing by, claimed he had killed him accidentally. On 23 October the three men set out for Fort Enterprise. Michel, stronger and better armed, became increasingly menacing. Richardson, the senior officer, executed him with a shot through the head, 'a dreadful act', he said, but necessary.

Weak and starving, Richardson and Hepburn struggled to Fort Enterprise, where they found the advance party in even worse condition than themselves, some dead, others subsisting on lichens and the larvae of insects. The supplies promised by the fur companies had never arrived. Akaicho, chief of the Copper Indians, was convinced that the explorers had perished, and failed to send supplies as arranged. When alerted by a search party under George

Back, he acted immediately, saving the lives of those who remained at Fort Enterprise.

The expedition returned to England in October 1822, having traversed some 5500 miles. Franklin was a national hero, Richardson a naturalist of consequence. Lady Franklin described him about this time as 'a middle-sized man … not well dressed … upon the whole rather plain, but the countenance thoughtful, mild and pleasing' (Johnson, 51). He had to face rumours of cannibalism and criticism of his shooting of Terohaute. Some wanted Richardson punished as a murderer. Franklin believed him justified. There was no official Admiralty inquiry and an account he sent privately to the Admiralty was modified before publication, so the matter remains unclear.

Richardson was granted leave to write up his sections of Franklin's narrative, published in 1823. In 1824 he was appointed surgeon to the marine division at Chatham, but was allowed to deputize his duties to accompany Franklin on a second expedition, which he saw as a chance to complete a definitive study of the plants and animals of the Canadian Arctic. All went well this time. Two trading companies whose feuding had hindered supplies and assistance to the earlier expedition were now at peace and provided support. Richardson had a young Scottish botanist, Thomas Drummond, to help with the collection of data and specimens. In the summer of 1826 he accompanied Franklin to the mouth of the Mackenzie River, where they separated, Franklin's group going 374 miles west, Richardson's group east to the mouth of the Coppermine River. With their earlier expedition, this accounted for 800 continuous miles of hitherto unmapped coastline. Richardson returned to England in 1827.

In 1828 Richardson was appointed chief medical officer of Melville Naval Hospital, Chatham, where he began the work that established him as a great naturalist, *Fauna Boreali-Americana* (1829–37). His first wife died on 25 December 1831 and on 8 February 1833 he married Mary Booth (1807–1845). She was a niece of Franklin and daughter of John Booth of Stickney, near Ingoldmells, Lincolnshire. They had seven children. In 1838 he was appointed senior physician at the Royal Naval Hospital Haslar, Gosport, and in 1840 he became inspector of hospitals. He made Haslar Library and Museum into an important centre for natural history, frequented by such distinguished figures as Darwin, Hooker the elder, Gray, and Lyell. Future scientists such as the younger Hooker and Thomas Henry Huxley came there to be trained.

In 1845 Franklin attempted his third search for the north-west passage, but Richardson's professional duties, the death of his second wife on 10 April 1845, and the care of his young children prevented his joining the expedition. By 1847, with no news from Franklin and anxiety mounting, the Admiralty authorized searches for the missing men. Richardson said that he had a sacred duty to help his old friend. Leaving his third wife, Mary (1802–1880), daughter of Archibald *Fletcher and Eliza *Fletcher, whom he had married on 4 August 1847, he set out with John Rae. In three boats, with eighteen men, they reached the mouth of the Mackenzie River in August 1848 and scouted eastward toward the Coppermine River. They had a difficult retreat across the Barren Lands to Great Bear Lake, where they wintered. Admitting that the task was too taxing for him, Richardson left the younger men to carry on, and returned to England in 1849; in 1851 he published *An Arctic Searching Expedition*.

Richardson's last years at Haslar were clouded. In 1853 Parry, his superior, with whom he worked happily, was transferred; the Crimean War brought an influx of sick and wounded; his youngest son died. When the director general of medical services retired, Richardson was not chosen to succeed him. Aged sixty-seven, he was said to be too old. He himself thought it was a question of favouritism, prestige, and money and decided to retire.

The family moved to Easedale, Westmorland, to the Lancrigg estate inherited by his third wife from her mother. Richardson continued his biological research as long as was practicable. He had been knighted in 1846 and in 1850 he became a companion of the Bath. In 1857 he was given an honorary LLD by Trinity College, Dublin. A fellow of the Royal Society since 1825, he received its Royal Medal in 1856.

In retirement Richardson occupied himself tramping over the Westmorland hills, touring Europe, gardening, calling on friends, maintaining a charity medical practice, and continuing a long-standing interest in philology. In 1861 he published *The Polar Regions*. He died at home in his bed on 5 June 1865, possibly after a recurrence of the 'spasms of the heart' from which he suffered in 1846 and 1848. He was buried at St Oswald's Church, Grasmere, on 7 June.

Richardson was eminent in medicine, exploration, and natural history. In medicine he held many advanced ideas. At Haslar he inaugurated regular routines, cleanliness, fresh air in the wards, general anaesthesia, nursing standards akin to those of Florence Nightingale (whom he knew), and humane treatment of the mentally ill. In *De febre flava* he came close to guessing the transmission of yellow fever. He proved, contrary to current opinion, that snow water was not the cause of goitre. He wrote a first-class description of protein-calorie malnutrition in men working under stress in the cold.

As an explorer, Richardson mapped with Franklin some 800 miles of coastline along the Polar Sea, more than any other team, and is remembered by Richardson's Mountain, Richardson's River, and Richardson's Point. His search for Franklin in 1847–9 was a model of careful planning and good execution, with no loss of life, no injuries, no shortages of food, and no lack of shelter. He shared the reasonable belief that some of Franklin's party survived the sinking of the *Erebus* and *Terror* and discovered the north-west passage before they died; and he argued for his old friend in *The Times* when McClure later claimed to have completed the discovery of the passage.

Richardson was pre-eminent in the natural history of the Canadian Arctic. His eight years of collecting and a lifetime of study are recorded in such eponyms of animals and plants as Richardson's goose, salmon, ground squirrel, gentian, aster, and locoweed. After 1837 he concentrated on ichthyology. Surgeon–naturalists from as far away as China, Japan, and New Zealand sent him specimens as he 'became *par excellence* the ichthyologist of England' (McIlraith, 277). He had over 100 publications to his name, many written in collaboration with distinguished scientists.

A twentieth-century tribute to Richardson by Dr D. A. Stewart aptly summed up his life: 'It is not every day that we meet in one person surgeon, physician, sailor, soldier, administrator, explorer, naturalist, author and scholar, who has been eminent in some roles and commendable in all' (Stewart, 1936, 16).

ROBERT E. JOHNSON and MARGARET H. JOHNSON

Sources J. McIlraith, *Life of Sir John Richardson* (1868) · R. E. Johnson, *Sir John Richardson. Arctic explorer, natural historian, naval surgeon* (1976) · C. S. Houston, ed., *Arctic ordeal: the journal of John Richardson, surgeon naturalist with Franklin* (1984) · W. J. Hooker and others, *Flora Boreali-Americana* (1840) · E. Fletcher, *Autobiography of Mrs. Fletcher of Edinburgh* (1874) · C. S. Houston, 'New light on Sir John Richardson', *Canadian Medical Association Journal*, 131 (1984), 653–60 · L. H. Neatby, *The search for Franklin* (1970) · R. Cyriax, *Sir John Franklin's last Arctic expedition* (1939) · D. A. Stewart, 'Sir John Richardson, surgeon, physician, sailor, explorer, naturalist, scholar', *Canadian Medical Association Journal*, 24 (1931), 292–7 · M. F. Curvey and R. E. Johnson, 'A bibliography of Sir John Richardson, (1787–1865)—printed books', *Journal of the Society of the Bibliography of Natural History*, 5 (1968–71), 202–7 · M. A. Huntley, R. E. Johnson, and A. P Bell, 'A bibliography of Sir John Richardson—articles in learned journals', *Journal of the Society of the Bibliography of Natural History*, 6 (1971–4), 98–117 · J. E. Gray, Gray Collection, NHM · D. A. Stewart, 'Sir John Richardson, surgeon, physician, sailor, explorer, naturalist, scholar', *Journal of the Royal Naval Medical Service*, 22 (July 1936), 181–7
Archives BM · Bodl. Oxf., corresp. · Chesham Bois, Buckinghamshire · Dumfries and Galloway Archives, Dumfries, letters, mainly to his sister, and papers · McGill University, Montreal, McCord Museum, corresp. and papers · NHM, notebook · NMM · RBG Kew · RGS, corresp. and papers · Saskatchewan University · Scott Polar RI, corresp. and papers · University of Illinois, Urbana-Champaign, journals and papers | Bath Royal Literary and Scientific Institution, letters to Leonard Blomefield · Derbys. RO, corresp. with Sir John Franklin · Linn. Soc., letters to William Swainson · NHM, corresp. with Sir Richard Owen and William Clift · PRO, letters to Sir John Ross, BJ2 · PRO, letters to Sir Edward Sabine, BJ3 · Royal Burgh Museum, Dumfries, Crombie bequest · Scott Polar RI, Mott MSS · U. Edin. L., letters to David Laing · U. St Andr. L., corresp. with James David Forbes · W. Sussex RO, letters to duke of Richmond
Likenesses T. Phillips, oils, 1825, Royal Naval Hospital, Gosport · B. Smith, plaster medallion, 1842, NPG [*see illus.*] · H. Smith, portrait medallion, 1842, Royal Borough Museum, Dumfries · S. Pearce, oils, 1850, NPG · crayon drawing, 1857, Richardson-Voss collection, Amersham, Buckinghamshire · photograph, 1862, Scott Polar Institute, Cambridge, Mott collection · L. Towers, photograph, 1864, Royal Borough Museum, Dumfries · photograph, 1864, Royal Borough Museum, Dumfries · S. Pearce, group portrait, oils (*The Arctic Council, 1851*), NPG · brass plaque, Haslar Hospital, Gosport
Wealth at death under £7000—in UK: probate, 10 July 1865, *CGPLA Eng. & Wales* · £8500: probate, McIlraith, *Life of Sir John*

Richardson, John (1797–1852), author, was born near Niagara Falls, Upper Canada. His father was Robert Richardson, a Scottish surgeon in the army, his mother, a Miss Askin, the daughter of a wealthy merchant then living in Detroit. John was the eldest of their six children. When he was young his father was posted to Amherstburg, where John spent a happy childhood. He served in the Canadian militia (41st regiment) during the Anglo-American War of 1812–14, and was taken prisoner at the battle of the Thames. After his liberation he entered the British army, and in 1815 went to England, where he married a woman from Essex. He spent part of his time in Paris, and in 1829 published *Écarté, or, The Salons of Paris*, which was poorly reviewed. In 1835 he joined the British Auxiliary Legion raised to fight in the Carlist War. He was appointed senior captain in the sixth Scots grenadiers, and in 1836 attained his majority and was made a knight of the military order of St Ferdinand by Queen Christina. But he quarrelled with his commander, George De Lacy Evans, to whose politics he was hostile, and pursued the grievance in his *Journal of the Movements of the British Legion* (1836). The matter was investigated by the House of Commons, and, the result not satisfying Richardson, he returned to the charge in his *Personal Memoirs* (1838). He also persuaded Theodore Hook to lampoon Evans and other officers in print, but this idea failed for want of a publisher.

Meanwhile, Richardson's tory politics recommended him to *The Times*, and in 1838 he agreed to become its correspondent in Canada, where Papineau's rebellion was in progress: but he so partisanly supported Lord Durham's arbitrary administration that he was dismissed. In 1840 he established, at Brockville, Ontario, a newspaper, the *New Era*, which lasted two years, and in 1843 he began to publish at Kingston, Ontario, the *Native Canadian*, in which he strongly supported Metcalfe's government. These were not particularly successful ventures and by 1845 Richardson had become a superintendent of police on the Welland Canal. The force was disbanded that year, and in 1848–9 Richardson moved to the United States, to live in New York city. He continued to write books and for the press until his death in poverty in that city in 1852. His *Wacousta, or, The Prophecy* (1832) was thought by contemporaries to be the best of his books and was popular. It drew on experiences from his early life in Amherstburg and his knowledge gained there of Indian life and customs. His *Wau-Nan-Gee* (1852) was also quite well liked. *Eight Years in Canada* (1847), although winning same praise for its account of life in the country, was mainly autobiographical and marred by Richardson's bitterness.

B. H. SOULSBY, rev. ELIZABETH BAIGENT

Sources J. Richardson, *Personal memoirs* (1838) · J. Richardson, *Eight years in Canada* (1847) · Allibone, *Dict.* · H. J. Morgan, *Sketches of celebrated Canadians, and persons connected with Canada* (1862) · A. MacMurchy, *A handbook of Canadian literature* (1906) · Boase, *Mod. Eng. biog.* · R. H. D. Barham, *The life and remains of Theodore Edward Hook*, new edn (1877)

Richardson, John (1817–1886), poet, was born on 20 August 1817 at Stone House (later called Piper House) in Naddle Vale, near Keswick, Cumberland, the son of Daniel Richardson, mason, and his wife Mary, *née* Faulder. He was educated under 'Priest' Wilson, who was master at the school of St John's in the Vale and incumbent of its little church. On leaving school Richardson followed his father's trade, and eventually became a builder. Among other works of a public character he rebuilt the church, the parsonage, and the schoolhouse of St John's in the Vale, where he was living. In 1840 he married Grace Birkett, who, with eight of their ten children, survived him. About 1857 he became master of the school, in which he laboured with untiring energy and remarkable success until partially disabled by a paralytic seizure about a year before his death.

Many of Richardson's writings, which are numerous, both in prose and verse, are rendered in the vernacular of the district of Cumberland in which he had spent his life. Besides his *Cumberland Talk* (1st ser., 1871; 2nd ser., 1876) Richardson read seven papers to the Keswick Literary Society, which were printed in the *Transactions of the Cumberland Association for the Advancement of Literature and Science*. In 1879 and 1880 he contributed to the *West Cumberland Times* a series of sketches, *Stwories 'at Granny Used to Tell*. He also contributed to various newspapers pieces of poetry and prose, some of them in the Cumberland dialect. Most of his compositions are characterized by humour and pathos. As a poet and songwriter he had a great local reputation. He died on the fellside, near his residence, Bridge House, on 30 April 1886.

ALBERT NICHOLSON, *rev.* S. R. J. BAUDRY

Sources private information (1896) [W. Routh Fitzpatrick, son-in-law] · H. D. Rawnsley, *Literary associations of the English Lakes* (1894), 2.234 · W. Andrews, *North country poets* (1888–9)

Wealth at death £281 9s. 6d.: administration, 12 July 1886, *CGPLA Eng. & Wales*

Richardson, Sir John Larkins Cheese (1810–1878), army officer and politician in New Zealand, the son of Robert Richardson of the Bengal civil service and his wife, Mary Anne, *née* Romney, was born in Bengal on 4 August 1810. He was sent to England to be educated for the East Indian military service, and in 1827 entered Addiscombe College. In 1828 he returned to India, and on 12 December joined the East India Company's service as a cadet in the Bengal artillery. He became lieutenant on 19 August 1837. He served in the Afghan campaign of 1842 and in the Anglo-Sikh wars. He was wounded at Ferozeshahr, and received medal and clasps (22 December 1845). On 21 August 1846 he was made commissary-general of ordnance and on 6 October 1846 he was promoted captain. He retired on 18 March 1852 and became major on 28 November 1854.

On 11 February 1834 Richardson had married Charlotte Laing at Agra; they had three children before Charlotte's death in 1842. In 1852 he travelled to New Zealand, with a view to settling his family there. He made a thorough tour of the colony, of which he gave, on his return to England, an informative account in *A Summer's Excursion in New Zealand ... by an Old Bengalee*. He also published a long poem on 'The first Christian martyr of the New Zealand church', which reflected his lifelong devoted allegiance to the Church of England.

In 1856 Richardson left England, with his children, as a pastoral settler, and after arriving at Port Chalmers in October purchased 150 acres in Otago, which he called Willowmead. He occasionally contributed to the *Otago Witness*, and in March 1860 became member, and subsequently speaker, of the Otago provincial council for his own district of Clutha. In May 1861 he was elected superintendent of Otago province, and drew on his military training to maintain public order in controlling the gold rush which took place in that year. He rapidly organized an effective police and personal security service, appointing experienced policemen from the Victoria goldfields, and prevented all trouble. In 1863 his opposition to political separation for the province led to his defeat in the new election for superintendent, but he was returned to the provincial council, of which he again became speaker; in October he also entered the house of representatives as member for Dunedin district. He continued to represent his own district in the provincial council until 1866, when he stood down, but he was instead elected for New Plymouth.

In November 1864 Richardson became postmaster-general in the Weld ministry, and in 1867, under Edward Stafford, Weld's successor, continued in office as legislative councillor without portfolio. He was largely responsible for legislation connected with the militia and the regulation of the goldfields. Between 1868 and 1878 he served as speaker of the legislative council, an office he filled with dignity and integrity, and in which he commanded great respect, but he was vilified in his home province because of the effects of the government's fiscal policy there. In 1875 he was knighted. He died at Dunedin on 6 December 1878, leaving his three children, who settled in New Zealand.

Richardson took particular interest in the educational progress of the young colony. In Dunedin he started the first public girls' high school in the southern hemisphere. Under his auspices as first chancellor, Otago became the first Australasian university to admit women students. He also campaigned in 1873 for shorter working hours for women in workshops.

C. A. HARRIS, *rev.* JANE TUCKER

Sources O. Trotter, 'Richardson, John Larkins Cheese', *DNZB*, vol. 1 · P. Mennell, *The dictionary of Australasian biography* (1892) · R. S. Hill, *Policing the colonial frontier: the theory and practice of coercive social and racial control in New Zealand, 1767–1867* (1986) · W. Gisborne, *New Zealand rulers and statesmen, 1840–1885* (1886) · B. J. Foster, 'Richardson, Sir John Larkins Cheese', *An encyclopaedia of New Zealand*, ed. A. H. McLintock, 3 (1966) · A. Lynch, 'The garden of Otago', MA diss., University of Otago, 1989 · *New Zealand Times* (8 Dec 1878)

Archives Otago Early Settlers Museum, Dunedin, New Zealand, personal and family papers

Likenesses two photographs, NL NZ, Turnbull L.

Wealth at death £5510 2s. 4d.—effects in New Zealand: probate and testamentary records, 1879, Archives New Zealand, Wellington

Richardson, John Wigham (1837–1908), shipbuilder, was born on 7 January 1837 in Torquay, Devon, where his family was spending the winter, the second son in the family of four sons and seven daughters of Edward Richardson (1806–1863), leather manufacturer, of Newcastle upon Tyne, from an old Yorkshire Quaker family in Whitby, and his wife, Jane, *née* Wigham (1808–1873) of Edinburgh. Richardson was educated at Dr Collingwood Bruce's academy in Newcastle, and at a private school in the home of J. D. Carr, the biscuit manufacturer, in Carlisle, before spending two years at Bootham School, the Quaker school in York. He left in 1852 to work as a ship's draughtsman for a few months for a relative, Senhouse Martindale, a Lloyds surveyor in Liverpool. In 1853 he took up an apprenticeship with Jonathan Robson, a builder of steam tugs in Gateshead, making iron ships and marine engines. After completing this in 1856, he spent a year at University College, London, studying Latin, German, English literature, and mathematics, and in the summer of 1857 he studied German in Tübingen. However, after the collapse of the Northumberland and District Bank, in which his father was a large shareholder, in the same year, he returned to Newcastle to a job in the machine-drawing office of the Forth Banks engine works of R. and W. Hawthorn (Robert Hawthorn was a neighbour). In 1864 he married Marian Henrietta (*b. c.*1845), eldest daughter of J. P. Thöl of Wycombe Marsh, Buckinghamshire; they had five sons and two daughters.

In 1860, with his father's help, Richardson bought Coutts's yard, a small shipyard at Walker, where the first iron ship on the Tyne had been launched in 1842, and founded the Neptune Works. He appointed John Denham Christie, a naval architect, as his assistant: Christie became his partner in 1862. The Neptune Works occupied a 4 acre site, with 100 yards' river frontage and three building berths, and employment for 200 men. The first ship to be built, the *Victoria*, was a small ferry-steamer for the Isle of Wight–Portsmouth route, but business was slow in the early years. Relying mainly on overseas customers, Richardson persevered, and in 1865 secured an order from the Prussian government for a steamer to carry railway trains across the Rhine, the first of many such ferries built by the yard. As business grew, thanks to Richardson's energetic pursuit of new orders, he decided to open his own marine-engine and boiler works in 1872, and in 1879 he appointed a marine-engine designer, John Tweedy. By the 1880s the yard was building every kind of ship except warships, and despite the slump of the mid-1880s the Neptune yard prospered, launching the steel-hulled *Alfonso XII* for the Spanish Compania Transatlantica in 1888, the largest non-warship built on the Tyne at that date. The yard built a number of Italian emigrant ships for the crossing from the Italian ports to South America, and in 1889 it launched its first refrigerated ship. By 1898, when the north yard was added, the firm had a workforce of 2000 and the capacity for 30,000 tons of shipping. In 1899 the company built the engines and boilers for the Russian ice-breaker *Angara*, which had to be transported out to Lake Baikal for fitting, and in 1902 it launched the 500 foot *Colonia*, a cable ship carrying 4000 miles of cable built for the Telegraph and Maintenance Company Ltd.

In 1899 a limited liability company, Wigham Richardson & Co. Ltd, was formed, with Richardson as chairman, and in 1903 the company amalgamated with Swan, Hunter of Wallsend to become Swan, Hunter, and Wigham Richardson Ltd, the largest merchant shipbuilding concern on the Tyne, which survived until nationalization of the shipbuilding industry in 1977. Richardson became vice-chairman of the new company. Later in 1903 the company bought the Tyne Pontoons and Dry Dock Company to give 4000 feet of continuous frontage along the Tyne.

Richardson was influential in the development of the shipbuilding industry in the north-east. As a result of his pamphlet *Lloyd's Register of Shipping: its Effect … upon the Art of Shipbuilding* (1874), the rules of Lloyds were modified. He was one of those who founded the journal *Shipping World* in Newcastle in 1882, and he was its first chairman. A founder member of the North East Coast Institution of Engineers and Shipbuilders in 1884, he served as president in 1890–92 and was a member of the North of England Institute of Mining Engineers and the Institution of Naval Architects, regularly contributing papers to all of these. He was president of the Newcastle Economic Society from 1896 to 1897. He also played an active part in local affairs as a member of Northumberland county council for many years, and as a JP for Northumberland he was chairman of the Castle ward licensing committee. An enthusiastic artist himself, he gave many paintings to the Walker Mechanics Institute, and donated a window in Christ Church, Walker, in memory of his elder sister, Anna Deborah Richardson. He was a director of the Walker and Wallsend Union Gas Company, and of the Tyne Pontoons and Dry Dock Company, and he was one of the first subscribers to the Tyneside Tramways and Tramroads Company, which opened in 1902.

Richardson was widely read and cultured. He liked to write Latin verses, and in the 1880s he held a series of evenings reading and translating the works of Virgil with a group of friends including the shipbuilder Sir Benjamin Chapman Browne and the banker Thomas Hodgkin. His interests included political economy and sociology, military and naval history, architecture—he designed a number of houses—and chess, and he became an expert on the construction of sundials, contributing an appendix to a new edition of Mrs Alfred Gatty's *Book of Sun-Dials* (1889). A good linguist, he travelled widely in Poland, Russia, Greece, and Turkey, and was particularly interested in visiting the battlefields of the Crimean and Franco-Prussian wars. He also went to North America, the West Indies, and Africa, making watercolour sketches of all his travels. As he grew older he turned to the Church of England, and attended Benwell church in Newcastle.

Richardson died suddenly on 15 April 1908 at 11 Nottingham Place, London, following an operation, and was buried on 18 April at Kensal Green cemetery. His wife survived him. *The Memoirs of John Wigham Richardson* were privately published in 1911.   ANNE PIMLOTT BAKER

Sources J. F. Clarke, *Building ships on the north east coast*, 1: *c.1640–1914* (1997) · *Launching ways: published on the occasion of their jubilee*, Swan, Hunter, and Wigham Richardson Ltd (1953) · *Memoirs of John Wigham Richardson* (1911) · W. Richardson, *History of the parish of Wallsend and Willington* (1923) · J. F. Clarke, 'Richardson, John Wigham', *DBB* · D. Dougan, *The history of north east shipbuilding* (1968) · L. A. Ritchie, ed., *The shipbuilding industry: a guide to historical*

records (1992) • 'John Wigham Richardson', *Mid-Tyne Link*, 2/7 (winter 1905–6), 145–51 • census returns, 1881 • *The Times* (16 April 1908) • *The Shipbuilder*, 3/9 (summer 1908) • *Engineering* (24 April 1908) • *Newcastle Weekly Chronicle* (18 April 1908) • *Newcastle Daily Journal* (16 April 1908) • *Transactions of the NE Coast Institution of Engineers and Shipbuilders*, 24 (1907–8) • d. cert.
Likenesses photograph, 1866, repro. in *Memoirs* • photograph, 1905, repro. in *Memoirs* • Bacon, photograph, repro. in *The Shipbuilder*
Wealth at death £92,001: Clarke, 'Richardson, John Wigham'

Richardson, Jonathan, the elder (1667–1745), portrait painter and writer, was born on 12 January 1667 in the parish of St Botolph without Bishopsgate, London, and baptized at St Botolph's on 17 January, the son of William Richardson (*c*.1620–1672), silk weaver and citizen of London, and his wife, Mary. Richardson's mother remarried, and about 1681 his stepfather apprenticed him to a scrivener. After six unhappy years he was released from his apprenticeship and began training to be a painter, for which he had a 'strong inclination' (Vertue, *Note books*, 3.23). His chosen master was the English-born portrait painter John Riley, with whom he lived until Riley's death in 1691. In early 1693 (in Lincoln's Inn chapel) he married Elizabeth Bray (*c*.1671–1726), a close relation of Riley's. Richardson may have taken over Riley's house and studio in Lincoln's Inn Fields, for from at least as early as 1703 (the date of the earliest extant list of occupants) until 1724 he lived in Holborn Row, Lincoln's Inn Fields. Elizabeth Richardson bore eleven children between 1694 and 1711, most of whom seem to have survived infancy; she died in January 1726. The eldest son, **Jonathan Richardson the younger** (1694–1771), who was born on 14 February 1694 and baptized the same day at St Giles-in-the-Fields, London, shared many of his father's literary and artistic interests. Although Horace Walpole states that he 'painted a little', and the sale catalogue of his collection included a few of his own drawings, Richardson the younger was raised as a gentleman, not a professional artist, and none of his works are identifiable today. His education included the acquisition of foreign and classical languages and, unlike his father, he travelled abroad (to Holland, Flanders, France, and Italy in 1716 and 1720).

Richardson the elder quickly established himself as a leading portraitist, and by 1705 was commanding prices for his pictures that were comparable to those of Sir Godfrey Kneller, the most fashionable portrait painter in England at the time. George Vertue placed Richardson, along with Kneller, Michael Dahl, and Charles Jervas, in the élite group of portraitists who led the field 'in great business and esteem amongst people of Quality' (Vertue, *Note books*, 3.138). He painted a wide range of aristocratic and professional sitters, including members of noble English and Scottish families (such as those of the first earl of Rockingham, the second earl of Oxford, the second duke of Queensberry, the first duke of Montrose, and the first duke of Roxburghe), eminent writers (including Alexander Pope, Matthew Prior, and Richard Steele), and prominent medical men such as Richard Mead, William Cheselden, and Sir Hans Sloane (whose full-length portrait by Richardson hangs in the examination schools,

Jonathan Richardson the elder (1667–1745), self-portrait, 1728

Oxford). Although he declined two invitations to be court painter, he executed a full-length portrait of Frederick, prince of Wales, in 1736 (now in Warwick Castle). In 1725 Richardson moved to Queen Square, Bloomsbury, where he lived for the rest of his life. After about 1730 his professional output of paintings decreased, and he gave up business entirely at the end of 1740. His students included Thomas Hudson (who married his daughter Mary), George Knapton, and the poet John Dyer.

Richardson was a productive and skilled draughtsman, especially during the last fifteen years of his life, when he executed numerous portrait drawings in two media: small lead-on-vellum studies, mainly of friends and family members; and larger chalk drawings (often on blue paper) which included many self-portraits and portraits of his eldest son. Very few of his drawings were preparatory sketches for paintings; they were finished works (sometimes derived from paintings or pencil sketches produced for his own retention. After being preserved by his son, they were sold with Richardson the younger's drawing collection on 5 February 1772. Numerous examples survive in the British Museum and elsewhere.

Richardson also collected drawings by earlier masters and by the time of his death had amassed one of the largest and finest collections in Britain, containing nearly 5000 examples which were carefully mounted, annotated, and methodically arranged. It contained works from the fourteenth to the seventeenth centuries, by Flemish, Dutch, British, and, above all, Italian artists. His collection was sold in 1747, and dispersed among numerous other collectors, including Thomas Hudson, the duke of Devonshire, and General John Guise. Drawings from Richardson's collection are identifiable by his distinctive collector's marks; some (including numerous examples at Christ Church, Oxford, from the Guise collection) still retain his mounts, on which he recorded attributions, shelf-marks, and observations about the drawings' provenance or significance.

Richardson was the most important and prolific English writer on art of the first half of the eighteenth century, publishing *An Essay on the Theory of Painting* (1715), *Two discourses: I. An essay on the whole art of criticism as it relates to painting, and II. An argument in behalf of the science of a connoisseur* (1719), and (with his son Jonathan the younger) *An account of some of the statues, bas-reliefs, drawings and pictures in Italy, &c. with remarks* (1722). Second editions of the first two books appeared in 1725, and a two-volume French translation of all three, with revisions and additions, was published in Amsterdam in 1728, entitled: *Traité de la peinture et de la sculpture*. In 1754 a second edition of *An account* was issued, followed by edited versions of *The Works of Jonathan Richardson* in 1778 and 1792. Richardson's books were widely read, and the influence of many of their central ideas can be traced in Sir Joshua Reynolds's *Discourses*.

Richardson wrote for a wide readership, at a time when middle-class as well as aristocratic English men and women were purchasing unprecedented numbers of pictures. While never belittling painting's decorative appeal and the requirement of skilled craftsmanship, he sought to educate English artists and consumers about the intellectual and instructional potential of painting. In many of its basic principles his art theory resembles that formulated in seventeenth-century academic French and Italian contexts, but Richardson used language and examples (notably Raphael's tapestry cartoons, displayed at Hampton Court) which were familiar to English readers. He also argued that portrait painting, the dominant genre practised by English artists, deserved higher esteem than its traditional placement below history painting. Richardson defended his countrymen's abilities as artists and connoisseurs against the established authority of continental taste. In doing so, he drew heavily upon the empirical philosophy of John Locke. For instance, in the first of his *Two discourses* he argued that anyone who could make methodical observations, compare ideas, and think rationally could learn to distinguish the quality, authorship, and originality of paintings. These principles were exemplified by *An account*, wherein Richardson, using notes taken by Jonathan the younger on a trip to France and Italy in 1720, disagreed with many accepted evaluations of ancient and modern artworks. Most contentiously, he pronounced Raphael's frescoes in the Vatican to be inferior to the cartoons at Hampton Court.

Throughout his life Richardson and his son Jonathan had literary interests and aspirations, which were encouraged by their friends Alexander Pope and Matthew Prior.

He was particularly devoted to John Milton's *Paradise Lost* and, partly in response to Richard Bentley's edition of the text in 1732, published *Explanatory Notes and Remarks on Milton's Paradise Lost* in 1734, written with Richardson the younger. The intimacy and harmony with which the Richardsons lived and collaborated was frequently commented upon by contemporaries, including Pope, who called them 'two such lovers of one another, and two such lovers of the fine arts' (*The Correspondence of Alexander Pope*, ed. G. Sherburn, 5 vols., 1956, vol. 2, pp. 140–41). The elder Richardson also wrote a copious body of poetry, selections from which were prepared for the press by Jonathan the younger and published posthumously as *Morning Thoughts* in 1776. Other poems, such as his lengthy 'Hymn to God', which he dedicated to his children in 1712, survive in manuscript.

Richardson died suddenly but peacefully in London (upon sitting down in his chair after his customary walk in St James's Park) at his home in Queen Square, Bloomsbury, on 28 May 1745. His friend Thomas Birch preached the funeral sermon, and Richardson was buried in the chancel of the church of St Michael, Wood Street, on 1 June 1745. In 1776 his son's *Richardsoniana, or, Occasional Reflections on the Moral Nature of Man*, was posthumously published, a volume incorporating observations from ancient and modern authors, and anecdotes about his father and other contemporaries. Richardson the younger died in London in June 1771 and was buried on 15 June in the church of St George the Martyr, London. He was unmarried.   CAROL GIBSON-WOOD

Sources Vertue, *Note books* · C. Gibson-Wood, *Jonathan Richardson: art theorist of the English Enlightenment* (2000) · will, PRO, PROB 11/740, fols. 247–8 · parish register, London, St Giles-in-the-Fields, 14 Feb 1694 [baptism, Jonathan Richardson jun.] · parish register, London, St George the Martyr, 15 June 1771 [burial, Jonathan Richardson jun.]
Archives Bodl. Oxf., letters to R. Palmer, MS Eng. Lett. C. 12, C.438
Likenesses J. Richardson, self-portrait, oils, *c*.1728, Polesden Lacey, Surrey · J. Richardson the elder, self-portrait, drawing, 1728, BM [*see illus.*] · J. Richardson, self-portrait, oils, *c*.1729, NPG · J. Richardson, double portrait, self-portrait, red chalk drawing (with his son), Montreal Museum of Fine Arts · J. Richardson, self-portraits, pencil and/or chalk drawings, AM Oxf.; Bodl. Oxf.; BM; Courtauld Inst., FM Cam., NG Scot., NPG, V&A, Yale U. CBA · J. Richardson the elder, drawings (Jonathan Richardson junior), BM, V&A · J. Richardson the elder, oils (Jonathan Richardson junior), priv. coll. · attrib. J. Richardson the elder, self-portrait, group portrait, oils, Capesthorne, Cheshire · R. Richardson the elder, drawings (Jonathan Richardson junior), Cornell University, New York
Wealth at death five houses in London; unspecified amounts of bank stock and South Sea investments: will, PRO, PROB 11/740, fols. 247–8

Richardson, Jonathan, the younger (1694–1771). *See under* Richardson, Jonathan, the elder (1667–1745).

Richardson, Joseph (1755–1803), writer and politician, was born at Hexham, Northumberland, the only son of Joseph Richardson (*d*. 1780?), tradesman of the town, and his wife, Frances, *née* Todd. He was educated at Haydon

Bridge School and admitted sizar at St John's College, Cambridge, on 4 July 1774, matriculating into the university in Michaelmas of that year. He was supported financially by Lady Boughton of Northumberland but her payments had stopped by 1778. Later described by one of his tutors at St John's (Dr Pearce, later dean of Ely) as 'having a talent for writing English verses', although 'no extraordinary Scholar' (Farington, *Diary*, 3.692), he was nevertheless placed in the highest class in college examinations of December 1776 and June 1777. There is no record of him for the examination of December 1777. Although he was readmitted as pensioner on 25 September 1780, he left the university without taking a degree.

During the break in his studies at Cambridge, Richardson started work for the *Morning Post*, reporting debates in the House of Lords. He obtained this position through 'a gentleman whom he had known at Cambridge', who 'afterwards furnished him with the means of becoming one of its proprietors' (Taylor, 2.164–5). This was probably Lord John Townshend, who matriculated at St John's in the term after Richardson. He was later described as being at this time a 'remarkably fine, showy young man', possessed of an 'admirable understanding', whose language displayed 'peculiar force and elegance' (ibid., 2.164). On 26 September 1780 he was listed by the *Morning Post* as one of its eight proprietors. Five days earlier he had fought a duel with the Revd Henry Bate Dudley, the newspaper's major shareholder and editor, because Bate Dudley had accused the other proprietors of cowardice for failing to support his attacks on the duke of Richmond. Richardson was wounded in the arm.

Richardson was admitted as a student at the Middle Temple on 24 March 1781, but continued to work as a journalist loyal to the Rockingham whigs. His allegiance to the whig party was fostered by Richard Brinsley Sheridan. Earl Fitzwilliam later remembered Richardson 'as far back as the American war' when he was 'editor, or chief manager, of the *English Chronicle*' (Aspinall, 452) offering, through Sheridan, to convert his paper into a strong supporter of the Rockinghamite whigs. Terms were agreed, but the paper subsequently lost circulation, causing financial loss for Richardson. He was recompensed by being paid £200 from the party's general subscription fund in return for continuing services as a political agent. Together with fellow proprietor Alderman Thomas Skinner, Richardson also attempted to make the *Morning Post* into a party paper, but success was limited to a brief period during the Fox–North coalition. He was called to the bar on 5 May 1786, but appeared as counsel only in a few contested election petitions, in which he is said to have excelled in cross-examination (*DNB*). His name was registered in *Browne's General Law List* from 1793 to 1797 and in John Hughes's *The New Law List* from 1799 to 1803.

In addition to his work with the *Morning Post* and the *English Chronicle*, Richardson contributed letters signed 'Englishman' to a paper called *The Citizen*, but much of his energy, after the establishment of Pitt's ministry, was devoted to political satire, published anonymously. He wrote numbers 4, 10, and 11 in *Criticisms of 'The Rolliad'*, part 1 (1784) and numbers 3 and 4 in part 2 (1785). He wrote numbers 4 and 19 in *Probationary Odes for the Laureateship* (1785), as well as much of the prose in that work (an attribution of these works can be found in an anonymous MS of 1785, inserted at the front of a combined edition, BL Catalogue G. 18972). He wrote *The Delavaliad* (1785), and *The Jekyll, a Political Eclogue* (1788), the latter a satire directed at the marquess of Lansdowne and his political adherents. He contributed to *Political Miscellanies* (1787) and also published, again anonymously, *The Complete Investigation of Mr Eden's Treaty* (1787), a serious political pamphlet which deployed historical argument and statistical evidence to support the whigs' attack on the commercial treaty with France.

Richardson was a founder member of the Whig Club (1784) and during the regency crisis was actively involved in the whigs' campaign to discredit Pitt. There were plans for Richardson to be made a commissioner of the stamp office in place of Sheridan's brother-in-law Richard Tickell if the whigs gained office. The three of them were now the closest of collaborators, politically and socially, with a penchant for playing practical jokes on each other. In the general election of 1790 Richardson was election agent for Sheridan in Stafford and for Ralph Noel Milbanke in co. Durham. He was a founder member of the Society of the Friends of the People and the Friends of the Liberty of the Press in 1792. With Fox's sponsorship he became a member of Brooks's Club on 24 April 1793.

Richardson's successful comedy *The Fugitive* was first performed by the Drury Lane Theatre company at the King's Theatre, Haymarket, on 20 April 1792, with a prologue by Richard Tickell and an epilogue by Burgoyne. Lampooning the absurdities of a value system based on birth and title ('the properties of the mind elude the frail laws of hereditary descent, and own no sort of obedience to their authority', *The Fugitive*, II, iii), the play elicited criticism from the duke of Portland for 'vilifying the aristocracy' (*HoP, Commons, 1790–1820*, 5.14–15). Richardson wrote the prologue to *The Glorious First of June*, an afterpiece performed at Drury Lane on 2 July 1794 for the benefit of the dependants of men who died in the naval engagement of that date, and he appears to have contributed some material to Sheridan's *Pizarro*, performed on 24 May at Drury Lane (R. B. Sheridan, *The Dramatic Works of Richard Brinsley Sheridan*, ed. C. Price, 2 vols., 1973, 2.627).

Richardson was Sheridan's closest friend after Tickell's death in 1793 and closely involved in the affairs of Drury Lane Theatre. As early as 1789 Sheridan conveyed a sixteenth share in the Drury Lane Theatre to Richardson. On 19 September 1795 Richardson became one of three managerial proprietors of the theatre, together with Sheridan and John Grubb, entitling him to a seventh share of the theatre's net profits. By 1796 Richardson was thought to have a £12,000 stake in the theatre (Farington, *Diary*, 2.468).

In 1796 Richardson was returned for the borough of Newport in Cornwall through the influence of the second duke of Northumberland. No doubt Richardson's candidature was advocated by Sheridan. The duke's electoral manager was Richard Wilson, whom Richardson might have known in Hexham, where Wilson had been articled to a solicitor. Richardson continued to represent Newport until his death, although he never spoke in the house, 'because he knew that his Northumberland accent might expose him to ridicule' (Taylor, 2.124). He did not join the Foxite secession from parliament, but appears to have remained on good terms with Fox, acting as his intermediary with the duke of Northumberland.

In 1799 Richardson married Sarah Fawcett, a descendant of Isaac Watts the dissenting divine and hymn writer. She was described as 'a remarkably intelligent woman' (Taylor, 2.124). Together they had four daughters, although it is clear from Richardson's will that they were all born before the marriage took place (HoP, Commons, 1790–1820, 5.15). The finances of the Drury Lane Theatre became increasingly chaotic, following the rebuilding by Henry Holland. On 1 February 1800 Richardson agreed to buy a quarter share worth £25,000. A subscription was raised, with contributions from the dukes of Bedford, Northumberland, and Devonshire, earls Thanet and Moira, and the banker Francis Baring. A further loan by the duke of Northumberland allowed the purchase to proceed by September 1801, giving Richardson an income of 15 guineas a week, but shortage of funds meant that his election expenses in 1802 had to be paid by the party. In February of that year the whigs considered raising an annuity of £300 for him.

In spite of declining health, Richardson attended to his parliamentary duties to the end of his life, voting with Fox in the minority on 24 May and 3 June 1803. He died on 9 June 1803 at The Wheatsheaf inn near Virginia Water, Surrey, after being taken ill the previous day. A distraught Sheridan, arriving with John Taylor after the burial on 13 June at Egham churchyard, insisted on the funeral service's being repeated (Taylor, 2.170). In his obituary notice it was said that Richardson possessed 'the merit of perfect consistency in his political conduct and faithful attachment, but not slavish devotion, to his party' (GM, 602–3). Lord John Townshend later wrote that he was 'an honest and excellent hearted fellow and the very staunchest Foxite I knew' (HoP, Commons, 1790–1820, 5.15). Political opponents esteemed him as 'the well-natured Richardson' in spite of his love of a good argument (Richardson, 16).

Richardson's widow continued to draw 10 guineas a week from Drury Lane Theatre; the duke of Northumberland cancelled the debt on his loan and money was raised for the family from subscriptions to Literary Relics of the Late Joseph Richardson (1807). The following year Sarah Richardson published her Original Poems, Intended for the Use of Young Persons, on a Plan Recommended by Dr Watts; and, again by subscription, Gertrude, a Tragic Drama (1809) and Ethelred, a Legendary Tragic Drama (1809). When the Drury Lane Theatre burnt down in 1809, destroying the family's finances, the whigs promoted a new subscription through William Adam and Lord John Townshend. Sarah Richardson later translated a novel, The Exile of Poland (1819), and published an Abridged History of the Bible, in Verse (1820–22). She died in 1824.   CHRISTOPHER CLAYTON

Sources DNB · J. Taylor, Records of my life, 2 vols. (1832) · S. Richardson, Literary relics of the late Joseph Richardson … with a sketch of the author (1807) · St John Cam., C 15.6, fols. 16, 17, 12v · R. F. Scott, ed., Admissions to the College of St John the Evangelist in the University of Cambridge, 4: July 1767 – July 1802 (1931) · Venn, Alum. Cant. · Admissions to the house, Middle Temple Archives, MT3 AHC 5 · Students' ledgers, Middle Temple Archives, MT 3/STL 3 · H. A. C. Sturgess, ed., Register of admissions to the Honourable Society of the Middle Temple, from the fifteenth century to the year 1944, 1 (1949) · A. Aspinall, Politics and the press, c.1780–1850, [2nd edn] (1973) · HoP, Commons, 1790–1820, vols. 1, 5 · The letters of Richard Brinsley Sheridan, ed. C. Price, 3 vols. (1966) · T. Moore, Memoirs of the life of the Rt. Hon. Richard Brinsley Sheridan, 2 vols. (1825) · The works of Samuel Parr … with memoirs of his life and writings, ed. J. Johnstone, 8 vols. (1828); vol. 7, pp. 320–22 · L. Werkmeister, The London daily press, 1772–1792 (1963) · Farington, Diary, vols. 2–3 · GM, 1st ser., 73 (1803), 602–3 · Betsy Sheridan's journal, ed. W. Lefanu (1960) · D. E. Ginter, ed., Whig organization in the general election of 1790: selections from the Blair Adam papers (1967) · D. E. Ginter, 'The financing of the whig party organization, 1783–1793', American Historical Review, 71 (1965–6), 421–40 · C. B. Hogan, ed., The London stage, 1660–1800, pt 5: 1776–1800 (1968)
Archives BL, Sheridan papers, letters, Add. MS 35118
Likenesses M. A. Shee, oils, 1792, repro. in Richardson, Literary relics · W. Ridley, stipple (after M. A. Shee), BM, NPG; repro. in Monthly Mirror, 800
Wealth at death see will, PRO, PROB 11/1395, sig. 568, cited in HoP, Commons, 1790–1820, 5.15 (1986), footnote 1 · Scott, ed., Admissions, 4.449

Richardson, Joseph (1814–1862), flautist, was born in London. He studied the flute with Charles Nicholson, and attended the Royal Academy of Music from January 1835 to June 1836, succeeding Nicholson as professor of the flute there in 1837. He became the most popular solo flautist of his day, and was engaged in most of the London orchestras. His many appearances included those at the Methodists' Club and the Società Armonica in 1836; he was also a member of the Liszt Concert Party in 1841. For many years he was the chief attraction at Jullien's Promenade Concerts, but, following claims of unfair treatment, he left to become principal flautist in the queen's private band on a smaller salary. It has been said that Richardson practised literally 'all day and every day' (Rockstro, 637) and attained an extraordinary neatness and rapidity of execution. Some, however, complained that his tone was hard and thin, and that he seldom played with musical feeling. The pieces with which he achieved the greatest success were Louis Drouet's Rule Britannia, Auber's Le Montagnard (1847), his own variations on 'There is Nae Luck' (1845), and the Russian national hymn. The last two remained popular with flautists after his death. He also composed many brilliant and difficult fantasias and variations for the flute, edited a volume of technical studies for the instrument (1844), and wrote waltzes for piano, as well as songs and other music. He died in London on 22 March 1862.   J. C. HADDEN, rev. DAVID J. GOLBY

Sources R. S. Rockstro, A treatise on the construction, the history, and the practice of the flute, 2nd edn (1928), 637–8 · Grove, Dict. mus.
Likenesses H. Watkins, print, c.1856–1859, NPG

Richardson, Josephine [Jo] (1923–1994), politician, was born on 28 August 1923 at The Gables, Elswick Road, Newcastle upon Tyne, the second among the three children of John Joseph Richardson, a textile manufacturer's agent, and his wife, Florence Rose, *née* Bicknell. Her father was a Methodist lay preacher whose children were obliged to go to church three times on Sundays. He stood unsuccessfully as a Liberal parliamentary candidate in Darlington in the 1930s. Florence Richardson, however, was a Labour supporter and a Congregationalist, and it was her influence that moulded her daughter's life, especially after John Richardson died, when Jo was sixteen. Much of Richardson's campaigning work on behalf of impoverished women caring for families was rooted in her mother's experience.

Josephine Richardson (1923–1994), by unknown photographer

Richardson left Southend-on-Sea High School for Girls at sixteen without distinction but with a dream of being a journalist. The Second World War intervened and she began work in the office of a steel foundry in Letchworth in 1939, becoming friends with trade unionists and joining the Labour Party at the end of the war. Her life changed in 1945, when she saw an advertisement in *The Tribune* for a secretary to Ian Mikardo, who had been elected MP for Reading that year, and she was selected from over 160 applicants. Her working partnership with Mikardo was the most important relationship of her adult life, one that took her to the heart of left-wing politics in post-war Britain. In her more than thirty years of service to Mikardo she also became secretary of the Keep Left group from 1947 to 1951; then of the larger grouping of Bevanites that took over from it; then of the Tribune group operating from 1964. Barbara Castle remarked of Richardson's early years in politics that she was 'a beautiful young woman who set the MPs' hearts aflutter' (Castle, 159), but she never married.

When Mikardo lost his seat in the general election of 1959 Richardson went with him to work first as secretary and then as co-director in his export business, which specialized in trade with eastern Europe. Mikardo found Richardson a better organizer than he 'and much more skilful at handling difficult situations and difficult people' (Mikardo, 116–7). Mikardo was returned to parliament in 1964, as MP for Poplar, but Richardson's political ambitions had been frustrated. She had been elected to Hornsey borough council in 1951, then unsuccessfully fought Monmouth in the general election of that year, did so again in 1955, then fought two constituencies that seemed to have better prospects for Labour—Hornchurch in 1959 and Harrow East in 1964—but with similar lack of success. She was inclined to abandon parliamentary hopes until her old Bevanite colleague Tom Driberg decided not to stand again in Barking and steered her towards the seat. She remarked, 'It was unheard of to have a woman trying for a seat in the East End at that time' (*The House Magazine*), but she was selected on the fifth ballot, by one vote. She was duly returned as MP for Barking at the general election of February 1974.

Much of Richardson's time in the following twenty years of representing Barking was engaged in persuading the Labour Party to take women's issues seriously. She was Labour's front bench spokesperson on women's rights from 1983, and in 1986 was finally able to persuade the party to adopt the creation of a ministry for women as policy. She played a leading part in campaigns in favour of abortion as a right, and for strengthening the law relating to domestic violence. Ever a 'conscience of the party', she was a leading member of the Campaign for Nuclear Disarmament and opposed the Falklands War. In the 1970s she was active in the campaign to make the leadership of the Labour Party more accountable to its members, and she backed Tony Benn's challenge for the deputy leadership of the party in 1981. She also supported a leadership challenge in 1983, but in 1988 left the Campaign Group amid some bitterness when it again backed Benn as a leadership candidate. She chaired the Labour Party conference in 1990, a performance notable for her refusal to call Tony Benn to speak against the Gulf War. Now she was no friend of the left nor sufficiently trusted by the right; she had lost her power base, and with it lost her seat on the national executive in 1991 (after twelve years of tenure) and on the shadow cabinet in 1992.

These were hard years: the decline in Richardson's political fortunes coincided with the illness and death, in 1993, of Ian Mikardo and a severe deterioration in the rheumatoid arthritis with which she was afflicted and for which she had a major spinal operation in 1993. Until the end of her life she continued to vote from a wheelchair in the House of Commons, arriving sometimes by ambulance, and was prominent in campaigning against the closure of St Bartholomew's Hospital, where she was being treated. She died, of respiratory failure, on 1 February 1994 at her home, 345 Latymer Court, Hammersmith Road, London.

JAD ADAMS

Sources *The House Magazine* (15 Jan 1988) · *The Times* (2 Feb 1994) · *The Independent* (2 Feb 1994) · B. Castle, *Fighting all the way* (1993) · I. Mikardo, *Back-bencher* (1988) · J. Adams, *Tony Benn: a biography* (1992) · T. Benn, *The end of an era: diaries, 1980–90* (1992) · *WWW* · b. cert. · d. cert.
Archives Labour History Archive and Study Centre, Manchester, minutes, corresp., and papers · Labour History Archive and Study Centre, Manchester, papers relating to Keep Left group

Richardson, (Sarah) Katharine [Katy] (1854–1927), mountaineer, was born on 24 April 1854, at Edlington, near Doncaster, Yorkshire, the second of five daughters of the Revd George Richardson, curate of Edlington and later vicar of Kilburn, Yorkshire, and his wife, Isabel Nussey. She first visited the Alps at the age of sixteen. After 1879 Katharine became a distinguished mountaineer, making 176 ascents over 11 climbing seasons, 116 of which were considered major ascents (including 6 first ascents and 14 first ascents by a woman). Although short, petite, and thin, her endurance and agility were remarkable. In 1882, for example, she climbed Zinal Rothorn, Weisshorn, Matterhorn, and Monte Rosa in eight days, and in 1889 she climbed the Aiguille Verte, Grand Dru, and Petit Dru in just three days. Michel Payot, a guide, said of her: 'she glides along the rocks like a lizard' (Paillon, 329).

Katharine Richardson's reputation as a climber often preceded her. In 1888 she made the first ascent of the Aiguille de Bionnassy, including a traverse to the Dôme du Goûter which had been considered impossible, and the first female ascent of Aiguilles des Charmoz. While still in Chamonix, she read in a newspaper that an Englishwoman had arrived in La Bérarde intending to make the first female ascent of the Meije. She quickly travelled to the Dauphiné, where she inquired as to the name of her compatriot and competitor. The name she was told, however, was none other than her own. Fulfilling the prophecy, she climbed the Meije with Pierre Gaspard and J. B. Bich, and observers below recognized her on the summit by her petite stature and skirt.

One of these observers was Mary Paillon (1848–1946), from a French medical family, who met Richardson afterwards and arranged to climb with her the following year. They became close friends and Richardson settled at Oullins, near Lyons, on the Paillon family estate, where she lived for the rest of her life. Richardson had a round face, full nose, green eyes, pulled her straight, brown hair back, and invariably wore a skirt while climbing. Paillon had high cheekbones, a thin, Gallic nose, close-cropped, wavy hair, wore a pince-nez, and was a strong advocate for women climbing in trousers. The two women often climbed together, including Pelvoux in 1897, one of the peaks of which was later named Pointe Richardson. After this ascent Paillon's eyesight began to fail and they attempted only less difficult walks. Richardson refused to climb peaks on which Paillon could not join her. They were both members of the Lyonnaise section of the Club Alpin Français, and they joined the Ladies' Alpine Club in 1908; Paillon was elected vice-president in 1910, and Richardson declined the presidency in 1912 and 1919. Richardson was also a distinguished watercolourist. She died on 20 August 1927 at the Paillon home, 48 rue de la République, Oullins, Rhône, France. Paillon wrote innumerable articles for climbing journals, including an obituary notice on Richardson that said she had been 'almost a sister to me' (Paillon, 326). Neither ever married.

PETER H. HANSEN

Sources M. Paillon, *La Montagne*, 23 (Nov 1927), 326–34 · E. Le Blond, 'In memoriam: Miss Katherine Richardson', *Alpine Journal*, 40 (1928), 160–62 · *Ladies Alpine Club Yearbook* (1948), 24–5 [obit. of Mary Paillon] · F. Gribble, 'Lady mountaineers', *Ladies Realm*, 2 (Oct 1897), 683–7 · private information (2004) · C. Williams, *Women on the rope* (1973) · R. W. Clark, *Victorian mountaineers* (1953) · *Alpine Journal*, 14 (1888–9), 150–51, 163, 498, 511–12 [accounts of expeditions] · *CGPLA Eng. & Wales* (1927) · M. Dronsart, *Les grandes voyageuses* (1894), 373–5
Archives Ladies' Alpine Club, London
Likenesses group photograph, 1890 (with Emile Rey and J. B. Bich) · photograph, c.1890–1899, repro. in Paillon, *La Montagne*, 324 · photograph, c.1890–1899, repro. in Gribble, 'Lady mountaineers', 686 · engraving, repro. in Dronsart, *Les grandes voyageuses*, 374
Wealth at death £6624 3s. 5d.: probate, 3 Nov 1927, *CGPLA Eng. & Wales*

Richardson, Lewis Fry (1881–1953), mathematician and pacifist, was born on 11 October 1881 at The Gables, Elswick Road, Newcastle upon Tyne, the youngest of the seven children of David Richardson (1835–1913) and his wife, Catherine (1838–1919), daughter of Robert and Jane Fry of Wellington, Somerset. His father was trained as a chemist and became a successful director of the family leather manufacturing business, developing improved methods of tanning to produce high quality leather. Both the parents were active members of the Society of Friends and they brought their children up in the best Quaker traditions.

After six years at local schools in Newcastle Richardson followed in the footsteps of his father and of three of his brothers by being sent to Bootham School in York, where he received every encouragement to pursue his interest in natural history. He continued his studies at the Durham College of Science in Newcastle (now Newcastle University) from where he gained a scholarship to King's College, Cambridge, in 1900. In the following ten years Richardson took a series of research and teaching posts, twice at the National Physical Laboratory, twice in industry, and twice in university physics departments. Of greatest significance for his future career was a spell with National Peat Industries from 1906 to 1907. Here he was asked to calculate how best to design drains in a peat moss, taking into account the annual rainfall. As the mathematical equations involved were not formally soluble, he was led to study approximate methods of solution, first graphical and then numerical. This resulted in the publication in 1910 of his first important paper 'The approximate solution by finite differences of physical problems involving differential equations'.

In 1909 Richardson married Dorothy (1885–1956), daughter of William *Garnett (after whom the Garnett College of Technology in Roehampton is named). Due to an incompatibility in their blood types, they were unable to have children of their own, but they adopted two boys and a girl between 1920 and 1927. Unlike her husband, who was shy and loved solitude, Dorothy was extrovert

Lewis Fry Richardson (1881–1953), by Walter Stoneman, 1931

and gregarious. Under his influence she left the Church of England to become an enthusiastic member of the Society of Friends. Throughout their happy marriage she was supportive of Lewis's pacifist views and helped him in his research work, for example by relieving him of some of the tedious arithmetic calculations.

Richardson realized that his method for obtaining approximate solutions to differential equations could have many practical applications, including weather prediction. His appointment in 1913 as the superintendent of Eskdalemuir observatory in Dumfriesshire and the encouragement of the director of the Meteorological Office, Sir Napier Shaw, at last gave him the opportunity to develop his ideas. By 1916, when he resigned from the Meteorological Office to join the Friends' Ambulance Unit, he had practically completed the first draft of his book *Weather Prediction by Numerical Process*. All that remained was to compute a weather forecast to demonstrate how his method would work. He made the necessary calculations while serving as an ambulance driver in France. His war experiences and Quaker beliefs led him at the same time to turn his thoughts to the causes of war and how to prevent them. He felt that it might be useful to tackle this problem by an objective scientific approach. His first paper on this subject, *Mathematical Psychology of War*, was published at his own expense in 1919. In it he postulated that the rate of increase of the warlike activity of one nation depended on the current activity of the opposing nation.

On returning to England in 1919 Richardson was reappointed by Shaw, this time to work at Benson Observatory with W. H. Dines on topics relating to numerical weather prediction. He experimented on measuring the vertical distribution of temperature and wind, atmospheric turbulence, and radiation. He derived a criterion, the 'Richardson number', for determining whether turbulence will increase or decrease.

In 1920 Richardson resigned again from the Meteorological Office because he felt unable to work directly for the armed services—the office had become part of the Air Ministry. From then until his retirement he worked in the education world, as lecturer in physics and mathematics at Westminster Training College until 1929 and then as principal of Paisley Technical College (now the University of Paisley).

Richardson's book on weather prediction was finally published in 1922. Although the pioneering nature of his method was widely recognized, the book had no practical impact: existing observing and computing facilities were very inadequate and his computed forecast was grossly in error. His ideas were taken more seriously in the 1950s thanks to the availability of better observations and much faster computers, and within a few years numerical methods had been introduced all over the world. In his early years at Westminster, Richardson continued his meteorological researches, especially on atmospheric diffusion. From his experiments he deduced a new law for the rate of diffusion; some twenty years later the same law was obtained independently on theoretical grounds.

While still a student at Cambridge, Richardson had decided to spend the first half of his life under the strict discipline of physics and then to apply this training to researches on living things. The change came in 1926 when he abandoned meteorology for psychology, immediately after being elected a fellow of the Royal Society. By 1929 he had already published the first of a series of papers on the quantitative estimation of perception, including brightness, colour, loudness, and pain. The accepted view at that time was that such measurements were meaningless but twenty years later his methods were being used widely by psychologists.

Another break came in 1935 when, after the failure of the disarmament conference in Geneva, Richardson decided to re-examine his earlier work on the causes of war. By using expenditure on arms as a measure of warlike activity, he showed that his simple mathematical model of an arms race corresponded roughly to what had happened in the run-up to both world wars. He next analysed statistically data on past wars and other deadly quarrels from a card catalogue which he himself had compiled, and found a number of significant relationships which he then tried to explain. As he was unable to find a publisher for the books containing all his findings, he published them himself on microfilm. Edited versions were published posthumously in 1960 under the titles *Arms and Insecurity* and *Statistics of Deadly Quarrels*. Another posthumous publication, *The Problem of Contiguity*, was influential in the development of fractals and of chaos theory.

In 1943 Richardson left Paisley for Hillside House, Kilmun, on the Firth of Clyde where he died in his sleep of a heart attack on 30 September 1953. His cremation at Maryhill, Glasgow, on 5 October was followed the same day by a memorial service of the Society of Friends in Glasgow. OLIVER M. ASHFORD

Sources O. M. Ashford, *Prophet—or professor: the life and work of Lewis Fry Richardson* (1985) · E. Gold, *Obits. FRS*, 9 (1954), 217–35 · *Collected papers of Lewis Fry Richardson*, ed. O. M. Ashford and others, 2 vols. (1993) · *Bootham School Register* (1935) · private information (2004)
Archives CUL, corresp. and papers · Lancaster University, Richardson Institute for Peace Studies · Meteorological Office, Bracknell, Berkshire · University of Paisley Library, papers
Likenesses W. Stoneman, photograph, 1931, NPG · W. Stoneman, photograph, 1931, RS [*see illus.*] · Elliott & Fry, three photographs, RS · glass engraving, Meteorological Office, Bracknell, Berkshire · photographs, CUL, Richardson MSS
Wealth at death £3726 18*s*. 1*d*.: confirmation, 16 Nov 1953, *CCI*

Richardson, Mary Raleigh (1882/3–1961), suffragette and political activist, though apparently born in Britain, was brought up by her Canadian mother in Belleville, Ontario, Canada, and her grandfather who was the local bank manager. She returned to Britain when she was sixteen, studying art and travelling to Paris and Italy. While living in Bloomsbury she undertook some freelance work as a journalist. A witness to the events of 'black Friday' (18 November 1910), in which the Women's Social and Political Union (WSPU) lobbied parliament and were brutally attacked by the police, she joined the WSPU and quickly engaged in militant activities. She described this change in her life as enlisting 'in a holy crusade' (Richardson, *Laugh a Defiance*, 6). She was arrested nine times, serving several sentences in Holloway prison for assaulting the police, breaking windows, and arson. She was often physically attacked while campaigning for the suffrage cause: her shoulder blade was broken and her clothing torn to shreds when she presented a petition to George V in Bristol in 1913. She campaigned with the socialist Sylvia Pankhurst in east London and was arrested and then imprisoned with her after a rally in Bromley by Bow in July 1913. She apparently also carried out orders from Christabel Pankhurst to enact daring deeds. Mary Richardson was one of the first two women to be force fed, under the 'Cat and Mouse Act' in 1913, having been arrested at the scene of an arson attack. She suffered extensive bruising and poor health as a result, writing about this experience as 'torture': 'forcible feeding is an immoral assault as well as a painful physical one' (Richardson, *Personal Experience*). When released in 1914 after a long period of forcible feeding to be operated on for appendicitis, she declared, 'The worst fight on record since the movement began is now raging in Holloway' (C. Pankhurst, 286). Mary Richardson was not the first, but the most famous, suffragette to slash a painting as a political protest. On 10 March 1914 she attacked Velázquez's *The Toilet of Venus* (the 'Rokeby Venus'), which had been acquired for the National Gallery through the National Art Collections Fund in 1906. She claimed that this act was perpetrated to draw attention to the plight of Emmeline Pankhurst, then on hunger strike

Mary Raleigh Richardson (1882/3–1961), by unknown photographer, *c*.1915

in Holloway prison, saying, 'You can get another picture but you cannot get a life, as they are killing Mrs Pankhurst' (*The Times*, 11 March 1914). For Mary Richardson, the most beautiful woman in art was of little significance compared with the life of Mrs Pankhurst, 'the most beautiful character in modern history' (ibid.). This action secured her notoriety, and eighteen months with hard labour. It also led to many museums' closing their doors to unaccompanied women.

On the outbreak of war in 1914 Mary Richardson resumed her literary career, publishing a novel, *Matilda and Marcus* (1915), and two volumes of poetry, *Symbol Songs* (1916) and *Wilderness Love Songs* (1917). Her third book of poetry, *Cornish Headlands*, appeared in 1920. In the 1920s and 1930s she stood several times as a parliamentary candidate. The first occasion was in November 1922 when she stood as Labour candidate in Acton, Middlesex, obtaining 26.2 per cent of the vote against the successful Conservative candidate. In October 1924 she stood for the same seat as an independent socialist against the official Labour candidate and received 7.6 per cent of the vote. Although adopted as a prospective parliamentary candidate for the rural constituency of Bury St Edmunds in 1926, she did not stand in the 1929 election. In 1931 she was adopted as a last-minute Labour candidate in Aldershot against Lord

Wolmer, the National Government incumbent, and lost heavily.

Although Mary Richardson had approached Sylvia Pankhurst with the idea of establishing a communist nunnery for social and religious service, she subsequently continued in public political life. First she joined the New Party, formed by Sir Oswald Mosley in 1932, and then, in 1934, at a time of significant membership growth, she joined the British Union of Fascists (BUF) as the organizing secretary of its women's section. Like many British fascists, she had been impressed by the work of Mussolini in Italy. She spoke extensively for the British Union of Fascists and wrote regularly for the fascist press. She frequently drew analogies between the current work of British fascists and those of the militant suffrage feminists before the First World War, controversially interpreting her fascist politics as the logical outcome of her suffrage past, 'I was first attracted to the Blackshirts because I saw in them the courage, the action, the loyalty, the gift of service, and the ability to serve which I had known in the suffrage movement' (*Blackshirt*, 29 June 1934, 3). She had left the BUF by 1935, having drawn hostility from Mosley's mother, who described her as full of 'dishonest inefficiency' (Mosley, 92).

Although single, after the First World War Mary Richardson adopted a son, Roger. In 1953 she published her autobiography, *Laugh a Defiance*, a sensationalist account of her time in the WSPU which was reticent about her later career. Mary Richardson died of heart failure and bronchitis, aged seventy-eight, on 7 November 1961 at her home in Hastings. Recently her time as a fascist has received attention from historians attempting to see the BUF as a movement in which feminist ideas were contested. Certainly in her autobiography she made no mention of this political activity and press coverage at the time of her death focused on her popular image as Slasher Mary.   HILDA KEAN

Sources M. Richardson, *Laugh a defiance* (1953) • H. Kean, 'Some problems of constructing and reconstructing a suffragette's life: Mary Richardson, suffragette, socialist and fascist', *Women's History Review*, 7 (1998), 475–93 • H. Kean, 'A study of Mary Richardson: suffragette, socialist and fascist', *Seeing through suffrage: new themes and directions in the study of British suffrage history*, ed. C. Eustance and J. Ryan (1999) • S. Cullen, 'Four women for Mosley', *Oral History*, 24 (spring 1996), 49–59 • R. Fowler, 'Why did suffragettes attack works of art?', *Journal of Women's History*, 2/3 (1991), 109–25 • M. Durham, 'Gender and the British Union of Fascists', *Journal of Contemporary History*, 27 (1992), 513–29 • E. S. Pankhurst, *The suffragette movement: an intimate account of persons and ideals* (1931) • *Calling All Women* (Feb 1962) • M. Richardson, *A personal experience of torture* [leaflet, Suffragette Fellowship collection, Museum of London] • *The Vote* (24 Sept 1926) • N. Mosley, *Beyond the pale* (1983) • C. Pankhurst, *Unshackled: the story of how we won the vote* (1959) • M. Durham, *Women and fascism* (1998) • d. cert.

Archives Museum of London, Suffragette Fellowship collection

Likenesses photograph, c.1915, NPG [*see illus.*] • photograph (as women's organizer of the British Union of Fascists), repro. in R. Thurlow, *Fascism in Britain* (1987), 142 • photograph (wearing suffragette prison medal), repro. in *Evening Standard* (7 Nov 1961) • photograph (being arrested), repro. in Pankhurst, *Unshackled*, 257 • photograph, repro. in *The Vote*

Richardson, Moses Aaron (1793–1871), antiquary, born in Newcastle upon Tyne, was the younger son of George Richardson (1749–1806), master of Blackett's charity school, Newcastle, who came of a family of small landed proprietors in north Tynedale. Having offended his parents by his first marriage, George had become a teacher and married secondly Jane Miles (*d.* 1830), Moses's mother. Moses's elder brother was Thomas Miles *Richardson (1784–1848), the artist.

Moses Richardson was educated at his father's school; he was interested from an early age in genealogy and local history. In 1818 he published by subscription *A collection of armorial bearings, inscriptions, &c., in the parochial chapel of St. Andrew, Newcastle-upon-Tyne*; it was illustrated with twenty-three plates of arms and a title-page by his brother. This was followed in 1820 by a larger work, in two volumes, about the church of St Nicholas, containing fifty engravings from drawings by his brother. In 1824 Richardson, with James Walker, brought out *The armorial bearings of the several incorporated companies of Newcastle-upon-Tyne, with a brief historical account of each company; together with notices of the Corpus Christi or miracle plays anciently performed by the trading societies of Newcastle-upon-Tyne*.

Meanwhile, Richardson had established a business in a shop at 5 Blackett Street, Newcastle, as a bookseller and music- and printseller. He subsequently moved to 101 Pilgrim Street and finally to 44 Grey Street, and, having added printing to his business, published a *Directory of Newcastle and Gateshead* for 1838. In the same year, when the British Association first visited Newcastle, Richardson issued *Richardson's Descriptive Companion* of the town and neighbourhood, with *An Inquiry into the Origin of the Primitive Britons*. This was reissued in 1846, when the Royal Agricultural Society held its annual show in Newcastle. In emulation of John Sykes's *Local Records*, issued in 1824 and 1833, Richardson next produced *The local historian's table book of remarkable occurrences, historical facts, legendary and descriptive ballads, &c., connected with the counties of Newcastle-upon-Tyne, Northumberland, and Durham*. This appeared in eight volumes between 1841 and 1846, illustrated by over 800 woodcuts. Although it was commercially unsuccessful, it was reissued by Bohn in 1846 under the title of *The Borderer's Table Book*. Richardson issued in seven annual volumes, from 1847 onwards, *Reprints of rare tracts and imprints of ancient manuscripts chiefly illustrative of the history of the northern counties*. He had the assistance of Joseph Hunter and other antiquaries, and produced the volumes in an edition limited to 100 copies on fine paper, well printed, with illuminated dedications and initials. For this work he was elected to the council of the Newcastle Society of Antiquaries. In 1849 Richardson emigrated to Australia on medical advice, and after initial financial success during the gold rush boom eventually became a rate-collector at Prahran, a suburb of Melbourne. Here, on 2 August 1871, he died; he was buried in the St Kilda cemetery in Melbourne.

Richardson and his wife, Anne Bewsher (1801–1875), had a son, **George Bourchier Richardson** (1822–1877), who was born in Newcastle upon Tyne on 26 October 1822. Educated at Bruce's academy in the city, he shared his father's tastes. He recorded in pencil and watercolour the decaying streets and buildings of Newcastle as the town was being redeveloped. He also executed woodcuts in the *Table Book* and the *Reprints*, lectured and wrote on local antiquities, and was a member of the Newcastle Society of Antiquaries and a fellow of the Society of Antiquaries of London. After his father's emigration, he failed to carry on his business with success, and followed his father in 1854 to Australia. He served for some time as librarian of the Melbourne Mechanics' Institute, but eventually became a journalist and editor of the *Wallaroo Times*. From 1874 he taught drawing and watercolour painting at Adelaide, where he died on 28 November 1877. He left a widow, Ellie (*d*. after 1909), but no children.

G. LE G. NORGATE, *rev.* C. M. FRASER

Sources R. Welford, *Men of mark 'twixt Tyne and Tweed*, 3 (1895), 294–8 · R. Welford, 'Art and archaeology: the three Richardsons [pt 2]', *Archaeologia Aeliana*, 3rd ser., 3 (1907), 135–51, esp. 141 · R. Welford, 'Art and archaeology: the three Richardsons [pt 8]', *Archaeologia Aeliana*, 3rd ser., 5 (1909), 197–202 · 'Biographies of contributors to the society's literature', *Archaeologia Aeliana*, 3rd ser., 10 (1913), 222–4 · M. Hall, *The artists of Northumbria*, 2nd edn (1982), 147–8 · minute books, Society of Antiquaries of Newcastle upon Tyne, Northumbd RO, 3g · parish register (baptism), Newcastle upon Tyne, St Andrew, 25 Aug 1793

Archives Northumbd RO, G. B. Richardson's sketchbooks, ZAN M13 F11–14

Likenesses photograph, *c*.1853 (George Bourchier Richardson), repro. in Welford, 'Art and archaeology ...', 198 [pt 8] · photograph, *c*.1870, repro. in Welford, 'Art and archaeology ...', 197 [pt 8]

Richardson, Muriel Elsa Florence, Lady Richardson (1913–2000). *See under* Richardson, Sir Ralph David (1902–1983).

Richardson, Sir Owen Willans (1879–1959), physicist, was born on 26 April 1879 in Blenheim Terrace, Dewsbury, Yorkshire, the eldest of the three children of Joshua Henry Richardson, woollen manufacturer, and his wife, Charlotte Maria Willans. From St John's Church day school, Dewsbury, Richardson won a scholarship to Batley grammar school in 1891. In 1897 he won another scholarship, to Trinity College, Cambridge, where he gained a first class in part one of the natural sciences tripos (with distinction in physics, chemistry, and botany, 1899) and proceeded in physics and chemistry to a first in part two in 1900. He was elected a fellow of Trinity in 1902, became Clerk Maxwell scholar in 1904, and was awarded the London DSc degree in the same year.

On graduating in 1900 Richardson began research at the Cavendish Laboratory under the supervision of J. J. Thomson, who suggested that he search for electrons blown out of a wire by a high-frequency alternating current. The results were negative and Richardson decided that:

> before starting another problem I would think over the whole field of opportunity and make my own decision as to what was the best thing for me to do and the best way to set about it, without asking anybody's advice. (Richardson to Rayleigh, 4 Dec 1940, Richardson MSS)

He began thinking about what the electrons were likely to

Sir Owen Willans Richardson (1879–1959), by Walter Stoneman, 1917

be doing inside a metal and why they did not get out more easily. As in much of his later work, he drew, for his theory, on classical thermodynamics and the kinetic theory of gases.

Richardson formulated a general theory of the process wherein electrons in the metal, responsible for its electrical conductivity, were regarded as evaporating through a potential barrier at its surface. 'It seemed to me that the real things to go for were the highest possible temperatures under the best attainable vacuum conditions', he wrote to Rayleigh, and he was encouraged by finding that McClelland, also at the Cavendish, had found the type of effect he expected using platinum. Richardson's detailed measurements on platinum, described in 'The electrical conductivity imparted to a vacuum by hot conductors' (*PTRS*, 201, 1903), fitted his formula

$$i = A_1 T^{1/2} e^{-\varphi/kT}$$

where A_1 is a constant, k is Boltzmann's constant, φ (the 'work function') is the energy needed to get the electrons over the barrier, i is the current, and T the temperature. However, difficulties in other fields of physics led to reconsideration of the theory from less specific thermodynamical approaches. As later described in his book *The Emission of Electricity from Hot Bodies* (1916), Richardson, Harold Albert Wilson, and several others at the Cavendish gradually improved the derivation of the emission formula obtaining

$$i = A_2 T^2 e^{-\varphi/kT}$$

which became known as Richardson's law, and which formed the basis for progress in radiotechnology. A_2 is a constant different from A_1. Experimentally the formulae are difficult to distinguish because of the overwhelming control by the exponential term. The second formula has withstood the test of experiment and time, being unaffected by changing views of the nature of the electron gas. The basic, evaporation-potential barrier, idea is retained. Richardson was able to use his theory to create a link with electrical and thermal conductivity in metals, and also with photoelectricity. His contribution in this field was recognized by the award of the Nobel prize in physics in 1928. He coined the word thermion, hence thermionics referring to the emission of electricity—negative or positive—by hot bodies, in 1909.

The difficulties encountered raised other questions. Mathematical studies of ionic recombination contributed to understanding of what was going on in the imperfect vacuum outside the emitting surface. Experimental and theoretical investigations of diffusion problems—such as hydrogen through palladium and platinum—contributed to ideas on what was going on inside metals. These seem to have been guiding principles for Richardson's further Cambridge researches in physics, but an element of indecision regarding his future course is evident from other investigations in physical chemistry and from a record of an application for a chair of physical chemistry at Liverpool.

In 1906 Richardson was appointed to the chair of physics at Princeton, and in the same year, on 12 June, married Lilian Maud (1875/6–1945), daughter of Albert William Wilson, goods manager to the North Eastern Railway Company at Darlington, and sister of his friend H. A. Wilson. The Richardsons had two sons and a daughter. At Princeton, Richardson built up a strong school of physics, A. H. Compton being his best-known pupil. His colleagues C. J. Davisson and O. Veblen married Richardson's two sisters. He continued to work on thermionic emission, looking at cooling and heating effects accompanying thermionic emission and absorption, reflection of slow electrons from metallic surfaces, theory of contact e.m.f. and thermo-electricity, and the emission of positive ions from heated salts. With F. C. Brown he verified that thermionic electrons have a Maxwellian velocity distribution. About the end of 1911 Richardson developed a theory of the photoelectric effect (in which electrons are emitted from a metal upon which ultraviolet light is falling). He again based his theory on the thermodynamics of the electrons, obtaining an emission law which was identical to Einstein's, but which did not require Einstein's assumption of the existence of light quanta—particles of light (*Philosophical Magazine*, 24, 1912). Concurrently he and his former student, K. T. Compton, in the most accurate experiments to date, verified the law predicted by both himself and Einstein (*Philosophical Magazine*, 24, 1912, and 26, 1913).

In broader fields of electron physics Richardson speculated on the possibility of explaining gravitation in terms of electron theory, and in 1908 predicted a rotational reaction on magnetization of iron. He failed to detect this effect, but it was observed by Einstein and De Haas in 1919

and has been called the Richardson–Einstein–De Haas effect. The converse phenomenon, observed by S. J. Barnett (1914), has been termed the Richardson–Barnett effect. These 'gyromagnetic' and 'magneto-mechanical' phenomena were more fully explained after the electron 'spin' concept had been introduced by Uhlenbeck and Goudsmit in 1925.

In 1913 Richardson was elected a fellow of the Royal Society, and the following year, after much deliberation, he returned to England to the Wheatstone chair of physics at King's College, London. His book *The Electron Theory of Matter* (1914), based on his Princeton lectures, provided the most comprehensive survey then available of electron theory and gave an even-handed treatment of both classical and modern theories. At King's, under the impact of the quantum theory and the stimulus of Bohr's explanation of the hydrogen spectrum, he began a protracted series of spectroscopic researches largely undertaken with C. B. Bazzoni, although thermionics, the photoelectric effect, metallic conduction, reflection of slow electrons from metals, emission of electrons in chemical reactions, and problems of theoretical physics continued to occupy him.

In 1924 Richardson was appointed Yarrow research professor of the Royal Society, being thereby relieved of teaching duties. He continued research, largely with T. Tanaka and later P. M. Davidson, primarily on the spectrum of molecular hydrogen, for which he had already published high resolution data. His book *Molecular Hydrogen and its Spectrum* (1934) is based on his Silliman memorial lectures at Yale in 1932. He acquired a magnificent reflection echelon with which he tested what have proved keystones of physics: theories of the spectra of atomic hydrogen and its isotopes. In 1940 he, with J. W. Drinkwater and W. E. Williams, published 'Determination of Rydberg constants, e/m, and fine structure of H_a and D_a with a reflexion echelon' (*PRS*, 174A, 164–88 and 175A, 345), which gave by far the most accurate wave number measurements of hydrogen spectrum lines hitherto made. These experiments were intended as a test of Dirac's theory but a flaw in the analysis of the fine structure components (probably occasioned by disruption of work due to the imminence of war) most regrettably obscured a vital feature only cleared up in 1947 by Lamb and Retherford. Richardson's greatest project, to use the echelon for measurements on the Lyman α-line, was abandoned because of the war, but before the evacuation of King's College in 1940 and the destruction of his laboratory by enemy action some measurements were obtained on fine structures in the molecular hydrogen spectrum which confirmed his previous work. With F. C. Chalklin and F. S. Robertson he studied the soft X-ray spectra of a number of metals, and in 1944 studied the reflection of very slow electrons by copper, with I. Gimpel. He continued scientific work long after retiring from his Yarrow professorship in 1944 and between 1901 and 1953 published, with his collaborators, more than 130 scientific papers.

Richardson received honorary degrees from Leeds, St

Andrews, and London, and was a fellow of King's College, London (1925), and an honorary fellow of Trinity College, Cambridge (1941). From the Royal Society he received the Hughes medal (1920) and a royal medal (1930). He was knighted in 1939. He was president of the Physical Society in 1926–8 and its honorary foreign secretary from 1928 to 1945.

Richardson was short, wiry, and sharp-featured. In his younger days he was fond of fell and mountain walking, sometimes alone, and could cover 40 miles in one day. He had been known to take a sleeper to Fort William, climb Ben Nevis, and return by the next sleeper. On returning to England in 1914 the Richardsons had settled in Hampstead, first in Cannon Place, and then at 45 Haverstock Hill. They had a home of extraordinary beauty containing the finest English period furniture and a wonderful collection of paintings by Dutch and other old masters. They kept a large and beautiful garden. They also maintained a country cottage in Sussex. Richardson had a fund of humorous after-dinner stories, sometimes told in the West Riding dialect, which he could speak perfectly. He had a hesitant but precise manner of speech. He kept a good table and a well-stocked cellar (wherein whisky was drawn from the wood). He rose late but seldom retired before 3 a.m.; this, he said, left it too late for burglars to start operations and he could work well in the early hours of the morning. He was a kindly man with much sympathy for refugees from totalitarian countries, whose misdirection of science he detested. He once remarked that he held practically no absolute conviction about anything except that science should be free. His work had practical applications in radio and other fields but he declined himself to be sidetracked from fundamental investigations.

In 1939 Richardson moved from Hampstead to Chandos Lodge, Alton, Hampshire. Partly as a war effort he bought a large farm at Medstead, nearby, which he supervised closely for several years. In 1945 his wife died and on 19 January 1948 he married Henrietta Maria Rupp (b. 1896/7), a physicist who was an early observer of electron diffraction. The divorced wife of E. Rupp, and daughter of an industrialist, J. Grunhut, she had been a family friend for many years. Richardson was president of the North-East Hampshire Agricultural Association in 1948–9. He died at home in Alton of a cerebral thrombosis on 15 February 1959; his wife survived him.

E. W. Foster, rev. Isobel Falconer

Sources W. Wilson, *Memoirs FRS*, 5 (1959), 207–215 · E. W. Forster, *Nature*, 183 (1959), 928–9 · *The Times* (16 Feb 1959) · *The Times* (21 Feb 1959) · personal knowledge (1971) · private information (1971, 2004) [O. Knudsen] · R. H. Stuewer, *The Compton effect: turning point in physics* (1975) · O. W. Richardson, letter to Lord Rayleigh, 4 Dec 1940, U. Texas, Richardson MSS · b. cert. · m. certs. · d. cert. **Archives** Ransom HRC, corresp. and papers [microfilm, Sci. Mus.] | University of Copenhagen, Copenhagen, Niels Bohr Institute for Astronomy, Physics and Geophysics, corresp. with Niels Bohr **Likenesses** W. Stoneman, photograph, 1917, NPG [*see illus.*] · photograph, repro. in *Memoirs FRS*, facing p. 207 **Wealth at death** £48,324 2s.: probate, 21 May 1959, CGPLA Eng. & Wales

Richardson, Philip John Sampey (1875–1963), journal editor and dance critic, was born on 17 March 1875 in Winthorpe, Nottinghamshire, the son of Edmund John Richardson, maltster, and of his wife, Margaret Sampey. He was educated at Beaumont College and University College School and had early experience in journalism. He married in 1909 Edith Aldersey (d. 1953), daughter of John Brough Hallem; there were no children.

Richardson found his vocation when, in 1910, he and the publisher T. M. Middleton bought the small house magazine of the Cavendish Rooms in London, called the *Dancing Times*, and transformed it into the first national British dance journal of the twentieth century, retaining its original title. Richardson became editor and Middleton took charge of the business affairs.

At first the magazine's pages were devoted mainly to social dancing and society news but the invasion of London by Russian dancers—Anna Pavlova and Diaghilev's Ballets Russes—whetted Richardson's enthusiasm for the art of ballet and more and more pages were devoted to news and reviews. Determined to learn more about the art form, he formed friendships with the leading dancers of the day and was at pains to discover more about the training methods of the great national schools—the Russian from Pavlova and Tamara Karsavina, the Danish from Adeline Genée, the French from Edouard Espinosa, and the Italian from the great pedagogue Enrico Cecchetti. He also enjoyed the friendship of a certain Mrs Stannus and took a keen interest in the progress of her young daughter, Edris, who, as Ninette de Valois, was to become a founding figure of the English national ballet which is today the Royal Ballet.

As early as 1912 Richardson began to have long talks with Espinosa about the need for proper codification of the intricacies of classical ballet training (known, in those days as 'operatic dancing'). In 1913 the *Dancing Times* began the publication of Espinosa's technical dictionary, one of the first of its kind to be published in English. In 1916 Richardson and Espinosa launched a campaign against faulty training by advocating, through the pages of the *Dancing Times*, the formation of an official examining body to certify teachers of dancing. This was in the middle of the First World War but the two men persevered, keeping up a barrage of publicity for their cause—and also a parallel campaign to recognize the merits of British dancers in the face of Russian domination. It took four years, but finally, in December 1920, the Association of Operatic Dancing of Great Britain (from 1936 the Royal Academy of Dancing, from 2000 the Royal Academy of Dance) was founded. Richardson and Espinosa headed the list of members as co-founders and Richardson became its secretary–treasurer (unpaid), operating from his desk at the *Dancing Times*. Adeline Genée became the first president, and the vice-presidents represented the national schools whose methods Richardson had so carefully studied.

Writing under the *nom de plume* the Sitter Out in his magazine, Richardson lost no opportunity not only of recognizing and saluting the great contribution of the Diaghilev Ballet but also of trumpeting the achievements of

British dancers. Diaghilev insisted on changing names—Lydia Sokolova, Anton Dolin, Ninette de Valois, Alicia Markova—but Richardson made sure his readers knew their true nationality.

As a critic, the Sitter Out was quick to recognize new choreography. In describing an early Balanchine ballet, *Barabau*, in 1925, he went so far as to say it contained sections 'which rise to the heights of genius' (*Dancing Times*, 16 Jan 1926, 438). In saluting the early ballets of Frederick Ashton he wrote, 'That hitherto mythical personage, a British choreographist [*sic*] of the first rank is amongst us' (*Dancing Times*, 21 Nov 1930, 126).

As practical encouragement of the infant British ballet companies being formed by Marie Rambert and Ninette de Valois, Richardson, together with his protégé Arnold Haskell and the music critic Edwin Evans, initiated the formation in 1931 of the Camargo Society, which aimed not only to sustain interest in ballet after the deaths of Diaghilev and Pavlova, but also to present performances in West End theatres which would prove conclusively that Britain had enough fine dancers and choreographers to present in a professional way both contemporary and classical ballets. Works by Ashton, de Valois, and Antony Tudor (some of them still danced today) represented native choreography. The presence of Olga Spesivtseva as guest, dancing with Anton Dolin, made possible the first British productions of *Giselle* and *Swan Lake*, Act 2. The dancing of Alicia Markova proclaimed a British ballerina of international repute.

In addition to these labours, Richardson early made his readers aware of the great traditions of ballet and its history. He not only published scholarly articles and translations of early writings, but also commissioned, from Cyril W. Beaumont, and published in instalments, a bibliography of dance materials in the British Museum. For his own use and interest he built up one of the most comprehensive private dance libraries on all forms of theatrical dance and was ever willing to share his treasures with young writers and historians.

Richardson's interest in and work for classical ballet was but one of his great contributions to dance in Britain. He was instrumental in founding, and became the first chairman of, the Official Board of Ballroom Dancing, to formulate and watch over the rules governing competitive ballroom dancing, and subsequently the International Council of Ballroom Dancing—bodies which, under various names, still regulate ballroom contests worldwide.

Richardson was an imposing figure, well over 6 feet tall, a little formidable at first meeting, but full of fun, enjoying good company, good food, good wine. His sight deteriorated in his later years but with the aid of a magnifying glass, which he called Cyclops, he invariably spotted any mistakes in his magazine which had slipped past the eyes of his successors. He remained chief editor until 1957 but served as chairman of the company until his death at his home, 22 Belsize Park Gardens, London, on 17 February 1963 (from pneumonia, caught a few days after attending a big ballroom function although suffering from a heavy

cold) and never lost his interest and enthusiasm. An inveterate chain smoker, he allowed the ash to drop not only on his jacket but also into his typewriter—it is preserved in the offices of the magazine and still emits clouds of ash when touched. He made one stage appearance. Accompanying a troupe of British dancers to Copenhagen in 1932, he was commandeered to fill the role of the godhead ('Job's spiritual self') in de Valois's masque for dancing, *Job*. He sensibly declared, with typical good humour, that any subsequent role would be a comedown.

Richardson's publications, in addition to innumerable articles, both signed and unsigned, were *Who's Who in Dancing* with Haskell, 1932; *The Art of the Ballroom* with Victor Silvester, 1936; *History of English Ballroom Dancing, 1910–1945*, 1946; and *Social Dances of the Nineteenth Century*, 1960. He was awarded the prize of the French ministry of arts in 1931, was appointed OBE in 1951, and was made a knight of the order of Dannebrog in 1952.   Mary Clarke

Sources *Dancing Times* (March 1963) · personal knowledge (2004) · G. B. L. Wilson, *A dictionary of ballet*, 3rd edn (1974) · *CGPLA Eng. & Wales* (1963) · *WWW* · b. cert. · d. cert. · *WW*
Likenesses C. Dobson, photographs, Dancing Times library, London
Wealth at death £25,465 2s. 0d.: probate, 15 May 1963, *CGPLA Eng. & Wales*

Richardson, Sir Ralph David (1902–1983), actor, was born on 19 December 1902 at Cheltenham, Gloucestershire, the third son and third and youngest child of Arthur Richardson, art-master at Cheltenham Ladies' College, and his wife, Lydia Susie, daughter of John Russell, a captain in the merchant navy. When Richardson was four his mother left his father and took him to live with her at Shoreham, Sussex, in a makeshift bungalow constructed out of two old railway carriages. Their allowance from her husband (with whom the two older boys remained) was £2 10s. a week, and on his own admission Richardson grew up as a 'mother's boy', educated by her at home and at the Xaverian College in Brighton, a seminary for those who intended to be priests, from which he soon ran away.

Richardson's education thereafter was erratic, and by 1917 he was working as an office boy for the Liverpool and Victoria Insurance Company in Brighton. Two years later, when his grandmother died leaving him £500 in her will, he resigned immediately from the office and enrolled at the Brighton College of Art. Once there, he rapidly discovered that he had no gift for painting; instead, he briefly considered a career in journalism but then, inspired by a touring production of *Hamlet* which had come to Brighton with Sir Frank Benson in the title role, decided that his future lay in the theatre.

Richardson joined a local semi-professional company run by Frank Growcott, who charged him 10s. a week to learn about acting with the understanding that, once he had learned how to do it, Growcott would in turn pay him the same amount to appear in his company. Richardson seldom saw the colour of Growcott's money but he did make his first stage appearances at Brighton having already created some memorable off-stage sound effects.

Sir Ralph David Richardson (1902–1983), by Dorothy Wilding, 1958

(As he said, 'I first burst on to the English stage as a bombshell'.) He then auditioned successfully for Charles Doran's touring players, with whom he stayed for five seasons while rising through the ranks to such roles as Cassio in *Othello* and Mark Antony in *Julius Caesar*.

On 18 September 1924 Richardson married the seventeen-year-old student actress Muriel Bathia Hewitt (d. 1942), daughter of Alfred James Hewitt, a clerk in the Telegraph and Cable Company; they had no children. The following year the pair joined the Birmingham Repertory Company and Richardson made his first London appearance for the Greek Play Society on 10 July 1926 as the stranger in *Oedipus at Colonus*.

Richardson spent the next four years largely in small West End roles in London, notably in two plays by Eden Phillpotts (*Yellow Sands* and *The Farmer's Wife*), and at the Royal Court where he spent much of 1928 in H. K. Ayliff's company, which also included a young Laurence Olivier. After touring South Africa in 1929, already aware that his young wife had contracted sleeping sickness (encephalitis lethargica), he returned in 1930 to join the Old Vic Company where he met John Gielgud for the first time. Of the three great actor knights of the mid-twentieth century (Richardson, Olivier, and Gielgud), Richardson was the eldest and the least predictable, the one who looked most like a respectable bank manager possessed of magical powers, and the one who had the most trouble with Shakespeare: the critic James Agate said that his 1932 Iago 'could not hurt a fly' and Richardson soon turned with what seemed a kind of relief to the modern dress of G. B. Shaw, W. Somerset Maugham, and James Bridie before starting in 1934 (with *Eden End*) an alliance with J. B. Priestley which was to lead to some of his best and most characteristic work.

A year later Richardson was on Broadway for the first time, playing Mercutio in *Romeo and Juliet* for Katharine Cornell's company, and in 1936 he returned to London for a long-running thriller, *The Amazing Dr Clitterhouse*, in which he was supported by the actress Meriel Forbes [*see below*], whom he married on 26 January 1944, two years after the death of his first wife in 1942.

By now a theory had developed in the theatre that Richardson was at his best playing 'ordinary little men', though as one critic later noted, anyone who believed that could seldom have met many ordinary little men. Those played by Richardson always had an added touch of magic, of something strange, though Agate was still not won over. When Richardson returned to the Old Vic in 1938 to play Othello in a production by Tyrone Guthrie, for which Olivier had elected to play Iago homosexually, much to his partner's horror, Agate simply noted, 'the truth is that Nature, which has showered upon this actor the kindly gifts of the comedian, has unkindly refused him any tragic facilities whatever. … He cannot blaze'.

Richardson returned to Priestley and triumph (*Johnson over Jordan*, 1939) and then, when the war came, rose to the rank of lieutenant-commander in the Royal Naval Volunteer Reserve where he was affectionately known as Pranger Richardson on account of the large number of planes which seemed to fall to pieces under his control.

It was in 1944, when he was released to form a directorate of the Old Vic with Olivier and John Burrell, that Richardson reached the height of his considerable form: over four great seasons at the New Theatre with Olivier, Dame Sybil Thorndike, and Margaret Leighton, he played not only the definitive Falstaff and Peer Gynt of the century but also the title role in Priestley's *An Inspector Calls*, Cyrano de Bergerac, Face in *The Alchemist*, Bluntschli in *Arms and the Man*, and John of Gaunt in *Richard II*, which he unusually also directed.

When the triumvirate was summarily sacked in 1947 by the Old Vic governors, who were uneasy about the Olivier and Richardson stardom in what was supposed to be a company of equals, Sir Ralph (it was also the year of his knighthood) returned to the life of a freelance actor, enjoying many more triumphs—as well as another Shakespearian defeat at Stratford upon Avon in the title role of *Macbeth* (1952).

The 1960s were highlighted by *Six Characters in Search of an Author* (1963), where in Pirandello, Richardson found an ethereal author to satisfy his own other-worldliness, and then in 1969 by a courageous move away from the classics and into the avant-garde as Dr Rance in *What the Butler Saw* by Joe Orton. A year later he was with Gielgud at the Royal Court in David Storey's *Home*, starting a late life partnership which took them on to Harold Pinter's *No Man's Land* (1975) in the West End and on Broadway, as well as to countless television interviews in which they appeared as two uniquely distinguished but increasingly eccentric brokers' men.

Richardson first joined the National Theatre in 1975, shortly after Olivier left it, as John Gabriel Borkman in Ibsen's play of that name, and it was there under Sir Peter Hall's administration that he was to do the best of his late work, which culminated a few months before his death in a haunting and characteristic final appearance as Don Alberto in Eduardo de Filippo's *Inner Voices*.

Deeply attached to his second wife, their only child, Charles (1945–1998), and a racing motor cycle on which he would speed across Hampstead Heath, Richardson achieved theatrical greatness by turning the ordinary into the extraordinary: on stage as off, he managed to be both unapproachable and instantly accessible, leaving, like Priestley's inspector, the impression behind him that perhaps he had not really been there at all, or that if he had, it was only on his way to or from somewhere distinctly unworldly.

Richardson turned somewhat uncertainly to the cinema in the 1930s, at the start of a long contract with Alexander Korda which led to such successes as *Things to Come* (1936), *The Four Feathers* (1939), *The Citadel* (1939), *The Fallen Idol* (1948), *An Outcast of the Islands* (1952), and *Richard III* (1955), before he went on to *Long Day's Journey into Night* (1962), *Doctor Zhivago* (1965), and *A Doll's House* (1973). It was with one of his very last screen roles, however, as the supreme being in *Time Bandits* (1980), that he achieved the perfect mix of the godly and the homespun which had always been at the heart of his acting.

Sir Ralph Richardson died in London on 10 October 1983 and was buried in Highgate cemetery; a memorial service was held in Westminster Abbey on 17 November. He left the memory of a great and mysterious theatrical wizard. At the National Theatre, and at his suggestion, a rocket is fired from the roof to denote first nights; it is known as Ralph's Rocket. Richardson was awarded the Norwegian order of St Olaf (1950) and the honorary degree of DLitt at Oxford (1969).

Richardson's second wife, **Muriel Elsa Florence Richardson** [*née* Muriel Elsa Florence Forbes-Robertson; *performing name* Meriel Forbes], Lady Richardson (1913–2000), actress, was born on 13 September 1913 at 302 Fulham Palace Road, Fulham, London, into a well-known theatrical family, the daughter of Frank Forbes-Robertson (*b.* 1885), actor–manager, and his wife, Honoria Helen, *née* McDermott. She was the great-niece of Sir Johnston Forbes-*Robertson (1853–1937), actor–manager. Educated in Eastbourne, Brussels, and Paris, from the age of sixteen she acted in a variety of plays, before and after marriage, latterly often with Richardson, and also in films—including *Oh! What a Lovely War* (1969)—and television. Vivacious and winsome, she excelled at light comedy, and her elegance and distinction led to many aristocratic roles. The Richardsons collected art, antiques, and memorabilia, and she keenly supported theatrical charities, by her will establishing an actors' benevolent fund, the Ralph and Muriel Richardson Foundation. She died of bronchopneumonia and cerebral ischaemia at her home, 19 Eaton Mews South, Westminster, on 7 April 2000. Her son, Charles, a television stage manager, predeceased her.

SHERIDAN MORLEY, rev.

Sources H. Hobson, *Ralph Richardson* (1958) · G. O'Connor, *Ralph Richardson* (1982) · J. Miller, *Ralph Richardson* (1995) · K. Tynan, *Show people* (1980) · T. Palmer, 'The importance of being Richardson', *Now!* (30 Nov 1979), 10–16 · *The Times* (11 Oct 1983) · *The Times* (18 Nov 1983) · I. Herbert, ed., *Who's who in the theatre*, 16th edn (1977) · WW · personal knowledge (1990) · private information (1990) · m. certs. · *CGPLA Eng. & Wales* (1983) · *Daily Telegraph* (14 April 2000) · *The Guardian* (17 April 2000) · G. Howell, 'The errant knight's tale', *Sunday Times Magazine* (7 April 2002), 20–29 · b. cert. [Muriel Forbes-Robertson] · d. cert. [Muriel Richardson]

Archives BL, papers, Dep 10035 | NL Scot., corresp. with William Douglas Home · Tate collection, corresp. with Lord Clark · Theatre Museum, London, corresp. with Christopher Fry | FILM BFI NFTVA, current affairs footage · BFI NFTVA, documentary footage · BFI NFTVA, news footage · BFI NFTVA, performance footage | SOUND BL NSA, *Desert island discs*, NP3529R BD1 · BL NSA, 'On looking back: a reading from his unfinished autobiography', M4879R BD1 · BL NSA, 'Richardson at 80', T5436WR TR1 · BL NSA, documentary recordings · BL NSA, performance recordings

Likenesses I. Penn, gelatine silver print, 1950, NPG · photograph, 1952, Hult. Arch. · D. Wilding, bromide print, 1958, NPG [*see illus.*] · M. Noakes, oils, 1961, NPG · A. Newman, bromide print, 1978, NPG

Wealth at death £1,291,468: probate, 6 April 1984, *CGPLA Eng. & Wales*

Richardson, Richard (1622/3–1689), Quaker administrator, of whose early life little is known, probably became a Quaker in the 1650s and is mentioned by George Fox in his journal as being at Swarthmoor Hall with him in 1660. After he became a Friend, Richardson, who was evidently well educated and of considerable learning, made his living as a schoolmaster. In 1670 he was tried at Chelmsford, Essex, for teaching without licence and, on refusing to take the oath of allegiance, was imprisoned for more than two years. He was freed under Charles II's charter of release in 1672.

Richardson seems to have moved to London soon afterwards, for in 1674 he was appointed as master of a school for the children of poor Friends being set up by London Friends at Devonshire House, Bishopsgate (the Quaker headquarters). Richardson was to receive a salary of £20 a year and fees when they could be afforded. The school taught Latin, writing, arithmetic, languages, and botany. On 23 May 1676 Richardson married Anne Mullins, formerly Blithe, (*c.*1633–1695), a widow of Bow, and they eventually settled in that district. She survived him but the couple do not appear to have had children.

On the death in 1681 of Ellis Hookes, the first recording clerk of the Society of Friends, Richardson took over his role. He became clerk to a variety of local and national meetings and soon also moved into Hookes's 'chamber'. This office, in Lombard Street, received reports of Friends' 'sufferings'—imprisonments and fines—and Richardson copied them into a central book with the assistance of Mark Swanner and later Benjamin Bealing. Richardson compiled a detailed index to the first two volumes. He was also instructed to collect two copies of every book written by Friends, and one copy of each book written against them; these books, together with the catalogue he compiled, laid the foundation of the library now in Friends' House, London.

Richardson was thus at the hub of the central organization of Friends in the capital. From 1675 he also wrote several polemical books, against oaths and tithes for example, and entered into spirited controversy with opponents of Quakerism such as Francis Bugg and William Rogers. George Fox used Richardson as a kind of research assistant, asking for references on subjects such as marriage which Fox himself did not have the education to pursue. Richardson and his assistants were also often requested to supply information at short notice—for example, lists of Friends who were being persecuted in particular areas—for those such as George Whitehead to use in petitions.

Although he was not called to public ministry, Richardson's writing and his administrative role were vital to the organization of Friends and he continued working long hours until a short time before his death. He died of consumption at Stratford-le-Bow on 14 June 1689 at the age of sixty-six, and was buried at Ratcliff Friends' burial-ground. He left several charitable bequests to Friends as well as a considerable number of his books.

GIL SKIDMORE

Sources N. Penney, 'Our recording clerks, ii: Richard Richardson', *Journal of the Friends' Historical Society*, 1 (1903–4), 62–8 · W. C. Braithwaite, *The second period of Quakerism*, ed. H. J. Cadbury, 2nd edn (1961) · J. Smith, *Catalogue of Friends' books* (1893)

Richardson, Richard (1663–1741), physician and botanist, was born at North Bierley, near Bradford, Yorkshire, on 6 September 1663. He was the eldest son of William Richardson (1629–1667) of North Bierley and Susannah (d. 1708), daughter of Gilbert Savile of Greetland, Elland, near Halifax, Yorkshire. William Richardson died intestate, but Richard inherited the family home and estate and provided for his sister and younger brother. He married Sarah, only daughter of John Crossley of Kerkshaw House, Halifax, at Luddenden Chapel, Halifax, on 9 February 1700. Sarah died on 21 October 1702, giving birth to a son (who died soon afterwards), and was buried in Bradford church. Richardson's second wife, whom he married at Kildwick in Craven on 27 December 1705, was Dorothy (1687–1763), second daughter of Henry Currer. Of their twelve children, seven survived. One son, also named Richard (d. 1776), continued his father's interest in horticulture at Bierley.

Richardson was educated at Bradford School, and on 20 June 1681 he matriculated at University College, Oxford, but left without a degree. On 10 November 1681 he was entered as a student at Gray's Inn. He spent three years at the University of Leiden, where he lodged with Paul Hermann, the professor of botany. He received his MD at Leiden in 1690; his thesis 'De febre tertiana' was printed with a dedication to Richard Thornton, 'amico et consanguineo suo' ('friend and relative'). After he returned to England and North Bierley, Richardson practised as a doctor, but, since he was a wealthy man, it has been suggested that most of his professional services were provided free.

Richardson was fascinated by plants and travelled widely in England, Wales, and Scotland in search of rare specimens, particularly cryptogams (mosses and lichens), and patronized less wealthy naturalists, gardeners, and collectors, including Samuel Brewer and Thomas Knowlton. He corresponded and exchanged plants with many well-known botanists and as a consequence his garden at Bierley Hall was rich in both native and foreign plants, and deservedly achieved a reputation as the best in the north of England. His garden was notable for its ponds and water features, and especially for its 'stove' or hothouse, considered to be among the first established in England. This enabled him to grow exotic fruits which he distributed to his friends—J. C. Loudon in 1828 mentioned a pineapple grown at Bierley being sent by Richardson to the ailing naturalist John Ray in 1698. A seedling cedar of Lebanon, sent to Richardson by Sir Hans Sloane, became in maturity a conspicuous feature at Bierley Hall and can be seen in the engravings made of his residence.

Richardson formed a valuable library of botanical and historical works, which passed to his descendant, Miss Frances Mary Richardson-Currer of Eshton Hall, who inherited both the Richardson and Currer estates. She also owned the two manuscripts written by Richardson, *De cultura hortorum* (1696) and *Index hort. Bierliensis* (1737), and twelve folio volumes of his correspondence which are now in the Bodleian Library, Oxford. Other letters survive at the Royal Society and the British Library.

Richardson corresponded with many of the most significant naturalists of his day, including Sir Hans Sloane, Dillenius, Gronovius, and Petiver. Many letters to and from him have been printed (Nichols, 1817; Smith, 1821; Turner, 1835; Henrey, 1986), and provide a fascinating glimpse of the scientific world at the beginning of the eighteenth century, when geographical exploration had provided a wealth of new material for the horticulturist and those biologists trying to create systems of classification for the natural world. It is noteworthy that Dillenius, in a letter to Richardson dated 25 August 1736, records 'A new Botanist is arisen in the North, founder of a new method, on the stamens and pistils, whose name is Linnaeus … He is a Swede, and has travelled over Lapland … I am afraid his method will not hold' (Smith, 152). Another of Richardson's correspondents, Thomas Knowlton, also expressed his dislike of the Linnaean system (Henrey, 150), and it is probable that Richardson too continued to follow Ray's method. The growing interest in natural history was also reflected in the growth of personal collections, and it is clear from the correspondence that Richardson played a significant role, amassing his own museum and donating specimens to the two most important of the day, made by Sloane and Petiver. He was elected FRS in 1712, and contributed several papers to the *Philosophical Transactions*.

Dillenius, who edited the third edition of John Ray's *Synopsis methodica stirpium Britannicarum*, identified Richardson and Sherard as the two men who, by their sustained botanical investigations throughout Britain, had most enlarged the list of species and identified the distribution and habitats of the flora. Dillenius also made particular reference in his *Historia muscorum* (1741) to Richardson's research on mosses. At the time when Richardson was travelling and botanizing, and collecting mosses and lichens, the taxonomy and biology of the cryptogams and the algae were little understood. Richardson's contribution should not therefore be underestimated—he is now considered the first Yorkshire naturalist to have collected lichens. The plant genera *Richardia* L. and *Richardsonia* Kunth. were named in his honour.

Richardson died at Bierley Hall on 21 April 1741 and was buried in Cleckheaton Chapel in Birstal, which he had had rebuilt. A monument with a Latin inscription was erected to his memory. W. P. COURTNEY, *rev.* PETER DAVIS

Sources R. Pulteney, *Historical and biographical sketches of the progress of botany in England*, 2 (1790), 185–8 · Nichols, *Illustrations*, 1.225–52 · *A selection of the correspondence of Linnaeus, and other naturalists, from the original manuscripts*, ed. J. E. Smith, 2 vols. (1821), vol. 1, p. vii; vol. 2, pp. 130–90 · B. Henrey, *No ordinary gardener: Thomas Knowlton, 1691–1781*, ed. A. O. Chater (1986) · J. C. Loudon, ed., 'Some account of Richard Richardson esq', *Gardener's Magazine*, 3 (1828), 127–8 · M. R. D. Seaward, '300 years of Yorkshire lichenology', *The Naturalist*, 112 (1987), 37–52 · F. A. Stafleu and R. S. Cowan, *Taxonomic literature: a selective guide*, 2nd edn, 4, Regnum Vegetabile, 110 (1983), 771–2 · Desmond, *Botanists*, rev. edn, 582 · J. Petiver, *Musei Petiveriai* (1695), 29 · H. E. Wroot, 'Notes on Yorkshire botany in 1727', *The Naturalist* (Aug 1906), 257–60 · E. J. L. Scott, *Index to the Sloane manuscripts in the British Museum* (1904), 452 · *Extracts from the literary and scientific correspondence of Richard Richardson*, ed. D. Turner (1835) · W. Claridge, *Origin and history of the Bradford grammar school* (1882), 36 · R. W. Innes Smith, *English-speaking students of medicine at the University of Leyden* (1932), 194 **Archives** BL, corresp. and notes, Add. MSS 4432, 4458 · Bodl. Oxf. · Eshton Hall, Yorkshire, corresp. · NHM, plant specimens · U. Oxf., Taylor Institution, botanical notes | BL, letters to James Petiver · BL, letters to Hans Sloane · Bodl. Oxf., letters to Edward Lhuyd **Likenesses** J. Basire, line engraving, 1817 (after portrait), NPG, BM; repro. in Nichols, *Illustrations*, 1.225 · W. O. Geller, print (after portrait), repro. in J. James, *The history and topography of Bradford* (1841), 388 · Graf and Soret, print (after portrait), repro. in Turner, *Extracts from … correspondence* · portrait; formerly in possession of Miss Currer, 1896 · portrait, Carnegie Mellon University, Pittsburgh, Hunt Botanical Library

Richardson, Robert (*d.* 1573), religious author and Church of England clergyman, is of unknown origins. He is first recorded as an Augustinian canon at Cambuskenneth, near Stirling, under Alexander Mylne, who was abbot from 1519; a Robert Richardson matriculated with other canons regular (given the honorific title *Dominus*) at St Andrews in 1525. At this time the abbey of St Victor in Paris was known for its reformed Augustinian observance and Richardson was accordingly sent there for study by Mylne. In Paris in early 1528 he helped the Piedmontese humanist Giovanni Ferrerio to become acquainted with Abbot Robert Reid, Ferrerio's future patron.

In early 1530 Richardson published at Paris his *Exegesis in canonem Divi Augustini*, Latinizing his surname as Richardinus. It is an orthodox and erudite commentary on St Augustine's rule, but its main feature is an unremitting catalogue of monastic behaviour, both community and individual, that is the very antithesis of what Augustine laid down. Its blanket condemnations and rhetoric, together with a lack of hard information, damage its credibility. Richardson's strictures on women and elaborate church music are particularly overstated.

Having studied under John Mair or Major and graduated BTh, Richardson returned to Scotland and in August 1531

was under monastic excommunication (exclusion from common table and choir) at Cambuskenneth for disobedience. Presumably he was the Robert Richardson (termed *Dominus*) who matriculated at St Andrews in 1531–2 and determined in arts in 1531, and also the Robert Richardson, *pauper*, licensed in 1532. In 1535 he was in Italy, visiting Rome, Bologna, Florence, and Pavia and having dealings with Cardinal Ghinucci, apparently in support of Henry VIII's divorce. He wrote to Thomas Cromwell in December, and having arrived in London wrote again in April 1536 seeking Cromwell's patronage and offering his services as political agent and go-between. He preached in London and, following the Pilgrimage of Grace in October 1536, proclaimed protestantism and submission to civil authority in Lincolnshire and further north. In January 1537 he again offered his services to Cromwell.

Richardson was naturalized as English in January 1540. In September 1541, however, the privy council meeting at York dismissed him with a safe conduct to Scotland; the purpose of this is not known. Early in 1543 he was sent by the English authorities to spy out the dispositions of Rouen and its district but was detained by the French. Then, freed in an exchange of prisoners, he was sent in May by the privy council to Scotland with letters from Henry. For a time he was in Governor Arran's favour during the latter's temporary *rapprochement* with protestantism, and he preached accordingly, until in November 1543 Arran's change of policy forced him to return to England.

Thereafter Richardson's career was mostly in London, as a churchman and royal chaplain, supported by various benefices. In 1545 he gave up the rectory of Stoke and he is probably the Robert Richardson, parson of Chelsea, disciplined in 1546 by Edmund Bonner, bishop of London, for light behaviour in matters of religion. During Mary's reign he was reader at Whittington College and was expected in 1555 to recant in a public sermon, but failed to do so clearly.

In 1559 Richardson was appointed parson of St Matthew's, Friday Street, London, a position he held until his death. He married soon afterwards, and a son was born in 1562, but tragedy struck in August 1570 when his maidservant, his daughter, and that son died in the same week. Three years later he died 'of very age' (Bannerman, 115); he was buried on 31 October 1573.

About 1570 Richardson published a short commentary on the psalm *De Profundis*, declaring it to be relevant to the living who feared God's judgment and not to the dead. Expounding this had been part of his ministry as he conducted funerals and memorial services in London. Death apparently loomed large in his outlook: his seal contained the Latin motto *Morieris* ('you will die') and his *Exegesis* describes a deathbed in stark detail.

MARK DILWORTH

Sources J. Durkan, 'Scottish evangelicals in the patronage of Thomas Cromwell', *Records of the Scottish Church History Society*, 21 (1981–3), 127–56 · G. G. Coulton, ed., *Commentary on the Rule of St. Augustine by Robertus Richardinus*, Scottish History Society, 3rd ser., 26 (1935) · *LP Henry VIII*, vols. 9–21 · R. Richardson, *A briefe and compendious exposition upon the psalme called Deprofundis* [1570] · *The diary of Henry Machyn, citizen and merchant-taylor of London, from AD 1550 to*

AD 1563, ed. J. G. Nichols, CS, 42 (1848) • J. M. Anderson, ed., *Early records of the University of St Andrews*, Scottish History Society, 3rd ser., 8 (1926) • A. M. B. Bannerman, ed., *The register of St Matthew, Friday Street, London, 1538–1812, and the united parishes of St Matthew and St Peter Cheap*, Harleian Society, register section, 63 (1933) • J. Durkan, 'The cultural background in sixteenth-century Scotland', *Essays on the Scottish Reformation, 1513–1625*, ed. D. McRoberts (1962), 274–331 • W. Page, ed., *Letters of denization and acts of naturalization for aliens in England, 1509–1603*, Huguenot Society of London, 8 (1893), 206 • D. S. Chambers, ed., *Faculty office registers, 1534–1549* (1966), 264 • W. D. Wilson, ed., *Ferrerii historia abbatum de Kynlos*, Bannatyne Club, 63 (1839), 39–40, 43

Richardson, Robert (d. 1578), prior of St Mary's Isle and administrator, was the son of Robert Richardson, burgess of Jedburgh (d. c.1556). The historian George Crawfurd asserts that he was descended 'of a stock of ancient and opulent burgesses of Edinburgh' (Crawfurd, 383), but there is little to connect him with the city before 1553, when he was made a burgess at the request of the fourth earl of Huntly. He matriculated at St Salvator's College, St Andrews, in 1531, and graduated MA in 1532. Nothing is known of his early career except that in April 1544 (along with the earl of Lennox) he was involved in armed opposition to the regent Arran at Glasgow, for which he later received remission. He was presented to the vicarage of Dunsyre in 1549 and held the vicarage of Eckford by 1552. In that year he was provided by the pope to the archdeaconry of Teviotdale, which he held until 1565 along with the appropriated parsonage of Morebattle. In 1558 he obtained crown presentation to the priory of St Mary's Isle, near Kirkcudbright, which he also resigned in 1565, retaining the usufruct.

Richardson's career as a royal official began around 1549 when he was comptroller clerk. In November 1552 he was an auditor of the treasurer's account. Gilbert Kennedy, third earl of Cassillis, appointed lord treasurer in April 1554, delegated the entire conduct of business to Richardson as treasurer clerk. After Cassillis's death in November 1558 Richardson continued as treasurer clerk and acting treasurer. It was probably in this capacity, rather than as 'Maister of the Cunze-hous' (*Works of John Knox*, 1.372), that he held the coining irons of the mint. In July 1559 the lords of the congregation seized these, along with great sums of money, claiming that they had done so to stop corruption of the coinage and that they had returned what they had seized, the irons being restored to him under an agreement between the lords and Mary of Guise.

Richardson sat as a prelate in the Reformation Parliament of 1560 and is listed by Knox among those 'that had renunceit Papistrie and oppinlie profest Jesus Chryst with us' (*Works of John Knox*, 2.88). Finally appointed lord treasurer on 5 March 1561, he sat in the privy council from 1561 to 1576. In 1562 he was named as one of the commissioners for receiving rentals of benefices and in October of that year was granted a pension of £1000 Scots from the thirds of benefices pending provision to a benefice of equal or greater value. The Reformation gave him further opportunities to add to the landed estate he had been acquiring since 1552, mainly in Haddingtonshire and Edinburghshire. Three charters by the commendator and convent of Dunfermline on 28 July 1563 conveyed to him extensive lands, mainly in Haddingtonshire, Edinburghshire, and Fife, amounting to no fewer than seventy-seven farms and scattered holdings. From September 1565 onwards he disposed of a large part of this property to the tenants, no doubt profitably. He retained lands and coalmines around Musselburgh, including Smeaton, where either he or his son built what in 1577 was described as a new house. He also acquired some small properties belonging to Jedburgh Abbey. Crawfurd wrote of Richardson:

> He appears to have been a very wise moderate man; for so far as I can observe from the history of these times, he kept himself more in a neutrality, and was less a party-man than any other that held any great office about the court. He was never violent against the Queen, tho' he complied with the Government under the young King. (Crawfurd, 383)

Richardson attended James VI's coronation in 1567, and in 1569 voted to refuse Mary's divorce from Bothwell. His support for the new regime is evidenced by a loan of £3000 to the regent Moray on 17 September 1567, secured on the royal jewels. In the following year, as he was 'greitlie superexpendit' as treasurer and unable to pay his creditors (Livingstone and others, 6, no. 259), Moray gave him the revenue arising from wards and marriages and vacant benefices. In January 1571 the lease of the mint which he had held since 1566 was renewed for three years, half the profits to be applied to paying off his 'super-expenses' as treasurer. According to a contemporary source, John Cunningham of Drumquhassle had been made 'half thesaurer, with Mr Robert Ritchartsone that wes thesaurer of befoir' (Thomson, *Diurnal*, 180) in July 1570, but Richardson remained in sole charge until 24 June 1571, when he was replaced by William, Lord Ruthven. He retained control of the mint until March 1573, his share of the profits amounting to more than £5400 Scots. Thereafter he continued to receive money from the mint to redeem the royal jewels that had been pledged to him, further payments being made to his sons after his death, which probably took place between May and November 1578.

Richardson was unmarried but four children, James, Robert, Stephen, and Elizabeth, were legitimated in 1552; another child may have been born in December 1563, when Randolph reported to Cecil that Richardson was to do public penance for getting a woman with child and Knox was to 'mayke the sermonde' (*Works of John Knox*, 6.527). James Richardson of Smeaton, the eldest of Richardson's children, received most of his father's lands; he married Elizabeth Douglas, and their second son, Sir Robert Richardson of Pencaitland, was created a baronet in 1630.

ATHOL MURRAY

Sources J. B. Paul and C. T. McInnes, eds., *Compota thesaurariorum regum Scotorum / Accounts of the lord high treasurer of Scotland*, 10–13 (1913–78) • M. Livingstone, D. Hay Fleming, and others, eds., *Registrum secreti sigilli regum Scotorum / The register of the privy seal of Scotland*, 4–8 (1952–82) • G. Crawfurd, *Lives of the officers of state in Scotland* (1726) • *The works of John Knox*, ed. D. Laing, 6 vols., Wodrow Society, 12 (1846–64) • T. Thomson, ed., *A diurnal of remarkable occurrents that have passed within the country of Scotland*, Bannatyne

Club, 43 (1833) · J. M. Thomson and others, eds., *Registrum magni sigilli regum Scotorum / The register of the great seal of Scotland*, 11 vols. (1882–1914), vol. 4 · J. M. Anderson, ed., *Early records of the University of St Andrews*, Scottish History Society, 3rd ser., 8 (1926), 231, 128 · M. H. B. Sanderson, *Scottish rural society in the sixteenth century* (1962) · protocol book of John Wilson, Jedburgh, 1550–72, NA Scot., B.38/1/1 · C. B. B. Watson, ed., *Roll of Edinburgh burgesses and guild-brethren, 1406–1700*, Scottish RS, 59 (1929) · *CSP Scot.*, 1547–74 · GEC, *Baronetage*, 2.380–03

Richardson, Robert (*bap.* 1731, *d.* 1781). *See under* Richardson, William (1698–1775).

Richardson, Robert (1779–1847), physician and traveller, was probably born in Stirlingshire. After leaving Stirling grammar school he studied arts at Glasgow University, though he graduated MD at Edinburgh on 12 September 1807. After practising for a time in Dumfriesshire, he became travelling physician to Charles John Gardiner, second Viscount Mountjoy (first earl of Blessington and husband of the famous countess). In 1816 he joined the party of Somerset Lowry Corry, second earl of Belmore, in a two-year tour through Europe, Egypt, and Palestine. While in Albania they had two interviews with Ali Pasha at Yanina. Having visited the pyramids and many places of interest on the Nile, as far as the second cataract, the party went on to Palestine, reaching Gaza in April 1818. Richardson claims to have been the first Christian traveller admitted to Solomon's mosque. At Tiberias the group were visited by Lady Hester Stanhope. Richardson's *Travels* were published in two volumes in 1822, with plans and engravings, to mixed reviews. Lady Blessington lent Byron the book, and he highly commended it, saying: 'The author is just the sort of man I should like to have with me for Greece—clever, both as a man and a physician' (Blessington, 330–31).

After his return to England, Richardson, who had become LRCP on 26 June 1815, settled in Rathbone Place, London, and obtained an extensive practice. He died in Gordon Street, Gordon Square, London, on 5 November 1847, and was buried in Highgate cemetery.

G. LE G. NORGATE, *rev.* ELIZABETH BAIGENT

Sources Munk, *Roll* · *GM*, 2nd ser., 28 (1847), 666 · Allibone, *Dict.* · M. Blessington, *A journal of the conversations of Lord Byron with the countess of Blessington* (1893)

Likenesses W. Brockedon, chalk drawing, 1826, NPG · C. Turner, mezzotint, 1842 (after S. Howell), Wellcome L.

Richardson, Samuel (*fl.* 1637–1658), writer, of Northamptonshire birth, was probably a soldier and an army preacher in the early part of the civil wars. In 1637 he was indicted for the distribution of puritan texts by Bastwick and Prynne. In his 1643 book *The Life of Faith* he speaks of a Mistress Ann Wilson as having oft refreshed him in the days of his pilgrimage. He became a leading member of one of the seven Baptist churches of London. In the three confessions of faith put forth by these churches in 1643, 1644, and 1646 Richardson's signature stands beside that of John Spilsbury, minister of the Baptist congregation at Wapping, and he may have been an elder or Spilsbury's colleague there. He ardently supported the action of the army and the government of Cromwell, to whom he had

open access. For a time he had scruples as to the title of protector, and told Cromwell of them to his face; but, on becoming convinced, he tried hard to reconcile Vavasor Powell and others to the protectorate. He was possibly the Samuel Richardson who on 21 July 1653 was appointed one of the committee for the hospitals of the Savoy and Ely House.

Richardson's numerous published works provide one of the core elements of Particular Baptist thinking in the 1640s and 1650s, and were instrumental in the delineation, defence, and subsequent revision of its confession of faith. Having himself felt the scourge of persecution in consequence of his beliefs, he also wrote extensively on toleration, culminating in his *Necessity of Toleration* of September 1647 in which he lambasted the empty legal formalism of the Westminster assembly's embryonic presbyterian church settlement. A supporter of the stance adopted by the New Model Army in summer 1647, Richardson also wrote in justification of Pride's Purge and sought to persuade the disgruntled Levellers to back the Commonwealth in the spring of 1649. Evidently having appreciated the advantages of such civic loyalism for those tender of conscience, Richardson later wrote in support of the protectorate, justifying the imprisonment of John Rogers and Christopher Feake, and criticizing the Fifth Monarchists who railed against Cromwell's betrayal of the 'good old cause'. Published in 1658, Richardson's final foray, although more obviously theological in content, may not have been entirely disconnected from his numerous excursions in print on behalf of successive regimes during the 1650s. *Of the Torments of Hell* repudiated the orthodox doctrine of eternal damnation as inconsistent with the goodness of God.

The date of Richardson's death is unknown; the administration of the estate of a Samuel Richardson of Berkshire was granted to his widow, Joane, on 10 June 1659.

W. A. SHAW, *rev.* SEAN KELSEY

Sources Greaves & Zaller, *BDBR*, pp. 93–5 · administration, PRO, PROB 6/35, fol. 209r

Richardson, Samuel (*bap.* 1689, *d.* 1761), printer and author, was baptized on 19 August 1689 at Mackworth, Derbyshire, the fourth of the nine children of Samuel Richardson (*fl.* 1667–1727), joiner, and his second wife, Elizabeth Hall (*fl.* 1682–1736).

Early years and education, 1689–1706 Richardson's forebears had been sturdy yeomen in Byfleet, Surrey, since at least the late sixteenth century, and four William Richardsons held in succession copyhold land on the royal manor of Byfleet. The last William, the author's grandfather, sent his son Samuel to London in 1667 where he became an apprentice to Thomas Turner, a joiner. The reason given by the novelist for this move is that his father's family had grown too numerous to live off the land and had to go into trades. Although Richardson's father had evidently become a successful joiner as well as draughtsman and was by 1678 a freeman of the Joiners' Company and of the City of London, for some unknown reason he chose to move into Derbyshire shortly before the novelist's birth.

Samuel Richardson (*bap.* 1689, *d.* 1761), by Mason Chamberlin, in or before 1754

In a letter to his Dutch translator, Johannes Stinstra, the only autobiographical account that we have, Richardson claimed that his father's known sympathies with the duke of Monmouth and the first earl of Shaftesbury prompted his move from the City at the time of Monmouth's execution in 1685 (Slattery, 23). To the end, however, Richardson was mysteriously silent about the circumstances of his birthplace and childhood years.

Richardson's siblings, not counting children who had died in infancy before he could have known them, included his half-sister, Elizabeth, daughter from his father's marriage to Elizabeth Lane, Mary and Anne, all born in London, and William, Sara, and another brother, name unknown, born in Derbyshire. His two youngest brothers were born in London—Benjamin, baptized in St Botolph's, Aldgate, on 4 October 1699, and Thomas, baptized on 14 January 1703, in the same church. An older brother, William, born in London, was buried in Derbyshire in September 1689. After returning to London, Richardson the elder lived in the area of Tower Hill, in Mouse Alley, a poor and dangerous neighbourhood. In 1703 he moved his family to a house nearby, on Rosemary Lane, which he continued to rent until 1727, the last record of his whereabouts.

Richardson's father had intended him for the church; but

> some heavy Losses having disabled him from supporting me as genteelly as he wished in an Education proper for the Function, he left me to choose at the Age of Fifteen or Sixteen, a Business; having been able to give me only common School-Learning. (Slattery, 24)

The question of Richardson's formal education may never be fully answered. We know nothing about the extent of his schooling during his ten years or so in Derbyshire. If the Samuel Richardson listed at the Merchant Taylors' School in 1701–2 is the novelist, he must have had at least enough tutelage to gain admission there. But he himself freely admitted that he knew only his native language.

By his own account, Richardson was a precocious letter writer. Even before he was eleven, he allegedly assumed the guise of an adult knowledgeable in the appropriate biblical texts and sent a letter to reprimand a widow nearly fifty years old, who under the pretence of religious zeal 'was continually fomenting Quarrels and Disturbances, by Backbiting and Scandal, among all her Acquaintance' (Slattery, 26). Without the interest in sports usual to boys his age, he gained the sobriquet of Serious and Gravity and preferred instead to become 'an early Favourite with all the young Women of Taste and Reading in the Neighbourhood' (Slattery, 26). While a small group of them were doing their needlework and with their mothers in attendance, he was often called upon to read to them and to make observations on the texts. When scarcely over thirteen he won the confidence of three of these young women to the extent of sharing their 'Love-Secrets, in order to induce me to give them Copies to write after, or correct, for Answers to their Lovers['] Letters' (Slattery, 27).

Apprenticeship and freedom, 1706–1721   To gratify his appetite for reading, he observed, Richardson chose to become a printer; and on 1 July 1706 he was apprenticed to John Wilde, a parsimonious master who begrudged giving his employees any rest at all but relented after their protests. Fearful of encumbering his master, who dubbed him 'The Pillar of his House', and even scrupulous to the extent of paying for his own candles, Richardson devoted his precious free time at night to reading literature and also to 'a Correspondence with a Gentleman greatly Superior in Degree, and /of ample/ Fortunes, who had he lived, intended high things for me' (Slattery, 25). The identity of this 'Master of the Epistolary Style' remains unknown. Since Wilde's business specialized in almanacs and jest books and such popular fiction as *The most Pleasant History of Tom A Lincoln*, it seems unlikely that Richardson's time spent working in the shop enhanced his interest in literature.

On 2 July 1713 Richardson completed his apprenticeship; and on 13 June 1715 he became freeman of the Stationers' Company and citizen of London. Thereafter he continued in Wilde's business as compositor and corrector until his master's death in January 1720. When Richardson married Wilde's daughter, Martha, in the Charterhouse chapel on 23 November 1721 the record mentions his belonging to St Bride's parish, the first trace of his residence in the Fleet Street neighbourhood where he spent the rest of his life. All the children from this marriage, five sons and one daughter, died in infancy, and Martha preceded her last born son in death on 23 January 1731. In 1748 Richardson reflected: 'I cherish the memory of my lost wife to this hour' (*Correspondence*, 4.226). Shortly after the death of his last infant Richardson married another printer's daughter, Elizabeth Leake (d. 1773), on 3 February 1733. Four daughters from this marriage outlived their father: Mary (Polly), Martha (Patty), Anne (Nancy), and Sarah (Sally). Their first born, Elizabeth, died in 1733, and a son, Samuel, died in 1739. Other than occasional tensions, Richardson seems to have enjoyed this marriage to the end.

On 5 March 1722 Richardson was granted the livery of the Stationers' Company. Besides his ties with his brother-in-law, Allington Wilde, who was admitted to the livery at the same time, Richardson was already associated with another printing establishment—that of John Leake and family. After John's death in February 1720, his widow, Elizabeth, carried on the business until her death in April 1721 when her son James acquired her share. But since James had already established a business as bookseller in Bath and moved there, Richardson stepped in to help manage the London shop; and throughout his life he was always on more intimate terms with James Leake than with Allington Wilde.

Early printing business and politics Already by 1722 when he was admitted to the livery, Richardson's printing business was prospering. Yet without the benefit of records comparable to those available for William Bowyer's press, the information about his printing activities remains patchy and until recently largely based upon the pioneering work of William Sale. But after careful study of the printer's many tell-tale ornaments, Keith Maslen has found that it was apparently Richardson's contracts for printing private bills, orders, and occasional reports for the House of Commons that enabled him to escape the usual dependence on booksellers. Since the bulk of the private bills printed involved such things as estate deeds, wills, and marriage settlements, Richardson gained considerable legal knowledge while representing the affairs of the upper classes, which doubtless provided the groundwork for his later development as a novelist.

Of the first books Richardson printed, *Poems on Various Occasions* (1721) by the Irish clergyman Jonathan Smedley even includes the printer's name on the title-page. Another early book is the translation of Fénelon's *Éducation des filles* (1721). As various newspaper advertisements in his name indicate, Richardson, besides printing, also occasionally acted as bookseller, publishing by subscription *Memoirs of the Reigns of Francis II and Charles IX of France* (1724), translated from the French of Michel de Castelnau, as well as the editions of Roger Acherley's *Britannic Constitution* (1727) and Joseph Morgan's *The History of Algiers* (1728–9).

In view of his later government contracts for printing the *Journals* of the House of Commons, it is noteworthy to find Richardson in his first years as printer being responsible for a number of publications against the ministry of Robert Walpole. During 1721–3, for instance, he printed pamphlets concerning government financial policies before and after the South Sea Bubble by the opposition tory member of parliament Archibald Hutcheson. Much

more risky were his associations with principals identified with the Jacobite *cause célèbre* of 1722—Francis Atterbury, bishop of Rochester, his amanuensis, the Reverend George Kelly, and the duke of Wharton. On 24 May 1723, soon after Atterbury was forced into exile, Richardson printed an edition of his *Maxims, Reflections and Observations*; in addition, he printed Kelly's speech before the House of Lords defending himself from his accusers, and later, while Kelly was in the tower, his translation of Castelnau.

Perhaps yet more daring was Richardson's involvement in printing Wharton's opposition paper, the *True Briton*. This mercurial aristocrat had lost much of his fortune in the South Sea Bubble and had subsequently allied himself with the City, becoming a member of the Waxchandlers' Company and editing this semi-weekly journal wittily satirical of Walpole's government. The seventy-four issues were published from 3 June 1723 to 17 February 1724. Richardson also printed the collected editions of the *True Briton* (1723–1732) that appeared in two volumes. Although at first posing as an old whig in defending Atterbury and Kelly in the House of Lords, Wharton eventually joined them in supporting the Pretender in France.

Richardson's first anonymous publications Despite John Nichols's belief, on John Duncombe's testimony, that Richardson was the author of the sixth issue of the *True Briton* (21 June 1723), modern biographers have discounted the attribution on stylistic grounds. What seems to have been ignored, however, is that this particular issue is mainly in the form of a letter signed by A. B., a pseudonym that Richardson used elsewhere, and that other letters with this signature appear in subsequent issues (numbers 9, 22, 23, and 24), all evidently written by the same person, according to the editor.

Besides printing the *True Briton* in 1723–4, Richardson was also responsible for the *Daily Journal* from its inception in 1720 to its demise in 1737. Here, too, we find numerous letters signed A. B. that appear to be his contributions, in some instances primarily advertisements puffing books that he was printing at the time. Moreover, in the *Daily Gazetteer* (9 January 1740) a letter with this same signature offers a proposal to rid the streets of prostitutes and to find the means of preserving the lives of the offspring of these women, a social problem that concerned Richardson to the end of his life. Perhaps the most telling instance of this signature appears in *The Apprentice's Vade Mecum* (1734), where Richardson produces a sample of an indenture, giving the hypothetical apprentice the initials N. N. and the citizen-printer, A. B. (p. 2). In view of Richardson's penchant for assuming the woman's voice, five other issues of the *True Briton* (numbers 28, 34, 45, 47, and 71) may well be his work.

Well before the general public knew him to be an author, Richardson's fellow printers admired his talents as a writer during his years in the newspaper business. In the January 1736 issue of the *Gentleman's Magazine*, Edward Cave, the editor, remarked that Richardson has 'often agreeably entertain'd with Elegant Disquisitions in Prose'. Among these anonymous works were doubtless the pamphlets *The Apprentice's Vade Mecum* and the *Seasonable Examination*, both of which concerned the well-being of the City working men and the evil influence from the theatre and other cultural diversions enjoyed by the upper classes in the West End. Originally written in the form of a personal letter to his nephew Thomas Verren Richardson (*Imperial Review*, 2, 1804, 609–16), who was to have begun as his apprentice in the printing trade, the *Vade mecum*, though only a modest success in the author's own lifetime, eventually became a standard reprint by the Stationers' Company down to the twentieth century. What is of particular interest in interpreting the provenance of the religious motifs in his novels is the third part that Richardson added while producing this cautionary manual. The main heads of this section inveigh against the 'Depravity of the present Age', attacking the allegedly rampant deism, scepticism, and libertinism of his society that threatened ruin to the young man starting out on his career.

Printing and editing in the 1730s During the 1730s Richardson expanded his business by printing bills and reports for the government. Nichols attributed to Arthur Onslow, speaker of the house, the lucrative contract in 1742 to print the *Journals* of the House of Commons, probably a reward for Richardson's long and tactful dealings with members of parliament. In addition to printing the *Daily Journal* he undertook the *Daily Gazetteer*, a newspaper that first appeared on 28 June 1735 and was designed to combine into one organ the three main pro-government papers—the *Daily Courant*, the *London Journal*, and the *Free Briton*. Although the *Daily Gazetteer* was begun by James Pitt (Francis Osborne) and William Arnall (Francis Walsingham), it was Ralph Courteville (R. Freeman) who soon became, according to James Ralph, its 'sole Director'. Originally intended as a platform to answer the devastating attacks by opposition writers, especially those in *The Craftsman*, thanks to Richardson's influence the *Daily Gazetteer* became increasingly less partisan and eventually included literary criticism, poems, moral essays, ship news, and other non-political matter. Some time in 1746 Richardson gave up his partnership with this paper, which lasted another two years before becoming the *London Gazetteer*.

Besides newspapers, Richardson also printed two periodicals—William Webster's *Weekly Miscellany* and Aaron Hill's *The Prompter*. He printed Webster's periodical from its inception on 16 December 1732 until 1736, during which time he generously absorbed the editor's mounting debts in this venture. Since the recurrent theme of the *Weekly Miscellany* laments the decline of religion and morality in the present age, a familiar stance in Richardson's correspondence and especially emphasized in *Clarissa*, it is not unlikely that he also contributed to this journal. In the issue for 11 October 1740, years after Richardson was no longer its printer, the *Weekly Miscellany* produced a letter, possibly by Webster himself, praising the manuscript of *Pamela* and urging the author to publish it, a letter included along with Hill's as advertisement for this novel. Associated already with Hill as the printer of his *Plain Dealer*, shortly after the demise of the *True Briton*, Richardson, in collaboration with William Popple, took on his friend's new paper, the twice-weekly *Prompter*, which began on 12 November 1734 and ended on 2 July 1736.

In addition to these printing activities Richardson was engaged in a number of editing projects. Some time in 1737 he helped the French Huguenot physician James Mauclerc to produce *The Christian's Magazine*. As in Webster's periodical, Mauclerc's stress on the orthodox Christian contempt of the world and preparation for death suited Richardson's own predilections when writing *Clarissa*. In the same year Richardson revised the fourth edition of Daniel Defoe's *Complete English Tradesman*, which includes a puff of Hill's *Plain Dealer* and of the *Apprentice's Vade Mecum*. Similarly, in 1738 Richardson revised and printed the second edition of Defoe's *Tour thro' the Whole Island of Great Britain*. At the end of 1739 Richardson produced an expurgated and abbreviated version of *Aesop's Fables*, based on Sir Roger L'Estrange's popular edition, originally published in 1692, which had already gone through an eighth edition in 1738.

Richardson still occasionally assumed the role of bookseller (i.e. publisher) as well as printer. In 1736 he was busy planning the *Universal History*, a multi-volume project that occupied him for the next twenty years. In the same year he became connected with the Society for the Encouragement of Learning, which was formed to publish scholarly books that booksellers were not willing to risk on the market. For this society Richardson published, partly at his own expense, the first volume of *The Negotiations of Sir Thomas Roe* in March 1740. Although widely advertised and handsomely printed, the *Negotiations* was a commercial failure, perhaps largely because of its high price, £1 7*s*. Nevertheless, the *History of the Works of the Learned* (May 1740) praised highly the editor's skill in organizing the diverse material in this book. During the 1740s Richardson had a brief acquaintance with the Society of Booksellers, a group interested in publishing learned works with unusually good terms for the authors concerned. For this society, as part owner as well as printer, Richardson produced Robert James's *Medicinal Dictionary* (1743–5).

Pamela During the autumn of 1739, Richardson turned to preparing a letter manual that was commissioned by the booksellers John Osborne senior, and Charles Rivington. In his letter to Hill (1 February 1741), Richardson recounts how he had long been urged by these business associates to 'give them a little book (which, they said, they were often asked after) of familiar letters on the useful concerns in common life' (*Correspondence*, 1.lxxiii). *Letters Written to and for Particular Friends, on the most Important Occasions* was published on 23 January 1741. While planning this manual, however, some time in November 1739, Richardson abruptly began writing the first draft of *Pamela*, completing it within about two months. Letters 138 and 139 from the manual, which represent the cautionary advice of a servant-girl's father after her master's 'vile attempt', and her dutiful reply about returning home, clearly anticipate the Pamela story. Rather than simply dream up the circumstances to generate the appropriate letter, Richardson seems to have benefited greatly from his long years of printing newspapers by grounding his fiction in reported experiences of the everyday world. Thus letter 62, 'A young Woman in Town to her Sister in the Country, recounting her narrow Escape from a Snare laid for her on her first Arrival, by a wicked Procuress', obviously a germ for the plot of Clarissa's abduction, may be a commonplace tale of the day, but Richardson enhances its uniqueness by an emphatic note: 'N. B. This shocking Story is taken from the Mouth of the young Woman herself, who so narrowly escaped the Snare of the vile Procuress; and is Fact in every Circumstance' (*Letters*, 84).

When *Pamela* appeared on 6 November 1740, only Richardson's wife and a few friends knew that he was the author. But gradually during the following year the secret was out; and the numerous letters witnessing this literary phenomenon, mostly of praise, may have prompted Richardson at this time to begin faithfully keeping his correspondence on record. Knightley Chetwood declared unabashedly that 'if all the Books in England were to be burnt, this Book, next the Bible, ought to be preserved' (V&A, Forster MSS, 27 Jan 1741, FM XVI, 1, fol. 43). But less sanguine responses faulted the 'warm scenes' as unfit for proper ladies. Yet, despite his own dissatisfaction with its 'lowness' and his continual revising of this novel until his death, Richardson made few changes to the erotic encounters. Despite previous assumptions that it was this novel's sexual explicitness which earned its place in the Index Librorum Prohibitorum by the Roman Catholic church, it seems more likely that the strongly protestant views of the heroine's economic 'salvation' were what gave most offence to the church authorities.

Pamela was an instant commercial success, going through five editions during its first year. As an indication of its popularity, numerous imitations of *Pamela* appeared almost immediately. The first, *An Apology for the Life of Mrs. Shamela Andrews*, published in April 1740, was written by Henry Fielding. With a focus on Pamela's own duplicitous narrative, following closely Mr. B.'s complaint about this 'artful Gypsy' (Richardson, *Pamela*, 40), it is a brilliant parody of the content and style of Richardson's novel. Unlike her predecessor, however, Shamela openly reveals her designs on her master: 'I thought once of making a little Fortune by my Person. I now intend to make a great one by my Vartue' (H. Fielding, *Joseph Andrews and Shamela*, ed. D. Brookes-Davies and T. Keymer, 1999, 329–30).

In the same month appeared *Pamela Censured*, which by contrast is a serious attack on the morality of the tale, urging the author to delete the objectionable, sexually explicit encounters and puns. On 28 May 1741 the first volume of John Kelly's *Pamela's Conduct in High Life* was published, and the second volume appeared in the following September. In June two more books appeared—Eliza Haywood's *Anti-Pamela, or, Feign'd Innocence Detected* and James Parry's *True Anti-Pamela*. Published in November 1741, Charles Povey's *The Virgin in Eden* repeats some of the negative criticism of *Pamela Censured* and recounts a virgin's pilgrimage from Sodom to Canaan after the manner of John Bunyan. On 22 February 1742 Fielding's *Joseph Andrews* was published with yet more parodic allusions to *Pamela*, especially in the early parts where Joseph writes to his sister, Pamela, of his employer Lady Booby's attempts on his virtue.

Stage versions of *Pamela* were also produced—the anonymous *Pamela, or, Virtue Triumphant* and Henry Giffard's *Pamela: a Comedy*, both published in November 1741. Voltaire adapted the story in *Nanine, ou, Le préjugé vaincu* (1749), and a year later Carlo Goldoni produced *Pamela nubile*, which by having the heroine eventually discovered to be the daughter of a Count Auspingh made the story more palatable to aristocratic audiences. Consequently, a French translation of this play by François de Neufchâteau was condemned after the Revolution and was required to be converted to its original Richardsonian version about a virtuous peasant girl.

Richardson followed all these developments with a mixture of disdain and appreciation. He never forgave Fielding for writing *Shamela*, and he was especially worried about attempts to exploit the success of his novel with counterfeit sequels. Dropping his pose as merely the editor, in an advertisement to the fourth edition of *Pamela*, Richardson refers to himself as 'the Author' while protesting against the spurious continuations. Upon the advice of such friends as Ralph Courteville, by April Richardson decided to proceed with his own sequel. After being widely advertised, Richardson's addition of two more volumes appeared on 7 December 1741, with the first instance of including his name along with the booksellers Rivington and Osborne. Without the appealing rusticity or suspense of the original, *Pamela II* nevertheless sold well enough to warrant a second duodecimo edition the following year. The third and fourth volumes were also printed together with the first two in a deluxe octavo edition.

Besides its many editions, translations, and stage adaptations, the Pamela vogue involved popular media such as waxworks, Francis Hayman's murals at Vauxhall Gardens, and illustrated fans for women. By coincidence, although Richardson had commissioned William Hogarth to design two frontispieces to *Pamela* but abruptly discarded them, unknown to him at the time Joseph Highmore was independently preparing twelve ambitious oil paintings illustrating scenes from the novel. After finally meeting Highmore, Richardson became good friends with the painter and his wife and daughter, both named Susanna, for the remainder of his life. Before that event, however, Richardson had paid Highmore's friend the French expatriate engraver Hubert Gravelot and his partner, Francis Hayman, to produce twenty-nine plates for the sixth edition of *Pamela*, published on 10 May 1742. Since Richardson had personally consulted these artists about the designs, it is these plates rather than Highmore's paintings, notwithstanding their high quality, which represent the author's graphic intentions. Later, again on his own initiative, Highmore illustrated the Harlowe family of Richardson's second novel and painted a full-length portrait of Clarissa that has since been lost. He also painted

Clementina della Porretta for Richardson's last novel, *Sir Charles Grandison*. In 1747 Highmore made pendant portraits of the novelist and his second wife, which had been acquired by the Stationers' Company in 1811. The portrait of Elizabeth, however, was destroyed in the Second World War by an enemy bomb.

Despite the pleasant distraction caused by the public success of *Pamela* and of his next very long novels, throughout the last decades of his life Richardson was hardly negligent toward his printing business. Against the tendency of literary scholars to downplay this aspect of his career, Maslen has shown, for instance, that as early as 1741, Richardson was printing the *Philosophical Transactions of the Royal Society* and continued to print them until his death in 1761. As Richardson remarked to Stinstra in 1753, 'My Business, Sir, has ever been my chief Concern. My Writing-time has been at such times of Leisure as have not interfered with that' (Slattery, 26). Richardson was apparently so efficient in running his large printing business, which included about 1500 private bills for both the Commons and the Lords, as well as the *Journals of the House of Commons*, volumes 1–28, that he was able to find the time to write some of the longest works of fiction in English and even correspond with his many readers in the process!

Clarissa To judge by letters exchanged with Edward Young and Hill, already by summer 1744 Richardson had conceived the overall plot of his second novel, and defended the character of Lovelace and the heroine's death. Not surprisingly, the 'prolixity' of this novel worried Richardson from the first, and he asked Hill for help in making abridgements, sending him portions of the manuscript at intervals. The surviving correspondence gives detailed accounts of the progress in the various stages of the revisions Richardson quietly made while pondering his readers' responses. But Hill's well-intentioned effort to rewrite the opening of *Clarissa* for the sake of reducing its length received a chilly reply and may have caused a nine-month lapse in their correspondence.

When the first two volumes appeared in November 1747 the novel was already complete in the author's mind. But Richardson was determined to test the water before submitting further volumes, and it was not until 28 April 1748 that the third and fourth volumes of *Clarissa* were published, which ended with the melodramatic plotting of the heroine's escape to Hampstead and in danger of being found out by her would-be seducer. By summer 1748 Richardson had revised the last three volumes of *Clarissa* enough to his satisfaction to advertise them in September, and on 6 December 1748 they were finally published.

Some two months before these final volumes appeared, Richardson gained a close friend and correspondent— Lady Bradshaigh. At about the age of forty and well connected during the time of their first encounter, Dorothy, *née* Bellingham, had married Roger Bradshaigh of Haigh, close to Wigan, in Lancashire, who had succeeded his father to the baronetcy in 1747. After disguising her identity in her first letters, she finally met Richardson on 6 March 1750. A few months earlier Richardson had described his appearance to enable her to recognize him:

> Short; rather plump than emaciated, notwithstanding his complaints: about five foot five inches: fair wig; lightish cloth coat, all black besides ... looking directly foreright, as passers-by would imagine, but observing all that stirs on either hand of him without moving his short neck; hardly ever turning back: of a light-brown complexion; teeth not yet failing him; smoothish faced, and ruddy cheeked: at sometimes looking to be about sixty-five, at other times much younger. (*Correspondence*, 4.290–91)

Like other readers Lady Bradshaigh protested against the imminent death of Clarissa and tried to persuade Richardson to reform Lovelace in the end. In addition to their lively correspondence, of considerable interest are their manuscript annotations to her copy of the first edition of *Clarissa* (Princeton University) and to her copy of the first edition of *Grandison*, of which only volume 7 survives (Hunt. L.).

Lady Bradshaigh's sister, Lady Echlin (*née* Elizabeth Bellingham), also proved to be an important friend and correspondent from 1753 until Richardson's death, though apparently they never met. Married to Sir Robert Echlin, with a seat near Dublin, Lady Echlin volunteered to help Richardson during the piracy of *Grandison*. In contrast to her rather lively sister in England, Lady Echlin was by her own account anything but a lady of fashion, preferring solitude and religious meditation to playing cards. Besides her letters objecting to the violence in *Clarissa*, she wrote an alternative version of the novel, shunning the rape of the heroine, who still dies but from the ill treatment by her family, and emphasizing Lovelace's conversion. Obviously impressed by her moral seriousness, Richardson responded in detail to her rewriting of the Clarissa story. After her husband's death, Lady Echlin eventually decided to move to England but declined Richardson's invitation to stay at Parson's Green until she could settle in a house of her own. To judge by his playful letters, Richardson seems to have enjoyed the rivalry between Lady Bradshaigh and Lady Echlin in gaining his attentions.

As in the composition of his first novel, Richardson kept revising *Clarissa*. Even the various introductory materials went through drastic changes, and his omission of William Warburton's preface to the third and fourth volumes of the first edition resulted in a breach of their friendship for years afterwards. To the London printer, anxious to be recognized as an original genius, Warburton's main error was probably in daring to hint that earlier French novelists may have been an influence.

Among the many responses to *Clarissa*, including letters written before and after the publication of the first volumes, Albrecht von Haller's review in a French periodical in Amsterdam and reprinted in the *Gentleman's Magazine* (19, June and August 1749, 245–6, 345–8) made trenchant comments on its strengths and weaknesses, the latter mainly about the coarseness of Lovelace and his associates at the brothel, Sinclair's death scene, Clarissa's delirium, and the nearly heroic death of the villain. At the end of the instalment in the August issue, Richardson appended detailed replies to the article.

As if confident that his audience would not only tolerate but also welcome a yet longer version after his initial worries over its length, for the third and fourth editions of *Clarissa* in 1751, Richardson restored much material previously withheld and also created further additions. To compensate the purchasers of his first and second editions, Richardson published separately (20 April 1751) *Letters and Passages Restored from the Original Manuscripts of the History of Clarissa*, comprising more than 300 pages, as a supplement to the earlier volumes.

As critics beginning with the author himself have stressed, the narrative gains the reader's credibility by its relentless particularity of description and sense of immediacy in the dramatic 'writing to the moment' strategy that emphasizes present over past time of reporting. In his preface to the novel, Richardson adapts a fertile quotation from Belford on the advantages of the temporal illusion of this narrative technique:

> *Much more* lively and affecting … must be the Style of those who write in the height of a *present* distress; the mind tortured by the pangs of uncertainty (the Events then hidden in the womb of Fate); *than* the dry, narrative, unanimated Style of a person relating difficulties and dangers surmounted, can be; the relator perfectly at ease; and if himself unmoved by his own Story, not likely greatly to affect the Reader!   (Richardson, *Clarissa*, 1.viii)

Apart from the technical skill of incorporating the chronicle of events within scenic moments, Richardson's narrative also invokes powerfully the major theme of *contemptus mundi* in orthodox Christian theology that opposes the temporal world to eternity and emphasizes the salvation of the individual by imitating Christ's journey to the cross. Numerous religious tracts could be adduced as sources for this theme, including Thomas à Kempis's *Imitation of Christ*, William Law's *A Serious Call*, and other titles advertised in the newspapers and periodicals printed by Richardson. In his postscript to the third edition of *Clarissa*, Richardson explicitly declared his intention of presenting a Christian tragedy, in which death comes as a deliverance, as a cheerful prospect for the future life. In both the first and third editions, Richardson inserted five meditations supposedly written by the heroine, culled from Job, Psalms, Ecclesiasticus, and the Wisdom of Solomon. Towards the end of 1749 he printed but never published *Meditations Collected from the Sacred Books*, which includes thirty-six meditations altogether, including the five printed within the novel.

If the first commentaries written on Richardson's masterpiece were not so numerous as those concerning *Pamela*, they were for the most part favourable, and this novel greatly enlarged his circle of friends and likewise his correspondence. He was especially proud to have received 'Letters from some of our gravest Divines and finest Writers', which brought him into personal acquaintance with five bishops (Slattery, 6). Edward Young judged *Clarissa* to be 'The Whole Duty of WOMAN' (Slattery, 41). Thomas Edwards praised *Clarissa* as a touchstone for determining one's sensibility:

> It is well for us, that you are of a Humane and gentle disposition, for you are so absolute a Master of the Heart,

that instead of swelling it with a noble grief, you could in numberless instances have torn it with intolerable anguish. (V&A, Forster FM XII, fol. 5 MSS, 26 Jan 1749)

In early January 1749, only a month after the final three volumes of *Clarissa* appeared, Sarah Fielding published anonymously her *Remarks on Clarissa* and gave a copy to Richardson. Evidently pleased with its defence of the novel against the various objections raised by its detractors, Richardson later sent a copy to Stinstra and declared that he had not seen this pamphlet before its publication.

One of the most hostile contemporary responses to Richardson—the anonymous pamphlet *Critical remarks on 'Sir Charles Grandison', 'Clarissa', and 'Pamela', enquiring whether they have a tendency to corrupt or improve the public taste and morals*, written by a 'Lover of Virtue' and published in 1754—condemned his novels for contributing to the decline of the English language and its literature. Despite this withering assault, in his *Dictionary* Samuel Johnson refers repeatedly to Richardson's writings to illustrate usage; and while introducing his friend's essay on women's decorum, *Rambler*, 97 (19 February 1751), he paid eloquent tribute to the author 'who has enlarged the knowledge of human nature, and taught the passions to move at the command of virtue' (S. Johnson, *Essays from the Rambler*, ed. W. J. Bate, vol. 4 of Yale Edition of Johnson, 1969, 153).

Sir Charles Grandison   Some time in 1749, largely in deference to Lady Bradshaigh, Richardson hesitantly undertook writing the story of a Good Man; and throughout most of 1750 he was soliciting advice from his circle of friends for the work in progress. Between November 1751 and January of the next year Catherine Talbot had read through ten manuscript volumes of the novel. By the end of the summer of 1752 Richardson was apparently writing the sixth volume but still without knowing how to end his story. Later, when it had reached almost the length of *Clarissa*, he deleted two whole volumes and continued to make further cuts in the remaining manuscript volumes.

But in early August, after having printed five entire volumes, and parts of the last two, Richardson was shocked to find that four Dublin booksellers had obtained these sheets from his shop. His first reaction was to stop the printing and thus inadvertently give the Irish pirates opportunity to gain an advantage over George Faulkner, the Dublin bookseller whom he had commissioned to publish *Grandison* in that country.

Faulkner's frank advice to Richardson to demand payment from the other booksellers touched a raw nerve and prompted the author to distribute *gratis* a complaint to the public—*The Case of Samuel Richardson, of London, Printer; with Regard to the Invasion of his Property* (14 September 1753), naming the four Irish pirates and detailing their treachery of corrupting his own journeymen. In the following October both the *Gentleman's Magazine* and *Gray's Inn Journal* denounced the theft. The Irish public, nevertheless, took a very different view of the matter and rejected the author's right of controlling the distribution of his work in their territory. After his Irish friend Philip Skelton made matters worse by insinuating that anyone purchasing the pirated edition would be as guilty as someone stealing a Bible, Richardson was even more disturbed and printed yet another document, a complaint against Faulkner (1 February 1754)—*An Address to the Public*—which was included at the end of *Grandison*. Despite the delay Richardson resumed printing the rest of the novel. The first four volumes were published on 13 November 1753, the next two on 11 December 1753, and the final volume on 14 March 1754.

Although most modern critics agree that this last novel does not equal the pastoral naïvety of the first or the other-worldly depth of the second, perhaps because of its focus on the more commonplace situations of daily life *Grandison* may have had the greatest impact on later novelists. Its documentary realism, for instance, is possibly more compelling than anything Richardson had tried before. Although Richardson was one of the least travelled authors, who seldom ventured very far from London, his rendering of Italy for the Clementina della Porretta episodes has impressed readers by its vivid fidelity. During her visit to Bologna Hester Piozzi was astonished to see how the city corresponded with Richardson's imaginary depiction of it. Leslie Stephen's observations on Richardson's possessing the 'extraordinary minuteness' of the Dutch painters attest to an inimitable trait of his narrative genius ('Richardson's Novels', *Cornhill Magazine*, 17, 1868, 55–6). When 2500 copies of the third edition in duodecimo appeared in March 1754 Richardson reported to Lady Bradshaigh that this novel had had much more success with the public than *Clarissa*. It met with enthusiastic responses from such diverse readers as William Cowper, who wrote an ode on its behalf, Edward Gibbon, and Lord Chesterfield.

Richardson's last literary activities After many years of enjoying his weekends at North End, where he composed his three novels, Richardson moved to a new country house at Parson's Green in October 1754. Here he entertained such friends as Speaker Onslow, the bishop of Oxford, the Talbots, and Susanna Highmore. Thomas Edwards and Margaret Dutton died there under his care. During the same year Richardson also moved into new quarters in Salisbury Court to accommodate his printing business in safer, if smaller, buildings. At this time he became first warden and then master of the Stationers' Company.

By 1754, at age sixty-five and in failing health, Richardson found holding a pen increasingly difficult. When Lady Bradshaigh urged him to try a chamber horse for exercise, he recalled the torturous regimen his old Scots friend Dr George Cheyne had recommended more than twenty years previously with little success. Concerned about Richardson's excessive flesh, Cheyne had urged him to abstain from meat and alcoholic drink, to practise thumb-vomits and purges regularly, and to exercise frequently by bouncing on a contraption with a suspended chair. From the 1750s until his death Richardson was a patient and

friend of the distinguished physician Dr William Heberden.

Reflecting on his literary achievement, Richardson was obviously proud of the sheer magnitude of his *œuvre*. He exclaimed to Sarah Wescomb: '19 Volumes in Twelves, close Printed—In Three Stories—Monstrous!—Who that sees them ranged on one Shelf, will forgive me?' (V&A, Forster MSS, 22 March 1754, FM XIV, 3, fol. 120). Partly to help his readers overcome the difficulties of mastering his voluminous study of 'Human Nature', since the summer of 1753 he had been hard at work—reluctantly, given his self-pitying complaints—on a compilation of the moral sentiments from the three novels. He had already provided a moral index for the third and fourth editions of *Clarissa*. After completing this tedious business by the following summer he was thanking Benjamin Kennicott, a fellow at Exeter College, Oxford, for his 'kind and friendly Preface' (26 Nov 1754, University of Pennsylvania) to the volume, which was finally published in March 1755 as *A collection of the moral and instructive sentiments, maxims, cautions, and reflexions, contained in the histories of Pamela, Clarissa, and Sir Charles Grandison*. Despite Dr Johnson's view that we should read Richardson 'for the sentiment, and consider the story as only giving occasion to the sentiment' (Boswell, *Life*, 2.175), the apparently unenthusiastic reception of this volume suggests that most readers did not follow his advice.

In 1755, at the urging of Catherine Talbot, who worried that his health would worsen if he ever gave up the pen for good, Richardson contemplated writing a life of Mrs Beaumont, a pseudonym for a friend from his early years, a widow who suffered hardship with exemplary fortitude. Later that year, after he abandoned this idea, Lady Bradshaigh coaxed him to write an autobiography. But Richardson was candid about his declining powers. On 21 October 1755, he confessed to her: 'I have, or seem to have, an unconquerable Aversion to the Pen! My Imagination on which you kindly compliment me, seems entirely quenched' (V&A, Forster MSS, FM XI, fol. 161). Over the following two years, however, he sometimes hoped that his muse would return for yet another novel even while his physical condition deteriorated.

In his last years Richardson's literary renown brought other writers to solicit his advice on their various projects. In January 1757, a Cleomira, who later identified herself as Anna Meades, daughter of William Meades, the vicar of Rampton, Cambridgeshire, wrote to Richardson for help in revising her novel in progress, called 'A Description of Modern Life' in manuscript. After apparently being edited by Thomas Hull, it was finally published in 1771 as *The History of Sir William Harrington*. At the time of her first letter to Richardson, Meades's *The history of Cleanthes, an Englishman of the highest quality, and Celemene, the illustrious Amazonian princess* had just been published anonymously. This romance is as remote from Richardson's concept of the realistic novel as possible. By contrast, however, in her next effort she was closely imitating Richardson's last two novels.

Besides Sarah Fielding, already mentioned, Catherine

Talbot, Elizabeth Carter, and Charlotte Lennox were frequent correspondents. After her resentment upon discovering her poem 'Ode to Wisdom' printed without her permission in the second volume of *Clarissa*, Carter later became reconciled to Richardson and earned £1000 from her edition of Epictetus, which he printed by subscription in 1758. At her own request, Lennox met Richardson through Johnson and paid tribute to both men in *The Female Quixote*, which was printed at Salisbury Court and published by Andrew Millar, Richardson's friend, in 1752. In striking contrast to Talbot, the granddaughter of the bishop of Salisbury and resident in the family of Thomas Secker, bishop of Oxford, Laetitia Pilkington, an Irish woman financially desperate after being divorced for infidelity, testified to Richardson's kindness and generosity in her *Memoirs*. Although the major bluestocking, Elizabeth Montague, gave only limited approval to Richardson's novels, Mrs Delany (*née* Mary Granville) was one of his most enthusiastic supporters.

In 1754 Richardson had offered substantial suggestions to Edward Young during the composition of the latter's satiric *The Centaur not Fabulous*. In early 1757 Richardson collaborated more extensively when Young was composing *Conjectures on Original Composition*, an attack on the Augustan ideal of imitation in favour of creative originality. Over the two years before its final publication, Young corresponded frequently with Richardson about the work and in parts quoted the latter's emendations verbatim.

Perhaps never having fully recovered from the traumatic experience with the Irish pirates, Richardson lived his last years clouded by depression and moments of paranoia. Unpaid debts by business clients and breaches of contract plagued him to the end. Even in the most profitable business of printing the *Journals* of the House of Commons Richardson encountered problems in being properly remunerated. By January 1759 his nervous tremors and insomnia were incapacitating him, and he had to enlist his nephew William to write letters for him. Yet in 1760 he was energetic enough to undertake a co-partnership in the law patent with his good friend Catherine Lintot, which gave them control over the printing of books on common law. On 28 June 1761, while having tea with Joseph Highmore, he suffered a stroke; and on 4 July that year he died at his house in Salisbury Court, Fleet Street, and was buried beside his first wife and dead children at the nearby St Bride's. With an estate worth about £14,000 Richardson enabled his widow and daughters to live comfortably for the rest of their lives.

Reputation and influence During his years of inventing 'a new species of writing', Richardson was continually irked by the popularity of his great rival, Henry Fielding, and even scolded Hill's daughters for their temerity in expressing a good opinion of *Tom Jones*. After his death critics carried on the tradition of comparing the two authors. In 1762 the *New and General Biographical Dictionary* attacked specifically 'all those effeminate and fantastic ideas of *sentiment*, *delicacy*, and *refinement*' that Richardson's novels represented and ends with a preference for Fielding's more compromising view of moral behaviour. To James

Boswell's bewilderment, Johnson extolled Richardson's psychological depiction of character over Fielding's flat comic types:

> In comparing these two writers, he used this expression; 'that there was as great a difference between them as between a man who knew how a watch was made, and a man who could tell the hour by looking on the dial-plate.' (Boswell, *Life*, 2.49)

From the beginning of his career as novelist, Richardson enjoyed a favourable audience in Europe. A German translation of *Clarissa* appeared almost immediately after the English original and inspired Friedrich Gottlieb Klopstock to write an ode, *Die todte Clarissa*. His wife, Meta, recounted to Richardson how his novels exerted a charm on their courtship and marriage. In 1754 Gotthold Ephraim Lessing ranked *Grandison* with *Clarissa*, and Christian Fürtegott Gellert wrote glowing verse for the second edition of the German translation of *Grandison*. As his contemporaries recognized, Gellert's novel *Leben der schwedischen Gräften von G.* (1747–8) has obvious parallels to Richardson's fiction.

The first French translation of *Clarissa*, by the Abbé Prévost, which appeared in 1751, made drastic cuts in the last two volumes of the original English text. Even though at this time Prévost was well known for his *Manon Lescaut*, *Cleveland*, *Le doyen de Killerine*, among other works, his service to a fellow novelist across the channel was hardly received as an honour. Besides being deeply disturbed that he had never been consulted beforehand, Richardson found Prévost's explanation for abridging and expurgating the original to suit French taste reprehensible. He told Stinstra:

> He has given his Reasons for his Omissions, as he went along; one of which is, The Genius of his Countrymen; a strange one to me! He treats the Story as a true one, and says, the English Editor has in many Places, sacrificed it to Moral Instruction, &c. (Slattery, 22)

On similar grounds Richardson objected to Prévost's translation of *Sir Charles Grandison*, published in 1755–6.

Despite the shortcomings of the abridged and expurgated French translations, Richardson still held sway along with Rousseau in France during the last decades of the century. It was in that country where he received after his death the most sustained and profound eulogy by Denis Diderot, printed in the *Journal Étranger* (January 1762):

> He carries his torch to the bottom of the cavern; and teaches you to discern the subtle and dishonourable incentives, concealing themselves from view behind honourable motives, that are eager to shew themselves foremost. He breathes on the sublime phantom, that presents itself at the mouth of the cavern: it vanishes, and the hideous Gorgon it masked appears to view. (S. Richardson, *Pamela*, ed. E. Mangin, 1811, 1.v.)

Diderot's *La religieuse* testifies to Richardson's influence in representing the sexual aspect of tyrannical institutions. No matter how far removed from the London printer's transparent didacticism, such French writers as Restif de la Bretonne, Choderlos de Laclos, and the marquis de Sade were surely in Richardson's debt. Even well into the next century, a very different kind of French novelist, Honoré de Balzac, exalted *Clarissa* as one of the greatest novels ever written.

Notwithstanding the enormous development of the English novel during the nineteenth century, when eighteenth-century literary culture had become largely a matter of nostalgia over the *ancien régime*, Richardson's novels were still continually reprinted. In her brother Henry's 'Biographical notice', appended to the posthumous edition of *Northanger Abbey* and *Persuasion* (1818), Jane Austen, we are told, knew Richardson by heart. Anna Laetitia Barbauld pronounced him to be 'the father of the modern novel of the serious or pathetic kind' (*Correspondence*, 1.xi). This judgement seems to have held throughout the twentieth century, when numerous editions and scholarly commentaries of his works have been published increasingly over the decades. Near the end of the century, both a fine opera and a film based on Richardson's masterpiece have appeared. On 18 May 1990 the première of Robin Holloway's *Clarissa* was performed by the English National Opera at the London Coliseum, with Vivien Tierney as Clarissa and Graeme Matheson-Bruce as Lovelace. In the following year Robert Bierman produced a film scripted by Janet Barron and David Nokes for British television that featured Sean Bean as Lovelace and Saskia Wickham as Clarissa. It was shown on American as well as on British television. JOHN A. DUSSINGER

Sources Nichols, *Lit. anecdotes* · *The correspondence of Samuel Richardson*, ed. A. L. Barbauld, 6 vols. (1804) · T. C. D. Eaves and B. D. Kimpel, *Samuel Richardson: a biography* (1971) · A. D. McKillop, *Samuel Richardson: printer and novelist* (1936) · W. M. Sale, *Samuel Richardson: a bibliographical record of his literary career with historical notes* (1936) · W. M. Sale, *Samuel Richardson: master printer* (1950) · W. C. Slattery, *The Richardson–Stinstra correspondence and Stinstra's prefaces to Clarissa* (1969) · J. Harris, introduction, in *Samuel Richardson's published commentary on Clarissa, 1747–65*, ed. T. Keymer, 1 (1998) · P. Sabor, introduction, in *Samuel Richardson's published commentary on Clarissa, 1747–65*, ed. T. Keymer, 2 (1998) · O. M. Brack, 'bibliographic essay', in *Samuel Richardson's published commentary on Clarissa, 1747–65*, ed. T. Keymer, 2 (1998) · [S. Richardson], *Samuel Richardson's published commentary on Clarissa, 1747–65*, 3 (1998) [incl. introduction by J. A. Dussinger and afterword by A. J. Van Sant] · S. Richardson, *One hundred and seventy-three letters written for particular friends, on the most important occasions, by the late Mr Richardson, author of Clarissa and Sir Ch. Grandison, directing not only the requisite stile and forms to be observed in writing familiar letters; but how to think and act justly and prudently, in the common concerns of human life*, 7th edn [n.d.] · *The true Briton: written by Philip, late duke of Wharton*, 2 vols. (1723–4) · *Daily Journal* (1720–1737?) · *Daily Gazetteer* (1735–48) [research pubns microfilm] · *Weekly Miscellany* (16 Dec 1732–27 June 1741) [research pubns microfilm] · S. Richardson, *The apprentice's vade mecum, or, Young man's pocket-companion* (1734) · S. Richardson, *A seasonable examination of the pleas and pretensions of the proprietors of, and subscribers to, play-houses* (1735) · S. Richardson, *Pamela, or, Virtue rewarded*, ed. T. C. Duncan Eaves and B. D. Kimpel (1971) · S. Richardson, *Clarissa, or, The history of a young lady*, 3rd edn (1751); facsimile (1990) [introduction F. Stuber] · S. Richardson, *The history of Sir Charles Grandison*, ed. J. Harris, 3 vols. (1972) · K. Maslen, 'Samuel Richardson as printer: expanding the canon', *Order and connexion: studies in bibliography and book history*, ed. R. C. Alston (1997), 1–16 · private information (2004) [T. Keymer, P. Sabor]

Archives Harvard U., Houghton L., letters · PRO, account books, C105/5 · Rice University, Houston, Texas, letters and literary drafts · V&A NAL, corresp. | BL, letters to Thomas Birch, Add. MS 4317 · BL, corresp. with Anne Meades, Add. MS 28097 [copies] · Bodl. Oxf., corresp. with Thomas Edwards · Stationers' Company, Stationers' Hall, London, Stationers' Company archives

Likenesses attrib. F. Hayman, group portrait, oils, *c.*1741; on loan to Holburne Museum of Art, Bath · J. Highmore, oils, 1747, Stationers's and Newspaper Makers' Company, London; version, NPG · J. Highmore, oils, 1750, NPG · M. Chamberlin, oils, in or before 1754, NPG [*see illus.*] · Stadler, coloured aquatint, pubd 1804 (after S. Highmore), NPG · S. Highmore, group portrait, drawing, Morgan L. · Stadler, engraving (after S. Highmore), repro. in Barbauld, ed., *Correspondence*, vol. 2 · C. Watson, engraving (after J. Highmore), repro. in Barbauld, ed., *Correspondence*, vol. 1

Wealth at death £14,000: Duncan Eaves and Kimpel, *Samuel Richardson*, 502

Richardson, Samuel (*d.* 1805), stenographer and Particular Baptist minister, was educated at the King's School in Chester, Cheshire, from 1736 to 1739. Lacking, however, the 'advantages of a liberal education', Richardson, as an older man, compensated by an 'intense application to study and reflection' (*GM*, 1.487), He had an academy in Foregate Street, Chester, and was pastor of a small congregation of Particular Baptists, a sect doctrinally Calvinistic. Late in life Richardson published two works. In the first, *An essay on the suretiship of Christ, in two parts: part I, the doctrine stated, part II, objections answered* (1796), he referred in his preface to the Scottish Baptist minister Archibald McLean, whom it is likely Richardson heard, and perhaps met, during one or more of McLean's visits to Chester.

About this time Richardson developed an original and innovative system of shorthand based on the 'stave or bar principle' (Paterson, 13), which employed three horizontal lines intersected by two perpendicular ones and required, like musical notation, the use of a specially ruled paper. This unusual system, published, according to Richardson, at the request of Edward Mainwaring, appeared in 1800 as *A new system of short-hand, by which more may be written in one hour, than in an hour and a half by any other system hitherto published* (five editions by 1811). It was 'improved' by stenographic disciples such as E. Hinton (1826), who adapted the system to James Henry Lewis's alphabet, and William Henshaw (1831), and was adapted to Welsh orthography and translated by Thomas Roberts in *Stenographia, neu, Law fer, yn ol trefn Mr. Samuel Richardson* (1839).

Richardson compared his system favourably with that of William Mavor, but, however ingenious, it never competed successfully with the popular and more legible systems of Mavor, Thomas Gurney, John Byrom, and Samuel Taylor. Richardson has sometimes been confused with another shorthand writer of the same name, who transcribed the trial of the abductors of Maria Glenn in 1818, and his shorthand system is not the 'Richardson's system' that was based on William Purton's system.

Richardson is said to have occasionally made unsigned contributions to various magazines and periodicals. He died at Chester on 21 March 1805 at his house in Pepper Street. PAGE LIFE

Sources *GM*, 1st ser., 75 (1805), 487 · J. E. Bailey, 'Samuel Richardson's shorthand, 1800–1810', *Shorthand: a Scientific Magazine*, 2

(1882), 12–17 • A. Paterson, 'Shorthand a hundred years ago', *Phonetic Journal*, 59 (1900), 13–14 • *DNB* • J. Westby-Gibson, *The bibliography of shorthand* (1887) • M. Levy, *The history of short-hand writing* (1862)

Archives NYPL, shorthand collection

Richardson, Sir Thomas (*bap.* 1569, *d.* 1635), judge, was baptized on 3 July 1569 at Hardwick, Norfolk, the son of William Richardson (*d. c.*1616), probably the curate there, and his first wife, Agnes (*d.* 1582). His father was one of the minority of the county's clergy who were both nongraduate and unlicensed to preach. Notwithstanding, in 1575 he was appointed by Sir Thomas Gresham to nearby Mulbarton, where he served as rector until his death; Agnes was buried there in April 1582.

Early career Perhaps helped by the Greshams, Thomas Richardson matriculated pensioner from Christ's College, Cambridge, in June 1584, then moved to Thavies Inn in preparation for admission to Lincoln's Inn on 5 March 1587. He was called to the bar in 1595. On 20 July that year he married Ursula (*d.* 1624), third daughter of John Southwell of Barham Hall, Suffolk, and thus became brother-in-law of another rising East Anglian lawyer, Thomas Bedingfield (1555–1636). In 1605 Richardson was appointed under-steward of Norwich Cathedral and counsel to its dean and chapter. He became a bencher of his inn in 1610 and was created serjeant-at-law in October 1614. By 1616 he was recorder of Bury St Edmunds, Suffolk, but he was never recorder of Norwich or Yarmouth as is sometimes stated, both being posts long held by Rice Gwynn.

Speaker of the House of Commons, 1621 By late November 1620 Richardson had risen sufficiently in his profession for the lord chancellor, Francis Bacon, Lord Verulam, to put his name to George Villiers, marquess of Buckingham, for James I's approval as the preferred of two candidates for speaker of the House of Commons in the forthcoming parliament, having secured the return of both men for his home borough of St Albans. Jocularly he recommended that the king should be asked for a prompt response as time pressed, and otherwise Bacon would not be able to dine with the new speaker 'for his drink will not be laid in tyme enough' (*Letters and Life of Francis Bacon*, 7.150). It is not clear when Richardson first knew his fate. For him time was of the essence for, alone of the ten speakers appointed between 1589 and 1628, he had never sat in parliament in the past. He sought familiarity with its ways by acquiring a large manuscript volume of Commons procedure and privileges, a copy of which is now in the British Library. His prolonged protestations of unfitness when he was dragged, sobbing, towards the chair early in February 1621 may well have been heartfelt, even though they were widely thought to be overdone. Arthur Goodwin, the lifelong friend of John Hampden, was sufficiently provoked to take him at his word and, interrupting his tearful protestations of unworthiness, bid him to be gone so that the house might proceed to the election of a more suitable speaker.

The agenda of the parliament of 1621 was bound to test a new speaker's bearing in the Commons chamber. Before it was a series of interrelated questions concerning funding the exchequer, reviving trade, and reducing patents and monopolies. There was also the issue of responding adequately to the loss of the palatinate and exile of its royal family, a problem which, given its religious and strategic dimensions, was always likely to complicate foreign policy, in particular proposals for a match between Charles and the Spanish infanta. For all its bulk Richardson's book of procedure and privileges was never likely to be sufficient. His behaviour as speaker soon began to attract criticism, and the Commons was quick to put him in his place. On the opening day of business, 5 February, after he had impetuously interrupted the secretary of state, Sir George Calvert, Sir Thomas Roe told him sharply that he had no right to speak unless called upon to do so, and later that day the house amended its procedure so that the speaker lost virtually all discretionary power over the order in which bills came forward for discussion. During its second session, on 3 December, James delivered from Newmarket 'so sharp a reprehension' at the way the Commons had encroached on his control of foreign policy that, in Calvert's words: 'it putt us instantly into disorder' (BL, Egerton MS 2595, fol. 8*v*). Shortly afterwards, within a week of prorogation, the Commons further disconcerted Richardson by approving a motion from William Mallory silencing the speaker for the whole day 'so that we might not be troubled' in the course of business (Zaller, 168). That James had knighted him on 26 March, just before the Easter recess, reflected relief at the temporary easing of tensions after the fall of the projector Sir Giles Mompesson and impending proceedings against Bacon rather more than any mark of confidence in the speaker, and he had done little to deserve it. But as John Chamberlain reflected, his 'divers bruske incounters and reprehensions' arguably proceeded 'rather [out] of ignorance than craft or cunning' (*Letters of John Chamberlain*, 2.358).

Chief justice Neither the fall of Bacon nor his own lack of political nous checked Richardson's professional and social advance. James appointed him a king's serjeant on 20 February 1625 and he became chief justice of common pleas on 22 November 1626 at a reported price of £17,000 for a post which had been vacant for almost a year. As his fellow judge and future executor, Sir Richard Hutton, noted afterwards, he still felt able to declare in his speech of acceptance that he had, on bended knee, begged the king not to promote him. If Richardson was indulging here in a clumsy attempt to suggest that he shared the doubts of others about his fitness for high office, his chances of convincing his hearers were severely reduced by rumours already in circulation about the size of the sum he had paid to attain it. In any case the context was suspicious. His wife Ursula having died on 11 June 1624, Richardson married, on 14 December 1626 at St Giles-in-the-Fields, Middlesex, the duke of Buckingham's cousin. His bride was Elizabeth (1576/7–1651) [*see* Richardson, Elizabeth], widow of Sir John Ashburnham and daughter of Sir Thomas Beaumont of Stoughton, Leicestershire. On 29 February 1628 she was created baroness of Cramond for life, with the remainder of the title to Richardson's heir at the time of her death.

Richardson joined a judiciary shaken by Charles I's recent dismissal from king's bench of its chief justice, Sir Randolph Crewe, for failing to endorse his case for the forced loan. Following the death of Crewe's pallid replacement, Sir Nicholas Hyde, in October 1631, Richardson became chief justice of king's bench, before his worst excesses had become apparent. John Nicholas, a seasoned observer on the western assize circuit, which Richardson was now riding, had however noted at Salisbury on 19 July that the judge was 'not a sownd man. Much alteracion ys observed in him, being nothing joviall as he was wont, but very melencolly and sad. He talked of going the whole circuyte, but yt ys thought he wyll not be able' (PRO, SP 16/196/93). He had come alone to Salisbury, but his judicial partner, Sir John Denham, soon caught up, and he managed to get round. On this evidence his problems, whether passing or longer term, were as likely to be mental as physical ones.

In his early years as chief justice Richardson demonstrated at times a fine appreciation of the bounds of the common law. He secured unanimity among the bench for ruling against the use of torture to extract information from John Felton, Buckingham's assassin, in answer to a question dutifully put by the king late in 1628. He also ruled against any attempt to interpret rash words spoken by Hugh Pyne against the monarchy as treasonable. But he could be perverse. The same year his insistence on exacting standards of proof at Middlesex sessions saved a group of suspected priests from conviction, and inflamed passions in the court room and later in parliament. Yet on other occasions he failed to make a stand. In 1634 he joined his fellow chief justice, Sir Robert Heath, in struggling to establish the intent of an opaque provision in the 1566 statute on sheriffs (8 Elizabeth c. 16), as Heath recounted in court during the star chamber prosecution of George Mynne, widely regarded as a particularly grasping clerk of hanaper in chancery and charged with extorting excessive fees. In his judgment Heath accordingly held that the relevant words were so confusing that Mynne should be excused his breach of their terms; but Richardson, following him and hearing adverse reactions in court to Heath's ruling, weakly contended otherwise and so undermined the colleague whose reservations he had appeared to share.

Controversy in London and in the provinces Richardson's fellow judges had always been inclined to take him lightly. When in November 1628 William Prynne had at a very late stage obtained a prohibition against further proceedings against him in high commission for publishing an anti-Arminian book, it had been granted by the three junior judges in common pleas, although Richardson 'had opposed it all he could' (Williams, 1.431–2). In the Easter law vacation in 1632 Richardson at his house in Chancery Lane surreptitiously bailed Sir Edward Heron, then in the Fleet for ignoring a recent exchequer judgment that he should pay his debt of 2000 marks (£1333 6s. 8d.) to John Bancroft, bishop-elect of Oxford. Helped no doubt by a timely intervention by the earl of Carlisle, Richardson managed to survive unscathed an early enquiry by the privy council at which Bishop William Laud and the earls of Arundel and Manchester were present. However, a further petition by Bancroft to the king in 1633 prompted Charles to refer the matter to the whole judicial bench. His fellow judges unanimously found against Richardson, concluding after a detailed comparison of his actions with those of Sir Edward Coke in a notorious case of bail taking some years earlier, that his 'abuse of his office … [was] farre greater' than ever Coke's had been (PRO, SP 16/340/13). They also pointed out that James I had fined Coke £2400, and although they did not recommend a sum for Richardson, William Whiteway of Dorchester later recorded in his diary that he had been ordered to pay £1500. A passage in Richardson's will referring to a sum of £1000 still owed by Heron may suggest that some agreed compensation for the fine was overdue.

Whiteway was doing no more than taking note of revealing news from Westminster concerning one of his county's current assize judges; but there is evidence that Richardson for his part was prepared to involve himself in country affairs once he had become a judge, riding one circuit or another without break for the last seven years of his life. When the recorder of Salisbury, the deeply Calvinist Henry Sherfield, was tried in star chamber in 1633 for breaking a stained glass window in his parish church, Richardson used his local knowledge to lend weight to his commendation of the character of his fellow bencher of Lincoln's Inn. 'To my knowledge' he told the court, Sherfield 'hath done good in that city since I went that circuit; so that there is neither beggar nor drunkard to be seen there'. In particular, he added

> for ecclesiastical government he is outwardly conformable: I have been long acquainted with him, he sitteth by me sometimes at church … [and] bringeth a bible … with him (I have often seen it) with the apocrypha and common-prayer book in it, not of the new cut. (*State trials*, 3, col. 545)

Other kinds of local involvement could prove more hazardous, however. On the western circuit it had become customary for its judges from time to time to provide instructions confirming strict limitations on wakes, revels, and church ales in the interests of good order and Sabbath observance, and in March 1632 Richardson's colleague, Denham, renewed one such order in Somerset, stipulating as usual that the minister in each parish should publicize the order on specified occasions, and that the high constables should report to the judges at Lent assizes annually that it had been done. Somehow Laud was alerted to what he now chose to interpret as a clash of jurisdictional authority, wrapped up in a regrettable expression of sabbatarian values. The agent was very probably Sir Robert Phelips, a Somerset JP whose papers still contain much information on these proceedings. Phelips badly needed to rehabilitate himself with potential allies at court and in the 1629 session of parliament had already been strongly critical of Richardson's refusal to admit the circumstantial evidence which had alone been brought against the Catholic suspects in Clerkenwell. It is not clear how far Richardson appreciated that Laud was always likely to cover his tracks, as no longer bishop of Bath and Wells and barely archbishop of Canterbury, while raising a jurisdictional issue in his old diocese between church government and common lawyers, and that he would seek to work through the king. It was in any case rash of him twice to ignore instructions from another royal servant, the lord keeper, Thomas Coventry, to countermand Denham's order, which would have allowed time for taking stock in changing times; and when at the Somerset summer assizes in 1633 he was finally obliged to do so, after direct intervention by King Charles, he chose to exacerbate matters by making his reluctance plain in court, while managing also to insult the Phelips family. Worse, he exploited local differences by inviting sympathetic JPs to his chamber afterwards to sign a petition of protest to the king, one apparently already prepared by Richardson's staff; twenty-five of them did so. The petition put reasonably enough the case for such restraint in the interests of local order, disregard for which had lately contributed to disturbances in the north of the county, and it supplied ample precedent dating back to the 1590s; but although Sir Ralph Hopton presented it to the king at Woodstock it was later bluntly endorsed 'stopt by the archbishop' (PRO, SP 16/255/40). Its fate made it plain that there were to be limits to how far common lawyers could intrude on the business of the church and give its ministers instructions to be read out periodically at their services. Shortly afterwards, on 18 October 1633, James's Book of Sports was reissued, restating the opportunities for approved leisure activities after divine worship on the sabbath. The point was driven home to Richardson during a dressing down by Archbishop Laud at a council hearing attended by the king. Through his ineptitude he had provided an opportunity for renewed restrictions on Calvinist preferences, and found himself demoted to the home circuit, the meanest of them all and an indignity last suffered by a chief justice (Sir Henry Hobart) eighteen years before.

Demotion and survival The punishment was a hard one for Richardson, who was capable of combining acute sensitivity to personal abuse with intermittent awareness of the dignity of his office. Yet he consistently lacked a sense of what was appropriate. Upset as he was by the prospect of the home circuit, he all too often failed to behave like a senior judge. Just months earlier, in June 1633, after a disagreement in his chamber at Chancery Lane with a former minor servant of the queen, he took himself off to Greenwich, where the privy council was gathering, in search of redress. The same year, during the course of a local dispute in king's bench with William Fanshawe, auditor of the duchy of Lancaster for northern parts, who lived near him in Chancery Lane, he assured the secretary of state, Coke, that he would deal with him as a neighbour and gentleman and 'be a means to work his reformation' (*Cowper MSS*, 2.46). But their differences soon multiplied to include a spell in King's Bench prison for Fanshawe, two petitions from him to the king, and a retaliatory suit by

Richardson in common pleas. Early in 1635 the chief justice, Sir John Finch, brokered an unconventional settlement in which Fanshawe withdrew all his objections except one which referred to Richardson as a blabber-lipped blockhead, an epithet soon in wider circulation. The king was reportedly furious over the whole business, but one of Richardson's long-suffering Norfolk neighbours then in town, Thomas Knyvett, wrote home in high good humour.

Yet, for all his excesses, and despite widespread rumours, Richardson was not dismissed from office. His wife's efforts may have saved him, and he was thought to be ageing fast; but the king and his advisers may well have calculated that a more suitable and exemplary punishment than dismissal or suspension would be to oblige Richardson, for the time he had left to him, to endure the increasing public disgrace into which he was bringing his office. Richardson acknowledged as much, but struggled on. In June 1634, before facing the home circuit for that summer's assizes, he got Lord Cottington to move the king, unsuccessfully, for his return to the western circuit, and afterwards continued to entertain hopes that he might be placed on another respectable circuit for the sake of the dignity of his office, if not the worthiness of his person. As late as December an unsolicited letter from Thomas Wentworth, Viscount Wentworth, at Dublin stirred his thoughts of further help, although without much justification. He remained active, sitting in the court of star chamber until at least 21 November 1634 and was still busy with Fanshawe in common pleas early in the following January.

Legacy and reputation By 16 January Richardson's thoughts had turned to making his will, 'drawn daily to the consideration of th[e] incertenty of this transitory life', and he died at his house in Chancery Lane on 4 February, removing all prospect of riding the home circuit for a third time (PRO, PROB 11/167, fol. 275v). He was survived by his son and heir, Thomas, and by four daughters: Ursula, wife of Sir William Yelverton; Mary, who married John Webb; Elizabeth, wife of Robert Wood, one of the executors of his will; and Susan. His childless second wife, whose barony of Cramond went on her death to his grandson, was left an annuity of £700, much of it from properties recently purchased in Norfolk; Richardson emphasized his hopes that she would remain true to his intentions. The will was carefully drawn, and left precise suggestions for his burial, depending on where he died: Norwich Cathedral if in Norfolk, the upper church at Bury St Edmunds if in Suffolk, and Westminster Abbey, if nearby. The abbey was made available, but the London newsletters were quick to point out that the occasion was no match for the splendour of its surroundings. His family saw that a monument, complete with a bronze portrait bust by Hubert Le Sueur, for which he had allowed £100 in his will, was erected in the south aisle of the abbey choir and soberly listed his offices and responsibilities. But if it aimed at modest respectability it did not at once succeed; and other judgements prevailed. 'Never sat there a judge in that court [of King's Bench] that was less respected', wrote George Garrard to Wentworth afterwards, 'and scarce a judge or any of his own profession to attend him to his grave. Yet he have left behind him an estate better than three thousand pounds a year' (*Strafford's Letters and Despatches*, 1.373). Knyvett could scarcely contain himself now that his 'great adversary' was 'deade as a dore naile. And buried, I knowe not howe, in a farr better place then he deserved ... I thinke no man (since Noahs flowdd) ever went out of the world with more joye to all mens hearts' (Schofield, 87–8).   BRIAN QUINTRELL

Sources CSP dom., 1619–35, esp. SP 14/119/67, SP 16/196/93, 255/40, 257/127, 340/13 · newsletters from London to John, Viscount Scudamore, 1630s, PRO, C 115/box 106 · will, PRO, PROB 11/167, fols. 275v–278r · Richardson's volume on House of Commons procedure and privileges, BL, Add. MS 36856 · George Calvert to earl of Carlisle, 27 Dec 1621, BL, Egerton MS 2595, fol. 8v · APC, 1613–31 · The manuscripts of the Earl Cowper, 3 vols., HMC, 23 (1888–9), vol. 2 · The manuscripts of the duke of Beaufort ... the earl of Donoughmore, HMC, 27 (1891) · GEC, Peerage [see under Cramond] · F. Blomefield and C. Parkin, An essay towards a topographical history of the county of Norfolk, [2nd edn], 11 vols. (1805–10) · The letters and life of Francis Bacon, ed. J. Spedding, 7 vols. (1861–74) · R. Zaller, The parliament of 1621: a study in constitutional conflict (1971) · W. Notestein, F. H. Relf, and H. Simpson, eds., Commons debates, 1621, 7 vols. (1935) · The Registrum vagum of Anthony Harison, ed. T. F. Barton, 2 vols., Norfolk RS, 32–3 (1963–4) · B. Schofield, ed., The Knyvett letters (1620–1644), Norfolk RS (1949) · T. G. Barnes, 'County politics and a puritan cause célèbre: Somerset churchales, 1633', TRHS, 5th ser., 9 (1959), 103–22 · G. Radcliffe, The earl of Strafforde's letters and dispatches, with an essay towards his life, ed. W. Knowler, 2 vols. (1739) · The works of the most reverend father in God, William Laud, ed. J. Bliss and W. Scott, 7 vols. (1847–60) · State trials, vol. 3 · W. R. Prest, The rise of the barristers: a social history of the English bar, 1590–1640 (1986) · W. J. Jones, Politics and the bench (1971) · T. G. Barnes, ed., Somerset assize orders, 1629–40, Somerset RS (1959) · J. S. Cockburn, ed., Western circuit assize orders, 1629–1648: a calendar, CS, 4th ser., 17 (1976) · J. S. Cockburn, A history of English assizes, 1558–1714 (1972) · E. Foss, Biographia juridica: a biographical dictionary of the judges of England ... 1066–1870 (1870) · The letters of John Chamberlain, ed. N. E. McClure, 2 vols. (1939) · [T. Birch and R. F. Williams], eds., The court and times of Charles the First, 2 vols. (1848) · William Whiteway of Dorchester: his diary, 1618 to 1635, Dorset RS, 12 (1991) · T. K. Rabb, Jacobean gentleman: Sir Edwin Sandys, 1561–1629 (1998) · DNB · Venn, Alum. Cant.

Archives University of Chicago, Joseph Regenstein Library, case papers | PRO, SP 14, C 115 · Som. ARS, Phelips MSS

Likenesses drawing, c.1621, NPG; repro. in A. I. Dasent, Speakers of the House of Commons (1911), facing p. 173 · H. le Sueur, bust on monument, Westminster Abbey · oils, Lincoln's Inn, London

Wealth at death £3000 p.a.; excl. estates devolved on heir in 1626: Knowler, ed., Strafford's letters, 1.373

Richardson, Thomas (1771–1853), financier and benefactor of Quaker institutions, son of Robert Richardson, formerly of Hull, and his wife, Caroline Garth, née Richardson, was born at Darlington on 15 September 1771. He was second cousin of George *Richardson and was related by marriage on his mother's side to Edward *Pease, Quaker woollen manufacturer and railway promoter. After a limited education at home, Thomas was apprenticed to a grocer in Sunderland. It is unknown how long he remained there, but at some point in the 1790s—probably in the earlier part of the decade—Edward Pease gave him money for a passage to London and an introduction to Messrs Smith, Wright, and Gray, Quaker financiers of Lombard Street, who engaged him as messenger, and then

as a clerk at a salary of £40 a year. He rose to be confidential manager. He married Martha, daughter of John Beeby of Allonby, Cumberland, in 1799; there were no children.

In 1802 Richardson alerted his employers to the fact that London merchants with bills for discount were habitually paying brokerage fees to bill brokers who secured accommodation for them. In recommending this practice to Smith, Wright, and Gray, Richardson claimed that country bankers dealing with the firm would be likely to take more bills, having been relieved of the payment for commission. Confronted by Smith, Wright, and Gray's rejection of his proposition, Richardson engaged in discussions with Gurneys of Norwich, the established Quaker bankers, with a view to sending them bills for discount, but without a commission charge. Gurneys' response was positive and from this reaction there developed the largest discount business in the country in the period to 1850. Smith, Wright, and Gray's objections to Richardson's approach to Gurneys (which threatened to undercut their business) were assuaged by an arrangement whereby bills submitted by Richardson had first to be approved by his former employers. In 1805, by which time his business with Gurneys was well established, Richardson joined with another former employee of Smith, Wright, and Gray—John Overend—to form Richardson, Overend & Co., bill brokers trading from a small upstairs room in Finch Lane, Cornhill, in the City of London. In 1807 the link with Gurneys' bank was strengthened when the new partnership was joined first by Samuel Gurney and then by his brother, John, who acted as the principal link with Norwich. By August 1808 the expanded partnership was responsible for supplying 42 per cent of Gurneys' London-acquired portfolio, including that of its branches. One year later, Richardson, Overend & Co. was transacting the whole of Gurneys' business, a fact which accounts in large measure for the firm's rapid rise to prominence in the London discount market. In 1810 Richardson twice gave evidence before the select committee of the House of Commons on the high price of bullion. He proved to be a highly effective advocate of the role of financial intermediaries, well represented in the case of Richardson, Overend & Co. According to his testimony, London bill brokers had proved instrumental in reducing the losses sustained on bills by country bankers, and in the case of his own firm, losses had been limited to 'a very small amount indeed'. Richardson also described how his firm took in bills from Lancashire before sending them on to discount in Norfolk, Suffolk, Sussex, and Essex. This was followed by the revelation that the annual turnover of his business was in the region of £7–8 million, with about £1.5 million out on loan at any one time.

As a wealthy member of the Quaker 'cousinhood', Richardson was one of a number of Friends with financial and banking interests to be recruited by Edward Pease as investors in the Stockton and Darlington Railway project, inaugurated in Darlington in 1818. As a founding shareholder, Richardson subscribed the sum of £10,000 to the railway before the official opening in September 1825. He then offered the equivalent sum as additional liquidity during the early phase of operations when traffic revenues were, as yet, uncertain. Richardson also provided significant capital funding in 1823 for the inauguration of Robert Stephenson & Co., locomotive builders of Newcastle upon Tyne, and in 1828 for the purchase of the Middlesbrough estate. The latter was a decisive development in the history of the Stockton and Darlington Railway in so far as it opened up the prospect of a profitable coastal trade in coal, in competition with long-established interests on the Tyne and Wear. Never an active participant in the managerial direction of the Stockton and Darlington company, Richardson sold the bulk of his shares to members of the Pease family in 1844, thereby confirming the Peases' status as the dominant managerial force.

Richardson retired from the bill-broking business in 1830, in the heyday of his firm's prosperity, and following his death in 1853 the name of the original partnership was changed to Overend, Gurney & Co., with its premises located at 65 Lombard Street in the City of London. In July 1865 the firm became a public limited liability company and it was in this form that it failed spectacularly in May 1866. The longer-term causes of the collapse can be traced to the firm's increasing commitment to speculative activities, compounded by a rise in the proportion of illiquid or 'lock-up' business. In the short term, the firm was adversely affected by the failure of associated concerns, one of whom—Watson, Overend & Co.—possessed a similar name. In these circumstances, the value of the firm's shares began to fall at the same time as there was a 'run' by anxious depositors in pursuit of liquidity. Failure, when it came, precipitated a rise in bank rate to the penal level of 10 per cent, as well as suspension of the Bank Act. In a long-term perspective the collapse of Overend, Gurney & Co. signalled the rise of the modern discount market. Domestic bills, which had brought the market into being, had virtually disappeared by 1914. Rediscounting by country banks declined dramatically after 1870 in response both to the rise of joint-stock banking and the spread of deposit banking at the local level. The latter development was of particular significance in so far as it facilitated the transfer of money balances around the country, thereby displacing the 'equalizing function' fulfilled by the discount market in the form of the domestic bill.

Richardson built for himself a handsome house at Stamford Hill, Great Ayton, Yorkshire, where he interested himself in establishing an agricultural school for the north of England, to be managed by Friends. To this he contributed about £11,000. He owned a second house at Allonby, Cumberland, and he was a generous benefactor to the neighbouring Friends' school at Wigton. Richardson died at Redcar, Yorkshire, on 25 April 1853, leaving by his will money for educational purposes in the Society of Friends.   M. W. KIRBY

Sources P. H. Emden, *Quakers in commerce: a record of business achievement* (1939) · A. O. Boyce, *Records of a Quaker family: the Richardsons of Cleveland* (1889) · M. W. Kirby, *The origins of railway enterprise: the Stockton and Darlington Railway, 1821–1863* (1993) · M. W. Kirby, *Men of business and politics: the rise and fall of the Quaker Pease dynasty of north-east England, 1700–1943* (1984) · *DNB* · J. G. Baker, *Friends' Quarterly Examiner* (Oct 1891) · W. T. C. King, *History of the London discount market* (1936) · G. A. Fletcher, *The discount houses in London* (1976) · W. M. Scammell, *The London discount market* (1968) · *The diaries of Edward Pease: the father of English railways*, ed. A. E. Pease (1907) · *Pease of Darlington* (privately printed, 1902) · d. cert. · M. Phillips, *Banks, bankers and banking in Northumberland, Durham and north Yorkshire* (1894), 347–9

Likenesses R. Dighton, caricature, coloured etching, NPG; repro. in Emden, *Quakers in commerce*

Richardson, Thomas (1816–1867), industrial chemist, was born on 8 October 1816 in Pilgrim Street, Newcastle upon Tyne, the first child of William Richardson (1793–1845), painter, decorator, and glass manufacturer, and Isabella (1792–1834), daughter of Henry French, glass manufacturer. His father was one of the few Conservative members of the reformed Newcastle town council from 1836. He was educated at Percy Street Academy, where John Collingwood Bruce, newly returned from Glasgow University, introduced a course of theoretical and practical chemistry in 1832. Richardson proceeded to Glasgow University to study chemistry under Thomas Thomson, winning several prizes. He went on to Liebig's laboratory in Giessen, researching the composition of coal and the use of lead chromate in organic analysis, and was awarded a PhD. He then completed his studies in Paris under Pelouze, with whom he published, in 1838, research on the action of water on cyanogen. He returned to Newcastle that year and served as a secretary of the chemistry section of the British Association meeting there, to which he contributed a paper on the composition of sphene.

Richardson then devoted his time to industrial chemistry, taking out a number of patents. In 1840, in partnership with George Currie, chemist and druggist, he established the Blaydon lead works, white lead manufacturers, removing impurities from 'hard' lead to convert it to 'soft' lead by means of oxidization, although John Percy claimed that the process had been patented by Walter Hall in 1814. Practical improvements by George Burnett resulted in the annual importation to the north-east of several thousand tons of Spanish lead. In 1844 Richardson introduced to Tyneside the manufacture of superphosphates, with works at Monkton near Hebburn. In 1848 he patented a method for condensing 'lead-fume' by means of steam. His lead refining business was still operating in 1851 and he continued the manufacture of fertilizers until his death.

On 20 May 1841 Richardson married Mary (*bap.* 1816, *d.* 1900), eldest daughter of Alderman William Brownsword Proctor, flax merchant and sail cloth manufacturer and sheriff of Newcastle in 1838, and his wife, Ann Currie, sister of Richardson's business partner. They had several children, of whom at least two daughters survived their father. With an inheritance of £4000 from his paternal grandfather, a successful painter and glazier, Richardson set up in business as an analytical chemist in September 1843 with a laboratory at his house in Portland Place, where he also offered private practical instruction. Thereafter he appears in Newcastle directories as an assayer and professional chemist, although his unfamiliar PhD was sometimes confused with an MD, leading to several listings as a physician or surgeon. His activities broadened to include consultancy, publication, and teaching. With Edmund Ronalds he translated a work by Knapp under the title *Technological Chemistry*, which was published between 1848 and 1851. A second edition, rewritten by Richardson in collaboration with Ronalds and then Henry Watts, published in 1856, became a standard work.

In 1848 Richardson was appointed lecturer in chemistry at the Newcastle School of Medicine and Surgery. On the temporary disruption of the school in 1851 he joined the majority of the lecturers in the Newcastle College of Medicine, which affiliated to the University of Durham in 1852. Richardson moved his laboratory into the college. In June 1856 he was awarded an honorary Durham MA and succeeded J. F. W. Johnston as lecturer in chemistry there, although his services were never much in demand at that essentially theological institution. In 1855, he and T. J. Taylor started compiling a history of industry on Tyneside. J. C. Stevenson, R. C. Clapham, and Thomas Sopwith later collaborated and they presented papers on the subject to the British Association meeting in Newcastle in 1863. These were incorporated in *The Industrial Resources of ... the Tyne, Wear and Tees*, edited by himself, W. G. Armstrong, Isaac Lowthian Bell, and John Taylor; two editions appeared in 1864.

With Armstrong and James Longridge he published in 1857-8 (reprinted 1859) three important reports on the use of Northumberland coal in steam boilers, containing a record of an extensive series of experiments. Their conclusions were opposed to those of Sir Henry De la Beche and Lyon Playfair, on whose recommendation Welsh steam coal had been exclusively adopted by the navy. In 1865 Richardson began similar investigations on Lancashire steam coal at Kirklees, near Wigan, published posthumously in 1867. He became an associate of the Institution of Civil Engineers on 3 May 1864, was elected FRS on 7 June 1866, and fellow of the Royal Society of Edinburgh in the same year. He was also a member of the Royal Irish Academy.

Richardson died of apoplexy at the Royal Hotel, Standishgate, Wigan, on 10 July 1867, and was buried in Newcastle general cemetery, Jesmond Road. He was said to be a man of singularly agreeable manner and generous and genial disposition with a large circle of friends. His library ranged from the scientific, including many works in French and German, to the theological. His principal contribution to Tyneside's industrial development was undoubtedly his painstaking and pioneering work as a professional chemical analyst. He published fifteen independent papers and six in collaboration with E. J. J. Browell (partner in his practice and fellow lecturer at the College of Medicine), John Lee, J. Pelouze, T. Sopwith, and R. D. Thomson, on various chemical questions.

C. D. WATKINSON

Sources Newcastle Daily Chronicle (13 July 1867) · M. S. Byrne, 'Thomas Richardson: his contribution to chemical education', *Durham Research Review*, 7 (1974), 944-8 · J. B. Morrell, 'The chemist breeders: the research schools of Liebig and Thomas Thomson', *Ambix*, 19 (1972), 1-46 · J. C. Bruce, *Memorials of John Bruce: schoolmaster in Newcastle-upon-Tyne and of Mary Bruce his wife*, ed. J. B. Williamson (1903) · *Durham Advertiser* (1832-44) · *Newcastle Courant* (1832-44) · *Newcastle Journal* (1832-44) · E. Dodds, 'Pedigrees from stones in All Saints churchyard', Newcastle City Libraries, Local Studies Library · parish register transcripts (baptisms), All Saints Church, Newcastle, 1816, Newcastle City Libraries, Local Studies Library · Newcastle Literary and Philosophical Society minute book, 1831-47, Newcastle Literary and Philosophical Society · E. Dodds, 'Westgate Hill cemetery epitaphs', Newcastle City Libraries, Local Studies Library · E. Dodds, 'Monumental inscriptions, general cemetery, Jesmond Road', Newcastle City Libraries, Local Studies Library · C. A. Russell, N. G. Coley, and G. K. Roberts, *Chemists by profession: the origins and rise of the Royal Institute of Chemistry* (1977) · W. A. Campbell, *A century of chemistry on Tyneside, 1868-1968* [1968] · *Newcastle street directories* (1790-1869) · d. cert. · *DNB* · *CGPLA Eng. & Wales* (1900) [Mary Richardson]

Archives Bayerische Staatsbibliothek, Munich, Germany, Liebigiana MSS, II B

Wealth at death under £600: probate, 28 Sept 1867, *CGPLA Eng. & Wales*

Richardson, Thomas Miles (1784-1848), landscape painter, was born at Newcastle upon Tyne on 15 May 1784, the eldest son of George Richardson (1749-1806), a grammar schoolmaster in the town, and his second wife, Jane Miles (1750-1830). Richardson early displayed a talent for art, and was at first apprenticed to the Newcastle engraver Abraham Hunter, and afterwards to the cabinet-maker William Pether. His father died in 1806 and Richardson was appointed his successor at the grammar school. He followed the profession of schoolmaster for some seven years, also giving private drawing lessons, then decided to become a full-time professional artist. In 1814 he had the first of thirteen works accepted by the Royal Academy: *A View of the Old Fish Market, Newcastle*, and in 1816, with the publisher William Dixon made his first of several ventures into antiquarian illustration: *Views of the architectural antiquities of Northumberland & Durham, from original pictures ... by T. M. R.* (1819-20). He soon became frustrated by the lack of a suitable place in Newcastle in which local artists might show their work, and together with Henry Perlee Parker and others, in 1822 founded the Northumberland Institution for the Promotion of the Fine Arts. While continuing to exhibit at the Royal Academy and subsequently the British Institution, he became a prolific exhibitor at the Northumberland Institution's annual exhibitions. After five years, however, he became so disillusioned with the latter's success in promoting the sale of exhibitors' work that together with Parker he decided to establish the Northern Academy, in Newcastle, staging its first exhibition in 1828. Its early exhibitions were supported by some of the best known names in contemporary British art, but by 1831 the academy found itself in considerable financial difficulties and had to be wound up. In 1833 Richardson was successful in selling to the corporation of Newcastle what is generally regarded as his finest landscape: *View of Newcastle from Gateshead Fell* (Laing Art Gallery, Newcastle upon Tyne). A second success came with the purchase by the corporation in 1835 of his *View of the Side*, and with his work now widely recognized he was able to live his remaining years in Newcastle in moderate prosperity. Throughout this period he continued to exhibit at the Royal Academy, the Royal Scottish Academy, the British

Institution, and at various Newcastle exhibitions, showing landscapes and occasional historical pictures. His last known exhibits, however, were those shown in Newcastle in 1846 at an exhibition of works by various members of his family. These artistically gifted members included Richardson's sons with his first wife, Margaret Shepherd whom he married on 12 January 1806: George Richardson (1807–1840), Edward Richardson (1810–1874), and Thomas Miles Richardson jun. (1813–1890); and with his second wife, Deborah Burdon (*c*.1796–1873) whom he married on 2 March 1824: Henry Burdon Richardson (1826–1874), Charles Richardson (1829–1908), and John Isaac Richardson (1836–1913). Richardson senior was the leading artist of the north-east of England in the early nineteenth century, and is generally regarded as 'The father of the fine arts in Newcastle' (*Durham Chronicle*, 10 July 1835), by virtue of his involvement in its various exhibitions from 1822 to 1843.

Although Richardson's best-known works were in oil he was a prolific and accomplished painter in watercolour, whose influence over the use of the medium by other artists in the north-east of England was considerable. In 1831 he founded the Newcastle Water-Colour Society, and as a teacher of drawing and painting encouraged many of his pupils to become proficient in its use. His exhibited work in the medium outside the north-east was, however, limited to some eleven works at the Society of Painters in Water Colours, twenty-three at the New Society of Painters in Water Colours (of which he was elected a member in 1840), and nineteen works at the Suffolk Street Gallery of the Society of British Artists. This resulted in his watercolour work remaining little known outside the north-east in his lifetime. Also he travelled very little to find subjects for his work, visiting only London, Scotland, Wales, Westmorland, Cumberland, Yorkshire, Northumberland, and Durham in his long career. However his watercolours of Durham city and Newcastle are among some of the most beautiful of their subjects ever painted, and what he may have missed in critical acclaim elsewhere in the country was more than adequately made up for by that which he received at the long succession of exhibitions at which his watercolours appeared in Newcastle and Carlisle from 1822 until his death. His subjects in the medium ranged from topographical works and marine compositions, to important state occasions like his *Scene at Greenwich on the River Thames, on the morning of Saturday 12th August, on which his most gracious majesty George IV embarked for Scotland* (1826; Laing Art Gallery, Newcastle).

While his main work was landscape painting Richardson's interest in antiquarian illustration continued throughout his life, his early work with Dixon being followed by *The Castles of the English and Scottish Borders* (1833), and together with Thomas Miles Richardson jun. in 1839, *Sketches at Shotley Bridge Spa and on the Derwent*, among several works etched, engraved or lithographed mainly by others. He also continued giving drawing lessons until close to his death at Newcastle on 7 March 1848, after a protracted illness. He was buried in Newcastle general cemetery, Jesmond. Richardson's work is frequently confused with that of his son, Thomas Miles Richardson junior, because of its similarities in style and signature. Examples of his work are in the British Museum and the Victoria and Albert Museum, London; the National Gallery of Ireland, Dublin; Cartwright Hall, Bradford; Derby City Art Gallery, and the Grosvenor Museum, Chester. Others are in regional galleries in Newcastle, Manchester, Liverpool, Leeds, Sunderland, Gateshead, Reading, and Portsmouth. MARSHALL HALL

Sources E. Mackenzie, *A descriptive and historical account of the town and county of Newcastle upon Tyne*, 1 (1827) · R. Welford, *Men of mark 'twixt Tyne and Tweed*, 3 vols. (1895) · M. Hall, *The artists of Northumbria*, 2nd edn (1982) · P. Usherwood and K. Bowden, *Art for Newcastle: Thomas Miles Richardson and the Newcastle exhibitions 1822–1843* (1984) [exhibition catalogue, Laing Art Gallery, Newcastle upon Tyne, 11 Oct – 2 Dec 1984] · *DNB* · T. M. Richardson, *Memorials of old Newcastle-upon-Tyne*, new edn (1897) · *Illustrated catalogue of the permanent collection of water colour drawings*, Laing Art Gallery, ed. C. B. Stevenson (1939) · M. Hardie, *Water-colour painting in Britain*, ed. D. Snelgrove, J. Mayne, and B. Taylor, 2: *The Romantic period* (1967), p. 230, pl. 218 · *Art Union*, 9 (1847), 389 · *Art Union*, 10 (1848), 195 · *The Studio*, 67 (1916), 251, 253
Likenesses T. Carrick, pencil drawing, Laing Art Gallery, Newcastle upon Tyne

Richardson, Vaughan (*d.* **1729**), organist and composer, was a child of the Chapel Royal under John Blow from at least 1678, and sang at the coronation of James II at Westminster Abbey in 1685. After his voice broke he became deputy organist of Worcester Cathedral, between Christmas 1686 and May 1688. Later he moved to Winchester Cathedral as organist (7 December 1692), lay vicar, and master of the choristers in succession to Daniel Roseingrave. He remained in these posts for the rest of his life. On 5 October 1710 he married a 'Mrs Apleford, of College Street' (Shaw, 299) at Winchester Cathedral.

Richardson is known to have written twenty-one anthems—some surviving in holograph (BL, Add. MSS 42065, 63490)—and a service in C, composed in 1713 to celebrate the treaty of Utrecht. According to *The Post Boy* of 15 February 1698, 'an Entertainment of New Musick, composed on the Peace [of Ryswick] by Mr Va[ugha]n Richardson, Organist of Winchester Cathedral' (Tilmouth, 22), was to be performed at York Buildings on 16 February 1698, with the 'Czar of Muskovy', Peter the Great, present. Richardson published *A Collection of New Songs* in 1701, which in addition to a few miscellaneous items contains an ode to St Cecilia (*Ye Tuneful and Harmonious Choir*), for soloists, chorus, and instruments. Whether this was given later at the St Cecilia's day concert at Wolvesey Castle, Winchester, in 1704 is not known, though it seems likely. *The Diverting Post* of 25 November 1704 reported:

> Last Wednesday the 22nd Instant … at Winchester, was performed a Consort of Vocal and Instrumental Musick, composed by Mr Valentine [*sic*] Richardson, organist there. Mr John Shore, the Famous Trumpeter, and Mr Elford [well-known countertenor], were sent down by the Gentlemen of the County. The whole Performance was very satisfactory, and received with general Applause of the Audience. (Tilmouth, 57)

One of Richardson's best anthems is 'O Lord, God of my

salvation', which has also been attributed to Jeremiah Clarke, but for the most part his music is rather bland. He died in 1729, in Winchester; his burial took place there on 9 May. He was survived by his daughter Laetitia, a minor.

IAN SPINK

Sources H. W. Shaw, *The succession of organists of the Chapel Royal and the cathedrals of England and Wales from c.1538* (1991), 299 · High-fill, Burnim & Langhans, *BDA*, 12.372–3 · A. Ashbee and D. Lasocki, eds., *A biographical dictionary of English court musicians, 1485–1714*, 2 vols. (1998) · M. Tilmouth, 'A calendar of references to music in newspapers published in London and the provinces (1660–1719)', *Royal Musical Association Research Chronicle*, 1 (1961), 22, 57

Richardson, William (1698–1775), antiquary and college head, was born at Wilstead, Bedfordshire, on 23 July 1698, the son of Samuel Richardson, vicar of Wilstead and prebendary of Lincoln, and Elizabeth, daughter of Samuel Bentham, rector of Knebworth and Paul's Walden, Hertfordshire. He was at school at Oakham and Westminster, and was admitted a pensioner at Emmanuel College, Cambridge, on 19 March 1716; soon afterwards he was elected scholar. He graduated BA in 1719 and proceeded MA in 1723, and DD in 1735, becoming fellow of the Society of Antiquaries in the same year. Richardson was ordained deacon in 1720 and priest in 1726. He served as curate (1723–6) and lecturer (1726–1734?) at St Olave's, Southwark; and was later a royal chaplain (1746–68). Richardson married Anne, daughter of William Howe and widow of Captain David Durell, in 1728; she died on 21 March 1759. They had one son, **Robert Richardson** (*bap.* 1731, *d.* 1781).

Richardson's uncle **John Richardson** (1647–*c.*1725) attended Emmanuel from 1665 to 1669, and had been a fellow of Emmanuel (1674–85) and rector of the college living of North Luffenham, Rutland (1685–1690) when he was ejected as a nonjuror. He wrote a *Vindication of the Canon of the New Testament Against Toland* (1700) and *Praelectiones ecclesiasticae triginta novem* delivered in Emmanuel College chapel (edited by William Richardson in 1726).

William Richardson early developed antiquarian tastes—William Stukeley recorded that he had 'a very good collection of coyns, British, Roman, English' (*Family Memoirs*, 2.38)—and was a strong tory. He moved to Cambridge in 1734 to pursue his scholarly work in the Cambridge libraries and to be near the leading Cambridge antiquary, the nonjuror Thomas Baker. Richardson had been encouraged by Bishops Edmund Gibson and John Potter to prepare a new edition of Francis Godwin's *De praesulibus Angliae commentarius*—a catalogue of English bishops with brief biographies establishing the episcopal succession. He engaged in a quantity of antiquarian endeavours, mostly concerning Cambridge and Emmanuel College, and left large unpublished collections of notes in Emmanuel and in the university registry; and a volume of brief biographies of Cambridge worthies, concluding with an autobiography (now in the university library). But the *De praesulibus* remains his chief literary monument. It is an odd work of scholarship, for Godwin's rambling, credulous introduction is preserved intact, and most of his text

likewise; but the dates and details were carefully corrected by reference to a wide range of original sources. The result—if used with care—was a remarkably accurate list of bishops, at least from the twelfth century on, and was the standard authority until William Stubbs's *Registrum sacrum Anglicanum* (1858)—though even in this work some erroneous dates of bishops' deaths survived from Richardson and were copied into twentieth century works of reference.

Richardson's strong tory principles and attachment to the Anglican establishment evidently commended him to the fellows of Emmanuel, who elected him master on 10 August 1736. He was vice-chancellor of the university twice, in 1737 and 1769. He remained the tory leader of a tory college, and as such canvassed for the prince of Wales against the duke of Newcastle in the election to the chancellorship of the university in 1748—though in the event the prince withdrew. In 1760 Charles Yorke helped Richardson to the precentorship of Lincoln, and this led him to support Yorke's brother, Lord Hardwicke, for the high stewardship in 1764–5—a brief lapse into Newcastle's camp.

At Emmanuel, Richardson proved a great builder. First of all he sponsored a scheme for a new western range by Sir James Burrough, the tory master of Gonville and Caius College and eminent amateur architect. This foundered because Richardson tried to incorporate the fellows' parlour in the master's lodge and give them new quarters at the other end of the hall—a fact which may lie behind the account of William Bennet, a fellow under Richardson from 1763, later tutor and bishop of Cork and Ross, and Cloyne, in Ireland: 'He was a most strict and unpleasant master to his fellows, but had a great regard for the prosperity of the body, with a gentleman-like behaviour, and a liberal mind' (Emmanuel College Archives, Col 9.1B, Bennet's Book II, 46). Bennet tells us that £10,000 was spent on building in Richardson's time, which 'reflects the greatest honour on Dr Richardson's mastership'—though he left the college in debt. An anonymous contemporary quoted in Nichols's *Literary Anecdotes* reversed the list of qualities: 'Dr Richardson was a good-humoured man, warmly attached to tory principles, and no less strict in the minutiae of College discipline' (Nichols, 2.619 n.). To Richardson the works of Burrough's professional pupil, James Essex, are due: the classical ornament of the college hall and the western range completing a very notable stone-faced court.

In 1724 Richardson had been appointed prebendary of Welton Rivall in Lincoln Cathedral in succession to his father. Under Archbishop Potter's will (1745) Richardson was commended to some of the patronage which Potter left in the hands of his executors; and in 1760, after a suit in the court of chancery, he became precentor of Lincoln Cathedral. To Lincoln he welcomed James Essex in 1761, and some of the credit for Essex's notable work at Lincoln is probably his. It is striking that all the work of Richardson and Essex in Emmanuel was classical—while Essex rendered Lincoln Cathedral more Gothic than ever before.

William Richardson died in Emmanuel on 14 March 1775, after a long illness, and was buried in the college chapel beside his wife. Their son Robert, who was to be awarded a DD in 1766, was baptized in April 1731 and attended Westminster School before continuing his education at Emmanuel College, Cambridge (1745–50). He rose to be fellow of Emmanuel in 1755, prebendary of Lincoln (1760–73), and royal chaplain; he was rector of Wallington, Hertfordshire, from 1759 to 1781, and during this period was also rector of All Hallows-the-Great, Thames Street (1776–8), and St Anne's, Soho (1778–81). He died at Dean Street, Soho, on 27 September 1781.

C. N. L. BROOKE

Sources account of Richardson's career in his own hand, CUL, MS Ff.3.32, fol. 111r, p. 427 · *DNB* · S. Bendall, C. Brooke, and P. Collinson, *A history of Emmanuel College, Cambridge* (1999), chaps. 11–12 · E. S. Shuckburgh, *Emmanuel College* (1904), 132–8 · *Fasti Angl.* (Hardy), 2.87, 113, 235 · Venn, *Alum. Cant.* · D. A. Winstanley, *The University of Cambridge in the eighteenth century* (1922), 38, 41, 43, 47, 130 n. 4, 136 n. 3 · Nichols, *Lit. anecdotes*, 2.619n.; 5.157–9 · Richardson's lists of college alumni, university lists, etc., Emmanuel College Archives, Cambridge, COL.9.2; UNI.1.1, 4, 5 · election of vice-chancellor, CUL, department of manuscripts and university archives, o.II.58 and misc. coll. 36, p. 56 · Emmanuel College Archives, Cambridge, COL.9.1B, Bennet's Book II · *The family memoirs of the Rev. William Stukeley*, ed. W. C. Lukis, 2, SurtS, 76 (1883), 38 · IGI
Archives BL, collections, notes, memoranda, etc., relating to Cambridge University, Add. MSS 5836, 5851–5852, 5879, 5885 · CUL, Degr. 1, 2, 4, 14 · CUL, MS Ff.3.32 · Emmanuel College Archives, Cambridge, COL.9.2; UNI.1.1, 4, 5 | BL, letters to C. Yorke, Add. MS 35640
Likenesses J. Freeman, portrait, 1775 (after Van der Myn), Emmanuel College, Cambridge · by or after H. van der Myn, oils, Emmanuel College, Cambridge; copy, NPG

Richardson, William (1740–1820), political activist and naturalist, was born probably at Castleroe, near Coleraine, co. Londonderry, the only son of Charles Richardson (*d.* 1743) and his wife, Sarah, daughter of Hercules Heyland of Coleraine. His father's family had, since 1729, been established on the nearby Somerset estate.

After early education under the Revd John Torrens at the diocesan school (later Foyle College, Londonderry), Richardson entered Trinity College, Dublin, as a scholar in 1761. He graduated BA in 1763 and MA in 1776 (the year in which he was appointed a fellow). In 1775 he graduated BD; his DD followed in 1778. In 1783 he was appointed to the college living of Clonfeacle on the border of counties Armagh and Tyrone. In 1785 he married Hannah (1749/50–1839), daughter of Mark McCausland and Elizabeth Heyland. The union may not have been untroubled, but the couple had at least two sons. In 1818 his second son was appointed to perpetual curacy of Moy, which was formed out of Clonfeacle.

The rector's tithes, probably exceeding £1000 yearly, and his glebes of over 500 acres, enabled Richardson to indulge his enthusiasm for geology and agricultural experimentation. His relative wealth enabled him to publish his works (and to distribute them liberally), to purchase military commissions for one (possibly two) sons, and to buy a private residence at Portrush—where he passed his summers. His position in society gained him the ear of influential men, many of whom had been his companions at the university. His second son, Thomas Wolfe, was named after Lord Kilwarden, clearly a close friend who in 1796, when attorney-general, accepted Richardson's advice to establish a force of mounted yeomanry in every district. Richardson encouraged magistrates in the northern counties to raise this force, formed to meet the threat of a French invasion, supported by a rising of United Irishmen, at a time troops could not be spared from Great Britain. This period is recounted in Richardson's *Origins of the Irish Yeomanry* (1801).

Despite his active writing and publishing of works by 1801, Richardson did not publicize his enthusiasm for geology, his opposition to the Huttonians and the Neptunians, nor his agricultural enthusiasm, until later. A committed opponent of the French Revolution, he associated the new ideas of the earth's structure with the revolutionaries, whom he abhorred as enemies of religion. Since he did not accept the new theories of the earth's formation, his work has long been disregarded, but it shows exceptional powers of observation and description. In 1808 he was one of the compilers of the earliest geological map of Ulster, presented to (but later lost by) the Geological Society of London by Babington. About this time he began to abandon geology as his main interest, concentrating instead on agricultural work.

Richardson experimented with sixteen grasses, as described in *An Elementary Treatise on the Indigenous Grasses of Ireland* (1806). From 1808 he was a zealous advocate of fiorin grass (Gaelic *fioreann*) (*Agrostis stolonifera* L) as food for animals, a preventive of famine, and a means of abating the poor laws. He believed it to be the most nutritious of grasses, with the advantages of late growth and harvesting; he pressed for its universal cultivation—mainly in the *Gentleman's Magazine* and *Philosophical Magazine*. Humphry Davy (whom Richardson had once piloted during a maritime exploration of the Causeway coast) supported his belief. He received gold medals from societies at Bath and in south-west Scotland for his work. When opposed, he accused seedsmen of selling as fiorin the roots of couch grass (*Agropyrum repens* Beauv.), and stewards of concealing their ignorance of grasses; but the expense of planting the stolons overcame the advantages and time confirmed his detractors' views. Richardson died at his home, Glebe House, Clonfeacle, on 14 June 1820. He was buried at Moy, co. Tyrone.

C. W. P. MAC ARTHUR

Sources W. Richardson, *Origin of the Irish yeomanry* (1801) · W. Richardson, 'On the volcanic theory: Part 1. Examination of Mr. Desmarest's memoir', *Transactions of the Academy of Sciences* (1771) · W. Richardson, 'On the volcanic theory: Part 2. Examination of the facts and opinions, given by different advocates for the volcanic origin of basalt, who followed Mr. Desmarest, to wit, Mr. Faujas de St. Fond, Mr. Dolomieu, Mr. Whitehurst, Bishop Troll, Abbé Spallanzani, and Dr. Hamilton. Part 3. Arguments against the volcanic origin of basalt, derived from its arrangement in the county of Antrim, and from other facts observed in that county, communicated by the Right Rev. the Lord Bishop of Dromore', *Transactions of the Royal Academy of Ireland*, 10 (1806), 35–108 · W. Richardson, *An elementary treatise on the indigenous grasses of Ireland, with a selection of those which promise to be most useful. Addressed to his agricultural friends* (1806) · W. Richardson, 'Memoir on fiorin grass', *Select Papers of the*

Belfast Literary Society (1808) · W. Richardson, *An Essay on Agriculture; containing an Introduction, in which the Science of Agriculture is pointed out, by a careful attention to the Works of Nature; also, the means of rendering barren soils luxuriantly productive, at a very moderate expense, and of beneficially employing the industrious and unoccupied poor. To which is added a Memoir, drawn up at the express wish of His Imperial Highness the Arch-duke John of Austria, on the nature and qualities of Fiorin Grass, with practical remarks on its abundant properties, and the best mode of cultivating that extraordinary vegetable* (1818) · W. Richardson, 'A letter on the alterations that have taken place in the structure of rocks, on the surface of the basaltic country in the counties of Derry and Antrim. Addressed to Humphry Davy, Esq., Sec. R.S.', *Philosophical Magazine*, 33 (1809), 102–16, 194–208 [from *Philosophical Transactions of the Royal Society of London* (1808)] · W. Riky, *The extraordinary conduct of the Rev. Doctor Richardson, Rector of the Parish of Clonfecle in the Diocese of Armagh, towards the curate of the said parish, briefly stated* (1807) · W. Richardson, 'An epitome of the very extraordinary habits, uses and properties of fiorin grass in a letter to Mr Malone', *GM*, 1st ser., 79 (1809), 133–4 · *GM*, 1st ser., 90/2 (1820), 88–9 · *Belfast News-Letter* (23 June 1820) · *DNB* · 'Richardson of Somerset', Young, *300 years in Inishowen* · J. B. Leslie, *Armagh clergy and parishes* (1911) **Archives** Linen Hall Library, Belfast, Joy MSS · PRO NIre., Macartney MSS · UCL, letters to Greenough **Likenesses** McCleary?, caricature, c.1809

Richardson, William (1743–1814), university teacher and literary scholar, was born on 1 October 1743 at Aberfoyle in Perthshire, the son of James Richardson (*d.* 1770), the Church of Scotland parish minister, and Jean Burrell (*d.* 1778), who came from Northumberland. At the age of seven he witnessed in his home the rape of Jean Key, or Wright, by Rob Roy McGregor's sons, which left a profound effect. Educated at the parish school, he was an able pupil with a gift for languages and entered the University of Glasgow in 1757. He was a distinguished student with a reputation for writing verse. After graduating in 1763 he abandoned his theological studies and accepted the post of tutor to the two eldest sons of Charles Cathcart, ninth Lord Cathcart, and his wife, Jane Hamilton, the sister of Sir William Hamilton. The family lived at Shaw Park in Cathcart, Renfrewshire, and Jane, like her brother, was a considerable scholar, also with an interest in modern languages. As was common at the time, Richardson spent two years with his charges at Eton where he became acquainted with several important families. When Lord Cathcart was appointed ambassador-extraordinary to Russia in 1768 Richardson sailed with the family and his pupils. He returned with the family in 1772 after Lady Cathcart's death in childbirth. He later published *Anecdotes of the Russian empire; in a series of letters, written, a few years ago, from St. Petersburg* (1784), which articulated forcefully the concerns he shared with Lady Cathcart about serfdom and the brutalities of the penal system. Although not much regarded at the time, it has come to be considered as 'a cogent and thorough account of Russia, presented with an unusual degree of sophistication', and 'a skeletal framework for a really synthetic interpretation of a whole society' (Cross, 348).

In 1773 Richardson secured the post of professor of humanity at Glasgow on the initiative of Cathcart, who had recently been elected rector of the university, and the duke of Montrose, the chancellor. The professors at Glasgow were badly paid (the stipend of the chair of humanity was only £30 a year) and they were expected to supplement their income from class fees for their lectures by taking boarding pupils and by publishing. Throughout his time at Glasgow, Richardson took boarders not just during the university year, but also in the summer months at his cottage at Croy. He attracted a galaxy of talent, including William Schaw Cathcart, his existing pupils, and the sons of Sir Robert Graham of Gartmore, of Sir Robert Dalyell, and of Henry Bathurst, second Earl Bathurst, the lord chancellor. He charged £75 for the university session, for which he provided an all-round education including visits to the theatre and physical training. He was a noted and popular lecturer; in 1788 he had 115 students and in 1807 he commented 'When I have done teaching and lecturing to near 500 young people, I am fit for nothing but to lay myself down and by resting in bed to regain my strength' (NL Scot., Add MS 22 4 7, fol. 161). What he did not say was that a class of this size provided him with an annual income of almost £1500. By this time his teaching extended beyond the Latin language and literature to include 'civil and political institutions, military customs and institutions, domestic manners and institutions and religious customs and institutions of the Romans' (Glasgow University Library, RB 1762). The course gives the impression of a wide range of non-literary sources, especially on the Roman army, in an age before corpora and handbooks made such knowledge easy to acquire. For example he drew on the artefacts discovered on the line of the Antonine wall that had been given to the faculty of arts.

From his student days Richardson had been interested in the work of the Foulis press and as a professor he acted as an editor of classical texts. One of his letters provides, perhaps, the best accounts of the Foulis brothers. He approved of Robert Foulis's 'great liking ... to converse on literary topics and even with persons much younger than himself' (W. J. Duncan, ed., *Notices and Documents Illustrative of the Literary History of Glasgow during the Greater Part of Last Century*, 1886, 41). He published five works of Shakespearian criticism and also maintained a lively interest in contemporary literature, reading widely, not only in English but in German, French, and Italian. He encouraged his boarders to do likewise. He was an active member of the Literary Society of Glasgow, which met in the university, and he claimed to have introduced Glasgow audiences to the poems of William Cowper. Although in writing about Russia he consistently described himself as English, he was an advocate for Scottish literature and published an essay in support of the authenticity of Macpherson's Ossian in 1807. He commented in 1787

One Burns a ploughman near Kilmarnock has lately published a volume of Poems that draw most attentions. They are wonderful for a mere ploughman ... Persons, who never read a verse before in their days, are all furiously fond of them. (W. Richardson to S. Rose, 1 Jan 1787, Glasgow University Library, MS gen. 520/2)

He helped Robert Anderson with his biography of Smollett and maintained a regular correspondence with his former pupil, the editor Samuel Rose, who assisted Cowper. He published his own rather ponderous elegiac verse, but he was better known as a critic than as an author.

The pressure of all this activity told on Richardson's health, and after 1803 he suffered from regular and increasingly severe bouts of gout. By the early 1810s he could get about only with difficulty. He died unmarried in Glasgow on 3 November 1814.　　MICHAEL S. MOSS

Sources H. J. Pitcher, 'A Scottish view of Catherine's Russia: William Richardson's *Anecdotes of the Russian empire* (London, 1784)', *Forum for Modern Language Studies*, 3 (1967) · P. Putnam, ed., *Seven Britons in imperial Russia, 1698–1812* (1952) · A. Cross, *By the bank of the Neva: chapters from the lives and careers of the British in eighteenth century Russia* (1997) · W. Richardson, letters, U. Glas. · W. Richardson's letters, NL Scot. · *DNB* · *Fasti Scot.*, new edn, 4.335 · W. I. Addison, ed., *The matriculation albums of the University of Glasgow from 1728 to 1858* (1913) · *GM*, 1st ser., 84/2 (1814), 509
Archives NL Scot., letters | NL Scot., letters to Robert Anderson · U. Glas. L., letters to Samuel Rose
Likenesses J. Graham-Gilbert, portrait (after H. Raeburn), Hunterian Museum and Art Gallery, Glasgow · H. Raeburn, oils, Dunedin Art Gallery, New Zealand · H. Raeburn, portrait, Hunterian Museum and Art Gallery, Glasgow · W. Ridley, stipple, BM, NPG; repro. in *Monthly Mirror* (1799)

Richardson, William (1768–1862), naval officer and author, was born in South Shields, co. Durham, and baptized on 22 July 1768 at the parish church of South Shields, the second of seven children of William Richardson, officer in the merchant navy, and Ann, *née* Tully (*d.* 1785), of Shields. His father spent most of his time at sea and William was much indulged by his mother, who allowed him to change between various local schools as the fancy took him. However, on one of his rare visits his father sent him to a boarding-school at West Boldon where he stayed for about three years until 1780, before going to Trinity School, Newcastle to study navigation, determined to follow a 'sailor's life' (W. Richardson, 3). On 16 January 1781 he was bound an apprentice for seven years to Captain Anderson in a collier, the *Forester*. On completing his apprenticeship his attempts to 'better himself' ended in a voyage as fourth mate in the slave trade under a sadistic captain who would 'flog a man as soon as look at him' (ibid., 51).

On arrival back in England in 1791 Richardson was pressed into the Royal Navy and served as an able seaman in the *London* for four months. On his discharge he briefly returned to the slave trade. There followed a time during which he served in several East Indiamen, but leaving Calcutta in the *Elizabeth* he was shipwrecked and cast adrift in an open boat. Fortunately Richardson was rescued but he was again impressed into the Royal Navy with only the shirt he stood up in; this time he was to serve for the remainder of his sea-going career. On his return to England he was drafted into the *Prompte* without a moment's liberty on shore. Here, however, his situation began to improve. In September 1795 he was appointed acting gunner, later confirmed, and on 23 July 1797 he married Sarah Thompson (*d.* in or before 1862), the daughter of a master

stonemason of Portsea. The *Prompte's* major role was convoying merchant vessels to and from the West Indies and she also captured a couple of prizes, one of which, a French schooner, foundered in a hurricane with the entire prize crew. This would have included Richardson had not one of the lieutenants asked to take command. Then, in 1799, he was promoted to the *Tromp*, and again returned to the West Indies but this time accompanied by his wife. This was to prove a far less happy commission owing to an outbreak of yellow fever on board. The majority of the ship's company died along with several of the wives and the vessel was converted into a prison ship. After a difficult two years they left for home but 'of those who left England in the ship, only my wife and I, with two others returned in her' (W. Richardson, 195).

With the renewal of the war with France, Richardson was appointed to the *Caesar* (80 guns) which pleased him greatly. In her he was involved in several major actions including Sir Richard Strachan's victory over a French squadron, the famous attack on the Basque Roads in 1809 and the unfortunate Walcheren expedition (1809). After a period in support of Wellington and the army off Lisbon the *Caesar* returned to England and was not to go to sea again. After appointments to two ships in ordinary, in 1819 Richardson was superannuated, much to his delight, receiving a pension of £65 per annum. He retired to Portsea with his wife.

Richardson's career was similar to that of many other pressed men, though he was clearly an excellent gunner and received very strong certificates and was reported as having a 'Very Good' character. However, significantly, he wrote an excellent account of his life, *A Mariner of England*, which was finally published in 1908. The book was clearly constructed from a diary that he seems to have kept for most of his career. It is remarkably dispassionate in that he analyses without rancour the unnecessary hardships imposed on seamen, though these refer as much to the merchant as to the Royal Navy. He makes it clear that in both services the comfort of those on board depended almost exclusively on the nature of the captain. In particular he criticized the refusal of many Royal Naval captains to allow leave on shore. All four of Richardson's brothers served in the navy during the war. He died on 4 August 1862 near Portsmouth, his wife having predeceased him.　　HENRY BAYNHAM

Sources W. Richardson, *A mariner of England*, ed. S. Childers (1908) · payment of superannuation, PRO, PMG 16/11 · dockyard surveys, PRO, ADM 11/35 · seniority list, PRO, ADM 118/354 · S. C. Richardson, 'Journal of William Richardson, who visited Labrador in 1771', *Canadian Historical Review*, 16 (1935), 54–61 · parish register, Durham RO [baptism]
Wealth at death under £200: probate, 2 Dec 1862, *CGPLA Eng. & Wales*

Richardson, William (*b.* 1796/7, *d.* after 1846), astronomer and accused murderer, was born in Pocklington, Yorkshire. With his friend and future brother-in-law William Rogerson of Leeds, he arrived in London without connections, but found temporary employment as a computer at

James South's first observatory in Blackman Street, Southwark, where South and John Herschel from 1821 to 1823 observed double stars. In 1822 he became a supernumerary computer at the Royal Greenwich Observatory, under John Pond. In 1824 he was promoted fourth assistant on the new salary scale of £100, rising by £10 per annum to a maximum of £300, to be one of Pond's 'indefatigable hard working and above all obedient drudges' for the 'forbidding task work' of dull calculation (Forbes, 170). Pond's effort in 1829 to obtain a £50 increase for the assistants was rejected by the Treasury. South praised Richardson as: 'attached to astronomy, but unable to maintain your family upon the *miserable* pittance allowed you by the government' (South, 165).

South referred to an extraordinary effort. In 1820 Pond had ordered Thomas Jones to replicate Edward Troughton's mural circle of 1812, and it was delivered in 1825. Richardson in leisure time used both circles to determine their errors, then between 1825 and 1828 made and reduced 4119 observations of fourteen selected stars, and determined a constant for the aberration of light of 20.505 seconds of arc for the Troughton and 20.502 for the Jones circles—a difference of only three-thousandths, and very close to the modern value of 20.5. For that 'immense labour' Richardson was awarded the 1830 gold medal of the Astronomical Society of London. Then from 1829 he alone reduced, edited, and brought to publication John Dunlop's nearly 40,000 observations of 7385 stars made between 1822 and 1826 at Sir Thomas Brisbane's observatory at Parramatta, Australia. That catalogue, involving much overtime at 4*d*. per hour in order to support his family, was published by the Admiralty under Richardson's name in 1835.

Those were the high points of Richardson's career. With Pond ill, after about 1829 the observatory degenerated until it was put under control by G. B. Airy in 1835. The Admiralty allowed Airy to dismiss the first assistant, Thomas Taylor, for abetting his son in falsifying data for Groombridge's star catalogue of 1832, publication of which Airy blocked. The Admiralty rejected his attempt to dismiss Richardson for collusion. Airy conceded: 'I shall endeavour to … secure the advantages of Mr. Richardson's abilities and will guard against the ill effects of his imperfect perception of honesty; arrangements in which I expect to have some trouble' (Meadows, 2). Richardson was apparently vindicated in 1838 when Airy noted that the bulk of the reductions had been well done. Meanwhile Airy brought in a Cambridge graduate, Robert Main, as first assistant at the Greenwich observatory at £400; the next two assistants received £150, and the fourth to sixth, including Richardson, £100. Annual increments became discretionary. A discreditably low level for arduous work, the new salary scale imposed a salary cut of £90 upon Richardson. By subservience and valuable work he was restored to £190 by 1841, and by 1845 was a senior assistant with £240 to support his wife, Ann, and nine surviving children at their home on Royal Hill, Greenwich, which suggests he was very fairly treated.

Night work of a different kind brought Richardson to his nadir. On 27 October 1845 'facts were brought', apparently by Main, to Airy's knowledge that Richardson had committed the loathsome act of fathering a child upon his 21-year-old spinster daughter, Anne Maria. Airy immediately suspended him, 'investigated' by what must have been a ghastly interview which obtained Richardson's admission, and dismissed him on 30 October (*The Times*, 26 Jan 1846, 7; Chapman, 126). On 22 January a man working on Richardson's cesspit found a child's coffin in it; by the 24th tests by two surgeons provided evidence of over four grains of arsenic in the remains, sufficient to cause a very painful death. Richardson was arrested in Pocklington. At 'the Greenwich murder' trial at the Old Bailey on 13 May, leading counsel said it was a horrific case 'almost without parallel', a father and daughter murdering a helpless child; he then left his junior to proceed. The story spilled out. Mrs Richardson had colluded, renting a room in Bermondsey for the lying-in, assisting the healthy birth on 16 October, and keeping 'dear Billy' informed. The child was unwell soon after Richardson's visit on the 23rd, screamed violently all night, and died on the 25th, certified as 'wasting away of vital powers'. The Greenwich surgeon said Richardson was depressed because his family faced poverty and the workhouse. A chemist's assistant 'believed' Richardson had bought arsenic 'about 12 September'; Anne Maria admitted an unregistered birth, and 'my father compelled me to … the connexion', but claimed the baby had been ill since birth. Richardson denied murder and concealment—'I could have procured secrecy for a few shillings'—had made no attempt at abortion, and denied buying arsenic; they had made every arrangement to preserve the child. The judge dismissed the case against Anne. The defence said that Richardson had admitted incest, but denied murder; there was no proof that poison caused the death, nor that he had bought or administered it. The evidence being circumstantial, Richardson was acquitted the same day.

An initiative and effort over thirteen years had displayed Richardson's talents and brought him honour unique at a public observatory before 1939 for one below the rank of first assistant. But 'the Greenwich murder' had been a sensation of the 'most orrible' kind. Richardson disappeared from the field of astronomy, his eventual fate as obscure as that of his family and infants.

ROGER HUTCHINS

Sources [J. South], 'Presidential address', *Monthly Notices of the Astronomical Society of London*, 5 (1830), 155–65 • E. G. Forbes, *Greenwich observatory*, 1: *Origins and early history (1675–1835)* (1975) • A. J. Meadows, *Greenwich observatory: the story of Britain's oldest scientific institution*, 2: *Recent history (1836–1975)* (1975) • *Memoirs, Astronomical Society of London*, 4 (1831), 59–128 • *History of the Royal Astronomical Society*, [1]: *1820–1920*, ed. J. L. E. Dreyer and H. H. Turner (1923); repr. (1987), 65 • G. B. Airy, 'Memo', 2 Feb 1846, CUL, RGO6, 73, 88 • *The Times* (26 Jan 1846), 7c • *The Times* (24 Feb 1846), 8d • *The Times* (26 Feb 1846), 8c • *The Times* (14 May 1846), 8c–d • census returns, 1841, PRO, HO 107/489, bk 9, fol. 18 • parish register, St Alphege, Greenwich, Kent • E. Dunkin, Autobiographical notes, 1894, RAS, MS Add. 54 • A. Chapman, 'Private research and public duty: G. B. Airy and the search for Neptune', *Journal for the History of Astronomy*, 19 (1988), 121–39, see also n. 25

Richardus Anglicus (*fl. c.*1180). *See under* Wendover, Richard of (d. 1252).

Riches, Sir Eric William (1897–1987), urological surgeon, was born on 29 July 1897 in Alford, Lincolnshire, the second of three children and elder son of William Riches, schoolmaster, and his wife, Kate Rowbotham. He was educated at St Dunstan's School, Alford, and Queen Elizabeth Grammar School, Alford, before securing an entrance scholarship to Christ's Hospital, Horsham, where he won a number of prizes. After a further entrance scholarship to the Middlesex Hospital, London, in 1915, he deferred his admission to join the army, serving first in the 10th Lincoln and then the 11th Suffolk regiments, in France and Flanders. Awarded the MC in 1917, he was demobilized in 1919 with the rank of captain and entered medical school, where he won a second-year exhibition, the Lyell gold medal in surgery, and the senior Broderip scholarship. He also played golf and rugby for the Middlesex Hospital. He obtained his MB, BS and MRCS, LRCP (both 1925), and his MS and FRCS (both 1927).

In 1925 Riches became surgical registrar to A. S. Blundell Bankart and Alfred Webb-Johnson, before his appointment to the surgical staff of the Middlesex in 1930. In 1928 he married Annie Margaret Sylvia (d. 1952), a doctor in general practice, daughter of Alexander Theodore Brand, medical practitioner, of Driffield, Yorkshire. They had two daughters, one of whom, Anne Riches, entered general medical practice. At the Middlesex, he began primarily as a general surgeon, with a special interest in urology, and was also appointed to the Hospital of St John and St Elizabeth (before 1930) and to St Andrew's, Dollis Hill. He was consultant urologist to the army and to the Royal Masonic Hospital, and consulting surgeon to the Ministry of Pensions spinal injuries centre.

Riches was a Hunterian professor at the Royal College of Surgeons in 1938, and both Hunterian professor and Jacksonian prizeman in 1942. He served six years on its court of examiners (1940–46) and sixteen years on the council, being vice-president in 1961–2. He was successively Bradshaw lecturer, Arnott demonstrator, and Gordon-Taylor lecturer. He developed a number of his own specialist surgical instruments and for many years acted as curator of historic surgical instruments at the Royal College of Surgeons.

Riches was a superb surgical technician and innovator. He was a most energetic man who took an enthusiastic interest in teaching his students and training young surgeons. He published many urological papers and wrote or contributed to several books, including *Modern Trends in Urology* (1953, 1960, and 1969) and *Tumours of the Kidney and Ureter* (1964). He was also a lively and effective speaker at the many societies he supported, being a founder member of council of the British Association of Urological Surgeons, its president in 1951, and St Peter's medallist (1964), president and Lettsomian lecturer (1958) of the Medical Society of London, and president and orator (1967) of the Hunterian Society. At the Royal Society of Medicine, of which he became an honorary fellow in 1966, he was a

vice-president and honorary librarian, and had been president of its urological, surgical, and clinical sections. He was chairman of the editorial committee and treasurer of the *British Journal of Urology*. His reputation was also international, for he was elected to the American Association of Genito-Urinary Surgeons in 1953, was vice-president of the International Society of Urology in 1961, and was president at that society's thirteenth congress in London in 1964. Riches retained a great love for Christ's Hospital, his old school, of which he became a governor in 1958 and a member of the council of almoners in 1960. He was knighted in 1958.

Riches, who went bald early, was a modest man of average height, with a friendly smile. He built up a large and highly successful private practice, which he continued for too many years after his retirement in 1962: indeed, he eventually had to be given very firm encouragement to stop operating. He included among his hobbies photography, golf, and music. In sad contrast to his lively character and exuberance in earlier times, he survived for the last few years of his life in poor and deteriorating health.

After the death of his first wife in 1952 Riches married in 1954 (Susan Elizabeth) Ann, a nurse at the Middlesex Hospital, daughter of Lieutenant-Colonel Leslie Holdsworth Kitton, regular army officer, of Wye, near Ashford, Kent. They had one daughter. Riches lived in retirement at Thames Bank, Goring, Oxfordshire; he died on 8 November 1987 at Thames Bank Nursing Home, Goring.

REGINALD MURLEY, *rev.*

Sources RCS Eng. • *BMJ* (5 Dec 1987), 1492 • *The Lancet* (5 Dec 1987), 1347 • *The Times* (10 Nov 1987) • personal knowledge (1996) • *CGPLA Eng. & Wales* (1988)
Wealth at death £244,121: probate, 13 Jan 1988, *CGPLA Eng. & Wales*

Richey, Alexander George (1830–1883), historian, was born in Dublin, the son of Alexander Richey, agent, of Mountemple, Coolock, co. Dublin, and his wife, Matilda Browne, whose sister Margaret married Henry, second son of the first earl and father of the third earl of Charlemont. He was educated at Dungannon Royal School, entered Trinity College, Dublin, in 1848, and was elected on the foundation in 1861. He graduated BA in 1854, winning the first gold medal in classics, LLB in 1855, and LLD in 1873. Richey married the elder daughter of Major-General Henry Smith of Bathboys, co. Wicklow. They had three sons, Henry, John, and James, and two daughters. Richey was called to the Irish bar in 1855, and took silk in 1871. In 1871 he was appointed deputy regius professor of feudal and English law at Trinity College, Dublin; he was also vice-president of the Royal Irish Academy, and an auditor and prizeman of the college historical society.

Richey published *Lectures on the History of Ireland* (2 vols., 1869–70). The first volume was based on a course delivered at Alexandra College, Dublin, covering the history of Ireland down to 1534; the second derived from lectures delivered at Trinity College and finished with the early seventeenth-century plantation of Ulster. These lectures, together with other occasional lectures, were collected in

A Short History of the Irish People, Down to the Date of the Planta-tion of Ulster (1887), edited, after Richey's death, by Dr Rob-ert Romney Kane. Richey also wrote *The Irish Land Laws* (1880), and edited and contributed prefaces to volumes 3 and 4 of the Brehon laws, produced under the commission for publishing the ancient laws and institutes of Ireland. He also contributed frequently to *The Athenaeum* and the *Saturday Review*. He was engaged on a more detailed his-tory of Ireland at the time of his death, but only one chap-ter had been written, which was incorporated in the *Short History* (1887). He was regarded by contemporaries as a pioneer in his field of study. J. P. Mahaffy, in his tribute to Richey, acknowledged his 'contact with Sir H. Main, Lave-leye, and other authorities of European fame', which enabled him 'to throw the light of parallel developments on the obscurities of Irish custom till then treated as an isolated growth'. Richey's work on the land law was subse-quently quoted by Gladstone in the debate on his land bill in 1881.

Richey died at his residence, 27 Upper Pembroke Street, Dublin, on 29 November 1883, and was buried on 3 Decem-ber in Mount Jerome cemetery.

A. F. POLLARD, rev. TERENCE A. M. DOOLEY

Sources *The Times* (4 Dec 1883) · *Daily Express* [Dublin] (4 Dec 1883) · *Irish Times* (4 Dec 1883) · Burtchaell & Sadleir, *Alum. Dubl.* · J. P. Mahaffy, 'Alexander George Richey', *The Athenaeum* (8 Dec 1883), 738–9 · A. G. Richey, *A short history of the Irish people down to the date of the plantation of Ulster*, ed. R. R. Kane (1887)

Wealth at death £2533 9s. 0d.: probate, 10 April 1884, *CGPLA Eng. & Wales*

Richey, James Ernest (1886–1968), geologist, was born on 24 April 1886 at Ballymully, co. Tyrone, the son of the Revd John Richey, priest in the Church of Ireland and rector of Desertcreat, and his wife, Susana Best. Educated at St Col-umba's College, Rathfarnham, and at Trinity College, Dublin, he obtained his BA degree in natural sciences in 1908 (with the award of a senior moderatorship and a gold medal) and his BAI in engineering in 1909. His published work gained him the ScD of Trinity in 1934.

After a period as demonstrator at Oxford (1910–11) under W. J. Sollas, Richey joined the geological survey in 1911 and was assigned as a geologist to the Scotland office in Edin-burgh. Richey went into the field under C. T. Clough (and later Edward Battersby Bailey) in Mull. It fell to Richey to complete the mapping of a broad dyke crossing Loch Bà; his meticulous work showed its annular, outward-dipping shape and provided the key to the principal structural element in the complex, a ring-fracture which had per-mitted the subsidence of a plug of rock more than 1 kilo-metre wide into the magma chamber below. It now began to emerge that a series of such ring-subsidences had taken place during the eruptive episode, and that a considerable variety of different rock-types had been emplaced in the fractures. The ring-dyke concept thus enabled successive foci to be defined, and the stages in the evolution of the magmas to be determined. Bailey had previously recog-nized what he called cauldron subsidence in the much older intrusive complex at Glencoe on the mainland. Now the way was open for the elucidation of the history of the

Tertiary volcanoes, the interiors of which had been exposed by erosion over the past 55 million years. A large share of this work fell to Richey, and he became the lead-ing figure in a subject that influenced work on volcanoes, ancient and modern, worldwide.

In the First World War, Richey was commissioned in the Royal Engineers in 1914, serving with the guards division in France, reaching the rank of captain, and gaining the MC. After the war, he began an investigation of the Ardna-murchan peninsula, where the ring form of the intru-sions is beautifully reflected in the topography, and by 1924 he had completed an extremely detailed 6 inch sur-vey. In the same year Richey married Henrietta Lily McNally from his own home county, and with his charm and Irish wit, sometimes mordant, they made an ideal couple. They later had three daughters.

The publication of Richey's Ardnamurchan map and descriptive memoir in 1930 was a landmark in the subject. However by then, although not entirely part of his official duties, he had begun to look at other volcanic centres on an axis which ran through Skye, Mull, and Arran, in order to reinterpret Harker's mapping in Skye and that of the geological survey of Ireland in Slieve Gullion and the Mourne Mountains. In an outstanding presidential address to the Geological Society of Glasgow in 1932 he was able to give a new conspectus of Tertiary vulcanicity in the British Isles, and he was later able to show that quiet upwelling of magnesian magmas alternated with violent periods of explosion when the magma became silica-rich.

Richey's geological interests were very wide. From 1925, when he became district geologist, he was actively engaged in the metamorphic areas of Morar, Moidart, and Morvern, and the granitic complex of Strontian. His col-laborators in this study included W. Q. Kennedy, J. B. Simp-son, and A. G. MacGregor. He contributed substantially to geological knowledge of Renfrewshire and Ayrshire, and later to the eastern midland valley of coalfield surveys in Scotland. After his retirement from the geological survey at the age of sixty, he set up as a consulting geologist and also gave lectures at Queen's College, Dundee. He wrote a number of papers, and also penned the foreword to the first issue of the *Quarterly Journal of Engineering Geology* (1967).

Richey's work achieved wide recognition. He received the Lyell medal of the Geological Society of London in 1933 and was elected FRS in 1938. The Geological Society of Edinburgh gave him their Clough medal in 1964, and the Royal Society of Edinburgh, of which he was a fellow (1927), general secretary (1946–56), and a vice-president (1956–9), awarded him its Neill prize in 1965. He became an honorary member of the Royal Irish Academy in 1967, and was an honorary fellow of the Geological Society of America (1948). The Society of Engineers awarded him its first Baker medal in 1954. His influential work on ancient volcanoes led to his election to the vice-presidency (1936–48) of the International Association of Volcanologists, a constituent body of the International Union of Geodesy and Geophysics. From 1950 to 1959 he was chairman of the Royal Society's committee on vulcanology. His presidencies included the geological societies of Glasgow and Edinburgh, and section C of the British Association for the Advancement of Science.

Richey was visited at his homes in Edinburgh and Monifieth, Angus, by geologists from all over the world. He was generous with his time and liked to encourage younger men to criticize and re-examine his work. Among his leisure interests, gardening was one of the chief. He had the charming custom of attaching names of friends he wished to remember to his rhododendron bushes. Richey died at Coleshill, Warwickshire, on 19 June 1968, survived by his wife.   KINGSLEY DUNHAM, rev.

Sources W. Q. Kennedy and A. G. MacGregor, *Memoirs FRS*, 15 (1969), 185–200 · A. G. MacGregor, *Year Book of the Royal Society of Edinburgh* (1967–8), 58–62 · A. G. MacGregor, *Proceedings of the Geological Society* (1969) · personal knowledge (1981)

Richmond. For this title name *see* Savoy, Peter of, count of Savoy and *de facto* earl of Richmond (1203?–1268); Brittany, John of, first earl of Richmond (1266?–1334); Montfort, John de, fourth earl of Richmond and duke of Brittany (d. 1399); Tudor, Edmund, first earl of Richmond (c.1430–1456); Beaufort, Margaret, countess of Richmond and Derby (1443–1509); Fitzroy, Mary, duchess of Richmond (c.1519–1555?); Stuart, Ludovick, second duke of Lennox and duke of Richmond (1574–1624); Stuart, Frances, duchess of Lennox and Richmond (1578–1639); Stuart, James, fourth duke of Lennox and first duke of Richmond (1612–1655); Villiers, Mary, duchess of Lennox and Richmond (1622–1685); Stuart, Charles, sixth duke of Lennox and third duke of Richmond (1639–1672); Stuart, Frances Teresa, duchess of Lennox and Richmond (1647–1702); Lennox, Charles, first duke of Richmond, first duke of Lennox, and duke of Aubigny in the French nobility (1672–1723); Lennox, Charles, second duke of Richmond, second duke of Lennox, and duke of Aubigny in the French nobility (1701–1750); Lennox, Charles, third duke of Richmond, third duke of Lennox, and duke of Aubigny in the French nobility (1735–1806); Lennox, Charles, fourth duke of Richmond and fourth duke of Lennox (1764–1819); Lennox, Charles Gordon-, fifth duke of Richmond and fifth duke of Lennox (1791–1860); Lennox, Charles Henry Gordon-, sixth duke of Richmond, sixth duke of Lennox, and first duke of Gordon (1818–1903).

Richmond and Somerset. For this title name *see* Fitzroy, Henry, duke of Richmond and Somerset (1519–1536).

Richmond, Alexander Bailey (*fl.* 1809–1834), spy, was a weaver by trade. By his own account he spent much of his early life in Ireland, where he was greatly affected by the people's distress. Between 1809 and 1812, when living in Pollokshaws in Renfrewshire, he took a leading part in the weavers' union societies and the agitation for the raising of wages. In January 1812, at a conference in Glasgow involving representatives of masters and operatives, Richmond was one of five spokesmen for the latter. During these meetings he met Kirkman Finlay (1773–1842), a leading Glasgow businessman, who made overtures to him on the government's behalf. The conference itself proved

fruitless and, following the advice of their counsel, Francis Jeffrey and Henry Cockburn, the operatives vainly applied to the law courts to put pressure on the magistrates to fix wages in accordance with an existing statute. A strike began at the close of 1812 and rapidly became general throughout the Scottish weaving industry. Richmond was arrested, charged with fomenting the strike, but released on bail; again he was approached by Finlay to work for the government, and was warned that, as a leader of the strike, he would be severely punished. The strike collapsed in February 1813, but the following month Richmond and others of the weavers' leaders were prosecuted for combination and conspiracy. On the advice of Jeffrey and Cockburn, Richmond did not appear, and was outlawed. He fled, via Lancashire, to Dublin, but returned to Scotland early in 1814, believing that he would be left alone as long as he remained quiet. The outlawry was not revoked and, while in hiding, Richmond fell seriously ill. In March 1815 he surrendered himself to the sheriff of Renfrewshire, and on 26 June, having pleaded guilty to the bulk of the indictment, was sentenced to a month's imprisonment.

In the spring of 1816, with capital lent him by Jeffrey, Cockburn, and others, Richmond set up his own warehouse in Glasgow for the sale of cotton and silk goods. That summer he wrote several letters to the *Glasgow Chronicle* on the need to assist the labouring classes; he also renewed his acquaintance with Finlay, now lord provost and MP for Glasgow, and frequently visited his house. According to Richmond, Finlay was convinced that there was a dangerous conspiracy being fomented by radicals; because he was sympathetic to reform, and feared that a plot might damage the cause, Richmond agreed to investigate it. Whatever the precise truth Finlay organized a spy network, and Richmond was his principal agent. On 22 February 1817 several prominent radical reformers were arrested while others took refuge in flight. Two trials followed: in the first the case was dismissed; in the second the case collapsed. Richmond subsequently protested that he was indignant at what had happened and offered to give evidence for the defence, but rumours circulated that he had manufactured the whole plot.

In May 1818 Richmond refused the government's offer, made through Finlay, of a grant of land in the Cape of Good Hope; he appears to have continued on the government's payroll at least into 1820. In 1821 he accepted a sum of money, and, owing to the hostility directed towards him in Glasgow, moved to Edinburgh. In 1824 he published an able defence of his conduct, which according to Cockburn, had 'a general foundation of truth in it'. A second edition appeared the following year. In 1825 Hugh Dickson, a Glasgow weaver, derided him as a contemptible informer in a pamphlet which was incorporated into *An Exposure of the Spy System … in Glasgow*, published in 1833. *Tait's Edinburgh Magazine* noticed the *Exposure* favourably, and Richmond prosecuted Tait's London agents, Simpkin and Marshall, for libel, claiming £5000 damages. The trial took place on 20 and 22 December 1834 in the court of exchequer, Guildhall, before Baron Parke and a special jury. Richmond conducted his own case. He described himself as a London parliamentary agent and explained that, in the previous year, he had served as a soldier at Antwerp. He spoke ably for four hours, but was nonsuited. Notwithstanding the issue of the trial, Jeffrey and Cockburn still expressed approval of Richmond's conduct, and Cockburn spoke of his 'gentleness and air of melancholy thoughtfulness'. Talfourd, who was counsel for the defence, told Cockburn he hated Richmond 'the spy' equally with 'the English courts, Tam Campbell and Brougham' (H. Cockburn, *Circuit Journeys*, 1983, 33). Nothing is known of Richmond after this period.

CLIVE EMSLEY

Sources P. B. Ellis and S. Mac A'Ghobhainn, *The Scottish insurrection of 1820* (1970) • A. B. Richmond, *Narrative of the condition of the manufacturing population* (1824) • [P. Mackenzie], ed., *An exposure of the spy system pursued in Glasgow during the years 1816–17–18–19 and 20 … edited … by a ten-pounder* (1832) • *The Times* (23 Dec 1834)
Likenesses portrait, repro. in Ellis and Mac A'Ghobhainn, *The Scottish insurrection of 1820*

Richmond, Bill (1763–1829), pugilist, was born on 5 August 1763 on Staten Island, New York. Either his enslaved Georgia-born black parents or their master, the Revd Richard Charlton, rector of St Andrew's Anglican Church, named him Richmond after the capital of Staten Island. During the American War of Independence St Andrew's continued to hold services but was also used as a hospital for the British sick and wounded, and Charlton acted as the chaplain of Lieutenant-Colonel Christopher Billopp's battalion of Staten Island loyalists. Whether through Charlton, or on his own initiative, the adolescent Richmond came to the attention and into the service of one of the British officers in occupied New York city. Hugh, Earl Percy (later the second duke of Northumberland), in 1777 took him to England, where he sent him to school in Yorkshire and later apprenticed him to a cabinet-maker in York. However, his career soon took a different turn.

The young Richmond attracted attention in York because he always prided himself on dressing smartly and cleanly after work. Insulted at a racetrack by a knife-grinder, George Moore, a 14 stone local bully, the shorter Richmond (at 10 stone 12 lbs) accepted a challenge from Moore; in the fight he blinded Moore. Soon thereafter Richmond beat two other soldiers who challenged him at the races. After being insulted and kicked by a 13 stone blacksmith, Richmond beat him as well. His next recorded victory was over a York brothel-keeper, who had called him a 'black devil' when he saw him walking down the street with a white female companion.

Richmond became a professional boxer when he moved to London at the beginning of the nineteenth century. Although he was beaten by George Maddox in three rounds at Wimbledon Common on 23 January 1804, the left-handed Richmond went on to a series of victories in 1805: over a whip-maker named Green in ten minutes at Islington Green on 12 April; the Jewish boxer Youssop in six rounds for a 10 guinea purse at Blackheath on 21 May; and Jack Holmes, known as the Coachman, in twenty-six

rounds at Cricklewood Green, near Kilburn Wells, on 8 July. But Richmond was defeated by the 14 stone 3 lb future heavyweight champion Tom Cribb in a ninety-minute fight at Hailsham, Sussex, for a 25 guinea purse.

Having temporarily retired from the ring, Richmond did not fight again until he beat Jack Carter at Epsom Wells in 29 minutes on 14 April 1808 for 15 guineas. He defeated Isaac Atkinson, a waterman, in 23 minutes for a subscription purse at Combe Wood on 9 April 1809. In a 100 guinea rematch with George Maddox near Margate on 9 August 1809, Richmond took his revenge in 52 minutes. He went on to beat Jack Power in 15 minutes for a £20 purse at Bob's chophouse, Holborn, in London on 1 May 1810.

Some time after his defeat of Power, Richmond became the popular publican of the Horse and Dolphin tavern on St Martin's Street, Westminster, from which he dispensed boxing advice as well as alcohol to aspiring fighters and celebrities, including Lord Byron and William Hazlitt. Richmond treated the young American-born former slave Tom Molineaux as his protégé, but was repaid with ingratitude. Richmond was known for his even temper in the face of taunts, though at least once he tossed out a young loudmouth. Besides occasionally giving exhibition fights in London theatres, he sometimes still fought professionally. For example, before a crowd of 10,000 spectators at Mousley Hurst, he beat Tom Shelton, half his age, for a £25 purse, after having threatened to withdraw if Shelton continued to refuse to shake his hand before the fight.

When he was fifty Richmond was said to look fifteen years younger because of his temperate lifestyle. He was a talkative man with a sense of humour. Aside from his talent for boxing, he was also a fine cricketer, despite a bad knee. He died in his house on Titchbourne Street, Haymarket, on 28 December 1829. According to his obituary, he spent his last evening, as he had many before, in the company of Tom Cribb, and although apparently in perfect health died in bed suddenly, after a coughing fit.

VINCENT CARRETTA

Sources *The fancy, or, True sportsman's guide: being authentic memoirs of the lives, actions, prowess, and battles of the leading pugilists, from the days of Figg and Broughton, to the championship of Ward*, 2 vols. (1826), 1.533–40 • P. Egan, *Boxiana, or, Sketches of ancient and modern pugilism*, 1 (1812), 440–49 • H. D. Miles, *Pugilistica: being one hundred and forty-four years of the history of British boxing*, 1 (1880), 289–301 • *The Times* (4 Jan 1830), 3e
Likenesses R. Dighton, portrait, 1810 (*A striking view of Richmond*), repro. in F. G. Stephens and others, eds., *Catalogue of prints and drawings in the British Museum*, 11 vols. (1870–1954), no. 11587 • T. Rowlandson, portrait, 1811 (*Rural sports. A milling match*), repro. in F. G. Stephens and others, eds., *Catalogue of prints and drawings in the British Museum*, 11 vols. (1870–1954), no. 11786

Richmond, Sir Bruce Lyttelton (1871–1964), journal editor, was born at Stafford Terrace, Kensington, London, on 12 January 1871, the only child of Douglas Close Richmond, who became secretary of the Charity Commission and comptroller in the Exchequer and Audit Office (1900–04) and his first wife, Margaret Cecilia, eldest daughter of Henry Austin *Bruce, first Baron Aberdare. He went to

Sir Bruce Lyttelton Richmond (1871–1964), by Walter Stoneman, 1946

Radcliffe's preparatory school in Fonthill, near East Grinstead, Sussex, and at the age of thirteen headed the scholarship roll at Winchester College, where he rose to become prefect of hall, a member of Lord's eleven, and winner of the prize for Greek prose. A scholar of New College, Oxford, he gained a first class in classical moderations in 1892. His second in Greats (1894) perhaps owed something to his having spent less effort on *literae humaniores* than on organizing chamber concerts and playing cricket for the university, though without achieving a blue. Called to the bar by the Inner Temple in 1897, Richmond made a mark by devilling for the editor of a legal textbook which attracted the notice of George Earle Buckle, editor of *The Times*, and led to Richmond's being engaged in 1899 as an assistant editor. In the autumn of 1902 he took over the editorship of the *Times Literary Supplement*, then only a few months old, from James Thursfield. Under his aegis in the next thirty-five years the *Lit. Sup.*—he never became reconciled to its later sobriquet, the *TLS*—achieved, in the words of George Gordon, a 'position of undisputed and ungrudged authority'. His task was not made easier by the threat, under which he worked daily and loyally for some years, of the sudden, arbitrary extinction of the *Supplement* by Lord Northcliffe. In 1913 Richmond married Elena Elizabeth (1878–1964), daughter of Blanche Marie Laling and William Gair Rathbone, of Liverpool. They were childless.

The Times's tradition of anonymity perfectly suited the confident but unassuming character of a man whose entry in *Who's Who*, to the day of his death, did not so much as mention his editorship of the *Supplement*. Apart from an occasional 'letter to the editor', signed Templar, on some point of scholarship, he never himself wrote in the *Supplement* and he enjoined strict secrecy on his reviewers, as much in their interest as in its own. These reviewers included many men and women already distinguished as divines or dons, in the services, in politics, and in literature. But his particular flair was for discovering, and encouraging, new talent. He gave Virginia Woolf and T. S. Eliot their first opportunities for serious critical work. If they both confessed to having fretted in the strait-jacket of '*The Times*'s style', Eliot was later to pay an impressive tribute to the mentor who had taught him 'the discipline of anonymity'. The anonymous writer, Eliot recognized,

> must subdue himself to his editor—but the editor must be a man to whom the writer can subdue himself and preserve his self-respect. … Good literary criticism requires good editors as well as good critics. And Bruce Richmond was a great editor. (*TLS*, 1961)

In a period before the proliferation of academic literary journals the *Supplement* under Richmond also enjoyed preeminence as a forum for the discussion, in signed articles and letters, of problems of literary history and textual criticism. He was not averse from allowing unsolicited contributors to expose their weaknesses. John Dover Wilson wrote to another regular writer on Shakespearian topics: 'What I admire about the *Lit. Sup.* is its intense impartiality. People growl to me, Why does the *Lit. Sup.* print letters from that ass—? But I think it is splendid of Richmond to do so, and *so* wise.'

Richmond contributed to the *Dictionary of National Biography* the notices of his editor, Buckle, and his friend John Fuller-Maitland, the music critic. His only separate publications were the brief anonymous guide to Bodiam Castle, in Sussex, and *The Pattern of Freedom* (1940), a prose and verse anthology inspired by the faith that a liberal spirit would outlast the war. Characteristically the anthology, which ranged from Homer, Ecclesiasticus, and Petronius to Henry James, Robert Bridges, and others of Richmond's *Supplement* contributor-friends, contained no editorial introduction or other overt justification of purpose.

In private life, besides authors, Richmond numbered among his friends many musicians, both professional and amateur. After literature, classical and modern, in both of which he was widely read, music was his chief abiding passion: he was a member of the executive committee of the Royal College of Music, as well as a vice-president of the Royal Literary Fund. He lived in simple elegance in South Kensington and also leased a small house outside Robertsbridge, in Sussex, where his male guests were inducted in all weathers, with a Henry Jamesian gesture of welcome, into the mystery of the earth closet some distance down the garden.

Richmond had a predilection, conservative almost to the point of prejudice, for Shakespearian acting as exemplified in Sir Henry Irving and Sir P. B. Ben Greet. Until after his ninetieth birthday he was still a familiar figure, with two sticks, and not always approving, at the theatre at Stratford upon Avon, where he seldom missed a new production of Shakespeare. He travelled little abroad until late in life, when his distaste for hotels was mitigated by the hospitality of friends, literary or diplomatic, in Italy, Greece, and Egypt.

Richmond received honorary doctorates of letters from the University of Leeds (1922) and from Oxford (1930). He was knighted in 1935, and on the last day of 1937 retired from *The Times* to live first in Netherhampton, in Wiltshire, and later at the Old Rectory, Islip, near Oxford, where he died on 1 October 1964. He was survived for only six days by his wife.

SIMON NOWELL-SMITH, *rev.* REBECCA MILLS

Sources F. C. Roberts, ed., *Obituaries from 'The Times', 1961–1970* (1975), 672–3 · *WWW, 1961–70* · [H. H. Child], 'The *Times Literary Supplement*: a record of its beginnings', *TLS* (18 Jan 1952), 33–9 · T. S. Eliot, 'Bruce Lyttelton Richmond', *TLS* (13 Jan 1961), 17 · *The Times* (2 Oct 1964) · personal knowledge (1981) · private information (1981) **Likenesses** F. A. de B. Footner, pencil drawing, 1937, priv. coll. · W. Stoneman, photograph, 1946, NPG [*see illus.*] · photograph, repro. in Eliot, 'Bruce Lyttelton Richmond' **Wealth at death** £12,571: probate, 15 Dec 1964, *CGPLA Eng. & Wales*

Richmond, George (1809–1896), portrait painter, fifth child of Thomas *Richmond (1771–1837), miniature painter, and his wife, Ann Coram (1772–1860), of 42 Half Moon Street, Mayfair, Westminster, was born on 28 March 1809, probably at Brompton. He was baptized on 1 May at St James's Church, Piccadilly, London.

Artistic training and involvement with the Ancients With his artistic family background (Thomas's great-grandfather was the miniaturist George Engleheart), and a gift for drawing strongly apparent by the age of twelve, it is not surprising that Richmond decided on a career in art. What other learning he received was at a dame-school in Soho; this limited elementary education explains his perennial difficulty with spelling, and his execrable handwriting. More important for his future were his regular visits to the British Museum to draw from the antique. He entered the Royal Academy Schools at Somerset House on 23 December 1824, and exhibited his first academy work, in tempera, in 1825: *Abel the Shepherd* (Tate collection). Among his older fellow pupils was a part-time student, Joseph Severn, a friend of John Keats, who had attended the poet's deathbed.

The most profound early influence on Richmond was that of William Blake, to whom he was introduced by John Linnell when he was sixteen; Richmond said that a conversation with Blake was like talking with the prophet Isaiah. He was at Blake's home, 12 Fountain Court, the Strand, on 12 August 1827, when Blake died, and he closed his eyes. A moving account of Blake's death, which Richmond sent to his friend Samuel Palmer, described how 'His countenance became fair—his eyes brightened and he burst out singing of the things he saw in Heaven. In truth he Died like a Saint' (G. E. Bentley, *Blake Records*, 1969, 346–7).

Blake had been the mentor to a group of young artists and friends which came to include Richmond. Palmer was the pivotal figure; the other members of the circle were Edward Calvert, Francis Oliver Finch, Henry Walter (1779–1849), Welby Sherman (*fl.* 1827–1834), Palmer's cousin John Giles (1810–1880), and two sons of the architect Charles Heathcote Tatham, Frederick (1805–1878) and Arthur (1809–1874). The Ancients, as they called themselves, met regularly, and frequently visited Shoreham in Kent, where Palmer's father lived and the painter himself owned a cottage. There they lived simply, bathing in the river, reading poetry, playing music, and discussing their work. Richmond recalled that, at Shoreham, he had managed to live on about 10s. a week. A simple piety animated the group: Richmond recollected how 'We all said our prayers attended church and Trusted wholly in God and were blessed in that Trust' (Richmond family MSS). They continued to meet regularly even into middle age.

Early career and marriage Wishing to broaden his artistic horizons, Richmond visited France from 1826 to 1829, supporting himself there by painting miniatures. Until the 1830s, in addition to portraits, he also engraved, drew, or painted religious and literary subjects set in landscapes reminiscent of Palmer's work. Among them were the engravings *The Shepherd* (1827; uncompleted) and *The Fatal Bellman* (1827), based on a passage in *Macbeth*; the paintings *Christ and the Woman of Samaria* (1828; Tate collection), and the numinous *The Eve of Separation* (1830; Ashmolean Museum, Oxford). Drawings in pen and ink, sometimes heightened with watercolour, include the Blake-like *A Damned Soul Hanging from a Gothic Building* (1823; priv. coll., England) and *The Angel and Elijah* (1824 or 1825; Tate collection).

About 1826 Richmond fell in love with Julia (1811–1881), the beautiful fourteen-year-old sister of the Tatham brothers, whose father had engaged Richmond to give her drawing lessons. Although old Tatham had encouraged the romance, his diminishing fortune brought a change of mind when a rich and elderly suitor expressed interest in Julia. Learning of this, the young couple—encouraged by Palmer, who loaned Richmond £40—eloped to Gretna Green, where they were married on 24 January 1831. Back in London, Richmond set up home at 27 Northumberland Street, New Road, sending Julia to stay for the time being with Palmer's father at Shoreham. Meanwhile John Linnell persuaded Tatham that Richmond had a promising future. Tatham forgave them, and within three weeks George and Julia were reunited: their marriage proved to be long and happy. They had fifteen children, of whom ten survived infancy; with this growing family Richmond needed a reliable income, and he spent most of his remaining working life painting portraits.

In the 1830s Richmond began to extend his social life; he was assisted by the tory politician Sir Robert Inglis, bt, who introduced Richmond to his circle. This included Inglis's second cousin William Wilberforce and the family of Henry Thornton. Inglis became guardian to Thornton's family after his death, and moved into the Thorntons' house, Battersea Rise, much frequented at that time by artists and thinkers. It was during a visit to Battersea Rise that Richmond was offered the chance to paint Wilberforce's portrait; timidity made him hesitate, but his wife insisted that he must do it. It was a turning point in his career: as an engraving by Samuel Cousins it sold well, enhancing both Richmond's reputation and his bank balance. By 1836 he was earning £1000 p.a. from portraits and enjoying considerable popularity. During the 1830s his sitters included the countess of Pembroke (1835), four reigning bishops—Chester (1833), Lichfield (1833), London (1833), and Montreal (1836)—the Revd Samuel Wilberforce (1834), later bishop of Oxford, and then of Winchester, Rowland Hill (1834), and Charles Darwin (1839).

Visit to Rome In 1837 Richmond and his wife, accompanied by the newly-weds Samuel and Hannah Palmer, visited Italy. The party embarked at Blackwall in October, and six weeks later entered Rome through the Porto del Popolo. Richmond lost no time in looking up his old fellow student Joseph Severn, now married and living in Rome. Severn later became British consul and was already moving in prestigious social circles, to which he introduced Richmond, as well as to other English artists working in the city. Among those with whom Richmond became thus acquainted were John Baring, of the banking dynasty, Sir Henry Russell, and Sir William Knight, son of the keeper of the privy purse under George IV. Among many social events during the coming months Richmond attended a party at the house of Torlonia, the Roman banker, where he saw the dukes of Devonshire and Sutherland and the Russian tsarevich. Severn also introduced Richmond to the young W. E. Gladstone, already at the age of twenty-nine an MP; with him the painter rode beyond the limits of the Roman states, where the young politician demonstrated his disapproval of the papal administration by throwing his hat in the air, crying 'long live liberty!'

However, the climate of Rome did not suit Richmond, who was anyway something of a hypochondriac. His eyes weakened, and for one period at least he was compelled temporarily to 'desist from night studies'. His fretfulness continued intermittently throughout the Italian visit, but he worked pertinaciously at such self-imposed tasks as copying Roman murals, and experimenting with technical devices, including an egg-yolk-based medium. He visited the Vatican to view Raphael's Loggia and the Sistine Chapel, recording the number of hours he spent sketching there. At the Sistine Chapel he obtained permission from Filippo Agricola, the managing artist, to erect scaffolding, so as to study more closely Michelangelo's frescoes. He studied carefully many other works, and attended life classes at the Rome Academy.

Further afield Richmond visited Naples, Pompeii, and Herculaneum, after which he travelled with Julia to Florence. There he threw himself with enthusiasm into the study of everything, from Michelangelo's *David* in the Accademia di Belli Arti to Leonardo's *Adoration of the Magi* in the Uffizi, and many works by the early Italian masters. Back in Rome, Richmond produced some original work, including landscapes and subject paintings, such as *The Journey to Emmaus*, commissioned by Baring. And there were portraits, enough to underline where his future lay:

'It will', he said in a note about 1841, 'be a long time before I shall earn equal reputation by historical art' (Richmond family MSS). Richmond and his wife finally left Rome on 22 June 1839, stopping at Florence for ten days, before setting off for Venice, where Richmond expressed himself 'less astonished than delighted'. Above all, he was able to study there the work of Titian, Veronese, and Tintoretto, and was impressed especially by the latter's awesome *Crucifixion* in the Scuola di San Rocco. The Richmonds left Venice for home in August 1839.

Success as a portrait painter In England, Richmond's portrait commissions multiplied. One of especial significance to his future career was a portrait of Thomas Dyke Acland, later eleventh baronet (1840), commissioned by the prestigious Grillion's Club, whose members were drawn from high strata of the aristocracy, politics, and professions. A portrait of each member was commissioned on his election: this opened a grand prospect for Richmond, who became for many years the club's portrait painter. In all, he painted seventy Grillion's portraits, and in 1861 was made an honorary member of the club. Richmond presented its members, many of them young MPs, as a high-minded élite; his drawings constitute one of the best series of British public-life portraiture.

Richmond visited Rome again in late 1840, and renewed acquaintance with much that he had seen during his previous visit, in addition to taking in much that was new to him. Characteristically, on this visit he pushed himself to study all he could during the daylight hours, and to study anatomy in the evening. As usual, this punishing regime led to depression and illness, which nevertheless abated whenever he received a letter from his wife. John Ruskin, then twenty-one years old, was in Rome at this time, and was introduced to Richmond by Joseph Severn. After visiting the Vatican with him, Richmond noted that Ruskin was 'not so open to receive impressions nor does he kindle readily at the sight of the great works' (Richmond family MSS, diary, 16 Dec 1840). Despite this artistic difference of opinion, Ruskin was devoted to Richmond for many years, and was influenced by him in the development of his own aesthetic awareness.

Richmond returned home early in 1841, having been away four months. He was immediately inundated with portrait commissions and was so busy that he was giving four or five sittings a day; before long his annual income exceeded £2000. With Richmond's ever expanding family, and an ever growing professional practice, a larger and more convenient house became necessary. Therefore, in 1833 the family moved to 16 Beaumont Street, London, where a son, William Blake *Richmond (1842–1921), was born, and then in 1843 to 10 (later renumbered 20) York Street, off Baker Street, where Richmond remained for the rest of his life.

Whenever possible Richmond turned to landscape, which was closer to his predilection than portraiture. There is no doubt that this imperative concentration on portraiture led to a neurotic inner struggle, and in turn to illness and depression. Despite his yearning for other subjects, however, Richmond was a superb portrait painter, his work refined by studies in Italy. If some of his portraits flattered somewhat, they were still, he said, 'the truth lovingly told' (E. T. Cook and A. Wedderburn, eds., *The Works of John Ruskin*, 36, 1909, xxvii). Such is his affectionate depiction of Samuel Palmer (1829; NPG), in which his friend's spiritual quality is fully captured, but his usually unkempt appearance is tactfully tidied. Occasionally—inspired no doubt by his strong evangelical beliefs—Richmond painted religious subjects, such as *The Agony in the Garden* (1858; Whitehaven Methodist Church, Cumberland).

Family, professional, social life, and other interests Richmond was a small man, but carried himself with dignity, and won much respect. As a family man he was a devoted husband and father, not averse to romping with his children. Yet he could be strict, even stern: when his son Willie ran away from home with Palmer's son, Thomas More, he was made to memorize scolding letters sent to him by his father's friends.

In 1844 Richmond was appointed by Gladstone to a seat on the School of Design council, vacated by Sir Augustus Callcott. In addition, he was making professional visits to Devon and Yorkshire, yet he still managed to attend the foregatherings of the Ancients. No doubt he was once again overworking, although he had breaks at Battersea Rise and in Kent, where he could indulge himself in landscape painting. But these short respites became increasingly difficult to arrange, and were almost impossible by 1847, in which year he painted nearly one hundred portraits. Throughout his life he continued to find time to study the technique of painting—his own work seldom, if ever, satisfied him and from the 1860s he added photography to his resources as an *aide-mémoire*.

Richmond's social life prospered: in addition to his honorary membership of Grillion's Club, he was elected a member of Johnson's Club (1860), the Athenaeum (1856), and of the Club of Nobody's Friends (1856). Professionally, he served on the royal commission for determining the site of the National Gallery, and in 1857 he was elected an associate of the Royal Academy, becoming an academician in 1866.

At infrequent intervals Richmond turned to sculpture, the technique of which he probably learned while a student at the Royal Academy. His most important sculpture—commissioned in 1859, and completed in 1867—was a recumbent effigy of his friend Charles James Blomfield, bishop of London, for his tomb in St Paul's Cathedral. From 1866 Richmond also began to undertake restorations, beginning with the full-length portrait of Richard II in Westminster Abbey. The earliest contemporary portrait of an English monarch, it had been inexpertly restored and overpainted in the eighteenth century, and was considered to be beyond repair. Richmond, feeling confident that he could restore it, offered his services to the dean; the work was successfully realized by Henry Merritt, the picture cleaner, under the artist's supervision. Following this triumph, Richmond received many similar commissions, the most spectacular of which was the restoration between 1872 and 1875 of Daniel Maclise's murals in the palace of Westminster, *Wellington Meeting with Blücher after the Battle of Waterloo* and *The Death of Nelson*.

Last years, death, and assessment During his final years Richmond worked largely on landscape, although he still painted a few portraits. The Ancients died: Henry Walter was the first to depart in 1849, Calvert the last in 1883; as the group's central figure, Samuel Palmer, lay on his deathbed in 1881, Richmond knelt in prayer beside him. Julia Richmond died in the same year. In old age he spent much time with his children and grandchildren. Surviving friends—among them Ruskin—kept in touch with him, but he had distanced himself from Gladstone because of what he considered to be mistaken policies towards Ireland and the Sudan.

Richmond received many honours, including honorary doctorates from the universities of Oxford and Cambridge, honorary fellowship of University College, London, and honorary associate membership of the Royal Institute of British Architects. Towards the end he became infirm and suffered frequent bouts of illness. He died at his home, 20 York Street, London, a few days before his eighty-seventh birthday, on 19 March 1896, and was buried in Highgate cemetery on 22 March.

As a portrait painter Richmond was undoubtedly a master, despite his preference for landscape and his forced overproductivity. His early pencil or chalk portraits, which closely resemble those of his contemporary Samuel Laurence, appear in technique to be based on the nets of lines and cross-hatchings of engraving, an art practised by Richmond early in his career. After studying in Italy, however, his oil paintings became enriched by splendid colouring which owed much to Veronese, while such devices as placing the sitter by an open window show the influence of Titian. This intelligent imitation of the Italian Renaissance masters served to lift Richmond's best works well above the common run of mid nineteenth-century portraiture.   RAYMOND LISTER

Sources priv. coll., Richmond family MSS · *The letters of Samuel Palmer*, ed. R. Lister, 2 vols. (1974) · R. Lister, *George Richmond: a critical biography* (1981) · A. Gilchrist, *Life of William Blake*, ed. R. Todd, [new edn] (1942) · A. M. W. Stirling, *The Richmond papers* (1926) · d. cert.
Archives priv. coll., family papers · University of North Carolina, Chapel Hill | BL, corresp. with W. E. Gladstone, Add. MSS 44358–44527 · Bodl. Oxf., letters to the Aclands · NA Scot., letters to Lady Mary Hamilton and Miss Hamilton · RA, corresp. with Sir William Richmond, etc.
Likenesses G. Richmond, self-portrait, miniature on ivory, 1830, priv. coll. · J. Denham, plaster cast, c.1834, NPG; bronze cast, NPG · G. Richmond, self-portrait, drawing, c.1840, AM Oxf. · G. Richmond, self-portrait, oils, 1840, FM Cam. · G. Richmond, self-portrait, oil on millboard, 1853, NPG · G. Richmond, self-portrait, oils, 1853, Stanford University Art Museum, California · G. Richmond, self-portrait, oils, 1854, Birmingham Museums and Art Gallery · G. Richmond, self-portrait, oil on board, 1858, Yale U. CBA, Paul Mellon collection · G. Richmond, self-portrait, oils, 1868, Uffizi Gallery, Florence, Italy · photograph, c.1883, NPG · H. J. Brooks, group portrait, oils (*Private view of the Old Masters Exhibition, Royal Academy, 1888*), NPG · Elliott & Fry, carte-de-visite, NPG · W. Holl, stipple (after Grillion's Club series by G. Richmond, 1863),

BM, NPG · G. Richmond, self-portrait, pencil drawing, NPG · Stephenson & Royston, line engraving (after W. Lovatt, 1842), NPG
Wealth at death £78,440 12s. 4d.: probate, 12 May 1896, CGPLA Eng. & Wales

Richmond, Sir Herbert William (1871–1946), naval officer and college head, was born at Beavor Lodge, Hammersmith, London, on 15 September 1871, the third child and second son of the artist Sir William Blake *Richmond (1842–1921) and his second wife, Clara Jane (d. 1916), daughter of William Richards of Cardiff. Herbert had first developed an interest in joining the navy when, at the age of ten, he had visited Portsmouth. He attended St Mark's School, near Windsor, and his brother wrote later that: 'He was not happy there. The complexities of Greek, Latin and mathematics worried him and confirmed him in his desire to go to sea' (Trevelyan, 326).

He entered the Royal Naval College, Dartmouth, in 1885; two years later he went to sea as a midshipman in the *Nelson*, flagship of the commander-in-chief on the Australia station. In 1892 he joined the hydrographic branch but lack of prospects there encouraged him to transfer to the torpedo branch in 1894. As a torpedo officer he served in several battleships, including two years in the *Majestic*, flagship of the channel squadron. In 1903 he was promoted commander and appointed to the naval ordnance department at the Admiralty in recognition of his technical expertise.

After a year in that department Richmond became executive officer of the *Crescent*, flagship of the commander-in-chief on the Cape of Good Hope station, for nearly three years before returning to the Admiralty where he became naval assistant to the second sea lord. On 8 July 1907 he married Florence Elsa (d. 1971), second daughter of Sir (Thomas) Hugh Bell, second baronet, of Rounton Grange, Yorkshire. They had one son and four daughters. Around this time Richmond's diary writings began to show the severely critical, and often arrogant, attitude he would adopt towards policies and individuals with whom he disagreed. In 1907 he characterized Admiralty organization as 'beneath contempt' and increasingly showed 'the intolerance he had for less gifted contemporaries—a certain prickliness of character that coloured most of his personal relationships' (Hunt, 2, 20).

Richmond was promoted captain in 1908 and in 1909 appointed to the command, for nearly two years, of the most famous ship in the navy of that day, the *Dreadnought*, then flagship of Sir William May, commander-in-chief of the Home Fleet. But by then his arrogance and intolerance had begun to cause him to be 'regarded as an unsettling gadfly, increasingly isolated and mistrusted by superiors' (Hunt, 25). He was consequently relegated to command only second-class cruisers for eighteen months from March 1911.

Despite his earlier dislike of school, Richmond had become increasingly intellectual in his interests and approach. During these commands he edited the Navy Records Society's volume on *The Loss of the Minorca* (1913), delivered a series of lectures on naval history at the Royal Naval War College, and completed a book, begun in 1907,

Sir Herbert William Richmond (1871–1946), by Henry Lamb, 1944

entitled *The Navy in the War of 1739–48*, which, however, was not published until 1920. At the War College he developed among the students the group of naval reformers later known as the Young Turks who advocated a much more offensive naval policy during the war.

In 1913 Richmond became assistant director of the operations division of the war staff at the Admiralty. In this role he was not afraid to attack bitterly the strategic plans of his superiors, including those of the first lord of the Admiralty, Winston Churchill. Arthur Marder suggests that in these circumstances 'the admiralty showed great forebearance indeed in continuing his employment' (Marder, *Dreadnought*, 1.404). But his career hardly prospered. He left the Admiralty in May 1915 to become liaison officer with the Italian naval command, a post which he held for four months before returning home to command the old battleship *Commonwealth* in the 3rd battle squadron. In April 1917 he was appointed to command the battleship *Conqueror* in the Grand Fleet, where he gained the support of Sir David Beatty, the commander-in-chief. By late 1917 the prime minister, Lloyd George, had become familiar with the ideas of the Young Turks. Through contacts, he and Richmond discussed naval issues and Richmond's career was revitalized. With Beatty's strong support in April 1918 he was selected as director of the newly formed training and staff duties division of the naval staff at the Admiralty. Richmond's ideas were in advance of his time, however, and practically all of his recommendations were vetoed; he was glad after a few months of frustration to return to the Grand Fleet, in command of the battleship *Erin*.

In 1920, after Beatty's appointment as first sea lord, Richmond was promoted to flag rank, and appointed to command the re-established Royal Naval War College to which flag officers and captains were sent to study the higher direction of war. There he was at last given the independence to promote his ideas. But when cutbacks occurred in the navy soon after, such studies were given low priority and his staff was severely reduced. He resumed work for the Navy Records Society, editing the *Spencer Papers* (vol. 4, 1924).

In 1923 Richmond was appointed commander-in-chief of the East India station. On his return to England at the end of 1925, he was kept from the higher level positions he would have expected by his continuing disagreement with current naval policy. In 1927, however, he was appointed commandant of the new Imperial Defence College where his views could perhaps be more safely expressed in training rather than command within the navy. His term there was brought to an end only by the standing rule which prescribed two years as its duration.

Richmond had been promoted vice-admiral in April 1925 and admiral in October 1929. But his unpopularity within the Admiralty was reinforced when, on the eve of the naval conference of 1930, Richmond contributed two articles to *The Times* (21 and 22 November 1929) on the subject of naval reduction, which proposed limitation in the size of ships rather than the official Admiralty plan of numerical reduction. This action, Marder suggests, 'virtually terminated his career on the active list' (Marder, *Portrait*, 29), and he was refused further employment. In April 1931, twelve months before the date on which he would have been subject to compulsory retirement under the standing regulations, he retired at his own request, and devoted himself to his work as a naval historian, which was, said George Trevelyan, his 'greatest service to this country' (Trevelyan, 332).

In 1931 Richmond published *The Navy in India, 1763–83*, which he had researched in the archives of Ceylon and Pondicherry eight years earlier, and a work on naval limitation under the title *Economy and Naval Security*. He also delivered a series of lectures at University College, London, and the Lees Knowles lectures at Trinity College, Cambridge, in 1932, published in book form as *Imperial Defence and Capture at Sea in War*. In 1933 he published a treatise, *Naval Training*, and the following year a more important work, *Sea Power in the Modern World*. In that year he was elected to the Vere Harmsworth chair of imperial and naval history at Cambridge, which Trevelyan, who was part of the electing body, said was a 'marked compliment to his eminence as a historian, for owing to the age limit affecting professorships he could only hold it for two years' (Trevelyan, 334). He was also made a professorial fellow of Jesus College. He was completely successful in the academic environment. At the close of his two years' tenure of the chair, he was elected to the mastership of Downing College, which had just fallen vacant.

On the outbreak of war in 1939 Richmond became chairman of the university joint recruiting board; he welcomed the establishment in his own college of the Cambridge

naval division, and he started a series of lectures on foreign affairs and the progress of the war for the junior combination room, afterwards continued and extended as the 'Richmond lectures'. But his greatest interest remained the promotion of ideas, learnt from history, of sea power and of a British strategy based on it. In 1941 he published, in the Cambridge Current Problems series, a booklet surveying British strategy from the days of Queen Elizabeth I; in 1943 he took the same theme for the Ford lectures which he delivered at Oxford, and these he afterwards expanded into his greatest work, *Statesmen and Sea Power*, published in 1946 only a few weeks before his death. A volume left in manuscript was edited by E. A. Hughes and published in 1953 as *The Navy as an Instrument of Policy, 1558–1727*.

Richmond was appointed CB in 1921 and promoted KCB in 1926. He was elected FBA in 1937 and was a fellow of the Royal Historical Society. On the establishment in 1934 of the National Maritime Museum at Greenwich he was appointed one of the trustees. He received the honorary degree of DCL from Oxford in 1939. He was forced by illness to give up all strenuous physical activity after 1940. He died of a heart attack at his home, the master's lodge, Downing College, on 15 December 1946, and was cremated at Cambridge on 18 December.

H. G. THURSFIELD, rev. MARC BRODIE

Sources *The Times* (17–18 Dec 1946) · B. D. Hunt, *Sailor-scholar: Admiral Sir Herbert Richmond, 1871–1946* (1982) · A. J. Marder, *Portrait of an admiral: the life and papers of Sir Herbert Richmond* (1952) · G. M. Trevelyan, 'Admiral Sir Herbert Richmond, 1871–1946', *PBA*, 32 (1946), 325–37 · A. J. Marder, *From the Dreadnought to Scapa Flow: the Royal Navy in the Fisher era, 1904–1919*, 5 vols. (1961–70) · M. H. Murfett, ed., *The first sea lords: from Fisher to Mountbatten* (1995) · personal knowledge (1959) · CGPLA Eng. & Wales (1947) · WWW · Burke, *Peerage*

Archives NMM, corresp., diaries, logbooks, and papers | BL, corresp. with Lord Keyes · CAC Cam., corresp. with A. V. Hill · JRL, letters to *Manchester Guardian* · King's Lond., Liddell Hart C., corresp. with Sir B. H. Liddell Hart · NA Scot., corresp. with Philip Kerr · NMM, corresp. with Sir Julian Corbett · NMM, corresp. with K. G. B. Dewar · U. Newcastle, Robinson L., corresp. with C. P. Trevelyan

Likenesses W. Stoneman, three photographs, 1921–43, NPG · W. G. de Glehn, oils, c.1942, Downing College, Cambridge · H. Lamb, oils, 1944, Downing College, Cambridge [*see illus.*] · photograph, repro. in *The Times*, 7 · photograph, repro. in Trevelyan, *PBA*, 32, facing p. 325

Wealth at death £2539 1s. 1d.: probate, 9 May 1947, CGPLA Eng. & Wales

Richmond, Sir Ian Archibald (1902–1965), archaeologist, was born on 10 May 1902 at Rochdale, Lancashire, the elder twin son of Daniel Richmond, medical practitioner, and his wife, Helen Harper. He was educated at Ruthin School and Corpus Christi College, Oxford (1920–24); his first publications appeared while he was still an undergraduate. They included a study of Ptolemy's *Geographia* on northern Britain. It was therefore no surprise that, despite a third in honour moderations (1922) and a second in *literae humaniores* (1924), he was awarded the Gilchrist scholarship to the British School at Rome, the Craven fellowship, and a Goldsmiths' senior studentship. His two years in Rome (1924–6), under the benevolent eye of

Thomas Ashby, developed that interest in Roman military architecture and the operations of the Roman army in the field which became his major research interest, although the range of his active work in archaeology would be wider than that of most of his contemporaries. As a young excavator he served his apprenticeship, first under Mortimer Wheeler, at Segontium (Caernarfon) and then in alliance with F. G. Simpson on the Roman works at Cawthorn, Yorkshire.

Richmond's first major work was an outstanding monograph, *The City Wall of Imperial Rome* (1930), illustrated by his own original plans and isometric drawings, a book which was the principal issue of his residence in Rome in 1924–6 and which is still a standard work. In 1926 he was appointed lecturer in classical archaeology and ancient history at the Queen's University, Belfast, a post which allowed him to spend half of each year on the continent or in Britain. Much of his summers he devoted to work on Hadrian's Wall, in conjunction with F. G. Simpson, R. G. Collingwood, and E. B. Birley. In 1930 he was the obvious choice to return to Rome as director of the British School, but two years later ill health caused him to resign. For nearly three years he was without a post, but he put his convalescence to good use, completing and seeing through the press the great work *The Aqueducts of Ancient Rome* (1935), which Thomas Ashby's premature death had left unfinished, and contributing a series of important papers on the western sector of Hadrian's Wall to the *Transactions* of the Cumberland and Westmorland Society.

In January 1935 Richmond was appointed to a lectureship in Romano-British history and archaeology at Armstrong College in Newcastle, part of the University of Durham. In 1938 he married Isabel Little, daughter of John Arthur Little, a woollen merchant in Newcastle upon Tyne; they had one son and one daughter. He remained in Newcastle, with a brief break for war service, until 1956. He was awarded a readership in 1943 and a personal chair in 1950, served a biennium as dean of the faculty of arts, and for several years was public orator. During his twenty-one years at Newcastle, Richmond directed a notable series of excavations, on Hadrian's Wall, at Corbridge, and at Fendoch, Newstead, and Inchtuthil in Scotland. His work at Inchtuthil, in partnership with J. K. St Joseph, continued until 1965, alongside his examination of the Roman fort at Hod Hill (Dorset) until 1958.

In 1956 Richmond had moved to Oxford as the first holder of the chair of the archaeology of the Roman empire with a fellowship at All Souls College. During his time there he trained and inspired many archaeologists who later achieved distinction and held major posts in the subject. In his last years he turned his attention to the Roman siege works at Masada in Israel and at Numantia in Spain. Had time allowed, he planned more work in Spain in the months before his death, though his work and advice for organizations and individuals continued unabated until the end.

Richmond would doubtless have written more, and more substantial, books but for his readiness to accept the countless calls upon his time. He accepted invitations from societies great and small; as he never drove a car, his travels could be protracted. When he visited one local society in the west country, he was met at a rural halt and driven to his destination by a pony and trap—this in 1960. He was a very dignified and eloquent public speaker, his addresses being notable for the elevation of their style, spoken deliberately as though he was seeking the exact word to match his meaning—even when the text had already been written out. But he could also lecture without notes and hold audiences in a spell. In private he would relax, full of fun and with a twinkle in his eye; there could be no greater contrast between his public and private images. A devout Anglican, he frequently attended chapel in All Souls.

Richmond's major books included *Roman Britain* (1947) and the first volume of the Pelican History of England on the same subject (1955), reissued in 1963. He edited three successive editions of John Collingwood Bruce's *Handbook to the Roman Wall* (1947, 1957, and 1966). At the time of his death he had completed a revised second edition of *The Archaeology of Roman Britain* by R. G. Collingwood, seen through the press by D. R. Wilson and published in 1969. His excavations at Hod Hill were published in 1968, those at Inchtuthil in 1985. But the great bulk of his original writings appeared in the publications of archaeological societies, particularly in *Archaeologia Aeliana* (Society of the Antiquaries of Newcastle upon Tyne) and the *Transactions* of the Cumberland and Westmorland Antiquarian and Archaeological Society, the *Proceedings of the Society of Antiquaries of Scotland*, and the *Journal of Roman Studies*. His major public lecture series included the Rhind lectures in Edinburgh (1933), the Riddell memorial lectures in Newcastle (1948), the Ford lectures in Oxford (1951), and the Gray lectures in Cambridge (1952). The Riddell lectures were published in the stimulating monograph *Archaeology and the after-Life in Pagan and Christian Imagery* (1950). The Ford lectures, on Britain in the third and fourth centuries, and the Gray lectures, on the Romano-British countryside, were edited by Professor Peter Salway and published in 1969.

Richmond gave unstinting service to many national and local organizations. From 1944 he served on the royal commissions on historical monuments, England and Scotland, contributing massively to their reports on Roman sites, notably in the English commission's volumes on Essex and York and the Scottish volumes on the county of Roxburgh. Elected a fellow of the Society of Antiquaries in 1931, he served as director of the society in 1959–64 and president from April 1964 until his death. No fellow had the interests of the society closer to his heart. He was also a pillar of the Society for the Promotion of Roman Studies, of which he was president in 1958–61. He was elected FBA in 1947 and received honorary doctorates from Edinburgh, Belfast, Leeds, Newcastle, Manchester, and Cambridge, and was a member of the German Archaeological Institute. He also served as president of the Society of Antiquaries of Newcastle and of the Bristol and

Gloucestershire Archaeological Society. He was appointed CBE in 1958 and knighted in 1964.

Ian Richmond was the most accomplished Roman archaeologist of his time and was recognized as such wherever the subject is pursued. He was as adept in reassessing earlier discoveries as in prosecuting new research aims. As an excavator he had the precious gift of visualizing how the Roman army would lay out its structures on a given site, so that his excavations could be carried out with unmatched economy of effort. His knowledge of Roman architecture and of the sculpted reliefs on the columns of Trajan and Marcus Aurelius, and on the triumphal monument at Adamklissi (Romania), added to his close familiarity with the literary sources, often caused his hearers to wonder whether he had not personally witnessed the Roman army at work. His writings were as notable as those of Francis Haverfield, his predecessor in the mastery of Romano-British archaeology, for their elegant style and for the care with which they were composed. He died at his home, 18 Farndon Road, Oxford, on 5 October 1965; he was survived by his wife.

ERIC BIRLEY, rev. MALCOLM TODD

Sources E. Birley, *PBA*, 52 (1966), 293–302 · *Journal of Roman Studies*, 55 (1965) · *The Times* (6 Oct 1965) · personal knowledge (1981, 2004) · *CGPLA Eng. & Wales* (1965)
Archives AM Oxf., notebooks, corresp., papers, photographs | Bodl. Oxf., letters to O. G. S. Crawford
Likenesses W. Bird, photograph, 1965, repro. in Birley, *PBA* · photograph, repro. in *Journal of Roman Studies*
Wealth at death £11,949: probate, 3 Dec 1965, *CGPLA Eng. & Wales*

Richmond, Legh (1772–1827), Church of England clergyman and writer, was born at Liverpool on 29 January 1772, the son of Henry Richmond (d. 1806), physician, and Catherine (1736–1819), daughter of John Atherton of Walton Hall, near Liverpool. The father, at one time fellow of Trinity College, Cambridge, practised as a physician at Liverpool, and afterwards at Bath. Legh Richmond was named after his grandfather, who was rector of Stockport from 1750 to 1769 and married Mary, eldest daughter of Henry Legh of High Legh.

Richmond's early education was impeded by an accident in childhood which rendered him permanently lame. After some time spent at Reading, where he was placed, in 1784, in care of a Mr Breach, and at a school at Blandford in Dorset, he entered Trinity College, Cambridge, in 1789, becoming a scholar on the foundation in the same year. At Cambridge he obtained considerable proficiency in the practice and theory of music. His health was weak, and he took an *aegrotat* degree as BA in 1794; he resided in Cambridge until 1797, collecting material for a book he intended to publish on the theory and history of music.

Richmond was ordained deacon in June 1797 and took his MA in July of the same year. On 22 July he married Mary Chambers (d. 1873), only daughter of James William Chambers, of Bath; they had twelve children. After his marriage he moved to the Isle of Wight and took up the

Legh Richmond (1772–1827), by William Finden, pubd 1833 (after Slater)

curacies of Brading (where he lived) and Yaverland on 24 July. He was ordained priest in February 1798.

Shortly afterwards Richmond first adopted those strictly evangelical views with which his name was thenceforth associated. He attributed the change to the influence of William Wilberforce's *Practical View of Christianity*, which led him to examine thoroughly the writings of the British and foreign reformers. While in the Isle of Wight, too, he collected, from local experiences, materials for his three famous tales of village life, 'The Dairyman's Daughter', based on the conversion of Elizabeth Wallbridge, 'The Young Cottager', and 'The Negro Servant'. Richmond wrote out the stories in 1809, after leaving the Isle of Wight, and they were all originally contributed by him, under the signature Simplex, to the *Christian Guardian* between 1809 and 1814. Their simple pathos and piety (Richmond refused to fictionalize or embellish the stories) won them instant popularity, and they were reprinted by the Religious Tract Society in 1814 under the general title of *The Annals of the Poor*. Of *The Dairyman's Daughter*, which Richmond greatly enlarged after its first publication, two editions of 20,000 copies each were printed in 1816. The book was translated into French, Italian, German, Danish, and Swedish, and it obtained a very wide circulation in America. It was calculated that in the lifetime of the author the number of copies printed in the English language alone amounted to 2 million. In 1822 Richmond revisited the Isle of Wight, and was present at the erection of memorials to the cottagers whom he had commemorated. (The cottage of the second tale's heroine, 'Little Jane', became a tourist attraction.) Although its cloying sentimentality can be distasteful to modern readers *Annals of the Poor* remains a significant evangelical publication.

After eight years spent in the Isle of Wight, and having refused Hannah More's invitation to accept the curacy of Cheddar, in the spring of 1805 Richmond became assistant chaplain to the Lock Hospital in London. Thenceforth the permanent chaplain, Thomas Fry, afterwards rector of Emberton, near Newport Pagnell, was his closest personal friend. But Richmond's stay in London was short. On 30 July 1805 he was inducted into the rectory of Turvey in Bedfordshire, in succession to Erasmus Middleton. He commenced his residence in the following October. At Turvey he speedily became popular as a preacher. Clergymen of ability holding evangelical views were rare, and many residents in neighbouring towns and villages attended his church. In the matter of parochial work he is largely remembered as an organizer of village benefit or friendly societies, agencies which he was among the earliest clergymen to initiate and encourage.

As Richmond's reputation extended, his services as a preacher were sought after beyond his own parish. He interested himself deeply in the establishment of the great evangelical societies like the British and Foreign Bible Society, the Church Missionary Society, and the Society for Promoting Christianity among the Jews. He lent all of them powerful aid, and frequently arranged extended and successful preaching tours in order to collect money for them. He acted for a time as joint secretary of the Religious Tract Society.

In 1806 Richmond undertook the editorship of a series of selections from the writings of the English reformers, in order to bring the principles of the Reformation more prominently before the public. The substance of the writings of William Tyndale, Nicholas Ridley, Hugh Latimer, Thomas Cranmer, John Hooper, John Bradford, John Jewell, and others was thus presented to English readers in eight large octavo volumes, which were published, at intervals between 1807 and 1812, under the general title of *Fathers of the English Church*. The outlay was considerable, and the venture proved unremunerative. In 1814 Richmond was with some difficulty relieved by his friends of heavy pecuniary embarrassments. *Fathers of the English Church* has since been recognized as an important work which 'must receive some of the credit for that return to the Reformed doctrines which characterized Anglican theology influenced by evangelicalism during the first quarter of the nineteenth century' (Lewis). Richmond also investigated and reported on Ann Moore, the 'fasting woman' of Tutbury (1813), and wrote some verse.

In 1814 the duke of Kent, who sympathized with Richmond's literary and religious views, appointed him his chaplain. Richmond also met at Portsmouth the Russian emperor Alexander whom he thanked for his interest in the Bible Society. In 1818 and 1820 he made preaching tours in Scotland on behalf of the religious societies with which he was connected. During 1820 he visited the island of Iona, which, although abounding in ruins of cathedrals

and churches, lacked a church of any kind and had no resident Christian minister. Richmond earnestly exerted himself to remove this anomaly, and raised a considerable sum of money. But the duke of Argyll, who owned the island, took the matter into his own hands, and built a church, minister's house, and school. Richmond's fund was consequently expended in establishing a free library for the island.

The death in 1825 of Richmond's younger son Wilberforce, at Turvey, was immediately followed by the loss of his eldest son, Nugent, who died at sea on his way home from India. These bereavements affected Richmond's health, and he died, probably of consumption, at Turvey on 8 May 1827. He was buried in Turvey church, where an epitaph was placed to his memory. Eight children survived him. Memorials of all of them were erected in Turvey church.

In 1833 Richmond's friend Thomas Fry published *Domestic Portraiture*, a description of Richmond's principles, as exemplified in his education of his family, and principally relating to his sons Wilberforce and Nugent.

G. F. W. MUNBY, *rev.* CLARE L. TAYLOR

Sources T. S. Grimshawe, *The life of Legh Richmond* (1828) · D. M. Lewis, ed., *The Blackwell dictionary of evangelical biography, 1730–1860*, 2 vols. (1995) · A. G. Newell, 'Early evangelical fiction', *The Evangelical Quarterly*, 38/2 (April–June 1966), 81–98
Likenesses W. Finden, line engraving, pubd 1828 (after Slater), NPG; repro. in T. S. Grimshawe, *A memoir of the Rev. Legh Richmond*, 9th edn (1837) · W. Finden, stipple engraving, pubd 1833 (after Slater), NPG [*see illus.*] · J. Collyer, line engraving (after R. Livesay), BM

Richmond, Nathaniel (1723/4–1784), landscape gardener and surveyor, was baptized on 8 December 1732, aged eight, at Christ Church, Spitalfields, London, the son of Joseph Richmond (*fl.* 1710–1760) and his wife, Mary (*fl.* 1710–1732). Nothing is known of his background, education, or early career, but by 1754 he was married to Susanna Richmond (*fl.* 1730–1806) and resident in Rickmansworth, Hertfordshire. In 1754 he began working with the landscape gardener Lancelot 'Capability' Brown. It is likely that he worked on Moor Park, Rickmansworth, supervising works for Brown until 1759. He had six daughters and two sons, but the two sons and a daughter died during 1757 and 1758. His second daughter, Mary, married Joseph Rose junior, the renowned plasterer, at St Marylebone on 15 December 1774.

In 1760 Richmond moved to Lisson Grove, Marylebone, where he leased property including a nursery, later run by his associate, Alexander Cunningham. His first independent commission was the modernizing of Marden Park, Surrey, for Sir Kenrick Clayton, bt, which he commenced in 1759. Further commissions followed, and in May 1763 his plan for Danson Park, Bexley, seat of John Boyd, was commented on favourably by Joseph Spence, the literary anecdotist and friend of Alexander Pope. From 1763 to 1769 major works at Shardeloes, Buckinghamshire, seat of Sir William Drake, were undertaken under his direction by John Hencher (Hensher, Henshaw), who later worked with Richmond at Saltram, Devon, on behalf of

John Parker in 1767–74. In 1765 he prepared a plan for improvements at Himley Hall, Dudley, for John Ward, first Viscount Dudley. At Danson, Shardeloes, and Himley, Richmond designed extensive lakes featuring unusual pincer-like lakeheads. At Shardeloes he naturalized the earlier formal layout by a substantial felling of timber.

At Saltram, Richmond also proposed designs for the greenhouse, which were carried out by the local builder, Stockman. His designs for walled gardens, pleasure grounds, and greenhouses form a notable element of his works. At Audley End, Essex, he prepared drawings in 1769 for the walled garden and greenhouse for Sir John Griffin Griffin. He made pleasure grounds at Badminton, Gloucestershire (1776–82); Gorhambury, Hertfordshire (date unknown); Hasells Hall, Hertfordshire (1766–8); Hitchin Priory, Hertfordshire (1764–75); and Lamer, Hertfordshire (1782–4). At Lamer, Humphry Repton was called in to complete the work, and in his red book of 1792 said: 'The pleasure ground has been made with so much good taste by Mr. Richmond that I should advise no alteration in what is already done' (Repton, 'Lamer').

At Lamer, Repton was critical of Richmond's drives and approaches generally, arguing that 'they are all circuitous and consequently generally neglected' (Repton, 'Lamer'). Repton made similar comments at Hewell Grange, Worcestershire, where Richmond had advised in 1770. Repton had nevertheless sketched Richmond's work (1773–8) at Beeston Hall, Norfolk, in 1781, and in 1788 wrote to Norton Nicholls, who admired Richmond's work at Shardeloes, that, 'the works of Kent, Brown and Richmond' were his 'places of worship' (Strand, 27). Later Repton criticized Richmond's work as 'technical and executive', though he continued to consider 'the late Mr. Richmond as the only person since the immortal Brown whose ideas were at all correct on the subject' (ibid., 28).

Horace Walpole admired Richmond's improvements at Lee Priory, Kent, when he visited in 1780. He wrote that 'Mr. Barrett has much improved the place under the direction of Richmond, Scholar of Browne, & has widened a little stream into a pretty River' (*Walpole Society*, 76–7). Richmond also advised at other sites, including Harleyford Manor, Buckinghamshire; Compton Place, Sussex; Stoke Park, Buckinghamshire; Terling Place, Essex; and Woodbury and Wratting Park in Cambridgeshire.

Richmond's contribution to the evolution of the urban villa garden can be seen in his pleasure grounds. He worked on a number of London town houses: these included Cremorne House, Chelsea; as well as the residences of John Walter at Battersea Rise and John Grimes at Teddington. It may be in this sphere that he most influenced Repton and others. It is not known when or where Richmond died but he was buried at St Marylebone on 28 February 1784. His wife and daughters inherited his possessions and the proceeds of his leasehold estate in Lisson Grove. DAVID A. BROWN

Sources Humphry Repton, 'Lamer' Red Book, 1792, priv. coll. · Drummonds Bank, account ledgers, 1754–1784, archives of Royal Bank of Scotland, London · Hoare's Bank, account ledgers, 1754–1784, archives of Hoare's Bank, London · R. W. King, 'Joseph Spence of Byfleet [pt 3]', *Garden History*, 8/3 (1980), 44–65, 77–114, esp. 87–9 · parish register, Rickmansworth, 1754–60, Herts. ALS · St Marylebone rate books, deed 456, 1760–84, LMA · will, PRO, PROB 10/2938/BP/99 · D. Jacques, *Georgian gardens* (1983), 84–5, 112, 113f, 134 · [J. Penn], *An historical and descriptive account of Stoke Park* (1813), 43 · C. Grimston, *A history of Gorhambury* (1821), 83 · D. Strand, *Humphry Repton* (1962) · baptismal register, Spitalfields, London, Christ Church, LMA, microfilm X24/1 · H. Walpole, 'Horace Walpole's journals of visits to country seats', *Walpole Society*, 16 (1927–8), 9–80, esp. 76–7

Archives Bexley local history library, Danson Park estate plan · Dudley local history library, Himley estate plan · Essex RO, Audley End estate records

Wealth at death see will, PRO, PROB 10/2938/BP/99

Richmond, Thomas (1771–1837), miniature painter, was born at Kew, Surrey, on 28 March 1771, the younger son of Thomas Richmond (1740–1794), originally from Bawtry, Yorkshire. His father was groom of the stables to the duke of Gloucester and proprietor of the Coach and Horses inn at Kew, and his mother, Ann Bone, was a cousin of the miniature painter George *Engleheart (1750–1829). Thomas Richmond consequently became Engleheart's pupil and also studied at St Martin's Lane Academy, London. He exhibited miniatures at the Royal Academy from 1795 to 1829, many of them in a style close to that of Engleheart but somewhat coarser. He practised from a studio at 42 Half Moon Street, Mayfair, Westminster, from 1800 to 1829 but also worked for a time from Portsmouth, and he appears to have established a large clientele of naval and army officers. As well as painting miniatures from life he also appears to have made copies after portraits by Richard Cosway and Engleheart, possibly for the royal family. He also copied in miniature many of the portraits by Sir Joshua Reynolds in royal collections. Although his miniatures were denigrated by the critic G. C. Williamson at the beginning of the twentieth century (Williamson, 2.37), they have been more favourably assessed in recent years, and he has been classed as 'a good artist who drew with strength and vitality' (Foskett, 627).

Richmond married, some time before 1802, Ann Coram (1772–1860), with whom he had two sons who both became artists. The elder, Thomas Richmond jun. (1802–1874), was a portrait painter in oils and watercolours who practised in Sheffield and London, exhibiting at the Royal Academy and the Society of British Artists from 1822 to 1860. He visited Rome with his brother George in 1840 and there made John Ruskin's acquaintance. The younger, George *Richmond (1809–1896), was a highly successful portrait painter in miniature, oils, watercolours, and crayons and was the father of the artist Sir William Blake Richmond (1842–1921).

Thomas Richmond died in London on 15 November 1837 and was buried in Paddington churchyard, near the grave of the actress Sarah Siddons. He was survived by his wife. ALBERT NICHOLSON, *rev.* V. REMINGTON

Sources private information (1896) · *Exhibition of miniatures by George Engleheart, J. C. D. Engleheart and Thomas Richmond* (1929), 7 [exhibition catalogue, V&A] · S. Edwards, *Miniatures at Kenwood: the Draper gift* (1997), 188 · D. Foskett, *Miniatures: dictionary and guide* (1987), 311, 313, 373, 627 · B. S. Long, *British miniaturists* (1929), 362 · L. R. Schidlof, *The miniature in Europe in the 16th, 17th, 18th, and 19th*

centuries, 2 (1964), 674 · G. C. Williamson, *The history of portrait miniatures*, 2 (1904), 37 · Graves, *RA exhibitors*
Likenesses T. Richmond, portrait, 1802; Sothebys, 28 Feb 1991, lot 349

Richmond, Sir William Blake (1842–1921), painter, was born at 10 York Street, London, on 29 November 1842, the second son of the painter George *Richmond (1809–1896) and his wife, Julia (1811–1881), daughter of Charles Heathcote *Tatham (1772–1842), architect. His second name and the choice of Samuel Palmer as his godfather shows that George Richmond destined this son from birth to follow in his artistic footsteps. The family home was a gathering-place for leading figures in the artistic community, including John Ruskin and J. E. Millais. Due to ill health William was educated at home, where he enjoyed the personal tutelage of Ruskin and the organist Edmund Kynvett. He developed a precocious artistic talent and a lifelong love of music. However, the handsome and wilful boy suffered under the harsh discipline of his father, and in the winter of 1857 he ran away from home with the equally unhappy More Palmer, Samuel's eldest son. The boys were caught by police, who had been alerted by their fathers, and were dragged home in ignominy. Richmond was thereafter prevented from seeing More, until, four years later, his friend lay dead. Gradually he forgave Samuel Palmer for his harshness, and both Palmer and Edward Calvert schooled the young artist in the idyllism prevalent in the early work of the Ancients, the brotherhood of artists who had flourished at Shoreham in Kent in the 1820s.

In 1858 Richmond entered the Royal Academy Schools where he won two silver medals, exhibiting his first portrait, of his brothers Walter and John (priv. coll.), at the Royal Academy show of 1861; it was there, and at the British Institution, that he exhibited various Pre-Raphaelite portraits, often of children, culminating in his outstanding conversation piece of Alice Liddell and her two sisters, *The Sisters* (exh. British Institution, 1865; priv. coll.). This has remained his masterpiece in portraiture. In 1866 his career shifted to Rome, where, for three years, he studied the old masters. His journey abroad was partly due to a domestic tragedy: on 21 October 1864 he had married Charlotte Foster (1841–1865), niece of the musician John Hullah, but she died from consumption on 13 December of the following year, having infected her husband with the disease and leaving him broken-hearted. The warmth and artistic inspiration of Rome contributed to Richmond's partial recovery. Under the influence of the landscape painter Giovanni Costa, and Frederic Leighton, the Royal Academy's budding classicist, he soon directed his artistic allegiance away from Pre-Raphaelitism to a form of classicism tempered, initially, by the mysticism of the Ancients and later by the aestheticism of Albert Moore, his fellow pupil at the Royal Academy Schools.

In 1869 Richmond exhibited again at the Royal Academy, showing *The Procession of Bacchus at the Time of the Vintage* (priv. coll.), a large classical processional scene influenced by Leighton but marked by the intensity of the

Deutsch-Römer, a group of German artists working in Rome. Paintings similar to theirs, such as *The Bowlers* (exh. RA, 1871; Downing College, Cambridge) and *The Lament of Ariadne* (exh. RA, 1872; Wigan metropolitan borough council), were severely criticized by traditional critics as un-English, having been inspired by continental classical friends. A relapse in health drove Richmond, in 1870, to Algeria. Here, thanks to the care of his second wife, Clara Richards (d. 1916), daughter of William Richards of Cardiff, whom he had met in Rome and married on 30 November 1867, he achieved a complete recovery.

On their return to England, accompanied now by their two children, it was evident that the young family would need accommodation outside York Street. Richmond purchased Beavor Lodge in the green riverside pastures of Hammersmith, where he remained for the rest of his life. The cost of rebuilding and adding a studio forced him back into portrait painting. Introductions made in Italy led to commissions for society portraits, such as the successfully aesthetic image of Lady Frederick Cavendish (exh. RA, 1871; Holker Hall, Lancashire), and his unappreciated likeness of the princess of Wales (exh. RA, 1873; Royal Collection). This earned Queen Victoria's disapproval, probably contributing to Richmond's failure to be elected an associate of the Royal Academy in 1876, the same year in which he exhibited his intensely atmospheric landscape *Near Via Reggio where Shelley's Body was Found* (exh. RA, 1876; Manchester City Galleries). Fortunately the Grosvenor Gallery, an exhibition venue more sympathetic to the aesthetic movement, opened in London in 1877. Richmond discontinued exhibiting at the Royal Academy until 1887, when his associateship of that body was assured for 1888.

At the Grosvenor Gallery further monumental mythological paintings were shown: the classically severe *Electra at the Tomb of Agamemnon* (exh. 1877; Art Gallery of Ontario, Toronto); *Sarpedon* (exh. 1879; Vancouver Art Gallery, British Columbia); and *An Audience in Athens* (exh. 1885; City of Birmingham Museum and Art Gallery), painted after Richmond's two extensive tours of Greece in 1882 and 1883. In 1880 at the same venue he showed *The Song of Miriam* (priv. coll., Australia), painted in the aesthetic manner using a lighter colour scheme. Various portraits and *The Bath of Venus* (exh. New Gallery, London, 1891; Aberdeen Art Gallery) were conspicuous for their abandonment of his traditional darker colours. In 1885, 1886, and 1887 he exhibited three mythological studies of the male nude, a daring subject in the 1880s: *Orpheus Returning from the Shades* (diploma work, Royal Academy of Arts), *Hermes* (exh. Grosvenor Gallery, London, 1886; priv. coll.), and *Icarus* (exh. Grosvenor Gallery, 1887; priv. coll.). They were not to everyone's taste: Mrs Douglas Freshfield, a sitter for one of Richmond's aesthetic portraits, described *Icarus* as 'most vile' (Reynolds, *William Blake Richmond*, 195). His masterpiece, the magnificent *Venus and Anchises* (Walker Art Gallery, Liverpool), depicting Venus's progress through the wintry wilderness turning winter into spring, was shown at the New Gallery in 1899. In 1879 and 1889 two life-sized sculptures were exhibited: *An Athlete* (exh. Grosvenor Gallery, 1879; St Peter's Square, Hammersmith, London) and *The Arcadian Shepherd* (des.); these and his *Memorial to Gladstone* of 1906 (Hawarden church, Flintshire) show no mean talent as a sculptor.

However, Richmond's success during his lifetime rested largely upon his portraiture. He first depicted pampered Victorian children, then glamorous, languid, and sensuous hostesses—the goddesses of society—such as Lady Mary Carr-Glyn (exh. Grosvenor Gallery, 1882; priv. coll.), the Countess Grosvenor (1888; priv. coll.), Viscountess Hood (exh. RA, 1888; priv. coll.), Mrs Ernest Moon (exh. RA, 1888; Tate collection), and Miss Muriel Wilson (exh. RA, 1899; Ferens Art Gallery, Hull). Like John Singer Sargent after him, he excelled as the portraitist to the 'Souls' for whom he could also paint Byronic male likenesses such as the portraits of George, thirteenth earl of Pembroke (exh. Grosvenor Gallery, 1887; Wilton House, Wiltshire), and Charles, fifth Lord Lyttelton (exh. Grosvenor Gallery, 1880; Hagley Hall, Worcestershire). He also depicted eminent statesmen, ecclesiastics, scientists, and artists, attributing to each the due solemnity, grandeur, vision, or artistic panache which might be appropriate to that sitter. He became a good friend of W. E. Gladstone, visited the monastery of Montecassino in Italy with him, and stayed at Hawarden Castle in Wales; he drew a memorial sketch of Gladstone's face just after his death. Richmond's portrait of Prince von Bismarck (exh. RA, 1888), which was instrumental to his participating in international exhibitions in Germany, is lost, but two likenesses of Gladstone (1867; exh. Grosvenor Gallery, 1881–2) exist at Hawarden Castle (though his portrait of Gladstone for Christ Church, Oxford, was turned down by the college); Charles Darwin's portrait (exh. Grosvenor Gallery, 1880) is in the department of zoology at the University of Cambridge; Andrew Lang's (exh. Grosvenor Gallery, 1884) is at the Scottish National Portrait Gallery, Edinburgh; and a likeness of William Morris (1882), two of William Holman Hunt (exh. Grosvenor Gallery, 1880 and 1900), and one of Robert Louis Stevenson (1886) are in the collections of the National Portrait Gallery, London. Richmond's portrait of Robert Browning (exh. Grosvenor Gallery, 1882) is at Waco, Texas, while that of Arthur Evans (exh. RA, 1907) is in the Ashmolean Museum, Oxford.

Richmond was also a master of the small oil landscape, painted directly from nature; many scenes are of Italy, where he travelled during most summers of his adult life. They earned him a little money in his later life when exhibited at the Fine Art Society in 1912 and 1914. He also designed two major sets of stained-glass windows, at Holy Trinity, Sloane Street, London (1908–10), and St Mary's Church, Stretton, Derbyshire (1896–7), while his only extant fresco design (1893–4) is that for Christ Church, Cheltenham, Gloucestershire. Other executed frescoes, along with his stained-glass windows in St Paul's Cathedral in London, have been destroyed.

Richmond's charm and erudition helped him towards achieving academic rewards: he held the Slade professorship at Oxford (1879–83) when Ruskin fell ill, and he was later awarded the honorary degrees of DCL at Oxford in 1896 and LLD at Cambridge. He became a Royal Academician in 1895 and was created KCB in 1897. During his later years he lectured widely on the somewhat divergent topics of art and of coal pollution and wrote three books: *Assisi: Impressions of Half a Century* (1919), illustrated with reproductions of his landscape paintings; *The Silver Chain* (1916), a novel; and *Democracy—False or True?* (1921). However, the crowning achievement which distinguishes him from the other polymaths of the Victorian Olympian tradition is his monumental decorative scheme in mosaic executed in St Paul's Cathedral.

The history of the decoration of St Paul's is one of English indecision: the high church attempted to enrich the cavernous interior while the low church tried to frustrate such efforts. In 1891 George Frederick Bodley, who had constructed the now demolished altar and reredos, invited Richmond to prepare cartoons for mosaic decoration of the apse and choir. These were accepted and Richmond duly commissioned to undertake the work. He chose the firm of Messrs James Powell of Whitefriars to produce the tesserae and, with a team of English workmen, to execute his designs in line with the production methods which had been used in the Byzantine churches he had visited in tours of Ravenna, Rome, and Palermo. Initially he attempted, unsuccessfully, to erect mosaic sections in his own studio at Hammersmith; having mastered the production techniques himself, he realized that future work had to be done *in situ*. The subject matter chosen was Christ in majesty, the creation, and related scenes from the Old Testament.

By 1895 much of the commissioned decoration, in a mixture between Byzantine and aesthetic styles, was in place and Richmond, voted further funds through the parliamentary intervention of W. E. Gladstone, set about decorating the aisles and eventually under the quarter-domes. By 1899 much of it was completed, but the recently knighted academician suddenly found himself exposed to a vicious attack in the newspapers criticizing the style and workmanship of the new mosaics. The low church combined with a powerful political lobby, architectural purists, and progressive art students such as Augustus John to spearhead their objections to the 'Romanizing' of Christopher Wren's classical masterpiece. With the Second South African War looming, funds dried up, and any prospect of extending decorative work into the nave was cancelled. The zenith of Richmond's creative career thus ended in ignominy.

In an attempt to reassert his threatened position in the art world, in 1900–01 Richmond mounted a vast one-man exhibition at the New Gallery, but popular taste, rejecting Victorian academia, had moved on to post-impressionism. Richmond, a large, bearded, ebullient man, fought a fierce rearguard battle against these new trends, earning himself the reputation of a political and artistic reactionary which, to this day, has hampered the overdue rehabilitation of his reputation. A damaged hand weakened his later paintings and, after the accidental death of his wife Clara in 1916, he retired into obscurity at

Beavor Lodge. Towards the end of his life—influenced by his friend Sir Hubert Parry—he began to compose music, an occupation which, along with writing, was less strenuous to his weakening heart than was painting. Richmond died at Beavor Lodge on 11 February 1921 and was buried alongside his wife at Chiswick, in the parish churchyard, on 16 February. He left four sons, including Herbert William *Richmond, and a daughter (one son having predeceased him in 1896), who soon sold the family home for demolition to make way for the construction of the A4.

SIMON REYNOLDS

Sources S. Reynolds, *William Blake Richmond* (1995) • S. Reynolds, *A companion to the mosaics of St Paul's Cathedral* (1994) • A. M. W. Stirling, *The Richmond papers* (1926) • [H. L. Lascelles], 'The life and work of Sir W. B. Richmond', *Christmas Art Annual* (1902) [whole issue] • W. B. Richmond, *Assisi: impressions of half a century* (1919) • W. B. Richmond, *The silver chain* (1916) • *The Times* (14 Feb 1921) • *Art Journal*, new ser., 10 (1890), 193–8, 236–9 • A. L. Baldry, 'Sir W. B. Richmond, KCB, R. A. 1901', *Art Magazine*, 146–50, 197–203 • Gladstone, *Diaries* • *DNB*

Archives Hammersmith and Fulham Archives and Local History Centre, London, corresp. • RA, corresp. and papers | BL, letters to W. E. Gladstone, Add. MSS 4459–4522 • JRL, letters to M. H. Spielmann • priv. coll., diary

Likenesses G. Richmond, oils, 1856, priv. coll. • W. B. Richmond, self-portrait, oils, 1880–83, priv. coll. • G. Phoenix, chalk drawing, 1893, NPG • F. Salisbury, oils, 1902, Art Workers' Guild • J. S. Sargent, charcoal drawing, 1910, priv. coll. • F. Salisbury, oils, 1913, priv. coll. • Elliott & Fry, cabinet photograph, NPG • Moffat, cabinet photograph, NPG • R. T., wood-engraving, NPG; repro. in *ILN* (5 May 1888) • R. W. Robinson, photograph, NPG; repro. in *Members and associates of the Royal Academy of Arts* (1891)

Wealth at death £9838 17s. 7d.: probate, 18 April 1921, *CGPLA Eng. & Wales*

Richson, Charles (1806–1874), educational reformer, was born at Highgate, Middlesex, the son of Richard Richson, a merchant of Clerkenwell, London. He became an usher in a school in Durham. In 1838, at an unusually late age, he entered St Catharine's College, Cambridge, graduating BA in 1842 and MA in 1845. He was ordained in 1841, when he became curate at Preston parish church. He moved to Manchester in 1843 to be clerk-in-orders at the collegiate church, later the cathedral. He held this position until December 1854, when he was appointed a canon residentiary of the cathedral and rector of St Andrew's, Ancoats, Manchester. Subsequently he was also subdean of the cathedral and a proctor in convocation.

For nearly thirty years Richson was one of the most prominent men in the public life of Manchester, especially devoting himself to education and sanitary reform. He was secretary of the Church Education Society founded in 1843 to support Anglican schools in the city following the defeat of Sir James Graham's factory bill. He was active in establishing the Manchester commercial schools, which long held a leading position among such institutions. His experience of running church schools for the poor soon convinced him that voluntary effort alone was inadequate to provide elementary schooling for all children. In 1848 he followed W. F. Hook, the vicar of Leeds, in advocating free schools funded by local rates. Three years later he was the instigator and principal organizer of the Manchester and Salford Committee on Education, which promoted a parliamentary measure to enable the inhabitants of the two boroughs to levy a rate to support schools. The bill, which countered an earlier proposal of the National Public School Association in favour of non-denominational schools, was referred in 1852 to a select committee, to which Richson gave evidence, and proceeded no further. He took a conciliatory approach towards the advocates of secular education, holding discussions with representatives of the rival association, including Richard Cobden and William Mckerrow, and succeeded in finding common ground between two bodies, reinforced at a joint meeting at the Manchester Free Trade Hall in 1857. In all essentials the ideas worked out at Manchester in this period formed the basis for organizing elementary education in England and Wales, and were embodied in W. E. Forster's Education Act of 1870. One of Richson's last acts in this connection was the drawing up of an important report (February 1870) for the convocation of York on primary education. His efforts on behalf of sanitary reform were almost equally vigorous, and with a few friends he founded the Manchester and Salford Sanitary Association in 1853.

Richson wrote a large number of pamphlets on popular education, several lesson-books on drawing and writing, papers on decimal coinage and the ruridecanal organization of dioceses, and some occasional sermons, including a remarkable one, the *Observance of Sanitary Laws* (1854), showing how modern public health legislation was foreshadowed by injunctions in the Old Testament on cleanliness, removal of waste, and healthy housing. Some of his papers were printed in the *Transactions of the Manchester Statistical Society*. Richson was married to Selina Sparke, daughter of Samuel Chambers of Brixton, Surrey. He died, after a long illness, on 15 May 1874, at his house, 31 Shakespeare Street, Ardwick, Manchester, and was buried at Birch church, near that city. His wife survived him; they had no children.

C. W. SUTTON, rev. M. C. CURTHOYS

Sources Boase, *Mod. Eng. biog.* • Venn, *Alum. Cant.* • *Manchester Courier* (16 May 1874) • *Manchester Guardian* (18 May 1874) • S. E. Maltby, *Manchester and the movement for national elementary education, 1800–1870* (1918) • *CGPLA Eng. & Wales* (1874)

Wealth at death under £3000: probate, 10 Sept 1874, *CGPLA Eng. & Wales*

Richter, Christian (1678–1732), miniature painter, was born in Stockholm, Sweden, the son of Hans Davidson Richter (d. 1695), the assessor of the Goldsmiths' corporation there, and Brita Bengtsdotter Selling. He came from a family of artists, and his brothers included the landscape painter Johann Richter and the medallist Bengt Richter, who visited England for a short time. Vertue (who referred to the latter as Rechter or Rector) recorded 'Medals in Silver … made of a Club of Several Gentlemen in London Sweeds. &c and english Gent … done by … Rechter. a Sweed … related to the limner' (Vertue, *Note books*, 4.108). Christian Richter's father had intended to enter him on the goldsmiths' lists but died in 1695 before this was done. His mother entered his name that same year, however, and he appears to have worked for his relative Frantz Boll. He was discharged as a journeyman in

1698, after less than three years, and with his brother Bengt went to study medal engraving with Arvid Karlsteen. About this time he took up miniature painting, and may have learnt to paint with Karlsteen (who is known occasionally to have painted miniatures) or possibly with Elias Brenner, the leading Swedish miniaturist of his day. Nisser noted that Richter's miniature of the Stockholm merchant Samuel Worster (1701) 'betrays a very great capacity' (Nisser, 165). Richter next visited Berlin and then proceeded to Dresden, where he had good introductions from Karlsteen. There he modelled a wax portrait of Augustus II, although his hope of an appointment at the court of Saxony remained unfulfilled, and he left for London.

Vertue notes that Richter arrived in England in 1702, having spent over two years in Dresden. A certificate dated 21 May 1702, probably intended for the passport authorities, confirms, however, that he was still in Sweden in 1702, and if his stay in Dresden lasted two years he could not have arrived in London until 1704. There he met his compatriots the painters Hans Huysing and Michael Dahl, and the enamellist Charles Boit. 'Mr Huysing … retaining much of the manner of Mr Dahl his Master … came to England in 1700. He was born at Stockholm—and in his youth Mr. Richter the limner. was companions' (Vertue, Note books, 3.44). Richter's skill in producing small limned copies of Dahl's and Huysing's oil paintings would undoubtedly have further promoted their reputations, while at the same time Vertue noted that Richter was:

> recommended to Mr Dahl. his countryman who encouraged him & promoted him all he cou'd by which means he became really an excellent Master coppying from several of our best painters, Vandyke Lilly Kneller Dahl. & others, & drawing from the life in a very just & good manner really better than any other of his contemporaries. (ibid., 25)

Of his copies Daphne Foskett noted that 'these are faithful replicas, but he had his own style and, therefore, earned his place as a first rate miniaturist' (Foskett, 627). Vertue observes 'His Manner of Painting very tender & Curious. His tincts had a great variety his pencil regular and neat. His lines of drawing very just & touch't with freedom' (Vertue, Note books, 3.63). A miniature dated 1719 (V&A) of Dr John Radcliffe, benefactor of the University of Oxford, who died in 1714 is a copy of a portrait by Kneller, which Dahl also copied (see Nisser, no. 19, p. 139 and pl. 59, and no. 122, p. 37). Five miniatures by Richter were exhibited in Edinburgh in 1965, including one of Sir James Thornhill (1718), another of John Churchill, first duke of Marlborough (1714), and one of Matthew Prior. Others remain in private collections, including one of Lady M. Harley, after Dahl. Commenting on the difficulties experienced by another foreign artist, 'Zurich', in attempting to establish himself in London in 1714–15 Vertue stated that he 'coud not rise in reputation equal to his Meritt' because of those 'established in reputation and merit, as Mr Bernard Lens. Mr. Rechter [sic]. Mr Zinke enamaller.' (Vertue, Note books, 3.76). These three artists dominated the market in London for small paintings in watercolour on vellum or ivory, and in enamel on metal.

At some point, presumably after this date, Richter succumbed to a disfiguring illness. While Richter was still alive Vertue noted only that 'his nose fall'n by some accident in ye Gardens of Venus made him look't on with a suspicious Eye, & did much prevent his publick appearance' (Vertue, Note books, 3.25). After his death Vertue recorded that Richter:

> had been many years in a bad state of health from an ill Curd Venereal distemper. which had fallen his nose & scarryfid his face which much depress'd his fortune & disperited his undertakings he seldom therefore appeared in public.

He added that 'tho' this blemish in his countenance appeared. he was Naturally a well meaning modest man' (ibid., 64). No longer presentable to his clients Richter ceased to paint from life, and copying became his only livelihood. The contemporary taste for collecting 'heads' of notable figures in English history brought him further commissions. He made at least two copies of Samuel Cooper's famous miniature of Cromwell, one of which is in the Wallace Collection, London; the other was formerly in the collection of Daphne Foskett.

Vertue also noted of Richter, late in his career, that:

> finding laterly that Enamelling was much encouraged & liked by Persons of fortune & Nobility he therefore set about the practice of it wherein tho' a begginner he succeeded so well that in time he might have arrivd to great perfection. (Vertue, Note books, 3.64)

Before this could happen, however, Richter 'dyd in Brewer Street near Golden Square, the second week of Nov. 1732' and was buried on 18 November 1732 in St James's churchyard, Piccadilly (ibid.). Enamels by Richter are rare; predominantly a copyist's art, enamelling would presumably have expanded his market. Further examples of his work are in the Victoria and Albert Museum and the National Portrait Gallery, London. Nisser's catalogue of Richter's works, published in 1927, remains the most comprehensive guide to his work. KATHERINE COOMBS

Sources Vertue, Note books · W. Nisser, Michael Dahl and the contemporary Swedish school of painting in England (1927) · DNB · D. Foskett, Miniatures: dictionary and guide (1987)

Richter, Hans [formerly Johann Baptist Isidor] (1843–1916), conductor, was born on 4 April 1843 at Raab, Hungary, the sole survivor of the four children of Anton Richter (1802–1854), an organist and choirmaster, and Josefine Czasensky (1822–1892), an opera singer and singing teacher. When his father died Richter was sent to Vienna as a choirboy in the Imperial Chapel and then to the conservatory. He graduated in 1862, joined the Kärthnerthor theatre as a horn player, and in 1866 was sent to Wagner to copy the score of Die Meistersinger. In June 1868 he assisted at the opera's première, and his musical versatility even enabled him to replace an indisposed singer at a performance. For a year he conducted in Munich, but in August 1869 he was sacked by King Ludwig for refusing to conduct Wagner's Das Rheingold (the staging was poor). Instead he went to Brussels to conduct the première there of Lohengrin. In 1871 he became music director at the Pest Opera, where he exerted a new musical discipline and raised standards. He

Hans Richter (1843–1916), by Barraud, pubd 1888

stayed until 1875, when he went to Vienna. On 27 January 1875 he married Mariska von Szitanyi (1854–1926), a singing pupil, and by 1882 they had six children. In the period 1875 to 1900 Richter increasingly dominated the musical life of Vienna as music director of the Vienna Philharmonic, as first Kapellmeister at the court opera, as Kapellmeister at the court chapel, and as conductor of the Gesellschaft der Musikfreunde from 1884. He gave world premières of symphonies by Brahms and Bruckner and Tchaikovsky's violin concerto, and championed Dvořák, who dedicated his sixth symphony to the conductor.

Meanwhile, Wagner's festival at Bayreuth began in 1876 with the first staging of *The Ring* cycle, which Richter conducted under the composer's supervision. To recoup its financial losses, Wagner's London supporters organized a festival at the Royal Albert Hall in 1877, when the composer's conducting so confused the orchestra that Richter took over most of the programmes, and had great success with both players and public alike. He returned in 1879 to conduct the first of what became the annual Richter Concerts, which for twenty-three years took place in the summer and/or autumn at St James's Hall and (after 1893) the Queen's Hall. His programmes were dominated by Wagner and Beethoven—the season usually concluded with the 'Choral' symphony—and orchestra and chorus were reconstituted annually, though they invariably had the same personnel. During these visits he toured with the orchestra throughout Britain. He was a fastidious orchestral trainer and a hard taskmaster, whose ear and eye missed nothing; such musical discipline and lack of rostrum showmanship had hitherto rarely been encountered. Because of Richter's reputation in and influence upon the musical life of London and Vienna, it became vital for the careers of solo instrumentalists and singers to appear under his baton and for composers to get their new works performed by him. Richter duly obliged with compositions by Parry, Stanford, Mackenzie, Cowen, and Elgar, whose *Enigma Variations* were first heard in June 1899. From 1885 to 1909 he led the Birmingham triennial festival, and in 1900 conducted Elgar's *Dream of Gerontius* there. In 1904 he gave a London Elgar festival, an unprecedented tribute to a living composer. After his own Richter Concerts ended in 1902 he formed a close association with the new London Symphony Orchestra, which he conducted in its first concert in June 1904 and in his own last concert, at Eastbourne in April 1911.

Richter loved the music of Wagner, whose operas from *Rienzi* to *The Ring* he conducted in both Vienna and London. From 1888 to 1912 he conducted either *Die Meistersinger* or *The Ring* at Bayreuth, and he gave the first *Die Meistersinger* (1882) and *Tristan und Isolde* (1884) in England. In 1903 he conducted at Covent Garden in the first of many German seasons, culminating in 1908 and 1909, when he gave *The Ring* in English, hoping (in vain) to develop an English National Opera. He took over the Hallé Orchestra in 1897, moving to Manchester in 1900 from Vienna, and introduced Strauss, Sibelius, Bartók, Debussy, and Glazunov to his programmes. He retired to Bayreuth in 1911 where he died on 5 December 1916. He was buried there on the 7th.

Despite Richter's gruff manner, his players and audiences alike held him in awed respect and genuine affection. His impact on British concert life was explosive, for his expectations of playing standards and demands for accurate orchestral scores and parts were unprecedented. Nineteenth-century conductors, often regarded by contemporary critics as mere time-beaters, were generally also composers or performers, but Richter, with his prodigious memory, his talent for playing every musical instrument except the harp, and his ability to make his players give of their best, concentrated solely on conducting and, although he made no recordings, built for himself an enduring international reputation.

CHRISTOPHER FIFIELD

Sources C. G. Fifield, *True artist and true friend: a biography of Hans Richter* (1993) · O. Strobel, 'Hans Richter', Bayreuth · private information (2004)
Archives BL, letters to Percy Pitt · U. Leeds, Brotherton L., Thompson MSS
Likenesses F. G. Papperitz, oils, 1885, Richard Wagner Gedenkstatte, Bayreuth · Barraud, photograph, pubd 1888, NPG [see illus.]

Richter, Henry James (1772–1857), artist and philosopher, was born in Newman Street, St Marylebone, Middlesex, on 8 March 1772. He was the second son of Mary Haig and John Augustus Richter, a native of Dresden, an artist, engraver, and scagliolist, well known for his works in imitation of marble. A brother, John *Richter (1769?–1830), was a prominent radical politician, and shared the reform views of John Horne Tooke, with whom he was committed to the Tower in 1794. Another brother, Thomas, was a director of the Phoenix Life Insurance Company. Richter was educated at Dr Barrow's school, Soho and St Martin's Library School, London. About 1787 he received tuition in art from his neighbour Thomas Stothard, with whom he remained a close friend, and through whom he became an intimate of William Blake. In 1788 he produced his first illustrations (to Shakespeare's plays), and first exhibited paintings, showing two landscapes at the Royal Academy, where he exhibited for many years. He became a student of the Royal Academy Schools in 1790, at which time he probably began his thorough study of anatomy.

Throughout the 1790s Richter worked mainly as an illustrator, demonstrating skills as both draughtsman and engraver; projects included editions of Samuel Richardson's *Sir Charles Grandison* and *Clarissa Harlowe* (with others, both 1793), Samuel Johnson's *Lives of the English Poets* (with others, 1797), and J.-H. Bernardin de Saint-Pierre's *Paul and Virginia* (1799). In 1809 Richter began to exhibit at the Associated Artists in Water Colours, Bond Street, becoming a member in 1810, and president in 1811–12. His most popular work at this stage was the genre subject *A Brute of a Husband*, though he also established himself as a literary painter, with depictions of such characters as Don Quixote and Falstaff, and became one of the few notable artists to paint historical subjects in watercolour. With the dissolution of the Associated Artists in Water Colours in 1812 he was elected a member of the Society of Painters in Oil and Water Colours, though he resigned his membership in December of the same year, and until 1820 was represented on its walls only as an exhibitor. (In that year the society returned to its original form as the Society of Painters in Water Colours.)

Richter was a pioneer in painting from nature, in both practice and theory. In 1812 he painted the oil *Christ Giving Sight to the Blind*, in bright sunlight on the roof of his house in Newman Street; the work was purchased by the trustees of the British Institution for 500 guineas and presented to the New Church, Greenwich. A second version, attempting to improve on its truth to nature, was exhibited four years later. Then, in 1817, he published the pamphlet *Daylight: a recent discovery in the art of painting, with hints on the philosophy of the fine arts, and on that of the human mind, as first dissected by Emmanuel Kant*. His more general ideas, including his approach to colour and use of models of his compositions in clay or wax, influenced other painters, notably the miniature painter James Holmes. *Daylight* combined his artistic interests with his study of metaphysical philosophy. (He was probably the author of the article entitled 'On Mr Hume's account of the origin of the idea of the necessary condition' (*Monthly Magazine*, 1797).) He also wrote part of the article 'Metaphysics' in the *Encyclopaedia Londonensis* and a paper, *German Transcendentalism* (1855). He was translating a metaphysical work by J. S. Beck, a former student of Kant, at the time of his death.

In 1821 Richter was again elected to the Society of Painters in Water Colours, though his membership and the frequency of his exhibits varied through the decade. But from 1829 until his death he was both a member and a frequent exhibitor. The subjects of his most ambitious paintings of this later phase were taken from Shakespeare. His work became highly popular through reproductive engravings and, from 1828, through the illustrations he produced for annuals such as the *Forget-me-Not*; one painting, *The School in an Uproar*, was even printed on pocket handkerchiefs. Examples of his work are in the British Museum.

Richter died at his home, 101 Lisson Grove, London, on 8 April 1857, leaving a widow, Charlotte Sophia. His daughter, Henrietta, was a successful amateur portrait painter.

L. H. Cust, rev. David Wootton

Sources A. T. Story, *James Holmes and John Varley* (1894) • Mallalieu, *Watercolour artists*, 2nd edn, vol. 1 • J. Gage, *A decade of English naturalism, 1810–1820* [1969] [exhibition catalogue, Norwich Castle Museum, 15 Nov – 15 Dec 1969, and V&A, 15 Jan – 28 Feb 1970] • M. Hardie, *Water-colour painting in Britain*, ed. D. Snelgrove, J. Mayne, and B. Taylor, 2nd edn, 3 vols. [1967–8] • H. Hammelmann and T. S. R. Boase, *Book illustration in eighteenth-century England* (1975) • Hume Archives, www.utm.edu/research/hume [administered by Jim Freser of the University of Tennessee at Martin] • S. M. Bennett, *Thomas Stothard: the mechanisms of art patronage in England, c. 1800* (1988) • G. E. Bentley, *The stranger from paradise: a biography of William Blake* (2001) • *Art Journal*, 19 (1857), 162 • M. H. Grant, *A dictionary of British landscape painters, from the 16th century to the early 20th century* (1952) • B. Stewart and M. Cutten, *The dictionary of portrait painters in Britain up to 1920* (1997) • D. Foskett, *Miniatures: dictionary and guide* (1987) • administration, PRO, PROB 6/233, fol. 337r

Archives V&A NAL, corresp.

Wealth at death £300: administration, PRO, PROB 6/233, fol. 337r

Richter, John (1769?–1830), radical and businessman, first appears in documentary records as a 21-year-old clerk in a London banking house in 1790. His is one of several tantalizingly shadowy careers in the radical politics of London in the decades between the French Revolution and the Great Reform Act of 1832. Like many of his associates, Richter lacked the means to give his political activities the time he might have wished, or to achieve the public prominence won by those more aristocratic scions who dabbled in metropolitan reform politics. He joined the London Corresponding Society (LCS) in 1792 and became an associate member of the Society for Constitutional Information. Both organizations were dedicated to the principles of an extended suffrage and an incorruptible constitution. In May 1794 he was arrested for high treason along with other leading members of the LCS, but was released without trial after Thomas Hardy and John Horne Tooke were acquitted.

At a public meeting of the LCS on 7 December 1795 Richter proposed a petition to the king for the defence of popular liberties. During the period of repression that followed, when most radicals retreated from open political activity, he presumably continued to make his living as an accountant or bank clerk, re-emerging onto the political scene as a member of the Westminster election committee in 1807. He and Francis Place together wrote an account of the 1807 election in which Sir Francis Burdett was returned as radical MP for Westminster. In 1808 he was a speaker at the Crown and Anchor tavern where the radicals celebrated the anniversary of their victory, and later in the same year he drafted public resolutions in support of Spanish independence: 'a people who will fight for their liberties are alone worthy of the friendship of a free nation' (Hone, 167).

Consistently involved in the organizing committee of Westminster radicals chaired by the glass manufacturer Samuel Brooks, Richter took a stern line with Burdett's fellow MP Lord Cochrane, exacting pledges on his radical principles in return for the committee's support at the election of 1812. In addition to fighting for constitutional freedoms at home and abroad, Richter's own practical version of radicalism led him to support two models of self-help and *laissez-faire* in which the Westminster election committee worked with others to achieve advancement for working people. One of these was the West London Lancasterian Association, which promoted schooling for artisans' children on the principles of Joseph Lancaster, and with which Jeremy Bentham was briefly associated. The association foundered on the issue, among other things, of whether or not to charge fees; the radicals' line being (as recounted by Francis Place) that any form of charity was demeaning, and therefore parents, however poor, ought to pay moderate fees. Richter also acted as secretary to the Association of Master Manufacturers, chaired by a fellow member of the Westminster committee who had also belonged to the LCS, Alexander Galloway. In 1814 they won abolition of the Elizabethan Statute of Artificers, which had perpetuated protection for skilled artisans in a period when industrial change was making such restrictions onerous to manufacturers. There is no evidence to show that Richter later became involved in the campaign of the mid-1820s to repeal the Combination Acts, which bore much more oppressively on workers' freedoms, but the principles he espoused in the earlier campaign were consistent with an overall guiding rule among his closest associates: to seek legislative freedoms in the workplace as much as in the political and constitutional arena.

By 1816 Richter appears to have been working as company secretary to a sugar refining company: a calling which left him little time for politics, but apparently was not remunerative. At his death in 1830 he left his widow, details of whom are unknown, in distressed circumstances, and Place and Galloway opened a subscription on her behalf.   ALICE PROCHASKA

Sources MSS confiscated from Richter at the time of his arrest in 1794, including an account of the progress of the French Revolution, PRO, TS11/951/3494 · BL, MSS of Francis Place (1771–1854), Add. MSS 27807–27850; 35151–35153 · F. Place and J. Richter, *An exposition of the circumstances which gave rise to the election of Sir Francis Burdett for the City of Westminster* (1807) · F. Burdett and W. Godwin, letters, Bodl. Oxf., MS Eng. lett. c. 64, fol. 73; MS Shelley Adds. c. 7, fol. 1 · *The autobiography of Francis Place, 1771–1854*, ed. M. Thale (1972) · J. A. Hone, *For the cause of truth: radicalism in London, 1796–1821* (1982) · D. Miles, *Francis Place, 1771–1854: the life of a remarkable radical* (1988)

Archives PRO, MSS confiscated from Richter

Rickards, Esther (1893–1977), surgeon and socialist activist, was born on 13 July 1893 at 13 James Street, Paddington, London, one of seven children of John Edward Rickards (d. 1903?), veterinary surgeon, and his wife, Annie, formerly Somers. John Rickards had converted to Judaism in order to marry.

Rickards was educated at the Regent Street Polytechnic, London, Birkbeck College, the London school of medicine, and St Mary's Hospital, London, the beginning of a long association with that institution. Although she had originally wished to be a veterinary surgeon like her father women at this time were not accepted into that profession. Consequently she chose medicine as her career, and became MB BS and MRCS LRCP (1920), MS (1923), and FRCS (1924). Rickards was one of the first women to become a fellow of the Royal College of Surgeons, and it was also unusual in this period for a woman to qualify as a master of surgery. In pursuing her medical education Rickards was supported by her only sister Phoebe, a schoolteacher, to whom she was close for her entire life.

Rickards achieved distinction as a medical student and she subsequently developed a particular expertise in gynaecology. Among her early posts were a residency at St Mary's, and as assistant medical officer for the London county council in Paddington. Following the creation of the National Health Service (NHS) she served as a member of the North-West Metropolitan Regional Hospital Board, subsequently as its vice-chairman, and was a governor of St Mary's Hospital, of which she became an honorary consulting surgeon in 1971. She was appointed OBE in 1966.

A defining feature of Esther Rickards's life was her commitment to socialism and a determination to see health care socialized. She retained these beliefs throughout her life, being, for example, a notable opponent of pay beds in NHS hospitals. Her socialism, which she claimed had worked against her in applications to posts at various London hospitals in the 1920s, led her to become a founding member, in 1930, of the Socialist Medical Association—indeed she chaired its inaugural meeting. This organization, which included other prominent socialist doctors such as Somerville Hastings and David Stark Murray, was affiliated to the Labour Party in 1931 and was, at least until 1945, instrumental in shaping Labour's health policy.

Rickards played a prominent part in the association. In addition to her role in formulating some of the association's early policy statements she also helped shape its position on maternal welfare, an important labour movement issue in the 1930s, given the high rate of maternal mortality. As a feminist, in the sense of someone who wanted to improve the condition of women, and as a medical practitioner professionally engaged with the issue, this was something about which Rickards felt very strongly. She was evicted from the gallery of the House of Commons for protesting about a public statement by Lord Cohen of Birkenhead on maternal mortality rates.

In 1928 Rickards became a member, and later alderman, of the London county council. This came under Labour control in 1934 and she was one of a group of Socialist Medical Association activists who played a crucial role in shaping the health policy of what was, at this time, the single largest provider of hospital beds in Britain, and possibly the world. It is evident that municipal politics was one of Rickards's primary concerns. She participated in Labour Party conferences and sat on the party's important public health advisory committee, both of which provided platforms from which to argue her own and the association's case for a socialized medical service.

In character Rickards was, as her professional and political careers might suggest, an extremely powerful personality. Small, bluff, determined, with a strong voice and an ironic sense of humour, she was always determined to get her own way in causes she thought just. This could, however, shade into stubbornness. On one occasion her sister Phoebe received a delegation of Rickards's colleagues seeking her help in overturning a medical decision she had come to and refused to change. At the outbreak of the Second World War, Rickards arrived at her clinic to find a sentry posted, much to her annoyance. The soldier was subsequently removed. A close relative has, understandably, described Esther Rickards as an 'irresistible force' (private information).

There was, however, more to her than simply an obstinate, if dynamic, medical practitioner and politician. Throughout her life she was interested in dogs, and in her retirement, which she spent in Windsor, she devoted herself to raising cocker spaniels. At the time of her death she was chairman of the London Cocker Spaniel Society. She founded the Windsor dog show, was pleased when the monarch became a patron, and travelled the world as a dog show judge. Esther and Phoebe were also great lovers of the music of Haydn and Mozart, and claimed to have the largest single collection of recordings of these composers' works in Britain. Both regularly attended concerts in Queen Elizabeth Hall. Such was her integration with the community in Windsor that Rickards, although a non-practising Jew, made kneelers for the parish church. This illustrates her interest in embroidery, further manifested by her work on the new presidential gown of the Royal College of Surgeons. Rickards never married, although she had at least one suitor as a young woman, and towards the end of her life was looked after by two airline pilots in Windsor. After a full, diverse, and active life, Esther died at the King Edward VII Hospital, Windsor, on 9 February 1977.   JOHN STEWART

Sources private information (2004) · E. H. Cornelius and S. F. Taylor, *Lives of the fellows of the Royal College of Surgeons of England, 1974–1982* (1988) · J. Stewart, *The battle for health: a political history of the Socialist Medical Association, 1930–51* (1999) · b. cert. · d. cert.
Archives U. Hull, Brynmor Jones L., Socialist Medical Association archive
Wealth at death £18,094: probate, 21 April 1977, CGPLA Eng. & Wales

Rickards, Sir George Kettilby (1812–1889), lawyer, was born in London on 24 January 1812, the eldest son of George Rickards of Ripley, Surrey, and Frances, daughter of Samuel Kettilby DD. On 10 July 1823 he was admitted to Westminster School, but left in 1824 for Eton. He matriculated from Balliol College, Oxford, on 6 April 1829, but

was elected scholar of Trinity College in the same year. His poem, 'African Desert', won the Newdigate prize in 1830. He graduated BA in 1833, taking a second class in classics, and proceeded MA in 1836. From 1836 to 1843 he was a fellow of Queen's College. He entered the Inner Temple as a student on 14 November 1831 and was called to the bar on 9 June 1837. He was elected a bencher of the Inner Temple in 1873. In 1851 he was appointed counsel to the speaker of the House of Commons. He was made KCB on resigning that post in 1882. Elected Drummond professor of political economy at Oxford in 1851, he held the chair until 1857, but made little contribution to the subject.

Rickards was twice married: first in 1842 to Frances Phoebe (d. 1859), daughter of John Henry George Lefroy of Ewshott House, Hampshire; second in 1861 to Julia Cassandra (d. 1884), daughter of Benjamin Lefroy, rector of Ashe, Hampshire.

Rickards was the author of several works, including some lectures on political economy and on translation of Virgil's *Aeneid* into blank verse. For the last seven years of his life he lived at Fyfield House, Oxford. He died suddenly at Hawkley Hurst, Liss, Hampshire, on 23 September 1889.   E. I. CARLYLE, rev. ERIC METCALFE

Sources J. Foster, *Men-at-the-bar: a biographical hand-list of the members of the various inns of court*, 2nd edn (1885), 392 · Foster, *Alum. Oxon.* · *The Times* (24 Sept 1889) · BL cat. · *Old Westminsters*, vols. 1–2 · R. Brent, 'God's providence: liberal political economy as natural theology at Oxford, 1825–1862', *Public and private doctrine: essays in British history presented to Maurice Cowling*, ed. M. Bentley (1993), 85–107 · Wellesley index
Wealth at death £18,113 0s. 6d.: probate, 30 Oct 1889, CGPLA Eng. & Wales

Rickards, Samuel (1796–1865), Church of England clergyman, was the son of Thomas Rickards of Leicester. He matriculated from Oriel College, Oxford, on 28 January 1813, graduating BA in 1817 and MA in 1820. He was a fellow there from 16 April 1819 to 6 October 1822, being contemporary with John Keble and John Henry Newman. He was Newdigate prizeman, 1815, for his 'Temple of Theseus', and English essayist, 1819, for 'Characteristic differences of Greek and Latin poetry'. From 1822 to 1832 he was the curate in charge of Ulcombe, Kent. J. H. Newman, while on a visit to him in September 1826, wrote his well-known verses 'Nature and art', and, during a second visit in October 1827, 'Snapdragon, a Riddle'. In 1832 he was presented by a college friend, Henry Wilson, to the rectory of Stowlangtoft, Suffolk, where he spent the remainder of his life.

Rickards was at first sympathetic to the Oxford Movement, but protested to Newman about Tract 10 and several other tracts. However, he submitted in September 1835 a tract on infant baptism—which was not included in the series—and he supported the publishing of the tracts financially, and paid some of the costs of Newman's church at Littlemore, near Oxford. He was instrumental in the publication of Keble's *Christian Year*, as a duplicate of the manuscript was lent to him by Keble, and, when Keble's own copy was lost in Wales, this was printed. A sound theologian of high character, many of Rickards's clerical brethren looked to him for counsel and guidance during the controversies by which his times were marked. Rickards was the author of *Hymns for Private Devotion for the Sundays and Saints' Days* (1825), *The Christian Householder, or, Guide to Family Prayer* (1830), and other small devotional works, as well as *Poems* (1870). He was known for reading character from handwriting. On 6 October 1821 Rickards married Lucy Maria; they had at least one child (a daughter, Lucy). He died on 24 August 1865 at Stowlangtoft rectory, survived by his wife and daughter.

G. C. BOASE, rev. H. C. G. MATTHEW

Sources *GM*, 3rd ser., 19 (1865), 650 · *Clergy List* (1864) · Foster, *Alum. Oxon.* · *Literary Churchman* (1 Feb 1858), 51 · *The letters and diaries of John Henry Newman*, ed. C. S. Dessain and others, [31 vols.] (1961–) · *N&Q*, 3rd ser., 8 (1865), 249, 357 · *N&Q*, 8th ser., 7 (1895), 149, 454 · CGPLA Eng. & Wales (1865)
Archives Birmingham Oratory, J. H. Newman MSS · Pusey Oxf., letters from J. H. Newman
Wealth at death under £7000: probate, 13 Oct 1865, CGPLA Eng. & Wales

Rickett, Sir Denis Hubert Fletcher (1907–1997), civil servant, was born on 27 July 1907 at Hawthorns, Overton Road, Sutton, Surrey, the second son and youngest of the three children of Hubert Cecil Rickett (1877–1947), a coal merchant, and his wife, Mabel (1875–1971), the daughter of Thomas Gerrard Fletcher. His father was chairman of Rickett, Cockerell & Co. Ltd, coal merchants, and a high sheriff of Surrey. Rickett was educated at Rugby School and Balliol College, Oxford, where he obtained first classes in classical moderations in 1927 and *literae humaniores* in 1929. In the latter year he was elected to a prize fellowship at All Souls College, which he retained for twenty years. Although he was offered a university lectureship in philosophy, and considered an academic career, a growing interest in economics led him in 1931 to join the staff of the newly created Economic Advisory Council, under the chairmanship of John Maynard Keynes. For the next eight years he combined that with academic work in Oxford.

On the outbreak of the Second World War, Rickett entered the permanent civil service and joined the staff of the War Cabinet Office. In 1943 he became private secretary to the minister of production, Oliver Lyttelton, and in 1945 he was appointed personal assistant (for work on atomic energy) to Sir John Anderson, chancellor of the exchequer. After the general election of 1945 Anderson continued to work in government as chairman of the advisory committee on atomic energy, and Rickett remained with him as his personal assistant until 1947. On 22 May 1946 he married (Ruth) Pauline (*b.* 1915), a medical doctor, the daughter of William Anderson Armstrong, solicitor, of South Shields, and formerly the wife of Alexander Duncan Campbell Peterson, educational reformer. They had three children: two sons and a daughter.

In 1947 Rickett joined the treasury as an under-secretary on the overseas finance side. In 1950 he was appointed principal private secretary to the prime minister, Clement Attlee, but when Winston Churchill became prime minister he wished to bring John Colville back into no. 10 as his joint principal private secretary, alongside David Pitblado. Rickett was sent to Washington as economic minister at the British embassy and head of the United Kingdom treasury and supply delegation. In 1955 he returned to the treasury as a third secretary in the overseas finance division, then succeeded Sir Leslie Rowan as second secretary in charge of the overseas finance division, serving in that capacity until his own retirement in 1968. He was made CMG in 1947, CB in 1951, and KCMG in 1956.

Rickett spent the last twenty years of his civil-service career (less the brief interlude in 10 Downing Street) in overseas finance. He became expert in the techniques, procedures, institutions, complexities, and problems of international finance, which came easily to his keen and precise intellect. He was one of the principal advisers on these matters to a succession of chancellors of the exchequer, from R. A. Butler to Roy Jenkins, closely involved in handling the various balance of payments and financial crises between 1955 and 1968, and representing the British government at many international financial meetings. He formed a close and friendly working partnership with Sir George Bolton, the director in charge of overseas finance at the Bank of England, and was widely recognized and respected among the government officials and bankers who made up the international financial community.

After he retired from the treasury, not long after the gold crisis of March 1968, Rickett went back to Washington as vice-president of the International Bank for Reconstruction and Development (the World Bank), where his principal responsibility was to raise money from the richer countries which could subsidize lending to less developed countries. He was also special adviser to the then president of the bank (Robert McNamara), and had particular responsibility for its Far Eastern activities. This appointment made good use of his negotiating skills and of what was by then his very large circle of contacts in the international financial world. On returning to London in 1974 he became a director of Schroder International, an adviser to J. Henry Schroder Wagg & Co. until 1979, and a director of De La Rue until 1977. He finally retired to live in a house in The Close at Salisbury.

Rickett's overriding private interest was music: he was a talented amateur pianist and a keen opera-goer. When Sir John Anderson was invited in 1946 to succeed Lord Keynes as chairman of the Royal Opera House Trust, he stipulated that Rickett (who was still working with him on atomic energy) should become the secretary of the trust. Rickett continued in that position, and then as secretary to the directors of the Royal Opera House Covent Garden Ltd, until 1968, thus establishing a tradition whereby a succession of treasury men acted as secretary to the Royal Opera House board for over fifty years.

With his high-powered intelligence, a considerable physical presence, and his great experience in international finance, Rickett could seem to some of the ministers whom he served, and even to colleagues who did not know him well, to be intimidating, not to say formidable;

this was enhanced by the air of detachment that he culti- vated. In private, however, and with friends and col- leagues with whom he felt comfortable, he was very good company: easy, relaxed, and entertaining. He died of heart failure at Milford House Nursing Home, Milford Mill Road, Salisbury, Wiltshire, on 26 February 1997, survived by his wife and their three children.

ROBERT ARMSTRONG

Sources *Daily Telegraph* (6 March 1997) · *The Times* (10 March 1997) · *WWW* · Burke, *Peerage* · personal knowledge (2004) · private information (2004) · b. cert. · m. cert. · d. cert.
Archives BLPES, corresp. with Lady Rhys Williams · Bodl. Oxf., corresp. with Attlee
Likenesses photograph, 1959, repro. in *Daily Telegraph* · photograph, repro. in *The Times*
Wealth at death £126,906: probate, 13 Oct 1997, *CGPLA Eng. & Wales*

Rickett, Josephine. *See* Doll, Josephine (1926–1988).

Rickett, Sir Raymond Mildmay Wilson (1927–1996), educationist, was born on 17 March 1927 in Fulham, Lon- don, the only son and younger of the two children of Mild- may Louis Rickett (1894–1967), barrister's clerk and later civil servant, and his wife, Winifred Georgina Ann, *née* Hazell (1900–1974). He spent his formative years at Whit- stable in Kent and was educated at Faversham grammar school. He suffered from a severe hearing defect which affected his early education and dogged him throughout his life, but such was his character and determination that he effectively overcame it. He left Faversham grammar school in 1946 and then served in the Royal Navy, on mine- sweepers, for his two years' national service. An ex-servicemen's grant enabled him to study at Medway Technical College, Chatham, between 1948 and 1953; there he took a London external degree in chemistry, fol- lowed by two years' research. From 1955 to 1959 he stud- ied in the USA at the Illinois Institute of Technology, where he was awarded a PhD in physical chemistry. While there he met and on 1 February 1958 married Naomi Nish- ida (*b*. 1930), a state-registered nurse of American- Japanese descent. They had two daughters, Kimiyo Megan (*b*. 1960) and Vanessa Reiko (*b*. 1963), and a son, Guy Masami (*b*. 1961).

Following his return to the United Kingdom, Rickett held a series of lecturing posts, at Plymouth College of Technology (1959), Liverpool College of Technology (1960– 62), West Ham College of Technology (1962–64), and Wol- verhampton College of Technology, where he was head of department (1965–6). In 1967 he was appointed vice- principal of Sir John Cass College. Following its amalgam- ation with the City of London College to form the City of London Polytechnic (later to become London Guildhall University), he was appointed vice-provost of the new institution (1969–72). In this post he enabled the City of London Polytechnic to become the first institution in the country approved to run a modular degree.

In 1972 Rickett was appointed director of Middlesex Polytechnic, a post he held until his retirement in 1991. What he found at Middlesex was a medley of six different further education institutions on twenty-three separate

sites spread over 100 square miles across three London boroughs, which had just been designated a polytechnic. During his period of tenure he moulded it into one of Brit- ain's leading polytechnics. His background (he was the first of his family to enter higher education) and his experience in the United States inspired him with three major objectives: first a belief that there should be oppor- tunities for wider participation in higher education (through part-time courses); second, to adopt modular degrees based on credit accumulation (enabling students to cover a number of different subjects in one degree and to accumulate credits which could be transferred to other higher education institutions); and third to achieve inter- national educational links. As director of Middlesex Poly- technic and also through the posts he held in the wider field of higher education, he had the opportunity to put these ideas forward. It was his belief that because of the existing system society wasted very valuable educational potential.

When Rickett retired in 1991 all three of his major objectives had been achieved. Under his leadership Middlesex took a leading role in introducing modular degrees, which were subsequently adopted by nearly all the other polytechnics. Many part-time courses were introduced, which enabled mature students to benefit from higher education. Middlesex also entered into agree- ments with a number of foreign higher education institut- ions, which enabled joint European degree courses to be established in conjunction with French, Spanish, and Ger- man institutions. In 1990 Rickett was awarded the Uni- lever prize for 'successful innovation and development in the setting up and improvement of undergraduate and post graduate programmes which require students to achieve operating competence in a European language, complimentary to a vocational education in the field of industry and commerce' (private information, Middlesex University press office). In December 1989 the *Times Higher Education Supplement* described him as an outspoken dir- ector who 'has observed—and often influenced—the Cinderella-like transformation of Polytechnics from poor cousins to … the higher education success story of the 1980s'.

Rickett opposed the binary system of higher education which distinguished between universities and the poly- technics, and fought to get equal funding for equal levels of work. He was twice chairman of the committee of the directors of the polytechnics, from 1980 to 1982 and again from 1986 to 1988. While in the post he advocated allow- ing polytechnics to award their own degrees and be known as universities. He had the satisfaction of seeing this achieved the year after he retired. After retiring from Middlesex he became the last chairman of the Council for National Academic Awards (1991–3), an organization which he had served for many years as a member of sev- eral committees, chairman of its policy committee and of its subcommittee on early entry qualifications, and a member of the advisory board for the accredited accumu- lation scheme. He was a member of the UNESCO advisory committee on higher education in Europe (1974–83) and was chairman of the UK advisory committee of the European Community Action Scheme for the Mobility of University Students, which provided grants for students to study in other EC countries (1988–91). He also had strong links with the British Council, being a member of the council board (1988–91), chairman of its committee for international co-operation in higher education, and a member of its inter-university and polytechnic council for higher education overseas and of its Gulf States committee. He was a member of the Council for Industry and Higher Education (1985–91), of the higher education review group for Northern Ireland (the Chilver committee) (1978–82), of the working group on management of higher education in the maintained sector (the Oakes committee) 1977–8), of the board of the National Advisory Body for Public Sector Higher Education (1982–7), and of the Open University council (1983–93). Among his outside interests were being a governor of the Hosting of Overseas Students Organisation and of the Yehudi Menuhin Live Music Now Scheme. He was chairman of the Mid Kent Healthcare Trust from 1992 until his death.

Rickett powerfully influenced the direction of higher education for twenty years. Kenneth Clarke, secretary of state for education from 1990 to 1992, described him as:

> one of the major advocates of the ending of the binary system, with its illogical separate status and funding systems for polytechnics and universities. He played quite a part in persuading me that this division was no longer relevant to a sensible system of higher education in this country.

In 1988 the German government awarded him the officer's cross of the order of merit of the Federal Republic of Germany. He was knighted for his services to education in 1990, having been made CBE in 1984. He died at the London Hospital on 6 April 1996 following a heart attack, and his ashes were interred in the cemetery of All Saints' Church, Whitstable, Kent; he was survived by his wife and three children.   LESLIE DUBOW

Sources personal knowledge (2004) · private information (2004) · *The Times* (2 May 1996) · *Daily Telegraph* (19 April 1996) · *The Independent* (22 April 1996) · *Times Higher Education Supplement* (Dec 1989) · WWW
Likenesses photograph, repro. in *The Times*
Wealth at death £45,091: probate, 30 July 1996, *CGPLA Eng. & Wales*

Ricketts, Charles de Sousy (1866–1931), artist and art collector, was born on 2 October 1866 at Maison Turretine, Grand Quai, Geneva, Switzerland, the only son of Charles Robert Ricketts (1838–1883), a retired English naval officer, and Hélène Cornélie de Soucy (1833/4–1880), daughter of Louis, marquis de Soucy. His mother was musical; his father, a painter of marine subjects. Ricketts spent his infancy in Lausanne and London, and his youth at Boulogne and Amiens in France, and was educated by governesses, except for a year at a French boarding-school near Tours. After his mother's death at Genoa in 1880, Ricketts, hardly able to speak English, returned to London with his father and his younger sister Blanche (1868–1903). Too delicate to attend school, he spent the next two years reading voraciously and 'basking' (*DNB*) in museums; he thus escaped being moulded along conventional

Charles de Sousy Ricketts (1866–1931), by Charles Haslewood Shannon, 1898 [*The Man in the Inverness Cape*]

lines. In 1882 he entered the City and Guilds Art School in Kennington, London, where he was apprenticed to Charles Roberts, a prominent wood-engraver. A year later his father died, and Ricketts lived on a quarterly allowance of £25 from his grandfather, Edmund Woodville Ricketts (1808–1895). On his sixteenth birthday he met his lifelong partner, the painter and lithographer Charles Haslewood *Shannon (1863–1937).

Ricketts and Shannon founded an occasional art journal, *The Dial* (1889–1897), which promoted a blend of English Pre-Raphaelitism and French symbolism, reflecting Ricketts's origins. The two artists also began designing and illustrating books, including *Daphnis and Chloe* (1893) and *Hero and Leander* (1894), which were unique in that the designs were cut by the artists who drew them, rather than by a professional engraver. Ricketts also worked for commercial publishers, designing books in an art nouveau style: his most famous were John Gray's *Silverpoints* (1893) and Oscar Wilde's *The Sphinx* (1895).

Meeting a wealthy barrister, Llewellyn Hacon, enabled Ricketts to realize his dream of being a publisher and he set up the Vale Press in 1894. An inheritance of £500 from his grandfather in 1895 was invested in it. For over eighty volumes, mostly reprints of English poetic classics, he designed three fonts and numerous decorations and illustrations. Although influenced by the aesthetic movement and by William Morris, whom he admired, his books are more classical than medieval in style. After a fire destroyed his stock and decorative material in 1899, he lost interest in publishing and closed the press with his *Bibliography of the Vale Press* (1904). Afterwards he designed books for friends such as Katherine Harris and Emma Cooper (who collaborated under the pseudonym Michael Field), and Gordon Bottomley.

Ricketts had already taken up painting and sculpture. Thomas Lowinsky points out how 'his books expressed in their pre-Raphaelitism the English side of his character, whilst his pictures, with their debt to Delacroix and Gustave Moreau, the French' (*DNB*). In the Symbolist tradition, his themes are tragic and romantic, and they focused on key moments in the destiny of his subjects, such as Salome, Cleopatra, Don Juan, Montezuma, and (though Ricketts was a non-believer) Christ, figures he admired for the way they courageously met their fates. Among his best paintings are *The Betrayal of Christ* (1904, Carlisle Museum and Art Gallery), *Don Juan and the Statue* (1905), *The Death of Don Juan* (1911, Tate collection), *Bacchus in India* (c.1913, Atkinson Art Gallery, Southport, Cheshire), *The Wise and Foolish Virgins* (c.1913, priv. coll.), *The Death of Montezuma* (c.1915, priv. coll.), *The Return of Judith* (1919), and *Jepthah's Daughter* (1924, Ashmolean Museum, Oxford). His great scholarship often inhibited his painting, before which he was often hesitant, and some paintings are overworked. His twenty or so sculptures, one of which, *Silence*, was a memorial to Oscar Wilde, are indebted to Rodin's smaller works. Bronzes such as *Orpheus and Eurydice* (Tate collection) and *Paolo and Francesca* (Fitzwilliam Museum, Cambridge) are powerful interpretations of their themes. In 1922 he was elected ARA and in 1928 RA.

In his lifetime Ricketts was probably best-known for his theatre designs. Here, his spontaneity, his sense of design and colour, and his understanding of the theatre united in harmony. His gift for linear arabesque, evident in his book illustrations, is also shown in the finished watercolours he drew from his designs. Among his most important productions were the first English production of Wilde's *Salomé* (1906), which was boycotted by the press; Shakespeare's *King Lear* (1909); W. B. Yeats's *The King's Threshold* (1914); Bernard Shaw's *Don Juan in Hell* (1907) and *Dark Lady of the Sonnets* (1909); John Masefield's *Philip the King* (1914) and *The Coming of Christ* (1928), the success of which initiated the Canterbury festival plays; the D'Oyly Carte Company's production of *The Mikado* (1926); the first production of Shaw's *Saint Joan* (1924), probably his greatest achievement; and Shakespeare's *Henry VIII* (1925). He did theatre work with gusto, often staying up all night to do the designs. The largest public collection of his designs is in the Victoria and Albert Museum, London.

Ricketts's great connoisseurship led to his being offered the directorship of the National Gallery in London, which he refused (and regretted later), to his acting as art adviser to the National Gallery of Canada in Ottawa (1924–31), and to his forming with Shannon a fine collection of French, English, and old master drawings and paintings, Greek and Egyptian antiquities, Persian miniatures, and Japanese prints and drawings. Never well off, they had in the early days made sacrifices to build their collection, which was left to museums, mainly the Fitzwilliam in Cambridge. Ricketts wrote *The Prado and its Masterpieces* (1903) and *Titian* (1910) which, though superseded by modern scholarship, remain among the most evocative books on art in English, and *Pages on Art* (1913), a selection of his articles. He also wrote and designed two collections of short stories, *Beyond the Threshold* (1928) and *Unrecorded Histories*

(1933), as well as *Recollections of Oscar Wilde* (1932), his memoir of the man he considered the most remarkable he had met.

Ricketts's last years were overshadowed by the illness and hostility of Shannon, whose brain was damaged in a fall in 1929. For once, his aesthetic values took second place, and to pay for Shannon's care he sold the Persian drawings for £4000. The strain of the situation and of overwork to escape it contributed to his death from angina pectoris at his home, Townshend House, Albert Road, Regent's Park, London, on 7 October 1931, six years before his partner. A memorial service was held at St James's, Piccadilly, on 12 October, after which he was cremated; his ashes were scattered in Richmond Park, London, and the remainder buried at Arolo, Lake Maggiore, Italy. His estate was valued for probate at £36,283.

Small in stature, Ricketts was 'a man of masterful personality' (*DNB*) and loved to influence people. He could be touchy and belligerent, and was implacably opposed to 'modern art' and especially to the influence of Cézanne. He was witty and a brilliant conversationalist. Although his quick mind and vivacity seemed more French than English, he resided in London. He lived entirely for art, not only for creating, collecting, or writing about it, but also for music and literature, which he read in five languages. When he travelled in Italy, Spain, Greece, Egypt, Tunisia, the USA, Canada, and other countries, it was to study or promote art. Shaw described him as 'the noble and generous Ricketts, who always dealt *en grand seigneur*, a natural aristocrat as well as a loyal and devoted artist' (ibid.).

There is a drawing (1899) and an oil painting (1898) of Ricketts by Shannon in the National Portrait Gallery, London, as well as a head (c.1920s) by Laura Anning Bell. A bust (1902) by Reginald Wells is a good likeness. In 1979 his work was exhibited in 'Charles Ricketts and Charles Shannon: an Aesthetic Partnership' at the Orleans House Gallery, Twickenham, London.   J. G. P. DELANEY

Sources BL, Ricketts and Shannon MSS, Add. MSS 58086–58109 · C. Lewis, ed., *Self-portrait: taken from the letters and journals of Charles Ricketts, R.A.* (1939) · J. G. P. Delaney, *Charles Ricketts: a biography* (1990) · J. Darracott, *The world of Charles Ricketts* (1980) · J. Darracott, ed., *All for art: the Ricketts and Shannon collection* (1979) [exhibition catalogue, Fitzwilliam Museum, Cambridge, 9 Oct – 3 Dec 1979] · T. S. Moore, *Charles Ricketts, R.A.: sixty-five illustrations* (1935) · E. Binnie, *The theatrical designs of Charles Ricketts* (1985) · S. Calloway, *Charles Ricketts: subtle and fantastic decorator* (1979) · J. G. P. Delaney, 'Ricketts, Shannon and his circle', *The last Romantics: the Romantic tradition in British art*, ed. J. Christian (1989), 39–45 [exhibition catalogue, Barbican Art Gallery, London, 9 Feb – 9 April 1989] · *CGPLA Eng. & Wales* (1931) · *DNB* · b. cert. · d. cert. [Hélène Cornélie Ricketts] · m. cert. [Charles Robert Ricketts and Hélène Cornélie de Soucy] · letters to 'Michael Field', BL, Add. MSS 58086–58089

Archives BL, Ricketts and Shannon MSS, Add. MSS 58085–58109 · FM Cam., Ricketts and Shannon collection · NRA, corresp. and papers · Theatre Museum, London, letters · U. Durham L., letters | AM Oxf., Pissarro MSS · BL, letters to Gordon Bottomley · BL, letters to Sir Sydney Cockerell, Add. MS 52746 · BL, letters to Mary, Lady Davis · BL, letters to George Bernhard Shaw, Add. MS 50548 · National Gallery of Canada, Ottawa, Brown MSS · U. Glas. L., letters to D. S. MacColl · V&A NAL, letters to H. Carter | FILM BFI NFTVA, documentary footage

Likenesses C. H. Shannon, lithograph, 1894, Carlisle City Art Gallery, V&A · A. Legros, silverpoint drawing, 1895, FM Cam. · W. Rothenstein, double portrait, lithograph, 1897 (with Shannon), NPG · C. H. Shannon, oils, 1898, NPG [*see illus.*] · C. Ricketts, self-portrait, chiaroscuro woodcut, *c*.1899, FM Cam. · C. H. Shannon, chalk drawing, 1899, NPG · R. Wells, bust, 1902, priv. coll. · G. C. Beresford, photograph, 1903 (with Shannon), NPG · C. Ricketts, self-portrait in group, oils?, *c*.1903, Carlisle City Art Gallery · J. E. Blanche, double portrait, oils, 1904 (with Shannon), Tate collection · F. Dodd, chalk drawing, 1905, BM · M. Beerbohm, caricature, watercolour and pen, 1907, FM Cam. · M. Beerbohm, double portrait, caricature, 1911 (with Shannon), Johannesburg Art Gallery, South Africa · E. Dulac, double portrait, caricature, watercolour and pen, 1914? (with Shannon), FM Cam. · C. H. Shannon, portrait, 1917, Art Gallery and Museum, Leamington Spa · L. A. Bell, pencil drawing, *c*.1920, NPG · E. Dulac, double portrait, caricature, 1920 (with Shannon), FM Cam. · G. C. Beresford, two photographs, NPG · K. Kennet, bronze statuette, Leeds City Art Gallery
Wealth at death £36,283 17*s.* 6*d.*: probate, 16 Dec 1931, *CGPLA Eng. & Wales*

Ricketts, Frederick Joseph [*pseud.* Kenneth J. Alford] (1881–1945), military band conductor and composer, was born on 21 February 1881 at 3 York Terrace, Ratcliff, Stepney, London, the fourth of five children of Robert George Ricketts, a coal merchant, and his wife, Louisa Alford. His mother, who came from Clerkenwell, may have been from a musical family. Ricketts's father died in 1888, and his mother, to whom he was especially close, died in 1895. He received some musical education as a church choirboy, learned to play the piano, and resolved on a career as a military musician. In 1895, having falsely told recruitment officials that he had been born on 5 March 1880 (the lowest age for entry to the military being fifteen), he enlisted in the Royal Irish regiment. He became a cornet player with the band of the 2nd battalion, and between 1895 and 1904 he had several postings, initially serving in Ireland, where his versatility as a musician became well respected.

In 1904 Ricketts entered the bandmaster's class in the Royal Military School of Music at Kneller Hall. He was young to be accepted on this course, but he graduated in 1906, having acquired a solid grounding in music theory to match his flair as a composer and arranger. Immediately after graduating he served for two years on the staff of the school as assistant to the director and as school organist. Ricketts married Annie Louisa Holmes at All Saints' parish church, Tooting Graveney, London, on 5 September 1907. She was the sister of a partner in the Walsh, Holmes & Co. publishing house. The couple had three sons and three daughters.

In 1907 Ricketts left Kneller Hall to become bandmaster of the 2nd battalion of Princess Louise's (Argyll and Sutherland Highlanders) regiment, which was then stationed near Bloemfontein, Orange Free State. He returned to Scotland with the band in 1910, and stayed with the regiment until 1927, when he was commissioned into the Royal Marines as lieutenant, director of music, at the Royal Marines depot at Deal. He took this post in preference to the directorship of the Royal Military School at Kneller Hall. Three years later Ricketts succeeded G. W. E.

Grayson as director of music of the Royal Marines at Plymouth, a post that he held until his retirement through ill health in April 1944.

Ricketts adopted the pen-name Kenneth J. Alford shortly after 1919. It derives from the name of his eldest son, his own middle name, and the maiden name of his mother. Under this name he wrote works in a variety of genres, and—as befitted a military band director—made a substantial number of arrangements. But it is for his eighteen marches that he is best remembered. He had a remarkable gift for this genre: his melodies are catchy, well shaped, and distinctive, and his ability to write for the medium of the military band was faultless. There is little doubt that he was the greatest English composer of marches, and many of his works have become woven into the culture of military band music. Among these the most famous is probably 'Colonel Bogey' (1914), so called (according to his widow) because of the composer's habit of whistling the B♭–G motif in moments of disappointment on the golf course. The fame of this march, particularly after its employment in the film *The Bridge on the River Kwai* (1957, directed by David Lean), has to an extent eclipsed his other great marches, such as 'The Great Little Army' (1916) and 'The Standard of St George' (1930), but his name is remembered each time a band of the Royal Marines performs, because of the adoption of his 'A life on the ocean wave' (1944) as their regimental march.

Many have drawn comparisons between Ricketts and the American march composer, John Phillip Sousa, and with good reason. Sousa published 136 marches, considerably more than Ricketts, but Ricketts's works compare with the very best of Sousa's, and many believe him to be the better composer. He certainly refined a distinctively English mode of composition, with finely detailed scoring and a dignified, even subtle approach to melody.

Ricketts was reputed to be a kindly and generous man, devoted to family life and apparently popular with service personnel of all ranks. The highest rank that he succeeded to was major, and he never received further honours in his lifetime. He died of stomach cancer at his home, 90 Blackborough Road, Reigate, Surrey, on 15 May 1945. Following his death a number of commemorative events were held, and in 1981, to celebrate his centenary, a postal cover was issued by the British Forces Post Office.

TREVOR HERBERT

Sources J. Trendell, *Colonel Bogey to the fore: a biography of Kenneth J. Alford* [1991] · *New Grove* · P. Gammond, *The Oxford companion to popular music* (1991) · www.total.net/~lanced/immscb.htm [International Military Music Society (IMMS), Canadian branch], 12 Oct 2000 [Kenneth J. Alford] · *CGPLA Eng. & Wales* (1945) · b. cert. · d. cert.
Likenesses photographs, repro. in Trendell, *Colonel Bogey* · photographs, Royal Marines School of Music, Plymouth
Wealth at death £3797 14*s.* 4*d.*: probate, 20 June 1945, *CGPLA Eng. & Wales*

Ricketts, Sir Henry (1802–1886), East India Company servant, third son of George William Ricketts and his wife, Letitia (*née* Meldmay), was born at Launceston House, near

Winchester, on 25 March 1802. He was educated at Winchester College and at the East India College at Haileybury, and entered the Bengal civil service in 1821. He married Jane, daughter of General George Carpenter of the East India Company, in 1823. He served initially in the Orissa division, where his linguistic skills and administrative competence distinguished him. He rose rapidly through the ranks, and in 1827 was appointed collector and magistrate of Cuttack district. The next year he was transferred to Balasore to conduct a land revenue settlement. While he was at Balasore, his district was hit by the hurricane and sea-inundation of 1831, which claimed more than 22,000 lives. Ricketts mounted a major relief operation, involving the distribution of food, clothing, cash, and seed for agricultural recovery. However, another hurricane in October 1832 destroyed much of his good work.

Balasore was also in an area known for the political turbulence of its tribal peoples and tributary states. Ricketts conducted a successful campaign against the states of Mayurbhanj and Nilghar. As a result, after only fifteen years' service, he was appointed commissioner of Cuttack in 1836. From here he led operations against the insurgent Gonds of Goomsur and attempted to suppress customs among them of human sacrifice. He was able to capture a leading rebel, Dora Dissoye, and to make some progress in persuading the tribes to abandon their custom, although not without encountering considerable resistance.

In 1840, after a furlough for ill health in England, Ricketts returned to work in the Bengal service. He was posted, first, to Chittagong, where he resettled the land revenue. He was then appointed, in 1849, to the board of revenue in Calcutta. It was as a member of the board that Ricketts's most significant contributions to government in India were made. In 1853, concerned at the decline in the standard of knowledge of native languages among junior civil servants, he designed an examination system to promote improvement. In 1856 he was appointed commissioner for the revision of civil salaries and establishments throughout India. He travelled extensively, interviewing officers at every level, and produced a major and highly controversial report. Not only did he propose plans for a reduction of nearly 1 million rupees a year in costs, but he also strongly recommended that the Indians themselves be given greater opportunities for advancement in the public service. His report, however, coincided with the Indian mutiny, after which British attitudes towards Indians became tainted with suspicion. His recommendations provoked bitter differences of opinion within the government and were never more than partially implemented.

In 1854 Ricketts declined the offer of promotion and transfer to another division as chief commissioner of the Nagpur territory in central India; and in 1858 he declined the offer of the lieutenant-governorship of the North-Western Provinces. He preferred to stay at the heart of government in Calcutta and was made a provisional member of the council at various times between 1854 and 1859. Most notably, in 1857 he resigned his seat in favour of Sir James Outram in order to strengthen the representation of the military on the council. Outram was a soldier whose subsequent role in quelling the Indian mutiny was to be extremely important. Ricketts was reappointed to a later vacancy and reorganized the management of the council's business, creating a quasi-cabinet system of government, which thereafter became firmly established.

In 1859 ill health forced Ricketts to resign the service and to return to England. He was highly praised by the then governor-general, and first viceroy, Lord Canning, who wrote to him: 'Of all the colleagues with whom I have been associated in the public service, either here or elsewhere, I have had none whose earnest, high-minded and able co-operation has been more agreeable to receive than yours.'

In spite of the reason for his retirement, Ricketts lived a further twenty-six years and published many pamphlets on the leading Indian questions of the day, not always supporting the policies of the government of India. He was not made a member of the Council of India but was created a knight commander in the Order of the Star of India in 1866. He died at his home, Oak Hill Grove, Surbiton, on 25 February 1886, and was buried in the churchyard at Twyford, near Winchester, where he had been brought up. He left one son, George H. M. Ricketts CB, who also entered the Bengal service, and three daughters.

Sir Henry Ricketts's career in India was distinguished by a dedication to the welfare of its native peoples, which showed itself particularly in an insistence that British officials should be thoroughly acquainted with their languages and customs. Shortly before his death he expressed the desire that an epitaph to himself, with the words 'He never forgot Balasore and the Ooriahs', should be inscribed on the monument he had put up to his wife, Jane, who had died at Balasore in 1830. The expense of the inscription was borne voluntarily by local Indian officials whose fathers and grandfathers had served with him.

DAVID WASHBROOK

Sources G. H. M. Ricketts, *Extracts from the diary of a Bengal civilian* [n.d., 1912?] · L. S. S. O'Malley, *Balasore* (1907) · L. Cobden-Ramsay, *Bengal gazetteer: feudatory states of Orissa* (1910)
Archives U. Edin., Dalhousie muniments
Wealth at death £20,554 9s. 11d.: administration with will, 21 April 1886, *CGPLA Eng. & Wales*

Ricketts, John William (1791–1835), social activist, the fourth and youngest child of Lieutenant John Henry Ricketts (1767–1792) and his Indian companion, Bibi Zeenut Ricketts (c.1770–1824), was born in October 1791. His father, the eldest son of an English surgeon, served as an engineer officer in the East India Company's army on survey work in Upper Bengal, where John William probably was born, and died on active service in the Carnatic.

Some years after the death of his father John William, together with his two elder brothers and sister, was brought to be educated at the Upper Military Orphanage, Calcutta. It had been founded in 1783 to care for the children of Bengal army officers who died while serving in India. Children of wholly European parentage were sent back to England, but those with Indian mothers were educated at the Calcutta orphanage. The four Ricketts children were baptized, together with the orphans of other officers, at Fort William, Calcutta, on 29 December 1796.

At fifteen Ricketts entered government service as an uncovenanted clerk, a conventional employment at the time for the Eurasian sons of British officers, and was posted in 1807 to Bencoolen in Sumatra. By 1810 he was serving on the staff of the British resident at Amboyna in the Moluccas, recently conquered from the Dutch. A youthful indiscretion, the birth of an illegitimate daughter, Amelia, to Ricketts and Mary Osborn in 1811, was followed soon after by a religious awakening. In 1814 Ricketts met Jabez, son of the Serampore Baptist missionary William Carey, on the latter's arrival at Amboyna. Jabez commended Ricketts, by now secretary of the local Bible Society, to his father for his seriousness and industry, and in 1816 Ricketts decided to abandon government service to become a Baptist missionary. That year, on 24 October, Ricketts married Sarah Catherine Gardiner (1799–1847), the daughter of James Gardiner, a British assistant surgeon of the East India Company, and an unknown Indian mother. She also had been educated at the Upper Military Orphanage, Calcutta. Sarah probably accompanied Ricketts to Murshidabad, where he served for two years as a missionary before ill health forced his return to Calcutta.

Back in Calcutta, Ricketts rejoined government service in the board of customs, and rose to become a deputy registrar. Throughout the 1820s he continued to support Baptist work in Calcutta, and, conscious of the unemployment and poverty already present among the large Eurasian population of the city, energetically promoted projects to provide apprenticeships and wider opportunities of employment for Eurasian youth. To Ricketts the provision of better education was a vital objective if mixed-race prospects were to be improved. The establishment of a school for Calcutta's Eurasian boys in 1823—the Parental Academic Institution—was to be his most enduring achievement. The Parental overcame the financial difficulties of its early years and, renamed the Doveton College following a generous bequest in 1853, survived into the early twentieth century.

Ricketts came publicly to the fore in 1829, when he took up the political grievances of Calcutta's Eurasians and promoted a petition, over the heads of the East India Company, to parliament at Westminster—the so-called East Indians' petition. It sought redress for Eurasian grievances at exclusion from appointments to the East India Company's covenanted civil service and its army, and for a variety of civil disabilities not suffered by British subjects. Ricketts volunteered himself as spokesman for the petition and sailed for England. In 1830 he gave evidence to both houses of parliament and returned the next year to a hero's welcome from the Eurasian communities of Madras and Calcutta, although the petition had failed in its primary purpose of obtaining official acceptance of Eurasians as British subjects. Ricketts, who had taken unpaid leave while abroad, returned to the board of customs and shortly afterwards was appointed a civil court judge (*sadr amin*) in up-country Bengal. He had never enjoyed robust health and died of a fever at Gaya, near Patna, on 28 July 1835. He was survived by seven of his children and his wife, Sarah, who lived in straitened circumstances at Calcutta until her own death in 1847.

John William Ricketts was the first, albeit unelected, spokesman for British India's Eurasian, later termed Anglo-Indian, community. A contemporary portrait shows a slim, dark-haired, and soberly dressed man of medium height. His library reflected his studious habits and religious interests. Although not credited by his contemporaries with charismatic qualities of leadership, Ricketts won respect as, with dogged determination, he pioneered the claims of his community for better education, wider employment, and access to government posts of greater responsibility. 'He was possessed of great moral courage, mental energy, and indomitable perseverance' ('Report of proceedings connected with the East Indians' petition', *Calcutta Review*, p. 76). Ricketts's untimely death left his community with no acknowledged spokesman to take his place. Half a century was to pass before formal Anglo-Indian community associations emerged, to articulate the concerns championed by Ricketts so many years before.

CHRISTOPHER HAWES

Sources 'Report of proceedings connected with the East Indians' petition to parliament', *Calcutta Review*, 11 (1849), 73–90 · 'East Indian education and the Doveton College', *Calcutta Review*, 24 (1855), 288–330 · *Report of proceedings connected with the East Indians' petition to parliament* (1831) · H. A. Stark, *John Ricketts and his times* (1934) · C. J. Hawes, *Poor relations: the making of a Eurasian community in British India* (1996) · J. W. Ricketts, *A series of letters and other matter regarding a scheme for forming a commercial and patriotic association avowedly for the public good of the East Indian community* (1828) · correspondence of Jabez Carey and John Marshman, Regent's Park College, Oxford, India missionary MSS · Doveton College reports, 1872, National Library, Calcutta · reports of the Calcutta Baptist Missionary Society, 1819–29, Regent's Park College, Oxford · E. Abel, *The Anglo-Indian community: survival in India* (1988) · *The Eurasian*, 3/3 (17 April 1909) [BL] · returns of baptisms, marriages, and burials, 1698–1969, BL OIOC · wills, probates, and administrations, 1774–1943, BL OIOC · V. C. P. Hodson, *List of officers of the Bengal army, 1758–1834*, 4 vols. (1927–47) · D. G. Crawford, ed., *Roll of the Indian Medical Service, 1615–1930* (1930) · *The Bengal obituary, or, A record to perpetuate the memory of departed worth*, Holmes & Co. (1851) · BL OIOC, Ricketts Family MSS, MS Eur. C347

Likenesses C. Pote, oils, *c*.1831, All-India Anglo-Indian Association, New Delhi

Wealth at death house at Bancorah; plate, cutlery, glass, household furniture; also library of 225 books; horse and buggy; personal clothing; all left to wife, incl. government pension of Rs50 a month: 1836, Bengal wills and inventories, BL OIOC, L/AG/34/29/57, pt. IV, p. 145; BL OIOC, L/AG/34/27/110, pt. I, pp. 181–8

Rickhill, Sir William (*d.* 1407), justice, was Irish by birth, according to Thomas Walsingham. Some support for this assertion may be found in the fact that he acted as an attorney for the earl of Ormond in 1379, 1380, and 1386, and he also had links with Thomas Morley, marshal of Ireland. In the 1380s, however, he was described as 'of London': he was an executor of William Walworth (lord mayor of London in 1381) who was godson to his eldest son, William, and he was also a friend of John Cheyne, recorder of London, whose son was to be one of his own executors. He had property in London, but his main residence was his manor of Islingham, near Rochester in Kent. By the end of his life he maintained a substantial establishment there, with numerous servants. He also held land in Surrey, the manor of Ditton Camoys in Cambridgeshire, and tenements in Northfleet in Kent, and he acted as feoffee for John, Lord Cobham, a prominent Kentish landowner. Rickhill's connection with Ormond, too, could have arisen from or been strengthened by his position in Kentish society, for Ormond held land in south-east England as well as in Ireland. Rickhill became a king's serjeant in 1383, and served as a justice of the peace in Kent, as a justice of assize and gaol delivery on the south-western circuit, and as a justice delivering Newgate gaol. On 20 May 1389 Richard II appointed him as one of the justices of the common pleas in place of one of the judges appointed by the lords appellant after the Merciless Parliament of the previous year. He was knighted by 1397.

For reasons which are not at all clear, Richard II chose Rickhill in September 1397 to go to Calais, where the duke of Gloucester was imprisoned. According to his own account, which he gave to parliament in two rather different forms in September 1397 and in November 1399, he was woken at midnight on 5 September at Islingham by a king's messenger with a writ dated 17 August ordering him to go to Calais with Thomas Mowbray, earl of Nottingham and captain of the town, and there, on pain of forfeiture, do what would be revealed to him on his arrival. He crossed to Calais on 7 September, and that evening Mowbray handed him another writ from the king ordering him to hold an interview with the duke of Gloucester and carefully report all that he should say to him. The following morning Rickhill was admitted to an interview with the duke in the castle. Before two witnesses, whose presence he insisted upon, Rickhill explained his commission and asked the duke to put what he had to say in writing. Late in the evening of the same day Gloucester, in the presence of the same witnesses, read a confession of nine articles which he then handed to Rickhill. Rickhill asked the duke if he had anything he wished to add, and Gloucester replied that he had omitted one matter. This was that he had told the king during the Merciless Parliament of 1388 that if he wanted to remain king he would have to stop interceding for the life of Simon Burley, who had been sentenced to death by that parliament. Two days later Rickhill returned to England, and took the precaution of obtaining a confirmation, under the great seal, of his commissions and the confession. A few days later Gloucester's death was announced in parliament, and Rickhill gave his account of the writing and delivery of the confession.

On Richard II's deposition Rickhill was arrested for his part in procuring Gloucester's confession and placed in custody in Rochester Castle. At the same time, however, Henry IV reappointed him as a justice of the common pleas, presumably not intending his disgrace to be permanent. The king ordered him to be brought to Lambeth on 18 October 1399 and handed over to the archbishop of

Canterbury. A month later, on 18 November, he was summoned before parliament to account for his part in the events at Calais. He was cross-examined by Walter Clopton, chief justice of the king's bench, and his story this time was more elaborate, and more self-exculpatory, than his account to the parliament of 1397. He now said that he had been greatly surprised by his commission to interview Gloucester, for he believed that the duke was already dead, and that his death had been notified to the people, but Mowbray had assured him that the duke was still alive. Rickhill's account of his interview with Gloucester was substantially the same as the one he had given earlier, but he now stated that at the end of the interview Gloucester asked him to return the following morning. He agreed to do so, but found the gates of the castle barred against him. Rickhill now told parliament that on his return to England he had obtained confirmation of the confession because he feared that the document might be tampered with. Rickhill concluded by pleading that he had done no more than carry out the orders which had been given to him; parliament accepted his account and acquitted him of any wrongdoing.

Rickhill continued his judicial duties in Henry IV's reign until early in the Trinity term of 1407, but was dead by 22 June of that year. In his will he expressed a wish to be buried in Rochester Cathedral. His wife, Rose, survived him, together with four sons and two daughters. His son William (who was not a beneficiary under his will) and another son John (who was a beneficiary) served as members of parliament for Kent in 1420 and 1423 respectively.

ANTHONY TUCK

Sources Baker, *Serjeants* · G. O. Sayles, ed., *Select cases in the court of king's bench*, 7 vols., SeldS, 55, 57–8, 74, 76, 82, 88 (1936–71), vols. 6–7 · A. E. Stamp, 'Richard II and the death of the duke of Gloucester [pt 1]', *EngHR*, 38 (1923), 249–51 · J. Tait, 'Did Richard II murder the duke of Gloucester?', *Owens College historical essays*, ed. T. F. Tout and J. Tait (1902), 193–216 · *HoP, Commons* · 'Annales Ricardi secundi et Henrici quarti, regum Angliae', *Johannis de Trokelowe et Henrici de Blaneforde … chronica et annales*, ed. H. T. Riley, pt 3 of *Chronica monasterii S. Albani*, Rolls Series, 28 (1866), 155–420 · *RotP* · Chancery records · register of Archbishop Arundel, LPL, microfilm in CUL, 1, fols. 243–5

Rickinghall [Rickinghale], **John** (*c*.1355–1429), bishop of Chichester, was ordained acolyte at Ely in 1376, but was probably born on the Bury St Edmunds Abbey manor of Rickinghall, Suffolk; it was certainly to that house that he owed his early career. His first cure, Thorpe Abbots in Norfolk (admitted 13 November 1381), was in Bury's gift. He came to the notice of Bishop Henry Despenser of Norwich, who by 1395 had collated him as dean of the college of St Mary-in-the-Fields in Norwich. In 1399 he sat as Despenser's assessor at the renunciation of heretical opinions by William Chatris of Bishop's Lynn. From 12 July to 17 August 1400 he acted as the bishop's commissary, apparently during the absence of the designated vicar-general (the bishop himself being then in custody). Rickinghall was to bequeath to Thorpe a vestment embroidered with the bishop's arms.

By 1405 Rickinghall was a doctor of theology of Cambridge University and was to serve as its chancellor for an almost unprecedented seven years from April 1415 to February 1422. In 1416 he became master of Gonville Hall, where he was sometimes in residence, until his resignation on 12 July 1426. He strenuously supported the university in its disputes with the town. On 7 May 1421 he and the chancellor of Oxford University petitioned in convocation for improvements in graduate promotion. Three weeks later he was an examiner there of the heretic William Taylor, and convicted him.

Meanwhile, after Bishop Despenser's death in 1406, Rickinghall had obtained the patronage of John, duke of Bedford, and received a handful of appointments in the northern province where the duke was in long-term royal service. In particular, on 5 December 1409 he became archdeacon of Northumberland and a prebendary of York, and on 15 September 1410 chancellor of York Minster; his benefices, which he was licensed to hold in plurality, were worth 250 marks. From his appointment, despite a licence for non-residence, Rickinghall conducted a vigorous campaign against Durham Cathedral priory's claim to archidiaconal jurisdiction over its churches in Northumberland, and its obstruction of his attempted visitation of them in 1410. His sponsorship by Bedford for Durham's rectory of Hemingbrough in Yorkshire in 1412 was perhaps part of a settlement; only on his promotion to the see of Chichester did Durham succeed in its struggle to convert Hemingbrough into a collegiate church. In this campaign he was supported by Archbishop Henry Bowet of York, who had also been in Despenser's service early in his career.

Rickinghall is said to have been in the royal delegation to the Council of Constance, but this requires further proof. Certainly he was abroad in 1424, very likely in attendance on Bedford, whose confessor he was at least between 19 August 1425 and 1428, but clearly with a personal association of much longer standing. His attorney during his absence in 1424 was the Norfolk serjeant William Paston. In March 1426 he wrote to his proctor in the curia from Norwich, so it seems that he still treated the deanery in St Mary's as his home base.

In a round of episcopal promotions managed by Bedford, Rickinghall was papally provided to Chichester on 27 February 1426, his likely elevation having been confidently rumoured amid the tangled politics surrounding these promotions during the previous year. He received the temporalities on 1 May and was consecrated at Mortlake on 30 June 1426. Rickinghall served as proctor at the curia on business concerning Lancastrian France in 1427–8 and was paid 300 marks by Bedford, its regent.

Rickinghall's short episcopate was, then, probably largely non-resident. He maintained his links with Bury and East Anglia to the end of his life. On 24 October 1427 he was named as co-supervisor with Sir Thomas Erpingham, a leading layman in the region, of the will of Ann, Lady Morley, a niece of his old patron, Bishop Despenser. In his own will (2 April 1429) he named as overseer John Doreward, the son of a former speaker of the Commons and steward of Bury's franchise, and left bequests to St Mary's College and two of his former benefices. However,

he was at Cakeham, Sussex, on 7 June and had remembered his cathedral in his will. He died on 29 June 1429 and was buried there, as he wished: the monument he specified survives. His nephew and only known kinsman, John Manning, was an executor.   CHRISTOPHER WHITTICK

Sources Emden, *Cam.* · Chancery records · R. B. Dobson, *Durham Priory, 1400–1450*, Cambridge Studies in Medieval Life and Thought, 3rd ser., 6 (1973), 91, 157–8 · C. N. L. Brooke, *A history of Gonville and Caius College* (1985), 38–9 · E. F. Jacob, ed., *The register of Henry Chichele, archbishop of Canterbury, 1414–1443*, 1, CYS, 45 (1943), xcii–xciv; 2, CYS, 42 (1937), 415–19 · BL, Cotton MS Faustina C.111, fols. 90v–91 · BL, Cotton MS Cleopatra C.IV fols. 167–172 · chancery, treaty rolls, PRO, C76/107 m 10 · LPL, ED 247, 450, 919, 951 · J. Hughes, *Pastors and visionaries: religion and secular life in late medieval Yorkshire* (1988), 239 · M. Hobbs, ed., *Chichester Cathedral: an historical survey* (1994) · [J. Challenor Smith], ed., *Index of wills recorded in the archiepiscopal registers at Lambeth Palace* (1919), 44
Likenesses L. Barnard, group portrait, painted panel on funeral monument, *c*.1535 (with bishops of Chichester), Chichester Cathedral; repro. in Hobbs, ed., *Chichester Cathedral*
Wealth at death bequests to Chichester Cathedral, former cures of Thorpe Abbots (Norfolk) and Fressingfield (Suffolk) and the college of St Mary in the Fields, Norwich: Jacob, ed., *Register of Henry Chichele*, vol. 2, pp. 415, 419

Rickman, John (1771–1840), statistician and civil servant, was born on 22 August 1771, the only son of Thomas Rickman, vicar of Newburn, Northumberland. He was educated at Guildford grammar school (1781–5), matriculated from Magdalen Hall, Oxford, in 1788, migrated to Lincoln College, and graduated BA in 1792. Rickman then joined his father, now in retirement at Christchurch, Hampshire, read widely, especially in economics, and served for a while as a private tutor. His attachment to his pupil's sister, later the marchioness of Ormond, led to Rickman's being named the marchioness's executor and being left a legacy of £7000 at her death in 1817.

Although Rickman edited the *Commercial, Agricultural, and Manufacturer's Magazine* until 1801, his most influential work was put forward, characteristically, in a private paper of 1796 where he developed the case for a census. Rickman correctly rejected the then modish view that population was falling, suggesting that a census would offer government an invaluable aid to effective military recruitment in the war with France, and by confirming growing national prosperity would also promote internal stabilization. He demonstrated that it was possible to derive population estimates from parish registers, thus facilitating a back-projection of demographic trends. Rickman's paper was shown to Charles Abbot by George Rose, MP for Christchurch, and in March 1801 Abbot steered the census bill to the statute book. Rickman had no hesitation in claiming credit; on 27 December 1801 he wrote to Robert Southey, 'At my suggestion, they have passed an Act of Parliament for ascertaining the population of Great Britain, and as a compliment (of course) have proposed me to superintend the execution of it' (Williams, 38). Rickman's career and posthumous reputation were thus determined. With considerable skill he conducted the first census, which confounded Malthus's fear of falling population, and then developed tolerably accurate estimates of eighteenth-century population trends.

John Rickman (1771–1840), by Samuel Bellin, pubd 1843 (after Samuel Lane, c.1831)

Rickman refined techniques in the 1811 and 1821 censuses, and in 1831 he considerably expanded both the scope of questions and the categorization of occupational groups. At the time of his death he was working on the still more ambitious 1841 census, which achieved a new sophistication in enumerators' returns.

In 1801 Rickman served briefly as personal secretary while Abbot was chief secretary for Ireland until, on Abbot's election to the speakership of the Commons, he accepted appointment as speaker's secretary. In 1803 he agreed to supervise the highly ambitious *Abstract of the Poor*, a survey of the incidence of poverty and expenditure under the poor laws. In 1805 Rickman married Susannah Postlethwaite (*d.* 1836) of Harting, Sussex, and, despite its formality, the marriage appears to have been happy. Rickman's salary as speaker's secretary was £300 per annum, supplemented by £1000–£1200 in election years. The post also carried a house adjacent to the speaker's official quarters, which Rickman occupied until the fire in the houses of parliament led to its demolition in 1835, when Rickman took Judge Jeffreys' House, 23 Duke Street, Westminster. Other official positions swelled Rickman's income. His secretaryship to the commission on the Caledonian Canal and highland roads brought him a further £400 a year until 1819 and a lifelong intimacy with Thomas Telford, and between 1815 and 1831 he received £100 per annum as secretary to the commission for building churches in the highlands and Ireland. In 1820 he was elevated to clerk assistant and an annual salary of £2500. No one did more to confound the reformers' notion of a sinecurist than Rickman. In 1817 he persuaded the house to simplify the procedure for recording votes and proceedings for the

Journals, a reform which resulted in votes being published the morning after they were cast. He produced an index of the statutes in 1818 and the *Journals* in 1825, and a catalogue of the Commons library in 1829. From 1817 he was producing annual poor law returns, and between 1816 and 1819 collated the statistics of local taxation, culminating in the authoritative *Local Taxation Return* of 1839.

Rickman was a man of passionate opinions, indirectly expressed. In private his high toryism, anti-Malthusianism, and antisemitism were forthright, in public carefully modulated. Perhaps because of his official position, Rickman was content to be an unacknowledged co-author. His friendship with the poet and critic Robert Southey, which began in 1797, was the pivotal intellectual and cultural relationship of his later life. Rickman regularly provided statistics, ideas, and material for Southey's articles in the *Quarterly Review*, and Southey's piece on the poor laws in the *Quarterly* of April 1818 was almost wholly Rickman's work. Had not Murray's financial difficulties intervened, Rickman and Southey would have collaborated in a sequel to Southey's *Colloquies* of 1829. Between 1829 and 1840 Rickman published on political, social, and archaeological topics.

As a statistician and public servant, Rickman was widely honoured. He was elected FRS in 1815 and an honorary member of the Institution of Civil Engineers in 1835. In 1820 Oxford University awarded him an honorary LLD, and in 1833 he was elected an honorary member of the Société Française de Statistique Universelle. Rickman was liable to depression, and in the 1830s his disposition was mirrored by his political distress as political reform and political economy displaced the striking blend of tory statistical positivism which Rickman had done much to promote. On 2 June 1840 Rickman fell ill with an ulcerated larynx, and he died at Judge Jeffreys' House on 11 August 1840. He was buried at St Margaret's, Westminster, beside his wife, who had died on 12 May 1836. His son and two daughters survived him. With genuine warmth Lord John Russell moved the tribute in the Commons, and Joseph Hume paid an amply justified tribute to Rickman's readiness 'to afford every information to others' and to his population returns which 'stand unrivalled in the amount of information and the concise manner in which he brought it before this house' (Williams, 319).

DAVID EASTWOOD

Sources O. Williams, *Lamb's friend the census-taker: life and letters of John Rickman* (1912) • M. J. Cullen, *The statistical movement in early Victorian Britain: the foundations of empirical social research* (1975) • *Selections from the letters of Robert Southey*, ed. J. W. Warter, 4 vols. (1856) • *New letters of Robert Southey*, ed. K. Curry, 2 vols. (1965) • D. V. Glass, *The development of population statistics* (1973) • D. V. Glass, *Numbering the people: the eighteenth-century population controversy* (1973)
Archives Hunt. L., corresp. • S. Antiquaries, Lond., papers relating to Avebury and Stonehenge | BL, letters to Thomas Poole and others • Hunt. L., letters, mainly to Robert Southey • NA Scot., corresp. with J. A. Stewart-Mackenzie • UCL, corresp. with Edwin Chadwick
Likenesses S. Lane, oils, c.1831, Palace of Westminster, London • S. Bellin, mezzotint, pubd 1843 (after S. Lane, c.1831), NPG [*see illus.*] • G. Hayter, group portrait, oils (*The House of Commons, 1833*),

NPG · A. Lefroy, watercolour, repro. in Williams, *Life and letters* · engraving, repro. in Williams, *Life and letters*

Rickman, Thomas (1776–1841), architect, was born on 8 June 1776 in Maidenhead, Berkshire, the eldest surviving son and third of the eleven children of Joseph Rickman (1749–1810) and Sarah Neave Rickman (1747–1809), members of the Society of Friends. His diaries in the library of the Royal Institute of British Architects, London, suggest that he remained an active Quaker throughout his life except for two periods: 1804–*c*.1812, on the occasion of his first marriage, and late in 1836, when he joined the Catholic Apostolic (Irvingite) church. Correspondence preserved in Rickman's notebooks in the British Museum reveal that he used the Quaker forms of address, *thee* and *thou*, throughout his career. His nonconformism is significant in the context of his mature career—namely, as a builder of Anglican churches for the government panel of church commissioners, and as a pioneering author on medieval architecture. There is no evidence to suggest that he saw any conflict between his faith and his professional activities, but he noted in his diary for 13 January 1822 that two brethren at meeting had characterized his building of Anglican churches as inconsistent with his faith. His reply was simply to describe how he had become fascinated by Gothic architecture, in the hope that others would understand this fascination.

Thomas Rickman's early career was a chequered one. His father, a surgeon and apothecary, trained him for a career in medicine in London from 1797 to 1801, and from 1801 to 1803 Rickman practised medicine in Lewes, Sussex, where his father had moved and where there were a large number of his relations. Disinclined to follow a medical profession, Rickman entered into partnership with a London corn factor, Samuel Burns, from 1803 to 1807. Contrary to the rules of the Society of Friends, he had married his first cousin Lucy Rickman (*c*.1773–1807) in 1804, provoking his first break with the Friends. The year 1807 was disastrous for Rickman, as his business failed, leaving him heavily in debt, and his wife, Lucy, died on 12 December. He moved to Liverpool in 1808, and found employment as a clerk in an insurance firm.

To the depression arising from this extremely difficult period has been attributed Rickman's passion for Gothic architecture, initiated during frequent sketching visits to old churches (Colvin, *Archs.*, 361). Rickman's son wrote that, 'from the time of his arrival in Liverpool he seems never to have missed a day or an hour which could be given to examining buildings' (T. M. Rickman, 6). By 1808 Rickman was collecting prints of Liverpool architecture, and the following year he met James Smith, the publisher. By 1812 Rickman had written an essay on Chester Cathedral (published posthumously in the *Journal of the Archaeological, Architectural, and Historic Society for the County of Chester*, 2, 1864), and he began writing an article on Gothic architecture for the first volume of Smith's *A Panorama of Arts and Sciences* (2 vols., Liverpool, 1815, copy in Liverpool Local History Library), which was to form the basis for his most important work, *An Attempt to Discriminate the Styles of English Architecture*, first published as a book in 1817 (2nd edn, 1819; 3rd edn, 1825). Rickman made some modifications to the fourth edition (1835), the last he saw through to publication, and three further editions appeared after his death, ending with the seventh edition of 1881, all of these published by the firm of the Oxford antiquary John Henry Parker. In the preface, Rickman said he intended the book to be 'a text-book for the architectural student', for the lack of one 'is generally acknowledged'. His object was to 'supply at a price which shall not present an obstacle to extensive circulation' ('Preface' to *An Attempt to Discriminate the Styles of English Architecture*, 2nd edn, 1819, iii–iv) an overview of medieval styles of architecture for restorers of ancient buildings and architects working in revived styles. Such an aim had been pursued by architectural writers and Gothic enthusiasts throughout the eighteenth century, beginning with Batty Langley's *Ancient Architecture Restored and Improved* (1741), but Rickman's *Attempt* was nothing less than the first accurate account of the history of medieval architecture in the British Isles. By establishing the chronology of the different medieval styles Rickman's account was a landmark in the history of the Gothic revival. *An Attempt* remained the standard reference on the subject of Gothic architecture throughout the nineteenth century and the nomenclature Rickman developed—Norman, Early English, Decorated, and Perpendicular—has remained in use ever since.

In writing his *Attempt*, Rickman succeeded where many others had failed, partly owing to his avoidance of contemporary debate over the origins and meaning of Gothic. It could be argued that his position as an outsider to the Church of England allowed him to be more objective than many of his contemporaries. Indeed, it has been suggested that Rickman's lack of a classical education meant he could not read medieval documents in Latin and therefore had to develop a visual method of approach (Baily, 148). His systematic, empirical approach to the subdivision and classification of architectural detail, since described as 'comparative taxonomy', enabled him to analyse the thousands of medieval structures he visited personally. By means of copious sketches and notes taken on site, he succeeded in constructing a coherent chronology of medieval architecture from the round-headed arches of the Normans to the broad, ogee'd arches of the Perpendicular Gothic. (This last term represents Rickman's original contribution to the nomenclature of medieval styles.)

Like many aspiring architects and designers, Rickman was able to found a career as a result of the success of his publication. He had written his essay on Chester Cathedral partly in response to the encouragement he received from George Harrison, an iron-founder in that town; in 1812 he met John Cragg, the ambitious owner of the Merseyside Iron Foundry, who commissioned him to design several churches in the Liverpool area, using cast iron as a principal building material. The first of these was the church of St George, Everton (1812–14), which was followed by St Michael, Toxteth (1814–15), and St Philip, Hardman Street, Liverpool (1815–16; dem. 1882). Cragg was able to reuse Rickman's designs for lace-like window tracery, 'vaulting', and thin, columnar supports in these churches, as the elements had been prefabricated in cast iron. Cast iron was not without its proponents at this time—the prince of Wales endorsed its use at Carlton House, London, and at the Royal Pavilion, Brighton—but the overt use of such an industrial material did not find favour with the church commissioners until the 1820s. Rickman himself preferred detailing in stone, and this interesting experiment with modern materials was not continued in his later career.

Rickman's first major domestic commission came through a Liverpool architect, John Slater, who needed assistance with Gothic designs for Scarisbrick Hall, Lancashire, where A. W. N. Pugin was also to begin his career as a domestic architect. Between 1813 and 1816 Rickman and Slater redesigned the rambling Elizabethan house, and some of Rickman's traceried windows and architectural details survive today. There is evidence to suggest that he also designed some furniture in the Gothic style for Scarisbrick, and that this may have been made by the Lancaster firm Gillows. On 22 October 1813 Rickman married second, in Liverpool, Christiana Hornor (c.1780–1814) of Hull, a teacher in the Quaker day school in Liverpool. This marriage also ended tragically when his wife died of puerperal fever nine days after giving birth to a daughter, Lucy (d. 1816). This second marriage led, however, to Rickman's reconciliation with the Society of Friends.

By December 1817 Rickman's new career was progressing sufficiently well for him to open an architectural office in Liverpool, and in 1818 he took as his first pupil the talented Henry Hutchinson (1800–1831), who became Rickman's partner in 1821 but whose career was cut short by an early death. With Hutchinson's assistance, Rickman was to execute the major buildings of his architectural career, most notably the church of St Peter, Hampton Lucy, Warwickshire (1822–6), the church of St John, Oulton, Yorkshire (1827–9), and the New Court of St John's College, Cambridge (1826–31), traditionally built stone structures lavishly decorated with the crisp, accurate Gothic detailing that Rickman knew intimately, and that Hutchinson could translate into beautifully rendered drawings.

Rickman's most reliable source of income during his architectural career was to come from the church commissioners, beginning with a commission for the church of St George, Birmingham (1819–22), which led to his opening an office at 5 Cannon Street in 1820, moved to 45 Ann Street in 1826. He moved to Birmingham in 1821 with Henry Hutchinson and Thomas Fuljames, while his brother Edwin Swan Rickman (1790–1873), assisted by John Broadbent, ran the Liverpool office. Just as St George's was finished, Rickman received the prestigious appointment of architect to Worcester Cathedral, as well as the commission for the church at Hampton Lucy, Warwickshire, his early masterpiece. The church, an exquisite jewel illustrating Rickman's Decorated Gothic, as defined in An Attempt, was built privately for the Revd George Lucy. It therefore received all the lavish detailing that the more economically built commissioners' churches were denied, and for which Rickman was sometimes unfairly criticized.

Rickman's architectural career was well established during the 1820s. As well as receiving a number of church commissions, he undertook a diverse range of work, including a country house for Mr Shirley at Lough Fea, Ireland (begun 1825), the modest town hall of Clitheroe, Lancashire (1820–1), and Matfen Hall, Northumberland (1832–5), for Sir Edward Blackett, in the Elizabethan style. By 1822 Rickman had begun work on the design of his next masterpiece, the New Court of St John's College, Cambridge, his largest building. This important commission involved the building itself, the romantic 'Bridge of Sighs' over the River Cam, which is generally ascribed to Hutchinson, and even interior fittings for the rooms of the college. Together with his unsuccessful but acclaimed designs for the Fitzwilliam Museum, the university library, and the hall of King's College, this project brought him into close contact with the university community, and a warm friendship was forged with William Whewell, fellow of Trinity College.

In the midst of so much activity Rickman married again on 20 January 1825. His third wife was a lively Scottish woman, Elizabeth Miller (b. c.1800) of Edinburgh, with whom he had two children. One of them was the architect Thomas Miller Rickman (1827–1912), later president of the Architectural Association in London. The family resided at 12 Islington Row, Edgbaston, Birmingham. Mrs Rickman took a keen interest in her husband's career, and her son records an incident in 1826 when she fell into a church vault while inspecting work at Handsworth church, Birmingham. Rickman himself apparently suffered a number of carriage accidents as a result of his constant professional travel, and in 1828 he fell off scaffolding while inspecting building work at St John's, Oulton, his masterpiece in the Early English style. His son described him as vigorous and energetic during most of his life.

The year 1830 was a watershed in Rickman's career. On 1 January he received notice of his election to the Society of Antiquaries of London, an indication of professional recognition by his colleagues. He had sufficient pupils and assistants to warrant building two houses for them on Islington Row, an indication of the size of his practice. Furthermore, in May that year he made the first of two visits to France, in the company of Henry Hutchinson. Rickman had long suspected that study of medieval buildings in France might illuminate the development of Gothic architecture, and this visit was to whet his appetite for a longer study tour of Picardy and Normandy in August 1832 in the company of William Whewell. The two met the eminent French antiquaries Augustin Le Prévost and Arcisse de Caumont, and Rickman sent back four letters to the president of the Society of Antiquaries, documenting their discoveries. His final letter contained careful sketches of French Flamboyant Gothic tracery.

Despite the fact that his health began to decline in 1834, Rickman was able to publish the fourth edition of An Attempt the following year, incorporating the results of his two visits to France. The existence of an extra-illustrated edition of his handbook in the Avery Library of Columbia University in New York suggests that, at the time of his death, he was working on a fifth edition. He also contributed in 1838 to the text of John Sell Cotman's *Specimens of Architectural Remains*. Thomas Miller Rickman later suggested that his father's scholarly activities increased as a result of his confinement to bed during the last years of his life. His architectural practice was busy preparing designs for the Palace of Westminster competition under the able direction of Richard Charles Hussey, who joined the firm in 1831 and became a partner in 1835, replacing Edwin Swan Rickman, who had begun to show the signs of mental illness that troubled several family members. Hussey's practical approach and sparsely ornamented style of Gothic architecture became increasingly evident in the firm's output of the later 1830s, during Rickman's final illness. On 4 January 1841 Thomas Rickman died of liver disease. He was buried in the grounds of St George's Church, Birmingham.

The life and career of Thomas Rickman demonstrate the power of an individual to triumph in seemingly unpromising circumstances. As a self-taught nonconformist, born into a large family of slender financial means and with a marked strain of mental illness, he was all the more remarkable for the double career he forged as the leading scholar of Gothic architecture in his day and as one of the most successful British architects during the first half of the nineteenth century. Writing to his aunt during his visit to France with Rickman in 1832, the antiquary William Whewell left the following description of his companion:

> He wears the Quaker dress, which of itself would draw some notice here, and being a little, round, fat man, with short, thick legs, and a large head, he sets off the dress to great advantage … he is perpetually running from one side of the street to the other to peep into whatever catches his attention … and we seldom move far without the honour of some special spectators … Notwithstanding this I like my companion very much. He is very good-humoured, and very intelligent and active, and I see more by travelling with him than I should do alone, besides understanding the architecture much better.   (Blamires, Greenwood, and Kerr, 120)

MEGAN ALDRICH

Sources Colvin, *Archs.* · J. Baily, 'Thomas Rickman, architect and Quaker: the early years to 1818', PhD diss., U. Leeds, 1977 · J. Turner, ed., *The dictionary of art*, 34 vols. (1996) · T. M. Rickman, *Notes on the life and on the several imprints of the work of Thomas Rickman* (1901) · M. Aldrich, 'Gothic architecture illustrated: the drawings of Thomas Rickman in New York', *Antiquaries Journal*, 65 (1985), 427–33 · A. Kerr, 'Thomas Rickman in France', *A Quaker miscellany for Edward H. Milligan*, ed. D. Blamires, J. Greenwood, and A. Kerr (1985) · J. S. B. S. [J. S. Boys Smith], 'Thomas Rickman, architect of the New Court', *The Eagle*, 67 (1974–7), 19–21 · M. Aldrich, 'Thomas Rickman (1776–1841) and architectural illustration of the Gothic revival', MPhil diss., Toronto University, 1983 · red catalogues, RS Friends, Lond.
Archives BL, drawings of churches and time books, Add. MSS 37793–37803 · BM, workbooks · Bodl. Oxf., notes and sketches of third edition of *Styles of English architecture* · Bodl. Oxf., sketches and drawings · RIBA BAL, diaries and architectural drawings · U. Birm. L., letters | BL, letters to Edward Blore, Add. MS 52587 · Northumbd RO, Newcastle upon Tyne, letters to Sir Edward Blackett · Trinity Cam., letters to William Whewell
Likenesses C. Barber, pen, ink, and wash caricature, *c.*1820 (with Henry Hutchinson), Athenaeum, Liverpool · Cruikshank, watercolour, 1826 · J. H. Beck, chalk sketch, 1888 (after Cruikshank), RS Friends, Lond.

Rickman, Thomas Clio (1761–1834), bookseller and reformer, was born on 27 July 1761 at The Cliffe, Lewes, the son of John Rickman and his wife, Elizabeth, *née* Peters. Both parents were Quakers and intended their son to enter the medical profession. Accordingly he was apprenticed to an uncle who practised as a doctor in Maidenhead. While revisiting Lewes at seventeen he began a lifelong friendship with the freethinker Thomas *Paine (1737–1809), who was employed there as an exciseman. Together they joined the Headstrong Club, which met at the White Hart inn at Lewes. Rickman became popular in the group with his poetry and historical reflections and was awarded the nickname Clio, which he subsequently added to his other names.

Continued friendship with Paine and marriage to a non-member of the group led the Sussex Friends to disown Rickman in 1783. In 1785 Rickman left Lewes to settle in London as a bookseller at 39 Leadenhall Street.

As a printer, Rickman published sheet music between 1788 and 1802, though he wrote satirical verses and prose for the *Black Dwarf* and other weekly journals. Many of his republican songs were published as broadsides with music. Rickman's name will be forever linked with Paine, for he 'was to Paine what Boswell was to Johnson' (Keane, xvi). They were close friends: Paine often, for example, teased Rickman about his excessive weight. Paine stayed as a lodger at the Rickmans' home in 1791 and 1792 and while there completed the second part of *The Rights of Man*. Rickman later fixed a tablet with an inscription on the small table at which Paine had worked. The two friends had a common interest in technology and Rickman assisted Paine in his inventions for iron bridges. He also patented his own signal trumpet. A circle of reformers soon developed around them, and frequent visitors to the Rickman home included Mary Wollstonecraft and Horne Tooke. Such was Rickman's dedication to Paine and his principles of liberty that his children were named Thomas Paine, Washington, Franklin, Rousseau, Petrarch, and Volney.

Rickman faced constant suspicion for selling Paine's books. He did not make matters easy for himself by composing and publishing songs in praise of political liberty and the French Revolution. In 1792 he had to be protected for a night by Maria Anne Fitzherbert for selling Painite literature and more than once he fled to Paris, where Paine had taken up residence to escape persecution. The situation became so difficult that the Rickmans moved to 7 Upper Marylebone Street, Middlesex, in 1798. When Paine began his final journey to America, Rickman left his wife and children to accompany his friend to Le Havre. On 1 September 1802 they parted for the last time. After years of deliberation and planning, Rickman published his chief work, *Life of Paine*, in 1819. It was one of three biographies of Paine published that year and was by far the most intimate and favourable.

Rickman died at his home at 7 Upper Marylebone Street on 15 February 1834. He was buried as a Quaker at the nonconformist graveyard at Bunhill Fields, London. He married twice but outlived both wives and most of his children. CHARLOTTE FELL-SMITH, *rev.* J.-M. ALTER

Sources M. D. Conway, *Life of Paine*, 2 vols. (1892) · T. Rickman, *Life of Paine* (1819) · *GM*, 2nd ser., 1 (1834) · I. Maxted, *The London book trades, 1775–1800: a preliminary checklist of members* (1977) · J. Keane, *Tom Paine* (1995) · J. Frushtman, *Thomas Paine* (1994)
Likenesses T. Holmes, stipple, pubd 1800 (after W. Hazlitt), BM, NPG · S. Springsguth junior, line engraving, pubd 1814, NPG · R. Dighton, portrait · W. Hazlitt, portrait

Rickword, (John) Edgell (1898–1982), poet and book reviewer, was born on 22 October 1898 at 28 Head Street, Colchester, the fifth and last child of George Rickword, borough librarian, and his wife, Mabel Thomas (née Prosser). From dame-school Rickword went to Colchester Royal Grammar School in 1908 and joined the Artists' Rifles in 1916, the earliest time at which he could have enlisted. Rickword was on active service in France for most of the last two years of the First World War and was awarded the Military Cross 'for conspicuous gallantry and initiative'. In the months after the armistice, he developed septicaemia which led to the removal of his left eye. Invalided out of the army, Rickword went up to Pembroke College, Oxford, in October 1919 to read modern languages, but left the next year without taking his degree. He became a contributor to the *Daily Herald* and the *New Statesman* and on 25 October 1920 married Margaret (Peggy) McGrath, daughter of John McGrath, farmer; their daughter had been born the previous month. Rickword's early married life, living in a succession of London flats and then in Chipstead, Surrey, was happy and productive. A second daughter was born in March 1922.

Rickword had been writing poetry since his mid-teens and published his first collection, *Behind the Eyes*, in 1921. His work as a literary journalist earned him recognition as an astute early interpreter of modernist poetry (see his anonymous review in the *Times Literary Supplement* of T. S. Eliot's *The Waste Land*). In 1923 he was contracted to write a biography of Arthur Rimbaud, whose poetry (of which Rickword made notable translations) had been highly influential on his own. By the time the Rimbaud book was published in 1924, Rickword had suffered a personal calamity when his wife had a nervous breakdown and the family broke up, Peggy going into a mental hospital and their daughters into foster homes.

Rickword moved into a flat in London with Bertram Higgins, together with whom and Douglas Garman he became founder of the short-lived but influential *Calendar of Modern Letters* (1925–7), 'a sort of discontented club' as Rickword himself described it many years later, 'discontented with all the established novelists and the literary cliques' (*Poetry Nation*, 78). Among the writers they published were D. H. Lawrence, Luigi Pirandello, Isaac Babel, Liam O'Flaherty, and the poets Robert Graves, John Crowe

Ransom, Allen Tate, and Hart Crane. He also edited two volumes of *Scrutinies* in this period (1928, 1931) and published two more volumes of poetry, *Invocations to Angels* (1928) and *Twittingpan* (1931), before he all but gave up the writing of verse. The abrupt end to his career as a poet has been attributed to his communist beliefs (Rickword joined the Communist Party in 1934), though Rickword himself explained it differently: 'I simply wasn't in a mind to write poems' (J. Lucas, *The 1930s: a Challenge to Orthodoxy*, 1978, 9–10).

In the 1930s and 1940s Rickword's energies were focused on political activism, as a founder and editor of *Left Review* (1934–8) and one of its successors, *Our Time* (1941–9). He was instrumental in the formation of the Left Book Club and the British section of the Writers' International, whom he represented as part of a delegation to the 1937 conference in Madrid during the Spanish Civil War. Described as 'one of the few really outstanding critical intelligences on the far Left' (R. Giddings, *Tribune*, 5 Jan 1979, 6), he was an inheritor of the English radical tradition of Marvell, Milton, Swift, and Hazlitt, all of whom he wrote about in publications ranging from the *Daily Worker* to the *Penguin Guide to English Literature*. As a poet he reacted strongly against the insipidity he perceived in the work of his contemporaries and strove to develop an aesthetic of 'negative emotions' deriving his use of form and symbol from the poets he specially admired, the French symbolists and English metaphysical poets—he was called by Herbert Palmer 'the only complete and satisfactory English symbolist' (H. Palmer, *Post-Victorian Poetry*, 1938, 256–8). In these tastes, and in his outstanding ability as an essayist and editor, he had more in common with Eliot than any other of his contemporaries. Rickword's poetry is trenchant, skilful, and encompasses a wide range of styles, from powerful satire to unusual and lyrical love poems. In metre and diction, as well as politically, he prefigured the Auden generation of poets, but unlike them wrote in an atmosphere of self-determined isolation. His absence from print hindered general recognition of his poetry, and the pared down *Collected Poems* that appeared in 1947 was not very well received. Rickword retired into a career as a bookseller, in Kent and later in London, with his second wife, Doris Russell (Jonny) Back (1899–1964) (they married on 24 July 1944 following Peggy's death in June that year), with whom he had been living since 1934; an artist and dressmaker, she was formerly the wife of Gilbert Back and was the daughter of Frederick Russell Quilter, civil engineer.

Rickword stuck to his Marxist principles, but left the Communist Party quietly after the Soviet invasion of Hungary in 1956. He was manager of Collet's bookshop in Hampstead from 1954. Jonny's health deteriorated after 1960 and she died in 1964 from a brain haemorrhage; a year later Rickword went to live with Beatrix Hammarling at 2 Hopping Lane, Islington, his home for the remaining seventeen years of his life. His sight, which had been weak for years, was lost completely by 1976. A revival of interest in his work began in the late 1960s with the republication of his *Collected Poems* and of *Left Review*; these were followed by his *Essays and Opinions* (1974), *Selected Poems and Translations* (1976) and collected prose, *Literature in Society* (1978).

Edgell Rickword died from carcinoma with obstructive jaundice on 15 March 1982 at the Whittington Hospital, Islington, London.   CLAIRE HARMAN

Sources C. Hobday, *Edgell Rickword: a poet at war* (1989) · E. Rickword, *Essays and opinions, 1921–31* (1974) · E. Rickword, *Literature in society* (1978) · *Poetry Nation*, 1 (1974) · *PN Review*, 6/1 (1979) · b. cert. · d. cert. · m. cert.
Likenesses C. Barker, photograph, repro. in C. Barker, *Portraits of poets*, ed. S. Barker (1986)
Wealth at death £25,121: probate, 12 Aug 1982, *CGPLA Eng. & Wales*

Ricraft, Josiah (*d.* 1688), author, was the son of James Ricraft of Stepney and his wife, Grace, daughter of John Mills, who were married at St Faith's, London, on 27 July 1622. Little is known about Ricraft's family, although his father was still alive in 1638 when he issued a petition in which he styled himself late pilot and factor of the ship *Elizabeth*. Josiah established himself as a merchant in Stepney, perhaps as an associate of the family of his kinsman Josiah Child. He witnessed the will of Child's father in 1639, and would name Sir Joshua Child as an overseer of his own will nearly fifty years later.

During the mid-1640s Ricraft emerged as a zealous parliamentarian, and as an activist and controversialist on behalf of the political and religious cause of the presbyterians. He was 'employed in several matters that concerned the Parliament' (Edwards, 2.100), and testimony was later given of his service in 'discovering of divers disaffected persons that have held correspondence with the enemy' (Ricraft, *A Nose-Gay*, A4v). That he was aligned with the presbyterians by the mid-1640s is evident from his first book, *A Looking Glasse for the Anabaptists* (September 1645), and his prominence within presbyterian circles is evident from his role in the November 1645 petition for the establishment of the London classes. He also provided evidence for Thomas Edwards's heresiography, *Gangraena*, by way of a letter outlining William Kiffin's role in sectarian meetings. Ricraft's enemies countered with allegations that he had sheltered a royalist who intended to murder the presbyterian minister Francis Roberts but such accusations were denied by both Ricraft and Roberts, who were probably friends. In May 1646 the daughter of Ricraft and his wife, Katherine (*d.* 1649), was baptized at Roberts's church, St Augustine, Watling Street, even though it was not in Ricraft's own parish. Ricraft also faced threats of violence, which prompted parliament to issue orders for his protection in May 1645.

In May 1646 Ricraft joined the literary battle between the presbyterians and Independents, with *A Nose-Gay of Rank-Smelling Flowers*, directed against John Goodwin, to which Edward Drapes replied in *A Plain and Faithfull Discovery*. The works for which he is best known, however, are his histories of the civil war, which first appeared in a triumvirate of broadsides in 1646, and which took the form of lists of parliamentarian victories. These were clearly biased towards the achievements of English and Scottish presbyterians, at a time when they were politically weak at Westminster, and they betrayed his hostility to religious Independency. Ricraft's allegiance to Robert Devereux, third earl of Essex, the leader of the English presbyterians, was also evident from his publication of a broadside *Funerall Elegy* after the lord-general's death. In December 1646, furthermore, Ricraft and other presbyterians were questioned by parliament for spreading rumours about threats made by Independents to deploy the army against the London presbyterians, and in the following year he served as scoutmaster to the presbyterian-controlled London militia. More importantly, 1647 also saw the appearance of Ricraft's most famous work, the extensive *A Survey of Englands Champions* (1647), in which he reprinted his lists of parliamentarian victories alongside a series of illustrated biographies of parliamentarian commanders. Once again, however, he exploited this format in order to stress the role played by his presbyterian heroes, both military and political, such as Essex and the earl of Manchester.

Ricraft, like many presbyterians, was less prominent during the republic. During the early 1650s he was living in the parish of St Benet Fink with his second wife, Hester, having buried his first wife there in October 1649. After the Restoration he returned to Stepney, where he was living when he married his third wife, Barbara Wood (*d.* in or after 1686), of Wapping, in July 1671. Although not politically active, Ricraft retained his religious zeal, notably after his appointment as a Middlesex JP in 1670, and his support for dissenters may also explain his removal from the bench during the tory purge in 1681. He died in January 1688, and was buried at St Dunstan-in-the-West, Stepney, on 23 January.   J. T. PEACEY

Sources J. Ricraft, *A looking glasse for the Anabaptists* (1645) · J. Ricraft, *A nose-gay of rank-smelling flowers* (1646) · J. Ricraft, *A survey of Englands champions, and truths faithfull patriots* (1647) · *CSP dom.*, 1638–81 · T. Edwards, *Gangraena, or, A catalogue and discovery of many of the errours, heresies, blasphemies and pernicious practices of the sectaries of this time*, 3 vols. in 1 (1646) · M. Mahoney, 'Presbyterianism in the City of London, 1645–1647', *HJ*, 22 (1979), 93–114 · *JHC*, 5 (1646–8) · J. C. Jeaffreson, ed., *Middlesex county records*, Middlesex County RS, 4 (1892) · will, PRO, PROB 11/391, fol. 183v [J. Child] · LMA, P93/DUN/280 · GL, MS 4097 · J. L. Chester and J. Foster, eds., *London marriage licences, 1521–1869* (1887)
Archives Hunt. L., MS, volume on civil war
Likenesses W. Faithorne, line engraving, NPG, BM; repro. in J. Ricraft, *The peculiar characters of the oriental languages* [1645] · engraving, repro. in Ricraft, *Survey*

Riddell, Charles James Buchanan (1817–1903), army officer and geophysicist, born at Lilliesleaf, Roxburghshire, on 19 November 1817, was the third son of Sir John Buchanan Riddell, ninth baronet, and his wife, Lady Frances Marsham, eldest daughter of Charles Marsham, first earl of Romney. With the exception of a year at Eton College, Riddell was educated at private schools. In 1832 he entered the Royal Military Academy, Woolwich, passing thence (1834) into the Royal Artillery as second lieutenant. The following year he was transferred to Quebec, and in

1837 received promotion as first lieutenant. After returning to England, he was ordered to Jamaica, but was invalided back a year later.

In 1839 Riddell began his scientific research. The Royal Society undertook to organize the British contribution to the worldwide survey of terrestrial magnetism initiated by Gauss; Riddell was chosen to superintend a magnetical and meteorological observatory at Toronto—a temporary station nearest to the magnetic north pole—under Edward Sabine. At the end of a year Riddell was invalided home, but he had done excellent service. Soon after, at Sabine's instance, he was appointed assistant superintendent of ordnance magnetic observatories at the Royal Military Repository, Woolwich. During his four years' tenure of this post he assisted Sabine in the reduction of magnetic data and the issue of results of observations made by the directors of the affiliated observatories. He was elected a fellow of the Royal Society on 13 January 1842. In 1844 the Admiralty issued Riddell's *Magnetical instructions for the use of portable instruments adapted for magnetical surveys and portable observatories, and for the use of a set of small instruments for a fixed magnetic observatory.*

Riddell was placed on the staff at Woolwich and during the Crimean War he was an efficient deputy assistant quartermaster-general. He served in the Indian mutiny in 1857–8, commanding the siege artillery of Outram's force at the siege and capture of Lucknow, and the artillery of Lugard's column at the engagement of the Tigree; he was three times mentioned in dispatches, was made a CB, and received the medal with clasps. He retired in 1866 with the rank of major-general. Afterwards he lived quietly at Oaklands, Chudleigh, Devon, where he owned and managed a farm, and undertook parochial and educational work. Riddell married, on 11 February 1847, Mary (d. 1900), daughter of Sir Hew Dalrymple *Ross; they had one daughter. He died at his home on 25 January 1903, and was buried at Chudleigh.   T. E. JAMES, rev. ELIZABETH BAIGENT

Sources *The Times* (26 Jan 1903) · Burke, *Peerage* · E. W. C., *PRS*, 75 (1905), 302–4 · *Nature*, 67 (1902–3), 421 · E. Sabine, *Observations made at the magnetical and meteorological observatory at Toronto*, 3 vols. (1845–57)

Wealth at death £13,726 18s. 11d.: resworn probate, 26 Feb 1903, *CGPLA Eng. & Wales*

Riddell [*née* Cowan], **Charlotte Eliza Lawson** [*pseud.* F. G. Trafford] (**1832–1906**), novelist, born on 30 September 1832 at The Barn (or Barn Cottage), Carrickfergus, co. Antrim, was the daughter of James Cowan (d. 1851), flax and cotton spinner of Carrickfergus, and his second wife, Ellen Kilshaw (d. 1856). She had one full brother, and a half-brother and six half-sisters from her father's first marriage. From her childhood her father was an invalid. On his death much of his property went, by her marriage settlement, to the family of his first wife; his widow had an annuity of £100 p.a. with which she and her daughter went to live on a small jointure at Dundonald, co. Down, the setting for Charlotte's novel *Berna Boyle* (1884). In 1855 they moved to London, where they knew no one, and Charlotte tried to earn money for herself and her dying

mother by writing, an experience she described in *A Struggle for Fame* (1883). Her first book, written as R. V. Sparling, was *Zuriel's Grandchild* (1856). Its publisher, to whom she long remained grateful, was Thomas Cautley Newby, better known, and often reviled, as the publisher of the first novels of Emily Brontë and Anthony Trollope. Her mother died on 16 December 1856 and did not profit from her daughter's first modest successes. As Rainey Hawthorne she published *The Ruling Passion* (1857), and as F. G. Trafford seven novels between 1858 and 1866. Of these the most successful, and indeed the most popular of all her many works, was *George Geith of Fen Court* (1864), a story of an unwittingly bigamous accountant—one of the sensation novels then in vogue, for which William Tinsley paid her £800, probably the best price she ever received. It went into several editions and was dramatized in 1883. Like many of her books, it is much preoccupied with the social status of the businessman. After 1866 all her novels appeared under the name Mrs J. H. Riddell, though many of her stories appeared anonymously in magazines.

On 24 September 1857 Charlotte Cowan married, at St Paul's, Covent Garden, London, Joseph Hadley Riddell (d. 20 March 1881), described in the register as a patent agent; he (or possibly his father and namesake) applied for several patents between 1856 and 1869, mostly for improvements to boilers and hot-water pipes, calling himself variously 'civil engineer', 'hot water engineer', 'boiler manufacturer', and 'American stove merchant'. The business was at 155 Cheapside, and it had collapsed by September 1871, when he petitioned the bankruptcy court for liquidation. The episode was acknowledged by his wife to have provided the background for her novel *Mortomley's Estate* (1874); it also left her with a husband (soon an invalid) to support and a burden of debt to discharge. The Riddells' financial problems may have antedated the actual bankruptcy. Charlotte Riddell's rate of production was high even in the 1860s, and she also edited for some time the *Home Magazine* (which ran from 1856 to 1866) and, from 1867, *St James's Magazine*, of which she was co-proprietor and in which her novel *A Life's Assize* ran from 1868 to 1870. But Harry Furniss recalled that she told him in 1873 that 'there is not a magazine in London paying, the libraries destroy the sale'.

In Charlotte Riddell's day she was known best as a novelist of commercial life, and she told an interviewer that 'all the pathos of the City, the pathos in the lives of struggling men, entered into my soul, and I felt I must write, strongly as my publisher objected to my subject'. However, her modern reputation rests on the revival of interest in her ghost stories (published in *Weird Stories*, 1882), largely owing to the work of E. F. Bleiler, who in 1977 collected and edited them as *Collected Ghost Stories*. The particular flavour of Riddell's writing comes from her atmospheric settings; the places she lived in—Ireland and various parts of London, especially the City in which she spent her early married life—are strongly evoked in various books. Further details are given by S. M. Ellis, who also records her many moves after 1870 around London's still semi-rural suburbs.

Much of Charlotte Riddell's work bears signs of hasty composition, for she was dogged by poverty. She was a friend of Dr George Harley (to whom she dedicated *The Nun's Curse*, 1888), whose daughter, the writer Ethel Tweedie, exerted herself to help Riddell in old age, obtaining grants for her from the Royal Literary Fund and the civil list, which, with some private donations, made up a pension fund administered by the Society of Authors; she was paid £60 p.a. from 1901, the society's first pensioner. She died, childless, at her home, 12 Lampton Road, Hounslow, London, on 24 September 1906, of breast cancer which had been diagnosed in 1892, and she was buried in Heston churchyard, near Osterley, London.

CHARLOTTE MITCHELL

Sources S. M. Ellis, *Wilkie Collins, Le Fanu, and others* (1931) · E. F. Bleiler, introduction, in *The collected ghost stories of Mrs J. H. Riddell*, ed. E. F. Bleiler (1977) · private information (2004) · H. C. Black, *Notable women authors of the day* (1893) · J. H. Riddell, patents, 1856–69 · *The Times* (28 Sept 1871) · *The Times* (26 Sept 1906) · Society of authors archive, BL, Add. MS 57113 and MS 57090 fol. 867 · Mrs A. Tweedie, *Thirteen years of a busy woman's life* (1912) · 'Lady novelists—a chat with Mrs J. H. Riddell', *Pall Mall Gazette* (18 Feb 1890), 3 · S. Paul, 'Charlotte Riddell', *British short-fiction writers, 1880–1914: the romantic tradition*, ed. W. F. Naufftus, DLitB, 156 (1996), 283–90 · H. Furniss, *Some Victorian women, good, bad, and indifferent* (1923) · will, PRO NIre., D 3855/1, A and B [James Cowan] · m. cert. · d. cert. · d. cert. [Joseph Hadley Riddell]

Likenesses W. F. Thomas, portrait, repro. in Black, *Notable women authors of the day*

George Allardice Riddell, Baron Riddell (1865–1934), by Sir William Orpen, 1919

Riddell, George Allardice, Baron Riddell (1865–1934), newspaper proprietor, was born at 2 Stanhope Place, Loughborough Road, Brixton Heath, London, on 25 May 1865, the only son of James Riddell, photographer, and his wife, Isabel Young. Educated privately, he was first employed as a clerk by a Bloomsbury solicitor who, impressed by Riddell's ability and promise, gave him his articles. In his final examinations he was placed first in all England and was admitted a solicitor in 1888. He became obsessively absorbed in his legal work. Later he developed a similar, all-consuming interest in the newspaper business. He told a friend that he had suddenly realized he was a slave to his work and was missing out on much life had to offer. He determined never to return to his office. Soon afterwards, the friend observed he devoted himself instead to the *News of the World*.

Riddell's association with the *News of the World* dated from 1891, when he had been the legal consultant to the consortium that purchased the ailing Sunday newspaper. He had already acquired a holding in the *Western Mail*. Shrewdly and constantly Riddell enhanced his shareholding in the *News of the World* and by 1903 was the managing director. In 1910 he secured the controlling interest in the failing publishing firm of George Newnes, and in quick succession added the publications *Country Life* and *John O'London's Weekly*. Before the First World War he secured most of the capital in C. Arthur Pearson Ltd, and in 1921 combined this firm with Newnes to which he later added London Opinion Ltd in 1924, and in 1929 Leach's Publications Ltd. But it was the *News of the World* that was the cornerstone of Riddell's fortune and influence. It was his

ingenuity and enterprise, particularly his appointment of agents to sell the paper directly throughout the country, that gave the first boost to sales. The paper's invariable priority was the 'solid, careful, objective presentation of police court reports of rape, seduction, violence and marital infidelity' (Williams, 235). Despite Riddell's support of the Judicial Proceedings (Regulation of Reports) Bill in 1926, designed to restrict the reporting of divorce case details, circulation continued to boom, from 30,000 copies when the newspaper was first acquired to more than 7 million.

Riddell's contribution to the paper's success was widely recognized by informed critics, as one acknowledged in 1933: 'The paper is uncommonly well managed with as perfect an organisation as can be made' (Blumenfeld, 161). Yet Riddell never readily acknowledged his connection with a newspaper that emphasized the sensational and the salacious. If, when he reached the gates of Heaven, St Peter frowned upon his association with the *News of the World*, he told Hamilton Fyfe, 'I will urge in extenuation my connection with *John O'London's Weekly* and *Country Life*' (Fyfe, 107–8).

In 1909 Herbert Asquith, advised that the support of the *News of the World* was a valuable asset to the Liberals, gave Riddell the knighthood he had been seeking. Among those who pressed the prime minister to reward Riddell was David Lloyd George. The politician and the newspaper proprietor were close friends for twenty years. Both men acknowledged, though no bargain was ever struck, the mutual advantage in working together. Riddell made himself indispensable to Lloyd George. He kept him well informed of all press gossip; he provided hospitality, holidays, a car, a house, the free tenancy of two country mansions, a golfing partner, and not least, constant, shrewd support in his newspaper. Lloyd George availed himself of his friend's consummate skills as a negotiator. In 1912 Riddell drafted the memorandum that settled the miners' strike and was the basis for the Miners' Minimum Wage Act. During the First World War, Riddell liaised between government and press, frequently chairing the press committee. At the peace conference he continued his work, establishing smooth relations between the British delegation and the press at various European locations in 1919, at Washington in 1921, and in 1927 at Geneva. For his public and private services Riddell was decorated by the French and Italian governments, and in 1918 made a baronet.

On 13 December 1888 Riddell had married Grace Edith Williams. They were divorced on 29 October 1900. Riddell never publicly acknowledged his first marriage. On 2 November 1900 he married his cousin, Annie Molison Allardice. In 1915, during the course of a heated newspaper exchange, Sir Hedley Le Bas made public Riddell's first marriage. Subsequently, George V rejected Riddell's nomination as a peer because he had been the guilty party in a divorce action. Lloyd George insisted upon his friend's elevation, and the king's reservations were finally overcome by letters from other press lords protesting Riddell's virtues as chairman of the Newspaper Proprietors' Association. He received a barony in 1920. So Riddell became the first divorced peer to enter the Lords, breaking a social and constitutional convention that, until then, had bound both houses of parliament.

After the Paris peace conference a rift began to develop between Lloyd George, who became bitterly anti-French, and Riddell, who was pro-French and disapproved of the government's Near Eastern policy. There is some dispute as to the cause of the final breach (R. Blake, *The Unknown Prime Minister: the Life and Times of Andrew Bonar Law, 1858–1923*, 1955), but the friendship was never repaired. Lloyd George resented Riddell's support for Andrew Bonar Law, and was persuaded, unfairly, that his erstwhile friend had no use for him once he had ceased to be prime minister (A. J. P. Taylor, ed., *Lloyd George: a Diary*, 1971).

No longer so engaged in the fortunes of high politics, Riddell concentrated his energies more upon his business interests, charitable activities, and least successfully upon writing. For someone who had, for years, contributed a regular newspaper column that was frequently lively and always informed, his books are surprisingly pedestrian, often as banal and jejune as their titles suggest, as in *Some Things that Matter* (1922) and *More Things that Matter* (1925). He churned out biography, company history, and a monograph on medical ethics. Altogether different in kind, style, and quality are the diaries he kept from 1908 to 1923, and published shortly before the end of his life in three volumes: *Lord Riddell's War Diary* (1933), *Lord Riddell's Intimate Diary of the Peace Conference and After* (1933), and *More Pages from my Diary, 1908–1914* (1934). They afford a most valuable guide to the politics of the period generally and to the career of Lloyd George in particular. The detailed

retailing of conversations, while not always appreciated by Riddell's interlocutors, has provided rich and entertaining pickings for historians.

Riddell's work for charity and his munificence were legion. He served as president, chairman, or treasurer on the boards of a score of disparate charitable boards. He had a particular concern for medical charities, and provided handsome endowments for the Royal Free Hospital, London, and the Eastman Dental Clinic. He was a generous and caring patron of the printing industry and a founder of the London School of Printing. Golf was his great recreation, and he wished that others might have the opportunity to share his passion for the game. With Sir Emsley Carr he founded the Artisans' Golf Association. He was closely associated with the golf course at Walton Heath, Surrey, and much preferred an austere room in the club house to any in his palatial mansion that overlooked St James's Park.

Riddell died at his home, Walton Heath House, Walton on the Hill, Banstead, Surrey, on 5 December 1934. Employees and friends alike remembered with affection the strange contradictions of Riddell's character. He was masterful yet extraordinarily considerate; sure of his own judgement yet always open to persuasion. Few rich men had so few wants. He was keenly interested in making money, but not in spending it upon himself. His clothes were shabby, he drank little, was indifferent to food, but smoked incessantly. A man of amazing industry, he had an insatiable curiosity, made manifest by cross-examining everyone with whom he came into contact. An editor noted that Riddell 'had an infinite capacity for asking never answering questions' (Dark, 18). He was consistently appreciative of service and good work by his employees. To his friends he was kindly, shrewd, invariably understanding, and helpful.   A. J. A. MORRIS

Sources D. Hopkin, 'Riddell, George Allardice', *DBB* · *DNB* · *The Riddell diaries, 1908–1923* (1986) · S. Dark, *Mainly about other people* (1925) · F. Stevenson, *Lloyd George: a diary*, ed. A. J. P. Taylor (1971) · F. L. Lloyd George, *The years that are past* (1967) · M. A. Beaverbrook, *Men and power, 1917–1918* (1956) · F. Owen, *Tempestuous journey: Lloyd George, his life and times* (1954) · Viscount Camrose [W. E. Berry], *British newspapers and their controllers* (1947) · F. Williams, *Dangerous estate: the anatomy of newspapers* (1957) · R. D. Blumenfeld, *The press in my time* (1933) · H. Fyfe, *Sixty years of Fleet Street* (1949) · *WWW* · b. cert. · m. certs. · d. cert.

Archives BL, diaries, Add. MSS 62955–62990 | BL, corresp. with Lord Northcliffe, Add. MS 62173 · HLRO, corresp. with Lord Beaverbrook · HLRO, corresp. with David Lloyd George | FILM BFI NFTVA, news footage

Likenesses W. Orpen, group portrait, oils, 1919 (*The signing of peace in the hall of mirrors, Versailles, 1919*), IWM · W. Orpen, oils, 1919, Scot. NPG [*see illus.*] · Lafayette, photograph, c.1920, NPG · W. R. Dick, bust, c.1931, Royal Free Hospital, London · D. Low, caricature, pencil sketch, NPG · W. Orpen, oils, second version of individual portrait, Stationers' Hall, London · M. L. Williams, oils (after photograph), NMG Wales

Wealth at death £1,838,901 16s. 9d.: probate, 14 Jan 1935, *CGPLA Eng. & Wales*

Riddell, Hannah (1855–1932), medical missionary, was born on 17 October 1855 at 9 The Barracks, Barnet, Hertfordshire, the only daughter of Daniel Riddle (1810–1889) (he always spelt his name differently from his wife and

Hannah Riddell
(1855–1932), by
unknown
photographer,
c.1906

daughter) and Hannah Wright (1814–1886), née Hunt. Daniel was born in Glasgow, the son of a weaver. He joined the army in 1837 and served in India and China. In 1853 he was appointed a staff sergeant in the militia and posted to Barnet. After retiring from the army in 1877 he took his family to live in Oystermouth near Swansea. Here they rented Russell House where Hannah ran a boarding-school for young ladies until she became bankrupt soon after her father's death in 1889. After release from bankruptcy she went to Liverpool in October 1889, where she was appointed deputy superintendent at the YMWCA.

Hannah was in Liverpool for less than a year before joining the Church Missionary Society (CMS) which in 1888 had decided to start sending women missionaries abroad. Apart from her orphaned niece, Ada Wright, to whom she was devoted, Hannah had few ties in England and accepted her posting to Japan with enthusiasm. She arrived in Kobe on 16 January 1891, where she stayed for several months before being sent to Kumamoto in Kyushu. A strong, forceful woman over 6 feet tall, Hannah was soon at odds with the small band of British missionaries stationed there, most of whom she regarded as lacking drive and ambition. They in turn found her pushy and extravagant, and disliked her practice of ignoring orthodox channels by writing directly to CMS headquarters in London in order to achieve her aims.

Soon after arriving in Kumamoto, Hannah visited the Honmyoji Temple, a favourite gathering place for lepers, where for the first time she encountered leprosy 'in every degree of loathsomeness' (report to CMS, 1 Dec 1891, Archives of the CMS). Profoundly shocked by the experience, she discovered that little or no provision was made for the victims of leprosy, a disease prevalent in Japan until effective drugs were developed in the 1940s.

Hannah decided to build a hospital in Kumamoto devoted to the care of lepers, and energetically set about raising the necessary funds. She received only lukewarm support from her fellow missionaries who felt that such a venture detracted from their primary task of converting the 'heathen' to Christianity. But, despite many difficulties, the Hospital of the Resurrection of Hope was finally opened on 12 November 1895.

Over the next few years Hannah's relations with her missionary colleagues steadily deteriorated. The CMS eventually decided to remove her altogether from Japan, but Hannah, determined not to abandon her patients, instead resigned from the society in 1900 and thereafter directed the hospital independently until her death. Money was a constant problem, but she established an impressive network of support, and donations (many of them very small) came in from Japan, England, and America. The hospital's precarious income did not deter Hannah from living in a lavish style that many people considered inappropriate for a missionary. She vigorously justified such expenditure by claiming that unless she appeared to be a lady of class and substance, she would not be taken seriously by those in a position to underpin her work.

Along with most of her contemporaries (including many distinguished doctors) Hannah had a minimal understanding of the pathology of leprosy. She erroneously asserted that the only way to eliminate the disease was by strict sex segregation. But she did influence official and public attitudes to leprosy. The result was more humane treatment of its victims. Thanks in part to her impassioned lobbying of the Japanese government the first legislation to provide for the care, rather than control, of lepers went through the Diet in 1907, and over the next few years five national leprosaria were built. She also initiated leper relief work in Kusatsu and Okinawa. Articulate and energetic, Hannah was a tireless traveller and lecturer in the promotion of her cause. She won both moral and financial support from many influential figures in Meiji Japan and, most important, from the imperial family. For her contribution to the fight against leprosy she was awarded the medal of the Blue Ribbon in 1906 and the order of the Sacred Treasure (sixth class) in 1922. Hannah died on 3 February 1932 at 436 Furushinyashiki, Kumamoto, and was buried in Kumamoto the following day. After her death the hospital was continued under the direction of her niece, Ada Wright, until its closure in 1941.   JULIA BOYD

Sources U. Birm. L., special collections department, Church Missionary Society archive · M. Uchida, *Yukari no minoru o michite: rideru to raito no shogai* (1990) · K. Aoki, *Mission to Okinawa* (Hong Kong, [1970]) · *Church Missionary Intelligencer*, 41–53 (1890–1902) · R. C. Hastings, ed., *Leprosy*, 2nd edn (1994) · J. Tobimatsu, *Hannah Riddell: known in Japan as the Mother of Lepers* (1937) · b. cert.
Archives U. Birm. L., special collections department, Church Missionary Society archive | Riddell-Wright Museum, Kumamoto, Kyushu, Japan
Likenesses photograph, c.1906, priv. coll. [*see illus.*]
Wealth at death resources entirely tied up with her hospital which continued after her death under direction of her niece; house and personal possessions to niece

Riddell, Henry Scott (1798–1870), poet, son of Robert Riddell, shepherd, and his wife, Agnes Scott, both of Teviotdale, was born at Sorbie, parish of Ewes, Dumfriesshire, on 23 September 1798. In his childhood his father worked as a shepherd and farmed in Dumfriesshire and Selkirkshire. Riddell's education progressed slowly; in summer he worked as a herder, and in winter he was either taught at home by a visiting master or was boarded in some village to secure school training. While the family lived at Eskdalemuir, Dumfriesshire, they were visited by James Hogg, who sang or recited to them his own lyrics. Riddell's love of reading and writing grew during his years of shepherd life and, on the death of his father in 1817, he attended the parish school of Biggar, Lanarkshire, for about two years. It was during this period that he wrote 'The Crook and the Plaid' and contributed border romances to the *Clydesdale Magazine*.

From 1819 to 1830 Riddell was a student at Edinburgh University, where he was befriended by Professor Wilson. His college course included a year at St Andrews (1830) under Thomas Chalmers and other eminent professors, and in 1830 he became a licentiate of the Church of Scotland. His poetry received recognition during these years as his work was printed in the collections of Scottish songs and poems edited by Robert Archibald Smith and Peter McLeod, the latter publishing what is perhaps his best-known song: 'Scotland yet'.

In 1831 Riddell settled with his eldest brother at Teviothead, Roxburghshire, and *Songs of the Ark*, a collection of his sacred pieces, was published. In 1833, he became incumbent of Caerlanrig Chapel. Soon afterwards he married Eliza Clark, the Eliza of his songs, daughter of a Biggar merchant. They were to have three sons, of whom two survived him. They lived near Hawick, 9 miles away from Caerlanrig; thus he conducted his work under difficult conditions until the duke of Buccleuch provided a suitable dwelling near the chapel, and for many years Riddell enjoyed prosperity and comfort. In 1841 shortly before he was due to receive ordination Riddell showed symptoms of mental illness, and for three years he was confined at the Crichton Royal Institution at Dumfries. Returning to Teviothead in 1844, he was enabled, by the generosity of the duke of Buccleuch, to retain his cottage while resigning his living; there he lived very quietly, occasionally lecturing at Hawick or elsewhere on behalf of some charitable object, but devoting himself mainly to the improvement of his house and its surroundings, and to literary work. In 1844 *Christian Politician* was published, a doctrinal volume displaying argumentative power, and the fruits of his convalescence appeared in 1847 as *Poems, Songs and Miscellaneous Pieces*. In the same year he wrote a discriminating biography of James Hogg for *Hogg's Instructor*.

In Riddell's last years, his interests were diverse. He involved himself closely with the Border Counties Association. He interested himself in local excavations, supported the Hawick Archaeological Society, and wrote a careful article, 'Cavers', for the *Statistical Account of Scotland*. He translated into lowland Scottish dialect in 1855 and 1857 respectively, the gospel of St Matthew and the Psalms of David, the latter for Prince Lucien Bonaparte. For the *Scottish Agricultural Journal*, in 1848–9 he wrote substantial papers entitled 'Store-farming in the south of Scotland', and about the same time received from the Highland and Agricultural Society a prize of £10 for his 'Essay on foot-rot in sheep'. Henry Scott Riddell died in

Teviothead Cottage on 30 July 1870 and was buried in Caerlanrig churchyard on 2 August. He was survived by his wife and two sons. *The Poetical Works of Henry Scott Riddell*, edited by James Brydon, was published in 1871.

T. W. BAYNE, *rev.* SAYONI BASU

Sources J. Brydon, 'Memoir', in *The poetical works of Henry Scott Riddell*, ed. J. Brydon, 1 (1871), ix–lxxv · C. Rogers, *The modern Scottish minstrel, or, The songs of Scotland of the past half-century*, 4 (1857) | brief autobiography until 1854] · J. C. Goodfellow, *Border biography* (1890)

Archives NL Scot., corresp., notes, and poems · U. Glas. L., letters and poems

Likenesses lithograph, repro. in Rogers, *Modern Scottish minstrel*, frontispiece · lithograph, BM · photograph, repro. in H. S. Riddell, *Poetical works* (1871), frontispiece

Riddell, James (d. 1674), merchant and manufacturer of soap and broadcloth, was the only son of James Riddell and his wife, Bessie Allan. The elder James Riddell was an English merchant descended from a landowning family, who traded in Cracow, Poland, and later moved to Edinburgh to become burgess and guild brother. In 1639 Riddell similarly became burgess and guild brother and tacksman of the lands of Kinglass, Linlithgowshire, in Bo'ness parish. He married Elizabeth Foulis (1620–1670), daughter of George Foulis, laird of Ravelston, on 15 October 1639.

Riddell appears to have been a skilled negotiator. He was useful to the Scottish army during its campaign in 1645, and during the English occupation of Scotland he was friendly with General Monck, a distant kinsman, and with Oliver Cromwell. He is said to have intervened to settle a clash between Monck and the minister of his parish, South Leith, when the minister incurred the governor's anger by praying for Charles II. He is also said to have obtained the discharge of several manufacturers from the army.

Riddell's business interests were varied. In 1645 he shared in setting up a broadcloth manufactory. In 1649 he obtained permission from the city council of Edinburgh for a soap works in Leith. In 1652 he received licence to sell naval stores from Norway in any English port, and was also importing oil for his soap works. His cargo was impounded by the commissioners at Leith and the ship declared forfeit, but with General Lilburne's help he obtained release of his goods. In September 1663, joined with the earl of Crawford, he received monopoly rights in Scotland for nineteen years in the manufacture of the cards used for tow and wool manufactures. In 1665 the trading hoy belonging to him and his partners was seized off Bremen by English privateers, who were subsequently ordered to release it. In 1668 he and several others, mostly miners, were involved in a rough confrontation with Dame Christian Forrester and her husband, the Revd John Waugh, even more strongly supported, over the rights to the drainage system of coal mines on the Grange estate at Kinglass. There was some fighting and stone throwing. Both sides complained at length to the privy council, who ordered the earls of Linlithgow and Kincardine to investigate the rival claims.

Riddell's high standing in the affairs of Leith is shown

by the fact that in March 1656, together with another burgess, Moses Trent, he represented the town in an unsuccessful attempt to persuade Edinburgh to surrender its superiority over Leith. It was probably he who became a merchant councillor in Edinburgh in 1672 and baron bailie for Leith in October 1673. Riddell's wife died on 10 June 1670 and was buried two days later in Leith; he himself died in 1674 and was buried on 29 December in Greyfriars churchyard, Edinburgh. They had four sons, James, Adam, George, and Andrew, and two daughters, Isabel and Agnes. James, who never married, was for a time a captain in the navy of the Netherlands. He is said to have encumbered his paternal estate. The family line was continued by George, whose grandson Sir James Riddell LLD, of Belton, England, re-established its landowning status in Scotland with an estate in Berwickshire and another in Ardnamurchan.

T. F. HENDERSON, rev. ROSALIND MITCHISON

Sources R. Douglas and others, The baronage of Scotland (1798) · M. Wood, ed., Extracts from the records of the burgh of Edinburgh, 1642–1655, [9] (1938) · M. Wood, ed., Extracts from the records of the burgh of Edinburgh, 1655–1665, [10] (1940) · M. Wood, ed., Extracts from the records of the burgh of Edinburgh, 1665–1680, [11] (1950) · CSP dom., 1652–4; 1664–7 · Reg. PCS, 3rd ser., vol. 2 · APS, 1661–9 · H. Paton, ed., Register of interments in the Greyfriars burying-ground, Edinburgh, 1658–1700, Scottish RS, 26 (1902) · C. B. B. Watson, ed., Roll of Edinburgh burgesses and guild-brethren, 1406–1700, Scottish RS, 59 (1929), pt 101 · H. Paton, ed., The register of marriages for the parish of Edinburgh, 1595–1700, Scottish RS, old ser., 27 (1905)

Riddell, James (1823–1866), classical scholar, was born on 8 June 1823, the eldest son of James Riddell (1796–1878), MA of Balliol College, rector of Easton, Hampshire, and Dorothy, daughter of John Foster, of Leicester Grange, Warwickshire. After spending seven years at Mr Browne's school at Cheam, Surrey, Riddell entered Shrewsbury School in 1838 as a pupil of Dr Kennedy. He gained a scholarship at Balliol in November 1840, and, leaving Shrewsbury as head boy in 1841, he began residence in Oxford in the Michaelmas term of that year. He was placed in the first class in literae humaniores. In the same year he was elected fellow of Balliol and, remaining unmarried, served his college as lecturer or tutor until his death. Among his tutorial pupils was the poet Gerard Manley Hopkins. It was probably Riddell's vote which secured the election of Robert Scott rather than Benjamin Jowett to the mastership in 1854. He was classical examiner in 1858–9, classical moderator in 1865–6, and senior proctor and select preacher in 1862. He died at Tunbridge Wells on 14 September 1866.

Riddell's fine scholarship was widely recognized. He was invited by the delegates of the university press to edit the Odyssey for their Oxford series; and Benjamin Jowett, who was planning an edition of Plato, entrusted to him the Apology, Crito, Phaedo, and Symposium. Both of these works were left incomplete. Riddell's commentary on Odyssey, i–xii, for which he had made large preparations, was completed by his friend and pupil, W. W. Merry (1876). Of his work on Plato he lived to finish only the Apology (1867). The edition is unusual for its date not only in its detailed use of contemporary European classical scholarship, but also for its lengthy introduction, which deals with Socrates' critical attitude to Athenian democracy and the detail of the procedure in his trial. Riddell's view of Socrates became influential through various school editions of the Apology which were based on his work. In the same volume appeared a 'Digest of Platonic idioms', which he left behind him, founded on a minute examination of the whole of Plato's works. This consists of over a hundred pages of instances where Plato breaks the rule of 'normal' grammar or which are otherwise linguistically remarkable. Although Riddell's principles of selection and arrangement have been superseded, the work is one of the earliest and fullest investigations of Platonic syntax.

Riddell's skill in Greek and Latin verse composition is shown in various translations in the Anthologia Oxoniensis and in Sabrinae corolla. These were collected, with additions, in a small volume of Reliquiae metricae (1867).

W. W. MERRY, rev. RICHARD SMAIL

Sources I. Elliott, ed., The Balliol College register, 1833–1933, 2nd edn (privately printed, Oxford, 1934) · Boase, Mod. Eng. biog. · F. Turner, The Greek heritage in Victorian Britain (1982)
Archives LPL, papers
Wealth at death under £6000: resworn probate, 1866, CGPLA Eng. & Wales

Riddell, John (1785–1862), lawyer and genealogist, was born on 4 October 1785, the eldest of four sons of Henry Riddell (1745–1801), of Little Govan, a Glasgow merchant, and his wife, Anne Glassford (d. 1827). His father was a scion of the Riddell family, baronets of Riddell, Roxburghshire. Riddell's education, before he was called to the bar in 1807, is not recorded, though he later showed himself to be an accomplished classical scholar.

Riddell made a special study of genealogy and peerage law. He assisted the philosopher Sir William Stirling Hamilton in the successful claim for his baronetcy in 1816, and he later succeeded in claiming the earldom of Crawford for the Lindsay family (though his efforts to establish their entitlement to the dukedom of Montrose were fruitless). He published a number of works on peerage and genealogical topics, of which the most substantial was Inquiry into the Law and Practice in Scottish Peerages before and after the Union (2 vols., 1842).

Riddell was friendly with J. G. Lockhart and it was the latter who recorded Sir Walter Scott's opinion that, among antiquaries, only Riddell and Thomas Thomson possessed a proper appreciation of pre-Reformation Scotland. Riddell's deep and extensive knowledge was derived from his familiarity with a wide range of public and private records and he was said to have inspected the contents of almost every principal charter-chest in Scotland. However, his pre-eminence in this field, combined with a volatile temperament, made him quick to enter into heated controversies with a younger generation of scholars, including Sir William Fraser, Cosmo Innes, and Mark Napier. Lord Lindsay noted that 'he occasionally attacked what he conceived to be a genealogical blunder or a legal heresy as if it had involved a moral delinquency'

(*Herald and Genealogist*, 540), and if this was his only fault it was certainly a conspicuous one.

Riddell died, unmarried, at his home, 57 Melville Street, Edinburgh, on 8 February 1862, and was buried locally in the Dean cemetery. The value of his extensive collection of notebooks and papers on peerage cases was immediately recognized and James Maidment published a catalogue of them in 1863. In due course they passed to the Advocates' Library, Edinburgh, and now reside in the National Library of Scotland.

LIONEL ALEXANDER RITCHIE

Sources *Herald and Genealogist*, 1 (1863), 538–45 · *Law Times* (28 March 1863), 290 · J. Maidment, *The Riddell papers: a catalogue of the annotated books and manuscripts of the late John Riddell, esq, advocate* (1863) · Burke, *Peerage* · *DNB* · *The Scotsman* (10 Feb 1862) · *Fasti Scot.*

Archives NL Scot., corresp., notebooks on peerage cases, and papers; memoranda and notes | Lpool RO, letters to Lord Stanley · Lyon Office Library, notes on Alexander Nisbet's *System of heraldry* [copy] · Stirling Central Regional Council Archives, letters and papers to Sir Archibald Edmonstone relating to Edmonstone genealogy · U. Aberdeen L., letters to William Innes relating to Sir Charles Forbes's claim to be Lord Forbes of Pitsligo · U. Edin. L., letters to David Laing

Likenesses photograph, repro. in Maidment, *Riddell papers*

Wealth at death £10,988 4s. 6d.: confirmation, 20 March 1862, NA Scot., SC70/1/111, 993–9

Riddell [*née* Woodley], **Maria** (1772–1808), poet, was born in England on 4 November 1772, the sixth of seven children and the youngest of the three daughters of William Woodley (1722–1793), a West Indian plantation owner, twice governor and captain-general of the Leeward Islands, and his wife, Frances Payne. She first demonstrated her literary bent at the age of fifteen, jousting in verse with Joseph Jekyll, a noted wit twice her age; her 'Inscription on an hermitage', written during a stay in the Caribbean in 1788, displays real poetical maturity. In the course of a second visit in 1790–91 she composed her *Voyages to the Madeira and Leeward Caribbean Isles: with sketches of the natural history of these islands* (1792), published with the help of the Edinburgh printer William Smellie, who praised its 'science, minute observation, [and] accurate description'.

On 16 September 1790, on St Kitts, Maria married a widower, Walter Riddell (1764–1802), lieutenant (on half pay), plantation owner on Antigua and the second son of Walter Riddell of Newhouse, a well-connected Dumfriesshire merchant, whose other son, Robert, of Glenriddell, was a noted antiquary and friend of Burns. They returned to Scotland, where Walter bought an estate near Dumfries. Renamed Woodley Park, it became the scene of many fashionable and literary gatherings. Two daughters, Anna Maria (1791–1859) and Sophia (1792–1797), were born before Walter departed in 1796 for Antigua, where he died.

Maria's acquaintance with Robert Burns, to whom she owed her introduction to Smellie, began in Dumfries in late 1791. Despite the 'Rape of the Sabines' episode during Christmas 1793, when a drunken Burns may have overstepped the bounds of propriety towards his hostess, and notwithstanding the lampoons with which he requited

Maria Riddell (1772–1808), by Sir Thomas Lawrence, *c*.1805

his subsequent exile from her house, the intimate friendship that Burns formed with this 'really first-rate woman' survived its year-long breach. She wrote a highly perceptive appreciation of Burns's character after his death in the *Dumfries Journal* (August 1796) and collaborated energetically with his biographer James Currie—thereby also effectively protecting her own interests and reputation.

Maria left Scotland in 1797 for London, where she remained until granted, in 1803, apartments in Hampton Court Palace. Intelligent, beautiful, and widely read in four languages, she cultivated men of 'unquestionable genius' such as Sir Thomas Lawrence and Henry Fuseli, whom she compared to Burns: his 'Lament for Maria' (1809?) was probably written in response to her death. Other literati who frequented her soirées included Sir James Mackintosh, Samuel Rogers, and 'Conversation' Richard Sharp. Her only other published work was *The Metrical Miscellany* (1802; 2nd edn, 1803), an anthology of fugitive verse by contemporary celebrities, in which she also published twenty of her own poems (among them the prefatory verses of 1802 by 'The Editor'). Of her prolific correspondence, little beyond that with William Roscoe and James Currie has survived. In 1808 Maria married Phillips Lloyd Fletcher (1782–1863), an officer of dragoons, of Gwernheylod, Ellesmere, Flintshire. She died on 15 December 1808 in Chester and was buried in the Fletcher family vault at Overton.

D. H. WEINGLASS

Sources H. S. Gladstone, 'Maria Riddell, the friend of Burns', *Transactions of the Dumfries and Galloway Antiquarian Society* (1915) · J. C. Ewing, ed., 'Maria Riddell's letters to James Currie', *Burns Chronicle* (1920–24) · J. M. Wood, *Robert Burns and the Riddell family* (1922) · A. Macnaghten, *Burns' Mrs. Riddell* (1975) · D. H. Weinglass, 'The painter's muse: Henry Fuseli and Maria Riddell', *Gazette des Beaux-Arts* (1978)

Archives Lpool RO, corresp. with William Roscoe
Likenesses T. Lawrence, oils, c.1805, Kingston Lacy, Dorset [see illus.]

Riddell, Robert, of Glenriddell (*bap.* **1755**, *d.* **1794**), antiquary and literary patron, born in Newhouse, Irongray, Dumfriesshire, and baptized at St Michael's Church, Dumfries, on 5 October 1755, was the eldest son and second of seven children born to Walter Riddell (1705–1788) of Newhouse and his wife and cousin, Anna Riddell, heir to the Glenriddell estate. Walter Riddell is best remembered as one of the two hostages taken by the Jacobite army in 1745. Anna Riddell succeeded to the Glenriddell estate in 1771 and Robert inherited it in 1788 following the death of his father. Subsequently he sold the estate but retained the territorial appellation. The family traced its descent from Gervase de Riddell, an Anglo-Norman official appointed sheriff of Roxburghshire. By the late seventeenth century the Riddells were one of the leading landed families in Glencairn parish, Dumfriesshire. Two brothers married into neighbouring families and established links which have strong connections with Robert *Burns: Robert Riddell (1700–1771) and Jean Fergusson of Craigdarroch were the parents of Anna Riddell, while her younger brother Walter Riddell married Katherine Laurie of Maxwelton. The family ties were strengthened by the marriage in 1709 of 'bonnie Annie Laurie' and Alexander Fergusson of Craigdarroch, aunt and uncle of Robert Riddell. The ancestral home of the Riddell family in Glencairn parish, Nithsdale, was no longer occupied by the middle of the eighteenth century and is now a picturesque ruin, near the ford across the Cairn Water.

Robert Riddell was educated at Dumfries Academy (where James Currie, the future biographer of Burns, was a classmate) and the universities of Edinburgh and St Andrews. Commissioned into the Scots Greys, on 17 November 1780, he became a captain in the 32nd (Cornwall) regiment of foot in Ireland and retired on half-pay at the end of the American War of Independence in 1783. On 31 October 1792 he joined the 12th (Prince of Wales's) regiment of light dragoons but did not see active service and spent most of his time on his country estate. On 7 November 1784 he married Elizabeth Kennedy (*d.* 1801), daughter of a Manchester merchant whose family had hailed from Lanarkshire. In the same year Riddell purchased the estate of Friars' Carse in Dunscore parish, Nithsdale, and settled there, devoting much of his time to antiquarian and literary pursuits.

Riddell published various papers in volumes 9 and 10 of *Archaeologia*, including 'An account of the ancient lordship of Galloway', 'Remarks on the title of thane and abthane', 'Of the ancient modes of fortification in Scotland', and 'Notices of fonts in Scotland'. He was a fellow of the Society of Antiquaries both of London and of Scotland, and a member of the Philosophical Society of Manchester. His illustrated description of Nithsdale was presented to the Society of Antiquaries in 1793, and volume 4 of the memoirs of the Manchester society contains his dissertations on the ancient carved stones in Scotland and on one in Dumfriesshire. Riddell gave much help to Francis Grose

who visited him at Friars' Carse in 1789, and he corresponded with Richard Gough and John Nichols. Riddell was granted the degree of LLD at Edinburgh in 1794.

An enthusiastic amateur musician and composer of some talent, Riddell was just the man who would be immediately drawn to Burns through a shared interest in Scottish song. About 1785 Riddell had compiled a volume entitled *New music for the piano forte or harpsichord composed by a gentleman consisting of a collection of reels, minuets, hornpipes, marches and two songs in the old Scotch taste, with variations to five favourite tunes* which was published by James Johnson, with whom Burns subsequently collaborated in the *Scots Musical Museum*. It may have been Johnson who introduced Burns and Riddell, although early biographers (unaware of this connection) assumed that they had been introduced by the poet's landlord, Patrick Miller of Dalswinton, at or about the time that Burns took up the lease of Ellisland Farm in June 1788.

Riddell, whose antiquarian enthusiasm occasionally outran his scientific approach to the subject, created a fake druids' circle and a hermitage, after the manner of the cell of a medieval anchorite. This folly, situated among the woods at the southern end of his estate, was close to the boundary of Ellisland Farm. Riddell gave the poet a key to this little summer house so that he could meditate therein whenever the mood took him. By 28 June 1788 this had yielded its first fruits, 'Verses in Friars' Carse Hermitage'. A substantially longer version was composed several months later. These poems were but the first of several inspired by the friendship of Burns and Riddell. Burns wrote the song 'The day returns' to a melody by Riddell to mark the latter's wedding anniversary (7 November 1788). Apart from a handful of letters and verse epistles addressed to Riddell, Burns undertook to prepare for his friend a collection of manuscripts. Riddell procured two handsome calf-bound quarto volumes which he passed to Burns with the intention that the first volume should contain poetry and the second a selection of the poet's letters. Work on the first volume, which eventually included fifty-seven unpublished poems as well as the long autobiographical letter to Dr John Moore, began about May 1789 and was completed on 27 April 1791. Work on the second volume, which eventually contained twenty-seven of the poet's most important letters, was still in progress at Christmas 1793 when it was abruptly terminated for reasons given below. After Riddell's death in 1794 Burns retrieved the first volume from his widow. After a long and chequered history the two volumes, now known as the Glenriddell manuscripts, were presented to the National Library of Scotland in 1926.

On 16 October 1789 Burns was a witness to a great drinking bout at Friars' Carse, when Riddell competed for a historic whistle with his cousins Sir Robert Laurie of Maxwelton and Alexander Fergusson of Craigdarroch. Fergusson was the victor, as Burns describes in 'The Whistle'. Riddell composed airs for several of Burns's songs, including 'The Whistle', 'The Banks of Nith', and 'The Blue-Eyed Lassie'. Burns assisted Riddell in founding the Monkland Free

Society, a parish circulating library; many of Burns's letters to the Edinburgh bookseller Peter Hill refer to books purchased for this library whose volumes are preserved at Ellisland. Riddell prevailed on his friend to add an account of the Monkland Free Society for Sir John Sinclair's *Statistical Account of Scotland* which he forwarded with a covering letter. This was subsequently published in volume 3 (1792, pp. 597–600).

In 1790 Riddell's brother Walter (1764–1802) married Maria Banks Woodley [see Riddell, Maria]. Walter took a lease of the estate near Dumfries called Goldielea and renamed it Woodley Park in honour of his young wife. Maria, though only nineteen, had already written a book about her travels in the West Indies. Burns, who was introduced to her at Friars' Carse, gave her a letter of introduction to his Edinburgh printer, William Smellie, on 22 January 1792, and as a result her book, entitled *Voyages to the Madeira and Leeward Caribbean Isles*, was published by Peter Hill and Thomas Cadell later that year. Burns wrote a number of songs in her honour, as well as at least twenty-five letters.

Even after he moved from Ellisland to Dumfries in November 1791 Burns remained on very close terms with Robert Riddell and his family, and named his daughter (born on 21 November 1792) Elizabeth Riddell Burns after Riddell's wife. Riddell, assisted by Burns, took a leading role in the foundation of the Theatre Royal in Dumfries which opened on 29 September 1792 and is the only surviving Georgian theatre in Scotland. Some time after Christmas 1793, however, at a party at Friars' Carse, there occurred a prank that badly misfired. After the ladies had withdrawn from the dining-room the men sat drinking. Somehow the Roman myth known as the rape of the Sabine women cropped up in conversation and somebody suggested that it would be rather a lark to re-enact the scene. Burns led the assault and grabbed hold of Maria Riddell, only to discover, to his horror, that he was alone, his fellow-conspirators having set him up. Burns was dismissed from the house. The following morning he wrote the so-called 'Epistle from hell' (one of the best descriptions of a hangover in literature) by way of apology to Elizabeth Riddell, his hostess. Unfortunately the rather jocular tone merely offended the lady and widened the rift. Maria Riddell was drawn into the squabble and her hostility drove Burns to pen the scurrilous verses 'Monody on a Lady Famed for her Caprice'.

Robert Riddell, whose part in the incident was by no means innocent, for he had plied Burns with too much drink, died at Friars' Carse on 21 April 1794 without any reconciliation having taken place. Nevertheless, Burns immediately published a sonnet on his late friend ('No more, ye warblers of the wood, no more'). Riddell was buried on 23 April 1794 in Dunscore parish churchyard; his grave is still preserved. When Robert Riddell died his brother Walter hoped to inherit Friars' Carse, or at least persuade the widow to surrender the estate in exchange for an annuity; but, according to Burns, Elizabeth Riddell hated her brother-in-law and refused to accede to his wishes. She died at Bath on 21 December 1801.

Riddell's library of books on antiquities was sold by Robert Ross in 1795; they included a manuscript, 'Collection of Scottish antiquities', containing journals of tours made with Francis Grose, illustrated by watercolours by Riddell. There were also manuscript collections of Scottish ballads, and glossaries and notes of families and peerages (N&Q, 3rd ser., 7.201). In May 1794, soon after his death, Riddell's posthumous volume *A Collection of Scots, Galwegian and Border Tunes* was published at Edinburgh.

JAMES A. MACKAY

Sources commissary records, Dec 1766–Dec 1809, Dumfries SCO · birth records, Glencairn RO · birth records, Irongray RO · birth records, Dumfries RO · marriage register, March 1784, Manchester Cathedral · marriage registers, Dumfries and Glencairn RO · *The songs of Robert Burns*, ed. D. A. Low (1993) · J. A. Mackay, *Burns-lore of Dumfries and Galloway* (1988) · J. A. Mackay, *Burns in Ellisland* (1989) · J. A. Mackay, *Burns, a biography of Robert Burns* (1993) · A. MacNaghton, *Burns's Mrs Riddell* (1975) · H. Gladstone, *Maria Riddell, the friend of Robert Burns* (1915) · J. Maxwell Wood, *Robert Burns and the Riddell family* (1922) · R. Thornton, 'Robert Riddell, antiquary', *Burns Chronicle* (1953), 44–67 · parish register, Bath, St James's [wife, death]

Archives Dumfries and Galloway Archives, Dumfries, commonplace book · National Museums of Scotland, Edinburgh, collections containing accounts of history, families, and antiquities of Dumfriesshire, Galloway, etc. · S. Antiquaries, Lond., MS on antiquities of Nithsdale | NL Scot., letters to G. Paton and R. Gough

Likenesses drawing, 1793, Society of Antiquaries of Scotland, Edinburgh, MS volume

Wealth at death conveyed Friars' Carse to Walter Riddell

Riddell, Sir Thomas (*bap.* 1602, *d.* 1652), royalist army officer, was baptized in St Nicholas's Church, Newcastle upon Tyne, on 14 February 1602, the second son of Sir Thomas Riddell (*c.*1568–1650) of Gateshead, co. Durham, and his wife, Elizabeth Conyers (*d.* 1631/2), daughter of Sir John Conyers of Sockburn, co. Durham, and his first wife, Agnes. The elder Riddell, with whom his son is often confused, was recorder and sheriff of Newcastle upon Tyne in 1601, mayor in 1604 and 1616, and MP for the borough in 1620–21, 1625, and 1627–8.

The younger Thomas Riddell was admitted to Emmanuel College, Cambridge, on 28 May 1617 (from where he matriculated but apparently did not graduate) and to Lincoln's Inn on 12 June 1619; he was called to the bar in 1626. On 13 April 1629 he married Barbara (*d.* 1673), widow of Ralph Calverley of Newcastle and daughter of Sir Alexander Davison of Blakiston, co. Durham; they had three sons and six daughters. Like his father Riddell became a wealthy landowner and collier. He held the manor of Softley, with further lands at Tonstall, Throston, Hamsterley, and Whickham. To distinguish him from his father, he is usually described as of Fenham, where he owned the lordship, including all the collieries and coalmines. He became recorder of Newcastle and was knighted on 1 April 1639. During the second bishops' war the Scots despoiled his father's estates, plundered his tenants, and laid waste his mills and coalmines; Riddell attempted to raise the town against them. He was MP for Newcastle in the Short Parliament of 1640.

Riddell, like his father, became an ardent royalist. Parliament ordered that he be apprehended as a delinquent on 20 September 1642, while he was subsequently added to the commission of array for Durham. He was among the most prominent Roman Catholics of the region, and was related to other Catholic royalists such as Sir Robert Clavering of Callaly, Northumberland, and John Forcer of Harbourhouse, co. Durham. The earl of Newcastle, the royalist general in the north, commissioned Riddell as colonel and appointed him governor of Tynemouth Castle. The earl's decision angered Sir John Marley, the governor of Newcastle upon Tyne, who later claimed that Riddell's service proved 'not much to my Lord's content nor to the advance of his Majesty's service' (Howell, 146). During February 1644 fifty of Riddell's musketeers unsuccessfully sallied from the castle to support the royalist army fighting the Scots. Marley surrendered Newcastle upon Tyne to the Scots on 22 October 1644, and some aldermen of Newcastle approached Riddell to yield at Tynemouth. Despite his initial answer that he 'durst not hazard his life in giving up the castle' (Sixth Report, House of Lords MSS, 33a), he surrendered the castle upon honourable terms on 27 October 1644. After Tynemouth's surrender, the 'bitter political antagonisms within Newcastle as much as Riddell's colonelcy and Catholicism drove him into exile' (Newman, The Old Service, 236). Parliament offered £1000 for his capture, but he escaped to the continent on a small fishing boat from Berwick.

Riddell could not compound for his estates because on 13 March 1649 he appeared on a list of royalists exempted from pardon. In November 1650 parliament again authorized his arrest and ordered that the council of state should prevent him from going into the north. On 1 July 1651 parliament ordered the sale of his confiscated estates. He died in Antwerp and was buried in the church of St Jacques there in April 1652. ANDREW J. HOPPER

Sources [R. Welford], ed., *Records of the committee for compounding, etc., with delinquent royalists in Durham and Northumberland during the civil war*, SurtS, 111 (1905) • Venn, *Alum. Cant.*, 1/3 • *A history of Northumberland*, Northumberland County History Committee, 15 vols. (1893–1940), vol. 4 • R. Surtees, *The history and antiquities of the county palatine of Durham*, 2 (1820) • P. R. Newman, *Royalist officers in England and Wales, 1642–1660: a biographical dictionary* (1981) • P. R. Newman, *The old service: royalist regimental colonels and the civil war, 1642–1646* (1993) • R. Howell, *Newcastle upon Tyne and the puritan revolution: a study of the civil war in north England* (1967) • DNB • J. Foster, ed., *Pedigrees recorded at the visitations of the county palatine of Durham* (1887) • Margaret, duchess of Newcastle [M. Cavendish], *The life of William Cavendish, duke of Newcastle*, ed. C. H. Firth, 2nd rev. edn (1906) • *JHC*, 2 (1640–42) • *JHC*, 3 (1642–4) • *JHC*, 6 (1648–51) • W. Dugdale, list of commissions of array, Northants. RO, Finch-Hatton papers, MS 133 • *Sixth report*, HMC, 5 (1877–8), 33
Wealth at death negligible: Welford, ed., *Records of the committee for compounding*, 320

Ridding, George (1828–1904), headmaster and bishop of Southwell, was born on 16 March 1828 in Winchester College, third son of Charles Henry Ridding (*d.* 1871), afterwards vicar of Andover, and his wife, Charlotte Stonhouse (*d.* 1832), daughter of Timothy Stonhouse-Vigor, archdeacon of Gloucester, and granddaughter of Sir James Stonhouse, eleventh baronet. George Isaac Huntingford,

bishop of Gloucester and Hereford and warden of Winchester, was his great-great-uncle and godfather. The death of his mother and his experience of religious conversion as a boy were crucial early influences. From 1840 to 1846 he was a scholar of Winchester (where his father had been second master), rising to be head of the school, while his three brothers won equal distinction as cricketers. In default of a vacancy at New College, Oxford, he matriculated as a commoner at Balliol, where he rowed in the college boat and gained the Craven scholarship, a first class in classics and a second in mathematics, and a mathematical fellowship at Exeter College (all in 1851). He won the Latin essay prize and proceeded MA in 1853; and took the degree of DD in 1869. From 1853 to 1863 he was tutor of Exeter, where he played a significant part in developing the modern tutorial system and in cultivating closer relations between undergraduates and dons. He was identified as on the liberal side of contemporary university controversies. His 1864 Oxford sermon on 'Liberty of teaching' stated his belief in free discussion and the open pursuit of truth. On 20 July 1858 he married Mary Louisa, third child of George *Moberly, headmaster of Winchester, and was one of the first married dons at Oxford. Devastated by his wife's early death, on the first anniversary of their marriage, he checked his grief by strength of will, which was already tested by a continual struggle against poor eyesight. To many he seemed a shy, austere character.

On 14 January 1863 Ridding was elected second master of Winchester; and on 27 September 1866 when Moberly, his father-in-law, resigned the headmastership, he was at once elected to succeed him. The Clarendon commission of inquiry into public schools had reported in 1864, and the time was ripe for reform. Carrying on the tradition initiated by Moberly, he established six additional boarding-houses. New classrooms were added, playing fields were acquired, and the chapel was rearranged. These additions to the facilities were personally financed by Ridding to the extent of £20,000, of which only about half was eventually repaid to him. Pupil numbers rose from about 250 to over 400, and might have grown further but for his conviction that a school should not exceed the number with which a headmaster could keep in personal touch.

Described as the 'second founder of Winchester', Ridding was one of the most prominent members of the generation of headmasters who created the public school system in its familiar form at the end of the nineteenth century. He attended the second meeting of the Headmasters' Conference, held at Sherborne in 1870, and was chairman of its standing committee until 1874. He was one of the founders in 1873 of the Oxford and Cambridge schools examination board, whose inspections and certificates averted the threat of state-controlled school examinations. Although he was a classicist, Ridding widened the curriculum at Winchester without relegating new subjects, such as history, modern languages, and natural science, to a separate 'modern side'. Following the example of Uppingham, he established a school mission, first in

1876 at Bromley in east London, and subsequently in 1882 at Landport in Portsmouth.

At Winchester, Ridding succeeded in carrying with him in a course of drastic reforms the co-operation and devotion of his assistant masters, whose numbers he doubled during his period of office. He often faced opposition from the fellows, who before 1871 constituted the governing body of the college, and was strenuously criticized by Wykehamists in general. His position as a Liberal did not stand easily with the Conservative predilections of both old boys and current pupils alike. A public controversy in November and December 1872, the so-called 'tunding row', tested his commitment to boy government. A fifth-former, William Charles Macpherson (1855–1936), later an Indian civil servant, was 'tunded' with a ground-ash wielded by a prefect for refusing to submit to a customary ritual. The extent of the injuries sustained by 'tunded Macpherson' was unclear, but the ensuing press outcry led to an inquiry by the school governors. Although the inquiry vindicated Ridding, the chairman of the governors, the fifteenth earl of Derby, and Stafford Northcote resigned in protest against the powers allowed to prefects. Ridding had originally attempted to allow the boys more freedom, but his anxiety about sexual vice among them, an issue on which he was particularly severe, led him to impose a more closely supervised regime after 1880.

Ridding married again on 26 October 1876; his second wife was Lady Laura Elizabeth Palmer [see Ridding, Lady Laura Elizabeth (1849–1939)], eldest daughter of Roundell *Palmer, first earl of Selborne. Lady Laura Ridding, whose diaries are preserved in the Hampshire Record Office, later wrote the biography of her husband, and published editions of his writings and visitation charges.

In 1884 Ridding was appointed the first bishop of Southwell, on the nomination of Gladstone whose inquiries had established Ridding to be 'one of those large minded men who will work on the one hand with great devotion and energy, on the other hand with a liberal and just regard to the various shades of sentiment and practice united in the communion of the Church' (Gladstone, *Diaries*, 11.113). He was consecrated on 1 May. Southwell was a new diocese, formed by separating the counties of Derby and Nottingham from the dioceses of Lichfield and Lincoln respectively. The cathedral town was so inaccessible that Ridding firmly declined to live in it, and rented Thurgarton Priory in Nottinghamshire as his residence in place of the ruined episcopal palace. In population the diocese was the fifth in England, but it had no chapter, no diocesan funds, no common organization; the two counties had diverse traditions, and much of the patronage remained in the hands of external bishops and chapters. Ridding's work was to bring unity and a corporate spirit out of diversity and jealousy, to create all kinds of diocesan organizations, to raise the intellectual standard of the clergy, and to stimulate spiritual life in neglected districts. As at Winchester, he was not understood at first, and encountered some opposition; but his sincerity, genuineness, and generosity (the whole of his official income was spent on the diocese) ultimately gained the affection and loyalty of both clergy and laity. Although he spoke, in 1888, of reunion between the Anglican church and dissent, he was emphatic in upholding the national church, and very definite in his advocacy of church principles. His independence and originality of thought made him a valued adviser of two successive archbishops of Canterbury; with Frederick Temple in particular he was united by cordial friendship, based on considerable resemblances of character. This same independence, on the other hand, often separated him from the main parties of church thought, and despite many similarities of outlook he was not formally identified with the broad-church party. During the controversy of 1902 on religious education, he was not in accord with either the government or the opposition of the day, but strenuously advocated a universal system of state schools, accompanied by universal liberty of religious teaching.

With the exception of a long holiday (necessitated by overwork) in Egypt and Greece from December 1888 to April 1889, Ridding's work in his diocese was unbroken. In 1891 he refused translation to Lichfield. In 1893, during the great strike in the coal trade, his efforts to restore peace were unceasing. In 1897 he presided at the Nottingham church congress, and in the same year became president of Nottinghamshire County Cricket Club. In July 1904, following repeated attacks of ill health, he tendered his resignation; but before it had taken effect an acute crisis supervened, and on 30 August he died at Thurgarton. He was buried just outside Southwell Minster.

Ridding published one volume of sermons, *The Revel and the Battle* (1897). His style, whether in writing or in speaking, was peculiar: full of thought, tersely and trenchantly expressed, but often difficult to follow from lack of connecting links and phrases. Contemporaries considered that this fault prevented him from exerting a wider influence (Headlam, 242). A former pupil recalled a 'keen, alert man, with handsome, mobile features, the curling black hair, the piercing eye, the eyeglass—now dropped, now fixed again, each time with queer but not inexpressive grimaces' (Bird, 733).

F. G. KENYON, rev. M. C. CURTHOYS

Sources L. Ridding, *George Ridding: schoolmaster and bishop* (1908) • [W. H. B. Bird], 'Bishop Ridding as head master', *Cornhill Magazine*, [3rd] ser., 17 (1904), 733–48 • [A. C. Headlam], 'George Ridding, first bishop of Southwell', *Church Quarterly Review*, 60 (1905), 241–85 • C. A. E. Moberly, *Dulce domum: George Moberly ... his family and friends* (1911) • personal knowledge (1912) • P. Gwyn, 'The "Tunding row": George Ridding and the belief in "boy-government"', *Winchester College: sixth-centenary essays*, ed. R. Custance (1982), 431–77 • Gladstone, *Diaries*

Archives Bodl. Oxf., corresp. and papers • Southwell Minster, Nottinghamshire, local history collections • Southwell Minster, Nottinghamshire, papers relating to reconstitution of chapter after 1884 • Southwell Minster, Nottinghamshire, rules and statutes • Southwell Minster, Nottinghamshire, scrapbooks of local events • Winchester College, corresp. and papers | Bodl. Oxf., annotated copy of Laura Ridding's *George Ridding* • Lancing College, West Sussex, letters to E. C. Lowe • LPL, corresp. about Association for the Furtherance of Christianity in Egypt • LPL, corresp. with Archbishop Benson

Likenesses Schemboche, photograph, *c*.1876 (with his wife, Laura Ridding), NPG; *see illus. in* Ridding, Lady Laura Elizabeth (1849–1939) • W. W. Ouless, oils, 1879, Winchester College • H. H.

Brown, portrait, 1896, priv. coll. • engravings, 1897 (after photographs) • engravings, 1904 (after photographs) • T. B. Carter, memorial brass, 1907, Winchester College • S. P. Hall, group portrait, watercolour (*The bench of bishops, 1902*), NPG • Hills & Saunders, carte-de-visite, NPG • F. W. Pomeroy, bronze statue, Southwell Minster • P. Rajon, engraving (after W. W. Ouless) • Spy [L. Ward], caricature, chromolithograph, NPG; repro. in *VF* (15 Aug 1901) • Spy [L. Ward], cartoon, repro. in *VF* (1891) • lithograph, BM • print, NPG • wood-engraving (after photograph by Schemboche), NPG; repro. in *ILN* (18 March 1884)

Ridding [*née* Palmer], **Lady Laura Elizabeth** (1849–1939), suffragist and philanthropist, was born on 26 March 1849 at Harley Street, London, the daughter of Roundell *Palmer (1812–1895), later the first earl of Selborne, and his wife, Lady Laura Waldegrave (1821–1885), the second daughter of William Waldegrave, eighth Earl Waldegrave. On 26 October 1876 she married the Revd Dr George *Ridding (1828–1904), who had been a widower for seventeen years. At that time he was headmaster of Winchester College; in 1884 he became the first bishop of Southwell. Their marriage was childless.

Laura Ridding was an advocate of women's suffrage for many years and was also involved in rescue work, temperance work, and nursing. In 1885 she and her husband founded Southwell House, a temporary rescue home for young women. She was also a member of a variety of committees and organizations: from 1895 to 1904 she was a poor-law guardian and rural district councillor for the Southwell union. In 1902 she was a member of the Nottinghamshire county education committee and in 1913 she joined the Hampshire county insurance committee. During the First World War she was active in a number of organizations: the Soldiers' and Sailors' Families Association; the Women's War Agricultural Committee; the YWCA Girls' Patriotic Club; and the Winchester Patrols.

One of Lady Laura's greatest achievements, however, was to establish, with Louise Creighton (1850–1936) and Emily Janes (1846–1928), among others, the National Union of Women Workers (NUWW) in 1895. This was an essentially conservative organization designed to co-ordinate women's philanthropic and charitable efforts throughout the country. From 1899 to 1910 Lady Laura was chair of the NUWW legislative committee. She also served on the executive committee and was vice-president before taking over as president in 1910. Her commitment to the NUWW was lifelong: although she did not attend London meetings after the First World War she was involved in her local Winchester branch up to her death in 1939.

All commentators on Lady Laura stress her intellectual ability: the writer of her obituary in *Women in Council*, who had worked with her on the NUWW legislative committee, felt that she 'had inherited her father's legal mind and brought a sound judgement to bear on all the problems that came before us. She had a delightful sense of humour and guided the Council with great skill, yet without imposing her will upon it'. In addition, 'No point was too small to be of interest and her thoroughness was realised by all who worked with her'. According to a piece in *The Times*, published the day after her funeral, she had 'a quick and ardent mind, full of interest and enthusiasm' (*The*

Lady Laura Elizabeth Ridding (1849–1939), by Schemboche, *c.*1876 [with her husband, George Ridding]

Times, 27 May 1939). Lady Laura clearly had a lighter side—*The Times* described her as 'a charming companion, an adoring wife, and a source of perpetual amusement' to her husband. She had an artistic ability, which was demonstrated by her skill in painting and 'the taste with which she arranged and adorned her three homes'. Despite a keen mind, she was decidedly emotional: her obituarist recalls 'her sympathy, her spontaneous gaiety, her affection for people and animals, her ready tears, her exaggerated apprehensions'. She was also held to have 'exhibited unaccountable foibles, which seemed to enhance rather than disfigure an essentially kind and really interesting and powerful personality, as occasional grotesqueness enhances some of the greatest classical art'. All her activities and characteristics were underpinned by a strong religious faith.

Lady Laura listed her recreations as gardening, the microscope, painting, the study of birds, and writing, and she was a member of the Ladies' Club in Winchester. Her publications included three biographies: of her husband, *George Ridding, schoolmaster and bishop, 43rd head of Winchester, 1866–1884, first bishop of Southwell, 1884–1904* (1908); of her nephew, Robert Palmer, who died in Mesopotamia in 1916, *The Life of Robert Palmer, 1888–1916* (1921); and of her sister, Lady Sophia Palmer, who married the comte de Franqueville in 1903 and died in 1915. She was also an occasional contributor to *The Times*. After her husband's death in 1904, she bought the Old Rectory at Wonston, Sutton

Scotney, Hampshire. It was there that she died on 22 May 1939 at the age of ninety. Although troubled by deafness, 'she retained her powers of mind unimpaired to the end' (*The Times*, 27 May 1939). She was buried in Southwell Minster on 26 May.   SERENA KELLY

Sources *The Times* (23 May 1939) · *The Times* (27 May 1939) · *Women in Council, the Magazine of the National Council of Women*, 17/5 (June 1939), 78–9 · C. Weir, *Women's history in Nottinghamshire* (1989) · A. J. R., ed., *The suffrage annual and women's who's who* (1913) · GEC, *Peerage*
Archives Hants. RO, diaries
Likenesses Schemboche, photograph, *c*.1876, NPG [*see illus.*]
Wealth at death £42,817 19*s*. 10*d*.: resworn probate, 25 July 1939, *CGPLA Eng. & Wales*

Ridding, (Caroline) Mary (1862–1941), Sanskrit and Pali scholar, was born on 30 August 1862 in Meriden, Warwickshire, the daughter of William Ridding (1830–1900), vicar of Meriden, who had been a notable cricketer, and his wife, Caroline Selina Caldecott. Her uncle was George Ridding, headmaster of Winchester College and later first bishop of Southwell, whose second wife, Lady Laura Ridding (the daughter of the first earl of Selborne), was close to the young woman. A Girton contemporary recalled that although Mary Ridding's mother came from an old Warwickshire family, her father was of modest means, so that she and her brother had to make their own way in the world.

Mary Ridding attended Bishopsgate Training College and in 1883 won a higher local scholarship to Girton College, Cambridge. She was placed in the second division of the second class in part one of the classical tripos, specializing in philology and Sanskrit, in 1886; she took her MA in 1923 after Cambridge University allowed women to receive titular degrees. At Girton, Ridding attended the lectures of Robert Alexander Neil, the university lecturer in Sanskrit, and met Edward Byles Cowell, the professor of Sanskrit, who at that time did not admit women to his university lectures. Soon afterwards, Cowell's wife wrote to her, 'we have not the heart to keep you from anything', which began a nineteen-year friendship lasting until Professor Cowell's death (*Cambridge Review*). Ridding later wrote 'Professor Cowell and his pupils' in *Indian Studies Presented to Professor Rapson*, volume 6 of the *Bulletin of the School of Oriental Studies* (1931).

After 1886 Ridding continued her studies, supporting herself by tutoring. In 1889 she was employed as a visiting classics mistress in London, living partly in Cambridge and partly in London before moving permanently to Cambridge. An extremely erudite scholar, Ridding knew Sanskrit, Pali, and some Bengali and Hindi. One of her first scholarly endeavours was to translate the Sanskrit romance *Kadambari* (Oriental Translation Fund publications, new ser., 11, 1896). She was particularly interested in Tibet, reviewing Tibetan books for the *Journal of Asiatic Studies* for many years. An Indian research student wrote of her, 'I had known of Miss Ridding's great reputation as an Orientalist in India, where her translation of the Sanskrit story Bana's Kadambari was justly famous … She loved India, and her appreciation of its philosophy touched me deeply' (*Girton Review*).

Perhaps Mary Ridding's greatest contribution to scholarship was her work as a cataloguer. After Cowell's death in 1903 she arranged the disposition of his books, and catalogued those that went to the Cambridge University Library. In this capacity, she was the first woman to be officially employed by the library. Of great use to scholars is her catalogue of the Sanskrit portion of the library's 'Hand-list of Oriental manuscripts'; she later began a complete catalogue, which was finished by Professor L. de la

(Caroline) Mary Ridding (1862–1941), by unknown photographer [front right, with the Girton students of the year 1883]

Vallée Poussin of Belgium. Equally important is her catalogue of the library's Tibetan block-printed books, hundreds of volumes comprising the Tibetan Buddhist canon, the *Kanjur*, along with other works.

Mary Ridding had many interests beyond her south Asian studies. She enjoyed travelling abroad to conferences, and in 1893 took a trip to Greece, suggested and partly arranged by her friend Emily Davies, the founder of Girton, in recognition of her achievements in a new field for women. Ridding loved classical music, particularly Beethoven, Schubert, and Chopin's works, which she played on the piano. She was a deeply committed Anglican, maintaining a close relationship with Edmund Gough de Salis Wood, vicar of St Clement's, Cambridge, her spiritual adviser. Contemporaries remembered her as a devoted friend and a true intellectual, but also as a born eccentric. In her last years she lived among clutter in a house above Market Hill in Cambridge, where she eschewed such modern conveniences as radios, telephones, and vacuum cleaners. She died in a nursing home in Cambridge on 9 November 1941. She left Girton College her south Asian books, as well as her valuable collection of first editions of her favourite writer, Charlotte Yonge. In her memory the college founded an annual prize for reading aloud.

FERNANDA HELEN PERRONE

Sources *Cambridge Review* (28 Feb 1942) · *Girton Review*, Michaelmas term (1942) · A. Adam, 'Notes on C. M. Ridding', 1942, Girton Cam. · K. T. Butler and H. I. McMorran, eds., *Girton College register, 1869–1946* (1948) · B. Stephen, *Emily Davies and Girton College* (1927) · Boase, *Mod. Eng. biog.* [William Ridding]
Archives Girton Cam.
Likenesses photograph, Girton College, Cambridge [*see illus.*]

Riddle, Edward (*bap.* 1786, *d.* 1854), mathematician and astronomer, was born at Troughend in Northumberland, the eldest son of John Riddle, an agricultural labourer, and his wife, Mary. He was baptized at the parish church of Elsdon, Northumberland, on 3 September 1786. After an elementary education at Troughend he went to a school at the nearby village of West Woodburn, kept by Cuthbert Atkinson, father of the mathematician Henry Atkinson, where he received a thorough training in mathematics.

When he was only eighteen Riddle became a schoolmaster at Shielyfield in Northumberland, and after a short time opened a school of his own at Otterburn. There he developed his interest in higher mathematics, and in the related disciplines of astronomy, navigation, and optics, through his friendship with James Thompson, well known locally for his scientific work. In 1807 he moved his school to Whitburn in Durham, and it was while he was living here that he married Eliza (Elizabeth) Wallace (*b. c.*1785) at All Saints' Church, Newcastle upon Tyne, on 30 April 1814. In 1810 he began contributing items on mathematics to the *Ladies' Diary*, winning in 1814 and 1819 the prizes given by the editor, Dr Charles Hutton. It was at Dr Hutton's suggestion that, in September 1814, Riddle was appointed master of the Trinity House School, Newcastle. While there he joined the Newcastle Literary and Philosophical Society, and attended the scientific lectures of the Revd William Turner. He also made an extensive series of observations to check the longitude of the school and the trustworthiness of certain lunar observations. His first child, John (1816–1862), was born in Newcastle. In September 1821, again through the recommendation of Dr Hutton, Riddle was appointed master of the upper mathematical school at the Royal Naval Hospital, Greenwich, where he remained until his retirement in September 1851. Shortly after moving there he was elected a fellow of the Royal Astronomical Society, to whose *Transactions* he contributed several valuable papers. From 1825 to 1851 he was an active member of its council.

Riddle's most valuable work was a *Treatise on Navigation and Nautical Astronomy* (1824), which provided a complete course of mathematics for sailors, combining theory and practice in a way which had not been attempted before. It became one of the standard textbooks for ships' masters, and went through numerous editions, the eighth and final one appearing in 1864. The tables of logarithms were issued separately in 1841 and 1851. He re-edited Hutton's *Mathematical Recreations* in 1840 and 1854. Between 1818 and 1847 he also published sixteen papers on astronomical subjects, of which eight were in the *Philosophical Magazine*, five in *Memoirs of the Royal Astronomical Society*, and three in *Monthly Notices of the Royal Astronomical Society*. His most important papers were on nautical astronomy and on chronometers. In 1821 the *Philosophical Magazine* published Riddle's article 'On the present state of nautical astronomy', and in 1829 the *Memoirs of the Royal Astronomical Society* included his piece on finding the rates of timekeepers, which was notable for showing how the going rates of chronometers could be determined without using a transit instrument. Riddle was considered by his contemporaries to be one of the leading teachers of nautical science, and after his retirement many of his friends and former pupils expressed their appreciation by presenting him with his bust in marble, sculpted by William Theed.

Riddle died from paralysis at his home, 3 Vansittart Terrace, Greenwich, on 31 March 1854 and was buried in the graveyard of the Royal Naval Hospital schools on 7 April. His son John was headmaster of Greenwich Hospital schools, and examiner in navigation to the Department of Science and Art. Edward Riddle was also survived by his wife, and by two married daughters, Jane and Eliza.

W. F. SEDGWICK, rev. GLORIA CLIFTON

Sources *GM*, 2nd ser., 41 (1854), 661 · *Memoirs of the Royal Astronomical Society*, 21 (1851–2), 176 · *Memoirs of the Royal Astronomical Society*, 24 (1854–5), 200–05 · R. Welford, *Men of mark 'twixt Tyne and Tweed*, 3 (1895), 311–14 · will, PRO, PROB. 11/2190, quire 315, fols. 120v–121r · death duty register, PRO, IR26/2007, fol. 353 · census returns for Greenwich, 1851, PRO, HO 107/1587, fols. 477–8 · T. Stephens, ed., *The register of baptisms, marriages and burials solemnized in the ancient parish church of Elsdon … from AD 1672 to AD 1812*, Society of Antiquaries of Newcastle upon Tyne (1903) · parish register (marriage), 30 April 1814, Newcastle upon Tyne, All Saints, Society of Genealogists, London, microfilm no. 1561 · *ILN* (29 May 1852), 436 · inscription on memorial to Edward and John Riddle, burial ground of Royal Hospital Schools, Greenwich [now Devonport House, Romney Road, Greenwich]
Likenesses W. Theed, marble bust, Devonport House burial ground, Romney Road, Greenwich · wood-engraving (after bust), NPG; repro. in *ILN* (1852)

Wealth at death £5797: PRO, death duty registers, IR 26/2007, fol. 353

Riddle, Joseph Esmond (1804–1859), classical scholar and Church of England clergyman, eldest of the eight children of Joseph Riddle of Old Market Street, Bristol, was born there on 7 April 1804. From Mr Porter's school in Bristol he was sent by the Bristol Clerical Society, which educated young men for the church, to H. M. Havergal at Astley rectory, Worcestershire for tuition in preparation for university. He matriculated from St Edmund Hall, Oxford, of which Havergal was a graduate, on 18 January 1825. Under the vice-principalship of John Hill the hall was the centre of evangelicalism in Oxford. Riddle obtained a first class in classics, graduating BA in Michaelmas term 1828, and MA in 1831.

From 1828 to 1830 Riddle lived at Ramsgate, where he took pupils and began a translation of Immanuel Scheller's folio Latin dictionary, *Lexicon totius Latinitatis*, which was published at the Clarendon Press, Oxford, in 1835. Several abridgements followed, and in 1838 he issued a *Complete English–Latin Dictionary*, and in 1849 *A Copious and Critical Latin-English Lexicon, Founded on the Dictionaries of Dr W. Freund*. Riddle was also joint editor of Latin dictionaries with John T. White, and of an *English–Latin Dictionary* with Thomas Kerchever Arnold.

Meanwhile, in 1830 Riddle was ordained deacon, and was successively curate of Everley, Upper Slaughter (from 1832), Reading, and All Souls, Marylebone. In 1836 he was assistant minister at Brunswick Chapel, Upper Berkeley Street, London, marrying in the same year Margaret Sharwood, who survived him, and with whom he had a son—Arthur Esmond Riddle (b. c.1843), rector of Tadmarton, Banbury—and a daughter. In 1837 he became curate of Harrow, where the vicar was J. W. Cunningham, a leading evangelical. He soon removed to Shipton Moyne, Gloucestershire. Subsequently he returned to Oxford in order to make use of the libraries. From 1840 until his death he was incumbent of St Philip's, Leckhampton, Gloucestershire.

Riddle was a painstaking and laborious scholar, a vigorous defender of evangelical principles against the Tractarian movement, and an earnest but unimpassioned preacher. He was appointed select preacher at Oxford in 1834 and 1854, and Bampton lecturer in 1852, the latter during the vice-chancellorship of R. L. Cotton. He published sermons and works on theology and ecclesiastical history on which he contributed two chapters to the *Encyclopaedia metropolitana*. His *Household Prayers* (1857) was reissued in 1887. Riddle died at his home, Tudor Lodge, Leckhampton, near Cheltenham, Gloucestershire, on 27 August 1859. E. C. MARCHANT, *rev.* M. C. CURTHOYS

Sources GM, 3rd ser., 7 (1859), 426–7 · private information (1887) · J. S. Reynolds, *The evangelicals at Oxford, 1735–1871: a record of an unchronicled movement*, [2nd edn] (1975) · Boase, *Mod. Eng. biog.*
Wealth at death under £3000: probate, 27 Sept 1859, CGPLA Eng. & Wales

Rideal, Sir Eric Keightley (1890–1974), physical chemist, was born on 11 April 1890 at Sydenham, Kent, the eldest in the family of four children (three sons and a daughter) of Samuel Rideal (1863–1929), public analyst, who devised the Rideal–Walker test for disinfectant activity, and his Irish wife, Elizabeth (Lilla), daughter of Samuel Keightley JP, of Bangor, co. Down. He was educated at Farnham grammar school and Oundle School. In 1907 he entered Trinity Hall, Cambridge, with an open scholarship in natural sciences. He graduated with first-class honours in both parts of the tripos (1910 and 1911). A lecturer in physiology, William Bate Hardy, kindled his interest in surface chemistry. Rideal then went to Aachen, transferring to Bonn to complete his PhD thesis on the electrochemistry of uranium in 1912, for which he received the gold medal of the Bonn Society of Engineers. He returned to England to enter his father's Westminster consulting practice, and at the outbreak of war in 1914 was in Ecuador dealing with water supply problems.

Rideal returned to England and joined the Artists' Rifles. After a spell of work on respirators he was transferred to the Royal Engineers as a captain, to supervise water supplies to Australian troops on the Somme. He was invalided out in 1916 and joined the nitrogen research laboratory at University College, London, where a team under J. A. Harker was working on the Haber process. Here he collaborated with H. S. Taylor on catalyst development and in their spare time the two wrote *Catalysis in Theory and Practice* (1919). Rideal's war work earned him appointment as MBE in 1918.

In 1919 Rideal was appointed visiting professor at the University of Illinois at Urbana, where he made contact with the leading American physical chemists and developed a lifelong interest in the USA. While returning by ship in 1920 he met Margaret Atlee (Peggy; *d.* 1964), daughter of Philip Nye Jackson, financier, of Princeton, New Jersey, and widow of William Agnew Paton, a Princeton professor. They married in 1921 and had one daughter, Mary, who married Lord Justice Oliver. The Rideals settled in Cambridge, at Thorndyke on the Huntingdon Road, where Rideal could indulge his interest in gardening.

In 1920 Rideal had been appointed H. O. Jones lecturer in physical chemistry and a fellow of Trinity Hall in Cambridge. There in the department of T. M. Lowry he built up a large, broadly based research group, covering electrochemistry, heterogeneous catalysis, colloid and surface chemistry, and kinetics spectroscopy. The first of his many research students, R. G. W. Norrish (joint Nobel prize-winner in 1967), described Rideal as 'bubbling with ideas, good and bad, but not strong on experimental detail, leaving the working out of his ideas to the (hopeful) ingenuity of his students, by whom he was much loved'.

In 1930 Rideal was elected FRS and made professor of colloid science, with his own laboratory of some 9000 square feet in Free School Lane. There in the years up to 1939 much progress was made in studying gas adsorption and catalysis, insoluble monolayers on water, and polymerization kinetics. During the Second World War the laboratory was largely devoted to classified work, on explosives, fuels, polymers, and other topics.

In 1946 Rideal left Cambridge (with an honorary fellowship at Trinity Hall), on accepting the Fullerian professorship and directorship of the Davy–Faraday Laboratory at the Royal Institution in London. Here he built up another thriving research laboratory, but finding the social duties onerous, he resigned in 1949. In 1950 he was appointed professor of physical chemistry at King's College, London, where in somewhat cramped conditions he assembled for the third time a large and active group of surface chemists. In 1955 came retirement, and he transferred to the chemistry department at Imperial College as senior research fellow. He continued active research and writing until the year of his death.

Rideal was knighted in 1951, and in the same year gave the Bakerian lecture to the Royal Society and received its Davy medal. He was elected a fellow of King's College, London, in 1963, and had honorary degrees from Dublin (1951), Birmingham (1955), Belfast (1960), Turin (1962), Bonn (1963), and Brunel (1967). During 1953–8 he was chairman of the Advisory Council on Scientific Research and Technical Development of the Ministry of Supply. He served terms as president of the Faraday Society, Society of Chemical Industry, and the Chemical Society. He published some three hundred papers and eight books. He died on 25 September 1974 in a nursing home at 20 Fitzjames Avenue, West Kensington, London and was probably buried at West Runton, Norfolk.   D. D. ELEY, rev.

Sources D. D. Eley, *Memoirs FRS*, 22 (1976), 381–413 · *The Times* (27 Sept 1974) · personal knowledge (1986) · private information (1986)
Archives CUL, corresp. with U. R. Evans and related papers · Royal Institution of Great Britain, London, MSS and corresp.
Likenesses W. Bird, photograph, c.1967, RS
Wealth at death £88,870: probate, 11 Dec 1974, *CGPLA Eng. & Wales*

Ridealgh [*née* Jewitt], **Mabel** (1898–1989), co-operator and politician, was born on 11 August 1898 at 19 Albert Terrace, Wallsend-on-Tyne, Northumberland, daughter of Mark Albert Jewitt, master butcher, and his wife, Lucy, formerly Burton. She was educated at elementary school and later attended evening classes, gaining a London University certificate. She worked as a civil servant in the income tax department until her marriage at Wallsend parish church on 14 June 1919 to Leonard Ridealgh (d. 1956), of Kentish Town, London, an engineer, the son of William Robert Ridealgh, also an engineer. They moved to Enfield, north London, in 1920 and had two children, a son and a daughter.

Ridealgh joined the Women's Co-operative Guild (WCG) in Enfield in 1920 and the Labour Party in 1921. One of the priorities of the WCG was to secure maximum support for the Co-operative Party, the political arm of the co-operative movement. She had political aspirations but because the WCG espoused absolute pacifism, she and other possible Co-operative–Labour Party candidates were barred from constituency lists when war threatened in 1939. She was one of two representatives of the guild on the central board for conscientious objectors.

During the Second World War, Ridealgh was honorary regional organizer for the Board of Trade's 'make-do and mend' initiative. She was also a member of the Ministry of Labour's national committee for the welfare of workers, the National Council of Social Service, the London Council of Social Service, and the London area committee of the Citizens' Advice Bureau. She was elected national president of the WCG for the year 1941–2, and campaigned for more women co-operators to take an active interest in politics and for more women in the police force. She represented the WCG at a meeting with Sir William Beveridge that called for a more effective and equitable method of fuel rationing.

In May 1944, when WCG members were finally accepted, Mabel Ridealgh was adopted as Labour–Co-operative candidate for the newly created constituency of Ilford North, which she won in the general election of 1945. Between the wars Labour had never won the previously undivided Ilford seat; in 1945 it won both of the new seats. Her maiden speech, in March 1946, was in support of the National Insurance Bill, on behalf of the sick, housewives, and spinsters. In 1947 she persuaded the chancellor of the exchequer to revoke the purchase tax he had imposed on electrical and gas apparatus, arguing that it was unfair to working-class housewives. Her other special interests were housing, spinsters' pension rights, nursery schools, compensation for war damage, the colonies, and post-war Europe. She was a member of parliamentary delegations to Belgium and Luxembourg and deputy delegate to the Council of Europe in 1949. She lost her Ilford seat decisively in the swing against Labour in London suburbia at the general election of 1950 and failed to regain it in 1951.

From 1953 until 1963 Ridealgh was the general secretary of the WCG, leading the guild's 'cost of living' and 'housing, rent, and repairs' campaigns and demonstrations, as well as those for nuclear disarmament and peace. The death of her husband in 1956 did not cause her to leave public life. In the late 1950s she was part of the 'Women's caravan of peace and friendship', supported the Campaign for Nuclear Disarmament, and was part of a 'committee of parents' deputation to Geneva to lobby foreign secretaries who were meeting there in 1958. In the 1960s she took part in the Aldermaston marches and led WCG members to present its anti-nuclear petition to MPs in 1962. She represented the WCG on the national joint committee of working women until 1970 (she was vice-president in 1956), was a member of the women's organizations committee of the cabinet economic unit in 1956, and the women's advisory committee of the British Standards Institution. She was a committed supporter of the International Co-operative Women's Guild until its demise in 1963, travelling widely to Europe and even China.

In her final year as general secretary Ridealgh was an *ex officio* member of a committee to modernize the constitution, which resulted in the WCG's name being changed to the Co-operative Women's Guild. When she left office, the annual report of 1963 noted that she was the 'chief official in the years of apathy and disillusionment that have characterised the affluent society', but praised her for keeping up the true spirit of the guild while building an up-to-date organization. She remained a member of her local guild and attended meetings until prevented by ill health. In 1983 she was a guest of honour at an 'at home' to celebrate the guild's centenary. She spent the last two years of her life in a residential home at 49 Eastwood Road, Goodmayes, Ilford, where she died of bronchopneumonia on 20 June 1989. She was cremated at the City of London crematorium.

JANET E. GRENIER

Sources *Annual Report* [Women's Co-operative Guild] (1941–63) · *Monthly Bulletins* [Women's Co-operative Guild] (1941–63) · J. Gaffin and D. Thoms, *Caring and sharing: the centenary history of the Co-operative Women's Guild* (1983) · C. Salt, P. Schweitzer, and M. Wilson, *Of whole heart cometh hope* (1983) · *Daily Telegraph* (1 Aug 1989) · *Ilford Recorder* (29 June 1989) · *WWBMP*, vol. 4 · G. Scott, *Feminism and the politics of working women: the Women's Co-operative Guild* (1998) · *Hansard 5C* (1945–50) · b. cert. · m. cert. · d. cert. · N. Black, *Social feminism* (1989) · *WWW*, 1981–90 · *Labour's election who's who*, Labour Party (1950), 87
Archives Bishopsgate Institute Library, London, Women's Co-operative Guild Annual Reports and Monthly Bulletins
Likenesses photograph, 1962, repro. in Salt, Schweitzer, and Wilson, *Of whole heart*, 311 · photograph, repro. in *Ilford Recorder* · photograph, Bishopsgate Institute; repro. in *Annual conference programme of WCG* (1942), cover
Wealth at death under £100,000: probate, 7 March 1991, *CGPLA Eng. & Wales*

Ridel, Geoffrey (d. 1120), justice, is of uncertain but possibly distinguished origins. There is a single reference in the Domesday survey of Norfolk to a man named Geoffrey Ridel, who is said to have come from Apulia with the brother of Roger (I) Bigod. A family named Ridel was prominent in southern Italy in the eleventh and twelfth centuries, and a Geoffrey Ridel who is mentioned between 1061 and 1084 as a lieutenant of Robert Guiscard became duke of Gaeta. That Geoffrey Ridel the justice was well connected is suggested by the fact that his brother Matthew was appointed to the important abbacy of Peterborough in 1102, while Geoffrey himself leased the manor of Pytchley from the abbey, originally, so the abbey claimed, for one year only, though he refused to give up the estate and was still in possession at the time of his death. It is about 1105 that Ridel begins to appear as a witness to royal documents. By 1106 he may already have received the lands of Robert de Buci centred on Great Weldon in Northamptonshire, for in that year he was included in the address of a royal precept relating to land in the county. In the same year he was appointed to a judicial panel inquiring into a complaint made against Osbert, sheriff of Yorkshire, and three years later he attended a royal council at Nottingham. About 1110 he was one of a group commissioned to inquire into the king's rights in Winchester, a city omitted from the Domesday Book, and in either 1110 or 1111 he was present when the king's court met before the Empress Matilda in the treasury at Winchester to deal with a case involving Abingdon Abbey, possibly an early reference to the court of the exchequer.

Ridel was one of those described by the chronicler Henry of Huntingdon as a 'justice of all England', a term which refers to the geographical scope of their authority as opposed to those who acted for the king in only one or two counties. But there is less evidence for his activities as a justice than for those of his colleague Ralph Basset: he does not appear as frequently in royal documents, and when he does it is often in a midlands context, from which it may be inferred that he was not constantly at court. The man named Warin Ridel who is recorded as a tenant of Richard *Basset in 1130 in Leicestershire as holding his land by the service 'of finding for the justiciar a messenger to go through the whole of England' (*Leicestershire Survey*, 15) may have been established by Geoffrey Ridel, Richard Basset's predecessor as overlord.

Ridel's wife, Geva, was a daughter of Hugh, earl of Chester. It has been surmised that she was illegitimate, but there is no evidence on this point, the fact that she did not succeed her brother in the earldom in 1120 being no proof of illegitimacy. Although Ridel did not attest documents issued by Henry I in Normandy, he was evidently returning to England with the royal court in 1120 when he lost his life on 25 November in the wreck of the *White Ship* off Barfleur in Normandy. His wife survived him and founded a priory at Canwell in Staffordshire; his daughter married Richard Basset, who succeeded to his lands.

JUDITH A. GREEN

Sources A. Farley, ed., *Domesday Book*, 2 vols. (1783) · *Reg. RAN*, vol. 2 · G. Barraclough, ed., *The charters of the Anglo-Norman earls of Chester, c.1071–1237*, Lancashire and Cheshire RS, 126 (1988), nos. 39, 40 · G. Loud, 'How "Norman" was the Norman conquest of southern Italy?', *Nottingham Medieval Studies*, 25 (1981), 22–3 · Ordericus Vitalis, *Eccl. hist.*, vol. 6 · *The chronicle of Hugh Candidus, a monk of Peterborough*, ed. W. T. Mellows (1949), 87 · *Storia de Normanni, di Amato di Montecassino: volgarizzata in antico francese*, ed. V. de Bartholomeis (Rome, 1935), 231, 237 · *Codex Diplomaticus Cajetanus*, 2 (Monte Cassino, 1891), 86 · W. T. Reedy, 'The origins of the general eyre in the reign of Henry I', *Speculum*, 41 (1966), 688–724 · C. F. Slade, ed., *The Leicestershire survey, c. AD 1130*, new edn (1956), 15 · Henry, archdeacon of Huntingdon, *Historia Anglorum*, ed. D. E. Greenway, OMT (1996) · R. C. van Caenegem, ed., *English lawsuits from William I to Richard I*, SeldS, 1, 106 (1990), nos. 194, 220

Ridel, Geoffrey (d. 1189), administrator and bishop of Ely, was probably a great-nephew of the royal justice Geoffrey Ridel (d. 1120), and therefore related to his namesake Geoffrey Ridel (son of Richard Basset and of Maud, daughter of the first Geoffrey Ridel) whose principal estates were in Northamptonshire. A royal charter issued before May 1173 names Galiena, daughter of William Blund, as his kinswoman, to whom he gave land in Exning in Suffolk on her marriage to Robert de Lisle. His early career can be traced in the royal chancery, where he witnessed charters immediately after Thomas Becket, the chancellor, c.1156–61. He acquired the church of Woolpit in Suffolk in 1161, became acting chancellor in 1162 on Becket's resignation, and archdeacon of Canterbury in early 1163, at the king's insistence, offices which he held until his election to the bishopric of Ely in 1173. Self-confident and ambitious—on one occasion he thrust his way into the royal council to proffer advice—he was closely identified with Henry II's policies against Thomas Becket throughout the controversy with the king, despite his standing surety for £100 of the fine imposed on Becket at Northampton. He represented Henry at the curia in 1164, appealed to the pope against Becket on 15 August 1166, urged Louis VII to expel him from his territories in summer 1169, and incurred excommunication on Ascension day 1169, from which he was temporarily released by the papal nuncios Vivian and Gratian at Bur-le-Roi (Calvados) on 1 September 1169. The sentence was reimposed in October 1169, however, following the failure of the negotiations for Becket's reconciliation with Henry II, which was attributed in part to Ridel's malign influence. Nevertheless Ridel continued to prosper in the king's service: a baron of the exchequer by September 1165, he was one of the justices ordered to impose royal decrees prohibiting the entry of papal and archiepiscopal mandates into England in late 1169; he was given charge of the vacant see of Ely in the same year; and he witnessed the royal writ announcing Becket's peace to Bishop Bartholomew of Exeter in July 1170.

But the man whom Thomas Becket called 'our archdevil', a play on 'archdeacon', remained an adamant opponent of the archbishop to the end, occupying the archiepiscopal church of Otford in Kent, raising difficulties even in the king's presence at Fréteval in July 1170, impeding the restoration of archiepiscopal properties in October 1170, and carrying from Archbishop Roger of York, Bishop Gilbert of London, and Bishop Jocelin of Salisbury to Henry, the Young King (Henry II's recently crowned son), the inflammatory message that 'the primate wanted to depose him' (Robertson and Sheppard, 7.406). In December he persuaded the Young King not to receive the archbishop, with the message, 'I know your father's wishes; and never will I be a party to admitting into your presence a man who purposes to disinherit you' (ibid., 1.111). In Normandy when Becket was murdered on 29 December, he was in Henry II's entourage in the following summer, and was elected bishop of Ely about 1 May 1173. Henry, the Young King, appealed to the pope against his election, accusing Ridel of 'many things', including complicity in Becket's murder and immorality, but he was supported by Bishop Gilbert of London, purged himself of the charges in September 1174 in St Katherine's Chapel, Westminster, in the presence of the new archbishop, Richard (d. 1184), and was consecrated at Canterbury on 6 October 1174. At least two contemporary witnesses remained hostile to him, however: Roger of Howden recounted an alleged conversation between the Young King's messenger and Pope Alexander III (r. 1159–81), in which Ridel's failure to go to the curia was excused on the grounds that 'he has taken a wife and therefore cannot come' (Chronica … Hovedene, 2.59); and Nigel of Canterbury recorded Roger of Worcester's refusal to participate in the consecration of a particular bishop, 'for reasons which you [Archbishop Richard] know' (Wireker, 1.198): the bishop was probably Geoffrey of Ely.

The chronicler Ralph de Diceto commented on the parallel advancement of Ridel's fellow archdeacon, Richard of Ilchester, 'contemporaneously holding the foremost rank at the court of the same sovereign, both archdeacons, both called to be bishops at the same time, consecrated together, enthroned in their respective sees on the same day, 13 Oct.' (Diceto … opera historica, 1.395). With this elevation, Ridel, like Richard, had achieved the pinnacle of his career, and thereafter played a full part in the affairs of church and kingdom. He attended the provincial Council of Westminster (11–18 May 1175), witnessed the treaty with the king of Connacht at Windsor on 6 October, and attended the legatine council at Westminster on 14–18 March 1176, where he defended the precedence of the archbishop of Canterbury so forcefully that the archbishop of York accused him of physical violence, against which he had to clear himself by oath in the king's presence at Winchester on 15 August. In July 1176 he compelled Cardinal Vivian, then en route for Scotland, to swear that he would not injure the rights of the English crown, and towards the end of the year he escorted the king's daughter Joanna as far as St Gilles in Provence, when she travelled to Sicily for her marriage to William II (r. 1166–89), returning to England before Christmas; and the honour of Eye was entrusted to his charge. In January 1177 Ridel was one of the prelates commissioned by Henry II to dissolve the college of secular canons at Waltham, after which he accompanied the archbishop of Canterbury on an embassy to the count of Flanders. In March he witnessed Henry II's adjudication of the dispute between the kings of Castile and Navarre; in June he was involved in missions from Henry II to the younger Henry and also to Louis VII of France; on 12 July, he was at Stansted when the king received news of a threatened interdict, unless the king would permit the consummation of Prince Richard's marriage to Princess Alix of France; and he occurs at the royal court at Winchester at Christmas 1178.

Ridel was active in the administration of justice throughout his career. In 1179 he was appointed—with associates who included his old colleague Richard of Ilchester—to be one of the chief justices who presided over a nationwide judicial visitation, his own responsibility being the midland circuit. From 1180 to 1185 he is frequently recorded either as a justice in the curia regis at Westminster or as a baron of the exchequer, while in February 1182 he was appointed an executor of the king's will. A witness to the marriage of the king of Scots at Woodstock on 5 September 1186, Ridel attended a royal council at Marlborough on 14 September, and attended the Christmas court at Guildford. In 1189 he held pleas in Lincolnshire, Derbyshire, and Cambridgeshire and attended the conference between Henry II and Louis VII at La Ferté Bernard on 4 June, but he had evidently returned to England before Henry II's death on 6 July, for he fell ill at Winchester, as he was 'hastening with a great train and full of pride' to greet the new king, Richard I, on his entry into the kingdom, and he died there on 20 or 21 August 1189 (Gesta … Benedicti, 2.78; Diceto … opera historica, 2.68). He was buried in Ely Cathedral. Since he left no will, his treasures, amounting to 3200 marks in coin and much gold and silver plate, horses, fine clothes, corn, and other stores, were seized for the king. At the enthronement of his successor on 6 January 1190 it was discovered that Ridel's tomb had been broken open, and his episcopal ring stolen. The Historia Eliensis describes Geoffrey Ridel as a benefactor of his cathedral church and monastery, to which he presented several rich vestments. He repaired the sides and part of the silver cover of St Etheldreda's shrine, 'painted the chair of the high altar and the middle part of the choir, and almost completed the new building to the west, with the tower' (Wharton, 1.631–2). Later rebuilding has destroyed some of the work, but the southern half of the western transept still remains (with a clerestory added later), together with the lower portions of the great west tower. A. J. DUGGAN

Sources D. M. Owen, ed., *Ely*, English Episcopal Acta [forthcoming] · R. W. Eyton, *Court, household, and itinerary of King Henry II* (1878) · J. C. Robertson and J. B. Sheppard, eds., *Materials for the history of Thomas Becket, archbishop of Canterbury*, 7 vols., Rolls Series, 67 (1875–85) · W. Stubbs, ed., *Gesta regis Henrici secundi Benedicti abbatis: the chronicle of the reigns of Henry II and Richard I, AD 1169–1192*, 2 vols., Rolls Series, 49 (1867) · *The chronicle of Jocelin of Brakelond: concerning the acts of Samson, abbot of the monastery of St Edmund*, ed. H. E. Butler (1949) · *Ann. mon.* · [H. Wharton], ed., *Anglia sacra*, 2 vols. (1691) · *Gesta abbatum monasterii Sancti Albani, a Thoma Walsingham*, ed. H. T. Riley, 3 vols., pt 4 of *Chronica monasterii S. Albani*, Rolls Series, 28 (1867–9) · *Pipe rolls* · H. Hall, ed., *The Red Book of the Exchequer*, 3 vols., Rolls Series, 99 (1896) · *Radulfi de Diceto ... opera historica*, ed. W. Stubbs, 2 vols., Rolls Series, 68 (1876) · L. Delisle and E. Berger, eds., *Recueil des actes de Henri II roi d'Angleterre et duc de Normandie, concernant les provinces françaises et les affaires de France*, 2–3 (Paris, 1916–20) · T. Madox, *Formulare Anglicanum* (1702) · *The historical works of Gervase of Canterbury*, ed. W. Stubbs, 2 vols., Rolls Series, 73 (1879–80) · D. Whitelock, M. Brett, and C. N. L. Brooke, eds., *Councils and synods with other documents relating to the English church, 871–1204*, 2 vols. (1981) · N. Wireker, *Tractatus Nigelli contra curiales et officiales clericos, The Anglo-Latin satirical poets and epigrammatists of the twelfth century*, ed. T. Wright, 1, Rolls Series, 59 (1872), 146–230 · *Fasti Angl., 1066–1300*, [St Paul's, London] · *Fasti Angl., 1066–1300*, [Monastic cathedrals] · *Fasti Angl., 1066–1300*, [Lincoln] · *Chronica magistri Rogeri de Hovedene*, ed. W. Stubbs, 4 vols., Rolls Series, 51 (1868–71) · *The letters of John of Salisbury*, ed. and trans. H. E. Butler and W. J. Millor, rev. C. N. L. Brooke, OMT, 2: *The later letters, 1163–1180* (1979) [Lat. orig. with parallel Eng. text] · M. G. Cheney, *Roger, bishop of Worcester, 1164–1179* (1980) · *Letters and charters of Gilbert Foliot*, ed. A. Morey and others (1967) · F. Barlow, *Thomas Becket* (1986), 81–3, 106, 144, 151, 169, index · C. Duggan, 'Richard of Ilchester, royal servant and bishop', *TRHS*, 5th ser., 16 (1966), 1–21, esp. 1–2, 5, 12–15, 21 · 'Richard of Ilchester, royal servant and bishop', C. Duggan, *Canon law in medieval England* (1982), no. 13
Wealth at death approx. 3200 marks—cash and valuables: *Historical works of Gervase of Canterbury*, 1.457; Wharton, ed., *Anglia sacra*, 1.631

Rider [Ryder], **John** (1562–1632), lexicographer and Church of Ireland bishop of Killaloe, was born in Carrington, Cheshire. He was educated at Jesus College, Oxford, where he graduated BA in February 1581 and MA in July 1583. He held the rectory of Waterstock, Oxfordshire, from September 1580 to the following year and that of South Ockenden from November 1583 to August 1590. He did not reside in either parish, but remained in Oxford teaching Latin grammar. In 1589 Rider published an English–Latin and Latin–English dictionary under the title *Bibliotheca scholastica*. Dedicated to Sir Francis Walsingham, this was printed in Oxford by Joseph Barnes. Some of Rider's contemporaries claimed that he had plagiarized his dictionary from the *Dictionarium linguae Latinae et Anglicanae* of Thomas Thomas published in Cambridge in 1587. The criticism was misplaced, however, since all Latin–English dictionaries of the period were based on Thomas Cooper's *Thesaurus linguae Romanae et Britannicae* (1565, 1573, 1584, and 1587) and Cooper himself based his

dictionary on the Latin–French dictionary of Robert Estienne, *Dictionarium Latino-Gallicum* (1552, 1561). A second edition of Rider's dictionary, revised and enlarged by Francis Holyoake, was published in London in 1606. It became a standard school textbook and was reprinted several times between 1612 and 1657. Geoffrey Keating, in the introduction to his *History of Ireland* (1628–34), quotes Rider's dictionary as an authority against Edmund Spenser (Comyn, 24–5).

From 1590 to 1597 Rider held the living of Bermondsey in Surrey. Having incurred great expense in publishing the first edition of his dictionary, he received financial help from the earl of Sussex and William Waad, a clerk of the privy council, as well as a number of Rider's parishioners in Bermondsey, and friends in Banbury, Oxfordshire. In 1597 through the influence of his patron, William, earl of Derby, he was appointed rector of the rich benefice of Winwick in Lancashire which he continued to hold until August 1615. He does not seem to have resided in Winwick, however, since in the same year he was appointed prebendary of St Patrick's Cathedral, Dublin, and dean shortly thereafter. In January 1598 he obtained the queen's licence to absent himself from Dublin in order to return to England, presumably in order to collect the income from his living in Winwick. He became prebendary of Geashill in the cathedral of Kildare in March 1599. In 1601 he published in London *The Coppie of a Letter ... Concerning the Newes out of Ireland*. In 1608 he exchanged the deanery of St Patrick's for the position of archdeacon of Meath, his place as dean being taken by Thomas Moigne. He continued to reside in Kildare for a while, however, for he is cited in a list of lords, knights, commons, and other officers in co. Kildare on 28 June 1608.

In Dublin, Rider engaged in a long and bitter theological controversy with the Irish Jesuit Henry Fitzsimon, who was imprisoned briefly in Dublin Castle for attempting to convert protestants. Rider published a pamphlet, *A Friendly Caveat to Irelands Catholickes*, in Dublin in 1602 in reply to six Catholic articles circulated in manuscript by Fitzsimon. Fitzsimon answered with *A Catholike Confutation of M. John Riders Clayme of Antiquitie* (1608). This tract of over 400 pages was printed in Rouen together with a shorter work, *Replie to Mr Rider's Rescript*. These rather disorganized works are notable for their attacks on Rider's character. Fitzsimon erroneously asserts that Rider graduated BA and MA in the same year and claims to quote Rider's erstwhile tutor in Oxford to the effect that Rider was the least able pupil he had ever taught and that Rider had passed his examinations dishonestly. Fitzsimon alleges that Rider was ignorant 'in scripture, in [church] fathers, in histories, in orthography, in Greek, in French, in Latin, in English and now in spelling' (Fitzsimon, 311)—an astonishing calumny against a lexicographer. Fitzsimon further relates that in May 1604 Dean Rider ordered his son to pull down an image but that the boy fell and was badly injured and at the same time Rider's servant was badly smitten with the plague; Fitzsimon takes these two misfortunes to be the righteous judgement of God. Fitzsimon also asserts that Rider, although very rich from his tithes, impoverished the bakers of Dublin by giving business to his sons-in-law:

> they being foreigners [i.e. Englishmen] and very flesh-worms in Dublin, such as neither bear cess nor press, watch nor award, toll nor custom, and in the meantime suck the juice of the City into their private purses under the warmth of your [Rider's] wings, to use your own phrase, and in the protection of your liberties. (ibid., 286)

In 1611 Rider was appointed bishop of Killaloe and was consecrated on 12 January 1613, his patent being dated 15 August 1612. In 1616, through the good offices of George Montgomery, bishop of Meath, Rider obtained from King James a letter ordering the restoration of lands belonging to the see. These included twenty-one quarters of plough-lands known as Tearmann Uí Ghrádaigh in the parish of Tuamgraney, near Scarriff, co. Clare. In 1622 he requested the royal commissioners, appointed to examine the state of his diocese, that he be allowed to repossess certain rectories which had been alienated to 'impropriators' during the long reign of his predecessor, Murtagh O'Brien. Rider's appeal was apparently successful. It is clear from Rider's own report on his diocese that he was very concerned about the loss of church lands to lay tenants, for many of these were Roman Catholics and failed in their duty to provide for the protestant clergy. The clergy were thus entirely dependent on such fees they could earn by baptizing, marrying, and burying. Interestingly it seems that many of the Church of Ireland clergy in the diocese of Killaloe at the time were of native origin and spoke Irish. Rider himself understood the importance of using Irish in ministering to his flock and it was probably the Irish-speaking clergy Rider had in mind when he suggested that recusancy fines in several parishes should be used to support such curates as read 'divine service in the Irish tongue unto their parishioners, that others by their example may be encouraged to the practice [of] the reading of the Irish language' (Phillips, 2.575).

Rider died in Killaloe on 12 November 1632 and was buried in the cathedral church of St Flannan. Lewis Jones, dean of Cashel, was appointed bishop to replace him. Rider was married and had two sons, John and Thomas, and at least two daughters. N. J. A. WILLIAMS

Sources H. Fitzsimon, *A Catholike confutation of M. John Riders clayme of antiquitie* (1608); repr. (1974) · *The whole works of Sir James Ware concerning Ireland*, ed. and trans. W. Harris, 2 vols. in 3 (1739–45, [1746]) · H. Cotton, *Fasti ecclesiae Hibernicae*, 1–5 (1845–60) · W. M. Mason, *The history and antiquities of the collegiate and cathedral church of St Patrick, near Dublin* (privately printed, Dublin, 1820) · J. S. Brewer and W. Bullen, eds., *Calendar of the Carew manuscripts*, 6: *Miscellaneous papers*, PRO (1873) · W. A. Phillips, ed., *History of the Church of Ireland*, 2 (1934) · D. T. Starnes, *Robert Estienne's influence on lexicography* (1963) · D. Comyn, *The history of Ireland by Geoffrey Keating, D.D.*, 1 (1902)

Rider [Ryder], **Sir William** (*c*.1544–1611), merchant and local politician, born about 1544 in Mucklestone, Staffordshire, was the grandson of Thomas Ryther of Lynstead in Kent and the son of Thomas Ryther, or Ryder, of Mucklestone; his mother also came from Staffordshire. He was

apprenticed to Thomas Burdet, a member of the Haberdashers' Company, of which he became free in 1569. He was a dealer in luxury cloths, and kept a shop in the Pawn of the Royal Exchange, the stock of which was valued at £3267 in 1592. Like many Londoners who prospered (Rider was already among the top 5 per cent of citizens in terms of his wealth by 1582), his business activities diversified. He became involved in the customs, holding the post of collector of the customs inwards from 1603 until 1610. From 1608 he enjoyed the lease of the imposts on sea coals as a member of a syndicate with Sir Thomas Bludder, John Trevor, and Marmaduke Darrell, and in the last year of his life he farmed the imposition on sugars with his son-in-law Sir Thomas Lake. He also speculated in crown lands, for example, by participating in a syndicate for the purchase and resale of £60,000-worth of lands in 1609.

For the early part of his career Rider lived in the parish of St Christopher-le-Stocks, but he seems to have moved into St Stephen Walbrook in 1599, and spent an increasing amount of time in Stepney. In 1609, shortly before his death, he inherited the manor of Leyton Grange in Low Leyton, Essex, from his financially embarrassed nephew and former apprentice, Edward Rider. He owned additional property at Greenwich, at Eythorne, and at the Mote near Maidstone in Kent, and also leased a manor at Dunmowe in Essex from the bishop of London. After serving the round of parish offices (collector for the poor in 1575–6 and churchwarden in 1580–81), he was elected to the common council for Cheapside ward in 1582. He was also active in the affairs of his livery company, serving as master on four occasions, the first in 1591. He was elected to the court of aldermen on 8 July 1591, and served successively in the wards of Bridge Without (1591–5) and Cornhill (1595–1611). His term as sheriff came in 1591–2, and he filled the office of lord mayor in 1600–01. As mayor Rider was remembered as a zealous reformer of weights and measures, seeking to establish uniform measures for sea coals, and becoming entangled in a protracted conflict with those who weighed the city's coal.

The most testing time of Rider's period of office came on Sunday 8 February 1601, when he was called from the sermon at Paul's Cross to deal with the irruption into the City of the earl of Essex at the head of about 140 followers, many of them of high rank. Essex probably planned to take the City and use it as a bargaining counter to remove his enemies from influence about the queen, but the rumours that twenty-one of the twenty-five aldermen would support him proved unfounded. Rider's strategy seems to have been to detach the earl from his followers by getting him indoors, either in his house or in that of the sheriff, Sir Thomas Smythe, and thereby giving the loyalist forces time to organize the defence of Whitehall and the City. The weeks which followed the revolt were tense, and Rider's energies were directed to surveillance and the pursuit of libellers against the now still more firmly entrenched Cecilian regime. He received the knighthood customarily given to the lord mayor in the early summer of 1601. For all the sympathy that the London élite and its favoured preachers had felt for the forward foreign policy with which Essex was associated, there was no way in which they could conceive of politics outside the framework of loyalty to the queen.

Rider's religious position seems to have been that of a conformist protestant, and there is little reason to connect him with the godly. He rebuilt the chancel of Leyton church, where he was buried. His largest charities were directed to the area where he had grown up. To the poor of Mucklestone he arranged for an annuity payable from property in Birchin Lane, London, while the inhabitants of Market Drayton were the beneficiaries of an annuity of £10 per annum to support their school for poor men's children, 'to thend they maie by their good teaching come to be putt forth apprentices and soe become good members in the Comon wealthe' (PRO, PROB11/118, fol. 281). Rider's bequests to charities were not, however, particularly large for a man of his wealth, and the bulk of his fortune passed to his two coheirs. He died at Leyton in September 1611, a few months after his wife, Elizabeth, the daughter of Richard Stone of Holme in Norfolk, whom he had married shortly before 1572. His funeral was celebrated on 19 November 1611 at St Olave, Hart Street, in the City. He was buried at Low Leyton church, where a monument to him was erected. The two daughters who survived him made good marriages—Mary (1575–1642) to Sir Thomas Lake in 1591 and Susanna (1577–1640) to the lawyer Thomas Caesar in 1593. On Rider's death the gossips noted that 'he died a richer man than ever he was esteemed', as Lake was allegedly the beneficiary through his wife of property valued at £20,000 (Letters of John Chamberlain, 1.316). Although it was Rider's intention to divide the property equally between his two daughters, they seem to have disputed the terms of the will.

IAN W. ARCHER

Sources G. E. Cokayne, *Some account of the lord mayors and sheriffs of the city of London during the first quarter of the seventeenth century, 1601–1625* (1897) · M. Benbow, 'Index of London citizens involved in city government, 1558–1603', U. Lond., Institute of Historical Research, Centre for Metropolitan History · A. B. Beaven, ed., *The aldermen of the City of London, temp. Henry III–[1912]*, 2 vols. (1908–13) · R. G. Lang, 'The greater merchants of London in the early seventeenth century', DPhil diss., U. Oxf., 1963 · will, PRO, PROB 11/118, sig. 94; sentence PROB 11/124, sig. 119 · subsidy assessments, PRO · journals, CLRO, court of common council · repertories of the court of aldermen, CLRO · *The letters of John Chamberlain*, ed. N. E. McClure, 2 vols. (1939) · *CSP dom.* · A. Poval, *The annals of the parishes of St Olave Hart Street and Allhallows Staining, in the City of London* (1894)

Rider, Sir William (d. 1669), merchant, was probably a native of Wembury, Devon, a place he would remember when making his will. From there he went to sea, spending much of his early life on trading voyages to the Mediterranean. He acquired the title of captain but there is no record of his service in the king's ships. He made a useful marriage to Priscilla, daughter of Roger Tweedy (commissioner of the navy, 1642–8). His father-in-law undoubtedly contributed to Rider's fortunes, but in the main he rose by his own skilful operations on the London exchange. By 1647 he had £1000 or more invested in the East India Company, on the strength of which he was elected to the company's committee of adventurers on 18 August; on 22 September he was admitted to the freedom of the company. He remained active in its affairs, being appointed to numerous committees and delegations and serving two terms as deputy governor. At various times he traded in cinnamon, indigo, tobacco, and wine; he also had a special 'sugar house' at Woolwich. In 1650–53 he was involved in a scheme for ransoming prisoners taken by the Barbary states.

The outbreak of war with the Dutch in 1652 heralded a shift in Rider's career; instead of the spices of the east, he came to specialize in those basic naval supplies—timber, pitch, and tar—for which the Baltic was the principal source. This brought him into close contact with successive governments and was the basis for his considerable prosperity. On 18 August 1655 he was named one of the commissioners for Cromwell's 'western design', the protector's cherished operation against the Spanish in the Caribbean. In the same year Rider was among those who petitioned the government for permission to sell the East India Company's saltpetre into Amsterdam, a controversial trade in the immediate aftermath of the First Anglo-Dutch War; permission was not given until 1658. Rider was also occasionally employed by the protectorate government in arbitration between other merchants. In November 1659 the East India Company appointed him to a committee for surveying all ships which it took into its service.

In March 1660 Rider was named a warden of Trinity House by the revived Rump Parliament. His services to Charles II's regime were recognized by a knighthood on 12 March 1661. On 17 April 1662 he was elected deputy governor of the East India Company for the following year. On 20 October he was appointed to the public committee of inquiry into the Chatham Chest, the seamen's charity. On 20 November he was named to the Tangier committee, and the following year he and Sir Richard Ford devised schemes for the civil administration and merchant law of England's new colony. In 1664 he was appointed to the corporation of the royal fishery. During the 1660s he made a succession of large contracts with the Navy Board, chiefly for timber, tar, and hemp. These were negotiated by Pepys, whom Rider had first met in January 1660 and with whom he developed a friendly, though never intimate, association. Rider taught the fledgeling naval official the complexities of marine insurance. Pepys would on one occasion denounce Rider as 'false' (Pepys, Diary, 6.170), but his criticisms amount to little. Ford and Rider were said to have defrauded the crown by taking more for the transport of soldiers to Tangier than they actually laid out. Pepys suspected Rider of complicity with his partner, William Cutler, in attempting a hike on the London exchange by inventing a story that the Stockholm tar house had been destroyed by fire. And Pepys detected Rider in persuading the board to buy sub-standard hemp which he himself had shipped and then dumped on a small-time operator: 'Here appears that merchants will be merchants, and Sir W. Rider will do as other men' (Latham, 75). Pepys, however, always took the view that tradesmen were adequately rewarded by the honour of supplying the crown and thought it impertinent of Rider and Ford to expect payment for goods already served to come in before a further contract was made. In 1664 it was suggested that Rider might go to Harwich as the Navy Board's resident commissioner; Sir William Coventry, to whom the bringing of any merchant into the public service was repugnant, warned darkly of 'the endeavours for Sir Wm Rider' (PRO, SP 29/104, no. 149), and no more is heard of his candidacy.

During the Second Anglo-Dutch War, Rider was a major supplier to the navy, having to bring in his goods across the battle zone. In 1665 he had the additional problem of his ships' being detained by the elector of Brandenburg, ostensibly to avoid contamination from the plague rampant in England. In August Rider warned the navy paymaster that his ships might have to return 'dead freight for want of monye', and gave notice that he would not expect to be blamed in consequence (PRO, SP 29/128, no. 80(i)).

Rider had bought an Elizabethan house, Kirby Castle, at Bethnal Green, already famous in popular ballads as the 'Blind Beggars' Palace'. Pepys had seen it for the first time in June 1663 and judged it 'a fine place', and the garden 'very pleasant', with 'the greatest quantity of strawberrys I ever saw, and good' (Pepys, Diary, 4.200). During the great fire in September 1666 many of Rider's friends, and indeed a more than welcome number of his remoter acquaintances, sent their valuables to safety there. Among those taking this precaution was Pepys, who deposited not only his cash and plate, but the four volumes which thus far comprised his diary. Rider had previously told Pepys that he had himself kept up a diary for the past forty years.

In October 1665 Rider was recommended by the duke of Albemarle for the victualling commission which Pepys had proposed. On 17 April 1667 he was elected for a further term as deputy governor of the East India Company, though in the course of his year of office he was in dispute with the company over cowries he had shipped. A larger concern came in June when, in his Trinity House capacity, he was ordered to see to the defences at Gravesend in the face of threatened Dutch invasion. He took up this duty with enthusiasm, but was later accused of sinking as blockships vessels laden with serviceable cargoes (possibly those of his commercial rivals).

Rider had lived comfortably on the proceeds of his success, and the onset of gout from 1664 was a predictable consequence. He had signalled his rise to the gentry by purchasing in 1666 a manorial licence to drive his carriage over Mile End Common to Stepney church. Rider died at Bethnal Green on 30 August 1669 and was buried at St Andrew Undershaft, London, on 9 September. His estate, which included over 1000 acres in Kent and Wiltshire, and £16,000 stock in the Royal African Company, passed chiefly to his widow and his elder son, Thomas. His younger son, William, received all 14,000 ducats which Rider had invested on the Venetian exchange. Other bequests were made to his daughter Elizabeth, her husband Richard Middleton, and their 'prettie babes' Richard, Elizabeth, and Mary, to his second daughter Priscilla and her husband, Richard Bayly, and to his unmarried daughters Mary, Anne, and Martha. Rider's will also mentions his sister Joan and her husband, Dr Joseph Crowther. Among colleagues remembered in the will were Captain Jeremy Blackman, Sir Richard Ford, and the lieutenant of the Tower, Sir John Robinson (PRO, PROB 11/331, fols. 153v–155v).

C. S. KNIGHTON

Sources E. B. Sainsbury, ed., *A calendar of the court minutes … of the East India Company*, 11 vols. (1907–38), vols. 3–11 · *The narrative of General Venables*, ed. C. H. Firth, CS, new ser., 60 (1900), 107 · Pepys, *Diary*, 1.14; 3.8, 114, 129–30, 238; 4.89, 200–01, 398, 426; 5.15, 52, 97, 136, 159; 6.191; 7.272, 283; 8.270–71; 9.354 · *Shorthand letters of Samuel Pepys*, ed. E. Chappell (1933), 34, 57 · *Samuel Pepys and the Second Dutch War: Pepys's navy white book and Brooke House papers*, ed. R. Latham, Navy RS, 133 (1995), 33–5, 60, 74–6, 99 [transcribed by W. Matthews and C. Knighton] · *CSP dom.*, 1651–2, 12, 371, 380, 433, 466; 1652–3, 318; 1655, 387; 1655–6, 127; 1656–7, 502; 1657–8, 338, 343, 380; 1658–9, 427; 1663–4, 84; 1665–8 · G. W. Hill and W. H. Frere, eds., *Memorials of Stepney parish* (privately printed, Guildford, 1890–91), p. 244, n. 1 · W. A. Shaw, *The knights of England*, 2 (1906), 233 · BL, Add. MS 9317, fol. 1 · *The diurnal of Thomas Rugge, 1659–1661*, ed. W. L. Sachse, CS, 3rd ser., 91 (1961), 58 · PRO, SP 29/104, no. 149 · PRO, SP 29/128, no. 80(1) · will, PRO, PROB 11/331, fols. 153v–155v
Archives PRO, letters (domestic, Charles II), SP 29
Wealth at death over 1000 acres; over £12,000 in cash bequests; £16,000 stock in Royal African Company; 14,000 ducats invested in Venetian exchequer at 6%: will, PRO, PROB 11/331, fols. 153v–155v

Rider, William (1723–1785), historian and writer, was baptized at St Botolph without Bishopsgate, London, on 14 May 1723, the son of John S. Rider, gentleman, and his wife, Fortune Perry. He was educated at Mr Watkin's academy in Spital Square. On 22 June 1739 he matriculated from St Mary Hall, Oxford, but moved to Jesus College, where he was a scholar from 1744 to 1749; he graduated BA in 1745, and was subsequently appointed chaplain of the Mercers' Company, lecturer of St Vedast, Foster Lane, and curate of St Faith's, London. He was also chaplain to St Paul's School, and in 1763 was appointed surmaster, a post from which he retired in 1783 on account of ill health.

Besides several individual sermons Rider undertook a translation of Voltaire's *Candide* in the year of its publication (1759). He also published a number of other literary works. *A Comment on Boadicia* (1754) was a call for the revival of the tragedy by Richard Glover which had played for nine nights at Drury Lane Theatre in December 1753. *A New Universal Dictionary, or, A Compleat Treasure of the English Language* (1759) was dedicated to William Pitt the elder. This was a scholarly work which demonstrated Rider's command of Anglo-Saxon, Welsh, and German, but which suffered by comparison with Johnson's *Dictionary*. Rider's other major work was *A New History of England* (50 vols., 1761–4), dedicated to George III. This work was designed to be an affordable and popular whig history of England, and contained lively engravings. It spanned the period from pre-Roman Britain to 1763. It was partly a compilation of primary sources and histories by T. Smollett and other secondary writers, but it also contained some original narrative and researches, notably on Celtic and Anglo-Saxon history. It was not a critical or commercial success, however. W. T. Lowndes, a later bibliographer, described it as one of the vilest Grub Street compilations ever published. In 1764 Rider published an atlas to accompany the work. *An Historical and Critical Account of the Lives and Writings of the Living Authors of Great Britain* (1762), published anonymously, was a short work containing accounts of, among others, Smollett, D. Hume, A. Young, and Samuel Johnson (with whom Rider was personally acquainted); it also carried a favourable notice of his own work. Another compilation, *The Christian Family's Bible* (1763-7), in three large folio volumes, contained lengthy comments by the editor. Rider also contributed verses to the *Gentleman's Magazine* under the pseudonym Philargyrus.

Rider died on 30 November 1785, leaving a widow, Hannah Rider, who received an allowance from the Mercers' Company until her death in 1809; a son, John Rider, who was a printer in Little Britain, died on 1 April 1800.

A. F. POLLARD, rev. KAREN O'BRIEN

Sources *GM*, 1st ser., 55 (1785), 1009 • Foster, *Alum. Oxon.* • R. B. Gardiner, ed., *The admission registers of St Paul's School, from 1748 to 1876* (1884), 1.84 • J. Hawkins, *The life of Samuel Johnson, LL.D*, ed. B. H. Davis (New York, 1961), 282 • Allibone, *Dict.* • Watt, *Bibl. Brit.* • W. D. Adams, *Dictionary of English literature*, rev. edn [1879-80] • *IGI* • Mercers' Company database

Ridevall [Musca], **John** (*d*. in or after **1340**), Franciscan friar and mythographer, is of unknown origins. The course of his life is unknown before his inception as a doctor of theology at Oxford, about 1331, when he became fifty-fourth lector of the Franciscan convent. He attended a general chapter of the Friars Minor at Basel on 28 October 1340, after which he passes from view. Several works, however, survive, all of which exemplify his interest in classical mythology and his ingenious moralizations of pagan deities for use in sermons. First, his Apocalypse commentary, which only survives in extracts in Venice, Biblioteca Marciana, MS Class. i.139, was probably the fruit of his doctoral lectures on scripture at Oxford *c*.1331. In it he indulged his taste for fantastic stories from ancient history, loosely related as *exempla* for sermons: he belonged therefore to the generation of 'classicizing' friars in Oxford and Cambridge among whom the Dominican Robert Holcot (*d*. 1349) was a leading voice. Second, he embarked on a commentary on Augustine's *De civitate Dei*, which shows the influence of another Dominican, Nicholas Trevet (*d*. 1328), but also his desire to improve on Trevet's commentary. A kind of critique of Trevet's work survives in Rome, *Tractatus additionum in expositione Trevet*; this was developed, probably in 1332, into a commentary on Augustine, intended to cover all twenty-two books, but of which only a prologue and books 1-3 and 6-7 are extant, in Corpus Christi College, Oxford, MSS 186-187.

This is a scholarly explanation of Augustine's allusions to pagan gods and ancient history. Ridevall exploited his limited library to the full; but he also used his vivid imagination to describe each of the twenty-two books of *De civitate Dei* as a critique of the cult of particular pagan deities. By the time he reached the sixth book he had read some of the development of Trevet's work by their contemporary Thomas Waleys, and thus had access to Waleys's larger body of source material. But he was more aware than either predecessor of Augustine's polemical purpose; as a critic, he understood the importance of his author's intention. In his *Fulgentius metaforalis*, evidently written in 1333, he developed his moralized exposition of classical mythology through an explanation of the *Mythologiae* of the fifth-century writer Fulgentius, which he knew in the enlarged version of Alberic of London. Ridevall's work was a handbook of myths moralized for the use of preachers; his technique was to draw a series of verbal pictures of pagan deities with their symbols, such as Venus in a sea shell. Though in some manuscripts of the work they were clumsily turned into illustrations, these verbal pictures were only rhetorical devices designed to stimulate the imagination of preachers. A shorter version of the work has been printed; its fuller form is extant in the Bodleian Library, MS Bodley 571.

Finally Ridevall commented upon Walter Map's satirical *Dissuasio Valerii de uxore non ducenda* (extant in Bodl. Oxf., MS Douce 147 and elsewhere). Like other commentators he took the work as a genuine work of Valerius Maximus, and commented on its abundant classical allusions. Lost works on Proverbs and the Song of Songs were owned by John Whethamstede (*d*. 1465) in the early fifteenth century, and Holcot cites another lost commentary on Augustine's *Confessions*. Ridevall took the indulgence of his fantastic visual imagination further than any of his contemporaries, in the service of lively preaching; at the same time, within the limits of the materials available to him he was scholarly in comparing texts and probing the intentions of the authors on whom he commented. His work had little circulation, mainly in Oxford and among Franciscans; his work on Augustine was eclipsed by the commentary of Trevet and Waleys. JEREMY CATTO

Sources J. Ridevall, Commentary on the Apocalypse, Biblioteca Marciana, Venice, MS Class i.139, fols. 110r-119r • J. Ridevall, 'Tractatus additionum in expositione Trevet', Archivum Generale Ordinis Fratrum Praedicatorum, Rome, MS xiv 28c, fols. 1r-9r • J. Ridevall, commentary on Augustine *De civitate Dei*, CCC Oxf., MSS 186-187 • J. Ridevall, commentary on *Dissuasio Valerii de uxore non ducenda*, Bodl. Oxf., MS Douce 147 • J. Ridevall, 'Fulgentius metaforalis', Bodl. Oxf., MS Bodley 571 • *Fulgentius metaforalis*, ed. H. Liebeschütz (1926) • B. Smalley, 'John Ridewall's commentary on *De civitate Dei*', *Medium Aevum*, 25 (1956-7), 140-53 • B. Smalley, *English friars and antiquity in the early fourteenth century* (1960) • T. Kaeppeli, 'Une critique du commentaire du Trevet sur le *Civitate Dei*', *Archivum Fratrum Praedicatorum*, 29 (1959), 200-05 • J. B. Allen, 'Commentary as criticism: the text, influence and literary theory of the "Fulgentius metaphored" of John Ridewall', *Acta conventus neo-Latini Amstelodamensis*, ed. P. Tuynman and others (1979), 29-47 • N. F. Palmer, 'Das "Exempelwerk der englischen Bettelmönchen"', *Exempel und Exempelsammlungen*, ed. W. Haug and B. Wachinger (1991), 137-72 • Emden, *Oxf.* • R. Sharpe and others, eds., *English Benedictine libraries: the shorter catalogues* (1996), 567

Archives Archivum Generale Ordinis Fratrum Praedicatorum, Rome, MS xiv 28c, fols. 1r-9r • Biblioteca Marciana, Venice, MS Class i.139, fols. 110r-119r • Bodl. Oxf., MS Bodley 571 • Bodl. Oxf., MS Douce 147 • CCC Oxf., MSS 186-187

Ridge, John (1589/90–1637?), Church of Ireland clergyman, was born at Oxford. He matriculated at St John's College, Oxford, on 16 June 1610, at the age of twenty, graduated BA on 23 May 1612, and was ordained deacon and priest by John Bridges, bishop of Oxford on, respectively, 8 March and 7 June 1612. Like many other English puritan clergy, Ridge chose to serve in the Church of Ireland, where subscription was not required, and was instituted to the vicarage of Antrim in the diocese of Connor on 7 July 1619 by the notably flexible bishop of Down and Connor, Robert Echlin, on the presentation of Arthur, Lord Chichester of Belfast. By this stage the diocese was the centre of extensive, if unofficial, Scottish settlement, which brought in its train a number of Scottish clergy, many committed presbyterians, some expelled from their homeland because of their radicalism; like Ridge, they were welcomed into the ministry of the Church of Ireland. One of these Scottish ministers, James Glendinning, began a popular religious revival in 1625. Since his hellfire preaching left his hearers terrified but uncomforted, Ridge, together with three Scottish clergy, Robert Blair, Robert Cunningham, and James Hamilton, organized that typically puritan institution, a series of monthly lectures by combination. These in turn led to the development of regular outdoor communions, lasting up to three days, when hundreds of people flocked from all over the region to hear sermons and be instructed.

Thus began the first Irish–Scottish religious revival, a precursor of the American great awakening of the eighteenth century. In a letter written about 1630 Ridge gave a sympathetic account of the enthusiasm and piety of his fellow clergy:

> the Lord hath exceedingly blessed their labours for they have brought a great number of people for 20 miles about them to as great a measure of knowledge and zeal in every good duty, as, I think, is to be found again in any part of Christendom. (NL Ire., MS 8014/i)

Though the Scottish ministers in their turn praised Ridge for charitable works, his humility, and his preaching, which they labelled unforgettable—though admittedly less for its brilliance than his constant repetition of salient points—there is no evidence that Ridge was a presbyterian, and he further differed with the Scots over the question of kneeling at communion.

Presbyterians and puritans alike, however, suffered at the hands of Lord Deputy Wentworth and Bishop John Bramhall, who, in the wake of the adoption of new canons at the 1634 Church of Ireland convocation, moved to impose subscription on the Irish clergy. At the regal visitation of 1634 Ridge was identified as a nonconformist. At his visitation in July 1636, the new and active bishop of Down and Connor, Henry Leslie, sentenced him and four Scottish ministers to perpetual silence within the diocese. When passing sentence after a lengthy debate, Leslie argued that Ridge's refusal to subscribe was a product of his melancholy nature, a charge denied by the minister who did, however, acknowledge that the bishop had given him a fair hearing. Though, as Leslie confessed, the people of Antrim continued to support and sympathize with the deposed clergy, most of the ministers left the diocese for Scotland, including Ridge, who reportedly died at Irvine, Ayrshire, in 1637.

Ridge, who was married, was survived by his daughters, one of whom, Susannah (d. 19 April 1693), was married on 30 September 1643 to Samuel Heathcote of Derby, and had ten children. A manuscript autographed by Ridge, 'Advice to his daughters', passed to her descendants.

ALAN FORD

Sources J. S. Reid and W. D. Killen, *History of the Presbyterian church in Ireland*, new edn, 1 (1867), 100, 201, 521 · J. Ridge, undated letter, NL Ire., MS 8014/i · *The life of Mr Robert Blair ... containing his autobiography*, ed. T. M'Crie, Wodrow Society, 11 (1848) · J. Livingstone, 'A brief historical relation of the life of Mr John Livingstone', *Select biographies*, ed. W. K. Tweedie, 1, Wodrow Society, 7/1 (1845), 127–97 · *Reports on the manuscripts of the earl of Eglinton*, HMC, 10 (1885), 46 · Foster, *Alum. Oxon.* · P. Adair, *A true narrative of the rise and progress of the Presbyterian church in Ireland (1623–1670)*, ed. W. D. Killen (1866), 16, 20, 53 · M. J. Westerkamp, *The triumph of the laity: Scots-Irish piety and the great awakening, 1625–1760* (1988) · A. Ford, 'The origins of Irish dissent', *The religion of Irish dissent, 1650–1800*, ed. K. Herlihy (1996), 9–30 · W. D. Bailie, *The Six Mile Water revival of 1625* (1976) · *DNB*

Archives NL Ire., letter

Ridge, William Pett (1859–1930), novelist and short-story writer, was born at Chilham, near Canterbury, Kent, on 22 April 1859, the son of James Ridge, a railway porter, and his wife, Elizabeth, *née* Pett. Very little is known of his early years, except that he was educated at Marden, Kent. When he went up to London in 1880 he attended evening classes at Birkbeck Literary and Scientific Institute (now Birkbeck College). During a long day from nine to seven o'clock he toiled as a clerk in the railway clearing house for 1 guinea per six-day week. Somehow he managed to find the energy to write, and in 1890 he published his first sketches of London life for the *St James Gazette* under the pseudonym Warwick Simpson.

Pett Ridge's first novel, *A Clever Wife* (1895), 'made more stir than most first novels do' (Adcock, 274), according to contemporary Arthur St John Adcock, but it was not until Pett Ridge's fifth, *Mord Em'ly* (1899), that he achieved popular success. Its appeal lay mainly in the feisty cockney protagonist, Em'ly, and her defiance of authority, particularly philanthropists bent on improving her lot. For Em'ly there is no better place than the East End, where she possesses an identity as a member of a female gang, in striking anticipation of contemporary urban life. Pett Ridge does not depict East End life in a grim or brutal way, however, as had Arthur Morrison in *A Child of the Jago* (1896). Instead, his East-Enders enjoy their amusements much more fully than his drab, boring middle-class characters. This attitude became the signature motif of the cockney school, and was initially received enthusiastically, with Pett Ridge 'boldly breaking away from the tragic convention of the slums' (Keating, 210). Cockney school novelists, including Henry Nevinson, Edwin Pugh, Arthur St John Adcock, and Pett Ridge did, however, owe a great deal to Dickens, particularly his portrayal of the virtuous poor; unlike Dickens, Pett Ridge explored the East End proper, that is, east of Aldgate pump. Later critics of Pett Ridge and the others saw their work as sentimental and facetious, an instrument for assuaging middle-class guilt.

On 28 February 1910 William Pett Ridge married Olga Hentschel (b. 1873/4), daughter of his friend Carl Hentschel, a newspaperman and editor of the London *Playgoer*. They had one son and a daughter. The other fictional terrain that Pett Ridge explored was suburbia, notably in *From Nine to Six-Thirty* (1910), and he became known for his portrayal of modern young women asserting their independence as clerks or typists.

Above all Pett Ridge was a humorist. This is captured in his description of meeting Mark Twain when he was introduced as 'the Mark Twain of England': '"What he meant to say", [Ridge] interrupted, "was that you are the Pett Ridge of America". "Ah", said the old man [Twain], taking my arm pleasantly, "now I know we shall get along together"' (Pett Ridge, 44). Pett Ridge's wit and geniality made him a popular after-dinner speaker and an eminently clubbable man; among others he joined the Yorrick and Boz clubs, was elected to the Garrick on nomination by J. M. Barrie, and latterly was president of the Omar Khayyam Club.

Pett Ridge had always taken an interest in children, especially those from the London slums, and he continued his charitable work there even after he moved his family to Ampthill, Willow Grove, Chislehurst, Kent, where he died on 29 September 1930. *The Times* obituary noted that he was an enthusiastic committee member of King Edward's Hospital Fund for London and observed that the capital would miss his 'kindly presence and never-failing humour' (quoted in Jasper, 303).

In photographs Pett Ridge, with his dark eyes and slightly hooded lids, seems solemn, and this deceptive appearance apparently served well his dry wit. Although he was prolific, producing over sixty novels and short-story collections as well as two charming memoirs, by the end of his career his literary following had drastically diminished. He is likely to remain a minor writer because he was innovative neither in style nor subject matter; his main flaw was that he ignored the devastating impact of severe deprivation on his east London characters and instead perpetuated the sentimental Victorian myth that cockneys with enough character could triumph over all obstacles. GEORGE MALCOLM JOHNSON

Sources M. Jasper, 'William Pett Ridge', *British short-fiction writers, 1880–1914: the realist tradition*, ed. W. B. Thesing, DLitB, 135 (1994), 298–303 · A. St John Adcock, *The glory that was Grub Street* [1928] · V. Brome, *Four realist novelists* (1965) · W. Pett Ridge, *A story teller* (1923) · P. J. Keating, *The working classes in Victorian fiction* (1971) · S. Kemp, C. Mitchell, and D. Trotter, *Edwardian fiction: an Oxford companion* (1997) · D. Trotter, *The English novel in history, 1895–1920* (1993) · *CGPLA Eng. & Wales* (1930) · b. cert. · d. cert.
Archives U. Leeds, Brotherton L., letters to Edward Clodd and Phyllis Clodd
Likenesses E. O. Hoppé, photograph, repro. in Adcock, *Glory that was Grub Street* · photograph, repro. in Jasper, 'William Pett Ridge', 298
Wealth at death £1848 11s. 7d.: probate, 18 Nov 1930, *CGPLA Eng. & Wales*

Ridgeway, Sir Joseph West (1844–1930), army officer, the second son of the Revd Joseph Ridgeway, rector of High Roothing, Essex, and his wife, Eliza Letitia Chambers, was born at High Roothing on 16 May 1844. Charles John Ridgeway (1841–1927), bishop of Chichester, and Frederick Edward Ridgeway (1848–1921), bishop of Salisbury, were his brothers. Educated at St Paul's School, London, he obtained a commission in the Bengal infantry at the age of sixteen. In 1869 the viceroy, Lord Mayo, selected him for civil employment in the central India and Rajputana agencies, and in 1873 he became an attaché in the Indian foreign department. He returned to Rajputana in 1875, serving as assistant agent to the governor-general and later as political agent of the eastern states. Late in 1879 he succeeded Henry Mortimer Durand as political secretary to Major-General F. S. Roberts, and accompanied him to Kandahar in August 1880. Ridgeway was mentioned in dispatches, promoted brevet lieutenant-colonel, and appointed under-secretary to the foreign department, government of India. He married in 1881 Carolina Ellen (known as Lina; d. 1907), younger daughter of Robert Calverley Bewicke of Coulby Manor, Middlesbrough, Yorkshire.

In 1884, owing to the Russian occupation of Merv in March and the continuous Russian advance towards Herat, a serious situation arose, and Britain and Russia agreed to send commissions to determine the ill-defined northern boundary of Afghanistan. Ridgeway commanded the Indian section of the commission, a force of about 1000 men. He successfully marched them from near Quetta, across difficult and dangerous territory, to join the chief commissioner, Sir Peter Stark Lumsden, at Kuhsan, north-west of Herat, in November.

Lumsden and Ridgeway had been told to expect a Russian boundary commission with a small military escort: they found, instead, a large military force hastening to occupy the territory in dispute. Consequently the work of the commission was held up, and Ridgeway remained for the winter with a small escort to keep the Turkoman population quiet and to give moral support to an Afghan force which was occupying the district of Panjdeh, south of Merv. By diplomacy and firmness he made friends with the Turkomans and held the Russians back throughout the winter; but on 29 March 1885, while he was in Herat reporting to Lumsden, the Russians under General Komarov attacked and defeated the Afghans at Panjdeh, which brought England and Russia close to war.

The work of the commission was resumed in November, Ridgeway succeeding Lumsden as chief commissioner. By June 1886 the boundary had been settled as far as Dukchi, 30 miles from the Oxus, but the line to the Oxus could not be agreed upon. In August the commission was recalled, and the British and Russian cabinets decided to determine for themselves the remaining frontier line. Ridgeway was made KCSI in November 1886. In April 1887 he was sent to St Petersburg to resume negotiations. He found the military party hostile, and on returning home to report progress was shocked to find that Lord Salisbury and his cabinet were apparently unconcerned, and it was only with the assistance of Sir Edward Bradford and the under-secretary at the Foreign Office, Sir Philip Currie, that he induced the government to continue negotiations. Nicholas II was in favour of a settlement, and a final agreement was reached in July 1887, defining the north-western frontier of Afghanistan between the Hari Rud and Oxus rivers. The treaty contented the amir Abdur Rahman and pleased the tribesmen by securing them their northern pasturelands. In 1887 Ridgeway was promoted colonel for distinguished service.

In the same year Ridgeway was appointed under-secretary for Ireland, and in 1889 was sworn of the Irish privy council. He held office under Balfour and his successor, Lord Allerton, and assisted in framing Balfour's Land Purchase Act of 1891. He was created KCB in 1891. Although Ridgeway's office was non-political, when the Liberals returned to power in 1892 he was removed, because he was so closely associated with Balfour's policy. His violent unionism and personal intransigence posed a considerable difficulty for W. E. Gladstone, the prime minister, who devoted much correspondence to the question of Ridgeway's future. After a special mission to the sultan of Morocco (1892–3) he was appointed governor of the Isle of Man from 1893 to 1895, and of Ceylon from 1896 to 1903. In Ceylon he reorganized the civil service, and by the waste lands ordinance protected crown lands from encroachment and crown forests from uncontrolled felling. In 1900 he was made GCMG.

Back in England, Ridgeway, a free-trader, the was unsuccessful Liberal candidate for the City of London in January 1906 and for London University in 1910. In March 1906 the Liberal government appointed him chairman of a committee of inquiry to go to South Africa and investigate the constitutions to be given to the Transvaal and Orange River Colony. Lord Selborne, the high commissioner, at first opposed granting responsible government, but Ridgeway was conciliatory; the home government supported him, and he and Selborne reached agreement. The commission gained the confidence of General Botha and other Boer leaders, and the committee reported in favour of immediate responsible government for both colonies, with white male franchises: non-whites continued to be excluded. The resulting Transvaal and Orange River Colony constitutions prepared the way for the Union of South Africa. In November 1906 Ridgeway was promoted GCB.

In 1910 Ridgeway became president of the British North Borneo Company. After inducing Sir Richard Dane to visit Borneo and make a report, he initiated changes in the civil service and the railway management there. Ridgeway was an honorary LLD of Cambridge and Edinburgh Universities and a vice-president of the Royal Geographical Society. He died suddenly at the Grosvenor Hotel, Victoria, London, on 16 April 1930, leaving one daughter.

E. I. CARLYLE, rev. JAMES LUNT

Sources *The Times* (17 May 1930) • A. C. Yate, *Travels with the Afghan boundary commission* (1887) • C. E. Yate, *Northern Afghanistan* (1888) • C. E. Yate, *Khurasan and Sistan* (1900) • *Annual Register* (1884), 340–50 • *Annual Register* (1885), 309–14 • *Annual Register* (1886), 413–17 • J. A. Spender, *The life of the Right Hon. Sir Henry Campbell-Bannerman*, 2 (1923) • P. Hopkirk, *The great game: on secret service in high Asia* (1990) •

Lord Roberts [F. S. Roberts], *Forty-one years in India*, 2 (1897) • M. Wilson and L. Thompson, eds., *The Oxford history of South Africa*, 2 vols. (1971), vol. 2 • Gladstone, *Diaries* • CGPLA Eng. & Wales (1930)
Archives NRA, priv. coll. | BL, corresp. with Arthur James Balfour, Add. MSS 49808–49812 • BL OIOC, corresp. with Sir Henry Durand, MS Eur. D 727 • BL OIOC, corresp. with Sir Alfred Lyall, MS Eur. F 132 • NL Scot., corresp., mainly with Lord Rosebery • PRO, corresp. with Sir Arthur Nicholson, PRO 30/81
Likenesses R. T., wood-engraving, NPG; repro. in *ILN* (20 Aug 1887)
Wealth at death £14,592 6s. 1d.: resworn probate, 14 May 1930, *CGPLA Eng. & Wales*

Ridgeway, Thomas, **first earl of Londonderry** (c.1565–1632), administrator and politician, was born either at Torwood or at Tor Abbey, the son and heir of Thomas Ridgeway (d. 1597) of Tor Mohun, Devon, and Mary, daughter of Thomas Southcote of Bovey Tracey in the same county. He matriculated from Exeter College, Oxford, on 17 November 1581, and was admitted a student of the Inner Temple, London, in 1583. Subsequently he was apparently appointed collector of customs at Exmouth. He married, probably about 1590, Cicely (d. 1627), sister and coheir of Henry Macwilliam, with whom he had five children. She was at one time maid of honour to Queen Elizabeth.

Ridgeway succeeded his father on 27 June 1597, and in July of that year fitted out a ship at his own cost to take part in the Azores expedition under the earl of Essex. He was high sheriff of Devon in 1600, and was knighted in the same year. He is said to have taken part in the wars in Ireland, and may possibly have done so under Lord Mountjoy. In 1603 he was appointed vice-treasurer and treasurer-at-wars in Ireland under Sir George Cary, whom he eventually succeeded as treasurer in April 1606, holding the office until 1616. He was returned MP for Devon on 28 February 1604. He was admitted to the privy council at Dublin on 20 October 1606. On 30 November following he submitted a project to the earl of Salisbury for increasing the crown revenues. On 18 December warrant was given to the lord chancellor to commission Ridgeway and others to inquire into abbey lands in co. Dublin. Ridgeway had apparently about this time been appointed master of the hawks and game in Ireland, an office formerly in the possession of Sir Geoffrey Fenton.

When the news of the rebellion of Sir Cahir O'Doherty and the burning of Derry reached Dublin in April 1608, the lord deputy, Sir Arthur Chichester, immediately dispatched a strong force into the north, under the marshal, Sir Richard Wingfield, and Sir Oliver Lambart, 'in which our noble treasurer', wrote Chichester, 'without my knowledge accompanied them' with a troop of horse, 'and rendered himself eminent by the rapidity with which he followed and subdued O'Dogherty'. Chichester regretted that 'he could give him no recompense but thanks', but he conferred the honour of knighthood on his eldest son, Robert, at that time sixteen years of age, who had accompanied him. Sir Thomas was one of several leading New English who pre-empted the official plantation of Ulster, building a bawn at Glaslough in co. Monaghan, alongside which a settlement of almost thirty houses was established by 1611. He subsequently assisted in the preliminary work of surveying the escheated counties, and urged on Salisbury the necessity of putting the plantation scheme into execution as speedily as possible. He was thanked by the king for his diligence, but the survey proved in many ways so imprecise that on 21 July 1609 a new commission was issued to Ridgeway and others, under the direction of Sir Josias Bodley. The commissioners were required to divide the counties into proportions and then to cast maps illustrating these divisions. On 31 July the commissioners set out from Dublin towards the north, returning about the beginning of October, but it was not until the end of February 1610 that the inquisitions taken by them were drawn up in legal form and the maps properly prepared. After arriving in London about 12 March with Sir John Davies, Ridgeway had an interview with Salisbury, and handed over to him all the documents connected with the survey. During the next few weeks he was busily engaged with Davies and the commissioners for Irish affairs before the lords of the council, helping to make a selection from the long lists of servitors willing to plant transmitted by Chichester and deciding the most suitable districts for locating the principal natives. He was detained in London until the beginning of July. Meanwhile new commissioners, of whom he was one, had been appointed to carry the scheme into execution. In order that his absence might not retard the work, Ridgeway, as soon as he was relieved from attendance on the council, 'put over in a small boat of seven or eight tons, a vessel', wrote Chichester, 'unfit for him to adventure in'.

Ridgeway's arrival helped expedite the plantation. He himself was assigned, as an undertaker, 2000 acres in the precinct of Clogher, co. Tyrone, lying on the south-eastern border of the barony of Clogher, adjoining that part of Monaghan known as the Trough, and represented on the map as well-wooded and containing little bog or wasteland. To this were subsequently added on 22 April 1613 the lands around Agher. Here he settled men from his native Devon, as well as several Londoners. Also assigned to him, as a servitor, was another estate of 2000 acres in the precinct of Dungannon, co. Tyrone, adjacent to that of Clogher. Lying along the upper course of the Blackwater, this additional estate is represented on the plantation map as abounding in woods and bog land. He was one of the first to take out his letters patent, and from a report made of the state of the plantation in 1611 he appears to have been fairly active in fulfilling his obligations as an undertaker. That year he was also one of the first to buy a baronetcy, obtained on 25 November for £1200, money which was intended for the upkeep of the militia in Ireland. A year later Ridgeway was made a burgess in the new borough of Ballynakill in Gallen-Ridgeway, Queen's county, created as part of the effort to secure a protestant majority in the parliament it was intended to assemble at Dublin in 1613. Elected MP for the borough in April, he was also returned as one of the knights of the shire for Tyrone. It was on Ridgeway's own motion that, when the parliament met, Sir John Davies was elected speaker, thus giving rise to the counter-election of Sir John Everard, and to

one of the most remarkable scenes in Irish parliamentary history, as the Catholic commoners installed their own nominee while the planters seated their own man in Everard's lap. In 1616 Ridgeway was discharged of the office of treasurer, some suspicion having been cast on his accounts during audit. On 25 May he was created Lord Ridgeway, baron of Gallen-Ridgeway. In 1619 Ridgeway was witness for the prosecution of the earl of Suffolk in Star Chamber, testifying that during his time as vice-treasurer he had never been able to obtain money needed for the public service unless his demand was accompanied by a bribe. On 19 August 1622 Ridgeway effectively purchased the earldom of Londonderry, in the gift of Sir James Erskine, to whom Ridgeway disposed his Ulster estate at Portclare and Ballykillygirie. Ridgeway's patent went out on 23 August 1623. His wife died in 1627; Londonderry himself died in London on 24 January 1632, and was buried in the south aisle of the parish church of Tor Mohun. His eldest son, Robert, succeeded him.

ROBERT DUNLOP, rev. SEAN KELSEY

Sources GEC, *Peerage* · T. W. Moody, *The Londonderry plantation, 1609–1641: the City of London and the plantation in Ulster* (1939) · P. S. Robinson, *The plantation of Ulster: British settlement in an Irish landscape, 1600–1670* (1984)
Archives BL

Ridgeway, William (1765–1817), law reporter and civil lawyer, was born in Dublin, eldest son of William Ridgeway (*fl.* 1730–1780), merchant, and his wife, Dorothy, *née* Tandy. Both his parents were Irish protestants; little else is known about them. He was educated at Trinity College, Dublin, which he entered in 1782, and where he graduated BA in 1787; he obtained the degree of LLB in 1790, followed in 1795 by that of LLD, which qualified him to practise in the civil law courts, namely ecclesiastical courts and the Irish court of Admiralty. He qualified as a barrister at the King's Inns, Dublin, in 1790. As a student for the Irish bar he also attended the Middle Temple in London. He married a daughter of the antiquary Edward Ledwich (her name is unknown) and left seven children, one of whom, named William, also attended Trinity College, Dublin. Whether it was because of family connections (through his mother he was related to James Napper Tandy, one of the founders of the society) or through personal political conviction, he joined the Dublin Society of United Irishmen in 1792. He seems to have played no active part in their proceedings.

Apparently, at the request of the Irish attorney-general he edited *Reports of cases argued and determined in the king's bench and chancery, during the time in which Lord Hardwicke presided in those courts*. These were printed at Dublin in 1794, the sheets being issued with a new title page in London later in the same year. The work was carefully done and was reprinted in the collection known as *English Trials*. Although a first printing in Dublin of English legal texts was not uncommon at the time, Ridgeway's work is unusual in that it also included notes referring to the decisions of Irish courts on issues raised before Lord Hardwicke.

Ridgeway began his career as a law reporter with a series

of reports of Irish cases, with the appearance in 1795 of *Reports of Cases upon Appeals and Writs of Error in the High Court of Parliament in Ireland*. The reports covered the period 1784–96. Although based largely upon the printed pleadings of parties appearing before the Irish House of Lords, they are an invaluable source of evidence for the work of the Irish final appellate court in this period. He also began an association with fellow barristers William Lapp and John Schoales, commencing with a joint report of the trial for treason of William Jackson in 1795. With the same colleagues he published *Irish Term Reports* in 1796. He had already published *A Report of the Proceedings in Cases of High Treason* (decided in Dublin) in December 1795. These trials were of 'defenders', members of a movement of agrarian protest. All these publications were no doubt facilitated by the emergence of an improved legal short-hand among Dublin lawyers, of which the most proficient practitioner was Ridgeway's contemporary William Sampson. Ridgeway himself made regular appearances as a crown prosecutor and so participated in the changing legal culture his reports reflected.

There followed during the period 1797–1817 reports of about thirty essentially political trials. One group of these, although published separately, was brought together under the title *A Report of the Proceedings in Cases of High Treason, at a Special Commission of oyer and terminer, Held in and for the County and City of Dublin* in 1798. These all arose out of the United Irish rising of that year. It is probable that these reports were initiated and subsidized by Robert Stewart, Viscount Castlereagh, the chief secretary to the viceroy in Dublin. This may have marked the beginning of the covert subsidization, for propaganda purposes, by the British government in Ireland, of reports of political trials. By the mid-nineteenth century such reports were published expressly on behalf of the British government. In 1803 Ridgeway was responsible for the publication of reports of the numerous trials arising out of the rising by Robert Emmet. The last report by Ridgeway was of the trial in 1817 of the radical Roger O'Connor, the eccentric father of Fergus O'Connor, the Chartist leader.

Ridgeway's reporting of trials was of a high order of accuracy and general impartiality. They remain a major source of information on Irish law and politics during the last decades of the eighteenth and the first decades of the nineteenth century. He died in Dublin on 1 December 1817, having contracted typhus while on circuit in Trim.

PAUL O'HIGGINS

Sources P. O'Higgins, 'William Ridgeway (1765–1817): law reporter', *Northern Ireland Legal Quarterly*, 18 (1967), 208–22 · P. O'Higgins, *A bibliography of Irish trials and other legal proceedings* (1986) · R. B. McDowell, ed., *Proceedings of the Dublin Society of United Irishmen*, IMC (1998) · Burtchaell & Sadleir, *Alum. Dubl.*, 2nd edn · E. Keane, P. Beryl Phair, and T. U. Sadleir, eds., *King's Inns admission papers, 1607–1867*, IMC (1982) · *State trials*, vol. 26 · *DNB*

Ridgeway, Sir William (1858–1926), classical scholar, was born on 6 August 1858, the youngest son of the Revd John Henry Ridgeway of Ballydermot, King's county, and Marianna, only daughter of Samuel Ridgeway of Aghanvilla, King's county. Ridgeway's forebears were from Devon, but

Sir William Ridgeway (1858–1926), by Richard Jack, 1921

settled in Ulster under James I. There they intermarried with Cromwellian settlers in King's county—'all first-class fighting men' in Ridgeway's words—and with Huguenot families round Portarlington. He belonged, therefore, to 'the pale', and believed that he had 'not a drop of Gaelic blood in his veins'. But from his earliest years he was surrounded by those who had plenty, and they contributed much to his personality and outlook. He was educated at Portarlington School and at Trinity College, Dublin, where he won all the chief classical prizes, studied Sanskrit, and graduated as senior moderator in both classics and modern literature. From Dublin he proceeded in 1876 to Peterhouse, Cambridge, migrating from there in 1878 to Gonville and Caius College, where he was subsequently elected a scholar. He was bracketed fifth in the classical tripos of 1880, and was elected a fellow of his college in the same year. That year he also married Lucy, eldest daughter of Arthur Samuels of Kingstown and sister of Arthur Warren Samuels, judge of the High Court of Justice in Ireland; they had one daughter. In 1881 a vacancy occurred in the classical staff of the college, but Ridgeway was not chosen. His disappointment was severe, and the partisan feeling then engendered delayed the recognition of his originality.

In 1883 Ridgeway was appointed to the chair of Greek at University College, Cork. This left him free to spend five months of every year in Cambridge. He published essays on the historical interpretation of Aristotle, on the size of the Homeric horse, and on the origin of the mathematical element in the teaching of Pythagoras. He was among the first British scholars to recognize the new scientific school of comparative philology in Germany, in marked contrast with the attitude prevailing at Cambridge as late as 1890. But he was deeply indebted to the Cambridge Philological Society and to the encouragement of Dr Henry Jackson. His discoveries, fiercely resisted, passed quickly into currency, and his fearless enquiry emancipated classical study in England from an unintelligent orthodoxy.

The turning point of Ridgeway's career was his appointment in 1892, after the publication of his first substantial book, to the Disney chair of archaeology at Cambridge and his re-election to a fellowship at his own college. Although the Disney chair was then poorly endowed, he resigned his chair at Cork, in which he had rendered important services to Irish education. But his appointment in 1907 to the Brereton readership in classics established his position in Cambridge. The university was then passing through a period of dissension, and Ridgeway's affection for the Anglican church and for the traditions of Cambridge scholarship limited his enthusiasm for reform. The bitter struggle about women's degrees separated him from some of his oldest friends. In the controversy on compulsory Greek he was again one of the opponents of change, but after the end of the First World War he was clear-sighted enough to discourage further resistance.

Ridgeway's first book, *The Origin of Metallic Currency and Weight Standards* (1892), attacked current theories of the purely religious origin of Greek coin types, and threw a flood of light on the early life of the Mediterranean lands: it identified the tuna fish, plant silphium, and ox (on early Athenian issues) not as objects of some unknown worship, but as recognized tokens of local commerce. In the first volume of his *Early Age of Greece* (1901) he drew a fundamental distinction between the Myceneans, associated by contemporary authors with bronze weapons, figure-of-eight shields, and southern ways of life, and the Achaeans of Homer, whom he proposed to identify with warrior immigrants of the early Iron Age who brought with them the round shields and long iron swords of central Europe and the sterner morals of the north. This work was never completed; of the second volume, parts already in type at his death (dealing with kinship and ancestor-worship in early Europe, and with Ireland in the heroic age) were published by friends in 1931, with an introduction exhibiting later developments of Ridgeway's doctrine. This book is Ridgeway's chief contribution to history. Its main doctrine secured wide acceptance, even among those who attacked it in detail. But the bitterness of the controversy took a tragic colour in Ridgeway's memory, and he retained the conviction that in certain quarters he would never be fairly treated.

In strict logic Ridgeway was weak. In support of a theory, of the truth of which he was convinced, he would use all kinds of evidence, strong and weak alike. Nor did he always give enough consideration to difficulties. But, to quote his pupil Professor D. S. Robertson:

his mind's eye surveyed so vast a range of facts that he saw in a flash the great lines of their connexion, and his lively knowledge of human nature kept him always within the limits of reasonableness and good sense … His words had a rough splendour that stamped them imperishably on his listeners' minds. He did not like formal lecturing; but round a table, with half a dozen students, he was incomparable. His vivid imagination, his width of view, his unbroken contact with reality kept one spellbound, as gems, coins, axeheads, totem-spoons tumbled on to the table from his inexhaustible pockets. He must always have had sensitive fingers, and as his sight failed he depended more and more upon touch. And he knew at once from the way in which new pupils handled and spoke of the stuff which he passed round the table, whether or no they had the makings of real archaeologists. (Quoted in *DNB*)

In *The Origin and Influence of the Thoroughbred Horse* (1905) Ridgeway showed the development of the horse from its small Homeric ancestor through admixture of zebraic blood by the horse-breeding Greeks of north Africa and their Muslim successors. This conclusion he reached almost simultaneously with, and independently of, the zoologists J. C. Ewart and H. F. Osborn, completing their zoological results by his historical study. His British Academy paper, *Who were the Romans?* (1907), revived by fresh evidence Schwegler's view of the racial distinction between the Sabine or patrician element in Rome, and the Latin or plebeian (cf. *Cambridge Ancient History*, 4, 1926, chap. 13). In *The Origin of Tragedy, with Special Reference to Greek Tragedians* (1910) Ridgeway argued that tragedy arose from the commemoration of local heroes at their tombs, the representations being later drawn into the ritual of Dionysus and combined with the satyric plays. In *Dramas and Dramatic Dances of Non-European Races* (1915) he confirmed his theory by comprehensive induction from China to Bolivia and Japan, from Australia and central Africa to Alaska. Other interests of his were represented by his studies of *Cuchulain* (1905 and 1907), and unpublished papers on the (Danish) origin of the Scots and on the origin of ballads in the praises of popular heroes (lecture delivered in 1926).

In later years Ridgeway was a frequent and valued correspondent of *The Times*, remarkable both for range of subject and vigour of style. To the last his enthusiasm for the great social ends of classical study remained unabated, and none of the honours that fell to him gave him more pleasure than his election as president of the Classical Association for 1914. The establishment of the Cambridge school of anthropology was a monument to another side of his influence. The general recognition of his work was marked on his sixtieth birthday (1913) by the presentation of a volume of *Essays and Studies* in his honour. Ridgeway was elected FBA in 1904, was president of the Royal Anthropological Institute from 1908 to 1910, and received honorary doctorates from the universities of Dublin (1902), Manchester (1906), Aberdeen (1908), and Edinburgh (1921). He was knighted in 1919.

No picture of Ridgeway's life would be complete which did not indicate the extraordinary stimulus which he exerted upon others, and his untiring interest in the research and the prospects of younger men. His home at Fen Ditton, about 4 miles from Cambridge, with its pleasant garden, was the constant resort of scholars engaged in many kinds of research, not merely in classical or anti-quarian learning. Such intercourse was only a part of his cordial acquaintance with all sorts and conditions of men.

The last months of Ridgeway's life were darkened by the sudden death of his wife in May 1926. His companion almost since his boyhood, she shared his ideals and was hardly less interested than he was in his work. His own death occurred suddenly at Fen Ditton on 12 August 1926, not quite three months after that of his wife.

Later developments in Ridgeway's two main fields, anthropology and the classics, have shown him to have been a less central figure than his contemporaries thought. He was, especially in his later work, too idiosyncratic and too much a prisoner of his time with his recurrent appeals to the image of 'tall, fair-haired men', to make seminal and lasting contributions. Reading with hindsight his exchanges with such figures as Malinowski, one is continually struck by the originality and learning behind his individual insights, yet uncomfortably aware of being in the presence of an isolated stream of thought.

R. S. CONWAY, *rev.* A. M. SNODGRASS

Sources R. S. Conway, 'Sir William Ridgeway, 1853–1926', *PBA*, 12 (1926), 327–36 · R. S. Conway, *Classical Review*, 40 (1926)
Archives U. Cam., Museum of Archaeology and Anthropology, corresp., notes, photographs, etc. | PRO NIre., corresp. with Edward Carson · Richmond Local Studies Library, London, Douglas Sladen MSS · U. Cam., Museum of Archaeology and Anthropology, letters to L. C. G. Clarke · University of Toronto, letters to James Mavor
Likenesses D. G. Lillie, watercolour drawing, 1909, NPG · V. H. Mottram, photograph, *c*.1909, NPG · J. P. Clarke, photograph, *c*.1920, U. Cam., Museum of Classical Archaeology · R. Jack, oils, 1921, Gon. & Caius Cam. [*see illus.*] · J. P. Clarke, photogravure photograph, NPG · portrait, repro. in *Royal Academy Illustrated* (1921)
Wealth at death £7668 9*s.* 5*d.*: probate, 5 Oct 1926, *CGPLA Eng. & Wales*

Ridgley [Rugeley], **Thomas** (*c*.1576–1656), physician, was the only son of Simon Rugeley, of Hawksyard, near Rugeley, Staffordshire, and his wife, Catherine, daughter of Augustine Babington, of Normanton, Derbyshire. He matriculated at St John's College, Cambridge, in 1594, taking his BA there in 1597 and MA in 1600. While an undergraduate he wrote verses to the memory of the master of St John's, William Whitaker, who died in 1595. Ridgley took his MD at the college in 1608. From 1608 to 1616 he was a country physician at Newark, Nottinghamshire. On 6 February 1608 he took out a Nottinghamshire licence to marry Anne Odingsells, daughter of Gabriel Odingsells of Epperstone and Bulcote, Nottinghamshire; they had four children, Thomas (*b*. 1613), Luke (*b*. 1615), George, and Mary.

In 1617 Ridgley moved to London. This would have enabled him to give greater attention to a lawsuit he was involved in and to increase his income. Intending to become a fellow of the College of Physicians, he made his first, unofficial appearance before the president and twelve fellows of the college, on 18 March 1617. His first formal appearance before the full *comitia* of the college

occurred on 3 June 1617. A letter from the chief royal physician, Theodore Turquet de Mayerne, to the president of the college recommended Ridgley and the college elected him a candidate. Mayerne's interest in Ridgley may have been sparked by their common interest in chemical medicine. Ridgley's reputation prompted a letter from Sir Gervase Clifton, which may perhaps be dated to this period, and which dealt with the value to sexual potency of a mercury derivative. Ridgley ridiculed the idea:

> Those Puritane Alchymists that talke so muche of separating the impure part from the pure cannot with all their art separate or extract anie thing out of Mercury … it being a simple homogeneous body never to be resolved into diverse natures. (Lansdowne MS 238, fol. 149)

In the same context, Ridgley also impugned the aphrodisiac benefits of the 'aurum potabile' preparation of Francis Anthony.

On 14 January 1619 Ridgley and Thomas Winston testified in the college against the medical activities of William Eyre. Despite these prerogatives of place, Ridgley was left to languish as a candidate for a number of years, still waiting to be elevated to a vacant fellowship. Rumour that Ridgley was to be passed over again in favour of a younger candidate caused James I to write to the college on Ridgley's behalf. In the letter, dated 7 March 1621, James argued 'that a man of whose merite yourselves are satisfied and we have receaved your good testimonie, should not be discouraged or kept back from such orderly prefermentes' (annals, RCP Lond., 3.143). The fellows vowed to elect him to the next open place, which they did on 28 November 1622. But their failure to elect him immediately irritated Ridgley; on 9 November 1621 the ill feeling between the fellows and Ridgley finally erupted, as the college demanded Ridgley's dues as a candidate:

> Dr Ridgley in his turn stood much upon his gentrye and knew none of us better: that he to paye was forced fowly and injuriously: but bids us keep our othe. Now he wanted moneye, but they pay more than the privilege is worth: He desiers no favour: but had brought the Kings letters: and it is not agenist his othe to bring the Kings letters. (ibid., 3.149)

The college censors were not impressed by Ridgley or Dr Diodati, who was also delinquent, and 'considered that an example ought to be made of them' (ibid.). Ridgley would not submit, and further letters of recommendation were sent by the earl of Rutland and Viscount Rocheford. Finally, on 28 November 1622, Ridgley 'humbled himself before the College', 'gave an ex tempore speech in good Latin and submissive in tone, following which he was more acceptable', and was elected a fellow by the votes of all present (ibid., 3.159).

Despite his initial problems with the college, Ridgley's time as a fellow gained him the respect of his colleagues. He was chosen as a censor in 1628, 1633, and 1638; and, according to Baldwin Hamey, did all that was asked of him without complaint. He was the model of the grave, learned physician, although at least one fellow, Peter Bowne, thought him too serious. But generally, the college and the public admired his honesty, his directness, his skill as a doctor, and the strong principles from which he seldom wavered. He was chosen as an elect on 2 September 1641; a supporter of the royalist cause, he resigned from this position on 24 May 1642 and withdrew from the college just as it was about to commit itself fully to parliament. He returned to the college in 1649.

As he was a physician of excellent reputation, Ridgley's comfortable income might have been greater, had he not limited the number of his patients. In 1618 he was among eighteen householders in Bassishaw ward who had 'taken the River Water into their houses'. In 1621 Ridgley made a voluntary contribution to aid the elector of the Palatinate at the beginning of the Thirty Years' War. When the common council of London assessed Bassishaw ward in 1624, of 108 persons so assessed, 23 were rated higher than Ridgley. In 1636 Ridgley was among forty residents of the ward contributing ship money; only eight others contributed more, this being perhaps an early indication of his loyalty to Charles I. In 1638 Ridgley's house in St Michael Bassishaw was valued at £26, a figure which placed him in the top 10 per cent of a large parish with perhaps 240 other householders.

Ridgley is best known as an early Helmontian or chemical physician. Samuel Hartlib wrote of him in 1654: 'Dr Ridgely an auncient physitian of the colledg the chiefest chymical doctor and preparing many excellent medicines … He bought up all Glauberian furnaces especially the 2nd with a new head, which Mr Boyle also hath' (Webster, 34). A 'Dr Ridgely' was also among the 'chemically given' physicians, named by George Starkey in 1657, who had repudiated Galenic medicine, although this may refer to Ridgley's son Luke, who shared the same chemical outlook.

Thomas Ridgley died at his house in London, possibly in the parish of St Sepulchre, on 21 June 1656 and was conveyed in a procession of college fellows, by candlelight, to the church of St Botolph's, Aldersgate, where he was interred. It was an honour that not even Sir Theodore Turquet de Mayerne or Thomas Winston had enjoyed. Ridgley's will, like the man, was short and direct. His money was to be divided into five equal parts, three-fifths going to his eldest son, Thomas, and two-fifths to his second son, Luke, who was also to receive 'all my books' and household goods, and the rest of the estate not otherwise bequeathed. Luke was made sole executor of the will, which he proved on 27 September 1656. Ridgley's other two children, George and Mary, alive in 1633, were not mentioned in the will.   WILLIAM BIRKEN

Sources Cooper, *Ath. Cantab.*, 2.496, 555 · Venn, *Alum. Cant.* · C. Webster, 'English medical reformers of the puritan revolution: a background to the "Society of Chymical Physitians"', *Ambix*, 14 (1967), 16–41, esp. 34 · *The Conway letters: the correspondence of Anne, Viscountess Conway, Henry More, and their friends, 1642–1684*, ed. M. H. Nicolson (1930), 71 · *Collections for a history of Staffordshire*, William Salt Archaeological Society, 5 (1884–5) · *Collections for a history of Staffordshire*, William Salt Archaeological Society, new ser., 6 (1903) · *The manuscripts of his grace the duke of Rutland*, 4 vols., HMC, 24 (1888–1905) · Munk, *Roll* · S. Erdeswick, *A survey of Staffordshire*, ed. T. Harwood, new edn (1844) · P. Bowne, *Pseudo-medicorum anatomia* (1624) · annals, RCP Lond. · B. Hamey, 'Bustorum aliquot reliquiae …', RCP Lond. · L. Hutchinson, *Memoirs of the life of Colonel Hutchinson*, ed. J. Hutchinson, 2nd edn (1808), 299 · *The visitation of London, anno Domini 1633, 1634, and 1635, made by Sir Henry St George*, 2, ed. J. J. Howard, Harleian Society, 17 (1883) · PRO, PROB 11/258/316 · Bodl. Oxf., MS Ashmole 834 · J. B. Whitmore and A. W. Hughes Clarke, eds., *London visitation pedigrees, 1664*, Harleian Society, 92 (1940)

Archives BL, Sloane MSS · BL, Ridgley's annotated copy of M. Sylvaticus, *Panlectae medicinae* (Leiden, 1541)

Ridgley, Thomas (1667–1734), Independent minister and tutor, was born in London; details about his parents and early life are unknown. He was educated for the ministry in Wiltshire, presumably at John Davison's academy at Trowbridge, and also at Islington under Thomas Doolittle. In 1695 he was made assistant to Thomas Gouge, minister of the Independent church at Three Cranes, Fruiterers' Alley, Thames Street, in London. On Gouge's death in 1700 he became the minister, a position he held until his death; according to Wilson, 'the congregation was in a low state … but under Ridgley it revived' (Wilson, 2.72). On 3 June 1712 he married Emlin Norris (*b.* 1687/8), who predeceased him; a daughter is mentioned in his will. In 1712, on the death of Isaac Chauncy, he became theological tutor at the Congregational Fund's academy in Tenter Alley, Moorfields, established in 1696. John Eames was appointed his assistant, and between them they created at Moorfields perhaps the most celebrated dissenting academy of its day. Their learning in the classics, theology, and the sciences attracted the most talented and able students for the ministry to their lectures.

Ridgley, a moderate Calvinist, was known for the depth and breadth of his thinking. 'He was accounted one of the most considerable Divines of his age … He thought for himself, and freely embraced what he conceived to be the truth, even though it might lay off the beaten track' (Wilson, 2.78). He published numerous sermons and religious works, and did not shy away from theological argument. 'The doctor entered deeply into the Arian controversy; and, ranking on the side of the subscribers (at Salters' Hall in 1719) appeared from the press in their defence' (Bogue and Bennett, 2.215–16). He was awarded the degree of DD by King's College, Aberdeen, in December 1728. He was Merchants lecturer at Salters' Hall and his Sunday evening lecture at Old Jewry was 'designed chiefly for the rising generation and was successful' (Wilson, 2.76).

The work for which Ridgley became known, *A Body of Divinity*, was first published in 1731 and subsequently went to numerous editions. Based on his lectures, the book expounded the catechism of the Westminster assembly, and 'was for long a popular presentation of Calvinistic theology' (McLachlan, 297). On 17 December 1731 he married Phoebe Brockatt, who is described in his will as 'my dear and loving wife'. He died on 27 March 1734 at Moorfields and was buried in Bunhill Fields burial-ground. His widow survived him and was executor of his will.

ALEXANDER GORDON, *rev.* ALAN RUSTON

Sources W. Wilson, *The history and antiquities of the dissenting churches and meeting houses in London, Westminster and Southwark*, 4 vols. (1808–14), vol. 2, pp. 72–81 · C. E. Surman, index to dissenting ministers, DWL, card R.715 · D. Bogue and J. Bennett, *History of dissenters, from the revolution in 1688, to … 1808*, 2nd edn, 2 (1833), 215–16 · H. McLachlan, *English education under the Test Acts: being the history of* *the nonconformist academies, 1662–1820* (1931), 10, 118, 297 • will, PRO, PROB 11/664, sig. 90 • IGI • J. A. Jones, ed., *Bunhill memorials* (1849), 230 • A. W. Hughes Clarke and R. H. D'Elboux, eds., *The registers of St Katharine by the Tower, London*, 7 vols., Harleian Society, register section, 75–81 (1945–52), vols. 4–5 • S. Peirce, *An account of Mr T. Ridgley* (1708)

Likenesses B. Dandridge, oils, DWL • J. Vandergucht, line engraving (after B. Dandridge, 1731), BM, NPG; repro. in T. Ridgley, *A body of divinity*, 2 vols. (1731)

Wealth at death see will, PRO, PROB 11/664, sig. 90

Ridley, (William) Arnold (1896–1984), actor and playwright, was born on 7 January 1896 at 4 Pera Place, Bath, the son of William Robert Ridley, drill instructor, and his wife, Rosa Caroline Morrish. The author of *The Ghost Train*, one of the most popular plays, and later films, of the first half of the twentieth century, Ridley had virtually a second coming when, in his seventies and eighties, he played the 'doddery and doubtfully continent' (*The Times*, 14 March 1984) Private Godfrey in the long-running BBC television series *Dad's Army*.

Ridley was educated at Clarendon School, Widcombe, and the City of Bath secondary school before studying for a certificate of the Board of Education in the elementary training department at Bristol University from 1914 to 1916. His first stage appearance was at the Theatre Royal, Bristol, in 1914 in *Prunella* by Laurence Housman and H. Granville Barker. Ridley enlisted in the Somerset light infantry in 1916, saw active service in France and in 1917 was discharged with injuries that left him prone to blackouts. He taught for a short period before joining first Birmingham Repertory Company (1918–20) and then the Plymouth Repertory Company (1920–21), but the severity of his war wounds led him to begin writing.

The Ghost Train, Ridley's second play, a comedy thriller, was written in 1923 while he was working as manager of his father's boot shop in Manvers Street, Bath, and was reputedly prompted by a four-hour wait at Mangotsfield Junction Station, Gloucestershire. Originally rejected, it was first put on at the Theatre Royal, Brighton, on 22 June 1925, and on the London stage at St Martin's Theatre on 23 November 1925. It transferred first to the Garrick Theatre, then to the Comedy Theatre, and in all ran for 655 West End performances. It became a favourite with provincial repertory companies and amateur dramatic groups, and was adapted as a musical, *Happy Holiday*.

Arnold Ridley wrote some thirty further plays, sometimes in collaboration with others. Among the most successful were *Third Time Lucky* (originally *Unholy Orders*), *Easy Money*, in which he played the original Philip Stafford, at the Grand Theatre, Blackpool, on 24 February 1947, and *Beggar My Neighbour*, all of which became films. His plays were described as 'tightly plotted, witty, compassionate, often exciting, about ordinary people doing extraordinary things' (*The Guardian*, 10 Jan 1976). In 1935 he formed his own short-lived film company, which produced *Royal Eagle*. His first marriage, to Hilda Mary Cooke, was followed by another, to Isola Strong.

Ridley enlisted in 1939 and went with the British expeditionary force to France as a public relations officer with the rank of major but was invalided out. For a few weeks in the 1940s he was a member of the Local Defence Volunteers at Caterham in Surrey. He joined the Entertainment National Service Association (ENSA) for which he directed *The Ghost Train*. Through this he met his third wife, Althea Parker, an actress; they were married in 1947 and had a son, Nicholas.

From 1942 to 1944 Ridley directed productions of the Malvern Company. He continued to act, sometimes in his own plays, and in 1953 took the part of Walter Gabriel in the stage adaptation of the BBC radio serial *The Archers* at the Theatre Royal, Birmingham; in the 1960s and 1970s he was heard as Doughy Hood in the radio broadcasts of the same serial. He was also the vicar in the television series *Crossroads*. His stage appearances included Juror no. 9 in *12 Angry Men* at the Queen's Theatre, London, in July 1964.

Ridley played Private Godfrey in the eighty *Dad's Army* television programmes, recorded between April 1969 and July 1977; in the stage version at the Shaftesbury Theatre, London, from 2 October 1975; and in its subsequent 27-week provincial tour. Ridley was the subject of the television programme *This is your Life* in March 1976. He was made an OBE in 1982.

Arnold Ridley described himself as 'always a repertory actor at heart' (*The Times*, 8 Jan 1976). He was regarded in the theatre as a 'disciplined person' who 'learnt his lines and moves very quickly' (Pertwee, 54). He claimed never to have missed a performance or arrived late for a rehearsal, and once said 'the one thing I can't stand is inefficiency' (*Freshview*, 5 Jan 1970). Off-stage his speech was 'brisk and schoolmasterly' and his eyes 'danced with humour and irony' (*The Guardian*, 10 Jan 1976).

Ridley had a lifelong interest in rugby football, joining Bath rugby club as a schoolboy in 1908. As its match secretary from 1929 to 1936 he 'did much to revise the fixture list and bring in the London clubs' (*Bath and West Evening Chronicle*). Ridley was its president from 1950 to 1952 and continued to support the side until 1982. He died on 12 March 1984 in hospital in Northwood; his funeral was held at St Anne's Church, Highgate, London, a week later.

C. M. P. TAYLOR

Sources J. Parker, ed., *Who's who in the theatre*, 10th edn (1947) • *The Times* (13 March 1984), 32 • *The Times* (14 March 1984), 18 • *Bath and West Evening Chronicle* (13 March 1984) • *Stage and Television Today* (29 March 1984) • *Freshview* (5 Jan 1970) • biographical file, Theatre Museum, London • B. Pertwee, *'Dad's army': the making of a television legend* (1989) • A. Nicoll, *English drama, 1900–1930* (1973) • K. Barker, *The Theatre Royal, Bristol, 1766–1966* (1974) • J. C. Trewin, *The Birmingham Repertory Theatre, 1913–1963* (1963) • CGPLA Eng. & Wales (1984) • *The Guardian* (10 Jan 1976) • *The Times* (8 Jan 1976) • *Daily Telegraph* (20 March 1976) • b. cert.

Archives FILM BFI NFTVA, performance footage |SOUND BL NSA, performance footage

Likenesses photographs, 1927–74, Hult. Arch. • photograph, repro. in Pertwee, *Dad's army*

Wealth at death under £4000: probate, 14 Sept 1984, CGPLA Eng. & Wales

Ridley, George [Geordie] (1835–1864), singer and songwriter, was born on 10 February 1835, in Gateshead, the eldest child of Matthew Ridley, ropemaker and sometime coalminer, born at Wrekenton near Gateshead about 1808, and his wife, Frances Stephenson (or Stevenson), born at Gateshead about 1812. George was baptized at St Mary's parish church, Gateshead, on 1 March 1835. He had five brothers and three sisters. A younger brother, John Stephenson Ridley, born about 1846, became the one-mile running champion of England in 1871.

George Ridley began work at Oakwellgate colliery, Gateshead, at the age of eight, and his publisher and biographer, Thomas Allan, later noted that his education 'must have been of the simplest'. He worked underground at Oakwellgate, then at the Goose pit, Gateshead, for ten years. About 1853 he moved to surface work as a wagon driver at Shipcote colliery, Gateshead. After three years he suffered an accident that was to change his life: a runaway wagon rolled over and left Ridley with severely crushed legs. Incapable of continuing pit work, he turned his hobby of entertaining as a vocalist into a full-time profession. His period of recuperation was lengthy, and it was not until the early 1860s that he began touring towns and villages north and south of the Tyne singing local and Irish songs.

By 1862, at the very latest, Geordie Ridley had begun to write his own songs, setting them, in both the early music-hall and ballad tradition of the period, to well-known tunes. His first song, 'Joey Jones', concerned the horse which won the Northumberland Plate or 'Pitman's Derby' of 1861. By the end of 1862 his songs had gained enough local popularity to persuade Thomas Allan to purchase ten of them and to produce *George Ridley's New Local Songbook*.

Although not included in this collection, Ridley's most celebrated work, 'The Blaydon Races', had already been written. It was first performed at Balmbra's Music Hall in the centre of Newcastle on 5 June 1862 at a benefit concert for the professional boat racer Harry Clasper. The following day the *Newcastle Daily Chronicle* recorded this first performance: 'Mr Ridley adapted to a popular air a ballad descriptive of a journey (in prospect) by road to the ensuing Blaydon Races'. The song was performed again, set to a tune called 'Brighton', on the actual day of the races, 9 June, and, after that event, a final verse was added.

There is no evidence that the song enjoyed any particular popularity in Ridley's lifetime or in the forty years after it was written, its fame being almost entirely a twentieth-century phenomenon. James Cosgrave, a Gateshead comedian, whose stage name was J. C. Scatter, featured it in his act during the early years of the reign of Edward VII, probably picking it up from one of Allan's later publications, in which it began to appear. Its recording on early 78 r.p.m. discs and its adoption by the followers of Newcastle United Football Club turned it into an anthem renowned worldwide in both tune and chorus.

Ridley himself had little over two years left to live after he composed 'The Blaydon Races'. During that time he wrote 'Cushie Butterfield', another song which gained popularity in the twentieth century, but at a much more local level. By the summer of 1864 his health was beginning to decline. Fellow entertainers and sportsmen, who featured in many of his songs, ran benefit concerts to help him, but he faded rapidly.

Ridley died, unmarried, at the family home, 1 Grahamsley Street, Gateshead, on 9 September 1864. The cause of death was recorded as 'cardiac dropsy', a heart condition probably accelerated by his accident. Local legend has the author of the most famous of Tyneside songs departing this world in abject poverty, although there is little evidence for this beyond the absence of any grant of probate and the balance of probabilities. He was buried at St Edmund's cemetery, Gateshead, on 11 September 1864.

KEITH GREGSON

Sources B. Fane, *A life of Ridley* (1985) · D. Harker, *Geordie Ridley sings The Blaydon races* (1973) · J. Gale, *The Blaydon races* (1970) · T. Allan and G. Allan, eds., *Illustrated editions of Tyneside songs* (1891) · T. Allan, ed., *Tyneside songs* (1862) · parish register (baptism) St Mary's church, Gateshead · d. cert.
Archives Newcastle Central Library, Allan MSS | SOUND Sunderland, Gregson 78 collection
Likenesses photograph, *c*.1862, repro. in Allan and Allan, eds., *Illustrated editions of Tyneside songs* · woodcut, *c*.1862 (as 'Johnny Luik-up the bellman'), repro. in Allan, ed., *Tyneside songs*; copy, Allan MSS, Newcastle Central Library
Wealth at death in poverty: most sources · successful: Harker, *Geordie Ridley*

Ridley, Glocester (1702–1774), writer, was a collateral descendant of Bishop Nicholas Ridley and son of Matthew Ridley, who, in April 1702, embarked with his pregnant wife to take up an appointment as East India Company factor at Bencoolen (Benkulen) in Sumatra. Their son was born later that year at sea on the East Indiaman after which he was named. Glocester was educated at Winchester College, becoming scholar in 1718, when he was described as of St Alban, Wood Street, London. He matriculated from Trinity College, Oxford, on 14 October 1721 (aged eighteen), but was admitted a scholar of New College on 1 September 1722, becoming a fellow on 18 June 1724; he graduated BCL on 29 April 1729. He enjoyed close friendships with Robert Lowth, Christopher Pitt, and Joseph Spence, all Wykehamists.

In youth Ridley enjoyed acting. In 1728 he and four friends wrote a tragedy, 'The Fruitless Redress', each man contributing one act; later he composed 'Jugurtha: a Philosophical Drama' in blank verse. Neither play was produced on the public stage or printed. Ridley's talent was such that Theophilus Cibber, actor and fellow Wykehamist, is said to have tried to persuade him to give up the church for the generally more highly paid profession of acting. Nevertheless Ridley was ordained and became curate to William Berriman (1688–1750), the Syriac scholar, at St Andrew Undershaft in the City of London. Later he preached Berriman's funeral sermon and was his executor. On 25 September 1728 the East India Company directors elected Ridley their chaplain at Poplar. His appointment was against the wishes of the local congregation (such conflicts between the company and the inhabitants of Poplar being common), but he lived and ministered at Poplar chapel until his death, during which time his salary rose from £20 to £50 p.a.

Glocester Ridley (1702–1774), by John Hall, pubd 1781 (after James Scouler)

In 1733 Ridley was presented by New College to the rectory of Weston Longville, Norfolk, worth £400 p.a.; he vacated his fellowship in the following year and soon afterwards married a woman named Ann. They had two sons (both of whom were at some time employed by the East India Company and predeceased their parents) and four daughters. Though his ministry at Weston is praised in John Whaley's 'Journey to Houghton' (J. Nichols, *Select Collection of Poems*, 1780–82, 6.189), Ridley lived mainly in Poplar. He became lecturer at St Anne's, Limehouse. In 1740 and 1741 he delivered a course of eight lectures endowed by Lady Moyer at St Paul's; his subject was the Holy Ghost but attendance from fellow clergy was poor (*GM*, 1741, 25). He published a little poetry: *Jovi eleutherio*, 'an Offering to Liberty' (1745), was reprinted in Dodsley's *Collection of Poems*, volume 3 (1748), together with *Psyche*, an allegory of the fall in Spenserian stanzas. An imitation of Horace's *Odes* iv.12, addressed to his friend Spence, appeared in Dodsley's *Museum*, volume 1 (1746), and he contributed to the preface to the *Works of Horace in English Verse* edited by the Duncombes (1757).

In 1748 Ridley was instituted as perpetual curate of Romford chapel, Essex, a New College living, which he vacated in 1762, when he was succeeded by his son James *Ridley, author of *Tales of the Genii* (in which Glocester appears as 'the Holy Dervise of Sumatra'). He continued to hold Weston Longville and to reside chiefly in Poplar. His (published) assize sermons were preached in Thetford and Norwich in 1753, but most of his two dozen sermons printed between 1736 and 1764 were delivered in London, where, to judge by the number of churches named (ten), he was much in demand. His experience as an actor gave him a 'judicious and graceful manner of speaking in the pulpit' (Nichols, *Lit. anecdotes*, 1.642). He gave the Boyle lectures (eight sermons annually) in 1772, 1773, and 1774, but they were never printed.

In the 1730s Ridley had obtained two manuscripts of parts of the sixth-century Syriac version of the New Testament attributed to Philoxenus, and, though he lacked even a knowledge of Syriac letters, he set about learning the language and preparing his manuscripts for publication. Among other deterrents was the expense of printing, so it was not until 1761 that his slim dissertation *De Syriacarum novi foederis versionum*, dedicated to Thomas Secker, archbishop of Canterbury, was published. Further work on the text was hindered by age and infirmities; Ridley was still transcribing Syriac in 1766, but he published no more. He gave the manuscripts to New College; they were edited by Joseph White (1745–1814) and published in 1778. In 1763 Ridley published his *Life of Bishop Ridley*, in which he revealed himself as 'a thorough master of the Popish controversy and an able advocate for the Reformation' (Nichols, *Lit. anecdotes*, 1.646). It was highly successful and enabled its author to invest £800 in the funds. Ridley's *Review* (1766) of the life of Cardinal Pole by Thomas Phillips is another work of protestant controversy.

Ridley's work on the Syriac New Testament was finally recognized when Archbishop Secker nominated him to the valuable prebend of Teinton Regis in Salisbury Cathedral (9 May 1766) and conferred upon him the degree of DD by diploma (25 February 1767). Secker also chose him to oppose Francis Blackburne (1705–1787) in print; so, with Secker as secret co-author, Ridley wrote three letters (1767) defending religious tests against the arguments in Blackburne's *Confessional*.

Ridley died at Poplar on 3 November 1774, aged seventy-two and infirm; he was buried on 10 November alongside his son James *Ridley in a family vault in Poplar chapel cemetery. By this time Poplar chapel was dilapidated and its roof was leaking: extensive repairs began in 1775. Ridley's successor at Weston was James Woodforde (1740–1803), the diarist, who was presented to the rectory on 15 December 1774. A dispute with Ridley's widow over dilapidations at Weston rectory was not settled until December 1776, when she paid him £115 12s. 4d. Ridley's longest poem, *Melampus, or, The Religious Groves*, a treatise on natural religion in Spenserian stanzas with copious notes, was published by subscription in 1781 for the benefit of his widow and daughters. Nine fables, seven other poems, and fragments of 'Jugurtha' were printed in Nichols's *Collection of Poems*, 8 (1782). Other poems remain unpublished: BL, Add. MS 28717 contains his early Latin and English verses and 'The Fruitless Redress'. Ann Ridley was still alive in 1784 and receiving a pension of £30 p.a. from the East India Company.

W. P. COURTNEY, rev. BRIDGET HILL

Sources Nichols, *Lit. anecdotes*, 1.641–9, 6.455, 8.410 · *GM*, 1st ser., 44 (1774), 505–8, 542, 554–5 · *GM*, 1st ser., 45 (1775), 9–10, 217–19, 269–71, 417–19, 471–4, 525–6, 631–2 · Foster, *Alum. Oxon.*, 1715–1886 · T. F. Kirby, *Winchester scholars: a list of the wardens, fellows, and scholars of … Winchester College* (1888), 227 · minutes of the court of directors, East India Company, BL OIOC, B/43/367, 390, 407; B/44/12; B/60/107–8 · minutes of the meetings of the inhabitants of the hamlet of Poplar and Blackwall, Tower Hamlets Local History Library, POP/455 • W. Foster, 'Poplar chapel', in W. Foster, *John Company* (1926), chap. 10 • S. Porter, ed., *Poplar, Blackwall and the Isle of Dogs: the parish of All Saints*, [1], Survey of London, 43 (1994), 103–4 • *The diary of a country parson: the Reverend James Woodforde*, ed. J. Beresford, 5 vols. (1924–31), vol. 1, pp. 171, 173, 187, 191, 194; vol. 5, pp. 417–18 • *Fasti Angl., 1541–1857*, [Salisbury], 78 • W. E. Buckley, 'Tales of the genii', *N&Q*, 7th ser., 1 (1886), 230 • *GM*, 1st ser., 11 (1741), 25 • *VCH Essex*, 8.84

Archives Yale U., Beinecke Rare Book and Manuscript Library, corresp. | BL, letters to Thomas Birch, Add. MS 4317 **Likenesses** J. Hall, line engraving, pubd 1781 (after J. Scouler), BM, NPG [*see illus.*] **Wealth at death** £721: will, 1774 • goods and chattels: will, 1774

Ridley, Henry Nicholas (1855–1956), economic botanist, was born on 10 December 1855 at West Harling Hall, Norfolk, the third child of the Revd Oliver Matthew Ridley and his wife, Louisa Pole, daughter of William Stuart, of Aldenham Abbey. He was a direct descendant of John Stuart, third earl of Bute (1713–1792), who also achieved botanical distinction and acted as scientific adviser to Princess Augusta when she was initiating the botanical gardens at Kew.

Ridley was educated at Haileybury College and at Exeter College, Oxford, where he obtained a second-class degree in natural science in 1878. In 1880 he was awarded the Burdett–Coutts scholarship in geology. However, the necessity of obtaining paid employment led him, in the same year, to take a position in the botanical department of the British Museum at South Kensington. There he began to develop an interest in the geographical distribution of plants. Seven years later he accompanied the Edinburgh zoologist G. A. Ramage on a Royal Society sponsored expedition to Brazil.

This tropical experience led to Ridley's selection, in 1888, as director of the botanical gardens at Singapore, where his responsibilities included the making of a preliminary forest survey. The survey, combined with his extensive exploration of the adjacent territories, provided much of the material and information which led to his *Flora of the Malay Peninsula* (5 vols., 1922–5). In addition to his travels within the Malay peninsula Ridley also visited Borneo and Sumatra (1897) and the Christmas and Keeling islands (1890–91). He was in Sarawak four times between 1903 and 1915. In 1911 he was in southern Siam. He retired from the Singapore gardens in the same year, but his botanical travels continued. In 1912 he was in Burma, India, and Egypt, in 1915 in Java, and a year later in Jamaica. From all these areas he took back material which enriched the collections at Kew and one genus, *Ranalisma*, is known only from the specimens which Ridley collected.

On his appointment to Singapore, Ridley found there seedlings of the Pará rubber tree which had been sent from Kew. Ridley's faith in the value of the Pará rubber as a plantation crop in Malaya led him to persuade planters to experiment with the new crop and to overcome a number of early difficulties. His services in establishing the rubber plantation industry were recognized by the award of the gold medal of the Rubber Planters' Association in

Henry Nicholas Ridley (1855–1956), by Walter Stoneman, 1917

1914 and fourteen years later by the award of the American Frank Meyer medal.

Ridley's active interest in the applied aspects of botany was further demonstrated by his initiation of the *Agricultural Bulletin of the Malay States* (for which he wrote many papers) and by his book, *Spices* (1912). He was also keenly interested in problems of plant dispersal, especially by animals and wind. This finally found expression in his book, *The Dispersal of Plants throughout the World* (1930), which he wrote in the years following his retirement. In 1941 he married his housekeeper, Lily Eliza, daughter of the late Charles Doran, builder.

Ridley was a versatile and entertaining conversationalist who, almost to the end of his days, enjoyed imparting his reminiscences to others. He was elected FRS in 1907, appointed CMG in 1911, and awarded the gold medal of the Linnean Society in 1950. On his hundredth birthday he received numerous tributes from home and overseas, among which was an appreciation from the president and council of the Royal Society. He was a prolific writer. On botanical subjects alone he wrote some 270 papers, and more than fifty others dealt with zoological topics; about ninety more were on agricultural and applied botanical subjects and a further forty on a variety of topics, geological, medical, ethnological, and biographical. Until he became bedridden he was a never-failing observer of the birds in Kew Gardens.

Ridley was short in stature and in later years distinctly rotund, but his appearance was not undistinguished because of the keen observant eyes. He died at his home, 7

Cumberland Road, Kew, on 24 October 1956, less than two months before his 101st birthday. He was the last surviving founder member of the Society for Psychical Research.　　　　　　　　　　　　　　E. J. SALISBURY, *rev.*

Sources E. J. Salisbury, *Memoirs FRS*, 3 (1957), 141–59 · personal knowledge (1971)
Archives RBG Kew, archives, corresp., and papers · RGS, papers relating to Pahang
Likenesses W. Stoneman, photograph, 1917, NPG [*see illus.*] · W. S. Stuart, photograph, 1928, RS · photograph, RS
Wealth at death £21,493 18*s.* 10*d.*: probate, 7 Feb 1957, *CGPLA Eng. & Wales*

Ridley, Humphrey (1653–1708), physician, son of Thomas Ridley of Mansfield, Nottinghamshire, matriculated from Merton College, Oxford, on 14 July 1671, but did not take a degree at Oxford, though he studied medicine there; in September 1679 he graduated MD at Leiden with a thesis, 'De lue venerea'. He was incorporated MD at Cambridge in 1688. He settled in London, became a candidate of the Royal College of Physicians on 30 September 1691, and was elected a fellow on 30 September 1692. He gave the Goulstonian lectures in 1694.

Ridley published in 1695 *The Anatomy of the Brain*, dedicated to the president and fellows of the Royal College of Physicians. The book was formally approved by the censors' board on 7 September 1694 and, although following so soon after the important writings of Thomas Willis and Raymond Vieussens, contains additions to their accounts of the brain. Ridley dissected the venous supply of the corpora striata more exactly than Willis, and demonstrated from observation in the engorged brains of men who had been hanged the lymph vessels, of which only one had been mentioned by Anthony Nuck in 1692. He was also the first to describe and name the circular sinus. His is the first English description of a sarcoma or new growth of the pineal gland (*Anatomy of the Brain*, 83). Ridley attacked the use of imagination in scientific writings, and gave anatomical reasons for doubting whether the soul was more seated in the brain than in the body at large. The figures which illustrate the book were drawn by William Cowper, the surgeon. A Latin translation was published at Leiden in 1725 by Langerak. On its title-page Ridley is erroneously named Henry, a mistake due to the fact that in his own book his initial only appears. In 1703 he published *Observationes quaedam medico-practicae et physiologicae*, which shows Ridley to have been as good a clinical observer as he was an anatomist. The observations, some of which are accompanied by accounts of autopsies, number more than thirty. The most interesting is that on hydrophobia in an English groom who accompanied his master to Ryswick in October 1697, when the peace was being concluded, and was there bitten by a Danish dog. Symptoms of hydrophobia developed on 11 December, and it was observed that in the convulsions his head was generally turned towards the wound, while just before his death difficulty of swallowing ceased and he took a large quantity of toast soaked in beer. Ridley died in April 1708, and was buried in St Andrew's Church, Holborn, on the ninth of that month.　　　　　NORMAN MOORE, *rev.* MICHAEL BEVAN

Sources Munk, *Roll* · Foster, *Alum. Oxon.* · *IGI* · Venn, *Alum. Cant.*
Archives BL, travel journal and medical papers, Sloane MSS 1502, 1504, 4033

Ridley, James (1736–1765), writer and Church of England clergyman, was born at Poplar, Middlesex (at that time a hamlet of Stepney, near London), in 1736, the elder son of Dr Glocester *Ridley (1702–1774) and his wife, Ann; he was baptized at St Dunstan and All Saints, Stepney, on 18 February of that same year. Ridley was educated at Winchester College, where he was elected scholar in 1749. He originally went up to University College, Oxford, on 25 May 1754, but soon after matriculation he moved to New College. He graduated BA in 1760, and held a fellowship at New College from 1755 to 1762. After taking orders, Ridley obtained a chaplaincy in the East India Company (the company maintained its own chapel and almshouse in Ridley's native Poplar), but relinquished the post to serve instead as chaplain to a marching regiment. Ridley accompanied the British expedition against Belle-Île in April 1761, and was present at the capture of the coastal citadel on 8 June of that year. Although the expedition succeeded in its immediate purpose of drawing off French forces from the Rhine (and, in so doing, helped to bring the Seven Years' War to its close), many of the troops participating in the siege subsequently suffered from dysentery. Ridley was among those confined for some weeks at the hospital in the harbour town of Le Palais; as Ridley's father later wrote, with reference to the period of his son's duty among the forces at Belle Île,

> he there laid the foundation of some disorders [from] which … he never recovered and which, some years after, being then happily married and preferred, put an early period to his life. (Nichols, *Lit. anecdotes*, 1.646)

Ridley appears to have returned to England some time late in 1761 or early in 1762; he probably soon thereafter married Ann, with whom he had three children, James John (*bap.* 1763), Ann (*b.* 1764), and Mary Judith (*b.* 1765).

It was only in the brief period extending from the end of 1761 to the earliest months of 1765 that Ridley was productive as a published author. His novel in four books, *The History of James Lovegrove, Esquire* (2 vols.), appeared in 1761. An earnest if generally unsuccessful effort, the novel anticipated something of the success of the later *Tales of the Genii*, if only in its sincere attempt to inculcate general moral lessons, and to impress upon its readers the desirability of submitting 'with Patience and Resignation' to 'the Designs of Providence' (Ridley, *James Lovegrove*, 9). Ridley likewise contributed a series of critical papers on contemporary topics to the *London Chronicle*. These same short essays were later (in 1763) published in a single volume edition under the title *The Schemer, or, Universal Satirist, by that Great Philosopher Helter Van Scelter*. Much in keeping with his earlier fiction, the conventional design of Ridley's satire was likewise 'to promote whatever is laudable and praise-worthy, and to disparage vice or folly'.

In 1762 Ridley obtained the reversion of his father's living at Romford in Essex; he died there in 1765. Although Ridley's death is recorded in the Romford register of burials, 1 March, Lysons notes that the author died on 24

February and was buried in the chapel cemetery at Poplar; Glocester Ridley likewise testified only weeks after his son's death that Ridley 'published his last number of The Tales of the Genii the first of February, in which month he died' (Nichols, *Lit. anecdotes*, 1.646–7).

Ridley's collection of oriental tales—*The Tales of the Genii, or, The Delightful Lessons of Horam, the Son of Asmar*—purported on its title-page to be 'Faithfully translated from the Persian Manuscript; and Compared with the French and Spanish editions Published at Paris and Madrid'. It was originally issued in shilling parts, and was reprinted in London for J. Wilkie in 1764 (2 vols.). The earliest editions of the *Tales* presented the collection as the transcription of 'Sir Charles Morell, Formerly Ambassador from the British Settlements in India to the Great Mogul'. Pointedly dedicated to the prince of Wales ('to promote the Cause of Morality'), Ridley's volumes of *Tales* also advertised themselves as together constituting

> a Book of great Note both at Ispahan and Constantinople, and frequently read by the religious Teachers of Mahomet to their Disciples, to excite them to Works of Morality and Religion. (J. Ridley, *Tales of the Genii*, ix)

All the stories in the collection were in fact the product of Ridley's own pen. Ridley modelled his tales on the interrelated narratives included in the anonymous early eighteenth-century translation (*c*.1704–1721) of Antoine Galland's *Mille et une nuits* (known to English audiences throughout the period as the *Arabian Nights' Entertainments*). Much like Joseph Addison, John Hawkesworth, Samuel Johnson, and Frances Sheridan, Ridley made use of the pretence of the exotic Eastern story to fashion his own, designedly more improving, if only pseudo-oriental, tales. The frame story of Ridley's *Tales* recounts the education of two young people—Patna and Coulor—who are the children of Giualar, the iman of Turkey. Within the security of the palace gardens, the pair are daily instructed by their well-meaning father in the paths of virtue. The children attract the further attention of a female genie by the name of Moang, who, though approving Giualar's general purpose, cautions the iman that such a cloistered education will prove of little practical value to his children in the real world; rather, the genie contends, 'they must be subject to Temptations ere their Worth be approved' (ibid., 4). The genie soon carries the students away to the noble palace inhabited by the race of genii, where they are instructed by means of a number of vivid, moral fables. Typical of the tales included in Ridley's collection is 'The Dervise Alfouran', in which the hypocrisy of a seemingly pious dervish is revealed by one of his former acolytes. The first edition of Ridley's collection was illustrated by the engravings of Anthony Walker (1726–1765).

The Tales of the Genii enjoyed a wide readership among children and adults alike, and was soon translated into French (1766) and German (1786). By the early decades of the nineteenth century it had already passed through at least ten separate English and American editions, and its influence began to manifest itself in the work of subsequent writers. One of Ridley's stories ('The Adventures of Abdullah the Merchant'), for example, appears to have

informed both the imagery and the specific language of Samuel Taylor Coleridge's 'Kubla Khan' (1816). Charles Dickens, too, confessed to having eagerly devoured the *Tales* as a child, and appears accurately to have recalled in later life that his very first composition—a juvenile piece called 'Misnar, the Sultan of India', written when he was only nine or ten years old for performance in his crudely made cardboard puppet theatre—had itself been based on material drawn from one of the extended stories (though primarily from 'The Enchanter, or, The Sultan of Misnar') in Ridley's collection. Dickens later referred to the collection in *Martin Chuzzlewit* (1844), and included a particularly telling allusion to its narrative at a climactic moment in *Great Expectations* (1861). Despite such influence, *The Tales of the Genii* has rarely been reprinted since the mid-nineteenth century; today the collection appears to be consulted only occasionally by literary historians and students of the English oriental tale.   ROBERT L. MACK

Sources Foster, *Alum. Oxon.* · T. F. Kirby, *Winchester scholars: a list of the wardens, fellows, and scholars of ... Winchester College* (1888) · *A catalogue of all graduates ... in the University of Oxford, between ... 1659 and ... 1850* (1851) · Nichols, *Lit. anecdotes*, 1.646–7; 2.376, 382 · W. Cushing, *Initials and pseudonyms: a dictionary of literary disguises* (1885), 504, 534 · J. Ridley, *The history of James Lovegrove, esquire*, 2 vols. (1761) · D. Lysons, *The environs of London*, 3 (1795), 464 · Allibone, *Dict.* · M. P. Conant, *The Oriental tale in England in the eighteenth century* (1908) · P. L. Caracciolo, *The Arabian nights in English literature* (1988) · R. Irwin, *The Arabian nights: a companion* (1994)

Ridley, John (*d.* 1782), bookseller and publisher, about whose background little is known, may have been related to booksellers of the same name recorded at Woodbridge in Suffolk from the 1750s. The earliest record of John Ridley as a London bookseller is in the imprint of a book published in 1763, where he is described as 'successor to the late Mr. Jackson' (Greene). Entries for Ridley can also be found in London trade directories from 1765, although his forename is occasionally given as 'James'. His premises were in St James's Street. In the *Eighteenth Century Short Title Catalogue* there are at least 180 imprints in which Ridley is mentioned, dated between 1763 and 1782. He appears to have been particularly closely associated with Sir John Hill, some thirty of whose works published between 1765 and 1775 bear Ridley's name in the imprint. During the 1770s, he also issued a number of pamphlets on American affairs.

Ridley's career as a bookseller is particularly well documented. He became the principal London bookseller to the university library at Göttingen in 1768 and continued to enjoy this position until his death. In contrast to the period after 1770 when only occasional letters are preserved, the first few years of Ridley's association with Göttingen are especially well documented, as his invoices and accompanying letters, all very neat and legible, were considered worthy of preservation with the original lists of orders in the library's archives. These provide a rare insight into the way a high-class London bookseller in the middle of the eighteenth century acted on behalf of a foreign institutional client.

Ridley's letters show that he acted not merely as a supplier of books to Göttingen but advised the library extensively on the contemporary London book trade. In selecting a bookseller to replace Thomas Osborne as Göttingen's principal supplier, Wilhelm Best, the Hanoverian diplomat charged with supervising Göttingen's dealings with London booksellers, may well have taken the convenient location of Ridley's shop into account: Ridley enjoyed the advantage of having premises a short distance from Best's own residence in St James's Place.

Ridley also brought to his work a knowledge of the current as opposed to the antiquarian trade. His emergence as Göttingen's principal supplier took place at a time when the library was gradually moving away from the selection of antiquarian books from catalogues to the acquisition of the most significant new publications. These were mostly ordered from Göttingen simply on the basis of brief book-trade announcements of forthcoming publications, and Ridley's advice on the status of such announcements proved invaluable. None of the 312 books that are known with certainty to have been supplied to Göttingen by Ridley was printed before 1701.

The earliest Ridley bill received by Best is apparently that of 21 November 1767. The bill dated 14 February 1768 might be considered typical of those that survive. It contains thirty-six items ranging in price from 1s. (for copies of John Windus's *Journey to Mequinez*, London, 1725; and *The Examination of Doctor Franklin*, London, 1767), to £3 3s. 0d. (for the tenth and eleventh volumes of Sir John Hill's *Vegetable System* in folio, published by Ridley himself). The total bill was for £27 10s. 6d., plus 15s. 6d. for packing. Göttingen normally placed four such orders each year. (Göttingen University Library, Bibl. Arch. 9a, fols. 42–3).

In the letter accompanying his bill of February 1768, Ridley points out 'some few mistakes', in the Göttingen order list 'with respect to prices' and describes in detail his reasons for not being able to supply certain titles (Göttingen University Library, Bibl. Arch. 9a, fol. 45). In October 1768 he refers to a thirteenth volume of the *Vegetable System* which he has ready for publication. He has 'therefore taken the first opportunity to send it, and it will probably be received before it is advertised in London' (ibid., fol. 59). Further evidence of the range of Ridley's contacts within the trade and beyond is found in other letters. Although these contacts do not appear to have extended to Scotland or Ireland, he was at least prepared to enter into correspondence on Göttingen's behalf with booksellers in Dublin, for example, or with authors about forthcoming publications. The standard of service and knowledge of the current trade shown in the correspondence contrast strongly with other London booksellers' communications in the library's archive, and show Ridley to have been the ideal bookseller for the university when there was a requirement for the rapid and efficient acquisition of new publications.

Ridley died on 22 February 1782 at his home, 77 St James's Street, London. In the same year Wilhelm Best retired to Hanover. Ridley's business was taken on by George Harlow, who appears to have continued to receive most of Göttingen's orders. Ridley's own family relationships are unknown, although diocesan records mention the death of his wife on 31 December 1774. It is possible that the Joseph Ridley who exhibited a printing press at the Royal Society of Arts in 1795 was also a relative.

GRAHAM JEFCOATE

Sources G. Jefcoate, 'Göttingen University library and the acquisition of books from London in the eighteenth century', *A catalogue of English books printed before 1801 held by the university library at Göttingen*, ed. B. Fabian, G. Jefcoate, and K. Kloth, 4 · I. Maxted, *The London book trades, 1775–1800: a preliminary checklist of members* (1977) · H. R. Plomer and others, *A dictionary of the printers and booksellers who were at work in England, Scotland, and Ireland from 1726 to 1775* (1932) · F. J. G. Robinson and others, *Eighteenth-century British books: an author union catalogue*, 5 vols. (1981) · E. B. Greene, *The tower: a poetical epistle, inscribed to John Wilkes* (1763) · Göttingen University Library, invoices and letters of John Ridley, Bibl. Arch. 9a · trade directories, London, 1765–

Archives Göttingen University Library, Bibl. Arch. 9a

Ridley, Lancelot (d. 1576), Church of England clergyman, is said to have been the son of John Ridley of Willimontswick in Northumberland, and Margaret, daughter of Richard Horton, and the nephew of Sir Nicholas Ridley, sheriff of Northumberland. Nicholas *Ridley, bishop of London, was his first cousin. He was educated at Clare College, Cambridge, and graduated BA early in 1524. He commenced MA in 1525–6, BTh in 1534–5, and DTh in 1540 or 1541. On the reorganization of the church of Canterbury under the king's charter of 8 April 1541 he was constituted, on Cranmer's recommendation, one of the six preachers of that cathedral. By May of the same year his preaching, and that of his fellow evangelical John Scory, had drawn a complaint from two conservative prebendaries. Cranmer took no action against either man. Controversial in print as well as in person, under both Henry VIII and Edward VI Ridley produced English scriptural commentaries (mainly on Pauline epistles) which commended the reading of scripture in the vernacular, attacked both Rome and the Anabaptists, and defended the doctrine of justification by faith alone. His opinions raised the concerns of the priest Henry Malet, who seems to have been given one of Ridley's books to approve for publication in 1539, and who expressed doubts about its compatibility with religious unity. One of the 'hereticall and noughty' books named by William Tolwyn in the confession of heresy extracted from him by Bishop Bonner of London at Paul's Cross in 1541 was Ridley's commentary on Ephesians (*The Declaracion Made at Poules Crosse*, B3v). The printed version of this confession drew a furious response from John Bale in 1543, which included a defence of Ridley's work. Ridley's commentary on Colossians (1548) contains a critique of the practice of teaching students 'heathen' philosophy before divinity: 'The Apostle would wee should, forme our judgementes, after holy scripture' (*An Exposicion in Englishe upon the Epistle of S. Paule to the Colossians*, J2r). Bishop Ridley seems to have considered promoting his cousin to the precentorship of St Paul's on hearing a rumour of Grindal's likely translation to a bishopric in November 1552. He was collated to the rectory of Willingham, Cambridge, on 10 June 1545. From this time on, the wills of Willingham parishioners show a tendency towards reformed religious opinions. He was also rector of Bluntisham, Huntingdonshire, from 1553 to 1554.

There are conflicting reports of Ridley's conduct during the Marian persecution. According to Strype he was pursued as a married clergyman by Bonner, and was deprived on 5 May 1554, one of only three clergymen in the diocese of Ely to suffer in this way. He was also reported to have put away his wife and returned to celibacy and the Roman obedience. He was notably absent from Nicholas Ridley's *A Friendly Farewel*. While he may have been less heroic in his response to the Marian regime than others, it seems unlikely that his renunciation of protestantism was either wholehearted or emphatic. His Catholic opponents would have made more of such an important conversion, and Ridley would surely have been rewarded with another benefice. Furthermore, a letter survives from William Turner to John Foxe, naming Ridley as a possible source for Foxe's account of Hugh Latimer. This suggests Ridley was not ostracized by the protestant exiles, as does the fact that under Elizabeth he quickly reappeared (in 1560) as one of the six preachers of Canterbury. He was also in the same year collated rector of Stretham, near Ely, where he died in 1576; he was buried there on 16 June.

Ridley married Mary, daughter of Christopher Paterson or Parkinson; among their six children were Lancelot, Henry, and the physician and scientist Mark *Ridley.

W. A. SHAW, *rev.* JASON YIANNIKKOU

Sources J. Hodgson, *A history of Northumberland*, 3 pts in 7 vols. (1820–58), pt 2, vol. 3, p. 340 · W. G. Searle, ed., *Grace book Γ* (1908), 210, 222, 298, 358 · *LP Henry VIII*, 14/1.561 · *The declaracion made at Poules Crosse … by Alexander Seyton and Mayster Willyam Tolwyn* [n.d., 1542?], B3v · J. Harryson [J. Bale], *Yet a course at the Romyshe foxe* (1543), 49r–v · *The works of Nicholas Ridley*, ed. H. Christmas, Parker Society, 1 (1841), 336–7, 494 · *VCH Cambridgeshire and the Isle of Ely*, 2.174, 176; 9.409–10 · *Ely Diocesan Remembrancer* (1913), 64 · *Transactions of the Cambridgeshire & Huntingdonshire Archaeological Society* (1908), 2.163 · L. Richmond, *The fathers of the English church* (1808), 2.10 · J. Strype, *Memorials of the most reverend father in God, Thomas Cranmer* (1694), 93–4, 329 · J. Strype, *The life and acts of Matthew Parker* (1711), 72 · F. Blomefield, *Collectanea Cantabrigiensa* (1750), 21 · G. Ridley, *The life of Dr Nicholas Ridley* (1763) · J. Ridley, *Nicholas Ridley: a biography* (1957)

Ridley, Mark (*b.* 1560, *d.* in or before 1624), physician and writer on magnetism, was born on 2 August 1560, and baptized on 18 August, at Stretham, Cambridgeshire, the second son of the six children of Lancelot *Ridley (*d.* 1576), rector of Stretham, and his wife, Mary. Having matriculated as a pensioner from Clare College, Cambridge, at Easter 1577, he graduated BA in 1581 and MA in 1584. On 25 September 1590 he was licensed by the College of Physicians to practise medicine, and from 26 June 1592 he is shown in the annals of the college as MD. On 28 May 1594 he was admitted as a fellow of the college, having been appointed the day before by Queen Elizabeth to serve the tsar of Russia, Feodor Ivanovich, who had written to the queen requesting the services of an English physician. William Cecil, Lord Burghley, was instrumental in the appointment.

Mark Ridley (*b.* 1560, *d.* in or before 1624), by unknown artist, *c.*1613

Ridley remained in Moscow for five years. Another of the tsar's physicians in 1594–7, simultaneously with him, was Baldwin Hamey the elder. Following the death of Tsar Feodor on 7 January 1598 Ridley was appointed to the service of his successor, Boris Godunov. At the request of Queen Elizabeth, however, he was given leave to return to England in 1599 and was present in London at a meeting of the College of Physicians held on 1 October that year. In a letter written to Elizabeth in May 1599 Boris Godunov commends Ridley for his faithful service and dismisses him 'with our princelie favour', but Timothy Willis, who was sent to Russia to replace Ridley, only to be rejected, refers cryptically to 'the manner of Dr Ridlies farewell without his wages due for the last year and the detayning some of his bookes' as reasons 'why it was not good to send anie physitione'.

On his return to England Ridley settled in London and on 12 August 1600 was admitted to Gray's Inn. He attended meetings of the College of Physicians regularly, and became active in its affairs. On 5 June 1607 he was elected censor of the college, and on 20 September 1609 he became one of the college's eight elects. Annually from 1609 to 1613 he was again elected censor and again in 1615 and 1618. He held the office of treasurer in 1610 and 1620, and was consiliarius in 1612–14, 1616–17, and 1621. In 1607–10 Ridley was a participant in proceedings initiated by the college against his former colleague in Moscow, Baldwin Hamey, who had arrived in London in 1597 and was practising medicine without a licence. Hamey was eventually licensed, but Ridley's part in moulding the college's policy towards him is imponderable.

Ridley's scientific interests extended beyond medical matters into magnetism, a subject on which he published two books: *A Short Treatise of Magneticall Bodies and Motions* (1613) and *Magneticall Animadversions: made by Marke Ridley, doctor in physicke, upon certaine magneticall advertisements, lately published, from Maister William Barlow* (1617). In the preface to *A Short Treatise* Ridley refers to William Gilbert, author of the classic *De magnete* (1600), as 'our friend and collegiate'. Following up Gilbert's work, Ridley gives directions for carrying out experiments on the loadstone, magnet, and terrella. He includes numerous engravings and descriptions of his improved instruments for determining the declination of the magnetic needle and for making use of the inclinatory needle for finding position at sea. Among the illustrations is a perspective of the southern hemisphere showing a continent denoted as 'Terra Australis'. The book's frontispiece is an engraved portrait of Ridley at the age of thirty-four, showing him with curly fair hair and a beard. He appears to have been of stocky build.

Three years after the appearance of his *A Short Treatise* Ridley was accused by William Barlow of plagiarism. In the introduction to his *Magneticall Advertisements* (1616) Barlow stated that some seven years before its publication a manuscript copy of this work had been 'either mislaied or embeseled' and that he had 'met with many portraitures of my Magneticall implements, and divers of my propositions set abroad in another mans name'. That the other man in question was Ridley was revealed by Ridley himself in his *Magneticall Animadversions*, in which he not only rejected the accusation, but also charged Barlow with having plagiarized both Gilbert's *De magnete* and his own *A Short Treatise*. In 1618 Barlow repeated the allegation that Ridley had lifted material from his stolen manuscript, and cast doubt on Ridley's claim to have been the tsar's principal physician.

To Ridley are attributed two manuscripts in the Bodleian Library, Oxford (MSS Laud misc. 47a and 47b): one is a Russian-English dictionary containing 7203 entries, entitled 'A dictionarie of the vulgar Russe tongue', the other an English-Russian dictionary (8113 entries), entitled 'A dictionarie of the Englishe before the vulger Russe tonnge'. The attribution depends primarily on comparison with an inscription by Ridley on the flyleaf of a Russian printed book (now in the library of Trinity College, Cambridge), presented by him in 1599 to Thomas Neville, dean of Canterbury and master of Trinity College. Being composed of words collected from the vernacular and uninfluenced by church Slavonic, the dictionaries often anticipate the evidence of other sources. They are not only the earliest dictionaries of Russian words with English equivalents, but also the first Russian dictionaries of any kind in the full sense, that is to say, arranged alphabetically and with the Russian words written in Cyrillic letters. A rudimentary Russian grammar on the first eight folios of the Russian-English dictionary is the earliest recorded. Both dictionaries also contain specialized vocabularies of words for birds, fishes, plants, and diseases.

The precise date of Ridley's death is not known, but he was certainly dead by 14 February 1624, when his successor as elect was appointed by the College of Physicians. He was not married and had no children.

GERALD STONE

Sources G. Stone, ed., *A dictionarie of the vulgar Russe tongue, attributed to Mark Ridley* (1996) · Munk, *Roll* · W. J. Harrison, *Clare College and its members, 1580–84* (1963) · J. J. Keevil, *Hamey the stranger* (1952) · Cooper, *Ath. Cantab.*, vol. 1 · Venn, *Alum. Cant.* · annals, RCP Lond., vol. 2 · will, Cambs. AS, VC16:160 1571 CW [Lancelot Rydley] · parish records, Stretham, Cambs. AS, P147/1/1 · M. Ridley, *Magneticall animadversions* (1617)
Archives Bodl. Oxf., Laud MSS
Likenesses pen-and-ink drawing, c.1613, NPG [*see illus.*] · line engraving, BM, NPG; repro. in M. Ridley, *A short treatise of magneticall bodies* (1613)

Ridley, Sir Matthew White, second baronet (1745–1813), land and coal owner and politician, was born on 28 October 1745 in Newcastle upon Tyne, the second of the twelve children of Matthew Ridley (1711–1778) of Heaton Hall and Newcastle, a landowner, coal magnate, and MP, though the eldest of Ridley's second wife, his first cousin Elizabeth (1722–1764), the daughter of Matthew White (1690–1750) of Blagdon. He had seven brothers and four sisters. He was educated at Newcastle Free School and Westminster School, and then went to Christ Church, Oxford, where he matriculated on 27 February 1764. At the age of seventeen he succeeded to the baronetcy of his maternal uncle, Sir Matthew White (1727–1763) of Blagdon.

Ridley was born into one of the dominant families of north-east England, and inherited a substantial landed estate in the south-east of Northumberland, lucrative investments in the coal, glass, and brewing industries, and an unassailable electoral interest in Newcastle upon Tyne. His family's pre-eminence dated from the later seventeenth century, when two Newcastle merchants, Nicholas Ridley (d. 1712) and Matthew White (d. 1716), began to invest heavily in the coal trade on the north bank of the Tyne, opening up collieries at Blaydon, Willington, Benton, Byker, Heaton, and Jesmond. Their effective business partnership was strengthened by the marriage of Nicholas Ridley's eldest son, Richard (1677–1739), to Matthew White's daughter Margaret, the first of a series of marriage alliances that left Sir Matthew White Ridley as the eventual heir to both families and both fortunes.

The steady growth of these fortunes was marked by the extension of their landed interests. Matthew White acquired the Blagdon estate to the north of the city in the 1690s, while his successors were able to take advantage of the forfeitures that followed the 1715 rebellion by purchasing the Heaton estate in 1719, followed in 1723 by the Newsham and Plessey estates further north on the Northumberland coast, which brought them effective control of the port of Blyth. These joint purchases allowed both families to construct substantial country seats, but their main importance lay in the commercial benefits to be gained from the valuable coal reserves that lay beneath the surface. In these early stages at least, agricultural rents made a relatively small contribution to the Ridleys' wealth: in fact both Matthew Ridley and Matthew White were chronically short of money in the 1740s, and borrowed heavily on the security of their land in order to develop their mining interests. It was the coal trade that supported their other business ventures, just as it supported the Ridleys' growing political influence.

This influence owed a great deal to Sir Matthew White Ridley's grandfather, Richard Ridley, who had built up a powerful body of support within Newcastle's entrenched and increasingly exclusive magistracy. Successive royal charters had contributed to placing complete control of the town in the hands of an oligarchy drawn from the Merchant Adventurers' Company, an oligarchy which safeguarded its members' economic interests by a virtual monopoly of places on the aldermanic bench. In a town which depended so completely on the coal trade, economic power and political influence went hand in hand: thus a politician who could summon sixty men on horseback and more than 300 on foot from among his own workforce to quell a demonstration against high food prices, as Matthew Ridley (Matthew White Ridley's father) did in 1740, was bound to win the support of his fellow magistrates. He was equally likely, however, to provoke hostility among the wider freeman electorate, and it took some time for Matthew Ridley to live down his father's reputation as 'the Terror of the Town' (Chicken, 4) and to build up a more broadly based electoral interest.

Although Sir Matthew White Ridley had been elected as MP for Morpeth in 1768, his political career began in earnest in 1774 when his father's declining health propelled him on to Newcastle's aldermanic bench and thence into the mayoralty and the parliamentary seat which his father had held unopposed since 1747, and which he was to hand on to his eldest son in 1812. In 1778 he succeeded his father as governor of the Merchant Adventurers' Company, another nominally elective position which in practice had become part of his family's patrimony, having been held by successive generations since 1715. In all these offices he followed family tradition by consistently representing the interests of the town's ruling oligarchy against those of 'the leather aprons' or 'raggamuffins', and he was equally consistent in his opposition to parliamentary reform. His electoral appeal outside the charmed circle of Newcastle's magistracy seems to have rested partly on tradition but mainly on his dominant position in the constituency's staple industry: an election song dating from 1784 made this abundantly clear by its crude but effective coupling of

Brandling for ever and Ridley for aye,
There's plenty of coals on our waggon way.
(Knox, 'Peace', 19)

In the Commons Ridley frequently voted with the whig opposition, but is best described as an independent; he took his own line on the main issues of the day, and intervened mainly to represent what he regarded as the best interests of his constituents.

Ridley portrayed himself in his correspondence and relatively infrequent speeches as a typical, plain-spoken, independent-minded country gentleman, and in some senses his background and education had prepared him for a conventional role in the landed gentry. Few county families, however, combined the quasi-feudal power of the Ridleys over their Newcastle fiefdom with the shrewd business sense that allowed each successive generation not simply to maintain their industrial inheritance but also to move into new and potentially lucrative areas of enterprise. Just as his father had reacted to the gradual decline of the Tyneside salt industry by diversifying into glass making, brewing, and tile making, so Ridley gradually extended his business interests into banking, insurance, and public utilities. In 1787, on the retirement of Ralph Carr, he became the leading partner in Newcastle's Old Bank, an investment which was not only profitable in itself but which allowed him to channel his own business through the bank free of charge. Within a few years the Old Bank had combined with one of its local rivals to establish an insurance company, the Newcastle Fire Office, which in 1797 acquired and extended the city's original waterworks, mainly in the interests of providing an adequate supply of water to protect the properties which it insured. In 1805 Ridley became a director of the Globe Insurance Company, drawing a salary of £150 a year, and in the later years of his life he acquired a portfolio of minor investments in transport improvements and government securities. His main sources of income, however, were still derived from the White and Ridley families' extensive holdings in the coal industry, from his partnership in the Northumberland Broad and Crown Glass Company, and from the Heaton and Blagdon estates.

Ridley married Sarah Colborne (d. 1806), the daughter and eventual heir of Benjamin Colborne of Bath, on 12 July 1777; they had five sons and one daughter. Sarah was described in 1778 as 'not the Pink of Gentility but very good humoured' (Elwin, 119), and it is to be hoped that she was also tolerant, since her husband was allegedly irresistible to women. In 1793 he was ordered to pay £400 in damages to one of his constituents after being caught *in flagrante delicto* with the latter's wife on the staircase of their house in Newcastle, a misfortune which seems to have had little effect on his local reputation for 'urbanity of manners and a most endearing condescension in his general intercourse with society' (Northumberland Record Office, ZRI 52/6). He died on 9 April 1813 in Portland Place, London, after a long illness, and was succeeded as third baronet by his eldest son, also Matthew White Ridley (1778–1836).

J. M. ELLIS

Sources G. T. Ridlon, *History of the ancient Ryedales, 860–1884* (1884) · L. Namier, 'Ridley, Sir Matthew White (1745–1813)', HoP, *Commons* · HoP, *Commons* · T. R. Knox, 'Popular politics and provincial radicalism: Newcastle upon Tyne, 1769–1785', *Albion*, 11 (1979), 224–41 · T. R. Knox, '"Peace for ages to come": the Newcastle elections of 1780 and 1784', *Durham University Journal*, 84/1 (1992), 3–19 · M. Phillips, *A history of banks, bankers and banking in Northumberland, Durham, and North Yorkshire* (1894) · E. Chicken, *No: this is the truth* (1740?), 4 · M. Elwin, ed., *The Noels and the Milbankes: their letters for twenty-five years, 1767–1792* (1967), 119 · *Newcastle Avertiser*, obit., 1813, Northumbd RO, ZRI 52/6 · parish register (baptism),

29/10/1745, All Saints', Newcastle upon Tyne · parish register (baptism), 26/11/1745, St John's, Newcastle upon Tyne

Archives Northumbd RO, Newcastle upon Tyne, corresp., diaries, and papers | Northumbd RO, Newcastle upon Tyne, letters to John Blackett

Likenesses J. Flaxman, statue, *c.*1813, St Nicholas's Church, Newcastle upon Tyne · J. Hoppner, portrait, Blagdon Hall, Seaton Burn, Newcastle upon Tyne · J. Zoffany, double portrait (with a friend), Blagdon Hall, Seaton Burn, Newcastle upon Tyne

Ridley, Matthew White, first Viscount Ridley (1842–1904), politician, born at 10 Carlton House Terrace, London, on 25 July 1842, was the elder son in a family of two sons and one daughter of Sir Matthew White Ridley, fourth baronet (1807–1877), of Blagdon, Northumberland, tory MP for North Northumberland. His mother was Cecilia Anne, eldest daughter of James *Parke, Baron Wensleydale. Ridley's mother died of tuberculosis in 1845 and his childhood at Blagdon was lonely and severe. At Harrow (1856–61) he was in the football and shooting elevens and became captain of the school. In 1860 he gained a classical scholarship at Balliol College, Oxford, and he matriculated on 12 October 1861. After taking a first class in classical moderations in 1863 and in the final classical school in 1865, he was elected a fellow of All Souls; he was admitted to the Inner Temple in 1864. His cousin Louisa Knightley described him in 1866 as 'rather handsome and exceedingly clever … [with] the extremely decided opinions of a very young, clever man who has lived in an intellectual set at Oxford and not yet learned to say "I don't know"' (*Journals of Lady Knightley*, 112). Ridley vacated his fellowship in 1874, after his marriage on 10 December 1873 to the Hon. Mary Georgiana (*d.* 1899), eldest daughter of Dudley Coutts Marjoribanks, first Baron Tweedmouth, with whom he had two sons and two daughters.

Destined for a political career, Ridley in 1868 succeeded his father as Conservative MP for North Northumberland, a seat he held until 1885. On his father's death in 1877 he succeeded as fifth baronet and owner of the family estates of over 10,000 acres. He was under-secretary to the Home Office from 1878 to 1880 in Beaconsfield's administration. From September 1885 to January 1886 he was financial secretary to the Treasury under Lord Salisbury. Meanwhile the Reform and Redistribution Acts of 1884 and 1885 changed the Northumberland constituencies, enfranchising nonconformist farmers and coal-miners; at the general elections in November 1885 and July 1886 he unsuccessfully stood for Hexham and Newcastle upon Tyne respectively. In August 1886 a by-election at Blackpool gave him an opening; he won, and retained the seat until he was raised to the peerage in 1900. Ridley did not receive office in the Salisbury government of 1886–92. He chaired the royal commission on civil establishments (1886–89), the so-called 'Ridley commission' which inquired into the work and organization of the Home Office. He was considered for the office of postmaster-general in the minor reshuffle of 1891, but he was not offered the job: Salisbury may have been dissuaded from promoting him by A. J. Balfour. A loyal party man, Ridley was on the squirearchical side of the party and he did not

Matthew White Ridley, first Viscount Ridley (1842–1904), by R. E. Ruddock

belong to the inner circle of Cecils and Souls. He was sworn of the privy council in 1892.

Although Ridley took little part in the debates of the house, he won its respect, and on 10 April 1895 he was put forward as the Conservative candidate for the speakership. On a division the Liberal candidate W. C. Gully was elected by 285 votes against 274 for Ridley. When Salisbury returned to office on 25 June 1895 Ridley became home secretary in the new government, holding the post until the dissolution of 1900. Ridley's administration of the Home Office was thoroughly safe and consequently attracted little attention. In 1897, when he released from prison some men convicted of dynamite outrages, he defended himself effectively against an attack from his own side, led by Henry Howorth and James Lowther. His most illustrious charge was Oscar Wilde, who was a prisoner in 1895–7; Ridley agreed to Wilde's requests for books, but he refused him early release. The appointment of his brother as a High Court judge in 1897 was unfortunate; Edward Ridley was a poor judge and his appointment exposed the home secretary to the charge of jobbery. Ridley was one of the two ministers to leave office when Salisbury reconstituted his government after the 1900 election (the other was Henry Chaplin). Ridley's dismissal was sometimes attributed to the malign influence of Balfour, but it seems likely that the decision was Salisbury's alone. On leaving office Ridley received a viscountcy. His last years were mainly spent at Blagdon.

True to his family tradition, Ridley was always active in the administration of his property. Known as an extremely capable man of business, he was long a director of the North Eastern Railway, and on the resignation of Sir Joseph Pease in 1902 he became chairman. He especially devoted himself to the development of the town of Blyth, which, originally part of the estates of the Radcliffe family but forfeited to the crown after the rising of 1715, had descended to Ridley with the other estates of Matthew White. After succeeding to the baronetcy in 1877, he carried a bill through parliament for the creation of a board of commissioners with powers to develop Blyth; as chairman of this board Ridley soon transformed the harbour and dock, from which (being principal proprietor) Ridley benefited largely, reviving his family fortunes at a time of agricultural depression. He contrived, however, that the inhabitants should share in the prosperity: he gave an open space for public recreation, which in 1904 he opened as the Ridley Park; he gave sites for a mechanics' institute, a church, and a hospital; and he was occupied until his death on a large scheme of planting trees in convenient places. Ridley was chairman of the Northumberland quarter sessions from 1873, and of the county council from 1889; but he resigned both offices in 1895 when he became home secretary. He joined the Royal Agricultural Society in 1869 and was its president in 1888, when the meeting was at Nottingham. He was also president of the National Union of Conservative Associations. He served as deputy lieutenant and JP for Northumberland and provincial grand master of freemasons for Northumberland (1885–1900), and he commanded the Northumberland yeomanry from 1886 to 1895. He was ecclesiastical commissioner for England in 1895–1904.

Ridley died at Blagdon on 28 November 1904, and was buried there. He was succeeded as viscount by his elder son, Matthew (1874–1916), Conservative MP for Stalybridge (1900–04) and chairman of the Tariff Reform League. His second son, Jaspar, became chairman of Coutts's Bank.

Ridley is remembered as being 'fairly stuffy and a huge eater', but his portly country gentleman's exterior masked disappointed ambition. It is to his credit that he advanced the standing and fortunes of his family at a time of aristocratic decline, leaving the Ridleys as second only to the Percys in Northumberland; but his political career failed to fulfil the promise of his youthful academic brilliance.   REGINALD LUCAS, rev. JANE RIDLEY

Sources U. Ridley, ed., *Cecilia* (1958) · *The Times* (29 Nov 1904) · E. Hughes, *North country life in the eighteenth century*, 1 (1952) · T. J. Nossiter, *Influence, opinion and political idioms* (1975) · N. McCord, *North-east England* (1979) · E. A. A. Douglas, *Chief whip* (1961) · *Salisbury–Balfour correspondence: letters exchanged between the third marquess of Salisbury and his nephew Arthur James Balfour, 1869–1892*, ed. R. H. Williams (1988) · J. Pellew, *The home office, 1848–1914* (1982) · R. F. V. Heuston, 'Lord Halsbury's judicial appointments', *Law Quarterly Review*, 78 (1962), 504–32 · P. Marsh, *The discipline of popular government: Lord Salisbury's domestic statecraft, 1881–1902* (1978) · private information (2004) · *The journals of Lady Knightley of Fawsley, 1856–1884*, ed. J. Cartwright (1915)

Archives Northumbd RO, Newcastle upon Tyne, corresp. and papers

Likenesses B. Stone, photograph, 1897, NPG · Ape [C. Pellegrini], chromolithograph cartoon, NPG; repro. in *VF* (23 July 1881), facing p. 51 · J. Brown, stipple (after H. T. Wells), BM · H. von Herkomer, portrait, Blagdon · R. E. Ruddock, photograph, NPG [*see illus.*] · carte-de-visite, All Souls Oxf. · etching (after photograph by R. E. Ruddock), NPG · wood-engraving, NPG; repro. in *ILN* (12 Feb 1876)

Wealth at death £535,615 14s.: probate, 20 Jan 1905, CGPLA Eng. & Wales

Ridley, Nicholas (c.1502–1555), bishop of London and protestant martyr, was born only a short distance away from Hadrian's Wall, near Willimontswick, to a Northumberland gentry family whose members were prominent in the life of the church, both before and during the Reformation. His father was Christopher Ridley of Unthank Hall; his mother is said to have been Anne Blenkinsop. Cuthbert Tunstall, bishop of London and later bishop of Durham, was a relative.

Education and evangelical conversion Much of Nicholas Ridley's early life and career were shaped by Cambridge University—'my loving mother and tender nurse' ('Last farewell', 91–2)—and his father's brother Robert *Ridley. Robert was Tunstall's secretary and a friend of Erasmus, but in his thinking (in keeping with the English style of humanism), classical and biblical studies were blended with medieval scholasticism. Terence professor in the faculty of arts in the first decade of the century, he was a considerable figure in the university and in the church at large, holding numerous livings in and near London and also a prebend in St Paul's. In some respects an ambivalent figure, he made strenuous efforts to combat heresy, but nevertheless encouraged the setting up of the university's first press. He was an important influence on Thomas Cranmer, and defrayed his nephew Nicholas's early expenses at Cambridge. Until his death, most likely in 1536, Robert Ridley probably loomed large in Nicholas's life.

After attending school at Newcastle upon Tyne, about 1518, in his middle to late teens, the young Nicholas Ridley entered Pembroke College, which he found to be 'studious, well learned, and a great setter forth of Christ's Gospel'. At the end of his life he remembered how, within the walls of its orchard, he had learned by heart the greater part of the epistles of St Paul, as well as much of the rest of the New Testament ('Last farewell', 92). His own zeal for learning was well rewarded. He received from the university every promotion that could be bestowed: including all of his degrees (BA, 1522; MA, 1525; BTh, 1537; DTh, 1541); a fellowship at Pembroke from 1524; a chaplaincy to the university in 1531; and a university professorship in Greek (from 1535 to 1537–8). Ultimately he became master of Pembroke (1540), a distinction he retained until his disgrace. He is also reported to have studied at Paris and Louvain.

With his many talents and superb connections, from the late 1530s Ridley began to receive ever more exalted attention from outside the university. In 1537 Archbishop Cranmer called him from Cambridge to be one of his chaplains, and also gave him his first cure, on 30 April 1538, by making him vicar of the 'worshipful and wealthy' parish of Herne in Kent ('Last farewell', 92). As with Thomas Cranmer and Hugh Latimer, Ridley's re-evaluation of Christian doctrine proceeded gradually.

Nicholas Ridley (c.1502–1555), by unknown artist, 1555

Initially the reformers stressed the great Pauline aspiration of 'preaching Christ', and they strove to disseminate the word of God through sermons and the printing press with the aim of bringing about a deep spiritual renewal throughout society. The distracting practices that the reformers felt had grown up in the Roman church in the post-apostolic centuries had to be identified and removed through self-referencing new interpretations of scripture, against which all doctrine and practices had to be judged. Much of the received wisdom of the Catholic church (including the sacraments) had to be re-examined, and where necessary cast aside. At this early period Ridley's views concerning the eucharist were conventional (by his own later admission), though his sermons had been strongly evangelical for some time. At Herne he encouraged the singing of the Te Deum in English, not Latin. The parish 'heard of my mouth ofttimes the word of god preached, not after the popish trade, but after the Christ's gospel'. He was gratified that 'godly virtue and zeal' was kindled among his parishioners, evident in the life and works of Lady Elizabeth Fyneux (the lady of the manor) and 'many other more' (ibid., 92–3).

Problems at Canterbury Ridley continued to adapt and expand his opinions as opportunity and circumstances allowed, in the face of resolute opposition from theological opponents and political enemies, and the complicating conservatism of the king. His arrival at Herne came at something of a high-water mark for evangelical reformers. After 1538 Henry VIII began to withdraw much of his previous support for doctrinal development, which he had backed until his supremacy over the English church was secured. The king encouraged the passage of the Act of the Six Articles in 1539, which demanded that all of his subjects believe that the natural body and blood of Jesus Christ was present under the form of the bread and wine, and that no other substance except Christ, God, and man remained in the sacrament of the altar. The six articles also stipulated that auricular confession was necessary in Henry's church. The new law, and the destruction of Thomas Cromwell that followed in 1540, applied a brake to Cranmer's long-term plans for the steady development of protestantism in England. For much of the 1540s the reformers had to be cautious in the face of continued opposition, much of it organized by bishops Stephen Gardiner of Winchester and Edmund Bonner of London.

One of the defeats that Cranmer suffered during these years concerned the refounding of Canterbury Cathedral. When the monastic foundation was dissolved in 1540 he wanted to recast the cathedral as a new seat of learning and preaching, staffed with twenty divines who would lecture their students in the sciences and tongues. Moreover, they would be gifted preachers who could bring the gospel to the people. And for the dean, who would round out and lead the chapter, Cranmer wished to have the 'most excellent' man he could find from the ancient universities, his old Cambridge friend Edward Crome (Cranmer, *Letters*, 396–7). But the new foundation, as it was actually instituted, disappointed the archbishop. Rather than a score of university-style teachers, the cathedral was provided with a dozen old-fashioned prebendaries, who were fairly divided (in accordance with the king's stipulations) between reformers and those of conservative religious opinion. Six were former monks from the old foundation, and they bitterly opposed reform. Cranmer managed to make Ridley one of the prebendaries, and he proved a valuable ally. Cranmer was also able to salvage part of his original programme in the creation of an innovative corps known as the 'six preachers', roving apostles of a special type who delivered sermons widely in Kentish parishes. Among them were John Scory (a former Dominican friar and future bishop of Hereford), and Ridley's cousin Lancelot. But even among the six preachers there were divisions. Two of them, Robert Searles and Edmund Shether, strongly opposed the archbishop's policies. The result was a mixed foundation that had been assembled by wrenching apart what had been one of the most glorious monasteries in Europe. On almost every issue the cathedral staff divided along doctrinal lines. To say, as one of the conservative prebendaries informed Bishop Gardiner, that 'sometimes they did not agree in preaching' was a vast understatement (*LP Henry VIII*, 18/2, 339).

The two Ridleys promoted the cautious reforms that Cranmer favoured, and they challenged some of the implications of the six articles. Nicholas preached that auricular confession was 'a godly mean' to bring the sinner to the priest for counsel, even though 'he could not find' its rationale in scripture. He also preached that many of the traditions of the church were but 'beggarly ceremonies' which detracted from the true meaning of Christ's sacrifice (*LP Henry VIII*, 18/2, 306). Not surprisingly, the two Ridleys were specially targeted by the cathedral's conservatives in 1543 in the attempt to ruin Cranmer and stop the Reformation completely, known now as the prebendaries' plot. In this they had the support of Stephen Gardiner, who heard Ridley preach and, not at all pleased, took him aside afterwards and severely admonished him. Eventually the plot failed and by the autumn the defeat of Gardiner and his supporters was assured. Had they succeeded, Ridley would probably have been swept away with Cranmer. But it is small wonder that he had little good to remember about his time in Canterbury. 'To speak of things pleasant' there, 'I dare not' ('Last farewell', 93).

Eucharistic thinking Over the next few years Ridley divided his time between Cambridge and Kent. He began a more mature assessment of the eucharist, centred on the question of the nature of Christ's presence in the supper that he had instituted. Was there or was there not any corporal presence of Christ's substance in the consecrated bread and wine? The Roman Catholic church taught that through the miraculous intervention of God, after the priest spoke the words of consecration, 'Hoc est corpus meum', the bread and wine were completely transformed into the self-same natural body that had been born of the Virgin Mary and hung upon the cross. The sacrament was an oblation offered daily on behalf of a sinful world. But the doctrine of transubstantiation had been heavily criticized by Luther and his followers from the second decade of the sixteenth century, and they deemed it improper to give the consecrated host the same honour that was due to Jesus himself. Luther argued that it was Christ's unique sacrifice on the cross that mattered for salvation, not the mass that re-enacted that one death. The bread and wine, with Christ's physical body and blood, were present simultaneously in the eucharist. After Luther's challenge a clear consensus about the nature of Christ's presence was slow to emerge. The Act of the Six Articles represented a fairly conservative interpretation of the issue. Although the statute did not mention transubstantiation, it did support the realist understanding that the body and blood of Christ alone were present after the consecration.

Ridley's own views were drawn from his careful study of the early fathers of the church, plus some eclectic choices, including the ninth-century monk Ratramnus of Corbie, who embraced a mystical understanding of the eucharist. Ridley's inquiries ultimately led him to relinquish the realist position, and to adopt the tenet that the nature of Christ's presence was spiritual. An exact time-frame for the stages of Ridley's gradual reassessment eludes complete precision, but some of the most important thinking was carried out in the quiet of his cure. Later he would write that he was Herne's 'debtor for the doctrine of the Lord's supper' ('Last farewell', 92–3). He preceded Cranmer to the belief that the eucharist represented the spiritual manifestation of Christ.

A new crisis broke in 1546, one that turned on the role of the mass in the English church. Henry's health was beginning to fail, and as Easter approached the evangelical reformers received what they understood to be new signals of support from him. In April, perhaps encouraged that the king was at last ready to enter a fresh phase of reforms, Crome preached that the mass was only a remembrance of Christ's death. He was arrested, and Bonner prepared a recantation for him to make at Paul's Cross, while Henry indicated that he wanted Crome to obey the law. But at the same time Latimer and other evangelical leaders urged Crome not to submit, and when he appeared at Paul's Cross on 9 May he announced that he would not recant. His stand triggered off a full-blown attack on the evangelicals, one that called into question the survival of the entire movement for reform. Consequently it became imperative that Crome submit, and the task of persuading him fell to Ridley. Among the ironies of the situation was that Ridley's own opinion might not have been far removed from Crome's. But vital though this issue was, personal considerations had to be pushed aside. Ridley and Richard Coxe, acting in their capacities as royal chaplains, examined Crome before the privy council. They reviewed his sermons point by point, noting every place where he had dissimulated. Ridley reminded Crome of the key strategy that all the reformers had to rely upon for the very survival of the protestant movement: their earnest obedience in doing the king's will. Crome was humiliated on 27 June at Paul's Cross, and by the middle of August Henry, who had been flirting with a *rapprochement* with the papacy, reversed once again, and began to make overtures to François I of France that they should work together to transform the mass into a communion service.

Henry's sudden oscillation may mark the opportunity that Cranmer and Ridley needed to move further away from the tenet of the real presence in the sacrament of the altar. When Cranmer was examined by the Marian authorities in 1555, he admitted that he had once 'believed otherwise than I do now', until Ridley 'did confer with me, and by sundry persuasions', developed from the doctors of the church, 'drew me quite from my opinion' (Cranmer, *Letters*, 218). Cranmer's thinking moved gradually in the weeks and months before the king's death, and continued to be revised into the new reign, under Ridley's guidance.

Bishop of Rochester The sacrifices of summer 1546 meant paradoxically that the reformers were well placed to gain complete control of government when Henry died in January 1547. The accession of the young Edward VI ushered in a new era. The time of equivocation and subterfuge, which had marked the evangelical movement in its dealings with the old king, was now past, and any further hesitation ended once conservative opposition was defeated. Bishops Gardiner and Bonner were arrested by the end of the summer. Among the earliest of Cranmer's acts was to issue a Book of Homilies, long in planning, that provided suitable material for the clergy to read in their parishes when preachers were unavailable. It was an evangelical *tour de force* that attempted to establish that the Christian was saved by faith in God's promise of redemption and forgiveness only. Every man or woman was justified not through any efforts of their own, but through the merciful generosity of God's supreme gift. Good works were not the means of salvation, but they were the fruit of faith.

On 4 September 1547 Ridley was elected bishop of Rochester, his first episcopal see. The royal assent was given on the 14th and he was consecrated on the 25th. He found 'much gentleness and obedience' as he promoted 'the trade of God's law' ('Last farewell', 93). Among his first public pronouncements as bishop was a sermon at Paul's Cross on the sacrament of the altar (now under reassessment in parliament), which attempted to find a careful balance that would distance the English church from the radical opinions of Anabaptists (who questioned the essential humanity and divinity of Christ), and the untried positions of the growing Calvinist movement. Ridley wished to 'rebuke the unreverend behaviour of certain evil disposed persons' who had spread 'railing' handbills against the dignity of the sacrament. It was 'truly and verily the body and blood of Christ, effectually by grace and spirit' (*Works*, 265). But the doctrine of a spiritual presence seemed new in 1547 (before the prayer book appeared), and so abstruse were the theological opinions involved that the people who crowded round the pulpit fastened upon the novel and shocking rather than on the substance of Ridley's meaning. He tried to deflect close questioning on the nature of the presence. Any who asked in crude terms how Christ was present, Ridley argued, were 'worse than dogs and hogs' in their ignorance (Foxe, ed. Townsend, 6.241). Overall his sermon was an indifferent success which left much confusion in its wake.

None the less further encouragement for Ridley and Cranmer to move beyond the realist view of the eucharist came late in November 1547, when Martin Bucer provided evidence, previously unknown, from a manuscript copy of one of John Chrysostom's epistles, showing that the saint had held that the bread remained after the consecration. This new evidence served to confirm Ridley's own readings in Ratramnus. Heinrich Bullinger was informed in September 1548 that Cranmer, following Ridley's lead, had rejected any remnant of Luther's thinking and now embraced the doctrine of the spiritual presence. The communion rite in the first Book of Common Prayer (1549) represented this view.

Elevation to London When Edmund Bonner was finally deprived in February 1550, Ridley was translated to the see of London. Among his earliest acts was an energetic visitation of the diocese. He ordered the destruction of altars, to 'turn the simple from the old superstitious opinions of the popish mass', and their replacement with 'honest' tables that would help to instil 'the right use of the Lord's supper' as a godly meal (*Works*, 319–21). By the end of the year every church in the city but one had a communion table. He examined every incumbent and curate for his learning, and threatened to 'eject' those who failed to come up to the standards he required. Whenever possible he promoted reformers to livings and offices. His task was complicated by the need to ensure that the reform movement in London was kept within the frame of Edward's church. Among the challenges he faced was one presented by London's two 'stranger' churches for foreigners,

who advocated faster and more complete changes in doctrine and practice: one congregation for refugees from France; and the other of merchants or exiles from the Low Countries and German-speaking regions. The Dutch church was led by the Polish theologian John à Lasco (Laski), who had strong links with John Calvin and represented a more aggressive and 'hotter' form of evangelism than anything Cranmer and Ridley ordinarily countenanced. His congregation remained seated to receive communion (in avoidance of any suggestion of idolatry), to the annoyance of Cranmer, whose prayer book specified that those 'minded' to receive should all be 'kneeling humbly upon their knees'. However, the archbishop invited Laski from Emden to provide a needed corrective against Anabaptism. For more than a year Ridley had led a series of English theologians in an effort to persuade the Anabaptist Joan Bocher to relinquish her heresies, without success. She was brought to the stake in May 1550 (Scory preached the sermon at her execution), one of only two heretics burnt under Edward's rule.

Ridley was also deeply concerned with the problems presented by John Hooper, who had been nominated in July 1550 to the bishopric of Gloucester, despite his impatience with the first prayer book. Encouraged by Laski, Hooper refused to be consecrated in the episcopal vestments that he dismissed as papistical remnants. The controversy pivoted upon the issue of adiaphora, of things indifferent, or trivial questions that were not subject to a standard determination. But Hooper's stance was a serious challenge to Cranmer's authority and a deep embarrassment to Edward's government, and also ill-timed following the initial violence that had met the 1549 prayer book in some parts of the realm. Ridley reasoned with him at length but at first in vain, and in January 1551 Hooper was confined in the Fleet. A month later he let himself appear in the hated garments, in a capitulation that represented a victory for Ridley's vision of the gradual reformation of the English church, inside (and distinct from) the international protestant movement.

A new threat arose in 1553 to the continuation of the reformation of the English church. Tuberculosis was stealing Edward's life although the king was only in his sixteenth year. In the previous September Ridley and his chaplain Edmund Grindal had paid a formal call upon Mary, the king's eldest half-sister and next heir, ostensibly to ask if the bishop could preach before her, but in reality to see how amenable she was to direction, and what course the future might bring. Edward had never succeeded in extinguishing her adherence to Catholicism. The pleasant countenance she initially showed Ridley changed when she heard his request. The door of the adjoining church shall be open to you, she replied, 'but neither I, nor none of mine shall hear you'. 'Madame', Ridley countered, 'I trust you will not refuse God's word'. Her reply was devastating: 'That is not God's word now, that was God's word in my father's days'. After this painful interview Ridley accepted a consoling drink, but suddenly he berated himself for forgetting his duty: 'Surely I have done amiss' to drink where the offer of God's word 'hath been refused'. He felt as if he should shake the dust from his feet (Foxe, 1583, 1396).

Arrest, trial, and martyrdom Convinced that the accession of Mary would overturn the reforms, Edward chose his cousin, the strongly evangelical Lady Jane Grey, as his new heir. Ridley, who had just been persuaded by the duke of Northumberland to replace the imprisoned Tunstall as bishop of Durham, did everything in his power to divert the succession. After the king died unexpectedly early on 6 July 1553, he preached vigorously in favour of Queen Jane. He proclaimed that neither Mary nor Elizabeth, who had been declared illegitimate by parliament during their father's lifetime, was eligible for the throne. It was an enormous gamble for England's religious identity, and it almost succeeded. Had Mary been secured before Edward died, Jane might have continued without insurmountable opposition. But Mary defended her right to inherit her father's throne and revivify her mother's religion. In a little over a week she mounted a successful coup against Jane and her supporters. Ridley was one of the first to be arrested as a traitor by the new regime. Bonner was immediately reinstated as bishop of London, and Ridley's register, interrupted in the full flow of diocesan business, survives as a witness to the calamity that overtook him.

At first Ridley was held in the Tower with Cranmer, Latimer, and John Bradford. In March 1554 the former bishops were taken to Oxford and imprisoned in the Bocardo, in preparation for a formal set-piece trial that was meant to discredit the entire reform movement from the 1520s onwards. In the following month Ridley defiantly entered into a lengthy disputation on the meaning of the eucharist.

In the time that remained to him Ridley wrote as often as he had paper and ink. He composed a *Brief Declaration of the Lord's Supper*, written in simple, accessible language for the widest possible readership. Latimer's servant, Augustine Bernher, smuggled goods and letters in and out of his prison chamber, and many of Ridley's exhortations reached Grindal's hands on the continent. Ridley's *Brief Declaration* and other writings were printed at Emden and distributed covertly in England soon after his execution. Records of his Oxford disputation and examination were eventually printed by John Foxe in his *Acts and Monuments*. Whenever possible, anguished people repaired to Ridley for advice on matters of belief and how they should behave towards the new regime.

In autumn 1555 Ridley and Latimer were put on trial. The final outcome was never in doubt. When on 15 October he was degraded from his office as bishop, Ridley refused to put on a surplice, associated as it now was with his persecutors. Towards the end he remembered those who had preceded him to the stake. Of his protégé Bradford he told Bernher that he was grateful 'that ever I had such a one in my house'. John Rogers, the first to die, had been 'one of my calling' as a prebendary preacher in London. And since Grindal had escaped into exile, Ridley wished to 'make up the trinity out of Paul's church, to suffer for Christ' (*Certain most Godly Letters*, 72–3).

The scene of the execution of Ridley and Latimer on 16 October 1555 in Oxford is one of the most distressing and moving episodes in all of Foxe's *Acts and Monuments*. Unlike Latimer, who quickly smothered at the stake, Ridley suffered cruelly in the flames, while a horrified Cranmer was forced to watch, in anticipation of his own burning only five months away. Foxe's account was much revised and improved over the years. Its most famous element, Latimer's final, defiant proclamation: 'Be of good comfort Master Ridley, and play the man: we shall this day light such a candle by God's grace in England, as (I trust) shall never be put out' (Foxe, 1583, 1770), was taken from Eusebius's story of the death of Polycarp. It was added in a later edition of Foxe's great work, and it may represent a general allusion to the vast procession of martyrs who have passed through the entire history of the church, rather than the event as it actually occurred. How much of Foxe's account was literal, and how much was art, will probably never be known. Foxe's Ridley, standing at the stake, was an ageing and vulnerable man, but not too removed from earthly concerns, even as he approached a fearful death, that he forgot to give his friends small coins and nutmegs as mementoes. His contributions to the Reformation had sprung from his unwavering commitment to the truth as he perceived it. Foxe's portrait reminded his readers of the humanity that also lay beneath Ridley's proud, scholarly reserve.

SUSAN WABUDA

Sources Augustine Bernher's collection of letters and theological tracts, Bodl. Oxf., MS Bodley 53 · R. Ridley, sermon collection, CUL, MS Dd.5.2 · Ridley's episcopal register, GL, MS 9531/12, pt 2, esp. fols. 275r–323r · 'Last farewell', *Certain most godly letters*, ed. M. Coverdale and [H. Bull] (1563), 25–113; repr. in *The works of Nicholas Ridley, sometime lord bishop of London, martyr, 1555*, ed. H. Christmas, Parker Society, 1 (1843), esp. 189–252, 380–81, 388, 395–418 · M. Bateson, ed., *Grace book B*, 2 (1905), 27 · *Miscellaneous writings and letters of Thomas Cranmer*, ed. J. E. Cox, Parker Society, [18] (1846), 396–7 · T. Cranmer, 'Defensio verae et catholicae doctrinae de sacramento corporis et sanguinis Christi', *Writings and disputations of Thomas Cranmer*, ed. J. E. Cox, Parker Society, 17 (1844) · *LP Henry VIII*, 18/2.291–378, esp. 300, 302–3, 306, 339, 368, 331–2, 334–7, 339, 346–7, 349–50, 354, 356, 361, 363–5, 367 · R. Morice, 'Anecdotes and character of Archbishop Cranmer', *Narratives of the days of the Reformation, chiefly from the manuscripts of John Foxe the martyrologist*, ed. J. G. Nichols, CS, old ser., 77 (1859), 234–72 · *State papers published under the authority of his majesty's commission* (1830), vol. 1, pt 2, 842–8 · J. Foxe, *Actes and monuments* (1563) · J. Foxe, *Actes and monuments*, 4th edn, 2 vols. (1583) · J. Foxe, *Acts and monuments*, ed. G. H. Townsend, 8 vols. (1843–9), vol. 6, pp. 125–6, 240–41, 437; vol. 7, pp. 406–583 · H. Robinson, ed. and trans., *Original letters relative to the English Reformation*, 1 vol. in 2, Parker Society, [26] (1846–7) · E. Cameron, *The European Reformation* (1991) · P. Collinson, *The Elizabethan puritan movement* (1967), 96 · P. Collinson, 'The protestant cathedral, 1541–1660', *A history of Canterbury Cathedral*, ed. P. Collinson, N. Ramsay, and M. Sparks (1995), 154–203 · P. Collinson, 'Truth and legend: the veracity of John Foxe's book of martyrs', *Elizabethan essays* (1994), 151–77 · T. Freeman, 'Texts, lies, and microfilm: reading and misreading Foxe's book of martyrs', *Sixteenth Century Journal*, 30 (1999), 23–46 · N. L. Jones, 'A bill confirming Bishop Bonner's deprivation and reinstating Bishop Ridley as the legal bishop of London, from the parliament of 1559', *Journal of Ecclesiastical History*, 33 (1982), 580–85 · D. R. Leader, *A history of the University of Cambridge*, 1: *The university to 1546*, ed. C. N. L. Brooke and others (1988), 76, 185, 189–90, 249–52, 300–

01, 318, 320, 323 · D. MacCulloch, *Thomas Cranmer: a life* (1996), 31, 180–83, 266, 284–7, 297–323, 354–8, 372–5, 378–83, 394, 410–21, 471–85, 560–74, 603–4 · A. Pettegree, *Marian protestantism: six studies* (1996), 28–9, 98, 124–5, 142–3 · J. Morris and T. Jones (1970) · S. Wabuda, 'Equivocation and recantation during the English Reformation: the "Subtle Shadows" of Dr Edward Crome', *Journal of Ecclesiastical History*, 44 (1993), 224–42 · S. Wabuda, 'Henry Bull, Miles Coverdale, and the making of Foxe's Book of martyrs', *Martyrs and martyrologies*, ed. D. Wood, SCH, 30 (1993), 245–58 · S. Brigden, *London and the Reformation* (1989) · F. Heal, *Of prelates and princes: a study of the economic and social position of the Tudor episcopate* (1980) · Venn, *Alum. Cant.*, 1/3.458 · J. Ridley, *Nicholas Ridley* (1957) · D. MacCulloch, *The boy king: Edward VI and the protestant reformation* (1999)

Likenesses oils, 1555, NPG [*see illus.*] · W. Passe and M. Passe, line engraving, 1620, BM, NPG; repro. in H. Holland, *Herōologia* (1620)

Ridley, Nicholas, Baron Ridley of Liddesdale (1929–1993), politician, was born on 17 February 1929 at Blagdon Hall, Seaton Burn, Northumberland, the younger son in the family of two sons and one daughter of Matthew White Ridley, third Viscount Ridley and seventh baronet (1902–1964), coal magnate, and his wife, Ursula (*d.* 1967), second of the four daughters of the architect Sir Edwin Landseer *Lutyens. He was the ninth member of his family to sit in parliament. His great-grandfather Matthew White Ridley, fifth baronet and first Viscount Ridley, was home secretary from 1895 to 1900, when he was ennobled.

Education and early career After Eton College—where he was neither successful nor popular—Ridley expressed to his father the desire to study architecture at Oxford. His father insisted that he embrace a more practical course of studies since, as the second son, he would have no great inheritance. So when he went up to Balliol he read mathematics and engineering, gaining a third in mathematical moderations in 1947 and a second-class degree in engineering science in 1951. His artistic bent was to express

itself for many years in his painting. Meanwhile he married, on 17 August 1950, the Hon. Clayre Campbell (*b.* 1927), second of the three daughters of Alistair Campbell, fourth Baron Stratheden and Campbell, army officer and public servant. There were three daughters of the marriage, Jane (*b.* 1953), Susanna (*b.* 1955), and Jessica Clayre (*b.* 1957).

On leaving Oxford, Ridley joined Brims & Co. Ltd in Newcastle upon Tyne as a civil engineering contractor, where he remained for nine years, being made a director after four years. It was during this period that he decided he would follow the family tradition and enter politics. His political instincts were honed in the traditional Conservative manner: he was adopted as the prospective parliamentary candidate for the unwinnable seat of Blyth in November 1952 at the age of twenty-three, and was badly beaten by Alf Robens in the general election of 1955. The scale of his defeat was, in some respects, a personal blow, for his family had developed the town as a port for the export of coal, and he felt that he had let his family down. However, he secured victory in the constituency of Cirencester and Tewkesbury in the general election of October 1959. This constituency he served until his retirement from the House of Commons in April 1992.

Initially Ridley made slow progress, although—oddly for one of his right-wing convictions—he served as parliamentary private secretary to the left-leaning minister of education, Sir Edward Boyle, from July 1962 to October 1964. They had in common only an Etonian background and their liking for argumentative conversation. Boyle was later to leave politics altogether (becoming vice-chancellor of Leeds University) because of his distress at what he saw as the right-wing tendency of the Conservative Party under Edward Heath. Concurrently with this appointment Ridley was a member of the British delegation to the Council of Europe and the Western European Union. In stark contrast to the political ideas he espoused

Nicholas Ridley, Baron Ridley of Liddesdale (1929–1993), by David Rose

in later life he was a staunch advocate of Britain's application to join the European Economic Community and was bitterly disappointed when President de Gaulle vetoed Britain's entry in January 1963. In April 1965 he was the co-author of a pamphlet for the Conservative Political Centre advocating a united Europe, *One Europe*. As late as 1971 he was a senior member of the Conservative Group for Europe and, in his capacity as one of the group's main spokesmen, took a leading part in the parliamentary debate on the terms of entry which Heath had negotiated in Brussels.

Ridley and Heath Despite the fact that he voted for Enoch Powell in the Conservative Party leadership contest of 1965, Ridley's pro-European credentials drew him to the friendly attention of Edward Heath, who won that contest. Heath's favourable opinion of Ridley at this time was enhanced by Ridley's frequent attacks from the back benches on Labour's economic policy, and his encouragement of the right-wing views of his own party. He harried the Labour minister for technology, Tony Benn, over proposals to subsidize Beagle Aircraft in February 1968, and he put forward detailed plans for the denationalization of British industry in January 1969. He remained close to Powell, and their views on British membership of the Common Market changed in tune with one another over the years. Nevertheless he was happy with Heath as leader, not only because of his European policy but because he seemed to Ridley's mind—and according to the party manifesto for the 1970 general election—a monetarist: that is, a politician who believed in an absolute minimum of state funding of government enterprises, including the National Health Service.

Against most expectations Heath won the general election of June 1970, and promptly gave Ridley his first taste of ministerial office as parliamentary secretary at the Ministry of Technology. Ridley immediately used his ministerial power to implement the policies of monetarism and, in spite of mounting difficulties, notably with the trade unions, insisted on the restriction of government expenditure. In particular he argued that companies which faced bankruptcy through giving in to excessive wage demands would not be bailed out by the state. With the absorption of the Ministry of Technology into the Department of Trade and Industry (DTI) in October 1970 he became parliamentary under-secretary of state at the DTI.

At that time, as well as sharing Heath's enthusiasm for British membership of the European Economic Community, Ridley took the view—which he believed Heath shared—that it would be necessary for the new government to break the power of the trade unions in order to implement the free market policies implied by the doctrines of monetarism. The election manifesto of 1970 contained a commitment to reform trade-union law so as to inhibit the power of the unions to bring their members out on strike, and to outlaw sympathetic strikes, whereby one union could strike in support of another. However, the worsening economic situation led Heath to conclude that he could not continue with his plans for 'the quiet

revolution' proclaimed to the Conservative Party conference of 1970.

1972 was a watershed in modern British political history. In the face of mounting economic difficulties Heath changed his mind on domestic economic policies. He and his closest colleagues—most notably James Prior and Peter Walker—had come to doubt their capacity to change the face of national politics. They had decided that no government could defeat the apparently entrenched power of the trade-union movement. Ridley, on the other hand, took the view that there was no point in being in politics if one sought only to retain office rather than to insist on acquiring the power to change things. The last straw for Ridley was the Industry Bill of 1972, which gave the government power to distribute large sums of public money to failing companies. Thus the consequences of the change of tack in 1972 were vastly increased public expenditure and burgeoning inflation.

Heath felt obliged to move Ridley from the Department of Trade and Industry—where his unbending monetarism was no longer acceptable—in his April 1972 reshuffle, and offered him instead the post of arts minister. Ridley's and Heath's accounts of this episode differed. Ridley felt that he could not serve in a government which was abandoning its policies. He therefore departed into the wilderness. This was described by Heath as a refusal to serve, and by Ridley as a resignation. In his autobiography, *The Course of my Life* (1998), Heath offered the judgement that Ridley was incompetent, but he did not deny that he offered him the job of minister for the arts. Ridley wrote:

> I could stand it no more. Ted Heath sent for me in 1972 when he had a reshuffle. I was on an official visit to Lisbon, and had to fly back in the middle of the night. He tried to move me sideways and asked me to become Minister for the Arts. I refused: I said I wanted to have no more to do with his Government. It was my first political resignation. It was a lonely experience.   (Ridley, 4)

The significance of Ridley's stand should not be underestimated. Ridley's was the only resignation from the Heath government on grounds of difference on economic policy. Thus Ridley knowingly deprived himself of any future prospect of office under Heath.

From 1972 to 1974 Ridley ceaselessly proclaimed his consistently stern views on economic policy. He was one of a handful of Conservative politicians who held to the principles laid down in the 1970 manifesto. But, like his friend John Biffen, he did not have the oratorical power to seize the public imagination; the only Conservative rebel who did have that power was Enoch Powell. During his time in exile, however, Ridley himself underwent a significant transformation in his own ideas, which was further to alienate him from Heath. From being an enthusiast for an ever closer union with Britain's partners in the European Economic Community, he came to distrust the motives of the western European continental powers, which he regarded as federalist in nature. Ridley, for all his earlier beliefs in European union, remained, at heart, a British nationalist. By the time Heath came to write his autobiography in 1998, he expressed himself with particular and lengthy bitterness about Ridley's change of heart on Europe: there were no fewer than six detailed hostile references to Ridley in it.

Heath never forgave those who changed their minds on British membership of the EEC. Thus it can readily be understood that between 1972 and 1974 Ridley's despair of his own political future was marked: he even contemplated resignation from the House of Commons. However, in this period he continued with great determination to pronounce, in terms adumbrated in the Conservative manifesto of 1970, on economic policy. He utterly opposed the introduction by the Heath government of a statutory incomes policy; he attacked the view that the government's increases in public expenditure would foster growth; and he criticized the weakness of the proposals for trade-union law reform introduced by the employment secretary, James Prior.

Ridley and Thatcher When, in February and October 1974, Heath went down to two successive general election defeats, Ridley saw the possibility of a change in his fortunes under a new leader, albeit in opposition. As he wrote at the beginning of his sole book, *'My Style of Government': the Thatcher Years*:

> One afternoon towards the end of 1974 I met Sir Keith Joseph in the Members' Lobby of the House of Commons. I asked him whether he was firm in his intention to challenge Edward Heath in the coming contest for the leadership of the Conservative Party. He replied that he had decided not to do so 'for personal reasons'. I was aghast. At last the opportunity had come to break with the miserable years of the past and secure a change of leader, and it was widely believed that it would be Keith Joseph who would make the challenge.
>
> 'I think Margaret will stand,' he said.
>
> I was amazed, because the news that Margaret Thatcher might stand hadn't reached my ears before. But I was relieved; at least there was a challenger. (Ridley, 1)

Ridley immediately sought out Margaret Thatcher and offered her his support in the leadership campaign. On 11 February 1975 she was elected leader of the Conservative Party, and Ridley was back in favour. Keith Joseph and the Institute of Economic Affairs were the major influences on Conservative Party policy formulation between 1975 and 1979. Ridley's distinction was less that of an influential force than that of a man who stood by his principles until the end of his House of Commons career. While in opposition he developed his business interests, which included directorships of Ausonia Finance and Marshall Andrew Ltd. He also married, on 16 February 1979 (his first marriage having ended in divorce in 1974), Judith Mary Augustine (Judy) Kendall, daughter of Dr Ernest Kendall of Epsom.

Following her election victory in May 1979, Margaret Thatcher appointed Ridley minister of state at the Foreign and Commonwealth Office (FCO). The truly difficult years of the first Thatcher government were between 1979 and 1981. Many of her cabinet colleagues were despairing of her determination to hold to monetarist policies. Ridley stood by the prime minister with resolution. His loyalty was to be richly rewarded. At the FCO he had proposed a resolution of the dispute with Argentina which provided for Argentinian sovereignty over the Falkland Islands in return for a lease-back agreement. Despite the fact that this was anathema to the prime minister, she recognized the steadfastness of his support of her domestic policy by making him financial secretary to the Treasury in September 1981. This job, which gave him a large say in the disposition of public spending, was delightful to Ridley. He was named a privy councillor in January 1983.

Ridley entered the cabinet in October 1983 as minister of transport, where he continued the policies that he had put forward at the Treasury, describing his department as 'the last bastion of the planned economy'. He announced his intention to privatize British Airways. He campaigned strenuously for cheaper air fares on European routes, and caused great offence by turning up at a meeting of British motor manufacturers in his newly purchased French car. He refused to supply government funds for the building of the channel tunnel, although he allowed work to start without a public inquiry, and he attacked the bus industry, again refusing public subsidy. In everything he did he was a proponent of free enterprise.

Ridley's promotion to be secretary of state at the Department of the Environment, in May 1986, was not simply a reward for his loyalty to the prime minister but an acknowledgement by her of his concern for matters rural. Initially his appointment was welcomed by the many and various campaigners for a cleaner and healthier rural Britain. They did not, however, realize that Ridley's overriding concern in all matters political was in the area of public expenditure. They were disappointed—and even enraged—by his determination to cut down any expenditure which helped rural preservation. Further spending in this area was, then, an immensely popular cause in the press and in the broadcast media. Ridley was immovable in the face of any criticism. He substantially reduced the budget of his new department and insisted on the diminution of public funding for environmental projects. His theory was that the countryside would best be served, not by government, but by private enterprise, and whatever unpopularity this attracted, it made no difference to him. One of the smaller matters which excited the hostility of environmental campaigners and the media alike was his decision to veto an application to build houses near his house in Stow on the Wold. Ridley was so irritated by opposition to his personal views that he simply walked out of a television interview in which he was challenged as selfish for preferring his own interests to those of the countryside at large. The hostility was exacerbated by the perceived double standards held by Ridley, since he had only a month earlier reproached a group of MPs for their 'not in my backyard' (NIMBY) attitudes. The acronym NIMBY was to haunt him in the closing years of his ministerial career. As secretary of state for the environment Ridley was also closely associated with the introduction of the community charge (poll tax). There was strong pressure from the Conservative party conference in 1987 for the tax to be introduced immediately rather than (as was proposed) phased in. Ridley had seen many of Thatcher's reforms opposed vigorously at the outset, only to win ultimate all-party acceptance, and assumed that this was another instance, so responded to the pressure. 'Every time I hear people squeal', he said on a television programme, 'I am more than ever certain that we are right' (*Daily Telegraph*, 26 March 1990, 17).

In July 1989 Thatcher appointed Ridley secretary of state at the Department of Trade and Industry, where his abrasive style could be more usefully employed against industrialists and trade unionists than against well-meaning environmentalists. This was to be Ridley's last major cabinet post. He told Mrs Thatcher that he wanted to retire from the House of Commons before the next general election, which was expected to be held late in 1990. Then, in July 1990, his capacity for indiscretion, coupled with a carefree attitude to the media, was exemplified in an interview he gave to the editor of *The Spectator*, Dominic Lawson. In this interview he denounced the members of the European Commission as 'seventeen unelected reject politicians', economic and monetary union as 'a German racket designed to take over the whole of Europe', and the French as Germany's 'poodles'. 'I'm not against giving up sovereignty, but not to this lot', he said. 'You might as well give it to Adolf Hitler, frankly' (*The Spectator*, 14 July 1990). When the interview was published it excited understandable anger among Britain's continental partners. Ridley believed that an interview given in good faith was used in bad faith. Mrs Thatcher offered to defend him against all odds, but Ridley did not want to cause her any further embarrassment and on 14 July resigned. He was the last instinctive Thatcherite in the cabinet, and his departure was damaging to her. Bracketing him with Keith Joseph in her memoirs, she wrote: 'In my experience there are few politicians for whom doing the right thing is of no importance, there are fewer still for whom it is the only consideration. Nick and Keith were among them' (Thatcher, 312).

Final years Ridley remained MP for Cirencester and Tewkesbury until the general election of April 1992. In 1991 he published '*My Style of Government': the Thatcher Years*, which, unlike the memoirs of many contemporaries, was not a self-justifying apologia but an analysis of Thatcher's policies and attitudes. The title of the book came from a speech she made in 1983. At Mrs Thatcher's behest Ridley was made a life peer in the 1992 dissolution honours. Even in retirement, however, he was prone to give offence. He chose as his title Baron Ridley of Liddesdale, which upset Scottish politicians because the river from which the title came is generally regarded as a Scottish river. Ridley replied to criticism by saying that one side of it was in England. He went on to make rebarbative speeches in the House of Lords on many matters of public concern until his final illness silenced him. Even when his doctors diagnosed the cancer which killed him he refused their advice to stop smoking, showing to the end a determination to resist all opinions other than his own. He died at his home, Kilnholme, Penton, Carlisle, on 4 March 1993, and was buried at Penton on 9 March 1993.

He was survived by his second wife and the three daughters of his first marriage. A memorial service was held at St Margaret's Church, Westminster, on 23 June 1993.

Ridley's arrogance of manner and insensitivity on matters of social concern made him an unpredictable colleague in an era of populist politics. The perceived hardness of his nature was, however, belied by his other career. He was a painter of real skill, devoting himself to the composition of the most delicate and elusive of watercolours. Unlike the many politicians who have taken to painting as a pleasurable pastime, Ridley could have made his mark as a professional painter. In summary, one can only say that his unfeeling attitude in his professional life was counterbalanced by the sensitivity of his art and the geniality of his private character. He was the most generous of hosts, and those who knew him well, and whom he liked, found him the most delightful and gregarious of companions.   PATRICK COSGRAVE

Sources N. Ridley, '*My style of government': the Thatcher years* (1991) • A. Roth, *Parliamentary profiles, L–R* (1990) • *The Times* (6 March 1993) • *The Independent* (6 March 1993) • *Wiltshire and Gloucestershire Standard* (11 March 1993) • *Sunday Times* (7 March 1993) • *The Guardian* (6 March 1993) • *Daily Telegraph* (6 March 1993) • M. Thatcher, *The Downing Street years* (1993) • E. Heath, *The course of my life: my autobiography* (1998) • J. Bruce-Gardyne, *Whatever happened to the quiet revolution?* (1974) • *WWW* • Burke, *Peerage*
Archives Glos. RO, letters | Glos. RO, constituency corresp. | SOUND BL NSA, current affairs recordings • BL NSA, documentary recordings • BL NSA, performance recording
Likenesses photographs, 1984–9, Hult. Arch. • D. Rose, photograph, repro. in *The Independent* [*see illus.*] • photograph, repro. in *The Times* • photograph, repro. in *Daily Telegraph* • photograph, repro. in *The Guardian* • photograph, repro. in *Wiltshire and Gloucestershire Standard* • photograph, repro. in *Sunday Times*
Wealth at death £698,428: probate, 2 June 1993, *CGPLA Eng. & Wales*

Ridley, Robert (*d.* 1536?), theologian, was a native of Northumberland (according to Leland, a relative of his lived in a tower on Hadrian's Wall); Nicholas *Ridley, later bishop of London, was his nephew. He studied at Cambridge (BA, 1496; MA, 1500; BTh, 1516; DTh, 1518; not to be confused with Cuthbert Ridley, a civil lawyer), where he became a fellow of the King's Hall, and also studied at Paris, probably in the years immediately following his graduation as MA. He lectured in philosophy (Thomas Cranmer, who was among his pupils, remembered him as an inspiring teacher), and was probably the Mr Ridley who was delivering 'ordinary lectures' in 1508–10. Named a university preacher in 1513–14, he was by this time a prominent figure at Cambridge, and was one of those commissioned to draft the statute that replaced customarily unruly proctorial elections with a system by which colleges nominated proctors on a rota. In 1521 he was among the theologians summoned from Oxford and Cambridge to consult Cardinal Wolsey and Henry VIII over the condemnation of Martin Luther.

This, together with the promotion of his relative Cuthbert Tunstall to the see of London that same year, launched Ridley's post-academic career. Tunstall made him his secretary, and presented him to a series of benefices in his diocese and cathedral. On a return visit to Cambridge at Christmas 1525, Ridley, together with Walter Preston (another of Tunstall's chaplains), instigated the accusations of heresy against Robert Barnes which led to the latter's public penance in London. Described by George Cavendish as 'a very small person in stature but sewerly a great & an excellent Clarke in dyvynytie' (Cavendish, 80), Ridley enjoyed a reputation for scholarship, assisting Polydore Vergil in his edition of Gildas, and appearing as a character in one of Vergil's dialogues.

The surviving remnants of Ridley's library (mostly found in Durham Cathedral Library) range from patristic and medieval authors to Catholic polemics against the Reformation (including Fisher's confutation of Luther). Ridley became a correspondent of the German Catholic polemicist Johannes Cochlaeus (who dedicated two books to him), and a stray letter from Ridley to Henry Gold details his criticisms of Tyndale's New Testament. As he is known to have preached in defence of relics, it can be conjectured that he preached against other aspects of the new doctrines. He assisted at numerous interrogations of heretics in London in the 1520s, including Robert Barnes and John Tewkesbury. Yet Ridley was by no means an uncritical supporter of the *status quo*. Barnes recalled how Ridley had once declared, in a conversation in the house of William Butts, that the bishops 'were clear out of order' (Barnes, fol. 29r). He showed similar bluntness in speaking on behalf of Katherine of Aragon in the divorce case, at the legatine tribunal in 1529. Rebuked by Cardinal Wolsey for his plain words, he roundly replied that 'an unreverent tale wold be onreverently answered' (Cavendish, 86). In 1531 he signed the protestation of a minority of convocation against the concession to Henry VIII of the title 'supreme head of the Church of England' (notwithstanding the proviso 'as far as the law of Christ allows'). Ridley accompanied his patron on the latter's translation to Durham in 1530. He may well have been the author of a letter (preserved in the Sanuto diaries) to Polydore Vergil, describing a whale which was beached at Tynemouth in 1532.

When suspicious royal agents raided Tunstall's palace at Bishop Auckland in 1534, as part of the campaign to secure acceptance of the oath of succession, they found in Ridley's room a critically annotated copy of *De vera differentia* (a propaganda tract advocating the royal supremacy), as well as a defence of the endowments of the clergy. Ridley was duly imprisoned, and may possibly have refused the oath of succession. He seems to have died in 1536 (when his benefices were filled as vacant by death), perhaps still in captivity, as with his arrest in 1534 he vanishes abruptly from the historical record. RICHARD REX

Sources M. Bateson, ed., *Grace book B*, 2 vols. (1903–5) · W. G. Searle, ed., *Grace book Γ* (1908) · Emden, *Cam.*, 480–81 [occasionally confuses Robert Ridley with Cuthbert Ridley] · J. Cochlaeus, *Aliquot articulis* (1527), dedication · Robert Barnes, *A supplicatyon* (1531), fols. 22v, 29r, 134v · P. Vergil, ed., *Gildas Britannus … de calamitate, excidio, & conquestu Britanniae* (1525), dedication · W. Friedensburg, 'Beiträge zum Briefwechsel der katholischen Gelehrten Deutschlands im Reformationszeitalter', *Zeitschrift für Kirchengeschichte*, 18 (1893), 261 · *LP Henry VIII*, 5, nos. 986–7; 14/2, no. 750 · letter to Henry Gold, BL, Cotton MS Cleo. E.v., fol. 392 · G. Cavendish, *The life and death of Cardinal Wolsey*, ed. R. S. Sylvester, EETS, original ser., 243 (1959), 79–80, 86 · *The acts and monuments of John Foxe*, new edn, ed. G. Townsend, 4 (1846), 689 · J. Cochlaeus, ed., *Beati Isidori … de ecclesiasticis officiis* (1534), dedication · G. Hennessy, *Novum repertorium ecclesiasticum parochiale Londinense, or, London diocesan clergy succession from the earliest time to the year 1898* (1898) · P. Friedmann, *Anne Boleyn: a chapter of English history, 1527–1536*, 1 (1884), 142 · *I diarii di Marino Sanuto*, ed. F. Stefani and others, 57 (Venice, 1902), col. 269–70 · *Joannis Lelandi antiquarii de rebus Britannicis collectanea*, ed. T. Hearne, [3rd edn], 6 vols. (1774), vol. 4, p. 42 · D. MacCulloch, *Thomas Cranmer: a life* (1996)

Ridley, Sir Thomas (*b.* before **1548**, *d.* **1629**), civil lawyer, was the second son of Thomas Ridley (*d.* 1548), yeoman, of Bouldon, Shropshire, and the Isle of Ely, and Alice, or Anne, daughter of Richard Day of Worfield, Shropshire. The younger Thomas Ridley was born at Ely before 1548. His paternal grandfather was possibly Lancelot *Ridley, the Elizabethan minister who was deprived during the Marian period. Ridley was also related to Nicholas Ridley, bishop of London, the Marian martyr. After his father's death in 1548 Ridley was brought up by his mother's family. His grandfather's kinsman William *Day, provost of Eton College, secured a place for him at Eton between 1562 and 1566, and later arranged for him to become provost there from 1579 until 1583. Ridley matriculated as a pensioner at King's College, Cambridge, in 1566, receiving the degrees of BA in 1571, MA in 1574, and LLD in 1583. He was a fellow from 1569 to 1579. He was admitted as an advocate of the arches on 13 October 1585 and entered Doctors' Commons on 10 October 1590. In 1590 he was granted an honorific admission to Gray's Inn. Day, who was also dean of Windsor, was responsible for Ridley's selection as MP from Chipping Wycombe, Buckinghamshire, in 1586. Ridley strengthened his relationship with Day by marrying his daughter, Alice, before 1596. After Day became bishop of Winchester in 1596, he appointed Ridley chancellor of the diocese, a position Ridley held until 1627. Ridley was a conscientious and able chancellor who performed most of his duties within the consistory court himself. He had a house at Owslebury, near Winchester, where he heard cases brought before the court. He also participated actively in the secular administration of his county. In addition to his work as chancellor, he served as JP for Hampshire and for Surrey from 1596 and he represented Lymington, which lay within Winchester diocese, in the parliament of 1601.

After 1604, Ridley spent more time in London, where he practised in the realm's principal ecclesiastical courts. His knowledge of the civil and ecclesiastical law led to his appointment, together with John Cowell and Sir Edward Stanhope, to revise the canons dealing with ecclesiastical procedure in 1604. Three years later he wrote *A View of the Civile and Ecclesiastical Law*, a vigorous defence of the autonomy of the ecclesiastical law at a time when the common law courts were using prohibitions to encroach upon the jurisdiction of the church courts. Law was derived from custom, statute and ultimately God. Ridley contended

that common law and ecclesiastical law were equally subject to royal jurisdiction so that there was no need for
writs of prohibition or actions of *praemunire* in which
common law courts pretended to control the ecclesiastical courts. The treatise, which was dedicated to James I,
lamented the current state of the civilians' profession,
which 'doth scarce keepe beggerie from the gate' (Ridley,
274). Among the common lawyers the book stimulated
fears that the civilians were attempting to strengthen the
civil law at their expense. James was so pleased 'that Sir
Edward Coke undertook from thence to prophecy the
decay of the common law' (Lloyd, 423).

In 1611 George Abbot, archbishop of Canterbury, named
Ridley as his vicar-general, and during his tenure in that
office, which lasted until his death in 1629, he was a member of the high commission. From 1609 until 1620 Ridley
also served as master in chancery in ordinary. He was
knighted at Greenwich Palace on 24 June 1619. His protestantism, reflected in his composition of verse for the 1576
edition of Foxe's book of martyrs, was never in doubt, but
his defence of ecclesiastical law made him vulnerable to
criticism from puritans. In 1644 William Prynne included
the second edition of Ridley's book (1634) among the
works published by the command of William Laud, archbishop of Canterbury, in defence of popish errors, super-
stitions, ceremonies, and practices. This edition, with
notes by John Gregory, was published in Oxford. Further
editions were published there in 1662 and 1675.

Having received a grant of arms in 1581, Ridley had accumulated considerable property in Hampshire, including
the manor of Baybridge, and purchased the manor of
Greane, Worcestershire. His second wife, Margaret,
daughter of Sir William Boleyn, inherited the manor of
Baybridge as well as a lease of the manor of Hoyle in
Middlesex. Ridley died on 23 January 1629. He was buried
at St Benet Paul's Wharf, the Doctors' Commons church,
on 27 January. In his will, proved on 23 January, he
explained that he had already bequeathed much of his
estates to his two daughters by his second wife, Anne and
Elizabeth.   BRIAN P. LEVACK

Sources HoP, *Commons, 1558–1603*, vol. 3 · B. P. Levack, *The civil lawyers in England, 1603–1641* (1973) · G. D. Squibb, *Doctors' Commons: a
history of the College of Advocates and Doctors of Law* (1977) · T. Ridley, *A
view of the civile and ecclesiastical law*, 2nd edn (1634) · Venn, *Alum.
Cant.* · J. Foster and W. H. Rylands, eds., *Grantees of arms named in
docquets and patents to the end of the seventeenth century*, Harleian Society, 66 (1915) · BL, Add. MS 12,496, fol. 115r · J. Foxe, *Actes and monu-
mentes*, 3rd edn, 2 vols. (1576) · W. Prynne, *Canterburies doome* (1644),
186, 218 · will, PRO, PROB 11/155, sig. 19 · will of Thomas Ridley
senior, PRO, PROB 11/32, sig. 12 · D. Lloyd, *State-worthies, or, the
states-men and favourites of England since the Reformation*, 2nd edn
(1670) · DNB
Wealth at death manor of Baybridge; lease of Poyle farm,
Middlesex: will, PRO, PROB 11/155, sig.19

Ridley, William Henry (1816–1882), Church of England
clergyman and author, born on 2 April 1816, was eldest son
of Henry Colborne Ridley (1780–1832), rector of Hambledon, near Henley-on-Thames, a descendant of the Ridleys
of Willimontswick. His mother was Mary, daughter of
James Ferrier of Lincoln's Inn Fields. He matriculated

from Christ Church, Oxford, on 15 May 1834, was a student
1836–41, and graduated BA in 1838 and MA in 1840. He succeeded to the family living of Hambledon on 25 July 1840,
and continued there until his death. He married, on 25
August 1841, Sophia Albertina, second daughter of
Charles Richard *Sumner, bishop of Winchester; they
had an only son, Henry Colborne Mannoir Ridley. In 1859
William Ridley became rural dean of Wycombe, and in
1871 an honorary canon of Christ Church, Oxford.

Ridley was a voluminous writer of theological literature, but many of his publications are only single sermons
and tracts. The latter include two *Plain Tracts on Confirmation* (1844 and 1862), which had a wide circulation. Other
publications of note are those on holy communion (1854;
3rd edn, 1860), the Crimea (1854), clerical incomes (1856),
and India (1857). Ridley was identified with the high-
church party, with a tinge of Tractarianism. He was an
advocate of personal confession. He died at Brighton on 17
February 1882; his wife died on 1 July 1884.

G. C. BOASE, rev. H. C. G. MATTHEW

Sources *The Guardian* (22 Feb 1882), 264 · *The Academy* (25 Feb
1882), 138 · *The Times* (22 Feb 1882)
Wealth at death £16,325 7s. 0d.: probate, 23 March 1882, CGPLA
Eng. & Wales

Ridolfi, Roberto di (1531–1612), merchant and conspirator, was born in Florence, Italy, on 18 November 1531, the
son of Pagnozzo di Giovanfrancesco Ridolfi and Madda-
lena Gondi. The ancient family of Ridolfi di Piazza enjoyed
an impressive heritage of civil service—Roberto's grandfather Giovanfrancesco and two uncles, Lucantonio and
Lodovico, were all Florentine senators. His family also
operated one of the largest banking houses in Florence.
Ridolfi cultivated many mercantile connections with London, settling there about 1562 to become a prosperous
merchant and a leading member of the Italian community in his own right. His employment as a financial agent
on behalf of William Cecil and other statesmen gave the
Florentine a position of influence and credibility at the
English court that for a time helped mask his conspiratorial activities. While he conducted business with protestants, as an ardent Catholic he preferred to socialize with
Catholics.

By the late 1560s Ridolfi's commercial interests had
been eclipsed by politics, and he soon became obsessed
with returning England to the Catholic fold by means of
foreign assistance, which he himself planned to muster.
He developed contacts by supplying information to the
French and Spanish ambassadors in London; he received
pensions from both in return. He also began acting as an
instrument of papal policy, reflected in his role as *nunzio
segreto*, or secret envoy, a designation he held from Pius V
from 1566. Ridolfi is known to have helped smuggle into
England and disseminate some eighty copies of *Regnans in
excelsis*, the papal bull of 1570 excommunicating Elizabeth
I. One of these copies was found nailed to the door of the
residence of the bishop of London on 25 May 1570. His
association with dissatisfied English Catholics resulted in
complicity in the 1569 rising of the northern earls, which

had the dual aims of restoring the ancient worship and releasing the imprisoned Mary Stuart from her captivity in Coventry. Wishing to aid the rebels, Pius V arranged for 12,000 crowns to be forwarded to and distributed by Ridolfi. Rumours of this dispersal brought the Florentine merchant to the attention of the English government, and in October 1569 he was summoned before Francis Walsingham. Ridolfi revealed little upon interrogation except to stress that the money was only an ordinary banking transaction. A suspicious Walsingham detained Ridolfi under house arrest and ordered that the Florentine's house and effects be searched under his own supervision. Nothing incriminating was found, and a month later Elizabeth requested that clemency be shown towards Ridolfi, who was released in January 1570. The leniency of his treatment at the hands of Elizabeth and her ministers has caused some scholars to suggest that during his house arrest Ridolfi was successfully 'turned' by Walsingham into a double agent who subsequently worked for, and not against, the Elizabethan government. Regardless of where his loyalty actually lay, Ridolfi's knowledge of foreign affairs was valuable enough for Cecil and Walsingham to consult him on English relations with Spain and the Low Countries.

While Ridolfi courted those in power at the English court, he continued to strengthen relations with individuals who might support a foreign invasion of England, including John Leslie, bishop of Ross and agent of Mary Stuart. More important, Ridolfi cultivated a relationship with Thomas Howard, duke of Norfolk, cousin to the queen and the highest ranking peer in England. After some persuasion he convinced Norfolk to sign a declaration stating that he was a Catholic and, if backed by Spanish militia, was willing to lead a revolt. Ridolfi also drew up a list of forty peers whom he believed would join the uprising. Mary's approval was acquired through her intermediary, the bishop of Ross. The plan, later to be known as the Ridolfi plot, was soon in place: a Catholic rising was to free Mary and then, with zealous Catholics as well as Spanish forces joining *en route*, bring her to London, where the queen of Scots would supplant Elizabeth. The English queen's ultimate fate was purposely left unclear for the benefit of those with tender consciences. Mary would then secure her throne by marrying Norfolk. The Ridolfi plot was ill conceived in the extreme and has been called 'one of the more brainless conspiracies' of the sixteenth century (Smith, 216). It was also destined to fail due to the personality of its originator, who, although undeniably persuasive, was also indiscreet enough to trumpet his scheme all over Europe.

The conspirators, unaware of Ridolfi's reckless streak, entrusted him to secure support in the guise of money and men from Pius V, Philip II of Spain, and the duke of Alva, governor-general of the Low Countries. Armed with letters from Norfolk and Mary Stuart authorizing him to speak on their behalf, Ridolfi left for the continent in March 1571. The English government was aware of his departure, but not of his intentions. He first arrived at Brussels and met Alva, who thought little of Ridolfi, considering him a 'new man' (*CSP Spain, 1568–79*, 133). Alva thought even less of his estimate of 8000 Spanish troops, a number he deemed inadequate to launch a rising. Ridolfi's reception in Rome was quite different, for Pius proved enthusiastic about any scheme to rid England of a protestant ruler. The pope immediately wrote letters to Mary Stuart and Philip declaring his support. Ridolfi also was warmly welcomed at the Spanish court. Philip invited the Florentine to a council meeting, where the pros and cons of Spanish involvement in the plot were discussed in detail. While the subject of Elizabeth I's assassination was raised, the Spanish did not sanction any such undertaking.

An excited Ridolfi wrote to the bishop of Ross and Mary Stuart in cipher and related his perceived success, but it was too late. While he was travelling through Europe his plot was uncovered by the English government. First, Ridolfi had been remarkably vocal about his mission. During his stay in Florence he told Grand Duke Cosimo (I) de' Medici, who immediately warned Elizabeth. Second, the English became aware of the plot as early as two weeks after Ridolfi's departure from England. At that time, a servant of Mary Stuart and the bishop of Ross named Charles Bailly had been arrested upon his arrival at Dover. A search of his baggage revealed that Bailly was carrying banned books as well as ciphered correspondence about the plot between Norfolk and his brother-in-law Lord Lumley. Another break came with the arrest of two of Norfolk's secretaries, who were conveying £600 in gold to Mary's Scottish supporters. The discovery of the money brought about the arrest of Ross and others, as well as the detainment, trial for treason, and execution of Norfolk.

Upon hearing of the unravelling of the plot, Ridolfi wrote to Mary from Paris on 30 September 1571, stating his inability to return to England. He nevertheless tried to resuscitate interest from his patrons, but was met on all sides with utter lack of interest. In a later memorial Ridolfi complained that the English government had confiscated his goods, which were valued at nearly £3000. After the death of Pius V he returned to his native Florence, where his expertise resulted in his employment by Grand Duke Francesco (I) de' Medici as one of his agents in Rome. In 1575 he was sent on a special embassy to Portugal and Spain on behalf of the grand duke. He held various administrative offices in Tuscany, including commissioner of Arezzo and governor of both Pisa and Pistoia, and he was appointed senator in 1600. Ridolfi died in Florence on 18 February 1612.

L. E. HUNT

Sources CSP dom., 1547–80 · CSP for., 1569–71 · CSP Rome, 1558–78 · CSP Scot. ser., 1589–1603, 905 · CSP Spain, 1568–79 · C. Roth, 'Roberto Ridolfi e la sua congiura', Rivista degli Archivi Toscani (April–June 1930), 119–27 · A. M. Crinò, 'Un altro memoriale inedito di Roberto Ridolfi', Fatti e figure del Seicento anglo-toscano: documenti inediti sui rapporti letterari, diplomatici e culturali fra Toscana e Inghilterra (Florence, 1957), 67–79 · F. Edwards, The marvellous chance: Thomas Howard, fourth duke of Norfolk, and the Ridolphi plot, 1570–1572 (1968) · J. H. Pollen, The English Catholics in the reign of Queen Elizabeth (1920) · 'Roberto Ridolfi', Enciclopedia Cattolica, 13 vols. (1949–54), 10.892–3 ·

N. Williams, *Thomas Howard, fourth duke of Norfolk* (1964) • L. Baldwin Smith, *The Elizabethan epic* (1969)

Archives Archivio di Stato, Florence, mediceo del principato

Ridpath, George (*d.* 1726), journalist and pamphleteer, may have been born in Berwickshire, the son of George Readpath, though further details of his origins are unknown. He remained with his mother at Colbrandspath, Berwickshire, where he was educated until he went to Edinburgh University. The name George Ridpath is listed as one of the graduates from Edinburgh in 1699 (*Catalogue of Edinburgh Graduates*, 1858, 163). In 1680–81 he was tutor, or servant, to the sons of a Mr Gray in Edinburgh and during this period engaged in anti-Catholic activities in the town. Robert Wodrow states that Ridpath 'had been very active in the project' of the 'boys of the college of Edinburgh' to burn an effigy of the pope on 25 December 1680 (Wodrow, *History of the Sufferings*, 3.344). He appears to have been a ringleader in these events as he was apprehended and imprisoned 'the very day before the design was to be executed' (ibid., 3.345). Then 'entering upon his philosophy' and a 'youth of promising genius', Ridpath was 'very hardly treated' for his part in these actions, receiving a beating from council servants (ibid.). He was kept in chains for some days, during which time he maintained that he was suffering for the protestant religion. Eventually charged with threatening to burn the provost's house, after five weeks' imprisonment he was banished from the country for, according to Wodrow, 'no other cause than his accession to this matter' (ibid.). He thereafter abandoned his plans to become a minister of the Church of Scotland and instead moved to London to earn his living by writing.

In 1687 Ridpath published a new method of shorthand, *Shorthand yet Shorter* (2nd edn, 1696), with a dedication to Philip, Lord Wharton, under whose roof the book had been written while Ridpath was 'one of his lordship's domestics'. The author also gave oral lessons in shorthand. Soon after the revolution of 1688 Ridpath became active as a journalist in the capital. Writing under the pseudonym Will Laick, in 1693 he made a violent attack on the episcopal party in Scotland in *An Answer to the Scottish Presbyterian Eloquence* and *A Continuation of the Answer*. These were criticized, with equal virulence, in Alexander Munro's *Apology for the Clergy of Scotland* and *The spirit of calumny and slander examined, chastised, and exposed, in a letter to a malicious libeller … addressed to Mr George Ridpath, newsmonger, near St Martins-in-the-Fields*, which identified Ridpath as 'the head of the presbyterian party in Scotland'. Ridpath subsequently responded in *The Scots Episcopal Innocence* and *The queries and protestation of the Scots clergy against the authority of the Presbyterian general assemblies* (both 1694). Two years later he was apparently involved in surveillance activities against the bishop of Glasgow and Alexander Munro.

Ridpath's next publications continued his defence of Presbyterianism: a translation of Sir Thomas Craig's *Scotland's Sovereignty Asserted* (1695), dedicated to the secretary of state, James Johnston; *Dialogue between Jack and Will, Concerning the Lord Mayor's Going to the Meeting-Houses* (1698),

defending the Presbyterian lord mayor, Sir Humphry Edwin; and in the previous year a translation of De Souligné's *Political Mischiefs of Popery*. In the wake of the failure of the Darien scheme and a growing crisis in Anglo-Scottish relations, Ridpath's writing came increasingly to focus on political matters, the author aligning himself with James Johnston in the production of a 'country party propaganda in support of the opposition's various schemes' (Riley, *King William*, 135). In *Scotland's Grievances Relating to Darien, Humbly Offered to the Consideration of the Parliament* (1700) he complained about external interference in the project at a time when the issue aroused intense political debate in the Scottish parliament. An anonymous pamphlet of the same year, *An Enquiry into the Causes of the Miscarriage of the Scots Colony at Darien*, has also often been attributed to Ridpath. In 1701 he extended his scope in his *Great Reasons and Interests Considered anent the Spanish Monarchy*, which considered the Spanish succession crisis and fears over the potential dynastic unification of the French and Spanish monarchies. By the following year Ridpath's focus was again Anglo-Scottish relations. His *Discourse upon the Union of Scotland and England … by a Lover of his Country* (1702) was critical of the benefits of union and of discussions held between the two governments from November 1702 to February 1703. Later in 1703 he gave the domestic crisis in Anglo-Scottish relations an important imperial and colonial dimension in *The Case of Scotsmen Residing in England and in the English Plantations*. Other pamphlets written at this time include a study of the historic powers of the Scottish parliament and *An Account of the Proceedings of the Parliament of Scotland*, detailing the turbulent session of the previous year. In 1704–5 he assisted James Anderson in the preparation of his *Historical Essay Showing that the Crown and Kingdom of Scotland is Imperial and Independent*. Ridpath also aroused controversy with his *Reducing of Scotland by Arms and Annexing it to England as a Province, Considered* (1705), a retrospective account of Anglo-Scottish relations since the dynastic union of 1603 in which he listed the supposed wrongs inflicted by England and considered the possibility of an English invasion of Scotland. According to one criticism of this account, *Remarks upon a Late Dangerous Pamphlet*, Ridpath's comments resulted in himself and his publisher being bound over to appear at the queen's bench bar. In the same year he also began a correspondence with the young historian Robert Wodrow in which both men expressed their mutual fears about the safety and future of Presbyterianism in the event of political union.

After the Union, Ridpath's energies were in part redirected towards matters religious. According to a note in the Advocates' Library, Edinburgh, Ridpath (along with William Carstares and Daniel Defoe) was responsible for *The Scots Representations to Her Majesty Against Setting up the Common Prayer Book in Scotland* (1711) and for *The Oath of Abjuration Considered*, written in 1712 after the oath's imposition on all ministers after the Toleration Act. This period also saw Ridpath contributing to several journals, including *History of the Works of the Learned* and *Medley*, as well as inventing the polygraphy—a writing engine moved by the foot by which one author could produce six copies—and engaging in furious debates with Abel Roper's tory *Post Boy.*

For some years Ridpath had also conducted a rival whig title, the *Flying-Post, or, Postman,* established in 1695. On 4 September 1712 William Hurt was arrested for printing in the paper scandalous and seditious reflections on Queen Anne and the Harley ministry. Ridpath was committed to Newgate on 8 September for being the author of three libels in the *Observator,* to which he became a contributor in succession to John Tutchin in 1712, and also in the *Flying-Post.* After being released on 23 October, he and Hurt appeared in the court of the queen's bench when their bail was extended. The tory satirist Jonathan Swift—one of Ridpath's frequent targets—damned the 'Scotch rogue' who continued to write following his release (Swift, *Journal to Stella,* ed. H. Williams, 1948, 2.568). On 19 February 1713 Ridpath was tried at the Guildhall in a case that quickly became a party political contest between the tories, who dominated the bench, and the whigs, whose new members were requested to donate 2 guineas to a fund in support of Ridpath. After an eight-hour trial the defendant was found guilty of two of the libels but avoided his sentence by fleeing London first for Scotland and then for the Netherlands.

Living in Rotterdam by 1713, Ridpath was, according to Swift, celebrated by the *Dutch Gazetteer* as 'one of the best pens in England' (*The Publick Spirit of the Whigs,* 1714, 1, quoted in *Swift's Political Tracts, 1713–1719,* ed. H. Davis and I. Ehrenpreis, 1953). In that year he published *Some thoughts concerning the peace and a series of observations on the address of the highlanders to Queen Anne* and prompted a retort in the form of *The honourable chieftains of the highland clans vindicated from the false aspersions … by Ridpath, the scandalous and justly condemned libeller.* In the following year Ridpath produced a more substantial, triumphalist study, *Parliamentary Right Maintained, or, The Hanoverian Succession Justified* in response to *Hereditary Right to the Crown of England Asserted* (attributed to Hilkiah Bedford). Ridpath returned to England after the accession of George I, and was made one of the patentees for serving the commissioners of the customs in Scotland with stationery wares. During 1717 he advised Robert Wodrow, who was then preparing his *History of the Sufferings of the Church of Scotland* and was himself proposing to write a continuation of George Buchanan's *History of Scotland.* Further anti-tory and anti-Jacobite attacks were levelled against rival journalists such as Nathaniel Mist. In Alexander Pope's view, 'To Dulness Ridpath is as clear as Mist' (*Dunciad,* 1.208).

In late 1722 and early 1723 Ridpath fell under the suspicion of the Hanoverian authorities for his involvement as secretary of a lottery in Harburg, Hanover, an organization which George I denied having authorized. After this date he avoided old friends and was said to be 'under some scandal', which at the time was rumoured to be bigamy. Whether or not the rumours were true, details of only one wife, Esther (*d.* in or after 1726), daughter of George Markland, are known. Ridpath's turning away from his former colleagues was not altogether mourned by those who

knew him: 'His memory is not savoury here. I'm sorry he's so vile, for once he did good service', commented Lord Grange (*Private Letters now First Printed, 1694–1732,* 1829). Ridpath died on 5 February 1726, the same day as his long-time rival Abel Roper. By his will, dated 29 January 1726, his estate passed entirely to Esther, their only son having died in 1706.

G. A. AITKIN, rev. JOHN R. YOUNG

Sources R. Wodrow, *The history of the sufferings of the Church of Scotland from the Restoration to the revolution,* ed. R. Burns, 4 vols. (1828–30) · *Miscellany of the Abbotsford Club* (1838) · *Early letters of Robert Wodrow, 1698–1709,* ed. L. W. Sharp, Scottish History Society, 3rd ser., 24 (1937) · *State papers and letters addressed to William Carstares,* ed. J. M'Cormick (1774) · *The life and errors of John Dunton,* [rev. edn], ed. J. B. Nichols, 2 vols. (1818) · *The Wentworth papers, 1705–1739: selected from the private and family correspondence of Thomas Wentworth, Lord Raby,* ed. J. J. Cartwright (1883) · *The tryal and conviction of Mr George Redpath* (1713) · *Daniel Defoe: his life, and recently discovered writings,* ed. W. Lee, 3 vols. (1869) · BL, Stowe MSS 225–227 · P. W. J. Riley, *King William and the Scottish politicians, 1689–1702* (1979) · P. W. J. Riley, *The Union of England and Scotland* (1978) · W. Ferguson, *Scotland's relations with England: a survey to 1707* (1977) · P. H. Scott, *Andrew Fletcher and the treaty of union* (1992)

Ridpath, George (1716?–1772), Church of Scotland minister and historian, was born at Ladykirk, Berwickshire, the eldest son of the Revd George Ridpath (*c.*1678–1740) and his wife, Ann Watson (*d.* 1765). Although his gravestone gives his birth as 24 November 1716, in his diary Ridpath makes reference to his birthday on 4 January. He had three brothers: Philip [*see below*] and William (1731–1797), like George, followed their father into the church; Thomas (*b.* 1724) may have died in infancy. Of his two sisters, Elizabeth (*b.* 1726) married Mr Waite, a Berwick merchant, while Ann, or Nancy (*b.* 1729), lived with George and their mother in Stichill manse until George's marriage. Ridpath attended Edinburgh University and was friendly with men of letters such as David Hume, William Robertson, and John Home. On 27 May 1740 he was licensed to preach at Chirnside, Berwickshire, and two years later was presented by George II and the earl of Home to the parish of Stichill and Hume. He was ordained on 16 February 1742 and remained there for the rest of his life.

A 'judicious and learned man' (*Fasti Scot.,* 2.475), Ridpath was an avid reader of the classics and of history, and was a member of the subscription library at Kelso. He kept a diary from April 1755 until January 1758 and from March 1758 to July 1761. Entries reveal a keen observer of human nature, a caring, tolerant, but not overly spiritual man. He was very sociable, exchanging frequent visits with colleagues and neighbours and enjoying the pleasures of the table. A friend of the local physician, Ridpath took a keen interest in medicine and was not above prescribing for parishioners who were unwell. His description of watching over his small niece as she died shows him to be a sensitive man, relied upon by his relatives in time of trouble. On 6 September 1764, four years after he had first proposed, he married Wilhelmina (Minna) Dawson (1732–1810), daughter of a Kelso merchant, William Dawson. They had three children: a daughter, Christian (*b.* 1766), George (*b.* 1769), of whom there is no further record, and Ann (*b.* 1770), who died aged ten.

Ridpath's first publication, a sermon entitled *Christian Liberty Opposed to Popish Tyranny and Superstition*, appeared in 1751. He admired the Scots scholar George Buchanan (1506–1582) and intended to write his biography, but abandoned this as impracticable. Instead, in March 1761, he began to compile a history of the borders and three years later announced a proposal for printing it by subscription. He was working on this book when he died, on 31 January 1772 in Stichill manse; he was buried in the kirkyard at Stichill. The history, dedicated to the duke of Northumberland, was edited by his brother Philip and published posthumously in 1776 under the title *The border-history of England and Scotland, deduced from the earliest times to the union of the two crowns*.

Philip Ridpath (1720–1788), Church of Scotland minister, was licensed to preach at Kelso, Roxburghshire, on 2 July 1745. When the Berwickshire parish of Hutton and Fishwick became vacant in 1756, he, supported by his brother George, solicited the help of local people of influence to secure the living. Lord Home considered himself patron of the parish and presented his own candidate, creating a conflict which continued for three years. Finally, the House of Lords decreed that, though Home was patron of Hutton, the king as patron of Fishwick had priority. Ridpath was ordained in May 1759 and his brother William became minister at nearby Edrom a month later. Philip's successor, Adam Landels, described him as 'a man of great worth and learning' (Sinclair, 3.215).

Philip Ridpath married Alison Hume (*d.* 1790) in October 1768; there were apparently no children of the marriage. In 1785 he published *Boethius's Consolation of Philosophy*, a work that his brother George records in his diary as having been begun in 1761. Philip died on 18 May 1788 at the manse at Hutton, Berwickshire; Alison died on 17 August 1790 at Eyemouth, Berwickshire, reportedly of spontaneous combustion.   AUDREY M. C. MITCHELL

Sources *Diary of George Ridpath, 1755–61*, ed. J. Balfour Paul (1922) • *Fasti Scot.*, new edn • *The Scotsman* (13 March 1922) [report on meeting of the Scottish Ecclesiological Society] • A. Jeffrey, *The history and antiquities of Roxburghshire*, 4 vols. (1857–64), 3.127 • P. Ridpath, preface, in G. Ridpath, *The border-history of England and Scotland*, ed. P. Ridpath (1776) • *Scots Magazine*, 34 (1772), 51 • J. Sinclair, *Statistical account of Scotland, 1791–1799*, [new edn], ed. D. J. Withrington and I. R. Grant, 3 (1979), 215 • *N&Q*, 2nd ser., 8 (1859), 227 • Watt, *Bibl. Brit.* • 'Ridpath, Rev. Philip', Allibone, *Dict.* • gravestone, kirkyard, Hutton, Berwickshire [P. Ridpath] • gravestone, kirkyard, Stitchell, Roxburghshire

Archives NA Scot., MSS journals, CH1/5/122–3

Ridpath, Philip (1720–1788). *See under* Ridpath, George (1716?–1772).

Rie [*née* Gomperz], **Dame Lucie** (1902–1995), potter, was born on 16 March 1902 in Vienna, the third and last child of Professor Benjamin Gomperz (1861–1936), an ear, nose, and throat specialist, and his wife, Gisela (1873–1937), daughter of Ignaz Wolf and his wife, Hermine. The Wolfs were a prominent Eisenstadt family whose fortune was based on wine production. The Gomperz family, too, was prosperous and Lucie's childhood was spent between their home in the Falkstrasse and the Wolfs' country

Dame Lucie Rie (1902–1995), by Hans Coper, *c*.1953

house at Eisenstadt. She was educated by a private tutor. Through her father, a friend of Sigmund Freud, and her uncle, the collector and Zionist historian Sandor Wolf, she was also in touch with the rich intellectual life of early twentieth-century Vienna. After contemplating a medical career she decided instead to enter the Kunstgewerbeschule, the art school attached to the Wiener Werkstätte, in 1922. There she was, she said, instantly 'lost' to the potter's wheel. She was taught by Michael Powolny, whose strengths as a ceramist were technical rather than aesthetic. Her work was nevertheless noticed by the co-founder of the Werkstätte, Joseph Hoffmann, who sent her pots to the Exposition des Arts Decoratifs et Modernes in Paris in 1925.

Over the next decade she developed her own style. She herself later said in an interview with the author that the work of these years was 'hardly at all important', but critics have disagreed (*The Guardian*, 31 Aug 1988). She combined a plain, modernist aesthetic with the technical daring that Powolny had encouraged in her, somewhat perversely, by telling her she would never be able to imitate ancient glazes. She used earthenware, raw glazing the pots, that is applying glaze to unfired clay. This ancient but difficult technique was at first a practical necessity as she had no kiln of her own and had to transport her work some distance to fire it. Raw glazing became, however, an essential feature of her pottery; form and glaze fused in a single firing. She was then, as always, interested in pots 'for the house'. Whether functional or decorative, her work was always concerned with the domestic interior.

In 1926 Lucie married Hans Rie (1901–1985), a young

businessman who worked in the Brüder Bohm hat factory. He was one of the Gomperz family circle, an easy-going man but with little in common with his wife beyond a fondness for skiing. The marriage never really took and Lucie Rie devoted herself increasingly to her work. She also became close to the architect Ernst Plishke, giving him one of his first commissions designing furniture for her apartment.

By 1938 Rie's refusal to take seriously the 'stupidity' of Nazism was no longer tenable. She and her husband escaped to England intending to move on to the United States. Her decision to stay in London, alone, determined the course of the rest of her life and work. She moved into a house in Albion Mews, Bayswater, where Freud's son, Ernst, adapted the interior for the Plischke furniture she had brought with her. Hans Rie went on to America and the couple were amicably divorced.

Rie found England stimulating after Vienna but not immediately receptive to her work. Her reputation had not reached England, and the revival of studio pottery there was dominated by Bernard Leach. The two became friends, but his heavier oriental and rustic aesthetic exerted an unhelpful influence on Rie at first. She later learned to take his advice selectively. The gallery owner Muriel Rose and William Honey, keeper of ceramics at the Victoria and Albert Museum, were early supporters. The prevailing mood in England was encouraging. There was an eagerness for design reform, cast in an English Arts and Crafts tradition, with an emphasis on the individual maker and on the social and moral value of craftsmanship. Rie benefited from this, but her own work remained cosmopolitan, urban, and informed by a view of craftsmanship rooted in architecture.

During and after the Second World War Rie made earthenware buttons and jewellery of great, if simple, charm. To these were added, in the mid- to late 1940s, a range of domestic wares. They included salad bowls pulled into oval shapes, their slight but decisive variations on conventional form showing how her strong formal intelligence could work easily within the limits of function.

In 1946 Hans *Coper (1920–1981), also a refugee from Nazi Germany, and trained as a textile engineer, came to Rie's studio looking for work. She taught him to make pottery and the two were soon working side by side. Coper counteracted the influence of Leach on Rie, who always regarded her former pupil as being in a higher category than herself. 'I am a potter', she said in the same interview, 'but he was an artist' (*The Guardian*, 31 Aug 1988). The two shared a workshop until 1958 and although their styles remained distinct the effect of each was critical on the other. Their friendship lasted until Coper's death in 1981.

In 1948 Rie acquired an electric kiln and began to make stoneware and porcelain in which a greater range of glaze effects was possible. It was from this point that she began to create the work that made her reputation. She continued to produce domestic ware as well as one-off pieces. She insisted that all her work was functional, yet a strongly sculptural sense of form runs through it. After a

visit to Avebury, Wiltshire, in 1948 she was inspired by prehistoric pots to use sgraffito in her own work. In this and in her use of subtly contrasting white glazes her work can be related to contemporary English abstraction, particularly the work of Ben Nicholson and Barbara Hepworth.

Recognition of Rie's work accrued slowly but steadily. She showed pots at the Festival of Britain in 1951 and in 1967 an Arts Council exhibition of her work established her importance in a broader context. It marked the acceptance of a potter whose work, as George Wingfield Digby wrote in the catalogue, went against the national grain by having 'no nostalgic undertones of folk art'. The following year she was made OBE, and in 1969 she received an honorary doctorate from the Royal College of Art. She was promoted CBE in 1981 and DBE in 1990.

Rie's work continued to develop. The flared bottle forms that are among her most characteristic pieces emerged only in the 1960s. These were thrown in two pieces and, after 1967, sometimes made with two clays, creating a spiral pattern within the body of the pot. Formally she drew on almost every ceramic tradition but depended on none. The qualities most often cited in relation to her work—restraint, elegance, and clarity—are not infrequently countered by moments of exuberance, even brashness in pink and turquoise volcanic glazes. In contrast to Coper she was prolific. Not every piece was a success and the standard of the work she chose to exhibit was sometimes uneven.

Rie never remarried. She had several close friendships with men over the years but she continued to live and work alone at Albion Mews. Although she was disparaging about Vienna and the Viennese she always retained the formal, somewhat severe manners she learned in childhood. She never lost her Austrian accent or her appetite for intellectual conversation, although she declined to discuss her own work in theoretical terms. 'I make pots, it's my profession', was her typical way of closing the subject.

Rie's standards were inflexible. She was too rigorous to be sympathetic to students, although she was a part-time tutor at the Camberwell School of Arts and Crafts from 1960 to 1971. As a member of the Design Council she caused embarrassment by rejecting the work of the potter Michael Cardew, and when collecting her OBE insignia she was disappointed by the standard of conversation at Buckingham Palace. She remained elegant, even pretty, into old age. Her somewhat steely courtesy did not preclude humour or warmth. She had a circle of close friends and always made time for anyone who took a serious interest in pottery.

Rie continued to exhibit and to work into her late eighties. In 1989 the Japanese fashion designer Issey Miyake arranged an exhibition of her pots alongside his own sculptural clothes in Tokyo and Osaka. Rie's work sat naturally with Miyake's. Despite the generations that separated them both were playing similarly on form and texture at the limits of tradition and function. After a series of strokes she was finally forced to stop working in the early

1990s. Lucie Rie died at her home, 18 Albion Mews, on 1 April 1995 and was cremated. Examples of her work are in the Victoria and Albert Museum, London, Dartington Hall, Devon, and Paisley Museum and Art Gallery.

ROSEMARY HILL

Sources T. Birks, *Lucie Rie* (1987) · T. Harrod, *Crafts*, 135 (1995), 42–7 · 'Hands on the wheel of fate', *The Guardian* (31 Aug 1988) [interview] · M. Coatts, *Lucie Rie and Hans Coper: potters in parallel* (1997) [exhibition catalogue, Barbican Art Gallery, London, February–May, 1997] · J. Houston and D. Cripps, *Lucie Rie* (1981) · Gallerie Besson, *Lucie Rie: 90th birthday exhibition* (1992) [exhibition catalogue, Galerie Besson, London] · personal knowledge (2004) · private information (2004) [Y. Mayer and M. Coatts] · *The Times* (3 April 1995)
Archives West Surrey College of Art and Design, Farnham, Crafts Study Centre | FILM probably NFTA, David Attenborough's documentary film (for television)
Likenesses H. Coper, bronze head, *c*.1953, priv. coll.; Bonhams, 13 June 1990, lot 202 [*see illus.*] · photographs, repro. in Birks, *Lucie Rie*

Riel, Louis David (1844–1885), leader of the métis in Canada, was born in St Vital parish, Red River colony (later Manitoba, Canada), on 22 October 1844, the first child of Louis Riel (1817–1864), a farmer and businessman of Red River, and his wife, Julie Lagimodière (*b.* 1822). Since his father was one-fourth native, Riel was one-eighth native. He grew up as part of the métis community. After early schooling in Red River, in 1858 he was sent to the Sulpician college in Montreal to study for the priesthood. He was gifted and performed well academically until 1865, when he began to flout rules and was expelled from the college. After a year without employment he studied law with a prominent radical lawyer and politician, but never completed his studies. After being severely disappointed in his desire to marry a non-native woman when her parents forbade the match, Riel left Montreal in mid-1866 and, apparently, wandered until he returned to Red River in July 1868.

Riel's return coincided with the emergence of crisis among the métis. In acquiring Rupert's Land from the Hudson's Bay Company, Canada failed to consult the local inhabitants about terms for annexing the region, and the Roman Catholic métis in particular felt insecure about their cultural institutions and customary land rights. Riel emerged as the leader of a resistance to Canada in the winter of 1869–70 that culminated in the negotiated entry of the region as the province of Manitoba in 1870. In the course of the resistance, a young Ontario Orangeman was put to death by the métis under Riel's leadership, and this miscalculation was to haunt Riel.

Although he expected praise for defending his community's interests, Riel soon found himself rebuffed and hunted. His disappointment was compounded by his failure to take a seat in parliament, to which he was elected several times, for fear of prosecution in eastern Canada. In the mid-1870s he travelled in the eastern states and Quebec, until in 1875 he succumbed to mental illness that led to his committal twice to asylums. At the time Riel believed he had received a mission from God to revitalize the Roman Catholic church in North America and to develop western Canada as a homeland for the world's oppressed. At this time he adopted the Biblical name David in acknowledgement that he was the 'Prophet of the New World'. In later years Riel would claim that he feigned madness to escape his persecutors by hospitalization, though he never abandoned his sense of divine mission.

After his discharge from asylum in 1878, Riel made his way to the American west. In 1875 the Canadian government had amnestied him for his role in the 1869–70 resistance on the condition that he endure five years' banishment from British territory. Riel eventually made his way to Montana, where he farmed and taught at a mission school. In April 1881 he married the métisse Marguerite Monet, called Bellehumeur, with whom he had a son, Jean, and a daughter, Marie-Angélique. However, he continued to believe in his mission, and as part of that he attempted unsuccessfully in 1879–80 to persuade Canada-based native leaders to join him in a campaign to conquer western Canada. He also became involved in territorial politics on behalf of the republicans, and in 1883 he became an American citizen.

During the summer of 1884 Riel and his family journeyed north to the Saskatchewan district in response to an invitation from a number of groups who had grievances with the Canadian government. The most important group among those who sought his help were the métis, whose complaints concerning lands received unsatisfactory responses from Canada. Their invitation to Riel was to lead a movement of peaceful protest, and for many months he did, culminating in a lengthy petition to the federal capital in December 1884.

As Canada failed to react, and then in March 1885 responded ineffectually, Riel veered from the peaceful path towards insurrection. Violence broke out on 26 March when armed métis clashed with mounted police near Duck Lake. Before the north-west rebellion was over in late spring, the métis had engaged in battles with Canadian police and militia at Fish Creek and Batoche. In addition, there were a number of minor assaults on European Canadians by groups of Indians, although the Indian nations collectively did not rise in support of the métis rebellion. The upshot of the affair was that Riel was tried for high treason in the summer of 1885. Although he rejected his lawyers' arguments that he should be acquitted for reason of insanity, Riel did not persuade the jury that he was innocent because rebellion was justified by government neglect. In spite of a jury recommendation for clemency, Riel was hanged at Regina gaol, Regina, Northwest Territories, on 16 November 1885 and interred on 12 December in the grounds of the basilica at St Boniface, in the heart of what had been the Red River colony.

In death Riel has been at least as controversial as he was in life. Historians have debated his motivation and contribution to Canadian history almost from the day he died. Defenders such as Sprague emphasize the government's culpability and depict Riel as the worthy champion of mistreated peoples. An interpretation developed by Flanagan in the 1970s stressed Riel's providential mission and portrayed him as a typical millenarian leader thrown up by a community experiencing dislocation. Scholars from the métis groups, such as Adams and McLean, cast Riel as the leader of native defence against Canadian government attack.

Politically, Riel has also been a focal point since his death. Nationalist francophones in Quebec seized on his fate immediately in 1886 and treated it as an example of the English-Canadian intolerance that threatened the distinctiveness of Quebec. Western regional politicians have emphasized his supposed role as a defender of prairie interests against eastern neglect. And radical students in the 1960s adopted Riel as a symbol of their causes, too. He has also been the subject of numerous stories, such as that by Rosenstock and Adair (1979), television movies, such as *Riel* by Roy Moore in 1978, and even an opera—*Louis Riel*, by Harry Somers (1975). In death, as in life, Louis Riel continues to fascinate many Canadians, while infuriating some.   J. R. MILLER

Sources G. F. G. Stanley, *Louis Riel* (Toronto, 1963) · T. Flanagan, *Louis 'David' Riel: prophet of the New World* (1979) · L. H. Thomas, 'Riel, Louis', *DCB*, vol. 11 · M. Siggins, *Riel: a life of revolution* (1994) · G. F. G. Stanley, *Louis Riel: patriot or rebel?* (1961) · G. F. G. Stanley, *The birth of western Canada: a history of the Riel rebellions* (1936) · G. Friesen, *The Canadian prairies: a history* (1984) · T. Flanagan, *Riel and the rebellion: 1885 reconsidered* (1983) · D. Owram, 'The myth of Louis Riel', *Canadian Historical Review*, 63 (1982), 286–97 · J. R. Miller, 'From Riel to the métis', *Canadian Historical Review*, 69 (1988), 1–20 · J. R. Miller, *Skyscrapers hide the heavens: a history of Indian–white relations in Canada* (1989) · H. Adams, *Prison of grass: Canada from the native point of view* (1975) · D. McLean, *1885: métis rebellion or government conspiracy?* (1985) · D. N. Sprague, *Canada and the métis, 1869–1885* (1988) · J. Rosenstock and D. Adair, *Riel* (1979) · T. Flanagan, *Louis Riel* (1992)
Archives NA Canada · Provincial Archives of Manitoba, Winnipeg | Archiepiscopal Archives of St Boniface, Manitoba, Taché MSS · NA Canada, Sir John A. Macdonald MSS
Likenesses portrait, *c.*1858, Archives de la Société historique de St Boniface, 0321 · portrait, 1864, NA Canada, C-1532 · portrait, 1869–70, Saskatchewan Archives Board, Regina, Saskatchewan, R-B684 · Notman Studios, portrait, 1873, NA Canada, C-2048 · portrait, *c.*1873–1874, Saskatchewan Archives Board, Regina, Saskatchewan, R-A2305 · portrait, *c.*1883, Saskatchewan Archives Board, Regina, Saskatchewan, R-A5680 · portrait, May 1885, Saskatchewan Archives Board, Regina, Saskatchewan, R-B2060 · portrait, Aug 1885, Saskatchewan Archives Board, Regina, Saskatchewan, R-B750 · wood-engraving (after sketch by H. de H. Haig), NPG; repro. in *ILN* (27 June 1885)

Rieu, Charles Pierre Henri (1820–1902), orientalist, born at Geneva on 8 June 1820, was the son of Jean Louis Rieu, first syndic of Geneva, whose memoirs he edited in 1870. His mother was Marie Lasserre. On leaving school, in November 1835 Rieu entered the Académie de Genève, where he studied philosophy and science. At Geneva he first took up oriental languages and became the pupil of Jean Humbert, who had studied under the French orientalist Sylvestre de Sacy. In 1840 Rieu proceeded to the University of Bonn, where he was inscribed in the philosophical faculty. There he read Sanskrit and Arabic, and at the same time acquired a thorough knowledge of German. On the completion of his studies in 1843 he received the degree of PhD and published his thesis, entitled *De Abul-Alae poetae arabici vita et carminibus secundum codices Leidanos et Parisiensem commentatio*. After a visit to Paris, where he

was elected a member of the Société Asiatique on 8 November 1844, he moved to St Petersburg; there, with Otto Boehtlingk, he edited with notes in German the text of 'Hemakandra's Abhidhânakíntâmani' or Sanskrit dictionary (1847). During this work he visited Oxford for the purpose of transcribing a unique manuscript in the Bodleian Library.

In 1847 Rieu settled in London and was appointed supernumerary assistant in the department of manuscripts at the British Museum, where in 1867 he became first holder of the office of keeper of oriental manuscripts. He was responsible for the second part of the *Catalogus codicum manuscriptorum orientalium* (1871), of which the first part (1846) had been compiled by William Cureton. These were followed by the *Catalogue of Persian Manuscripts* (3 vols., 1879–83; suppl., 1895), the *Catalogue of Turkish Manuscripts* (1888), and the Arabic supplement (1894). These seven volumes were seen as a monumental achievement which confirmed Rieu's position as an orientalist of the first rank, his reputation based on his distinction as a scholar no less than on his helpfulness as a curator.

In 1871 Rieu married Agnes Hisgen, the daughter of Julius Heinrich Hisgen; they had five sons and two daughters, the translator Emile Victor *Rieu (1887–1972) being their youngest child. Rieu was also for many years professor of Arabic and Persian at University College, London. On the jubilee of his doctorate, 6 September 1893, he received a congratulatory address from the University of Bonn. In 1894, notwithstanding his advanced age, he was elected by invitation to Sir Thomas Adam's professorship of Arabic at Cambridge, in succession to William Robertson Smith. He resigned his post at the museum in 1895, and died at his home, 28 Woburn Square, London, on 19 March 1902, after a brief illness.

G. S. WOODS, *rev.* NILANJANA BANERJI

Sources *The Times* (21 March 1902) · *The Athenaeum* (29 March 1902), 405 · E. G. Browne, 'Professor Charles Rieu', *Journal of the Royal Asiatic Society of Great Britain and Ireland* (1902), 718–21 · private information (1912)
Wealth at death £1458 10*s.* 8*d.*: administration, 18 June 1902, CGPLA Eng. & Wales

Rieu, Emile Victor (1887–1972), literary scholar and translator, was born in London on 10 February 1887, the fifth son and seventh and youngest child of Charles Pierre Henri *Rieu (1820–1902), of Geneva, keeper of oriental manuscripts at the British Museum, and later professor of Arabic at Cambridge, and of his wife, Agnes, daughter of Julius Heinrich Hisgen, of Utrecht. Rieu held scholarships at St Paul's School and Balliol College, Oxford, and took a first in classical honour moderations (1908). After a year's travel abroad for health reasons, he left Oxford.

Rieu joined the Oxford University Press in 1910 and in 1912 was appointed manager in India with instructions to open a branch in Bombay. In 1914 he married Nelly, daughter of Henry Thomas Lewis, businessman, of Pembrokeshire; they had two sons and two daughters. He was commissioned in the 105th Maratha light infantry in 1918, but returned to his work in Bombay in 1919, and left India the same year after repeated attacks of malaria.

Emile Victor Rieu (1887–1972), by Walter Bird, 1957

In 1923 Rieu became educational manager of Methuen & Co. and held the post with distinction, editing the Methuen's Modern Classics series (with Peter Wait), for which he compiled two volumes of *Essays by Modern Masters* (1926, 1934). He was promoted to managing director in 1933, but was less happy in this post and resigned in 1936, though he remained an academic and literary adviser to the firm, editing (again with Wait) *Modern Masters of Wit and Laughter* (1938), and returning to full-time work in 1940. He also served as a major in the Home Guard from 1944.

Only after 1936 did Rieu truly fulfil his promise as a classical scholar, though he had edited a well-chosen textbook anthology (*A Book of Latin Poetry*) for Methuen in 1925. He formed the habit of translating aloud to his wife, and her interest in the *Odyssey* encouraged him to start polishing and writing his version. After the interruptions of the war years he offered it to Allen Lane, the owner of Penguin Books. Despite his editorial board's initial reservations about Rieu's lack of scholarly experience and the financial viability of the proposed translation, Lane published Rieu's *Odyssey* in 1946 (early copies misdated 1945). Penguin's editor-in-chief, William Emrys Williams, observed that Rieu had 'made a good book better' (Morpurgo, 216), and the *Odyssey* became the first of a new series, Penguin Classics in Translation, which Rieu edited until his retirement in 1964.

Rieu went on to translate the *Pastoral Poems of Virgil* (1949), the *Iliad* (1950), and Apollonius Rhodius's *Argonautica* as *The Voyage of Argo* (1959). All exemplified his firm belief that translation should be into contemporary but not too topical prose, readily intelligible to all. This approach certainly played an important part in the remarkable success of Penguin Classics. By 1964 the *Odyssey* had sold over 2 million copies, and the translations numbered 200. Rieu had sometimes appeared uneasy in business relations, but the growing prestige of Penguin Classics, and the satisfaction he derived from it, made him a relaxed and genial editor who inspired affection and respect from his translators.

Despite his family's Franco-Swiss background, Rieu could seem very much an Englishman of his generation in his attachment to British institutions; he was proud to be both a British subject and a citizen of Geneva. At the age of sixty, Rieu embraced the Anglican church, and went on to prepare his translation of *The Four Gospels* (1952), and to sit on the joint churches' committee for the *New English Bible*.

Although basically serious in his temperament and beliefs, Rieu delighted in verbal wit, and wrote light verse in the best English tradition: *Cuckoo Calling* was published in 1933 and reissued with additional poems in 1962 as *The Flattered Flying Fish, and other Poems*. His output was modest but well crafted, and a selection was included in *A Puffin Quartet of Poets* in 1958.

Rieu took unaffected pleasure in the public honours of his later years, perhaps as the result of his early academic disappointment. He was made an honorary LittD (Leeds) in 1949, and appointed CBE in 1953, and was happy in his recognition by the Royal Society of Literature, of which he was a fellow from 1951, vice-president in 1958, and recipient of the Benson silver medal in 1968. He was also president of the Virgil Society in 1951 and was awarded the golden jubilee medal of the Institute of Linguists in 1971. Rieu died in his home, 31 Hurst Avenue, London, on 11 May 1972.

P. J. CONNELL

Sources *The Times* (13 May 1972) · J. E. Morpurgo, *Allen Lane, King Penguin: a biography* (1979) · 'E. V. Rieu', *Proceedings of the Virgil Society*, 12 (1972–3), 57 · DNB · CGPLA Eng. & Wales (1972)
Archives Royal Society of Literature, London, letters to the Royal Society of Literature
Likenesses R. Moynihan, group portrait, 1955–6 (*After the Conference*), repro. in Morpurgo, *Allen Lane* · W. Bird, photograph, 1957, NPG [*see illus.*] · W. Stoneman, photograph, 1957, NPG
Wealth at death £77,604: probate, 17 Oct 1972, CGPLA Eng. & Wales

Rievaulx, Ailred of. *See* Ailred of Rievaulx (1110–1167).

Rigaud, John Francis (1742–1810), history and decorative painter, was born at Turin, Piedmont, on 18 May 1742 and baptized on 9 September 1742 at the protestant church of La Tour in the valley of Lucerne in Piedmont, the second son of James Dutilh or Rigaud (1705–1764), merchant of Turin, and his wife, Jeanne Françoise, *née* Guiraudet (d. 1744). His paternal grandfather, Jacques Dutilh (1655–1705), was a descendant of an ancient family of Clairac, Guyenne, and a merchant at Lyons, who married Elizabeth, daughter of Jean Rigaud, a merchant of Crest in Dauphiné. Jacques Dutilh, a protestant, fled with his wife to Geneva after the revocation of the edict of Nantes but died *en route*. His wife then assumed her maiden name, by which their son was also known.

Rigaud was intended to share his father's commercial business, but showing artistic abilities was placed with Chevalier Beaumont of Turin, historical painter to the king of Sardinia. Leaving his master, he travelled in Italy, visiting Florence and Bologna, where he was made a member of the Accademia Clementina in 1766. He then went to Rome, but was recalled to Turin for family reasons. He left Turin again in January 1768, travelling to Piacenza, Parma, and Bologna before settling in Rome in February. He was then occupied with studying in the city's life-drawing schools and copying old masters. He also produced a life-scale picture of *Hercules Resting from his Labours*, which he considered one of his most important works. In Rome he struck up friendships with a number of artists, notably the Swedish sculptor Johan Tobias Sergel (1740–1814) and the Irish painter James Barry (1741–1806). In April 1770 he left Rome with Barry, travelling to Florence, Bologna, and Turin. Rigaud then went on to Paris for a short period, before arriving in London in December 1771, bringing with him the *Hercules*, which he exhibited at the Royal Academy in 1772. He was elected an associate of the Royal Academy in November 1772. On 21 July 1774 he married Mary (1740?–1808), second daughter of John Williams of Haverfordwest. They had three daughters and one son, the historical and decorative painter Stephen Francis Dutilh *Rigaud (1777–1861).

Throughout his career, Rigaud exhibited subject pictures and portraits at the Royal Academy, but his most lucrative and engrossing employment was decorative painting for the town and country houses of the nobility, including Lord Gower, Lord Sefton, and the earl of Aylesford. In particular, the architect Sir William Chambers provided him with a number of such commissions, including, in London, work at Lord Melbourne's house in Piccadilly (1772 and 1774) and Somerset House (1780). He also carried out decorative work for the common council chamber of the Guildhall, London (1794), and for Trinity House (1796). These works were all executed in the fashionable Italian style of G. B. Cipriani and Biagio Rebecca, being mostly classical figures and imitations of bas-reliefs. Rigaud also produced historical paintings of classical, literary, and historical subjects, notably the *Entry of the Black Prince into London with his Royal Prisoner* (exh. RA, 1775; Christies, 1955) and a number of pictures for the commercial galleries run by T. Macklin, R. Bowyer, and S. Boydell in the late 1780s. On two occasions he received commissions for religious paintings: a *Descent from the Cross* for the Roman Catholic chapel of the Sardinian embassy in London in 1780, and an *Accession* for St Martin's Outwich in 1797 (both des.). In general, his historical paintings were not well received.

Rigaud produced a large number of portraits, including the group portraits of Francesco Bartolozzi, Agostino Carlini, and G. B. Cipriani, exhibited in 1777 (NPG) and of Sir Joshua Reynolds, Sir William Chambers, and Joseph Wilton, exhibited in 1782 (NPG). In 1781 he painted for Captain W. Locker small portraits of naval heroes, including Nelson (National Maritime Museum, Greenwich). His portraits tend to be strongly characterized and boldly conceived, even occasionally eccentric, such as the picture of *Captain Lunardi with George Biggin and Mrs Sage in a Balloon* (1785; Yale Center for British Art, New Haven). In addition to these mainstream artistic activities, Rigaud also produced transparencies and other paintings for the popular mechanical exhibitions of the time.

Rigaud was elected a Royal Academician on 10 February 1784, presenting a picture of *Samson Breaking his Bands* as his diploma work. Although he never achieved senior office, he served on the council and as a visitor in the life schools on a number of occasions. In 1795, probably by virtue of his old friendship with Sergel, he was appointed historical painter to Gustavus IV of Sweden and was made a member of the Royal Academy of Stockholm. Rigaud and his son were prominent members of the Marylebone Volunteers on their being mustered in 1799.

After 1800 Rigaud's career as a painter seems to have declined. In 1802 his translation of Leonardo da Vinci's *A Treatise on Painting* was published. He became more occupied as a restorer of old decorative work, being employed at Greenwich Hospital and Montague House, London. Rigaud's wife died in 1808 and in his last years he lived with his son. Rigaud died suddenly from apoplexy on 6 December 1810 at Packington Hall, Warwickshire, the seat of Lord Aylesford, and was buried in Packington.

L. H. CUST, rev. MARTIN MYRONE

Sources S. F. D. Rigaud, 'Facts and recollections of the XVIIIth century in a memoir of John Francis Rigaud', ed. W. L. Pressly, *Walpole Society*, 50 (1984), 1–164 · E. Croft-Murray, *Decorative painting in England, 1537–1837*, 2 (1970) · minutes of council, RA · minutes of the General Assembly, RA · *GM*, 1st ser., 80 (1810), 596
Archives RA, papers · Yale U., Beinecke L., memoirs
Likenesses J. F. Rigaud, group portrait, 1782 (with family); [lost]; photograph, National Gallery of Art, Washington, DC · J. F. Rigaud, group portrait, 1784–8 (with family); Christies, 1970 · G. Dance, drawing, 1793, RA · H. Singleton, group portrait, oils (*Royal Academicians*, 1793), RA
Wealth at death £1500: administration, 15 Feb 1811, PRO, PROB 6/187/299

Rigaud, Stephen Francis Dutilh (1777–1861), painter, only son of John Francis *Rigaud (1742–1810), history and portrait painter, and his wife, Mary, *née* Williams (1740?–1808), was born at 44 Great Titchfield Street, London, on 26 December 1777. As related in the father's entry, the family name was originally Dutilh. Stephen Rigaud, father of Stephen Peter Rigaud, future Savilian professor of astronomy at Oxford, was one of his godfathers. A sister, Miss E. A. Rigaud, exhibited watercolour portraits at the Royal Academy from 1797 to 1800. The young Stephen Rigaud was admitted to the Royal Academy Schools in 1792, and in 1794 he won the silver palette from the Society of Arts for a classical group. He won the gold palette for a historical painting in 1799, and in 1801 was awarded the gold medal of the Royal Academy for *Clytemnestra*. In April 1798 he visited the Revd Robert Nixon, rector of Foots Cray, Kent, an accomplished amateur artist and brother of the caricaturist John Nixon. Together with J. M. W. Turner, who is said to have produced his first oil painting at

Nixon's rectory, they made a sketching tour through the county. He also assisted his father with decorative paintings at several locations including the earl of Aylesford's Packington Hall in Warwickshire and Windsor Castle.

In April 1805 Rigaud was one of the six artists to join the ten founders of the Society of Painters in Water Colours in their first exhibition, and he remained a member of the society, latterly serving as treasurer, until the temporary dissolution in 1812. In 1807 he painted *The Genius of Painting Contemplating the Rainbow* in commemoration of the establishment of the society, to which he presented it. It is conceived in the grandest allegorical terms and, although Rigaud was primarily a figure painter, he acknowledges in it the importance of landscape to the society as a whole. He specialized in religious, classical, and literary subjects, which may have since climbed a little from the depth of disfavour they received in the mid-twentieth century, when Williams could write of *Telemachus Discovering the Priest of Apollo*: 'It is a pretentious and heavy-handed work, which makes no appeal to the taste of today' (I. A. Williams, *Early English Watercolours*, 1952, 223). About the time of his marriage to Margaret, daughter of John Davies of Milford Haven, Pembrokeshire, on 1 January 1808, he moved from the family home in Great Titchfield Street to 48 London Street, Fitzroy Square, and later to 19 Upper Thornhaugh Street, Brunswick Square. In 1817, owing to his wife's ill health, he gave up professional work as a painter, and they moved to Pembrokeshire. After her death on 1 January 1839, he returned to London, settling for a time at 9 Woburn Buildings, Tavistock Square, before moving out to 4 Wellington Street, Islington. In 1849 he made a tentative enquiry about rejoining his colleagues in the re-formed Old Watercolour Society. He appears to have had little further success as an artist, and in 1860 he made a final move to 1 Pleasant Row, Shacklewell Green, in Hackney, London, where he died on 4 January 1861, leaving under £1500 to be administered by his late wife's niece. He was buried in Abney Park cemetery, London. There are examples of his work in the British Museum and the Victoria and Albert Museum, London, and the National Museum and Gallery of Wales, Cardiff. His manuscript memoir of his father is now in Yale University Library. HUON MALLALIEU

Sources S. F. D. Rigaud, 'Facts and recollections of the XVIIIth century in a memoir of John Francis Rigaud', ed. W. L. Pressly, *Walpole Society*, 50 (1984), 1–164 · J. L. Roget, *A history of the 'Old Water-Colour' Society*, 1 (1891), 199, 276 · Mallalieu, *Watercolour artists* · *CGPLA Eng. & Wales* (1861)
Wealth at death under £1500: resworn probate, Aug 1861, *CGPLA Eng. & Wales*

Rigaud, Stephen Jordan (1816–1859), bishop of Antigua, eldest son of Stephen Peter *Rigaud (1774–1839) and his wife, Christian (d. 1827), eldest daughter of Gibbes W. Jordan, a barrister, was born at Westminster, London, on 27 March 1816, and educated at Greenwich. He matriculated from Exeter College, Oxford, on 23 January 1834, and graduated BA (1841), MA (1842), and DD (1854). He took a double first in 1838 and was elected fellow of his college on 30 June, and he was appointed mathematical lecturer

in 1840. He was ordained deacon in 1840 and priest in 1841. In the same year he resigned his fellowship on his marriage on 6 July to Lucy Frances, only daughter of Benjamin Lewis Vulliamy of Pall Mall, London. However, he was appointed tutor of the college in 1842.

In September 1846 Rigaud, who had formed a great friendship with Henry George Liddell, went to Westminster School as Liddell's senior assistant master. While he lived in London he was appointed domestic chaplain to the duke of Cambridge, and in 1850 he was elected headmaster of Queen Elizabeth's School, Ipswich. In 1856 he was select preacher at St Mary's, Oxford, and published *The Inspiration of the Holy Scripture* (1856) and several other similar works.

In 1858 Rigaud was chosen bishop of Antigua; he was consecrated on 2 February at Lambeth Palace and went out to his diocese almost immediately. He began active work with the inspection of all the schools in Antigua, and on 11 July he held his first confirmation at St John's. On the 15th he started a tour of his diocese, going first to Tortola; he then visited each island in turn. On 17 May 1859 he died in Antigua of yellow fever, his wife surviving him. His journal, published in the *Colonial Church Chronicle* (vol. 13, 1859), contains excellent descriptions of some of the less known West Indian islands.

C. A. HARRIS, *rev.* H. C. G. MATTHEW

Sources *GM*, 3rd ser., 7 (1859), 83 · *Colonial Church Chronicle* (1858–9) · *N&Q*, 5th ser., 12 (1879), 495 · S. J. Rigaud, *Testimonials addressed to the … electors of Rugby School in favour of … S. J. Rigaud* (1849) · *CGPLA Eng. & Wales* (1859)
Archives BL, letters to Philip Bliss, Add. MSS 34575–34580
Likenesses T. H. Maguire, lithograph, BM; repro. in T. H. Maguire, *Portraits of honorary members of the Ipswich Museum* (1852)
Wealth at death under £4000: administration, 17 Aug 1859, *CGPLA Eng. & Wales*

Rigaud, Stephen Peter (1774–1839), astronomer, was born on 12 August 1774 at Powell's Row (later Old Palace Terrace), Richmond, Surrey, the son (there was also a daughter) of Stephen Rigaud (d. 1814), observer at the King's Observatory, Kew, and his wife, Mary, daughter of Stephen Charles Triboudet *Demainbray (1710–1782). Both families were of ancient French origins. Rigaud was educated at Mr Delafosse's school, Richmond, and in April 1791 he entered Exeter College, Oxford, where he made his first astronomical observations in 1793. In the following year (while still an undergraduate) he was elected a fellow; he graduated BA in 1797 and proceeded MA in 1799. At the age of forty Rigaud married, in June 1815, Christian, the eldest daughter of Gibbes W. Jordan, a barrister.

Rigaud tutored at Exeter College. From about 1805 he deputized for the ailing Thomas Hornsby, the Savilian professor of astronomy and reader in experimental philosophy, by giving his lectures. On Hornsby's death in 1810 Abram Robertson was elected to his chair; Rigaud replaced Robertson as Savilian professor of geometry and was also appointed reader in experimental philosophy. By this time Rigaud was already a distinguished scholar, a fellow of the Royal Society since 1805, and, since his father's death in 1814, joint observer with his grandfather at the

Stephen Peter Rigaud (1774–1839), by unknown artist

King's Observatory at Kew. Therefore, when Robertson died in 1827 and the university transferred Rigaud from the Savilian chair of geometry to that of astronomy, the Radcliffe trustees accepted him without question as their observer. They made up his salary to £300, with free accommodation, and during the 1820s (when attendance averaged forty) the fees from his experimental philosophy lectures in the Ashmolean museum were substantial.

Within a year the honour of succeeding to the chair and observership was shattered. Rigaud's beloved young wife died, on 26 March 1827, leaving him with seven small children. Bereft, his black hair 'turned swiftly to grey' (Guest, 257). He immersed himself in the care and education of his children, and work. With one assistant, Angel Lockey, he supervised continuation of the meteorological observations commenced in 1816, and the regular meridian observations with the John Bird instruments of 1772–3. The latter work alone, if reduced for timely publication, would have been as much as two men could manage, and though Rigaud was a practical astronomer by training and tradition, his and Robertson's observations were 'overtaken by more accurate work' (Thackeray, 9) elsewhere and were never published. Notably, his books and all but one of his papers published outside Oxford were written after his arrival at the observatory. Meanwhile he was responsible for the observatory's first major new instrument, by Thomas Jones, transitional in design between a mural circle and a meridian circle, requested from the trustees. Rigaud oversaw its installation in 1836, tested it in 1837 and 1838, but died before he could bring it into use.

Rigaud had a passion and skill for scientific history, and after the loss of his wife became the foremost historian of astronomy and mathematics in his generation. He had a large library of his own, after 1834 supplemented annually by the trustees. His delight was to recover from oblivion the details of biography and invention, and the processes of discovery. Having rediscovered Bradley's original observations and correspondence, his first major work was an acclaimed edition of both (1831). Other publications on Newton's *Principia*, and on Thomas Harriot's

observations, were considered important. Rigaud saw his projected life of Halley as 'a duty, to rescue his memory' (Rigaud, 11), but this massive effort was never completed. Those motives underlay his transcription of nearly a thousand pages of *Letters of Scientific Men* of the seventeenth century (1841, 2nd edn 1862).

A conservative in politics Rigaud served four monarchs, but he was independent and never self-seeking. He was a devout Anglican, and studied scripture. Of a sensitive and rather anxious nature, but amiable, modest, and renowned for his personal and scholarly integrity, Rigaud was a founder of the Ashmolean Society in Oxford. He published numerous papers on subjects as diverse as meteorology, Greek mathematics, steam engines, topography, and historical observations in its *Proceedings*, and twenty in the *Journal of the Royal Institution*, *Edinburgh Philosophical Journal*, *Journal of Science*, *Philosophical Magazine*, and others. Sometime proctor and delegate to the university press, he was one of the first public examiners in 1801, 1806, and 1835 for the university's mathematics scholarship. Rigaud was one of the first to collect systematically scientific ephemera and prints, contemporary and historical, now mostly in the Museum of the History of Science, Oxford.

Rigaud was a member of the board of longitude criticized by Francis Baily in 1822 as containing learned professors who seldom attend (Dreyer, 57). Although domestic circumstances after 1827 partly explain his absence from the learned societies, arguably this deprived Oxford science of a potential motive force, although he served as vice-president of the Royal Society for 1837–8. But his real interests lay elsewhere. In 1839 Rigaud was still transcribing letters, working on the papers of Savery and Halley, and revising lectures. While staying with his friend, the clockmaker Benjamin Vulliamy, in Pall Mall, Rigaud was taken ill and after eighteen hours of intense suffering died on 16 March 1839, probably of a burst appendix. He was buried in St James's churchyard, Piccadilly.

After Rigaud's death the university appointed a mathematician without astronomical experience to the Savilian chair. The trustees declined to appoint him as their observer, preferring a young astronomer of their own choice, Manuel Johnson, to work their expensive new instrument. For the ensuing thirty-five years the professors had neither instruments nor observatory for research. From Exeter College, Rigaud's eldest son, Stephen Jordan *Rigaud (1816–1859), became a headmaster, then, in 1857, bishop of Antigua. Rigaud's fourth son, John, became a fellow of Magdalen College until his death in 1888. Another son, Gibbes (d. 1885), rose to the rank of major-general.   ROGER HUTCHINS

Sources *Monthly Notices of the Astronomical Society of London*, 5 (1839–43), 22–4 • [J. Rigaud], *Stephen Peter Rigaud M.A., FRS.: a memoir* (1883) • I. Guest, *Dr John Radcliffe and his trust* (1991) • A. V. Simcock, *The Ashmolean Museum and Oxford science, 1683–1983* (1984) • *History of the Royal Astronomical Society*, [1]: 1820–1920, ed. J. L. E. Dreyer and H. H. Turner (1923); repr. (1987) • R. J. Beevor, *Inventory of Rigaud papers in the Bodleian Library* (1905) • Foster, *Alum. Oxon.* • A. D. Thackeray, *The Radcliffe Observatory, 1772–1972* (1972) • C. Knight, ed., *The*

English cyclopaedia: biography, 3 (1856) · Ward, *Men of the reign* · *DNB* · A. A. Rambaut, 'Note on the unpublished observations made at the Radcliffe Observatory, Oxford, between the years 1774 and 1838', *Monthly Notices of the Royal Astronomical Society*, 60 (1899–1900), 265–93 · *GM*, 1st ser., 85/1 (1815), 562 · *GM*, 1st ser., 97/1 (1827)

Archives Bodl. Oxf., corresp. and MSS · Bodl. Oxf., MSS relating to Savilian Foundation · Oxf. U. Mus. NH, corresp. and MSS · Oxf. U. Mus. NH, observatory notebooks with Jones's circle, MS RAD 41 | BL, letters to P. Bliss, Add. MSS 34568–34572 · Man. CL, Manchester Archives and Local Studies, letters, mainly to W. R. Whatton · RS, corresp. with Sir John Herschel · Trinity Cam., corresp. with William Whewell

Likenesses bust, Exeter College, Oxford · portrait, repro. in Guest, *Dr. John Radcliffe and his Trust*, facing p. 273 · silhouette, Exeter College, Oxford, MHS Oxf. [*see illus.*] · silhouette, Radcliffe Observatory, Oxford

Rigby, Alexander (*bap.* 1594, *d.* 1650), politician and parliamentarian army officer, was baptized on 9 July 1594 at Flixton, Lancashire, the eldest son of Alexander Rigby (*d.* 1621) of Wigan, merchant and landowner, and his first wife, Alice, daughter of Leonard Ashawe of Shaw Hall, Flixton. The parliamentarian army officer Joseph *Rigby was a younger brother, as was the lawyer George *Rigby. Alexander the younger matriculated from St John's College, Cambridge, in 1610, graduated BA in 1614, and was created MA in 1615 on the king's visit. He pursued a legal career, being admitted to Gray's Inn on 1 November 1610 and called to the bar on 19 November 1617. On 4 May 1638 he became an ancient of Gray's Inn where he kept a chamber in 1642. During the 1630s Rigby combined the law with activity in his native county. He had inherited considerable estates from his father, with his main seat at Middleton in the parish of Goosnargh in the north-west of the county. He acquired militia experience, in 1634 serving in the trained band for Lonsdale hundred. In addition the Rigby family had a tight grip on the office of clerk of the peace for the county from 1608.

In the late 1610s Rigby married Lucy (*bap.* 1596, *d.* 1644), daughter of Sir Urian Legh of Adlington, Cheshire; their eldest son, Alexander, was baptized at the Legh parish church of Prestbury on 20 August 1620; two more sons, one of whom died in infancy, and a daughter followed. Following Lucy's death in February or March 1644 and that of her eldest brother, the royalist Colonel Thomas Legh, at the end of that year, Rigby married the latter's widow, Anne (*d.* 1676), daughter of John Gobert of Coventry and Bosworth, Leicestershire. After Rigby's death Anne married about 1659 Sir John Booth of Woodford, Cheshire. In due course Rigby's son Alexander maintained the family connection with the Leghs by taking as his second wife his cousin and stepsister, Thomas's daughter, Anne.

Elected to the Short Parliament as member for Wigan on 17 March 1640, and to the Long Parliament the following November, Rigby quickly emerged as an active member serving on several committees. He investigated the judicial abuses of the Star Chamber and was a member of a committee which examined the position of Archbishop Laud. Thereafter Rigby served on so many committees that he was quite possibly the most industrious MP of the 1640s. He was especially noted as a prime leader of the war party in the Commons between 1643 and 1645.

Rigby was also the chief spokesman for Lancashire at Westminster. He obtained men and money from parliament for the county, sponsored the legislation which would benefit the county, and acted as a channel of communication between Lancashire and Westminster. In 1643, perhaps as a financial speculation, Rigby purchased a lapsed patent, known as the Plough patent, at Sagadahook in New England. The patent gave Rigby lordship of the province of Lygonia in Maine in 1646. On his death his title fell to his eldest son.

Rigby's prominence in parliament was combined with local responsibility in his native county. Already a JP, he became deputy lieutenant on 24 March 1642. Along with his colleagues John Moore and Ralph Assheton he helped organize the parliamentarian war effort. In June 1642 he put the militia ordinance into execution and during the summer he attempted to counter the activities of James Stanley, Lord Strange, soon to be the seventh earl of Derby. Rigby was in London during the crucial siege of Manchester in late September 1642 but returned north in the spring of 1643. As a member of the Lancashire county committee and colonel for the hundreds of Leyland and Amounderness, Rigby organized recruitment in the previously unengaged western parts of the county. He issued numerous commissions and raised a sizeable foot regiment. He also took over Richard Shuttleworth's horse regiment on his return from Westminster. Rigby's successful campaign of summer and autumn 1643 culminated in a victory in Furness over the north Lancashire and Cumbrian royalists on 1 October 1643. This and the subsequent capture of Thurland Castle on 7 October attracted wide attention especially as his reputation had been built on legal not military foundations.

Despite strategic misgivings Rigby was persuaded to send forces to Cheshire to raise the siege of Nantwich which was achieved by the defeat of Byron on 25 January 1644. Less impressive was his attempt to capture the royalist stronghold of Lathom House. The siege was brought to an abrupt end on the arrival of Prince Rupert in May 1644. Falling back on Bolton, Rigby was fortunate to escape when the town was attacked on 28 May 1644. Following this alarm Rigby returned south to parliament. In all, between September 1642 and December 1645 he spent only nine months in his native county. Yet such was his reputation that on his return to the county Rigby was immediately accepted as one of the leading deputy lieutenants and committee members. There is no evidence that his frequent absences in London were viewed critically within Lancashire parliamentarian circles. Indeed, along with William Ashurst, Rigby's role as county spokesmen in parliament served to enhance his personal standing.

Rigby resumed his political prominence at Westminster following Charles I's defeat in the summer of 1646. On 21 March 1646 Rigby had been among the MPs who supported the earl of Warwick as admiral and governor in chief on all foreign plantations planted by the English. On

11 July he was appointed a commissioner for the conservation of peace between England and Scotland and on 21 May 1647 he served on a committee to relieve persons sued for any act done by the authority of parliament. In late 1648 his radicalism was witnessed to when he was one of the four 'honest men' from the Commons appointed to the committee of sixteen to negotiate a new agreement of the people between representatives of the army, the City and parliamentary Independents, and the Levellers. Rigby appears to have sat little or not at all on the committee, where the only MP who regularly attended was Henry Marten. Rigby's standing in the spring of 1649 was nevertheless high enough with the Leveller leaders (by now imprisoned in the Tower) for them to suggest that he and Marten act as sympathetic umpires to broker their differences with Oliver Cromwell and Henry Ireton. John Lilburne later portrayed Rigby differently, as having acted as the mouthpiece of the army's grandees who tried unsuccessfully to buy off the Levellers with lavish offers of preferment on the day that the Commons sent them to the Tower. In December 1648 Rigby was himself nominated one of the judges for the king's trial, but he did not attend. On 1 June 1649 Rigby was made baron of the exchequer and began a career as a judge.

Meanwhile Rigby had distinguished himself by galvanizing resistance in Lancashire to the Scots invasion of 1648, though it was his eldest son, Alexander, who exercised military command during the Preston campaign. Rigby's reputation was further enhanced by his appointment as parliamentarian emissary to the west country where his aim was to improve the popular perception of parliament through, among other measures, the abolition of free quarter. Rigby seems to have presided at the Lancaster assizes in September 1649 and on 1 April 1650 was one of four commissioners named in the act for establishing the high court of justice.

The following August Rigby fell ill while presiding at the Essex assizes at Chelmsford; the court adjourned to escape the disease—quite possibly gaol fever picked up from the prisoners—and moved on to Surrey: too late for Rigby, his fellow judges, and most of the officers of the court, all struck down with 'a most violent pestilential fever' (Vicars, 13). Desperately ill, Rigby was brought from Croydon to London where he died on 18 August 1650. After lying in state at Ely Place, Holborn, his body was taken back up north and he was buried at Preston on 9 September 1650.

Alexander Rigby proved to be one of the most committed parliamentarians and radicals of the 1640s. His energy was remarkable and displayed itself in his expert juggling of legal, political, and military roles. His contribution to the parliamentarian war effort in Lancashire from June 1642 onwards was a crucial factor in its initial survival and eventual success, while his legal and communication skills were much to the fore at Westminster. In 1647 Rigby claimed that such commitment had carried a heavy cost. Because his estate had been plundered by the royalists he had been forced to live as an ordinary soldier. He never received relief from parliamentary funds nor appropriated any money from the estates and goods of delinquents. Initially a presbyterian, Rigby emerged in the 1640s as a revolutionary Independent and 'A most desperate Enemy to the Presbyterians Church Discipline' (Vicars, 12).

Essentially a war party man, Rigby wanted a determined prosecution of the war with no holds barred, leading to a dictated peace. His manoeuvring in December 1648 indicates that he accepted Pride's Purge and was in favour of taking part in preliminary proceedings against Charles. However, Rigby's non-participation in the king's execution seems to imply his preference for a deposition.

MALCOLM GRATTON

Sources Greaves & Zaller, BDBR · J. M. Gratton, 'The parliamentarian and royalist war effort in Lancashire, 1642–1651', PhD diss., University of Manchester, 1998 · Keeler, Long Parliament · DNB · Palatine Note-Book, 3 (1883) · E. Robinson, A discourse of the warr in Lancashire … betweene King Charles and the parliament, ed. W. Beamont, Chetham Society, 62 (1864) · B. G. Blackwood, The Lancashire gentry and the great rebellion, 1640–60, Chetham Society, 3rd ser., 25 (1978) · G. Ormerod, ed., Tracts relating to military proceedings in Lancashire during the great civil war, Chetham Society, 2 (1844) · D. Underdown, Pride's Purge: politics in the puritan revolution (1971) · S. Barber, 'The people of northern England and attitudes towards the Scots, 1639–1651: "the lamb and the dragon cannot be reconciled"', Northern History, 35 (1999), 93–118 · R. Halley, Lancashire: its puritanism and nonconformity, 2 vols. (1869) · J. Vicars, Dagon demolished (1660) · IGI [Flixton, Lancashire] · W. Dugdale, The visitation of the county palatine of Lancaster, made in the year 1664–5, ed. F. R. Raines, 3, Chetham Society, 88 (1873), 245–6 · Venn, Alum. Cant. · J. P. Earwaker, East Cheshire: past and present, or, A history of the hundred of Macclesfield, 2 (1880), 213, 243, 252 · W. Haller and G. Davies, eds., The Leveller tracts, 1647–1653 (1944) · D. M. Wolfe, ed., Leveller manifestoes of the puritan revolution, another edn (1967) · B. Taft, 'The council of officers', Agreement of the people, 1648/9', HJ, 28 (1985), 169–85
Archives Lancs. RO, lieutenancy book · NRA, priv. coll., letters | Lancs. RO, corresp. with George Rigby
Likenesses engraving, repro. in J. Croston, Nooks and corners of Lancashire and Cheshire (1882)

Rigby, Christopher Palmer (1820–1885), diplomatist and army officer, was born on 18 January 1820 at Yately Lodge, Yately, Hampshire, the youngest son and sixth of the eight children of Tipping Thomas Rigby (1774–1862), barrister and recorder of Wallingford, and his wife, Ann Eliza, née Cousins. Educated at Abingdon grammar school (1831–3) and at Addiscombe College (1834–5), Rigby began his military career in 1836, as an ensign in the 5th regiment of native infantry stationed in Poona. He remained in India, except for a posting in Aden from 1840 to 1843, until 1850—with one leave in England. During these years of service overseas he acquired fluency in eight oriental and African languages, and wrote a number of erudite articles which appeared in the Transactions of the Bombay Geographical Society.

Rigby returned to India in April 1854—to Bombay—and soon afterwards was appointed president of the examination committee for native languages—his latest recreation being the study of Turkish. At this period relations between Persia and Britain were worsening on account of

Afghanistan. Accordingly, in September 1854 Britain dispatched an expeditionary field force to the Persian port of Bushehr, with Rigby as interpreter and, later, superintendent of police—with himself the only policeman in the town.

After returning to Bombay early in 1858 Rigby was appointed the East India Company's agent in Zanzibar and British consul, the previous consul having died at his post thirteen months previously. On 27 July 1858, the day of his arrival in Zanzibar, Rigby called on the sultan, Majid bin Saʿid al-Busaʾidi, aboard his flagship and was given a royal salute. The sultanates of Muscat and Zanzibar had recently been separated by the terms of the Canning award, but Majid's position remained insecure; in 1859 his half-brothers Thwain of Muscat and Baragash, who was to succeed Majid as sultan, attempted to capture Zanzibar. However, at Rigby's instance, the Royal Navy gave Majid the necessary support and the insurrection failed, Baragash being sent to Bombay where he was compelled to remain for eighteen months.

While serving in Zanzibar, Rigby met and assisted several celebrated explorers: Sir Richard Burton (who was to be accused by Rigby of withholding payment from porters and other members of the expedition to Lake Tanganyika—an accusation which was denied by Burton), J. H. Speke, and David Livingstone. In particular, he befriended James A. *Grant.

Atkins Hamerton, Rigby's predecessor in Zanzibar, had signed a treaty with Majid's father in 1845; this restricted, but did not abolish, the east African slave trade. Rigby worked with ardour to suppress the traffic in slaves and his efforts to enforce the 1845 treaty were unremitting. Furthermore, he ordered the emancipation of all slaves owned by British subjects residing in Zanzibar; it is estimated that he set free 8000 slaves up to the time of his leaving Zanzibar.

In 1861 the Bombay government published Rigby's *Report on the Zanzibar Dominions*, a comprehensive and informative survey of the sultanate. On 5 September 1861 Rigby left Zanzibar because of ill health and returned to England. In January 1864 he was appointed commissioner for the settlement of boundary disputes between the states of Baroda and Jamnagar. On 27 June 1867, in London, he married Matilda, *née* Prater. They had two sons (one of whom was killed in action in the First World War) and two daughters (one of whom died in infancy). Their daughter Lillian (1875–1949) became a follower of Albert Schweitzer and was his first British assistant at Lambarené.

Rigby resigned from the army in August 1867 with the rank of major-general. Shortly before his death he lost all his savings in the collapse of the Oriental Bank. He died at his home, 14 Portland Place, London, on 14 April 1885; he was survived by his wife. His daughter Lillian translated his philosophical lectures and edited, as C. E. B. Russell, *General Rigby, Zanzibar and the Slave Trade* (1935). A photograph of Rigby, taken by Grant in Zanzibar in 1860, was left to the Royal Geographical Society.

P. J. L. FRANKL, *rev.*

Sources *The Times* (16 April 1885) · *Proceedings* [Royal Geographical Society], new ser., 7 (1885) · C. E. B. Russell, ed., *General Rigby, Zanzibar and the slave trade* (1935) · *CGPLA Eng. & Wales* (1885)
Likenesses J. A. Grant, photograph, 1860, RGS
Wealth at death £4629 1s.: probate, 6 May 1885, *CGPLA Eng. & Wales*

Rigby [*née* Rayner], **Edith** (1872–1950), suffragette, was born on 18 October 1872 at 1 Pole Street, Preston, Lancashire, the second of seven children of Alexander Clement Rayner (1841/2–1916), surgeon, and his wife, Mary, *née* Pilkington Sharples (known as Polly). She was educated at Preston high school from 1883 to 1885, and Penrhos College in north Wales from 1885 to 1890. On 7 September 1893 she married Charles Samuel Alfred Rigby (1858–1926), a doctor, and took up residence at 28 Winckley Square, Preston. The couple adopted a two-year-old baby, Arthur (known as Sandy), in December 1905.

Edith Rayner came from a poor but middle-class family. Her father's patients were mainly Preston's working classes, which gave her an early awareness of social and economic inequalities. On her marriage to Charles Rigby, she began to engage in philanthropic and reform activities. She joined the Independent Labour Party in 1905, and in 1906 formed a branch of the Women's Labour League in Preston and served on the league's national executive council. In January 1907 she formed a Preston branch of the militant suffragettes' organization, the Women's Social and Political Union (WSPU).

From 1907 until 1913 Edith Rigby was the mainstay of Preston's WSPU. She recruited a number of women who went on to become actively militant suffragettes, and was herself one of the most committed members of the local union. Her suffragette activity included two London deputations in 1907 and 1908, in which she was arrested and served two weeks and four weeks in prison respectively for obstruction, and a protest at a meeting addressed by Winston Churchill in Preston in 1909, in which she was again arrested. On her release, she followed Churchill to Waterloo in Liverpool, and smashed a window at the local police station. For this she was sentenced to two weeks in prison, during which time she took up the hunger strike and was forcibly fed. Edith Rigby was again arrested for window-breaking on a London deputation in 1911, and served three weeks in Holloway prison. In 1913 she was briefly imprisoned in Manchester for throwing a black pudding at a Labour MP and in July of the same year she undertook more serious suffragette action. She placed a bomb (which did not detonate) in the Liverpool Cotton Exchange, and three days later set fire to the holiday home of Preston's local soap powder entrepreneur, Sir William Lever. The following day, she surrendered to the police, admitting arson and incendiarism. There followed a lengthy court case, in which she was sentenced to nine months in prison. She again took up the hunger strike, but under the new 'Cat and Mouse' system, was allowed to starve herself until she was physically debilitated, then released to allow for her recuperation, and brought back into custody when her health began to improve. Between 9 July and 20 October Edith Rigby had served only thirty-five days in custody, and it became clear that serving the whole nine-month sentence under this system would take years, and probably kill her in the process. She went missing after her fifth release on 20 October, probably escaping to Ireland where she remained in hiding until mid-1914, when she returned to Preston. No attempt was made to rearrest her.

During the First World War Edith Rigby was involved in the Women's Land Army, and was nominally a secretary for the Preston branch of the independent WSPU, a rebel branch of the Pankhursts' WSPU. With the outbreak of war, the Pankhursts had ordered that all suffrage work be dropped so that WSPU members could put their energies into supporting the war effort. The minority of women who formed the independent WSPU disagreed with this strategy and continued the campaign for the vote, threatening to resume militant action against the government. Once the war was over, Edith Rigby turned her attentions to her natural environment, to wholefoods, and to the works of Rudolph Steiner. When Charles Rigby retired in 1926, the pair built a new home, Erdmuth, in the fields near Llan-rhos, Caernarvonshire, but Charles died before the building work was finished and Edith spent the rest of her life in retreat there, with regular visits from friends and relatives. In 1931 she published *Man and Animal*, her translation from the German of Herman Poppelbaum's work. She died on 23 July 1950 at Erdmuth.

Edith Rigby's life was a rejection of conventional beliefs about women. She refused to wear styles of female dress appropriate to her era, often preferring men's clothes, and always chose footwear for comfort rather than fashion. Her life was less about an adherence to feminist beliefs than an expression of independence of mind and a courage in her own convictions that was rare for women of this time. She was an individual with a charisma that made her memorable, and was renowned for the limits to which she was prepared to push herself. Edith Rigby is remembered for her sacrifices to the suffrage movement, yet the years of fighting for the vote were only one of many phases of her life. She was resolute, independent, and thoroughly unpredictable.   HELOISE BROWN

Sources P. Hesketh, *My aunt Edith* (1966); repr. (1992) · A. J. R., ed., *The suffrage annual and women's who's who* (1913) · O. Banks, *The biographical dictionary of British feminists*, 2 (1990) · R. Fulford, *Votes for women: the story of a struggle* (1957) · b. cert. · m. cert. · *CGPLA Eng. & Wales* (1950)
Likenesses photographs, repro. in Hesketh, *My Aunt Edith*
Wealth at death £10,061 11s. 9d.: probate, 29 Dec 1950, *CGPLA Eng. & Wales*

Rigby, Edward (1747–1821), physician, son of John Rigby, and his wife, Sarah (*c*.1724–1773), daughter of John *Taylor (1694–1761), the hebraist, and his wife, Elizabeth, was born at Chowbent, Lancashire, on 27 December 1747. His sister Sarah married Caleb Hillier Parry, and was mother of Sir William Edward Parry, the Arctic explorer. Educated at Dr Priestley's school at Warrington, Rigby was apprenticed in 1762 to David Martineau, surgeon, of Norwich, and afterwards studied in London and was admitted a member of the Company of Surgeons on 4 May 1769. In

the same year he married his first wife, Sarah, coheir of John Dybal; they had two daughters. In 1803 he married Anne (1777–1872), daughter of William Palgrave of Yarmouth; they had twelve children, four of whom, three girls and a boy, were the production of one birth on 15 August 1817. Among his children were Edward *Rigby and Elizabeth *Eastlake, Lady Eastlake.

In 1776 Rigby published *An Essay on the Uterine haemorrhage which precedes the Delivery of the Full-Grown Foetus*. This work was translated into French and German, and placed Rigby in the first rank of his profession. He added to his reputation by *An essay on the theory and production of animal heat, and on its application in the treatment of cutaneous eruptions, inflammations, and some other diseases* (1785), and *Chemical Observations on Sugar* (1788). In 1786 he played an important role in establishing the Norfolk Benevolent Society for the relief of the widows and orphans of medical men. In July 1789 he visited France and other parts of the continent. His *Letters from France*, addressed to his wife in 1789, were first published by his daughter Elizabeth, Lady Eastlake, in 1880. Written from Paris at the outbreak of the French Revolution, Rigby's letters provide a firsthand account of what he described as being 'the most extraordinary revolution that perhaps ever took place in human society' (Rigby, 1880, 28). They are also a useful supplement to Arthur Young's observations on the agriculture and the peasantry of France at that time. A practical agriculturist, Rigby was the friend of Thomas William Coke of Holkham, afterwards earl of Leicester, and experimented on his own farm at Framingham, about 5 miles from Norwich. A 'whig of the old stamp', in 1783 he became a member of the corporation of guardians of Norwich, and promoted the economical administration of the poor laws. But, after meeting with strong opposition, he resigned in the following year, when he was presented by the people of Norwich with a service of plate, in recognition of his efforts. He became alderman in 1802, sheriff in 1803, and mayor of Norwich in 1805. He is said to have made local manufacturers aware of the flying shuttle, and to have introduced vaccination into the city. He died on 27 October 1821, and was buried at Framingham.

    W. A. S. HEWINS, *rev.* MICHAEL BEVAN

Sources E. Rigby, *An essay on the uterine haemorrhage*, 6th edn (1822) [incl. a memoir by J. Cross] · E. Rigby, *Letters from France … in 1789*, edited by his daughter Lady Eastlake (1880) · *Annual Register* (1821), 244 · W. Wadd, *Nugae chirurgicae, or, A biographical miscellany* (1824), 138 · J. Donaldson, *Agricultural biography* (1854), 110
Likenesses D. Turner, etching, 1816 (after M. Sharp, 1815), BM, Wellcome L.

Rigby, Edward (1804–1860), obstetrician, was born with a twin sister on 1 August 1804, the son of Edward *Rigby (1747–1821), a prominent Norwich physician, and his second wife, Anne (1777–1872), the daughter of William Palgrave. Elizabeth *Eastlake, Lady Eastlake, was his younger sister. Educated at the grammar school, Norwich, he attended Norfolk and Norwich Hospital in 1821 and the following year matriculated at Edinburgh University. He graduated MD on 1 August 1825, with a dissertation entitled 'De Iodino'. After graduation he spent some time in Dublin, taking advantage of its facilities for dissection, and in 1826 went to Berlin University to study midwifery. From Berlin he passed to Heidelberg, and studied under C. F. Naegele. In 1829 he published *An Essay on the Mechanism of Parturition*, from the German of Naegele, which greatly advanced the science of midwifery in England. In 1830 he became a house pupil at the General Lying-in Hospital in York Road, Lambeth, where he later held the appointments of junior and senior physician. In 1831 he was admitted a licentiate of the Royal College of Physicians, and in 1843 became a fellow.

In 1831 Rigby began to lecture on midwifery at St Thomas's Hospital, and from 1838 to 1848 he lectured on the same subject at St Bartholomew's Hospital. He was examiner in midwifery in London University from 1841 to 1860. He was regarded as the pre-eminent obstetric physician in London after Sir Charles Locock retired from practice. When the Obstetrical Society was founded in 1859 he was elected its first president. He was a fellow of the Linnean Society, and a member of many foreign medical societies.

In September 1838 Rigby married Susan (*d.* 1841), daughter of John Taylor FRS FGS; they had a daughter. In 1851 Rigby married his second wife, Marianne (*d.* 1853), the eldest daughter of S. D. Darbishire of Pendyffrin, north Wales; they had two daughters.

Rigby also wrote on midwifery, his most successful work being *Memoranda for Young Practitioners in Midwifery* (1837) which ran to four editions. Rigby died on 27 December 1860 at his home in Berkeley Square, London.

E. I. CARLYLE, *rev.* MAX SATCHELL

Sources Munk, *Roll* · *BMJ* (1861), 17–18 · *Nomina eorum, qui gradum medicinae doctoris in academia Jacobi sexti Scotorum regis, quae Edinburgi est, adepti sunt, ab anno 1705 ad annum 1845*, University of Edinburgh (1846), 246 · *Medical Times and Gazette* (5 Jan 1861), 24–5 · *CGPLA Eng. & Wales* (1861)
Likenesses oils, Royal Society of Medicine, London
Wealth at death under £18,000: probate, 18 Jan 1861, *CGPLA Eng. & Wales*

Rigby, George (*bap.* 1602, *d.* 1644), lawyer, was the third surviving son of Alexander Rigby (*d.* 1621) of Wigan and Peel, Lancashire, and his wife, Alice, daughter of Leonard Ashawe of Shaw Hall, Flixton, Lancashire. He was baptized on 21 February 1602. His father was a common law attorney, clerk to Sir Gilbert Gerard, master of the rolls, and clerk of the peace for the county from 1612 to 1621; his mother was a sister of Leonard Ashawe, a busy JP in Salford hundred. Alexander *Rigby and Joseph *Rigby were his brothers. Rigby was admitted to Gray's Inn on 21 February 1618, shortly before matriculating at St John's College, Cambridge, where he left furniture and other belongings in the care of his college tutor when he began his training as a common law attorney. He remained at Gray's Inn and then Lincoln's Inn until 1627, despite his father's death, confident that his brother-in-law Robert Mawdesley of Wigan, then deputy clerk of peace, was fulfilling the responsibilities of the office and secure in the knowledge that he could take up his duties as clerk of the peace when he was ready.

That Rigby could do so was an unintended consequence of another branch of the family overreaching itself. The Rigbys of Burgh had taken a firm hold of the clerkship of the crown in 1570; and in 1589 Roger Rigby, brother of Edward, then the county's clerk of the crown, acquired the grant of the clerkship of the peace for life as well. The administration of assizes and quarter sessions, and all the influence and profit that went with it, was thus in the hands of one branch of the Rigbys. But Roger was not a lawyer, and soon called on the professional services of George's father, Alexander, who served as deputy for more than twenty years before taking advantage of Roger's financial ineptitude to displace him. By letters patent in January 1612 Alexander Rigby senior secured from the crown the clerkship of peace for his own life and that of his eldest son, another Alexander. A further grant in June 1615 added a reversionary interest for George and his other son, Joseph. When Alexander senior died in April 1621, he made it clear that he intended the clerkship to go to George, the principal executor of his will, and nominated his son Alexander, by now a rising barrister, as trustee for George until he was ready to take over. Alexander made sure that he received such profits as were due to him during the time he was away from Lancashire. George formally entered office on 6 July 1627 and, as his title now rested on the original grant, assigned that of 1615 to his friend Thomas Pigott of Booths in Worsley, for safe keeping. He intended to provide against the possibility of having to surrender both patents; but his action was later to provoke hard-fought litigation. After George's death Joseph, by fair means or foul, managed to insert himself into the clerk's office under the 1615 terms; and Roger Kenyon of Parkhead, Whalley, who married George's only surviving daughter in 1657, had to draw heavily on purse and patience before Joseph was finally detached from the clerkship in 1663 after suits in the duchy court and at assizes. The Kenyons, with their own roots deep in local government service and as litigious as the Rigbys, maintained their life interest through three generations until 1780; meanwhile the Burgh line continued to monopolize the clerkship of the crown for Lancashire, holding it, apart from three short breaks, from 1570 to 1710. Such continuity may suggest a settled local community; but it is more likely to illustrate the acquisitive character of Lancashire's senior legal families, developed by opportunities available to them in both duchy and palatine administration and hardened by domestic infighting. While there are some signs of long-held clerkships of peace elsewhere in England by the 1630s, none seems to rival that of Lancashire in duration or to reveal such detail of its tenure. Nevertheless, as George's career was to show, the quality of county government did not necessarily suffer by the Rigbys' dominance.

After his return to Lancashire, George Rigby in 1630 married Beatrice, daughter of William Hulton, whose sister's husband was the future Commonwealth official William Jessop. They settled at Peel, Little Hulton. By 1634 he had built Peel Hall, with a traditional central hall but possessing a 'studied symmetry and rather fanciful character [which was] typically Jacobean', later known as Kenyon Peel Hall (Fleetwood-Hesketh, 151). As clerk of the peace he attended, with his deputy and cousin Alexander Tompson of Langho and their staff, no fewer than eighteen formal sessions of JPs' proceedings each year: four meetings of quarter sessions (at Lancaster, Preston, Wigan or Ormskirk, and Salford) each quarter and a business meeting of the county's JPs at the sheriff's table on the first evening of each assizes week at Lancaster. He was responsible for convening most of them and kept the records for all, including the sheriff's table, for which individual orders, complete with their elaborate heading, were available to interested parties by 1627. Rigby's extant correspondence as clerk of peace, amounting to almost a thousand letters, illustrates the range of his activities and the pivotal importance of his office in administering a county not by nature centralized. It is likely that the profits from process were substantial; Kenyon later calculated that, even in the 1650s, they had been worth £200 p.a. to Joseph Rigby.

In the civil war Rigby, a sound Calvinist, was involved from the start in rallying support for the parliamentary cause, unlike his royalist Burgh cousins, and later served as captain of one of the south Lancashire companies, probably under his brother Colonel Alexander Rigby. He died in April 1644 during the siege of Lathom House, after some months' illness. By then one of his four children, all daughters, was already dead; another predeceased his widow, Beatrice, who died in 1648; a third followed in 1656. But when the survivor, Alice, married Roger Kenyon in June 1657 she revived the prospect of the Peel Rigbys' continuing association with Lancashire's clerkship of the peace. In all, eight members of the Rigby–Kenyon affinity served the clerkship in unbroken sequence between 1589 and 1780.

BRIAN QUINTRELL

Sources Lancs. RO, Kenyon of Peel papers, DDKe 1–7, 9, 13 • *The manuscripts of Lord Kenyon*, HMC, 35 (1894) • C. W. Brooks, *Pettyfoggers and vipers of the Commonwealth* (1986) • R. Somerville, *History of the duchy of Lancaster, 1265–1603* (1953) • R. Somerville, *Office-holders in the duchy and county palatine of Lancaster from 1603* (1972) • J. J. Bagley, 'Kenyon v. Rigby: the struggle for the clerkship of the peace in Lancashire in the seventeenth century', *Transactions of the Historic Society of Lancashire and Cheshire*, 106 (1954), 35–56 • D. Wilkinson, 'The justices of the peace and their work in Lancashire, 1603–1642', MLitt diss., U. Oxf., 1982 • B. W. Quintrell, ed., *The proceedings of the Lancashire justices of the peace at the sheriff's table during assizes week, 1578–1694*, Lancashire and Cheshire RS, 121 (1981) • E. Stephens, ed., *The clerks of the counties, 1360–1960* (1961) • J. Harland, *The Lancashire lieutenancy under the Tudors and Stuarts*, Chetham Society, 49–50 (1859) • R. St George, *Visitation of the county palatine of Lancaster, made in the year 1613*, ed. F. R. Raines, Chetham Society, 82 (1871) • F. Gastrell, *Notitia Cestriensis, or, Historical notices of the diocese of Chester*, ed. F. R. Raines, 2/2, Chetham Society, 21 (1850) • P. Fleetwood-Hesketh, *Murray's Lancashire architectural guide* (1955) • Venn, *Alum. Cant.* • J. Foster, *The register of admissions to Gray's Inn, 1521–1889, together with the register of marriages in Gray's Inn chapel, 1695–1754* (privately printed, London, 1889)

Archives Lancs. RO, Kenyon MSS

Likenesses oils, *c*.1642–1643, priv. coll.; repro. in Bagley, 'Kenyon v. Rigby'

Wealth at death comfortable; modest property at Farington (leased out); had spent heavily on Peel; bulk of income probably from clerk of peace's office

Rigby, Sir John (1834–1903), judge, was born at Runcorn, Cheshire, on 4 January 1834, the second son of Thomas Rigby of Runcorn and his wife, Elizabeth, daughter of Joseph Kendall of Liverpool. Sent first to the collegiate institution in Liverpool (which afterwards became Liverpool College), he was admitted on 20 February 1852 to Trinity College, Cambridge, where he was elected to an open scholarship in 1854. In 1856 he graduated as second wrangler and second Smith's prizeman, taking a second class in the classical tripos. He was a fellow of his college for about ten years from 1856, and took his MA in 1859.

Rigby entered as a student at Lincoln's Inn on 17 October 1855, and was called on 26 January 1860. Starting as 'devil' (junior counsel) in the chambers of Richard Baggallay QC, one of the leaders of the Chancery bar, he rapidly acquired a large practice both in chambers and in court, and in 1875 Sir Richard Baggallay, then attorney-general, made him junior equity counsel to the Treasury, a regular stepping-stone to the judicial bench. Rigby, however, was not content to wait; he took silk in 1880 and attached himself to the court of Mr Justice Kay, where he obtained a complete ascendancy both over his rivals and over the judge himself, who was susceptible to his brand of quasi-preacherly rhetoric. Within a few years he was able to confine his practice to the appeal courts, only appearing at first instance for a special fee. His fees in general were none the less reckoned moderate in view of his eminence. He was especially in demand for property and patent cases, where his chief rivals were Horace Davey, Edward Macnaghten, and Montague Cookson. He owed his success to his mastery of equity, to his ingenuity and pertinacity, and to an impressive personality which lent force to a style 'in which his fervid utterance seemed to contend with an almost pedantic desire to measure his words and give weight to every syllable.' He was 'an incomparable advocate in a bad case' (*The Times*, 27 July 1903). He was on the bar committee from 1883 and in May 1884 he was made a bencher of his inn.

In December 1885 Rigby entered parliament as a Liberal for the Wisbech division of Cambridgeshire, but, following Gladstone when the party split over the Home Rule Bill (he made a powerful speech on the second reading), he lost his seat at the general election of 1886. He did not return to the House of Commons until July 1892, when he was elected for Forfarshire, presumably to enable him to be made solicitor-general, as he was by Gladstone on 20 August 1892; he was knighted on 26 November. He gave invaluable assistance to Sir William Harcourt with the intricate details of the Finance Act of 1893 but was not a success in parliament. His unconventional ways, apparent lack of humour, and somewhat uncouth exterior at first provoked the ridicule of opponents, and though he gradually won some popularity, his courtroom style was ill-suited to the Commons. Moreover, his utter inexperience in criminal trials exposed him to a humiliating failure when he conducted the unsuccessful prosecution of the directors of the Hansard Union in 1893. After a brief term as attorney-general from 3 May 1894 in succession to Sir Charles Russell, he was appointed on 19 October 1894 to the Court of Appeal on the promotion of Davey, and made a privy councillor.

On the bench Rigby did not justify the high expectations his admirers had of him. He displayed his accustomed skill and ingenuity in unravelling complicated and contradictory statutes; he showed characteristic independence and individuality in reaching his conclusions, and his dissenting judgments were sometimes found persuasive by the House of Lords. But his intellect, which was massive rather than flexible, failed to adapt itself to new demands. Near the end of the century his powers showed a perceptible decline, believed to be the effect of a severe fall. He at length resigned on 2 November 1901 and died at his London home, Carlyle House, Chelsea, on 26 July 1903. He was buried at Marylebone cemetery, Finchley. He was unmarried. A son of his cousin, Rigby Swift, became a High Court judge. J. B. ATLAY, *rev.* PATRICK POLDEN

Sources *The Times* (27 July 1903) · private information (1912) · Venn, *Alum. Cant.* · J. Foster, *Men at the bar: a biographical hand list of the members of the various inns of court*, 2nd edn (1885) · *Law Times* (1 Aug 1903), 335 · *Law Journal* (1 Aug 1903), 400 · F. W. S. Craig, *British parliamentary election results, 1832–85*, 2nd edn (1989) · Viscount Alverstone [R. E. Webster], *Recollections of bar and bench* (1914), 227 · A. T. C. Pratt, ed., *People of the period: being a collection of the biographies of upwards of six thousand living celebrities*, 2 vols. (1897) · E. S. Fay, *Life of Mr Justice Swift* (1939) · Sainty, *Judges* · Sainty, *King's counsel*
Likenesses A. T. Nowell, oils; formerly in possession of the family, 1912 · Spy [L. Ward], caricature, chromolithograph, NPG; repro. in *VF* (28 March 1901) · Stuff [H. C. Sepping Wright?], watercolour caricature, NPG; repro. in *VF* (31 Aug 1893) · A. Trevelyan, oils, Lincoln's Inn
Wealth at death £212,859 15s. 9d.: resworn probate, Dec 1903, *CGPLA Eng. & Wales*

Rigby, Joseph (*d.* 1671), parliamentarian army officer and poet, was the third (but second surviving) son of Alexander Rigby (*d.* 1621), merchant and gentleman, and his first wife, Alice, daughter of Leonard Ashawe of Shaw Hall, near Flixton, Lancashire. His eldest brother was the noted parliamentarian officer Colonel Alexander *Rigby (*bap.* 1594, *d.* 1650); George *Rigby was a younger brother. Joseph attended Eton College between about 1614 and 1618. He was admitted to Gray's Inn in February 1618, but went on to matriculate at St John's College, Cambridge, in Michaelmas 1618, and graduated BA in 1622. He was appointed under-sheriff of Lancashire in November 1640. After the outbreak of the civil war he progressed rapidly up the parliamentarian military hierarchy. Styled captain in December 1643, he had risen to major by March 1644, serving in that capacity in the regiments of his brother Alexander and George Dodding. In the following September he was commander-in-chief at the siege of Greenhalgh Castle.

Rigby became a captain in Colonel Oughtred Shuttleworth's foot regiment after the reorganization of Lancashire parliamentarian forces in the spring of 1645. At this time he proved most assiduous in the discovery of 'cancelled delinquent's estates', the royalist Alexander Rigby of Layton being a particular target. During the war of 1648 Joseph Rigby served as lieutenant-colonel to Colonel Richard Standish and held the same rank in the newly formed county militia of 1650. His offer to serve in Ireland, made

in April 1650, came to nothing. In common with many parliamentarian officers, Rigby sought to improve his financial prospects following the royalist defeat. He acquired crown land and also farmed sequestrated property.

Rigby was embroiled in an acrimonious dispute regarding the clerkship of peace for Lancashire. Traditionally held by the Rigby family, the office was assigned to him as early as April 1621. His hold was challenged by his nephew Roger Kenyon and, after extensive litigation from 1651 to 1663, Kenyon assumed office by a court order. During the dispute, in April 1654, Rigby was committed for contempt over his refusal to hand over books and papers, but by June 1654 he was at liberty.

Rigby, who lived at Aspull near Wigan, was a fervent puritan with literary talent. About 1650 he produced 'Concerning the Lord's prayer and repentence'. His only published work, a duodecimo volume of verse, *The Drunkards' Prospective, or, Burninge Glasse* (1656), warned against the evils of alcohol. This was followed by 'Pride, Sensualitie, Whoredom and Bloodshed' in 1660. His manuscript works survive in the possession of the Wigan library service. Rigby died in November 1671; he had married Margaret Houghton, daughter of Gabriel Houghton of Knowsley, Lancashire. She was a Roman Catholic—an unusual choice for a mid-seventeenth-century Lancashire puritan. MALCOLM GRATTON

Sources *DNB* · Lancs. RO, Kenyon of Peel papers, DDKe · E. Robinson, *A discourse of the warr in Lancashire … betweene King Charles and the parliament*, ed. W. Beamont, Chetham Society, 62 (1864) · B. G. Blackwood, *The Lancashire gentry and the great rebellion, 1640–60*, Chetham Society, 3rd ser., 25 (1978) · *CSP dom.*, 1644–63 · J. M. Gratton, 'The parliamentarian and royalist war effort in Lancashire, 1642–1651', PhD diss., University of Manchester, 1998 · PRO, Commonwealth Exchequer papers, SP 28/211/287; SP 28/300/215, 219, 222 · A. J. Hawkes, 'Wigan's part in the civil war', *Transactions of the Lancashire and Cheshire Antiquarian Society*, 47 (1930–31), 84–138 · B. G. Blackwood, 'The Catholic and protestant gentry of Lancashire during the civil war period', *Transactions of the Historic Society of Lancashire and Cheshire*, 126 (1976), 1–29 · W. A. Shaw, ed., *Minutes of the Manchester presbyterian classis*, 3 vols., Chetham Society, new ser., 20, 22, 24 (1890–91) · trustees for the sale of crown lands, certificates, PRO, E 121/5/7 · Venn, *Alum. Cant.* · W. Sterry, ed., *The Eton College register, 1441–1698* (1943)

Rigby, Richard (1722–1788), politician, was born at Mistley Hall, Essex, in February 1722, the only son among the three children of Richard Rigby (*d.* 1730) and his wife, Anne Perry (*d.* 1741). His paternal grandfather, Edward, a London draper, had acquired his Essex estate in 1703 from the last de Vere earl of Oxford. His father disposed of the drapery business and prospered as a South Sea Company factor, and built a mansion at Mistley.

Rigby, heir at the age of eight to a rent roll of £1100 a year, entered Corpus Christi College, Cambridge, and the Middle Temple in 1738, but proceeded, without qualifications, on the grand tour, returning in 1742. He joined White's Club in London in 1744, with his friend (until 1756) Horace Walpole, whose brother Robert, second earl of Orford, brought Rigby into parliament on a vacancy for his borough of Castle Rising on 24 October 1745, ignoring a complaint that Rigby had assaulted an Oxford University proctor. His gambling made inroads on his fortune, and he fell under the influence of the cynical Thomas Winnington, on whose death in 1746 he transferred his attention to Frederick, prince of Wales. The latter induced him to contest Sudbury in the 1747 election, in which he was successful, surviving a petition against his return that alleged intimidation. Promised £1000 by the prince of Wales for his expenses, he obtained most of it and an assurance of appointment as groom of the bedchamber. When, two years later, the prince chose another man, Rigby fell out with him, although Frederick had intended to make him clerk of the green cloth, if possible.

Rigby's next allegiance was to John Russell, fourth duke of Bedford, whose addiction to country sports he shared, and whom he went on to rescue from an unruly mob at Lichfield races (1752). In 1756 a loan from the duke paid Rigby's debts. It was on the Bedford interest that he sat in parliament for Tavistock from 1754 after he had lost Sudbury and failed to win as the duke's candidate at Newport, Cornwall. Bedford was then in opposition, and Rigby became the boatswain of the 'Bloomsbury crew', as the duke's personal adherents were called. Well built, high spirited, personable when he chose, but in general brash, vehement, and disdainful of his opponents, Rigby obtained a seat at the Board of Trade in December 1755 following Bedford's alliance with Henry Fox, which association he had recommended to the duke. When Bedford became lord lieutenant of Ireland in January 1757 he named Rigby as his secretary. Rigby's conviviality was appreciated in Dublin, but he did make enemies, not least as the Dublin Castle spokesman in the Irish parliament, where he sat as member for Old Leighlin. He fell foul of a Dublin mob that was incensed by rumours of Irish union in 1759: they had threatened him with the gallows. He informed William Pitt that the rioters were probably the pawns of a French invasion scheme. In November 1759 he obtained the sinecure Irish mastership of the rolls in preference to a senior Irish lawyer, and vacated his Board of Trade seat. In June 1760 he became an Irish privy councillor.

Displaced from Ireland in March 1761 with Bedford, Rigby angled for further office. Bedford was prepared to see him made speaker of the Commons, but Rigby would have preferred a seat at the Treasury board. The duke of Newcastle was prepared to place him at the Admiralty board. Joining Bedford in denunciation of the protraction of the Seven Years' War for purely German objectives in 1762, Rigby was regarded in September as a likely secretary at war to reduce the army, but he opted for a less onerous Irish appointment, as joint vice-treasurer. He was Bedford's intermediary with Bute's administration when the duke was negotiating peace in Paris. On Bute's resignation in 1763, Rigby quarrelled with Henry Fox over Fox's refusal on obtaining a peerage to surrender the paymastership of the forces to him. As Rigby had championed Fox in debate, the latter was deeply hurt: but Rigby also savaged George Grenville in debate in November 1763, after previously backing his resistance to popular radicalism. The house cautioned Grenville against retaliation, and Rigby, who readily fought a duel with Lord Cornwallis

instead, spent part of 1764 on the continent, regaling Bedford with his adventures. He opposed the Rockingham ministry's repeal of the Stamp Act and was critical of American defiance during 1765 and 1766. He went into opposition to the Chatham administration, despite his patron's readiness to negotiate with them, and publicly ridiculed the 'annual ministries' of that decade in a debate on 13 May 1767, Chatham having ignored Bedford's recommendation of Rigby for office. He tried unsuccessfully to unite the opposition factions until the Bedford group joined the Grafton ministry in November 1767. In January 1768 he was restored to the Irish joint vice-treasurership that he had forfeited in July 1765 and obtained a promise of the paymastership of the forces, which he secured the following June.

His ambition realized, Rigby was a committed supporter of Lord North's administration. At the pay office his hospitality to congenial cronies was notorious: at Mistley Hall, too, they drank freely. Junius, in his *Letters*, mocked Rigby's purple face. In 1769 Rigby was a prominent opponent of the radical John Wilkes, and organized an Essex petition which was a subject of caricature. In January 1771 Bedford died, disclaiming Rigby's debts to him. Rigby had opposed Grenville's campaign against election bribery in 1770, and went on to oppose further attempts to secure parliamentary and economical reform: he defended the *status quo*, warts and all. In 1783 he defended two of his own officials against charges of malversation. He could not resist intriguing, and despite his staunch support of the suppression of the American rebellion he saw that military ineptitude and mounting expense would lose the war. Privately critical of North, he clung to office: over half a million pounds of surplus public money was in his custody, and he was said to lend it out liberally. He lost office with North in March 1782, despite his professions of support for the succeeding ministries of Rockingham and Shelburne which wound up the war.

Rigby's animosity toward the house of Pitt led him to oppose Pitt the younger's administration from 1783 onwards. On 23 February 1784 he was required to pay interest on outstanding balances from his paymastership tenure: four years later £156,000 was still owing. He came in for Tavistock again in 1784, despite the dowager duchess of Bedford's disinclination to return him: he toyed with Harwich, but had never exerted his electoral interest in Essex. In May 1785 he rallied to Pitt's Irish commercial propositions, but his political career was halted by failing health. Gout ridden, he gave up residence in St James's Place, London, and on medical advice retired to Bath, where he died of dropsy on 8 April 1788. He was buried at Mistley. He had clung to his seat in parliament. In his will, dated 31 December 1781, no mention is made of any debt to the public. Unmarried, he left legacies to his illegitimate daughter Sarah Lucas and her mother at Ipswich (an illegitimate son had predeceased him) and £100 a year to another mistress, Jenny Pickard of Colchester. His chief eventual beneficiary was Francis Hale, the son of his sister Martha, who took the additional name of Rigby.

Benjamin Disraeli, in *Coningsby* (1844), gave the name

Rigby to a political intriguer and parasite. By then Mistley Hall, which Rigby had landscaped and embellished, had been demolished. ROLAND THORNE

Sources L. B. Namier, 'Rigby, Richard', HoP, *Commons, 1754–90* · R. R. Sedgwick, 'Rigby, Richard', HoP, *Commons, 1715–54* · *GM*, 1st ser., 58 (1788), 369–71 · *Correspondence of John, fourth duke of Bedford*, ed. J. Russell, 2–3 (1842–6) · *Correspondence of William Pitt, earl of Chatham*, ed. W. S. Taylor and J. H. Pringle, 4 vols. (1838–40) · *The Grenville papers: being the correspondence of Richard Grenville … and … George Grenville*, ed. W. J. Smith, 2 (1852); 3 (1853), 389, 391–2; 4 (1853), 57, 61, 196 · *Additional Grenville papers, 1763–1765*, ed. J. R. G. Tomlinson (1962), 37, 89, 247 · earl of Ilchester [G. S. Holland Fox-Strangways], *Henry Fox, first Lord Holland, his family and relations*, 2 (1920), 257, 301 · P. Morant, *The history and antiquities of the county of Essex*, 1 (1768), 460, 462 · Walpole, *Corr.*, vols. 9, 21–2, 30, 37–8 · H. Walpole, *Memoirs of King George II*, ed. J. Brooke, 3 vols. (1985) · PRO, PROB 11/1166/173 · *DNB* · Venn, *Alum. Cant.*

Archives BL, corresp. with George Grenville and Lord Temple, Add. MSS 42084–42085, 57811 · BL, corresp. with Lord Holland, Add. MS 51385 · BL, letters to Sir Robert Keith, Add. MSS 35510–35536, *passim* · BL, corresp. with duke of Newcastle, etc., Add. MSS 32863–32987, *passim* · BL, letters to Lady Spencer · NA Scot., corresp. with Henry Dundas · NMM, corresp. with Lord Sandwich · priv. coll., corresp. with Robert FitzGerald · PRO, corresp. with Lord Stafford, PRO 30/29 · PRO NIre., corresp. with Lord Gosford · U. Mich., Clements L., corresp. with Thomas Gage · Yale U., Hanbury Williams MSS

Likenesses J. Sayers, caricature, etching, pubd 1782, NPG

Wealth at death £25,000: will, PRO, PROB 11/1166/173 · *c*.£150,000 in debt to the public

Rigg, Ambrose. *See* Rigge, Ambrose (*c*.1635–1705).

Rigg, Caroline Edith (1852–1929), headmistress, the eldest of three children, was born on 26 August 1852 in Guernsey, where her father, Dr James Harrison *Rigg (1821–1909), was Wesleyan minister. Her mother, Caroline (*d*. 1889), was daughter of John Smith, alderman of Worcester. James McMullen *Rigg was her younger brother. Caroline was educated at private schools until her father moved to London in 1867, when she attended the City of London College for Ladies in Finsbury Circus. This was modelled on Queen's College, Harley Street, and, as that drew on the staff of King's College, this City 'branch' utilized the staff of the City of London Boys' School, the model secondary school of the Taunton commissioners. In 1868 Dr Rigg became principal of Westminster Training College, and in 1872 continued his daughter's careful preparation 'for the instruction of others' by arranging for her to attend the sister college, Southlands, then in Battersea, as an out-student for one year's training, which she passed in division 1. Caroline was a born teacher, and she was born into teaching.

From 1873 Caroline Rigg was head of a board school in Hammersmith, until in 1877 she was appointed headmistress of the new Mary Datchelor Girls' School. This was the first use of an obsolete City parochial charity for girls' education of the new kind. The endowment in the parish of St Andrew Undershaft had increased dramatically by the sale of a coffee house in Threadneedle Street, and the charity commissioners appointed parochial trustees to administer the funds for a girls' school. Camberwell in south London, with a growing middle-class population, was selected as the location, and land and buildings acquired in Grove Lane. Of this enterprise Miss Rigg was appointed headmistress at the age of twenty-five. Her salary was £100 with capitation fees, which brought a total then considered generous for a woman.

One pupil remembered her mother's words on the opening day, 'I hope Clara won't be in her class—the little fair lady with curls; she looks far too young'. 'Little did she realise', her daughter added, 'the greatness of her personality and her many gifts' (Pearse, 27). In her application Miss Rigg said: 'Teaching with me is a passion and a pleasure' (ibid., 26). Many pupils testified to this. 'She had immense dignity and authority. Her absolute integrity, the unconscious influence of a dedicated personality, made it impossible to take an interview with her lightly' (ibid., 58). Her scripture and literature lessons were especially memorable, and many spoke of her beautiful voice. As the governors provided her with a secretary, she was able to teach an unusually full timetable, including Latin with the matriculation class.

Success depended on sheer persistent hard work and dedication. To Miss Rigg the school was her life. As well as her teaching, the organization and administration were formidable. The school opened with thirty pupils, aged eight to sixteen. Five months later there were 100, and by its fourth year 324, and no room for more. New buildings were required. The governors, to whom Miss Rigg reported monthly, were supportive. She had all the qualities of a pioneer, but the youthful headmistress was not quite of the pioneering generation. Experience of the new kind of girls' school was accumulating and these schools were using the system Miss Rigg designed for Datchelor. This was a broad academic curriculum, including science, leading to public examinations, with thorough attention to music and art, non-sectarian religious education, proper physical education, and training in social responsibility (there was a much-loved Dorcas Society). Girls were encouraged to aim at higher education and careers. Miss Rigg was always in the forefront of experiment, but her successor spoke of her 'power of remaining unchanged through change' (Dr Brock's memorial address, *Datchelor School Magazine*, 44, 1929, 9–10).

It was in her attitude to her staff that Miss Rigg can be classed not so much with the pioneering as with the professional generation of women educationists. As headmistress of a secondary school she was unusual, even unique, in that she had both professional training in, and experience of, elementary school teaching. Although academically qualified members of staff, even graduates, became available, Miss Rigg wanted professional training for her staff as well. Encouraged by the inspector, she began from 1879 to select pupils to train herself, perhaps using the model of the pupil teachers of the elementary system. Several so trained became members of staff, and as the demand grew senior girls were awarded 'student-teacherships', and then passed on to Maria Grey College, the only one then available for this purpose. In 1888 Miss

Rigg persuaded the trustees to open a training department at Datchelor, with herself as principal. A mistress of method was appointed and a lecturer in educational science. Students were admitted from other schools. Recognition by the Cambridge training syndicate was granted in 1899; in 1902 the college was inspected and recognized by the Board of Education, and from 1908 became eligible for its grants. In 1905 Miss Rigg and her vice-principal were recognized as teachers in pedagogy in the University of London, and the students became its internal students.

The Clothworkers' Company replaced the parochial trustees as governors of Datchelor in 1894–5, and proved generous guardians. In 1909 a new scheme enabled the London county council (since 1903 the local education authority) to be represented on the governing body. School board scholars had already been admitted, and from 1909 Datchelor accepted the county council's eleven-year-old scholarship holders. By 1914 these outnumbered the fee payers by 267 to 207. Throughout her long tenure Miss Rigg kept her vision of a less socially divided school system. She herself manifested the non-sectarian nature of girls' secondary schooling, for she was a Wesleyan headmistress of a school using old endowments from an Anglican parish. An inspection of 1915 reported that Datchelor

> maintains the well-deserved reputation for earnest, high-minded work which it has gained, above all, through the long unwearying services of the Head Mistress, who shows no trace of declining energy and enthusiasm, and who continues to have the support of a loyal and most capable staff. (Pearse, 70)

Miss Rigg served for ten years on the executive of the Association of Head Mistresses, which she represented on the board of examiners for education handwork (for she gave great importance to practical subjects).

Miss Rigg resigned in 1917, having over forty years built up Datchelor into one of the leading secondary schools, not only in London but in the country. She died at her home, 79 Brixton Hill, Brixton, London, on 16 December 1929. While her father was at Westminster, Miss Rigg attended the Horseferry Road Wesleyan church. When he moved to Brixton they went to the Brixton Hill church, where her memorial service was held. In the parish of St Mark, Camberwell, where Datchelor girls had been encouraged to give active social service, they proposed to place a memorial of her 'in the All Saints Corner of our Church'. In her will Miss Rigg left bequests to the Wesleyan Methodist Missionary Society, and to the Clothworkers' Company to provide scholarships to help girls who 'desire to proceed to a University' (*Datchelor School Magazine*, 44, 1929, 3).   MARGARET BRYANT

Sources R. N. Pearse, ed., *The story of the Mary Datchelor School, 1877–1977*, new edn (1977) · *WWW* · Clothworkers' Hall, London, Datchelor archives · *Datchelor School Magazine*, 22 (1918) · *Datchelor School Magazine*, 44 (1929) · M. E. Bryant, *The London experience of secondary education* (1986) · *VCH Middlesex*, vol. 1 · M. Bryant, *Private education* (1900) · b. cert. · d. cert. · 'The Datchelor Collegiate School and Training College', *Women's Herald* (25 May 1893), 221 · *CGPLA Eng. & Wales* (1930)

Archives Clothworkers' Hall, City of London, Datchelor archives

Likenesses R. Peacock, oils, 1901, Clothworkers' Hall, London · photograph, repro. in Pearse, ed., *Story of the Mary Datchelor School*

Wealth at death £24,515 14s. 1d.: probate, 9 Jan 1930, *CGPLA Eng. & Wales*

Rigg, James Harrison (1821–1909), Wesleyan Methodist minister and educationist, was born at Newcastle upon Tyne on 16 January 1821, the second son and third child of John Rigg (1786–1857), a Wesleyan Methodist minister there, and his second wife, Anne (*b.* 1797), daughter of James McMullen, Irish Methodist missionary at Gibraltar. Brought up in straitened circumstances, the boy was for five years (1830–35) a pupil and for four years (1835–9) a junior teacher at the Kingswood School for preachers' sons near Bristol. In 1839 he became assistant in the Revd Mr Firth's academy, Hartstead Moor, near Leeds, and having made an unsuccessful effort to conduct a school of his own in Islington, London, he became in 1843 classical and mathematical master at John Conquest's school at Biggleswade. In July 1845 he entered the Wesleyan Methodist ministry as probationer and, being ordained on 1 August 1849, served in Wesleyan circuits until 1868.

From an early date Rigg read widely and wrote much on religious and theological themes. A vigorous and clear style gave his writings influence in his denomination. He was a chief contributor to the *Biblical Review* (1846–9), and frequently wrote in the Wesleyan newspaper *The Watchman*. Having contributed to the first number of the *London Quarterly Review*, a Wesleyan Methodist periodical, in September 1853, he soon joined its editorial staff (1868), was co-editor with Dr William Burt Pope (1883–6), and ultimately sole editor (1886–98). Rigg explained his theological position in three volumes: *Principles of Wesleyan Methodism* (1850; 2nd edn, 1851), *Wesleyan Methodism and Congregationalism Contrasted* (1852), and *Modern Anglican Theology* (1857; 3rd edn, 1880). In the last he ably criticized the broad-church teaching of Maurice, Kingsley, and Jowett as being pervaded with a non-Christian Neoplatonism, but his differences with Kingsley were so considerately expressed that Kingsley sought his acquaintance. In 1866 he republished many periodical articles as *Essays for the Times on Ecclesiastical and Social Subjects*. His literary work was early valued in America. He acted as English correspondent of the *New Orleans Christian Advocate* (1851) and of the *New York Christian Advocate* (1857–76). In 1865 he received the degree of DD from Dickinson College, USA, and in 1877 from Edinburgh.

In 1868 Rigg was appointed principal of the Westminster (Wesleyan) Training College for day-school teachers, and he held that post until 1903. In matters of education he acquired an expert knowledge and was an active controversialist. When the first Elementary Education Act was passed in 1870 Rigg took the traditional Wesleyan view, opposing secularism and favouring denominational schools, although without sympathy for sectarian exclusiveness. He was opposed by William Arthur and Hugh Price Hughes, who supported the transfer of Wesleyan schools to the school boards created in 1870. He pressed his views, in correspondence, on the attention of Gladstone and W. E. Forster, and the Wesleyan conference supported him. From 1870 to 1876 he served as a member for Westminster on the first London school board. With the help of Professor Thomas Huxley and W. H. Smith MP he secured the provision of a syllabus of religious instruction. He advocated a broad curriculum open to girls as well as boys. He was a member of the royal commission on elementary education (1886–8), known as the Cross commission, which reported in favour of the school board management as against the voluntary system.

In the general administration of Wesleyan affairs Rigg was recognized to be a statesman-like leader of liberal-conservative temper. He was successively chairman of the Kent and second London districts (1865, 1877), and in 1878 and 1892 was president of the Wesleyan conference. From 1881 to 1909 he was treasurer of the Wesleyan Missionary Society. In controversies concerning the internal organization of the Wesleyan church Rigg took a middle course. He accepted the addition of a representative lay session of conference, but in 1890 successfully advocated its insertion between two sessions restricted to ministers, so that the pastoral element should predominate. Rigg's proposal of 1894, supported by the 'progressive' party under Hugh Price to exempt chairmen of districts from circuit duties and leave them free to exercise supervision over the district, was rejected by the conference from a suspicion that Rigg's 'separated chairmen' had a colour of episcopacy. With Hughes and the progressive party Rigg's relations were often strained. Writing privately to Cardinal Manning, a colleague on the education commission, on the education question on 17 December 1888, he described Hughes as 'your intemperate temperance coadjutor, our methodist firebrand' (Smith, 212). The unauthorized publication of the letter in Purcell's *Life* of the cardinal (1895) led to reprisals by Hughes, who wrote in the *Methodist Times* an article entitled 'The self-revelation of Dr Rigg' (described by a friend of Rigg as 'unscrupulous' and 'mendacious'; Methodist Archives, MAM PLP 89-39-2). At Rigg's request the letter was withdrawn from later editions of Purcell's book, and Hughes and he were reconciled.

Rigg never abated his literary energies amid his varied activities. For many years he was a member of the committee of the London Library. To an earlier study entitled *The Churchmanship of John Wesley* (1869, 1879) he added *The Living Wesley* (1875; reissued as *The Centennial Life of Wesley* in 1891). The former played down Wesley's high-church characteristics in the light of current Wesleyan suspicions of Anglo-Catholicism. The latter attempted a fuller account of Wesley's private life. Rigg's *Oxford High Anglicanism and its Chief Leaders* (1895; 2nd edn, 1899) is apparently the only attempt made by a nonconformist to write a history of the Oxford Movement. Rigg was a severe critic of Newman, but especially emphasized the influence of Pusey on the development of Anglo-Catholicism. There followed *Reminiscences Sixty Years Ago* (1904), covering only his early life; a sympathetic biography of Jabez Bunting (1905); and the article 'Methodism' in the *Encyclopaedia Britannica* (9th edn).

Rigg married, on 17 June 1851, Caroline Smith (*d.* 17 Dec 1889), the daughter of John Smith, alderman of Worcester. They had two schoolmistress daughters (the elder, Caroline Edith *Rigg, became a renowned headmistress and the younger married Rigg's biographer, John Telford) and a barrister son, James McMullen *Rigg, who contributed many articles to the *Dictionary of National Biography*. Short, rotund, and bearded, Rigg was aggressive and self-confident, especially in controversy (some compared him to Dr Johnson). Yet he was also an able compromiser in negotiation. He was kindly to individuals and devoted to his wife, who was often in poor health.

For many years Rigg dominated Wesleyan educational policy, which was directed at developing denominational middle-class as well as elementary education. A major influence on policy, however, was fear of Roman and Anglo-Catholic advance (and 'infidelity'). This can be seen in Rigg's advocacy of Wesleyan schools, his writings on Anglicanism, and his interpretations of John Wesley. These fears weakened Rigg's inherited conservative Wesleyan sympathies with Anglicanism, and strengthened his assertion of the superiority of Wesleyan doctrine and polity, though he disliked aggressive nonconformity. Both he and Hughes wished to protect Wesleyan children from Roman and Anglo-Catholic 'perversion', though they differed on the best policy for achieving this: the mixed 'denominational and secular' system secured in 1870 (Rigg) or a purely 'secular' one (Hughes). Both insisted that the secular schools must include non-denominational religious instruction. In Rigg's last years Hughes's more nonconformist policies were clearly gaining ground in Wesleyanism. Rigg died on 17 April 1909 at 79 Brixton Hill, London, and was buried in the city's Norwood cemetery.

C. H. IRWIN, *rev.* HENRY D. RACK

Sources J. Telford, *Life of J. H. Rigg, 1821–1909* (1909) · J. T. Smith, *Methodism and education, 1849–1902: J. H. Rigg, Romanism and Wesleyan schools* (1998) · R. E. Davies, A. R. George, and G. Rupp, eds., *History of Methodism in Great Britain*, 2 (1978), 244–5 · R. E. Davies, A. R. George, and G. Rupp, eds., *History of Methodism in Great Britain*, 3 (1983), 161, 186, 194–6, 296 · JRL, Methodist Church Archives, letters of J. H. Rigg, MAM PLP 89-39 · D. P. Hughes, *The life of Hugh Price Hughes* (1904) · E. S. Purcell, *Life of Cardinal Manning*, 2 vols. (1895) · *Men and women of the time* (1899) · 'Royal commission to inquire into … elementary education: final report', *Parl. papers* (1888), vol. 35, C. 5485 [England and Wales]
Archives JRL, Methodist Archives and Research Centre, corresp.
Likenesses three photographs, 1852–1901, repro. in Telford, *Life of J. H. Rigg*, pp. 94, 276, and frontispiece · Adams-Acton, bust, 1892; formerly in Westminster College, Oxford · Adams-Acton, marble medallion, priv. coll. · oils, Westminster College, Oxford · woodengraving (after photograph by Appleton & Co.), NPG; repro. in *ILN* (10 Aug 1878)
Wealth at death £6557 15s. 6d.: probate, 17 May 1909, CGPLA Eng. & Wales

Rigg, James McMullen (1855–1926), biographer and historian, the son of James Harrison *Rigg (1821–1909), principal of the Wesleyan college, Westminster, and his wife, Caroline (*d.* 1889), daughter of John Smith, alderman of Worcester, was born at Brentford on 28 September 1855. He was educated at the City of London School under Dr E. A. Abbott and at St John's College, Oxford, of which he was a scholar. He obtained a second class in classical moderations in 1876 and a third class in *literae humaniores* in 1878. He entered Lincoln's Inn in 1880, and was called to the bar in November 1881. He soon abandoned law entirely, and devoted the rest of his life to literary work.

In 1885 Rigg began to write articles for the *Dictionary of National Biography*, to which he contributed more than 600 entries, mainly on the judiciary. Some of his assessments of recent judges were regarded as being rather bold. Besides editing Sir Thomas More's translation of the Latin life of Pico della Mirandola (1890) and writing a study of St Anselm as thinker and writer (1896) he published valuable editions of the plea rolls of the exchequer of the Jews, covering the thirteenth century, first for the Selden Society (1902) and then for the Jewish Historical Society (1905, 1910). In 1909 Rigg was appointed by the deputy keeper of the records to research in the Vatican archives, and spent nine months of each of the years 1909 to 1915 in Rome. His two volumes of *A Calendar of State Papers … Rome* (vol. 1, 1558–71; vol. 2, 1572–8) were published in 1916 and 1926. All Rigg's editorial work was distinguished by accurate scholarship. He also published a translation of Boccaccio's *Decameron* (1903).

In appearance Rigg was spare and ascetic, in manner shy and reserved. He usually spoke abruptly and emphatically, yet in friendly surroundings he was an excellent talker. His greatest interest in life was the history and philosophy of religion. In spite of his Wesleyan origins he seemed to be pleased when anybody mistook him for a Roman Catholic. He died at his home, 79 Brixton Hill, London, on 14 April 1926. He was unmarried, and lived with the elder of his two sisters, Caroline Edith *Rigg, headmistress for forty-one years of the Mary Datchelor School, Camberwell.   G. J. TURNER, *rev.* G. MARTIN MURPHY

Sources private information (1937) · personal knowledge (1937)
Wealth at death £13,126 5*s.* 1*d.*: administration, 1 June 1926, *CGPLA Eng. & Wales*

Rigge [Rigg], **Ambrose** (*c.*1635–1705), Quaker preacher and writer, was born at Bampton, Westmorland. After studying at the Bampton Free School, he became a schoolmaster at Grayrigg, Westmorland. When in 1652 or 1653 he became a Quaker after hearing George Fox preach near Sedbergh, Yorkshire, his parents renounced him. With Thomas Robertson, Rigge preached in Kent, Surrey, Sussex, and Hampshire, and they were imprisoned together for fifteen weeks at Basingstoke for refusing to take the oath of abjuration in the summer of 1655. The following March, Rigge was whipped and incarcerated at Southampton, and in 1657 he was gaoled at Dorchester and, with Thomas Salthouse, at Southwark. A prolific author, his earliest works included *Of Perfection* (1657), composed in Dorchester prison and addressed to presbyterians, Independents, Baptists, and seekers, all of whom he accused of repudiating the biblical doctrine of perfection. The same year he published *The Banner of Gods Love*, denouncing persecutors and 'cruel oppressors, who grinde the faces of the poore' (A. Rigge, *The Banner of Gods Love*, 1657, 10). In 1658 he had entrails thrown at him in Henley-on-Thames, Oxfordshire, was imprisoned on the Isle of Wight, and

was whipped and transported in a dung cart at Southampton. Against this background he castigated the professional clergy in *To All Hireling Priests* (1659), called on MPs and magistrates to suppress violence and spoliation of the people in *Oh ye Heads of the Nation* (July 1659), and insisted that Friends were innocent of all plotting and relied wholly on spiritual weapons in *To All who Imprison & Persecute* (1659).

After the Restoration, Rigge continued to preach in southern England. At Southampton in December 1660 he wrote *To the Whole Flock of God*, describing himself as 'a Souldier in the Army of the Lamb', and exhorting Friends to be courageous despite being 'compassed about with many Enemies' (A. Rigge, *To the Whole Flock of God*, 1660, 2, 8). On 11 January 1661 he was arrested in Hampshire and gaoled for more than four months at Winchester after refusing the oath of allegiance, and his books were seized and sent to Sir Edward Nicholas. Apprehended again, this time at Hurstpierpoint, Sussex, on 20 May 1662, he refused to take the oath of allegiance, was convicted of *praemunire*, and spent ten years and four months in Horsham gaol. From his cell he appealed publicly to Charles II in *A Visitation of Tender Love* (September 1662), arguing that the king had violated his pledge of liberty to tender consciences and warning of divine punishment unless he repented. A private but futile appeal followed on 16 February 1663. In June Rigge completed *A True Prospect*, in which he condemned numerous Anglican practices as unscriptural and averred that Quakers should be protected by law. He also engaged in a debate with the vicar of Horsham, Leonard Letchford, especially over the Quaker doctrine of perfection, denouncing his views in *A Standard of Righteousness* (October 1663) and *The Serpent's Subtilty Discovered* (1663). On 6 September 1664 Rigge married a fellow inmate, Mary (d. 1689), daughter of Captain Thomas Luxford of Hurstpierpoint, with whom he was to have five children. Mary was prosecuted by Letchford for refusing to pay tithes, and had furniture and cooking utensils seized from her cell.

In *A Lamentation over England* (August 1665) Rigge donned Jeremiah's mantle to declaim against England's iniquity and urge repentance. He argued in *The Good Old Way* (1669), which included a biographical postscript by Rebecca Travers, that Quaker opposition to tithes and oaths followed early Christian practice, a thesis reinforced with appeals to church history and law. Although a warrant for his release was issued on 12 May 1669, he remained in prison. After further appeals to the king, including one on 27 October 1671 which he claimed Christ had commanded him to make, Rigge was released in February 1672. For a while he remained at Horsham, where he hosted William Penn in September 1672; three years earlier Penn had distributed some of Rigge's tracts in Ireland. Penn's influence was undoubtedly responsible for Rigge's acquisition of 5000 acres in Pennsylvania, though he never emigrated.

Rigge left Horsham, where he had been clerk of the monthly meeting, for Gatton, Surrey, and again was a schoolmaster. His pedagogical interests are reflected in *A*

Scripture-Catechism for Children (1672), a lengthy series of questions and answers about the Bible. In 1674 the minister of Gatton, Robert Pepys, prosecuted him in the exchequer for refusing to remit tithes, and in July 1676 he was imprisoned for recusancy. At Southwark on 24 November 1676 he finished *A Premonition to the Bishops and Priests*, explaining why Friends refused to attend parish services, in part because they were held in what had been the Roman Catholics' 'Idolatrous Houses' (A. Rigge, *A Premonition to the Bishops*, 1676, 13). The extensive quotations from the patristics in *True Christianity Vindicated* (November 1678) indicate that he spent time studying, and in *A Brief and Serious Warning* (January 1679) he articulated a code of ethics for Quaker merchants, warning them not to 'borrow upon the Truth's Credit' (A. Rigge, *A Brief and Serious Warning*, 1679, 4). As Pepys continued to prosecute him, he lost eight cows valued at £32 in 1681 for refusing to pay tithes, and he was cited in the exchequer for recusancy in 1683. He protested against the suffering inflicted on Quakers in *To the Magistrates, Governors & Rulers* (June 1682), and again in a petition submitted with Nathaniel Owen and George Beale to Surrey MPs in 1685. Yet he continued to suffer, losing hops and other goods worth £5 10s. between 1686 and 1690.

Following the death in January 1689 of Mary, Rigge married Ann Bax of Capel, Surrey, on 12 May 1690; they had no children. He remained active in the 1690s, speaking at Fox's funeral and publishing *The Spiritual Guide of Life* (1691), which dealt with the Holy Spirit's inward teaching. By November 1692 he had moved to Reigate, Surrey, where he wrote *An Epistle from our Monthly Meeting* (1692) on the importance of raising children as Quakers and excluding people whose conduct was inappropriate. He was a signatory of George Whitehead's *The Christian Doctrine* (1693). In his late works he provided spiritual counsel to families in *A General Epistle of Universal Love* (1698), reiterated the doctrine of perfection in *A Testimony to True Christianity* (1703), and offered guidance for obtaining spiritual knowledge in *A Treatise Concerning the Internal Word* (1704).

Rigge died at Reigate on 31 January 1705 and was buried at Guildford on 4 February. His children by his first marriage included a son, Thomas, of Lewis, Suffolk; a daughter who married Thomas Penny of London; a daughter who wed Samuel Sandys of London; and his youngest daughter, Elizabeth, who married John Trevor of Stepney, Middlesex. Some of Rigge's writings, edited by Whitehead, were published as *Constancy in the Truth Commended* (1710). RICHARD L. GREAVES

Sources RS Friends, Lond., Swarthmore MSS, 1.162 · G. F. Nuttall, ed., *Early Quaker letters from the Swarthmore MSS to 1660* (1952) · PRO, SP 29/68/74; 29/292/113, 114 · *The journal of George Fox*, ed. N. Penney, 2 vols. (1911) · *CSP dom.*, 1660–61, 473–4; 1663–4, 50; 1668–9, 323; 1671–2, 170 · J. Besse, *A collection of the sufferings of the people called Quakers*, 1 (1753), 228–31, 699, 702, 705–7, 713, 715, 717 · *DNB* · N. Penney, ed., 'The first publishers of truth': being early records, now first printed, of the introduction of Quakerism into the counties of England and Wales* (1907) · W. C. Braithwaite, *The beginnings of Quakerism*, ed. H. J. Cadbury, 2nd edn (1955) · *The papers of William Penn*, ed. M. M. Dunn, R. S. Dunn, and others, 1 (1981), 109, 246, 652 · will, PRO,

PROB 11/480, sig. 38 · *The short journal and itinerary journals of George Fox*, ed. N. Penney (1925), 176, 342–3, 353
Archives PRO, MSS, PRO 30/8/72 · RS Friends, Lond., letters and MSS
Wealth at death £136; plus household goods, books, MSS, and other unspecified possessions: will, PRO, PROB 11/480, sig. 38

Rightwise, John (*c*.1490–1533), grammarian, was born at Sall, Norfolk. He was educated at Eton College and King's College, Cambridge (BA, 1513; MA, 1516), where he held a fellowship until 1524. In 1517 Rightwise was engaged by John Colet as surmaster (second master) for his new foundation of St Paul's School. The high-master was the more eminent grammarian William Lily, whose daughter Dionysia Rightwise married. He was elected to the high-mastership upon Lily's retirement in 1522, but the appointment was not a success, and there were persistent complaints alleging increasing negligence of his duties in the school. He was eventually dismissed in December 1532, and granted a pension from school funds.

Rightwise is known as a grammarian through his contributions towards the augmentation of Lily's Latin grammar, consisting of verses relating to the treatment of nouns and verbs in the *Brevissima institutio*. Since no dramatic writings attributed to him are known to exist, it is not certain that he can also be described as a dramatist. There are, however, records that show him to have been actively involved in the direction and staging of Latin plays, performed by the boys of St Paul's, under the patronage of Cardinal Wolsey. On 10 November 1527 Rightwise and his boys enacted a flattering topical allegory before the king, Wolsey, and the court at Greenwich, of which interesting details have been preserved. It featured characters such as Religion, Heresy, False Interpretation, Curruptio Scriptoris, Luther, Wolsey, the pope, the dauphin and his brother, the emperor's chancellor, and a number of others (BL, Egerton MS 2605, fol. 37). At some time between 1522 and 1530 a 'tragedy of Dido, out of Virgil' was also performed for Wolsey, the composition of which has traditionally been attributed to Rightwise, though one source suggests that it was the work of his wife, Dionysia (BL, Cole MSS, vol. 12, fol. 150).

Shortly before his dismissal from St Paul's, Rightwise had petitioned the crown for financial support, claiming hardship on account of illness, and noting that he had 'by command of the King and Council played Comedies before ambassadors and others visiting the realm' (*LP Henry VIII*, addenda, 1929, 1/1.242). His health may indeed not have been good, for he died a few months after his dismissal, some time between 12 July and 20 August 1533, in the parish of St Botolph, Aldersgate. He was remembered in some verses by John Leland. RICHARD BEADLE

Sources Wood, *Ath. Oxon.*, new edn, 1.35 · W. Sterry, ed., *The Eton College register, 1441–1698* (1943), 281 · Venn, *Alum. Cant.*, 1/3.460 · M. McDonnell, ed., *The registers of St Paul's School, 1509–1748* (privately printed, London, 1977), 18–19 · I. Lancashire, *Dramatic texts and records of Britain: a chronological topography to 1558* (1984), 62–3, 144, 195 · E. K. Chambers, *The medieval stage* (1913), 2.196, 215, 219 · *LP Henry VIII*, 4/2, nos. 3563–4 (pp. 1603–6); addenda 1/1, no. 717 (p. 242) · BL, Egerton MS 2605, fol. 37 · BL, Cole MSS, vol. 12, fol. 150 · will, PRO, PROB 11/25, sig. 5

Rignold [Rignall], **George Richard** (1839–1912), actor and theatre manager, was born in Leicester, the second son of the actors William Ross Rignold (1813–1883) and his wife, Patricia Blaxland (1800–1888). Music was George Rignold's first love and he became an accomplished violinist, but his father encouraged him to take to the stage, which offered better financial prospects. After early experience at the Theatre Royal, Birmingham, Rignold joined J. H. Chute's company in Bath and Bristol. In the production of *A Midsummer Night's Dream* with which the new Theatre Royal, Bath, opened on 4 March 1863 Rignold played Theseus in a notable cast, which included his elder brother William (1836–1904) as Lysander, Charles Coghlan as Demetrius, Henrietta Hodson as Oberon, Ellen Terry as Titania, and the father and daughter William and Madge Robertson (later Dame Madge Kendal) as Egeus and Second Singing Fairy respectively.

In March 1869, following further engagements with Chute and others in Plymouth, Swansea, and Manchester, Rignold progressed to the metropolis, to the Queen's Theatre, Long Acre, where E. J. Young's company included Henrietta Hodson, Mrs Stirling, and Charles Wyndham. Rignold made his mark in a range of parts: Sir John Bridges in Tom Taylor's *'Twixt Axe and Crown* and Father Isambard in the same author's *Joan of Arc*; William in Douglas Jerrold's *Black-Eyed Susan*, which he also played at the Holborn Theatre; and Shakespeare's Caliban (28 October 1871), Posthumus (30 March 1872), and Romeo, to Adelaide Neilson's Juliet (14 September 1872). Roles in contemporary plays followed: Westland Marston's *Put to the Test* at the Olympic Theatre in February 1873, Herman Merivale's *The White Pilgrim* at the Court Theatre in February 1874, and the first provincial tour of Taylor's *Clancarty* in the same year, but it was his casting as Henry V in New York in 1875 that proved to be the turning point in Rignold's career.

Charles Calvert's revival of *Henry V* had been such an outstanding success at the Prince's Theatre, Manchester, in 1872 and subsequently on tour that it had been bought by the New York managers Jarrett and Palmer. Calvert supervised the staging at Booth's Theatre in February 1875, but, because of his poor health, stepped down from the title role and cast Rignold in his stead. Calvert's elaborate stagecraft and detailed realization of medieval pageantry and warfare were a revelation to New Yorkers. Rignold's Henry V, though it lacked the subtlety of Calvert's own interpretation, impressed American audiences, for whom Henry James can stand as a spokesman: 'He plays the part in a most natural fashion, looks it and wears it to perfection, and declaims its swelling harangues with admirable vigour and taste. He is worth looking at and listening to' (*The Nation*, 11 March 1875). Now dubbed Rignold Rex and Handsome George, Rignold was fêted by lady admirers—his wooing of Princess Katherine was considered to be his finest scene—and his photographs by Sarony sold in huge quantities.

Rignold took *Henry V* across America, from the east coast to Salt Lake City and on to San Francisco, and thence to Australia and New Zealand. Acclaim was universal: 'His interpretation in every sense of the word is perfection' (*Wellington Evening Chronicle*, 27 Dec 1878). It was not just the influence of England's theatre that Rignold was spreading across the globe, but also, especially with such a patriotic play as *Henry V*, her history and culture. The success of *Henry V* had encouraged Rignold to add Macbeth to his repertory at Booth's Theatre in May 1875, but this served only to reveal his limitations as an actor. Even with Henry V the more exacting London critics expressed reservations when Rignold appeared at Drury Lane in November 1879: 'He does but small justice to the noble words put into his mouth. His elocution is imperfect, often incorrect in emphasis, too hurried, and deficient in kingly dignity. He seems too anxious to get over the speeches and come to the fighting' (*The Times*, 6 Nov 1879).

The strictures of the London critics, compared with the plaudits of their American and Australian counterparts, no doubt influenced Rignold's decision to pursue his career in Australia. On 25 March 1882 he appeared in Melbourne as Frank Darlington in Augustus Harris's Drury Lane success *Youth*, and, following a brief business trip to England to buy plays and other requisites, Rignold went into partnership with James Allison at Her Majesty's Opera House, Melbourne. Later the two men took Her Majesty's Theatre in Sydney, of which, following Allison's death in 1895, Rignold assumed sole charge. During the nine years from 1888 Rignold mounted plays from the English repertory: melodramas such as Watts Phillips's *The Dead Heart* and Charles Reade's *The Lyons Mail*, Gilbert Parker's version of Goethe's *Faust*, and Shakespeare. He performed in most of the productions himself and attracted several notable English actors to his theatre, playing Mark Antony to J. F. Cathcart's Brutus, Master Ford to his brother William's Falstaff, and Macbeth to Janet Achurch's Lady Macbeth. Rignold proclaimed: 'I made Shakespeare pay. I never lost a farthing over any of my revivals, and I did the pieces as well as it was possible with all the best attainable effects electric and otherwise' (*The Era*, 8 Nov 1902). In an age in which international copyright was more honoured in the breach than the observance Rignold was scrupulous in remunerating living authors.

Rignold returned to London in 1902 to appear in a benefit performance for his, by then blind, brother William. Rignold's first wife, whom he married on 28 September 1865, the actress Marie Braybrook Henderson, had supported him in his various enterprises, and died in Australia on 26 February 1902. His second marriage, on 3 October 1907, was to Georgina Harriet Dora Coppin (1864–1911), the daughter of the Australian politician and theatre manager George Selth *Coppin. He had no children from either marriage. Rignold lived quietly at his property on the beautiful shore of Sydney's Middle Harbour, though he made a return to the Melbourne stage in 1907 as Jason in Hall Caine's *The Bondsman*. He died in a Sydney nursing home, Charlemont Private Hospital, Darlinghurst, on 16 December 1912. His death was extensively reported in his home country, but had he remained there he would not have achieved as great an eminence as he did in Australia:

'He trained as far as possible an Australian company of players, and throughout his career set up a high artistic standard which did much to place the Australian stage in its present position' (*The Times*, 17 Dec 1912).

RICHARD FOULKES

Sources *The Era* (22 Feb 1896) · *The Era* (8 Nov 1902) · *The Era* (19 Dec 1912) · *The Stage* (19 Dec 1912) · *The Times* (17 Dec 1912) · J. Parker, ed., *The green room book, or, Who's who on the stage* (1909) · J. Parker, ed., *Who's who in the theatre* (1912) · J. Parker, ed., *Who's who in the theatre*, 10th edn (1947) · C. E. Pascoe, ed., *The dramatic list* (1879); repr. (1971) · D. Mullin, ed., *Victorian actors and actresses in review: a dictionary of contemporary views of representative British and American actors and actresses, 1837–1901* (1983) · A. Wade, ed., *Henry James: the scenic art* (1957) · G. C. D. Odell, *Annals of the New York stage*, 15 vols. (1927–49) · *AusDB* · B. Burke, *A genealogical and heraldic history of the colonial gentry*, 2 (1895) · *CGPLA Eng. & Wales* (1913)
Archives Harvard TC | Folger, prompt book, Her Majesty's Theatre, Sydney, *Julius Caesar*, 24 Aug 1889
Likenesses ceramic sculpture, 1879 (as Henry V) · portrait, 1879 (as Henry V, programme cover for Drury Lane Theatre), Theatre Museum, London · Sarony, portrait; copies, Lincoln Center, Performing Arts Library, New York · portrait (as Othello), repro. in *The Era* (8 Nov 1902) · prints, Harvard TC
Wealth at death £11,000: Parker, ed., *Who's who in the theatre*, 10th edn · £4626 5s. 10d.: resworn probate, 1913, *CGPLA Eng. & Wales*

Rijens, Jan. *See* Reynes, John (*d.* 1545).

Riley. *See also* Reilly, Ryley.

Riley, Henry Thomas (1816–1878), literary scholar and translator, was born on 29 June 1816, the son of Henry Riley, an ironmonger in Borough High Street, London, and Caroline Parker. He was educated at a boarding-school in Ramsgate before attending Charterhouse School as a day boy (1832–4). In 1834 he entered Trinity College, Cambridge, but migrated to Clare College, where he was elected a scholar on 24 January 1835. He won a Latin essay prize in 1838 and graduated BA in 1840. He received his MA in 1859 before moving to Corpus Christi College. On 16 June 1870 he was incorporated at Exeter College, Oxford.

Riley married Ellen, the daughter of Richard V. Windsor, a law stationer in Chancery Lane, on 14 July 1838 at St George's, Bloomsbury. According to his obituarists, Riley 'was forced to toil for the booksellers in order to gain a livelihood'. This is an exaggeration, though he spent many years translating classics and medieval chronicles for Henry Bohn. He is said to have translated the *Olynthiacs* of Demosthenes as early as 1836, but this is unproven. For several years Riley was a schoolteacher, from 1839 at the recently erected City of London School. In 1841 he was appointed headmaster of Morpeth grammar school, Northumberland, where he remained until 1856. Riley translated Ovid's works for Bohn's Classical Library (*Metamorphoses*, *Fasti*, and *Tristia* in 1851, and the *Heroïdes* in 1852). The *Comedies* of Plautus appeared in 1852, Lucan's *Pharsalia*, the *Comedies* of Terence, and the *Fables* of Phaedrus in 1853, and, with Dr John Bostock, the *Natural History* of the elder Pliny in 1855–7 (6 vols.). For Bohn's Antiquarian Library he translated Roger of Howden's *Annals* (1853), and in 1854 the spurious *Chronicle of the Abbey of Croyland* by Ingulph. Riley helped to establish the latter as a medieval forgery, though later editors have disputed his dating.

Bohn also published Riley's *Dictionary of Latin Quotations* (1856).

Riley was called to the bar at the Inner Temple on 23 November 1847 and was recorded as an equity draftsman and conveyancer. He was also a member of the Fan Makers' Company. Although he returned to London in 1856 and is later described as a barrister, it is unlikely that he often practised this calling, for he devoted the later 1850s and the 1860s to the task of editing and partly translating the medieval records of the corporation of London, on which his scholarly reputation deservedly rests. For the twelfth volume of the master of the rolls' series of chronicles Riley edited the corporation's *Liber albus* (1859) and the *Liber custumarum* (1860), with a translation of the Anglo-Norman passages (1862); the *Liber Horn* was to have been included but was omitted. He translated the *Liber albus* (1861) and the Latin and Anglo-Norman *Chronicles of the Mayors and Sheriffs of London, 1188–1274*, [with] *The French Chronicle of London, 1259–1343* (1863). And in 1868 he published *Memorials of London and London Life … Extracts from the Archives, 1276–1419*.

Riley further edited for the Rolls Series (vol. 28, published in 12 vols., 1863–76) the *Chronica monasterii S. Albani*, comprising the annals of John Amundesham and the works of Thomas Walsingham, John de Trokelowe, Henry Blaneforde, and William Rishanger, and the register of John Wethamsted. Riley's scholarship was generally sound, though he was criticized for some of his opinions, for instance by V. H. Galbraith in his *The St Albans Chronicle, 1406–1420* (1937, 11–12). When the Historical Manuscripts Commission was established in 1869, Riley was appointed to inspect the archives of municipal corporations, the muniments of Oxford and Cambridge colleges, and the registries of several bishops and chapters. His well-researched accounts appear in the first six reports of the commission, published between 1874 and 1877.

Riley wrote for *The Athenaeum* and the *Gentleman's Magazine*, and on both Plinys for the eighth edition of the *Encyclopaedia Britannica*. An indefatigable editor, he died at his home, Hainault House, The Crescent, Selhurst, Croydon, on 14 April 1878 from illness caused, it was said, by 'hard mental work'. He was survived by his wife.

W. P. COURTNEY, rev. K. A. MANLEY

Sources Venn, *Alum. Cant.* · *The Times* (16 April 1878) · *The Athenaeum* (27 April 1878), 542 · parish register (birth and baptism), St George the Martyr, Southwark, London, 29 June 1816 – 13 July 1816 · parish register (marriages), St George's, Bloomsbury, London, 14 July 1838 · T. Walsingham, *The St Albans chronicle, 1406–1420*, ed. V. H. Galbraith (1937) · *CGPLA Eng. & Wales* (1878)
Wealth at death under £8000: probate, 9 May 1878, *CGPLA Eng. & Wales*

Riley, John (1646–1691), portrait painter, was born, according to his friend and earliest biographer, Richard Graham, 'in the City of *London*, *Anno*, 1646' (Graham, 347). In the second volume of his *Note Books* George Vertue transcribed Graham's account verbatim, but, in recording further information from Riley's pupil Anthony Russel, he also noted 'Bishopsgate Church [St Botolph's where] Mr Roily painter [was] buried. His father and mother lived in this parish where he was born' (Vertue, *Note books*, 4.43). In his will, Riley calls himself 'John Riley Junior, Bachelor' and mentions 'John Riley Senior his ffather, Jochebed Riley his Mother and Thomas Riley his brother' (will, PRO, PROB 11/404, sig. 71). Jochebed Riley (d. 11 Jan 1693) was probably Riley's stepmother, since she was apparently only eleven years old at the time of his birth. This record of his parentage confirms that he was not the John Riley, son of the Lancaster herald William Riley (d. 1667), mentioned in a Herald's College manuscript that led James Dallaway in his edition of Horace Walpole's *Anecdotes of Painting in England* to identify Riley 'as one of the several sons of William Riley, Lancaster Herald' (Walpole, 2.221). This error has subsequently been repeated in the literature concerning Riley. It is conceivable, however, that the herald was Riley's grandfather, and this might explain Riley's later entry into court circles, and how he came to paint the Windsor herald Elias Ashmole twice. But Riley is hardly an uncommon name; and Graham does not mention such a connection.

An early anonymous source states 'Mr. Hale that Stuttered, used to temper colours for Mr Reyley, that learnt … first of Mr. Fever' [William Fever, who is totally obscure] (Whinney and Millar, 188, n. 1). Graham says that John Riley 'was instructed in the first Rudiments of *Painting* by Mr. *Zoust* [Gerard Soest (c.1605–1681)] and Mr. *Fuller* [Isaac Fuller (1606–1672)] but left them while he was very *Young*, and began to practise after the *Life*' (Graham, 347). There is little trace of Fuller in Riley's work, but much of Soest, a portrait painter from Westphalia, who was probably trained in the Netherlands and worked in London from the 1640s. He was a very accomplished artist who attained a good practice among the gentry and aristocracy. But his unidealized, eccentric, melancholy characterizations of his sitters set him apart from the fashionable, flattering styles, such as that of Sir Peter Lely, favoured in court circles.

That Riley could begin practising 'very young' suggests that he had independent wealth, of which there are other indications. In November 1681 Mary Beale saw at the picture restorer Parry Walton 'the Lady Carnarvons picture H.L. [half length] by Vandyck. in blew satin … lately bought by Mr Riley for 3511 [pounds]' (Vertue, *Note books*, 4.175), a large sum at the time. On 15 September 1682 Riley acquired the freedom of the Painter–Stainers' Company of London 'by redemption', that is by payment.

Riley, says Graham:

acquir'd no great *Reputation*, till, upon the Death [30 Nov 1680] of Sir *Peter Lely*, [Riley's] Friends being desirous that he should succeed that excellent *Master* in the Favour of King *Charles* II. engag'd Mr. *Chiffinch* [William Chiffinch, (c.1602–1688), keeper of the king's jewels and of his majesty's closet] to sit to him for his *Picture*. (Graham, 347–8)

The portrait (Dulwich Art Gallery), Riley's first-known work, is a bust showing the sitter wearing his own hair. The drapery is Soest-like, if less stylish, and the head has a Soestian gravity, and also a shyness which characterizes Riley's best heads.

With the Chiffinch portrait, says Graham, Riley:

perform'd so well, that the King, upon sight of it, sent for [Riley] and having employ'd him in drawing the Duke of *Grafton's Portrait*, and soon after his own, took him into his *Service*, honour'd him with several obliging *Testimonies* of his *Esteem*, and withal gave this Character of his *Works*, that *he painted both Inside and Outside*. (Graham, 348)

Riley's pupil Thomas Murray (1663–1735) gave a very different account of his master's encounter with the king:

when [Riley] drew King Charles the Seconds picture. when his Majesty look'd at it. & said is this like me. (odds fish) then I'me an ugly fellow. this so much damp't Mr. Roilys spirit that he never coud endure to look at the picture. tho' a Noble man bought it & payd well for it. the King had it not. (Vertue, *Note books*, 4.28)

Nevertheless, Riley was 'sworne Painter & Picture drawer in Ordinary' to the king on 23 April 1681 (Gibson, 214).

Murray also told Vertue that Riley refused to allow even his students to watch him while he was painting 'from the life' (Vertue, *Note books*, 4.28). If sitters criticized his work:

this would mortify him to such a degree that he woud go out of the room & go into an other were his scholars were & vent his passion or uneasiness in til he had eas'd himself & then return to the company. put on an obliging agreable air. (ibid.)

Riley's secrecy contrasted with the practice of Godfrey Kneller, his rival in the 1680s. With his cosmopolitan background, including study with Rembrandt and Bernini, the German was confident and open: 'he let any body see & be by him—painters or others often or casually any of his scholars' (Vertue, *Note books*, 4.29). That Riley practised successfully for a decade as a fashionable London painter shows tenacity of spirit, the more so as he had grave technical deficiencies.

Bainbrigg Buckeridge says that Riley's 'excellence was confined to a head' (Buckeridge, 415). Richard Graham also claimed that 'that which eminently distinguished [Riley] from all his *Contemporaries* was his *peculiar Excellence* in a *Head*; and especially the *Colouring part*' (Graham, 348). In addition, wrote Graham, Riley, 'by studying the Life, rather than following a particular *Manner*, arriv'd to a pleasant and most agreeable *Style* of *Painting*' (ibid.). Graham's later statement is special pleading, doubtless designed to account for the eclecticism of the designs of the figures in Riley's portraits.

The heads in Riley's bust portraits of men are honest and discerning in character and have an attractive, melancholy reticence. That of *John Maitland, 1st Duke of Lauderdale* (c.1680–82, exh. RA, 1960; priv. coll.) conveys the latent power of this Scottish aristocrat. *Elias Ashmole* (1687; AM Oxf.), with its cool mauve drapery and silvery-toned hair and face, is a probing study of an aged intellectual. Of the same year, his portrait of Charles II's master of ceremonies, Sir Charles Cotterell (priv. coll.), is a grave yet genial portrayal of an elderly courtier. Like Soest, Riley seldom painted women, but his bust of Lady Verney in widow's weeds (Claydon House, Buckinghamshire) has the dignified simplicity of his best male heads; and his bust of the playwright Aphra Behn, known only from Robert White's engraving, has an engaging shyness.

Riley could not, however, represent convincingly anything more in space than a bust: his larger works all have structural weaknesses. His three-quarter length *Scullion* (Christ Church, Oxford) is unusual, being a portrait of a servant, and the head is full of character. Yet the poorly drawn figure fits awkwardly into the pictorial space. The three-quarter length *Lady Spencer and Child* (1683; ex Sothebys, 10 July 1985) is documented in the sitter's diary as by Riley; its design is a flattened derivation from Soest's *Unknown Lady with her Son* (ex Christies, 18 March 1949). Other clumsy designs include the three-quarter lengths *Charles II* (Bodl. Oxf.) and *Elias Ashmole* (1683; AM Oxf.). Riley's three-quarter length *Prince George of Denmark* (1687; Royal Collection) is an adaptation of a late design by Lely, but with the head and body awkwardly joined, probably because two painters were involved. Riley recognized his technical weaknesses and hired Jan Baptiste Gaspars (*fl.* 1641–1692) to paint 'postures' (Vertue, *Note books*, 2.135). (On 25 November 1681 the Painter–Stainers' Company asked Riley and Gaspars to paint a portrait of the duchess of York for them.) Gaspars had painted 'postures' for Lely and was also to do so for Kneller. But they, like most artists who ran fashionable studios, still designed their postures, even if they used assistants to help them paint them. However, Riley apparently used his assistants (Gaspars and others) to design as well as paint postures and background settings. This was the case with the Riley–Closterman partnership, involving Riley with one, or perhaps two artists—John *Closterman, who came to England with his brother John Baptist Closterman (a much inferior painter) in 1680. Vertue gives a confused account of the 'partnership', claiming that it started with Closterman's arrival in England and 'held about two years only', yet stating that it was so disadvantageous to Closterman that 'had not Riley died [in 1691] he [Closterman] might well have been in debt' (Vertue, *Note books*, 1.61). Thus Vertue was not clear when the partnership began. Also, because the two Clostermans were thought from the early eighteenth century until 1964 to be one artist, we cannot be certain whether one, or perhaps both, were involved in the partnership.

The three-quarter length portrait of Katherine Elliott (*d.* 1688) in the Royal Collection is described in a Queen Anne inventory as 'Ryley ye Head Closterman ye Drapery' (Millar, no. 331). As in Riley's *Prince George of Denmark*, the head and body are awkwardly joined. The portrait traditionally attributed to Riley of Bridget Holmes (1686; Royal Collection; inscribed with an apparently strengthened Riley 'signature'), an elderly royal servant, is, however, a sophisticated, accomplished piece, far beyond the powers of Riley, but entirely consonant with independent works by John Closterman.

At Belton House, Lincolnshire, there are four full-length portraits of two generations of Brownlows which are generally recognized as products of the Riley–Closterman partnership. The female portraits are far superior in structure to those of the males, suggesting that the former may have been painted by John Closterman and the latter by his brother John Baptist. Riley may have painted the heads. It was also probably Riley who received the commission, since the Brownlows had patronized Soest.

There were additional reasons for Riley's success as a fashionable portrait painter. 'He was', says Graham, 'a *Gentleman* extremely *Courteous* in his Behaviour, *Obliging* in his *Conversation* … He was never guilty of a peice of *Vanity* (too common amongst *Artists*) of saying *mighty things* on his *own* Behalf [and was] *Prudent* in all his *Actions*' (Graham, 348–9). Thomas Murray's account corroborates this, showing how Riley could hide his feelings and be agreeable. He was a good dissembler, and he knew his limitations.

Riley's English birth was also an asset. From the early seventeenth century, because of their superior training and knowledge of the latest styles, foreigners had dominated fashionable painting in England. By the latter part of the century this had provoked discontent and the puffing up of English artists. William Aglionby touted the sculptor Grinling Gibbons as a potential '*Northern Michelangelo*' and lamented the absence of 'any of note, that was an Englishman, that pretended to History Painting', attributing this to the nation's preference for portraits: 'in that part we have had some who have proved most Excellent Artists … even at this time Mr Riley, who undoubtedly deserves his Character of the first and best Painter for Portraits in our Age' (Aglionby, preface). There is no mention of Van Dyck, Lely, or Kneller, because Aglionby was considering only painters of English birth. (It is surprising that he elevated Riley above John Michael Wright.) Richard Graham's fulsome biography of Riley, published in 1695, is further evidence of this nationalistic trend.

Riley is not known to have travelled abroad, nor are there any known portraits by him of foreign visitors. Thus Graham's statement about Riley's '*Works* … being plentifully distributed over *other Nations*, as well as *our own*' (Graham, 349) is inexplicable. Riley's career culminated on 24 July 1689 in his joint appointment with Kneller as 'Principal Painter' to William III and Queen Mary (Gibson, 216), though there are no known portraits by Riley of either as sovereign. According to Graham, 'He had for several years been violently persecuted by the *Gout*; which after many terrible *Assaults*, flying up at last into his *Head*, brought him to his *Grave*' (Graham, 349). He dictated a brief will on 3 March 1691 at his house in Holborn Row, Lincoln's Inn Fields, London, leaving his property to John Riley senior, Jochebed Riley, and his brother Thomas, also a painter. He died at home on 27 March 1691 and was buried on 30 March at St Botolph without Bishopsgate.

Riley's pupils included Anthony Russell (1663?–1742), Edward Gouge (*fl.* 1715), Thomas Murray, and the elder Jonathan Richardson. The last named recorded Riley's will, became his administrator, and sold Riley's collection of pictures and drawings in two sales in February and April 1693. There is no drawing certainly by Riley himself (Croft-Murray and Hulton, 1.470). Riley occupies an honourable but minor place in the history of painting in England. Richardson was the teacher of Thomas Hudson, who in turn taught Sir Joshua Reynolds. Yet to see this progression as an 'apostolic succession' (Whinney and Millar, 188) is a false metaphor. The real development of painting in

England, the 'handing on of keys' was from Van Dyck and Lely to Kneller, and then to Hogarth, Reynolds, and Gainsborough.   J. DOUGLAS STEWART

Sources [R. Graham], 'A short account of the most eminent painters, both ancient and modern', in C. A. Du Fresnoy, *De arte graphica / The art of painting*, trans. J. Dryden (1695), 227–355 · Vertue, *Note books* · B. Buckeridge, 'John Riley esq', *An essay towards an English school of painting* (1706); repr. (1969) · H. Walpole, *Anecdotes of painting in England: with some account of the principle artists*, ed. J. Dallaway, new edn, 3 vols. (1849); repr. (1976) · C. H. C. Baker, *Lely and the Stuart portrait painters: a study of English portraiture before and after van Dyck*, 2 vols. (1912) · C. Gibson-Wood, *Jonathan Richardson, art theorist of the English enlightenment* (2000) · M. Whinney and O. Millar, *English art, 1625–1714* (1957) · *The age of Charles II* (1960) [exhibition catalogue, Royal Academy of Arts, London, 1960] · *British portraits* (1956) [exhibition catalogue, Royal Academy of Arts, London, 1956] · O. Millar, *The Tudor, Stuart and early Georgian pictures in the collection of her majesty the queen*, 2 vols. (1963) · C. Lloyd, *The queen's pictures: royal collectors through the centuries* (1991) · W. Aglionby, *Painting illustrated* (1686) · E. Croft-Murray and P. H. Hulton, eds., *Catalogue of British drawings*, 1 (1960) · E. Waterhouse, *Painting in Britain, 1530–1790*, 4th edn (1978) · E. K. Waterhouse, *The dictionary of British 16th and 17th century painters* (1988) · Mrs R. Lane Poole, ed., *Catalogue of portraits in the possession of the university, colleges, city and county of Oxford*, 3 vols. (1912–25) · J. Haydn, *The book of dignities: containing lists of the official personages of the British empire*, ed. H. Ockerby, 3rd edn (1894); repr. as *Haydn's book of dignities* (1969) · J. D. Stewart, *Sir Godfrey Kneller and the English baroque portrait* (1983) · D. Piper, *Catalogue of seventeenth-century portraits in the National Portrait Gallery, 1625–1714* (1963) · P. Murray, *The Dulwich picture gallery: a handlist* (1980) · K. Gibson, '"Best belov'd of kings": the iconography of King Charles II', PhD diss., Courtauld Inst., 1997 · will, PRO, PROB 11/404, sig. 71

Likenesses J. Richardson junior, drawing, 1734 (after self-portrait by J. Riley?), BM

Sir Ralph Riley (1924–1999), by unknown photographer

Riley, Sir Ralph (1924–1999), plant geneticist, was born on 23 October 1924 at Dybdale Nursing Home, West Street, Scarborough, Yorkshire, the youngest child in the family of two sons and one daughter of Ralph Riley (d. 1924), a builder from Oldham, Lancashire, who had moved to Scarborough after going bankrupt, and his wife, Clara, née Urmson (d. 1942). Riley's father died three months before Riley was born, and his mother moved the family to live with her father in Manchester. He was educated at Audenshaw grammar school in Manchester, leaving in 1941, after taking his school certificate, for a job in the local public reference library. He was called up in 1943 and served in the infantry. He was wounded in Germany in 1945, and left the army as a captain in 1947 after serving in Palestine. He then entered the University of Sheffield, and graduated with a first-class degree in botany in 1950. On 21 July 1949 he married Joan Elizabeth Norrington (b. 1924/5), a teacher, and daughter of Howard Norrington, a garage proprietor; they had two daughters.

Remaining at Sheffield, Riley worked on molecular genetics for a PhD which was awarded in 1955, but in 1952 he was recruited to a research position at the Plant Breeding Institute, which was moving out of Cambridge to its new Trumpington site after severing its links with the university to become a separate research institute administered by the Agricultural Research Council. In 1954 Riley became head of the new cytogenetics department. For twenty years he worked on the genetics of wheat, investigating the mechanisms by which genetic characteristics are transferred from one plant to another. In 1957 he discovered the *Ph* gene, which controls the means by which chromosomes from related plants join to form new strains. This enabled him to introduce genes from wild varieties of wheat into the wheat crop, and he was able to isolate genes for desirable properties including disease resistance, to create new varieties of wheat. In the 1970s improved varieties of wheat developed at the Plant Breeding Institute accounted for 75 per cent of wheat production in the United Kingdom, and wheat yields increased from 4 to 6 tons per hectare: this increase continued into the 1980s, reaching 8.4 tons per hectare in 1984. Riley's methods were adopted in cereal breeding programmes all over the world, especially in developing countries, and made an important contribution to the 'green revolution' of the 1960s and 1970s. He was elected a fellow of Wolfson College, Cambridge, in 1967, and a fellow of the Royal Society in the same year.

Struggling with the problem of poor eyesight caused by the onset of diabetes, Riley found it hard to continue his microscopic experimentation, and moved into administration in 1971 when he accepted the directorship of the Plant Breeding Institute. He was successful in attracting the funding to build up its reputation as an international centre for research into plant molecular biology, and under his directorship the institute twice received the queen's award for industry: in 1973 for technological innovation in the breeding of varieties of winter wheat, and in 1975 for improvements in the breeding of brassica crops. During this time he was also secretary of the International Genetics Federation from 1973 to 1978, and special professor of botany at the University of Nottingham from 1970 to 1978. In 1978 he left the Plant Breeding Institute to become secretary to the Agricultural and Food Research Council, where he remained until he retired in 1985; he was also deputy chairman from 1983 to 1985. His responsibilities included the funding of basic research in agriculture in Britain, and working with industry to apply the results of this research: under his secretaryship plant biotechnology developed in British universities and research institutes.

In retirement Riley became more involved in developing agriculture in the third world. In 1989 he led a United Nations Development Programme team to increase grain production in Bangladesh. He was a member of the board of trustees of the International Rice Research Institute, in the Philippines, and the International Center for Agricultural Research in Dry Areas, both under the auspices of the World Bank, as well as a member of the technical advisory committee of the Rockefeller Foundation rice biotechnology programme; and he was president of the seventeenth International Congress of Genetics, held in Birmingham in 1993. He was enthusiastic about developments in genetic engineering: whereas all his work in the 1950s and 1960s involved the transfer of genetic material between related plants, his successors in the 1980s developed the techniques for taking genes from one species and introducing them into another, making it possible to design new crop plants with increased yields and reduced need for herbicides and pesticides. He was convinced that these advances would enable the developing world to become self-sufficient in food production. He was co-editor, with J. C. Waterlow and others, of *Feeding a World Population of More than Eight billion People* (1998). He was knighted in 1984 for services to agriculture. Other awards included the Royal Society's royal medal in 1981, and the Wolf international prize in agriculture in 1986. He died at Addenbrooke's Hospital, Cambridge, on 27 August 1999, following a stroke, and was buried on 8 September. He was survived by his wife and their two daughters.

ANNE PIMLOTT BAKER

Sources *The Plant Breeding Institute: 75 years, 1912–1987* (1987) · *The Independent* (10 Sept 1999) · *The Guardian* (13 Oct 1999) · *WW* · private information (2004) [Lady Riley] · b. cert. · m. cert. · d. cert. · R. Flavell, *Memoirs FRS*, 49 [forthcoming]
Likenesses photograph, repro. in *The Guardian* · photograph, repro. in *The Independent* · photograph, John Innes Centre, Norwich [*see illus.*]
Wealth at death £271,246—gross; £267,632—net: probate, 8 June 2000, *CGPLA Eng. & Wales*

Rimbault, Edward Francis [*pseud.* Franz Nava] (1816–1876), writer on music and antiquary, born in Soho, London, on 13 June 1816, was the son of Stephen Francis Rimbault (1773–1837), organist of St Giles-in-the-Fields, a descendant from a Huguenot refugee family. After learning the elements of music from his father, he became the pupil of Samuel Wesley and William Crotch, and at the age of sixteen he was appointed organist of the Swiss church, Soho. In 1838 he lectured in London on the history of music, then an unusual subject, and two years later, with Edward Taylor (1784–1863), Gresham professor of music, and William Chappell (1809–1888), he helped to found the Musical Antiquarian Society, of which he became secretary, and for which he edited a number of works. At the same time he assisted in the foundation of the Percy Society, of which he also became secretary. In 1841 he became editor of the Motet Society's publications. A year later he was elected FSA and a member of the Academy of Music, Stockholm, and was offered, but declined, the chair of music at Harvard University. Also in 1842 he edited for the Percy Society five *Ancient Poetical Tracts of the Sixteenth Century*. In 1844 he joined the committee of the Handel Society, for whom he edited *Messiah*, *Samson* and *Saul* (1850, 1852, and 1854). In 1848 he lectured at the Royal Institution. Subsequently he occupied himself with his duties as organist of various churches, including St Peter's, Vere Street, and St John's Wood Presbyterian Church, and in editing musical journals and arranging music.

The *Catalogue of Printed Music in the British Library to 1980* devotes twelve double-column pages to a list of works, original and arranged or edited by Rimbault, and a further three pages to works he edited or arranged under his pseudonym, Franz Nava. Significant publications include Byrd's mass for five voices (1841), a new edition of Samuel Arnold's *Cathedral Music* (1843), Roger North's *Memoirs of Musick* (1846), the *Bibliotheca madrigaliana* (1847); with Dr E. J. Hopkins, *The Organ: its History and Construction* (1855); *The Pianoforte* (1860), *Early English Organ Builders* (1864), and *The Old Cheque Book of the Chapel Royal* (1872) for the Camden Society. His chief literary achievements outside musical topics were an edition of Sir Thomas Overbury's *Miscellaneous Works* (1856) and *Soho and its Associations*, edited by George Clinch (1895). Rimbault possessed a wide rather than deep knowledge of the history of music in the sixteenth and seventeenth centuries. His few musical compositions are unimportant: they include an operetta, *The Fair Maid of Islington* (1838), and a musical drama, *The Castle Spectre* (1839), which at one time enjoyed a great vogue. He made a large number of pianoforte scores of operas by Louis Spohr, William Vincent Wallace, Michael Balfe, and others, and was an admirable harmonium player. Rimbault died at 29 St Mark's Terrace, Regent's Park, London, on 26 September 1876, leaving a widow and two children. He was buried at Highgate cemetery on 30 September. His large library was sold, after his death, at Sothebys for nearly £2000.

R. H. LEGGE, *rev.* RICHARD TURBET

Sources *Musical Standard* (30 Sept 1876) · *The Athenaeum* (7 Oct 1876), 442, 473 · *The Athenaeum* (14 Oct 1876), 449 · D. Baptie, letter to editor, *Musical World* (7 Oct 1876), 671 · W. Chappell, *Musical World* (21 Oct 1876), 707 · P. A. Scholes, *The mirror of music, 1844–1944: a century of musical life in Britain as reflected in the pages of the Musical Times*, 2 vols. (1947) · A. H. King, *Some British collectors of music, c.1600–1960* (1963) · W. G. Hiscock, 'Christ Church missing books, II: printed music', *TLS* (11 Feb 1939), 96 · *Catalogue of the valuable library of the* *late Edward Francis Rimbault* (1877); facs. edn with introduction by A. H. King (1975) • R. Turbet, 'The Musical Antiquarian Society, 1840–1848', *Brio*, 29 (1992), 13–20 • L. Baillie and R. Balchin, eds., *The catalogue of printed music in the British Library to 1980*, 62 vols. (1981–7)

Archives BL, Novello archive

Wealth at death under £3000: resworn probate, Feb 1878, *CGPLA Eng. & Wales* (1876)

Rimington, Claude (1902–1993), biochemist and poet, was born on 17 November 1902 in London, the youngest of three children of George Garthwaite Rimington, a businessman, and his wife, Matilda Isabel, *née* Klyne, who was artistically inclined. When he was three the family moved to rural Hertfordshire, where Claude grew up. A lonely boy, he developed an intense interest in nature. He read poetry and prose voraciously, particularly on his long train journeys from home to Haberdashers' Aske's Boys' School, then at Cricklewood. Chemistry (but not physics) was another early love.

As a boy during the First World War he assisted at a canteen for the troops at King's Cross. Shortly afterwards, while preparing to apply for an open scholarship to Cambridge, he suffered a serious breakdown of health which interrupted his studies for a year—its nature remains unknown. Fully recovered by 1921, he entered Emmanuel College, Cambridge, where he obtained a first-class degree in biochemistry, only recently recognized as separate from chemistry. He was particularly influenced by J. B. S. Haldane, reader in the department.

Rimington's first topic of serious research, on phosphoproteins and protein-bound carbohydrate complexes, led to his London PhD in 1928. He also paid the first of a lifelong series of visits to Norway and Denmark. He rapidly learned the languages and underwent total immersion in their poetry, prose, and science. The high spot of his trip was hearing a lecture by Marie Curie.

Back in Cambridge (1926–8) the constellation of biochemical pioneers—Gowland Hopkins, J. H. Quastel, Joseph Needham, J. B. S. Haldane, and Albert Szent-Gyorgyi to mention but a few—was dazzling. Even so, Rimington decided to accept a post in Leeds to set up a biochemical department for the Wool Research Association. In the same year (1929) he married Soffi, daughter of Clement Andersen, a young Norwegian from the island of Askerøy, near Lyngør, whom he had met in London. They had one daughter, Greta, who survived them both, and a son who died in infancy during the tenure of Rimington's next post, a research scholarship in Pretoria.

In South Africa, Rimington began work on the sheep disease Geeldikkop ('yellow thick head'), which initiated him into porphyrin studies. Sir Arnold Theiler, lately director of the institute in Pretoria, greatly influenced Rimington's scientific thought. He had received some strange specimens from farms in Swaziland: chocolate-brown bones which Rimington recognized as similar to those seen in the human disease congenital erythropoietic porphyria. Rimington's discovery of animal porphyria was seminal and became the main scientific focus in his life.

In 1937 Sir Henry Dale offered Rimington a post at the National Institute for Medical Research at Hampstead. There he studied the copper-containing red porphyrin complex from the wing feathers of the turaco, a South American bird. The Nobel laureate Hans Fischer, the acknowledged expert in this area, claimed that the porphyrin was a uroporphyrin I but Rimington rather courageously showed it to belong to the isomeric series III. This was later confirmed by other workers.

In 1937 Rimington and his wife built a house in Askerøy, and while they were on holiday there in 1939 war broke out. Leaving his wife and six-year-old daughter there to enjoy a few more weeks' relaxation, Rimington returned to England. The family was overtaken by events: the German invasion of Norway severed all communications between them and made her return impossible.

After the war—Rimington had joined the Home Guard—his wife and daughter returned. He accepted the chair of chemical pathology at University College medical school. By an oversight Rimington's old teacher at Cambridge, J. B. S. Haldane (then professor of biometrics at University College), had not been invited to his inaugural lecture. Haldane took this as a personal affront and blamed Rimington—which caused him deep distress.

As time went by, Rimington built up a department renowned throughout the world for research on pyrrole pigment metabolism. Shortly before he retired he embarked on a collaboration with Ida Macalpine and Richard Hunter suggesting that the hereditary illness affecting several European royal houses, and focusing on the madness of George III, was likely to be a form of porphyria. Relatively unsuccessful efforts were made to obtain samples of urine and faeces from royalty or their close relatives. Without them, however, the hypothesis remained controversial.

When Rimington retired in 1968 the only difference was his release from departmental responsibility, which he did not relish in any case. He travelled extensively to centres of scientific excellence and continued to produce high-calibre publications. He was elected a fellow of the Royal Society in 1954 and became an honorary fellow of the Royal College of Physicians of Edinburgh (1966), an honorary member of the Biochemical Society, a member of the Norwegian Academy of Science and Letters, and a holder of the Norwegian order of merit (1989).

Rimington had an impeccable knowledge of Norwegian. He wrote poetry in it and translated much Norwegian poetry into English. Scientist and poet, he was also a deeply religious Christian and recognized no conflict between these aspects of his life. On first contact this tallish man appeared remote, formal, and austere but, on further acquaintance, his charm and simplicity shone through. Despite his scientific pre-eminence, he was quick to put young collaborators at their ease and treated them as equals. He died on 8 August 1993 at his island home on Askerøy. MERTON SANDLER

Sources A. Neuberger and A. Goldberg, *Memoirs FRS*, 42 (1996), 365–78 • *The Independent* (13 Aug 1993), 12a • *The Times* (23 Aug 1993), 12a • *WWW* • personal knowledge (2004) • private information (2004)

Archives Trinity Cam., corresp. with R. L. M. Synge
Likenesses photograph, repro. in *The Independent* · photograph, repro. in *The Times*
Wealth at death £156,609—in England and Wales: probate, 25 Aug 1994, *CGPLA Eng. & Wales*

Rimington, Samuel (1739/40–1826), army officer, of whose parents nothing is known, joined the Royal Artillery as a matross in January 1757. Commissioned a second lieutenant on 15 March 1771, he embarked for Quebec and the following August took a detachment to Niagara. Having returned to England, he went recruiting in December 1775 and in March 1776 sailed back to Quebec with four companies of artillery. He saw action against the Americans on 8 June at Three Rivers, and commanded a gunboat on Lake Champlain at the battle of Valcour Island (11 October 1776). In 1777, as part of General Burgoyne's expedition from Canada, he acted as a commissary of horse before being captured along with the rest of the army at Saratoga. Promoted lieutenant while still captive on 7 July 1779, he served in New York following his exchange in 1781; he was appointed captain-lieutenant on 1 December 1782. In 1783 he was sent to Bermuda to inspect the garrison battalion before its disbandment.

After three years' home service, Rimington set sail for Canada once again in April 1787. He remained there two years. Appointed captain of no. 8 company, 4th battalion, on 24 March 1791, he commanded the artillery in Scotland for the next eleven years, rising to the rank of lieutenant-colonel. It was probably during this period that he married Ann (1763/4–1825), daughter of Captain Thomas Hosmer (1737/8–1805), of the Royal Artillery, and his wife, Mary (1743/4–1814); they had five children. On 10 February 1802, being unfit for foreign service, Rimington retired to the invalid battalion at Woolwich, with which he remained until promoted major-general on 4 June 1811. His final promotion, to lieutenant-general, was dated 19 July 1821. Rimington died at Woolwich (his home was in Prospect Place) on 23 January 1826, aged eighty-six. He was interred in the burial-ground of St Alfege, Greenwich, five days later. B. H. SOULSBY, *rev.* ALASTAIR W. MASSIE

Sources J. Philippart, ed., *The royal military calendar*, 3rd edn, 5 vols. (1820) · J. Kane, *List of officers of the royal regiment of artillery from the year 1716 to the year 1899*, rev. W. H. Askwith, 4th edn (1900) · will, 1825, PRO, PROB 11/1709, fol. 111 · *GM*, 1st ser., 96/1 (1826), 274 · parish register, Greenwich, St Alfege, LMA [burial] · St Alfege, Greenwich, burial-ground inscriptions, copied 1912 and 1922, typescript, Greenwich Local History Library · F. Duncan, ed., *History of the royal regiment of artillery*, 2nd edn, 2 vols. (1874)
Wealth at death see will, 1825, PRO, PROB 11/1709, fol. 111

Rimmer, Alfred (1829–1893), artist and writer, was born on 9 August 1829 in Liverpool, the son of Thomas Rimmer, timber merchant, and his wife, Mary, née Burroughs. He was educated at Liverpool College when the Revd John Saul Howson (1816–1885), later dean of Chester, was senior classics master. He was articled to a Liverpool architect named Cunningham, and then practised as an architect. He published *Ancient Halls of Lancashire, from Original Drawings* (1852) and contributed two articles to the *Transactions of the Historic Society of Lancashire and Cheshire* (1850–52). On 5 August 1858 in Childwall parish church, Lancashire,

he married Frances (*b.* 1839/40), daughter of John Parkinson, an engineer: they had five sons and two daughters. In the same year he moved to Canada, where he engaged in trade and became consul-general for Denmark and justice of the peace in Montreal. He returned to England in 1870, settling in Chester, where he worked with Dean Howson, illustrating *Chester as it Was* (1872) and *The River Dee: its Aspect and History* (1875). His other books included *Ancient Stone Crosses of England* (1875), *Ancient Streets and Homesteads of England* (1877), *Pleasant Spots around Oxford* (1878), *Our Old Country Towns* (1881), *Rambles about Eton and Harrow* (1882), *The Early Home of Prince Albert* (1882), *About England with Dickens* (1883), *Stonyhurst Illustrated* (1884), *Summer Rambles Round Manchester* (1890), and *Rambles Round Rugby* (1892). All these he illustrated himself.

Rimmer received a grant of £100 from the royal bounty fund in 1892. He died on 27 October 1893 at his home, 13 Crook Street, Chester.

C. W. SUTTON, *rev.* ANNE PIMLOTT BAKER

Sources *The Times* (20 Oct 1893) · Boase, *Mod. Eng. biog.* · census returns, 1881 · BL cat. · *Chester Chronicle* (28 Oct 1893) · *Chester Courant* (1 Nov 1893) · *Chester Courant* (12 June 1895) · private information (1896) [John H. Rimmer, T. M. Wilcock] · S. Houfe, *The dictionary of 19th century British book illustrators and caricaturists*, rev. edn (1996) · m. cert.
Archives Ches. & Chester ALSS, architectural and antiquarian papers
Wealth at death £93 6s. 10d.: administration, 6 Dec 1893, *CGPLA Eng. & Wales*

Rimmer, William (1861–1936), bandmaster and composer, was born in Southport and was to live there for the whole of his life. Encouraged by his father, Thomas Rimmer, bandmaster of the local volunteer regiment, to develop his musical skills, he learned the piano at the age of nine, joined the band as drummer at fifteen, and emerged as an accomplished cornet player by his early twenties. The brass-band movement, whose heartland lay in the textile and mining communities of north-west England, was then in its heyday, and William Rimmer was soon in demand, first as a soloist and then as conductor, by the area's leading contesting bands. In the early 1890s he abandoned his trade as a painter for a full-time career as a band trainer and contest adjudicator.

By the first decade of the twentieth century Rimmer had come to dominate the British brass-band world, both because of his outstanding record of contest successes and because of the growing popularity of his compositions and arrangements. Between 1905 and 1909 bands under his direction consistently took first prize at both the British Open (Belle Vue, Manchester) and the National (Crystal Palace) championships. In twenty years of contesting he coached dozens of northern bands, but he had particularly fruitful associations with Wingates, Irwell Springs, Black Dyke, and Fodens. The work of a professional band trainer was physically and mentally demanding, and involved constant travelling to intensive and repetitive rehearsals. It was not unknown for Rimmer to tutor three different bands in the course of a single evening, or to conduct six bands at the same one-day contest. Indifferent health had earlier ended his appearances as a soloist, and in 1909 he announced his retirement from all contest work. He could now afford to opt for an easier life: he had secured a five-year appointment as conductor of the Southport municipal band for the regular summer season, was under exclusive contract as arranger and composer to the London-based music publisher Richard Smith & Co., and had been commissioned by them to compose the championship test piece for Crystal Palace for three years starting in 1910. When this last agreement acrimoniously expired in 1913, Rimmer teamed up with Smith's leading provincial rivals, Wright and Round. He became a director of the firm, and continued to compose for their *Liverpool Journal*—an annual collection of 'new' music, to which many bands subscribed—for the rest of his life. More than 300 pieces were published under his own name, and countless others under various aliases; until the 1950s a brass-band concert programme without at least one item by Rimmer would have been unthinkable. Most of his original compositions were tuneful, conventional in structure and harmony, undemanding on the ear, and eminently forgettable. However, his arrangements and selections from nineteenth-century classical composers were important in popularizing 'serious' music among audiences who never saw the inside of an opera house or concert hall, while the best of his many marches can stand comparison with those of the American J. P. Sousa.

After giving up contesting, Rimmer lived quietly in Southport, where he enjoyed a modest local fame and contributed to the wider musical life of the town. His achievements were never recognized by the British musical establishment, but to devotees of the brass-band movement at home and throughout the empire he was 'the king'. Endowed with a handsome presence but a retiring disposition, he personified the human qualities most admired in this vast but self-contained segment of the musical world; he was fair, forthright, affable, meticulous, and utterly dependable. William Rimmer died at his home in Belmont Street, Southport, after a short illness, on 9 February 1936, leaving a widow, Mary, and three daughters.

DUNCAN BYTHELL

Sources *Southport Guardian* (2 June 1900) · *Southport Visiter* (11 Feb 1936) · *Brass Band News* (1896) · *Brass Band News* (1909) · *Brass Band News* (1913) · *Brass Band News* (1936) · *British Bandsman* (1909) · *British Bandsman* (1936) · A. R. Taylor, *Brass bands* (1979) · T. Herbert, ed., *The British brass band: a musical and social history* (2000) · D. Russell, *Popular music in Britain, 1840–1941: a social history* (1987) · D. Bythell, 'Provinces *versus* metropolis in the British brass band movement: the case of William Rimmer and his music', *Popular Music*, 16/2 (1997), 151–64

Archives Southport Public Library, local history collection |SOUND Southport Public Library, local history collection, 10 recordings with Southport Municipal Band, Columbia Records, 1913

Wealth at death £11,138 16s.: probate, 13 May 1936, *CGPLA Eng. & Wales*

Rimmington, Samuel. *See* Rimington, Samuel (1739/40–1826).

Rimston, William. *See* Rymington, William (*d.* in or after 1385).

Ring, John (*bap.* **1752**, *d.* **1821**), surgeon and vaccinator, was born in Wincanton, Somerset, and baptized on 21 August 1752, the son of Richard Ring. Nothing is known of the family beyond that they were people of some position. Certainly, they were able to provide their son with a good education. John Ring attended Winchester College for two years from 1765 before travelling to London where he trained under some of the most eminent practitioners of the day—Percivall Pott and William and John Hunter—and attended St George's Hospital. Ring received the diploma of the Surgeons' Company in 1774 and set up practice as a surgeon and accoucheur in Swallow Street, London.

Ring was a man of extraordinary energy. He was an active member of his profession: he held the prestigious post of surgeon to St Thomas's Hospital and was a member of the medical societies of London and Paris and the Physical Society of Guy's Hospital. He published two works on the treatment of gout and another on dropsy, and briefly ventured into medical politics with a pamphlet criticizing the leadership of the Surgeons' Company over their attempt to achieve collegiate status.

However, Ring's career was dominated by his advocacy of smallpox vaccination. In 1799, one year after Edward Jenner published the first description of vaccination, Ring responded to an attack on the new procedure by Benjamin Moseley. This won him an introduction to Jenner and Ring was drawn into a loyal circle of Jenner's admirers and supporters. Ring quickly became the leading voice among the pro-vaccination camp, and over the next sixteen years produced a prodigious flow of pamphlets and contributions to the medical press, particularly the *Medical and Physical Journal*. Ring was highly sensitive to criticism and he clearly developed a strong personal identification with Jenner and with vaccination. Even after his friendship with Jenner lapsed in 1812 Ring acted as his bulldog, swiftly and vigorously repudiating the slightest criticism of vaccination or of Jenner's opinions.

Although Ring had an extensive, partly private, partly charitable, vaccination practice, his writings and journal articles contain no original observations on the procedure. His major work on vaccination, the two-volume *Treatise on the Cow Pox* (1801–3), was a compilation of reports of successful practice. He summarily dismissed Benjamin Moseley's fears of introducing an animal disease into the human frame (which inspired the famous cartoon by James Gillray of vaccinated patients sprouting cows' heads), declaring that Moseley had no experience of vaccination and no understanding of the procedure. When faced with more sombre claims that patients had suffered smallpox after vaccination, Ring's tactic was to cast doubt on the original vaccination—questioning the skill of the vaccinator, the manner in which the operation had been performed, the viability of the vaccine used— or the diagnosis of the subsequent complaint.

Ring was not above launching virulent personal attacks in a style more usually associated with seventeenth- and eighteenth-century polemicists. When Jenner and John

Walker, the chief vaccinator to the Royal Jennerian Society, became embroiled in a bitter dispute, ostensibly over vaccination technique, Ring produced a sequence of anonymous pamphlets entitled *The Vaccine Scourge* (1809, 1810) which even Jenner felt went beyond the bounds of polite and reasoned discourse. Ring also sought to promote vaccination in a more positive fashion. In 1800 he used his professional contacts to encourage London's most prominent practitioners to lend their names to a testimonial in favour of vaccination. Two years later he testified in favour of the procedure before a parliamentary committee of inquiry, thus helping to secure a government grant for Jenner in recognition of the public benefit derived from vaccination.

Before the dispute between Jenner and Walker brought the Royal Jennerian Society to an ignominious end, Ring had been one of the organization's leading lights. Established in 1803 under distinguished patronage the society provided free vaccination to the poor through vaccine stations scattered over London. Ring attended the station at Marylebone, sat on the society's medical committee, and served on two committees which investigated reported vaccination failures in Hampshire and Cambridge. In 1807, when the society fell into disarray, Jenner suggested that Ring should be appointed as chief vaccinator to the new, government sponsored National Vaccine Establishment. However, the president of the new body was determined that the staff should be drawn from all of London's various and jealously competitive vaccination institutions. For this reason most of Jenner's candidates, including Ring, were rejected.

Ring's activities were not confined to medicine. He published a poetic tribute to George Handel which ran to two editions and his Latin verse appeared in various periodicals. Adverse reviews again brought out the confrontational side to Ring's talents, prompting him to publish *The Beauties of the 'Edinburgh Review' alias the Stinkpot of Literature* (1807). His reputation as a fine Latinist was established in 1820 by a widely praised translation of Virgil which won him election to the Royal Society of Literature. Ring died of apoplexy on 7 December 1821 at his home for over twenty years in New Street, Hanover Square, London.

DEBORAH BRUNTON

Sources R. B. Fisher, *Edward Jenner* (1991) · J. Baron, *The life of Edward Jenner*, 2 vols. (1827–38) · *GM*, 1st ser., 91/2 (1821), 643–4 · *London Medical and Physical Journal*, 47 (1822), 165 · J. Watkins, *The universal biographical dictionary*, new edn (1821) · J. Ring, *An answer to Mr Goldson* (1804) · J. Ring, *An answer to Dr Moseley* (1805) · DNB

Likenesses J. Rogers, stipple, pubd 1821, BM · J. Rogers, stipple, pubd 1824, NPG · R. J. Lane, lithograph, NPG · J. Rogers, engraving (after T. S. Drumond), RCS Eng., Wellcome L.; repro. in *New European Magazine*

Ringer, Sydney (1835–1910), physician and physiologist, was born in Norwich, the second of three sons of John Manstripp Ringer, a Norwich tradesman, and his wife, Harriet. His elder brother, John Melancthon, and younger brother, Frederick, were successful merchants in Shanghai and Japan. Ringer was educated at private schools, and after a brief apprenticeship to a doctor in Norwich he

entered University College, London, in 1854, to study medicine; he became MB (1860) and MD (1863), and MRCP (1863) and FRCP (1870). At University College Hospital, Ringer became, successively, resident medical officer (1861), assistant physician (1863), physician (1866), and consulting physician (on his retirement in 1900). He was also assistant physician at Great Ormond Street Children's Hospital from 1864 until 1869. At University College, Ringer was professor of materia medica, pharmacology, and therapeutics (1862–78), professor of the principles and practice of medicine (1878–87), and Holme professor of clinical medicine (1887–1900). He became a member of the Physiological Society in 1884 and was elected FRS in 1885; and he was an honorary member of the New York Medical Society and a corresponding member of the Academy of Medicine in Paris.

Ringer was the author of *A Handbook of Therapeutics* (1869), and *On the Temperature of the Body as a Means of Diagnosis of Phthisis, Measles and Tuberculosis* (1865), and he contributed articles to J. R. Reynolds's *System of Medicine* (vol. 1, 1886) and to medical and scientific journals. Although a poor lecturer Ringer was an excellent bedside physician and teacher, bringing his knowledge to bear in a systematic and lucid way on the cases presented to him. However, he is best remembered for his research, which was carried out in the physiological laboratory of University College, his love of research probably being first stimulated by William Sharpey, professor of anatomy and physiology at University College, and then by Michael Foster. Ringer studied the effects of drugs and poisons on the tissues of the body; he also studied the clotting of blood, the function of peripheral nerves, and the contraction of muscle. His most important observations were on the effects of a number of ions, including sodium, potassium, and calcium ions, on the contraction of the heart. In particular, he described a solution containing these ions which can sustain living tissues removed from the body. The term 'Ringer's solution' is still used widely for such solutions. He also showed the vital role of calcium ions for the contraction of the heart. This work anticipated modern understanding of the physiological importance of these ions, and it was published in a series of papers in the *Journal of Physiology* between 1875 and 1895.

Ringer's character was the product of a severe nonconformist upbringing. He was noted for his punctuality, his kindness—which was frequently practical and anonymous—and his love of music. Although physically and mentally vigorous, he was shy, nervous, and socially retiring, and led a simple life. His eminence and outstanding achievements in clinical practice and research were consequences of his ability for rapid thought and the energy he devoted to a life dedicated to his work. His morning hospital visit would conclude with a visit to the physiological laboratory which, to the laboratory assistant, 'came not unlike electric shocks, from which he would scarcely have recovered before he would find that it was all over … a tracing taken, various suggestions made, and off he was again [to the morning's consulting work]' (*BMJ*, 1384–6).

The afternoon would be filled with clinical work, followed, whenever possible, by another visit to the laboratory.

Ringer married Ann (1833–1897), daughter of Henry Brewster Darley (d. 1860), of Aldby Park, in York on 8 August 1867. They had two daughters: Annie (1868–1875), in whose memory they restored the St Mary's Church at Lastingham in the North Riding of Yorkshire, and Hilda. Sydney Ringer died as a result of a stroke on 14 October 1910 at Lastingham, where he was buried with his wife, alongside their daughter Annie, in St Mary's churchyard.

C. H. Orchard

Sources BMJ (29 Oct 1910), 1384–6 · The Lancet (5 Nov 1910), 1386–7 · E. A. S., PRS, 84B (1911–12), i–iii · Nature, 84 (1910), 540 · DNB · Walford, County families (1898) · churchyard register, St Mary's, Lastingham, north Yorkshire · m. cert. · W. B. Fye, 'Sydney Ringer, calcium, and cardiac function', Circulation, 69 (1984), 849–53 · B. Moore, 'In memory of Sidney Ringer', The collected papers of Sydney Ringer, 3 (1912) · 'Sydney Ringer (1835–1910), clinician and pharmacologist', Journal of the American Medical Association, 206 (1968), 2515–6 [editorial] · K. H. Schnepp, 'Sydney Ringer, 1835–1910', Bulletin, Sangamon County Medical Society, 38 (1973), 2–10 · R. A. Chapman, 'The effect of lime and potash on the frog heart: an imaginative reconstruction of a paper presented by Sydney Ringer to the Physiological Society on 9th December 1882', The calcium channel: structure, function and implications, ed. M. Morad, W. Nayler, S. Kazda, and M. Scramm (1988) · W. J. O'Connor, Founders of British physiology: a biographical dictionary, 1820–1885 (1988), 153–5

Archives UCL, certificates and papers · Wellcome L.

Likenesses photograph, repro. in E. A. S., PRS

Wealth at death £54,895 7s. 9d.: resworn probate, 7 Dec 1910, CGPLA Eng. & Wales

Ringrose, Basil (d. 1686), buccaneer, left no details of his birth or education. He may have taken part in the assault on Porto Bello in 1679 before joining a party of some 330 buccaneers who, under Captain Peter Harris, landed at Golden Island on 5 April 1680 with the intention of marching over the Isthmus of Darien to sack Panama. On 15 April he was active in the assault on the Spanish town of Santa Maria and later was in a sea battle in the Bay of Panama when three armed Spanish vessels were seized. Thus equipped to mount unlimited operations against the Spaniards, and under the new leadership of Captain Bartholomew Sharpe, the buccaneers scoured the length of the Pacific coast of America in pursuit of prizes. Ringrose seems to have held a position of trust on board the Trinity, Sharpe's only vessel from May 1680. On 12 September 1680 Ringrose calculated the ship's longitudinal position from an eclipse of the sun, indicating that he was highly trained as a navigator.

On 28 July 1681 Sharpe seized a Spanish vessel named Rosario off the Ecuadorian coast which carried a derrotero, or waggoner, which tabled pilotage instructions for the whole Pacific coastline of America, a world jealously guarded by Spain and closed to foreigners. Ringrose made a copy of the waggoner, probably after his return to England on 30 January 1682. He was also one of five buccaneers, including William Dampier and Lionel Wafer, who kept a journal of the expedition. His narrative is by far the most detailed account of the voyage and it was published as the second volume of A. O. Exquemelin's Bucaniers of America (1685). The publisher's preface summed up Ringrose's achievement very fairly:

> [he] not only fought with his sword in the most desperate engagements and battles of the Buccaneers against the Spaniards, but with his pen gave us a true account of those transactions, and with his pencil has delineated unto us the very scenes of those tragedies. (Exquemelin, 2.290)

Ringrose's intelligence and sensitivity are qualities which permeate his narrative. Entries like that for 26 August 1680, where Ringrose recoils from an atrocity committed on board a prize vessel, reveal a man at odds with his employment. 'Such cruelties', he wrote, 'I abhorred very much in my heart', after Sharpe's men shot the ship's chaplain in the back, casting him overboard before he was dead (Exquemelin, 2.360). It is therefore surprising that he, unlike Dampier, Wafer, and so many others, stayed on board for the entire voyage. Ringrose was in the Trinity when she passed round Cape Horn en route for the Caribbean in January 1682. This was the first time any English vessel made the transit in an easterly direction. On 11 February, Ringrose took passage from Nevis in the Lisbon Merchant (Captain Robert Porteen), landing at Dartmouth on 26 March 1682.

On 1 October 1683 Ringrose embarked as supercargo in the Cygnet (Captain Swan), bound for the south seas on a trading voyage. Dampier remarks that Ringrose 'had no mind to this Voyage; but was necessitated to engage in it or starve' (Dampier, 272). On 2 October 1684 the Cygnet, having already abandoned lawful trade to go on the account, joined forces with the Batchelor's Delight commanded by Captain Edward Davis. Together they launched attacks against towns on the mainland before assembling with a force of nearly a thousand buccaneers in the Bay of Panama to intercept the plate fleet. In May 1685 the fleet arrived, having already disposed of its treasure. After an inconclusive battle the Cygnet and the Batchelor's Delight mounted an abortive attack on Léon. On 26 August 1685 Dampier transferred from the Batchelor's Delight to the Cygnet to be reunited with Ringrose for a voyage to the East Indies. Ringrose never returned to England. On 19 February 1686 Dampier's 'ingenious friend Mr. Ringrose' was killed in an ambush mounted by the Spanish troops following a raid on a small town, possibly Tepic, near Santiago in Mexico (ibid., 271).

Ringrose's legacy is unquestionably his journal. Complementing Wafer's famous study of the Cuna Indians of Darien, Ringrose offers his own, more pointed, analysis which has received too little attention. Ringrose depicts the Cuna as shrewd and manipulative. They co-opted the unsuspecting buccaneers as mercenaries and with slick administrative procedures they managed to sustain the movement and resupply of a small army across the region. In directing the attack on Santa Maria, the Indians brought modern weapons technology to bear upon their Spanish adversaries. With their war aims achieved the Indians simply melted into the forest leaving the buccaneers with no option but to paddle downstream towards the Bay of Panama. Thus, the Indians effectively disposed of a second unwanted power. Ringrose's narrative offers a radical perspective to challenge the view that Native Americans were politically innocent, and incapable of effective resistance during the early phases of European occupation.   JAMES WILLIAM KELLY

Sources B. Ringrose, 'South sea waggoner', [n.d., in or before 1682–1683], NMM, P.32 · Basil Ringrose's journal (holograph), undated but written in or before 1683, BL, Sloane 3820 · B. Ringrose, *Bucaniers of America: the second volume, containing the dangerous voyage and bold attempts of Captain Bartholomew Sharp and others* (1685) · W. Dampier, *A new voyage around the world* (1697) · L. Wafer, *A new voyage and description of the isthmus of America* (1699) · a copy of Ringrose's journal by Phillip Dassigny with illustrations by William Hack, BL, Sloane MS 48 · presentation copy of *derrotero* for Charles II by William Hack, BL, K. Mar. VIII 15 (7 TAB 123) · a copy of Sharpe's journal, c.1685, BL, Sloane MS 46A · a copy of Sharpe's journal, 1683, BL, Sloane MS 46B · *The voyages and adventures of Capt. Barth. Sharp and others in the south sea* (1684) · W. Hacke, ed., *A collection of original voyages* (1699) · unpublished biographical description of a Spanish *derrotero* sold at auction at Christies, 13–14 June 1979, as lot 175 (possibly the original document taken by Sharpe from the *Rosario*) · D. Howse and N. J. W. Thrower, eds., *A buccaneer's atlas: Basil Ringrose's South Sea waggoner* (Berkeley, CA, 1992) · G. Williams, *The great South Sea: English voyages and encounters, 1570–1750* (1997) · P. T. Bradley, 'Sharp and company: the first of the buccaneers, 1679–82', *The lure of Peru: maritime intrusion into the south sea, 1598–1701* (1989), 103–28 · P. Edwards, *The story of the voyage* (1994) · N. J. W. Thrower, ed., *The compleat plattmaker: essays on chart, map, and globe making in England* (1978) · T. R. Adams, 'William Hack's manuscript atlases of "The great south sea of America"', *John Carter Brown Library Annual Report: 1965–6* (1967), 45–52 · E. Lynham, 'William Hack and the south sea buccaneers', *The mapmaker's art: essays on the history of maps* (1953) · G. Williams, '"The inexhaustible fountain of gold": English projects and ventures in the south seas, 1670–1750', *Perspectives of empire: essays presented to Gerald S. Graham*, ed. J. E. Flint and G. Williams (1973), 27–52
Archives BL, holograph journal, Sloane MS 3820

Ringstead, Thomas (*d.* 1366), bishop of Bangor and author, was probably a native of Ringstead in Norfolk. He was said by John Bale to have been educated at the University of Cambridge, where he graduated MA and DTh. He became a member of the Dominican convent at Cambridge in January 1346 and was still there in 1348, during which period he was licensed to hear confessions in Ely diocese. He subsequently studied in France and Italy, and in 1353 he was in residence at the papal court at Avignon, where he was penitentiary of England. In 1356 he was employed by Pope Innocent VI as a papal messenger to Edward III concerning peace in France.

When the diocese of Bangor became vacant in 1357 it was Ringstead's standing with the pope which led Innocent to set aside the claims of Ithel ap Robert, an influential local candidate who had been elected by the chapter, and provide Ringstead to the see on 21 August 1357.

Consecrated at Avignon about September 1357, he received the spiritualities on 15 November 1357. He was admitted a portioner of Llandinam, Montgomeryshire, c.1360, and he vacated that benefice in 1363. He died at Shrewsbury convent on 8 January 1366, and was buried either at Blackfriars, London, or else in the Dominican friary at Huntingdon, where, according to Thomas Tanner (*d.* 1735), his parents were also buried. In his will he left £100 to his cathedral, but enjoined that this was not to be paid if

his successor was Welsh. He also bequeathed the sum of £100 to maintain five poor scholars from his diocese at either Oxford or Cambridge, but stipulated that it should on no account be distributed by a Welshman, and he may also have intended that the recipients should be drawn from among the English-speaking inhabitants of his diocese.

Ringstead was a scholar of distinction in his own right as well as being a patron of learning. He is claimed as the author of a number of theological writings. Several copies of his readings on the *Sentences* of Peter Lombard survive. One copy of his readings on the Proverbs, originally delivered as lectures at Cambridge, existed in the library of Canterbury College, Oxford, and is now Bodleian MS 829 (2720). Similar copies are extant in other Oxford colleges: Balliol (MS 34), Lincoln (MS 86), and Trinity (MS 35). Its title is variously given as *Expositio super parabolas Salamonis*, *Super Salamonis proverbia*, and *Postilla super 29 capitula parabolarum*. These have generally been considered separate works, without good ground, as the opening words of two of the manuscripts are identical. A note, added by a later hand to one of the manuscripts, stating that it was written in London in 1461, points to the author having perhaps been a later Thomas Ringstead who held prebends in Lincoln Cathedral between 1440 and 1452. John Bale also credited the earlier Thomas Ringstead with a number of theological works and sermons, all of which are now lost.

GLANMOR WILLIAMS

Sources Bale, *Cat.* · Bale, *Index* · Emden, *Cam.* · *Fasti Angl., 1300–1541*, [Welsh dioceses] · F. Stegmüller, ed., *Repertorium biblicum medii aevi*, 11 vols. (Madrid, 1950?–1980) · J. R. L. Highfield, 'The English hierarchy in the reign of Edward III', *TRHS*, 5th ser., 6 (1956), 115–38 · G. Williams, *The Welsh church from conquest to Reformation*, rev. edn (1976) · B. Willis, *A survey of the cathedral church of Bangor* (1721) · W. Hughes, *Bangor* (1911)
Archives Balliol Oxf., MS 34 · Bodl. Oxf., MS 829 (2720) · Lincoln College, Oxford, MS 86 · Trinity College, Oxford, MS 35
Likenesses T. Ringstead, possibly self-portrait, pencil drawing, NPG
Wealth at death two bequests of £100 each

Rintoul, Robert Stephen (1787–1858), journal editor, was born at Tibbermore, in Perthshire. He was educated at the parish school of Aberdalgie and apprenticed as a printer in Edinburgh. His career as a journalist started in April 1809, when he became a printer for the *Dundee Advertiser*. Within two years, in January 1811, he became its editor. From 1811 to 10 February 1825 the *Dundee Advertiser* was 'edited, printed, and published by R. S. Rintoul'. Given the journalistic practices of the time, it was probably also principally written by him. His regular calls for municipal reform in the *Advertiser* eventually brought him into association with some of Scotland's leading liberals, including Douglas Kinnaird, Francis Jeffrey, Henry Cockburn, and James Moncreiff. For reasons not explained, Rintoul left Dundee for London in 1825, and by 1826 had become editor of *The Atlas*, a well-written, Benthamite newspaper with a strong literary bent. After three years, however, he resigned over an attempt, as he put it, to 'vulgarise and betwaddle the "Atlas"—contrary to our compact and to

Robert Stephen Rintoul (1787–1858), by David Octavius Hill and Robert Adamson, 1843–8

the line of conduct which gave that paper its literary character' (letter to William Blackwood, 7 July 1828). He managed to take the entire literary staff with him, and, with his own money and backing from Kinnaird and a few others, he founded *The Spectator* on 6 July 1828.

Although he was editor and publisher of *The Spectator*, and as such one of the more important people of his time, little is known of his private life. He was obviously a talented journalist. He must have had a powerful personality to inspire the kind of loyalty he did among his writers. Edward Gibbon Wakefield's niece remembered him as gentle-mannered, and Wakefield himself found him the most charming and helpful of men, except on Fridays, when *The Spectator* was being put together. Although he claimed to be above politics his philosophical radicalism informed most of *The Spectator's* political positions and played a major role in influencing important mid-century legislation.

Despite his claims to the contrary, Rintoul was not apolitical; rather, he was a rarity of the time, an editor who had not allied himself with any party. In 1857 the *Newspaper Press Directory* could speak of *The Spectator's* 'utter independence of, and indifference to, any particular class, sect, or party; and this feature, associated also with certain characteristic individuality (the result, no doubt, of the existence, at this moment in full force, of the same energetic influence [namely Rintoul] which imparted its earlier impulses) stamps its opinions and views with an impressive and striking originality' (Mitchell, 28). Rintoul

challenged both of the leading parties on such vital issues as reform (1832), the abolition of slavery (1832), corn law repeal (1848), and emigration reform (1830–50). In fact, as Alexander Hastie Millar notes in the *Dictionary of National Biography*, 'The "Spectator" took a prominent part in the discussion of every important reform, social or political, achieved during the thirty years that he acted as its editor'.

Both Millar and Leigh Hunt, who succeeded Rintoul as editor, claimed that Rintoul's 'suave personality and brilliant talents' (*DNB*) attracted some of the best minds in London to write for the paper—men such as Jeremy Bentham, and John Stuart Mill—and thus he wrote little himself. Instead, he supposedly suggested topics and treatments, supervised the writing, and kept a clear and consistent editorial position. To some extent, all editors do those things. However, the fact that he devoted almost all of his time to the paper, not even taking a vacation until 1842 (when he left Hunt in charge), argues that he was doing a good share of the writing, both for the 'middles' (the editorials) and in other areas. And although his political pages were, indeed, consistent, his editorial page often clashed with other pages. Rintoul was, for example, a passionate advocate of the abolition of slavery in the colonies, and on 7 April 1832 he wrote a scorching editorial attacking those who would slow down abolition, concluding that 'there is no use in disputing whether West Indian slavery is worse than African freedom, or whether the owners abuse their property'; rather, one must support 'a sudden redemption of slavery' because 'bit-by-bit emancipation will only make things worse' (*The Spectator*, 7 April 1832, 325). And on 8 September 1832, in 'Sugar and slavery', he concluded that 'slavery is an unmanly and detestable vice of society—let it be extinguished' (ibid., 8 Sept 1832, 849). Yet his book reviewer, commenting on 'Murray on colonial slavery' on 14 July 1832, criticized Murray for 'ranting' against slavery and contended that a 'graduated scale of enfranchisement' over the next fourteen years was preferable to sudden abolition. And again, in a review of the novel *The System* on 1 September 1832, he said that although slavery might be evil, the planters were as much victims of the system as the slaves were.

Rintoul established himself as an important national voice in the debate over the Reform Bill of 1831–2, coining the phrase 'The Bill, the Whole Bill, and Nothing but the Bill' in its defence. His championing of the Reform Bill boosted *The Spectator's* sales and embellished its reputation as a literate, independent, unique voice in the world of the London press, a periodical which combined extensive coverage of current affairs with a large section devoted to the arts and an editorial department devoted to 'the people'. The paper got a further boost through Rintoul's support of Edward Gibbon Wakefield's scheme of colonial reform from 1830 to 1850. In *The Story of 'The Spectator'* William Beach Thomas credits Rintoul with 'the winning idea that produced Greater Britain. The foundation of South Australia and New Zealand, the settlement of Canada, all in different degrees owe something to his constructive imagination as well as to his valorous support' (Thomas, 144). As in his support of the Reform Bill (and later the repeal of the corn laws), Rintoul's position was a result of his dedication to 'improving the condition of the working classes in their domestic life even more than in their political status' (Escott, 238).

Rintoul kept his private life intensely private. None of the secondary accounts about him mention his wife or children, yet his will reveals that he had a wife, Henrietta, a son, Robert, who was a lieutenant in Her Majesty's 4th regiment of dragoon guards, and a daughter, also Henrietta, who was unmarried at the time of his death. His circle of friends included reform politicians such as Sir William Molesworth and Charles Buller; social reformers such as Wakefield (a friend for over twenty years); poets and writers such as Robert Browning, Alfred Tennyson, Laman Blanchard, and Brian W. Procter; the economist Joseph Hume; actors such as William Charles Macready; and influential clerics such as Thomas Chalmers. His health failing, Rintoul sold *The Spectator* in 1858 to a group of Americans whose major investor seemed to be Benjamin Moran, secretary to the American legation. He died on 22 April 1858 at his home at 9 Wellington Street, Savoy, London. RICHARD D. FULTON

Sources DNB · *The Spectator* (1 May 1858) · *Daily News* (24 April 1858) · W. B. Thomas, *The story of The Spectator, 1828–1928* (1928) · P. Bloomfield, *The Spectator* (18 April 1958) · T. H. S. Escott, *Masters of English journalism* (1911) · J. Grant, *The newspaper press: its origin, progress, and present position*, 3: *The metropolitan weekly and provincial press* (1872) · A. J. Harrap, 'Rintoul and Wakefield', *The Spectator* (3 Nov 1928) · *The diaries of William Charles Macready, 1833–1851*, ed. W. Toynbee, 2 vols. (1912) · Mrs Oliphant, *William Blackwood and his sons* (1897), vols. 1–2 of *Annals of a publishing house* (1897–8) · C. Mitchell, *The newspaper press directory* (1857) · *The journal of Benjamin Moran*, ed. S. A. Wallace and F. E. Gillespie (1948) · D. Griffiths, ed., *The encyclopedia of the British press, 1422–1992* (1992) · CGPLA Eng. & Wales (1858)
Likenesses D. O. Hill and R. Adamson, photograph, 1843–8, NPG [*see illus.*] · woodcut, repro. in Thomas, *Story of 'The Spectator'* (1928)
Wealth at death under £7000: probate, 20 May 1858, CGPLA Eng. & Wales

Rinuccini, Giovanni Battista [Gianbattista] (1592–1653), archbishop of Fermo and papal diplomat, was born in Rome on 15 September 1592.

Family and Italian career Rinuccini's father, Camillo, was a Florentine patrician, and his mother, Virginia, was the daughter of PierAntonio Bandini and the sister of Cardinal Ottavio Bandini. His brother Tomasso later became the chief gentleman of the bedchamber of the grand duke of Tuscany. Rinuccini's early education was at the hands of the Jesuits in Rome. He studied law in the universities of Bologna and Perugia, before receiving a doctorate of canon and civil law (*utrumque ius*) from the university of Pisa. The doctorate in canon law was a classical stepping-stone to a variety of important ecclesiastical careers. Although Rinuccini was appointed as secretary of the congregation of rites in Rome, it appears that his legal activities in Rome were of far greater importance. On 26 February 1622 he was made a referendary in the two most important courts in Rome, the *segnatura di giudizio* and (in breach of regulations) the *segnatura di grazie*. In 1623 he

became a *giudice civile* in the special tribunal of the cardinal vicar of Rome. His uncle Cardinal Bandini had previously been archbishop of Fermo but had resigned the see in favour of one of his nephews, Alessandro Strozzi. On Strozzi's death, another nephew, Pietro Dini, acquired the archdiocese, and when he died in August 1625, it was Rinuccini, presumably at his uncle's instigation, who was offered the see. After a swift ordination, Rinuccini was promoted to the archbishopric on 17 November 1625 having acquired a dispensation from the minimum six-month interval between priestly orders and consecration as a bishop. The see initially yielded him 1000 scudi (about £250) per annum, though after Bandini's death in 1629, this apparently increased to 5000 scudi.

Rinuccini proved a devoted pastor. He was deeply committed to his archdiocese (he refused to leave it for the more prestigious see of Florence in 1631) and considered it a bishop's personal responsibility to ensure the salvation of the souls entrusted by God to his care. He had a varied authorial career, producing works on philosophy, rhetoric, history, and geography, but considered his religious writings as fundamentally more important, particularly the two-volume *Della dignita et offitio dei vescovi: discorsi quaranta di Monsignor Gio. Battista Rinuccini, arcivescovo e prencipe di Fermo* (1651), a discussion of the pastoral bishop which he regarded as the consummation of his published output. In terms of readership, however, the immensely popular *Il cappuccino scozzese*, a romantic novel-like text loosely based on the life of a Scottish friar, George Lesley, which was published in at least twenty-six editions in the course of the seventeenth century, dwarfed anything else that he produced.

The Irish nunciature Rinuccini was officially confirmed as nuncio to the confederate Catholics in March 1645, but the decision to appoint him was evidently taken by the newly installed Pope Innocent X no later than early January of that year. Rinuccini was a somewhat unlikely figure for the post. He recalled the nuncios of the immediate post-Tridentine era, a pastoral archbishop rather than a career diplomat of the type that had become more usual by the mid-seventeenth century. His mission was publicized as a particularly meritorious ecclesiastical venture, and its genesis owed much to the circumstances surrounding Innocent X's controversial elevation to the throne of St Peter. In the wake of his bitterly contested election, the new pope evidently wished to demonstrate his religious credentials for office. The plan of sending a nuncio and funds to Ireland, despite the confederate supreme council's lack of interest in receiving one, was intended as a bold statement of pontifical solicitude for the Catholics of Ireland, who were widely regarded in Europe as a particularly oppressed religious community. By directing the new nuncio's route through Paris, Innocent was also able to introduce one of his own ministers into France, whose regency government had reacted with extreme hostility to his election but could hardly decline to receive a nuncio engaged in such a praiseworthy mission.

Rinuccini arrived in Paris in May 1645 and did not leave

until September, but had little success in thawing relations between Mazarin's government and Rome. On the sea-journey to Ireland his frigate was subjected to a prolonged chase by a larger hostile vessel, which had been alerted to his probable arrival by news of his slow and well-publicized journey through Italy and France to La Rochelle. A fire in the pursuing ship's galley, which the nuncio interpreted as divine intervention, eventually saved the expedition. Blown west of Waterford, he eventually made landfall in Kenmare, where he and his party were impressed by the religious knowledge, hospitality, and respect accorded them by the remote rural community there. He proceeded to Limerick, where he encountered his predecessor as papal representative, Pierfrancesco Scarampi, and was finally received in what was effectively the confederate capital, Kilkenny, on 12 November 1645.

Rinuccini and the Ormond peace When Rinuccini reached Ireland the confederates, the oath-bound association which had emerged following the rising of 1641, had been engaged for over two years in peace negotiations with Charles I and his lord lieutenant in Ireland, the marquess of Ormond. By May 1645 three critical issues had emerged as the chief obstacles to a settlement: the protection of Catholics from the penal elements of the reformation legislation; the right of the Catholic clergy to exercise a jurisdiction derived from Rome; and the future of the churches and church livings which had been transferred from the protestant clergy to their Catholic counterparts since the rising of 1641. The second and third of these issues were of urgent concern only to the Catholic clergy, but they constituted a formidable interest group and during summer 1645 proved capable of preventing the conclusion of a treaty. The impasse, however, was apparently broken by the mission of the earl of Glamorgan. Dispatched by Charles with a private mandate to supplement the lord lieutenant's public authority, he arrived in Ireland in July 1645 and in September entered into a secret additional agreement with the confederates which offered to secure for the Catholic clergy their chief objectives. Difficulties in ensuring that details of the published treaty did not contradict Glamorgan's secret protocol nevertheless continued to delay the conclusion of peace until Rinuccini's arrival.

Rinuccini found the composite settlement unsatisfactory, but was pessimistic about his chances of preventing its completion. Consequently, he extracted some further concessions from Glamorgan and informed his superiors that there was little else that he could do. Two factors swiftly radicalized his position, however. The first was Glamorgan's imprisonment in Dublin, the result of the publication in London of details of his agreement with the confederates. In an effort to limit the damage to the king's reputation, Ormond and George Digby, the king's secretary, accused the earl of high treason. Rinuccini argued for an immediate attack on Dublin but was forced to content himself with the convocation of a general assembly, the quasi-parliament of the confederates, to discuss the issue.

The second factor in hardening his position was the communication to him from Italy of a draft treaty negotiated between the pope and Sir Kenelm Digby, Queen Henrietta Maria's envoy to Rome, which offered substantially better conditions than Glamorgan's for Catholics in the Stuart dominions in general, and Ireland in particular.

Glamorgan's release on parole from Dublin none the less offered the supporters of the Ormond peace an opportunity to resuscitate it. They were deeply unwilling to gamble the fruit of sustained negotiation on the uncertain venture of the Roman treaty, but the nuncio's addresses to the assembly in February 1646 revealed his capacity to stir support and the political folly of ignoring him. Eventually a bargain was reached on 19 February: the conclusion of the Ormond peace would be delayed until 1 May to allow an official copy of the papal peace to arrive. If it did not, Rinuccini would rest content with the Glamorgan protocol. The confederate peace party, however, deceived the nuncio by concluding the peace on 28 March, just before the elapse of Ormond's mandate, although in deference to Rinuccini the treaty was not published.

Rinuccini received nothing further concerning the papal peace before the deadline of 1 May and eventually had to accept that the Roman treaty had collapsed. Once again, despite the news which had reached Ireland in March that Charles also had disowned Glamorgan, he decided to offer no overt opposition to the Ormond peace—which he still did not know had been concluded—if the confederates chose to ignore his advice concerning its inadvisability.

However, a succession of developments operated to harden Rinuccini's attitude again. On 13 June he received news of Owen Roe O'Neill's victory at Benburb. This inaugurated a period of confederate military success which included the capture of Roscommon and Bunratty. Rinuccini had a direct influence on these events. He had left Rome with approximately 50,000 scudi (*c*.£12,500) and received additional monies in France. Up to a third of this money was subsequently lost in the shipwreck of one of his agents, Carlo Invernizzi, but he was still able to furnish O'Neill with 16,000 scudi in money and arms, and approximately twice this sum to the Leinster army under Preston. Thus papal funds were largely responsible for the successes of Benburb and Roscommon, while Rinuccini himself played a critical role in galvanizing the confederates into the successful assault on Bunratty. These victories boosted Rinuccini's confidence and made him believe that a militant policy in Ireland was practicable. He believed that, until a peace settlement satisfactory to the clergy was on offer, the confederates should prosecute their war vigorously and attempt to conquer the entire island.

The confederate peace party consistently opposed this logic, but their position was weakened by the king's declaration on 11 June against any treaty in Ireland. Ormond consequently was unwilling to publish the peace. Ultimately, only a major application of French influence, and a public declaration from Digby that it was consonant with the king's will, impelled Ormond to allow the promulgation of the long-concluded agreement on 30 July. No opposition was anticipated from Rinuccini, but in little over a month he orchestrated the destruction of the settlement.

Rinuccini's distrust of elements on the confederate supreme council was intense, and it was increased by his realization in June that he had been hoodwinked concerning the conclusion of the treaty. Other less important deceptions had also occurred. He had previously convoked a legatine synod at Waterford for early August and this now became the forum for resistance to the peace. Rinuccini clearly did not act unilaterally: a broad consensus existed among the Irish clergy concerning the inadequacy of the settlement which encouraged the nuncio to lend his leadership to a programme of opposition. Rinuccini's task was greatly eased by the power vacuum which developed in Kilkenny with the lapse of confederate government. Ormond responded to the escalation of the crisis rather slowly, though belatedly the lord lieutenant did try everything in his power to protect the peace. A major deficiency of the settlement was the failure to offer significant posts to the generals of the two principal confederate armies, O'Neill and Preston. This contributed to their support of the clergy. The populations of the confederate towns also proved unwilling to dare the interdict issued by the clergy in Waterford, and the combination of ecclesiastical, urban, and military pressure ultimately ensured the collapse of the settlement. Rinuccini returned to Kilkenny in September, the principal authors of the peace were imprisoned, and a new supreme council, with the nuncio as president, was created.

The most important policy adopted by the new council was an attack on Dublin, which evidently reflected Rinuccini's own preoccupation with eliminating the influence of Ormond among the confederates and his belief that a striking success would attract additional subsidies from Rome. It was probably his most significant mistake during his nunciature. The campaign was a dismal failure, compromised from the beginning by the mutual distrust of Preston and O'Neill, to whom it had been jointly entrusted. Rinuccini showed considerable personal bravery and psychological insight in preventing Preston's defection from the confederates, but the collapse of the assault severely diminished his prestige and influence.

Nicholas French, the bishop of Ferns, and Nicholas Plunkett now came to the fore as architects of a fresh, more moderate, strategy. Another general assembly was convoked which confirmed the rejection of the peace but which exonerated its chief authors from the charge of perjury of the confederate oath of association that had previously been made against them. A new supreme council was elected, largely favourable to clerical interests, and Rinuccini, to his superiors' relief, renounced his presidency. Plunkett and Bishop French were now the major influences on the confederate council, and Rinuccini, who trusted both men, concentrated more of his energies on ecclesiastical concerns. Plunkett, Bishop French, and their supporters attempted to stabilize the association in the course of 1647 but numerous problems confronted them. Ormond was not prepared to deal with the confederates except on the basis of the rejected peace. Since his quarters around Dublin had been comprehensively ravaged, he saw little alternative when the assembly endorsed the repudiation of the peace but to turn to the English parliament, which he had initially contacted during Rinuccini's campaign. He was eventually replaced in Dublin by a formidable army under Michael Jones in August 1647.

With Rinuccini's acquiescence, Plunkett and Bishop French devoted a great deal of attention to strengthening Preston's army and enjoyed considerable success. Appalled at the devastation which the Ulster army had created in the province and eager to conciliate moderate opinion, they refused to allow O'Neill to remain in the east but detailed him for service in Connaught. They and Rinuccini suffered a crushing set-back, however, when Jones outmanoeuvred and routed the Leinster forces at Dungan's Hill, leading to the hurried recall of the Ulster army. In Munster also a succession of disasters occurred. The clerical coup of 1646 had derailed plans for an attack on the parliamentarian enclave under Inchiquin's command in Cork. With increased supplies and eager to protect his position from English criticism, Inchiquin adopted an aggressive strategy in 1647. He was helped by considerable confederate disarray in the province. Anti-Rinuccini figures in Munster, led by Viscount Muskery, were bitterly unhappy with the rejection of the treaty, and the provincial army provided them with a basis for resistance against the supreme council. Prolonged dissension led first to the paralysis of the army, which contributed to the free hand which Inchiquin enjoyed early in the year, and finally to a June mutiny which resulted in Muskery's reinstallation as commander. Rinuccini argued for firm measures against the viscount, but the moderate voices on the council rejected his advice. In the event, Rinuccini's suggested course of action was probably wiser because, under the control of first Muskery and then his ally Viscount Taaffe, the Munster army did nothing to confront Inchiquin for most of the summer. Instead they became involved in plans to desert to French service. As a consequence, confederate Munster was comprehensively devastated. Only in November, when hopes of transfer to France had been dashed, did Taaffe seek to engage Inchiquin, but his forces were routed at the battle of Knocknanuss.

These military defeats undermined the policy which Plunkett and Bishop French had pursued over the previous twelve months. Their attempts to reintegrate the confederate association, by refusing to make peace without the clergy's agreement, while conciliating the supporters of peace and marginalizing the Ulster army, foundered because of a combination of poor generalship, parliamentarian strength, and the refusal of Ormond's confederate partisans to co-operate with their strategy, particularly in Munster.

The end of the nunciature By November 1647 the military prospects of the confederate association appeared bleak and what strength it possessed depended largely on the widely resented Ulster army. Crucially, however, Rinuccini did not share the common view that the year's setbacks had proved the inability of the association to pursue a militant policy. Although his confidence had been shaken, he ascribed the defeats which had occurred to God's punishment for the sins of dissension which the confederates had committed. He was convinced that greater unity of purpose could have prevented the disasters in Leinster and Munster, and believed that a sizeable donation of money from Rome could still rescue the situation in Ireland. Unlike many of the confederates, who viewed the English parliament with hardly less horror, he had little difficulty in placing his reliance on the Ulster army. The second general assembly of 1647 revealed how sharply the association was now divided: indeed the civil war which erupted the following year was almost ignited at this point. Ultimately the confederates chose to seek a foreign protector, and the moderate influence of Plunkett and Bishop French was removed when they were chosen for the mission to Rome. The composition of the supreme council also changed, with some of Rinuccini's most inveterate opponents, such as Richard Bellings, Gerald Fennell, and Sir Lucas Dillon, returning to its ranks.

By March 1648 Rinuccini was strongly tempted to leave Ireland. Since his arrival in Ireland he had pleaded with Rome to supply him with additional funds but his hesitant and parsimonious master was reluctant to invest in Ireland until he saw evidence of some prestigious progress. Eventually, the rejection of the first Ormond peace in 1646 persuaded him to loosen the purse strings again. This money, however, on which Rinuccini counted desperately, was delayed in France for almost a year and contributed to the confederate *annus horribilis* by rendering Rinuccini incapable of assisting the military. Eventually, the remnant of the money arrived in March 1648 but the 30,000 scudi was too small a sum to allow a dramatic alteration of circumstances. Feelings of loyalty and solidarity with O'Neill and some Irish bishops, none the less, impelled Rinuccini to remain in Ireland, and his distrust of the supreme council led to his gradual embroilment in the controversy of the Inchiquin truce. Rinuccini's opposition to the suggested truce with the recently turned royalist Inchiquin had little to do with the merits of the agreement, but rather concerned his justified suspicions that it was intended as part of a process leading to the reintroduction of the Ormond peace. In May, fearful for his safety, he fled from Kilkenny to the Ulster camp at Maryborough, and on the 29th, in a somewhat panicky attempt to protect O'Neill's position, he ignited a confederate civil war with a declaration of excommunication against the supporters of the truce.

This proved Rinuccini's last truly decisive act in Ireland. O'Neill lacked the resources to achieve victory, and Rinuccini's inability to assemble a synod to ratify his actions, which confirmed his belief in the turpitude of those who prevented him, meant Rinuccini could provide little additional support. Ormond arrived in Ireland in September and opened negotiations with a new general assembly. By November Rinuccini was a marginalized figure in Galway. In that month Plunkett and Bishop French, having been frustrated of all expectation of papal aid, returned from Rome and threw their energies into an attempt to secure acceptable conditions in the new treaty of peace with Ormond. Rinuccini rather bitterly accepted this turn of events and put no further obstacle in the way of the negotiation of the treaty. He left Ireland in February 1649 following the conclusion of the second Ormond peace, but was unable to remain in France to oversee Irish affairs and returned to Italy. He compiled a long report of his mission, rejected the offer of the secretaryship of the *propaganda fide*, which he contrived to have given to his close subordinate, Massari, and by August 1650 had returned to Fermo. In that year he decided to publish a history of Irish affairs during the period of his nunciature, a project which ultimately resulted in the *Commentarius Rinuccinianus*. His health was not good and seems to have broken down almost completely towards the end of 1651. Rinuccini spent much of 1652 completely absent from his see for reasons of ill health, though he did return to the archdiocese prior to his death there on 13 December 1653. He was buried later that month in the cathedral in Fermo.

Significance, historical standing, and personality Rinuccini is a highly significant figure in the history of the 1640s, chiefly because of the manner in which he helped to delay the completion of a peace settlement between the royalist and confederate parties in Ireland. Without his influence it seems probable that an anti-parliamentarian union with secure control of Dublin would have been established in 1646.

Rinuccini polarized opinion among both his contemporaries and later historians. One consistent strand of historical opinion has branded him as a rash, intransigent, and unrealistic zealot. A more sympathetic view, emphasizing his devotion to the Catholic cause, has also been widely disseminated by nationalist historians. Contemporary evaluations have generally attempted to establish a more balanced portrait, in particular by highlighting his often justified distrust of elements of the confederate association, which was critical in causing him to adopt certain positions. Recent work also has attempted to situate him in a wider European context and to supplement personal criticism with analysis of the forces of which Rinuccini was a product and which materially dictated his behaviour in Ireland.

Rinuccini's personal characteristics, however, evidently cannot be ignored in assessing his activities. He was a very frail figure throughout his life, and endured the miseries of repeated bronchial illnesses and what may have been a tapeworm during his sojourn in Ireland. He was highly intelligent, psychologically shrewd, meticulous, persistent, and an inspiring orator in both Italian and Latin. His passionate religious convictions and his belief in an interventionist deity meant that, while often adept at political manipulation, at bottom he was no politician. This ultimately proved crucial in his marginalization and failure.

TADHG Ó HANNRACHÁIN

Sources B. O'Ferrall and D. O'Connell, *Commentarius Rinuccinianus de sedis apostolicae legatione ad foederatos Hiberniae Catholicos per annos 1645–1649*, ed. J. Kavanagh, 6 vols., IMC (1932–49) · G. Aiazzi, *Nunziatura in Irlanda di Monsignor Gio. Battista Rinuccini* (Florence, 1844) · T. Ó hAnnracháin, *Catholic reformation in Ireland: the mission of Rinuccini, 1645–9* [forthcoming] [incl. detailed bibliography] · nunziatura d'Inghilterra, Biblioteca Apostolica Vaticana, Vatican City, vol. 8 · miscellaneae varie, Archivio della Sacra Congregazione di Propaganda Fide, Rome, vol. 9 · *History of the Irish confederation and the war in Ireland … by Richard Bellings*, ed. J. T. Gilbert, 7 vols. (1882–91) · J. T. Gilbert, ed., *A contemporary history of affairs in Ireland from 1641 to 1652*, 3 vols. (1879–80) · acta vicecancellarii, Archivio Segreto Vaticano, Vatican City, 17 · processus episcoporum sacrae consistorialis, Archivio Segreto Vaticano, Vatican City, 21 · correspondance politique, Angleterre, Archives du Ministère des Affaires Étrangères, Paris, vols. 48–9, 51–2, 54–5, 57, 60 · [U. de Burgh, earl of Clanricarde], *Letter-book of the Earl of Clanricarde, 1643–47*, ed. J. Lowe, IMC (1983) · D. Cregan, 'The confederation of Kilkenny: its organisation, personnel and history', PhD diss., National University of Ireland, 1947 · P. J. Corish, 'Ormond, Rinuccini, and the confederates, 1645–9', *A new history of Ireland, ed. T. W. Moody and others*, 3: *Early modern Ireland, 1534–1691* (1976), 317–35 · J. Lowe, 'Charles I and the confederation of Kilkenny', *Irish Historical Studies*, 14/53 (March 1954), 1–19 · J. Lowe, 'The Glamorgan mission to Ireland', *Studia Hibernica*, 4 (1964), 155–96 · M. Ó Siochrú, *Confederate Ireland, 1642–1649: a constitutional and political analysis* (Dublin, 1999) · M. Capucci, 'Caratteri e fortune di un cappuccino scozzese', *Studi Secenteschi*, 20 (1979), 43–88 · miscellanea, medicea, Archivio di Stato di Firenze, Florence, 436 ins 19 · P. J. Corish, 'Bishop Nicholas French and the second Ormond peace', *Irish Historical Studies*, 6 (1948–9), 83–100 · M. Hynes, *The mission of Rinuccini: nuncio extraordinary to Ireland, 1645–1649* (Louvain, 1932)

Archives Archivio Arcivescovile di Fermo, Italy, iii c/10, iii c/11, iii c/13 · Archivio Storico, Milano, Biblioteca Trivulziana, Codice 1958, 1963, 1964 · Archivio Vaticano, Vatican City, lettere di Vescovi e Prelati | Biblioteca Apostolica Vaticana, Vatican City, Nunziatura d'Inghilterra, 8 · extracts by Thomas Birch from Holkham Hall transcript of Rinuccini's 'Nuncio's memoirs'

Rinvill, Samuel. *See* Norton, Samuel (1548–1621).

Riollay, Francis William (*c*.1748–1797), physician, was the son of Christopher Riollay of Guingamp, France, and was born in Brittany. He was educated at Trinity College, Dublin, where he devoted himself to classical studies and graduated BA. He published at Oxford in 1776 a student's edition of the text with Reitzius's Latin version of Lucian's *Pōs dei historian syngraphein*, dedicated to his friend Thomas Winstanley. Riollay was incorporated at Hertford College, Oxford, on 13 January 1777, proceeded MA on 29 April 1780, and began to practise medicine at Newbury, Berkshire. He published in 1778 in London *A Letter to Dr Hardy on the Hints he has Given Concerning the Origin of Gout*. In this he suggested that gout is a disease of the nervous system, but failed to provide any anatomical evidence, relying as he did on observation and not experimentation. James Hardy published a reply in 1780. Riollay graduated MB at Oxford in March 1782, and MD on 13 July 1784. He moved to London, where he lived in Hart Street, Bloomsbury, and in 1783 published *The Doctrines and Practice of Hippocrates in Surgery and Physic*, an abstract of the Hippocratic writings, with a complete translation of the aphorisms. He became a candidate or member of the Royal College of Physicians on 9 August 1784, and was elected a fellow on 15 August 1785. In 1787 he delivered the Goulstonian lectures on fever. They were published, with a Latin preface, in 1788, and contain a clear account of the classical, medieval, and then existing doctrines as to fever, without any clinical illustrations or personal observations. His *Critical Introduction to the Study of Fevers* appeared in 1788. He also gave the Harveian oration in 1787, and was Croonian lecturer in 1788, 1789, and 1790. He went to live at Margate, Kent, in 1791, and probably died there, in 1797.

NORMAN MOORE, *rev.* CLAIRE L. NUTT

Sources Munk, *Roll* · Foster, *Alum. Oxon.* · H. A. Waldron, 'James Hardy and the Devonshire colic', *Medical History*, 13 (1969), 74–81 · P. J. Wallis and R. V. Wallis, *Eighteenth century medics*, 2nd edn (1988)

Riou, Edward (1762–1801), naval officer, was born on 20 November 1762 at Mount Ephraim, Faversham, Kent, the second of three children who survived infancy of Captain Stephen Riou (1720–1780), an officer in the Grenadier Guards descended from a Huguenot family, and his wife, Dorothy (*d*. 1801), daughter of George Dawson of North Ferriby Grange, Yorkshire. Riou joined the Royal Navy at the age of twelve, before serving in the *Barfleur* at Portsmouth and the *Romney* on the Newfoundland station. In 1776 he sailed as a midshipman in the *Discovery* (Captain Charles Clerke) which accompanied the *Resolution* (Captain James Cook) on Cook's third voyage to the south seas. After Cook's death Riou transferred with Clerke to the *Resolution* to continue exploration in the Arctic seas.

In October 1780, after his return to England, Riou was promoted lieutenant, and between 1780 and 1784 he served in the *Scourge* in the West Indies, the *Mediator* in the channel, and the guardship *Ganges* at Portsmouth. He spent two years on half pay before joining the *Salisbury* on the Newfoundland station. Through the patronage of the Townshend family, in 1789 Riou was given command of the converted frigate *Guardian*, bound for Port Jackson, carrying twenty-five convict artisans and a full cargo of urgently needed stores for the new Australian convict settlement. He sailed from Spithead on 8 September. On Christmas eve, thirteen days out from the Cape of Good Hope and not far from Marion Island, the *Guardian* struck the submerged spur of a massive iceberg which tore away her rudder and much of her keel. Half the ship's company took to the boats, but only fifteen of them survived to carry the news of the disaster back to Britain.

Riou was left with only sixty men—the boatswain and carpenter, three midshipmen, and an unruly crew of seamen, supernumeraries, and twenty-one convicts—to work the waterlogged and rudderless ship. With superb seamanship, steering mostly with the tattered sails and keeping his exhausted and mutinous crew at the pumps by combined persuasion and force, Riou brought the *Guardian* within sight of the Cape of Good Hope on 21 February 1790. She was towed into Table Bay where she was found to be damaged beyond repair, beached, and broken up. The surviving convicts (for whom Riou requested and obtained pardons) and salvaged stores were sent on to Port Jackson when the ships of the Second Fleet called at the Cape.

Riou returned to England to find that the *Guardian*'s epic

Edward Riou (1762–1801), by Samuel Shelley, *c.*1796

voyage had made him a popular hero. He underwent a formal court martial for the loss of a king's ship, was honourably acquitted, and soon afterwards promoted commander and then post captain (4 June 1791). As commander of the frigate *Rose* (28 guns) and subsequently the *Beaulieu* (40 guns) he saw action in the West Indies campaign of 1794 under Sir John Jervis. After being invalided home he was appointed to command the royal yacht *Princess Augusta*, and he served on the courts martial following the mutiny of 1797. In 1799 Riou commissioned the frigate *Amazon* (38 guns), and in 1801 he sailed with the Baltic fleet under Sir Hyde Parker, with Lord Nelson as second in command. A squadron of ships was detached under Nelson to attack Copenhagen, and the *Amazon* was employed to reconnoitre the Danish defences and to lead the squadron through the narrow northern channel to its anchorage 2 miles from the enemy's line. This was Riou's first meeting with Nelson, whom he impressed with his discipline and seamanship. After the signal had been made to prepare for action, Nelson entertained his senior officers to dinner on board his flagship. Afterwards Riou stayed on to assist Nelson with the orders for the next day's battle. Riou himself was given command of the frigates and smaller craft.

The attack began on the morning of 2 April against a strong Danish defence. Riou brought his three frigates under heavy fire in a brave attempt to replace ships of the line that had gone aground. In the thick of the battle, thinking the British were facing defeat, Admiral Parker made the signal to discontinue action. Nelson ignored it and went on to win the day; Riou reluctantly obeyed the signal and hauled off. As the *Amazon* showed her stern to the shore batteries Riou, already wounded, was killed by a raking shot. Nelson mourned the death of 'the gallant and good Captain Riou' (*Dispatches and Letters*, 4.314). A monument was erected to Riou in St Paul's Cathedral, and his heroism was acclaimed by the poet Thomas Campbell in his ballad 'The Battle of the Baltic'. He never married, and left his small estate to his mother, his brother and sister, and his 'dearest friend', Mrs Charlotte Hartwell (PRO, PROB 11/1356).

Riou was a tall man of unusually strong physique, with a deserved reputation for courage, resourcefulness, and devotion to duty. Jacob Nagle, a seaman in the *Ganges*, described him as a strict disciplinarian with a fanatical regard for cleanliness. His manner was reserved, but his letters to his family reveal an affectionate son and brother with a lively sense of humour and deeply held Christian faith.   M. D. Nash

Sources *DNB* · NMM, Riou family MSS, RUSI/NM/235/R · M. D. Nash, ed., *The last voyage of the Guardian: Lieutenant Riou, Commander, 1789–1791*, Van Riebeeck Society (1990) · *The dispatches and letters of Vice-Admiral Lord Viscount Nelson*, ed. N. H. Nicolas, 7 vols. (1844–6), vol. 4, pp. 299–315 · PRO, PROB 11/1356, fols. 350–52 · pedigree of Riou, UCL, Huguenot Library, Wagner collection · *The journals of Captain James Cook*, ed. J. C. Beaglehole, 3/1, Hakluyt Society, 36a (1967), xcviii · *Letters and papers of Admiral of the Fleet Sir Thos. Byam Martin, GCB*, ed. R. V. Hamilton, 1, Navy RS, 24 (1903), 43–8 · *The Nagle journal*, ed. J. C. Dann (1988), 73–6 · W. L. Clowes, *The Royal Navy: a history from the earliest times to the present*, 7 vols. (1897–1903), vol. 4 · W. James, *The naval history of Great Britain, from the declaration of war by France in 1793, to the accession of George IV*, [3rd edn], 6 vols. (1837), vol. 1, pp. 212–13 · W. Manchée, 'Marylebone, and its Huguenot associations', *Proceedings of the Huguenot Society*, 11 (1915–17), 58–128

Archives Mitchell L., NSW, family collection, ML MS 5711 · NMM, corresp. and papers, journals; letter-book · PRO, admiralty records

Likenesses oils, 1776, on loan to NMM · S. Shelley, miniature, oils, *c.*1796, NMM [*see illus.*] · S. Shelley and J. Heath, engraving, pubd May 1801 (after miniature in oils by S. Shelley), Museum Africa, Johannesburg, South Africa · J. Heath, stipple (after S. Shelley), BM · J. C. Rossi, monument (with Captain Rosse), St Paul's Cathedral, London · oils?, repro. in *Proceedings of the Huguenot Society*, 10 (1914), facing p. 241; priv. coll. · pencil?, repro. in Dann, ed., *The Nagle journal*

Wealth at death £2000: will, PRO, PROB 11/1356, fols. 350–52

Ripa, Walter de (*fl.* 1218–1227), goldsmith and maker of seals, was probably a Londoner—the name de Ripa was fairly common in the early thirteenth-century city. Two entries in the close rolls name him in connection with the production of the king's seal, and on the basis of the lettering and figure-style on the seal it is possible to attribute others to him. Taken together, these show that over a decade he attracted a range of important patrons.

It is clear from the first of the close roll entries, in early November 1218, which specifies at 5 marks the weight of silver for which Walter was reimbursed, that he had made a great seal comprising two substantial matrices. A month later he was paid the considerable sum of 40s. for the work. Although the matrices were destroyed in October 1260, many impressions survive of Henry III's first great seal to testify to the artistry of its maker. The style shows the mature classicism of the 'transition' between Romanesque and Gothic. Moreover, the side showing the king enthroned was influential on European royal seals from Spain (Jaume I of Aragon, 1213–1276) to Norway (Haakon Haakonson, 1217–1263).

Perhaps as a result of this commission, Walter de Ripa provided seals for a wide range of patrons in the south and east of England. Among those which can be attributed to him, the most spectacular is the two-sided seal of the barons of London, possibly in use by 1219, showing St Paul standing within the city on its main face, and St Thomas Becket enthroned receiving the prayers of the citizens on the reverse. By 1223 Walter had also produced a seal for the Augustinian canons of St Botolph's, Colchester, and later (apparently by 1226) one for the bailiffs of Norwich; both of these derive in part from the London design.

The aristocracy also sought Walter out. Hugh Bigod, earl of Norfolk from 1221 to 1225, had a seal made by him, as too, probably in 1227, did Henry III's brother, Richard, count of Poitou and earl of Cornwall (d. 1272). Walter may have died in the late 1220s as no later work by him has yet been discovered.   T. A. HESLOP

Sources T. D. Hardy, ed., *Rotuli litterarum clausarum*, RC, 1 (1833), 381, 383 · A. B. Wyon and A. Wyon, *The great seals of England* (1887), 21–2, 149–50 · Birch, *Seals*, vol. 1, nos. 100–17, 2985; vol. 2, nos. 5068, 5234, 6328–9 · J. Alexander and P. Binski, eds., *Age of chivalry: art in Plantagenet England, 1200–1400* (1987), nos. 144, 193, 453 [exhibition catalogue, RA] · J. Tait, *The medieval English borough* (1936), 236, 266, 303, 314 · N. J. M. Kerling, ed., *Cartulary of St Bartholomew's Hospital, founded 1123* (1973)

Ripley, Dorothy (1767–1831), missionary, was born on 24 April 1767 in Whitby, Yorkshire, the second daughter in the large family of Dorothy and William Ripley (1739–1784), of Whitby. Her father was a master mason and a Methodist minister. Dorothy learned to pray at two or three, and felt chosen to preach the gospel to the heathen from eleven. Her teenage years were turbulent, marked by a suicide attempt in 1783, and in 1784 the death of her beloved father. At about twenty, on her way 'to meeting', she encountered a group of sailors who had just stripped, tarred, and feathered a beautiful girl 'ruined by a snare'. Ripley 'became servant to this miserable female', helped her on with borrowed clothes, 'lifted up my eyes to Heaven, and asked, Why is this not me Lord?' Later, in her prison visiting, she always sought out prostitutes for kindness.

In 1802, already a minister for ten years, Dorothy Ripley set out to preach to 'Ethiopia's children' living under 'base tyranny' in 'the large cities of America'. Several times she returned home because of illness, but never for long. She maintained links with the Quakers but made a point of religious independence: 'As I am not a member of any community, no society can answer for my irregular conduct.' She valued herself on being self-supporting, 'enabled to pay my own expenses many times, at Inns, by printing'. At Chester in England in October 1807 she spent two days editing a slim volume of letters addressed to her by several 'Africans and Indians', including a black bishop, proto-feminist Indian women, and a convicted felon.

In New York in 1810 Ripley issued her *Extraordinary conversion, and religious experience … with her first voyage and travels in America*. She stated that this was the first volume and reprinted it in London in 1817, but never produced a second volume. A similar work prepared for the press soon after this one appeared only in 1819, in Philadelphia, as *The Bank of Faith and Works United*. That year she also published an account of a nineteen-year-old woman executed for arson. Her memoirs in jaunty verse (including 'A Hymn from my Nativity', written in 1819) and prose (written in late 1821, in Mythe near Tewkesbury) appeared together at Bristol as *An Address to All in Difficulties*. A second, revised and expanded edition of *The Bank* in 1822 earned her a passage to the southern states of America, her ninth Atlantic crossing. On yet another voyage, from New York to France in 1826, she found time to write a preface to her father's recently discovered memoirs, published in Philadelphia in 1827.

Ripley's texts reflect the contradictions of her career. The language of her faith and preaching was otherworldly, yet she was deeply concerned with social issues and the roots of crime and poverty. She was selfless in religious commitment, yet delighted in displaying herself in print as a spiritual heroine. Dorothy Ripley died on 23 December 1831 in Mecklenburgh, Virginia. She was unmarried.   ISOBEL GRUNDY, *rev.*

Sources D. Ripley, *The bank of faith and works united* (1819) · D. Ripley, *The extraordinary conversion, and religious experience of Dorothy Ripley* (1810) · J. Smith, ed., *A descriptive catalogue of Friends' books*, 2 vols. (1867); suppl. (1893)

Ripley, George (d. c.1490), alchemist and Augustinian canon, is of obscure origins. According to his own account, given at the end of his *Medulla philosophiae chemicae*, he was descended from a gentry family, with branches in Lincolnshire and north Yorkshire. His family was well represented in the vicinity of Hull, an important local centre of intellectual as well as commercial exchange, and he himself became a canon at Bridlington, about 25 miles from Hull. There is no evidence that he took a degree at an English university, but according to the *Medulla* he studied in Italy. In the dedication to Edward IV of *The Compound of Alchymy*, Ripley says that it was on the king's instruction that he perfected his alchemical craft at the University of Louvain, a destination for students from throughout Europe who wished to study with the astrologer Spiricus. Louvain was an especially appropriate place to study because the duchy of Burgundy was the home of the order of the Golden Fleece, whose Argonautic ideology had as its objective the same uncorrupted golden age that was sought through alchemy.

The detail of Ripley's political connections is unclear. The epistle of dedication for the *Compound*, which was presented to Edward IV in 1471, suggests some level of personal contact with the king. In it Ripley claims to have sent Edward secret alchemical information from Louvain and promises to reveal the full secret of alchemy in a private demonstration. His medical advice warning against excess hints at some direct knowledge of the king's state

George Ripley (*d. c.*1490), tinted manuscript drawing

of health. There is no evidence of any personal remuneration, but in 1468, the year of the marriage between Edward's sister and Charles of Burgundy and therefore a plausible date for the secondment to Louvain, Edward pardoned Bridlington Priory all its outstanding debts to the crown. It would thus appear that during the quarrel between Edward and the earl of Warwick, Ripley put royal preferment before loyalty to the Nevilles, who had long-standing ties with Bridlington. His evident relief in his letter of dedication for the *Compound*, that Edward had ended 'old ranchors' (Ashmole, 109), may be a sign of this conflicted allegiance. Yet in 1476 he dedicated his *Medulla* to George Neville, archbishop of York, at a time when the latter's health and political influence were in sharp decline. The explanation may be that Edward had become disillusioned with Ripley or simply that dedications should always be read as demands for advancement.

When Ripley died, probably about 1490, he was buried in Bridlington Priory. BL, Cotton MS Vit. E.x, a compilation of chronicles and other documents, gives a drawing of his tomb, probably no later than the 1490s, with no effigy, just a cross, on its top, but with a prominent display round the sides of alchemical symbols, including crossed knives, and serpents and peacocks with intertwining necks, and sun and moon heads. This suggests how far Ripley's alchemy had managed to fit alongside conventional Christianity. Thereafter colourful traditions accumulated around Ripley's name; but there is no evidence that he became chamberlain to Pope Innocent VIII, still less that fumes from his laboratory at Bridlington drew complaints

from the local populace, or that he visited Rhodes and helped the knights hospitaller to resist the Turks by making gold to the value of £100,000 a year. This last apocryphal tale illustrates the quality of service to Christendom and the community which validated Western alchemy at the end of the fifteenth century.

In England the belief that the secret of the philosophers' stone would be reserved to those distinguished by spiritual merit is usually associated with the revival of interest in the works of the thirteenth-century Franciscan Roger Bacon. However, Ripley was most influenced by the alchemical works posthumously and erroneously attributed to the thirteenth-century Catalan philosopher Ramon Lull. The most important of these pseudo-Lullian texts, the *Testamentum*, is thoroughly in this moral tradition, presenting alchemy as a means of liberating the world from postlapsarian impurity; and Ripley followed the pattern when he offered Edward IV the secrets of alchemy 'sith I see that God you guideth and that ye be vertuous' (Ashmole, 109). The Lullian tradition also placed particular emphasis on sexual union as a metaphor for the alchemical process. By popularizing this ideology Ripley helped to set the tone for the alchemical literature of the sixteenth and seventeenth centuries, which dwelt increasingly on the sexual idiom, especially once printing had facilitated the reproduction of complex iconography. More immediately, Ripley was the author and practitioner who contributed most to the revival of the craft of alchemy in late fifteenth-century England following the relaxation, under Henry VI, of the prohibitions instituted by Henry IV.

The survival of over 200 manuscripts of his writings provides strong evidence for Ripley's immediate and enduring popularity. *The Compound of Alchymy* exists in seven fifteenth-century manuscript versions, his verse song, the *Cantilena*, in five. Copies proliferated in the sixteenth century, and the *Compound* was printed by Ralph Rabbards in 1591. His collected works were not published until 1649, when they appeared in Kassel. In England the great part of his opus appeared in 1652, during the vogue for alchemy which followed the civil war, when Ashmole published *Theatrum chemicum Britannicum*. Further editions of his works appeared in Amsterdam, Nuremberg, and Vienna, as well as in London. In addition Ripley was cited as a source of authority by sixteenth- and seventeenth-century alchemists. Thomas Charnock (1526–1581) claimed that he had studied with William Holleway, prior of Bath, who told him that he had learned the craft from a servant of Ripley. Later, George Starkey (*d.* 1665), an American alchemist resident in England, writing under the pseudonym Eireneaus Philalethes, presented some of his theories as tributes to Ripley in *Ripley Reviv'd* (1678) and *Sir George Ripley's Epistle to King Edward Expounded*.

ANTHONY GROSS

Sources E. Ashmole, ed., *Theatrum chemicum Britannicum* (1652) · G. Roberts, *The mirror of alchemy* (1994) · F. S. Taylor, 'George's Ripley's song', *Ambix*, 2 (1938–46), 177–81 · E. J. Holmyard, *Alchemy* (1957) · D. W. Singer and A. Anderson, *Catalogue of Latin and vernacular alchemical manuscripts in Great Britain and Ireland, dating from*

before the XVI century, 3 vols. (1928–31) • J. Greatrex, *Biographical regis-ter of the English cathedral priories of the province of Canterbury* (1997) • W. R. Newman, *Gehennical fire: the lives of George Starkey, an American alchemist in the scientific revolution* (1994) • *CPR, 1467–77,* 111 • W. Dugdale, *The visitation of the county of Yorke,* ed. R. Davies and G. J. Armytage, SurtS, 36 (1859) • BL, Cotton MS Vit. E.x
Archives Biblioteca Universitaria, Bologna, MS 109 vol. 2 • BL, Stowe MS 1070 • Derby Local Studies Library, Derby, 1491 • LPL, 'Alchima' and 'Medulla philosophie' • Royal College of Physicians of Edinburgh, alchemical scroll • Trinity Cam., MSS 1312, 1400
Likenesses tinted manuscript drawing, Bodl. Oxf., Bodley Rolls 1 [*see illus.*]

Ripley, Thomas (*bap.* 1682, *d.* 1758), architect, son of Leonard Ripley, was baptized on 12 February 1682 in the parish of Rillington, near Malton in the East Riding of Yorkshire. It is probable his family were the yeoman farmers of that name living at Scampston. Although he is said to have walked to London to seek his fortune, it is possible that he was introduced to Sir Robert Walpole by Sir William St Quintin, who lived in Scampston and who, as well as being a supporter of Walpole, held various lucrative government appointments, including lord of the Treasury (1714–17). Ripley married one of Sir Robert's servants (*d.* 1737) and his appointment in 1715 as labourer in trust at the Savoy marked the beginning of a steady rise through the ranks of the office of works; in 1726 he succeeded Vanbrugh as comptroller of the works and in 1729 Walpole engineered an additional appointment as surveyor of Greenwich Hospital.

Buildings for the government included the custom house (1718–25) and the Admiralty (1723–6) in London as well as the Queen Mary block and chapel at Greenwich (1729–50). In 1739 he was collaborating with William Kent on designs for the new houses of parliament and between 1750 and 1754 he made a number of changes to Kent's designs for the Horse Guards. In 1720 his appointment as executant architect at Houghton, Norfolk, was the first of a number of Walpole commissions. Here his responsibility for setting back the portico and the opening of the colonnades to the garden on the west side demonstrated that he was more than a project manager. From 1725 he designed and built Wolterton, Norfolk, for Sir Robert's brother Horatio, the first Lord Walpole, and was chiefly responsible for converting the formal park into a naturalized landscape. Until 1731 he was in charge of the major alterations at Raynham, Norfolk, for the Townshend family.

Ripley was involved in various speculative adventures. In 1726 he was the original lessee of the west side of Grosvenor Square, and although his contribution there was limited to 16 Grosvenor Street, he built a number of other houses in central London. In 1732 James Brydges, first duke of Chandos, commented, 'he is very rich and though he is in good employment he continues still this type of business' (Colvin, *Archs.,* 819). Ripley was active in promoting the scheme to build Westminster Bridge and was involved in Richard Holt's failed attempt to develop artificial stone. Nevertheless he appears to have been an astute investor: he was one of the few to make money out of the South Sea Bubble.

Ripley's reputation with his contemporaries was not high. Vanbrugh commented that on seeing Ripley's name 'such a laugh came upon me I had like to Beshit my Self' (*Complete Works,* 138), while the Burlington circle's contempt was publicized by Alexander Pope's stinging couplets and his view that Ripley was 'a carpenter, employed by a first Minister who raised him to an Architect, without any genius in the art' (Pope).

But despite the dull and sometimes ill-proportioned character of Ripley's public works this is too harsh a judgement. His pragmatic approach and undoubted skill at managing large projects ensured that Greenwich was completed and fulfilled its function. He supported Nicholas Hawksmoor and John James out of his own pocket when they were not paid. At his insistence the chapel was built and, owing to his astute exploitation of bureaucratic loopholes, the underground link with the hall was completed. Ripley always retained a craftsman's concern for practicality; in his words he 'was for the plain and simple thing' (*A Short Narrative,* 32). At Wolterton this resulted in a building of controlled austerity which demonstrated how convenience and dignity could be achieved through subtle planning.

On 17 November 1737 Ripley's first wife died and on 22 April 1742 he married Sarah Bucknall (*d.* 1752) of Hampton, Middlesex, an heiress said to be worth £40,000. She predeceased Ripley, who died at his house in Old Scotland Yard on 10 February 1758, leaving three sons and four daughters. He was buried in Hampton church on 18 February, but no memorial survives.

A. O. C. RICKETTS and AXEL KLAUSMEIER

Sources A. Klausmeier, *Thomas Ripley, Architekt: Fallstudie einer Karriere im 'Royal Office of the King's Works' im Zeitalter des Neopalladianismus* (Frankfurt am Main, Berlin, New York, and Paris, 2000) • A. Klausmeier, 'Wolterton Hall in Norfolk von Thomas Ripley: zum Hauptwerk eines von der Architekturgeschichte verstoßenen', *Architectura,* 28/1 (1998), 62–84 • Colvin, *Archs.* • H. M. Colvin and others, eds., *The history of the king's works,* 5 (1976), 347–8 • J. Bold, *Greenwich: an architectural history of the Royal Hospital for Seamen and the Queen's House* (2000) • A. Bowett, 'Thomas Ripley and the early use of mahogany', *Georgian Group Journal,* 7 (1997) • A. Pope, *An epistle to Richard Boyle, 3rd earl of Burlington* (1731) • *A short narrative of the proceedings of the gentlemen concerned in obtaining the act for building a bridge at Westminster, and of the steps, which the honourable commissioners, appointed by that act, have taken to carry it into execution* (1738) • *The complete works of Sir John Vanbrugh,* ed. G. Webb, 4: *The letters* (1928) • V. E. Whiting, ed., *The parish registers of Rillington 1638–1812,* Yorkshire Parish Register Society (1948), 18 • *The Builder,* 9/413 (1851), 3 • *GM,* 1st ser., 7 (1737), 702 • *GM,* 1st ser., 12 (1742), 274 • *London Chronicle* (11–14 Feb 1758), 146 • GL, MS 4335/2, fol. 36 • PRO, T53.37, fol. 131 • PRO, Cres 6/37, fols. 109, 123 • PRO, 6152, fol. 437
Archives Houghton Hall, Norfolk • PRO • Wolterton Hall, Norfolk
Likenesses J. Highmore, oils, 1746, NPG
Wealth at death see will, Feb 1758, PRO, PROB 11/836/53

Ripon. For this title name *see* Robinson, Frederick John, first Viscount Goderich and first earl of Ripon (1782–1859); Robinson, George Frederick Samuel, first marquess of Ripon (1827–1909).

Ripon, Stephen of. *See* Stephen of Ripon (*fl. c.*670–*c.*730).

Rippingille, Edward Villiers (*c.*1790–1859), genre and portrait painter, is recorded in early dictionaries as having been born in 1798 the son of a farmer of King's Lynn in Norfolk. However, the poet John Clare, a close friend of Rippingille in the 1820s, recalled that in 1807 or 1808 he had seen a bookseller's window full of the artist's pictures in Wisbech where, he says, Rippingille was painting portraits and giving drawing lessons. In 1813 Rippingille exhibited *The Ramblers* at the Norwich Society of Artists and he showed *Enlisting* and *The Cheat Detected* at the Royal Academy in 1813 and 1814, respectively. The earlier birth date of about 1790 is confirmed by the obituary notice in the *Art Journal* (probably written by Rippingille's friend Samuel Carter Hall, the editor) in which it is stated that Rippingille 'had almost, if not quite, reached the allotted term of life—the three score years and ten'.

By 1817 Rippingille was living in The Mall, Clifton, then just outside Bristol. Within a year he was painting portraits of local gentry, including Charles Abraham Elton (1778–1853), scholar and poet and later sixth baronet, and Dr John King (1776–1846), surgeon and friend of Dr Thomas Beddoes, Humphrey Davy, S. T. Coleridge, and Robert Southey. His first notable success came in 1819 with the exhibition at the Royal Academy of *A Country Post Office* (copy by the artist in Leeds City Art Gallery). The retired writer on art George Cumberland commented:

> A Mr Rippingale here has found out Bird's secret from chosen models by working with him and attending to his method of invention etc. He has done a Post office full of humour and will crop his teacher's laurels without ever thanking him or acknowledging it. (BL, Add. MS 36514, fol. 269)

It is unlikely that Rippingille was a formal pupil of Edward Bird RA (1772–1819) and his fine and intimate portrait of Bird in his studio (priv. coll., USA) suggests a respectful friendship. In 1822 Rippingille showed *The Recruiting Sergeant* (Bristol City Museum and Art Gallery) at the Royal Academy where David Wilkie had created such unprecedented excitement the previous year with *Chelsea Pensioners Reading the Gazette of the Battle of Waterloo*. Rippingille's painting depicts a crowded village gathering at which soldiers tempt gullible young men with the king's shilling. It lacks the compositional coherence and swirling triumphalism of Wilkie's masterpiece, but it has a more sensitive observation of the variety of human character and was a biting commentary on the mistreatment of soldiers who had fought in the Napoleonic wars. It is Rippingille's most original work. On 22 March 1822 George Cumberland had written to his son in London describing the painting, as 'a fine picture in Bird's style or better perhaps' (BL, Add. MS 36509, fol. 42). He related that he had given Rippingille a letter of introduction to Thomas Stothard RA, and proudly noted that he was depicted in the painting. In the same letter he described Rippingille as 'a sour-tempered and unpolished being with little religion and little regard for anyone. He keeps no friends and his politics are radical in the extreme, but he don't want for talent in painting' (ibid.). In fact Rippingille had a wide circle of acquaintances and friends, although he exasperated many of them by his wayward behaviour. Probably through Elton he had met Mrs Emmerson, patron of John Clare, the poet.

Early in June 1822 Rippingille spent two weeks with Clare in London. They met again in late June and July 1824, visiting ale houses, prize fights, Astley's Amphitheatre, and the French Playhouse, where they both fell for a beautiful actress. With Elton they called on Deville, the phrenologist, and Rippingille took Clare to the studio of Sir Thomas Lawrence, the president of the Royal Academy who, as Clare recorded,

> paid Rip several fine compliments about his picture of the breakfast at an Inn and told him of his faults in a free undisguised manner but with great kindness … told him that the Royal Family … took more notice of his picture than all the rest—but Rip would not own it for he affects a false appearance of such matters. (Clare, 153–4)

The painting in question is Rippingille's best-known work, *The Stage Coach Breakfast* (RA, 1824; Clevedon Court, Somerset). It records, with deliberate nostalgia, Bristol's remarkable literary associations a quarter-century earlier, including portraits of Coleridge, Lamb, Southey, and Wordsworth, of Elton and his family, and of others including John Gibbons, Rippingille's patron, and of Rippingille himself ironically being offered the bill.

Rippingille reluctantly left Clare in London and hurried back to Bristol to prepare a series of lectures on art delivered at the Bristol Institution. John King noted a great drop in attendance between the first and second lectures, but an improvement in his delivery despite long-winded digressions. King had earlier lamented that 'authorship, lecturing and music are too many pursuits to be carried on with habits of late rising etc' (John King to John Gibbons, 18 Jan 1823, Gibbons papers). Rippingille continued to lecture—for example at Gloucester and Worcester in 1829—and his writing later much increased. His punning and salacious poem 'Address to Echo' was published in the *London Magazine* in August 1824. He founded the *Artist and Amateur's Magazine*. Twelve monthly numbers were produced from March 1843 with much of the content written by Rippingille. After its demise the *Art Union* gloated that it had been aimed too much at the professional. A series of articles by Rippingille entitled 'Personal reflections of artists' was published, mostly posthumously, in the *Art Journal*. Among them is the famous description of J. M. W. Turner on varnishing day at the Royal Academy. He wrote tales of brigands for *Bentley's Magazine* and appeared regularly in the role of Pictor in the Revd John Eagles's articles for *Blackwood's Edinburgh Magazine* between 1833 and 1835. He had earlier illustrated Eagles's satirical poem *Rhymes, Latin and English by Themaninthemoon*, published in Bristol in 1826.

In the 1820s Rippingille undertook a number of ambitious historical paintings of medieval subjects, of which the finest was *The Funeral Procession of William Canynge to St Mary Redcliffe, 1474* (RA, 1822; Clevedon Court). The iron-founder D. W. Acraman unsuccessfully offered it to the newly founded Bristol Institution in the hope of prompting the formation of a collection of works by Bristol artists. In 1829 the institution did acquire Rippingille's model for his sculpture *Sleep*, but only after insisting that the subject's bosom was covered in drapery. The subscription that had been raised to buy the finished work was directed to a commission to paint *The Temptation of Christ* in order to enable Rippingille to travel to Italy; neither the sculpture nor the painting, which was completed in 1836, have survived. Rippingille, who set out for Italy in 1830, got no further than Germany. He finally moved from Bristol to London in 1832, and married his long-suffering mistress, Sarah Reedman, mother of three of his seven children:

> while at Bristol it did not matter whether or not she was my wife: on leaving Bristol I knew it would be likely we shall be thrown into another sort of company and in order not to compromise my friends ... I have married her.   (E. V. Rippingille to John Gibbons, 30 May 1832, Gibbons papers)

His four daughters with Mary Jellds—Mary, Olivia, Ellen, and Emma—had been baptized in St Paul's Church, Bristol, on 4 November 1825. His three children with Sarah Reedman—Fanny, Catherine, and Thornton—were baptized in the same church on 12 May 1830.

In 1832 Rippingille spent six weeks in France with the Bristol artist James Baker Pyne. By the winter of 1834–5 Rippingille's wife and family had moved there, but the artist himself was living in London with his model, a Miss Smith. In 1836 he sold the series of six paintings *The Progress of Intemperance* (Walker Art Gallery, Liverpool) for £300, perhaps prompting his journey to Italy in 1837. After stays in Paris and Florence, he arrived in Rome at Christmas at the height of the cholera epidemic and he may have remained there until 1841. In 1843 he won a prize in the Westminster Hall fresco competition, but no commission followed. He continued to exhibit regularly at the Royal Academy until 1849 and intermittently thereafter until 1857. He died suddenly at the railway station at Swan Valley in Staffordshire on 22 April 1859. Many years later his close friend S. C. Hall wrote:

> Poor wayward RIPPINGILLE! Always struggling against a conviction that fate withheld from him the greatness that was his right! ... A constitutional irritability, a proneness to debate, and that which is very dangerous to artists—a liking to use the pen—stood terribly in his way; and he never fulfilled ... the promise he had given in youth.   (Hall, 491)

John Clare, who had no doubts about Rippingille's genius, described him with affection as 'a rattling sort of odd fellow with a desire to be thought one' (Clare, 138). But it is his own words that best express both his humour and his cussedness: 'It is a fact that has been ascertained by actual experiment, that artists will die if they are not fed' (*Felix Farley's Bristol Journal*, 26 Feb 1825).

FRANCIS GREENACRE

Sources Bristol RO, Gibbons papers, 41197 · P. Cox, '"A liking to use the pen": Edward Villiers Rippingille (*c.* 1790–1859) and John Clare', *John Clare Society Journal*, 17 (July 1998), 17–23 · F. Greenacre, *The Bristol school of artists: Francis Danby and painting in Bristol, 1810–1840* [1973], 120–39 [exhibition catalogue, City Museum and Art Gallery, Bristol, 4 Sept–10 Nov 1973] · *Art Journal*, 21 (1859), 187 · *The Athenaeum* (7 May 1859), 614 · S. C. Hall, *A book of memories of great men and women of the age*, 2nd edn (1877), 491 · R. Redgrave and S. Redgrave, *A century of painters of the English school*, 2 vols. (1866) · E. Adams, *Francis Danby: varieties of poetic landscape* (1973) · B. Stewart and M. Cutten, *The dictionary of portrait painters in Britain up to 1920* (1997) · [J. Clare], *John Clare by himself*, ed. E. Robinson and D. Powell (1996) · directories, Bristol, 1817–31

Archives Bristol Museum and Art Gallery · Clevedon Court, Somerset · V&A NAL, letters and notes · Walker Art Gallery, Liverpool | BL, letters to George Cumberland and others · Bristol RO, Gibbons papers, letters to John Gibbons, 41197

Likenesses E. V. Rippingille, self-portrait, pencil and watercolour drawing, 1811, Bristol City Museum and Art Gallery · E. V. Rippingille, self-portrait, oils, 1821 (*Settling the account*); Sothebys, 15 July 1992, lot 161 · E. V. Rippingille, self-portrait, oils, 1822 (*The artist's studio*), Clevedon Court, Somerset · E. V. Rippingille, self-portrait, oils, 1824 (*The stage coach breakfast*), Clevedon Court, Somerset · E. V. Rippingille, self-portrait, oils, *c.*1830, Bristol City Museum and Art Gallery · E. V. Rippingille, self-portrait, oils (*The paternity suit*); Christies, 21 Nov 1986, lot 69

PICTURE CREDITS

Randolph, Peyton (1721/2–1775)—The Virginia Historical Society, Richmond, Virginia

Randolph, Thomas (*bap.* 1605, *d.* 1635)—© National Portrait Gallery, London

Ranjitsinhji Vibhaji, maharaja jam sahib of Navanagar [Ranjitsinhji or Ranji] (1872–1933)—Michael Carr-Archer / Beldam Collection / Popperfoto

Rank, (Joseph) Arthur, Baron Rank (1888–1972)—© Karsh / Camera Press; collection National Portrait Gallery, London

Rankine, (William John) Macquorn (1820–1872)—© National Portrait Gallery, London

Ransome, Arthur Michell (1884–1967)—Garrick Club / the art archive

Rapin de Thoyras, Paul de (1661–1725)—© National Portrait Gallery, London

Rashdall, Hastings (1858–1924)—© National Portrait Gallery, London

Rassam, Hormuzd (1826–1910)—© National Portrait Gallery, London

Rathbone, (Philip St John) Basil (1892–1967)—© National Portrait Gallery, London

Rathbone, Eleanor Florence (1872–1946)—© National Portrait Gallery, London

Rathbone, William (1819–1902)—© National Portrait Gallery, London

Rathborne, Aaron (*b.* 1571/2)—© National Portrait Gallery, London

Rattigan, Sir Terence Mervyn (1911–1977)—© Karsh / Camera Press; collection National Portrait Gallery, London

Raven, Dame Kathleen Annie (1910–1999)—Getty Images – Hulton Archive

Ravenstein, Ernst Georg (1834–1913)—The Royal Geographical Society, London

Raverat, Gwendolen Mary (1885–1957)—© Estate of Sir Geoffrey Keynes

Ravis, Thomas (*b.* in or before 1560, *d.* 1609)—Christ Church, Oxford

Rawlings, Sir (Henry) Bernard Hughes (1889–1962)—© National Portrait Gallery, London

Rawlings, Margaret Lilian (1906–1996)—© Tom Hustler / National Portrait Gallery, London

Rawlinson, Henry Seymour, Baron Rawlinson (1864–1925)—© National Portrait Gallery, London

Rawlinson, Richard (1690–1755)—© National Portrait Gallery, London

Rawsthorne, Alan (1905–1971)—© Cecil Beaton Archive, Sotheby's; collection National Portrait Gallery, London

Ray, Edward Rivers [Ted] (1877–1943)—© Empics

Ray, Gabrielle (1883–1973)—© National Portrait Gallery, London

Ray, John (1627–1705)—© National Portrait Gallery, London

Ray, Martha (1742?–1779)—Christie's Images Ltd. (2004)

Ray, Ted (1909–1977)—© National Portrait Gallery, London

Rayner, Derek George, Baron Rayner (1926–1998)—© News International Newspapers Ltd

Read, Sir William (*d.* 1715)—Wellcome Library, London

Reade, Charles (1814–1884)—© National Portrait Gallery, London

Redgrave, Sir Michael Scudamore (1908–1985)—© National Portrait Gallery, London

Redgrave, Richard (1804–1888)—© National Portrait Gallery, London

Redhead, Brian Leonard (1929–1994)—Nils Jorgensen / Rex Features

Redmayne, Sir Richard Augustine Studdert (1865–1955)—courtesy of the Institution of Civil Engineers Archives

Redmond, John Edward (1856–1918)—National Gallery of Ireland

Redmond, William Hoey Kearney (1861–1917)—© National Portrait Gallery, London

Redpath, Anne (1895–1965)—Scottish National Portrait Gallery

Redwood, Sir (Thomas) Boverton, first baronet (1846–1919)—© National Portrait Gallery, London

Rée, Harry Alfred (1914–1991)—© News International Newspapers Ltd

Reece, Sir Gerald (1897–1985)—© National Portrait Gallery, London

Reed, Sir Carol (1906–1976)—© Kenneth Hughes / National Portrait Gallery, London

Reed, Sir Edward James (1830–1906)—© National Portrait Gallery, London

Reed, (Thomas) German (1817–1888)—© National Portrait Gallery, London

Reed, Talbot Baines (1852–1893)—© National Portrait Gallery, London

Rees, Abraham (1743–1825)—by permission of Dr Williams's Library

Rees, David James [Dai] (1913–1983)—Getty Images – Hulton Archive

Rees, Sarah Jane [Cranogwen] (1839–1916)—by courtesy of the National Library of Wales

Reeve, Henry (1813–1895)—© National Portrait Gallery, London

Reeve, Sir Thomas (1672/3–1737)—Graves Art Gallery, Sheffield; photograph National Portrait Gallery, London

Reeves, John (1752–1829)—© National Portrait Gallery, London

Reeves, John (1774–1856)—© Fitzwilliam Museum, University of Cambridge

Reeves, (John) Sims (1818–1900)—© National Portrait Gallery, London

Reeves, William Pember (1857–1932)—© National Portrait Gallery, London

Reid, Beryl Elizabeth (1919–1996)—Getty Images – Hulton Archive

Reid, Elisabeth Jesser (1789–1866)—© National Portrait Gallery, London / Oxford University Press

Reid, John (1722?–1807)—courtesy of the University of Edinburgh's Collections

Reid, Robert Threshie, Earl Loreburn (1846–1923)—The Masters of the Bench of the Inner Temple. Photograph: Photographic Survey, Courtauld Institute of Art, London

Reid, Thomas (1710–1796)—photograph by kind permission of The National Trust for Scotland

Reid, Sir Thomas Wemyss (1842–1905)—© National Portrait Gallery, London

Reilly, Sir (D'Arcy) Patrick (1909–1999)—© National Portrait Gallery, London

Reilly, Thomas Rundle (1919–2000)—© News International Newspapers Ltd

Reinagle, Ramsay Richard (1775–1862)—private collection; photograph © Sotheby's Picture Library, London

Reinhardt, Max (1873–1943)—Getty Images – Hulton Archive

Reinhold, Frederick Charles (1741–1815)—Garrick Club / the art archive

Reith, John Charles Walsham, first Baron Reith (1889–1971)—© National Portrait Gallery, London

Rejlander, Oscar Gustaf (1813–1875)—Royal Photographic Society

Relph, Harry [Little Tich] (1867–1928)—Mander & Mitchenson Theatre Collection

Renard, Simon (*c.*1513–1573)—Lauros / Girandon / Bridgeman Art Library

Rendall, Montague John (1862–1950)—© Estate of Glyn Philpot

Rendel, Harry Stuart Goodhart- (1887–1959)—RIBA Library Photographs Collection

Rendel, James Meadows (1799–1856)—© National Portrait Gallery, London

Rendel, Stuart, Baron Rendel (1834–1913)—Getty Images – Hulton Archive

Rennell, James (1742–1830)—© National Portrait Gallery, London

Rennie, George (1791–1866)—© National Portrait Gallery, London

Rennie, John (1761–1821)—Scottish National Portrait Gallery

Rennie, Sir John (1794–1874)—V&A Images, The Victoria and Albert Museum

Rennie, Sir John Ogilvy (Jack) (1914–1981)—private collection

Repington, Charles À Court (1858–1925)—© National Portrait Gallery, London

Repton, Humphry (1752–1818)—© Copyright The British Museum

Reuter, (Paul) Julius de, Baron de Reuter in the nobility of Saxe-Coburg and Gotha (1816–1899)—© National Portrait Gallery, London

Revere, Paul (*bap.* 1734, *d.* 1818)—Copyright 2004 Museum of Fine Arts, Boston; gift of Joseph W. Revere, William B. Revere and Edward H. R. Revere

Revett, Nicholas (1721–1804)—RIBA Library Photographs Collection

Revie, Donald (1927–1989)—Getty Images – Hulton Archive

Reynolds, John Hamilton (1794–1852)—© National Portrait Gallery, London

Reynolds, Sir Joshua (1723–1792)—© Royal Academy of Arts, London

Reynolds, Richard (1735–1816)—© National Portrait Gallery, London

Reynolds, Samuel William (1773–1835)—© National Portrait Gallery, London

Reynolds, Stephen Sydney (1881–1919)—© National Portrait Gallery, London

Reynolds, Walter (*d.* 1327)—by kind permission of the Dean and Chapter of Canterbury; photographer: Mrs Mary Tucker

Reynolds, William (1758–1803)—© Ironbridge Gorge Museum Trust

Rhodes, Cecil John (1853–1902)—© National Portrait Gallery, London

Rhodes, Francis William (1851–1905)—© National Portrait Gallery, London

Rhodes, Wilfred (1877–1973)—from the Bob Appleyard Collection

Rhŷs, Sir John (1840–1915)—© National Portrait Gallery, London

Ricardo, David (1772–1823)—© National Portrait Gallery, London

Rice, Sir Cecil Arthur Spring- (1859–1918)—Getty Images – Hulton Archive

Rice, Thomas Spring, first Baron Monteagle of Brandon (1790–1866)—© National Portrait Gallery, London

Rich, Henry, first earl of Holland (*bap.* 1590, *d.* 1649)—© National Portrait Gallery, London

Rich, John (1692–1761)—Garrick Club / the art archive

Rich, Mary, countess of Warwick (1624–1678)—© National Portrait Gallery, London

Rich, Sir Nathaniel (*c.*1585–1636)—private collection; photograph National Portrait Gallery, London

Rich, Richard, first Baron Rich (1496/7–1567)—The Royal Collection © 2004 HM Queen Elizabeth II

Rich, Robert, second earl of Warwick (1587–1658)—The Metropolitan Museum of Art, The Jules Bache Collection, 1949. (49.7.26) Photograph © 1998 The Metropolitan Museum of Art

Rich, Sir Robert, fifth baronet (1717–1785)—King's Own Royal Regiment Museum, Lancaster

Richard, first earl of Cornwall and king of Germany (1209–1272)—Landeshauptarchiv, Koblenz, Best. 133 Nr. 18

Richard I (1157–1199)—photograph: AKG London

Richard II (1367–1400)—© Dean and Chapter of Westminster

Richard III (1452–1485)—Society of Antiquaries of London